D1242451

CONTEMPORARY POETS

Contemporary Writers of the English Language

Contemporary Poets

Contemporary Novelists
(including short story writers)

Contemporary Dramatists

Contemporary Literary Critics

CONTEMPORARY POETS

THIRD EDITION

PREFACE TO THE FIRST EDITION
C. DAY LEWIS

PREFACE TO THE THIRD EDITION
MARJORIE PERLOFF

EDITOR
JAMES VINSON

ASSOCIATE EDITOR
D. L. KIRKPATRICK

ST. MARTIN'S PRESS
NEW YORK

 For information write:
ST. MARTIN'S PRESS
175 Fifth Avenue
New York, New York 10010

ISBN 0 312 16836 5
Library of Congress Catalog Card Number 78-165556

First edition published 1970; second edition published 1975.

Printed in Great Britain by
REDWOOD BURN LIMITED
Trowbridge & Esher

CONTENTS

PREFACE
to the first edition

I have been asked to say something, by way of a preface, about what the writing and reading of poetry have meant to me in my own life. Writing it, which I did copiously from 14 or 15, must presently become either a way of life or a pleasant occasional pastime. For me it became the former: in my teens I wanted nothing so much as to be a Poet, and I firmly believed that I would never be capable of doing anything but write poetry: this is a good start, since it concentrates any powers one may have and sets up a strong initial momentum. Art cannot be a substitute for religion; but the habit of poetry has something in common with the habit of prayer – through it we search the unknown and search our own heart, to praise and to understand; we submit ourselves to a discipline which is partly a discipline of meditation and partly one of craft, of making language adapt itself to the conveying of states of mind incommunicable in any other way. The meditation and the craft are interfused, for his craft is the poet's mode of meditation.

Since words are what he works in, the young poet should always be extending his knowledge of them and of the way other poets have used them. He should read a page or two of the dictionary every day, as a priest reads his breviary. I wish I had done so myself. The colour, configuration, connotations of a single word may be the seed of a poem. Equally, he will read the work of poets living and dead, to learn what poetry is and gradually to understand how difficult it is to write a good poem. At school I read poetry because I wanted to be different, a one-man élite – it was a kind of social protest – Swinburne, Masefield, the early Yeats, and I was also attracted to Virgil, Wordsworth, Keats and Tennyson. What drew me – a raw, dreamy, provincial boy – was the sound of words, the shapes of lyric writing, the sense that I was on the brink of a glorious mystery, and my own feeling for nature reflected back and as it were justified by the poems of other men.

Just as in early manhood one makes the most lasting friendships, so one receives the strongest impressions from poetry: though I have admired many poets since my Oxford days, it is the ones I read there to whom I most often return: the later Yeats, Owen, Frost, Emily Dickinson, Hardy, the Meredith of *Modern Love*, Pope, the Metaphysicals. I was fortunate in getting to know a number of coaevals who wrote poetry. I was no less fortunate in being susceptible to their enthusiasms but not overwhelmed by them: Donne and Eliot were two of these; but, making nothing of them at first, I put them aside and was able to return to them later when I was ripe for them.

Most poets' reading is a desultory affair, not a diligent and orderly course of "required reading." The books he requires are those of poets who, at any given stage of his life, can offer him encouragement, new ways of approaching poetry and new technical possibilities which present both a challenge and a way in to some new phase of his own work. This is the meaning of tradition, the right use of influences. A mediating power.

I was also lucky to be one of a group (it was never consciously a "movement") of young men who came from not dissimilar environments and responded keenly to one another's work and to the weather of the times. A considerable momentum is set up when a group of poets is pulling in roughly the same direction: but the degree of the momentum cannot be gauged until each of the group has cast off from the others and is pursuing an individual course. That course is unpredictable. With certain poets – I am not one of them – hindsight reveals a continuity of development: my own work, though I can see its obsessive and recurrent themes, appears to me a hand-to-mouth affair – a seizing upon any subject which comes my way and trying to make something of it. "Making something" of a subject means the deepening of its implications: but if one carries the deepening beyond what the subject will allow, the poem gets out of its depth and becomes an incoherent, echoing void filled with empty poeticisms.

One thing I have begun to learn from the reading and writing of poetry is level – the level at which a given poem should work. If we take such dissimilar objects as the writings of the Caroline poets and Clough's *Amours de Voyage*, we see how delicately these poets have adjusted their treatment to the weight of theme their verse can bear, never tempted into profundities where their subject would go astray and be lost. As we do not always want to be reading Shakespeare or Dante, so we should not always be pining to write the great poem. When I was young, I wished to write a better poem than Auden; later, I wanted each poem I was writing to by my best: now, I want to write another poem.

In the writing, I have always been so captivated by the charms and possibilities of more-or-less strict verse form that I very seldom have attempted the larger liberties of "free verse." It is as difficult to handle as the Protestant conscience – only a few poets in England and America have produced a first-class body of work in this medium. It may be that the poetry of the future will more and more be written in this formless form: we are told it enables the poem to be truly "organic" – whatever that may mean. But for me the endless fascination of verse, of organising a poem in metre and rhyme, outweighs any advantage that could be gained from the free way of writing. Form is not something a poet imposes on a poem: it is worked out by him in collaboration with the growing poem – its needs and nuances – as the meaning of that poem little by little becomes clear to him. I believe every artist is required to make coherent patterns out of chaos, not to reproduce it.

Nevertheless, one cannot have read poetry for fifty years, even in the specialised way poets read, without knowing that time and again the value of the great technical innovators has gone unrecognised by their contemporaries. The innovation of free verse as we know it, dating only from Whitman, is still resisted – if only by reactionary poets like myself. But so long as its practitioners can communicate in a memorable as well as a novel way, their work will justify itself: new forms will be seen to have emerged from behind the apparent formlessness, and the core of the poetic tradition be felt beneath a multiplicity of seemingly heterodox and even anarchic poems.

The present volume, which contains material about some thousand living poets from all over the world who write in English, is more than a handbook of information, less than a definitive roll of honour. We cannot tell how many of these names will survive through their work even beyond their own lifetime: 10%? 1%? Nevertheless, the book does honour to poetry, and provides a mass of information. It offers the serious reader a conspectus of representative writers from many countries, and so encourages him to extend his curiosity and broaden his reading. More important still, the book is a witness to the remarkable diversity of talents, the vigour and the inventiveness which poetry can command, even in a bitter, bewildering age when its sources are muddied or obstructed, "under conditions that seem unpropitious."

C. DAY LEWIS

PREFACE
to the third edition

Reading poetry in 1980, one often has the uneasy feeling that the revolution known as Modernism never occurred, that Ezra Pound never talked of "Direct treatment of the 'thing,' " or the "VORTEX" as "a radiant node or cluster ... from which, and through which, and into which, ideas are constantly rushing"; that Eliot never referred to "the law that poetry must not stray too far from the ordinary everyday language which we use and hear," or talked about the "intensity of the poetic process" and the need for "clear visual images." Consider the following poem:

At Claybank

Your parents lie buried
Under emblems of waves.
Cold surges of granite
Secure the ancient graves.

After pain and blindness,
With clouds closing in,
Summer lightning and rain,
We bring you to your kin.

What you asked is done.
You lie in their pure flood.
The rain washes the clay
Above it, dark as blood.

This little lyric has all the hallmarks of *fin de siècle*: the orderly quatrains of iambic trimeter, the semantically neutral rhymes ("waves"/"graves"; "flood"/"blood"), the use of abstract nouns, the vaguely mournful theme presented by means of ominous but unspecified nature images, the absence of what Yeats, himself a survivor of *fin de siècle*, called "dramatic tension" or the rhythm of "passionate, normal speech." But "At Claybank" was written neither by John Davidson nor by W. E. Henley. Its author is a very contemporary John Finlay, and it appeared in a 1979 issue of *Poetry Nation Review*.

Hard to believe? Here is a related example, this time from Anthony Hecht's *The Venetian Vespers*, which was extravagantly praised by Christopher Ricks on the front page of the *New York Times Book Review* (2 December 1979) and has been nominated for the annual Book Critics Circle Award:

Still Life

Sleep-walking vapor, like a visitant ghost,
    Hovers about a lake
Of Tennysonian calm just before dawn.
Inverted trees and boulders waver and coast
In polished darkness. Glints of silver break
Among the liquid leafage, and then are gone....

Like Rimbaud's "Le Dormeur du Val," this is a nature poem with a surprise ending: the idyllic setting is deceptive, for, as we learn in the last stanza, "I stand beneath a pine-tree in the cold,/Just before dawn, somewhere in Germany,/A cold, wet, Garand rifle in my hands." But unlike Rimbaud's poem, in which every image is functional, Hecht's is mostly window-dressing; it recalls such Georgian poets as Edward Thomas and J. C. Squire, poets who were the targets of such well-known Poundian dicta as "Don't chop your stuff into separate IAMBS": "A rhyme must have in it some slight element of surprise if it is to give pleasure"; "Use no superfluous word, no adjective which does not reveal something. Don't use such an expression as 'dim lands of *peace*'. It dulls the image." Hecht's "Tennysonian calm" is made up of just such "expression(s) as 'dim lands of *peace*' ": for example, "Sleep-walking vapor," "visitant ghost," "Glints of silver," "polished darkness," "liquid leafage." And neither the rhymes – "ghost"/"coast"; "lake"/"break" – nor the conventionalized iambic pentameter can be said to create any particular "surprise."

The nostalgia for the peaceful decades before the First World War is everywhere with us. An apt emblem of that nostalgia is the recent BBC serialization of the life of Lily Langtry, the most celebrated of Edward VII's mistresses. The film *Lily* juxtaposes Whistler interiors in which Oscar Wilde is engaged in witty repartee with fellow poets and painters, to such idealized Edwardian images as the Garden Party, the Tryst in the Hunting Lodge, the Morning Ride in Hyde Park, the Presentation to the Queen. Furthermore, there is the ubiquitous presence of the servants, those humble, supportive, and charming folk who people the "upstairs and downstairs" of the Victorian and Edwardian celluloid world. Just so, in Anthony Hecht's "The Grapes," the speaker is a chambermaid who suddenly discovers, as she contemplates the light on the grapes in a bowl, that "There was nothing left for me now, nothing but years."

But nostalgia, no matter how strong, never reproduces the original. Despite the current conservatism of our literary quarterlies and publishing houses, despite the seeming preference for the safe, the orderly – the "cooked," as Philip Rahv called it – to the experimental, the messy, the "raw," there continues to be exciting experimentation in the poetry of our own *fin de siècle*, a poetry that is postmodern rather than neo-Victorian or Edwardian.

Consider, in the first place, the transformation of the long poem. Late Modernist long poems were almost invariably sequences: Robert Lowell's *Life Studies* (1959) and *Notebook* (1970), Charles Olson's *Maximus* (1960–68), Galway Kinnell's *The Book of Nightmares* (1971), Ted Hughes's *Crow* (1971), A. R. Ammons's *Sphere: The Form of a Motion* (1974). "The modern sequence," writes M. L. Rosenthal in *Contemporary Literature* (Summer 1977), "is a grouping of mainly lyric poems and passages, rarely uniform in pattern, tending to interact as an organic whole. It usually includes narrative and dramatic elements ... but its ordering is finally lyrical, a succession of *affects*." It is just such a "succession of *affects*" that poets are now questioning. John Cage puts it very cunningly in an essay called "The Future of Music" (1974):

> We will continue to "wrestle with the Daimonic".... But more and more this concern with personal feelings of individuals, even the enlightenment of individuals, will be seen in the larger context of society. We know how to suffer or control our own emotions. If not, advice is available. There is a cure for tragedy. The path to self-knowledge has been mapped out by psychiatry, by oriental philosophy, mythology, occult thought, anthroposophy, and astrology. We know all we need to know about Oedipus, Prometheus, and Hamlet. What we are learning is how to be convivial. "Here Comes Everybody."

Tongue-in-cheek as these remarks are, there is an important truth behind them. If self-knowledge and self-projection seem less important than they did to poets in the past, it is not because there is, in fact, "a cure for tragedy" (Cage knows better), but because, given the context of experience in the late 20th century, individual tragedy no longer seems quite plausible or real: we can, after all, turn on the television and watch the same things that trouble us happening to everyone else. "Learning how to be convivial" thus becomes a central element, and "Here Comes Everybody" involves narrative.

Thus James Merrill's celebrated "Book of Ephraim" (*Divine Comedies*, 1975) and its sequel *Mirabell: Book of Numbers* (1978) renounce the lyric sequence in favor of old-fashioned plot and a list of "Dramatis Personae" that include "Auden, W(ystan) H(ugh), 1907–/73, the celebrated poet," and "Deren, Eleonora ('Maya'),/1917–61, doyenne of our/American experimental film." At the opening of "Ephraim," the poet begins by disarming the reader's possible objections to a long narrative poem, full of events, information, and obscure references to the supernatural:

> Admittedly I err by undertaking
> This in its present form. The baldest prose
> Reportage was called for, that would reach
> The widest public in the shortest time.

And from here we move quickly to the scene: JM (Merrill) and DJ (his friend David Jackson) seated at the Ouija Board, calling up the spirit of Ephraim, a Greek Jew born in A.D. 8 and a favorite of the Emperor Tiberius, a character who proceeds to instruct the two protagonists on the meaning of history, philosophy, and especially the modern science of biology. Merrill's is a poetry that subordinates the Romantic image to the play of ideas, and so, in Aristotelian terms, it marks a return to the precedence of Mythos over Ethos, and of Dianoia over Melopoiea. "Ephraim" has brilliant buried rhymes and a panoply of clever verbal devices, but it is certainly not a musical or lyric poem.

The same turn from lyric to narrative can be found in other poems quite different from the elegant "Ephraim" and *Mirabell*. Contemporary narrative poems range from Ted Hughes's allegorical treatment of evil in *Gaudete* (1977), a violent and, I think, ultimately pretentious tale about an Anglican clergyman replaced by a changeling who seduces, one by one, all the good ladies of the parish until their men seek revenge and restore the "real" Reverend Lumb; to Ed Dorn's brilliant assemblage of cowboy epic, science fiction, drug culture *argot*, and Wittgensteinian logic in *Gunslinger* (1975); to the "exemplary narratives" embedded in the extraordinary "talk poems" of David Antin (*Talking at the Boundaries* [1976] and *Tuning* [1980]). A recent circular issued by the Poetry Project at St. Mark's-in-the-Bowery announced a reading by Howard A. Norman, "translator of *The Wishing Bone Cycle, Narrative Poems of the Swampy Cree Indians*":

> *The Wishing Bone Cycle* takes its name from the remarkable series of poem-stories that begin this book. Howard A. Norman, a young Canadian poet, first learned these poems about a wishing bone – capable of changing itself into various characters, objects and circumstances – from the venerable Swampy Cree Indian Jacob Slowstream. In addition to the thirty poems of this cycle, Norman has included a series of name-origin poems, a long animal-origin prose tale, and a group of songs and lullabies.

I cite this circular because it designates so clearly a kind of event that is taking place in our poetry world, a world that no longer worries much about the boundaries between poetry and prose, lyric and narrative. Howard A. Norman is a practitioner of a lively new discipline called *ethnopoetics*, which involves the transcription, translation, and discussion of the spoken and chanted word, especially the oral tradition of tribal peoples. The journal *Alcheringa: Ethnopoetics* publishes the work of Gary Snyder, Robert Kelly, Nathaniel Tarn, and Jerome Rothenberg, who is its leading spokesman. Rothenberg's own long poems – *Poland/1931* and *Seneca Journal* – as well as his distinctive anthologies – *Revolution of the Word, Technicians of the Sacred, America a Prophecy* – have made a great impact on younger poets. Indeed, Rothenberg's own collage-anthology *The Big Jewish Book* can be regarded as an intriguing postmodern narrative in its own right.

John Ashbery's latest collection, *As We Know* (1979), contains what I take to be the finest narrative poem of recent years, the 68-page "Litany." Written in double columns (which can be read both "across" and "down"), containing stories that fade in and out, overlap, mirror one another, or, on the contrary, cancel out each other's meanings, "Litany" beautifully exemplifies what Ashbery himself has called, in his *Three Poems* (1972), "an open field of narrative possibilities." We may, for example, read in the left-hand column:

> Just as everything seemed about to go wrong
> The music began; later on, the missing
> Refreshments would be found and served,
> The road turned caramel just as the first stars
> Were putting in a timid appearance, like snowdrops.

while the right-hand column presents a parody lecture on the sorrows of contemporary criticism:

Just one minute of contemporary existence
Has so much to offer, but who
Can evaluate it, formulate
The appropriate apothegm, show us
In a few well-chosen words of wisdom
Exactly what is taking place all about us?
Not critics, certainly, though that is precisely
What they are supposed to be doing....

Even these short passages will indicate to the reader that the narrative contained in "Litany" is fragmented and enigmatic. As Ashbery says of Gertrude Stein (in *Poetry*, July 1957):

> *Stanzas in Meditation* gives one the feeling of time passing, of things happening, of a "plot," though it would be difficult to say precisely what is going on. Sometimes the story has the logic of a dream.... But it is usually not events which interest Miss Stein. Rather it is their "way of happening," and the story of *Stanzas in Meditation* is a general, all-purpose model which each reader can adapt to fit his own set of particulars.

I cite these remarks at some length because they bring me to a related point about the poetry of the present. If narrative is, as I have been positing, once again central to poetry, this is not to say that it is the narrative of a William Morris or an Edwin Arlington Robinson. Postmodern narrative poetry is characterized by its peculiar indeterminacy, what Tzvetan Todorov has called its "undecidability" and other critics its "suspensiveness." Surely it is no coincidence that Ashbery's "Litany" appeared just a few years after Derrida's *Glas* (a critical commentary that has more in common with poetic discourse than with philosophy, and which is also written in double columns, the two voices ostensibly being those of Hegel and Genet), for Derrida's treatment of the absence of the signifier, if not applicable to poetry in general, is curiously applicable to the contemporary situation. In the enigma poetry of John Ashbery, a signal seems to be emitted, but the receiver's connection with the transmitter would seem to be on a faulty line. The poem is thus poised between sense and nonsense; it simultaneously discloses and conceals its meaning. This revelation/reveiling paradigm can be discovered not only in the word of Ashbery and his followers, but also in the Surrealist poetry of J. H. Prynne and Tom Raworth, the "Objectivist" lyric of Louis Zukofsky and George Oppen, and the performance art of John Cage and David Antin. The poetry of indeterminacy can be traced back, as I suggest in my new book on the subject, to the verbal constructions of Beckett, and before him of Pound, Stein, and their French precursors both in poetry and in painting. I call this particular mode Rimbaldian because its first exemplar was the Rimbaud of the *Illuminations*.

"An open field of narrative possibilities," indeterminacy, the free play of ideas that refuses to harden into "statement – this refusal to create the dense Symbolist network of High Modernist poetry is what I find especially exhilarating in the most interesting poetry of our own time. And here some related developments deserve discussion.

In "The ABC of Contemporary Reading" (*Esthetics Contemporary*, 1978), Richard Kostelanetz remarks: "The major esthetic innovations of recent art extend from three generative principles: minimalism, overload, and intermedia." Let me expand on some of Kostelanetz's suggestive generalizations.

Minimalism, "the principle of reducing the amount of surface content in a work – painting with only one color, say, or sculpture with smooth rectangular shapes, or fictions with very few words, or poems with a severely limited vocabulary" – is perhaps most obviously exemplified by the poetry of Robert Creeley, whose newest book, *Later* (1979), contains such lyrics as "Speech":

Simple things
one wants to say
like, what's the day
like, out there –
who am I
and where.

Such reductiveness is dangerous: the poem all but melts away. A very different minimalism is that of Geoffrey Hill in "The Pentecost Castle" (*Tenebrae*, 1978):

shadows warned him
not to go
not to go
along that road

or of George Oppen in "Of Being Numerous" (*Collected Poems*, 1974):

It is the air of atrocity,
An event as ordinary
As a President.

A plume of smoke, visible at a distance
In which people burn.

And in the avant-garde journal *L = A = N = G = U = A = G = E*, a group of poets, most of whom are still too young and too little known to be represented in this volume – Charles Bernstein, Ray di Palma, Steve McCaffrey, Douglas Messerli, Michael Lally – as well as some more familiar ones like Larry Eigner, Tom Clark, Michael Brownstein, and Jackson Mac Low – are performing experiments with the decomposition of language, the dismantling of normal syntax and word usage so as to create a new language field. The *L = A = N = G = U = A = G = E* poets look both to Gertrude Stein and to William Carlos Williams as their models, but perhaps the greatest Minimalist of all is the Beckett of "Ping," "Imagination Dead Imagine," "Fizzles," or "Lessness" – works that students of poetry (as opposed to drama and fiction) have oddly ignored.

"The contrary motive of overload," writes Kostelanetz, "informs such serial compositions as Milton Babbitt's *Relata 1* (1964), which presents an awesomely large number of discrete musical events in remarkably few minutes, or James Joyce's *Finnegans Wake*, where several stories, in several languages, are rendered on a single page." Overload is, in other words, simply the reverse side of minimalism. *Gunslinger*, mentioned earlier, is a prime example, but so are the "novels" and parodic poems of the New York School: for example, James Schuyler's *The Home Book* (1977), Barbara Guest's *Seeking Air* (1978), and the recent prose poems of Kathleen Fraser. John Ashbery's cut-up poem "Europe," dismissed by certain critics as excessively disorderly and pointless, is a fine example of overload.

Intermedia, to my mind the most significant of Kostelanetz's "three generative principles," refers to "the new art forms that were invented by marrying the materials and/or concepts of one traditional genre with another (or others), or by integrating art itself with something previously considered nonartistic." Concrete Poetry was, of course, an early manifestation of the belief that the typography and lay-out of poetic texts creates its own range of meanings, a doctrine that can be traced back to Dada. But in the past decade, the more extreme forms of Concretism (as in the poetry of Ian Hamilton Finlay, bp Nichol, Aram Saroyan, and Mary Ellen Solt) have given way to a broader interest in what is now called Visible Language, a phenomenon not at all restricted to Minimalist forms. The publication of Zukofsky's *"A"* in the year of the poet's death in 1978, will undoubtedly lead to some interesting studies of Visible Language, and the *L = A = N = G = U = A = G = E* group discussed above is, as its very name indicates, committed to the verbal-visual conjunction.

The relation of word to image is also found in the genre called "the artist's book," a genre that again can be traced back to Dada and Surrealism. Charles Tomlinson's collage-drawings in *In Black and White* are closely related to his sequence of prose poems called "Processes," although they are not printed in the same volume. Richard Howard's *Misgivings* (1979) contains a series of dramatic addresses to famous 19th-century figures photographed by Nadar, each poem being placed on the facing page of the Nadar photograph in question. Or again, in the delightful *Mobile Homes* (1980), Rudy Burkhardt takes portfolios of his own earlier photographs and juxtaposes them to pieces of a journal, prose sketches, poems, and playlets. Ron Padgett's *Tulsa Kid* (1980) creates a similar collage using cartoons rather than photographs. The artist's book will surely become an important genre in the years to come.

Meanwhile, intermedia involving word and music has given us what is now known as Sound Poetry. The father of Sound Poetry is surely John Cage; such performances as *Empty Words*, made up of sentences, phrases, words, and syllables taken from the journals of Thoreau, is at once musical and "poetic" – the verbal configurations, ever shifting and continually surprising in their variousness, are sometimes mimetic, sometimes abstract; they employ such "musical" devices as intervals and scales. In England, Michael Horovitz has worked with sound poetry, and there are now regular sound poetry festivals in many parts of the world, for example, "The Four Horsemen" in Toronto.

This brings me to a larger question: the role of *free verse* in late 20th-century poetry. Most theorists agree, I believe, that free verse is no longer a mode of defamiliarization, that it has become, on the contrary, the tedious norm. We are now as accustomed to free-verse poems, relating a particular personal experience in Imagist terms, as the Elizabethans were to the Petrarchan sonnet. To innovate in 1980 means, accordingly, to go beyond the free verse aesthetic of the 1960's: the breathless, end-stopped lines of Robert Bly or James Wright. One way to get around the "free verse problem" is to play off the linear base against the overriding syntax of the sentence and paragraph, much as earlier poets played off the speech rhythms of free verse against the iambic pentameter norm. A poem like Robert Hass's "Meditation at Lagunitas" calls attention to itself as a single, coherent paragraph, whose elements are always in tension with the line. Other poets, as diverse as Russell Edson, W. S. Merwin, Michael Benedikt, and Larry Eigner, have turned to the prose poem as a way out of the free verse impasse. Again, a "talk poet" like David Antin will utilize what Northrop Frye calls the "associative rhythm," his norm being not the sentence or verse line but the short fragmentary unit of ordinary speech, placed in the repetitive patterns of seemingly natural (but actually formalized in subtle ways) discourse. Still other poets – Donald Davie, Geoffrey Hill, Thom Gunn, Seamus Heaney – are returning to traditional metres and stanza forms: the ballad, the villanelle, the sestina, even the sonnet. At its best, as in Davie's "Three for Watermusic," a set of subtle and intricate meditations on our capacity to create myths and to believe in them, such recreation of fixed forms (here, heroic couplets, five-line trimeter stanzas rhyming abcb, and so on) is surely an example of Making It New.

Such consideration of traditionalism brings me back full circle to the point where I began: the neo-Edwardian or neo-Victorian lyric of a John Finlay or an Anthony Hecht. By now it will, I hope, be evident that the poetry of 1980 can only be "traditional" with a difference. To write a quatrain poem today involves a self-consciousness quite uncharacteristic of even the more mannered *fin-de-siècle* poets; its use requires the special tact of a Davie or a Hill. In the context of composition by field and fragmented narrative, of indeterminacy and suspensiveness, of visible language, sound poetry, performance art, of prose compositions that insist on being read as "poetry" and of ethnopoetics, the "traditional" poems currently most fashionable begin to remind one of the "Gothic" facades of Viollet-le-Duc. Behind those impressively intricate towers and turrets, the language of poetry is being recharged. For the Arthur Rackham fairy-tale castle we long for in our more nostalgic moments is, as John Ashbery puts it in "Valentine," "a house of cards.... and it is also built on/Shifting sands."

MARJORIE PERLOFF

EDITOR'S NOTE

The selection of poets included in this book is based upon the recommendations of the advisers listed on page xvii.

The entry for each poet included consists of a biography, a full bibliography, a comment by the poet on his verse if he chose to make one, and a signed critical essay on his work.

Only those critical studies recommended by the entrant have been listed. British and United States editions of all books have been listed; other editions are listed only if they are the first editions.

An appendix of entries has been included for some 22 poets who have died since 1950 but whose reputations are essentially contemporary.

We would like to thank the entrants and contributors for their patience and cooperation in helping us compile this book.

ADVISERS

Donald Allen
James Bertram
Earle Birney
Edward Kamau Brathwaite
Hayden Carruth
John Robert Colombo
John Cotton
James A. Emanuel
G. S. Fraser
Donald Hall
Thomas Kinsella
Maurice Lindsay
Edward Lucie-Smith
Roland Mathias
Ralph J. Mills, Jr.
John Montague
William Plomer
Arthur Ravenscroft
Howard Sergeant
Martin Seymour-Smith
Thomas W. Shapcott
A. J. M. Smith
C. K. Stead
Douglas Stewart
Allen Tate
Anthony Thwaite
Robert Vas Dias

CONTRIBUTORS

Abdul Majid Bin Nabi Baksh
Duane Ackerson
Fleur Adcock
James Aitchison
Peter Alcock
Michael André
David Astle
Jane Augustine
Houston A. Baker, Jr.
Roger Baker
Bruce Beaver
D. R. Beeton
Charles G. Bell
Leonidas V. Benesa
Carol Bergé
Bernard Bergonzi
James Bertram
Jennifer Birkett
Harold Bloom
Carl Bode
Walter Bode
Elmer Borklund
Corrine E. Bostic
Robert Boyers
Gaynor F. Bradish
Edward Kamau Brathwaite
Lloyd W. Brown
Alan Brownjohn
George Bruce
Joseph Bruchac
Jim Burns
George F. Butterick
Don Byrd
Edward Callan
Rivers Carew
Hayden Carruth
D. D. C. Chambers
Samuel Charters
Paul Christensen
Richard Church
Alan Clark
Austin Clarke
Anne Cluysenaar
Arthur A. Cohen
John Robert Colombo
William Cookson
John R. Cooley
Seamus Cooney
Neil Corcoran
John Cotton
Patricia Craig
Tony Curtis
Richard Damashek
Michael Davidson
Anthony Delius
R. H. W. Dillard
Dale Doepke
Max Dorsinville
David Dowling
Charles Doyle
Louis Dudek
Douglas Dunn
Gavin Ewart
Lloyd Fernando
Ian Fletcher
G. S. Fraser

Norman Friedman
Robin Fulton
Sally M. Gall
Norman T. Gates
Edward B. Germain
S. R. Gilbert
Michael Gnarowski
Lois Gordon
Alvin Greenberg
Thom Gunn
Ralph Gustafson
Rodney Hall
Ruth Harnett
David M. Heaton
Geof Hewitt
William Heyen
Douglas Hill
John Hinchey
Philip Hobsbaum
Jacqueline Hoefer
Daniel Hoffman
Jan Hokenson
Eric Homberger
Theodore R. Hudson
Charles L. James
Louis James
Elizabeth Jennings
Eldred D. Jones
Nancy Keesing
Burton Kendle
Brendan Kennelly
James Korges
Richard Kostelanetz
Norbert Krapf
Stanley W. Lindberg
Carl Lindner
Maurice Lindsay
Edward Lucie-Smith
Glenna Luschei
Dennis Lynch
Michael Lynch
Norman MacCaig
Roy Macnab
Roland Mathias
William Matthews
John Matthias
E. L. Mayo
George McElroy
David Meltzer
Ralph J. Mills, Jr.
Robert Miola
Shankar Mokashi-Punekar
John Mole
Charles Molesworth
John Montague
Edwin Morgan
Norman Moser
Meenakshi Mukherjee
Rosalie Murphy
S. Nagarajan
Rudolph L. Nelson
John Newlove
Leslie Norris
Robert Nye
William Oxley
Jerry Paris
Joseph Parisi
Derek Parker
Jay S. Paul
E. Pereira
Marjorie Perloff
Kirsten Holst Petersen
William Plomer
Peter Porter
John Press
Dudley Randall
Julia Randall
David Ray
J. C. Reid
John M. Reilly
Colin Rickards
James K. Robinson
Alan Roddick
Judith Rodriguez
Lawrence Russ
Anna Rutherford
Carol Lee Saffioti
Andreas Schroeder
Alexander Scott
Peter Scupham
Howard Sergeant
Martin Seymour-Smith
Thomas W. Shapcott
David Shapiro
J. N. Sharma
Alan R. Shucard
Jon Silkin
A. J. M. Smith
Stan Smith
Kendrick Smithyman
Radcliffe Squires
William Stafford
Donald Barlow Stauffer
C. K. Stead
Carol Simpson Stern
Holly Stevens
Joan Stevens
Anne Stevenson
Douglas Stewart
Mark Strand

Lucien Stryk
Rosemary Sullivan
William Sylvester
Julian Symons
John Taggart
Henry Taylor
Myron Taylor
Arthur Terry
Edwin Thumboo
Anthony Thwaite
Anne Tibble
Saundra Towns
John Tripp
Michael True
Constantine Trypanis
James Tulip
Roland Turner
John Van Domelen
Mark Van Doren
Robert Vas Dias
K. Venkatachari
Linda Wagner
Diane Wakoski
William Walsh
Eliot Weinberger
James Whitehead
John Stuart Williams
Margaret Willy
Joseph Wilson
George Woodcock
Judith Wright
Leopoldo Y. Yabes
Steven Young

CONTEMPORARY POETS

Dannie Abse
Chinua Achebe
Milton Acorn
Helen Adam
Léonie Adams
Perseus Adams
Robert Adamson
Fleur Adcock
Rewi Alley
A. Alvarez
Kingsley Amis
A. R. Ammons
Michael Anania
Jon Anderson
Carlos A. Angeles
David Antin
Sarah Appleton
John Ashbery
Margaret Atwood
Alvin Aubert
Margaret Avison
Kofi Awoonor

Howard Baker
Gavin Bantock
Douglas Barbour
George Barker
Gene Baro
Taner Baybars
Bruce Beaver
Samuel Beckett
John Beecher
Patricia Beer
Henry Beissel
Ben Belitt
Charles G. Bell
Marvin Bell
Michael Benedikt
Louise Bennett
Asa Benveniste
Anne Beresford
Stephen Berg
Carol Bergé
Bill Berkson
Daniel Berrigan
Ted Berrigan
Francis Berry
Wendell Berry
James Bertolino
John Betjeman
Earle Birney
Elizabeth Bishop
Bill Bissett
David Black
Robin Blaser
John Blight

Robert Bly
Charles Boer
Alan Bold
Martin Booth
Philip Booth
Keith Bosley
Ronald Bottrall
George Bowering
Edgar Bowers
Kay Boyle
John Brandi
Edward Kamau Brathwaite
Richard Emil Braun
Richard Brautigan
Ray Bremser
Kwesi Brew
Elizabeth Brewster
John Malcolm Brinnin
Edwin Brock
David Bromige
William Bronk
Gwendolyn Brooks
James Broughton
George Mackay Brown
Sterling Brown
Wayne Brown
Michael Dennis Browne
Alan Brownjohn
Michael Brownstein
George Bruce
Dennis Brutus
Tom Buchan
George Buchanan
Vincent Buckley
Charles Bukowski
Michael Bullock
Basil Bunting
William Burford
Kenneth Burke
Jim Burns
Stanley Burnshaw
Guy Butler

Alistair Campbell
David Campbell
Donald Campbell
George Campbell
Paul Carroll
Hayden Carruth
Martin Carter
Michael Casey
Charles Causley
Syl Cheyney-Coker
John Ciardi
John Pepper Clark
Leonard Clark

Tom Clark
Gillian Clarke
Jack Clemo
Lucille Clifton
Sydney Clouts
Anne Cluysenaar
Bob Cobbing
Frederick Cogswell
Leonard Cohen
Barry Cole
Elliott Coleman
Laurence Collinson
Frank A. Collymore
John Robert Colombo
Alex Comfort
Stewart Conn
Tony Connor
Robert Conquest
Anthony Conran
Stanley Cook
Clark Coolidge
Jane Cooper
Hilary Corke
Cid Corman
Alfred Corn
Sam Cornish
John William Corrington
Gregory Corso
John Cotton
Henri Coulette
Jeni Couzyn
Malcolm Cowley
Louis Coxe
Robert Creeley
Judson Crews
Kevin Crossley-Holland
Victor Hernández Cruz
Marcus Cumberlege
J. V. Cunningham
Allen Curnow
R. N. Currey

Peter Dale
Ruth Dallas
Robert Dana
Roy Daniells
D. K. Das
Kamala Das
Frank Davey
Michael Davidson
Donald Davie
Peter Davison
Bruce Dawe
Robert Dederick
Anthony Delius
Ricaredo Demetillo
James Den Boer
Babette Deutsch
James Dickey
R. P. Dickey
William Dickey
Patric Dickinson
R. H. W. Dillard
Diane di Prima
Rosemary Dobson
Ed Dorn
Basil Dowling
Freda Downie
Charles Doyle
Norman Dubie
Louis Dudek
Alan Dugan
Robert Duncan
Ronald Duncan
Douglas Dunn
Stephen Dunn
Lawrence Durrell
Geoffrey Dutton
Bob Dylan

Charles Edward Eaton
Richard Eberhart
Michael Echeruo
George Economou
Russell Edson
Larry Eigner
George P. Elliott
Kenward Elmslie
James A. Emanuel
William Empson
Paul Engle
Maurice English
D. J. Enright
Theodore Enslin
Clayton Eshleman
Federico Espino
Abbie Huston Evans
Mari Evans
Gloria Evans Davies
Ronald Everson
William Everson
Peter Everwine
Gavin Ewart
Nissim Ezekiel

Ruth Fainlight
John Fairfax
Colin Falck
Elaine Feinstein
Irving Feldman
James Fenton
Lawrence Ferlinghetti

Thomas Hornsby Ferril
Doug Fetherling
Edward Field
John Figueroa
Robert Finch
Donald Finkel
Ian Hamilton Finlay
Joan Finnigan
Roy Fisher
Robert Fitzgerald
Robert D. FitzGerald
Ian Fletcher
Charles Henri Ford
R. A. D. Ford
Gene Fowler
Janet Frame
Robert Francis
G. S. Fraser
Kathleen Fraser
Christopher Fry
John Fuller
Roy Fuller
Robin Fulton

Vi Gale
Tess Gallagher
Isabella Stewart Gardner
Roger Garfitt
Robert Garioch
Raymond Garlick
George Garrett
David Gascoyne
Gary Geddes
Karen Gershon
Brewster Ghiselin
Zulfikar Ghose
Monk Gibbon
Ruth Gilbert
David Gill
Valerie Gillies
Allen Ginsberg
Nikki Giovanni
Robert Gittings
John Glassco
Duncan Glen
Denis Glover
Louise Glück
Michael Gnarowski
Denis Goacher
Patricia Goedicke
Albert Goldbarth
Giles Gordon
Phyllis Gotlieb
Henry Graham
W. S. Graham
Robert Graves

Jonathan Greene
Arthur Gregor
Horace Gregory
Jonathan Griffin
Bryn Griffiths
Geoffrey Grigson
Frederick Grubb
Peter Gruffydd
Barbara Guest
Harry Guest
Charles Gullans
Thom Gunn
Ralph Gustafson
Don Gutteridge

Marilyn Hacker
John Haines
Donald Hall
J. C. Hall
Rodney Hall
Daniel Halpern
Michael Hamburger
Ian Hamilton
Christopher Hampton
Kenneth O. Hanson
Pauline Hanson
Michael S. Harper
Wilson Harris
Jim Harrison
Keith Harrison
Tony Harrison
David Harsent
William Hart-Smith
Michael Hartnett
Gwen Harwood
Lee Harwood
Robert Hass
Robert Hayden
H. R. Hays
Samuel Hazo
Seamus Heaney
John Heath-Stubbs
Anthony Hecht
Michael D. Heller
David Helwig
Hamish Henderson
A. L. Hendriks
Adrian Henri
Rayner Heppenstall
Calvin C. Hernton
Phoebe Hesketh
Dorothy Hewett
Geof Hewitt
John Hewitt
William Heyen
Charles Higham

Geoffrey Hill
Daryl Hine
Jack Hirschman
George Hitchcock
Philip Hobsbaum
Sandra Hochman
Daniel Hoffman
David Holbrook
Molly Holden
John Hollander
Anselm Hollo
Geoffrey Holloway
John Holloway
Edwin Honig
Jeremy Hooker
A. D. Hope
Frances Horovitz
Michael Horovitz
Katherine Hoskins
dom Sylvester Houédard
Richard Howard
Anthony Howell
Barbara Howes
Harry Howith
Andrew Hoyem
Alejandrino G. Hufana
Robert Huff
Glyn Hughes
Ted Hughes
Richard Hugo
Sam Hunt
Pearse Hutchinson
Daniel Huws

David Ignatow
Kenneth Irby
Kevin Ireland
Valentin Iremonger

Alan Jackson
Paul Jacob
Josephine Jacobsen
David Jaffin
Peter Jay
Elizabeth Jennings
Judson Jerome
Louis Johnson
Ronald Johnson
George Johnston
George Jonas
Brian Jones
D. G. Jones
Evan Jones
Glyn Jones
LeRoi Jones
Erica Jong
June Jordan
Jenny Joseph
M. K. Joseph
Donald Justice

Lenore Kandel
P. J. Kavanagh
Lionel Kearns
Richard Kell
Robert Kelly
X. J. Kennedy
Brendan Kennelly
Milton Kessler
Keorapetse Kgositsile
Galway Kinnell
Thomas Kinsella
James Kirkup
Carolyn Kizer
Etheridge Knight
John Knoepfle
Bill Knott
Kenneth Koch
Arun Kolatkar
James Koller
Bernard Kops
Richard Kostelanetz
Shiv K. Kumar
Maxine Kumin
Stanley Kunitz
Joanne Kyger

P. Lal
Philip Lamantia
Patrick Lane
Joseph Langland
Philip Larkin
Richmond Lattimore
James Laughlin
Irving Layton
Dennis Lee
Don L. Lee
Laurie Lee
Owen Leeming
Geoffrey Lehmann
John Lehmann
Tom Leonard
Douglas LePan
Laurence Lerner
Christopher Levenson
Denise Levertov
Peter Levi
Philip Levine
Larry Levis
John L'Heureux
Laurence Lieberman
Lyn Lifshin

Maurice Lindsay
Lou Lipsitz
Dorothy Livesay
Douglas Livingstone
Taban lo Liyong
Liz Lochhead
Ron Loewinsohn
John Logan
Christopher Logue
Michael Longley
Audre Lorde
Edward Lowbury
Edward Lucie-Smith

Lewis MacAdams
George MacBeth
Norman MacCaig
Gwendolyn MacEwen
Alastair Mackie
Alasdair Maclean
Archibald MacLeish
Joseph Macleod
Jackson Mac Low
Roy Macnab
Jay Macpherson
Barry MacSweeney
Charles Madge
Wes Magee
Derek Mahon
Clarence Major
David Malouf
Eli Mandel
Bill Manhire
John Manifold
Jack Marshall
Sid Marty
Harold Massingham
William H. Matchett
Roland Mathias
William Matthews
Gerda Mayer
Seymour Mayne
E. L. Mayo
James J. McAuley
Michael McClure
Ronald McCuaig
Roger McDonald
David McFadden
Roy McFadden
Roger McGough
Thomas McGrath
Tom McKeown
Anthony McNeill
Sandra McPherson
George McWhirter
Matthew Mead

Arvind Krishna Mehrotra
David Meltzer
William Meredith
James Merrill
W. S. Merwin
Bert Meyers
Robert Mezey
James Michie
Christopher Middleton
Josephine Miles
Vassar Miller
Eric Millward
Ewart Milne
Adrian Mitchell
David Mitchell
John Moat
Judith Moffett
Shankar Mokashi-Punekar
John Mole
John Montague
Nicholas Moore
Dom Moraes
Edwin Morgan
Frederick Morgan
Pete Morgan
Robert Morgan
Howard Moss
Stanley Moss
Oswald Mtshali
Ian Mudie
Paul Muldoon
Richard Murphy
Les A. Murray
Susan Musgrave

Pritish Nandy
Leonard Nathan
Adèle Naudé
Larry Neal
Howard Nemerov
John Newlove
Barrie Phillip Nichol
Norman Nicholson
John Frederick Nims
Leslie Norris
Harold Norse
Kathleen Nott
Alden Nowlan
Jeff Nuttall
Robert Nye

Philip Oakes
Ned O'Gorman
Desmond O'Grady
John Okai
Gabriel Okara

Elder Olson
Toby Olson
Michael Ondaatje
George Oppen
Joel Oppenheimer
John Ormond
Frank Ormsby
Simon J. Ortiz
Vincent O'Sullivan
Rochelle Owens
William Oxley

Robert Pack
Ron Padgett
P. K. Page
Michael Palmer
Thomas Parkinson
R. Parthasarathy
Betty Parvin
Linda Pastan
Alistair Paterson
Brian Patten
Raymond R. Patterson
Tom Paulin
Basil Payne
Okot p'Bitek
Grace Perry
Lenrie Peters
Donald Petersen
Paul Petrie
W. H. Petty
Tom Pickard
Marge Piercy
William Pillin
Christopher Pilling
Robert Pinsky
Kenneth Pitchford
Ruth Pitter
Allen Planz
Stanley Plumly
Ralph Pomeroy
Hal Porter
Peter Porter
A. Poulin, Jr.
Craig Powell
Neil Powell
F. T. Prince
Frederic Prokosch
J. H. Prynne
A. G. Prys-Jones
Sally Purcell
Al Purdy
Rodney Pybus

Craig Raine
Kathleen Raine

Carl Rakosi
A. K. Ramanujan
Paul Ramsey
Dudley Randall
Julia Randall
Margaret Randall
Tom Raworth
David Ray
James Reaney
Peter Redgrove
Henry Reed
Ishmael Reed
F. D. Reeve
Alastair Reid
Kenneth Rexroth
Adrienne Rich
Edgell Rickword
Laura Riding
Anne Ridler
Philip Roberts
Roland Robinson
Jeremy Robson
Paul Roche
Alan Roddick
Stephen Rodefer
Carolyn M. Rodgers
Edouard Roditi
Judith Rodriguez
Alan Rook
William Pitt Root
Raymond Roseliep
Joe Rosenblatt
M. L. Rosenthal
Alan Ross
Jerome Rothenberg
David Rowbotham
J. R. Rowland
A. L. Rowse
Larry Rubin
Anthony Rudolf
Muriel Rukeyser
Peter Russell
Vern Rutsala

Bruce St. John
Sonia Sanchez
Ed Sanders
Stephen Sandy
Reg Saner
Aram Saroyan
May Sarton
Teo Savory
Vernon Scannell
James Schevill
Michael Schmidt
Dennis Schmitz

Andreas Schroeder
James Schuyler
Armand Schwerner
Alexander Scott
F. R. Scott
Tom Scott
E. J. Scovell
James Scully
Peter Scupham
Frederick Seidel
Howard Sergeant
A. J. Seymour
Martin Seymour-Smith
Thomas W. Shapcott
David Shapiro
Harvey Shapiro
Karl Shapiro
Richard Shelton
Judith Johnson Sherwin
Penelope Shuttle
Glen Siebrasse
Jon Silkin
Alan Sillitoe
Charles Simic
James Simmons
Louis Simpson
R. A. Simpson
Keith Sinclair
C. H. Sisson
Sacheverell Sitwell
Robin Skelton
Knute Skinner
David Slavitt
A. J. M. Smith
Dave Smith
Iain Crichton Smith
John Smith
Ken Smith
Michael Smith
Vivian Smith
William Jay Smith
Elizabeth Smither
Kendrick Smithyman
W. D. Snodgrass
Gary Snyder
Mary Ellen Solt
Gilbert Sorrentino
Raymond Souster
Wole Soyinka
Barry Spacks
Muriel Spark
Francis Sparshott
Charles Spear
Stephen Spender
Radcliffe Squires
William Stafford
Jon Stallworthy
Ann Stanford
George Stanley
George Starbuck
C. K. Stead
Stephen Stepanchev
Alan Stephens
Meic Stephens
Gerald Stern
Peter Stevens
Anne Stevenson
Douglas Stewart
Harold Stewart
Adrien Stoutenburg
Randolph Stow
Mark Strand
Lucien Stryk
Dabney Stuart
Andrew Suknaski, Jr.
Hollis Summers
Robert Sward
May Swenson
Julian Symons

John Tagliabue
Nathaniel Tarn
James Tate
Andrew Taylor
D. M. Thomas
R. S. Thomas
Derick S. Thomson
Anthony Thwaite
Edith Tiempo
Terence Tiller
Richard Tillinghast
Charles Tomlinson
Rosemary Tonks
Emmanuel Torres
Shirley Toulson
Philip Toynbee
John Tranter
Sydney Tremayne
John Tripp
Constantine Trypanis
Lewis Turco
Gael Turnbull
W. Price Turner
Hone Tuwhare

John Updike
Constance Urdang

Jean Valentine
Mona Van Duyn
Monika Varma
Robert Vas Dias

Peter Viereck
José Garcia Villa
R. G. Vliet

Miriam Waddington
David Wagoner
John Wain
Diane Wakoski
Derek Walcott
Anne Waldman
Margaret Walker
Ted Walker
Chris Wallace-Crabbe
Chad Walsh
Francis Warner
Rex Warner
Robert Penn Warren
Lewis Warsh
Robert Watson
Roderick Watson
Wilfred Watson
Tom Wayman
Harri Webb
Phyllis Webb
Richard Weber
Ian Wedde
Theodore Weiss
Daniel Weissbort
James Welch
Anne Welsh
David Wevill
Philip Whalen
Peter Whigham
Laurence Whistler
Thomas Whitbread
Ivan White
Kenneth White
James Whitehead
Ruth Whitman
Reed Whittemore
John Wieners
Richard Wilbur
Peter Wild
Nancy Willard
C. K. Williams
Emmett Williams
Gwyn Williams
Herbert Williams
Hugo Williams
John Stuart Williams
Jonathan Williams
Miller Williams
Margaret Willy
Keith Wilson
Sheila Wingfield
Hubert Witheford
Wong May
Wong Phui Nam
George Woodcock
John Woods
Charles Wright
David Wright
James Wright
Judith Wright
Kit Wright

J. Michael Yates
Al Young
David Young
Ian Young

Marya Zaturenska
Paul Zimmer
Harriet Zinnes
Lotte Zurndorfer

APPENDIX

W. H. Auden
James K. Baxter
John Berryman
Paul Blackburn
Jean Garrigue
Randall Jarrell
Patrick Kavanagh
Robert Lowell
Frank O'Hara
Christopher Okigbo
Charles Olson
Kenneth Patchen
Sylvia Plath
Theodore Roethke
Delmore Schwartz
Anne Sexton
Burns Singer
Stevie Smith
Sydney Goodsir Smith
Jack Spicer
Vernon Watkins
Louis Zukofsky

ABSE, Dannie. Welsh. Born in Cardiff, Glamorgan, 22 September 1923. Educated at St. Illyd's College, Cardiff; University of South Wales and Monmouthshire, Cardiff; King's College, London; Westminster Hospital, London; qualified as physician, M.R.C.S., L.R.C.P. Served in the Royal Air Force, rising to the rank of Squadron Leader. Married Joan Mercer in 1951; three children. Writer-in-Residence, Princeton University, New Jersey, 1973–74. Since 1978, President, Poetry Society. Recipient: Foyle Award, 1960; Welsh Arts Council award, for verse, 1971. Agent: (drama) Margery Vosper Ltd., Suite 8, 26 Charing Cross Road, London WC2H 0DE; (literary) Anthony Shiel Associates Ltd., 2–3 Morwell Street, London, WC1B 3AR. Address: 85 Hodford Road, London N.W.11, England.

PUBLICATIONS

Verse

After Every Green Thing. London, Hutchinson, 1949.
Walking under Water. London, Hutchinson, 1952.
Tenants of the House. London, Hutchinson, 1957; New York, Criterion, 1958.
Poems, Golders Green. London, Hutchinson, 1962.
Dannie Abse: A Selection. London, Studio Vista, 1963.
A Small Desperation. London, Hutchinson, 1968.
Selected Poems. London, Hutchinson, and New York, Oxford University Press, 1970.
Funland: A Poem in Nine Parts. Portland, Oregon, Portland University Press, 1971.
Corgi Modern Poets in Focus 4, with others, edited by Jeremy Robson. London, Corgi, 1972.
Funland and Other Poems. London, Hutchinson, and New York, Oxford University Press, 1973.
Lunchtime. London, Poem-of-the-Month Club, 1974.
Penguin Modern Poets 26, with D. J. Enright and Michael Longley. London, Penguin, 1975.
Collected Poems 1948–1976. London, Hutchinson, and Pittsburgh, University of Pittsburgh Press, 1977.

Recording: *Poets of Wales*, Argo, 1972.

Plays

Fire in Heaven (produced London, 1948). London, Hutchinson, 1956; revised version, as *Is the House Shut?* (produced London, 1964); revised version, as *In the Cage*, in *Three Questor Plays*, 1967.
Hands Around the Wall (produced London, 1950).
House of Cowards (produced London, 1960). Included in *Three Questor Plays*, 1967; in *Twelve Great Plays*, edited by Leonard F. Dean, New York, Harcourt Brace, 1970.
The Eccentric (produced London, 1961). London, Evans, 1961.
Gone (produced London, 1962). Included in *Three Questor Plays*, 1967.
The Joker (produced London, 1962).
Three Questor Plays (includes *House of Cowards*, *Gone*, *In the Cage).* London, Scorpion Press, 1967.
The Dogs of Pavlov (produced London, 1969; New York, 1974). London, Vallentine Mitchell, 1973.
The Courting of Essie Glass (broadcast, 1975). Published in *The Jewish Quarterly* (London), 1972.
Funland (produced London, 1975).
Pythagoras (produced Birmingham, 1976). London, Hutchinson, 1979.
Gone in January (produced London, 1978).

Radio Plays: *Conform or Die*, 1957; *No Telegrams, No Thunder*, 1962; *You Can't Say Hello to Anybody*, 1964; *A Small Explosion*, 1964; *The Courting of Essie Glass*, 1975.

Novels

Ash on a Young Man's Sleeve. London, Hutchinson, 1954; New York, Criterion, 1955.
Some Corner of an English Field. London, Hutchinson, 1956; New York, Criterion, 1957.
O. Jones, O. Jones. London, Hutchinson, 1970.

Other

Medicine on Trial. London, Aldus Books, 1967; New York, Crown, 1969.
A Poet in the Family (autobiography). London, Hutchinson, 1974.

Editor, with Howard Sergeant, *Mavericks.* London, Editions Poetry and Poverty, 1957.
Editor, *European Verse.* London, Studio Vista, 1964.
Editor, *Corgi Modern Poets in Focus 1, 3, 5.* London, Corgi, 1971–73.
Editor, *Thirteen Poets.* London, Poetry Book Society, 1973.
Editor, *Poetry Dimension 2–5: The Best of the Poetry Year.* London, Robson, 1974–78; New York, St. Martin's Press, 1976–79; *The Best of the Poetry Year 6: Poetry Dimension*, 1979.

Critical Studies: Interviews in *Jewish Quarterly* (London), Winter 1962–63, *Flame* (Wivenhoe, Essex), March 1967, *Anglo-Welsh Review* (Tenby), Spring 1975, and *Three Poets, Two Children*, edited by Desmond Badham-Thornhill, Gloucester, Thornhill Press, 1975; "Poet on Poet" by Fleur Adcock, in *Ambit* (London), 1970; by Jeremy Robson, in *Corgi Modern Poets in Focus 4*, 1972; "In Celebration" by Renee Winegarten, in *Jewish Chronicle Literary Supplement* (London), 10 June 1977; "The Poetry of Dannie Abse" by Howard Sergeant, in *Books and Bookmen* (London), July 1977; "Predicament of Otherness" by John Pikoulis and "Dannie Abse Revisited" by John Tripp, both in *Poetry Wales* (Swansea), October 1977; by Raymond Gardner, in *The Guardian* (London), 31 January 1978.

* * *

After Every Green Thing, Dannie Abse's first book of poems, was declamatory, full of an eloquence natural to his gifted Jewish family background. His elder brother Leo, still and for many years M.P. for Pontypool, often spoke from a soap-box in Llandaff Fields and Dannie himself, a combative Socialist in a Catholic school, saw poetry as a generalised exposition of ideals and experiences, in which repetition and rhetoric were dominant features. When he became a medical student, first at Cardiff and then in London, the back pages of his notebooks were always "noisy with poems." This first work, notwithstanding its eloquent verbosity and the "publicness" of its poetic attitude (extended by Dannie's early practice in reading poetry to an audience), is attractive even when flawed, and his second book, *Walking under Water*, with its rejection of naivete and its much greater formal control, is at first sight a disappointment. But behind the new discipline, in which a variable refrain is often used to indicate the steps of the poetic argument and in which symbols as well as words are rigorously organised, the successes of the future were being prepared.

With *Tenants of the House* Dannie Abse emerged as a poet of undoubted significance. In this volume his hortatory intention is provided with a satisfactory vehicle and an understood destination. Briefly, an extended symbolic concept, itself the main or entire structure of the individual poem, uses the existing knowledge of the reader to make the narrative line or the poetic argument absolutely clear, enabling even the uninitiate among readers to "get at" the second level of meaning. Thus "Social Revolution in England" overtly presents a picture of a bewildered aristocratic household emptied by the bailiffs. His fondness for refrain, too, brought Abse at this stage to the discovery of a rhythmic structure which would carry the message of the poem just as well as an understood "picture." The nursery-rhyme basis of "The Trial" – "I'll sum up, the severe Judge moans/showing the white of his knucklebones" – provides an area of unconscious suggestion in which the "meaning" is far more easily grasped.

Always remarkable for the sensitivity and honesty of his search for poetic experience, Dannie Abse, in his next volume, *Poems, Golders Green*, moved back to quieter and more personal country. This collection was perhaps less uniformly successful than its predecessor, but it contains some halfdozen very fine poems, amongst which "Return to Cardiff" (most of all for the scrupulousness of its "point") is outstanding:

> Unable to define anything I can hardly speak
> and still I love the place for what I wanted it to be
> as much as for what it unashamedly is
> now for me, a city of strangers, alien and bleak.

In *A Small Desperation* he made more obvious both the width of his interest and the variety of formal treatment he was prepared to give to poetry. The original eloquence entirely "gritted down," he brought his vocational knowledge of medicine into greater play, and his self-criticism, amused as well as searching, gave him an approach to "the condition of man" which is as little limited as are his moods. *Funland and Other Poems*, while making use of the title sequence to return to the extended allegory, an irreverent and surrealist picture of modern substitutes for faith, also went back to Wales more often. In this volume are to be found some of Dannie Abse's most memorable short poems (like "A New Diary" and "An Old Commitment") and the few additions to *Collected Poems* confirm that his costive publication (no more than five or six poems a year) is making less and less fallible the amalgam of irony, wit, and irreducible sentiment which the imagination he applies to simple and colloquial language so marvellously shapes. That he takes risks and pulls them off "Cousin Sidney" (with its repeated "silly ass") admirably illustrates, and his dream of Nell Gwynn in "The Test" points his success in keeping both preciousness and portentousness out of his writing. Dannie Abse's poetry is humane without being predictable, sensitive without seeking to screw the language tight on the reader's thumb. In all that he writes he is his own man, an important voice out of the midst of a confused generation.

—Roland Mathias

ACHEBE, Chinua. Nigerian. Born Albert Chinualumogu in Ogidi, 16 November 1930. Educated at Government College, Umuahia, 1944–47; University College, Ibadan, 1948–53, B.A. (London) 1953. Married Christie Okoli in 1961; four children. Talks Producer, Lagos, 1954–57, Controller, Enugu, 1958–61, and Director, Lagos, 1961–66, Nigerian Broadcasting Corporation. Chairman, Citadel Books Ltd., Enugu, 1967. Since 1967, Senior Research Fellow, University of Nigeria, Nsukka. Visiting Professor, University of Massachusetts, Amherst, 1972–75, and University of Connecticut, Storrs, 1975–76. Since 1962, Founding

Editor, Heinemann African Writers series, and since 1970 Director, Heinemann Educational Books (Nigeria) Ltd., and Nwankwo-Ifejika Ltd., later Nwamife, publishers, Enugu. Since 1971, Editor, *Okike*, an African journal of new writing. Member, University of Lagos Council, 1966; Chairman, Society of Nigerian Authors, 1966. Recipient: Margaret Wrong Memorial Prize, 1959; Nigerian National Trophy, 1960; Rockefeller Fellowship, 1960; UNESCO Fellowship, 1963; Jock Campbell Award (*New Statesman*), 1965; Commonwealth Poetry Prize, 1973; Neil Gunn International Fellowship, 1974. D.Litt.: Dartmouth College, Hanover, New Hampshire, 1972; University of Southampton, 1974; University of Ife, 1978; D. Univ.: University of Stirling, 1974; LL.D.: University of Prince Edward Island, Charlottetown, 1976; D.H.L.: University of Massachusetts, 1977. Honorary Fellow, Modern Language Association of America, 1974. Address: University of Nigeria, Nsukka, Nigeria.

PUBLICATIONS

Verse

Beware Soul-Brother and Other Poems. Enugu, Nwankwo-Ifejika, 1971; revised edition, Enugu, Nwamife, and London, Heinemann, 1972.
Christmas in Biafra and Other Poems. New York, Doubleday, 1973.

Novels

Things Fall Apart. London, Heinemann, 1958; New York, McDowell Obolensky, 1959.
No Longer at Ease. London, Heinemann, 1960; New York, Obolensky, 1961.
Arrow of God. London, Heinemann, 1964; New York, Day, 1967.
A Man of the People. London, Heinemann, and New York, Day, 1966.

Short Stories

The Sacrificial Egg and Other Stories. Onitsha, Etudo, 1962.
Girls at War. London, Heinemann, and New York, Doubleday, 1972.

Other

Chike and the River (juvenile). London and New York, Cambridge University Press, 1966.
How the Leopard Got His Claws (juvenile). Enugu, Nwamife, 1972; New York, Third Press, 1973.
Morning Yet on Creation Day: Essays. London, Heinemann, and New York, Doubleday, 1975.
In Person: Achebe, Awoonor, and Soyinka at the University of Washington. Seattle, University of Washington African Studies Program, 1975.
The Flute (juvenile). Enugu, Fourth Dimenson, 1977.
The Drum (juvenile). Enugu, Fourth Dimension, 1977.

Editor, *The Insider: Stories of War and Peace from Nigeria.* Enugu, Nwankwo-Ifejika, and Chatham, New Jersey, Chatham Booksellers, 1971.
Co-Editor, *Don't Let Him Die.* Enugu, Fourth Dimension, 1978.

Critical Studies: *Chinua Achebe* by Arthur Ravenscroft, London, Longman, 1969; *Chinua Achebe* by David Carroll, New York, Twayne, 1970; *Chinua Achebe* edited by Bernth Lindfors and C. L. Innes, London, Heinemann, and Washington, D.C., Three Continents Press, 1978.

Chinua Achebe comments:

I am a political writer. My politics is concerned with universal human communication across racial and cultural boundaries as a means of fostering respect for all people. Such respect can issue only from understanding. So my primary concern is with clearing the channels of communication in my own neighbourhood by hacking away at the thickets that choke them.

Africa's meeting with Europe must be accounted a terrible disaster in this matter of human understanding and respect. The nature of the meeting precluded any warmth of friendship. First Europe was an enslaver; then a colonizer. In either role she had no need and made little effort to understand or appreciate Africa; indeed she easily convinced herself that there was nothing there to justify the effort. Today our world is still bedevilled by the consequences of that cataclysmic encounter.

I was born into the colonial era, grew up in the heady years of nationalist protest and witnessed Africa's resumption of independence. (It was not, however, the same Africa which originally lost her freedom that now regained it, but a different Africa created in the image of Europe – but that's another story.) So I have seen in my not very long lifetime three major eras in precipitate succession, leaving us somewhat dazed. My response as a writer has been to try to keep pace with these torrential changes. First I had to tell Europe that the arrogance on which she sought to excuse her pillage of Africa, i.e., that Africa was the Primordial Void, was sheer humbug; that Africa had a history, a religion, a civilization. We reconstructed this history and civilization and displayed it to challenge the stereotype and the cliché. Actually it was not to Europe alone I spoke. I spoke also to that part of ourselves that had come to accept Europe's opinion of us. And I was not alone nor even the first.

But the gauntlet had barely left our hands when a new historic phase broke on us. Europe conceded independence to us and we promptly began to misuse it, or rather those leaders to whom we entrusted the wielding of our new power and opportunity. So we got mad at them and came out brandishing novels of disenchantment. Actually we had all been duped. No independence was given – it is never given but taken, anyway. Europe had only made a tactical withdrawal on the political front and while we sang our anthem and unfurled our flag she was securing her iron grip behind us in the economic field. And our leaders in whose faces we hurled our disenchantment neither saw nor heard because they were not leaders at all but marionettes.

So the problem remains for Africa, for black people, for all deprived peoples and for the world. And so for the writer, for he is like the puppy in our proverb: that stagnant water in the potsherd is for none other but him. As long as one people sit on another and are deaf to their cry, so long will understanding and peace elude all of us.

* * *

With the publication of *Christmas in Biafra*, Chinua Achebe showed the kind of mature and sensitive voice which might make his book the kind of landmark in African writing which his first novel, *Things Fall Apart*, was fourteen years earlier.

Coming out of the incredible tragedy of a civil war, the poems show remarkable restraint, their language simple and careful, yet never lacking in depth. Their imagery, as in the first few lines of "After a War," is exact and intense: "After a war life catches/desperately at passing/hints of normalcy like/vines entwining a hollow/twig...." Many of the poems make use of biting irony, as in "Christmas in Biafra" where the seasonal music broadcast over the radio bears messages of "pure transcendental hate" and the starving mothers and children stare mutely at a manger where Jesus lies "plump-looking and rose-cheeked."

Not all of the poems are about the Biafran conflict, for Achebe ranges from personal statements to far-reaching satirical comments on Western foreign policy as in "He Loves Me; He Loves Me Not": "Harold Wilson he loves/me he gave me/a gun in my time/of need to shoot/my rebellious brother...." But Achebe's subject matter, as in his other writings, is rooted in the confused landscape of post-colonial Africa, where rotten politics and international deals affect the lives of people who still follow traditional paths. One of his best poems, "Beware, Soul Brother," which begins

> We are the men of soul
> men of song we measure out
> our joys and agonies
> too, our long, long passion week
> in paces of the dance

is a reminder to the African reader of his connection with the earth and warns against those "lying in wait leaden-footed, tone deaf/passionate only for the deep entrails/of our soil ...," yet it is also a poem for all human beings who remember

> where a man's
> foot must return whatever beauties
> it may weave in air, where
> it must return for safety
> and renewal of strength....

—Joseph Bruchac

ACORN, Milton. Canadian. Born in Charlottetown, Prince Edward Island, in 1923.

PUBLICATIONS

Verse

In Love and Anger. Privately printed, 1956.
The Brain's the Target. Toronto, Ryerson Press, 1960.
Against a League of Liars. Toronto, Hawkshead Press, 1960.
Jawbreakers. Toronto, Contact Press, 1963.
I've Tasted My Blood: Poems 1956 to 1968, edited by Al Purdy. Toronto, Ryerson Press, 1969.
I Shout Love and Shaving Off His Beard. Toronto, Village Book Store Press, 1971.
More Poems for People. Toronto, NC Press, 1972.
Jackpine Sonnets. Toronto, Steel Rail, 1977.

* * *

Milton Acorn, after serving in the Canadian armed forces in World War II, gravitated to Montreal where he settled in the 1950's. Here, he published his first book, and, with two other writers, the poet Al Purdy and the poet/novelist Gwen MacEwen (whom he later married) he edited the little magazine, *Moment* (1960–1962). Acorn moved to Toronto in the early 1960's, and established himself as a figure of some prominence in the freer and less "established" sectors of that city's literary life. One of the first "public" poets and readers on the coffee house poetry reading scene in Canada in the 1950's, Acorn used to frequent and was variously associated with some of the great coffee houses of the period: *viz.* L'Echourie,

El Cortijo, The Place, The Bohemian Embassy. He was honoured in a dramatic but genuine gesture by Canadian poets who presented him with the first Canadian Poets' Award in May of 1970 as an act of defiance and reproach aimed at the Governor General's Awards Committee which, with an American academic on its panel, had given the annual award to George Bowering and Gwendolyn MacEwen.

Milton Acorn is a poet of realistic statement and strong political feelings. A carpenter by training, he sees himself as a workingman's poet, and has taken a strong left-wing and nationalist stance. He says: "I have called myself many things; but I guess the one that sticks best is 'revolutionary poet' – that is 'revolutionary' in the political sense, not the poetic sense." From the outset, Acorn has written a poetry of direct, almost commonplace rhetoric, relying on hard, driving rhythms, and a near-palpable physicality of image. In scanning his own performance, Acorn has suggested that: "My own poetry, from 1956 on, has been built around the voice. I originally patterned the voice rhythm of my poems around that of the most intelligent (because the best-travelled and the best-read) of workers at that time – the merchant seamen."

Acorn's full range extends appreciably beyond the poetry of social and socialist concerns. He has a fine sense of locale which is revealed in his better poems which have to do with Maritime Canada; a certain lyrical bent which slides easily into his own peculiar kind of introspectiveness and poetic home-spun. Cragginess, a cragginess of mind and spirit, is Acorn's best quality:

> Since I'm Island-born home's as precise
> as if a mumbly old carpenter,
> shoulder-straps crossed wrong,
> laid it out,
> refigured to the last three-eighths of a shingle.

—Michael Gnarowski

ADAM, Helen (Douglas). British. Born in Glasgow, Lanark, 2 December 1909. Educated at Seymour Lodge; Navin Academy; University of Edinburgh for two years. Journalist in Edinburgh and London during the 1930's; moved to the United States in 1939, and worked at various office jobs in New York until 1949, then lived in California. Address: 223 East 82nd Street, New York, New York 10028, U.S.A.

PUBLICATIONS

Verse

The Elfin Pedlar and Tales Told by Pixy Pool. London, Hodder and Stoughton, 1923; New York, Putnam, 1924.
Charms and Dreams from the Elfin Pedlar's Pack. London, Hodder and Stoughton, 1924.
Shadow of the Moon. London, Hodder and Stoughton, 1929.
The Queen o' Crow Castle. San Francisco, White Rabbit Press, 1958.
Ballads. New York, Acadia Press, 1964.
Counting-Out Rhyme. New York, Interim, 1972.

Selected Poems and Ballads. New York, Helikon Press, 1974.
Ghosts and Grinning Shadows. Brooklyn, New York, Hanging Loose Press, 1977.
Turn Again to Me and Other Poems. New York, Kulchur, 1977.

Play

San Francisco's Burning, with Pat Adam (produced New York, 1966). Berkeley, California, Oannes, 1963.

* * *

Helen Adam was 30 before she emigrated from Scotland with her mother and sister. Born in Glasgow, she grew up in the coastal farming region of upper north Scotland, in Nairnshire, on Moray Firth, with its Neolithic ruins, its low-lying ground, and large private forests, the imagery and landscape of most of her poems. She worked as a journalist in Edinburgh and London before emigrating, and finally settled in San Francisco in 1953, where a poetic renaissance was in full flower. Her work gradually drew the attention of other poets, especially the appreciation of Robert Duncan, who has frequently praised her curious themes and ideas as a singular expression of the inner life. Indeed, she is without parallel in recent poetry in her recreation of medieval balladry and narrative – she writes in a patois of old Scots dialect and modern English, sounding very much like a transliteration of the old literature. But in fact her ballads and songs are entirely of her own composing and constitute a new extension of ballad tradition.

Her primary theme is love and the curious sort of underworld of spirits, demons, and allegorical monsters that inhabit the unconscious mind of any lover. Her landscapes are the forests and dark caves of medieval romance, the realm of unicorns, angels, mysterious gardens, all described with skillful allegorical awareness. In her recent *Selected Poems and Ballads* Adam chose poems that concentrate exclusively on the terror and grief of love – the havoc of jealousy, the desolation of stranded women, the powers of lust, the awesome and ghoulish revenge of the unrequited and jilted, the primal urgings of incest and cannibalism. All of these elements come together in a brief poem, "A Tale Best Forgotten," which narrates the awful fate of a male lover (most victims of her verse are males) who comes between a father and his daughter:

In the garden, in the garden, while the river slowly ran,
Walked the daughter, and her lover, and the dog-headed man.
The daughter, and her lover, and the dog-headed man!
It's a tale best forgotten, but before the tale began
His daughter, by the river that reflected as it ran,
Fed the bones of her lover to the dog-headed man.

Most of her narratives end in the death of either one or both lovers, who then go on restlessly haunting the living or, as in "I Love My Love," pull the living into their graves. "I Love My Love" is especially gruesome as a tale of unrequited desire, in which a man slays his wife and buries her, and is then swept to his death by the tangle of her still-growing hair. "Doll Song" is the most stunning performance of *Selected Poems and Ballads*, in which a young girl models two dolls from clay and calls them Love and Hate. They grow into demons when the girl falls in love and become her ruthless guardians thereafter. The tale allegorizes the real emotions of a young girl maturing, who then lives in the exile of adulthood with these immense emotions to rule and torment her. The magical landscape glitters with psychological mystery throughout the poem, and the narrator widens the incident to universality by closing with images of other youths innocently making their own small dolls for their pillows.

Adam is an uncanny magician of the romantic and supernatural, but her purposes are grounded in a real earth of psychological facts. Her archaisms and dialect, her ancient landscapes and quaint plots, are all meant to heighten and illustrate themes that could be treated in other ways, of course, but not with the same poignancy and startling power as her damp, desolate Scottish moors create. Adam is a very modern poet in her perceptions of irrational processes, and in her sophisticated grasp of instinct and primal urge. But she is especially timely in her depiction of very powerful females and beautiful, but somehow vague, male suitors, a perspective of many contemporary women poets – who are exploring the mythos of their sex as the privileges and powers of gender in society shift base.

—Paul Christensen

ADAMS, Léonie (Fuller). American. Born in Brooklyn, New York, 9 December 1899. Educated at Girls' High School; Barnard College, New York, B.A. (magna cum laude) 1922 (Phi Beta Kappa). Married the writer William Troy in 1933 (died, 1961). Bookshop Assistant, Best and Company, New York, 1922–23; Research Secretary, Yale University Law School, New Haven, Connecticut, 1923–24; Editorial Assistant, Wilson Publishing Company, New York, 1924; Editor, *Measure*, New York, 1924–25; English Teacher, Hamilton Institute for Girls, New York, 1925; Editorial Assistant, Metropolitan Museum of Art, New York, 1926–28; Instructor, Washington Square College, New York, 1930–32, Sarah Lawrence College, Bronxville, New York, 1933–34, and Bennington College, Vermont, 1935–37, 1941–45; Lecturer, New Jersey College for Women, New Brunswick, 1946–48, and Columbia University, New York, 1947–68; Consultant in Poetry, 1948–49, and Fellow in American Letters, 1949–55, Library of Congress, Washington, D.C.; Lecturer, New School for Social Research, New York, 1952–53; Fulbright Professor, France, 1955–56; Visiting Professor, Trinity College, Hartford, Connecticut, Summer 1960, University of Washington, Seattle, 1960, 1968–69, and Purdue University, Lafayette, Indiana, 1971–72. Recipient: Guggenheim Fellowship, 1928, 1929; National Institute of Arts and Letters grant, 1949; Harriet Monroe Poetry Award, 1954; Shelley Memorial Award, 1955; Bollingen Prize, 1955; Academy of American Poets Fellowship, 1959; National Endowment for the Arts grant, 1966; Brandeis University Creative Arts Award, 1968. D.Litt.: New Jersey College for Women, 1950. Secretary, National Institute of Arts and Letters, 1959–61. Address: Candlewood Mountain, R.R.2, New Milford, Connecticut 06776, U.S.A.

PUBLICATIONS

Verse

Those Not Elect. New York, McBride, 1925.
Midsummer. Privately printed, 1929.
High Falcon and Other Poems. New York, Day, 1929.
This Measure. New York, Knopf, 1933.
Poems: A Selection. New York, Funk and Wagnalls, 1954.

Other

Editor, and translator with others, *Lyrics of François Villon.* Croton Falls, New York, Limited Editions Club, 1933.

Manuscript Collection: Beinecke Library, Yale University, New Haven, Connecticut.

Critical Studies: by Eda Low Walton, in *The Nation* (New York), 1930; "Three Younger Poets" by Louis Untermeyer, in *The English Journal* (Champaign, Illinois), 1932; *Poetry in Our Time* by Babette Deutsch, New York, Holt, 1952, revised edition, 1963.

Léonie Adams comments:

Lyric Poetry, in largely traditional forms. At formative period influenced by Elizabethan, early Romantic and, through Yeats largely, Symbolist poetry.

My work has been described sometimes as "metaphysical" and sometimes as "romantic." It is perhaps some sort of fusion. Though its images are largely from nature (and tradition of Nature), I have tended in my better work toward a contemplative lyric articulated by some sort of speech music. To find my "figurative language" in the natural scene was less a literary habit I think than one absorbed from my mother, in whom the traditional American experience of nature remained unbroken by her translation from rural Maryland to the city. It was only thus I could catch and keep the tune. As for the other and larger modes I could admire, and (hopefully) possess, their use by others.

* * *

The poetry of Léonie Adams is very traditional: the poet's imagery derives from careful observations of beauty in nature. Her diction is strongly reminiscent of the Romantics: possibly to accommodate rhyme, normal sentence structure is often ignored ("Those not Elect"):

> Never, being damned, see paradise.
> The heart will sweeten at its look;
> Nor hell was known, till paradise
> Our senses shook.

At times, this device is bothersome, and combined with the heavy emphasis on traditional, romantic subjects, results in archaic textures ("Words for the Raker of Leaves"):

> Birds are of passage now,
> Else-wending; where
> (Songless, soon gone of late)
> They night among us,
> No tone now upon grass
> Downcast from hedge or grove
> With goldening day invites.

In counterpoint, the best of Adams's work incorporates traditional concerns with a contemporary vision. The reader has been lulled by her lyrics (which are varied enough rhythmically that their lulling is accomplished by subject, not tedious sing-song). "Ghost Tree" begins as a typically romantic ode: "Oh beech, unbind your yellow leaf, for deep/The honeyed time lies sleeping, and lead shade/Seals up the eyelids of its golden sleep." Suddenly, the poet abandons the multi-syllabic adjectives and allows the scene to describe its own potential:

> And here is only the cold scream of the fox,
> Only the huntsman following on the hound;
> While your quaint-plumaged,
> The bird that your green summer boughs lapped round,
> Bends south its soft bright breast.

These poems are meticulously crafted. Nowhere does the reader feel that the poet has abandoned her poem in favor of a digressive second look at the subject. This single-mindedness sometimes results in an almost too-predictable unity to Adams's work, but the energy with which she welds her vision to her art provides an oasis for those who thirst after a time when the poem was a song of life, neither contradictory nor simple.

—Geof Hewitt

ADAMS, Perseus. Pseudonym for Peter Robert Charles Adams. South African. Born in Cape Town, 11 March 1933. Educated at Cambridge, East London, and Sea Town high schools, Cape Town; University of Cape Town, B.A. in psychology and English. Has worked as a journalist, psychologist, clerk, and English teacher in six countries. Address: 7 New End, Hampstead, London N.W.3, England.

PUBLICATIONS

Verse

The Land at My Door. Cape Town, Human and Rousseau, 1965.
Grass for the Unicorn. Cape Town, Juta, 1975.

Perseus Adams comments:

(1970) Major themes: 1) subjects where the life-death, light-dark juxtaposition is sharply counterpointed; 2) creatures, people or animals, who have been robbed by life; 3) a metaphysical probing to discover our rightful place in the universe.

I employ a free verse with powerful resonant rhythms and complex tones. My style can be harshly decisive or gently lyrical – depending on the subject matter or mood. I have been called my country's "foremost lyricist," but this is not a title I care for.

* * *

Perseus Adams is essentially a lyric poet and even where he has grouped his poems under objective, thematic headings, the personal and subjective element comes through in the rhythms, texture, and structure of his verse. The mood varies from a Hopkinsian delight in nature and the joyful spontaneity of youth, to a more introspective frame of mind in which the lessons of experience are mulled over. If this results at times in too explicitly didactic a strain, the poet's seriousness of purpose and lyrical intensity rescue his work from the commonplace or trivial. His first volume, *The Land at My Door*, with its division of poems into "Morning" and "Afternoon," reflects the two contrasting moods postulated above – a grouping reminiscent of Blake's "Songs of Innocence and of Experience," though with none of the latter's conscious parallelism and antithesis. The mood of the "Morning" poems is closer to a Wordsworthian sense of awe, as in the closing section of the sonnet "Dawn on Table Mountain":

> Nor has there ever been a presence of air to match
> That tumult of impending absence that is

An African sky, and blue, so blue you feel
You are gazing at innocence and sacredness blended.
Now under that dome of an incandescent eye, three play
Their parts on this altar above the world: Grass, dew and sun
While joy shivers a watching bush-dove with supernal lightning.

The poems of this first volume are characterized by a somewhat indiscriminate abundance and variety of images which give, at times, an impression of contrived ingenuity. The sentiment, too, can be forced and stilted, imposed on rather than issuing from the poetic experience: this is true particularly of the closing lines of "Widow" and the self-consciously didactic "A Sky's Blue Innocence." It is worth noting that these failures of tone and technique occur mainly in poems whose subject-matter lies outside the writer's range of experience: the clichés and ritual gestures of "The War Veteran," for instance, reveal a sensibility not fully engaged by its subject. Against these, one can place poems such as "Crying Baby in a Grocer Shop," where the apparently commonplace is experienced in a way that invests it with a humane profundity, of "My Grandmother," where the closing stanzas present a beautifully sustained and entirely convincing vision of age advancing towards death and decay.

In *Grass for the Unicorn*, published ten years later, the verbal profusion of the earlier volume has given way to a markedly sparer style and a more austere, controlled expression of feeling. An empathic mode of perception is one of Perseus Adams's strengths as a poet; this is finely realized in "Mountain Protea," which illustrates also his flexible but highly functional command of form:

If – as I'm inclined to believe –
empathy is the art that comes
most naturally to the deeply quiet
spiralling out –
this sun pyx has it: high on Devil's Peak
with watch-fire head, all ears pricked
it unfolds
to enter into leopard and hawk
accenting their speed, a fleck in their sight
its tense repose, its dovetailing jet
theirs when they hunt....

Many of Perseus Adams's poems are inspired by his native Cape Town, its environs and peoples. He observes keenly but with a sense of humility and awe, as in the fine (and Frost-like) lines of "Bird Shrine," where the teacher-pupil roles are reversed as the normally backward class truant is transfigured by the "feathered glory" of his pigeons. Satire and protest are foreign to Adams's genius and when, as in "Indigenous and "Woltemade" he resorts to overt social or political comment, he reduces the force and expansiveness of his lyrical gift. Similarly, though his metrical virtuosity is amply illustrated in *Grass for the Unicorn*, his experiments with typography and visual effect are extrinsic to his essentially metaphoric style and have little but novelty to commend them. The precision, force, and clarity encapsulated in a poem such as "Sea Scalpel" point to one salient aspect of Adams's poetry – his craftsmanship – and explain why he selected as motto for his second volume the remark by the Argentinian poet, Arturo Aquino, that he preferred poetry to prose because "poetry drops like an eagle and stabs before you know." The other major feature of Adams's poetry is his humanistic vision: he never forgets the Wordsworthian admonition that the poet is a man speaking to men. It is this probing but sympathetic awareness that informs his most successful efforts, as in the poignant "Elegy for the Pure Act," and gives an earnest of his still-developing powers.

—E. Pereira

ADAMSON, Robert. Australian. Born in Sydney, 17 May 1943. Married Cheryl Adamson in 1973. Worked as a pastry cook, fisherman, and journalist in the 1960's; Associate Editor, 1968–70, Editor, 1970–75, and Assistant Editor, 1975–77, *New Poetry* magazine, Sydney; Editor and Director, Prism Books, Sydney, 1970–77. Since 1979, Founding Editor and Director, with Dorothy Hewett, Big Smoke Books, Sydney. Designer for Prism Books and *New Poetry* magazine since 1970, and since 1979, Designer for Big Smoke Books. Recipient: Australia Council Fellowship, 1976, 1977; Grace Leven Prize, 1977. Address: 1/2 Billyard Avenue, Elizabeth Bay, New South Wales 2011, Australia.

PUBLICATIONS

Verse

Canticles on the Skin. Sydney, Illumination Press, 1970.
The Rumour. Sydney, New Poetry, 1971.
Swamp Riddles. Sydney, Island Press, 1974.
Theatre I–XIX. Sydney, Pluralist Press, 1976.
Cross the Border. Sydney, New Poetry, 1977.
Selected Poems. Sydney, Angus and Robertson, 1977.
Where I Come From. Sydney, Big Smoke, 1979.

Novel

Zimmer's Essay, with Bruce Hanford. Sydney, Wild and Woolley, 1974.

Manuscript Collection: Australian National Library, Canberra.

Critical Studies: by Dorothy Hewett in *New Poetry 27* (Sydney), no. 1; interview with John Tranter in *Makar 1* (Brisbane), 1979.

* * *

With five major collections (plus a *Selected Poems*) published between 1970 and 1979, Robert Adamson has claimed for himself a central position among Australian poets of his generation – a generation that, in 1968, accomplished a remarkable revitalisation of poetic energies in this country. His work over this period has balanced an overt need to surprise or challenge (or even shock) the reader, with an ongoing discovery of sources of creative nourishment from personal experience and from his Hawkesbury River regional background. Adamson is not, however, a regional or a confessional poet. His most recent volume, *Where I Come From*, would seem to be a collection of autobiographical pieces about parents, childhood, and a delinquent adolescence, related with a sort of deadpan selectivity. It is a carefully contrived game, exploring ways of approaching the self (and themes already uncovered in earlier volumes) that imply a complex relationship not only with the reader, but with the possibility of ever realising a state beyond "the lie" of the conscious artist. In all his verse Adamson has sought to transcend the easily ironic stance (or the glibly petulant). His poetry constantly undercuts its own pretentions, but the effect is lacerating, not denigratory. Its surface may range from the artful *simpliste* chronicler of *Where I Come From* to the arty fabulist of "The Grail Poems," but the masks are worn with a wholehearted willingness, a risk-taking, that drags us into the exploration – and the search. Adamson's work is, in the best sense, self-conscious. It is also consistent in its deeply felt need to seek out (if not to find) some transforming quality from the rawness of observed data and experience.

His first book, *Canticles on the Skin*, established all the ongoing concerns he has subsequently followed: poems of prison experience (notably the opening sequence, pointedly titled "The Imitator" and bearing an inscription from St. Paul that still illuminates Adamson's approach to art: "For though I be free from all men, yet have I made myself servant unto all, that I might gain the more"); poems of literary homage; poems of landscape homage; and those nervous drug/car/energy poems that were probably his most immediate successes. It was followed by *The Rumour* in 1971, with its long title centrepiece, pivotal poems of the early 1970's in Australia (the other two being John Tranter's "Red Movie" and Martin Johnston's "The Blood Aquarium"). Though its derivations are clear, "The Rumour" reveals a sense of intense purpose and a drive that carries it into areas almost unexplored in Australian verse. *Swamp Riddles*, though diffuse, prints the first outstanding group of Hawkesbury poems, and a much acclaimed set of elegies for his contemporary, Michael Dransfield. *Cross the Border*, ambitious and uneven, attempts a large synthesis, but survives through individual achievements. *Where I Come From* is a deliberate turning away from this aesthetic experiment in a (self-claimed) "New Romanticism." It is immediately gripping, and seemingly accessible. It is also a progress report.

As editor of the magazine *New Poetry* in Sydney, Robert Adamson has been intensely involved in the politics of poetry; his personal influence has been considerable. But it is the capacity to transform his own restless energy to lyrical and celebrative experiments that has given Adamson's own work a depth and overriding intensity unique among poets of his generation in Australia.

—Thomas W. Shapcott

ADCOCK, Fleur. British. Born in Papakura, New Zealand, 10 February 1934; emigrated to the United Kingdom in 1963. Educated in England, 1939–47; Wellington Girls' College and Victoria University of Wellington, New Zealand, M.A. (honours) in classics. Married Alistair Campbell, *q.v.*, in 1952 (divorced, 1957); two sons. Temporary Assistant Lecturer in Classics, University of Otago, New Zealand, 1958. Held library posts at the University of Otago, 1959–61, and at Turnbull Library, Wellington, 1962. Since 1963, Assistant Librarian, Foreign and Commonwealth Office Library, London. Arts Council Creative Writing Fellow, Charlotte Mason College of Education, Ambleside, Cumbria, 1977–78. Recipient: Festival of Wellington Prize, 1961; New Zealand State Literary Fund Award, 1964; Buckland Award, 1967; Jessie MacKay Award, 1968, 1972; Cholmondeley Award, 1976. Address: 14 Lincoln Road, London N2 9DL, England.

PUBLICATIONS

Verse

The Eye of the Hurricane. Wellington, Reed, 1964.
Tigers. London, Oxford University Press, 1967.
High Tide in the Garden. London, Oxford University Press, 1971.
Corgi Modern Poets in Focus 5, with others, edited by Dannie Abse. London, Corgi, 1973.
The Scenic Route. London, Oxford University Press, 1974.
A Morden Tower Reading 5, with Gavin Ewart. Newcastle upon Tyne, Morden Tower, 1977.
The Inner Harbour. London, Oxford University Press, 1979.
Below Loughrigg. Newcastle upon Tyne, Bloodaxe, 1979.

Other

Editor, with Anthony Thwaite, *New Poetry 4*. London, Hutchinson, 1978.

Critical Study: Introduction by Dannie Abse to *Corgi Modern Poets in Focus 5*, 1973.

Fleur Adcock comments:

I can't give a code of my poetic practice or a set of rules by which I have operated; I can only point to certain tendencies and outline an attitude. Poetry is a search for ways of communication; it must be conducted with openness, flexibility, and a constant readiness to listen. The content of my poems is the content of those parts of my life which are directly experienced: relationships with people or places; images and insights which have presented themselves sharply from whatever source, conscious or subconscious; the investigation of certain ideas. The voice has to be my own and has to carry the weight of whatever I want to say and whatever in addition the poem may want to say for me. Therefore I take care to be honest, not to use tricks or masks or to act as a ventriloquist. For this reason my language tends to be plain, syntactically conventional, and, I hope, accessible.

My verse forms are relatively traditional (traditions alter). In general they have moved away from strict classical patterns in the direction of greater freedom – as is usual with most artists learning a trade. It takes courage, however, to leave all props behind, to cast oneself, like Matisse, upon pure space. I still await that confidence. In the meantime I continue to learn; and sometimes find it fruitful to return to a rigid metrical form as a discipline and for a different kind of exploration.

I write primarily for the printed page, not for performance (regarding poetry readings as the trailer, not the movie). But because the sound of words is central to the experiencing of a poem I read my work aloud as it develops and try to remove anything which is clumsy or unacceptable to the ear. As for the eye, the patterns of lines in type don't particularly interest me; words, not their shape on the page, are what matter. If one is fortunate their destination, like their origin, will be as voices speaking in the mind.

* * *

Fleur Adcock generally writes within a tradition of English poetry which is distinguished by its clarity, fastidiousness, and sharp observation of scenes and events. A kind of emotional toughness and an innate reticence underlie the surface candour, and the combination is often extremely effective. It's the ironical aspect of personal relations that interests her, along with its proper mode of expression, pointed understatement. She is by turns amused, expectant, and self-effacing, but always composed and vigorous – if she assumes, for example, a posture of wilful bafflement it is probably because she's in a sceptical humour: "I do not understand your arrangements." The last line of this poem ("Hauntings"), "You needn't think I am here to stay," reads like a warning issued by someone who is very much in control; this is a characteristic stance.

One of the protective measures which places distance between the poet and the grotesque or threatening image is a certain jauntiness of tone ("Grandma"); another is the kind of salutary ruthlessness conveyed in "Think Before You Shoot": "They've eaten all the squirrels. They want you,/And it's no excuse to say you're only children./No one is on your side. What will you do?" If the central metaphor occasionally seems a little too contrived or expected, the poet is apt, with grace, to acknowledge this herself in the last verse – "Gardens are rife with sermon-fodder" – a trick which indicates self-awareness at the very least. More often, however, the comparison makes a deft summing-up of the theme and adds an oblique comment on it: in "Against Coupling," for example, "Pyramus and Thisbe are dead, but/The hole in the wall can still be troublesome."

Fleur Adcock nearly always writes well about New Zealand, and about Ulster, another starting point for the ex-patriot's concern with origins, settled principles, and continuity. She distinguishes, however, between the backward look which is essentially disabused, and the retrogressive tendency which implies nostalgia. In "Please Identify Yourself," a remarkably economical and satisfactory poem, she is making fun of the civilized person exposed to bigotry, who can do nothing but align herself with the other side – "I scrawl incredulous notes under my hymnbook/And burn with Catholicism." In a recent pamphlet, *Below Loughrigg*, the scene has moved to the Lake District where the poet is lucky enough to overhear a deep voice bellowing "Wordsworth" – an incident sufficiently odd and felicitous to work its own effect. But it is the more formal, intricate and condensed "Ex-Queen among the Astronomers" (in *The Inner Harbour*) that seems to me her most impressive work to date; this shows how a near-metaphysical conceit may be presented without laboriousness or affectation.

—Patricia Craig

ALLEY, Rewi. New Zealander. Born in Springfield, Canterbury, 2 December 1897. Educated at Christchurch Boys High School. Served in the New Zealand Expeditionary Force during World War I: Military Medal. Sheep farmer, 1920–26. Has lived in China since 1926: Factory Inspector, Shanghai, 1927–38, then active in Gung Ho Cooperatives Movement; Director of Baillie Industrial School, Sandan, 1941–45; later New Zealand representative for the Asian and Pacific Peace Liaison Committee. D. Litt.; Victoria University of Wellington, 1971. Address: 1 Tai Chi Chang, Peking, China.

PUBLICATIONS

Verse

Gung Ho, edited by H. Winston Rhodes. Christchurch, Caxton Press, 1948.
Leaves from a Sandan Notebook (includes prose), edited by H. Winston Rhodes. Christchurch, Caxton Press, 1950.
This Is China Today, edited by H. Winston Rhodes. Christchurch, Rewi Alley Aid Group, 1951.
Fragments of Living Peking and Other Poems, edited by H. Winston Rhodes. Christchurch, New Zealand Peace Council, 1955.
Beyond the Withered Oak Ten Thousand Saplings Grow, edited by H. Winston Rhodes. Christchurch, Caxton Press, 1962.
Who Is the Enemy? Peking, New World Press, 1964.
The Mistake. Christchurch, Caxton Press, 1965.
For the Children of the Whole World. New York, Far East Reporter, 1966.
In Southeast Asia Today: The United States, Vietnam, China: Four Poems. New York, Far East Reporter, 1966.
What Is Sin? Christchurch, Caxton Press, 1967.
Twenty-Five Poems of Protest. Christchurch, Caxton Press, 1968.
Upsurge: Asia and the Pacific. Christchurch, Caxton Press, 1969.
73—Man to Be. Christchurch, Caxton Press, 1970.
Winds of Change. Christchurch, Caxton Press, 1972.
Poems for Aotea Roa. Auckland, New Zealand China Society, 1972.
Walkabout: 52 Poems of Australia. Canterbury, New Democratic Publications, 1973.

Hills of Blue. Christchurch, Caxton Press, 1974.
Over China's Hills of Blue: Unpublished Poems and New Poems. Christchurch, Caxton Press, 1974.
Today and Tomorrow. Christchurch, Caxton Press, 1975.
Snow over the Pines. Christchurch, Caxton Press, 1977.
The Freshening Breeze. Peking, New World Press, 1977.

Other

The Chinese Industrial Cooperatives. Chungking, China Information, 1940.
Two Years of Indusco. Hong Kong, Chinese Industrial Cooperatives, 1940.
Yo Banfa! (We Have a Way!), edited by Shirley Barton. Shanghai, China Monthly Review, 1952.
The People Have Strength: Sequel to "Yo Banfa!" Peking, New World Press, 1954.
Man Against Flood: A Story of the 1954 Flood on the Yangtse and of the Reconstruction That Followed It. Peking, New World Press, 1956.
Spring in Viet-Nam: A Diary of a Journey. Christchurch, Raven Press, 1956.
Land of the Morning Calm: A Diary of Summer Days in Korea. Christchurch, Raven Press, 1956.
Buffalo Boys of Viet-Nam. Hanoi, Foreign Languages Publishing House, 1956.
Journey to Outer Mongolia: A Diary with Poems. Christchurch, Caxton Press, 1957.
Human China: A Diary with Poems. Christchurch, New Zealand Peace Council, 1957.
Peking Opera: An Introduction Through Pictures. Peking, New World Press, 1957.
Children of the Dawn: Stories of Asian Peasant Children. Peking, New World Press, 1957.
Stories out of China. Peking, New World Press, 1958.
Sandan: An Adventure in Creative Education. Christchurch, Caxton Press, 1959.
Towards a People's Japan. Christchurch, Caxton Press, 1960.
China's Hinterland in the Leap Forward. Peking, New World Press, 1961.
3 Conferences at Cairo, New Delhi, and Bandung.... Christchurch, Caxton Press, 1961.
Land and Folk in Kiangsi: A Chinese Province in 1961. Peking, New World Press, 1962.
Amongst Hills and Streams of Yunan in the Fall of 1962. Peking, New World Press, 1963.
Our Seven – Their Five: A Fragment from the Story of Gung Ho. Peking, New World Press, 1963.
Co-operative Management, with Shou Tseng Meng. New Delhi, National Co-operative Union of India, 1964.
In the Spirit of Hunghu: A Story of Hupeh Today. Peking, New World Press, 1966.
Fruition: The Story of George Alwin Hogg. Christchurch, Caxton Press, 1967.
Oceania. Christchurch, Caxton Press, 1971.
Taiwan: A Background Study. Auckland, China Society, 1972.
Chinese Children: A Book of Photographs. Christchurch, Caxton Press, 1972.
The Prisoners. Christchurch, Caxton Press, 1973.
The Rebels. Christchurch, Caxton Press, 1973.
Travels in China 1966–1971. Peking, New World Press, 1973.
A Highway and an Old Chinese Doctor. Christchurch, Caxton Press, 1973.
China: The Quality of Life, with Wilfred Burchett. London, Penguin, 1976.

Translator, *Peace Through the Ages: Translations from the Poets of China.* Peking, 1954.
Translator, *The People Speak Out: Translations of Poems and Songs of the People of China.* Peking, 1954.
Translator, *Lament of the Soldier's Wife,* by Dang-Tran-Con. Hanoi, Foreign Languages Publishing House, 1956.

Translator, *The People Sing: More Translations of Poems and Songs of the People of China.* Peking, 1958.
Translator, *Poems of Revolt: Some Chinese Voices over the Last Century.* Peking, New World Press, 1962.
Translator, *Selected Poems*, by Tu Fu. Peking, Foreign Languages Press, 1962.
Translator, *Not a Dog: An Ancient Thai Ballad.* Peking, New World Press, 1962.
Translator, *The Eighteen Laments*, by Ts'ai Wenchi. Peking, New World Press, 1963.

Manuscript Collection: University of Canterbury Library, Christchurch.

Rewi Alley comments:

As I have been in China for 52 years, I feel that I should try in the interests of a working internationalism to make better known the China I have travelled and worked in.

* * *

Rewi Alley's verse (whether in his own spasmodic lyrics, or in translations from the Chinese) is the by-product of an intensely active life as a pioneer social worker, organiser of industrial co-operatives, and propagandist of the Chinese Revolution. No westerner has been so intimately linked with the struggles of the Chinese people since 1927 as this stocky New Zealander who has tramped the hills and fields of every province, and now lives as an honoured sage in the old Legation Quarter of Peking.

Alley has the broad vision of a poet, with few of the niceties of the craft. A self-made writer, he is far more concerned with content than with form, and can turn out political verses that are mere lists of slogans. But when he is writing directly about people and places, things seen and done, his warm human sympathy and creative response to experience find their own natural eloquence.

His free-verse jottings (generally made on the spot, and seldom revised) chart with vivid immediacy the landscape, the lives, and the longings of ordinary people confronting war, revolution and social change. More recently, he has written as vividly of scenes and people in his native New Zealand. Because of his unrivalled familiarity with the Chinese vernacular and terrain, and his historical understanding, his translations from classical and modern Chinese poetry have a force and vigour seldom achieved by more academic scholars.

In verse as in prose, Alley can be very uneven. Yet when passionate conviction touches his superb firsthand material into imaginative life, he becomes a direct popular writer (in eastern or western traditions) of a very high order indeed.

—James Bertram

ALVAREZ, A(fred). British. Born in London, 5 August 1929. Educated at Oundle School, Northamptonshire; Corpus Christi College, Oxford (Senior Research Scholar, 1952–53, 1954–55), B.A. 1952, M.A. 1956; Princeton University, New Jersey (Procter Visiting Fellow, 1953–54). Married 1) Ursula Barr in 1956 (marriage dissolved, 1961), one son; 2) Anne Adams, 1966, one son and one daughter. Gauss Lecturer, Princeton University, 1957–58; Visiting Professor, Brandeis University, Waltham, Massachusetts, 1960, and State University of New York, Buffalo, 1966. Advisory Poetry Editor, *The Observer*, London, 1956–66; Editor, *Journal of Education*, 1957; Drama Critic, *New Statesman*, London,

1958–60. Since 1965, Advisory Editor, Penguin Modern European Poets in Translation. Recipient: Rockefeller Fellowship, 1955; D. H. Lawrence Fellowship, 1958; Vachel Lindsay Prize (*Poetry*, Chicago), 1961. Address: c/o The Observer, 160 Queen Victoria Street, London E.C.4, England.

PUBLICATIONS

Verse

(Poems). Oxford, Fantasy Press, 1952.
The End of It. Privately printed, 1958.
Twelve Poems. London, The Review, 1968.
Lost. London, Turret, 1968.
Penguin Modern Poets 18, with Roy Fuller and Anthony Thwaite. London, Penguin, 1970.
Apparition. Brisbane, University of Queensland Press, 1971.
The Legacy. London, Poem-of-the-Month Club, 1972.
Autumn to Autumn and Selected Poems 1953–1976. London, Macmillan, 1978.

Play

Screenplay: *The Anarchist*, 1969.

Novels

Hers. London, Weidenfeld and Nicolson, 1974; New York, Random House, 1975.
Hunt. London, Macmillan, 1978; New York, Simon and Schuster, 1979.

Other

The Shaping Spirit: Studies in Modern English and American Poets. London, Chatto and Windus, 1958; as *Stewards of Excellence: Studies in Modern English and American Poets*, New York, Scribner, 1958.
The School of Donne. London, Chatto and Windus, 1961; New York, Pantheon, 1962.
Under Pressure: The Artist and Society: Eastern Europe and the U.S.A. London, Penguin, 1965.
Beyond All This Fiddle: Essays 1955–1967. London, Allen Lane, 1968; New York, Random House, 1969.
The Savage God: A Study of Suicide. London, Weidenfeld and Nicolson, 1971; New York, Random House, 1972.
Beckett. London, Fontana, and New York, Viking Press, 1973.

Editor, *The New Poetry: An Anthology.* London, Penguin, 1962; revised edition, 1966.

Critical Study: Interview with Ian Hamilton, in *New Review* (London), March 1978.

* * *

The published poetry of A. Alvarez is slight indeed in volume, but rich in its economy. *Autumn to Autumn and Selected Poems* contains 37 poems, 16 published for the first time. Of the new poems, only eight have been written since 1974, seven of them comprising the section called "Autumn to Autumn."

It is a shame that Alvarez, who has done so much to cultivate a climate receptive to the confessional poetry of Lowell, Berryman, and Plath – even though his essay on Plath in *The*

Savage God could be criticized for feeding the public's nearly insatiable appetite to feast upon a poet's life to understand her art – and whose writings on Donne and Eliot have done much to clarify their place in the history of contemporary poetry, should be so restrained in his practice of poetry. Perhaps he is too wary of rendering a poetry in the style of the Movement which he so aptly described in his essay, "The New Poetry; or, Beyond the Gentility Principle." Does he fear that he cannot heed his own warning and remain "immune" to gentility? He complained of the nine poets who formed the Movement that their "academic-administrative verse, polite, knowledgeable, efficient, polished, and, in its quiet way, even intelligent," practiced its own pieties and strove too hard to make the poet appear like the man next door. Alvarez has found his own, colloquial, modern voice and a hard-to-find originality in his novel, *Hers*, but in his poetry he clings to a compression of style and formality of verse that seem ultimately to inhibit him. Perhaps the standard he sets in the close of the above-mentioned essay is too high. There he asks that contemporary poetry be like "Coleridge's Imagination," that it "reconcile a 'more than usual state of emotion' with more than usual order."

Alvarez's new poems continue the strain and form of the poems in *Lost*. They are poems of ephemera. Briefly an emotion is isolated, felt, and wafted away, leaving the persona with a sense of perplexity and regret. Often he depicts mates inhabiting their "grey untender rooms," divided by fears and dreams. In "He Said, She Said" from *Autumn to Autumn*, a scent and a presence pass through the bedroom as two autumnal lovers lie together. He names the smell "hawthorn" and says it beckons, "Come"; she scoffs and says it said "Gone." Alvarez closes the poem characteristically with a note of mild irony:

> A flicker of gold, a smile, a far voice calling
> Confusedly, "Come," "Gone," "Come." The jumbled scents
> of Spring on the autumn night. "Our last chance," he said
> And she answered, "You take it without me."

More than a decade earlier, in another poem of dialogue, "Autumn Marriage," the wife's words were equally matter-of-fact and loveless. Alvarez's range continues to be narrow. This volume, containing poetry of two decades, reflects his admiration for Eliot, Frost, and Donne, and for Plath and Hughes. Several of the poems written in the late 1950's and early 1960's recall Plath's stridency and savage treatment of love's anger. "Sunstruck" is such a poem, "Anger" another. "Operation," "Back," and "The Nativity in New Mexico" recall Plath's "Tulips" or "Cut." They shed a harsh, clinical light on a grinning midwife and thighs sticky with afterbirth. Others use an economy of words to call up ordinary scenes, closing time in a park, a sleeper awakening, the coming of old age. His preoccupation with dreams, restlessness, and disintegration mark his modernity; his verse forms and gift for understatement recall the traditional British poetry of the early 20th century.

—Carol Simpson Stern

AMIS, Kingsley (William). British. Born in London, 16 April 1922. Educated at City of London School; St. John's College, Oxford, M.A. Served in the Royal Corps of Signals, 1942–45. Married 1) Hilary Ann Bardwell in 1948 (marriage dissolved, 1965); 2) the novelist Elizabeth Jane Howard, 1965; three children, including the writer Martin Amis. Lecturer in

English, University College, Swansea, Wales, 1949–61; Fellow in English, Peterhouse, Cambridge, 1961–63. Visiting Fellow in Creative Writing, Princeton University, New Jersey, 1958–59; Visiting Professor, Vanderbilt University, Nashville, Tennessee, 1967. Recipient: Maugham Award, 1955; *Yorkshire Post* award, for fiction, 1974; Campbell Memorial Award, for fiction, 1977. Agent: A. D. Peters, 10 Buckingham Street, London WC2N 6BU, England.

PUBLICATIONS

Verse

Bright November. London, Fortune Press, 1947.
A Frame of Mind. Reading, Berkshire, University of Reading School of Art, 1953.
(Poems). Oxford, Fantasy Press, 1954.
A Case of Samples: Poems 1946–1956. London, Gollancz, 1956; New York, Harcourt Brace, 1957.
The Evans Country. Oxford, Fantasy Press, 1962.
Penguin Modern Poets 2, with Dom Moraes and Peter Porter. London, Penguin, 1962.
A Look round the Estate: Poems 1957–1967. London, Cape, 1967; New York, Harcourt Brace, 1968.
Collected Poems 1944–1979. London, Hutchinson, 1979.

Recordings: *Kingsley Amis Reading His Own Poems*, Listen, 1962; *Poems*, with Thomas Blackburn, Jupiter, 1962.

Plays

Radio plays: *Something Strange*, 1962; *The Riverside Villas Murder*, from his own novel, 1976.

Television Plays: *A Question about Hell*, 1964; *The Importance of Being Harry*, 1971; *Dr. Watson and the Darkwater Hall Mystery*, 1974; *See What You've Done (Softly, Softly* series), 1974; *We Are All Guilty* (*Against the Crowd* series), 1975; *Break In*, 1975.

Novels

Lucky Jim. London, Gollancz, and New York, Doubleday, 1954.
That Uncertain Feeling. London, Gollancz, 1955; New York, Harcourt Brace, 1956.
I Like It Here. London, Gollancz, and New York, Harcourt Brace, 1958.
Take a Girl Like You. London, Gollancz, 1960; New York, Harcourt Brace, 1961.
One Fat Englishman. London, Gollancz, 1963; New York, Harcourt Brace, 1964.
The Egyptologists, with Robert Conquest. London, Cape, 1965; New York, Random House, 1966.
The Anti-Death League. London, Gollancz, and New York, Harcourt Brace, 1966.
Colonel Sun: A James Bond Adventure (as Robert Markham). London, Cape, and New York, Harper, 1968.
I Want It Now. London, Cape, 1968; New York, Harcourt Brace, 1969.
The Green Man. London, Cape, 1969; New York, Harcourt Brace, 1970.
Girl, 20. London, Cape, 1971.
The Riverside Villas Murder. London, Cape, and New York, Harcourt Brace, 1973.
Ending Up. London, Cape, and New York, Harcourt Brace, 1974.
The Alteration. London, Cape, 1976; New York, Viking Press, 1977.
Jake's Thing. London, Hutchinson, 1978; New York, Viking Press, 1979.

Short Stories

My Enemy's Enemy. London, Gollancz, 1962; New York, Harcourt Brace, 1963.
Penguin Modern Stories 11, with others. London, Penguin, 1972.
Dear Illusion. London, Covent Garden Press, 1972.
The Darkwater Hall Mystery. Edinburgh, Tragara Press, 1978.

Other

Socialism and the Intellectuals. London, Fabian Society, 1957.
New Maps of Hell: A Survey of Science Fiction. New York, Harcourt Brace, 1960; London, Gollancz, 1961.
The James Bond Dossier. London, Cape, and New York, New American Library, 1965.
Lucky Jim's Politics. London, Conservative Political Centre, 1968.
What Became of Jane Austin? and Other Questions. London, Cape, 1970; New York, Harcourt Brace, 1971.
On Drink. London, Cape, 1972; New York, Harcourt Brace, 1973.
Kipling and His World. London, Thames and Hudson, 1974; New, York, Scribner, 1976.

Editor, with James Michie, *Oxford Poetry 1949*. Oxford, Blackwell, 1949.
Editor, with Robert Conquest, *Spectrum: A Science Fiction Anthology*. London, Gollancz, 1961; New York, Harcourt Brace, 1962. (and later volumes.)
Editor, *Selected Short Stories of G. K. Chesterton*. London, Faber, 1972.
Editor, *Tennyson*. London, Penguin, 1973.
Editor, *Harold's Years: Impressions from the New Statesman and The Spectator*. London, Quartet, 1977.
Editor, *The New Oxford Book of Light Verse*. London and New York, Oxford University Press, 1978.
Editor, *The Faber Popular Reciter*. London, Faber, 1978.

Bibliography: *Kingsley Amis: A Checklist* by Jack Benoit Gohn, Kent, Ohio, Kent State University Press, 1976.

Manuscript Collection: State University of New York, Buffalo.

Kingsley Amis comments:

I used to be lumped into the "Movement" of the 1950's. No doubt I have, or had, something in common with some of the other poets lumped into it.

* * *

Although Kingsley Amis's most celebrated work is his fiction, he began as a poet, continues to write and publish poems, and is unambiguously convinced that poetry is a higher form of art. His first book (*Bright November*) was decent but quite unremarkable, though it included one poem – "Beowulf" – which he has reprinted and which sits happily enough with his later work. The first clearly Amisian poems appeared in *A Frame of Mind*, most of the contents of which were collected in *A Case of Samples: Poems 1946–1956*. There is a good deal of variety here, both in form and content, and some evidence of well-learned and well-digested influence from Auden, Graves, and Amis's own admired contemporary, Philip Larkin. The plain-man stance is apparent, with a distrust of extremes and a reliance on disabused commonsense; but this is managed with more gravity, more mutedly, than in the novels. "Against Romanticism" sets the tone well, in its steady-eyed wish for a landscape

> not parched or soured by frantic suns
> Doubling the commands of a rout of gods,
> Nor trampled by the havering unicorn;
> Let the sky be clean of officious birds
> Punctiliously flying on the left;
> Let there be a path leading out of sight,
> And at its other end a temperate zone:
> Woods devoid of beasts, roads that please the foot.

The novelist of *Lucky Jim* and its successors is more recognizable in *A Look round the Estate: Poems 1957–1967*, particularly in the sequence of coarse and comical vignettes, "The Evans Country," with its sly and almost admiring delineation of Dai Evans, South Walian hypocrite and lecher. "What about you?" – the question with which both the opening and closing poems end – is a clear invitation not to cast the first stone at Dai before having a good look at oneself.

The love poems are less individual, and in fact the hand of Graves is too obvious in them. In general, though, the later poems seem intelligent, witty, concentrated, and essentially light by-products of the impulse that has made the Amis novels. They compare favourably with Larkin's rather similar lighter poems (such as "Naturally the Foundation Will Bear Your Expenses"), but with one early exception (the poem "Masters," which was first published in 1949), Amis has never approached the measured grandeur of Larkin's best work.

—Anthony Thwaite

AMMONS, A(rchie) R(andolph). American. Born in Whiteville, North Carolina, 18 February 1926. Educated at Wake Forest College, North Carolina, B.S. 1949; University of California, Berkeley, 1950–52. Served in the United States Naval Reserve, 1944–46. Married Phyllis Plumbo in 1949; one child. Principal, Hatteras Elementary School, North Carolina, 1949–50. Executive Vice-President, Friedrich and Dimmock, Inc., Millville, New Jersey, 1952–62. Since 1964, Member of the Faculty, Associate Professor, 1969–71, since 1971, Professor of English, and since 1973, Goldwin Smith Professor of English, Cornell University, Ithaca, New York. Visiting Professor, Wake Forest University, 1974–75. Poetry Editor, *Nation*, New York, 1963. Recipient: Bread Loaf Writers Conference Scholarship, 1961; Guggenheim Fellowship, 1966; American Academy of Arts and Letters Travelling Fellowship, 1967; Levinson Prize (*Poetry*, Chicago), 1970; National Book Award, 1973; Bollingen Prize, 1975; National Institute of Arts and Letters award, 1977. D.Litt.: Wake Forest University, 1972; University of North Carolina, Chapel Hill, 1973. Address: Department of English, Cornell University, Ithaca, New York 14850, U.S.A.

PUBLICATIONS

Verse

Ommateum, with Doxology. Philadelphia, Dorrance, 1955.
Expressions of Sea Level. Columbus, Ohio State University Press, 1964.
Corsons Inlet. Ithaca, New York, Cornell University Press, 1965.

Tape for the Turn of the Year. Ithaca, New York, Cornell University Press, 1965.
Northfield Poems. Ithaca, New York, Cornell University Press, 1966.
Selected Poems. Ithaca, New York, Cornell University Press, 1968.
Uplands. New York, Norton, 1970.
Briefings: Poems Small and Easy. New York, Norton, 1971.
Collected Poems 1951–1971. New York, Norton, 1972.
Sphere: The Form of a Motion. New York, Norton, 1974.
Diversifications. New York, Norton, 1975.
The Snow Poems. New York, Norton, 1977.
The Selected Poems 1951–1977. New York, Norton, 1977.
Highgate Road. Ithaca, New York, Inkling Press, 1978.
Six-Piece Suite. Ithaca, New York, Palaemon Press, 1979.

Critical Studies: "A Poem Is a Walk" by the author, in *Epoch* (Ithaca, New York), Fall 1968; "A. R. Ammons: When You Consider the Radiance" by Harold Bloom, in *The Ringers in the Tower*, Chicago, University of Chicago Press, 1971; "A. R. Ammons Issue" of *Diacritics* (Ithaca, New York), 1974; *A. R. Ammons* by Alan Holder, Boston, Twayne, 1978.

* * *

A. R. Ammons is an American Romantic in the tradition of Emerson and Whitman. He is committed to free and open forms, to the amassing of the exact details experience provides rather than the extrusion therefrom of any *a priori* order. His favorite subject is the relation of a man to nature as perceived by a solitary wanderer along the beaches and rural fields of New Jersey, where Ammons grew up. Because of the cumulative nature of his technique, Ammons's work shows to best advantage in poems of some magnitude. Perhaps the best, and best known, of these is the title poem from *Corsons Inlet*, in which, describing a walk along a tidal stream, he says,

I was released from forms,
from the perpendiculars,
straight lines, blocks, boxes, binds
of thought
into the hues, shadings, rises, flowing bends and blends of sight....

Ammons here as elsewhere accepts only what is possible to a sensibility attuned to the immediacy of experience, for he admits that "Scope eludes my grasp, that there is no finality of vision,/that I have perceived nothing completely,/that tomorrow a new walk is a new walk."

Another kind of poem characteristic of Ammons is the brief metaphysical fable, in which there are surprising colloquies between an interlocutor and mountains, winds, or trees, as in "Mansion":

So it came time
for me to cede myself
and I chose
the wind
to be delivered to.
The wind was glad
and said it needed all
the body
it could get
to show its motions with....

The philosophical implications in these poems are explicit in "What This Mode of Motion

Said," a meditation upon permanence and change phrased as a cadenza on Emerson's poem "Brahma."

Ammons's *Collected Poems* was chosen for the National Book Award in 1973. Not included in this compendious volume is his book-length *Tape for the Turn of the Year*, a free-flowing imaginative journal composed in very short lines, written on a roll of adding-machine tape. The combination here of memory, introspection and observation rendered in ever-changing musical phrasing is impressive. Such expansiveness is Ammons's métier. *Sphere: The Form of a Motion* is a long poem in 155 12-line stanzas which comprise one unbroken sentence. Taking Whitman and Stevens as his models, Ammons combines the all-inclusive sensibility of the one with the meditative philosophical discourse of the other, as these excerpts may suggest:

> ... the identifying oneness of populations, peoples: I
> know my own – the thrown peripheries, the stragglers, the cheated,
> maimed, afflicted (I know their eyes, pain's melting amazement),
>
> the weak, disoriented, the sick, hurt, the castaways, the
> needful needless: I know them: I love them, I am theirs ...
>
> the purpose of the motion of a poem is to bring the focused,
> awakened mind to no-motion, to a still contemplation of the
> whole motion, all the motions, of the poem ...
>
> ... by intensifying the alertness
>
> of the conscious mind even while it permits itself to sink,
> to be lowered down the ladder of structured motions to the
> refreshing energies of the deeper self ...
> the non-verbal
> energy at that moment released, transformed back through the
> verbal, the sayable poem ...

Ammons's work is consistent in its experimentation with open forms and its celebration of living processes and the identity of man with nature.

—Daniel Hoffman

ANANIA, Michael. American. Born in Omaha, Nebraska, 5 August 1939. Educated at the University of Nebraska, at Lincoln, 1957–58, at Omaha, B.A. 1961; State University of New York, Buffalo, Ph.D. 1969. Married Joanne Oliver in 1960. Bibliographer, Lockwood Library, State University of New York, Buffalo, 1963–64; Instructor in English, State University of New York, Fredonia, 1964–65, and Northwestern University, Evanston, Illinois, 1965–68. Instructor, 1968–70, and since 1970, Assistant Professor of English, University of Illinois, Chicago. Poetry Editor, *Audit*, 1963–64, and Co-Editor, *Audit/Poetry*, 1963–67, Buffalo. Since 1968, Literary Editor, Swallow Press, Chicago; since 1971, Member, Board of Directors, and since 1972, Member, Executive Committee, Coordinating Council of Literary Magazines. Recipient: Swallow Press New Poetry Series Award, 1970. Address: Department of English, University of Illinois at Chicago Circle, Chicago, Illinois 60680, U.S.A.

PUBLICATIONS

Verse

The Color of Dust. Chicago, Swallow Press, 1970.
Set/Sorts. Chicago, Wine Press, 1974.
Riversongs. Urbana, University of Illinois Press, 1978.

Other

Editor, *New Poetry Anthology I* and *II*. Chicago, Swallow Press, 1969, 1972.

* * *

In *The Color of Dust*, Michael Anania traces his passage from the timeless to the contemporary, from small-town life by the Missouri River to a state of mind questioning national myths and the consequences of war. By evoking a sense of the land and people, and by recognizing the permanence and the regenerative powers of the river, he demonstrates how identity stems from the knitting together of person and place ("We are not confused,/we do not lose our place"). But self-definition may be accomplished only one moment at a time and periods of doubt inevitably occur ("Am I a songster or a dealer?"). So, too, in his calling, the poet attempts to capture and maintain, thereby creating his own dilemma; the writing of a poem means the wresting of something from its organic context. But it is the nature of the creator to utter his vision and, in doing so, to preserve what he perceives. Time and again the poet must confront the realization that all things change; in Robert Creeley's words, "Everything is water/if you look long enough." Anania's attempts to preserve the interrelatedness of experience may be seen metaphorically in "The Fall" and dramatically in his war pieces. In the latter, he presents the survivors – those men with fragments of mind and those who suffer physical decay. Here Anania successfully weaves a living tapestry as he reveals the tragic operation of causality in human lives. Time goes on and man improves – his weapons; he progresses from shrapnel to napalm. The American hero, manifestation of national power, propagated by the media, wears "the satin cape/the big red S/meaning, after all, better than." Superman's cool efficiency and superior strength symbolize the power of a machine-driven culture.

In *Riversongs* the meaning and metaphor of the river is extended to encompass a sense of the historical past, the passage of time to the present, and the inevitable flow toward death. "The Riversongs of Arion," the ten-poem sequence which gives the book its name, recounts a recent attempt to retrace the Lewis and Clark journey; incorporated are excerpts drawn from Lewis's *Journals*. The river of historical time flows into now and becomes one with the mind of the persona. After all, the first rule – of river and mind – is motion. "... In time/the river sidewinds its banks./Never the same soil...." Elements of the historical past, of the struggle to settle the frontier, clarify how human experience is continuous and intertwined as it flows into contemporary America; Lewis's words mingle with references to Billy the Kid, John Wesley Hardin, Wild Bill Hickok, Sacajawea, and Huck Finn. The poem's movement resembles the outward rippling caused by a stone dropped in water and, simultaneously, a deepening, for every journey is a life quest, individual, uncertain –

each night I read my Journals
like a novel, seeking some
inevitability of plot, a hint
of form pointing toward an end

The river of memory floats the persona back to the dead fathers of his family ("Reeving") and forward to time-present ("News Notes, 1970").

Poetry is music that moves like a river, a liquid music flowing and changing. In the play of liquid and light, illuminations sparkle like sunlight on wave-tips. In *Riversongs*, the best of Anania's poems embody the endurance of water wedded to the delicacy of light – things come in waves, they stream past the beholding eye, and they are gone. In the river's continuity and the light playing on its surface, Anania captures and preserves "Those shafts of light/the soul is mirror to."

—Carl Lindner

ANDERSON, Jon (Victor). American. Born in Somerville, Massachusetts, 4 July 1940. Educated at Northeastern University, Boston, B.S. 1964; University of Iowa, Iowa City, M.F.A. in creative writing 1968. Married 1) Nancy Garland in 1964 (marriage dissolved); 2) Linda Baker in 1967 (marriage dissolved); 3) Barbara Hershkowitz in 1971. Instructor, later Assistant Professor of Creative Writing, University of Portland, Oregon, 1968–72; Assistant Professor of Creative Writing, Ohio University, Athens, 1972–73, and University of Pittsburgh, 1973–76. Since 1976, Assistant Professor of Creative Writing, University of Iowa. Recipient: Borestone Mountain Award, 1964; Oscar Blumenthal Prize (*Poetry*, Chicago), 1970; Guggenheim Fellowship, 1976. Address: Department of English, University of Iowa, Iowa City, Iowa 52240, U.S.A.

PUBLICATIONS

Verse

Looking for Jonathan. Pittsburgh, University of Pittsburgh Press, 1968.
Death and Friends. Pittsburgh, University of Pittsburgh Press, 1970.
In Sepia. Pittsburgh, University of Pittsburgh Press, 1974.
Counting the Days. Lisbon, Iowa, Penumbra Press, 1974.

* * *

Jon Anderson's *Looking for Jonathan* is principally a search for identity, both the poet's and our own. The formal, the christened, name seems to signify the essential person. The work belies that easy idea, however, by discovering that change is the human condition. Finally, being and becoming are identified, but this poetry elaborates the moribund nature of human metamorphosis. Images of light and metaphors of dark drive the poems, just as Anderson sees us forging through experience from illusion to disillusion.

"It Is Morning; the Animals" opens the collection wonderfully. The paradisaical beasts are characterized by a uniquely tainted innocence which is the blessing of undeluded animality. The lion is central, as is the lamb, Christ, in the title poem of the second section, "The Summer Deaths." In a blazing sun the lion ironically, but gently, explains a sleeping man:

This is my peaceable son;
my fond intention, dreaming,
even unto death.

Man's ignorance of his animal endowment forces him forever to dream (especially the illusion of his benignity). His dreaming may even be suicidal. Yet the poem concludes with a brilliant ambiguity that also allows us to see ourselves as the lion's progenitor:

The man disappears, as though
he was not ever in that house at all,
but was invisible, or asleep
deep in the lion's dark belly,
or was the lion, dreaming of him.

Man's animality and spirituality are dreams of each other; yet the verse arrangement and syntax leave no doubt that both dreams are possible, in reality.

The second group mainly traces various vanishings, of experiences, relationships, whole persons. All drop into the wake of the speaker's progress, which is leading to "The New World," both a hope and a poem, which adroitly prefigures the book's finale. The third and last section is dominated by movement in deep shadow, erosion, and barren resignation. These poems culminate in the piece which gives the volume its title, a work prepared for by the psychological "clarity" of a self now borne "with ... indifference." Seeing himself, the poet perceives not a "new world" but a weary America and his own industrially stained home town. Once-fecund religious myths yield here to a more difficult vision:

When I saw America, she had danced all night,
she was chalk-white,
leaning on her husband's arm.

I could see
the orange home town, coming.
I leaned honestly
into my own reflection.
I had no more stories of God.

In *Death and Friends* Anderson finds himself immersed in and then nearly drowned by myriad deaths. In the ragged separateness of all things he locates the veritable model of Donne's "pictures" of death. Not only does the grave take our friends, but Death's compatriots, like the "Angel of Departures" in *Looking for Jonathan*, are at work dissolving all connections, human and temporal. Personal and cosmic discontinuity merge. The poet sees the always travelling "Trucker" with a history of years

... like the stars
he watched from the speeding cab,
spaced unevenly ...
so many particular events.

The individual is no less fractured than the past. But now Anderson sometimes discovers that while the disconnected phases of our years and our own disparate personalities are unknowable to our friends, they are "friends" to each other and a source of that strange human unity Montaigne discerned in our constant inconsistency. This line of feeling is initiated in the first poem, "The Parachutist," and brought to fruition in "The Photograph of Myself," a poem at least as good as Adrienne Rich's "The Evil Eye." Addressing the image of his childhood self with wit, irony and a touch of Wordsworth's "the child is father of the man," the speaker allows that: "Good friend, believe me,/here I am, perhaps your best intention."

Anderson's third book, *In Sepia*, is a retrospect, a work of and for the memory. Reflection (the philosophic cast of mind, light upon surfaces, the mirror's image) is of the essence. The absolute terminus of life looms, especially as engulfing water or blackening forest. And across darkness, fragments of light (headlights on bridges, moon glimmerings in branches) pulse messages of life's ephemerality. But the poet now fraternizes with time and struggles to make his losses a "progress from judgment to compassion." The yellow-brown, autumnal stain is cast on the mind's memories of all seasons, but with a paradoxical ardor: "We who have changed, & have/No hope of change, must now love/The passage of time." The "Years" and one's friends are so many "Stories," but:

... the stories they lived
Were not the same,
Many were distracted into love,
Slept, & woke alone, awhile serene.

Wordsworth has it that "Our birth is but a sleep and a forgetting." Anderson sees that, but he wants to know the dream of that sleep and its strange final memory, not before we are transported back into an eternal day, but as we sink into true darkness.

—David M. Heaton

ANGELES, Carlos A. Filipino. Born in Tacloban City, Philippines, 25 May 1921. Educated at the University of the Philippines, Diliman, Quezon City. Married to Concepcion Reynoso; seven children. Chief of Bureau, International News Service, Manila, 1948–58. Philippine Presidential Press Assistant, 1958–59. Since 1959, Public Relations Manager, Pan American World Airways, Manila. Recipient: United States State Department grant, 1958; Philippine Cultural Heritage Award, 1964; Palanca Memorial Award, 1964. Address: 141 Pinatubo Street, Mandaluyong, Rizal, Philippines; or, Post Office Box 172, Manila, Philippines.

PUBLICATIONS

Verse

A Stun of Jewels. Manila, Alberto S. Florentino, 1963.

Critical Study: Introduction by Leonard Casper to *A Stun of Jewels*, 1963.

* * *

Carlos A. Angeles's reputation depends on a volume of his collected poems, *A Stun of Jewels*, and a number of other pieces which have been anthologised. His poetry attaches value to everyday commonplace experiences but the banality is deceptive. "Highway," for example, operates at different levels; the description of the winding road is a search for truth; its being couched in the terminology of the chase makes it a metaphor of the quest for sexual fulfilment while the intensity of the quest is responsible for the success of his best poetic pieces. His quartet "Poems for My Psychiatrist's Future Reference" takes its origin in trivial incidents but goes on to trace a pattern of specific human emotions. His other poems develop similarly. Each explores a central idea through concrete images. In "Landscape" the sun becomes an eye; in "The Eye," the eye is likened to the sun; and each by piercing the centre of reality becomes the stronghold of reality. Actually, Angeles does not plumb the depths of his subject. He presents not the realised experience but the experience itself moving towards definition. It is the immediacy distilled by this "poetry-in-progress" that makes Angeles's poems such pleasing pieces.

—Abdul Majid bin Nabi Baksh

ANTIN, David. American. Born in New York City, 1 February 1932. Educated at City College, New York, B.A. 1955; New York University (Lehmann Fellow), 1964–66, M.A. in linguistics 1966. Married to Eleanor Antin; one son. Free-lance editor and translator, 1956–57; Chief Editor and Scientific Director, Research Information Service, New York, 1958–60; free-lance editor and consultant, Dover Press, New York, 1959–64; Curator, Institute of Contemporary Art, Boston, 1967. Director of the University Art Gallery and Assistant Professor of Visual Arts, 1968–72, and since 1972, Professor of Visual Arts, University of California, San Diego. Former Editor, with Jerome Rothenberg, *Some/Thing*, New York; Contributing Editor, *Alcheringa*, New York; Member of the Editorial Board, *New Wilderness*. Recipient: Longview Award, 1960; Guggenheim Fellowship, 1976. Address: P.O. Box 1147, Del Mar, California 92014, U.S.A.

PUBLICATIONS

Verse

Definitions. New York, Caterpillar Press, 1967.
Autobiography. New York, Something Else Press, 1967.
Code of Flag Behavior. Los Angeles, Black Sparrow Press, 1968.
Meditations. Los Angeles, Black Sparrow Press, 1971.
Talking. New York, Kulchur, 1972.
After the War (A Long Novel with Few Words). Los Angeles, Black Sparrow Press, 1973.
Talking at the Boundaries. New York, New Directions, 1976.

Other

Translator, *100 Great Problems of Elementary Mathematics: Their History and Solution*, by Heinrich Doerrie. New York, Dover, 1965.
Translator, *The Physics of Modern Electronics*, by W. A. Guenther. New York, Dover, 1967.

Critical Studies: "John Cage, Buckminster Fuller, and David Antin" by Barry Alpert, "Some Notes Toward a Discussion of the New Oral Poetry" by George Economou, and "A Correspondence Between the Editors Robert Kroetsch and William Spanos and David Antin," all in *Boundary 2* (Binghamton, New York), Spring 1975; interview with Barry Alpert, and articles by Gilbert Sorrentino, Hugh Kenner, Toby Olson, and David Bromige, in *Vort* (Silver Spring, Maryland), Winter 1975.

* * *

Classical poetic theory regularly distinguished between the three terms *poeta* (the maker), *poesis* (the process of making), and *poema* (the thing which has been made). Modern theory, whether New Critical, Structuralist, or Post-Structuralist, is narrowly concerned with the third of these three terms: the poem as *text*. Further, because most discussion of contemporary poetry is still narrowly Romantic, it is taken for granted that a poem is a text expressing personal feelings, "emotion recollected in tranquillity." Turn the pages of any poetry magazine and you will quickly come upon the now-formulaic lyric poem in which an "I," standing in a wheat-field or crossing a brook or suddenly meeting someone loved long ago, ruminates on his or her personal experience and has an appropriate epiphany.

In such a context, it is not surprising that David Antin's extraordinary improvisations – he calls them "talk pieces" or "talk poems" – have been greeted with some hostility in establishment quarters. For the talk poems are improvised for particular occasions in particular places, recorded on tape, and only later transcribed on the typewriter. The written texts, collected in *Talking at the Boundaries* and elsewhere, are described by Antin as "the notations of scores of oral poems with margins consequently unjustified." As scores of actual talks, these texts obviously lack verse form: they do away not only with meter, but even with that last stronghold of free verse – lineation. To make matters worse, Antin has expressed a "distrust of ideas of interiority and the whole rhetorical ensemble of notions about 'feelings and emotions.' " Rather, he regards the "art of talking" as essentially the *language* art, and he is less interested in *ethos* or *pathos* than in *dianoia*, which Aristotle defines as "all the thought that is expressed or effected by the words," or again, as "the ability to say what is possible and appropriate."

Is an Antin composition, then, written in "normal" prose? Not at all. "Prose," says Antin, "is an image of the authority of 'right thinking,' conveyed primarily through right printing – justified margins, conventional punctuation, and regularized spelling." The distinction between Antin's "talking" and "prose" was established in the early 1960's by Northrop Frye (in *The Well-Tempered Critic*):

> One can see in ordinary speech ... a unit of rhythm peculiar to it, a short phrase that contains the central word or idea aimed at, but is largely innocent of syntax. It is much more repetitive than prose, as it is in the process of working out an idea, and the repetitions are largely rhythmical filler.

This "associative rhythm" as Frye calls the rhythm of speech, may be conventionalized in two ways:

> One way is to impose a pattern of recurrence on it; the other is to impose the logical and semantic pattern of the sentence. We have verse when the arrangement of words is dominated by recurrent rhythm and sound, prose when it is dominated by the syntactical relation of subject and predicate.

All three of these "primary rhythms of verbal expression" belong to *poesis* though not, of course to *poema*. The interchange between the three provides the combinations which give literature its variety and complexity. When, for example, the "associative rhythm" is influenced, but not quite organized by, the sentence, we get what Frye calls "free prose," a form that develops much earlier than free verse: witness the associative monologue found in the personal letter, the diary, in Swift's *Journal to Stella*, and in *Tristram Shandy*. Beckett's *The Unnamable* is an important modern example.

There is thus a sense in which David Antin is a perfectly traditional poet; it is just that his tradition is no longer that of Romanticism and its Symbolist offshoots. The talk poems bypass Romanticism and return to a more classical notion of *poesis* as *making*. Frye remarks that "the associative rhythm represents the process of bringing ideas into articulation in contrast to prose or verse, which normally represent a finished product." Just so, Antin's "poetry," even his earlier, more conventionally lineated poems, like the elegy "Definitions for Mendy," is a process-oriented art.

How does it work in practice? Pieces like "is this the right place?" or "what am i doing here?" are, I think, governed by certain implicit rules:

(1) Just as there are no margins, so there are no complete sentences, the trick being to "keep it moving," in Charles Olson's words. Consider the following passage about cross-country jet travel:

> when i got on the plane i had the feeling   i started out early in the
> day   it was about 12 oclock   to be on a plane   12 oclock on a plane is in
> some ways the worst possible time to get on a plane because   what happens
> is   you start out in the daylight and you wind up in the night and there never
> was any day   and its odd you feel that youre travelling into the past

Notice that the first "when" clause is never completed by a main clause, for the speaker immediately interests himself in what it was like *when* he got on. Again, the proposition "it was about 12 oclock" leads, not to the expected account of what happened at twelve o'clock, but to a comic sequence about the peculiar feelings attendant upon boarding an East-bound flight at noon. And so it goes with rapid-fire shifts from one image or idea to another. The text is a transcription, not of a character's speech as one might find it in, say, a novel, but of David Antin's *talk*.

But if it's just "talk," what makes it *art*? Here three other rules come in.

(2) The talk poem incorporates as many different threads as can allow it to retain its improvisatory quality, yet those threads are all relational. The analogy is to a juggling act: as we watch Antin juggle the balls, we gradually realize that they will – or at least should – all be caught. So, in "Real Estate," the inquiry into the meaning of the words "real estate" and "currency" seems to get lost as we are given a series of comic narratives about various Antin relatives who did or did not own real estate. These "stories" are fun in themselves but, in considering in what sense, if any, a little hotel in the Catskills, bought by his eccentric uncle, is a "real" estate, Antin leads us right back to the possible meanings of his title.

Such three-ring performance is not easy. At one extreme, the talk may be too linear, too concerned with the exposition of a particular theme. At the other, the diverse materials – childhood memories, anecdotes about art shows, speculations on Homeric narrative, and so on – may fail to generate the necessary cross-references. So the successful talk poem is one that maintains a balance between leaving-out and putting-in.

(3) Closely related to (2): narrative (but not fiction) is an integral part of the talk poem. Pure exposition, rumination, meditation – these undercut the poet's emphasis on *poesis*, on the ongoing process of discovery in which one creates the self. Antin's narratives function as parodic examples; they prove the points the speaker is making but only because he wants them to, not because they have any sort of objective validity.

(4) The generation of a particular *voice* is the one fictional element Antin allows himself. If, for example, one were to become ill while visiting San Diego and phoned David Antin for advice and help, he would undoubtedly be able to furnish some useful medical information. In a talk poem, however, a "medical center" is decomposed. Here is Antin's account of what happened when he and his family first arrived in Southern California and found that his little boy was sick:

> and i said to somebody in a shoestore "what do you do if somebody gets sick during lunch?" and they said "theres a medical center right up the hill" and i drove to the medical center and there was a medical center in california a medical center is unlike anything youve ever seen unless youre a californian medical centers depend on redwood trees because theyre made out of redwood trees and ice plant because what they do is level off an area whatever was there they take a bulldozer and level it off if there were eucalyptus trees they knock them down they push things out of the way and then what they dont cover with redwood and blacktop they cover with iceplant wherever you go theres iceplant

This is a good example of what the Russian Formalists called *defamiliarization*. Who else would define a medical center as a place made of redwood and iceplant? It has nothing to do with informational content but everything to do with the poet's first impressions of the strange new world which is Southern California.

The voice of the talk poems can describe persons, places, and events in the most minute detail, but a detail that would never do for, say, a newspaper article. We don't *know* Dick Berlinger or the Uncle from Argentina or even the poet's wife "elly" (or "ely"); we merely witness certain fragmented gestures, words, or actions that provide a matrix for the speaker's talking. The mode here is synecdochic but the parts refer to no whole. Behind the manic behavior of "Dick," at the wheel of the 53 Chrysler or Candy's rejection of her would-be lover because of his cherry tattoo, there is an absent totality.

The refusal to claim knowledge either of himself or of his characters has suggested to some readers that Antin is unfeeling, that he refuses to take life "seriously." This is to misunderstand the nature of the talk poems completely. In adopting the stance of puzzled observer, of the unhabituated eye that sees persons and places as if for the first time, Antin can convey to us how the mind actually does experience the outside world. He can, moreover, embed such general questions as he does wish to raise – for example, is the photograph a true reproduction of visual reality? – in a set of images or narrative contexts so that the audience shares his own process of discovery. Antin's *dianoia* thus becomes ours. As he says: "now if you freeze life   its like frozen food," but "when you translate something it changes."

—Marjorie Perloff

ANTONINUS, Brother. See EVERSON, William O.

APPLETON, Sarah (Sherman). American. Born in New York City, 14 April 1930. Educated at Vassar College, Poughkeepsie, New York, B.A. 1952; University of Iowa, Iowa City, 1952; Ohio State University, Columbus, M.A. 1957, Ph.D. 1961. Married Joseph G. Weber in 1965; one daughter and one son. Teaching Assistant, Ohio State University, 1955–61; Instructor in English, Smith College, Northampton, Massachusetts, 1962–65; Poetry Editor, *Literature East and West*, College Park, Maryland, 1966–68; Fellow, Bunting Institute, Radcliffe College, Cambridge, Massachusetts, 1970–72; Member of the Adjunct Faculty, Syracuse University, New York, 1977. Recipient: Yaddo Fellowship, 1974, 1975, 1976, 1977; Creative Artists Public Service grant, 1975. Address: 124 Dorset Road, Syracuse, New York 13210, U.S.A.

PUBLICATIONS

Verse

The Plenitude We Cry For. New York, Doubleday, 1972.
Ladder of the World's Joy. New York, Doubleday, 1977.

Other

Theology and Poetry in the Middle English Lyric: A Study of Sacred History and Aesthetic Form (as Sarah Appleton Weber). Columbus, Ohio State University Press, 1969.

Sarah Appleton comments:

Both my life and professional career have developed from writing poetry and the study of poetic form. My work as a poet began in 1952 when I was a senior at Vassar College and began to study with Elizabeth Sewell. I realized that the life of the imagination exacted the same terms as life itself, and I left formal academic study until 1955.

It was while I was teaching at Smith College that I wrote *The Plenitude We Cry For*, a long poetic sequence on the growth forms of a horse chestnut. The poem, which started out as a personal experiment, proved to be the opening up of an inexhaustible source of instruction and poetry. *Ladder of the World's Joy* continues the pursuit of poetry through plant life and evolution. The long title poem was written from the energy and joy in my discovery, through reading Teilhard de Chardin's *Le Phénomène Humain*, of the coherence of creation. The poem follows the rebirth of my understanding as it experiences the evolutionary birth of the universe. Its sections are musical sequences which move outward toward a mystery, what is partially known, so that individual poems catch moments, insights, glints of the whole.

Since 1975 I have been working on a series of poems and sentences called "Book of My Hunger/Book of the Earth," a journey step-by-step of sentences given release by my understanding of the earth. At the same time it follows the movement of my autobiography. The sections are a kind of fiction, a wedding of my words with what I speak of: the fiction gives each section life, quality, and creates the steps of the work. The energy, the transforming power of poetry, its breath, makes the way and allows the fragility that never breaks.

* * *

Sarah Appleton might be considered a female Joyce Kilmer (she's even published in *Trees*), sharing as she does his love of nature and religious sensibilities, but without rhyme, and sometimes the same reason. Indeed, Appleton's reasons are quite personal and therefore elusive. Her first book records a "double life": that of the horse chestnut tree whose branches reach to her second-story writing-room window, and that of herself "interpreting with the tree's life." *The Plentitude We Cry For*, she explains, is a "series of notes imitating the stages of the tree's growth: reflective, concentrated and elliptical, exploding, enumerative, suspending, dispersing, in summer spare and mechanical." Thus, in place of mere logic, she strives for philosophical insight or "poetical" effect, but not without strain. For her reflections are often as banal as her images are hackneyed, and her pastoral vision is often blurred by tortuous syntax and apparent uncertainty about the basic meanings of words. Her favorite devices, typical of the "nature poet," are facile personification and pervasive pathetic fallacies. These are warmed up with (one fears, not unintentional) sexual metaphors, producing a steamy atmosphere more reminiscent of the hothouse than the great outdoors. As with other authors blessed with mystical sensibilities, Appleton presumes to know the mind of God, as well: "God demands that poetry should burn," she tells us, supporting the assertion with a nonsequitur: "This thought came from spring rain." Amid descriptive lists, other pithy observations abound; as, for example: "Death is/absolute mutation."

In *Ladder of the World's Joy*, Appleton turns her talents to meditations upon Teilhard de Chardin's *The Phenomenon of Man*, while the reader turns the book sideways to read her long lines. Here technical characteristics are even more pronounced than in her first book: rationale is more evasive, fragments more oddly juxtaposed, contortions more mannered (or manneristic). However, the resulting collage effect (which gives the impression of notes toward a poem) and the incompleteness are appropriate to her theme. Commenting on "the birth of man within the evolution of the earth," she offers "sequences" (titled as seven "Periods") which ignore impersonal, naturalistic, Darwinian implications in favor of her *maître*'s mystical meanings. An evident sincerity runs through her ruminations on birds, bees, stars, sun, moon, and the elementary aspects of this life. And when she turns to loving relations of men and women and children, her lines are frequently touching. For those who find her private symbols and significances difficult to follow, as in her earlier book the poet offers a concluding summary explication in prose.

—Joseph Parisi

ASHBERY, John (Lawrence). American. Born in Rochester, New York, 28 July 1927. Educated at Deerfield Academy, Massachusetts; Harvard University, Cambridge, Massachusetts (Member of the Editorial Board, *The Harvard Advocate*), B.A. in English 1949; Columbia University, New York, M.A. in English 1951; New York University, 1957–58. Copywriter, Oxford University Press, New York, 1951–54, and McGraw-Hill Book Company, New York, 1954–55; Art Critic, European Edition of *New York Herald Tribune*, Paris, 1960–65, and *Art International*, Lugano, Switzerland, 1961–64; Editor, *Locus Solus* magazine, Lans-en-Vercors, France, 1960–62; Editor, *Art and Literature*, Paris, 1963–64; Paris Correspondent, 1964–65, and Executive Editor, 1965–72, *Art News*, New York. Since 1974, Professor of English, Brooklyn College. Since 1976, Poetry Editor, *Partisan Review*, and since 1978, Art Critic, *New York* magazine. Recipient: Fulbright Fellowship, 1955, 1956; Yale Series of Younger Poets Award, 1956; Poets Foundation grant, 1960, 1964; Ingram Merrill Foundation grant, 1962, 1972; Harriet Monroe Memorial Prize, 1963, Union League Civic and Arts Foundation Prize, 1966, and Levinson Prize, 1977 (*Poetry*, Chicago); Guggenheim Fellowship, 1967, 1973; National Endowment for the Arts grant, 1968, 1969; National Institute of Arts and Letters award, 1969; Shelley Memorial Award, 1973; Frank O'Hara Prize, 1974; Harriet Monroe Poetry Award, 1975; National Book Critics Circle Award, 1976; Pulitzer Prize, 1976; National Book Award, 1976; Rockefeller grant, for playwriting, 1978. D.Litt.: Long Island University, Southampton, New York, 1979. Agent: Georges Borchardt Inc., 136 East 57th Street, New York, New York 10022, U.S.A.

PUBLICATIONS

Verse

Turandot and Other Poems. New York, Tibor de Nagy, 1953.
Some Trees. New Haven, Connecticut, Yale University Press, 1956.
The Poems. New York, Tiber Press, 1960.
The Tennis Court Oath. Middletown, Connecticut, Wesleyan University Press, 1962.
Rivers and Mountains. New York, Holt Rinehart, 1966.
Selected Poems. London, Cape, 1967.
Sunrise in Suburbia. New York, Phoenix Book Shop, 1968.
Three Madrigals. New York, Poets Press, 1968.
Fragment. Los Angeles, Black Sparrow Press, 1969.
The Double Dream of Spring. New York, Dutton, 1970.
The New Spirit. New York, Adventures in Poetry, 1970.
Penguin Modern Poets 19, with Lee Harwood and Tom Raworth. London, Penguin, 1971.
Three Poems. New York, Viking Press, 1972.
The Vermont Notebook. Los Angeles, Black Sparrow Press, 1975.
Self-Portrait in a Convex Mirror. New York, Viking Press, and London, Penguin, 1976.
Houseboat Days. New York, Viking Press, and London, Penguin, 1977.
As We Know. New York, Viking Press, and London, Penguin, 1979.

Plays

The Heroes (produced New York, 1952). Included in *Three Plays*, 1978.
The Compromise (produced Cambridge, Massachusetts, 1956). Included in *Three Plays*, 1978.
Three Plays (includes *The Heroes*, *The Compromise*, *The Philosopher*). Calais, Vermont, Z Press, 1978.

Novel

A Nest of Ninnies, with James Schuyler. New York, Dutton, 1969.

Other

Editor, with others, *American Literary Anthology I.* New York, Farrar Straus, 1968.
Editor, *Penguin Modern Poets 24.* London, Penguin, 1973.
Editor, *Muck Arbour*, by Bruce Marcus. Chicago, O'Hara, 1974.

Translator, *Melville*, by Jean-Jacques Mayoux. New York, Grove Press, 1960.
Translator, *Alberto Giacometti*, by Jacques Dupin. Paris, Maeght, 1963.

Bibliography: *John Ashbery: A Comprehensive Bibliography* by David K. Kermani, New York, Garland, 1976.

Critical Studies: *John Ashbery: An Introduction to the Poetry* by David Shapiro, New York, Columbia University Press, 1979; *John Ashbery* edited by David Lehman, Ithaca, New York, Cornell University Press, 1979.

* * *

John Ashbery, who is now emerging as the outstanding poet of his generation, is still suspect in the eyes of those who long nostalgically for a poetry of statement. In a long review for the *Times Literary Supplement* (1978), Robert Boyers observed: "If we take meaning to refer to the possibility of shared discourse in which speaker and auditor may participate more or less equally," then Ashbery is "an instance of a poet who, through much of his career, eliminates meaning without achieving any special intensity.... Meaning is often left out of an Ashbery poem ... to ensure the continuity of a quest for which ends are necessarily threatening." This is to regard *meaning* as some sort of fixed quantity that the poet as speaker can either "leave out" or proffer to the expectant auditor with whom he is engaged in "shared discourse." But what if there are other ways of "meaning"? Ashbery's penchant for *trompe l'oeil*, for "shifting sands," for rooms whose "fourth wall is invariably missing," is born of a conviction that, as he puts it in *Three Poems*, "the magic world really does exist," that to escape "the familiar interior which has always been there ... is impossible outside the frost of a dream, and it is just this major enchantment that gave us life to begin with." But, he adds in the next breath, "Life holds us, and is unknowable."

Dream is thus regarded as the source of our energy, our élan, of life itself, and yet that life remains curiously "unknowable." This paradox is at the heart of Ashbery's poetry and accounts for his preoccupation with dream structure rather than dream content. Not *what* one dreams but *how* – this is the domain of Ashbery, whose stories "tell only of themselves," presenting the reader with "an open field of narrative possibilities." Again and again in Ashbery's poems, the "I" (or "you" or "we" or "he," for Ashbery tends to use these pronouns interchangeably) moves in and out of dream; his are visions that are, in the words of a recent title, "Lost and Found and Lost Again." Indeed, in a new 50 page poem called "Litany," each page has two columns of verse (the prayer and response form of the genre), and although each column is to be read independently, as one moves from page to page, it is often possible to move from left to right (or right to left), creating alternate plots or thought processes, each equally tantalizing and equally possible.

Such indeterminacy has no real precedent in Anglo-American poetry. Wallace Stevens is regularly cited as Ashbery's central precursor, and the early poetry does have the phrasing and accent of the late Stevens, but the two poets have very different sensibilities. A closer model is the Auden of the "Bucolics" and "In Praise of Limestone" – "Rivers and Mountains," for example, echoes Auden's "Mountains" – but Ashbery's landscape is like a comic-strip version of Auden's. In his introduction to the *Collected Poems* of Frank O'Hara,

Ashbery describes the New York climate of the early 1960's, in which O'Hara came of age, as "Picasso and French poetry, de Kooning and Guston, Cage and Feldman...." This was also Ashbery's own artistic climate: Cage, for instance, is surely a source for the two-column strategy of "Litany." Having lived in Paris for a decade (1955–65), Ashbery cast a cold eye on the Neo-Symbolism of his American contemporaries, their mania for what he called "over-interpretation" or "objective correlativitis." In an essay written in French for the special Reverdy issue of the *Mercure de France* (1962), he argued that, whereas Eliot and his followers insisted on endowing each word or phrase with symbolic significance, Reverdy's images existed in their own right as "living phenomena," their main characteristic being "transparency." Again, the quirky texts of Raymond Roussel are praised for their "mysteries of construction." Roussel's language, says Ashbery, "seems always on the point of revealing its secret, of pointing the way back to the 'republic of dreams' whose insignia blazed on his forehead."

Language on the point of revealing its secret without ever actually doing so – this is what we find in Ashbery's own enigma texts. Symbolist poetry, we know, is difficult, but it is not impossible to decode; behind the intricate collage of, say, *The Waste Land*, there is, after all, a coherent core of relational meanings. Ashbery takes poetry a step further. When we read a poem like "On the Towpath" (in *Houseboat Days*), we are confronted by a series of arresting, palpable images that seem to coalesce for a moment, about to disclose a hidden meaning. But here the ambiguity is not of the Empsonian kind; it is, rather, irreducible. As Ashbery puts it, in talking of Gertrude Stein's *Stanzas in Meditation*:

> *Stanzas in Meditation* gives one the feeling of time passing, of things happening, of a "plot," though it would be difficult to say precisely what is going on. Sometimes the story has the logic of a dream ... at other times it becomes startlingly clear for a moment, as though a change in wind had suddenly enabled us to hear a conversation that was taking place some distance away.... But it is usually not events which interest Miss Stein, rather it is their "way of happening," and the story of *Stanzas in Meditation* is a general, all-purpose model which each reader can adapt to fit his own set of particulars. The poem is a hymn to possibility.

To create such "hymns to possibility" is by no means easy, as anyone who has read the countless imitations of Ashbery currently breaking into print knows. Too much disclosure produces contrivance; too much concealment, unintelligibility and boredom. Spell out the *content* of the dream and it loses its strangeness; conceal all clues, on the other hand, and you may lose your reader. In *The Tennis Court Oath* (1962), concealment is sometimes excessive. In such cut-up poems as "America" or "Europe," for example, even the "way of happening" becomes obscure. But, from the time of "These Lacustrine Cities" (1966), perhaps his first great "dream song," Ashbery creates a verbal landscape that reminds one of the Proustian magic-lantern show that enchants the child of *Swann's Way*. In the recent book *Houseboat Days* Ashbery's landscapes of desire are increasingly presented in the guise of what O'Hara called "charming artifice." Medieval romance, Elizabethan pageant, comic books, Arthur Rackham fairy-tale, Disney World T-shirts, flowered wallpaper, frosted wedding cakes, stage machinery, "grisaille shepherdesses," "terrorist chorales" – all these coalesce in the dream theater of *Houseboat Days*.

Not surprisingly, one of the finest poems in the book is called "Pyrography"; the process of burning designs on wood and leather with a heated tool here becomes the process of imprinting burning traces of memory and vision on a consciousness so fluid and amorphous that the "heated tool" is likely to slip on its surface. The scene of the poem is "Cottage Grove" (Chicago), the heart of the nation ("This is America calling"), but curiously it is also a fairy-tale world in which "The carriages/Are drawn forward under a sky of fumed oak." This contrast of old and new is nicely reflected in the stanza's rhythm which oscillates between the formality of "In service stairs the sweet corruption thrives," a perfect iambic pentameter line with inverted word order and heavy alliteration, and the prosaic inflection of "The page of dusk turns like a creaking revolving stage in Warren, Ohio."

In the second stanza, the "we" who are also "they" set out on a journey across the great American continent, first by boxcar through the "gyrating fans of suburbs" and "the darkness of cities," and then the scene suddenly dissolves and the travellers are moving up the Pacific coast to Bolinas, where "The houses doze and seem to wonder why." Along the way, they meet, in an echo of Baudelaire's "Le Voyage," the "disappointed, returning ones," but "the headlong night" beckons and it is too late to take warning and turn back. Indeed, as the journey continues, one proceeds, not westward or north to Canada, but into an imaginary world. A city has evidently been erected, "built ... Partly over with fake ruins in the image of ourselves:/An arch that terminates in mid-keystone a crumbling stone pier/For laundresses, an open-air theater, never completed/And only partially designed." Where are we? Like Rimbaud's "Villes," or Ashbery's own "lacustrine cities," these cities cannot be specified; they emerge as part of a theater decor upon which the curtain may fall any minute. So the poet asks:

> How are we to inhabit
> This space from which the fourth wall is invariably missing,
> As in a stage-set or dollhouse, except by staying as we are,
> In lost profile, facing the stars....

This question has haunted Ashbery from the beginning. He has known, all along, that "Everything has a schedule, if you can find out what it is," the difficulty being that you can't find out. Just so, the question posed in "Pyrography" is rhetorical, for the poet knows that the only way to inhabit a "space from which the fourth wall is invariably missing" is to accept it as the "stage-set or dollhouse" it really is, to realize that, in Yeats's words, "Man can embody truth but he cannot know it."

—Marjorie Perloff

ATWOOD, Margaret (Eleanor). Canadian. Born in Ottawa, Ontario, 18 November 1939. Educated at Victoria College, University of Toronto, B.A. 1961; Radcliffe College, Cambridge, Massachusetts, A.M. 1962; Harvard University, Cambridge, Massachusetts. Lecturer in English, University of British Columbia, Vancouver, 1964–65; Instructor in English, Sir George Williams University, Montreal, 1967–68. Recipient: E. J. Pratt Medal, 1961; President's Medal, University of Western Ontario, 1966; Governor-General's Award, 1967; Centennial Commission prize, 1967; Union League Civic and Arts Foundation Prize (*Poetry*, Chicago), 1969. Lives in Ontario. Address: c/o Oxford University Press, 70 Wynford Drive, Don Mills, Ontario, Canada.

PUBLICATIONS

Verse

Double Persephone. Toronto, Hawkshead Press, 1961.
The Circle Game. Bloomfield Hills, Michigan, Cranbrook Academy of Art, 1964; revised edition, Toronto, Contact Press, 1966.
Talismans for Children. Bloomfield Hills, Michigan, Cranbrook Academy of Art, 1965.
Kaleidoscopes: Baroque. Bloomfield Hills, Michigan, Cranbrook Academy of Art, 1965.

Speeches for Doctor Frankenstein. Bloomfield Hills, Michigan, Cranbrook Academy of Art, 1966.
The Animals in That Country. Toronto, Oxford University Press, 1968; Boston, Little Brown, 1969.
Five Modern Canadian Poets, with others, edited by Eli Mandel. Toronto, Holt Rinehart, 1970.
The Journals of Susanna Moodie. Toronto, Oxford University Press, 1970.
Procedures for Underground. Toronto, Oxford University Press, and Boston, Little Brown, 1970.
Power Politics. Toronto, Anansi, 1972; New York, Harper, 1973.
You Are Happy. Toronto, Oxford University Press, and New York, Harper, 1974.
Selected Poems. Toronto, Oxford University Press, 1976; New York, Simon and Schuster, 1978.
Two-Headed Poems. Toronto, Oxford University Press, 1978.

Recording: *The Poetry and Voice of Margaret Atwood*, Caedmon, 1977.

Novels

The Edible Woman. Toronto, McClelland and Stewart, London, Deutsch, and Boston, Little Brown, 1969.
Surfacing. Toronto, McClelland and Stewart, 1972; London, Deutsch, and New York, Simon and Schuster, 1973.
Lady Oracle. Toronto, McClelland and Stewart, and New York, Simon and Schuster, 1976; London, Deutsch, 1977.
Life Before Man. New York, Simon and Schuster, 1979.

Short Stories

Dancing Girls and Other Stories. Toronto, McClelland and Stewart, 1977.

Other

Survival: A Thematic Guide to Canadian Literature. Toronto, Anansi, 1972.
Up in the Trees (juvenile). Toronto, McClelland and Stewart, 1978.

Manuscript Collection: University of Toronto.

Critical Study: *A Violent Duality* by Sherril Grace, Montreal, Vehicule Press, 1979.

Margaret Atwood comments:

I feel that the task of criticizing my poetry is best left to others (i.e., critics) and would much rather have it take place after I am dead. If at all.

* * *

Margaret Atwood has justly been described as "the most discussed and widely read writer in Canada." She has distinguished herself as a poet, novelist, and critic, and has emerged in the 1960's and 1970's not only as a best-selling author but also as a spokeswoman for both Canadian literature and feminist concerns. Her accomplishment is all the more surprising in that the outlook of her work could best be described as unpromising and uncompromising – ironic, detached, suggestive, intellectual, essentially poetic. Who would have believed the public was prepared for such a private person? The 125 poems in Atwood's *Selected Poems* reveal no thematic development but they do display a stylistic movement in the direction of poetry that is even more spare and economic, even delphic in deft indirection. Her recent *Two-Headed Poems* may be read as being about personal relationships, but also as about the continual dialogue between French-speaking Quebec and the rest of English-speaking Canada:

Your language hangs around your neck,
a noose, a heavy necklace;
each word is empire,
each word is vampire and mother.

As for the sun, there are as many
suns as there are words for sun;

true or false?

The dialogue breaks down into a monologue and then comes together again as "a duet": "This is not a debate/but a duet/with two deaf singers." The conceptions of the two countries or communities within Canada may not be new, but the intensity with which a writer is defining them and the wide currency they are receiving are new. The poems go beyond the political and the social analogue into the psychological and metaphysical realm of duality, for one poem "The Right Hand Fights the Left" concludes: "The right hand holds the knife,/the left hand dances."

—John Robert Colombo

AUBERT, Alvin. American. Born in Lutcher, Louisiana, 12 March 1930. Educated at Southern University, Baton Rouge, Louisiana, B.A. 1959; University of Michigan, Ann Arbor (Woodrow Wilson Fellow), A.M. 1960; University of Illinois, Urbana, 1963–64, 1966–67. Married 1) Olga Alexis (divorced), one daughter; 2) Bernadine Tenant in 1959; two daughters. Instructor, 1960–62, Assistant Professor, 1962–65, Associate Professor of English, 1965–70, Southern University; Visiting Professor of English, University of Oregon, Eugene, Summer 1970. Since 1970, Associate Professor of English, State University of New York, Fredonia. Editor, *Obsidian* magazine, and Advisory Editor, *Drama and Theatre*, both Fredonia, New York. Recipient; Bread Loaf Fellowship, 1968: National Endowment for the Arts grant, 1973; Coordinating Council of Literary Magazines grant, 1979. Address: 10 George's Place, Fredonia, New York 14063, U.S.A.

PUBLICATIONS

Verse

Against the Blues. Detroit, Broadside Press, 1972.
Feeling Through. Greenfield Center, New York, Greenfield Review Press, 1975.

Critical Studies: by J. B., in *Kliatt* (West Newton, Massachusetts), November 1972; James Shokoff, in the *Buffalo Courier-Express*, 8 June 1973; Herbert W. Martin, in *Three Rivers Poetry Journal* (Pittsburgh), November 1978.

Alvin Aubert comments:

A poem is a verification (in every sense of the word) of experience in thought and feeling, but mostly the latter, for feeling is the means by which essential experience is transmitted. If the feeling is "right" the intellectual content is "right" also, which is to say that in the poem that works there takes place a mutual verification of thought by feeling, feeling by thought. From another perspective, a successful poem embodies an ordering of external data (experience), a forming of it to facilitate a significant connection of externals and internals, the data out there and the data within. I am an Afro-American, one who is very much aware of his roots in that somewhat unique region of the U.S., south Louisiana, with its French influence. But I am above all an Afro-American of African descent, and the two terms constitute a reality far beyond their sum. Thus, there is no question as to the source of that experience which verifies, as well as finds its verification in, a poem of mine. As for my thematic concerns, I concur in James Shokoff's assessment: "His themes are death, the shapes of the past, the terror of existence, and the pain of endurance, yet [hopefully] the poems are neither depressing nor pessimistic."

* * *

The title of Alvin Aubert's first book of poetry, *Against the Blues*, directs us to read his verse against a background of recalled popular sources. For example, "Whispers in a Country Church" simulates an exchange of worldly gossip among the, no doubt, pious; "De Profundis" relates the practical plea of a drinker for some sign, less miraculous than a burning bush, to move him to sobriety. These stock comic figures are matched in a pair of poems, opening the book, that invoke Bessie Smith in an allusion to the muse and announce the news of the dispensation of the blues. None of the poems is long. All have the apparent simplicity of direct statement. And except for the references to Bessie Smith and, in another poem, Nat Turner, the immediate subjects are personal experiences. Just like the blues! The singer/poet presents first-person experiences in ways that will make them typical.

As both singer and poet know, it is not so much the experience itself, though that is surely familiar, as the form in which it is rendered that makes the song and poem typical. Thus, Aubert typifies his poems through the patterns of language. The characters of Zenobia in "Photo Album" or "Uncle Bill" and "Granny Dean" are familiar not only because we may know people like them, but because the poet's lines about his characters approximate the habits of speech. Often a use of negatives or identical rhymes echoes the oral games of Black English. Sometimes, as in "Garden Scene," the verse nearly assumes the form of anecdotal *exemplum*. Yet, of course, it is not to imitate, even the patterns of spoken language, that Aubert writes. The typicality provided by linguistic patterns acknowledged by poet and reader serves as subject for creative imagination.

Aubert opens his second book of poetry with "Black Aesthetic," a poem that proposes to reverse Duchamp's *Nude Descending a Staircase* so that it would portray a black man going up, not down. And out. "Feeling Through," the title poem of the second book, illustrates Aubert's point, pulling experience up into reflective consciousness and setting it out as the new experience of a poem. With a characteristic syntactic economy, now become almost elliptical, Aubert establishes a situation. He, or his persona, sits on a porch swing, looking through a window at the reflection in a mirror of a carnival photograph. A partial dialogue is overheard but quickly displaced, so that wonder about the old photograph is transformed into soliloquy on the problem of recapturing the past. The scene and events of "Feeling Through" are the material of a family story. Narrative, however, remains inchoate as the poetic voice plays feelings held in the foreground of mind over the background of anecdote. The poem is, thus, both a gloss on the latent tale of the photograph and the expression of a newly defined experience.

Increasingly Aubert attaches subjective significance to his imagery. In poems such as "Economics" from the first volume or "The Opposite of Green" from the second details explain the mundane appearance of racism, but "Nightmare" and "Levitation," both in the second book, have highly personal references. Still, the tactics of language are consistent throughout Aubert's work. The texts of his poems maintain a continuity with Afro-American tradition by simulation and innovation that become a commentary on the richness of his sources and evidence of authentic re-creation.

—John M. Reilly

AVISON, Margaret (Kirkland). Canadian. Born in Galt, Ontario, 23 April 1918. Educated at the University of Toronto, B.A. 1940. Recipient: Guggenheim Fellowship, 1956; Governor-General's Award, 1961. Address: 17 Lascelles Boulevard, Apartment 108, Toronto M4V 2B6, Canada.

PUBLICATIONS

Verse

Winter Sun. Toronto, University of Toronto Press, and London, Routledge, 1960.
The Dumbfounding. New York, Norton, 1966.
Sunblue. Hantsport, Nova Scotia, Lancelot Press, 1978.

Other

The Research Compendium, with Albert Rose. Toronto, University of Toronto Press, 1964.

* * *

Although her poems have been appearing in literary magazines and anthologies since the early 1940's, Margaret Avison did not publish a volume until 1960, when *Winter Sun* appeared, to be followed in 1966 by *The Dumbfounding*. With these, the reputation she had already acquired among a small group of critical readers as an original and significant modern poet was confirmed by an almost universal sanction.

Avison's originality lies partly in the stylistic and organizational boldness with which she gives expression to an extraordinary sensibility. This is first and most strikingly a visual one. Her poetry "begins (and often ends)," wrote the critic Milton Wilson, "with the perceptive eye." Problems of focus, structure, and design – intellectual, emotional, and moral – are everywhere at the heart of her early poems and persist with an added congruence into the later. Such titles as "Geometaphysics," "Perspective," and "Meeting Together of Poles and Latitudes" are indicative of this preoccupation. Her perceptive eye, however, is also a contemplative eye, metaphysical as well as physical, and it is not the eye alone that is made the instrument of critical awareness but the organs of the more intimate senses of smell, taste, and touch as well.

There are some literary affinities here perhaps, a hint occasionally of Wallace Stevens or Marianne Moore, of Herbert or Hopkins, but they are of little significance when set against the gnarled syntax and conglomerate diction she has forged out for herself. No single adjective is adequate to describe her diction: it is erudite, complex, archaic, simple, modern – an amalgam of the scientific and philosophical with the familiar and the new, a high style and a low, pillaged and put to work. Her poems come to terms with a reality that is heterogeneous and explosive. They set up a constant tension between a grainy local foreground and an eternal circumambiance of space and time.

In her second book Avison goes beyond perception and philosophy into a pure Christian poetry that brings something of the grace and humility of George Herbert easily and naturally into the modern world and into her own personal experience. "The Word," "The Dumbfounding," "Person, or a Hymn on and to the Holy Ghost," "Searching and Sounding," and the remarkable dramatic dialogue "A Story" are acts of submission and worship as well as poems. They are the result of a precisely dated mystical experience. I believe they have a validity as firm as the religious poetry of Hopkins or Eliot.

—A. J. M. Smith

AWOONOR, Kofi. Ghanaian. Born in Wheta, 13 March 1935. Educated at the University of Ghana, Accra, B.A. 1960; University of London (Longmans Fellow, 1967–68), M.A. 1968. Married; three children. Research Fellow, Institute of African Studies, Legon, 1960–64; Director, Ghana Ministry of Information Film Corporation, 1964–67. Since 1968, Poet-in-Residence, State University of New York, Stony Brook. Visiting Professor, University of Texas, Austin, 1972–73. Past Editor, *Okyeame*, Accra, and Past Co-Editor, *Black Orpheus*, Ibadan. Detained on suspicion of treason, Ghana, 1975–76. Recipient: Gurrey Prize, 1959. Address: c/o Loretta Barrett, Doubleday Publishing Company, 245 Park Avenue, New York, New York 10017, U.S.A.

PUBLICATIONS

Verse

Rediscovery and Other Poems. Ibadan, Mbari, and Evanston, Illinois, Northwestern University Press, 1964.
Night of My Blood. New York, Doubleday, 1971.
Ride Me, Memory. Greenfield Center, New York, Greenfield Review Press, 1973.
The House by the Sea. Greenfield Center, New York, Greenfield Review Press, 1978.

Plays

Ancestral Power, and *Lament*, in *Short African Plays*, edited by Cosmo Pieterse. London, Heinemann, 1972.

Novel

This Earth, My Brother: An Allegorical Tale of Africa. London, Heinemann, 1970; New York, Doubleday, 1971.

Other

In Person – Achebe, Awoonor, and Soyinka at the University of Washington. Seattle, University of Washington African Studies Program, 1975.
The Breast of the Earth: A Survey of the History, Culture, and Literature of Africa South of the Sahara. New York, Doubleday, 1975.

Editor, with George Adali-Martty, *Messages: Poems from Ghana*. London, Heinemann, 1970; New York, Humanities Press, 1971.
Editor, *Guardians of the Sacred Word: Ewe Poetry*. New York, Nok, 1974.

Kofi Awoonor comments:

Traditional oral poetry of the Ewes with its emphasis on lyricism, the chant, repetition of lines, symbolism and imagery transfused into English through the secondary influence of Pound, Dylan Thomas, etc.

* * *

Educated almost exclusively in Africa, Kofi Awoonor has been less influenced by the poetic traditions of Britain and America than many of his African contemporaries, though his work makes it obvious that he has read widely and he does not hesitate to use biblical references and echoes where he deems it necessary to his purpose. From the beginning of his poetic career, Awoonor made it his aim to write poetry in which genuine African experiences are communicated, in a language which owes something to the African vernaculars, even when writing in English (and he also writes in Ewe, his native tongue). So that when he says "In our beginnings lies our journey's end" ("Salvation"), the phrase is appropriate to the poem and the reader appreciates that the thought has not been taken over from Eliot, but derived from the actual experience of the Ghanaian poet; he has arrived at the same destination as Eliot from a completely different direction. He has, in fact, perceived the significance and value – both for his own writing as well as that of other poets – of the rich oral and folk traditions of Africa, and has experimented, not always successfully, with them in his poetry. Where other poets, and especially those educated in Britain and America, have felt alienated and have experienced an acute sense of conflict between the imposed values of western society and those of Africa, so that it became incumbent on them to emphasise their "African-ness," Awoonor has been able to be his natural self, without shouting the odds about Africa, to go on writing quite unperturbed by the conflicts around him (or so it might seem from his work). The title of his volume *Rediscovery* has implications at two levels – firstly, it celebrates the need to rediscover the African traditions of thought and way of life, which entails a knowledge of both the past and the present; secondly, it expresses the urge of the poet himself towards self-identification in terms of his own environment. At both levels he draws freely upon ideas and imagery from African rituals and ceremonies – sacrificial offerings, altars, bitter herbs, drums, purification rites, etc., abound in his work, to merge occasionally with specifically Christian images (as in "That Which Flesh Is Heir to") – and by a technique he describes as "transliteration of thoughts" introduces literally translated vernacular expressions and coinages into his English, which adds both freshness and meaning to his work. Although several of the poems in *Rediscovery* have been much anthologised, Awoonor has made rapid progress in the development of an individual style since the publication of his first volume. Amongst later poems are "Songs of Sorrow," based on an Anlo dirge, "The Sea Eats the Land at Home" and, one of his most ambitious and best-sustained efforts to date, the long poem entitled "I Heard a Bird Cry."

—Howard Sergeant

BAKER, Howard (Wilson). American. Born in Philadelphia, Pennsylvania, 5 April 1905. Educated at Whittier College, California, B.A. 1927; Stanford University, California,

M.A. 1929; Sorbonne, Paris, 1929–31; University of California, Berkeley (Phelan Fellowship, 1933–35), Ph.D. 1937 (Phi Beta Kappa). Married 1) the novelist Dorothy Dodds in 1931 (died, 1968); 2) Virginia De Camp Beattie, 1969; two daughters. Briggs-Copeland Instructor, Harvard University, Cambridge, Massachusetts, 1937–43; Visiting Professor, University of California, Berkeley, 1958–59, Davis, 1963–66. Editor, with Yvor Winters and Janet Lewis, *Gyroscope*, Palo Alto, California, 1929–30. Founding Member, The Barn Theatre, Porterville, California. Olive and orange grower: Director, Lindsay Ripe Olive Company, Lindsay, California, 1956–57; President of the Board of Directors, Grand View Heights Citrus Association, 1962–73, and Tulare-Kern Citrus Exchange, 1969–73; Member, Citrus Advisory Board of California. Recipient: Guggenheim Fellowship, 1944. Agent: Lucille Sullivan, R.R.2, Box 171, West Brattleboro, Vermont 05301. Address: Route 1, Box 11, Terra Bella, California 93270, U.S.A.

PUBLICATIONS

Verse

A Letter from the Country and other Poems. New York, New Directions, 1941.
Ode to the Sea and Other Poems. Denver, Swallow, 1966.

Recording: *Ode to the Sea*, Library of Congress, 1949.

Plays

Trio, with Dorothy Baker (produced New York, 1944; as *Two Loves I Have*, produced London, 1952).
The Ninth Day, with Dorothy Baker (televised, 1957; produced Dublin, 1962). Dixon, California, Proscenium Press, 1967.

Television Play: *The Ninth Day*, 1957.

Novel

Orange Valley. New York, Coward McCann, 1931.

Other

Induction to Tragedy: A Study in the Development of Form in Gorboduc, The Spanish Tragedy, and Titus Andronicus. Baton Rouge, Louisiana State University Press, 1939.

Critical Study: by William Van O'Connor, in *Poetry* (Chicago), January 1967.

Howard Baker comments:

Since our poetry begins with Homer, if you are going to be a poet, the best place to begin, ideally, is in the Epics and the Hymns. For me, living in the country in California, though the ideal was always present, the fulfillment was far beyond my capacities. But this was for the best, possibly, because, with a little digging into the poetry of Homer, the farm and the farm workshop, the seasons for hunting and fishing, and the astonishing sights that were to be met in the mountains and on the beaches, and in the crowded places where men congregate, became more freshly Homeric, I think, than the unvaried application to the Homeric text could have made them. The natural unavoidable impact of the past on the present, and the present on the past, with no forced applications of the one on the other, is good for poets, and I would imagine for everyone. The ideal to be strived for is the scope of the Renaissance Man; and of the pre-Renaissance, pre-Socratic viewer of many races and many cities.

May I restate all this by quoting from the title poem in *A Letter from the Country*?

Be muched hedged in. Rehearse the ancient ways
Till to your strong windbreak on wholesome days,
  Timid, to fright still uninured,
  Comes Amaryllis, reassured;

Comes softly, briar-scratched, with tangled hair
Leading those others who wait and shyly stare –
  Masters who fled the savage wave,
  Returned unkempt from their high cave.

Then lean your head to their slow syllables:
Whispering deep seas beneath the fleeting gulls:
  The torch of Hecuba, the birth,
  Ruined Ilium fading into earth....

* * *

Among the pungent footnotes to Yvor Winters's important essay, "Problems for the Modern Critic of Literature," is the famous second, referring to one of Winters's best students, a poet and scholar who, after teaching at Harvard for three years became disgusted with academic politics and wastefulness of Departmental Life. The unnamed talented poet withdrew from the Academy, having decided there is more profit (and more intellectual honesty) in raising olives and oranges in a California valley. The unnamed subject of that footnote was Howard Baker. Recently Baker agreed to leave his orchards, giving a few lectures at a California university. He has also published recently some essays on classical subjects, essays which are stimulating as well as being learned. Since he does not have to "publish or perish," he publishes only what he thinks worthy of print. His standards tend to be higher than those of the academic marketplace.

Baker's "Advice to a Man Who Lost a Dog" (in a difficult stanza form) may remind readers of Winters's celebrated "Elegy on a Young Airedale Bitch Lost Some Years Since in the Salt-Marsh." Unfortunately Baker's poems is almost unknown; here is one of the seven stanzas:

Think, when you hunt him on the windy brow
Where the lean settler led his shaggy cow
And questioning yielded to the tranquil plow,
  That that fine poise bequeathed alone
  A cellar overgown.

And of course, neither poem is about a dead dog at all. The sonnet "Dr. Johnson" is one of Baker's best poems, tragically concluding: "We are all Boswells harkening the worms." The intelligence and the prosodic brilliance which inform his best poems make them models of their kind. At times, in the lesser poems, the irony may be easy; but there is scarcely a fault in "Pont Neuf." That poems about response to a public statue have become almost "set piece" now should not dull our response to Baker's poem, an almost perfect example of the kind. Other poems one wishes more people knew are "Quiet Folk," "The Passing Generation," and, despite Winters's objections to its associational technique, the long "Ode to the Sea":

Conserving sea! To what auroral plains
Have you consigned the meaning of the names

Augustine, Abelard,
Aquinas, Bede, Bernard?
Permanent, Lossless, undiminished Sea,
Change is the law of your stability!

Although Baker's poems tend to be passed over by anthologists who favor more showy pieces, his poems will remain a delight and an instruction to discriminating readers.

—James Korges

BANTOCK, Gavin (Marcus August). British. Born in Barnt Green, near Birmingham, Warwickshire, 4 July 1939. Educated at King's Norton Grammar School; New College, Oxford, M.A. (honours) in English Language and Literature 1964. Head of English department in various private secondary schools in England. Since 1969, Lecturer in English, Reitaku University, Kashiwa-shi, Chiba-ken, Japan. Recipient: Richard Hillary Memorial Prize, 1964; Alice Hunt Bartlett Prize, 1966; Eric Gregory Award, 1969. Agent: Peter Jay, 69 King George Street, London SE10 8PX. Address: The Grey Cottage, 36 Bittell Road, Barnt Green, near Birmingham, England.

PUBLICATIONS

Verse

Christ: A Poem in Twenty-Six Parts. Oxford, Donald Parsons, 1965.
Juggernaut. London, Anvil Press Poetry, 1968.
A New Thing Breathing. London, Anvil Press Poetry, 1969.
Anhaga. London, Anvil Press Poetry, 1970.
Gleeman. Cardiff, Second Aeon, 1972.
Eirenikon. London, Anvil Press Poetry, 1972.
Isles. Feltham, Middlesex, Quarto Press, 1974.
Dragons. London, Anvil Press Poetry, 1979.

Play

The Last of the Kings: Frederick the Great (produced Edinburgh, 1969).

Other

Land of the Setting Sun. Tokyo, Kinseido, 1973.
Disunited Kingdom. Tokyo, Kinseido, 1974.
Twenty Eggs in One Basket. Tokyo, Kinseido, 1975.
Nobler in the Mind. Tokyo, Kinseido, 1976.
Ten-Year Gaijin. Tokyo, Kinseido, 1979.
Pioneers of English Poetry. Tokyo, Kinseido, 1979.

Gavin Bantock comments:

Themes and subjects: In *Christ* – Jesus as a man suffering human emotions and human love – a tragic, yet optimistic, interpretation of the Gospel Christ.

In middle-length poems, "Hiroshima," "Juggernaut," "Ichor," and "Person" – examination of the human predicament, in a world of intense suffering where there is no God, except violence and destruction, and where life is lived only in the present with no possible planned future. Condemnation of narrow-minded and blindly orthodox people.

Eirenikon is an attack on all those crying for peace, and on this rotten western, capitalistic society – of which the U.S.A. is the chief culprit. Most evils of modern society originate in the U.S.A.

Dragons is a collection of poems, some with Japanese background, emphasizing the unknown behind the known, deepening one's concepts of seemingly ordinary things.

Verse forms etc.: Usually disciplined free verse, based on somewhat elevated speech rhythms; perhaps too much rhetorical usage; trying to eliminate this. (Much early practice in iambic English verse forms.)

Main sources and influences: Anglo-Saxon (I've made numerous translations), The Bible, Ezra Pound, Dylan Thomas, Ted Hughes. *Other strong interests*: Beethoven, Einstein, Astronomy, Dictators, Pipe-organs, Japanese archery, gardening, Shakespeare production.

My chief aims are to expose the short-comings of people who live narrow lives, who are unconscious of the strength of simplicity and of the practical wisdom of the much-damned attitude of loving-kindness. My attitude to such people is ruthless when they will not listen and sympathetic when they cannot listen. I have great admiration for people with strong wills and powers of endurance; I despise idleness and escapism and irresponsible action in human affairs.

Artistically, I hope to help maintain modern poetry steady in strength and efficiency of words used, in logical forms and order and in importance of subject. Too much poetry today is formless, trivial, arbitrary, small-minded, and does not make use of words or images designed to *develop* the language – too much of the language of modern poetry is dead and dull.

I believe writing poetry is a skilled craft, and must be learned. Too many people write lines of verse without ever making poetry, or make "poetic" utterances without knowing a thing about versification.

I am trying to make a distinction between the versifying of hippies and layabouts and the making of good poetry by dedicated poets. The public seem to be confused about the values of both.

* * *

Gavin Bantock's poetry has always been unfashionably rhetorical; his imagination centres on moral and often religious themes. His long poem *Christ*, which won both the Richard Hillary and Alice Hunt Bartlett awards, has many passages of considerable power; but those who found its rhetoric distasteful will not have been comforted by his more recent poetry. *Juggernaut*, *Anhaga*, and *Eirenikon*, written after a long stay in Japan, continue to use language forcefully, making points often by devices (such as repetition) used today by few poets of standing. But Bantock's irony never deserts him, and is sharp and bitter enough to give his verse considerable muscle even when its form seems a little heavy:

> Rejoice and be exceeding glad for great is your reward
> surely his goodness and mercy shall grant you
> a cup of tea and a biscuit in the interval.

One of the difficulties facing Bantock as a communicator is that his poems are long (*Christ* has some 7,000 lines), though extremely dense, when his rhetoric is under proper control. A further refinement of his technique will no doubt bring him within range of readers who at present find his poetry somewhat unapproachable, and indeed will do that poetry no harm. The passages one remembers are those furthest from bellowing:

And the last dragon on its back coiled in divine agony
offers its silken belly to sword or feather-duster and lies there
dying of uncontrollable laughter and a surfeit of greenhorn spells.

—Derek Parker

BARAKA, Amiri. See **JONES, LeRoi.**

BARBOUR, Douglas. Canadian. Born in Winnipeg, Manitoba, 21 March 1940. Educated at Acadia University, Wolfville, Nova Scotia, B.A. in English 1962; Dalhousie University, Halifax, Nova Scotia, M.A. in English 1964; Queen's University, Kingston, Ontario (Canada Council Doctoral grant, 1967–68), Ph.D. in English 1976. Married Sharon Nicoll in 1966. Assistant Professor, 1969–76, and since 1977, Associate Professor of English, University of Alberta, Edmonton. Editor, *Quarry*, Kingston, for three years; Member of the Editorial Board, *White Pelican*, Edmonton, 1971–76. Since 1978, Poetry Editor, *Canadian Forum*, Toronto; since 1978, Member of the Editorial Board, NeWest Press, Edmonton. Address: 10808 75th Avenue, Edmonton, Alberta T6E 1K2, Canada.

PUBLICATIONS

Verse

Land Fall. Montreal, Delta Canada, 1971.
A Poem As Long As the Highway. Kingston, Ontario, Quarry Press, 1971.
White. Fredericton, New Brunswick, Fiddlehead, 1972.
Songbook. Vancouver, Talonbooks, 1973.
He & She &. Ottawa, Golden Dog Press, 1974.
Visions of My Grandfather. Ottawa, Golden Dog Press, 1977.
Shore Lines. Winnipeg, Turnstone Press, 1979.

Other

World Out of Words: The SF Novels of Samuel R. Delany. Hayes, Middlesex, Bran's Head, 1979.

Editor, *The Story So Far 5.* Toronto, Coach House Press, 1978.

Douglas Barbour comments:

My poetry has moved from an attempt to articulate the outer landscape in the best words I could find to the more various and complex attempt to articulate the inner landscape that *is* both the best words I can discover at the moment of writing and me and my friends, our relations. So that: in fact, language *is* the landscape, richly inhabited, I now seek to explore in my poems.

Rime, in all its guises, rhythm (that "absolute rhythm" of which Ezra Pound wrote) and *sound*: these are central to what poetry is about, and it goes about playing, most seriously (though not solemnly) with these and with the many multifaceted relationships language can map.

To explore, anything, is the great game of making poems. I try.

* * *

Douglas Barbour is one of the younger generation of poets who emerged in the later 1960's, and whose work is distinguished by open if intensely self-contained forms, and a new eclecticism as far as related or absorbed influences are concerned. Not directly descended from any one of the three major movements in contemporary Canadian poetry, he has combined an awareness of the speaking voice in the poem with a somewhat more tenacious reliance on form, albeit open form, which in its turn is more disciplined than the compositional openness of the "field" theorists. In his first slim collection, *Land Fall*, Barbour moved between examples of prefigured concreteness and what one reviewer described as his "mindscapes." In his second volume the process of the poem became dependent on the physical tracings of a cross-country journey in which geography buttressed perception, and the act of travelling issued its summons to the imagination. *Songbook*, Barbour's fourth book, is a collection of lyrical jottings which, by virtue of being part impression and part reminiscence, strikes one as somewhat less imaginatively secure, although it has fine moments in which the sensuous and the personal are challenged by the unpunctuated austerities of lower-case statement, and the lonely sharpness of mind-images.

—Michael Gnarowski

BARKER, George (Granville). British. Born in Loughton, Essex, 26 February 1913. Educated at Marlborough Road School, Chelsea, London; Regent Street Polytechnic, London. Married Elspeth Langlands in 1964; several children. Professor of English Literature, Imperial Tohoku University, Sendai, Japan, 1939–41; Visiting Professor, New York State University, Buffalo, 1965–66; Arts Fellow, York University, 1966–67; Visiting Professor, University of Wisconsin, Madison, 1971–72. Patron of the Poetry Society, Oxford University, 1953. Recipient: Royal Society of Literature bursary, 1950; Guinness Prize, 1962; Levinson Prize (*Poetry*, Chicago), 1965; Borestone Mountain Poetry Prize, 1967; Arts Council bursary, 1968. Address: Bintry House, Itteringham, Aylsham, Norfolk, England.

PUBLICATIONS

Verse

Thirty Preliminary Poems. London, Parton Press, 1933.
Poems. London, Faber, 1935.
Calamiterror. London, Faber, 1937.

Elegy on Spain. London, Parton Press, 1939.
Lament and Triumph. London, Faber, 1940.
Selected Poems. New York, Macmillan, 1941.
Sacred and Secular Elegies. New York, New Directions, 1943.
Eros in Dogma. London, Faber, 1944.
Love Poems. New York, Dial Press, 1947.
The True Confession of George Barker. London, Fore, 1950; augmented edition, New York, New American Library, 1964; London, MacGibbon and Kee, 1965.
News of the World. London, Faber, 1950.
A Vision of Beasts and Gods. London, Faber, 1954.
Collected Poems 1930–1955. London, Faber, 1957; New York, Criterion, 1958.
The View from a Blind I. London, Faber, 1962.
Penguin Modern Poets 3, with Charles Causley and Martin Bell. London, Penguin, 1962.
Collected Poems 1930–1965. New York, October House, 1965.
Dreams of a Summer Night. London, Faber, 1966.
The Golden Chains. London, Faber, 1968.
At Thurgarton Church. London, Trigram Press, 1969.
Runes and Rhymes and Tunes and Chimes (for children). London, Faber, 1969.
What Is Mercy and a Voice. London, Poem-of-the-Month Club, 1970.
To Aylsham Fair (for children). London, Faber, 1970.
The Alphabetical Zoo (for children). London, Faber, 1970.
Poems of Places and People. London, Faber, 1971.
III Hallucination Poems. New York, Helikon Press, 1972.
In Memory of David Archer. London, Faber, 1973.
Dialogues etc. London, Faber, 1976.
Seven Poems. Warwick, Greville Press, 1977.
Villa Stellar. London, Faber, 1978.

Plays

Two Plays (*The Seraphina* and *In the Shade of the Old Apple Tree*). London, Faber, 1958.

Radio Plays: *The Seraphina*, 1956; *Oriel O'Hanlon* (published as *In the Shade of the Old Apple Tree*), 1957.

Novels

Alanna Autumnal. London, Wishart, 1933.
Janus (two novellena). London, Faber, 1935.
The Dead Seagull. London, Lehmann, 1950; New York, Farrar Straus, 1951.

Other

Essays. London, MacGibbon and Kee, 1970.

Editor, *Idylls of the King and a Selection of Poems*, by Alfred, Lord Tennyson. New York, Doubleday, 1961.

Manuscript Collections: University of Texas, Austin; Lockwood Memorial Library, State University of New York, Buffalo; Berg Collection, New York Public Library.

Critical Studies: "A Prolegomena to George Barker" by Patrick W. Swift, in *X* (London), 1960; *English Poetry 1900–1950* by C. H. Sisson, London, Hart Davis, 1971; *Homage to*

George Barker on His 60th Birthday, edited by John Heath-Stubbs and Martin Green, London, Martin Brian and O'Keeffe, 1973.

* * *

During his poetic career, George Barker's reputation has perhaps suffered on two counts. First, he emerged as a poet at the same time as Dylan Thomas, and at almost exactly the same age. From the beginning they were often linked by critics as being in some sense "romantic," as poets of personal concern and extravagant gesture, somehow seen in opposition to the supposedly more social concerns of Auden, Spender, and MacNeice. And though the essays in Francis Scarfe's *Auden and After* (a book which gives a fair picture of critical orthodoxies in the early 1940's) give equal prominence to Barker and Thomas, Thomas's later reputation, particularly after his death, seems to have obscured Barker's. Second, the anti-romantic tide in the mid-1950's turned against Barker, making him seem a period figure and wrongly lumping him indiscriminately with the New Apocalyptics and the wholly inflated tone which was taken to be the mark of the bad old wartime days.

In fact Barker's development has been much more interesting than this. There is an awkward Miltonic grandeur about some of the early work in *Thirty Preliminary Poems* and *Poems*, expressed in flowing and serpentine syntax, and a heady rhetoric which was given a more extended outing in his long poem *Calamiterror*. But the first fully achieved books are *Lament and Triumph* and *Eros in Dogma*, particularly in those poems (such as "Allegory of the Adolescent and the Adult," "Resolution of Dependence," and the much-anthologised "To My Mother") which show an effort of concentration on some external object or narrative.

With *News of the World*, there begins a relaxation of tone and a greater linguistic simplicity which Barker has continued through his later books. His themes were by this time established: elegies, both particular and general; the furies and betrayals of love; celebration and disgust. All reached their most concentrated, ambitious and notorious expression in *The True Confession of George Barker*, a long poem in which Barker seemed to take a baleful delight in trying on the various masks (Villon and Baudelaire, for example) of a damned, despairing but nevertheless jaunty creature:

I know only that the heart
   Doubting every real thing else
Does not doubt the voice that tells
   Us that we suffer. The hard part
At the dead centre of the soul
   Is an age of frozen grief
No vernal equinox of relief
   Can mitigate, and no love console.

The View from a Blind I shows two more recent manners, in his sardonic or satirical ballads (such as "The Ballad of Yucca Flats" and "Scottish Bards and an English Reviewer"), and in the limpid and sometimes even conversational "Roman Poems." The heavy rhetorical tread of the early poems has been replaced by something much more spontaneous and lyrical, though equally copious – and sometimes, even now, prolix, as in parts of the recent loosely-connected sequence of quatrains in *The Golden Chains*. Barker's faults of verbal absurdity and self-indulgence are plain for all to see, but the compensations of energy and eloquence have not sufficiently been noticed.

(1980) In *Poems of Places and People*, *In Memory of David Archer*, *Dialogues*, and *Villa Stellar*, George Barker has continued to follow chiefly the "limpid and sometimes even conversational" style noted above in *The View from a Blind I*. The tone is often one of puzzled plain questioning, of the past and of past mistakes, of human frailty and absurdity, relieved with something more sardonic and ironical. Interleaved with such poems are elegies for dead friends and artists, meditations on death, and some purely lyrical poems of a kind one can recognise in much earlier Barker books. The recent work is sometimes self-lacerating and self-puncturing, sometimes bewildered and humble in a way that is certainly quite different from the jauntily aggressive persona he once donned; the danger is that some of it sounds like prosaic muttering. But at his best Barker is still producing effects which are astonishingly direct and exaltedly eloquent: one might note particularly, from *Villa Stellar*, the poem numbered 44, which begins "To all appearances the life serene."

Barker is still as prolific as ever, after over 45 years of production, and perhaps because of this copiousness his reputation is still uncertain: for some time, it has probably been higher in the United States than in Britain. But even if only as a type-case, perhaps the last survivor of the romantic, bohemian, self-condemned and yet dedicated poet, he has a unique position in poetry written in English.

—Anthony Thwaite

BARO, Gene. American. Born in New York City, in 1924.

PUBLICATIONS

Verse

Northwind and Other Poems. New York, Scribner, 1959.
A View of Water. Leeds, Northern House, 1965.
Claes Oldenberg and Gene Baro. New York, Wittenborn, 1968.

Other

Editor, *Beat Poets.* London, Vista, 1961.
Editor, *Famous American Poems.* London, Vista, 1962.
Editor, *After Appomattox: The Image of the South in Its Fiction 1865–1900.* New York, Corinth, 1963.
Editor, *Modern American Stories.* London, Faber, 1963.

* * *

A distinction increasingly being made in criticism is that between history and myth, between facts in related sequence, and the concept behind "events"; between distinct occurrences in sequence, and the everlasting moment that erases the lineal idea of time. The first attitude is Judaic, and the second belongs to the Greeks. If we say Yeats fits more readily into the second of these, it can be seen that to conceptualize with passion involved elegance; and if we consider these two as inseparable, then passionate elegance is that Yeatsian mode which best describes Gene Baro's work. Narrative does not concern Baro. It is the timeless, fixed moment, the moment in which all the strands implied by narrative are brought into intense, significant conjunction, with which Baro is concerned. This Byzantine preoccupation produces at its best a sense of both permanence and hazard. The images (and it is essentially an image-orientated position) strike into the sense creating the illusion of permanence by their intense isolate quality. At the same time, this sense of isolation suggests vulnerability, lack of physical connection and support – from the world. Thus it is not accidental that Baro's creatures are often seen in postures of duress, and suffering. The preoccupation perhaps chooses the mode of expression. In "Sebastian":

Focus of eyes, focus of arrows:
this is the plot the body demanded,
young captain and hero.
... Yet of all this the increment
is death, the gift but an infant
corruptible and triumphant.

And again in "The Laundresses":

Plunging their arms in steam,
as martyrs take hold of their fires, ...
the laundresses mightily
hunch at buckets and tubs,
heave and lunge.

Assuming that some must bear suffering, and many more inflict it, taking for granted the desire for purification as fundamental, Baro can concern himself with the intensity and elegance with which all this is rendered. The position is traditional, concerned as it is with detail only as it subscribes to the lasting moment, and as it perfects an area previously worked and defined by other poets.

—John Silkin

BAYBARS, Taner. British. Born in Nicosia, Cyprus, 18 June 1936. Educated privately, and at the Turkish Lycée, Nicosia. Married to Kristin Baybars (divorced, 1977); one daughter. Since 1956, Member of the Staff, and since 1972, Head of the Overseas Reviews Scheme, British Council, London. Address: 69 Onslow Gardens, London N10 3JY, England.

PUBLICATIONS

Verse

Mendilin Ucundakiler (in Turkish). Nicosia, Cyprus, Çardak Yayinevi, 1953.
To Catch a Falling Man. Lowestoft, Suffolk, Scorpion Press, 1963.
Susila in the Autumn Woods. Rushden, Northamptonshire, Sceptre Press, 1974.
Narcissus in a Dry Pool. London, Sidgwick and Jackson, 1978.

Novel

A Trap for the Burglar. London, Peter Owen, 1965.

Other

Plucked in a Far-Off Land: Images in Self Biography. London, Gollancz, 1970.

Editor, with Osman Türkay, *Modern Turkish Poetry.* London, Modern Poetry in Translation, 1971.

Translator, *Selected Poems of Nazim Hikmet.* London, Cape, 1967; New York, Humanities Press, 1968.
Translator, *The Moscow Symphony and Other Poems*, by Nazim Hikmet. London, Rapp and Whiting, 1970; Chicago, Swallow Press, 1971.
Translator, *The Day Before Tomorrow*, by Nazim Hikmet. Oxford, Carcanet Press, 1972.

Critical Studies: "Voice Production" by Frederick Grubb, in *Poetry Review* (London), 1964; "Bigger Than Both of Us" by Bernard Share, in *Irish Times* (Dublin), 12 June 1965; *The Poet Speaks* by Peter Orr, London, Routledge, 1966; "Plucked Untimely" by Raymond Gardner, in *The Guardian* (London), 19 May 1970; "Flame by Flame" by Peter Lewis, in *Times Literary Supplement* (London), 3 October 1978.

Taner Baybars comments:

I try to express experiences without turning them into "stories"; I try to select images which should convey something without verbal stuffing – to be able to say more by leaving quite a lot out of the poem. Themes: human relationships, fears and the significant aspect of the commonplace; scientific mysticism.

* * *

Taner Baybars is a Cypriot whose first book of poems, written in Turkish, was published in Nicosia in 1953. Coming to England 12 years later with the expressed intention of studying Law (he soon gave up that idea), he decided to stay in London and has adopted English as his literary language with quite remarkable effect. If he experienced any difficulties in writing his poems in a second language, he has enjoyed an advantage over his British contemporaries in that he has remained free of group pressures and influences, and has never shown the slightest inclination to follow prevailing fashions in diction or style. His poems, successful, or otherwise, have always been quite unlike anyone else's.

The poems in his *To Catch a Falling Man* are arranged in chronological order so that it is possible to trace his development as a poet throughout the volume. The collection begins with the description of a cycle journey through the English countryside and these early pieces reflect a simplicity or clarity of vision allied to an unusually sophisticated and well-informed outlook, reinforced by a creative mind that enables him to evoke the scene in such phrases as "the coquettish wind perambulating in the wheels" or "the waves unkiss the cliff." Though his themes are quotidian – the demolition of an old house, taking barbitone for sleep, the end of a musical concert, spelling out his name, chopping down a tree, or even the sound of a key turning in the lock – he somehow contrives to surround them with a sinister atmosphere, as in his poem about a computer, "The Oracle":

> We are much honoured; we hold conferences and
> discuss what the most fitting question should be;
> when we find it we march and surround the machine;
>
> the problem is fed in, the drone irregularly
> distends, no answer is laid. We grow old and visit
> everyday, the clean compact brain and wait.

In his later work the simplicity of his earlier style gives way to a search for the unexpected, for what goes on below the surface of human relationships, for the motives beneath the conversation, for the realities underlying appearances. "Demolishing a House" demonstrates Baybars's skill at piling detail upon detail without overwhelming the poem:

Yet while I ate and poised the fork in the air,
the noise of a drill shivered the glass facade,
the fake plants shook, too, a little afraid.
I had to open my mouth to let the noise out.
Then I heard the crash of another falling wall.

Narcissus in a Dry Pool begins where *To Catch a Falling Man* concludes, stylistically. The individual nature of Baybars's enquiry into the phenomena of existence and his odd and sometimes bizarre approach to his subject lends a sort of piquancy to his poetry. For a single volume there is a wide range of styles and types of writing, from the three-line haiku, to a series of love poems, "Explorations," to "The Loneliness of Columbus," a dramatic monologue. The description of a boy's "Circumcision Just Before Puberty" leaves nothing to the imagination, but is nevertheless handled with extraordinary delicacy and understanding. The group of poems "for Susila Jane," his daughter, manifest a new preoccupation, that of observing his daughter's gradual introduction to the external world and her development through touch, taste, sight and smell:

Seeing your own reflection on a doorknob
you begin to utter your name, then stop
in that conflux of brass stained by my hand.
Who? I hold you against the windowglass.

You exclaim: Dark! I put you down. You live
in a galaxy of sounds absorbed by your tongue
and keeping your name a secret to your tongue
and grow in full awareness of others.

What seems to impress him most in this exploration of infancy and childhood is the paradox of innocence combining with an almost frightening kind of inner certainty arising from the need for self-fulfilment.

Perhaps most interesting of all are the poems devoted to the relationship between man and woman, the man always being Baybars himself and the woman a particular woman drawn from his private circle; they are, of course, love poems in every sense of the word, yet for Baybars the love relationship is complicated, for his partners are not merely women or lovers, but each, willingly or unwillingly, acquires a symbolistic quality which takes its idiosyncratic scope from some aspect of Baybars's experience – his native country, his childhood, his family, his adolescence, etc. – and which, inevitably defines the relationship for him.

—Howard Sergeant

BEAVER, Bruce (Victor). Australian. Born in Sydney, New South Wales, 14 February 1928. Educated at Manly Public School and Sydney Boys' High School. Married to Brenda Beaver. Lived in New Zealand, 1958–62. Currently, Free-lance Journalist. Recipient: *Poetry Magazine* Award, Sydney, 1963; Commonwealth Literary Fellowship, 1967; Captain Cook Bi-Centenary Prize, 1970; Grace Leven Prize, 1970; Poetry Society of Australia Award, 1970. Address: 14 Malvern Avenue, Manly, New South Wales 2095, Australia.

PUBLICATIONS

Verse

Under the Bridge. Sydney, Beaujon Press, 1961.
Seawall and Shoreline. Sydney, South Head Press, 1964.
Open at Random. Sydney, South Head Press, 1967.
Letters to Live Poets. Sydney, South Head Press, 1969.
Lauds and Plaints: Poems (1968–1972). Sydney, South Head Press, 1974.
Odes and Days. Sydney, South Head Press, 1975.
Death's Directives. Sydney, Prism Poets, 1978.
As It Was. Brisbane, University of Queensland Press, 1979.
Selected Poems. Sydney, Angus and Robertson, 1979.

Novels

The Hot Spring. Sydney, Horvitz, 1965.
You Can't Come Back. Adelaide, Rigby, 1966.

Critical Studies: *New Impulses in Australian Poetry*, edited by Thomas Shapcott and Rodney Hall, Brisbane, University of Queensland Press, 1968; "Gift-Bearing Hands: The Poetry of Bruce Beaver" by Craig Powell, in *Quadrant* (Sydney), XII, 5, 1978; "Bruce Beaver's Poetry" by R. D. FitzGerald in *Meanjin* (Melbourne), September 1969; "New Australian Poetry" by James Tulip, in *Southerly* (Sydney), 1970; *Poets on Record 7*, Brisbane, University of Queensland Press, 1972; "The 'Livres composés' of Bruce Beaver" by J. and R. M. Beston, in *WLWE* (Perth), April 1975.

* * *

Something of a maverick among Australian poets, Bruce Beaver is an original and idiosyncratic writer whose reputation has grown with the appearance of each new book. A first collection of poems, *Under the Bridge*, was published in 1961 to some critical acclaim and not a little grumbling. Though his work was said to be colourful and lively in its descriptions of landscapes and regional settings, the human element touched on throughout was vaguely eccentric and even in part perverse; it certainly does not have the dryly humorous to openly heroic characterisation that appeals to so many Australian poets.

In his second book he consolidated the thematic development of 20th century man in and sometimes versus a landscape. In "A View from the Bridge-rail" and "Letters from Sydney" he stressed the relative brevity and existential pressures of human life, setting these against a Heraclitean background of flux and fusion in the book's title poem "Seawall and Shoreline." An impressive sequence entitled "Harbour Sonnets" describes with a lyrical fervour the landscape near his home at Manly, N.S.W.

The same attachment, almost obsessional, to an intimate landscape is seen in the opening pages of his third book, somewhat diffidently entitled *Open at Random*, in poems such as "Excursion" and "Remembering." Again the critics were divided in their estimates of this non-conforming talent. Some found the characterisation too splenetic, others remarked on the apparent opacity of some of the verses, yet the book has had its share of praise and an elder poet of stature, R. D. FitzGerald, has stated that he considers one of the poems, "The Killers," as among the best poems written in Australia.

—Staff of *Poetry Australia*

BECKETT, Samuel (Barclay). Irish. Born near Dublin, 13 April 1906. Educated at Portora Royal School, County Fermanagh; Trinity College, Dublin, B.A. in French and Italian 1927, M.A. 1931. Worked at the Irish Red Cross Hospital, St. Lô, France, 1945. Married Suzanne Dechevaux-Dumesnil in 1948. French teacher, Campbell College, Belfast, 1928; Lecturer in English, Ecole Normale Supérieure, Paris, 1928–30; Lecturer in French, Trinity College, Dublin, 1930–31. Closely associated with James Joyce in Paris in the late 1920's and the 1930's. Settled in Paris in 1938, and has written chiefly in French since 1945; translates his own work into English. Recipient: *Evening Standard* award, for drama, 1955; Obie Award, for drama, 1958, 1960, 1962, 1964; Italia Prize, 1959; International Publishers Prize, 1961; Prix Filmcritice, 1965; Tours Film Prize, 1966; Nobel Prize for Literature, 1969. D.Litt.: Dublin University, 1959. Address: c/o Editions de Minuit, 7 rue Bernard-Palissy, Paris 6, France.

PUBLICATIONS

Verse

Whoroscope. Paris, Hours Press, 1930.
Echo's Bones and Other Precipitates. Paris, Europa Press, 1935.
Gedichte (collected poems in English and French, with German translations). Wiesbaden, Limes Verlag, 1959.
Poems in English. London, Calder, 1961; New York, Grove Press, 1963.
Collected Poems in English and French. London, Calder, and New York, Grove Press, 1977.

Plays

Le Kid, with Georges Pelorson (produced Dublin, 1931).
En Attendant Godot (produced Paris, 1953). Paris, Editions de Minuit, 1952; translated by the author as *Waiting for Godot: Tragicomedy* (produced London, 1955; Miami and New York, 1956), New York, Grove Press, 1954; London, Faber, 1956.
Fin de Partie: Suivi de Acte sans Paroles (produced London, 1957). Paris, Editions de Minuit, 1957; translated by the author as *Endgame: A Play in One Act; Followed by Act Without Words: A Mime for One Player* (*Endgame*, produced New York and London, 1958; *Act Without Words*, produced New York, 1960), New York, Grove Press, and London, Faber, 1958.
All That Fall (broadcast, 1957). New York, Grove Press, 1957; as *All That Fall: A Play for Radio*, London, Faber, 1957.
Krapp's Last Tape (produced London, 1958; New York, 1960). Included in *Krapp's Last Tape and Embers*, 1959; in *Krapp's Last Tape and Other Dramatic Pieces*, 1960.
Embers (broadcast, 1959). Included in *Krapp's Last Tape and Embers*, 1959; in *Krapp's Last Tape and Other Dramatic Pieces*, 1960.
Krapp's Last Tape and Embers. London, Faber, 1959.
Act Without Words II (produced New York, 1959; London, 1960). Included in *Krapp's Last Tape and Other Dramatic Pieces*, 1960; in *Eh Joe and Other Writings*, 1967.
Krapp's Last Tape and Other Dramatic Pieces (includes *All That Fall*, *Embers*, *Act Without Words I* and *II*). New York, Grove Press, 1960.
Happy Days (produced New York, 1961; London, 1962). New York, Grove Press, 1961; London, Faber, 1962; bilingual edition, edited by James Knowlson, Faber, 1978.
Words and Music (broadcast, 1962). Included in *Play and Two Short Pieces for Radio*, 1964; in *Cascando and Other Short Dramatic Pieces*, 1968.
Cascando (broadcast, in French, 1963). Paris, Editions de Minuit, 1963; translated by the author as *Cascando: A Radio Piece for Music and Voice* (broadcast, 1964; in

Beckett 3, produced London, 1970; produced New York, 1976), included in *Play and Two Short Pieces for Radio*, 1964; in *Cascando and Other Short Dramatic Pieces*, 1968.

Play (produced Ulm-Donau, 1963; New York and London, 1964). Included in *Play and Two Short Pieces for Radio*, 1964; in *Cascando and Other Short Dramatic Pieces*, 1968.

Play and Two Short Pieces for Radio (includes *Words and Music* and *Cascando*). London, Faber, 1964.

Eh Joe (televised, 1966). Included in *Eh Joe and Other Writings*, 1967; in *Cascando and Other Short Dramatic Pieces*, 1968.

Come and Go: Dramaticule (produced Paris, 1966; Dublin, 1968; London, 1970; New York, 1974). London, Calder and Boyars, 1967; in *Cascando and Other Short Dramatic Pieces*, 1968.

Eh Joe and Other Writings (includes *Act Without Words II* and *Film*). London, Faber, 1967.

Cascando and Other Short Dramatic Pieces (includes *Words and Music*, *Eh Joe*, *Play*, *Come and Go*, *Film*). New York, Grove Press, 1968.

Film. New York, Grove Press, 1969; London, Faber, 1971.

Breath (produced Oxford, 1970). Included in *Breath and Other Shorts*, 1971.

Breath and Other Shorts (includes *Come and Go*, *Act Without Words I* and *II*, and the prose piece *From an Abandoned Work*). London, Faber, 1971.

Not I (produced New York, 1972; London, 1973). London, Faber, 1973; in *First Love and Other Shorts*, 1974.

Tryst (televised, 1976). Included in *Ends and Odds*, 1976.

That Time (produced London and Washington, D.C., 1976; New York, 1977). London, Faber, 1976; in *Ends and Odds*, 1976.

Footfalls (also director: produced London, 1976; Washington, D.C., 1976; New York, 1977). London, Faber, 1976; in *Ends and Odds*, 1976.

Ends and Odds: Dramatic Pieces (includes *That Time*, *Footfalls*, *Tryst*, *Not I*). New York, Grove Press, 1976; London, Faber, 1977.

Screenplay: *Film*, 1965.

Radio Plays: *All That Fall*, 1957; *Embers*, 1959; *Words and Music*, 1962; *Cascando*, 1963.

Television Plays: *Eh Joe*, 1966; *Tryst*, 1976; *Shades* (*Ghost Trio*, *Not I*, and ... *But the Clouds* ...), 1977.

Novels

Murphy. London, Routledge, 1938; New York, Grove Press, 1957.

Molloy. Paris, Editions de Minuit, 1951; translated by the author and Patrick Bowles, Paris, Olympia Press, and New York, Grove Press, 1955; London, Calder, 1959.

Malone meurt. Paris, Editions de Minuit, 1951; translated by the author as *Malone Dies*, New York, Grove Press, 1956; London, Calder, 1958.

L'Innommable. Paris, Editions de Minuit, 1953; translated by the author as *The Unnamable*, New York, Grove Press, 1958; London, Calder, 1959.

Watt (written in English). Paris, Olympia Press, 1953; New York, Grove Press, 1959; London, Calder, 1963.

Comment C'Est. Paris, Editions de Minuit, 1961; translated by the author as *How It Is*, New York, Grove Press, and London, Calder, 1964.

Mercier et Camier. Paris, Editions de Minuit, 1970; translated by the author as *Mercier and Camier*, London, Calder and Boyars, 1974; New York, Grove Press, 1975.

Short Stories and Texts

More Pricks Than Kicks. London, Chatto and Windus, 1934; New York, Grove Press, 1970.
Nouvelles et Textes pour Rien. Paris, Editions de Minuit, 1955; translated by the author and Richard Seaver as *Stories and Texts for Nothing*, New York, Grove Press, 1967; in *No's Knife: Selected Shorter Prose, 1945–1966*, 1967.
From an Abandoned Work. London, Faber, 1958.
Imagination morte imaginez. Paris, Editions de Minuit, 1965; translated by the author as *Imagination Dead Imagine*, London, Calder and Boyars, 1965.
Assez. Paris, Editions de Minuit, 1966; translated by the author as *Enough*, in *No's Knife*, 1967.
Bing. Paris, Editions de Minuit, 1966; translated by the author as *Ping*, in *No's Knife*, 1967.
Têtes-Mortes (includes *D'Un Ouvrage Abandonné, Assez, Bing, Imagination morte imaginez*). Paris, Editions de Minuit, 1967; translated by the author, in *No's Knife*, 1967.
No's Knife: Selected Shorter Prose, 1945–1966 (includes *Stories and Texts for Nothing, From an Abandoned Work, Imagination Dead Imagine, Enough, Ping*). London, Calder and Boyars, 1967.
L'Issue. Paris, Georges Visat, 1968.
Sans. Paris, Editions de Minuit, 1969; translated by the author as *Lessness*, London, Calder and Boyars, 1971.
Séjour. Paris, Georges Richar, 1970.
Premier Amour. Paris, Editions de Minuit, 1970; translated by the author as *First Love*, London, Calder and Boyars, 1973.
Le Dépeupleur. Paris, Editions de Minuit, 1971; translated by the author as *The Lost Ones*, London, Calder and Boyars, 1972.
The North. London, Enitharmon Press, 1972.
First Love and Other Shorts. New York, Grove Press, 1974.
Fizzles. New York, Grove Press, 1976.
For to End Yet Again and Other Fizzles. London, Calder, 1976.
All Strange Away. New York, Gotham Book Mart, 1976; London, Calder, 1979.
Four Novellas (The Expelled, The Calmative, The End, First Love). London, Calder, 1977.
Six Residua. London, Calder, 1978.

Other

"Dante ... Bruno. Vico .. Joyce," in *Our Exagmination round His Factification for Incamination of Work in Progress*. Paris, Shakespeare and Company, 1929; London, Faber, 1936; New York, New Directions, 1939.
Proust. London, Chatto and Windus, 1931; New York, Grove Press, 1957; with *Three Dialogues with Georges Duthuit*, London, Calder, 1965.
Bram van Welde, with others. Paris, Georges Fall, 1958; translated by the author and Olive Classe, New York, Grove Press, 1960.
A Samuel Beckett Reader. London, Calder and Boyars, 1967.
I Can't Go On: A Selection from the Work of Samuel Beckett, edited by Richard Seaver. New York, Grove Press, 1976.

Translator, *Anthology of Mexican Poetry*, edited by Octavio Paz. Bloomington, Indiana University Press, 1958; London, Thames and Hudson, 1959.
Translator, *The Old Tune*, by Robert Pinget. Paris, Editions de Minuit, 1960; in *Three Plays*, by Robert Pinget, New York, Hill and Wang, 1966; in *Plays*, London, Calder and Boyars, 1966.

Translator, *Zone*, by Guillaume Apollinaire. Dublin and London, Dolmen Press – Calder and Boyars, 1960.
Translator, *Drunken Boat*, by Arthur Rimbaud, edited by James Knowles and Felix Leakey. Reading, Whiteknights Press, 1977.

Bibliography: *Samuel Beckett: His Work and His Critics: An Essay in Bibliography* by Raymond Felderman and John Fletcher, Berkeley, University of California Press, 1970 (through 1966).

Manuscript Collections: University of Texas, Austin; Ohio State University, Columbus; Washington University, St. Louis, Missouri; Dartmouth College, Hanover, New Hampshire; Reading University, England.

Theatrical Activities:

Director: **Plays** – *Come and Go*, Paris, 1966; *Endgame*, Berlin, 1967; *Krapp's Last Tape*, Berlin, 1969; *Krapp's Last Tape* and *Act Without Words*, Paris, 1970; *Krapp's Last Tape* and *Endgame*, London, 1971; *Happy Days*, Berlin, 1971, London, 1979; *Waiting for Godot*, Berlin, 1975, New York, 1977; *Krapp's Last Tape* and *Not I*, Paris, 1975; *Footfalls*, London, 1976; *Krapp's Last Tape*, Berlin, 1977, and London, 1978. **Television** – *Eh Joe*, 1966 (Germany).

* * *

Samuel Beckett published two very short volumes of verse in his youth, each with minority presses, *Whoroscope* and *Echo's Bones*. They attracted no critical attention at all and when in 1962 he was a very famous writer indeed, and John Calder brought out the bulk of these early poems as *Poems in English*, so far as I know I was the only reviewer to write about them, and that briefly and anonymously. They are, indeed, minor poems as Joyce's are, but, like Joyce's poems at their best (and like those plays of Beckett's, *All That Fall* and *Embers*, for instance, which were not translated from Beckett's French but written directly in English – Irish English – for radio), they express the author's intimate feelings with a certain concentration and they have a rooted feeling, a local lovingness, they offer some intimate clues to Beckett's bitterness. It is impossible for anybody to be as chillingly negative in verse, consistently, as Beckett is in prose. He is a great master of prose and, like Joyce, only a rather small and precious master in verse, and very much in the Irish tradition of the glumps, or melodious subjective gloom. In verse, unlike prose, the writer has to expose, or give away, the intimate hurts of the inner heart. And these, for Beckett as for most people, are the hurts of lost or rejected love, and the self-disgust, or the self-despisal, that goes with rejection:

> the churn of stale words in the heart again
> love love love thud of the old plunger
> pestling the unalterable
> whey of words

The metaphor is from butter-making and one seems to smell the stale milk smells of a dairy. The Anglo-Irish aspirate *w* where the English do not and in standard English "whey of words" becomes "way of words." *Plunger* and *pestling* and *unalterable*, like *churn*, suggest a mechanical, desperate, barren sexuality. But the most moving short poem in the book is one of a set on Dieppe, written first in French, and then in very traditional Irish English, echoing Synge and Lady Gregory, in Kiltartan or *Playboy of the Western World* language, one might say:

> I would like my love to die
> and the rain to be falling on the graveyard

and on me walking the streets
mourning the first and last to love me.

These four lines have lasted in my memory with a hurting poignancy. I spoke of them, when I wrote my too brief review, as expressing "the quiet persistence of loving self-hurt, the innocent, exorbitant, childish bitterness preserved and hardened in manhood and used to claw down the world."

—G. S. Fraser

BEECHER, John. American. Born in New York City, 22 January 1904. Educated at Virginia Military Institute, Lexington, 1919–20; Cornell University, Ithaca, New York, 1921–24; University of Alabama, University, 1924–25, A.B. 1925; Harvard University, Cambridge, Massachusetts, 1926–27; University of Paris, 1928; University of Wisconsin, Madison, 1929–30, M.A. 1930; University of North Carolina, Chapel Hill, 1933–34. Served in the United States Maritime Service during World War II: Combat Medal. Married Barbara Marie Scholz in 1955; five children. Chemist, 1918–19, Steel Worker, 1920–21, 1923–24, and Open Hearth Metallurgist, 1928–29, U.S. Steel Corporation, Birmingham, Alabama. Instructor in English, Dartmouth College, Hanover, New Hampshire, 1927, and University of Wisconsin, 1929–33; United States government administrator, in the South, New York, and New England, 1934–43; Director, Displaced Persons Program, UNRRA, Stuttgart, Germany, 1945; Chief, National Institute of Social Relations Editorial Section, Washington, D.C., 1946–47; Assistant Professor of Sociology, San Francisco State College, 1948–50; Rancher and Fine Press Operator, Sebastopol, California, 1951–58; Lecturer in English, Arizona State University, Tempe, 1959–61; Poet-in-Residence, University of Santa Clara, California, 1963–65; Visiting Professor, Miles College, Birmingham, Alabama, 1966–67; Poet-in-Residence, North Shore Community College, Beverly, Massachusetts, 1969–71; Campus Visitor, Association of American Colleges Arts Program, New York, 1969–72; Poet-in-Residence, Saint John's University, Collegeville, Minnesota, 1970, and Assumption College, Worcester, Massachusetts, 1971. Since 1973, Visiting Scholar, Duke University, Durham, North Carolina. Correspondent and Staff Writer, San Francisco *Chronicle*, Birmingham *Age-Herald* and *News*, *New York Post*, 1943; Associate Editor, *Ramparts Magazine*, San Francisco, 1959–63. Recipient: Ford Fellowship, 1951; National Endowment for the Arts grant, 1976. L.H.D.: Illinois College, Jacksonville, 1948. Address: Route 1, Box 35, Burnsville, North Carolina 28714, U.S.A.

PUBLICATIONS

Verse

And I Will Be Heard. New York, Twice a Year Press, 1940.
Here I Stand. New York, Twice a Year Press, 1941.
Land of the Free: A Portfolio of Poems on the State of the Union. Oakland, California, Morning Star Press, 1956.
Observe the Time: An Everyday Tragedy in Verse. San Francisco, Morning Star Press, 1956.
Just Peanuts. San Francisco, Morning Star Press, 1957.
Inquest. San Francisco, Morning Star Press, 1957.

Moloch. San Francisco, Morning Star Press, 1957.
In Egypt Land. Scottsdale, Arizona, Rampart Press, 1960.
Homage to a Subversive. Scottsdale, Arizona, Rampart Press, 1961.
Phantom City. Scottsdale, Arizona, Rampart Press, 1961.
Report to the Stockholders and Other Poems 1932–1962. New York, Monthly Review Press, 1962.
Undesirables. Phoenix, Rampart Press, 1962.
Bestride the Narrow World. Phoenix, Rampart Press, 1963.
Conformity Means Death. Phoenix, Rampart Press, 1963.
On Acquiring a Cistercian Breviary. Phoenix, Rampart Press, 1963.
Yours in the Bonds. Phoenix, Rampart Press, 1963.
An Air That Kills. Phoenix, Rampart Press, 1963.
A Humble Petition to the President of Harvard. Phoenix, Rampart Press, 1963.
Undesirables (collection). Lanham, Maryland, Goosetree Press, 1964.
To Live and Die in Dixie and Other Poems. Birmingham, Red Mountain, 1966.
Hear the Wind Blow! Poems of Protest and Prophecy. New York, International, 1968.
Collected Poems 1924–1974. New York, Macmillan, and London, Collier Macmillan, 1974.

Recording: *To Live and Die in Dixie*, Folkways, 1968.

Other

All Brave Sailors: The Story of the S.S. Booker T. Washington. New York, Fischer, 1945.

Bibliography: "Homage to a Crusader: John Beecher and His Rampart Press in Arizona" by James S. Fraser, in *Arizona Librarian* (Tempe), Winter 1967.

Critical Studies: "The Poetry of John Beecher" by Leslie Woolf Hedley, in *Mainstream* (New York), September 1962; "If I Forget Thee, O Birmingham" by Cornelia Jessey, in *Way* (San Francisco), April 1967; Introduction by Maxwell Geismar to *Hear the Wind Blow!*, 1968; "Hear the Wind Blow!" by Donald Demarest, in *Way* (San Francisco), March 1969; "America's Poetic Voice of Protest" by Edgar Battle, in *Irish Independent* (Dublin), 15 July 1970; "Here I Stand" by Clayton Barbeau, in *San Francisco Magazine*, April 1973.

John Beecher comments:

I am known principally as a poet of social protest. My very earliest published work, which appeared in the Twenties, dealt with the injustice I encountered when I worked 12-hour shifts in the steel mills of Alabama as a youth of 16. My heritage may also have influenced me. I am descended from Abolitionists and social reformers. Harriet Beecher Stowe was a great-great aunt. In the Thirties I was involved with the poor – the unemployed city workers, sharecrop farmers and uprooted migrants, disadvantaged blacks and chicanos, Jews barred from jobs because of their religion. After the great war for freedom was over I refused to sign an unconstitutional "loyalty" oath and was blacklisted myself, becoming a rancher when my profession as a college teacher was closed to me. All these experiences have made me the kind of poet I am. Fortunately I lived through it all and find today that even my work of the Twenties and Thirties meets with a better response and deeper understanding than when I first wrote it. But I am not a poet of the Twenties and Thirties primarily. I am a poet also of the Forties, Fifties, Sixties and Seventies. I have been writing poems for 50 years now. My *Collected Poems* will I hope show the continuity. My autobiography is to follow.

* * *

John Beecher is the stuff of legends: his abolitionist heritage (Henry Ward Beecher and Harriet Beecher Stowe), his personal history of protest, and especially his poems, have attracted an enthusiastic audience. The poems chronicle the desperation and tragedy of the poor, and the crimes of man to men from the Thirties into the present.

Beecher's poems are not "literary" but stress an incantatory voice of preacher or prophecy; the narratives are expansive and (unfortunately) timeless, but his heroes and sympathies remain individual: there is an epic quality and effort in, for example, "In Egypt Land."

Beecher's view of nature and man is Romantic while society is starkly and brutally political. Overlying the poems is a heavy and *credible* shadow of physical danger; within the poems a frustration, as tactile as that of Steinbeck's famous *The Grapes of Wrath*, threatens to explode.

Beecher concentrates on three topics: laborers (steelworkers, especially), blacks (farmers and the civil rights movement), and political liberty. Although recent poems are occasionally weakened by a discomforting note of self-righteousness ("A Commemorative Ode," "A Humble Petition ..."), the poet deals with a history which textbooks have failed to present and still are trying to accomplish, too slowly Beecher knows ("After Eighty Years"). Even though his anger occasionally overwhelms his vision, and a prose rhetoric covers some poems with preachment, it is always to Beecher's credit as a poet – and as a "radical" and human – that he at least makes us seriously wonder if such passion may not be as good as inevitable. In these poems the enemy is immediate, obvious, physical, and simple. There is little of the subtle maneuvering and abstraction one has come to associate with much of the "protest" art of the middle class in America. This is direct rage: Beecher's poems are of the uneducated poor who do not deal in abstractions, but suffer the immediate danger of the "foremen" and the "agents" of abstractions.

—Joseph Wilson

BEER, Patricia. British. Born in Exmouth, Devon, 4 November 1924. Educated at Exmouth Grammar School; Exeter University, B.A. (honours) in English (London); St. Hugh's College, Oxford, B.Litt. Married to the architect Damien Parsons. Lecturer in English, University of Padua, 1946–48, British Institute, Rome, 1948, and Ministero Areonautica, Rome, 1950–53; Senior Lecturer in English, Goldsmiths' College, London, 1962–68. Address: 1 Lutton Terrace, Flask Walk, London N.W.3, England.

PUBLICATIONS

Verse

Loss of the Magyar and Other Poems. London, Longman, 1959.
The Survivors. London, Longman, 1963.
Just Like the Resurrection. London, Macmillan, and Chester Springs, Pennsylvania, Dufour, 1967.
The Estuary. London, Macmillan, 1971.
Spanish Balcony. London, Poem-of-the-Month Club, 1973.
Driving West. London, Gollancz, 1975.
Poems 1967–1979. London, Hutchinson, 1979.

Novel

Moon's Ottery. London, Hutchinson, 1978.

Other

Mrs. Beer's House (autobiography). London, Macmillan, 1968.
An Introduction to the Metaphysical Poets. London, Macmillan, and Totowa, New Jersey, Rowman and Littlefield, 1972.
Reader: I Married Him. London, Macmillan, and New York, Barnes and Noble, 1974.

Editor, with Ted Hughes and Vernon Scannell, *New Poems 1962.* London, Hutchinson, 1962.
Editor, *New Poems 1975.* London, Hutchinson, 1975.
Editor, with Kevin Crossley-Holland, *New Poetry 2.* London, Arts Council, 1976.
Editor, *Poetry Supplement.* London, Poetry Book Society, 1978.

Patricia Beer comments:

In my opinion my verse has changed radically since the publication of *Loss of the Magyar* in 1959. I do not repudiate my early work but I am now aiming at something quite different. I am trying to break away from the limitations imposed by traditional metres and have been turning increasingly to free verse and syllabics. I am also aiming at using less obvious metaphor.

The writing of my autobiography has influenced my work in two ways: the intensive use of prose has made me try for greater precision in my poetry; and since the publication of the autobiography I have felt able to deal poetically with subjects of a more overtly personal nature. I am not speaking in terms of confessional poetry because that is a mode which, though I respect it, is not for me. But I find I have less need to present my themes objectively by the use of, for example, legend.

The poets whom, currently, I most admire are Yeats, Robert Lowell, Ted Hughes.

* * *

Patricia Beer's poems may seem at first glance to have something literary and secondhand about them, in that many of them are pegged to romantic myths, legends, historical anecdotes; and literariness of this sort is rightly distrusted. But what is remarkable is that, starting out from such received themes, and using repeatedly such words as "love," "blood," "joy," "grief," "bone," "gold," she transcends the derivative and the tiresomely plangent. She is neatly eloquent, with a fine control of syntax and structure.

The most ambitious poem in her first book was the title one, "The Loss of the Magyar," a sequence of eight pieces, varied in form, on the sinking of the small Devon ship of which her great-grandfather was Master and in which all the crew was drowned. "The Loss of the Magyar" showed from the start that Patricia Beer could handle plain stuff plainly (the second and third sections, for example) as well as the more heightened rhetoric of the close. Another good poem in this book, and one which gains from its close circumstantial detail, is "The Fifth Sense."

Birth and death – again, common themes but seldom handled by Miss Beer as if they were commonplace – are the substance of the poems in *The Survivors.* "Gynaecological Ward," "Life Story," "New Year," "Next of Kin," "Out of Season," and most notably "Death of a Nun," are all good poems drawing on these two great facts. Here and there (as in *Loss of the Magyar*) there are chant-like cadences that remind one uncomfortably of Yeats, but more generally there is a freshness and individuality in her measures, well demonstrated in "The Gorilla," which takes the creature in his cage in the zoo and ends:

And yet my human fantasy
Imagines in him wrath at more
Than being trapped, involuntary
Anger at his successors' dullness
Who do not understand his wholeness,

As if some black prophetic rage
At the mistaking of his nature
Had gripped him from an early age
With knowledge that through all his future
People would talk before his cage
Clothed and upright, would turn and pass
Saying how like a man he was.

Just Like the Resurrection shows no startling development, but she now seems more prepared to risk lack of resonance for a more glancing effect, using a looser line and sometimes syllabics. There is more room in these poems for the casual, the trivial and the whimsical; and though the danger, of course, is *mere* whimsy (as in "Foam: Cut to Any Size"), she shows that she can handle an odd insight with economy and wit, as in the nine-line poem "Scratchpath."

(1980) The free style I noted above in *Just Like the Resurrection* has continued in *The Estuary* and *Driving West*, and Patricia Beer now seems completely at ease with it, able to encompass a wide range of subject-matter and tone, from the flatly written yet piercingly moving "After Death" (about finding a dead bird in a locked-up house) to such wistful and even humorous reminiscences of childhood as "John Milton and My Father" and "Called Home," in the same vein as that exploited so well in her volume of autobiography, *Mrs. Beer's House*. Anecdotal, conversational, but very seldom slackly self-indulgent or merely whimsical in the way that I noted earlier as possibly dangerous, the quiet craftsmanship of Patricia Beer is unobtrusive but pervasive. Subjects are appraised, inspected, commemorated, with the wry self-confidence of a good storyteller.

—Anthony Thwaite

BEISSEL, Henry (Eric). Canadian. Born in Cologne, Germany, 12 April 1929; emigrated to Canada in 1951: naturalized, 1956. Educated at the University of Cologne, 1948–50; University College, London, 1950–51; University of Toronto (Epstein Award, 1958; Davidson Prize, 1959), 1957–60, B.A. 1958, M.A. 1960. Packer, salesman, and clerk, in Canada, 1951–54; free-lance writer and film-maker, Canadian Broadcasting Corporation, 1954–58; Lecturer, University of Munich, 1960–62, University of Alberta, Edmonton, 1962–64, and University of the West Indies, Trinidad, 1964–66. Assistant Professor, 1966–68, Associate Professor, 1968–76, and since 1976, Professor of English, Sir George Williams University, now Concordia University, Montreal. Editor, *Edge* magazine, Montreal, 1963–69. Recipient: Canada Council grant, 1967, 1968, 1969, 1971, 1973, 1974 (2 grants). Address: Ayorama Cottage, R.R. 5, Alexandria, Ontario K0C 1A0, Canada.

PUBLICATIONS

Verse

Witness the Heart. Toronto, Green Willow Press, 1963.

New Wings for Icarus: A Poem in Four Parts. Toronto, Coach House Press, 1966.
The World Is a Rainbow (for children), music by W. Bottenberg. Toronto, Canadian Music Centre, 1969.
Face on the Dark. Toronto, New Press, 1970.
Quays of Sadness. Montreal, Delta Press, 1973.
The Salt I Taste. Montreal, DC Books, 1975.

Plays

The Curve, adaptation of a play by Tancred Dorst (produced Edmonton, 1963). Included in *Three Plays*, 1976.
Skinflint: A Marionette Play (produced Montreal, 1969; London, 1971).
A Trumpet for Nap, adaptation of a play by Tancred Dorst (produced London, 1970). Toronto, Playwrights Co-op, 1973.
Inook and the Sun (produced Stratford, Ontario, 1973; London, 1974). Toronto, Playwrights Co-op, 1974.
Three Plays (*The Curve, A Trumpet for Nap, Grand Tirade at the Town-Wall*), by Tancred Dorst. Toronto, Playwrights Co-op, 1976.
Goya (produced Montreal, 1976). Toronto, Playwrights Co-op, 1978.
For Crying Out Loud, in *Cues and Entrances*, edited by Henry Beissel. Toronto, Gage, 1977.
Under Coyote's Eye (produced Chicago, 1978).

Other

Introduction to Spain (filmstrip and text). London, Common Ground, 1955.

Editor, *Cues and Entrances: 10 Canadian One-Act Plays.* Toronto, Gage, 1977.

Translator, *The Price of Morning: Selected Poems*, by Walter Bauer. Vancouver, Prism International Press, 1968.
Translator, *A Different Sun*, by Walter Bauer. Ottawa, Oberon Press, and London, Dobson, 1976.

* * *

Henry Beissel is a poet whose considerable interest in drama is readily apparent in his work. He is immensely conscious of the poet's role, both in the practice of his art and in relation to the society in which he finds himself. This consciousness has found expression in various acts of protest or strong social comment which should be linked to Beissel's views on poetry which he has made known at poetry readings and in his editorial in *Edge 7* (Winter 1967–68). He has summarised his own and the poet's function in the following excerpt: "On the other hand the poet as myth-maker: all art, as Yeats said, is founded upon personal vision, and myth is the embodiment of man's vision of himself and his world. It is this vision that distinguishes man from all other forms of being. And here too, in a time like ours determined to pervert the individual and to obscure all true vision, the poet's task is of especial magnitude." Beissel's first, noteworthy statement is contained in *New Wings for Icarus*, a book-length poem in four parts in which his personal vision works to telescope time and experience in what is, on occasion, a critical but generally affirming comment on the human process: "... to render us human/for the one night in which we bloom." *Face on the Dark* is a more personal and more intimately considered collection of poems. Again, there is something of the conscious poetic *persona* operating in the verse, and there is a good deal of drawing on travel as an ordering experience. Social comment crops up in one or two rather tense poems. Otherwise, the line has become longer, the poems, structurally more complex.

As a more recent development, Beissel has shifted his energy into drama. His translation of the German poems of Walter Bauer was widely and favourably reviewed.

—Michael Gnarowski

BELITT, Ben. American. Born in New York City, 2 May 1911. Educated at the University of Virginia, Charlottesville, B.A. 1932 (Phi Beta Kappa), M.A. 1934, 1934–36. Served in the United States Infantry, 1942–44; Editor-Scenarist, Signal Corps Photographic Center Combat Film Section, 1945–46. Assistant Literary Editor, *The Nation*, New York, 1937–38. Since 1938, Member of the English Department, and currently Professor of literature and languages, Bennington College, Vermont. Taught at Mills College, Oakland, California, 1939, and Connecticut College, New London, 1948–49. Recipient: Shelley Memorial Award, 1937; Guggenheim Fellowship, 1945; Oscar Blumenthal Award, 1957, and Union League Civic and Arts Foundation prize, 1960 (*Poetry*, Chicago); Brandeis University Creative Arts Award, 1962; National Institute of Arts and Letters award, 1965; National Endowment for the Arts grant, 1967. Address: Department of English, Bennington College, Bennington, Vermont 05201, U.S.A.

PUBLICATIONS

Verse

The Five-Fold Mesh. New York, Knopf, 1938.
Wilderness Stair. New York, Grove Press, 1955.
The Enemy Joy: New and Selected Poems. Chicago, University of Chicago Press, 1964.
Nowhere But Light: Poems 1964–1969. Chicago, University of Chicago Press, 1970.
The Double Witness: Poems 1970–1976. Princeton, New Jersey, Princeton University Press, 1978.

Other

Adam's Dream: A Preface to Translation. New York, Grove Press, 1978.

Editor and Translator, *Poet in New York: Federico García Lorca.* New York, Grove Press, 1955; London, Thames and Hudson, 1956.
Editor and Translator, *Selected Poems of Pablo Neruda.* New York, Grove Press, 1961.
Editor and Translator, *Juan de Mairena and Poems from the Apocryphal Songbooks.* Berkeley, University of California Press, 1963.
Editor and Translator, *Selected Poems of Rafael Alberti.* Berkeley, University of California Press, 1966.
Editor and Translator, *A New Decade: Poems 1958–67*, by Pablo Neruda. New York, Grove Press, 1969.
Editor and Translator, *Splendor and Death of Joaquín Murieta*, by Pablo Neruda. New York, Farrar Straus, 1972; London, Alcove Press, 1973.
Editor and Translator, *New Poems 1968–1970*, by Pablo Neruda. New York, Grove Press, 1973.
Editor and Translator, *Five Decades: Poems 1925–1970*, by Pablo Neruda. New York, Grove Press, 1974.

Translator, *Four Poems by Rimbaud: The Problem of Translation.* Denver, Swallow, 1947; London, Sylvan Press, 1948.

Translator, with others, *Cántico: Selections*, by Jorge Guillén. Boston, Little Brown, 1965.

Translator, *Poems from Canto General*, by Pablo Neruda. New York, Racolin Press, 1968.

Translator, with others, *Selected Poems 1923–1967*, by Jorge Luis Borges. New York, Delacorte Press, 1972.

Translator, *A la pintura*, by Rafael Alberti. West Islip, New York, Universal Art Editions, 1972.

Bibliography: "Ben Belitt Issue" of *Voyages* (Washington, D.C.), Fall 1967, and of *Modern Poetry Studies* (Buffalo), 1976.

Manuscript Collections: University of Virginia Library, Charlottesville; State University of New York Library, Buffalo; Mugar Memorial Library, Boston University.

Critical Studies: "In Search of the American Scene" by the author, in *Poets on Poetry*, edited by Howard Nemerov, New York, Basic Books, 1965; "The Fascination of What's Difficult" by Howard Nemerov, in *Reflexions on Poetry and Poetics*, New Brunswick, New Jersey, Rutgers University Press, 1972; "Antipodal Man: An Interview with Ben Belitt" by Joan Hutton, in *Quadrille* (Bennington, Vermont), Spring 1973; "A Wild Severity: The Poetry of Ben Belitt" by Joan Hutton, in *Salmagundi* (Saratoga Springs, New York), April 1973; "Confronting Nullity: The Poetry of Ben Belitt" by Robert Boyers, in *Sewanee Review* (Tennesee), Fall 1973.

Ben Belitt quotes from "In Passing," in *Voyages* (Washington, D.C.), Fall 1967:

Perhaps the best way of accounting for my purpose as a poet at the present time is to say that I intend more poems. I can add to that an increased sense of wonder with regard to the forms, sounds, dimensions, and subjects my poems may take in the future; for more than ever I realize that the whole realm of *subject* – the occasions which produce poems, or which are created by poems – needs to be extended, imagined, wondered at. In the past, I have been preoccupied with the factor of *place – real* places lived in, with their genius for crystallizing experience, testing identity, specifying – as the source of the poet's opportunity: the "world's body" as an inalienable aspect of his subject. In this belief, I have kept my geography mobile – exchanged Vermont for Block Island or New Mexico, New Mexico for Old Mexico, Granada for Florence, the Alhambra for the Uffizi, the new world for the old: all in the hope of reassembling my identity in the "place" which matters to me most – some new poem I will inhabit for myself or leave as a trust for whomsoever it may concern. For this reason, I suppose, I have come to look upon poetry as a series of "departures," arranged my books in colors and areas like a map-maker, found no substitute for the specificities of the substantive world.

I shall go on doing so; but after ten years, Vermont and Mexico (between which most of my poems have been recently strewn) are not half heterogeneous enough. They have, however, helped me to keep antipodal, pointed my head two ways, allowed me to walk under and over my subject, wrenched my inner ear. A collateral aspect of my concern for place, over the years, has been a concern for the *language* of the place, domestic or exotic – English, Spanish, Italian, French – as well as its spirit; and a further consequence for poetry has been my concern for the translation of that language. It is this kind of deployment and displacement which has brought me to the translation into English of selected works from Federico García Lorca, Antonio Machado, Pablo Neruda, Borges, Jorge Guillén, Rafael Alberti, Arthur Rimbaud, and incidental lyrics by Montale, Quasimodo, Valéry, as well as to certain prosodic and textural reverberations which have helped to translate me to myself.

I am curious about matters which lie suspended between myself and the world outside me. I would like to search for a subject at the heart of the poetic function itself for which there is perhaps no given "place," on the Augustinian hunch that "place there is none: we go backward and forward, and there is no place." I long to live on the "invisible edge" of Things, to write poems which coincide exactly with the time that induced them, and thereby create a subject which is *time's* – uniquely time's – and thus gives the spirit a further dimension to move in.

* * *

Ben Belitt extends and enriches a tradition in which the eccentric particular flourishes, and in which the line between will and fancy, on the one hand, and responsible imagination, on the other, is consistently challenged, though rarely obscured. We experience in reading Belitt's verse "the fascination of what's difficult," to borrow the title of Howard Nemerov's 1964 essay on Belitt; but what is difficult in Belitt seems also necessary, if not perfectly inevitable. That is to say, the texture of Belitt's verse is characteristically dense in a way that compels strict attention to details even as those details beckon towards others which seem not so much predicated by their earlier counterparts as waywardly implied. We are not tempted, really, to stop at particular images for very long, for we believe the poet knows just where he is going and where he can confidently take us, and we feel we ought somehow to let ourselves be guided. We learn gradually to anticipate not the inevitable but the relevant particular, the word or image that surprises us by revealing a significant pattern we had not expected but had only minimally apprehended. Rarely in Belitt does the extravagant detail disturb the reader's developing or retrospective experience of the poem as a whole. Always the function of the vivid metaphor, the strange idiom, the rare and chiselled phrase, is to enlarge the context of the poem, or to clothe an abstraction in the flesh of an unmistakable object. Verbal feeling, an at least partial reliance on the sound and texture of words in themselves, does not in Belitt vie with sense, with the content of the poem, for, as in Stevens, the processes of the poem's composition are very largely what the poem deals in. What we value above anything else in our experience of the poetry of a Belitt is the pleasure of making our way through the obliquities of syntax and imagery and diction, for we recognize throughout that the obliquity is no evasive stratagem contrived to throw us off the trail of meaning, whatever that may be. We accept in reading this sort of work that poetry evokes a complex state of consciousness of which ideas and reductive meanings are a very limited part. Probably it is useful to say that certain poets require to be read only by a certain kind of reader, to be confronted by an intelligence to whom the idea of an equilibrium perilously approached and maintained continues to be beautiful.

Belitt is determined through his work to live in the spirit, and to make it possible for his readers at least temporarily to do so. This is a very special sort of thing in Belitt, for Belitt's is no moral vision, no saintly pursuit, no trance-like reduction of self to a still-point stripped of instinct and content with waiting for some ultimate deliverance. For Belitt, to live in the spirit is nothing less than the conception of a poetic idiom so finely modulated that it constitutes a system of notations far removed from practical language. This is in no way to suggest that the raw materials with which the poet works are to be discounted, or tolerated only so that they may be transformed. What Belitt loves are the things *and* the transformative urgency he must at once yield to and control. What we wonder at in reading Belitt is that he transmutes his raw materials, the stuff of reality as we generally acknowledge it, as completely as the grape is transmuted in its conversion to a fine wine, and yet the original elements remain. In fact, they are felt with greater force and clarity than they were before their translation into the specifically poetic medium.

Associated with all this is Belitt's marvellous evocation of dream-like longings without the accompanying fuzziness of patently poetical dream states. Occasionally the mind is made to boggle a bit before it can get at the sense of a poem, but such disorientation as a reader may experience has more to do with the laxness of conventional discourse than with the excessive rigors of Belitt's. The late R. P. Blackmur once wrote of Stevens that his "ambiguity is that of a substance so dense with being, that it resists paraphrase and can be truly perceived only in the form of words in which it was given." It is what one feels compelled to say of whatever seems inscrutable or at least resistant to paraphrase in Belitt. In his work, possibility is evoked by means of that tenuous equilibrium which the words of a language conspire at once to establish and to unsettle. In his power to make us wonder at the extraordinary things poetry can do, Belitt is truly one of our greatest modern masters.

—Robert Boyers

BELL, Charles G(reenleaf). American. Born in Greenville, Mississippi, 31 October 1916. Educated at the University of Virginia, Charlottesville, B.A. 1936; Oxford University (Rhodes Scholar, 1936–38), B.A. 1938, B.Litt. 1939, M.A. 1966. Married 1) Mildred Cheatham Winfree in 1939 (divorced, 1949), three daughters; 2) Diana Mason in 1949, two daughters. Instructor in English, Blackburn College, Carlinville, Illinois, 1939–40; Instructor and Assistant Professor of English, Iowa State College, Ames, 1940–45; Assistant Professor of English, Princeton University, New Jersey, 1945–49; Assistant Professor of Humanities, University of Chicago, 1949–56; Tutor, Saint John's College, Annapolis, Maryland, 1956–67. Since 1967, Tutor, Saint John's College, Santa Fe, New Mexico. Guest Professor, University of Frankfurt, 1952; Guest Professor and Director of the Honors Program, University of Puerto Rico, Mayaguez, 1955–56; Fulbright Professor, in art and philosophy, Technische Hochschule, Munich, 1958–59; Poet-in-Residence, University of Rochester, New York, Spring 1967; Guest Professor, in philosophy, State University of New York, Old Westbury, Spring 1970. Recipient: Rockefeller Fellowship, 1948; Ford Fellowship, 1952. Address: 1260 Canyon Road, Santa Fe, New Mexico 87501, U.S.A.

PUBLICATIONS

Verse

Songs for a New America. Bloomington, Indiana University Press, 1953; revised edition, Dunwoody, Georgia, Norman S. Berg, 1966.
Delta Return. Bloomington, Indiana University Press, 1956; revised edition, Dunwoody, Georgia, Norman S. Berg, 1969.

Novels

The Married Land. Boston, Houghton Mifflin, 1962.
The Half Gods. Boston, Houghton Mifflin, 1968.

Manuscript Collection: Boston University.

Critical Study: "A Poet of Re-Attachment" by Galway Kinnell, in *Modern Age* (Chicago), Summer 1958.

Charles G. Bell comments:

My style grew out of the older tradition: Wordsworth, Blake, Milton, then the

Elizabethans, then Middle English, then Dante in Italian, Goethe and Hölderlin in German, all memorized *in extenso*; I never read any moderns until after my own manner was more or less formed. My preoccupation from the first was philosophic and discursive, aimed at a long poem, or at the shorter formed poem of controlled statement and apocalyptic intimation.

From Stringfellow Barr at Virginia I took (1934) the challenge of cyclical history, which drove me to study great books, language, and the arts, and which put me in my earliest published poems (1938–9) on more or less the same ground of meaning that Yeats had occupied in his last, though I was not aware of that at the time. My treatment of the cyclical theme had two distinct phases, from the war years and after: as I have written in the preface of the revised edition of *Songs for a New America*:

> It was a temptation to arrange the pieces chronologically. For they reflect ten years' struggle with notions of life and death in history, which, in an age like ours, one did not have to read Spengler to be haunted by; and they run the gamut from Augustinian despair of time and search for faith, to romantic affirmation of the moment in which it seemed our greatness to burn.

My second book, *Delta Return*, attempted an organic manifold of self and world, based on the play of polarities, a dialectic of symbolic forces, light–dark, east–west, north–south, earth–water, etc. As I wrote in the foreword to the revised edition:

> These poems arose from a trip I made in June of 1953 to visit my mother in my home town of Greenville, Mississippi. I had sent off my first book, in which the title poem, "Songs for a New America," celebrated the tragic daring of the flight west. Here that Promethean theme yields to the water-death and ebbing of the motion south and home. Though, as with other underworld journeys, what is sought is not death simply, but some ambivalent, regenerative sign.

In the last years, having deflected some of the larger urge into my novels (which in a sense are vastly expanded prose poems), I have been refining a purer verse concentrate – though it remains philosophical:

MAN

Two, subconscious of each
Other, one waking
While the other sleeps.

To reach out and touch
The double above our waking,
The One, who sleeps.

* * *

The best poems in Charles G. Bell's first collection, *Songs for a New America*, are accomplished and attractive enough to make readers regret that there has been no new volume since 1956. Cast in a variety of traditional metrical patterns, the *Songs* are essentially lyrical and meditative responses to the problem of change, the loss of past forms and sanctions, and the crude excesses of technology and "progress." Looking down from a plane in cross-continental flight Bell wonders (as Chicago fades from view)

> is this curse of earth and air
> And water, this rearward ugliness the cost
> Of every embodied dream and act of power?

"We build as we destroy," he reflects at first, "consummately," a people "involved in the doom/Of shifting things, knowing no permanent goods." The controlling metaphor of one of the most effective poems, "These Winter Dunes," is that of a sensitive man watching the endless movement of the sand:

If there are strangers still coming to this great land,
Tell them out of pity, and make it plain,
Not to love what they find; or if love surprise
(As we are weak), let it be of a special kind,
Quick and evasive; for here all things will change
Before the fruit can ripen on the vine.

But Bell's final conclusions are far from being tragic, or even much more than sadly nostalgic for the old civilities and an unspoiled countryside. Change means challenge and the possibility of new growth (the precedent, after all, seems to be on our side):

The impossible future holds
No more impossible miracle than we own
Here in this present – out of the fall and rain
Of energy, building of atoms and cells,
Desperate chances of reptiles, mammals and men,
This present we have won, unbelievable,
This gift, this now.
The property of spirit
Is transcendence. We have much to transcend.

The later poems in this volume depart, quite literally, from America, with their fond picture-postcard recollections of Como, Königstein, Le Havre, and other places cherished by the cultivated tourist. There are a few experiments with dramatic monologues, but whatever the scene or poetic mode, the refrain is always the same: "Life is a wave that moves by breaking." The sum of wisdom is acceptance – not only acceptance of change but the joyful anticipation of what change may offer. The truly wise man is like the skillful rider: "Perceptive spirit rides with loosened rein."

The freshness of the *Songs* is largely absent from the poems in *Delta Return*, at least in part because Bell has forced his themes into an obsessively rigid pattern of three five-part cantos, divided into five subsections, each in turn divided into five five-line iambic pentameter stanzas, irregularly rhymed. The occasion for the cycle is Bell's return from the energetic, constructive "North" to his home town, Greenville, Mississippi – a symbolic "ebbing to passivity, a dissolving." The motion is neither sentimental, however, nor regressive: the journey is that of the eternal return, the descent into one's past necessary for renewal and reemergence. The dialectic is modish but not inherently unpoetic. Bell's problem is not so much his model as the extreme unevenness of his diction, which ranges from rhetorical posturing to banal flatness, and his forcing of personal experience to take on the weight of impersonal, mythic significance.

—Elmer Borklund

BELL, Marvin (Hartley). American. Born in New York City, 3 August 1937. Educated at Alfred University, New York, B.A. 1958; Syracuse University, New York, 1958;

University of Chicago, M.A. 1961; University of Iowa, Iowa City, M.F.A. 1963. Served as a Foreign Military Training Officer in the United States Army 1963–65. Married 1) Mary Mammosser in 1958; 2) Dorothy Murphy in 1961; two sons. Visiting Lecturer, 1965, Assistant Professor, 1966–69, Associate Professor, 1969–75, and since 1975, Professor of English, University of Iowa. Visiting Professor, Oregon State University, Corvallis, Summer 1969, and Goddard College, Plainfield, Vermont, Summer 1972. Editor, *Statements* magazine, 1959–64; Poetry Editor, *North American Review*, Mount Vernon, Iowa, 1964–69, and *Iowa Review*, 1969–71. Since 1975, Columnist ("Homage to the Runner"), *American Poetry Review*, Philadelphia. Recipient: Lamont Poetry Selection Award, 1969; Bess Hokin Prize (*Poetry*, Chicago), 1969; Emily Clark Balch Prize (*Virginia Quarterly Review*), 1970; Guggenheim Fellowship, 1975; National Endowment for the Arts grant, 1978. Address: Writers Workshop, University of Iowa, Iowa City, Iowa 52242, U.S.A.

PUBLICATIONS

Verse

Two Poems. Iowa City, Hundred Pound Press, 1965.
Things We Dreamt We Died For. Iowa City, Stone Wall Press, 1966.
Poems for Nathan and Saul. Mount Vernon, Iowa, Hillside Press, 1966.
A Probable Volume of Dreams. New York, Atheneum, 1969.
The Escape into You: A Sequence. New York, Atheneum, 1971.
Woo Havoc. Somerville, Massachusetts, Barn Dream Press, 1971.
Residue of Song. New York, Atheneum, 1974.
Stars Which See, Stars Which Do Not See. New York, Atheneum, 1977.

Other

Editor, *Iowa Workshop Poets 1963.* Iowa City, Statements-Midwest Magazine, 1963.

Critical Studies: "The Poetry of Marvin Bell" by Peter Elfed Lewis, in *Stand* (Newcastle upon Tyne), xiii, 4, 1972; "Marvin Bell: 'Time's Determinant/Once, I Knew You' " by Arthur Oberg, in *American Poetry Review* (Philadelphia), May–June 1976.

* * *

For *A Probable Volume of Dreams*, his first full-length collection of poems, Marvin Bell drew heavily on his own early experience as a Jew, the son of a Jew. Bell's approach, for which the reader is prepared at the outset by Yiddish proverbs ("Sleep faster, we need the pillows") is easy, almost too smooth. The poems, like a stand-up comedian, come close to naming some essential areas of experience: they sober up just long enough to provide serious relief before the earnest frown fades back to be replaced by smiles. The throwaway line undercuts the poem, and a tension is created between Bell the poet and Bell the entertainer, as in the last half of "A Poor Jew":

Either way, he looks forward
to an inevitable fixing-up –
that settling of his mind and body
amid great welcome –
but at great expense.
And he goes about getting fixed
to afford it. Love is
alright, genes

are to be expected, also
toys, games, plans and fate
are worth looking into.
But with money in your pocket,
you are wise and you are
handsome and you sing well too.

In some of these poems, the play of language, a proliferation of puns, threaten to obscure any real feeling other than mild amusement, and the end result is that they seem too consciously crafted, too pat: "Finally, I am clearing out/by marking down./And I am for hire,/who cannot keep Father's/glass front firm ..." ("In Memory of H. G. Grand"). Bell's sense of humor has wrought one of literature's finest beginnings for a marriage poem: "It is customary to conceive/of the bride in white,/dressed to merit pleasure/and holier than thou" (Section 1 of "A Bride in White"). The same volume contains "Toward Certain Divorce," where Bell encounters squarely all that is serious and doubting and searching:

I am afraid I have only the casual prophecy
and not the life of the word, that energy,
within me, though I have sworn to seek it.
Swear to me, that you leave to seek it too.

The Escape into You carried out the promise of his earlier meditational poems. A sequence of 54 18-line poems, the book confronts identity less obliquely than *A Probable Volume*, with bigger belly laughs and greater moments of despair. The form curiously loosens the language and these poems have a wonderful mixture of the colloquial and the formal ("The Children):

The death of the father is my shepherd
he maketh me three versions of wanting.
He giveth back my shadow; he restores.
He pays out and pays out the darkness.
How much does it cost to keep silence?

Bell knows the ultimate identity of absurdity and pathos, but *The Escape into You* does not accept or write off such wisdom, but comes instead to war it.

He is a funny man, but unlike most, his wit wakens the reader an hour overdue with the nagging memory of a euphoric giggle. Wondering, "did he mean something else by that ... ?" the reader goes back to the poem and learns that just behind the smile, the seemingly easy language, the quick laugh, is something deeper, a challenge far greater:

"The Pornographic But Serious History"

of myself, begging your pardon, as a
young man, quick to draw arms, quick
to take a fence for daggers toward my
heart, quick to shoot from the hip,
fast to let fly in all directions
as if to injure fatally the unsettled

just recognized in myself, which is why
in the end I take myself for example
though what the new critic says isn't proof
and the thin line is shifting again
between comic and tragic, body and spirit,
and the wife doesn't know her husband.

Not to fill up with history but no ideas,
not to merely *see* life and think it images,
not to think morality a bad medicine
does the husband offer his boyhood to his
wife's mouth, the words are a white balm,
the self heated to the temper of its time.

—Geof Hewitt

BENEDIKT, Michael. American. Born in New York City, 26 May 1935, Educated at New York University, B.A. 1956; Columbia University, New York, M.A. 1961. Served in the United States Army, 1958–59. Associate Editor, Horizon Press, publishers, 1959–61; New York Correspondent, *Art International*, Lugano, 1965–67. Associate Editor, *Art News* magazine, New York, 1963–72. Instructor in Language and Literature, Bennington College, Vermont, 1968–69; Poet in Residence, Sarah Lawrence College, Bronxville, New York, 1969–73; Associate Professor of Arts and Humanities, Hampshire College, Amherst, Massachusetts, 1973–75; Associate Professor, Vassar College, Poughkeepsie, New York, 1976–77; Visiting Professor, Boston University, 1977–79. Poetry Editor, *Paris Review*, 1974–78. Recipient: Bess Hokin Prize (*Poetry*, Chicago), 1968; Guggenheim Fellowship, 1969. Address: 315 West 98th Street, New York, New York 10025, U.S.A.

PUBLICATIONS

Verse

Serenade in Six Pieces. Privately printed, 1958.
Changes. Detroit, New Fresco, 1961.
8 Poems. Privately printed, 1966.
The Body. Middletown, Connecticut, Wesleyan University Press, 1968.
Sky. Middletown, Connecticut, Wesleyan University Press, 1970.
Mole Notes. Middletown, Connecticut, Wesleyan University Press, 1971.
Night Cries. Middletown, Connecticut, Wesleyan University Press, 1976.

Recording: *Today's Poets 5*, Folkways, 1968.

Plays

The Vaseline Photographer (produced New York, 1965).
The Orgy Bureau, in *Chelsea* (New York), 1968.
Box (produced New York, 1970).

Other

Editor, with George E. Wellwarth, *Modern French Theatre: The Avant-Garde, Dada and Surrealism.* New York, Dutton, 1964; as *Modern French Plays: An Anthology from Jarry to Ionesco*, London, Faber, 1965.
Editor, with George E. Wellwarth *Postwar German Theatre: An Anthology of Plays.* New York, Dutton, 1967; London, Macmillan, 1968.

Editor and Translator, *Ring Around the World: The Selected Poems of Jean L'Anselme.* London, Rapp and Whiting, 1967; Denver, Swallow, 1968.
Editor, *Theatre Experiment: New American Plays.* New York, Doubleday, 1967.
Editor, with George E. Wellwarth, *Modern Spanish Theatre: An Anthology of Plays.* New York, Dutton, 1968.
Editor, *22 Poems of Robert Desnos.* Santa Cruz, California, Kayak, 1971.
Editor, *The Poetry of Surrealism: An Anthology.* Boston, Little Brown, 1974.
Editor, *The Prose Poem: An International Anthology.* New York, Dell, 1976.

Manuscript Collection: Humanities Research Center, University of Texas, Austin.

Critical Studies: *Benedikt: A Profile*, Tucson, Grilled Flowers Press, 1978.

Michael Benedikt comments:

(1970) Major theme is probably the relationship of matter and spirit; sometimes the sensual and the "pure." General sources and influences: the French Symbolists and Surrealists until about 1968; most recently, the English romantic poets. Stylistically, I am interested in the treatment of "difficult" subjects with clarity, since their reality *is* very clear (at least to me). I am probably as much influenced by contemporary painting, film, and theatre as I am by any movement in poetry. I have become interested in the possibilities of the poem in prose as well as verse.

(1980) Newer work is largely in verse, concerned with the incorporation of more "realistic" material in the above context. Titles of work-in-progress: "Family Blessings, Family Curses" and "Dear Alice."

* * *

There are many ways to imagine The Poet; warbling his native woodnotes wild, legislating unknown to the rest of us, speaking in the language that men do know, giving to airy nothing a local habitation and a name, making things that are palpable and mute. Michael Benedikt typifies the poet as the eternal outsider, the poet against the world. And what a world it is, filled with "traditional poets," "collegiate English instructors" "Women of the Earth" (who use their snatches "to snatch at people with"), "Power People" (who shout through loudspeakers "Get up off your asses and make a revolution!"), guests at garden parties in Scarsdale, "X" (whose lovers are dull: "so that others glimpsing them, and after conversation, would remark: 'Agh! phooey! you wouldn't catch us talking to them at even the dullest cocktail party ever thrown!' ..." ["For Love or Money"]). So many cocktail parties, so many references to the upper west side of New York; a whole poem devoted to sneering at Troy, New York, which all New York poets know is Nowheresville. I sense in this work a life dedicated to chastising opponents of true culture, true art, true life, whatever *that* is. In his book *Mole Notes* there is one passage that for me sums up Benedikt's work, expresses the stance he takes toward the world: "Also, at this very moment, there is someone in a Civilian Submarine at the bottom of the Gulf of Mexico whose actions affect us all with their secluded elegance' their secret grandeur, grace, and repose" ("Molar Advent in Retrospect"). In poem after poem Benedikt takes the position of the commander of that submarine, alternately raving about his enemy the world, or lamenting its abysmal ignorance, or pitying its failure to be sensitive, graceful, grand, or elegant. Submarines keep appearing throughout his work, always as out-moded vehicles of transport, "civilian" or "pleasure" submarines, the very latest model for the year 1915. These and other images and objects in the work give it a dated air, reminding me of those Surrealist collages that juxtapose steam engines and harpies, corset ads and patent velocipedes.

Benedikt has translated a great deal of Surrealist poetry, and edited *The Poetry of Surrealism*. It would be surprising if this interest weren't reflected in his own poetry. But what does it mean to be writing Surrealist poetry in the 1970's, to be guided by an avant-garde esthetic now a half a century old? The very objects in many of these poems recall the interiors of early 20th-century Europe: umbrella stands, mirrors, bowler hats, decolletage. I don't mean to say that Benedikt is a kind of verbal Edward Gorey, camping out among the Edwardiana, for many of his poems are set firmly in the present. It's just that he hasn't always been able to resist using the same *things* that are familiar to us from that earlier work, and so his poems necessarily partake of that earlier poetry's peculiar historical "feel."

Some of his poems read like exercises in Surrealism. "The European Shoe," for example, consists of 15 short sections, each having The European Shoe as its subject: "Tears fall from the eye of the European Shoe as it waves goodbye to us/ from the back balcony of the speeding train" (The Body). The use of the same incongruous object in a repetitive pattern; the animation of the inanimate (or the other way around); these are devices made familiar to us by the Surrealists, and to find them in a contemporary poem is to be reminded of the poet's forebears, and also to perceive the poem as a crafted thing, a consciously made artifact. Hence my difficulty with this and other poems in *The Body* and *Air*, for the Surrealists despised the idea of art as craftsmanship. We are confronted here with something that seems very much like the anti-Surrealist Surrealist poem. This destruction of what one wishes to celebrate must necessarily come along with the use of Surrealism as a style. In "A Beloved Head," Benedikt employs the Surrealist device of turning something organic into something mechanical: here Surrealism exists only at the surface of the poem, decorating the straightforward idea that some men manipulate women as if they were machines. André Breton would not have approved.

Mole Notes, an elegantly printed volume of short prose pieces, seems a logical development in Benedikt's work. In *The Body* and *Sky* there is a gradual but noticeable drift toward the long line, a growing sense of paragraphs rather than stanzas, or stanza-like forms. But the tone of *Mole Notes* remains consistent with the earlier work, the sense of a series of collisions, of unexpected juxtapositions. In some of the pieces the comic and the serious can work beautifully together ("The Bewitched Lover"):

> And whenever you carry me away, it is as if you
> were bringing me something! O come to me, true
> beloved, so that you can go away in a hurry again!

Here there is a kind of fusion, or better, an alternating current that expresses exactly the attraction and repulsion cycle of love. But the common problem of poets who turn to short prose works appears here as well, the sense that in writing prose the poet can be unbuttoned, casual, and kick over the traces of form. Many of these mole notes seem loose to the point of carelessness. "The Secret of Scotch" and "The Pain Alarm" strike me as being very good stand-up comic routines, and no doubt they lay them in the aisles at readings, but they disappoint the reader.

—Steven Young

BENNETT, Louise. Jamaican. Educated at primary and secondary schools in Jamaica; Royal Academy of Dramatic Art, London (British Council Scholarship). Worked with the BBC (West Indies Section) as resident artist, 1945–46 and 1950–53, and with repertory companies in Coventry, Huddersfield, and Amersham. Returned to Jamaica, 1955. Drama Specialist with the Jamaica Social Welfare Commission, 1955–60; Lecturer in drama and Jamaican folklore, Extra-Mural Department, University of the West Indies, Kingston, 1959–61. Lecturer and radio and television commentator. Represented Jamaica at the Royal Commonwealth Arts Festival in Britain, 1965. Recipient: Silver Musgrave Medal of the

Institute of Jamaica; Norman Manley Award of Excellence. M.B.E. (Member, Order of the British Empire); Order of Jamaica. Address: Enfield House, Gordon Town, St. Andrew, Jamaica.

PUBLICATIONS

Verse

Dialect Verses. Kingston, Gleaner, 1940.
Jamaican Dialect Verses. Kingston, Gleaner, 1942; expanded version, Kingston, Pioneer Press, 1951.
Jamaican Humour in Dialect. Kingston, Gleaner, 1943.
Miss Lulu Sez. Kingston, Gleaner, 1948.
Anancy Stories and Dialect Verse, with others. Kingston, Pioneer Press, 1950.
Laugh with Louise: A Potpourri of Jamaican Folklore, Stories, Songs, Verses. Kingston, Bennett City Printery, 1960.
Jamaica Labrish. Kingston, Sangster's Book Stores, 1966.
Anancy and Miss Lou. Kingston, Sangster, 1979.

Recordings: *Jamaican Folk Songs,* Folkways, 1954; *Jamaican Singing Games,* Folkways, 1954; *West Indies Festival of Arts,* Cook, 1958; *Miss Lou's Views,* Federal, 1967; *Listen to Louise,* Federal, 1968.

Critical Study: Introduction by Rex Nettlefold, to *Jamaica Labrish,* 1966.

Louise Bennett comments:

I have been described as a "poet of utterance performing multiple roles as entertainer, as a valid literary figure and as a documenter of aspects of Jamaican life, thought, and feeling." I would not disagree with this.

* * *

Louise Bennett is to Jamaica what the calypsonian The Might Sparrow is to Trinidad and Tobago: an articulate voice of the people, a political commentator, a satirist, and, in many ways, a social historian. The difference between them is the difference between the traditional Trinidadian calypso and the traditional Jamaican mento. The calypso, however, when set down in the cold light of print, loses its sparkle and its inflections and becomes dull and often meaningless, because it has lost its music. The mento, on the other hand, can be understood and enjoyed merely from the printed page.

The "West Indian English" which is in common use, and in which Miss Bennett works, is gradually being recognised by anthropologists and linguistic specialists as a language with its own grammar, syntax and rules, rather than as a mere dialect. "English," the Barbadian poet and novelist George Lamming has said, "is a West Indian language." "West Indian English" – called Creole in some islands, Patois in others (especially those which have been, for periods in their history, French) – has enabled Louise Bennett to get many points across in pithy phrases which would have taken a whole paragraph to say in dictionary terms. It has the kind of racy flavour which suits her style, and she has been quick to use, too, some of the words and phrases in common daily use which go back to the standard English of Elizabethan and Cromwellian times.

Louise Bennett's researches have rescued from oblivion, often from extinction, a number of the island's folk songs, stories and sayings, and her stage productions have put Jamaican vernacular before large audiences.

There is a mass of her writing scattered about, very largely in Jamaica's newspapers and magazines over the years, and much of it was collected into a book entitled *Jamaica Labrish* (a dialect word meaning chatter or gossip) in 1966.

No subject has been too sacred for her fancy and biting wit. She has tackled the changing city, the war, Jamaican history, politics, middle-class attitudes, immigration and many other things, and no poet in Jamaica has a better understanding of the island and its people.

—Colin Rickards

BENVENISTE, Asa. British. Born in New York City, 25 August 1925; emigrated to England in 1950, became British subject in 1965. Educated at James Monroe High School, New York; New School for Social Research, New York, B.A. 1948; Sorbonne, Paris, 1950. Served as a Radio Operator in the United States Army Infantry, 1943–46. Married Pip Walker in 1949; three stepsons. Researcher, Jewish News Agency, New York, 1947; Co-Editor, *Zero Quarterly*, Paris, Tangier, and London, 1948–56; Correspondent, *Nugget Magazine*, London, 1956–57; Copy Editor, Doubleday and Company, publishers, New York, 1957–58; Senior Art Editor, Paul Hamlyn Ltd., publishers, London, 1959–61; Senior Editor, Studio Vista Ltd., publishers, London, 1961–63. Since 1965, Staff Member, and currently Executive Editor, Trigram Press Ltd., London. Address: 22 Leverton Street, London N.W.5, England.

PUBLICATIONS

Verse

Poems of the Mouth. London, Trigram Press, 1966.
A Word in Your Season: A Portfolio of Six Seriagraphs, with Jack Hirschman. London, Trigram Press, 1967.
Count Three. Berkeley, California, Maya, 1969.
The Atoz Formula. London, Trigram Press, 1969.
Free Semantic No. 2. London, Wallrich, 1970.
Umbrella. London, Wallrich, 1972.
Time Being, with Ray Di Palma and Tom Raworth. London, Trigram Press, 1972.
Blockmakers Black. London, Steam Press, 1973.
Certainly Metaphysics. London, Trigram Press, 1973.
It's the Same Old Feeling Again. London, Trigram Press, 1973.
Edge. London, Joe DiMaggio Press, 1974.
Dense Lens, with Brian Marley. London, Trigram Press, 1975.
A Part Apart. Middlesex, White Dog Press, 1975.
Listen. Bowling Green, Ohio, Doones Press, 1975.
Poems. London, Joe DiMaggio Press, 1976.
Loose Use. Newcastle upon Tyne, Pig Press, 1977.

Plays

Radio Plays: *Tangier for the Traveller*, 1956; *Piano Forte*, 1957.

Other

An Introduction to Brothers and Sisters, a Novel by Ivy Compton-Burnett. New York, Zero Press, 1956.
Autotypography: A Book of Design Priorities. London, Latimer New Dimensions, 1974.

Manuscript Collection: Washington University, St. Louis.

Critical Study: "Great Rejoicing" by Anselm Hollo, in *Ambit 41* (London), 1969.

Asa Benveniste comments:

Environmentalists will agree: describe the situation and you describe yourself. It's become clearer that poets mainly function within two areas: description or language. Most English poets fall within the former range ("Breakfast in the morning, then how do I compare with everyone else's corn flakes"). I can see how this might have a narrowing effect on the employment of language – and usually does, all around us. You can tell from the first line what the last line will read like. It's that prelude to tedium: To Thine Own Self Be True. Good enough for my aunt, good enough for me. Housman, Tennyson, after all, *are* good poets.

The second kind of work verges on the hysterical. Logic, clarity, description, narration, connecting links, have to make it as best they can, so long as they don't interfere with the *other* exercise, the possibility of hitting psychic accuracy and the sheer pleasure of two words coming together for the first time ever, and miraculously. For example: Robert Fludd, John Clare, Blake, Novalis, Zukofsky. Language for itself, and then its by-products like meaning, truth, perspicacity, play, pleasure, secret rejoicing. But it's dense material to work with, and anyone who argues publicly in favor of it, is bound to lose.

* * *

Asa Benveniste writes with light. Illuminates poems. Clear, subtle, lucid. I often imagine that even his punctuation marks become prisms on the page.

He is able to verify the mystical vision and tradition in poems often as simple as breath – and that's the essence of their power and immediacy. He is able to give added dimension to the real and enhance commonplace objects with mystery. Conversely he makes real and accessible the remote symbols of the Kabbalah and gives them face and form.

Tradition tells us that the great secrets and mysteries exist beyond the book and can only be exchanged from teacher to disciple through speech. Much of the available literature demonstrates the difficulty of verbalizing the inner journey and its unfolding, and of balancing the visible with the invisible and delineating the continual interplay between these two realities.

Therefore, Asa Benveniste's two books of poetry – *Poems of the Mouth* and *The Atoz Formula* – must be considered as valuable guides to the creative use of the process. They are sparks and must be cherished for their clarity.

Each volume develops possibilities inherent in a given mystical realm. *Poems of the Mouth* expands a proposition in the *Sefer Yetsira*, a primary Kabbalist textbook. *The Atoz Formula* explores the Hebrew Alphabet and the metaphorical/meta-actual progression of symbols enclosed within the cards of the Tarot.

It must also be noted that Asa Benveniste is an imaginative and elegant printer. The books he has issued from the Trigram Press are of consistently high quality.

—David Meltzer

BERESFORD, Anne. British. Born in Redhill, Surrey, 10 September 1929. Educated privately, and at Central School of Speech Training and Dramatic Art, London. Married Michael Hamburger, *q.v.*, in 1951 (divorced, 1970); remarried Michael Hamburger in 1974; three children. Former stage actress and BBC broadcaster. Teacher at the Poetry Workshop, Cockpit Theatre, London, 1971–73. Since 1969, drama teacher, Wimbledon High School; since 1970, extra-mural teacher of drama and elocution. London. Address: Marsh Acres, Middleton, Saxmundham, Suffolk IP17 3NH, England.

PUBLICATIONS

Verse

Walking Without Moving. London, Turret, 1967.
The Lair. London, Rapp and Whiting, 1968.
Footsteps in Snow. London, Agenda, 1972.
Modern Fairy Tale. Rushden, Northamptonshire, Sceptre Press, 1972.
The Courtship. Brighton, Unicorn Bookshop, 1972.
The Curving Shore. London, Agenda, 1975.
Words, with Michael Hamburger. East Bramley, Surrey, Words Press, 1977.
Unholy Giving. Knotting, Bedfordshire, Sceptre Press, 1977.

Plays

Radio Plays: *Struck by Apollo*, with Michael Hamburger, 1965; *The Villa*, 1968.

Other

Translator, *Alexandros: Selected Poems*, by Vera Lungu. London, Agenda, 1974.

Manuscript Collection: Humanities Research Center, University of Texas, Austin.

Critical Studies: review by Christopher Levenson, in *Queen's Quarterly* (Kingston, Ontario), September 1971; review in *Times Literary Supplement* (London), 13 October 1972.

* * *

Ezra Pound wrote: "Our life is, in so far as it is worth living, made up in great part of things indefinite, impalpable; and it is precisely because the arts present us these things that we – humanity – cannot get on without the arts" (*Selected Prose*, London, Faber, 1973, p. 33). Much of the subtlety of Anne Beresford's poetry stems from her attempts to define moments and states of mind of this nature – those aspects of consciousness and daily life which are most impatient of words. Anne Beresford's "Heimweh" is short enough to give in its entirety:

a thrush sings
every evening
in the ash tree

it has been singing
for as long
as I can remember
only then
the tree was probably
an oak

the song
aches and aches
in the green light
if I knew
where it was
I would go
home

Anne Beresford seldom overstates, but is reticent and elliptical. This gives her work an impersonal quality which is rare. At its best her writing expresses an imagination (*not* fancy) unlike that of any other contemporary poet. This is connected, in a strange way, with humour and satire. Her irony succeeds because it is not obvious.

A fault present in some poems is a tenuousness of rhythm, where the emotions don't seem strong enough to generate sufficient rhythmic energy. But this is sometimes offset by a clarity and simplicity of imagery which evoke much, particularly if these poems are lived with rather than read quickly: "outside, high on the mountains/is the great plain with wild flowers/wild flowers and air so fresh/one's head goes light." ("Eurydice"). At times the imagery is menacing: "You have come to a tower of slate/crumbling into grey sky./Don't climb, not there ..." ("Half-Way"). This is not poetry which strives for immediate effect; hence a first reading often misses how much meaning her usually very simple words contain.

Anne Beresford uses dream and myth to express states of mind which are real, never as ornament or literary device. Her most recent work makes use of dramatic monologue and shows an historical consciousness which raises her poetry above that of contemporary writers of the short poem who seem to be incapable of embodying subjects other than the personal and the incidentals of everyday life. I shall close these notes by quoting "Nicodemus" in full:

Keeping a sense of proportion
lip service to what is considered correct
I have brought what is needed to bury the dead.
Once again I come to you by night.
This time to take away all visible proof of my understanding.
In secret I have applied myself
to seek out wisdom
to know what is before my face –
the inside and the outside are reversed
that which is
has become that which is not –
displaced, troubled
I live naked in a house that is not my own
and the five trees of Paradise evade me.

—William Cookson

BERG, Stephen. American. Born in Philadelphia, Pennsylvania, 2 August 1934. Educated at the University of Pennsylvania, Philadelphia; Boston University; University of Iowa, Iowa City, B.A. 1959; University of Indiana, Bloomington. Married Millie Lane in 1959; two daughters. Formerly Instructor in English, Temple University, Philadelphia. Currently, Assistant Professor, Philadelphia College of Art. Poetry Editor, *Saturday Evening*

Post, Philadelphia, 1961–62; Editor, with Stephen Parker and Rhoda Schwartz, *The American Poetry Review*, Philadelphia. Recipient: Rockefeller-Centro Mexicano de Escritores grant, 1959–61; National Translation Center grant, 1969; Frank O'Hara Prize (*Poetry*, Chicago), 1970; Guggenheim Fellowship, 1974; National Endowment for the Arts grant, 1976; Columbia University Translation Center award, 1976. Address: 2005 Mt. Vernon Street, Philadelphia, Pennsylvania 19130, U.S.A.

PUBLICATIONS

Verse

Berg Goodman Mezey. Philadelphia, New Ventures Press, 1957.
Bearing Weapons. Iowa City, Cummington Press, 1963.
The Queen's Triangle: A Romance. West Branch, Iowa, Cummington Press, 1970.
The Daughters. Indianapolis, Bobbs Merrill, 1971.
Grief: Poems and Versions of Poems. New York, Grossman, 1975.

Other

Editor, with Robert Mezey, *Naked Poetry: Recent American Poetry in Open Forms.* Indianapolis, Bobbs Merrill, 1969.
Editor, with S. J. Marks, *Between People.* Chicago, Scott Foresman, 1972.
Editor, with S. J. Marks, *About Women.* New York, Fawcett, 1973.
Editor, with S. J. Marks, *Doing the Unknown.* New York, Dell, 1974.
Editor, with Robert Mezey, *The New Naked Poetry.* Indianapolis, Bobbs Merrill, 1976.

Translator, with others, *Cántico: Selections*, by Jorge Guillén. Boston, Little Brown, 1965.
Translator, *Nothing in the Word: Versions of Aztec Poetry.* New York, Grossman, 1972.
Translator, with others, *Clouded Sky*, by Miklos Radnoti. New York, Harper, 1972.
Translator, with Diskin Clay, *Oedipus the King*, by Sophocles. New York and London, Oxford University Press, 1978.

Manuscript Collection: Mugar Memorial Library, Boston University.

Stephen Berg comments:

Non-theoretical: all comments on my work – such as the introductions to *Nothing in the Word*, *Clouded Sky*, and *Grief* – are random and apply only to the particular books and poems in question. Some remarks in the essay "Hands and Feet," the introduction to *Between People*, and an essay on French Poetry in *Poetry* (Chicago), May 1970, may shed some light.

* * *

Many of the poems in Stephen Berg's large collection *The Daughters* break forth with an almost breathless fury of speech, the expression of an agonized, compassionate mind and sensibility confronting the bitter realities of modern existence:

We, the dooms, your future, the bloody fire
between places, dancers on the corpses of who,
we eat what there is. Are you
sitting at a table? Is there food? Us,

the zero washing itself, bones entering the floor,
leaves zigzagging down through silt, through farms
in the lone face of a mirror.

Berg appears to write with the example of such poets as Neruda, Vallejo, Patchen, among others, behind him. Like them he strives for a language and imagery that will encompass the irony, fatality, and suffering of a life everywhere overshadowed by mortality, a life unredeemed and unaccounted for either by reason or by any known God. In this endeavour Berg often stretches words and syntax to their extreme limits; frequently his means of progression – more evident, naturally, in his longer pieces, where there are greater space and freedom – are elliptical and associative rather than logical or merely sequential. Sometimes his poems surge and lash out seemingly uncontrollably; yet this is never the case, I think, for a strong, inventive imagination operates constantly, drawing together disparate details, linking objects and bodies, love and death, pain and anger, until the reader feels himself inside a poetic universe which lights up his own sense of the world with sudden, vivid and terrible lightning strokes of vision. To be sure, Berg's poetry has at times its lapses, excesses, and repetitions, but these are minor in comparison with the ambitiousness and force of what he attempts, and recent, as yet uncollected poems, show a calmer, more reflective side to his writing. Berg is an energetic and highly talented poet, translator, and editor of whom considerable accomplishment may be expected. "I can go anywhere, I can let go forever/and live in the middle of fire, in silence...."

—Ralph J. Mills, Jr.

BERGÉ, Carol. American. Born in New York City, 4 October 1928. Educated at New York University, 1946–52; New School for Social Research, New York, 1952–54. Has one son, Peter. Editorial assistant, Syndicate Publications, Simon and Schuster, publishers, *Forbes* magazine, and Hart Publishing Company, New York, 1950–54; Assistant to the President, Pendray Public Relations, New York, 1955. Member of the Board of Directors, COSMEP, 1971–73; lecturer at Thomas Jefferson College, Allendale, Michigan, 1975–76, Goddard College, Plainfield, Vermont, 1976, University of California, Berkeley, 1976–77, Indiana University, Bloomington, 1977, University of Southern Mississippi, Hattiesburg, 1977–78, University of New Mexico, Albuquerque, 1978–79, and Wright State University, Dayton, Ohio, 1979. Since 1971, Editor, *Center* magazine. Contributing Editor, *Woodstock Poetry Review*; Editor, *Paper Branches*, Albuquerque; Editor-in-Chief, *Mississippi Review*, Hattiesburg, 1977–78. Recipient: MacDowell Fellowship (four times); New York State Council on the Arts grant, for editing, 1971, for fiction, 1974. Agent: R. Weyr, William Morris Agency Inc., 1350 Avenue of the Americas, New York, New York 10019, U.S.A.

PUBLICATIONS

Verse

Four Young Lady Poets, with others, edited by LeRoi Jones. New York, Totem-Corinth, 1962.
The Vulnerable Island. Cleveland, Renegade Press, 1964.
Lumina. Cleveland, Flowers Press, 1965.

Poems Made of Skin. Toronto, Weed/Flower Press, 1968.
Circles, As in the Eye. Santa Fe, Desert Review Press, 1969.
An American Romance. Los Angeles, Black Sparrow Press, 1969.
The Chambers. Aylesford Priory, Kent, Aylesford Review Press, 1969.
From a Soft Angle: Poems about Women. Indianapolis, Bobbs Merrill, 1972.
The Unexpected. Milwaukee, Membrane Press, 1976.
Rituals and Gargoyles. Bowling Green, Ohio, Newedi Press, 1976.
A Song, A Chant. Albuquerque, Amalgamated Sensitivity Publications, 1978.
Alba Genesis. Woodstock, New York, Aesopus Press, 1979.
Alba Nemesis: The China Poems. Albuquerque, Amalgamated Sensitivity Publications, 1979.

Novel

Act of Love: An American Novel. Indianapolis, Bobbs Merrill, 1973.

Short Stories

The Unfolding. New York, Theo Press, 1969.
A Couple Called Moebius. Indianapolis, Bobbs Merrill, 1972.
Timepieces. Union City, California, Fault, 1977.
The Doppler Effect. Berkeley, California, Effie's Press, 1979.
Remembrance of Things to Come. New York, Theo Press, 1979.

Other

The Vancouver Report: A Report and Discussion of the Poetry Seminar at the University of British Columbia. New York, Peace Eye, 1964.
A Chronograph of the Poets: A History of the "Deux Mégots Poets" from 1959–1965. New York, Island Press, 1965.

Manuscript Collection: Humanities Research Center, University of Texas, Austin.

Critical Studies: by Hayden Carruth, in *Hudson Review* (New York), 1969; Howard McCord, in *Measure* (Pullman, Washington), 1970; Ishmael Reed, in Washington, D.C., *Post*, 1973.

Carol Bergé comments:

I worked in poetry through 1968 and had been moving more and more into prose as the Big Challenge since 1965. With the publication of the 190-page collection, *From a Soft Angle*, in 1972, a book that encompasses work from 1959 through 1971, I feel the work in that field is wrapped up, and am working almost solely in prose now. The book of stories *A Couple Called Moebius* has been well-received and reviewed and I'm content to be represented by the stories therein. The novel *Acts of Love* is as well-made as I can achieve at this time: it operates on at least three levels: that of a sociological/historical novel, that of a description of contemporary life, and that of an interesting and occasionally amusing fiction. It was a joy to write, I am now working on a third novel (the first novel, unpublished, needs revision); this one is concerned with the alternatives offered to Singles, a subdivision of which I have been a part for a long time. I hope to be as good a writer as Isak Dinesen, as Kobo Abe, as Jacov Lind, as Margaret Mitchell, as lady Murasaki. There is no separating the life from the work. These days, I will write perhaps one poem every two months or so; therefore, I no longer feel I can be classified as a poet, but as a novelist.

* * *

Female intensities, of wit, of lust, tenderness, the intelligence of the body, its groping, the ravage and despair, and all in language as varied as the weather, formalities of basic talk, spontaneous yet out of much reading, responding, looking: this is Carol Bergé's poetry. But foremost and always female, in her own voice or in dozens of personae, the terrible endlessness of sexual need, loving, hating, fighting, forgiving:

> The women breast to breast across empty
> across lava-strewn bitter plains
> facing lidless eyes of the majestic surgeons
> who demand they empty their wombs
> of the quintuplet dolls shaped like "husband"
> Women offering full teats to
> men with infant faces who drink with mouths
> the violet of sleep or of healed circumcision

And so on and on, the hurt imagination putting out, but not sloganizing or attitudinizing – at least not much. And then the nuances of observances of self:

> these days
> when you draw back
> as I reach for you
> it is an old wound you rip
> open ...

Bergé can be, and often is, talkative. Her poems sometimes seem put together from random images, broken by unlikely shifts of tone and texture, with little attempt at lyric unity. But her talk is intelligent, tough, urbane, and original, which is more than can be said for a good deal of poetry. And when she breaks through her talk into genuine poems of her own, they are moving and lucid, and they show a degree of maturity that most writing by other self-conscious female poets today cannot approach.

—Hayden Carruth

BERKSON, Bill. American. Born in New York City, 30 August 1939. Educated at Brown University, Providence, Rhode Island, 1957–59; New School for Social Research, New York (Dylan Thomas Memorial Award, 1959); Columbia University, New York, 1959–60; New York University Institute of Fine Arts. Editorial Associate, *Portfolio and Art News Annual*, New York, 1960–63; Associate Producer, *Art-New York* series, WNDT-TV, New York, 1964–65; taught at the New School for Social Research, 1964–69; Guest Editor, Museum of Modern Art, New York, 1965–69; Editor, *Best and Company* magazine, 1969; Teaching Fellow, Ezra Stiles College, Yale University, New Haven, Connecticut, 1969–70. Since 1972, Editor, *Big Sky* magazine and Big Sky Books, Bolinas, California. Since 1976, teacher, California Poetry-in-the-Schools Program. Recipient: Poets Foundation grant, 1968; Yaddo Corporation grant 1968; Coordinating Council of Literary Magazines grant, 1973–77; National Endowment for the Arts grant, 1977. Address: Box 389, Bolinas, California 94924, U.S.A.

PUBLICATIONS

Verse

Saturday Night: Poems 1960–61. New York, Tibor de Nagy, 1961.
Shining Leaves. New York, Angel Hair, 1969.
Recent Visitors. New York, Boke, 1971.
Two Serious Poems and One Other, with Larry Fagin. Bolinas, California, Big Sky, 1972.
Recent Visitors (collection). New York, Angel Hair, 1973.
Ants. Berkeley, California, Arif Press, 1974.
Quiet World. San Francisco, Grape Press, 1974.
Hymns of St. Bridget, with Frank O'Hara. New York, Adventures in Poetry, 1974.
100 Women. Chicago, Simon and Schuchat, 1974.
Enigma Variations. Bolinas, California, Big Sky, 1975.
Blue Is the Hero: Poems 1960–1975. Kensington, California, L Publications, 1976.
Parts of the Body. Bolinas, California, Tombouctou, 1979.

Other

Editor, *In Memory of My Feelings*, by Frank O'Hara. New York, Museum of Modern Art, 1967.
Editor, with Irving Sandler, *Alex Katz.* New York, Praeger, 1971.
Editor, with Joe LeSueur, *Homage to Frank O'Hara.* Bolinas, California, Big Sky, 1978.

Manuscript Collection: University of Connecticut, Storrs.

* * *

Bill Berkson is a late arrival to the New York Ferment that produced such poets as Frank O'Hara, Kenneth Koch, John Ashbery, and James Schuyler in the 1950's, when abstract expressionism released new energies of awareness for poets as well as painters. Jackson Pollock and Willem de Kooning were giants at the center of this creative apocalypse and their projections through paint of various states of conscious (and unconscious) experience liberated art from its old logical categories. Suddenly free and fluid forms of self-expression became the norm of such art, and by the mid-1950's poets applied to syntax and diction the same release and invented a fresh discourse. Frank O'Hara is the reigning figure of this revolution in poetics, who, as associate curator of the Museum of Modern Art, served as liaison between painting and writing.

Berkson is from the next generation, but his credentials were good: born in New York to upper-class parents, private-school education, writer for *Art News*, occasional work with the Museum of Modern Art. In addition, Berkson edited a book of O'Hara's poems, *In Memory of My Feelings*, and collaborated with him on a second, *Hymns to St. Bridget*. Details of a life, but they add up to a sophisticated apprenticeship to writing a certain style of poetry, one that requires considerable daring and finesse, since much of it is calculated to swing into and well out of ordinary sense. There is about the New York style a punning sense of reality, that objects and events are only tenuously situated in fixity, and that the whole texture of one's certainty is as easily disturbed as a creek bed. A delicate, sometimes foolish humor overtakes such lyric, but behind it is a philosophical impetus – a gnawing frustration with the usual and the vague, a repressed but squirming vitality beneath the mundane and the actual, as in "Leave Cancelled":

What we need is a great big vegetable farm!
Every vegetable to stand up and be counted,
and all the farmers to love one another
in their solid, lazy dreams.

Then this would be all knowledge,
all hygiene, and the plants we feel,
and it comes down to Boy and Dad and kind
balloons of sight. The sky's neat sweep,

the irrational, would be this butterfly dish
where lovely woman stacks her arms....

Berkson only narrowly skirts sense in his own work, now collected in *Blue Is the Hero*, and this sets up an interesting tension in reading him. Although the language often seems to be a runaway *logopoeia* – words ordered by sounds alone – with a little scrutiny the thread of a reasoning process is discernible, as in this typical passage:

Are you different from that shelter you
Built for knives? On the side walk, sapphires.
On the fifth floor, fungus was relaxing. I have put on
The crimson face of awareness you gave me.
What is the heart-shaped object that thaws your fingers?
It is a glove and in it a fist.

Sometimes Berkson's experiments break through to a new level of metaphor that ties extraordinary words together ("In the Mean"):

Running water –
it makes you think of all you didn't do
but not regret it, no: *de ma jeunesse.*
You didn't know I was the President
of a great cloud of falling bricks, did you?
Zoom. Bent. The bare stalk of the corn tree plant
of October thirty-one, of November one, November two....

In such work, however, the strain for novelty can become an effort, and there is much dogged flippancy in Berkson:

What am I indicting that heads off gardenia?
  green green stove-pipe
  arm around me stalk wherein pegged a relax bus
  globule of often-candelabra in the cake
  of soap ...

and so on. The intention, we might suppose, is to draw attention to the maker, to the process of mind that gives rise to words, or even more precisely, the compromising nature of words as indications of a consciousness words can only guess at. The intellection of lines such as these would suggest more than one process is at work although words themselves track a single linear reasoning. But then the poetic itself has only found the fault of language, not its virtues and possibilities. Taken far enough, this kind of experiment produces a stingy nonsense, and Berkson mercifully backs off and pursues more often a lyric of genuine feeling.

—Paul Christensen

BERRIGAN, Daniel J., S.J. American. Born in Virginia, Minnesota, 9 May 1921. Educated at Weston (Jesuit) Seminary, Massachusetts; ordained Roman Catholic priest, 1952. Taught French and philosophy, Brooklyn Preparatory School, New York, 1954–57; Professor of New Testament Studies, LeMoyne College, Syracuse, New York, 1957–63; Director of United Christian Work, Cornell University, Ithaca, New York, 1967–68. Jailed for anti-war activities, 1968. Recipient: Lamont Poetry Selection Award, 1957; Thomas More Association Medal, 1970; Melcher Book Award, 1971. Address: 99 Claremont Avenue, New York, New York 10027, U.S.A.

PUBLICATIONS

Verse

Time Without Number. New York, Macmillan, 1957.
Encounters. Cleveland, World, 1960.
The World for Wedding Ring: Poems. New York, Macmillan, 1962.
No One Walks Waters. New York, Macmillan, 1966.
False Gods, Real Men: New Poems. New York, Macmillan, 1966.
Love, Love at the End: Parables, Prayers, and Meditations. New York, Macmillan, 1968.
Night Flight to Hanoi: War Diary with 11 Poems. New York, Macmillan, 1968.
Crime Trial. Boston, Impressions Workshop, 1970.
Trial Poems. Boston, Beacon Press, 1970.
Selected and New Poems. New York, Doubleday, 1973.
Prison Poems. Greensboro, North Carolina, Unicorn Press, 1973.
Prison Poems. New York, Viking Press, 1974.

Recording: *Not Letting Me Not Let Blood: Prison Poems*, National Catholic Reporter, 1976.

Play

The Trial of the Catonsville Nine (produced New York and London, 1971). Boston, Beacon Press, 1970.

Other

The Bride: Essays in the Church. New York, Macmillan, 1959.
The Bow in the Clouds: Man's Covenant with God. New York, Coward McCann, and London, Burns and Oates, 1961.
They Call Us Dead Men: Reflections on Life and Conscience. New York, Macmillan, 1966.
Consequences: Truth and .... New York, Macmillan, and London, Collier Macmillan, 1967.
Go from Here: A Prison Diary (includes verse). San Francisco, Open Space, 1968.
No Bars to Manhood. New York, Doubleday, 1970.
The Dark Night of Resistance. New York, Doubleday, 1971.
The Geography of Faith: Conversations Between Daniel Berrigan, When Underground, and Robert Coles. Boston, Beacon Press, 1971.
Absurd Convictions, Modest Hopes: Conversations after Prison with Lee Lockwood. New York, Random House, 1972.
America Is Hard to Find. New York, Doubleday, 1972; London, SPCK, 1973.
Jesus Christ. New York, Doubleday, 1973.
Lights On in the House of the Dead: A Prison Diary. New York, Doubleday, 1974.

The Raft Is Not the Shore: Conversations Toward a Buddhist/Christian Awareness. Boston, Beacon Press, 1975.
A Book of Parables. New York, Seabury Press, 1977.
Uncommon Prayers: A Book of Prayers. New York, Seabury Press, 1978.
Beside the Sea of Glass: The Song of the Lamb. New York, Seabury Press, 1978.

* * *

In spite of his Jesuit training there is little in Daniel Berrigan's poetry to remind one of so conspicuously available a model as Gerard Manley Hopkins. Reading the *Imprimaturs* and the *Nihil Obstats* on the early volumes is surprising to the reader who has come to Berrigan from his later work where such marks of orthodoxy are so conspicuously absent, perhaps even unavailable. Hopkins was probably too abstractly theological to be a model for Dan Berrigan's taste. Berrigan's early poems have more the feel of 17th-century English devotional verse. His references to Simone Weil suggest an indebtedness to her favorite poet among the English writers – George Herbert. The early volumes brought quick success to Berrigan as a poet:

> Style
> envelops a flower like its odor;
> bestows on radiant air
> the spontaneous word that greets and makes a king.

An early poem addressed to Wallace Stevens interestingly accepts the techniques but repudiates the metaphysics that was a part of the Stevens aesthetic:

> Awakening
> When I grew appalled by love
> and promised nothing, but stood, a sick man
> first time on feeble knees
> peering at walls and weather
> like the feeble minded –
> the strange outdoors, the house of strangers –
> there, there was a beginning.

But even the early poems were dedicated to Dorothy Day, the quiet figure so central to the life of radical Catholicism in America – *beata pauperes spiritu* and *beata pacifici* they intone in their dedications, and Berrigan was to take the words seriously.

His opposition to the Vietnam War led him to found Clergy and Laymen Concerned about Vietnam when he returned to the U.S. This ecumenical action so enraged Cardinal Spellman that he exiled Berrigan to South America, a move that proved so unpopular that the Cardinal was quickly forced to rescind the action. But the tour through South America – the response to the appalling poverty he saw there – brought him back to the U.S. a convinced religious radical. *Consequences: Truth and* ... is the record of his spiritual and political development during that period.

A post as professor of religion and poetry at Cornell University did not dampen his growing involvement with his brother Philip in active opposition to the war. Pouring blood on draft files led on to the burning of draft files in Catonsville, Maryland. As he turned increasingly to direct action, he also turned to prose. His poetry was used to focus his personal reaction to the events he experienced. In *Night Flight to Hanoi* he wrote of holding one child saved from bombing:

> Children in the Shelter
> Imagine; three of them.
> As though survival

were a rat's word,
and a rat's end
waited there at the end
And I must have
in the century's boneyard
heft of flesh and bone in my arms
I picked up the littlest
a boy, his face
breaded with rice (his sister calmly feeding him
as we climbed down)
In my arms fathered
in a moment's grace, the messiah
of all my tears. I bore, reborn
a Hiroshima child from hell.

The Trial of the Catonsville Nine brought Berrigan to world-wide attention, and his prison journals were among the eloquent publications of the last years of the 1960's. *The Dark Night of Resistance*, published in that period, illustrated the growing influence on Berrigan of St. John of the Cross. Read in the 1950's by poets influenced by the religious revival of that period, one has a sense that Berrigan came to understand him in the late 1960's. He found St. John of the Cross in his prison experience a model to be lived rather than a style to be imitated.

Berrigan remains a Roman Catholic and a Jesuit. He is less active in writing poetry now, and more active in building a society that can be honestly celebrated in poetry. Despite the serious moral and political issues he forced through his personal involvement, there remains throughout his poetry a sustained joyousness – a marked characteristic of all his work.

—Myron Taylor

BERRIGAN, Ted (Edmund Joseph Michael Berrigan, Jr.). American. Born in Providence, Rhode Island, 15 November 1934. Educated at the University of Tulsa, Oklahoma, B.A. 1959, M.A. 1962. Served in the United States Army, 1954–57. Married to Sandra Alper; two children. Editor of "*C*" magazine and "C" Press, New York, Taught in the Poetry Workshop at the St. Mark's Arts Project, New York, 1966–67; Visiting Lecturer, University of Iowa, Iowa City, 1968–69. Recipient: Poetry Foundation Award, 1964. Address: 911 West Diversey Parkway, Chicago, Illinois 60614, U.S.A.

PUBLICATIONS

Verse

The Sonnets. New York, "C" Press, 1964.
Many Happy Returns to Dick Gallup. New York, Angel Hair, 1967.
Bean Spasms, with Ron Padgett. New York, Kulchur Press, 1967.
Some Thing, with Joe Brainard and Ron Padgett. Privately printed, n.d.
Living with Chris. New York, Boke, n.d.
Many Happy Returns: Poems. New York, Corinth, 1969.

Fragment for Jim Brodey. London, Cape Goliard Press, 1969.
Memorial Day, with Anne Waldman. New York, Poetry Project, 1971; London, Aloes, 1974.
In the Early Morning Rain. London, Cape Goliard Press, 1970; New York, Grossman, 1971.
Back in Boston Again, with Tom Clark and Ron Padgett. Philadelphia, Telegraph, 1972.
A Feeling for Leaving. New York, Frontward, 1975.

Plays

Seventeen: Collected Plays, with Ron Padgett. New York, "C" Press, 1965.

Ted Berrigan comments:

I'm a sophisticated American
Primitive. I make up each
poem (i.e. "verse form") as
it arrives by putting
things where they have to go
tho I sometimes vary this by putting
things where they don't have to go.

My influences are obvious and I put
them in too, just like
everybody else does.

* * *

In "Tambourine Life" Ted Berrigan quotes Yeats's remark that out of our quarrels with ourselves we make poetry, and he adds, "Yes, that is true." Berrigan uses not only his quarrels with himself to make poetry, but any and every facet of his life. As a result, a reader of Berrigan's will know seemingly all there is to know about the poet: everything from who his lovers and friends are (the latter include Allen Ginsberg, Ron Padgett, and Philip Whalen), to his various residences, his pill-popping habit, his all-night writing sessions, and even his habitual Pepsi at 8 a.m. Berrigan's poetry, then, is intensely, almost exclusively, inner-directed. This type of writing, of course, has a long tradition. Most recently, the best of the confessional poets, such as Lowell and Plath, have shown how wonderful extremely intimate poems can be. At its finest, Berrigan's work is just as powerful.

For example, "Things to Do on Speed" is a long, effective catalogue which begins rather humorously listing such activities as "clean/all desk drawers, arrange all/pens & pencils in precise parallel patterns"; it continues with such things as "Dismantle 12 radios/string beads interminably/empty your purse," and, picking up speed, it ends darkly with

Notice that tiny bugs are crawling over your whole body
around, between and over your many new pimples.
Cut away pieces of bad flesh.
Discuss mother's promiscuity
Sense the presence of danger at the movies
Reveal
get tough
turn queer
In the winter, switch to heroin, so you won't catch pneumonia.
In the Spring, go back to speed.

Elsewhere, Berrigan's work has at times a fine lyric quality, as in the closing lines of "American Express," about the poet's experiences walking around New York City in a coat borrowed two years previously:

> The mist of May
> is on the gloaming
> & all the clouds
> are halted, still
> fleecey
> & filled
> with holes.
>
> They are alight with borrowed warmth,
> just like me.

Frequently, however, Berrigan's work suffers from leaving too much unsaid. For instance, the cause of his drug habit is never explained; as a result, it is hard to understand his problems or to have much sympathy for him. A poem like "As Usual" ("Take off your hat & coat & give me all your money/I have to buy some pills & I'm flat broke") brings us no closer to comprehending the author's condition, nor does "Matinee," which reads, "Morning/(ripped out of my mind again!)." The two pieces just quoted are hardly impressive bits of writing, and they point to one of Berrigan's major faults: a terrible inability, especially in his early work, to self-edit. Berrigan at times appears to feel that anything he writes can pass as poetry. To his credit, though, he parodies this tendency in another part of "Tambourine Life":

> Now I'm going to read 3 cereal poems:
> CORN FLAKES
> OATMEAL
> RY-KRISP
> thank you
> they were composed
> excuse me
> I mean NOT composed
> using the John-Cage-Animal-Cracker
>
> Method of Composition
> (this seems to be mushrooming into a
> major work
> of high
> seriousness)

As this poem shows, Berrigan's writing can often give delight, a delight also found in "Something Amazing Just Happened," a whimsical fantasy in which he dreams of spending a Guggenheim Grant, in "Three Sonnets and a Coda for Tom Clark," a collage of the most memorable lines (and there are many) from his earlier poems, and in his marvelous short prose pieces, the best of which, "Che Guevara's Cigars," anticipated a technique E. L. Doctorow later used in *Ragtime*. For the reader this delight outweighs the faults of Berrigan's poetry, such as occasional triteness and frequent name-dropping. Berrigan has not as yet produced a "major work of high seriousness," but one feels he gets closer with each volume. And what Berrigan has produced so far is some of the most entertaining poetry to come out of the American counterculture.

—Dennis Lynch

BERRY, Francis. British. Born in Ipoh, Malaya, 23 March 1915. Educated at Hereford Cathedral School; Dean Close School; University of London, B.A. 1949; University of Exeter, M.A. 1960. Served in the British Army, 1939–46. Married 1) Nancy Melloney Graham in 1947 (died), one son and one daughter; 2) Patricia Thomson in 1970 (marriage dissolved); 3) Eileen Lear. Articled clerk, 1931. Assistant Lecturer, Lecturer, Senior Lecturer, Reader, and Professor of English, University of Sheffield, 1947–70. Since 1970, Professor of English, Royal Holloway College, University of London, Egham, Surrey. Visiting Lecturer, Carleton College, Northfield, Minnesota, 1951–52, and University of the West Indies, Jamaica, 1957; British Council Lecturer in India, 1966–67; Visiting Lecturer in Germany, 1972; Visiting Fellow, Australian National University, Canberra, 1979. Fellow, Royal Society of Literature, 1969. Address: Department of English, Royal Holloway College, University of London, Egham, Surrey, England.

PUBLICATIONS

Verse

Gospel of Fire. London, Mathews and Marrott, 1933.
Snake in the Moon. London, Williams and Norgate, 1936.
The Iron Christ: A Poem. London, Williams and Norgate, 1938.
Fall of a Tower and Other Poems. London, Fortune Press, 1943.
Murdock and Other Poems. London, Dakers, 1947.
The Galloping Centaur: Poems 1933–1951. London, Methuen, 1952.
Morant Bay and Other Poems. London, Routledge, 1961.
Ghosts of Greenland. London, Routledge, 1966.

Plays

Radio Plays: *Illnesses and Ghosts at the West Settlement*, 1965; *The Sirens*, 1966; *The Near Singing Dome*, 1971.

Novel

I Tell of Greenland. London, Routledge, 1977.

Other

Herbert Read. London, Longman, 1953; revised edition, 1961.
Poets' Grammar: Person, Time and Mood in Poetry. London, Routledge, 1958; Westport, Connecticut, Greenwood Press, 1974.
Poetry and the Physical Voice. London, Routledge, and New York, Oxford University Press, 1962.
The Shakespeare Inset: Word and Picture. London, Routledge, 1965; New York, Theatre Arts, 1966; revised edition, Carbondale, Southern Illinois University Press, 1971.
John Masefield: The Narrative Poet (lecture). Sheffield, University of Sheffield, 1968.
Thoughts on Poetic Time (lecture). Abingdon-on-Thames, Berkshire, Abbey Press, 1972.

Editor, *Essays and Studies 22.* London, Murray, 1969.

Manuscript Collections: Lockwood Memorial Library, State University of New York, Buffalo; Sheffield Public Library.

Critical Study: "Francis Berry" by G. Wilson Knight, in *Neglected Powers*, London, Routledge, 1971.

Francis Berry comments:

Have been deeply enchanted by geography – the Mediterranean, the West Indies, Greenland – for the settings it supplies for human actions. Strongest emotion used to be fear in its varieties, especially around sunset or in the night. But even strong noontide sunlight provoked anxiety. Cruelty figures in early poems because I am frightened of cruelty. Have felt responsive to other times as well as other places: so history and myths are also poetic preoccupations. I believe the dead might still care, and would not hurt them. It is a gratification to have written any poem that I think is good enough, but the long poem, narrative or dramatic, of lively structure, compact, of varied rhythm, and vivid images, is what I would most delight in making: its making would sustain the maker day after day during its making and render tolerable the return of first consciousness each morning.

* * *

Francis Berry is a master of the long poem, and his finest work is in that genre. Because of this, he has been under-represented in magazines and anthologies and his reputation has yet to match the opinion which such critics as G. Wilson Knight and Donald Davie have formed of his work.

The Iron Christ tells of a statue made from the guns of the frontier fortresses of Chile and Argentina and the attempt to erect this on the highest point of the Andes as a symbol of peace. The struggle up the mountain is rendered graphically:

The driver turns his face, his arm to throttle
Levering steam, but, with a cursing, spin
The driving-wheels, skidding upon raw rails,
Circuiting vainly, then grab, heel over rods,
Pistons pant, valves hiss, wheels grip, groan, grab ...

Fall of a Tower shows a town dominated and overshadowed by a church, and the attempt of a man, Edmund, to blow that church up:

Struts straddle; West Front
Walks apart, begins ungainly waddle,
Collapses on its face; brick and mortar
Flee yelling from their stocks ...

Murdock chronicles the unending affray of two ghostly brothers:

We of this Village know our heavy Wood
Haunted by Brothers in their furious Mood.
Two Brothers, locked and pledged to nightly Duel,
Fight under Trees, hidden at fullest moon.
Though dumb, their Blows do toss upon the Gale;
Their Groans disturb us at our Murdock fires;
Their sobs are heard through Falls of Autumn Rain ...

Morant Bay deals with a negro uprising in Jamaica, put down ruthlessly by Governor Eyre in 1865. The exotic coloration is instantly compelling:

... On the other side of the ravine
Rises the opposing flank of another spur,
Its sandstone swooned from the blurs of that sun,
Dotted with thorned scrub, roots bedded in stone,
On which the red spider darts or the lizard waits
Before his next scurry with a sobbing throat ...

Equally compelling are the different voices that interweave the narration. One thinks of the diatribe which emanates from the black Deacon Bogle. He denounces the governor and is echoed by the impassioned responses of his congregation:

"Der he be
In dat King's House, an' he eat" –
In dat King's House, an' he eat.
"He eat fishes an' he eat meat,"
He eat fishes an' he eat meat,
War-o, heavy war-o ...

Because he uses the voices of his protagonists, Berry is able to enter into their characters and see all sides of this question – Eyre, courageous but bigoted; the coloured Gordon, intelligent and envious; Deacon Bogle, personification of the superstitious blacks. What is so impressive about this poem upon a vexed subject – race hatred – is that it does not take sides. Instead, it seeks to understand the difficulty of a situation. In many ways, *Morant Bay* is a great Catholic poem. It sees the massacre at Morant Bay in terms of original sin, an obeah "Whose magic undergoes all manner of transfer/But cannot be cast out."

In *Illnesses and Ghosts at the West Settlement*, Berry's recreation of voices takes a further step and enters a new terrain. This is the Greenland colonized at the end of the first millenium A.D. by Erik the Red. Plague strikes down the little settlement, smashing the sanctions that govern even this primitive society. The remnant of people staying there becomes demoralized. The whole poem is couched in terms of a recollection by the various ghosts hovering above the colony where they suffered so dreadfully a thousand years ago. Erik's daughter-in-law, Gudrid, is the central character. Her voice comes across the centuries in characteristically tentative metres, recreating a woman's agony in the face of male intransigence:

Illnesses and ghosts.
You founded Greenland. I've seen enough of your Greenland
And I want the sun for a while, husband or no husband.
I want the sun because I am so cold, you know I am so cold,
That I could hear that particular sound again
Oh, I am so old
Before I am hardly girl. Dear Father, Father-in-law, help me ...

It is questionable whether any contemporary poet can show so great a range of technique and subject-matter. And the characteristically exotic settings are a means of staging a penetration into the motives behind human affection and human action. The story doesn't end with Greenland, however. Francis Berry's most recent major work, not yet published, was broadcast in the summer of 1971. It concerns Shah Jehan who built the Taj Mahal in memory of his wife. Here is the voice of another woman: the dead Mumtaz accusing her husband of wishing her dead in order to erect his immemorial dome:

I died because you wanted me to die.
Or thought you did ... Sometimes. For I could read
That silent thought in the way you looked
At me ... sometimes. It made me sad – for you,

Because I surmised you would be desolate
And helpless ... I gone. And that you would regret
That thought you had allowed me to discern ...
Sometimes ... though you should have not ...

This is a sparser, more austere verse than we are used to from Berry. And indeed *The Near Singing Dome* may still be part of a work in progress. The reputation of the man who wrote this, and *Illnesses and Ghosts*, *Morant Bay*, *Murdock*, *Fall of a Tower* and *The Iron Christ*, may continue to grow slowly, as great reputations will. But the admirers of Francis Berry believe that his work will certainly endure.

—Philip Hobsbaum

BERRY, Wendell (Erdman). American. Born in Henry County, Kentucky, 5 August 1934. Educated at the University of Kentucky, Lexington, A.B., M.A. Married Tanya Amyx in 1957; one daughter and one son. Member of the English Department, University of Kentucky, 1964–77. Since 1977, staff member, Rodale Press, Emmaus, Pennsylvania. Recipient: Guggenheim Fellowship, 1951; Rockefeller Fellowship, 1965; Bess Hokin Prize (*Poetry*, Chicago), 1967; National Endowment for the Arts grant, 1969. Address: Port Royal, Kentucky 40058, U.S.A.

PUBLICATIONS

Verse

November Twenty-Six, Nineteen Hundred Sixty-Three. New York, Braziller, 1964.
The Broken Ground. New York, Harcourt Brace, 1964; London, Cape, 1966.
Openings. New York, Harcourt Brace, 1969.
Findings. Iowa City, Prairie Press, 1969.
Farming: A Hand Book. New York, Harcourt Brace, 1970.
The Country of Marriage. New York, Harcourt Brace, 1973.
An Eastward Look. Berkeley, California, Sand Dollar, 1974.
To What Listens. Crete, Nebraska, Best Cellar Press, 1975.
Horses. Monterrey, Kentucky, Larkspur Press, 1975.
Sayings and Doings. Lexington, Kentucky, Gnomon, 1975.
The Kentucky River: Two Poems. Monterrey, Kentucky, Larkspur Press, 1976.
Three Memorial Poems. Berkeley, California, Sand Dollar, 1977.
Clearing. New York, Harcourt Brace, 1977.

Novels

Nathan Coulter. Boston, Houghton Mifflin, 1960.
A Place on Earth. New York, Harcourt Brace, 1967.
The Memory of Old Jack. New York, Harcourt Brace, 1974.

Other

The Rise. N.p., Graves Press, 1968.

The Long-Legged House. New York, Harcourt Brace, 1969.
The Hidden Wound. Boston, Houghton Mifflin, 1970.
The Unforeseen Wilderness: An Essay on Kentucky's Red River Gorge. Lexington, University Press of Kentucky, 1971.
A Continuous Harmony: Essays Cultural and Agricultural. New York, Harcourt Brace, 1972.
The Unsettling of America. San Francisco, Sierra Club, 1977.

* * *

The most important fact about Wendell Berry is that, except for brief periods of study and teaching, he has stayed close to his own place on earth, in Kentucky, on the Kentucky River not far from where it flows into the Ohio. Berry's poetic world is largely the physical and social world of his native region. Berry is a regionalist, not a provincialist. A deep sense of his native place animates all his works, the poetry, the essays, the novels. He knows the land literally at first hand, for he farms it. He understands the cycle of the seasons, planting, tending, harvesting, animal husbandry, country people. Because his ancestors have been in his region for two centuries, he has a strong feeling for ancestral inheritance. He enunciates the familial bond in "The Gathering" (*The Country of Marriage*):

At my age my father
held me on his arm
like a hooded bird,
and his father held him so....
My son
will know me in himself
when his son sits hooded on
his arm and I have grown
to be brother to all
my fathers, memory
speaking to knowledge
finally, in my bones.

Like Edwin Muir, whose poetry and prose Berry has publicly praised, Berry conveys the story of his life in the context of a fable of a family: faithful watchers guard the traditional day.

Berry's seriousness about small farming is informed and passionate. He is the first real farmer-poet of stature in American history. He sees clearly and tells us forthrightly how Kentucky land has been overworked and ruined by greedy men and is now being dehumanized by agribusinessmen forcing crops and polluting soil and air with chemical fertilizers and huge machines.

Berry's central subjects are central subjects: love and death. There is no contemporary American poet more inclined to, or successful with, the elegy. Berry first attracted national notice with *November Twenty-Six, Nineteen Hundred Sixty-Three*, the only successful elegy, in this writer's opinion, prompted by the death of President Kennedy. There have followed at least three other important elegies: "Elegy: Pryor Thomas Berry" (*The Broken Ground*), "In Memory: Stuart Egnol" (*Openings*), and "Elegy" (on Owen Flood), the first section of *Three Memorial Poems*. Poems on love are numerous, many deeply serious, some light and witty, like "The Mad Farmer's Love Song" (*The Country of Marriage*), here quoted in full:

O when the world's at peace
and every man is free
then will I go down to my love

O and I may go down
several times before that.

Berry's style is deceptively simple. Though his language is not actually the language of Kentuckians, it sounds authentic. It would hardly be mistaken, say, for that of a New Englander or a Westerner. His prosody is mainly open form or "naked," though occasionally, especially in most recent work, there are rhymes and meter. The characteristic mode is didactic. Berry goes behind the nature of things to assert the causes of things. His poetry has not changed markedly in theme, style or intention since he began publishing. But it has grown in sureness, in power, in passionate directness.

—James K. Robinson

BERTOLINO, James. American. Born in Hurley, Wisconsin, 4 October 1942. Educated at the University of Wisconsin, Stevens Point, Madison, and Oshkosh, B.S. in English and art, 1970; Washington State University, Pullman, 1970–71; Cornell University, Ithaca, New York, 1971–73, M.F.A. 1973. Married the artist Lois Behling in 1966. Teaching Assistant, Washington State University, 1970–71; Teaching Assistant, 1971–73, and Lecturer in Creative Writing, 1973–74, Cornell University. Editor, *Abraxas* magazine and Abraxas Press, Madison, Wisconsin, and Ithaca. New York, 1968–72; Editor, Stone Marrow Press, Ithaca, New York, 1970–72; Assistant Editor, *Epoch* magazine, Ithaca, New York, 1971–73. Recipient: Book-of-the-Month Club Award, 1970; Coordinating Council of Literary Magazines grant, 1970; YM-YWHA Poetry Center Discovery Award, 1972; National Endowment for the Arts grant, 1974. Address: Department of English, Cornell University, Ithaca, New York 14850, U.S.A.

PUBLICATIONS

Verse

Day of Change. Milwaukee, Gunrunner Press, 1968.
Drool. Madison, Wisconsin, Quixote Press, 1968.
Mr. Nobody. Marshall, Minnesota, Ox Head Press, 1969.
Ceremony: A Poem. Milwaukee, Morgan Press, 1969.
Maize: A Poem. Madison, Wisconsin, Abraxas Press, 1969.
Stone Marrow. Madison, Wisconsin, Anachoreta Press – Abraxas Press, 1969.
Becoming Human. Oshkosh, Wisconsin, Road Runner Press, 1970.
The Interim Handout. Privately printed, 1972.
Employed. Ithaca, New York, Ithaca House, 1972.
Edging Through. Berkeley, California, Serendipity, 1972.
Soft Rock. Tacoma, Washington, Charas Press, 1973.
Making Space for Our Living. Port Townsend, Washington, Copper Canyon Press, 1975.
Terminal Placebos. New York, New Rivers Press, 1975.
The Gestures. Providence, Rhode Island, Bonewhistle Press, 1975.
New and Selected Poems. Pittsburgh, Carnegie Mellon University Press, 1978.

Other

Editor, *Quixote: Northwest Poets.* Madison, Wisconsin, Quixote Press, 1968.

Editor, *Provisions*, by Anselm Parlatore. Berkeley, California, Serendipity, 1971.
Editor, *The Abraxas/5 Anthology*. Ithaca, New York, Abraxas Press, 1972.

Manuscript Collection: Murphy Library, University of Wisconsin, La Crosse.

Critical Studies: "Three Good Prospects" by James Naiden, in *Granite* (Hanover, New Hampshire), Autumn 1972; "Observations on a Book of Poetry" by Steven Granger, in *Seizure* (Eugene, Oregon), Fall–Winter 1972; "Employed" by Ripley Schemm, in *Bartleby's Review 2* (Machias, Maine), 1973.

James Bertolino comments:

My recent work in poetry, 1971–73, has been characterized by each poem being a series of rapidly accelerating images which, though often discordant, are forced to cohere due to the speed at which the reader is propelled through them. The poems, then, when experienced properly by the reader, become something akin to psychic depth-charges. That is, though they "meaningfully" cohere under the pressure of their lyric-kinetic structure, once they've been driven through the protective walls of the psyche, they explode like fragmentation bombs, the disparate images like pieces of shrapnel lodging in the most sensitive areas.

I know this sounds rather brutal, but clearly the poems aren't "nice" and aren't satisfied with titillating the surface-level pre-conception of many readers of poems.

My work in *Granite* (numbers 4, 5, and 6) is indicative of this phase of my work.

* * *

Poised precariously between innocence and wisdom, James Bertolino's poems may run the risk of being taken for the expression of an artless naivete. Actually, there is no doodling with abstractions, no aimless stream-of-consciousness in his work. Here everything is pared to the quick, every syllable functional. Consider in these lines from "The Old Clearing" –

a gentle force
the morning draws me here
place I've never off dusty road
under carefully the
barbed-wire
miles from how I've walked here

– how "carefully" suggests the physical movements of the sleepwalker with the obstruction, and "barbed-wire" the persistence of the real. No line of Bertolino's has more than six words in it, most only three. And although he never makes use of formal meter, not syllable count but *stress* (as in W. C. Williams) is the secret of all his rhythmic effects.

Each poem, moreover, is not so much a picture (as in Pound, H.D., etc.) as it is an *event*. In a series of images embracing all the senses including the kinesthetic *something happens*. Perhaps it is Bertolino's verbal parsimony that makes us realize how terrible and precise a single word standing alone (but drawing strength from a sparse context) can be. For instance:

a green Mack truck
(with no trailer)
bore down upon a preoccupied
wren
& before the feathers
had settled,
three sparrows &
the rest
of the wrens
were singing again.

One notices the assonantal "en" melody which makes the poem end in song (and yet this is free verse!) and how the single word "wren" upon the page becomes the bird itself, and how the Mack truck's having no trailer gives a kind of factual authenticity to the event. So in "Design" two sharp details lead us to a startling recognition: "Worms hole/flower petals/ with composition//the sun/free/below." There is a lot of joy in these poems, joy in nature and joy in love, a surprising circumstance perhaps in view of the times in which we live. But the second section of *Employed*, entitled "The Executrix of Weirds" is Bertolino's descent into Hell, and his emergence from it. Here his imagery at times brings us close to nausea, and we no longer doubt, if we had before, the presence of evil in the world. Yet in these poems too we find the same precise workmanship, beauty of form, control.

Intensity is the norm in these poems, each of which seems to be an event encapsulated out of time. Furthermore, Bertolino knows exactly what he is doing. In an interview (in *The Outer Circle 4*, Fall 1973), Bertolino remarked:

> I think I've always had an impulse toward condensation, making a poem very tight and clear and small, and, by the same token, emphasizing or zeroing in on the essential small details of an experience ... a concern with finding ... where the spaces between objects and details are that open up into something else, the larger experience.

—E. L. Mayo

BETJEMAN, John. British. Born in Highgate, London, 1906. Educated at Marlborough; Magdalen College, Oxford. Served as Press Attaché, Dublin, 1941–42; in the Admiralty, 1943. Married Penelope Valentine Hester in 1933; one son and one daughter. Book reviewer, *Daily Herald*, London; radio and television speaker. Columnist ("City and Suburban"), *Spectator*, London, 1954–58. Founder, Victorian Society. Member, Royal Fine Art Commission; Governor, Pusey House (Church of England). Recipient: Heinemann Award, 1949; Foyle Poetry Prize, 1955, 1959; Loines Award (USA), 1956; Duff Cooper Memorial Prize, 1958; Queen's Gold Medal for Poetry, 1960; Companion of Literature, Royal Society of Literature, 1968. LL.D.: Aberdeen University; D.Litt.: Oxford, Reading and Birmingham universities. Honorary Associate, Royal Institute of British Architects. Honorary Member, American Academy of Arts and Letters, 1973. C.B.E. (Commander, Order of the British Empire), 1960; Knighted, 1969. Named Poet Laureate, 1972. Address: 29 Radnor Walk, London S.W.3, England.

PUBLICATIONS

Verse

Mount Zion; or, In Touch with the Infinite. London, James Press, 1931; New York, St. Martin's Press, 1975.
Continual Dew: A Little Book of Bourgeois Verse. London, Murray, 1937.
Sir John Piers (as Epsilon). Mullingar, Ireland, Westmeath Examiner, 1938.
Old Lights for New Chancels: Verses Topographical and Amatory. London, Murray, 1940.
New Bats in Old Belfries. London, Murray, 1945.
Slick But Not Streamlined: Poems and Short Pieces, edited by W. H. Auden. New York, Doubleday, 1947.

Selected Poems, edited by John Sparrow. London, Murray, 1948.
A Few Late Chrysanthemums. London, Murray, 1954.
Poems in the Porch. London, S.P.C.K., 1954.
Collected Poems, edited by the Earl of Birkenhead. London, Murray, 1958; Boston, Houghton Mifflin, 1959; revised edition, 1962, 1972, 1979.
(*Poems*). London, Hulton, 1958.
Summoned by Bells (verse autobiography). London, Murray, and Boston, Houghton Mifflin, 1960.
A Ring of Bells, edited by Irene Slade. London, Murray, 1962; Boston, Houghton Mifflin, 1963.
High and Low. London, Murray, 1966; Boston, Houghton Mifflin, 1967.
Six Betjeman Songs, music by Mervyn Horder. London, Turret, 1967.
A Wembley Lad, and The Crem. London, Poem-of-the-Month Club, 1971.
A Nip in the Air. London, Murray, 1974; New York, Norton, 1975.
Betjeman in Miniature: Selected Poems. Paisley, Renfrewshire, Gleniffer Press, 1976.
Metro-land: Selected Verses from His Commentary for the Film. London, Warren, 1977.
The Best of Betjeman, edited by John Guest. London, Murray, 1978.

Plays

Television Documentaries: *The Stained Glass at Fairford*, 1955; *Pity about the Abbey*, with Stewart Farver, 1965; *Metro-Land*, 1973; *A Passion for Churches*, 1974; *Vicar of This Parish*, 1976.

Other

Ghastly Good Taste; or, A Depressing Story of the Rise and Fall of English Architecture. London, Chapman and Hall, 1933; revised edition, 1970
Devon. London, Architectural Press, 1936.
An Oxford University Chest: Comprising a Description of the Present State of the Town and University of Oxford, with an Itinerary Arranged Alphabetically. London, J. Miles, 1938; New York, Oxford University Press, 1980.
Antiquarian Prejudice. London, Hogarth Press, 1939.
Vintage London. London, Collins, 1942.
English Cities and Small Towns. London, Collins, 1943.
John Piper. London, Penguin, 1944.
Murray's Buckinghamshire [Berkshire, Shropshire] Architectural Guide, with John Piper. London, Murray, 3 vols., 1948–51.
First and Last Loves (essay on architecture). London, Murray, 1952.
The English Town in the Last Hundred Years (lecture). Cambridge, University Press, 1956.
Collins Guide to English Parish Churches, Including the Isle of Man. London, Collins, 1958; as *An American's Guide to English Parish Churches*, New York, McDowell Obolensky, 1959; revised edition as *Collins Pocket Guide to English Parish Churches*, Collins, 2 vols., 1968.
Ground Plan to Skyline (as Richard M. Farren). London, Newman Neame, 1960.
English Churches, with Basil Clarke. London, Studio Vista, 1964.
Cornwall. London, Faber, 1964.
The City of London Churches. London, Pitkin Pictorials, 1965.
London's Historic Railway Stations. London, Murray, 1972.
A Pictorial History of English Architecture. London, Murray, and New York, Macmillan, 1972.
West Country Churches. London, Society of SS. Peter and Paul, 1973.
A Plea for Holy Trinity Church, Sloane Street. London, Church Union, 1974.

Archie and the Strict Baptists (juvenile). London, Murray, 1977; Philadelphia, Lippincott, 1978.

Editor, *Cornwall Illustrated: In a Series of Views of Castles, Seats of the Nobility, Mines, Picturesque Scenery, Towns, Public Buildings, Churches, Antiquities, Etc.* London, Architectural Press, 1934.
Editor, *A Pickwick Portrait Gallery, from the Pens of Divers Admirers.* London, Chapman and Hall, and New York, Scribner, 1936.
Editor, *Selected Poems*, by Sir Henry Newbolt. London, Nelson, 1940.
Editor, with Geoffrey Taylor, *English, Scottish and Welsh Landscape, 1700-ca. 1860* (verse anthology). London, Muller, 1944.
Editor, with Geoffrey Taylor, *English Love Poems.* London, Faber, 1957.
Editor, *Altar and Pew: Church of England Verses.* London, Hulton, 1959.
Editor, with Sir Charles Tennyson, *A Hundred Sonnets*, by Charles Tennyson Turner. London, Hart Davis, 1960.
Editor, with Winifred Hindley, *A Wealth of Poetry.* Oxford, Blackwell, 1963.
Editor, *Victorian and Edwardian London from Old Photographs.* London, Batsford, 1968; New York, Viking Press, 1969.
Editor, with J. S. Gray, *Victorian and Edwardian Brighton from Old Photographs.* London, Batsford, 1972.
Editor, with A. L. Rowse, *Victorian and Edwardian Cornwall from Old Photographs.* London, Batsford, 1974.
Editor, *John Masefield: A Selection of Poems.* London, Heinemann, 1978.

Bibliography: *John Betjeman: A Bibliography of Writings by and about Him* by Margaret L. Stapleton, Metuchen, New Jersey, Scarecrow Press, 1974.

* * *

John Betjeman is of the same generation as W. H. Auden, a contemporary at Oxford, but his name has never been bracketed with those of other poets as that of a partner in some real or supposed school or movement. He has affinities with certain other poets of his time but it would be hard to name a single one of them who could speak of Isaac Watts, Dyer, or Mickle as "easily among my favourites," or even of Praed and Hood, still less of John Mason Neale. His taste for certain lesser poets of the 18th and 19th centuries, as well as for such great ones as Tennyson and Hardy, is partly, he has said, topographical. He admires in them particularly their ability "to catch the atmosphere of places and times," which can be seen as one of his own chief aims and successes.

No English poet of his generation seems to have been more deeply enchanted by the atmosphere of places known in childhood. Betjeman's impressionability in the North London suburb where his well-to-do and conventional parents brought him up, and on the North Cornish coast to which he was taken in summertime, was so intense that in his poetry he is able to recall these places with a precision of detail hardly to be matched among poets of English life in the early part of this century.

His lifelong love-affair with Edwardian England (in many ways the last period of Victorian England) has included old churches, old railways, old gaslit streets, old country-towns, old dons, and old invalids; it has also given him a distaste for much of what is supposed to represent progress. Narrow judgments may write him off as a backward-looking sentimentalist, too traditional in his interests and beliefs, and in his forms, rhythm, and diction, to be taken seriously as a poet in the 1960's; but poetry is not invalidated by retrospection, and one of the things he has done better than anybody else is to give form in poetry to the affectionate sadness inherent in all those old enough and feeling enough to have known happiness in an England now only vestigial, after two World Wars and political, economic, social, and technological revolutions.

One effect of Betjeman's poetry has been so to heighten general consciousness of what excites his own admiration that it has done much to cause a revolution (or should one say a counter-revolution?) in English taste. Manifestations, particularly in church architecture, of Victorian and Edwardian religious faith, fantasy, art, and craftsmanship, formerly taken for granted, condemned as ugly aberrations, or simply ignored, are now far better appreciated and understood. He is much more than "the Laureate of the suburbs and the Gothic Revival." Among the conspicuous qualities of his work are humanity, euphony, and a playful wit. No doubt among the main causes of his popularity, these qualities are not always discernible in contemporary poetry. What is more, they do not always appear appreciable by certain of the newer species of academic pedants and prigs, who parade their limitations and prejudices in literary journalism, but whose hack work, or hatchet work, is seldom heeded or even seen by the "common reader" of poetry. Whether from envy of the poet or a feeling of intellectual superiority towards his admirers, they seem to regard his popularity (enlarged and strengthened by his later career in television) as a serious weakness. As for his playfulness and wit, these things always disconcert earnest dogmatists, who wrongly suppose them incompatible with gravity.

The appeal of Betjeman's poetry is no doubt greater to older than to younger readers, if only because in it he shows himself moved by memories, scenes, associations and beliefs less familiar and less poignant to later generations than his own. There is nothing international about him except his humanity. He has not shown any concern with or even consciousness of world-wide revolutionary tendencies, intellectual fashions, the atomic danger, space travel, or Chairman Mao. Why should he?

Betjeman's poetic technique has shown no signs of being open to American influences, or to fashionable trends or doctrines. Lecturing in 1968, Roy Fuller, a poet only a few years younger than Betjeman, spoke of "the need to break away from the tyranny of the iambic line." One can suppose that this phrase would astonish Betjeman, who, never having felt any such tyranny, could feel no need to break away from it. His use of iambics suggests that he finds them not only traditional but idiomatically natural for the utterance of an English poet. In his long autobiographical poem, *Summoned by Bells*, he has used blank verse, with rhymed interludes, so effectively and skilfully that it is impossible to imagine how any other metre could have suited his purpose.

Summoning bells, like the sound of the sea, are often and variously to be heard in his poems. When he was a boy, church bells in England, as I myself remember, used to ring louder and longer than they do now, and almost everywhere. To some the sound of them was and is melancholy, vexing, and anachronistic, but Betjeman's poems show that they have never rung in vain for him. His interest in churches is not merely aesthetic; he is in fact a religious poet, a practising member of the Church of England, whose poetry shows him to be a believer in the reality of evil, in the need for self-questioning, in prayer, grace, hope, and charity – a charity which means giving not merely alms but one's imagination and, if need be, one's whole self.

Betjeman is at times, a satirical poet, and can be found attacking cruelty, want of imagination, and (as in his "In Westminster Abbey") a combination of stupidity and hypocrisy with racial, social, and personal self-complacency. The people in his poems tend to be old and sad and helpless, or young and vigorous in a breezy way (like Joan Hunter Dunn), or falsely genteel and emptily materialistic, accepters of cheap shoddiness and up-to-date cant, given to reckless driving and low standards of taste and manners. There are an exceptional gentleness and good nature in his affection for "ordinary," marginal people and in his understanding of, for example, the deceased secretary of a golf club, lonely business girls in Camden Town, or a Platonist bank-clerk. That he is not self-important appears from certain poems about humiliating moments in his own life; and his ironic wit is inseparable from his humour, which can turn into the joviality of old-fashioned song, as in a piece like his "A Shropshire Lad." That is one of the "tales in verse" included by John Sparrow in Betjeman's *Selected Poems*. Another, "Sir John Piers," is both the most concentrated expression of Betjeman's recurrent response to the "ruins and rain" of Ireland and one of his most dramatic poems. In these "tales," and indeed throughout his work, there is a dramatic, novelistic element.

In *Summoned by Bells* the character drawing of his father and mother brings them freshly to life, and the self-portrait in the same poem is no less lifelike. Betjeman has always felt vividly, and conveyed vividly, the stimulus of the particular. He is as little given to general statements or vague rhetoric as to trendiness. His acute sensibility to the past has prevented his being recognized as an innovator: his themes are in fact as curiously his own as his orchestration of detail, his fluency, and his honesty. A few low-voltage passages in his work are perhaps the result of an over-simplification of thought. He is at his best in unravelling the complexities of a vanished or vanishing England to which he seems, unmistakably, devotedly, and sadly, to be saying good-bye.

—William Plomer

BIRNEY, Earle. Canadian. Born in Calgary, Alberta, 13 May 1904. Educated at the University of British Columbia, Vancouver, B.A. 1926; University of Toronto, M.A. 1927, Ph.D. 1936; University of California, Berkeley, 1927–30; Queen Mary College, London, 1934–35. Served in the Canadian Army, in the reserves 1940–41, and on active duty 1942–45: Major-in-Charge, Personnel Selection, Belgium and Holland, 1944–45. Married Esther Bull in 1940; one child. Instructor in English, University of Utah, Salt Lake City, 1930–34; Lecturer, later Assistant Professor of English, University of Toronto, 1936–42; Supervisor, European Foreign Language Broadcasts, Radio Canada, Montreal, 1945–46; Professor of Medieval English Literature, 1946–63, and Professor and Chairman of the Department of Creative Writing, 1963–65, University of British Columbia; Writer-in-Residence, University of Toronto, 1965–67, and University of Waterloo, Ontario, 1967–68; Regents Professor in Creative Writing, University of California, Irvine, 1968. Since 1968, free-lance Writer and Lecturer. Literary Editor, *Canadian Forum*, Toronto, 1936–40; Editor, *Canadian Poetry Magazine*, Edmonton, 1946–48; Editor, *Prism International*, Vancouver, 1964–65; Advisory Editor, *New: American and Canadian Poetry*, Trumansburg, New York, 1966–70. Recipient: Governor-General's Award, 1943, 1946; Stephen Leacock Medal, 1950; Borestone Mountain Poetry Award, 1951; Canadian Government Overseas Fellowship, 1953, Service Medal, 1970; Lorne Pierce Medal, 1953; President's Medal, University of Western Ontario, 1954; Nuffield Fellowship, 1958; Canada Council Senior Arts Fellowship, 1962, 1974, Medal, 1968, Special Fellowship, 1968, 1978, and Travel Award, 1971, 1974. LL.D.: University of Alberta, Calgary, 1965. Fellow, Royal Society of Canada, 1954. Address: c/o McClelland and Stewart, 25 Hollinger Road, Toronto, Ontario M4B 3G2, Canada.

PUBLICATIONS

Verse

David and Other Poems. Toronto, Ryerson Press, 1942.
Now Is Time. Toronto, Ryerson Press, 1945.
Strait of Anian: Selected Poems. Toronto, Ryerson Press, 1948.
Trial of a City and Other Verse. Toronto, Ryerson Press, 1952.
Ice Cod Bell or Stone. Toronto, McClelland and Stewart, 1962.
Near False Creek Mouth. Toronto, McClelland and Stewart, 1964.
Selected Poems 1940–1966. Toronto, McClelland and Stewart, 1966.
Memory No Servant. Trumansburg, New York, New Books, 1968.
Poems of Earle Birney. Toronto, McClelland and Stewart, 1969.

Pnomes, Jukollages and Other Stunzas. Toronto, Gronk Press, 1969.
Rag and Bone Shop. Toronto, McClelland and Stewart, 1971.
Four Parts Sand: Concrete Poems, with others. Ottawa, Oberon Press, 1972.
The Bear on the Delhi Road. London, Chatto and Windus, 1973.
What's So Big about Green? Toronto, McClelland and Stewart, 1973.
Collected Poems. Toronto, McClelland and Stewart, 2 vols., 1975.
The Rugging and the Moving Times: Poems New and Uncollected 1976. Coatsworth, Ontario, Black Moss Press, 1976.
Alphabeings and Other Seasyours. London, Ontario, Pikadilly Press, 1976.
Ghost in the Wheels: Selected Poems 1920–1976. Toronto, McClelland and Stewart, 1977; London, Canadabooks, 1978.
Fall by Fury. Toronto, McClelland and Stewart, 1978.

Recordings: *David*, 1964; *Earle Birney Reads His Poems*, Barnet, 1970; *Birney*, Ontario Institute for Studies in Education, 1971.

Play

The Damnation of Vancouver: A Comedy in Seven Episodes (broadcast, 1952). Included in *Trial of a City*, 1952; revised version (produced Seattle, 1957; Vancouver, 1978), in *Selected Poems*, 1966.

Radio Play: *The Damnation of Vancouver*, 1952.

Novels

Turvey: A Military Picaresque. Toronto, McClelland and Stewart, 1949; London and New York, Abelard Schuman, 1959; as *The Kootenay Highlander*, London, Four Square, 1960.
Down the Long Table. Toronto, McClelland and Stewart, 1955; London, Abelard Schuman, 1959.

Short Stories

Big Bird in the Bush. Ottawa, Mosaic Press, 1979.

Other

The Creative Writer. Toronto, CBC, 1966.
The Cow Jumped over the Moon: The Writing and Reading of Poetry. Toronto, Holt Rinehart, 1972.

Editor, *Twentieth Century Canadian Poetry.* Toronto, Ryerson Press, 1953.
Editor, *Record of Service in the Second World War.* Vancouver, University of British Columbia, 1955.
Editor, with others, *New Voices.* Vancouver, Dent, 1956.
Editor, with Margerie Lowry, *Selected Poems of Malcolm Lowry.* San Francisco, City Lights, 1962.
Editor, with Margerie Lowry, *Lunar Caustic*, by Malcolm Lowry. New York, Grossman, 1963; London, Cape, 1968.

Bibliography: by Peter C. Noel-Bentley and Earle Birney in *Essays in Canadian Writing* (Toronto), 1980.

Manuscript Collection: Fisher Library, University of Toronto.

Critical Studies: *Earle Birney* by Richard Robillard, Toronto, McClelland and Stewart, 1971; "Maker of Order, Prisoner of Dreams: The Poetry of Earle Birney" by W. H. New, in *Articulating West*, Toronto, New Press, 1973; *Earle Birney*, edited by Bruce Nesbitt, Toronto, McGraw Hill Ryerson, 1974; "A Stubborn Master: The Poetry of Earle Birney" by William Walsh, in *Lugano Review* (Switzerland), 1975; "Visual Poetry in Canada: Birney, Bissett, and bp" by Jack David, in *Studies in Canadian Literature* (Fredericton), Summer 1977; "Poet on Poet" by Kevin Crossley-Holland, in *Ambit 74* (London), 1978; "Birney's Makings" by George Woodcock, in *Ontario Review* (Windsor), Fall–Winter 1978–79; *Earle Birney* by Peter Aichinger, Boston, Twayne, 1979.

Earle Birney comments:

In the last 25 years I have been successively influenced by Beat, Projectivist, Concretist, and Sound poetry, and I hope to remain responsive – but eclectic – in relation to contemporary change and experimentation. I believe that poetry is both an oral entertainment and a visual notation.

I write out of compulsion to talk to another man within me, an intermittent madman who finds unpredictable emblems of the Whole in the trivia of my experience, and haunts me with them until I have found a spell of words and rhythms to exorcise these ghosts and, for the moment, appease him. For me, the hauntings and the exorcizings are happenings so intense as to be beyond pleasure or pain – ends in themselves. But I go on to publish some of the result because I believe that my poems are the best proof I can print of my Humanness, signals out of the loneliness into which all of us are born, and in which we die, affirmations of kinship with all the other wayfarers.

I have tried to develop an ability to read my own poetry effectively, and I have sought audiences wherever there was a knowledge of the English language. In Canada I have many times toured the universities and colleges from Vancouver Island to Newfoundland, and have also read to students in high schools, and to audiences in art galleries and public libraries. With the help of Canada Council grants I have sounded my work and that of other living Canadians in most of the universities of Australia and New Zealand, Chile, Peru, Mexico, the University of the West Indies, and about 30 universities in the U.S.A. I have also read in Japan, Hong Kong, Singapore, Malaya, Sri Lanka, India, Tanzania, Uganda, Egypt, Kenya, Nigeria, Ghana, Sierra Leone, Gambia, and at the University of Bordeaux. I have given readings in Dublin and in the chief cities of England and Scotland, especially to workingclass groups and in public houses. Recently I have been performing sound-poems in company with a percussion group and dancers.

* * *

The earliest of the poems which Earle Birney included in his most recent selection from a life's work, *Ghost in the Wheels*, was written, at least in first draft, in his teens, but his first book of verse, *David*, was not published until 1942, when he was already 38. He came into prominence as one of the generation of the 1940's, following on the pioneer work of Smith, Scott, and Pratt, yet one of the influences that permanently affected his writing was the political radicalism of the 1930's. His academic speciality, Old and Middle English, also deeply influenced his choice of form and language – even now one observes in kennings and alliterations the lingering debt he owes to the Anglo-Saxon scops. Finally, an acute consciousness of the physical environment, bred in a childhood lived in the Rockies, has given a peculiarly topographical nature to a great deal of his poetry.

This characteristic has been intensified by Birney's love of travel, and by the way in which each phase of wandering seemed to mark a period of his writing. He himself divided his *Collected Poems* according to region, and the arrangement throws into highlight the remarkable poems – among the best he ever wrote – that came out of travel in Asia and Latin America during the late 1950's and early 1960's, poems like "A Walk in Kyoto," "Cartagena de Indias," and the splendid "Bear on the Delhi Road," observing Kashmiri hunters trying to teach a bear they have captured to dance:

> It is no more joyous for them
> in this hot dust to prance
> out of reach of the praying claws
> sharpened to paw for ants
> in the shadows of deodars
> It is not easy to free
> myth from reality
> or rear this fellow up
> to lurch, lurch with them
> in the tranced dancing of men

In these travel poems Birney develops a characteristic stance, that of the observer who appears as a character in the poem and so emphasizes the strangeness of the bridges by which two cultures meet.

One is aware, all the time, of a man observing and reflecting on his world, on other worlds, on himself, and one of the most striking features of the process is the way the voices and manner change according to the situation. When he writes poems about America and Americans, his voice often takes on an emphatic jerkiness, often spasmodic, which affects the visual shape of the poem as well as its sound when read. In other poems, particularly those he wrote during the 1960's, the voice slows down, broadening its flow, taking a narrative pace in the travel poems, and assuming an eloquent loping rhythm in that magnificent meditation on human destiny, "November Walk near False Creek Mouth," with its notable ending:

> But still on the highest shelf of ever
> washed by the curve of timeless returnings
> lies the unreached unreachable nothing
> whose winds wash down to the human shores
> and slip showing
>
> into each thought nudging my footsteps now
> as I turn to my brief night's ledge
>
> *in the last of warmth*
> *and the fading of brightness*
> *on the sliding edge of the beating sea*

One characteristic of Birney as a poet is his disinclination to be definite and final. This means that when he republishes his poems, from collection to collection, they are often radically revised, so that the version we finally have may have been 20 years in the writing, though the best of his poems – the fine travel poems – have usually been written in a force of feeling that refuses revision. Related to his desire to change and improve is his restless urge to experiment in form and language. From Joycean experiments in the 1940's he came to dabblings in concrete poetry in the 1960's, and his recent book *Fall by Fury* is a strange combination of typographical patterns and the vulnerable love poems of old age:

> Loving you is beyond wings
> is to sway with primal weed
> is to dance with fins
> in a joy too salt
> for sounding

—George Woodcock

BISHOP, Elizabeth. American. Born in Worcester, Massachusetts, 8 February 1911. Educated at Vassar College, Poughkeepsie, New York, A.B. 1934. Lived in Brazil for 16 years. Consultant in Poetry, Library of Congress, 1949–50. Teacher, University of Washington, Seattle, 1966, 1973. Since 1970, Lecturer in English, Harvard University, Cambridge, Massachusetts. Recipient: Houghton Mifflin Fellowship, 1944; Guggenheim Fellowship, 1947; Lucy Martin Donnelly Fellowship, 1951; National Institute of Arts and Letters grant, 1951; Shelley Memorial Award, 1953; Pulitzer Prize, 1956; *Partisan Review* Fellowship, 1956; Amy Lowell Traveling Fellowship, 1957; Chapelbrook Fellowship, 1962; Academy of American Poets Fellowship, 1964; Rockefeller Fellowship,1967; Ingram Merrill Foundation grant, 1969; National Book Award, 1970; Harriet Monroe Poetry Award, 1974; *Books Abroad* – Neustadt International Prize, 1976; National Book Critics Circle Award, 1976. LL.D.: Smith College, Northampton, Massachusetts, 1968; Rutgers University, New Brunswick, New Jersey, 1972; Brown University, Providence, Rhode Island, 1972; Adelphi University, Garden City, New York, 1977; Brandeis University, Waltham, Massachusetts, 1978; Dalhousie University, Halifax, Nova Scotia, 1979; Princeton University, New Jersey, 1979. Chancellor, Academy of American Poets, 1966; Member, American Academy of Arts and Letters, 1976; American Academy of Arts and Sciences. Order of Rio Branco (Brazil), 1971. Address: c/o Farrar Straus and Giroux, 19 Union Square West, New York, New York 10003, U.S.A.

PUBLICATIONS

Verse

North and South. Boston, Houghton Mifflin, 1946.
Poems: North and South – A Cold Spring. Boston, Houghton Mifflin, 1955.
Poems. London, Chatto and Windus, 1956.
Questions of Travel. New York, Farrar Straus, 1965.
Selected Poems. London, Chatto and Windus, 1967.
The Ballad of the Burglar of Babylon (juvenile). New York, Farrar Straus, 1968.
The Complete Poems. New York, Farrar Straus, 1969; London, Chatto and Windus, 1970.
Poem. New York, Phoenix Book Shop, 1973.
Geography III. New York, Farrar Straus, and London, Chatto and Windus, 1977

Other

Brazil, with Emanuel Brasil. New York, Time, 1962.

Editor and Translator, *Anthology of Contemporary Brazilian Poetry*, volume 1. Middletown, Connecticut, Wesleyan University Press, 1972.

Translator, *The Diary of Helena Morley.* New York, Farrar Straus, 1957; London, Gollancz, 1958.

Critical Study: "Elizabeth Bishop Issue" of *World Literature Today* (Norman, Oklahoma), Winter 1977.

Elizabeth Bishop comments:

All my life I have lived and behaved very much like [the] ... sandpiper – just running along the edges of different countries and continents, "looking for something" ... having spent most of my life timorously pecking for subsistence along coastlines of the world.

* * *

Elizabeth Bishop's poetic landscapes are reminiscent of Marianne Moore's, for they abound in the concrete details of realistic experience, to which she adds an extraordinary wit and fancifulness. It is the world indeed that fills these meticulously detailed landscapes – from Nova Scotia and Jerusalem to Brazil, New York, Paris, and Mexico. Within these poems, most importantly, is the poet's keen sense of the unusual or terrifying within the familiar and ordinary, as well as the converse, the recognizable or banal within the otherwise unfamiliar or terrifying.

Unlike those of so many of her contemporaries, Bishop's landscapes are not primarily symbolic statements of the poet's struggles for personal and spiritual wholeness. Her seascapes, rivers, harbors, and roads – note how the titles of her volumes reflect her geographical interests – contain the *quidditas* of specific place, and yet the vast potential of mystery contained therein. As John Ashbery remarked when she received the Books Abroad Neustadt Award, "It is this continually renewed sense of discovering the strangeness, the unreality of our reality at the very moment of becoming conscious of it *as* reality, that is the great subject for Elizabeth Bishop."

Bishop's morality urges moderation and courage, the conviction that we ought to indulge in, enjoy, and appreciate the little things in life, the domesticity of home and family. Courage in the face of ultimate annihilation is the hard-won prize attainable – yes, attainable – through experience itself. Humor, manners, pride in accomplishment, and reasonableness – these are her values within poetic forms as classical in their proportion and verbal precision as in their statement. Hers is a form where good sense and exactness abound. Bishop's skill in verbal pruning is as typically impressive in the following lines as her precise use of sense details: "the palm trees clatter in the stiff breeze/like the bills of the pelicans."

"The Map" exemplifies Bishop's descriptive skills, where vastness is first localized and then generalized. Particular locales are described through color and shape which reveal their inhabitants' activities, and these combinations bring the reader into the otherwise strange and exotic world:

> The shadow of Newfoundland lies flat and still.
> Labrador's yellow, where the moony Eskimo
> has oiled it. We can stroke these lovely bays,
> under a glass as if they were expected to blossom,
> or as if to provide a clean cage for invisible fish.
> The names of seashore towns run out to sea,
> the names of cities cross the neighboring mountains
> – the printer here experiencing the same excitement
> as when emotion too far exceeds its cause.
> These peninsulas take the water between thumb and
> finger
> like women feeling for the smoothness of yard-goods.

The world beckons Bishop to chart it; many of her poems reflect her ambivalence in so doing: "My eyes bulge and hurt. They are my one great beauty, even so" ("Giant Toad"). She would "open the book" of knowledge ("Holy Land"), of origins and significances, of all things human and alive to understand them and write of them: "Thus should have been our travels;/serious, engravable." At times she realizes that ultimate meaning is elusive: "Should we have stayed at home," she writes, "wherever that may be?" ("Questions of Travel"). After all:

> The Seven Wonders of the world are tired
> and a touch familiar, but the other scenes,
> innumerable, though equally sad, and still,
> are foreign.

In "Holy Land" she would travel back to and recreate the history and myth of the Birth of Christ, for if she gazed long enough, perhaps the ecstasy of identification with that moment – that blending of the ordinary within the extraordinary, might be an exorcism for the relentless need for discovery: "Open the heavy book. Why couldn't we have seen/ this old Nativity while we were at it? .../ – and looked and looked our infant sight away." For knowledge one would sacrifice all: "We'd rather have the iceberg than the ship/Although it meant the end of travel" ("The Imaginary Iceberg").

In her more domestic scenes, the ordinary and strange again intermingle. A young girl (a frequent persona in the poems) sits in the dentist's waiting room, her aunt inside. Reading the *National Geographic*, she is disturbed by the photos of foreign lands, the "black, naked women with necks/wound round and round with wire/like the necks of light bulbs./Their breasts were horrifying" ("In the Waiting Room"). But she is simultaneously disturbed by the strangeness of her aunt's cries from within. The girl feels faint, as though she were about to fall off the "round, turning world/into cold, blue-black space." The fusion of the magazine's images with her own vertigo is juxtaposed against her instinctive thrust to hold on to the familiar things of her world: "trousers and skirts and boots/and different pairs of hands/lying under the lamps." A "cry of pain" intrudes upon her – not just "my aunt or me, or anyone." Her world is forever changed, and she is left speechless "How – I didn't know any/word for it. ..."

In the well-known "The Fish" the simple experience of catching a fish becomes a moment of transfiguration wherein the poet simultaneously sees the universal vulnerability of all living things and her intellectual superiority over brute force. Through such knowledge – concretely, that she has indeed the power to outwit and catch "the tremendous fish" – comes humility and charity: "I let the fish go."

Caught without a struggle, the fish hangs "battered," "Venerable," and "homely," a triad that becomes the metaphorical conceit that ties the victim to his victor. She would look into his eyes, which are "far larger than mine," but they are "shallower." She has observed in remarkable detail the fish both externally and internally – utilizing color and flower images – and she expresses a great admiration for this aged ruin, whose body scars reveal its resistance to capture many times. At last she realizes their common victory in survival; she proclaims her superiority of vision: "I stared and stared," and awed by her vision, the boat fills with a rainbow. The colors of the fish she has so vividly described now blend with those of the "bilge," of rust, of "everything" in the "little rented boat," and extend to vaster, more mysterious nature, until "everything/was rainbow, rainbow, rainbow" and "I let the fish go." Her sense of victory and humility, of proportion and modesty, have lent her vision grace, in the radiant image of the rainbow.

—Lois Gordon

BISSETT, Bill. Canadian. Born in Halifax, Nova Scotia, 23 November 1939. Since 1962, Editor and Printer, Blewointmentpress, Vancouver. Artist: One-Man Shows – Vancouver Art Gallery, 1972, and Western Front Gallery, Vancouver, 1977. Recipient: Canada Council grant, 1967, 1968, 1972, 1975, 1977, bursary and travel grant, 1971, 1977. Address: Box 8870, Station Bentall, Vancouver 5, British Columbia, Canada.

PUBLICATIONS

Verse

Th jinx ship nd othr trips: pomes-drawings-collage. Vancouver, Very Stone House, 1966.
we sleep inside each other all (with drawings). Toronto, Ganglia Press, 1966.
Fires in th Tempul (with drawings). Vancouver, Very Stone House, 1967.
where is miss florence riddle. Toronto, Luv Press, 1967.
what poetiks. Vancouver, Blewointmentpress, 1967.
(th) Gossamer Bed Pan. Vancouver, Blewointmentpress, 1967.
Lebanon Voices. Toronto, Weed/Flower Press, 1967.
Of th Land/Divine Service Poems. Toronto, Weed/Flower Press, 1968.
Awake in the Red Desert! Vancouver, Talonbooks, 1968.
Killer Whale. Vancouver, See Hear Productions, 1969.
Sunday Work? Vancouver, Blewointmentpress-Intermedia Press, 1969.
Liberating Skies. Vancouver, Blewointmentpress, 1969.
The Lost Angel Mining Co. Vancouver, Blewointmentpress, 1969.
A Marvellous Experience. Vancouver, Blewointmentpress, 1969(?).
S th Story I to. Vancouver, Blewointmentpress, 1970.
Th Outlaw. Vancouver, Blewointmentpress, 1970.
blew trewz. Vancouver, Blewointmentpress, 1970.
Nobody Owns th Earth. Toronto, House of Anansi, 1971.
air 6. Vancouver, Air, 1971.
Tuff Shit Love Pomes. Windsor, Ontario, Bandit/Black Moss Press, 1971.
dragon fly. Toronto, Weed/Flower Press, 1971.
Rush what fukin thery. Vancouver, Blewointmentpress, 1971.
drifting into war. Vancouver, Talonbooks, 1971.
Four Parts Sand: Concrete Poems, with others. Ottawa, Oberon Press, 1972.
th Ice bag. Vancouver, Blewointmentpress, 1972.
pomes for yoshi. Vancouver, Blewointmentpress, 1972.
air 10–11–12. Vancouver, Air, 1972.
Pass th Food, Release th Spirit Book. Vancouver, Talonbooks, 1973.
th first sufi line. Vancouver, Blewointmentpress, 1973.
Vancouver Mainland Ice & Cold Storage. London, Writers Forum, 1973.
what. Vancouver, Blewointmentpress, 1974.
drawings. Vancouver, Blewointmentpress, 1974.
Medicine my mouths on fire. Ottawa, Oberon Press, 1974.
space travl. Vancouver, Air, 1974.
yu can eat it at th opening. Vancouver, Blewointmentpress, 1974.
Living with the Vishyun. Vancouver, New Star, 1974.
IBM. Vancouver, Blewointmentpress, n.d.
Th fifth sun. Vancouver, Blewointmentpress, 1975.
Image being. Vancouver, Blewointmentpress, 1975.
stardust. Vancouver, Blewointmentpress, 1975.
Venus. Vancouver, Blewointmentpress, 1975.
th wind up tongue. Vancouver, Blewointmentpress, 1976.
Plutonium Missing. Vancouver, Intermedia, 1976.
An Allusyun to Macbeth. Coatsworth, Ontario, Black Moss Press, 1976.
sailor. Vancouver, Talonbooks, 1978.
Beyond Even Faithful Legends. Vancouver, Talonbooks, 1979.

Plays

Television Documentaries: *In search of innocence*, 1963; *Strange grey day this*, 1964; *Poets of the 60's*, 1967.

Critical Study: "The Typography of bill bissett" by bpNichol, in *we sleep inside each other all*, 1966.

Bill Bissett comments:

poet and painter: abt equal time nd involvment, been merging th fields for sum time now, since abt '62 nd previous with concrete poetry, which i early got into with lance farrell, allowing th words to act visually on th page, was aware of such effects before i cud accept th use of say grammatical thot in writing as such appeard too limiting to th singularly amazing development of th person.

spelling – mainly phonetic

syntax – mainly expressive or musical rather than grammatic

visual form – apprehension of th spirit shape of th pome rather than stanzaic nd rectangular

major theme – search for harmony within th communal self thru sharing (dig Robin Hood), end to war thereby – good luck

characteristic stylistic device – elipse

favorite poet – mick jagger

general source – there is only one, nd th variation that spawnd th fingrs of night woven grace issue (romanticism or elevation, i don't feel th I, i.e. ME writes but that i transcribe indications of flow mused spheres sound), from a hoop

* * *

I like Bill Bissett's poetry when it's most woolly. He admits he can't spell or write right: "the way is clear, the free hard path, no correct spelling, no grammar rules." Puns seem to replace meter: "hes closin in all the doors then iul open them yer all stond." Drugs seem to replace vision. The language is dialect, what's known around here as the Southwestern Ontario Rock 'n Roll Accent. Stupidity, almost, is faked, as in Chaucer, adding a little, as in Chaucer, to the difficulty of the dialect of speeding speech:

> did yu blow cock eat cunt make a good
> business deal and still relate were yu are
> yu happy were yu good just once did yu today
> have an existential moment in no time were yu
> normal today did yu screw society but found
> sum innocent outlets like no one knew or evry
> one knew did yu buy sum orange pop sticks green
> ones did yu have a treat and were clean were yu
> a dirty outlet for a while managin at th same
> time to find pleasure in nature and read a thot
> conditionin book by a provocative author did. ...

Bissett asks a lot of questions. His monologues are unpunctuated but best when interrogatory. It's exuberant. It's genuinely written by someone who is outside himself, making rapid connections. Perhaps calling popsicles pop sticks is a trifle cutesy. Bissett draws, writes narrative, political and concrete poetry and chants. But there is sadness, still interrogatory:

> why just when my body nd souls startin to fit
> sum they rip it all up mother i was happy
> in sum of those open spaces why hard times
> again did yu catch me foolin with th images
> now how can i carry any once cross this
>
> swamp ium sinkin in th deep mud myself

Hopkins? There is a religious aspect, drugs seem a mere polite excuse for vision. Analogously, Warhol's starting to look like Burroughs, and gets sadder, and sadder, and lines form. It's not poetry, those lines. Bissett wears a mask in his poetry; the art in a man's face, the lines, are not fictive, which is why I wish I knew Bissett personally. Still, Burroughs and Warhol are distant from Bissett. Bissett's *Nobody Owns th Earth* values the earth, love and country. Did I say cliché? Not really, just downhome talk. Smart people, like Chaucer, know the difference between cliché and proverb; Canadians are a young people like Chaucer's English were. Nevertheless, I prefer New Yorkers, and wonder if it is precisely the provinciality of Canada that pushes Bissett beyond sadness into heavy hopelessness:

there is
nothing
to hope

th candul
yu lit it
is going

there is
nothing
to hope

shut out
the wind
flame

there is
nothing
to hope

a sea of
skulls in
th harbor

These lines are from a chant in which Bissett turns from a benign "mother" to give some orders to "flame." Bissett's assertive mood is heavy. When he stops asking and hoping, he starts hinting at an apocalypse. Of course, that hinting is itself a hoping, the hope for an end.

—Michael André

BLACK, David (Macleod). Scottish. Born in Wynberg, South Africa, 8 November 1941. Educated at Edinburgh University, M.A. in philosophy 1966; University of Lancaster, M.A. in religious studies. Recipient: Scottish Arts Council prize, 1968, and publication award, 1969; Arts Council of Great Britain bursary, 1968. Lives in London.

PUBLICATIONS

Verse

Rocklestrakes. London, Outposts, 1960.

From the Mountains. London, Outposts, 1963.
Theory of Diet. London, Turret, 1966.
With Decorum. Lowestoft, Suffolk, Scorpion Press, 1967.
A Dozen Short Poems. London, Turret, 1968.
Penguin Modern Poets 11, with Peter Redgrove and D. M. Thomas. London, Penguin, 1968.
The Educators: Poems. London, Barrie and Rockliff-Cresset Press, 1969.
The Old Hag. Preston, Lancashire, Akros, 1972.
The Happy Crow. Edinburgh, Lines Review, 1974.
Gravitations. Edinburgh, Lines Review, 1979.

Critical Study: "The World of D. M. Black" by John Herdman, in *Scottish International 13* (Edinburgh), February 1971.

David Black comments:

My verse is currently undergoing a lot of change, and I can't say too much that'll be at all useful. What I've published so far has been mainly a kind of surrealist-ish narrative poetry; I'm now moving from that to a simpler and more daylit subject-matter which (hopefully) will be seen to be a move from concern primarily with effects to concern primarily with some such question as "how to live in the world as it is." But I think that at bottom that was always the concern. Let the change be symbolized by the fact that I am descending from the heights of my initials, and shall publish in future under the name of David Black.

* * *

The 1960's saw a revived interest in surrealism, and no doubt David Black's earlier poetry reflected this, but it was a surrealism of a modified type, laced by side-shrieks from George MacBeth's poetry of cruelty, tinged by science-fiction and mythmaking, and peppered by the place-names of a hallucinatory Edinburgh. The heady mixture was poured into a flat, deadpan, jerkily enjambed free verse which at moments of stress could take off into lyrical humours and mild, almost pop horror. Long exotic narratives like "Theory of Diet," "Without Equipment," and "The Rite of Spring," which refuse to come into clear focus, present nightmare explorations of cannibal islands, dwarfs speaking dwarf language, a prince whose mother is devoured by ants. Among the shorter poems, violent and extraordinary fantasies are more successfully related to a ruling idea: in "My Species" it is artificial insemination, in "The Educators" it is the generation gap, in "The Fury Was on Me" it is the transforming power of anger, in "The Eighth Day" it is the revenge of fruitfulness on asceticism. In some of the most attractive poems, fantasy shades off towards reality: "Leith Docks" and "The Red Judge" with their evocation of the dramatic northernness and Calvinist tensions of Edinburgh, "With Decorum" celebrating the mysterious sense of renewal in death like a 28-line *Finnegans Wake*, "Clarity" turning a track-suited lout into a dancer:

Open the
windows, Jock! My
beauties, my
noble horses – yoked in
pairs, white horses, drawing my great
hearse, galloping and
frolicking over the cropped turf.

In his later work he has made rather a specialty of the long poem, with a clarifying of style and a leaning towards myth, romance, and fairy-tale. In *The Happy Crow*, "Peter MacCrae

Attempts the Active Life" deals with an incestuous brother-sister relationship, and "Melusine," in a variant of a medieval French legend, tells the story of the Count's wife who periodically turns into a fish. In *Gravitations*, other long poems start off from Grimm's fairy-tales and the Sumerian Gilgamesh cycle, or give the tormented Browningesque confessions of a monk. These are poems of psychological and metaphysical search; their unusualness can sometimes make them seem to promise more than they actually deliver; but the attempt to revive narrative poetry is to be applauded. Black continues to develop. He refreshingly, if at times unaccommodatingly, goes his own way.

—Edwin Morgan

BLASER, Robin (Francis). Canadian. Born in Denver, Colorado, 18 May 1925; naturalized Canadian citizen, 1972. Educated at Northwestern University, Evanston, Illinois, 1943; College of Idaho, Caldwell, 1943–44; University of California, Berkeley, B.A. 1952, M.A. 1954, M.L.S. 1955. Librarian, Harvard University Library, Cambridge, Massachusetts, 1955–59; Assistant Curator, California Historical Society, 1960–61; Librarian, San Francisco State College Library, 1961–65. Lecturer, 1966–70, and since 1970, Professor of English, Simon Fraser University, Burnaby, British Columbia. Co-Founder, *Measure*, Boston, 1957; Editor, *Pacific Nation*, Vancouver, 1967–69. Recipient: Poetry Society Award, 1965; National Endowment for the Arts grant, 1968; Canada Council award, 1970. Address: Simon Fraser University, Burnaby, British Columbia V5A 1S6, Canada.

PUBLICATIONS

Verse

The Moth Poem. San Francisco, Open Space, 1964.
Les Chimères (versions of Gérard de Nerval). San Francisco, Open Space, 1965.
Cups. San Francisco, Four Seasons, 1968.
The Holy Forest Section. New York, Caterpillar, 1970.
Image-nations 1–12, and The Stadium of the Mirror. London, Ferry Press, 1974.
Image-nations 13–14. Vancouver, Cobblestone Press, 1975.

Other

Editor, *The Collected Books of Jack Spicer.* Los Angeles, Black Sparrow Press, 1975.
Editor, *Troilus*, by Jack Spicer. Los Angeles, Black Sparrow Press, 1975.

Robin Blaser comments:

I have had two great companions in poetry, Jack Spicer and Robert Duncan. And there is a real debt to Charles Olson.

I have insisted in my work upon a poetry which in its imagery is cosmological. I have tried to include, take in, and bring over in the content of that work images of those worlds to which one is given the possibility of entrance.

I am interested in a particular kind of narrative – what Jack Spicer and I agreed to call in our own work the serial poem – this is a narrative which refuses to adopt an imposed story line, and completes itself only in the sequence of poems, if, in fact, a reader insists upon a definition of completion which is separate from the poems themselves. The poem tends to act as a sequence of energies which run out when so much of a tale is told. I like to describe this in Ovidian terms, as a *carmen perpetuum*, a continuous song, in which the fragmented subject matter is only apparently disconnected. I believe a poet must reveal a mythology which is as elemental as air, earth, fire, and water; and that the authors who count take responsibility for a map of those worlds that is addressed to companions of the earth, the world, and the spirit.

* * *

Literature misses a lot of things. Of course, people miss a lot of literature. They missed Robin Blaser. He's an unknown classic – some of the people in this book are classic unknowns, so that's a small and utter difference.

But literature does miss a lot of things. Robin Blaser, besides an audience, missed the future. I'm talking about his style, about:

above

This poem is doubtless something archaic, something free versey, and something symbolic, not something "avant-garde." I have not yet looked at the poem you have looked at, above. This poem was selected at random by pointing my finger at a passage in a random Blaser book.

Dear Mr. Blaser, Why don't you answer your mail? Here you see an example of the truth of the aleatory mode. Are you at all familiar with this? I am a great fan of yours. I worry, though, that you imagine you write perfectly – but perfect writing is not marred by insensitive attitudes, and is more adventurous than yours.

Still, Blaser has written some superb poems. Here is the beginning of Poem 8 from *Cups*:

There is no salutation. The
harvesters with gunny sacks
bend picking up jade stones

(Sure that Amor would appear
in sleep. Director. Guide.)

Secret borrowings fit into their hands.

Cold on the tongue
White flecks on the water.

These jade pebbles are true green
when wet.

On the seventh night, the branches parted.
                    The other replied,
How photographic. Amor doesn't appear
on demand. He's more like a snake skin.
If he fits, he lets you in
or sheds your body against the rocks.

—Michael André

BLIGHT, John. Australian. Born in Unley, South Australia, 30 July 1913. Educated to secondary school level; qualified in accountancy. Married to Madeline D'Arcy Irvine; two daughters. Worked as a clerk, orchardist and swagman, and later as a public servant. Retired as secretary to a sawmilling company. Member, The Timber Inquiry Commission, 1949–50. Recipient: Myer Award, 1965; Australia Council Writers Senior Fellowship, 1973–75, 1976–79; National Book Council Award, 1976; Patrick White Literary Award, 1976; Grace Leven Prize, 1976. Address: 34 Greenway Street, The Grange, Brisbane, Queensland, Australia.

PUBLICATIONS

Verse

The Old Pianist. Sydney, Dymock's Book Arcade, 1945.
The Two Suns Met: Poems. Sydney, Edwards and Shaw, 1954.
A Beachcomber's Diary: Ninety Sea Sonnets. Sydney, Angus and Robertson, 1964.
My Beachcombing Days: Ninety Sea Sonnets. Sydney, Angus and Robertson, 1968.
Hart. Melbourne, Nelson, 1974.
Selected Poems 1939–1975. Melbourne, Nelson, 1976.
Pageantry for a Lost Empire. Melbourne, Nelson, 1977.
The New City Poems. Melbourne, Nelson, 1979.

Critical Studies: *Preoccupations in Australian Poetry* by Judith Wright, Melbourne and London, Oxford University Press, 1965; "John Blight: An Elder Practising Poet's Point of View," in *Southerly* (Sydney), 1974; "Two Views of the Poetry of John Blight" by Bruce Beaver and David Malouf, in *Southerly* (Sydney), 1976.

John Blight comments:

I have written published poetry for over 40 years. In that time I have written as I would speak, with the difference that when I write a poem my vision is naturally heightened by aftersight, and my speech, therefore, becomes more intense. The poem pronounces with certitude upon an aspect of life. The success of the poem is relative to the acuteness of the vision.

Goethe comes closest for me in his definition of poetry – a criticism of life. If you are looking for theme in my poetry, take heed of Goethe's definition. I like to examine closely this quality of matter – life. It is simple then to become intense and excited about it – to become poetical.

In the past I have deliberately chosen the sonnet as the vehicle for my poetry. I have adapted it to suit my purpose, not deeming it relevant to conform to Elizabethan or Wordsworthian patterns. I have striven to use it allegorically rather than lyrically.

It has benefited my work by avoidance of the abstract, in concentrating illumination of the subject, holding it before one for a brief space of time like life itself.

* * *

In the early 1970's, nearly 30 years after his first book, John Blight's poetic career seemed established and well-understood. His was one-topic, regional, and on both counts minor poetry – poetry of the Queensland sea-coast. Distinguished contemporaries – Judith Wright and Douglas Stewart – appreciated the scope Blight found in his subject, and the vivid plainness of his talk. Still, "Becalmed," chosen by Stewart for a 1964 anthology, shows Blight's kinship with ten-year-old work by Wright, say, and even Hope, rather than his individual touch. It goes through the motions of reasoning, to approach a dreamily-imaged metaphysical puzzle:

"Which of us now is you, is me?"
Everything double under the sun;
And doubly doubled to prove which one
Is under which, which sun above.
"God, if the counterpart would move."
But movement there or here is none.

For a majority of readers Blight was a one-poem poet; "Death of a Whale" was repeatedly anthologized and "set," and attempts were made in a thousand schoolrooms to beg the conclusion, for children to whom Hitler's ways with Jews were the latest but also the last example of genocide, amply bewept: " – Sorry we are, too when a child dies;/But at the immolation of a race, who cries?"

By 1968 (*My Beachcombing Days*) Blight was confirmed as Australia's most obstinate sonneteer. His were felt to be rough-hewn attempts. The sonnet in those years was well-behaved, and mostly in the hands of second-rate writers, though a much younger Queensland writer of note, Thomas Shapcott, persisted in using it. Not till six years later did Les Murray publish his notable couplet-rhymed "spiral of sonnets" on the University ("Sidere Mens Eadem Mutato"); it was another four years before John Tranter, another cult-leader, published a book of one hundred sonnets. By then, Blight had moved on. His sonnets always kept in touch with actual language and living.

Blight a decade later – a new poet! With talk in Sydney and Melbourne about "the New Poetry" it is a dangerous term, for Blight made course with no-one. Only Brisbane-based *Makar*, among "New" periodicals, published any of the poems in *Hart*. Yet with *Hart*, and his *Selected Poems* a year later, Blight broke the strait-jacket of generalizations about him. "It finished their writing when we dirtied the surf" Blight begins an unrhymed fourteen lines entitled "His Best Poems Are about the Sea." The new subject matter is personal, but also open-eyed, social, even polemic:

I am too old to advantage myself of its beauty
which I find now synthetic with the purchase
of sand for its far-famed beaches, at approximately
a dollar a grain ... and those kids constantly
riding the surf – the surfies off the headlands
where the great grey-nurses paraded and even
seasonal whales.
... Blue, pure and beautiful!
Blue skies of the tourist brochure, I am beginning
to loathe that colour with its aura of beauty contests;
seeing the winners, knowing their fuck is not far away.

Once his new work was seen in quantity, there was recognition for the strength of Blight's ambling, sometimes Frostian observations about the world's habits and happenings. Any game people play, and anything, is fit for comment – an idiomatic phrase, ship's rubbish spewed into the sea, bubbles growing and breaking, modesty, the bomb, old furniture, a plane-flight, racial prejudice, people known ... clearly, Blight's collected poems will need an index of topics.

For Blight, his new-found poetic life has been exhilarating. All but one poem in *Pageantry for a Lost Empire* were written in one year. It is hard to say what outside factors have contributed – he is no disciple. Blight has had ready for 1970's Australia a habit of mind it relishes; but this is not to say he has stood still. He has emerged into freer forms; he is ready to hop, skip, and jump, to play or plod, according to the proper impulse of the poem. Blight engages large issues, often challenging the evaluation of a topic as "large" or "small"; and, caring little for the poet's dignity, he cares greatly for poetry's ("Anthology," "Burnt Poems," "The Poet at Work").

In his gusto, and the fruitful wedding of features of prose and poetry, Blight knowingly runs the risks of triviality and looseness. But his best is worth risks ("The Gold Watch"):

> I touch it
> knowing it will always last, although
> the silly little trickling minutes which coursed
> through it have passed. What-ho for Uncle! I
> remember him now. Could I beg such a monument?

or "Old Man and Tree":

> This, I gave courage as the seedling;
> now there sits a song for me on
> every bough; and longer as
> I live, companionship, shade, and
> comfort on the hottest day. ...

Among senior Australian poets, only David Campbell rivals Blight in his openness to life.

—Judith Rodriguez

BLY, Robert (Elwood). American. Born in Madison, Minnesota, 23 December 1926. Educated at St. Olaf College, Northfield, Minnesota, 1946–47; Harvard University, Cambridge, Massachusetts, B.A. (magna cum laude) 1950; University of Iowa, Iowa City, M.A. 1956. Served in the United States Navy, 1944–46. Married Carolyn McLean in 1955; four children, Mary, Bridget, Noah, and Micah. "I earn my living giving readings at American colleges and universities, and translating." Founding-Editor, since 1958, *The Fifties* magazine (later *The Sixties* and *The Seventies*), and The Fifties Press (later The Sixties and The Seventies Press), Madison, Minnesota. Recipient: Fulbright Fellowship, 1956; Amy Lowell Traveling Fellowship, 1964; Guggenheim Fellowship, 1964; National Institute of Arts and Letters grant, 1965; Rockefeller Fellowship, 1967; National Book Award, 1968. Address: Odin House, Madison, Minnesota 56256, U.S.A.

PUBLICATIONS

Verse

The Lion's Tail and Eyes: Poems Written Out of Laziness and Silence, with James Wright and William Duffy. Madison, Minnesota, Sixties Press, 1962.
Silence in the Snowy Fields. Middletown, Connecticut, Wesleyan University Press, 1962; London, Cape, 1967.
The Light Around the Body. New York, Harper, 1967; London, Rapp and Whiting, 1968.
Chrysanthemums. Menomenie, Wisconsin, Ox Head Press, 1967.
Ducks. Menomenie, Wisconsin, Ox Head Press, 1968.
The Morning Glory: Another Thing That Will Never Be My Friend: Twelve Prose Poems. San Francisco, Kayak, 1969; revised edition, 1970; complete version, New York, Harper, 1975.

The Teeth Mother Naked at Last. San Francisco, City Lights, 1970.
Poems for Tennessee, with William E. Stafford and William Matthews. Martin, Tennessee Poetry Press, 1971.
Water under the Earth. Rushden, Northamptonshire, Sceptre Press, 1972.
Christmas Eve Service at Midnight at St. Michael's. Rushden, Northamptonshire, Sceptre Press, 1972.
Jumping Out of Bed. Barre, Massachusetts, Barre, 1973.
Sleepers Joining Hands. New York, Harper, 1973.
The Dead Seal near McClure's Beach. Rushden, Northamptonshire, Sceptre Press, 1973.
The Hockey Poem. Duluth, Minnesota, Knife River Press, 1974.
Point Reyes Poems. San Francisco, Mudra, 1974.
Grass from Two Years, Let's Leave. Denver, Ally Press, 1975.
Old Man Rubbing His Eyes. Greensboro, North Carolina, Unicorn Press, 1975.
This Body Is Made of Camphor and Gopherwood: Prose Poems. New York, Harper, 1977.
This Tree Will Be Here for a Thousand Years. New York, Harper, 1979.

Recording: *Today's Poets 5*, with others, Folkways.

Other

A Broadsheet Against the New York Times Book Review. Madison, Minnesota, Sixties Press, 1961.
Talking All Morning: Collected Conversations and Interviews. Ann Arbor, University of Michigan Press, 1979.

Editor, with David Ray, *A Poetry Reading Against the Vietnam War.* Madison, Minnesota, American Writers Against the Vietnam War, 1966.
Editor, *The Sea and the Honeycomb: A Book of Poems.* Madison, Minnesota, Sixties Press, 1966.
Editor, *Forty Poems Touching on Recent American History.* Boston, Beacon Press, 1970.
Editor, *Leaping Poetry: An Idea with Poems and Translations.* Boston, Beacon Press, 1975.
Editor, *Selected Poems*, by David Ignatow. Middletown, Connecticut, Wesleyan University Press, 1975.
Editor, *News of the Universe: Poems of Twofold Consciousness.* San Francisco, Sierra Club Books, 1979.

Translator, *The Illustrated Book about Reptiles and Amphibians of the World*, by Hans Hvass. New York, Grosset and Dunlap, 1960.
Translator, with James Wright, *Twenty Poems of Georg Trakl.* Madison, Minnesota, Sixties Press, 1961.
Translator, *The Story of Gösta Berling*, by Selma Lagerlöf. New York, New American Library, 1962.
Translator, with James Wright and John Knoepfle, *Twenty Poems of César Vallejo.* Madison, Minnesota, Sixties Press, 1962.
Translator, with Eric Sellin and Thomas Buckman, *Three Poems*, by Tomas Tranströmer. Lawrence, Kansas, T. Williams, 1966.
Translator, *Hunger*, by Knut Hamsun. New York, Farrar Straus, 1967; London, Duckworth, 1974.
Translator, with Christina Paulston, *I Do Best Alone at Night*, by Gunnar Ekelöf. Washington, D.C., Charioteer Press, 1967.

Translator, with Christina Paulston, *Late Arrival on Earth: Selected Poems of Gunnar Ekelöf.* London, Rapp and Carroll, 1967.
Translator, with others, *Selected Poems*, by Yvan Goll. San Francisco, Kayak, 1968.
Translator, with James Wright, *Twenty Poems of Pablo Neruda.* Madison, Minnesota, Sixties Press, and London, Rapp and Whiting, 1968.
Translator, *Forty Poems of Juan Ramón Jiménez.* Madison, Minnesota, Sixties Press, 1969.
Translator, *Ten Poems*, by Issa Kobayashi. Privately printed, 1969.
Translator, with James Wright and John Knoepfle, *Neruda and Vallejo: Selected Poems.* Boston, Beacon Press, 1971.
Translator, *Twenty Poems of Tomas Tranströmer.* Madison, Minnesota, Seventies Press, 1971.
Translator, *The Fish in the Sea Is Not Thirsty: Versions of Kabir.* Ithaca, New York, Lillabulero Press, 1971.
Translator, *Night Vision*, by Tomas Tranströmer. Ithaca, New York, Lillabulero Press, 1971; London, London Magazine Editions, 1972.
Translator, *Ten Sonnets to Orpheus*, by Rainer Maria Rilke. San Francisco, Sephyrus Image, 1972.
Translator, *Lorca and Jiménez: Selected Poems.* Boston, Beacon Press, 1973.
Translator, *Elegy, Some October Notes*, by Tomas Tranströmer. Rushden, Northamptonshire, Sceptre Press, 1973.
Translator, *Basho.* San Francisco, Mudra, 1974.
Translator, *Friends, You Drank Some Darkness: Three Swedish Poets, Henry Martinson, Gunnar Ekelöf, Tomas Tranströmer.* Boston, Beacon Press, 1975.
Translator, *Try to Live to See This: Versions of Kabir.* Rushden, Northamptonshire, Sceptre Press, and Denver, Ally Press, 1976.
Translator, *The Kabir Book.* Boston, Beacon Press, 1977.
Translator, *The Voices*, by Rainer Maria Rilke. Knotting, Bedfordshire, Sceptre Press, and Denver, Ally Press, 1977.
Translator, *Twenty Poems of Vicente Aleixandre.* Madison, Minnesota, Seventies Press, 1977.
Translator, *Twenty Poems of Rolf Jacobson.* Madison, Minnesota, Seventies Press, 1977.
Translator, *Selected Poems*, by Rainer Maria Rilke. New York, Harper, 1979.

Bibliography: Robert Bly Checklist by Sandy Dorbin, in *Schist 1* (Willimantic, Connecticut), Fall 1973.

Critical Studies: *Alone with America* by Richard Howard, New York, Atheneum, 1969; *The Inner War: Forms and Themes in Recent American Poetry*, Philadelphia, Fortress Press, 1972; "Robert Bly Alive in Darkness" by Anthony Libby, in *Iowa Review* (Iowa City), Summer 1972; "Robert Bly: Radical Poet" by Michael D. True, in *Win* (Rifton, New York), 15 January 1973; *The Emotive Imagination: A New Departure in American Poetry* by Ronald Moran and George Lensing, Baton Rouge, Louisiana State University Press, 1976; "Domesticity to Sublime: Bly's Later Poems" by Charles Molesworth, in *Ohio Review* (Athens), Fall 1978.

* * *

Robert Bly emerged from the early 1960's as one of the more stubbornly independent and critical poets of his generation, boldly stating positions against war and corporate monopoly, broadening federal powers, crassness in literature wherever forums were open to him. He was a dominating spokesman for anti-war groups during the Vietnam War, staging readings around the United States and compiling (with David Ray) extraordinary poetic protests in the anthology *A Poetry Reading Against the Vietnam War.* Throughout his career, he has been a cranky but refreshing influence on American thought and culture, as much for the grandeur of his positions as for the force of his artistic individuality.

Although Bly's output has been relatively small in an era of prolific poets, his books follow a deliberate course of deepening conviction and broader conceptions. *Silence in the Snowy Fields*, his first book, is a slender collection of polished, mildly surreal evocations of his life in Minnesota and of the northwestern landscape, with its harsh winters and huddled townships. Bly's brief poems impute to nature a secret, willful life-force, as in this final stanza from "Snowfall in the Afternoon:"

> The barn is full of corn, and moving toward us now,
> Like a hulk blown toward us in a storm at sea:
> All the sailors on deck have been blind for many years.

Silence in the Snowy Fields has an immediacy of the poet's personal life that reflects the inward shift of poetry during the late 1950's and early 1960's, a direction that Bly then actively retreated from, claiming poetry deserved a larger frame of experience than the poet's own circumstances and private dilemmas.

The Light Around the Body moves into the political and social arena with poems against corporate power and profiteering, presidential politics, and the Vietnam War. These poems are more boldly imaginative and take reckless leaps into a surreal mode of discourse. The poems fuse together the banal and the bizarre: "Accountants hover over the earth like helicopters,/Dropping bits of paper engraved with Hegel's name" ("A Dream of Suffocation") and "Filaments of death grow out./The sheriff cuts off his black legs/and nails them to a tree" ("War and Silence").

To explain his poetic and to give it context, Bly edited an interesting volume of poems entitled *Leaping Poetry* where he argued that consciousness had now expanded to a new faculty of the brain where spiritual and supralogical awareness is stored. His commentary is wonderfully speculative and vivid, but bluffly assertive of its premise. A subsequent elaboration of this thesis appears in the essay, "I Came Out of the Mother Naked," included in the book of poems *Sleepers Joining Hands*, where he suggests that society is now returning to a matriarchal order, in which sensuous awareness and synthetic reason will replace the old patriarchal emphasis on rationality and analysis. *The Kabir Book*, Bly's translations of the 15th-century Indian mystic, are, in Lowell's sense, imitations of the work of a poet who "leaps" in his poetry and manifests the androgynous sensibility Bly has championed recently.

In the prose poems of *This Body Is Made of Camphor and Gopherwood* Bly has become a master of his own sensuous self-awareness, creating in a dreamy language states of consciousness that unite self and nature, mind and viscera. The illustrations of Gendron Jensen show a snail shell progressively turning through a single revolution, just as the poems appear to turn round for us the human inner life through a revolution of emotions. Bly seems to have found a means of linking primal thought to contemporary verse, and the resulting lyric is profoundly moving.

Bly continues to read poetry on the university circuit and to translate Scandinavian literature as his livelihood, but even in these facets of his life he has rooted his new convictions. His readings are now made dramatic with primitive masks, chanting, and extemporaneous lectures on the new mind he feels is remaking the culture of the West.

—Paul Christensen

BOER, Charles. American. Born in Cleveland, Ohio, 25 June 1939. Educated at Western Reserve University, Cleveland, 1957–61, A.B. 1961; University of Florence (Fulbright

Fellow), 1961–62; Harvard University, Cambridge, Massachusetts (Woodrow Wilson Fellow, 1962–63); State University of New York, Buffalo, 1963–66, Ph.D. in comparative literature 1967. Assistant Professor, 1966–70, Associate Professor, 1970–75, and since 1975, Professor of English, University of Connecticut, Storrs. Recipient: Swallow Press New Poetry Series Award, 1969. Address: Box 69, Pomfret Center, Connecticut 06258, U.S.A.

PUBLICATIONS

Verse

The Odes. Chicago, Swallow Press, 1969.
Varmint Q: An Epic Poem on the Life of William Clarke Quantrill. Chicago, Swallow Press, 1972.

Other

Charles Olson in Connecticut (biography). Chicago, Swallow Press, 1975.

Editor, with George Butterick, *The Maximus Poems of Charles Olson, Volume Three.* New York, Grossman, 1975.

Translator, *The Homeric Hymns.* Chicago, Swallow Press, 1971; revised edition, Dallas, Spring Publications, 1975.
Translator, *The Bacchae of Euripides*, in *An Anthology of Greek Tragedy.* Indianapolis, Bobbs Merrill, 1972.

* * *

Classicist Charles Boer puts the ancient forms of ode and epic, now largely fallen into disuse, in the service of perennial themes of war, love, and loss, but with a contemporary mood. Predominantly serious in tone, his score of irregular odes follow English tradition in variety but favor fragmentary colloquialism in grammatical structure. In apostrophes to sea nymphs, movie stars, a Wagnerian soprano, in scenes of wartime Europe and a nameless French river, classical allusions resonate within the matrix of the modern idiom. Unhampered by frequent punctuation, run-on lines drive a sometimes breathless lyric, while ambiguity and repetition give phrase and verse an oracular air, though at the price of dissipating force by frequently choppy caesurae and by strained and jerky syntax. Eschewing the confessional mode, Boer's lines lack the precision and polish of Allen Tate's and the charm of Frank O'Hara's. Individual images – petals and the four elements, especially fiery sun and timeless ocean, are his favorites – strike vividly, but the impression is often blunted by a nebulous context or a too-sudden shift of subject. Classical metaphor can control by maintaining distance, but it can also mask the personal. When the difficult or obscure is avoided, and the poet speaks directly, as in "The Water Ode," his voice is more affecting.

Varmint Q., "an epic poem on the life of William Clarke Quantrill," mocks epic conventions with wry humor but fits more comfortably with picaresque fiction. The history and myth of Q., alias Charley Hart, alias Capt. Quantrill, of the "peculiar eyes" are told through poetry interlarded with the sometimes semi-literate narratives and letters of his accomplices and antagonists, forming a novelistic composite of contrasting points-of-view. Boer sets the ironic tone with "An Invocation to John Greenleaf Whittier As an Aside" and with a genealogy of Q.'s fraudulent, forging kin (incidentally having Mary Quantrill snatch from the "old gray head" of Barbara Frietchie, Whittier's heroine, the honor of saving the flag at Frederick). In contrast to Whittier's high-toned narratives, Boer portrays the violent career of a juvenile delinquent whose sadistic tendencies held him in good stead as Indian-fighter, Civil War guerilla, and tutor of Cole Younger and the James Boys. Q.'s own letters to his mother reveal a poetic sensibility, unfortunately belied by ox-theft, gambling, attempted and successful murder, among other things. Having fun with folklore, Boer plays ironic counterpoint throughout by recounting conflicting reports of Q.'s treacherous exploits (for example, he helps the Underground Railroad steal slaves to freedom then sells them back, after setting up the massacre of the Abolitionists) and by adding a descant of asides and rhetorical questions. Spurred on by his adulterous muse, Annie Walker (invoked under her other name, A. Slaughter), Q.'s odyssey surveys the deadly life of the Western underworld, in which the scoundrel-hero can and does take both sides. Even the epic "game" is disreputable, a horse race in which Q.'s filthy steed wins by a mile, and a ruse. In his final madness, Q. offers as a hecatomb the massacre and burning of Lawrence, Kansas, and he dreams of assassinating Lincoln. Ill-omened and too late for that, he dies ingloriously, but not without the poet's reflections on the demise of the wild West by urbanization and on the making of an American myth.

—Joseph Parisi

BOLD, Alan (Norman). Scottish. Born in Edinburgh, 20 April 1943. Educated at Broughton Secondary School, Edinburgh; Edinburgh University (travelling scholarship in fine art, 1964), 1961–65. Married Alice Howell in 1963; one daughter. Editor, *Gambit*, 1963, 1965, and *Rocket*, 1965–66, Edinburgh; Member of the Editorial Staff, *Times Educational Supplement*, London, 1966–67. Recipient: Scottish Arts Council bursary, 1967, 1974, 1979. Address: Balbirnie Burns East Cottage, near Markinch, Fife, Scotland.

PUBLICATIONS

Verse

Society Inebrious. Edinburgh, Mowat Hamilton, 1965.
The Voyage, adaptation of a poem by Baudelaire. Edinburgh, M. Macdonald, 1966.
To Find the New. London, Chatto and Windus-Hogarth Press, 1967; Middletown, Connecticut, Wesleyan University Press, 1968.
A Perpetual Motion Machine. London, Chatto and Windus-Hogarth Press, and Middletown, Connecticut, Wesleyan University Press, 1969.
Penguin Modern Poets 15, with Edward Brathwaite and Edwin Morgan. London, Penguin, 1969.
The State of the Nation. London, Chatto and Windus-Hogarth Press, and Middletown, Connecticut, Wesleyan University Press, 1969.
He Will Be Greatly Missed: A Poem. London, Turret, 1971.
The Auld Symie. Preston, Lancashire, Akros, 1971.
A Century of People. London, Academy, 1971.
A Pint of Bitter. London, Chatto and Windus, and Middletown, Connecticut, Wesleyan University Press, 1971.
A Lunar Event: A Poem and a Drawing. Richmond, Surrey, Keepsake Press, 1973.
Scotland, Yes: World Cup Football Poems. Edinburgh, Paul Harris, 1978.
This Fine Day. Dunfermline, Fife, Borderline Press, 1979.

Short Stories

Hammer and Thistle, with David Morrison. Wick, Caithness Books, 1974.

Other

Art and Action (lecture). London, Peter Moran, 1965.
Bonnie Prince Charlie. London, Pitkin Pictorials, 1973.
Robert Burns. London, Pitkin Pictorials, 1973.
Scottish Clans. London, Pitkin Pictorials, 1973.
Thom Gunn and Ted Hughes. Edinburgh, Oliver and Boyd, 1976.
Mary Queen of Scots. Hove, Sussex, Wayland, 1977.
Scottish Tartans. London, Pitkin Pictorials, 1978.
Robert the Bruce. London, Pitkin Pictorials, 1978.
George Mackay Brown. Edinburgh, Oliver and Boyd, 1978.
The Ballad. London, Methuen, 1979.

Editor, *The Penguin Book of Socialist Verse*. London, Penguin, 1970.
Editor, *Cambridge Book of English Verse 1939–1975*. Cambridge, University Press, 1976.
Editor, *The Martial Muse: Seven Centuries of War Poetry*. Exeter, Wheaton, 1976.
Editor, *Making Love: The Picador Book of Erotic Verse*. London, Pan, 1978.
Editor, *The Bawdy Beautiful*. London, Sphere, 1979.

Critical Study: "Poet in Search of a Public" by Philip Oakes, in *Sunday Times* (London), 8 February 1970.

Alan Bold comments:

(1970) I am mainly concerned in my poems to explore the insights made available to modern man through scientific research and political change. However, I do not limit myself to one type of poem such as the discursive epic or the short satirical poem. I believe that modern poetry should be judged by the same rigorous standards we apply to the literature of the past and consequently I have made it my business to equip myself with the full range of poetic forms. In this way I am able to emphasise thematic unity by the use of formal variety. Most modern poetry is timid, pretentious, incompetent and inadequate. I would like to see instead of the present fashions – confessional verse, concrete poetry etc. – a poetry of precision which tested the authenticity of its emotion against the observable world of fact. I want poetry to be more ambitious than the novel and the play and to win a new mass audience. And I would like to contribute to this process.

(1974) When I look at my statement in the 1970 edition it seems to suggest that poetry is simply a mechanical process of perfecting a technique and then applying it to all and sundry subjects. I now see that technical expertise is but a beginning and that it can never be fully attained, as each *real* poem demands its own particular technical as well as emotional solution. Thus my poetry has become more experimental (using the word in its scientific sense as the exploration of possibilities, not its lit. crit. sense) and more personal as I feel less inclined to pontificate on the world and more sure of my own feelings. Not that I intend to produce a self-pitying form of versified pessimism but I am now more likely to create a poem in and through personally meaningful language whereas before I would think of something to say and then execute it in poetry. I still feel contemporary English poetry (and that includes Scottish poetry in English, of course) is inadequate: a safety-first response to life in timid and academically acceptable phraseology. I want to write poems that have a life of their own and that reflect life in general and not books or other men's styles. Probably the most significant recent development in my books has been my entry into the visual field. In 1972 I had six exhibitions: of etchings, drawings, paintings and Illuminated Poems. These Illuminated Poems are a combination of original manuscript and watercolour illustration.

(1980) Since making the above statements (which ring together with the absolutist chime of a final Credo) I have discarded my urban environment and come to terms with rural life in a cottage on a Dantean wood in Fife. The impact of this change has been vital; giving me a new lease of creative life. Coming to live in Balbirnie was, in many ways, a revolutionary experience for me. Before that, like most urban poets from Baudelaire downwards, I was expected to produce work that was personal to the point of solipsism – the city as mere backdrop to the historic and omnipotent "I" – and deracinated to the point of vacuity. Now I feel a part of (not apart from) a total process of growth and natural creativity. As a result my poetry is no longer a matter of factual statement but a question of suggestion. Altogether more sensuous, more integrated, more joyous. I still regard poetry as the most *memorable* form of literature; an artistic idiom that gives full scope to inventive ingenuity, inspirational insights, and technical expertise. But in the past I was conscious of a desire to display the structural complexity of a poem whereas now my priority is the achievement of a natural fluency so that the poems, at their best, speak eloquently for themselves.

* * *

Alan Bold was brought up in a "typically anti-social, anti-cultural working class environment," as he described it, which he categorises as "an oppressive prison." His resistance to this condition is the basic motivation of his poetry. The title of his first collection of poetry, *Society Inebrious*, describes the characteristic response of the "prisoners" to their social condition. At the age of 22 Bold had embarked on creating a poetry of social protest. In his second book, *To Find the New*, he wrote: "Damn it!/Our voices are not made for singing now/But for straight talking." There were good precedents for a declaratory poetry in the Scottish literary tradition from Dunbar to MacDiarmid, the vitality of the tradition being ensured by the Scots tongue, a more communal vehicle than English. Bold's poetry of protest, however, has been made in English, which has put his larger utterances at risk. Such lines as

When
Was the world more in need of poetry?
Real poetry – the kind that sings
The facts and yells the truth

presume an effect which their rhetoric fails to carry, while there is the presumption of youth in the didacticism of "I come with a message on the state of the nation/on the definition of our moment," which begins Bold's book-long poem *The State of the Nation*. The blurb for the poem claims: "An enormous variety of moods, verse-techniques and subjects are interwoven and sustained to re-create for the reader an impression of the epic potential of a world increasingly perceived as a single nation." This focuses attention on an effect which is not achieved, but several passages witness to a vigorous intelligence which has already absorbed a wide range of literary experience – a mind impatiently seeking out a rationale which will take account of the cruelties and distortions to life of which Bold is acutely conscious. When that mind moves from the hortatory to deal with given, particular experience, in some cases painful experience, it has the necessary detachment, and poetic technique. I have in mind the admirable tragic poem "A Memory of Death," a narrative of the death of his father. The death is seen through several perspectives. The poet begins by placing it in a historical perspective: "Nineteen fifty six was a momentous year,/The year of Suez and Hungary and the death/Of my father. I was thirteen. He was forty-nine." Here are firmness, courage, and compassion – the right words in the right place. As impressive as the straight telling is the shifting context provided by voices off in the form of interpolations in prose, one officially recording the death, others being passages from letters of sympathy.

There are other achievements in the area of portrayal, such as "Old Nell," the ironic, competent "Portrait of Norbert," and "That's Life" about the death of a tramp in Princes Street, Edinburgh, in which the suppressed rage of the writer against the indifference of society comes through. It is a poem after the style of MacDiarmid, though Bold has made it his own. These three poems appear in *To Find the New*. Even so the tendency to use a spent idiom in the presence of the "great event" has not been eradicated by 1969, in which year a fine poem, "1 June at Buchenwald" (in *A Perpetual Motion Machine*), was flawed by such lines as, "We are not helpless/Creatures crashing onwards irresistibly to doom." But the range of experience under control by this date has widened. "A Memory of Death" is in this collection, and also a charming "Dedicatory Poem, For my daughter, Valentina," which has these lines:

The earth turns round and tells that our
  Precarious point in space
Is not forever – but these sour
Predictions vanish every hour
    We chatter face to face.

Once Bold has used a form – and the variety is wide – it will return with variants. In a little anthology, *Poets and Peasants* (1978), there is this stanza in Bold's poem "Poverty":

Poverty is a dank and darkened room
Situated almost anywhere;
There is a stench in the gloom
And you can taste despair.

Social concern remains the prime consideration, but the approaches to it run from tender feeling for the disadvantaged to comic portrayals. He puts himself at the centre of a comic, ironic fantasy in "The Day I Committed ..." (suicide) (in *A Pint of Bitter*). The flow and rhyming of the poem are exhilarating, but a serious attack is being made on a society which will not support real values. Bold's comic creation of the town councillor – "He will be greatly missed" – whose bigotry extends to the football team he supports, who "Whistles green whistles, shouts green shouts," exhibits a characteristic form of Scottish, myopic mindlessness. To create poetry from such roughage is no small achievement – and Bold feels for and against this society. To judge by Bold's statements, he may not have cast himself in the role of an interpreter of character and a creator of characters, but his main contribution to literature may be along these lines.

—George Bruce

BOOTH, Martin. British. Born in Lancashire, 7 September 1944. Educated at King George V School, Hong Kong; Trent Park College of Education, now Enfield Polytechnic, Barnet, Hertfordshire. Founder, 1968, Sceptre Press, Frensham, Surrey, later Rushden, Northamptonshire, now Knotting, Bedfordshire. Former editor, Fuller d'Arch Smith Ltd. and Omphalos Press, London; Schoolmaster Fellow, St. Peter's College, Oxford, 1973. Poetry critic, and rock music critic, *Tribune*, London, and literary critic, *Pacific Quarterly*. Member of the Executive and General councils, Poetry Society, London, 1968–74. Recipient: Guinness Award, 1970; Gregory Award, 1971; Greenwood Prize, 1971. Agent: A. M. Heath & Co. Ltd., 40–42 William IV Street, London WC2N 4DD, England.

PUBLICATIONS

Verse

Paper Pennies and Other Poems. Privately printed, 1967.
Supplication to the Himalayas. Frensham, Surrey, Sceptre Press, 1968.
In the Yenan Caves. Frensham, Surrey, Sceptre Press, 1969.
The Borrowed Gull: After Virginia Woolf. Frensham, Surrey, Sceptre Press, 1970.
A Winnowing of Silence. Richmond, Surrey, Keepsake Press, 1971.
The Crying Embers. London, Fuller d'Arch Smith, 1971.
Pilgrims and Petitions. Birmingham, Aquila, 1972.
On the Death of Archbishop Broix. Cardiff, Second Aeon, 1972.
Nature Study. St. Ives, Cornwall, Poetry St. Ives, 1972.
Teller. London, Poet and Printer, 1972.
Coronis. St. Brelade, Jersey, Channel Islands, Andium Press, 1973.
Spawning the Os. Feltham, Middlesex, Quarto, 1974.
Yogh. Denver, Ally Press, 1974.
Brevities. New Rochelle, New York, Elizabeth Press, 1974.
Snath. London, Oasis, 1975.
In Her Hands. Rushden, Northamptonshire, Sceptre Press, 1973.
Two Boys and a Girl, Playing in the Churchyard. Hitchin, Hertfordshire, Mandeville Press, 1975.
Hands Twining Grasses. Godalming, Surrey, Words Press, 1975.
Rider and Horse. Richmond, Surrey, Keepsake Press, 1976.
The Knotting Sequence. New Rochelle, New York, Elizabeth Press, 1977.
Extending upon the Kingdom. London, Poets Yearbook, 1978.
The Dying. Knotting, Bedfordshire, Sceptre Press, 1978.
The Earth Man Dreams of a Turned Sod. Higham Ferrers, Northamptonshire, Greylag Press, 1978.
The Cnot Dialogues. New Rochelle, New York, Elizabeth Press, 1979.

Plays

Television Plays (juvenile): *John of Badsaddle, Mary Mad, The Claw of Mammon, Beth and the Hand of Glory, The Winter Warrior*, 1976–78.

Novel

The Carrier. London, W. H. Allen, 1978.

Other

White Bat (juvenile). London, Macmillan, 1974.

Editor, *Unpublished Poems and Drafts of James Elroy Flecker.* Richmond, Surrey, Keepsake Press, 1971.
Editor, with George MacBeth, *The Book of Cats.* London, Secker and Warburg, 1976; New York, Morrow, 1977.

Translator, *Stalks of Jade: Renderings from the Chinese.* London, Menard Press, 1976.

Manuscript Collection: National Manuscript Collection of Contemporary Writers, University of Birmingham.

Critical Studies: in *Palantir* (Preston, Lancashire), March 1977, May 1978.

Martin Booth comments:

I am a writer concerned with the relationship between the child who is father of the man and that man himself: I work within historical contexts and am concerned with the development of language as an arm of realties, both inner and outer.

* * *

From the start of his literary career Martin Booth had a fine command of language and an ear for rhythm and music. In many of his early poems his style was very compressed and elliptic. He was inclined to leave too much to the reader. Despite his remarkable descriptive and lyrical gifts, many of the separate pieces seemed like extracts from a longer sequence, so that, read in isolation, they failed to make the impact they might otherwise have had. One must obviously exclude from this generalisation such admirable poems as "Cathedral Starlings," "Hunt," "The Black Cranes," and "Dismissal at the Building of the Tower of Babel."

With the publication of *The Crying Embers* his intentions became a good deal clearer and it is possible to discern the unity of his work, which draws substantially on dream imagery. The best thing in this volume is "Orbis Picture," a series of emblem poems based upon woodcuts from Comenius's pedagogical work published in Nuremberg in 1658. Although largely descriptive, the significant details have been selected to recreate the atmosphere of the printshop; each section is as stark and clearly defined as the woodcut concerned and the language is perfectly controlled.

Coronis, divided into three sections and containing the ambitious long poem "On the Death of Archdeacon Broix," shows the distance Booth has travelled and confirms the promise of his early work. His best poems written between 1971 and 1973 are included.

Individual poems appear in magazines and anthologies which have not yet been collected in more permanent form. "Letter from the Gone Before" (for Robin Skelton) provides a new aspect of his work: "take my hand/for I bear no dull messages/see in me/no pity or exactitude/of love/I am not here to blind you/or to crack your double joints...."

The Knotting Sequence is paradoxically concerned with the Bedfordshire hamlet of Knotting, where Martin Booth lives. To draw closer to the land and its history, Booth recreates the persona of Cnot, the Anglo-Saxon founder of the hamlet. From Chenotinga to Knotting "they have called/this the/Place of/the Sons/of Cnot." As if to imply the tenuous relationship between the poet and the Anglo-Saxon forerunner, and the effort required in communication with a spirit from the past, the language is sparse and fragmented, almost like echoes at times. The longest piece, "Noises from the Wold," is reminiscent of Ted Hughes's "Crow's Account of the Battle" and depicts a skirmish between the local Belgae and the Roman invaders. Needless to say, Cnot seems to show the same instinct for survival as Crow – although

"the local
tribe were resoundingly
defeated

I remember *that*
Cnot says

I didn't go
to help

no sense in drawing
them over here

he counted his
wives again and
a new
moaning washed
across the evening"

Gradually Cnot gives way to the poet, who secures his rights of possession through his feelings for the landscape and its inhabitants.

Extending upon the Kingdom, together with *The Knotting Sequence*, marks a clear stage in the poet's development. "Replicas" and "Shooting a Fox" in this volume are keenly observed and demonstrate the new power of Booth's writing.

—Howard Sergeant

BOOTH, Philip. American. Born in Hanover, New Hampshire, 8 October 1925. Educated at Dartmouth College, Hanover, A.B. 1948; Columbia University, New York, M.A. 1949. Served in the United States Army Air Force, 1944–45. Married Margaret Tillman in 1946; three daughters. Instructor, Bowdoin College, Maine, 1949–50; Assistant to the Director of Admissions, 1950–51, and Instructor, 1954, Dartmouth College; Assistant Professor, Wellesley College, Massachusetts, 1954–61. Associate Professor, 1961–65, and since 1965, Professor of English and Poet-in-Residence, Syracuse University, New York. Taught at the University of New Hampshire Writers Conference, Durham, 1955; Spencer Memorial Lecturer, Bryn Mawr College, Pennsylvania, 1959; taught at Tufts University Poetry Workshop, Medford, Massachusetts, 1960, 1961. Phi Beta Kappa Poet, Columbia University, 1962. Recipient: Bess Hokin Prize (*Poetry*, Chicago), 1955; Lamont Poetry Selection Award, 1956; *Saturday Review* prize, 1957; Guggenheim Fellowship, 1958, 1965; Emily Clark Balch Prize (*Virginia Quarterly Review*), 1964; National Institute of Arts and Letters grant, 1967; Rockefeller Fellowship, 1968; Theodore Roethke Prize (*Poetry Northwest*), 1970. D.Litt.: Colby College, Waterville, Maine, 1968. Address: Castine, Maine 04421, U.S.A.

PUBLICATIONS

Verse

Letter from a Distant Land. New York, Viking Press, 1957.
The Islanders. New York, Viking Press, 1961.
North by East. Boston, Impressions Workshop, 1966.
Weathers and Edges. New York, Viking Press, 1966.
Margins: A Sequence of New and Selected Poems. New York, Viking Press, 1970.
Available Light. New York, Viking Press, 1976.

Recording: *Today's Poets 4*, with others, Folkways.

Other

Editor, *The Dark Island.* Lunenberg, Vermont, Stinehour Press, 1960.
Editor, *Syracuse Poems, 1965, 1970, 1973, 1978.* Syracuse, New York, Syracuse University Department of English, 1965, 1970, 1973, 1978.

Manuscript Collections: State University of New York, Buffalo; University of Texas, Austin; Dartmouth College, Hanover, New Hampshire.

* * *

Beginning in the 1950's with somewhat formal poems, then moving toward freer but still concise, controlled statements, Philip Booth has made himself the poet of the Maine coast: "Crouched hard on granite,/facing a weathered sea,/I breathe as slow as rock." It is his home, important to him not simply as home – place of sea and stone, gull and bellbuoy, weather and poor washed towns – but as the edge of land, the margin. Again and again he returns to the idea of man at the brink of the sea:

> The late fog, lifting.
> A first wind, risen.
> The long tide, at ebb.
>
> And cast off finally,
> into that routine hope,
> the fishboats: going out.

Booth's poems, even the long ones, are laconic in manner, suggesting the speech of Maine; suggesting, too, the hard-bitten quality of mind that casts off into a "routine hope." His fishermen and coastal farmers, who carry the Yankee tradition into the machine age, are skeptics, despairers, silent sufferers, intensely human – alive in their particularities of speech and culture; and the wry poems which celebrate them, Booth's elegies of the verge, have won a distinct place in the varied literature of New England.

—Hayden Carruth

BOSLEY, Keith. British. Born in the Thames Valley, 16 September 1937. Educated at Borlase School, Marlow, Buckinghamshire, 1949–56; the universities of Reading, Paris, and Caen, 1956–60, B.A. (honours) in French 1960. Married Helen Sava in 1962; one son. Recipient: Finnish State Prize, for translation, 1978. Address: 108 Upton Road, Slough SL1 2AW, England.

PUBLICATIONS

Verse

The Possibility of Angels. London, Macmillan, 1969.
Dark Summer. London, Menard Press, and Berkeley, California, Serendipity, 1976.
The Three Houses. Knotting, Bedfordshire, Sceptre Press, 1976.
Stations. London, Anvil Press Poetry, 1979.

Play

The Last Temptations, adaptation of an opera by Joonas Kokkonen (produced Savonlinna, Finland, 1977).

Other

Tales from the Long Lakes: Finnish Legends from the Kalevala (juvenile). London, Gollancz, 1966; as *The Devil's Horse: Tales from the Kalevala*, New York, Pantheon, 1971.
And I Dance: Poems Original and Translated (juvenile). London, Angus and Robertson, 1972.

Editor, *The Elek Book of Oriental Verse*. London, Elek, 1979.

Translator, *Russia's Other Poets*. London, Longman, 1968; as *Russia's Underground Poets*, New York, Praeger, 1969.
Translator, *An Idiom of Night*, by Pierre Jean Jouve. London, Rapp and Whiting, 1969.
Translator, *The War Wife: Vietnamese Poetry*. London, Allison and Busby, 1972.
Translator, *Snake Charm: From the Kalevala*. London, Menard Press, 1972.
Translator, *The Song of Aino: From the Kalevala*. High Wycombe, Buckinghamshire, Moonbird, 1973.
Translator, *The Song of Songs*. Andoversford, Gloucestershire, Whittington Press, 1976.
Translator, *Finnish Folk Poetry: Epic*. Helsinki, Finnish Literature Society, and London, Hurst, 1977.
Translator, *The Poems*, by Stephane Mallarmé. London, Penguin, 1977.
Translator, *A Round O: Eighteen Poems*, by André Frenaud. Egham, Surrey, Interim Press, 1977.
Translator, *Lament: From the Kamassian*. London, Menard Press, 1977.
Translator, *Whitsongs*, by Eino Leino. London, Menard Press, and Berkeley, California, Serendipity, 1978.

Critical Study: "Keith Bosley: A Poet on the Problems of Translation: Interview by Erkki Toivanen," in *Books from Finland* (Helsinki), 1979.

* * *

Keith Bosley is a poet of considerable charm and much technical ability. At his best, he achieves a tender lyricism rare in this violent age ("The Smoke"): "Summer persists./The smoke/from that squat chimney climbs/into a perfect sky/this still October, trees/hang yellow against blue/longing for leaf fall...." Again, at his best Bosley can manage a clear plot-line better than many of his contemporaries. This is true of "The Unknown Language" where the speaker mysteriously picks up on the 16-metre band of his radio the tongue of the ancient Incas. It is true also of "Haunted" – a poem about a mad grandmother sniped at by soldiers who are imaginary and who go away after her death – which is real.

Very strikingly, the argument commands attention in "Wind at Midnight":

> The night I was away you said the wind
> vaulted the horizon, tore overland
> snatched at the trees and stole their dark green sleep
> fingered the river and set it gasping
>
> and then walked to our house, quite quietly
> to where you lay alone....

The wind behaves like an interloper, howling to get in, sighing when excluded, going away as disappointed as a man. Then

Tonight we are together. Listen: your
horizon, land, trees, river move. I stand
shut in my tomb or kennel at the door
real and whimpering as any wind.

In a more recent work, *Dark Summer*, Bosley voices characteristic themes of disillusion, loneliness, despair. This is a sequence drawing quite explicitly upon poets of other tongues – Jouve, Montale, Hölderlin, Stefan George most notably of all, Dante. The fact that he tends to assimilate all their idioms to the same hushed minor key does not diminish the candour and authenticity of the verse:

Sorry it's been so long in coming back –
the note is not signed, but the hand is hers.
Forgotten books, forgotten borrowers:
a parcel, a replacing on the rack ...

This is moving enough, with its quiet play upon words. But it also acts as a kind of footnote to the story of Paolo and Francesca who in Dante first kiss over a book which itself tells of a guilty love.

It seems that Bosley's original work has learned a good deal from his translations. There are a good many of them – this, from Ransetsu, for example, "The house is locked up:/ around a paper lantern/the bats are dancing." Bosley shows considerable felicity in his verse renderings of Ransetsu, and Ransetsu's master, Bashō. He is equally at home with that very European elegist, Lorca, and with the ellipses of Mallarmé. We owe him a particular debt for his versions of less familiar material, for example, the Vietnamese translations in *The War Wife*. In our age of disruption and violence Keith Bosley is not only a technically adept poet but a distinguished practitioner of the civilised art of translation.

—Philip Hobsbaum

BOTTRALL, (Francis James) Ronald. British. Born in Camborne, Cornwall, 2 September 1906. Educated at Redruth County School; Pembroke College, Cambridge (Foundress' Scholar; Charles Oldham Shakespeare Scholar, 1927), M.A. (honours); Princeton University, New Jersey (Commonwealth Fund Fellowship, 1931–33). Served with the Air Ministry, 1940–41. Married 1) Margaret Florence Saumarez Smith in 1934 (marriage dissolved, 1954), one son; 2) Margot Pamela Samuel in 1954. Lector in English, University of Helsingfors, Finland, 1929–31; Johore Professor of English Language and Literature, Raffles College, Singapore, 1933–37; Assistant Director and Professor of English, British Institute, Florence, 1937–38; Secretary, School of Oriental and African Studies, London University, 1939–45. British Council Representative in Sweden, 1941; Italy, 1945; Brazil, 1954; Greece, 1957; Japan (and Cultural Counsellor, Tokyo), 1959–61. Chief, Fellowships and Training Branch, Food and Agricultural Organization of the United Nations, Rome, 1963–65. Reviewer, *Times Literary Supplement*, London, 1965–74. Recipient: Coronation Medal, 1953; Syracuse International Poetry Prize, 1954. Fellow, Royal Society of Literature, 1955. Grand Officer of the Order of Merit, Italy, 1973. C.B.E. (Commander, Order of the British Empire), 1949. Knight Commander, Order of St. John of Jerusalem, 1977. Address: c/o FAO, AGOX, Viale delle Terme di Caracalla, 00153 Rome, Italy.

PUBLICATIONS

Verse

The Loosening and Other Poems. Cambridge, Gordon Fraser, 1931.
Festivals of Fire. London, Faber, 1934.
The Turning Path. London, Arthur Barker, 1939.
Farewell and Welcome. London, Editions Poetry London, 1945.
Selected Poems. London, Editions Poetry London, 1946.
The Palisades of Fear. London, Editions Poetry London, 1949.
Adam Unparadised. London, Verschoyle, 1954.
The Collected Poems of Ronald Bottrall. London, Sidgwick and Jackson, 1961.
Day and Night. London, London Magazine Editions, 1973.
Poems 1955–1973. London, Anvil Press Poetry, 1974.

Other

Rome. London, Joseph, and Cleveland, World, 1968.

Editor, with Gunnar Ekelöf, *Dikter*, by T. S. Eliot. Stockholm, Albert Bonniers Förlag, 1942.
Editor, with Margaret Bottrall, *The Zephyr Book of English Verse.* Stockholm, Zephyr, 1945.
Editor, with Margaret Bottrall, *Collected English Verse.* London, Sidgwick and Jackson, 1946.

Manuscript Collections: State University of New York, Buffalo; University of Texas, Austin; British Museum, London.

Critical Studies: Preface to *Selected Poems* by Edith Sitwell, 1946; *The Modern Writer and His World* by G. S. Fraser, London, Verschoyle, 1953; *The Present Age: From 1920* by David Daiches, London, Cresset Press, 1958; Introduction to *Collected Poems* by Charles Tomlinson, 1961; *Guide to Modern World Literature* by Martin Seymour-Smith, London, Wolfe, 1973.

Ronald Bottrall comments:

At the beginning one has plenty of thematic material but only after trial and error can one use it effectively. In mid-career things coalesce and clarify and when situations present themselves one has the technique and experience to deal with them to the best of one's ability. In later years the technical skill is still there, but the situations are harder to grasp and transmute into poetry. My imagery derives from my early years in Cornwall in the country and by the sea. Later from my extensive travels. The greatest influence on my early poetry was Ezra Pound's *Hugh Selwyn Mauberley*. In the course of my work I have used a great many metrical forms, including, from 1946, syllabic verse. An ability to make use of metrical forms is most important for a poet.

* * *

(1970) Ronald Bottrall's reputation as a poet has suffered a great deal through his being tipped off, in the early 1930's, by Dr. F. R. Leavis as the most rangingly intelligent of the younger poets at that time. His early poetry owes a great deal to the example of Ezra Pound, on whose early *Cantos* he wrote a most acute critical study in *Scrutiny*, and, having spent most of his life in such diverse places as Scandinavia, Italy and Brazil, working for the British

Council, he is like Pound a cosmopolitan and multi-lingual poet, full of oblique allusions; he is like Pound also in his learning: in the BBC volume of translations from Dante's *Inferno* his opening ones were perhaps the best. These preoccupations and also perhaps a tendency to write too rapidly and fluently made him seem apart from the mainstream of British verse in the 1930's. And when, at the end of the 1940's, younger poets like John Wain rediscovered the equally learned and obscure poetry of Bottrall's Cambridge friend and contemporary, William Empson, they did not rediscover Bottrall.

Yet a selection of his best poems would be an impressive volume. Always very much in the thick of the world of cultural poses and pretensions, he has a gift for satirising this, in an oblique way, borrowed from Pound's *Hugh Selwyn Mauberley*, that includes a great deal of self-satire. But he has also a directly lyrical gift, for modulation and phrasing. In spite of his Cambridge connections, he was much admired by Dame Edith Sitwell, and the free, loose rhythmical movement of many of his later poems has something in common with her work. A certain roughness, hastiness, or impatience of workmanship flaws many of his later poems; a natural fluency makes it hard for him to eliminate and condense. Nor is there any final philosophy of life in his poetry except that of the sceptical, disabused, but always eager and curious spectator and critic of life, an urbane cynic coupled with a lyrical celebrator. One of his best poems is on the primitive painter, Arnold Wallis, like himself a Cornishman, like himself of working-class origin. Bottrall was to move on from such origins to explore all the splendours of the world. But it may be that it is a certain wistfulness for a lost simplicity and innocence that gives his overabundant, always accomplished but always uneven verse its most poignant moments.

(1974) Since I wrote the above, Bottrall, at sixty-seven, has had an extraordinary new burst of creativity. This began with a group of short poems, which occurred to him just as he was waking in the morning, and then were immediately written down. They have a quality of condensed mysteriousness. He has also written his longest poem to date, *Talking to the Ceiling*, an extremely vivid, loving and Chaucerianly humorous evocation of his Cornish childhood and his father, sixty years ago. It is a poet's late assertion of the sacredness of roots, the strength of family ties, and the richness of life, a kind of counterblast to *The Waste Land*. These poems, which I have been privileged to see in the process of composition, are now being published, along with a number of other new ones. In bulk they are almost equivalent to his earlier *Collected Poems* and they have a new serenity, simplicity, and directness. Bottrall's intelligence and skill had been highly praised in the 1930's by F. R. Leavis, in the 1940's by Edith Sitwell, and in the 1960's by Charles Tomlinson. Three such different critics, two of them poets – and very different poets – cannot, between them, have been entirely wrong. This late flowering should restore Bottrall to a central position in the poetic scene.

—G. S. Fraser

BOWERING, George. Canadian. Born in Keremeos, British Columbia, 1 December 1938. Educated at Victoria College, British Columbia; University of British Columbia, Vancouver, B.A. 1960, M.A. 1963; University of Western Ontario, London. Served in the Royal Canadian Air Force, 1954–57. Married 1) Angela Luoma in 1962; 2) Thea Claire Bowering in 1971. Has worked for the British Columbia Forest Service and for the Federal Department of Agriculture. Assistant Professor, University of Calgary, Alberta, 1963–66; Writer-in-Residence, 1967–68, and Assistant Professor of English, 1968–72, Sir George Williams University, Montreal. Since 1972, Associate Professor of English, Simon Fraser University, Burnaby, British Columbia. Editor, *Imago* magazine, Vancouver. Recipient: Canada Council grant, 1968, 1971; Governor-General's Award, 1969. Agent: Linda

McCartney, 104 Lyndhurst Avenue, Toronto, Ontario M5R 2Z1. Address: 2499 West 37th Avenue, Vancouver 13, British Columbia, Canada.

PUBLICATIONS

Verse

Sticks and Stones. Vancouver, Tishbooks, 1963.
Points on the Grid. Toronto, Contact Press, 1964.
The Man in the Yellow Boots. Mexico City, El Corno Emplumado, 1965.
The Silver Wire. Kingston, Ontario, Quarry Press, 1966.
Baseball. Toronto, Coach House Press, 1967.
Two Police Poems. Vancouver, Talonbooks, 1968.
Rocky Mountain Foot: A Lyric, A Memoir. Toronto, McClelland and Stewart, 1968.
The Gangs of Kosmos. Toronto, Anansi, 1969.
Sitting in Mexico. Montreal, Imago, 1970.
George, Vancouver: A Discovery Poem. Toronto, Weed/Flower Press, 1970.
Geneve. Toronto, Coach House Press, 1971.
Touch: Selected Poems 1960–1970. Toronto, McClelland and Stewart, 1971.
The Sensible. Toronto, Massasauga, 1972.
Layers 1–13. Toronto, Weed/Flower Press, 1973.
Curious. Toronto, Coach House Press, 1973.
In the Flesh. Toronto, McClelland and Stewart, 1974.
Allophanes. Toronto, Coach House Press, 1976.
Poems and Other Baseballs. Coatsworth, Ontario, Black Moss Press, 1976.
The Catch. Toronto, McClelland and Stewart, 1976.
The Concrete Island: Montreal Poems 1967–1971. Quebec, Vehicule Press, 1977.

Plays

A Home for Heroes, in *Prism International* (Vancouver), 1962.

Television Play: *What Does Eddie Williams Want?*, 1965.

Novels

Mirror on the Floor. Toronto, McClelland and Stewart, 1967.
A Short Sad Book. Vancouver, Talonbooks, 1977.
Concentric Circles. Coatsworth, Ontario, Black Moss Press, 1977.

Short Stories

Flycatcher. Ottawa, Oberon Press, 1974.
Protective Footwear. Toronto, McClelland and Stewart, 1978.

Other

How I Hear "Howl". Montreal, Sir George Williams University, 1968.
Al Purdy. Toronto, Copp Clarke, 1970.
Autobiology. Vancouver, Vancouver Writing Series, 1972.
At War with the U.S. Vancouver, Talonbooks, 1974.

Editor, *Vibrations: Poems of Youth.* Toronto, Gage, 1970.
Editor, *The Story So Far.* Toronto, Coach House Press, 1971.

Manuscript Collection: Douglas Library, Queen's University, Kingston, Ontario.

Critical Study: Introduction by the author to *Touch: Selected Poems*, 1971.

George Bowering comments:

I don't think that I will make a "personal statement introducing my work" because I don't write personal poetry. In fact when personal poetry gets to be confessional poetry I turn it off & reach for the baseball scores. I'll share with you what I wrote as notes 2 days ago: The snowball appears in hell every morning at seven. Dr Babel contends about the world's form, striking its prepared strings endlessly, a pleasure moving rings outward thru the universe. All sentences are to be served. You've tried it & tried it & it cant be done, you cannot close your ear – i.e. literature must be thought, now. Your knee oh class equal poet will like use a simile because he hates ambiguity. The snowball says it: all sentences are imperative.

* * *

"I was all those things that other poets always are on the dust jackets before they became poets." George Bowering's boast must be true, for his work is immensely various and the poet himself seems at times a powder-keg of energy. Wondering what Bowering will publish next is almost a pastime in Canadian poetry circles.

Bowering's work is terribly uneven, however, and irritatingly bad when it is poor. The virtues and vices are both found in *Touch: Selected Poems 1960–1970*, which includes poems from his earlier books, including *Rocky Mountain Foot* for which he received the Governor-General's Award in 1969. This last book is the first that groups poems thematically rather than chronologically, for as he explained, "Now nearly all I work on are books themselves."

A few of the vices include his misspelled words; his endless egotism; his philistinism; his ultra-radical chic. Some of his virtues are a vivid sense of space and time; a lyricism that is capable of sprouting wings; a happy-go-lucky sensibility (when not radicalized); an instant sympathy for the oppressed. It could be said his work has more tone that taste.

"Emphasis is on voice," Bowering wrote, and his poetry does have a decided cadence, a nonchalance of its own, and a quickness that is characteristic and enjoyable. Perhaps the spirit of his work can best be caught in a poem like "Grandfather" which begins:

> Grandfather
>
> Jabez Harry Bowering
>
> strode across the Canadian prairie
>
> hacking down trees
>
> & building churches
>
> delivering personal baptist sermons in them
>
> leading Holy holy holy lord god almighty songs in them.

The poem does not conclude so much as end: "Till he died the day before his eighty fifth birthday/in a Catholic hospital of sheets white as his hair." The need to create a personal mythology is here, as it is in Whitman's verse, and Bowering's poems all seem interconnected in some vast Life of the Western Canadian Poet.

Perhaps Hugh MacCallum best summed Bowering's work up when he wrote: "The speaker in these poems achieves at times an almost bardic simplicity of manner that allows him to revel in the ordinary, the commonplace, the self-evident. But there is also a kind of wonder at the fullness and assertiveness of phenomena. Energy is the thing that arouses the poet's imagination – energy in landscape, man, or woman."

—John Robert Colombo

BOWERS, Edgar. American. Born in Rome, Georgia, 2 March 1924. Educated at the University of North Carolina, Chapel Hill, B.A. 1947; Stanford University, California, M.A. 1949, Ph.D. 1953. Served in the United States Army, 1943–46. Instructor, Duke University, Durham, North Carolina, 1952–55; Assistant Professor, Harpur College, Binghamton, New York, 1955–58. Since 1958, Member of the English Department, and currently Professor of English, University of California, Santa Barbara. Recipient: Swallow Press New Poetry Series Award, 1955; Guggenheim Fellowship, 1958, 1969; *Sewanee Review* Fellowship; Fulbright Fellowship; Edward F. Jones Foundation Fellowship; University of California Institute of Creative Arts Fellowship; Ingram Merrill award, 1974. Address: 1502 Miramar Beach, Santa Barbara, California 93108, U.S.A.

PUBLICATIONS

Verse

The Form of Loss. Denver, Swallow, 1956.
Five American Poets, with others, edited by Ted Hughes and Thom Gunn. London, Faber, 1963.
The Astronomers. Denver, Swallow, 1965.
Living Together: New and Selected Poems. Boston, Godine, 1973; Manchester, Carcanet Press, 1977.

Critical Studies: *Forms of Discovery* by Yvor Winters, Denver, Swallow, 1967; *Alone with America* by Richard Howard, New York, Atheneum, 1969; "The Theme of Loss in the Earlier Poems of Catherine Davis and Edgar Bowers," in *Southern Review 9* (Baton Rouge, Louisiana), and "Contexts for 'Being,' 'Divinity,' and 'Self' in Valéry and Edgar Bowers," in *Southern Review 13*, both by Helen A. Trimpi.

* * *

Sometimes a major poet may be ignored by the majority of readers, so that he must content himself with fit audience, though few. Sometimes a major poet may seem less "important" than more public figures, for instance, poets who disturb political conventions or march on the Pentagon, or who titillate the public with confessional songs and sonnets. No matter how worthy their causes or how honest their confessions, poets must be judged by their poems, not their activities or biographies. Edgar Bowers has not sought publicity, nor has he achieved notoriety. He has not written in the modish confessional manner of divorce, madness, and self-advertisement. He has simply written some of the great poems of our time. One needs to read his work slowly and carefully; his poems are worth taking the time to understand.

Bowers' powerful treatment of themes of deception and honesty, of shadow and lucidity, of loss and form can be found in his earliest poems; but his depth and range have grown, with no diminution of his prosodic mastery. A chief characteristic of his poems, as Yvor Winters pointed out, is that "sensory perception and its significance are simultaneous." This is especially true of "Autumn Shade," a sequence of ten poems that ends *The Astronomers* and that Winters mistakenly slighted. The sequence begins with a sense of destiny which amounts almost to predestination, a sense that appears in other poems by Bowers:

Now, toward his destined passion there, the strong,
Vivid young man, reluctant, may return
From suffering in his own experience
To lie down in the darkness.

The young man wakes, he works, he sleeps again; but the first poem ends with a chilling image: "The snake/Does as it must, and sinks into the cold." In another poem the young man lights a fire as the night grows cold:

Gently
A dead soprano sings Mozart and Bach.
I drink bourbon, then go to bed, and sleep
In the Promethean heat of summer's essence.

This is pentameter so subtle in modulation that one may miss a good deal of the technical virtuosity which makes the apparently colloquial notation of actions possible. So much is packed into the subdued, suggestive style that one may overlook the complexity of life and of emotional response to sensations being presented: perception and significance are simultaneous, statement and meaning coincide. The young man of the sequence is aware that the things "I have desired/Evade me, and the lucid majesty/That warmed the dull barbarian to life./So I lie here, left with self-consciousness." One of Winters' mistakes in reading the sequence seems to have been a confusion of "self-consciousness" with solipsism. Within the sequence, the young man's books, his old neighbor who drives through rain and snow, the recollection of Hercules (though the young man does not try for the great task), and of his own father (a form of loss), and his view out the window of a Cherokee trail ("I see it, when I look up from the page"), all indicate the reality of the external world. The density of reference suggests the presence of the past, and the complexity of a man's perceptions. The young man is trying in this dark night, during these seasons of the soul, to understand his own past and thus his present. His old neighbor's driving in snow recalls to him his own driving in war:

Was this our wisdom, simply, in a chance
In danger, to be mastered by a task,
Like groping round a chair, through a door, to bed?

Not many poets in the language could have written those lines. The verbal precision evokes deep resonance of response. His firm control, his stylistic brilliance permit Bowers a potentially dangerous ending for the sequence: it would be trite, after this night of darkness and cold to have the sunlight transform the room, so that even shadows become "substantial light." But like all masters, Bowers takes the potentially trite and makes it hugely moving. The man of the sequence survives: "I stay/Almost as I have been, intact, aware,/Alive, though proud and cautious, even afraid." This ending is indicative of one of Bowers' strengths, as man and as poet: his refusal to be deceived, his almost desperate honesty.

The dramatic monologue "The Prince" is a major examination of what we term "German war guilt"; in it, familial relations become the vehicle for a poetic rendering of moral relations:

My son, who was the heir
To every hope and trust, grew out of caring
Into the form of loss as I had done,
And then betrayed me who betrayed him first.

Likewise, in another fine poem, "From J. Hayden to Constanze Mozart (1791)," a verse letter expressing grief becomes a meditation on the rare fusion of mind and body, sense and reason that Mozart's music embodies: "Aslant at his clavier, with careful ease,/To bring one last enigma to the norm,/Intelligence perfecting the mute keys." These poems, along with "Amor vincit omnia" (the greatest poem on the theme of the Magi since Yeats's), "The Mountain Cemetery," and "The Astronomers of Mont Blanc" are part of the enduring body of work that distinguishes Edgar Bowers' books. One can return to these poems as one returns to Campion, Donne, or Landor: to clear one's sense of language. For in Bowers we have a poet at once exact and exciting in his use of language. The word always fits the sense; and the sense never exceeds what language is capable of doing: "Whereof we cannot speak, thereof we must be silent."

—James Korges

BOYLE, Kay. American. Born in St. Paul, Minnesota, 19 February 1902. Educated at the Cincinnati Conservatory of Music; Ohio Mechanics Institute, 1917–19. Married 1) Richard Brault in 1923 (divorced); 2) Laurence Vail in 1931 (divorced); 3) Baron Joseph von Franckenstein (died, 1963); six children. Lived in Europe for 30 years. Foreign Correspondent, *The New Yorker* magazine, 1946–53. Since 1963, Professor of English, San Francisco State College. Lecturer, New School for Social Research, New York, 1962; Fellow, Wesleyan University, Middletown, Connecticut, 1963; Director, New York Writers Conference, Wagner College, New York, 1964; Fellow, Radcliffe Institute for Independent Study, Cambridge, Massachusetts, 1964–65; Writer-in-Residence, University of Massachusetts, Amherst, 1967, and Hollins College, Virginia, 1970–71. Recipient: Guggenheim Fellowship, 1934, 1961; O. Henry Award, for short story, 1935, 1941. D.Litt.: Columbia College, Chicago, 1971; Skidmore College, Saratoga Springs, New York, 1977. Member, American Academy of Arts and Letters. Address: c/o A. Watkins Inc., 77 Park Avenue, New York, New York 10016, U.S.A.

PUBLICATIONS

Verse

A Statement. New York, Modern Editions Press, 1932.
A Glad Day. New York, New Directions, 1938.
American Citizen: Naturalized in Leadville, Colorado. New York, Simon and Schuster, 1944.
Collected Poems. New York, Knopf, 1962.
Testament for My Students. New York, Doubleday, 1970.

Novels

Plagued by the Nightingale. New York, Cape and Smith, and London, Cape, 1931.
Year Before Last. New York, Smith, and London, Faber, 1932.
Gentlemen, I Address You Privately. New York, Smith, 1933; London, Faber, 1934.
My Next Bride. New York, Harcourt Brace, 1934; London, Faber, 1935.
Death of a Man. New York, Harcourt Brace, and London, Faber, 1936.
Monday Night. New York, Harcourt Brace, and London, Faber, 1938.
Primer for Combat. New York, Simon and Schuster, 1942; London, Faber, 1943.
Avalanche. New York, Simon and Schuster, and London, Faber, 1944.
A Frenchman Must Die. New York, Simon and Schuster, and London, Faber, 1946.
1939. New York, Simon and Schuster, and London, Faber, 1948.
His Human Majesty. New York, McGraw Hill, 1949; London, Faber, 1950.
The Seagull on the Step. New York, Knopf, and London, Faber, 1955.
Generation Without Farewell. New York, Knopf, 1960.
The Underground Woman. New York, Doubleday, 1975.

Short Stories

Short Stories. Paris, Black Sun Press, 1929.
Wedding Day and Other Stories. New York, Cape and Smith, 1930; London, Pharos, 1932.
The First Lover and Other Stories. New York, Smith and Haas, 1933; London, Faber, 1937.
The White Horses of Vienna and Other Stories. New York, Harcourt Brace, 1936; London, Faber, 1937.
The Crazy Hunter: Three Short Novels. New York, Harcourt Brace, 1940; as *The Crazy Hunter and Other Stories*, London, Faber, 1940.
Thirty Stories. New York, Simon and Schuster, 1946; London, Faber, 1948.
The Smoking Mountain: Stories of Post War Germany. New York, McGraw Hill, 1951; London, Faber, 1952.
Three Short Novels. Boston, Beacon Press, 1958.
Nothing Ever Breaks Except the Heart. New York, Doubleday, 1966.

Other

The Youngest Camel (juvenile). Boston, Little Brown, and London, Faber, 1939; revised edition, New York, Harper, 1959; Faber, 1960.
Breaking the Silence: Why a Mother Tells Her Son about the Nazi Era. New York, Institute of Human Relations Press-American Jewish Committee, 1962.
Pinky: The Cat Who Liked to Sleep (juvenile). New York, Crowell Collier, 1966.
Pinky in Persia (juvenile). New York, Crowell Collier, 1968.
Being Geniuses Together, with Robert McAlmon. New York, Doubleday, 1968; London, Joseph, 1970.
The Long Walk at San Francisco State and Other Essays. New York, Grove Press, 1970.
Four Visions of America, with others. Santa Barbara, California, Capra Press, 1977.

Editor, with Laurence Vail and Nina Conarain, *365 Days.* New York, Harcourt Brace, and London, Cape, 1936.
Editor, *The Autobiography of Emanuel Carnevali.* New York, Horizon Press, 1967.
Editor, with Justine Van Gundy, *Enough of Dying! An Anthology of Peace Writings.* New York, Dell, 1972.

Translator, *Don Juan*, by Joseph Delteil. New York, Cape and Smith, 1931.
Translator, *Mr. Knife, Miss Fork*, by R. Crevel. Paris, Black Sun Press, 1931.
Translator, *The Devil in the Flesh*, by Raymond Radiguet. New York, Smith, 1932; London, Grey Walls Press, 1949.

Ghost-writer for the books *Relations and Complications: Being the Recollections of H. H. the Dayang Muda of Sarawak*, by Gladys Palmer Brooke, London, Lane, 1929, and *Yellow Dusk*, by Bettina Bedwell, London, Hurst and Blackett, 1937.

Manuscript Collection: Morris Library, Southern Illinois University Library, Carbondale.

Kay Boyle comments:

Although I have published over twenty books of short stories and novels, I consider myself primarily a poet.

[My poetry] is extremely personal in motivation and deals in the main with social and political problems. I have been influenced by William Carlos Williams, D. H. Lawrence, James Joyce, and Padraic Colum.

* * *

Kay Boyle has been an important novelist, short story writer, and poet since the expatriate generation of the 1920's, and her fiction and poetry have enriched one another. Perhaps the distinguishing formal characteristic of her poetry has been her emphasis upon the implied narrative occasion of most lyric poems. In her work this narrative framework, which incites the lyric response, has been handled in contrasting ways. In certain poems, and these extend throughout her career, the story-telling elements are deliberately made obvious to the point that the poems contain passages of both prose and verse, with the prose usually presenting more factual material and the verse intensifying it to poetic significance. The complex, macabre, and splendid "A Complaint for Mary and Marcel" is an arresting variation of this technique. The opposite method is also used. In these poems the narrative or plot elements are withheld but assumed, and the poems have the mysterious immediacy of overheard conversation. The poems, also characteristic of her work throughout, give an up-to-date, "coded" quality to her writing and seem to anticipate the work of such recent poets as James Merrill.

In content Boyle's poems, taken as a whole, expand the personal emotion of private relationships toward a strong communal and political consciousness, with an accompanying stress upon the social role of the artist. Over the years she has focused her sensibilities and quiet outrage upon political injustice, from the victims of the Fascists to the problems of American students in the 1960's. But her point of view was and remains positive. There is a strong emphasis upon youth and death in her poetry, but her frequent use of images of nature, and the importance of spring and renewal in her work, point to a kind of informed Shelleyan optimism and place her in the mainstream of American romanticism. If her poetry is sometimes more effusive that current taste prefers, Kay Boyle represents nevertheless the testament of a committed artist to an active belief in the possibilities of a heightened human identity, which has been after all the great and underlying theme of poetry since its beginning.

—Gaynor F. Bradish

BRANDI, John. American. Born in Los Angeles, California, 5 November 1943. Educated at California State College, Northridge, B.F.A. 1965. Married Gioia Tama de Brandi in 1968; two children. Member, Peace Corps, South America, 1965–68. Artist and bookmaker: has exhibited paintings in the United States and Mexico. Recipient: *Portland State Review Prize*, for prose, 1971. Address: Box 356, Guadalupita, New Mexico 87722, U.S.A.

PUBLICATIONS

Verse

Poem Afternoon in a Square of Guadalajara. San Francisco, Maya, 1970.
Emptylots: Poems from Venice and LA. Bolinas, California, Nail Press, 1971.
San Francisco Lastday Homebound Hangover Highway Blues. Bolinas, California, Nail Press, 1973.

A Partial Exploration of Palo Flechado Canyon. Bolinas, California, Nail Press, 1973.
The Phoenix Gas Slam. Bolinas, California, Nail Press, 1974.
Firebook. Virgin River, Utah, Smoky the Bear Press, 1974.
In a December Storm. Bowling Green, Ohio, Tribal Press, 1975.
Looking for Minerals. Cherry Valley, New York, Cherry Valley Editions, 1975.
Smudgepots: For Jack Kerouac. Guadalupita, New Mexico, Nail Press, n.d.
Poems from Four Corners. Fort Kent, Maine, Great Raven, 1978.
Andean Town Circa 1980. Guadalupita, New Mexico, Tooth of Time Press, 1978.

Other

Desde Alla. Santa Barbara, California, Christopher's Press, 1971.
One Week of Mornings at Dry Creek. Santa Barbara, California, Christopher's Press, 1971.
Towards a Happy Solstice: Mine, Yours, Everybody. Santa Barbara, California, Christopher's Press, 1971.
Y Aun Hay Mas: Dreams and Explorations: New and Old Mexico. Santa Barbara, California, Christopher's Press, 1972.
Narrowgauge to Riobamba. Santa Barbara, California, Christopher's Press, 1975.
Memorandum from a Caribbean Isle. Brunswick, Maine, Blackberry, 1977.
Diary from Baja California. Santa Barbara, California, Christopher's Press, 1978.
Diary from a Journey to the Middle of the World. Berkeley, California, Figures, 1979.

Manuscript Collection: University of California, Davis.

John Brandi comments:

Desde Alla and *Narrowgauge to Riobamba* are two books akin to two separately painted panels translating the one-same diorama, that of isolated hamlets in the inter-mountain basins of the remote Andes where I spent a few years living with Quechua-speaking peasants.

Whenever I journey, I travel in two separate vehicles. One over the physical landscape, the other within the meta-physical. My writing and painting link the two spheres, migrating back and forth between inner and outer geographies.

That's what my books are about. They're geography books. Earth primers.

* * *

John Brandi is a prolific and energetic writer/artist. He has filled journal after journal with writings, poems, drawings, collages. His work seeks source and renewal in new geographies and in the act of travel with its inevitable encounters, mysteries, and misunderstandings. He's a spy of sorts who looks, listens, takes notes, sketches interesting sights with a flair. Because he is an accomplished graphic artist, Brandi is able to describe the jungles of Ecuador or the mesas of New Mexico or Alaska's endless night with rich visual attention to physical detail. There are both a naivety and a shrewd persona present in his writing. Sometimes it reads like a curious union of *Candide* and Céline. Not unlike many writers born in post-World War II urban sprawl, Brandi attempts self-geography which sometimes gets in the way of his text and diminishes the nuances of his writing.

Brandi's work exemplifies the impressionistic postcard travel-writing style established by Jack Kerouac. The surfaces are often extremely attractive, and poverty and suffering are dealt with in near-romantic detail. Depth is often absent in visceral celebrations of place. As strangers, we bring expectations to a place and its people which, as artists, we hope to translate into myth. Travel writing, in many cases, becomes an elusive form of colonialism, though in Brandi's case his books of travel remain essentially the record of a search, a quest. He is the artist-wanderer (or fool-monk) on the road to enlightenment which, as it is rumoured, is being totally awake in the present – no matter where one is. Despite his often finely stated descriptions of place, Brandi makes clear that these books of travel are a continuing inward journey, portraits of the artist as a young man, filled with self-revelation, examination, self-doubt, dreams, and theories.

His verse is not as sure as his prose. There is a confusion as to where the prose ends and the poem begins. His eye and ear seem tuned to the rhythms of prose. Up to 1976 his poems were mainly long-lined Ginsbergian chants of dissatisfaction with the U.S.A. and of journeys taken to Ecuador, Alaska, Mexico, and of his home environment of Los Angeles. Generally the tone of these poems remains similar to that of his prose. It's as if he merely chopped prose into poetic lines to highlight the content of a piece.

Since that time his lines have shortened into compact lyrics, sometimes terse and direct, dealing with love, landscape, domestic realities, social occasions. Though they fail to project the music of poetry, they do demonstrate Brandi's development as a poet and do bear indications of a growing lyric simplicity, and an emerging sureness of style and verbal sensitivity.

—David Meltzer

BRATHWAITE, Edward Kamau. Barbadian. Born in Bridgetown, Barbados, 11 May 1930. Educated at Harrison College, Barbados; Pembroke College, Cambridge (Barbados Scholar), 1950–54, B.A. (honours) in history 1953, Cert.Ed. 1954; University of Sussex, Falmer, 1965–68, D. Phil. 1968. Married Doris Monica Welcome in 1960; one son, Michael Kwesi. Education Officer, Ministry of Education, Ghana, 1955–62; Tutor, University of the West Indies Extra Mural Department, St. Lucia, 1962–63. Lecturer, 1963–76, and since 1976, Reader in History, University of the West Indies, Kingston. Plebiscite Officer in the Trans-Volta Togoland, United Nations, 1956–57. Founding Secretary, 1966, Caribbean Artists Movement. Since 1970, Editor, *Savacou* magazine, Mona. Recipient: Arts Council of Great Britain bursary, 1967; Camden Arts Festival prize, London, 1967; Cholmondeley Award, 1970; Guggenheim Fellowship, 1972; City of Nairobi Fellowship, 1972; Bussa Award, 1973; Casa de las Americas Prize, 1976. Address: Department of History, University of the West Indies, Mona, Kingston 7, Jamaica.

PUBLICATIONS

Verse

The Arrivants: A New World Trilogy. London and New York, Oxford University Press, 1973.
Rights of Passage. London, Oxford University Press, 1967.
Masks. London, Oxford University Press, 1968.
Islands. London, Oxford University Press, 1969.
Penguin Modern Poets 15, with Alan Bold and Edwin Morgan. London, Penguin, 1969.
Panda No. 349. London, Royal Institute for the Blind, 1969.
Days and Nights. Mona, Jamaica, Caldwell Press, 1975.
Other Exiles. London and New York, Oxford University Press, 1975.
Black + Blues. Havana, Casa de las Americas, 1976.
Mother Poem. London, Oxford University Press, 1977.

Recordings: *The Poet Speaks 10*, Argo, 1968; *Rights of Passage*, Argo, 1969; *Masks*, Argo, 1972; *Islands*, Argo, 1973; *The Poetry of Edward Kamau Brathwaite*, Casa de las Americas, 1976.

Plays

Four Plays for Schools (produced Saltpond, Ghana, 1961–62). London, Longman, 1964.
Odale's Choice (produced Saltpond, Ghana, 1962). London, Evans, 1967.

Other

The People Who Came 1–3 (textbooks). London, Longman, 1968–72.
Folk Culture of the Slaves in Jamaica. London, New Beacon, 1970.
The Development of Creole Society in Jamaica 1770–1820. Oxford, Clarendon Press, 1971.
Caribbean Man in Space and Time. Mona, Jamaica, Savacou, 1974.
Contradictory Omens: Cultural Diversity and Integration in the Caribbean. Mona, Jamaica, Savacou, 1974.
Our Ancestral Heritage: A Bibliography of the Roots of Culture in the English-Speaking Caribbean. Kingston, Carifesta, 1976.
Wars of Respect: Nanny, Sam Sharpe, and the Struggle for People's Liberation. Kingston, API, 1977.
Jamaica Poetry: A Checklist, Slavery to the Present. Kingston, Jamaica Library Service, 1979.

Editor, *Iouanaloa: Recent Writing from St. Lucia.* Castries, University of the West Indies Department of Extra-Mural Studies, 1963.

Bibliography: in *Savacou Bibliographical Series 2* (Mona, Jamaica), 1973.

Critical Studies: "The Poetry of Edward Brathwaite" by Jean D'Costa, in *Jamaica Journal* (Kingston), September, 1968; *The Chosen Tongue* by Gerald Moore, London, Longman, 1969; "Brathwaite's Song of Dispossession" by K. E. Senanu, in *Universitas* (Accra), March 1969; "The Poetry of Edward Brathwaite" by Damian Grant, in *Critical Quarterly* (London), Summer 1970; "Dimensions of Song" by Anne Walmsley, in *Bim 51* (Bridgetown, Barbados), July–December 1970; "Three Caribbean Poets" by Maria K. Mootry, in *Pan-Africanist*, ii, 1, 1971; "This Broken Ground" by Mervyn Morris, in *New World Quarterly* (Kingston), v, 3, 1971; "Islands" by Gordon Rohlehr, in *Caribbean Studies* (Rio Piedras, Puerto Rico), January 1971; "Walcott Versus Brathwaite" by Patricia Ismond, in *Caribbean Quarterly 17* (Kingston), September–December 1971; "A Study of Some Ancestral Elements in Brathwaite's Trilogy" by Samuel Asein, in *African Studies Association of the West Indies Bulletin 4* (Mona, Jamaica), December 1971; "Edward Brathwaite y el neoafricanismo antillano" by G. R. Coulthard, in *Cuadernos Americanos* (Mexico City), September–October 1972; "Odomankoma Kyerema se: A Study of *Masks*" by Maureen Warner, in *Caribbean Quarterly* (Kingston), June 1973.

Edward Kamau Brathwaite comments:

the texture and life-style of peoples: seen as dialectic of motion: history as achievement: failure: equilibrium/catastrophe
in this context we might try to understand the new world of the caribbean (the new world and the caribbean): what explosions occurred to create the symbolic fragments of continent: el dorado: lost atlantis: prospero's drowned island etc.

what caused the death of the amerindians: the holocaust of slavery: the birth of tom and caliban
in terms of my weltanschaung: my culture-view: it all began with the fall of the roman empire: this imperial achievement had created an equilibrium of material/spirit: metropole/ province: law/chaos: which made possible a definition of values with the decline and fall of rome: flux appeared: movements of magic into the metropole: custom replaced statute: gargoyle replaced statue
the vikings moved in from the north: the goths, huns, magyars came on from the east; the crescent of islam curved north; african and aztec civilizations began to prophesy disaster
christianity (the holy roman empire) attempted to restore/retain the equilibrium but it was impossible: there were too many alternatives: there was mohamet: there were magi: there was the new science of copernicus, the natural philosophers, the medical school at salerno, there was a choice: galilee or galileo: emperor or pope: priest or politician
and then money became the centre of this shattered universe: market, bourg, bourse: commerce, ship, merchant, bank: middle class, taxes, nations, mercantilism: travel to new lands: control of new markets: the shift of authority outwards: supported by bullet and bible: but no prayer: but purse: not custom anymore, but curse
marco polo overland to china; the portuguese by stepping stone to africa; columbus to san salvador
moctezuma collapsed: chichen itza defeated: geronimo doomed: saskatchewa: mohican: esquimo and ewe whale-worshippers: timbucto, kumasi, ile-ife, benin city, zimbabwe
caribs moving towards malaria and syphilis; cherokees moving towards the horse, the weston rifle, the waggon train; ibo and naga to slave ships; zulus towards the locomotive tank; masai towards the jumbo jet, caliban to new york, paris, london town. so that here in the caribbean we have people without (apparent) root: values of whip, of bomb, of bottle: the culture of materialism, not equilibrium
food, flesh, house, harbour: not stone, demon, wilderness, space: extermination of the arawaks
first 10, then 20
first 20, then 200
first 200 then 200,000 africans: slaves, lukumi, tears
200,000: 300,000: 400,000: a million: tears, tears, lukumi
1 million: 2 million: 3 Million: 4 Million: materialism buildings hotels, plantation houses
10 million: 20 million: lukumi: lukumi: tears
30 million: 40 million: 50 million: we could go on counting: men: money: materialism: tears: tears: lukumi
the spaniards drained the lake of mexico away: the modern city sited in the dust bowl
where are the bison of the prairies: leviathan of the pacific indians
where are those 50 million africans: without tongue, without mother, without god *can you expect us to establish houses here?*
to build a nation here? where
will the old men feed their flocks?
where will we make our markets? (*Masks*, p. 21)
the history of catastrophe requires such a literature to hold a broken mirror up to broken nature.

* * *

Edward Kamau Brathwaite's solid reputation as a major West Indian poet rests largely on the well-known trilogy *Rights of Passage*, *Masks*, and *Islands* – reprinted in one volume as *The Arrivants*. But since the publication of the trilogy two other volumes of poetry have appeared – *Other Exiles* and *Mother Poem* – together with a Spanish translation of selected poems, published in Cuba as *Black + Blues*.

Of these five major collections *Other Exiles* spans a considerable period of Brathwaite's activity as a poet, 25 years to be exact, prior to its actual publication. In these circumstances it is not surprising that it is a rather varied collection, reflecting that diversity of interests and techniques which is characteristic of Brathwaite's work as a whole, but which is often obscured by a prevailing tendency to see him, on the basis of *The Arrivants*, as the monolithic, collective voice of the "Black Diaspora." The collection actually ranges from the exile's intense sense of personal isolation in Europe ("The Day the First Snow Fell") to the satirically detached portrait of the growth of an archetypal young colonial ("Journeys"). In "Conqueror" the personal voice shifts from that of the colonial governor in the Caribbean to the collective consciousness of an emerging Caribbean nationalism, one that has emerged with the West Indian's step from "slave to certain owner."

The collection is also Brathwaite's most uneven work, a reflection, perhaps, of the degree to which it spans his development from inexperienced writer to mature artist. The precisely drawn portrait of the colonial psyche in "Journeys" is therefore far superior to the self-indulgence and flabbiness of language which mar the word pictures of jazz artists in "Blues." Similarly "Conqueror" demonstrates an acute ear for the discriminating and the effectively appropriate use of language, a quality that is lacking in rather sentimental pieces like "At the Death of a Young Poet's Wife" and "Schooner." On the whole *Other Exiles* is significant in that it reflects, at its best, those qualities which have become the hallmarks of Brathwaite's mature poetry – the enormous suppleness of language which facilitates a deceptive ease of transition from one viewpoint to the other ("Conqueror"), the complex sense of personality which allows the poet to develop his persona both as a distinctive individual and as the archetype of a collective experience ("Journeys"), the imaginative handling of folk language as the expression of a distinctive West Indian culture, and, even in the badly flawed "Blues," a crucial interest in the expressive significance of music in the history and culture of Blacks inside and outside the Caribbean.

These are all the qualities that underly the success of the trilogy. The ambiguity of Brathwaite's poetic "I" (as both private individual and collective archetype) is perfectly adapted to the poet's exploration of the Caribbean experience in both its private dimension and in its significance to an inclusive West Indian culture. And in turn that ambiguity pinpoints the role of the poet himself – voicing his vision in personal terms that are analogous to and comparable with those of musicians and other artists. And at the same time the terms of that personal vision symbolize a group experience in which the creative energies of the culture – like the poetic imagination itself – represent and celebrate the vitality that has persisted in spite of slavery and colonialism.

Rights of Passage, the first section of the trilogy, concentrates on Blacks in the Americas, moving from the West Indies to North America and back. In the process the poet discovers affinities between the songs, dances, and language forms through which Blacks have responded to a common history, not only in the New World but also in Africa. The exploration of these connections in *Rights of Passage* amounts to a prelude of sorts to the themes of *Masks* where the poet reverses the historical Middle Passage of slavery by returning from the New World to Africa.

Africa is the source of much that has been explored in *Rights of Passage*, and here in *Masks* the poet expands upon that sense of a common source. The continent is simultaneously the historical root and the contemporary essence of a global Black presence. The sense of affinities is not only geographical but temporal: the New World Black's return to West Africa is therefore described in terms which recall the forcible departure of the visitor's ancestors into New World slavery, and the sights and sounds of pre-colonial Africa are at times indistinguishable from those of both contemporary Africa and the modern Caribbean. The past and the present also co-exist in *Islands* where the poet returns to the contemporary West Indies after symbolically retracing the original voyages of enslavement. Here the images of slavery and colonialism are juxtaposed, for the purposes of dramatic contrast, with symbols of the new West Indian nationalism.

Finally, the self-conscious use of a variety of language forms (West Indian and Black American as well as West African) is fundamental to Brathwaite's themes throughout the trilogy. The very variety of language enforces the poet's vision of West Indian culture as the diverse product of several sources – Africa, Europe, Asia, and the New World itself. In a similar vein the journey themes which dominate the narrative design of the trilogy reinforce a sense of cultural and historical continuities as we move with the poet, through space and time, from one point of the Black diaspora to another. And this impression of continuous movement also dramatizes that cultural and psychic progression which gradually culminates, in the trilogy, in the emergence of a national consciousness that displaces traditional self-hatred and entrenched colonial values.

Mother Poem is actually an intensified and detailed continuation of the themes of *The Arrivants*, for here the progression from a destructive past to a future of creative possibilities is concentrated in Barbados. The mother image that dominates the work (a long continuous poem) is a dual one: it connotes a personal mother and it reflects the perception of Barbados itself as a mother country, as a cultural source of the poet's perception of self and society. This duality intensifies the vision of growth and change: the progression is simultaneously cultural in a broad social sense and deeply personal. And in turn this sustained duality attests to the persistence of one of Brathwaite's most important assets as poet – his ability to integrate the personal and public voices into a complex poetic language which allows each voice to remain distinctive.

—Lloyd W. Brown

BRAUN, Richard Emil. American. Born in Detroit, Michigan, 22 November 1934. Educated at the University of Michigan, Ann Arbor, 1952–59, A.B. 1956, A.M. 1957; University of Texas, Austin, 1960–62, 1968, Ph.D. 1969. Lecturer, 1962–64, Assistant Professor, 1964–69, Associate Professor, 1969–76, and since 1976, Professor of Classics, University of Alberta, Edmonton. Recipient: President's Medal, University of Western Ontario, London, 1965; Bread Loaf Writers Conference Robert Frost Fellowship, 1968; Canada Council bursary, 1969. Agent: Joan Daves, 515 Madison Avenue, New York, New York 10022, U.S.A. Address: Department of Classics, University of Alberta, Edmonton, Alberta T6G 2E5, Canada.

PUBLICATIONS

Verse

Companions to Your Doom. Detroit, New Fresco, 1961.
Children Passing. Austin, University of Texas Press, 1962.
Bad Land. Penland, North Carolina, Jargon, 1971.
The Foreclosure. Urbana, University of Illinois Press, 1972.

Other

Editor, *Satires*, by Juvenal, translated by Jerome Mazzaro. Ann Arbor, University of Michigan Press, 1965.

Translator, *Antigone*, by Sophocles. New York, Oxford University Press, 1973; London, Oxford University Press, 1974.

Translator, *Rhesos*, by Euripides. New York, Oxford University Press, 1978; London, Oxford University Press, 1979.

Bibliography: *Journal of Modern Literature 6* (Philadelphia), no. 4, 1977.

Manuscript Collection: Humanities Research Center, University of Texas, Austin.

Critical Studies: "Putting It Together: The Poetry of Richard Emil Braun" by Jerome Mazzaro in *Modern Poetry Studies 5* (Buffalo), Winter 1974; "Deceptive Symmetry: Classical Echoes in the Poetry of Richard Emil Braun" by Roy Arthur Swanson, in *Modern Poetry Studies 7* (Buffalo), Winter 1976; *The Art of the Real* by Eric Homberger, London, Dent, 1977.

Richard Emil Braun comments:

1) I suggest that a reader go through my books from front to back, since I mean them to be read that way. *Bad Land* has been called a "verse novel." *Children Passing* and *The Foreclosure* are selections (*not* collections) of poems placed in a formal order.

2) My "ethical" aims may, in great part, be learned from Richard Ellmann's introduction to his *Selected Writings of Henri Michaux.* Ellmann says, "With dreams and nightmares to corroborate him, he [Michaux] has seemed to suggest that if any formula can be elicited from experience, it is that the unexpected happens to the unready." He reports a remark of Gide's that Michaux makes us feel "both the strangeness of natural things and the naturalness of strange things." And last: "His *saeva indignatio* ... is usually concealed, and he is less explicit than Swift or Voltaire in describing what man might be.... But his standards are, like theirs, medicinal; good and evil fall into place."

3) My manner of writing is the opposite of Michaux's, however. Michaux rejects construction and tradition. In my view, disorders of experience demand methodical exposition. I think that non-conformity may best operate through parody, or willful misuse, of traditional forms and notions; that is, by tactics of subversion.

I aim at progressively tighter integration of larger and more varied mixtures of subject matter, and at fast-linked schemes of metaphor and image; and aim to eliminate local metaphors and merely illustrative comparisons.

The tradition I parody and abuse is that of naturalism. Thus I employ what seems to be informative or atmospheric description; but my "details" are symbolic emblems or poetic images which work with others, never singly. Discursive, dramatic, and narrative structures are really camouflaged juxtapositions which have metaphoric force, or act as imagistic or symbolic arrangements. Therefore, argumentation may be cogent or illogical, dialogue either true or stilted, and any real-life plot may be interrupted by fantasy, according to the needs of the large scheme or of emotional tensions which pervade it. Even when I approximate fiction, the characters and their stories belong more to the world of dream (and of vaudeville) than to that of the realistic novel.

Finally, the verses themselves. Most are composed in authentic verse-modes, where sounds are counted predictably; but the style often mocks some conventional pattern (a pentameter that is not iambic, or a ballad bared of rhyme). At all times – even (or especially) when the subject matter is humorous, grotesque, or downright horrible – the lyricist's phonemic blendings and the dramatist's rhythmic periods abound.

* * *

Richard Emil Braun writes a massive, highly sculptured poetry, moulded equally by classical forms and philosophy (he is a professor of classics at the University of Alberta) and those of modern prose, and their echoes in the surrealism of Henri Michaux and the classicism of John Crowe Ransom and Robert Frost. The delicate balance thus achieved makes great demands on the reader, who would do well to bear in mind the opening lines of "Against Nature":

To combat
nature, not man,
is what men do which is most concordant
with nature.

In Braun's poetry, the accidental coincidences and anonymous consequences of nature (i.e., everything that is not self, as with Rilke) require the action of a mind watching them, and the structure of a poetic "conscience of identities" to record them.

To engage this combat with nature, Braun turns most frequently to the epic form of narration and episode, told through interior monologue. The narrator's highly specific point of view watches, records, and transforms:

Now I am old you'll look to me for beauty;
you'll want a metric close, a final turn
to ground suspended cadences. I warn
you, though: clear statement isn't clarity.

he says in "Late Promenades," one of his earliest published poems. In this coupled, doubled vision of the poem and the narrator, the events of reality begin to shimmer and dissolve, allowing us to peer dimly through them, to "actively invert to core/that is the real external."

In close conjunction with the multiple points of view, the poems themselves reorganize reality, by means of both their overall shape and their specific detail. *Bad Land* is an epyllion, or epic lyric, seven long, interconnected poems that recount forty years in the lives of John Greer and John Harlan and their wives and families, travelling to and from two cities "in the geometrical center of the United States." The classical balance and formal organization of this sequence has been explicated by Roy Arthur Swanson and Jerome Mazzaro in its rich internal symmetries, and echoes of the *Iliad.* Such links of places and ages are not irrelevant to Braun's poetry: as John Greer meditates, "What God once was, we are now./Whatever God today is, we will one day be."

The formal organization of *Bad Land* resonates in detail throughout Braun's work. Ellie H., Harlan's daughter and Greer's wife, reappears, like a musical theme, in "Listening," the opening poem of *The Foreclosure*. Here, she squats, nearly immobile, unblinking, "listening for the possibilities of sight." The narrator, "to spare you pain," warns her of the distortions of funhouse mirrors, but seeing her,

as I brag
("You'll never see some of yourself,
Louella, as so
fine as reflected in my eyes")

he realizes that her tears "are for me,/for my, my pain."

These recurrences enlarge the breadth of the poems, just as Braun's poetry provides a musical background for his themes and variations. In the ambiguous rhyme scheme of "Late Promenades," the *abba* scheme in the four lines quoted above becomes so elusive later that it can be read as a different, harmonic scheme. In "Listening," the assonances and consonances of "yourself/Louella," "as so," and "fine ... my eyes" hint at the detailed craftsmanship of his work. Throughout his work, Braun presents a unique and deeply considered way of seeing, describing the shapes of essences, until (as in "Ties That Bind") "The arcs join,/mend a circle. We are upon it./The circle, like us, has a memory."

—Walter Bode

BRAUTIGAN, Richard. American. Born in Tacoma, Washington, 30 January 1933. Recipient: National Endowment for the Arts grant, 1968. Address: c/o Delacorte Press, 1 Dag Hammarskjold Plaza, New York, New York 10017, U.S.A.

PUBLICATIONS

Verse

The Return of the Rivers. San Francisco, Inferno Press, 1957.
The Galilee Hitch-Hiker. San Francisco, White Rabbit Press, 1958.
Lay the Marble Tea: Twenty-Four Poems. San Francisco, Carp Press, 1959.
The Octopus Frontier. San Francisco, Carp Press, 1969.
The Pill Versus the Springhill Mine Disaster (Poems 1957–1968). San Francisco, Four Seasons, 1968; London, Cape, 1971.
The San Francisco Weather Report. Goleta, California, Unicorn, 1969.
Rommel Drives On Deep into Egypt. New York, Dell, 1970.
Loading Mercury with a Pitchfork. New York, Simon and Schuster, 1975.
June 30th, June 30th. New York, Delacorte Press, 1978.

Novels

In Watermelon Sugar. San Francisco, Four Seasons, 1964; London, Cape, 1970.
A Confederate General from Big Sur. New York, Grove Press, 1965; London, Cape, 1971.
Trout Fishing in America. San Francisco, Four Seasons, 1967; London, Cape, 1970.
The Abortion: An Historical Romance. New York, Simon and Schuster, 1971; London, Cape, 1973.
The Hawkline Monster: A Gothic Western. New York, Simon and Schuster, 1974; London, Cape, 1975.
Willard and His Bowling Trophy: A Perverse Mystery. New York, Simon and Schuster, 1975; London, Cape, 1976.
Sombrero Fallout: A Japanese Novel. New York, Simon and Schuster, 1976; London, Cape, 1977.
Dreaming of Babylon: A Private Eye Novel 1942. New York, Delacorte Press, 1977; London, Cape, 1978.

Short Stories

Revenge of the Lawn: Stories 1962–1970. New York, Simon and Schuster, 1971; London, Cape, 1972.

* * *

The Pill Versus the Springhill Mine Disaster, his first collection of poems, confirmed for Richard Brautigan in poetry the same place *Trout Fishing in America* had won him in fiction. His work, characterized by spare form and cool reserve, is extremely popular on American college campuses, and he rates with Hesse and Tolkien as an underground literary favorite.

Brautigan's poems, like epitaphs, tell more about what's under them than about the man who carved the words. His work is popular, but not because of the easy sentimentality that distinguishes the poetry of other commercially successful "poets." In comparison to other best-sellers, Brautigan's books are refreshing; his poems have true intelligence, the dash of impeccable inspiration-imagination:

When you take your pill
it's like a mine disaster.
I think of all the people
lost inside of you.

That is the title poem in its entirety. We see the precision with which the mason has cut the words. His imagery is sharp and beautifully rendered, and when connected to something of consequence, especially memorable: he describes himself and a harbor "that does not know/ where your body ends/and my body begins": "Fish swim between our ribs/and sea gulls cry like mirrors/to our blood" ("The Harbor"). That final stanza, with its continued identity-suggestion of the mirrors, and the internal-tactile association of fish in the ribs, completes the suggestion of the poet's unity with his environment. The poem thus becomes a whole realization, a wonderfully understated acid trip.

Brautigan's second collection of poems, *Rommel Drives On Deep into Egypt*, continues in the same vein, but fewer poems strike such moments of brilliance. The title poem is as flashy as "The Pill ...," but significantly, it suggests a lighter view of consequence, reflective of the entire collection:

Rommel is dead.
His army has joined the quicksand legions
of history where battle is always
a metal echo saluting a rusty shadow.
His tanks are gone.
How's your ass?

This sort of vision is enticing because it suggests the ultimate powerlessness of the military. But it is not, I'm afraid, of much value to us of this world which can be powdered instantly by any of many frustrated generals. At times Brautigan's offhandedness becomes annoying, which I believe is ultimately less harmful than the seduction also occurring in *Rommel Drives On*. Four pages of the book are blank, except for titles at the top of the page: the first, on page two, works, but thereafter the joke begins to pale. Here are the four "poems," complete with titles, squeezed into less space than they claim in the book: "A 48-Year-Old-Burglar from San Diego"; "1891–1944"; "8 Millimeter (mm)"; " '88' Poems."

His cleverness, at this point, seems to work against him. Reading *Rommel Drives On*, I feel less and less that he is writing for me, an individual reader; more and more the poems seem aimed at an audience of semi-literate flower children. And I envision them thinking: this stuff's not deep enough.

Another possibility is that Brautigan's immersion in absurdity will not last forever, and that the flash will ignite a greater warmth. One cannot question his imaginative ability, nor the unpretentiousness of those poems consisting of more than a title. At the same time, one wishes that he would come to poetry with more commitment than that of a story teller anxious to dump his less-promising thoughts.

—Geof Hewitt

BREMSER, Ray. American. Born in Jersey City, New Jersey, 22 February 1934. Served in the United States Air Force. Married Bonnie Frazer in 1959; one child. Served prison sentences for armed robbery, parole violation, and bail jumping.

PUBLICATIONS

Verse

Poems of Madness. New York, Paper Book Gallery, 1965.
Angel: The Work of One Night in the Dark, Solitary Confinement, New Jersey State Prison, Trenton. New York, Tompkins Square Press, 1967.
Drive Suite: An Essay on Composition, Materials, Reference, Etc. San Francisco, Nova Broadcast Press, 1968.
Black Is Black Blues. Buffalo, New York, Intrepid Press, 1972.
Blowing Mouth: The Jazz Poems 1958–1970. Cherry Valley, New York, Cherry Valley Editions, 1978.

* * *

The best of Ray Bremser's poetry is a celebration of life as it is lived by some of the denizens of our 20th century cities, a wild, swinging (in the jazz sense) discourse on the ups and downs, and the joys and sorrows, of the streets and apartments and prisons which – in Bremser's case, at least – form such an integral part of the total experience. And it's fitting that the language of the poems is often as chaotic and colourful as the subject-matter, as varied and sometimes shocking as Bremser's own activities.

It is language which is the key factor in the poems, and it can move within a single stanza from a knowing patter redolent of street corners and jazz cellars and prison cells to an articulate imagery which displays a highly-developed awareness of the impact of the pure sound of words. And it is always rhythmic. It would not be absurd to suggest that Bremser's work is best read to a background of fast-moving jazz records.

In suggesting that his main attribute is a penchant for lively language one doesn't wish to play down his knowledge, unpolished and fragmentary though it may often be. He was once described as an "American primitive," and it is an accurate summing-up of his general position. One sees him as wandering through the city, occasionally involved in its quick pleasures, and then again capable of grassroots flashes of insight which highlight the pain and corruption also to be found there.

True, Bremser has certain basic faults. He can be tasteless, and his verbal trickiness can lead to passages which, rhythmic though they are, have little of substance in them. One accepts them in the context of the poems, just as one accepts tawdry advertisements found in parts of a city, but there is nothing to be learned from them. They are, to be fair, a part of the whole scene, but one moves on to more profitable things. Bremser's lapses should be ignored, if possible, and his less-frenetic expressions studied with care. When he succeeds he offers a personal view of life which, despite its limitations, is often more accurate and honest than that proposed by poets with seemingly-superior techniques.

—Jim Burns

BREW, O. H. Kwesi. Ghanaian. Born in Cape Coast, Ghana, in 1928. Educated at schools in Cape Coast, Kumasi, Tamale and Accra; University College of the Gold Coast (now the University of Ghana). Entered the Administrative Service in 1953; Government Agent at Keta for nearly two years, then Assistant Secretary in the Public Service Commission. Now in the Ghana Foreign Service: has been Ambassador for Ghana to England, France, India, Germany, the U.S.S.R., and Mexico. Currently, Ambassador to Senegal. Recipient: British Council Prize. Address: c/o Foreign Office, Accra, Ghana.

PUBLICATIONS

Verse

The Shadows of Laughter. London, Longman, 1968.
Pergamon Poets 2: Poetry from Africa, with others, edited by Howard Sergeant. Oxford, Pergamon Press, 1968.

Play

Screenplay: *The Harvest.*

* * *

Kwesi Brew has a much wider range, both of subject and style, than most of his African contemporaries, and over the years he has developed a voice inherently his own. He has written poems about childbirth ("Gamelli's Arm Has Broken into Buds"), childhood memories, youthful indiscretions, and middle-age reflections ("The Middle of the River"), as well as some of the most tender love poems to come out of Africa ("Flower and Fragrance," "The Two Finds," "The Mesh," etc.). Ghanaian folk song and customs are intricately woven into the tapestry of his poetry and since Brew has exceptional descriptive gifts the Ghanaian landscape and idiom come suddenly to life for non-African readers when he makes use of them, as he frequently does as a background element. If he has written about such specifically traditional subjects as ancestor-worship ("Ancestral Faces") and the passing of the fighting tribes ("Questions of Our Time"), he has not hesitated to deal with a recent event of great significance for his country – the downfall of President Nkrumah – in a poem entitled "A Sandal on the Head." In this fascinating poem, which appeared in *Outposts* shortly after the event it celebrates, Brew maintained a careful distance from his subject by employing an objective correlative appropriate to the situation in the Ghanaian custom of touching the head of a chief with one of his own sandals to declare him "de-stooled." "Ghost Dance," "The Master of the Common Crowd," "The Secrets of the Tribe," "A Plea for Mercy," "The Harvest of Our Life," and many other poems draw strongly upon the African way of life and present the conflict between old and new, between tribal instinct and national aspiration, and between the regional and the universal.

—Howard Sergeant

BREWSTER, Elizabeth (Winifred). Canadian. Born in Chipman, New Brunswick, 26 August 1922. Educated at the University of New Brunswick, Fredericton, B.A. 1946; Radcliffe College, Cambridge, Massachusetts, M.A. 1947; University of Toronto (Pratt Gold Medal and Prize, 1953), B.L.S. 1953; Indiana University, Bloomington, Ph.D. 1962. Cataloguer, Carleton University Library, Ottawa, 1953–57, and Indiana University Library, 1957–58; Member of the English Department, Victoria University, British Columbia, 1960–61; Reference Librarian, Mount Allison University Library, Sackville, New Brunswick, 1961–65; Cataloguer, New Brunswick Legislative Library, Fredericton, 1965–68, and University of Alberta Library, Edmonton, 1968–72; Visiting Assistant Professor of English, University of Alberta, 1970–71. Assistant Professor, 1972–75, and since 1975, Associate Professor of English, University of Saskatchewan, Saskatoon. Recipient: Canada Council award, 1971, 1976, 1978. Address: Department of English, University of Saskatchewan, Saskatoon, Saskatchewan, Canada.

PUBLICATIONS

Verse

East Coast. Toronto, Ryerson Press, 1951.
Lillooet. Toronto, Ryerson Press, 1954.
Roads and Other Poems. Toronto, Ryerson Press, 1957.
Five New Brunswick Poets, with others, edited by Fred Cogswell. Fredericton, New Brunswick, Fiddlehead, 1962.
Passage of Summer: Selected Poems. Toronto, Ryerson Press, 1969.
Sunrise North. Toronto, Clarke Irwin, 1972.
In Search of Eros. Toronto, Clarke Irwin, 1974.
Sometimes I Think of Moving. Ottawa, Oberon Press, 1977.

Novel

The Sisters. Ottawa, Oberon Press, 1974.

Short Stories

It's Easy to Fall on the Ice. Ottawa, Oberon Press, 1977.

Critical Study: "The Poetry of Elizabeth Brewster" by Desmond Pacey, in *Ariel* (Calgary, Alberta), July 1973.

* * *

"I have written poems principally to come to a better understanding of myself, my world, and other people," Elizabeth Brewster has explained. Her work does dramatize (again in her own words) "the struggle to lead a human rational life in a world which is increasingly inhuman and irrational."

This credo applies particularly to *Passage of Summer: Selected Poems*, which brings together the best poems of the New Brunswick-born writer's earlier collections. These poems are sometimes slight and always sentimental, celebrating as they do life in "one of its gentler moods" (as Miss Brewster wrote on one occasion). The poet's early memories are brought to life and given an overall structure in "Lillooet," a poem about a Maritime village written in twenty pages of rhyming couplets. The poem concludes: "No matter where I live, my neighbour still/Will be Miss Ruby Mullins or Peter Hill." It is a moving experience to read "Lillooet," but it is not a particularly memorable work.

The poems of Miss Brewster's more recent book, *Sunrise North*, are less concerned with the past and more focused on the present and the future. They display to advantage a new facet of the poet's personality: a delightful, rather pixie-like, sense of humour. There is a poem called "Munchausen in Alberta" which ends: "That's the only time/I was ever a fire-eater." And in "Gold Man" she concludes: "Next time I am born/I intend to come/from a different country."

The forms of the new poems are all free and flowing, rather in the manner of Raymond Souster. They are Souster-ish, too, in that the lyric spirit takes off imaginatively from an anecdote or an incongruity observed by the poet. The poems are quiet but somewhat fanciful, as if the author has been freed to some extent from her earlier credo ("human *rational* life") and may now explore less rational realms of desire and imagination.

One does not expect Miss Brewster to turn into a Confessional poet, but she has become a truly contemporary poet. She is beginning to write more out of her personality, and it is interesting to note the last line of "Advice to the Fearful Self": "If necessary, scream." One wonders whether or not she will.

—John Robert Colombo

BRINNIN, John Malcolm. American. Born in Halifax, Nova Scotia, Canada, 13 September 1916. Educated at the University of Michigan, Ann Arbor, B.A. 1941; Harvard University, Cambridge, Massachusetts, 1941–42. Associate Editor, Dodd Mead, publishers, New York, 1948–50. Taught at Vassar College, Poughkeepsie, New York, 1942–47, and at the University of Connecticut, Storrs, 1951–62. Director, YM-YWHA Poetry Center, New York, 1949–56. State Department Lecturer and Delegate in Europe in 1954, 1956 and 1961. Since 1961, Professor of English, Boston University. Recipient: Levinson Prize (*Poetry*, Chicago), 1943; Poetry Society of America Gold Medal, 1955; National Institute of Arts and Letters grant, 1968. Address: Duxbury, Massachusetts 02332, U.S.A.

PUBLICATIONS

Verse

The Garden Is Political. New York, Macmillan, 1942.
The Lincoln Lyrics. New York, New Directions, 1942.
No Arch, No Triumph. New York, Knopf, 1945.
The Sorrows of Cold Stone: Poems 1940–1950. New York, Dodd Mead, 1951.
The Selected Poems of John Malcolm Brinnin. Boston, Little Brown, and London, Weidenfeld and Nicolson, 1963.
Skin Diving in the Virgins and Other Poems. New York, Delacorte Press, 1970; London, Macmillan, 1974.

Other

Dylan Thomas in America: An Intimate Journal. Boston, Little Brown, 1955; London, Dent, 1956.
The Third Rose: Gertrude Stein and Her World. Boston, Little Brown, 1959; London, Weidenfeld and Nicolson, 1960.
William Carlos Williams: A Critical Study. Minneapolis, University of Minnesota Press, 1961.
Arthur: The Dolphin Who Didn't See Venice (juvenile). Boston, Little Brown, 1961.
William Carlos Williams. Minneapolis, University of Minnesota Press, 1963.
Dylan. New York, Random House, 1964.
The Sway of the Grand Saloon: A Social History of the North Atlantic. New York, Delacorte Press, 1971.

Editor, with Kimon Friar, *Modern Poetry: American and British.* New York, Appleton Century Crofts, 1951.
Editor, *A Casebook on Dylan Thomas.* New York, Crowell, 1960.
Editor, *Poems*, by Emily Dickinson. New York, Dell, 1960.
Editor, with Bill Read, *The Modern Poets: An American-British Anthology.* New York, McGraw Hill, 1963; revised edition, 1970.

Editor, *Selected Operas and Plays of Gertrude Stein.* Pittsburgh, University of Pittsburgh Press, 1970.

Editor, with Bill Read, *Twentieth Century Poetry, American and British (1900–1970): An American-British Anthology.* New York, McGraw Hill, 1971.

Critical Study: by the author, in *Poets on Poetry*, edited by Howard Nemerov, New York, Basic Books, 1965.

* * *

It is obvious enough that the surface of John Malcolm Brinnin's verse has caught something of the tone of both Dylan Thomas and of Theodore Roethke; but this has tended to mislead readers – especially at that level of discussion which, while it doesn't reach print, makes or mars reputations – from his own qualities. I doubt if he is a poet much actually read except in anthologies; and this is unjust. For, unlike Thomas (who was not an intellectual at all), and in a manner totally different from Roethke's, Brinnin works very hard, and with persistent intelligence, to control his verbally excited surface. This amounts to a method – not to an excess – and it is a method that is instructive. Whether it is entirely successful is another matter; but poetry, at much cost to the individual poet, thrives on failure. Brinnin is consistently interesting and serious: his poetry deserves to be better known than his famous *Dylan Thomas in America*, and this is not the case.

Brinnin is infinitely better educated than Thomas (which does sometimes add an unnecessary dimension of literary rhetoric to his work, but also gives it greater coherence) and less violently self-centred than Roethke. A better clue to the nature of his work, however, is to be found in his admiration of, and fine translation from, the poetry of the gifted Ecuadorian Jorge Carrera Andrade – who was one of the favourite poets of William Carlos Williams, on whom Brinnin has written a book. Andrade, who employed surrealism but was not a surrealist, learned much from the early poetry of Francis Jammes, and one of Brinnin's qualities is the possession of a Jammesian gentleness and melancholy. He thus has two distinct styles (his capacity for pastiche is a third that is avowedly less serious): the Bardic-religious, with overtones of Thomas, of which "The Worm in the Whirling Cross" is the most representative example, and a more pellucid, direct and humorous manner. There is no doubt that the latter comes more naturally to him; but the former is (and understandably) more ambitious. Thus, the language of "The Worm in the Whirling Cross" cannot quite match up to its highly complex content, and even falls back on Hopkins (a surprising fault in a poet already mature):

No further, fathering logos, withering son,
Shall I my sense for want of grace confess,
But vouch this matter of decaying green
That with a shark's-tooth grin
Hinges the rooftree of my dwelling place....

He is more effective, and in fact as profound, when he is less ambitious, as in "Architect, Logician," the little poem about a snail: "Architect, logician, how well the snail/Narrates his tenuous predicament!/... Each hauls his house; the trick's to live in it."

Brinnin's ultimate problem as a poet is the introduction of himself – as any kind of entity other than a literary one – into the work: he seems not to exist in his poems, to evade the quality of his own feeling. This strategy sometimes does, of course, reveal the poetic personality, and one may point to him as a composer of very superior literary artifacts. But poetry requires something more, and here Brinnin (so far) has only shown himself in a few, and too widely dispersed, lines.

—Martin Seymour-Smith

BROCK, Edwin. British. Born in London, 19 October 1927. Educated at state primary and grammar schools. Served in the Royal Navy, 1945–47. Married 1) Patricia Brock in 1959 (marriage dissolved, 1964); 2) Elizabeth Brock in 1964; three children. Editorial Assistant, Stonhill and Gillis, London, 1947–51; Police Constable, Metropolitan Police, London, 1951–59; Advertising Writer, Mather and Crowther, 1959–63, J. Walter Thompson, 1963–64, and Masius Wynne-Williams, 1964, all London; Creative Group Head, S. H. Benson, London, 1964–72. Since 1972, Free-lance Writer, Ogilvy Benson and Mather, London. Since 1960, Poetry Editor, *Ambit* magazine, London. Agent: David Higham Associates Ltd., 5–8 Lower John Street, Golden Square, London W1R 4HA. Address: The Granary, Lower Tharston, Norwich NR15 2YN, England.

PUBLICATIONS

Verse

An Attempt at Exorcism. London, Scorpion Press, 1959.
A Family Affair: Two Sonnet Sequences. London, Scorpion Press, 1960.
With Love from Judas. Lowestoft, Suffolk, Scorpion Press, 1963.
Penguin Modern Poets 8, with Geoffrey Hill and Stevie Smith. London, Penguin, 1966.
Fred's Primer: A Little Girl's Guide to the World Around Her. London, Macmillan, 1969.
A Cold Day at the Zoo. London, Rapp and Whiting, 1970.
Invisibility Is the Art of Survival: Selected Poems. New York, New Directions, 1972.
The Portraits and the Poses. London, Secker and Warburg, and New York, New Directions, 1973.
I Never Saw It Lit. Santa Barbara, California, Capra Press, 1974.
Paroxisms: A Guide to the ISMS. New York, New Directions, 1974.
The Blocked Heart. London, Secker and Warburg, 1975; New York, New Directions, 1976.
Song of the Battery Hen: Selected Poems 1959–1975. London, Secker and Warburg, 1977.
The River and the Train. London, Secker and Warburg, and New York, New Directions, 1979.

Plays

Radio Play: *Night Duty on Eleven Beat*, 1960.

Television Play: *The Little White God*, 1964.

Novel

The Little White God. London, Hutchinson, 1962.

Other

Here. Now. Always (autobiography). London, Secker and Warburg, and New York, New Directions, 1977.

Manuscript Collection: State University of New York, Buffalo.

Critical Studies: *The New Poets* by M. L. Rosenthal, New York, Oxford University Press, 1967; Introduction by Alan Pryce-Jones to *Invisibility Is the Art of Survival*, 1972.

Edwin Brock comments:

One of the more embarrassing chores foisted by publishers upon their writers is that of writing the autobiographical note for the book's jacket; writing an introduction to one's work runs it a very close second. On one such jacket-note I said recently that I have spent the years since 1927 waiting for something to happen, and that poetry is the nearest thing to an activity I have yet found. This statement was not as flip as it sounds: I believe that most activity is an attempt to define oneself in one way or another: for me poetry, and only poetry, has provided this self-defining act. With such an attitude, it was inevitable that my early poetry would be autobiographical; and, indeed, there is still an autobiographical core to most of my writing. But self-examination is an open-ended process: there comes a point at which if one is to "make" or define oneself, one has first to make or define a Maker. It is this which provided the content of most of my recent work. "Consequently I rejoice, having to construct something/Upon which to rejoice," said the maestro, and this seems, to me, to be a role of the artist. If this sounds a self-centred, non-communicating attitude for a writer, I would add that it is only when the process of defining/making/constructing results in something which has an objective "shareable" reality that it becomes exciting – both for the writer and the reader.

So far, critics have traced the following influences in my work: Dylan Thomas, Robert Graves, Philip Larkin, Edmund Blunden, Ted Hughes, Thomas Hardy, and William Blake. To find a common factor in that lot, you have to be ... another critic!

* * *

It might be said that all Edwin Brock's poetry is concerned with the vital question of personal identity, and most of the poems in his first two books, *An Attempt at Exorcism* and *A Family Affair*, are directly autobiographical. In an attempt to define his own identity he writes about his relationships with his grandparents and parents, about growing up with a working-class background in South London, about his brother in a military prison, about his wife and children, and falling in and out of love – but always there is sense of guilt present in greater or less degree. Perhaps he had still to come to terms with the mother symbol:

I have loved
all mothers from time to time: mother
Church, mother Hubbard and poor old
mother Brock, yet I will never understand
why every woman taking my dumb hand
between her own remains so true to type:
many-mouthed, loudly critical, alone,
declaring that the best is always past
and swearing that each mouthful is my last.

He evinces the same preoccupations in *With Love from Judas*, and, despite so many poems in which he denies the reality of God ("An Ordered Sabbath"), he constantly reverts to God: "Dear God, accepting that you cannot win/without my intervention, can't we, as/fathers, settle for a non-aggression pact?" In the title poem, again as a result of conflicts with his children, we have:

I watch tears
run from my daughter's side, showing her
no mercy. Repentance later will decide
but, for this moment, Christ is dead

and in the group of poems on the break-up of his marriage, he simply cannot keep God out of it, though even there he is forcefully insisting that his wife carries her dead god to church "like a decayed foetus" and links it with the death of love. But *With Love from Judas* marks an important stage in Brock's development, not only because he has found a natural and less formal mode of expression, but because, in a poem entitled "Five Ways to Kill a Man" (a poem much-anthologized) he turns outward from his private obsessions to a public theme and shows how admirably he can deal with it:

These are, as I began, cumbersome ways
to kill a man. Simpler, direct, and much more neat
is to see that he is living somewhere in the middle
of the twentieth century, and leave him there.

An even better poem on a subject particularly appropriate to our age is his "Song of the Battery Hen":

You can tell me: if you come by
the North Door, I am in the twelfth pen
on the left-hand side of the third row
from the floor; and in that pen
I am usually the middle one of three.
But even without directions, you'd
discover me. I have the same orange-
red comb, yellow beak and auburn
feathers; but as the door opens and you
hear above the electric fan a kind of
one-word wail, I am the one
who sounds loudest in my head....
God made us all quite differently,
and blessed us with this expensive home.

Although disposed of in earlier books, God is much in evidence in *The Portraits and the Poses* and the poet tells us that he abandoned God for "bicycles, filmstars, Glenn Miller/and my penis", yet paradoxically, in "Five Exposures" admits later that "superstitiously/I touch prayer/to make/a photograph/for God/to love." If in *The Portraits and the Poses* Brock is still trying to find himself and claim an identity in his own inner world, in *The Blocked Heart* he attempts to explore the external world with the same objectives. Since he is an advertising executive (he was a policeman when he first started to write), it is hardly surprising that he turns, with some disquiet, to the adman's sphere of marketing, products, market research and techniques, commodities and consumers: "and inasmuch as you/will climb to heaven/on a neighbour's neck/I will sell you spiked climbing boots."

Brock has undoubtedly been more influenced by American poetry than almost any other British poet, both in the confessional style of writing and in the adoption of very short lines – what Peter Porter has described as "extraordinarily pure, almost abstract language." His latest book, *The River and the Train*, is more assured and more compassionate in the poet's acceptance of his place by the river (East Anglia), in the train on his regular visits to London, in his daily occupations, and more important, in relation to at least one other person:

"My love, it is no longer dialogue but
myself entering home again and again
to make this beginning which is this
becoming which is this continuous end."

Now that Brock seems to have found himself and his own place in the scheme of things, perhaps we can look forward to the major work of which he is capable and for which he has acquired, by a painful process, the understanding, the language and the skill.

—Howard Sergeant

BROMIGE, David (Mansfield). Canadian. Born in London, England, 22 October 1935. Educated at Haberdashers' Aske's School for Boys, London; University of British Columbia, Vancouver, B.A. 1962; University of California, Berkeley (Woodrow Wilson Fellow, 1962–63; Poet Laureate Competition prize, 1964; Phelan Award, 1968), M.A. 1964. Married 1) Ann Livingston in 1957 (divorced, 1961); 2) Joan Peacock in 1961 (divorced, 1970), one son; 3) Sherril Jaffe in 1970. Dairy farm worker, 1950–53; mental hospital attendant, 1954–55; elementary school teacher, in England, 1957–58, and in British Columbia, 1959–62; free-lance reviewer, Canadian Broadcasting Corporation, 1960–62; Instructor in English, University of British Columbia, Summer 1964. Teaching Assistant, 1965–69, and Instructor in English, 1969–70, University of California, Berkeley. Since 1970, Assistant Professor of English, California State College, Sonoma. Editor, *Raven* magazine, 1960–62; Poetry Editor, *Northwest Review*, Eugene, Oregon, 1963–64; Editor, *R. C. Lion*, Berkeley, 1966–67. Recipient: Canadian Broadcasting Corporation prize, 1961; KVOS-TV prize, for play, 1962; Canada Council grant, 1965, 1966, and bursary, 1971; National Endowment for the Arts grant, 1969. Address: 880 First Street, Sebastopol, California 95472, U.S.A.

PUBLICATIONS

Verse

The Gathering. Buffalo, New York, Sunbooks, 1965.
Please, Like Me. Los Angeles, Black Sparrow Press, 1968.
The Ends of the Earth. Los Angeles, Black Sparrow Press, 1968.
The Quivering Roadway. Berkeley, California, Archangel Press, 1969.
In His Image. Berkeley, California, Twybyl Press, 1970.
Threads. Los Angeles, Black Sparrow Press, 1971.
The Fact So of Itself. Los Angeles, Black Sparrow Press, 1971.
They Are Eyes. San Francisco, Panjundrum Press, 1972.
Birds of the West. Toronto, Coach House Press, 1973.
Tight Corners and What's Around Them. Los Angeles, Black Sparrow Press, 1974.
Spells and Blessings. Vancouver, Talonbooks, 1974.
Out of My Hands. Los Angeles, Black Sparrow Press, 1974.
Ten Years in the Making: Selected Poems, Songs, and Stories 1961–1970. Vancouver, New Star, 1974.

Plays

Radio and Television Plays: *Palace of Laments*, 1957; *The Medals*, 1959; *The Cobalt Poet*, 1960; *Save What You Can*, 1961.

Short Stories

Three Stories. Los Angeles, Black Sparrow Press, 1973.

David Bromige comments:

Primary among my associations in the field of poetry is the work of Robert Creeley, Charles Olson, and Robert Duncan – particularly Duncan – and therefore those poets they draw on, and those who share certain terms of the poem with the three named. But I use whatever I can, I can see, wherever.

I would sooner not state what, to my mind, are my major themes, preferring to leave that up to the reader. Again, he will be the best judge of my so-called stylistic devices – though I would draw attention to the note at the end of my book *The Ends of the Earth*. I have no usual verse forms, although no doubt patterns are apparent; certainly I love rime as passionately as I deplore (unless that *is* the concern of the specific poem) a mindless regularity of meter.

I am not interested in poetry as vehicle for ideas but rather as speech arising from dumb desire and passion and arousing further word clusters until constellations emerge I had previously no knowledge were within me. Nor, in a sense, were they: speaking, we enter a Speech, and though we may think we sit each in his aloneness, yet the words which then enter bear news of others; I was not born with that vocabulary, nor were those who, reading my poems, make of them something more than I could ever plan to give. In the instant when I had assumed I had understood certain linguistic and philosophical arguments intended to destroy faith in language – "we must all be talking about a different place," one recent poet put it – I found their flaw. Seekers after "the truth" who, in order to keep clear their minds, would dismiss much that is imagination's creation, choose not to see the prior acts of their own imaginations which have created so singular a notion of the truth.

I believe a poet is one both by birth and nurture; I don't believe that everyone can be a poet; nor can I see why anyone should *want* to be. There are obsessions which weigh less heavily and constantly upon a life. This is no request for gratitude. One is what one is and is used accordingly. However, there are poets who, because they wrote, and published, have enabled me to go on living; that is enough for me.

* * *

David Bromige's work comes out of Black Mountain via the Vancouver nexus of poets around the magazine *Tish*. His dissertation (in progress) is on Duncan and Creeley, but already in his first book, *The Gathering*, he had written some of the best Creeley criticism I know – criticism in the form of poems which elucidate Creeley's techniques by intelligent adaptation. There was more to the book than this, of course – among other things the first workings in an area of subject matter he has continued to mine, personal erotic-psychological experience, and long narrative-based poems which have also continued. Less elusively than many of Creeley's, Bromige's poems too, even when they do subsume a narrative element, always locate their action on the page, not in some anterior "real" world. Always, too, they have more than one kind of interest: feeling, tone, music, logopoeia, and (a particular strength of his) a rapidly eliding muscular syntax which keeps pace with the mind's play rather than imposing too neat an order on a linguistic end-product. The results are invigorating and delightful. I wish I could quote several poems to show his range – from *The Gathering*: "She Rose Up Singing" for its lovely music, "We Could Get a Drink" for its energetic use of an Olson-like open structure, and "The Sign" for its humor; from *The Ends of the Earth*: "A Call" and "Forgets Five" as short and long examples of his convincing dream poems, and "A Kind Numbness" for its tender and traditional imagery (interestingly – and oddly – comparable to Larkin's "At Grass"); and from *Threads*: "For –" with its erotic tribute to the muse-goddess. And many others. Space being limited, here is one short piece to give a glimpse of his wit:

"I can see arguments for both sides"
how impressive this intelligence
where will its weight be placed –
in this scale here
in that scale here ...

—Seamus Cooney

BRONK, William. American. Born in Fort Edward, New York, 17 February 1918. Educated at Dartmouth College, Hanover, New Hampshire, A.B. 1938. Served in the United States Army, 1941–45. Owns and manages a lumber business, Hudson Falls, New York. Address: 57 Pearl Street, Hudson Falls, New York 12839, U.S.A.

PUBLICATIONS

Verse

Light and Dark. Ashland, Massachusetts, Origin Press, 1956.
The World, The Worldless. New York and San Francisco, New Directions – San Francisco Review Press, 1964.
The Empty Hands. New Rochelle, New York, Elizabeth Press, 1969.
That Tantalus. New Rochelle, New York, Elizabeth Press, 1971.
To Praise the Music. New Rochelle, New York, Elizabeth Press, 1972.
Utterances. Providence, Rhode Island, Burning Deck, 1972.
Looking at It. Rushden, Northamptonshire, Sceptre Press, 1973.
Silence and Metaphor. New Rochelle, New York, Elizabeth Press, 1975.
The Stance. Port Townsend, Washington, Graywolf Press, 1975.
My Father Photographed with Friends and Other Pictures. New Rochelle, New York, Elizabeth Press, 1976.
The Meantime. New Rochelle, New York, Elizabeth Press, 1976.
Finding Losses. New Rochelle, New York, Elizabeth Press, 1976.
Twelve Losses Found. Lincoln, Grosseteste Press, 1976.
That Beauty Still. Providence, Rhode Island, Burning Deck, 1978.
The Force of Desire. New Rochelle, New York, Elizabeth Press, 1979.

Other

The New World (essays). New Rochelle, New York, Elizabeth Press, 1974.
A Partial Glossary: Two Essays. New Rochelle, New York, Elizabeth Press, 1974.

Critical Studies: in *Grosseteste Review 5* (Pensnett, Staffordshire), Spring 1972; interview with Robert Bertholf, in *Credences 3* (Kent, Ohio), 1976; article by Felix Stefanile, in *Parnassus 5* (New York), Spring-Summer 1977.

* * *

William Bronk has lived most of his life in Hudson Falls, a small town in upstate New York, where he has owned and operated a lumber yard. His sophisticated, intelligent, pessimistic poems seem to be moments of crisis in an on-going monologue. It doesn't occur to the reader to ask whom he is talking to; it is so obviously himself.

In his work Bronk shares little with his contemporaries. Of a generation for which Pound's dictum, "Go in fear of abstraction," was law, he uses the poem as a register of thought. Of a generation obsessively concerned with poetic form, Bronk sees forms as a practical matter. Staying for the most part with a line which at least suggests pentameter, he writes poems which are tight, neatly crafted, and logical. He is not a formal experimenter or innovator. Although his early work shows clear signs of Wallace Stevens's influence, the voice which emerged in the late 1950's was distinctively his own. In his more recent work, he has pared his most characteristic moves down to the barest essentials. "Spring Storm" is typical of his attempts to get down to the minims of both his style and his themes:

I heard two claps of thunder this afternoon.
I didn't see the lightning. Well, we hear
– sometimes we see, which doesn't say there is
a world or we are. But something is.

Bronk is a transcendentalist, of sorts, but the contact between the lived world and the real one is extremely tenuous. He is a twentieth-century version of Carlyle rather than of Emerson. In a short essay, "Costume as Metaphor," he writes, "Clothing as metaphor not to dress ourselves nor to say what the world is if we knew but to praise that world however it might be." There is much contemporary poetry in which metaphor seems nothing but decoration to sentiments which carry no conviction as mere statement. The crucial difference between Bronk's poetry and the merely decorative is that Bronk is decorative with a vengeance. In "Corals and Shells," for example, a nine-line poem, there are only four concrete nouns. The poem's statement is complete and meaningful without the phrase from which it takes its title. The poem concludes: "Alive, we couldn't endure it; we die to endure,/ endure to die. It kills us. We are glad it does./Corals and shells. Shall we ever cover a land?" The corals and shells are in one sense mere decoration. They are not, in fact, invoked by the organic demands of the poem. In another sense, however, they provide the terms of the dissonance which is most characteristic of Bronk's work. Many of Bronk's poems end with a shudder which results from the sudden recognition that the concrete world is *only* decoration. It has a structure which is vaguely rational, it is a place in which it is possible to create certain fictions, but at every turn the rationality and the fiction collapse, leaving us in precisely the most frightening and desirable place: confronting the unspeakable reality, with the full realization that *no* fiction or logic is supreme.

Bronk is a poet who deserves more attention than he has received. His is a chilling vision, but it is his assumption that we must somehow snatch a life out of the awe-fullest possibilities.

—Don Byrd

BROOKS, Gwendolyn. American. Born in Topeka, Kansas, 17 June 1917. Educated at Wilson Junior College, Chicago, graduated 1936. Married Henry L. Blakely in 1939; two children. Publicity Director, NAACP Youth Council, Chicago, in the 1930's. Taught at Northeastern Illinois State College, Chicago, Columbia College, Chicago, Elmhurst College, Illinois, and University of Wisconsin, Madison; Distinguished Professor of the Arts, City College, City University of New York, 1971. Recipient: Guggenheim Fellowship, 1946, 1947; National Institute of Arts and Letters grant, 1946; Eunice Tietjens Memorial Prize (*Poetry*, Chicago), 1949; Pulitzer Prize, 1950; Anisfield-Wolf Award, 1968; Shelley Memorial Award, 1976. L.H.D.: Columbia College, 1964; D.Litt.: Lake Forest College, Chicago, 1965; Brown University, Providence, Rhode Island, 1974. Poet Laureate of Illinois, 1969. Address: 7428 South Evans Avenue, Chicago, Illinois 60619, U.S.A.

PUBLICATIONS

Verse

A Street in Bronzeville. New York, Harper, 1945.
Annie Allen. New York, Harper, 1949.

Bronzeville Boys and Girls (juvenile). New York, Harper, 1956.
The Bean Eaters (juvenile). New York, Harper, 1960.
Selected Poems. New York, Harper, 1963.
In the Time of Detachment, In the Time of Cold. Springfield, Illinois, Civil War Centennial Commission of Illinois, 1965.
In the Mecca. New York, Harper, 1968.
For Illinois 1968: A Sesquicentennial Poem. Chicago, Illinois Sesquicentennial Commission, 1968.
Riot. Detroit, Broadside Press, 1969.
The Wall. Detroit, Broadside Press, n.d.
Family Pictures. Detroit, Broadside Press, 1970.
Aloneness. Detroit, Broadside Press, 1971.
Aurora. Detroit, Broadside Press, 1972.
Beckonings. Detroit, Broadside Press, 1972.

Novel

Maud Martha. New York, Harper, 1953.

Other

A Portion of That Field, with others. Urbana, University of Illinois Press, 1967.
The World of Gwendolyn Brooks (miscellany). New York, Harper, 1971.
Report from Part One: An Autobiography. Detroit, Broadside Press, 1972.
The Tiger Who Wore White Gloves; or, What You Are You Are (juvenile). Chicago, Third World Press, 1974.

Editor, *A Broadside Treasury.* Detroit, Broadside Press, 1971.
Editor, *Jump Bad: A New Chicago Anthology.* Detroit, Broadside Press, 1971.

* * *

In what has now become a well-known episode, Gwendolyn Brooks describes an auspicious turning point in her career, a turning point that came in 1967 when she attended the Second Black Writers' Conference at Fisk University in Nashville. The Pulitzer-Prize winning poet was stunned and intrigued by the energy and electricity generated by LeRoi Jones (Amiri Baraka) and Ron Milner, among others, on that predominantly black campus. The excitement was at once surprising and stirring and contagious, and Brooks admits that from that moment she entered a "new consciousness." What had occurred in fact is that Brooks discovered a "new" audience: young people full of a new spirit and ready, as she characterized them, to take on the challenges. The sturdy ideas that she earlier held were no longer valid in this "new world" and several years later she would untendentiously remark: "I am trying to weave the coat that I shall wear."

The older coat that Gwendolyn Brooks doffed is made of the material for which she is best known: such vignettes of ghetto people in Chicago as "The Anniad," "The Sundays of Satin-Legs Smith," "The Bean Eaters," or "We Real Cool," for example. They are works of a poet who brings a patrician mind to a plebeian language; a poet always in search for the stirring, unusual coloration of words; the poet in whom Addison Gayle, Jr., has noted what he calls "a tendency towards obscurity and abstraction" and "a child-like fascination for words." But like Emily Dickinson, Brooks was in constant search for fresh sounds and imagery produced by word clusters that startled rather than obscured:

> Let it be stairways, and a splintery box
> Where you have thrown me, scraped me with your kiss,
> Have honed me, have released me after this
> Cavern kindness, smiled away our shocks.

Most of her poems written before 1967, before the Fisk conference, are her "front yard songs," poems whose making reflects the self-consciousness of a poet whose audience seeks lessons in a lyric that ostensibly transcends race. They are solid, highly imaginative poems, and if they suggest comparisons with Wallace Stevens, as several critics have noted, they also recall for this eye Emily Dickinson's ingenuity with language, her ironic ambiguities:

A light and diplomatic bird
Is lenient in my window tree.
A quick dilemma of the leaves
Discloses twist and tact to me.

They recall as well the "grotesques" who habituate the fictional world of Sherwood Anderson's *Winesburg, Ohio*:

True, there is silver under
The veils of the darkness,
But few care to dig in the night
For the possible treasure of stars.

But above all, there is the unmistakable rhythmic shifting – "My hand is stuffed with mode, design, device./But I lack access to my proper stone" – and the haunting incongruities – "Believe that even in my deliberateness I was not deliberate."

The startling Fisk conference, however, may be metaphorically viewed as Brooks's peek at "the back yard" ("Where it's rough and untended and hungry weed grows"), the escape, as George Kent says, from the highly ordered and somewhat devitalized life of her "front yard training." The backyard offers a new vitality, a new consciousness. Gwendolyn Brooks, beyond age 50, strikes up a dialogue in free verse with the subjects of her earlier poetry. The distances narrow and the angles flatten: "we are each other's/harvest:/we are each other's/business:/we are each other's magnitude and bond."

The angles of vision have changed to suit what Brooks describes as "my newish voice": "[It] will not be an imitation of the contemporary young black voice, which I so admire, but an extending adaptation of today's G.B. [sic] voice." So there is something of a near elegiac tone in Brooks's "transcendence" of her poetic past; but it is elegy without regrets, for she has moved from a place of "knowledgeable unknowing" to a place of "Know-now" preachments

I tell you
I love You
and I trust You.
Take my Faith.
Make of my Faith an engine.
Make of my Faith
a Black Star. I am Beckoning.

—Charles L. James

BROUGHTON, James (Richard). American. Born in Modesto, California, 10 November 1913. Educated at Stanford University, California, B.A.; New School for Social Research, New York. Married to Suzanna Broughton (divorced, 1978); two children, Serena and Orion. Worked in the merchant marine, and as a printer, waiter, and ghost-writer; book reviewer, New York *Herald-Tribune*; resident playwright, San Francisco Playhouse, 1958–64; Lecturer, San Francisco State University, 1966–76. Since 1968, Lecturer, San Francisco Art Institute. Since 1948, Director, Farallone Films. Recipient: Phelan Award, 1948; Avon Foundation grant, 1968; Guggenheim Fellowship, 1970, 1973; National Endowment for the Arts grant, 1976; film awards in Edinburgh, 1953, Cannes, 1954, and Oberhausen, 1968, and from *Film Culture Magazine*, 1975. Address: P.O. Box 183, Mill Valley, California 94941, U.S.A.

PUBLICATIONS

Verse

Songs for Certain Children. San Francisco, Adrian Wilson, 1947.
The Playground. San Francisco, Centaur Press, 1949.
The Ballad of Mad Jenny. San Francisco, Centaur Press, 1950.
Musical Chairs: A Songbook for Anxious Children. San Francisco, Centaur Press, 1950.
An Almanac for Amorists. Paris, Olympia Press, 1954; New York, Grove Press, 1955.
True and False Unicorn. New York, Grove Press, 1957.
The Water Circle: A Poem of Celebration. San Francisco, Pterodactyl Press, 1965.
Tidings. San Francisco, Pterodactyl Press, 1967.
Look In Look Out. Eugene, Oregon, Toad Press, 1968.
High Kukus. Highlands, North Carolina, Jargon, 1969.
A Long Undressing: Collected Poems 1949–1969. Highlands, North Carolina, Jargon, 1971.
Going Through Customs. San Francisco, Arion Press, 1976.
Erogeny. San Francisco, ManRoot, 1977.
Odes for Odd Occasions. San Francisco, ManRoot, 1977.
Song of the Godbody. San Francisco, ManRoot, 1978.
Hymns to Hermes. San Francisco, ManRoot, 1979.

Recording: *The Bard and the Harper*, MEA, 1965.

Plays

A Love for Lionel (produced New York, 1944).
Summer Fury (produced Palo Alto, California, 1945). Published in *The Best One-Act Plays of 1945*, edited by Margaret Mayorga, New York, Dodd Mead, 1946.
Burning Questions (produced San Francisco, 1958).
The Last Word. Boston, Baker, 1958.
The Rites of Women (produced San Francisco, 1959).
How Pleasant It Is to Have Money (produced San Francisco, 1964).
Bedlam; or, America the Beautiful Mother (produced Waterford, Connecticut, 1969).

Films: *The Potted Psalm*, 1946; *Mother's Day*, 1948; *Adventures of Jimmy*, 1950; *Four in the Afternoon*, 1951; *Loony Tom the Happy Lover*, 1951; *The Pleasure Garden*, 1953; *The Bed*, 1968; *Nuptiae*, 1969; *The Golden Positions*, 1970; *This Is It*, 1971; *Dreamwood*, 1972; *High Kukus*, 1973; *Testament*, 1974; *The Water Circle*, 1975; *Erogeny*, 1976; *Together*, 1976; *Windowmobile*, 1977; *Song of the Godbody*, 1978; *Hermes Bird*, 1979.

Novel

The Androgyne Journal. Oakland, California, Scrimshaw Press, 1977.

Other

The Right Playmate. London, Hart Davis, and New York, Farrar Straus, 1952; revised edition, San Francisco, Pterodactyl Press, 1964.
Seeing the Light. San Francisco, City Lights, 1977.

Manuscript Collection: Special Collections, Kent State University, Ohio.

Critical Studies: *Visionary Film* by P. Adams Sitney, New York, Oxford University Press, 1974; "James Broughton Issue" of *Film Culture 61* (New York), 1975; "Celebration" by Terry Sheehy, in *Film Quarterly* (Berkeley), Summer 1976; "Quest for the Ecstatic" by Robert Lipman, in *Credences* (Kent, Ohio), March 1978.

James Broughton comments:

Although I have done as much work in theater and cinema forms as I have in pure verse, I consider myself first and foremost a poet, for all my work is motivated by a poet's view and attitude. I have been associated with various San Francisco groups since 1949, but I do not belong to any school of poetry.

The greatest influences upon my poetry: Bach, Blake, Mother Goose, Shakespeare, Stravinsky, Yeats, Joyce, Firbank, Stein, and folk song.

Fellow poets who have personally taught me the most: Auden, Cummings, Robert Duncan, Dylan Thomas.

Poetry is a search for essence, becomes an essence, remains an essential.

The poet has to allow everything to happen to him, or he can make nothing happen. The poet has to let go in order to hold on.

A poet is in the service of something larger than his personal life, his craft, or his published works. Poetry is an act of love, it asks no rewards.

To live poetically is more important than to write good poems.

Poetry may be a criticism of life, as Arnold said, but life triumphs over all criticism.

Poetry is a quest for liberation. But it must be limited in order to be liberated. A poem is a uniqueness defined by its limitations.

A poem is a stone, a wind, a glass of water, a fire on the plain.

Writing the poem is not difficult except that the poet must know and must not know what he is doing. Poets are both more irrational and more conscious than other human beings.

Without joy there is no wonder, and without wonder there is no magic, and without magic there is no poem.

A book of poems is a seed catalogue, a tarot pack, a package of dynamite, a menu for gourmets, a field of stars, a map of the sea floor.

A poem can be about anything if it is not about anything but itself.

Poetry is always both sense and nonsense: the sense in nonsense, and the nonsense of sense.

There is an enormous difference between art and self-expression.

Poetry is a confessional, but it is also an altar. It is a vessel of transformation, it is the host and the communion cup. But it is also the fly on the windowpane.

Poetry is impersonal about the personal, personal about the non-personal, and personably transpersonal.

A poem is, was, and will be. It is of the present only if it is connected to the past and to the future. A contemporary poem needs some fragrance of the ancient, an echo of the primordial, a taste of the everlasting: otherwise it has no parents nor progeny.

A poem can be what it always is when it can become what it already was. "Attain the inevitable!"

Poets are defined by businessmen, as everything is defined by its opposite. And opposites always need each other, else there is no wholeness nor texture.

In school time learn, in love time sing, in wisdom ripen. Allness is ripe.

Do you ever hear it?
Do you know
what your voice is
always singing?
Listen!
It sings
(like everything)
as if no song
were ever sung before like
this
It
is the song you have been singing
all your life.

* * *

James Broughton has always been considered a San Francisco poet, though as he says himself he has ranged over the world both as traveler and as artist. In the years after the second World War – during what was called the San Francisco poetry renaissance – he and, among many others, Kenneth Rexroth and Weldon Kees, were at the center of San Francisco's creative life, and his plays and films were as widely known as his poetry. He approaches life with a sensitive, often outraged humanism that expresses itself in poems that are sometimes angry and hard, dense and difficult, but with a surface simplicity that leads the eye into the poem, even when there is no sureness as to where it's being led. He is brought up against the cruel reality of the modern world time and time again. "Did you ever try embracing a hangman?" he asks in one poem. At best he allows himself a bare, dangerous optimism. You can almost feel him walking a grim, trembling tight rope when he lets himself hope:

I stopped where I stepped, sleep I dared not,
I waited awake – then was banged overside
by shepherd that grew utter beast on a cord.

Often his imagery centers on innocent animals, as often on the death and corruption of the body and the flesh. It is poetry of emotional thrusts and hard questioning, that always comes back again to his anger at the ferocity of the world around him, because it is love that he wants to return to. Wherever he begins, whatever he forces himself, and us, to look at, he returns again and again to the place he has described as "where the birth and the death and the life are one/and the last word I speak is Love."

—Samuel Charters

BROWN, George Mackay. British. Born in Stromness, Orkney, Scotland, 17 October 1921. Educated at Stromness Academy; Newbattle Abbey College; Edinburgh University,

M.A. 1960. Recipient: Arts Council Award, 1966; Society of Authors Travel Award, 1968; Scottish Arts Council Literature Prize, 1969; Katherine Mansfield Menton Short Story Prize, 1971. M.A.: Open University, 1976; LL.D.: University of Dundee, 1977. O.B.E. (Officer, Order of the British Empire), 1974. Address: 3 Mayburn Court, Stromness, Orkney, Scotland.

PUBLICATIONS

Verse

The Storm. Kirkwall, Orkney, Orkney Press, 1954.
Loaves and Fishes. London, Hogarth Press, 1959.
The Year of the Whale. London, Hogarth Press, 1965.
The Five Voyages of Arnor. Falkland, Fife, K. D. Duval, 1966.
Twelve Poems. Belfast, Festival, 1968.
Fishermen with Ploughs: A Poem Cycle. London, Hogarth Press, 1971.
Poems New and Selected. London, Hogarth Press, 1971; New York, Harcourt Brace, 1972.
Lifeboat and Other Poems. Crediton, Devon, Gilbertson, 1971.
Penguin Modern Poets 21, with Iain Crichton Smith and Norman MacCaig. London, Penguin, 1972.
Winterfold. London, Hogarth Press, 1976.
Selected Poems. London, Hogarth Press, 1977.

Plays

Witch (produced Edinburgh, 1969). Included in *A Calendar of Love*, 1967.
A Spell for Green Corn (broadcast, 1967; produced Edinburgh, 1970). London, Hogarth Press, 1970.
Loom of Light (produced Kirkwall, 1972).
The Storm Watchers (produced Edinburgh, 1976).
The Martyrdom of St. Magnus, music by Peter Maxwell Davies, adaptation of the novel *Magnus* by Brown (produced Kirkwall and London, 1977). London, Boosey and Hawkes, 1977.
The Two Fiddlers, music by Peter Maxwell Davies, adaptation of the story by Brown (produced London, 1978). London, Boosey and Hawkes, 1978.

Radio Play: *A Spell for Green Corn*, 1967.

Television Plays: Three stories from *A Time to Keep*, 1969; *Orkney*, 1971; *Miss Barraclough*, 1977; *Four Orkney Plays for Schools*, 1978.

Novels

Greenvoe. London, Hogarth Press, 1972; New York, Harcourt Brace, 1973.
Magnus. London, Hogarth Press, 1973.

Short Stories

A Calendar of Love. London, Hogarth Press, 1967; New York, Harcourt Brace, 1968.
A Time to Keep. London, Hogarth Press, 1969; New York, Harcourt Brace, 1970.
Hawkfall and Other Stories. London, Hogarth Press, 1974.
The Sun's Net and Other Stories. London, Hogarth Press, 1976.
Witch and Other Stories. London, Longman, 1977.

Other

An Orkney Tapestry. London, Gollancz, 1969.
The Two Fiddlers (juvenile). London, Chatto and Windus, 1974.
Letters from Hamnavoe (essays). Edinburgh, Wright, 1975.
Edwin Muir: A Brief Memoir. West Linton, Peeblesshire, Castlelaw Press, 1975.
Pictures in the Cave (juvenile). London, Chatto and Windus, 1977.

Manuscript Collections: Scottish National Library, Edinburgh; Edinburgh University.

Critical Study: *George Mackay Brown* by Alan Bold, Edinburgh, Oliver and Boyd, 1978.

George Mackay Brown comments:

Themes: mainly religious (birth, love, death, resurrection, ceremonies of fishing and agriculture). Verse forms: traditional stanza forms, sonnets, ballads, *vers libre*, prose poems, runes, choruses, etc. Sources and influences: Norse sagas, Catholic rituals and ceremonies, island lore.

* * *

In the preface to *Winterfold*, George Mackay Brown insists that "It should not be obligatory for poets to celebrate, as best they can, only the greyness of contemporary life. Some of the poems in this book are swatches cut from here and there in one weave of time." This seems to me very precisely to suggest both the scope of his achievement and its severe limitations. In his best work he does, indeed, produce a dramatic, historically dense poetry feeding off legend, saga, and myth which remind us of our origins in a pre-sophisticated, homogeneous, rural culture imaginatively expressing itself in religion, rune, and ritual. But there is always the nagging doubt that he is too ready to presume the "greyness" of the contemporary, too little willing to search out what sustenance there is in the life of his own time, and, as a result, capable not exactly of romanticising the past, but of being too resolutely *intended* about it. The actual poetry itself sometimes seems too thin to cope with the obvious richness of the imaginative conception behind it. The schematic push is more recognisable than the realised form.

This "schematic push," in which Brown self-consciously attempts to recreate something of the ancient bardic function of the poet, focuses most intensely on the history and legends of the Orkney islands, the community of fishermen and farmers into which he was born and in which he has chosen to continue to live; and on the tradition of Roman Catholicism, the religion he chose to enter in 1961. He creates, in his work, a composite "mythology" of a place he calls "Hamnavoe" in which man is situated in his most essential, elemental condition – working the difficult, resistant ground and the treacherous sea for his food; praying to the gods for comfort; enacting the processes of generation; succumbing to decay and death.

In the long poem-cycle *Fishermen with Ploughs* this "mythologising" extends from the first settlements on Orkney in the 9th century, through its present depopulation, to an imagined resettlement after a nuclear holocaust. The visionary poetic energy of the section of the poem dealing with this post-nuclear world is intense, and is by far the best thing in the book; it suggests, perhaps, that Brown's imagination is most at home when most unhampered by the need to deal with ordinary social contingency. When it does have to respond to this need, there is often something static and tableau-like about his presentation of historical moments, and something perfunctory about his characterisation, that make for a certain lack of vitality in his verse. For all its obsession with elemental man, situated "between crib and coffin," there is little of that tension and pain which other mythologising and historicising poets such as Geoffrey Hill, Seamus Heaney, and David Jones have found in their material and embodied in their language. To be too certain of the "greyness" of the contemporary is to miss the opportunity for real richness in one's own work, which must, of necessity, be written out of contemporary experience, however much it attempts to disguise the fact.

But at his best Brown is a poet extraordinarily full of reverence and tenderness for animal and human life, and for the processes of ritual and religion. This tenderness is apparent particularly in his many poems about, or addressed to, the Virgin Mary, and in his whole feeling for women, in their creative fecundity and in their possession of natural wisdom unknown to men. This feeling informs these lines from "The Death of Thorkeld," which also suggest the quiet, meditative rhythm at the heart of Mackay Brown's work:

They are glad, all women, at a man's stillness –
In the cradle lying, quiet as apples,
In the trance after love,
Even carried in from boarfang or whalequake:
In wombfold again laid, her utter man.

This is perhaps the kind of poetry Brown describes, in "The Poet," as the poet's "true task": it is the "interrogation of silence."

—Neil Corcoran

BROWN, Sterling (Allen). American. Born in Washington, D.C., 1 May 1901. Educated at public schools in Washington, D.C.; Williams College, Williamstown, Massachusetts, A.B. 1925 (Phi Beta Kappa); Harvard University, Cambridge, Massachusetts, A.M. 1930. Married Daisy Turnbull in 1919. Teacher at Virginia Seminary and College, Lynchburg, 1923–26, Lincoln University, Jefferson City, Missouri, 1926–28, and Fisk University, Nashville, Tennessee, 1929. Since 1929, Professor of English, Howard University, Washington, D.C. Visiting Professor, New York University, New School for Social Research, New York, Sarah Lawrence College, Bronxville, New York, and Vassar College, Poughkeepsie, New York. Literary Editor, *Opportunity* magazine, Washington, D.C., in the 1930's; Editor of *Negro Affairs* for the Federal Writers' Project, 1936–39. Recipient: Guggenheim Fellowship, 1937. Address: 1222 Kearny Street N.E., Washington, D.C. 20017, U.S.A.

PUBLICATIONS

Verse

Southern Road. New York, Harcourt Brace, 1932.
The Last Ride of Wild Bill and Eleven Narrative Poems. Detroit, Broadside Press, 1975.

Recording: *16 Poems*, Folkways, 1973.

Other

Outline for the Study of the Poetry of American Negroes (study guide for James Weldon Johnson's *The Book of American Negro Poetry*). New York, Harcourt Brace, 1931.
The Negro in American Fiction. Washington, D.C., Associates in Negro Folk Education, 1937.

Negro Poetry and Drama. Washington, D.C., Associates in Negro Folk Education, 1937.

James Weldon Johnson, with A. B. Spingarn and Carl Van Vechten. Nashville, Fisk University Department of Publicity, 1941(?).

The Negro in Washington, with *Negro Newcomers in Detroit*, by George Edmund Haynes. New York, Arno Press, 1969.

Editor, with Arthur P. Davis and Ulysses Lee, *The Negro Caravan: Writings by American Negroes.* New York, Dryden Press, 2 vols., 1941.

* * *

Essentially a traditional song-maker and story teller, Sterling Brown has witnessed cross-currents of American literature, and chooses in his poetry to depict blacks and the clash of their roles with those of whites in the variegated society of the American South, particularly in the time caught between two world wars.

His poetry has been collected in anthologies as early as James Weldon Johnson's *The Book of American Negro Poetry* (1922), and, like Johnson himself and Langston Hughes, he set about disrupting the patently false and banal image of the docile American Negro with his charming *patois*, artificially stylized and mimicked by the whites in the minstrel shows still popular in the 1920's and 1930's. Johnson says in his preface of Hughes and Brown that they "*do* use a dialect, but it is not the dialect of the comic minstrel tradition or the sentimental plantation tradition: it is the common, racy, living, authentic speech of the Negro in certain phases of real life."

Brown uses original Afro-American ballads such as "Casey Jones," "John Henry," and "Staggolee" as counterpoint for his modern ones, but the portent of his ironic wit should not be underestimated, for it is actually a tool to shape an ironic, infernal vision of American life as Hades: "The Place was Dixie I took for Hell," says Slim in "Slim in Hell." The American Negro is heralded not as Black Orpheus but as modern tragic hero Mose, a leader of *all* people while futilely attempting to save his own: "A soft song, filled with a misery/Older than Mose will be." In "Sharecropper" he is broken as Christ was broken; his landlord "shot him in the side" to put him out of his misery; he is lost and wild as Odysseus in "Odyssey of a Big Boy"; and found again:

Man wanta live
Man want find himself
Man gotta learn
How to go it alone.

Though minimal in quantity, Brown's poetry is epic in conception; his ballad, blues, and jazz forms are the vehicles for creative insight into themes of American life.

—Carol Lee Saffioti

BROWN, Wayne. Trinidadian. Born in Trinidad, 18 July 1944. Educated at the University of the West Indies, Kingston, Jamaica, 1965–68, B.A. (honours) in English 1968. Married Megan Hopkyn-Rees in 1968. Staff Journalist, 1963–65, Art Critic, 1970–71, *Trinidad Guardian*; Schoolteacher, Jamaica, 1969, Trinidad, 1970–71. Recipient: Jamaican Independence Festival Poetry Prize, 1968; Commonwealth Poetry Prize, 1972. Address: c/o André Deutsch, 105 Great Russell Street, London WC1B 3LJ, England.

PUBLICATIONS

Verse

On the Coast. London, Deutsch, 1972.

Other

Edna Manning: The Private Years 1900–1938. London, Deutsch, 1976.

Editor, with Tom Wharton, *21 Years of Poetry and Audience.* Solihull, Warwickshire, Aquila, 1976.

Critical Studies: "Coming to Terms with Major Issues of Modern West Indies" by Lee Johnson, in *Trinidad Sunday Guardian*, 25 February 1973; "In Cold Rage," in the *Times Literary Supplement* (London), 4 May 1973; "Marine Depths" by John Carey, in *London Magazine*, June 1973; "Below the Surface" by Mervyn Morris, in the *Sunday Gleaner* (Kingston, Jamaica), 16 September 1973.

* * *

Wayne Brown is outstanding amongst West Indian poets, even considered in the context of so good an anthology as Andrew Salkey's *Breaklight*. Brown's *On the Coast* confirms the impression that he is capable of sophisticated and powerful original statements, as in the remarkable "Soul on Ice" with its flow of un-Jamaican imagery and unexplained, but totally communicative, exclamations: an assured, moving projection of personal, local dilemmas into terms that can form the objective correlative for quite other pressures and yet, of course, by that very fact, make real to the reader experiences he may never know more directly. Brown is already a poet who can use his art as a means of, in Solzhenitsyn's words, performing "the miracle of overcoming man's characteristic weakness of learning only by his own experience, so that the experience of others passes him by."

—Anne Cluysenaar

BROWNE, Michael Dennis. American. Born in Walton-on-Thames, Surrey, 28 May 1940; naturalized American citizen, 1978. Educated at St. George's College, Weybridge, Surrey; Hull University, 1958–62, B.A. (honours) in French and Swedish 1962; Oxford University, 1962–63, Cert. Ed. 1963; University of Iowa, Iowa City (Fulbright Scholar, 1965), 1965–67, M.A. in English 1967. Visiting Lecturer in Creative Writing, University of Iowa, 1967–68; Adjunct Assistant Professor, Columbia University, New York, 1968–69; member of the English Department, Bennington College, Vermont, 1969–71. Staff member, since 1971, currently Associate Professor, University of Minnesota, Minneapolis. Recipient: Hallmark Prize, 1967; National Endowment of the Arts grant, 1977, 1978. Address: Department of English, Lind Hall, 207 Church Street S.E., Minneapolis, Minnesota 55455, U.S.A.

PUBLICATIONS

Verse

The Wife of Winter. London, Rapp and Whiting, 1970; revised edition, New York, Scribner, 1970.
Fox. Duluth, Minnesota, Knife River Press, 1974.
Sun Exercises. Loretto, Minnesota, Red Studio Press, 1976.
The Sun Fletcher. Pittsburgh, Carnegie Mellon University Press, 1978.

Plays

How the Stars Were Made (cantata for children), music by David Lord (produced Farnham, Surrey, 1967). London, Chester, 1967.
The Wife of Winter (song cycle), music by David Lord (produced Aldeburgh, Suffolk, 1968). London, Universal, 1968.
The Sea Journey (cantata for children), music by David Lord (produced Farnham, Surrey, 1969). London, Universal, 1969.
Nonsongs, music by David Lord. London, Universal, 1973.
Carol of the Candle, music by Stephen Paulus. N.p., AMSI, 1977.
Carol of the Hill, music by Stephen Paulus. N.p., Hinshaw, 1977.

Michael Dennis Browne comments:

(1974) Since my first book, I have become very interested in material very dangerous and pretentious, and maybe also essential, for a young writer to approach. Writers like Jung (always), Erich Neumann, Joseph Campbell. I am finally reading *The Golden Bough*.... I come to this material by way of my dreams, which have presented me with images of such power I have had to follow them out into contexts much larger than my own individual life. I hope that I will always write poems which are lyrical, vivid, and happy; I want also to find forms, find the music, for the deeper motions I find beginning to move in myself. I hope, as does any poet who plans to grow, to be able to make larger and more visionary discoveries and statements in my work. But I love clarity in poetry and hope to keep my work, in the best sense, *clear*. I am also beginning to write fables, children's stories, where there are few rhetorical comforts, and all that is required of the writer is invention!

Finally, I am excited by the landscapes I am beginning to see. Whether or not I can reach them, I do not know.

(1980) This last year I have been on sabbatical and have been building a house in the north woods of Minnesota. This activity and landscape have given me a great many things to write about and I hope that my new work, to be in my third book, will have at least some of the vividness of this exceptional territory.

* * *

Michael Dennis Browne is a poet of hard, surprising images. The clarity and suddenness of imagery make real the dreams that fill *The Wife of Winter*: the order of reality is successfully inverted and the crazy world of the dream is the real, the normal, and not at all nightmarish.

Browne's voice affirms with a kind of joy – although there is a sardonic edge to the war poems and the Michael Morley sequence; he dreams and sings in face and spite of some nameless, abstract things which underlie the world of the poems:

> And you can forget the poems
> that have run away from you in horror
> like headless birds in the dark
> you have not quite killed,

because in this house and place
there are good fresh ghosts,
there are small & near ones here.

The poems are not preoccupied with traditional "themes" and grand ideas ("The Terrible Christmas"), but focus on the naming of things to create his world. He praises a woman, because "When the king of ideas advanced through the wood/you fed him an image and he went away." Another woman, the speaker of the excellent title sequence, the "Wife of Winter," finds that waking and the morning are

Dark. A new dark. I am dropped
from the high claw of a dream. Fox

retrieves me, wolf waits.
Who is the owl with wings of snow?
And where is my eagle now?
He is not here, my lady they cry.

Browne leaps past prose with recurring, angry eagles, apples, Fox, snow, images which may attain the symbolic in much the same way that Roethke – one of Browne's strongest influences – created symbols. Browne has learned much from Roethke. It is readily apparent in his rhythms and the song-like quality of many of his poems, even in an occasional image, but Browne's own voice remains clear.

—Joseph Wilson

BROWNJOHN, Alan (Charles). British. Born in Catford, London, 28 July 1931. Educated at Brownhill Road School, London; Brockley County School, London; Merton College, Oxford, 1950–53, B.A. 1953, M.A. 1961. Married 1) Shirley Toulson, *q.v.*, in 1960 (divorced, 1969), one son; 2) Sandra Willingham in 1972. Wandsworth Borough Councillor, London, 1963–65; Labour Party Parliamentary Candidate, Richmond, Surrey, 1964. Since 1965, Senior Lecturer in English, Battersea College of Education, now Polytechnic of the South Bank, London. Poetry Critic, *New Statesman*, London, 1968–72. Member of the Arts Council Literature Panel, 1968–72; Chairman of the Greater London Arts Association Literature Panel, 1973–77. Since 1979, Deputy Chairman, Poetry Society. Recipient: Cholmondeley Award, 1979. Address: 2 Belsize Park, London N.W. 3, England.

PUBLICATIONS

Verse

Travellers Alone. Liverpool, Heron Press, 1954.
The Railings. London, Digby Press, 1961.
The Lions' Mouths. London, Macmillan, and Chester Springs, Pennsylvania, Dufour, 1967.
Oswin's Word (libretto for children). London, BBC, 1967.
Woman Reading Aloud. Oxford, Sycamore Press, 1969.
Being a Garoon. Frensham, Surrey, Sceptre Press, 1969.

Sandgrains on a Tray. London, Macmillan, and Chester Springs, Pennsylvania, Dufour, 1969.
Penguin Modern Poets 14, with Michael Hamburger and Charles Tomlinson. London, Penguin, 1969.
A Day by Indirections. Frensham, Surrey, Sceptre Press, 1969.
Brownjohn's Beasts (for children). London, Macmillan, and New York, Scribner, 1970.
Synopsis. Frensham, Surrey, Sceptre Press, 1970.
Frateretto Calling. Frensham, Surrey, Sceptre Press, 1970.
Transformation Scene. London, Poem-of-the-Month Club, 1971.
An Equivalent. Rushden, Northamptonshire, Sceptre Press, 1971.
Warrior's Career. London, Macmillan, 1972.
She Made of It. Rushden, Northamptonshire, Sceptre Press, 1974.
A Song of Good Life. London, Secker and Warburg, 1975.

Other

To Clear the River (novel for children; as John Berrington). London, Heinemann, 1964.
The Little Red Bus Book. London, Inter-Action, 1972.
Philip Larkin. London, Longman, 1975.

Editor, *First I Say This: A Selection of Poems for Reading Aloud.* London, Hutchinson, 1969.
Editor, with Seamus Heaney and Jon Stallworthy, *New Poems 1970–1971.* London, Hutchinson, 1971.
Editor, with Maureen Duffy, *New Poetry 3.* London, Arts Council, 1977.

Manuscript Collection: Manor House Library (Lewisham Public Library), London.

Critical Studies: Review by Peter Porter, in *London Magazine*, October 1969; *The Society of the Poem* by Jonathan Raban, London, Harrap, 1971; by Roger Garfitt, in *British Poetry since 1960*, edited by Michael Schmidt and Grevel Lindop, Oxford, Carcanet Press, 1972.

Alan Brownjohn comments:

In consulting with Peter Digby Smith, the publisher of my first hardback volume of verse, *The Railings*, I evolved for the dust-jacket the simple statement "Poems concerned with love, politics, culture, time."

I think this still defines the themes of my verse, with one or other of these four dominant at different moments. But they all, of course, intersect and interrelate: states of politics or culture affect the values of love; love and time constantly stare at one another, amused, shame-faced or fatalistic; time watches politics rise to honourable humane achievement, or decline into vanity.

I've come to some recent conclusions about the language, tone and temperament of my poetry which critics might confirm; or contradict. Although I am quietly, but very seriously, atheist, socialist and internationalist, it's the English-ness of what I write that strikes me most as I look back at it – the use of language, the attitudes rehearsed, the codes of honour and styles of reticence employed. I don't feel like making apology for this, because I greatly admire certain English puritan values and feel that English rationalism, democracy and humanity would be our best post-imperial contribution to the world at large; the vehicle for transmission of these values being the English language.

Every poet would like to feel he was writing for, communicating to, the world; and if I ever succeed in doing that, in any thing at all, I'd like to feel it was in the above terms, and transmitting the above values. "The world," incidentally, is not the European Economic Community.

* * *

Though the subject matter of Alan Brownjohn's poetry ranges widely, taking in such traditional themes as love and childhood, it is his expression of his concern for social issues that marks his poetry out as specially his own. His poem "Knightsbridge Display Window" ends "Sometime we'll get perhaps/A commonwealth of sense, and not with guns" which is in line with his statement that the poem aims "at a kind of cheerful democratic puritanism." An ideal not without a degree of paradox; but that may well be in the nature of most ideals. In his first collection, *The Railings*, Brownjohn's concern can be seen from the beginning as very much a poet's concern:

Don't look for hunger and disease before
You blame a country. Stop and listen, now,
For the unquestioned currency of talk
Its people handle.

This is a standpoint from which a society is to be judged by the quality of life it engenders. In *The Lions' Mouths* this concern is pursued, and we find that while it is compassionate it is, nevertheless, allied to an uncompromising critical stance. "Why shouldn't they do as they like?" asks the "Fool-libertarian voice" in the poem "A Hairdressers." "No," the poet replies, "I can't wish I were as liberal as that." Here is the puritan speaking, a voice which persists, and which we find in his more recent collection, *A Song of Good Life*, where he writes sadly, even harshly, of modern development and New Towns "In Hertfordshire":

It has fangs of reinforced concrete and triple glazing,
Its eyes are huge stacks of strip-light in Industrial Areas
Refining precisions to blur life, imprinting so tidily on
Clicking cards the specific patterns of your death.

Yet the human spirit is more robust than that, as in the same collection his group of poems on the wiles and adventures of the Old Fox would suggest.

In all Brownjohn's poetry there is the same sharp mind probing and enquiring. The poem "For a Journey" explores the significance of what at first seems an unlikely subject, the naming of country fields – "Topfield," "Third field," and the like – to conclude: "Who knows what could become of you where/No one has understood the place with names?" This need for Brownjohn to analyse is reflected in the language he uses. On occasions it can become as complex as the line of thought he pursues.

It is with metaphor
We can assuage, abolish and
Create. I will apologise
With metaphors

he writes in "Apology for Blasphemy," and the tendency is for such poetry to become abstract in both content and form. Yet in *Sandgrains on a Tray* we find him successfully combating this, and developing a clarity and directness which give added strength and purpose to his work, as does his deliberate avoidance of decoration or embellishment. The words are made to work in their own right, consistent again with his cheerful puritanism.

In his collection *Warrior's Career*, poems such as "Ode to Centre Point" and "A Politician" see him making his points much more directly, and a new, more personal element is to be observed emerging in the section of love poems. Meanwhile the thread of social concern continues in the group of poems in *A Song of Good Life* which presents a picture of life in the 1970's through their observation of modern habits and fashions. In this Brownjohn is very much a poet of his time and one of our best social poets. He is also a continually developing one.

—John Cotton

BROWNSTEIN, Michael. American. Born in Philadelphia, Pennsylvania, 25 August 1943. Educated at Antioch College, Yellow Springs, Ohio; New School for Social Research, New York. Taught creative writing, University of Colorado and Naropa Institute, Boulder, 1976–77. Recipient: Poets' Foundation Grant, 1966; Fulbright Scholarship, 1967; Frank O'Hara Award, 1969. Address: 33 St. Mark's Place, New York, New York 10003, U.S.A.

PUBLICATIONS

Verse

Behind the Wheel. New York, "C" Press, 1967.
Highway to the Sky. New York, Columbia University Press, 1969.
Three American Tantrums. New York, Angel Hair, 1970.
30 Pictures. Stinson Beach, California, Grape Press, 1972.
Strange Days Ahead. Calais, Vermont, Z Press, 1975.

Novel

Country Cousins. New York, Braziller, 1974.

Short Stories

Brainstorms: Stories. Indianapolis, Bobbs Merrill, 1971.

* * *

Highway to the Sky, Michael Brownstein's first collection, is cryptic, elliptical, ironic, witty, occasionally symbolic or surreal; it's also inbred and a bit smartassed. "Genius," he says, is "to eat and mumble in peace." His poems about poetry are not the usual jejune praise:

Life is beautiful.   However

The only truly human, American expressions
    of its staggering rich moments
  (two baby bulldogs in open window, 3:17 a.m.)
Aren't really forms of expression like language, but

The only truly human, American expressions
    of its staggering rich moments
  (two baby tomatoes in open window, 3:17 a.m.)
Aren't really forms of expression like language, but

Parallels manifesting themselves right alongside
Those moments, like music.

Brownstein is his most brilliant when he concentrates on what something represents or, that horrid word, "symbolizes." "The method must be purest meat, and no symbolic dressing," Ginsberg says, speaking for many of his generation. In his usual weird tone, Brownstein deadpans agreement with this Beat and Black Mountain formula:

A naturalist witnessing the scene begins to weep
for joy. A small child of either sex joins him:
it's a tableau, simple and real.
No "symbols," no straining after a meaning
that wasn't there in the beginning, obvious to all,
before the first walrus appeared ...

His assent is mitigated by that last line and the gratuitously bizarre and generalized "small child of either sex." Brownstein's second book, in fact, consists of prose poems of mythic, symbolic and even (cf. Empson) ambiguous import. "The Overcoat," for instance, contrasts the political and sexual implications of a preference for overcoats over t-shirts. In "Who Knows Where the Time Goes" a mythy figure of magic asks the persona of the poem more and more curious questions till finally the persona wearily indicates he's merely a Bowery bum giving a good rap for his dime. The stone outlaw seems tougher and more impassive than the other outlaws in his gang till it transpires, finally, that he is a literal statue. Brownstein's recent work in fiction suggests that though he struck a tone in poetry, for its blossoming he needs the larger forms of prose.

—Michael André

BRUCE, George. British. Born in Fraserburgh, Aberdeenshire, Scotland, 10 March 1909. Educated at Fraserburgh Academy; Aberdeen University, M.A. (honours) in English. Married Elizabeth Duncan in 1935; one son, David, and one daughter, Marjorie. Taught English and history, Dundee High School, 1933–46. General Programmes Producer, Aberdeen, 1946–56, and since 1956, Documentary Talks Producer, BBC, Edinburgh. Fellow in Creative Writing, Glasgow University, 1971–73; Visiting Professor, Union Theological Seminary, Richmond, Virginia, 1974; Writer in Residence, Prescott College, Arizona, 1974; Visiting Professor of English, College of Wooster, Ohio, 1976–77. Recipient: Scottish Arts Council award, 1968, 1971. Litt.D.: College of Wooster, 1977. Address: 25 Warriston Crescent, Edinburgh 3, Scotland.

PUBLICATIONS

Verse

Sea Talk. Glasgow, Maclellan, 1944.
Selected Poems. Edinburgh, Oliver and Boyd, 1947.
Landscapes and Figures: A Selection of Poems. Preston, Lancashire, Akros, 1967.
The Collected Poems of George Bruce. Edinburgh, Edinburgh University Press, 1970.

Plays

To Scotland, With Rhubarb (produced Edinburgh, 1965).

Radio Play: *Tonight Mrs. Morrison*, music by David Dorward, 1968.

Other

Scottish Sculpture, with T. S. Halliday. Dundee, Findlay, 1946.
Neil M. Gunn. Edinburgh, National Library of Scotland, 1971.
Anne Redpath. Edinburgh, Edinburgh University Press, 1974.
The City of Edinburgh: A Historical Guide. London, Pitkin Pictorials, 1974; revised edition, 1977.
Festival in the North: The Story of the Edinburgh Festival. London, Hale, 1975.
Some Practical Good: The Cockburn Association 1785–1975. Edinburgh, Cockburn Association, 1975.
William Soutar: The Man and the Poet. Edinburgh, National Library of Scotland, 1978.

Editor, *The Exiled Heart: Poems 1941–1956*, by Maurice Lindsay. London, Hale, 1957.
Editor, with Edwin Morgan and Maurice Lindsay, *Scottish Poetry One* to *Six*. Edinburgh, Edinburgh University Press, 1966–72.
Editor, *The Scottish Literary Revival: An Anthology of Twentieth Century Poetry*. London, Collier Macmillan, and New York, Macmillan, 1968.

Manuscript Collections: State University of New York, Buffalo; National Library of Scotland, Edinburgh.

Critical Studies: *The Scottish Tradition in Literature* by Kurt Wittig, Edinburgh, Oliver and Boyd, 1958; *The Scots Literary Tradition* by John Spiers, London, Faber, 1962; "Myth-Maker: The Poetry of George Bruce" by Alexander Scott, in *Akros* (Preston, Lancashire), December 1975.

George Bruce comments:

(1970) I belong, I suppose, to the current Scottish Literary Revival, though I believe I owe nothing in style to any of my Scottish contemporaries. I have learned the craft of verse especially from Ezra Pound.

From about 1941 to 1953 the main subject-matter was life in a sea town and the environment of that life. The approach was definitive rather than descriptive: I was concerned to establish the extraordinary nature of the case, that people continued to believe in life and to make a particular thing of it in circumstances that might have warranted despair; but then should one not despair in any case of human life which is, *ipso facto*, precariously placed between light and dark.

I came to this subject when the war seemed to confirm by its explicit outrage on human dignity the evidence of Eliot's *The Waste Land*. In these circumstances I found myself – for I did not seek to do so – making a statement in verse about the establishing of life on a minimal basis. I noted the fishermen whose lives were almost continuously threatened by the life giving and killing element from which they drew their livelihood. To their adaptation to, and acceptance of, their situation they added an apparently unreasonable belief in a personal God. I could not identify myself with their attitudes, nor with them. But in looking with particularity at them the sense of a separate existence came home at a time when the word "object" was almost meaningless to me. I had found an "objective correlative."

I proceeded to apply a craft of verse that I had learned from Ezra Pound, particularly from *Mauberley*, with, as far as I could, clinical exactness. Just as much of my country was mere rock so my language should be, so the rhythms short and vigorous. When I applied my ear to what I had written I found the tone and accent and articulation of the words and sentences related more closely to the manner of speech of the community in which I had been brought up (and to some extent continued about me, for I believe there is a tendency in educated Scottish speech, in English, to certain general characteristics) than to the implied accent of Pound or to the speech of Southern England. A strong emphasis on consonants and a high articulation is characteristic. In my more successful poems of this period I think these elements are present. This was a point of beginning. All my poems were in English.

Then I became increasingly interested in the idea of order. That aspect of nature I knew best, and the irregular characteristics of growth itself threatened order. My poem about St. Andrews, "A Gateway to the Sea," is written as an exposition on the order of a mediaeval town which embodies theological concepts of order in its structure, an order that is threatened by men and by the ravages of the sea. This interest is subordinated in several poems to a rejoicing in the irregularity and variety of creation. It is easy enough to accept that variety as one looks back in history; it is more difficult to accept when the force of life expresses itself in what appears to be brashness and vulgarity. This is the main concern of my poem *Landscapes and Figures*.

(1980) In the 1970's there have been two new developments in my poetry. The one is the use of contemporary events, social and political, as material, on which I have made generally satiric comment; the other is the writing of poetry in Scots, which medium I have also applied to the current social scene. This had led Alexander Scott to comment on my having "an uproarious sense of sardonic humour."

* * *

The term "regional poet" can either mean a minor writer who celebrates his locality with a certain amount of enthusiasm and charm, or a writer who uses the sights and smells and sounds of his native district as imaginative material for containing problems and predicaments that are humanity's. It is in this second, good sense, that George Bruce is the poet of the North East of Scotland, with its cold farm-lands, its rugged cliffscapes, and its dour and tenacious fishermen.

That tenacity, that necessary continuing belief in life at its basic food-winning level during the early years of the second World War, inspired some of the poems in Bruce's first book, *Sea Talk*. His technique he learned to some extent from Eliot, though principally from Pound, especially *Mauberley*. But the tone and timbre of the application of that technique are very much his own, relating to those durable qualities among which he had been brought up. "Just as much of my country was mere rock," the poet has explained, "so my language should be, so the rhythms short and vigorous." Comparing the graciousness which allowed Gothic spires to flourish in wind-swept Balbec and Finistère with the granite knuckle-thrust where the Buchan fisherman has his being, Bruce exclaims:

> To defend life thus and so to grace it
> What art! but you, my friend, know nothing of this,
> Merely the fog, more often the east wind
> That scours the sand from the shore,
> Bequeathing it to the sheep pasture,
> Whipping the dust from fields,
> Disclosing the stone ribs of earth –
> The frame that for ever presses back the roots of corn
> In the shallow soil. This wind,
> Driving over your roof,
> Twists the sycamore's branches
> Till its dwarf fingers shoot west,
> Outspread on bare country, lying wide.
> Erect against the element
> House and kirk and your flint face.

Just as the relentless action of wind and waves has shaped his coastline, so past generations have moulded his North East character:

> This which I write now
> Was written years ago
> Before my birth
> In the features of my father.
>
> It was stamped
> In the rock formations
> West of my hometown.
> Not I write
>
> But perhaps, William Bruce,
> Cooper....

The poet's words become "the paint/Smeared upon/The inarticulate."

Against this backcloth of the elements, Bruce sets the hero, determinedly going about his business, doing what needs to be done: "The short man waves his hand,/Half turns, and then makes off./He is going to the country...."

Such experiences, as Kurt Wittig has remarked, spring from specific moments of the poet's personal life, and are "explained in very personal symbols (such as the curtain half way up the stairs) and seen in flashes of very personal and momentary observation."

Perhaps because of the role of impresario to other poets which Bruce's post as a BBC Producer has imposed on him, he has published all too little. Twenty-three years lie between *Sea Talk* and *Landscapes and Figures*. By the second collection, the range and power of the verse have deepened. There is still the hero, "a man of inconsequent build," his "Odyssey the trains between/Two ends of telephone...." He is still

> ... the small man
> With broad pale brow lined deep as if the pen
> Held tight in hand had pressed its ink
> In strokes.

There are also clear, objective recollections of the details of childhood, as in the much-praised "Tom." In one part of this sequence, "Tom on the Beach," the poet asks himself:

> How many years since with sure heart
> And prophesy of success
> Warmed in it
> Did I look with delight on the little fish,
>
> Start with happiness, the warm sun on me?
> Now the waters spread horizonwards,
> Great skies meet them,
> I brood upon uncompleted tasks.

Now Bruce occasionally uses Scots, though usually only for special colloquial effects in the counterpart of his verse's rugged music. Henry Moore's sculpture, the impact of distant wars through the television screen and the experience of an Italian sojourn have given him new thematic material. When eventually a fuller collection of Bruce's work is published, though there will undoubtedly be surprises and fresh riches discovered, I doubt if anything will surpass "A Gateway to the Sea," his elegy for the changelessness of change. The "gateway" leads to ruined St. Andrew's Cathedral, where once there was living gossip:

... Caesar's politics.
And he who was drunk last night;
Rings, diamants, snuff boxes, warships,
Also the less worthy garments of worthy men!

Here once:

The European sun knew these streets
O Jesu parvule; Christus Victus: Christus Victor.
The bells singing from their towers, the waters
Whispering to the waters, the air tolling
To the air – the faith, the faith, the faith.

But "All that was long ago. The lights/Are out, the town is sunk in sleep...."
And yet:

Under the touch the guardian stone remains
Holding memory reproving desire, securing hope
In the stop of water, in the lull of night.
Before dawn kindles a new day.

I know of no other "regional" poet whose treatment of the oldest and most Universal theme of all is as powerfully affecting as Bruce's in this poem. The voice is Scottish, but the words are warmed into poetry by a European mind.

—Maurice Lindsay

BRUTUS, Dennis (Vincent). British (South African). Born in Salisbury, Rhodesia, 28 November 1924. Educated in South Africa at Paterson High School; Fort Hare University, Alice, B.A. in English 1947; Witwatersrand University, Johannesburg, 1963–64. Married May Jaggers in 1950; eight children. High school teacher and journalist for 14 years. Served 18 months in Robben Island Prison, for opposition to apartheid, 1964–65. Left South Africa in 1966. Director, Campaign for Release of South African Political Prisoners, London, 1966–71; Staff Member, International Defence and Aid Fund, London, 1966–71. Visiting Professor, University of Denver, 1970. Since 1971, Professor of English, Northwestern University, Evanston, Illinois. Visiting Professor, University of Texas, Austin, 1974–75. Since 1959, Secretary, South African Sports Association; since 1963, President, South African Non-Racial Olympic Committee; since 1972, Chairman, International Campaign Against Racism in Sport; Council Member, Emergency World Government. Director, Troubadour Press; Member of the Editorial Board, *Africa Today*. Recipient: Mbari Prize, 1962. Address: 18 Hilton Avenue, London N.12, England; or, 624 Clark Street, Evanston, Illinois 60201, U.S.A.

PUBLICATIONS

Verse

Sirens, Knuckles, Boots. Ibadan, Mbari, 1963; Evanston, Illinois, Northwestern University Press, 1964.

Letters to Martha and Other Poems from a South African Prison. London, Heinemann, 1968.
The Denver Poems. Denver, University of Denver, 1969.
Poems from Algiers. Austin, University of Texas, 1970.
Thoughts Abroad (as John Bruin). Del Valle, Texas, Troubadour Press, 1971.
A Simple Lust: Selected Poems. London, Heinemann, and New York, Hill and Wang, 1973.
China Poems. Austin, University of Texas, 1975.
Strains, edited by Wayne Kamin and Chip Dameron. Austin, Texas, Troubadour Press, 1975.
Stubborn Hope. London, Heinemann, and Washington, D.C., Three Continents Press, 1977.

Manuscript Collection: Northwestern University Library, Evanston, Illinois.

Critical Studies: *Introduction to African Literature* by Ulli Beier, Evanston, Illinois, Northwestern University Press, 1967; *Who's Who in African Literature* by Janheinz Jahn, Tübingen, Germany, Horst Erdman Verlag, 1972; *African Authors* by Herdeck, Washington, D.C., Black Orpheus Press, 1973; *The Black Mind* by O. R. Dathorne, Minneapolis, University of Minnesota Press, 1974.

Dennis Brutus comments:

A lyrical poet: "protest" elements are only incidental, as features of the South African scene obtrude. Favourite poets: John Donne, Browning, Hopkins.

* * *

It is hardly surprising that the earliest poetry of Dennis Brutus should be marked by expressions of anger, bitterness and frustration, and that the images employed in his poems should be taken direct from his South African environment:

investigating searchlights rake
our naked unprotected contours ...
under jackboots our bones and spirits crunch.
police cars cockroach through the tunnelled streets ...

Brutus has, in fact, been criticized on this score by some West African critics, but surely it is understandable that a young poet in his situation, living in a police state and constantly harassed by the authorities for his anti-apartheid activities, should feel the need to express himself in such direct terms, rather than through the medium of a polite literary language acceptable to those who have not shared his experience. To know his poetry is to know the man. As he said in a speech at a conference held in Stockholm in 1967, "I am not concerned with how a man expresses his involvement: I am desperately concerned that he should."

Brutus was born of South African parents in Rhodesia. After graduating from Fort Hare University College he took up a teaching post at Port Elizabeth; but, as President of the South African Non-Racial Olympic Committee, his protests against racialism in sport and his campaign for the exclusion of South Africa from the Olympic Games soon brought him into conflict with the authorities and he was barred from teaching. He was arrested in 1963 and escaped while still on bail, and though he possessed a Rhodesian passport, the Portuguese Secret Police in Mozambique handed him over to the South African Security Police. He was shot down while attempting to escape again and on recovery was sentenced to eighteen months hard labour at the notorious Robben Island. His first book, *Sirens, Knuckles, Boots*, was published by Mbari while he was in prison. He wrote the poems of his second book,

Letters to Martha, after his release from prison but during the period in which he was not allowed to write anything of a publishable nature, so that his poems had to be devised as "letters" to his sister-in-law. He would be a curious poet indeed if this experience was not reflected in his work.

Nevertheless, if Dennis Brutus has expressed his rage at times his craftsmanship has been apparent from the beginning. In "Erosion: Transkei" he uses the subject – the erosion of the land – as an objective correlative and describes his own feelings, so that the poem has meanings at more than one level. Examples of his method of interweaving image and idea can be found in poem after poem, and he frequently deploys language in a new and significant way. Take, for instance, the poem "This Sun on This Rubble":

> – sun-stripped perhaps, our bones may later sing
> or spell out some malignant nemesis
> Sharpevilled to spearpoints for revenging
> but now our pride-dumped mouths are wide
> in wordless supplication
> – are grateful for the least relief from pain
> – like this sun on this debris after rain.

The coinage here, "Sharpevilled," is more than a clever gimmick, and in its context, "Sharpevilled to spearpoints for revenging" is extremely apt, adding tremendous power to what is being said. In other poems he writes of "Saracened arrest," "quixoting," etc. But there is always anger beneath the surface of the poem, finding its way even into the most tender of his love poems:

> we found a poignant edge to tenderness,
>
> and, sharper than our strain, the passion
> against our land's disfigurement and tension;
> hate gouged out deeper levels for our passion –
>
> a common hate enriched our love and us.

One third of the poems in *Letters to Martha* are directly concerned with his prison experience and these poems tend, on that account, to be somewhat restricted in range and tone. If there is "the sense of challenge of confrontation, vague heroism mixed with self-pity," there is more often fear, humiliation, and the sense of vulnerability. But in the rest of the volume there is a wide variety of mood and subject. "The Mob" describes a crowd of whites who attacked those protesting against the Sabotage Bill. There are landscapes and seascapes, poems written on a train journey and in flight over the Atlantic. "Blood River Day" deals ironically with the annual celebration of the Battle of Blood River (1838) in which the Boers commemorate their triumph over the black Africans in their trek northwards from British control:

> Each year on this day
> they drum the earth with their boots
> and growl incantations
> to evoke the smell of blood
> for which they hungrily sniff the air ...

Finally, there is the long "Our Aims Our Dreams Our Destinations," in which the poet agonises over the human condition and questions his own religious faith:

Can we find hope
in thinking that our pain
refines us of our evil dross,
prepares us for a splendid destiny?

or in a fellow-link
a shared enterprise
the splendid Gethsemane
which must purchase redemption for the world
and by our agony
pay debts to buy
the pardon for the world....

—Howard Sergeant

BUCHAN, Tom (Thomas Buchanan Buchan). Scottish. Born in Glasgow, 19 June 1931. Educated at Jordanhill College School; Balfron High School; Aberdeen Grammar School; University of Glasgow, 1947–53, M.A. (honours) in English 1953. Married Emma Chapman in 1962; three children. Teacher, Denny High School, Stirlingshire, 1953–56; Lecturer in English, University of Madras, India, 1957–58; Warden, Community House, Glasgow, 1958–59; Teacher, Irvine Royal Academy, 1963–65; Senior Lecturer in English and Drama, Clydebank Technical College, Glasgow, 1967–70. Since 1970, Free-lance Writer. Partner, Poni Press, Offshore Theatre Company, and Arts Projects, all in Edinburgh. Recipient: Scottish Arts Council award, 1969, and bursary, 1971. Address: 10 Pittville Street, Edinburgh EH15 2BY, Scotland.

PUBLICATIONS

Verse

Ikons. Madras, Tambaram Press, 1958.
Dolphins at Cochin. London, Barrie and Rockliff-Cresset Press, and New York, Hill and Wang, 1969.
Exorcism. Glasgow, Midnight Press, 1972.
Poems 1969–1972. Edinburgh, Poni Press, 1972.

Plays

Tell Charlie Thanks for the Truss (produced Edinburgh, 1972).
The Great Northern Welly Boot Show, lyrics by Billy Connolly (produced Glasgow and London, 1972).
Knox and Mary (produced Edinburgh, 1972).

Novel

Makes You Feel Great. Edinburgh, Poni Press, 1971.

Other

Editor, with Nora Smith and John Forsyth, *Genie: Short Stories*. Edinburgh, Edinburgh University Press, 1974.

Tom Buchan comments:

Considered chronologically, my poetry shows a steady progression from traditional forms, through traditional forms used in unconventional ways, to open verse. In poetry, I am rapidly approaching what seems to be a formal impasse, and my writing in this medium is becoming increasingly fragmented. I hope that beyond this impasse lie new forms appropriate to our times.

Partly because of this, I am developing my work as writer/director/actor in the theatre, and am presently engaged also in writing fiction and multi-media entertainments.

My early work was political and polemical. My most recent work is difficult to categorize – "spiritual," "religious," "metaphysical" or "mystical" would be too precious a description – but I am pressing on with my own inner development and at the same time trying to make a combination which anyone could enjoy.

* * *

Tom Buchan's poetry shows a distinctive and consistent development from his first collection, *Dolphins at Cochin*, to his most recent *Poems 1969–1972*. His distinction, in the first instance, is in his making a true aesthetic response to machine imagery of the twentieth century. He in no way indulges this response, but it provides the cutting edge to his satire. Thus he depicts "The White Hunter" in *Dolphins at Cochin*:

The white hunter in his newly laundered outfit
emerges from the acacias hung about with guns,
compasses, bandoliers, belts, charms, binoculars,
Polaroid sun-specs, cameras and a shockproof watch.

The more vividly the equipment displays itself the greater the doubt cast on the reality of the person encased in it. Buchan's effects are immediate; their impact is decisive. "The Everlasting Astronauts" begins:

These dead astronauts cannot decay –
they bounce on the quilted walls of their tin grave
and very gently collide with polythene balloons
full of used mouthwash, excrements and foodscraps.

The hallucinatory effect of the floating bodies is captured, but the emphasis is on doubt as to the values of the achievement of modern man. The nausea suggested in the last line of the quatrain becomes in Buchan's second collection a more important factor in a book which exhibits passionate indignation, disgust and contempt at the hypocrisy and callousness of officials in power in modern society. The achievement is in the creation of a nightmare world inhabited by politicians who seem to be caricatures of actual persons. These creations induce belief. They are seen as we know them projected on screens of the cinema and television. He presents "Mister Nixon President" thus:

announces the U.S. invasion of Cambodia
(Cambodia) on TV and sincerely his sincere right eye
fixes the poor old silent US majority
with Operation Total Myopic Solemnity.

The observation is cruel, comic and with some truth in it. Buchan's stated "subversive" intention does not limit him to satirising capitalist politicians. In the same poem he hits off Brezhnev:

> meanwhile dateline moss-cow Comrade Leonid
> Nebuchadnezzar Brezhnev in a weird soft hat
> reviews the latest lumpen May Day
> parade with a stiff diminutive wave
> reminiscent of our own dear Queen....

The poet undermines the reader's sense of the truth of the observation by injecting into his text such references as CUT and CAM 2, reminding him that for him these are shadows on a screen. He uses the idea of our seeing the object through a camera lens to a more subtle and profound purpose in his very fine poem, "The Flaming Man," in which we seem to witness the death of a man by burning napalm in slow motion.

Indignation in this poem gives way to compassion. This is Buchan at his best. Occasionally he resorts to political campaigning and to an indulgence in nausea, which characteristics manifest themselves in a strident rhetoric. But for the greater part Buchan's rhetoric gives a sinewy strength to his verse.

—George Bruce

BUCHANAN, George (Henry Perrott). British. Born in Kilwaughter, County Antrim, Northern Ireland, 9 January 1904. Educated at Campbell College and Queen's University, Belfast. Served in the Royal Air Force Coastal Command, 1940–45. Married 1) Mary Corn in 1938 (marriage dissolved, 1945); 2) Noel Beasley in 1949 (died, 1951); 3) Janet Margesson in 1952 (died, 1968); two daughters, Florence and Emily; 4) Sandra McCloy in 1974. Reviewer for the *Times Literary Supplement*, London, 1928–40; on the editorial staff, *The Times*, London, 1930–35; Columnist and Drama Critic, *News Chronicle*, London, 1935–38. Chairman, Town and Country Development Committee, Northern Ireland, 1949–53. Since 1954, Member of the Executive Council of the European Society of Culture, Venice. Address: 27 Ashley Gardens, London S.W.1, England.

PUBLICATIONS

Verse

Bodily Responses. London, Gaberbocchus, 1958.
Conversation with Strangers. London, Gaberbocchus, 1961.
Annotations. Oxford, Carcanet Press, 1970.
Minute-Book of a City. Oxford, Carcanet Press, 1972.
Inside Traffic. Manchester, Carcanet Press, 1976.

Plays

Dance Night (produced London, 1934). London, French, 1935.
A Trip to the Castle (produced London, 1960).
Tresper Revolution (produced London, 1961).
War Song (produced London, 1965).

Novels

A London Story. London, Constable, 1935; New York, Dutton, 1936.
Rose Forbes: The Biography of an Unknown Woman (part 1). London, Constable, 1937.
Entanglement. London, Constable, 1938; New York, Appleton Century, 1939.
The Soldier and the Girl. London, Heinemann, 1940.
Rose Forbes (parts 1 and 2). London, Faber, 1950.
A Place to Live. London, Faber, 1952.
Naked Reason. New York, Holt Rinehart, 1971.

Other

Passage Through the Present: Chiefly Notes from a Journal. London, Constable, 1932; New York, Dutton, 1933.
Words for Tonight: A Notebook. London, Constable, 1936.
Serious Pleasures: The Intelligent Person's Guide to London. London, London Transport, 1938.
Green Seacoast (autobiography). London, Gaberbocchus, 1959; New York, Red Dust, 1968.
Morning Papers (autobiography). London, Gaberbocchus, 1965.
The Politics of Culture. London, Menard Press, 1977.

Critical Studies: "George Buchanan Special Supplement" of *Honest Ulsterman 59* (Belfast), 1978.

George Buchanan comments:

The book titles suggest preoccupations: passage through the present, bodily responses, conversation with strangers – mainly to do with the role of the imagination in submerged mass-life in a city ("I am in the poem, not the poem in me"). Which implies also a permanent intention. ("Perhaps poetry is/our desires expressed as laws./We desire what is absolutely necessary./... The next line may be the next line.")

The Russian Formalists saw that writers often took a subliterary genre and turned it to literature (e.g., Pushkin and the *vers de société*). We may take the subliterary genre of intelligent conversation and turn it, if we can, to poetic speech.

* * *

George Buchanan is a quirky, eccentric poet: a man with something quite specifically different to say, and with a different way of saying it. In his earlier small volumes, such as *Bodily Responses* and *Conversation with Strangers*, the footnotes are larger and better (in the sense of being epigramatically provocative) than the poems, which are both lightweight and themselves prosy. This is partly because he tended towards the use of a line whose length he was not adept at handling: the genuinely epigrammatic effect of his footnotes is lost in arhythmic drag:

> Sneering at the sheer number of others is a drug for self-cultivators
> Who are also (they won't believe it) particles of the mass.
> All of us are; and are filled with that million-made blaze.

The footnotes are those of a very odd-man-out indeed: a man whose intelligence is refreshingly angled to the stream of fashion. Much more of this emerges in the recent poetry of *Minute-Book of a City* (no footnotes), in the poems of which form plays an important part in the creation of tension, leading to a sharper and more effective wit – as in "Anger":

> Cut out feeling (they say) yet often
> policy is the expression of a bad temper:
> when feeling's excluded, anger is the exception.
> We're at the mercy of official tempers.
> Irritable statesmen set the tone.
> Would well-intentioned villagers
> form a milder Cabinet,
> or would their rural eyes flash
> in ultra defiance even more animal?

—Martin Seymour-Smith

BUCKLEY, Vincent (Thomas). Australian. Born in Victoria, 8 July 1925. Educated at St. Patrick's (Jesuit) College, East Melbourne; University of Melbourne, B.A., M.A.; Cambridge University. Married; three daughters. Lockie Fellow, 1958–60, Reader, 1960–67, and since 1967, Professor of English, University of Melbourne. Formerly, Member of the Editorial Board, *Prospect* magazine. Recipient: Australian Literature Society Gold Medal, 1959; Myer Award, 1967. Lives in Melbourne.

PUBLICATIONS

Verse

The World's Flesh. Melbourne, Cheshire, 1954.
Masters in Israel. Sydney, Angus and Robertson, 1961.
Arcady and Other Places. Melbourne, Melbourne University Press, and London, Cambridge University Press, 1966.
Golden Builders and Other Poems. Sydney, Angus and Robertson, 1976.

Other

Essays in Poetry, Mainly Australian. Melbourne, Melbourne University Press, 1957.
Poetry and Morality: Studies on the Criticism of Matthew Arnold, T. S. Eliot, and F. R. Leavis. London, Chatto and Windus, 1959.
Henry Handel Richardson. Melbourne, Lansdowne Press, 1961.
Poetry and the Sacred. London, Chatto and Windus, and New York, Barnes and Noble, 1968.

Editor, *The Incarnation in the University: Studies in the University Apostolate.* Melbourne, University Catholic Federation of Australia, 1955; London, International Movement of Catholic Students, and Chicago, Young Christian Students, 1957.
Editor, *Australian Poetry 1958.* Sydney, Angus and Robertson, 1958.
Editor, *The Campion Paintings*, by Leonard French. Melbourne, Gayflower Press, 1962.
Editor, *Eight by Eight.* Brisbane, Jacaranda Press, 1963.

* * *

Of the many Australian poets who work as teachers of literature, Vincent Buckley has been perhaps the most successful in performing the functions of both professions. A respected teacher, he has broken new ground – always by way of self-preparation – in his published criticism, beginning, bravely for the time, with the field of Australian poetry. Hindsight and their later work would qualify his judgment of contemporaries, but his affirmation of, for instance, the visionary value of C. J. Brennan's poetry illuminated both Brennan criticism and Buckley's large preoccupations. The holder, like Brennan, of a personal chair at his university, Buckley has written searchingly of culture in Australia and has scathing epigrams upon the pretensions which attend it ("Margins").

The early books of poems declared force, wit, and craftsmanship. They owed a debt to the English poets of the 1930's, witness their firm diction, controlled forms, and the intensifying interaction of social comment and personal obsession ("Secret Policeman"):

Pledge me: I had the hangman for a father
And for my mother the immortal State;
My playground was the yard beside the lime-pit,
My play-songs the after-cries of hate ...

The dead eyes point the way I go,
The dead hands presage me in air.
I run on shifting pavements, by fired walls
Falling, and weighted lamp-posts everywhere.

But, also in *Arcady and Other Places*, the first considerable achievement was the sequence "Stroke." Here Buckley found his own voice, precisely in confronting his father's death and the heritage of a native place, a temperament, and mortality.

Every clod reveals an ancestor.
They, the spirit hot in their bodies,
Burned to ash in their own thoughts; could not
Find enough water; rode in a straight line
Twenty miles across country
For hatred jumping every wire fence ...
Remembering always, when I think of death,
The grandfather, small, loveless, sinister,
    ["The most terrible man I ever seen,"
    Said Joe, who died thin as rice paper]
Horse-breaker, heart-breaker, whose foot scorches,
Fifty years after, the green earth of Kilmore.
It's his heat that lifts my father's frame
Crazily from the wheel-chair, fumbles knots,
Twists in the bed at night,
Considers every help a cruelty.

This voice, humane and precise, speaks still in "Golden Builders," whose 27 sections, in forms varying from Blakean quatrains to very free verse, first appeared in *Poetry Australia* in 1972, in the same issue as Murray's "Walking to the Cattle Place." It was an impressive juxtaposition: large utterances both, Buckley's strictly urbane, keeping in the whole Christian-European experience, asking after the City of God from the streets of Carlton in inner Melbourne. This, the precinct of the University of Melbourne, in years of unrest pointed by disgust with the Vietnam war participation, was a heavily migrant-populated district of rooming-houses, cafés and billiard-rooms, where personal crisis was the more easily seen as social emergency, both figured for Buckley in the barking of the dogs kept for experiments in biology. Not only in the epigraph and the poem called "Blake in the Body," Buckley walks by the London prophet.

This great poem, so various that quotation must be unjust, is of that kind that gives literary and visionary existence to a place and its people, by invoking wider relevance. An important poem in the same book is "Ghosts, Places, Stories, Questions," which talks of belief and "the few poems/that are the holy spaces of my life"; and in several shorter poems about horses and riders, weather and travel, Buckley strikes out, in extraordinary lines and half-lines, peculiar kinetic presence:

and the horse at dawn
breathing and stamping   touching
        the cold air with his whole body
            hair swinging like rain

the whistling weight of leather, children
darkening by the roadside,
cars barbed with sun, the shimmering
late odour of traffic

Since this book, Buckley's interest has steered back beyond his Australian forbears to his background in Ireland, where he plans an extended stay, and of which he writes as a homeland. He plans a book on Metaphor ("It won't be an academic book"). These are fresh directions but consistent, striking deeper; there is a mild irony in the arrival of Buckley, a pioneer in the serious criticism of Australian poetry, at this point just as the academic generality turns to Aust-Lit conferencing. Buckley's movement, however, is a controlled progression, no mere trendiness.

Buckley's output has been comparatively small. His qualities are an authority which is not unacademic, a native force that bulges the utterance, and occasionally a deftly placed, uplifting sweetness. The possibility of his surprising us with new work on a large scale should not be discounted.

—Judith Rodriguez

BUKOWSKI, Charles. American. Born in Andernach, Germany, 16 August 1920; emigrated to the United States in 1922. Attended Los Angeles City College, 1939–41. Divorced; one child. Formerly, Editor, *Harlequin*, Wheeler, Texas, then Los Angeles, and *Laugh Literary* and *Man the Humping Guns*, both in Los Angeles. Columnist ("Notes of a Dirty Old Man"), *Open City*, Los Angeles, then *Los Angeles Free Press*. Ricipient: Loujon Press award. Address: P. O. Box 132, San Pedro, California 90731, U.S.A.

PUBLICATIONS

Verse

Flower, Fist and Bestial Wail. Eureka, California, Hearse Press, 1959.
Longshot Poems for Broke Players. New York, 7 Poets Press, 1961.
Run with the Hunted. Chicago, Midwest, 1962.
Poems and Drawings. Crescent City, Florida, Epos, 1962.
It Catches My Heart in Its Hands: New and Selected Poems, 1955–1963. New Orleans, Loujon Press, 1963.

Cold Dogs in the Courtyard. Chicago, Chicago Literary Times, 1965.
Crucifix in a Deathhand: New Poems, 1963–65. New Orleans, Loujon Press, 1965.
The Genius of the Crowd. Cleveland, 7 Flowers Press, 1966.
True Story. Los Angeles, Black Sparrow Press, 1966.
On Going Out to Get the Mail. Los Angeles, Black Sparrow Press, 1966.
To Kiss the Worms Goodnight. Los Angeles, Black Sparrow Press, 1966.
The Girls. Los Angeles, Black Sparrow Press, 1966.
The Flower Lover. Los Angeles, Black Sparrow Press, 1966.
2 by Bukowski. Los Angeles, Black Sparrow Press, 1967.
The Curtains Are Waving. Los Angeles, Black Sparrow Press, 1967.
At Terror Street and Agony Way. Los Angeles, Black Sparrow Press, 1968.
Poems Written Before Jumping Out of an 8-Story Window. Berkeley, California, Litmus, 1968.
If We Take.... Los Angeles, Black Sparrow Press, 1969.
The Days Run Away Like Wild Horses over the Hills. Los Angeles, Black Sparrow Press, 1969.
Penguin Modern Poets 13, with Philip Lamantia and Harold Norse. London, Penguin, 1969.
Another Academy. Los Angeles, Black Sparrow Press, 1970.
Fire Station. Santa Barbara, California, Capricorn Press, 1970.
Mockingbird Wish Me Luck. Los Angeles, Black Sparrow Press, 1972.
Me and Your Sometimes Love Poems. Los Angeles, Kisskill Press, 1972.
While the Music Played. Los Angeles, Black Sparrow Press, 1973.
Love Poems to Marina. Los Angeles, Black Sparrow Press, 1973.
Burning in Water, Drowning in Flame: Selected Poems 1955–1973. Los Angeles, Black Sparrow Press, 1974.
Africa, Paris, Greece. Los Angeles, Black Sparrow Press, 1975.
Tough Company, with *The Last Poem*, by Diane Wakoski. Santa Barbara, California, Black Sparrow Press, 1976.
Scarlet. Santa Barbara, California, Black Sparrow Press, 1976.
Maybe Tomorrow. Santa Barbara, California, Black Sparrow Press, 1977.
Love Is a Dog from Hell. Santa Barbara, California, Black Sparrow Press, 1977.

Novels

Post Office. Los Angeles, Black Sparrow Press, 1971; London, London Magazine Editions, 1974.
Factotum. Los Angeles, Black Sparrow Press, 1975.
Women. Santa Barbara, California, Black Sparrow Press, 1978.

Short Stories

Notes of a Dirty Old Man. North Hollywood, California, Essex House, 1969.
Erections, Ejaculations, Exhibitions and General Tales of Ordinary Madness. San Francisco, City Lights, 1972.
South of No North. Los Angeles, Black Sparrow Press, 1973.
Life and Death in the Charity Ward. London, London Magazine Editions, 1974.

Other

Confessions of a Man Insane Enough to Live with Beasts. Bensenville, Illinois, Mimeo Press, 1965.
All the Assholes in the World and Mine. Bensenville, Illinois, Open Skull Press, 1966.
A Bukowski Sampler, edited by Douglas Blazek. Madison, Wisconsin, Quixote Press, 1969.

You Kissed Lilly. Santa Barbara, California, Black Sparrow Press, 1978.

Editor, with Neeli Cherry and Paul Vangelisti, *Anthology of L.A. Poets.* Los Angeles, Laugh Library, 1972.

Bibliography: *A Bibliography of Charles Bukowski* by Sanford Dorbin, Los Angeles, Black Sparrow Press, 1969.

Manuscript Collection: University of California, Santa Barbara.

* * *

When, around the bend of the Fifties, an almost aging prose-fiction writer emerged from a ten-year bout with bottles and bar-rooms and burst into flame, the prophecy of a San Francisco journalist-poet had come true: There was indeed, a need for a "crude disheveled kind of poetry." The man was Charles Bukowski. "Poetry is going into the streets, into the whorehouses, into the sky ... into the whiskeybottle. The fraud is over –" says Bukowski, in *Ole*'s "monster-review" edition (no. 7).

For this new giant, poetry is just "too fine/and lacks the coarseness/of gamble" (from "The Last Round"). This is no poetic image: Bukowski prides himself on his horse-playing abilities. Here is a poet who is obviously at one with the experiences in his poems, a crucial point when you think of most other poets. To this day, he drinks and brawls as wildly as ever, and as far as I know, still plays the horses. His tough-guy image, however, is only partly true; in person, he is most generous and trusting. If he belongs to any school, it'd be the School of Funk!

His best poems aren't word-games. In rough-hewn, gasping and gaping lines he wraps his guts around a tree, then calmly walks off. You can call it protest poetry, you can call it some of the most hilarious sado-masochistic satiric plunges poetry ever saw. Sometimes it's both. For at least a decade he's been ripping out the likes of "Singing Is Fire":

... not enough water to save the burning
birds   and *they* are telling me now:
        FLAME! FLAME! FLAME!
as old trains move through the
deserts
as the schoolboys dream of laborless
love
        the birds BURN and
        die before me
        they
fly away done
leaving the grass for what's left of the
worms ...

Few poets manage such complete release with anything like Bukowski's ferocity. Why? The risks are too great. His work has the power of "forcing the hidden psychopath in us back to reality," says a midwest poet-editor in *The Outsider*'s famous Bukowski celebration-issue (no. 3). Joe Friedman, once editor of the fine magazine *Venture*, adds that his laughter is often meant to be offensive, "*offensive* to connote attack, an impertinent zany attack on death, for ... he is keenly sensitive to the innermost innards of being alive." This rings well. It can also be, with only slight modification, said of the foremost of his many imitators, among whom Doug Blazek is the best and most original.

It is, of course, possible to point to several poets Bukowski is fond of and roughly similar to – Jeffers, Pound and Ginsberg, whom he kids: "the Whitmanesque prophet rantings of the later Ginsberg." Strange, since these two poets are perhaps his closest spiritual companions, although in Bukowski there is no hint of homosexuality. Certainly, many of his long rambling prose-poems can only be called Whitmanesques. Here, too, no double-dealing: He owns up to the outrageous badness of a considerable number of these poems. It might help to remember Neruda's concept of Impure Poetry, Henry Miller's analogy of the supreme imperfection of both art *and* life, or Jackson Pollock's approach to painting. One rather famous poet-editor (who also spans both decades) still finds Bukowski's main contribution to be in his prose. Well, if you call *all* his poems prosepoems, a small measure of truth might be lurking somewhere here; but it is just this kind of hokum or petty professional jealousy that so turns Bukowski (and me) off the "literary scene" here and in England. Long after, I feel, the pretty, precious verses of 90 per cent of the name poets of 20th century U.S. and British poetry have ceased to have interest to anyone but the narrowest of scholars, lines like these will still clearly stand out – for their flamelike intensity and searing honesty ("Like a Flyswatter"):

some day I will walk into a cage with a bear
look at Him, light a cigarette
and He will sit down and cry,
40 billion people watching without sound
as the sky turns upside down and
splits the backbone
open

—Norman Moser

BULLOCK, Michael (Hale). British. Born in London, 19 April 1918. Educated at Stowe School, Buckinghamshire; Hornsey College of Art, London. Married Charlotte Schneller in 1941; two children. Chairman, Translators Association, London, 1964–67. McGuffey Visiting Professor of English, Ohio University, Athens, 1968. Since 1969, Professor of Creative Writing, University of British Columbia, Vancouver. Founding Editor, *Expression* magazine, London; Member of the Editorial Board, *Canadian Fiction Magazine*, Vancouver. Recipient: Schlegel-Tieck Translation Prize, 1966. Agent: International Copyright Bureau, 26 Charing Cross Road, London W.C.2, England. Address: 3836 West 18th Avenue, Vancouver, British Columbia V6S 1B5, Canada.

PUBLICATIONS

Verse

Transmutations (as Michael Hale). London, Favil Press, 1938.
Sunday Is a Day of Incest. London and New York, Abelard Schuman, 1961.
World Without Beginning, Amen! London, Favil Press, 1963.
Zwei Stimmen in Meinem Mund (bilingual edition, translated by Hedwig Rohde). Andernach, Germany, Atelier Verlag, 1967.
A Savage Darkness. Vancouver, Sono Nis Press, 1969.
Black Wings White Dead. Fredericton, New Brunswick, Fiddlehead, 1978.
Last Message Through Rain. Vancouver, Intermedia, 1979.

Plays

Not to Hong Kong (produced London, 1972). Published in *Dialogue and Dialectic*, Guelph, Ontario, Alive Press, 1973.
The Island Abode of Bliss (produced Vancouver, 1972).

Novel

Randolph Cranstone and the Glass Thimble. London, Boyars, 1977.

Short Stories

Sixteen Stories as They Happened. Vancouver, Sono Nis Press, 1969.
Green Beginning Black Ending. Vancouver, Sono Nis Press, 1971.
Randolph Cranstone and the Pursuing River. Vancouver, Rainbird Press, 1975.

Other

Translator, with Jerome Ch'ên, *Poems of Solitude*. London and New York, Abelard Schuman, 1961.
Translator, *The Tales of Hoffman*. London, New English Library, 1962; New York Ungar, 1963.
Translator, with Jerome Ch'ên, *Mao and the Chinese Revolution, With 37 Poems by Mao Tse-Tung*. London, Oxford University Press, 1965.
Translator, *The Stage and Creative Arts*. Greenwich, Connecticut, New York Graphic Society, 1969.
Translator, *Foreign Bodies*, by Karl Krolow. Athens, Ohio University Press, 1969.
Translator, *Invisible Hands*, by Karl Krolow. London, Cape Goliard Press, and New York, Grossman, 1969.
Translator, with Jagna Boraks, *Astrologer in the Underground*, by Andrzej Busza. Athens, Ohio University Press, 1971.
Translator, *Stories for Late Night Drinkers*, by Michel Tremblay. Vancouver, Intermedia, 1977.

Other translations include novels and plays by Max Frisch and over 130 other French and German books.

Critical Studies: by John Ditsky, in *Canadian Forum* (Toronto), February 1971; Richard Hopkins, in *British Columbia Library Quarterly* (Victoria), January 1972; "Light on a Dark Wood" by John Reid, in *Canadian Literature* (Vancouver), Autumn 1972; interview with Richard Hopkins, in *British Columbia Library Quarterly* (Victoria), June 1973.

Michael Bullock comments:

I consider myself a surrealist, or at least a neo-surrealist, in that I base my work upon the free play of the imagination without, however, sacrificing clarity of expression. I seek to use vivid and striking imagery to convey states of mind and emotion and to create an autonomous world freed from the restrictions and limitations of everyday existence. This world and the means I use to give it form remain the same whether I am writing verse, prose or drama. I believe that my writing in all three genres can with almost equal right be described as poetry. All of it is a vehement rejection of realism. I like to hope that there is some truth in the comment of a reviewer who wrote that my fables "bear witness to one of the most wildly imaginative minds ever to reach the printed page" and in Anaïs Nin's description of my work as "a liberating expansion of what is reality." The two remarks together sum up what I am trying to do.

* * *

In the poem "Escape" (*A Savage Darkness*), which might easily stand as his personal manifesto, Michael Bullock explains:

The real surrounds me
with its barbed wire entanglements
Leaping upwards I clutch at a cloud
and stuff it into my head

In a blue haze
figures emerge
and drift
in an endless floating dance

Women with streaming hair
fall downwards
holding burning flowers
Flocks of eyes fly around gazing
and flapping their lids

Stretched out
on the cloud in my mind
I wait for the approach
of the ultimate dream ...

The poem continues, but the most important catch-phrase has occurred: "the ultimate dream." For Michael Bullock is a Surrealist, an almost orthodox one in fact, and both his poetry and his prose insist entirely on the freedom, the total possibility which is the dream – both as a source and as mode. Bullock's poems are associative, fantastical, alogical; they leap and swirl to the arabesques of the imagination like a free-form dance. Through his writings Bullock re-enacts creation according to his own laws, according to a triumphantly lyrical, non-lineal progression both in time and space:

Out of the air I draw the memory of a bird.
Out of the earth I draw the memory of a tree.
From the memory of the bird
and the memory of the tree
I make the memory of a poem
that weighs lighter than air
and floats away without wind ...

The result is that Bullock's poetry almost always departs from unexpected places and arrives at unfamiliar destinations. And the means by which it gets there is, needless to say, no less unpredictable.

—Andreas Schroeder

BUNTING, Basil. British. Born in Scotswood on Tyne, Northumberland, 1 March 1900. Educated at a Quaker public school; London School of Economics. Jailed as a conscientious objector during World War I. Married 1) Marian Culver in 1930; 2) Sima Alladadian in 1948; two children. Assistant Editor, *Transatlantic Review*, Paris, in the 1920's; Music Critic, *The Outlook*, London; lived in Italy and the United States in the 1930's; Persian Correspondent for *The Times*, London, after World War II; Sub-Editor, Newcastle *Chronicle*, for 12 years. Taught at the University of California, Santa Barbara; Poetry Fellow, universities of Durham and Newcastle, 1968–70; taught at the universities of British Columbia, Vancouver, Binghamton, New York, and Victoria, British Columbia. President, The Poetry Society, London, 1972–76, and Northern Arts, 1974–78. Recipient: Levinson Prize (*Poetry*, Chicago), 1966; Arts Council bursaries. D.Litt.: Newcastle, 1971. Address: 107 Stridingedge, Blackfell, Washington, Tyne and Wear, England.

PUBLICATIONS

Verse

Redimiculum Matellarum. Milan, Grafica Moderna, 1930.
Poems 1950. Galveston, Texas, Cleaners' Press, 1950.
First Book of Odes. London, Fulcrum Press, 1965.
Loquitur. London, Fulcrum Press, 1965.
The Spoils: A Poem. Newcastle-upon-Tyne, Morden Tower, 1965.
Ode II/2. London, Fulcrum Press, 1965.
Briggflatts. London, Fulcrum Press, 1966.
Two Poems. Santa Barbara, California, Unicorn Press, 1967.
What the Chairman Told Tom. Cambridge, Massachusetts, Pym Randall Press, 1967.
Collected Poems. London, Fulcrum Press, 1968; revised edition, London and New York, Oxford University Press, 1978.
Version of Horace. London, Holborn, 1972.

Other

Descant on Rawthey's Madrigal (Conversations with Jonathan Williams). Lexington, Kentucky, Gnomon Press, 1968.

Editor, *Selected Poems*, by Ford Madox Ford. Cambridge, Massachusetts, Pym Randall Press, 1971.
Editor, *Selected Poems*, by Joseph Skipsey. Sunderland, Ceolfrith Press, 1976.

Bibliography: *Basil Bunting: A Bibliography of Works and Criticism* by Roger Guedalla, Norwood, Pennsylvania, Norwood Editions, 1973.

Basil Bunting comments:

Minor poet, not conspicuously dishonest.

* * *

"With sleights learned from others and an ear open to melodic analogies I have set down words as a musician pricks his score, not to be read in silence, but to trace in the air a pattern of sound that may sometimes, I hope, be pleasing." Thus Basil Bunting defines his purpose in the Preface to his *Collected Poems*, adding, characteristically, "Unabashed boys and girls may enjoy them. This book is theirs." Bunting has learnt from many others, and he is generous in his acknowledgments; but it is from Ezra Pound and the "sterner, stonier" Louis Zukofsky that he derived this essentially Renaissance pre-occupation with an art which, like music or sculpture, aims first of all to delight before it can instruct, and which delights by the sheer candour of its cadence and contour. Bunting describes his major poem, *Briggflatts*, as "an autobiography, but not a record of fact.... The truth of the poem is of another kind"; and indeed, it is the articulation of image and theme in a "Flexible, unrepetitive line/... laying the tune on the air,/nimble and easy as a lizard" that brings together the poet, his Northumbrian landscape, and the history that lies behind them. Speaking in the persona of the Japanese poet Chomei in another poem, Bunting defines the distinctive combination of parochial and universal (so much larger than the cosmopolitan) which characterizes *Briggflatts*:

> Neither closed in one landscape
> nor in one season
> the mind moving in illimitable
> recollection.

Briggflatts opens with the stonemason's inscription of a name on a tombstone: "the stone spells a name/naming none,/a man abolished." By the end of the poem, it is clear that this is not just the poet's own literal epitaph but also an analogy for that literary death-in-life by which a man is translated into language, into words that inscribe not only his labour but that of all the hands that go to make a finished book. In a lambent metaphor, the traces which record our disappearance are compared to the light from a star which, taking 50 years to reach us, compacts time, as, throughout the poem, the brutal Anglo-Saxon world of Eric Bloodaxe and the Celtic lament for the slain of Aneurin pervade the personal present and mingle with the poet's regrets for a lost love:

> Then is Now. The star you steer by is gone ...
>   light from the zenith
> spun when the slowworm lay in her lap
> fifty years ago.
> The sheets are gathered and bound,
> the volume indexed and shelved,
> dust on its marbled leaves.

The slowworm, with its obvious phallic imagery, in its blind relentless progress through the poem, makes another correlation, between sexuality and artistic creation. *Briggflatts* returns repeatedly to a kind of poetic *tristitia post coitum* in which the poet laments the "flawed fragments" of his labours, never able to consummate the perfect match of form and content: "He lies with one to long for another .../obstinate, mating/beauty with squalor to beget lines still-born." Yet this struggle with the intractable is the highest task of the artist. Like Schoenberg rather than Monteverdi, the poet tells us, his task is to "entune a bogged orchard,/its blossom gone,/fruit unformed, where hunger and/damp hush the hive." Throughout *Briggflatts* there is a powerful counterpoint of the demotic and the aesthetic, the monosyllabic beat of Anglo-Saxon noun and verb in tight-packed proximity and a heavy alliterative metre with a larger, more elaborate vocabulary, syntax, and rhythm. Stylistically this reinforces the urgency with which, in the image of the sweating Pasiphaë mounted by the bull-god, a major theme is presented: the holiness of the bestial, that sordid material being which is the groundbass of all our finer tones.

Bunting's progress from his earliest poems, the odes he wrote in the 1920's, has indeed been a retreat from an orotund latinity, excessively adjectival in style, to the tangible, concrete immediacy of his latest work. The odes written during the 1930's suggest that it was not only the tradition of Modernism, mediated by Pound, Eliot, and Auden, but also the actual social experience of the period which effected this change. These 1930's poems are full of a sense of the human locked in effort, struggle, hard material labour, "resigned to/anything except your own numb toil, the/seasonal plod to spoil the land alone" (*"O ubi campi!"*). But the obverse of this is a solidarity between poet and *menu peuple* which is expressed in sexual terms in "The Orotava Road," which speaks of his encounter with young peasant girls on donkeys:

You can guess their balanced nakedness
under the cotton gown and thin shift....
They say "Adios!" shyly but look back
more than once, knowing our thoughts
and sharing our
desires and lack of faith in desire.

This last note is characteristic: like Chomei, in Bunting's own words, he has an "urbane, sceptical and ironical temper" which prevents him from ever "preaching the simple life." Unequivocally rooted, Bunting's poetry is nevertheless, like Hugh MacDiarmid's, heir to world literature, as his translations ("Overdrafts" he calls them, thereby signalling an ironic relationship to his inheritance) and his complex allusiveness within the body of his poems to Oriental, Persian, Classical, and Renaissance literature all indicate. An irony that can transcend archness or cynicism is rare in modern poetry, but Bunting's is finally rich and affirmative, as is revealed most succinctly perhaps, in the short and apparently simple lyric which opens his *Second Book of Odes*, where the last line invites us to re-view the lines which precede it, offering a balanced comment on the poetic and the human vocations:

A thrush in the syringa sings.

"Hunger ruffles my wings, fear,
lust, familiar things.

Death thrusts hard. My sons
by hawk's beak, by stones,
trusting weak wings
by cat and weasel, die.

Thunder smothers the sky.
From a shaken bush I
list familiar things,
fear, hunger, lust."

O gay thrush!

—Stan Smith

BURFORD, William (Skelly). American. Born in Shreveport, Louisiana, 20 February 1927. Educated at Amherst College, Massachusetts (Glasscock Memorial Award, Mount Holyoke College, 1949), B.A. (magna cum laude) 1949 (Phi Beta Kappa); the Sorbonne, Paris, 1950–52 (Fulbright Scholar); Johns Hopkins University, Baltimore, M.A. 1956, Ph.D. 1966. Served in the United States Army, 1945. Married Lolah Egan in 1956; three daughters. Assistant to the President, Richardson Refining Company, Texas City, 1949–50. Instructor in English, Southern Methodist University, Dallas, 1950–51, 1952–54, and Johns Hopkins University, 1955–58; Assistant Professor, 1958–64, and Associate Professor of English, 1964–65, University of Texas, Austin; Associate Professor of Humanities, University of Montana, Missoula, 1966–68; Professor of English, Texas Christian University, Fort Worth, Texas, 1968–72. Since 1972, teacher in the National Endowment for the Arts Poetry-in-the-Schools Program. Poet-in-Residence, Evergreen State College, Olympia, Washington, 1974.

Recipient: Walt Whitman Memorial Award, 1962. Address: 3000 West Gambrell, Fort Worth, Texas 76133, U.S.A.

PUBLICATIONS

Verse

Man Now. Dallas, Southern Methodist University Press, 1954.
Faccia della Terra/Face of the Earth (bilingual edition). Bologna, Libreria Antiquaria Palmaverde, 1960.
A World. Austin, University of Texas Press, 1962.
A Beginning. New York, Norton, 1966.
Gymnos. N.p., Four Mountains Press, 1973.

Other

The Art of Anaïs Nin, with *On Writing*, by Nin. Yonkers, New York, Baradinsky, 1947.

Editor and Translator, with Christopher Middleton, *The Poet's Vocation: Selections from the Letters of Hölderlin, Rimbaud, and Hart Crane.* Austin, University of Texas Press, 1967.
Editor and Translator, with Jean Autret, *On Reading*, by Marcel Proust. New York, Macmillan, and London, Souvenir Press, 1972.

Manuscript Collection: Lockwood Library, State University of New York, Buffalo.

Critical Study: Review by David Ignatow, in *The New York Times*, 6 January 1967.

William Burford comments:

Poetry, at least as I have learned to want to write it, is a way of giving reality and even courage to the life a man senses within himself, and which he knows, by living among other men, is their chief possession also. The poetry which seems to me the most admirable is characterized by a certain firm delicacy, a style which at once both moves and instructs the sense of life in us. If a man writes poems for any length of time, he learns how much experience of both life and art is required to achieve this style, how few men have been masters of it, and these few seemingly by some grace of nature or intelligence or artistic perception, that cannot be willed by himself into his own possession but only perhaps gradually approached if he has a view of the goal.

* * *

In scenes of childhood innocence, in cities of youthful pleasure lurk recurring forms of terror, loneliness, and melancholy. A childish game destroys a harmless life. A boy, frightened by his nurse's disfigured face, marks his fate with clocks ticking the hours of a father's absence. A father bids his son remove annoying sparrows which return in nightmare as birds of prey. In sunlit Paris the youth denies the phantom of himself. He finds Venice "sunk to a sewer." In Amsterdam an old man tells him: "To live is to persist." The poet sees with the eyes of the painter; indeed, paintings become subjects for some of his strongest lines. The once-benevolent surgeon's scalpel stabs the brain that was a world. The sensuous face of the sexless monk mocks the artist. Stones arranged like human bones spell out station-names in fields lying in ashes. Images of frost, marble waves, slivers of glass quickly etch vignettes made even more poignant by the poet's delicate, controlling hand. Yet William Burford's incisive, sombre scenes do not depress but comfort and enlighten; for usually a calm instilled by oblique and muted Christian symbolism pervades and promises hope, which in later poems finds fruition in the loving presence of a sleeping wife and awkward grace of an adolescent son.

Burford seeks to capture "that moment fatal in our lives" by asking: "Where does one go for love these days?" This probing for the fundamental gives his poetry a continuity of theme and purpose (and several early poems reappear, revised, in later volumes); he traces the private world of child and youth as it opens to the social consciousness of maturity. But early he learned that passion is "aged to a patience." He cried, "My name is man, and I am dumb from pain." "In an ironic age," he discovers, "reasonable men" are hospitable to the Devil they do not believe in; judges behind their tinted glass are still "hypnotizing existence." Solipsistic man thinks his body is the world, "And so a final philosophy." The perfect young dancer thinks himself immortal, though destruction waits in the wings. The poet, too, has "measureless privacy," but he turns his penetrating eye upon the ephemeral and finds the "self is strong, unisolated,/And from its birth forms bonds throughout all." Unlike the windy, undisciplined, but fashionable voices decrying a fractured world in despair, Burford depicts in short, polished verse a destructive universe still capable of meaning through humanity and faith.

—Joseph Parisi

BURKE, Kenneth (Duva). American. Born in Pittsburgh, Pennsylvania, 5 May 1897. Educated at Peabody High School, Pittsburgh; Ohio State University, Columbus, 1916–17; Columbia University, New York, 1917–18. Married 1) Lily Mary Batterham in 1919 (divorced); 2) Elizabeth Batterham in 1933; five children. Research Worker, Laura Spelman Rockefeller Memorial, New York, 1926–27. Music Critic, *Dial*, New York, 1927–29, and *The Nation*, New York, 1934–35. Editor, Bureau of Social Hygiene, New York, 1928–29. Lecturer, New School for Social Research, New York, 1937; University of Chicago, 1938, 1949–50; Bennington College, Vermont, 1943–61; Princeton University, New Jersey, 1949, 1975; Kenyon College, Gambier, Ohio, 1950; Indiana University, Bloomington, 1953, 1958; Drew University, Madison, New Jersey, 1962, 1964; Pennsylvania State University, University Park, 1963; Regents Professor, University of California at Santa Barbara, 1964–65; Lecturer, Central Washington State University, Ellensburg, 1966; Harvard University, Cambridge, Massachusetts, 1967–68; Washington University, St. Louis, 1970–71; Wesleyan University, Middletown, Connecticut, 1972; University of Pittsburgh, 1972. Recipient: *Dial* Award, 1928; Guggenheim Fellowship, 1935; National Institute of Arts and Letters grant, 1946, and Gold Medal, 1975; Princeton Institute for Advanced Study Fellowship, 1949; Stanford University Center for Advanced Study in the Behavioral Sciences Fellowship, 1957; Rockefeller grant, 1966; Brandeis University Creative Arts Award, 1967; National Endowment for the Arts Award, 1968. D.Litt.: Bennington College, 1966; Rutgers University, New Brunswick, New Jersey, 1968; Dartmouth College, Hanover, New Hampshire, 1969; Fairfield University, Connecticut, 1970; Northwestern University, Evanston, Illinois, 1972; University of Rochester, New York, 1972. Member, American Academy of Arts and Letters; American Academy of Arts and Sciences. Address: R. D. 2, Andover, New Jersey 07821, U.S.A.

PUBLICATIONS

Verse

Book of Moments: Poems 1915–1954. Los Altos, California, Hermes, 1955.
Collected Poems 1915–1967. Berkeley, University of California Press, and London, Cambridge University Press, 1968.

Novel

Towards a Better Life: Being a Series of Epistles or Declamations. New York, Harcourt Brace, 1932; revised edition, Berkeley, University of California Press, and London, Cambridge University Press, 1966.

Short Stories

The White Oxen and Other Stories. New York, Boni, 1924.
The Complete White Oxen: Collected Shorter Fiction. Berkeley, University of California Press, 1968.

Other

Counter-Statement. New York, Harcourt Brace, 1931; revised edition, Berkeley, University of California Press, and London, Cambridge University Press, 1968.
Permanence and Change: An Anatomy of Purpose. New York, New Republic, 1935; revised edition, Los Altos, California, Hermes, 1954.
Attitudes Towards History. New York, New Republic, 2 vols., 1937; revised edition, Los Altos, California, Hermes, 1959.
The Philosophy of Literary Form: Studies in Symbolic Action. Baton Rouge, Louisiana State University Press, 1941; revised edition, New York, Random House, 1957; London, Peter Smith, 1959.
A Grammar of Motives. New York, Prentice Hall, 1945; London, Dobson, 1947.
A Rhetoric of Motives. New York, Prentice Hall, 1950; London, Bailey Brothers and Swinfen, 1955.
The Rhetoric of Religion: Studies in Logology. Boston, Beacon Press, 1961.
Perspectives by Incongruity, edited by Stanley Edgar Hyman. Bloomington, Indiana University Press, 1964.
Press, 1964.
Language as Symbolic Action: Essays on Life, Literature and Method. Berkeley, University of California Press, and London, Cambridge University Press, 1966.
Dramatism and Development. Worcester, Massachusetts, Clark University Press, 1972.
Ideas for Environment [*Reading and Writing, Science, Spelling and Phonics, Sports, American History, Americans – All, Consumer Education, Men and Women of the World, World History*], with Julie Kranhold. Belmont, California, Lear Siegler Fearon, 10 vols., 1973–74.

Translator, *Death in Venice*, by Thomas Mann. New York, Knopf, 1925; revised edition, New York, Modern Library, 1970.
Translator, *Genius and Character*, by Emil Ludwig. New York, Harcourt Brace, 1927; London, Cape, 1930.
Translator, *Saint Paul*, by Emile Baumann. New York, Harcourt Brace, 1929.

Kenneth Burke comments:

In calling my theory of language as symbolic action "Dramatistic" (as contrasted with "Scientistic") I have in mind a distinction that boils down to this: A "Scientistic" approach centers in "It is/it is not"; a "Dramatistic" approach centers in "Do/don't." My aim is to develop a theory of language in general, with emphasis upon its application to specific texts.

* * *

My favorite among Kenneth Burke's *Collected Poems 1915–1967* is a 17-page poem in 5 parts entitled "Tossing on Floodtides of Sinkership: A Diaristic Fragment." Driving across the country, the speaker floats on a turbulent sea of memories, reflections, and feelings – the dangers of traffic, the power of the machine, pollution, reactions to America's face and fate, politics, Vietnam, his own inner conflicts – but concludes with the stubborn persistence of spring and of the sunrise. Now Burke writes most frequently about our public life, but what I find distinctive in this poem is the way in which the public is seen in terms of the personal, for not only do the larger issues arise naturally and dramatically out of the particular situation, but they are also seen *in relation* to the speaker and his own turmoil. He sees the destructiveness of highspeed autos in political terms – the easy manipulation of such vicarious power may tend to make us docile citizens – and he feels the fascination of his own suicidal urge to spin off the road as well. He sees the deterioration of the land, and he senses a connection with his own desolation: "half experimental animal,/half control group./I am mine own disease." And when he comes to the Vietnam issue, he not only vents his indignation – "Cook them with napalm in the name of freedom/tear up their way of life" – he also confronts his own hesitation – "Gad! I couldn't tell them that!" – and concludes this section (IV) with the wry admission that "To be safe in striking at the powerful/make sure that your blows are powerless."

It is not, alas, always thus. Too often his poems are simply public statements without either tension or intensity. Excellent critic that he is, Burke offers a Foreword and various explanatory prose excursions, whose gist is that, contrary to our common assumptions, prose is more subtle, conditional, and qualified than lyric poetry. Criticism, he says in "Extraduction from What?," is "moderate in tone and at least theoretically charitable.... The very attempt to be circumspect in criticism could make one, by rebound, at least *wish* for *some* verse in the style of a news broadcast blasting forth pellets...." And therein lies the problem, for the very life of the lyric depends upon its stemming from and embodying a sense of personal urgency, it seems to me, and if you would write the unqualified sort, as E. E. Cummings does, for example, your sense of self must be intense, accepting, intuitive, passionate, and transcendent, so that when it confronts the troublesome public world it will do so on the basis of inner confidence. Yet, in "Extraduction," he speaks of "my morbid Selph, lost among the monsters of machinery and politics." And in his admiring elegy on Cummings, he takes pleasure in opining that Cummings had more brains than he admitted to – "you secretly, like the scholastics' God,/an intellectual" – as if to say that Cummings' mysticism was less than whole-hearted.

An instructive contrast to the Vietnam section of "Tossing" is found in another, shorter poem on the same subject, "The Great Debate," which is in this "news broadcast" style, and which concludes:

> But time is running out.
> Where we but increase our forces
> the enemy escalates.
>
> Give us an honorable peace
> And we'll stop
> Our dishonorable war.
>
> (There's shouting in the streets – and I wanna go home)

There is irony here, of course, but it is still, as is the rest of the poem, rather flat, and the final line is an ineffectual attempt to supply a dramatic base, for it is a deliberately forlorn gesture and is simply stuck on at the end – quite different in function and effect from the similar conclusion of Cummings' "pity this busy monster, manunkind": "listen: there's a hell/of a good universe next door; let's go."

One would think, then, that Burke would be more at home in writing the qualified sort of lyric, as in "Tossing," in which the sense of personal urgency arises from tension, conflict, intelligence, consideration, and self-confrontation, and one recalls Yeats's sobering remark that we make rhetoric out of our quarrel with others, but poetry out of our quarrel with ourselves. But Burke's poetic self is just as tenuous when confronting itself as the public world, betraying its uncertainties and avoidances in a wobbly style which skitters from the melodic to the prosaic, and touches doggerel, slang, nonsense, and puns along the way. And self-knowledge rarely gets in touch either with the possibility that the public is an extension of ourselves or that it becomes internalized and sticks within as a part of ourselves.

It is this awareness which surfaces but seldom in Burke's poetry, and when it does it finds its only acknowledged symptom in insomnia. Nevertheless, in six successive lyrics entitled "On a Photo of Himself," "Self-Portrait," "Know Thyself," "Now I Lay Me," "On the Reflexive," and "Personality Problem," the speaker presents himself with gentleness, wit, and frankness as sleepless and aging:

One-third insomnia
One-third art
One-third The Man
With the Cardiac Heart....

I'm flunking my Required Course
In Advanced Burkology.

This is less powerful than "half experimental animal, etc.," but it is effective in its own way. And he can on occasion combine self-study with social criticism, as in "Photo," which concludes:

Bring on your bombs, your bugs, and the trick chemicals.
Get this damned business done

But in the interim
Curse me for a not-yet-housebroken cur
And rub my nose in filthy lucre.

And "L'Auberge" is a lovely counterpart, in its depiction of a respite at an inn while traveling, to the similar concluding section of Part I of "Tossing," but it drives even deeper into the recesses of the self. Here and throughout he appears as an engaged and engaging poet indeed, more moderate and charitable than he seems to think he is. I could only wish that he did not feel his poetry represented an escape from his more brilliant and arduous critical work.

—Norman Friedman

BURNS, Jim. British. Born in Preston, Lancashire, 19 February 1936. Educated at local schools. Served in the British Army, 1954–57. Divorced; two sons. Editor, *Move* magazine,

Preston, 1964–68. Since 1964, regular contributor, *Tribune*, London; since 1978, Editor, *Palantir*, Preston. Address: 7 Ryelands Crescent, Larches Estate, Preston, Lancashire, England.

PUBLICATIONS

Verse

Some Poems. New York, Crank, 1965.
Some More Poems. Cambridge, R Books, 1966.
My Sad Story and Other Poems. Chatham, Kent, New Voice, 1967.
The Store of Things. Manchester, Phoenix Pamphlet Poets Press, 1969.
A Single Flower. St. Brelade, Jersey, Channel Islands, Andium Press, 1972.
Leben in Preston. Cologne, Palmenpresse, 1973.
Easter in Stockport. Sheffield, Rivelin Press, 1975.
Fred Engels in Woolworths. London Oasis, 1975.
Playing It Cool. Swansea, Galloping Dog Press, 1976.
The Goldfish Speaks from Beyond the Grave. London, Salamander, 1976.

Other

Cells: Prose Pieces. Lincoln, Grosseteste Press, 1967.
Saloon Bar: 3 Jim Burns Stories. London, Ferry Press, 1967.
Types: Prose Pieces and Poems. Cardiff, Second Aeon, 1970.

Critical Studies: "The American Influence" by the author, in *New Society* (London), 7 December 1967; "Exit to Preston" by Raymond Gardner, in *The Guardian* (London), 10 August 1972; "A Poet in His Northern Corner" by Bel Mooney, in *Daily Telegraph Magazine* (London), 2 March 1973; "Jim Burns' Poems" by John Freeman, in *Cambridge Quarterly*, 1975; "Mit Poesie Kannst Du Kein Auto Fahren" by Michael Buselmeir, in *Frankfurter Rundschau*, 8 April 1978.

Jim Burns comments:

(1970) I suppose my main subject-matter tends towards the "domestic," i.e., that which I know best and experience personally. Brevity and wit are attributes I admire in a poet and I think (or hope) that some of this comes in some of my own work.

My main influences have been contemporary American and English poets, and some translations from the Chinese and Japanese. I like the directness in these latter. If asked to single out one poet whose work I particularly like and find stimulating I would name Kenneth Rexroth.

I have a deep feeling that the most significant ideas can be expressed in direct and clear language, and that the unusual and significant are in the obvious.

The reader may also get an idea of my leanings from the opinions expressed in the articles I have contributed (since 1964) to *Tribune* on little-magazines and related publications.

(1974) In the past three or four years, my poetry has, I think, tended to diversify, both in form and content. I still like brevity and wit, but have found that, in order to deal with matters outside the domestic concerns my poems once related to, I've had to become perhaps more discursive. In a sense, as the subject-matter widens, so do the forms I use. The lines tend to be longer, the rhythm less precise. Interestingly enough, however, I find that when I do revert to "domestic" concerns the form tightens again.

* * *

If one had to find a single word to describe Jim Burns' poems it would be "anecdotal." Each poem tells a story and the tone adopted is that of the raconteur where the impetus relies more on the narrative flow and the ultimate making of a point than on language or rhythm as such. What informs each story is the persona adopted, that of the wryly candid man who, though beguiled by the romantic, is never taken in by it; whether it be romantic love – "Better to make love in bed, turn/your back afterwards. Sleep easy" ("The Way It Is") – or the pretentiousness of romantic politics ("Meanwhile"):

The left wing intellectuals
had fought the Paris Commune, the
General Strike, the Spartacist uprising
and the Spanish Civil War all over
again and would have sung the Red Flag
had they known the words or tune.
Instead, they ordered another round
and the landlord rubbed his hands
and then called time. For everyone

Indeed, it seems to be Burns' mission to gently deflate the phoney and the ostentatious; gently because he too knows the temptations and has some sympathy with those who succumb. For this reason the language used avoids the "high flown" to the point of flatness; Burns' sense of rhythm and the narrative flow carrying the poems on. Nevertheless, the truth must out. "Is a man any less a poet/ because he stays at home/with his wife and children" he asks in "A Single Flower." Poetry stands or falls by what is on the page; it is irrelevant if the author washes himself, sleeps with his sister or has two heads, if he is an arch bishop or an arch-Villon:

I once slept out all night
with the homeless, and although
it taught me pity
it did not teach me poetry.

And he is right; though there are some who will not forgive him for that! But self-depreciatory, honest and always caring as he is, one cannot help liking the man behind the poems.

—John Cotton

BURNSHAW, Stanley. American. Born in New York City, 20 June 1906. Educated at Columbia University, New York, 1924; University of Pittsburgh, B.A. 1925; University of Poitiers, 1927; University of Paris, 1927–28; Cornell University, Ithaca, New York, M.A. 1933. Married 1) Madeline Burnshaw in 1934 (divorced); 2) Lydia Powsner in 1942; one daughter, Valerie, and two stepchildren, Amy and David. Advertising Assistant, Blaw-Knox Company, Blawnox, Pennsylvania, 1925–27; Advertising Manager, The Hecht Company, New York, 1928–32; Co-Editor and Drama Critic, *The New Masses*, New York, 1934–36; Editor-in-Chief, The Cordon Company, publishers, New York, 1937–39; President and Editor-in-Chief, Dryden Press, New York, 1939–58; Vice-President, 1958–66, and Consultant to the President, 1966–68, Holt, Rinehart and Winston Inc., publishers, New

York. Lecturer, New York University, 1958–62. Founding Editor (and hand setter), *Poetry Folio* magazine, and Folio Press, Pittsburgh, 1926–29. Contributing Editor, *Modern Quarterly*, 1932–33, and *Theatre Workshop* magazine, 1935–38. Director, American Institute of Graphic Arts, 1960–61. Recipient: National Institute of Arts and Letters award, 1971. Address: Lamberts Cove, Martha's Vineyard, Massachusetts 02568, U.S.A.

PUBLICATIONS

Verse

Poems. Pittsburgh, Folio Press, 1927.
The Great Dark Love. Privately printed, 1932.
The Iron Land: A Narrative. Philadelphia, Centaur Press, 1936.
The Revolt of the Cats in Paradise: A Children's Book for Adults. Gaylordsville, Connecticut, Crow Hill Press, 1945.
Early and Late Testament. New York, Dial Press, 1952.
Caged in an Animal's Mind. New York, Holt Rinehart, 1963.
The Hero of Silence. Privately printed, 1965.
In the Terrified Radiance. New York, Braziller, 1972.
Mirages: Travel Notes in the Promised Land: A Public Poem. New York, Doubleday, 1977.

Play

The Bridge (in verse). New York, Dryden Press, 1945.

Novel

The Sunless Sea. London, Davies, 1948; New York, Dial Press, 1949.

Other

A Short History of the Wheel Age. Pittsburgh, Folio Press, 1928.
André Spire and His Poetry: Two Essays and Forty Translations. Philadelphia, Centaur Press, 1933.
The Seamless Web: Language-Thinking, Creature-Knowledge, Art-Experience. New York, Braziller, and London, Allen Lane, 1970.

Editor, *Two New Yorkers* (Kruse lithographs and Kreymborg poems). New York, Bruce Humphries, 1938.
Editor, with others, *The Poem Itself: 45 Modern Poets in a New Presentation.* New York, Holt Rinehart, 1960; London, Penguin, 1964.
Editor, with T. Carmi and Ezra Spicehandler, *The Modern Hebrew Poem Itself: From the Beginnings to the Present: Sixty-Nine Poems in a New Presentation.* New York, Holt Rinehart, 1960.
Editor, *Varieties of Literary Experience: Eighteen Essays in World Literature.* New York, New York University Press, 1962; London, Peter Owen, 1963.

Critical Studies: "The Great Dark Love" by André Spire, in *Mercure de France* (Paris), 1 December 1933; "The Poem Itself" by Lionel Trilling, in *The Mid-Century* (New York), August 1960; "On Translating Poetry" by Herbert Read, in *Poetry* (Chicago), April 1961; "The Poet Is Always Present" by Germaine Brée, in *The American Scholar* (Washington, D.C.), Summer 1970; "In the Terrified Radiance" by James Dickey, in *New York Times Book Review*, 24 September 1972.

Stanley Burnshaw comments:

Poetry is the expression of the creator's total organism – or, as I say at the beginning of *The Seamless Web*:

> Poetry begins with the body and ends with the body. Even Mallarmé's symbols of abstract essence lead back to the bones, flesh, and nerves. My approach, then, is "physiological," yet it issues from a vantage point difference from Vico's when he said that all words originated in the eyes, the arms, and the other organs from which they were grown into analogies. My concern is rather with the type of creature-mind developed by the evolutionary shock which gave birth to what we have named self-consciousness. So far as we know, such biological change failed to arise in any other living creature. So far as we can tell, no other species, dead or alive, produced or produces the language-think of poetry. We are engaged, then, with a unique phenomenon issuing from a unique physiology which seems to function no differently from that of other animals – in a life-sustaining activity based on continuous interchange between organism and environment.

Poetry begins with the body and ends with the body – *The Seamless Web* pursues and confronts the implications of this statement from three different vantage points: 1) Language-Thinking, 2) Creature-Knowledge, 3) Art-Experience. The Third (Art-Experience) offers the clearest introduction to my poetry, especially for the reader who has at hand a copy of my *Caged in an Animal's Mind*: there are numerous references to the pages in that volume of my poems.

* * *

Writing of man's struggle through science and technology to master Nature, and the culmination of that struggle in the discovery and use of atomic power, Stanley Burnshaw says: "The war against Nature had been confidently waged and won; and we post-moderns, of 1945-and-after, breathe the spirit of a different epoch, and we have a different terror on our minds: Now that man is victorious, how shall he stay alive?"

This question is a recurring one in his poems, as death, love, and life wage unceasing war, observed by a coal-hard intellect striving relentlessly to illuminate the world, "this eden," through a sense of its kinship with the world of nature. In his forty-year-long poetry-writing career, Burnshaw has remained contemporary, and in his view of the urgency of confronting man's imminent self-annihilation through the destruction of nature he is in agreement with many poets younger than himself. His latest collection, *In the Terrified Radiance*, gives us those parts of his earlier work he wants us to remember, and his *oeuvre* is made to seem remarkably of a piece. From the beginning, he has filled his lyrics with stones, flames, wind, trees, singing, and blood – an imagery suggestive at times of Robinson Jeffers and at others of Theodore Roethke; in all of them, however, Burnshaw is distinctively (if somewhat monotonously and humorlessly) himself.

In his dense, hard-surfaced poems one encounters a harsh, relentless, and totally committed intelligence fronting with mind and senses the inexorable facts of death and life. The effect is a seamless web (to borrow the title of his book about the physiological origins of the creative act) of images of storm, fire, growth, destruction, and the nourishment of creativity by the forces that destroy. These are not simply poems about the "good that comes from evil" or of the cyclical quality of nature; there is something much more elemental in their feeling of primordial unity. Burnshaw, in a paradox of cerebral style and physiological message – what he refers to as creature-knowledge – seems a solemn shaman preserving his intellectual detachment whilst in an ecstasy of sympathy with the tides of being.

—Donald Barlow Stauffer

BUTLER, (Frederick) Guy. South African. Born in Cradock, Cape Province, 21 January 1918. Educated at local high school; Rhodes University, Grahamstown, M.A. 1939; Brasenose College, Oxford, M.A. 1947. Served in World War II in the Middle East, Italy, and the United Kingdom. Married; four children. Taught at the University of Witwatersrand, Johannesburg, 1948–50. Currently, Professor of English at Rhodes University, Grahamstown, South Africa. D.Litt.: University of Natal, Durban, 1968. Address: Department of English, Rhodes University, Grahamstown, South Africa.

PUBLICATIONS

Verse

Stranger to Europe: Poems 1939–1949. Cape Town, Balkema, 1952; augmented edition, 1960.
South of the Zambezi: Poems from South Africa. London, Abelard Schuman, 1966.
On First Seeing Florence. Grahamstown, South Africa, New Coin-Rhodes University, 1968.
Selected Poems. Johannesburg, Donker, 1975.
Songs and Ballads. Cape Town, David Philip, 1978.

Plays

The Dam (produced Cape Town, 1953). Cape Town, Balkema, 1953.
The Dove Returns (produced Cape Town, 1956). Cape Town, Balkema, and London, Fortune Press, 1956.
Take Root or Die (produced Grahamstown, 1966). Cape Town, Balkema, 1970.
Cape Charade (produced Cape Town, 1968). Cape Town, Balkema, 1968.

Other

An Aspect of Tragedy. Grahamstown, Rhodes University, 1953.
The Republic of the Arts. Johannesburg, Witwatersrand University Press, 1964.
Karoo Morning: An Autobiography 1918–35. Cape Town, David Philip, 1977.

Editor, *A Book of South African Verse.* London, Oxford University Press, 1959.
Editor, *When Boys Were Men.* Cape Town, Oxford University Press, 1969.
Editor, with Tim Peacock, *Plays from Near and Far: Twelve One-Act Plays.* Cape Town, Maskew Miller, 1973(?).
Editor, *The 1820 Settlers: An Illustrated Commentary.* Cape Town, Human and Rousseau, 1974.
Editor, with Christopher Mann, *A New Book of South African Verse.* Cape Town, Oxford University Press, 1979.

Manuscript Collection: Thomas Pringle Collection for English in Africa, Rhodes University, Grahamstown.

Guy Butler comments:

Much of my poetry – but by no means all – is generated by the European–African encounter as experienced by someone of European descent, who feels himself to belong to Africa. I am, I think, a product of the old, almost forgotten Eastern Cape Frontier tradition, with its strong liberal and missionary admixture. The nature of the frontier has changed and spread, until all articulate men, but particularly artists, are frontiersmen and/or interpreters.

English, as the chosen language of literature of millions of Blacks, has a great and exciting future in Africa; and I've made it my life's business to encourage its creative use in this corner of the world.

* * *

Guy Butler's work is a sustained endeavour to distinguish and reconcile the two strains of Europe and Africa – chiefly, but not merely, the southern part of the continent; to record and interpret the local scene; to find appropriate media – vocabulary, imagery, forms – through which to discover and express something of the African essence and primitive consciousness; to establish an African mythology and archetypes (Livingstone, Camoens, the last Trekker); to acclimatize as far as possible "the Grecian and Mediaeval dream." Orpheus has an "African incarnation" ("Myths"), Apollo must come to "cross the tangled scrub, the uncouth ways" ("Home Thoughts") and join the Dionysian dance.

Africa almost becomes an image for a state of mind in which the poet's imagination tries to find dwelling and the human being strives to come to terms with himself, a testing ground for his beliefs and values. The inescapable preoccupation of the modern artist, to find his place in his world, is, for the English poet in Africa, sensitive to European history, art and thought, perhaps more dramatically evident than for his British counterpart. The struggle to articulate, clarify, harmonize and balance contending forces, and be true to experience, informs Butler's poetry with tension and some anguish, and lifts it above trivialities. Circumstances tempt the South African writer to exploit rather than explore his material, to be self-conscious or self-pitying, to address too limited a home audience, to slide into fashionable political or literary cant. Butler rarely succumbs.

T. S. Eliot observes of the genuine poet that "his strict duty is to his *language*, first to preserve, and second to extend and improve." Butler's responsible and experimental use of language is grounded in such an awareness of literary tradition. This leads him to genres other than the ubiquitous meditative lyric – ballad, song, sonnet, elegy, narrative, metaphysical debate, in a variety of measures; and particularly the long poem where he shows a not inconsiderable architectonic skill. Besides verse drama, there is the seemingly casual free verse anecdote ("Sweet-Water") and the formal symphonic poem in fairly elaborate stanzas ("Bronze Heads"). With an understanding of neoclassic decorum, he uses a range of styles, language prismatic or transparent, speaking voice or singing robes. Sometimes regarded as an old-fashioned versifier playing safe, he is in fact often taking risks, with rhyme, intricate verse and image patterns, colloquialisms, cliché, plain statement or rhetorically splendid utterance. The long poem "On First Seeing Florence" is a complex structure of varied styles, rhythms and images which eloquently presents a moment of vision.

Because of this readiness to undertake the hazardous and difficult, this range, breadth, and technical skill, and because he has something to say, Butler is possibly the most considerable poet now writing in South Africa. Others may reach greater heights in individual poems; few can present a body of work which has such a wholeness, complexity, variety and approachableness. Nor is his appeal merely local, though certain poems will have a particular poignancy for his countrymen. A lyric like "Stranger to Europe," a meditation like "Myths," will be read wherever poetry is recognized.

—Ruth Harnett

CAMPBELL, Alistair (Te Ariki). New Zealander. Born in Rarotonga, Cook Islands, 25 June 1925; emigrated to New Zealand in 1933. Educated in Otago Boys' High School, Dunedin; Victoria University of Wellington, B.A. in Latin and English. Married 1) Fleur Adcock, *q.v.*, in 1952 (divorced, 1957), two sons; 2) Meg Anderson in 1958, three children.

Editor, Department of Education School Publications Branch, Wellington, 1955–72. Since 1972, Senior Editor, New Zealand Council for Educational Research, Wellington. President, P.E.N. New Zealand Centre, 1976–79. Recipient: La Spezia Film Festival Gold Medal, 1974. Address: 4 Rawhiti Road, Pukerua Bay, Wellington, New Zealand.

PUBLICATIONS

Verse

Mine Eyes Dazzle: Poems 1947–49. Christchurch, Pegasus Press, 1950; revised edition, 1951, 1956.
Sanctuary of Spirits. Wellington, Victoria University-Wai-te-ata Press, 1963.
Wild Honey. London, Oxford University Press, 1964.
Blue Rain. Wellington, Wai-te-ata Press, 1967.
Drinking Horn. Paremata, Bottle Press, 1970.
Walk the Black Path. Paremata, Bottle Press, 1971.
Kapiti: Selected Poems 1947–71. Christchurch, Pegasus Press, 1972.
Dreams, Yellow Lions. Waiura, Alister Taylor, 1975.

Recording: *The Return and Elegy*, KIWI.

Plays

When the Bough Breaks (produced Wellington, 1970). Published in *Contemporary New Zealand Plays*, edited by Howard McNaughton, Wellington, Oxford University Press, 1974.

Radio Plays: *The Homecoming, The Proprietor, The Suicide, The Wairau Incident, Death of the Colonel.*

Television Documentary: *Island of Spirit*, 1973.

Other

The Fruit Farm (juvenile). Wellington, School Publications Branch, 1953.
The Happy Summer (juvenile). Christchurch, Whitcombe and Tombs, 1961.
New Zealand: A Book for Children. Wellington, School Publications Branch, 1967.
Maori Legends. Wellington, Seven Seas, 1969.

Critical Studies: by James Bertram, in *Comment* (Wellington), January–February 1965; "Alistair Campbell's *Mine Eyes Dazzle*: An Anatomy of Success" by David Gunby, in *Landfall* (Christchurch), March 1969; "Alistair Campbell's *Sanctuary of Spirits*" by Frank McKay, in *Landfall* (Christchurch), September 1978.

Alistair Campbell comments:

Primarily a lyric poet. My early verse, written in a variety of mainly regular verse forms, shows the influence of such poets as Tennyson, Yeats, Pound, and Edward Thomas. More recently, Latin-American and Spanish poets, among others, have shown me how to write with a new freedom and spontaneity, while Maori history has provided me with new themes.

* * *

Alistair Campbell was born in Rarotonga of Scottish sailor father and a Polynesian mother of chiefly rank. The early deaths of both parents led to his upbringing as orphan and exile in New Zealand. Such radical uprooting, joined with the failure of his first marriage to Fleur Adcock (subsequently a talented poet in her own right), as well as major problems of mental health for both partners of his subsequent marriage, have left conspicuous traces through his poetry. These have been movingly presented, as to his parentage in four "Personal Sonnets" and, in respect of marriage, notably in his play *When the Bough Breaks* (based on his earlier *The Homecoming*) and in a number of poems of which some are incorporated in that play (e.g., "Why Don't You Talk to Me?"). Campbell's other radio drama deals with schizophrenia (*The Suicide*), marital breakdown based on Greek myth in absurdist style (*The Proprietor*) and Maori–European clash (*The Wairau Incident*). His hillside coastal home presents a commanding view of the island of Kapiti, now a bird sanctuary, once the island citadel of Maori warrior chief ("the Maori Napoleon") Te Rauparaha. Both island and chief are potent entities in several poems, notably the sequence *Sanctuary of Spirits* with its terrifying ending

The wind rises,
lifts the lid off my brain –

Madman, leave me alone!

This biographical clearing of the ground seems necessary preparation for entry into a world musical, often hedonist, of brief and personal, often haunted, lyric of love, of nature and, increasingly in recent years, of traditional Maori culture.

Campbell's first volume – brief, rich, formal, ultra-Romantic, or late Victorian lyrics – was somewhat of a *succès d'estime*. It was notable for "Elegy" (on a friend killed climbing) – a highly animistic lyric sequence – and his mysterious and atavistic "The Return" that presents below "the long pouring headland" and "on the surf-loud beach" both "men ... moving between the fires" and "Their heads finely shrunken to a skull, small/And delicate, with small black rounded beaks/... rain-jewelled, leaf green/Bodies ... Plant gods, tree gods," together with "Face downward/And in a small creek mouth all unperceived;/The drowned Dionysus...." Crisis and transition characterize *Sanctuary of Spirits*. Commissioned for radio, this book (like the related television documentary a decade later) is "more a series of images than a documentary" and culminates in "Against Te Rauparaha" which Campbell himself calls "an exorcism." Frank McKay, however, doubts its efficacy and, more positively, suggests "that subconsciously at least desire to belong to a tribe lies behind these poems." Certainly from here on the Georgian formalism of Campbell's earlier work, though never abandoned, is definitively transcended and his approximation to Maori and Polynesian oratory may be thought to have both psychologically freed his style and enabled him more fully to use both Polynesian content and, presumably, attitudes. Examples include "Reflections on Some Great Chiefs," "Waiting for the Pakeha," and most recently the plangent "Friend":

This is the dearest of my wishes,
The last leaf shaken from the tree –
Sow the South Wind with my ashes
To fall in tears on Kapiti.

In general the more brooding personal lyrics of the 1960's seem left behind in recent poetry that, along with the nihilism of, say, "Walk the Black Path," embraces also the (very Maori) fantasy cowboy myth in "The Gunfighter," surrealist abreaction of "The Manner Is to Be Deplored," humane rebuke of "Memo to Mr. Auden" – "Mr. Auden ... You are the delicate/ Expensive ship that sees something amazing, perhaps/Even tragic – a boy falling out of the sky,/But you have a poem to finish and sail calmly on" – and his unfailing gift for nature lyric in "Flowering Apple," and sensitively mature personal reaction in "The Australian

Girl." His neighbour, the younger poet Sam Hunt, has spoken usefully of Campbell's gifts for natural imagery, for "the whimsical and earthy," and adds: "something which is rarely mentioned in such discussion – and, along with some other critics, we believe it to be the key to Campbell's best work – is the *duende* of the poems.... The Spanish poet Lorca described that power as being 'the spirit of the earth.' " Campbell's total poetic output is slender; his uncomplex prosody, early and late, runs largely to short lines and quatrains; *Sanctuary of Spirits*, happy coincidence of radio needs and oral inheritance, has "freed" much of his later work; "the earthy" in his work never for long precludes the somewhat dandiacal aesthete.

—Peter Alcock

CAMPBELL, David (Watt Ian). Australian. Born in Ellerslie, Adelong, New South Wales, 16 July 1915. Educated at King's School, Parramatta; Jesus College, Cambridge, B.A. Served in the Royal Australian Air Force during World War II: Distinguished Flying Cross and Bar. Farmer. Address: The Run, Queanbeyan, New South Wales 2620, Australia.

PUBLICATIONS

Verse

Speak with the Sun. London, Chatto and Windus, 1949.
The Miracle of Mullion Hill. Sydney, Angus and Robertson, 1956.
Poems. Sydney, Edwards and Shaw, 1962.
Selected Poems 1942–1968. Sydney, Angus and Robertson, 1968.
The Branch of Dodona and Other Poems. Sydney, Angus and Robertson, 1970.
Selected Poems 1942–1970. Sydney, Angus and Robertson, 1973.
Starting from Central Station: A Sequence of Poems. Canberra, Brindabella Press, 1973.
Devils' Rock and Other Poems 1970–1972. Sydney, Angus and Robertson, 1974.
Deaths and Pretty Cousins. Canberra, Australian National University Press, 1975.
Words with a Black Orpington. Sydney, Angus and Robertson, 1978.
The Man in the Honeysuckle. Sydney, Angus and Robertson, 1979.

Short Stories

Evening under Lamplight. Sydney, Angus and Robertson, 1959.
Flame and Shadow: Selected Stories. Brisbane, University of Queensland Press, 1976.

Other

The History of Australia, with Keith Looby. Sydney, Macleay Museum, 1976.

Editor, *Australian Poetry 1966.* Sydney, Angus and Robertson, 1966.
Editor, *Modern Australian Poetry.* Melbourne, Sun, 1970.

Translator, with Rosemary Dobson, *Moscow Trefoil.* Canberra, Australian National University Press, 1975.
Translator, with Rosemary Dobson, *Seven Russian Poets.* Brisbane, University of Queensland Press, 1979.

Manuscript Collection: National Library, Canberra.

Critical Study: "David Campbell: *Selected Poems 1942–1968*" by Leonie Kramer, in *Southerly* (Sydney), 1969.

* * *

Though there is a wide variety in his poetry, especially in his later books, ranging from studies in haiku form of the aboriginal rock carvings around Sydney to love poems and poems of his travels in Europe, from family portraits in their historical setting to poems from the Russian of Anna Akhmatova and Osip Mandelstam, David Campbell is probably best known in Australia as the poet of the Monaro. If, beyond that, he is more properly to be regarded simply as one of the finest lyric poets Australia has produced, nevertheless it is in the Monaro that he has lived and found his distinctive imagery.

This is the district where he lives, having for its centre the national capital, Canberra. It is a beautiful, unspoilt countryside of sheep and cattle stations, rising from the low rolling hills near Canberra – patrolled by flocks of white cockatoos, and the hawks with which as an ex-airman and a descendant of Highland chieftains, Campbell has always shown some affinity – to the granite uplands of the Snowy Mountains. Since World War II, Campbell has farmed three properties in the Monaro, and, from his first book to his latest, his love of the land shows as the central stream of his poetry. It is a love for the small flowers and creatures of the earth, down to the very stones in its creeks:

Stones come alive
In your hands in water;
Dive and feel
In the cobbled green runs....

It is a love for his own sheep and lambs:

But in the evening light the lambs
Forget their hillward-munching dams;
To cuckoo-pipes their dances start
And fill and overflow the heart ...

for the land itself:

Sweet rain, bless our windy farm,
Sweeping round in skirts of storm
While these marble acres lie
Open to an empty sky ...

and for the people of the Monaro seen in a variety of moods from the comic ballad of "Jack Spring" to the archetypal figure of Peter Quinn

Who, from the pools of Dairyman,
Has learned the dreamer's power
To shut up mountains in his mind
As the seed holds the flower.

Campbell himself of course has this same "dreamer's power"; and ultimately his creatures of the Monaro, while cherished for their own sakes, become symbols of some principle of joy infusing and indeed creating the universe: a magpie sings in the moonlight

And to the heartbeats of the light
Now from the deepness of the glade
Well up the bubbles of delight:
Of such stuff the stars were made.

—Douglas Stewart

CAMPBELL, Donald. Scottish. Born in Wick, Caithness, 25 February 1940. Educated at Boroughmuir Senior Secondary School, Edinburgh. Married Jean Fairgrieve in 1966; one son. Writer-in-Residence, Edinburgh Education Department, 1974–75. Recipient: Scottish Arts Council bursary, 1973. Agent: Joanna Marston, Rosica Coley Ltd., 4 Hereford Square, London SW7 4TU, England. Address: 53 Viewforth, Edinburgh, Scotland.

PUBLICATIONS

Verse

Poems. Preston, Lancashire, Akros, 1971.
Rhymes 'n Reasons. Edinburgh, Reprographia, 1972.
Murals: Poems in Scots. Edinburgh, Lothlorien, 1974.

Plays

The Jesuit (produced Edinburgh, 1976). Edinburgh, P. Harris, 1976.
Somerville the Soldier (produced Edinburgh, 1978). Edinburgh, P. Harris, 1978.
Widows of Clym (produced Edinburgh, 1979).

Critical Studies: "The Progress of Scots" by John Herdman, in *Akros* (Preston, Lancashire), 1972; "The MacDiarmid Makars" by Alexander Scott, in *Akros* (Preston, Lancashire), 1972.

Donald Campbell comments:

The bulk of my work is written in Scots – that is to say, in the language which is, to a greater or lesser extent, the language of the greater part of the Scottish people. Now, this in itself probably requires a great deal of explanation – but, without going into a mass of detail, I will be as brief as possible. Most people who know little of Scots poetry appear to assume that Scots is a language (like English or Spanish) which died out years ago and that the work of the Modern Scots poets is no more than a sentimental attempt to revive or re-create it. This is not the case. Scots has never been subject to formal documentation like most other modern languages and survives for two reasons (a) its proximity to English (most English speakers can, with little difficulty, learn to read and understand Scots) and (b) because it has been sustained for over seven centuries by its own distinctive literary tradition. It is within this tradition that I appear to work. The advantages for a poet who is working in Scots (and who can work in Scots) are that he is not restricted by so many "rules of language" and that, although there is a great deal of poetry in our tradition, there are vast uncharted areas of poetic possibility that have never been explored. For instance, although we have had many poets who have written what you might call poems of "direct statement," not much work has been done with the use of images in Scots. We have had many great formal craftsmen (Dunbar, Henrysoun, Fergusson, etc.) but very few who can handle free verse.

My work as a poet does not start and end with Scots however. That is only the tool. I have no concise aims (poets should never have aims) but what I am against *as a man* is the erection of barriers among men. This may seem paradoxical unless you realise that Standard English is a great barrier in Scotland. The inability to speak "correct" English often prevents our people from realising their full potential – and I am naturally against that not simply because they are Scottish but because they are human beings. I want to help exorcise the shame of having for your most natural speech a language which is not recognised as an official language but is, as often as not, not recognised as a language at all. I think all this shows in my poems.

My influences have been mostly foreign – the main ones being the Russian Mayakovsky, the Frenchman Jacques Prévert, and the English poet Gerard Manley Hopkins. Scots poets who have influenced me have been Hugh MacDiarmid, Sydney Goodsir Smith, Robert Garioch, and, most important of all, both the Alexander Scotts – the medieval love poet from Dalkeith and the modern poet and dramatist from Aberdeen. I am also a great admirer of the artistry and language of Norman MacCaig.

* * *

In Donald Campbell's first pamphlet, *Poems*, all the verse was in Scots, and its energy and contemporary concern suggested better work to come when those qualities were combined with greater self-criticism and technical care. This combination has been achieved in a majority of the poems in *Rhymes 'n Reasons*. The characteristic Scottish expression of tenderness through the medium of a darkly-ironical apparent callousness is a difficult mode to master, but Campbell brings it off with fine panache in "Vietnam on My Mind," while in another political – or anti-political – poem, "Bangla Desh," he accomplishes the even trickier feat of expressing sympathy through its seeming denial. This command of ambiguity finds a subject in itself in "Ye Say 'Glass,' " and enables a love-poem, "You're the Warst," to end a series of amusing paradoxes by becoming a savage hate-poem too. Yet Campbell is also capable of restraint, and the quietness of "At a Party" is fairly appropriate to its desolate theme of two lovers failing to meet. His few poems in English, sharing the human sympathy expressed in such Scots work as "Keelie" and "Communion at Dunkirk," have a nice delicacy of under-emphasis.

Although *Murals* contains only 14 poems, these still range widely in content, mood and style. An ironical beast-fable, "Jist Shows Ye!," on the theme of the early bird and the worm, combines comedy and pathos in its quaint reversal of the customary moral; a satirical dramatic monologue, "Hauf-roads up Schiehallion," demonstrates an impeccable ear for the nuances of contemporary Scots speech as well as insight into the tragi-comic complexities of adolescent passion; "Betrayal in Morninside" makes effective – and unusual – use of the reductive idiom in order to reduce the stature of the writer himself; and "In the Tenement of My Mind" dares to employ the actualities of tenement existence in singing a lament for "the long littleness of life." Other verses display a kind of brash rhetoric lacking the sensitivity to evoke a poetic response, but when Campbell eschews exclamation and allows his subject to speak for themselves he achieves a striking interplay between the imaginative and the real.

—Alexander Scott

CAMPBELL, George. Jamaican. Born in Panama, 26 December 1916. Educated at St. George's College, Kingston, Jamaica; New School for Social Research, New York. Married Odilia Crane in 1948; four daughters. Journalist, *Jamaica Daily Gleaner*, Kingston, and an editor in the Jamaican welfare department; secretary with the little theatre movement, Jamaica; Program Director, Jewish centers, New York, for 30 years. Currently, Publications Consultant, Institute of Jamaica, Kingston. Address: Institute of Jamaica, 5 East Street, Kingston, Jamaica, West Indies.

PUBLICATIONS

Verse

First Poems. Privately printed, 1945.

Play

A Play Without Scenery (produced Kingston, 1947). Published in *Focus* magazine (Kingston).

George Campbell comments:

Much of my early poetry is identified by critics with the struggle for Jamaican independence, a struggle that lasted from the late 1930's until separation from British colonial rule in 1962. The publication of *First Poems* was considered something of a "landmark"; it was recognised as a break away from Victorian poetry and as a valid usage of free verse. It influenced Jamaican and other Caribbean poets (one of the poems, "Litany," was used as a symbol for the first "Carifesta," held in Guyana in 1972). The themes of my poems vary: as Louis Simpson wrote in *Air with Armed Men*, they deal with the beauty of people, protest, and love. The more recent poetry is philosophical, and about nature and love.

* * *

George Campbell is one of the most important figures in the transition from colonial apprenticeship to a sense of the autochthonous and its expression. His work dominates Edna Manley's *Focus*, one of the four locally based West Indian journals which provided a forum for the emerging Caribbean writers of the 1930's and early 1940's (the others were the *Beacon* in Trinidad, *Bim* in Barbados and *Kyk-over-al* in Guyana).

As with most West Indian poets, especially those of the transitional period (1900–50), nature appears as the first inspiration for Campbell's poetry, with, as with M. G. Smith, E. M. Roach, and H. M. Telemaque, a strong sense of the pantheistic about it (see "Litany," "Essential," "Infinity," "Hymn to Being," among others). Love, a certain social optimism, and a feeling for the League of Nations of all peoples, leading to a kind of Christian Socialism – even his patriotism within a multi-racial plural society – all stem from this vision of original nature. The pity is that Campbell (again, like most poets of this period) hardly ever found the sustained language to move the body of his poetry out of the post-Victorian into the modern Caribbean. Although there is a certain arresting Imagism, it is strongly coloured, as with McKay's Jamaican poems, with romanticism: "These people with their scarlet heads/Bear baskets of their golden fruit/Down blue streets/Into market beds/Of leaf green heaps/And crimson blaze,/They stoop before their golden fruit." At his best, Campbell transcended these limitations through developing a sense of form (in "Litany," "Last Queries," and "History Makers") where word/sound combine with social criticism and vision to create:

Women stone breakers
Hammers and rocks
Tired child makers
Haphazard frocks.

Strong thigh
Rigid head
Bent nigh
Hard white piles
Of stone
Under hot sky
In the gully bed.

No smiles
No sigh
No moan.

Women child bearers
Pregnant frocks
Wilful toil sharers
Destiny shapers
History makers
Hammers and rocks.

But even this is not his finest achievement. Campbell may have started as an Imagist, and developed, given his place and time, an acute and important social criticism; but more than any other poet of the 1930's he was also involved in the struggle for and articulation of political autonomy for the Caribbean. The popular uprisings throughout the archipelago led to the formation of militant nationalist parties and the promise, wrenched from the Mother Country, of self-rule and eventual Independence. It was at this juncture that Campbell's talents responded most securely to the movement of his time, calling out of himself an enduring eloquence he had not known before ("On This Night"):

On this momentous night O God help us.
With faith we now challenge our destiny.
Tonight masses of men will shape, will hope,
Will dream, with us; so many years hang on
Acceptance. Who is that knocking against
The door? Isle of Jamaica is it you
Looking for a destiny, or is it
Noise of the storm?...
Wind where cometh the fine technique
Of rule passing through me? My hands wet with
The soil and I knowing my world.

—Edward Kamau Brathwaite

CARROLL, Paul. American. Born in Chicago, Illinois, 15 July 1927. Educated at the University of Chicago, M.A. in English 1952. Served in the United States Naval Reserve, 1945–46. Married Inara Birnbaum in 1964 (divorced, 1973); one son. Poetry Editor, *Chicago Review*, 1957–59; Editor, *Big Table Magazine*, Chicago, 1959–61; Editor, Big Table Books, Follett Publishing Company, Chicago, 1966–71. Visiting Professor of English, University of Iowa, Iowa City, 1966–67; Professor of English and Chairman of The Program for Writers, University of Illinois, Chicago, 1968–73; Poet-in-Residence, Branford College, Yale

University, New Haven, Connecticut, Spring 1969. Address: 7737 North East Lake Terrace, Chicago, Illinois 60626, U.S.A.

PUBLICATIONS

Verse

Odes. Chicago, Follett, 1968.
The Luke Poems. Chicago, Follett, 1971.

Other

The Poem in Its Skin. Chicago, Follett, 1968.

Editor, *The Edward Dahlberg Reader.* New York, New Directions, 1967.
Editor, *The Young American Poets.* Chicago, Follett, 1968.

Paul Carroll comments:

I can't imagine life without poetry.

* * *

Paul Carroll's esthetic understanding abruptly flowered in three volumes of 1968–69. *The Poem in Its Skin* analyzed ten poems by, to Carroll's eyes, the ten leading American poets. *The Young American Poets*, an anthology of 54 poets, encouraged and further directed young poets. *Odes*, Carroll's own selected poems, promulgates in verse the same sensibility and fashions as the essays and anthology.

In the essay on James Wright in *The Poem in Its Skin*, Carroll characterizes Wright's poem as a hip or "impure" homage to Po Chu-i. Similar homage is a motive in Carroll's own odes, though Carroll offers homage not to past poets like Trakl or Po Chu-i but to leading contemporaries like Dickey, Ginsberg, Logan, Wright, and, especially, Neruda. *Odes* owes its title and certain techniques to Neruda's *Odas Elementales*; Carroll acknowledges this explicitly by offering an "Ode to Neruda." "Ode on My 40th Birthday," the opening poem, reworks the theme of Dickey's "Heaven of Animals," a poem Carroll analyzed in *The Poem in Its Skin.* Dickey typically divides life between predator and prey, and reconciles them in a "ritual" hunt. Carroll, spiritually a Catholic, finds a Saint Francis who succumbs less to ritual than "role," becoming, briefly, the glint-toothed, priestly predator:

Francis free finally to be
the timber wolf he's feared in dreams
because its teeth and fur are yours
slaughters the lamb for the feast reciting
the prayer at the top of his voice.

Some lines later Carroll dextrously invokes Dickey's antithesis, the Buddhist Allen Ginsberg:

Do you dance
on your own body throughout eternity
as your new lover Allen Ginsberg says?

Carroll's earliest poems depend, significantly, on the literally Catholic and allusive manner of Lowell's *Lord Weary's Castle*. An "Ode to Claes Oldenburg" alerts us that the "impure poem" – a poem, celebrated in Carroll's criticism, which is markedly contemporaneous – derives from Pop art. Carroll's musical odes appeal to the kindly, well-dressed mandarin-about-town.

—Michael André

CARRUTH, Hayden. American. Born in Waterbury, Connecticut, 3 August 1921. Educated at the University of North Carolina, Chapel Hill, B.A. 1943; University of Chicago, M.A. 1947. Served in the United States Army Air Corps during World War II. Married 1) Sara Anderson in 1943; 2) Eleanore Ray in 1952; 3) Rose Marie Dorn in 1961; two children. Editor, *Poetry*, Chicago, 1949–50; Associate Editor, University of Chicago Press, 1950–51, and Intercultural Publications Inc., New York, 1952–53. Visiting Professor, Johnson State College, Vermont, University of Vermont, Burlington, and St. Michael's College, Winooskie, Vermont. Since 1978, Professor of English, Syracuse University, New York. Currently, Member of the Editorial Board, *Hudson Review*, New York; since 1979, Poetry Editor, *Harper's*, New York. Recipient: Bess Hokin Prize, 1954, Vachel Lindsay Prize, 1956, Levinson Prize, Eunice Tietjens Memorial Prize, and Morton Dauwen Zabel Prize, 1968 (*Poetry*, Chicago); Harriet Monroe Award, 1960; Bollingen Fellowship, 1963; Carl Sandburg Prize, 1963; Emily Clark Balch Prize (*Virginia Quarterly Review*), 1964; Guggenheim Fellowship, 1965, 1979; National Endowment for the Arts grant, 1966, 1968, 1974; Shelley Memorial Award, 1978. Address: Department of English, Syracuse University, Syracuse, New York 13210, U.S.A.

PUBLICATIONS

Verse

The Crow and the Heart, 1946–1959. New York, Macmillan, 1959.
Journey to a Known Place. New York, New Directions, 1961.
The Norfolk Poems, 1 June to 1 September 1961. Iowa City, Prairie Press, 1962.
North Winter. Iowa City, Prairie Press, 1964.
Nothing for Tigers: Poems 1959–1964. New York, Macmillan, 1965.
Contra Mortem. Johnson, Vermont, Crow's Mark Press, 1967.
For You. New York, New Directions, 1970; London, Chatto and Windus, 1972.
The Clay Hill Anthology. Iowa City, Prairie Press, 1970.
From Snow and Rock, From Chaos: Poems 1965–1972. New York, New Directions, and London, Chatto and Windus, 1973.
Dark World. Santa Cruz, California, Kayak, 1974.
The Bloomingdale Papers. Athens, University of Georgia Press, 1974.
Loneliness: An Outburst of Hexasyllables. West Burke, Vermont, Janus Press, 1976.
Aura. West Burke, Vermont, Janus Press, 1977.
Brothers, I Loved You All. New York, Sheep Meadow Press, 1978.

Novel

Appendix A. New York, Macmillan, 1963.

Other

After "The Stranger": Imaginary Dialogues with Camus. New York, Macmillan, 1965.

Editor, with James Laughlin, *A New Directions Reader*. New York, New Directions, 1964.
Editor, *The Voice That Is Great Within Us: American Poetry of the Twentieth Century*. New York, Bantam, 1970.
Editor, *The Bird/Poem Book: Poems on the Wild Birds of North America*. New York, McCall, 1970.

Manuscript Collection: University of Vermont, Burlington.

* * *

At this point in his poetic career we can begin to see the emerging shape of Hayden Carruth's work. At the center of his first book, *The Crow and The Heart*, is his important long poem "The Asylum" which establishes one of the central themes and concerns of his poetry: the interplay between (so-called) madness and sanity. Like most of his early work, "The Asylum" is tightly controlled verse dominated by iambic lines and rhymed couplets. He describes a long winter spent in a mental institution. Like Roethke, Carruth struggles through nightmare and chaos; "how hard the search here for the self at last!" He comes to the painful conclusion that, if nothing else is possible, "*Save thou thyself.*" The poem slowly enlarges to encompass America in her own illness ("This land once was asylum when we came..."). But madness and decay now grow throughout the land. Leaving the asylum, he rebuilds his life "on a windy knoll," held in check now by labor and the land. He discovers that in this "house of pain" called life, we each have "our particular hells" to endure. On this foundation of pain and understanding he rebuilds: "we lie all nailed and living, love's long gain." "The Asylum," even in its later, revised form, is not, I think, so good as Roethke's "The Lost Son," but it is comparable. Certainly Carruth's windswept Vermont farm country is as important to his restoration and vision as was the greenhouse to Roethke. This poem is also central to our engagement with his later work, for it establishes Carruth's crucial and complex interplay between chaos and order, between the nighmare of the asylum and the relative control that comes from farm labor and the cycle of the seasons.

Throughout his work Carruth has returned, again and again, to the form of the long poem, usually containing many parts and often many voices. It is a form which serves him admirably, allowing sufficient room for the loose, imagistic form in which he excels. *For You* is his richest exploration of the long poem form. It opens with a revised and extended version of "The Asylum," containing the essential core of the earlier poem, but ending with the unsettling, but perhaps more honest lines, "here am I, drowned, living, loving, and insane." "North Winter" is the central poem of this volume; its unleashed, icy blasts seem to chill all that surround it. "North" and "winter" are many things to Carruth, but above all they are states of mind. "North is a horror from which a horror grows...." Later we find that, in addition to horror, "north is the aurora north is/ deliverance emancipation .../ north is ... nothing...." With *For You* Carruth's poetry begins to extend strongly beyond the self and the region, speaking to issues both national and human. As Adrienne Rich expressed it, "his poetry is radical in its need for roots, and its hatred of the rootless shifting opportunism and greed and dishonor which are wasting our country...."

From Snow and Rock, From Chaos is a collection of Carruth's shorter poems. We learn a landscape of Vermont place-names and farm labors, and meet more than one "tough minded Yankee." Carruth manages, despite the omnipresence of Robert Frost, to make the familiar topics of farming fresh with life, and with a voice quite his own. His poems here are like fragments wrested, torn from tree, rock, and earth, and forced into poems – like a leaf torn in two, " one leaf/ torn to give you half/ showing ... love's complexity in an act...." In many of these poems we witness pain being endured through suffering and waiting, until the release that brings wider vision and moments of intense love.

Brothers, I Loved You All contains some of Carruth's finest work yet. He captures here, as in many earlier poems, sharply etched images of momentary events. Some of these, notably the long poem "Vermont," and several that follow it, are very Frostian in theme. The volume ends with "Paragraphs," a 28-part poem in improvisational style, which honors Carruth's favorite musicians. But his subject is best expressed by the line, "RAVAGE, DEVASTATE, SACK." With shock and rage, he sees even the pastoral hills of Vermont ravaged and devastated by the greedy and shortsighted. He reproaches his neighbors, by name, for selling their farms to make way for stores and trailer parks, and "for a hot pocketful of dollars." Through them he accuses all America: "your *best* is what you gave them/ o my friends –/ your lives, your farms." With this poem a much more direct and forceful public voice emerges, one we need identify with Gary Snyder and most particularly with Wendell Berry, as poets crying forcefully against the environmental destructiveness of our culture. Thus we see Hayden Carruth not only as a survivor of chaos, but also as a revolutionary poet who sees "all dark ahead and behind, his fate/ a need without hope: *the will to resist*."

—John R. Cooley

CARTER, Martin (Wylde). Guyanan. Born in Georgetown, British Guiana, now Guyana, in 1927. Educated at Queen's College, Georgetown. Worked as a clerk in the Civil Service for four years: forced to resign as a result of his political activities. Currently, representative for Guyana at the United Nations.

PUBLICATIONS

Verse

The Hill of Fire Glows Red. Georgetown, Miniature Poets, 1951.
To a Dead Slave. Privately printed, 1951.
The Kind Eagle. Privately printed, 1952.
The Hidden Man. Privately printed, 1952.
Poems of Resistance from British Guiana. London, Lawrence and Wishart, 1954.
Poems of Succession. London, New Beacon, 1977.

Other

Man and Making – Victim and Vehicle (lecture). Georgetown, National History and Art Council, 1971.

* * *

Apart from contributions in the now defunct Guyanese journal, *Kyk-over-al*, the main significant body of Martin Carter's work is to be found in *Poems of Resistance* (1954) and "Jail Me Quickly," five poems first published in 1964 by the *New World Fortnightly*.

Carter's specific concern is with politics, political revolution and colonial oppression. *Poems of Resistance* was written when the poet was placed in detention for his political views in 1953. "Jail Me Quickly" is a direct response to the political crisis in Guyana in 1962, when the Guyanese Constitution, under Dr. Cheddi Jagan, was suspended by the British Government and British troops were moved in to uphold "law and order" in the country ("Black Friday 1962"):

were some who ran one way.
were some who ran another way.
were some who did not run at all.
were some who will not run again.
and I was with them all,
when the sun and streets exploded,
and a city of clerks
turned a city of men!

This is Carter's hope – that the individual man may become an aware and fully rounded person, despite the horrors and failures of his colonial past ("I Come from the Nigger Yard"):

I come from the nigger yard of yesterday
leaping from the oppressor's hate
and the scorn of myself;
from the agony of the dark hut in the shadow
and the hurt of things ...

But Carter's poetry reveals little *substantial* awareness of the past. He asserts that he will "turn to the histories of men and the lives of the peoples"; but unlike his older contemporary, A. J. Seymour, he has produced no work of reconstruction. Because of this shallow soil of heritage, Carter, poet of the revolution, has really only himself and the revolution and a hope for the future to sustain his vision ("The Knife of Dawn"):

The sharp knife of dawn glitters in my hand
but how bare is everything – tall tall tree
infinite air, the unrelaxing tension of the world
and only hope, hope only, the kind eagle soars and wheels in flight.

What is more fully realized in his poetry is an apprehension of terror (here he reminds us of Yeats), of hopelessness and futility: "And I have seen some creatures rise from holes,/and claw a triumph like a citizen,/and reign until the tide!" ("Black Friday").

But this hopelessness and terror and futility are transformed through Martin Carter's energy of image and metaphor into a triumph of the writer's art; the elevation of a single mind against the world ("University of Hunger"):

The long streets of night move up and down
baring the thighs of a woman
and the cavern of generation.
The beating drum returns and dies away
the bearded men fall down and go to sleep
the cocks of dawn stand up and crow like bugles.

And again ("I Come from the Nigger Yard"):

O it was the heart like this tiny star near to the sorrows
straining against the whole world and the long twilight
spark of man's dream conquering the night
moving in darkness stubborn and fierce
till leaves of sunset change from green to blue
and shadows grow like giants everywhere.

—Edward Kamau Brathwaite

CASEY, Michael. American. Born in Lowell, Massachusetts, in 1947. Educated at Lowell Technological Institute, B.S. 1968; State University of New York, Buffalo, M.A. 1973. Served in the United States Army. Research Assistant, State University of New York, Buffalo, 1972–73; Guest Editor, *Rapport*, Buffalo, Summer 1973. Since 1972, Editorial Adviser, Alice James Press, Cambridge, Massachusetts. Recipient: Yale Series of Younger Poets Award, 1971. Address: c/o Yale University Press, 92a Yale Station, New Haven, Connecticut 06520, U.S.A.

PUBLICATIONS

Verse

Obscenities. New Haven, Connecticut, Yale University Press, 1972.
On Scales. Buffalo, New York, Lockwood Memorial Library, 1972.
My Youngest That Tall. Buffalo, New York, Slow Loris Press, 1972.
My Brother-in-Law and Me. Cambridge, Massachusetts, Pomegranate Press, 1974.
The Company Pool. Pittsburgh, Slow Loris Press, 1976.

Critical Study: by A. Poulin, Jr., in *Modern Poetry Studies* (Buffalo, New York), iii, 4, 1972.

* * *

Any critical statement on the poetry of Michael Casey must be drawn from his single collection, *Obscenities*, and must therefore be qualified – despite its having won the Yale Series of Younger Poets award. It is a slim book, well received by most critics and definitely showing promise; it also, however, shows Casey operating within a relatively narrow range, both technically and thematically.

Obscenities is a product of the war in Vietnam: "a kind of anti-poetry," Stanley Kunitz asserts in the Foreword, "that befits a kind of war empty of any kind of glory." Avoiding all traditional rhetorical stances toward war, Casey presents a series of short anecdotes about army life and the war in Vietnam as seen from his somewhat peripheral position as a military policeman. These anecdotes are related with economy and with maximum use of crude but authentic G.I. slang. They are witty, often ironic, occasionally moving or disturbing. And they entertain.

At his best (e.g., in "Learning" and "On What the Army Does to Heads") Casey goes far beyond mere entertainment, of course, transcending surface simplicity and moving toward ambiances that resonate, reward. But all too many of these poems are already time-bound; in his attempt to avoid cant, he simply adopts a different but equally limiting argot. After a while his poems tend to sound alike, gimmicky, almost formulaic; and like most pop art, many fail to invite or sustain subsequent readings.

Despite these reservations, one senses that Michael Casey is a poet worth watching in the future. His first volume shows clear potential and some fine moments within its limited boundaries. As one of the youngest poets ever to win the Yale award, Michael Casey has time on his side. One hopes that he can find new strategies to mature beyond this successful beginning.

—Stanley W. Lindberg

CAUSLEY, Charles (Stanley). British. Born in Launceston, Cornwall, 24 August 1917. Educated at Launceston National School; Horwell Grammar School; Launceston College;

Peterborough Training College. Served in the Royal Navy, 1940–46. Taught in Cornwall, 1947–76. Honorary Visiting Fellow in Poetry, University of Exeter, 1973–74. Literary Editor of BBC radio magazines, *Apollo in the West* and *Signature*, 1953–56. Member of the Arts Council Poetry (later Literature) Panel, 1962–66. Vice-President, West Country Writers' Association; Vice-President, The Poetry Society, London. Recipient: Society of Authors travelling scholarship, 1954, 1966; Queen's Gold Medal for Poetry, 1967; Cholmondeley Award, 1971. Fellow, Royal Society of Literature, 1958. D.Litt.: University of Exeter, 1977. Agent: David Higham Associates Ltd., 5–8 Lower John Street, Golden Square, London W1R 3PE. Address: 2 Cyprus Well, Launceston, Cornwall, England.

PUBLICATIONS

Verse

Farewell, Aggie Weston. Aldington, Kent, Hand and Flower Press, 1951.
Survivor's Leave. Aldington, Kent, Hand and Flower Press, 1953.
Union Street. London, Hart Davis, 1957; Boston, Houghton Mifflin, 1958.
The Ballad of Charlotte Dymond. Privately printed, 1958.
Johnny Alleluia. London, Hart Davis, 1961.
Penguin Modern Poets 3, with George Barker and Martin Bell. London, Penguin, 1962.
Ballad of the Bread Man. London, Macmillan, 1968.
Underneath the Water. London, Macmillan, 1968.
Figure of 8: Narrative Poems. London, Macmillan, 1969.
Figgie Hobbin: Poems for Children. London, Macmillan, 1970; New York, Walker, 1973.
Pergamon Poets 10, with Laurie Lee, edited by Evan Owen. Oxford, Pergamon Press, 1970.
Timothy Winters, music by Wallace Southam. London, Turret, 1970.
The Tail of the Trinosaur (for children). Leicester, Brockhampton Press, 1973.
As I Went Down Zig Zag (for children). London, Warne, 1974.
Six Women. Richmond, Surrey, Keepsake Press, 1974.
Collected Poems 1951–1975. London, Macmillan, and Boston, Godine, 1975.
Here We Go Round the Round House (juvenile). Leicester, New Broom Press, 1976.
The Hill of the Fairy Calf (juvenile). London, Hodder and Stoughton, 1976.
The Animals' Carol. London, Macmillan, 1978.
St. Martha and the Dragon. London, Oxford University Press, 1978.

Recordings: *Here Today 1*, Jupiter; *The Poet Speaks 8*, Argo; British Council tapes, 1960, 1966, 1968; *Causley Reads Causley*, Sentinel, 1975; *Pushing the Business On*, Plant Life, 1977.

Plays

Runaway. London, Curwen, 1936.
The Conquering Hero. London, Curwen, and New York, Schirmer, 1937.
Benedict. London, Muller, 1938.
How Pleasant to Know Mrs. Lear. London, Muller, 1948.
The Ballad of Aucassin and Nicolette, music by Stephen McNess (produced London, 1978). London, Penguin, 1979.
The Gift of a Lamb. London, Robson, 1978.

Short Stories

Hands to Dance. London, Carroll and Nicholson, 1951; augmented edition, as *Hands to Dance, and Skylark*, London, Robson, 1979.
When Dad Felt Bad (juvenile). London, Macmillan, 1975.
Dick Whittington (juvenile). London, Penguin, 1976.
Three Heads Made of Gold (juvenile). London, Robson, 1978.
The Last King of Cornwall (juvenile). London, Robson, 1978.

Other

Editor, *Peninsula: An Anthology of Verse from the West-Country.* London, Macdonald, 1957.
Editor, *Dawn and Dusk: Poems of Our Time.* Leicester, Brockhampton Press, 1962; New York, Watts, 1963.
Editor, *Rising Early: Story Poems and Ballads of the 20th Century.* Leicester, Brockhampton Press, 1964; as *Modern Ballads and Story Poems*, New York, Watts, 1965.
Editor, *An Octave*, by Siegfried Sassoon. London, Arts Council, 1966.
Editor, *Modern Folk Ballads.* London, Studio Vista, 1966.
Editor, *In the Music I Hear: Poems by Children.* Gillingham, Kent, ARC Press, 1970.
Editor, *Oats and Beans and Barley: Poems by Children.* Gillingham, Kent, ARC Press, 1971.
Editor, *Selected Poems*, by Frances Bellerby. London, Enitharmon Press, 1971.
Editor, *The Puffin Book of Magic Verse.* London, Penguin, 1974.
Editor, *The Puffin Book of Salt-Sea Verse.* London, Penguin, 1978.
Editor, *The Batsford Book of Stories in Verse.* London, Batsford, 1979.

Manuscript Collections: State University of New York, Buffalo; University of Exeter Library, Devon.

Critical Studies: *Poetry Today 1957–60* by Elizabeth Jennings, London, Longman, 1961; "Of Tigers and Trees" by John Pett, in *The Guardian* (London), 15 January 1965; *Poets of the 1939–1945 War* by R. N. Currey, London, Longman, 1967; "Charles Causley Talks to Peter Orr", on British Council Tape Recording 1390, 1968; "Haiku in the Park" by Norman Hidden, in *The Times Educational Supplement* (London), 17 November 1972; *Poetry Today 1960–73* by Anthony Thwaite, London, Longman, 1973; "The Poetry of Charles Causley" by Edward Levy, in *PN Review* (London), v, 2, 1978; *An Introduction to 50 Modern British Poets* by Michael Schmidt, London, Pan, 1979.

* * *

Charles Causley's poems are not the sort of work that would readily attract the adjective "pioneer": most of them are, or seem to be, utterly traditional. Yet Causley's handling of ballad and lyrical forms, and his jaunty, vivid, humorous way with language, seem – in a way not often acknowledged – to lie behind much of the "pop" poetry of the late 1960's: a poetry intended to be spoken aloud, to be grasped immediately and cheerfully by a mass audience.

Causley was writing such poems before many of his debtors were born. *Farewell, Aggie Weston* and *Survivor's Leave* contain work which could easily fit into his later book, *Underneath the Water*; and their simple ballad rhythms, their hyperbolic images and their spry blending of old and new imagery could sit comfortably in such a collection as *Love Love Love* – though they are considerably better written and more intelligent:

I saw a shot-down angel in the park
His marble blood sluicing the dyke of death,
A sailing tree firing its brown sea-mark
Where he now wintered for his wounded breath.

These early poems also remind one sometimes of Roy Campbell, but they lack the often oppressive (and aggresive) personality of Campbell. In fact, a legitimate charge against much of Causley's work up until *Underneath the Water* would be that it is too blandly and automatically anonymous, a voice without a man behind it: an attractive but rather irrelevant voice. There was also a feeling that sombre and complex subjects were being prettified and over-simplified, as in "Recruiting Drive":

Down in the enemy country
  Under the enemy tree
There lies a lad whose heart has gone bad
  Waiting for me, for me.

All these are justifiable objections, but they do not take in the whole of Causley, by any means. From the beginning, he could break away from lilting measures and gaudy diction when it suited him, as in "Chief Petty Officer," which is an excellent comic sketch in free verse, and – in a more traditional mode – he could be weighty, as in "I Am the Great Sun." More impressively, *Underneath the Water* contains poems drawing more closely from the personal and the circumstantial, with the old lyrical sweetness but with new depths: for example, "Conducting a Children's Choir":

I bait the snapping breath, curled claw, the deep
And delicate tongue that lends no man its aid.
The children their unsmiling kingdoms keep,
And I walk with them, and I am afraid.

Causley's wartime experiences in the Navy, the mundane stuff of his childhood and present life as a teacher, are handled with a brisk attention to real detail. Yet the "folk" properties and the oral narrative characteristics are still there as plainly and successfully as ever, in "By St. Thomas Water," "Reservoir Street," "In Coventry," "Lord Sycamore" and "Ballad of the Bread Man." These poems are not artless: what Roy Campbell wrote of Causley several years ago is still true: "The poems have an apparent freshness and spontaneity about them which, with their fine finish, could never have been attained without the most careful work and subtle refinement." His work has an initial availability (often to children as well as to adults) which, unlike that of some more recent popular poets, bears re-hearing and re-reading: the rhythms and images work their way into the memory, and earn their keep there.

—Anthony Thwaite

CHEYNEY-COKER, Syl. Sierra Leonean. Born in Freetown, 28 June 1945. Educated at the University of Oregon, Eugene; University of California, Los Angeles; University of Wisconsin, Madison. Has been a drummer, radio producer, factory worker and dock worker. Journalist, Eugene, Oregon, 1968–69; Teaching Assistant, University of Wisconsin, 1971. Recipient: Ford grant, 1970. Lives in Freetown.

PUBLICATIONS

Verse

Concerto for an Exile. New York, Africana, 1972; London, Heinemann, 1973.
The Graveyard Also Has Teeth. London, New Beacon, 1974.

Syl Cheyney-Coker comments:

I hold the terrible distinction of being the only poet from my country who has published a sizeable volume of poems. I say terrible not in the pejorative sense but from a feeling of painful awareness that before my appearance, my country was a ghetto of silence.

A popular awareness of self and the creation of different modes of expression of our social and cultural needs seem to me to be the immediate task of the Sierra Leonean writer. We are a strange people; our history, language and culture are not to be confused with those of other English-speaking Africans.

The admixture of English philanthropy and African exotica that has produced and shaped the Sierra Leonean Creole is for me the makeup of any genuine Sierra Leonean Literature.

My "Afro-Saxon" heritage has meant a lot for me as I summarize my passion and I hope it will convey something of the strangeness of my people to the reader.

* * *

The question of ancestry is a central concern in the writing of many Third World poets. In the poems of Syl Cheyney-Coker, especially those collected in his book *Concerto for an Exile*, this concern becomes a fixation, his

... Creole ancestry
which gave me my negralised head
all my polluted streams

providing the impulse for poems which, in the extravagance and precise violence of their imagery, match some of the best writing of Vallejo and U'Tamsi, two poets whom Cheyney-Coker acknowledges as influences.

There are also definite echoes of the Negritude school and the poems of David Diop. The "Africa, my Africa" of Diop's poems has, however, been narrowed down to a specific nation, Sierra Leone, the land of freed slaves where a patois language, Creole and a Western influenced capital, Freetown, are ironic heritages of the colonial era:

In my country the Creoles drink only
Black and White with long sorrows
hanging from their colonial faces ...

Cheyney-Coker's poems are cries of bitter agony and bright illumination at one and the same time. They present the picture – as in "Agony of the Dark Child" or in "Misery of the Convert" with its lines:

I was a king before they nailed you on the cross
converted I read ten lies in your silly commandments
to honour you my Christ
when you have deprived me of my race ...

– of a nation and a poet tortured by a culture and a religion imposed upon them, a nation and a poet who may find salvation through defiance.

Painful is a word which can be readily applied to much of Syl Cheyney-Coker's writing, just as another word – truthful – can also be applied to the same poems. He attempts, through a wrenching examination of personal and national histories, to create a new vision, a more honest world. In his poem "Guinea," written on the unsuccessful invasion of that nation by Portuguese mercenaries, he defines his role:

I am not the renegade
who has forsaken your shores
I am not the vampire
gnawing at your heart
to feed capitalist banks
I am your poet
writing No to the world.

—Joseph Bruchac

CIARDI, John (Anthony). American. Born in Boston, Massachusetts, 24 June 1916. Educated at Bates College, Lewiston, Maine, 1934–36; Tufts College, Medford, Massachusetts, A.M. (magna cum laude) 1938 (Phi Beta Kappa); University of Michigan, Ann Arbor (Hopwood Award, 1939), 1939. Served in the United States Army Air Force, 1942–45: Air Medal, Oak Leaf Cluster. Married Myra Judith Hostetter in 1946; three children. Instructor, University of Kansas City, Missouri, 1940–42; Briggs Copeland Instructor in English, 1946–48, and Assistant Professor, 1948–53, Harvard University, Cambridge, Massachusetts; Lecturer, 1953–54, Associate Professor, 1954–56, and Professor of English, 1956–61, Rutgers University, New Brunswick, New Jersey; Lecturer, 1947–73, and Director, 1956–72, Bread Loaf Writers Conference, Vermont. Editor, Twayne Publishers, New York, 1949; Lecturer, Salzburg Seminar in American Studies, 1951; Poetry Editor, *Saturday Review*, New York, 1956–73; Host, *Accent* program, CBS-TV, 1961–62. Since 1973, Contributing Editor, *World Magazine*, New York. Recipient: Oscar Blumenthal Prize, 1943, Eunice Tietjens Memorial Prize, 1944, Levinson Prize, 1946, and Harriet Monroe Memorial Prize, 1955 (*Poetry*, Chicago); New England Poetry Club Golden Rose, 1948; American Academy in Rome Fellowship, 1956; Boys' Clubs of America Junior Book Award, 1962. D.Litt.: Tufts College, 1960; Ohio Wesleyan University, Delaware, 1971; Washington University, St. Louis, 1971; Hum.D.: Wayne University, Detroit, 1963; LL.D.: Ursinus College, Collegeville, Pennsylvania, 1964; D.L.H.: Kalamazoo College, Michigan, 1964; Bates College, 1970. Member, National Institute of Arts and Letters, and American Academy of Arts and Sciences. Address: 359 Middlesex Avenue, Metuchen, New Jersey 08840, U.S.A.

PUBLICATIONS

Verse

Homeward to America. New York, Holt, 1940.
Other Skies. Boston, Little Brown, 1947.
Live Another Day: Poems. New York, Twayne, 1949.

From Time to Time. New York, Twayne, 1951.
As If: Poems New and Selected. New Brunswick, New Jersey, Rutgers University Press, 1955.
I Marry You: A Sheaf of Love Poems. New Brunswick, New Jersey, Rutgers University Press, 1958.
39 Poems. New Brunswick, New Jersey, Rutgers University Press, 1959.
In the Stoneworks. New Brunswick, New Jersey, Rutgers University Press, 1961.
In Fact. New Brunswick, New Jersey, Rutgers University Press, 1962.
Person to Person. New Brunswick, New Jersey, Rutgers University Press, 1964.
The Strangest Everything. New Brunswick, New Jersey, Rutgers University Press, 1966.
An Alphabestiary: Twenty-Six Poems. Philadelphia, Lippincott, 1967.
A Genesis: 15 Poems. New York, Touchstone Publications, 1967.
The Achievement of John Ciardi: A Comprehensive Selection of His Poems with a Critical Introduction, edited by Miller Williams. Chicago, Scott Foresman, 1969.
Lives of X. New Brunswick, New Jersey, Rutgers University Press, 1972.
The Little That Is All. New Brunswick, New Jersey, Rutgers University Press, 1974.
For Instance. New York, Norton, 1979.

Recording: *As If*, Folkways.

Other

The Reason for the Pelican (verse for children). Philadelphia, Lippincott, 1959.
Scrappy the Pup (juvenile). Philadelphia, Lippincott, 1960.
I Met a Man (verse for children). Boston, Houghton Mifflin, 1961.
The Man Who Sang the Sillies (verse for children). Philadelphia, Lippincott, 1961.
You Read to Me, I'll Read to You (verse for children). Philadelphia, Lippincott, 1962.
The Wish-Tree (juvenile). New York, Crowell Collier, 1962.
Dialogue with an Audience. Philadelphia, Lippincott, 1963.
Poetry: A Closer Look, with James M. Reid and Laurence Perrine. New York, Harcourt Brace, 1963.
John J. Plenty and Fiddler Dan: A New Fable of the Grasshopper and the Ant (verse for children). Philadelphia, Lippincott, 1963.
You Know Who (juvenile). Philadelphia, Lippincott, 1964.
The King Who Saved Himself from Being Saved (verse for children). Philadelphia, Lippincott, 1965.
The Monster Den; or, Look What Happened at My House – and to It (verse for children). Philadelphia, Lippincott, 1966.
Someone Could Win a Polar Bear (verse for children). Philadelphia, Lippincott, 1970.
Manner of Speaking (*Saturday Review* columns). New Brunswick, New Jersey, Rutgers University Press, 1972.
Fast and Slow (verse for children). Boston, Houghton Mifflin, 1975.

Editor, *Mid-Century American Poets.* New York, Twayne, 1950.
Editor, *How Does a Poem Mean?* Boston, Houghton Mifflin, 1960; revised edition, with Miller Williams, 1975.

Translator, *The Inferno*, by Dante. New Brunswick, New Jersey, Rutgers University Press, 1954.
Translator, *The Purgatorio*, by Dante. New York, New American Library, 1961.
Translator, *The Paradiso*, by Dante. New York, New American Library, 1970.

Bibliography: *John Ciardi: A Bibliography*, by William White, Detroit, Wayne State University Press, 1959.

John Ciardi comments:

Poetry, for me, finds voices, but the aim should not be an idiosyncratic single voice immediately recognizable as the voice of a given man (style as signature). Something of that sort is bound to happen as a man learns to write into himself; there will be some of the lub-dub of his own heart if the writing lives at all. I take that personalization to be essential and inevitable but secondary. The ideal accomplishment of a poem may be put as *homo fecit*. A man did it, and any man may say it of himself as one of the voices of his humanity, of his humanity quickened to itself.

* * *

Poet, teacher, acerbic commentator on contemporary life, John Ciardi has created one of the major careers in modern American poetry. His importance does not depend upon the significance of individual poems nor is it marred by the occasional redundancy of others. The frequent, short volumes of his poetry compose an unannounced but inevitably accumulating journal of a sensitive everyman who, in the tradition of Wordsworth and Whitman, but in a different age and in a highly individual voice, links the personal to the universal, the present imperfect to the ideal, and by "what light there is" seeks to discern from the fragments of closely observed experience some certitude in a larger design.

Ciardi's poetic method, with its continuing and controlling metaphors combining the personally important and timely with the generally significant and timeless, is evident in the opening lines of his early collection *Other Skies*: "Delicatessen and Carnival, the beach/ Slopes under the continental shelf" ("Record Crowds at Beaches"). Here and throughout the poem a contemporary genre scene and its present participants ironically expand into the reaches of an evolutionary landscape and a distant, mythic reality. Subsequently, expanding settings and characters are usually more directly autobiographical. Recollections of growing up ("A Knothole in Spent Time"), his marriage ("Men Marry What They Need. I Marry You"), war service ("Death of a Bomber"), children ("Two Poems for Benn"), death of family and friends ("Aunt Mary," "Elegy, for Kurt Porjescz, Missing in Action, 1 April 1945"), all the commonplaces of everyday life, are constantly placed in larger contexts and examined by the comparison.

But these commonplaces of everyday life that are so persistently the points of departure for his poems' encompassing metaphors nevertheless represent, in the constant presence of the ideal they prefigure, imperfection. It is Ciardi's acceptance of this imperfection of present experience that gives to his work its most characteristic tension and that helps to define as well his concept of the poet. The disparities between the flawed and the sought-after perfection are presented somewhat abstractly in the figures of the Damaged Angel and the Improved Ape in "A Dialogue in the Shade" and in the modern debate of Body and Soul in "Tenzone." But in his portraits of his father and his "friend and teacher, John Holmes" ("The Poet's Words") he offers both a more personal version and one that centers upon acceptance. He acknowledges "My father died imperfect as a man" and in the significantly titled latter poem concludes that "The best of a man/is what he thought of and could not be." And it is here that he suggests as well the complementary and paradoxical role of the imperfect poet. Although "Language ends in the tongue's clay pit," it is this same "Language" that must be "the wind/that brings all thought to mind."

If Ciardi's own poems move inevitably toward a larger coalescence, his concerns with the universal and the ideal move as well toward order and certitude, a tendency not emphasized but not unexpected in so distinguished a translator of Dante. The design his poems sketch out by allusion is not the orthodox one of Dante's time, however, but a less secure modern order based on his references to evolution, to myth, to the cosmic regularity of tides, seasons, day and night. A splendid example is provided in lines from one of his finest poems, "Poem for My Twenty-Ninth Birthday," in the eerie and lovely double image of death plane and sun rising:

We take our places while a switch is pressed,
And sun and engines rise from the hillside –
A single motion and a single fire
To burn, return, and live upon desire.

—Gaynor F. Bradish

CLARK, John Pepper. Nigerian. Born in Kiagbodo, 6 April 1935. Educated at Warri Government College, Ughelli, 1948–54; Ibadan University, 1955–60, B.A. (honours) in English 1960; Princeton University, New Jersey (Parvin Fellowship), 1962–63; Ibadan University (Institute of African Studies Research Fellowship, 1963–64). Married; four children. Nigerian Government Information Officer, 1960–61; Head of Features and Editorial Writer, *Daily Express*, Lagos, 1961–62. Founding-Editor, *The Horn* magazine, Ibadan. Since 1965, Member of the English Department, and currently Professor of English, University of Lagos. Founding Member, Society of Nigerian Authors. Address: Department of English, University of Lagos, Lagos, Nigeria.

PUBLICATIONS

Verse

Poems. Ibadan, Mbari, 1962.
A Reed in the Tide: A Selection of Poems. London, Longman, 1965; New York, Humanities Press, 1970.
Casualties: Poems 1966–1968. London, Longman, and New York, Africana, 1970.

Plays

Song of a Goat (produced Ibadan, 1961; London, 1965). Ibadan, Mbari, 1961; in *Three Plays*, 1964.
Three Plays: Song of a Goat, The Raft, The Masquerade. London, Oxford University Press, 1964.
The Masquerade (produced London, 1965). Included in *Three Plays*, 1964.
The Raft (broadcast, 1966; produced New York, 1978). Included in *Three Plays*, 1964.
Ozidi. Ibadan, London, and New York, Oxford University Press, 1966.
The Ozidi Saga. London, Oxford University Press, 1979.

Screenplay: *The Ozidi of Atazi.*

Radio Play: *The Raft*, 1966.

Other

America, Their America. London, Deutsch-Heinemann, 1964; New York, Africana, 1969.
The Example of Shakespeare: Critical Essays on African Literature. London, Longman, and Evanston, Illinois, Northwestern University Press, 1970.
The Ozidi Saga. Ibadan, Ibadan University Press, 1977; London, Oxford University Press, 1979.
The Hero as a Villain. Lagos, University of Lagos Press, 1978.

John Pepper Clark is a dramatist as well as a poet, but whereas his drama production is held together by a certain unity of theme and style, his poetry is not. *A Reed in the Tide* is a collection of occasional poems. Each poem seems to be inspired by an actual occurrence in the poet's life such as watching Fulani cattle, seeing a girl bathing in a stream, or flying across America. The incident takes on a symbolic and sometimes a moral value, and this is worked out in the poem, partly through description and partly through explicit commentary; "Agbor Dancer" is a good example of this. Seeing a girl dance the traditional Agbor dance, Clark describes the event. "See her caught in the throb of a drum ... entangled in the magic maze of music ...," and this leads him to a feeling of loss because he can no longer do the dance, i.e., he is alienated from tribal life. This in turn leads to a wish for reintegration. "Could I, early sequester'd from my tribe,/Free a lead-tether'd scribe/I should answer her communal call...." The theme of cultural integration which runs through some of the poems is supported by the poems dealing with traditional African themes like "Abiku" and also by the poems which evoke Clark's native Nigerian town and landscape; this last section contains the most successful poems of the collection. Both the Ezra Pound-inspired poem about Ibadan and the very sensitive evocation of the wet tropical Niger delta in "Night Rain" are excellent visual descriptions which gain much from not having any philosophy tagged onto them. The poems dealing with modern American life provide a logical contrast to the loving concern with traditional life. Here Clark dwells on the alienating effect of technology like the slot-machine ("Service") and the underground train ("Cave Call").

Clark's next collection, *Casualties*, deals with the Biafran War and can thus be said to have a unified theme. Clark took a personal part in the war, intervening on behalf of a friend, and he also was personally acquainted with several of the most important leaders in the conflict. An intimate knowledge of the details of the war is necessary for an understanding of the poetry which is mainly narrative/argumentative, and Clark has felt obliged to provide footnotes to most of the poems, to explain, for instance, that the crocodile in "The Reign of the Crocodile" is Major-General Ironsi who carried a stuffed crocodile as a swagger-stick. The collection suffers badly from this concern with the actual details of the war. One can only agree with Clark when he writes in the Preface to Notes that "I sometimes wish I had written in prose this personal account...." Some of the poems, however, are transfused with a sadness which transcends the details and brings across not just the misery of war, but the particular misery of civil war where friendships and family ties are tested and broken.

—Kirsten Holst Petersen

CLARK, Leonard. British. Born in St. Peter Port, Guernsey, 1 August 1905. Educated at Monmouth School, 1917–22; Normal College, Bangor, Caernarvonshire, 1928–30, Cert. Ed. 1930. Served in the Home Guard, Devon Regiment, 1940–43. Married Jane Callow in 1954; one son and one daughter. Taught in Gloucestershire, 1922–28, and London, 1930–36; Inspector of Schools, Devon, Yorkshire, and London, 1936–70. Since 1970, Editor, Longmans Poetry Library series (64 titles); currently, Consultant Editor, Chatto and Windus Poetry Books for the Young, London, and Thornhill Press, Gloucester. Member, Arts Council Literature Panel, 1965–69. Liveryman of Haberdashers' Company, 1965. Freeman of City of London, 1965. Honorary Associate, London Academy of Music and Dramatic Art, 1969. Fellow, Royal Society of Literature, 1953. Knight of the Order of St. Sylvester, 1970. O.B.E. (Officer, Order of the British Empire), 1966. Address: 50 Cholmeley Crescent, London N6 5HA, England.

PUBLICATIONS

Verse

Poems. London, Fortune Press, 1940.
Passage to the Pole and Other Poems. London, Fortune Press, 1944.
Rhandanim. Leeds, Salamander Press, 1945.
The Mirror and Other Poems. London, Allen Wingate, 1948.
XII Poems. Birmingham, City of Birmingham School of Printing, 1948.
English Morning and Other Poems. London, Hutchinson, 1953.
Selected Poems, 1940–1957. London, Hutchinson, 1958.
Daybreak: A First Book of Poems for Children. London, Hart Davis, 1963.
The Year Round: A Second Book of Poems for Children. London, Hart Davis, 1966.
Fields and Territories. London, Turret, 1967.
Good Company: Poems for Children. London, Dobson, 1968.
Near and Far: Poems for Children. London, Hamlyn, 1968.
Here and There: Poems for Children. London, Hamlyn, 1969.
Walking with Trees. London, Enitharmon Press, 1970.
Every Voice. Guildford, Surrey, Words Press, 1971.
Secret as Toads: Poems for Children. London, Chatto and Windus, 1972.
Singing in the Streets: Poems for Christmas. London, Dobson, 1972.
The Broad Atlantic: Poems for Children. London, Dobson, 1974.
Four Seasons: Poems for Children. London, Dobson, 1974.
The Hearing Heart. London, Enitharmon Press, 1974.
Collected Poems and Verses for Children. London, Dobson, 1975.
Winter to Winter and Other Poems. London, Dobson, 1977.
The Tale of Prince Igor. London, Dobson, 1977.
Silence of the Morning. London, Enitharmon Press, 1978.
Twelve Poems from St. Bartholomew's. Privately printed, 1978.
Stranger Than Unicorns. London, Dobson, 1978.
The Singing Tree: Poems for Children. London, Hodder and Stoughton, 1979.

Other

Alfred Williams: His Life and Works. Oxford, Blackwell, 1945; New York, A. M. Kelly, 1969.
Ideas in Poetry. Birmingham, City of Birmingham School of Printing, 1947.
Sark Discovered: Prospect of an Island: Being a Literary and Pictorial Record of the Island of Sark. London, Dent, 1956; revised edition, London, Dobson, 1971, 1979.
Walter de la Mare: A Checklist. Cambridge, University Press, 1956.
Walter de la Mare. London, Bodley Head, 1960; New York, H. Z. Walck, 1961; revised edition, 1968.
Green Wood: A Gloucestershire Childhood. London, Parrish, 1962.
Andrew Young. London, Longman, 1964.
When They Were Children (juvenile). London, Parrish, and New York, Roy, 1964.
A Fool in the Forest (autobiography). London, Dobson, 1965.
Robert Andrew Tells a Story [and Tiffy, by the Sea, and the Holy Family, and the Red Indian Chief, and Skippy, in the Country] (juvenile). Leeds, E. J. Arnold, 7 vols., 1965–66.
Prospect of Highgate and Hampstead. London, Highgate Press, 1967.
Grateful Caliban (autobiography). London, Dobson, 1967.
A Tribute to Walter de la Mare, with Edmund Blunden. London, Enitharmon Press, 1974.
Mr. Pettigrew's Harvest Festival [Train, and the Bellringers] (juvenile). Gloucester, Thornhill Press, 3 vols., 1974–75.

St. Felix and the Spider (juvenile). London, Catholic Truth Society, 1974.
St. Patrick (juvenile). London, Catholic Truth Society, 1974.
St. Anthony of Egypt (juvenile). London, Catholic Truth Society, 1974.
St. Dorothea and the Flowers of Paradise (juvenile). London, Catholic Truth Society, 1974.
The Inspector Remembers (autobiography). London, Dobson, 1976.
Writing for the Public. Gloucester, Thornhill Press, 1976.
The Story of Rahere. Privately printed, 1978.

Editor, *The Magic Kingdom: An Anthology of Verse for Seniors.* London, Mathews and Marrot, 1937.
Editor, *The Open Door: Anthology of Verse for Juniors.* London, Mathews and Marrot, 1937.
Editor, *The Kingdom of the Mind: Essays and Addresses 1903–1937 of Albert Mansbridge.* London, Dent, 1944.
Editor, *Andrew Young: Prospect of a Poet: Essays and Tributes by Fourteen Writers.* London, Hart Davis, 1957.
Editor, *Quiet as Moss: Thirty Six Poems*, by Andrew Young. London, Hart Davis, 1959.
Editor, *The Collected Poems of Andrew Young.* London, Hart Davis, 1960.
Editor, *Drums and Trumpets: Poetry for the Youngest.* London, Bodley Head, 1962; Chester Springs, Pennsylvania, Dufour, 1963.
Editor, *Common Ground: An Anthology for the Young.* London, Faber, 1964.
Editor, *Selected Poems by John Clare, 1793–1864.* Leeds, E. J. Arnold, 1964.
Editor, *All Things New: An Anthology.* London, Constable, 1965; Chester Springs, Pennsylvania, Dufour, 1968.
Editor, *The Poetry of Nature.* London, Hart Davis, 1965.
Editor, *Following the Sun: Poems by Children.* London, Odhams, 1967.
Editor, *Flute and Cymbals: Poetry for the Young.* London, Bodley Head, 1968; New York, Crowell, 1969.
Editor, with others, *The Complete Poems of Walter de la Mare.* London, Faber, 1969.
Editor, *Sound of Battle.* Oxford, Pergamon Press, 1969.
Editor, *Poems by Children.* London, Studio Vista, 1970.
Editor, *All Along Down Along: A Book of Stories in Verse.* London, Longman, 1971.
Editor, *The Complete Poems of Andrew Young.* London, Secker and Warburg, 1973.
Editor, *Poems of Ivor Gurney 1890–1937.* London, Chatto and Windus, 1973.
Editor, *Tales from the Panchatantra.* London, Evans, 1979.
Editor, *The Way the Wind Blows: An Anthology for the Young.* London, Evans, 1979.

Leonard Clark comments:

I have been described as a "Neo-Blake Imagist" and as "of the company of Traherne and Clare." But my themes are nature (whether in town or country), religion, childhood, and love. I have tried most verse forms, but my more recent work is of its own day – unrhyming but strong and subtle rhythmic and sound effects. I have been influenced by Edward Thomas, de la Mare, Hardy, Andrew Young and by some of my younger contemporaries. I have been trying to master the English language for forty years, developing slowly, with my best work still to come. I have tried to keep a sense of wonder and my belief in a few eternal values, forgetting the unhappier aspects of living. I believe I have a special gift for writing poetry for the young and am seeking to develop this by greater insight, and technical power. I am essentially a countryman, wherever I happen to live, with a strong feeling for history and music.

* * *

Leonard Clark is one of those poets who, familiar with the experience in versification of the past half-century, and to some extent profiting by this, remains at heart a Georgian poet, with many of the virtues of that school and few of its vices. He is primarily a nature poet, who began by writing poems celebrating the English landscape ("Forest Pools," "High Beeches," "Abyss"); as time has passed, his poems have become more personal, more mystical, but if anything simpler in expression. Both in those verses written specifically for children and in others, his language is perfectly straightforward – sometimes seeming almost too simplistic, remaining one (as in "Men as Trees") of Victorian hymns. But when, as in "Golden Eagle," he combines a deeply personal vision with a sharply observant eye, the result is a poem which is memorable. Technically, Clark uses often a loose form within which he can move easily; very occasionally in early poems the apparently deliberate use of somewhat archaic language can jar. But in his latest work he uses a sure ear to make carefully judged effects which round his poems off into well-shaped wholes, only now and then betraying their subjects by seeming oversmooth. The body of his work shows a mind moving within certain bounds, but surveying the ground completely and thoroughly. Few poets have been so successful in restricting their themes so deftly, in order to avoid over-reaching themselves.

—Derek Parker

CLARK, Tom. American. Born in Chicago, Illinois, 1 March 1941. Educated at the University of Michigan, Ann Arbor (Hopwood Prize, 1963), B.A. 1963; Cambridge and Essex universities (Fulbright Fellow, 1963–65). Married Angelica Heinegg in 1968; one child. Poetry Editor, *Paris Review*, 1963–73; Instructor in American Poetry, University of Essex, Wivenhoe, 1966–67. Since 1978, Senior Writer, *Boulder Monthly*, Colorado. Recipient: Bess Hokin Prize, 1966, and George Dillon Memorial Prize, 1968 (*Poetry*, Chicago); Poets Foundation Award, 1967; Rockefeller Fellowship, 1968; Guggenheim Fellowship, 1970. Address: 744 University, Boulder, Colorado 80302, U.S.A.

PUBLICATIONS

Verse

Airplanes. Brightlingsea, Essex, Once Press, 1966.
The Sand Burg: Poems. London, Ferry Press, 1966.
Bun, with Ron Padgett. New York, Angel Hair, 1968.
Stones. New York, Harper, 1969.
Air. New York, Harper, 1970.
Green. Los Angeles, Black Sparrow Press, 1971.
John's Heart. London, Cape Goliard Press, and New York, Grossman, 1972.
Back in Boston Again, with Ted Berrigan and Ron Padgett. Philadelphia, Telegraph Books, 1972.
Smack. Los Angeles, Black Sparrow Press, 1972.
Blue. Los Angeles, Black Sparrow Press, 1974.
Suite. Los Angeles, Black Sparrow Press, 1974.
Chicago. Los Angeles, Black Sparrow Press, 1974.
At Malibu. New York, Kulchur, 1975.
Baseball. Berkeley, California, Figures, 1976.

35. Berkeley, California, Poltroon Press, 1977.
How I Broke In/Six Modern Masters. Bolinas, California, Tombouctou, 1978.
When Things Get Tough on Easy Street: Selected Poems 1963–1978. Santa Barbara, California, Black Sparrow Press, 1978.

Play

The Emperor of the Animals. London, Goliard Press, 1967.

Novel

Who Is Sylvia? Eugene, Oregon, Blue Wind Press, 1979.

Other

Neil Young. Toronto, Coach House Press, 1971.
Champagne and Baloney: The Rise and Fall of Finley's A's. New York, Harper, 1976.
No Big Deal, with Mark Fidrych. Philadelphia, Lippincott, 1977.
The World of Damon Runyon. New York, Harper, 1978.
One Last Round for the Shuffler: A Blacklisted Ball Player's Story. St. Paul, Minnesota, Truck, 1979.

Manuscript Collection: University of Connecticut, Storrs.

* * *

Tom Clark's poetry published in the 1960's can give the impression of the man who got on his horse and rode off in all directions at once. The "look" of the poems is frequently reassuring, the lines of more-or-less equivalent length grouped into equivalent units on the page, promising a rational structure. But within these units chaos can sometimes reign. The thin, or non-existant punctuation often creates syntactical confusions. There is also a certain fondness for quirky modifiers, as though the poet were a computer choosing at random from a bank of nouns and a bank of adjectives and combining the result. To place a "secretive tambourine" and a "sober dog" back-to-back in the poem "Comanche" from the same collection suggests an interest more in the way words can collide than in their potentiality for pleasing combinations. This fondness for playing with words also surfaces in some poems in the form of a jingly sound effects. Also, Clark seems fond of the chain poem, where repetition of a single word or phrase in each section ties the whole together, as in his brash parody of Wallace Steven's famous Blackbird poem, "Eleven Ways of Looking at a Shit Bird" (*Stones*).

The poems published during the 1970's move away from the scattergun effects I've described. This work seems clearer, cleaner, though with the same drive and energy, the general feeling that Clark is perpetually *en route*. Also, the range of subjects widens here, the introspection of the earlier work giving way to concern with things and people in the world. One of my favorites is "To Kissinger" (*When Things Get Tough on Easy Street*), a wacky series of insults that makes a forceful political point with humor. There are a number of poems about running in the same collection, some short, throwaway pieces, others, such as "Morning Leaves Me Speechless," expressing beautifully the euphoria that can appear on the other side of physical exertion.

In a number of books published during this time Clark seems overly fond of the tiny poem. *Green* and *Blue* contain a number of poems that consist of one sentence, or even less; *Smack* is made up entirely of single sentences arranged vertically on the page. These efforts at minimal art via the word aren't always successful; they give the impression of notebook jottings, casual ideas that might grow into poems. There is a throwaway streak in Clark's work, a willingness to let things go, to gallop on to the next poem, to get on down the road. While this tendency may undermine the shorter poems, in the longer ones where there is room for discursive, casual, or colloquial effects, it can produce exciting poetry. A good example of this is "Chicago" (*When Things Get Tough on Easy Street*), an extended recollection of the poet's youthful experiences as an usher at various stadiums, ball-parks, and convention halls in the Chicago area that ends up by evoking an entire era – that strange period of American History known as "the fifties." There is an interesting and unexpected idea implied in this poem, that poets and ushers have something in common. Both are employed spectators, in it for more than entertainment.

Clark is a world-class spectator, his work a grand record of his passionate looking-on. In many of his sports poems, especially those dealing with baseball, he tries to invest the game with meaning far beyond its position in American society as an entertainment. Clark is a *Fan*; he doesn't write about baseball, he celebrates it. These poems belong to the tradition of the encomium, and the names of the players ring through them like a Homeric roll-call: Orestes Minoso, Catfish Hunter, Vida Blue, Bert Campaneris, Bill Lee. The poem on Bill Lee is perhaps the best of these, a long, warm appreciation of that player's eccentric intelligence.

In his most recent poems, Clark seems to have abandoned baseball as a subject, perhaps because he has been able to celebrate the sport in prose in a number of books and articles, but his fondness for the encomium persists in a group of poems about artists – two on Reverdy, one each on Ungaretti, Vuillard, Kafka, and Lenny Bruce. But this recent work isn't all hero worship; in "How I Broke In," the poem sequence that concludes *When Things Get Tough on Easy Street*, Clark shuffles and reshuffles a number of images, allusions, individual lines, upping the ante in each section, increasing the pressure until I began to wonder how he could sustain it and keep going. To read this sequence is to confront something powerful, even dangerous, barely held in control. The experience is exhilarating.

—Steven Young

CLARKE, Gillian (née Williams). Welsh. Born in Cardiff, Glamorgan, 8 June 1937. Educated at St. Clare's Convent, Porthcawl, Glamorgan; University College, Cardiff, B.A. in English 1958. Since 1975, Lecturer in Art History, Gwent College of Art and Design, Newport. Since 1976, Editor, *Anglo-Welsh Review*, Cardiff. Recipient: Welsh Arts Council Prize, 1979. Agent: David Thomas, 1 Padarn Terrace, Llanbadarn, Aberystwyth, Dyfed. Address: 1 Cyncoed Avenue, Cyncoed, Cardiff, Glamorgan, Wales.

PUBLICATIONS

Verse

Snow on the Mountain. Swansea, Christopher Davies, 1971.
The Sundial. Llandysul, Dyfed, Gwasg Gomer, 1978.

Plays

Radio Poems: *Talking in the Dark*, 1975; *Letter from a Far Country*, 1979.

* * *

Making her first appearance in print in 1970, Gillian Clarke has now a firm reputation in literary Wales. She has written two successful short verse plays for radio but continues to publish poetry infrequently. *The Sundial* brings together 39 poems and, as in the work of Dylan Thomas, the basic properties of stone, sea, sun, survival, growth, and fertility abound. Gillian Clarke goes too for the big ending, an epiphany or, at least "significance," and so occasionally risks the reader's sympathy: "Neatly, slowly I folded/Clothes, and survived ("Lines"). And again: "its stone/Profile of an ancient priest/Preaches continually/In the face of turning tides" ("St. Augustine's Penarth"). But at her best, and that means in at least half of the poems in this collection, the conception is underpinned by a force of language that is fulfilling and, at times, astonishing, as in "Harvest at Mynachlog":

We talk
Of other harvests. They remember
How a boy, flying his plane so low
Over the cut fields that his father

Straightened from his work to wave his hat
At the boasting sky, died minutes later
On an English cliff, in such a year
As this, the barns brimming gold.

We are quiet again, holding our cups
In turn for the tilting milk, sad, hearing
The sun roar like a rush of grain
Engulfing all winged things that live
One moment in the eclipsing light.

The transference of the grain's fruitful rush back to the heat of the sun is an exciting use of language, and allows one to forget the excesses of "boasting sky" and "tilting milk." Here is a real talent. The extent to which that gift blossoms would appear to be in Gillian Clarke's own hands.

—Tony Curtis

CLEMO, Jack (Reginald John Clemo). British. Born in St. Austell, Cornwall, 11 March 1916. Educated at Trethosa Village School. Married Ruth Grace Peaty in 1968. "A dreamer and social misfit, I had already spent five years as an unemployable hermit mystic before partial deafness increased my isolation." Recipient: Atlantic Award, Birmingham University, 1948; Arts Council Festival Prize, 1951; Civil List pension, 1961, supplemented in 1966 and 1969. Address: Goonamarris, St. Stephen's, St. Austell, Cornwall, England.

PUBLICATIONS

Verse

The Clay Verge. London, Chatto and Windus, 1951.
The Map of Clay. London, Methuen, 1961; Richmond, Virginia, John Knox Press, 1968.
Penguin Modern Poets 6, with Edward Lucie-Smith and George MacBeth. London, Penguin, 1964.

Cactus on Carmel: Poems. London, Methuen, 1967.
The Echoing Tip. London, Methuen, 1971.
Broad Autumn. London, Eyre Methuen, 1975.

Novel

Wilding Graft. London, Chatto and Windus, and New York, Macmillan, 1948.

Other

Confession of a Rebel (autobiography). London, Chatto and Windus, 1949.
The Invading Gospel (theology). London, Bles, 1958; revised edition, London, Morgan Marshall and Scott, 1972; Old Tappan, New Jersey, Fleming Revell, 1973.
Clay Phoenix. London, Gollancz, 1979.

Critical Studies: *Rule and Energy* by John Press, London, Oxford University Press, 1963; *Religious Trends in English Poetry*, vol. 6, by Hoxie N. Fairchild, New York, Columbia University Press, 1968; *The Ironic Harvest* by Geoffrey Thurley, London, Arnold, 1974.

Jack Clemo comments:

(1970) I intended to be chiefly a prose writer, but the loss of my sight in 1955 forced me to restrict myself to composing verse.

Apart from a few poems describing the Cornish clay district, my poetry reflects various phases of Christianity as an experience of personal conversion. Its main themes are the Christian view of "fallen nature," the sacrament of marriage, and the place of suffering in the achievement of true happiness. There are also some fierce Barthian strictures on religious humanism, and a realistic Evangelical optimism akin to Browning's. My first two collections of verse were chiefly odes in the Francis Thompson vein, though grimmer and bleaker because I used the imagery of clay-mining. In my later work, I have developed a more modern imagist technique with sprung rhythm and a minimum of rhyme; the symbols are more frequently drawn from nature, and I show a deep affinity with primitive Catholic visionaries like Bernadette. This, however, does not involve any discarding of my earlier creed or my taste for stark aesthetic patterns. I write entirely on spiritual inspiration and do not consciously choose either the subject or the style of my poems. My erotic mysticism, though it answers D. H. Lawrence, was spontaneously evolved under the pressure of my emotional crises. Incidents from my own life are often depicted in my verse, and the range is widened by dramatic monologues and tributes to various writers, saints and preachers. I think that my four collections make a fairly complete statement of my philosophy, but the physical handicaps of my mature years have restricted my output and are too often dragged in by critics to explain my beliefs and attitudes which I had already adopted while unhandicapped.

* * *

Jack Clemo is a Cornish poet whose early faith appears to have been nourished in all the paraphernalia of the local clay-pits – the dumps, cinder heaps, the snow-covered quarries – rather than the natural beauty of his native countryside; there has always been a sense of conflict between his attitude to nature and his concept of divine grace. That is because his early spiritual struggles were conducted against such a background. In his prose volume, *The Invading Gospel*, which might be described as his testament of faith, he tells us that he had "to fight among the clay-kilns and refuse-barrows of mid-Cornwall the same sort of battle as D. H. Lawrence fought among the headstocks and slagheaps of the Derbyshire collieries." It is a kind of landscape which seems to reflect in some ways the personal experience of a poet who has been stone-deaf for most of his life, and who, after spells of blindness during his schooldays, has suffered from blindness since 1955.

In his first book of poems, *The Clay Verge*, he has little to say in favour of nature and he will have nothing to do with the God of nature-worshippers. His Calvinistic creed and the almost savage mythology expressed in this volume are likely to antagonize those who have been conditioned to respond in a particular way whenever the "mysteries of Nature" are mentioned. But the puritanical strength and the intensity of vision underlying these poems, and the organic unity and content, can hardly be ignored. It is a poetry not merely of renunciation, but of vilification of the natural world. Here and there the technical influences of both Hardy and Lawrence can be discerned, but they are not obtrusive. It is precisely because of his own sensitivity to sense impressions and fears that his spiritual life may be imperilled by undue attachment to "Nature's teeming perfidies" that he reacts so violently. This over-emphasis upon isolated points of belief, together with the harsh symbolism of the clay-pits tended to distort the ideas he was trying to present, yet his concept of Christianity as a "redemptive invasion of nature by the divine grace which is outside nature" would probably be acceptable to most Christians.

There is a strong sexual element in all Clemo's poetry, whether he is referring to human relationships or not. In his earliest poems he was inclined to equate sexual feeling with the corruption to be found in nature, and this set up a sense of conflict since it involved his own instincts as well as his religious concepts. In "The Plundered Fuchsias," where the conflict is most clearly marked, he finds a grim satisfaction in the destruction of the flowers by his lady companion, apparently without appreciating the sensual symbolism of the act itself, and then proceeds to indulge his own nature:

She marred the rhythm of soil,
  She checked fertility
And then, the last flower trampled on,
  She turned more naughtily
  And gave her lips to me.

Clemo's second collection traces his development, step by step, from the isolationist position he had taken up after his conversion to the more enlightened state in which he recognized the need for solidarity with other Christians. In "The Broadening Winter" he compares the experience of C. H. Spurgeon with that of his own – Clemo's views on predestination approach those of Barth and Spurgeon, whom he has studied to some effect. Clemo's most revitalizing influences, however, have been visiting American evangelists, Renee Martz, the child evangelist, and Billy Graham, in particular. In *The Map of Clay* a new "jazz" phraseology begins to replace that previously drawn from the Cornish clayworks – "God's jazzdrums seemed to thunder ..." or "Hot ragtime stains the austere track ..." – to match the new mood of pentecostal gaiety.

Most of the poems in *The Echoing Tip* were written after his marriage in 1968, and it is noticeable that the sexual element has been subdued and almost replaced by a preoccupation with "objective portraiture" (there are reflective poems on Beethoven, Helen Keller, Simone Weil, and "The Death of Karl Barth"). The clay-pit symbolism has disappeared altogether and there is a revealing poem, "Wedding Eve," in celebration of his forthcoming marriage: "And I feel in your flushed curves,/In your kiss, the world-renouncing nun."

In *Broad Autumn* he refers to his own pilgrimage in the title poem, and his resolution of his personal conflicts allows him to turn outwards to the problems and experiences of others – Gerard Manley Hopkins, John Clare, Kagawa, Joseph Hocking, John Wesley, Donne, and Mary Slessor. It can now be said that as a religious poet, and as a landscape poet, Jack Clemo has few challengers. It remains to be seen how his work will develop in the future.

—Howard Sergeant

CLIFTON, Lucille. Afro-American. Born in Depew, New York, 27 June 1936. Educated at Howard University, Washington, D.C., 1953–55. Married Fred J. Clifton in 1958; six children. Formerly, Visiting Writer, Columbia University School of the Arts, New York. Since 1971, Poet-in-Residence, Coppin State College, Baltimore. Recipient: YM-YWHA Poetry Center Discovery Award, 1969; National Endowment for the Arts grant, 1969. Agent: M. Marlow, Curtis Brown Ltd., 575 Madison Avenue, New York, New York 10022. Address: 2605 Talbot Road, Baltimore, Maryland 21216, U.S.A.

PUBLICATIONS

Verse

Good Times. New York, Random House, 1969.
Good News about the Earth. New York, Random House, 1972.
An Ordinary Woman. New York, Random House, 1974.

Other (juvenile)

Some of the Days of Everett Anderson. New York, Holt Rinehart, 1970.
The Black BC's. New York, Dutton, 1970.
Everett Anderson's Christmas Coming [Year, Friend, 1–2–3, Nine Month Long]. New York, Holt Rinehart, 5 vols., 1972–78.
All Us Come cross the Water. New York, Holt Rinehart, 1973.
Don't You Remember? New York, Dutton, 1973.
The Boy Who Didn't Believe in Spring. New York, Dutton, 1973.
The Times They Used to Be. New York, Holt Rinehart, 1974.
My Brother Fine with Me. New York, Holt Rinehart, 1975.
Three Wishes. New York, Viking Press, 1976.
Generations of Americans: A Memoir (for adults). New York, Random House, 1976.
Amifika. New York, Dutton, 1977.
The Lucky Stone. New York, Delacorte Press, 1979.

Lucille Clifton comments:

I am a black woman poet, and I sound like one.

* * *

Two things are apparent in the poetry of Lucille Clifton – that she is Black and that she is a woman. Her Blackness becomes evident mainly in her themes and insights. Characteristically, in "After Kent State" she writes, "white ways are/the way of death/come into the/Black/and live," and in an untitled poem she states, "listen children/... we have never hated black/... always/all ways/... we have always loved each other/... pass it on." Seeing with clarity the bitterness, ugliness, and adversity wrought by racism, she nevertheless is constructive and optimistic. There is celebration, affirmation, of Black life in her poems. Her Black perception also manifests itself in the heroes that she poetically portrays, such as Fred Clifton (her husband), Little Richard, Angela Davis, and in her creative reactions to biblical personages and events in the "Some Jesus" section of her *Good News about the Earth*.

Mrs. Clifton's femininity is revealed by her dignity and poise and by her themes. Poems such as "the lost baby poem," about an aborted baby, and "Mary," an empathetic depiction of the Virgin Mary, could have been written only by a lady. Her womanly sensitivity, however, is not one of weak softness, protected reclusion, cloying sentimentality, or shielded vision. For example, in "Admonitions" she says, "girls/first time a white man/opens his fly/like a good thing/we'll just laugh."

Lucille Clifton's poems are short, graceful, incisive, usually with pointed conclusions which sometimes come to the reader as a re-reaction. Her lines, usually short, are sinewy, lithe. Her diction is plain; she only occasionally employs so-called Black grammar or dialect. Her characterizations are precise and economical. She uses both poetic indirection and flat statement effectively, employs understated or subtle metaphorical language skillfully.

—Theodore R. Hudson

CLOUTS, Sydney (David). South African. Born in Cape Town, 10 January 1926. Educated at South African College School; University of Cape Town, B.A. Married; three sons. Since 1969, Research Fellow of the Institute of the Study of English in Africa. Recipient: Olive Schreiner Award, 1968; Ingrid Jonker Prize, 1968. Address: c/o Rhodes University, Grahamstown, South Africa.

PUBLICATIONS

Verse

One Life. Cape Town, Purnell, 1966.

Other

Editor, *Among Stones*, by Jean Lipkin. Cape Town, David Philip, 1975.

* * *

I believe Sydney Clouts to be a truly great poet, this in spite of the fact that he is not a "name" even in his own country and he has written only one volume, *One Life*. There is an inevitability about his best poems that resists analysis. Yet to me there is nothing cold about his sheerness, nothing hard in his brilliancy. His talent is almost heathen – in his wish simply to *be* – as the pebble he describes in "Of Thomas Traherne" is heathen. "Heathen" here has an unaffected self-possession:

> Obscure vermilion heats the dim pebble I hold.
> ... I have read firm poems of God.
> Good friend, you perceived bright angels.
> This heathen bit of world lies warm in my palm.

His quality is immediately apprehended in his crystalline imagery, but it is often best seen in the quieter shades of his perception: "firm poems" – this economical phrasing is neither too delicate nor too confident; a sure balance has been kept by a gift that knows itself. Traherne's "Contentments," and their opposite – the sense of communion with, and separation from, the spirit moving in nature – are evident in Clouts's own work, though here they are transmuted into the paradox of his succinct imagery, and, in particular, his unforgettable closing lines. The concluding – "and the sea came by/the breaking sea came by" – in "After the Poem" conveys a sense of existence outside life, and yet the poet, by identifying his perception, defines the wonder of being and its important connection with consciousness.

Clouts can be quite dazzling, as in the following stanzas from "Prince Henry the Navigator":

Through the leafy Lisbon trees I heard
the frogless ocean whiten wild as flutes.

... silent I prayed, my task began
I cross the deliberate gulf of man

or quietly eloquent, as in his address to "Marge" in "The Sleeper":

When you awake
gesture will waken
to decisive things.
Asleep, you have taken
motion and tenderly laid it within,
deeply within you.

But both in dazzling imagery and quiet attitude the fusion of honesty and affection (with Clouts one hesitates to use so ostentatious a word as "love") makes for his inviolable quality.

The poet is highly aware of the excitements and grandeurs of Africa, particularly of the Cape of Good Hope. We see this in "Prince Henry the Navigator" and in "After the Poem." In "The Discovery" his link between Portugal and Africa is poetically forged: "Rounding the Cape, the sodden/wooden grumble of the wheel." Here the prosaic touch, the low-toned "grumble," counterpoints the splendour of its context.

Clouts is also aware of the tragic divisions of his country, for example in the two "Roy Kloof" poems, where a boy of mixed origin, of confusing pride and shame, cries out: "My country has given me flint for a soul." The readily discernible complexities of Roy Kloof's condition would lead to the far more impenetrable human condition indicated by a piece such as "Within," which in the striking power of its closing lines shows the verbal "purity" I have been trying to characterize:

flat is the world you'd find:
a row of wooden rooftops
that can easily topple
and bring the heart down
and bring down the mind.

It is not only in this kind of imagery that his exploration of the human condition signals itself. In "The Game" at one level – and a very real level – he takes part in the child's game of hide and seek, but the closing lines give the clue to another dimension: "I'll find myself as well,/hidden where truth has eyes."

The finally undissectible sheerness of his texture indicates why it is necessary for him to write poetry and not anything else, a necessity that shares humility with greatness. In him we are induced to believe that sheerness explains and seeks generosity amidst the overwhelming conditions of existence:

Flowers are toppling
the earth burbles blood.
O scholars of Mercy
interpret the flood!

—D. R. Beeton

CLUYSENAAR, Anne (Alice Andrée). Irish. Born in Brussels, Belgium, 15 March 1936. Educated at Trinity College, Dublin (Vice-Chancellor's Prize, 1956). Married. Reader to the writer Percy Lubbock for one year. Taught at universities of Manchester, Aberdeen, and Lancaster, and at Trinity College, Dublin; Huddersfield Polytechnic, 1972–73; University of Birmingham, 1973–78. Since 1978, Member of the Department of English, Sheffield City Polytechnic. Address: Woodend Farm, Joan Royd Road, Pennistone, Sheffield, South Yorkshire, England.

PUBLICATIONS

Verse

A Fan of Shadows. Manchester, David Findley Press, 1967.
Nodes. Dublin, Dolmen Press, 1969.
Poetry Introduction 4, with others. London, Faber, 1978.

Other

Introduction to Literary Stylistics: A Discussion of Dominant Structure in Verse and Prose. London, Batsford, 1976; as *Aspects of Literary Stylistics*, New York, St. Martin's Press, 1976.

Editor, *Selected Poems*, by Burns Singer. Manchester, Carcanet Press, 1977.

* * *

Anne Cluysenaar's earlier poetry belongs to the school of Valéry and Beckett. Her poems evoke formally what it is to "be" human – the perceiving centre, constantly changing, of a universe itself in a constant state of flux. *Fan of Shadows* is a collection of models of the human condition, explained in appended notes as figures of "continuous creation," or "radiations from an occasionally moving centre." In "Figures," the image of Derwentwater is "love's point of balance" between opposites – stillness and movement, presence and absence, love and solitude, liquid and solid:

The variant self awakes
To hills, fields, open water,
Newly aware of their stillness.

Between a kiss and the stillness
Of lonely thought, water
Off balance on a stony shore.

In "Sea," the stillness of mid-ocean is complemented by the moving tides; in "Petrarch," the "still pool" is speechless, and only knows itself in its overflow, "river-song." The sameness of experience is underlined by the accumulation of archetypes of desire – Orpheus, Laura, Balder – and by a repetition of words, phrases, and whole verses which in several poems dictates the entire structure. The love-lyric "Sea" falls into two near-mirror halves; "Epithalamium" opens as "The rings of the sun rise" to close on an echo: "The rings of a winter sunrise." The details of the difference are what makes the present moment, which Cluysenaar seeks to flesh out, charting, in the words of the more recent "La Belle Otero," what she calls "The strangely similar gaze in two chance moments."

The changes in the quality of her perceptions of the present are what distinguish her development – and progress – as a poet. In her earlier work, she doesn't always successfully cross the divide between eternal verity and dead cliché. Her landscapes remain abstract, shot through by mind rather than sensuous matter. A poem like "Figures" can in its separate moments pinpoint an interesting and self-defining interpenetration of thinker and perceived world:

A slim wave's shadow
Sinks into the hammered gold
Of dry stone creased with water.

Fish becomc concentrations
Of light, on which waves wind
Tongue-rolls of clear water.

But the vein it works is limited, and the strain of avoiding the twin evils of banality and preciosity constantly shows through. In later works, there is more warmth, and a personal voice finally makes itself heard. "Maker" recognises the poet's problem – the distance between the vivid colour of the real world and the abstractly arid version on the dead paper before him. "The May Fox" solves it; a surprise confrontation with death (the narrow escape of a fox, caught in the car's headlights) turns into love, a moment of shared human and animal warmth which dramatically re-enacts the exchange of meaning between man, nature, and the ideas and objects of man's creation. "Walt" blends her own voice with those of others, past and present, in an assertion of the human community rooted in specific place, family, neighbourhood and nation:

Not sure what I had in mind,
I do know that behind the message
lies a way of life whose voice,
newly mine, was always the speech
of those who had somewhere to live.

"Woodend Farm" knows now "what dwelling means"; it's finding a particular place in the meshes of time and space, evoking "the stream/whose tiny, illegal trout/come to fingers patient with memories." These two recent poems form part of a new project for a "meditative documentary diary" whose personal reminiscences, sparked off by letters, photographs, family souvenirs, chart "the secret ground of a shared life," still understanding the abstract patterns underlying our existence as humans, but now firmly emphasising their embodiment in an immediate and sensuous reality: "Affections share us, though we fail to name them,/ and ground relations in more than relationship."

—Jennifer Birkett

COBBING, Bob. British. Born in Enfield, Middlesex, 30 July 1920. Married; five children. Formerly, teacher and bookshop manager. Publisher, Writers Forum, London. Performer with the abAna group, and with Konkrete Canticle. Chairman, Association of Little Presses. Recipient: C. Day Lewis Fellowship, Goldsmiths' College, London, 1973. Address: 262 Randolph Avenue, London W.9, England.

PUBLICATIONS

Verse

Massacre of the Innocents, with John Rowan. London, Writers Forum, 1963.
Sound Poems: An ABC in Sound. London, Writers Forum, 1965.
Eyearun. London, Writers Forum, 1966.
Chamber Music. Stuttgart, Editions Hansjörg Mayer, 1967.
Kurrirrurriri. London, Writers Forum, 1967.
SO: Six Sound Poems. London, Writers Forum, 1968.
Octo: Visual Poems. London, Writers Forum, 1969.
Whisper Piece. London, Writers Forum, 1969.
Why Shiva Has Ten Arms. London, Writers Forum, 1969.
Whississippi. London, Writers Forum, 1969.
Etcetera: A New Collection of Found and Sound Poems. Cardiff, Vertigo, 1970.
Kwatz. Gillingham, Kent, ARC Publications, 1970.
Sonic Icons. London, Writers Forum, 1970.
Kris Kringles Kesmes Korals. Cardiff and London, Vertigo-Writers Forum, 1970.
Three Poems for Voice and Movement. London, Writers Forum, 1971.
Konkrete Canticle. London, Covent Garden Press, 1971.
Beethoven Today. London, Covent Garden Press, 1971.
Spearhead. London, Writers Forum, 1971.
Five Visual Poems. London, Writers Forum, 1971.
The Judith Poem. London, Writers Forum, 1971.
Poster No. 2. Brighton, Judith Walker Posters, 1971.
Songsignals. Cardiff, Second Aeon Publications, 1972.
Tomatomato. Kettering, Northamptonshire, All-In, 1972.
15 Shakespeare-Kaku. London, Writers Forum, 1972.
Trigram. London, Writers Forum, 1972.
E colony. London, Writers Forum, 1973.
Circa 73–74. London, Writers Forum, 1973.
Alphapitasuite. London, Writers Forum, 1973.
In Any Language. London, Writers Forum, 1973.
The Five Vowels. London, Writers Forum, 1974.
Picture Sheet One. London, Good Elf, 1974.
A Winter Poem. London, Writers Forum, 1974.
Five Performance Pieces. London, Writers Forum, 1975.
Yedo Keta Waro. London, Writers Forum, 1975.
Hydrangea. London, Writers Forum, 1975.
Kyoto to Tokyo. London, Good Elf, 1975.
A Round Dance. Stockholm, Writers Forum, 1976.
Poems for the North West Territories. London, Writers Forum, 1976.
Bill Jubobe: selected texts 1942–1975. Toronto, Coach House Press, 1976.
Jade-Sound Poems. London, Writers Forum, 1976.
Furst Fruts Uv 1977, with Lawrence Upton. London, Good Elf – Writers Forum, 1977.
Title: Of the Work. London, Writers Forum, 1977.
Number Structures. Stockholm, Writers Forum, 1977.
Tu To Ratu: Earth Best. London, Writers Forum, 1977.
Cygnet Ring: collected poems 1. London, Tapocketa Press, 1977.
And Avocado. London, Writers Forum, 1977.
Bob Cob's Rag Bag. London, Writers Forum, 1977.
Anan An' Nan. London, Writers Forum, 1977.
Scorch Scores. London, Writers Forum, 1977.
Citycisms. London, Writers Forum, 1977.

Windwound. London, Writers Forum, 1977.
Voice Prints. London, Writers Forum, 1977.
Janus. London, Writers Forum, 1977.
Fingrams. London, Writers Forum, 1977.
Fracted. London, Writers Forum, 1977.
Cuba. London, Writers Forum, 1977.
A Movie Book. London, Writers Forum, 1978.
Two Leaf Book. London, Writers Forum, 1978.
Found: Sound. London, Tapocketa Press, 1978.
Principles of Movement. London, Writers Forum, 1978.
Meet Bournemouth. London, Writers Forum, 1978.
Fugitive Poem No. X. London, Writers Forum, 1978.
Game and Set. London, Writers Forum, 1978.
Ginetics. London, Writers Forum, 1978.
A B C/Wan Do Tree: collected poems 2. London, El Uel Uel U, 1978.
Sensations of the Retina. Toronto, Gronk, 1978.
A Peal in Air: collected poems 3. Toronto, AnonbeyondgrOnkontaktewild Presses, 1978.
Fiveways. Toronto, Writers Forum, 1978.
Niagara. London, Writers Forum, 1978.
Grin. London, Writers Forum, 1979.
A Short History of London, with Jeremy Adler. London, Writers Forum, 1979.
The Kollekted Kris Kringle (collected poems 4). London, Anarcho Press, 1979.

Recordings: *An ABC in Sound*, with Ernst Jandl, Writers Forum, 1965; *Chamber Music*, Swedish Radio-Fylkingen, 1968; *Whississippi*, Swedish Radio-Fylkingen, 1969; *Marvo Moves Natter* and *Spontaneous Appealinair Contemprate Apollinaire*, Ou, 1969; *Variations on a Theme of Tan*, Stedelijk Museum, Amsterdam, 1970; *As Easy*, Swedish Radio-Fylkingen, 1971; *Ga(il s)o(ng)*, *Suesequence*, *Poem for Voice and Mandoline and Poem for Gillian*, *Hymn to the Sacred Mushroom*, Arts Council, 1971; *Khrajrej*, Opus Magazine, 1973; *E colony*, Typewriter Magazine, 1973; *Hymn to the Sacred Mushroom*, CBS/Sugar, 1975; *Portrait of Robin Crozier*, Fylkingen, 1977; *15 Shakespeare-kaku*, with Laurence Casserley, Cramps, 1978.

Other

Editor, *Gloup and Woup: A Folio of English Concrete Poetry.* Todmorden, Lancashire, ARC Publications, 1974.
Editor, with Peter Mayer, *Concerning Concrete Poetry.* London, Writers Forum, 1978.

Critical Studies: by Dom Sylvester Houédard, in "Bob Cobbing Issue," *Extra Verse 17* (London), 1966; by Eric Mottram, in *Second Aeon 16–17* (Cardiff), 1973; *Bob Cobbing and "Writers Forum"* edited by Peter Mayer, Sunderland, Ceolfrith Press, 1974.

Bob Cobbing comments:

My earlier poems "might seem to be conventionally linear; but their urge is towards stabilized diagram, intemized pieces of information in a spatial lay-out which is, in fact, the syntax" (Eric Mottram). In later poems, the dance of letters, half-letters, syllables and words on the page is score for "a ballet of the speech organs" (Victor Shklovsky). In still later poems, the scores are for instrumental as well as vocal poetry; for a ballet of the whole body and not just the voice.

I have been described as "a lettriste, thirty years out of date" (François Dufrêne), and it is true that I value lettriste principles, but not solely. My work derives equally from Joyce, Stein and the Kerouac of "Old Angel Midnight"; from François Dufrêne's post-lettriste cri-rythmes and the vocal micro-particles of Henri Chopin. This leads Dom Sylvester Houédard to note the range of my personal scale (a) from eye to ear, (b) from most to least abstract.

At present I am working on single-voice poems; multi-voiced poems; poems based on words; poems not using words or even letters; poems for electronic treatment on tape; poems for "voice as instrument and instruments as speaking voices" (*Time Out* magazine, concerning the group abAna with which I perform); poems as scores for dance or drama, invitations to act out an event in space, sound and choreography.

"History points to an origin that poetry and music share in the dance that seems to be a part of the make-up of homo sapiens and needs no more justification or conscious control than breathing" (Basil Bunting). This attitude is worth exploring again and means both a going back and a going forward.

* * *

The claim that Bob Cobbing is the leading British exponent of Sound Poetry is not an unreasonable one. Certainly he has been an indefatigable worker and propagandist in this country for that international flowering of abstract poetry which has been a distinctive phenomenon in the last two decades. The steady flow of publications from his Writers Forum Press, the exhibitions he has organised, are part of an energetic campaign to put such poetry on the British map.

It was W. H. Auden, when once describing his method of composition, who said, in essence, that unless he abandoned some of his poems he would never cease revising them. In a contrary way Bob Cobbing subscribes to such a view, in that far from abandoning his poems he is to be seen constantly revising them or, to put it better perhaps, constantly producing new versions of them. Thus one of the more successful of his visual poems, "Are Your Children Safe in the Sea?," is to be found in many versions. The copy I have before me at the moment is a folded card "triptych" described as "one of several eye interpretations of the poem." The poem itself is a five lined verbal poem of which *Extra Verse 17*, for example, contains another and completely different visual interpretation. "Wowromwrormm (Worm)," an attempt to balance the appeal between eye and ear using Apollinaire's "Rain" as a jumping off point, is another poem to be found in various versions on cards, folders or in books. Other visual poems are described as "typographic interpretations of sound poems" where Cobbing keeps worrying a theme into a variety of mediums.

The sound poems themselves are often composed directly onto tape recorders and then interpreted or re-interpreted by use of superimposition, play-back and other electronic recording techniques. Here Cobbing's technical skill is undeniable, and often his sound poems, such as "Tan Tandinanan," with their almost obsessive repetition, can be seen to be paralleled in the Mantras. Another relationship might be that concrete poetry is to the visual arts as sound poetry is to music. Though I imagine Bob Cobbing might see that as too facile a formula.

But is it poetry? If we accept the validity of what Cobbing is doing we could still deny that it is poetry and categorize it instead as one of the visual arts or music. The telling argument against abstraction in general is to me, a poet working in a traditionally verbal medium, that it can be seen as an attempt to dehumanize the arts. To this the answer is given that the more the artist abstracts the less he becomes mimetic, descriptive and consequently deceptive, and the more his art becomes concretely truthful and, it follows, of human value. Bob Cobbing himself says he is working towards "a new abstract entity – the re-amalgamation of poetry with music and dance," an attempt to transcend intellect which will "reunite poetry with music."

But if one refuses, as one should, to accept the frontiers of art as inviolable, and acknowledges the valuable contribution of past experimentation in the arts, then one must but recognize the pioneering work of Bob Cobbing and his colleagues.

—John Cotton

COGSWELL, Frederick (William). Canadian. Born in East Centreville, New Brunswick, 8 November 1917. Educated at the University of New Brunswick, Fredericton, B.A. 1949, M.A. 1950; University of Edinburgh, Ph.D. 1952. Served in the Canadian Army, 1940–45. Married Margaret Hynes in 1944; two daughters. Assistant Professor, 1952–57, Associate Professor, 1957–61, and since 1961, Professor of English, University of New Brunswick. Editor, *Fiddlehead* magazine, 1952–66, and *Humanities Association Bulletin*, 1967–72, both in Fredericton. Since 1960, Editor, Fiddlehead Poetry Books, Fredericton. Recipient: Nuffield Fellowship, 1959; Canada Council Fellowship, 1966. Address: 769 Reid Street, Fredericton, New Brunswick, Canada.

PUBLICATIONS

Verse

The Stunted Strong. Fredericton, New Brunswick, Fiddlehead, 1954.
The Haloed Tree. Toronto, Ryerson Press, 1956.
Descent from Eden. Toronto, Ryerson Press, 1959.
Lost Dimension. London, Outposts, 1960.
Five New Brunswick Poets, with others, edited by Frederick Cogswell. Fredericton, New Brunswick, Fiddlehead, 1962.
Star-People. Fredericton, New Brunswick, Fiddlehead, 1968.
Immortal Plowman. Fredericton, New Brunswick, Fiddlehead, 1969.
In Praise of Chastity. Fredericton, New Brunswick, Chapbooks, 1970.
The Chains of Liliput. Fredericton, New Brunswick, Fiddlehead, 1971.
The House Without a Door. Fredericton, New Brunswick, Fiddlehead, 1973.
Light Bird of Life: Selected Poems. Fredericton, New Brunswick, Fiddlehead, 1974.
Against Perspective. Fredericton, New Brunswick, Fiddlehead, 1978.

Other

Editor, *A Canadian Anthology.* Fredericton, New Brunswick, Fiddlehead, 1960.
Editor, *Five New Brunswick Poets.* Fredericton, New Brunswick, Fiddlehead, 1962.
Editor, with Robert Tweedie and S. W. MacNutt, and contributor, *The Arts in New Brunswick.* Fredericton, University of New Brunswick Press, 1966.
Editor, with Thelma Reid Lower, *The Enchanted Land: Canadian Poetry for Young Readers.* Toronto, Gage, 1967.
Editor, *The Home Place*, by Marion McLellan. Charlottetown, Prince Edward Island 1973 Centennial Commission, 1973.
Editor and Translator, *The Poetry of Modern Quebec.* Montreal, Harvest House, 1975.

Translator, *The Testament of Cresseid*, by Henryson. Toronto, Ryerson Press, 1957.
Translator, *One Hundred Poems of Modern Quebec.* Fredericton, New Brunswick, Fiddlehead, 1970.
Translator, *A Second Hundred Poems of Modern Quebec.* Fredericton, New Brunswick, Fiddlehead, 1971.
Translator, *Confrontation*, by G. Lapointe. Fredericton, New Brunswick, Fiddlehead, 1973.

Frederick Cogswell comments:

My poetry is a response, as a rule, to direct personal experience. It finds its own form instinctively out of the various forms which I have encountered either traditional or modern. It is marked by directness, economy, sincerity, and the avoidance of long words.

* * *

"It is marked by directness, economy, sincerity, and the avoidance of long words." This is not a critic dissecting Frederick Cogswell's verse, but the poet himself discussing his own work. The statement displays all the characteristic self-deprecation of the poet. For many years Cogswell has tirelessly served the interests of fellow writers, as a teacher of English, as the publisher of *The Fiddlehead*, the best magazine of poetry in the Maritimes, and now as the publisher of Fiddlehead Poetry Books, a seemingly endless stream of chapbooks devoted in the main to the work of new young poets.

All along Cogswell has been publishing a rivulet, if not a stream, of booklets of brief poems. His first publication, *The Stunted Strong*, is a series of arresting vignettes dramatizing the negative aspects of life in the small communities that make up Atlantic Canada; the collection had a decided influence on the early work of Alden Nowlan and was widely read across the country. The early phase of biographical and autobiographical poems ended in the publication of *Descent from Eden*, a kind of selected poems. Since then the poems have been elliptical and epigrammatic as well as lyric, as two recent publications, *The Chains of Liliput* and *The House Without a Door*, demonstrate.

"It was the chains of Liliput/Taught Gulliver he was a giant," Cogswell explains. The poet cannot resist a too-easy parody called "Spiv's Innisfree" which begins: "I will arise and go to a pub in Piccadilly/And six quick ones will I down there, of Scotch and soda made." His strengths are shown in this verse from "Unhappy Clown":

I smile and I sing,
And I laugh like a king
For the same reason as you,
To be part of the show.

One is always aware, reading a Cogswell poem, that the poet is aware of writing it. Sometimes the poet is able to make this work to his – and the reader's – advantage, as it does in this sincere poem "In Defence of Rosaries":

and God whose stillness
speaks as loud as noise
will understand
my private prayer

—John Robert Colombo

COHEN, Leonard (Norman). Canadian. Born in Montreal, Quebec, 21 September 1934. Educated at McGill University, Montreal, B.A. 1955; Columbia University, New York. Composer and Singer: has given concerts in Canada, the United States and Europe. Artist-in-Residence, University of Alberta, Edmonton, 1975–76. Recipient: McGill University Literary Award, 1956; Canada Council Award, 1960; Quebec Literary Award, 1964. D.L.: Dalhousie University, Halifax, Nova Scotia, 1971. Lives in Montreal and Greece. Address: c/o Martin J. Machat, 1501 Broadway, 30th Floor, New York, New York 10036, U.S.A.

PUBLICATIONS

Verse

Let Us Compare Mythologies. Montreal, Contact Press, 1956.

The Spice-Box of Earth. Toronto, McClelland and Stewart, 1961; New York, Viking Press, 1965; London, Cape, 1971.
Flowers for Hitler. Toronto, McClelland and Stewart, 1964; London, Cape, 1973.
Parasites of Heaven. Toronto, McClelland and Stewart, 1966.
Selected Poems 1956–1968. Toronto, McClelland and Stewart, and New York, Viking Press, 1968; London, Cape, 1969.
Leonard Cohen's Song Book. New York, Collier, 1969.
Five Modern Canadian Poets, with others, edited by Eli Mandel. Toronto, Holt Rinehart, 1970.
The Energy of Slaves. Toronto, McClelland and Stewart, and London, Cape, 1972; New York, Viking Press, 1973.

Recordings: *The Songs of Leonard Cohen*, Columbia, 1968; *Songs from a Room*, Columbia, 1969; *Songs of Love and Hate*, Columbia, 1971; *Live Songs*, Columbia, 1973; *New Skin for the Old Ceremony*, Columbia, 1974; *Death of a Lady's Man*, Warner Brothers, 1977; *Recent Songs*, CBS, 1979.

Plays

The New Step (produced London, 1972).
Sisters of Mercy: A Journey into the Words and Music of Leonard Cohen (produced Niagara-on-the-Lake, Ontario, 1973).

Novels

The Favorite Game. New York, Viking Press, and London, Secker and Warburg, 1963.
Beautiful Losers. Toronto, McClelland and Stewart, and New York, Viking Press, 1966; London, Cape, 1970.

Critical Studies: *Leonard Cohen* by Michael Ondaatje, Toronto, McClelland and Stewart, 1970; *Leonard Cohen: The Artist and His Critics* edited by Michael Gnarowski, Toronto, McGraw Hill, 1976.

* * *

The figures of Leonard Cohen's poems rise like figures in Chagall, transformed from the ordinary, surprised into a world of visionary experience. Out of the junk of the everyday – "the garbage and the flowers" – the magical world of the imaginative is created. There is a strong sense in which his poetry is a prodigious search of experience for the exit from the ordinary. But it is not always violently so. Some of the earlier lyrics – "Go by Brooks," for instance – have a simple lyricism that is also intense. Occasionally, it slopes off into a wry humour that is characteristic of him; more often its apparent Emily Dickinson simplicities conceal a toughness and a danger for which only the ballad form is adequate. And it is in the ballads that his greatest strength lies. The concentration of the imagery and the force of the rhyme give a telling intensity to the surrealist experiences of his imagination – an intensity that becomes at times almost gnomic:

History is a needle
for putting men asleep
anointed with the poison
of all they want to keep.

Certain themes continue to pre-occupy Cohen as certain images haunt his imagination. His search is for the sensual heaven of "The Sisters of Mercy," not the skeletal world of the ideal, the astringent dead world of "I Have Not Lingered in European Monasteries." Indeed, his religion is the rejection of the suffering ascetic – "I disdain God's suffering./Men command sufficient pain" – for a priapic world in which the liturgical celebrations are the extreme of physical – a "constant love/and passion without flesh" – that is not a bloodless mysticism but the apogee of the physical, almost like "high." But even in the physical world his fear of entrapment by the deadly females of such poems as "The Unicorn Tapestries" or "I Long to Hold Some Lady" is strong. They become in his poetic fabric the creatures – associated with doctors, rabbis, and priests – of the liturgy of death. "The Story of Isaac" lurks behind the sacrificial metaphors to which he recurs. What is most telling in this balladic pre-occupation with the undefined horror is Cohen's recognition of it not as external to himself, but part of his own psyche. Dachau is everyday Montreal; the amatory is also the murderous "tasting blood on your tongue/does not shock me." So the poetry (of *Flowers for Hitler* especially) is exculpatory, and the desire to escape from the "ape with angel glands" the more intense.

In his later poetry there is a sense of imminence. The partisan's retreat is more embattled even than "the small oasis where we lie" of his earlier love poems. His concern with freedom, his feeling of the "incomparable sense of loss" to which he refers in "Queen Victoria and Me," is more than nostalgia for a lost land of freedom and the spirit. It is a matter of skirmishes in the hills "on the side of the ghost and the king," a matter of escaping from the horrific city whose terrors are also the terrors of "the armies marching still" towards the war that must surely come.

A mode like Ferlinghetti's prevents such poems as "The killers that run other countries" from sentimentalism. And Cohen's "Song for My Assassin" (another ballad) has the same wryness as his love songs – a wryness that recognizes that the pretty fictions (even his women) are in large measure self-amusements. Occasionally he slips from his customary Horatian tone to a heavy-handed Juvenalian, and when feeling is too close to be contained the poem can be very flat indeed. But even in the ostensible absence of the muse Cohen can write a fine poem, of which "The poems don't love us anymore" (in *The Energy of Slaves*) is a good example.

Cohen's voice is most sympathetic and most telling, not in his escapes from the horror and the junk into the fashionable "pot" world of despair, but in his celebrations of the poet's capacity not only to hold out against the faceless butchers but to make acclaim of "orange peels,/cans, discarded guts." The gaiety of vision is also his *seigneur*, and the surrealism that is so much a part of the Canadian sensibility provides him with a new way of seeing the ordinary transformed: "One of the lizards/was blowing bubbles/as it did pushups on the carpet." The conclusion to that poem is "I believe the mystics are right/when they say we are all One." The Prophets and *The Song of Songs* inform this voice. Its celebration is of a beauty, entirely human, that prevails over "the clubfoot crowds." Its affirmation is that not only all poets but "all men will be sailors."

—D. D. C. Chambers

COLE, Barry. British. Born in Woking, Surrey, 13 November 1936. Served in the Royal Air Force for two years. Married Rita Linihan in 1958; three daughters. Worked in the Central Office of Information, London, 1965–70. Northern Arts Fellow in Literature, universities of Newcastle upon Tyne and Durham, 1970–72. Address: 18A Great Percy Street, London W.C.1, England.

PUBLICATIONS

Verse

Blood Ties. London, Turret, 1967.
Ulysses in the Town of Coloured Glass. London, Turret, 1968.
Moonsearch. London, Methuen, 1968.
The Visitors. London, Methuen, 1970.
Vanessa in the City. London, Trigram Press, 1971.
Pathetic Fallacies. London, Eyre Methuen, 1973.
The Rehousing of Scaffardi. Richmond, Surrey, Keepsake Press, 1976.
Dedications. Nottingham, Byron Press, 1977.

Novels

A Run Across the Island. London, Methuen, 1968.
Joseph Winter's Patronage. London, Methuen, 1969.
The Search for Rita. London, Methuen, 1970.
The Giver. London, Methuen, 1971.
Doctor Fielder's Common Sense. London, Methuen, 1972.

Barry Cole comments:

The subjects of my poems are myself, love, my wife; the world I know I see and the world I think I see. My verse forms are neither traditional nor *avant garde*, but of my own time at any given moment. Sometimes they rhyme, sometimes they don't, but I try for precision, brevity and clarity. The poems aim at wit and intelligence, though they may hit none or any of these. Their sources are my own felt and thought experiences and those of sympathetic antecedents and contemporaries. Influences are few and unrecognizable.

* * *

Barry Cole has, in recent years, been a prolific novelist. The novels have an instantly recognisable atmosphere – one of strangeness rooted in the ordinary, as if a different order, with totally different rules, subsumed the mundane world we see, and manifested itself unexpectedly at moments of crisis. The atmosphere in Cole's most interesting poems is exactly the same as that which we discover in the novels – they are, in fact, capsule versions of the stories he tells in prose. The thing that counts is the total image; not the individual line. Quoted in fragments, the poetry often seems flat. It is only when we read the poem through as a narrative that we see what the poet's purpose is.

—Edward Lucie-Smith

COLEMAN, Elliott. American. Born in Binghamton, New York, 26 September 1906. Educated at Wheaton College, Illinois, B.A. 1926; Princeton Theological Seminary, New Jersey; General Theological Seminary, New York; St. Stephen's House, Oxford. Ordained to the Diaconate of the Episcopal Church, 1942. Master, Asheville School, North Carolina, 1928–40. Worked for Henry Holt and Company, publishers, 1943, and Doubleday and Company, publishers, 1944, both in New York. Since 1945, Member of the English

Department, currently Professor of English and Director of the Writing Seminars, Johns Hopkins University, Baltimore. Address: Department of English, Johns Hopkins University, Baltimore, Maryland 21218, U.S.A.

PUBLICATIONS

Verse

The Poems of Elliott Coleman. New York, Dutton, 1936.
An American in Augustland. Chapel Hill, University of North Carolina Press, 1940.
Pearl Harbor. Privately printed, 1942.
27 Night Sonnets. Milan, Scheiwiller, 1949.
A Glass Darkly: New Sonnets. Baltimore, Contemporary Poetry, 1952.
33 Night Sonnets. Baltimore, Contemporary Poetry, 1955.
Sonetti (bilingual edition, translated by Alfredo Rizzardi). Bologna, Italy, Libreria Antiquaria Palmaverde, 1959.
Mockingbirds at Fort McHenry. Pamplona, Spain, Atlantis, 1963.
Broken Death. Baltimore, Linden Press, 1964.
Rose Demonics 1936–1966. Baltimore, Linden Press, 1967.
One Hundred Poems. Chapel Hill, North Carolina, Tinker Press, 1972.
The Tangerine Birds. Baltimore, Harbor House, 1973.
In the Canyon. Baltimore, Bay Press, 1974.
Oxford Flow. Oxford, Duns Scotus Press, 1976.
Poems from the Chilton Seminars. N.p., Hill Press, 1979.
Four Counties of Youth. N.p., Hill Press, 1979.

Other

The Golden Angel: Papers on Proust. New York and Sacramento, Coley Taylor-Academy Guild, 1954.

Editor, *Lectures in Criticism.* New York, Pantheon, 1949.
Editor, *Poems of Byron, Keats and Shelley.* New York, Doubleday, 1968.

Translator, with the author, *Studies in Human Time*, by Georges Poulet. Baltimore, Johns Hopkins University Press, 1956.
Translator (unrhymed portions only), *The Mad Poet*, by Pierre Emmanuel. Baltimore, Contemporary Poetry, 1956.
Translator, with the author, *The Interior Distance*, by Georges Poulet. Baltimore, Johns Hopkins University Press, 1959.
Translator, with the author, *Towns of This World*, by Alfredo Rizzardi. Baltimore, Contemporary Poetry, 1962.
Translator, with the author and Mrs. Carley Dawson, *The Metamorphoses of the Circle*, by Georges Poulet. Baltimore, Johns Hopkins University Press, 1967.
Translator, with the author, *Proustian Space*, by Georges Poulet. Baltimore, Johns Hopkins University Press, 1977.

Elliott Coleman comments:

Very few of the earliest poems – influenced by Virgil, Shelley, Wordsworth, Browning, Brooke and Hardy – are worth saving.

In a middle period, two books of sonnets experimented impetuously with the Shakespearean form.

Later work – *Mockingbirds at Fort McHenry, Rose Demonics* – was in large part a taking of fragmentary dictation from the pre-conscious.

The latest stuff, a reflective series of Proses, is the most strangely imagined of all.

Intention: Hoping never to write anything else that is boring, not just now concerned about writing anything else at all, I still should pray for a few more interesting catches, early in the morning.

* * *

Two of the most eminent poets in America, A. R. Ammons and Josephine Jacobsen, have written at length about the quality of Elliott Coleman's poetry. Jacobsen has written that one leaves the reading of a book of Coleman's poetry with the "feeling that one has stumbled about the earth with half-shut eyes. There is a preoccupation with light which verges on color on the one hand, and on the religious and mystical on the other...." A. R. Ammons has written that Coleman's poems "search out the deeper elements of the mind that are at once sharp reality and vision. It is as if in rejecting the control of his experience by archetypes – he has discovered the elements archetypes are made of without any loss to their luminosity and suggestiveness. Because of this, poems that derive from particular experience generalize spontaneously into a community of insight and feeling. The total body of Mr. Coleman's work represents one of the supreme poetic achievements of our time." The respect that both of these poets have for Elliott Coleman's poetry is shared by a good number of poets in both England and America. Coleman has never courted poetic fame. Nor has he been ever the reflection of a given school of poetics. One realizes in reading Coleman's poems that the range and depth of his poetry are enormous. From his earliest sonnets, he has moved from an impeccable classicism into a poetic territory that has been truly the creation of his own exploration. In his poem "Scattered Proses" Coleman experiments with language and form:

sands wide enough for two   and nothing possible but silence
lighted rooms one may not enter   but music and then voices
the old prairie and the old car   and bumping the end of the sun

In his more recent poetry one senses that Coleman is attempting to define and crystalize the language into the simplest, most elemental thing; where once he expanded the form and the language with experiment, dissatisfied with the accepted ironies of traditional non-conformism, now the expression in its most graceful truth is equivalent to a sudden and unexpected simplicity. From the poem "White Coral":

star coral
sea pen
sea fan
live flower

dead men's fingers
rigid
sharp
sway light itself

she who gave it

white coral spray
   dear skeleton

More recently, in his books written in England, Coleman has moved even further into the language or voice of the poet, at the same time attempting to go beyond the literary or poetic fluid within which the written voice of the contemporary poet often hides itself. There is nothing "poetic" now, in the sense of a deliberate artifice. The poet speaking, the poet listening, the poet seeing, the poet expressing are all one. This is what separates Coleman from the majority of contemporary poets. He is attempting to express a truth that even he is not sure exists. He is struggling with the invisibility of a gracefulness that he seeks to make visible and that he calls now a song, a voice, a simple object or movement. In one of his latest poems he writes:

On a winter night in 1979,
When it had cooled down to 2 degrees below
absolute zero,
The Church of St. Mary the Virgin, Chilton
exploded....
The nave was hydrogen light.
The chancel was voices.
Saxon voices
Roman voices
Norman voices
Elizabethan voices
Modern voices
Young voices
Then it was dark and morning,
dark and day.

—Michael Lynch

COLLINSON, Laurence (Henry). British. Born in Leeds, Yorkshire, 7 September 1925. Educated at various Australian primary schools; Brisbane State High School; Dalby High School, Queensland; University of Queensland, Brisbane; Julian Ashton Art School, Sydney; Mercer House, Melbourne, teaching diploma 1955. Freelance radio, magazine and newspaper writer until 1954; English and Maths teacher in Victoria secondary schools, 1956–61; Editor, *The Educational Magazine*, Melbourne, teachers' journal of the Victorian Education Department, 1961–64. Also acted, directed and wrote for various Australian little theatres up to 1956. Sub-Editor, IPC Magazines Ltd., London, 1965–73. Recipient: Society of Australian Authors prize, London, 1969; Australian Council of the Arts special grant and fellowship, 1973. Lives in London. Agent: Margery Vosper Ltd., Suite 8, 26 Charing Cross Road, London WC2H 0DG, England.

PUBLICATIONS

Verse

Poet's Dozen. Privately printed, 1952.
The Moods of Love. Melbourne, Overland, 1957.
Who Is Wheeling Grandma? Melbourne, Overland, 1967.
Hovering Narcissus. London, Grandma Press, 1977.

Plays

Friday Night at the Schrammers' (produced Brisbane, 1949). Published in *Australian*

One-Act Plays, Book 2, edited by Greg Branson, Adelaide, Rigby, 1962.
No Sugar for George (produced Brisbane, 1949).
The Zelda Trio (produced Melbourne, 1961; London, 1974).
A Slice of Birthday Cake (broadcast, 1963). Published in *Eight Short Plays*, Melbourne, Nelson, 1965.
The Wangaratta Bunyip, in *Plays for Young Players*, edited by Colin Thiele and Greg Branson. Adelaide, Rigby, 1970.
Thinking Straight (produced London, 1975). Published in *Homosexual Acts*, London, Inter-Action, 1975.
One Penny for Israel (produced London, 1978).

Screenplays: Two *Export Action* series documentaries, 1964.

Radio Plays: *A Slice of Birthday Cake*, 1963 (Australia); *The Slob on Friday*, 1969 (Canada).

Television Plays: *Uneasy Paradise*, 1963 (Australia); *Nude with Violin*, 1964 (Australia); *The Audition*, 1964 (Australia); *The Moods of Love*, 1964 (Australia); *Number Thirty Approximately*, 1968 (UK); *Loving Israel*, 1968 (UK); *The Girl from Upstairs*, 1971 (UK).

Novel

Cupid's Crescent. London, Grandma Press, 1973.

Manuscript Collections: Eunice Hangar Memorial Library, University of Queensland, Adelaide; National Library, Canberra.

Critical Studies: "Writer and Critic" by John Barnes, in *Westerly 3* (Perth), 1958; *Queensland and Its Writers* by Cecil Hadgraft, Brisbane, University of Queensland Press, 1959; "Laurence Collinson: A Poet in Development" by Pauline M. Kirk, in *Overland 49* (Melbourne), 1971.

Laurence Collinson comments:

I write poems only when compelled to by some kind of "inner necessity." The impulse may derive from a subjective emotion or an external situation; my two primary subjects in 30 years of writing have been physical love and the self-deception that pervades our personal and social lives. Once the "poetic" idea comes into my consciousness, I try my best to shape the poem according to the needs of the subject and my desire to communicate pleasurably – formal pleasure being essential whether the subject is tragic or comic or something in between. I still adhere to the pronouncement of one of my high-school English teachers that the principal elements of a poem are its music and imagery. The freedom from form that many "contemporary" poets demand in order to allow themselves full "self-expression" seems to me unrewarding for both writer and reader: I believe with other Marxists that "freedom is the recognition of necessity," and the limitations imposed on a subject by the use of even the simplest of traditional forms create an infinitely more complex, gratifying, and precious object than the wildest expressionist verses. When I read the work of other poets, what delights and moves me more than anything else is to come across an astonishing and absolutely right image and to feel also that the poet has set down an experience in such a way that I can recognise and share it with him totally. And this is what I would like other readers to find in my own poetry.

* * *

Laurence Collinson was born in England, but with his family moved to Australia when he was very young. Education, outlook and basic perceptions are, therefore, influenced by Australia, and Collinson identifies himself with that country. Almost all his published verse first appeared in Australian magazines and anthologies and his two major collections were published by the Melbourne publisher Overland. This identification is not, however, jingoistic in any sense – Collinson claims he feels no urge to assert any specific Australianness. Some poets have driven powerful (and some bathetic) work out of the landscape and names of Australia; Collinson only allows a precise sense of place to emerge when it is necessary to the wider movement of a poem. Most of his work could have been written anywhere where the English language is spoken and respected.

Collinson's first collection of poems, *The Moods of Love*, was published in 1957 when he was already well-known as one of the more important younger poets working in Australia. Critics were sharply divided in their reactions, mostly (seen at this distance) on trivial issues. But one thing does emerge from that response, and which is relevant to any consideration of Collinson's poetry, is that many critics were made uneasy by the strong social/political comment implicit in much of the verse. At the time of the volume's publication, Collinson wrote about "a world duped and doped by commercialism, dulled by education (such as we know it), broken by war and oppression...." His work is never didactic on these themes; but neat, observed pieces such as "Suburban Party" and "The Clerk's Prayer" make their points through satire and a sardonic wit. The sonnet sequence that gives the book its title explores, often with great intensity, the responsiveness of one human being to the contact of love. The tone is often deceptively conversational ("I think I love you all the ways there are") which serves only to underscore the personal involvement and technical control of the work.

The second major volume, *Who Is Wheeling Grandma?*, was published in 1967. A sense of political commitment is still present in some poems, notably in "Aspects of Modern Education," a sequence subtitled "Double Standards in Search of a Schoolboy." The overall feel is darker, however, and "the lover drowns as dreams capsize." The poems are generally shorter, and tighter. Collinson has always been a highly disciplined writer; he believes that shape and form are as important as content, and his very concise imagery and perfectly balanced lines do, indeed, give a great deal of pleasure.

—Roger Baker

COLLYMORE, Frank A(ppleton). British (West Indian). Born in Barbados, 7 January 1893. Educated at Combermere School, Barbados, 1903–09. Married 1) Gwendolyn Hutchinson in 1917; 2) Ellice Lorna Honychurch in 1947; four daughters. Teacher, 1910–49, 1958–63, and Deputy Headmaster, 1949–58, Combermere School. Editor, *Bim* magazine, Bridgetown, Barbados, 1943–73. Amateur actor. M.A.: University of the West Indies, Kingston, 1968. O.B.E. (Officer, Order of the British Empire), 1958. Address: Woodville, Chelsea Road, St. Michael, Barbados, West Indies.

PUBLICATIONS

Verse

Thirty Poems. Bridgetown, Barbados, Advocate, 1944.
Beneath the Casuarinas. Bridgetown, Barbados, Advocate, 1945.
Flotsam. Bridgetown, Barbados, Advocate, 1948.

A Dozen Short Poems. Georgetown, Guyana, Miniature Poets, 1952.
Collected Poems. Bridgetown, Barbados, Advocate, 1959.
Rhymed Ruminations on the Fauna of Barbados. Bridgetown, Barbados, Advocate, 1969.
Selected Poems. Bridgetown, Barbados, Coles, 1971.

Other

Notes for a Glossary of Words and Phrases of Barbadian Dialect. Bridgetown, Barbados, Advocate, 1953; revised edition, 1957, 1965, 1970.

Frank A. Collymore comments:

I had always enjoyed the reading of poetry and had on several occasions tried to write verse unsuccessfully. In the early forties, I happened to be living alone, and the reading of the poetry of Day Lewis, W. H. Auden, and Louis MacNeice seemed to act as stimulus to whatever dormant muse may have been awaiting expression. During the forties and early fifties I wrote continuously – I suppose well over 200 poems – and encouraged by some friends, I ventured to have them published.

I am afraid that since that period my muse has forsaken me, although I have from time to time written some light verse.

* * *

Frank A. Collymore is essentially a "Nature" poet, "Georgian" in mode. His themes are landscape, love, beauty, mutability, reflections on an empire of the mind in which man's perceptions were once whole, as in "Mutability":

All that our mortal hands have wrought
Upon time's wide and fleeting range
Enjoy but brief integrity,
Soon suffer change.

Even the temple that we rear
To love, so proud against the sky,
May not prevail o'er transience,
For love must die.

But though he is very conscious of the fragility of things, Collymore is not a sentimentalizer. His perception of love and beauty is often fixed within tight, exact images; and his landscapes are often fully realized. The sea, for example, is "crisscrossed with stillness" in lines which use the overtly ordinary "lazylapping," "windruffed" and "aglitter" in a combination which produces effects more memorable and accurate than might, on the surface, be expected ("Hymn to the Sea"):

Always, always, the encroaching sea,
Eternal, lazylapping, crisscrossed with stillness;
Or windruffed, aglitter with gold; and the surf
Waist-high for children, or horses for Titans ...

In "Blue Agave," from *Flotsam*, this language takes on the hard, harsh, barren quality of the seaside plant:

Perched between stones, rooted in rock;
Thriving in drought and seablast ...

The bunched fingers spiked, at first
Resentful, now drooping as fountains drip
...; reptilian leaves armoured
Against the unknown foe ...

Avid the pronged claws, the idle
Teeth; and the uncoiling leaves, stark
And impervious as shark's hide, bear
The imprint of tooth and claw upon them ...

Armoured against forgotten fate
They score the low horizon ...

No other West Indian poet, not even Derek Walcott in *The Castaway*, has captured the desolation of the windward Caribbean coasts as precisely and as symbolically as Collymore in this poem. And as the West Indian archipelago is a fragment of a continent, and our history a fragment of a lost and possible whole, so Collymore's sensibility perceives the splinters ("Words Are the Poem"):

Words – words are the poem,
The incalculable flotsam;
That which bore them vanished beneath
The hurrying drift of time.

How shall they speak, how tell
Of the ship and the lost crew?
Each plank a splinter,
Each splinter enough for memory?

This sense of fragment, of ruin, the loss of something that was once beautiful, receives its fullest social expression in "Old Windmill":

... Once she was the focused joy
Of the countryside, her mighty sails unfurled:

Queen of the trades, a good ship manned
By her pressed crews to ride the surge and swell
Of the blue days ...

Then there was singing, there was laughter, delight
In her life's blood ...

Desolate now; only the empty eyes
Forever framed within the past ...
Under windswept skies
The sloven tractors shamble to the factory.

But to appreciate properly the achievement of Frank Collymore, one must read him alongside the "older" generation of West Indian poets – Tom Redcam, Claude McKay, Clare McFarlane, and those others who appear in *A Treasury of Jamaican Poetry* (1949). His "Blue Agave" must be compared with, say, McKay's "Spanish Needle": "Lovely, dainty Spanish Needle/With your yellow flower and white,/Dew-bedecked and softly sleeping,/Do you think of me tonight?" The differences are devastating. The point is that Collymore transcends the verse of his "Georgian" contemporaries. While they attempted to "sing" like Tennyson, he was learning from the discoveries of T. S. Eliot. He is the great poet of the West Indian transition. He is not yet concerned with social reality, however. "The Windmill" looks back to a golden time before mechanization, but gives no hint, except in "pressed crews," of the plantation system of which it is also a symbol. This failure to come to terms with this central area of West Indian experience is perhaps responsible for a certain lack of development in his poetry. One feels that, with his talents, he has consciously limited himself. On the other hand, he transforms an apparently everyday world which the poets of the "revolution" have often forgotten or have had little time for. More surely than most of his contemporaries of both generations, he can move from "Chanson Triste" – "Are you loved?/Weep; for the doll may never return/The kisses its mother/Bestows ..." – to "voici la plume de mon oncle":

> See how nicely his tie sits underneath his collar...
> You can always tell an educated man if you know where to look.
> See, he takes his hat off when the band is playing
> The National Anthem! That man's no bloody fool:
> He owns three houses and a drugstore in Porkmarket;
> He has learnt to use both edges of the Golden Rule.

—Edward Kamau Brathwaite

COLOMBO, John Robert. Canadian. Born in Kitchener, Ontario, 24 March 1936. Educated at Waterloo College, Ontario, 1956–57; University College, University of Toronto, B.A. 1959, 1959–60. Married to Ruth Brown; three children. Editorial Assistant, University of Toronto Press, 1959–60; Assistant Editor, Ryerson Press, 1960–63; Senior Advisory Editor, McClelland and Stewart, Toronto, 1964–70. Former Editor, *The Montrealer* and *Exchange*. Since 1959, Managing Editor, *Tamarack Review*, Toronto. Occasional Instructor, York University, Toronto, 1963–66; Writer-in-Residence, Mohawk College, Hamilton, Ontario, 1978. Member, Canada Council Arts Advisory Panel, 1968–70. Recipient: Canada Council grant, 1967, 1971; Centennial Medal, 1967. Member, Academy of Canadian Writers, 1977. Address: 42 Dell Park Avenue, Toronto M6B 2T6, Canada.

PUBLICATIONS

Verse

Fragments. Privately printed, 1957.
Variations. Kitchener, Ontario, Hawkshead Press, 1958.
This Citadel in Time. Kitchener, Ontario, Hawkshead Press, 1958.
This Studied Self. Kitchener, Ontario, Hawkshead Press, 1958.
In the Streets (as Ruta Ginsberg). Toronto, Hawkshead Press, 1959(?).
Poems and Other Poems. Toronto, Hawkshead Press, 1959.
Two Poems. Toronto, Hawkshead Press, 1959.
This Is the Work Entitled Canada. Toronto, Purple Partridge Press, 1959.
Fire Escape, Fire Esc, Fire. Toronto, Hawkshead Press, 1959.
The Impression of Beauty. Toronto, Hawkshead Press, 1959.

Poems to Be Sold for Bread. Toronto, Hawkshead Press, 1959.
Lines for the Last Day. Toronto, Hawkshead Press, 1960.
The Mackenzie Poems. Toronto, Swan, 1965.
The Great Wall of China: An Entertainment. Montreal, Delta Canada, 1966.
Abracadabra. Toronto, McClelland and Stewart, 1967.
Miraculous Montages. Toronto, Heine, 1967.
John Toronto: New Poems by Dr. Strachan, Found by John Robert Colombo. Ottawa, Oberon Press, 1969.
Neo Poems. Vancouver, Sono Nis Press, 1970.
The Great San Francisco Earthquake and Fire. Fredericton, New Brunswick, Fiddlehead, 1971.
Praise Poems and Leonardo's Lists. Toronto, Weed/Flower Press, 1972.
Translations from the English. Toronto, Peter Martin, 1974.
The Sad Truths. Toronto, Peter Martin, 1974.
Mostly Monsters. Toronto, Hounslow Press, 1977.
Variable Cloudiness. Toronto, Hounslow Press, 1977.
Private Parts. Toronto, Hounslow Press, 1978.

Other

Editor, *Rubato: New Poems by Young Canadian Poets.* Toronto, Purple Partridge Press, 1958.
Editor, *The Varsity Chapbook.* Toronto, Ryerson Press, 1959.
Editor, with Jacques Godbout, *Poésie 64/Poetry 64.* Toronto and Montreal, Ryerson Press-Editions du Jour, 1963.
Editor, with Raymond Souster, *Shapes and Sounds: Poems of W. W. E. Ross.* Toronto, Longman, 1968.
Editor, *How Do I Love Thee: Sixty Poems of Canada (and Quebec)....* Edmonton, Hurtig, 1970.
Editor, *New Directions in Canadian Poetry.* Toronto, Holt Rinehart, 1970.
Editor, *Rhymes and Reasons: Nine Canadian Poets Discuss Their Work.* Toronto, Holt Rinehart, 1971.
Editor, *An Alphabet of Annotations.* Montreal, Gheerbrant, 1972.
Editor, *Colombo's Canadian Quotations.* Edmonton, Hurtig, 1974; *Concise Canadian Quotations*, 1976.
Editor, *Colombo's Little Book of Canadian Proverbs, Graffiti, Limericks, and Other Vital Matters.* Edmonton, Hurtig, 1975.
Editor, *Colombo's Canadian References.* Toronto, Oxford University Press, 1976; London and New York, Oxford University Press, 1977.
Editor and Translator, with Nikola Roussanoff, *The Balkan Range: A Bulgarian Reader.* Toronto, Hounslow Press, 1976.
Editor, *East and West: Selected Poems*, by George Faludy. Toronto, Hounslow Press, 1978.

Translator, *From Zero to One*, by Robert Zend. Vancouver, Sono Nis Press, 1973.
Translator, with Nikola Roussanoff, *Under the Eaves of a Forgotten Village: Sixty Poems from Contemporary Bulgaria.* Toronto, Hounslow Press, 1975.
Translator, with Nikola Roussanoff, *The Left-Handed One*, by Lyubomir Levchev. Toronto, Hounslow Press, 1977.
Translator, with Nikola Roussanoff, *Remember Me Well*, by Andrei Germanov. Toronto, Hounslow Press, 1978.
Translator, with Nikola Roussanoff, *Depths*, by Dora Gabe. Toronto, Hounslow Press, 1978.

Manuscript Collection: Mills Memorial Library, McMaster University, Hamilton, Ontario.

Critical Studies: by Northrop Frye, in *University of Toronto Review*, July 1959; Alfred Purdy, in Toronto *Globe and Mail*, 4 June 1966; George Woodcock, in *Canadian Literature* (Vancouver), Summer 1966; Louis Dudek, in Montreal *Gazette*, 22 October 1966; Miriam Waddington, in Toronto *Globe and Mail*, 18 March 1967; Hugh MacCallum, in *University of Toronto Review*, July 1967 and July 1968.

John Robert Colombo comments:

Poetry can be written in the language of song, which is verse, or in the language of speech, which is prose. In my original poems, and especially in my found poetry, I am exploring the rhythms of the poem-as-prose. I prefer the authentic effect of prose to the artifice of a poem. I want the reader or listener to be so startled by the poem he will regard the world itself as a work of art – as a Great Collage. Favourite writers include Jorge Luis Borges, Nicanor Parra, Rainer Maria Rilke, Wallace Stevens, Francis Ponge, Constantine Cavafy, Jozsef Attila, Miroslav Holub, Zbigniew Herbert, etc. They are always with me.

* * *

The appearance of John Robert Colombo's *Abracadabra* in 1967 marked a welcome return by him to a poetry whose resonances were familiar and whose values were less stridently asserted – closer to the central human experience. To use his own lines: "What is immensely important here is life itself: man/feeding on the world." It is that affirmation that one finds celebrated in the *Abracadabra* volume – the more than cerebral apprehension of terror in "There Is No Way Out," for instance.

Not all his celebrations are as fortunate, however. "The hot wells of your flowing kidneys" must surely be classed among the great lines of "unredeemed poetry." And the preciocity incumbent upon a sustained attention to works of art bespeaks, and is exacerbated by, the leaden "relevances" of a naive and isolated provincialism often present in his work.

This feeling of the provincially claustrophobic is present in *The Mackenzie Poems*. There is a sense in which these pieces of "found poetry" or "redeemed prose" are made to assume the mantle of a Canadian Gettysburg, and they (even as prose) will not stand the strain. If there is something sympathetic and attractive in the firebrand character of Mackenzie's life it is not an attractiveness that his prose conveys. Ultimately the factiousness becomes tedious, and, worse, the limitations of Mackenzie's imagination ("System is everything") work at variance to the larger mundo of poetry.

Coleridge said that the power of poetry "reveals itself in the balance or reconciliation of opposite or discordant qualities; ... a more than usual state of emotion, with more than usual order." The emotion in these poems, unfortunately, is scarcely ever above the pedestrian. This is not the politically visionary stuff of Blake or Milton, or even Pope. At its best it is Felix Holt. And when the order is "more than usual" it is so because the prose itself has a rhetorical (e.g. Ciceronian) structure that encourages the transformation into poetry.

No such structure underlies the private and public letters of Bishop Strachan – the raw material of Colombo's next volume *New Poems by Dr. Strachan*. Strachan and Mackenzie were adversaries in the early polity of Upper Canada – Strachan as resolutely Church of England establishment as Mackenzie was non-conformist radical. *New Poems* was announced as a book that "tells the other half of the story," but one wonders, remembering Arnold's observations on the turgid flatulence of Victorian Toronto society, whether "the story" was worth the candle – let alone two volumes of poetry.

Something of the deadness of Strachan's position (let alone the issues) is conveyed in the "poem" "Universal Corruption": "I am still the same Tory/that you knew me to be/forty years ago." This is a man who can refer to the magnificent wilderness, still unspoiled, as "a dismal wood." Even Mr. Casaubon in all his dullness was not arrayed so drably as this. Minds as lapidary as Strachan's are not creative of great prose, let alone poetry. Even in his private reflections we have the sense of a man dead at the centre – the complacent (and complaisant) voice of orotund establishment, feeding its piety with goose dinners and Addisonian maxims, assured that the business of religion is in dispensing the unquestionable intellectual and moral superiority of the British nation.

The reader has a similar sense of weighty indigestion in *The Great Wall of China* but there the weariness comes from a weight of accumulated statistic and observation, lightened only occasionally by such magical poems as "The Legendary Mound of Ch'in." For there the felicities are of the realm of the lyrical imagination as the pleasures of "Arabesque" (another poem in the sequence, taken from Maugham) are the rhetorical enchantments of a high order of descriptive prose.

In *Neo Poems* again one has the sense of a notebook full of possible poems, never quite realised. Many if not most are collections of para-Haiku, at their best finely descriptive: "the sea drifts into France" or "The mind has/a tongue in both its cheeks." But Colombo is not alone among Canadian poets in allowing the gnomic to become merely the cute. "I want to scribble passionate marginalia all through the Book of Life" is too close to Rod McKuen for comfort of mind.

Part of Colombo's problem here is a distinctively Canadian one – a rather adolescent stridency that tends to a chauvinism that is both personal and national. (Often they tend to become confused.) Quoting with approval Symons's "it is not natural to be what is called 'natural' any longer," the poet assumes the role of exile-in-one's-own-country and exalts the sententious and truistic to the level of the profound. We are offered "In all literature, the traditional must expose the actual" as if that statement (piece of poetry?) meant something.

This is a pity, for Colombo is a good poet and a fine wit – a poet who has yet to find a medium appropriate to his sensibility. For ultimately it is not his "found poetry" but his "made poetry" that has the greater stature. And it is in this mode that (as he says of Wyeth) "a detail becomes a dimension" because the imaginative life that sustains it is not fortuitous or ideologically strident but integral and creative, and affirmative of life at its highest pitch.

—D. D. C. Chambers

COMFORT, Alex(ander). British. Born in London, 10 February 1920. Educated at Highgate School, London; Trinity College, Cambridge (Styring Scholar; Senior Scholar), M.B., B.Ch. 1944, M.A. 1945; London Hospital (Scholar), D.C.H. 1945, Ph.D. (biochemistry) 1949, D.Sc. (gerontology) 1963; M.R.C.S., L.R.C.P. Married 1) Ruth Muriel Harris in 1943 (marriage dissolved, 1973), one son; 2) Jane Tristram Henderson in 1973. House Physician, London Hospital, 1944; Resident Medical Officer, Royal Waterloo Hospital, 1944–45; Lecturer in Physiology, 1945–51, Honorary Research Associate, Department of Zoology, 1951–73, Director of Research on the Biology of Ageing, 1966–73, University College, London. Since 1974, Lecturer in Psychiatry, Stanford University, California; since 1975, Senior Fellow, Institute for Higher Studies, Santa Barbara, California; since 1976, Professor of Pathology, University of California School of Medicine, Irvine. Editor, Poetry Folios, 1942–46. President, British Society for Research on Ageing, 1967. Recipient: Ciba Foundation Prize, 1958; Karger Memorial Prize in Gerontology, 1969. Address: 683 Oak Grove Drive, Santa Barbara, California 93108, U.S.A.

PUBLICATIONS

Verse

France and Other Poems. London, Favil Press, 1941.

Three New Poets, with Roy McFadden and Ian Serraillier. Billericay, Essex, Grey Walls Press, 1942.
A Wreath for the Living. London, Routledge, 1942.
Elegies. London, Routledge, 1944.
The Song of Lazarius. Barnet, Hertfordshire, Poetry Folios, and New York, Viking Press, 1945.
The Signal to Engage. London, Routledge, 1946.
And All But He Departed. London, Routledge, 1951.
Haste to the Wedding. London, Eyre and Spottiswoode, 1962; Chester Springs, Pennsylvania, Dufour, 1964.
All But a Rib: Poems Chiefly of Women. London, Mitchell Beazley, 1973; as *Coming Together: Poems Chiefly about Women*, New York, Crown, 1975.
Poems for Jane. London, Mitchell Beazley, 1978; New York, Crown, 1979.

Plays

Into Egypt: A Miracle Play. Billericay, Essex, Grey Walls Press, 1942.
Cities of the Plain: A Democratic Melodrama. London, Grey Walls Press, 1943.

Television Play: *The Great Agrippa*, 1968.

Novels

The Silver River: Being the Diary of a Schoolboy in the South Atlantic 1936. London, Chapman and Hall, 1938.
No Such Liberty. London, Chapman and Hall, 1941.
The Almond Tree: A Legend. London, Chapman and Hall, 1942.
The Power House. London, Routledge, 1944; New York, Viking Press, 1945.
On This Side Nothing. London, Routledge, and New York, Viking Press, 1949.
A Giant's Strength. London, Routledge, 1952.
Come Out to Play. London, Eyre and Spottiswoode, 1961.

Short Stories

Letters from an Outpost. London, Routledge, 1947.

Other

Peace and Disobedience. London, Peace News, 1946.
Art and Social Responsibility: Lectures on the Ideology of Romanticism. London, Falcon Press, 1946.
The Novel and Our Time. Letchworth, Hertfordshire, Phoenix House, and Denver, Swallow, 1948.
Barbarism and Sexual Freedom: Six Lectures on the Sociology of Sex from the Standpoint of Anarchism. London, Freedom Press, 1948.
First-Year Physiological Techniques. London, Staples Press, 1948.
The Pattern of the Future. London, Routledge, and New York, Macmillan, 1949.
The Right Thing to Do, Together with the Wrong Thing to Do. London, Peace News, 1949.
Authority and Delinquency in the Modern State: A Criminological Approach to the Problem of Power. London, Routledge, 1950.
Sexual Behaviour in Society. London, Duckworth, and New York, Viking Press, 1950; revised edition, as *Sex in Society*, Duckworth, 1963; New York, Citadel Press, 1966.
Delinquency (lecture). London, Freedom Press, 1951.

Social Responsibility in Science and Art. London, Peace News, 1952.
The Biology of Senescence. London, Routledge, and New York, Rinehart, 1956; revised edition, as *Ageing: The Biology of Senescence*, 1964; revised edition, Edinburgh, Churchill Livingston, 1979.
Darwin and the Naked Lady: Discursive Essays on Biology and Art. London, Routledge, 1961; New York, Braziller, 1962.
The Process of Ageing. New York, New American Library, 1964; London, Weidenfeld and Nicolson, 1965.
The Nature of Human Nature. New York, Harper, 1965; as *Nature and Human Nature*, London, Weidenfeld and Nicolson, 1966.
The Anxiety Makers: Some Curious Preoccupations of the Medical Profession. London, Nelson, 1967.
What Rough Beast? and What Is a Doctor? (lectures). Vancouver, Pendejo Press, 1971.
The Joy of Sex: A Gourmet's Guide to Love Making. New York, Crown, and London, Quartet, 1973.
More Joy: A Sequel to "The Joy of Sex." London, Mitchell Beazley, and New York, Crown, 1974.
A Good Age. New York, Crown, 1976; London, Mitchell Beazley, 1977.
A Practise of Geriatric Psychiatry. New York, Elsevier, 1979.
The Facts of Love: Living, Loving, and Growing Up (juvenile), with Jane Comfort. New York, Crown, and London, Mitchell Beazley, 1979.
I and That. London, Mitchell Beazley, and New York, Crown, 1979.

Editor, with Robert Greacen, *Lyra: An Anthology of New Lyric.* Billericay, Essex, Grey Walls Press, 1942.
Editor, with John Bayliss, *New Road 1943* and *1944: New Directions in European Art and Letters.* London, Grey Walls Press, 1943, 1944.
Editor, *History of Erotic Art, I.* London, Weidenfeld and Nicolson, and New York, Putnam, 1969.
Editor, *Sexual Consequences of Disability.* Philadelphia, Stickley, 1978.

Translator, with Allan Ross Macdougall, *The Triumph of Death*, by C. F. Ramuz. London, Routledge, 1946.
Translator, *The Koko Shastra.* London, Allen and Unwin, 1964; New York, Stein and Day, 1965.

Bibliography: "Alexander Comfort: A Bibliography in Progress" by D. Callaghan, in *West Coast Review* (Burnaby, British Columbia), 1969.

Critical Studies: *The Freedom of Poetry* by Derek Stanford, London, Falcon Press, 1947; "The Scientific Humanism of Alex Comfort" by Wayne Burns, in *The Humanist* (London), November–December 1951; "The Anarchism of Alex Comfort" by John Ellerby, "Sex, Kicks and Comfort" by Charles Radcliffe, and "Alex Comfort's Art and Scope" by Harold Drasdo, all in *Anarchy* (London), November 1963; *Alex Comfort* by Arthur E. Salmon, Boston, Hall, 1978.

* * *

Alex Comfort's best known poems are concerned with sexual love – with a sometimes tender, sometimes bawdy exploration of the sexual impulse in man and woman. If other poets have occasionally explored this area, Dr. Comfort is (apart from his contemporary, Gavin Ewart) the only poet who is known almost exclusively for it – partly no doubt because of his extrapoetic writing, often about sexual psychology and physiology, and partly through the continual anthologisation of his fine poem "For Ruth" ("There is a white mare that my love keeps/unridden in a hillside meadow ...").

Comfort's earlier poems, owing much (as whose did not?) to Eliot, consisted often of meditations on death – not only on violent death in war (as in *Elegies*), but death seen lurking in the natural world of landscape: "The condemned cell of the woods lies round our doors,/ the trees are bars, and barbs the bramble carries...." His later war poems (in *The Signal to Engage*) were as bitter as those of Siegfried Sassoon, a generation earlier, who sometimes seems indeed to have been a direct influence (cf. "Song for the Heroes").

But it was later, within the last twenty years, that Dr. Comfort found the theme and the style, sometimes extrovert, sometimes interior, which was to enable him to write the poems in which he is seen at his most amusing, accomplished and wise. His range, within that theme, is considerable, from the lyrical to the epigrammatic ("Babies' and lovers' toes express/ecstasies of wantonness./That's a language which we lose/with the trick of wearing shoes").

Comfort's technical range is not great, yet he does command a technique which enables him to make his points in a sinewy and terse language which only occasionally is marred by sentimentality. His anecdotes, often telling a short story which might have appealed to Maupassant (cf. "The Charmer"), are succinct, and if he turns his hand to a purpose-made piece, as in the epithalamion *Haste to the Wedding*, the note is never false and invariably lively.

His attitude to love, now increasingly shared by his younger readers, is celebrated in poetry like none that has been written since the Restoration: direct and uncompromising, a note of wholehearted enjoyment: he is tired of "the best pentameters," of "eloquence overdone": "That first act of our own/is still the best act left. Let's go to bed." Of course this means there are limitations: Dr. Comfort has never perhaps wholly recaptured the tenderness of "For Ruth." But many other poets have written single poems of considerable beauty; not so many have written, for instance, a complaining elegy on bed-manufacturers: "Surely the trade has one Stradivarius?/If not, I know why in Neolithic days/the Goddess was steatopygic./For the meantime let us unroll the rug."

His later love poems succeed perhaps *because* they lack the painful intensity of longing that pierces the verse of poets both less happy as lovers and more intent on their poetry. Comfort's verse celebrates, not mourns nor yearns. His words "serve to fill the space/between meeting and meeting –/this is the eloquent thing/that they are celebrating/and nothing that we write/myself or any other/matches the fine content/of what we do together."

—Derek Parker

CONN, Stewart. British. Born in Glasgow, Scotland, 5 November 1936. Educated at Kilmarnock Academy and Glasgow University. National Service: Royal Air Force. Married Judith Clarke in 1963; two sons. Since 1962, Radio Drama Producer, BBC, Glasgow. Literary Adviser, Edinburgh Royal Lyceum Theatre, 1973–75. Recipient: Gregory Poetry Award, 1963; Scottish Arts Council Poetry Prize and Publication Award, 1968, award, 1979. Lives in Edinburgh. Agent: Mrs. Nina Froud, Harvey Unna Ltd., 14 Beaumont Mews, Marylebone High Street, London W1N 4HE, England.

PUBLICATIONS

Verse

Thunder in the Air. Preston, Lancashire, Akros, 1967.
The Chinese Tower. Edinburgh, M. Macdonald, 1967.
Stoats in the Sunlight. London, Hutchinson, 1968; as *Ambush and Other Poems*, New York, Macmillan, 1970.

Corgi Modern Poets in Focus 3, with others, edited by Dannie Abse. London, Corgi, 1971.
An Ear to the Ground. London, Hutchinson, 1972.
Under the Ice. London, Hutchinson, 1978.

Plays

Break-Down (produced Glasgow, 1961).
Birds in a Wilderness (produced Edinburgh, 1964).
I Didn't Always Live Here (produced Glasgow, 1967). Included in *The Aquarium, The Man in the Green Muffler, I Didn't Always Live Here*, 1976.
The King (produced Edinburgh, 1967; London, 1972). Published in *New English Dramatists 14*, London, Penguin, 1970.
Broche (produced Exeter, 1968).
Fancy Seeing You, Then (produced London, 1974). Published in *Playbill Two*, edited by Alan Durband, London, Hutchinson, 1969.
Victims (includes *The Sword, In Transit*, and *The Man in the Green Muffler*) (produced Edinburgh, 1970). *In Transit* published New York, Breakthrough Press, 1972; *The Man in the Green Muffler* included in *The Aquarium, The Man in the Green Muffler, I Didn't Always Live Here*, 1976.
The Burning (produced Edinburgh, 1971). London, Calder and Boyars, 1972.
A Slight Touch of the Sun (produced Edinburgh, 1972).
The Aquarium (produced Edinburgh, 1973). Included in *The Aquarium, The Man in the Green Muffler, I Didn't Always Live Here*, 1976.
Thistlewood (produced Edinburgh, 1975).
Count Your Blessings (produced Pitlochry, Perthshire, 1975).
The Aquarium, The Man in the Green Muffler, I Didn't Always Live Here. London, Calder, 1976.
Play Donkey (produced Edinburgh, 1977).
Billy Budd, with Stephen Macdonald, adaptation of the novel by Melville (produced Edinburgh, 1978).

Radio Plays; *Any Following Spring*, 1962; *Cadenza for Real*, 1963; *Song of the Clyde*, 1964; *The Canary Cage*, 1967.

Television Plays: *Wally Dugs Go in Pairs*, 1973; *The Kite*, 1979.

Other

Editor, *New Poems 1973–74.* London, Hutchinson, 1974.

Manuscript Collection: Scottish National Library, Edinburgh.

Critical Studies: Interviews with James Aitchison in *Scottish Theatre* (Edinburgh), March 1969; introduction by Dannie Abse to *Corgi Modern Poets in Focus 3*, 1971; interview with Allen Wright in *The Scotsman* (Edinburgh), 30 October 1971.

Theatrical Activities:

Director: **Radio**– *Armstrong's Last Goodnight* by John Arden, 1964; *The Anatomist* by James Bridie, 1965; *My Friend Mr. Leakey* by J. B. S. Haldane, 1967; *Mr. Gillie* by James Bridie, 1967; *Happy Days Are Here Again* by Cecil P. Taylor, 1967.

* * *

Unexpectedly early in his poetic career, by 1963, Stewart Conn had written two poems, "Todd" and "Simon," completely themselves in style, and of such visionary intensity and sensuous richness as to suggest that a new poet had found himself. The sap and vitality of a country childhood and the experience of being a minister of the gospel's son are the roots of the success of the poems, in which Conn yokes together the actual and the legendary in his brief portrayals of the two country characters. "Todd" begins:

My father's white uncle became
   Arthritic and testamental in
Lyrical stages. He held cardinal sin
      Was misuse of horses, then any game
Won on the Sabbath....

Intimate and physical words from the stable about this horse-obsessed man mingle with the rhetoric of pulpit and Bible. The poem implies an affirmation of life of wide tolerance. Even when Conn describes the nauseous in nature, there is a sense of marvelling at its fecundity. His poem "Plague" (*Thunder in the Air*) begins:

The fox lies by the roadside,
Its belly gutted. Maggots
Breed in their millions.
In that area the earth moves.

Cruelty is one of Conn's main themes. When he treats it in historic episodes, which he simplifies to make dramatic points, one is conscious of contrivance, the detached style sounding olympian; but when he deals with the indifferent cruelty of nature, as when it affects members of his family, then the fine temper of the mind of this poet gives the situation appropriate expression. "To My Father" begins by sketching a picture of secure middle-class life in the early 1940's, and then dramatic information is slipped in undramatically:

Each year we picnicked on the lawn;
Mother crooking her finger
As she sipped her lime. When
They carried you out on a stretcher
She knew you'd never preach again.

The conventional manners are linked to a firmness of character which does not allow terrible sorrow to destroy the social texture. It is the last verse, however, which shows the poet possesses a medium capable of reflecting his more complex integrity, in which he scrutinizes his motives for failing to visit his dying father. The poem ends:

If we come over
Tonight, there will be the added irony
In proving my visit isn't out of duty
When, to myself, I doubt the dignity
Of a love comprising so much guilt and pity.

This is admirably expressed, but however well done the poetry is made out of a society which did not question its own validity. In Conn's most recent book, *Under the Ice*, he investigates our present condition. When he now tells a horror story, as in "Reawakening," it relates to the frightening unguided missile in which we travel through space and time. The burden of the perplexities of urban man today is accepted into the verse. When an affirmation is proposed, such as the love between two people, it is presented in a context which casts doubt on its efficacy. Such writing, discreet, perceptive, and above all humane, is a rare achievement.

—George Bruce

CONNOR, Tony (John Anthony Augustus Connor). British. Born in Manchester, Lancashire, 16 March 1930. Left school at fourteen. Served as a tank driver in the 5th Royal Inniskilling Dragoon Guards, 1948–50. Married Frances Foad in 1961; three children. Textile Designer, Manchester, 1944–60. Assistant in Liberal Studies, Bolton Technical College, 1961–64; Visiting Poet, Amherst College, Massachusetts, 1967–68. Visiting Poet and Lecturer, 1968–69, and since 1971, Professor of English, Wesleyan University, Middletown, Connecticut. Visiting Playwright, Oxford Playhouse, England, 1974–75. M.A.: Manchester University, 1968; Wesleyan University, 1971. Fellow, Royal Society of Literature. Address: 44 Brainerd Avenue, Middletown, Connecticut 06457, U.S.A.

PUBLICATIONS

Verse

With Love Somehow. London, Oxford University Press, 1962.
Lodgers. London, Oxford University Press, 1965.
Poems: A Selection, with Austin Clarke and Charles Tomlinson. London and New York, Oxford University Press, 1964.
12 Secret Poems. Manchester, MICA, 1965.
Kon in Springtime. London, Oxford University Press, 1968.
In the Happy Valley. London, Oxford University Press, 1971.
The Memoirs of Uncle Harry. London, Oxford University Press, 1974.
Seven Last Poems from the Memoirs of Uncle Harry. Newcastle upon Tyne, Northern House, 1974.
City of Strangers. Walton on Thames, Outposts, 1975.
To a Friend, Who Asked for a Poem. Knotting, Bedfordshire, Sceptre Press, 1975.
Twelve Villanelles. Derry, Pennsylvania, Rook Press, 1977.

Recording: *Poems*, with Norman Nicholson, Argo, 1974.

Plays

Billy's Wonderful Kettle (produced Manchester, 1971).
I Am Real and So Are You, A Visit from the Family, and Crewe Station at 2 A.M. (produced London, 1971).
The Last of the Feinsteins (produced London, 1972).
A Couple with a Cat (produced London, 1972).
Otto's Interview (produced London, 1973).
Dr. Crankenheim's Mixed-Up Monster (produced Oxford, 1974). London, Dobson, 1975.
David's Violin, adaptation of a Yiddish play (produced New York, 1976).

Other

Translator, with George Gomöri, *Love of the Scorching Wind*, by Laszlo Nagy. London, Oxford University Press, 1973.

Tony Connor comments:

There are no critical studies of Tony Connor's work, which has received scant and condescending attention from English reviewers. In U.S.A., however, he is considered "one of the poets now bringing new life to English verse" (M. L. Rosenthal, *Saturday Review*, 1968) and "undoubtedly one of the best and most authentic of recent British poets" (*Poetry*, January 1969).

His poetry is unacademic, independent and original and uses domestic themes and imagery in a free-flowing, at times surrealistic, manner. The moral ambiguity of Mr. Connor's apparent simplicities reminds one of Frost more than of any modern English poet, and this, perhaps, helps to explain the fact that his reputation stands higher in the United States than in his own country.

* * *

Tony Connor has established himself as one of the best of the numerous domestic poets now writing in England. Ordinary incidents of family life, the rubs of marriage, even memories of National Service, supply him with material for poems which are usually strongly and logically constructed and economically if rather conventionally written. Recent attempts to extend his range, and to write more complex work, have been less successful. But his more characteristic poetry is often attractive – earthy, straightforward, convincingly truthful, and far less monotonous than the restricted subject matter might suggest.

—Edward Lucie-Smith

CONQUEST, (George) Robert (Acworth). British. Born in Great Malvern, Worcestershire, 15 July 1917. Educated at Winchester College; Magdalen College, Oxford, B.A. 1939; University of Grenoble. Served in the Oxfordshire and Buckinghamshire Light Infantry, 1939–46. Married 1) Joan Watkins in 1942 (divorced, 1948), two sons; 2) Tatiana Mihailova in 1948 (divorced, 1962); 3) Caroleen Macfarlane in 1964 (divorced, 1978). Member of the U.K. Diplomatic Service, 1949–56; Fellow, London School of Economics, 1956–58; Lecturer in English, University of Buffalo, 1959–60; Literary Editor, *The Spectator*, London, 1962–63; Senior Fellow, Columbia University, New York, 1964–65; Fellow, Woodrow Wilson Center, Washington, D.C., 1976–77; Senior Research Fellow, Hoover Institution, Stanford, California, 1977–79. Recipient: P.E.N. prize, 1945; Festival of Britain prize, 1951. M.A. 1972, and D.Litt., 1974: Oxford University. Fellow, Royal Society of Literature, 1972. O.B.E. (Officer, Order of the British Empire), 1955. Address: 28 Shawfield Street, London S.W.3, England.

PUBLICATIONS

Verse

Poems. London, Macmillan, and New York, St. Martin's Press, 1955.
Between Mars and Venus. London, Hutchinson, and New York, St. Martin's Press, 1962.
Arias from a Love Opera. London, Macmillan, and New York, Macmillan, 1969.
Casualty Ward. London, Poem-of-the-Month Club, 1974.
Forays. London, Chatto and Windus, 1979.

Novels

A World of Difference. London, Ward Lock, 1955; New York, Ballantine, 1964.
The Egyptologists, with Kingsley Amis. London, Cape, 1965; New York, Random House, 1966.

Other

Where Do Marxists Go from Here? (as J. E. M. Arden). London, Phoenix House, 1958.
The Soviet Deportation of Nationalities. London, Macmillan, and New York, St. Martin's Press, 1960.
Common Sense about Russia. London, Gollancz, and New York, Macmillan, 1960.
Courage of Genius: The Pasternak Affair. London, Collins-Harvill Press, and Philadelphia, Lippincott, 1961.
Power and Policy in the U.S.S.R. London, Macmillan, and New York, St. Martin's Press, 1962.
The Last Empire. London, Ampersand, 1962.
Marxism Today. London, Ampersand, 1964.
Russia after Krushchev. London, Pall Mall Press, and New York, Praeger, 1965.
The Great Terror: Stalin's Purge of the Thirties. London, Macmillan, and New York, Macmillan, 1968; revised edition, 1973.
The Nation Killers: The Soviet Deportation of Minorities. London, Macmillan, and New York, St. Martin's Press, 1970.
Lenin. London, Fontana, and New York, Viking Press, 1972.
Kolyma: The Arctic Death Camp. London, Macmillan, and New York, Viking Press, 1978.
Present Danger: Towards a Foreign Policy. Oxford, Blackwell, 1979.
The Abomination of Moab. London, Temple Smith, 1979.

Editor, *New Lines I* and *II.* London, Macmillan, 1956, 1963.
Editor, *Back to Life* (anthology). London, Hutchinson, and New York, St. Martin's Press, 1958.
Editor, with Kingsley Amis, *Spectrum: A Science Fiction Anthology.* London, Gollancz, 5 vols., 1961–66; New York, Harcourt Brace, 5 vols., 1962–67.
Editor, *Soviet Studies Series.* London, Bodley Head, 8 vols., 1967–68; New York, Praeger, 8 vols., 1968–69.
Editor, *Pyotr Yakir.* London, Macmillan, 1972; New York, Coward McCann, 1973.
Editor, *The Robert Sheckley Omnibus.* London, Gollancz, 1973.
Editor, *The Russian Tradition*, by Tibor Szamuely. London, Secker and Warburg, 1974; New York, McGraw Hill, 1975.

Translator, *Russian Nights*, by Alexander Solzhenitsyn. London, Collins-Harvill Press, 1977; New York, Farrar Straus, 1978.

Critical Studies: in *The Times Literary Supplement* (London), 30 May 1955; by D. J. Enright, in *The Month* (London), May 1956; by John Holloway, in *Hudson Review* (New York), xiv, 4, 1961; by Thom Gunn, in *The Spectator* (London), 4 May 1962.

Robert Conquest comments:

I suppose my main theme is the poet's relationship to the phenomenal universe – in particular to landscape, women, art and war. Forms usually, though not always, traditional. Sometimes straight lyric, more often with development of a train of thought: an attempt to master, or transmit, a presented reality in intellectual and emotive terms simultaneously. The vocabulary often runs to words – not specialist ones – drawn from the technical, scientific and philosophical spheres, and mediatised into the ordinary language.

Since all this is in principle a complex and difficult process, a strong effort goes into keeping it as comprehensible as possible, avoidance of forced obscurities, and provision of a rigorous guidance of sound and structure.

* * *

Although as a very young man in the late thirties Robert Conquest had contributed some Audenesque exercises to *Twentieth Century Verse*, he did not emerge as a mature poet until his first collection, *Poems*, came out in 1955. A year later Conquest edited *New Lines*, an anthology of the poets of the so-called "Movement," and his own poetry exhibited the favoured qualities of that school: exactness of form, intellectual structure, emphasis on empiricism and common-sense values, and a certain preoccupation with the nature of the poetic process. But Conquest was distinguished from the other contributors to *New Lines* by the greater range of his subject matter. He wrote love poems and poems about Eastern Europe and the Mediterranean, and philosophical reflections on the nature of perception. And in "The Landing in Deucalion" Conquest wrote the first of several poems inspired by his abiding interest in science fiction. *Poems* was an enjoyable, even distinguished first collection. It presented the reader with an urbane and civilized mind, widely read and widely travelled, sympathetically curious about most forms of human activity. The poetic influences were from Auden and Robert Graves, but they were well assimilated, and Conquest's voice was highly personal, however much he employed the general idiom of the Movement. Formal precision was combined with delicacy of response, and though feeling was controlled it was unmistakably present. The qualities of Conquest's best poetry can be seen in his sonnet, "Guided Missiles Experimental Range," where he responds to a modern, technological subject with a precisely deployed classical reference. Here is the sestet:

> Stronger than lives, by empty purpose blinded,
> The only thought their circuits can endure is
> The target-hunting rigour of their flight;
>
> And by that loveless haste I am reminded
> Of Aeschylus' description of the Furies:
> "*O barren daughters of the fruitful night.*"

If most of the poems in the book are in traditional metres and rhyme schemes, one of the finest, "Near Jakobslev," is in free verse, a beautifully rendered account of a sub-arctic landscape in summer.

Conquest's later poetry continues the subjects of his first book: love, landscapes, science fiction, poetry itself. But it is generally less rewarding; the precision of the verse has become a little mechanical, and the pressure of feeling to be contained is less immediate. There is a heavy reliance on certain recurring key words – "love," "poem," "girl" – and an air of self-imitation. Even so, the craftsmanship remains admirable at a time when the formal virtues that Conquest argued for and exhibited in the mid-fifties have been disregarded by many younger poets. And he remains capable of formidable feats of skill, as in his recent completion of two fragments of verse from a Housman manuscript, turning them into finished poems in the form and metre of Housman's drafts ("Two Housman Torsos," *Times Literary Supplement*, October 19, 1973). One regrets, though, that so gifted a poet has remained content with his own gifts, and developed them so little.

—Bernard Bergonzi

CONRAN, Anthony. British. Born in Kharghpur, India, 7 April 1931. Educated at University College of North Wales, Bangor, B.A. (honours) in English and philosophy, M.A. in English. Since 1957, Research Fellow and Tutor, University College of North Wales. Recipient: Welsh Arts Council award, 1960, and bursary, 1968. Address: 1 Frondirion, Glanrafon, Bangor, Gwynedd, Wales.

PUBLICATIONS

Verse

Formal Poems. Llandybie, Carmarthenshire, Christopher Davies, 1960.
Metamorphoses. Pembroke Dock, Pembrokeshire, Dock Leaves Press, 1961; revised edition, Market Drayton, Shropshire, Tern Press, 1979.
Icons. Privately printed, 1963.
Asymptotes. Privately printed, 1963.
A String o Blethers. Privately printed, 1963.
Sequence of the Blue Flower. Privately printed, 1963.
The Mountain. Privately printed, 1963.
For the Marriage of Gerard and Linda. Privately printed, 1963.
Stelae and Other Poems. Oxford, Clive Allison, 1965.
Guernica. Denbigh, Gee, 1966.
Collected Poems. Oxford, Clive Allison, 1 vol., 1966; Denbigh, Gee, 3 vols., 1966–68.
Claim, Claim, Claim. Guildford, Surrey, Circle Press, 1969.
Spirit Level and Other Poems. Llandybie, Carmarthenshire, Christopher Davies, 1974.
Poems 1951–67. Bangor, Deiniol Press, 1974.
Life Fund. Llandysul, Dyfed, Gomer, 1979.

Other

On to the Fields of Praise: Essays on the English Poets of Wales. Aberystwyth, Planet Press, 1979.

Editor and Translator, *The Penguin Book of Welsh Verse.* London, Penguin, 1967.

Translator, *Eighteen Poems of Dante Alighiere.* Market Drayton, Shropshire, Tern Press, 1975.

Critical Studies: by Gwyn Thomas, in *Poetry Wales* (Cardiff), Spring 1967; Jeremy Hooker, in *Anglo-Welsh Review* (Tenby), Spring 1975.

Anthony Conran comments:

I regard myself as a poet of Wales, though I write in English. Behind me are Anglo-Welsh poets like Hopkins, Idris Davies, Dylan Thomas, and R. S. Thomas; but also I have felt the groundswell of the age-old Welsh tradition, from Taliesin in the 6th century to Bobi Jones in the 20th.

I write poems when people seem to want them. The demands of what they want form the co-ordinates of my poems.

* * *

Anthony Conran is one of the foremost translators of Welsh poetry and has edited the *Penguin Book of Welsh Verse*, doing valuable work in bringing a number of masterpieces before a wider audience.

His own collected poems, *Spirit Level*, cover the years 1956–68, including a section of experiments in strict metre from Chinese, Japanese, Provençal, and Celtic, which are certainly different and partly successful. He also includes his "gift-poems" – pieces of praise, and celebrations of other people's marriages (given as presents on wedding-days) and the births of their children. Conran dedicates many of his poems to friends and writers, alive and dead. He says that the giving and receiving of gifts and odes formed the "central arch of

Welsh civilisation," and he should know, because he is steeped in it. There are plenty of these poems in his volumes, following a groove of sentimentality, and leaving a slightly syrupy taste in the mouth.

Conran favours custom and ceremony, ritual, elegy, tradition, and the formal language-splash of Dylan Thomas, to whose memory he dedicates an earlier poem in which he employs Thomas compounds, like "womblight," "dreamdank," "outwombward," "chapeldownunder" (which sounds a reference to an Australian church), "gift of gab devil" and "steepled town." Elsewhere, although originally a stranger and outsider to Wales who sank eagerly into its culture, he writes of his "Lineage":

My lineage is kingly. Once, my fathers ruled
The broad acres of an island sweet with grass
And climbed the volcanic hills, through dingle
Of birch and pinetree, scrubland where wild deer
Picked out their path to the bald peak:
There the visiting gods conversed, who came
As friends to friends with the kings my fathers....

And these lines to a Welsh potter:

And the racks in your front-room shop
No longer fill
Quietly, quietly, with the cups and jugs
Of your fingers' skill;

And because now, though the potter's gone
And the clay dries dead,
We are glad that the love of a bride
Has graced your bed –

Of Conran's erudition, stockpiled classical allusions, intermittent elegance and varied technical skill, one has no doubt, but these frequently run into the sand, or explode in trivial puffs of smoke which soon drift away. All that scholarly brilliance still has a whiff of the midnight-candle about it, as if plotted from an ivory-tower above a quadrangle. A measure of fustian also inhabits his work, loading some thin subject-matter that simply cannot carry the weight.

As a critic, he has a reputation for severity, often using a sledgehammer to crack a nut by bringing the considerable weapons of his armoury to bear on marginal work. He interpolates rare and precious words of praise into devastating, remorseless hatchet-jobs, which are often massacres disguised as reviews. He also has a weakness for fashionable psychology-based criticism, which occasionally leads him into a weird area of precipitate assumption, odd parallels and comparisons, and manufactured mysteries where none exist. It is a perilous area, which temptingly invites hasty surmise in the absence of evidence, and dramatic overstatement, as well as the inaccurate analysis of sexual imagery.

Conran's premier accomplishment as a translator ranges from Taliesin (late 6th century) to the excellent moderns, such as R. Williams Parry, Saunders Lewis, Gwenallt Jones, Euros Bowen, and Waldo Williams. He is adept at assessing what some mistakenly consider to be a minor and ancillary literature, about which no general opinion has previously been built up. His main purpose has been to make poetic sense, in English, of sometimes very difficult poems, and to this end he has stated that he often departed further from the literal meaning than would easily be justifiable were his purpose purely scholarly – though he has always attempted to be literal. In his extremely knowledgeable introduction to the Penguin selection, he also makes it clear that the special relationship which the Welsh-language "bard" has with his public is very different from the English poet's connection with his minority audience. The Welshman is something of a leader within his own community, often a national figure who appears at public functions and is constantly asked to give opinions on poetry, political matters, and even international affairs, knowing that many "influential" people are going to listen. As Anthony Conran adds: "No English poet has been able to do this since Tennyson."

—John Tripp

COOK, Stanley. British. Born in Austerfield, Yorkshire, 12 April 1922. Educated at Doncaster Grammar School, 1933–40; Christ Church, Oxford, 1940–44, B.A. in English language and literature 1943, M.A. 1948. Married Kathleen Mary Daly in 1947; two daughters and one son. Assistant Master, Barrow-in-Furness Grammar School, 1944–48; Sixth Form English Master, Bury Grammar School, 1948–55; Senior English Master, Firth Park School, Sheffield, 1955–68. Since 1969, Lecturer in English, The Polytechnic, Huddersfield. Recipient: Hull Arts Centre-BBC Competition Prize, 1969; Cheltenham Festival Competition Prize, 1972. Address: 600 Barnsley Road, Sheffield S5 6UA, England.

PUBLICATIONS

Verse

Form Photograph. Stockport, Cheshire, Harry Chambers, 1971.
Signs of Life. Manchester, E. J. Morten, 1972.
Staff Photograph. Stockport, Cheshire, Harry Chambers, 1976.
Alphabet. Stockport, Cheshire, Harry Chambers, 1976.
Woods Beyond a Cornfield. Richmond, Surrey, Keepsake Press, 1979.

Other

Seeing Your Meaning: Concrete Poetry in Language and Education. Huddersfield, The Polytechnic, 1975.
Come Along: Poems for Younger Children. Privately printed, 1978.
Word Houses: Poems for Juniors. Privately printed, 1979.

Critical Studies: by Robert Nye, in *The Times* (London), 10 February 1972; *Critical Quarterly* (Manchester), Spring 1972; *The Teacher* (London), 3 March 1972; Colin Bulman, in *The Teacher* (London), 27 October 1972; "Signs of Life" in *The Times* (London), 14 December 1972; *Times Literary Supplement* (London), 17 August 1973.

Stanley Cook comments:

My attitude to my poetry is expressed in the Introduction to *Form Photograph*:

> You live with your subject matter for years; one day something puts it into your head to write about it. After that it is simply a case of stating accurately what you have observed. Of course you have observed inaccurately and the accurate recording of the distinctive inaccuracies of which you are unaware is the theme of your poems. There ought to be more in a poem than you are conscious of expressing and more than your reader is conscious of receiving.

> As far as style is concerned, I hope the steelworker and his wife next door would never need a dictionary to read my poems. I like to feel, too, that I have been as practical and unsentimental with a poem as if I had farmed, smithed or carpentered it – that the rest of the family would think I had done some "real work" and had not let them down.

Assuming I have written that kind of poem in the past, I have kept on writing it. If my work has developed, I hope this has been not by altering but by adding. I am now very interested in the visual impact of printed literature on the reader's unconscious, largely destroyed by the utilitarian format of paperbacks. My concrete poems aim to test-drill for such impacts.

I have come to realise that the Augustans were roughly right: Dryden to Crabbe is the greatest period of our poetry. One can't lecture on it without learning from it; and until one is learning from it one can't lecture on it.

Still suffering from provincial isolation, I have had to publish *Come Along* and *Word Houses* myself. I can see that eventually most of the poems in "Come Along" will have been anthologised by various publishers, none of whom was willing to publish the collection. The all-or-nothing reaction of the children for whom they were written is refreshingly different.

* * *

For many years Stanley Cook was a schoolmaster in Sheffield. His two main themes are Yorkshire and education. The metre he characteristically uses is a roughened blank verse. This is conducive to the description of exact minutiae that make up his world. It has taken some years for his work to gain a hearing, for his qualities are not the obvious ones. His tone is subdued, his day overcast, his walks through depressed areas and neglected parks. Cook is at his best when his landscapes are equipped with figures. The murderer, Charles Peace, gives him a cue for black comedy; so does his mother's landlord. That other Sheffield poet, James Montgomery, merits only satire for his lack of an eye to the world about him – that Sheffield world of rain and railings which Cook observes with acquaintance and insight. The most moving poems are those about the author's family, especially those who had to endure the hungry thirties. The one about his father is, in middle age, also about himself:

> My body is buried, when I used to be my father,
> In the overspill from the village churchyard
> Into a field, where a single electrified wire
> Keeps back the cows but not the grass or flowers.
> Now he is I he waits for a worthwhile task
> In which to succeed, better than the water towers
> And colliery washers bulky as beer-drinkers
> He built as foreman. Pity everyone
> Who had, like him, to swim for it in the Thirties,
> Fully clothed in the nation's economy.
> Those days when he sat in his chair with nothing to smoke
> And dressed in his best suit weekly to draw the dole
> Pared people down to their character …

Read on. The verse is never as simple as it seems. Cook's voice inflects and turns with the independence of its native speech. Glamour, romance and melodrama are not his stock in trade: his power is in his redoubtable honesty. No critic can sum up Cook as well as he can himself: "I promised myself this walk in a minor key/Along the old canal dismissed from its trade…."

—Philip Hobsbaum

COOLIDGE, Clark. American. Born in Providence, Rhode Island, 26 February 1939. Attended Brown University, Providence, 1956–58. Married to Susan Hopkins; one daughter, Celia Elizabeth. Editor, *Joglars* magazine, Providence, 1964–66. Recipient: National Endowment for the Arts grant, 1966; New York Poets Foundation Award, 1968. Lives in Hancock, Massachusetts. Address: Box 224, New Lebanon, New York 12125, U.S.A.

PUBLICATIONS

Verse

Flag Flutter and U.S. Electric. New York, Lines, 1966.
(Poems). New York, Lines, 1967.
Ing. New York, Angel Hair, 1969.
Space. New York, Harper, 1970.
The So. New York, Boke, 1971.
Moroccan Variations. Bolinas, California, Big Sky, 1971.
Suite V. New York, Boke, 1973.
The Maintains. San Francisco, This Press, 1974.
Polaroid. New York, Boke, 1975.
Quartz Hearts. San Francisco, This Press, 1978.
Own Face. Lenox, Massachusetts, Angel Hair, 1978.

Play

To Obtain the Value of the Cake Measure from Zero, with Tom Veitch. San Francisco, Pants Press, 1970.

Critical Studies: "Clark Coolidge Issue" of *Big Sky 3* (Bolinas, California), 1972; interview, in *This 4* (San Francisco), Spring 1973; *The End of Intelligent Writing* by Richard Kostelanetz, New York, Sheed and Ward, 1974; "A Symposium on Clark Coolidge," in *Stations 5* (Milwaukee), Winter 1978.

Clark Coolidge comments:

The context of my works is the Tonality of Language (seen, heard, spoken, thought) itself, a tonality that centers itself in the constant flowage from meaning to meaning, and that sideslippage between meanings. All the books we shall perhaps never read again form a constant background of reference points. We are free now to delight in the Surface of Language, a surface as deep as the distance between (for instance) a noun (in the mind) (in a dictionary) and its object somewhere in the universe.

* * *

None of the young experimental poets in America has been as various, intelligent and prolific as Clark Coolidge, who also edited one of the few genuinely avant-garde literary magazines of the sixties, *Joglars*. His opening book, *Flag Flutter and U.S. Electric*, collected his early forays into post-Ashberyan acoherence, where the poet tries to realize the semblance of literary coherence without resorting to such traditional organizing devices as meter, metaphor, exposition, symbolism, consistent allusion, declarative statements or autobiographical reference. (The key Ashbery work in this vein is "Europe," 1960, collected in *The Tennis Court Oath*, 1962.) In a theoretical statement contributed to Paul Carroll's anthology of *The Young American Poets* (1968), Coolidge wrote that "Words have a universe of qualities other than those of descriptive relation: Hardness, Density, Sound-Shape, Vector-

Force, & Degrees of Transparency/Opacity," and his earlier poems revealed rather exceptional linguistic sensitivities, especially regarding the selection and placement of words. The intelligence informing his creative processes is radically poetic, precisely because it is *not* prosaic.

In his subsequent work Coolidge pursued not just varieties of acoherence, but reductionism, joining Kenneth Gangemi and Robert Lax among America's superior minimal poets. In the back sections of Coolidge's fullest retrospective, *Space*, are several especially severe examples, such as the untitled poem, beginning "by a I" which contains individually isolated words, none more than two letters long, that are scattered across the space of a single page (which has so far been Coolidge's primary compositional unit). These words are nonetheless related to each other – not only in terms of diction and corresponding length (both visually and verbally), but spatial proximity; for if the individual words were arranged in another way, both the poem and the reading experience would be different. It should also be noted that Coolidge's work extends radically the Olsonian traditions both of "composition by field," as opposed to lines, and of emphasizing syllable, rather than rhyme and meter.

Like all genuinely experimental artists, Coolidge accepted the challenge of an inevitable next step, extending his delicate reductionist technique into two of the most remarkable long poems of the past decade: "AD," originally published in *Ing* and then reprinted in *Space*; and *Suite V*, which appeared as a booklet in 1973, although it was initially composed several years before. "AD" begins in the familiar Coolidgean way, with stanzas of superficially unrelated lines, but the poetic material is progressively reduced over twenty pages (thereby recapitulating Coolidge's own poetic development, in a kind of formalist autobiography) until the poem's final pages contain just vertically ordered fragments of words. *Suite V* is yet more outrageously spartan, containing nothing more than pairs of three-letter words in their plural forms, with one four-letter word at the top and the other at the bottom of otherwise blank pages.

Coolidge has scattered his writings through numerous periodicals and anthologies, as well as small-press booklets, and much of his work remains unpublished. The best introduction to his excellences is not *Space*, which also suffers from ineptly tiny typography, but the third issue of *Big Sky*, a periodical edited by Bill Berkson. The poetry collected there is far more various and, for that reason, more indicative of Coolidge's experimental temper. It is my considered opinion that he is the most extraordinary American poet of our mutual generation.

—Richard Kostelanetz

COOPER, Jane (Marvel). American. Born in Atlantic City, New Jersey, 9 October 1924. Educated at Vassar College, Poughkeepsie, New York, 1942–44; University of Wisconsin, Madison, B.A. 1946; University of Iowa, Iowa City, M.A. 1954. Since 1950, Member of the English Department, Sarah Lawrence College, Bronxville, New York. Recipient: Yaddo grant, 1958, 1967, 1968; Guggenheim Fellowship, 1960; MacDowell Colony grant, 1965; Lamont Poetry Selection Award, 1968; National Endowment for the Arts grant, 1969; Ingram Merrill Foundation grant, 1971. Address: Department of English, Sarah Lawrence College, Bronxville, New York 10708, U.S.A.

PUBLICATIONS

Verse

The Weather of Six Mornings. New York, Macmillan, 1969.

Maps and Windows. New York, Macmillan, 1974.
Calling Me from Sleep: New and Selected Poems 1961–1973. Bronxville, New York, Sarah Lawrence College, 1974.

Jane Cooper comments:

My earliest poems (largely unpublished) were heavily metrical. I thought of writing a book of war poems from the point of view of a woman, a non-combatant. What concerned me was what could survive in the way of an individual feeling, or moral life, in a world at war. There is no longer a specific war in most of the poems I write now, but there is the same conviction that we live in a very stripped-down landscape. At the same time joy, if not happiness, is important. Many of my poems have to do with deaths; others with love, the life of the physical world in and around us, and above all with the possibility of writing, of speaking out.

Poetry is a kind of non-abstract musical composition. In my latest work, I am interested in a more open American speech line and in the activity that goes on between lines and even words of a poem, almost more than in what is "said." Pasternak is an influence, in his emphasis on the poem happening *now*. The long poem has always been a challenge. I like trying sequences of shorter poems, almost apparently unrelated; what is their effect on one another? I want to get more fluidity into single pieces now; the self is variable, places change and disappear. I should like to write city poems – another version of life fragmented as if by war.

* * *

Jane Cooper's first volume of poems represents her creative efforts over a period exceeding ten years. Although she has no radical experiments in form, her poems demonstrate a versality ranging from highly patterned to spare, free verse. And though her images are seldom vivid or startling, she employs them, most notably images of weather, with precision and appropriateness.

Most of her poems, and her best, are drawn from the intimate reserves of her own experience: memories of her childhood, of her mother, her loves, her encounters with death, and most effectively her moments of loss, regret, and loneliness. Cooper's poems seldom function as a single, unambiguous perception of an experience. Her poems, as she says in "A Letter for Philo Buck," leave "the tongue unraveling sweets from sours." Many poems seem balanced between emotional polarities of release and joy (the ecstasy of "Morning on the St. John's") and restraint and resignation (the advice in "A Little Vesper" to "bed with what we are"). A poem recalling the childhood rapture of collecting butterflies is entitled "Practising for Death"; and one of her most successful poems, "Obligations," images the speaker and her lover "wrapped in the afternoon/As in a chrysalis of silken light" awaking reluctantly to "the long war, and shared reality,/And death and all we came here to evade."

The inescapable reality of time and change and memory seems increasingly to concern Jane Cooper. "Once you leave the landing," she says in "Leaving Water Hyacinths," "Your whole life will be sailing back."

—Dale Doepke

CORKE, Hilary. British. Born in Malvern, Worcestershire, in 1921. Educated at Charterhouse; Christ Church, Oxford. Served in the Royal Artillery, 1941–45. Married to the poet Sylvia Bridges; four children. Lecturer, Cairo University, two years, and the University of Edinburgh, four years. Since 1956, Free-lance Writer. Lives in Abinger Hammer, Surrey, England.

PUBLICATIONS

Verse

Epithalamium, The Nightfearers. West Worthing, Sussex, Fantasma, 1948.
Adam Awake. Privately printed, 1961.
The Early Drowned and Other Poems. London, Secker and Warburg, 1961.

Other

Editor, with William Plomer and Anthony Thwaite, *New Poems 1961.* London, Hutchinson, 1961.

Translator, *Poems in the Rough*, by Paul Valéry. London, Routledge, 1969; New York, Pantheon, 1970.

* * *

Hilary Corke first became known as a literary critic who used his wit and verbal ingenuity to distinguish the real thing from the pretense. These talents and this interest, along with a power of lyric melody, are present in his poetry. Corke's early poems are often celebrations of sexual love. There is much ardor, and there is much enjoyment of the classics in English love poetry. In "Sleeping," for example, he presents his own version of Donne's intricate conceits. In "Oiseuse," he makes something of his own out of Eliot's "Fire Sermon" in *The Waste Land.* Corke's linguistic virtuosity appears also in his rich, sometimes witty, musical rhetoric. The wit often serves as a kind of check on the ardor with which the rhetoric praises love, but it is sometimes difficult to tell just how seriously that ardor is meant to be taken. One has the sense of a poet who has yet to find his own voice.

In the later poems, love is viewed from a perspective of loss and suffering, as Corke shifts his attention to experience that is, as in "The Evening Walk," at once personal and part of contemporary history:

> Have you noticed, by the way, it is growing chilly?
> That could be predicted. Are you done predicting?
> And we old. Let us speak of details.
>
> That, when you come down to it, is all.
> A question of region ...

The region in question is England in the 1950's and early 1960's; it is also the particularity of the poet's own situation. A kind of imitation of earlier poets remains. Some of these poems – in their now often conversational qualities, their moral landscapes and their sense of the generally ominous – recall poetry written between the two World Wars by W. H. Auden. Others recall Yeats's attempt to create poetry out of his own situation in history. Yet the necessity in the face of pain and loss to define one's own bearings leads Corke in these later poems to speak with a modest, authorative voice of his own.

—Jerry Paris

CORMAN, Cid (Sidney Corman). American. Born in Boston, Massachusetts, 29 June 1924. Educated at Boston Latin School; Tufts College, Medford, Massachusetts, B.A. 1945; University of Michigan, Ann Arbor (Hopwood Award, 1947), 1946–47; University of North Carolina, Chapel Hill, 1947; the Sorbonne, Paris, 1954–55. Married. Poetry Broadcaster, WMEX, Boston, 1949–51. Since 1951, Editor, *Origin* magazine and Origin Press, Kyoto, Japan. Recipient: Chapelbrook Foundation grant, 1967–69; National Endowment for the Arts grant, 1974; Lenore Marshall Memorial Prize, 1975. Address: Fukuoji-cho 82, Utano-ku, Kyoto 616, Japan.

PUBLICATIONS

Verse

subluna (juvenilia). Privately printed, 1945.
Night Claims (song), music by Hugo Calderón. New York, Schirmer,1950.
A Thanksgiving Eclogue from Theocritus. New York, Sparrow Press, 1954.
Ferrini and Others, with others. Berlin, Gerhardt, 1955.
The Precisions. New York, Sparrow Press, 1955.
The Responses. Ashland, Massachusetts, Origin Press, 1956.
Stances and Distance. Ashland, Massachusetts, Origin Press, 1957.
The Marches. Ashland, Massachusetts, Origin Press, 1957.
Clocked Stone. Ashland, Massachusetts, Origin Press, 1959.
A Table in Provence. Kyoto, Origin Press, 1959.
The Descent from Daimonji. Kyoto, Origin Press, 1959.
For Sure. Kyoto, Origin Press, 1960.
For Instance. Kyoto, Origin Press, 1960.
For Good. Kyoto, Origin Press, 1961.
Sun Rock Man. Kyoto, Origin Press, 1962; New York, New Directions, 1970.
In No Time. Kyoto, privately printed, 1963.
In Good Time. Kyoto, Origin Press, 1964.
All in All. Kyoto, Origin Press, 1965.
Nonce. New Rochelle, New York, Elizabeth Press, 1965.
For You. Kyoto, Origin Press, 1966.
For Granted. New Rochelle, New York, Elizabeth Press, 1966.
Stead. New Rochelle, New York, Elizabeth Press, 1966.
Words for Each Other. London, Rapp and Carroll, 1967.
& Without End. New Rochelle, New York, Elizabeth Press, and London, Villiers Publications, 1968.
No Less. New Rochelle, New York, Elizabeth Press, 1968.
Hearth. Kyoto, Origin Press, 1968.
No More. New Rochelle, New York, Elizabeth Press, 1969.
Plight. New Rochelle, New York, Elizabeth Press, 1969.
Nigh. New Rochelle, New York, Elizabeth Press, 1970.
Livingdying. New York, New Directions, 1970.
Of the Breath of. Berkeley, California, Maya, 1970.
For Keeps. Kyoto, Origin Press, 1970.
For Now. Kyoto, Origin Press, 1971.
Out and Out. New Rochelle, New York, Elizabeth Press, 1972.
Be Quest. New Rochelle, New York, Elizabeth Press, 1972.
A Language Without Words. Saffron Walden, Essex, Byways, 1973.
So Far. New Rochelle, New York, Elizabeth Press, 1973.
Poems: Thanks to Zuckerkandl. Rushden, Northamptonshire, Sceptre Press, 1973.
Breathings. Tokyo, Mushinsha, 1973.
Three Poems. Rushden, Northamptonshire, Sceptre Press, 1973.

Yet. New Rochelle, New York, Elizabeth Press, 1974.
RSVP. Knotting, Bedfordshire, Sceptre Press, 1974.
O/I. New Rochelle, New York, Elizabeth Press, 1974.
For Dear Life. Los Angeles, Black Sparrow Press, 1975.
Once and for All: Poems for William Bronk. New Rochelle, New York, Elizabeth Press, 1975.
'S. New Rochelle, New York, Elizabeth Press, 1976.

Other

At: Bottom. Bloomington, Indiana, Caterpillar, 1966.
William Bronk: An Essay. Carrboro, North Carolina, Truck Press, 1976.
Word for Word: Essays on the Art of Language. Santa Barbara, Black Sparrow Press, 1977.

Editor, *The Gist of "Origin": An Anthology*. New York, Grossman, 1975.

Translator, *Cool Melon*, by Basho. Ashland, Massachusetts, Origin Press, 1959.
Translator, *Cool Gong*. Ashland, Massachusetts, Origin Press, 1959
Translator, with Kamaike Susumu, *Selected Frogs*, by Shimpei Kusano. Kyoto, Origin Press, 1963.
Translator, *Back Roads to Far Towns*, by Basho. Tokyo, Mushinsha, 1967.
Translator, with Kamaike Susumu, *Frogs and Others: Poems*, by Shimpei Kusano. Tokyo, Mushinsha, 1968; New York, Grossman, 1969.
Translator, *Things*, by Francis Ponge. Tokyo, Mushinsha, and New York, Grossman, 1971.
Translator, *Leaves of Hypnos*, by René Char. Tokyo, Mushinsha, and New York, Grossman, 1973.
Translator, *Breathings*, by Philippe Jaccottet. New York, Grossman, 1974.

Bibliography: by John Taggart, New Rochelle, New York, Elizabeth Press, 1975.

Manuscript Collections: University of Texas, Austin; Kent State University, Ohio; Indiana University, Bloomington; New York University; State University of New York, Buffalo.

Cid Corman comments:

My work has developed from the pioneer poetry of Pound-Williams-Stevens, but much also from contact with French poetry. No forms, but a strict sense of the sounded meaning of words, pauses, verses, etc., and the felt thought that poetry is. Brevity, immediacy, clarity. A poetry that makes the role of the critic pointless, needless. The ideal, always, to join that most human society of poets whose work is published under the title of ANON.

Poetry calls for anonymity. It appeals, in short, to the each in all and the all in each. Its particularity must become yours. Autobiography is implicit in anyone's work and may be taken for granted, but what has been realized and so set out as to be shared loses itself in the self that is found extended without end in song.

As the author has elsewhere put it: *If I have nothing to offer you in the face of death – in its stead – the ache behind every ache, the instant man knows, I have no claim as poet. My song must sing into you a little moment, stay in you what presence can muster – of sense more than meaning, of love more than sense, of giving the life given one with the same fulness that brought each forth, each to each from each, nothing left but the life that is going on.*

* * *

Cid Corman's poems are tight, reticent, and resonant. He has learned (from the Japanese principally, one assumes) how evocative the minimal registration of specifics can be, and he has combined with this his own life-long concern for the sound of poetry, syllable by syllable (Zukofsky is for him, as for Creeley, a measure of such possibilities). The result, both in the longer more discursive poems of *Sun Rock Man* or *& Without End* and in the short haiku-like poems of such books as *Nonce*, *Stead*, and *Nigh*, is a poetry of considerable grace and strength.

As one reads the early poems now, they seem to cry out for the compression of the later style. "First Farm North" from *The Precisions* begins: "I stood above at the bathroom window" and goes on, in leisurely anecdotal style, to evoke a mood by careful accumulation of detail, ending:

The mirror was thawed into the scene
and the brightness of the morning
pressed a cool handful of water
into my eyes and my pulse raced song.

Corman is already free of iambic regularity while retaining a sense of measure in these lines, but the poem, though charming, is diffuse. In other poems one notices 1950's elegance ("Leaves discuss the wind") consorting somewhat uneasily with touches of what has come to seem Corman's characteristic sensibility ("It takes all my time, and my father's,/to let life go").

Between such early work and the development seen in *Sun Rock Man* there intervenes the first stay in Japan and the translations from Bashō and others published in *Cool Gong* and *Cool Melon*. A gain in expressive means – shorter lines, barer statement, more fluid syntax – is seen throughout the 1962 book. Here is "The Gift":

First night in a
strange town to
be going home

passing a
strange girl saying
goodnight to me

how night is
when she says so
suddenly good

The line breaks are like Creeley's, the syntax with its dangling participles and the canny deployment which gets the clinching phrase at the end owes something to Williams (cp. "Poem": "As the cat/climbed over ...") and the syllabic grid (4–3–4; 3–4–4; 3–4–4) suggests Marianne Moore. But the poem is, in its feelings, wholly Corman's. And the entire book, its sum exceeding its parts as a tribute to a place and people – the Italian town where the poet spent a year teaching English – marks the emergence of Corman's mature voice.

In the next book, *For Instance*, one finds more specific oriental influences in content, tone, and technique. Number 7 reads:

gong gone
odor of cherry tolling
eventide

Though a haiku translation, the juxtaposed verbless phrases evoking that mood of contemplative harmony with natural surroundings that one associates with Japanese poetry, this is nevertheless a western poem in its reliance on metaphor, assonance, and connotative language (who'd have thought it possible to rescue "eventide" for a modern poem?).

Corman's work has continued along the lines of the two books just mentioned. It cannot be denied that his emotional range is narrow and that his tone can verge on too easy a plangency, too self-indulgent an acquiescence in the drift towards dissolution. "The Mystery," for instance, from *In Good Time*, ends (speaking of swallows): "How each/ pursues//each,/pursued/by a green sky/as the sun settles,//desperate/to let themselves/go, O/against night." Unfair, of course, to crowd it like that, but it may be agreed that the melodramatic "desperate" and the moaning "o" sounds produce too facile a pathos and distract attention from the things seen to the emoting observer. Contrast the restraint of a successful poem on roughly the same thing:

Someone will
sweep the fallen
petals away

away. I know,
I know. Weight of
red shadows.

Here the talking voice is never swamped and the tone plays against and makes more convincing the feelings that weigh on the speaker. Even more fully impersonal is the following, also from *Nonce*:

The leaf that moved with the wind
moves
with the stream.

The energy is released by so simple a means as a change in tense. And the emotional effect is complex – transience is recognized but also cyclical renewal – and all is made to inhere in the thing seen, not worked up by the sensibility of the poet. When he writes like this, and he does it often enough for every book to be rewarding, Corman's is a voice that earns our careful attention.

—Seamus Cooney

CORN, Alfred. American. Born in Bainbridge, Georgia, 14 August 1943. Educated at Emory University, Atlanta, 1961–65, B.A. in French 1965; Columbia University, New York (Woodrow Wilson Fellow; Faculty Fellow), 1965–67, M.A. 1967; Fulbright Fellow, Paris, 1967–68. Married Ann Jones in 1967 (divorced, 1971). Preceptor, Columbia University, New York, 1968–70; Associate Editor, *University Review*, New York, 1970; Staff Writer, DaCapo Press, New York, 1971–72; Assistant Professor, Connecticut College, New London, 1978. Visiting Lecturer, 1977, 1978, and 1979, Yale University, New Haven, Connecticut. Recipient: Ingram Merrill Fellowship, 1974; George Dillon Prize, 1975, and Oscar Blumenthal Prize, 1977 (*Poetry*, Chicago). Address: 1806 Yale Station, New Haven, Connecticut 06520, U.S.A.

PUBLICATIONS

Verse

All Roads at Once. New York, Viking Press, 1976.
A Call in the Midst of the Crowd. New York, Viking Press, 1978.
The Various Light. New York, Viking Press, 1980.

Critical Study: "Alfred Corn's Speaking Gift" by George Kearns, in *Canto* (Andover, Massachusetts), Fall 1978.

Alfred Corn comments:

My poems have often been compared to those of Elizabeth Bishop, John Ashbery, and James Merrill; but perhaps just as useful a comparison could be made with the trio that figured importantly in their own development – Marianne Moore, Stevens, Auden. Subject matter favored: human relationships, especially love; landscape and cityscape; the arts; the difficult fitting between poetry and truth; the poet's vocation; the search for response in an inanimate world with no (at least denominational) religious dimension; suffering and death; social injustice; historical events and persons; childhood; imagination and introspective life.

In my first book I tried several tones of voice, still hewing fairly close to the ideal of speechly sound, middle diction, and the avoidance of syllable-stress meter. These tendencies continue in the second volume, which, in addition to an opening suite of lyrics, includes the long seasonally arranged title poem (with historical prose extracts interpolated) on New York City. (A precedent, on a somewhat smaller scale, was the sequence, "Pages from a Voyage," in the first book, a meditation on Darwin's round-the-world expedition, contemporary civilization, and personal fate.) In my third book, landscape came to replace cityscape in importance; and syllable-stress meter and rhyme are frequently used. Many of the poems might be described as late-Symbolist or simply introspective, notably, the 200-line (roughly) "Lacrimae Rerum," a meditation on sensory, and impalpable, reality.

* * *

"Getting Past the Past" is both a title and a leitmotif in Alfred Corn's impressive first book, *All Roads at Once.* Both in style and subject matter, past is present – or, as he puts it, "the past is a project/To be continued" – viewed and revised by a keenly individual sensibility: "We invent/The world and a wide cup to catch it in." Whether remembering childhood reading of and identification with fairy tales or traveling in Italy, France, and the Caribbean, the poet is caught by an evanescent past beyond recapture, if not recall, by the gift of imagination: "Yet somehow it's lost./The instinct to save, to fix in words,/Drains color, excitement dying to be/Art for others, from which you withdraw,/Victim of an imagination." Thus the artist's awareness of his vocation, and his ambivalence about it, joy and inevitable disappointment, and meanwhile the hope in this "double life, to be read and dreamed/Until the secret order appears."

Creating "poems across the trenches/of time" is one way to impose an order on "the curve of history," while waiting for the indefinite future. And already Corn demonstrates master craftsmanship in the traditional poetic forms. If in his sophistication he sometimes sounds too world-weary, even languid, the sharpness of his observations and apercus, his wit and word-play (often twisting clichés and turning puns into newer and neater truisms) prevent these poems from being merely facile, though not always from being mannered. Corn's verbal ability and technical virtuosity are reminiscent of James Merrill, as his gift for evoking associative meaning through catalogue and astute juxtaposition owe more than a little to John Ashbery. The weights of tradition, however, like those of his own past, are not so much burdens as influences transformed into a distinctive identity. Thus, Hart Crane's *The Bridge* helps Corn make his own philosophical and spiritual connections; while "Passages from a Voyage," the brilliantly sustained long poem which concludes the volume, uses Darwin's account of his journey as a base for personal, poetic explorations of the duality of man's life, the ambiguity of consciousness and the body's "ignorant optimism," and mutability and its terrors, the whole becoming an "experience arranged in a splendid contraption."

With *A Call in the Midst of the Crowd*, Corn continues to develop his themes of love and loss, but here self-assuredness replaces the self-consciousness of his earlier work. Again we find the subtle allusions to illustrious predecessors, the bright phrases and descriptive catalogues; but now the abstract and concrete combine in lyrics capable of capturing even the most elusive mood – or the immensity and diversity of a great city. Once again, too, travel is a subject, the dislocation provoking unease as "thoughts come stunned/And out of order." But the very disarray proves a creative stimulus. Though the "world of objects perpetually/Closes in," Corn has many a "rare moment when seeing comes of age," particularly in the long title poem on New York City which makes up most of the book. The four-part poem is itself half made up of astutely selected and cleverly arranged quotations from Crane, Henry James, Poe, Melville, Whitman, de Tocqueville, Wallace Stevens, whose comments play counterpoint to Corn's own observations about the city, its effect on the individual adventurer (or exile) there, and the course of a broken then mended romance. As the poem progresses, often ironically, through the seasons of love, it reveals the infinite possibilities, for achievement and failure, the chaos, distractions, and sheer abundance that make the excitement and danger of the city. As long urban history merges with the individual present with oblique significance, we are told "Our births choose us; then our lives; then our deaths." But, for all that, the city grants freedom to the poet, for here he is "Free once more to stroll where I'm drawn, hero/Of my own story." The promise Corn finds in the city is the same this book holds for its author: "The speaking gift that falls to one who hears/A word shine through the white noise of the world."

—Joseph Parisi

CORNISH, Sam(uel James). American. Born in Baltimore, Maryland, 22 December 1935. Educated at Booker T. Washington High School, Baltimore. Served in the armed service, 1958–60. Married Jean Faxon in 1967. Former Editor of the Enoch Pratt Library publication *Chicory*, Baltimore. Currently, Editor, *Mimeo* magazine. Consultant in elementary-school teaching, Central Atlantic Regional Educational Laboratories Humanities Program. Recipient: National Endowment for the Arts grant, 1967, 1969.

PUBLICATIONS

Verse

In This Corner: Sam Cornish and Verses. Baltimore, Fleming McAllister, 1961.
People Beneath the Window. Baltimore, Sacco, 1962.
Generations. Baltimore, Beanbag Press, 1964.
Angles. Baltimore, Beanbag Press, 1965.
Winters. Cambridge, Massachusetts, San Souci Press, 1968.
Short Beers. Cambridge, Massachusetts, Beanbag Press, 1969(?).
Generations: Poem. Boston, Beacon Press, 1971.
Streets. Chicago, Third World Press, 1973.

Sometimes: Ten Poems. Cambridge, Massachusetts, Pym Randall Press, 1973.
Sam's World. Washington, D.C., Decatur House, 1978.

Other

Your Hand in Mine. New York, Harcourt Brace, 1970.
Grandmother's Pictures (juvenile). Lenox, Massachusetts, Bookstore Press, 1974.
Walking the Street with Mississippi John Hurt (juvenile). Scarsdale, New York, Bradbury Press, 1978.

Editor, with Lucian W. Dixon, *Chicory: Young Voices from the Black Ghetto.* New York, Association Press, 1969.
Editor, with Hugh Fox, *The Living Underground: An Anthology of Contemporary American Poetry.* East Lansing, Michigan, Ghost Dance Press, 1969.

Critical Study: Introduction by Ron Schreiber to *Winters*, 1968.

Sam Cornish comments:

Most of my major themes are of urban life, the negro predicament here in the cities and my own family. I try to use a minimum of words to express the intended thought or feeling, with the effect of being starkly frank at times. Main verse form is unrhymed, free. Main influences – Lowell, T. S. Eliot, LeRoi Jones.

* * *

Sam Cornish's inclusion in nearly all major anthologies of new black poetry, including the one edited by Clarence Major, indicates his rapidly growing stature among contemporary Black American poets and points to richer future achievement. Cornish feels that T. S. Eliot, Robert Lowell, and LeRoi Jones have influenced him and this influence is evident in his affinity with Jones in his themes and the subtle irony of his poetry, a quality so significant in Eliot and Lowell. The three dominant themes in his poetry are urban life, the situation of the Negro, and his own family. In form, his poetry is strikingly concise, even terse, and his verse unrhymed. The short poem "Sam's World" is a representative sample of the poet's sharp consciousness of the Blacks' plight and, simultaneously, his perception of the identity and dignity possible even in that plight:

sam's mother has
grey combed hair

she will never touch
it with a hot iron

she leaves it
the way the lord
intended

she wears it proudly
a black and grey
round head of hair

In his comments on his well-known "Generations 1," Cornish says that he "walked to the east side Baltimore trying to find and remember the boys that grew up with me and were still living on the streets: laughing, talking and thinking about the streets, the playgrounds that had turned into parking lots, or weeded places after the riots. The poem grew out of those meetings and remembering what it was like to grow up alone, how I felt about women, the church, what I wanted to do with my life." Remembered, re-lived, and reflected-upon events provide a major basis for his poetry. But the unrecognizable and beautiful transformations of these events into poetry will be obvious to anyone reading "Generations 1." Specific details about the familiar figures of everyday life become highly generalised and evocative in such lines as these:

he would come into her cold apartment
wondering if he had the special knowledge
that women wanted from men
endured the pain she moaned
the odor between her breasts

and wanted god to remember
he was young
and in much trouble

with himself

Cornish's poetry shows an intense awareness of what it means to be human and, especially, to be black in contemporary America. It fuses in a complex way a tender awareness of intimate man-woman relations, close family ties, and a sympathy and understanding for fellow blacks. As a black poet, Cornish suffers the anguish of his people and writes about it in a way that combines the immediacy of one sharing the experience and the control of the detached observer. It is this tone of wistfulness and this control that make his poetry deeply moving without being shriekingly militant.

—J. N. Sharma

CORRINGTON, John William. American. Born in Memphis, Tennessee, 28 October 1932. Educated at Centenary College, Shreveport, Louisiana, A.B. 1956; Rice University, Houston, M.A. 1958; University of Sussex, Falmer, D.Phil. 1964; Tulane University Law School, New Orleans, J.D. 1975. Married Joyce Elaine Hooper in 1959; four children. Taught at Louisiana State University, Baton Rouge; Loyola University, New Orleans; University of California, Berkeley, 1968; practiced law, 1975–78. Recipient: Charioteer Prize, 1962; National Endowment for the Arts grant, 1966. Address: 1724 Valence Street, New Orleans, Louisiana 70115, U.S.A.

PUBLICATIONS

Verse

Where We Are. Washington, D.C., Charioteer Press, 1962.
The Anatomy of Love and Other Poems. Fort Lauderdale, Florida, Roman, 1964.
Mr. Clean and Other Poems. San Francisco, Amber House Press, 1964.
Lines to the South and Other Poems. Baton Rouge, Louisiana State University Press, 1965.

Plays

Screenplays, with Joyce H. Corrington: *Richthofen or Brown*, 1970; *The Omega Man*, 1970; *Box Car Bertha*, 1972; *The Arena*, 1973; *Battle for the Planet of the Apes*, 1973.

Television Plays: *The Killer Bees*, 1974; *Search for Tomorrow* series, with Joyce H. Corrington, 1978–.

Novels

And Wait for the Night. New York, Putnam, and London, Blond, 1964.
The Upper Hand. New York, Putnam, 1967; London, Blond, 1968.
The Bombardier. New York, Putnam, 1970.

Short Stories

The Lonesome Traveler and Other Stories. New York, Putnam, 1968.
The Actes and Monuments. Urbana, University of Illinois Press, 1978.

Other

Editor, with Miller Williams, *Southern Writing in the Sixties.* Baton Rouge, Louisiana State University Press, 2 vols., 1966–67.

John William Corrington comments:

(1970) I am primarily a novelist. Poetry served me chiefly as a school in which to learn the intensive use of figurative language – as opposed to analytical and metaphysical language. My work in poetry gave me a far greater sensitivity to form and style than an apprenticeship in prose fiction would have produced.

The larger part of my work, looked at in retrospect, seems to be composed of brief dramatic monologues, narratives of an elliptical nature, more or less sly jokes, and textured obscenities – none of these taken to exclude the others.

Again, in retrospect, it would appear that I am something of a religious maniac, an overwhelming percentage of my poetry in one way or another dealing with theological matters. This mania would unnerve me if it were not for the fact that, in the twentieth century, a religious nut seems among the least objectionable kind, and of a certain antiquarian interest and value.

My chief influences seem to have been Browning, Auden, Cummings, Wallace Stevens and Lawrence Ferlinghetti. I would add the name of James Dickey, but that would be hubris. His work is too good to digest.

I have written chiefly fiction over the past four years, but hope to remember soon how to write a poem. Perhaps I am too wise to write poetry now. Or perhaps not.

(1980) A great deal has happened since my last appearance here. Law School, more or less permanent employment in television, the practice of law, publication in political philosophy, and a renewal of my first love – music. The writing has taken on new influences, far more fugitive than those before: above all, the thought of Eric Voegelin, through his *Order and History*, the literature and mode of thought of the bar, and the music of Mozart. Such peculiar connexities are troublesome only if one is determined to "make something" of influences. Fortunately, the plenum of consciousness is not exhausted by understanding, but only by the limits of expression. I have begun to see the analogies between poetry and music, and to touch the shadow of Heraclitus's *logos*, the non-rational order of the cosmos which applies to Lex and Physis, to Musaeus, as well as to the making of poets. It turns out Coleridge was right: there is a "fugitive logic" there.

* * *

The central drama of Christianity, recurring or perpetually present, dominates the characteristic Corrington poem. The "messianic sun" and a "bronzejawed noncom/his arm a clutter of/roman stripes" ("It Happens Every Spring") are the eternal antagonists. Military life is the most obvious image of commitment to death: in "Corps Commander at Anzio," the officer boasts "... Now they realize my map – carve projected/salients in flesh and iron, murder my/statistics into fact"; in "Lines to the South," a statue of General Sherman sits astride a pony "whose shoulders/withers/flank/shrink from their burden/ooze metallic shame/whose blind sculptured eyes/look southward with/brute sympathy –." "Prayers for a Mass in the Vernacular" explores the sources of this lethal dedication: fallen man, who worships a "chrome madonna," perverts meaning in the guise of creating it ("then we communicated"), and celebrates The Word "in other words." Distortion of meaning is also the theme of "The Anatomy of Love," a series of vignettes which test varieties of modern love by their approximation to "the same standard," presumably that of the crucifixion scenes that begin and end the poem. As usual, Corrington's language is precise, exciting, and his spare lines carry each episode to an appropriate, often shocking, climax. But as in the other ambitious long poems, "Prayers for a Mass in the Vernacular," and "Communique," "Anatomy" inadequately dramatizes its personae, in this instance characters articulating the obsessive power of profane love. Thus, the poem is more successful in satirizing these proponents of the secular than in sustaining a tension between them and the implicit spiritual criterion. "Communique," an eclectic poem in three parts (which reads like a more accessible version of Pound's *Cantos*), so skillfully fuses its Eliotesque "fragments" from history, literature, and folklore into a controlled and consistently ironical picture of the consequences of the loss of faith that it fails to generate a sense that the evil embodied in the archetypal "commander grinly" could accomplish its destructive ends. Despite Corrington's wonderful play on "absolutely" in a variety of sexual and military contexts, the poem creates no Paolo and Francesca to make sin a live option, and no Capaneus to suggest the temptation of defiant violence. Corrington is stronger with the cosmic aftermath of the failure of faith in "Pastoral," where a Japanese farmer feels "the breath of armageddon/on his neck," and sees "a brook leap into stream," and "the city being eaten by the sun."

Though he has not yet written his *Waste Land*, Corrington's wit and often dazzling imagery and word-play animate both his pervasive motifs and his straightforward love poems and Audenesque explorations of neurosis like "An Exemplary Fiction." Familiar themes of the perversion of meaning, the atrophy of love and attendant burgeoning of egoism, often in military guise, explode powerfully from the image of Lucifer "wrapped in a banner of pronouns" ("Lucifer Means Light"). In "The Portable Goya," the gnomic verse that simultaneously mocks and reinforces the picture of the artist become a "giltframed classic" epitomizes the ambition and daring of Corrington's own poetry:

there is no art without risk
as dr frankenstein
wheezed dying to a
village constable.

—Burton Kendle

CORSO, (Nunzio) Gregory. American. Born in New York City, 26 March 1930. Married 1) Sally November in 1963 (divorced), one daughter; 2) Belle Carpenter in 1968, one daughter. Manual laborer, 1950–51; Reporter, Los Angeles *Examiner*, 1951–52; merchant seaman, 1952–53. Member of the English Department, State University of New York,

Buffalo, 1965–70. Recipient: Longview Foundation Award; Poetry Foundation Award. Address: c/o Phoenix Bookshop, 18 Cornelia Street, New York, New York 10014, U.S.A.

PUBLICATIONS

Verse

The Vestal Lady on Brattle and Other Poems. Cambridge, Massachusetts, Richard Brukenfeld, 1955.
Gasoline. San Francisco, City Lights, 1958.
Bomb. San Francisco, City Lights, 1958.
A Pulp Magazine for the Dead Generation: Poems, with Henk Marsman. Paris, Dead Language, 1959.
The Happy Birthday of Death. New York, New Directions, 1960.
Minutes to Go, with others. Paris, Two Cities, 1960.
Long Live Man. New York, New Directions, 1962.
Selected Poems. London, Eyre and Spottiswoode, 1962.
Penguin Modern Poets 5, with Lawrence Ferlinghetti and Allen Ginsberg. London, Penguin, 1963.
The Mutation of the Spirit: A Shuffle Poem. New York, Death Press, 1964.
There Is Yet Time to Run Back Through Life and Expiate All That's Been Sadly Done. New York, New Directions, 1965.
10 Times a Poem. New York, Poets Press, 1967.
Elegiac Feelings American. New York, New Directions, 1970.
Egyptian Cross. New York, Phoenix Book Shop, 1971.
Ankh. New York, Phoenix Book Shop, 1971.
The Night Last Night Was at Its Nightest. New York, Phoenix Book Shop, 1972.
Earth Egg. New York, Unmuzzled Ox, 1974.

Plays

This Hung-Up Age (produced Cambridge, Massachusetts, 1955).
That Little Black Door on the Left, in *Pardon Me Sir, But Is My Eye Hurting Your Elbow?*, edited by Bob Booker and George Foster. New York, Geis, 1968.

Novel

The American Express. Paris, Olympia Press, 1961.

Other

The Minicab War (parodies), with Anselm Hollo and Tom Raworth. London, Matrix Press, 1961.

Editor, with Walter Höllerer, *Junge Amerikanische Lyrik.* Munich, Carl Hanser Verlag, 1961.

Gregory Corso comments:

[I am a] mental explorer, un-Faustian.
[My verse is] hopeful – naive – strange – sweet – soon smart – why not.

* * *

To say that Gregory Corso is a member of the Beat Generation might be thought to say it all. But even though he was one of its most ardent apologists, he is no more typical than any of the others: Ginsberg, Ferlinghetti, Kerouac, Snyder. Still, they all shared that anti-social, apocalyptic, love-centered, freedom-loving mystique that has become so familiar to us. With Ginsberg and Kerouac, Corso was part of a kind of Beat triumvirate, each encouraging and supporting the other and his work. If Kerouac was the father-figure and Ginsberg the rabbi-figure, Corso was the child-figure and the clown.

Born into a poor immigrant family in Manhattan, Corso grew up as an underprivileged kid and became a juvenile delinquent who before he was 20 spent three years in prison for attempted robbery. He read widely and voraciously in prison, and after his release eventually found his way to the Harvard Library, where he continued his self-education and was taken up by local students and writers, who subsidized and saw through the press his first book of poems, *The Vestal Lady on Brattle*. It was at this point that Ginsberg and Kerouac "discovered" him.

Corso's poems are a mixture of powerful statement and bombast. He can be funny, maudlin, original, hackneyed, outrageous, sentimental – sometimes all in one poem. His stance is that of the sophisticated child, looking about him at a world gone mad and wondering why he is here. But madness is also a virtue, in the Blakean sense, since it is a response to and release from the sanity and conformity of the suburban fifties against which the Beats were reacting. As Corso puts it, "Man is great and mad, he was born mad and wonder of wonders the sanity of evolution knoweth not what to do."

Corso thinks of himself rather self-consciously as a poet, which leads him into excesses of language, archaisms, "poetic" phrasing, and unusual words. As one might expect of an autodidact, he wears his learning rather heavily, scattering literary and mythological allusions through his work. He likes to use words like "swipple," "precocial," "spatchcock," and the like; he can use a word like "writ" without apparent irony, and he seems to want such lines as "Life has meaning and I do not know the meaning" to be taken at face value. We can see the strong influence of Kerouac at work here, with his belief in letting it all hang out and writing without revision. This hit-or-miss technique of composition sometimes results in powerfully expressed feelings and ideas, but they often fall wide of the mark. He is not afraid to take chances, and there is something both endearing and annoying about the mixture of prosy language and verbal excess. Here is a typical piece of fustian taken at random:

> O walking crucifixes hooded and bowed
> treking catacombic apothecaries
> Grains drams and ounces of aphasia
> Etherized Popes their desperado nods
> raise welts of confessional memories on my lips

His subjects include large ones, like the plight of man and American society, Zen Buddhism, Egyptian religion, and Art, and smaller ones, like travel in Europe and Africa, his childhood, and the literary life. His most frequently anthologized poem is his best: that funny-sad meditation called "Marriage." The famous "Bomb" poem, printed in the shape of a mushroom cloud, shows a richness of invention which is one of his hallmarks, and an obsession with death, which is another. The title of one of his collections is *The Happy Birthday of Death*, a title ostensibly chosen at random from among a long list of such possibilities as Fried Shoes, Gargoyle Liver, The Rumpled Backyard, Radiator Soup, etc. Other good poems include "Giant Turtle," which describes a turtle laying eggs, "Hair," another repetitious but inventive poem, and "Seed Journey." Two long efforts in *Elegiac Feelings American* should be noted. The title poem, inscribed "for the dear memory of John Kerouac," is an attack on America and its destruction of Kerouac, rather incoherent in its excesses and logical inconsistencies. "The Geometric Poem" is a facsimile reproduction of a long handwritten manuscript complete with cartoon-like illustrations and hieroglyphics drawn by the poet; it is an elaborate and not wholly successful evocation of Egyptian culture and religion.

It is difficult not to like Corso as a person seen through his poetry: he is the perennial bad boy, jack-off (a recurrent but minor theme), hipster, clown, rebel, and misty-eyed romantic. Already, though, much of his poetry seems rather dated and quaint, and one wonders whether this 50-year-old child will be able to continue mining the same vein and whether the poems themselves will survive the era in which they were written.

—Donald Barlow Stauffer

COTTON, John. British. Born in London, 7 March 1925. Graduate of London University, B.A. (honours). Served as an officer in the Royal Naval Commandos in the Far East during World War II. Married Peggy Cotton in 1948; two sons. Since 1947, teacher, and since 1963, headmaster of a comprehensive school, Hertfordshire. Founder, with Ted Walker, and Editor, 1962–72, *Priapus* magazine. Since 1969, Editor, *The Private Library*; since 1975, Publisher, Priapus Press. Chairman, The Poetry Society, 1972–74, 1977, London. Recipient: Arts Council award, 1971. Address: 37 Lombardy Drive, Berkhamsted, Hertfordshire HP4 2LQ, England.

PUBLICATIONS

Verse

Fourteen Poems. Berkhamsted, Hertfordshire, Priapus Press, 1967.
Outside the Gates of Eden and Other Poems. Bushey Heath, Hertfordshire, Taurus Press, 1969.
Ampurias. Berkhamsted, Hertfordshire, Priapus Press, 1969.
Old Movies and Other Poems. London, Chatto and Windus-Hogarth Press, 1971.
The Wilderness. Berkhamsted, Hertfordshire, Priapus Press, 1971.
Columbus on St. Dominica. Rushden, Northamptonshire, Sceptre Press, 1972.
A Sycamore Press Broadsheet. Oxford, Sycamore Press, 1973.
Preludes: San Martin. Rushden, Northamptonshire, Sceptre Press, 1973.
Kilroy Was Here: Poems 1970–74. London, Chatto and Windus-Hogarth Press, 1975.
Places. Berkhamsted, Hertfordshire, Priapus Press, 1976.
Fragments 11, 12, and 13. Knotting, Bedfordshire, Sceptre Press, 1976.
Powers. Berkhamsted, Hertfordshire, Priapus Press, 1977.
A Berkhamsted Three, with Fred Sedgwick and Freda Downie. Berkhamsted, Hertfordshire, Priapus Press, 1978.
Piers. Leicester, New Broom Press, 1979.

Other

British Poetry since 1965. London, National Book League, 1973.

Critical Studies: in *Poetry Book Society Bulletin 69* and *84* (London), 1971, 1975; by Anne Cluysenaar, in *Stand* (Newcastle-upon-Tyne), xiv, 1, 1972.

John Cotton comments:

Overstatement is the obvious and inherent peril in writing a piece of this kind. Yet if it sounds pretentious to say that my pursuit of the art basically constitutes an exploration of that area between our wish to make it last forever and our consciousness that it never can, I can plead that it is the nearest I can get to an explanation of what I attempt to do. Having gone thus far, I may as well compound things by saying that with Aristotle I look upon one of the purposes of our fictions as a means of bringing order to the plethora of disparate experiences to which we are subjected. In mitigation I would add that while I take the art seriously, I do not take myself so.

* * *

John Cotton's writing presents a persistent, unspectacular search for consistency of awareness despite the complex conditions of human living:

Innocence, as all things
With man, has to be attained

At once brisk and delicate in observation, his poems attempt balance and sanity in the face of an acute sense of the disparateness of experience (a sense which the quietness of his manner never exploits). So he may speculate on the social motives that lead the Romans to heave "great stones ... into a wall" and find time to notice, by the side of the wall, "a hundred whitening snails" clustering "on a single stem to conserve moisture." The bringing together of these observations on different scales is, in Cotton, more than a device to relate man's attempt at order and life with nature's: it demonstrates a willingness to be comprehensive in his conception of order, and to reject idealism for a harder form of innocence, encompassing both the commonplace and the inevitable.

—Anne Cluysenaar

COULETTE, Henri (Anthony). American. Born in Los Angeles, California, 11 November 1927. Educated at Los Angeles State College, B.A. 1952; University of Iowa, Iowa City, M.F.A. 1954, Ph.D. 1959. Served in the United States Army, 1945–46. Married Jacqueline Meredith in 1950. Lecturer, University of Iowa, 1957–59. Since 1959, Member of the English Department, and currently Professor of English, California State University, Los Angeles. Associate Editor, *Midland* magazine. Recipient: Lamont Poetry Selection Award, 1965; Phelan Award, 1966; Order of the Black Rose, Krakow, Poland, 1972; Guggenheim Fellowship, 1976. Address: 475 Madeline Drive, Pasadena, California 91105, U.S.A.

PUBLICATIONS

Verse

The War of the Secret Agents. New York, Scribner, 1966.
The Family Goldschmitt. New York, Scribner, 1971.

Other

Editor, with Paul Engle, *Midland: Twenty-Five Years of Fiction and Poetry Selected from Writing Workshops of the State University of Iowa.* New York, Random House, 1961.

Editor, with Philip Levine, *Character and Crisis: A Contemporary Reader.* New York, McGraw Hill, 1966.

Editor, *The Broken Lyre: Interviews with 14 Poets.* Washington, D.C., National Endowment for the Arts, 1971.

Henri Coulette comments:

I consider myself a *maker* rather than a *bard.* From this consideration, all else follows. I am interested in technique, and take pride in demonstrating it: in traditional meter, syllabics, accentuals. I like to think that I bear witness to my experience; i.e., that my subject matter is being me, here, now. I hope that I may rise above these limitations, but I have no illusions about being a spokesman for others, or of possessing the truth. Limitation is mystery, and I try to live with the excitements and discomforts thereof.

* * *

Henri Coulette, particularly in *The War of the Secret Agents*, displays a definite predilection for oddities, for people and things "... like old streetcars buried at sea,/In the wrong element, with no place to go." He shows an allegiance and affection for things the world at large might consider neither proper, practical, nor valuable. He writes about an imagined fifth season, about neglected attic treasures, about a soldier who falls asleep during a mock battle and is killed when he falls from his truck, about "gentle kooks" and mild failures.

"The War of the Secret Agents" itself is about events surrounding a group of amateur agents for the Allies in World War II, about whom Coulette writes, "They will appeal to lovers of the absurd," being like "debutantes slumming on Skid Row." The 35-page poem, title-piece of the book for which Coulette was awarded the Lamont Poetry Selection Award, is wonderful. Written in a syllabic scheme appropriately odd (stanzas of 11–5–7–9–11–7), the poem captures the hypocrisy and duplicity of modern nations, and the lives of people trapped in their collectivist webs, dramatizing them with a kind of subtlety, humor, irony, and sympathy that runs contrary to present literary fashions. The language of the poem, if not fashionable, is thoroughly contemporary; Coulette has a marvelous ear for the natural speaking voice.

In *The Family Goldschmitt* Coulette has turned away from the matter and rhyme of his first book, but the poems still give the impression of being more formal than most recent poetry. The book, though it does contain fine poems, seems a drop-off from his first, with nothing that approaches "War of the Secret Agents" or the force of this short poem from the first book:

Robert Roger Coulette, Musician

He plays no more
Whose play was need,
The darkened score,
The broken reed.

—Lawrence Russ

COUZYN, Jeni. South African. Born in South Africa, 26 July 1942. Educated at the University of Natal, B.A. 1962, B.A. (honours) 1963. Drama Teacher, Rhodesia, 1964;

Producer, African Music and Drama Association, Johannesburg, 1965; Teacher, Special School, London, 1966; Poetry Organiser and Gallery Attendant, Camden Arts Centre, London, 1967. Since 1968, Free-lance poet, lecturer, and broadcaster. Recipient: Arts Council grant, 1971, 1974; Canada Council grant, 1977. Address: 17 Willow Road, London N.W.3, England.

PUBLICATIONS

Verse

Flying. London, Workshop Press, 1970.
Monkeys' Wedding. London, Cape, 1972.
Christmas in Africa. London, Heinemann, 1975.
House of Changes. London, Heinemann, 1978.
Life by Drowning. London, Heinemann, 1980.

Other

Editor, *Twelve to Twelve: Poems Commissioned for Poetry D-Day, Camden Arts Festival 1970.* London, Poets' Trust, 1970.

Jeni Couzyn comments:

I am interested in using symbol rather than image, and tend to write with as much clarity as I can. I am at times monosyllabic, and look for the shortest and simplest words I can find. I believe poetry should be "true" at the deepest possible level, and dislike the kind of poetry that appears to be complex on the surface, crammed with learned references and tricky images, but which finally has little to say.

I write in free verse, using rhythm and stress to underline meaning and to counterpoint the sense whenever I can. Similarly I use rhyme for surprise and emphasis rather than in any metrical pattern. I am particularly fond of imperfect rhymes, especially where the rhyming syllable falls on the unstressed part of the word.

I believe that poetry should be spoken, and read on the page only as a kind of specialised reference – as music is written to be played and listened to. Reviewers at this time in the history of poetry use the words "poetry circuit" as a dirty word, as though it were some kind of big roundabout that only the common and the simple people climbed aboard. The simply expressed but profound truth of a poem like Robert Frost's "Nothing Gold Can Stay" is what I most admire in poetry and most seek for. The criteria I use to judge my own work are: is it interesting; is it relevant to other people's lives; is it music; is it true in the deepest sense – in a lasting way. To the extent that these criteria are approached, I am pleased or displeased with a poem.

In sound I have been most influenced by Dylan Thomas – not so much in his technique as in his courage in defying the dry tradition of poetry he was born into.

That I am a poet in an age where the "unintellectual" (i.e., almost everybody) think of poetry as something they didn't like when they were at school, and the intellectual think it something the masses should be excluded from, is sad for me. This age has too much reverence for poetry, and too little respect – for by the same token it is very difficult indeed to earn a living from poetry. Nor are poets considered valid members of the community – you will never see a panel set up to discuss drug usage, for example, or terrorism in Ireland, with a poet among the psychiatrists, students, businessmen, clergy and housewives being asked to give their view.

For me being a poet is a job rather than an activity. I feel I have a function in society, neither more nor less meaningful than any other simple job. I feel it is part of my work to make poetry more accessible to people who have had their rights withdrawn from them. Standing in the way of this are the poetry watchdogs who bark in the Sunday reviews, trying to preserve their sterile territory. Also it is necessary to overcome the apathy and ignorance of a whole society with a totally untrained ear and a profoundly sluggish imagination.

* * *

Jeni Couzyn's first book, *Flying*, came as a surprise even to readers who thought themselves sophisticated. Few of the poems contained in it had reached the usual magazines and anthologies, though Couzyn was known for her appearances on the recital circuits. *Flying* consisted, among other things, of reflections upon her South African background, descriptions of London's grey suburbia, dramatisations of love relationships, and revelations of mental stress. These last were at their best when the author expressed her internal conflicts by way of her flow of exotic imagery. For example, "The Farm" deals with what looks like a depressive illness, but it does so in terms almost of a child's holiday.

On the farm there are two
cows.
And there are a lot of
trees. They change their leaves
whenever they like. When they change their leaves you
know
that it is autumn. The two cows have a calf and then you
know
that it is spring.
You can take your cat with you to the farm or whatever
you like. You can take your
bicycle
or your
typewriter
or all your books
you can take whatever you like with you to the farm...

These patient monosyllables ratify a childish acceptance of what becomes more abnormal the further the poem proceeds. The resultant conflict, between the innocent and the sinister, sets up an uneasy tension, too, in the reader. Couzyn, when she projects a parable of the mind's cliffs of fall, is a distinguished poet.

But her second book, *Monkeys' Wedding*, suffers from over-explicitness. Many of the attitudes are straight out of Women's Lib. The collection contains some powerful work; perhaps most notably "The Babies," a painful poem about contraception and abortion: "On the table the baby lay/pulped like a water-melon, a few/soft bits of skull protruding from the mush...." One may feel here, however, that the skin of fiction is stretched too thin over the agony. We are more conscious of outcry than of experience. Emotion of this sort demands an objective correlative if it is not to seem shrill.

Such a correlative is sought for in *Christmas in Africa*. Couzyn makes considerable use of science fiction, notably the work of Brian Aldiss: "I am your priest and your prophet./May the long journey end/may the ship come home...." But this would be obscure to a reader who did not know *Non-Stop*. And the reader who does know that remarkable book may wonder why he has need of Couzyn's poem. More striking are what seem to be reminiscences of Couzyn's childhood in South Africa, e.g., "In the House of the Father":

The snakes were the price. In their hundreds they inhabited
our world at Christmas. They were the hazard
in the garden. And they were everywhere
tangled in undergrowth, slithering over your feet in the pathway

stretched across doorways in the sun
lurking under the banana plant and nesting in the luckybean tree....

But, sharp though these details are, they don't have the pressure of implication that we find in the African imagery of *Flying*. Nor are they contained within a sufficiently decisive form: the verse is discursive.

In *House of Changes* we are, for the most part, deprived even of sharp details. Imagery gives way to incantation: "Leprechaun take back thy curse/Leprechaun take back thy curse...." This seems to be wrenched from a context, but no adequate context is given to us in the book. There are more science fiction poems, but they are even more dependent upon Philip K. Dick than the earlier ones were upon Brian Aldiss. Only occasionally do the two interrelate –

Insatiable one, I'm exhausted with eating
I'm a bag of stones, I am all stomach. Bloated
I lie here unable to move in my sea of flesh.
My thighs and breasts flow without shape
my head sags in a heap of chins
I lie here defiled in a mound of
self-disgust, in a pool of half-digested fluids
yet you hunger and hunger in me.
I was a woman once....

This is from a poem called "I and Wolverine" which I take to be a dialogue between an exhausted woman and the unappeasable sexuality that devours her. It suggests that Couzyn is by no means at the end of her poetic range. Yet one is conscious, in all her books, of a gap between potentiality and achievement. Though she has touched notes beyond the set register of her early work, Couzyn cannot really be said to have improved her tessitura. No fiction has quite replaced her early formalism as a correlative for incipient violence and hysteria. The science fiction analogues and the incantations alike show that she is still in search of a form that will also be a plot. Her many admirers will follow her future explorations in the hope of sharing in a fresh sense of discovery.

—Philip Hobsbaum

COWLEY, Malcolm. American. Born in Belsano, Pennsylvania, 24 August 1898. Educated at Peabody High School, Pittsburgh; Harvard University, Cambridge, Massachusetts (Editor, *The Advocate*, 1919), A.B. (cum laude) 1920 (Phi Beta Kappa); University of Montpellier, Diplome 1922. Served in the American Ambulance Service in France, 1917, and the United States Army, 1918; Office of Facts and Figures, Washington, D.C., 1942. Married Muriel Maurer (second wife) in 1932; one son, Robert. Associate Editor, *Broom* magazine, New York, 1923; Literary Editor, *New Republic*, New York, 1929–44. Visiting Professor: University of Washington, Seattle, 1950; Stanford University, California, 1956, 1959, 1960–61, 1965; University of Michigan, Ann Arbor, 1957; University of California, Berkeley, 1962; Cornell University, Ithaca, New York, 1964; University of Minnesota, Minneapolis, 1971; University of Warwick, England, 1973. Since 1948 Literary Adviser, The Viking Press, New York. Director of the Yaddo Corporation. Recipient: Levinson Prize, 1927, and Harriet Monroe Memorial Prize, 1939 (*Poetry*, Chicago); National Institute of Arts and Letters grant, 1946; National Endowment for the Arts grant, 1967; Signet Medal, 1976. Litt.D.: Franklin and Marshall College, Lancaster, Pennsylvania, 1961;

Colby College, Waterville, Maine, 1962; University of Warwick, Coventry, 1975. President, 1956–59, 1962–65, National Institute of Arts and Letters; Chancellor, American Academy of Arts and Letters, 1967–76. Address: Sherman, Connecticut 06784, U.S.A.

PUBLICATIONS

Verse

Blue Juniata. New York, Cape and Smith, 1929.
The Dry Season. New York, New Directions, 1941.
Blue Juniata: Collected Poems. New York, Viking Press, 1968.

Other

Racine. Paris, Union, 1923.
Exile's Return: A Narrative of Ideas. New York, Norton, 1934; London, Cape, 1935; revised edition, as *Exile's Return: A Literary Odyssey of the 1920's*, New York, Viking Press, 1951; London, Bodley Head, 1961.
The Literary Situation. New York, Viking Press, 1954.
Black Cargoes: A History of the Atlantic Slave Trade, 1518–1865, with Daniel P. Mannix. New York, Viking Press, 1962; London, Longman, 1963.
The Faulkner-Cowley File: Letters and Memories, 1944–1962. New York, Viking Press, and London, Chatto and Windus, 1966.
Think Back on Us: A Contemporary Chronicle of the 1930's, edited by Henry Dan Piper. Carbondale, Southern Illinois University Press, 1967.
A Many-Windowed House: Collected Essays on American Writers and American Writing. Carbondale, South Illinois University Press, 1970.
A Second Flowering: Works and Days of the Lost Generation. New York, Viking Press, and London, Deutsch, 1973.
And I Worked at the Writer's Trade: Chapters of Literary History 1918–1978. New York, Viking Press, 1978.

Editor, *Adventures of an African Slaver, Being a True Account of the Life of Captain Theodore Canot*, by Brantz Mayer. New York, Boni, and London, Routledge, 1928.
Editor, *After the Genteel Tradition: American Writers since 1910.* New York, Norton, 1937; revised edition, Carbondale, Southern Illinois University Press, 1964.
Editor, with Bernard Smith, *Books That Changed Our Minds.* New York, Doubleday, 1939.
Editor, *The Portable Hemingway.* New York, Viking Press, 1944.
Editor, with Hannah Josephson, *Aragon: Poet of the French Resistance.* New York, Duell, 1945; as *Aragon: Poet of Resurgent France*, London, Pilot Press, 1946.
Editor, *The Portable Faulkner.* New York, Viking Press, 1946; revised edition, 1966; London, Chatto and Windus, 1967.
Editor, *The Portable Hawthorne.* New York, Viking Press, 1948; revised edition, 1969; London, Penguin, 1977.
Editor, *The Complete Poetry and Prose of Walt Whitman.* New York, Pellegrini and Cudahy, 1948; as *The Works of Walt Whitman*, New York, Funk and Wagnalls, 1968.
Editor, *Stories*, by F. Scott Fitzgerald. New York, Scribner, 1951.
Editor, *Great Tales of the Deep South.* New York, Lion, 1955.
Editor, *Writers at Work: The "Paris Review" Interviews.* New York, Viking Press, and London, Secker and Warburg, 1958.
Editor, *Leaves of Grass, The First (1855) Edition*, by Walt Whitman. New York, Viking Press, 1959.

Editor, with Robert Cowley, *Fitzgerald and the Jazz Age*. New York, Scribner, 1966.
Editor, with Howard E. Hugo, *The Lessons of the Masters: An Anthology of the Novel from Cervantes to Hemingway*. New York, Scribner, 1971.

Translator, *On Board the Morning Star*, by Pierre MacOrlan. New York, Boni, 1924.
Translator, *Joan of Arc*, by Joseph Delteil. New York, Minton Balch, 1926.
Translator, *Variety*, by Paul Valéry. New York, Harcourt Brace, 1927.
Translator, *Catherine-Paris*, by Marthe Lucie Bibesco. New York, Harcourt Brace, 1928.
Translator, *The Green Parrot*, by Marthe Lucie Bibesco. New York, Harcourt Brace, 1929.
Translator, *The Sacred Hill*, by Maurice Barrès. New York, Macaulay, 1929.
Translator, *The Count's Ball*, by Raymond Radiguet. New York, Norton, 1929.
Translator, *Imaginary Interviews*, by André Gide. New York, Knopf, 1944.
Translator, with James R. Lawler, *Leonardo Poe Mallarmé*, by Paul Valéry. Princeton, New Jersey, Princeton University Press, 1972.

Bibliography: *Malcolm Cowley: A Checklist of His Writings*, by Diane U. Eisenberg, Carbondale, Southern Illinois University Press, 1975.

Manuscript Collection: Newberry Library, Chicago.

Critical Studies: Introduction by Henry Dan Piper to *A Many-Windowed House*, 1970; by Lewis P. Simpson, in *Sewanee Review* (Tennessee), Autumn 1974.

Malcolm Cowley comments:

I am sorry to record that my principal theme has been nostalgia: for the countryside where I was born, for the easier society in which I came to manhood, for the friends of my younger days. I try to make each poem an action complete in itself; to let it discover its own form, often by patient revision. I am more interested in sound than sight, in tonal qualities than in images. I believe that every successful poem is a charm or mantra in which every word has become unchangeable.

* * *

Malcolm Cowley's output as a poet has never been copious. Throughout a long and distinguished literary career he has been known primarily as a critic and historian of American literature rather than a poet. Nevertheless, *Blue Juniata*, the 1968 volume of collected poems, shows that Cowley's talents as a poet are real and unforced, however infrequently he may have exercised them. He sees his poems as expressions and illustrations of his personal and intellectual history, beginning in a Pennsylvania childhood in the opening years of this century; an attachment to country life and the natural world is a recurring theme in his poetry. But as well as its personal dimension, Cowley's poetry also documents and crystallizes crucial moments in modern American history. Thus, "Chateau de Soupir: 1917" is a sharp recollection of the First World War; "Ezra Pound at the Hotel Jacob" recalls the expatriate Parisian literary life of the 1920's; "Tomorrow Morning" reflects the political passions of the 1930's and the impact of the Spanish Civil War. Most recently, "Here with the Long Grass Rippling" looks in passing at the Vietnam war.

Cowley's poetry is not dramatic or particularly vivid in its language. But it possesses the solid virtues of craftsmanship, urbanity, controlled lyricism, and exact observation of the physical world.

—Bernard Bergonzi

COXE, Louis (Osborne). American. Born in Manchester, New Hampshire, 15 April 1918. Educated at St. Paul's School, Concord, New Hampshire; Princeton University, New Jersey, B.A. 1940. Served in the United States Navy, 1942–46. Married Edith Winsor in 1946; four children. Instructor, Princeton University, 1946; Briggs-Copeland Fellow, Harvard University, Cambridge, Massachusetts, 1948–49; Assistant Professor, then Associate Professor, University of Minnesota, Minneapolis, 1949–55. Professor of English, 1955–56, and since 1956, Pierce Professor of English, Bowdoin College, Brunswick, Maine. Fulbright Lecturer, Trinity College, Dublin, 1959–60, and University of Aix-Marseilles, 1971–72. Recipient: Donaldson Award, for drama, 1952; *Sewanee Review* Fellowship, 1956; Brandeis University Creative Arts Award, 1960; National Endowment for the Arts award, 1977; Academy of American Poets Prize, 1977. Address: Department of English, Bowdoin College, Brunswick, Maine 04011, U.S.A.

PUBLICATIONS

Verse

The Sea Faring and Other Poems. New York, Holt, 1947.
The Second Man and Other Poems. Minneapolis University of Minnesota Press, 1955.
The Wilderness and Other Poems. Minneapolis, University of Minnesota Press, 1958.
The Middle Passage. Chicago, University of Chicago Press, 1960.
The Last Hero and Other Poems. Nashville, Tennessee, Vanderbilt University Press, 1965.
Nikal Seyn, Decoration Day: A Poem and a Play. Nashville, Tennessee, Vanderbilt University Press, 1966.
Passage: Selected Poems 1943–1978. Columbia, University of Missouri Press, 1979.

Plays

Billy Budd, with Robert Chapman, adaptation of the story by Herman Melville (as *Uniform of Flesh*, produced New York, 1949; revised version, as *Billy Budd*, produced New York, 1951). Princeton, New Jersey, Princeton University Press, 1951; London, Heinemann, 1966; as *The Good Sailor* (produced London, 1956).
The General (produced Cambridge, Massachusetts, 1954).
The Witchfinders (produced Rochester, Minnesota, 1955; New York, 1958).

Other

Christianity and Education. Brunswick, Maine, St. Paul's Episcopal Church, 1958.
Edwin Arlington Robinson. Minneapolis, University of Minnesota Press, 1962.
Edwin Arlington Robinson: The Life of Poetry. New York, Pegasus, 1969.
Enabling Acts: Selected Essays in Criticism. Columbia, University of Missouri Press, 1976.

Editor, *Chaucer.* New York, Dell, 1963.

* * *

The Sea Faring, the title of his first book, is also Louis Coxe's favorite theme. The sea acts not only as a setting for individual displays of courage and villainy but also as a powerful metaphor for the universal struggles endured in man's precarious moral voyages. The poet frames his astute observations with skilful verse forms, but several early and some later works suffer from a hypercerebral tone, overly technical terminology, and complex and constricting syntax; what might be music is muffled by a heavy academic pall, which also gives the impression of greater profundity than actually lies beneath the convoluted surface. Even here, however, the search for fundamentals, for the eternal designs behind the ephemeral, gives Coxe's lines their particular strength. The persona asks, "How shall he tell you: Mac, the war/Was rugged?" and answers through descriptions of strategic maneuvers and vignettes of warship personnel, for brief and vivid abstracts best convey the fearful order in the larger strife. Later, in the panoramic treatment of a disastrous naval battle, "The Strait," he commemorates the "Thousands who burned or drowned died to no end ... far from imagined loves" at Pearl Harbor and in the South Pacific, and reveals the deadly artistry behind apparent chaos.

Coxe's sense of history – as a cyclic, usually violent, seldom redemptive process – underlines and unifies the several strands in his work. The harsh Colonial past is peopled by the likes of Hannah Dustin, who castrates and scalps her Indian rapist with his own knife; by Samuel Sewall, late witch-burner now obsessed with guilt and possessed by the Devil; by Thomas Jefferson, imposing his classical designs upon the treacherous wilderness that is the young country – and the heart of man. Salem and Boston send forth handsome sailing ships, whose "wrecks grow timber out of shale." The greed, destructiveness, and sexual perversion behind the Puritan facade of salty self-reliance is most brilliantly revealed in the long blank-verse narrative, *The Middle Passage.* A shrewd but seemingly innocent nineteen-year-old, Canot, soon commandeers *The Happy Delivery*, a slaveship disguised as a whaler, half outwits its crafty Yankee owners, but experiences a sea-change; the filthy but lucrative business exacts its toll, 300 blacks drowned and the loss of Canot's soul in an orgy of sadistic lust, drink, and drugs, culminating in grand theft and murder: "New Englanders don't damn/The easy way...." But all is part of the pattern. The sins of the Forefathers breed the current misery of the cities: "We are strangers on the earth,/To one another, and lament a private loss." We are left with "separate lives inside, grown separate hells." "Progress" is merely repetition of original sin, a myth amounting to a moral stand-still.

Despite the seriousness of most of Coxe's verse, its effect is not gloomy. He has a gift for dramatic exposition. Even when the perhaps inexplicable motivations of the "heroes" of *The Middle Passage* and *Nikal Seyn* remain murky, we share the fascination of the limited and unreliable narrators with their flamboyant adventures. Poems celebrating nature, particularly flights of birds, rise with lyrical power. Several portraits strip historical personages to the core: Dean Swift, "Who studied hate lest pity turn him mad"; Ambrose Bierce, of whom Coxe asks, "Yet how can sworn enemy/of corruption rot/embalmed by hate?" Often poignant and witty, especially in "personal" poems dedicated to family and friends, Coxe's best lines give the satisfaction that comes when problems and paradoxes are subtly restated and elegantly shaped by art.

—Joseph Parisi

CREELEY, Robert (White). American. Born in Arlington, Massachusetts, 21 May 1926. Educated at Holderness School, Plymouth, New Hampshire; Harvard University, Cambridge, Massachusetts, 1943–46; Black Mountain College, North Carolina, B.A. 1955; University of New Mexico, Albuquerque, M.A. 1960. Served with the American Field Service in India and Burma, 1944–45. Married twice; six children. Taught on a finca in Guatemala for two years; Instructor, Black Mountain College, Spring 1954, Fall 1955; Visiting Lecturer, 1961–62, and Lecturer, 1963–66, 1968–69, University of New Mexico; Lecturer, University of British Columbia, Vancouver, 1962–63. Visiting Professor, 1966–67, Professor, 1967–78, and since 1978, Gray Professor of Poetry and Letters, State University of New York, Buffalo. Visiting Professor, San Francisco State College, 1970–71, and University of New Mexico, 1978, 1979. Operated the Divers Press, Palma de Mallorca, 1953–55. Editor, *Black Mountain Review*, North Carolina, 1954–57, and associated with *Wake*, *Golden Goose*, *Origin*, *Fragmente*, *Vou*, *Contact*, *CIV/n*, and *Merlin* magazines in the early 1950's, and other magazines subsequently. Recipient: Levinson Prize, 1960, Oscar Blumenthal Prize, 1964, and Union League Civic and Arts Foundation Prize, 1967 (*Poetry*, Chicago); D. H. Lawrence Fellowship, 1960; Guggenheim Fellowship, 1964, 1971; Rockefeller Fellowship, 1965. Lives in Placitas, New Mexico. Address: Department of English, State University of New York, Buffalo, New York 14260, U.S.A.

PUBLICATIONS

Verse

Le Fou. Columbus, Ohio, Golden Goose Press, 1952.
The Kind of Act of. Palma, Mallorca, Divers Press, 1953.
The Immoral Proposition. Karlsruhe-Surlach, Germany, Jonathan Williams, 1953.
A Snarling Garland of Xmas Verses. Palma, Mallorca, Divers Press, 1954.
All That Is Lovely in Men. Asheville, North Carolina, Jonathan Williams, 1955.
Ferrini and Others, with others. Berlin, Gerhardt, 1955.
If You. San Francisco, Porpoise Bookshop, 1956; London, Lion and Unicorn Press, 1968.
The Whip. Worcester, Migrant Press, and Highlands, North Carolina, Jonathan Williams, 1957.
A Form of Woman. New York, Jargon-Corinth, 1959.
For Love: Poems 1950–1960. New York, Scribner, 1962.
Distance. Lawrence, Kansas, Terrence Williams, 1964.
Two Poems. San Francisco, Oyez, 1964.
Hi There! Urbana, Illinois, Finial Press, 1965.
Words. Rochester, Minnesota, Perishable Press, 1965.
About Women. Los Angeles, Gemini, 1966.
Poems 1950–1965. London, Calder and Boyars, 1966.
For Joel. Madison, Wisconsin, Perishable Press, 1966.
A Sight. London, Cape Goliard Press, 1967.
Words. New York, Scribner, 1967.
Robert Creeley Reads (with recording). London, Turret-Calder and Boyars, 1967.
The Finger. Los Angeles, Black Sparrow Press, 1968.
5 Numbers. New York, Poets Press, 1968.
The Charm: Early and Uncollected Poems. Mount Horeb, Wisconsin, Perishable Press, 1968; London, Calder and Boyars, 1971.
The Boy. Buffalo, Gallery Upstairs Press, 1968.
Numbers. Stuttgart and Dusseldorf, Edition Domberger-Galerie Schmela, 1968.
Divisions and Other Early Poems. Mount Horeb, Wisconsin, Perishable Press, 1968.
Pieces. Los Angeles, Black Sparrow Press, 1968.
Hero. New York, Indianakatz, 1969.
A Wall. New York and Stuttgart, Bouwerie-Edition Domberger, 1969.
Mary's Fancy. New York, Bouwerie, 1970.
In London. Bolinas, California, Angel Hair, 1970.
The Finger: Poems 1966–1969. London, Calder and Boyars, 1970.
For Betsy and Tom. Detroit, Alternative Press, 1970.
For Benny and Sabina. New York, Samuel Charters, 1970.
As Now It Would Be Snow. Los Angeles, Black Sparrow Press, 1970.
America. Miami, Press of the Black Flag, 1970.
Christmas: May 10, 1970. Buffalo, State University of New York at Buffalo Lockwood Memorial Library, 1970.

St. Martin's. Los Angeles, Black Sparrow Press, 1971.
Sea. San Francisco, Cranium Press, 1971.
1.2.3.4.5.6.7.8.9.0. Berkeley, California, and San Francisco, Shambala-Mudra, 1971.
For the Graduation. San Francisco, Cranium Press, 1971.
Change. San Francisco, Hermes Free Press, 1972.
One Day after Another. Detroit, Alternative Press, 1972.
A Day Book (includes prose). New York, Scribner, 1972.
For My Mother. Rushden, Northamptonshire, Sceptre Press, 1973.
Kitchen. Chicago, Wine Press, 1973.
His Idea. Toronto, Coach House Press, 1973.
Sitting Here. Storrs, University of Connecticut Library, 1974.
Backwards. Knotting, Bedfordshire, Sceptre Press, 1975.
Thirty Things. Santa Barbara, California, Black Sparrow Press, 1976.
Away. Santa Barbara, Black Sparrow Press, and Solihull, Warwickshire, Aquila, 1976.
Selected Poems. New York, Scribner, 1976.
Myself. Knotting, Bedfordshire, Sceptre Press, 1977.
Hello: A Journal, February 23–May 3, 1976. New York, New Directions, and London, Boyars, 1978.
Later. West Branch, Iowa, Toothpaste Press, 1978.
Desultory Days. Knotting, Bedfordshire, Sceptre Press, 1978.
Later: New Poems. New York, New Directions, 1979.

Recordings: *Today's Poets 3*, with others, Folkways; *Robert Creeley Reads*, Turret-Calder and Boyars, 1967.

Play

Listen (produced London, 1972). Los Angeles, Black Sparrow Press, 1972.

Novel

The Island. New York, Scribner, 1963; London, Calder, 1964.

Short Stories

The Gold Diggers. Palma, Mallorca, Divers Press, 1954.
Mister Blue. Frankfurt, Insel, 1964.
The Gold Diggers and Other Stories. London, Calder, and New York, Scribner, 1965.
Mabel: A Story, and Other Prose. London, Boyars, 1976.

Other

An American Sense (essay). London, Sigma, 1965(?).
Contexts of Poetry. Buffalo, Audit, 1968.
A Quick Graph: Collected Notes and Essays. San Francisco, Four Seasons, 1970.
A Day Book. Berlin, Graphis, 1970; New York, Scribner, 1972.
Notebook. New York, Bouwerie, 1972.
A Sense of Measure (essays). London, Calder and Boyars, 1972.
The Creative. Los Angeles, Black Sparrow Press, 1973.
Contexts of Poetry: Interviews 1961–1971, edited by Donald Allen. Bolinas, California, Four Seasons, 1973.
Inside Out: Notes on the Autobiographical Mode. Los Angeles, Black Sparrow Press, 1973.
Presences: A Text for Marisol. New York, Scribner, 1976.

Was That a Real Poem and Other Essays, edited by Donald Allen. Bolinas, California, Grey Fox Press, 1978.

Editor, *Mayan Letters*, by Charles Olson. Palma, Mallorca, Divers Press, 1953; London, Cape, and New York, Grossman, 1968.
Editor, with Donald Allen, *New American Story*. New York, Grove Press, 1965.
Editor, *Selected Writings*, by Charles Olson. New York, New Directions, 1966.
Editor, with Donald Allen, *The New Writing in the U.S.A.* London, Penguin, 1967.
Editor, *Whitman*. London, Penguin, 1973.

Bibliography: *Robert Creeley: An Inventory 1945–1970* by Mary Novik, Montreal, McGill-Queen's University Press, 1974.

Manuscript Collection: Washington University, St. Louis.

Critical Studies: Review by Robert Duncan, in *New Mexico Quarterly* (Albuquerque), xxxii, 3–4, 1962–63; "Introduction to Robert Creeley" by Charles Olson, in *Human Universe and Other Essays*, New York, Grove Press, 1967; Louis B. Martz, in *Yale Review* (New Haven, Connecticut), 1969; "Address and Posture in the Poetry of Robert Creeley" by Kenneth Cox, in *Cambridge Quarterly*, iv, 3, 1969; *Three Essays on Creeley* by Warren Tallman, Toronto, Coach House Press, 1973; "Robert Creeley's *For Love: Poems 1950–1960*" by Charles Olson, in *Additional Prose*, San Francisco, Four Seasons, 1974; "Robert Creeley Issue" of *Boundary 2* (Binghamton, New York), Spring–Fall 1978; *Robert Creeley's Poetry* by Cynthia Edelberg, Albuquerque, University of New Mexico Press, 1978; *Robert Creeley* by Arthur Ford, Boston, Twayne, 1968.

Robert Creeley comments:

I write to realize the world as one has come to live in it, thus to give testament. I write to move in *words*, a human delight. I write when no other act is possible.

* * *

Rarely has a living poet enjoyed the wide critical attention Robert Creeley now receives. Book-length critical studies are beginning to appear, and essays analyzing all aspects of his writing abound in current literary journals. He has been interviewed with wearying frequency, but through it all Creeley has responded with unusual charm and freshness. Clearly Creeley has touched a nerve of life in such a way as to provoke this intensity of response. That nerve may be his own inner life, which Creeley has plumbed with rare precision and thoroughness. His language is a delicate x-ray of the emotions under the stress and near madness of marriages gone wrong. This lyric self-analysis has exposed the masculine uncertainty rife in the age, and has also called into question the very substance of reality lying beyond and around self. His canon seems a clearing house of issues that have troubled literature since the close of World War II – dilemmas of identity and relationship to others. Hence the critical furor to pinpoint the work to certain formulable ideas which its processual nature has so far eluded.

Creeley's early poems, collected in *For Love: Poems 1950–1960*, are intensely formal in their compactness and closure. Many tend toward epigram in their brevity and pithy advice. A typical instance is "The Warning":

For love – I would
split open your head and put
a candle in
behind the eyes,

Love is dead in us
if we forget
the virtue of an amulet
and quick surprise.

The best of the short poems define the self from an oblique but penetrating angle of insight, as in the three couplets of "The End":

When I know what people think of me
I am plunged into my loneliness. The grey

hat bought earlier sickens.
I have no purpose no longer distinguishable.

A feeling like being choked
enters my throat.

Creeley's marital theme is expressed in the majority of poems in *For Love*, but "The Whip," "A Form of Women," "The Way," "A Marriage," and "Ballad of the Despairing Husband" capture its dilemmas with great clarity. Other poems in this large collection depict the female as more than sexual partner, but as a force or element necessary to sustain male consciousness. "The Door," among the longest and most ambitious of these poems, explores the female in her divine and archetypal aspect.

Recently, Creeley has dissolved the formalisms of his verse in order to create verse fields in book-length serial compositions, in the manner of Charles Olson and Robert Duncan. He has abandoned the structural neatness of his earlier verse, and the more fluid compositions of *Words*, *Pieces*, and *A Day Book* tend to scrutinize the fine filaments of consciousness in tiny fragments of lyric. A new book, *Away*, marks a regretful close to his second marriage and may signal an end to this long preoccupation with marriage crises. A brief pamphlet of poems in sequence entitled *Later* already shows steps of this departure with its reminiscences on childhood.

His prose work, the short fiction collected in *The Gold Diggers*, a novel *The Island*, the first half of *A Day Book*, and more recently, *Marisol*, a long commentary on the sculptor, all follow the themes of his verse. The novel closely recounts the last year of marriage to his first wife. Creeley's prose is unique in modern fiction: his use of detail is extraordinarily delicate and precise, producing an uncanny perceptiveness in his narrators. Self-absorption in *The Island* is all the more compelling as the narrator dismantles his own thinking process to inspect the deterioration jealousy causes in him. Although a highly provocative writer of prose, his poetry has had a more pervasive influence on younger writers.

In his criticism, *A Quick Graph*, and in interviews, collected in *Contexts of Poetry*, he has proved an astute chronicler of modern poetry, particularly on the work and influence of Charles Olson, with whom he lauched the movement now known as Black Mountain poetry.

—Paul Christensen

CREWS, Judson C. American. Born in Waco, Texas, 30 June 1917. Educated at La Vega High School, Waco; Baylor University, Waco, A.B. 1941, M.A. in sociology and psychology 1944, graduate work in art, 1946; Kinzinger Field School of Art, Taos, New Mexico, 1947. Served in the United States Medical Corps, 1942–44. Married Mildred Tolbert in 1947; two daughters. Graduate Assistant in Sociology, Baylor University, 1941–42. Consumer Market Researcher, Stewart Dougal and Associates, New York, 1948; Printer and Publisher, Taos *Star*, *El Crepusculo*, Taos *News*, 1948–66. Former Caseworker, El Paso County Child Welfare Unit, Texas; former Instructor in Sociology and Psychology, Wharton County Junior College, Texas. Intensive Care Unit Director, State Training School for Girls, Chillicothe, Missouri, 1973; Lecturer in Social Development Studies, University of Zambia, Lusaka. During the 1930's, 1940's, and 1950's, Editor, *Vers Libre*, *Taos*, *Motive*, *The Flying Fish*, *Suck-Egg Mule*, *The Deer and Dachshund*, *Poetry Taos*, and *The Naked Ear* magazines. Address: P.O. Box 40011, Albuquerque, New Mexico 87196, U.S.A.

PUBLICATIONS

Verse

Psalms for a Late Season. New Orleans, Iconograph Press, 1942.
No Is the Night. Privately printed, 1949.
A Poet's Breath. Privately printed, 1950(?).
Come Curse the Moon. Privately printed, 1952(?).
The Anatomy of Proserpine. Privately printed, 1955.
The Wrath Wrenched Splendor of Love. Privately printed, 1956.
The Heart in Naked Hunger. Ranches of Taos, New Mexico, Motive Book Shop, 1958.
To Wed Beneath the Sun. Privately printed, 1958(?).
A Sheaf of Christmas Verse. Washington, D.C., Three Hands, n.d.
The Ogres Who Were His Henchmen. Eureka, California, Hearse Press, 1958.
Inwade to Briney Garth. Taos, New Mexico, Este Es Press, 1960.
The Feel of Sun and Air upon Her Body. Eureka, California, Hearse Press, 1960.
A Unicorn When Needs Be. Taos, New Mexico, Este Es Press, 1963.
Hermes Past the Hour. Taos, New Mexico, Este Es Press, 1963.
Selected Poems. Cleveland, Renegade Press, 1964.
You, Mark Antony, Navigator upon the Nile. Privately printed, 1964.
Angels Fall, They Are Towers. Taos, New Mexico, Este Es Press, 1965.
Three on a Match, with Wendell B. Anderson and Cerise Farallon. Privately printed, 1966.
The Stones of Konarak. Santa Fe, New Mexico, American Poets Press, 1966.
Notions and Peoples. Cherry Valley, New York, Cherry Valley Editions, 1976.
Nolo Contendere. Houston, Wings Press, 1978.
Selected Poems. Berkeley, California, Thorpe Springs Press, 1979.

Other

The Southern Temper. Waco, Texas, Motive Book Shop, 1946.
Patocinio Barela: Taos Wood Carver, with Mildred Crews and Wendell B. Anderson. Taos, New Mexico, Taos Recordings and Publications, 1955; revised edition, 1962.

Manuscript Collections: University of Texas, Austin; University of California, Los Angeles; Yale University, New Haven, Connecticut.

Critical Study: *A Critical Analysis of Poems by a Contemporary Poet of the Avant-Garde: Judson Crews*, by Wendell B. Anderson, Rindge, New Hampshire, Franklin Pierce College, unpublished thesis, 1969.

* * *

In the poetry of Judson Crews, the imagination of a man of the Southwestern United States comes into contact with the poetic innovations of Pound, Williams, Charles Olson and Wallace Stevens. Crews's response to these innovations is original and idiosyncratic. He is something of a primitive poet, doggedly pursuing his own way. Mostly short lyrics, his poems range from simple songs to abstract meditations. Verbal experiment is used both for its own sake and as a kind of exploration into the sources of creative life.

Often Crews begins a poem with a striking, sometimes strange phrase ("No wail it went the gladsome son"), and pursues its meanings through the use of language generated by similarity of sound or by a kind of verbal inventiveness ("he sought the wicked in the middle heart/night was lonelier than a restless wing"). Many poems are brief, often zany fables that reach towards mythic realities, towards dimly grasped terrors and possibilities of courage. Language is pushed to hyperbole, even to nonsense, for the sheer sake of celebration. It is true that at times the language is too "poetic" and that the poems at times move with rhythmical monotony and a kind of glibness. The lyric extravagance allows the inclusion of much that is banal. But beyond the affectation and excess are a rambunctious kind of humor and an eager, open sense of wonder.

This humor and this wonder seem rooted in the man himself and in his region. The young Crews, wrote Henry Miller, "reminded one, because of his shaggy beard and manner of speech, of a latter-day prophet." And there is something larger than ordinary life in the energy and constant power of invention present in Crews's poetic career. Certainly his imagination is indiscriminate; but it is also prolific. And he writes with a gusto that is rare in contemporary American poetry.

—Jerry Paris

CROSSLEY-HOLLAND, Kevin (John Williams). British. Born in Mursley, Buckinghamshire, 7 February 1941. Educated at Bryanston school; St. Edmund Hall, Oxford, B.A. (honours) in English language and literature. Has two sons. Editor, Macmillan and Company, publishers, London, 1962–71. Gregory Fellow, University of Leeds, 1969–71. Talks Producer, BBC, London, 1972. Editorial Director, Victor Gollancz Ltd., publishers, London, 1972–77. Currently, English lecturer, University of Regensburg. Recipient: Arts Council award, for children's book, 1968. Agent: Deborah Rogers Ltd., 5–11 Mortimer Street, London, W1N 7RH, England.

PUBLICATIONS

Verse

On Approval. London, Outposts, 1961.
My Son. London, Turret, 1966.
Alderney: The Nunnery. London, Turret, 1968.
Norfolk Poems. London, Academy, 1970.
A Dream of a Meeting. Frensham, Surrey, Sceptre Press, 1970.
Confessional. Frensham, Surrey, Sceptre Press, 1970.
More Than I Am. London, Steam Press, 1971.
The Wake. Richmond, Surrey, Keepsake Press, 1972.
The Rain-Giver. London, Deutsch, 1972.
Petal and Stone. Knotting, Bedfordshire, Sceptre Press, 1975.
The Dream-House. London, Deutsch, 1976.

Other

Havelok the Dane (juvenile). London, Macmillan, 1964; New York, Dutton, 1965.
King Horn (juvenile). London, Macmillan, 1965; New York, Dutton, 1966.
The Green Children (juvenile). London, Macmillan, 1966; New York, Seabury Press, 1968.
The Callow Pit Coffer (juvenile). London, Macmillan, 1968; New York, Seabury Press, 1969.
Wordhoard: Anglo-Saxon Stories (juvenile), with Jill Paton Walsh. London, Macmillan, and New York, Farrar Straus, 1969.
The Pedlar of Swaffham (juvenile). London, Macmillan, 1971; New York, Seabury Press, 1972.
Pieces of Land: Journeys to Eight Islands. London, Gollancz, 1972.
The Sea-Stranger (juvenile). London, Heinemann, 1973; New York, Seabury Press, 1974.
The Fire-Brother (juvenile). London, Heinemann, and New York, Seabury Press, 1975.
Green Blades Rising: The Anglo-Saxons (juvenile). London, Deutsch, 1975; New York, Seabury Press, 1976.
The Earth-Father (juvenile). London, Heinemann, 1976.
The Wildman (juvenile). London, Deutsch, 1976.

Editor, *Winter's Tales for Children 3.* London, Macmillan, 1967.
Editor, *Running to Paradise: An Introductory Selection of the Poems of W. B. Yeats.* London, Macmillan, 1967; New York, Macmillan, 1968.
Editor, *Winter's Tales 14.* London, Macmillan, 1968.
Editor, with Patricia Beer, *New Poetry 2.* London, Arts Council, 1976.
Editor, *The Faber Book of Northern Legends.* London, Faber, 1977.

Translator, *The Battle of Maldon and Other Old English Poems.* London, Macmillan, and New York, St. Martin's Press, 1965.
Translator, *Beowulf.* London, Macmillan, and New York, Farrar Straus, 1968.
Translator, *Storm and Other Old English Riddles.* London, Macmillan, and New York, Farrar Straus, 1970.
Translator, *The Exeter Riddle Book.* London, Folio Society, 1978.

Kevin Crossley-Holland comments:

If the society reflected in Old English poetry now seems alien, many of its moods are wholly familiar, essentially English: an out-and-out heroism, a dogged refusal to surrender, a love of the sea, an enjoyment of melancholy, nostalgia. In translating it, my staple diet has been a non-syllabic four-stress line, controlled by light alliteration. There are plenty of cases, though, where I have not conformed to this pattern; my concern has been to echo rather than slavishly to imitate the originals. My diction inclines to the formal, though it certainly is less formal than that of the Anglo-Saxon poets; it seemed to me important at this time to achieve truly accessible versions of these poems, that eschewed the use of archaisms, inverted word orders, and all "poetic" language. I have not gone out of my way to avoid words that spring from Latin roots, but the emphasis has fallen naturally on words derived from Old English. My translations are, I believe, faithful by and large to the letter of the originals, but it is the mood I have been after. And if I have not caught anything of it, then I have not succeeded in my purpose.

* * *

Kevin Crossley-Holland's poetry seems to me a particularly successful example of the "middle style" written by many British poets of the post-war period. This style was basically the invention of the poets of the Movement, but subsequent practitioners have moved away from Movement tenets. They have been attracted, especially, by some of the better Georgians, notably Edward Thomas and Edmund Blunden. Blunden, in fact, supplies a happy comparison where Crossley-Holland is concerned. In both poets there are a natural decorousness and gentleness, a refusal to show off. The result can occasionally be dull, but it is always honest and often tender. In Crossley-Holland's case, the style is leavened by his interest in Anglo-Saxon poetry – he has made many translations from the Anglo-Saxon, including a new version of *Beowulf* and a selection of Anglo-Saxon riddles. Despite this affection for the heroic age, he is not a poet who willingly raises his voice. His tone can perhaps be represented by the brief poem, "A Plea," I quote here:

> This is the time to reduce the volume.
> Listen. You can still just walk
> In the diminishing peaceable-enough copse
> Through green light, amongst under-surfaces.
>
> It is time to do this. Take the leaf
> A singular oblique sunshaft lit
> And come back listening for difference.
> Sound not the screams but each distress.

—Edward Lucie-Smith

CRUZ, Victor Hernández. Puerto Rican. Born in Aguas Buenas, 6 February 1949; emigrated to the United States in 1954. Educated in public schools in New York City. Married; one son. Formerly, Editor, *Umbra* magazine, New York, Instructor, San Francisco State University, lecturer, University of California, Berkeley, and employed by San Francisco Art Commission. Address: c/o Severo Merced, Jardines Country Club, Calle 34 A.N. 10, Loiza Station, Santurce, Puerto Rico.

PUBLICATIONS

Verse

Papo Got His Gun. New York, Calle Once, 1966.
Snaps. New York, Random House, 1969.
Mainland. New York, Random House, 1973.
Doing Poetry. Berkeley, California, Other Ways, n.d.
Tropicalization. Berkeley, California, Reed Cannon and Johnson, 1976.

Other

Editor, with Herbert Kohl, *Stuff: A Collection of Poems, Visions and Imaginative Happenings from Young Writers in Schools – Opened and Closed*. Cleveland, World, 1970.

Victor Hernández Cruz comments:

I sit on a fence between two languages, thus I write in three simultaneously: Spanish as base, English as usage, and Bilingual when the occasion merits. From the mixture a totally new language emerges, an intense collision, not just of words but of attitudes. My situation is that of the emigrant which in a way is the story of our time, migration, escape from choking conditions into the cosmopolity – but always with a strange nostalgia for the original beans. Hispano-America is the result of years and years of racial and cultural mixture; my mind is creole and can fuse many unlikely things together: outer variety, inner unity; we are an experiment in communications; I am now moving towards writing more in Spanish and translation.

* * *

Some of Victor Hernández Cruz's poems exhibit the urgency of the new world poets to write stirring and highly motivated work. Others seem vehicles of the poetic-political meld to be read silently, or aloud, throughout the Third and transcending worlds. Such poetry demands validation of older new world ideals:

when they stop poems
in the mail & clap
their hands or dance to
them
when women become pregnant
by the side of poems
the strangest sounds making
the river go along.

Mr. Cruz was born in Puerto Rico. However, he grew up in New York City, and much of his work reflects a bilingual ease: "thoughts in Spanish run through/the mind/the buildings seem broken English." With a combination Latin/Anglo imagery he creates a tense warm lyricism:

Que Pasa?
Y los palos
do not feel at home anymore La luna
goes round the star dotted cielo? Let's watch
In this part of Mexico
Se habla inglish

The poetry of Cruz is filled with humorous, angry, brilliant imagery that makes him one of America's finest young poets.

—Corrine E. Bostic

CUMBERLEGE, Marcus (Crossley). British. Born in Antibes, France, 23 December 1938. Educated at Sherborne School, Dorset; St. John's College, Oxford, B.A. Married Maria Lefever (second marriage) in 1973; one daughter by previous marriage. Worked for the British Council in Lima, Peru, 1957–58, 1962–63; Advertising Executive, Ogilvy and

Mather, London, 1964–68; has taught at the Lycée International, St. Germain-en-Laye, and the universities of Lugano and Antwerp; Editor, with Scott Rollins, *Dremples*, Amsterdam, 1977; Founder, Bruges Poetry Collective, 1978. Member of the Advisory Panel, *Skrip*, Bruges. Recipient: Eric Gregory Award, 1967. Address: Westmeers 84, 8000 Bruges, Belgium.

PUBLICATIONS

Verse

Oases. London, Anvil Press Poetry, 1968.
Poems for Quena and Tabla. Oxford, Carcanet Press, 1970.
Running Towards a New Life. London, Anvil Press Poetry, 1972.
Firelines. London, Anvil Press Poetry, 1977.
The Poetry Millionaire. Swanage, Dorset, Dollar of Soul Press, 1977.
La Nuit Noire. Bruges, Manufaktuur, 1977.
XX Vriendelijke Vragen. Bruges, Ganzespel, 1977.
Bruges/Brugge, with Owen Davis. Bruges, Orion, 1978.

Marcus Cumberlege comments:

Major influences: César Vallejo, the French Symbolists, Lorca, Blake, Rilke, Eliot, Yeats. Later influences: Gautier, Pessoa, Van Ostaijen and Flemish Expressionism; Basho, Wang Wei, Rumi; Mellie Uyldert and Henri van Praag.

Earlier themes: (1) survival of "human beings" in urban society, compassion for the former while satirizing shortcomings of the latter; (2) automatic poetry attempting to situate the poet geographically and define his role as interpreter of mysteries; (3) original poetry in Spanish, French, and Dutch; translation from contemporary Latin American poets. Recent themes: Connemara and West Flanders: haiku; he remains an experimentalist in practice and his poetry is concerned with changing the quality of life at an environmental level, partly through direct co-operation with musicians and graphic artists. He is conscious of poetry's educational function, and although he treats writing as an act of personal spiritual discipline, he regards his books as an extended physical manifestation of his own personality, seeking through publication to serve, delight, and ultimately enlighten others.

* * *

Marcus Cumberlege had been writing poems for about ten years before the publication of his first major collection, *Running Towards a New Life*, though his smaller collections, *Oases* and *Poems for Quena and Tabla*, had introduced his work to the public. During that period it seemed that he was working towards the development of an individual style, experimenting with styles, ideas, forms, and the use of language to obtain different effects. The result was that *Running Towards a New Life*, covering the whole of that period, gives the impression that his work was a great deal more uneven than it had become by the time of publication.

Sometimes the influences are a little too obvious in the earlier poems – one can identify the Auden style and the Brian Patten manner, for instance – but there is a calm assurance about the latest poems in the book, which has a roughly chronological sequence. Nevertheless, whatever the style or tone, Cumberlege has always written civilised verse, work that is witty, sophisticated, and rooted in European poetry, demonstrating a wide reading of classical and modern poetry. The polished couplets of "Mural for the Country Residence of a Latin American President," with its deliberate connection with Eliot's "Prufrock" at the beginning, is still one of the best things he has done. His knowledge of technique is remarkable, but his most striking characteristic is a capacity for finding the startlingly apt image or metaphor;

when he manages to combine these qualities with a driving theme he can be quite superb. In "There Are Days" he shows his real potentiality.

Having worked his way systematically through the relatively long process of experimentation, Cumberlege appears to be reaping the benefit, if one can judge from his second major collection, *Firelines*. The volume is divided into five sections – "The Sun-Dial," "The Ram," "Harmonia's Necklace," "The Murmuring Branches," and "Errisberg" – each with its dedication, epigraph, and poetic style. He exerts a firmer control over his material, manipulates language in a more effective manner, and gives more attention to precision of statement, while demonstrating his versatility in a range of styles. The first section is more structured than the rest and more traditionally lyrical –

No South or North. I turn.
Sun breathes, warm as a dog
Chasing sheep into rock. The moon
Thrusts its slane into the bog

– but one might hazard a guess that these poems are from an earlier phase. "Oasis" and "Lord Dunsany" were, in fact, included in *Oases*, published nine years earlier. Certainly one cannot imagine that Cumberlege would not now be content with the following stanza from "Hesperides":

Sun dips a brush in darkness.
The paintbox in the west
Closing, one drop of scarlet
Splashes the robin's breast.

Still, there are some attractive pieces in which the rhyming or half-rhyming pattern lends deceptive simplicity ("Eclipse"):

The river clambers to its source,
Apples awaken as they fall.
Ghosts of the famine stalked our house
And whispered through a moonlit wall.

"The Ram" section, which links astrological symbols, Tarot concepts, with "fierced-eyed Mrs. Mop," "the Connaught moon," the "Moorish dreams of Potocki," "the Western Buddha," "The House of Opposites," and St. John, has striking phraseology here and there, but with its slightly surrealistic use of imagery is likely to be inaccessible to many readers. The most outstanding poems are all collected in the "Harmonia's Necklace" section – "The Connemara Cradle," "A Hot Chestnut," "Questions for Goldilocks," "The Perfect Man," and "Coole Park and Ballylee, Winter."

Cumberlege lived part of his childhood in Ireland and later spent some time on the West Coast of Ireland. It is not surprising, then, that this experience seems to have made a strong impact upon his poetry. "The Murmuring Branches" section contains his fine translations from the Spanish of Lorca (including "The Faithless Wife") and Carlos Bousoño, the Flemish of Herman Leys, and the French of Jacques Prévert.

—Howard Sergeant

CUNNINGHAM, J(ames) V(incent). American. Born in Cumberland, Maryland, 23 August 1911. Educated at St. Mary's College, Kansas, 1928; Stanford University, California,

A.B. 1934, Ph.D. 1945. Married 1) the poet Barbara Gibbs in 1937 (divorced, 1942); 2) Dolora Gallagher in 1945 (divorced, 1949); 3) Jessie MacGregor Campbell in 1950; one daughter. Instructor, Stanford University, 1937–45; Assistant Professor, University of Hawaii, Honolulu, 1945–46, University of Chicago, 1946–52, and University of Virginia, Charlottesville, 1952–53. Professor of English, 1953–76, and since 1976, University Professor, Brandeis University, Waltham, Massachusetts. Visiting Professor, Harvard University, Cambridge, Massachusetts, 1952, University of Washington, Seattle, 1956, Indiana University, Bloomington, 1961, University of California, Santa Barbara, 1963, and Washington University, St. Louis, 1976. Recipient: Guggenheim Fellowship, 1959, 1967; National Institute of Arts and Letters grant, 1965; National Endowment for the Arts grant, 1966; Academy of American Poets Fellowship, 1976. Address: Department of English, Brandeis University, Waltham, Massachusetts 02154, U.S.A.

PUBLICATIONS

Verse

The Helmsman. San Francisco, Colt Press, 1942.
The Judge Is Fury. New York, Swallow Press-Morrow, 1947.
Doctor Drink. Cummington, Massachusetts, Cummington Press, 1950.
Trivial, Vulgar, and Exalted: Epigrams. San Francisco, Poems in Folio, 1957.
The Exclusions of a Rhyme: Poems and Epigrams. Denver, Swallow, 1960.
To What Strangers, What Welcome: A Sequence of Short Poems. Denver, Swallow, 1964.
Some Salt: Poems and Epigrams.... Madison, Wisconsin, Perishable Press, 1967.
The Collected Poems and Epigrams of J. V. Cunningham. Chicago, Swallow Press, and London, Faber, 1971.
Selected Poems. Mount Horeb, Wisconsin, Perishable Press, 1971.

Recording: *J. V. Cunningham Reading at Stanford*, Stanford University, 1974.

Other

The Quest of the Opal: A Commentary on "The Helmsman." Denver, Swallow, 1950.
Woe or Wonder: The Emotional Effect of Shakespearean Tragedy. Denver, University of Denver Press, 1951.
Tradition and Poetic Structure: Essays in Literary History and Criticism. Denver, Swallow, 1960.
The Journal of John Cardan: Together with The Quest of the Opal and The Problem of Form. Denver, Swallow, 1964.
The Collected Essays of J. V. Cunningham. Chicago, Swallow Press, 1976.

Editor, *The Renaissance in England.* New York, Harcourt Brace, 1966.
Editor, *The Problem of Style.* New York, Fawcett, 1966.
Editor, *In Shakespeare's Day.* New York, Fawcett, 1970.

Bibliography: *A Bibliography of the Published Writings of J. V. Cunningham* by Charles Gullans, Los Angeles, University of California Library, 1973.

Critical Studies: *The Poetry of J. V. Cunningham* by Yvor Winters, Denver, Swallow, 1961; *Connoisseurs of Chaos* by Denis Donoghue, New York, Macmillan, 1965; "The Poetry of J. V. Cunningham" by Patrick Cosgrave, in *Spectator* (London) 23 October 1971; "The Collected Poems and Epigrams" by John Hollander, in *New York Times Book Review*, 21 November 1971; "A Location of J. V. Cunningham" by Hayden Carruth, in *Michigan*

Quarterly Review (Ann Arbor), Spring 1972; "The Collected Essays" by Denis Donoghue, in *New York Times Book Review*, 7 August 1977; "The Poetry of J. V. Cunningham" by Robert Pinsky, in *New Republic* (Washington, D.C.), 28 January 1978.

J. V. Cunningham comments:

I have a prejudice for brevity.

* * *

In *The Quest of the Opal* J. V. Cunningham comments that the later poems in his first book, *The Helmsman*, "were direct statements of something he had to say, given form and definitiveness by the technique of verse." Throughout his career, especially when he is writing in a less serious vein, he achieves a finely chiseled definitiveness – indeed a lapidary style – that reminds us that light verse need not be lightweight. Cunningham writes effectively in the tradition of the Greek Anthology or of the Latin and Renaissance epigrammatists. Take, for example, his exuberant portrayal of a young man's sexual awakening: "*Arms and the man I sing*, and sing for joy,/Who was last year all elbows and a boy." This ear-pleasing heroic couplet – Pope has few things finer – represents the poet at his epigrammatic best: two perfectly crafted decasyllables, the opening trochaic reversal stressing the key word "arms," the masterful handling of stress and pause in the second highlighting the antithetical "elbows." Also, the witty epic allusion suggests the consuming subjective importance of a first love experience, and at the same time slyly hints that to the rest of the world it may not be of quite such heroic proportions. Note too how the obvious enjoyment of linguistic manipulation for its own sake serves as an additional device for projecting the new sophistication of a boy recently become a man.

In his other 99 or so epigrams Cunningham is generally more cynical, sardonic, satirical, or scurrilous than in "*Arms and the man*": "Mistress of scenes, good-by. Your maidenhead/ Was fitter for the couch than for the bed," or "I married in my youth a wife./She was my own, my very first./She gave the best years of her life./I hope nobody gets the worst." But counter this blast at domestic bliss with his delightfully complimentary lyric to his wife, "The Metaphysical Amorist."

Actually, Cunningham's lyric impulse has something of the compression of the epigram, so that one or two lines – especially the first – frequently capsulize the lyric heart of a poem. He may wander thereafter into the aridity that sometimes accompanies an overemphasis on statement in poetry, or into unearned desolation, or into a hard-boiled stance that is finally too limited to engage our full sympathy. But back to first lines: "I drive Westward. Tumble and loco weed/Persist," "On either side of the white line," "In a few days now when two memories meet," "You have here no otherness,/Unadressed [sic] correspondent," "The soft lights, the companionship, the beers." These are from the first five poems of his most ambitious venture, the sequence *To What Strangers, What Welcome*. Cunningham's collected poems and epigrams run to only 142 pages, and his venture into the genre of the modern lyric sequence is correspondingly minimal – 15 short poems. (Compare *The Waste Land* or Yeats's Irish civil war sequences, much less *Song of Myself* or *The Cantos*.) At the heart of this little tale of love recaptured and lost by the Pacific is a bleakness familiar from the earlier "Montana Pastoral," where the poet finds "no images of pastoral will,/But fear, thirst, hunger, and this huddled chill," and "Horoscope," where he sees "Neither Venus nor Mars" in his heaven. In *To What Strangers* a humiliated and lonely sensibility is presented more nakedly:

> We neither give nor receive:
> The unfinishable drink
> Left on the table, the sleep
> Alcoholic and final
> In the mute exile of time.

On the other hand, the sequence also projects moments of considerably higher morale – "Innocent to innocent,/One asked, What is perfect love," "Hemming a summer dress as the tide/Turns at the right time" – and a cool, defining clarity: "Good is what we can do with evil," "A premise of identity/Where the lost hurries to be lost." Such evocative and incisive lines, together with his consistently high craftsmanship and sharp wit, are the hallmark of Cunningham's best work.

—Sally M. Gall

CURNOW, Allen. New Zealander. Born in Timaru, 17 June 1911. Educated at Christchurch Boys' High School, 1924–28; University of Canterbury, 1929–30, University of Auckland, 1931–38, B.A. 1938; St. John's College (Anglican theological), Auckland, 1931–33. Married 1) Elizabeth J. LeCren in 1936, three children; 2) Jennifer Mary Tole in 1965. Cadet Journalist, *Sun*, Christchurch, 1929–30; Reporter and Sub-Editor, 1935–48, and Dramatic Critic, 1945–47, *The Press*, Christchurch; Member of the News and Sub-Editorial Staff, *News Chronicle*, London, 1949. Lecturer in English, 1951–66, and Associate Professor of English, 1967–76, University of Auckland. Recipient: New Zealand State Literary Fund travel award, 1949; Carnegie grant, 1950; New Zealand University Research Committee grant, 1957, 1966; Jessie Mackay Memorial Prize, 1957, 1962; Institute of Contemporary Arts Fellowship, Washington, D.C., 1961; Whittall Fund award, Library of Congress, 1966. Litt.D.: University of Auckland, 1966. Address: 62 Tohunga Crescent, Parnell, Auckland 1, New Zealand.

PUBLICATIONS

Verse

Valley of Decision. Auckland, University College Press, 1933.
Three Poems. Christchurch, Caxton Press, 1935.
Another Argo, with Denis Glover and A. R. D. Fairburn. Christchurch, Caxton Press, 1935.
Enemies: Poems 1934–36. Christchurch, Caxton Press, 1937.
Not in Narrow Seas. Christchurch, Caxton Press, 1939.
A Present for Hitler and Other Verses (as Whim-Wham). Christchurch, Caxton Press, 1940.
Recent Poems, with others. Christchurch, Caxton Press, 1941.
Island and Time. Christchurch, Caxton Press, 1941.
Verses, 1941–42 (as Whim-Wham). Christchurch, Caxton Press, 1942.
Verses 1943 (as Whim-Wham). Wellington, Progressive, 1943(?).
Sailing or Drowning. Wellington, Progressive, 1943.
Jack Without Water. Christchurch, Caxton Press, 1946.
At Dead Low Water, and Sonnets. Christchurch, Caxton Press, 1949.
Poems 1947–57. Wellington, Mermaid Press, 1957.
The Hucksters and the University. Auckland, Pilgrim Press, 1957.
Mr. Huckster of 1958. Auckland, Pilgrim Press, 1958.
The Best of Whim-Wham. Hamilton, Paul's Book Arcade, 1959.
A Small Room with Large Windows: Selected Poems. Wellington and London, Oxford University Press, 1962.

Trees, Effigies, Moving Objects: A Sequence of Poems. Wellington, Catspaw Press, 1972.
An Abominable Temper and Other Poems. Wellington, Catspaw Press, 1973.
Collected Poems 1933–73. Wellington, Reed, 1974.
An Incorrigible Music: A Sequence of Poems. Auckland, Auckland University Press-Oxford University Press, 1979.

Plays

The Axe: A Verse Tragedy (produced Christchurch, 1948). Christchurch, Caxton Press, 1949.
Moon Section (produced Auckland, 1959).
The Overseas Expert (broadcast, 1961). Included in *Four Plays*, 1972.
Doctor Pom (produced Auckland, 1964).
The Duke's Miracle (broadcast, 1967). Included in *Four Plays*, 1972.
Resident of Nowhere (broadcast, 1969). Included in *Four Plays*, 1972.
Four Plays (includes *The Axe*, *The Overseas Expert*, *The Duke's Miracle*, and *Resident of Nowhere).* Wellington, Reed, 1972.

Radio Plays: *The Overseas Expert*, 1961; *The Duke's Miracle*, 1967; *Resident of Nowhere*, 1969.

Other

Editor, *A Book of New Zealand Verse 1923–45.* Christchurch, Caxton Press, 1945; revised edition, 1951.
Editor, *The Penguin Book of New Zealand Verse.* London, Penguin, 1960.

Critical Studies: "Allen Curnow's Poetry (Notes Towards a Criticism)" by C. K. Stead, in *Landfall* (Christchurch), March 1963; "Conversation with Allen Curnow: Interview by MacDonald P. Jackson," in *Islands* (Auckland), Winter 1973; "Allen Curnow: Forty Years of Poems" by Terry Sturm, in *Islands* (Auckland), Autumn 1975.

Allen Curnow comments:

I don't know of any school I would care to belong to. New Zealand is difficult enough for me.

I don't know anything about "themes," "subjects," etc., only that "occasions" for poems or plays crop up, as one feels a need (intermittently) to touch something, to check on its existence or one's own.

I don't know about influences either, but sometimes think of Yeats's dictum, "All that is personal soon rots; it must be packed in ice or salt. Ancient salt is best packing." This is bound to be misinterpreted. I would like to be a poet writing verse so radically old that it looks radically new. I would have to be a much better poet than I am.

Twenty years ago I wrote a good few poems "about" New Zealand, as much to find out what I was, as what it was. Worry about one's country is one of the major human worries; of course, one can think of "universality" and worry about that instead, but it's an arid ground for poetry. One learns to live with the oddity of one's country, like Byron's lame foot or Wallace Stevens's insurance company, and these "universal" poems record the learning-process. Poetry won't bear too much accidental stuff, but must have some. Warning: do not exceed the stated dose.

* * *

Allen Curnow has been a central figure in modern New Zealand poetry. His *A Book of New Zealand Verse 1923–1945*, a selection of poems supported by an impressive introduction, made apparent for the first time that New Zealand's modern poets had produced the beginnings of a distinct tradition. The period of colonial literature was over – this was Curnow's point, demonstrated by the fact that the poets were no longer romanticising their environment with an eye to, or with the eyes of, English readers, but coming to terms with it as it was. Curnow's argument was further supported by an enlargement of his anthology in 1951, and extended in his 1960 *Penguin Book of New Zealand Verse*.

The critical writing went hand in hand with the writing of his poetry, contributing to the development of his subject matter, which had always, however personal its origins, reached towards public statement. In the 1930's, while still finding his voice, he wrote political and social satire. But his characteristic middle style as he found it in the 1940's, was one of ironic perplexity, brooding over one or another distinctly New Zealand scene or historical event, making its detail sharply present to the senses, yet working at it verbally until its particulars rendered up some broader significance. A sonnet in memory of a cousin killed in North Africa begins: "Weeping for bones in Africa, I turn/Our youth over like a dead bird in my hand." By the end, the dead soldier has assumed, not heroic, but national proportions:

> But O if your blood's tongued it must recite
>
> South Island feats, those tall, snow-country tales
> Among incredulous Tunisian hills.

A recording of a Beethoven quartet becomes "Your 'innermost Beethoven' in the uttermost isles." The skeleton of the extinct moa "on iron crutches" in a museum suggests a vision of the New Zealand poet: "Not I, some child, born in a marvellous year/Will learn the trick of standing upright here." Even in his more difficult poems Curnow's gift for dazzling phrase arrests and holds attention. His lines have the ring of major statement: "Small gods in shawls of bark, blind, numb and deaf,/But buoyant, eastward, in the blaze of surf."

In poems written, most of them, in the mid-1950's, very different occasions or "subjects" seem to have led Curnow consistently to the same preoccupation, weighing objective against subjective, real against ideal. In the real – the present time and place – and in that alone, our salvation, or more simply our satisfaction, lies. It is the pursuit of the ideal that will damn us. The self is discovered and defined only as it confronts what exists *out there*:

> A kingfisher's naked arc alight
> Upon a dead stick in the mud
> A scarlet geranium wild on a wet bank
> A man stepping it out in the distance
> With a dog and a bag.

In the 1950's Curnow's anthologies brought him into conflict with a younger generation of poets. Then (the two facts are not necessarily connected) for fifteen years from 1957, he published almost no new poems. In 1972 (the year of James K. Baxter's death) came Curnow's sequence *Trees, Effigies, Moving Objects*, which put him right back into the centre of new developments in New Zealand poetry. This was followed by a less striking collection, *An Abominable Temper*, in 1973; and in 1979 by the extraordinary and powerful sequence, *An Incorrigible Music*. In this latter book Curnow juxtaposes images of coastal New Zealand with modern urban Italy, and a Borgia murder with that (exactly 500 years later) of the Italian statesman Aldo Moro. The mind and the poetic skills are cast out wide to bring together these various realities, each of them a means of confronting death in a new way. Curnow has never written better.

—C. K. Stead

CURREY, R(alph) N(ixon). British. Born in Mafeking, South Africa, 14 December 1907. Educated in South Africa; Kingswood School, Bath; Wadham College, Oxford, 1927–30, M.A. (honours) in modern history 1930. War Service, 1941–46: Commissioned with the Royal Artillery, Staff Major after 1945, writing and editing Army Bureau of Current Affairs publications. Married the playwright Stella Martin Currey in 1932; two sons. Senior English Master, 1946–72, and Senior Master for Arts Subjects, 1964–72, Royal Grammar School, Colchester, Essex. Since 1967, President of the Suffolk Poetry Society, Ipswich. Recipient: Viceroy's Prize, 1945; South African Poetry Prize, 1959. Fellow, Royal Society of Literature, 1970. Address: 3 Beverley Road, Colchester, Essex CO3 3NG, England.

PUBLICATIONS

Verse

Tiresias and Other Poems. London, Oxford University Press, 1940.
This Other Planet. London, Routledge, 1945.
Indian Landscape: A Book of Descriptive Poems. London, Routledge, 1947.
The Africa We Knew. Cape Town, David Philip, 1973.

Plays

Radio Plays: *Between Two Worlds*, 1948; *Early Morning in Vaaldorp*, 1961.

Other

Poets of the 1939–1945 War. London, Longman, 1960; revised edition, 1967.

Editor, with R. V. Gibson, *Poems from India by Members of the Forces.* Bombay, Oxford University Press, 1945; London, Oxford University Press, 1946.
Editor, *Letters and Other Writings of a Natal Sheriff: Thomas Phipson, 1815–1876.* Cape Town and London, Oxford University Press, 1968.

Translator, *Formal Spring: French Renaissance Poems of Charles d'Orléans and Others.* London, Oxford University Press, 1950.

Critical Studies: *A Critical Survey of South African Poetry in English* by G. M. Miller and Howard Sergeant, Cape Town, Balkema, 1957; by W. G. Saunders, in *South African Poetry: A Critical Anthology*, edited by D. R. Beeton and W. D. Maxwell-Mahon, Pretoria, University of South Africa Press, 1966.

R. N. Currey comments:

It takes a lifetime to discover what kind of poet one is. I appear to be an occasional poet, having written much more at some periods of my life than at others.

In the war I found myself placed, quite unprepared by any previous technical training, in a highly technical branch of warfare, in which destruction was carried out impersonally at a distance. I received from this experience an intense impression of what I take to be the likely warfare of the future, in which it will require a strong effort of imagination on the part of the killer to realize what he is doing. I wrote of this in *This Other Planet* and in *Between Two Worlds*, and am intrigued to find that some of the poems in which I tried to express my response to this are now being anthologized more often than the conventional war poems that found more favour at the time.

When I was posted to India, I found there, still going on, the Middle Ages I had read about when studying History at Oxford. Indians still went on pilgrimage, as people did in the England of Chaucer's time, and my anti-aircraft gunners, who had the same names as the gods in the Indian temples, belonged to the same pre-industrial world. The excitement of this theme is still with me, and I hope to write about it again. Translating French poems, of the Renaissance and Middle Ages, has also given me an entry into those pre-industrial times; and I am glad to find that these poems, too, have the vitality that gets them reprinted many years after first being published.

I have written other topographical poems about places of special importance to me. South Africa, where I spent my boyhood, and where I have a long family connexion, has underlined contrasts and aroused tensions of the sort that produce poetry. *The Africa We Knew* is a book of South African poems, most of which have been printed and broadcast both in England and in South Africa. I recently edited the letters of a great-grandfather who went to South Africa in 1849, and found much that called for a poetical rather than a historical treatment. This I hope to give it at some time. Meanwhile I have completed a biographical study of a pioneer, Thomas Vinnicombe (1854–1932) who kept a *verse* account of a lifetime spent in many of the places where South African history was made; he found verse (for mnemonic reasons) more suitable to a life often spent on horseback and in covered waggons where writing is often impracticable.

I find that I have to go to a new country to discover the one in which I live, to move for a while into a different period in order to come to terms with the present. Both North Africa and the Western United States have given me new viewpoints from which to see the imperial world in which I grew up.

I have published poems, at different times in my life, in different countries, mainly in England, but also in the United States, India, South Africa and Ireland. For many years I have done my writing and broadcasting alongside teaching English and running an English Department at a grammar school, but have now retired to do more writing. There is a great deal that I want to do.

* * *

T. S. Eliot said of R. N. Currey that he was the best war-poet, in the precise sense of the word, that World War II produced. This was high praise since between 1939 and 1945 some very distinguished verse appeared in the little reviews and the numerous anthologies of the period. But the war poems, collected in his volume *This Other Planet*, reconsidered after nearly a quarter of a century, seem still to hold the essence of their period, in what was felt and thought by those who were the *dramatis personae* of "this damned unnatural sort of war," where so much was remote and impersonal. Like the enemy pilot:

To us he is no more than a machine
Shown on an instrument; what can he mean
In human terms? – a man, somebody's son,
Proud of his skill; compact of flesh and bone,
Fragile as Icarus – and our desire
To see that damned machine come down on fire.

It was as a war poet that Currey really established his reputation, and it is significant that he was chosen by the British Council to write their publication *Poets of the 1939–1945 War*. Nevertheless, it is largely as a South African poet that he has developed, finding his themes in, and feeding his imagination on, the physical Africa that he knew as a boy and on the history of men and things in that complicated but fascinating Eur-African world with its odd duality: "Eating our Christmas pudding beneath the grace/Of feminine willows on the vivid grass" or "My father, all that tawny homeward run,/Remembering snow as I remember sun."

Although Currey has lived most of his adult life in Britain, he goes home from time to time, and his long work, *Early Morning in Vaaldorp*, successfully broadcast by the BBC, is in a sense of a tribute to his South African *oeuvres*, "which could not have been written if I had not come from a long South African tradition and spent most of my impressionable years there." North Africa, particularly Morocco, has been responsible for other impressive poems by Currey, who claims to be able to see the Southern Cross from both ends of the Dark Continent, a kind of unifying light in his work. India, too, where much of his war was spent, makes a further link in this chain of poetic topography.

Some of his most memorable poems, of love particularly, have a lyric poignancy that, devoid of any particular context of time or place, achieves a universality of appeal. Such is his beautifully constructed "Song," revealing how truth emerges only from the tug-of-war of contrasts:

> There is no joy in water apart from the sun,
> There is no beauty not emphasized by death,
> No meaning in home if exile were unknown;
> A man who lives in a thermostat lives beneath
> A bell of glass alone with the smell of death.

In such poems as these, Currey reveals himself as a poet of considerable artistry, taking infinite pains with his verse-making to derive the maximum impact from word or image, an observer of life or landscape with very particular vision.

—Roy Macnab

DALE, Peter (John). British. Born in Addlestone, Surrey, 21 August 1938. Educated at Strode's School, Egham, Surrey; St. Peter's College, Oxford, 1960–63, B.A. (honours) in English 1963. Married Pauline Strouvelle in 1963; two children. English Master, 1965–71, and Head of English, 1971–72, Glastonbury High School, Sutton, Surrey. Since 1972, Head of English, Hinchley Wood School, Esher, Surrey. Since 1971, Associate Editor, *Agenda* magazine, London. Recipient: Arts Council bursary, 1969. Agent: David Higham Associates, 5–8 Lower John Street, Golden Square, London W1R 3PE. Address: 10 Selwood Road, Sutton, Surrey, England.

PUBLICATIONS

Verse

Nerve. Privately printed, 1959.
Walk from the House. Oxford, Fantasy Press, 1962.
The Storms. London, Macmillan, and Chester Springs, Pennsylvania, Dufour, 1968.
Mortal Fire. London, Macmillan, and Chester Springs, Pennsylvania, Dufour, 1970; revised edition, London, Agenda, and Athens, Ohio University Press, 1976.
Cross Channel. Sutton, Surrey, Hippopotamus Press, 1977.
One Another: A Sonnet Sequence. London, Agenda, 1978.

Other

Translator, *The Legacy and Other Poems of François Villon.* London, Agenda, 1971; revised edition, as *The Legacy, The Testament, and Other Poems*, London, Macmillan, and New York, St. Martin's Press, 1973.

Translator, *The Seasons of Cankam.* London, Agenda, 1974.
Translator, *Selected Poems of Villon.* London, Penguin, 1978.

Critical Studies: "Notes on the Poetry of Peter Dale" by William Cookson, in *Agenda* (London), viii, 3–4, 1970; "The Poetry of Peter Dale" by Terry Eagleton, in *Agenda* (London), xiii, 3, 1975; "Father's Story" by Donald Davie, in *The Listener* (London), October 1976; "The Poetry of Ordinariness," in *Agenda* (London), xiv, 4–xv, 1, 1977, and "Fathers and Sons: Peter Dale's *Mortal Fire*," in *Southern Review* (Baton Rouge, Louisiana), Winter 1979, both by William Bedford.

Peter Dale comments:

Reason tells one when a phase of the work is finished; the publishing history of my work shows how often reason had reckoned wrong – as would the variorum of Auden or Lowell's work. So I cannot really make about my work any statement which would be much use. I have no confidence that I should agree with it fully by the time this volume is published. It would not be wise to try to guess what one's skills and learnings were, and hazardous to listen too intently to what critics may assert. It is therefore foolish to prognosticate. Skills one has mastered are no longer necessarily relevant to the making of new poems and to rationalise about them and make them self-conscious could hinder and ossify one's approach and progress. (I've just finished a sonnet-sequence and wasted a year trying to avoid the form.) Yet I would not like to imply that poetry is entirely intuitive or instinctive. Coleridge's set of paired opposites best describes it; the creative and critical faculties are concurrent in composition. The poems will have to speak for themselves.

* * *

Peter Dale took as epigraph to his first hardback collection, *The Storms*, a line of William Blake, "The most sublime act is to set another before you." He is obsessed with two things in his poetry: the problem of suffering and the problem of "knowing" another person. The first is worked out in various poems based on jobs in hospitals; the second in love poems and friendship poems. His early booklet, *Walk from the House*, criticizes the Christian view: "I would erect suffering into a belief...." This idealisation is rejected and other poems in that book and *The Storms* set suffering sometimes savagely in its animal/human context. "Just Visiting" represents the human difficulties in attending the sick:

> And some of them have indolent golden hair.
> Over there a woman is dying, the line
> of used laughter hung in bands on the lean
> bones. And what you say I cannot hear.

In this context, the poetry is more and more concerned with the uselessness of compassion to alleviate pain, to "know" another's suffering. "Passing the Gates" and "Patient in a Ward" are two poems that analyse this.

The problem of knowing another person runs through the same books and is perhaps best summed up in "The Storms" that deals with a painter and writer who tried to "record" the same tree and their troubled friendship. The theme occurs more fully in "Having No Alternative" (*Mortal Fire*), where drug addiction strains a friendship to breaking point. The final poem in the sequence, "Thinking of Writing a Letter," ends with a sense of loneliness, distances, and desolation which is deeply moving.

Old themes, but what is fresh is the obsessive power of the poems, their direct yet subtle unfolding of the situations. Peter Dale is a realist and portrays the world, recognisable and tragic. There are a hardness and honesty about his poetry which preclude sentimentality. Work which is rootedly personal and yet never runs the risk of embarrassing the reader is rare. What T. S. Eliot has called "private experience at its greatest intensity becoming universal" seems an appropriate description. Much of this power comes from the quiet, concealed control of technique. The central prosodic quality of these poems is freedom within form. The forms range from traditional stanzas through experiments with various rhyme techniques to a free verse which owes little to Pound, Eliot, or Williams. And always there is the individual tone of a voice talking quietly with a great force of controlled emotion behind the words, as in "Unaddressed Letter":

> Now it is autumn ... And rain ... Big drops you can trace.
> I notice how one drop's enough to tear
> an amber leaf out of the brittle trees.
> I suppose much the same happened last year,
> but it is now I notice watching a caricature
> of your face talking to myself as I stare
> out of the window where the puddles stir.

Along with the range of forms goes a range of approach and tone. Dale can manage dramatic monologue with great variety: there is the detached irony of "Afternoon Operating List" – early version in *Walk from the House* – and the powerful involvement of "It Is Finished" (*Mortal Fire*). There are the humorous "Obtainable at All Good Herbalists," the quiet gratitude of "Dedication," and the Imagist concision of "Last Respects."

The directness of the finest of Peter Dale's poems often veils a more subtle undercurrent to the feeling and the thought. They stand the acid tests that, once read, they remain in the mind, and, reread, they do not bore, but gain in strength. The blurb of *The Storms* suggests that while the poems are haunting, there are no memorable lines. This is partly due to method; the shifting caesuras and constant overrunning of lines prevent this. But what is memorable is the clarity and delicacy of the imagery: "and underwings extend wood-ember white," or "Across the playing fields the amber leaves/shine oldgold through the frost," or "Your presence, love,/like the underlight of trees/within a wood."

The revised and much improved 1976 edition of *Mortal Fire*, which is really a selected poems, contains a powerful sequence of love poems, "The Going," which further explores, in a highly rhythmic and controlled free verse, the problem of knowing another person I've already referred to. Spare and uncluttered by rhetoric, these lyrics are informed by a new richness of metaphor: "Scotch fir, the trunk/staked in the still pools of its boughs/on the old hill." "The Going" has a simplicity akin to Dale's version from the Tamil, *The Seasons of Cankam*, a beautiful little book, which has qualities in common with Pound's translations from the Chinese.

Since *Mortal Fire* Dale has further widened his scope by translating almost the complete works of François Villon. This is a strict metrical translation which faithfully reproduces the rhyme schemes of the original – an incredibly difficult task in English. By this method, Dale has recreated the spirit of Villon with sometimes electric energy. He has written, in my opinion, the finest English Villon we are likely to get – certainly no other version has expressed with such power the humour, word-play, and swift changes of tone of the French together with its elegiac lyricism. The difference between Dale's Villon and his own poetry is a good measure of the breadth and versatility of his writing.

Dale's most recent work, *One Another*, is a sequence of 62 sonnets. Tracing the relationship of a man and woman through many years, these are poems to be lived with and experienced slowly: the images interweave and shed light on each other in a complex pattern, so that each rereading gives a sense of discovery. Possessing the truth of the imagination, the most moving sonnets are the final group, which express the man's memories and responses to the woman's death: "Now, love, you are the north/my memory steers from, late, so very late."

Peter Dale has probably produced a greater variety and extent of work which will endure than other poets of his generation. Undeflected by fashions and influences, his poetry is instantly recognisable. The loudest voices soon grow hoarse.

—William Cookson

DALLAS, Ruth. Pseudonym for Ruth Mumford. New Zealander. Born in Invercargill, New Zealand, 29 September 1919. Recipient: New Zealand Literary Fund Achievement Award, 1962; Robert Burns Fellowship, University of Otago, 1968; New Zealand Book Award, 1977; Buckland Literary Award, 1979. Litt.D.: University of Otago, Dunedin, 1978. Address: 448 Leith Street, Dunedin, New Zealand.

PUBLICATIONS

Verse

Country Road and Other Poems 1947–52. Christchurch, Caxton Press, 1953.
The Turning Wheel. Christchurch, Caxton Press, 1961.
Experiment in Form. Dunedin, Otago University Bibliography Room, 1964.
Day Book: Poems of a Year. Christchurch, Caxton Press, 1966.
Shadow Show. Christchurch, Caxton Press, 1968.
Walking on the Snow. Christchurch, Caxton Press, 1976.
Songs for a Guitar and Other Songs, edited by Charles Brasch. Dunedin, University of Otago Press, 1976.

Other

Sawmilling Yesterday. Wellington, School Publications, 1958.
The Children in the Bush (juvenile). London, Methuen, 1969.
Ragamuffin Scarecrow (juvenile). Dunedin, Otago University Bibliography Room, 1969.
A Dog Called Wig (juvenile). London, Methuen, 1970.
The Wild Boy in the Bush (juvenile). London, Methuen, 1971.
The Big Flood in the Bush (juvenile). London, Methuen, 1972; New York, Scholastic, n.d.
The House on the Cliffs (juvenile). London, Methuen, 1975.
Shining Rivers (juvenile). London, Methuen, 1979.

Manuscript Collection: Hocken Library, University of Otago, Dunedin.

Critical Studies: by James Bertram, in *Landfall 29* and *62* (Christchurch), March 1954 and June 1962; Introduction by Charles Brasch to *Songs for a Guitar*, 1976; "The Rhythm of Change: Comments on the Work of Ruth Dallas" by John Gibbs, in *Pilgrims* (Dunedin), iii, 1–2, 1978.

Ruth Dallas comments:

I am sometimes rather frowningly called a "nature poet"; but I have never lived in a large city and been separated from the life of the earth and the coming up and going down of the sun in unpolluted skies; so I take my imagery where I find it. I have tried to keep in the forefront of my mind my position in space and time; I want never to forget that I am on a remote small planet in space, and never to forget that I am on it at present and must soon leave. And who is to say that I am to write 20th-century poetry, or any other kind of poetry? It is chance that I was born in the 20th century and not the 10th, and chance that I was born in New Zealand and not Scandinavia or China. I care nothing for fashion in poetry and think a poem should be as free as one of the far-ranging seabirds I have watched by the hour flying in storm and calm about the coasts of New Zealand. A bird is not always flying; when it is still it is very still; but you know what it can do. Perhaps for this reason I have been attracted to the ancient meditative poems of the Chinese and Japanese, who used words with as much thought as they used the brush-strokes from which their poems are hardly separable. I, too, like to use words sparingly, and to make them carry as many overtones as possible, but all should seem spontaneous. A poem is a human utterance, like dance and song, or an involuntary cry. What would please me most would be to find that my poems appeared effortless, however hard I work on them. But if I fail, it is difficult to believe that it matters. Poetry runs in our veins, and over the centuries will flower now here, now there. If it does not come from my pen it will come from another's.

* * *

Ruth Dallas first became known as a regional poet, a meditative recorder of rural life and incident in Southland, the lonely province at the bottom of New Zealand that looks inland to small farms, mountain lakes, and brooding beech-forests, and south to Antarctica. This is hard country (Central Otago concentrates wilderness, fruitlands, and climatic extremes), and a girl growing up in intellectual isolation, threatened with blindness and with an ailing mother to care for, had to develop her own inner discipline and self-reliance. The result was a lyrical poetry of plain statement and diction, responsive to the play of natural and historical forces on human lives: *Country Road* has several poems ("Milking Before Dawn," "Grandmother and Child," "The World's Centre") that soon became stock New Zealand anthology pieces, and Ruth Dallas was conveniently typed as a nature poet with a limited range.

Eight years later, however, *The Turning Wheel* revealed a more restless and capacious mind. The title-sequence is still concerned with seasonal growth and change, but the "Letter to a Chinese Poet" (Po Chü-I) is a much more ambitious sequence in which local and personal material is assimilated into a cultural and metaphysical synthesis of real power and intensity. An autobiographical essay, "Beginnings" (*Landfall*, December 1965), describes the independent reading which led to a new interest in Buddhist influences in Indian, Chinese, and Japanese literature: "Through my lack of formal, dogmatic education, there were no walls to break down, and I was able to pass as freely into one culture as into another." Ruth Dallas's first writing in Invercargill had been encouraged by the critic and editor M. H. Holcroft; when she moved to Dunedin she began a long association with the poet Charles Brasch in the editing of *Landfall* which is clearly traceable in the development of her thought. It would be misleading to describe her as a philosophical poet; she is no system-maker, her best work remains concentrated in short lyrical forms. But like Ruth Pitter, perhaps, Ruth Dallas has produced a considerable body of lyrical work, often experimental in shape and texture and apparently purely decorative or musical, which carries a gravity of thought and perception quite disproportionate to its limited compass.

During the 1970's, Ruth Dallas had some international success with her stories for children, and must now be considered a creative prose-writer as well as a poet. Yet her verse volume *Walking in the Snow* won the New Zealand Book Award for Poetry in 1977, and there is evidence of a steadily widening appreciation of her distinctive lyrical achievement. She is one of the most independent and unfashionable of New Zealand writers; but her purity of diction and clear singing note seem likely to preserve her work when more aggressively modern verse is forgotten. She has no doubts about what she is striving for – the unassuming mastery of a Japanese jar glimpsed in a pottery film: "The jar was uneven, casual, easy, nonchalant; it seemed almost accidental, but was not. That's how I should like my finished work to appear."

—James Bertram

DANA, Robert (Patrick). American. Born in Allston, Massachusetts, 2 June 1929. Educated at Drake University, Des Moines, Iowa, B.A. 1951; University of Iowa, Iowa City, M.A. 1953. Served as a radioman in the United States Navy, 1946–48. Married Mary Kowalke in 1951; two daughters and one son. Instructor in English and Journalism, 1954–58, Assistant Professor, 1958–62, Associate Professor, 1962–68, and since 1968, Professor of English, Cornell College, Mt. Vernon, Iowa. Editor, Hillside Press, 1957–67, and *The North American Review*, 1964–68, Mt. Vernon, Iowa. Recipient: Danforth grant, 1959; Rinehart Foundation Fellowship, 1960; Ford-ACM grant, 1966. Address: R.R. 1, Box 99, Solon, Iowa 52333, U.S.A.

PUBLICATIONS

Verse

My Glass Brother and Other Poems. Iowa City, Constance Press, 1957.
The Dark Flags of Waking. Iowa City, Qara Press, 1964.
Journeys from the Skin: A Poem in Two Parts. Iowa City, Hundred Pound Press, 1966.
Some Versions of Silence: Poems. New York, Norton, 1967.
The Power of the Visible. Chicago, Swallow Press, 1971.
The Watergate Elegy. Chicago, Wine Press, 1973.
Tryptych. Chicago, Wine Press, 1974.
In a Fugitive Season. Athens, Ohio, Swallow Press, 1978.

Bibliography: *Voyages to the Inland Sea III*, edited by John Judson, La Crosse, University of Wisconsin Press, 1973.

Critical Study: "A World That Comes Apart like a Surprise" by Anselm Hollo, in *New Letters* (Kansas City, Missouri), Summer 1973.

Robert Dana comments:

I see myself as a poet – I don't believe in poets as prophets, or priests, or even as people of superior intelligence and feeling. Though I'm sure I once did and once in a while still do. Ultimately, I think, I believe what Auden and Cunningham have believed before me – that the poet's only magic is with words. He begins life with a natural gift for handling them and hearing them. He loves them for their sounds, their taste, their soft or their steel feel. And for their enduring strangeness. Each word has, for him, its own perfect story.

Much later, when the poet begins to develop a style, he comes to recognize that style is not just a way of saying things but a way of seeing things. And seeing them with the whole being at once. Poetry is felt thought, Eliot once said. And so it is. But being both at once, it is neither. A poem is an experience of a total kind in which the transitory in our existence passes into permanence.

* * *

Robert Dana crafts in irony the perishing world as it becomes part of his inner-life, charting this country's taste for concrete in images "Unlikely as Chicago," the American view of nature: "Pigs blister the hillside .../Morning may strike us anywhere."

Separate, but not separated from that, as in a never-consummated divorce, Dana looks for balance in another direction, towards the T'ang poets he translates or to

> The grace of simple food ...
> ... the table wooden as the loneliness of plain fact

And bread for the moon
the heart's small loaf.

Sometimes the tension between these worlds is manifest in his silences, sometimes it's in the "zag zag zag of sodium lamps/blue across the causeways," sometimes it's in the precision of an elegant image. His technical skill carries it through a range of modern poetic strategies.

In Pound's terms, Robert Dana is a master rather than an inventor, moving through a variety of techniques and images, frequently using them better than their originators. His first book contains a tense world, sparse, attenuated details of vivid intensity, controlled word-by-word, his technique at its best nearly equal to Creeley's at *his* best. Dana works primarily with resonances, articulate matter accusing itself across silences.

In his second book, the poetry becomes metamorphic, turns toward dreams:

And I am driving into my own sleep
of white chickens
past barnyard harvests of junked cars
the wind slumps through the empty eyes of cows.

The landscape begins to flash surrealistically, Los Angeles slumps into the ocean after nine days rain, Kennedy is assassinated again, "razors could not cut the rain from the glass." Without reveling in vatic zeal or surreal petulance, however, the poet "whistles under the true sky of his troubles/walking slowly/inside himself," realizing that regardless of the emotions that flood him, he gains only a measured wisdom:

I see that I am what I always was
that ordinary man on his front steps
bewildered under the bright mess of the heavens
by the fierce indecipherable language of its stars.

It is this balance, or candidness, that more and more characterizes Dana's recent poetry, with its growing breadth of concern, its remarkable sureness of technique: one learns to have confidence in this voice.

—Edward B. Germain

DANIELLS, Roy. Canadian. Born in London, England, 6 April 1902; emigrated to Canada in 1910. Educated at the University of British Columbia, Vancouver, B.A. 1930; University of Toronto, M.A. 1931, Ph.D. 1936. Married Laurenda Francis in 1948; two children. Head of the Department of English, University of Manitoba, Winnipeg, 1937–46. Head of the Department of English, 1948–65, and University Professor of English, University of British Columbia, 1965–74, now retired. Recipient: Lorne Pierce Medal, 1970; Canadian Cultural Institute in Rome Fellowship, 1974. LL.D.: University of Toronto, 1964; Queen's University, Kingston, Ontario, 1964; D.Litt.: McMaster University, Hamilton, Ontario, 1970; University of Windsor, Ontario, 1971. President, Royal Society of Canada, 1970–71. Companion of the Order of Canada, 1972. Address: 1741 Allison Road, Vancouver V6T 1S7, Canada.

PUBLICATIONS

Verse

Deeper into the Forest. Toronto, McClelland and Stewart, 1948.
The Chequered Shade. Toronto, McClelland and Stewart, 1963.

Other

The University and the Impending Crisis (lecture). Fredericton, University of New Brunswick, 1961(?).
Milton, Mannerism and Baroque. Toronto, University of Toronto Press, 1963.
Alexander Mackenzie and the North West. London, Faber, and New York, Barnes and Noble, 1969.

Editor, *A Serious and Pathetic Contemplation of Mercies of God, in Several Most Devout and Sublime Thanksgivings for the Same* ..., by Thomas Traherne. Toronto, University of Toronto Press, 1941.
Editor, with others, and contributor, *Literary History of Canada.* Toronto, University of Toronto Press, 1965.

Roy Daniells comments:

Strongest influences have been religion, Canadian history and travel in Europe. Most poems are sonnets. The influence of Milton and Marvell is apparent.

* * *

Roy Daniells is a scholar and a critic, a Miltonist who has also written eloquently on the Canadian traveller Alexander Mackenzie, and this breadth of interest not only defines the quality of his humanism, but also reflects the apparent contradictions within his poetry. In poetry, as in scholarship, he appears at first to be a traditionalist, until one discovers that, just as his thought roves over whole Canadas of speculation, so his verse achieves, through the use of tried forms, that idiosyncratic quality which marks the work of all truly religious poets. His history of publication spans from the Forties to the Sixties, but he belongs to no school and is hard to place securely in any decade. His output has been small and slow – one book, *Deeper into the Forest*, published when he was 46, and a second, *The Chequered Shade*, published when he had just passed 60. *Deeper into the Forest* contained one memorable long poem in quatrains, "Farewell to Winnipeg," in which Daniells built, around the Canadian folk hero Louis Riel, an elaborate meditation on the world in his time, but most of his poems have been sonnets, and he has adapted this form to his own uses with a virtuosity rare among modern poets. Undoubtedly the best of his sonnets are those in *The Chequered Shade*; the form is traditional, but the way of speaking is contemporary, and the human predicament is seen within the frame and form with the eyes of a modern man. Particularly in the central sequence, based on texts from The Psalms and the New Testament, the agony of endurance that marks man's relationship to whatever is not himself is celebrated, often with an irradiating humour, always with a curiously irreverent reverence.

—George Woodcock

DAS, D(eb) K(umar). Indian. Born in Calcutta, 22 December 1935. Educated at St. Xavier's College, Calcutta University (Quinlan Medallist, 1955; Tata Fellowship, 1955), B.A. (honours) 1955; Queens' College, Cambridge, B.A. 1958, M.A. 1962. Management Staff, I.C.I., Calcutta, 1959–61; Teaching Assistant, University of Washington, Seattle, 1961–63; Instructor, then Superintendent, S.O.I.C., Seattle, 1967–70; Deputy Director, then Director of Research and Planning, State Board for Community College Education, Seattle, 1970–72. Since 1972, director and evaluator of federal projects in education and community development, Seattle. Broadcaster, Viewpoint radio program, for two years. Paintings exhibited in India and the United States. Agent: P. Lal, c/o Writers Workshop, 162–92 Lake Gardens, Calcutta 45, India. Address: 3105½ Eastlake Avenue E., Seattle, Washington 98102, U.S.A.

PUBLICATIONS

Verse

The Night Before Us. Calcutta, Writers Workshop, 1960.
Through a Glass Darkly. Calcutta, Writers Workshop, 1965.
The Eyes of Autumn: An Experiment in Poetry. Calcutta, Writers Workshop, 1968.
The Four Labyrinths. Calcutta, Writers Workshop, 1969.
The Fire Canto. Calcutta, Writers Workshop, 1971.
The Winterbird Walks. Calcutta, Writers Workshop, 1976.
Always Once Was: Experiments in Metapoetics. Calcutta, Writers Workshop, 1977.

Other

Navbharat Papers: A Political Programme for a New India. Seattle, San Vito Press, 1968.
Freedom and Reality, Parts I to VI. Privately printed, 1968.
The First Philosopher: Yajñavalka. Seattle, San Vito Press, 1971.
The Agony of Arjun and Other Essays. Privately printed, 1971.
Svatvavāda: Towards a Theory of Property, 2000 B.C.–1800 A.D.: An Essay in Three Parts. Privately printed, 1972.
An Essay on the Forms of Individualism. Seattle, SFSC Press, 1973.
What Final Frontier? or, The Future of Man in Space. Seattle, SFSC Press, 1973.
Beginnings of Human Thought: The Rig Vedas. Seattle, SFSC Press, 1973.

Translator, *Two Upanisads: Iśa and Kena.* Calcutta, Writers Workshop, 1969.
Translator, *Sankarāchārya: A Discourse on the Real Nature of Self.* Calcutta, Writers Workshop, 1970.
Translator, *Jabala and Paingala Upanisads.* Calcutta, Writers Workshop, 1979.

D. K. Das comments:

My interest is divided about equally between *writing* (in all forms), *painting* (have had several one-man exhibitions in India and U.S.A.), and *research/teaching* in mathematics/economics.

Conflict is a basic theme in my poetry; that between past and future, order and anarchy, passion and reason – with war as an extension of this contemporary human condition. My pre-suppositions are those of the *Bhagavad Gita*; by image as well as reference, I have tried to translate into contemporary terms its message that centrality, being, even meaning, can be found in the *heart* of conflict; the "eye of the storm," its still centre. Space exploration and technological images/themes appear frequently in my poetry, because of my search for modern metaphors, and a contemporary frame of reference. Other than Indian philosophy (especially Vedanta), the strongest influences on my work were undoubtedly T. S. Eliot and W. H. Auden; my mathematical training also influenced my language and "poetic logic"; Albert Camus' *Myth of Sisyphus* also entered many of my poetic intuitions. I am also experimenting with poetic form, trying to create small and large poetic formats capable of carrying poetic *as well as* metaphysical meaning.

* * *

Writer, poet, and economist, D. K. Das, in 1958, helped found Calcutta's Writers Workshop whose purpose was to discuss, encourage and publish Indo-English writing. Exceptionally, he often used traditional verse-forms – most successfully, blank verse, though rhyme sometimes adds irony or piquancy.

He acknowledges influences from Eliot, Auden, and Camus, but more basically the Bhagavat-Gita and Vedanta classics (he has translated upanisads, and Sankarāchārya's *A Discourse on the Real Nature of Self*). He uses his logical-mathematical training to organize poems as penetrations from conflicts and paradoxes into cores of central meaning – the "still point" at the heart of every storm. This may be sardonic – to improve the army computer, which, one factor missing, fire-bombs its own unit then duly notifies next-of-kin, he suggests creating "a special digit/for machine error's contradiction .../a voice that click-clacked error, to the last." More seriously, in "Descartes' God" God's "death" might logically prove Descartes did not exist – or was he wrong, for the wrong reasons, and so logically, right: "Man's mind was a parasite/In symbiosis with a word called God."

Words, like God, are matters of faith. Poets coin names to keep events whole, lest historians simplify them – yet in saying they "mean" feelings or facts, "we are only/crossing our fingers –/Praying that those three blind/movings/(words, feelings, facts)/Are moving Together, finitely."

The Fire Canto, Das's most successful attempt at combining "poetic ... [and] metaphysical meaning," finds Fire the primal substance, man's mind the "Fire of this forever universe," whose burning, "we being merely Fire-bearers must affirm; in order to be and to become Ourselves."

Das found it increasingly hard to so affirm in India's "clockwork existence"; it had "too many anxious excuses for everything/Except the freedom of the firefly's search/... Truth repeated two hundred thousand times/until its words were only incantations." In 1968 he went to Seattle to teach economics and math to ghetto children. He continued to send to Writers Workshop poems, stories and translations, but – no doubt for this desertion – Pritish Nandy pointedly omitted him from his 1972 anthology of Indo-English poetry.

—George McElroy

DAS, Kamala. Pseudonym: Madhavikutty. Indian. Born in Malabar, South India, 31 March 1934. Privately educated. Married K. Madhava Das in 1949; three sons. Recipient: P.E.N. Prize, 1964; Kerala Sahitya Academy Award, for fiction, 1969. Address: c/o K. Madhava Das, The Reserve Bank of India, Bombay 1, India.

PUBLICATIONS

Verse

Summer in Calcutta: Fifty Poems. Delhi, Everest Press, 1965.

The Descendants. Calcutta, Writers Workshop, 1967.
The Old Playhouse and Other Poems. Madras, Longman, 1973.

Novel

Alphabet of Lust. New Delhi, Orient, 1977.

Short Stories

Pathu Kathakal (Ten Stories), *Tharisunilam* (Fallow Fields), *Narachirukal Parakkumbol* (When the Bats Fly), *Ente Snehita Aruna* (My Friend Aruna), *Chuvanna Pavada* (The Red Skirt), *Thanuppu* (Cold), *Rajavinte Premabajanam* (The King's Beloved), *Premathinte Vilapa Kavyam* (Requiem for a Love), *Mathilukal* (Walls). Trichur, Kerala, Current Books, 1953–72.
A Doll for the Child Prostitute. New Delhi, India Paperbacks, 1977.

Other

Driksakshi Panna (Eyewitness) (juvenile). Madras, Longman, 1973.
My Story. Jullandur, Stirling, 1976; London, Quartet, 1978.

Critical Study: Review by John Bernard, in *Journal of Commonwealth Literature* (Leeds), 1967.

Kamala Das comments:

(1970) I began to write poetry with the ignoble aim of wooing a man. There is therefore a lot of love in my poems. I feel forced to be honest in my poetry. I have read very little poetry. I do not think that I have been influenced by any poet. I have liked to read Kalidasa. When I compose poetry, whispering the words to myself, my ear helps to discipline the verse. Afterwards, I count the syllables. I like poetry to be tidy and disciplined.

(1974) My grand-uncle is Nalapat Narayana Menon, the well-known poet-philosopher of Malabar. My mother is the well-known poetess Nalapat Balamani Amma. I belong to the matriarchal community of Nayars. Our ancestral house (Nalapat House) is more than 400 years old and contains valuable palm-leaf manuscripts like the *Varahasamhita, Susrutha Samhita*, and books of mantras.

As I have no degree to add to my name, my readers considered me in the beginning like a cripple. My writing was like the paintings done by "foot and mouth" painters or like the baskets made by the blind. I received some admiration, but the critics, well-known academicians, tore my writing to shreds. This only made my readers love me more. All I have wanted to do is to be real and honest to my readers.

* * *

Kamala Das is an intensely, and consciously, subjective poet. Her own experience – a rich, love-filled childhood, a marriage that failed to provide emotional fulfilment and autonomy and growth to her "self," and her restless longing for a fulfilling relationship – is the dominant subject-matter of her poetry. As she says in "The Old Playhouse," a barely veiled address to her own man,

> It was not to gather knowledge
> Of yet another man that I came to you but to learn
> What I was, and by learning, to learn to grow, but every
> Lesson you gave was about yourself.

This ardent yearning for a love complete with sexual fulfilment but offering more is expressed in "The Freaks," one of her best poems, where the man can only excite physical passion, none too strongly; whose "Nimble finger-tips unleash/Nothing more alive than the/ Skin's lazy hungers?"; who fails to evoke or match the woman's "Flamboyant lust," which is the poet's ideal of love between man and woman.

Kamala Das's almost pathological obsession with her own feelings, urges, and frustrations makes her poetry thematically narrow and repetitious not in the poems' concerns alone but in the phrases and metaphors as well. At the same time, this obsession makes her poetry disturbingly spontaneous and gives her metaphors and images a striking vitality and freshness. Early critics were quick to note the unstrained candour of her sexual views – shocking for an upper-class married Indian woman – and this candour gives authenticity and power to her poetry. Though her movingly fierce emotionalism is the force behind her poems, they are not, as many critics think they are, crude in form. Many of them conceal a subtle craftsmanship, a care in achieving compression and vividness without diluting the strength of the emotion.

Juxtaposed with present yearnings and frustrations in her poetry is a nostalgia for a time and place that fill life with beauty, excitement, and love – the ancestral house in Kerala and the fond grandmother, who understood the child's needs and lavished tender care on her: the "house now far away where once/I received love.... That woman died,/The house withdrew into, silence...." And the house where, she asks the reader if he would believe, "I lived ... and/Was proud, and loved.... I who have lost/My way and beg now at strangers' doors to/Receive love, at least in small change?"

At its best Kamala Das's language is not recognizably Indian English; and yet occasionally her phrases and lines have an Indian flavour that need not bother either the poet or the reader, for it only enhances the authenticity of the expression of an Indian sensibility whose responses to the world around as well as within have established their universal interest. Her prose fiction is chiefly an extension, barely competent, of themes which her poetry has already treated much more beautifully. Her interest and power as a writer remain essentially in her intense personality, as brought out in her poetry and in her exceptionally frank, sometimes over-sentimental, over-dramatic, autobiography, *My Story*.

—J. N. Sharma

DAVEY, Frank(land Wilmot). Canadian. Born in Vancouver, British Columbia, 19 April 1940. Educated at the University of British Columbia, Vancouver, 1957–63, B.A. 1961, M.A. 1963; University of Southern California, Los Angeles, 1965–68, Ph.D. 1968. Married 1) Helen Simmons in 1962 (divorced, 1969); 2) Linda McCartney in 1969; one son and one daughter. Teaching Assistant, University of British Columbia, 1961–63; Lecturer, 1963–66, and Assistant Professor, 1967–69, Royal Roads Military College, Victoria, British Columbia; Writer-in-Residence, Sir George Williams University, Montreal, 1969–70. Since 1970, Associate Professor, and Coordinator of the Creative Writing program, 1976–79, York University, Toronto. Editor, *Tish* magazine, Vancouver, 1961–63. Since 1973, General Editor, Quebec Translations series, and since 1975, Member of the Editorial Board, Coach House Press, Toronto; since 1977, General Editor, New Canadian Criticism series, Talonbooks, Vancouver. Recipient: Humanities Research Council of Canada grant, 1974; Canada Council Fellowship, 1974; Canadian Federation for the Humanities grant, 1979. Address: 104 Lyndhurst Avenue, Toronto, Ontario M5R 2Z7, Canada.

PUBLICATIONS

Verse

D-Day and After. Vancouver, Tishbooks, 1962.
City of the Gulls and Sea. Privately printed, 1964.
Bridge Force. Toronto, Contact Press, 1965.
The Scarred Hull. Calgary, Imago, 1966.
Four Myths for Sam Perry. Vancouver, Talonbooks, 1970.
Weeds. Toronto, Coach House Press, 1970.
Griffon. Toronto, Massasauga, 1972.
King of Swords. Vancouver, Talonbooks, 1972.
L'An Trentiesme: Selected Poems 1961–1970. Vancouver, Community Press, 1972.
Arcana. Toronto, Coach House Press, 1973.
The Clallam; or, Old Glory in Juan de Fuca. Vancouver, Talonbooks, 1973.
War Poems. Toronto, Coach House Press, 1979.

Other

Five Readings of Olson's "Maximus." Montreal, Beaver Kosmos, 1970.
Earle Birney. Toronto, Copp Clark, 1971.
From There to Here: A Guide to English-Canadian Literature since 1960. Erin, Ontario, Press Porcépic, 1974.

Editor, *Tish 1–19.* Vancouver, Talonbooks, 1975.
Editor, *Mrs. Dukes' Million*, by Wyndham Lewis. Toronto, Coach House Press, 1977.

Manuscript Collection: Simon Fraser University, Burnaby, British Columbia.

Critical Studies: Interviews with Elizabeth Komisar in *White Pelican* (Edmonton, Alberta), 1975, and with George Bowering in *Open Letter 4* (Toronto), Spring 1979; "Frank Davey Finding Your Voice to Say What Must Be Said" by Douglas Barbour, in *Brave New Wave* edited by Jack David, Windsor, Black Moss Press, 1978.

* * *

Frank Davey is best known for his espousal of Black Mountain poets in Canada, introduced through the monthly mimeographed newsletter *Tish*, continued through the triannual *Open Letter* (from 1968), and embodied in his own teaching and in articles, reviews, and the pages of *From There to Here*, a useful though opinionated handbook. Davey's own poetry, judged by *L'An Trentiesme: Selected Poems* and *Arcana*, is not at all doctrinaire, but light and lyrical (contrary to what George Bowering is quoted as saying in *There to Here*): "description/is a bird who comes down/all too easy." This comes from "out &/on," a poem from the "Bridge Force" part of the selected poems. The other volume includes occasional poems plus meditations on the Tarot cards. It could be argued that Davey is basically an occasional poet. He has written semi-documentary, semi-lyrical poems on a number of marine disasters, culminating in *The Clallam*, a long poem that recreates a sinking of a ship most successfully. Perhaps his credo is best summed up in "The Mirror XIV" from *Arcana*:

I write these words
that someone, will remember me,
or at least finding me here
poisd, burnd, loved, unloved, will see words
moving.

—John Robert Colombo

DAVIDSON, Michael. American. Born in Oakland, California, 18 December 1944. Educated at San Francisco State University, 1963–67, B.A. 1967; State University of New York, Buffalo, 1967–71, Ph.D. Lecturer, San Diego State University, 1973–76. Since 1975, Research Historian, and since 1976, Assistant Professor, University of California at San Diego, La Jolla. Recipient: National Endowment for the Arts grant, 1976. Address: 5804 Camino de la Costa, La Jolla, California 92037, U.S.A.

PUBLICATIONS

Verse

Exchanges. Los Angeles, Prose and Verses Press, 1972.
Two Views of Pears. Berkeley, California, Sand Dollar, 1973.
The Mutabilities, and The Foul Papers. Berkeley, California, Sand Dollar, 1976.

Critical Studies: reviews by Robert Bertholf in *Credences 5–6* (Kent, Ohio), and Jed Rasula in *Open Letter 8* (Toronto), Spring 1978.

Michael Davidson comments:

My first encounters with poetry occurred, as they did for most of my generation, via Brooks and Warren's *Understanding Poetry*. As I remember, "classic" poems were presented followed by four or five seminal questions which, once answered by the bright literature student, would solve the curious riddle hidden (intentionally, no doubt) in the poem. Such an approach to poetry was pretty intimidating for a young writer; after all, the poet presumably had thought these strategies out before sitting down to write, and my early practice simply involved writing "toward" some vaguely formed idea. The Brooks and Warren method of literary analysis was accompanied in Creative Writing workshops by stern lectures on what was then called the "craft" of poetry – that is, the poet's ability to exert his will to power over form. The supreme poet, then, was one who could channel the multifarious happenings of daily life into a series of discrete, oblique figures, usually involving some part of the poet's inner organs or perhaps his ancestral origins. This rather inhospitable atmosphere was an important formulating experience for my own work but, under the salutary influence of the poetry renaissance of the late 1950's and early 1960's in San Francisco, I resumed the practice of writing "toward" some vaguely formed idea.

I would like to think of my work as an interrogation or exploration of its own processes – not for the sake of formalist exercise but in order to test the thresholds of meaning. In this sense, poetry is a profoundly human activity since it refuses to take the world for granted while believing utterly in its multi-faceted character. The most difficult task for the poet, as Jack Spicer pointed out, is avoiding what YOU want to say since this invariably results in a trivializing of that initial charge that drove you to write in the first place. And oddly enough, the result is something extremely personal if only because the writing embodies the wandering, desultory quality of one's thoughts. At times this "tracing" involves areas of interruption and semantic breakdown since it is often where language fails to provide necessary information (or where it provides the unwanted figure, slip of tongue or typo) that it most reveals. How, then, to capture that quality? At the simplest level, by being open to the qualities and textures and confusions of one's own language as it struggles with difficult material, and alternately by avoiding the lure of an imperializing rhetoric which yearns to "temper" that experience by subordinating its semantic plurality. This may not be a practical solution, but it is at least the atmosphere in which the various solutions offered in my writing have been nurtured.

* * *

"To 'do' one's art," Michael Davidson writes, "means to solve problems in a language which the art establishes as it is being created. Its grammar and lexicon emerge less as a result of a commitment to prior forms and more as a response to immediate necessity." The locus of interest in Davidson's *The Mutabilities* is precisely in watching the response to immediate necessity unfold. The poems are, as it were, live performances.

The epigraph to the volume is from *Tristram Shandy*, and the pervading tone is Shandean. Davidson's poetry turns on a sense of language as a persistent but unreliable medium. Above all, "I" – that sign which traditionally holds a privileged place in language, as the center of control – is very slippery and unstable. It would not be an oversimplification to say that Davidson's work is an investigation of language in which the "I" becomes as much a matter of conjecture as everything else:

Marking this way
as a direction one comes to know
one is known,
hence you are still you
and I
am not so sure.

Lacking a dependable ordering ego, the poems are variations on unstated (and unstatable) themes, or, as in "Often he felt uncomfortable," on a theme which is itself mutable. The idiomatic phrase, "to come out," is loaded with ambiguities, and in this poem Davidson uses it in a half-dozen or more different senses. The central matter of conjecture, however, is how *words* come out. Of all things their coming out is most mysterious: "and the vipers and bats and lizards come out of nowhere/ which is a word out of which other words come out." The origins of language are completely concealed by the fact that whatever they might be can only be stated in language:

in the beginning was the word and when it was out
there was a space projected like a little star
out of which all the light we have ever seen came pouring
one word at a time.

There is nothing occult, nothing hidden, in Davidson's poetry. It is, like the poetry of Michael Palmer, a poetry of surfaces.

"The Foul Papers" (*The Mutabilities*) are prose poems, but their strategies are fundamentally like those found in Davidson's other work. In the title piece of this section, for example, there are seven paragraphs about some unnamed "he" who is, however, "close to," if not identical with, the "I" who gives the account. Although the paragraphs are very loosely organized, they do have centers of concerns: the first is about his loss of virginity, the second a concert by the Coasters, the third his "47 Plymouth with blue Satin seat covers," the fourth the cat odors in his house, the fifth is a list of things which he has to do on some relatively uneventful day, the sixth is about a love affair (perhaps with the woman with whom he speaks in the second), and the last about a conversation with another woman. Although it is possible to trace several lines of connection through the piece, one of the primary conjectural centers has to do with smells. The piece concludes: "so their conversation draws on into empty night, the prospect emptying itself into their conversation until only smells remain and which, in time, take on the unexpected pressure of beauty." It is just that "unexpected pressure of beauty," issuing from what seems rather unpromising material, which is the dominant effect of Davidson's work.

—Don Byrd

DAVIE, Donald (Alfred). British. Born in Barnsley, Yorkshire, 17 July 1922. Educated at Barnsley Grammar School; St. Catharine's College, Cambridge, B.A. 1947, M.A. 1949, Ph.D. 1951. Served in the Royal Navy, 1941–46. Married Doreen John in 1945; three children. Lecturer in English, 1950–57, and Fellow of Trinity College, 1954–57, Dublin University; Lecturer in English, 1958–64, and Fellow of Gonville and Caius College, 1959–64, Cambridge University; Professor of English, 1964–68, and Pro-Vice-Chancellor, 1965–68, University of Essex, Wivenhoe. Professor of English, Stanford University, California, 1968–78. Since 1978, Andrew W. Mellon Professor of Humanities, Vanderbilt University, Nashville. Visiting Professor, University of California, Santa Barbara, 1957–58; British Council Lecturer, Budapest, 1961; Elliston Lecturer, University of Cincinnati, 1963. Recipient: Guggenheim Fellowship, 1973. D.Litt.: University of Southern California, Los Angeles, 1978. Honorary Fellow, St. Catharine's College, Cambridge, 1973; Fellow, American Academy of Arts and Sciences, 1973; Honorary Fellow, Trinity College, Dublin, 1978. Address: 4400 Belmont Park Terrace, Nashville, Tennessee 37235, U.S.A.; or, 31 Fore Street, Silverton, Exeter, Devon, England.

PUBLICATIONS

Verse

(Poems). Oxford, Fantasy Press, 1954.
Brides of Reason. Oxford, Fantasy Press, 1955.
A Winter Talent and Other Poems. London, Routledge, 1957.
The Forests of Lithuania, adapted from a poem by Adam Mickiewicz. Hessle, Yorkshire, Marvell Press, 1959.
A Sequence for Francis Parkman. Hessle, Yorkshire, Marvell Press, 1961.
New and Selected Poems. Middletown, Connecticut, Wesleyan University Press, 1961.
Events and Wisdoms: Poems 1957–1963. London, Routledge, 1964; Middletown, Connecticut, Wesleyan University Press, 1965.
Poems. London, Turret, 1969.
Essex Poems 1963–1967. London, Routledge, 1969.
Six Epistles to Eva Hesse. London, London Magazine Editions, 1970.
Collected Poems 1950–1970. London, Routledge, and New York, Oxford University Press, 1972.
Orpheus. London, Poem-of-the-Month Club, 1974.
The Shires. London, Routledge, 1974; New York, Oxford University Press, 1975.
In the Stopping Train and Other Poems. Manchester, Carcanet Press, 1977.

Recording: *Donald Davie Reading at Stanford*, Stanford University, 1974.

Other

Purity of Diction in English Verse. London, Chatto and Windus, 1952; New York, Oxford University Press, 1953.
Articulate Energy: An Enquiry into the Syntax of English Poetry. London, Routledge, 1955; New York, Harcourt Brace, 1958.
The Heyday of Sir Walter Scott. London, Routledge, and New York, Barnes and Noble, 1961.
The Language of Science and the Language of Literature 1700–1740. London and New York, Sheed and Ward, 1963.
Ezra Pound: Poet as Sculptor. London, Routledge, and New York, Oxford University Press, 1964.
Thomas Hardy and British Poetry. New York, Oxford University Press, 1972; London, Routledge, 1973.

Poetry in Translation. Milton Keynes, Buckinghamshire, Open University, 1975.
Pound. London, Fontana, 1975; New York, Viking Press, 1976.
The Poet in the Imaginary Museum: Essays of Two Decades, edited by Barry Alpert. Manchester, Carcanet Press, 1976; New York, Persea Press, 1977.
A Gathered Cloud: The Literature of the English Dissenting Interest 1700–1930. London, Routledge, and New York, Oxford University Press, 1978.
Trying to Explain. Ann Arbor, University of Michigan Press, 1979.

Editor, *The Late Augustans: Longer Poems of the Later Eighteenth Century.* London, Heinemann, and New York, Macmillan, 1958.
Editor, *Poems: Poetry Supplement.* London, Poetry Book Society, 1960.
Editor, *Poetics Poetyka.* Warsaw, Panstwowe Wydawn, 1961.
Editor, *Selected Poems of Wordsworth.* London, Harrap, 1962.
Editor, *Russian Literature and Modern English Fiction: A Collection of Critical Essays.* Chicago, University of Chicago Press, 1965.
Editor, with Angela Livingstone, *Pasternak.* London, Macmillan, 1969.
Editor, "Thomas Hardy Issue" of *Agenda* (London), Spring–Summer 1972.
Editor, *Augustan Lyric.* London, Heinemann, 1974.
Editor, *The Collected Poems of Elizabeth Daryush.* Manchester, Carcanet Press, 1975.
Editor, *Collected Poems*, by Yvor Winters. Manchester, Carcanet Press, 1978.
Translator, *The Poems of Doctor Zhivago*, by Boris Pasternak. Manchester, Manchester University Press, and New York, Barnes and Noble, 1965.

Manuscript Collection: University of Essex, Wivenhoe.

Critical Studies: by Calvin Bedient, in *The Iowa Review* (Iowa City), 1971; "A Breakthrough into Spaciousness" by Donald Greene, in *Queen's Quarterly* (Kingston, Ontario), 1973; by Martin Dodsworth, Michael Schmidt, and G. Dekker, in "Donald Davie Issue" of *Agenda* (London), Summer 1976.

* * *

The poet comments: "A good poem is necessarily a response to a human situation. To make poetry out of moral commonplaces, a poet has to make it clear that he speaks not in his own voice ... but as the spokesman of a social tradition." When one considers the *oeuvre* of Donald Davie, the terms formal elegance, urbane wit, meticulous syntax, restraint, plain diction – the Neo-Augustan – come to mind. Dedicated to a chastely austere poetry, Davie, always the British professor, critic, and historian, treats the contemporary need for personal moderation and restraint in forms that reflect his vision. It is the word itself – indeed language – which requires purification, and if the poet can purify the dialectic of the tribe, perhaps the values of propriety and control, those moral values that inspire integrity and courage, may return to the decadent modern world. Man may as well better understand his proper place in the scheme of things – personal and perhaps even metaphysical.

In his earliest work Davie was associated with the *New Lines* anthology and the 1950's "the Movement." His name was often linked with Wain, Amis, Larkin, Gunn, Conquest, Enright, and the other "reactionary" poets who stood against the romantic excesses of the British poets of the 1940's, e.g., Dylan Thomas, and the early Anglo-American moderns. *Brides of Reason*, basically in traditional meter, appeals to the "logic" in man: "So poets may astonish you/With what is not, but should be, true,/And shackle on a moral shape." The poet's social function is clear: "The practice of ... [my] art/is to connect all terms/into the terms of art" ("Hypochondriac Logic").

Influenced especially by the Augustans Johnson, Cowper, and Goldsmith, as well as by Pound, Pasternak, and Yvor Winters, Davie has evolved a poetry often compared to Charles Tomlinson's, in his insistence upon the connection between form and morality. Davie has stood fast against his fashionable contemporaries – the confessional Roethke, Plath, Lowell –

and even the great mythmakers of the century, Yeats and Eliot. Although Davie's aims are not unlike theirs – to inspire action and change in a philistine and unimaginative contemporary world (in Davie's case, most often, post-imperial Britain), he would accomplish this not through his reader's imaginative, impassioned immersion in myth, but through inspiring his readers toward conscious control. Through Davie's example of proper rhyme, meter, and syntax, for example, one might feel himself affirming the proper values of his more stable and civilized past. In "Vying" he writes:

> I, the sexton, battle
> Earth that will overturn
> Headstones, and rifle tombs,
> and spill the tilted urn.

Over the years Davie has moved toward shorter, brisker lines, and a less obscure poetry; there has been an increasing emotional involvement with the landscapes, metaphors, and even history. His abhorrence of a poetry consumed with the poet's "messy ego" has been absolute, however, like his insistence that language is at the root of England's moral decay. He will not follow current usage: "the stumbling, the moving voices," "the Beat and post-Beat poets,/the illiterate apostles" ("Pentecost"). What is always needed is reasonableness, "common values" ("The Garden Party"), and "a neutral tone" ("Remembering the Thirties").

Six Epistles to Eva Hesse, Pound's translator, is a sort of "Essay on Criticism" ("Heroic comedy, I suggest,/Fits American history best"), in which he again utilizes the verse epistle form. Typically, Davie goes back in history to contemplate old and new values:

> Confound it, history ... [sic] We transcend it
> Not when we agree to bend it
> To this cat's cradle or that theme
> But when, I take it, we redeem
> This man or that one, La Pérouse
> Lives when he's no longer news.

One associates most of Davie's subjects with England, and the *Collected Poems* contains his statement of "faith that there are still distinctively English – rather than Anglo-American or 'international' – ways of responding imaginatively to the terms of life in the twentieth century." Many of his poems compare the Mediterranean and Northern worlds, yet Davie has as well composed "The Forests of Lithuania," which, as he tells us in a prefatory note, is based on Mickiewicz's *Pan Tadensz*, and deals with Lithuania during its Russian Occupation in 1811–12. Another of these long and well-sustained historical, political, and personal commentaries, "A Sequence for Francis Parker," deals with Davie's response to North America. His *tour de force*, however, entirely about England, is "The Shires," which consists of 40 poems, one for each county in England (arranged in alphabetical order, from Bedfordshire to Yorkshire). "Shires" contains the poet's revery about the English landscape, culture, and history itself. Davie traverses England and fills his landscapes with autobiographical information and reminiscences. At times he is profoundly serious, even bitter, about the problems of his world; at other times, he is wry, and witty. In "Suffolk" he writes: "My education gave me this bad habit/Of reading history for a hidden plot/And finding it; invariably the same one,/Its fraudulent title always, 'Something Gone.' " The poems are suffused with historical figures – Bunyan, Calvin, Drake, Hawkins, and literary figures, Hamburger, Housman, Auden, Blake, Smart, John Fowles. Man is described in terms of his relationship with his past: "We run through a maze of tunnels for our meat/As rats might .../Drake, This is the freedom that you sailed from sure/To save us for?"

The extraordinary "Trevenen" is a verse biography, a narrative tragedy, of the late 18th-century Cornish naval officer who, after a heroic career, was used, abused, and driven mad by those he served. Trevenen lived in "an age much like our own;/As lax, as vulgar, as confused;/Its freedoms just as much abused/... Where personalities were made,/And makers of them plied a trade/Profitable and esteemed;/Where that which was and that which seemed/Were priced the same;/where men were duped/And knew they were." Davie's portrayal of Trevenen's heroic life, basic naivety, and final death are among his most moving lines:

> Aware man's born to err,
> Inclined to bear and forbear.
> Pretense to more is vain.
> Chastened have they been.
> Hope was the tempter, hope.
> Ambition has its scope
> (Vast: the world's esteem);
> Hope is a sickly dream.

Although Davie has recently moved toward a more open and personal poetry, his concern with perfect language and syntax remains, that which, in an essay on Pound, he calls the connection between politics and form, for "to dislocate syntax is to threaten the rule of law in the community."

—Lois Gordon

DAVISON, Peter (Hubert). American. Born in New York City, 27 June 1928. Educated at the Fountain Valley School, Colorado Springs; Harvard University, Cambridge, Massachusetts, A.B. (magna cum laude) 1949 (Phi Beta Kappa); St. John's College, Cambridge (Fulbright Scholar), 1949–50. Served in the United States Army, 1951–53. Married Jane Truslow in 1959; two children. Page in the United States Senate, 1944. Editorial Assistant, 1950–51, and Assistant Editor, 1953–55, Harcourt Brace, publishers, New York; Assistant to the Director, Harvard University Press, 1955–56. Associate Editor, 1956–59, Executive Editor, 1959–64, and since 1964, Director, Atlantic Monthly Press, Boston. Since 1972, Poetry Editor, *Atlantic Monthly*, Boston. Recipient: Yale Series of Younger Poets Award, 1964; National Institute of Arts and Letters award, 1972. Address: 11 Mellen Street, Cambridge, Massachusetts 02138, U.S.A.

PUBLICATIONS

Verse

The Breaking of the Day and Other Poems. New Haven, Connecticut, Yale University Press, 1964.
The City and the Island. New York, Atheneum, 1966.
Pretending to Be Asleep. New York, Atheneum, 1970.
Dark Houses. Cambridge, Massachusetts, Halty Ferguson, 1971.
Walking the Boundaries: Poems 1957–1974. New York, Atheneum, and London, Secker and Warburg, 1974.
A Voice in the Mountain. New York, Atheneum, 1977.

Other

Half-Remembered: A Personal History. New York, Harper, 1973; London, Heinemann, 1974.

Editor, *Hello Darkness: The Collected Poems of L. E. Sissman.* Boston, Little Brown, 1978.

Manuscript Collection: Beinecke Library, Yale University, New Haven, Connecticut.

Critical Study: Foreword by Dudley Fitts to *The Breaking of the Day and Other Poems*, 1964.

* * *

Most of Peter Davison's poetry has an even, gem-like quality that typifies intelligent, academic verse. Davison's work, generously laden with mythical allusions, is often rhymed and carefully metered. At its best, the poetry illuminates a moment or an observation from the poet's life without straining towards an undeserved depth. In "Lunch at the Coq D'Or," Davison portrays a fancy restaurant where "Each noon at table tycoons crow/And flap their wings around each other's shoulders." He is waiting for an associate, Purdy, who eventually "is seated with his alibis":

> I know my man. Purdy's a hard-nosed man.
> Another round for us. It's good to work
> With such a man. "Purdy," I hear myself,
> "It's good to work with you." I raise
> My arm, feathery in the dimlight, and extend
> Until the end of it brushes his padded shoulder.
> "Purdy, how are you? How you doodle do?"

Here, Davison has included himself among the blamed by repeating the feather-wing imagery of the tycoons and then his own arm of luncheon goodwill. The humor of his concluding line emphasizes the nonsense encountered in daily business intercourse.

Too often, Davison lacks this detachment; he becomes merely a clever man with a pen, rhyming when he should be working his guts in ink. His position is ambiguous: surely, "Conviction Means Loss of License" deals with a serious subject, but Davison seems only to consider the fatal car crash of three brothers an opportunity to exercise his wit. And worse, he preaches in the sardonic manner of a radar cop:

> For they were faithful to the plan
> That nature must make way for man
>
> And fed their faith in this great cause
> By putting speed above the laws
> Designed to neither help nor hurt.
>
> Inertia rendered them inert.

In other poems, particularly "Intacta," (where he tells the familiar story of a seemingly virginal, but permissive girl) and "Winter Fear," which ends, "The weather tells of famine and defeat,/Of lying leaves and how we were betrayed/By spring. But winter never yet has won," he seems too pat. How, after all, does he know that the girl of "Intacta" is loose unless he's been in her pants? And, although it's true that winter "never yet has won," neither has any season (or condition of mind, the poem suggests to me) triumphed over winter. In short, Davison refuses to confess his own possible guilt or confusion.

These comments are perhaps unfairly negative, for there is much to admire in the body of Davison's work. "The Breaking of the Day," title poem of his first collection, is a perfect refutation of the criticisms I levy against the least successful poetry. Here, the poet takes the risk of baring himself to the reader, acknowledging his doubts: "I shall never know myself/ Enough to know what things I half believe/And, half believing, only half deny." In a poem such as this, the fusion of craft and insight is fully realized, and Davison proves himself the poet of skill his reputation holds him to be.

Dark Houses is a seven-part retrospective in verse on the life of his father, poet Edward Davison, whose presence is fully documented in Peter Davison's *Half-Remembered*, an autobiography. *Dark Houses* is a very fine poem, crafted with a precision less and less evident among contemporary poets:

And now his thirsty body
Is part of the land at last, land of his children,
Where the grey ungiving stone can always stand
For fathers, thrusting up above the fields
Not ever his own, though dearer than the land
That gave him birth but never knew his name.

—Geof Hewitt

DAWE, (Donald) Bruce. Australian. Born in Geelong, Victoria, 15 February 1930. Educated at Northcote High School; Melbourne University; Queensland University, Brisbane, B.A., M.A.; University of New England, Armidale, New South Wales, Litt.B. 1973. Served in the Royal Australian Air Force for nine years. Married Gloria Desley; four children. Worked as labourer, gardener, postman. Currently, Senior Lecturer in Literature, Darling Downs Institute of Advanced Education, Darling Heights, Toowoomba. Recipient: Myer Prize, 1966, 1969; Ampol Arts Award, 1967; Mary Gilmore Medal, 1973. Address: 30 Cumming Street, Toowoomba, Queensland, Australia.

PUBLICATIONS

Verse

No Fixed Address. Melbourne, Cheshire, 1962.
A Need of Similar Name. Melbourne, Cheshire, 1965.
An Eye for a Tooth. Melbourne, Cheshire, 1968.
Beyond the Subdivision. Melbourne, Cheshire, 1969.
Heat-Wave. Melbourne, Sweeney Reed, 1970.
Condolences of the Season. Melbourne, Cheshire, 1971.
Just a Dugong at Twilight: Mainly Light Verse. Melbourne, Cheshire, 1975.
Sometimes Gladness: Collected Poems 1954–1978. Melbourne, Longman Cheshire, 1978.

Other

Editor, *Dimensions.* Sydney, McGraw Hill, 1975.

Manuscript Collection: Fryer Library, University of Queensland, Brisbane.

Critical Studies: *The Man down the Street*, edited by Ian V. Hansen, Melbourne, V.A.T.E., 1972; *Times and Seasons: An Introduction to Bruce Dawe* by Basil Shaw, Melbourne, Cheshire, 1974.

Bruce Dawe comments:

The themes I deal with are the common ones of modern civilization, loneliness, old age, death, dictatorship, love. I like the dramatic monologue form, and use it in free, blank and rhymed verse-forms, attempting at the same time to capture something of the evanescence of contemporary idiom, which is far richer and more allusive than the stereotyped stone-the-crows popular concept of Australian speech would have people believe.

* * *

Bruce Dawe has been certainly the most central and pivotal poet in Australia during the decade of the 1960's. His work first appeared in Melbourne in the late 1950's and broke through to a wide audience with *No Fixed Address*, his first collection. *No Fixed Address* displayed a freshness and gaiety quite unusual in Australian literature at the time, and, more importantly, demonstrated a highly developed sense of local speech cadence and inflection. Bruce Dawe has always been concerned with the celebration of the maligned denizens of the great sprawl of outer suburbs that surround our cities. He views them with affection, sympathy and wit, and an ear attuned to natural speech rhythms that is more precise and more immediately convincing than that of any other poet. This perceptiveness is coupled with a brilliant feeling of language and, particularly, of image.

Dawe broke through to a whole new generation of Australian readers, and his popularity has been gained without any loss of integrity or style; indeed, because of the genuineness of his essential attitudes, such popularity is a natural aspect of his poetic justification. Over recent years, and in his later volumes, Bruce Dawe has been concerned with developing his initial vision and perceptions. He has been one of the few Australian poets who has found a convincing method of dealing with current political events and issues without loss of poetic validity. This is an area where Australian poetry has always been backward and undeveloped. In 1972 a selected volume *Condolences of the Season* offered readers a summary of Dawe's work. His later poems tend to employ a more elegiac cadence, but though the subject matter is often eclectic and wide flung, it would seem, still, that his contribution related primarily to the admission into the corpus of Australian poetry of an area of suburban reality and liveliness that had only been approached in the most awkward and uncomfortable way by his predecessors.

—Thomas W. Shapcott

DEDERICK, Robert. British. Born in Manchester, Lancashire, 27 September 1919. Educated at Taunton School, Somerset. Served in South Africa during World War II. Married in 1949; four children. Solicitor in England, 1947–51; moved to South Africa in 1951. Since 1952, Member of the legal staff, South African BP Group. Recipient: State Poetry Prize, 1967; Pringle Award, 1971. Address: 82 Camp Ground Road, Rondesbosch, South Africa.

PUBLICATIONS

Verse

The Quest and Other Poems. Cape Town, Purnell, 1968.
Bi-Focal. Cape Town, David Philip, 1974.

Robert Dederick comments:

(1970) I use more than a trace of pantheistic agnosticism (if that isn't too much of a contradiction in terms). Stars, in which my interest is amateur and aesthetic, play a big part in the poems. I seem to think that man is (as someone else has said) guilty but insane; but to me neither the guilt nor the insanity rules out humour. My verse forms are broadly traditional but fairly flexible; I have no taste for writing free verse. Hardy and Housman have influenced me, massively reinforced by Frost; Betjeman is by no means to be sneezed at. I try to make my work pithy and epigrammatic, its themes extracted from everyday scenes and things. I try to make it lucid and comprehensible, without (I hope) being obvious.

(1980) The writing of poems is to me – in the first instance – a self-indulgence. There is a tremendous "kick" in producing even a little order out of the chaos of memories and associations, etc. I am therefore much in sympathy with Frost's famous remark about the writing of free verse – that he'd "as lief play tennis with the net down." Speaking of Frost: he's a dangerous man to admire because he can all too easily move into one's work and *take over*. Yet I do admire him, not least for his wit, irony, wryness, humour, and superficial appeal – all of which serve a purpose which is anything but superficial, and all of which are dolefully out of fashion in poetry these days. As is, of course, form.

I would say that of about 250 or 300 of my poems now in print, there are perhaps six that I would regard as (to quote Frost again) "my best bid for remembrance." And of these six, four are in the later book. Hardly a fanfare for "development" is it? But I'm not dismayed at this. I was 41 when my first work was accepted for publication; so I have no *published* juvenilia to regret and suppress.

* * *

Robert Dederick's first volume of verse, *The Quest and Other Poems*, showed him to be an ironic observer of the human condition, rendering his perceptions in verse which is often taut, epigrammatic, and thought-provoking, as in "Looking up is looking back":

Because that haze high over me
left Orion's Great Nebula
in Herod's eventful century

And all those flashes to my right
were, when Canopus sent them out,
pre-Raphael light,

there is an almost neighbourly glow
to Alpha Centauri, skimming low,
only four years away and ago.

The antithetical style can, however, easily degenerate into mere word-play, and in retrospect *The Quest* fails to transcend the writer's preoccupation with pun and paradox. Despite its South African locale and flavour, much of the social satire in this volume harks back to Auden and the "English tradition" of the 1930's:

I awoke, this morning, wanting my Muse.
I knew, while brushing my hair and my shoes,
That many fine things today could be seen,
But not from the windows of the 8.14.

The Quest is characterized by a journalistic element – evident in much of the headline-inspired or topical verse – which, together with the trivializing effect of the word-play, tends to subvert the poet's more serious attempts at meaningful expression. Yet these are poems of undoubted promise and a refreshing directness of engagement, and in "The Pont at Malgas" – one of the few sustained lyrical evocations in the volume – Dederick successfully fuses English tradition and South African experience. In his best work paradox operates implicitly through the sense and structure of the verse: "Poem on a Slate" shows how technique can be subordinated to poetic purpose and a finely honed sensibility.

Word-play and epigram also characterize Dederick's second volume, *Bi-Focal*, but here they are used with a greater measure of restraint and, consequently, poetic effectiveness. This is evidenced by poems such as "The Present Imperative" and the short but significant title poem:

> Some survey the wood beyond the trees.
> Do not, while seeing eye to eye with these,
> Overlook those whose scrutiny perceives
> Within the trees within the wood the leaves.

There are in this volume poems which reflect more ingenuity than thought, and Dederick has not altogether avoided the tendency to versify events; in general, however, the somewhat slick satire of *The Quest* has given way to a more personal, reflective mood. Childhood memories achieve in retrospect a new relevance (the "bi-focal" vision of the poet is often brought to bear on family photograph or diary) and there are both tenderness and expansiveness of spirit in a poem such as "Blanketed ... Mantled," which links Dederick, at his unsentimental best, with Frost. In very different vein are the (literally) "fifty lines" of the poem of that title – a successful adaptation of a theme popularized by Spender, Day Lewis, and Vernon Scannell:

> *I must not day-dream during class*
> *I must not* but the trouble was
> that bee fizzing about the window
> suggesting stamens made me wonder
> was it male or female or
> *I must not* and I was with her
> *I must not* swish of stocking-tops
> a hint of crossing-straps and lips'
> slow parting *I must not* when what
> began her moan became a shout
> from Honks: "Repeat the question, boy!" ...

In *Bi-Focal* the kaleidoscopic range of *The Quest* has narrowed down to the juxtaposition of youth and age, not as an exercise in nostalgia, but as a means of coming to terms with the passage of time and achieving a new sense of perspective. Poems in which these concerns are treated directly, as in "Shadows and Echoes" and "Perspective," tend to be unrealised and didactic: Dederick is most impressive when his insights are arrived at through the exploration of mood and image, and the greater lyrical emphasis of *Bi-Focal* gives scope to this aspect of his poetic impulse. He is also more of a craftsman in *Bi-Focal*: not only are there fewer lapses of tone and technique, but greater variety and flexibility in his use of rhyme and verse-form. This, together with the greater concentration of subject-matter, has resulted in an altogether richer and poetically more satisfying volume.

—E. Pereira

DELIUS, Anthony (Ronald St. Martin). South African. Born in Simonstown, 11 June 1916. Educated at St. Aidan's College, Grahamstown; Rhodes University, Grahamstown, B.A. 1938. Served in the South African Intelligence Corps, 1940–45. Married in 1941; two children. Staff Member, Port Elizabeth *Evening Post*, 1947–50; Parliamentary Correspondent, *Cape Times*, Cape Town, 1951–54, 1958–67. Banned from the South Africa House of Assembly for his *Cape Times* political commentary. Writer, BBC Africa Service, London, 1968–77. Since 1977 free-lance writer. Former Co-Editor, *Standpunte*, Cape Town. Since 1962, Member of the Editorial Board, *Contrast* magazine, Cape Town. Address: 30 Graemesdyke Avenue, London SW14 7BJ, England.

PUBLICATIONS

Verse

An Unknown Border: Poems. Cape Town, Balkema, 1954.
The Last Division. Cape Town, Human and Rousseau, 1959.
A Corner of the World: Thirty-Four Poems. Cape Town, Human and Rousseau, 1962.
Black South-Easter. Grahamstown, New Coin, 1966.

Play

The Fall: A Play about Rhodes. Cape Town, Human and Rousseau, 1957.

Novels

The Day Natal Took Off: A Satire. Cape Town, Human and Rousseau, and London, Pall Mall Press, 1963.
Border. Cape Town, David Philip, 1976.

Other

The Young Traveller in South Africa. London, Phoenix House, 1947; revised edition, 1959.
The Long Way Round (travel in Africa). Cape Town, Howard B. Timmins, 1956.
Upsurge in Africa. Toronto, Canadian Institute of International Affairs, 1960.

Manuscript Collection: Rhodes University, Grahamstown.

* * *

Anthony Delius has described himself as one of the most indoctrinated of South Africans, a misleading description, since it would imply an acceptance of current socio-political attitudes in his country which would be the opposite of the truth. What one can properly infer, however, is that of the poets of his country writing in English he is probably the most consciously South African. It is an identification with *A Corner of the World* – the title of his 1964 collection – that is his own but it is more than a country, rather the African continent as a whole, many of his poems reflecting his travels there. From his early poems, including the long, impressive "Time in Africa" written during the Second World War, Delius has shown himself fascinated by what living in Africa has accumulated over the centuries, seeing history as a continuous process working on his own contemporary experience and on into the future like a prophecy.

In "Black South-Easter," probably the best long poem produced by a South African, in a generation, Delius, twenty years after "Time in Africa," succeeded in using history as a poet should, taking imagination as catalyst to produce a recipe for the making of myth. The poet, struggling through the windy Cape night, is confronted by historical ghosts, by symbolical figures of contemporary values, the millionaire and the actress and by his own many-sidedness, his own "Indian file of selves," while his mind and memory are swept dramatically on a course of their own through a wider and deeper disorder of time and circumstance – for instance, seeing the Fifteenth Century navigator Diaz thus:

His niche was the stern
Of a torpedoed tanker, cliff-hung
Like an opera box.

Here is a tremendously ambitious poem; that it succeeds is the measure of the poet's power to use language to control a variety of influences working on the imagination at the same time. If Delius has proved his staying power in attempting the long distances (since *The Lusiads*, the Cape presents a surviving challenge to South African poets to go for the big theme), yet his enduring reputation may well lie among some of his short poems, such as the exquisite "The Gamblers," about Cape Coloured fishermen, a popular anthology piece since it first appeared in *The New Yorker*:

Day flips a golden coin – but they mock it.
With calloused, careless hands they reach
Deep down into the sea's capacious pocket
And pile their silver counters on the beach.

"Deaf and Dumb School" is another poem beautifully conceived to express the poet's compassion: "Silence like a shadow shows the room/Of minds that make their signs and mouth their cries."

There is another kind of compassion, perhaps of the best kind, that which comes after very clear vision has stripped away from situations and people what humbug, false myth and sloth have accumulated about them. In this process satire acts like a paint-stripper, and Delius, as satirist, has long been active in the South African context. Though echoes of Roy Campbell sometimes interrupt originality, there are parts of *The Last Division* (1959) whose humour will preserve it long after the lampooned figures of politics have been forgotten.

—Roy Macnab

DEMETILLO, Ricaredo. Filipino. Born in Dumangas, Iloilo, 2 June 1920. Educated at Silliman University, Dumaguete City, A.B. in English; University of Iowa, Iowa City, M.F.A. in English and creative writing. Married to Angelita Demetillo; four children. Assistant Professor, 1959–70, Chairman of the Department of Humanities, 1961–62, Associate Professor, 1970–75, and since 1975, Professor of Humanities, University of the Philippines, Diliman, Quezon City. Recipient: Rockefeller Fellowship, 1952; University of the Philippines Golden Jubilee Award; Philippines Republic Cultural Heritage Award, 1968. Address: T 1416, Area 14, University of the Philippines, Diliman, Quezon City, Philippines.

PUBLICATIONS

Verse

No Certain Weather. Quezon City, Guinhalinan Press, 1956.

La Via: A Spiritual Journey. Quezon City, Diliman Review, 1958.
Daedalus and Other Poems. Quezon City, Guinhalinan Press, 1961.
Barter in Panay. Quezon City, University of the Philippines Office of Research Coordination, 1961.
Masks and Signature. Quezon City, University of the Philippines Press, 1968.
The Scare-Crow Christ. Quezon City, Diliman Review, 1973.
The City and the Thread of Light and Other Poems. Quezon City, Diliman Review, 1974.
Lazarus, Troubadour. Quezon City, New Day, 1974.
Sun, Silhouettes, and Shadow, photographs by B. David Williams, Jr. Quezon City, New Day, 1975.

Play

The Heart of Emptiness Is Black (produced Quezon City, 1973). Quezon City, University of the Philippines Press, 1975.

Other

The Authentic Voice of Poetry. Quezon City, University of the Philippines Office of Research Coordination, 1962.

Critical Studies: "The Wounded Diamond" by Leonard Casper, in *Bookmark* (Manila), 1964; by Leonard Casper, in *Solidarity Magazine* (Manila), 1968.

Ricaredo Demetillo comments:

(1970) My poetry has been much influenced by the New Criticism in America, but I don't belong to any "school."

My poetry has been concerned with the following major themes: the rebellion of the young against the conventional values of an overly repressive society; the modern journey of the individual from lostness to wholeness and fullest creativity; the rise and fall of civilization using the myth of Daedalus in ancient Crete to objectify and evoke the human condition; and the important position of the artists as the bearers and the creators of volumes necessary to the renewal of society. To project all these themes, I have used the lyric, the elegiac, the poetic essay, the epic, etc., with relatively good success. Always, I have been concerned with the human condition and also celebrated the hierarchy of light. Strongest influences: Homer, Dante, Baudelaire, Dylan Thomas, W. B. Yeats and Auden, not to mention myths of all sorts, including the Filipino ones.

(1974) My recent book, *The Scare-Crow Christ*, was written mostly during the troubled period of student activism in Manila and contains poems objectifying the poverty and the spiritual confusion of the time. One poem speaks of the indifference of the average man to the welfare of the "diminished, unfulfilled" man and asks: "Are you not Judas to his scare-crow Christ?"; still another one pays "tall tribute to the hardihood of man" that is able to survive the horrors of war (in Vietnam and elsewhere).

But these new poems are evocations, not propagandistic statements.

My forthcoming verse drama, *The Heart of Emptiness Is Black*, really a sort of sequel to *Barter in Panay*, deals centrally with the conflict between tribalism and emergent individualism; which may have relevance to the present situation of the Philippines under martial law. I chose the drama as a form so that I can be heard by the public, for poetry locally is mostly unheard and unread, if not dead.

The forthcoming *The City and Other Poems* objectifies or evokes the lostness of man in the modern city and the poet's search for any available meaning in the human condition today.

* * *

Ricaredo Demetillo is dedicated to overcoming modern man's bewilderment in a world of changing values. In *No Certain Weather*, he asserts his right to destroy traditional norms, "To breathe the ordered Word into psychic strife" ("Baudelaire"), in order to forge his own values. The iconoclastic wit of *La Via* is directed at the cant and humbug of society. Actually, the new order he envisions is unexcitingly obvious and reactionary. This becomes explicit in *Daedalus and Other Poems*, where his being "a part of one vast whole" ("Sonnet") causes joy. The self-concern is finally dispersed in *Barter in Panay*, a loose adaptation of the folk-odyssey *Maragtas* and the first Filipino epic in English. It suggests that life can be meaningful only through identification with the community.

Demetillo's language which throughout approximates to well-written prose reflects the enlarging of his vision. The stridency of such early images as "What cuckold's voice announced the crib of Christ ...?" ("Baudelaire") is, however, progressively modulated; the serenity in *Daedalus*, of having been "a part of one vast whole" becomes more pronounced in *Barter in Panay* which has, in addition, the detachment and urbanity of the philosopher who has realised his quest. Demetillo's high place among Filipino poets is assured if his development is consistent.

—Abdul Majid bin Nabi Baksh

DEN BOER, James (Drew). American. Born in Sheboygan, Wisconsin, 21 August 1937. Educated at Calvin College, Grand Rapids, Michigan, A.B. 1960; University of California, Santa Barbara, M.A. 1969. Served in the United States Naval Reserve, 1955–63. Married 1) Daphne Kirgma in 1961 (divorced, 1969), one daughter; 2) Emily Cady Williams in 1970, one son. Field Epidemiologist, New Jersey State Department of Health, Trenton, 1962–63; Writer and Editor, United States Public Health Service, Washington, D.C., 1963–67; Deputy Director, White House Conference on Children and Youth, Washington, D.C., 1970–71; Free-lance Consultant, Santa Barbara, 1972–73. Since 1973, Research Information Officer, University of California, Santa Barbara. Assistant Director, Unicorn Press, 1968–70, and Editor, *Spectrum*, Santa Barbara, 1969. Since 1966, Associate Editor, *Voyages* magazine, and since 1971, Editor-at-Large, *Black Box* magazine, Washington, D.C. Recipient: International Poetry Forum Award, 1967; National Endowment for the Arts grant, 1971, 1976; National Institute of Arts and Letters grant, 1971; Author's League of America grant, 1973; Carnegie Foundation grant, 1973. Address: 288 Ortega Ridge Road, Santa Barbara, California 93108, U.S.A.

PUBLICATIONS

Verse

Learning the Way. Pittsburgh, University of Pittsburgh Press, 1968.
Trying to Come Apart. Pittsburgh, University of Pittsburgh Press, 1971.
Nine Poems. Santa Barbara, California, Christopher's, 1972.

James Den Boer comments:

(1970) Bah – who knows what tomorrow's poems will be like; I don't want to be limiting. Poetic *ideals* are a different thing: I'd like my poems to look spare, be direct, colloquial when necessary, a touch surreal, compassionate, courageous, tender, magnanimous – one could go on – the language always fresh and energetic. Themes, subjects, sources probably would reduce to being the same for all poets – what one sees and feels; forms are what happens to happen on the page, and never are "usual."

(1974) I'm not given to placing my poetry within the boundaries of a "school" or particular group of American poets – in many ways, I've deliberately avoided such placing. My major concerns have been with the physical world: woods, water, trees, animals; but within that context it is the human response that matters most – how is it that we relate to the world, what place do we have in it, what succor can we give or take from it, what is our appropriate relationship to it? By "appropriate" I mean a relationship that is primarily non-destructive, that recognizes differences but celebrates congruence, that affords the most insight and the highest degree of transcendant experience. I am not an urban poet, to be most succinct, although that is not deliberate choice but a function of personal happenstance. As to form, I want my poems to be open, colloquial, organic; in the past year or so I have been attempting to write poems that will hold real trees and animals and at the same time deal with ideas – that is, ideas as real as trees and animals. My reading is largely in the life sciences and philosophy; that kind of knowledge brackets my work, however spontaneously or emotionally the poems are triggered.

* * *

James Den Boer's *Learning the Way* and *Trying to Come Apart* present evidence for the emergence of an important talent. In both books, Den Boer draws heavily on autobiographical material, and displays a rare ability to look at his life without flinching.

As the title of *Learning the Way* hints, the poems in this book comprise a sort of itinerary of places and events from the first 30 years of the poet's life. In fact, the book can almost be read as an episodic autobiographical novel, though the episodes are poems, and none of the events seems fabricated; Den Boer writes with the assurance of having lived through every one, and done so from the skin down to wherever genuine poems are born. The experiences form the poems instead of being embedded and half-concealed in poems like pebbles in conglomerate. This nakedness, even more apparent in dealing with the more harrowing experiences (marital breakup, for example) that form *Trying to Come Apart*, is counterpointed by careful organization in this first book, from the first, and title poem, set in the childhood of the poet along Lake Michigan, where he plays at being an Indian, and "tested the limits/of my cunning in isolation," through to the last, "The Jar," in which he declares:

I have been promised
help, despite myself,

and have seen
in the depth of glaze

all I lack – not of color
but of depth –

creator, there are many
flaws. I cross the room
to touch orange, centering.

"The Jar," in addition to expressing an assessment of his life and work at that moment, bringing to at least a temporary terminus the movement started in "Learning the Way," does several other things: "I cross the room/to touch orange, centering" also suggests, in terms of Den Boer's itinerary, his arrival in California, the destination suggested several poems earlier in "The Summons" ("I reach across/the continent, my hand touches California"). "Creator, there are many/flaws" could be an address to himself, an assessment of his book, or an address to God, a half-humorous reproach for creating a poet with all his human imperfections; actually, it's probably both, and in the light of the latter implication, Den Boer himself becomes the "one jar, thrown/on a stranger's wheel" and is, in centering the jar, centering on himself, trying to go deeper for the next journey, the new book.

That next book, *Trying to Come Apart*, does go deeper, especially in a long, powerful poem sequence, "Muttering," about the breakup of the poet and his wife. The book seems an attempt not so much to exorcise, or rationalize, the pain of such experiences, as to deal with it, honestly and openly. The line length of the poems, and the length of the poems themselves, tend to be longer than in the earlier book, and Den Boer tends to see the poems in more and longer sequences than in the first book. The over-all effect is choppier, more discontinuous, than in the first book, as even the title should suggest. The first section opens the book on a hopeful note: the couple, settling in the wilds, hoping for a new life, though this hope is shattered in the second section, "Muttering." The last two sections seem to be an attempt to cope with past experience, to heal and put it in perspective, by accepting the hurt and "trying to come apart." Necessarily, this book does not have the neat sense of design of the first, but there is the exciting sense here of a man not merely viewing his life as potential material for art, but attempting to use his art to heal his life. Den Boer's search is open-ended, without clear resolutions, as is that of most honest men. Those who realize the value lies in the journey, rather than its destination, will want to continue to travel with him in the future.

—Duane Ackerson

DEUTSCH, Babette. American. Born in New York City, 22 September 1895. Educated at Barnard College, New York, B.A. 1917. Married Avrahm Yarmolinsky in 1921; two sons. Taught at the New School for Social Research, New York, 1933–35, and Columbia University, New York, 1944–71. Honorary Consultant to the Library of Congress, Washington, D.C., 1960–66. Recipient: *Nation* prize, 1926; Ford Foundation Prize, 1941; William Rose Benét Memorial Award, 1957. D.Litt.: Columbia University, 1946. Member, American Academy of Arts and Letters. Chancellor, Academy of American Poets. Address: 300 West 108th Street, New York, New York 10025, U.S.A.

PUBLICATIONS

Verse

Banners. New York, Doran, 1919.
Honey out of the Rock. New York and London, Appleton, 1925.
Fire for the Night. New York, Cape and Smith, 1930.
Epistle to Prometheus. New York, Cape and Smith, 1931.
One Part Love. New York, Oxford University Press, 1939.
Take Them, Stranger. New York, Holt, 1944.
Animal, Vegetable, Mineral. New York, Dutton, 1954.
Coming of Age: New and Selected Poems. Bloomington, Indiana University Press, 1959; London, Oxford University Press, 1960.
Collected Poems 1919–1962. Bloomington, Indiana University Press, 1963.
The Collected Poems of Babette Deutsch. New York, Doubleday, 1969.

Novels

A Brittle Heaven. New York, Greenberg, 1926.

In Such a Night. New York, Day, and London, Secker, 1927.
Mask of Silenus: A Novel about Socrates. New York, Simon and Schuster, 1933.
Rogue's Legacy: A Novel about François Villon. New York, Coward McCann, 1942.

Other

Potable Gold: Some Notes on Poetry and This Age. New York, Norton, 1929.
This Modern Poetry. New York, Norton, 1935; London, Faber, 1936.
Heroes of the Kalevala, Finland's Saga (juvenile). New York, Messner, 1940; London, Methuen, 1941.
Walt Whitman: Builder for America. New York, Messner, 1941.
It's a Secret! (juvenile). New York and London, Harper, 1941.
The Welcome (juvenile). New York, Harper, 1942.
Only the Living. New York, Emergency Committee to Save the Jewish People of Europe, 1943.
The Reader's Shakespeare. New York, Messner, 1946.
Poetry in Our Time. New York, Holt, 1952; revised edition, New York, Doubleday, 1963.
Tales of Faraway Folk (juvenile), with Avrahm Yarmolinsky. New York, Harper, 1952.
Poetry Handbook: A Dictionary of Terms. New York, Funk and Wagnalls, 1957; London, Cape, 1958; revised edition, Funk and Wagnalls, 1962, 1969, 1974; Cape, 1965.
More Tales of Faraway Folk (juvenile), with Avrahm Yarmolinsky. New York, Harper, 1963.
I Often Wish (juvenile). New York, Funk and Wagnalls, 1966.

Editor, with Avrahm Yarmolinsky, and Translator, *Contemporary German Poetry.* New York, Harcourt Brace, 1923.
Editor, *Poems of Samuel Taylor Coleridge.* New York, Crowell, 1967.

Translator, with Avrahm Yarmolinsky, *The Twelve*, by Alexander Blok. New York, Heubsch, 1920.
Translator, *Modern Russian Poetry*, edited by Avrahm Yarmolinsky. New York, Harcourt Brace, 1921; London, Lane, 1923; revised edition, as *Russian Poetry*, New York, International, 1927; as *A Treasury of Russian Verse*, New York, Macmillan, 1949.
Translator, *Crocodile*, by K. I. Chukovsky. Philadelphia, Lippincott, 1931.
Translator, *Rosh Hashanah L'Ilanoth (The Trees' New Year's)*, by Solomon Blumgarten, music by Leo Low. New York, Transcontinental, 1940.
Translator, *Poems from "The Book of Hours,"* by Rainer Maria Rilke. New York, New Directions, 1941; London, Vision, 1947; revised edition, New Directions, 1969.
Translator, *Eugene Onegin*, by Alexander Pushkin, edited by Avrahm Yarmolinsky. New York, Heritage Press, 1943; London, Penguin, 1965.
Translator, with Avrahm Yarmolinsky, *The Steel Flea*, by N. Leskov. New York, Harper, 1943; revised edition, 1964.
Translator (verse only), *Selected Writings of Boris Pasternak.* New York, New Directions, 1949.
Translator, *Jean sans Terre*, by Yvan Goll. New York and London, Yoseloff, 1958.
Translator, *Elegy of Ihpetonga*, by Ivan Goll. Kentfield, California, Allen Press, 1962.
Translator, *Two Centuries of Russian Verse*, edited by Avrahm Yarmolinsky. New York, Random House, 1966.
Translator, *There Comes a Time* (juvenile), by Elisabeth Borchers. New York, Doubleday, 1969.

Critical Study: "The Naked Voice" by George Garrett, in *Virginia Quarterly* (Charlottesville), Spring 1964.

Babette Deutsch comments:

The most "personal statement" concerning my work is in the poems themselves. My hope is (as I have written on poetry elsewhere) that my poems "realize an unusually comprehensive experience more intensely" or "realize an unusually intense, if sometimes trivial, experience more comprehensively."

* * *

Babette Deutsch, whose first book of poems appeared in 1919, has published eight more in the fifty years since then, along with novels, books for children, and critical works of commanding importance. She remains primarily a poet, and because her mind is of the very finest grain, and because the range of her interests is unlimited, she continues to occupy a high, unique place among her peers. She is one of the most intelligent poets who ever wrote, and one of the most toughly sensitive, with an unimpeachable seriousness which humor keeps always sweet. Her phrasing is brilliant and swift, but her chief charm is in the completeness with which she realizes and renders a subject. For example, "Lizard at Pompeii":

Little finger of fiery green, it
flickers over stone. Waits
in a weed's shadow.
Flashes emerald –
is gone.

Here once horror poured so hot, heavy, thick,
everyone was dead before he was sick.
Now here is no heat but the sun's
on old stone treads;
no motion but that rippling inch of whip:
yours, you little live jewel, who slipped away
into silence. Yet stay on to haunt memory,
like those dead.

Or "History":

History
Coming too close
Is monstrous, like a doll
That is alive and bigger than the child
Who tries to hold it.
It is a clock that tolls the thirteenth hour.
It is a theatre
On fire.

Or "To the Moon, 1969": "Now you have been reached, you are altered beyond belief –/... a planet that men have, almost casually, cheapened." Babette Deutsch has been valuable as a translator of Russian, German, and French poetry; and certainly she has been valuable as a critic; but her permanent gift to us is the pleasure we derive from the play of her mind over truths of the heart she has known how to make finally plain.

—Mark Van Doren

DICKEY, James (Lafayette). American. Born in Atlanta, Georgia, 2 February 1923. Educated at Clemson College, South Carolina, 1942; Vanderbilt University, Nashville, Tennessee, B.A. (magna cum laude) 1949 (Phi Beta Kappa), M.A. 1950. Served in the United States Army Air Force during World War II and in the Air Force during the Korean War. Married 1) Maxine Syerson in 1949 (died, 1976), two sons; 2) Deborah Dodson in 1976. Taught at Rice University, Houston, 1950, 1952–54, and the University of Florida, Gainesville, 1955–56; Poet-in-Residence, Reed College, Portland, Oregon, 1962–64, San Fernando Valley State College, Northridge, California, 1964–66, and the University of Wisconsin, Madison, 1966. Consultant in Poetry, Library of Congress, Washington, D.C., 1967–69. Since 1969, Professor of English and Writer-in-Residence, University of South Carolina, Columbia. Recipient: *Sewanee Review* Fellowship, 1954; Union League Civic and Arts Foundation Prize (*Poetry*, Chicago), 1958; Vachel Lindsay Prize, 1959; Longview Foundation Award, 1960; Guggenheim Fellowship, 1961; Melville Cane Award, 1966; National Book Award, 1966; National Institute of Arts and Letters grant, 1966. Address: 4620 Lelia's Court, Lake Katherine, Columbia, South Carolina 29206, U.S.A.

PUBLICATIONS

Verse

Into the Stone and Other Poems. New York, Scribner, 1960.
Drowning with Others. Middletown, Connecticut, Wesleyan University Press, 1962.
Helmets. Middletown, Connecticut, Wesleyan University Press, and London, Longman, 1964.
Two Poems of the Air. Portland, Oregon, Centicore Press, 1964.
Buckdancer's Choice. Middletown, Connecticut, Wesleyan University Press, 1965.
Poems 1957–1967. Middletown, Connecticut, Wesleyan University Press, and London, Rapp and Carroll, 1967.
The Achievement of James Dickey: A Comprehensive Selection of His Poems, with a Critical Introduction, edited by Laurence Lieberman. Chicago, Scott Foresman, 1968.
The Eye-Beaters, Blood, Victory, Madness, Buckhead and Mercy. New York, Doubleday, and London, Hamish Hamilton, 1970.
The Zodiac. Bloomfield Hills, Michigan, Bruccoli Clark, 1976; revised edition, New York, Doubleday, 1976; London, Hamish Hamilton, 1977.
The Strength of Fields. Bloomfield Hills, Michigan, Bruccoli Clark, 1977; revised edition, New York, Doubleday, 1979.

Recordings: *Poems*, Spoken Arts; *James Dickey Reads His Poetry*, Caedmon Tapes.

Plays

Screenplay: *Deliverance*, 1972.

Television Play: *The Call of the Wild*, from the novel by Jack London, 1976.

Novel

Deliverance. Boston, Houghton Mifflin, and London, Hamish Hamilton, 1970.

Other

The Suspect in Poetry. Madison, Minnesota, Sixties Press, 1964.
A Private Brinksmanship. Pasadena, California, Castle Press, 1965.

Spinning the Crystal Ball: Some Guesses at the Future of American Poetry. Washington, D.C., Library of Congress, 1967.
Metaphor as Pure Adventure (lecture). Washington, D.C., Library of Congress, 1968.
Babel to Byzantium: Poets and Poetry Now. New York, Farrar Straus, 1968.
Self-Interviews, edited by Barbara and James Reiss. New York, Doubleday, 1970.
Sorties (essays). New York, Doubleday, 1971.
Exchanges ...: Being in the Form of a Dialogue with Joseph Trumbull Stickney. Bloomfield Hills, Michigan, Bruccoli Clark, 1971.
Jericho: The South Beheld, paintings by Hubert Shuptrine. Birmingham, Alabama, Oxmoor House, 1974.
God's Images: The Bible: A New Vision, illustrated by Marvin Hayes. Birmingham, Alabama, Oxmoor House, 1977.
Tucky the Hunter (juvenile). New York, Crown, 1978.

Translator, *Stolen Apples*, by Evgenii Evtushenko. New York, Doubleday, 1971; London, W. H. Allen, 1972.

Critical Study: Introduction by Laurence Lieberman to *The Achievement of James Dickey*, 1968.

Theatrical Activities:
Actor: **Film** – *Deliverance*, 1972.

James Dickey comments:

I like to think the major theme, if there is one, is continuity between the self and the world, and the various attempts by men to destroy this (wars, and so on: heavy industry and finance and the volume-turnover system). I try to say something about the individual's way, or ways, of protecting this sense of continuity in himself, or of his attempts to restore it. Much of my work deals with rivers, mountains, changes of weather, seas and the air. I am lately trying to move into a kind of poetry in which the exchanges between people – rather than between one person and, say, the landscape – will have more part.

* * *

The emergence and growth of James Dickey as a poet in a little more than a decade is a remarkable phenomenon, a testimony to his enormous drive and the extraordinary powers of his imagination. As if this accomplishment were not sufficient in itself, his collected reviews and essays on contemporary verse, *Babel to Byzantium*, clearly place him as one of the three or four excellent practical critics of poetry now functioning.

In his essay "The Poet Turns on Himself," Dickey has observed that he did not begin to write poems until the age of 24, and then with no particular knowledge of the various formal techniques available from the English poetic tradition. Instead, his concentration was upon "the individually imaginative or visionary quality" that might be attained in the effort to render with immediacy and force the most intense moments of experience. He came also to realize that his own life, its love affairs and deaths, its periods spent in two wars as a combat pilot, an inclination toward athletics and motorcycle riding in youth, a fascination with hunting animals using only bow and arrow, was the richest potential material for his art; and so Dickey has carried that life experience into poetry, but has so beautifully and amazingly transformed it through language, image, rhythm, through his seemingly endless imaginative resources and capacity for extending the range of his feelings, that to encounter one of his poems is to enter the realms of myth or dream. The universe of Dickey's poetry is charged with hidden energies; things exist in secret relation with one another; here everything is possible, for the imagination which brings these images to birth is both sophisticated and primitive, animistic. Not only that, but the individual or self in his poems continually manifests the ability to reach out and participate in the being of others: two boys in a tree house at night simply by their presence summon their dead brother to join them; the hunter senses within himself the existence of the animal he tracks; the shadows of people seated on a lighted screened porch are cast upon the surrounding grass of the yard inhabited by chirping night insects, and mysteriously these human shadows bring the souls of the people with them into the grass so that the two worlds of the living momentarily coalesce:

> Where the people are lying,
> Emitted by their own house
> So humanly that they become
> More than human, and enter the place
> Of small, blindly singing things,
> Seeming to rejoice
> Perpetually, without effort,
> Without knowing why
> Or how they do it.

More recently, Dickey has been exploring the possibilities of some longer poems, and while they still exemplify his strengths and vision, they tend at times to become wordy and diffuse. Though his writing is uniquely his own, Dickey stands in a line of poetic descent from Whitman and Roethke, both of whom he admires greatly, and perhaps has learned from Rilke and other modern European poets. Among contemporaries, his closest literary affinities are with Robert Bly, James Wright, Louis Simpson, and W. S. Merwin, though each poet bears his own distinctive manner, has his own particular interests.

—Ralph J. Mills, Jr.

DICKEY, R(obert) P(reston). American. Born in Flat River, Missouri, 24 September 1936. Educated at the University of Missouri, Columbia, B.A. 1968, M.A. 1969. Served in the United States Air Force, 1954–56. Married the poet Victoria McCabe in 1969 (divorced, 1976), one son. Instructor, University of Missouri, 1967–69; Assistant Professor, Southern Colorado State College, Pueblo, 1969–73. Since 1975, Assistant Professor of Creative Writing, Pima College, Tucson. Since 1966, Founding Editor, *Poetry Bag Magazine*. Recipient: Swallow Press New Poetry Series Award, 1969. Agent: Charles R. Byrne, 1133 Avenue of the Americas, New York, New York 10036. Address: Pima College, West Campus, Tucson, Arizona 85709, U.S.A.

PUBLICATIONS

Verse

Four Poets, with others. Pella, Iowa, C.U.I. Press, 1967.
Running Lucky. Chicago, Swallow Press, 1969.
Acting Immortal. Columbia, University of Missouri Press, 1970.
Concise Dictionary of Lead River, Mo. Taos, New Mexico, Black Bear Press, 1972.
The Basic Stuff of Poetry. Dubuque, Iowa, Kendall Hunt, 1972.
Life-Cycle of Seven Songs. Taos, New Mexico, Talmaneh Press, 1972.

McCabe Wants Chimes. Taos, New Mexico, Talmaneh Press, 1973.
The McCabes: A Family Sketch. Privately printed, 1973.
Drunk on a Greyhound. Shawnee Mission, Kansas, BkMk Press, 1973.
One Man in Pueblo. Privately printed, 1973.

Plays

This Is Our Living Room (produced Denver, 1971).
Concise Dictionary of Lead River, Mo., music by Carol Ann Plonkey (produced Pueblo, Colorado, 1973). Taos, New Mexico, Black Bear Press, 1973.
Minnequa, music by Gerhard Track (produced Pueblo, Colorado, 1976).

Critical Studies: Reviews in *Sou'wester* (Edwardsville, Illinois), Winter 1970, Winter 1971; *Times-Union* (Rochester, New York), 28 January 1970; *Contempora* (Atlanta), May–June 1970; *Choice* (Chicago), July–August 1970; *Library Journal* (New York), 1 October 1970, September 1972; *South Dakota Review* (Vermillion), Winter 1970–71; *Western Humanities Review* (Salt Lake City), Winter 1971; *December* (Western Springs, Illinois), xiii, 1–2, 1971; *Poetry* (Chicago), July 1971; *Western American Literature* (Fort Collins, Colorado), v, 1.

R. P. Dickey comments:

I consider myself primarily a poet. Roughly 75% of my poems are in the prose mode, 25% in the verse mode. I didn't plan it, but as I check out my books, it seems that I use rhyme in about 15% of my poems, for whatever that might be worth. I have written about thirty short stories and published exactly one; about fifty reviews and published all of them except one – the editor said it was "intemperate," which was what I had considered its central virtue. Several critical articles of mine have been published, but the less said on that the better. I tend to agree with the late Win Scott when he said, "Criticism is dead the minute it's written and buried the minute it's published." I completed my first novel after seven years of false starts and woeful ignorance of technique, in 1971. Called *Clarkey's Itinerary*, it's my *Inferno* of the times and so far (*circa*, March, 1973) hasn't found the proper publisher. It has done me for the prose end of the continuum for a while. One of these days I may write my *Purgatorio*, but just now I'm back into my true love, poetry, and working slowly on a new play. Plays, like public readings (I've given nearly 200 since 1966), are among other things, sobering; they get one in touch with a healthy objectivity of a kind we all need. Such activities can be rescue jobs from the narcissistic subjectivity and self-pity all of us wallow in, alas, too much of the time.

It seems that the peculiar quality of a poem, as such, resides in the tension which exists because on one level the poem is calling attention to itself, to itself as *language* formally organized, and on another level is directing the reader's attention away from itself, out of things and actual events, is pointing away from itself, is making itself into as transparent a medium as it can in order that the reader may see through it to the enduring truth and universals it points to with its marshalling of particulars. Something like that. I believe that whatever the truth is, it is both manifold and one, and that the medium of poetry exists in order to help get us in touch with it, to help us get with it. I believe that the truth – again, whatever it is in any final description – is not dependent nor any way reliant upon the observer, the poet. It is the poet's difficult job to get with *it*, as much as he can.

What makes poetry important as a body of knowledge is that nowhere else can a reader go to find out how people *really* feel about things; that makes poetry unique. The poet has a duty, a responsibility to what John Ciardi has called that "midnight man" of 100 years from now who will be rummaging through a shelf of books of poems trying to find some hard, clear, complex, honest help in answering the question of who he is. Saul Bellow or R. G. Collingwood, one of them said that art is a medicine for society's disease of stupidity, and of course sometimes medicine is hard to swallow or comes in the form of a bitter pill. The poet, like anyone trying to be worth his salt, looks for what is good; but he must record, not what he is looking for, but what he actually *finds*. It follows that simplism is the poet's main enemy as he makes his forms.

I like to extend myself and try longer things sometimes, but these days I find myself writing mostly short poems, meditative if not lyric, but more and more, influenced by Browning, dramatic instead of meditative. Pound and Yeats have been my major literary influences and I suspect continue to be so. (I am both bothered and embarrassed when thoughtless people say, of some poet or other, that he was "all right for his time, but is outdated now," etc., forgetting that they are talking about art as if it were journalism. The two profoundly wise aphorisms by Pound which they need to remember in this context are these: "Literature is news that stays news"; and, in art "All ages are contemporaneous.") I still like to experiment with traditional structures and rimes, slant-rimes mostly, but less and less. At the risk of sounding hopelessly didactic, I agree with Rilke's archaic torso of Apollo that a great work of art tells you, among other things, that you must change your life. The best poems happen to you, you have to write them; but in between there is the necessary difficulty of keeping the pencil sharp for those infrequent good ones, by writing bad ones, Parnassian ones, practice ones, whatever, just to keep writing, to keep sane so you might be able to handle the next bout of inspiration or madness. And you read, and reread. I reread a lot in Ted Hughes, Larkin, Lowell, James Dickey, Leonard Cohen, Browning, Shakespeare, Dante, Pound, Yeats, Bellow, the King James Bible, and C. S. Lewis's non-fiction, among others.

* * *

The title poem to R. P. Dickey's first volume, "Running Lucky," exemplifies the tone of much of his poetry – ironic, self-mocking, and rebellious: "I run with shabby baggage,/a toy for some god that won't grow up./And yet I feel I'm lucky." The extent of his luck is to have escaped being nailed "to that well-built cross/on which the stricken and hopeless hang."

Dickey's escape, always provisional, rests upon an allegiance to personal feelings and values as they are related to his surroundings (principally, the central Missouri area) and to the men and women who give significance to his life. Many of the poems, especially in the second volume, *Acting Immortal*, are about friends or dedicated to them. They speak persuasively for the belief that intimate contact is the foundation of living. In this regard, Dickey attaches special importance to sensory experience; some of his best poems record his delight with the human body and the experience of love.

He uses effectively natural speech rhythms, breath phrasing, short lines, expressive word positioning, and compressed syntax in the experimental tradition of Cummings, Williams, and, more recently, the Projectivist poets. When least successful, the style is self-conscious and contrived; when most successful, the controlled casualness of his style reflects Dickey's theme of confronting life honestly and without pretense.

—Dale Doepke

DICKEY, William. American. Born in Bellingham, Washington, 15 December 1928. Educated at Reed College, Portland, Oregon, B.A. 1951 (Phi Beta Kappa); Harvard University, Cambridge, Massachusetts, M.A. 1955; University of Iowa, Iowa City, M.F.A. 1956; Jesus College, Oxford (Fulbright Scholar), 1959–60. Married Shirley Ann Marn in 1959 (divorced, 1972). Instructor, Cornell University, Ithaca, New York, 1956–59; Assistant Professor, Denison University, Granville, Ohio, 1960–62. Since 1962, Member of the

English Department, and currently Professor of English, San Francisco State University. Visiting Professor, University of Hawaii, Honolulu, Spring 1973. Formerly, Managing Editor, *Western Review*, and Editorial Assistant, *Civil War History*. Recipient: Yale Series of Younger Poets Award, 1959; Union League Civic and Arts Foundation Prize (*Poetry*, Chicago), 1962; National Endowment for the Arts fellowship, 1977; University of Massachusetts Press Juniper Prize, 1978. Address: 121 Liberty Street, San Francisco, California 94110, U.S.A.

PUBLICATIONS

Verse

Of the Festivity. New Haven, Connecticut, Yale University Press, 1959.
Interpreter's House. Columbus, Ohio State University Press, 1963.
Rivers of the Pacific Northwest. San Francisco, Twowindows Press, 1969.
More under Saturn. Middletown, Connecticut, Wesleyan University Press, 1971.
The Rainbow Grocery. Amherst, University of Massachusetts Press, 1978.

William Dickey comments:

I am closest to various poets who studied at the Writers Workshop of the University of Iowa in the 1950's; but I don't know that it would be recognized as a school.

* * *

William Dickey's first book was W. H. Auden's last selection as editor of the Yale Younger Poets, and the older poet was clearly one of the chief influences on the then neophyte:

And through the morns the ample ladies gather
The ribbons of their lives and press them dear.
They are intrinsic selves and need no other
Posture to arrive and interfere.

Dickey's book overflows with the posturings of several selves, and often the several postures of the individual divided against himself. But such division is always controlled, always measured. The title poem of this volume is elaborately rhymed with simple words and concerns the speaker's inanition, his fear of the potential disruption of love, but it also reveals an awe of communication mingled with doubt of its efficacy ("And all the words my mouth has ever said/Will fail to tell us whether we live or die"). The poems are learned, but not to a fault, though too often they form a commentary on experience rather than a presentation of it. As such, the book stood at the end of a decade whose poetic idiom, replete with irony and balanced wit, it substantially epitomized.

His latest book, *More under Saturn*, differs radically from the first; an aesthetic of openness, of imaginative suddenness, has replaced the earlier, formalistic decorum. Now we have Macy's department store instead of Caesar's Gallic Wars, an almost surreal jangle of images in place of the structured rhetoric, and a coarse colloquial ear keeping measure, rather than the polished flow of iambs. Here is a poem, complete, called "The Instructor Has Not Followed the Lesson Plan Very Carefully":

The motor grinds & won't catch.
Nowhere worth going to: so the car thinks.

And I think. Once there was punctuation
worth listening to. I was used to that & I said:

Here are all the commas you will use up in a normal life.
The students bit at my wrists & ankles &

A wild deer burst into the office & bled to death
Kicking the files to mush.

The irony is still there, but now instead of bringing things into focus, it's employed to break open the closures of the poems, to celebrate madness rather than to contain neurotic stasis. The ampersand and the colon have replaced the comma, and, instead of assured articulation, we are offered, almost threatened with, insistent juxtapositions.

Dickey's startling development, or devolution if looked at from another angle, is symptomatic of changes in American poetry throughout the 1960's. As the Eliotic-Audenesque hegemony broke apart, the dominant idiom splintered, and many poets, certainly Dickey among them, were set adrift. His career is too heterogeneous to judge easily, and his main strengths at this point are his quiet responsiveness and his continued responsibility to use language to sharpen the contours of his experience. This may require release as well as concision for the moment. He is a poet in mid-stride, though obviously very capable of energetic movement.

—Charles Molesworth

DICKINSON, Patric (Thomas). British. Born in Nasirabad, India, 26 December 1914. Educated at St. Catharine's College, Cambridge (Crabtree Exhibitioner), B.A. (honours) in English and classics 1936. Served with the Artists' Rifles, 1939–40. Married the anthologist Sheila Shannon in 1947; two children. Schoolmaster, 1936–39. Producer, 1942–45, and Poetry Editor, 1945–48, BBC, London. Since 1948, Free-lance Writer. Gresham Professor of Rhetoric, City University, London, 1964–67. Recipient: Atlantic Award, 1948; Cholmondeley Award, 1973. Address: 38 Church Square, Rye, Sussex, England.

PUBLICATIONS

Verse

The Seven Days of Jericho. London, Dakers, 1944.
Theseus and the Minotaur, and Poems. London, Cape, 1946.
Stone in the Midst and Poems. London, Methuen, 1948.
The Sailing Race and Other Poems. London, Chatto and Windus, 1952.
The Scale of Things. London, Chatto and Windus, 1955.
The World I See. London, Chatto and Windus-Hogarth Press, 1960.
This Cold Universe. London, Chatto and Windus-Hogarth Press, 1964.
Selected Poems. London, Chatto and Windus, 1968.
More Than Time. London, Chatto and Windus-Hogarth Press, 1970.
A Wintering Tree. London, Chatto and Windus-Hogarth Press, 1973.
The Bearing Beast. London, Chatto and Windus-Hogarth Press, 1976.
Our Loving John. London, Chatto and Windus, 1979.

Plays

Theseus and the Minotaur (broadcast, 1945). Included in *Theseus and the Minotaur, and Poems*, 1946.

Stone in the Midst (produced London, 1949). Included in *Stone in the Midst and Poems*, 1948.
Robinson, adaptation of a play by Jules Supervielle (produced London, 1953).
The Golden Touch (produced Wolverhampton, Staffordshire, 1959; London, 1960).
A Durable Fire (produced Canterbury, 1962; London, 1963). London, Chatto and Windus, 1962.
Pseudolus, adaptation of the play by Plautus (produced Stoke on Trent, 1966).
Ode to St. Catharine, music by Bernard Rose (produced Cambridge, 1973).
Creation, music by Alan Ridout (produced Ely, 1973).
The Miller's Secret, music by Stephen Dodgson (produced Cookham, Berkshire, 1973).

Radio Plays and Documentaries: *Theseus and the Minotaur*, 1945; *The First Family*, 1960; *Wilfred Owen*, 1970; *The Pensive Prisoner*, 1970; *Phaeton*, music by Alan Ridout, 1977.

Television Play: *Lysistrata*, from the play by Aristophanes, 1964.

Other

A Round of Golf Courses: A Round of the Best Eighteen. London, Evans, 1951.
The Good Minute: An Autobiographical Study. London, Gollancz, 1965.

Editor, *Soldiers' Verse.* London, Muller, 1945.
Editor, *Byron: Poems.* London, Grey Walls Press, 1949.
Editor, with Erica Marx and J. C. Hall, *New Poems 1955.* London, Joseph, 1955.
Editor, *Poetry Supplement.* London, Poetry Book Society, 1958.
Editor, with Sheila Shannon, *Poems to Remember* (juvenile). London, Harvill Press, 1958.
Editor, with Sheila Shannon, *Poets' Choice: An Anthology of English Poetry from Spenser to the Present Day.* London, Evans, 1967.
Editor, *C. Day Lewis: Selections from His Poetry.* London, Chatto and Windus, 1967.

Translator, *Aristophanes Against War: Three Plays.* London, Oxford University Press, 1957.
Translator, *The Aeneid of Virgil.* New York, New American Library, 1961.
Translator, *The Complete Plays of Aristophanes.* London, Oxford University Press, 2 vols., 1971.

Manuscript Collections: British Library, London; Birmingham University; Humanities Research Center, University of Texas, Austin.

Patric Dickinson comments:

Bias towards country subjects since I live in the country. No "usual" verse forms: a tendency to invention. General sources: English poetry from 1500. Influences in youth: Yeats, Frost, Edward Thomas, in particular. Stylistic devices: a continual attempt at greater honesty, clarity, and conciseness.

* * *

The essential Patric Dickinson is a stubborn lyricist who thrives on paradox. He seems endlessly surprised by emblematic landscapes, refining them into "a particular/Sharp agony of atmosphere," and his most successful poems are (to borrow from a title) passionate, graceful distillations of Outsight to Insight. Their impact derives from the tension between fear and affirmation, loss and gratitude, a cold impersonal universe and the intimacy of "our sweet immediate life." Some of the early work gestures too largely; the influence of Yeats is conspicuous and there are strong echoes of late-1930's Auden: "Against you all I set up love/ And cry it in your teeth." Here it is the *poetry* that is set up, a willed confrontation in the grand manner of romantic stoicism sharpened by contemporary reference, but Dickinson worked this need to posture out of his system quickly, and by the time he published his excellent 1948 collection, *Stone in the Midst*, he had become altogether more subtle. In one of this book's best poems, "The Ammonite," he considers "how we/Are riddled with creation," and in that challenging pun lies the ambiguity which remains at the centre of his subsequent achievement; to live is to suffer, and suffering gives the edge to love. The riddle is the actual pain and the illusive mystery. Here is a complete, and characteristic, short poem, "Winter Sun" (*The Scale of Things*):

Out of the sea the sun
Rose into cloudlessness.
All that the heart could tell
Of certainty was there
In the pure blessing air.
No need for poetry, peace
Between symbol and real was signed
By the thrush in the bare tree
And the mind in its life-cell.

But the grief-divining ray
Aware of its nakedness
Wove round itself a cloud –
That tribute of small tears
No day is day nor love
Is daily love without.

Time and again, Dickinson insists upon "how lonely all men are" among the bewildering generosities of nature, how this loneliness both intensifies our awareness of beauty (he's a poet who is neither afraid of that word nor uses it sentimentally) and agitates us towards destruction: "all nature's/A prisoner on parole/To our violence." Above all, though, despite the grim recesses of the human condition, he never turns away towards an easier, more diffuse light or indulges in melancholy: it is "The dark sea bed of the soul where move/All the creative impulses of love," and, as he remarks in "A Wintering Tree," it is "The condition of being rooted/That gives a creature worth." This strong sense of particularity is what gives his finest poems their resonant firmness and a memorable context for their weightier generalisations. A stanza may begin "Walking together through time," courting the portentousness of abstraction, but on that journey "every cobblestone snaps down/A lid as a foot falls," giving an immediacy to the experience which is simply (though not easily achieved) the hallmark of true poetry.

If Dickinson's work is characterised by the thematic tensions noted at the beginning, it must in the end be emphasised that what gives so many of the poems their force is the precision and accuracy of their notation. There have been patches of meandering dullness in several of the books, but these are outnumbered by the elegant, moving lyrics in which an individual, lovingly troubled voice is clearly heard:

But if a secret is born of a secret
And kept to the very death
Of itself and you within and without,
It is indeed the proof
In mortal man
Of divinity enough.

—John Mole

DILLARD, R(ichard) H(enry) W(ilde). American. Born in Roanoke, Virginia, 11 October 1937. Educated at Roanoke College, Salem, Virginia, 1955–58, B.A. 1958 (Phi Beta Kappa); University of Virginia, Charlottesville (Woodrow Wilson Fellowship, 1958–59; DuPont Fellowship, 1959–61), M.A. 1959, Ph.D. 1965. Married Cathy Hankla (second marriage) in 1979. Instructor in English, Roanoke College, Summer 1961, and University of Virginia, 1961–64. Assistant Professor, 1964–68, Associate Professor, 1968–74, since 1971, Chairman of the Graduate Program in Contemporary Literature and Creative Writing, and since 1974, Professor of English, Hollins College, Virginia. Since 1973, Vice President, *The Film Journal*, New York. Contributing Editor, *The Hollins Critic*, Hollins College, Virginia, 1966–77. Recipient: Academy of American Poets Prize, 1961; Ford grant, 1972. Agent: Blanche C. Gregory, 2 Tudor City Place, New York, New York 10017. Address: Box 9671, Hollins College, Virginia 24020, U.S.A.

PUBLICATIONS

Verse

The Day I Stopped Dreaming about Barbara Steele and Other Poems. Chapel Hill, University of North Carolina Press, 1966.
News of the Nile. Chapel Hill, University of North Carolina Press, 1971.
After Borges. Baton Rouge, Louisiana State University Press, 1972.

Play

Screenplay: *Frankenstein Meets the Space Monster*, with George Garrett and John Rodenbeck, 1966.

Novel

The Book of Changes. New York, Doubleday, 1974.

Other

Horror Films. New York, Monarch Press, 1976.

Editor, with Louis D. Rubin, Jr., *The Experience of America: A Book of Readings.* New York, Macmillan, and London, Collier Macmillan, 1969.
Editor, with George Garrett and John Rees Moore, *The Sounder Few: Essays from "The Hollins Critic."* Athens, University of Georgia Press, 1971.

R. H. W. Dillard comments:

Although I have thought a good deal about what I am doing in my poems, I don't know that I really am able to express the results of that thinking very clearly, except (I hope) in the poems themselves. Allow me, then, to offer in place of an introductory statement about my poetry, excerpts from three poems which might do the job.

The first, from the poem "News of the Nile," is just a description of the source of my poems – experience in the broadest sense: "All these things I have read and remembered,/ Witnessed, imagined, thought and written down...."

The second, from the poem "Construction," may be a bit more helpful, for it is as close as I've come to an explicit esthetic statement, and it also makes explicit my central concern with the vital involvement of seeing and saying, of action and belief:

To say as you see. To see as by stop-action,
Clouds coil overhead, the passage of days,

Trees bend by the side of the road
Like tires on a curve, plants uncurl,

How the world dissolves in the water of the eye:
The illusion speed produces. The reality of speed.

A result: to see as you say,
As gravity may bend a ray of light.

To say the earth's center is of fire:
Life leaps from the soil like sun flares.

To see the world made true,
An art of rocks and stones and trees,

Real materials in real space,
L'esthétique de la vitesse.

The third, from the long poem *January: A Screenplay*, is a prayer which states briefly the faith and the humility which I hope is at the heart of everything I do:

For my sorrow in this depth of joy,
Gift beyond reward, I'm sorry.
For the joy I feel in this broken world,
This sorrow, this woe, I thank you,
I thank you.

* * *

Each of R. H. W. Dillard's three fine volumes is an important contribution to American poetry. The first, *The Day I Stopped Dreaming about Barbara Steele*, despite its echoes of Williams, Auden, Stevens, Ransom and Tate, is a highly sophisticated, humorous and unique representation of experience. The most traditionally formal of the three volumes, it is most impressive in its sardonic rendering of a wide range of "things." Mr. Dillard, fascinated by the power of his imagination, transforms into objects of beauty things – objects, emotions, experiences – that might otherwise be ephemeral or unnoticed. The wit in this volume does not diminish the sense of tragedy but as in Williams' "Pictures from Brueghel: Landscape with the Fall of Icarus," enlarges it by placing it in a comic context. At the same time it should be emphasized that the "thinginess" is definitely not that of the empiricist, realist or naturalist, but more that of the esthete.

News of the Nile, his second volume, is a further development of a distinctive voice. The See-er of visions of the imagination, intellectualized and witty, becomes autobiographical, personal, subjective, troubled. The models shift to Lowell and Roethke. Perhaps too much influenced by his study of horror movies, Mr. Dillard examines the perverse in human nature and experience – blood lust, cannibalism, the macabre. Poems such as "Night of the Living Dead," "Event; A Gathering; Vastation," "Act of Detection," studies of the predatory and bestial nature of man, revel in visions of horror. Other poems, much lighter, struggle in the poet's soul to deal honestly with the substance of his own time and place and his relationship to it.

Mr. Dillard's third volume, *After Borges*, represents a mature achievement. The title signals a profound experience with the work of the Argentine writer, Jorge Luis Borges. The shock of a recent discovery of evil of too many of the poems in *News of the Nile* has given way to the good humor and wit of the first volume. Poems such as "Round Ruby," "What Can You Say to Shoes," "Sweet Strawberries," and "Wings" express a new found and authentic joy in life, its triviality, absurdity, beauty and pathos. Others, such as "Limits," "The Other Tiger," "Argumentum Ornithologicum," and "Epilogue" which purport to be "after the Spanish of Jorge Luis Borges," are more serious and complex. At the base of these poems is an extreme solipsism. Thus "Epilogue" tells us of the poet who sets "out to shape a world," and finds at the end of his work a "face, wearing/And worn, warm as worn stone,/A face you know: your own." The tension in this and other poems is based on the conflict of ego struggling to see through, beyond, or around itself, its face, to another self or world which seems inaccessible. Perhaps most important about the direction of these latest poems is that, if his work is becoming more psychological and personal, it is also more conscious of the psyche in history. Mr. Dillard's discovery of Borges's labyrinth helped him to see himself in a deeper and richer, if more difficult, context.

—Richard Damashek

---

di PRIMA, Diane. American. Born in New York City, 6 August 1934. Attended Swarthmore College, Pennsylvania, 1951–53. Married Alan S. Marlowe in 1962; five children. Contributing Editor, *Kulchur* magazine, New York, 1960–61; Co-Editor, with LeRoi Jones, 1961–63, and Editor, 1963–69, *Floating Bear* magazine, New York; also associated with *Yugen*, *Guerilla*, San Francisco *Sunday Paper*, and *Rallying Point*. Publisher, with Alan S. Marlowe, Poets Press, New York, 1964–69, and since 1974, Eidolon Editions, San Francisco. Co-Founder, New York Poets Theatre, 1961. Since 1971, teacher in the Poetry-in-the-Schools Program; since 1974, teacher at the Naropa Institute, Boulder, Colorado. Artist-in-Residence, Napa State Hospital, 1976–77. Recipient: National Endowment for the Arts grant, 1966, 1973; Coordinating Council of Little Magazines grant, 1967, 1970. Address: 263 Laguna Street, San Francisco, California 94102, U.S.A.

PUBLICATIONS

Verse

This Kind of Bird Flies Backward. New York, Totem Press, 1958.
The Monster. New Haven, Connecticut, Penny Poems, 1961.
The New Handbook of Heaven. San Francisco, Auerhahn Press, 1963.
Unless You Clock In. Palo Alto, California, Patchen Cards, 1963.
Combination Theatre Poem and Birthday Poem for Ten People. New York, Brownstone Press, 1965.
Poems for Freddie. New York, Poets Press, 1966.
Haiku. Topanga, California, Love Press, 1967.
Earthsong: Poems 1957–59, edited by Alan S. Marlowe. New York, Poets Press, 1968.
Hotel Albert. New York, Poets Press, 1968.
New Mexico Poem, June–July 1967. New York, Roodenko, 1968.
The Star, The Child, The Light. Privately printed, 1968.
Revolutionary Letters. New York, Long Hair, 1969.
L.A. Odyssey. New York, Poets Press, 1969.
New As.... Privately printed, 1969.

Notes on a Summer Solstice. Privately printed, 1969.
The Book of Hours. San Francisco, Brownstone Press, 1970.
Kerhonkson Journal 1966. Berkeley, California, Oyez, 1971.
Prayer to the Mothers. Privately printed, 1971.
So Fine. Santa Barbara, California, Yes Press, 1971.
XV Dedications. Santa Barbara, California, Unicorn Press, 1971.
The Calculus of Letters. Privately printed, 1972.
Loba, Part 1. Santa Barbara, California, Capra Press, 1973.
Freddie Poems. Point Reyes, California, Eidolon, 1974.
Selected Poems 1956–1975. Plainfield, Vermont, North Atlantic, 1975.
Loba as Eve. New York, Phoenix Book Shop, 1975.
Loba, Part 2. Point Reyes, California, Eidolon, 1976.
Loba, Parts 1–8. Berkeley, California, Wingbow Press, 1978.

Plays

Paideuma (produced New York, 1960).
The Discontent of the Russian Prince (produced New York, 1961).
Murder Cake (produced New York, 1963).
Like (produced New York, 1964).
Poets Vaudeville, music by John Herbert McDowell (produced New York, 1964). New York, Feed Folly Press, 1964.
Monuments (produced New York, 1968).
The Discovery of America (produced New York, 1972).
Whale Honey (produced San Francisco, 1975; New York, 1976).

Novels

The Calculus of Variation. New York, Poets Press, 1966.
Spring and Autumn Annals. San Francisco, Frontier Press, 1966.
Memoirs of a Beatnik. New York, Olympia Press, 1969.

Short Stories

Dinners and Nightmares. New York, Corinth, 1961; revised edition, 1974.

Other

Editor, *Various Fables from Various Places.* New York, Putnam, 1960.
Editor, *War Poems.* New York, Poets Press, 1968.
Editor, with LeRoi Jones, *The Floating Bear: A Newsletter, Numbers 1–37.* La Jolla, California, Laurence McGilvery, 1974.

Translator, *Seven Love Poems from the Middle Latin.* New York, Poets Press, 1965.

Manuscript Collection: Southern Illinois University, Carbondale.

* * *

With the publication of Diane di Prima's *Selected Poems* and *Loba, Parts 1–8* we are provided with the opportunity to see the full form of her work to date. In all its progressions and occasional regressions, what is visible remains a consistent and inventive level of excellence.

Di Prima's work is an uncompromising history of herself as woman, mother, citizen, artist, and mythmaker. From the early works in *This Kind of Bird Flies Backwards* and

Earthsong and their refinement in *Freddie Poems*, to the in-progress (or in-process) exploration of a feminine archetype, *Loba*, her work retains clarity and unity of purpose. Though the work is diverse, there are no contradictions as to its totality. The magical poems in *The New Handbook of Heaven* in no way betray the straightforward practical polemics of *Revolutionary Letters*; the exact and lyric *Kerhonkson Journal* complements the erotic vaudevilles in *Memoirs of a Beatnik*. There remains in all of her work a forthright, tender, and emotional honesty which continues to develop as the power of her art does.

Loba is a culmination of the works preceding it and enters more deeply into the realms of mystery. In this case, the mystery is the feminine, the myths embodied in the wolf Loba, Lilith, the vengeful first bride of Adam, Eve, Persephone, Iseult. Di Prima's poetic language affirms and expands the strength and spirit of the feminine without exploiting them. She restores the myth-making powers of the feminine by often using literary and mythic examples from a past created for the most part by males in male-dominated cultures. She presents these myths from the center of the feminine and reveals the realms of woman's spiritual reality active in the mysteries and the realities. Whether in childbirth, or blessing a daughter's entry into womanhood, or as succubus or divine beloved, woman remains complete within her domain. *Loba* is a deeply rendered and richly annotated work.

—David Meltzer

DOBSON, Rosemary. Australian. Born in Sydney, New South Wales, 18 June 1920. Educated at Frensham, Mittagong, New South Wales; Sydney University. Married A. T. Bolton in 1951; one daughter and two sons. Recipient: *Sydney Morning Herald* prize, 1946; Myer Award, 1966. Address: 61 Stonehaven Crescent, Deakin, Canberra, ACT 2600, Australia.

PUBLICATIONS

Verse

Poems. Mittagong, New South Wales, Frensham Press, 1937.
In a Convex Mirror. Sydney, Dymock's Book Arcade, 1944.
The Ship of Ice and Other Poems. Sydney, Angus and Robertson, 1948.
Child with a Cockatoo and Other Poems. Sydney, Angus and Robertson, 1955.
(*Poems*), selected and introduced by the author. Sydney, Angus and Robertson, 1963.
Cock Crow: Poems. Sydney, Angus and Robertson, 1965.
Rosemary Dobson Reads from Her Own Work (with recording). Brisbane, University of Queensland Press, 1970.
Selected Poems. Sydney, Angus and Robertson, 1973.
Greek Coins: A Sequence of Poems. Canberra, Brindabella Press, 1977.
Over the Frontier. Sydney, Angus and Robertson, 1978.

Other

Focus on Ray Crooke. Brisbane, University of Queensland Press, 1971.
A World of Difference: Australian Poetry and Painting in the 1940's (lecture). Sydney, Wentworth Press, 1973.

Editor, *Australia, Land of Colour, Through the Eyes of Australian Painters.* Sydney, Ure Smith, 1962.

Editor, *Songs for All Seasons: 100 Poems for Young People.* Sydney, Angus and Robertson, 1967.

Editor, *Australian Voices: Poetry and Prose of the 1970's.* Canberra, Australian National University Press, 1975.

Translator, with David Campbell, *Moscow Trefoil.* Canberra, Australian National University Press, 1975.

Translator, with David Campbell, *Seven Russian Poets.* Brisbane, University of Queensland Press, 1979.

Manuscript Collections: National Library of Australia, Canberra; Fryer Memorial Library, University of Queensland, Brisbane.

Critical Studies: "Rosemary Dobson: A Portrait in a Mirror" by A. D. Hope, in *Quadrant* (Sydney), July–August 1972; "The Poetry of Rosemary Dobson" by James McAuley, in *Australian Literary Studies* (Hobart), May 1973.

* * *

Rosemary Dobson wrote, designed, and printed her first collection of poems in 1937, while she was still at school. They are juvenilia, but already apparent is a sense of purpose, and also a quiet elegance: it is a beautifully designed small volume. *In a Convex Mirror* is to a large extent made up of poems originally published in the Sydney *Bulletin*, and which had attracted considerable interest by their vivacity and concern with an immediately experienced world without loss of lyric poise. The title poem, which takes as its starting-point a famous Vermeer interior, is significant also for its preoccupation with time, a subject that became of overriding concern for a number of poets in this period of dramatic upheaval. For Rosemary Dobson, time was most fully explored in the long title poem of her next collection, *The Ship of Ice*, which begins: "Time is a thief at the end of a road, is a river," and maintains a fine balance between wit and tension. This book also contains the vivacious sequence "The Devil and the Angel" which broke new ground in Australian writing of that period, with its joyful irony and alert conversational tone. But it was in her next volume, *Child with a Cockatoo*, that Rosemary Dobson fully explored what has become her most admired achievement, the "Poems from Paintings." Art had always played an important part in her concerns, and its particular capacity to exist, as it were, outside time provides the essential frisson behind these witty and perceptive poems. The underlying sensibility remains elegant and alert, though perhaps the poems in monologue form most sharply retain that particular freshness which made their first appearance so notable.

It was to be ten years before Rosemary Dobson's next publication, *Cock Crow*. There is a considerable deepening of feeling in the opening poems, "Child of Our Time" and "Out of Winter," poems of personal apprehension reminiscent perhaps of the work of Judith Wright. Rosemary Dobson has always been careful about intruding the naked personality into her poems, and the first section of *Cock Crow* represents, through its very attempts at overcoming a natural reticence, a moving testament to the poet's inner agony. The second section of the book is more playful, especially in the poems that translate figures from classical mythology into thoroughly Australian settings.

Another long period of silence intervened before the publication of *Selected Poems*. This contained 26 new poems, some written in England and some from Greece and Crete. Their firm lyrical tone and occasional moments of witty observation place them securely in the characteristic Dobson style. *Over the Frontier* is her most recent collection. Its most engaging quality is still that carefully modified informality, as in "Callers at the House" or "Oracles for a Childhood Journey," as well as the more overtly lyrical "Canberra Morning" or poems that explore classical, literary, and even scientific themes. Her recent translation, with David

Campbell, of contemporary Russian poets, *Moscow Trefoil*, has added a subtle flavour and tension to the best of the recent work (and most notably in the title poem of this collection), though the centrepiece is the sequence "Poems from Pausanias." Attracted by the immediate vividness of Pausanius's *Guide to Greece* she has utilised her own response to re-negotiate its immediacy; thus the theme of time, always essential to her vision, becomes a subtly recurring third theme explored here. The reader becomes part of an ongoing chain of recognition and discovery.

—Thomas W. Shapcott

DORN, Ed(ward Merton). American. Born in Villa Grove, Illinois, 2 April 1929. Educated at the University of Illinois, Urbana; Black Mountain College, North Carolina. Married Jennifer Dunbar. Visiting Professor of American Literature (Fulbright Lecturer, 1965–66, 1966–67), University of Essex, Wivenhoe, 1965–68, 1974–75; Visiting Poet, University of Kansas, Lawrence, 1968–69. Taught at Idaho State University, Pocatello. Editor, *Wild Dog* magazine, in the mid-1960's. Recipient: National Endowment for the Arts grant, 1966, 1968; D. H. Lawrence Fellowship, 1969. Lives in San Francisco.

PUBLICATIONS

Verse

The Newly Fallen. New York, Totem Press, 1961.
Hands Up! New York, Totem Press, 1964.
From Gloucester Out. London, Matrix Press, 1964.
Idaho Out. London, Fulcrum Press, 1965.
Geography. London, Fulcrum Press, 1965.
The North Atlantic Turbine. London, Fulcrum Press, 1967.
Gunslinger, Book I. Los Angeles, Black Sparrow Press, 1968.
Gunslinger, Book II. Los Angeles, Black Sparrow Press, 1969.
Gunslinger, Books I and II. London, Fulcrum Press, 1969.
Twenty-Four Love Songs. San Francisco, Frontier Press, 1969.
The Midwest Is That Space Between the Buffalo Statler and the Lawrence Eldridge. Lawrence, Kansas, T. Williams, 1969.
The Cosmology of Finding Your Spot. Lawrence, Kansas, Cottonwood, 1969.
Songs: Set Two, A Short Count. West Newbury, Massachusetts, Frontier Press, 1970.
Spectrum Breakdown: A Microbook. LeRoy, New York, Athanor, 1971.
A Poem Called Alexander Hamilton. Lawrence, Kansas, Tansy-Peg Leg Press, 1971.
The Cycle. West Newbury, Massachusetts, Frontier Press, 1971.
The Hamadryas Baboon at the Lincoln Park Zoo. Chicago, Wine Press, 1972.
Gunslinger, Book III: The Winterbook Prologue to the Great Book IV Kornerstone. West Newbury, Massachusetts, Frontier Press, 1972.
Recollections of Gran Apacheria. San Francisco, Turtle Island, 1974.
Gunslinger, Books I, II, III, IV. Berkeley, California, Wingbow Press, 1975.
The Collected Poems 1956–1974. Bolinas, California, Grey Fox Press, 1975.
Manchester Square, with Jennifer Dunbar. London, Permanent Press, 1975.
Hello, La Jolla. Berkeley, California, Wingbow Press, 1978.
Selected Poems, edited by Donald Allen. Bolinas, California, Grey Fox Press, 1978.

Recording: *Edward Dorn Reads from "The North Atlantic Turbine,"* Livingdiscs, 1967.

Short Stories

Some Business Recently Transacted in the White World. West Newbury, Massachusetts, Frontier Press, 1971.

Other

What I See in the Maximus Poems. Worcester, Migrant Press, 1960.
Prose 1, with Michael Rumaker and Warren Tallman. San Francisco, Four Seasons, 1964.
The Rites of Passage: A Brief History. Buffalo, New York, Frontier Press, 1965; revised edition, as *By the Sound*, Mount Vernon, Washington, Frontier Press, 1971.
The Shoshoneans: The People of the Basin-Plateau. New York, Morrow, 1966.
Views and Interviews, edited by Donald Allen. Bolinas, California, Grey Fox Press, 1978.

Translator, with Gordon Brotherston, *Our Word: Guerilla Poems from Latin America.* London, Cape Goliard Press, and New York, Grossman, 1968.
Translator, with Gordon Brotherston, *Tree Between Two Walls*, by José Emilio Pacheco. Los Angeles, Black Sparrow Press, 1969.
Translator, with Gordon Brotherston, *Selected Poems*, by César Vallejo. London, Penguin, 1976.
Translator, *Images of the New World: The American Continent Portrayed in Native Texts*, edited by Gordon Brotherston. London, Thames and Hudson, 1979.

Bibliography: "Ed Dorn: A Checklist" by George F. Butterick, in *Athanor* (Clarkson, New York), Winter 1973.

Manuscript Collection: Northwestern University, Evanston, Illinois.

Critical Study: "An Interview with Edward Dorn," in *Contemporary Literature* (Madison, Wisconsin), xv, 3.

* * *

Ed Dorn's work has been widely praised in both England and America. Russell Banks, writing in *Lillabulero*, has compared him, not invidiously, with Olson, Williams, and Pound. In England, A. Alvarez decided that Dorn has produced "a handful of beautifully pure and unaffected love-songs, and an intriguing long poem about a drive, 'Idaho Out,' in which cultural worry loses out to a kind of anarchic, footloose vitality and a feeling for the vast, frozen emptiness of the American West." Dorn's work reminds Alvarez of Hemingway, and it is true that Dorn is concerned with capturing idiomatic speech accurately; but he also indulges a kind of jam-pack jumbling of observations that is more the poetic counterpart of exuberant and excited writers like Thomas Wolfe. Dorn's recall of childhood, his feeling for places and writers, his political convictions, his tourism, all find their way, in cascades of energy, into his loose, straying verse – though it is only fair to say that there is, supposedly, some underlying structure based more or less on "projective verse" sympathies.

Dorn's reactions to England, where he lived for some time, are particularly sensitive:

As we go
through Sussex, hills are round
bellies are the downs
pregnantly lovely

the rounds of them, no towns
the train passes
shaking along the groove
of the countryside.

He purports "to love/that, and retain an ear for/the atrocities of my own hemisphere," criticizing, with simplistic pessimism, almost everything about America:

The thorn however
remains, in the desert
of american life, the thorn
in the throat of our national hypocrisy.

And yet he is also sentimental at will about his land: "And yes Fort Benton is lovely/and quiet, I would gladly give it as a gift/to a friend/...." Indeed, at his best, Dorn is a sentimentalist for the America he denounces:

Bitterly cold were the nights.
The journeymen slept in the lots of filling stations
and there were the interrupting lights
of semis all night long as those beasts
crept past or drew up to rest their motors
or roared on.

And his *Gunslinger* must be built on these strong native feelings: it is an effort at building a comic epic on the Western, for Dorn finds there the archetypal characters and enthusiasms that reveal America. For painting and wit, the commendable:

And why do you have a female horse
Gunslinger? I asked. Don't move
he replied
the sun rests deliberately
on the rim of the sierra.

This work also moves away from the Ego as center, which was getting to be a problem in long poems in which Dorn spoke as a seer; it is only to be hoped that he does not lose other qualities of his earlier work – exuberance, puritanical anger, authority about his enthusiasms.

—David Ray

DOWLING, Basil (Cairns). British. Born in Southbridge, Canterbury, New Zealand, 29 April 1910. Educated at St. Andrew's College; Canterbury University College, Christchurch, New Zealand, M.A.; Otago University, Dunedin; Cambridge University. Married to Margaret Wilson; one son and two daughters. Librarian at Otago University, Dunedin, 1947–52; Assistant Master, Downside School, Surrey, England, 1952–54. Assistant Master, 1954–65, and, since 1965, Head of English Department, Raine's Foundation Grammar School, London. Recipient: Jessie Mackay Memorial Prize, New Zealand, 1954. Address: 12 Mill Road, Rye, Sussex, England.

PUBLICATIONS

Verse

A Day's Journey. Christchurch, Caxton Press, 1941.
Signs and Wonders: Poems. Christchurch, Caxton Press, 1944.
Canterbury and Other Poems. Christchurch, Caxton Press, 1949.
Hatherley: Recollective Lyrics. Dunedin, University of Otago Bibliography Room, 1968.
A Little Gallery of Characters. Christchurch, Nag's Head Press, 1971.
Bedlam: A Mid-Century Satire. Christchurch, Nag's Head Press, 1972.
The Unreturning Native. Christchurch, Nag's Head Press, 1973.
The Stream. Christchurch, Nag's Head Press, 1979.

Manuscript Collections: State University of New York, Buffalo; Hocken Library, Otago University, Dunedin, New Zealand; Alexander Turnbull Library, Wellington, New Zealand.

Critical Studies: *Recent Trends in New Zealand Poetry* by James K. Baxter, Christchurch, Caxton Press, 1951; "Unreturning Native: The Poetic Achievement of Basil Dowling" by David Dowling, in *Landfall* (Christchurch), March 1979.

Basil Dowling comments:

[My poetry] has been said to be at its best when descriptive of the New Zealand landscape, more particularly that of Canterbury. Certainly, landscape, both for its own sake and as a background to human life and history, has been a main preoccupation, but many of my poems have had philosophical overtones, and perhaps something reminiscent of the English metaphysical poets of the seventeenth century. I have been influenced most, I should say, by Hardy, Edward Thomas, Robert Frost and Andrew Young, and to some extent by Wilfred Owen and Siegfried Sassoon. As for method and manner, I like metrical variety, lightness of touch, however serious the subject, and, most of all, precision and economy of statement.

* * *

Basil Dowling's poems are traditional in form, technically neat, and somewhat Georgian in their general flavour. The prevailing mode is New Zealand pastoral – contemplative description lit with verbal felicities – although there is an epigrammatic wryness in some of his shorter lyrics and his range extends also to the deservedly much-anthologized ballad "The Early Days."

Mr. Dowling was prolific in the nineteen-forties, coming into his full powers in *Canterbury and Other Poems*, but he has published relatively little since; he appears to have suffered a poetic amputation when he cut himself off from the South Island environment which so profoundly permeated his most vigorous work. His poems about the Canterbury landscape are full of crisp, accurate visual details, beautiful and often exultant descriptions of scenes and weathers, gentle pictures of birds, animals, trees. He is compassionate when he writes (more rarely) of people, and calm when he writes (even less frequently) about his personal life; but there is a deep pessimism underlying all but the most sunfilled of his poems. This becomes most intense in *Bedlam: A Mid-Century Satire*, written in 1958, in which the Christian philosophy of his earlier work has given way to gloomy fatalism.

In his recent book, *A Little Gallery of Characters*, he returns to his "holy land of childhood," a peopled place this time, to portray sympathetically or with half-wistful humour the more memorable acquaintances of his early youth.

—Fleur Adcock

DOWNIE, Freda (Christina). British. Born in London, 20 October 1929. Educated at schools in England and Australia. Married. Has worked for music publishers and art agents, and at a bookshop, all in London. Recipient: Stroud Festival prize, 1970; Arts Council prize, 1977. Address: 32 Kings Road, Berkhamsted, Hertfordshire HP4 3BD, England.

PUBLICATIONS

Verse

Night Music. Hitchin, Hertfordshire, Mandeville Press, 1974.
A Sensation. Hitchin, Hertfordshire, Cellar Press, 1975.
Night Sucks Me In. Berkhamsted, Hertfordshire, Priapus, 1976.
A Stranger Here. London, Secker and Warburg, 1977.
A Berkhamsted Three, with Fred Sedgwick and John Cotton. Berkhamsted, Hertfordshire, Priapus, 1978.
Man Dancing with the Moon. Hitchin, Hertfordshire, Mandeville Press, 1979.

* * *

Though Freda Downie was born in 1929, her poems have appeared sparingly, gathered in the last few years into pamphlets and one substantial collection: their number is relatively small, the possibility of seeing a changing, developing talent in those which have been published is slight. These poems, though, veil and reveal an intelligence and sensitivity of remarkable quality. She is a formalist, an apparent mandarin, a writer whose syntax is easy and conversational, but whose vocabulary shows a refinement of epithet and habit of exactitude which ensure that her work rarely falls below a level where the reader must keep alert and supple. She creates a world of nuance; there are always a grace and play about the poems which rarely fall into preciosity or fine writing. The interplay between the precisions of her aesthetic sense and the dark, indifferent spaces of the world is central to her craft:

And that tiny boat there is not rocking on an
Armful of jewels, but proceeds with audacity
Across the cold arena like a butterfly
Moving over the green gravel of a formal grave.

The dark spaces are stitched together, in part, by the sufficient worlds of music and painting. Their enigmatic consolations are real, their effects ambiguous. When the running thread of music closes "The empty bandstand still wears its steady crown/Prolonging a silent music/And the damp grass bends its perfume." These arts have been a part of Freda Downie's life – she has worked for a music publisher and art agent – and the poems frequently move between a posed landscape, a fiction which shimmers, dissolves, and re-forms, and the rough unfocused directions of life. Her poems may suggest a glass perfection – worlds proper to Chagall, Corot, Oriental silk painting, the Douanier – but the key word is "suggest." The artists do not remove her from life; they transfigure and clarify life for her, as " Meister Bertram 1345–1415," where Christ appears

Then red robed again, on a shrewd ass,
Sadly entering Jerusalem
And adored by devout gentlemen,
While others hurrah Him with wrong leaves,
Or show stylish legs in smart blue hose
From a good view in intricate trees.

These exquisite errors find Him.
All mine, less bright, leave me where I am.

Freda Downie's world, cleansed and lit by art, is a personal world: a world of properly human pleasures and pains. Life is celebrated with an adroit and witty affection; she has a clear-sighted admiration for codes of stoical behaviour and for those strategies of style by which life is given a substantial meaning. Her father and a swan mirror each other in an old photograph, "And my father has one hand in his pocket/As though he, too, were unacquainted with base emotion/And incapable of sudden flight." Always in her work there is a bed-rock knowledge that under that agreeable armful of jewels life is a rough passage, whatever the possibilities of redemption, through halls of loss and indifference,

> While the occupants of that tiny boat cast out
> Their hopes, and knowing the balm of occupation,
> Drag abundant sustenance from the wet charnel
> Of lives and voyages lost in dark inundation.

—Peter Scupham

DOYLE, Charles (Desmond). Pseudonym: **Mike Doyle.** British. Born in Birmingham, Warwickshire, 18 October 1928. Educated at Wellington Teachers College, New Zealand, Dip. Teach. 1956; Victoria University College, University of New Zealand (Macmillan Brown Prize, 1956), B.A. 1956, M.A. 1958; University of Auckland, Ph.D. Served in the Royal Navy. Married Doran Ross Smithells in 1959 (second marriage); three sons and one daughter. Taught at the University of Auckland; Visiting Fellow, Yale University, New Haven, Connecticut (American Council of Learned Societies Fellowship), 1967–68. Currently, Professor of English, University of Victoria, British Columbia. Editor, *Tuatara* magazine. Recipient: Jessie Mackay Memorial Prize, 1955; UNESCO Creative Artist Fellowship, 1958. Address: Department of English, University of Victoria, Victoria, British Columbia, Canada.

PUBLICATIONS

Verse

A Splinter of Glass: Poems 1951–55. Christchurch, Pegasus Press, 1956.
The Night Shift: Poems on Aspects of Love, with others. Wellington, Capricorn Press, 1957.
Distances: Poems 1956–61. Auckland, Paul's Book Arcade, 1963.
Messages for Herod. Auckland, Collins, 1965.
A Sense of Place. Wellington, Wai-te-ata Press, 1965.
Earth Meditations: 2. Auckland, Aldritt, 1968.
Noah, with *Quorum*, by Robert Sward. Vancouver, Soft Press, 1970.
Earth Meditations. Toronto, Coach House Press, 1971.
Abandoned Sofa. Victoria, British Columbia, Soft Press, 1971.
Earthshot. Exeter, Exeter Books, 1972.
Preparing for the Ark. Toronto, Weed/Flower Press, 1973.
Planes. Toronto, Seripress, 1975.
Stonedancer. Auckland, Auckland University Press – Oxford University Press, 1976.

Other

Small Prophets and Quick Returns: Reflections on New Zealand Poetry. Auckland, New Zealand Publishing Society, 1966.
R. A. K. Mason. New York, Twayne, 1970.
James K. Baxter. Boston, Twayne, 1976.

Editor, *Recent Poetry in New Zealand.* Auckland, Collins, 1965.
Editor, *William Carlos Williams: The Critical Heritage.* London, Routledge, 1979.

Manuscript Collection: Hocken Library, Otago University, Dunedin, New Zealand.

Critical Studies: *Aspects of New Zealand Poetry* by James K. Baxter, Christchurch, Caxton Press, 1967; "Earth Meditations One to Five" in *Quarry* (Kingston, Ontario), Summer 1972; "Quiet Islands," in *Anthos* (Ottawa), Winter 1978; "Poetic Journeys," in *Canadian Literature 79* (Vancouver), 1979.

* * *

Because of his residence in Britain, New Zealand, America, and Canada, and his occupation as academic, critic, and editor, Charles Doyle's poetic career might well be described in the words of an acknowledged master, W. C. Williams, as the attempt to "find a local speech." The sense of geographical displacement in the 1950's is exchanged for a sense of intellectual displacement in the 1960's, while in the 1970's the search for poetic form has dominated. His best poetry is when a balance between inventive form, philosophical reflection, and deeply felt personal experience is achieved.

His earlier lyrics contrast Europe ("our derelict hearts abandoned in distant places") with New Zealand (he wonders why "in a green country/where the cricket sings/there is such heartache/at the heart of things"). When he does attempt to verbalise the here and now, the real says "I am a thing, and that/Defeats you utterly." In *Messages for Herod* Doyle is vividly capable of evoking the present in dramatic lyrics, like the one when the clear smile of a hitch-hiker is glimpsed from a car window. But the title poem shows the poet's dread of the personal as the parochial: Herod slaughters the children because one of them denies that Auckland is the centre of the universe.

Doyle seeks a solution in a Yeatsian Byzantium – "To make is to discover." *Earth Meditations* is a sustained intellectual mosaic, like *The Waste Land* welding together disparate fragments of form – concrete, imagist, lyric – and aesthetic idea – Magritte ("woid voice us imidge"), Joyce, Spinoza, Butler – in a search for meaning. For all its linguistic inventiveness, the sequence affirms the real in theory ("Could you have made/that same daub/without the dame?" the poet asks Magritte) and in practice, in autobiography (life in New Zealand as sitting on "a cairn/of sheep currants").

More arid experimentation is found in *Earthshot* and *Noah*, another long sequence which betrays Doyle's occasional mawkish naivety ("all that water?" and "Perhaps paradise/is always/what is lost?"). Yet even here there are those superb moments when emotion is crisply captured: when lamenting separation from his love "arms in my head/grow long three thousand miles," or in *Noah*, "Even the windowpanes/wept."

All these volumes may be seen as a long apprenticeship for the recent flowering of *Stonedancer*. In a remarkable variety of forms, these poems are wedded to occasional as well as more profound meditations with the sculptural simplicity, grace, and rightness of the Gaudier-Brzeska work of the title. A comparison of the title poem of Doyle's first volume –

> I have shed an abstruse skin, and my bone's necrosis
> Leaves Love's uncomplicated land to rediscover
> Simple as still water or a moving tree

– with the last poem of *Stonedancer*, "The Journey of Meng Chiao" –

I must leave you here by the pinewoods under the sky.
I must go now. What do I hope to find when I arrive?
If I am lucky, the pinewoods under the sky

– shows Doyle's advance in philosophy and technique. An oriental simplicity of form and acceptance of emotion pervade the volume, as in "Shen Kua's Specifications for Travel" or the bliss of fulfilled love: "And on the hill slope, look/at the beautiful skiers./See them go, see them go/over the frozen snow."

So much of this volume achieves Doyle's new ideal of the "poem as breathing" ("I dig those small/thin poems" he says) but also as "Dionysiac ravings." Fortunately Doyle escapes mystic platitudes by retaining that vigorous engagement with the world which has always marked his poetry. There is a superb poem about the torture of an innocent African, for example, which ends: "It was nobody's fault/that, as far as life is concerned, by the end of it/ he knew everything else there was to know."

The volume suggests that Doyle "may have saved/the fullest wine until/gross appetite's discarded/its first, careless edge"; his speech is local to each poem, like a unique bouquet. Such versatility in thought, feeling, and technique as Doyle shows is rare among modern poets. For all his academic fluency, he can always be relied upon to give us in each poem Williams's ideal – "a new world that is always 'real.' "

—David Dowling

DRINAN, Adam. See **MACLEOD, Joseph (Todd Gordon).**

DUBIE, Norman (Evans, Jr.). American. Born in Barre, Vermont, 10 April 1945. Educated at Goddard College, Plainfield, Vermont, 1964–69, B.A. 1969; University of Iowa, Iowa City, 1969–71, M.F.A. 1971. Married 1) Francesca Stafford in 1969 (divorced, 1973); one daughter; 2) Pamela Stewart in 1974 (divorced, 1979). Teaching Assistant, 1969–71, and Lecturer in Creative Writing, 1971–74, University of Iowa; Assistant Professor, Ohio University, Athens, 1974–75. Writer-in-Residence, 1975–76, Director of the Graduate Writing Program, 1976–77, and since 1978, Associate Professor, Arizona State University, Tempe. Poetry Director, Prison Writers and Artists Workshop, Iowa City, 1973–74. Recipient: Bess Hokin Prize (*Poetry*, Chicago), 1976; Guggenheim grant, 1977. Address: Department of English, Arizona State University, Tempe, Arizona 85281, U.S.A.

PUBLICATIONS

Verse

The Horsehair Sofa. Plainfield, Vermont, Goddard Journal, 1969.
Alehouse Sonnets. Pittsburgh, University of Pittsburgh Press, 1971.
The Prayers of the North American Martyrs. New York, Penumbra Press, 1975.

Popham of the New Song and Other Poems. Port Townsend, Washington, Graywolf Press, 1975.
In the Dead of the Night. Pittsburgh, University of Pittsburgh Press, 1975.
The Illustrations. New York, Braziller, 1977.
A Thousand Little Things and Other Poems. Omaha, Cummington Press, 1978.
Odalisque in White. Seattle, Porch, 1978.
The City of the Olesha Pruit. New York, Doubleday, 1979.
Comes Winter, The Sea Hunting. Tucson, Maguey Press, 1979.
The Everlastings. New York, Doubleday, 1979.

Manuscript Collection: University of Iowa Special Collections, Iowa City.

Critical Study: Interview in *American Poetry Review* (Philadelphia), July–August 1978.

* * *

Norman Dubie writes a rich, evocative poetry that is sensuous and intricate. Each poem creates a world both complete and vastly larger than itself. Dubie recreates places, events, and people with an ear and eye that are remarkably deft and skillful. He works with remote times and places much as Borges does in his fiction. Yet these little worlds and brief lives, that seem so exotic and foreign to our own, are not so, and bear up the endless commonality of human situations. Dubie's individuals struggle for freedom and further understanding, and despite their frequent failures he treats them with compassion and understanding. The poems have apppropriately been called "realizations of history." His voice is so convincing there is little doubt he has visited Hedda Gabler, gotten drunk with William Hazlitt, traveled with runaway slaves. His poems are convincing moments in the amber of time, so brightly illuminated they are their own reason for being.

Alehouse Sonnets is a series of related poems circling the life and circumstances of English critic William Hazlitt. At times the poet is Hazlitt's drinking partner; occasionally the voice is Hazlitt's interior monologue; at times we hear a contemporary voice explaining our world to the Englishman ("And, yes, we have new weapons;/tanks, flame-throwers, bomb squadrons,/choking gas with the odor of horseradish, the H-bomb ..."). This is an impressive first book, both in its sustained use of the sonnet, and in its re-creation of a historical figure. One is driven forward, as if reading a novel, and rewarded with memorable images, such as "my wife comes spilling from the pond/fresh buckets of water for our bath." Still, I found myself tiring of the drunken revelries of Dubie and Hazlitt, and of the inevitable aftermath: "Hazlitt, we'll spend the night curled/up in a sheep's head like two fat/round worms."

In the Dead of the Night presents a much wider range of lives and voices. Dubie transports us, with equal ease to a Pennsylvania battlefield in 1774, or to "Genoa where sailboats smell of barns." He gives us here a remarkably wide range of voices that might have been far away and long ago, but that speak timelessly and remind us of our commonality ("It is another century; things are/not better or worse ..."). Dubie's voice is often omniscient and editorial, as in "I didn't tell you the blind soldier had shot *himself*." His re-creation of historical moments reminds me in subject, but not in style, of Robert Lowell's strong historicity. A further and fundamental quality of his poetry is his philosophy of correspondences. Dubie gives us great insight into the parallels and interrelationships of living things. (As a priest walks home at night, "he picks up his robes, they leave/a figure in the snow/like when a rabbit is grabbed by a snare....") History often intrudes upon us in these poems with unexpected violence, or tenderness: "A giant with black hair has kicked through the double doors;/with a machine gun sprays you back and forth. And then tosses/a flower onto the floor."

The Illustrations contains Dubie's finest work yet. His poems are longer and more memorable; his voice has greater authority and control. His poems affirm life, even in its most terrible moments. To live is to struggle, these poems so often say, but the struggle also has its brief rewards, its moments of pleasure, its illuminations. His poetry does not give us the unity of a single place and time, but it gives a unity nonetheless. From separate, seemingly disparate images, he presents a unifying tableau of humanity, from its tragic to its humorous guises. ("The bald heads of two priests can be seen/like the white buttocks of the lovers fleeing into the trees.") One of Dubie's personae comments, "I want to know what is going/ to happen to everyone" – a statement that is close to the heart of Norman Dubie's imaginative brilliance.

—John R. Cooley

DUDEK, Louis. Canadian. Born in Montreal, Quebec, 6 February 1918. Educated at Montreal High School; McGill University, Montreal, B.A. 1939; Columbia University, New York, M.A. in history 1946, Ph.D. in English and comparative literature 1955. Married; one son. Instructor in English, City College of New York, 1946–51. Since 1951, Member of the English Department, and currently Greensheilds Professor of English, McGill University. Associated with *First Statement* magazine, 1941–43; Editor, *Delta* magazine, 1957–66; former Publisher, Contact Press, Toronto, and Delta Canada Press, Montreal. Currently, Publisher, DC Books, Montreal. Director-at-Large, Canadian Council of Teachers of English. Member, Humanities Research Council of Canada. Recipient: Quebec Literary Award, 1968. Address: 5 Ingleside Avenue, Montreal 215, Quebec, Canada.

PUBLICATIONS

Verse

Unit of Five, with others, edited by Ronald Hambleton. Toronto, Ryerson Press, 1944.
East of the City. Toronto, Ryerson Press, 1946.
The Searching Image. Toronto, Ryerson Press, 1952.
Cerberus, with Irving Layton and Raymond Souster. Toronto, Contact Press, 1952.
Twenty-Four Poems. Toronto, Contact Press, 1952.
Europe. Toronto, Laocoon Press, 1954.
The Transparent Sea. Toronto, Contact Press, 1956.
En México. Toronto, Contact Press, 1958.
Laughing Stalks. Toronto, Contact Press, 1958.
Atlantis. Montreal, Delta Canada, 1967.
Collected Poetry. Montreal, Delta Canada, 1971.
Epigrams. Montreal, DC, 1975.
Selected Poems. Montreal, DC, 1975.

Recording: *The Green Beyond*, CBC, 1973.

Other

Literature and the Press: A History of Printing, Printed Media, and Their Relation to Literature. Toronto, Ryerson Press, 1960.
The First Person in Literature. Toronto, Canadian Broadcasting Corporation, 1967.
DK: Some Letters of Ezra Pound. Montreal, DC, 1974.

Editor, with Irving Layton, *Canadian Poems 1850–1952*. Toronto, Contact Press, 1952.

Editor, *Selected Poems*, by Raymond Souster. Toronto, Contact Press, 1956.

Editor, *Poetry of Our Time: An Introduction to Twentieth Century Poetry, Including Modern Canadian Poetry.* Toronto, Macmillan, 1966.

Editor, with Michael Gnarowski, *The Making of Modern Poetry in Canada: Essential Articles on Contemporary Canadian Poetry in English.* Toronto, Ryerson Press, 1967.

Editor, *All Kinds of Everything.* Toronto, Clarke Irwin, 1973.

Translator, *Montreal, Paris d'Amérique*, by Michel Régnier. Montreal, Editions du Jour, 1961.

Critical Studies: "Louis Dudek as Man of Letters," in *Canadian Literature* (Vancouver), Autumn 1964; "Louis Dudek Issue" of *Yes 14* (Montreal); *The Oxford Anthology of Canadian Literature*, Toronto, Oxford University Press, 1973.

* * *

I hate travel
but all the poetry I've ever written
seems to be about travel.

Louis Dudek was born in Montreal; lives in Montreal; always returns to the harbour of his birthright and local knowledge. And with all this adherence to place, to the environment which formed him and the context which identifies him, he is constant voyager. He is the true Balboa of Canada; eternally discovering his Pacifics with courage and resourcefulness and accumulation of stubborn wonder.

His outer life is witness to this. He is the instigator to farther horizons. He brings back his horizons to where he lives with others; teaching the young, instituting vehicles of expression, implementing starting-points. He is a professor of European literature and modern poetry at McGill University; he set up in type and launched ten years of excitement in his magazine *Delta*; helped found and keep alive for new books of poetry Contact Press, and his present Delta Press. His energy is witnessed in a hundred places.

His poetry is witness. The energy and driving aesthetic are put into his books for anyone to have; shaped, committing, intellectual and passionate. Nine volumes, starting way back a quarter of a century ago. He was written off by the pundits on his seventh, 15 years ago. What did they know? What does anyone know about a poet's timing? His genius is to stop the clocks. Dudek has always stopped clocks. He stops them always at the present. For ten years he watched the hands turn; then stops us at the present again in his eighth book, *Atlantis.*

In *Atlantis* we have the accumulated wisdom and resolutions of the eternal voyager, this Canadian of regional placement shaping in poetry his Pacific. Cosmic regionalism the university tailors of literature call it, stitching on their labels. Dudek takes a trip and comes up with a contemporary epic; goes to Naples, Rome, Paris and London, and brings them back to Montreal. A Ulysses and his Ithaca. He is after what is worth of the past for the illumination of the present. Others have poetically descended from Ezra Pound but none has practised Pound with more affinity and cogency than Dudek. What's more, his pound is his own weight:

Today we passed over Atlantis,
which is our true home.
We live in exile
waiting for that world to come.

And what is Dudek's City of Dioce whose walls are seven of seven colours? First, and a first which makes the others of little matter, first: all-encompassing love, Walt Whitman's love, love that is human compassion – and love not left romantic. Dudek has sufficient knowledge of the negative that is everywhere, alas:

> The price is suffering,
>   it doesn't matter.
> "We've had it, Chiquita."
>   (The waste is frightening.)
> What does matter is the dawn,
> the nimbus, the brief light of love.
> Try standing in the sun for a minute once a day.

And there Dudek does stand, his minute in the sun, before the horrendous world innocent so that he can have wonder. He has the answer, this poet of Canada:

> Always everywhere
>   to treat everyone as a person
> worthy and serious, and vulnerable to love.

—Ralph Gustafson

DUGAN, Alan. American. Born in Brooklyn, New York, 12 February 1923. Educated at Queens College, New York; Olivet College, Michigan; Mexico City College, B.A. 1951. Served in the United States Army Air Force during World War II. Married to Judith Shahn. Worked in advertising, publishing, and for a medical supply company; taught at Sarah Lawrence College, Bronxville, New York, 1967–71. Since 1971, Staff Member for Poetry, Fine Arts Work Center, Provincetown, Massachusetts. Recipient: Yale Series of Younger Poets Award, 1961; Pulitzer Prize, 1962; National Book Award, 1962; American Academy in Rome Fellowship, 1962; Guggenheim Fellowship, 1963, 1972; Rockefeller Fellowship, 1966; Levinson Prize (*Poetry*, Chicago), 1967. Address: Box 97, Truro, Massachusetts 02666, U.S.A.

PUBLICATIONS

Verse

General Prothalamion in Populous Times. New Haven, Connecticut, privately printed, 1961.
Poems. New Haven, Connecticut, Yale University Press, 1961.
Poems 2. New Haven, Connecticut, Yale University Press, 1963.
Poems 3. New Haven, Connecticut, Yale University Press, 1967.
Collected Poems. New Haven, Connecticut, Yale University Press, 1969; London, Faber, 1970.
Poems 4. Boston, Little Brown, 1974.
Sequence. Cambridge, Massachusetts, Dolphin, 1976.

* * *

Alan Dugan is a fine poet who has created a significant body of work while cultivating a confining style and exercising his caustic intelligence on a relatively narrow range of subjects. One does not get terribly excited about his work, but one nevertheless returns to it with increasing regularity, for it successfully inhabits that middle ground of experience which our best poets today seem to loathe to admit. In Dugan, at least, if one is able to hope at all, he hopes to endure rather than to triumph. If one feels trapped, he will strive not for ultimate freedom and total independence, but for the sensation of freedom, temporary, imperfect, illusory. Dugan's spirit is best expressed in the conditional, which is to say that nothing he feels or thinks is very far removed from regret for what might have been. It has been generally accepted that Dugan is something of a moralist, and I suppose it is possible to go along with such a view if we understand a moralist to be someone who experiences convulsive fits of nausea from time to time, whenever he remembers what he is and to what he has given his approval if only by means of undisturbed acquiescence. Dugan's is an intensely private, almost a claustrophobic vision, and his poems usually communicate small perceptions appropriate to the lives of small people, so that we listen not because of any glittering eye, but because we feel we should. The voice that apprehends us is as earnest as any we might hope to encounter, and the combination of brittle surfaces and an underlying warmth is relentlessly imposing.

Dugan's poems have variety, but they might all be drawn together as a single long poem. The same alert but static sensibility is operant in all of them, and the speaker rarely indulges the sort of emotional extremism which might distinguish his more inspired from his more characteristically quotidian utterances. Particulars in the work are easily reducible to an elementary abstraction in which polarities are anxiously opposed until, under the wry focus of Dugan's imagination, they somehow coalesce. Alternatives become merely matters of perspective, and the wise man gradually learns that as between one choice and another, we had best avoid choices altogether.

The predictable, low-keyed humor, so often remarked upon by others, does little to mitigate the stinging venom of self-contempt that courses through so much of Dugan's work. His is a bitter eloquence. If the cadence is austere, it is rarely impoverished, and the muscular flow of his terse diction is rarely purchased at the expense of complexity. Dugan invites us to witness with him, without any redemptive qualification, the sordid spectacle of our common humiliation. It is a strangely unimpassioned witnessing, but the amusement of ironic detachment has much to recommend it, or so it would seem. What Dugan fears most is that neutrality which predicts the death of the spirit, but more and more it appears to him that this is indeed his most authentic reality.

—Robert Boyers

DUNCAN, Robert (Edward). American. Born Edward Howard Duncan in Oakland, California, 7 January 1919; adopted in 1920 and given name Robert Edward Symmes. Educated at the University of California, Berkeley, 1936–38, 1948–50. Editor, *The Experimental Review*, 1938–40, *Phoenix*, and *The Berkeley Miscellany*, 1948–49, all in Berkeley. Lived in Mallorca, 1955–56. Taught at Black Mountain College, North Carolina, 1956; Assistant Director of the Poetry Center (Ford grant), 1956–57, and Lecturer in the Poetry Workshop, 1965, San Francisco State College; Lecturer, University of British Columbia, Vancouver, 1963. Recipient: Union League Civic and Arts Foundation Prize, 1957, Harriet Monroe Memorial Prize, 1960, Levinson Prize, 1964, and Eunice Tietjens Memorial Prize 1967 (*Poetry*, Chicago); Guggenheim Fellowship, 1963; National Endowment for the Arts grant, 1966 (two grants). Address: 3267 20th Street, San Francisco, California 94110, U.S.A.

Publications

Verse

Heavenly City, Earthly City. Berkeley, California, Bern Porter, 1947.
Poems 1948–1949. Berkeley, California, Berkeley Miscellany, 1950.
Medieval Scenes. San Francisco, Centaur Press, 1950.
The Song of the Border-Guard. Black Mountain, North Carolina, Black Mountain College, 1952.
Caesar's Gate: Poems 1949–1950. Palma, Mallorca, Divers Press, 1955.
Letters. Highlands, North Carolina, Jargon, 1958.
Selected Poems. San Francisco, City Lights, 1959.
The Opening of the Field. New York, Grove Press, 1960; London, Cape, 1969.
Roots and Branches. New York, Scribner, 1964; London, Cape, 1970.
Writing, Writing: A Composition Book of Madison 1953, Stein Imitations. Albuquerque, New Mexico, Sumbooks, 1964.
Wine. Berkeley, California, Oyez, 1964.
Uprising. Berkeley, California, Oyez, 1965.
A Book of Resemblances: Poems 1950–1953. New Haven, Connecticut, Henry Wenning, 1966.
Of the War: Passages 22–27. Berkeley, California, Oyez, 1966.
The Years As Catches: First Poems 1939–1946. Berkeley, California, Oyez, 1966.
Fragments of a Disordered Devotion. San Francisco, Gnomon Press, 1966.
Boob. Privately printed, 1966.
Epilogos. Los Angeles, Black Sparrow Press, 1967.
The Cat and the Blackbird. San Francisco, White Rabbit Press, 1967.
Christmas Present, Christmas Presence! Los Angeles, Black Sparrow Press, 1967.
Bending the Bow. New York, New Directions, 1968; London, Cape, 1971.
My Mother Would Be a Falconess. Berkeley, California, Oyez, 1968.
Names of People. Los Angeles, Black Sparrow Press, 1968.
The First Decade: Selected Poems 1940–1950. London, Fulcrum Press, 1968.
Derivations: Selected Poems 1950–1956. London, Fulcrum Press, 1968.
Play Time, Pseudo Stein. New York, Poets Press, 1969.
Achilles' Song. New York, Phoenix Book Shop, 1969.
Poetic Disturbances. San Francisco, Maya, 1970.
Bring It Up from the Dark. Berkeley, California, Cody's Books, 1970.
Tribunals: Passages 31–35. Los Angeles, Black Sparrow Press, 1970.
In Memoriam Wallace Stevens. Storrs, University of Connecticut, 1972.
An Ode and Arcadia, with Jack Spicer. Berkeley, California, Ark Press, 1974.
Dante. Canton, New York, Institute of Further Studies, 1974.
The Venice Poem. Sydney, Prism, 1975.

Recording: *Letters*, Stream.

Plays

Faust Foutu (produced San Francisco, 1955; New York, 1959–60). Published as *Faust Foutu: Act One of Four Acts: A Comic Mask*, San Francisco, White Rabbit Press, 1958; complete edition, as *Faust Foutu: An Entertainment in Four Parts*, Stinson Beach, California, Enkidu Surrogate, 1960.
Medea at Kolchis: The Maiden Head (produced Black Mountain, North Carolina, 1956). Berkeley, California, Oyez, 1965.

Other

The Artist's View. Privately printed, 1952.

On Poetry (radio interview with Eugene Vance). New Haven, Connecticut, Yale University, 1964.
As Testimony: The Poem and the Scene. San Francisco, White Rabbit Press, 1964.
The Sweetness and Greatness of Dante's "Divine Comedy," 1265–1965. San Francisco, Open Space, 1965.
Six Prose Pieces. Rochester, Michigan, Perishable Press, 1966.
The Truth and Life of Myth: An Essay in Essential Autobiography. New York, House of Books, 1968.
65 Drawings: A Selection of 65 Drawings from One Drawing-Book: 1952–1956. Los Angeles, Black Sparrow Press, 1970.
Notes on Grossinger's "Solar Journal: Oecological Sections." Los Angeles, Black Sparrow Press, 1970.
An Interview with George Bowering and Robert Hogg, April 19, 1969. Toronto, Coach House Press, 1971.

Manuscript Collection: Bancroft Poetry Archive, University of California, Berkeley.

* * *

Following 25 years of intense activity in the life of poetry, relatively little has been heard from Robert Duncan in the 1970's, seemingly because of a private decision to publish little for a long period (15 years, it has been said). Duncan retreated to "Ground Work," to what he called, in an unpublished piece, "speculations and appreciations, associations, rantings if need be, phantasies, lectures, nocturnes and mind soul and spirit dances and inventions." Much of this locates both the nature, and the problems, of his work, most of the best of which is in three volumes, *The Opening of the Field*, *Roots and Branches* and *Bending the Bow*, all collections first published in the 1960's, when the Black Mountain poets, among whom Duncan is a leading figure, were at the height of their energy and influence.

A desire for privacy, an obliqueness, which is a central feature even of his technique, has always been part of Duncan's enigmatic "presence" as a writer. In *The Years as Catches*, which gathers work from his earlier career (1939–46), he says: "From the beginning I had sought not the poem as a discipline or paradigm of my thought and feeling but as a source of feeling and thought, following the movement of an inner impulse and tension rising in the flow of returning vowel sounds and in measuring stresses that formed phrases of a music for me, having to do with mounting waves of feeling and yet incorporating an inner opposition of reproof of such feeling." He speaks of poetry as "at once a dramatic projection and ... a magic ritual," of himself as a poet of "many derivations" and as one whose faith is in "the process of poetry itself."

Curiously, when seen in the long perspective of his work, Duncan's first book, *Heavenly City, Earthly City*, was influenced by the British poet George Barker, a romantic *poète maudit*, of whose verse he said later that it "agreed with Freud's concept of the underlying disturbed and disturbing bisexuality of man's nature." Equally, however, Duncan was influenced by the musical metrics of the Elizabethans Wyatt and Surrey. Both influences fed his own early-formed sense of the poem as manipulative magic.

The important influence of Ezra Pound was also present in Duncan's work from very early, combining with that of a little-known poet, Sanders Russell, to develop in Duncan an aesthetic, almost a mystique, of awareness. Pound's middle cantos (LII–LXXI) helped strengthen Duncan's already acute musical sense, as is manifest in the early "Persephone":

memory: farfields of morning,
  maimd winter, wheel & hoofhammerd weeds,
bare patches of earth. We heard rumor of the rape
among the women who wait at the wells with dry urns,
talk among leaves and among the old men
who sift tincans and seashells searching for driftwood
to make fires on cold hearthstones.

(The spelling here, the elided "e," is a convention adopted later.) Duncan makes a related point, made earlier by Eliot and Valéry: "When a rhythm began in my writing it would career me on into a dimension in which fantasy, the glow and fusion of images ... would take over." Later, stating his aesthetic for Donald Allen's *The New American Poetry 1945–60*, Duncan showed that his position was fundamentally the same – poetry as ritual emerging from a deeper, perhaps divine, level. Meantime he had been saved from total introversion by perceiving his own life as part of a larger human life and in opposition to American capitalism and world *realpolitik*. An early reading of Lorca, and particularly "Ode to the King of Harlem," helped merge in Duncan's psyche the realms of fantasy and reality.

Duncan sees poems as "intentions" towards the one great poem. A certain literariness, derivativeness from other poems or works of art, is paradoxically part of his openness and spontaneity. A further paradox is that he sees art as an alternative reality, a "made" reality (this is explored in the sequence "The Structure of Rime") and yet as part of the process which is the universal whole. In "Rites of Participation" he consents to the insight of Paracelsus, that "the key to man's nature is contained in the larger nature," and his best work gradually enriches and amplifies this insight.

Duncan once cited with approval Gertrude Stein's remark in *Composition as Explanation* that, "The composition is the thing seen by everyone living in the living they are doing." Duncan has shared this sense of process with Charles Olson and Robert Creeley, and like them he is concerned with open form, though the texture of his poetry has the air, at least, of being more traditional. Like Olson, he derives from Edward Sapir the idea that a shared language is a shared experience, so (in a sense) no experience is purely individual and experience has a kind of flowing quality *through* individuals. Duncan's sense of himself as poet is of one joining in a participation mystique (here he is influenced by Geza Roheim's work on the Australian aborigines). In the autobiographical essay "Towards an Open Universe," he has said: "Our consciousness and the poem as a supreme effort of consciousness comes in a dancing organization between personal and cosmic identity." He is fond of using the dance of the bees as a relevant figure. Following Erwin Schrodinger's *What Is Life?* he sees life as interaction between matter and environment, an orderly disequilibrium, which "to the poet means that by its nature life is orderly and that the poem might follow the primary processes of thought and feeling, the immediate impulse of psychic life."

The sheer music of Duncan's best work, combined with what M. L. Rosenthal rightly terms "mystical directness," is exemplified in "Often I Am Permitted to Return to a Meadow," and in the musical qualities especially in, say, "Food for Fire, Food for Thought" and the well-known "A Poem Beginning with a Line by Pindar." Duncan is a flowing, musing poet, the impact of whose work is in its totality rather than in set pieces. Partly this is because he is less interested in statement and meaning than in evocation and incantation. Yet, in the greatest poetry, the two are not inevitably separated. Certainly, "one may lose sight of the target in order to gain insight of the target," as Duncan once observed in a piece on Olson's Maximus, but this is somewhat like his preference for intuition over wisdom. Need one choose?

Stating these perceived limitations is uncomfortable, for (especially to those engaged in the life of poetry) Duncan's work and example are enormously engaging. There is a kind of modesty, as well as pride, in the way he has presented himself and his work over the years. Among American poets of the last 30 years he is one of the most naturally gifted, and it would be against the grain of those gifts to expect from him a larger quota of "finished" poems, or gilt-edged anthology pieces. Despite a certain lack of imagistic presence, *The Opening of the Field* and *Roots and Branches* are among the richest books of their period in poetic fibre.

—Charles Doyle

DUNCAN, Ronald (Frederick Henry). British. Born in Salisbury, Rhodesia, 6 August 1914. Educated in Switzerland and at Downing College, Cambridge, M.A. 1936. Married Rose Marie Theresa Hansom in 1941; two children. Editor, *The Townsman*, London, 1938–46; Columnist ("Jan's Journal"), *Evening Standard*, London, 1946–56. Has farmed in Devon since 1939. Founder, Devon Festival of the Arts, Bideford, 1953; Co-Founder, English Stage Company at the Royal Court Theatre, London, 1955. Agent: Eric Glass Ltd., 28 Berkeley Square, London W.1. Address: Welcombe, Bideford, Devon, England.

PUBLICATIONS

Verse

Postcards to Pulchinella. London, Fortune Press, 1941.
The Mongrel and Other Poems. London, Faber, 1950.
The Solitudes. London, Faber, 1960.
Judas. London, Blond, 1960.
Unpopular Poems. London, Hart Davis, 1969.
Man, part 1. London, Rebel Press, 1970.
Man, part 2. Welcombe, Devon, Rebel Press, 1972.
Man, part 3. Welcombe, Devon, Rebel Press, 1972.
Man, parts 4 and 5. Welcombe, Devon, Rebel Press, 1974.
For the Few. Welcombe, Devon, Rebel Press, 1977.
Auschwitz. Welcombe, Devon, Rebel Press, 1979.

Plays

Birth (produced London, 1937).

The Dull Ass's Hoof (includes *The Unburied Dead; Pimp, Skunk and Profiteer; Ora Pro Nobis*). London, Fortune Press, 1940.

This Way to the Tomb: A Masque and Anti-Masque, music by Benjamin Britten (produced London, 1945; New York, 1961). London, Faber, 1946; New York, Theatre Arts, 1967.

The Eagle Has Two Heads, adaptation of a play by Jean Cocteau (produced London, 1946; New York, 1947). London, Vision Press, and New York, Funk and Wagnalls, 1948.

The Rape of Lucretia, music by Benjamin Britten, adaptation of a play by André Obey (produced Glyndebourne, Sussex, 1946). London, Boosey and Hawkes, 1946; augmented edition, London, Lane, 1948.

Amo Ergo Sum (cantata), music by Benjamin Britten (produced London, 1948).

The Typewriter, adaptation of a play by Jean Cocteau (produced London, 1950). London, Dobson, 1948.

Stratton (produced Brighton, 1949; London, 1950). London, Faber, 1950.

St. Spiv (as *Nothing up My Sleeve*, produced London, 1950; revised version, as *St. 'Orace*, music by Jerry Wayne, produced London, 1964). Included in *Collected Plays*, 1971.

Our Lady's Tumbler, music by Arthur Oldham (produced Salisbury, Wiltshire, 1950). London, Faber, 1951.

Don Juan (produced Bideford, Devon, 1953; London, 1956). London, Faber, 1954.

The Death of Satan (produced Bideford, Devon, 1954; London, 1956; New York, 1960). London, Faber, 1955; in *Satan, Socialites, and Solly Gold: Three New Plays from England*, New York, Coward McCann, 1961.

A Man Named Judas, adaptation of a play by C. A. Puget and Pierre Bost (produced Barnstaple, 1956).

The Cardinal, with Hans Keuls, adaptation of a play by Harald Bratt (produced Cambridge, 1957).

The Apollo de Bellac, adaptation of a play by Jean Giraudoux (produced London, 1957). London, French, 1958.
The Catalyst (produced London, 1958; revised version, as *Ménage à Trois*, produced London, 1963). London, Rebel Press, 1964; New York, Theatre Arts, 1967.
Christopher Sly, music by Thomas Eastwood (produced London, 1960).
Abelard and Heloise: A Correspondence for the Stage (produced London, 1960). London, Faber, 1961.
The Rabbit Race, adaptation of a play by Martin Walser (produced Edinburgh, 1963). Published in *Plays, vol. 1* by Martin Walser, London, Calder, 1963.
O-B-A-F-G$_{S}^{K\text{-}M}$*R-N: A Play in One Act in Stereophonic Sound* (produced Exeter, Devon, 1964). London, Rebel Press, 1964; New York, Theatre Arts, 1967.
The Trojan Women, adaptation of a play by Jean-Paul Sartre based on the play by Euripides (produced Edinburgh, 1967). London, Hamish Hamilton, and New York, Knopf, 1967.
The Seven Deadly Virtues: A Contemporary Immorality Play (produced London, 1968). Included in *Collected Plays*, 1971.
The Gift (produced Exeter, Devon, 1968). Included in *Collected Plays*, 1971.
The Rehearsal (as *Still Life*, televised 1970). Included in *Collected Plays*, 1971.
Collected Plays (includes *This Way to the Tomb, St. Spiv, Our Lady's Tumbler, The Rehearsal, The Seven Deadly Virtues, O-B-A-F-G, The Gift*). London, Hart Davis, and New York, Theatre Arts, 1971.

Screenplay: *Girl on a Motorcycle*, 1969.

Television Plays: *The Portrait*, 1954; *The Janitor*, 1955; *Preface to America*, 1959; *Not All the Dead Are Buried*, 1960; *The Rebel*, music by Thomas Eastwood, 1969; *Still Life*, 1970; *Mandala*, 1972.

Novels

The Last Adam. London, Dobson, 1952.
Saint Spiv. London, Dobson, 1961.

Short Stories

The Perfect Mistress and Other Stories. London, Hart Davis, 1971.
A Kettle of Fish. London, Hart Davis, 1971.
Tale of Tales: Ten Fables. London, Elephant Press, 1977.
Mr. and Mrs. Mouse. Welcombe, Devon, Rebel Press, 1977.

Other

The Complete Pacifist. London, Boriswood, 1937.
The Rexist Party Manifesto (as the Bishop of Marsland). London, Townsman, 1937.
Strategy in War (as Major-General Marsland). London, Townsman, 1937.
Journal of a Husbandman. London, Faber, 1944.
Home-Made Home (on architecture). London, Faber, 1947.
Jan's Journal 1. London, William Campion, 1949.
Tobacco Cultivation in England. London, Falcon Press, 1951.
The Blue Fox (newspaper articles). London, Museum Press, 1951; New York, Oxford University Press, 1952.
Jan at the Blue Fox (newspaper articles). London, Museum Press, 1952.
Where I Live. London, Museum Press, 1953.

Jan's Journal 2. London, Museum Press, 1954.
All Men Are Islands: An Autobiography. London, Hart Davis, 1964.
Devon and Cornwall. London, Batsford, and New York, Hastings House, 1966.
How to Make Enemies (autobiography). London, Hart Davis, 1968.
Obsessed (autobiography). London, Joseph, 1975.
Benjamin Britten: A Personal Memoir. London, Faber, 1979.

Editor, *Songs and Satires of John Wilmot, 2nd Earl of Rochester*. London, Forge Press, 1948.
Editor, *Selected Poems*, by Ben Jonson. London, Grey Walls Press, 1949.
Editor, *Selected Writings of Mahatma Gandhi*. London, Faber, and Boston, Beacon Press, 1951.
Editor, with the Countess of Harewood, *Classical Songs for Children*. London, Blond, and New York, Potter, 1965.
Editor, with Marion Harewood, *The Penguin Book of Accompanied Songs*. London, Penguin, 1973.
Editor, with Miranda Weston-Smith, *The Encyclopaedia of Ignorance*. Oxford, Pergamon Press, 2 vols., 1977.
Editor, with Miranda Weston-Smith, *Lying Truths*. Oxford, Pergamon Press, 1979.

Translator, *Diary of a Film: La Belle et la Bête*, by Jean Cocteau. London, Dobson, 1950.

Manuscript Collection: Humanities Research Center, University of Texas, Austin.

Critical Studies: *Ronald Duncan* by Max Walter Haueter, London, Rebel Press, 1969 (includes bibliography); *Ronald Duncan* by William Wahl, Salzburg, Salzburg University Press, 1973; *Tribute to Ronald Duncan* by Lord Harewood and others, London, Harton Press, 1974.

Theatrical Activities:
Director: **Play** – *Abelard and Heloise*, London, 1973.

* * *

Although there was a period when Ronald Duncan was so in fashion that his poems almost seemed pastiches ("Passion's no prince,/is the maimed mind's blindness"), he has, over thirty years, pursued his own course. His interest in music provoked (or resulted from?) verse forms which have always been disciplined, even when apparently at their loosest; and a strong note of sensuality has sometimes found a beautifully cool expression: "Oh Rose Marie if you make yourself/ As naked and smooth as the moon/ I will become the softest mist/ And cover you." Some of the verse has worn badly (cf. the once much-admired libretto for Britten's *Rape of Lucretia*); but, in a harsher timbre, the love poems in *The Solitudes*, written in loneliness and despair, are almost totally successful, and perhaps represent Duncan at his most approachable. With *Judas*, Duncan turned to a longer form, and during the past ten years has concentrated on *Man*, a long poem tracing "emergent consciousness in man," having concluded that "90% of poetry is no more than a mating call. That may be sufficient for adolescents." *Man*, much concerned with science, is by no means an unapproachable poem; it has been insufficiently examined by critics, for it is in fact one of the more serious examples recently published of a sustained long poem, and has passages of great intensity. If the reader is forced to consider, in the end, whether Duncan has in fact chosen the right setting for his speculations, he has undeniably written an original long poem which is discernibly an exploration of form as well as subject; and such truly exploratory verse in our time is rare.

—Derek Parker

DUNN, Douglas (Eaglesham). British. Born in Inchinnan, Renfrewshire, 23 October 1942. Educated at Renfrew High School; Camphill School, Paisley; Scottish School of Librarianship; University of Hull, 1966–69, B.A. in English 1969. Married Lesley Balfour Wallace in 1964. Library Assistant, Renfrew County Library, Paisley, 1959–62, and Andersonian Library, Glasgow, 1962–64; Assistant Librarian, Akron Public Library, Ohio, 1964–66; Librarian, Chemistry Department Library, University of Glasgow, 1966; Assistant Librarian, Brynmor Jones Library, 1969–71, and Fellow in Creative Writing, 1974–75, University of Hull; Poetry Reviewer, *Encounter* magazine, London, 1971–78. Recipient: Eric Gregory Award, 1966; Scottish Arts Council award, 1970; Maugham Award, 1972; Faber Memorial Prize, 1976. Address: c/o Faber and Faber Ltd., 3 Queen Square, London W.C.1, England.

PUBLICATIONS

Verse

Terry Street. London, Faber, 1969; New York, Chilmark Press, 1973.
Corgi Modern Poets in Focus 1, with others, edited by Dannie Abse. London, Corgi, 1971.
Backwaters. London, The Review, 1971.
Night. London, Poem-of-the-Month Club, 1971.
The Happier Life. London, Faber, 1972; New York, Chilmark Press, 1972.
Love or Nothing. London, Faber, 1974.
Barbarians. London, Faber, 1979.

Plays

Screenplays (verse commentary): *Early Every Morning*, 1975; *Running*, 1977.

Radio Play: *Scotsmen by Moonlight*, 1977.

Television Play: *Ploughman's Share*, 1979.

Other

Editor, *New Poems 1972–73.* London, Hutchinson, 1973.
Editor, "British Poetry Issue" of *Antaeus 12* (New York), 1973.
Editor, *A Choice of Byron's Verse.* London, Faber, 1974.
Editor, *Two Decades of Irish Writing.* Manchester, Carcanet Press, and Philadelphia, Dufour, 1975.
Editor, *What Is to Be Given: Selected Poems of Delmore Schwartz.* Manchester, Carcanet Press, 1976.
Editor, *The Poetry of Scotland.* London, Batsford, 1979.

Manuscript Collection: Brynmor Jones Library, University of Hull.

* * *

Douglas Dunn's first poems to appear in such anthologies as *Scottish Poetry* gave evidence of a talent for accurately-observed sensuous imagery as it reflects from the surface of things. The best section of his first book, *Terry Street*, related this talent to the setting and the way of life of a working-class street in Hull, as in "From the Night-Window":

The night rattles with nightmares,
Children cry in the close-packed houses,
A man rots in his snoring.
On quiet feet, policemen test doors.
Footsteps become people under streetlamps.

Sometimes the effect of active engagement with the urban scene is got simply by a kind of cumulative cataloguing, redeemed from being a series of prose statements by a personal rhythmic tone:

On the quiet street, Saturday night's fag-packets,
Balls of fish and chip newspaper, bottles
Placed neatly on window sills, beside cats.

A street of oilstains and parked motorbikes,
Wet confectionery wrappers becoming paste,
Things doing nothing, ending, rejected.

To some extent this is Larkin without either the tension or the compassion. But since at any rate many Scots readers still applaud most loudly those among their poets who write of lonely places and aspects of dying peripheral cultures, any poet who tries to come to terms with the urban situation of the majority as successfully as does Dunn in *Terry Street* must be respected.

Unfortunately, having re-created in poetry's terms a mirror-image of this situation, albeit as an expatriate – yet one who, in "Ships," can still write evocatively of his native Clydeside:

A fine rain attaches itself to the ship like skin.
The lascars play poker, the Scottish mate looks
At the last lights, one that is Ayrshire,
Others on lonely rocks, or clubfooted peninsulas

– what does the poet do next? The *Terry Street* Room-at-the-Top Dunn becomes, in *The Happier Life*, his second volume, Life-at-the-Top Dunn: and all he seems to want to do is snipe and sneer at everything that comes within range of his cleverness, from "Ted Heath's Britain" (an image as meaningless and vague as "Harold Wilson's Britain" or "Lord Palmerston's Britain"), to Irish girls come to town in search of a fuller life, who can be bought for an hour for ten pounds ("essentially rural whores, essentially innocent"), sportsmen ("scum, they have fast cars and money"), and "the rising young executives." An attempt is made to deal with the problem of a cohesing tension by resorting either to rhyming couplets or to formal stanzas. Sicanus, Thucydides, Ceres, and other literary allusions, are also used to help out when the pressure of something to say is low.

I do not mean to suggest that *The Happier Life* is wholly without interest. Cleverness abounds, like the detailed, formal expression of the disgust of a poor young man who nevertheless remains the kept pimp of a rich older woman ("Morning Bedroom"); and the more direct final section of the poem "Fixed." But ultimately the overall impression is of a staleness as flat as a copy of last Sunday's *News of the World*.

His third collection, *Love or Nothing*, marked a considerable advance, a rise in poetic pressure accompanied by an increasing mastery of formal constructions so that they often attain a fluidity of expression as rewarding as the range of his sometimes surprising imagery. But in spite of his increasing sophistication, he still sees himself as an outsider.

In your culture, I am a barbarian,
But I'm that here, and everywhere,
Lulled by alien rites, lullabyed with remorse
Here on the backstreets of the universe

he tells us in "The Wealth," from his fourth collection, *Barbarians*. However, he keeps up his excessive hatred of the myth-symbols, past or present, of every sort of "establishment" (other than that of his own political reality) and this leads him into over-simplification, as in "Warriors" ("In no war would I bleed"). But there is also a moving sense of compassion, as in "Ballad of the Two Left Hands," in which, when struck by the cruel fate of redundancy:

> ... men of several trades
> Stood there on Clydeside Street
> Stood staring at each new left hand
> That made them obsolete ...
>
> Such dignity, so many lives,
> Even on Clydeside Street
> When mind and heart together ask
> "Why are we obsolete?"

Perhaps Dunn's compassion will continue to broaden, so that he will no longer be interested in hanging even "my Lord ... somewhere in the shade."

—Maurice Lindsay

DUNN, Stephen. American. Born in New York City, 24 June 1939. Educated at Hofstra University, Hempstead, New York, 1958–62, B.A. in history 1962; New School for Social Research, New York, 1964–66; Syracuse University, New York, 1968–70, M.A. in creative writing 1970. Served in the United States Army. Married Lois Kelly in 1964; two daughters. Professional basketball player for the Williamsport Billies, Pennsylvania, 1962–63; Copywriter, National Biscuit Company, New York, 1963–66; Assistant Editor, Ziff-Davis, publishers, New York, 1967–68; Assistant Professor of Creative Writing, Southwest Minnesota State College, Marshall, 1970–73. Since 1974, Associate Professor, Stockton State College, New Jersey. Visiting Poet, Syracuse University, 1973–74, and University of Washington, Seattle, Winter 1979. Recipient: Academy of American Poets prize, 1970; National Endowment for the Arts Fellowship, 1973; Bread Loaf Writers Conference Robert Frost Fellowship, 1975; Theodore Roethke Prize (*Poetry Northwest*, Seattle), 1977; New Jersey Arts Council fellowship, 1979. Address: 224 Key Drive, Absecon, New Jersey 08201, U.S.A.

Publications

Verse

Five Impersonations. Marshall, Minnesota, Ox Head Press, 1971.
Looking for Holes in the Ceiling. Amherst, University of Massachusetts Press, 1974.
Full of Lust and Good Usage. Pittsburgh, Carnegie Mellon University Press, 1976.
A Circus of Needs. Pittsburgh, Carnegie Mellon University Press, 1978.

Other

Editor, *A Cat of Wind, An Alibi of Gifts* (anthology of children's poetry). Trenton, New Jersey State Council on the Arts, 1977.

Editor, *Silence Has a Rough, Crazy Weather* (poems by deaf children). Trenton, New Jersey State Council on the Arts, 1979.

Stephen Dunn comments:

I write what I discover to be true or effective or moving in the act of writing. Then I rewrite for coherence and, ideally, beauty. Certain obsessions emerge. I have a vague idea what they are, but I don't wish to know them too consciously. I want the poem to emerge from my own imperatives and reach out to the reader, naturally, clearly, as if I had cut through all the sanctioned lies, and was simply speaking.

* * *

The voice of Stephen Dunn's poems is sure, lyric, and comic, with just the proper mixture of love and of distance from those nearest him. There is also a persistent note of joy in his work, even as he struggles to feel at home in an occasionally inhospitable world. In "Truck Stop: Minnesota," for example, "The waitress looks at my face as if it were a small tip," the customer says, trying to win a friendly response from a woman treated familiarly by regular customers, the truckers, who call her "Sweetheart,... Honey. Doll." "She is the America I would like to love," the speaker admits, warily. "I'm full of lust and good usage, lost here."

It is Dunn's lust for life that makes him ill-at-ease, when he insists upon saying hello to everyone on Main Street in "Small Town: The Friendly" and in wanting to know, as he stalks the beach, in "A Private Man Confronts His Vulgarities at Dawn," "how/to cherish all of this, and just how many debts/a body is allowed." Not surprisingly, he feels most at home among salesmen and degenerates, "men with raincoats/on their laps, who chew their sleeves," as they watch a pornographic film, in "Visiting the City Again":

> We are comrades in a way; alone, embarrassed
> when the lights go on.
> I step into the men's room to pee and wash up.
> There are four feet in one stall, their owners
> have heard me and are still.
> I do what I came for, quickly,
> and walk out into the cold Minneapolis air,
> inexplicably pleased.

The joy of Dunn's poems grows out of their insistence on the "this-ness" of the body, a refusal to ignore its pleasures, in the midst of awkwardness and pain. The speaker wants to wear his body naturally and pleasantly, but someone or something reminds him continually that it just won't do. In "Modern Dance Class," for example, "the instructor looks at me/the way gas station attendants/look at tires whose treads are gone." And the dancer, who knows "grace/is what occurs after technique/has been loved a long while/and then forgotten," tries hard to pull himself together. The reader's enjoyment of such poems is a direct result of the poet's successful rendering of his and of our difficulty in doing so.

Stephen Dunn has accurately described the speaker in his poems as "the normal man, gone public," the person whose "private little efforts/to fulfill himself/are/not unlike yours, or anyone's." And there is something approaching perfecton in the way his work combines appreciation and satire, with its simplicity of language and intelligence of style. His poems of love and recollection, including "Those of Us Who Think We Know" and "The Visitant," are as beautiful, in their rightness, as the comic poems. After three books of short lyrics, he is presently engaged in writing a book-length poem that promises a new range in style and subject matter.

—Michael True

DURRELL, Lawrence (George). British. Born in Julundur, India, 27 February 1912. Educated at the College of St. Joseph, Darjeeling, India; St. Edmund's School, Canterbury, Kent. Married 1) Nancy Myers in 1935 (divorced, 1947); 2) Eve Cohen in 1947 (divorced); 3) Claude Durrell in 1961 (died, 1967); 4) Ghislaine de Boysson in 1973 (divorced, 1979); two children. Has had many jobs, including jazz pianist (Blue Peter nightclub, London), automobile racer, and real estate agent. Lived in Corfu, 1934–40. Editor, with Henry Miller and Alfred Perlès, *The Booster* (later *Delta*), Paris, 1937–39; Columnist, *Egyptian Gazette*, Cairo, 1941; Editor, with Robin Fedden and Bernard Spencer, *Personal Landscape*, Cairo, 1942–45; Special Correspondent in Cyprus for *The Economist*, London, 1953–55; Editor, *Cyprus Review*, Nicosia, 1954–55. Taught at the British Institute, Kalamata, Greece, 1940. Foreign Press Service Officer, British Information Office, Cairo, 1941–44; Press Attaché, British Information Office, Alexandria, 1944–45; Director of Public Relations for the Dodecanese Islands, Greece, 1946–47; Director of the British Council Institute, Cordoba, Argentina, 1947–48; Press Attaché, British Legation, Belgrade, 1949–52; Director of Public Relations for the British Government in Cyprus, 1954–56. Andrew Mellon Visiting Professor of Humanities, California Institute of Technology, Pasadena, 1974. Recipient: Duff Cooper Memorial Prize, 1957; Prix du Meilleur Livre Etranger, 1959. Fellow, Royal Society of Literature, 1954. Has lived in France since 1957. Address: c/o National and Grindlay's Bank, 13 St. James's Square, London S.W.1, England.

PUBLICATIONS

Verse

Quaint Fragment: Poems Written Between the Ages of Sixteen and Nineteen. London, Cecil Press, 1931.
A Ballade of Slow Decay. Privately printed, 1932.
Ten Poems. London, Caduceus Press, 1932.
Bromo Bombastes: A Fragment from a Laconic Drama by Gaffer Peeslake. London, Caduceus Press, 1933.
Transition. London, Caduceus Press, 1934.
Mass for the Old Year. Privately printed, 1935.
Proems: An Anthology of Poems, with others. London, Fortune Press, 1938.
A Private Country. London, Faber, 1943.
The Parthenon: For T. S. Eliot. Privately printed, 1945(?).
Cities, Plains, and People. London, Faber, 1946.
Zero, and Asylum in the Snow: Two Excursions into Reality. Privately printed, 1946; Berkeley, California, Circle, 1947.
On Seeming to Presume. London, Faber, 1948.
A Landmark Gone. Privately printed, 1949.
Deus Loci. Ischia, Italy, Di Mato Vito, 1950.
Private Drafts. Nicosia, Cyprus, Proodos Press, 1955.
The Tree of Idleness and Other Poems. London, Faber, 1955.
Selected Poems. London, Faber, and New York, Grove Press, 1956.
Collected Poems. London, Faber, and New York, Dutton, 1960; revised edition, 1968.
Penguin Modern Poets 1, with Elizabeth Jennings and R. S. Thomas. London, Penguin, 1962.
Poetry. New York, Dutton, 1962.
A Persian Lady. Privately printed, 1963.
Beccafico Le Becfigue (English, with French translation by F.-J. Temple). Montpellier, France, La Licorne, 1963.
La Descente du Styx (English, with French translation by F.-J. Temple). Montpellier, France, La Murène, 1964.
Selected Poems 1935–63. London, Faber, 1964.

The Ikons and Other Poems. London, Faber, 1966; New York, Dutton, 1967.
The Red Limbo Lingo: A Poetry Notebook for 1968–1970. London, Faber, 1971.
On the Suchness of the Old Boy. London, Turret, 1972.
Vega and Other Poems. London, Faber, 1973.
The Plant Magic Man. Santa Barbara, California, Capra Press, 1973.
Lifelines. Edinburgh, Tragara Press, 1974.
Selected Poems, edited by Alan Ross. London, Faber, 1977.

Plays

Sappho: A Play in Verse (produced Hamburg, 1959; Edinburgh, 1961; Evanston, Illinois, 1964). London, Faber, 1950; New York, Dutton, 1958.
Acte (produced Hamburg, 1961). London, Faber, 1965; New York, Dutton, 1966.
An Irish Faustus: A Morality in Nine Scenes (produced Sommerhausen, Germany, 1966). London, Faber, 1963; New York, Dutton, 1964.

Screenplays: *Cleopatra*, with others, 1963; *Judith*, with others, 1966.

Television Script: *The Lonely Road*, 1971.

Recording: *Ulysses Come Back: Sketch for a Musical* (story, music and lyrics by Lawrence Durrell), 1971.

Novels

Pied Piper of Lovers. London, Cassell, 1935.
Panic Spring (as Charles Norden). London, Faber, and New York, Covici Friede, 1937.
The Black Book: An Agon. Paris, Obelisk Press, 1938; New York, Dutton, 1960; London, Faber, 1973.
Cefalû. London, Editions Poetry London, 1947; as *The Dark Labyrinth*, New York, Ace, 1958.
White Eagles over Serbia. London, Faber, 1957; New York, Criterion Books, 1958.
The Alexandria Quartet. London, Faber, and New York, Dutton, 1962.
Justine. London, Faber, and New York, Dutton, 1957.
Balthazar. London, Faber, and New York, Dutton, 1958.
Mountolive. London, Faber, 1958; New York, Dutton, 1959.
Clea. London, Faber, and New York, Dutton, 1960.
The Revolt of Aphrodite. London, Faber, 1974.
Tunc. London, Faber, and New York, Dutton, 1968.
Nunquam. London, Faber, and New York, Dutton, 1970.
Monsieur; or, The Prince of Darkness. London, Faber, 1974; New York, Viking Press, 1975.
Livia; or, Buried Alive. London, Faber, 1978; New York, Viking Press, 1979.

Short Stories

Esprit de Corps: Sketches from Diplomatic Life. London, Faber, 1957; New York, Dutton, 1959.
Stiff Upper Lip: Life among the Diplomats. London, Faber, 1958; New York, Dutton, 1959.
Sauve Qui Peut. London, Faber, 1966; New York, Dutton, 1967.
The Best of Antrobus. London, Faber, 1974.

Other

Prospero's Cell: A Guide to the Landscape and Manners of the Island of Corcyra. London, Faber, 1945; with *Reflections on a Marine Venus*, New York, Dutton, 1960.
Key to Modern Poetry. London, Peter Nevill, 1952; as *A Key to Modern British Poetry*, Norman, University of Oklahoma Press, 1952.
Reflections on a Marine Venus: A Companion to the Landscape of Rhodes. London, Faber, 1953; with *Prospero's Cell*, New York, Dutton, 1960.
Bitter Lemons (on Cyprus). London, Faber, 1957; New York, Dutton, 1958.
Art and Outrage: A Correspondence about Henry Miller Between Alfred Perlès and Lawrence Durrell, with an Intermission by Henry Miller. London, Putnam, 1959; New York, Dutton, 1960.
Groddeck (on Georg Walther Groddeck). Wiesbaden, Limes, 1961.
Briefwechsel über "Actis", with G. Gründgens. Hamburg, Deutsches Schauspielhaus, 1961.
Lawrence Durrell and Henry Miller: A Private Correspondence, edited by George Wickes. New York, Dutton, and London, Faber, 1963.
Spirit of Place: Letters and Essays on Travel, edited by Alan G. Thomas. London, Faber, and New York, Dutton, 1969.
Le Grand Suppositoire (interview with Marc Alyn). Paris, Editions Pierre Belfond, 1972; as *The Big Supposer*, London, Abelard Schuman, 1973; New York, Grove Press, 1974.
The Happy Rock (on Henry Miller). London, Village Press, 1973.
Blue Thirst. Santa Barbara, California, Capra Press, 1975.
Sicilian Carousel. London, Faber, and New York, Viking Press, 1977.
The Greek Islands. London, Faber, and New York, Viking Press, 1978.

Editor, with others, *Personal Landscape: An Anthology of Exile.* London, Editions Poetry London, 1945.
Editor, *A Henry Miller Reader.* New York, New Directions, 1959; as *The Best of Henry Miller*, London, Heinemann, 1960.
Editor, *New Poems 1963: A P.E.N. Anthology of Contemporary Poetry.* London, Hutchinson, 1963.
Editor, *Lear's Corfu: An Anthology Drawn from the Painter's Letters.* Corfu, Corfu Travel, 1965.
Editor, *Wordsworth.* London, Penguin, 1973.

Translator, *Six Poems from the Greek of Sekilanos and Seferis.* Privately printed, 1946.
Translator, with Bernard Spencer and Nanos Valaortis, *The King of Asine and Other Poems*, by George Seferis. London, Lehmann, 1948.
Translator, *The Curious History of Pope Joan*, by Emmanuel Royidis. London, Verschoyle, 1954; revised edition, as *Pope Joan: A Personal Biography*, London, Deutsch, 1960; New York, Dutton, 1961.

Bibliography: by Alan G. Thomas, in *Lawrence Durrell: A Critical Study* by G. S. Fraser, London, Faber, 1968.

Manuscript Collections: University of California, Los Angeles; University of Illinois, Urbana.

Critical Studies: *The World of Lawrence Durrell* edited by Harry T. Moore, Carbondale, Southern Illinois University Press, 1962; *Lawrence Durrell and the Alexandria Quartet* by Alan Warren Friedman, Norman, University of Oklahoma Press, 1970; *Lawrence Durrell Newsletter* (Kelowna, British Columbia).

* * *

Lawrence Durrell's world fame is based on his series of novels of the 1950's, *The Alexandria Quartet*, but critics like Francis Hope, who dislike these and also the subterranean novel of the late 1930's, published in Paris, *The Black Book*, see his real achievement in his poems and in his three travel books, which have much of the quality of his poems, about Corfu before the Second World War, Rhodes during its post-war Allied occupation, and Cyprus during the troubles of the early 1950's. Those who feel that as a novelist Durrell is over-rated would probably say that in *The Alexandria Quartet* the set scenes, the landscapes, the evocations of local atmosphere are the work of a poet but that the handling of incident and character is excessively romantic, in a "story-book" sense. It is oddly true that the tone and diction of the poems are quieter, more subdued, much less boldly coloured than much of the prose of *The Alexandria Quartet* and *Tunc*: Durrell does not seem to be trying so hard, straining his resources so much, and it may be therefore that as a poet he is at his most convincing.

There is not much development in the poetry, and in his collected and selected poems Durrell rightly arranges the poems according to affinities of kind, tone, or subject-matter rather than in chronological order. Though he is very obviously a "modern" poet, he owes a great deal to two of his favourite poets of the nineteenth century, Landor and Browning. In short lyrics like "Water Music" he aims at, and often achieves, a Landorian perfection of form. Longer poems about characters or places have deliberately a certain Browningesque looseness or roughness of texture, and resemble Browning's dramatic monologues in setting great figures of the past, Byron, Horace, Rochefoucauld, in a perspective of ambiguous self-questioning; but more obviously than Browning, influenced perhaps by Browning's disciple Ezra Pound, Durrell is using such figures to express or sometimes to reject aspects of his own nature.

Poems about places, like the effective "Alexandria," written in war-time, similarly use a place and sometimes friends and enemies in a place to concretise a creative mood. The place becomes, as in the good little poem about the cold chaste beauty of the English West Country, "Bere Regis," a symbol for a whole complex of attitudes to be savoured, appreciated, perhaps finally to be relegated to the large category of attitudes which, for Durrell, are not finally adequate. Durrell is not an objective poet of landscape like his friend, that fine, neglected poet, Bernard Spencer, but a poet of what may be called moodscape.

A third category of poems is what Robert Graves calls "satires and grotesques": humorous and fantastic poems, but always in the end affectionate rather than sharply satirical, like "Uncebunke" or "The Ballad of the Good Lord Nelson." There are some poems like the early "Sonnet of Hamlet" or the later short "Nemea" where the main interest seems to be in the poetry of vocabulary, in surprising collocations or strange and beautiful echoings of words: such poems are perhaps the equivalent of what T. S. Eliot called "five-finger exercises."

The total impression that one derives from Durrell's poems is of a benign quietism, something like that of a humorous Chinese sage gazing on waterfalls from a hut on a mountain. Born in India, Durrell has always been deeply interested in Eastern thought, in what he calls the "expurgation" of the self, in the achievement of states of calm contemplation. This spiritual bent is expressed, however, in scene or anecdote, strange joke, or hushed and gentle lyric rather than in abstract or dogmatic terms. The sage is strangely married, also, to the literary dandy. Durrell's kind of poetry is today distinctly unfashionable; it is not confessional, it is not socially committed, its language and attitudes may seem excessively "literary." It never clamours for attention. Yet it has always pleased good critics and it will last.

—G. S. Fraser

DUTTON, Geoffrey (Piers Henry). Australian. Born in Anlaby, South Australia, 2 August 1922. Educated at Geelong Grammar School, Victoria, 1932–39; University of Adelaide, 1940–41; Magdalen College, Oxford, 1946–49, B.A. 1949. Served as a Flight Lieutenant in the Royal Australian Air Force, 1941–45. Married Ninette Trott in 1944; three children. Senior Lecturer in English, University of Adelaide, 1954–62; Visiting Lecturer in Australian Literature, University of Leeds, 1960; Visiting Professor, Kansas State University, Manhattan, 1962. Editor, Penguin Australia, Melbourne, 1961–65. Since 1965, Editorial Director of Sun Books Pty. Ltd., Melbourne. Co-Founder, *Australian Letters*, Adelaide, 1957, and *Australian Book Review*, Kensington Park, 1962. Member of the Australian Council for the Arts, 1968–70, and Commonwealth Literary Fund Advisory Board, 1972–73. Since 1973, Member, Australian Literature Board. Address: Old Anlaby, Kapunda, South Australia 5373, Australia.

PUBLICATIONS

Verse

Nightflight and Sunrise. Melbourne, Reed and Harris, 1945.
Antipodes in Shoes. Sydney, Edwards and Shaw, 1955.
Flowers and Fury. Melbourne, Cheshire, 1963.
On My Island: Poems for Children. Melbourne, Cheshire, 1967.
Poems Soft and Loud. Melbourne, Cheshire, 1968.
Findings and Keepings: Selected Poems 1940–1970. Adelaide, Australian Letters, 1970.
New Poems to 1972. Adelaide, Australian Letters, 1972.
A Body of Words. Sydney, Edwards and Shaw, 1977.

Novels

The Mortal and the Marble. London, Chapman and Hall, 1950.
Andy. Sydney and London, Collins, 1968.
Tamara. Sydney and London, Collins, 1970.
Queen Emma of the South Seas. Melbourne and London, Macmillan, 1976; New York, St. Martin's Press, 1978.

Other

A Long Way South (travel). London, Chapman and Hall, 1953.
Africa in Black and White. London, Chapman and Hall, 1956.
States of the Union (travel). London, Chapman and Hall, 1958.
Founder of a City: The Life of William Light. Melbourne, Cheshire, and London, Chapman and Hall, 1960.
Patrick White. Melbourne, Lansdowne Press, 1961; London and New York, Oxford University Press, 1971.
Walt Whitman. Edinburgh, Oliver and Boyd, and New York, Grove Press, 1961.
Paintings of S. T. Gill. Adelaide, Rigby, 1962.
Russell Drysdale (art criticism). London, Thames and Hudson, 1962.
Tisi and the Yabby (juvenile). Sydney and London, Collins, 1965.
Seal Bay (juvenile). Sydney and London, Collins, 1966.
The Hero as Murderer: The Life of Edward John Eyre, Australian Explorer and Governor of Jamaica, 1815–1901. Melbourne, Cheshire, and London, Collins, 1967.
Tisi and the Pageant (juvenile). Adelaide, Rigby, 1968.
Australia's Last Explorer: Ernest Giles. London, Faber, 1970.
Australia since the Camera: From Federation to War 1901–14. Melbourne, Cheshire, 1972.

White on Black: The Australian Aborigine Portrayed in Art. Melbourne, Macmillan, 1974.
A Taste of History: Geoffrey Dutton's South Australia. Adelaide, Rigby, 1978.
Patterns of Australia, with Harri Peccinotti. Melbourne, Macmillan, 1979.

Editor, *The Literature of Australia.* Melbourne, Penguin, 1964; revised edition, 1976.
Editor, *Modern Australian Writing.* London, Fontana, 1966.
Editor, *Australia and the Monarchy: A Symposium.* Melbourne, Sun, 1966.
Editor, with Max Harris, *The Vital Decade: 10 Years of Australian Art and Letters.* Melbourne, Sun, 1968.
Editor, with Max Harris, *Sir Henry Bjelke, Don Baby, and Friends.* Melbourne, Sun, 1971.
Editor, *Republican Australia?* Melbourne, Sun, 1977.

Translator, with Igor Mezhakoff-Koriakin, *Bratsk Station*, by Yevgeny Yevtushenko. Melbourne, Sun, 1966; New York, Doubleday, 1967; London, Hart Davis, 1968.
Translator, with Igor Mezhakoff-Koriakin, *Fever and Other New Poems*, by Bella Akhmadulina. Melbourne, Sun, 1968; New York, Morrow, 1969; London, Peter Owen, 1970.
Translator, *Kazan University and Other New Poems*, by Yevgeny Yevtushenko. Melbourne, Sun, 1973.

Geoffrey Dutton comments:

My poetry began in the turmoil of war, and the *Angry Penguins* period of modernism in Australia; my poetic thinking was heavily influenced by modern French and German as well as the English and American poetry. I was fortunate enough to be in close contact with a remarkable group of poets in Adelaide in the 1940's, which included Donald Kerr, Max Harris, and Paul Pfeiffer; both Kerr and Pfeiffer were killed in the R.A.A.F. during the war. In Melbourne in 1944 I shared my ideas with the poet Alister Kershaw and the painters Arthur Boyd and Sidney Nolan.

Six years in Oxford, London and France after the war, and friendship with Roy Campbell and Richard Aldington, made me work towards a greater clarity and technical control. My wandering life and return to Australia were reflected in my poems.

In the early 1960's I was much influenced towards attempting a more complex human response to my own country by studying Walt Whitman. In the late 1960's I met and travelled in Russia with the poet Yevgeny Yevtushenko, having with Igor Mezhakoff-Koriakin translated a large number of his poems; with Igor Mezhakoff-Koriakin I also translated Bella Akhmadulina's new poems, and met her on my visits to Russia in 1966 and 1967. In these visits I discovered the vast field of modern Russian poetry, and have learnt a great deal from the modern Russian poets about the relation between poetry and the modern world on both sides of the so-called iron curtain. Also the importance of rhyme and rhythm in Russian has helped shore up my technical beliefs in them at a time when regular rhyme and rhythm have been unpopular.

I think many of the poems which are nearest to what I had hoped they might be are to do with love; it is difficult to write anything about these.

I welcome what has been called the new nationalism in Australia, not for narrow pseudo-patriotic reasons, but because it may help give Australian poets confidence in welcoming the nourishment most good poets draw from the soil in which they grew.

* * *

Remarkable for its intrinsic light-heartedness, the poetry of Geoffrey Dutton has tended to be under-rated by most critics while a growing audience of appreciative readers testifies to its inherent qualities.

Despite the light-heartedness, this poet is capable of extended lyrical meditations of a uniquely beautiful nature. His best work to be found in poems such as "Abandoned Airstrip, Northern Territory" in which he recapitulates his memories as a flyer in the Second World War; "Night Fishing," a long nocturne celebrating the shared lives and joys of an Australian couple in love and experiencing the primal mateship of hunters alone in an eternally providing world; and "The Smallest Sprout," a poem written in memory of his mother in which his natural lyricism is enriched by elegiacal overtones.

His recent work has been spread evenly among suites and individual pieces descriptive of his travels in Russia – elsewhere his versions of Yevtushenko are noteworthy – and America, equally appreciative of the most positive as well as the negative aspects of both countries and the inhabitants, and in tart and pungent satires criticising and ridiculing the tasteless and the chauvinistic in modern Australia. His comments in verse on the Vietnamese war show him to be capable of clear-headed and compellingly written poems of protest, but it is in the longer autobiographical poem imbued with lyrical insights and quiet humour that this fine poet's best work is found.

—Bruce Beaver

DYLAN, Bob. American. Born Robert Zimmerman in Duluth, Minnesota, 24 May 1941. Educated at the University of Minnesota, Minneapolis, 1960. Composer and Performer: concert appearances in the United States, 1961–66, 1971, 1974, and in Europe and Australia, 1964–66. Recipient: Emergency Civil Liberties Committee Tom Paine Award, 1963. D.Mus.: Princeton University, New Jersey, 1970. Address: P.O. Box 264, Cooper Station, New York, New York 10003, U.S.A.

PUBLICATIONS

Verse

Tarantula. New York, Macmillan, 1966.
Approximately Complete Works. Amsterdam, De Bezige Bij-Thomas Rap, 1970.
Poem to Joanie. London, Aloes Press, 1972.
Words. London, Cape, 1973.
Writings and Drawings. New York, Knopf, and London, Cape, 1973.
The Songs of Bob Dylan 1966–1975. New York, Knopf, 1976.

Scores: *The Bob Dylan Songbook*, New York, Witmark, 1963; *Songs for Voice and Guitar*, New York, Witmark, 2 vols., 1968; *Bob Dylan's Songs for Harmonica*, New York, Witmark, 1968; *Song Book*, Witmark, 1970.

Recordings: *Bob Dylan Himself*, Columbia, 1962; *The Freewheelin' Bob Dylan*, Columbia, 1963; *The Times They Are A-Changin'*, Columbia, 1963; *Another Side of Bob Dylan*, Columbia, 1964; *Bringing It All Back Home*, Columbia, 1965; *Highway 61 Revisited*, Columbia, 1965; *Blonde on Blonde*, Columbia, 1966; *Bob Dylan's Greatest Hits*, Columbia, 1967; *John Wesley Harding*, Columbia, 1968; *Nashville Skyline*, Columbia, 1969; *Self Portrait*, Columbia, 1970; *New Morning*, Columbia, 1970; *Bob Dylan's Greatest Hits, vol. 2*, Columbia, 1971; *Dylan*, Columbia, 1974; *Planet Waves*, Island, 1974; *Before the Flood*, Asylum, 1974; *Blood on the Tracks*, Columbia, 1975;

The Basement Tapes, CBS, 1975; *Desire*, Columbia, 1976; *Hard Rain*, CBS, 1976; *Street Legal*, CBS, 1978; *Bob Dylan at Budokan*, 1979; *Slow Train Coming*, 1979; incidental music for the film *Pat Garrett and Billy the Kid*, 1972.

Theatrical Activities:

Actor: **Films** – *Don't Look Back*, 1965; *Eat the Document*, 1966; *Pat Garrett and Billy the Kid*, 1972; *Renaldo and Clara*, 1978.

* * *

Bob Dylan's lyrics spring from two regions of the mind – the Minnesota "North Country" that stands still in time and New York City, the magnification of change. And to Dylan in the late 1950's, constancy seemed oppressive. He went to New York, taking along rhythms and motifs absorbed from folk songs and blues. He wrote of Minnesota and events of the City, but compared to his later verse, these songs were tame. For three reasons: the subjects were not widely known, the persona sounded too vulnerable and was prone to melodrama, and Dylan had not learned to integrate images from various sources into a single poem.

He pitched his young voice toward the Byronic, becoming old beyond his years, "an arch criminal who'd done no wrong." Singing like one of the changing instilled confidence:

My road it might be rocky,
The stones might cut my face.
But as some folks ain't got no road at all,
They gotta stand in the same old place.
Hey, hey, so I guess I'm doin' fine.

Satire and protest allowed him to speak vehemently without revealing himself. Encountering bizarre individuals ("I Shall Be Free") or atomic holocaust ("Talking World War III Blues"), he played a victim as irrepressible as Chaplin:

Well, I rung the fallout shelter bell
And I leaned my head and I gave a yell,
"Give me a string bean, I'm a hungry man."
A shotgun fired and away I ran.
I don't blame him too much, though,
He didn't know me.

"I don't like to be stuck in print," he admitted in "11 Outlined Epitaphs." He preferred to watch the night "unwind" because "there's no end t' it/and it's so big." The songs became "nothin' but the unwindin' of/my happiness."

By his fifth album, *Bringing It All Back Home*, Dylan was comfortable with the rhetoric of existentialism. "i accept chaos," he wrote for the liner notes; "i am not sure whether it accepts me." "The/Great Books've been written"; art had to be change, action. This urgency required dynamic language, lucid, rapidly shifting images. The results ranged from the frenetic "Subterranean Homesick Blues" ("Get sick, get well/ Hang around the ink well") to "Mr. Tambourine Man" and (perhaps the tightest poem) "Love Minus Zero/ No Limit":

The bridge at midnight trembles,
The country doctor rambles.
Bankers' nieces seek perfection,
Expecting all the gifts that wise men bring.
The wind howls like a hammer,
The night blows cold and rainy.
My love she's like some raven
At my window with a broken wing.

Then *Highway 61 Revisited* intensified his achievement. "Like a Rolling Stone" raised pointlessness one power to invisibility. The iconoclast verged on insanity ("Tombstone Blues"). Riding the mailtrain, the wanderer wearily mused, "I went to tell everybody,/But I could not get across." Dylan called the songs "exercises in tonal breath control ... the subject matter – though meaningless as it is – has something to do with the beautiful strangers." Indeed, with "Desolation Row" and "Highway 61 Revisited" his early efforts culminated in a visionary intensity.

Most of Dylan's recent lyrics are not compelling poetry. He is more interested, these days, in performance – experimenting with instrumentation, singing *to* an audience rather than protesting *at* them. The elusiveness is gone, the mystique of the seer. When, as in "Lily, Rosemary, and the Jack of Hearts" (*Blood on the Tracks*), he articulates a vision, it is one of compassion. The fast-talking irreverence has given way to a quiet, even grieving voice.

The only sustained handling of this theme of compassion remains *John Wesley Harding* (1968). With parable and heroic folk song for antecedents, Dylan sings his empathy for the oppressed rather than implying it, as before, through attacks on the oppressors. In "I Pity the Poor Immigrant" he creates an outcast who spends himself without assurance of comfort. The suffering figure in "I Dreamed I Saw St. Augustine" moves the singer to tears. "All Along the Watchtower" acknowledges that all is far from well, but insists on affirmation. "There are many here among us who feel that life is but a joke," Dylan advises, harkening to his theme of absurdity; "But you and I, we've been through that, and this is not our fate." Even though there is a sense of foreboding, the watchers are patient, not angry or jeering.

On such occasions, Dylan finds his way back to the North Country, singing griefs that are timeless instead of the grievances that belong to the moment.

—Jay S. Paul

EATON, Charles Edward. American. Born in Winston-Salem, North Carolina, 25 June 1916. Educated at Duke University, Durham, North Carolina, 1932–33; University of North Carolina, Chapel Hill, 1933–36, B.A. 1936 (Phi Beta Kappa); Princeton University, New Jersey, 1936–37; Harvard University, Cambridge, Massachusetts, 1938–40, M.A. in English 1940. Married Isabel Patterson in 1950. Instructor, Ruiz Gandia School, Poncé, Puerto Rico, 1937–38; Instructor in Creative Writing, University of Missouri, Columbia, 1940–42; Vice Consul, American Embassy, Rio de Janeiro, Brazil, 1942–46; Professor of Creative Writing, University of North Carolina, 1946–51. Free-lance Writer and Art Critic, and Organizer of Art Shows. Recipient: Bread Loaf Writers Conference Robert Frost Fellowship, 1941; Boulder, Colorado, Writers Conference Fellowship, 1942; Ridgely Torrence Memorial Award, 1951; Gertrude Boatwright Harris Award, 1954; *Arizona Quarterly* Award, 1956, 1977; New England Poetry Club Golden Rose, 1972; O. Henry Award, for fiction, 1972; Alice Fay di Castagnola Award, 1974. Address: Merlin Stone, Woodbury, Connecticut 06798, U.S.A.

PUBLICATIONS

Verse

The Bright Plain. Chapel Hill, University of North Carolina Press, 1942.
The Shadow of the Swimmer. New York, Fine Editions Press, 1951.
The Greenhouse in the Garden. New York, Twayne, 1955.
Countermoves. New York and London, Abelard Schuman, 1962.
On the Edge of the Knife. New York and London, Abelard Schuman, 1969.
The Man in the Green Chair. South Brunswick, New Jersey, A. S. Barnes, and London, Yoseloff, 1977.
Colophon of the Rover. South Brunswick, New Jersey, A. S. Barnes, 1980.

Play

Sea Psalm (produced Chapel Hill, North Carolina, 1933). Published in *North Carolina Drama*, Richmond, Virginia, Garrett and Massie, 1956.

Novel

A Lady of Pleasure. Lunenburg, Vermont, North Country, 1972.

Short Stories

Write Me from Rio. Winston-Salem, North Carolina, John F. Blair, 1959.
The Girl from Ipanema. Lunenburg, Vermont, North Country, 1972.
The Case of the Missing Photographs. South Brunswick, New Jersey, A. S. Barnes, 1978.

Other

Charles and Isabel Eaton Collection of America Paintings. Chapel Hill, University of North Carolina Art Department, 1970.
Karl Knaths. Washington, Connecticut, Shiver Mountain Press, 1971.
Karl Knaths: Five Decades of Painting. Washington, D.C., International Exhibitions Foundation, 1973.
Robert Broderson: Paintings and Graphics. Washington, Connecticut, Shiver Mountain Press, 1975.

Manuscript Collections: (Verse) Southern Historical Collection, University of North Carolina, Chapel Hill; (Prose) Mugar Memorial Library, Boston University.

Critical Studies: by Louis Untermeyer, in *Yale Review* (New Haven, Connecticut), Winter 1944; by Robert Hillyer, in *New York Times Book Review*, 22 July 1951; "The Poetry of Charles Edward Eaton" by W. W. Davidson, in *Georgia Review* (Athens), Spring 1956; by Gerard P. Meyer, in *Saturday Review* (New York), 31 March 1956; in *Booklist* (Chicago), 1 May 1956; by May Swenson, in *Poetry* (Chicago), March 1957; "The Greenhouse in the Garden" by William Carlos Williams, in *Arizona Quarterly* (Tucson), Spring 1957; by Wallace Fowlie, in *New York Times Book Review*, 12 May 1963; by John Engels, in *Poetry* (Chicago), September 1963; by F. C. Flint, in *Virginia Quarterly Review* (Charlottesville), Autumn 1963; "Betwixt Tradition and Innovation" by Robert D. Spector, in *Saturday Review* (New York), 26 December 1970; "The Crisis of Regular Forms" by John T. Irwin, in *Sewanee Review* (Tennessee), Winter 1973; by Robert Miola, in *Commonweal* (New York), 18 August 1978.

Charles Edward Eaton comments:

Though I am resistant in general to definitions of poetry and poets as too limiting, if pressed, I might admit to being a modern formalist, but I should insist on the importance of the qualifying adjective. I compose in a number of verse forms, and write lyrical as well as dramatic poetry, but I do not lean on any poet of the past or present for technical inspiration. I believe that each poet must develop his own organic sense of form and adapt even the most conventional meter to his personal rhythm. For example, a number of my poems are written in triptychs, their long lines rhyming every other line, modulated in an entirely individual way. William Carlos Williams, in a study of my work, called this three line stanza an Americanization of *terza rima*. Perhaps he felt it was very American in its love of freedom and yet somewhat European in its formal allegiance. There is no doubt that I like poetry that is both vigorous and controlled.

In this respect, I think the best short statement about my work has been made by Robert D. Spector in *The Saturday Review*: "Charles Edward Eaton may not belong at all in the category of unconventional poets, and yet, it seems to me, his use of conventions becomes a very personal thing that removes him from tradition.... If Eaton's poetry, with its use of rhymed stanzas, appears superficially to belong to a formal tradition, his long, free lines and sometimes brutal imagery and diction, pushing his feelings to their limit, suggest otherwise. *On the Edge of the Knife* combines conventional and unconventional in such a way that it is finally the poet's own work. Perhaps, after all, that is the way of poetry. Whether bound to tradition or not, its value rests on the peculiar virtues of the poet."

I am in emphatic accord with any statement about my work which indicates that I believe in working powerfully and freely on one's own terms within the entire range of poetry. I am in no sense a reductionist, but have confidence in the fundamental richness of poetry and the surprise lurking in its possibilities. Form should be an energetic expression of the poet's own psychology not an artificial imposition, and the poem should convey some sense of the struggle which went into the formal achievement:

> I have a powerful nature in pursuit of pleasure,
> Peace, good will, and I do not share
> My time's contempt for passion balanced by strict measure.

An extension of what is involved in this position is given at the conclusion of "The Turkey":

> So the bird I know is like a gaudy catafalque.
> If you should carry a secret hump upon your back,
> You, too, would have a burdened and uncertain walk.
>
> This is what it is to spread an image in the sun –
> This is how we teach thick, precarious balance as if the land moved like a ship
> And one set sail heavily, slowly, encumbered with imagination.

As to my subject matter, it is greatly influenced by where I am living and what I am doing at any given time. In this sense, it is always around me, and it moves forward with me as I go along. Almost every poem, hidden though it may be to the reader, has its *donnée* from some aspect of my experience. Landscape wherever I have lived (North Carolina, Puerto Rico, Brazil, Connecticut, etc.) comes strongly into my work, but I do not consider myself a nature poet. Animals and flowers are continuous with and contiguous to my interest in human beings, and are a constant motif in my work, but I am not interested in fauna or flora *per se*, and am in no sense a botanical or zoological poet. All of my subjects are finally a way of talking about people in the expanding enclave of interest and experience I have chosen to explore. I have been amused by one magazine editor's recognition of my predilection for "all things, great and small" in welcoming a new submission as another poem from "the Garden of Eaton."

Painting has been another seminal influence, and I have long enjoyed what John Singleton Copley called "the luxury of seeing." This interest is the specific motivation in such poems as "The Gallery," "The Museum," "Homage to the Infanta," and "Nocturne for Douanier Rousseau," among others, but it is a constantly underlying, energizing source. "Five Etudes for the Artist" (*Art International*, November 1972) is an extended statement of this pictorial dedication which has been noted by numerous artists, including the New England painter Karl Knaths who has commented at length on the "vital imaginative reality" of the visual qualities of the poems.

The intellectual content of my poetry and of its final outlook and credo has been greatly strengthened by the study of philosophy. Writing in the *New York Times* about *Countermoves*, Wallace Fowlie recognized this influence when he said: "Charles Eaton demonstrates an admirable technical control over the effects he wishes to make, and a clear awareness of at least one major function of poetry. This would be the art of questioning everything, and of questioning in particular the power of poetry."

Fowlie's acknowledgment of the power of sentiment as balancing the intellectual in the poetry is reflected in a line from my long poem, "Robert E. Lee: An Ode": "I believe in the world seen through a temperament." I am certain that it is always the task of the writer to give us his personal vision of reality. This means an uncommon dedication, a determination to keep the fine arts fine, a perpetual sense of renewal and reaffirmation. One must constantly ask oneself in times of discouragement: Who will do my particular kind of writing if I don't? Who will take care of my dreams when I am gone? In our dispersive time, it is not easy to keep a sense of personality and purpose, and, as a consequence, attention to the disciplines of character is equally important with ability. Probably more writers fail through lack of character than of ability. Morale is one of the essential fibres of a meaningful life. Cézanne reminded himself every morning to be *"Sur le motif!"* So must the poet.

* * *

The poetry of Charles Edward Eaton ranges from the quiet, reflective, and calmly precise to the colorful, daring, gripping, and raw. The best of his work provides the reader with a delightful though sometimes disturbing experience: he advances confidently, secure in the carefully controlled rhythms, the superbly disciplined energies of syntax, until of a sudden he loses his balance. Upon recovering it the reader discovers that he has been walking on a tightrope, stretched precariously between the world as he usually sees it and the world as it really is.

Eaton is a poet who allows his mind and heart to play upon experience. He sings of ordinary things: the amber light of the sun, the fading fragrance of purple lilacs, the red fire of October, the bodies of swimmers, golden and hard-muscled, a day in spring, "... like a bell/Rung suddenly in many tones of green,/Sprung full and clear-toned well/Into the rounded air...." He sings also of extraordinary things: the Giggler, Voyeur, Centaur, Eunuch, Cowboy, Woman with a Scar, and Madame Midget, "Her tiny heart, loaded with feeling close as a plum is to its stone." Repeatedly, through skillful use of conventional form and variations, the poet demonstrates how tenuous and fluctuating is the distinction between the two. For Eaton all experience, the ordinary as well as the extraordinary, the painful as well as the pleasant, is matter for poetry to assimilate and rearrange. "From bee-sting, spider-bite, thorn-prick, hammer-bruise," no less than from "lip-brush" and "hand-grasp," the flesh learns and "grows wise."

Eaton's most recent volumes, *On the Edge of the Knife* and *The Man in the Green Chair*, explore with increasing boldness and vigor the abnormality of the normal. They reveal the bestial power of Eros and they descend into the primitive darkness deep within each of us. The verse, like the song of the Tree Frog, is often "raw with harsh and heartfelt music," a music which reverberates through the intelligent verse paragraphs, the chiselled quatrains, the unorthodox, long-lined triptychs. Such rawness never chafes or offends. For the mastery of form, achieved by years of experience and adopted to the distinctive sound of the poet's individual voice, finally teaches the heart the lesson it learns in "Della Robbia in August," not only to grieve, but to rise "in a brilliant form of care."

—Robert Miola

EBERHART, Richard (Ghormley). American. Born in Austin, Minnesota, 5 April 1904. Educated at the University of Minnesota, Minneapolis, 1922–23; Dartmouth College, Hanover, New Hampshire, B.A. 1926; St. John's College, Cambridge, B.A. 1929, M.A. 1933; Harvard University, Cambridge, Massachusetts, 1932–33. Served in the United States Naval Reserve, 1942–46: Lieutenant Commander. Married Helen Butcher in 1941; two children. Tutor to the son of King Prajadhipok of Siam, 1930–31. English Teacher, St. Mark's School, Southboro, Massachusetts, 1933–41, and Cambridge School, Kendal Green, Massachusetts, 1941–42. Assistant Manager to the Vice-President, Butcher Polish Company, Boston, 1946–52; now honorary Vice-President and Member of the Board of Directors. Visiting Professor, University of Washington, Seattle, 1952–53, 1967, 1972; Professor of English, University of Connecticut, Storrs, 1953–54; Visiting Professor, Wheaton College, Norton, Massachusetts, 1954–55; Resident Fellow and Gauss Lecturer, Princeton University, New Jersey, 1955–56. Professor of English and Poet-in-Residence, 1956–68, Class of 1925 Professor, 1968–70, and since 1970, Professor Emeritus, Dartmouth College. Elliston Lecturer, University of Cincinnati, 1961; Visiting Professor, Columbia University, New York, 1975, University of California, Davis, 1975, and University of Florida, Gainesville, winter term, 1974–79. Founder, 1950, and First President, Poets' Theatre, Cambridge, Massachusetts; Member, 1955, and since 1964, Director, Yaddo Corporation. Consultant in Poetry, 1959–61, and Honorary Consultant in American Letters, 1963–69, Library of Congress, Washington, D.C. Recipient: Guarantor's Prize, 1946, and Harriet Monroe Memorial Prize, 1950 (*Poetry*, Chicago); New England Poetry Club Golden Rose, 1950; Shelley Memorial Award, 1952; Harriet Monroe Poetry Award, 1955; National Institute of Arts and Letters grant, 1955; Bollingen Prize, 1962; Pulitzer Prize, 1966; Academy of American Poets Fellowship, 1969; National Book Award, 1977. D.Litt.: Dartmouth College, 1954; Skidmore College, Saratoga, New York, 1966; College of Wooster, Ohio, 1969; Colgate University, Hamilton, New York, 1974; Franklin Pierce College, Rindge, New Hampshire, 1978. Poet Laureate of New Hampshire, 1979. Since 1972, Honorary President, Poetry Society of America. Member, National Institute of Arts and Letters, 1960, and American Academy of Arts and Sciences, 1967. Address: 5 Webster Terrace, Hanover, New Hampshire 03755, U.S.A.

PUBLICATIONS

Verse

A Bravery of Earth. London, Cape, 1930; New York, Cape and Smith, 1931.
Reading the Spirit. London, Chatto and Windus, 1936; New York, Oxford University Press, 1937.
Song and Idea. London, Chatto and Windus, 1940; New York, Oxford University Press, 1942.
A World-View. Medford, Massachusetts, Tufts College Press, 1941.
Poems, New and Selected. New York, New Directions, 1944.
Rumination. Hanover, New Hampshire, Wayzgoose Press, 1947.

Burr Oaks. New York, Oxford University Press, and London, Chatto and Windus, 1947.
Brotherhood of Men. Pawlet, Vermont, Banyan Press, 1949.
An Herb Basket. Cummington, Massachusetts, Cummington Press, 1950.
Selected Poems. New York, Oxford University Press, and London, Chatto and Windus, 1951.
Undercliff: Poems 1946–1953. London, Chatto and Windus, 1953; New York, Oxford University Press, 1954.
Great Praises. New York, Oxford University Press, and London, Chatto and Windus, 1957.
The Oak: A Poem. Hanover, New Hampshire, Pine Tree Press, 1957.
Collected Poems 1930–1960, Including 51 New Poems. New York, Oxford University Press, and London, Chatto and Windus, 1960.
The Quarry: New Poems. New York, Oxford University Press, and London, Chatto and Windus, 1964.
The Vastness and Indifference of the World. Milford, New Hampshire, Ferguson Press, 1965.
Fishing for Snakes. Privately printed, 1965.
Selected Poems 1930–1965. New York, New Directions, 1965.
Thirty One Sonnets. New York, Eakins Press, 1967.
Shifts of Being. New York, Oxford University Press, and London, Chatto and Windus, 1968.
The Achievement of Richard Eberhart: A Comprehensive Selection of His Poems, edited by Bernard F. Engle. Chicago, Scott Foresman, 1968.
Three Poems. Cambridge, Massachusetts, Pym Randall Press, 1968.
Fields of Grace. New York, Oxford University Press, and London, Chatto and Windus, 1972.
Two Poems. West Chester, Pennsylvania, Aralia Press, 1975.
Collected Poems 1930–1976, Including 43 New Poems. New York, Oxford University Press, and London, Chatto and Windus, 1976.
Poems to Poets. Lincoln, Massachusetts, Penmaen Press, 1976.
Ways of Light. New York, Oxford University Press, and London, Chatto and Windus, 1980.

Recording: *Richard Eberhart Reading His Own Poems*, Caedmon, 1966.

Plays

The Apparition (produced Cambridge, Massachusetts, 1951). Included in *Collected Verse Plays*, 1962.
The Visionary Farms (produced Cambridge, Massachusetts, 1952). Included in *Collected Verse Plays*, 1962.
Triptych (produced Chicago, 1955). Included in *Collected Verse Plays*, 1962.
The Mad Musician, and Devils and Angels (produced Cambridge, Massachusetts, 1962). Included in *Collected Verse Plays*, 1962.
Collected Verse Plays (includes *Triptych*, *The Visionary Farms*, *The Apparition*, *The Mad Musician*, *Devils and Angels*, *Preamble I and II*). Chapel Hill, University of North Carolina Press, 1962.
The Bride from Mantua, adaptation of a play by Lope de Vega (produced Hanover, New Hampshire, 1964).

Other

Poetry as a Creative Principle (lecture). Norton, Massachusetts, Wheaton College, 1952.

Of Poetry and Poets. Urbana, University of Illinois Press, 1979.

Editor, with others, *Free Gunner's Handbook*, revised edition. Norfolk, Virginia, Naval Air Station, 1944.
Editor, with Selden Rodman, *War and the Poet: An Anthology of Poetry Expressing Man's Attitude to War from Ancient Times to the Present.* New York, Devin Adair, 1945.
Editor, ... *Dartmouth Poems.* Hanover, New Hampshire, Dartmouth Publications-Butcher Fund, 12 vols., 1958–59, 1962–71.

Manuscript Collection: Dartmouth College Library, Hanover, New Hampshire.

Critical Studies: "Richard Eberhart" by Ralph J. Mills, Jr., in *Contemporary American Poetry*, New York, Random House, 1960; *Richard Eberhart* by Ralph J. Mills, Jr., Minneapolis, University of Minnesota Press, 1966; Introduction by Bernard F. Engle to *The Achievement of Richard Eberhart*, 1968; "The Cultivation of Paradox: The War Poetry of Richard Eberhart" by Richard J. Fein, in *Forum* (Muncie, Indiana), Spring 1969; *Richard Eberhart: The Progress of an American Poet* by Joel Roache, New York, Oxford University Press, 1971; *Richard Eberhart* by Bernard F. Engle, New York, Twayne, 1972; *Richard Eberhart* (film), directed by Samuel Mandelbaum, New York, Tri-Pix, 1972; *Richard Eberhart* (film), directed by Irving Broughton, Seattle, University of Washington, 1974.

Richard Eberhart comments:

My poetry celebrates life, which does not last long, and mankind, which is temporal as well, through understanding and perception of my times, insofar as I am able to create poems which may communicate values and meanings I can know.

* * *

The poet comments: "Divisive man can know unity only at death (or so he can speculate), and he cannot know what kind of unity that is. He lives in continuous struggle with his imperfection and the imperfection of life. If one were only conscious of harmony, there would be no need to write."

Throughout the 50 years of his career Richard Eberhart has been consumed with the extremes of Romantic vision – wonder, ecstasy, emptiness, isolation, and despair. Often, the poet sings of a radiance in nature, and exultant joy, as he feels a harmony with all living things and Spirit. Through the splendid imagination, he writes, "You breathe in maybe God," and then write "with a whole clarity." Hence he writes in "This Fevers Me":

This fevers me, this sun on green,
On grass glowing, this young spring.
The secret hallowing is come,
Regenerate sudden incarnation,
Mystery made visible
In growth ...

In "The Groundhog," observing the groundhog's disintegration and absorption into nature, the poet experiences a deep sense of man's "naked frailty," which arouses a "passion of the blood," a "fever," which transforms into "a flame/... Immense energy in the sun." He simultaneously identifies with "Alexander," "Montaigne," and "Saint Theresa," who similarly suffered vision, through imaginative realization of man's mortality.

Witnessing the wild "Ospreys in Cry," Eberhart again identifies in the birds his own mortality, while proclaiming his inspired role:

I felt a staggering sense
Of the victor and of the doomed,
Of being one and the other,
Of being both at one time,
I was the seer
And I was revealed.

What moves the spirit is the fusion of imagination with a "divine" force emanating from nature: "our wills are with hers [nature] fused/And we would impregnate her with our shape"; in the "great moments of being, something/Beyond our wills, is the prime Mover" ("Necessity").

Although death may be the moment of revelation, of "wordless ecstasy/Of mystery" ("The Soul Longs to Return Whence It Came"), there are moments when the transcendent joy and sense of unity desert Eberhart, when the poet laments that understanding, and perhaps vision itself, is impossible, and in these often blunt portraits of man's mortality and the finality of all things, resound the moving strains of man's weary and lonely old age, and his ultimate loneliness and despair in the face of an indifferent universe. "A name may be glorious but death is death," writes the poet ("I Walked over the Grave of Henry James"). When intellect rules spirit, "the hard intellectual light/That kills all delight/... brings the solemn, inward pain/Of truth into the heart again" ("In a Hard Intellectual Light"). Thus, Eberhart may yearn for "the incomparable light," "Where everything is as it was in my childhood," and he may ask: "Oh where/Has gone that madness wild?" In "Flux" he says: "There is a somber, imponderable fate./Enigma rules, and the heart has no certainty."

Eberhart acknowledges man's fallen state, the cruelty he is capable of enduring and imposing. In "The Fury of Aerial Bombardment" he asks: "Was man made stupid to see his own stupidity?" But because he would wish humanity to embrace love – to Eberhart human love "concrete, [and] specific" is the primary human experience – his work is filled with the rhetorical "Am I My Brother's Keeper?" Love is "discoverable here/Difficult, dangerous, pure, clear,/The truth of the positive hour/Composing all of human power" ("The Goal of Intellectual Man").

The *Collected Poems 1930–1976* contains 43 new poems, many of which again concern the poet's visionary powers and yet his sense of limited selfhood, his joy and fear in the presence of a beautiful but indifferent world. In "Trying to Hold It All Together," a poem on Auden's death he writes:

We are faced with the hard facts of time,
Beyond any man ...
We cannot hold it all together, the depth,
We cannot trick it out with word embroidery,
Time is the master of man, and we know it.

In "Usurper" he speaks of being captured in nature and how "art momentarily" controls "myths of consciousness"; he cries:

Not to be supine! Not to lie
On the face of the earth dreaming
As a boy as you used to be,
Your eyes full of sensual hope,
But to stand up to nature,
To stand up to time, and say
I seize your power, I am.

"Mind and Nature" celebrates both the immutability of nature and the mortality and transcendent imagination of man:

No resolution! The mind
Is a play of lightning, a happy change,
While the duration of the earth, fixed,
Makes us one with the bee, the ant.

In "Big Rock" Eberhart returns once again to a scene in nature to mark both its change and his attitude toward it: "I have sat in this garden yearly/With an eye to the changes of nature." Nature, he continues, "goes on changing, wryly,/Indifferent to my attitude," and it is this, says the poet, that "excites me." It is man's discerning mind that creates nature and acknowledges and appreciates its powers: "I claim that I make nature alive/Because if it were not for the human predicament/Nobody would know what nature was like"; and finally, illustrating man's power, his imagination within nature, his mythic inventiveness:

I can imagine anything I can imagine,
Nature is not my lover, I am the lover of nature,
I kick the boulder with the foot of Hercules,
The boulder sits, but I can walk around it.

"Big Rock" contains the simple, direct language we associate with the great Eberhart, as he transforms keenly felt experience through its very language into larger, more metaphysical, even mystical, experience. The poet, Eberhart has said, "makes the world anew; something grows out of the old, which he locks in words."

Man is chosen, however; all men are chosen, for

In the secret heart all are free
Each has a secret heart of pure imagination.
Each man struggles with reality.

—Lois Gordon

ECHERUO, Michael (Joseph Chukwudalu). Nigerian. Born in Umunumo, Mbano Division, 14 March 1937. Educated at Stella Maris College, Port Harcourt, 1950–54; University College, Ibadan, 1955–60, B.A. (honours) 1960; Cornell University, Ithaca, New York (Phi Beta Kappa), 1962–65, M.A. 1963, Ph.D. 1965. Married Rose N. Echeruo in 1968; four children. Lecturer, Nigerian College of Arts and Technology, Enugu, 1960–61. Lecturer, 1961–70, Senior Lecturer, 1970–73, and Professor, 1973–74, University of Nigeria, Nsukka. Since 1974, Professor of English, and since 1978, Dean of the Postgraduate School, University of Ibadan. Since 1977, Founding Resident, Nigerian Association for African and Comparative Literature. Recipient: All-Africa Poetry Competition Prize, 1963. Address: Department of English, University of Ibadan, Ibadan, Nigeria.

Publications

Verse

Mortality: Poems. London, Longman, 1968.

Distanced: New Poems. Enugu, I. K., 1975.

Other

Joyce Cary and the Novel of Africa. London, Longman, and New York, Africana, 1973.
Victorian Lagos. London, Macmillan, 1977.
The Conditioned Imagination from Shakespeare to Conrad: Studies in the Exo-Cultural Stereotype. London, Macmillan, 1978.
Joyce Cary and the Dimensions of Order. London, Macmillan, 1979.

Editor, *Igbo Traditional Life, Literature, and Culture.* Austin, Texas, Conch, 1972.

* * *

Michael Echeruo, like his late countryman Christopher Okigbo, has forged, from the crossroads experience of an African heritage and a "European" education, poetry which is wide-ranging, deceptively simple and highly individual. Although the poems in his first volume *Mortality* often come out of his experiences as an M.A. and Doctoral student in the United States, they are still like trees with their roots deep in African soil, no matter how high their branches reach into a foreign sky. The return to Africa, whether physically or metaphorically, is implicit, as in the first poem in the book, "Debut":

Have we not looked the whole world out,
searched the whole hearth out
till we saw the palm-nuts again
by which we were to live?

It is, therefore, no accident that an entire section of his book is titled "Defections" and that he says in the poem "Harvest time": "Village maidens/are the bearers of my harvest...."

Wit and irony also figure strongly in Echeruo's poetry, along with a sense of what it is to be an African poet in a foreign land:

... like an unfeathered bird
in their spring –
white and spruce and clean –
... like an unclassified gift
to their museums
where they spin out fine tall tales
all day long
amid the blistering flurries
of their bleak December days.

Though his Nigeria figures strongly in his verse, Echeruo also ranges, capably, throughout Western literature, bringing in such diverse sources as the Bible, D. H. Lawrence, Joyce and St. John of the Cross. His poem "The Signature," which revolves around the figure of O'Brien (who seems to be an Irish priest like the Flannagan of Chris Okigbo's "Limits"), draws a picture of African ceremonies in conjunction with Catholic rites and draws the conclusion that "The priests and elders of my past/would love to see O'Brien's paradise."

There is one last quality about Echeruo's poetry which should be taken note of. Whether ironic or celebratory, whether a poem of love or a poem of satire, there is a current of lyricism which runs through all of Echeruo's verse, a lyricism which can be felt in these lines from his poem "Wedding," lines which speak of birth and stress again his ties to the soil:

Tap roots beneath the giant
speak like the gods
and life comes
like a spasm of light....

—Joseph Bruchac

ECONOMOU, George. American. Born in Great Falls, Montana, 24 September 1934. Educated at Colgate University, Hamilton, New York, A.B. 1956; Columbia University, New York, M.A. 1957, Ph.D. 1967. Married Rochelle Owens, *q.v.*, in 1962. Lecturer, Wagner College, New York, 1958–60. Since 1961, Member of the English Department, and currently Professor of English, Long Island University, Brooklyn, New York. Editor, *Chelsea Review*, New York, 1958–60; Editor, *Trobar*, New York, 1960–64. Field Editor for Old and Middle English, Twayne English Authors. Recipient: American Council of Learned Societies Fellowship, 1975; Creative Artists Public Service Fellowship, 1976. Address: 606 West 116th Street, New York, New York 10027, U.S.A.

PUBLICATIONS

Verse

The Georgics. Los Angeles, Black Sparrow Press, 1968.
Landed Natures. Los Angeles, Black Sparrow Press, 1969.
Poems for Self-Therapy. Mount Horeb, Wisconsin, Perishable Press, 1972.
Ameriki: Book One and Selected Earlier Poems. New York, Sun, 1977.

Other

The Goddess Natura in Medieval Literature. Cambridge, Massachusetts, Harvard University Press, 1972.

Co-Editor, *In Pursuit of Perfection: Courtly Love in Medieval Literature.* Port Washington, New York, Kennikat, 1975.
Editor, *Geoffrey Chaucer: A Collection of Criticism.* New York, McGraw Hill, 1975.
Editor, *Proensa: An Anthology of Troubadour Poetry Selected and Translated by Paul Blackburn.* Berkeley, University of California Press, 1978.

Critical Studies: reviews by Harry Lewis, in *Mulch* (Amherst, Massachusetts), Spring 1972, and in *San Francisco Review of Books*, 1978; by Gerald Dorset, in *Northeast Rising Sun* (Cherry Valley, New York), Fall 1978.

George Economou comments:

(1970) Major themes – Nature, the great one we live in and the small ones that are myself and those I love.

(1980) I want to explore the landscapes of America and Americans in my poems. Their forms are determined by my responses to their discovered topographical and psychological models.

* * *

George Economou is most closely associated with poetry of the "deep image," and for a time co-edited, along with Robert and Joan Kelly, *Trobar*, the "deep image" poetry journal. Robert Kelly defined "deep image" as poetry filled with "intensity and immediacy," and "containing the primal gestures of language." First referred to in Jerome Rothenberg's *Poems for the Floating World*, the "deep image" comes from dream, from the invisible pull and tug of life. It is a poetry charged with the rough, raw energy transmitted by direct and primal human actions. Most of these qualities are present in George Economou's poetry. His poems contain the facts and rituals of life close to the earth; earth rhythms and surprises animate it.

Economou's *The Goddess Natura in Medieval Literature* illuminates his frequent poetic reference to his muse and patron, the goddess Natura. She is the allegorical personification of nature in classic and medieval literature, and also an intermediary between man and God. Like Chaucer's "Nature" in *The Parliament of Fowls*, Economou's goddess presides over a harmonious landscape, and fruitfulness in love and romance. In "Prayer of a Natural Man" he asks Natura to set his heart high, to let him "be the sure handler/of every bird and snake it finds...." Economou's poems are informal and conversational – the words of a poet who walks for his health, talks to himself, invokes muses and animal spirits. The poet's "secret life" in nature is everywhere present: "I am a magnificent animal ..."; "I become wolf/I become wolf man...." The first portion of *Landed Natures* is composed of eight "Georgics," and even though the landscape is the American West there are thematic connections with Virgil's *Georgics*. Economou, as earth husband, consoles the "poor earth we live off/nobody here loves you...." He advises the shepherd in us to love our flock:

caress them daily and be
kind as you can,
enter their dumb world
without a word or thought.

There are qualities here reminiscent of the earth poems of Gary Snyder, and, to a lesser degree, of Galway Kinnell and James Dickey, but Economou is not at this point up to the calibre of such poets. Yet there is a compelling directness in these conversations between poet and reader. Earth guide, mystic traveler, George Economou speaks as one who has been to the territory and who, given a chance, will reveal some of nature's finest mysteries.

—John R. Cooley

EDSON, Russell. American. Born 9 April 1935. Educated at the Art Students League, New York; New School for Social Research, New York; Columbia University, New York; Black Mountain College, North Carolina. Married to Frances Edson. Recipient: Guggenheim Fellowship, 1974; National Endowment for the Arts grant, 1976. Agent: Georges Borchardt Inc., 145 East 52nd Street, New York, New York 10022. Address: 149 Weed Avenue, Stamford, Connecticut, 06902, U.S.A.

PUBLICATIONS

Verse

Appearances: Fables and Drawings. Stamford, Connecticut, Thing Press, 1961.
A Stone Is Nobody's: Fables and Drawings. Stamford, Connecticut, Thing Press, 1961.
The Boundry (sic). Stamford, Connecticut, Thing Press, 1964.
The Very Thing That Happens: Fables and Drawings. New York, New Directions, 1964.
The Brain Kitchen: Writings and Woodcuts. Stamford, Connecticut, Thing Press, 1965.
What a Man Can See. Highlands, North Carolina, Jargon, 1969.
The Childhood of an Equestrian. New York, Harper, 1973.
The Clam Theatre. Middletown, Connecticut, Wesleyan University Press, 1973.
The Intuitive Journey and Other Works. New York, Harper, 1976.
The Reason Why the Closet-Man Is Never Sad. Middletown, Connecticut, Wesleyan University Press, 1977.

Plays

The Falling Sickness: A Book of Plays. New York, New Directions, 1975.

Critical Studies: *A Prose Poem Anthology*, edited by Duane Ackerson, Pocatello, Idaho, Dragonfly Press, 1970; "Prose Poems" by William Matthews, in *New: American and Canadian Poetry 15* (Trumansburg, New York), 1971; "I Am Sure Happiness Is Not Too Far Away" by Thomas Meyer, in *Parnassus* (New York), ii, 1, 1974.

Russell Edson comments:

I write short prose pieces which are neither fiction nor reportage. Perhaps the currently popular term in America (although we certainly didn't originate it), *prose poem*, is vague enough to describe the blurred borders of my gross generality. But, as soon as I say this I want to shout that I refuse to write prose poems, that I want to write the work that is always in search of itself, in a form that is always building itself from the inside out.

In that I am more at home in my work than in describing it, I offer an example below, "A Chair":

A chair has waited such a long time to be
with its person. Through shadow and fly buzz
and the floating dust it has waited such a
long time to be with its person.
What it remembers of the forest it forgets,
and dreams of a room where it waits – Of the
cup and the ceiling – Of the animate one.

* * *

In an introduction to his first major book, *The Very Thing That Happens*, Denise Levertov says this of Russell Edson: "Russell Edson is one of those originals who appear out of the loneliness of a vast, thronged country to create a peculiar and defined world." Several books later, this impression of Edson's eccentric genius (as perhaps all true genius appears eccentric) remains as strong as ever. His is the world seen from all the frightening, and funny, perspectives adults so often forget to see, or choose to forget: worlds seen through the wrong end of the spyglass, or through the looking glass, where everything pursues a strange, relentless logic of its own. His soap bubble worlds refuse to pop, returning us, like the knowledge we have had a dream, to the reassuring; instead, the world they reflect comes apart in the face of dream logic. A man's hand is a white spider, and, driven by the necessity of such metamorphoses, suspends the man eventually from the ceiling by the spider webs it has woven. Edson's prose poetry is more carefully wedded to metaphor, and the pursuit of metaphor to its sometimes ludicrous, sometimes lovely ends, than most verse, as in "Antimatter," where Edson manages a fine blend of both:

> On the other side of a mirror there's an inverse world,
> where the insane go sane; where bones climb out of the earth
> and recede to the first slime of love.
> And in the evening the sun is just rising.
> Lovers cry because they are a day younger, and soon
> childhood robs them of their pleasure.
> In such a world there is much sadness which, of course,
> is joy....

Edson is also a playwright, and the earlier poems of *What a Man Can See* and *The Very Thing That Happens* are like miniature theatre-of-the-absurd plays, vignettes of family life in which everyone converses in shouts and parents pass on parental wisdom untouched by human thought. Though the humor touches on cartoons (Edson's father was a famous cartoonist) and the black humor of the absurd, there is an undercurrent of pathos reminiscent of Chekhov and O'Neill; these prose poems and fables constitute *A Long Day's Journey into Night* without the tedium.

Edson's range is considerable, from these exchanges to still-life portraits like "A Chair" ("A chair has waited such a long time to be/with its person ...") or beast fables tinged with melancholy, like "How a Cow Comes to Live with Long Eared Ones," in which an over-inquisitive cow is kidnapped by a rabid rabbit. Edson pulls such antics off, and creates a real slapstick tragedy, the sort of thing other American artists like Chaplin have been drawn to attempt. Sometimes, the moral explicitness we might expect from the traditional fable is there (though more often, as in "A Journey by Water," Edson creates a sort of anti-fable that satirizes didacticism), as in "A Lovely Man":

> A man is such a lovely man; he really is if you'll only
> look past him into the flower garden.
> Wait, shall he move so that you can look more fully
> into the garden?
> Shall he die and be put under the flower garden to nourish
> beauty and never to be in the way of it again?

The prevailing mood of many of these poems is melancholy, but it's a darkness defined by quick lightning streaks of humor, like a figure in a cubistic woodcut (which Edson's drawings in his various collections resemble) cracking a grin. Edson's prose poems tend to attack the false security and self satisfaction by which we too often live, to dismantle our umbrellas and let us see the storm that is always raging. They throw off just enough light to let us see that black sky overhead again.

—Duane Ackerson

EIGNER, Larry (Lawrence Joel Eigner). American. Born in Lynn, Massachusetts, 7 August 1927. Educated at home; Massachusetts Hospital School, Canton, 2 years; correspondence courses from University of Chicago. Palsied from birth. Address: 1770 La Loma, Berkeley, California 94709, U.S.A.

PUBLICATIONS

Verse

From the Sustaining Air. Palma, Mallorca, Divers Press, 1953; augmented edition, Eugene, Oregon, Toad Press, 1967.
Look at the Park. Privately printed, 1958.
On My Eyes. Highlands, North Carolina, Jargon, 1960.
The Music, The Rooms. Albuquerque, New Mexico, Desert Review Press, 1965.
The Memory of Yeats, Blake, DHL. London, Circle Press, 1965.
Six Poems. Portland, Oregon, Wine Press, 1967.
Another Time in Fragments. London, Fulcrum Press, 1967.
The-/Towards Autumn. Los Angeles, Black Sparrow Press, 1967.
Air the Trees. Los Angeles, Black Sparrow Press, 1967.
The Breath of Once Live Things, In the Field with Poe. Los Angeles, Black Sparrow Press, 1968.
A Line That May Be Cut. London, Circle Press, 1968.
Valleys, Branches. London, Big Venus, 1969.
Flat and Round. New York, Pierrepont Press, 1969.
Over and Over, Ends, As the Wind May Sound. Cambridge, Massachusetts, Restau Press, 1970.
Poem Nov. 1968. London, Tetrad Press, 1970.
Circuits: "A Microbook, A Microbook." LeRoy, New York, Athanor Press, 1971.
Looks Like Nothing, The Shadow Through Air. Guildford, Surrey, Circle Press, 1972.
What You Hear. London, Edible Magazine, 1972.
Selected Poems, edited by Samuel Charters and Andrea Wyatt. Berkeley, California, Oyez, 1972.
Words Touching Ground Under. Belmont, Massachusetts, Hellric, 1972.
Shape Shadow Elements Move. Los Angeles, Black Sparrow Press, 1973.
Things Stirring Together or Far Away. Los Angeles, Black Sparrow Press, 1974.
Anything on Its Side. New Rochelle, New York, Elizabeth Press, 1974.
No Radio. Boulder, Colorado, Lodestar Press, 1974.
My God the Proverbial. Kensington, California, L, 1975.
Suddenly It Gets Light and Dark in the Streets: Poems 1961–74. Winchester, Green Horse Press, 1975.
The Music Variety. Newton, Massachusetts, Roxbury, 1976.
The World and Its Streets, Places. Santa Barbara, California, Black Sparrow Press, 1977.
Watching How or Why. New Rochelle, New York, Elizabeth Press, 1977.
Cloud, Invisible Air. Rhinebeck, New York, Station Hill Press, 1978.
Flagpole Riding. Alverstoke, Hampshire, Stingy Artist, 1978.
Running Around. Providence, Rhode Island, Burning Deck, 1978.
Heat Simmers Cold. Malakoff, France, Orange Export, 1978.
Time Details of a Tree. New Rochelle, New York, Elizabeth Press, 1979.

Play

Murder Talk: The Reception: Suggestions for a Play; Five Poems, Bed Never Self Made. Placitas, New Mexico, Duende, 1964.

Short Stories

Clouding. New York, Samuel Charters, 1968.
Farther North. New York, Samuel Charters, 1969.

Other

Selected Prose, edited by Garrett Watten. San Francisco, This Press, 1978.

Bibliography: *A Bibliography of Works by Larry Eigner, 1937–1969* by Andrea Wyatt, Berkeley, California, Oyez, 1970.

Manuscript Collection: Kenneth Spencer Research Library, University of Kansas, Lawrence.

Larry Eigner comments:

Maybe the most that you can do with verse is assess things come to or arrived at, the line (/) or stanza (//) break providing the emphasis, mostly anyway, this being a potential when there are no natural stresses to obscure, interfere with it (there's lacuna, indent, and whatever else, typography can't be ignored much as long as you have writing on paper) – or, since there's no ranking, to realize (the weight or import of) things. You'd think more than two or three things have to be together enough to make a whole, for there to be a weighing, but a poem can stop at any point, after a few words. While a prose piece has to be of some length, has to be continuous. Prose is fairly indeterminate, unbounded, informal; it's the way people run on.

* * *

For Larry Eigner the circumstances of his life have given a form and a shape to his poetry. He is a spastic, and his life has been spent in a glassed-in front porch of a frame house on a side street of a small Massachusetts town. Through the windows – and through the window of his bedroom – he follows the world of the seasons, the sky, the birds, the trees. There has been some travel – to visit his brothers in San Francisco and Missouri – and smaller trips into Boston or further along Cape Ann to see other poets. And despite the limits of his physical world he is part of the community of younger American poets through a wide and open correspondence, and continued reading of the books and magazines that pile up on his desk. He has always thought of himself as close to the poets who broke from the Anglo-American tradition, and there are clear elements of style from Williams, Olson, and Creeley in his poetry – though he doesn't work in the larger forms that characterize the work of Olson – or of Pound, another poet Eigner thinks of as a source. His prose pieces, which tie closely to the poetry and have their own distinct presence, have some correspondences to the Gertrude Stein of the *Autobiography*. The intense use of the immediate image is at the center of his work, and in poem after poem he has framed the physical world he sees through his windows. He can write a poem complete within a few words, so total is his glimpse of this world: "the wind masses such birds/green inside the tree." There is excitement in the poetry about his surroundings – fire engines go by, cars pass in the night, storms grip the trees, birds come, children play loudly – but a dominating theme in his evocation of this scene is a nostalgia at the impermanence of it,

two big pigeons on the new roof
below which he grew corn
                    ten years back, one year

a nostalgia that becomes sad, musing: "But I grow old/because I was too much a child." And even though much of his published work was written while he was still in his twenties and thirties he has had to spend too many hours in hospitals, and he is deeply conscious of the presence of death: "once a man is born he has to die/and that is time." A poem that is often quoted:

> the knowledge of death, and now
> the knowledge of the stars
>
> there is one end
>
> and the endless
> Room at the center
> passage/in no time
> a rail thickets hills grass

But as often as the mood is subdued the poems more often have an open, direct optimism. They have also a lightness, a deftness, but with such care in their detail that he can make sudden emphases, sudden shifts of meaning with only a few words. He does not insist on his own presence in the work – there is an essential modesty in the poetry, as well as a large intelligence that he uses only to keep the elements of the poem in easy balance with each other. There is much of Eigner's work published, all of it with his distinctive voice and style. The longer poems of a few years ago have given way to short, almost haiku-like poems of recent collections, but this has not been an intentional shift in direction, only an intuitive strengthening and purifying of his line. The work will continue, and the new direction could as well be back to the longer poem. It is this strength of his response – the persistence of it – that will go on in the poetry. As he says:

> The fountain of youth is a poetry
> and whether we are one minute older
> the present always arrives.

—Samuel Charters

ELLIOTT, George P(aul). American. Born in Knightstown, Indiana, 16 June 1918. Educated at the University of California, Berkeley, A.B. 1939, M.A. 1941. Married Mary Emma Jeffress in 1941; one child. Assistant Professor, St. Mary's College, California, 1947–55, 1962–63, Cornell University, Ithaca, New York, 1955–56, and Barnard College, New York, 1957–60; Lecturer, University of Iowa, Iowa City, 1960–61, and University of California, Berkeley, 1962. Since 1963, Professor of English, Syracuse University, New York. Since 1965, Member of the Corporation of Yaddo. Recipient: Albert Bender grant, 1951; Fund for the Advancement of Education Fellowship, 1953; *Hudson Review* Fellowship, 1956; Guggenheim Fellowship, 1961, 1970; D. H. Lawrence Fellowship, 1962; Ford Fellowship, for theatre, 1965; National Institute of Arts and Letters grant, 1969. Address: Department of English, Syracuse University, Syracuse, New York 13210, U.S.A.

PUBLICATIONS

Verse

Fever and Chills. Iowa City, Stone Wall Press, 1961.

Fourteen Poems. Lanham, Maryland, Goosetree Press, 1964.
From the Berkeley Hills. New York, Harper, 1969.
Reaching. Northridge, California, Santa Susana Press, 1979.

Novels

Parktilden Village. Boston, Beacon Press, 1958.
David Knudsen. New York, Random House, 1962.
In the World. New York, Viking Press, 1965.
Muriel. New York, Dutton, 1972.

Short Stories

Among the Dangs. New York, Holt Rinehart, 1961; London, Secker and Warburg, 1962.
An Hour of Last Things and Other Stories. New York, Harper, 1968; London, Gollancz, 1969.

Other

A Piece of Lettuce: Personal Essays on Books, Beliefs, American Places and Growing Up in a Strange Country. New York, Random House, 1964.
Conversions: Literature and the Modernist Deviation (essays). New York, Dutton, 1971.

Editor, *Fifteen Modern American Poets.* New York, Rinehart, 1956; London, Peter Smith, 1963.
Editor, *Types of Prose Fiction.* New York, Random House, 1964.
Editor, *Selected Poems of Winfield Townley Scott.* New York, Doubleday, 1967.
Editor, *Syracuse Poems 1966–67.* Syracuse, New York, Syracuse University, 1967.

Manuscript Collection: Washington University Library, St. Louis.

Critical Study: "Recurrences" by X. J. Kennedy, in *Nation* (New York), 30 March 1970.

George P. Elliott comments:

I function best as a narrative poet using syllabic verse. Usually I operate in the regions of lower rhetorical and prosodic intensity. I commonly employ verse as a way of heightening the story, the ideas, the imagined experience, rather than using these as material for pure poetry.

* * *

George P. Elliott has worked with alacrity in a variety of forms since he began writing poetry in 1942. Always sensitive to the depth effects of the aural, he has mastered rhymed, regular but unrhymed, and free verse alike. Highly controlled, his poems are very rarely self-conscious. His syntax is, however, occasionally convoluted so that while it suits psychological complexities it skirts the voice's natural timbre. He has achieved a subtle control of his line, displaying a consistent precision for letting enjambments carry a significant but not heavy burden of ambiguity and irony. His dramatic monologues and narrative poems spring from a compelling curiosity about the psychology of intense confrontations.

Elliott often juxtaposes life as we actually feel it with rational and scientific "truth," whether constituted by the facts of chromosomes or interstellar space. His tone can be quietly epiphanal when a common-place marvel of the natural or affectional order seizes his fancy. Thus he can ponder the Kingfisher and its mysterious origins: "What is the bow, blue arrow, that flashed you by?" And as regards a man's child, he remarks what the "rationalistic eye" of a camera never could: "Tosses of laughter, his daughter just turned from waving."

He records, also, the extreme feelings which come with the ruination of domestic peace, ranging from the mild and the torturing ambivalences of infidelities to the blank withdrawals of nervous collapse and schizophrenia. Pre-eminently, though, his poetry elaborates the vicissitudes of marital and romantic love and especially moments of enlightening if painful realization. In this sphere he is nowhere better than in "Three in the Morning," the adroit title of which complements its fine delineation of a woman's tormented relation to husband and lover and to her own ineffectual "will." It is likewise in this sphere that his imagery is so often poignantly evocative, as when, in "Seen Through a Doorway," the speaker glimpses within a sun-drenched room, "charged with powers of gold," a woman's "bite of melon poised/ Chartreuse in a dazzling spoon."

—David M. Heaton

ELMSLIE, Kenward. American. Born in New York City, 27 April 1929. Educated at Harvard University, Cambridge, Massachusetts, B.A. 1950. Worked with the Karamu Inter-Racial Theatre, Cleveland. Art Critic, *Art News*, New York, 1966–67. Since 1972, Editor, Z Press, Calais, Vermont. Recipient: Ford grant, 1964; National Endowment for the Arts grant, 1966, 1978; Frank O'Hara Award, 1971. Address: 104 Greenwich Avenue, New York, New York 10011, U.S.A.

PUBLICATIONS

Verse

Pavilions. New York, Tibor de Nagy, 1961.
The Power Plant Poems. New York, "C" Press, 1967.
The Champ. Los Angeles, Black Sparrow Press, 1968.
Album. New York, Kulchur, 1969.
Circus Nerves. Los Angeles, Black Sparrow Press, 1971.
Motor Disturbance. New York, Columbia University Press, 1971.
Girl Machine. New York, Angel Hair, 1971.
Penguin Modern Poets 24, with Kenneth Koch and James Schuyler. London, Penguin, 1973.
ZZ. Calais, Vermont, Z Press, 1974.
Tropicalism. Calais, Vermont, Z Press, 1975.
Communications Equipment. Providence, Rhode Island, Burning Deck, 1979.

Plays

Unpacking the Black Trunk, with James Schuyler (produced New York, 1965).
Lizzie Borden, music by Jack Beeson (produced New York, 1965). New York, Boosey and Hawkes, 1965.
Miss Julie, music by Ned Rorem (produced New York, 1965). New York, Boosey and Hawkes, 1965.

The Sweet Bye and Bye, music by Jack Beeson (produced Kansas City, 1973). New York, Boosey and Hawkes, 1966.
The Grass Harp, music by Claibe Richardson, adaptation of the novel by Truman Capote (produced New York, 1971). New York, French, 1971.
City Junket (produced New York, 1974). New York, Boke, 1972.
The Seagull, music by Thomas Pasatieri, adaptation of the play by Chekhov (produced Houston, 1974). Melville, New York, Belwin Mills, 1974.
Washington Square, music by Thomas Pasatieri, adaptation of the novel by James (produced Detroit, 1976). Melville, New York, Belwin Mills, 1976.

Novel

The Orchid Stories. New York, Doubleday, 1973.

Other

The Baby Book. New York, Boke, 1965.
The 1967 Gamebook Calendar. New York, Boke, 1967.
Shiny Ride. New York, Boke, 1972.
The Alphabet Work. Washington, D.C., Titanic Press, 1978.

Critical Studies: "Poetry and Public Experience" by Stephen Donadio, in *Commentary* (New York), February 1973; "Figure in the Carport" by John Ashbery, in *Parnassus* (New York), Summer 1976.

Kenward Elmslie comments:

Since about 1961, I've considered myself primarily a poet; before that I thought of myself, and *was*, primarily a writer of lyrics for songs. I have continued to write for the theatre, and have now completed a novel, but I feel most centred (as a writer) when working on a poem. I am sometimes listed as a member of the New York School of Poets, and I've been involved with Koch, Ashbery, and the late Frank O'Hara, the "School's" founders, but the word "school" seems somehow awfully serious.

I haven't thought much about "major themes" etc. – I've tried to describe places I've been, moods I've been in, people I've been close to. Some of my poems are lectures, or appreciations, or gossip – I like some sort of stanza form to fit the words into, but I don't go in for "formal" dum-dum-di-dum poems. I have written one *sestina*, and enjoyed doing so. I've been influenced by, mainly, Koch, Ashbery, O'Hara, Wallace Stevens, James Schuyler, Jane Bowles, Joe Brainard, John Latouche, Ron Padgett, Bert Brecht, Evelyn Waugh, Gogol, Kafka, S. J. Perelman, W. C. Williams.

* * *

Kenward Elmslie has reached a plateau, asking with Wittgenstein, "What, me worry?" There is no discrepancy between what he means and what he says. He means business about pleasure.

In *Lizzie Borden*, an Elmslie libretto, Lizzie is denied money and freedom (pleasure) by her father, so Lizzie gives the fellow forty-one whacks with an axe, and Elmslie approves. In *The Seagull*, based on the Chekhov downer, Constantine is denied love and respect by his mother and step-father figure and, in a typical bourgeois confusion, commits not murder but suicide. In the musical *The Grass Harp*, a spinster behaves unpleasantly, so her family goes to live in a treehouse.

Just what is so much fun? Spectacle, firstly. I see no spectacle, no panoramic imagination, in other members of the New York School (except in the prose of Harry Mathews).

In the lush, sly drama, *City Junket*, the family of a middle class bumpkin visits the New York metropolis of 1889. I acted in one production with Kenward, Anne Waldman, Joe Brainard and John Ashbery, and had occasion, as well, to view it. The audience was engulfed. Giant slides by Larry Rivers mapped rich verbal vistas which at once transfigure and travesty.

The texture of the writing ranges from delicate to concrete. He likes Hollywood and Scientific Americana. A Romantic stanza imitates, concretely, Busby Berkeley:

what a life,   just falling in and out of
what a life,   just falling in and out of
                              swimming pools
xylophones   WANTED   xylophones
WANTED   female singer   WANTED
bigtime floorshow   bigtime floorshow
bigtime floorshow   bigtime floorshow.

What else is fun? Elmslie will get into the act even in pastorals:

    Around here, all is simpler. Down the paths whistling minks
rush unafraid. Too clumsy to shy at the beauty of bodies,
    they never pay for the damage they do – trampled mushrooms
bruised raspberries. And the storms never pay for the damage *they* do.

The role is fatherly but in grander, surreal transformations, it becomes childlike. Beyond dreams, where do dreams begin? "Shirley Temple Surrounded by Lions" opens:

    In a world where kapok on a sidewalk looks like an "accident" –
innards – would that freckles could enlarge, well, meaningfully,
    into kind of friendly brown kingdoms, all isolate,
with a hero's route, feral glens,
    and a fountain where heroines cool their mouths.

It would be well to contrast this with the large scale of New York painting, the long poems of Olson and others, Manhattan skyscrapers, and of course Cinemascope.

—Michael André

EMANUEL, James A(ndrew, Sr.). American. Born in Alliance, Nebraska, 15 June 1921. Educated at Alliance High School, 1935–39; Howard University, Washington, D.C., 1946–50, B.A. (summa cum laude) 1950; Northwestern University, Evanston, Illinois, 1950–53, M.A. 1953; Columbia University, New York, 1953–62, Ph.D. 1962. Served in the 93rd Infantry Division, United States Army, 1944–46: Army Commendation Ribbon. Married Mattie Johnson in 1950; one son. Canteen Steward, Civilian Conservation Corps, Wellington, Kansas, 1939–40; Elevator Operator, Des Moines, Iowa, 1940–41; Weighmaster, Rock Island, Illinois, 1941–42; Confidential Secretary, Office of the Inspector General, United States War Department, Washington, D.C., 1942–44; Civilian Chief, Pre-Induction Section, Army and Air Force Induction Station, Chicago, 1951–53; Instructor, Harlem YWCA Business School, New York, 1954–56. Instructor, 1957–62, Assistant Professor, 1962–70, Associate Professor, 1970–72, and since 1972, Professor of English, City College of New York. Fulbright Professor of American Literature, University of Grenoble,

France, 1968–69, University of Toulouse, France, 1971–73, and University of Warsaw, 1975–76. General Editor, Broadside Press "Critics Series," Detroit. Recipient: John Hay Whitney Fellowship, 1952; Saxton Memorial Fellowship, 1965. Address: Department of English, City College of New York, Convent Avenue, New York, New York 10031, U.S.A.

PUBLICATIONS

Verse

The Treehouse and Other Poems. Detroit, Broadside Press, 1968.
At Bay. Detroit, Broadside Press, 1969.
Panther Man. Detroit, Broadside Press, 1970.
Black Man Abroad: The Toulouse Poems. Detroit, Lotus Press, 1978.

Other

Langston Hughes. New York, Twayne, 1967.
How I Write 2, with MacKinlay Kantor and Lawrence Osgood. New York, Harcourt Brace, 1972.

Editor, with Theodore L. Gross, *Dark Symphony: Negro Literature in America.* New York, Free Press, 1968.

Manuscript Collection: Jay B. Hubbell Center, Duke University Library, Durham, North Carolina.

Critical Studies: *Road Apple Review* (Oshkosh, Wisconsin), Winter 1971–72; "James A. Emanuel: The Perilous Stairs," in *Caliban*, n.s. xii, 1976, and "Black Man Abroad: James A. Emanuel," in *Black American Literature Forum*, Fall 1979, both by Marvin Holdt; *Black American Poetry: A Critical Commentary* by Ann Semel and Kathleen Mullen, New York, Monarch Press, 1977.

James A. Emanuel comments:

(1974) Some of the personal history, and many of the ideas, reflected in my poetry can be found in my contribution to the book *How I Write 2.* By now, writing poetry is my principal method of finding and expressing what life means. From the time that I began to write poetry steadily, in the late 1950's, the exacting labor and the large mysteries of that activity – usually carried on late at night – have centered upon vital, everyday matters. The categories into which my poems can be divided describe areas of experience and thought with which ordinary men are well acquainted (and I have wanted my poetry to be fundamentally clear to the largest possible audience): recurrent subjects are youth (centrally my son, James) and miscellaneous Black experience; other subjects include writers, anti-Semitism, blues, war, etc.; the lyrics continue philosophical, descriptive, and personal themes; the tone is usually serious, sometimes satirical, once in a while humorous; the form varies from strict sonnets to free verse that attempts to catch nuances of Black American speech patterns that might be heard on a Harlem street. My poetry runs roughly parallel to my life: a movement from the reflective traditional to the compressed tensions of the 1970's, with inevitably special emphasis on racism, but also with constantly interspersed lyrics that have little to do with our perilous decades. Thus I hope that my poetry, in its unplanned evolution and variety, attests the crucial, dual role of the Black poet: to struggle as embroiled man, but to reflect as clear Mind; to denude and expose as destroyer, yet to clothe and grace as creator; to live as Black and therefore made for the wide world, yet American and therefore made for the narrow cauldron that our nation has become.

My latest work, especially "The Toulouse Poems" and generally those written in and after 1972, might well suggest that three loves develop in my work: parental, racial, and romantic. These common passions are the staple of my poetry. Trying to fathom them and to transform them into art. I am content to be judged by that mass of readers who feel as strongly as they think and who are drawn to what I want increasingly to keep in my poetry: the bite and song of reality.

(1980) Reviewing my poems written recently in London and Paris, I find experiments with anti-realism coming into my work – perhaps as an intensification of my grappling with such subjects as tyranny, art, and time.

* * *

James A. Emanuel's sympathies are clear even without his statement in *Panther Man* that young people are "the only people whom I tend to respect as a group." Poems like "A Clown at Ten," "The Young Ones, Flip Side," "Fourteen," "Sixteen, Yeah," and "Fisherman" celebrate with an understanding smile the passion and energy of youth while they steer clear of Housmanian idolatry and pathos. Young adulthood is pain, punching, and confusion for the poet, the hopeful stage through which the world passes to confrontation. Behind it stretches the pre-lapsarian vista of childhood. The poet captures the antics of the bathtub sailor in "The Voyage of Jimmy Poo," a time of sterling memory in "I Wish I Had a Red Balloon," and the joy of answering children's questions in "For the 4th Grade, Prospect School: How I Became a Poet."

Manhood brings a different order: understanding, rebellion, militancy, anguish, and death. "Emmett Till," "Where Will Their Names Go Down," and "For Malcolm, U.S.A." pay tribute to the victims, while "Panther Man," "Animal Tricks," "Crossover: for RFK," and "Black Man, 13th Floor" speak in strident (sometimes black, idiomatic) tones of the growth of a generation of men who are rising to take control.

Surrounding and undergirding all stages, however, is the essential romantic humanism of the poet. "Nightmare" and "Christ, One Morning" let us know that all is in the hands of man; there is no God who can be trusted. And ceaselessly, Emanuel reaffirms the power of the imaginative intellect to scale the heights of its own treehouse and dream ("A Negro Author" and "The Treehouse"), or to bring the authoritarian assumptions of the world down with a wince ("Black Poet on the Firing Range"). Two new poems from Toulouse show a sweep and maturity that combine this essential vision with a firm formal mastery.

—Houston A. Baker, Jr.

EMPSON, William. British. Born in Yokefleet, East Yorkshire, 27 September 1906. Educated at Winchester College, Hampshire; Magdalene College, Cambridge, B.A. in mathematics 1929, M.A. 1935. Married Hester Henrietta Crouse in 1941; two sons. Taught English Literature, Tokyo National University, 1931–34, and National University, Peking, 1937–39, 1947–52. Member of the Monitoring Service, 1940, and Chinese Editor, Far Eastern Section, 1941–46, BBC, London. Taught at Kenyon College, Gambier, Ohio, summers 1948, 1950, 1954. Professor of English Literature, Sheffield University, 1953–71; since 1971, Emeritus Professor. Recipient: Ingram Merrill Foundation Award, 1968. Litt.D.: University of East Anglia, Norwich, 1968; Bristol University, 1971; Sheffield University, 1974. Knighted, 1979. Address: Studio House, 1 Hampstead Hill Gardens, London N.W.3, England.

PUBLICATIONS

Verse

Letter IV. Cambridge, Heffer, 1929.
Poems. Privately printed 1934.
Poems. London, Chatto and Windus, 1935.
The Gathering Storm. London, Faber, 1940.
Collected Poems of William Empson. New York, Harcourt Brace, 1949; London, Chatto and Windus, 1955; revised edition, Harcourt Brace, 1961.

Recording: *Poems*, Listen, 1961.

Other

Seven Types of Ambiguity. London, Chatto and Windus, 1930; New York, Harcourt Brace, 1931; revised edition, Chatto and Windus, and New York, New Directions, 1947; Chatto and Windus, 1953; New York, Noonday Press, 1955; London, Penguin-Chatto and Windus, 1963.
Some Versions of Pastoral. London, Chatto and Windus, 1935; New York, New Directions, 1950; as *English Pastoral Poetry*, New York, Norton, 1938.
Shakespeare Survey, with George Garrett. London, Brendin, 1937.
The Structure of Complex Words. London, Chatto and Windus, and New York, New Directions, 1951.
Milton's God. London, Chatto and Windus, 1961; New York, New Directions, 1962; revised edition, Chatto and Windus, 1965.

Editor, *The Outlook of Science*, by J. B. S. Haldane. London, Routledge, 1935.
Editor, *Science and Well-Being*, by J. B. S. Haldane. London, Routledge, 1935.
Editor, *Shakespeare's Poems*. New York, New American Library, 1969.
Editor, with David Pirie, *Coleridge's Verse: A Selection*. London, Faber, 1972; New York, Schocken Books, 1973.

Critical Studies: *William Empson: The Man and His Work*, edited by Roma Gill, London, Routledge, 1974.

William Empson comments:

(1974) Most of the poets who were starting to write around 1930 hoped to learn methods and techniques from the French Symbolists and also the seventeenth-century English Metaphysicals; but Mallarmé would consider it vulgar to argue, if ever confronted with argufying in poetry, whereas Donne did it all the time. The young Eliot was large-minded and courageous, I still think, to write so much (in his prose) recommending Donne, a poet so very remote from his own practice; and I suppose he was merely being charitable or reassuring to his disciples when he told them they needn't actually bother about the arguments.

I imitated Donne only, which made me appear pointlessly gawky or half undressed; but I still think that the two methods cannot be combined – you cannot write both like Mallarmé and like Donne at the same time, or anyway not energetically enough. So, though grateful for the generous and sympathetic remarks of my old friend George Fraser, I cannot really feel pleased when he tells you at the end not to bother about the arguments. They are what the poetry is made out of, whether the result is good or bad.

* * *

William Empson's great reputation and influence as a poet are based mainly on his volume of 1935, *Poems*, and his volume of 1940, *The Gathering Storm*. The *Collected Poems* of 1955 contain only a few more short poems and a masque written mainly by Empson's students at Sheffield for a visit by the Queen to the university there, a masque to which Empson himself contributed only a few lines. The poems in the first volume reflect very much the influence of Donne, who remains Empson's favourite English poet. The style is terse, riddling and elliptical, there are many metaphors as in Donne from astronomy, biology, and the other natural sciences, the mood is one of witty desperation, or even despair; many of the poems are love poems, others are about the neutrality and indifference of the outer universe to man's predicament. Though the influencc of Donne is the most obvious one, there is a touch, in the general attitude to life, of ironic defiance or slightly swaggering pessimism, that might recall A. E. Housman, who is also one of Empson's favourite poets. There is a sense of an intricate, witty, and deliberately puzzling form being imposed on a massive and almost unbearable personal unhappiness. With all the intricacy, there is an odd rough directness in the tone of voice.

The Gathering Storm, by contrast, is in the main a poem of public events and the public tone of voice. In the intervening years Empson had taught both in Japan and in China, at the time of the Japanese invasion of Manchuria. Fleeing, as he puts it in one of the finest poems in the volume, "Aubade," from the disorder and injustice of Europe, he had found in the Far East "only the same war on a stronger toe." Yet his very experience of violence had oddly strengthened him: "The heart of standing is we cannot fly." The poems suggested a deep trust in the fundamental, sane anti-Fascism of the British people – when tested by the Hoare-Laval pact, for instance, the "thing has answered like a gong" – and in a combination of prudence and courage in facing Axis aggression. There is nothing of the rather naive belief of Auden (mocked at in "Just a Smack at Auden") either that Western civilization is automatically running to an end or that we shall have Utopia tomorrow. The voice has a tart and humorous authority. The tone suggests political poets of the Restoration, like Dryden, Rochester, or Marvell in his satires much more than Donne; there is a kind of bulldog sturdiness in it, and in a way it was appropriate that Churchill should choose the same title, *The Gathering Storm*, for his volume of memoirs about the 1930's. The tone of tense and intricate personal despair is replaced by one of humorous combative stoicism. Technically, what is notable is the use of forms like the *villanelle* involving the use of a refrain or repeated lines, in a way that gives a twist or change of emphasis at each repetition. There is also a very effective use of a deliberate colloquial flatness and terseness. Both the diction and the verse forms were borrowed extensively by the young "Movement" poets of the early 1950's, notably John Wain, who also, at the end of the 1940's, wrote the first proper appreciation of Empson's poetic achievement so far. But Edwin Muir noted that these young disciples tended to lack the element that transforms Empson's poetry, passion. The strength of the later Empsonian style is the sense that so much is held in reserve, so many fires are banked under: "You don't want madhouse and the whole thing there." For all their intelligence, and the brilliance of Empson's own prose notes on them, these poems, so unlike anybody else's, do not lend themselves to simple summary in terms of theme: irony and ambiguity, hurdles for the reader's intelligence, are everywhere. Donald Davie has suggested that Empson is predominantly a poet of *tone*, of tact and skill in channelling and modifying the reader's responses. A dominating personality certainly comes through, as it does also in his prose criticism: and a peculiar flavour, tart, fibrous, captivating, like that of a quince or a crab apple. What one remembers in the end of Empson perhaps is "a taste in the mind."

—G. S. Fraser

ENGLE, Paul (Hamilton). American. Born in Cedar Rapids, Iowa, 12 October 1908. Educated at Coe College, Cedar Rapids, B.A. 1931 (Phi Beta Kappa); University of Iowa, Iowa City, M.A. 1932; Columbia University, New York, 1932–33; Merton College, Oxford (Rhodes Scholar), B.A. 1936, M.A. 1939. Married to Hualing Nieh; two daughters and three grandchildren. Director of the Creative Writing Program, 1937–65, Professor of English, 1946–77, and Director of the International Writing Program, 1966–77, University of Iowa. Member of the Advisory Commission on the Arts, and the National Council on the Arts. Recipient: Yale Series of Younger Poets Award, 1932; Guggenheim Fellowship, 1953; Lamont Poetry Selection Award, 1962; Rockefeller Fellowship; Ford Fellowship. D.Litt.: Coe College, 1946; LL.D.: Monmouth College, Illinois, 1949; L.H.D.: Iowa Wesleyan College, Mount Pleasant, 1956. Agent: William Morris Agency Inc., 1350 Avenue of the Americas, New York, New York 10019. Address: 1104 North Dubuque, Iowa City, Iowa 52240, U.S.A.

PUBLICATIONS

Verse

Worn Earth. New Haven, Connecticut, Yale University Press, 1932.
American Song. New York, Doubleday, 1934; London, Cape, 1935.
Break the Heart's Anger. New York, Doubleday, and London, Cape, 1936.
Corn. New York, Doubleday, 1939.
New Englanders. Muscatine, Iowa, Prairie Press, 1940.
West of Midnight. New York, Random House, 1941.
American Child. Privately printed, 1944.
American Child: A Sonnet Sequence. New York, Random House, 1945; revised edition, as *American Child: Sonnets for My Daughter, with Thirty Six New Poems,* New York, Dial Press, 1956.
The Word of Love. New York, Random House, 1951.
Book and Child: Three Sonnets. Iowa City, Cummington Press, 1956.
Poems in Praise. New York, Random House, 1959.
Christmas Poems. Privately printed, 1962.
A Woman Unashamed and Other Poems. New York, Random House, 1965.
Embrace: Selected Love Poems. New York, Random House, 1969.

Plays

For the Iowa Dead, music by Philip Bezanson. Iowa City, State University of Iowa, 1956.
Golden Child, music by Philip Bezanson (televised, 1960). New York, Doubleday, 1962.

Novels

Always the Land. New York, Random House, 1941.
Golden Child. New York, Dutton, 1962.

Other

Robert Frost. Iowa City, State University of Iowa Library, 1959.
A Prairie Christmas. New York, Longman, 1960.
Who's Afraid? (juvenile). New York, Crowell Collier, 1963.
An Old-Fashioned Christmas. New York, Dial Press, 1964.
Portrait of Iowa, photographs by John Zielinski. Minneapolis, Adams Press, 1976.

Women in the American Revolution. Chicago, Follett, 1976.

Editor, with Harold Cooper, *West of the Great Water: An Iowa Anthology.* Iowa City, Athens Press, 1931.
Editor, *Ozark Anthology*, by G. F. Newburger. Cedar Rapids, Iowa, Torch Press, 1938.
Editor, *Prize Stories: The O. Henry Awards.* New York, Doubleday, 6 vols., 1954–59.
Editor, with Warren Carrier, *Reading Modern Poetry.* Chicago, Scott Foresman, 1955; revised edition, 1968.
Editor, *Homage to Baudelaire, on the Centennial of "Les Fleurs du Mal," from the Poets at the State University of Iowa.* Iowa City, Cummington Press, 1957.
Editor, with Henri Coulette and Donald Justice, *Midland: Twenty-Five Years of Fiction and Poetry from the Writing Workshops of the State University of Iowa*, and *Midland II.* New York, Random House, 1961, 1970.
Editor, with Joseph Langland, *Poet's Choice.* New York, Dial Press, 1962.
Editor, *On Creative Writing.* New York, Dutton, 1964.

Translator, with Hualing Nieh, *Poems of Mao Tse-Tung.* New York, Dell, 1972; as *The Poetry of Mao Tse-tung*, London, Wildwood House, 1973.

Manuscript Collection: University of Iowa Library, Iowa City.

Paul Engle comments:

My poetry tries to find the most concentrated human feeling in the fewest words. It was a sprawling effort in the early years and has tightened up in the later years. The poems about Edmund Blunden at Oxford University represent the struggle to absorb direct experience into direct language. Emotion without sentimentality, images containing the emotion as object. Rilke and Yeats the greatest influences.

* * *

Paul Engle has been a major figure in American poetry for thirty years and more. As a principal in the founding and development of the famous Writers Workshop at the University of Iowa, as a teacher and editor, he has been an important and encouraging influence for many young poets: several are important contemporary voices. Engle's current efforts are largely directed toward the development of a Translation Workshop, also at the University of Iowa.

As a poet, Engle's reputation is based on more than ten volumes published since 1932. It is perhaps not surprising to note that these contain consistently energetic poems of affirmation. It is an optimistic verse which frequently states its opposition to the modern voice of despair and makes use of so-called "American themes": *Corn*, and *A Prairie Christmas*, "Coney Island," "American Harvest." It is a verse which, like his titles, and even in the later volumes which reach outside of America for some subject matter, is direct and uncomplicated:

Her spine curves like a C,
But does it therefore beg
For pity and despair
Like Lautrec's crooked leg?

No! For the food she grows
That Tokyo may eat,
Comes from determination
Perfect and complete.

A poet of Engle's ability and temperament has apparently had to answer some hard questions: How is one to affirm in a world where despair is more obvious and cynicism seems safer? How do we have a popular poetry, of good taste, in a nation where the real has so often been merely vulgar?

Engle has proclaimed and praised with control and clear speech in each of his volumes. His subjects and attitudes are occasionally close to Whitman or Sandburg or Lindsay, but it would be wrong to say Engle sings or celebrates. The tone of his early poems is reminiscent of the Georgians and, in later volumes, several reviewers have noted that the poems are nostalgic although occasionally "worn" or "repetitive."

He is at his best when his verse is simplest:

That was a shocking day
When we watched, lying prone,
The two trout sidle under
The underwater stone ...

And in "Pair":

Nothing can live alone,
Two are behind each birth.
Every fallen stone
Lies on the rock of earth.

Never a single thing
Has the whole power to be.
Always the wind must bring
Pollen from tree to tree.

A man is how he stands,
Thrust of foot in shoe.
I am my own long hands
And their live touch of you.

But in the eagerness to attack despair, too often there are lines which are prosaic or merely sentimental:

There is a primitive old strength of heart
Men have called courage and that we call guts,
It bore the Crucifix and warped the wagons
Of Boone's men westward through the frozen ruts ... (1939)

or "Abruptly in her black and grateful eyes/The red firecrackers of her heart explode (1965).

One of the excellences of contemporary poetry has been its recognition that there are moments of special emotion when the poet should be struck speechless, and his poem communicate that "silence between the words." It is the essayist or teacher who explains, or over-explains, and too often explains away, but the essayist or teacher is seeking a different, and predominantly intellectual, credibility.

Engle's technique has been markedly influenced by several poets: Shelley in the early volumes, Donne's use of paradox and metaphor, Eliot in several poems (e.g., "Harlem Airshaft"), Auden's Christmas oratorio, Frost, and his former teacher at Oxford, Edmund Blunden. Like Blunden he keeps a distance from the physical – and from his subjects – which is often as aristocratic as aesthetic. Engle's best poems for the contemporary ear are lyric and personal, avoiding strong masculine rhymes, similes, and deliberate iambics. "Kaarlo in Finland" is a sensitive sequence of "letters" around the "Russo-Finnish" war. The title sequence of *A Woman Unashamed* and "In a Bar near Shibuya Station, Tokyo" are good examples of his best work in which there is a striking delicacy: "As if on a summer day, in the dazzle of noon,/One snowflake fell on my astonished hand."

—Joseph Wilson

ENGLISH, Maurice. American. Born in Chicago, Illinois, 21 October 1909. Educated at Harvard University, Cambridge, Massachusetts, A.B. 1933 (Phi Beta Kappa). Married Fanita Blumberg in 1945; two children. Free-lance Journalist in the United States and Europe, 1933–54; Editor-in-Chief, International Division, NBC, 1941–43. Editor and Publisher, *Chicago Magazine*, 1954–58. Managing Editor, 1961–63, and Senior Editor, 1963–69, University of Chicago Press. Founding Director, Temple University Press, Philadelphia, 1969–76. United States Delegate to Les Biennales Internationales de Poésie, Knokke-le-Zoute, Belgium, 1965. Recipient: Fulbright Fellowship, 1966. Address: 724 Pine Street, Philadelphia, Pennsylvania 19102, U.S.A.

PUBLICATIONS

Verse

Midnight in the Century. Park Forest, Illinois, Prairie School Press, 1964.
A Savaging of Roots. Waterloo, Ontario, Pasdeloup Press, 1974.

Other

Editor, *The Testament of Stone: Themes of Idealism and Indignation from the Writings of Louis Sullivan*. Evanston, Illinois, Northwestern University Press, 1963.

Translator, with others, *Selected Poems of Eugenio Montale*. New York, New Directions, 1967.

Critical Studies: by Ralph J. Mills, Jr., in *Tri-Quarterly* (Evanston, Illinois), Spring 1965; by Peter Michelson, in *Chicago Maroon Literary Supplement*, 1965.

Maurice English comments:

Peter Viereck once wrote that I was the "post-modern" poet who had most successfully assimilated lessons from such divergent sources as Eliot and Hart Crane; I hope he is right; I share in the universal debt to the French poets from Baudelaire on, and owe a particular one to Eugenio Montale, whose poetry I first read, with revivifying effect on my own, while learning Italian and (under the tutelage of the late Renato Poggioli) translating it into English.

My major themes and characteristic subjects are both indicated by the title of my book of poems *Midnight in the Century*. Nearly all the poems I most value have been compelled into existence; I have been essentially a medium for them.

* * *

Action/contemplation, passion/premeditation, impulse/custom, chaos/order, "all the fanged opposites," form the continuing theme and structure of Maurice English's poems. Though he perceives the dualities in his subjects, balance in the expression does not result: the latter halves of the oppositions usually dominate. He begins his volume with the apologia: "I have put on these masks to show you my face." But the reserved temperament permits only a filtered vision; the cautious persona emerges just on the brink of revelation. Not that the poet is cold (or coy); but he is, above all, controlled. The poems under the heading of a Social Security number invite autobiographical interpretation. The first, a précis of the standard saga of callow youth – education, travel (flight), return – ends in middle-aged repose with "fat decanter" and hope of son and daughter sharing the "rare flotsam of my joy." "Form Was the World" marks the passage from a boy's love of geometric perfection to a man's appreciation of natural spontaneity. "Thalassa" tells how a sea unseen is traded for life in an inland city, how profferred grace is denied in favor of "the El, the grassless yard." "I turned away a manic guide," he explains in "Acrophobia II," "To travel by the urge of brain and bone." But, weary of intellection, the "annihilating eye," and afraid of the "dangerous voyages" of the heart, he cries: "Blessed are those who do not understand." He comforts Narcissus: "You have no knowledge, and are therefore wise." This and other paradoxes are the logical products of a love of contrasts. Likewise, the cerebral poet expresses conflict and contradiction in parables, further reduced to a pithy "Epitaph" and witty "Biography," and still further compressed in clever aphorisms. His agile pen is honed to a cutting edge when he writes "Against Elders" or indicts with easy sarcasm a Pope who can forget Guernica as he blesses the Spanish generals.

Despite his strong voice, a sense of impotence breaks through, the feeling of inadequacy in "Healing sick passion with sick wit." This may explain his championing of men of daring and action, partisans and soldiers who fight the restraining forces. Hence, too, the engrossing fascination in "The House of Mirrors," a five-part dramatic poem depicting a murder-suicide in a cathouse from several perspectives. A news item introduces the question whether "*Pity, though meant to cure*" can prove a butchery. The supercilious newspaperman jokes as he phones in his report, oblivious to the agony of the victims, a tart plagued daily by brutish "tricks" and haunted nightly by dreams of childhood violation, and her would-be savior, the whorehouse pianist driven by paranoid fantasies to slay her and himself, thus releasing them from their separate demons. Confronting the internal conflicts and expressing the self-destructive dichotomies in our natures, lucidly and without sentimentality, the poet can evoke our sympathies. In the strength of honest lines he achieves his "hope to breed/A passion that is purpose and some power."

—Joseph Parisi

ENRIGHT, D(ennis) J(oseph). British. Born in Leamington, Warwickshire, 11 March 1920. Educated at Leamington College; Downing College, Cambridge, B.A. (honours) in English 1944, M.A. 1946; University of Alexandria, Egypt, D.Litt. 1949. Married Madeleine Harders in 1949; one daughter. Lecturer in English, University of Alexandria, 1947–50; Extra-Mural Lecturer, Birmingham University, England, 1950–53; Visiting Professor, Konan University, Kobe, Japan, 1953–56; Gastdozent, Free University, West Berlin, 1956–57; British Council Professor of English, Chulalongkorn University, Bangkok, 1957–59; Professor of English, University of Singapore, 1960–70. Temporary Lecturer in English, University of Leeds, Yorkshire, 1970–71. Since 1975, Professor of English, University of Warwick, Coventry. Co-Editor of *Encounter* magazine, London, 1970–72. Editorial Advisor, 1971–73, and since 1973, Member, Board of Directors, Chatto and Windus, publishers, London. Recipient: Cholmondeley Award, 1974. Fellow, Royal Society of Literature, 1961. Address: Chatto and Windus Ltd., 40–42 William IV Street, London WC2N 4DF, England.

PUBLICATIONS

Verse

Season Ticket. Alexandria, Editions du Scarabee, 1948.
The Laughing Hyena and Other Poems. London, Routledge, 1953.
The Year of the Monkey. Privately printed, 1956.
Bread Rather Than Blossoms. London, Secker and Warburg, 1956.
Some Men Are Brothers. London, Chatto and Windus, 1960.
Addictions. London, Chatto and Windus, 1962.
The Old Adam. London, Chatto and Windus, 1965.
Unlawful Assembly. London, Chatto and Windus, and Middletown, Connecticut, Wesleyan University Press, 1968.
Selected Poems. London, Chatto and Windus, 1969.
The Typewriter Revolution and Other Poems. New York, Library Press, 1971.
In the Basilica of the Annunciation. London, Poem-of-the-Month Club, 1971.
Daughters of Earth. London, Chatto and Windus, 1972.
Foreign Devils. London, Covent Garden Press, 1972.
The Terrible Shears: Scenes from a Twenties Childhood. London, Chatto and Windus, 1973; Middletown, Connecticut, Wesleyan University Press, 1974.
Rhyme Times Rhyme (for children). London, Chatto and Windus, 1974.
Sad Ires and Others. London, Chatto and Windus, 1975.
Penguin Modern Poets 26, with Dannie Abse and Michael Longley. London, Penguin, 1975.
Paradise Illustrated. London, Chatto and Windus, 1978.
A Faust Book. London, Oxford University Press, 1979.

Novels

Academic Year. London, Secker and Warburg, 1955.
Heaven Knows Where. London, Secker and Warburg, 1957.
Insufficient Poppy. London, Chatto and Windus, 1960.
Figures of Speech. London, Heinemann, 1965.

Other

A Commentary of Goethe's "Faust." New York, New Directions, 1949.
The World of Dew: Aspects of Living Japan. London, Secker and Warburg, 1955; Chester Springs, Pennsylvania, Dufour, 1959.
Literature for Man's Sake: Critical Essays. Tokyo, Kenkyusha, 1955; Philadelphia, West, 1976.
The Apothecary's Shop. London, Secker and Warburg, 1957; Chester Springs, Pennsylvania, Dufour, 1959.
Robert Graves and the Decline of Modernism (address). Singapore, Craftsman Press, 1960; Folcroft, Pennsylvania, Folcroft Editions, 1974.
Conspirators and Poets. London, Chatto and Windus, and Chester Springs, Pennsylvania, Dufour, 1966.
Memoirs of a Mendicant Professor. London, Chatto and Windus, 1969.
Shakespeare and the Students. London, Chatto and Windus, 1970; New York, Schocken, 1971.
Man Is an Onion: Essays and Reviews. London, Chatto and Windus, 1972; LaSalle, Illinois, Library Press, 1973.

A Kidnapped Child of Heaven: The Poetry of Arthur Hugh Clough (lecture). Nottingham, University of Nottingham, 1972.
The Joke Shop (juvenile). London, Chatto and Windus, 1976.
Wild Ghost Chase (juvenile). London, Chatto and Windus, 1978.
Beyond Land's End (juvenile). London, Chatto and Windus, 1979.

Editor, *Poets of the 1950's: An Anthology of New English Verse.* Tokyo, Kenkyusha, 1955.
Editor, with Takamichi Ninomiya, *The Poetry of Living Japan.* London, Murray, and New York, Grove Press, 1957.
Editor, with E. de Chickera, *English Critical Texts: 16th Century to 20th Century.* London and New York, Oxford University Press, 1962.
Editor, *Rasselas*, by Samuel Johnson. London, Penguin, 1976.

Critical Study: *D. J. Enright: Poet of Humanism* by William Walsh, London, Cambridge University Press, 1974.

* * *

The chief stimulus for the highly individual talent of D. J. Enright has been the landscape and people of the countries, mainly in the Far East, where he has spent most of his working life. Some characteristic attitudes were, however, already apparent in early poems about his native Black Country (in, for example, his pointing the incongruity between the idyllic name and dreary reality of Swan Village); and have persisted in later work like the disenchanted cameos of commuter London in *Sad Ires* or of the contemporary English scene satirized in *Paradise Illustrated.*

But it is through his pictures of life abroad that his sense of ironic contrast is most memorably communicated, as in "The Beach at Abousir" between holidaymakers and those "pointed shapes, like trees in winter –/Aged men and ancient children," patiently waiting their chance to pilfer from the prosperous. In Japan the cherry "comes to its immaculate birth" amidst poverty, hunger, and disease. A beautiful peasant girl is found a perfect subject by film-makers "except for the dropsy/Which comes from unpolished rice" (the grim word-play of the title, "A Polished Performance," is typical). Ragged subway sleepers, tensely "hectic rice-winners" commuting on the underground, the ragman who "picks his comfort" in the gentle beauty of the Kyoto autumn, make their silent but uncompromising comment on a society of extremes. In "A Pleasant Walk," contrasting the rows of banks lining "a noble promenade ... paved in gold from every nation" with "the brutal village sunk in slush," Enright bitterly observes: "High commerce civilizes, there's no doubt of that." The banker of "Happy New Year," bemoaning the falling yen as he shows off his opulent house and art treasures, is relentlessly juxtaposed with the empty-pocketed "masters of their fourpenny kites/That soar in the open market of the sky"; the "moderate ambitions" of princes and generals for an air-conditioned palace, a smarter G.H.Q., with the refugees of "Brush-Fire" in flight from their burning shacks, pushing bicycles piled with small bundles. The controlled anger of "The Monuments of Hiroshima" is matched by the deadly fairy-tale idiom employed to recount a bombing error in "The Pied Piper of Akashi."

To Enright's acute, compassionate eye, the great enemy is indifference to suffering, whether in the anonymous multitude or the individual tragedy like that of the 13-year-old suicide who found rat poison cheaper than aspirin. In his dry, amused relish of the ludicrous he can often be very funny; but it is a humour, as in the caustic comment of "Public Address System" on the grotesqueries of excessive official politeness, from which the biting edge is seldom absent. "Simply, he was human, did no harm, and suffered for it" is his epitaph for the poor and oppressed; his sense of the common sadness of the human condition most poignantly crystallized in the diffident, fragile nocturnal melody, at once elegiac and celebrating survival, of "The Noodle-Vendor's Flute."

The shock of large-scale misery and squalor to a caring Western sensibility is frequently registered through the accent of deliberate, almost casual understatement which allows the recorded fact to speak for itself; and this powerful restraint serves to intensify by contrast the impassioned force of the writer's pity and indignation. In common with his fellows of the "Movement," Enright has resolutely refused to sentimentalize the apparently picturesque – rejecting "Epochs of parakeets, of peacocks, and paradisaic birds" for unembellished "images that merely were." This is reflected in his astringent advice in "Changing the Subject," and the wry self-mockery of an acknowledged poetic temptation in "Displaced Person Looks at a Cage-Bird"; while both "Nature Poetry" and the enchanting "Blue Umbrellas" survey our distortions of reality by "the dishonesty of names."

Slyly quizzical, irreverent, socially inconvenient in his impatience of humbug, Enright directs the same remorseless wit towards his own shortcomings (in "The Fairies," "The Ageing Poet," and "A Commuter's Tale") as barbs his scrutiny of the human sham from minister of state to theorizing anarchist or romanticizing poet. A sceptical inner voice prompts him to question whether his own persistent choice of exotic backgrounds might not represent an escapist "rest from meaning." The answer is provided by his characteristic affirmation that "Nothing is exotic, if you understand,/If you stick your neck out for an hour or two." The special tone of this civilized, ironic, unostentatious voice is invoked in "Elegy in a Country Suburb":

> Wholly truthful, intimate
> And utterly unsparing,
> A man communing with himself.

—Margaret Willy

ENSLIN, Theodore (Vernon). American. Born in Chester, Pennsylvania, 25 March 1925. Educated in public and private schools; studied composition with Nadia Boulanger. Married 1) Mildred Marie Stout in 1945 (divorced, 1969), one daughter and one son; 2) Alison Jane Jose in 1969, one son. Recipient: National Endowment for the Arts grant, 1976. Address: Box 522, Temple, Maine 04984, U.S.A.

PUBLICATIONS

Verse

The Work Proposed. Ashland, Massachusetts, Origin Press, 1958.
New Sharon's Prospect. Kyoto, Japan, Origin Press, 1962.
The Place Where I Am Standing. New Rochelle, New York, Elizabeth Press, 1964.
This Do (and The Talents). Mexico City, El Corno Emplumado, 1966.
New Sharon's Prospect and Journals. San Francisco, Coyote's Journal, 1966.
To Come To Have Become. New Rochelle, New York, Elizabeth Press, 1966.
The Four Temperaments. Privately printed, 1966.
Characters in Certain Places. Portland, Oregon, Prensa da Lagar-Wine Press, 1967.
The Diabelli Variations and Other Poems. Annandale-on-Hudson, New York, Matter, 1967.
2/30–6/31: Poems 1967. Cabot, Vermont, Stoveside Press, 1967.
Agreement and Back: Sequences. New Rochelle, New York, Elizabeth Press, 1969.
The Poems. New Rochelle, New York, Elizabeth Press, 1970.

Forms, Part One: The First Dimension. New Rochelle, New York, Elizabeth Press, 1970.
Views 1–7. Berkeley, California, Maya, 1970.
The Country of Our Consciousness. Berkeley, California, Sand Dollar, 1971.
Forms, Part Two. New Rochelle, New York, Elizabeth Press, 1971.
Forms, Part Three. New Rochelle, New York, Elizabeth Press, 1972.
Etudes. New Rochelle, New York, Elizabeth Press, 1972.
Views. New Rochelle, New York, Elizabeth Press, 1973.
Forms, Part Four. New Rochelle, New York, Elizabeth Press, 1973.
Sitio. Hanover, New Hampshire, Granite, 1973.
In the Keepers House. Dennis, Massachusetts, Salt Works Press, 1973.
With Light Reflected. Fremont, Michigan, Sumac Press, 1973.
The Swamp Fox. Dennis, Massachusetts, Salt Works Press, 1973.
The Mornings. Berkeley, California, Shaman/Drum, 1974.
Fever Poems. Brunswick, Maine, Blackberry, 1974.
The Last Days of October. Dennis, Massachusetts, Salt Works Press, 1974.
The Median Flow: Poems 1943–1973. Los Angeles, Black Sparrow Press, 1974.
Synthesis 1–24. Plainfield, Vermont, North Atlantic, 1975.
Ländler. New Rochelle, New York, Elizabeth Press, 1975.
Papers. New Rochelle, New York, Elizabeth Press, 1976.

Other

Mahler. Los Angeles, Black Sparrow Press, 1975.
The July Book. Berkeley, California, Sand Dollar, 1976.

Editor, *The Selected Poems of Howard McCord 1961–1971.* Trumansburg, New York, Crossings Press, 1975.

Manuscript Collection: Fales Collection, New York University Libraries.

Critical Study: "The Frozen State" by the author in *Elizabeth* (New Rochelle, New York), 1965.

Theodore Enslin comments:

I suppose I would classify as a "non-academic," and have been allied with those who broke with the "New Criticism" in the early fifties.

Perhaps, as Cid Corman once said, I write more "you" poems than anyone else now alive. My "themes" are what I find around me, and since I live in the country, this has sometimes led to thinking that I am in some way a "nature poet." I heartily disavow this. My poems are intensely introspective from which I attempt to produce the impersonality/personality which I feel necessary to any valid work of art. My formal structure is based on sound, and I feel that my musical training has shaped this more than anything else. The line breaks/stresses are indicated as a type of notation, something which concerns me, since I believe we have no adequate notation for poetry, and I conceive of any poem as requiring a performance. It should be read aloud. In ways, some important to me, and some to the work itself, I would say that Rilke, W. C. Williams, Thoreau, and latterly Louis Zukofsky, were influences. The rest must be said in the poems themselves.

* * *

Theodore Enslin's work became known in the pages of *Origin*, the seminal magazine edited by Cid Corman, who also published Enslin's first book. It's not surprising, then, to find a continuity between the work of the two men. Both write spare, quiet, post-Williams poems grounded in a shared respect for the otherness and autonomy of natural things and a distrust of the romantic ego. A basic premise is that sufficiently careful naming of phenomena can by itself energize attention. But Enslin is more diffuse than Corman. Many of his poems, read quickly, seem merely flat, no more than prose jottings. Reread, however, with due attention to the lineation and sound, the best of them take on a pondered weight and become meditations rather than mere statements. His method of condensing daily experience and observation into poems can be seen in the charming *New Sharon's Prospect*, which gives both the prose anecdotes and sketches and the poems which crystallize out of them. Enslin's work is filled with the places, people, and things of rural New England, where he lives. If at times it reminds you of a Frost landscape, it is free of Frost's often intrusive "personality." Others of his poems are more abstract notations of emotion or of the problematic relations of observer and external reality; this one is from *The Place Where I Am Standing*:

I turned once to the window
and once
to you
            not here.
I would have shown you
a world I see there,
but it would not have been your world.
It is better this way.
In absence, you come to the window,
look out on just those things
I have shown you.

Recently Enslin has published the first four of what are to be five volumes of *Forms*, a long open-structure poem, the product of "sixteen years of experiment and discovery" which he describes as "my apperception of art, of history, of experience, whatever any of it may have been worth, and no matter how limited." First acquaintance suggests that it is less rewarding than the short poems, but the interest of the latter is grounds enough for thinking the long work will deserve frequentation.

—Seamus Cooney

ESHLEMAN, Clayton. American. Born in Indianapolis, Indiana, 1 June 1935. Educated at Indiana University, Bloomington, 1953–61, B.A. in philosophy, M.A. in English. Married 1) Barbara Novak in 1961 (divorced, 1967), one son, Matthew; 2) Caryl Eshleman. Instructor, University of Maryland Eastern Overseas Division, Japan, 1961–62; Instructor in English, Matsushita Electric Corporation, Osaka, Japan, 1962–64; lived in Peru, 1965; Instructor, New York University American Language Institute, 1966–68; Member of the School of Critical Studies, California Institute of the Arts, Valencia, 1970–72; taught at University of California, Los Angeles, 1975–77; taught in a black ghetto high school in Los Angeles (California Arts Council grant), 1977–78; Dreyfuss Poet-in-Residence, California Institute of Technology, Pasadena, 1979–80. Editor and Publisher, *Caterpillar* magazine, New York, 1967–70, and Sherman Oaks, California, 1970–73. Recipient: Union League Civic and Arts Foundation Prize (*Poetry*, Chicago), 1968; National Translation Center awards; National Endowment for the Arts grant, 1969; Coordinating Council of Literary

Magazines grant, 1969, 1970, 1971; Guggenheim Fellowship, 1978; National Book Award, for translation, 1979. Address: c/o Black Sparrow Press, Box 3993, Santa Barbara, California 93105, U.S.A.

PUBLICATIONS

Verse

Mexico and North. Privately printed, 1962.
The Chavin Illumination. Lima, Peru, La Rama Florida, 1965.
Lachrymae Mateo: 3 Poems for Christmas 1966. New York, Caterpillar, 1966.
Walks. New York, Caterpillar, 1967.
The Crocus Bud. Reno, Nevada, Camels Coming, 1967.
Brother Stones. New York, Caterpillar, 1968.
Cantaloups and Splendour. Los Angeles, Black Sparrow Press, 1968.
T'ai. Cambridge, Massachusetts, Sans Souci Press, 1969.
The House of Okumura. Toronto, Weed/Flower Press, 1969.
Indiana. Los Angeles, Black Sparrow Press, 1969.
The House of Ibuki: A Poem, New York City, 14 March–30 Sept. 1967. Fremont, Michigan, Sumac Press, 1969.
Yellow River Record. London, Big Venus, 1969.
A Pitchblende. San Francisco, Maya, 1969.
The Wand. Santa Barbara, California, Capricorn Press, 1971.
Bearings. Santa Barbara, California, Capricorn Press, 1971.
Altars. Los Angeles, Black Sparrow Press, 1971.
The Sanjo Bridge. Los Angeles, Black Sparrow Press, 1972.
Coils. Los Angeles, Black Sparrow Press, 1973.
Human Wedding. Los Angeles, Black Sparrow Press, 1973.
The Last Judgment: For Caryl Her Thirty-First Birthday, The End of Her Pain. Los Angeles, Plantin Press, 1973.
Aux Morts. Los Angeles, Black Sparrow Press, 1974.
Realignment. Providence, Rhode Island, Treacle Press, 1974.
Portrait of Francis Bacon. Sheffield, Rivelin Press, 1975.
The Gull Wall: Poems and Essays. Los Angeles, Black Sparrow Press, 1975.
Cogollo. Newton, Massachusetts, Roxbury, 1976.
The Woman Who Saw Through Paradise. Lawrence, Kansas, Tansy Press, 1976.
Grotesca. London, New London Pride, 1977.
On Mules Sent from Chavin: A Journal and Poems 1965–66. Swansea, Galloping Dog Press, 1977.
Core Meander. Santa Barbara, California, Black Sparrow Press, 1977.
The Gospel of Celine Arnauld. Willits, California, Tuumba Press, 1978.
The Name Encanyoned River. Providence, Rhode Island, Treacle Press, 1978.
What She Means. Santa Barbara, California, Black Sparrow Press, 1978.
A Note on Apprenticeship. Chicago, Two Hands Press, 1979.

Other

Editor, *A Caterpillar Anthology: A Selection of Poetry and Prose from Caterpillar Magazine.* New York, Doubleday, 1971.

Translator, *Residence on Earth*, by Pablo Neruda. San Francisco, Amber House, 1962.
Translator, with Denis Kelly, *State of the Union*, by Aimé Césaire. Bloomington, Indiana, Caterpillar, 1966.
Translator, *Seven Poems*, by César Vallejo. Reno, Nevada, Quark, 1967.

Translator, *Poémas Humanos/Human Poems*, by César Vallejo. New York, Grove Press, 1968; London, Cape, 1969.

Translator, with José Rubia Barcia, *Spain, Take This Cup from Me*, by César Vallejo. New York, Grove Press, 1974.

Translator, *Letter to André Breton*, by Antonin Artaud. Los Angeles, Black Sparrow Press, 1974.

Translator, with Norman Glass, *To Have Done with the Judgement of God*, by Antonin Artaud. Los Angeles, Black Sparrow Press, 1975.

Translator, with Norman Glass, *Artaud the Momo*, by Antonin Artaud. Santa Barbara, California, Black Sparrow Press, 1976.

Translator, with José Rubia Barcia, *Battles in Spain*, by César Vallejo. Santa Barbara, California, Black Sparrow Press, 1978.

Translator, with José Rubia Barcia, *The Complete Posthumous Poetry*, by César Vallejo. Berkeley, University of California Press, 1978.

Translator, with Annette Smith, *Notebook of a Return to the Native Land*, by Aimé Césaire. New York, Montemora, 1979.

Manuscript Collections: Lilly Library, Indiana University, Bloomington; Special Collections Library, New York University; University of California, San Diego.

Critical Studies: by Hayden Carruth, in *New York Times Book Review*, 13 February 1972; Introduction by the author to *Coils*, 1973; by Robert Peters, in *Margins 24–26* (Milwaukee); by Eric Mottram, in *Margins 27* (Milwaukee); by Diane Wakoski, in *Iowa Review* (Iowa City), Winter 1975; by Paul Zweig, in *New York Times Book Review*, 1 February 1976; "Clayton Eshleman Issue" of *Oasis 19* (London), 1977; by Alan Williamson, in *Parnassus* (New York), Spring 1979.

Clayton Eshleman comments:

As species disappear, the paleolithic grows on us; as living animals disappear, the first outlines become more dear, not as reflections of a day world, but as the primal contours of psyche, the shaping of the underworld, at the point Hades was an animal. The new wilderness is thus the spectral realm created by the going out of animal life and the coming in of these primary outlines. Our tragedy is to search further and further back for a common non-racial trunk in which the animal is not separated out of the human while we destroy the turf on which we actually stand.

* * *

Clayton Eshleman is unusual among his contemporaries because he did not start writing poetry until he was in college, whereas most poets are composing little masterpieces to the rose bush or their puppies before they are seven and often have written an entire body of work before they are 30. And part of the fascination of Eshleman's poetry is its organic relationship to his life. He has created a poetry which embodies the struggles of transformation from an insulated bourgeois business administration student from the Mid-West into a poet of raw and brutal self-revelations.

Taking as his mentor William Blake, Eshleman has commenced a spiritual journey, in an attempt to purge the clogging murky insulation of his early life and create a poetry out of the new revealed personality. Eshleman is an archetypal poet, looking for the everyman in his experiences, looking for the primal sources in himself and trying to locate the self in poetry. His work is obsessively self-involved, filled with minute details of his personal observations, and almost cruelly willing to reveal every impression of the self in hopes that such bareness will finally discover the rich spirit of poet in each person.

His most powerful book to date, *Coils*, is a rare document combining his own sense of the mythic self with the autobiographical Clayton Eshleman from Indiana, U.S.A. His poems are filled with a sensuousness that transcends the most painful moments. His ability to describe the textures of a world seen as a thrillingly beautiful place, surface as magic moments which almost deny the purposes of the poems and yet give the poet precisely what he is looking for – the poetry of existence.

Eshleman's career as a poet has been intertwined with that of a magazine he founded and published, called *Caterpillar*. This magazine created a forum for Eshleman and his colleagues who write longer poems in open forms. The inspiration for this magazine (and for much of his work, Eshleman claims) was Cid Corman, an American editor who founded *Origin* magazine.

—Diane Wakoski

ESPINO, Federico (Licsi, Jr.). Filipino. Born in Pasig, Rizal, 10 April 1939. Educated at the University of Santo Tomas, Manila, B.A. in journalism 1959. Assistant Editor, *Mirror Magazine*, Manila, 1969–72. Recipient: Asia Foundation-Silliman University Fellowship, 1966; Palanca Memorial Award, 1967, 1969, 1972; *Free Press* Short Story Prize, 1972; *Graphic* Short Story Prize, 1972. Address: 178 Marcelo H. del Pilar, Pasig, Rizal, Philippines.

PUBLICATIONS

Verse

In Three Tongues: A Folio of Poems in Tagalog, English, and Spanish. Quezon City, Bustamante Press, 1963.
Apocalypse in Ward 19 and Other Poems. Quezon City, Journal Press, 1965.
The Shuddering Clavier. Quezon City, Journal Press, 1965.
Sa Paanan ng parnaso. Quezon City, Journal Press, 1965.
Toreng Bato, Kastilyong Pawid. Quezon City, Journal Press, 1966.
Balalayka ni Pasternak at iba pang tula (in Tagalog and English). Manila, Pioneer Press, 1967.
A Rapture of Distress. Manila, Pioneer Press, 1968.
Alak na buhay, hinog na abo, phoenix na papel (in Tagalog and English). Manila, Pioneer Press, 1968.
Dark Sutra. Quezon City, Pioneer Press, 1969.
Burnt Alphabets: Poems in English, Tagalog, and Spanish. Manila, Pioneer Press, 1969.
Dawn and Downsitting: Poems. Quezon City, Pioneer Press, 1969.
Counterclockwise: Poems 1965–1969. Quezon City, Bustamante Press, 1969.
A Manner of Seeing: A Folio of Poems. Privately printed, 1970.
Caras y Caretas de Amor. Quezon City, Bustamante Press, 1970.
The Winnowing Rhythm. Quezon City, Bustamante Press, 1970.
Makinilya at lira, tuluyan at tula. Manila, Pioneer Press, 1970.
From Mactan to Mandiola: A Poem of Protest, and Others. Quezon City, Manlapaz, 1971.
Twinkling: A Sheaf of Poems. Privately printed, 1972.
Letters and Nocturnes: Poems 1972–1973. Manila, Pioneer Press, 1973.
Puente del Diablo: A Poem in Three Movements. Manila, Pioneer Press, 1973.

Makabagong panulaan. Quezon City, Manlapaz, 1974.
In the Very Torrent. Privately printed, 1975.
Opus 27. Manila, Pioneer Press, 1976.
Tambor de Sangre. Bilbao, Ayala, 1977.

Short Stories

The Country of Sleep. Quezon City, Bustamante Press, 1969.
Percussive Blood: Selected Stories. Manila, Pioneer Press, 1972.

Critical Study: "Philippine Poetry in English: Some Notes for Exploration" by Cirilo Bautista, in *Solidarity Magazine* (Manila), December 1970.

Federico Espino comments:

I have been compared to the French Symbolists though the affinity I have with them is only a matter of subject matter, not of form. I do not, however, believe in a Rimbaudian derangement of the senses or in the Baudelairean theory of correspondences and I eschew the celebration of neurosis, though in my stories I write about neurotic people. The psychological minorities interest me only in relation to a Catholic frame of reference.

* * *

Federico Espino is not only an English language poet: he has the distinction of being the leading Filipino writer in Tagalog, which is the language of Manila and its environs, and which forms the basis of the artificial national language. Nothing that he has done in English verse is as good as the short stories collected in *The Country of Sleep*; but he shows signs of development. His English poetry is often too obviously derivative and self-consciously experimental, and he seems to have been over-influenced by his important compatriot José Garcia Villa (although Villa, strangely, is generally much disliked in his native country): various sorts of technical effects, often well-executed, tend to swallow up or diminish the content of his poems. He is at his best when his subject is the actual problem of poetic procedure, with which he is honestly and unpretentiously concerned. His use of Lowell and Stevens has been unproductive: but Guillén, with his sonorous, nostalgic toughness, has been a valuable influence. His difficulties may originate in his bilingualism: there is not really a large or appreciative audience for Tagalog writing, and it is natural enough that an author with a perfect command of English should turn to the latter language. The decision has been successful in the realm of short fiction; but one is bound to wonder if Espino's Tagalog poetry is not better than his English: more authentically his own.

—Martin Seymour-Smith

EVANS, Abbie Huston. American. Born in Lee, New Hampshire, 20 December 1881. Educated at Radcliffe College, Cambridge, Massachusetts, B.A. 1913 (Phi Beta Kappa), M.A. 1918. Member of the Staff, the Settlement Music School, Philadelphia, 1923–53. Recipient: Guarantor's Prize (*Poetry*, Chicago), 1931; Loines Memorial Award, 1960; New England Poetry Club Golden Rose, 1965. Litt.D.: Bowdoin College, Brunswick, Maine, 1961. Address: 404 North Walnut Street, West Chester, Pennsylvania 19380, U.S.A.

PUBLICATIONS

Verse

Outcrop. New York and London, Harper, 1928.
The Bright North. New York, Macmillan, 1938.
Fact of Crystal. New York, Harcourt Brace, 1961.
Collected Poems. Pittsburgh, University of Pittsburgh Press, 1970.

Other

Editor, with Florence S. Esdall, *The Poems of Jean Batchelor.* New York, Rockport Press, 1947.

Critical Study: *Quintet: Essays on Five American Women Poets* by George Brandon Saul, The Hague, Mouton, 1967.

Abbie Huston Evans comments:

Most recent work reflecting increasingly contemporary discoveries in Natural Science.

* * *

Abbie Huston Evans is so reticent a poet – she published no book between *The Bright North* (1938), her second volume, and *Fact of Crystal* (1961) – that her name was scarcely known to readers of contemporary verse when she received the Loines Award for Poetry from the National Institute of Arts and Letters in 1960. Her *Collected Poems* appeared in 1970.

When Abbie Evans grew up in Camden, Maine, where her father was the Congregational minister, among her Sunday School pupils was a gifted girl named Edna St. Vincent Millay. While still at college Millay burst into print, but Miss Evans, who has said "Words have to ripen for me," did not publish until after her former student was famous. In her foreword to Miss Evans's first book, *Outcrop*, Millay wrote, "Read these poems too swiftly, or only once, and your heart may still be free of them. Read them again, with care, and they will lay their hands upon you."

Of her late-blooming poetry Miss Evans has said, "I must hold the record for slowness.... Three of four short things are my output." Her patience and persistence are rewarded when she writes lovingly of her heritage – her father had been a coal miner in Wales at the age of seven – and of the Maine mountains and the sea. Perhaps her father's life in the mines and her own experience after World War I as a social worker in a Colorado mining camp have made her so imaginatively responsive to rocks, to crystals, to geologic time. Miss Evans is that rare thing, a nature poet who does not sentimentalize her subjects but acknowledges their power, vastness, and mystery. Whether she writes of frost on the bunchberry or of rocks as old as the stars, her language, like a "fact of crystal," is "grappled into jewel."

For many years Miss Evans taught dancing, art and dramatics at the Settlement Music School in Philadelphia. (Half of the members of the Philadelphia Orchestra are said to have been her students.) In these lines, published in her ninetieth year, Miss Evans has the grace, the courage, and the joy to say, "To a Poet Yet Unborn":

> No one but you can help us much. Subdue what blasts. Dare do it.
> Ride formlessness, word wordlessness. Be not aghast. Be poet.

—Daniel Hoffman

EVANS, Mari. African-American. Born in Toledo, Ohio. Attended the University of Toledo. Writer-in-Residence, Indiana University-Purdue University, Indianapolis, 1969–70; Northwestern University, Evanston, Illinois, 1972–73; Assistant Professor, Purdue University, West Lafayette, Indiana, 1978–80. Producer, Writer, and Director, The Black Experience television program, Indianapolis, 1968–73. Recipient: John Hay Whitney Fellowship, 1965; Woodrow Wilson Foundation grant, 1968. Address: P.O. Box 483, Indianapolis, Indiana, 46206, U.S.A.

PUBLICATIONS

Verse

Where Is All the Music? London, Paul Breman, 1968.
I Am a Black Woman. New York, Morrow, 1970.
Whisper. Berkeley, University of California Center for African American Studies, 1979.

Other

JD (juvenile). New York, Doubleday, 1973.
I Look at Me. Chicago, Third World Press, 1973.
Rap Stories. Chicago, Third World Press, 1973.
Singing Black. Indianapolis, Reed, 1976.
Jim Flying High (juvenile). New York, Doubleday, 1979.

* * *

Though she was born during the Harlem Renaissance, Mari Evans' poetry reveals little of the inclination toward compromise with white values and forms that was cherished by most black intellectuals of that period. Quite the contrary, her work is informed by the uncompromising black pride that burgeoned in the 1960's, and she stands tall with Don Lee, Nikki Giovanni, Sonia Sanchez, and the resuscitated Gwendolyn Brooks as a powerful poetic proclaimer of the new black awareness.

That she is conscious of the change in black stance is demonstrated by the deliberate contrast she achieves between Countée Cullen's famous plaint of the mid-1920's "Yet Do I Marvel" and her "Who Can Be Born Black." Where Cullen constructs a Shakespearian sonnet replete with classical allusions to express his wonder at God's great capacity to create horror, the most amazing example of which is "To make a poet black, and bid him sing," she responds briefly and without apparent artifice:

Who
can be born black
and not
sing
the wonder of it
the joy
the
challenge

Who
can be born black
and not exult!

Mari Evans, like the best of the new black poets, usually keeps close to the bone of black experience and frequently works through the rhythms of its speech and music. Hopefully a non-black will find that experience, as filtered through her poetry, a paradigm of the human condition, but it is clear that she is unconcerned about the feelings of those who are too opaque to find it so.

—Alan R. Shucard

EVANS DAVIES, Gloria. British. Born in Maesteg, Glamorgan, 17 April 1932. Educated at schools in Wales and Bristol. Recipient: Gulbenkian Foundation grant; Royal Literary Fund grant. Address: 25c High Street Superior, Brecon, South Wales.

PUBLICATIONS

Verse

Words – For Blodwen. London, Chatto and Windus, 1962.
Her Name Like the Hours. London, Chatto and Windus, 1974.

* * *

Within Wales, the standing of Gloria Evans Davies as a poet is a strange one. Although she has published poems elsewhere, she has been largely unacknowledged in her own country, and her obvious accomplishment almost ignored. This may well be because she lives and writes – in the mountain township of Brecon – in some isolation from the main urban centres of Welsh life and culture, though it is also possible that her work has simply not appealed to the editors of certain magazines through the past few years.

In her second collection, *Her Name Like the Hours*, fresh, original images are drawn from the mountain and coastal landscape, comprising a number of sharp, visual details played off one against the other in rather curious sequences. She conveys clear impressions of sea, shore and hills with accuracy and precision, each line intense and concentrated in its effects. In one short poem, "West Wales Coast," she gives a feeling of both heat and weight, combining to produce a vision of time past:

Waves are heavy with the deep,
The heat scalds though the sun
Is a pressed fern against its own light.

Forests smell of sawdust,
Villages crust with houses;
A leaf turns to flame and to leaf again.

Gloria Evans Davies writes with an instinctive sense of rhythm, perhaps more like a musician, which she once wanted to become, than a conventional poet. The phrasing and structure link smoothly with the meaning – which is rarely obscure – as seen in such a poem as "Breconshire":

Rain runs along the silver wire of dawn,
And already the tourists on the Usk,
Beacons and Llangorse lake;
Trees show more scratches from cats
Than leaves ...

Because of rain all week
One is not crowded into a standstill
Except by sheep in the town centre ...

Slate roofs turn mauve in a shower.

The basic unit of meaning in her poems is the image; an obvious example comes from an earlier, four-line poem, "Peace":

The sun sets into a moon. Trees let birds in.
Wish we could put a name to what peace can begin.

The waves hunt Summer to the shore and defeat,
Where down corridors of mist gun to gun we meet.

Here, after celebrating harmonious nature, the shock last line – against man's spoiling – pulls the reader up short. The fragility of peace, like an armed truce, is shattered by the destructive element in human relations.

Gloria Evans Davies's range may not be very wide, but her vision is deep, and her modest achievement distinctive. It is impressive because of a quality of authenticity ("hammering out a simplicity," as she says), and there can be little doubt – though recognition is still late in coming – as to her poetic merit.

—John Tripp

EVERSON, Ronald (Gilmour). Canadian. Born in Oshawa, Ontario, 18 November 1903. Educated at the University of Toronto, 1923–27, B.A. 1927; Upper Canada Law Society, 1927–30; called to the Ontario Bar 1930. Served with British Security Co-ordination, 1940–45. Married Lorna Jean Austin in 1931. Managing Director, 1936–47, and President, 1947–63, Johnston, Everson and Charlesworth Ltd., Toronto. Chairman, Communications-6 Inc., Montreal, 1964–66. Co-founding Director, Delta Canada Books, Montreal, 1960–63; Director, Ryerson Press, Toronto, 1960–65; Co-founder, League of Canadian Poets, 1966. Address: 4855 ch. Côte St.-Luc, Montreal, Quebec, Canada.

PUBLICATIONS

Verse

Three Dozen Poems. Montreal, Cambridge Press, 1927.
A Lattice for Momos. Toronto, Contact Press, 1958.
Blind Man's Holiday. Toronto, Ryerson Press, 1963.
Four Poems. Norwich, Vermont, American Letters Press, 1963.
Wrestle with an Angel. Montreal, Delta Canada, 1965.
Incident on Côte des Neiges. Amherst, Massachusetts, Green Knight Press, 1966.

Raby Head and Other Poems. Amherst, Massachusetts, Green Knight Press, 1967.
The Dark Is Not So Dark. Montreal and Santa Barbara, California, Delta Canada-Unicorn, 1969.
Selected Poems 1920–1970. Montreal, Delta Canada, 1970.
Indian Summer. Ottawa, Oberon Press, 1976.
Carnival. Ottawa, Oberon Press, 1978.

Other

Of This and That, with J. G. Johnston and J. L. Charlesworth. Privately printed, 1940.

Bibliography: in *Salt* (Moose Jaw, Saskatchewan), Summer 1973.

Critical Studies: by Margaret Avison in *Poetry* (Chicago), June 1959; by James Dickey, in *Sewanee Review* (Tennessee), Autumn 1960, and in *Poetry* (Chicago), February 1964; by Munro Beattie, in *Literary History of Canada*, Toronto, University of Toronto Press, 1965; by M. J. Sidnell, in *Canadian Forum* (Toronto), January 1966; by Robert Gibbs, in *Fiddlehead* (Fredericton, New Brunswick), April 1970; by Al Purdy in *Quarry* (Kingston, Ontario), Spring 1970; by Ralph Gustafson, in *Canadian Literature* (Vancouver), Summer 1971; by William Dickey, in *Hudson Review* (New York), April 1971; by Charles Molesworth, in *Poetry* (Chicago), May 1972.

* * *

"I admire poetry that risks going out beyond the end of thinking," Ronald Everson has written. Everson published his first book in 1927; his second appeared over thirty years later when he was fifty-four years old. But the Montreal poet has made up for lost time, for since then the former public-relations consultant has gained the admiration of James Dickey who perceptively noted that Everson "thinks of practicality as one of the greatest of the artistic virtues, and as underlying all real imagination."

After a reading of his *Selected Poems 1920–1970*, it is difficult not to see Everson as the perfect embodiment of his United Empire Loyalist ancestors. He is his own man, like the New England farmer. A true "U.E.L.," he retains a realistic approach to life without requiring the consolations of compromise or moral superiority. He seems to be an agnostic, but not an atheist, for he can write: "I do not know where we are/None knows where we are."

Everson is knowledgeable without being pedantic, shrewd without being cutting, worldly-wise without being sophisticated. He is a great traveller, yet his poems about the places he has been are neither anecdotal nor picturesque, and hence escape the label "travel poetry." Instead they are splendid and precise evocations, in the imagistic manner, of the associations that a modest and reasonable man would have in the presence of the unyielding world.

Everson's particular stamping ground is the Maritimes and rural Ontario, although he has written about other parts of Canada as well. In "Love Poem," he writes about having "given up on the salvation of mankind." Perhaps this accounts for his mellow outlook. In another poem, he meditates on "a field of Ontario Quaker graves." The poem comes to a magnificent conclusion:

No new graves
Congregation gone
Religion gone
They entered underground to lie unknown
on their own plan
I stare at the chance-taking dead.

—John Robert Colombo

EVERSON, William (Oliver). American. Born in Sacramento, California, 10 September 1912. Educated at Fresno State College, California, 1931, 1934–35. Conscientious objector during World War II: spent three and a half years in work camps in Oregon. Co-Founder, Untide Press, Waldport, Oregon. Dominican lay brother, 1951–69 (Brother Antoninus). Since 1971, Poet-in-Residence, Kresge College, University of California, Santa Cruz. Recipient: Guggenheim Fellowship, 1949; Shelley Memorial Award, 1978. Address: 312 Swanton Road, Davenport, California 95017, U.S.A.

PUBLICATIONS

Verse (as William Everson)

These Are the Ravens. San Leandro, California, Greater West, 1935.
San Joaquin. Los Angeles, Ward Ritchie Press, 1939.
The Masculine Dead: Poems 1938–1940. Prairie City, Illinois, James A. Decker, 1942.
X War Elegies. Waldport, Oregon, Untide Press, 1943.
Waldport Poems. Waldport, Oregon, Untide Press, 1944.
War Elegies. Waldport, Oregon, Untide Press, 1944.
Residual Years: Poems 1940–1941. Waldport, Oregon, Untide Press, 1945.
Poems MCMXLII. Waldport, Oregon, Untide Press, 1945.
The Residual Years: Poems 1934–1946. New York, New Directions, 1948.
A Privacy of Speech: Ten Poems in Sequence. Berkeley, California, Equinox Press, 1949.
Triptych for the Living. Oakland, California, Seraphim Press, 1951.
There Will Be Harvest. Berkeley, California, Albion Press, 1960.
The Year's Declension. Berkeley, California, Albion Press, 1961.
The Blowing of the Seed. New Haven, Connecticut, Henry W. Wenning, 1966.
Single Source: The Early Poems of William Everson 1934–1940. Berkeley, California, Oyez, 1966.
In the Fictive Wish. Berkeley, California, Oyez, 1967.
The Springing of the Blade. Reno, Nevada, Black Rock Press, 1968.
The Residual Years: Poems 1934–1948. New York, New Directions, 1968.
Tendril in the Mesh. Aromas, California, Cayucos, 1973.
Black Hills. San Francisco, Didymus Press, 1973.
Man-Fate: The Swan Song of Brother Antoninus. New York, New Directions, 1974.
River-Root: A Syzygy for the Bicentennial of These States. Berkeley, California, Oyez, 1976.
Missa Defunctorum. Santa Cruz, California, Lime Kiln Press, 1976.
The Mate-Flight of Eagles. Newcastle, California, Blue Oak Press, 1977.
Blackbird Sundown. Northridge, California, Lord John Press, 1978.
Rattlesnake August. Northridge, California, Santa Susana Press, 1978.
The Veritable Years: Poems 1949–1966. Santa Barbara, California, Black Sparrow Press, 1978.
Cutting the Firebreak. Swanton, California, Kingfisher Press, 1978.
Blame It on the Jet Stream! Santa Cruz, California, Lime Kiln Press, 1978.
The Masks of Drought. Santa Barbara, California, Black Sparrow Press, 1979.

Verse (as Brother Antoninus)

At the Edge. Oakland, California, Albertus Magnus, 1958.
A Fragment for the Birth of God. Oakland, California, Albertus Magnus, 1958.
An Age Insurgent. San Francisco, Blackfriars, 1959.
The Crooked Lines of God: Poems 1949–1954. Detroit, University of Detroit Press, 1959.

The Hazards of Holiness: Poems 1957–1960. New York, Doubleday, 1962.
The Poet Is Dead: A Memorial for Robinson Jeffers. San Francisco, Auerhahn Press, 1964.
The Rose of Solitude. Berkeley, California, Oyez, 1964.
The Rose of Solitude (collection). New York, Doubleday, 1967.
The Vision of Felicity. Cambridge, Massachusetts, Lowell House, 1967.
The Achievement of Brother Antoninus: A Comprehensive Selection of His Poems with a Critical Introduction, by William E. Stafford. Chicago, Scott Foresman, 1967.
A Canticle to the Waterbirds. Berkeley, California, Eizo, 1968.
The City Does Not Die. Berkeley, California, Oyez, 1969.
The Last Crusade. Berkeley, California, Oyez, 1969.
Who Is She That Looketh Forth as the Morning. Santa Barbara, California, Capra Press, 1972.

Recording: *Savagery of Love*, Caedmon, 1968.

Other

The Dominican Brother: Province of the West. Privately printed, 1967.
Robinson Jeffers: Fragments of an Older Fury. Berkeley, California, Oyez, 1968.
If I Speak Truth: An Inter View-ing, with Jerry Burns. San Francisco, Goliards Press, 1968.
Earth Poetry. Berkeley, California, Oyez, 1971.
Archetype West: The Pacific Coast as a Literary Region. Berkeley, California, Oyez, 1976.
Earth Poetry: Essays and Interviews. Berkeley, California, Oyez, 1979.

Editor, *Cawdor and Medea*, by Robinson Jeffers. New York, New Directions, 1970.
Editor, *Californians*, by Robinson Jeffers. Aromas, California, Cayucos, 1971.
Editor, *The Alpine Christ*, by Robinson Jeffers. Aromas, California, Cayucos, 1973.
Editor, *Tragedy Has Obligations*, by Robinson Jeffers. Santa Cruz, California, Lime Kiln Press, 1973.
Editor, *Brides of the South Wind*, by Robinson Jeffers. Aromas, California, Cayucos, 1974.
Editor, *The Double Axe and Other Poems*, by Robinson Jeffers. New York, Liveright, 1977.

Bibliography: *William Everson: A Descriptive Bibliography* by Lee Bartlett and Allan Campo, Metuchen, New Jersey, Scarecrow Press, 1977.

Manuscript Collections: (earlier work) William Andrews Clark Library, University of California, Los Angeles; (middle period) Bancroft Library, University of California, Berkeley.

Critical Studies: *William Everson: Poet from the San Joaquin* by Allan Campo, D. A. Carpenter, and Bill Hotchkiss, Newcastle, California, Blue Oak Press, 1978; *Benchmark and Blaze: The Emergence of William Everson* edited by Lee Bartlett, Metuchen, New Jersey, Scarecrow Press, 1979.

William Everson comments:

(1970) I was born William Oliver Everson, the son of Louis Waldemar Everson, an immigrant Norwegian musician and composer, and Francelia Maria Herber, a Minnesota farm girl of German-Irish extraction who was twenty years his junior. With an older sister and younger brother I grew up in the little town of Selma, California, where our father was bandmaster. My mother had been born a Catholic, but left that faith to marry my father; we children were brought up as Christian Scientists. In adolescence I became an agnostic, but at Fresno State College, I encountered the verse of Robinson Jeffers, whose mystical pantheism opened my soul to the constitutive religious reality sustaining the cosmos, and I dropped out of college to go back to the land and become a poet in my own right, to plant a vineyard, commune with nature, and marry my highschool sweetheart.

In World War II I was drafted as a conscientious objector and spent three and a half years in the work camps of Oregon. At Waldport I headed a Fine Arts Program and helped establish the Untide Press, one of the few experimental presses of the war period. After release I migrated to San Francisco, joining the group of anarchists and poets around Kenneth Rexroth. I remarried, this time to the writer Mary Fabilli. Through her hands I encountered Catholicism, and we separated to enter the Roman Catholic Church in 1949. There followed a year on a Guggenheim Fellowship, and another year of troubled interior search; I served with the Catholic Worker movement in the Oakland slums, and resolved to leave the world to find my vocation as a monk, just as I had once left college to find my vocation as a poet.

Thus I became a Dominican lay brother in 1951, receiving the name of Brother Antoninus and for seven years of monastic withdrawal disappeared from the literary scene. I re-emerged with the San Francisco Renaissance in the late fifties, identifying with the Beat Generation because it proclaimed against a triumphant American pragmatism the necessity for mystical vision, and because as a literary movement it launched dionysian revolt against that pretentious highbrow formalism which, owing to the disassociation between the American poet and the American people, is always able to pass itself off as genuine tradition. Resuming publication, I used the detached freedom possible in monastic life to spend long periods on the poetry reading circuits, developing my own platform style based on oracular Beat intensity as befitting the prophetic mission of the poet, but embodying my own sense of the encounter which has, since Isaiah, constituted the archetype of religious awareness whenever a poet and his people confront.

I began as a nature poet with religious overtones but upon embracing Catholicism began to write a poetry of emphatic religious content etched against the immense backdrop of the American West. It is not surprising, then, that stylistically I favor a more rhetorical idiom than is currently fashionable. Rhetoric is the vehicle of consequence. That it can be faked does not dispense us from its essential use, for life is consequential, existence is infinitely consequential. The area of deepest consequence I believe to be the sexual exaltation and travail between man and woman, insofar as this encounter is the analogue of the exaltation and travail between man and God. I believe that the solution to the problem of violence is found only in the Cross, but I also believe that the poet alone can accommodate the violence of his age to the Cross. This for me constitutes his archtypal role as prophet to his time. It is his failure, and it is awesome, that sends the best minds of his generation in search of solutions where none can ever be found.

(1974) In 1969 I left the Dominican Order to marry Susanna Rickson, and spent two years with her and her infant son Jude at Stinson Beach, north of San Francisco. In 1971 I became Poet in Residence at Kresge College, University of California, Santa Cruz. My preoccupation with the Cross as solution to the mystery of violence, noted above, has not abated, but in the ecological crisis has shifted to the numen subsistent in Nature, as totem, or metaphor, in the encounter between man and God. Rational European theological speculation exhausted the human and divine aspects of the Incarnation. It remains now to recover the atavistic implications inherent in the flesh of Christ. Thus in the final phase of my life now opening I look for aboriginal modes of response to the fact of existence on this continent, and in my work will seek to recover the pertinence of Wilderness as purifier to the corrupt civilized dream.

(1980) The publication of *The Veritable Years* in 1978 finally placed before the public the shape of my overall endeavor, the lifetime trilogy I have chosen to call *The Crooked Lines of God.* Composed of three related volumes, *The Residual Years: Poems 1934–1948*, *The Veritable Years: Poems 1949–1966*, and *The Integral Years: Poems 1966–*, it constitutes a sort of Hegelian triad in its accent of thesis, antithesis, and synthesis. Thus, the primal preoccupation with Nature in *The Residual Years* was followed by a corresponding preoccupation with God in *The Veritable Years*, emerging as a consequent preoccupation with God-in-Nature in *The Integral Years*, as indicated in my 1974 statement above.

Just as the first two volumes were composed of private printings, booklets and broadsides issued as I went along, so with *The Integral Years*, now in progress. Its chief components so far are the collections *Man Fate* and *The Masks of Drought*, but the individual poems *Tendril in the Mesh*, *The City Does Not Die*, and *Blame It on the Jet Stream!* will all take their place within it. For across the whole span of *Crooked Lines* the thematic disposition is markedly chronological. And this in turn is because the abiding force is confessional, whether as thesis, antithesis, or synthesis. It is this confessional attitude that meets the issue of relevance to the central concern of contemporary poetry. As M. L. Rosenthal has written, "To build a great poem out of the predicament and horror of the lost Self has been the recurrent effort of the most ambitious poetry of the last century." Hence it is the attitude of existential confrontation, whether with Man or God or Nature, that both shapes the trilogy in its thrust towards wholeness and denotes its relevance to its time.

* * *

Slowly, from various outposts he found during the 1940's, William Everson began to send out his own kind of direct, emphatic poems of social judgment. Though he listed no church affiliation when he was held as a conscientious objector in work camps in Oregon and California during World War II, his writings – like those of Robinson Jeffers, who influenced him greatly – were always moral and principled, and serious; and by the time those poems came into general notice in the early 1950's William Everson had become Brother Antoninus, a Dominican lay brother, and one of the early and influential participants in the "San Francisco Group" of "Beat Poets."

In his career since that early seasoning, when he actually had to live outside American society and look at it long, Brother Antoninus has continued his measured assessment, in many periodicals and many books and many public readings. His language has taken on religious tonality but in a way to make ritual violently confront jagged experience. His progression has not been so much toward leaving the Robinson Jeffers non-human stance as it has been toward combining the brute world and the church. He hammers the language of religion into statements that create shock: bleak juxtapositions, stern assertions. In his most characteristic works, the landscapes and the creature-scapes of a rugged coastal region get yoked into a chant of judgment, as in *A Canticle to the Waterbirds*:

> Clack your beaks you cormorants and kittiwakes,
> North on those rock-croppings finger-jutted into the rough Pacific surge ...
> Break wide your harsh and salt-encrusted beaks unmade for song
> And say a praise up to the Lord.

—William Stafford

EVERWINE, Peter (Paul). American. Born in Detroit, Michigan, 14 February 1930. Educated at Northwestern University, Evanston, Illinois, B.S. 1952; Stanford University, California, 1958–59; University of Iowa, Iowa City, Ph.D. 1959. Served in the United States Army, 1952–54. Divorced; two children. Instructor in English, University of Iowa, 1959–62. Since 1962, Professor of English, California State University, Fresno. Recipient: Lamont Poetry Selection Award, 1972. Address: 2645 Moroa, Fresno, California 93704, U.S.A.

Publications

Verse

The Broken Frieze. Mt. Vernon, Iowa, Hillside Press, 1958.
In the House of Light: Thirty Aztec Poems. Iowa City, Stone Wall Press, 1970.
Collecting the Animals. New York, Atheneum, 1973.
Keeping the Night. New York, Atheneum, 1977.

* * *

The quantity of Peter Everwine's poetry is slight; the quality is gem-like. Some of the poems in *Keeping the Night* were collected earlier in *The New Naked Poetry*; "nude" would have been a more fitting adjective to describe his art. His poetry is neither raw, nor bare. It is subtler – precise, but unadorned; palpable and dumb. It achieves its effect slowly. It wants to be read over and over. It unfolds in silence and in empty spaces. "Night" from *Keeping the Night* is typical of Everwine's manner; it is quite like Haiku:

In the lamplight falling
on the white tablecloth
my plate
my shining loaf of quietness.

I sit down.
Through the open door
all the absent I love enter
and we eat.

At its best, Everwine's poetry is deceptively simple. Largely monosyllabic, invariably brief, his poems mold speech to express unspoken, deeply-felt truths found in moments selected from ordinary life, either his own or that of his kin.

The earlier volume *In The House of Light* is comprised of his translations of Spanish transcriptions of poems of the Nahuatl Indians in Mexico. Everwine observed that one of the words used to mean poet in Nahuatl is "tlamatine: one who knows something," and in his verse translations he offers "an attempt to locate that ancient presence in my own speech" (*Collecting the Animals*). He succeeds excellently.

The seeming simplicity of his poetry establishes an aura of trust and candor rarely found in contemporary poetry. His poetry is unmarred by self-consciousness. There is no stridency, no verbal fireworks, no exhibitionism. Nor is there any hint of sentimentality in the many memories he evokes. In "Drinking Cold Water" (*Collecting the Animals*) his recreation of his tough-spirited grandmother who "lay down in the shale hills of Pennsylvania" 20 years ago is completely authentic:

all I can think of is your house –
the pump at the sink
spilling a trough of clear
cold water from the well –
and you, old love,
sleeping in your dark dress
like a hard, white root.

His Italian grandfather who emigrated to the United States and spat in the wind, quit his job, and returned to Italy every time his bosses maddened him is depicted with equal vividness in "Paola Castelnuova" (from *Keeping the Night*) which ends with the grandson, the persona, penning the will the old man did not leave:

I, Paola, give my stone to the priests.
Tell them to make it bread.

Water I give to those loving how money sweats.

Fire I leave to my children

As for air,
give it to the buzzard who is the first
and last of kings.

The other portraits in *Keeping the Night* and *Collecting the Animals*, of Dorothy, "her ass rubbed raw through half the fields in Armstrong County," of his emigrant mother who was never really American until grass closed over her gravestone, of his sons, are equally precise and real.

Whether Everwine searches for a language to hold night's secrets, or childhood recollections, or the paradoxical condition of man who eats dinner talking with his guests of the past dead and never looking at "the axe lying in the courtyard, a crust of blood and feathers on its edge" ("The Dinner," *Keeping the Night*), he catches exactly the experience he knows. He has learned his experience and his craft "hand over hand," as he says in another poem in a slightly different context.

—Carol Simpson Stern

EWART, Gavin (Buchanan). British. Born in London, 4 February 1916. Educated at Wellington College; Christ's College, Cambridge (Exhibitioner), B.A. (honours) in English 1936. Served in the Royal Artillery during World War II. Married; two children. Worked for the British Council, 1946–52; advertising copywriter, 1952–71. Since 1971, Free-lance Writer. Recipient: Cholmondeley Award, 1971; Eric Gregory traveling scholarship, 1977. Address: 57 Kenilworth Court, Lower Richmond Road, London S.W.15, England.

PUBLICATIONS

Verse

Poems and Songs. London, Fortune Press, 1939.
Londoners. London, Heinemann, 1964.
Throwaway Lines. Richmond, Surrey, Keepsake Press, 1964.
Two Children. Richmond, Surrey, Keepsake Press, 1966.
Pleasures of the Flesh. London, Alan Ross, 1966.
The Deceptive Grin of the Gravel Porters. London, Alan Ross, 1968.
Twelve Apostles. Belfast, Ulsterman, 1970.
Folio, with others. Frensham, Surrey, Sceptre Press, 1971.
The Gavin Ewart Show. London, Trigram Press, 1971.
Venus. London, Poem-of-the-Month Club, 1972.
The Select Party. Richmond, Surrey, Keepsake Press, 1972.
Alphabet Soup. Oxford, Sycamore Press, 1972.
Penguin Modern Poets 25, with B. S. Johnson and Zulfikar Ghose. London, Penguin, 1974.

Be My Guest! London, Trigram Press, 1975.
A Question Partly Answered. Knotting, Bedfordshire, Sceptre Press, 1976.
No Fool Like an Old Fool. London, Gollancz, 1976.
A Morden Tower Reading 5, with Fleur Adcock. Newcastle upon Tyne, Morden Tower, 1977.
Or Where a Young Penguin Lies Screaming. London, Gollancz, 1977.
The First Eleven. London, Poet and Printer, 1977.
All My Little Ones: The Shortest Poems of Gavin Ewart. London, Anvil Press Poetry, 1978.

Play

Tobermory, music by John Gardner, adaptation of the story by Saki (produced London, 1977).

Other

Editor, *Forty Years On: An Anthology of School Songs.* London, Sidgwick and Jackson, 1964.
Editor, *The Batsford Book of Children's Verse.* London, Batsford, 1976.
Editor, *New Poems 1977–78.* London, Hutchinson, 1977.
Editor, *The Batsford Book of Light Verse for Children.* London, Batsford, 1978.

Manuscript Collections: National Library of Scotland, Edinburgh; Humanities Research Center, University of Texas, Austin; Brynmor Jones Library, University of Hull.

Critical Study: by David Montrose, in *Honest Ulsterman* (Belfast), Spring 1978.

Gavin Ewart comments:

Formal. Rhyming. More recently – experimental in vocabulary and form. Alliterative. Subjects mainly concerned with the pressures and pleasures of contemporary urban life.

The "school" of Auden was from the start a major influence.

* * *

Gavin Ewart began precociously early. In 1933, at the age of seventeen, he was contributing assured and witty poems to Geoffrey Grigson's *New Verse.* They included "Phallus in Wonderland," a set of epigrams and short poems written in skilful pastiche of Pound, Eliot, Auden and other contemporaries, and "Audenesque for an Initiation," which showed Ewart to be an early if critical admirer of the dominating English poet of the thirties. As a young poet in the pre-war years Ewart exhibited the social and political concerns of the age, though in a wryly individual voice. What is striking about his subsequent career is that more than forty years later Ewart is still writing in much the same way about similar subjects: the occasional splendours and frequent absurdities of sex; himself, as *l'homme moyen sensuel*; and the kaleidoscope surface of modern urban life. From the beginning Ewart has been the master of a kind of writing that is posed between amusing light verse and an authentic poetry of serious social comment or personal reflection. When the poise fails he is inclined to fall into slack triviality on the one hand or neat sentimentalities on the other. He has a good ear and can write memorable lines and elegant lyrics. At the same time, he is rather complacently attached to his favourite stylistic devices; having found that "kisses" makes an effective rhyme for "cissies" in a poem published in 1937 he is still using the same rhymes in poems in *The Gavin Ewart Show* in 1971.

Thematically, too, there is variation rather than great development. In his earliest poems

Ewart treated sexual subjects with the characteristic bravado and anxiety of adolescence. "Young Blondes: A Religious Poem" is a crisp and poignant instance from the forties. In the sixties and seventies similar themes are presented with the more urgent anxiety of middle-age, often rather tastelessly. If there is a new element in Ewart's poetry it is a greater compassion that undercuts his characteristic tone of cool ironic comment on human folly. A striking example of this quality is "The Gentle Sex" (1974), a horrified and horrifying account of an atrocity in Northern Ireland. Increasingly his greatest irony is directed at himself, as in "The Ewart Organization" or the delightful "2001: The Tennyson/Hardy Poem" which looks forward to a time when the poet will have outlived all his contemporaries. Here Ewart once more displays his skill as a writer of pastiche, this time of Thomas Hardy:

Soon comes the day when the stream runs dry
And the boat runs back as the tide is turning,
The voice once strong no more than a sigh
By the hearth where the fire is scarcely burning.
Stiff in my chair like a children's guy,
Simply because I have no seniors
The literati will raise the cry:
Ewart's a genius!

Ewart preserves in a remarkably pure form the positive qualities of the poetry of the thirties: the wit, the formal skill, the willingness to combine comic means and serious ends, and, at his best, an attractive intellectual gaiety.

—Bernard Bergonzi

EZEKIEL, Nissim. Indian. Born in Bombay, 16 December 1924. Educated at the University of Bombay (Lagu Prize, 1947), 1941–47, M.A. 1947. Married Daisy Jacob in 1952; two daughters and one son. Lecturer, Khalsa College, Bombay, 1947–48; Professor of English and Vice-Principal, Mithibai College, Bombay, 1961–72. Since 1972, Reader in American Literature, Bombay University. Visiting Professor, University of Leeds, 1964, and University of Chicago, 1967. Editor, *Quest* magazine, 1955–57; Associate Editor, *Imprint* magazine, 1961–67; Art Critic, *The Times of India*, Bombay, 1964–67. Lived in London, 1948–52. Recipient: Farfield Foundation travel grant, 1957. Address: The Retreat, Bellasis Road, Bombay 400008, India.

PUBLICATIONS

Verse

A Time to Change and Other Poems. London, Fortune Press, 1952.
Sixty Poems. Bombay, Strand Bookshop, 1953.
The Third. Bombay, Strand Bookshop, 1958.
The Unfinished Man: Poems Written in 1959. Calcutta, Writers Workshop, 1960.
The Exact Name: Poems 1960–1964. Calcutta, Writers Workshop, 1965.
Pergamon Poets, with others, edited by Howard Sergeant. Oxford, Pergamon Press, 1969.
Hymns in Darkness. New Delhi and London, Oxford University Press, 1976.

Plays

Three Plays (includes *Nalini, Marriage Poem, The Sleepwalkers*) (produced Bombay, 1969). Calcutta, Writers Workshop, 1969.

Other

The Actor: A Sad and Funny Story for Children of Most Ages. Bombay, India Book House, 1974.

Editor, *A New Look at Communism.* Bombay, Indian Committee for Cultural Freedom, 1963.
Editor, *Indian Writers in Conference.* Mysore, P.E.N. All India Writers Conference, 1964.
Editor, *Writing in India.* Lucknow, P.E.N. All India Writers Conference, 1965.
Editor, *An Emerson Reader.* Bombay, Popular Prakashan, 1965.
Editor, *A Martin Luther King Reader.* Bombay, Popular Prakashan, 1969.
Editor, *All My Sons*, by Arthur Miller. Madras, Oxford University Press, 1972.

Critical Studies: *The Poetry of Nissim Ezekiel* by Meena Belliapa and Rajeev Taranath, Calcutta, Writers Workshop, 1966; student edition of *The Unfinished Man*, Calcutta, Writers Workshop, 1969; by Rajeev Taranath in *Quest 74* (Bombay), January–February 1972; *Nissim Ezekiel: A Study* by Chetan Karnani, New Delhi, Arnold-Heinemann, 1974; "Nissim Ezekiel Issue" of *Journal of South Asian Literature* (Rochester, Michigan), September–December 1974.

Nissim Ezekiel comments:

I do not identify myself with any particular school of poetry. Labelled "Indo-Anglian" or "Indo-English," i.e., an Indian poet writing in English, I accept the label. I am satisfied at present to be included among the poets of the Commonwealth, but hope to be better known in the U.K. and U.S.A. as an *Indian* poet. I consider myself a modernist but not avant-garde.

I have written in the traditional verse forms as well as in free verse. Major influences: Pound, Eliot, Auden, MacNeice, Spender, Yeats and modern English and American poetry in general. My latest poetry, 1966–73, is beyond all influences. Some of my recent poems are in Indian English. I have written "found" poems on scientific subjects and several on newspaper reports and personal letters. Major themes: love, personal integration, the Indian contemporary scene, modern urban life, spiritual values. I aim at clarity above all, claim never to have written an obscure poem. I like to make controlled, meaningful statements, avoiding extremes of thought and expression.

* * *

In the foreword to *Sixty Poems*, Nissim Ezekiel confesses that his main reason for publishing the poems is that he has not the courage to destroy them. "There is in each line or phrase, an idea or image which helps me to maintain some sort of continuity in my life. If I could transcend the personal importance of these poems, I would not publish them.... [The present collection] does not claim to be poetry, but it reveals a few small discoveries in the pursuit of poetry." What makes Ezekiel worthy of the respect of students of contemporary Indian poetry is this dedication. His scrupulousness is both aesthetic and moral. He is deeply concerned with the craftsmanship of his poems and with self-understanding. While there is much in his early volumes that is crude in thought, feeling and expression, with *The Exact Name* Ezekiel achieved a fine combination of freedom and discipline, of alertness and relaxation: "To force the pace and never to be still/Is not the way of those who study birds/

Or women." (The poem from which this quotation comes, "Poet, Lover, Birdwatcher," is itself a fine example of this development.) There is still an occasional line or two in this collection that does not quite fit in – for example, the line "Exactly as described in books on Indian birds" in the otherwise excellent poem "Paradise Flycatcher." Ezekiel's recent collection *Hymns in Darkness* bears ample testimony to the steady development of his poetic personality: a fine sense of rhythm; an exact diction, sparing of adjectives; utter clarity; a clear eye both for the external world and the internal; and a genuinely sincere self-appraisal which is different in kind from the attitudinizing of some of his contemporaries with whom such self-introspection is a mode of hedging their bets. Many of the poems in this collection delicately etch a scene or character in such a way that the "comment on experience" is both unobtrusive and irresistible ("Ganga").

Ezekiel is an Indian Jew, and a certain measure of cultural isolation is perhaps unavoidable in the circumstances. While this isolation has sharpened his powers of observation and inclined him towards rationalism and humanism, several of the poems express an unfulfilled desire to discover religious values also. He is aware that he has been clinging "too long to the same static vision" ("The Room"). He is aware that his prayers have been those of an egoist. The "Hymns" end with the declaration: "Belief will not save you,/nor unbelief.//All you have/is the sense of unreality,/unfathomable/as it yields its secrets/ slowly/one/by/one." The connexion between belief and a sense of reality is left unexplored. It is also not clear whether reality simply "is," or whether it has "secrets" that have to be wrested; and how reality differs from the romantic ego's perceptions of the external world and of itself. These dilemmas confront every sensitive poet who is unable to acquire a sense of tradition. Since Ezekiel rarely repeats himself, his next collection will be of the greatest interest to students of Indian poetry in English.

—S. Nagarajan

FAINLIGHT, Ruth. American. Born in New York City. Educated at schools in America and England. Address: 14 Ladbroke Terrace, London W.11, England.

PUBLICATIONS

Verse

A Forecast, A Fable. London, Outposts, 1958.
Cages. London, Macmillan, 1966; Chester Springs, Pennsylvania, Dufour, 1967.
18 Poems from 1966. London, Turret, 1967.
To See the Matter Clearly and Other Poems. London, Macmillan 1968; Chester Springs, Pennsylvania, Dufour, 1969.
Poems, with Alan Sillitoe and Ted Hughes. London, Rainbow Press, 1971.
The Region's Violence. London, Hutchinson, 1973.
21 Poems. London, Turret, 1973.
Another Full Moon. London, Hutchinson, 1976.
Two Fire Poems. Knotting, Bedfordshire, Sceptre Press, 1977.
The Function of Tears. Knotting, Bedfordshire, Sceptre Press, 1979.
Sibyls and Other Poems. London, Hutchinson, 1980.
Sibyls. Northampton, Massachusetts, Gehenna Press, 1980.

Plays

All Citizens Are Soldiers, with Alan Sillitoe, adaptation of a play by Lope de Vega (produced London, 1967). London, Macmillan, and Chester Springs, Pennsylvania, Dufour, 1969.

Short Stories

Penguin Modern Stories 9, with others. London, Penguin, 1971.
Daylife and Nightlife. London, Deutsch, 1971.

* * *

Though married to Alan Sillitoe, the English novelist and poet, Ruth Fainlight is nevertheless American by birth. As such she is one of a small but distinguished group of American women poets, expatriated by marriage. The most famous number of this group is, of course, Sylvia Plath, with whom Ruth Fainlight was on close terms. Surprisingly, one has to hunt quite hard to find the Plath influence in Fainlight's poetry. Essentially, hers is a much quieter voice. Though it sometimes speaks of desperation, the despair is stubbornly combatted; if possible, the energies it generates are turned into something useful – an attitude well summed up in two lines from Ruth Fainlight's most recent collection: "The poem, though derived from suffering, does/Not describe its chill of death." On the whole, this poet does not as yet enjoy the reputation she deserves – partly because her development has been a gradual one; partly because she displays an uncomfortable honesty about aspects of character – aggressive impulses, for example – which many readers would prefer not to confront.

—Edward Lucie-Smith

FAIRFAX, John. British. Born in London, 9 November 1930. Educated at public school and by private tutors. Married; two sons. Editor of *Nimbus* magazine in the early 1950's. School teacher, 1955–62. British Editor, *Panache* magazine, New York. Since 1967, Director, Phoenix Press, Newbury, Berkshire. Since 1968, Co-Founding Director, Arvon Foundation, Devon. Recipient: Society of Authors award; Arts Council grant. Address: The Thatched Cottage, Hermitage, Newbury, Berkshire, England.

PUBLICATIONS

Verse

This I Say: Twelve Poems. Newbury, Berkshire, Phoenix Press, 1967.
The 5th Horseman of the Apocalypse. Newbury, Berkshire, Phoenix Press, 1969.
Double Image, with Michael Baldwin and Brian Patten. London, Longman, 1972.
Adrift on the Star Brow of Taliesin. Newbury, Berkshire, Phoenix Press, 1975.

Other

Editor, *Listen to This: A Contemporary Anthology*. London, Longman, 1967.
Editor, *Stop and Listen: An Anthology of Thirteen Living Poets*. London, Longman, 1969.

Editor, *Frontier of Going: An Anthology of Space Poetry.* London, Panther, 1969.
Editor, *Horizons.* London, Arnold, 1971.

Critical Studies: by Graham Fawcett, in *Southern Arts Review* (Winchester, Hampshire), March and May 1970; by Roger Garfitt, in *London Magazine*, August–September 1975.

John Fairfax comments:

My style has been called "analogical." I go along with this. Form tending to be traditional. I write for the ear and voice as well as for the reading eye. Rhythm is very important. I like my work to be read aloud. I am concerned with a magical and spell-casting quality in poetry – with the power to encompass myth and mystery.

* * *

John Fairfax's juxtaposition of space-age philosophy and rural concerns is an interesting one; but it has not too often manifested itself in his poems, whose general weakness is that they cannot sustain the reader's interest by rhythmical or linguistic means. His most ambitious and successful poem is the relatively long *The 5th Horseman of the Apocalypse*, which runs to over 600 short lines. One wonders if the author had Blok's extraordinary *The Twelve* in mind, even though its style has not influenced him. For here, too, his men "Hack through dead cities." In this poem as a whole, Fairfax has subsumed his dark theme under an imaginative language far more effective than anything found in his earlier poems; his handling of the short line is reasonably deft and sure:

Four horsemen and hounds
Belong to the crossed master
Of hounds and horse.
They are photographed by dazzling
Kodacolours of a magnifying
Eye which repeats
The image into new birth
Until nothing exists....

This vision is sustained, and the ambiguous figure of the fifth horseman is introduced with proper dramatic effect. Furthermore, the performance of the poem does add a genuine, and not merely rhetorical, dimension to it.

—Martin Seymour-Smith

FALCK, Colin. British. Born in London, 14 July 1934. Educated at Christ's Hospital; Magdalen College, Oxford, B.A. in philosophy, politics and economics 1957, B.A. in philosophy, psychology and physiology 1959. Served in the British Army, 1952–54. Lecturer in Sociology, London School of Economics, 1961–62; part-time lecturer in literature, London and Hertfordshire, 1962–64. Since 1964, Lecturer in Humanities, Chelsea College, London. Associate Editor, *The Review*, Oxford and London, 1962–72. Agent: John Johnson, 51–54 Goschen Buildings, 12–13 Henrietta Street, London WC2E 8LF. Address: 16 St. Augustine's Road, London NW1 9RN, England.

PUBLICATIONS

Verse

The Garden in the Evening, adaptations of poems by Antonio Machado. Oxford, The Review, 1964.
Promises. London, The Review, 1969.
Backwards into the Smoke. Cheadle, Cheshire, Carcanet Press, 1973.
In This Dark Light. London, TNR, 1978.

Other

Editor, with Ian Hamilton, *Poems since 1900: An Anthology of British and American Verse in the Twentieth Century.* London, Macdonald and Jane's, 1975.

Colin Falck comments:

Writing a poem means persuading the semi-verbal impulses which start up at the back of one's mind under the pressure of some insistent emotion to arrange themselves poetically on the page. By doing this one discovers more about what the emotion was. The only test I can find for a poem's validity is that it should be moving – should generate the distinctive feeling or *frisson* (cf. Housman and others) which signals the presence of poetry. For me this has a lot to do with rhythm and sound-texture – but no analysis seems to take one very near to understanding what is really going on.

The poems I have written so far are quite short. I could wish they were longer, but the writing of short poems has been – for me – a bottleneck that has to be gone through. I would like to be able to get through it and to move on from poems of straightforward mood and atmosphere to poems which handle larger amounts of material and more public themes – but which handle them poetically, rather than merely versifying attitudes and opinions or stringing out a lot of images on one long idea (this may be some kind of reaction to the poetry which was prevalent in Britain during the 1950's). *Backwards into the Smoke* is a mood-sequence, to do with learning to accept life, learning where one's more negative and irrational impulses can lead, hoping to accept such impulses and remain dedicated to life and humanity. I would like, before very long, to be able to write poems which look more obviously adequate to such heavyweight preoccupations, and have perhaps begun to do so in one or two poems included in the pamphlet *In This Dark Light.*

* * *

Colin Falck is one of a group of poets and critics associated during the nineteen-sixties with the English magazine, *The Review*, who made a deliberate attempt to revive Imagism as a poetic discipline and a mode of imaginative apprehension. Falck is an explicit theorist in criticism and he has argued that Imagism continues the essential insights of Romanticism: a poem, whatever else it does, must articulate the emotion of a particular moment as truthfully as possible. Falck's own poems present Imagist notations of encounters and places. They are calculatedly small-scale and, in a sense, insubstantial; sometimes they remain merely frail and even trivial, but at other times they achieve a haunting resonance with a very few words. In his love poems Falck is courageously vulnerable; where they succeed they are tremulously beautiful and where they fail they tumble into bathos. He is literally on firmer ground in his poems based on places, such as "Central Ohio," "End of the Summer Term at Christ's Hospital," "Box Hill" and "Lyme Regis Station." He is considerably influenced by modern Spanish poetry, and has published a set of exquisite translations of poems by Antonio Machado.

—Bernard Bergonzi

FEINSTEIN, Elaine. British. Born in Bootle, Lancashire, 24 October 1930. Educated at Wyggeston Grammar School, Leicester; Newnham College, Cambridge. Married Dr. Arnold Feinstein in 1956; three sons. Editorial Staff Member, Cambridge University Press, 1960–62; Lecturer in English, Bishop's Stortford Training College, Hertfordshire, 1963–66; Assistant Lecturer in Literature, University of Essex, Wivenhoe, 1967–70. Recipient: Arts Council grant, 1970; Daisy Miller Award, for fiction, 1971; Kelsus Prize, 1978. Agent: (verse) Olwyn Hughes, 100 Chetwynd Road, London N.W.5; (fiction) Hilary Rubinstein, A. P. Watt and Son, 26–28 Bedford Row, London WC1R 4HL. Address: c/o Hutchinson Publishing Group Ltd., 3 Fitzroy Square, London W1P 6JD, England.

PUBLICATIONS

Verse

In a Green Eye. London, Goliard Press, 1966.
The Magic Apple Tree. London, Hutchinson, 1971.
At the Edge. Rushden, Northamptonshire, Sceptre Press, 1972.
The Celebrants and Other Poems. London, Hutchinson, 1973.
Some Unease and Angels: Selected Poems. London, Hutchinson, and University Center, Michigan, Green River Press, 1977.

Play

Television Play: *Breath*, 1975.

Novels

The Circle. London, Hutchinson, 1970.
The Amberstone Exit. London, Hutchinson, 1972.
The Glass Alembic. London, Hutchinson, 1973; as *The Crystal Garden*, New York, Dutton, 1974.
Children of the Rose. London, Hutchinson, 1975.
The Ecstasy of Dr. Miriam Garner. London, Hutchinson, 1976.
The Shadow Master. London, Hutchinson, 1978; New York, Simon and Schuster, 1979.

Short Story

Matters of Chance. London, Covent Garden Press, 1972.

Other

Editor, *Selected Poems of John Clare.* London, University Tutorial Press, 1968.
Editor, with Fay Weldon, *New Stories 4.* London, Hutchinson, 1979.

Translator, *The Selected Poems of Marina Tsvetayeva.* London, Oxford University Press, 1971.
Translator, *Three Russian Poets: Margarita Aliger, Yunna Moritz, Bella Akhmadulina.* Manchester, Carcanet Press, 1978.

Manuscript Collection: Cambridge University.

Critical Study: *British Poetry since 1960*, edited by Michael Schmidt and Grevel Lindop, Oxford, Carcanet Press, 1972.

Elaine Feinstein comments:

When I began writing in the early sixties I felt the influence of the Americans (Stevens and perhaps even Emily Dickinson as much as W. C. Williams); and I suppose the turning point in finding a voice of my own arose, paradoxically, from working on the translations of Marina Tsvetayeva and other modern Russian poets. And perhaps also from writing prose, which began at first as an extension of the poetic impulse, but (after four novels) works as a channel for the exploration of my humanist concerns, and leaves me freer now to take greater risks with language when I choose to write lyric poetry. Perhaps both experiences have encouraged me to write longer poems (such as the title poem of *The Celebrants*), and to find longer lines and new rhythms, as well as richer subject matter.

* * *

"Anniversary," which opens the collection *The Magic Apple Tree*, makes the act of faith in humanity on which all Elaine Feinstein's poetry is posited:

Listen, I shall have to whisper it
into your heart directly: we are all
supernatural/every day
we rise new creatures/cannot be predicted.

Confronting the banal, flat surfaces of modern existence, symbolised by the mud, mists and rain of the East Anglian fens, "our brackish waters" ("The Magic Apple Tree"), she acknowledges the limitations set to the human by "the tyranny of landscape" ("Moon") and by our rooting in a particular and all-pervasive present: "How do you change the weather in the blood?" ("I Have Seen Worse Days Turn"). The techniques of poetry are the "alembic," the alchemist's vessel which effects a transformation which is not the transcendence but a sharpening of the real, the celebration of "what in the landscape of cities/has to be prized" ("Some Thoughts on Where"). Feinstein shares with the reader the liberating power of new perceptions: "We have broken some magic barrier" to become "open to the surprises of the season" ("Renaissance February 7"). She delights in the surprises of imagery, colour, syntax, tone, and rhythms which set "your own East Anglian children/... dancing. To an alien drum" ("Moon"). "Our Vegetable Love Shall Grow" develops the surrealist quality of Marvell's image, in the mock-horror of a vampire crocus, grotesquely yoking the energies of nature and the city to drain away the lesser vitality of the human. Black humour is the vehicle for modern man – and woman – to reassert dominance of a reality that threatens to overwhelm. The invocation of Buster Keaton ("Out") is no accident; nor is the marvellous, punning cynicism of "West," whose hesitating and stabbing rhythms embrace exactly the bitterly revealing twists of Mae West's comedy.

Beyond the struggle, the creative effort for freedom, what is sought is a sense of repose – "to live freely in silver light/here a visitor" ("Some Local Resistance"), experiencing "the peculiar joy of abandoning restlessness" which is generated by the icon, or by the "infantine" vision of Samuel Palmer's painting ("The Magic Apple Tree"). Feinstein moves incessantly between the turmoil and the sense of peace, carrying the poet's burden of personal responsibility for the remaking of harmony and unity out of a torn, disjointed world. The broken utterances of "Marriage" catch the pain of human separateness on an intensely personal note:

tender whenever we touch   what
else we share   this flesh   we
bring together   it hurts to
think of dying as we lie close

In the realm of private loves, Feinstein can convey the kind of raw emotion she found in

Tsvetayeva, whom she praised in the introduction to her translations for the "wholeness of her self-exposure." She also, however, goes beyond the purely personal. *At the Edge* evokes the new understanding reached through the "lyric daze" of carnal passion, but makes it clear that the knowledge gained at these frontiers can only be kept through the interpretative but distancing medium of poetic language: "We were washed in salt on the same pillow together/and we watched the walls change level gently as water...."

The title poem of *The Celebrants* recounts man's perpetual quest for meaning through love, science, art, and religion, seeking to evade the limits of death and corruption bounding the world of the body, waiting for the gratuitous moment of poetic surprise "to free us from the/black drama/of the magician." The other poems in this volume have a darker tone than earlier work, a deeper and richer seriousness, and a more biting and bitter humour. But still the abiding note struck is one of an optimism which finds in given reality not only its torment but its reassurance: "the earth has another language, we have been/given complexities of the soil against the taste of the grave" ("A Ritual Turning," dedicated to Octavio Paz). Her recent volume *Some Unease and Angels*, essentially a well-chosen retrospect with some new poems, confirms her determination to create through language a new balance of man and his world with nature and its warring elements, as in "Watersmeet":

> everywhere plant flesh
> and rich ores had eaten into each other, so that
> peat, rain, green leaves and August fused
> even the two of us together; we took
> a new balance from the two defenceless
> kingdoms bonded in hidden warfare underfoot.

—Jennifer Birkett

FELDMAN, Irving (Mordecai). American. Born in Brooklyn, New York, 22 September 1928. Educated at the City College of New York, B.S. 1950; Columbia University, New York, M.A. 1953. Married Carmen Alvarez in 1955; one son. Taught at the University of Puerto Rico, Rio Piedras, 1954–56, University of Lyons, France, 1957–58, and Kenyon College, Gambier, Ohio, 1958–64. Since 1964, Professor of English, State University of New York, Buffalo. Recipient: Jewish Book Council of America Kovner Award, 1962; Ingram Merrill Foundation grant, 1963; National Institute of Arts and Letters grant, 1973; Guggenheim Fellowship, 1973. Address: 349 Berryman Drive, Buffalo, New York 14226, U.S.A.

PUBLICATIONS

Verse

Work and Days and Other Poems. Boston, Little Brown, and London, Deutsch, 1961.
The Pripet Marshes and Other Poems. New York, Viking Press, 1965.
Magic Papers and Other Poems. New York, Harper, 1970.
Lost Originals, New York, Holt Rinehart, 1972.
Leaping Clear. New York, Viking Press, 1976.
New and Selected Poems. New York, Viking Press, 1979.

Critical Study: *Alone with America*, by Richard Howard, New York, Atheneum, 1969.

* * *

Irving Feldman has always been a Jewish poet, which is to say that his work has been typically marked by an ardent spirituality tending frequently toward verbal abstraction and vaguely detailed suffering. Like Randall Jarrell, he has had a strong feeling for dream-states, though without Jarrell's ear for and sensitivity to the language of dreams. Richard Howard has described his mature verse as "the expression of a full heart" committed to the examination of loss. This sense of loss, and of faith at odds with obvious circumstance, is so consistently and impressively felt in Feldman's work that one hesitates to demand particulars by way of substantiation. What we've lost, according to Feldman, is precisely those objects of faith which make us feel at home with our longings and comfortably warm, rather than a little queasy, in our affections.

In one of his early volumes, Feldman spoke of his desire to teach his fathers – the insulted and injured – of a Jewish past it is this poet's function to reclaim and repossess, "the light-hearted dance," but he is not authentically of the light-hearted. He is in fact endowed with much the same spirit that illuminates the work of others more fatally bound and defined by blood and tradition. Feldman is a singer of hope and modest suffering in the service of vision. What he aims at is the change of heart which is nothing so grand as those transformations of character or of the human condition which a great many American poets have taken as their burden. Feldman's change of heart is typically more modest, a desire not for light-heartedness which would be a function of absolute self-mastery or self-effacement, but for that temporary lightness which involves at once accommodation to things as they are and a refusal of slavish acquiescence. Feldman's work represents what is best in the contemporary Jewish tradition, which is a combination of earnestness, faithfulness in search of suitable objects, and lucidity.

Sometimes, Feldman seems more in perfect control of his materials than we'd expected, and we feel a little suspicious – we know, of course, that the poet must be in charge, must master the materials of his vision, but ordinarily we like to feel that the poet is also himself possessed in a way that might almost be thought subversive to the purposes of craftsmanship and routine orderliness or coherence. We want the communicated impression that the poet is deeply moved by his vision, that in his desire to manifest it he will allow it to develop a momentum of its own. In reading Feldman, we sometimes want to ask whether he is expressing a passing fancy or a more permanent intuition of things.

At his best, Feldman manages a tone that is sharply ironic and commiserating by turns, or that rings with a prophetic authority that distinguishes him from any of his contemporaries. Some of Feldman's poems are conceptually intricate and sustained in a remarkable way, replete with verbal felicities of great wit and variety. More surprising, Feldman is an accomplished poet whose work clearly reveals a whole range of borrowed cadences, in his recent work from the late Randall Jarrell. These cadences are an aspect of Feldman's gift for ventriloquism, his inclination towards dramatic utterance. Though Feldman has more and more come to speak in his own voice, this voice has remained various, the expression of alternating masks. In working through these masks, Feldman betrays nothing of that anxiety which so pollutes the exchanges between other poets – one thinks for example of the altogether more tense and problematic borrowings that characterize the relation between Roethke and Yeats. Feldman's poetry works through tension and uncertainties, rather than allowing them to fester. In so doing, Feldman manages a complex evocation of the contemplative urgency of the faithful heart.

—Robert Boyers

FENTON, James (Martin). British. Born in Lincoln, 25 April 1949. Educated at Durham Chorister School; Repton School; Magdalen College, Oxford (Newdigate Prize, 1968), B.A. 1970. Assistant Literary Editor, 1971, Member, Editorial Staff, 1972–73, and since 1976, political columnist, *New Statesman*, London. Recipient: Eric Gregory Award, 1973. Address: c/o New Statesman, 10 Great Turnstile, London W.C.1, England.

PUBLICATIONS

Verse

Our Western Furniture. Oxford, Sycamore Press, 1968.
Put Thou Thy Tears into My Bottle. Oxford, Sycamore Press, 1969.
Terminal Moraine. London, Secker and Warburg, 1972.

James Fenton comments:

Eclectic, serious, should go far.

* * *

Immediately, James Fenton's verse has two striking features. The first is his technical skill, for he already sees more virtue in the labours of craftsmanship than many other young poets are prepared to. In his first collection we can follow this through from his varied handling of the sonnet in "Our Western Furniture" (21 sonnets) to the consciously smart performance of "Open Letter to Richard Crossman," with 25 stanzas rhyming abababcc. In the latter, even modesty is part of the smartness – "And I've failed even to twit/You in this style, by AUDEN out of BYRON."

The second feature is the considerable extent to which the substance of his poetry is detailed, factual and documented, as if his poetic function were primarily to fashion into verse the ideas and information culled by a voracious reader. Thus we have the biological material incorporated in "Frog" and "The Fruit-Grower in War-Time," and the reminiscences of the first Americans in Japan in "Our Western Furniture," the closing lines of which aptly describe his method: "we offer you an almost-fiction/Constructed on a grid of contradiction."

That poets should be willing to meet and utilise the multifarious information which is so accessible to the modern reader is vitally important for this is one of the ways in which poetry can prevent its confinement to a marginal role. An extreme instance of course is Hugh MacDiarmid, in whose work the numerous spoils from numerous worlds of knowledge are caught up in an impetuous imaginative driving-force. For Fenton, at the beginning of his career, the highly referential nature of his poetry may well serve as a prop, so it will be interesting to see how he uses his skills when he moves (if he does) into more difficult areas of personal commitment where the raw material is not, *a priori*, clear-cut.

—Robin Fulton

FERLINGHETTI, Lawrence (Mendes-Monsanto). American. Born in Yonkers, New York, 24 March 1919. Educated at the University of North Carolina, Chapel Hill, A.B.; Columbia University, New York, M.A. 1948; the Sorbonne, Paris, Doctorat de l'Université

1951. Served in the Naval Reserve, 1941–45: Lieutenant-Commander. Married Selden Kirby Smith in 1951; two children, Lorenzo and Julie. Worked for *Time* magazine, New York, in the 1940's. Co-Founder, 1952, with Peter L. Martin, and since 1953, Owner and Editor-in-Chief, City Lights Books. Delegate, with Allen Ginsberg, to the Pan American Cultural Conference, University of Concepción, Chile, 1960. Address: City Lights Books, 261 Columbus Avenue, San Francisco, California 94133, U.S.A.

PUBLICATIONS

Verse

Pictures of the Gone World. San Francisco, City Lights, 1955.
A Coney Island of the Mind. New York, New Directions, 1958.
Tentative Description of a Dinner Given to Promote the Impeachment of President Eisenhower. San Francisco, Golden Mountain Press, 1958.
One Thousand Fearful Words for Fidel Castro. San Francisco, City Lights, 1961.
Berlin. San Francisco, Golden Mountain Press, 1961.
Starting from San Francisco. New York, New Directions, 1961; revised edition, 1967.
Penguin Modern Poets 5, with Allen Ginsberg and Gregory Corso. London, Penguin, 1963.
Where Is Vietnam? San Francisco, City Lights, 1965.
To Fuck Is to Love Again; Kyrie Eleison Kerista; or, The Situation in the West; Followed by a Holy Proposal. New York, Fuck You Press, 1965.
An Eye on the World: Selected Poems. London, MacGibbon and Kee, 1967.
After the Cries of the Birds. San Francisco, Dave Haslewood Books, 1967.
Moscow in the Wilderness, Segovia in the Snow. San Francisco, Beach Books, 1967.
Reverie Smoking Grass. Milan, East 128, 1968.
The Secret Meaning of Things. New York, New Directions, 1969.
Tyrannus Nix? New York, New Directions, 1969.
Back Roads to Far Places. New York, New Directions, 1971.
Love Is No Stone on the Moon: Automatic Poem. Berkeley, California, Arif Press, 1971.
Open Eye, Open Heart. New York, New Directions, 1973.
Director of Alienation. Clinton, New Jersey, Main Street, 1976.
Who Are We Now? New York, New Directions, 1976.
Northwest Ecolog. San Francisco, City Lights, 1978.
Landscape of Living and Dying. New York, New Directions, 1979.

Recordings: *Poetry Readings in "The Cellar,"* with Kenneth Rexroth, Fantasy, 1958; *Tentative Description of a Dinner to Impeach President Eisenhower and Other Poems*, Fantasy, 1959; *Tyrannus Nix? and Assassination Raga*, Fantasy, 1971; *The World's Greatest Poets 1*, with Allen Ginsberg and Gregory Corso, CMS, 1971.

Plays

The Alligation (produced San Francisco, 1962; New York, 1970). Included in *Unfair Arguments with Existence*, 1963.
Unfair Arguments with Existence: Seven Plays for a New Theatre (includes *The Soldiers of No Country, Three Thousand Red Ants, The Alligation, The Victims of Amnesia, Motherlode, The Customs Collector in Baggy Pants, The Nose of Sisyphus*). New York, New Directions, 1963.
The Customs Collector in Baggy Pants (produced New York, 1964). Included in *Unfair Arguments with Existence*, 1963.
The Soldiers of No Country (produced London, 1969). Included in *Unfair Arguments with Existence*, 1963.

3 by Ferlinghetti: Three Thousand Red Ants, The Alligation, The Victims of Amnesia (produced New York, 1970). Included in *Unfair Arguments with Existence*, 1963.
Routines (includes 13 short pieces). New York, New Directions, 1964.

Novel

Her. New York, New Directions, 1960; London, MacGibbon and Kee, 1967.

Other

Howl of the Censor, edited by J. W. Ehrlich. New York, Nourse, 1961.
Dear Ferlinghetti/Dear Jack: The Spicer-Ferlinghetti Correspondence. San Francisco, White Rabbit Press, 1962(?).
The Mexican Night: Travel Journal. New York, New Directions, 1970.

Editor, *Beatitude Anthology.* San Francisco, City Lights, 1960.
Editor, with Michael McClure and David Meltzer, *Journal for the Protection of All Beings.* San Francisco, City Lights, 1961.
Editor, *City Lights Journal.* San Francisco, City Lights, 4 vols., 1963–73.
Editor, *Panic Grass*, by Charles Upton. San Francisco, City Lights, 1969.
Editor, *City Lights Anthology.* San Francisco, City Lights, 1974.

Translator, *Selections from Paroles by Jacques Prévert.* San Francisco, City Lights, 1958; London, Penguin, 1963.

Manuscript Collection: Bancroft Library, University of California, Berkeley.

* * *

Lawrence Ferlinghetti is a writer whose work remains as exciting today as it was in the 1950's when he was one of the founders and the chief impresario of the Beat group of poets. While most of the other Beats have died or have gradually drifted away from the literary world, Ferlinghetti remains a powerful force on the poetic scene, not only as an author, but also as an editor who has encouraged and published numerous young authors, and as the proprietor of the City Lights Bookstore.

Like Walt Whitman, Ferlinghetti believes that the poet should be an agitator whose message should reach the great masses of people too often ignored by more traditional poets; like Whitman, Ferlinghetti has had great success at this. Ferlinghetti's *A Coney Island of the Mind* remains one of the all-time bestsellers for a volume of poetry. Part of its success was no doubt due to its experimental technique (which owed much to E. E. Cummings) and to its use of some shocking (for the time of publication) words. Published during a time of great conventionality, Ferlinghetti's book provided a rousingly vigorous alternative view of life. The book celebrates love, sex, and freedom and attacks the crass materialism which, as these lines from "Christ Climbed Down" indicate, controls society:

Christ climbed down
from His bare Tree
this year
and ran away to where
no intrepid Bible salesmen
covered the territory
in two-tone Cadillacs

This godless society is the frequent target of Ferlinghetti's satiric attacks. "Beat is the soul of beatific," Jack Kerouac said, and all the Beats had a strong concern for the spiritual side of man. Ferlinghetti's poetry stems from his intense moral concern about where "the Bosch-like world" is heading.

"When the guns are roaring the Muses have no right to be silent," writes Ferlinghetti, and during the violence-filled 1960's he continued to make his voice heard. His poetry took on a surrealistic edge, in part because of the surreal rush of events in the decade. "Some days I'm afflicted/with Observation Fever/omnivorous perception of phenomena" begins "Buckford's Buddha," and in the world of "death TV" sensory overload ensues. About this time some of Ferlinghetti's poems were written under the influence of LSD, a drug the poet took not because of hedonism but instead, in the words of one volume's title, to find "the secret meaning of things." The poems of this period are more fragmented than his earlier work, but their message, as expressed in "Assassination Raga," a powerful elegy for the Kennedys, remains the same: "There is no god but Life ... love love and hate hate."

In the 1970's Ferlinghetti's technical experiments involved working with the prose poem and creating Indian chants and mantras in English. He continued to keep an "open eye, open heart" on his society and to condemn "a world awash with fascism and fear." For Ferlinghetti there was no middle-aged mellowing or watering-down of his ideals. A few lines from "Overheard Conversation" indicate how little his concept of poetry changed in two decades: "And still the whole idea of poetry being/to take control of life/out of the hands of/the Terrible People." On rare occasions the Terrible People Ferlinghetti attacks are hackneyed subjects, as in the long poem "Vegas Tilt" which exposes the materialism of Las Vegas, hardly a novel or challenging concept; but more frequently his adversaries are well chosen. With Whitman, Vachel Lindsay, and Carl Sandburg, Ferlinghetti stands in the great line of American poets who have been gadflies, yea-sayers to humanity, nay-sayers to the forces of repression. One of his finest and most recent poems, "Populist Manifesto," expresses Ferlinghetti's ideas about and hopes for poetry. It is a clarion call: "Poets, come out of your closets..../You have been holed-up too long/in your closed world." It continues by stating that poetry has become too stifling. Ironically echoing his friend Allen Ginsberg, Ferlinghetti writes, "We have seen the best minds of our generation/destroyed by boredom at poetry readings," and after a Whitman-like catalogue of all the various schools of poetry flourishing today, Ferlinghetti exhorts other writers, crying

Poets, descend
to the street of the world once more
And open your minds and eyes
with the old visual delight
Clear your throat and speak up,
Poetry is dead, long live poetry
with terrible eyes and buffalo strength.

Lawrence Ferlinghetti practices what he preaches. One only wishes that more poets would write with his immediacy, power, and passion.

—Dennis Lynch

FERRIL, Thomas Hornsby. American. Born in Denver, Colorado, 25 February 1896. Educated at East Denver High School; Colorado College, Colorado Springs, A.B. 1918. Served as an Officer in the Signal Corps Aviation Section, 1918. Married Helen Drury Ray in 1921 (died, 1978); one daughter. Drama Critic, Denver *Times*, 1919–21; worked in motion picture advertising, 1921–26; Editor, *Through the Leaves* and *The Sugar Press*, 1926–68, for Great Western Sugar Company; Editor and Publisher, with his wife, *The Rocky Mountain Herald* weekly newspaper, 1939–72. Columnist ("Western Half-Acre"), *Harper's Magazine*, New York. Associated with the Colorado University Writers Conference since its inception, and other conferences. Recipient: Yale Series of Younger Poets Award, 1926; *Nation* prize, 1927; Oscar Blumenthal Prize (*Poetry*, Chicago), 1937; Denver *Post*-Central City Opera House Association Prize, 1958; Robert Frost Poetry Prize, 1960; Ridgely Torrence Prize, 1963. Honorary Degrees from Colorado College, Colorado University, Boulder, and Denver University. Honorary Member, Phi Beta Kappa, Denver University, 1955. Address: 2123 Downing Street, Denver, Colorado 80205, U.S.A.

PUBLICATIONS

Verse

High Passage. New Haven, Connecticut, Yale University Press, 1926.
Westering. New Haven, Connecticut, Yale University Press, 1934.
Trial by Time. New York and London, Harper, 1944.
New and Selected Poems. New York, Harper, 1952.
Words for Denver and Other Poems. New York, Morrow, 1966.

Plays

... And Perhaps Happiness (produced Central City, Colorado, 1958).
Ferril, Etc. (produced Denver, 1972).

Musical Collaborations with Cecil Effinger performed and published.

Other

I Hate Thursday (essays). New York and London, Harper, 1946.

Editor, with Helen Ferril, *The Rocky Mountain Herald Reader*. New York, Morrow, 1966.

Manuscript Collection: Denver Public Library.

Critical Study: *The Poetry of Thomas Hornsby Ferril* by Robert Fulton Richards, Columbia University, New York, unpublished dissertation, 1960.

* * *

Thomas Hornsby Ferril for years has pursued a course somewhat apart from the mainstream of modern American poetry. He has been an individualist of the old stripe, eschewing all cliques and cults and academic auspices. The result is that his poetry took a long time finding a place among the works of his generation, though by now it is firmly established. For many years Ferril and his wife published the *Rocky Mountain Herald*, a weekly newspaper, far better edited than most, which celebrated the mountains of Colorado and adjoining regions. At the same time Ferril himself became an amateur scholar of mountain folklore and culture, while he wrote his poems about life in the high country.

Ferril's characteristic poem is in slackened but recognizably traditional meter, incorporating the colloquial diction of his region. His characteristic theme is the speed of change in a frontier culture. In one of his best poems, "Waltz Against the Mountains," he writes:

I was pulling hair from the trunk of a cottonwood tree
The longhorn cattle rubbed when a sudden man
Started tossing red-hot rivets up through the leaves,
Scorching the amber varnish of the leaves.
He made the red-hot rivets stick to the sky.

Anyone in western America knows that longhorn cattle haven't been raised in that region since the days of the frontier, seventy or eighty years ago. Yet now one of the greatest cities of America, Denver, sprawls against the mountainside, its sky-scrapers lifting their lights toward the sky. The swiftness of time, the pathos of loss, the fear of impermanence, the courage of resistance – these are the typically western motifs of Ferril's poetry, bringing into clear relationship the frontier and the existentialist homeland of modern Europe.

—Hayden Carruth

FETHERLING, Doug. Canadian. Born in Ohio County, West Virginia, United States, 1 January 1947; emigrated to Canada in 1967; naturalized citizen. Left school at age 16. Worked as tree trimmer, bartender, reporter. Editor, House of Anansi Press, Toronto, 1968–69; Script Writer and Consultant, Canadian Broadcasting Corporation, Toronto, 1969–70; Book Page Editor, Toronto *Star*, 1973; Associate Editor, Books in Canada, Toronto, 1974. Recipient: Canada Council and Ontario Arts Council grants. Address: Box 367, Station F, Toronto, Ontario M4Y 2L8, Canada.

PUBLICATIONS

Verse

The United States of Heaven. Toronto, Anansi, 1968.
My Experience in the War. Toronto, Weed/Flower Press, 1970.
Our Man in Utopia. Toronto, Macmillan, 1971.
Eleven Early Poems. Toronto, Weed/Flower Press, 1972.
Café Terminus. Toronto, Missing Link Press, 1973.
Achilles' Navel: Throbs, Laments and Vagaries. Toronto, Press Porcépic, 1974.

Other

Hugh Garner. Toronto, Forum House, 1972.
The Five Lives of Ben Hecht. Toronto, Lester and Orpen, 1977.

Editor, *Thumbprints: An Anthology of Hitchhiking Poems*. Toronto, Peter Martin, 1969.
Editor, *A Caricature History of Canadian Politics*. Toronto, Peter Martin, 1974.
Editor, *The Four Jameses*, by W. A. Deacon. Toronto, Macmillan, 1974.

* * *

Doug Fetherling, the Toronto poet and cultural journalist, published his first collection of poems when he was twenty-one. *The United States of Heaven* was heavily influenced by "the greatest English language poet of all time, Allen Ginsberg, to whom this is dedicated." The poems, made up of discontinuous words and images, read like jottings taken down while descending the rings of some metropolitan inferno. A taste of the book as a whole can be conveyed by quoting a single line: "i fully expect to be dead be4 im 30."

Our Man in Utopia, the title of Fetherling's next major collection, conveys the notion that the poet is a correspondent, rather than a participant, right down to the device of calling the poems "Dispatch Number Two," "Dispatch Number Twenty-One," etc. The poet has a new beat now, an inner one, and he is not unduly concerned that

> Every thirteen minutes somewhere
> in this troubled world rioters
> are taking over the post office
> while we lie here relishing the
> night or cursing the morning.

The poet-correspondent is able to "sidestep all their/politics like puddles" and maintain "an involvement with more/than they have to offer." Here are poems, evocative and sensitive to the nuances of speech, that are as well-written as prose.

Fetherling's next – and most recent – collection is archly entitled *Achilles' Navel*. The archness extends to the subtitle (*Throbs, Laments and Vagaries*) and demonstrates the distance Fetherling has travelled from the "surrealist hell" (Raymond Souster's description of the world of his first book) to the more meditative world he now inhabits. The book opens on the macabre image of a child playing with a human skull and closes on an ironic love poem written "in the manner of Irving Layton." In between there are poems that show an awareness of history, of uncertain relationships, and of possibly difficult futures. Fetherling treats imaginatively the ghost of W. L. Mackenzie (a nineteenth-century revolutionary), the film actor Leslie Howard, and civilized values in a poem about a poet who is "au courant with emptiness." There is even a meditation on the passing years:

> Twice, for instance, while combing my hair,
> my hand has touched a bald spot I knew did not exist,
> and more than once an older face has sprung up
> in the mirror.

It is hard to believe this is the voice of a poet of 27, who fully expects "to be dead be4 im 30."

—John Robert Colombo

FIELD, Edward. American. Born in Brooklyn, New York, 7 June 1924. Attended New York University. Served in the United States Army Air Force, 1942–45. Lecturer, YM-YWHA Poetry Center, New York. Recipient: Lamont Poetry Selection Award, 1962; Guggenheim Fellowship, 1963; Shelley Memorial Award, 1975. Address: 463 West Street, New York, New York 10014, U.S.A.

PUBLICATIONS

Verse

Stand Up, Friend, With Me. New York, Grove Press, 1963.

Variety Photoplays. New York, Grove Press, 1967.
Sweet Gwendolyn and the Countess. Gulfport, Florida, Konglomerati Press, 1977.
A Full Heart. New York, Sheep Meadow Press, 1977.
Stars in My Eyes. New York, Sheep Meadow Press, 1977.

Other

Editor and Translator, *Eskimo Songs and Stories, Collected by Knud Rasmussen on the Fifth Thule Expedition.* New York, Delacorte Press, 1973.
Editor, *A Geography of Poets: An Anthology of New Poetry.* New York, Bantam, 1979.

Critical Studies: Review by Robert Mazzocco, in *New York Review of Books*, 1967; *Alone with America* by Richard Howard, New York, Atheneum, 1969.

* * *

Edward Field writes poems for which the reader is honestly grateful. They are heart-felt. Straightforward and unadorned, they have little or no figurative language, but are conversational and colloquial. The speaker may be humble, sad, funny (ribald, witty, wry), and self-deprecating. And there is unabashed sentimentality. At the same time Field manages to control and distance intensely personal material. He understates, he responds, he perceives. And, finally, he joins, brings together. As he expresses those feelings of shame and frustration which characterized his childhood years, he opens the door to his private hell – "the terror and guilt/and self-loathing" he felt in his father's house.

Field's hopes for himself and the world are centered in the triumph of love, the gifts of affection and sexuality. The freedom to feel, to be natural and uninhibited – the freedom to be – these are his concerns. And so he attempts to bring people together, to overcome distances, to bring down barriers. By inviting the reader to share intimacies, by embracing the reader, Field resembles a Jewish Walt Whitman. In his emphasis on companionship and sexuality, on love above all, he is most Whitmanesque.

Gentle, yearning, believing that "all men and women are my brothers and sisters now" ("Visiting Home"), Field writes confessional poetry. Because it is personal, it cannot help but be. It is a poetry of skepticism, of cautious hope, of the sorrow of estrangement and alienation, of the search for one's way in the world. One must be one's own guru: "you have to trust to your heart/Which often needs more than one lifetime to make a man" ("Union City").

The courage of the heart is what Field's poetry is most about. He is not afraid to be himself, to reveal his weaknesses, his fears, his humiliations ("Unwanted"):

> His aliases tell his history: Dumbell, Good-for-nothing
> Jewboy, Fieldinsky, Skinny, Fierce Face, Greaseball, Sissy.
>
> Warning: This man is not dangerous, answers to any name
> Responds to love, don't call him or he will come.

Through his unassuming honesty, he touches the reader with prose-poetry. Field's humor is effective and genuinely funny. Laughter – as device and response – enables him to avoid falling into the slough of selfpity. Laughter is a great leveler; not surprisingly, Field's bawdiness serves a democratic function. It reminds us that we all eat, excrete, copulate: "As the smile is to the face/the hard-on is to the body" ("Chopped Meat").

In *Variety Photoplays*, he uses humor to offset maudlin sentiment as he discovers in old movies the familiar and universal themes – frustrated love, alienation, loneliness, prejudice, force of circumstance. His three Frankenstein poems are especially admirable. "He is pursued by the ignorant villagers,/Who think he is evil and dangerous because he is ugly and makes ugly noises." Finally the majority – the real beast – succeeds in creating a monster worse than the Baron: "He was out to pay them back/to throw the lie of brotherly love/in their white Christian teeth." The poem arrives at a moment of triumph:

So he set out on his new career
his previous one being the victim,
the good man who suffers.

Now no longer the hunted but the hunter
he was in charge of his destiny.

Cinema creates and shapes the fairy-tales of American culture. The gothic motifs, the soap opera, the happily-ever-after quality which deceives the audience and often the actors – all are treated by Field with wry clarity and sad-eyed humor. If there is nostalgia, a sharp realization of the brevity of youth and fame ("Whatever Happened to May Caspar"), there is also the poet's unique parable, *Sweet Gwendolyn and the Countess*. This poem depicts the victimization of innocence and beauty by power and aggression; Field implies that as long as "innocence" refuses to see and participate in the real world, refuses to be active rather than passive, it will not only continue to be victimized but actually be contributing to its own subjugation and demise.

A Full Heart has clear moments of joy, of exuberance. The book is more genuinely happy for there are the fulfillment of love and the quickening of life that accompanies it. No longer the outsider, Field has been invited to the party. And when love is lost, he can console himself for his having had it. Field begins this collection by celebrating "New York" – "I live in a beautiful place, a city/... this is a people paradise." Nothing is too little or ugly to praise: "Thank God for dogs, cats, sparrows, and roaches."

A Full Heart shows how Field goes forward and how sometimes this requires a going backward first. In "Pasternak: In Memoriam" Field stresses personal fulfillment as opposed to heroism:

You were right:
This real person in my arms
is who I want
not the moment of passion on the barricades
not the dream of the ideal
love in a perfect world.

Survive in this world
love as you can
and go on with your work.

This is what the poet has come to learn. And in such poems as "Both My Grandmothers" and "Visiting Home" he deals with the need for roots, for a sense of origin. His Jewishness – tradition and culture more than a particularized system of belief – helps him to realize his identity in a shifting and arbitrary world. If, in the second of these poems, he acknowledges the severe difficulties visited upon him by his father, he can also say "thank God I am my mother's son too/for what she gave me/is what I survived by." Suffering and love – the two are wedded in this world and in Field's. He is a poet whose heart is "full" and, in sharing, he fills the reader's heart as well.

—Carl Lindner

FIGUEROA, John (Joseph Maria). Jamaican. Born in Kingston, Jamaica, 4 August 1920. Educated at schools in Jamaica; Holy Cross College, Worcester, Massachusetts; London University; degrees: A.B., M.A., L.H.D. Married Dorothy Grace Murray Alexander; four sons and three daughters. Teacher and Lecturer in the United States; Lecturer in English and Philosophy, University of London; Sports Reporter, 1946–60, and Broadcaster, BBC, London. Formerly, Dean and Professor of Education, University of the West Indies, Kingston, Professor of English, University of Puerto Rico, Rio Piedras, and Professor of Education, University of Jos, Nigeria. Recipient: British Council Scholarship, 1946; Carnegie Award, 1960; Guggenheim Fellowship, 1964. Address: c/o J. Edward Milner, 60 Crouch Hall Road, London N.8, England.

PUBLICATIONS

Verse

Blue Mountain Peak. Kingston, Gleaner, 1944.
Love Leaps Here. Kingston, C. Tinling, 1962.
Ignoring Hurts. Washington, D.C., Three Continents Press, 1976.

Other

Staffing and Examinations in Secondary Schools in the British Caribbean. London, Evans, 1964.
Society, Schools and Progress in the West Indies. Oxford, Pergamon Press, 1971.

Editor, *Caribbean Voices: An Anthology of West Indian Poetry.* London, Evans, 2 vols., 1966–70; Washington, D.C., Luce, 1973.

Critical Studies: Reviews by Derek Walcott, in *Trinidad Guardian*, 1962, and by Cecil Gray, in *Bim 55* (Bridgetown, Barbados), July–December 1972.

John Figueroa comments:

I hope that [my verse] is influenced by Horace and Virgil and Sappho as well as by our Jamaican speech rhythms and Trinidadian calypsoes. But I'm hardly the one to say. Once in the early days a well-known critic excused himself from commenting (in a broadcast) on the verse, on the grounds that it was "very religious." Perhaps he was being tactful. On the other hand, I have been called "basically a love poet."

* * *

John Figueroa is well-known throughout the Caribbean as poet, editor, critic and educationalist. However, his poetry is not as widely known outside the West Indies as it ought to be. Figueroa is certainly an original poet at his best and quite unlike any other West Indian poet. He is actually aware of the physical world and responds to contrasts of one kind or another – contrasts of place, as in his "At Home the Green Remains," contrasts of colour, and even contrasts in modes of living. He constantly seems to be relating one thing to another, the known to the unfamiliar, darkness to light, and rough to smooth.

An eminent scholar, Figueroa has obviously read widely. His influences might be said to be partly environmental (i.e., Jamaican speech rhythms, Trinidadian calypsoes, etc.) and partly classical (Virgil, Sappho, and particularly Horace, a good deal of whose verse he has translated). Indeed, in his poetry there seems to be some kind of conflict between the two, so that the struggle to achieve a balance between the urge to express his own individual experience and the need for technical control, is not easily resolved. At times, the academic pressures seem to prevent him from speaking in his own voice.

John Figueroa has a wide range of styles and subjects, but his work falls into five broad categories: 1) reflective poems, 2) poems with a religious theme or insight, 3) poems arising out of experiences in other countries, 4) personal and anecdotal poems, and 5) translations. His greatest strength, however, lies in his reflective and philosophical poetry. In such poems as "On Hearing Dvorak's 'New World' Symphony," "Other Spheres," "Green Is the Colour of Hope," "The Three Epiphanies," "From the Caribbean with Love," and "Columbus Lost," one finds significant utterance combined with unusual craftsmanship.

—Howard Sergeant

FINCH, Robert (Duer Claydon). Canadian. Born in Freeport, Long Island, New York, United States, 14 May 1900. Educated at the University of Toronto (Jardine Memorial Prize, 1924), B.A. 1925; the Sorbonne, Paris, 1928; studied music with Alberto Guerrero and Wanda Landowska. Painter: exhibitions in Toronto, Paris, New York. Member of the French Department, 1928, and since 1968, Professor Emeritus, University College, University of Toronto. Recipient: Governor-General's Award, 1947, 1962; Lorne Pierce Medal, 1968. LL.D.: University of Toronto, 1973. Fellow, Royal Society of Canada, 1963. Address: Massey College, 4 Devonshire Place, Toronto, Ontario M5S 2E1, Canada.

PUBLICATIONS

Verse

Poems. Toronto, Oxford University Press, 1946.
The Strength of the Hills. Toronto, McClelland and Stewart, 1948.
Acis in Oxford and Other Poems. Oxford, privately printed, 1959; Toronto, University of Toronto Press, 1961.
Dover Beach Revisited and Other Poems. Toronto, Macmillan, 1961.
Silverthorn Bush and Other Poems. Toronto, Macmillan, 1966.

Play

A Century Has Roots (produced Toronto, 1953). Toronto, University of Toronto Press, 1953.

Other

The Sixth Sense: Individualism in French Poetry 1686–1760. Toronto, University of Toronto Press, 1966.

Editor, with C. R. Parsons, *René*, by Chateaubriand. Toronto, University of Toronto Press, 1957.
Editor, with Eugène Joliat, *French Individualist Poetry 1686–1760: An Anthology.* Toronto, University of Toronto Press, 1971.
Editor, with Eugène Joliat, *Sir Politick Would-Be*, by Saint-Evremond. Geneva, Droz, 1978.
Editor, with Eugène Joliat, *Les Opéra*, by Saint-Evremond. Geneva, Droz, 1979.

* * *

Literary verse is infrequently attempted presently in Canada, that area of verse-making where the form commands the content, where the thought is sophisticate, the metaphor more cogent than daring. It is an area out of fashion, an area dangerous and difficult to achieve success in – dangerous since to fail is to leave the literary rather than the vital effect; difficult, for it demands that the formality become necessary to the communication.

Robert Finch dares the hazards of this kind of poetry and proves them surmountable. Amid the turbulence of the world, he dares to write sonnets; his adherence to grace of thought demands his formality. It is a poetry of pensive mood and sensitive craftsmanship. To read his books is to have walked, aware of the melancholy world outside, in a garden of Le Nostre.

Finch first found assertion long ago in that watershed of an anthology, *New Provinces*. His presentation then was as an Imagist when Imagism and the French Symbolists might not have existed as far as Canadian awareness was concerned: "Lacks a blue buck bearing vermilion horns/led by a groom in tightest daffodil?" Finch soon established himself with a poetry of precision and form and accurate detailed sensuousness. The definition is not surprising. Finch is a skilled musician, painter – and professor of French in Toronto. His eye is that of the painter:

The dark green truck on the cement platform
is explicit as a paradigm.
Its wheels are four black cast-iron starfish ...
The truck holds eleven cakes of ice,
each cake a different size and shape.
Some look as though a weight had hit them.
One, solid glass, has a core of sugar.
They lean, a transitory Icehenge.

This imagist stasis is deceived into movement. The movement proceeds by paradox; the logic, by metaphor. He is as fond of variations as a musician is. His book *Dover Beach Revisited and Other Poems* contains eleven variations on the theme of Matthew Arnold's poem. It witnesses the quality of his mind, a quiet perception of tides and time in a verse of intellectual lyricism. The passage of the seasons is everywhere evident. Reliance on the variations in weather to express mood and emotion is to admit the usual conventional dangers. Finch startles in his best poems of this kind by concurrent, spare intellectualism, a sophistication of taste and perception. The happy wind, the pensive trees

have all gone and we are far away
Where every season is a winter's day
That comes and goes and always is the same

Except that we, more than its atmosphere,
Still know and feel and see and breathe and hear
That wind, that grass, those trees, that eager stream.

Finch's poetry is a poetry of personality, seasoned, spare yet sensuous, astringent yet warm with humility and compassion. Its effect is that of a resolution in music, inevitable and "Building with Euclidean grace."

—Ralph Gustafson

FINKEL, Donald. American. Born in New York City, 21 October 1929. Educated at Columbia University, New York, B.S. in philosophy 1952 (Phi Beta Kappa), M.A. in literature 1953. Married Constance Urdang, *q.v.*, in 1956; three children. Instructor, University of Iowa, Iowa City, 1957–58, and Bard College, Annandale-on-Hudson, New York, 1958–60. Since 1960, Poet-in-Residence, Washington University, St. Louis. Visiting Lecturer, Bennington College, Vermont, 1966–67. Visited Antarctica, 1969–70, at invitation of National Science Foundation. Recipient: Helen Bullis Prize (*Poetry Northwest*), 1964; Guggenheim Fellowship, 1967; National Endowment for the Arts grant, 1969, 1973; Ingram Merrill Foundation grant, 1972; Theodore Roethke Memorial Prize, 1974. Address: 6943 Columbia Place, St. Louis, Missouri 63130, U.S.A.

PUBLICATIONS

Verse

The Clothing's New Emperor and Other Poems. New York, Scribner, 1959.
Simeon: Poems. New York, Atheneum, 1964.
A Joyful Noise. New York, Atheneum, 1966.
Answer Back. New York, Atheneum, 1968.
The Garbage Wars. New York, Atheneum, 1970.
Adequate Earth. New York, Atheneum, 1972.
A Mote in Heaven's Eye. New York, Atheneum, 1975.
Going Under, and Endurance: An Arctic Idyll: Two Poems. New York, Atheneum, 1978.

Play

The Jar (produced Boston, 1961).

Manuscript Collection: Washington University Library, St. Louis.

Critical Study: *Alone with America*, by Richard Howard, New York, Atheneum, 1969.

* * *

"Plain speech is out of place in the pulpit,/poetry is out of place in the square," writes Don Finkel, who in his works has attempted to combine prose and poetry, and the religious and the secular worlds. As an early poem like "Hands" indicates, Finkel is a strong believer in the power of poetry, even though he is not totally happy with its present condition:

The poem makes truth a little more disturbing
like a good bra, lifts it and holds it out
in both hands. (In some of the flashier stores
there's a model with the hands stitched on, in red or black.)

Lately the world you wed, for want of such hands,
sags in the bed beside you like a tired wife.
For want of such hands, the face of the moon is bored,
the tree does not stretch and yearn, nor the groin tighten.

Devious or frank, in any case,
the poem is calculated to arouse.
Lean back and let its hands play freely on you:
there comes a moment, lifted and aroused,
when the two of you are equally beautiful.

The struggle to make poetry once again a force capable of arousing and disturbing us has led Finkel in his later work to increased experimentation. This began with the use of the collage technique in his long sequence "Three for Robert Rauschenberg" (*A Joyful Noise*), but this innovation seems pale next to what Finkel attempts in his later books. In these amazing volumes Finkel manages to develop a voice and a technique uniquely his own.

Answer Back is an astonishing book arranged around the metaphor of cave exploration. It has six sections, each of which is named after a particular part of Mammoth Cave. Speleology, though, is only one of Finkel's concerns here: his other topics include Vietnam, the relation of the sexes, the nature of religion, the function of poetry, the origins of the universe, and much more. His voice modulates from biblical tones to satiric ones, and his verse ranges from lyrics to doggerel. Interspersed between the bits of poetry are passages of prose, about two per page, from such varied sources as Lenny Bruce, Admiral Byrd, Camus, Heraclitus, Hoyle, the *I Ching*, Jesus, Kafka, the *Kama Sutra*, the Missouri State Penitentiary, *Playboy*, Pound, and Lord Raglan. Needless to say, the whole effect is rather staggering. While one is impressed with Finkel's erudition and is often amused by the clever juxtaposition he creates, one also feels that the poet has been too unrestrained and has produced a poem too fragmented.

Like *Answer Back* the long poem "Water Music" in *The Garbage Wars* has a controlling metaphor (experimentation on dolphins) and it, too, uses many prose borrowings. Yet here Finkel has refined his technique and uses it more subtly. His next book, *Adequate Earth*, is his masterpiece. Once again Finkel is daring in his choice of subject, for this book is a series of seven long poems about Antarctica. Finkel spent a month on that continent in 1969 and his experiences form the basis of some of the sections. Other parts have as a narrative frame the explorations of Amundsen, Byrd, and others. As usual Finkel interpolates prose passages from various authors, but here it is more tightly focused than previously. And, as usual, Finkel tries to bring everything into his poetry, from science to theology to politics to psychology. Here, though, he has finally chosen a subject which can stand all this weight and at the same time offer great narrative potentiality. As a result, *Adequate Earth* is one of the few fine contemporary epic poems. It has a vast sweep: part of it is myth-making, as Finkel "takes the liberty of quoting at length throughout from the gospels of the Emperor Penguins," a remarkably allegorical document; part of it is devastating satire, such as the section "Pole Business," which is a bitter attack on the commercialism encroaching on our planet's last wilderness; part of it is tragedy in its accounts of ill-fated attempts to explore the polar regions; and all of it is a tribute to man's ability to endure in even the harshest of worlds:

> We'll get used to that bite in the air
> soon enough; we'll get used to
> everything. It's what we do:
> the adaptable animal, whelped in the time
> of ice, we adapt to anything.

Full justice cannot be done to Finkel's work by brief quotations from it; like a collage its power comes not from any one part alone but from the interaction of all its parts. Finkel's collages are daring attempts to bring unity to the world's chaos through art. At his worst he can be obscure and pedantic; at his best he can produce works of startling resonance.

Interestingly, Finkel returns to the metaphors of exploring caves and Antarctica in his latest book(s) *Going Under* and *Endurance*, a volume which is literally two books in one. Finkel, who has constantly confounded expectations about the proper subjects for poetry, here confounds expectations about the very way a book is printed and presented. The result is a bibliographer's nightmare but a reader's delight. Fortunately, these poems give the reader none of the disappointment one often feels in reading sequels. Indeed, each work is in some way superior to its predecessor because each has a much sharper narrative focus; *Going Under* centers on the strange lives of two Mammoth Cave explorers, *Endurance* on one doomed polar expedition. It is no surprise that Don Finkel is so intrigued by the stories of adventurers; few writers are as ambitious and daring as he.

—Dennis Lynch

FINLAY, Ian Hamilton. Scottish. Born in Nassau, Bahamas, 28 October 1925. Left school at 13. Married to Susan Finlay; two children, Eck and Ailie. Concrete Poetry exhibited at Axiom Gallery, London, 1968, Scottish National Gallery of Modern Art, Edinburgh, 1972, National Maritime Museum, Greenwich, 1973, Southampton Art Gallery, 1976, Graeme Murray Gallery, Edinburgh, 1976, Kettle's Yard, Cambridge, 1977, Serpentine Gallery, London, 1977; Sundials: University of Kent, Canterbury, in Biggar, Lanarkshire, Royal Botanic Garden, Edinburgh; Poems designed for Max Planck Institute, Stuttgart. Editor, *Poor. Old. Tired. Horse*, Dunsyre, Lanarkshire; Publisher, with Sue Finlay, Wild Hawthorn Press, Edinburgh, 1961–66, Easter Ross, 1966, and since 1969, Dunsyre, Lanarkshire. Recipient: Scottish Arts Council bursary, 1966, 1967, 1968; Atlantic-Richfield Award (USA), 1968. Address: Stonypath, Dunsyre, Lanarkshire, Scotland.

PUBLICATIONS

Verse

Books and booklets (all published by Wild Hawthorn Press unless otherwise noted): *The Dancers Inherit the Party*, Worcester, Migrant Press, 1960; *Glasgow Beasts, an a Burd*, 1961; *Concertina*, 1962; *Rapel*, 1963; *Canal Stripe Series 3* and *4*, 1964; *Telegrams from My Windmill*, 1964; *Ocean Stripe Series 2* to *5*, 1965–67; *Cythera*, 1965; *Autumn Poem*, 1966; *6 Small Pears for Eugen Gomringer*, 1966; *6 Small Songs in 3's*, 1966; *Tea-Leaves and Fishes*, 1966; *4 Sails*, 1966; *Headlines Eavelines*, Corsham, Wiltshire, Openings Press, 1967; *Stonechats*, 1967; *Canal Game*, London, Fulcrum Press, 1967; *The Collected Coaltown of Callange Tri-kai*, Newport, Monmouthshire, Screwpacket Press, 1968; *Air Letters*, Nottingham, Tarasque Press, 1968; *The Blue and The Brown Poems*, New York, Atlantic Richfield-Jargon Press, 1968; *After the Russian*, Corsham, Wiltshire, Openings Press, 1969; *3/3's*, 1969; *A Boatyard*, 1969; *Lanes*, 1969; *Wave*, 1969; *Rhymes for Lemons*, 1970; *"Fishing News" News*, 1970; *30 Signatures to Silver Catches*, Nottingham, Tarasque Press, 1971; *Poems to Hear and See*, New York, Macmillan, 1971; *A Sailor's Calendar*, New York, Something Else Press, 1971; *The Olsen Excerpts*, Göttingen, Verlag Udo Breger, 1971; *A Memory of Summer*, 1971; *From "An Inland Garden,"* 1971; *Evening/Sail 2*, 1971; *The Weed Boat Masters Ticket, Preliminary Text (Part Two)*, 1971; *Sail/Sundial*, 1972; *Jibs*, 1972; *Honey by the Water*, Los Angeles, Black Sparrow Press, 1973; *Butterflies*, 1973; *A Family*, 1973; *Straiks*, 1973; *Homage to Robert Lax*, 1974; *A Pretty Kettle of Fish*, 1974; *Silhouettes*, 1974; *Exercise X*, 1974; *So You Want to Be a Panzer Leader*, 1975; *Airs Waters Graces*, 1975; *The Wild Hawthorn Wonder Book of Boats*, 1975; *A Mast of Hankies*, 1975; *The Axis*, 1975; *Trombone Carrier*, 1975; *Homage to Watteau*, 1975; *Three Sundials*, Exeter, Rougemont Press, 1975; *Imitations, Variations, Reflections, Copies*, 1976; *The Wild Hawthorn Art Test*, 1977; *Heroic Emblems*, Calais, Vermont, Z Press, 1977; *The Boy's Alphabet Book*, Toronto, Coach House Press, 1977; *The Wartime Garden*, 1977; *Trailblazers*, 1978; *Homage to Poussin*, 1978; *Peterhead Fragments*, 1979; *"SS"*, 1979; *Dzaezl*, 1979; *Woods and Seas*, 1979; *Two Billows*, 1979.

Some 200 cards, folding cards, and poem/prints published by Wild Hawthorn Press.

Short Stories

The Sea-Bed and Other Stories. Edinburgh, Alna Press, 1958.

Manuscript Collection: Lilly Library, University of Indiana, Bloomington.

Critical Studies: "Ian Hamilton Finlay Issue" of *Extra Verse 15* (London), Spring 1965; by Bryan Robertson, in *Spectator* (London), 6 September 1968; *Ian Hamilton Finlay* by Francis Edeline, Paris, Atelier de l'Agneau, 1978; exhibition catalogues by Stephen Bann, Scottish National Gallery of Modern Art, Edinburgh, 1972, Stephen Scobie, Southampton Art Gallery, 1976, Stephen Bann and others, Kettle's Yard, Cambridge, 1977, and Stephen Bann, Serpentine Gallery, London, 1977.

Ian Hamilton Finlay comments:

(1970) As a "concrete" poet I am interested in poetry as "the best words, in the best possible order" ... *in the best materials*, i.e., such as glass or stone for interiors of gardens. I have been described as "the leading concrete poet now writing in English." But "concrete" has no meaning nowadays. What is concrete?

My verse is not a *single* thing since it has changed over the years. On the other hand, I have usually tried for the same ends – lucidity, clarity, a resolved complexity. I have used many forms, from traditional rhymed verse to poems designed as entire gardens (such as the poem I prepared for the American architect John Johansen). I consider that the seasons, nature, inland waterways, and oceans are proper themes for poetry. I do not expect poems to solve my problems. I do not believe in "the new man." Possibly A. Alvarez is the stupidest writer I have ever come across. I admire the poems of George Herbert. In the context of this time, it is not the job of poetry to "expand consciousness" but to offer a modest example of a decent sort of order.

(1980) The subject of my work is culture, without any undemocratic distinction between past and present. Besides, though one "knows" the past is past one may *experience* it as present, as Nietzsche (for example) did when he was writing on the Greek Pre-Socratics. Recently I have taken to publishing the bibliographies of my seemingly "graphic" works, in part to "categorise" them as "poetry," in part to alert the viewer (reader?) to the subject beyond the object – to Plutarch in the case of the "E" (aircraft carrier) series, or to the European emblem tradition (see Praz, *Studies in Seventeenth Century Imagery*), in such reliefs as "Woodland Is Pleasing to the Muses" (see my *Heroic Emblems*). It is relevant to note that the old emblematists used bibliography less as a particular illumination than as a means of "splicing" the emblem to a concept of classical culture as a whole. —1977.

To my original list of "proper themes" for poetry I should now add *culture* (not excluding warships, aircraft carriers, and warplanes). Increasingly, as our culture abandons its own traditional perspectives, the idea of a poet's "statement" (of his intentions?) becomes a perplexing one. To whom is such a statement actually addressed? To the public – as was peremptorily demanded of me by the Scottish Arts Council – though even in 1800 Friedrich Schlegel was unable to believe in a "public" except as an "idea"? (Today the "public" would be 50,000 "ideas.") Or is one expected to "communicate" with our secularising Arts Council art-bureaucrats, public art gallery "keepers," and publishers, as if they had some essential (actual) concern with culture, history, and truth? "Only through the relationship to the infinite do content and utility arise" – Schlegel once again. Where truth has ceased to be an aspiration and has become a synonym for The Convenient (as "nice" for "pure," "depression" for "despair," and so on), statements become a matter of dramatic allegory: the life is not the work but it is the only possible commentary *on* the work; the commentary "neither uttered nor hidden" is revealed by biography – event as "Event." —1979

* * *

Ian Hamilton Finlay's poetry has undergone a considerable evolution, but the movements in that evolution are not random or (in the wrong sense) "experimental." The main driving-force behind his work may be called classical, if classicism implies a deliberate search for order, form, and economy, yet his classicism is accompanied by obviously romantic and playful elements. He indicated something of this in sub-titling his collection *Rapel* "10 fauve and suprematist poems." The fauve element preserves his work from frigidity, as the suprematist element preserves it from clutter and indulgence.

His first book, *The Dancers Inherit the Party*, contained short poems of much charm and humour, in traditional rhyming verse, about love, people, fishing, Orkney. The brevity of many of these poems was taken a step farther in his next two productions, *Glasgow Beasts* and *Concertina*, both of which had illustrations closely tied to the text. As well as the enhanced visual presentation, there was again a strong infusion of humour in both books.

The visual element, and the movement towards verbal economy, both predisposed Finlay to react with enthusiasm to the international development known as concrete poetry, which he learned about in 1962. Most of his work from *Rapel* (1963) onwards has been received and discussed under the "concrete" label, unsatisfactory and amorphous as that term has now become. Essentially it should signify (to quote the Brazilian Poets' "Pilot-Plan for Concrete Poetry" of 1958) a poetry that "begins by being aware of graphic space as structural agent" and is "against a poetry of expression, subjective and hedonistic." To Finlay, it was a poetry that would link back to the purity and harmony of artists like Malevich and Mondrian, and in general to those Constructivist ideals of half a century ago which had been sterilized by a new wave of expressionism. Painter as well as poet, he found no difficulty in seeing and accepting this formal extension of a verbal art into a visual domain; that many people do find it difficult he has had to admit. But whether his work is to be called "poetry" or something else, it will win over most unprejudiced eyes by its beauty and complete integrity.

"Little Calendar" could be quoted as representing his concrete approach at its most transparent:

april	light	light	light	light
may	light	trees	light	trees
june	trees	light	trees	light
july	trees	trees	trees	trees
august	trees'	light	trees'	light
september	lights	trees	lights	trees

But from this basis, which is still that of the poem printed on the page, Finlay evolved a range of ancillary conceptions of the poem: standing poems (printed on specially folded cards), poster poems, "kinetic" poems which release a serial meaning through the act of turning over the pages of a book, and three-dimensional poem-objects and poem-environments involving the use of metal or stone or glass and produced in cooperation with craftsmen in these materials. These meticulously designed and striking objects (especially successful are *Autumn Poem* and *Ocean Stripe 5* among the "kinetic" books, and "Wave/Rock" and "Seas/Ease" among the three-dimensional poems) have a characteristic distinction of using the simplest of means, and often a very Scottish and homely simplicity – rocks and water, boats and fishing-nets, canals and tugs, stars and potato-fields – to bring out patterns, harmonies, analogies, and meanings that transcend their strongly local and native roots.

Much of his effort has gone into making his own home environment at Stonypath a garden of emblems and symbols. Trees and water, plants and flowers, are brought into intimate relationship with inscribed slabs, benches, sundials, and other objects in such a way as to suggest new perspectives, and to restore old echoes, of the relation between man and nature. A slab inscribed with Albrecht Dürer's monogram is placed in a setting reminiscent of an actual Dürer water-colour; an aircraft-carrier carved out of stone and set on a plinth becomes a bird-bath, with real birds as imaginary aeroplanes; the slate conning-tower of a nuclear submarine stands black and sinister at the edge of a pond; the network of lines on a stone sundial suggests fishermen's nets on the sea. The recurrent use he makes in some of these works, and in other works of the 1970's, of formalized and emblematic military images, generally from the Second World War, raises questions of response, about which much remains to be written. But whatever questions his work gives rise to, it continues to exert its own distinctive fascination.

—Edwin Morgan

FINNIGAN, Joan. Canadian. Born in Ottawa, Ontario, 25 November 1925. Educated at Carleton University, Ottawa; Queen's University, Kingston, Ontario, B.A. Widow of Charles Grant MacKenzie (died, 1965); three children. Formerly, school teacher, and reporter for the Ottawa *Journal*. Since 1965, Free-lance Writer, for the National Film Board of Canada and the Canadian Broadcasting Corporation, Toronto. Recipient: Borestone Mountain Poetry Prize, 1959, 1961, 1963; Canada Council grant, 1965, 1967, 1968, 1969, 1973; Centennial Prize, 1967; President's Medal, University of Western Ontario, 1968; Etrog Award, for screenplay, 1969. Address: Harrowsmith, Ontario, Canada.

PUBLICATIONS

Verse

Through the Glass, Darkly. Toronto, Ryerson Press, 1957.
A Dream of Lilies. Fredericton, New Brunswick, Fiddlehead, 1965.
Entrance to the Green-house. Toronto, Ryerson Press, 1968.
It Was Warm and Sunny When We Set Out. Toronto, Ryerson Press, 1970.
In the Brown Cottage on Loughborough Lake. Toronto, CBC Learning Systems, 1970.
Living Together. Fredericton, New Brunswick, Fiddlehead, 1976.
A Reminder of Familiar Faces. Toronto, NC Press, 1978.

Plays

Up the Vallee (produced Ottawa, 1978).

Screenplay: *The Best Damn Fiddler from Calabogie to Kaladar*, 1969.

Other

Canada in Bed (as Michelle Bedard). Toronto, Pagurian Press, 1967.
Kingston: Celebrate This City. Toronto, McClelland and Stewart, 1976.
I Come from the Valley. Toronto, NC Press, 1976.
Canadian Colonial Cooking. Toronto, NC Press, 1976.
Canada: Country of the Giants. Toronto, NC Press, 1979.

Manuscript Collection: Queen's University, Kingston, Ontario.

Joan Finnigan comments:

Since I was seven I have been writing poetry. At forty I came to creative film-scripts and so began to write long poems. My poetry always veered towards the dramatic and my film-scripts are strongly poetic. The reason a creative film-script, done with integrity, is like a long poem is that both are condensations of intensity, a boiling down to the quintessence, a search for ultimate essence. I had matured enough to move from the short form – the poem – to the one requiring greater sustaining power – the screenplay – when the National Film Board of Canada began commissioning me to work for them.

* * *

That "poetry is not a turning loose of emotion but an escape from emotion" has become axiomatic in the criticism and the writing of modern poetry. Such a statement finds support in the general scientific and philosophic evolution of the age, and it informs the modern poetical canon's scepticism towards the perception of Nature as a paradigm for benevolent humanism or the articulation of traditional themes (love, birth, death, marriage) through the filter of sensibility removed from the conditioning factors of man-made environment. In Canada, this consciousness is central to the work of an E. J. Pratt and the poets of The McGill Movement, and it is emblematized in the wilderness-garden mythos of the Frye school of poets from D. G. Jones to Margaret Atwood. The rejection of facile romanticism at the core of Eliot's pronouncement was germane to the poetics initiated in the Twenties in Canada as a reaction against the nineteenth century Confederation Poets. At any rate, it is a commonplace now that the eternal verities can be improved by being expressed in diction and vision attuned to the age.

With these considerations in mind, it is no small surprise to encounter the poetry of Joan Finnigan celebrating a domestic world revolving around family life, the family cottage, the family friends, love and nature rendered in language free from sophistication. An openness toward self and others characterizes an outlook whose subjective correlative is the operations of benevolent Nature. The world is Edenic and pristine in her first three books, dominated by radiant colors and cheerful sounds controlled by the key symbol of the sun shining at the height of summer. There exudes a feeling of oneness with the elements culminating in transcendental intimations of immortality, no doubt sincerely felt by the poetess. Eve-like, but unlike Eve since her boundless innocence cannot precipitate any Fall of Man, she celebrates a garden whose paradisiacal emoluments she has no reason to suspect. To be sure, a few queries are raised ("Oh, who in all of heathendom,/Is half so sad as I?"), but they pose no threat of disruption to this Arcadia where no vital concerns are entertained.

Miss Finnigan's two favorite themes – love and nature – recur in her last books. The related feelings of nostalgia, flight of time, urbanophobia conveying an undercurrent of sweet melancholy are now accentuated with the intrusion of death. In *It Was Warm and Sunny When We Set Out*, the theme is, at first, embarrassingly stated – "And I think perpetually now of your dead HEART (for no one could get directions to that place, not even yourself) ..." – in the not surprising ingenuous confessional style – "Who, who could ever believe our private murders or the possibility of this revenge?" – which the poetess delights in. It finds a more felicitous expression, however, in the contrasting use of symbols. The sun that hitherto glowed on a bountiful world presently reflects the destruction of the Covenant: it is blinding, bleeding, mocking, scorching. Though the diction falters – "If people really love one another,/snow, why do they die?" – one finds interesting, nonetheless, the substitution of the symbolic winter grip for the vision of warmth generated by summer. The intensity of personal suffering finally yields through visceral apprehension a sober consciousness structured by a lucid polarization of the universals in Miss Finnigan's 1970 book, *In the Brown Cottage on Loughborough Lake*. In a book markedly contrasting with her early work, the weaving of alternating polarities (light and dark, summer and autumn, outer life and inner life, life and death, happiness and sorrow) germinates in the mature expression of pain endured, challenged and possibly conquered. Her beloved Nature is still there, as anthropomorphic as ever, the language is still mined with clichés, the world as restricted as usual. But this elegy, which can all too easily be assigned to the Wordsworthian canon, is quite moving in its expression of emotions barely recovering from the trauma of exposure to the existence of pain and cruelty. Even fractionally the poetess has been able to master and contain pain and bear witness to this control over emotion by finding a structure of objective correlatives, making this her best work to date. Maybe Eliot was not wrong after all.

—Max Dorsinville

FISHER, Roy. British. Born in Handsworth, Birmingham, Warwickshire, 11 June 1930. Educated at Wattville Road Elementary School; Handsworth Grammar School; Birmingham University, B.A., M.A. Married Barbara Venables in 1953; two sons. Pianist with jazz groups since 1946. School and college teacher, 1953–63; Principal Lecturer and Head of the Department of English and Drama, Bordesley College of Education, Birmingham, 1963–71. Since 1971, Member of the Department of American Studies, University of Keele, Staffordshire. Recipient: Andrew Kelus Prize, 1970. Address: Department of American Studies, University of Keele, Keele, Staffordshire ST5 5BG, England.

PUBLICATIONS

Verse

City. Worcester, Migrant Press, 1961.
Ten Interiors with Various Figures. Nottingham, Tarasque Press, 1967.
The Memorial Fountain. Newcastle upon Tyne, Northern House, 1967.
Collected Poems 1968: The Ghost of a Paper Bag. London, Fulcrum Press, 1969.
Correspondence. London, Tetrad Press, 1970.
Matrix. London, Fulcrum Press, 1971.
Also There. London, Tetrad Press, 1972.
Bluebeard's Castle. Guildford, Surrey, Circle Press, 1972.
Cultures. London, Tetrad Press, 1975.
Neighbours! Guildford, Surrey, Circle Press, 1976.
Nineteen Poems and an Interview. Pensnett, Staffordshire, Grosseteste, 1976.
Four Poems. Newcastle upon Tyne, Pig Press, 1976.
Widening Circles: Five Black Country Poets, with others, edited by Edward Lowbury. Stafford, West Midland Arts, 1976.
Barnardine's Reply. Knotting, Bedfordshire, Sceptre Press, 1977.
Scenes from the Alphabet. Guildford, Surrey, Circle Press, 1978.
The Thing about Joe Sullivan: Poems 1971–1977. Manchester, Carcanet Press, 1978.

Other

Then Hallucinations: City 2. Worcester, Migrant Press, 1962.
The Ship's Orchestra (prose poem). London, Fulcrum Press, 1966.
Titles. Nottingham, Tarasque Press, 1969.
Metamorphoses (prose poems). London, Tetrad Press, 1971.
The Cut Pages (prose poems). London, Fulcrum Press, 1971.

Critical Studies: "Resonances and Speculations upon Reading Roy Fisher's *City*" by Gael Turnbull, in *Kulchur 7* (New York), 1962; by Stuart Mills and Simon Cutts, in *Tarasque 5* (Nottingham), 1967; "Roy Fisher's Work" by Eric Mottram, in *Stand* (Newcastle upon

Tyne), xi, 1, 1969; "Roy Fisher: An Appreciation" in *Thomas Hardy and British Poetry* by Donald Davie, New York, Oxford University Press, 1972, and London, Routledge, 1973; Preface by Jon Silkin to *Poetry of the Committed Individual*, London, Gollancz-Penguin, 1973.

* * *

In a poem about Joe Sullivan, Roy Fisher evokes the pleasure which a listener experiences as his own perceptions, following Joe Sullivan's "through figures that sound obvious/find corners everywhere,/marks of invention, wakefulness;/the rapid and perverse/tracks that ordinary feelings/make when they are driven/hard enough against time." The reader, following through Roy Fisher's poems "the dry track of half a voice," finds that this poet preserves visual details of life with such accuracy – the winter afternoon sunlight on a slope "clear and pale like a redcurrant" – that an absolute confidence is built up as to the eventual emergence of significance, even when this is elusive: the poems are a triumph of conveying without saying. One could say that there are three movements in reading Fisher: first, intensely objective "language," verbal and perceptual; second, intensely subjective awareness of a state of mind, the "meaning" of the riddle; last, a joyful, objective recognition of the meeting of separate minds, vouched for by the emergence of that awareness. Two classicisms on either side of a romanticism.

Perhaps it is always true of a good poem that it is, at some level, a riddle whose meaning has to be incarnated in the reader but eludes paraphrase. With Fisher, though, the matching of awareness through the medium of art seems to occupy the philosophical centre. Although he is not a poet who is often explicit about his intentions – "What kind of man/comes in a message?" – there are passages throughout his work which indicate this clearly. True responses, *true* in the fullest sense, are for him both problematic and vitally important. The source of joy in art is precisely that, following the "dry track" left by the artist, we become aware, simultaneously, of his and our own struggle for clean, attentive life, issuing in the success of the work as direct experience.

The core of Fisher's writing, whether in prose or verse, is in this sense positive, though never brashly optimistic. There is sadness, even bitterness, concerning the attitudes our culture induces: "What's now only disproved/was once imagined." But "a genuine poet," as Goethe said, "always feels a call to fill himself with the glory of the world," and in *City* Fisher wrote: "Once I wanted to prove the world was sick. Now I want to prove it healthy." Tempted, one guesses, to "go mad after the things which are not," and yet determined not to be "able to feel only vertically, like a blind wall, or thickly, like the tyres of a bus," Fisher inhabits a ground of perceptual precisions made taut by a heart-rending, though quiet, sense of inexplicable significance beyond. The more one reads him, the more one wants to read, tantalised as by one's own immediate experience. "If you take a poem/you must take another/and another/till you have a poet," he has written. As one does so, one's moral and aesthetic response is increasingly to a man, an approach to living, rather than to isolated utterances.

Fisher's fineness lies in the extraordinary intimate communication he achieves, through the medium of a sophisticated, well-mannered art whose illusory coldness is the sign of a real respect for his own and his reader's individuality.

—Anne Cluysenaar

FITZGERALD, Robert (Stuart). American. Born in Geneva, New York, 12 October 1910. Educated at Springfield High School, Illinois; Choate School, Wallingford, Connecticut; Harvard University, Cambridge, Massachusetts, 1929–31, 1932–33, A.B. 1933;

Trinity College, Cambridge, 1931–32. Served in the United States Naval Reserve, 1943–46. Married Sarah Morgan in 1947 (separated, 1974); six children. Reporter, New York *Herald-Tribune*, 1933–35; Staff Writer, *Time* magazine, 1936–40, 1941–43, 1946–49. Instructor, Sarah Lawrence College, Bronxville, New York, 1946–53, and Princeton University, New Jersey, 1950–52; Poetry Reviewer, *New Republic*, Washington, D.C., 1948–52. Lived in Italy, 1953–64. Visiting Professor, Notre Dame University, Indiana, 1957, University of Washington, Seattle, 1961, and Mount Holyoke College, South Hadley, Massachusetts, 1964. Since 1965, Boylston Professor of Rhetoric, Harvard University. Since 1951, Fellow, Indiana University School of Letters, Bloomington. Recipient: Midland Author's Prize (*Poetry*, Chicago), 1931; Guggenheim Fellowship, 1952, 1971; Shelley Memorial Award, 1956; National Institute of Arts and Letters grant, 1957; Ford grant, 1959; Bollingen Award, for translation, 1961; Bollingen Fellowship, 1965; National Endowment for the Arts grant, 1969, 1972; Ingram Merrill Foundation grant, 1973, and award, 1978; London Translation Award, 1976; New England Poetry Club Golden Rose, 1976. D.Litt.: Holy Cross College, Worcester, Massachusetts, 1967; Rosary College, Rochester, New York, 1976; Loyola University, Chicago, 1976. Member, National Institute of Arts and Letters, 1961; Member, American Academy of Arts and Sciences, 1962. Chancellor, Academy of American Poets, 1968. Address: 3 Warren House, Harvard University, Cambridge, Massachusetts 02138, U.S.A.

Publications

Verse

Poems. New York, Arrow, 1935.
A Wreath for the Sea. New York, Arrow, 1943.
In the Rose of Time: Poems 1931–1956. New York, New Directions, 1956.
Ombra di Primavera (bilingual edition). Milan, Edizioni del Triangolo, 1959.
Spring Shade: Poems 1931–1970. New York, New Directions, 1971.

Other

Editor, *The Aeneid of Virgil, Translated by John Dryden.* New York, Macmillan, 1965.
Editor, *The Collected Poems of James Agee.* Boston, Houghton Mifflin, 1968.
Editor, *The Collected Short Prose of James Agee.* Boston, Houghton Mifflin, 1968; London, Calder and Boyars, 1972.
Editor, with Sally Fitzgerald, *Mystery and Manners: Occasional Prose*, by Flannery O'Connor. New York, Farrar Straus, 1969.
Editor, *In Another Country: Poems 1935–1975*, by James Laughlin. San Francisco, City Lights, 1978.

Translator, with Dudley Fitts, *Alcestis*, by Euripides. New York, Harcourt Brace, 1936.
Translator, with Dudley Fitts, *Antigone*, by Sophocles. New York, Harcourt Brace, 1939.
Translator, *Oedipus at Colonus*, by Sophocles. New York, Harcourt Brace, 1941; London, Faber, 1957.
Translator, with Dudley Fitts, *Oedipus Rex*, by Sophocles. New York, Harcourt Brace, 1949; London, Faber, 1950.
Translator, with Dudley Fitts, *The Oedipus Cycle.* New York, Harcourt Brace, 1958.
Translator, *Amphion*, *Semiramis*, and *The Narcissus Cantata*, in *Plays*, by Paul Valéry. New York, Pantheon, and London, Routledge, 1960.
Translator, *The Odyssey*, by Homer. New York, Doubleday, 1961; London, Heinemann, 1962.

Translator, *Chronique*, by St. John Perse. New York, Pantheon, 1961.
Translator, *Birds*, by St. John Perse. New York, Pantheon, 1965.
Translator, *Dante*, in *Two Addresses*, by St. John Perse. New York, Pantheon, 1966.
Translator, *Deathwatch on the Southside*, by Jorge Luis Borges. Cambridge, Massachusetts, Grolier Book Shop, 1968.
Translator, *The Little Passion: 37 Wood-cuts by Albrecht Dürer ... with the Latin Poems of Benedictus Chelidonius....* Verona, Italy, Officina Bodoni, 1971.
Translator, *The Iliad*, by Homer. New York, Doubleday, 1974.

Manuscript Collections: Houghton Library, Harvard University, Cambridge, Massachusetts; Berg Collection, New York Public Library.

Robert Fitzgerald comments:

I have been independent and trustful of my own powers. Poetry can be at least an elegance, at most a revelation, and I have worked as opportunity offered between these limits. Eliot was and remains a great touchstone and irritant. The Greek Masters have been before me often, and more lately so has Dante. I hold by constructive beauty, energy of language, depth of life.

* * *

Robert Fitzgerald's original poetry has probably not had the attention it deserves because (ironically) of his great distinction as a teacher and as a translator. Furthermore, as Donald Davidson wrote in reviewing his first book – one of, he claimed, "major" accent – Fitzgerald's "subject and form are minor."

As befits one of this century's finest translators of Greek in the English language, Fitzgerald's sense of form – best described as pliant rather than free – is highly developed. From the beginning his poems, whatever their scope, were word perfect, rhythmically impeccable. In an early poem "In This House," the enjambements already display a practised and craftsmanlike poet:

In this house of the untidy lamp, a
Man is leafing lexicons, his
Limpid fingers in forgotten
Brains....

Who dreamt he bedded with a whore
's face, body of a child....

There is here already, too, a somewhat over-bookish, though never dry, quality, which has characterized all Fitzgerald's poetry. He is nothing if not a literary poet. However, and again in poetry of the first half of the Thirties, he anticipated many aspects of post-war poetry – aspects that were not to be confined to English poetry. Sometimes he is merely mannered ("... Keenly/Clenching the eye push into bone wisp, see/How thick the shadow is, teems, is prodigious,/Stored with time ...") but at others he is genuinely concerned with the interior of the mind – in a manner somewhat akin to that of the Swedish poet Ekelöf in his immediately post-surrealist "suicidal" phase of the mid-Thirties. Thus he could produce, before 1935, a line such as "Between dinner and death the crowds shadow the loom of steel" – and that this is "Park Avenue" (the title) does not diminish, but rather reinforces, the inner resonances.

Fitzgerald's post-war poetry became more rhetorical, more cultural (in the "American-in-Europe" sense), a little simpler: the poems are not perhaps as suggestive as the earlier, but the ear has remained as sure, and one is always in the presence of an elegant and educated sensibility. "The Painter" thus packs in much comment on its subject, and is as intellectually calculated as it is eloquent, as its opening stanza shows:

On bluish inlets bristling
Black in the tall north,
Like violet ghosts risen
The great fish swam forth,
And hoary blooms and submarine
Lightning in the cradling west
Lent summer her vivid sheen
For the deep eye's interest.

—Martin Seymour-Smith

FitzGERALD, Robert D(avid). Australian. Born in Hunters Hill, New South Wales, 22 February 1902. Educated at Sydney Grammar School; Sydney University, 1920–21; Fellow, Institution of Surveyors. Married Marjorie-Claire Harris in 1931; four children. Surveyor, FitzGerald and Blair, 1926–30; Native Lands Commission Surveyor, Fiji, 1931–36; Municipal Surveyor, 1936–39; Surveyor, Australian Department of the Interior, 1939–66, now retired. Visiting Lecturer, University of Texas, Austin, 1963. Recipient: Australian Sesqui-Centenary Poetry Prize, 1938; Australian Literature Society Gold Medal, 1938; Grace Leven Prize, 1952, 1959, 1962; Fulbright grant, 1963; Encyclopedia Britannica Award, 1965. O.B.E. (Officer, Order of the British Empire), 1951. Address: 4 Prince Edward Parade, Hunters Hill, New South Wales 2110, Australia.

PUBLICATIONS

Verse

The Greater Apollo. Privately printed, 1927.
To Meet the Sun. Sydney, Angus and Robertson, 1929.
Moonlight Acre. Melbourne, Melbourne University Press, 1938.
Heemskerck Shoals. Melbourne, Mountainside Press, 1949.
Between Two Tides. Sydney, Angus and Robertson, 1952.
This Night's Orbit: Verses. Melbourne, Melbourne University Press, 1953.
The Wind at Your Door: A Poem. Sydney, Talkarra Press, 1959.
Southmost Twelve. Sydney, Angus and Robertson, 1962.
Of Some Country: 27 Poems. Austin, University of Texas, 1963.
(*Poems*), selected and introduced by the author. Sydney, Angus and Robertson, 1963.
Forty Years' Poems. Sydney, Angus and Robertson, 1965.
Product. Sydney, Angus and Robertson, 1978.

Other

The Elements of Poetry. Brisbane, University of Queensland Press, 1963.
Of Places and Poetry. Brisbane, University of Queensland Press, 1976.

Editor, *Australian Poetry 1942.* Sydney, Angus and Robertson, 1942.
Editor, *Selected Verse*, by Mary Gilmore. Sydney and London, Angus and Robertson, 1948; revised edition, 1969.
Editor, *The Letters of Hugh McCrae.* Sydney, Angus and Robertson, 1970.

Critical Studies: *Six Australian Poets* by T. Inglis Moore, Melbourne, Robertson and Mullen,

1942; *Literature of Australia* edited by Geoffrey Dutton, Melbourne, Penguin, 1964; *Preoccupations in Australian Poetry* by Judith Wright, Melbourne, Oxford University Press, 1965; *Robert D. FitzGerald* by A. Grove Day, New York, Twayne, 1973.

* * *

The outstanding characteristics of Robert D. FitzGerald's poetry are his command of technique and, in Matthew Arnold's term, his "high seriousness." His verse is plain, bare, without ornament and almost without adjectives, taking its life from his vigorous individual speech rhythm and the controlled emotional intensity of his thought; and his thought is concerned with Australia's national destiny in this place "which lay, unleased,/beneath its empty centuries and stars turning,/... waking under his love"; with the aspiration that has taken mankind into far places and far thoughts and achievements:

the necessity in men, deep down, close cramped,
not seen in their own hearts, for some attempt
at being more than ordinary men,
rising above themselves;

and ultimately, because both national destiny and worthwhile achievement depend upon it, with human integrity:

Attitude matters: bearing. Action in the end
goes down the stream as motion, merges as such
with the whole of life and time; but islands stand:
dignity and distinction that attach
to the inmost being of us each.
It matters for man's private respect that still
face differs from face and will from will.

It is important how men looked and were.
Infirm, staggering a little as Hastings was,
his voice was steady as his eyes. Kneeling at the bar
(ruler but late of millions) had steeled his poise;
he fronted inescapable loss
and thrown, stinking malice and disrepute,
calmly, a plain man in a plain suit.

Though he has written many admirable short poems, from his early lyrical reflections on life and landscape set in Fiji (where he spent some years as a surveyor) to the more recent profound meditations of *Product*, his reputation rests chiefly on a number of medium-length and long poems. Among these, "The Hidden Bole" is a curious exploration of the banyan tree for the "hidden bole," the central principle hidden in the complexity of existence. "Essay on Memory," which won the poetry prize in the Australian sesqui-centenary competition, deals with the influence of the past in human history upon the present. "The Face of the Waters," unusually fluid in technique, is an extraordinary vision of the creation and perpetual recreation of the universe. *Between Two Tides*, a poem of book length, is an epic of tribal war in Tonga, by implication a commentary on power politics and corruption by power. And "Heemskerck Shoals" (about the navigator Abel Janszoon Tasman), "Fifth Day" (about the shorthand writer who recorded the trial of Warren Hastings), and "The Wind at Your Door" (about the convicts and their masters who were the first settlers of Australia) are poems of that middle length in which his powers of sustained thought and construction and the portrayal of character in action have reached their most impressive combination.

—Douglas Stewart

FLETCHER, Ian. British. Born in London, 22 August 1920. Educated at Dulwich College, London; Goldsmiths' College, University of London; University of Reading, Berkshire, Ph.D. 1965. Served in the Middle East in the Ministry of Information and Forces Broadcasting, 1942–46. Married Loraine Hollyman in 1965; two children. Children's Librarian, Lewisham Borough Council, 1946–55. Since 1965, Reader in English Literature, University of Reading. Address: Faculty of Letters, The University, Whiteknights Park, Reading, Berkshire, England.

PUBLICATIONS

Verse

An Homily to Kenneth Topley. Privately printed, 1945.
Orisons, Picaresque and Metaphysical. London, Editions Poetry London, 1947.
The Lover's Martyrdom: Translations from the Italian of Dante, Guarini, Tasso, and Marino with Original Texts. Oxford, Fantasy Press, 1957.
Motets: Twenty One Poems. Reading, University of Reading, 1962.
The Milesian Intrusion: A Restoration Comedy Version of Iliad XIV. Nottingham, Byron Press, 1968.

Plays

A Passion Play. Khartoum, Sudan Bookstore, 1943.
Get Up What Stairs?, with Peter Myers (produced London, 1948).

Other

Partheneia Sacra. Aldington, Kent, Hand and Flower Press, 1950.
Walter Pater. London, Longman, 1959; revised edition, 1971.
A Catalogue of the Imagist Poets, with Wallace Martin. New York, J. H. Woolmer, 1966.
Beaumont and Fletcher. London, Longman, 1967.
Swinburne. London, Longman, 1973.

Editor, with G. S. Fraser, *Springtime: An Anthology of Young Poets and Writers.* London, Peter Owen, 1953.
Editor, *The Complete Poems of Lionel Johnson.* London, Unicorn Press, 1953.
Editor, *Romantic Mythologies.* London, Routledge, and New York, Barnes and Noble, 1967.
Editor, *Meredith Now.* London, Routledge, and New York, Barnes and Noble, 1971.
Editor, *Selections from British Fiction 1880–1900.* New York, New American Library, 1972.
Editor, *Poems of Victor Plarr.* London, E. and J. Stevens, 1974.
Editor, *Collected Poems of John Gray.* London, Cecil Woolf, 1974.
Editor, *Fifty Renascence Love Poems*, translated by Edwin Morgan. Reading, Whiteknights Press, 1975.
Editor, *Decadence and the Eighteen-Nineties.* London, Arnold, 1979.

Manuscript Collections: State University of New York, Buffalo; University of Kansas, Lawrence; University of Reading, Berkshire.

Ian Fletcher comments:

Dualism; topographical and architectural topics; moderately strict verse forms. Influence, Yeats; I like trying my hand at free translation. Syllabics need not apply.

Ian Fletcher was one of the most interesting poets to reach maturity during the Forties, and some critics have expressed regret that he seems to have half-abandoned his career – whether this is so or not, he has certainly published much less in recent years. But some of this strongly-thewed and energetic later work shows signs of a development towards a greater directness and increase in purely descriptive power. His early poems were highly involute, well-made, reflecting an intelligence engaged with problems of culture, often expressed in terms of the past, and with the significance of religious change. *The Maenad under the Cross*, the title of a projected volume that never appeared, aptly sums up his position. His best-known poem, "Adolescents in the Dusk" is the apogee of his earlier manner, and well illustrates his technical control, subtle use of metaphor, and the metaphysicality that underlies his pictorial imagination:

About this time when dusk falls like a shutter
Upon the decomposition of the time
Eliding eye and day and surfaces and shapes,
Whitening of faces like stoles in the twilight ...
When the gardens between the houses are rose –
Encumbered with sidereal roses
And the roads like gorges grey in the tired light of falling....

The new poems are less involute, more confident, stronger in thrust – but they do not sacrifice the old subtlety. Fletcher was once a leading poet of his generation, and a serious one; it is to be hoped that current fashions will not obscure his earlier or his later achievement, and that he will be encouraged to put himself forward, once again, as the owner of a distinctive voice and manner.

—Martin Seymour-Smith

FORD, Charles Henri. American. Born in Hazlehurst, Mississippi, 10 February 1913. Lived in Paris in the 1920's. Editor, *Blues*, Columbus, Mississippi, 1929–30; *View*, New York, 1940–47. Photographer and Painter: One-Man Shows – Institute of Contemporary Arts, London, 1955; Galerie Marforen, Paris, 1956; Galerie du Dragon, Paris, 1957, 1958; Cordier and Ekstrom Gallery, New York, 1965; New York Cultural Center, 1975; Carlton Gallery, New York, 1975. Agent: Oscar Collier, 280 Madison Avenue, New York, New York 10016. Address: 1 West 72nd Street, New York, New York 10023, U.S.A.

PUBLICATIONS

Verse

A Pamphlet of Sonnets. Mallorca, Caravel Press, 1936.
The Garden of Disorder and Other Poems. New York, New Directions, and London, Europa, 1938.
ABC's. Prairie City, Illinois, James A. Decker, 1940.
The Overturned Lake. Cincinnati, Little Man Press, 1941.
Poems for Painters. New York, View, 1945.
The Half-Thoughts, The Distances of Pain. New York, Gotham Bookmart, 1947.
Sleep in a Nest of Flames. New York, New Directions, 1949.
Spare Parts. New York, New View, 1966.

Silver Flower Coo. New York, Kulchur, 1968.
Flag of Ecstasy: Selected Poems, edited by Edward B. Germain. Los Angeles, Black Sparrow Press, 1972.
On Krishna. Cherry Valley, New York, Cherry Valley Editions, 1978.

Play

Screenplay: *Johnny Minotaur*, 1971.

Novel

The Young and Evil, with Parker Tyler. Paris, Obelisk Press, 1933; New York, Arno Press, 1973.

Other

Editor and Translator, *The Mirror of Baudelaire.* New York, New Directions, 1942.
Editor, *A Night with Jupiter and Other Fantastic Stories.* New York, View, 1945; London, Dobson, 1947.

Manuscript Collection: University of Texas, Austin.

Critical Studies: Introduction by William Carlos Williams to *The Garden of Disorder and Other Poems*, 1938; Introduction by Edith Sitwell to *Sleep in a Nest of Flames*, 1949.

* * *

When he began publishing in 1929, Charles Henri Ford was unique: America's surrealist poet. In retrospect, he is seminal. His first two books create American surrealism. *Garden of Disorder* welds together radio jazz and iambic pentameter, surrealist conceits and the sonnet form. *The Overturned Lake* shows Ford as influenced by Whitman, Poe, and Mother Goose as by Breton, Reverdy, and Eluard, employing a freer line and lyric forms. It demonstrates Ford's forte: the surrealist image. In one poem, Ford transforms the day from a poem into a horse. He turns the sky into an arm, a mouth, a man, a thief, and then into an enormous face. The sun, he makes into a wound, a jewel, an equation, an eye, a tear. Night is a ditch. All in eight lines, with obvious ease, and clarity.

The "New York School" centered around Frank O'Hara and John Ashbery owes something to these early surrealist lyrics. During World War II, Ford encouraged young poets, like Philip Lamantia, in the pages of his influential surrealist magazine, *View* – the first literary magazine to publish Allen Ginsberg. Ford himself began writing longer poems at this time, typically part dream or ghost-story, part amoral allegory, filled with convulsive imagery and sexual themes. Often parts of these poems are greater than their whole. The self-conscious mannerism implicit in many of them surfaces in Ford's next two books, *Spare Parts* and *Silver Flower Coo*, collage poems which are exercises in gratuitous eroticism. Another, far more interesting series, written but not published during this period, are Ford's prose-poems and found-poetry, represented in the "Drawings" section of his selected poems.

Ford's best work lies predominantly with the rather narrow lyric form in his early books. Some of these poems, "Plaint" for example, are among the most evocative and moving short lyrics of our century. In most, Ford creates wonder, wit, and a sensuous beauty free from the predictable tropes and rapacious glibness of much surrealist-influenced poetry of the 1960's and 1970's.

—Edward B. Germain

FORD, R(obert) A(rthur) D(ouglass). Canadian. Born in Ottawa, Ontario, 8 January 1915. Educated at the University of Western Ontario, London, B.A. 1937; Cornell University, Ithaca, New York, M.A. 1940. Married Maria Thereza Gomes in 1946. Member of the History Department, Cornell University, 1938–40. Joined the Canadian Department of External Affairs, 1940; served in Rio de Janeiro, Moscow, and London, 1940–51; Head of the European Division, Ottawa, 1954–57; Ambassador to Colombia, 1957–58, to Yugoslavia, 1959–61, and to the United Arab Republic, 1961–63. Since 1964, Canadian Ambassador to the Soviet Union. Recipient: Governor-General's Medal, 1957. D.Litt.: University of Western Ontario, 1965. Companion of Order of Canada, 1971. Address: Canadian Embassy, Moscow, U.S.S.R.

PUBLICATIONS

Verse

A Window on the North. Toronto, Ryerson Press, 1956.
The Solitary City. Toronto, McClelland and Stewart, 1969.
Holes in Space. Toronto, Hounslow Press, 1979.

* * *

The poetic canon of R. A. D. Ford is relatively small, but one clear voice emerges. These are quiet, serious poems, lyric rather than dramatic, but always restrained. They explore around the edges of emotion, seldom taking risks. They offer little irony, less of the comic, very few surprises. And yet they are nearly all worth reading – consistently competent, sincere, quietly rewarding.

A sense of isolation pervades Ford's poems, whether in the loneliness of open spaces or the equally barren "landscape of the past." Also regularly present – especially in *A Window on the North* – is an oppressive sense of the Cold, silently "smothering the world," pressing into rooms and lives, invading

> The sanctity of man propped lone on
> The plain edge of winter, not
> Day but the dull half white dawn
> Of the never-ending snow night....

For the most part Ford's poetry is marked by clear statement and traditional meters. He sometimes employs rhyme effectively (as in "Avoiding Greece"), but usually when rhyme is present, too much else appears sacrificed to it. This intrusion of technique is, somewhat surprisingly, more common in *The Solitary City* than in his first book. Fortunately, he avoids rhyme in most of his poems, and the best of his later work demonstrates a growing freedom from form and a more successful, more believably earned realization of experience (as in "The Thieves of Love" and "How Doth the Solitary City Stand").

Ford's translations deserve special note, for they demonstrate both fidelity to the spirit of the originals and a view of Ford's abilities that remain hidden behind self-imposed restraints in much of his own poetry. The quality of the translations and adaptations appears consistently high, and the range of his interests (from the Russian of Pasternak, Akhmatova, Yessenin, and others, to Brazilian Portuguese, French, and Serbo-Croatian) is in itself impressive. Together they reinforce the impression one has from Ford's own poems, that the deeply quiet, unpretentious voice of R. A. D. Ford is one worth hearing.

—Stanley W. Lindberg

FOWLER, Gene. American. Born in Oakland, California, 5 October 1931. High school education. Served in the United States Army, three years. Served five years in San Quentin Prison. Poet-in-Residence, University of Wisconsin, Milwaukee, Summer 1970. Recipient: National Endowment for the Arts grant, 1970. Address: 463–C 61st Street, Oakland, California 94609, U.S.A.

PUBLICATIONS

Verse

Field Studies. El Cerrito, California, Dustbooks, 1965.
Quarter Tones. Grande Ronde, Oregon, GRR Press, 1966.
Shaman Songs. El Cerrito, California, Dustbooks, 1967.
Her Majesty's Ship. Sacramento, California, Grande Ronde Press, 1969.
Fires. Berkeley, California, Thorp Springs Press, 1971.
Vivisection. Berkeley, California, Thorp Springs Press, 1974.
Felon's Journal. San Francisco, Second Coming Press, 1975.
Fires: Selected Poems 1963–1976. Berkeley, California, Thorp Springs Press, 1975.

Critical Study: by James K. Bell, in *Eikon* (Ogunquit, Maine), i, 1, 1967.

Gene Fowler comments:

There are no "positions" for non-academic poets. Officially, I am illiterate. Not qualified to teach the use of language, existing literature or other such.

I am not and have never been a member of a school of poetry – though reviewers have tried to stuff me into one or another. I battle against such entities.

Whitman wrote critical analysis of his own work – but under other names. I've done what amounts to c. a. in letters. But, here, I'll say only what I believe I'm up to. I want to write poems that when recalled are confused with the reader's own experiences, not recalled – at first – as "something read" but as "something that happened." Fighting against myth perpetuated by both outlaws and academics that craft is the same thing as academic tone. I take the Orphic myth literally. Believe words can induce and manipulate perceptions. Intend, in my poems, to prove this.

* * *

Gene Fowler is a contemporary symbolist, a maker of surprising equations. In poems like "The Lover," these equations develop dramatically, become revelations; the body of the beloved is the earth. "The Words" is a little allegory about writing:

I carry boulders across the day
From the field to the ridge,
And my back grows tired ...
I take a drop of sweat
Onto my thumb,
Watch the wind furrow its surface,
Dream of a morning
When my furrows will shape this field,
When these rocks will form my house.
Alone, with heavy arms,
I listen through the night to older farms.

Unlike Creeley, who has a collection titled *Words*, Fowler finds writing a heavy labor. His rhythms, in poems like "Venus Returns to the Sea," are heavy (though that is not a literal deduction from a symbolic equation). What happens to words transmuted into poems? They grow hot, like coals or fires: "i come upon stones/in the wind shoved grasses//they wait/tensed/curled in on themselves//i reach out to touch/sun warmed quiet and flame/jumps to scorch my fingers."

Fowler's first major collection is called *Fires*. The symbols are systematically deployed. "Shaman Songs," collected in *Fires* (though mangled by the publisher), compares society to an Indian tribe and the poet to a neglected shaman. The songs rise above symbol and allegory to ritual and magic, as in "on taking coal from the fire in naked fingers": "The word/is in the hand./Under the moon/in the hand./At the head of the valley/in the hand./It glows in the hand./Here!/Look here/in the hand./Look at the word/in the hand./It glows./A great translucence/in the hand./Go thru the translucence/in the hand./Into the world/in the hand."

—Michael André

FRAME, Janet. New Zealander. Born in Dunedin, 28 August 1924. Educated at Oamaru North School; Waitaki Girls' High School; Otago University Teachers Training College, Dunedin. Recipient: Church Memorial Award, 1951, 1954; New Zealand Literary Fund Award, 1960; New Zealand Scholarship in Letters, 1964; Robert Burns Fellowship, Otago University, 1965. D.Litt.: Otago University, 1978. Address: c/o Brandt and Brandt, 101 Park Avenue, New York, New York 10017, U.S.A.

PUBLICATIONS

Verse

The Pocket Mirror. New York, Braziller, and London, W. H. Allen, 1967.

Novels

Owls Do Cry. Christchurch, Pegasus Press, 1957; New York, Braziller, 1960; London, W. H. Allen, 1961.
Faces in the Water. Christchurch, Pegasus Press, and New York, Braziller, 1961; London, W. H. Allen, 1962.
The Edge of the Alphabet. Christchurch, Pegasus Press, New York, Braziller, and London, W. H. Allen, 1962.
Scented Gardens for the Blind. Christchurch, Pegasus Press, and London, W. H. Allen, 1963; New York, Braziller, 1964.
The Adaptable Man. Christchurch, Pegasus Press, New York, Braziller, and London, W. H. Allen, 1965.
A State of Siege. New York, Braziller, 1966; London, W. H. Allen, 1967.
The Rainbirds. London, W. H. Allen, 1968; as *Yellow Flowers in the Antipodean Room*, New York, Braziller, 1969.
Intensive Care. New York, Braziller, 1970; London, W. H. Allen, 1971.
Daughter Buffalo. New York, Braziller, 1972; London, W. H. Allen, 1973.
Living in the Maniototo. New York, Braziller, 1979.

Short Stories

The Lagoon: Stories. Christchurch, Pegasus Press, 1951; revised edition, as *The Lagoon and Other Stories*, 1961.
The Reservoir: Stories and Sketches. New York, Braziller, 1963.
Snowman, Snowman: Fables and Fantasies. New York, Braziller, 1963.
The Reservoir and Other Stories. Christchurch, Pegasus Press, and London, W. H. Allen, 1966.

Other

Mona Minim and the Smell of the Sun (juvenile). New York, Braziller, 1969.

Bibliography: by John Beston, in *World Literature Written in English* (Austin, Texas), November 1978.

* * *

Janet Frame is best known as a novelist. She has published only one collection of poems – *The Pocket Mirror.* It has the appearance, not of a nervous slim volume of carefully selected, carefully worked samples of the writer's best, but of a file of poems, each hastily written and quickly forgotten, taken up and sent to the publisher without revision, perhaps to be rid of them. All their strengths and limitations depend on the casual indifference with which they have been written. Janet Frame is not indifferent to her subject matter but to the art of poetry itself. She is also immensely talented, endlessly inventive, fluent, and has a good ear. Her natural mode of thinking is not abstract but in images. So her poems are mostly "thoughts," "ideas," put down in the form of free verse. Their weakness is often that they are neither fish nor fowl – too abstract for the images to seem solid, hard, irreducible reality; and not rigorous enough to seem more than whimsical when considered as ideas. They are also a kind of verbal conjuring, the images conjured into being as an illustration of her thought rather than convincingly confronted in nature. Thus Miss Frame has primacy over Nature, which seems the wrong way about.

But Miss Frame has the enviable freedom of a talented writer not wholly committed to poetry. To compare her with another New Zealand woman poet, Fleur Adcock, is instructive. There can be no doubt that Miss Adcock's poems are better made – yet her work can seem crabbed and cramped when set alongside the novelist's casual fluency, which can afford so many misses and still score enough remarkable hits to make her presence as a poet felt.

—C. K. Stead

FRANCIS, Robert (Churchill). American. Born in Upland, Pennsylvania, 12 August 1901. Educated at Harvard University, Cambridge, Massachusetts, A.B. 1923, Ed.M. 1926. Phi Beta Kappa Poet, Tufts University, Medford, Massachusetts, 1955, and Harvard University, 1960. Recipient: Shelley Memorial Award, 1939; New England Poetry Club Golden Rose, 1942; American Academy in Rome Fellowship, 1957; Jennie Tane Award (*Massachusetts Review*), 1962; Amy Lowell Traveling Scholarship, 1967; Brandeis University Creative Arts Award, 1974. L.H.D.: University of Massachusetts, Amherst, 1970. Address: Fort Juniper, 170 Market Hill Road, Amherst, Massachusetts 01002, U.S.A.

PUBLICATIONS

Verse

Stand with Me Here. New York, Macmillan, 1936.
Valhalla and Other Poems. New York, Macmillan, 1938.
The Sound I Listened For. New York, Macmillan, 1944.
The Face Against the Glass. Amherst, Massachusetts, privately printed, 1950.
The Orb Weaver: Poems. Middletown, Connecticut, Wesleyan University Press, 1960.
Come Out into the Sun: Poems New and Selected. Amherst, University of Massachusetts Press, 1965.
Like Ghosts of Eagles: Poems 1966–1974. Amherst, University of Massachusetts Press, 1974.
Collected Poems 1936–1976. Amherst, University of Massachusetts Press, 1976.

Recordings: *Today's Poets 1*, with others, Folkways, 1967; *Robert Francis Reads His Poems*, Folkways, 1975.

Novel

We Fly Away. New York, Swallow Press, 1948.

Other

The Satirical Rogue on Poetry (essays). Amherst, University of Massachusetts Press, 1968.
The Trouble with Francis: An Autobiography. Amherst, University of Massachusetts Press, 1971.

Editor, *A Time to Talk: Conversations and Indiscretions*, by Robert Frost. Amherst, University of Massachusetts Press, 1972; London, Robson Books, 1973.

Critical Studies: "Constants Carried Forward: Naturalness in the Poetry of Robert Francis" by John Holmes, in *Massachusetts Review* (Amherst), Summer 1960; by Albert Stewart, in *Masterplots: 1967 Annual*, New York, Salem Press, 1967.

Robert Francis comments:

Neither avant-garde nor traditional. Less and less dependence on accepted forms while stressing form itself, the forming of the poem. Early poems, quiet and brooding; later poems, more active and colorful. During the 60's some poems in a new technique I call "word-count." Still more recently poems that explore surface fragmentation to intensify impact of total poem.

* * *

Robert Francis is a balanced poet, both in art and sensibility. Although his rhythms are variable, his rhyming flexible, his language fresh, and his world is an out-of-doors and immediate universe, his poems are carefully structured, often too carefully structured. And, although his outlook is mature and in some ways profound, it is more placid and complacent than intense and compelling. Each poem represents a serene process of unfolding rather than a shocking flash of revelation, suffering from a kind of overdevelopment caused by excessive explicitness in dealing with the material and drawing out its meaning. And this in turn, paradoxically, seems to be the effect of a certain limitation of insight, as if over-explicitness were a compensation for deficiency of vision and passionate involvement.

The first section of *The Orb Weaver*, for example, deals largely with skill and the analogies the poet sees between various bodily skills and those of art. He writes about boys riding horses, baseball players, wrestlers, divers, swimmers, and so on. And his interest lies in the tension of balance that such skills must sustain between opposing forces. And yet, as in "Two Wrestlers," all is too perfectly balanced and worked out; he at once says too much and implies too little. The second section is mainly about Nature – her fruits, seasons, mountains, creatures, and so on. These are good poems, and they speak movingly of fulness. "Waxwings," for example, depends more for its effect on imagery and less on explanation than usual: "Four Tao philosophers as cedar waxwings/chat on a February berrybush/in sun, and I am one." Section III is primarily concerned with the relation of people to Nature. "The Revellers" is one of the most effective, portraying crowds joyously enthralled by summer, and so is reminiscent of Stevens' "Sunday Morning" and "Credences of Summer," but it is, alas, almost entirely without the greater poet's depth and intensity. The fourth section gets darker, dwelling more on the side of night and winter, and the stanza-patterns become more regular, perhaps as a sign of the need to control a threatening mood. "Three Darks Come Down Together" is quite good. The fifth and final section is darker still, dealing with death, winter, and loss. Robert Frost is a strong influence, and this becomes most specific in the title poem, "The Orb Weaver," which is about a ghastly spider much like the one in Frost's "Design." A reading of Francis' conclusion, however, will not sustain the comparison: "I have no quarrel with the spider/But with the mind or mood that made her/To thrive in nature and in man's nature." "Two Bums Walk Out of Eden," though, is interesting, and "Cold," which describes a freeze, is excellent:

Under the glaring and sardonic sun,
Behind the icicles and double glass
I huddle, hoard, hold out, hold on, hold on.

Collected Poems 1936–1976 contains *The Orb Weaver*, all of his previous volumes, plus his most recent ones, *Come Out into the Sun* and *Like Ghosts of Eagles*. His development, as he says in his Preface, is becoming "bolder and livelier," and it is true that his recent work shows significant signs of diversification in mood, style, and structure. He is experimenting with word count, fragmented surface, and fused syntax. And yet he remains by and large objective and impersonal, not in the modernist sense of integrating the intensely subjective into the controlling structure of the poem, but rather in the sense of being simply an observer – acute, perceptive, witty, but with neither an anguished self that must wrestle with experience nor an ability to blend with and dramatize the anguish of others. Too much of his autobiography is kept from his poems; indeed, much of it is rather low-keyed in *The Trouble with Francis*, his autobiography, itself.

—Norman Friedman

FRASER, G(eorge) S(utherland). British. Born in Glasgow, Scotland, 8 November 1915. Educated at Glasgow Academy; Aberdeen Grammar School; St. Andrews University, M.A. 1937. Served in the Middle East, 1939–45. Married Eileen Lucy Andrew in 1946; two daughters and one son. Journalist, Aberdeen *Press and Journal*, 1937–39. Free-lance Journalist, 1946–59. Cultural Adviser to the UK Liaison Mission in Japan, 1950–51. Regular Reviewer and Leaderwriter, *Times Literary Supplement*, London. Reviewer, *New Statesman*, London, and "New Poetry" broadcaster on BBC radio, in the 1950's. Lecturer, 1959–63, and Reader in Modern English Literature, 1964–79, University of Leicester. Visiting Professor, Rochester University, New York, 1963–64. Recipient: Hodder and Stoughton bursary, 1946. *Died 3 January 1980.*

PUBLICATIONS

Verse

The Fatal Landscape and Other Poems. London, Editions Poetry London, 1943.
Home Town Elegy. London, Editions Poetry London, 1944.
The Traveller Has Regrets and Other Poems. London, Harvill Press-Editions Poetry London, 1948.
Leaves Without a Tree. Tokyo, Hokuseido Press, 1956.
Conditions: Selected Recent Poetry. Nottingham, Byron Press, 1969.

Other

Vision of Scotland. London, Elek, 1948.
News from South America (travel). London, Harvill Press, 1949; New York, Library Publishers, 1952.
Post-War Trends in English Literature. Tokyo, Hokuseido Press, 1950.
Impressions of Japan and Other Essays. Tokyo, Asahi-Shimbun-Sha, 1952.
Three Philosophical Essays. Tokyo, Eibunsha, n.d.
The Modern Writer and His World. London, Verschoyle, 1953; New York, Criterion, 1955; revised edition, London, Deutsch, 1964; New York, Praeger, 1965; London, Penguin, 1968.
W. B. Yeats. London, Longman, 1954; revised edition, 1962, 1965.
Scotland. London, Thames and Hudson, and New York, Studio, 1955.
Dylan Thomas. London, Longman, 1957; revised edition, 1964.
Vision and Rhetoric: Studies in Modern Poetry. London, Faber, 1959; New York, Barnes and Noble, 1960.
Ezra Pound. Edinburgh, Oliver and Boyd, 1960; New York, Grove Press, 1961.
Lawrence Durrell: A Critical Study. London, Faber, 1968; New York, Dutton, 1969; revised edition, Faber, 1973.
Lawrence Durrell. London, Longman, 1970.
Metre, Rhythm, and Free Verse. London, Methuen, 1970.
P. H. Newby. London, Longman, 1974.
Essays on Twentieth-Century Poets. Leicester, Leicester University Press, and Totowa, New Jersey, Rowman and Littlefield, 1977.
Alexander Pope. London, Routledge, 1978.
A Short History of English Poetry. London, Open Books, 1979.

Editor, with John Waller, *The Collected Poems of Keith Douglas.* London, Editions Poetry London, 1951; revised edition, with Waller and J. C. Hall, London, Faber, 1966; New York, Chilmark Press, 1967.
Editor, with Ian Fletcher, *Springtime: An Anthology of Young Poets and Writers.* London, Peter Owen, 1953.
Editor, *Poetry Now: An Anthology.* London, Faber, 1956.
Editor, *Selected Poems of Robert Burns.* London, Heinemann, and New York, Macmillan, 1960.
Editor, *Vaughan College Poems.* Leicester, University of Leicester, 1963.
Editor, with John Waller and J. C. Hall, *Alamein to Zem Zem*, by Keith Douglas. London, Faber, 1966; New York, Chilmark Press, 1967.

Translator, *The Dedicated Life in Poetry, and The Correspondence of Laurent de Cayeux*, by Patrice de la Tour du Pin. London, Harvill Press, 1948.
Translator, *The Mystery of Being*, by Gabriel Marcel. London, Harvill Press, 1950.
Translator, *Men Against Humanity*, by Gabriel Marcel. London, Harvill Press, 1952.

Translator, *Pascal: His Life and Works*, by Jean Mesnard. London, Harvill Press, 1952.

Translator, with E. de Mauny, *Béla Bartók*, by S. Moreux. London, Harvill Press, 1953.

Translator, with others, *Dante's Inferno*. London, BBC, 1966.

Critical Studies: in *Time Literary Supplement* (London), 1944; *Poetry in Our Time* by Babette Deutsch, New York, Doubleday, 1963.

G. S. Fraser comments:

(1970) [Poetry is] my main gift. But to earn a living I became first a literary journalist, then a university teacher, and now teaching, especially the teaching of poetry, has become as true a vocation as writing poetry.... Like many Scottish poets I am old-fashioned in my taste for strict metrics and explicit poetic statement.

I think my best poems have been, in a sense, "occasional," responses to particular scenes and situations (Egypt in the second World War) of a partly reflective, partly descriptive kind. The feelings tend to be subjective and personal and for that very reason I usually need a strict form and a clear pattern of statement. Lately I have become much more experimental, particularly in the use of unrhymed syllabic verse. I am very conscious of the poem as something to be read aloud, though not in an over-dramatic manner. I worry most about the true modulation of feeling in verse. I am a rather intermittent writer, never trying to "force" a poem. I think my productivity was cut down a great deal in the 1950's and after, first by reviewing much current verse, later by teaching students to appreciate great poetry: I have grown more and more fastidious about my own poems, though not in the least dispirited about the best of them. I have thought of myself as a rather forgotten poet, but have been pleased in recent years to find that many people know some of my poems and that students seem to respond to them.

(1980) In the last two or three years, I have compensated for tiredness brought on by teaching by a new energy and confidence in writing verse. It is now less "occasional." Typical titles are "Memory" and "Alder."

* * *

G. S. Fraser first appeared in the rather strange company of the writers of that Second World War movement which called itself "The New Apocalypse." There was nothing remarkable about this association, since during the early 1940's the New Apocalyptics virtually dominated the poetry-magazine scene. Yet Fraser's work stood out from that of other members of the group by virtue of its elegant clarity, qualities appropriate to one on whom the influence of Yeats was apparent.

In his early work, much of it written while he was serving in the Middle East, he captured with great delicacy the innocent sensuousness of youth; the sharpness of its pangs, whether of joy or sorrow; above all, its evanescence. So, from Egypt, he remembers aspects of his native Aberdeen:

I think of the glitter of granite and distances
And against the blue air the lovely and bare trees,
And slippery pavements spangled with delight
Under the needles of a winter's night,
And I remember the dances, with scarf and care,
Strolling home in the cold with the silly refrain
Of a tune by Cole Porter or Irving Berlin
Warming a naughty memory up like gin,
And Bunny and Sheila and Joyce and Rosemary

Chattering on sofas or preparing tea,
With delicate voices and their small white hands.
This is the sorrow everyone understands
More than Rostov's artillery....

But it is also a sorrow which, in Fraser's case, related not only to the down on the cheeks of college-girls, but to Scotland and, in particular, to less pleasing qualities met with in his native city:

Here, where the baby paddles in the gutter,
  Here, in the slaty greyness and the gas,
Here, where the women wear dark shawls and mutter
  A hasty word as other women pass.

Telling the secret, telling, clucking and tutting
  Sighing, or saying that it served her right,
The bitch! – the words and weather both are cutting
  In Causewayend, on this November night.

Fraser became an expatriate, not only from his own country – a parting from the sense of people which he celebrates with the movingly beautiful lyric "The Traveller Has Regrets," a remarkable technical achievement in that it consists of one long, musical sentence – but, as everybody must, from the sharp edges of his youth.

His most recent volume, *Conditions*, widens his range to take in the philosophical preoccupations of middle life, the cynicism of ideals bent back upon themselves, as in "The Insane Philosophers" and "On the Persistence of Humanity." But it is these poems using his familiar technique of building up detail, layer upon layer, sometimes with the odd colloquial Byronic rhyme, conserving the whole ambience of an age-group, that he is at his most successful. One such poem is "For Tilly, Sick, with Love": "People don't give such parties now. The young men are/Busy with social do-gooding or class self-importance:/More on the make than we were, if all were told."

Elegiac sadness is one of life's universal experiences. It has rarely been captured as gracefully or as gently as it is in one of the best of Fraser's later poems, "Autumnal Elegy": "These are the words that moved us long ago/And now like smiles through smoke in public-houses/Can reassure us of a warmth we know." They are the words, too, of a poet who a quarter of a century earlier made plain a standpoint, from which he has never departed, either in his criticism or in his poetry:

What a race has is always crude and common,
  And not the human or the personal:
I would take sword up only for the human,
  Not to revive the broken ghosts of Gael.

—Maurice Lindsay

FRASER, Kathleen. American. Born in Tulsa, Oklahoma, 22 March 1937. Educated at Occidental College, Los Angeles, B.A. in English 1959; Columbia University and New School for Social Research, both New York, 1960–61; San Francisco State University, 1976–77, Doctoral Equivalency in creative writing. Married Jack Marshall, *q.v.*, in 1961 (divorced, 1970); one son. Visiting Professor, Writers Workshop, University of Iowa, Iowa City, 1969–71; Writer-in-Residence, Reed College, Portland, Oregon, 1971–72. Director of the Poetry Center, 1972–75, and since 1975, Associate Professor of Creative Writing, San Francisco State University. Recipient: YM-YWHA Discovery Award, 1964; National Endowment for the Arts grant, 1969, and Fellowship, 1978. Address: 554 Jersey Street, San Francisco, California 94114, U.S.A.

PUBLICATIONS

Verse

Change of Address and Other Poems. San Francisco, Kayak, 1966.
In Defiance of the Rains. Santa Cruz, California, Kayak, 1969.
Little Notes to You from Lucas Street. Iowa City, Penumbra Press, 1972.
What I Want. New York, Harper, 1974.
Magritte Series. Willits, California, Tuumba Press, 1978.
New Shoes. New York, Harper, 1978.

Other

Stilts, Somersaults, and Headstands: Game Poems Based on a Painting by Peter Breughel (juvenile). New York, Atheneum, 1968.
Adam's World: San Francisco (juvenile), with Miriam F. Levy. Chicago, Whitman, 1971.

Kathleen Fraser comments:

My poetry has moved from girlish, Plath-fed lyrics, first published in the mid-1960's, towards a recognition – inside the poem – of life as a more undecided and precarious process. Language is, for me, exploratory – the fluid and changing record of daily risk-taking. I use my writing to locate myself in particular, to catch the multiplicity, the layering of thoughts, feelings, visual impressions experienced simultaneously. Writing is, in a sense, taking a reading on what has thus far transpired and what my attitude toward it is ... there is, hopefully, a movement back and forth. I use my poetry as my most serious way of paying attention to the world outside of my own interior struggle. The poems begin as acts of attention and try to allow in whatever is there waiting to make itself heard. And seen. I regard the ability to write as a gift which must be honored with the utmost seriousness. My great permission-giver, in learning to use that gift, was Frank O'Hara. He still appears in my dreams as a guide and friend. I am also deeply indebted to Virginia Woolf and Gertrude Stein, for complexity. American jazz (particularly Eddie Jefferson's lyrics and Betty Carter's scat) has made a much greater range of tonalities and movements available to me. Painting has always been important and often provides paths to unconscious material which I bring into the poetry. Surely my father's early chanting of limericks and lyrics from *Alice* and *Through the Looking-Glass* will always be there as playful resonance in my work. And my mother's singing. To catch the exact angle of light as two planes shift. To catch the unbroken moment between two people and speak it.

* * *

Kathleen Fraser's subjects are those of many of the women poets of her generation: sexual love, marriage, divorce, motherhood – the business of day-to-day survival in a busy and confusing world. The special distinction Fraser brings to these subjects is one of *tone*: an unusual attentiveness coupled with a nice comic detachment, a buoyancy and warmth that make the most ordinary incidents seem special.

Fraser's command of the ethical argument had to be learned; her early poems do not always avoid a self-conscious Sylvia Plath note: "Feelings stick to me like expensive glue," or, in a poem about pregnancy, "Is it you? Are you there,/thief I can't see ... New mystery floating up my left arm, clinging to the curtain." Such metaphors are merely clever, and Fraser soon turned from the elaboration of metaphysical conceits to the surrealistic image, the boundary between what really happens and what one imagines dissolving:

But over here, where it's dark out,
I'm just me
feeling uneasy in these nights
cold and black.
I turn the heat up
higher
thinking other people's lives
are warmer....

The playful self-mockery of this passage recalls Frank O'Hara as well as Kenneth Koch with whom Kathleen Fraser studied. From both these poets, she learned, in the words of Charles Olson's "Projective Verse," how to "keep it moving." In "Because You Aren't Here to Be What I Can't Think Of," for instance, Fraser invents a dazzling inventory, reminiscent of Koch's "Sleeping with Women" or O'Hara's "Having a Coke with You." In this catalogue poem, the speaker blithely tries to convince herself that she is *not* going to care about her lover's involvement with someone else, all the while doing everything in her power to conjure up his presence. The distance between the lovers takes on fantastic proportions: "Because the moon's another streetlight and your lights are off, and on in someone else's," or "Because there's a saxophone playing between our telephones but you can't pick it up." Yet, injured party that she is, the speaker wryly and wisely concludes that, life being what it is, things could be worse: "because I'm not on a dancefloor with you, but here,/hanging out with my shadow over a city of windows,/lit-up, imagining another kind of life almost like this one." The lover's absence is irritating but not, finally, tragic. The same rueful comedy is found in "The Fault," in which the poet watches another woman make the wrong moves to a man she herself has not hitherto paid much notice, but whom she now suddenly finds an attractive challenge:

I felt myself in love with him watching his tongue run over his lips
and remembered Fredericka

always keeping the tube of vaseline in her purse
always gliding it over her mouth should there be someone to kiss

and thought how I liked space and long unending lines, how my life
was that way, without visible connections or obvious explanations

how I was glad
I'd washed my hair

This is a witty analysis of a woman's momentary self-satisfaction, of the pleasure that fortuitous circumstances sometimes bring. Other poems in her recent book *New Shoes*, most notably the "Magritte Series," give this kind of material more complex treatment. The Magritte poems are not "about" the paintings that give them their titles; rather, Fraser uses a given Magritte as a stimulus for psychological exploration. Take "L'Invention Collective/Collective Invention," which is based on Magritte's grotesque and haunting image of a sort of reverse-mermaid: a fish with human legs, slender and feminine, and pubic hair. In Magritte's painting, the fish-woman is oddly erotic and repulsive; the single blank fish eye confronts the beholder, whose eye is drawn downward to her (its?) lower parts. She lies on the edge of the beach, the white-caps of a silly blue ocean beating pointlessly behind her. Fraser invents a narrative that can incorporate this image: her story is of a tacky, domestic heroine, part comic-book, part fairy-tale, whose role in life is to keep things "neat and tidy," so that she is quite unable to "see/her seducers in a line and shaking their fingers." Only in her dreams, does she see herself lying "at the edge of the waters," the sand scratching her body, and watches herself turn into a fish: "a face cut deep with gills and the sad eyes panting/and the absolute quiet of something about to arrive." What this something is we don't know but it is frightening, in the poem as well as in the Magritte painting. The pose of the figure invites rape, but what would that mean in this context? Fraser is playing with notions of smugness and self-deception, exploring the fantasy life of the little woman who wanted life for herself and her little boy to be "as fresh as Watermelon slice."

In her recent prose poems – for example, "Green and Blue Piece for Francie Swimming, in Which Grace Enters" – Fraser is moving further in the direction of the "painterly" poem, the text as elaborate word-system in which a fixed number of items, here the colors "blue" and "green," the "body swimming," the words of Grace and the paint strokes of Francie, undergo a series of permutations until nothing remains what it once was. If "Green and Blue Piece" is less jaunty than Fraser's previous work, it has a new explanatory quality, probing behind the surfaces of personal relationships. As she puts it in one of the Magritte poems, "The secrets between men and women are of peculiar fascination."

—Marjorie Perloff

FRY, Christopher. British. Born in Bristol, 18 December 1907. Educated at Bedford Modern School, 1918–26. Served in the Non-Combatant Corps, 1940–44. Married Phyllis Marjorie Hart in 1936; one son. Teacher, Bedford Froebel Kindergarten, 1926–27; Actor and Office Worker, Citizen House, Bath, 1927; Schoolmaster, Hazelwood School, Limpsfield, Surrey, 1928–31; Secretary to H. Rodney Bennett, 1931–32; Founding Director, Tunbridge Wells Repertory Players, 1932–35; Lecturer and editor of schools magazine, Dr. Barnardo's Homes, 1934–39; Director, 1939–40, and Visiting Director, 1945–46, Oxford Playhouse; Visiting Director, 1946, and Staff Dramatist, 1947, Arts Theatre Club, London. Also composer. Recipient: Shaw Prize Fund Award, 1948; Foyle Poetry Prize, 1951; New York Drama Critics Circle Award, 1951, 1952, 1956; Queen's Gold Medal for Poetry, 1962; Heinemann Award, 1962. Fellow, Royal Society of Literature. Agent: ACTAC Ltd., 16 Cadogan Lane, London S.W.1. Address: The Toft, East Dean, near Chichester, Sussex, England.

PUBLICATIONS

Verse

Root and Sky: Verse from the Plays of Christopher Fry, edited by Charles E. and Jean G. Wadsworth. Cambridge, Rampant Lions Press, and Boston, Godine, 1975.

Plays

Youth and the Peregrines (produced Tunbridge Wells, Kent, 1934).
To Sea in a Sieve (as Christopher Harris) (revue; produced Reading, 1935).
She Shall Have Music (lyrics only, with Ronald Frankau), book by Frank Eyton, music by Fry and Monte Crick (produced London, 1934).

The Open Door (produced London, 1936). Goldings, Hertfordshire, Printed by the Boys at the Press of Dr. Barnardo's Homes, n.d.

The Boy with a Cart: Cuthman, Saint of Sussex (produced Coleman's Hatch, Sussex, 1938; London, 1950; New York, 1953). London, Oxford University Press, 1939; New York, Oxford University Press, 1951.

The Tower (pageant; produced Tewkesbury, Gloucestershire, 1939).

Thursday's Child: A Pageant, music by Martin Shaw (produced London, 1939). London, Girls' Friendly Society, 1939.

A Phoenix Too Frequent (produced London, 1946; Cambridge, Massachusetts, 1948; New York, 1950). London, Hollis and Carter, 1946; New York, Oxford University Press, 1949.

The Firstborn (broadcast, 1947; produced Edinburgh, 1948). Cambridge, University Press, 1946; New York, Oxford University Press, 1950; revised version (produced London, 1952; New York, 1958), London and New York, Oxford University Press, 1952, 1958.

The Lady's Not for Burning (produced London, 1948; New York, 1950). London and New York, Oxford University Press, 1949; revised version, 1950, 1958.

Thor, With Angels (produced Canterbury, 1948; Washington, D.C., 1950; London, 1951). Canterbury, H. J. Goulden, 1948; New York, Oxford University Press, 1949.

Venus Observed (produced London, 1950; New York, 1952). London and New York, Oxford University Press, 1950.

Ring round the Moon: A Charade with Music, adaptation of a play by Jean Anouilh (produced London and New York, 1950). London and New York, Oxford University Press, 1950.

A Sleep of Prisoners (produced Oxford, London and New York, 1951). London and New York, Oxford University Press, 1951.

The Dark Is Light Enough: A Winter Comedy (produced Edinburgh and London, 1954; New York, 1955). London and New York, Oxford University Press, 1954.

The Lark, adaptation of a play by Jean Anouilh (produced London, 1955). London, Methuen, 1955; New York, Oxford University Press, 1956.

Tiger at the Gates, adaptation of a play by Jean Giraudoux (produced London and New York, 1955). London, Methuen, 1955; New York, Oxford University Press, 1956.

Duel of Angels, adaptation of a play by Jean Giraudoux (produced London, 1958; New York, 1960). London, Methuen, 1958; New York, Oxford University Press, 1959.

Curtmantle (produced Tilburg, Holland, 1961; London, 1962). London and New York, Oxford University Press, 1961.

Judith, adaptation of a play by Jean Giraudoux (produced London, 1962). London, Methuen, 1962.

The Bible: Original Screenplay, assisted by Jonathan Griffin. New York, Pocket Books, 1966.

Peer Gynt, adaptation of the play by Ibsen (produced Chichester, 1970). London and New York, Oxford University Press, 1970.

A Yard of Sun: A Summer Comedy (produced Nottingham and London, 1970; Cleveland, 1972). London and New York, Oxford University Press, 1970.

The Brontës of Haworth (televised, 1973). London, Davis Poynter, 2 vols., 1974.

Cyrano de Bergerac, adaptation of the play by Edmond Rostand (produced Chichester, 1975). London and New York, Oxford University Press, 1975.

Paradise Lost, music by Penderecki, adaptation of the poem by Milton (produced Chicago, 1978). London, Schott, 1978.

Screenplays: *The Beggar's Opera*, with Denis Cannan, 1953; *The Queen Is Crowned* (documentary), 1953; *Ben Hur*, 1959; *Barabbas*, 1962; *The Bible: In the Beginning*, 1966.

Radio Plays: for *Children's Hour* series, 1939–40; *The Firstborn*, 1947; *Rhineland Journey*, 1948.

Television Plays: *The Canary*, 1950; *The Tenant of Wildfell Hall*, 1968; *The Brontës of Haworth* (four plays), 1973; *The Best of Enemies*, 1976; *Sister Dora*, from the book by Jo Manton, 1977.

Other

An Experience of Critics, with *The Approach to Dramatic Criticism* by W. A. Darlington and others, edited by Kaye Webb. London, Perpetua Press, 1952; New York, Oxford University Press, 1953.
The Boat That Mooed (juvenile). New York, Macmillan, 1966.
Can You Find Me: A Family History. London, Oxford University Press, 1978; New York, Oxford University Press, 1979.

Translator, *The Boy and the Magic*, by Colette. London, Dobson, 1964.

Incidental Music: *A Winter's Tale*, London, 1951, recorded by Caedmon.

Bibliography: "A Bibliography on Fry" by B. L. Schear and E. G. Prater, in *Tulane Drama Review 4* (New Orleans), March 1960.

Critical Studies: *Christopher Fry* by Derek Stanford, London, Longman, 1954; *The Drama of Comedy: Victim and Victor* by Nelson Vos, Richmond, Virginia, John Knox Press, 1965; *Creed and Drama* by W. M. Merchant, London, SPCK, 1965; *The Christian Tradition in Modern Verse Drama* by William V. Spanos, New Brunswick, New Jersey, Rutgers University Press, 1967; *Christopher Fry: A Critical Essay* by Stanley M. Wiersma, Grand Rapids, Michigan, Eerdmans, 1970.

Theatrical Activities:
Director: **Plays** – *How-Do, Princess?* by Ivor Novello, toured, 1936; *The Circle of Chalk* by James Laver, London, 1945; *The School for Scandal* by Sheridan, London, 1946; *A Phoenix Too Frequent*, Brighton, 1950; *The Lady's Not for Burning*, toured, 1971; and others.
Actor: **Plays** – in repertory, Bath, 1937.

Christopher Fry comments:

Influences are difficult to pin-point. Certainly, as it must be with anyone of my generation, T. S. Eliot was a releasing factor. In the plays I have tried to work towards an end which I broadly expressed in a lecture: "No event is understandable in a prose sense alone. Its ultimate meaning (that is to say, the complete life of the event, seen in its eternal context) is a poetic meaning." I have tried to shape a verse form (a metrical system) which could contain both the "theatrical" elements (rhetoric, broad colours, etc.) and the rhythms and tone of the colloquial, which would work for the "artificial comedy," or the historical, or the conversation of the present time.

* * *

It was Christopher Fry (and, later, T. S. Eliot) who led the short revival of interest in the poetic drama during the decade or so after the second world war – an interest which now seems completely dead. *A Phoenix Too Frequent*, an imperfect sentimental farce, attracted some attention in 1946; and with *The Lady's Not for Burning* Fry captured the imagination of the critics, and of a potentially large audience. The most obviously brilliant of Fry's plays, it was fortunate in an impeccable production by John Gielgud, and a fine cast, headed by Pamela Brown, Claire Bloom, Richard Burton and Gielgud himself. Its amusing plot and the natural yet highly decorated language, finely characterised and supremely dramatic (Fry himself was for some time an actor), were a revelation after the dryness and aridity of the language of wartime drama. Over-succulent on the page, the verse (especially when delivered in the romantic style of acting still predominant in the late 1940's) seemed irresistible in performance.

But as Fry's technical assurance grew, so critical and public interest waned. *Venus Observed*, written for Laurence Olivier, was a critical and to some extent public failure; a graver comedy of autumn, its language was more disciplined and restrained, still often witty, but quieter and without the obvious verbal fireworks of its predecessor. In *A Sleep of Prisoners*, perhaps his most entirely successful piece, Fry turned to wholly serious matters, and most obviously to his perennial theme of "the growth of vision: the increased perception of what makes for life and what makes for death." Prisoners-of-war penned up in a Church explore each other's personalities in their dreams. It is a moving and totally realised poetic drama. *The Dark Is Light Enough*, a winter play based on Fabre's parable of the butterfly making its way through storm and profound darkness to arrive brightly inviolate at its destination, was written for Edith Evans and staged in 1954. It was disliked both by critics and by the public. Since its production Fry has concentrated for the most part on translation (from Anouilh and Giraudoux, for instance) and film scripting. He has, however, written a play which completes the quartet of plays of the seasons – a comedy of high summer.

His place in the theatre is perhaps ephemeral; he has been compared, damagingly, to the Victorian poetic dramatist Stephen Phillips, whose *Paolo and Francesca* seemed at the turn of the century to be a masterpiece, but is now almost totally forgotten. The comparison seems unfair; Fry is more accomplished both as poet and dramatist than Phillips. His language is, on the page, overblown, and seems lacking in muscle and discipline. But in performance it is always amusing and dramatically viable; and its sentiment is at worst harmlessly touching. It is strange now to remember that many critics found Fry "difficult" in the 1940's and 50's. Whatever he is, he is not that. Accused of over-writing ("Too many words!") Fry replied (in *An Experience of Critics*, 1952): "It means, I think, that I don't use the same words often enough; or else, or as well, that the words are an ornament on the meaning and not the meaning itself. That is certainly sometimes – perhaps often – true in the comedies, though almost as often I have meant the ornament to be, dramatically or comedically, an essential part of the meaning; and in my more sanguine moments I think the words are as exact to my purpose as I could make them at the time of writing."

Posterity may find this claim to be true. It is unlikely that he is in any sense a major writer, but within his own set limits Fry is a craftsman of considerable accomplishment, and where he is most successful, he is memorable.

—Derek Parker

FULLER, John (Leopold). British. Born in Ashford, Kent, 1 January 1937; son of Roy Fuller, *q.v.* Educated at St Paul's School; New College, Oxford (Newdigate Prize, 1960), B.A. 1960, M.A. 1964, B.Litt. 1965. Married Cicely Prudence Martin in 1960; three children. Visiting Lecturer, State University of New York, Buffalo, 1962–63; Assistant Lecturer, Manchester University, 1963–66. Since 1966, Fellow of Magdalen College, Oxford. Publisher, Sycamore Press, Oxford. Recipient: Richard Hillary Memorial Prize, 1961; Eric Gregory Award, 1965; Faber Memorial Prize, 1974; Prudence Farmer Prize (*New Statesman*), 1975. Address: 4 Benson Place, Oxford, England.

PUBLICATIONS

Verse

Fairground Music. London, Chatto and Windus-Hogarth Press, 1961.
The Tree That Walked. London, Chatto and Windus-Hogarth Press, 1967.
The Art of Love. Oxford, The Review, 1968.
The Labours of Hercules: A Sonnet Sequence. Manchester, Manchester Institute of Contemporary Arts, 1969.
Three London Songs, music by Bryan Kelly. London, Novello, 1969.
Annotations of Giant's Town. London, Poem-of-the-Month Club, 1970.
The Wreck. London, Turret, 1970.
Cannibals and Missionaries. London, Secker and Warburg, 1972.
Boys in a Pie. London, Steam Press, 1972.
Hut Groups. Hitchin, Hertfordshire, Cellar Press, 1973.
Penguin Modern Poets 22, with Adrian Mitchell and Peter Levi. London, Penguin, 1973.
Epistles to Several Persons. London, Secker and Wärburg, 1973.
Poems and Epistles. Boston, Godine, 1974.
Squeaking Crust (juvenile). London, Chatto and Windus, 1974.
A Bestiary. Oxford, Sycamore Press, 1974.
The Mountain in the Sun. London, Secker and Warburg, 1975.
Bel and the Dragon. Oxford, Sycamore Press, 1977.
The Wilderness. Buffalo, Lockwood Memorial Library, 1977.
Lies and Secrets. London, Secker and Warburg, 1979.

Plays

Herod Do Your Worst, music by Bryan Kelly (produced Thame, Oxfordshire, 1967). London, Novello, 1968.
Half a Fortnight, music by Bryan Kelly (produced Leicester, 1970). London, Novello, 1973.
The Spider Monkey Uncle King, music by Bryan Kelly (produced Cookham, Berkshire, 1971). London, Novello, 1975.
Fox-Trot, music by Bryan Kelly (produced Leicester, 1972).
The Queen in the Golden Tree, music by Bryan Kelly (produced Edinburgh, 1974).
How Did You Get Here, Jonno?, music by Bryan Kelly (produced Wolverhampton, 1975).
The Ship of Sounds, music by Bryan Kelly (produced Leicester, 1975).
Adam's Apple, music by Bryan Kelly (produced Abingdon, Oxfordshire, 1975).
Linda, music by Bryan Kelly (produced Reading, 1975).

Other

A Reader's Guide to W. H. Auden. London, Thames and Hudson, and New York, Farrar Straus, 1970.
The Sonnet. London, Methuen, 1972.
The Last Bid (juvenile). London, Deutsch, 1975.
Carving Trifles: William King's Imitation of Horace (lecture). London, Oxford University Press, 1976.

Editor, with others, *Light Blue Dark Blue: An Anthology of Recent Writings from Oxford and Cambridge Universities.* London, Macdonald, 1960.
Editor, *Oxford Poetry 1960.* Oxford, Fantasy Press, 1960.
Editor, *Poetry Supplement.* London, Poetry Book Society, 1962.

Editor, with Harold Pinter and Peter Redgrove, *New Poems 1967.* London, Hutchinson, 1968.
Editor, *Poetry Supplement.* London, Poetry Book Society, 1970.
Editor, *Nemo's Almanac.* Oxford, Sycamore Press, 1971.

Critical Study: "The Poetry of John Fuller" by Edward Mendelson, in *New Republic* (Washington, D.C.), 28 May 1977.

* * *

In reviewing John Fuller's second book of poems, *The Tree That Walked*, Stephen Wall wrote, in a generally favourable review: "the poems ... are oddly tangential to some of the central commonplaces of human feeling. The impression of a rooted reticence has something to do with the sense of powers not only excellently under control but also sometimes too tightly restrained." And Fuller himself has disparaged "powerful feelings and simplicity"; poetry, he feels, "must perform its moral function." From this, it is easy to infer that he is not a "confessional" or a lyrical poet. One or two of the poems collected in his first book, *Fairground Music*, do contain lines that can be (and by one critic have been) compared to Rupert Brooke; but this element has very carefully and deliberately been purged from the poems of his second volume.

Notwithstanding the "Georgian" element in his earliest poems – which is hardly unusual – Fuller is and always has been a markedly intellectual poet whose main source of literary inspiration is the eighteenth century. His first book was characterized by wit, playfulness, sophistication and by a tendency towards melodrama that sometimes seemed inconsistent with his anti-romanticism.

In the best poems of his second book, which reveals a considerable development of his talent, he has often succeeded in achieving a style that better suits his extremely cerebral content. One of his most admired and serious poems, "Hedge Tutor," combines one side of Marvell's anthropocentric genius with Augustan descriptive virtues in a manner that has not yet been seen in modern poetry. The subject is the Marvellian one of the relationship between people and landscape, and the restraint and elegance of its surface are beautifully achieved:

Consulting the calendar of hedges
Banked up higher than your head,
We seem to share the surprise of walking
Upon a riverbed....

... we lean to ourselves, and to
These rituals that love condemns
Us to, gathering until the hand
Is hot with stems.

Fuller's virtues include intelligence, technical control and grace. His chief recurring fault is probably that where his subject is fantastic or frivolous his elegance tends to degenerate into a decadent rococo. But he remains an assured craftsman, in whose poetry learning is natural and never pretentious.

—Martin Seymour-Smith

FULLER, Roy (Broadbent). British. Born in Failsworth, Lancashire, 11 February 1912. Educated at Blackpool High School, Lancashire; qualified as a solicitor, 1934. Served in the Royal Navy, 1941–46; Lieutenant, Royal Naval Volunteer Reserve. Married Kathleen Smith in 1936; one son, John Fuller, *q.v.* Assistant Solicitor, 1938–58, Solicitor, 1958–69, and since 1969, Director, Woolwich Equitable Building Society, London. Chairman of the Legal Advisory Panel, 1958–69, and since 1969, a Vice-President, Building Societies Association. Professor of Poetry, Oxford University, 1968–73. Chairman, Poetry Book Society, London, 1960–68; Governor, BBC, 1972–79; Member, Arts Council of Great Britain, and Chairman of the Literature Panel, 1976–77 (resigned). Recipient: Arts Council Poetry Award, 1959; Duff Cooper Memorial Prize, for poetry, 1968; Queen's Gold Medal for Poetry, 1970. M.A.: Oxford University. Fellow, Royal Society of Literature, 1958. C.B.E. (Commander, Order of the British Empire), 1970. Address: 37 Langton Way, Blackheath, London S.E.3, England.

PUBLICATIONS

Verse

Poems. London, Fortune Press, 1940.
The Middle of a War. London, Hogarth Press, 1942.
A Lost Season. London, Hogarth Press, 1944.
Epitaphs and Occasions. London, Lehmann, 1949.
Counterparts. London, Verschoyle, 1954.
Brutus's Orchard. London, Deutsch, 1957; New York, Macmillan, 1958.
Collected Poems 1936–1961. London, Deutsch, and Chester Springs, Pennsylvania, Dufour, 1962.
Buff. London, Deutsch, and Chester Springs, Pennsylvania, Dufour, 1965.
New Poems. London, Deutsch, and Chester Springs, Pennsylvania, Dufour, 1968.
Pergamon Poets 1, with R. S. Thomas, edited by Evan Owen. Oxford, Pergamon Press, 1968.
Off Course. London, Turret, 1969.
Penguin Modern Poets 18, with A. Alvarez and Anthony Thwaite. London, Penguin, 1970.
To an Unknown Reader. London, Poem-of-the-Month Club, 1970.
Song Cycle from a Record Sleeve. Oxford, Sycamore Press, 1972.
Tiny Tears. London, Deutsch, 1973.
An Old War. Edinburgh, Tragara Press, 1974.
Waiting for the Barbarians: A Poem. Richmond, Surrey, Keepsake Press, 1974.
From the Joke Shop. London, Deutsch, 1975.
The Joke Shop Annexe. Edinburgh, Tragara Press, 1975.
An Ill-Governed Coast: Poems. Sunderland, Ceolfrith Press, 1976.
Re-treads. Edinburgh, Tragara Press, 1979.

Novels

The Second Curtain. London, Verschoyle, 1953; New York, Macmillan, 1956.
Fantasy and Fugue. London, Verschoyle, 1954; New York, Macmillan, 1956.
Image of a Society. London, Deutsch, 1956; New York, Macmillan, 1958.
The Ruined Boys. London, Deutsch, 1959; as *That Distant Afternoon*, New York, Macmillan, 1959.
The Father's Comedy. London, Deutsch, 1961.
The Perfect Fool. London, Deutsch, 1963.
My Child, My Sister. London, Deutsch, 1965.
The Carnal Island. London, Deutsch, 1970.

Other

Savage Gold (juvenile). London, Lehmann, 1946.

With My Little Eye (juvenile). London, Lehmann, 1948; New York, Macmillan, 1957.
Catspaw (juvenile). London, Alan Ross, 1966.
Owls and Artificers: Oxford Lectures on Poetry. London, Deutsch, and La Salle, Illinois, Library Press, 1971.
Seen Grandpa Lately? (juvenile). London, Deutsch, 1972.
Professors and Gods: Last Oxford Lectures on Poetry. London, Deutsch, 1973; New York, St. Martin's Press, 1974.
Poor Roy (juvenile). London, Deutsch, 1977.
The Other Planet (juvenile). Richmond, Surrey, Keepsake Press, 1979.

Editor, *Byron for Today*. London, Porcupine Press, 1948.
Editor, with Clifford Dyment and Montagu Slater, *New Poems 1952*. London, Joseph, 1952.
Editor, *The Building Societies Acts 1874–1960: Great Britain and Northern Ireland*, 5th edition. London, Frayney, 1961.
Editor, *Supplement of New Poetry*. London, Poetry Book Society, 1964.

Manuscript Collections: State University of New York, Buffalo; British Library, London.

Critical Studies: "Private Images of Public Ills: The Poetry of Roy Fuller" by George Woodcock, in *Wascana Review* (Regina, Saskatchewan), iv, 2, 1970; *Roy Fuller* by Allen E. Austin, Boston, Twayne, 1979.

* * *

The themes of Roy Fuller's earliest poetry, which was very much influenced by poets of the 1930's, are largely social and political, though they do not describe particular events or issues. His style, too, was markedly Audenesque, as in, for instance, "August 1938" with its references to "the sexy lighthouse" beneath "the usual sky" and "the pleasure towns where most/Have come to live or die." Some of these verbal mannerisms and social themes persist for some time after the war, but increasingly the poems are about personal fears and anxieties. Indeed the principal subject of the war poems is the worries, the boredom, the sense of loneliness of servicemen separated by the War from loved ones. As the war closes one poem ("During a Bombardment by V-Weapons") notes the return of the "real" world:

And love I see your pallor bears
A far more pointed threat than steel
Now all the permanent and real
Furies are settling in upstairs.

A persistent theme, however, of his poetry since the war has been his sense of the imminence of world disaster ("Doom, total of the human race," "Obituary of R. Fuller"). "The Lake" envisages a later Gibbon by Lake Geneva translating "Our frightful end to ornamental prose." He is continually aware of the frailty of life and the nightmare of possible human disaster. There is some consolation to be found in nature's capacity for survival ("The Lawn, Spring and Summer"). But even this hope is tentative – life is so frail, and, in any case, man's successor may prove even more of an oppressor: "Though who's to say the formic city less/Unjust than ours, and that the dove, evolved/Wouldn't impose tyrannical modes of love?" ("Elephant, Ants, Doves"). The images used in connection with this theme are often autumnal or of disease, and a parallel is frequently drawn between our world and the last days of the Roman Empire threatened by barbarian invasion.

Another major theme running throughout Fuller's poetry is art. Many of the poems draw their subjects from the worlds of art, literature, and music, and are preoccupied with the creative process, the function of art, and particularly the relation of art to life. Poetry tries to be exact and truthful but inevitably it falsifies the reality it seeks to portray. The successful image pleases but distorts in the very process of producing art: "words alone/... are, like all art, condemned/To failure in the sense that they succeed" ("Expostulation and Inadequate Reply"). All the artist can do is attempt to be as truthful as possible.

In "Dedicatory Epistle" (*Collected Poems*) Fuller describes his style as "a muted, sparse accompaniment" to the times we live in, and certainly his poetry does not contain many vivid and sensuous phrases. The tone is generally thoughtful, sometimes self-mocking and sardonic. Frequently his technique is to begin a poem with a minute and particular description of an object, a landscape, a bird or animal, and to use this as a starting-point for his thoughts on some general aspect of human behaviour and emotion. So in "Ambiguities" he notes a blackbird suffering from "some malignancy" catch a caterpillar, and this begins a contemplation of the "ambiguities of pain and greed." A number of subjects are often woven together and the similarities and differences are juxtaposed for the purposes of comparison and contrast. A good example of this technique is "On Reading *The Bostonians* in Algeciras Bay" in which his thoughts on James's novel, memories of the Spanish Civil War, and observation of an old man sitting near him are threaded together with his thoughts and feelings about society and change. This is also his first use of syllabic verse. He has always used a wide variety of forms in his poetry, but the 11 or 13 syllabic line, he feels, has allowed him greater freedom in his use of subject-matter, while at the same time imposing a rigorous and disciplined pattern on his poetry.

Fuller has always insisted on the importance of discipline, order, and coherence in poetry, and has criticised in his Oxford lectures the lack of this in contemporary "so-called" poetry. Certainly care and intellect are characteristics of both his poetry and novels.

—David Astle

FULTON, Robin. Scottish. Born in the Isle of Arran, Scotland, 6 May 1937. Educated at Edinburgh University, M.A. 1959, Ph.D. 1972. Editor of *Lines Review*, Edinburgh, 1967–76. Recipient: Eric Gregory Award, 1966; Edinburgh University Writer's Fellowship, 1969–71; Arts Council bursary, 1972; Swedish Authors' Fund bursary, 1973, 1976; Artur Lundkvist Award, for translation, 1977; Swedish Academy Award, for translation, 1978. Lives in Scandinavia.

PUBLICATIONS

Verse

A Matter of Definition. Edinburgh, Giles Gordon, 1963.
Instances. Edinburgh, M. Macdonald, 1967.
Inventories. Thurso, Caithness Books, 1969.
The Spaces Between the Stones. New York, New Rivers Press, 1971.
Quarters. West Linton, Peeblesshire, Castlelaw Press, 1971.
The Man with the Surbahar. Edinburgh, M. Macdonald, 1971.
Tree-Lines. New York, New Rivers Press, 1974.
Music and Flight. Knotting, Bedfordshire, Sceptre Press, 1975.
Between Flights: Eighteen Poems. Egham, Surrey, Interim Press, 1976.
Places to Stay In. Knotting, Bedfordshire, Sceptre Press, 1978.

Other

Contemporary Scottish Poetry: Individuals and Context. Edinburgh, M. Macdonald, 1974.

Editor, *Trio: New Poets from Edinburgh.* New York, New Rivers Press, 1971.

Translator, *An Italian Quartet: Versions after Saba, Ungaretti, Montale, Quasimodo.* London, Alan Ross, 1966.
Translator, *Blok's Twelve.* Preston, Lancashire, Akros, 1968.
Translator, *Selected Poems*, by Lars Gustafsson. New York, New Rivers Press, 1972.
Translator, *Selected Poems*, by Gunnar Harding. London, London Magazine Editions, 1973.
Translator, *Selected Poems*, by Tomas Tranströmer. London, Penguin, 1974.
Translator, *Citoyens*, by Tomas Tranströmer. Rushden, Northamptonshire, Sceptre Press, 1974.
Translator, *Selected Poems*, by Osten Sjöstrand. Cambridge, Oleander Press, 1975.
Translator, *Selected Poems*, by Werner Aspenström. London, Oasis, 1976.

* * *

Robin Fulton is a delicate and fastidious poet. His craftsmanship does not show itself in regular or conventional verse forms, but arises from the exacting objectives of his art. In "A Lifework" he writes:

to say what you mean is hazardous
to sort out and plainly describe
one mere subdivision
of a minor species takes more
than a homemade poet with a simple lens.

At his simplest he is, as he entitles a poem, "A Meticulous Observer," in which he writes:

he watched boys with almost pre-
hensile feet on high walls
where they risked their short lives
for reasons no-one else would appreciate

he watched girls with newly-shaped
bodies advertising themselves
without guile in the summery light
and without needing a reason to guide them.

The detached tone is equable to the point of the poems becoming clinical studies. The movement of the verse never reflects the shocks to life nor bodily sensations. What the mind's eye sees is all important. He notes appearances, placing them judiciously, as a means of discovering truths. He has created a flexible, exact art, in which by subtle shifts of tone and viewpoint he exposes a mental condition. In his poem, "forecast for a quiet night," he moves from witty talk to humane concern, as these lines witness:

by dawn too a generation of mice
will have been snipped by a night-shift of owls
working separately and almost in silence

and the mild local disturbance behind the eyes
of the invalid
will have been noted only by the next of kin.

Fulton has made a means of inquisition which he uses gently, but by which he may penetrate deeply. He is a humane intellectual, conscious of the burden of being true to what he creates and examines. This is increasingly matter of consequence. The following lines are from "the survivors begin again" in his collection, *The Spaces Between the Stones*:

we huddle in our old-fashioned coats watching
our thin smoke bend as the mist breathes
and one of us points to a green mist in the trees –
small leaves prick through the peeling rust

soon our blades will be sharp enough to let blood.

—George Bruce

GALE, Vi. American. Born in Noret, Dala-Jarna, Sweden; emigrated to U.S. in 1929: naturalized, 1940. Educated at the University of Oregon, Eugene; Lewis and Clark College, Portland, Oregon; Portland State University; University of Colorado, Boulder. Married to James C. Gale. Since 1962, Director, YWCA Writing Workshops and currently, conducting Community Program, Portland. Writer-in-Residence, Eastern Oregon College, La Grande, Summer 1968, and Clatsop Community College, Astoria, Oregon, Summer 1969. Recipient: Swallow Press New Poetry Series Award, 1958. Address: 11519 N. E. Prescott, Portland, Oregon, 97220, U.S.A.

PUBLICATIONS

Verse

Several Houses. Denver, Swallow, 1959.
Love Always. Denver, Swallow, 1965.
Nineteen Ing Poems. Portland, Press-22, 1970.
Clouded Sea. Portland, Press-22, 1971.
Clearwater. Chicago, Swallow Press, 1974.

Critical Studies: Reviews by Dudley Fitts, in *Saturday Review* (New York), 1959, and Bruce Berlind, in *Poetry* (Chicago), February 1960.

* * *

Vi Gale's poems since her 1959 collection, *Several Houses*, have, like much American poetry moving from the rigid academic poetry so prevalent in the fifties to the freer poetic climate of the sixties, become more relaxed, more conversational, and more interesting. This is especially true of one of her longer collections, *Love Always*, published by Alan Swallow, the publisher for the earlier collection as well. The latter book contains such effective poems as "Did You Hear?," "Orange," "Today, in the Obituaries," and "Pattern Pretty Much

Established." Ms. Gale's poems are strongly autobiographical and personal, dealing frequently with her experiences, friends, and relatives. They risk – and sometimes succumb to – sentimentality. Unlike the poems mentioned above, some in *Love Always*, and *Nineteen Ing Poems*, an even more recent collection, finally fail ("Hunters" is one example of this) to draw potentially interesting material together; Ms. Gale is strongest when she sticks close, as she frequently does, to personal material, weakest when she fails to let the experience speak for itself, tacking on an unprepared-for leap into universality. The fine, homely and well-observed details of hunters' preparations for a plunge into the wilds are undercut in "Hunters," for example, by the last two lines ("Slow the fleeing deer./Let these driven hunters kill what stalks us down"), as the entirety of "Don't Eat the Snow" is marred by the attempt to make it a protest against the radiation pollution; in either case, we're much more able to respond to the personal death or injury, the boy drowned at the end of "Did You Hear?" (one of her most powerful poems), than to such generalizations. Ms. Gale is best in her personally observed and felt responses to people and nature (of which she is a keen and well-informed observer, like many good Northwest poets). The personal experience – two experiences, actually, nature the link – speaks evocatively and well for her in "Orange," from which the first and third stanzas:

> Once the long season had us in its reach
> our miracles were few. On the Christmas Eve
> that an uncle came traveling, traveling on skis
> with the gift of an orange, my brother and I
> went wild in our marveling.
>
> Halfway around the world one later December
> on a day so mild that we'd sunned in Los Angeles,
> I reached easily into the boughs, into rich leaves;
> pulled out a childhood of long snow,
> the far sound of skis.

—Duane Ackerson

GALLAGHER, Tess. American. Born in Port Angeles, Washington. Educated at the University of Washington, Seattle, B.A., M.A. 1970; University of Iowa, Iowa City, M.F.A. 1974. Has been married twice (both marriages dissolved). Taught at St. Lawrence University, Canton, New York, 1974–75; Kirkland College, Clinton, New York, 1975–77; University of Montana, Missoula, 1977–78; University of Arizona, Tucson, 1979–80. Recipient: Creative Artists Public Service grant, 1976; Elliston Award, 1976; National Endowment for the Arts grant, 1977; Guggenheim Fellowship, 1979. Address: 2485 Bay Street, Port Angeles, Washington 98362, U.S.A.

PUBLICATIONS

Verse

Stepping Outside. Lisbon, Iowa, Penumbra Press, 1974.
Instructions to the Double. Port Townsend, Washington, Graywolf Press, 1976.
Under Stars. Port Townsend, Washington, Graywolf Press, 1978.
Portable Kisses. Seattle, Sea Pen Press, 1978.

Critical Studies: Reviews by Hayden Carruth in *Harper's* (New York), April 1979, and Peter Davison, in *Atlantic Monthly* (New York), May 1979; interview in *Ironwood* (Tucson), October 1979.

Tess Gallagher comments:

When I was a young girl salmon fishing with my father in the Straits of Juan de Fuca in Washington State I used to lean out over the water and try to look past my own face, past the reflection of the boat, past the sun and the darkness, down to where the fish were surely swimming. I made up charm songs and word-hopes to tempt the fish, to cause them to mean biting my hook. I believed they would do it if I asked them well and patiently and with the right hope. I am writing my poems like this. I have used the fabric and the people of my life as the bait. More and more I have learned how to speak for the others, the ones who do not speak in poetry though their lives are of it. What do I write about? The murder of my uncle by thieves in the night, the psychic death of my husband in the Viet Nam war, walking through Belfast in 1976, a horse with snow on its back circling a house where the dancers have fallen to the floor by daybreak. I have wanted the words to go deep. I have wanted music and passion and human tenderness in the poems. Intelligence and loss. Only in the language I have made for myself in the poems am I in touch with all the past, present, and future moments of my consciousness and unconsciousness. The poem is the moment of all possibilities where I try to speak in a concert of tenses, to reflect the intersection of the various time-zones of actualities and imaginative transformations. I don't want to disappear into the present tense, the awful NOW. I want to survive it and to take others with me. I am more concerned about the kind of writing that will allow WITH than I was in the beginning. Not just TO or FOR or AT. The Irish have no word for "mine" or for "wife" ... only "he or she who goes along with me." *My* poetry. I can't say that. Only "that which goes along with me."

* * *

Born in the Pacific Northwest, the oldest of five children of a logger turned longshoreman, Tess Gallagher was a member of the last class taught by Theodore Roethke at the University of Washington, and also a student there of David Wagoner. That is not to say her work bears theirs much resemblance beyond great vitality and an obsessive desire to make words count.

Instructions to the Double is full of doubles, doubles of two kinds: persons with whom the speaker closely identifies – father, mother, uncle, husband – and likenesses – reflections in a mirror, water, or eyes, resemblances, shadows, ghosts, photographs. Whichever the kind, the poems which disappoint are those whose subjects remain generalized. The most successful are concrete, rooted in intimate and intimately felt family experience: "Two Stories," about an uncle murdered by thieves, "Coming Home," "The Woman Who Raised Goats," "Black Money," and "Time Lapse with Tulips." This last is one of Gallagher's best; it brilliantly considers and rejects illusion and fixes on a passionate reality. The wedding photograph which is the occasion for the poem is illusory in at least two senses: a photographic image is an illusion, and the particular image "preserves/a symmetry of doubt with us/at the center." The poem has its own symmetry of statement. The first stanza retrospectively denies the impact of a marital kiss and the prospects of living in connubial bliss into old age. The second stanza denies the assumptions of tulips that they will be accepted by the bride, the third the uncertainties of the wedding guests, the "symmetry of doubt." The turn suggested in stanza two ("But they are wrong") is declared at the beginning of stanza four: "Whatever the picture says, it is wrong." The real picture is something else, something not doubtful. Instead of what the photograph portrays, passion suppressed, is passion ready to be released, passion comprehending love and death:

> Inside, the rare bone of my hand and that harp
> seen through a window suddenly so tempting

you must rush into that closed room, you must
tear your fingers across it.

Symmetry and harmony are about to be achieved.

After *Instructions to the Double*, *Under Stars* is a letdown. The first half of the book, "The Ireland Poems," derives from Gallagher's travels in Ireland in 1976. A traveller's impressions, even those of a sensitive poet with ethnic affinities for the land visited, almost inevitably disappoint. After reading Seamus Heaney, say, with his profoundly apprehended vision of the Irelands, one is tempted to characterize Gallagher's poems, especially such ones as "Disappearances in the Guarded Sector" and "The Ballad of Ballymote," with their eternal notes of sadness, as simply more news from that unhappy land. The second half of the book, "Start Again Somewhere," is not so much a second start as a return to subjects explored in *Instructions to the Double*; for instance, there are such poems as "3 A.M. Kitchen: My Father Talking" and "My Mother Remembers That She Was Beautiful." Yet even in these less successful poems Gallagher is clearly a strong young poet: passionate, elegant, painstaking.

—James K. Robinson

GARDNER, Isabella Stewart. American. Born in Newton, Massachusetts, 7 September 1915. Educated at Foxcroft School, Middleburg, Virginia, 1931–33; Leighton Rollins School of Acting, East Hampton, New York; Embassy School of Acting, London, 1937. Married 1) Harold Van Virk in 1938, one daughter; 2) Maurice Seymour in 1943 (divorced, 1947), one son; 3) Robert H. McCormick III in 1947 (divorced, 1957); 4) Allen Tate in 1959 (divorced, 1966). Professional Actress; occasional reader for publishers. Associate Editor, with Karl Shapiro, *Poetry*, Chicago, 1952–56.

PUBLICATIONS

Verse

Birthdays from the Ocean. Boston, Houghton Mifflin, 1955.
Un Altra Infanzia (bilingual edition, translated by Alfredo Rizzardi). Bologna, Libreria Antiquaria Palmaverde, 1959.
The Looking Glass: New Poems. Chicago, University of Chicago Press, 1961.
West of Childhood: Poems 1950–1965. Boston, Houghton Mifflin, 1965.

Manuscript Collection: Washington University, St. Louis.

Critical Studies: "The Celebration of Birthdays" by John Logan, in *Sewanee Review* (Tennessee), Winter 1956; *Contemporary American Poetry* by Ralph J. Mills, Jr., New York, Random House, 1965; *The Poem in Its Skin* by Paul Carroll, Chicago, Follett, 1968.

Isabella Stewart Gardner comments:

My poems celebrate and affirm life, but they are also elegiac. My central theme is the interpersonal failure of love, the failure of the I-Thou relationship. They are the poems of a poet who is woman first and poet second. My content determines my prosody. I use many verse forms including, recently, syllabic verse. My poems, while often romantic and erotic, are also often ironic. I am politically engaged but seldom write polemically.

* * *

The mature woman in the arts achieves the stature of Myth within the lifetime; but Isabella Stewart Gardner is the woman behind the myths: alive here, classic, modern, ageless, in rooms and at tables as real as flesh: tall, long-limbed, the strength and soft-edged energy flowing where she walks. Or sits, decidedly graceful, sorrel hair, natural colors, with live blossoms, geodes, shells arrayed to give information about her spirit ... She chooses a certain blue-green, intense, and umbers, earth-colors that appear in the poems front-and-center, rather than as backdrop. ... And always the flesh-tones, bright faces, her own, her children's, her friends' and her students' in a comforting ring ... one is, as a poet, always alone. The warmth of friends and children and lovers near. But not in the making of the page. The solitary process. After which the faces reappear, conjured whole in the wrought words....

Having begun the craft early; left it "because I was too facile" in her early teens; stopped reading (contemporary) poetry; leaned the talents into acting and followed this, in character parts where her shy stutter would be less liable to obtrude (and burrs and brogues: the devices), until the children were born. And back then into writing: "the courage and energy" entailed and finally faced.

So few books over the past fifteen years. Not a productive fountain: her work is edited before it reaches paper, then wrought and hewn to the precision, the *forms*, necessary. (This is a Virgo lady: who shapes with honor.) In a time where a thousand poets cry for notice, leafleting the world with accidental prosodies ... "the challenge of form." Precision, gift for the gestures of language.

A woman, writing of the soft and tough consciousness. Love of earth's good presences (that angular sight into others' lives never achieved by the arrogant or the haughty), talk in the poems of the daughter, the son, their fathers; sweet, dark liturgies of loss; her voice's timbre unmistakable, on or off the page. A voice the color of her auburn hair. The Boston accent, "*Poet*," not poetess, said softly clearly hard, like quartzite formed.

Explains carefully (with *care*!) that she may pass the friends without acknowledging them if they are too far for her eyes to see clearly; nor can she recall names of the myriad friends and acquaintances of her years: stumbles for their names, not wishing to slur, and is SHY, thus with a fierce respect for your, and her, privacy of soul and motion. The word "discretion." How we choose chambers, and then shape them to fit: the friends today are rarely those of earlier years; the Setting a protection, that the poet may continue; and only part of it is "how," agreeing that the poet is the child who has no one to talk with: that gap is filled by the inner sounds of poetry (at first an interior dialogue). And the process brings it through and out, distills the voices, the clarity, brings vision in ... Belle Gardner, as transmuter, witch, reading, listening, above all seeing as if the eyes, the ears, the skin itself were all tender antennae.

The eyes, as readers: voraciously, at first; then, not at all; now, when accomplished, selectively, solemnly, seldom. But always with care. Caring. Who will trouble to read all friends' poems and to give of time. As an editor of *Poetry*, reached out to a new poet with encouragement, though the poems were not accepted there, referred the woman to a Dylan Thomas anthology being done at Yale; twenty years later, this poet recalls Isabella Gardner as "someone I owe all of it to: my beginnings; a wonderfully kind, warm person; imagine, taking the trouble to send me a telegram about that anthology! – and soon, my poems appearing next to hers in it! I'd never even read my poems to anybody!" Spoken with respect and affection....

Generous, in the life and in chance-taking: seeking, working with the voice of the self. "Not that oneself is better than another but that the self is all that the poet knows acutely, it is for him the burning glass and the prism."

And the modesty, before which must stand the "necessary nakedness" required of the poet: that risk of confrontation, of honesty. Of the assumption of the work, follow-through, development of a form visibly one's own, through the imperative solitary strengths ... recognition of, absorption of, defiance of the possibilities for failure. A gambling-game, see her fine poem "Writing Poetry": "it's the gamblers wearing their own hides who shoot/the moon rocketing on unprotected feet to outer space ..." for the sake of all men. This concern, with craft and with fellow-workers. She will quote those she admires for their desire for oneness with all men, *einfuhlung*, as Keats has it, or Unamuno, or the "failure of the love which is ... recognition of one human being by another. Communication. The meeting, greeting, acknowledging, the outstretched hand, the asking and accepting voice, the eye that really looks and really sees, the democracy of universal vulnerability...." This is the stance of the woman in her own rooms and spaces. She has succeeded in defining herself, and in the definition has succeeded in the communication of love.

—Carol Bergé

GARFITT, Roger. British. Born in Melksham, Wiltshire, 12 April 1944. Educated at Tiffin School, Kingston upon Thames, Surrey, 1955–62; Merton College, Oxford, 1963–68, B.A. (honours) 1968. Secretary, Oxford Community Workshop, 1969–70; English Teacher, Ousedale School, Newport Pagnell, Buckinghamshire, 1970–71, and Bicester School, Oxfordshire, 1971–72; Arts Council Creative Writing Fellow, University College of North Wales, Bangor, 1975–77; Writer-in-Residence, Sunderland Polytechnic, Tyne and Wear, 1978–80. Poetry Critic, *London Magazine*, 1973–76. Since 1978, Editor, *Poetry Review*, London. Recipient: Guinness Award, 1973; Eric Gregory Award, 1974. Address: c/o Carcanet Press, 330 Corn Exchange Buildings, Manchester M4 3BG, England.

PUBLICATIONS

Verse

Caught on Blue. Oxford, Carcanet Press, 1970.
West of Elm. Cheadle, Cheshire, Carcanet Press, 1974.
Unwritten Histories. Manchester, Carcanet Press, 1980.

Roger Garfitt comments:

My early poems began as a direct response to landscape, and especially to the play of light on a landscape. I tried to recreate in language the quality and intensity of that light. Recently I have become more interested in the landscape as a register of the lives lived there and in particular the unacknowledged lives of the majority of us. History, as it has generally been written, is the business of kings and ministers, of manufacturers and merchants: if we look instead at the unwritten histories, at the lives of the working people, our perspective is completely changed. To write those unwritten histories is to unwrite the official histories.

* * *

It would be too easy to slip Roger Garfitt's poetry into place somewhere in the long tradition of English pastoral poetry and leave it at that. He can certainly write skilfully and feelingly of the countryside, of the world of cattle in "Spring Grazing" – "The bullocks back and churn in a mill by the gate/Their breath hangs in snarls in the unravelling mist./They balk at the open field" – and he has a fine eye for the landscape of agriculture – "The harvest field shelved away, a bare shelf/set with a trap: white-rimmed stumps, pebbles and cracked soil" ("Out of a Clear Blue Sky") – or for the dunes and the sea – "Sand gathers grass. Mud grows samphire./The seven silences of water/turn to the one silence of earth" ("Titchwell").

But the urban poems, "Equinox," "Born 1940," "The Hitch-Hiker," and the group of poems written for Shelter, are all equally as well observed and as sensitively written. Can these two aspects of Roger Garfitt's works be reconciled? Is there a common factor besides that of authorship? Indeed, there is and it is that most English of preoccupations, the seasons. That aspect of external nature which affects the lives of country and town dweller alike. The shorter of the poems written for Shelter, "Spring Greens," illustrates this clearly where the climate is related to the keenest of urban images:

> Whiskers on the moss. Rust
> burns beneath the overflow. In the tenements
> the damp is changing seasons.
> And all the tins in Tesco's sharpen their colours.

Here the movement of the seasons is as essential to the town dweller as to the cattle in "Spring Grazing." There is winter in the city: "dropping over the roofs a husk of twilight/caught neatly up by magnesium fans/into circle and black," or summer at Bablock Hyth: "Out of hours, the road is warm stone/a basking place beside the stream." The titles too reveal this essential pivot on which the world of Garfitt's poetry turns: "Winter Economy," "September Morning," "Trees in City Winter," as well as the others already mentioned. It is the element in which we are all caught and involved, the climatic environment that shapes our lives, our moods, and our outlook.

Roger Garfitt's poetry is quietly voiced. It eschews verbal fireworks, but is the more effective for that, working gently as it does towards atmosphere and significance.

—John Cotton

GARIOCH, Robert (Sutherland). Scottish. Born in Edinburgh, 9 May 1909. Educated at Royal High School, Edinburgh; University of Edinburgh, 1927–31, M.A. (honours) in English. Served in the Royal Signals, 1941–46: Prisoner of War, 1942–45. Married Margaret Sutherland in 1941; two children. School master in Edinburgh, London, and Kent; now retired. Since 1965, Lexicographer, Dictionary of the Older Scottish Tongue, and Transcriber with the School of Scottish Studies. Writer-in-Residence, University of Edinburgh, 1971–73. Recipient: Sloan Prize, for verse in Scots, 1930; Scottish Arts Council Award, 1968, 1977. Address: 4 Nelson Street, Edinburgh 3, Scotland.

PUBLICATIONS

Verse

17 Poems for 6d: In Gaelic, Lowland Scots and English, with Somhairle MacGhill-Eathain. Edinburgh, Chalmers Press, 1940.
Chuckies on the Cairn: Poems in Scots and English. Edinburgh, Chalmers Press, 1949.
The Masque of Edinburgh. Edinburgh, M. Macdonald, 1954.

Jephthah and the Baptist, Translatit frae Latin in Scots, by George Buchanan. Edinburgh, Oliver and Boyd, 1959.
Selected Poems. Edinburgh, M. Macdonald, 1966.
The Big Music. Thurso, Caithness Books, 1971.
Doktor Faust in Rose Street. Edinburgh, M. Macdonald-Lines Review, 1973.
Collected Poems. Edinburgh, M. Macdonald, 1977.

Other

Two Men and a Blanket: Memoirs of a Captivity. Edinburgh, Southside, 1975.

Editor, *Made in Scotland: An Anthology of Poems.* Cheadle, Cheshire, Carcanet Press, 1974.

Manuscript Collection: National Library of Scotland, Edinburgh.

Robert Garioch comments:

In general, I am a Scottish writer belonging to the Lowlands, knowing no Gaelic, but aware that the Gaelic culture also is part of the Scottish environment. Accustomed in childhood to hearing more Scots than English spoken, I spoke school-English consciously as required; this is, or was then, a usual experience, and not injurious, except to those who try to cultivate a kind of West-end London accent, which can sound ludicrous and has given rise to many jokes. Like everyone else, I suffer more or less from belonging to a half-nation betrayed to and taken over by the English government of 1707. So there is a political reason for writing in Scots, but poetical reasons come first in poetry, I hope, and I write in English when it seems more suitable for reasons not always arguable, but possibly valid for all that.

* * *

The largest part of Robert Garioch's poetry, and certainly the best of it, is in Scots. He is one of the most fluent and convincing users of the Scottish tongue in recent literature, and much of the pleasure his work gives to a Scottish reader comes from the way in which he handles the language. But his genius is essentially comic and the enjoyment of his high spirits, of a satire that is never harsh but often very telling, easily communicates itself to readers and audiences outside Scotland. Like his beloved predecessor, Robert Fergusson of the eighteenth century, he is particularly a poet of Edinburgh, and this is seen both in extended entertainments like "Embro to the Ploy" (on the Edinburgh Festival) and *The Masque of Edinburgh* (a dramatic fantasy) and in the more tightly controlled and remarkable series of "Edinburgh Sonnets" where he tilts with laconic ingenuity and glorious rhymes against the bailies of the city, the local brands of casual violence, the anti-pleasures of northern religion, the enthusiasms of the avant-garde, and his own uneasy position as teacher, observer and bard. A play with a religious theme is eagerly argued over by its Saturday-night audience, but:

It seemed discussion wad last out the nicht,
hadna the poliss, sent by Mrs Grundy
pitten us out at twelve. And they were richt!
Wha daur debait religion on a Sunday?

The wry humour of a reticent autobiographer is glimpsed through fables like "The Percipient Swan" and "Sisyphus." The man of his time brooding on science and suffering shows (less successfully, but interestingly) in "The Muir" and "The Wire." The skill of the patient craftsman makes fine translations from Pindar and Belli and George Buchanan.

The publication of his prose memoirs of wartime experience as a P.O.W., *Two Men and a Blanket*, and of his *Collected Poems*, widened and confirmed our view of his entertaining, perceptive, and original talent. Complaints that have been voiced at times about his "jokiness" or his "parochialism" could no doubt find chapter and verse, but that he is a poet who can write with perfect seriousness within an ironic mode is shown clearly in a poem like "Brither Worm," where he watches a worm poke its head ("if he had yin") through a tiny crack in the paving-stones and meditates on the strange persistence of the apparently frail non-human life that is part of the substratum of even great cities and has here "sent out a spy." But more:

> I watched, and thocht lang of the ferlies of Naitur; I didna muve;
> I thocht of the deeps of the soil, deeper nor the sea. I made nae sound.
>
> A rat raxt frae a crack atween two stanes.
> I shuik wi sudden grue. He leukit at me, and wes gane.

—Edwin Morgan

GARLICK, Raymond (Ernest). Welsh. Born in London, 21 September 1926. Educated at the University College of North Wales, Bangor, 1944–48, B.A. 1948. Married Elin Jane Hughes in 1948; one son and one daughter. Taught in Wales, 1948–59, and the Netherlands, 1960–67. Senior Lecturer in English, 1967–72, and since 1972, Director of Welsh Studies and Principal Lecturer, Trinity College, Carmarthen. Founding Editor, *Dock Leaves*, later *The Anglo-Welsh Review*, Pembroke Dock, 1949–60. Recipient: Welsh Arts Council Prize, 1969, 1973, 1977. Member of the Welsh Academy. Address: 30 Glannant House, College Road, Carmarthen SA31 3EF, Wales.

PUBLICATIONS

Verse

Poems from the Mountain-House. London, Fortune Press, 1950.
Requiem for a Poet. Pembroke Dock, Dock Leaves Press, 1954.
Poems from Pembrokeshire. Pembroke Dock, Dock Leaves Press, 1954.
The Welsh-Speaking Sea. Pembroke Dock, Dock Leaves Press, 1954.
Blaenau Observed. Pembroke Dock, Dock Leaves Press, 1957.
Landscapes and Figures: Selected Poems 1949–63. London, Merrythought Press, 1964.
A Sense of Europe: Collected Poems 1954–1968. Llandysul, Dyfed, Gomer, 1968.
A Sense of Time: Poems and Antipoems 1969–1972. Llandysul, Dyfed, Gomer, 1972.
Incense: Poems 1972–1975. Llandysul, Dyfed, Gomer, 1976.

Recording: *Poets of Wales* series, Argo.

Other

An Introduction to Anglo-Welsh Literature. Cardiff, University of Wales Press, 1970; revised edition, 1972.

Editor, *Poetry from Wales.* Brooklyn, Poetry Book Magazine, 1954.

Bibliography: in *A Bibliography of Anglo-Welsh Literature, 1900–1965* by Brynmor Jones, Swansea, Library Association, 1970.

Manuscript Collection: National Library of Wales, Aberystwyth.

Critical Studies: "The Poetry of Raymond Garlick" by John Hill, in *The Anglo-Welsh Review* (Pembroke Dock), Summer 1972; statement by the author, in *Artists in Wales 2*, edited by Meic Stephens, Llandysul, Dyfed, Gomer, 1973; by Anthony Conran, in *Poetry Wales* (Swansea), Winter 1977; by Tony Bianchi, in *Planet* (Llangeitho, Dyfed), November 1977.

Raymond Garlick comments:

Major themes: Wales and Europe, landscapes and figures, justice and non-violence, art and time. Preoccupation with English as a language of Wales, clarity of communication, poetry as structure and shape. General influence: Anglo-Welsh poetry from the late fifteenth century onwards.

* * *

Raymond Garlick is a central figure in Anglo-Welsh literature in that he founded, in 1949, *Dock Leaves*, later *The Anglo-Welsh Review*, a magazine that was to present the best writing from Wales. He is totally committed to the concept of Anglo-Welsh literature, and through his editorship and other critical writings was a major contributor to the growth of interest and debate about the tradition of writing in English from Wales. His *Introduction to Anglo-Welsh Literature* is as a useful survey of that tradition.

His *Collected Poems 1954–1968* carries the title *A Sense of Europe*, and the book emphasises both the poet's seven years' teaching in Holland and his continuing commitment to Europe as a real entity, expressing real values and underlying unities. That said, for Garlick his adopted country Wales is the focus of his ideas and their expression in poetry. He has learned Welsh and lives in the Welsh-speaking town of Carmarthen. Also, his has been one of the strongest literary voices in promoting Welsh nationalism. He castigates the old enemy England at every opportunity, as in "Waterloo":

I didn't know before
that any Dutch were near the place.
I'd always thought it was
just French and Prussians face to face –
and the English of course,
that other violent race.

As he says at the end of *A Sense of Europe*, "My poems/are speeches,/clumsy speeches for Wales" ("Clues"). The implications of that self-proclamation are profound: the political poet is invariably more political than poet. Certainly, there are "poems and anti-poems" in *A Sense of Europe* that fail as pieces of writing because the poetic structure and invention are swamped by the anger of the politics. In one such poem, "Passion 72," the Welsh Language Society protestors are spoken of in terms of Christ: "The police/are always with us,/Roman, Dyfed-Powys,/and the Passion/unfolds before us/in unchanging fashion." Many readers would find that extremity in the writing to be ludicrous. How much more controlled and effective are poems such as "View from Llansteffan" and "Agincourt." This is the dilemma facing the politically con mitted writer, and one hopes that Raymond Garlick moves towards a resolution in his future work. Certainly, recent magazine publications indicate a more personal subject-matter, moving towards the confessional stance. Whether or not one is carried along by his anger, Garlick is clearly to be viewed as one of the most interesting of poets at present active in Wales.

—Tony Curtis

GARRETT, George (Palmer, Jr.). American. Born in Orlando, Florida, 11 June 1929. Educated at Sewanee Military Academy; The Hill School; Princeton University, New Jersey, 1947–48, 1949–52, B.A. 1952, M.A. 1956; Columbia University, New York, 1948–49. Served in the Field Artillery, United States Army, 1952–55. Married Susan Parrish Jackson in 1952; three children. Assistant Professor, Wesleyan University, Middletown, Connecticut, 1957–60; Visiting Lecturer, Rice University, Houston, 1961–62; Associate Professor, University of Virginia, Charlottesville, 1962–67; Writer-in-Residence, Princeton University, 1964–65; Professor of English, Hollins College, Virginia, 1967–71; Professor of English and Writer-in-Residence, University of South Carolina, Columbia, 1971–73; Senior Fellow, Council of the Humanities, Princeton University, 1974–77; Adjunct Professor, Columbia University, 1977–78; Writer-in-Residence, University of Michigan, Ann Arbor, 1979. Since 1979, Professor of English, Bennington College, Vermont. President of Associated Writing Programs, 1971–73. United States Poetry Editor, *Transatlantic Review*, Rome (later London) and New York, 1958–71; Contemporary Poetry Series Editor, University of North Carolina Press, Chapel Hill, 1962–68; Co-Editor, *Hollins Critic*, Virginia, 1965–71. Since 1970, Contributing Editor, *Contempora*, Atlanta; since 1971, Assistant Editor, *The Film Journal*, Hollins College, Virginia; since 1972, Co-Editor, *Worksheet*, Columbia, South Carolina. Recipient: *Sewanee Review* Fellowship, 1958; American Academy in Rome Fellowship, 1958; Ford grant, in drama, 1960; National Endowment for the Arts grant, 1967; *Comtempora* award, 1971; Guggenheim Fellowship, for fiction, 1974. Agent: Perry Knowlton, Curtis Brown Ltd., 60 East 56th Street, New York, New York 10022. Address: York Harbor, Maine 03911, U.S.A.

PUBLICATIONS

Verse

The Reverend Ghost. New York, Scribner, 1957.
The Sleeping Gypsy and Other Poems. Austin, University of Texas Press, 1958.
Abraham's Knife and Other Poems. Chapel Hill, University of North Carolina Press, 1961.
For a Bitter Season: New and Selected Poems. Columbia, University of Missouri Press, 1967.
Welcome to the Medicine Show: Postcards, Flashcards, Snapshots. Winston-Salem, North Carolina, Palaemon Press, 1978.

Plays

Sir Slob and the Princess: A Play for Children. New York, French, 1962.
Garden Spot, U.S.A. (produced Houston, 1962).

Screenplays: *The Young Lovers*, 1964; *The Playground*, 1965; *Frankenstein Meets the Space Monster*, 1966.

Novels

The Finished Man. New York, Scribner, 1959; London, Eyre and Spottiswoode, 1960.
Which Ones Are the Enemy? Boston, Little Brown, 1961; London, W. H. Allen, 1962.
Do, Lord, Remember Me. New York, Doubleday, and London, Chapman and Hall, 1965.
Death of the Fox. New York, Doubleday, 1971; London, Barrie and Jenkins, 1972.
Magic Striptease. New York, Doubleday, 1973.

Short Stories

King of the Mountain. New York, Scribner, 1958; London, Eyre and Spottiswoode, 1959.
In the Briar Patch. Austin, University of Texas Press, 1961.
Cold Ground Was My Bed Last Night. Columbia, University of Missouri Press, 1964.
A Wreath for Garibaldi. London, Hart Davis, 1969.

Other

Editor, *New Writing from Virginia.* Charlottesville, Virginia, New Writing Associates, 1963.
Editor, *The Girl in the Black Raincoat.* New York, Duell, 1966.
Editor, with W. R. Robinson, *Man and the Movies.* Baton Rouge, Louisiana State University Press, 1967.
Editor, with R. H. W. Dillard and John Moore, *The Sounder Few: Essays from "The Hollins Critic."* Athens, University of Georgia Press, 1971.
Editor, with O. B. Hardison, Jr., and Jane Gelfman, *Film Scripts One, Two, Three,* and *Four.* New York, Appleton Century Crofts, 1971–72.
Editor, with William Peden, *New Writing in South Carolina.* Columbia, University of South Carolina Press, 1971.
Editor, with John Graham, *Craft So Hard to Learn.* New York, Morrow, 1972.
Editor, with John Graham, *The Writer's Voice.* New York, Morrow, 1973.
Editor, with Walton Beacham, *Intro 5.* Charlottesville, University Press of Virginia, 1974.
Editor, with Katherine Garrison Biddle, *The Botteghe Oscure Reader.* Middletown, Connecticut, Wesleyan University Press, 1974.
Editor, *Intro 6: Life As We Know It.* New York, Doubleday, 1974.
Editor, *Intro 7: All of Us and None of You.* New York, Doubleday, 1975.
Editor, *Intro 8: The Liar's Craft.* New York, Doubleday, 1977.
Editor, with Michael Mewshaw, *Intro 9.* Austin, Texas, Hendel and Reinke, 1979.

Bibliography: in *Seven Princeton Poets*, Princeton, New Jersey, Princeton University Library, 1963; "George Garrett: A Checklist of His Writings" by R. H. W. Dillard, in *Mill Mountain Review* (Roanoke, Virginia), Summer 1971.

Manuscript Collections: University of Virginia, Charlottesville; Wesleyan University, Middletown, Connecticut.

Critical Studies: "George Palmer Garrett, Jr." by James B. Meriwether, in *The Princeton University Library Chronicle* (New Jersey), xxv, 1, 1963; "The Poetry of George Garrett" by Henry Taylor, in *Latitudes* (Houston), ii, 2, 1968; "The Poetry of Garrett" by R. H. W. Dillard, in *Masterpieces of World Literature 6*, New York, Salem Press, 1968; "The Poetry of George Garrett" by Richard Moore, in *Mill Mountain Review* (Roanoke, Virginia), Summer 1971.

George Garrett comments:

All of my work in all forms, including the verse, is part and parcel of the same voice. I make no distinction in the voice only the forms.

* * *

George Garrett's poetry shares much of the character of his fiction. His language is free and colloquial, but always strictly under control and serving the larger ends of his thought and feeling. He is personal without being confessional, and his vision is Christian without being pietistic. His work is composed upon a framework of contradictions, of polarities. The sinner who is a saint, the wounding truth that finds its only anodyne in a lie, the spirit trapped in the cage of flesh which discovers moral freedom in physical action, the cruel and painful joy (and mystery) of love – these are some of the enigmas upon which Garrett builds the lively textures of his poems.

The world of George Garrett's seeing and saying is a fallen one, a world of clenched fists and dark bruises where we all still suffer the consequences of Adam's fall in bone and flesh, and where we act out that fall again and again each passing day. His Salome describes that world in the important poem that bears her name:

A bad marriage from the beginning,
you say, a complete mismatch.
Flesh and spirit wrestle
and we call it love.

We couple like dogs in heat.
We shudder and are sundered.
We pursue ourselves,
sniffing, nose to tail
a comic parade of appetites.

That is the truth,
but not the whole truth.
Do me a little justice.
I had a dream of purity
and I have lived in the desert ever since.

In the desert, one holds to what he has (and what he had), learning like Adam and Eve after they were cast out of the garden "to lie a little and to live together." That learning is not always serious, and Garrett is capable of writing comic poems, some of which satirize our vice and folly and others of which celebrate our vital foolishness (particularly as it expresses itself in the relationships between men and women). But the tone and substance of his poetry are perhaps best expressed by the closing stanza of "For My Sons," a poem which figures importantly in the novel *Death of the Fox*:

Nothing of earned wisdom I can give you,
nothing save the old words like rock candy
to kill the taste of dust on the tongue.
Nothing stings like the serpent, no pain greater.
Bear it. If a bush should burn and cry out,
bow down. If a stranger wrestles, learn his name.
And if after long tossing and sickness you find
a continent, plant your flags, send forth a dove.
Rarely the fruit you reach for returns your love.

—R. H. W. Dillard

GASCOYNE, David (Emery). British. Born in Harrow, Middlesex, 10 October 1916. Educated at Salisbury Cathedral Choir School; Regent Street Polytechnic, London. Married Judy Tyler in 1975. Lived in France, 1937–39, 1954–65. Recipient: Rockefeller-Atlantic Award, 1949. Fellow, Royal Society of Literature, 1951. Address: 48 Oxford Street, Northwood, Cowes, Isle of Wight, United Kingdom.

PUBLICATIONS

Verse

Roman Balcony and Other Poems. London, Lincoln Williams, 1932.
Man's Life Is This Meat. London, Parton Press, 1936.
Hölderlin's Madness. London, Dent, 1938.
Poems 1937–1942. London, Editions Poetry London, 1943.
A Vagrant and Other Poems. London, Lehmann, 1950.
Night Thoughts. London, Deutsch, and New York, Grove Press, 1956.
Collected Poems, edited by Robin Skelton. London, Oxford University Press-Deutsch, 1965.
Penguin Modern Poets 17, with Kathleen Raine and W. S. Graham. London, Penguin, 1970.
The Sun at Midnight: Notes on the Story of Civilisation Seen as the History of the Great Experimental Work of the Supreme Scientist. London, Enitharmon Press, 1970.
Collected Verse Translations, edited by Robin Skelton and Alan Clodd. London, Oxford University Press-Deutsch, 1970.
Three Poems. London, Enitharmon Press, 1976.

Play

The Hole in the Fourth Wall; or, Talk, Talk, Talk (produced London, 1950).

Novel

Opening Day. London, Cobden Sanderson, 1933.

Other

A Short Survey of Surrealism. London, Cobden Sanderson, 1935.
Thomas Carlyle. London, Longman, 1952.
Paris Journal 1937–1939. London, Enitharmon Press, 1978.

Editor, *Outlaw of the Lowest Planet*, by Kenneth Patchen. London, Grey Walls Press, 1946.

Translator, *Conquest of the Irrational*, by Salvatore Dali. New York, Levy, 1935.
Translator, with Humphrey Jennings, *A Bunch of Carrots: Twenty Poems*, by Benjamin Péret. London, Roger Roughton, 1936; revised edition, as *Remove Your Hat*, 1936.
Translator, *What is Surrealism?*, by André Breton. London, Faber, 1936.

Bibliography: "David Gascoyne: A Checklist" by A. Atkinson, in *Twentieth-Century Literature 6* (Los Angeles), 1961.

Manuscript Collections: British Library, London; University of Tulsa, Oklahoma; State University of New York, Buffalo; New York Public Library.

Critical Studies: by Edwin Muir, in *The Observer* (London), December 1950; "Poetry and

Ideas II: David Gascoyne" by Anthony Cronin, in *London Magazine*, July 1957; "The Restoration of Symbols" by Kathleen Raine, in *Every Changing Shape*, London, Deutsch, 1961; "A Voice from the Darkness" by Gavin Ewart, in *London Magazine*, November 1965; "David Gascoyne and the Prophetic Role" by Kathleen Raine, in *Defending Ancient Springs*, London, Oxford University Press, 1967; *David Gascoyne: The Evolution of the Ideas of a Surrealist Poet* by Michel Rémy, University of Nancy, unpublished thesis, 1968.

* * *

David Gascoyne began his literary career precociously early. Whilst still in his teens he was an active propagandist for the Continental surrealist movement, and was one of the few English poets to produce work in the surrealist manner that still looked like genuine poetry. Gascoyne's surrealist apprenticeship gave him a feeling for the arresting image, and for the way in which unexpectedly juxtaposed images can produce a disturbing but memorable effect. In the late thirties and early forties Gascoyne produced the major phase of his work; the poems he wrote at that time were collected in his *Poems 1937–1942*, which remains one of the few distinguished collections of the decade. In these poems Gascoyne was preoccupied with several recurring themes: a sense of personal anguish expressed in the terms of existential philosophy, as in such poems as "Noctambules," "A War-Time Dawn" and "The Gravel-Pit Field"; an awareness of a world first threatened by war and then overwhelmed by it; and a deep interest in the central symbols of Christianity. Gascoyne used these very effectively in a sequence of poems called "Miserere," though his interest in the Christian religion was that of a poetic mythologizer rather than that of an orthodox believer. The opening of "Pieta" from this sequence shows Gascoyne's ability to express intense feeling in vivid images, in a verse that is mannered and yet at the same time highly controlled:

Stark in the pasture on the skull-shaped hill,
In swollen aura of disaster shrunken and
Unsheltered by the ruin of the sky,
Intensely concentrated in themselves the banded
Saints abandoned kneel.

Elsewhere, in "Snow in Europe," which is dated "Christmas, 1938," Gascoyne shows both his awareness of the pressures of history and his adroit handling of images:

The warring flags hang colourless a while;
Now midnight's icy zero feigns a truce
Between the signs and seasons, and fades out
All shots and cries. But when the great thaw comes,
How red shall be the melting snow, how loud the drums!

Gascoyne's post-war poetry is, by comparison, less intense and generally less interesting. *Night Thoughts*, a long semi-dramatic poem intended for radio, may have come across effectively in that medium, but is flat and diffuse on the page.

—Bernard Bergonzi

GEDDES, Gary. Canadian. Born in Vancouver, British Columbia, 9 June 1940. Educated at the University of British Columbia, Vancouver, 1958–62, B.A. !962; Reading

University, Berkshire, 1963–64, Dip. Ed. 1964; University of Toronto, 1964–68, M.A. and Ph.D. Married Jan Geddes in 1973; three daughters. Visiting Assistant Professor, Trent University, Peterborough, Ontario, 1968–69; Lecturer, Carleton University, Ottawa, 1971–72, and University of Victoria, British Columbia, 1972–74; Writer-in-Residence, 1976–77, and Visiting Associate Professor, 1977–78, University of Alberta, Edmonton. Visiting Associate Professor, 1978–79, and since 1979, Associate Professor of English, Concordia University, Montreal. General Editor, Studies in Canadian Literature series, Douglas and McIntyre, publishers, Vancouver. Address: Department of English, Concordia University, 1455 de Maisonneuve Boulevard West, Montreal, Quebec H3G 1M8, Canada.

PUBLICATIONS

Verse

Poems. Waterloo, Ontario, Waterloo Lutheran University, 1970.
Rivers Inlet. Vancouver, Talonbooks, 1972.
Snakeroot. Vancouver, Talonbooks, 1973.
Letter of the Master of Horse. Ottawa, Oberon Press, 1973.
War and Other Measures. Toronto, Anansi, 1976.

Play

Les Maudits Anglais, with the Theatre Passe Muraille (produced Montreal, 1978).

Short Stories

The Unsettling of the West. Ottawa, Oberon Press, 1980.

Other

Conrad's Later Fiction. Montreal, McGill-Queen's University Press, 1980.

Editor, *20th-Century Poetry and Poetics.* Toronto, Oxford University Press, 1969.
Editor, with Phyllis Bruce, *15 Canadian Poets.* Toronto, Oxford University Press, 1970.
Editor, *Skookum Wawa: Writings of the Canadian Northwest.* Toronto, Oxford University Press, 1975.
Editor, *Divided We Stand.* Toronto, Martin Associates, 1977.
Editor, *Love, Lust, and Laughter* (anthology of erotic verse). Toronto, Jonathan James, 1980.

Gary Geddes comments:

My poetry begins as an effort to come to terms with the influence of family and place in my life. Eventually it broadens out to include history generally, moving from lyric to narrative in order to accommodate anecdote and story. Unformed historical fragments (the Spanish conquests, the fall of Hong Kong, a reported journey of Chinese Buddhists to North America centuries ago, etc.) seem to give my imagination all it needs to work on. At the moment I am moving back and forth between poetry and fiction, writing short stories and exploring the fruitful ground between the two genres in longer forms, trying perhaps to write an epic for our times. Robert Kroetsch has said of *War and Other Measures* that it "builds, incredibly builds, it's the kind of long poem poets are only supposed to be able to dream." The trick is to combine the intensity of the lyric with the comprehensiveness of the epic. The lyrics continue to come, though, and the recent poem on the killings at Kent State, "Sandra Lee Scheuer," shows where my voice goes; Al Purdy has said of this poem that it is the kind of piece poets wait a lifetime for, and some never achieve.

* * *

Gary Geddes is one of those people for whom the world is not quite acceptable as it is. As an anthologist, he argues for regionalism in *Skookum Wawa* and for nationalism in *Divided We Stand*, straining to find the meeting – if not the breaking – point for these opposites, wherever that may be. In his poetry, especially in his longer poems, he takes pains to contrast the world's bright appearance with its grim reality. In *Letter of the Master of Horse* "bright plumes, scarlet tunics" are stripped away to reveal "yellow teeth, bloody gums," so that the poet may pose the rhetorical question in the back of his mind: "What is the shape of freedom/after all?" On 18 May 1966, one Paul Joseph Chartier tried to blow up the Parliament Building in Ottawa and succeeded only in killing himself. Out of this anarchistic act, Geddes has written *War and Other Measures*, an episodic long poem full of narrative and nuance: "It's all a matter/of roots, etymologies./Dynamite: from the Greek/*dynamos*, meaning power." Pondering the problem of the just and equitable use of power, Geddes finds in violent acts a *rationale* all their own – short on reason perhaps, but strong on emotion:

> Out of this blood another rose
> will burst, its fragrance
> confound the universe.
>
> History is being made,
> I am the materials.

So Geddes, as anthologist and poet, is both activist and analyst. The two passions come to an equipoise in his most successful poems.

—John Robert Colombo

GERSHON, Karen. British. Born in Bielefeld, Germany, 29 August 1923; emigrated to England in 1938, to Israel in 1969. Married; four children. Recipient: Arts Council bursary, 1967; *Jewish Chronicle* prize, 1967; President of Israel's grant, 1967; Pioneer Women Award, 1968. Lives in Jerusalem, Israel.

PUBLICATIONS

Verse

New Poets 1959, with Christopher Levenson and Iain Crichton Smith. London, Eyre and Spottiswoode, 1959.
Selected Poems. London, Gollancz, and New York, Harcourt Brace, 1966.
Legacies and Encounters: Poems 1966–1971. London, Gollancz, 1972.
First Meeting. Richmond, Surrey, Keepsake Press, 1974.
My Daughters, My Sisters and Other Poems. London, Gollancz, 1975.
Jephthah's Daughter. Knotting, Bedfordshire, Sceptre Press, 1978.

Other

Coming Back from Babylon. London, Gollancz, 1979.

Editor, *We Came as Children: A Collective Autobiography.* London, Gollancz, and New York, Harcourt Brace, 1966.
Editor, *Postscript: A Collective Account of the Lives of Jews in West Germany since the Second World War.* London, Gollancz, 1969.

Translator, *Obscene: The History of an Indignation*, by Ludwig Marcuse. London, MacGibbon and Kee, 1965.

Karen Gershon comments:

All my work is largely autobiographical; until now it has concerned mainly minority experiences (especially the holocaust). More recently, in family poems, I have begun writing about experiences shared by everybody. And I have extended my experimentation with counter-rhythm and free rhyme.

Being in a position rather like Conrad's, I long ago adapted to myself his saying: "And it is thus, with poignant grief in my heart, that I write [poems] to amuse the English." But now the moving force had ceased to be grief.

* * *

Karen Gershon was born in Germany, of Jewish parentage, and was one of the German Jewish children who were saved at the last moment from the Nazis. Her parents were left behind to die. Jewishness, the sense of exile, guilt for the past, the search for an identity in the changed circumstances of the present – these form the subject-matter of her poems. The search has been pursued in reality as well as in literature. At one time the poet went to Israel to live, but has now returned to England. Though there are occasions when she refers to herself as "exiled" in language, her poems belong very much to the English tradition. Wilfred Owen, in particular, has been an important influence. Her ideal is the plain style which has maximum emotional impact. Her work can be criticised, quite justly, for technical limitations – notably an over-use of jog-trot rhythms – and for a certain monotony of feeling, but she nevertheless remains, in my view, one of the few really interesting "confessional" poets to have flourished in England.

—Edward Lucie-Smith

GHISELIN, Brewster. American. Born in Webster Groves, Missouri, 13 June 1903. Educated at the University of California, Los Angeles, A.B. 1927; University of California, Berkeley, M.A. 1928, 1931–33; Oxford University, 1928–29. Married Olive F. Franks in 1929; two sons. Instructor in English, University of Utah, Salt Lake City, 1929–31; Assistant in English, University of California, Berkeley, 1931–33. Instructor, 1934–38, Lecturer, 1938–39, Assistant Professor, 1939–46, Associate Professor, 1946–50, Director of the Writers' Conference, 1947–66, Professor of English, 1950–71, Distinguished Research Professor, 1967–68, and since 1971, Professor Emeritus, University of Utah. Poetry Editor, 1937–46, and Associate Editor, 1946–49, *Rocky Mountain Review*, later *Western Review*, Salt Lake City and Lawrence, Kansas. Recipient: Ford Fellowship, 1952; Ben and Abby Grey

Foundation Award, 1965; National Institute of Arts and Letters grant, 1970; Oscar Blumenthal Prize, 1973, and Levinson Prize, 1978 (*Poetry*, Chicago). Address: Department of English, University of Utah, Salt Lake City, Utah 84112, U.S.A.

PUBLICATIONS

Verse

Against the Circle. New York, Dutton, 1946.
The Nets. New York, Dutton, 1955.
Images and Impressions, with Edward Lueders and Clarice Short. Salt Lake City, University of Utah Printmaking Department, 1969.
Country of the Minotaur. Salt Lake City, University of Utah Press, 1970.
Light. Omaha, Abattoir, 1978.
Windrose. Salt Lake City, University of Utah Press, 1979.

Other

Writing. Washington, D.C., American Association of University Women, 1959.

Editor, *The Creative Process: A Symposium.* Berkeley, University of California Press, 1952.

Manuscript Collection: Lockwood Memorial Library, State University of New York, Buffalo.

Critical Studies: *Spinning the Crystal Ball* by James Dickey, Washington, D.C., Library of Congress, 1967; "An Earthen Vessel" by William Ralston, in *Sewanee Review* (Tennessee), Summer 1969; by Radcliffe Squires, in *Concerning Poetry* (Bellingham, Washington), Fall 1970; by Kathleen Raine, in *Sewanee Review* (Tennessee), Spring 1971; by Samuel French Morse, in *Michigan Quarterly Review* (Ann Arbor), Fall 1971; by Henry Taylor, in *Masterplots: 1971 Annual*, New York, Salem Press, 1971; "The Long and Short of It" by Robert B. Shaw, in *Poetry* (Chicago), March 1972; "The Needle and the Garment" by X. J. Kennedy, in *Counter/Measures 3* (Bedford, Massachusetts), 1974.

Brewster Ghiselin comments:

Like almost every poet, I feel that my poetry can live only in being heard – that it must be given the body of life, as sensation of sound and of vibration and movement of the articulating voice. Though I have used a great variety of forms and measures, I have never written free verse. The measure I have most often found right is *accentual*, a strongly stressed and syllabically various flow that I first heard clearly when I read *Beowulf* in Old English, and turned to my own freer use, long before I read any of Gerard Manley Hopkins.

In my writing of poetry, all considerations of verse form arise from the fact that the shaping of verse is the shaping of breath – the breath of life in every sense. If a poet says that "The poetry does not matter," as T. S. Eliot did in one context, meaning, I suppose, that nothing matters except what has been called "the ground of being," he simply reminds me of the vast importance of poetry, which only through accord with that inexhaustible attains whatever life it has. In the degree that poetry is realization and communion, it is false to say that it does not matter:

The poetry matters:
Whom the wind scatters
Breath makes one again.

My central subject is men's struggle for breath, for being and light. Under the universal necessity of change, which sweeps away all form, man can have integrity and wholeness only through ceaseless shaping and reshaping of himself and his course and of those perspectives of vision that direct it. What draws my interest most and gives me matter and theme is the passion of living creatures to transcend the limits that choke them, and to find and enjoy the limits that, each in changing succession, are the freeing form of a moment of breath.

* * *

Brewster Ghiselin's two early collections offered many poems whose parts were so polished that it was difficult to grasp the whole. The effect was that of Byzantine mosaics seen close, an effect of brilliant yet disparate atomies rather than of anatomy. Yet in his later collection, *Country of the Minotaur*, the opposite is true. The parts are still burnished, but the confluence of a tidal rhythm, an audacious language, and important themes distances the poems, so that one sees their integrity and strength, as Yeats saw the integrity and strength of the lofty mosaics at Ravenna. This virtuous distance has come because Ghiselin has developed into one of the few poets today whose faith rests in universals. Because his quandaries are eternal they remain pure, for they remain unresolved. Because his passions are conceived as parallels of the passions of vast energies, like sea and land, they remain at peace; most at peace when most violent.

Passion and peace define the boundaries of his poems, and the field within the boundaries is that Nature which modern science has made both more heartless and more mysteriously beautiful than the Nature Wordsworth knew. It is a Nature that can only be understood as a broad order which barely superintends random movement, fluctuation. Except for St. John Perse I can think of no one who is so majestically at home in this nomadic drift-land. And in some ways Ghiselin is the better poet, for he varies his focus, and Perse does not.

—Radcliffe Squires

GHOSE, Zulfikar. British. Born in Sialkot, Pakistan, 13 March 1935. Educated at Keele University, England, B.A. in English and philosophy 1959. Married in 1964. Cricket Correspondent for *The Observer*, London, 1960–65. Teacher in London, 1963–69. Since 1969, Lecturer in English, University of Texas, Austin. Recipient: Arts Council of Great Britain bursary, 1967. Agent: Harold Matson Company Inc., 22 East 40th Street, New York, New York 10016. Address: Department of English, University of Texas, Austin, Texas 78712, U.S.A.

PUBLICATIONS

Verse

The Loss of India. London, Routledge, 1964.
Jets from Orange. London, Macmillan, and Chester Springs, Pennsylvania, Dufour, 1967.
The Violent West. London, Macmillan, 1972.
Penguin Modern Poets 25, with Gavin Ewart and B. S. Johnson. London, Penguin, 1974.

Novels

The Contradictions. London, Macmillan, 1966.
The Murder of Aziz Khan. London, Macmillan, 1967; New York, Day, 1969.
The Incredible Brazilian, Book I. London, Macmillan, and New York, Holt Rinehart, 1972.
Crump's Terms. London, Macmillan, 1975.
The Beautiful Empire. London, Macmillan, 1975.
A Different World. London, Macmillan, 1978.

Short Stories

Statement Against Corpses, with B. S. Johnson. London, Constable, 1964.

Other

Confessions of a Native-Alien (autobiography). London, Routledge, 1965.
Hamlet, Prufrock, and Language. London, Macmillan, 1978.

* * *

Like several of his distinguished contemporaries from the Commonwealth, the Pakistani poet Zulfikar Ghose combines sophistication of technique with a sense of deracination. His gift for the rendering of minutiae is considerable, as in "Getting to Know Fish":

> Bombay's famous fish is called Bombay Duck.
> Slim and lazy-eyed like English haddock,
> it is a small fish, dried in the sun,
> hanging, hooked to string, among coconut trees.
> It stinks. When dry, it is boiled and eaten
> with rice; through the hollows of its eyes
> its bone-juice is pressed out, salted and spiced ...

Such particularity has, for a Western reader, an attraction beyond its grip on circumstance. What is matter-of-fact for Ghose is, for his audience in the West, exotic. Thus, in speaking realistically of his childhood, Ghose commands a colour and romance over and above his ostensible subject. It would be deprecating Ghose's intelligence to assume that he is unaware of the fascination of his subject matter. He appears himself in his careful verses as an alien presence; he calls attention to his crooked nose, his "morose-Ghose face." But the point about Ghose is that he is alien everywhere. He looks for his roots ("To My Ancestors"); he loses India ("The Loss of India"); he falls in love with England ("This Landscape, These People"). Yet he is not at home there: English tolerance permits an air of drought between himself and the natives ("The Alien"); he cries "I belong to this landscape but not to these people" ("Marriages"). Zulfikar Ghose is a poet, not of love, but of distance; not of belonging but of alienation.

This indicates the presence of a dichotomy deep down in the plasm of his verse. He has adopted a language so completely that he must be regarded as one of its modern masters. Yet his precision of detail is a pattern about a void. This is seen quite clearly when Ghose attempts a major theme, as in "War in India":

> In Delhi I saw this:
> a man, yes a man and not a reptile,
> crawl from the bank of the pavement to defile
> the streamlined river of traffic with his
>
> blood....

There is a disparity between the theme and its expression. The technique, adequate for tourist sketches and domestic settings, unintentionally reduces its subject matter. It is as though the eye, unsteadied by what it perceives, slides from the battle to the peripheries. A tank, immobilised, is seen as a crab upside down; the valleys, policed with air-strips, seem to Ghose like bowls scoured of ice. Restricted by sensibility or by technique, it seems that Ghose cannot rise far beyond the recording of minutiae.

All the poems quoted so far occur in Zulfikar Ghose's first collection, *The Loss of India*. It is a fine book, but it has the limitations of its fineness. Deracination seems to have set limits to Ghose's imaginative horizons. And the subsequent collections extend those horizons only nominally. *Jets from Orange* brings in France ("Choosing a Language," "Of Animate and Inanimate Matter") but in much the same externalising way as the first book brought in Britain. *The Violent West* evokes America, but it is an America of the yellow butterflies of Lake Travis, the brown earth of Texas. In both books there are Indian poems, and it is they that act as the real attraction. "The Attack on Sialkot," "The Kleptomaniac," "In the Desert" have something of the intensity and the nostalgia of the poems about India in the first collection. But, if the considerable distinction of Zulfikar Ghose is not to depend on one book only he will have to find ways of integrating his past with his present experience. Already he has done extraordinarily well in pitting an alien background against a metropolitan technique. His admirers will look forward to his future work in the hope of seeing him attain an even greater degree of wisdom, balance, and fusion.

—Philip Hobsbaum

GIBBON, (William) Monk. Irish. Born in Dublin, 15 December 1896. Educated at St. Columba's College, Rathfarnham; Keble College, Oxford (Open History Exhibitioner); Dublin University, Ph.D. Served as an Officer in the Royal Army Service Corps, 1914–18. Taught at Chateau d'Oex, Switzerland; Oldfeld School, Swanage, Dorset; Clive House, Prestatyn; Aravon School, Bray, County Wicklow; Brook House, Monkstown, County Dublin. Tredegar Lecturer, Royal Society of Literature, 1952; Tagore Centenary Lecturer, Abbey Theatre, 1961. Recipient: Tailteann Games Silver Medal, 1928. Fellow, Royal Society of Literature, 1950. Member, 1960, and Vice-President, 1967, Irish Academy of Letters. Address: 24 Sandycove Road, Sandycove, County Dublin, Ireland.

PUBLICATIONS

Verse

The Tremulous String: Poems in Prose. Fair Oak, Hampshire, At the Sign of the Grayhound, 1926.
Wise Small Birds. Dublin, Cuala Press, 1926.
The Branch of Hawthorn Tree. London, Grayhound Press, 1927.
Within a Little Field. Dublin, Cuala Press, 1927.
For Daws to Peck At. London, Gollancz, and New York, Dodd Mead, 1929.
A Ballad. Winchester, Hampshire, Grayhound Press, 1930.
Now We'll Forget the Windy Hill. Dublin, Cuala Press, 1931.
Seventeen Sonnets. London, Joiner and Steele, 1932.
This Insubstantial Pageant: Collected Poems in Verse and Prose. London, Phoenix House, and New York, Devin Adair, 1951.
The Velvet Bow and Other Poems. London, Hutchinson, 1972.

Other

The Seals (autobiography). London, Cape, 1935.
The Stapleton Children in Jersey. Privately printed, 1938.
Mount Ida (autobiography) London, Cape, 1948.
The Red Shoes Ballet: A Critical Study. London, Saturn Press, and New York, Auvergne, 1948.
Swiss Enchantment. London, Evans, 1950.
The Tales of Hoffman: A Study of the Film. London, Saturn Press, 1951.
An Intruder at the Ballet. London, Phoenix House, 1952.
Austria. London, Batsford, 1953.
In Search of Winter Sport. London, Evans, 1953.
Western Germany. London, Batsford, 1955.
The Rhine and Its Castles. London, Putnam, 1957; New York, Norton, 1958.
The Masterpiece and the Man: Yeats As I Knew Him. London, Hart Davis, 1959; New York, Macmillan, 1960.
Netta (biography of Henrietta Franklin). London, Routledge, 1960.
The Climate of Love (autobiography). London, Gollancz, 1961.
Inglorious Soldier (autobiography). London, Hutchinson, 1968.
The Brahms Waltz (autobiography). London, Hutchinson, 1970.

Editor, *The Living Torch: An Anthology of Prose by AE, Principally Drawn from "Irish Statesman."* London, Macmillan, 1937; New York, Macmillan, 1938.
Editor, *Poems from the Irish*, by Douglas Hyde. Dublin, Allen Figgis, 1963.
Editor, *The Poems of Katherine Tynan*. Dublin, Allen Figgis, 1963.
Editor, *Thy Tears Might Cease*, by Michael Farrell. London, Hutchinson, and New York, Knopf, 1964.

Bibliography: *Monk Gibbon: A Bibliography* by Alan Denson, in *Dublin Magazine*, Autumn–Winter 1966.

Critical Studies: "Metanoia" by Alan Denson, in *Irish Press* (Dublin), 8 July 1972; "The Treason of Memory" by Eavan Boland, in *Irish Times* (Dublin), 5 August 1972.

Monk Gibbon comments:

A poet can be lucky enough to be borne along upon the contemporary tide, or it may happen to have set against him. Herbert Palmer described me in a review as "one of the most neglected of poets today whose work is of consequence." He meant that I was not "with it." My own view is that a poem, even when topical, should lie outside time. My earlier poetry is very simple, my later a good deal more complex; but I have had a few venerated readers who could take both sorts. It is hard not to be influenced by fashion, but I think that readers should be completely above all poetic snobbery. I am lost in admiration for Dylan Thomas's allusive "Fern Hill." But that doesn't prevent me thinking Housman and W. H. Davies superb poets. Poetic coteries fight hard for their own – which is laudable – and even harder against their opposites – which is contemptible.

I try in my verse to crystallise certain moments of vision, delight, or mere contemplation. I try quite often to embalm the past: I try to give an inkling of how profoundly our emotions can record, transmute or interpret the external world.

* * *

Compared to much present-day poetry Monk Gibbon's inevitably appears old-fashioned. Though he has experimented successfully with free verse, by far the greater part of his poetry has been written in strict metrical forms. His diction and syntax make few concessions to modern colloquial usage and his subject-matter is rooted in an earlier tradition. The list of touchstones in "Ultimates" illustrates Monk Gibbon's traditional approach to his craft:

All else passes
These remain
Sun's warmth,
Wind, rain;

Grass underfoot
Cloud overhead
Birds in flight,
Man's slow tread ...

Throughout his career Monk Gibbon has remained detached from the mainstream of modern poetry, concentrating on his own exploration of traditional themes and on the preservation of an individual and distinctive voice. The theme to which he returns most often is the celebration of beauty, mainly as embodied in woman. It follows that a good deal of his output consists of love poems. These are generally tender and reflective, poems of admiration rather than of passionate involvement, though at times passion breaks through. "The Black Heart" presents a finely controlled statement of polarities in love:

So all night long we spell
Love's language slowly out,
Who have forgotten that theft
Ends always as great drouth.

For theft is always loss –
"Yet theft is ecstasy?"
This, at the mouth of hell,
My black heart says to me.

Monk Gibbon's pre-occupations are generally private rather than public, metaphysical rather than actual. Often there is a troubled awareness of the fragility of man's consciousness, floating for a while on a tide of sensation between dark and dark:

My life is like a dream:
I do not know
How it began, nor yet
How it will go.

Out of the night a bird
Has quickly flown
Across the lighted room
And now is gone

Into the dark again
From whence it came ...

Monk Gibbon's poetry demonstrates only a modest degree of involvement with the Ireland of tradition or of the present day, although social and political comment does find a place in his later poetry. Some of the more recent poems and the collection of sonnets dating from 1932 show him technically at his most ambitious, but when he attempts to fill the larger or more difficult structures the inspiration is not always sufficient to meet the demands made upon it. He is generally most satisfying when writing economically and the finest of the simple lyrics from the earlier collections, *The Branch of the Hawthorn Tree* and *For Daws to Peck At* are still among his best.

—Rivers Carew

GILBERT, (Florence) Ruth. New Zealander. Born in Greytown, 26 March 1917. Educated at Hamilton High School; Otago School of Physiotherapy, Dunedin. Married to Dr. John Bennett Mackay; two daughters and two sons. Formerly, Physiotherapist, Otago School of Physiotherapy. Recipient: Jessie Mackay Memorial Award, 1948, 1949, 1967. Address: 83 Donald Street, Karori, Wellington, New Zealand.

PUBLICATIONS

Verse

Lazarus and Other Poems. Wellington, Reed, 1949.
The Sunlit Hour. London, Allen and Unwin, 1955.
The Luthier. Wellington, Reed, 1966.

Manuscript Collection: Turnbull Library, Wellington.

Ruth Gilbert comments:

My chosen forms are the lyric and the quatrain, and my aim in writing: clarity, simplicity, economy. The brevity of the quatrain appeals to me, while the lyric holds the music which my ear demands. Should my subject need more room I find the lyric sequence, which I use often, the perfect medium. Poetry is my only form of creative writing.

* * *

Ruth Gilbert's talent is for the straightforward evocation of brief moments of emotion, particularly those of the child or the woman, within the tradition of the romantic lyric. For her, the poetry seems to lie more in the words themselves than in the experiences; she is willing to take over poetic resonances established by others, reshuffling them for her own purposes:

> How steeped in beauty these old names are:
> Saffron, Sandalwood, Cinnibar ...

This is a Georgian attitude, resulting in low-pressure poems of simple statement. If she has a poetic ancestor, it is Walter de la Mare, who is close at hand in "Phobia," "Legendary Lady" and "Portrait."

Some of these moments of emotion are as imagined in the lives of others, particularly within Bible stories, where such figures as Joseph, Rachel and Lazarus are sympathetically probed. Some are personal to the poet, as "Sanatorium" and nearer to the bone, "Fall Out." Some are crystallised into small perfection, as in "Li Po," "Metamorphosis" and "The Trees of Corot."

Ruth Gilbert has made several attempts to increase her scale, by binding lyrics into a sequence. Of these the most successful is *The Luthier*, which, even if conventionally romantic in essence, has the merit of a more vigorous vocabulary, and more complex rhythms than she has commanded elsewhere.

At her best, she can set up quiet ripples – never disturbing ones – which take her meaning beyond the sensitive but unadventurous moment which she describes. Her later work, however, suggests a growing awareness of the forces to be tapped when the form has been hammered out by the pressure of the content and is not a mere relaxed rehandling of old worlds and shapes. There may therefore be different work ahead of her. But her natural place is with the Georgians.

—Joan Stevens

GILL, David (Lawrence William). British. Born in Chislehurst, Kent, 3 July 1934. Educated at Chislehurst and Sidcup Grammar School; University College, London, B.A. (honours) in German 1955, B.A. (honours) in English 1970; Birmingham University, Cert.Ed. 1959. Served in the Royal Signals, 1955–57. Married Irene Zuntz in 1958; three children. Taught at Bedales School, Hampshire, 1960–62, Nyakasura School, Fort Portal, Uganda, 1962–64, and Magdalen College School, Oxford, 1965–71. Since 1971, Lecturer, Newland Park College of Education, Chalfont St. Giles, Buckinghamshire. Recipient: Birmingham *Post* Prize, 1959. Address: 25 Redriff Close, Maidenhead, Berkshire, England.

PUBLICATIONS

Verse

Men Without Evenings. London, Chatto and Windus-Hogarth Press, 1966; Middletown, Connecticut, Wesleyan University Press, 1967.
The Pagoda and Other Poems. London, Chatto and Windus-Hogarth Press, 1969; Middletown, Connecticut, Wesleyan University Press, 1970.
Peaches and Aperçus. London, Poet and Peasant, 1974.
The Upkeep of the Castle. Bakewell, Derbyshire, Hub, 1976.

Other

Editor and Translator, *In the Eye of the Storm: Fifty Years of Poetry*, by Ondra Lysohorsky. Bakewell, Derbyshire, Hub, 1976.

David Gill comments:

(1970) I began writing verse as a schoolboy on chemistry labs, daffodils, gym masters, myself, love and other universal topics. A late developer, I wrote one good poem at university. The influences of my German reading – Rilke, Stefan George, as well as Welsh idols such as Dylan Thomas and Wilfred Owen – had a delayed action. Rilke's *Dinggedichte* plus a certain mistrust of the abstract brought home to me the importance of things at the centre of poems, visual things like roundabouts, pagodas, punch-and-judy shows, cartwheels, missiles.

In 1958 I became involved in the struggle against nuclear weapons, and, in poetry, in a parallel struggle to tame proud and angry feelings in a cage of words. At the same time (1959–62) I wanted to say quieter things about the Hampshire hangers and beech-forests near Selbourne, and became aware of the truth that poems are ways of stating the contrasts that bother the mind, the contrast of present and past ("On the Cathedral Floor"):

Bunches of angels hang from exploding branches
Watching the aisles. Six hundred years below
My son makes progress on the gothic floor,
Ant-explorer, crawling to and fro
Between the massive trees.

Or the contrast of here and elsewhere in the world-village ("I Must Withdraw"):

This day as every day my clock-shod mind
Has tramped to crises in the Timbuctoos,
Tibets and Thailands of the headlined news,
But only at such frontiers to find
The vultures knife-eyed; victims small and blind.

The shape of my verse has travelled from quatrains to more complex stanzas to a kind of free-verse, which at times goes near to prose. Preoccupations with people, politics, landscape, animals, dominate the collection of poems written in Uganda and entitled *Men Without Evenings*. Of these poems the *Guardian* critic Bernard Bergonzi wrote: "His poems are immersed in the colours, sounds, and smells of that country, but they have an intelligent moral dimension which makes them something more than touristic snapshot verse."

(1980) During the early 1970's I began to take part in public poetry readings, writing more for the straining ear, and with greater directness. The need to express feelings against my natural drift to elegy has led me to invest in disguises and dramatic monologues. In my latest book I vanish into a hunch-backed Archduke, the poet Edmund Waller, and the last unpolluted man on earth.

* * *

David Gill's poetry describes and comments but seldom enacts or explores. The range of subject-matter is considerable, attesting for instance to wide travel, but in a sense this very richness of his raw material draws attention to the relatively meagre use he makes of it poetically. For it *remains* subject-matter, safely beyond the reader's capacity for surprise. Whether the ostensible subject is political prisoners, children, historical figures or exotic landscapes, the ready adjective and the banal (if admirably sensible) observation screen us from any sense of discovery or presentness. Descriptions of animals for example have none of the inventive flair we would find in, say, Norman MacCaig's animals. And, more seriously, the effort to mould his verse into the shape he wants can sometimes blind him to a betrayal of a doubtless sincere feeling, as in the conclusion of "Beatrix Potter," or lines like these:

Will you not think, you gentle theologians,
of what has been expunged from these calm walks?
The buddhist priests bleeding in burning pagodas,
and clouds of helicopters hanging like hawks.

This may well mean no more than that Gill accepts a limited function for his poetry, but in the context of a survey such as this the point must be made. His own description of his writing, made with reference to the craft of a wheelwright, clarifies the issue:

the bark of images is stripped to show
the dead-straight grain of relevance behind,
and soon the jobbing words begin the slow

and careful fashioning of stalwart verse ...

The imagination has a way, unfortunately, of eluding the most carefully fashioned invitations.

—Robin Fulton

GILLIES, Valerie (née Simmons). Scottish. Born in Edmonton, Alberta, Canada, 4 June 1948. Educated at Trinity Academy, Edinburgh, 1953–66; University of Edinburgh, 1966–70, 1972–74, M.A. 1970, M.Litt. 1974; University of Mysore, India, 1970–71. Married William Gillies in 1972; one son and one daughter. Writer-in-Residence, Boroughmuir School, Edinburgh, 1978–79. Recipient: Scottish Arts Council bursary, 1976; Eric Gregory Award, 1976. Address: 50 Comiston Drive, Edinburgh EH10 5QS, Scotland.

PUBLICATIONS

Verse

Trio: New Poets from Edinburgh, with Roderick Watson and Paul Mills, edited by Robin Fulton. New York, New Rivers Press, 1971.
Each Bright Eye: Selected Poems. Edinburgh, Canongate, 1977.

Plays

Radio Plays: *Rabbits*, 1978; *Stories of the Mountains*, 1979; *The Ballad of Tam Lin*, 1979.

Other

Editor, *Scottish Short Stories 1979* and *1980.* London, Collins, 2 vols., 1979–80.

Valerie Gillies comments:

I first began writing at about the age of 14. A poem would come into my head while I was out walking: I'd write it down when I got back, altering it here and there. This is my method of composition still. I like to fool around with words, to play with half-rhymes. I write in strict form and in freer verse too. About the time I went to India I was experimenting with the poetry of meditation. The denser poems in *Each Bright Eye* are a result of that kind of concentration. The love poem and the divine poem were my first preoccupations, and I have written enough animal poems to begin a bestiary. I am not afraid of ideas, and I like to make them strike sparks off one another in the old metaphysical way, but I am working towards a clearer, simpler voice in my poems today.

*   *   *

Canadian-born Valerie Gillies grew up and was educated in Scotland and at the University of Mysore. The influences both of India and the Scotland in which she has now married and settled are apparent in her verse. Unlike some women poets, she is capable of a keen objectivity that is matched by the lithe strength of her poetic structures. She favours *vers libre*, varied occasionally with a kind of lolloping casual rhyme or half-rhyme. Her best free-verse poems hold together, so to say, from the centre.

It is difficult for any poet other than a master of the first order to capture and convey the "feel" of an alien country. Gillies's poems with Indian subject-matter are thus, not surprisingly, her least successful, partly because the sense of someone "outside looking-in" results in a certain sense of verbal opacity, not helped by the now-and-then use of Indian terms or experiences unlikely to be understood by a non-Indian reader. When she is writing of people, whether of her grandfather, minded "to make a crook and staff," or Indians like "Mister B. Rajan, diamond buyer" in "Fellow Passenger," or, even more vividly, in "The Piano-Tuner," she captures, not just the pathos of the unsuccessful disguise of unadmitted personal limitation in her subject, but the lingering echoes of the vanished British Raj culture:

> Two hundred miles, he had come
> to tune one piano, the last hereabouts.
> Both of them were relics of imperial time:
> the Anglo-Indian and the old upright knockabout.
>
> He peered, and peered again
> into its monsoon-warped bowels.
> From the flats of dead sound he'd beckon
> a tune on the bones out to damp vowels.
>
> His own sounds were pidgeon....

She has written both love poems and poems about birth. The former are seriously tender, concentrating on the nature of the association that binds lovers together rather than on anatomical detail; the latter, delicately original, as "For a Son's First Birthday": "Your first breath/blew you up so pink/you were ragged robin in the marshes.//What I forget/is your first sound:/loud, brilliant and reedy." That double meaning of the word "reedy" binds the images together, aligns them to complement each other, like glasses in a telescope, and reveals the technique of a true poet.

Gillies's real strength, however, shows itself to strongest advantage in her animal poems. It is one of the received Eng. Lit. myths of our time that every poet who writes about animals must in some way be under the influence of Ted Hughes: absurd, of course, since many older poets were well aware of what goes on in the forests of the night. Gillies's special concern is with animals in motion, as in "The Greyhound," "The Salmon-Loup" (in which the comparison between the salmon about to make "his curve of a fish-leap" and her lover, "newly arrived in fresh sight/ A silverskin of atlantic littoral" is beautifully made), and in her picture of "Deerhounds": "Long dogs, you move with air/belling the vault of your ribcage./ You subdue the miles below your hocks .../The bracken hurdles below your height,/the rushes make way for you;/your hard eye holds in sight the rapid hills...."

—Maurice Lindsay

GINSBERG, Allen. American. Born in Newark, New Jersey, 3 June 1926. Educated at Paterson High School, New Jersey; Columbia University, New York, B.A. 1948. Served in the Military Sea Transport Service. Associated with the Beat movement and the San Francisco Renaissance in the 1950's. Widely travelled: has participated in many poetry readings and demonstrations. Lived in the Far East, 1962–63. Since 1971, Director, Committee on Poetry Foundation, New York; Director, Kerouac School of Poetics, Naropa Institute, Boulder, Colorado. Recipient: Guggenheim Fellowship, 1965; National Endowment for the Arts grant, 1966; National Institute of Arts and Letters grant, 1969; National Book Award, 1974. Member, National Institute of Arts and Letters, 1973. Address: P.O. Box 582, Stuyvesant Station, New York, New York 10009, U.S.A.

PUBLICATIONS

Verse

Howl and Other Poems. San Francisco, City Lights, 1956; revised edition of *Howl*, as *Howl for Carl Solomon*, San Francisco, Grabhorn Hoyem, 1971.
Siesta in Xbalba and Return to the States. Privately printed, 1956.
Empty Mirror: Early Poems. New York, Totem-Corinth, 1961.
Kaddish and Other Poems 1958–1960. San Francisco, City Lights, 1961.
A Strange New Cottage in Berkeley. San Francisco, Grabhorn Press, 1963.
Reality Sandwiches 1953–60. San Francisco, City Lights, 1963.
Penguin Modern Poets 5, with Lawrence Ferlinghetti and Gregory Corso. London, Penguin, 1963.
The Change. London, Writers Forum, 1963.
Kral Majales. Berkeley, California, Oyez, 1965.
Prose Contribution to Cuban Revolution. Detroit, Artists' Workshop Press, 1966.
Wichita Vortex Sutra. London, Peace News Poetry, 1966.
T.V. Baby Poems. London, Cape Goliard Press, 1967; New York, Grossman, 1968.
Wales – A Visitation, July 29, 1967. London, Cape Goliard Press, 1968.
Scrap Leaves, Hasty Scribbles. New York, Poets Press, 1968.
Message II. Buffalo, Gallery Upstairs Press, and London, Ad Infinitum, 1968.
Planet News 1961–1967. San Francisco, City Lights, 1968.
Airplane Dreams: Compositions from Journals. Toronto, Anansi, 1968; San Francisco, City Lights, 1969.
Ankor-Wat. London, Fulcrum Press, 1969.
The Moments Return. San Francisco, Grabhorn Hoyem, 1970.
Notes after an Evening with William Carlos Williams. New York, Charters, 1970.
Iron Horse. Toronto, Coach House Press, 1972; San Francisco, City Lights, 1974.
The Fall of America: Poems of These States 1965–1971. San Francisco, City Lights, 1972.
The Gates of Wrath: Rhymed Poems 1948–1952. Bolinas, California, Grey Fox Press, 1972.
Open Head, with *Open Eye*, by Lawrence Ferlinghetti. Melbourne, Sun, 1972.
New Year Blues. New York, Phoenix Book Shop, 1972.
Bixby Canyon Ocean Path Word Breeze. New York, Gotham Book Mart, 1972.
Sad Dust Glories. Berkeley, California, Workingman's Press, 1975.
First Blues: Rags, Ballads, and Harmonium Songs 1971–74. New York, Full Court Press, 1975.
Mind Breaths: Poems 1972–1977. San Francisco, City Lights, 1978.
Poems All Over the Place: Mostly Seventies. Cherry Valley, New York, Cherry Valley Editions, 1978.
Selected Gay Poems and Correspondence, with Peter Orlovsky, edited by Winston Leyland. San Francisco, Gay Sunshine Press, 1979.

Recordings: *Howl and Other Poems*, Fantasy-Galaxy, 1959; *Kaddish*, Atlantic Verbum,

1966; *William Blake's Songs of Innocence and Experience Tuned by Allen Ginsberg*, MGM, 1970.

Plays

Don't Go Away Mad, in *Pardon Me, Sir, But Is My Eye Hurting Your Elbow?*, edited by Bob Booker and George Foster. New York, Geis, 1968.
Kaddish (produced New York, 1972).

Other

The Yage Letters, with William S. Burroughs. San Francisco, City Lights, 1963.
Notes on an Interview with Allen Ginsberg, by Edward Lucie-Smith. London, Turret, 1965.
Indian Journals: March 1962–May 1963: Notebooks, Diary, Blank Pages, Writings. San Francisco, Dave Haselwood, 1970.
Improvised Poetics, edited by Mark Robison. Buffalo, Anonym Press, 1971.
Allen Verbatim: Lectures on Poetry, Politics, Consciousness, edited by Gordon Ball. New York, McGraw Hill, 1974.
The Visions of the Great Rememberer (on Jack Kerouac). Amherst, Massachusetts, Mulch Press, 1974.
Chicago Trial Testimony. San Francisco, City Lights, 1975.
To Eberhart from Ginsberg. Loncoln, Massachusetts, Penmaen Press, 1976.
As Ever: The Collected Correspondence of Allen Ginsberg and Neal Cassady, edited by Barry Gifford. Berkeley, California, Creative Arts, 1977.
Journals: Early Fifties–Early Sixties, edited by Gordon Ball. New York, Grove Press, 1977.

Bibliography: *A Bibliography of the Works of Allen Ginsberg* by George Dowden, San Francisco, City Lights, 1970.

Manuscript Collections: Columbia University, New York; University of Texas, Austin.

Critical Studies: *Allen Ginsberg in America* by Jane Kramer, New York, Random House, 1968; *Scenes Along the Road*, edited by Ann Charters, New York, Gotham Book Mart, 1971; *Allen Ginsberg in the 60's* by Eric Mottram, Brighton, Sussex, Unicorn Bookshop, 1972.

Allen Ginsberg comments:

(1970) Beat-Hip-Gnostic-Imagist.

Major themes: transformation of consciousness to include visionary gleam of planet-light in Eternity before death. Characteristic subject: my own body or imagistic body of planet. Usual forms and sources: Bible and Kit Smart, parallelism and litany. Sources in Whitman, Rimbaud, Shakespeare, Blake above all, Pound, Jack Kerouac, and W. C. Williams. Influenced by "Black Mountain" poets, Olson, Creeley, Duncan. Travels and music of Orient leading into Mantra chanting reflect back on poesy as prophetic Shamanistic Chaunt. I have achieved the introduction of the word *fuck* into texts inevitably studied by schoolboys.

(1974) A.D. 1973 studying poetics and meditation in the whispered transmission school of Mila Repa (12th century Tibetan Buddhist yogi-poet) with Rimpoche Chögyam Truagpa Lama, also a poet; tendency of my poetry practice last 2 years has been toward natural minded improvisation, taking for granted that "first thought is best thought," an attitude necessary for the realization of spontaneous flow of rhymed lines; presently in U.S. black Blues form and wedded to traditional triple-chord (CFG or GCD etc.) Western Blues. This is outgrowth of a decade's monochord practice mantra-chanting, followed by several years tuning Blake's lyrics to actual song (restoring the words to song, so to speak).

The tradition of improvising poems on the spot in communal situations is I believe older than the written tradition and perhaps more distinguished – as in the work of Homer or the much more ancient oral epic tradition of Australian Aborigine Song Men with whom I've had some brief contact Spring 1972. In any case it may be appropriate to restore facility in the bardic improvised manner in this over-civilized day and age when we are not sure that the supply of electric or paper will outlast the century, outlast our own lives. So as a conservation of viable poetries independent of material base (printed book) in case of, just in case of, historical necessity, and as outgrowth of Beat-hip-gnostic-imagistic spontaneous mind style, I am practicing improvised poetry.

* * *

Allen Ginsberg is perhaps the crucial figure in the revival of American poetry in the 1950's and 1960's. His intellectual contributions to the new American poetry are not as important as Charles Olson's; his technical contributions are not as important as Robert Duncan's; his work may not in the long-run be as satisfying as Edward Dorn's, John Ashbery's, Jack Spicer's, or Robert Creeley's. It was, however, Ginsberg who created the public image of the poet for his generation. Seldom have previous generations been so fortunate, to be represented in the public eye by a poet of his abilities. It is difficult to sort out Ginsberg the phenomenon from Ginsberg the poet. He is, however, a genuine poet whose achievement cannot be doubted.

Post-Whitmanian poetry – and it is Whitman's tradition the poets of the 1950's renewed – is a poetry which recognizes the perpetual state of crisis in which language exists. That is, it appeals to precisely the fact which poetry has traditionally attempted to diminish by the ritualization of itself and of experience. The new American poetry, though it often has an important religious concern, is timely rather than eternal, political rather than religious, immediate rather than ritualized. The apparent ritual of a Ginsberg performance – the chanting and the priest-like presence of the poet himself – has a totally non-ritual meaning: the destiny of this poetry is to *discover* its destiny syllable by syllable and line by line. Ginsberg created this poetry for the popular audience, without compromising it. Never has such a dense, difficult, and learned poetry had such a vast appeal.

That Ginsberg is a learned poet is a point worth emphasizing. It is impossible to read through his work without being aware that he knows the literary tradition thoroughly. He is widely read in philosophy, eastern religion, and history. His knowledge of current politics is neither casual nor merely fashionable. When he speaks in *Howl* of the poets "who studied Plotinus Poe St. John of the Cross telepathy and bop kaballa because the cosmos instinctively vibrated at their feet in Kansas," he might have been speaking about Allen Ginsberg and Paterson, N. J. Ginsberg's strategy is to call both the private and the public crisis into the critical space of the poem. He insists that language register the flow and feel of consciousness which does not allow itself the comfort of ritualizing itself. The uncertainties and ambiguities of sexual identity, the possibilities for consciousness opened by drugs, the sense that religious and visionary experience is at most fleeting, and the overt, obvious dangers of political life are brought to bear on the immediate occasion of speech and perception. Although they may outrage traditional notions of poetric craftsmanship, Ginsberg's compositions on a tape recorder are no less demanding of attention and care than the most polished poems. He has an impeccable ear. Many poets who endlessly revise their work write more dull, lifeless lines than Ginsberg does.

In *Indian Journals*, Ginsberg writes, "We think in blocks of sensation & images. IF THE POET'S MIND IS SHAPELY HIS ART WILL BE SHAPELY. That is, the page will have an original but rhythmic shape – inevitable thought to inevitable thought, lines dropping inevitably in place on the page, making a subtle infinitely varied rhythmic SHAPE." The poem, in other words, cannot be dissociated from spiritual discipline as a whole, and Ginsberg's world-wide quest for spiritual guidance is a poetic quest. His work is one of the clearest records we have of the quest for a shapely mind.

Ginsberg is not a poet who should be read for great passages or anthology pieces. The most interesting fact of his work is that he has been able to *sustain* his energies. The Ginsbergian flow of speech is always available as an energy source.

—Don Byrd

GIOVANNI, Nikki (Yolande Cornelia Giovanni). American. Born in Knoxville, Tennessee, 7 June 1943. Educated at Fisk University, Nashville, Tennessee, 1960–61, 1964–67, B.A. (honors) in history 1967; University of Pennsylvania School of Social Work, Philadelphia; Columbia University, New York. Has one son. Assistant Professor of Black Studies, Queens College, Flushing, New York, 1968; Associate Professor of English, Livingston College, Rutgers University, New Brunswick, New Jersey, 1968–70. Editorial Consultant, *Encore* magazine, Albuquerque, New Mexico. Recipient: Ford grant, 1968; National Endowment for the Arts grant, 1969. D.H.: Wilberforce University, Ohio, 1972; D. Litt.: University of Maryland, Princess Anne, 1974; Ripon University, Wisconsin, 1974; Smith College, Northampton, Massachusetts, 1975. Address: c/o Glickman, 24 West 40th Street, New York, New York 10018, U.S.A.

PUBLICATIONS

Verse

Black Judgement. Detroit, Broadside Press, 1968.
Black Feeling, Black Talk. Detroit, Broadside Press, 1968.
Re: Creation. Detroit, Broadside Press, 1970.
Black Feeling Black Talk/Black Judgement. New York, Morrow, 1970.
Poem of Angela Yvonne Davis. New York, TomNik, 1970.
My House. New York, Morrow, 1972.
The Women and the Men. New York, Morrow, 1975.
Cotton Candy on a Rainy Day. New York, Morrow, 1978.

Recordings: *Truth Is on Its Way*, Right On, 1971; *Like a Ripple on a Pond*, Niktom, 1973; *The Way I Feel*, Niktom, 1975; *Legacies*, Folkways, 1976.

Other

Spin a Soft Black Song (juvenile). New York, Hill and Wang, 1971.
Gemini: An Extended Autobiographical Statement on My First Twenty-Five Years of Being a Black Poet. Indianapolis, Bobbs Merrill, 1971; London, Penguin, 1976.
Ego Tripping and Other Poems for Young Readers. Westport, Connecticut, Lawrence Hill, 1973.
A Dialogue: James Baldwin and Nikki Giovanni. Philadelphia, Lippincott, 1973.
A Poetic Equation: Conversations Between Nikki Giovanni and Margaret Walker. Washington, D.C., Howard University Press, 1974.

Editor, *Night Comes Softly* (anthology). New York, TomNik, 1970.

Manuscript Collection: Mugar Memorial Library, Boston University.

* * *

After awaking to "the possibility of/Blackness/and the inevitability of/Revolution"; after dispensing with refined language for colloquial talk ("Can a nigger kill the Man/Can you kill nigger/Huh?"); after using that power to deal with social issues and at the same time whispering a desire to do something "counterrevolutionary" like making love ("Seduction"); after committing herself to a life of encounter, abandoning bourgeois ways to become "a for real Black person who must now feel/and inflict/pain," and admonishing all Blacks to do the same ("You must invent your own games," she advises in "Poem for Black Boys," "and teach us old ones/how to play"); after celebrating Blackness in "Nikki-Rosa," "Beautiful Black Men" and "Ego Tripping"; Nikki Giovanni published an autobiography, *Gemini*, and conducted a tour through *My House*, a place rich with family remembrance, distinctive personalities, and prevailing love, where

> the old man said my time is getting near
> the old man said my time
> is getting near
> he looked at his dusty cracked boots to say
> sister my time is getting near
> and when i'm gone remember i smiled
> when i'm gone remember
> i smiled
> i'm glad my time is getting near

and where if, "the revolution screeeeeeeeeeeeching/to a halt," the dream was dead, there was "a free future"; if she was disappointed, she was going to live on lovingly. But the latest look into her private life, *Cotton Candy on a Rainy Day*, revealed discouragement and fatigue, Giovanni likening herself to "the unrealized dream of an idea unborn," thinking "I should write a poem/but there's almost nothing/that hasn't been said/and said and said," finally saying in "Being and Nothingness," "i don't want to exert anything."

In *The Women and the Men*, her richest collection of poems, the women can "sit and wait" for love, or resent one another, or keep their integrity into old age, or aspire to greatness, or be assertive to men. "The Women Gather" shows their effectuality. Preparing for a funeral, in a time when "we are no longer surprised/that the unfaithful pray loudest," the women leave off being selfish to be merciful and loving. Despite the tendency to forgive "because we have trespassed" and comfort "because we need comforting,"

> the women gather
> with cloth and ointment
> their busy hands bowing to laws that decree
> willows shall stand swaying but unbroken
> against even the determined wind of death.

"Because it is not unusual to know [a man] through those who love him," we judge, but by being merciful we make a more generous accounting of "dreams" and "deeds," of "intent" and "shortcomings." The women "sift/ through ashes/and find an unburnt picture."

For Giovanni a poem, "pure energy/horizontally contained/between the mind/of the poet and the ear of the reader," is vital for touching others and preparing the young for their lives. As Paula Giddings puts it, in her Introduction to *Cotton Candy*, Giovanni is "a witness," whose poems are "souvenirs extracted from the site of a precious moment" rather than "flawless gems." Power prevails in Giovanni's world, but she sustains the hope for love having effect. "i dream of black men and women walking/together side by side into a new world."

—Jay S. Paul

GITTINGS, Robert (William Victor). British. Born in Portsmouth, Hampshire, 1 February 1911. Educated at St. Edward's School, Oxford; Jesus College, Cambridge (Chancellor's Medal, 1931), B.A. 1933, M.A. 1936. Married 1) Katharine Edith Cambell in 1934 (marriage dissolved); 2) Joan Grenville Manton in 1949; two sons and one daughter. Research Student and Research Fellow, 1933–38, and Supervisor in History, 1938–40, Jesus College, Cambridge. Producer and Scriptwriter, BBC, 1940–63. Visiting Professor, Vanderbilt University, Nashville, Tennessee, Summer 1966, Boston University, 1970, and University of Washington, Seattle, 1972, 1974. Recipient: Heinemann Award for non-fiction, 1955, 1979; Phoenix Trust Award, 1963; Smith Award, for non-fiction, 1969; Christian Gauss Award, 1975; Black Memorial Prize, for non-fiction, 1979. Litt.D.: Cambridge University, 1970. Fellow, Royal Society of Literature. C.B.E. (Commander, Order of the British Empire), 1970. Address: The Stables, East Dean, Chichester, Sussex, England.

PUBLICATIONS

Verse

The Roman Road and Other Poems. London, Oxford University Press, 1932.
The Story of Psyche. Cambridge, University Press, 1936.
Wentworth Place. London, Heinemann, 1950.
Famous Meeting: Poems, Narrative and Lyric. London, Heinemann, 1953.
This Tower My Prison and Other Poems. London, Heinemann, 1961.
Matters of Love and Death. London, Heinemann, 1968.
American Journey: Twenty-Five Sonnets. London, Heinemann, 1972.
Collected Poems. London, Heinemann, 1976.

Plays

The Seven Sleepers (produced London, 1950).
The Makers of Violence. London, Heinemann, 1951.
Through a Glass, Lightly. London, Heinemann, 1952.
Man's Estate: A Play of Saint Richard of Chichester, in *Two Saints Plays*, edited by Leo Lehman. London, Heinemann, 1954.
Out of This Wood: A Country Sequence of Five Plays (includes *The Brontë Sisters*, *Our Clouded Hills*, *Parson Herrick's Parishioners*, *Thomas Tusser's Wife*, *William Cowper's Muse*). London, Heinemann, 1955.
Love's a Gamble: A Ballad Opera, music by Doris Gould. London, Oxford University Press, 1961.
This Tower My Prison (produced London, 1961). Included in *This Tower My Prison and Other Poems*, 1961.
Conflict at Canterbury: An Entertainment in Sound and Light (produced Canterbury, 1970). London, Heinemann, 1970.

Son et Lumière scripts: *This Tower My Prison*, 1961; *St. Paul's*, 1968; *Conflict at Canterbury*, 1970.

Radio Writing: Adaptations and Features, 1939–63, including *Famous Meetings* series, 1948–51.

Other

The Peach Blossom Forest and Other Chinese Legends, with Jo Manton. London, Oxford University Press, 1951.

John Keats: The Living Year, 21 September 1818 to 21 September 1819. London, Heinemann, and Cambridge, Massachusetts, Harvard University Press, 1954.
The Mask of Keats: A Study of Problems. London, Heinemann, and Cambridge, Massachusetts, Harvard University Press, 1956.
Windows on History, with Jo Manton. London, Hulton, 4 vols., 1959–61.
Shakespeare's Rival: A Study in Three Parts. London, Heinemann, 1960; Westport, Connecticut, Greenwood Press, 1976.
The Story of John Keats (juvenile), with Jo Manton. London, Methuen, 1962; New York, Dutton, 1963.
The Keats Inheritance. London, Heinemann, 1964; New York, Barnes and Noble, 1965.
Makers of the Twentieth Century, with Jo Manton. London, Hulton, 1966.
John Keats. London, Heinemann, and Boston, Little Brown, 1968.
The Odes of Keats and Their Earliest Known Manuscripts in Facsimile. London, Heinemann, and Kent, Ohio, Kent State University Press, 1970.
Young Thomas Hardy. London, Heinemann, and Boston, Little Brown, 1975.
The Flying Horses: Tales from China (juvenile), with Jo Manton. London, Methuen, and New York, Holt Rinehart, 1977.
The Older Hardy. London, Heinemann, 1978; as *Hardy's Later Years*, Boston, Little Brown, 1978.
The Nature of Biography. London, Heinemann, and Seattle, University of Washington Press, 1978.
The Second Mrs. Hardy, with Jo Manton. London, Heinemann, and Seattle, University of Washington Press, 1979.

Editor, *The Living Shakespeare.* London, Heinemann, 1960; New York, Fawcett, 1961.
Editor, with Evelyn Hardy, *Some Recollections*, by Emma Hardy. London, Oxford University Press, 1961.
Editor, *Selected Poems and Letters of John Keats.* London, Heinemann, and New York, Barnes and Noble, 1966.
Editor, *Omniana; or, Horae otiosiores*, by Robert Southey and Samuel Taylor Coleridge. London, Centaur Press, 1969.
Editor, *Letters of John Keats: A New Selection.* London, Oxford University Press, 1970.

Robert Gittings comments:

I have tried to use, so far as one ever consciously does, the best, or what seems to me best, of what is old and what is new.

Major themes are probably indicated by the title of my book of verse, *Matters of Love and Death.*

I do not feel I have fully achieved this, but am still trying.

Technically, I am interested in the use of verse for dramatic and narrative purposes, have written verse-plays and verse-scripts for Son et Lumière productions and for broadcasting.

* * *

There can be little doubt that Robert Gittings's reputation as a critic and, in particular, his study of John Keats, has overshadowed his attributes as a poet in his own right. In his earliest work he tended to write in an unfashionably traditional mode, though at any other period his poems would have attracted attention. Since then, however, he has produced several volumes of poetry and developed a personal style and approach, and it is high time that his poetic talents were properly recognised. In his narrative vein he is quite unlike any other poet, for most of his contemporaries have found it extremely difficult to write convincing narrative verse. Robert Gittings can and does – with a quite extraordinary flair. This is probably best demonstrated in *Famous Meeting* which contains nine narrative poems on such diverse subjects as the meeting between Wellington and Nelson, Livingstone, Boswell's "London Journal," and a lost explorer in the Australian desert. His next volume, *This Tower My Prison*, takes its title from the dramatic monologue between Robert Carr, Earl of Somerset, and Frances Howard, on the murder of Sir Thomas Overbury and makes skilful use of the historic present.

Gittings's understanding of character and his dramatic gifts are to be discerned, once again, in the long poems included in his *Matters of Love and Death*: "Antony and Cleopatra," "The Secret Mistress," and "By the Lake" (a sequence on D. H. Lawrence and Frieda). Each of these volumes also contains a number of lyrics which, if assembled in a single collection, would be enough to establish a sound reputation for any poet. Amongst these are to be found such admirable poems as "The Guillemot's Egg," "Kilvert at Clyro," "A Breath of Air," "A Daughter," and "The Middle-Aged Man." *American Journey* is a collection of 25 sonnets, all competently executed, inspired by a winter journey by air to America.

—Howard Sergeant

GLASSCO, John (Stinson). Canadian. Born in Montreal, Quebec, 15 December 1909. Educated at Selwyn House School, Montreal; Bishop's College School, Lennoxville, Quebec, 1923–24; Lower Canada College, Montreal, 1924–25; McGill University, Montreal, 1925–28. Married 1) the dancer Elma von Colmar in 1963 (died, 1971); 2) Marion McCormick in 1974. Councillor, 1948–52, and Mayor, 1952–54, Village of Foster, Quebec. Founder, 1951, and Honorary Chairman, 1964, Foster Horse Show. Recipient: Quebec Provincial Prize, 1961; Canada Council Senior Arts Fellowship, 1966, and grant, 1974; Governor-General's Award, for verse, 1972, for translation, 1976. Address: Jamaica Farm, Foster, Quebec, Canada.

PUBLICATIONS

Verse

Conan's Fig. Paris, Transition, 1928.
The Deficit Made Flesh. Toronto, McClelland and Stewart, 1958.
A Point of Sky. Toronto, Oxford University Press, 1964.
Square Hardman (as George Colman). Waterloo, Quebec, Pastime Press, 1966.
Selected Poems. Toronto, Oxford University Press, 1971.
Montreal. Montreal, Delta Canada, 1973.

Novels

Contes en Crinoline (as Jean de Saint-Luc). Paris, Gaucher, 1930.
Under the Hill (completion of the unfinished novel by Aubrey Beardsley). Paris, Olympia Press, 1959; London, New English Library, 1966; New York, Grove Press, 1967.
The English Governess (as Miles Underwood). Paris, Olympia Press, 1960; as *Under the Birch*, Paris, Ophelia Press, 1965; as *Harriet Marwood, Governess* (published anonymously), New York, Grove Press, 1967.

Fetish Girl (as Sylvia Bayer). New York, Grove Press, 1972.
The Fatal Woman: Three Tales. Toronto, Anansi, 1974.

Other

Memoirs of Montparnasse. Toronto and New York, Oxford University Press, 1970.

Editor, *English Poetry in Quebec* (Proceedings of the Foster Poetry Conference). Montreal, McGill University Press, 1965.
Editor, *The Poetry of French Canada in Translation.* Toronto, Oxford University Press, 1970.
Editor, *The Temple of Pederasty*, by Ihara Saikaku. North Hollywood, California, Essex House, 1970.

Translator, *The Journal of Saint-Denys Garneau.* Toronto, McClelland and Stewart, 1962.
Translator, *Lot's Wife*, by Monique Bosco. Toronto, McClelland and Stewart, 1974.
Translator, *The Complete Poems of Saint-Denys Garneau.* Ottawa, Oberon Press, 1975.
Translator, *Venus in Furs*, by L. von Sacher-Masoch. Vancouver, Blackfish Press, 1977.
Translator, *The Manitou*, by Jean-Yves Soucy. Toronto, McClelland and Stewart, 1979.

Manuscript Collections: McGill University Library, Montreal; National Archives of Canada, Ottawa.

Critical Studies: Interviews in *Time* (New York), 2 December 1974; *Maclean's* (Toronto), August 1975; *The Canadian* (Toronto), 21 February 1976.

* * *

John Glassco is an elegiac poet in the classic tradition who has found a subject-matter for his philosophical and evocative verses in the rural life of the Eastern Townships of his native province of Quebec. A little pocket of country isolation, of run-down farms and stony pastures, is presented as symbolic of a kind of forlorn and heroic rejection of the mechanization and success-worship of the acquisitive society. In such poems as "The Entailed Farm," "The Rural Mail," or "Deserted Buildings under Shefford Mountain," the spirit of John Clare or Edward Thomas has been introduced into Canadian poetry.

Besides his eclogues and bucolic verses John Glassco has written witty and sophisticated poems of a personal and psychological nature which testify to the wide range of his experience and the eclecticism of his literary taste. The irony and stylistic elegance found in his prose *tour de force*, the completion of Aubrey Beardsley's unfinished *Under the Hill*, and in several *novellas* published by the Olympia Press, is seen also in metaphysical love poems like "A Devotion" and mordant satires like "Brummell at Calais," "Utrillo's World," or "The Screaming Child." In these poems, technically strict and carefully shaped, a modern consciousness that shares something of the allusive richness of Proust has found its most natural expression in a traditional style that manages to be at once local and universal. This is especially true of the three or four philosophical meditations on death which give a peculiar distinction to the collection, *A Point of Sky*. They demonstrate clearly that the tradition of Matthew Arnold, Robert Bridges and E. A. Robinson is still capable of producing work that is personal, intense and thoroughly alive.

—A. J. M. Smith

GLEN, Duncan. Scottish. Born in Cambuslang, Lanark, 11 January 1933. Educated at West Coats School, Cambuslang, 1938–46; Rutherglen Academy, 1946–49; Heriot-Watt College, Edinburgh, 1950–53; Edinburgh College of Art, 1953–56. Served in the Royal Air Force, 1956–58. Married Margaret Eadie in 1957; one son and one daughter. Typographic Designer, Her Majesty's Stationery Office, London, 1958–60; Lecturer in Typographic Design, Watford College of Technology, 1960–63; Editor, Robert Gibson and Sons Ltd., publishers, Glasgow, 1963–65; Senior Lecturer in Graphic Design, Preston Polytechnic, Lancashire, 1965–78. Since 1978, Head of the Department of Visual Communications, Trent Polytechnic, Nottingham. Since 1965, Owner, Akros Publications, and Editor, *Akros*, Preston, later Nottingham. Editor, *Knowe*, 1971, and *Graphic Lines*, 1975–78, both Preston. Fellow, Society of Industrial Artists and Designers. Address: 21 Cropwell Road, Radcliffe on Trent, Nottingham NG12 2FJ, England.

PUBLICATIONS

Verse

Stanes. Kinglassie, Fife, Duncan Glen, 1966.
Idols: When Alexander Our King Was Dead. Preston, Lancashire, Akros, 1967.
Kythings and Other Poems. Thurso, Caithness Books, 1969.
Sunny Summer Sunday Afternoon in the Park? Preston, Lancashire, Akros, 1969.
Unnerneath the Bed. Preston, Lancashire, Akros, 1970.
In Appearances. Preston, Lancashire, Akros, 1971.
Clydesdale: A Sequence o Poems. Preston, Lancashire, Akros, 1971.
Feres. Preston, Lancashire, Akros, 1971.
A Journey Past: A Sequence o Poems. Preston, Lancashire, Akros, 1972.
A Cled Score. Preston, Lancashire, Akros, 1974.
Mr. and Mrs. J. L. Stoddart at Home. Preston, Lancashire, Akros, 1975.
Buits and Wellies; or, Sui Generis. Preston, Lancashire, Akros, 1975.
Follow! Follow! Follow! and Other Poems. Preston, Lancashire, Akros, 1976.
Spoiled for Choice. Preston, Lancashire, Akros, 1976.
Weddercock. Privately printed, 1976.
Gaitherings. Preston, Lancashire, Akros, 1977.
Traivellin Man. Preston, Lancashire, Harris Press, 1977.
In Place of Wark; or, Man of Art. Preston, Lancashire, Akros, 1977.
Of Philosophers and Tinks. Preston, Lancashire, Akros, 1977.
The Inextinguishable. Preston, Lancashire, Herbert, 1977.
Ten Sangs. Preston, Lancashire, Akros, 1978.
Ither Sangs. Preston, Lancashire, Akros, 1978.
Ten Bird Sangs. Preston, Lancashire, Akros, 1978.
Ten Sangs of Luve. Preston, Lancashire, Akros, 1978.

Other

Hugh MacDiarmid: Rebel Poet and Prophet, A Short Note on His Seventieth Birthday. Hemel Hempstead, Hertfordshire, Drumalban Press, 1962.
Hugh MacDiarmid and the Scottish Renaissance. Edinburgh, Chambers, 1964.
The Literary Masks of Hugh MacDiarmid. Glasgow, Drumalban Press, 1964.
Scottish Poetry Now. Preston, Lancashire, Akros, 1966.
An Afternoon with Hugh MacDiarmid. Privately printed, 1969.
A Small Press and Hugh MacDiarmid: With a Checklist of Akros Publications 1962–1970. Preston, Lancashire, Akros, 1970.
The MacDiarmids: A Conversation Between Hugh MacDiarmid and Duncan Glen with Valda Grieve and Arthur Thompson. Preston, Lancashire, Akros, 1970.

The Individual and the Twentieth Century Scottish Literary Tradition. Preston, Lancashire, Akros, 1971.
A Bibliography of Scottish Poets from Stevenson to 1974. Preston, Lancashire, Akros, 1974.
Preston's New Buildings, with John Brook. Preston, Lancashire, Harris Press, 1975.
Five Literati. Preston, Lancashire, Harris Press, 1976.
Forward from Hugh MacDiarmid; or, Mostly Out of Scotland, Being Fifteen Years of Duncan Glen/Akros Publications, with a Check-List of Publications August 1962–August 1977. Preston, Lancashire, Akros, 1977.
Hugh MacDiarmid: An Essay for 11th August 1977. Preston, Lancashire, Akros, 1977.

Editor, *Poems Addressed to Hugh MacDiarmid and Presented to Him on His Seventy-Fifth Birthday.* Preston, Lancashire, Akros, 1967.
Editor, *Selected Essays of Hugh MacDiarmid.* London, Cape, 1969; Berkeley, University of California Press, 1970.
Editor, *The Akros Anthology of Scottish Poetry 1965–1970.* Preston, Lancashire, Akros, 1970.
Editor, *Whither Scotland? A Prejudiced Look at the Future of a Nation.* London, Gollancz, 1971.
Editor, *Hugh MacDiarmid: A Critical Survey.* Edinburgh, Scottish Academic Press, and New York, Barnes and Noble, 1972.
Editor, with Nat Scammacca, *La Nuova Poesia Scozzese.* Palermo, Celebes, 1976.
Editor, *Preston Polytechnic Poets.* Preston, Lancashire, Harris Press, 1977.
Editor, *Graphic Designers as Poets.* Preston, Lancashire, Harris Press, 1977.
Editor, *Typoems.* Preston, Lancashire, Harris Press, 1977.

Critical Studies: by Paul Duncan, in *Sou' Wester* (Carbondale, Illinois), Summer 1970; Sam Adams, in *Anglo-Welsh Review* (Pembroke Dock, Wales), Autumn 1970; John C. Weston, in *Akros* (Preston, Lancashire), April 1971; Anne Cluysenaar, in *Stand* (Newcastle upon Tyne), xii, 4, 1971; "Meaning and Self" by Walter Perrie, in *Chapman* (Hamilton, Lanarkshire), Spring 1972; "The Progress of Scots" by John Herdman, in *Akros* (Preston, Lancashire), December 1972; *Two Younger Poets: Duncan Glen and Donald Campbell* by Leonard Mason, Preston, Lancashire, Akros, 1976; *Our Duncan, Who Art in Trent: A Festschrift for Duncan Glen* edited by Philip Pacey, Preston, Lancashire, Harris Press, 1978.

* * *

Duncan Glen belongs to that important community of Scottish writers who have developed a style in Scots (or Lallans – the fashionable term) on a prose base. Glen, one feels, or his people, might speak with the same calculated understatement or with the not unkindly irony of his poetry. His idiom allows him to sketch the picture of his dead father in his poem, "My Faither," with a sense of truth, respect and manliness. The poem begins:

Staunin noo aside his bress-haunled coffin
I mind him fine aside the black shinin range
In his grey strippit troosers, galluses and nae collar
For the flannel shirt. My faither.

(Standing now beside his brass handled coffin
I remember him well beside the black shining range
In his grey striped trousers, braces and no collar
For the flannel shirt. My father.)

This honest, modest achievement is characteristic of a deal of the rather better writing in Scots, but Glen goes beyond this in his finer poems. In the last verse of "My Faither" the writer looks down on the body, "laid oot in the best/Black suitin...." This father ("My father") – he uses the English spelling – he does not know. The solid, known person becomes dramatically unknowable.

The domestic imagery in Scots is Glen's point of beginning. His poem "Progress" begins from naive statement, bouncing along like a nursery rhyme, but there is a remorseless logic in it. It proceeds thus: "Is not nature wonderful/We cam oot heid first – get a slap/and oor mither toungue." By the end one is aware Glen is applying a kind of Socratic dialogue to the argument. The bright tone darkens. He takes this development further in "Bacchae in Suburbia." Written in a homely Scots ("You are feart son?"), one hears, as it were, behind the words, the knock on the door that might mean death or torture, as it has done for many in Europe in our time.

So far the concentration and intensity achieved in the poems referred to have been rare. It may be that the diffuse verse written by Duncan Glen mainly in English has been due to time spent generously in publishing and editing known and unknown writers. This has been a very valuable service, but the cultivation of his own markedly individual talent may well be rewarding to Scottish letters.

—George Bruce

GLOVER, Denis (James Matthews). New Zealander. Born in Dunedin, 10 December 1912. Educated at Auckland Grammar School; Christ's College; Canterbury University College, A.B. Served as an officer in the Royal Navy during World War II: Distinguished Service Cross. Married 1) Mary Granville in 1936, one son; 2) Lyn Cameron in 1972. Taught English at Canterbury University, 1936–38, and typography at the Technical Correspondence Institute, Wellington. Founder, Caxton Press, Christchurch, 1936; joined Pegasus Press, 1953, and Wingfield Press, 1955. Formerly, journalist, *The Press*, Christchurch. Former President, New Zealand P.E.N., and Friends of the Turnbull Library, Wellington; Member of The Canterbury University Council, and of the New Zealand State Literary Fund Committee. Recipient: Jessie Mackay Award, 1960. Address: 4/537 Broad Way, Wellington 3, New Zealand.

PUBLICATIONS

Verse

Short Reflection on the Present State of Literature in This Country. Christchurch, Caxton Club, 1935.
Another Argo, with Allen Curnow and A. R. D. Fairburn. Christchurch, Caxton Club, 1935.
Thistledown. Christchurch, Caxton Club, 1935.
Six Easy Ways of Dodging Debt Collectors. Christchurch, Caxton Press, 1936.
A Caxton Miscellany, with others. Christchurch, Caxton Press, 1937.
The Arraignment of Paris. Christchurch, Caxton Press, 1937.
Thirteen Poems. Christchurch, Caxton Press, 1939.
Cold Tongue. Christchurch, Caxton Press, 1940.
Recent Poems, with others. Christchurch, Caxton Press, 1941.
The Wind and the Sand: Poems 1934–44. Christchurch, Caxton Press, 1945.
Summer Flowers. Christchurch, Caxton Press, 1946.
Sings Harry and Other Poems. Christchurch, Caxton Press, 1951.

Arawata Bill: A Sequence of Poems. Christchurch, Pegasus Press, 1953.
Since Then. Wellington, Mermaid Press, 1957.
Poetry Harbinger, with A. R. D. Fairburn. Auckland, Pilgrim Press, 1958.
Enter Without Knocking: Selected Poems. Christchurch, Pegasus Press, 1964; augmented edition, 1972.
Sharp Edge Up: Verses and Satires. Auckland, Blackwood and Janet Paul, 1968.
Myself When Young. Christchurch, Nag's Head Press, 1970.
To a Particular Woman. Christchurch, Nag's Head Press, 1970.
Diary to a Woman. Wellington, Catspaw Press, 1971.
Dancing to My Tune, edited by Laurie Edmond. Wellington, Catspaw Press, 1974.
Wellington Harbour. Wellington, Catspaw Press, 1974.
For Whom the Cock Crows. Dunedin, McIndoe, 1976.
Or Hawk or Basilisk. Wellington, Catspaw Press, 1977.
Come High Water. Palmerston North, Dunmore Press, 1977.
Clutha River. Dunedin, McIndoe, 1978.

Plays

Screenplays: *The Coaster*, 1951; *Mick Stimson*, with John Lang, 1972.

Radio Play: *They Sometimes Float at Sea*, 1970.

Short Stories

3 Short Stories. Christchurch, Caxton Press, 1936.
Till the Star Speak. Christchurch, Caxton Press, 1939.

Other

D Day. Christchurch, Caxton Press, 1944.
A Clutch of Authors and a Clot. Wellington, Wingfield Press, 1960.
Hot Water Sailor. Wellington, Reed, 1962.
Denis Glover's Bedside Book. Wellington, Reed, 1963.

Editor, with Ian Milner, *New Poems.* Christchurch, Caxton Club, 1934.
Editor, *The Disadvantages of Being Dead and Other Sharp Verses*, by A. R. D. Fairburn. Wellington, Mermaid Press, 1958.
Editor, *Cross Currents*, by Merrill Moore. Christchurch, Pegasus Press, 1961.
Editor, *Collected Poems*, by A. R. D. Fairburn. Christchurch, Pegasus Press, 1966.
Editor, with Geoffrey Fairburn, *The Woman Problem and Other Prose*, by A. R. D. Fairburn. Auckland, Blackwood and Janet Paul, 1967.

* * *

Denis Glover was one of the group of New Zealand poets whose work began to appear in the 1930's. He was also a printer, and his founding of the Caxton Press in Christchurch established what has become a tradition of fine printing in New Zealand, particularly in the production of editions of poetry. This is characteristic of the boldness with which Glover and his friend Allen Curnow set out on their poetic careers. Where there was no publisher for poetry they became publishers themselves. Where there was no interest in poetry they created it. Where there was no criticism they wrote it. In Glover's early poetry there is a double sense of excitement: that which was in the air of the time everywhere; and that which belongs peculiarly to a moment in New Zealand's literary history. There are many echoes in his early work of the Auden group – both in his political beliefs and in his technical innovations:

Rolling along the roads on holiday wheels
Now wonder at their construction, the infinite skill
That planned the road to the gradient of the hill,
The precision, the planning, the labour it all reveals.

An unremembered legion of labourers did this....

These men we should honour above the managers of banks....

But there was also a freshness in the writing that came from a consciousness that he and his contemporaries in purely New Zealand terms were opening up territory to poetry that had previously been closed to it; that they were turning their backs not merely on Georgianism in the broadest sense, but on the local Georgianism that looked to England as "Home." Colonial versifying was over:

I do not dream of Sussex downs
Or quaint old England's quaint old towns:
I think of what will yet be seen
In Johnsonville and Geraldine.

Glover's collected poems would read like a handbook of good writing without containing anything that lays claim to being "major." Glover himself seldom appears and this is perhaps a limitation. The scene, the event, the "subject" are ruggedly presented to us, without a word wasted. But the poet who felt moved to write is withdrawn. Instead there is often a persona – his fictional "Harry," who sings in the windbreak; the historical figure of the prospector, "Arawata Bill"; or simply the voice of an observer who remains distinct from the poet because he is detached – sometimes irritable, sometimes preposterous, often funny, but never revealing himself fully.

Glover has written some of New Zealand's finest descriptive verse, and some of its most beautiful lyrics:

Once the days were clear
Like mountains in water.
The mountains were always there
And the mountain water ...

And here is Glover the satirist, catching at once the flavour of New Zealand life and that of its literature, holding them both up to gentle ridicule:

The Centennial Baths
(Horace III, 13, O Fons Bandusiae)

O municipal baths with your gleaming tiles,
Most worthy I find you of praise,
Of tribute worthy in a column of news.

Tomorrow to you do I vow
My virginal togs; in your coolness
How brightly their colours will glow!

In vain do the nor'-westers beat
On your surface that offers delight
To the weary, the restless crowd on the street.

And you among noble baths will take station
When I sing of the flagpole above your tiles
And your waters loquacious with motion.

—C. K. Stead

GLÜCK, Louise (Elisabeth). American. Born in New York City, 22 April 1943. Attended Sarah Lawrence College, Bronxville, New York; Columbia University, New York. Married 1) Charles Hertz, Jr., in 1967 (divorced), one son; 2) John Dranow in 1977. Visiting lecturer, Goddard College, Plainfield, Vermont, 1971–72, 1973–74, University of North Carolina, Greensboro, 1973, University of Virginia, 1975, University of Iowa, Iowa City, Columbia University, New York; Elliston Professor of Poetry, University of Cincinnati, 1978. Recipient: Academy of American Poets prize, 1966; Rockefeller Fellowship, 1967; National Endowment for the Arts grant, 1969; Eunice Tietjens Memorial Prize (*Poetry*, Chicago), 1971; Guggenheim Fellowship, 1975. Address: West Hill Pond Road, Cabot, Vermont 05647, U.S.A.

PUBLICATIONS

Verse

Firstborn. New York, New American Library, 1968; London, Anvil Press Poetry, 1969.

The House on Marshland. New York, Ecco Press, 1974; London, Anvil Press Poetry, 1976.

The Garden. New York, Antaeus, 1976.

Critical Studies: by Calvin Bedient, in *Sewanee Review* (Tennessee), Spring 1976; Joan Hutton Landis, in *Salmagundi* (Saratoga Springs, New York), Winter 1977; Helen Vendler in *New Republic* (Washington, D.C.), 17 June 1978.

* * *

Louise Glück's firstborn volume, *Firstborn*, does not lack for influences, as discerning critics have been quick to remark. Most obvious are the traces of Stanley Kunitz, with whom she studied at Columbia University, and of early Robert Lowell. There are also indications that she has gone to school to Plath and Sexton, Hart Crane, Jarrell, and Dugan. "My Life Before Dawn," with its emphasis on sexual violence and on male mental cruelty, may well represent the first manner. The poem begins,

Sometimes at night I think of how we did
It, me nailed in her like steel, her
Over-eager on the striped contour
Sheet (I later burned it) and it makes me glad
I told her – in the kitchen cutting bread –
She always did too much – I told her Sorry baby you have had
Your share (I found her stain had dried into my hair.).

Here, already, is a subtle command of a basically five-beat line, of slant rhyme, of a *persona* sharply conceived and convincingly rendered.

The House on Marshland is decisively Glück's own. Its pervasive theme is loss. The obsessive feeling is pain experienced in relationships with men. The triumphant achievement is the balancing of an almost misogynist bitterness with an undeterrable hopefulness. Most of the poems are in the confessional tradition, though there is no reason to assume they are autobiographical. "The Letters," "The Apple Tree," and "School Children" are outstanding examples. Paradoxically, Glück, like Tennyson and many another before them, writes most powerfully when she turns away from presumably private or personally apprehended experience. The less personal the experience the more intense is the feeling with which its expression is charged. "All Hallows" seems to derive from a landscape painting; a scene of "barrenness/of harvest or pestilence" suggests a question to a wife leaning out of a window: amid all this barrenness, can she be fertile? "Brennende Liebe – 1904" is a poetized love letter from an aristocratic lady in which the mood of love longing is elegantly conveyed. If the supposed writer was an ancestor, one can understand why Glück has retained her umlaut. The most psychologically penetrating and striking poem is "Abishag." The account in *I Kings* of the young woman brought to King David's bed is from David's perspective. So have been treatments by such poets as Rilke, the Hebrew Fichman, the French Spire. Glück offers Abishag's voice and perspective: recollection is dreamlike; only a colon impedes the flow of the opening stanza. The concluding stanza of the first section, however, is firmly end-stopped, staccato, bitter: "They took me as I was./Not one among the kinsmen touched me,/no one among the slaves./No one will touch me now." Abishag has a classical feminine oedipal fantasy. She rages at her father for letting her be taken by someone other than himself. The second and final section deserves quotation in full:

In the recurring dream my father
stands at the doorway in his black cassock
telling me to choose
among my suitors, each of whom
will speak my name once
until I lift my hand in signal.
On my father's arm I listen
for not three sounds: *Abishag.*
but two: *my love* –

I tell you if it is my own will
binding me I cannot be saved.
And yet in the dream, in the half-light
of the stone house, they looked
so much alike. Sometimes I think
the voices were themselves
identical, and that I raised my hand
chiefly in weariness. I hear my father saying
Choose, choose. But they were not alike
and to select death, O yes I can
believe that of my body.

Rage at father has become hatred of self for having imagined she has been used.

In *The Garden* Glück may be signalling a new phase. As she has written, "The impulse to write is usually spent in a brief lyric." "Abishag" is 49 lines long, by far the longest poem in *The House on Marshland. The Garden* is half again as long. Consisting of five almost independent lyrics about fear, *The Garden* is a coherent, powerful whole, perhaps Glück's highest achievement to date.

Glück has clearly begun what can no longer be called merely a promising career. Her command of voices, diction, rhythm is great. Command of a wider range of feeling and theme will doubtless follow.

—James K. Robinson

GNAROWSKI, Michael. Canadian. Born in Shanghai, China, 27 September 1934. Educated at McGill University, Montreal, B.A.; University of Montreal, M.A.; University of Ottawa, Ph.D. Married; three children. Formerly, Associate Professor, and Coordinator of Canadian Studies, Sir George Williams University, Montreal. Currently, Professor of English, Carleton University, Ottawa. Editor, Critical Views Series, Tecumseh Press, Ottawa; General Editor, Carleton Library Series, Macmillan, Toronto. Founding Co-Editor, *Canadian Poetry*. Address: 15 Ossington Avenue, Ottawa, Ontario, Canada.

PUBLICATIONS

Verse

Postscript for St. James Street. Montreal, Delta Canada, 1965.
The Gentlemen Are Also Lexicographers. Montreal, Delta Canada, 1969.

Other

Canadian Poetry: A Supplementary Bibliography, with George Ross Roy. Quebec, Culture, 1964.
An Index to "Direction." Quebec, Culture, 1965.
Index to CIV/n. Quebec, Culture, 1965.
Contact 1952–1954 (index). Montreal, Delta Canada, 1966.
A Concise Bibliography of English-Canadian Literature. Toronto, McClelland and Stewart, 1973; revised edition, 1978.
Theses and Dissertations in Canadian Literature (English): A Preliminary Check List. Ottawa, Golden Dog Press, 1975.

Editor, with Louis Dudek, *The Making of Modern Poetry in Canada: Essential Articles on Contemporary Canadian Poetry in English.* Toronto, Ryerson Press, 1967.
Editor, *The Rising Village of Oliver Goldsmith: A New Edition.* Montreal, Delta Canada, 1968.
Editor, *Three Early Poems from Lower Canada.* Montreal, Lande Foundation, 1969.
Editor, *Archibald Lampman.* Toronto, Ryerson Press, 1970.
Editor, *Selected Stories of Raymond Knister.* Ottawa, University of Ottawa Press, 1972.
Editor, *The City of the End of Things*, by Archibald Lampman. Ottawa, Golden Dog Press, 1972.
Editor, *New Provinces: Poems of Several Authors.* Toronto, University of Toronto Press, 1976.
Editor, *Leonard Cohen: The Artist and His Critics.* Toronto, McGraw Hill, 1976.

Michael Gnarowski comments:

Influenced by the "Montreal School" of Dudek, Layton, etc., and particularly by Wallace Stevens as the major external influence. Major themes, or, more accurately, major concerns could be said to be related to urban realism and the response of the individual to the complexity of modern business and its society.

* * *

Michael Gnarowski's poetry is deceptively modern, steeped in the technological urban world, in a search for humanist values denied relevance in an ecology of bankers, developers, brokers and other captains of the marketplace – the battering rams of material progress. The sensibility is attuned to the age, and, though the locus for reflection is specific, St. James Street is paradigmatic of the Wall Streets and the Bond Streets that rule over the quality of modern man's life. Gnarowski does not make concessions to the reader, using a tightly-controlled verbal medium, self-reflexive in tonality, imagery and symbolism. The structure is thematically consistent. The world of the city, concrete, physical, heavy with cement and mammoth steel and glass monuments to itself, weighs on its human architects and pillars as leaden and mute as their constructions blotting out the natural cycle whose destroyed wilderness has yielded a factory-made garden. The necessary counterpoise of a felt sensibility – be it the archetypal pioneer past or the reassuring atmosphere of an old Church, the free play of the senses or the recollection of the dream of immigrants who came to the New World in search of innocence and vitality – is evoked as a vision betrayed: "You'all must come and visit me/in my New World of small inventions/and turned away/dispensing such new wisdom/as gallonage of pumps/and tachometric spec of old machines." Always the vision is made poignant in the face of the irreconcilability of urban desolation and corporate anonymity. Loneliness, alienation prevail. Even in poems where the land is addressed, the image of virginal splendor and purity is deflated by its larger perception as a "white asylum." The wilderness is within as well as without.

Gnarowski functions evidently in the poetic tradition of the Eliot-Stevens-Williams school where verbal economy and self-reliance become their own structure of meaning. But in a number of poems, particularly in his second book of poetry, there lurk yearnings for the celebration of love, warmth and gentleness binding the poet to his fellowman. Deflected, they signal a possible flaw: the apparent indebtedness of the poet's sensibility to the Fifties' "lonely crowd" mythos. The poet's strategy in the face of defeat is to seek refuge behind words whose increasing obscurity and gratuitousness ironically imply that the technology and the plasticity previously denounced now claim the poet as victim when language becomes sound or noise with no referential point. Admittedly, the irony can be at the expense of the reader. Gnarowski's second book may be a sign of artistic evolution when it is understood that the emblematic arrangement of typography is a conceit of "pure poetry" substituted for the early thematic order. Yet, the poet's original vision is that of a moralist subtly summoning the age to account for its failures and betrayals. As such, his last book leaves one unsatisfied; the more so when one of the greatest tragedies of our time, Vietnam, is suggested only as a sign of the ambient technological nightmare and not explored as a nexus of a general moral crisis.

The decade when Vietnam came to dominate our consciousness, the Sixties, saw the parallel emergence of a novel sense of self that spread across North America and Europe. Beyond its symbol in the revolution of the young, the temper of the Sixties affirmed the need to invade the wilderness and the africas within and without. New Forces were released, defiant rages vented, but a belief in the celebration of the Dionysian imperative was also expressed denying that despair was an inevitable and inescapable condition for technological man. This affirmation is belied in Gnarowski's refuge in "pure poetry," if not silence. Too bad.

—Max Dorsinville

GOACHER, Denis. British. Born in London, 9 June 1925. Has three children. Address: Dioné House, Wembworthy, Chulmleigh, North Devon, England.

PUBLICATIONS

Verse

The Marriage Rite, with Peter Whigham. Ditchling, Sussex, Ditchling Press, 1960.
Logbook. Kingswinford, Staffordshire, Grosseteste, 1972.
Transversions. Kingswinford, Staffordshire, Grosseteste, 1973.
Night of the 12th, 13th. Rushden, Northamptonshire, Sceptre Press, 1973.
Three Songs from the Romany King of Wembworthy. Knotting, Bedfordshire, Sceptre Press, 1976.

Other

Editor, *Soldier On* (autobiography of Colonel Sir Mike Ansell). London, Peter Davies, 1973.

Translator, *Inferno* (Cantos 29–31), by Dante. London, BBC, 1965.

Denis Goacher comments:

The rapidly increasing tendency of "poets" to give prose reductions of their poetic aims makes their function, as poets, increasingly preposterous.

For myself, the aim and aspiration can be entirely deduced from my published collections – to those who can *read*. Alas, that skill, like that of the wheelwright, the stonemason and the butcher, is now quite rare.

* * *

Denis Goacher's poems have a sense of style, and contain some freshly perceptive and original lines. He is elliptical, and it is clearly a problem to him as to how to preserve the sound of his own voice and yet to maintain the communicability he seeks. In the first three lines of "Dead Friends" – "How many years?/My capsule holds a smeary track/signals pass" – he succeeds because of the resonances set up by the evocative second line, and the rhythmical assuredness. Elsewhere he does preserve his own way of speaking (and hearing), but at the expense of failing to achieve coherence. But the praise he has received from Basil Bunting and Herbert Read has been deserved: this is a positive and entirely honest response, and a voice (as Bunting has pleaded) that is original:

I touched a buttercup petal fell
not far
saw the shrew dead on her back
then blessed one foxglove gave my finger
luck
and heart's ease....

—Martin Seymour-Smith

GOEDICKE, Patricia. American. Born in Boston, Massachusetts, 21 June 1931. Educated at Middlebury College, Vermont, B.A. 1953 (Phi Beta Kappa, 1952); Ohio University, Athens, M.A. 1963. Married Leonard Wallace Robinson in 1971. Editorial Assistant, Harcourt Brace and World, publishers, New York, 1953–54, and T. Y. Crowell, publishers, New York, 1955–56. Instructor in English, Ohio University, 1962–68, and Hunter College, New York, 1969–71. Since 1972, Instructor in Creative Writing, Instituto Allende, San Miguel de Allende, Mexico. Recipient: National Endowment for the Arts grant, 1969, 1976; William Carlos Williams Award (*New Letters*, Kansas City), 1976. Address: Apdo. 462, San Miguel de Allende, Guanajuato, Mexico.

PUBLICATIONS

Verse

Between Oceans. New York, Harcourt Brace, 1968.
For the Four Corners. Ithaca, New York, Ithaca House, 1976.
The Trail That Turns on Itself. Ithaca, New York, Ithaca House, 1978.
The Dog That Was Barking Yesterday. Amherst, Massachusetts, Lynx House Press, 1979.

Critical Studies: "The Fruit of Her Orchard" by Tom O'Grady and Shirley Bossert, in *New Letters* (Kansas City), Fall 1977; "A Bow to Women for Poetic Providing Wealth" by G. E. Murray, in *Sun-Times* (Chicago), 9 July 1978; "The Trail That Turns on Itself" by Peter Schjedahl, in *New York Times Book Review*, 17 December 1978; "The Desperate Tongue" by Ron Slate, in *Three Rivers Poetry Journal* (Pittsburgh), March 1979.

Patricia Goedicke comments:

As the daughter of a psychiatrist, I have subjected myself to so much self-analysis that I prefer to confine any general analysis of my poetry to specific poems. People I have admired and learned from are W. H. Auden, Hollis Summers, Robert Frost, Dylan Thomas, William Carlos Williams, Charles Olson, Patricia Grean, Leonard Wallace Robinson, and many others. I try to tell the truth in my poetry; I try to make it sing. I believe that metaphor-making is the way all of us come to know the true nature of the world. Verse forms are free.

* * *

Patricia Goedicke writes relatively little, one assumes, her single collection having included work from a ten year period. Many of her poems are occasional, dealing with experiences of girlhood, love, marriage, death, while others are more like self-imposed literary exercises, often on themes from what Larkin calls "the myth kitty." The poems of the first kind show her at her weakest. They are marred by disconcerting coyness ("Yet my lord husband/Loves me, loves this dizzy daisy/Picking itself to pieces!") or pretentious solemnity ("To wake up in the night/Terrified, trembling, to think/Of Beowulf, and Christ, and Homer gone/Is natural ...") and seem uncomfortably vulnerable. There are exceptions, however. Two longer poems, "Stranger in the House" (about the recurrent awareness of death from childhood on) and "At the River: For Nicholas" (about the death of a son), despite their unevenness, engage one's sympathies by their subject matter, and "The Thunder," on the same subject as "At the River," is all the better for touching on it indirectly. It speaks of having tape-recorded bird song while a storm approached, and ends:

Now, on the playback,
One of us having
Lost his voice forever,

Out of the balloon of silence,
In a rumor of distant birds

We do not ask for wisdom, we keep
Listening to the thunder.

The poems of the second sort, many using personages from myth and fairy tale, are more frequently successful, perhaps because attempting less. "The Prodigal" shows the haunting presence within the young man of the family he has deserted. "Cassandra" evokes well the prophetic mood of terrified insight and powerlessness to communicate it to others. And the following poem, despite the triteness of "highways of the year" and the echo of Stevens' "The Emperor of Ice Cream" at the end, is charmingly effective in its concrete imagery and represents the writer at her best. It is called "Goldilocks":

Between the bricks the warmth.
Crumble of weeds. Clay. The honey husk of nuts.

Sunshine after a bitter night.
Like pots of herbs the odors cluster

But the days are getting colder.
Darkening along the highways of the year

Oak leaves, arthritic, stiffen.
The heel of morning hardens

O but listen, call Goldilocks!
Such a little jug of jelly, so sweet –

Call the silly liar, one last time
Let her display the whiteness of her feet.

—Seamus Cooney

GOLDBARTH, Albert. American. Born in Chicago, Illinois, 31 January 1948. Educated at University of Illinois, Chicago, B.A. 1969; University of Iowa, Iowa City, M.F.A. 1971; University of Utah, Salt Lake City, 1973–74. Instructor, Elgin Community College, Illinois, 1971–72, Central YMCA Community College, Chicago, 1971–73, and University of Utah, Salt Lake City, 1973–74; Assistant Professor, Cornell University, Ithaca, New York, 1974–76; Visiting Professor, Syracuse University, New York, 1976. Since 1977, Assistant Professor of Creative Writing, University of Texas, Austin. Advisory Editor, *Seneca Review*, Geneva, New York. Recipient: Theodore Roethke Prize (*Poetry Northwest*, Seattle), 1972; National Endowment for the Arts grant, 1974. Address: 710 West 14th, Apartment B, Austin, Texas 78710, U.S.A.

PUBLICATIONS

Verse

Under Cover. Crete, Nebraska, Best Cellar Press, 1973.
Coprolites. New York, New Rivers Press, 1973.
Opticks: A Poem in Seven Sections. New York, Seven Woods Press, 1974.
Jan. 31. New York, Doubleday, 1974.
Keeping. Ithaca, New York, Ithaca House, 1975.
Comings Back: A Sequence of Poems. New York, Doubleday, 1976.
Curve: Overlapping Narratives. New York, New Rivers Press, 1977.
Different Fleshes. Geneva, New York, Hobart and William Smith Colleges Press, 1979.
Eurekas. Memphis, St. Luke's Press, 1980.

Other

Editor, *Every Pleasure: The "Seneca Review" Long Poem Anthology.* Geneva, New York, Seneca Review Press, 1979.

Albert Goldbarth comments:

I don't much care to turn my poems over and study their undersides: motives, influences, psychic needs filled. I'd rather go on to a new poem instead. What can be said briefly, and I think truly, is that my interest in the long poem and its possibilities grows stronger. By this I don't mean to turn my back on the shorter poem – *Comings Back*, though it included the 15-page "Letter to Tony," included a 6-line poem I like as well. But the extended poem that includes narrative, or has scope enough to play with large bodies of time, or that finds room for dialogue or quoted source materials, that can build up litany or weave motifs in and out with the huge sweep a suite has.... *Different Fleshes*, for instance, is a "novel/poem" and is one book-length piece of alternating prose and poetry sections, which is able – happily, I think – to allow moments of pure lyric visionary intensity to take place within a novel-like framework: plot, historic and invented characters, quoted conversation. My hope is that some of its best moments have learned from, even include, the concentration and connotation one expects from a brief poem – but that those moments accumulate toward, and then take place within, an even richer context. In any case, that's the challenge I feel right now, and I suspect my next few efforts will record how well or poorly I've faced it.

* * *

Albert Goldbarth is bent on restoring some useful clutter to American lyric – for years now the tendency has been to keep stripping down language to some ultimate essence, some vital center where all the truth may be put down in a phrase or a word. Most lyric language since World War II has been as gaunt as winter branches. Charles Olson stretched the line longer and freighted it with more content, Robert Lowell crabbed syntax and meter, and other poets have managed to spread language more thickly along the line, but Goldbarth has about him a certain genius to patter on indefinitely and keep it interesting.

His poems open any subject and become pretexts for labyrinthine monologues; his logic is a bramble bush of interconnections. Goldbarth's poetic, if one may hazard discerning it, is to pull everything around him into the form at hand. In one way, his mode is high parody of our universal lust to consume, to own, to put it all into the shopping cart even if the money runs out. The poem comes back to its premise eventually, but the means is primary for a Goldbarth poem – the joy is in watching him drown in chatter and float back up again with a point.

Jan. 31 departs somewhat from this florid verse style, but the leaner lyric has some advantage for Goldbarth – he shows himself a moving, tensely emotional observer of the cold weather of Chicago, which he makes his vortex for a close commentary on love, love-making, survival, friendship, urban squalor, isolation, thinking, and finally hopefulness. Much of the book is written at half his range, however, and as a journal of poetic notations and some fully fledged poems, it lacks the delirious variety of his more exuberant, free-form explosions.

Albert Goldbarth renews poetic discourse by dropping back in time into the grandiloquent style of Elizabethan verse – Shakespeare's and Jonson's – and he does it shamelessly, lavishing on his verse all the naive punning and word play, sonorous embellishment, exaggeration, polysyllabia that geysered up at the birth of English dialect. Laid over this older baroque is Goldbarth's sure touch with American slang, and the pastiche works, as in "A Week on the Show":

> CORRECT-O! The Lung is the Foot on the Breath-Stop!
>   Gwendolyn
> Halverstrom, clovequeen and fingerwhorls etched with spittle
> turning Newark's alley-cobbles to delta with life electrode in you
> as in cue-chalk, skewering, shewering, NOW
> for the slats are down and the scent of muff of Gazelle, as the hand
> prongs five is the fifth of the gift and Luck the gland the Lord forgot:
> What astronomical body circles the earth and has phases?

But there is more to Goldbarth than mere verbal performance. His poems are nearly desperate about language and the need to keep talking, the need to explain the slightest facet of personal history with all the terminological armament of science and philosophy. His most fully conceived book, *Comings Back*, is also the clearest instance of how Goldbarth intends his poetry to be a point of convergence between the individual and the immense culture heaped around him. Perhaps Goldbarth intends us to see that we are again at a birth of language, a dawning of new technological speech which he dares to use as his own personal utterance. *Comings Back* is charged with scientific lore, with facts of all sorts, with statistical junk, heaps of otherwise useless information, all put to lyric use.

His persona is chameleon, dropping into other periods and other voices at whim, and seems also to suggest how the poet now may not have a culture to possess personally – he may plunder its codes and some of its lesser secrets in swashbuckling verse, but he too is a drifter in a much larger and increasingly impersonal human realm. Unlike the vast majority of other poets now writing, Goldbarth is not interested in staking out some part of the human realm as his own – his attention wanders from old lovers to friends, to the deep past, to fragments of experience belonging to all of human experience.

A poetic vision more in-the-making than fully formed lies below the verbal froth of his recent books – Goldbarth has been doggedly pursuing a certainty that life is a Moebius strip. "History repeats itself," he blandly declares at one point of *Jan. 31*, but that theme is pervasive in *Comings Back*, and is the whole point of a recent chapbook, *Curve: Overlapping Narratives*. This premise dominates contemporary thought and art, but Goldbarth makes it his personal discovery in the range and depth of his own writing, with its seemingly inexhaustible energy to find new metaphors for capturing it.

—Paul Christensen

GORDON, Giles (Alexander Esme). British. Born in Edinburgh, 23 May 1940. Educated at Edinburgh Academy, 1948–57. Married Margaret Anna Eastoe in 1964; two sons and one daughter. Advertising Executive, Secker and Warburg, publishers, London, 1962–63; Editor, Hutchinson Publishing Group, London, 1963–64, and Penguin Books, London, 1964–66; Editorial Director, Victor Gollancz, publishers, London, 1967–72. Since 1972, Partner, Anthony Sheil Associates, literary agents, London. Lecturer in Creative Writing, in London, for Tufts University, Medford, Massachusetts, 1971–76; C. Day Lewis Fellow in Writing, King's College, London, 1974–75. Member, Arts Council of Great Britain Literature Panel, 1966–69; Member, Society of Authors Committee of Management, 1973–75. Member of the Governing Board, Writers' Guild of Great Britain. Recipient: *Transatlantic Review* prize, for fiction, 1966; Scottish Arts Council grant, 1976. Address: 9 St. Ann's Gardens, London NW5 4ER, England.

PUBLICATIONS

Verse

Landscape Any Date. Edinburgh, M. Macdonald, 1963.
Two and Two Make One. Preston, Lancashire, Akros, 1966.
Two Elegies. London, Turret Books, 1968.
Eight Poems for Gareth. Frensham, Surrey, Sceptre Press, 1970.
Between Appointments. Frensham, Surrey, Sceptre Press, 1971.
Twelve Poems for Callum. Preston, Lancashire, Akros, 1972.
One Man Two Women. London, Sheep Press, 1974.
Egyptian Room, Metropolitan Museum of Art. Rushden, Northamptonshire, Sceptre Press, 1974.
The Oban Poems. Knotting, Bedfordshire, Sceptre Press, 1977.

Novels

The Umbrella Man. London, Allison and Busby, 1971.
About a Marriage. London, Allison and Busby, and New York, Stein and Day, 1972.
Girl with Red Hair. London, Hutchinson, 1974.
100 Scenes from Married Life: A Selection. London, Hutchinson, 1976.
Enemies: A Novel about Friendship. Hassocks, Sussex, Harvester Press, 1977.

Short Stories

Pictures from an Exhibition. London, Allison and Busby, and New York, Dial Press, 1970.
Penguin Modern Stories 3, with others. London, Penguin, 1970.
Farewell, Fond Dreams. London, Hutchinson, 1975.
The Illusionist and Other Fictions. Hassocks, Sussex, Harvester Press, 1978.
Couple. Knotting, Bedfordshire, Sceptre Press, 1978.

Other

Book 2000: Some Likely Trends in Publishing. London, Association of Assistant Librarians, 1969.
Walter and the Balloon (juvenile). London, Heinemann, 1973.
Beyond the Words: Eleven Writers in Search of a New Fiction. London, Hutchinson, 1975.

Editor, with Alex Hamilton, *Factions: Eleven Original Stories.* London, Joseph. 1974.

Editor, with Michael Bakewell and B. S. Johnson, *You Always Remember the First Time.* London, Quartet, 1975.
Editor, with Dulan Barber, *Members of the Jury: The Jury Experience.* London, Wildwood House, 1976.
Editor, *Prevailing Spirits: A Book of Scottish Ghost Stories.* London, Hamish Hamilton, 1976.
Editor, *A Book of Contemporary Nightmares.* London, Joseph, 1977.
Editor, with Fred Urquhart, *Modern Scottish Short Stories.* London, Hamish Hamilton, 1978.

Manuscript Collection: National Library of Scotland, Edinburgh.

Giles Gordon comments:

I fear my poetry becomes less important to me as my prose fiction becomes more important to me. I seem to be able to use prose in a more flexible way than I am able to use poetry. I think it is important (for one's self respect, if nothing else) to recognise one's limitations as a writer by the time one is, say, thirty. My limitations as a poet are considerable, and I doubt whether I shall publish in future more than the occasional new poem. If it isn't impossibly arrogant (which it is), I like to think that my real poetry is in my prose. Which is not to say that I write "poetic prose"; quite the contrary.

* * *

As a novelist and short-story writer Giles Gordon is courageously experimental, being obsessed both by the feeling that "the world is not for us" (i.e., he is interested in giving non-anthropomorphic accounts of events) and by questions of identity that can best be described as Pirandellian. Yet, though his attempts to work out these themes in prose are valuable and intelligent, and will in due course play their part in his work, his most memorable prose has been written when he was directly moved (an article on the loss of a child; an account of his friend and fellow-writer B. S. Johnson's suicide and funeral), and is itself direct and moving. The foregoing remarks are relevant to his poetry: while he fully understands the different role of the poem – by virtue of the rhythm and, in particular, its line – we find a similar dichotomy between the intellectual and the directly emotional (though by no means uncontrolled), and a similar promise of a future reconciliation between the two attitudes.

But the poems in *Two and Two Make One* nonetheless go beyond his prose in finding, in landscape (of Provence), mysterious although significant parallels to human experience. Unlike the bulk of his fiction, these poems sometimes seem to be trying to ask the question, "How is the world for us?" rather than making the statement that it *is* not; at other times he sees (interestingly) people *as* landscapes:

All things are in two, have sides or halves,
one always complementary to the other.
In the sky, sun and moon; man and woman
on earth....

In *Twelve Poems for Callum* he becomes more direct. These celebrate the birth of a son against the hideous background of world events, and in them the author is simply asking the question of how he can reconcile his delight with the horrors perpetrated by the world of which he – and now his son – are a part. As the doomed Dubcek returns from Moscow to Prague the child

cries in his sleep
mutters in his growing
convinces my dreams
that something
is real.

—Martin Seymour-Smith

GOTLIEB, Phyllis (Fay, née Bloom). Canadian. Born in Toronto, Ontario, 25 May 1926. Educated at public schools in Toronto; University of Toronto, B.A. in English language and literature 1948, M.A. 1950. Married Calvin Gotlieb in 1949; three children. Address: 29 Ridgevale Drive, Toronto, Ontario M6A 1K9, Canada.

PUBLICATIONS

Verse

Who Knows One? Toronto, Hawkshead Press, 1962.
Within the Zodiac. Toronto, McClelland and Stewart, 1964.
Ordinary, Moving. Toronto, Oxford University Press, 1969.
Doctor Umlaut's Earthly Kingdom. Toronto, Calliope Press, 1974.
The Works: Collected Poems. Toronto, Calliope Press, 1978.

Plays

Doctor Umlaut's Earthly Kingdom (broadcast, 1970; produced Ontario, 1972). Published in *Poems for Voices*, Toronto, CBC, 1970.
Garden Varieties (broadcast, 1973; produced Ontario, 1973).

Radio Plays: *Doctor Umlaut's Earthly Kingdom*, 1970; *Garden Varieties*, 1973.

Novels

Sunburst. New York, Fawcett, 1964; London, Coronet, 1966.
Why Should I Have All the Grief? Toronto, Macmillan, 1969.
O Master Caliban! New York, Harper, 1976.

Critical Studies: Reviews by Fred Cogswell, in *Canadian Literature* (Vancouver); by Mary Keyes, in *Canadian Forum* (Toronto), January 1970; by Michael Hornyansky, in *University of Toronto Quarterly*, July 1970; by Louis Martz, in *Yale Review* (New Haven, Connecticut), Summer 1970; by Daisy Alden, in *Poetry* (Chicago), April 1971; "A Cornucopia of Poems" by Douglas Barbour, in *Tamarack Review* (Toronto), Winter 1979.

Phyllis Gotlieb comments:

My work, poetry or prose, makes use of any aspect of human culture and experience I can manage to find out about: family, childhood, growing up in Toronto; Jewish background, either learned or experienced, Talmud or Kabbala, rational or mystic; early interests in Greek and Roman cultures; folklore all over the world; enthusiasms for as much science as I can understand: biology, medicine, astronomy, anthropology; painting, sculpture. I'd like to call myself a universalist except that the abstract leaves me floundering. Humanity is my department.

* * *

Phyllis Gotlieb has written in two, seemingly disparate sub-genres: science fiction stories and a novel, and poems of a more esoteric focus. Yet the common theme which binds the two strains and which is most easily seen in *Within the Zodiac*, is also appropriate to each. In all her work there is a preoccupation with the unity of all things in the universe and an exploration of the energy which binds them. Such a concern pertains naturally enough to the science fiction stories and these need not be considered as more than largely well-written examples of the school. It is not, however, a theory which is so easily situated in literary forms which look away from the explicatory for their narrative or stylistic emphasis. And in dealing with her theory in such contexts, Gotlieb meets with varied success.

In *Within the Zodiac*, for example, the early poems are marred by a dry style and the essentially cerebral and yet curiously over-clear statements in which they attempt to objectify the myriad, incongruous aspects of the universe. These early poems lack any poetic rhythm and any personal response to the universe they so dispassionately detail. In the poem "Day Falcon," however, Gotlieb seeks in memory for congruity within this apparent incongruity, developing her personal myth in brilliant, naturalistic description. And, as a result, the poem rises above the others. Like "Day Falcon," the later poems in the collection open the more personal avenues of memory ("A Bestiary of the Garden for Children Who Should Know Better") and the Jewish tradition ("Who Knows One"). The point-of-view to which these final *Zodiac* poems lean is more fully assumed in *Ordinary, Moving*, a vastly more successful collection of poems.

In *Ordinary, Moving*, Gotlieb becomes more intimate with her creation, while maintaining an intellectual reserve and without becoming sentimental. She still considers ideas that are metaphysical and catholic but now views them as weighted equally with skeletal parts, bricks and old telephone numbers. Indeed, by grounding her musings in homely objects, she simultaneously strengthens her myth of unity and avoids the aridity of the *Zodiac* poems. Here, the rhythms are actively present and if the musical patterns (as well as the sense of family memory) is Jewish in sensibility, it is nevertheless accessible to gentile readers. This is not to suggest that Gotlieb's characteristic economy of words, sparsity of figures and avoidance of allusions have been altered. Rather, her personal myth has been expanded and made sufficiently comprehensible that it supersedes the need for more traditional links. At last in *Ordinary, Moving*, the reader not only understands what Gotlieb is saying, but feels he has himself experienced it before.

The novel *Why Should I Have All the Grief?*, however, lies outside the experience of most readers. It cannot be denied that the suffering of the Jews fits into Gotlieb's spectrum of universality, but its expression in this novel is too strongly dependent on a response to Jewish sentiment to appeal to those who lack it. Moreover, Gotlieb worries over her plot with an attention bordering on hysteria and the denouement is very early given away. Unable to do his own thinking and stranger in an alien, Talmudic culture, the reader cannot identify as he does with the *souvenirs* of the *Ordinary, Moving* poems, cannot associate himself with the joys and sufferings of the fictional world presented or the larger universe assumed, and quickly loses interest.

That he is not disinterested in the *Ordinary, Moving* poems is a significant statement of the appeal of anchoring the suggested in the familiar. The collage of *Ordinary, Moving* demonstrates that Gotlieb did, indeed, "like all writers [spend her youth] listening in buses, cars & cafes/trams & subways/streets & alleyways...." And furthermore, it celebrates the concentric concatenation of energies in which all that she overheard is joined and in which the reader by the last line also becomes part of the unity and then "begin[s] again."

—S. R. Gilbert

GRAHAM, Henry. British. Born in Liverpool, Lancashire, 1 December 1930. Educated at Liverpool College of Art. Painter: exhibitions in London and Northern England; gave up painting for poetry at the age of 30. Since 1969, Lecturer in Art History, Liverpool Polytechnic. Poetry Editor, *Ambit* magazine, London. Recipient: *Ambit* prize, 1968; Arts Council award, 1969, 1971.

PUBLICATIONS

Verse

Soup City Zoo, with Jim Mangnall. London, Anima Press, 1968.
Good Luck to You Kafka/You'll Need It Boss. London, Rapp and Whiting, 1969.
Passport to Earth. London, Rapp and Whiting-Deutsch, 1971.

Henry Graham comments:

My early influences in writing were the modern American poets, Pound, Olson, Duncan, etc. But now the Englishness of all the English arts interests me more; Auden, for instance, is one of the poets I admire most. The arts, and especially poetry, are not an attempt on my part to communicate, but are a way of looking into myself and the universe. If, as sometimes seems to happen, others are interested in and find in me what lies outside themselves, good; if not, good.

* * *

Henry Graham is a poet who never formed part of the so-called "Liverpool Scene," though he is sometimes included in anthologies of Pop Poetry. His background, however, is much like that of the other Liverpool poets who emerged in the late 1960's. He is a painter, and has worked as a jazz-musician. Experience of the other arts seems to have turned him, not towards popular materials, but towards an attempt at hermetic synthesis, of the sort one finds in poetry by Frenchmen such as Blaise Cendrars and Pierre Reverdy. Graham is by no means an even writer, nor is he a particularly prolific one. But he has produced a handful of poems with real control and authority. Perhaps the following lines will give an idea of what he can do on top form:

A soprano sings. The poem
limps on. The cat yawns. It feels
the air with the fine
wires on its nose. It yearns
to wear away the white
marble of milk it commands
morning and evening....

—Edward Lucie-Smith

GRAHAM, W(illiam) S(ydney). British. Born in Greenock, Renfrewshire, Scotland, 19 November 1918. Educated at Greenock High School; Workers Educational Association

College, Newbattle Abbey, Edinburgh, 1 year. Married. Lecturer, New York University, 1947–48. Recipient: Atlantic Award, 1947. Address: 4 Mountview Cottages, Madron, Penzance, Cornwall, England.

PUBLICATIONS

Verse

Cage Without Grievance. Glasgow, Parton Press, 1942.
The Seven Journeys. Glasgow, Maclellan, 1944.
2nd Poems. London, Editions Poetry London, 1945.
The Voyages of Alfred Wallis. London, Anthony Froshaug, 1948.
The White Threshold. London, Faber, 1949; New York, Grove Press, 1952.
The Nightfishing. London, Faber, and New York, Grove Press, 1955.
Malcolm Mooney's Land. London, Faber, 1970.
Penguin Modern Poets 17, with David Gascoyne and Kathleen Raine. London, Penguin, 1970.
Implements in Their Places. London, Faber, 1977.
Collected Poems 1942–1975. London, Faber, 1979.

Manuscript Collection: National Library of Scotland, Edinburgh.

Critical Studies: "Notes on a Poetry of Release" by the author, in *Sewanee Review* (Tennessee), 1947; "W. S. Graham's Threshold" by Edwin Morgan, in *Nine 3* (London), Spring 1950; *Babel to Byzantium* by James Dickey, New York, Farrar Straus, 1968.

W. S. Graham comments:

I do recognise a Scots timbre in my "voice" although I can't see myself, in any way, as characteristic of Scots poetry.

Major themes: The difficulty of communication; the difficulty of speaking from a fluid identity; the lessons in physical phenomena; the mystery and adequacy of the aesthetic experience; the elation of being alive in the language.

Although I love the ever-present metronome in verse, I am greedy for my rhythmic say. The gesture of speech often exists, moving seemingly counter to the abstract structure it is in. The three-accent line, not specially common in the body of English poetry, even a kind of strait-jacket, interested me enough for me to keep to it for a bit and try to ring the changes within.

As far as I can discern, my verse is influenced by the prose of Joyce and Beckett and by the verse of Marianne Moore, Pound and Eliot. And the textures of my verse shows, I think, a fondness for Anglo-Saxon and Scandinavian roots, also for translations of early Jewish and Scottish Gaelic verse.

* * *

Probably because he was one of the most verbally gifted poets of his generation in Scotland, W. S. Graham had a struggle to clarify a personal style that first carried large acknowledgements of other wordsmiths like Dylan Thomas, Gerard Manley Hopkins, and James Joyce. His early volumes – *Cage Without Grievance*, *The Seven Journeys*, and *2nd Poems* – have a tendency to thrash around with adjectives and to produce obscurely exciting effects, yet his devotion to the *word*, and his sense of the poem as a voyage of discovery, were not perverse. In exploring the self, and the poet's relation to his living audience and the audience of all the dead, Graham was working within a network of image and reference that was anchored to his Clydeside upbringing – indeed all his poetry is haunted by sea and shipyards, and by place-names from the countryside around Glasgow. The best of the early poems shows a distinctive lyricism ("O Gentle Queen of the Afternoon") and a deepening sense of mortality ("Many Without Elegy").

In *The White Threshold* and *The Nightfishing* Graham produced a very remarkable poetry, strong, musical, and intense, where the central sea imagery feeds a range of subtly related themes: his autobiography, wartime shipwrecks and drownings, fishing, and the metaphorical "white threshold" of all life and death which Herman Melville had tried to plumb before him. Apart from the two long title-pieces in these volumes, there are several shorter poems of great beauty and force: "Listen. Put on Morning," "Gigha," "Men Sign the Sea," "Night's Fall Unlocks the Dirge of the Sea," and "Letter VI." A growing lucidity humanizes the verse, but without removing its obsessional preoccupation with the endless dyings and metamorphoses of the self:

I bent to the lamp, I cupped
My hand to the glass chimney.
Yet it was a stranger's breath
From out of my mouth that
Shed the light.

After a 15-year silence, Graham published two new collections in the 1970's. Continuity with the earlier work, in both themes and technique, was clear, but to the younger generation of poets and critics, to whom his earlier poetry was perhaps little known, these two volumes came across with considerable impact and gave his reputation – for integrity, for craftsmanship – a new boost. Among poems on places and persons in Cornwall (where he had been living) and poems on the difficulty and necessity of communication (his most recurrent theme), there are some particularly fine poems of memory, or a mingling of memory and imagination, or memory and dream, in which he evokes his family and his childhood on Clydeside. "The Dark Dialogues," "Greenock at Night I Find You," and "To Alexander Graham" have a firm, reserved pathos which is very impressive:

See, I am back. My father turned and I saw
He had the stick he cut in Sheelhill Glen.
Brigit was there and Hugh and double-breasted
Sam and Malcolm Mooney and Alastair Graham.
They all were there in the Cartsburn Vaults shining
To meet me but I was only remembered.

—Edwin Morgan

GRAVES, Robert (Ranke). British. Born in London, 24 July 1895. Educated at Charterhouse School, Surrey; St. John's College, Oxford, B.Litt. 1926. Served with the Royal Welch Fusiliers in World War I; was refused admittance into the armed forces in World War II. Married 1) Nancy Nicholson; 2) Beryl Pritchard; seven children. Professor of English, Egyptian University, Cairo, 1926. Settled in Deyá, Mallorca, in 1929; with the poet Laura Riding established the Seizin Press and *Epilogue* magazine. Left Mallorca during the Spanish Civil War: settled in Glampton-Brixton, Devon during World War II; returned to Mallorca after the war. Clark Lecturer, Trinity College, Cambridge, 1954; Professor of Poetry, Oxford

University, 1961–66; Arthur Dehon Little Memorial Lecturer, Massachusetts Institute of Technology, Cambridge, 1963. Recipient: Bronze Medal for Poetry, Olympic Games, Paris, 1924; Hawthornden Prize, for fiction, 1935; Black Memorial Prize, for fiction, 1935; Femina Vie Heureuse-Stock Prize, 1939; Russell Loines Poetry Award, 1958; National Poetry Society of America Gold Medal, 1960; Foyle Poetry Prize, 1960; Arts Council Poetry Award, 1962; Italia Prize, for radio play, 1965; Queen's Gold Medal for Poetry, 1968; Gold Medal for Poetry, Cultural Olympics, Mexico City, 1968. M.A.: Oxford University, 1961. Honorary Member, American Academy of Arts and Sciences, 1970. Address: c/o A. P. Watt and Son, 26–28 Bedford Row, London W.C.1, England.

PUBLICATIONS

Verse

Over the Brazier. London, Poetry Bookshop, 1916; New York, St. Martin's Press, 1975.
Goliath and David. London, Chiswick Press, 1916.
Fairies and Fusiliers. London, Heinemann, 1917; New York, Knopf, 1918.
Treasure Box. London, Chiswick Press, 1919.
Country Sentiment. London, Secker, and New York, Knopf, 1920.
The Pier-Glass. London, Secker, and New York, Knopf, 1921.
Whipperginny. London, Heinemann, and New York, Knopf, 1923.
The Feather Bed. Richmond, Surrey, Hogarth Press, 1923.
Mock Beggar Hall. London, Hogarth Press, 1924.
Welchman's Hose. London, The Fleuron, 1925; Folcroft, Pennsylvania, Folcroft Editions, 1971.
(*Poems*). London, Benn, 1925.
The Marmosite's Miscellany (as John Doyle). London, Hogarth Press, 1925.
Poems (1914–1926). London, Heinemann, 1927; New York, Doubleday, 1929.
Poems (1914–1927). London, Heinemann, 1927.
Poems 1929. London, Seizin Press, 1929.
Ten Poems More. Paris, Hours Press, 1930.
Poems 1926–1930. London, Heinemann, 1931.
To Whom Else? Deyá, Mallorca, Seizin Press, 1931.
Poems 1930–1933. London, Barker, 1933.
Collected Poems. London, Cassell, and New York, Random House, 1938.
No More Ghosts: Selected Poems. London, Faber, 1940.
(*Poems*). London, Eyre and Spottiswoode, 1943.
Poems 1938–1945. London, Cassell, and New York, Creative Age Press, 1946.
Collected Poems (1914–1947). London, Cassell, 1948.
Poems and Satires 1951. London, Cassell, 1951.
Poems 1953. London, Cassell, 1953.
Collected Poems 1955. New York, Doubleday, 1955.
Poems Selected by Himself. London, Penguin, 1957; revised edition, 1961, 1966, 1972.
The Poems of Robert Graves. New York, Doubleday, 1958.
Collected Poems 1959. London, Cassell, 1959.
More Poems 1961. London, Cassell, 1961.
Collected Poems. New York, Doubleday, 1961.
New Poems 1962. London, Cassell, 1962; as *New Poems*, New York, Doubleday, 1963.
The More Deserving Cases: Eighteen Old Poems for Reconsideration. Marlborough, Marlborough College Press, 1962; Folcroft, Pennsylvania, Folcroft Editions, 1978.
Man Does, Woman Is 1964. London, Cassell, and New York, Doubleday, 1964.
Love Respelt. London, Cassell, 1965.
Collected Poems 1965. London, Cassell, 1965.

Seventeen Poems Missing from "Love Respelt". Privately printed, 1966.
Collected Poems 1966. New York, Doubleday, 1966.
Colophon to "Love Respelt". Privately printed, 1967.
(*Poems*), with D. H. Lawrence, edited by Leonard Clark. London, Longman, 1967.
Poems 1965–1968. London, Cassell, 1968; New York, Doubleday, 1969.
Poems about Love. London, Cassell, and New York, Doubleday, 1969.
Love Respelt Again. New York, Doubleday, 1969.
Beyond Giving. Privately printed, 1969.
Poems 1968–1970. London, Cassell, 1970.
Advice from a Mother. London, Poem-of-the-Month Club, 1970.
The Green-Sailed Vessel. Privately printed, 1971.
Corgi Modern Poets in Focus 3, with others, edited by Dannie Abse. London, Corgi, 1971.
Poems 1970–1972. London, Cassell, 1972; New York, Doubleday, 1973.
Deyá. London, Motif Editions, 1973.
Timeless Meeting: Poems. London, Bertram Rota, 1973.
At the Gate. London, Bertram Rota, 1974.
Collected Poems 1975. London, Cassell, 2 vols., 1975.
New Collected Poems. New York, Doubleday, 1977.

Recordings: *Robert Graves Reading His Own Poems*, Argo and Listen, 1960; *Robert Graves Reading His Own Poetry and The White Goddess*, Caedmon; *The Rubaiyat of Omar Khayyam*, Spoken Arts.

Plays

John Kemp's Wager: A Ballad Opera. Oxford, Blackwell, and New York, T. B. Edwards, 1925.

Radio Play: *The Anger of Achilles*, 1964.

Novels

No Decency Left, with Laura Riding (as Barbara Rich). London, Cape, 1932.
The Real David Copperfield. London, Barker, 1933; as *David Copperfield by Charles Dickens, Condensed by Robert Graves*, edited by Merrill P. Paine, New York, Harcourt Brace, 1934.
I, Claudius: From the Autobiography of Tiberius Claudius, Emperor of the Romans, Born B.C. 10, Murdered and Deified A.D. 54. London, Barker, and New York, Smith and Haas, 1934.
Claudius the God and His Wife Messalina: The Troublesome Reign of Tiberius Claudius Caesar, Emperor of the Romans (Born B.C. 10, Died A.D. 54), As Described by Himself; Also His Murder at the Hands of the Notorious Agrippina (Mother of the Emperor Nero) and His Subsequent Deification, As Described by Others. London, Barker, 1934; New York, Smith and Haas, 1935.
"*Antigua, Penny, Puce.*" Deyá, Mallorca, Seizin Press, and London, Constable, 1936; as *The Antigua Stamp*, New York, Random House, 1937.
Count Belisarius. London, Cassell, and New York, Random House, 1938.
Sergeant Lamb of the Ninth. London, Methuen, 1940; as *Sergeant Lamb's America*, New York, Random House, 1940.
Proceed, Sergeant Lamb. London, Methuen, and New York, Random House, 1941.
The Story of Marie Powell: Wife to Mr. Milton. London, Cassell, 1943; as *Wife to Mr. Milton: The Story of Marie Powell*, New York, Creative Age Press, 1944.
The Golden Fleece. London, Cassell, 1944; as *Hercules, My Shipmate*, New York, Creative Age Press, 1945.

King Jesus. New York, Creative Age Press, and London, Cassell, 1946.
Watch the North Wind Rise. New York, Creative Age Press, 1949; as *Seven Days in New Crete*, London, Cassell, 1949.
The Islands of Unwisdom. New York, Doubleday, 1949; as *The Isles of Unwisdom*, London, Cassell, 1950.
Homer's Daughter. London, Cassell, and New York, Doubleday, 1955.

Short Stories

The Shout. London, Mathews and Marrot, 1929.
¡Catacrok! Mostly Stories, Mostly Funny. London, Cassell, 1956.
Collected Short Stories. New York, Doubleday, 1964; London, Cassell, 1965; as *The Shout and Other Stories*, London, Penguin, 1978.

Other

On English Poetry. New York, Knopf, and London, Heinemann, 1922.
The Meaning of Dreams. London, Cecil Palmer, 1924; New York, Greenberg, 1925.
Poetic Unreason and Other Studies. London, Cecil Palmer, 1925.
My Head! My Head! Being the History of Elisha and the Shunamite Woman; With the History of Moses as Elisha Related It, and Her Questions to Him. London, Secker, and New York, Knopf, 1925.
Contemporary Techniques of Poetry: A Political Analogy. London, Hogarth Press, 1925; Folcroft, Pennsylvania, Folcroft Editions, 1977.
Another Future of Poetry. London, Hogarth Press, 1926.
Impenetrability; or, The Proper Habit of English. London, Hogarth Press, 1926.
The English Ballad: A Short Critical Survey. London, Benn, 1927; revised edition, as *English and Scottish Ballads*, London, Heinemann, and New York, Macmillan, 1957.
Lars Porsena; or, The Future of Swearing and Improper Language. London, Kegan Paul Trench Trubner, and New York, Dutton, 1927; revised edition, as *The Future of Swearing and Improper Language*, Kegan Paul Trench Trubner, 1936.
A Survey of Modernist Poetry, with Laura Riding. London, Heinemann, 1927; New York, Doubleday, 1928.
Lawrence and the Arabs. London, Cape, 1927; as *Lawrence and the Arabian Adventure*, New York, Doubleday, 1928.
A Pamphlet Against Anthologies, with Laura Riding. London, Cape, 1928; as *Against Anthologies*, New York, Doubleday, 1928.
Mrs. Fisher; or, The Future of Humour. London, Kegan Paul Trench Trubner, 1928; Folcroft, Pennsylvania, Folcroft Editions, 1974.
Goodbye to All That: An Autobiography. London, Cape, 1929; New York, Cape and Smith, 1930; revised edition, New York, Doubleday, and London, Cassell, 1957; London, Penguin, 1960.
T. E. Lawrence to His Biographer Robert Graves. New York, Doubleday, 1938; London, Faber, 1939.
The Long Week-end: A Social History of Great Britain 1918–1939, with Alan Hodge. London, Faber, 1940; New York, Macmillan, 1941.
Work in Hand, with others. London, Hogarth Press, 1942.
The Reader over Your Shoulder: A Handbook for Writers of English Prose, with Alan Hodge. London, Cape, 1943; New York, Macmillan, 1944.
The White Goddess: A Historical Grammar of Poetic Myth. London, Faber, and New York, Creative Age Press, 1948; revised edition, Faber, 1952, 1966; New York, Knopf, 1958.
The Common Asphodel: Collected Essays on Poetry 1922–1949. London, Hamish Hamilton, 1949; Folcroft, Pennsylvania, Folcroft Editions, 1971.
Occupation: Writer. New York, Creative Age Press, 1950; London, Cassell, 1951.

The Nazarene Gospel Restored, with Joshua Podro. London, Cassell, 1953; New York, Doubleday, 1954.
The Crowning Privilege: The Clark Lectures 1954–1955; Also Various Essays on Poetry and Sixteen New Poems. London, Cassell, 1955; as *The Crowning Privilege: Collected Essays on Poetry*, New York, Doubleday, 1956.
Adam's Rib and Other Anomalous Elements in the Hebrew Creation Myth: A New View. London, Trianon Press, 1955; New York, Yoseloff, 1958.
The Greek Myths. London and Baltimore, Penguin, 2 vols., 1955.
Jesus in Rome: A Historical Conjecture, with Joshua Podro. London, Cassell, 1957.
They Hanged My Saintly Billy. London, Cassell, 1957; as *They Hanged My Saintly Billy: The Life and Death of Dr. William Palmer*, New York, Doubleday, 1957.
Steps: Stories, Talks, Essays, Poems, Studies in History. London, Cassell, 1958.
5 Pens in Hand. New York, Doubleday, 1958.
Food for Centaurs: Stories, Talks, Critical Studies, Poems. New York, Doubleday, 1960.
The Penny Fiddle: Poems for Children. London, Cassell, 1960; New York, Doubleday, 1961.
Greek Gods and Heroes. New York, Doubleday, 1960; as *Myths of Ancient Greece*, London, Cassell, 1961.
Selected Poetry and Prose, edited by James Reeves. London, Hutchinson, 1961.
The Siege and Fall of Troy (juvenile). London, Cassell, 1962; New York, Doubleday, 1963.
The Big Green Book. New York, Crowell Collier, 1962; London, Penguin, 1978.
Oxford Addresses on Poetry. London, Cassell, 1961; New York, Doubleday, 1962.
Nine Hundred Iron Chariots: The Twelfth Arthur Dehon Little Memorial Lecture. Cambridge, Massachusetts Institute of Technology, 1963.
The Hebrew Myths: The Book of Genesis, with Raphael Patai. New York, Doubleday, and London, Cassell, 1964.
Ann at Highwood Hall: Poems for Children. London, Cassell, 1964.
Majorca Observed. London, Cassell, and New York, Doubleday, 1965.
Mammon and the Black Goddess. London, Cassell, and New York, Doubleday, 1965.
Two Wise Children (juvenile). New York, Harlin Quist, 1966; London, W. H. Allen, 1967.
Poetic Craft and Principle. London, Cassell, 1967.
Spiritual Quixote. London, Oxford University Press, 1967.
The Poor Boy Who Followed His Star (juvenile). London, Cassell, 1968; New York, Doubleday, 1969.
The Crane Bag and Other Disputed Subjects. London, Cassell, 1969.
On Poetry: Collected Talks and Essays. New York, Doubleday, 1969.
Poems: Abridged for Dolls and Princes (juvenile). London, Cassell, and New York, Doubleday, 1971.
Difficult Questions, Easy Answers. London, Cassell, 1972; New York, Doubleday, 1973.

Editor, with Alan Porter and Richard Hughes, *Oxford Poetry, 1921.* Oxford, Blackwell, 1921.
Editor, *John Skelton (Laureate), 1460(?)–1529.* London, Benn, 1927.
Editor, *The Less Familiar Nursery Rhymes.* London, Benn, 1927.
Editor, *The Comedies of Terence.* New York, Doubleday, 1962; London, Cassell, 1963.

Translator, with Laura Riding, *Almost Forgotten Germany*, by Georg Schwarz. Deyá, Mallorca, Seizin Press, London, Constable, and New York, Random House, 1936.
Translator, *The Transformations of Lucius, Otherwise Known as The Golden Ass*, by Apuleius. London, Penguin, 1950; New York, Farrar Straus, 1951.

Translator, *The Cross and the Sword*, by Manuel de Jésus Galván. Bloomington, Indiana University Press, 1955; London, Gollancz, 1956.
Translator, *The Infant with the Globe*, by Pedro Antonio de Alarcón. London, Trianon Press, 1955; New York, Yoseloff, 1958.
Translator, *Winter in Majorca*, by George Sand. London, Cassell, 1956.
Translator, *Pharsalia: Dramatic Episodes of the Civil Wars*, by Lucan. London, Penguin, 1956.
Translator, *The Twelve Caesars*, by Suetonius. London, Penguin, 1957.
Translator, *The Anger of Achilles: Homer's Iliad.* New York, Doubleday, 1959; London, Cassell, 1960.
Translator, with Omar Ali-Shah, *Rubaiyat of Omar Khayyam.* London, Cassell, 1967; New York, Doubleday, 1968.
Translator, *The Song of Songs.* New York, Clarkson Potter, and London, Collins, 1973.

Bibliography: *A Bibliography of the Works of Robert Graves* by Fred H. Higginson, London, Nicholas Vane, 1966.

Manuscript Collections: Lockwood Memorial Library, State University of New York at Buffalo; New York City Public Library; University of Texas Library, Austin.

* * *

The poetry of Robert Graves may, allowing for anticipations and regressions, be divided into four main phases: from his schoolboy beginnings in 1906 until his discovery of the poetry of the American poet Laura Riding (now Laura Jackson) in 1925; the duration of his literary and personal association with Miss Riding (1926–39); the period of his war-time sojourn in a South Devon farmhouse and of the first years of his return to Mallorca (1939–56); and what may be called the years in which he entered into world fame. The two main events in his poetic life have been the impact upon him of four years' trench warfare in World War I, and his response to the poetry and personality of Laura Riding. While the effect of Graves's war experiences has been adequately appreciated by his critics, the influence of Miss Riding has been very seriously underestimated, owing, one feels, to failure to understand her poetry. Whether the general verdict on this poetry will be reversed or not (one suspects that it may be, from the private interest that has been shown in it), it is certainly true to say that no one who will not make the effort to understand Miss Riding's poetry (she stopped writing it in 1939) can hope to understand Graves's. (That this is a statement he himself fully endorses does not prove it to be correct, but it is a fact not irrelevant for students of his poetry.)

As Graves has written in a note to the 1965 English edition of his *Collected Poems*, "... I always aimed at writing more or less as I still do." This is only another way of saying that his development has been less a matter of a series of fresh inventions, or successions of changed attitudes, than of a continuously expanding awareness of his purposes as a poet. His faith in the poem he has to write – although not attended by any careless arrogance about his capacities to write it – has been as great as that of any English poet, perhaps greater. In this sense the poem, for Graves, is a thing outside himself, a task of truth-telling – and not a thing to be invented or "composed." Poem-writing is a matter of absolute truthfulness to the emotional mood of self-revelation. Graves is not a craftsman who invents shapes in stone, to his own desires; but one who seeks, by means of intuition, to discover the exact shape in the middle of the stone, in which he has absolute faith.

If one of the signs of a major as distinct from a minor poet is development, then Graves is certainly a major poet. Yet his experiments have always been within the limits of tradition. As a schoolboy he worked on hosts of complicated rhyme-schemes and verse-forms, including the Welsh *englyn*, as well as with assonance and dissonance. For his subject-matter he drew on the worlds of chivalry, romance and nursery rhyme. Much of his technical facility and his capacity to use folk-themes without parodying them he owed to his father, Alfred Perceval Graves, who was a graceful minor Irish poet.

Graves was one of a group of war-poets which included Sassoon and Owen; but unlike theirs his poetry did not mature during the war, and he has rejected nearly all his war poetry. Much of his immediately post-war poetry, written under the twin (and opposing) influences of war-trauma and pastoral marriage, he has also rejected. It is technically accomplished, charming, and with an underlying complexity that is not as typically Georgian as is its surface. Graves was at this time working – under the influence of W. H. R. Rivers, the anthropologist – on the Freudian theory that poetry was therapeutic, a view he largely abandoned in the later Twenties.

Little of the poetry of Graves's first period has been preserved in his *Collected Poems*; but its main positive features – delight in nonsense, preoccupation with terror, the nature of his love for women – have survived into his later poetry. What was purged was softness and cloying over-sweetness. A poem (preserved) such as *The Pier-Glass* (1921) perfectly illustrates the qualities of the early poems and at the same time delineates the area that the later poems were to explore so meticulously and movingly. Written in the person of a lonely female ghost doomed to wander a lonely mansion, it conjures up a picture of utter lifelessness, so that the ghost cries to her "sullen pierglass, cracked from side to side" for "one token" this life exists, "So be it only this side Hope"; anything but "this phantasma." Graves was to explore the life "this side Hope," only to find it dangerous and phantasmagoric; but his poetry gained immensely in vitality and depth.

Laura Riding was on the fringes of the American Fugitive Group (which included John Crowe Ransom, Allen Tate and Robert Penn Warren) and it was in *The Fugitive* that Graves first encountered her work. What influenced him was not her procedures – which were, rhythmically, totally unlike his – but the content of her poems and the personality that went with this. The poems of his maturity are in no sense at all imitations of hers; but her remarkably complicated view of life (and therefore the work in which she expressed this) are relevant to them: he shared, or rather, attempted devotedly to learn, this view, and the material of the poems is his struggle to accommodate himself lovingly to it and to her. The process proved impossible in the end, as he foresaw in "Sick Love," written in the late Twenties: "O Love, be fed with apples while you may," this begins; and it ends: "Take your delight in momentariness,/Walk between dark and dark – a shining space/With the grave's narrowness, though not its peace." The poems Graves wrote in his second period record, with great directness and in a diction of deliberate hardness and strength, the nerve-strains of impossible love ("To the galleys, thief, and sweat your soul out" one begins) and his attempt to achieve an existence that accorded with the goodness that Graves and (at that time) Laura Riding saw as residing in poetry above every other human activity. These are therefore extremely "existential" poems, and to be understood they must be read in this way: they are at once an account of a condition of romanticized devotedness, of a search for perfection (always tempered with ironic realism and earthly masculine robustness) and of human failures. Poems such as "The Legs" describe the distractions that Graves saw as tempting him from the concentration his single-minded quest for poetic wisdom required. His "historical grammar of poetic myth," *The White Goddess*, is essentially a generalization from his experiences of these years of devoted struggle to serve a savagely demanding muse, whom in "On Portents" he has seen as a vast propeller, a "bladed mind" strongly pulling through the "ever-reluctant element" of Time. These poems, by which – together with those of the succeeding phase – Graves will probably be chiefly remembered, provide what will almost certainly become the classic latter-day record of romantic love; this is so not least because of their unsentimentality, their tough and unidealistic acceptance of the author's strong masculine recalcitrance. Thus, his mood changes from confidence, as in "End of Play" –

> We tell no lies now, at last cannot be
> The rogues we were – so evilly linked in sense
> With what we scrutinized that lion or tiger
> Could leap from every copse, strike and devour us.

– to zestful gloom, as in "The Succubus":

> Yet why does she
> Come never as longed-for beauty
> Slender and cool, with limbs lovely to see ...?

As he wrote in 1965, "My theme was always the practical impossibility, transcended only by miracle, of absolute love continuing between man and woman." It is the tension between "practical impossibility" and "miracle," a tension reflected in universal experience, that gives Graves's poetry its unique power.

The poems of Graves's third phase, written when he had abandoned his prodigious enterprise of creating – with Laura Riding – an existence in which poetry and what it represents would be a natural way of life (for more details of this, see Laura Riding's Introduction to her *Collected Poems*, 1938), reflect upon the meaning of his experience ("A Love Story"):

> her image
> Warped in the weather, turned beldamish.
> Then back came winter on me at a bound,
> The pallid sky heaved with a moon-quake.
>
> Dangerous had it been with love-notes
> To serenade Queen Famine....

They also discover new love, in some of the most beautiful love lyrics in English: "Have you not read/The words in my head,/And I made part/Of your own heart?" ("Despite and Still"). Finally they humorously state his position and accept that fame has caught up with him, as in "From the Embassy," where he refers to himself as "ambassador of Otherwhere/ To the unfederated States of Here and There."

The poetry of Graves's most recent phase has continued to develop. More technically impeccable than ever, more consciously cunning in its artistry than anything that has gone before it, it lacks the tension of the earlier work – but never the convincing tone of a man in love. It owes a good deal to the Sufist ideas by which Graves has been influenced in recent years, and it discovers the peaceful figure of the Black Goddess who lies behind the crueller one of the White Goddess. Love, to Graves in these new poems, walks "on a knife-edge between two different fates": one fate is to consort with the White Goddess, and is physical; the other, more difficult yet more rewarding, to find peace in the domains of the Black Goddess. Frequently the poems are so lapidary as to remind the reader of Landor; but they reach a greater power than ever Landor achieved when they envisage the hell of a world made dead by a too great reliance upon physical passion. Of one who is trapped in this hell, who in departing too casually has said, "I will write," he says in a poem of the same title: "Long letters written and mailed in her own head –/There are no mails in a city of the dead." Graves's latest poems provide, in their explorations of the possibilities of a world purged of what he calls "the blood sports of desire," and of the agonies of alienation from such a world, a fitting sequel to those of his earlier years. He will be, perhaps, the last romantic poet to operate within wholly traditional limits – and his mastery of these is not in question.

—Martin Seymour-Smith

GREENE, Jonathan (Edward). American. Born in New York City, 19 April 1943. Educated at Bard College, Annandale-on-Hudson, New York, B.A. Married; two daughters. Since 1965, Founding Editor, Gnomon Press, Lexington, later Frankfort, Kentucky. Apprentice Printer, then Assistant Production Manager, and Production Manager and Designer, University Press of Kentucky, 1966–75. Recipient: National Endowment for the Arts grant, 1969, 1978. Address: P.O. Box 106, Frankfort, Kentucky 40602, U.S.A.

PUBLICATIONS

Verse

The Reckoning. Annandale-on-Hudson, New York, Matter, 1966.
Instance. Lexington, Kentucky, Buttonwood Press, 1968.
The Lapidary. Los Angeles, Black Sparrow Press, 1969.
A 17th Century Garner. Lexington, Kentucky, Buttonwood Press, 1969.
An Unspoken Complaint. Santa Barbara, California, Unicorn Press, 1970.
Scaling the Walls. Lexington, Kentucky, Gnomon Press, 1974.
Glossary of the Everyday. Toronto, Coach House Press, 1974.
Once a Kingdom Again. Berkeley, California, Sand Dollar, 1978.
Peripatetics. St. Paul, Minnesota, Truck Press, 1978.
Quiet Goods. Monterey, Kentucky, Larkspur Press, 1979.

Other

Translator, *The Poor in Church*, by Arthur Rimbaud. Lexington, Kentucky, Polyglot Press, 1973.

Jonathan Greene comments:

(1970) Friendships early on with "deep image" poets important; close ties with Robert Kelly, Robert Duncan and Robin Blaser.

No school, but a tradition involving individual poets felt strongly: Blake, Yeats and more recent incarnations.

(1980) My recent work has delved into psychological/philosophical ruminations as well as being concerned with living in a rural setting.

* * *

Jonathan Greene may be placed among the group of writers affiliated (through shared concerns rather than "influence") with Robert Kelly. (Others include Charles Stein and Harvey Bialy and the prose writer Richard Grossinger.) Kelly published and wrote the introduction for Greene's first book and was his teacher and friend at Bard College. The hermetic tradition as mediated through such writers as Blake, H.D., and Robert Duncan is a major informing presence in Greene's work. One consequence is a frequently baffling abstractness and allusiveness, but even in the obscurest poems there is evident a care for the weight and sound of each syllable. Greene speaks of "the work,/which is/love/persistent" and of how "the *care-/takers*/portion out/their harvests,/the bounty." The bounty for us, in the most successful poems, is a delicate but tough lyricism – see, for example, "The Definition" from *The Lapidary.* Much influenced by Jung, Greene writes out of a sense of poetry as "given" from a source "beyond" and thus inevitably dealing in archetypal material. "A Palimpsest" opens:

The old story keeps writing itself.
Dark woods & the turn of the road
again. I do not write it. A *turn*
of the road, writes itself. *A*
changed life, interpolates from
an unknown source. Underneath,
the writing still goes on.
The true writing.

And a haiku-like poem from *Instance* puts it more imagistically: "the old tales are told,/ migratory birds/come home to/the heart."

It should be added that Greene's uncollected recent work shows a welcome inclusion of more directly personal subject matter, while retaining the qualities of ear and of access to depth evidenced in his earlier books.

—Seamus Cooney

GREGOR, Arthur. American. Born in Vienna, Austria, 18 November 1923; emigrated to the United States, 1939, naturalized, 1945. Educated at Newark College of Engineering, New Jersey, B.S. in electrical engineering 1945. Engineer, Electronic Transformer Corporation, New York, 1945–54; Editor, Whitney Publications, New York, 1955–61; Senior Editor, Macmillan Company, publishers, New York, 1962–70; Visiting Professor, California State University, Hayward, 1972–73. Since 1973, Professor and Director of the Creative Writing Center, Hofstra University, Hempstead, New York. Recipient: First Appearance Prize (*Poetry*, Chicago), 1948; Palmer Award, 1962. Address: 131 West 78th Street, New York, New York 10024, U.S.A.

PUBLICATIONS

Verse

Octavian Shooting Targets. New York, Dodd Mead, 1954.
Declensions of a Refrain. New York, Poetry London-New York Books, 1957.
Basic Movements. New York, Gyre Press, 1966.
Figure in the Door. New York, Doubleday, 1968.
A Bed by the Sea. New York, Doubleday, 1970.
Selected Poems. New York, Doubleday, 1971.
The Past Now: New Poems. New York, Doubleday, 1975.

Plays

Continued Departure (produced New York, 1968). Published in *Accent* (Urbana, Illinois), 1951.
Fire (produced Urbana, Illinois, 1952).
The Door Is Open (produced New York, 1970).

Other

1 2 3 4 5 (juvenile). Philadelphia, Lippincott, 1956.

The Little Elephant (juvenile). New York, Harper, 1956.
Animal Babies (juvenile). New York, Harper, 1959.

Manuscript Collection: Mugar Memorial Library, Boston University.

Critical Studies: Reviews by Laurence Lieberman, in *Yale Review* (New Haven, Connecticut), Spring 1968; Hayden Carruth, in *Hudson Review* (New York), Spring 1968; Robert A. Carter, in *Modern Poetry Studies* (Buffalo, New York), Autumn 1971; Thomas Lask, in *The New York Times*, 9 December 1971; Christopher Collins, in *The Nation* (New York), 15 February 1972; F. D. Reeve, in *Poetry* (Chicago), January 1973; Josephine Jacobsen, in *Nation* (New York), 9 October 1976; James Finn Cotter, in *Hudson Review* (New York), Spring 1978.

Arthur Gregor comments:

I have tried to explore and to articulate what I consider the poetic reality in myself – a reality which lies in all. My influences have been art, nature, and those in whom throb powerfully the magic, the mystery of life.

* * *

During a time when the evolution of American poetry has been defined by large movements with clearly directed aims, Arthur Gregor has followed a decidedly independent, sometimes contrary course. In part it is a question of his European origin. He was born and raised in Vienna, and has traveled extensively in the Old World; his poetry relies upon images and allusions drawn from European history and culture. But the distinction is more basic than this. If we agree that the great movement of American poetry in the past 25 years has been away from the symbolist tradition and the dominance of such poets as Eliot and Yeats, and toward a poetry based not only on native themes and idioms but on an objectivist view of reality (which does not preclude mythic values), then Gregor has clearly stood against the main stream with his insistence upon the continuing human validity of symbolist modes of perception. It has not been an argued insistence. Though Gregor has been a journalist and editor, as well as an engineer, he has rarely resorted to theoretical statements about his own work. But in his poetry his philosophical affinities are clear: they are with the great symbolists of the European tradition, and particularly with such poets of the richly colored, central European imagination as Rilke and Hofmannsthal.

It is easy to overemphasize the programmatic importance of these distinctions, however. Gregor fits comfortably enough in the present American literary scene. In tone and verbal texture his verse resembles the contemporary free-form writing of most American poets. In fact from his first poems in the 1940's Gregor used a freer, more flexible line that the formalist conventions of that period sanctioned. He could never have been classed with the academics. On the other hand his early work did show an ornateness of diction and figure which seemed very baroque at the time, as if this European poet had taken the manner of Wallace Stevens and converted it to foreign ends, though the actual influence of Stevens, if it existed at all, was superficial. From these beginnings Gregor moved toward quieter, gentler poems that reached ever farther into his mystical view of experience. An evocation of unseen presences, a realization of history or of the minds of ancestors, a glimpse of the "elsewhere" that lies somehow within the defined particulars of each new place: these and similar themes occupied him more and more. It is difficult to say precisely what his religious orientation may be; his poems are written always obliquely, as if alongside the standard forms of spiritual evolution, not within them. Allusions can be detected to Hebrew, Christian, Gnostic, and Vedantic motifs, but they are allusions of feeling, not form, of spirit, not substance. His vision is clearly his own. And in his poems about people, though they are often richly erotic, it is the essential mystery of the person toward which the vision aspires.

The danger of Gregor's vision is that words will fail its mysteriousness and turn into mere talk – talking about what cannot be sufficiently embodied, the failure of symbolism. It is a danger that Gregor has not always surmounted. But in his best poems – some of those about his parents and his travels – his vision is conveyed intact. It is a private vision, hence in some sense exclusive or even elitist, at odds with the prevailing temper of the age. Yet Gregor's work has a gentleness and seriousness which have won it considerable popularity in recent years, especially among young people, and his somewhat alien voice has become a distinct and useful element in the American literary sensibility of the time.

—Hayden Carruth

GREGORY, Horace (Victor). American. Born in Milwaukee, Wisconsin, 10 April 1898. Educated at the Milwaukee School of Fine Arts, Summers 1913–16; German-English Academy, Milwaukee, 1914–19; University of Wisconsin, Madison, B.A. 1923. Married Marya Zaturenska, *q.v.*, in 1925; two children. Free-lance Writer, New York and London, 1923–34. Member of the English Department, 1934–60, and since 1960, Professor Emeritus, Sarah Lawrence College, Bronxville, New York. Associate Editor, *Tiger's Eye* magazine, New York. Recipient: Lyric Prize, 1928, Levinson Prize, 1934, and Union League Civic and Arts Foundation Prize, 1951 (*Poetry*, Chicago); Levinson Award, 1936; Loines Award, 1942; Guggenheim Fellowship, 1951; Academy of American Poets Fellowship, 1961; Bollingen Prize, 1965. D.Litt.: University of Wisconsin, Madison, 1977. Member, National Institute of Arts and Letters. Address: Palisades, Rockland County, New York 10964, U.S.A.

PUBLICATIONS

Verse

Chelsea Rooming House. New York, Covici Friede, 1930; as *Rooming House*, London, Faber, 1932.
No Retreat. New York, Harcourt Brace, 1933.
A Wreath for Margery. New York, Modern Editions Press, 1933.
Chorus for Survival. New York, Covici Friede, 1935.
Poems 1930–1940. New York, Harcourt Brace, 1941.
Selected Poems. New York, Viking Press, 1951.
Medusa in Gramercy Park. New York, Macmillan, 1961.
Alphabet for Joanna: A Poem (juvenile). New York, Holt Rinehart, 1963.
Collected Poems. New York, Holt Rinehart, 1964.
Another Look. New York, Holt Rinehart, 1976.

Other

Pilgrim of the Apocalypse: A Critical Study of D. H. Lawrence. New York, Viking Press, 1933; London, Secker, 1934; revised edition, as *D. H. Lawrence: Pilgrim of the Apocalypse*, New York, Grove Press, 1957.
The Shield of Achilles: Essays on Beliefs in Poetry. New York, Harcourt Brace, 1944.
A History of American Poetry 1900–1940, with Marya Zaturenska. New York, Harcourt Brace, 1946.
Poet of the People: An Evaluation of James Whitcomb Riley, with James T. Farrell and Jeanette Covert Nolan. Bloomington, Indiana University Press, 1951.

Amy Lowell: Portrait of the Poet in Her Time. New York, Nelson, 1958.
The World of James McNeill Whistler. New York, Nelson, 1959; London, Hutchinson, 1961.
The Dying Gladiators and Other Essays. New York, Grove Press, 1961.
Dorothy Richardson: An Adventure in Self-Discovery. New York, Holt Rinehart, 1967.
The House on Jefferson Street: A Cycle of Memories. New York, Holt Rinehart, 1971.
Spirit of Time and Place: Collected Essays of Horace Gregory. New York, Norton, 1973.

Editor, with Eleanor Clark, *New Letters in America.* New York, Norton, 1937.
Editor, *The Triumph of Life: Poems of Consolation for the English-Speaking World.* New York, Viking Press, 1943.
Editor, *Critical Remarks on the Metaphysical Poets*, by Samuel Johnson. Mount Vernon, New York, Golden Eagle Press, 1945.
Editor, *The Portable Sherwood Anderson.* New York, Viking Press, 1949.
Editor, *Snake Lady*, by Violet Paget. New York, Grove Press, 1954.
Editor, *Selected Poetry*, by Robert Browning. New York, Rinehart, 1956.
Editor, with Marya Zaturenska, *The Mentor Book of Religious Verse.* New York, New American Library, 1957.
Editor, with Marya Zaturenska, *The Crystal Cabinet: An Invitation to Poetry.* New York, Holt Rinehart, 1962.
Editor, with others, *Riverside Poetry 4: An Anthology of Student Verse.* New York, Twayne, 1962.
Editor, *Evangeline and Selected Tales and Poems of Longfellow.* New York, New American Library, 1964.
Editor, *Selected Poems*, by E. E. Cummings. New York, Harcourt Brace, 1965.
Editor, with Marya Zaturenska, *The Silver Swan: Poems of Romance and Mystery.* New York, Holt Rinehart, 1966.
Editor, *Selected Poems of George Gordon, Lord Byron.* New York, Crowell, 1969.

Translator, *The Poems of Catullus.* New York, Covici Friede, 1931.
Translator, *Poems*, by Catullus. New York, Grove Press, and London, Thames and Hudson, 1956.
Translator, *The Metamorphoses*, by Ovid. New York, Viking Press, 1958.
Translator, *Love Poems of Ovid.* New York, New American Library, 1964.

Critical Studies: "Horace Gregory Issue" of *Modern Poetry Studies* (Buffalo, New York), May 1973.

* * *

Horace Gregory is perhaps best known as the translator of Catullus and Ovid. But he has also published critical studies on Amy Lowell, D. H. Lawrence, James McNeill Whistler and others, as well as collaborating with his wife, the poet Marya Zaturenska, on *A History of American Poetry 1900–1940*, and on the editing of an anthology for young readers, *The Crystal Cabinet: An Invitation to Poetry.*

Elizabeth Drew has written that his "emotional range is perhaps the most comprehensive among modern poets," and Louis Untermeyer wrote that Gregory "does not share Eliot's disillusions or Crane's disorganization," a statement that is unfair to all three poets. However, poems like "Valediction to My Contemporaries" compare interestingly with Hart Crane's "The Bridge" in their language, their idealism, their purposes; and many of Gregory's efforts to recapture in monologues the pathos and cacophony of life in the modern city remind one of Eliot. In the final analysis, however, authenticity and integrity may not be enough; subtleties of syntax, powers of condensation, originality of imagery, distinguish Eliot and Crane from those who wrote with comparable verve.

Gregory is academic, ordered, descriptive, even-paced; he might be quite properly compared with MacLeish for his intellectual ambition, rhetorical power, and sense of American history. Most of his poems are based on classical subjects in one way or another, though he often juxtaposes classical imagery with modernistic impressions; he also has many poems about paintings, European scenes, and – like MacLeish – his country's cultural history. His well-known poem on Emerson recapitulates Emerson's life in an investigation of the intellectual's role ("To know too well, to think too long") in a land where action and immortality are even more akin than rhetoric and relevance. Gregory, like MacLeish, bears a heavy weight of idealism at all times, perhaps more than his country's history can support. Because the idealism is more muted in his Chelsea rooming house poems, they are perhaps more appealing than his poems with more epic ambitions. In poems like "McAlpin Garfinkel, Poet" and "Time and Isidore Lefkowitz," Gregory seems to have absorbed the influence of Edwin Arlington Robinson and to have looked forward to the work of poets like Kenneth Fearing:

> Look at Isidore Lefkowitz,
> biting his nails, telling how
> he seduces Beautiful French Canadian
> Five and Ten Cent Store Girls,
> beautiful, by God, and how they cry
> and moan, wrapping their arms
> and legs around him
> when he leaves them....

In an age when we have come to think of poems as the swiftly captured sound of madness, Gregory's work stands as a celebration of order, with the glimpsed backstreet life crying out to have a part of that order and the consideration due to it:

> How can I unlearn
> the arts of love within a single hour;
> how can I close my eyes before a mirror,
> believe I am not wanted, that hands, lips, breast
> are merely deeper shadows behind the door
> where all is dark?

—David Ray

GRIFFIN, Jonathan. Pseudonym for Robert John Thurlow Griffin. British. Born in Worthing, Sussex, in 1906. Educated at Radley School; New College, Oxford, B.A. Married 1) Joan Scudamore Creyke (marriage dissolved); 2) Kathleen Evelyn Willson. Director of European Intelligence, BBC, London, 1940–44; Second Secretary, British Embassy, Paris, 1945–51. Address: c/o Brookside Press, Villiers Publications Ltd., Ingestre Road, London NW5 1UL, England.

PUBLICATIONS

Verse

The Rebirth of Pride. London, Secker and Warburg, 1957.

The Oath and Other Poems. London, Gordon, 1963.
In Time of Crowding: Selected Poems 1963–1974. London, Brookside Press, 1975.
In This Transparent Forest. University Center, Michigan, Green River Press, 1977.
Outsing the Howling: An Interlude. London, Permanent Press, 1979.
The Fact of Music. London, Menard Press, 1980.

Plays

The Master of Santiago, and *Malatesta*, adaptations of plays by Henry de Montherlant (produced London, 1957). Included in *The Master of Santiago and Four Other Plays*, London, Routledge, and New York, Knopf, 1951.
The Hidden King: A Poem for the Stage in the Form of a Trilogy (produced Edinburgh, 1957). London, Secker and Warburg, 1955.
The Cardinal of Spain, adaptation of a play by Henry de Montherlant (produced Guildford, Surrey, 1969). Published in *Plays of the Year 37*, London, Elek, 1969.
The Prince of Homburg, adaptation of a play by Heinrich von Kleist (produced Manchester, 1976). Published in *Plays of the Year 36*, London, Elek, 1969.
Break of Noon, adaptation of a play by Paul Claudel (produced Ipswich, 1972).
The Deep Man, adaptation of a play by Hugo von Hofmannsthal (produced Manchester, 1979).

Screenplay: *Diary of a Country Priest* (English version), 1950.

Other

Britain's Air Policy: Present and Future. London, Gollancz, 1935.
Alternative to Re-armament. London, Macmillan, 1936.
Glass Houses and Modern War. London, Chatto and Windus, 1938.
The Czechoslovak-German Frontier: Its Strategic Importance. London, Czechoslovak Broadsheets, 1938.
Lost Liberty? The Ordeal of the Czechs and the Future of Freedom, with Joan Griffin. London, Chatto and Windus, 1939.

Translator, *The Hussar on the Roof*, by Jean Giono. London, Museum Press, 1953; as *The Horseman on the Roof*, New York, Knopf, 1954.
Translator, *Christ Recrucified*, by Nikos Kazantzakes. Oxford, Cassirer, 1954; as *The Greek Passion*, New York, Simon and Schuster, 1954.
Translator, *Freedom and Death*, by Nikos Kazantzakes. Oxford, Cassirer, 1956; as *Freedom or Death*, New York, Simon and Schuster, 1956.
Translator, *The Roots of Heaven*, by Romain Gary. London, Joseph, and New York, Simon and Schuster, 1958.
Translator, *For the Time Being*, by Vercors. London, Hutchinson, 1960.
Translator, *Fernando Pessoa I-IV.* Oxford, Carcanet Press, 1971.
Translator, *Selected Poems*, by Fernando Pessoa. London, Penguin, 1974.
Translator, *Camões: Some Poems.* London, Menard Press, 1976.
Translator, with Mary Ann Caws, *Poems of René Char.* Princeton, New Jersey, Princeton University Press, 1976.

Many other translations published.

Jonathan Griffin comments:

If I write true poems, I learned it from Arthur Schnabel. I first met him in (I think) 1931. I was not a good enough pianist to be a pupil of his: he read my thoughts and invited me to his master classes as a listener. What he taught, by speech and example, was to find how the great music is made and what it says, combining truthfulness and passion. So he lit every art.

I still waited about 16 years – did not have enough to say. I wanted to include and go beyond politics. The idea of *The Hidden King* came as my liberation. The questions which most people desperately want answered have no evident answer: if there is a truth about these questions, a play may take us nearer to it through clashes between imaginary living people. A similar way may be to bring together poems that interact.

Every true poem, however light, is committed; yet a distinction between politically committed and pure poems has been found helpful. I am impelled to write poems of both kinds, and it seems to me good, when publishing, to mix them.

Though love poetry has a big part in *The Hidden King*, I have written hardly any love poems. The things lovers say to each other are mostly trite, discoveries to them: to make beautiful poems of such words was customary, but by now they have been that-much-more "done to death." Poems to a girl were a part of courtship, now young men and girls hurry to the point. The great love poems of recent times have tended (Williams, "O asphodel ..."; George Oppen, "Anniversary Poem"; Basil Bunting, *Briggflatts*; Peter Whigham, *The Ingathering of Love*) to be by older men about a remembered love or a love which has endured until the parting by natural death seems near.

Details of my own life are rather rare in my poems: I live it with zest but am short on the feeling that whatever has happened to me must interest other people. Also, privacy is a precious freedom – more threatened, in some places, than freedom of speech. Yet my poems are mine and passionate –

my pure joys yes
hardly won barely held
faith yes not sins and glosses ...
In my art I evade my evasions
I go away and rise above myself

Ambition: to sing truth. One must keep faith with doubt and, if a grand poem which is honest comes, dare it.

I am driven to write about my neighbour rather than myself, my neighbour in the future as well as now. As I grow older I become more firmly a modern poet: forward-looking. To waste life on feelings of guilt about old wrongs is absurd and a parasitic indulgence, since our guilt about the present is to be looked at, and lessened. But the injuries being done to our successors and to Earth are even greater – their (if possible) reversal more urgent. (One instance: the continuing crime in Brazil, against the rain forests and their soil, is Hitlerian, and international corporations are in it.) Shame makes me write love poems to Earth and poems of solicitude for wronged posterity.

* * *

The card catalogue of the New York Public Library assumes that there are three Jonathan Griffins: the English poet, the 1930's journalist and expert on military affairs, and the translator of a shelf-full of books from seven European languages. To these we might add the "would-be" pianist who studied with Schnabel in Berlin in the early 1930's, the director of BBC European Intelligence during World War II, the diplomat in Paris, the screenwriter in Rome, the playwright featured at the Edinburgh Festival in 1957. But amidst this flock of public Griffins, the poet – the one whose work will last – has scarcely been visible. The poems rarely appear in magazines; the later books are published by the smallest of small presses. Other than a few short reviews, there has been no critical attention. One poem was anthologized once; no survey of contemporary writing has hitherto mentioned his name. He is, in short, one of Britain's secret treasures, perhaps the finest unknown poet in our language today.

The voice is unique, and even at first glance a Griffin poem is unmistakable: titles which seem to come from nowhere, catching the reader off-guard ("You May Come Out"; "Ear to House –"; "3 Angels in Supernova"; "Into the Straight"; "At the Crucifixion of One's Heirs"; "The World Is Bugged"); rhymes that appear and disappear; neologisms (*breathprint*, *terracide*, *gravechill*, *brainstone*); rhythms like shattering glass; breath-pauses presented on the page through a system of line indentation he has apparently invented. The music can be as dense as the later Bunting; the language as personal as that of David Jones (though unlike Jones, Griffin never displays his erudition – the poems are entirely without literary reference). "The syntax," George Oppen has commented, "moves of its own force, moves in the force of the world, it restores light and space to poetry. It is what the poetry of England has lacked for – how long?"

He was first published in his (and the century's) fifties, and the work contains none of the indulgences of younger poets. There is wit but never cleverness, no fanciful speculation, no anecdote, few occasional pieces and – other than some recent meditations on death – no autobiography, no confession. The "I" of the poem, when it appears, is linked only to verbs of thought, declaration or perception. Griffin's nuclear words are *man*, *God*, *music*, *pride*, *humility*. There is always the sense that the poet has been impelled to speech.

This may be the first poetry to contemplate seriously the new vision of earth given us by the lunar missions. It is a poetry of planetary consciousness, but without the occultism and nostalgia for a Golden Age that has recently characterized more popular writing. Accordingly, given the times, the vision is double; the poet's response both ecstasy and rage. The intense lyrics in celebration of natural beauty – some of the loveliest in the language – are almost eclipsed by the bleak and apocalyptic meditations. Griffin is one of the few poets today who is confronting, in the poem, this earth of pesticide, radiation, holocaust, overpopulation, deforestation, chemical waste – the way we live now, in the first age to devastate the future. His is a voice at world's end: "We need no prophets We know what is coming/but can we live with it?"

Although the poems continue the English spiritual tradition (and indeed Griffin seems closer to Vaughan, Herbert and Traherne, Hopkins and Dixon, than to any poet of this century) the God of organized religion never enters these contemplations. Griffin's God is idiosyncratic and complex: a divine force which is either destructive or does not exist; a God that is the Goddess, planet earth; a God that "is men making music." One of his darkest lines simply states: "Entropy is God."

In the absence of a creator God, the poetry becomes spiritual in the broadest sense: the spirit of incantation, incantation meaning music, poetry, prayer ("I believe in prayer not in God"). In a world where "we voted with our feet a deadness to live in," Griffin's prayer is a grim one: "for/Earth to be saved from Man." He writes: "I believe in man but not much."

2000 years ago, Wei Hung stated: "The music of an age on the verge of ruin is mournful and thoughtful." Griffin's music is both and, yet, given his vision, strangely ecstatic. For Jonathan Griffin, the "fact of music" – that it is there, that we are capable of making it – may be, in the end, all that matters:

> Is it too late? Before it is too late
> remember the great music. Because small
> mammals dreamed it, because it is at all,
> preserve the world, continue Man. Let great
> work, by the few unlikely, inseminate
> silence – the private silences, the All
> Silence – with new music: to the still, small
> tune of Man the last waste reverberate.

—Eliot Weinberger

GRIFFITHS, Bryn(lyn David). Welsh. Born in Swansea, West Glamorgan. Left school at age 14; attended Coleg Harlech, Merioneth, 1961–62. Served in the Merchant Navy for 7 years. Free-lance writer. Lives in Wales and Western Australia. Address: c/o J. M. Dent and Sons Ltd., Aldine House, 26 Albemarle Street, London W1X 4QY, England.

PUBLICATIONS

Verse

The Mask of Pity. Llandybie, Dyfed, Christopher Davies, 1966.
The Stones Remember. London, Dent, 1967.
Scars. London, Dent, 1969.
At the Airport. Frensham, Surrey, Sceptre Press, 1971.
The Survivors. London, Dent, 1971.
Beasthoods: Poems. London, Turret, 1972.
Starboard Green. Blackwood, Monmouthshire, Imble, 1973.
The Dark Convoys: Sea Poems. Solihull, Warwickshire, Aquila, 1974.

Recording: *The Stones Remember*, with Bryan Walters, Argo, 1974.

Plays

Radio Plays: *The Sailor*, 1967; *The Dream of Arthur*, 1968.

Other

Editor, *Welsh Voices: An Anthology of New Poetry from Wales.* London, Dent, 1967.

Bryn Griffiths comments:

I am primarily concerned with the present of man and his future, and particularly the symbiotic relationship of mankind with other life on this planet. I also draw on my Welsh background for themes – sources from Celtic myth and history – and am trying, slowly, to hammer out, through syllabic structures of words, a personal poetic vision of our world.

* * *

After a somewhat mixed experience as a welder, painter, labourer, seaman and car-tester, Bryn Griffiths started his writing career at a time when, partially as a result of the activities of the "pop" poets, the general public was being persuaded to take an increasing interest in poetry readings – an interest which Griffiths has subsequently done a good deal to encourage and sustain. As his poetry is pithy, down-to-earth, and direct in impact, it is hardly surprising that, from the beginning, it has had a great appeal for listeners, as well as readers. In fact, his earliest work seems to reflect both the strength and weakness of the poet whose platform performance is almost equal to his technical skill – the ability to communicate a rich variety of thought and feelings to a wide audience, combined with an occasional tendency to content himself with superficial impressions.

With the publication of his second volume, *The Stones Remember*, it became apparent that Griffiths was undergoing a period of rapid development and exploring his own experience at great depth. He has always been preoccupied with the landscape, people and traditions of his native Wales, but with this volume, and *Scars*, which followed two years later, he produced clear evidence of having found an individual voice. *The Survivors* is largely concerned with his experiences on two trips to Australia, but even in that vast continent, impressed as he is by the strange grandeur of his new environment, he looks back to his native country: "I take you with me, Wales, wherever I go."

—Howard Sergeant

GRIGSON, Geoffrey (Edward Harvey). English. Born in Pelynt, Cornwall, 2 March 1905. Educated at St. Edmund Hall, Oxford. Married 1) Frances Galt (died, 1937), one daughter; 2) Berta Kunert (marriage dissolved), one son and one daughter; 3) Jane McIntyre, one daughter. Formerly, Staff Member, *Yorkshire Post*, Leeds, and Literary Editor, *Morning Post*, and BBC, London. Founding Editor, *New Verse*, London, 1933–39. Recipient: Duff Cooper Memorial Prize, 1971; Oscar Blumenthal Prize (*Poetry*, Chicago), 1971. Agent: David Higham Associates Ltd., 5–8 Lower John Street, London W1R 4HA. Address: Broad Town Farm, Broad Town, Swindon, Wiltshire, England.

PUBLICATIONS

Verse

Several Observations: Thirty Five Poems. London, Cresset Press, 1939.
Under the Cliff and Other Poems. London, Routledge, 1943.
The Isles of Scilly and Other Poems. London, Routledge, 1946.
Legenda Suecana: Twenty-Odd Poems. Privately printed, 1953.
The Collected Poems of Geoffrey Grigson 1924–1962. London, Phoenix House, 1963.
A Skull in Salop and Other Poems. London, Macmillan, and Chester Springs, Pennsylvania, Dufour, 1967.
Ingestion of Ice-Cream and Other Poems. London, Macmillan, 1969.
Discoveries of Bones and Stones. London, Macmillan, 1971.
Penguin Modern Poets 23, with Edwin Muir and Adrian Stokes. London, Penguin, 1973.
Sad Grave of an Imperial Mongoose. London, Macmillan, 1973.
The First Folio. London, Poem-of-the-Month Club, 1973.
Angles and Circles and Other Poems. London, Gollancz, 1974.
The Fiesta and Other Poems. London, Secker and Warburg, 1978.

Other

Henry Moore. London, Penguin, 1943.
Wild Flowers in Britain. London, Collins, and New York, Hastings House, 1944.
Samuel Palmer: The Visionary Years. London, Kegan Paul, 1947.
The Harp of Aeolus and Other Essays on Art, Literature, and Nature. London, Routledge, 1948.
An English Farmhouse and Its Neighbourhood. London, Parrish, 1948.
The Scilly Isles. London, Elek, 1948; revised edition, London, Duckworth, 1977.
Places of the Mind. London, Routledge, 1949.
The Crest on the Silver: An Autobiography. London, Cresset Press, 1950.
Flowers of the Meadow. London, Penguin, 1950.
Wessex. London, Collins, 1951.

A Master of Our Time: A Study of Wyndham Lewis. London, Methuen, 1951; New York, Gordon Press, 1952.
Essays from the Air (broadcasts). London, Routledge, 1951.
West Country. London, Collins, 1951.
Gardenage; or, The Plants of Ninhursaga. London, Routledge, 1952.
The Female Form in Painting, with Jean Cassou. London, Thames and Hudson, and New York, Harcourt Brace, 1953.
Freedom of the Parish. London, Phoenix House, 1954.
Gerard Manley Hopkins. London, Longman, 1955; revised edition, 1962.
The Englishman's Flora. London, Phoenix House, 1955.
English Drawing from Samuel Cooper to Gwen John. London, Thames and Hudson, 1955.
The Shell Guide to Flowers of the Countryside [*Trees and Shrubs*, *Wild Life*]. London, Phoenix House, 3 vols., 1955–59; in *The Shell Nature Book*, 1964.
Corot. New York, Metropolitan Museum, 1956.
Painted Caves. London, Phoenix House, 1957.
England. London, Thames and Hudson, 1957; New York, Studio, 1958.
Fossils, Insects, and Reptiles. London, Phoenix House, 1957; in *The Shell Nature Book*, 1964.
Art Treasures of the British Museum. London, Thames and Hudson, and New York, Abrams, 1957.
The Wiltshire Book. London, Thames and Hudson, 1957.
The Three Kings. Bedford, Gordon Fraser, 1958.
English Villages in Colour. London, Batsford, 1958.
Looking and Finding and Collecting and Reading and Investigating and Much Else (juvenile). London, Phoenix House, 1958; revised edition, London, Baker, 1970.
A Herbal of All Sorts. London, Phoenix House, and New York, Macmillan, 1959.
English Excursions. London, Country Life, 1960.
Samuel Palmer's Valley of Vision. London, Phoenix House, 1960.
Christopher Smart. London, Longman, 1961.
The Shell Country Book. London, Phoenix House, 1962.
The Shell Book of Roads. London, Ebury Press, 1964.
Shapes and Stories: A Book about Pictures (juvenile), with Jane Grigson. London, Baker, and New York, Vanguard Press, 1964.
The Shell Nature Book. London, Phoenix House, and New York, Basic Books, 1964.
The Shell Country Alphabet. London, Joseph, 1966.
Shapes and Adventures (juvenile), with Jane Grigson. London, Marshbank, 1967; as *More Shapes and Stories: A Book about Pictures*, New York, Vanguard Press, 1967.
Shapes and People: A Book about Pictures (juvenile). London, Baker, and New York, Vanguard Press, 1969.
Poems and Poets. London, Macmillan, and Chester Springs, Pennsylvania, Dufour, 1969.
Notes from an Odd Country. London, Macmillan, 1970.
Shapes and Creatures (juvenile). London, Black, 1973.
The Contrary View: Glimpses of Fudge and Gold. London, Macmillan, and Totowa, New Jersey, Rowman and Littlefield, 1974.
A Dictionary of English Plant Names and Some Products of Plants. London, Allen Lane, 1974.
Britain Observed: The Landscape Through Artists' Eyes. London, Phaidon, 1975.
The Goddess of Love: The Birth, Triumph, Death, and Return of Aphrodite. London, Constable, 1976; New York, Stein and Day, 1977.

Editor, with others, *The Year's Poetry.* London, Lane, 1934.
Editor, *The Arts Today.* London, Lane, 1935.
Editor, with Denys Kilham Roberts, *The Year's Poetry 1937–38.* London, Lane, 1938.

Editor, *New Verse: An Anthology.* London, Faber, 1939.
Editor, *The Journals of George Sturt.* London, Cresset Press, 1941.
Editor, *The Romantics: An Anthology.* London, Routledge, 1942; Cleveland, World, 1962.
Editor, *Visionary Poems and Passages; or, The Poet's Eye.* London, Muller, 1944.
Editor, *The Mint: A Miscellany of Literature, Art, and Criticism.* London, Routledge, 2 vols., 1946–48.
Editor, *Before the Romantics: An Anthology of the Enlightenment.* London, Routledge, 1946.
Editor, *Poems of John Clare's Madness.* London, Routledge, 1949.
Editor, *Poetry of the Present: An Anthology of the Thirties and After.* London, Phoenix House, 1949.
Editor, *Selected Poems of William Barnes 1800–1866.* London, Routledge, and Cambridge, Massachusetts, Harvard University Press, 1950.
Editor, *Selected Poems*, by John Clare. London, Routledge, 1950.
Editor, *Selected Poems*, by John Dryden. London, Grey Walls Press, 1950.
Editor, *Poems*, by George Crabbe. London, Grey Walls Press, 1950.
Editor, *The Victorians: An Anthology.* London, Routledge, 1950.
Editor, *Thornton's Temple of Flora*, by Robert John Thornton. London, Collins, 1951.
Editor, *Poems*, by Samuel Taylor Coleridge. London, Grey Walls Press, 1951.
Editor, *About Britain* series. London, Collins, 13 vols., 1951.
Editor, with Charles Harvard Gibbs-Smith, *People, Places and Things.* London, Grosvenor Press, and New York, Hawthorn Press, 4 vols., 1954.
Editor, *The Three Kings: A Christmas Book of Carols, Poems, and Pieces.* Bedford, Gordon Fraser, 1958.
Editor, *Country Poems.* London, Hulton, 1959.
Editor, *The Cherry Tree: A Collection of Poems* (juvenile). London, Phoenix House, and New York, Vanguard Press, 1959.
Editor, *Poets in Their Pride* (juvenile). London, Phoenix House, 1962; New York, Basic Books, 1964.
Editor, *The Concise Encyclopaedia of Modern World Literature.* London, Hutchinson, and New York, Hawthorn Books, 1963; revised edition, Hutchinson, 1970; Hawthorn Books, 1971.
Editor, *O Rare Mankind! A Short Collection of Great Prose* (juvenile). London, Phoenix House, 1963.
Editor, *Poems*, by Walter Savage Landor. London, Centaur Press, 1964; Carbondale, Southern Illinois University Press, 1965.
Editor, *The English Year: From Diaries and Letters.* London, Oxford University Press, 1967.
Editor, *A Choice of William Morris's Verse.* London, Faber, 1969.
Editor, *A Choice of Thomas Hardy's Poems.* London, Macmillan, 1969.
Editor, *A Choice of Robert Southey's Verse.* London, Faber, 1970.
Editor, *Thirty-Eight Poems*, by Pennethorne Hughes. London, Baker, 1970.
Editor, *Rainbows, Fleas, and Flowers* (juvenile). London, Baker, 1971; New York, Vanguard Press, 1974.
Editor, *Unrespectable Verse.* London, Allen Lane, 1971.
Editor, *The Faber Book of Popular Verse.* London, Faber, 1971; as *Gambit Book of Popular Verse*, Boston, Gambit, 1971.
Editor, *The Faber Book of Love Poems.* London, Faber, 1973.
Editor, *Cotton.* London, Penguin, 1974.
Editor, *The Penguin Book of Ballads.* London, Penguin, 1975.

Manuscript Collections: British Museum, London; Birmingham University Library.

Critical Study: in *Times Literary Supplement* (London), 31 July 1969.

Geoffrey Grigson comments:

I deduce from my poems that I write by this conviction: graces enter and exist in living; they start up, vanish, and are seen again in glimpses. It is sentimental treason to suppose that we can be anaesthetized or satisfied by these graces, but the grand treason, realizing the constancy of the bad and the worst, is not as well to admit and celebrate and be thankful for these consolatory graces, or viaticum.

* * *

Geoffrey Grigson is one of the most interesting of the so-called "Auden generation" of English poets who began writing in the 1930's; but his merits as a poet have always been overshadowed by his activities as an entrepreneur of letters. For several years in the thirties Grigson was editor of the influential magazine *New Verse*, and throughout his life he has been an active and polemical critic. His early poetry was marked by its precise, imagistic observations of the contemporary scene; Grigson was a believer in the brief snapshot of reality, presented without elaboration or comment, though the political preoccupations so evident in the poetry of Auden or Spender were often implicitly present in his verse. These early poems were redeemed from flatness by Grigson's delicate and very personal sense of rhythm. They can still be read with pleasure, although at the same time they are very much of their period, when poets were following up Eliot's fascination with urban landscape, and were actively interested in sociological enquiry: the 1930's movement called Mass Observation echoes the title of Grigson's book of poems *Several Observations*.

His later poetry, though still anchored to the discipline of exact description, is less austere and more overtly emotional. In addition to his original discipleship of Auden and the Imagists, Grigson developed a great admiration for John Clare, and much of his description of natural objects recalls the precise botanical observations of Ruskin or Hopkins. Although Grigson remains what he has always been, a writer of short poems, there are pieces in his *Collected Poems* that show he has occasionally been more ambitious, like the short verse play "The Islanders," and a rather impressive sequence of love poems called "Legenda." Yet a brief poem like "Elms under Cloud" remains most typical of Grigson's art:

Elms, old-men with thinned-out hair,
And mouths down-turned, express
The oldness of the English scene:

And up the hill a pale road reaches
To a huge paleness browned with scattered,
Irritated cloud....

A poem in Grigson's latest collection, *The Fiesta*, provides a sad, ironic companion piece, "Driving Through Dead Elms," a response to the ravages of elm disease in the English countryside. *The Fiesta* is characteristic Grigson in its imagistic observations, and sour, sometimes cryptic epigrams, though the passions and disillusionments of a poet in his seventies bring an unsettling resonance to Grigson's small, precise notations of experience.

—Bernard Bergonzi

GRUBB, Frederick (Crichton-Stuart). British. Born near Salisbury, Wiltshire, 18 June 1930. Educated at Trinity College, Cambridge, M.A. 1960; London University, Ph.D.

Recipient: Arts Council bursary, 1966. Address: 243 Haverstock Hill, London N.W.3, England.

PUBLICATIONS

Verse

Title Deeds and Other Poems. London, Longman, 1961.
September Sun. Frensham, Surrey, Sceptre Press, 1969.
Frog. Rushden, Northamptonshire, Sceptre Press, 1972.

Other

A Vision of Reality: A Study of Liberalism in Twentieth Century Verse. London, Chatto and Windus, and New York, Barnes and Noble, 1965.

Frederick Grubb comments:

Descendant of Lord Bute who was satirised by Charles Churchill and whose inept policies did Britain the service of losing the American colonies. Never "educated" but played pub darts at a "public" school, attended Trinity College, Cambridge (M.A.), has Ph.D., London, for research on "Relation Between Feeling and Values in T. S. Eliot," and lives by work and the dole.

Socialist (i.e. fights capitalism), enjoys (red) wine if cheap, travels (frugally) in remote areas of Latin countries, prefers a pub to a club and a workers caff to a restaurant and a bedsitter to a flat. Unlikely to be invited to a Foyles Literary Lunch: he expropriated the expropriators.

Agrees with T. S. Eliot that "art is not a career, it's a mug's game." Is not a member of any organization or committee, neither owns, attends, hears nor sees telly, radio, discs, cinema, theatre, concerts, galleries, newspapers, junkets, house, or car, dislikes all ornaments, and believes that art is an individual activity with (one hopes) social meaning and culture is individuals communicating to (one hopes) individuals. A revival of satire of the Augustan type is needful.

Prefers Russian literature, British poetry to Byron, the best 1930's work to current writing. Loathes Hardy, but likes Larkin, Nicholson, Hughes, Middleton, Hamburger, Martin Bell, and thirty others, often Scots or Welsh. His poems were fussy and elaborate, but does not agree with W. H. Auden that poems can be rewritten – or withdrawn. Now aims at clarity, austerity, moments of vividness and force in resolutely structured or free designs with unity of thought-form and feeling-pattern.

* * *

The poetry of Frederick Grubb is made up of maddening starts and stops. In his output there is scarcely one complete poem. Grubb's erudition has been proverbial for some years now, and he was advocating Yeats, Rilke, Valéry and Péguy as long ago as 1953 when he was still an undergraduate. Yet all his study of literature has not served to show him how to shape a line or frame an image as adeptly as the newcomer who went down last year.

Perhaps the answer to this puzzle is that Grubb is grappling with concerns more difficult than the deftness of lines or the immediate appeal of imagery. There is a dichotomy in the author of *A Vision of Reality*, and it is a curiously post-Romantic one. As an artist and critic of literature Grubb seems to attach himself to works which are self-substantive and finely wrought; the poems of Valéry, Rilke and Yeats, in fact. But as a socialist and social critic he seeks to subjoin such grecian urns to the soiled crockery of humanity as a means of making it whole. In other words, he has trouble in relating his aesthetic and political concerns.

This dilemma is not new. It accounts for the vagueness of Shelley, the triviality of Wilde, the evasiveness of Auden. Other practitioners have compounded their honour with their safety and set politics at a considerable remove from art. Yet *A Vision of Reality* is a critical book that only a poet could have written, and the same is true of Grubb's poetry.

If we read it, we read it as fragments. Thus:

Landscape already tinged with regret
How shall we keep you, externally passing away
Clouds drift into clouds, trees to another forest
Caves into cathedrals, rivers into seas ...
—from "The Imperfect Day"

Anyone could walk in. The gates creaking.
The parterre mature if not overblown.
The orangery reeks ...
—from "The Hall of Mirrors in the Evening"

The ice that froze his uncle's ambition
Thawed, burned in him: his Moscow was the throne ...
—from "Napoleon III"

Uncommon people? Yes, but commonness
Is not so rare you cannot breed from it ...
—from "Talented Families"

Lascaux was closed, the taint of breath
– First since the last, that dried the paint –
Mildewed the pigments ...
—from "Cave"

Under drizzle,
Among taffic, dominated by constructions
The spirit
Is at a solemn music but not for long ...
—from "A Short View of Music"

Two moving dots, slow, sure, dutiful, go
Along the row of elms, to pealing bells.
An ageing couple
My parents worship in the church below ...
—from "Elegy"

The poetry does not last as long as the prose sense of these pieces, the prose sense seldom as long as the external form. But among much that is tortuous, certain lines, like the ones quoted, stand out clear. They survive, wrenched out of context, because the context does little to help them.

It would appear that this student of mythopoeic poetry is in search of a myth for himself. He may disturb the conventional reader by his refusal to take an easy way out of his intellectual labyrinth. But it must be said that the tortuosities of Frederick Grubb carry more conviction than the dexterity of many rivals who on the surface seem more accomplished.

—Philip Hobsbaum

GRUFFYDD, Peter. British. Born in Liverpool, Lancashire, 12 April 1935. Educated at University College of North Wales, Bangor, 1957–60, B.A. (honours) in English 1960. Served in the British Army, 1955–57. Lecturer in Liberal Studies, Rochdale College of Art, Lancashire, 1965–67; taught English, Volkhochschule, Munich, 1970–72. Free-lance writer, translator, and actor. Recipient: Gregory Award, 1963; Welsh Arts Council award, 1968; Arts Council of Great Britain award, 1972. Address: Grosvenor Hotel, Llanberis, Carnarvonshire, North Wales.

PUBLICATIONS

Verse

Triad: Thirty-Three Poems, with Harri Webb and Meic Stephens. Merthyr Tydfil, Glamorganshire, Triskel Press, 1963.
The Shivering Seed. London, Chatto and Windus, and Middletown, Connecticut, Wesleyan University Press, 1972.

Play

Radio Play: *The Cuckoo*, 1968.

Peter Gruffydd comments:

I am, and have always felt myself to be, a lone wolf – with no labels, manifestos, or luggage other than words.

My poems involve cyclic themes of life, birth, death, love, individuals in everyday or esoteric "environments."

It seems to me that any modern poet has the whole scope of techniques and stylistic devices, the poet's tool bag, in English, from Chaucer to now, at his fingertips – should he either need or care to use them. The field is completely open.

What I try to achieve in poetry is truth to the object and the image in "true" words.

No modern poet expects to live by selling his work, but the standard of payment (in the few that do pay) is unspeakably low in British periodicals. *C'est la vie!*

* * *

Many of Peter Gruffydd's poems are about Wales, particularly in his last collection, *The Shivering Seed.* Some are evocations of place, the accumulation of sharp details of a scene where he employs vivid images: "the dog which, deaf,/Maps out again its world of odours"; "this fire-flicked/Brasswink and elbow-kept room"; "the sour steel sky." Other Welsh poems are "exposures" of the more corrupt, confused and unintelligent of his compatriots, and these rather bitter indictments have been criticised as stale and pompous – best left to other writers with a closer, wittier knowledge of the much-battered targets flayed by Gruffydd. But he is not without a sense of irony (unusual in Celtic practitioners), and is occasionally very funny at the expense of the narrower specimen of Welshman.

His main talent consists in describing objects and landscape, rather than in forming significant conclusions about them. Often he stretches his material too thinly over too many lines, being consciously "poetic" while evading the necessity of asking himself what a particular experience may signify.

Gruffydd is effective as a sensitive observer of childhood, recording a sense of awe in the face of nature and capturing a child's first shock of wonder or apprehension. Though at his best his language has a tautness, richness and density, it is possible to detect influences – such as, inevitably, Dylan Thomas's – on Gruffydd's work which have not yet been completely assimilated into his own, original voice. There is much, however, in his work that is impressive, promising a distinctive accomplishment in the future.

—John Tripp

GUEST, Barbara. American. Born in Wilmington, North Carolina, 6 September 1920. Educated at the University of California, Berkeley, A.B. 1941. Married 1) Lord Haden-Guest in 1948 (divorced, 1954); 2) Trumbull Higgins in 1954; two children. Editorial Associate, *Art News*, New York, 1951–54. Recipient: Yaddo Fellowship, 1958; Longview Foundation Award, 1960. Address: 1148 Fifth Avenue, New York, New York 10028, U.S.A.

PUBLICATIONS

Verse

The Location of Things. New York, Tibor de Nagy, 1960.
Poems: The Location of Things, Archaics, The Open Skies. New York, Doubleday, 1962.
The Blue Stairs. New York, Corinth, 1968.
I Ching: Poems and Lithographs, with Sheila Isham. Paris, Mourlot, 1969.
Moscow Mansions. New York, Viking Press, 1973.
The Countess from Minneapolis. Providence, Rhode Island, Burning Deck, 1976.
The Turler Losses. Montreal, Mansfield, 1979.

Plays

The Ladies Choice (produced New York, 1953).
The Office (produced New York, 1963).
Port (produced New York, 1965).

Novel

Seeking Air. Santa Barbara, California, Black Sparrow Press, 1978.

Other

Robert Goodnough, with B. H. Friedmann. Paris, G. Fall, 1962.

Manuscript Collections: University of Kentucky, Lexington; Lockwood Memorial Library, State University of New York, Buffalo.

* * *

The poems of Barbara Guest ignore almost every convention in metrics in English and American poetry – past and present; this fact can create difficulties for the reader and leaves one searching for analogies in painting, the art which she has been closely identified with as editor and commentator, in order to describe her work. Paintings are her subject in several poems, their effect reminiscent of the full bright canvasses of Matisse, without frames. In "Passage," for John Coltrane, she compares the two arts directly:

Words
  after all
are syllables *just*
and you put them
    in their place
    notes
    sounds
a painter using his stroke ...
slashed as it was with cólor
  called "being"
  or even "it"

A typical poem by Barbara Guest is a pastiche of colors, shapes, natural setting in which the objects create the mood. She constantly explores problems in aesthetics, how beauty makes itself felt, enjoying "the transformed colors and shapes that the imagination makes possible," as William Van O'Connor once said of Wallace Stevens' work. Her poems are a search for a definable form, as if she were discovering the shape of things for the first time. She tells the painter Robert Motherwell, for example, in "All Elegies Are Black and White": "(How wise you are to understand/the use of orange with blue./'Never without the other.')" For all their distinctive charm, however, a reader may wonder how concretely the poems relate to this world, this time, and how as reader, viewer, audience, one can participate in the poet's original discovery, in the poetic excitement and awe and wonder that prompted her highly imaginative and impressionistic response. Many of the poems lack moral weight, a social or ethical grounding.

Guest writes as if the Imagist movement began yesterday, saying "no ideas but in things," moving persistently toward some revelation no one else has discovered. At its best, her poetry brings together the Imagist delight in objects, landscapes, and seascapes, and the uneasiness of a person attuned to suffering, anxiety, pain. At one point, she wonders "if this new reality is going to destroy me." But the dominant note, as in "Now," is one of joy and confidence in the lyrical beauty that surrounds her:

It's Autumn
It's Fall. A red cloth with
Yellow leaves is chosen. And the
Sophisticated color of mauve
Burnt orange for the touch. To affect
A change. Where the ripe dawn
Hurries a red is.

—Michael True

GUEST, Harry (Henry Bayly Guest). British. Born in Penarth, Glamorganshire, Wales, 6 October 1932. Educated at Malvern College, Worcestershire, 1946–50; Trinity Hall, Cambridge, 1951–54, B.A. in modern languages 1954; the Sorbonne, Paris, 1954–55, D.E.S. 1955 (thesis on Mallarmé). Married Lynn Guest in 1963; one daughter and one son. Assistant Master, Felsted School, Essex, 1955–61; Head of Modern Languages Department, Lancing College, Sussex, 1961–66; Assistant Lecturer, Yokohama National University, Japan, 1966–72. Since 1972, Head of French Department, Exeter School. Address: 1 Alexandra Terrace, Exeter, Devon EX4 6SY, England.

PUBLICATIONS

Verse

Private View. London, Outposts, 1962.
A Different Darkness. London, Outposts, 1964.
Arrangements. London, Anvil Press Poetry 1968.
The Cutting-Room. London, Anvil Press Poetry, 1970.
Penguin Modern Poets 16, with Jack Beeching and Matthew Mead. London, Penguin, 1970.
The Place. Rushden, Northamptonshire, Sceptre Press, 1971.
Text and Fragment, The Inheritance, Miniatures. Southampton, Hampshire, Earth Ship 13, 1972.
The Achievements of Memory. Rushden, Northamptonshire, Sceptre Press, 1974.
The Enchanted Acres. Knotting, Bedfordshire, Sceptre Press, 1975.
Mountain Journal. Sheffield, Rivelin Press, 1975.
A House Against the Night. London, Anvil Press Poetry, 1976.
English Poems. London, Words Press, 1976.
Two Poems. Knotting, Bedfordshire, Sceptre Press, 1977.
The Hidden Change. Higham Ferrers, Northamptonshire, Greylag Press, 1978.
Zeami in Exile. Knotting, Bedfordshire, Sceptre Press, 1978.

Plays

The Inheritance (broadcast, 1973). Included in *Text and Fragment, The Inheritance, Miniatures*, 1972.

Radio Plays: *Beware of Pity*, translation of a play by Stefan Zweig, 1962; *Trial of Strength*, translation of a play by G. A. Golfar, 1964; *The Inheritance*, 1973; *The Emperor of Outer Space*, 1976.

Novel

Days. London, Anvil Press Poetry, 1978.

Other

Another Island Country (essays). Tokyo, Eikôsha, 1970.

Editor and Translator, with Lynn Guest and Kajima Shozo, *Post-War Japanese Poetry.* London, Penguin, 1972.

Harry Guest comments:

(1970) Lyrical analysis of personal relationships, bisexual love, landscapes, etc. Certain amount of intellectual demand: European rather than transatlantic: syllabics or stress-length lines: high premium on musicality.

I admire Klee, the early Godard, Debussy's piano music.

(1974) *Private View* is a poem in XIV sections dealing with the relationships between art and reality, imagination and love. "Matsushima" (1967) examines the shadow-line crossed when death is felt in the marrow as inevitable. "Metamorphoses" (1968) uses a highly condensed, elliptical language for its "Six Poems on Related Themes." *The Place* is 15 connected meditations about a holiday on the west coast of Japan, and *Miniatures* is 36 brief poems recording a visit with the poet's daughter to a volcanic island.

The short poems in various structural forms are primarily lyrical or narrative – love-poems like "The Summers of Nowhere" or "At Shoreham"; problems of perception like "Allegories," "Autumns," or "Nocturnes for the Dead of Winter"; or of art – "The Painter ...," "Cinema."

The kind of poetry that most appeals to me has music and density, appeals to the senses as much as to the mind and spirit.

* * *

Harry Guest was first introduced to the reading public with two booklet collections in the *Outposts Modern Poets Series* – *Private View* and *A Different Darkness*. *Private View* is a series of reflective poems arising out of a visit to an art exhibition, largely concerned with the relationship between the artist and his subject, as well as the part played by the artist himself:

> If I could catch his eye, we'd bolt for the pub
> And over Guinness alternate the old crude gags
> With laments for oh the brevity of beauty,
> The change within a year of the expression on flesh,
> The slender moving to the coarse,
> Metamorphoses of the delicate.

Though he treats his theme with respect his sense of humour does not allow him to become unduly earnest.

Like much of his poetry, *Private View* makes its impact by means of skilfully manipulated images and association of ideas. In *Arrangements* the poems are divided under such headings as "Problems," "Relationships," "Criticisms," "Narratives," and "Techniques," but this classification tends to obscure his real strengths and virtues as a poet. One might remark upon his skill and note the interest he displays in the techniques of other writers, reflected in such poems as "Statement," "About Baudelaire," and "Elegy for Jean Cocteau." "Sterility and regret are the only muse," he says in one of these poems, and this would seem to be true for Harry Guest, for he writes most effectively about his regrets for lost opportunities, situations not grasped, failures of communication and response. Some critics have praised his "travel" poems, but he has a style all his own and rarely writes a simple descriptive piece. "Matsushima" and "A Bar in Lerici" demonstrate his use of the environment to effect new insights into the human situation:

> We talk of love,
> Balanced as always between the recollection –
> The afternoon spent across the bay in sunlight –
> And anticipation of the stars
> Tending to disappoint.
> Darkness
> After being born should be familiar
> And natural as the scenery of the Milky Way.

Perhaps best of all are his poems celebrating the man-woman relationship, the marital relationship in particular, on which he can be lyrical and tender without losing control over his material.

In *The Cutting Room*, written in Japan, Guest extended his range of subject and treatment, and produced his most ambitious work up to that time, the "Metamorphoses" sequence of six poems, but again the more personal references to lover, wife, and daughter show his capacity for dealing with intimate relationships. *A House Against the Night* collects the poems written between 1969 and 1973. It is perhaps most noticeable that, continuing his experiments with form and diction, Guest has adopted a much shorter line and exercises far tighter control of both diction and imagery, and, except in "Anniversary," seems deliberately to avoid the warmer aspects of human relationships. "I am a man for whom the external world exists," he said in an earlier poem, and he would appear to be exploring the external world at much greater depth than before in order to find himself and to define his own psychological limits, as in "Lacunae":

These distant images bring pain.
The tors stood out,
first greyness on the silence.
If there was laughter
the echoes carried isolation,
companionship
struck stone.

All this adds up to an unusual austerity reflected to a lesser extent in the later pamphlets.

—Howard Sergeant

GULLANS, Charles (Bennett). American. Born in Minneapolis, Minnesota, 5 May 1929. Educated at the University of Minnesota, Minneapolis, B.A. 1948, M.A. 1951; King's College, Durham (Fulbright Fellow, 1953–55); Stanford University, California (Fellow in Creative Writing, 1952), Ph.D. 1956. Taught at the University of Washington, Seattle, 1955–61. Since 1961, Member of the English Department, Associate Professor, 1965–72, and since 1972, Professor of English and Director of Creative Writing, University of California, Los Angeles. Recipient: University of California Institute of Creative Arts Fellowship, 1965. Address: 1620 Greenfield, Los Angeles, California 90025, U.S.A.

PUBLICATIONS

Verse

Moral Poems. Palo Alto, California, John Hunter Thomas, 1957.
Arrivals and Departures. Minneapolis, University of Minnesota Press, 1962.
Imperfect Correspondences. Los Angeles, Symposium Press, 1978.

Other

The Decorative Designers, 1895–1931: An Essay. Los Angeles, University of California Library, 1970.
A Bibliography of the Published Writings of J. V. Cunningham. Los Angeles, University of California Library, 1973.

Editor, *The English and Latin Poems of Sir Robert Ayton.* Edinburgh, Blackwood, 1963.
Editor, with John Espey, *A Checklist of Trade Bindings Designed by Margaret Armstrong.* Los Angeles, University of California Library, 1968.

Translator, with Franz Schneider, *Last Letters from Stalingrad.* New York, Morrow, 1962.

Manuscript Collection: University of California, Los Angeles.

Critical Study: "A Study of the Poetry of Charles Gullans" by Mary Cecile Caestecker, in *The Barat Faculty Review* (Lake Forest, Illinois), January 1966.

* * *

Published in 1962, Charles Gullans' *Arrivals and Departures* remains one of the best books of poems of our period. Volumes by other poets contain individual poems as good or better than any of Gullans'; yet few can equal *Arrivals and Departures* as a book, whole and unified in its diversity and variety. The book is divided into three sections: "Love and Landscapes," "Friends and Relations," and "Metaphysicians and Marvels." The progression is not an arbitrary grouping of poems with similar themes, as in most books of verse. One needs to read the poems in the order printed; not because they form a sequence, but because of the deliberate arrangement, each poem and each section informing the rest. The book is a sort of record or impression of a wholly civilized man: almost fragile love poems can stand with bitter satire; poems of great originality can bear the comparison one inevitably makes with his translations from Rilke, Petrarch, José-María de Heredia, and Nietzsche. It takes a man of courage and equal talent to put his own poems beside those of masters; but the poems of Gullans can bear such comparison; and the translations show another dimension of his mind, his understanding, his gift. They are part of the contents of an urbane, educated, aware mind; and that is one thing the book is about.

I cannot do justice to Gullans in this short notice. Only a close examination of his stylistic virtues, his intellectual and emotional integrity, and his poetic virtuosity could do such justice. His translation of Rilke's "The Panther" is the finest I know in English; and he boldly follows it with one of his own best poems, "First Love," a beautifully rendered piece. Other good poems include "After Analysis" and the two poems titled "Midsummer Day" and "Autumn: An Ode." His "Autumn Burial: A Meditation" is a great poem.

—James Korges

GUNN, Thom(son William). British. Born in Gravesend, Kent, 29 August 1929. Educated at University College School, London; Trinity College, Cambridge, B.A. 1953, M.A. 1958; Stanford University, California, 1954–55, 1956–58. Served in the British Army, 1948–50. Member of the English Department, University of California, Berkeley, 1958–66. Poetry Reviewer, *Yale Review*, New Haven, Connecticut, 1958–64. Since 1966, Free-lance Writer. Recipient: Levinson Prize (*Poetry*, Chicago), 1955; Maugham Award, 1959; Arts Council of Great Britain award, 1959; National Institute of Arts and Letters grant, 1964; Rockefeller award, 1966; Guggenheim Fellowship, 1971. Address: 1216 Cole Street, San Francisco, California 94117, U.S.A.

PUBLICATIONS

Verse

(*Poems*). Oxford, Fantasy Press, 1953.
Fighting Terms. Oxford, Fantasy Press, 1954; revised edition, New York, Hawk's Well Press, 1958; London, Faber, 1962.

The Sense of Movement. London, Faber, 1957; Chicago, University of Chicago Press, 1959.
My Sad Captains and Other Poems. London, Faber, and Chicago, University of Chicago Press, 1961.
Selected Poems, with Ted Hughes. London, Faber, 1962.
A Geography. Iowa City, Stone Wall Press, 1966.
Positives, photographs by Ander Gunn. London, Faber, 1966; Chicago, University of Chicago Press, 1967.
Touch. London, Faber, 1967; Chicago, University of Chicago Press, 1968.
The Garden of the Gods. Cambridge, Massachusetts, Pym Randall Press, 1968.
The Explorers. Crediton, Devon, Gilbertson, 1969.
The Fair in the Woods. Oxford, Sycamore Press, 1969.
Poems 1950–1966: A Selection. London, Faber, 1969.
Sunlight. New York, Albondocani Press, 1969.
Last Days at Teddington. London, Poem-of-the-Month Club, 1971.
Moly. London, Faber, 1971.
Corgi Modern Poets in Focus 5, with others, edited by Dannie Abse. London, Corgi, 1971.
Poem after Chaucer. New York, Albondocani Press, 1971.
Moly, and My Sad Captains. New York, Farrar Straus, 1973.
Mandrakes. London, Rainbow Press, 1973.
Songbook. New York, Albondocani Press, 1973.
To the Air. Boston, Godine, 1974.
Jack Straw's Castle. New York, F. Hallman, 1975.
Jack Straw's Castle (collection). London, Faber, and New York, Farrar Straus, 1976.
The Missed Beat. Sidcot, Somerset, Gruffyground Press, and West Burke, Vermont, Janus Press, 1976.
Games of Chance. Omaha, Abattoir, 1979.
Selected Poems 1950–1975. London, Faber, and New York, Farrar Straus, 1979.

Other

Editor, *Poetry from Cambridge 1951–52: A Selection of Verse by Members of the University.* London, Fortune Press, 1952.
Editor, with Ted Hughes, *Five American Poets.* London, Faber, 1963.
Editor, *Selected Poems of Fulke Greville.* London, Faber, and Chicago, University of Chicago Press, 1968.
Editor, *Ben Jonson.* London, Penguin, 1974.

Bibliography: *Thom Gunn: A Bibliography 1940–1978* by W. C. Jack and George Bixby, London, Bertram Rota, 1979.

Manuscript Collection: University of Maryland, College Park.

Critical Studies: by Martin Dodsworth, in *The Survival of Poetry*, London, Faber, 1970; essay by the author in *Corgi Modern Poets in Focus 5*, 1971; "The Stipulative Imagination of Thom Gunn" by John Miller, and "A Critical Performance of Thom Gunn's *Misanthropos*" by Merle E. Brown in *Iowa Review* (Iowa City), Winter 1973; "My Suburban Muse" by the author, in *Seven Modern Poets*, edited by Geoffrey Summerfield, London, Penguin, 1974; Introduction by the author to *Thom Gunn: A Bibliography*, 1979.

* * *

In one of his early poems, Thom Gunn observes, famously, that Elvis Presley "turns revolt into a style." Elaborating this in the poem's final stanza, Gunn provides a peg on which we can, if we like, hang the immense variety of his own work:

Whether he poses or is real, no cat
Bothers to say: the pose held is a stance,
Which, generation of the very chance
It wars on, may be posture for combat.

A "pose" – apparently superficial, a matter, possibly, of advertising, of presenting the self for sale – solidifies into a "stance," a relation between the self and the world that has a more achieved and focused integrity; and this, as a "posture for combat," may embrace a political or philosophical relation.

The title of Thom Gunn's fifth collection, *Moly*, takes its name from the herb which Hermes offered Ulysses to keep him proof against transformation into one of Circe's pigs. And, while Gunn has not, of course, transformed himself into a pig, he has certainly never protected himself against the processes of metamorphosis. Geographically, he has moved from England to America, more specifically from 1950's Cambridge to 1960's San Francisco; metrically, he has moved from highly disciplined traditional forms, through syllabics to a very loose kind of free form; and thematically, he has made use of such widely varied influences as French existentialist thought and American lysergic acid. And, even emotionally and sexually, Gunn has moved from poems overtly addressed to women to openly frank homosexual poems. He is, altogether, a poet difficult to get clear and difficult to get whole.

There is also the further difficulty that, if one appreciates the strenuous energy under control, the formal stanzaic grandeur of poems like "On the Move" or "In Santa Maria del Popolo," it is difficult not to feel that the later work is often sentimental or downright silly. (The latter criticism seems almost mild against the poem, "Listening to Jefferson Airplane," which reads, in its entirety, "The music comes and goes on the wind,/Comes and goes on the brain.") But one can be generous even about these poems, perhaps, if one sees Gunn's whole enterprise as a series of "poses" creating a "stance" of combative self-definition in relation to society and to the world. The poems' "posturing" may then be seen as a kind of moral assertion. Gunn's ultimate "carnal knowledge," in the well-known poem of that title, is that "Even in bed I pose"; and knowledge – of oneself, as well as of others – is an infinitely recessive series ("You know I know you know I know you know I know," contained only by its pentameter bounds) in which one *is* what one presents oneself as. Gunn's poems are, as he has himself described some of them, "a debate between the passion for definition and the passion for flow."

Some of his most recent poems are an explicit examination of these processes and passions. The sequence "The Geysers," for instance, situates Gunn in a state between sleep and waking, between water and air, in the bath house of the geysers in Sonoma County, California. The poem mimics the processes occurring on the frontiers of consciousness:

I am part of all
          hands take
                    hands tear and twine

I yielded
     oh, the yield
               what have I slept?
my blood is yours the hands that take accept ...

torn from the self
          in which I breathed and trod
I am

     I am raw meat

          I am a god

Some of Gunn's best effects are achieved, as they are here, when language, still disciplined and restrained, spreads and spills to accommodate the phases of "definition and flow." In the act of love and in sleep these processes are at their most immediate: one is both defined in one's own being, and involved in the being of others. The act of love and the moment of sleep are returned to again and again in Thom Gunn's work, and they come together at the conclusion of the marvellous poem "Touch":

> What is more, the place is
> not found but seeps
> from our touch in
> continuous creation, dark
> enclosing cocoon round
> ourselves alone, dark
> wide realm where we
> walk with everyone.

—Neil Corcoran

GUSTAFSON, Ralph (Barker). Canadian. Born in Lime Ridge, Quebec, 16 August 1909. Educated at Bishop's University, Lennoxville, Quebec, B.A. 1929, M.A. 1930; Oxford University, B.A. 1933. Married Elisabeth Renninger in 1958. Taught at Bishop's College School, 1930, and St. Alban's School, Brockville, Ontario, 1934. Worked for the British Information Services, 1942–46. Since 1960, Music Critic, Canadian Broadcasting Corporation. Since 1963, Professor of English and Poet-in-Residence, Bishop's University. Recipient: Prix David, 1935; Canada Council Senior Fellowship, 1959, award, 1968, 1971; Governor-General's Award, 1974; A. J. M. Smith Award 1974; Queen's Silver Jubilee Medal, 1978. M.A.: Oxford University, 1963; D.Litt.: Mount Allison University, Sackville, New Brunswick, 1973; D.C.L.: Bishop's University, 1977. Address: P.O. Box 172, North Hatley, Quebec, Canada.

PUBLICATIONS

Verse

The Golden Chalice. London, Nicholson and Watson, 1935.
Alfred the Great (verse play). London, Joseph, 1937.
Epithalamium in Time of War. Privately printed, 1941.
Lyrics Unromantic. Privately printed, 1942.
Flight into Darkness: Poems. New York, Pantheon, 1944.
Rivers among Rocks. Toronto, McClelland and Stewart, 1960.
Rocky Mountain Poems. Vancouver, Klanak Press, 1960.
Sift in an Hourglass. Toronto, McClelland and Stewart, 1966.
Ixion's Wheel: Poems. Toronto, McClelland and Stewart, 1969.
Themes and Variations for Sounding Brass. Sherbrooke, Quebec, Progressive, 1972.
Selected Poems. Toronto, McClelland and Stewart, 1972.
Fire on Stone. Toronto, McClelland and Stewart, 1974.
Corners in the Glass. Toronto, McClelland and Stewart, 1977.
Soviet Poems. Winnipeg, Turnstone Press, 1978.

Gradations of Grandeur. Victoria, British Columbia, Sono Nis Press, 1979.
Sequences. Toronto, Black Moss Press, 1979.
Stars and Carpets. Toronto, McClelland and Stewart, 1980.

Short Stories

The Brazen Tower. Tillsonburg, Ontario, Roger Ascham Press, 1974.

Other

Poetry and Canada. Ottawa, Canadian Legion Educational Service, 1945.

Editor, *Anthology of Canadian Poetry (English).* London, Penguin, 1942.
Editor, *A Little Anthology of Canadian Poets.* New York, New Directions, 1943.
Editor, *Canadian Accent: A Collection of Stories and Poems by Contemporary Writers from Canada.* London, Penguin, 1944.
Editor, *The Penguin Book of Canadian Verse.* London, Penguin, 1958; revised edition, 1967, 1975.

Bibliography: "Ralph Gustafson: A Bibliography in Progress" by L. M. Allison and Wendy Keitner, in *West Coast Review* (Burnaby, British Columbia), June 1974.

Manuscript Collections: State University of New York, Buffalo; Queen's University, Kingston, Ontario; University of Saskatchewan, Saskatoon.

Critical Studies: *Literary History of Canada*, Toronto, University of Toronto Press, 1966; *Oxford Companion to Canadian History and Literature*, Toronto, Oxford University Press, 1968; "Ralph Gustafson: A Review and Retrospect" by Robin Skelton, in *Mosaic* (Winnipeg, Manitoba), 1974; "Gustafson's Double Hook" by Wendy Keitner, in *Canadian Literature* (Vancouver), February 1979; *Ralph Gustafson* by Wendy Keitner, Boston, Twayne, 1979.

Ralph Gustafson comments:

Those interested might see my "Foreword to the Revised Edition" of *The Penguin Book of Canadian Verse*, 1975, especially p. 36. Some aphorisms to my "Towards a Noticeable Notebook" run as follows:

Poetry is not only a way of happening; it is a way of
concluding.
Poetry can't wind clocks – but it tells the time.
Poetry is a verbal rite, if it is right.
Science tries hard; poetry understands.
Poetry is exalted pragmatism.
Poetry faces truth without make-up.
Present poets? Too much I am in their iamb.
Ironic comedy is the only mode possible.

* * *

Ralph Gustafson is one of the most prolific, various and technically accomplished of contemporary Canadian poets. After a somewhat unpromising start with a volume of romantic lyrics and sonnets and a poetic play on the subject of King Alfred in the mid-thirties, Ralph Gustafson found an original style and an individual voice in the sardonic and tender poetry produced during and after World War II. *Flight into Darkness* assimilated, rather than shook off, influences of Hopkins and Donne and demonstrated the relevance of the metaphysical dialectic to the problem of preserving an individual integrity in the kaleidoscopic new world of the post-war breakdown.

The poet's elliptical and intensely allusive style took on a new subtlety and his work a wider field of interest in three volumes published since 1960, *Rivers among Rocks*, *Rocky Mountain Poems* and *Sift in an Hourglass*. In these, travel across Canada, especially to the Rockies and the mountains of the north-west coast, and to Italy, Greece and Scandinavian countries, has provided the stimulus for a prolific outburst of poetry in which the themes of nature, art, history, love and sex are given a highly individual treatment. As Professor Earle Birney has written: "Ralph Gustafson has a way all his own of fusing music and passion with sophisticated feeling and graceful craft.... A stylist given to paradox and poetic wit, he is nonetheless serious, and his sensitive judgments rise from a warm heart."

Mr. Gustafson has written also a number of prize-winning short stories and has edited three influential anthologies.

—A. J. M. Smith

GUTTERIDGE, Don(ald George). Canadian. Born in Point Edward, Ontario, 30 September 1937. Educated at the University of Western Ontario, London, 1956–60, 1962–63, B.A. (honours) 1960. Married Anne Barnett in 1961; one daughter and one son. English teacher, Elmira School Board, Ontario, 1960–62; Teaching Fellow, University of Western Ontario, 1962–63; Head of the Department of English, Ingersoll School Board, Ontario, 1963–64, and London Board of Education, Ontario, 1964–68. Since 1968, Professor of English Methods, University of Western Ontario. Recipient: President's Medal, University of Western Ontario, 1971; Canada Council Travel Grant, 1973. Address: 114 Victoria Street, London, Ontario N6A 2B5, Canada.

PUBLICATIONS

Verse

The Brooding Sky. Privately printed, 1960.
New Poems 1964. Privately printed, 1965.
Other Woods: New Poems. Privately printed, 1966.
Intimations of Winter: Poems for the Latter Half of 1966. New York, Bitterroot Press, 1967.
Riel: A Poem for Voices. Fredericton, New Brunswick, Fiddlehead, 1968; revised edition, Toronto, Van Nostrand Reinhold, 1972.
The Village Within: Poems Toward a Biography. Fredericton, New Brunswick, Fiddlehead, 1970.
Death at Quebec and Other Poems. Fredericton, New Brunswick, Fiddlehead, 1971.
Perspectives. London, Ontario, Pennywise Press, 1971.
Saying Grace: An Elegy. Fredericton, New Brunswick, Fiddlehead, 1972.
Coppermine: The Quest for North. Ottawa, Oberon Press, 1973.
Borderlands. Ottawa, Oberon Press, and London, Dobson, 1975.
Tecumseh. Ottawa, Oberon Press, 1976.
A True History of Lambton County. Ottawa, Oberon Press, 1977; London, Dobson, 1978.

Novel

Bus-Ride. Nairn, Ontario, Nairn Publications, 1973.

Other

Language and Expression: A Modern Approach (textbook). Toronto, McClelland and Stewart, 1970.

Critical Studies: *Survival: Themes in Canadian Literature* by Margaret Atwood, Toronto, Anansi, 1971; "Rivering of Vision" by David Cavanagh, in *Alive* (Guelph, Ontario), August 1973; "*Tecumseh*" by D. H. Sullivan, in *West Coast Review* (Burnaby, British Columbia), January 1978.

Don Gutteridge comments:

One of our poets has called Canada a "country without a mythology"; little wonder, then, that my work – like that of many Canadian writers – is concerned with the sense of place and the perspective of time, with roots into the past and what myths can be made in the face of such vast geography and empty stretches of history. My work takes two forms: personal poems about my childhood village and narrative poems on Canadian historical figures (real and imagined). Though quite different in content and form, these two types are related in that they share my concern for making something of my own past as well as that of my country, and my belief, however naive, that the two are somehow connected.

*   *   *

"History is the biography of great men," Carlyle once said, and Don Gutteridge would probably agree with him, for to the teacher (who was born in an historic section of Ontario and teaches in the old city of London, Ontario) history and biography are very much a unity. So far he has published poems of two types: historical and autobiographical.

The historical poems are the more familiar, although to date these have not won him too many readers. His widest read work, *Riel: A Poem for Voices*, might at first glance seem an ideal script for a radio documentary about the leader of the two Métis uprisings on the Canadian prairies, for the long poem is constructed, as a mason would construct a wall, of bits and pieces – editorials, letters, lyrical interludes.

Gutteridge promises to tell "what Riel really was in Canadian terms," and the short lyric poems are always on the verge of revealing some psychological or universal truth:

When my body
swings like a
dead tongue
from the white-man's
scaffolding,
will there be
an eloquence
to tell....

Riel remains an enigma wrapped up in a mystery swinging from the white man's scaffolding. *Riel* is a labour of love, but essentially a pastiche, and as such unrevealing and undramatic.

The same might be said of *Death at Quebec and Other Poems* and *Coppermine: The Quest for North* which attempt to build dramatic monologues on the personalities of early missionaries and explorers as revealed through their writings. Gutteridge deserves credit for spotting the poetic possibilities in these figures from the past, but the language he uses is neither of the period nor particular to the person, and so seems inappropriate.

Although the historical poems are so far more adventurous than the autobiographical poems, it is perhaps in this latter area that Gutteridge may develop in the future. *Saying Grace: An Elegy* is a short, impressionistic poem written on the death of his mother. It includes these moving lines, somewhat quirky, yet moody and effective: "Death does not/'take us,' it/moves into the/waiting spaces//is welcome."

—John Robert Colombo

HACKER, Marilyn. American. Born in New York City, 27 November 1942. Educated at Bronx High School of Science, New York; Washington Square College, New York University; Art Students League, New York. Has one daughter. Has worked as a teacher; mail sorter; editor of books, magazine, and trade journals; and antiquarian bookseller. Recipient: Lamont Poetry Selection Award, 1973; National Endowment for the Arts grant, 1974; National Book Award, 1975. Address: c/o Alfred A. Knopf Inc., 201 East 50th Street, New York, New York 10022, U.S.A.

PUBLICATIONS

Verse

The Terrible Children. Privately printed, 1967.
Highway Sandwiches, with Thomas M. Disch and Charles Platt. Privately printed, 1970.
Presentation Piece. New York, Viking Press, 1974.
Separations. New York, Knopf, 1976.

Recording: *The Poetry and Voice of Marilyn Hacker*, Caedmon, 1976.

* * *

Marilyn Hacker's poems combine the classical rhyming forms of sestina, sonnet, and villanelle with a blunt terse declarative sentence-structure to express the deranged black richness of contemporary experience. More than any other poet currently writing, Hacker has employed the sestina as vehicle for display of the lurid and quirky obsessions of contemporary minds. Her language is jewel-encrusted, reminiscent of Jacobean drama and the early Robert Lowell; it resonates thoroughly with the excesses of over-ripe technological civilization. Cities built of concrete and metal, ominous and harshly-lit, often supply both backdrop and metaphor for a devastated inner world of difficult loving, tangled sexuality, and the cool torture generated by convoluted relationships. The act of converting these horrors into elegant rhymed poems appears to be the only consolation for this poet as she travels through the landscape of nightmare. Her intelligence refuses to overlook – indeed has some fascination for – terrifying situations: a *ménage à trois*, death of a young self-destructive lover, betrayals, loneliness, and the encroaching debris of junkies and lunatics on New York and San Francisco streets. Such self-exposure takes guts, and it cannot be labelled "confessional," because no guilt or self-pity muddies the poet's objective view of the way the world manifests, not as she designed it. Still it comprises the milieu she is committed to, and she directs her energy to it.

Fear, alienation, and rejection are hard stones for her sculptor's tools. Her poems therefore come to resemble great baroque jewels, blood-red or purple in craggy settings. She often uses semi-precious gems – onyx, amethyst, alexandrite – as metaphors for the hardness, mystery, and rich perverse intensity of experience. Lured by whatever is foreign and strange, Hacker invents vaguely Latin-American scenes of revolution and insurrection to reflect restless social chaos. She invents "imaginary translations" which allow her to play with exotic locales and overblown emotions. While these poems almost seem experiments, *tours de force*, they lead into the deepest, most essential employment of her craft and intellect, which is to elucidate her own intense passions, both sexual and moral. The realism of "The Callers" is a grotesque "translation" of the usual mother-child relationships, though it reads as a word-for-word tape recording of an interview with a madwoman. "Prism and Lens" has the detail and flavor of Hacker's personal experience, but these do not differ greatly from the "fiction" of such poems as "La Vie de Château" and "After the Revolution."

But since form is inseparable from function, the sequence entitled "Separations," written in sonnet form, de-emphasizes obsession and becomes a graceful, almost Shakespearean delineation of the aspects of love. If love always springs lively and ubiquitous in Hacker, despite difficulties, then death also surrounds her all-pervadingly. The intertwining of love and death is the note on which *Presentation Piece* opens. There she speaks of "the skull of the beloved" as a brooding nobleman in a Jacobean play addresses the skull of his dead mistress. Death is the gruesome smog we must all breathe; Hacker enters its presence with the weapon of language even while knowing she can't win. The powerful ten-poem sequence "The Navigators" in *Presentation Piece* is prelude and foreshadowing to the heartbroken elegy "Geographer" in *Separations*, a poem which unites in formal sestina-like word repetition her continuing themes of death, cities, gems, language, obsession and painful but persisting love:

I have held your death the way I hold my child,
but it has no weight and no voice. The death
of a red begonia from frost, the hibernal death
of the Heath horse-chestnuts, colored, odored words
pile up. But I have not found the words
to thread the invisible waste of your death;
the quicksilver veins threading the way of the city,
till the lights all froze out, all over the city.

Hacker's poetry welds strong intellect to consummate language skill, and brave vision to humane commitment. She is able to draw on the rich resources of English literature as she explores the ambiguous gifts of contemporary life. Such a combination is extremely unusual and makes Marilyn Hacker an outstanding figure in American writing today.

—Jane Augustine

HAINES, John (Meade). American. Born in Norfolk, Virginia, 29 June 1924. Educated at art schools in Washington, D.C., and New York. Served in the United States Navy, 1943–46. Married 1) Jo Ella Hussey in 1960; 2) Jane Everett in 1970; four step-children. Homesteaded in Alaska, 1947–69. Free-lance Writer. Poet-in-Residence, University of Alaska, Anchorage, 1972–73, University of Washington, Seattle, 1974, and University of Montana, Missoula, 1975. Recipient: Corcoran Gallery Sculpture Prize, 1948; Jennie Tane Award (*Massachusetts Review*), 1964; Guggenheim Fellowship, 1965; National Endowment for the Arts grant, 1967; Amy Lowell Traveling Scholarship, 1976. Address: P.O. Box 25, Indianola, Washington 98342, U.S.A.

PUBLICATIONS

Verse

Winter News. Middletown, Connecticut, Wesleyan University Press, 1966.
Suite for the Pied Piper. Menomonie, Wisconsin, Ox Head Press, 1967.
The Mirror. Santa Barbara, California, Unicorn Press, 1971.
The Stone Harp. Middletown, Connecticut, Wesleyan University Press, and London, Rapp and Whiting-Deutsch, 1971.
The Legend of Paper Plates. Santa Barbara, California, Unicorn Press, 1970.
Twenty Poems. Santa Barbara, California, Unicorn Press, 1971.
Leaves and Ashes. Santa Cruz, California, Kayak, 1974.
In Five Years Time. Missoula, Montana, SmokeRoot Press, 1976.
The Sun on Your Shoulder. Privately printed, 1976.
Cicada. Middletown, Connecticut, Wesleyan University Press, 1977.
In a Dusty Light. Port Townsend, Washington, Graywolf Press, 1977.

Play

Television Documentary: *The River Is Wider Than It Seems*, 1979.

Other

Translator, *El Amor Ascendia*, by Miguel Hernández. Menomonie, Wisconsin, Ox Head Press, 1967.

Manuscript Collection: University of Alaska Library, Fairbanks.

Critical Studies: Review by Paul Zweig, in *The Nation* (New York), 27 March 1967; Ira Sadoff, in *Seneca Review* (Geneva, New York), April 1971; William Witherup, in *Kayak* (Santa Cruz, California), 1972; Paul Zweig, in *Parnassus* (New York), Winter 1972–73; "John Haines Issue" of *Stinktree* (Memphis), November 1972; by the author, in *Cutbank 6*, Spring 1976; Sam Hamill in *Cutbank 10*, Winter 1979.

John Haines comments:

The early poems for which I am perhaps best known (*Winter News*) grew out of my experience in the Alaskan wilderness. It is a poetry of solitude – to say it oversimply – but a peopled solitude. The subject matter is drawn mainly from nature and its citizens – animals, birds, trees, ice and weather, and the occasional human traveler. These things had their counterpart in my imagination – the durable stuff of childhood fantasies of life in the great north woods – and that as much as anything else gives the poems what significance they may have. They can be read as part of a continuing interior monologue, but it seems to me that they contain plenty of actual sticks and stones to stumble on and be bruised by.

For a time in the late 1960's I was preoccupied with events in the outside world – politics, social conflict, all that absorbed so many of us at the time. I tried to deal with these things in my poems (*The Stone Harp*). In a few of them I think I was successful, but on the whole I was too far from the events themselves for them to dominate my poems as convincingly as the wilderness world had up until that time.

For a number of reasons I became dissatisfied with the isolation I have been living in, and made a decisive break with it in 1969. The poems I have published since then have ranged more widely in their materials. *Cicada* contained a number of poems addressed to or directly concerned with individuals. In some ways this book marks the close of a line of thought, or development, and appears to open the possibility of another. *In a Dusty Light* returns to something like the world of *Winter News*, but here the subject matter is drawn not only from Alaska, but from Montana and the Northwest, and from events generally.

Writing continues to be for me a necessary undertaking, a means by which I place myself in the world. I am still interested in the long poem, in its modern form as sequence. I write considerably more prose than I used to, and I'm preparing a book of essays for publication. I have also begun a long prose work, an account of my Alaska years, and which I hope will turn out to be a useful meditation on wilderness, as well as a book on life generally.

* * *

John Haines homesteaded in Alaska in 1947 at a place over sixty miles from Fairbanks. All through the 1950's and into the 1960's he and his wife lived there in a house they built. In some seasons they lived off the country, but as time went on and recognition came – a Guggenheim grant and steady publication – the Haineses ranged farther and lived more easily.

John Haines's work recurrently links to the animals and the land: moose, caribou, owls; snow, wind, cold. In the literature of our time, he evokes a totem feeling.

His presence in the American scene slowly became known through the 1950's and then more rapidly in the 1960's, through work in little magazines of small circulation but special reputation: *The Sixties*, *Kayak*, *Chicago Choice*, *The San Francisco Review*. Where these magazines do circulate, they count; and in them the poems of John Haines, trenchant but quiet, appear. And now and then the Haines criticism drops into place, a voice distanced, serious, uncompromising – different, but carefully not part of any coterie.

From a few poetry readings, down country, "in the lower 48," his reputation grew; by 1969 with a conference of Alaska writers at Alaska Methodist University in which his accomplishment was celebrated, he began to go national in reputation. In recent years, he had resided prevalently in California, from whence he currently operates, with readings all over the nation and with occasional guest professorships at colleges and universities.

—William Stafford

HALL, Donald (Andrew, Jr.). American. Born in New Haven, Connecticut, 20 September 1928. Educated at Phillips Exeter Academy, New Hampshire; Harvard University, Cambridge, Massachusetts (Garrison and Sergeant prizes, 1951), B.A. 1951; Oxford University (Henry Fellow; Newdigate Prize, 1952), B.Litt. 1953; Stanford University, California (Creative Writing Fellow), 1953–54. Married Jane Kenyon in 1972; two children. Junior Fellow, Society of Fellows, Harvard University, 1954–57; Assistant Professor, 1957–61, Associate Professor, 1961–66, and Professor of English, 1966–75, University of Michigan, Ann Arbor. Poetry Editor, *Paris Review*, Paris and New York, 1953–62; Member of the Editorial Board for Poetry, Wesleyan University Press, 1958–64. Literary Consultant, Harper and Row, publishers, New York. Lived in England, 1959–60, 1963–64. Recipient: Lamont Poetry Selection Award, 1955; Edna St. Vincent Millay Memorial Prize, 1956; Longview Foundation Award, 1960; Guggenheim Fellowship, 1963, 1972. Address: Eagle Pond Farm, Danbury, New Hampshire 03230, U.S.A.

PUBLICATIONS

Verse

(*Poems*). Oxford, Fantasy Press, 1952.

Exile. Privately printed, 1952.
To the Loud Wind and Other Poems. Cambridge, Massachusetts, Harvard Advocate, 1955.
Exiles and Marriages. New York, Viking Press, 1955.
The Dark Houses. New York, Viking Press, 1958.
A Roof of Tiger Lilies. New York, Viking Press, and London, Deutsch, 1964.
The Alligator Bride. Menomonie, Wisconsin, Ox Head Press, 1968.
The Alligator Bride: Poems New and Selected. New York, Harper, 1969.
The Yellow Room Love Poems. New York, Harper, 1971.
A Blue Tit Tilts at the Edge of the Sea: Selected Poems 1964–1974. London, Secker and Warburg, 1975.
The Town of Hill. Boston, Godine, 1975.
Kicking the Leaves. Mount Horeb, Wisconsin, Perishable Press, 1975.
Kicking the Leaves (collection). New York, Harper, 1978; London, Secker and Warburg, 1979.

Recording: *Today's Poets 1*, with others, Folkways, 1967.

Play

An Evening's Frost (produced New York, 1965).

Other

Andrew the Lion Farmer (juvenile). New York, Watts, 1959; London, Methuen, 1961.
String Too Short to Be Saved: Childhood Reminiscences. New York, Viking Press, 1961; London, Deutsch, 1962.
Henry Moore: The Life and Work of a Great Sculptor. New York, Harper, and London, Gollancz, 1966.
Marianne Moore: The Cage and the Animal. New York, Pegasus, 1970.
As the Eye Moves: A Sculpture by Henry Moore. New York, Abrams, 1970.
The Gentleman's Alphabet Book. New York, Dutton, 1972.
Writing Well. Boston, Little Brown, 1973; revised edition, 1976, 1979.
A Writer's Reader, with D. L. Emblen. Boston, Little Brown, 1976; revised edition, 1979.
Dock Ellis in the Country of Baseball, with Dock Ellis. New York, Coward McCann, 1976.
Riddle Rat (juvenile). New York, Warne, 1977.
Remembering Poets: Reminiscences and Opinions – Dylan Thomas, Robert Frost, T. S. Eliot, Ezra Pound. New York, Harper, 1978.
Goatfoot Milktongue Twinbird: Interviews, Essays, and Notes on Poetry 1970–6. Ann Arbor, University of Michigan Press, 1978.

Editor, *The Harvard Advocate Anthology.* New York, Twayne, 1950.
Editor, with Robert Pack and Louis Simpson, *New Poets of England and America.* Cleveland, Meridian, 1957; *Second Selection*, with Pack, 1962.
Editor, *Whittier.* New York, Dell, 1961.
Editor, *Contemporary American Poetry.* London, Penguin, 1962; revised edition, 1971.
Editor, *A Poetry Sampler.* New York, Watts, 1962.
Editor, with Stephen Spender, *The Concise Encyclopedia of English and American Poets and Poetry.* London, Hutchinson, and New York, Hawthorn, 1963; revised edition, 1970.
Editor, with Warren Taylor, *Poetry in English.* New York, Macmillan, 1963; revised edition, 1970.

Editor, *The Faber Book of Modern Verse*, revised edition. London, Faber, 1965.
Editor, *A Choice of Whitman's Verse*. London, Faber, 1968.
Editor, *The Modern Stylists: Writers on the Art of Writing*. New York, Free Press, 1968.
Editor, *Man and Boy: An Anthology*. New York, Watts, 1968.
Editor, *American Poetry: An Introductory Anthology*. London, Faber, 1969.
Editor, *The Pleasures of Poetry*. New York, Harper, 1971.

Critical Studies: by Ralph J. Mills, Jr., in *Iowa Review* (Iowa City), Winter 1971; "Donald Hall Issue" of *Tennessee Poetry Journal* (Martin), Winter 1971.

* * *

Donald Hall lives with his wife, the poet Jane Kenyon, in his ancestral farm house in New Hampshire. Through the zero winters they burn wood in ancestral woodstoves – eight cords, cut, split, delivered in the fall. Don rises in the night to stoke the fires. In the summers Jane grows a garden. The farm grows hay, which others cut. The barn is dilapidated now, the old buggy still inside which Don's grandfather drove to church three-quarters of a century ago. In New England no one throws much away. Upstairs are spinning wheels, wedding dresses, a churn. The main floor is filled with books, hundreds of feet of bookshelves added in 1975 when Hall left a professorship at the University of Michigan to come to this place and live by writing.

He writes every day from 6 or so until noon: essays, reviews, short stories, plays, textbooks, and poems. He writes about the house, about the fathers who have lived there before. "Naming the Horses" eulogizes generations of horses that worked the farm. Other poems make eulogies to grandparents, their lives, the vanishing rural occupations, shearing sheep, making ox carts. He and Jane hunt through a grave yard for his grandfather's grave. They find it. They don't find it. Different poems.

He watches his dreams. His grandparents come back to the house "laughing with pleasure at our surprise." He wakes again "hearing a voice from sleep: 'The blow of the axe resides in the acorn,' " and he writes it down.

Hall is returned, fully mature, to a well-spring of themes and values. He is not sentimental and his poetry is not pastoral; it is tinged with the politically alert, ironic restlessness of an urban, sophisticated mind. He looks from a window at Boston lawyers' summer places "with swimming pools cunningly added to cowsheds," but he knows "we are all of us sheep, and death is our shepherd,/and we die as the animals die."

Hall has learned to build poems centrifugally from chance beginnings. This takes time – two years per poem on the average, lines breaking and reforming. He has become willing to give over everything written so far to the next shaping impulse, to the new image, to the dream-self if it surfaces in the poem. He discovers "meaning" last. "In recent years," Hall writes, "I have come to accept the beginning of a poem, or even a whole draft, without the slightest clue to the subject matter.... The process of writing a poem is a process of shaping the words which the poem begins with...." This process produces poetry of a complete pattern, at its best, as in "Naming the Horses," symphonic – layers of music: the last, elegiac line – "O Roger, Mackerel, Riley, Ned, Nellie, Chester, Lady Ghost" – names the horses, recapitulating and resolving the progressions of assonance that structure the poem. It is a powerful conclusion, with more than the spirits of the horses lingering in the last name.

Hall grew up in metrics. His grandfather recited set-pieces to him as they did chores in the summer – "Casey at the Bat," "Over the Hills to the Poor House." He grew up with his grandfather's New England morality, but aware of its limitations. His first book of poems reiterates one theme: whether posed by the witty and ironic voice of the student ("The Lone Ranger") or by the reflective, uncertain graduate ("Exiles"), the problem is how to reach one's deep selves, the anima, dreams; how even to begin to understand the inner "world that must remain unvisited" since "no man can knock his human fist upon/the door...." All of Hall's subsequent work has struggled with that problem.

Partly because of his education (Exeter, Harvard, Oxford), Hall stayed in "careful ignorance" of the Black Mountain poets and the Beats until the late 1950's. In his third book of poems, metrics alternate with open forms for 44 pages until a sequence of poems on the sculpture of Henry Moore. Here images, not ideas, predominate. Immediately, the functioning of the image changes.

In the next pages the assassination of John F. Kennedy becomes an image of how Hall had let the requirements of his daily, mechanical life kill off his dreams. He accepts this responsibility for the first time ("I squeeze slowly" on the trigger). Images show him a well of sexual fear; he climbs out. Crashed airplanes have recurred in his poems. Now the pilot's spirit revives in the "narrow cockpit/although his muscles are stiff." He starts his plane and flies "in a beam of the late sun" to join the souls of the human race.

Hereafter images become more accessible to latent (unconscious) information, expecially in Hall's next book, *The Alligator Bride*, with its aura of surrealism. Puzzling over the change in his poetry, Hall produced a remarkable essay on the creative process, "The Vatic Voice," which concludes: "I truly think that to clear the passageway to the insides of ourselves, to allow the vatic voice to speak through us, is the *ultimate* goal to which men must address themselves. It is what to live for, it is what to live by." The vatic voice probably speaks inside every man. Keats heard it (negative capability); so did André Breton. By 1969, Hall heard it. It shaped his decision to return to the ancestral farm. It shaped his poems. But he was not and will not be a surrealist poet. His inward journey extends only to that point where we fear to lose our identity in the inner chaos of faces and animals and confused scenes. Of this area, this passageway, Hall is a precise mapmaker.

With the publication of *Kicking the Leaves*, Hall steps away from the direct influence of any movement, poet, or school. His poems are still concerned with self-revelation, but the Self is extended now. It reaches to Hall's youth and childhood and to the lives of others who have touched him. The mature voice speaks with compassion and humor. Its tone is typically elegiac (even to a mock-heroic elegy for cheeses) and full of the music of American speech. He has written again on creativity; "Milktongue, Goatfoot, Twinbird" finds the psychic origins of creativity in the baby-self and locates the experience of a poem in the mouth and body as well as in the mind. It is an essential primer on his own work and on art as "regression in the service of the ego."

Hall is becoming one of the best American poets. He is a superb reader. Summing up his work-to-date, he writes: "The poem is a vehicle for self discovery.... The premise is that if you discover something that is deep enough inside yourself, it's going to be a part of other people's insides, too, and reveal themselves to themselves."

—Edward B. Germain

HALL, J(ohn) C(live). British. Born in London, 12 September 1920. Educated at Leighton Park, Reading, Berkshire; Oriel College, Oxford. Has two children. Formerly, a book publisher. Since 1955, Member of the Staff, *Encounter* magazine, London. Address: 198 Blythe Road, London W14 0HH, England.

PUBLICATIONS

Verse

Selected Poems, with Keith Douglas and Norman Nicholson. London, John Bale and Staples, 1943.

The Summer Dance and Other Poems. London, Lehmann, 1951.
The Burning Hare. London, Chatto and Windus–Hogarth Press, 1966.
A House of Voices. London, Chatto and Windus–Hogarth Press, 1973.

Other

Edwin Muir. London, Longman, 1956.

Editor, *Collected Poems of Edwin Muir 1921–1951.* London, Faber, 1952; New York, Grove Press, 1957; revised edition, Faber, 1960; New York, Oxford University Press, 1965.
Editor, with Patric Dickinson and Erica Marx, *New Poems 1955.* London, Joseph, 1955.
Editor, with G. S. Fraser and John Waller, *The Collected Poems of Keith Douglas*, revised edition. London, Faber, 1966.
Editor, with G. S. Fraser and John Waller, *Alamein to Zem Zem*, by Keith Douglas. London, Faber, 1966; New York, Chilmark Press, 1967.

* * *

J. C. Hall's early poems, collected in *The Summer Dance*, though reflective and carefully formed, lack any strongly individual quality. As he himself acknowledged: "All these long years I've pondered how to make/A poetry I could truly call my own." In the next volume, *The Burning Hare*, the influence of Edwin Muir is all-pervasive. "Before This Journeying Began" and "The Double Span" are dedicated to him, and "The Island" reads like a pastiche of Muir. Hall is a conservative poet, conscious of his debt to literary tradition, and "The Playground by the Church," with its allusions to Valéry, is typical of his meditative poetry, which questions and explores the world of ideas and of philosophical apprehensions.

His latest book, *A House of Voices*, relies less than the previous collections on myth and symbol, although Hall remains aware of their potency. The tone of the verse is more relaxed, and the poems are more firmly rooted in the world of everyday experience. In "The Double" Hall ends on a note of metaphysical speculation, but the first three stanzas are more humorous and colloquial than anything in his earlier work:

I often wonder what he was really like,
That identical boy – whether he knew of me
Taking the rap, riding round on my bike
Secretly proud of the devil I dared not be.

Hall's patient search for a poetry truly his own appears finally to have been successful.

—John Press

HALL, Rodney. Australian. Born in Solihull, Warwickshire, England, 18 November 1935; emigrated to Australia during his childhood. Educated at City of Bath Boys' School; Brisbane Boys' College; University of Queensland, Brisbane, B.A. 1971. Married to Maureen Elizabeth MacPhail; three daughters, Imogen, Delia, Cressida. Free-lance Scriptwriter and Actor, 1957–67, and Film Critic, 1966–67, Australian Broadcasting Commission, Brisbane. Tutor, New England University School of Music, Armidale, New South Wales, Summers

1967–71; Youth Officer, Australian Council for the Arts, 1971–73. Since 1962, Advisory Editor, *Overland* magazine, Melbourne; since 1967, Poetry Editor, *The Australian* daily newspaper, Sydney. Travelled in Europe, 1958–60, 1963–64, 1965, and the United States, 1974. Australian Department of Foreign Affairs Lecturer in India, 1970, and Malaysia, 1972. Recipient: Australian National University Creative Arts Fellowship, Canberra, 1968; Commonwealth Literary Fund Fellowship, 1970; Literature Board Fellowship, 1973. Address: c/o University of Queensland Press, P.O. Box 42, St. Lucia, Queensland 4067, Australia.

PUBLICATIONS

Verse

Penniless till Doomsday. London, Outposts, 1962.
Four Poets, with others. Melbourne, Cheshire, 1962.
Forty Beads on a Hangman's Rope: Fragments of Memory. Newnham, Tasmania, Wattle Grove Press, 1963.
Eyewitness. Sydney, South Head Press, 1967.
The Autobiography of a Gorgon. Melbourne, Cheshire, 1968.
The Law of Karma: A Progression of Poems. Canberra, Australian National University Press, 1968.
Heaven, In a Way. Brisbane, University of Queensland Press, 1970.
A Soapbox Omnibus. Brisbane, University of Queensland Press, 1973.
Selected Poems. Brisbane, University of Queensland Press, 1975.
Black Bagatelles. Brisbane, University of Queensland Press, 1978.

Recording: *Romulus and Remus*, University of Queensland Press, 1971

Novels

The Ship on the Coin: A Fable of the Bourgeoisie. Brisbane, University of Queensland Press, 1972.
A Place among People. Brisbane, University of Queensland Press, 1976.

Other

Social Services and the Aborigines, with Shirley Andrews. Canberra, Federal Council for Aboriginal Advancement, 1963.
Focus on Andrew Sibley. Brisbane, University of Queensland Press, 1968.

Editor, with Thomas W. Shapcott, *New Impulses in Australian Poetry.* Brisbane, University of Queensland Press, 1968.
Editor, *Australian Poetry 1970.* Sydney, Angus and Robertson, 1970.
Editor, *Poems from Prison.* Brisbane, University of Queensland Press, 1974.
Editor, *Australians Aware: Poems and Paintings.* Sydney, Ure Smith, 1975.
Editor, *Voyage into Solitude*, by Michael Dransfield. Brisbane, University of Queensland Press, 1978.

Rodney Hall comments:

I suppose the only way I'd be prepared to describe my own work is to say that it is basically non-confessional. It is my hope that each poem may take on an independent life of its own. If this is possible the emotional experience, it would seem to me, becomes available to the reader in a far more pure and direct form than is generally possible with confessional poetry, where the poet as a person perpetually obtrudes and everything is limited to his vision of himself. My experiences are nearly always projected into imaginary situations – often in an attempt to relate them back to that skeleton of our world-view, legends and myths.

I have also concentrated on a special form, which I call a Progression. This consists of many short poems, each capable of standing alone, tightly inter-related so that they become something akin to a single long poem with all the peaks left in and the discursive passages cut. I have published five of these progressions so far. The average length is forty poems, the largest is sixty-six.

* * *

Of Australian poets who came to prominence in the early 1960's, only Rodney Hall and Bruce Beaver have achieved, to date, a fully creative integration in their work of the two very opposed cultural stress-points of the 1960's and the 1970's – and the work of Beaver, in the 1960's, is more peripheral to its period than is Hall's output of early maturity.

Penniless till Doomsday, published in England in 1962, aroused immediate attention in Hall's adopted country, Australia. Its qualities of wit, wry appraisal, and implicit social involvement were exactly what the new decade, in Australia, was seeking – a way out of the cultural impasse of tired regionalism and provincial introversion that was the thinning out of the important 1940's "new *Bulletin* school" energies into a 1950's caution and intellectual sloth. Rodney Hall was one of the contributors to *Four Poets* (1962), the collection that made an important claim for a new group of Brisbane poets at this time, when Sydney was also being challenged by Melbourne as the centre of Australian poetry. Hall's regional – Brisbane – associations were essentially peripheral to his real poetic concerns, which were ambitiously developed in his succeeding volumes. He has been a prolific writer, and these collections reveal a restless and sometimes strenuously alert intelligence preoccupied by the allure of invention. *Eyewitness* holds on to models of detachment and observation, and some of its individual poems still attack the reader with their terse exactitude and surprise. But the two extended sequences *The Autobiography of a Gorgon* and *The Law of Karma* present, in a very real way, the culmination of the 1960's in Australian poetry. *The Autobiography of a Gorgon*, shorter, encapsuled in a tight case of irony and deliberate self-regard, is, I contend, the masterpiece of its decade. *The Law of Karma* is a deliberate attempt at a schematic poem, and its self-conscious virtuosity in fact mitigates against its final effect, substituting the power to impress for the power to move. Yet it remains a minefield of expressive force. The 1970's has emphasised the impromptu and the immediate in poetry; *The Law of Karma* is deliberate, terrifyingly insistent upon inexorable processes. In a sense it codifies the very order that was, in the year of its composition and publication, to be overthrown by a new generation.

It is interesting to note that Rodney Hall, as poetry editor for the national newspaper *The Australian*, was to become central in recognising the emerging forces of this succeeding generation of poets, and in making their work available. *The Law of Karma* is built upon a premise of social observation and indeed responsibility – something the oncoming "generation of 1968" (as it has, retrospectively, been termed) was to make central in their concerns, tightened by the Vietnam conscription commitment of the Australian government of the day. Hall's next two books, *Heaven, In a Way* and *A Soapbox Omnibus*, can be seen, now, as transition pieces, where the poet, acutely sensitive to the dynamics of life around him and bounded, finally, by his very virtuosity of technical accomplishment (many of the pieces here are almost rigid in their cleverness, many are acutely moving in their interplay of tensions), tries out various structures and forms to weld together his intellectual and his responsive abilities in confrontation with this turning point in the culture's history. "Folk Tales," the concluding sequence of *A Soapbox Omnibus*, points decisively to a pedal-point in Hall's work. *Selected Poems* is perhaps the most remarkable of its kind in Australian literary history, as it is nearly half given over to a long new sequence ("The Owner of My Face") that would seem almost entirely unprepared for in any of the earlier work. Hall had very early on developed what he called a "progression" of poems – *The Law of Karma* was the most fully extended of these. But "The Owner of My Face" broke radical new ground, in that it explored states of subjective being and intuitive response – almost a direct opposition to his prior command of authorial irony and interplay of controlled nuances ("walking the tightrope of passion and detatchment" he once called it). *Black Bagatelles* expands further this area of subjective vulnerability in Hall's work, but with important modifications: his sense of theatre, of event, is given free play (the work is a series of dialogues with Death), and his sense of irony is counterpointed (often brilliantly) with the very willingness to be "open" that is at the heart of the 1970's exploration. It is a work that allows Hall's brilliance, and his deep humanity, full play, and interplay. It is also a work of deep pain, one of the high points of its decade in Australian poetry.

—Thomas W. Shapcott

HALPERN, Daniel. American. Born in Syracuse, New York, 11 September 1945. Educated at San Francisco State College, 1963–64; California State University, Northridge, 1966–69, B.A. in psychology 1969; Columbia University, New York (Woolrich Fellow), 1970–72, M.F.A. 1972. Since 1969, Editor, *Antaeus* magazine, New York; since 1971, Editor-in-Chief, Ecco Press, New York; since 1978, Director, National Poetry Series, New York. Instructor, New School for Social Research, New York, 1971–76; Visiting Professor, Princeton University, New Jersey, 1975–76. Since 1976, Assistant Professor, and Acting Chairman, 1978–79, Columbia University School of the Arts. Recipient: Rehder Award (*Southern Poetry Review*, Raleigh, North Carolina), 1971; YM-YWHA Discovery Award, 1971; National Endowment for the Arts Fellowship, 1973, 1974; Bread Loaf Writers Conference Robert Frost Fellowship, 1974; Creative Artists Public Service grant, 1978. Address: 1 West 30th Street, New York, New York 10001, U.S.A.

PUBLICATIONS

Verse

Traveling on Credit. New York, Viking Press, 1972.
The Keeper of Height (as Angela McCabe). New York, Barlenmir House, 1974.
The Lady Knife-Thrower. Binghamton, New York, Bellevue Press, 1975.
Treble Poets 2, with Gerda Mayer and Florence Elon. London, Chatto and Windus, 1975.
Street Fire. New York, Viking Press, 1975.
Life among Others. New York, Viking Press, 1978.

Other

Editor, with Norman Thomas di Giovanni and Frank MacShane, *Borges on Writing.* New York, Dutton, 1973; London, Allen Lane, 1974.
Editor, *The American Poetry Anthology.* Boulder, Colorado, Westview Press, 1975.

Translator, *Songs of Mririda, Courtesan of the High Atlas*, by Mririda n'Aït Attik. Greensboro, North Carolina, Unicorn Press, 1974.

* * *

Highly educated, moderately successful as an author, editor, and translator, Daniel Halpern is caught in the alienation, isolation, and yearning for spontaneous feeling that incites much contemporary poetry. "The Ethnic Life," the first poem in his first book of poetry, *Traveling on Credit*, begins "I've been after the exotic/For years" and ends "For years I've lived simply/Without luxury –/With the soundness of the backward/Where the senses can be heard." The headlong rush to identify ethnic and exotic with simple still leaves Halpern stopped, as he so often is, at the sense, stranded between objective sensations and subjective feelings.

Traveling on Credit and *Street Fire* are carefully arranged into sections by topic: places are seen with a fine precision of mood; the vagaries of affection between men and women rise up out of stillness; the small rituals of daily life and social gatherings ward off larger fears. The language of both books hews to a clear speech neither too idiomatic nor too elevated, set in lines of regular length. Throughout, Halpern aims at a middle road, oscillating between melancholy lyricism and bemused objectivity.

Wary of extremes in emotional life and of the norms of accepted tradition, Halpern concentrates on the seductive pull of the imagination. "Aubade" (*Life among Others*) modifies its traditional form by being neither particularly joyous, wholly of the morning, nor precisely of lovers parting. It begins at night with the lovers going to bed: "It is when I fall to dream in your arms/that I climb into the arms of another:/... until I am back again beside you/in the first light, the morning of the different day." The protagonist of Halpern's poems is a man to whom life, and especially women, has come easily, but this ease has spawned a restless investigation into the ambiguities and difficulties of communication.

Life among Others focuses more directly on the dimensions of these difficulties, addressing openly the isolation which was held at arm's length in his earlier work. The first section puts into service the delicate atmospheric descriptions of *Traveling on Credit* to present the loneliness of the traveler's rooms:

I sit in front of my window, I tempt
the solitary lights that go on and off
on the water: lights of boats, cape lights,
the lights across the water. They pile up
in darkness here. It is a collection, a pastime.
Now I have the chance to speak – not to explain
but to return everything – your bright lives
rooted to nothing more than a light seen at a distance
that diminishes as it moves closer and closer.

The desire for speech comes in such moments, but its consummation escapes him. The others remain nameless and faceless. The poems of the second section spring from memories and images, moments of pain and loss when the protagonist tries to accept his isolation, or at least to understand it. The final four interconnected poems – "White Tent," "White Train," "White Contact," and "I Am a Dancer" – envelope his isolation in a series of images:

White, the color of clarity
where nothing has to live.
It matches everything and can go
anywhere. It fits in and is nothing.
White contact in a house where nothing
is said.

The tent of dream
is a privacy, the bird a way out,
the train, power to keep on. I'm
not really unpleasant, and there is no crime
committed against others.

However, this neat summary belies the strength of the attempt, and the sentences are too coolly structured to give us the feeling of a break in the protagonist's intellectual reserve. Despite this, the book is a clear step forward. Halpern seems a patient poet, and his patience may yet be further rewarded.

—Walter Bode

HAMBURGER, Michael (Peter Leopold). British. Born in Berlin, 22 March 1924; emigrated to England in 1933. Educated at schools in Germany; George Watson's School, Edinburgh; The Hall, Hampstead, London; Westminster School, London; Christ Church, Oxford, B.A. in modern languages, M.A. 1948. Served as an infantryman, non-commissioned officer, and lieutenant, Royal Army Educational Corps, 1943–47. Married Anne Beresford, *q.v.* in 1951 (marriage dissolved, 1970); remarried Anne Beresford, 1974; three children. Assistant Lecturer in German, University College, London, 1952–55; Lecturer, then Reader in German, University of Reading, Berkshire, 1955–64; Florence Purington Lecturer, Mount Holyoke College, South Hadley, Massachusetts, 1966–67; Visiting Professor, State University of New York, Buffalo, 1969, and Stony Brook, 1970, Wesleyan University, Middletown, Connecticut, 1971, University of Connecticut, Storrs, 1972, University of California, San Diego, 1973, University of South Carolina, Columbia, 1973, Boston University, 1975, 1977, and University of Essex, Wivenhoe, 1978. Recipient: Bollingen Fellowship, 1959, 1965; Deutsche Akademie für Sprache und Dichtung Translator's Prize, 1964; Schlegel-Tieck Prize, for translation, 1967, 1978; Arts Council translation prize, 1969; Levinson Prize (*Poetry*, Chicago), 1972; Institute of Linguists Gold Medal, 1977; Wilhelm-Heinse Prize, 1978. Address: Marsh Acres, Middleton, Saxmundham, Suffolk, England.

PUBLICATIONS

Verse

Later Hogarth. London, Cope and Fenwick, 1945.
Flowering Cactus: Poems 1942–49. Aldington, Kent, Hand and Flower Press, 1950.
Poems 1950–1951. Aldington, Kent, Hand and Flower Press, 1952.
The Dual Site. New York, Poetry London–New York, 1957; London, Routledge, 1958.
Weather and Season: New Poems. London, Longman, and New York, Atheneum, 1963.
In Flashlight. Leeds, Northern House, 1965.
In Massachusetts. Menomonie, Wisconsin, Ox Head Press, 1967.
Feeding the Chickadees. London, Turret, 1968.
Travelling: Poems 1963–68. London, Fulcrum Press, 1969.
Penguin Modern Poets 14, with Alan Brownjohn and Charles Tomlinson. London, Penguin, 1969.
Home. Frensham, Surrey, Sceptre Press, 1969.
In Memoriam Friedrich Hölderlin. London, Menard Press, 1970.
Travelling I–V. London, Agenda, 1972.
Ownerless Earth: New and Selected Poems 1950–1972. Cheadle, Cheshire, Carcanet Press, and New York, Dutton, 1973.

Conversations with Charwomen. Rushden, Northamptonshire, Sceptre Press, 1973.
Babes in the Wood. Knotting, Bedfordshire, Sceptre Press, 1974.
Travelling VI. London, I.M., 1975.
Travelling VII. Luxembourg, Club 80, 1976.
Real Estate. London, Anvil Press Poetry, 1977.
Real Estate (collection). Manchester, Carcanet Press, 1977.
Palinode: A Poet's Progress. Knotting, Bedfordshire, Sceptre Press, 1977.
Moralities. Newcastle upon Tyne, Morden Tower, 1977.

Plays

The Tower, adaptation of a play by Peter Weiss (produced New York, 1974).

Radio Play: *Struck by Apollo*, with Anne Beresford, 1965.

Other

Reason and Energy: Studies in German Literature. London, Routledge, and New York, Grove Press, 1957; revised edition, London, Weidenfeld and Nicolson, 1971; as *Contraries: Studies in German Literature*, New York, Dutton, 1971.
Hugo von Hofmannsthal: Zwei Studien. Göttingen, Sachse and Pohl, 1964; translated as *Hofmannsthal: Three Essays*, Princeton, New Jersey, Princeton University Press, 1970; Cheadle, Cheshire, Carcanet Press, 1974.
From Prophecy to Exorcism: The Premisses of Modern German Literature. London, Longman, 1965.
Zwischen den Sprachen: Essays und Gedichte. Frankfurt, Fischer, 1966.
The Truth of Poetry: Tensions in Modern Poetry from Baudelaire to the 1960's. London, Weidenfeld and Nicolson, 1969; New York, Harcourt Brace, 1970.
A Mug's Game: Intermittent Memoirs 1924–1954. Cheadle, Cheshire, Carcanet Press, 1973.
Art as Second Nature: Occasional Pieces 1950–1974. Manchester, Carcanet Press, 1975.

Editor and Translator, *Beethoven: Letters, Journals, and Conversations.* London, Thames and Hudson, and New York, Pantheon, 1951; revised edition, London, Cape, 1966.
Editor, and Translator with others, *Poems and Verse Plays*, by Hugo von Hofmannsthal. New York, Pantheon, and London, Routledge, 1961.
Editor and Translator, with Christopher Middleton, *Modern German Poetry, 1910–1960: An Anthology with Verse Translations.* London, MacGibbon and Kee, and New York, Grove Press, 1962.
Editor, and Translator with others, *Selected Plays and Libretti*, by Hugo von Hofmannsthal. New York, Pantheon, and London, Routledge, 1963.
Editor, *Das Werk: Sonette, Lieder, Erzählungen*, by Jesse Thoor. Frankfurt, Europäische Verlagsanslalt, 1965.
Editor and Translator, *East German Poetry: An Anthology in German and English.* Oxford, Carcanet Press, and New York, Dutton, 1972.
Editor, *Selected Poems*, by Thomas Good. London, St. George's Press, 1973.

Translator, *Poems*, by Hölderlin. London, Nicholson and Watson, 1943; revised edition, as *Hölderlin: His Poems*, London, Harvill Press, 1952; New York, Pantheon, 1953; revised edition, as *Selected Verse*, London, Penguin, 1961; revised edition, as *Poems and Fragments*, London, Routledge, 1966; Ann Arbor, University of Michigan Press, 1967.

Translator, *Twenty Prose Poems of Baudelaire.* London, Editions Poetry London, 1946; revised edition, London, Cape, 1968.

Translator, *Decline: 12 Poems*, by Georg Trakl. St. Ives, Cornwall, Latin Press, 1952.

Translator, *The Burnt Offering*, by Albrecht Goes. New York, Pantheon, and London, Gollancz, 1956.

Translator, *Egmont*, by Goethe, in *Classic Theatre 2*, edited by Eric Bentley. New York, Doubleday, 1959.

Translator, with Yvonne Kapp, *Tales from the Calendar*, by Bertolt Brecht. London, Methuen, 1961.

Translator, with Christopher Middleton, *Selected Poems*, by Günter Grass. London, Secker and Warburg, and New York, Harcourt Brace, 1966.

Translator, *Poems*, by Hans Magnus Enzensberger. Newcastle upon Tyne, Northern House, 1966.

Translator, *Lenz*, by Georg Büchner, with *Immensee* by Theodor Storm and *A Village Romeo and Juliet* by Gottfried Keller. London, Calder and Boyars, 1966; in *Leonce and Lena, Lenz, Woyzeck*, 1972.

Translator, with others, *O the Chimneys*, by Nelly Sachs. New York, Farrar Straus, 1967; as *Selected Poems, Including the Verse Play "Eli,"* London, Cape, 1968.

Translator, with Jerome Rothenberg and the author, *Poems for People Who Don't Read Poems*, by Hans Magnus Enzensberger. New York, Atheneum, and London, Secker and Warburg, 1968; as *Poems*, London, Penguin, 1968.

Translator, *And Really Frau Blum Would Very Much Like to Meet the Milkman: 21 Short Stories*, by Peter Bichsel. London, Calder and Boyars, 1968.

Translator, *Journeys: Two Radio Plays: The Rolling Sea at Setúbal, The Year Lacerta*, by Günter Eich. London, Cape, 1968.

Translator, with Christopher Middleton, *Poems*, by Günter Grass. London, Penguin, 1969.

Translator, with Matthew Mead, *The Seeker and Other Poems*, by Nelly Sachs. New York, Farrar Straus, 1970.

Translator, *Stories for Children*, by Peter Bichsel. London, Calder and Boyars, 1971.

Translator, with Christopher Middleton, *Selected Poems*, by Paul Celan. London, Penguin, 1972.

Translator, *Leonce and Lena, Lenz, Woyzeck*, by Georg Büchner. Chicago, University of Chicago Press, 1972.

Translator, *Selected Poems*, by Peter Huchel. Manchester, Carcanet Press, 1974.

Translator, *German Poetry 1910–1975*. New York, Urizen, 1976; Manchester, Carcanet Press, 1977.

Translator, with Christopher Middleton, *In the Egg and Other Poems*, by Günter Grass. New York, Harcourt Brace, 1977; London, Secker and Warburg, 1978.

Translator, *Texts*, by Helmut Heissenbüttel. London, Boyars, 1977.

Translator, with André Lefevere, *Seedtime* (*La Semaison*)*: Extracts from the Notebooks 1954–1967*, by Philippe Jaccottet. New York, New Directions, 1977.

Translator, *Poems*, by Franco Fortini. Todmorden, Lancashire, Arc, 1978.

Manuscript Collections: University of Texas, Austin; Lockwood Memorial Library, State University of New York, Buffalo; University of Reading, Berkshire.

Critical Studies: "The Subject Beneath the Subject" by the author, in *Christian Science Monitor* (Boston), 31 January 1967; "Across Frontiers: Michael Hamburger as Poet and Critic" by Jon Glover, in *Stand* (Newcastle upon Tyne), 1970; "Rhythm" by the author, in *Agenda* (London), x, 4–xi, 1, 1972–73; "More New Poetry" by Terry Eagleton, in *Stand* (Newcastle upon Tyne), 1973; "Forward, Ay, and Backward" by Martin Dodsworth, in *The Guardian* (London), 5 April 1973; "Ownerless Earth" by Donald Davie, in *New York Times Book Review*, 28 April 1974; "Travellers" by John Matthias, in *Poetry* (Chicago), April 1974.

* * *

Michael Hamburger's is a poetry of ideas made as sensuous as possible by being passed through images of nature, tinged very frequently with a decent uncloying melancholy. The turning point in his poetry is made in *Weather and Season* in which all the traditionally metrical and rhyming forms have almost entirely been disbanded because, as he stated in the reading he gave at the University of Iowa in 1969 (and I paraphrase) "in my previous books I used the traditional forms to protect myself from the pressure and intensity of my feelings; whereas I subsequently came to feel that, in writing the later poems, I no longer wished to evade or mask these feelings." This frank, direct criticism of an earlier stance, together with his decision to shuck off the encrustments of such forms, has brought rewards.

The poetry has two contexts. One is that of men socialized into a dilemma which may be resolved only by using the charged, moral conscience ("In a Cold Season"); the other context is nature, although as one critic has recently, and justly, pointed to some affinity with Edward Thomas, so I suggest that he is no more a nature poet than Thomas is. Leavis in *New Bearings* has indicated that for Thomas nature was used as the arena of delicate and scrupulous psychological re-enactment, and for Hamburger this is also valid. Many of the poems in his pamphlet *In Flashlight* cohere to form an exploration of the use and stamina of memory. A capacity for valuation, issuing directly from responsive memory which absorbs the two nodes of experience seen here as change through exploration and settled recurrence, is examined in "Tides" and "The Road" (*Weather and Season*). In the latter, memory is the recognising faculty by which the conscious mind penetrates its unconscious, to find natural images built there into an ideal country – an absolute, alluring and unattainable – and which the teller does "not look for ... when awake."

The question of identity, subsumed in the role of poet in "Man of the World" (*Weather and Season*), is more inclusively embodied in "The Search" (*Weather and Season*). In that search, "as commanded," the familiar country of the man's origins is discovered as alien, and when, through tracts of nature, he reaches the village, the symbolic ideal is released to him, to be discovered as actual, in its alien quality as "Why, Mors, need we tell you, mors, MORS." Expectedly enough this is the last poem of *Weather and Season*.

The extrapolation from biography into criticism is dubious, but I think it's relevant here to indicate that Hamburger is a Jew, of German birth, and that he with most of his family emigrated to England in the year of Hitler's rise to power, and averted for themselves the Nazi holocaust. Hamburger is acutely fitted to write such a poem as "The Search," with all its narrower, more defined implications. It is the Jewish component of this poet that hiddenly but with integrated power explores the landscape of nature and village and finds that the search discovers his origins and death to be identical. The same qualification permits him to write of the issues of conscience in relation to Eichmann.

Eliot has declared in another context that "Humankind cannot bear very much reality," but it is Hamburger's alert and intelligent contention that it is the burden of humanity as well as its necessary precondition for survival that it use language as searchingly as possible and with as faithful a rendering of the referents in experience, and interpretation of them, as can be. Mercy, honesty and perception are in this context integral: "Dare break one word and words may yet be whole." Hamburger's language is quiet and naturally spoken, even when speaking of violence. The intensity of the poetry is in the *un*extraordinary and seemingly non-manipulative but exact use of ordinary language – "the sea, that basher of dumb rock" – and its unassumingly painful exploration of painful experience ("For a Family Album"). Metaphoric imagery is used rarely. The images are visually referential; or else the metaphors live in consideration of the metaphysical data as if the data was actual, or physically tangible. And these are fed through hovering, tentative but persistent rhythms fitted to their unrhymed, speech-moulded cadences.

Hamburger has shown a preference for the comforting rural (or even cultivated) natural phenomena of creature and plant. This desire for their presence as a sanitive has continued. It is this poet's matrix, on which everything else is sounded, and often judged. Perhaps such a preference accounts, in part, for the slow-moving rhythms of much of his verse.

A collection called *Travelling* contained a poem of that name, and this has been the seed of Hamburger's most interesting, ambitious, and sustained poem to date – with the possible exception of "In a Cold Season." In this early version, the poem is in two sections. In *Real Estate* the poem has a third section, and the whole has become the first of a suite of 11 poems under the same title. In the "Envoi" to *Travelling*, Hamburger wrote: "Goodbye, words..../ Go out and lose yourselves in a jabbering world,/Be less than nothing." The injunction is only half-true for Hamburger. The "jabbering world" of which he complains, has, in the full version of "Travelling," become more acutely judged – an earth committed to (human) acquisition and possession. It is a human world that must give up what it possesses in order to enter into what cannot be possessed either, although supremely desired – love given to and received from another: "The place that, holding you still,/Could fill and affirm your name." "Still" means both unmoving and a condition continuous in time. Travelling involves the need for a fixed point of return (the compasses image in Donne's "A Valediction: Forbidding Mourning"). At that point of return one realises that to be in that "place" is not to possess it ("Ownerless Earth"): "Last of my needs, you/I'll unlearn, relinquish/If that was love. Too late,/Let you go, return, stay/And move on."

The close-grained, almost possessed energy of Hamburger's earlier poems tends, in "Travelling," to become something other. There is an almost invariably direct syntax, and a greater rhythmical assurance both in line length and enjambments. Some of this assurance is obtained by a "likeable" repetition: there are pairs or triads of things – "sand, pebble, rock," "On cobbles, on brick, on slabs," or of verbs, such as "Propel, transmute; and create/again"; in this last example development is described (not enacted). This triadic formation also tends to occur in the rhythmic structure of a line, producing a wavering, wave-like movement, at once "tentative and persistent"; and therein lies Hamburger's enacted argument with himself. Linguistically, that argument tends to get dissolved in a resolute search for, and an achievement of, clarity. The clarity sometimes irons out, or expunges, what one senses as greater tensions or antagonisms beneath the surface. The achievement of "Travelling" (and its synonym *Real Estate*) is, nevertheless, high and consistent. The long poem (a risk these days) sustains itself round the go/stay, fixed/moving paradox where abnegation and love form the field of the drama. Even the determination to be plain and understandable have for the reader a moving vulnerability; it may not be a central part of the poem, but it is a bonus – surely not what the poet had meant us to observe: a struggling to "get it right."

—Jon Silkin

HAMILTON, (Robert) Ian. British. Born in King's Lynn, Norfolk, 24 March 1938. Educated at Darlington Grammar School; Keble College, Oxford, B.A. Married; has one son. Editor, *Tomorrow*, Oxford, 1959–60. Since 1962, Editor, *The Review*, later *The New Review*, London. Since 1965, Assistant Editor, *Times Literary Supplement*, London, and Poetry Reviewer, *The Observer*, London. Recipient: Gregory Award, 1963. Address: 18 Dorset Square, London N.W.1, England.

PUBLICATIONS

Verse

Pretending Not to Sleep. London, The Review, 1964.
The Visit: Poems. London, Faber, 1970.
Anniversary and Vigil. London, Poem-of-the-Month Club, 1971.

Other

A Poetry Chronicle: Essays and Reviews. London, Faber, and New York, Barnes and Noble, 1973.
The Little Magazines: A Study of Six Editors. London, Weidenfeld and Nicolson, 1976.

Editor, *The Poetry of War, 1939–45.* London, Alan Ross, 1965.
Editor, *Selected Poetry and Prose*, by Alun Lewis. London, Allen and Unwin, 1966.
Editor, *The Modern Poet: Essays from "The Review."* London, Macdonald, 1968; New York, Horizon Press, 1969.
Editor, *Eight Poets.* London, Poetry Book Society, 1968.
Editor, *Selected Poems*, by Robert Frost. London, Penguin, 1973.
Editor, with Colin Falck, *Poems since 1900.* London, Macdonald and Jane's, 1975.

* * *

Response in our time to the problem of how to render intimate and profound emotion in poetry has been extremely varied; often confused. Some poets have preferred to keep off the terrain almost altogether, sublimating pure feeling while employing it as the driving-force for a poetry which makes general, impersonal statements of another kind. Some have taken masks to disguise it, expressing it obliquely or with ironic detachment. Others have adopted the very direct, confessional manner, holding nothing back, hoping that the raw, detailed truth of their utterances will validate the poetry which contains them. Ian Hamilton's achievement has been to establish an alternative different from any of these: an area where personal feeling can be expressed not only with vividness and fidelity to experience but also with a subtlety and a reticence which do not diminish its force. It is a very private, very individual mode of writing; but the emotions are recognizable and universal.

Hamilton's output has been small. His one volume, *The Visit*, contained some thirty poems only, written during seven years; and beyond it, there are so far only a few uncollected new poems printed in magazines, or as yet unpublished. All the poems are short, none exceeding twenty lines. They are most of them direct and simple; or simple once the situation – between father and son, poet and wife, poet and child – has been grasped. Dwelling on significant human moments has been a very deliberate choice. In a note in the *Bulletin* of the Poetry Book Society (Summer 1970), Hamilton defines his poems as "dramatic lyrics ... the intense climactic moment of a drama." The reader must supply "the prose part ... the background data" from clues inside the brief statements the poems make. Yet reading Hamilton is never a matter of puzzling out a wilfully cryptic technique. The authenticity and strength – and the interest and relevance for the reader – of the emotions, are immediately apparent. Re-reading gradually uncovers the full situation, the exact intention, affording an increasing sense of the scrupulousness and delicacy with which he handles images and verbal effects.

Sorrow, alarm, tragedy are never far away in Hamilton's verse, but they are contained (in both senses) in small human gestures or minute, careful observations of objects: the movements of hands, or hair, or breath, the play of light in a room, a sudden scent. In "Trucks," the light from the vehicles at night "Slops in and spreads across the ceiling,/ Gleams, and goes." The sick, or dreaming, loved one speaks suddenly: "You're taking off, you say,/And won't be back./Your shadows soar." But her remoteness from him will turn again into a kind of closeness, if he can only wait: "Very soon/The trucks will be gone. Bitter, you will turn/Back again. We will join our cold hands together." An entire situation is caught in 13 very simple lines in which images of light and shadow, the gestures of hands, enact its "climactic moment"; sensitive judgment of punctuation and line-endings captures a speaking tone which movingly renders both the intimacy and the alarm. In "Father, Dying," petals from a rose suggest the dying flower, but act also, in words of quiet yet intense physical immediacy, as images for the dying man: "Trapped on your hand/They darken, cling in sweat, then curl/Dry out and drop away." The end of the poem, as the man's hand bleeds from the thorns on the bare stem, suggests effects in the poetry of Sylvia Plath: " 'My hand's/ In flower,' you say, 'My blood excites/This petal dross. I'll live.' " There is a certain debt here to a more florid confessional poetry; but the economy and precision, the avoidance of overt drama, are something only Hamilton achieves.

The poems towards the end of *The Visit* are no less moving and arresting, but tend even more towards the laconic; as if the poet feels he can suggest all the more by saying even less. Hamilton's immense skill (very much a personal technical skill) in writing short poems of great tenderness and resonance has tempted many imitators who lack his resource and judgment. As a poet who has helped to keep certain areas of personal sensitivity open at a time when crudity and rhetoric have invaded so much personal verse, his place is assured. But the difficulty of emulating him should be clearly demonstrated by the fine complexity and irony of "Friends," an uncollected poem in which even the plain-looking title contributes a dimension of bitter meaning:

> "At one time we wanted nothing more
> Than to wake up in each other's arms."
> Old enemy,
> You want to live forever
> And I don't
> Was the last pact we made
> On our last afternoon together.

—Alan Brownjohn

HAMPTON, Christopher. British. Born in London, 3 May 1929. Educated at Ardingly College, Sussex, 1944–46; Guildhall School of Music, London (Piano Prize, 1953, Principal's Prize, 1954), 1948–53, A.G.S.M. (Associate, Guildhall School of Music) 1953. Married Kathleen Hampton in 1956; one daughter. Pianist, accompanist, proof-reader, 1954–61; Director of Studies, Shenker Institute, Rome, 1962–66; Teacher, Davies School of English, London, 1966–67. Since 1968, Lecturer, Polytechnic of Central London. Recipient: Cobbold Prize, 1972. Address: 161 Southwood Lane, London N6 5TA, England.

PUBLICATIONS

Verse

An Exile's Italy. Leiston, Suffolk, Stuart Thonnesen, 1972.

Other

Island of the Southern Sun (juvenile). London, Chatto and Windus, 1962.
The Etruscans and the Survival of Etruria. London, Gollancz, 1969; as *The Etruscan Survival*, New York, Doubleday, 1970.

Editor, *Poems for Shakespeare.* London, Globe Playhouse Trust, 1972.
Editor, *Poems for Shakespeare 6.* London, Globe Playhouse Trust, 1978.

Translator, *The Fantastic Brother* (juvenile), by René Guillot. London, Methuen, 1961; Chicago, Rand McNally, 1963.

Christopher Hampton comments:

Since each of us carries within himself, at least potentially, those obscure intangibles and myths that determine the underlying rhythms of identity and being, we have to find ways of getting at them and making something of them. They have to be transposed, caught and held within the forms of another and less fugitive reality, symbolic and imaginative, or let go. And for me poetry is a reality of this order. Poems are mediators, transmitters of the essences of feeling. In a world in which time and change put each of us continually at risk and in doubt, a poem is one way to reflect on and to embody the discoveries and rewards of the struggle. What one is after is an exact correspondence, a verbal equivalent that will mirror the rhythms of the life within and around one. A poem is a way of recording and of celebrating the impact of momentary vision; of getting at roots and sources; of attempting some kind of affirmation. As I see it:

The attempt's what matters – against time's slow attritions
To pit memory and feeling and to hold intact
Snatched fragments, building from them what we can.

An Exile's Italy, the collection from which this fragment comes, is a sequence of 34 poems, embodying at different levels both the metaphor implicit in the title and the experience of the place itself. In its metaphorical sense, the idea of exile involves the recognition that dispossession, loss, captivity, exclusion are terms of existence that one has to live with and accept. But the awareness of this underlying condition also inevitably involves one in the search for place, equilibrium and identity. In face of the alienating facts of time, of change, of familiarity, of strangeness, one is in pursuit, "*Cosi l'animo preso entra in desire ... e mai non posa/fin che la cosa amata il fa gioire*," as Dante had it in the lines from *Purgatorio* that I have used as an epigraph. "The committed spirit, possessed by desire ... can know no rest till the loved object be enjoyed entire" – this is the feeling that governs all the poems. In the search for possession one has to register the fact that all that is most worth having must always remain in the deepest sense beyond possession, or that it can be possessed only in terms of the moment, unless in the poem itself. For what else can one do with the marvellous quivering presences around one except to try and live them through "as constancies between death's stopped notes, held/High up and uncorrupted as life sheds its moment"; and then let them go? Yet, having known them, having been marked by them, broken into, made to see, we may (perhaps) absorb them as potentiality, as sources of the energy and vividness we are after. And maybe then a little of the intangible vitality of the external world will have got into us – which we have to find the voice, the sensuous equivalent for, somehow, if we can. All that is lost is there, waiting for us. We have an inheritance, if we can free ourselves from the blunting routines, the rule of "the weak and the tame." Waking the dead, we become lovers and are changed by what we've stirred, referred back to the vitality and vividness in things, and so potentially at least to ourselves. Though dispossession and defeat are there for many, perhaps even for all (whether as victims of puritan oppression or of the intolerance of the system, as in a number of the monologues in my book, or in the act of life itself), beyond this there is also the hurt of the search for possession. These are conditions we have to face and meet, if possible, since they define the terms of the struggle for survival and for solvency, for continuity and replenishment. Death is always coming at us, to deny and to haunt; but also as part of the pattern of life, which is there to be celebrated through the intangible gifts of Being. Alive, we

bear the hurt of contact
Like a voice between us who know –
Though caught in the glare of sun and stone – this keeps us
Close to love, and will not let us go.

* * *

Christopher Hampton was trained as a musician at the Guildhall School of Music and Drama but after working for a time as pianist and conductor, he abandoned music in order to concentrate upon a writing career, though he has published a number of musicological articles. Before he went to Italy in 1962 he was an active and enthusiastic member of the Group, the gathering of poets who met regularly to discuss and analyse each other's poems, and he was represented in *A Group Anthology*, edited by Edward Lucie-Smith and Philip Hobsbaum.

Hampton's poems have been published in a large number of British and American periodicals and for his first collection, *An Exile's Italy*, he was awarded first prize at the East Anglian Festival of poetry and the arts. He has also published two children's books as well as a book on the art and culture of the Etruscans, *The Etruscans and the Survival of Etruria*.

As might be expected, the poems which make up the sequence *An Exile's Lady* were inspired by his experience as a teacher in Italy. In a way this is unfortunate since many of Hampton's best poems, such as "The Grandmother," "Home for Incurables," and "The Man with the Club Foot," are not (at the time of writing) yet available in volume form, and to appreciate Hampton's stature as a poet his work must be seen as a whole. Be that as it may, *An Exile's Italy* is an interesting sequence which admirably sets the modern Italy in sharp juxtaposition with the ancient world of Cato and Cicero. "A Non-Roman Asserts His Independence" is a satirical piece on the ancient scene; "Cato Castigates the Fish-Breeders" ridicules the effeminacy and extravagances evident in the years between the Punic Wars; and in "The Veteran Takes a Disaffected View of Britain" the Roman soldier stationed in Britain complains about life in 44 A.D. "Forgotten on the fringe of things."

—Howard Sergeant

HANSON, Kenneth O. American. Born in Shelley, Idaho, 24 February 1922. Educated at schools in Shelley; University of Idaho, Pocatello and Moscow, B.A. 1942; University of Washington, Seattle. Since 1956, Professor of Literature and Humanities, Reed College, Portland, Oregon. Delegate to the first Institute in Chinese Civilization, Formosa (Fulbright Fellowship), 1962. Recipient: Bollingen award, 1962; Rockefeller Award, 1966; Lamont Poetry Selection Award, 1966; Asia Society award, 1971; Amy Lowell Traveling Scholarship, 1973; National Endowment for the Arts grant, 1976. Address: Reed College, Portland, Oregon 97202, U.S.A.

PUBLICATIONS

Verse

8 Poems 1958. Privately printed, 1958.
Poems. Portland, Oregon, Portland Art Museum, 1959.
Five Poets of the Pacific Northwest, with others, edited by Robin Skelton. Seattle, University of Washington Press, 1964.
The Distance Anywhere. Seattle, University of Washington Press, 1967.
Saronikos and Other Poems. Portland, Oregon, Press-22, 1970.
The Uncorrected World. Middletown, Connecticut, Wesleyan University Press, 1973.
Portraits: Friends: Artists, prints by LaVerne Krause. Portland, Oregon, Press-22, 1978.

Other

Editor, *Clear Days: Poems by Palamás and Elytis, in Versions by Nikos Tselepides*. Portland, Oregon, Press-22, 1972.

Translator, *Growing Old Alive: Poems*, by Han Yü. Port Townsend, Washington, Copper Canyon Press, 1978.

Critical Study: "On Translation," interview with William Stafford, in *Madrona* (Seattle), Summer 1973.

Kenneth O. Hanson comments:

Chief influences on my work have been Pound, Williams, the Chinese language, the Greek landscape, Prévert, Cavafy, and my third-grade teacher Miss Warwas, who taught me how to pay attention.

* * *

The first poem in Kenneth O. Hanson's *The Distance Anywhere* describes a skin-diver who hangs "hours on the surface of one world/and stares into another." A frequent visitor to Greece and a serious student of classical Chinese culture, Hanson might in those lines be describing a central situation in his poems. As an observer he likes to be inconspicuous ("Beginning the day with ouzo/you're one jump ahead./I stick to beer"), and reticent ("Sometimes/a thing can be made/too clear").

His rhetoric is colloquial, understated. His more formal tone, usually elegiac, is closer to Waley's and Rexroth's translations from Chinese poetry than to British or American models: "What is empty? What is full? Only/the four corners of the past stand pat."

Most of *The Uncorrected World* is set in Greece; a few poems at the book's end long for Greece and meditate on what it means to be a traveller, and to be back in America. Throughout the book age-old Greece and its current political situation collide:

This rocky
landscape Hesiod how could he
plow a straight furrow?
Three thousand years.
Sun. Moon. Stone. Sky.
Against the whitewashed wall.
Official pronouncements.

But the world is uncorrected, and Greek political life is a manifestation, rather than a cause, of that fact. Hanson in Greece is a shrewd version of the American innocent abroad, but Hanson even at home is a traveller, because we all are:

We like to seem importunate

before this world of change.
O plains o vasty deep o marge and void
etc. We move but not through distance

into time, as if the fatal toad
in time's thin stone still faintly ticked
somewhere beyond. Aficionados of the moon!

O distances we gaze into!

—William Matthews

HANSON, Pauline. American. Born in Massachusetts. Since 1950, Assistant to the Director, Yaddo, Saratoga Springs, New York. Recipient: Eunice Tietjens Memorial Prize (*Poetry*, Chicago), 1965; National Endowment for the Arts grant, 1972; National Institute of Arts and Letters award, 1972. Address: Yaddo, Saratoga Springs, New York 12866, U.S.A.

PUBLICATIONS

Verse

The Forever Young. Denver, Swallow, 1948.
The Forever Young and Other Poems. Denver, Swallow, 1957.
Across Countries of Anywhere. New York, Knopf, 1971.

* * *

The landscape of Pauline Hanson's poetry is stark, vast, and abstract; seasons slip into seasons, years into centuries, one dead into many, the flesh into spirit – and all are unspecified. Frequently, the nameless persona stands before the altars of the night ("Like Anyone Who Waits Here" from *Across Countries of Anywhere* or "Poems for the Night" from *The Forever Young and Other Poems*) and struggles to think her way out of the silence and into a knowledge of death, love, and her place in the scheme of things. The roads she travels are time and space; the people she meets are spectres and shadows, as in "The Ways":

And once, beyond the words of it,
slowly then all suddenly,
imagined in the longest night
the way, the only way, was time ...

When you touched me, when I touched you,
when your shadows, when my shadows,
shimmered into the sensuous flesh
of my body, of your body:
lust into lust we moved and then –
then dreamed from every secret self
of our remembering, it was
like lost ... like found ... like always love.

Whether Hanson practices a mental athleticism as she speculates on atomic theory, astrophysics and Hindu mysticism in "The Questions of the One Question," or whether in her less pretentious long poem, "The Forever Young and Never Free" (originally titled "The Forever Young"), she fashions her story in the form of arduous questionings, she characteristically leads her reader through tight paradoxes and tortured syntax unrelieved by conventional imagery to an understanding of life's mysteries.

In "The Forever Young" and many other of her poems, it is a particular death, the death of her lover, that lies behind all the deaths she probes and gives her verse its poignancy and power. This lover also figures in poems where the living and dead are fused in love and love transcends the bonds of time: "Love is to the farthest place –/love is to so far a place/from always its greater distances,/to see where death was, I look back" ("And I Am Old To Know"). Hanson's refusal to employ figurative language and her insistence on a limited vocabulary of familiar but haunting words used repetitively contribute to the ritualistic, hypnotic quality of her poetry: "Where the constant winter was,/where stricken from myself I went/into the cold and colder sweep/of snow on snow already deep" ("The Ways"). At times her heavy dependence upon repetition coupled with her habit of leaving her pronouns without referents renders her verse unintelligible rather than ambiguous; but generally, her craft does not falter and the austere language is poetically effective. That she can evoke concrete images is illustrated in several of her poems. Eager to celebrate the living and contrast it to the unknown, she recalls a "small bird's crimson flight" ("The Forever Young"). In "So Beautiful Is the Tree of Night" the arched branches of the great tree are etched against the sky. In the grotesque lines of "We Meet," she appalls us with her piteous image of the hanging jew child:

> .... Of God who for these hours is to let him hang here –
> with his hands tied, with his feet tied – put here for others to look at –
> put up here as high as he has seen at home branches hang and
> he reached up his hand but could not touch the flowers on them,
> could not touch the shining apples on them.

But these images are rare. Generally, her poetry is one of questioning, examining life's paradoxes. Like Gerontion, she keeps reminding her reader and herself to "think now." Her setting is astral; the ways she travels take her beyond time; and her place is nowhere and anywhere as she tries to answer "Who I am?"

—Carol Simpson Stern

HARPER, Michael S(teven). American. Born in Brooklyn, New York, 18 March 1938. Educated at City College of Los Angeles, A.A. 1959; California State University, Los Angeles, B.A. 1961, M.A. in English 1963; University of Iowa, Iowa City, M.A. 1963; University of Illinois, Urbana, 1970–71. Married Shirley Ann Buffington in 1965; one daughter and two sons. Taught at Contra Costa College, San Pablo, California, 1964–68; Reed College and Lewis and Clark College, Portland, Oregon, 1968–69; California State University, Hayward, 1970. Since 1971, Professor of English, Brown University, Providence, Rhode Island. Recipient: National Institute of Arts and Letters Award, 1972; Black Academy of Arts and Letters Award, 1972; Guggenheim Fellowship, 1976; National Endowment for the Arts grant, 1977; Melville-Cane Award, 1977. Address: Box 1852, Brown University, Providence, Rhode Island 02912, U.S.A.

PUBLICATIONS

Verse

Dear John, Dear Coltrane. Pittsburgh, University of Pittsburgh Press, 1970.
History Is Your Own Heartbeat. Urbana, University of Illinois Press, 1971.
Photographs: Negatives: History as Apple Tree. San Francisco, Scarab Press, 1972.
Song: I Want a Witness. Pittsburgh, University of Pittsburgh Press, 1972.
Debridement. New York, Doubleday, 1973.
Nightmare Begins Responsibility. Urbana, University of Illinois Press, 1974.
Images of Kin: New and Selected Poems. Urbana, University of Illinois Press, 1977.

Other

Editor, *Heartblow: Black Veils* (anthology). Urbana, University of Illinois Press, 1975.
Editor, with Robert B. Stepto, *Chant of Saints: A Gathering of Afro-American Literature, Art, and Scholarship.* Urbana, University of Illinois Press, 1979.

* * *

Michael S. Harper's collections reveal a broad diversity of themes and his disparate interests, ranging from music (jazz and blues), to nature (birth and death), to history and myth. But it is soon apparent that they are manifestations of a highly sensitized Black witness within whom all these themes coalesce and then are transposed into emotional and spiritual expressions. Harper states that "relationships between speech and body, between men, between men and cosmology are central to my poetry."

In certain respects his poetry defies characterization for it is controlled by intensely personal rhythms emanating from his deeply rooted jazz and blues impulses. (He tells us for example that "Billie Holiday played piano in my family's house when I was 12.") At the same time the scope of his writing is atuned to a historical sense of moment, something of what T. S. Eliot called a perception not only of the pastness of the past, but of its presence. Harper sets out to affirm his conviction that man must not allow himself to be dislocated from his historical continuum: "When there is no history there is no metaphor." It is with such conviction that his poetry at once synthesizes and articulates this sensibility. And it is out of his own Blackness as well as his own humanness that Africa is viewed as the "potent ancestor" providing "a strong ancestral base that reflects the African spirit wherever it is located":

And we go back to the well: Africa,
the first mode, and man, modally,
touched the land of the continent,
modality: we are one; a man is another
man's face, modality, in continuum,
from man, to man, contact-high, to man....

It is out of this spiritual and historical consciousness as well that Michael Harper defines relationships between people and the cosmos, and generates metaphor:

This suture is race
as it is blood,
long as the frozen
lake building messages
on typewritten paper,
faces of my ancestors,
warm in winter only
as their long scars touch ours.

Conviction of course means responsibility; Harper's responsibility as poet is to take on "the very tenuous 'business' of operating on historical legacies," creating a "clinical imagery to draw attention, to shock a reader with a detailed, medical closeness and approximation." Thus, when surgeon is poet and flesh is landscape with its history, tradition and myth, debridement becomes metaphor and restoration becomes image. In this sense Michael Harper's poems may be perceived as "healing songs."

Ragboned Bob Hayden, shingled in slime,
reaches for his cereus ladder of midnight flight,
his seismographic heartbeats
sphinctered in rhiney polygraphs of light;
Dee-troit born and half-blind
in diction of arena and paradise,
his ambient nightmare-dreams streak his tongue;
mementos of his mother, of Erma, he image-makes
peopling the human family of God's mirror,
mingling realities, this creature of transcendence
a love-filled shadow, congealed and clarified.

—Charles L. James

HARRIS, (Theodore) Wilson. British. Born in New Amsterdam, British Guiana, now Guyana, 24 March 1921. Educated at Queen's College, Georgetown. Married to Margaret Whitaker. Government Surveyor, in the 1940's, and Senior Surveyor, 1955–58, Government of British Guiana. Visiting Lecturer, State University of New York at Buffalo, 1970; Writer-in-Residence, Scarborough College, University of Toronto, 1970; Commonwealth Fellow in Caribbean Literature, Leeds University, Yorkshire, 1971; Visiting Professor, University of Texas, Austin, 1972, and Yale University, New Haven, Connecticut, 1979. Delegate to the National Identity Conference, Brisbane, 1968; to UNESCO Symposium on Caribbean Literature, Cuba, 1968. Recipient: Arts Council grant, 1968, 1970; Guggenheim Fellowship, 1973; Henfield Writing Fellowship, 1974; Southern Arts Writing Fellowship, 1976. Address: c/o Faber and Faber Ltd., 3 Queen Square, London WC1N 3AU, England.

PUBLICATIONS

Verse

Fetish. Privately printed, 1951.
The Well and the Land. Georgetown, Magnet, 1952.
Eternity to Season. Privately printed, 1954; revised edition, London, New Beacon, 1979.

Novels

The Guiana Quartet:
Palace of the Peacock. London, Faber, 1960.
The Far Journey of Oudin. London, Faber, 1961.
The Whole Armour. London, Faber, 1962.
The Secret Ladder. London, Faber, 1963.
Heartland. London, Faber, 1964.
The Eye of the Scarecrow. London, Faber, 1965.
The Waiting Room. London, Faber, 1967.
Tumatumari. London, Faber, 1968.
Ascent to Omai. London, Faber, 1970.
Black Marsden: A Tabula Rasa Comedy. London, Faber, 1972.
Companions of the Day and Night. London, Faber, 1975.
Da Silva Da Silva's Cultivated Wilderness, and Genesis of the Clowns. London, Faber, 1977.
The Tree of the Sun. London, Faber, 1978.

Short Stories

The Sleepers of Roraima. London, Faber, 1970.
The Age of the Rainmakers. London, Faber, 1971.

Other

Tradition and the West Indian Novel (lecture). London, New Beacon, 1965.
Tradition, The Writer and Society: Critical Essays. London, New Beacon, 1967.
History, Fable, and Myth in the Caribbean Guianas. Georgetown, Ministry of Information and Culture, 1970.
Fossil and Psyche (lecture on Patrick White). Austin, University of Texas, 1974.

Manuscript Collections: University of the West Indies, Mona, Kingston, Jamaica; University of Texas, Austin; University of Indiana, Bloomington; University of Guyana, Georgetown.

Critical Studies: "The Necessity of Poetry" by Louis James, and "Kyk-over-Al and the Radicals" by Edward Brathwaite, in *New World* (Georgetown), 1966; *The Naked Design* by Hena Maes-Jelinek, Aarhus, Denmark, Dangaroo Press, 1976.

Wilson Harris comments:

Fetish and *Eternity to Season*, along with other miscellaneous poems of the early 1950's, stand at the beginning of an exploration which extends deeper and further at a later stage in my work in the novel over the 1960's. The development of the novels is foreshadowed, to some extent, in the earlier poems. Constant to that exploration within poem and novel is the use I continue to make of the brooding continental landscape of Guiana as a gateway of memory between races and cultures, Amerindian, European, African, Asian.

* * *

The poetry of Wilson Harris, like his contribution to the art of the novel since 1960 (he has published no poetry since this date), is outside the present mainstream of Caribbean writing in English. Like Martin Carter, also of Guyana, his metaphorical perception and expression are more akin to that of the Martiniquan poet Aimé Césaire and the Cuban writer Alejo Carpentier. One does not find in Harris's work the clear air of the anglophone islands' poets. His sensibility has been formed by the world of the Guyanese forest and its rivers, its complexities and contradictions ("Amazon"):

> The world-creating jungle
> travels eternity to season. Not an individual artifice
> this living movement
> this tide
> this paradoxical stream and stillness rousing reflection.

Harris's poetry is to be found in *Kyk-over-Al* and in the privately published *Eternity to Season*, which contain his most important poems. He does not concern himself with social conditions, individual problems, the "historical" colonial past, or a possible or impossible future. His themes are time (into which he subsumes history), creation, separation and unity. His burden is not the Faustian ego but the environmental collective. There is some evidence of the operation of a Hegelian/Marxist dialectic in his poems. When individuals appear in his poetry, they are gigantic mythologized figures like Hector "hero of time," Agamemnon, Achilles (the great runner) and Teiresias. Harris uses these figures, and simple material existences like rice, water and charcoal to initiate journeys both (and often simultaneously) into cosmic space and human time. Because of the nature of Harris's perception, some of his poetry is obscure (although most of it deposits its meaning after repeated reading) and sometimes (perhaps through the need to make meaning clear) Harris eschews metaphor for "prose" statement:

> But earth cannot simply be
> a cosmic and arbitrary discovery! what of its changing roots
> and purposive vitality? External and internal
> forces are separate illusions that move
> beyond the glitter and the gloom with a knife to cut inner and outer times
> from each other
> as they weave and interweave in the tapestry of life....

Earlier in this same poem, "Amazon," this *statement* had been already almost magically expressed as:

Branches against the sky smuggle to heaven the extreme beauty
of the world: the store-house of that very heaven
breaks walls to drop tall streams like falls.

The green islands of the world
and the bright leaves lift their tender blossom of sunrise
to offset arenas of sunset
and wear a wild rosette like blood.

This self same blossom burns the clouds....

Nor is Harris alone in this paradoxical riverain and arboreal continuum. Two hundred years before his time, George Pinckard, an English army doctor, travelling on Guyanese water, received and recorded the same kind of environmental breakdown and unification that Harris has transmuted into poetry (*Notes on the West Indies*, 1806, vol. 2, pages 470–71):

> The watery medium made no impression upon the eye, but the open azure expanse was seen the same, whether we looked upwards or downwards. We seemed suspended in the centre of a hollow globe, having the same concave arch above and below, with an inverted and an upright forest on either hand. At one spot we met a huge mass of earth resembling a small island, floating down the silent river, with a variety of plants and shrubs growing upon it; and from the water being invisible, the perfect reflection of this little plantation gave it the appearance of a clump of young trees calmly moving in a wide vacuum, with each plant growing perpendicularly upward and downward, in precise resemblance. If we held out a hand or an oar ... the same was seen below, without discovering the limpid medium between them. In short we seemed to move, like our globe itself, in ethereal space.

From this world, Harris has derived his sensibility. His achievement has been the creation of it into poetry. And at its best, this poetry moves even beyond recreation into enactment; so that often we are able to participate in the creation (out of elements of space, time and material) of the poet's vision ("Vision at the Well"):

Touched by vision
the light fingertips of rain pass softly
to change the stone and burden of her perfection
into rapt walls that house joy and pain and living imperfection.
Her cheeks are the dark glow of blood
beneath the frail temper of space and eternity, the history
of her flesh and blood is strange and new.

—Edward Kamau Brathwaite

HARRISON, Jim (James Thomas Harrison). American. Born in Grayling, Michigan, 11 December 1937. Educated at Michigan State University, East Lansing, B.A. 1960; M.A. in comparative literature 1964. Married Linda King in 1960; two daughters. Formerly, Assistant Professor of English, State University of New York, Stony Brook. Now lives on a farm in Michigan. Recipient: National Endowment for the Arts grant, 1967, 1968, 1969;

Guggenheim Fellowship, 1969. Agent: Robert Datilla, 225 East 49th Street, New York, New York. Address: Box 120a, Lake Leelanau, Michigan 49653, U.S.A.

PUBLICATIONS

Verse

Plain Song. New York, Norton, 1965.
Locations. New York, Norton, 1968.
Walking. Cambridge, Massachusetts, Pym Randall Press, 1969.
Outlyers and Ghazals. New York, Simon and Schuster, 1971.
Letters to Yesenin. Fremont, Michigan, Sumac Press, 1973.

Novels

Wolf. New York, Simon and Schuster, 1971.
A Good Day to Die. New York, Simon and Schuster, 1973.
Farmer. New York, Viking Press, 1976.

Jim Harrison comments:

I write "free verse" which is absurdly indefinite as a name for what any poet writes. I consider myself an "internationalist" and my main influences to be Neruda, Rilke, Yeats, Bunting, Lorca, and, in my own country, Whitman, Hart Crane, Robert Duncan and Ezra Pound. Not that this helps much other than to name those I esteem, and, perhaps vacantly, wish to emulate. Most of my poems seem rural, vaguely surrealistic though after the Spanish rather than the French. My sympathies run hotly to the impure, the inclusive, as the realm of poetry. A poet, at best, speaks in the "out loud speech of his tribe," deals in essences whether political, social or personal. All of world literature is his province though he sees it as a "guild" only to be learned from, as he must speak in his own voice.

* * *

Jim Harrison seems most at home in his poems when he is alone in the woods of Northern Michigan, where he lives. He is a poet of the physical world and the natural world. His work is immersed in sensations – the taste of blackberry brandy, the smell of manure and kerosene – and many of his most forceful poems show a close observation of animals and a great sympathy for them, for starving swans, for wolves turned mad or murderous by the imprisonment men impose upon them.

Harrison's is a grainy, tactile kind of writing. An increased adeptness and richness of description are the primary gains that resulted from his work with longer forms in *Locations*. That talent for description serves him well in his professed intention to write about "audible things, things moving/at noon in full raw light"; still, one could wish that Harrison were more concerned with spiritual matters, that he had more of the religious tenderness possessed by a poet like Roethke. Largely in the ghazals which comprise the most of *Outlyers* an adolescent and cruel side of Harrison surfaces. The ghazals are pervaded by a kind of sneering humor, an American tough-guy stance that can be ugly, especially when he deals with women. In countless couplets Harrison either insults, ogles, or accuses women, and continuously pictures or imagines females suffering a myriad of indignities and cruelties.

In a series of poems, *Letters to Yesenin*, that has appeared since *Outlyers*, Harrison confesses to having reached an emotional dead-end, unable to love, exhausted and inured. The poems, however, are encouraging not only because they have a feel of genuine honesty in contrast to the locker-room honesty of the ghazals, but because in them Harrison seems to have found a form that suits his considerable talent, especially his facility for creating a sense of natural speech.

—Lawrence Russ

HARRISON, Keith (Edward). Australian. Born in Melbourne, Victoria, 29 January 1932. Educated at Trinity Grammar School, Melbourne; Melbourne Teachers' College, 1951; University of Melbourne (Masefield Prize, 1954), 1952–54, B.A. in English and French 1954; University of Iowa, Iowa City, 1966–67, M.A. 1967. Married Inger Christina Götesdotter Haglund in 1965; two daughters. High school teacher, Victoria, 1954–57; lecturer, City Literary Institute, London, 1959–63; Tutor, University of London Extra-Mural Department, 1963–65; Visiting Poet, University of Iowa, 1966; Lecturer in English, York University, Toronto, 1966–68. Assistant Professor, 1968–74, and since 1974, Associate Professor of English, and since 1970, Director of the Arts Program, Carleton College, Northfield, Minnesota. Recipient: Canada Council grant, 1968; Department of Health, Education, and Welfare Seminar on South Asian Studies Fellowship, 1969, 1970; Arts Council of Great Britain award, 1972. Address: Route 1, Northfield, Minnesota 55057, U.S.A.

PUBLICATIONS

Verse

Points in a Journey and Other Poems. London, Macmillan, 1966; Chester Springs, Pennsylvania, Dufour, 1967.
Two Variations on a Ground. London, Turret, 1968.
Songs from the Drifting House. London, Macmillan, 1972.
The Basho Poems. Iowa City, Cyathus Press, 1975.

Manuscript Collection: Carleton College Library, Northfield, Minnesota.

Critical Studies: Reviews by Mingo Jones, in *Saturday Night* (Toronto), April 1967, Stan Fefferman, in *Toronto Telegram*, April 1967, and Carl Harrison-Ford, in *New Poetry* (Sydney), April 1973.

Keith Harrison comments:

Teaching still seems to me the best and worst job for a poet. Young people are so starved at their high schools for good literature – good art of any kind – that introducing them to poetry both at an interpretive and a creative level is an urgent necessity, as well as an exciting challenge. The trick is to find enough time for your own work – and no university poet whom I know has solved that one, except by becoming a public institution, an "instant personality."

To get to more substantial matters; I think there are stable mythic patterns. Chiefly: to grow, it would seem that artists, as well as everybody else, have to go through hell. Modern man is a neurotic mess and that is the ground we have to stand on. The evasive strategies of madness, suicide or incoherence simply won't do. The difficult thing, the damnably difficult thing, is to take one's private predicament and by imaginative heat to forge something hard and emblematic out of it. One hopes that on the other side of all that one will be able to write a poetry that is full of sunlight and broad humour (there is too little *pleasure* in contemporary poetry) – but there is no easy way out of hell. I have just finished a book of very dark poems and I hope the darkness is made acceptable by the validity and accuracy of the language. (I also hope it's the last dark thing that I ever do.)

Poetry readings are currently the dullest and most ill-organized form of entertainment we have. I would like, both as a writer and a reader to improve them to the level of, say, a concert given by a group of bright young musicians. The whole art of poetry – writing, understanding, reading aloud – is still in its infancy in this country, and in most others.

* * *

An Australian, Keith Harrison has lived and studied in both England and America for a considerable number of years. Like so many poets, he has found it necessary to work through the experiences of childhood before being able to experiment with new styles and ideas. His first book, *Points in a Journey*, records in an eight-part autobiographical poem, the discoveries he has made about himself, his family and his background. The second part of this book consists of a series of dramatic monologues of which the most outstanding is "Leichardt in the Desert" (Leichardt was a nineteenth-century German explorer who died while attempting to cross the Australian desert):

> I did not choose to make this westward journey
> Into the dry rock country of the dead
> Where in the torpid light the lizards
> Flick from our tracks into the mean rock shadows;
> To slash that tunnel through the mountain forest,
> Cross the grasslands, wade the inland rivers –
> I did not choose; say rather I was called....

Other pieces of interest are "The Island Weather of the Newly Betrothed," "Wife Waiting" and "Dentist at Work." The third section contains more formal experiments, set in Spain and London, and these poems are not quite so successful as the rest.

In *Songs from the Drifting House*, Keith Harrison still persists in the role of ironic observer, commenting upon life as he sees it on his travels. "Swedish Vignettes" and "Midwestern Blues" make their point with due economy. The title of the book is taken from a series of lyrics which are pleasant enough but in no way outstanding. There are some competent translations from Ronsard, Baudelaire and Rimbaud, but overall one gains the impression of a poet lacking a real sense of direction. Harrison undoubtedly has talent, but so far his promise is greater than his achievement.

—Howard Sergeant

HARRISON, Tony. British. Born in Leeds, Yorkshire, 30 April 1937. Educated at Cross Flats County Primary, Leeds, 1942–48; Leeds Grammar School, 1948–55; University of Leeds, 1955–60, B.A. in classics, Postgraduate Diploma in linguistics. Married Rosemarie Crossfield in 1962; one daughter and one son. Lecturer in English, Ahmadu Bello University, Zaria, Northern Nigeria, 1962–66, and Charles University, Prague, 1966–67; Editor, with Jon Silkin and Ken Smith, *Stand*, Newcastle upon Tyne, 1968–69; Resident

Dramatist, National Theatre, London, 1977–78. Delegate, Conference on Colonialism and the Arts, Dar-es-Salaam, Tanzania, July 1971. Recipient: Northern Arts Fellowship, 1967, 1976; Cholmondeley Award, 1969; UNESCO Fellowship, 1969; Faber Memorial Award, 1972; Gregynog Fellowship, 1973. Address: 9 The Grove, Gosforth, Newcastle upon Tyne NE3 1NE, England.

PUBLICATIONS

Verse

Earthworks. Leeds, Northern House, 1964.
Newcastle Is Peru. Newcastle upon Tyne, Eagle Press, 1969.
The Loiners. London, London Magazine Editions, 1970.
Corgi Modern Poets in Focus 4, with others, edited by Jeremy Robson. London, Corgi, 1971.
Ten Poems from the School of Eloquence. London, Rex Collings, 1976.
The School of Eloquence and Other Poems. London, Rex Collings, 1978.

Plays

Aikin Mata, with James Simmons, adaptation of *Lysistrata* by Aristophanes (produced Zaria, Nigeria, 1965). Ibadan, Oxford University Press, 1966.
The Misanthrope, adaptation of a play by Molière (produced London, 1973; Washington, D.C., and New York, 1975). London, Rex Collings, 1973; New York, Third Press, 1974.
Phaedra Britannica, adaptation of the play by Racine (produced London, 1975).
Bow Down, music by Harrison Birtwhistle (produced London, 1977). London, Rex Collings, 1977.
The Passion, from the York Mystery Plays (produced London, 1977). London, Rex Collings, 1977.
The Bartered Bride, adaptation of an opera by Sabina, music by Smetana (produced New York, 1978). New York, Schirmer, 1978.
Oresteia, adaptation of the play by Aeschylus (produced London, 1979).

Other

Translator, *Poems*, by Palladas. London, Anvil Press Poetry, 1975.

Manuscript Collections: University of Newcastle upon Tyne; Newcastle Literary and Philosophical Society.

Critical Studies: by James Simmons, in *The Honest Ulsterman* (Belfast), September–October 1970; Jeremy Robson, in *Corgi Modern Poets in Focus 4*, 1971.

* * *

Tony Harrison, who has been described by the poet, critic and discriminating editor David Wright as "the white hope of English poetry," is certainly one of the most accomplished technicians of his generation. His brilliant translation of Molière, a deserved success on the stage, aptly demonstrates that form, intelligently and experimentally employed, is still viable. His use of "the floating s" (the transfer of an apostrophe s to the following line), his vigour and nerve and faith to the spirit of the original: all these contribute to one of the greatest successes in translation of recent years. It is as readable as it is performable. His skill as a translator is also to be seen in his versions of Palladas and in his contributions to Peter Jay's *Greek Anthology*.

Harrison is not a poet who works from the excitement words create in him; he begins, rather, with an idea or a theme and then clothes it with his verbal imagination. One may (so far) miss in him the kind of richness that is to be found in some of the best Latin American poetry (from some of the *Modernistas* onward); but that one should think of missing it at all is tribute to his very evident potentialities. His caution, at a time when complete carelessness and the tendency to splurge on without thought is perfectly acceptable, is, in any case, admirable; his well-judged daring in translation shows that he has the capacity to do justice to his linguistic resources, which are considerable.

As it is, Harrison's elegant and originally angled poems work primarily by means of wit (in the Empsonian sense), and their emotional substance is conveyed by means of carefully chosen modes of tone and the force of particular lines. He is an intellectual, though never a cold, poet – one would suspect that the influence of Empson, though never disastrous as in the case of the early John Wain, has been a strong one. He shows something of Empson's ability to clothe a complex idea in a form of words that is passionate and yet not over-emotional; he has Empsonian restraint, and one suspects that his political position is somewhat near to Empson's at least in the sense that his powerful feelings are as powerfully restrained by intelligence – an intelligence so acute that it is sometimes felt as despair. Harrison is refreshing because he turns his energies, which are considerable, not to the fashionable literary world or what it may vaguely feel it wants at any given time, but to the exploration of what can be done with the colloquial and the unfamiliar. This suggests that he may soon feel ready to plunge more directly into his own imagination, which may have positively startling results on a poetic scene that is still dominated – in terms of gifts – by Philip Larkin. "On Not Being Milton," aside from its subtle puns, its characteristic wit and its strong sense of history, contains hints of the latent power that I have suggested Harrison possesses:

Read and committed to the flames, I call
these sixteen lines that go back to my roots,
my *Cahier d'un retour au pays natal*,
my growing black enough to fit my boots.

The stutter of the scold out of the branks
Of condescension, class and counter-class
thickens with glottals to a lumpen mass
of Ludding morphemes closing up their ranks.
Each swung cast-iron Enoch of Leeds stress
clangs a forged music on the frames of Art,
the looms of owned language smashed apart!

Three cheers for mute ingloriousness!

Articulation is the tongue-tied's fighting.
In the silence round all poetry we quote
Tidd the Cato Street conspirator who wrote:

Sir, I Ham a very Bad Hand at Righting.

Not all that Harrison writes is as effectively compressed and moving and sardonic as this fine poem; but much is. In him, for the first time for many years, we have an intellect combined with what was once called a heart. It is cheering that even at his weakest he has no trace of sentimentality; that almost all he writes is worthy of discussion at a high critical level.

—Martin Seymour-Smith

HARSENT, David. English. Born in Devonshire, 9 December 1942. Works in publishing. Recipient: Gregory Award, 1967; Arts Council bursary, 1969; Faber Memorial Award, 1978. Address: c/o Oxford University Press, 37 Dover Street, London W1X 4AH, London. Lives in Buckinghamshire.

PUBLICATIONS

Verse

Tonight's Lover. London, The Review, 1968.
A Violent Country. London, Oxford University Press, 1969.
Ashridge. Oxford, Sycamore Press, 1970.
After Dark. London, Oxford University Press, 1973.
Truce. Oxford, Sycamore Press, 1973.
Dreams of the Dead. London, Oxford University Press, 1977.

* * *

David Harsent's first collection of poetry, *A Violent Country*, contains poems about madness and death, a series of love poems deeply veined with sadness and terror, and a sequence in which a woman probes her anguished existence.

There is, obviously, little easy terrain in this country, and Harsent does not flinch from penetrating the deepest undergrowth. Occasionally he revels in the gore and desolation, and then the poems seem contrived and over-sentimental. But for the most part, Harsent writes with harsh accuracy, richly conveying the violence: "the crushed/head, the raw/excresence at/the gaping jaw –/rubbery bleb/of its own/congealing guts" ("The Woman and the Cat").

But Harsent's major talent lies in the exactness and authority with which he communicates the deep crises raging within – a dreamlike, obsessive world of impotence, hopelessness, and madness. In "The Woman and the Cat," the real horror is not the eyes of the cat cracking "like a trodden grape," but the woman's eyes, like a camera, recording every detail, visualising the moment of impact, picturing precisely the process of death.

The series of poems about the woman are among the most powerful and disturbing that Harsent has written. Moving slowly through her house and garden – reminiscent of an Ingmar Bergman movie – the woman's mind is full of blood imagery, guilt, and doom. Through meticulous examination of objects, soft words and stillness, she exorcises both pain and passion; but waking in the morning, her words – real or dreamed – return to haunt her through the day, until: "That evening, tired of speech/she tests/the astringency of song" ("The Woman's Soliloquies").

Pain and anguish are less blatant in *After Dark*, but uncertainties linger and the poignancy remains intense. The poems are generally softer, more reflective and more obviously personal. The poet lives quietly in the country ("After Dark"):

I have bogged down in this odd village;
my children belong to the place.
At night I can hear the cows
coughing in a field behind the house.

I close my eyes
and invent arrivals.

Harsent is constantly reminded of his childhood – strange, passionate, less ordered than the present, it underlines the inadequacies of his adult life. Perhaps the strongest "presence" is the austere landscape – a wildness surrounding his neat interior, reflecting his love and his solitude in its bleak depths ("Figures in a Landscape"):

Too tired for sleep and knowing of no way
to quieten you, I've walked to this cold bench.

Above the fields
mountains of purple cloud lumber through drizzle.

Between your open window and this place
the land is dark and wringing wet.

Later in the volume the uncertainties harden; there is less looking back. He begins to anticipate death, lured by signs of withering skin, "insights of fatigue," a switchblade drawn across the palm. The volume ends with a poem about a suicide. Hurtling towards the street, the man's last glimpse is of the sky: "a fractured blue, and clouds/like dark pools where his other lives submerged" ("Leap Off the City Skyline").

There are no half measures for Harsent. Death is the totality, and suffering the way toward it. How vital then, to remember passion, to always hope for love ("Acid Landscapes"):

... how lovers might
suffer the fierce light flensing their lives

of all but one bald fact;
how they might lie awake by those blunt hills
breathing each other's breath
and feeling the island slipping with the tides.

There is an extraordinary power in Harsent's poetry. If he can withstand a slight tendency to sentimentalize, he will undoubtedly emerge as a major poet of his generation.

—Roland Turner

HART-SMITH, William. Australian. Born in Tunbridge Wells, Kent, England, 23 November 1911; emigrated to New Zealand in 1924, and to Australia in 1936. Educated in Scotland; St. Clair, Walmer, Kent; Gunnersbury Preparatory School, London; Belmont Primary School, Auckland; Seddon Memorial Technical College, Auckland. Served in the Australian military forces, 1941–43. Married 1) M. Wynn in 1939 (marriage dissolved, 1949); 2) P. A. McBeath in 1949 (separated); four children. Clerk, New Zealand Shipping Company, Auckland, 1926–27; Radio Salesman and Mechanic, Wisemans Ltd., Auckland, 1927–30; Radio Serviceman, Auckland, 1930–36, and Baden-Cameron Company, Hobart, Tasmania, 1936–37; Radio Copywriter and Announcer, Station 2CH, Sydney, 1937–44; Free-lance Writer, Sydney, 1944–47; Tutor Organizer, Adult Education Department, Canterbury, New Zealand, 1948–55; Advertising Copywriter, Jack Penny Ltd., Christchurch, 1956–60; Manager, Christchurch Office, 1960–62, and Advertising Manager, Sydney, 1962–66, Charles Kidd and Company; Radio Technician, Amalgamated Wireless of Australasia, Sydney, 1966–70; clerk and part-time tutor, Western Australian Institute of Technology, Perth, 1972–78. President, Poetry Society of Australia, 1963–64. Recipient: Crouch Memorial Medal, 1959; Grace Leven Prize, 1966; three Australian Arts Council fellowships, 1973–78. Agent: Angus and Robertson Ltd., 102 Glover Street, Cremorne, New South Wales 2090, Australia.

PUBLICATIONS

Verse

Columbus Goes West. Adelaide, Economy Press, 1943.
Harvest. Melbourne, Georgian House, 1945.
The Unceasing Ground. Sydney, Angus and Robertson, 1946.
Christopher Columbus: A Sequence of Poems. Christchurch, Caxton Press, 1948.
On the Level: Mostly Canterbury Poems. Timaru, New Zealand, Timaru Herald, 1950.
Poems in Doggerel. Wellington, Handcraft Press, 1955.
Poems of Discovery. Sydney, Angus and Robertson, 1959.
The Talking Clothes. Sydney, Angus and Robertson, 1966.
Poetry from Australia: Pergamon Poets 6, with Judith Wright and Randolph Stow, edited by Howard Sergeant. Oxford, Pergamon Press, 1969.
Minipoems. Perth, Western Australian Institute of Technology, 1974.
Let Me Learn the Steps: Poems from a Psychiatric Ward, with Mary Morris. Privately printed, 1977.

Manuscript Collection: Fisher Library, University of Sydney.

Critical Studies: *Australian Literature* by E. Morris Miller and F. T. Macartney, revised edition, Sydney, Angus and Robertson, 1956; by Sister Veronica Brady, in *Westerly* (Perth), March 1976.

William Hart-Smith comments:

Began reading widely, age of 19. Shortly after 21st birthday made a definite decision to be a poet and stay with it at all costs, earning a living as best I could. Have travelled widely both in Australia and New Zealand, so that "landscape and spirit of place" are strongly in evidence. Was closely associated with an Australian nationalist movement, "Jindyworobak," early 1940's. Have experimented with form, style, and method a great deal. Strongest early influences were from two New Zealand poets, Gloria Rawlinson and D'Arcy Cresswell; later, in Australia, matured suddenly, particularly because of the profound effect the Australian environment had on me. Main literary influences would be D. H. Lawrence, Ezra Pound, and modern American poetry in general which gave me carte blanche to experiment. Read much of the Imagists so that the main aim would appear to be to concentrate with an almost painterly eye on the concrete visual image. However prime intention is, using the Sufi approach, to let the image itself and the reader's enjoyment of it as an image per se, to disguise, or merely hint at, what the visual image is really trying to say, or stand in for. Many poems, therefore, are little parables, or poems using the device of parable. It's the only way I can find effectively to verbalise moments of insight and intuition. Another aim has been extreme compression, at the same time to listen to the verbal music the words make. The poems are never just dashed off as some may think: the original draft is only the starting point of an attempt to give even the shortest, Zen-like poem a strictly disciplined structure of interlocking rhyme and para-rhyme, assonance and dissonance. In other words, no matter how compressed the poem may be, how sparingly the words are used, the aim is to retain the poem's authenticity as a work of thorough craftsmanship and be a pleasure to the ear as well as the eye; or, act as a stimulus to the reader's *own* imagination, no matter on what level of consciousness he can reach. Most of my poems record brief moments of extreme joy and delight. Insights, Discoveries, moments of Understanding.

* * *

Over the years since 1936, William Hart-Smith, who left England at the age of twelve, has consistently written of his adopted country, Australia, and sometimes of New Zealand where he has also lived some years. His spare economy of language, the simple, usually free, shapes of his poems and the lucidity and apparent casualness of their statements have kept his work from becoming fashionable, but also lent it strength. He seems to have found his way easily into both his new countries as providers of symbol and background, and his pithy conversational rhythms have much in common with their speech.

Few of his poems take much space to make their point. His one long poem, *Christopher Columbus*, consists of forty-three short poems, few of more than page-length, each devoted to some aspect of Columbus' story and each complete in itself. Comment is kept at a minimum; with Hart-Smith, it is selection that does the commenting; and he chooses his momentary glimpses of the voyages, or his quotations from the documents, much as a good documentary film-maker does, for their visual or human illuminations.

There is, indeed, something of document in many of his poems, directed as they are towards objects, events or persons. To write this kind of verse, into which the poet as person intrudes so minimally, is not easy, if the poet is to avoid a cool pedestrianism of vision. This danger for Hart-Smith's poetry is increased by the fact that though his vision is individual, ironic and continually interesting, it does not seem to be directed through any deep interior conviction or world-view. This apparent lack of thematic connection between separate poems is reinforced by the lack of much change or apparent poetic development over the years, though there has been a perceptible increase in tautness of manner, a sharpening of his use of language, and a lessening in his earlier more lyrical attack.

An important influence in his work was the "Jindyworobak" movement, through which a group of Australian poets attempted to work their way into a "native" attitude to Australian themes. Hart-Smith was one of the most distinguished of the poets in the movement, and his verse still displays some of their characteristic tenets. In a comment on the movement's achievement, he once wrote: "It is more than a few rather fanatical individuals trying to be exclusively and most Aboriginally Australian in the English language; it's a case of a number of creative writers pointing the way back to ... the childhood of the human race, 'to a land that is common to us all.' " His poems, he says, are "poems of discovery," "attempts to record moments of understanding." Their concentration on objects and events of the outer world is motivated by this attempt to re-see them in a fresh light.

At his best, he does this with memorable individuality. Such poem-titles as "Boomerang," "Bathymeter," "A Snail," "Number," "Candles" indicate the directions in which he turns the searchlight of his verse.

Though he has published a number of books of verse, no complete collection has yet appeared. When this happens, it will be possible to see that, instead of a succession of descriptive and commentary verses, he has produced a gallery of portraits and still-lifes that illuminate the world from the viewpoint of an original and ironic mind.

—Judith Wright

HARTNETT, Michael. Irish. Born in County Limerick, 18 September 1941. Educated at Newcastle West Secondary School; University College, Dublin; Trinity College, Dublin. Married; one daughter. Has worked as civil servant, dishwasher, postman, tea-boy, housepainter, telephonist; currently teacher, National College of Physical Education, Limerick. Contributor to *The Irish Times*, Dublin, and Radio Eireann. Editor, with James Liddy and Liam O'Connor, *Arena*, Dublin, 1963–65. Recipient: Irish American Cultural Institute Award, 1975; Irish Arts Council Award, 1975.

PUBLICATIONS

Verse

Anatomy of a Cliché. Dublin, Dolmen Press, 1968.
Selected Poems. Dublin, New Writers Press, 1971.
Cula Ide, The Retreat of Ita Cagney (Gaelic and English). Dublin, Goldsmith Press, 1975.
A Farewell to English and Other Poems. Dublin, Gallery Press, 1975; revised edition, 1978.
Poems in English. Dublin, Dolmen Press, 1977.
Prisoners. Deerfield, Massachusetts, Deerfield Press, 1978.
Adharca Broic (Gaelic). Dublin, Gallery Press, 1978.
Daoine (Gaelic). Dublin, Gallery Press, 1979.

Other

Editor, with Desmond Egan, *Choice.* Dublin, Goldsmith Press, 1970.

Translator, *The Hag of Beare: A Rendition of the Old Irish.* Dublin, New Writers Press, 1970.
Translator, *Gipsy Ballads*, by Lorca. Dublin, Goldsmith Press, 1970.
Translator, *Tao: A Version of the Tao Te Ch'ing.* Dublin, New Writers Press, 1972.

Critical Study: Interview in *The Poet Speaks*, edited by Peter Orr, London, Routledge, and New York, Barnes and Noble, 1966.

Michael Hartnett comments:

Major themes: The woman as human being; deaths (not *Death*); "nature" in human terms.
Characteristic Subjects: Love Poems; the hunting of animals; wake poems.
Usual Verse Forms: Lyric, syllabic, assonantal, rhyme (sparingly), metric (rarely in the classical sense); developing more complex forms.
General Sources and Influences: Mainstream English poetry; Gaelic poetry.
Characteristic Stylistic Devices: Compound words; anglosaxon (*not* in the D. H. Lawrence sense) vocabulary; the animal as symbol.

* * *

Michael Hartnett's achievement as a poet so far has been distinguished by its emotional intensity, its scrupulous attention to the subtleties of craftsmanship, its thematic variety, and its essentially experimental and adventurous character. In his work, intelligence and music play equally important parts. There is no arid intellectualizing, no meaningless melody. Reading through his output so far, one has the sense of a dedicated artist who refuses to admit anything shabby or shoddy into his work. Some critics in fact say that Hartnett is fastidious to the point of being finicky, that his obsession with technique conceals very serious emotional limitations. This, to my mind, is a complete misreading of Hartnett's purpose and achievement. Hartnett, as far as I can see, has the full equipment for a poet of stature. He is well on his way to becoming a master of language, his *own* language; he has a keen ear for the subtlest rhythms; almost everything he writes haunts the reader for its cutting insight expressed in appropriate verbal music; and, above all, his poems at their best have that quiet authority which is the surest mark of confidence.

Take, for example, the last of "Four Sonnets," from *Selected Poems*:

I saw magic on a green country road –
That old woman, a bag of sticks her load,

Blackly down to her thin feet a fringed shawl,
A rosary of bone on her horned hand,
A flight of curlews scribing by her head,
And ashtrees combing with their frills her hair.

Her eyes, wet sunken holes pierced by an awl,
Must have deciphered her adoring land:
And curlews, no longer lean birds, instead
Become ten scarlet comets in the air.

Some incantation from her canyoned mouth,
Irish, English, blew frost along the ground,
And even though the wind was from the South
The ashleaves froze without an ashleaf sound.

The picture of that old woman is completely, yet concisely, imagined. The form is old enough for anyone's taste; but the diction is novel and energetic. This blend of the old and the new is reflected in the imagery of the poem: "curlews, no longer lean birds, instead/Become ten scarlet comets in the air."

In his vision of the past as a source of vitality and inspiration, Michael Hartnett has produced a moving, elegant version of the Chinese classic, the *Tao*, and a magnificent translation of the greatest of Old Irish poems, *The Hag of Beare*. This latter poem shows Hartnett's technical dexterity at its most brilliant. He makes a fine, sustained attempt to convey something of the rhythms of the original by interlocking assonance and by alliteration. Many Irish poets have tried to translate this marvellous lament for lost youth, this outcry against the ravages of time. I think that Michael Hartnett's is the best.

Very fine, too, are his translations of the *Gipsy Ballads* of Garcia Lorca. It is obvious that no translator can fully capture Lorca's magic; all he can hope to do, at best, is to suggest something of its nature and effects. In his versions of Lorca's "The Flight," "San Miguel," "Gabriel," and "Ballad of the Black Sorrow," Michael Hartnett succeeds in making precisely that suggestion.

What have we then? We have a gifted and dedicated poet, as intensely interested in the cultures of other lands as in that of his own. Hartnett is one of the most accomplished and enterprising poets now writing in Ireland.

—Brendan Kennelly

HARWOOD, Gwen(doline Nessie). Australian. Born in Taringa, Queensland, 8 June 1920. Educated at Brisbane Girls' Grammar School. Married Frank William Harwood in 1945; four children. Formerly, Organist at All Saints' Church, Brisbane, and Secretary to a Consultant Physician, Hobart. Recipient: *Meanjin* prize, 1958, 1959; Commonwealth Literary Fund grant, 1973; Grace Leven Prize, 1975; Robert Frost Award, 1977; Patrick White Award, 1978. Address: Kettering, Tasmania 7155, Australia.

PUBLICATIONS

Verse

Poems. Sydney, Angus and Robertson, 1963.
Poems: Volume Two. Sydney, Angus and Robertson, 1968.
Selected Poems. Sydney, Angus and Robertson, 1975.

Plays

The Fall of the House of Usher, music by Larry Sitsky (produced Hobart, 1965).
Commentaries on Living, music by James Penberthy (produced Perth, 1972).
Lenz, music by Larry Sitsky, adaptation of the story by Georg Büchner (produced Sydney, 1974).
Sea Changes, music by Ian Cugley (produced Hobart, 1974).
Fiery Tales, music by Larry Sitsky (produced Adelaide, 1976).

Manuscript Collections: Australian National Library, Canberra; Fryer Memorial Library, University of Queensland, Brisbane.

Critical Studies: by David Moody, in *Meanjin* (Melbourne), no. 4, 1963; "The Poet as Döppelganger" by Dennis Douglas, in *Quadrant* (Sydney), April 1969; "Gwen Harwood and the Professors" by A. D. Hope, in *Australian Literary Studies* (Hobart), 1972, and a reply to Professor Hope by Dennis Douglas, May 1973; "Artists and Academics in the Poetry of Gwen Harwood" by John B. Beston, in *Quadrant* (Sydney), 1974; "Truth Beyond the Language Game: The Poetry of Gwen Harwood" by N. Talbot, in *Australian Literary Studies* (Brisbane), May 1976; "Worlds Beyond Words: Gwen Harwood's *Selected Poems*" by D. Dodwell, in *Westerly* (Perth), June 1977; "A Fire-Talented Tongue: Some Notes on the Poetry of Gwen Harwood" by R. F. Brissenden, in *Southerly* (Sydney), March 1978.

Gwen Harwood comments:

My major themes are music and musicians; the celebration of love and friendship. I write in a number of styles but the qualities I value most in poetry are power and clarity. I want my poems "to shape joy from the flux of sense."

* * *

Since 1963 Gwen Harwood has been delighting Australian readers with a steady flow of excellent poems written under her own and at least two pen names. Though not stylistically adventurous she is a virtuoso of the character study, choosing her subjects and sometimes victims from a milieu of outwardly polite, inwardly primitive middle-class Australians, often with academic backgrounds.

Her two chief poetic protagonists through whose reactions she sifts and analyses both blatant and subtle aspects of a predominantly bourgeois morality are Professor Eisenbart, a middle-aged academic, and Kröte, an aging declassé music teacher. Though in her satirical manner and expert use of the iambic line she may be said to resemble superficially A. D. Hope, the true affinity of her poetry is with the scarifying humour and intricate characterisation of the fiction of Patrick White.

In her first book, simply entitled *Poems*, surrounded by a body of perfectly wrought individual pieces of the calibre of the philosophical "Hesperian," the scathingly witty "Critic's Nightwatch" and the beautiful, compassionate "At the Sea's Edge," is the central sequence "Professor Eisenbart." Here in eight self-contained yet thematically linked poems she depicts the arrogant yet vulnerable professor seduced at a prize-giving concert – "a sage fool trapped/by music in a copper net of hair" – caught napping at a visit to the zoo, lecturing his mistress on elementary physics at the seaside and so on, "Too old to love, too young to die."

Kröte the musician is the central character of her second book *Poems: Volume Two*. He, like Eisenbart, brings a cultured European consciousness to bear on the not-quite-barbarous wilderness of Australian society in the Sixties. In his isolated crises of suffering and near despair he becomes a persona of the poet in a largely unsympathetic environment.

Gwen Harwood's innate love of music sounds throughout her books. Whether she is examining the spectacle of domesticity versus art, as in "Burning Sappho," or poking sophisticated fun at pedantic get-togethers, "Academic Evening" and "Cocktails at Seven," music is invariably invoked as a saving grace and guardian angel of the embattled, non-conforming poet-witness of the contemporary scene.

—Bruce Beaver

HARWOOD, Lee. British. Born in Leicester, 6 June 1939. Educated at state schools; Queen Mary College, London, B.A. (honours) in English 1961. Married to Jud Walker; two sons and one daughter. Monumental mason's mate, 1961; library and museum assistant, 1962–64, 1965–66; packer, 1964; assistant, 1966–67, and manager of the poetry department, 1971, Better Books, London; bus conductor, Brighton, 1969; lived in the United States, 1970, 1972–73; Writer-in-Residence, Aegean School of Fine Arts, Paros, Greece, Summer 1971, 1972; post office worker, Brighton, 1973–77. Editor, *Night Scene* magazine, London, 1963; Co-Editor, *Night Train* magazine, London, 1963; Editor, with Johnny Byrne, *Horde* magazine, London, 1964; Editor, with Claude Royet-Journoud, *Soho* magazine, London and Paris, 1964; Editor, *Tzarad* magazine, London and Brighton, 1965–69; Co-Editor, *Boston Eagle*, 1973–74. Recipient: Poets Foundation Award (USA), 1966; Alice Hunt Bartlett Award, 1976. Address: c/o 9 Highfield Road, Chertsey, Surrey, England.

PUBLICATIONS

Verse

Title Illegible. London, Writers Forum, 1965.
The Man with Blue Eyes. New York, Angel Hair, 1966.
The White Room. London, Fulcrum Press, 1968.
The Beautiful Atlas. Brighton, Kavanagh, 1969.
Landscapes. London, Fulcrum Press, 1969.
The Sinking Colony. London, Fulcrum Press, 1970.
Penguin Modern Poets 19, with John Ashbery and Tom Raworth. London, Penguin, 1971.
The First Poem. Brighton, Unicorn Bookshop, 1971.
New Year. London, Wallrich, 1971.
Captain Harwood's Log of Stern Statements and Stout Sayings. London, Writers Forum, 1973.
Freighters. Newcastle upon Tyne, Pig Press, 1975.
H.M.S. Little Fox. London, Oasis, 1976.
Boston – Brighton. London, Oasis, 1977.
Old Bosham Bird Watch and Other Stories. Newcastle upon Tyne, Pig Press, 1977; revised edition, 1978.

Recording: *Landscapes*, Stream, 1968.

Other

Tristan Tzara: A Bibliography. London, Aloes, 1974.

Translator, *A Poem Sequence*, by Tristan Tzara. Gillingham, Kent, ARC Publications, 1969; revised edition, as *Cosmic Realities Vanilla Tobacco Drawings*, 1975.
Translator, *Destroyed Days*, by Tristan Tzara. Colchester, Essex, Voiceprint Editions, 1971.
Translator, *Selected Poems*, by Tristan Tzara. London, Trigram Press, 1975.

Critical Studies: review in *Records and Recording* (London), April 1969; by Raymond Gardiner, in *The Guardian* (London), 8 July 1970; interview with Victor Bockris, in *Pennsylvania Review 1* (Philadelphia), 1970; *The Ironic Harvest: English Poetry in the 20th Century* by Geoffrey Thurley, London, Arnold, 1974; interview with Eric Mottram, in *Poetry Information 14* (London), Winter 1975–76; "The Illusions of Freedom: The Poetry of Lee Harwood" by Paul Selby, in *Poetry Information 15* (London), 1976.

Lee Harwood comments:

Schools of poetry seem totally irrelevant today when "new writing" is becoming more and more international, both in its aspirations and its audiences. My explaining my own work would be ridiculous – if one can explain art, why bother to create it? Long live the object – which is common property.

* * *

"I just want to tell you the truth," says Lee Harwood's voice in *Boston – Brighton* – not through self-conscious symbols, but with "the small daily details." And if the reader objects: "There's no pleasing some folks./You pays your money/and you takes your choice." Observing process is Harwood's forte. How seeing "rows of white houses" evolves into a song title. How hearing the song brings or does not bring the houses back into view. How we compose a reality out of fragments, and within this "picture," how everyone goes or does not go about his own way – and the "strange pleasures" we find "inside it all."

He makes no statements about Fate or Meaning. Whereas, say, Robert Frost sets an eternal, metaphysical watch at the ocean's edge for people who can see "Neither Out Far Nor In Deep," Harwood simply sets up what you might expect:

a lone freighter
silhouetted
maybe three freighters
with crews and cooks and captains
are silhouetted
are even clear out to sea
                                        there
I point in front of my face.

That awareness, an ordinary alertness "so that no thoughts are [supernaturally] clear, and, therefore, obsessive," an accessible curiosity. Postcards from Boston full of practical history; drawings of the earth's substrate supporting the Thames valley; sketches of positions the River Adur has occupied since the 13th century: this is part of what *Boston – Brighton* contains.

This world has formed on the edge of the "ghost" world of the past. Yet in it we become what we "choose" and face an "exciting ... Progress" "out to the possible – no bounds...." What interests Harwood most in this world of tempered optimism is motion – motion between the past and present, between the unconscious and conscious and back again. *H.M.S. Little Fox* began charting that world, reckoning with ghosts (Rilke, de Chirico, Stendhal) and their dreams that move through him (choose him?). He seeks a clear representation of "the process/to live on land the roots growing down/in one place a movement, yes/but a constant – that simplicity."

Given our unconscious/ghost roots, poems happen when you rub a pencil over grain you didn't know was there. Life itself is "a bare canvas, but not empty –/all there under the surface." Harwood reveals this life by exposing movements; sometimes he sees himself as a ship, or as a fox precariously crossing a river on a log. It's as though we are all "passengers," "like accomplices in the dream/we all know," yet as we move in any direction, we feel the wind ruffle our hair.

H.M.S. Little Fox acknowledges itself as an historical romance integrating dream and fairy tales sparingly into its story of a love affair. Not merely his lady's house, for example, but "the small and isolated fortress/that lies to the north/where you are left." Harwood creates a mutable reality here that changes as his mind adjusts its focal length. We read backward into time and so see the world become what it was. By section IV we are in 1969–70 where Harwood is using masks, inhabiting other voices (chance overhearings, phrases in books), walking in a world that threatens to become a hieroglyph for himself, to become "a matter of lists/that act as buttresses, even defenses" behind which he (we) play at being ourselves.

This world frequently achieves the intensity of myth, both symbolically, through allusions to the Egyptian gods the lovers imitate or that once stood as expressions of such a love, and naively, when love integrates and focuses the world of the lovers so that "a cool breeze comes up the river/and ruffles your hair." But the "Image is the ultimate enemy," as Harwood has more recently written: "pictures of ourselves distract/abstract us from being ourselves. The final section of *H.M.S. Little Fox* shows a sequence of returning heroes in ironic perspectives ("the returned astronaut waves/a *handkerchief* from the capsule's door"). Each is a different mask of the poet; each leaves "the prison of images pursuing ... the hero of the ritual." Elsewhere, Harwood has investigated that "prison." In *The Sinking Colony* and *Landscapes*, for example, he finds in precise detail the connections between the images in our eyes and the images coming from our minds. Here, he moves away from this ritual obsession; it was "about time/I woke up ... and appreciated the possible/sincerity of ... people and bodies." It was about time that he met his lady; she puts him in a "Dazzle" and threads together the poems of *H.M.S. Little Fox*. She is "REAL" and she helps him to see it is about time that he get an answer to a simple question: "I mean what is happening? – NOW!" She makes it possible for him to say, seven years later, "I just want to tell you the truth."

The question comes in the penultimate poem of *H.M.S. Little Fox*. The final poem is a sequence of satires on surrealism, from which Harwood appears to have turned away. The question may be a turning point for him; certainly it is a beginning for the reader. We have been reading backwards, into ghost roots. Now the question requires us to turn this all around, to put it together going in the other direction – as Harwood did. This chronological strategy is unusual and successful: the poems come to life.

—Edward B. Germain

HASS, Robert. American. Born in San Francisco, California, 1 March 1941. Educated at St. Mary's College, Moraga, California, B.A. 1963; Stanford University, California

(Woodrow Wilson Fellow; Danforth Fellow), 1964–67, M.A. 1965. Married Earlene Leif in 1962; three children. Has taught at the State University of New York, Buffalo, University of Virginia, Charlottesville, St. Mary's College, and Goddard College, Plainfield, Vermont; Poet-in-Residence, The Frost Place, Franconia, New Hampshire, 1978. Recipient: Yale Series of Younger Poets Award, 1972; US–UK Bicentennial Exchange Fellowship, 1976; Guggenheim Fellowship, 1979. Address: c/o Ecco Press, 1 West 30th Street, New York, New York 10001, U.S.A.

PUBLICATIONS

Verse

Field Guide. New Haven, Connecticut, Yale University Press, 1973.
Winter Morning in Charlottesville. Knotting, Bedfordshire, Sceptre Press, 1977.
Praise. New York Ecco Press, 1979.
Five American Poets, with others. Manchester, Carcanet Press, 1979.

* * *

Robert Hass's poetry moves quietly through a landscape of natural life and rhythm, until it arrives in a world of personal feeling and intimate reflection. Hass reexamines some of the central problems of the Romantic imagination, using the unforced order of nature as a lens with which to focus on the effects of time and death in man's life, and the inescapable division between consciousness and the pulse of the created world. In accepting this separation of the natural and imaginal worlds, Hass finds a potentially rich source of understanding. In *Field Guide* the poet is constantly outdoors, walking the California coast where he grew up, the upstate New York city where he taught, or even the landscape of literature – in the group of poems which form the central section of the volume. These last poems mark the crossroads of Hass's concerns, where (in "Measure") "Last light/rims the blue mountain/and I almost glimpse/what I was born to/not so much in the sunlight/or in the plum tree/as in the pulse/that forms these lines." While a great many of the poems in *Field Guide* recall Lowell in the attempt to situate the poet in historical time and place, Hass has none of Lowell's intense need for confrontation. More like Stevens or perhaps Roethke in tone, Hass attempts to integrate past and present as the two arms of a single balance.

Hass's painterly descriptions of the natural world flood the poems, and flow naturally into observations of how consciousness transforms that world. In "Songs to Survive the Summer," a gentle meditation on death's presence in life, he describes a summer that is both backdrop and reflecting mirror:

> These are the dog days,
> unvaried
> except by accident,
>
> mist rising from soaked lawns,
> gone world, everything
> rises and dissolves in air,
>
> whatever it is would
> clear the air
> dissolves in air and the knot
>
> of days unties
> invisibly like a shoelace.

Hass measures the shape and weight of feeling in its place, its season, temperature, and texture. The poems are a measure in themselves, and Hass's natural unit of writing is the thought. He uses typographical lines to divide, recombine, and link thoughts with their fellows. Rhythm provides another measure of the poem's activity, whether it is the short, steady pulse of the lines above, or the slow, solid pounding of the tides. With these simple cadences, Hass adjusts the speed of our association of words, allowing him to use a simple vocabulary divorced from its usual banality through line and rhythm.

Death

in the sweetness, in the bitter
and the sour, death
in the salt, your tears,

this summer ripe and overripe.
It is a taste in the mouth,
child.

"Songs to Survive the Summer" is Hass's longest published poem, and the longer form seems to allow him to relax more comfortably into his own particular atmosphere. The shorter poems frequently attempt to condense recognitions into a single word, resulting in an abrupt shift in the level of awareness that is little consonant with the general feeling of the poem. The longer poems have a greater fullness and body due to the more complete evolution of feeling in them.

In his work since *Field Guide*, Hass seems to be advancing more deeply into the seasons of the mind. While carrying with him the careful modulation of tone and atmosphere and the meticulous observation of the earlier poems, he is more concerned with imaginative objects rather than concrete ones. In "Heroic Simile" an Akira Kurosawa film calls up a vision of a poor woodsman and his uncle chopping at a monumental log: "They have stopped working/ because they are tired and because/I have imagined no pack animal/or primitive wagon." Though the woodsmen are patient and the poet concerned, he concludes "There are limits to the imagination."

Yet Hass is not uncomfortable with limits. He acquiesces to them, even celebrates them with the gentle good humor and watchful restraint typical of his work. Above all, it is his sense of balance, whether on tiptoe or firmly on his feet, that gives Robert Hass's poetry the warmth of life.

—Walter Bode

HAYDEN, Robert (Earl). American. Born in Detroit, Michigan, 4 August 1913. Educated at public schools in Detroit; Detroit Institute of Musical Art; Detroit City College, now Wayne State University, 1932–36, B.A. 1942; University of Michigan, Ann Arbor (Hopwood Award, 1938, 1942), M.A. 1944. Married Erma Inez Morris in 1940; one daughter. Teaching Fellow, University of Michigan, 1944–46; Assistant Professor, 1946–54, Associate Professor, 1954–67, and Professor of English, 1967–69, Fisk University, Nashville. Visiting Professor, 1968, and since 1969, Professor of English, University of Michigan. Poet-in-Residence, Indiana State University, Terre Haute, Summer 1967; Bingham Professor, University of Louisville, Spring 1969; Visiting Poet, University of Washington, Seattle,

Summer 1969, and Connecticut College, New London, Spring 1974. Consultant in Poetry, Library of Congress, Washington, D.C., 1976–78. Since 1970, Consultant, Scott Foresman, publishers, Glenview, Illinois. Member, and Poetry Editor, *World Order*, Baha'i Faith. Recipient: Rosenwald Fellowship, 1947; Ford grant, 1954; Dakar Arts Festival prize, 1966; Russell Loines Award, 1970; Academy of American Poets Fellowship, 1975. D.Litt.: Grand Valley State College, Allendale, Michigan, 1975; Brown University, Providence, Rhode Island, 1976; Benedict College, Columbia, South Carolina, 1977; Wayne State University, 1977. Member, National Institute of Arts and Letters, 1979. Address: 1201 Gardner Avenue, Ann Arbor, Michigan 48104, U.S.A.

PUBLICATIONS

Verse

Heart-Shape in the Dust. Detroit, Falcon Press, 1940.
The Lion and the Archer, with Myron O'Higgins. Nashville, Counterpoise Press, 1948.
Figures of Time: Poems. Nashville, Hemphill Press, 1955.
A Ballad of Remembrance. London, Paul Breman, 1962.
Selected Poems. New York, October House, 1966.
Words in the Mourning Time: Poems. New York, October House, 1970.
The Night-Blooming Cereus. London, Paul Breman, 1972.
Angle of Ascent: New and Selected Poems. New York, Liveright, 1975.
American Journal. Taunton, Massachusetts, Effendi Press, 1978.
The Legend of John Brown, prints by Jacob Lawrence. Detroit, Detroit Institute of Arts, 1978.

Recording: *Today's Poets*, with others, Folkways, 1967.

Play

In Memoriam Malcolm X, music by T. J. Anderson (produced New York, 1974).

Other

How I Write 1, with Judson Philips and Lawson Carter. New York, Harcourt Brace, 1972.

Editor, *Kaleidoscope: Poems by American Negro Poets.* New York, Harcourt Brace, 1967.
Editor, with David J. Burrows and Frederick R. Lapides, *Afro-American Literature: An Introduction.* New York, Harcourt Brace, 1971.
Editor, "Modern American Poetry," in *The United States in Literature.* Chicago, Scott Foresman, 1972.

Critical Studies: Review by Julius Lester, in *The New York Times Book Review*, 24 January 1971; "Robert Hayden's Use of History" by Charles T. Davis, in *Modern Black Poets*, edited by Donald B. Gibson, Englewood Cliffs, New Jersey, Prentice Hall, 1973; *Interviews with Black Writers* by John O'Brien, New York, Liveright, 1973; by Michael S. Harper, in *New York Times Book Review*, 22 February 1976; *Chant of Saints: A Gathering of Afro-American Literature, Art, and Scholarship* edited by Michael S. Harper and Robert E. Stepto, Urbana, University of Illinois Press, 1979.

Robert Hayden quotes a conversation in *How I Write 1*, 1972:

I write poetry because I prefer it to prose, for one thing. Because, for another, I'm driven, impelled to make patterns of words in the special ways that poetry demands. Maybe whatever it is I'm trying to communicate I can most truthfully express in poems. I think I have other reasons, too. At best, though, I can make only very tentative statements, and they're subject to change without notice. I suppose I could say, with fear of contradicting myself later, that writing poetry is one way I have of coming to grips with both inner and external realities. I also think of my writing as a form of prayer – a prayer for illumination, perfection. No, I'm not satisfied with any of this. It's all beginning to sound pompous, highfalutin, but it's about as close as I can come to an answer. Most poets don't consciously analyze their reasons for being poets anyway. One doesn't choose to be a poet any more than he chooses to be born. If one could answer the question, "Why do you go on living?" then perhaps one could come up with a convincing answer to "Why do you write poetry?"

* * *

In his first book, *Heart-Shape in the Dust*, Robert Hayden foreshadowed his later themes. There were poems in the racy language of urban Blacks, like "Bacchanal," poems of personal emotion like "Obituary," written for his father, poems of social import like "Speech." This book established Hayden's reputation as one of the most promising of the younger poets. His language was simple, colorful, and direct. His fluid verse encompassed the ballad, blank verse, the sonnet, and free verse. His themes covered the personal, the social, local color, and world events. This wide range showed that from the beginning he was "opposed to the doctrinaire and the chauvinistic."

In *The Lion and the Archer* (with Myron O'Higgins) Hayden writes in a denser, more baroque style, abandoning the dialect and colloquialism of his first book. "A Ballad of Remembrance" has a surreal effect, with glittering, whirling, nightmare images. "Homage to the Blues" adds to his pictures of Black life, and like Sterling Brown's "Ma Rainey" was one of the earliest tributes to a specific Black singer. "Magnolias in Snow" is one of his simpler, more direct lyrics, but is moving in its personal emotion.

Hayden's movement toward a more complex poetry was confirmed in *A Ballad of Remembrance*, which won him the grand prize for poetry in English at the first World Festival of Negro Arts at Dakar, Senegal in 1966. The book contained two long poems which are among his finest achievements. "Middle Passage" depicts the horrors of the slave ships and the seizure of the *Amistad* by Cinquez and other captives. "Runagate Runagate" is a narrative of escape from slavery celebrating Harriet Tubman who led more than three hundred slaves to freedom. In these poems Hayden speaks with varied voices, using compelling rhythms, irony, and allusions.

Selected Poems, *Words in the Mourning Time*, and *The Night-Blooming Cereus* are more recent books. All along Hayden has written poems hinting of nightmare and evil, such as "The Wheel," but in *Cereus* the tone of the whole book has this disquieting quality. It is most evident in "Ballad of the True Beast," where the suspicion of the villagers toward two men who had seen a fabled monster and reported it as harmless caused the villagers to persecute the two, and the two men themselves to become bosom enemies.

Hayden's poetry is characterized by flexibility and control of rhythms, sensuous images, a Negro folk quality, and allusiveness. He has written of Negro history and folk lore and also of world events and personal feelings. At times he writes with directness and simplicity as in "Those Winter Mornings," "The Web," and "The Wheel." At other times he writes in a baroque, richly ornamented manner. He has created his own stanza forms with patterns of lines of varying length, in flexible rhythms, unrimed or with imperfect rimes. His best poems are an enduring contribution to American poetry.

—Dudley Randall

HAYS, H(offman) R(eynolds). American. Born in New York City, in 1904. Educated at Cornell University, Ithaca, New York, B.A.; Columbia University, New York, M.A.; University of Liège, Belgium. Married to Juliette Levine; two children. Acting Head of Drama Department, Fairleigh Dickinson University, Rutherford, New Jersey, 1960–63; Coordinator of the Drama Program, Southampton College, Long Island University, New York, 1965–69. Recipient: Putnam Award, 1964. Address: Box 22, Baiting Hollow Road, East Hampton, New York 11937, U.S.A.

PUBLICATIONS

Verse

Strange City. Boston, Four Seas, 1929.
Selected Poems 1933–1967. San Francisco, Kayak, 1968.
Inside My Own Skin. Santa Cruz, California, Kayak, 1974.
Portraits in Mixed Media. Oceanside, New York, Survivors Manual, 1978.

Plays

Medicine Show; or, Death Is a Statistician, with Oscar Saul, music by Hanns Eisler (produced New York, 1940).
Vincent van Gogh, in *The Best Television Plays 1950–1951*, edited by William I. Kauffman. New York, Merlin Press, 1952.

Novels

Stranger on the Highway. Boston, Little Brown, 1943; London, Hale, 1947.
Lie Down in Darkness. New York, Reynal, 1944; London, Hale, 1948.
The Takers of the City. New York, Reynal, 1946; London, Sampson Low Marston, 1947.
The Envoys. New York, Crown, 1953.

Other

From Ape to Angel: An Informal History of Social Anthropology. New York, Knopf, 1958, London, Methuen, 1959.
In the Beginnings: Early Man and His Gods. New York, Putnam, 1963.
The Kingdom of Hawaii. Greenwich, Connecticut, New York Graphic Society, 1964.
The Dangerous Sex: The Myth of Feminine Evil. New York, Putnam, 1964; London, Methuen, 1966.
Charley Sang a Song, with Daniel Hays. New York, Harper, 1964.
Explorers of Man: Five Pioneers in Anthropology. New York, Crowell Collier, 1971.
Birds, Beasts, and Men: A Humanistic History of Zoology. New York, Putnam, 1972; London, Dent, 1973.
Children of the Raven: The Seven Indian Nations of the Northwest Coast. New York, McGraw Hill, 1975.

Editor and Translator, *12 Spanish American Poets: An Anthology.* New Haven, Connecticut, Yale University Press, 1943.

Translator, *The Trial of Lucullus: A Play for Radio*, by Bertolt Brecht. New York, New Directions, 1943; in *Plays of Brecht*, London, Methuen, 1960.
Translator, *Selected Poems of Bertolt Brecht.* New York, Reynal, 1947.
Translator, *The Selected Writings of Juan Ramón Jiménez.* New York, Farrar Straus, 1957.

Translator, *The Selected Poems of Jorge Carrera Andrade.* New York, New York University Press, 1972.

Critical Studies: by Millen Brand and Allen Planz, in "H. R. Hays Issue" of *Voyages* (Washington, D.C.), Winter 1969; "H. R. Hays and Spanish America," in *Street* (Port Jefferson, New York), ii, 3, 1978.

H. R. Hays comments:

I don't use "verse forms," don't have characteristic subjects, belong on the whole to the generation which developed out of imagism after William Carlos Williams, Pound, Eliot, etc. I suppose W. C. Williams, Latin-American and French surrealism are the chief influences. My poetry adds up to an autobiography of my reactions to the world in which I have found myself.

* * *

H. R. Hays is one of the hidden poets of America. I say hidden because, beyond his reputation as the author of some books on anthropology for the general reader, his most widely known appearance as a poet occurs in his role as translator, a role in which he must *seem* to be invisible or transparent, subordinating himself to the effort of transmitting another man's poetry. His endeavors in this area have been exemplary and influential. The recently reissued *12 Spanish American Poets*, originally published in 1943 and difficult to obtain, has been acknowledged by such poets as James Wright, David Ignatow, and Robert Bly as an important discovery for them in terms of their own art. Hays' volumes of Brecht and Jiménez translations are likewise highly regarded.

Accomplished translating of this sort is, of course, a poetic achievement, a genuine literary contribution to the language; but Hays is a fine poet in his own right as well. His selected work of thirty-four years, gathered in a small, handsome book, reveals a poetry that is subtle, meditative, often calm, full of the closest observation of objects, the life of nature, and seasonal change: "... the iris blades/Emerge/Sharp, green,/From old trash,/Warm with/Secret life." Throughout his work there is evident a deep sense of history and its ironies, of social and political injustice, of the failures and delusions of modern life. Like the Latin American poets he admires, Hays speaks out on these matters, sometimes in direct fashion, at other times in an exaggerated irrational mode appropriate to the realities he must cope with. Recurrently one encounters – particularly, though not exclusively, in later poems – an infusion of elements of the mysterious, the dreamlike, the surreal:

Oh there are marvels in the souls of children –
Prophetic insects, stones that grow. They see
Life in a drowned hair
And know that death flies into rooms
On a bird's wings.

Writing in a manner both precise and perceptive, Hays has produced a number of handsome and moving poems which deserve the attention of more readers.

—Ralph J. Mills, Jr.

HAZO, Samuel (John). American. Born in Pittsburgh, Pennsylvania, 19 July 1928. Educated at Notre Dame University, Indiana (Mitchell Award, 1948), B.A. (magna cum laude) 1948; Duquesne University, Pittsburgh, M.A. 1955; University of Pittsburgh, Ph.D. 1957. Served in the United States Marine Corps, 1950–53. Married to Mary Anne Sarkis; one son. Instructor, Shady Side Academy, 1953–55. Since 1955, Member of the English Department, Dean of the College of Arts and Sciences, 1961–66, and since 1965, Professor of English, Duquesne University. Visiting Professor, University of Detroit, 1968. Since 1966, Director, International Poetry Forum, Pittsburgh. Contributing Editor, *Mundus Artium* magazine, Athens, Ohio; Poetry Editor, *America*, Washington, D.C. United States State Department Lecturer in the Middle East and Greece, 1965, in Jamaica, 1966. Recipient: Pro Helvetia Foundation grant (Switzerland), 1971. D.Litt.: Seton Hill College, Greensburg, Pennsylvania, 1965. Address: 785 Somerville Drive, Pittsburgh, Pennsylvania 15243, U.S.A.

PUBLICATIONS

Verse

Discovery and Other Poems. New York, Sheed and Ward, 1959.
The Quiet Wars. New York, Sheed and Ward, 1962.
Listen with the Eye, photographs by James P. Blair. Pittsburgh, University of Pittsburgh Press, 1964.
My Sons in God: Selected and New Poems. Pittsburgh, University of Pittsburgh Press, 1965.
Blood Rights. Pittsburgh, University of Pittsburgh Press, 1968.
The Blood of Adonis, with Adonis (Ali Ahmed Said). Pittsburgh, University of Pittsburgh Press, 1971.
Twelve Poems, with George Nama. Pittsburgh, Byblos Press, 1972.
Seascript: A Mediterranean Logbook. Pittsburgh, Byblos Press, 1972.
Once for the Last Bandit: New and Previous Poems. Pittsburgh, University of Pittsburgh Press, 1972.
Quartered. Pittsburgh, University of Pittsburgh Press, 1974.
Inscripts. Athens, Ohio University Press, 1975.

Novel

The Very Fall of the Sun. New York, Popular Library, 1978.

Other

Hart Crane: An Introduction and Interpretation. New York, Barnes and Noble, 1963; revised edition, as *Smithereened Apart: A Critique of Hart Crane,* Athens, Ohio University Press, 1978.

Editor, *The Christian Intellectual: Studies in the Relation of Catholicism to the Human Sciences.* Pittsburgh, Duquesne University Press, 1963.
Editor, *A Selection of Contemporary Religious Poetry.* Glen Rock, New Jersey, Paulist Press, 1963.

Translator, with Beth Luey, *The Growl of Deep Waters: Essays,* by Denis de Rougemont. Pittsburgh, University of Pittsburgh Press, 1976.

Critical Study: "Swimming in Sharkwater: The Poetry of Samuel Hazo" by R. H. W. Dillard, in *Hollins Critic* (Hollins College, Virginia), February 1969.

Samuel Hazo comments:

Suffice it to say that I regard poetry as the best form of conversation with largely unknown readers or hearers whose answer is hopefully their attention and assent. The rest is for critics to discover and evaluate.

* * *

Samuel Hazo's first two collections, *Discovery* and *The Quiet Wars*, introduced a meditative Christian poet concerned with the tough and enduring realities of death and suffering. He displayed the technical mastery necessary to avoid portentousness and unearned statement; his style is at once traditional and colloquial – that of a thinking modern man's believable metrical utterance.

Listen with the Eye, a small collection of poems with accompanying photographs by James Blair, involves a technical departure of some importance; many of the poems are cast in a strongly iambic free verse. The result is not so much rhythmic freedom as it is a stronger sense of the weight of each line. This quality distinguishes the new poems of *My Sons in God*, a collection of new and selected earlier poems in which the union of style and theme marks the arrival of an important American poet. Among the new poems is a group of "transpositions" from the Arabic of Ali Ahmed Said, the contemporary Lebanese poet; here again this fresh technical influence brings to Hazo's own poems an additional firmness of line. A larger selection of Said's poems, *The Blood of Adonis*, appeared in 1971.

Once for the Last Bandit: New and Previous Poems hones down the selection of early poems which appeared in *My Sons in God*; it includes generous selections from that book and from *Blood Rights*. Nearly half of the book is given over to the title sequence, a group of poems having some qualities of a journal, or as Hazo calls it, "an almanac of a penman in transit." The sinuous, heavily iambic free verse is a genuine new direction for Hazo; while his themes of loss, God, and persistence are still central, a larger variety of starting points and tones has become available to this very resourceful, still vitally developing poet.

—Henry Taylor

HEANEY, Seamus (Justin). Irish. Born in Castledawson, County Derry, 13 April 1939. Educated at Anahorish School; St. Columb's College, Derry; Queen's University, Belfast, B.A. (honours) in English 1961. Married Marie Devlin in 1965; two sons and one daughter. Teacher, St. Thomas's Secondary School, Belfast, 1962–63; Lecturer, St. Joseph's College of Education, Belfast, 1963–66; Lecturer in English, Queen's University, 1966–72; Guest Lecturer, University of California, Berkeley, 1970; moved to County Wicklow, 1972, did regular radio work and teaching at various American universities. Since 1975, Teacher at Carysfort Training College, Dublin. Recipient: Eric Gregory Award, 1966; Cholmondeley Award, 1967; Faber Memorial Prize, 1968; Maugham Award, 1968; Irish Academy of Letters Award, 1971; Denis Devlin Memorial Award, 1973; American-Irish Foundation Award, 1975; National Institute of Arts and Letters E. M. Forster Award, 1975; Duff Cooper Memorial Award, 1976; Smith Literary Award, 1976. Lives in Dublin. Address: c/o Faber and Faber Ltd., 3 Queen Square, London WC1N 3AU, England.

Publications

Verse

Eleven Poems. Belfast, Festival, 1965.
Death of a Naturalist. London, Faber, and New York, Oxford University Press, 1966.
Room to Rhyme, with Dairo Hammond and Michael Longley. Belfast, Arts Council of Northern Ireland, 1968.
A Lough Neagh Sequence. Manchester, Phoenix Pamphlet Poets Press, 1969.
Door into the Dark. London, Faber, and New York, Oxford University Press, 1969.
Night Drive: Poems. Crediton, Devon, Gilbertson, 1970.
Boy Driving His Father to Confession. Frensham, Surrey, Sceptre Press, 1970.
Land. London, Poem-of-the-Month Club, 1971.
Wintering Out. London, Faber, 1972; New York, Oxford University Press, 1973.
North. London, Faber, and New York, Oxford University Press, 1975.
Bog Poems. London, Rainbow Press, 1975.
Stations. Belfast, Ulsterman, 1975.
Field Work. London, Faber, and New York, Farrar Straus, 1979.

Other

The Fire i' the Flint: Reflections on the Poetry of Gerard Manley Hopkins (lecture). London, Oxford University Press, 1975.
Robert Lowell: A Memorial Lecture and an Eulogy. Privately printed, 1978.

Editor, with Alan Brownjohn and Jon Stallworthy, *New Poems 1970–1971.* London, Hutchinson, 1971.
Editor, *Soundings 2.* Belfast, Blackstaff Press, 1974.

* * *

As an Ulster Catholic, Seamus Heaney has always been aware of the complex and violent history that has gone to shape modern Ireland. In "Shoreline" (*Door into the Dark*) he hears in the tide, "rummaging in/At the foot of all fields," echoes of successive waves of invaders, Celts, Danes, Normans; in *North* he writes of "those fabulous raiders," the Vikings, "ocean-deafened voices/warning me, lifted again/in violence and epiphany." Elsewhere in the same volume, "Ocean's Love to Ireland" recalls, in a sinister compounding of copulation and murder which is a recurring motif, the complicity of courtier-poet Ralegh in the Irish massacres: while "Bog Oak" (*Wintering Out*) with a cool obliqueness insinuates, into the "dreaming sunlight" of Edmund Spenser's pastoral, hints of the atrocities he supervised. "For the Commander of the 'Eliza' " and "At a Potato Digging" evoke the Great Hunger and the ruthless expediencies of British rule in 1845. "Docker," with a forced but urgent understanding, depicts the Northern Protestant not only to recall past bigotry but to offer, in 1966, prophetic anticipation of its renewal ("That fist would drop a hammer on a Catholic –/ Oh yes, that kind of thing could start again").

From his first volume onwards, Heaney has written extensively of the strenuous, unremitting life of rural labour in County Derry and beyond. Many of the poems celebrate the people, crafts, and skills which sustain communal life; others, such as "The Wool Trade" or "Traditions," explore the linguistic and commercial nexus that "beds us down into/the British isles." In many poems Heaney effects a remarkable transition between manual and mental labour, the currencies of material life and of language. In "Digging," the first poem of his first volume, this theme is already enunciated: the poet digs with his pen as father and grandfather dug with their spades the rich peat of Ireland. Violence is hinted at by the simile which adds a third implement to the human repertoire ("The squat pen rest; snug as a gun"). The title poem of *Death of a Naturalist* extends this menace, recalling the poet as a boy sickened by the pools of frogspawn which tell of a repulsive world beyond the human: "The great slime kings/Were gathered there for vengeance and I knew/That if I dipped my hand the spawn would clutch it." Throughout this volume tha water-rat recurs as image of an alien yet terrifyingly familiar world, a world finally admitted, in "Personal Helicon," to be close to the poet's own creative springs, as, "pry[ing] into roots ... finger[ing] slime," this "big-eyed Narcissus" is startled by a rat that "slapped across my reflection." Poetry itself is a "door into the dark" where we seek our own carnal origins, and "Bogland" and "Bann Clay" stress this symbolic digging for a lost, primordial centre of being: "Under the humus and roots/This smooth weight. I labour/Towards it still. It holds and gluts." The very language in which Heaney writes partakes of this glutinous physical presence. There is a tactile, viscous quality to his words, speaking of "the sucking clabber" of water, the "soft gradient/of consonant, vowel-meadow," or "the tawny guttural water" which "spells itself." "Anahorish," "Toome," "Broagh" (*Wintering Out*) explore the very sounds of the old Irish words, stressing their status as material utterance, the muscular effort of a "guttural muse" whose "uvula grows/vestigial" ("Traditions"). In poems such as "Gifts of Rain" or "Oracle" the human organs of communication are in turn transferred to nature ("small mouth and ear/in a woody cleft,/lobe and larynx/of the mossy places"). Throughout *North* language is equated with the rich, secretive loam of the Irish bog, which engulfs and preserves, but can be kindled over and over into meaning, as the title poem indicates:

> Lie down
> in the word-hoard, burrow
> the coil and gleam
> of your furrowed brain.
>
> Compose in darkness.

The whole volume is as much about the difficulty of poetic composition as about the fratricidal decomposition of Ireland: death and love, language, poetry and politics, converge in poem after poem. Several, developing the insight of "Tollund Man" (*Wintering Out*), draw upon P. V. Glob's book *The Bog People* for a potent imagery of atrocity. In Glob's photographs of those ancient human sacrifices, preserved by the "dark juices" of the Danish peat bog, Heaney finds an analogy to the role of the modern Irish poet, the "artful voyeur" who is both an accomplice and helpless witness to "the exact/and tribal, intimate revenge" spoken of in a poem such as "Punishment." Superficially much influenced by Ted Hughes, Heaney perhaps in this double understanding of complicity and betrayal, establishes his own distinctive moral and emotional stance. Unlike Hughes, he is finally concerned with the redemption, not the dismissal, of the human, its exhumation from a "mother ground/... sour with the blood/of her faithful."

—Stan Smith

HEATH-STUBBS, John (Francis Alexander). British. Born in London, 9 July 1918. Educated at Queen's College, Oxford, B.A. (honours) in English 1942, M.A. 1972. English teacher, Hall School, Hampstead, London, 1944–45; Editorial Assistant, Hutchinson and Company, publishers, London, 1945–46. Gregory Fellow in Poetry, Leeds University, 1952–55; Visiting Professor of English, University of Alexandria, Egypt, 1955–58, and the University of Michigan, Ann Arbor, 1960–61. Lecturer in English, College of St. Mark and

St. John, London, 1963–72. Recipient: Arts Council bursary, 1965; Queen's Gold Medal for Poetry, 1974; Oscar Williams-Jean Derwood Award, 1978. Fellow, Royal Society of Literature, 1953. Address: 35 Sutherland Place, London W.2, England.

PUBLICATIONS

Verse

Wounded Thammuz. London, Routledge, 1942.
Beauty and the Beast. London, Routledge, 1943.
The Divided Ways. London, Routledge, 1946.
The Charity of the Stars. New York, Sloane, 1949.
The Swarming of the Bees. London, Eyre and Spottiswoode, 1950.
A Charm Against the Toothache. London, Methuen, 1954.
The Triumph of the Muse and Other Poems. London, Oxford University Press, 1958.
The Blue-Fly in His Head. London, Oxford University Press, 1962.
Selected Poems. London, Oxford University Press, 1965.
Satires and Epigrams. London, Turret, 1968.
(*Selected Poems*), with Thomas Blackburn. London, Longman, 1969.
Artorius, Book I. Providence, Rhode Island, Burning Deck, 1970; London, Enitharmon Press, 1973.
Penguin Modern Poets 20, with F. T. Prince and Stephen Spender. London, Penguin, 1971.
Four Poems in Measure. New York, Helikon Press, 1973.
A Parliament of Birds (juvenile). London, Chatto and Windus, 1975.
The Watchman's Flute: New Poems. Manchester, Carcanet Press, 1975.
The Mouse, The Bird, and the Sausage. Sunderland, Ceolfrith Press, 1978.

Plays

The Talking Ass (produced London, 1953). Included in *Helen in Egypt and Other Plays*, 1958.
Helen in Egypt and Other Plays (includes *The Talking Ass*, *The Harrowing of Hell*). London, Oxford University Press, 1958.

Other

The Darkling Plain: A Study of the Later Fortunes of Romanticism in English Poetry from George Darley to W. B. Yeats. London, Eyre and Spottiswoode, 1950; Norwood, Pennsylvania, Norwood Editions, 1975.
Charles Williams. London, Longman, 1955.
The Verse Satire. London, Oxford University Press, 1969.
The Ode. London, Oxford University Press, 1969.
The Pastoral. London, Oxford University Press, 1969.

Editor, *Selected Poems of Shelley.* London, Falcon Press, 1947.
Editor, *Selected Poems of Tennyson.* London, Falcon Press, 1947.
Editor, *Selected Poems of Swift.* London, Falcon Press, 1947.
Editor, with David Wright, *The Forsaken Garden: An Anthology of Poetry 1824–1909.* London, Lehmann, 1950.
Editor, *Mountains Beneath the Horizon: Selected Poems*, by William Bell. London, Faber, 1950.
Editor, *Images of Tomorrow: An Anthology of Recent Poetry.* London, SCM Press, 1953.

Editor, with David Wright, *The Faber Book of Twentieth Century Verse: An Anthology of Verse in Britain 1900–1950*. London, Faber, 1953; revised edition, 1965, 1975.
Editor, *Selected Poems of Alexander Pope*. London, Heinemann, 1964; New York, Barnes and Noble, 1966.
Editor, with Martin Green, *Homage to George Barker on His 60th Birthday*. London, Martin Brian and O'Keeffe, 1973.

Translator, *Poems from Giacomo Leopardi*. London, Lehmann, 1946.
Translator, *Aphrodite's Garland*. St. Ives, Latin Press, 1952.
Translator, with Peter Avery, *Thirty Poems of Hafiz of Shiraz*. London, Murray, 1955.
Translator, with Iris Origo, *Selected Poetry and Prose*, by Giacomo Leopardi. London, Oxford University Press, 1966; New York, New American Library, 1967.
Translator, *The Horn/Le Cor*, by Alfred de Vigny. Richmond, Surrey, Keepsake Press, 1969.
Translator, with Shafik Megally, *Dust and Carnations: Traditional Funeral Chants and Wedding Songs from Egypt*. London, TR Press, 1977.
Translator, with Peter Avery, *The Ruba'iyat of Omar Khayyam*. London, Allen Lane, 1979.
Translator, with Carol Whiteside, *Anyte*. Warwick, Greville Press, 1979.

Manuscript Collections: Humanities Research Center, University of Texas, Austin; Claude Colleer Abbott Memorial Library, State University of New York, Buffalo.

Critical Studies: *Poetry and Personal Responsibility* by George Every, London, SCM Press, 1948; "John Heath-Stubbs: A Poet in Alexandria" by Shafik Megally, in *Cairo Bulletin of English Studies*, 1959; *The Price of an Eye* by Thomas Blackburn, London, Longman, and New York, Morrow, 1961; *Rule and Energy* by John Press, London, Oxford University Press, 1963; "John Heath-Stubbs Issue" of *Aquarius 10* (London), 1978; "Triad from Great Britain" by Tony Stoneburner, in *The Poetics of Faith*, Missoula, Montana, Scholars Press, 1978.

John Heath-Stubbs comments:

Influenced at Oxford by teaching of C. S. Lewis and Charles Williams; also by friendship with fellow undergraduate poets Sidney Keyes, Drummond Allison, and William Bell.

* * *

There is a certain Byzantine quality in much of John Heath-Stubbs's poetry. An encyclopaedic knowledge of past cultures and a continual application of this knowledge is reminiscent of Byzantium. It is significant that Heath-Stubbs wrote a poem about Alexandria, that other great centre of Hellenistic and early Christian culture. "Alexandria" is, significantly, the longest poem in *The Swarming of the Bees*. The poem summarizes much of Heath-Stubbs's early poetry. It displays his use of a rather recondite knowledge of myth and legend and his blending of the humanistic and Christian traditions, and it demonstrates his highly sophisticated, stylized technique. His preference for the past is also revealed: the poet carries his account of Alexandria down only to early Christian times.

Heath-Stubbs is a poet of the modern city as well. In *A Charm Against the Toothache*, the megalopolis is modern London. In the same volume the poet begins to speak in his own voice. "Poem after Solstice" is a reaction to the termination of an unfortunate and unsatisfactory love; and in "Address Not Known," more direct and conversational, a failure of earthly love is revealed. In Heath-Stubbs's poetry there is a continual contrast between the *civitas dei* and the *civitas mundi*, divine love and earthly love.

Yet it would be erroneous to assume that his early poems were mere exercises in virtuosity, while the later poetry alone reveals the artist's private experience. Heath-Stubbs has been labelled a neo-Romantic on the basis of early poems, such as some of those included in *The Divided Ways*. One of the poems in *The Divided Ways*, "The Hill," is an account of a profoundly personal religious experience. The hill of the title is a spiritual vantage point, perhaps associated with Golgotha, where the protagonist is dissolved by the heat of the sun. This heat, at first suggestive of the justice of God, eventually proves to be his Love, but not before the speaker has undergone a profound change accompanied by fear and suffering.

John Heath-Stubbs's poetry is conspicuous for its erudition; its technical virtuosity, partly dependent upon the poet's sensitive musical ear; and a strong critical sense that is especially evident in his satire. He is at his best when he is using his sense of history and his moral sensitivity to reveal the shoddiness of modernity.

—John Van Domelen

HECHT, Anthony (Evan). American. Born in New York City, 16 January 1923. Educated at Bard College, Annandale-on-Hudson, New York, B.A. 1944; Columbia University, New York, M.A. 1950. Served in the United States Army during World War II. Married 1) Patricia Harris in 1954 (divorced, 1961); 2) Helen D'Alessandro in 1971; three sons. Taught at Kenyon College, Gambier, Ohio, 1947; University of Iowa, Iowa City, 1948; New York University, 1949; Smith College, Northampton, Massachusetts, 1956–59; Bard College, 1962–67. Since 1967, Member of the English Department, Rochester University, New York. Hurst Professor, Washington University, St. Louis, 1971. Recipient: American Academy in Rome Fellowship, 1951; Guggenheim Fellowship, 1954, 1959; *Hudson Review* Fellowship, 1958; Ford Fellowship, for drama, 1960, for verse, 1968; Brandeis University Creative Arts Award, 1964; Rockefeller Fellowship, 1967; Loines Award, 1968; Pulitzer Prize, 1968; Academy of American Poets Fellowship, 1969. Chancellor, Academy of American Poets, 1971. Member, National Institute of Arts and Letters. Address: 19 East Boulevard, Rochester, New York 14610, U.S.A.

PUBLICATIONS

Verse

A Summoning of Stones. New York, Macmillan, 1954.
The Seven Deadly Sins. Northampton, Massachusetts, Gehenna Press, 1958.
Struwwelpeter. Northampton, Massachusetts, Gehenna Press, 1958.
A Bestiary, illustrated by Aubrey Schwartz. Los Angeles, Kanthos Press, 1962.
The Hard Hours. New York, Atheneum, and London, Oxford University Press, 1967.
Aesopic: Twenty Four Couplets.... Northampton, Massachusetts, Gehenna Press, 1967.
Millions of Strange Shadows. New York, Atheneum, and London, Oxford University Press, 1977.
The Venetian Vespers. New York, Atheneum, and London, Oxford University Press, 1979.

Other

Editor, with John Hollander, *Jiggery-Pokery: A Compendium of Double Dactyls.* New York, Atheneum, 1967.

Translator, with Helen Bacon, *Seven Against Thebes*, by Aeschylus. New York, Oxford University Press, 1973.

* * *

It is strange to confront a contemporary who actually admits God. Anthony Hecht believes not only in Jehovah, but in Satan. His poems question not the existence of Evil and Death, but their perpetuation before an allegedly Just and hopefully Merciful God. Hecht has a powerful sense of death, and as poet he renders Death more immediate, nearer than Life; with his old Jew, "He is saying a prayer for all whom this room shall kill."

There are a classic intensity and expansiveness in his poems. At best the distant voice also achieves a profound personal, but never incredible, honesty. His is the kind of poem many have tried to "make," usually through some "revolutionary" technique which affects one more as a mistake than a mode. Hecht's poetry is not "revolutionary"; he works squarely within tradition.

It would be as impossible as undesirable to escape the consciousness of antiquity. Poems are titled to Jason and Adam (who, while they *are* the poet's sons, rely on their mythic namesakes for poetic existence); *Seven Deadly Sins* focused on nearly-medieval, sometimes epigrammatic, descriptions of the archetype sins, with accompanying woodcuts.

Hecht's technique is traditional. He is fond of the narrative element, the decasyllabic line, and in general works unabashedly, audibly with accentual-syllabic verse. He even writes sonnets, and without the euphemisms of elaborate typography or convoluted structure.

What is noteworthy is not Hecht's control of the conventions – many have shown their ability at "exercises" – or even his probable refusal to let the conventions control *him*. Rather, one notices the form, the craft or ingenuity not at all and senses the mode of the poem is not only transparent, but inevitable.

Hecht's poems especially achieve impact through unexpected juxtapositions of imagery, clashes which spark new imaginings for the reader. In the poem "Jason" the untouchable myth in golden rooms of the reader's imagination is suddenly destroyed:

Dream how a little boy alone
With a wooden sword and the top of a garbage can
Triumphs in gardens full of marigold.

At times, especially in *The Hard Hours*, Hecht can bespeak the entire horror of the Jewish experience; or again, the vision is the personal, and at its poetic best, timeless experience of dying. The mode of the poems arises, finally and appropriately, with the energy and voice of Old Testament prophecy, the product of a vision which is at once confessional and cultural.

—Joseph Wilson

HELLER, Michael D. American. Born in New York City, 11 May 1937. Educated at Miami Beach Senior High School, graduated 1955; Rensselaer Polytechnic Institute, Troy, New York (Managing Editor, *Rensselaer Engineer*, and Editor, *Bachelor* magazine), B.S. in management engineering 1959; City College, New York 1961–63; New School for Social Research, New York (Coffey Prize, 1964), 1963–64; New York University, 1970–71. Married 1) Doris C. Whytal in 1962 (divorced, 1978), one son; 2) the writer Jane Augustine in 1979. Chief Technical Writer, Norelco Corporation, New York, 1963–65; part-time teacher in Spain, 1965–66; free-lance industrial and advertising writer, 1966–67. Since 1967,

Member of the Faculty, now Master Teacher, American Language Institute, New York University. Since 1970, teacher with New York State Poetry in the Schools program. Adjunct Lecturer in Developmental Skills, New York City Community College, 1973. Contributing Editor, *Montemora* magazine and staff member, Montemora Foundation, New York. Recipient: Creative Artists Public Service grant, 1975; National Endowment for the Humanities grant, 1979. Address: P.O. Box 981, Stuyvesant Station, New York, New York 10009, U.S.A.

PUBLICATIONS

Verse

Two Poems. Mount Horeb, Wisconsin, Perishable Press, 1970.
Accidental Center. Fremont, Michigan, Sumac Press, 1972.
Figures of Speaking. Mount Horeb, Wisconsin, Perishable Press, 1977.
Knowledge. New York, Sun Press, 1979.

* * *

The publication in 1972 of *Accidental Center* announced an authentic, hard-edged, meditative poet of truly contemporary sensibility who worked in the Objectivist manner, a poet who exemplified Oppen's "sense of the poet's self among things" and Reznikoff's detailed, literal, compassionate witnessing of the modern city dweller, a poet who knew that

the words
are precipitates
– in themselves
precipitous
rare and expensive dust
desperately grasped
in the amalgam.

For Michael D. Heller, the words represent a process of distillation: they are hard-won, to be treasured and used sparingly. At the same time, there's a willingness to follow where the words lead, into darkness, mystery; this is a fundamental recognition, based on his awareness of physical principles, of "how each/word is a shift of matter."

Accidental Center was remarkable in that, unlike most first books, there was a complete absence of that "overwriting" which masks lack of assurance and control. The poems result from an intense concentration, a focusing on the objective, in Zukofsky's early formulation of Objectivist poetry. In fact, the photo-image is prevalent in the book – "the moment in the sense" caught and held – almost as if Objectivist principles were being given a technical underpinning. *Accidental Center* is a serious book that takes language seriously. The method of many of the poems is to proceed by means of simple, declarative constructs to form an image as proposition – a logic based on the "thingness of things," on exact observation. The poems are often based on the paradoxical image, provoking us to respond to the artifact as material for a contemporary mythology. Numerous references employing the terms of astrophysics, chemistry, and biology function almost as a traditional mythic or religious gloss, amplifying and expanding the particular emotive context ("Operation Cicero"):

writing of the great light of cities
... these are entropic times
and those bright clusters
in our lives
in their rot

are black bodies
and absorb it all
like a woman
on one's bed
who cannot bear the light

The paradoxical quality results also from the contrast between the precision of the scientific terms, economy of language, the short lines and spare style – and the genuine acceptance of a sort of negative capability: things, ideas, emotions – oneself in the world – are not rendered simplistically but exactly as a measure of their subtle relativity and mystery: what we know is a function of how we know.

Heller expresses throughout the poems of *Accidental Center* an explicit or implicit ontological concern, not in the form of abstract disquisition, but as speculation on the objects which relate to and define the self. The finest example of a poem given over wholly to this concern is the impressive "Meditation on the Coral," in which our existence as city-dwellers is explored in terms of the coral, symbolizing in its cellular structure our dependent and communal way of life but also, in its origins in the sea, our atavistic urges, "and the warm saline/– as of the birth sac/still a dream."

Heller's second major collection, *Knowledge*, contains in addition to the speculative poetry which characterized the earlier book, poems which are more discursive, leisurely, descriptive – though no less formal in intent. Having settled into a style, he is now able to accommodate more immediate and personal concerns without, however, sacrificing intensity. Thus, events which mark the perception of both continuity and change in family relationships – with father, mother, wife, son – become occasions for poems in which the occasion makes its own space and pace. Literalness coexists with irony in a number of these poems, producing a gentle humor. "Bialystok Stanzas" recalls the incisiveness, objectivity, and compassion of Reznikoff's depictions of traditional Jewish life and the holocaust. But in even as occasional a poem as "On the Beach," Heller never relaxes his gaze; though the occasion may seem commonplace – "watching square yards of such flesh/Baste itself with oil" – nevertheless, "Even here, amid these minor increments/of peril, one is consoled. In this/Careless resort of life of beaches/Deceptions themselves are a kind of truth."

The energy which informs Heller's poems – and the reason he is so rewarding as a poet – derives from "the world alreading existing / without a name," in which the impulse is to question, to take nothing for granted, while perceiving what is there, in a very real sense, for all to know. The concluding section of "At Albert's Landing (with my son)" specifies the process of that special knowledge:

Different as the woods are
This is no paradise to enter or leave.
Just the real, and a wild nesting
Of hope in the real
Which does not know of hope.
Things lean and lean, and sometimes
Words find common centers in us
Resonating and filling speech.
Let me know a little of you.

—Robert Vas Dias

HELWIG, David (Gordon). Canadian. Born in Toronto, Ontario, 5 April 1938. Educated at the University of Toronto, B.A. 1960; University of Liverpool, M.A. 1962. Married Nancy Keeling in 1959; two children. Assistant Professor of English, Queen's University, Kingston, Ontario. Address: 73 Baiden Street, Kingston, Ontario, Canada.

PUBLICATIONS

Verse

Figures in a Landscape. Ottawa, Oberon Press, 1967.
The Sign of the Gunman. Ottawa, Oberon Press, 1969.
The Best Name of Silence. Ottawa, Oberon Press, 1972.
Atlantic Crossings. Ottawa, Oberon Press, 1974.
A Book of the Hours. Ottawa, Oberon Press, 1979.

Play

A Time in Winter (produced Kingston, Ontario, 1967). Included in *Figures in a Landscape*, 1967.

Novels

The Day Before Tomorrow. Ottawa, Oberon Press, 1971.
The Glass Knight. Ottawa, Oberon Press, 1976.
Jennifer. Ottawa, Oberon Press, 1979.

Short Stories

The Streets of Summer. Ottawa, Oberon Press, 1969.

Other

A Book about Billie (documentary). Ottawa, Oberon Press, 1972.

Editor, with Tom Marshall, *Fourteen Stories High: Best Canadian Stories of 71.* Ottawa, Oberon Press, 1971.
Editor, with Joan Harcourt, *72, 73, 74,* and *75: New Canadian Stories.* Ottawa, Oberon Press, 4 vols., 1972–75.
Editor, *Words from Inside.* Kingston, Ontario, Prison Arts, 1972(?).

Critical Studies: "Spells Against Chaos" by Tom Marshall, in *Quarry* (Kingston, Ontario), Spring 1968; "David Helwig's New Timber," in *Queen's Quarterly* (Kingston, Ontario), Summer 1974.

* * *

David Helwig's recent muse is less violent and political than in some of his earlier poetry. In *The Sign of the Gunman*, for instance, there was a curious stridency and rhetorical pose that seemed artificial and laboured: "They are burning our cities/They are shooting at us with bullets." This is not good poetry and it goes hand in hand with occasional distasteful revelling in sutures and seared flesh that reminds one of nothing so much as the songs of Tom Lehrer: "Somewhere is a photograph/of a man in two pieces/burned until he is only/two pieces of a cooked man." When the violence is necessary to greatness, as it is in his "Apollo and Daphne," it is right, and felt as a conclusion to the poem. Helwig, however, does not escape the fashionable Canadian taste for Frye-esque mythology where Harlequin and the acrobat, like the Zeus of his "Metamorphosis," appear to stand for more than they are, gesturing for significance.

In *Atlantic Crossings*, however, the four poems that comprise the collection are not racked by symbol. The image of the louse, in the Columbus section, moving "off the edge of my swollen brain/into a new world" has an appropriately Donnean quality. It is indicative of what preserves this collection from mere indulgence in the horrific world of madness through which it travels.

The strength of Helwig's earliest poetry is present again in his more recent work – a strength that owes much to a fine-edged description. Helwig's admiration for Andrew Wyeth is evident in his "After Brueghel" where winter is a season "of sudden long white distances/ that empty the mind." There is something of the Pacific NorthWest School (William Stafford, for instance) in Helwig's "Still Life" or "Sunday Breakfast":

Orange, one egg, tea in a cup
of blue and white, composing silences
against the hurt nerves fluttering.

Although some of the poems in Helwig's latest collection (*A Book of the Hours*) come perilously close to McKuen, his affection for the familial and domestic is rarely sentimental. A classic of toughness is his poem "A Shaker Chair":

I see in the Shaker rocking chair
stillness turning, stillness moving,
comtemplation and silent standing,
even the denial of the body.

Occasionally, too, one senses Helwig's debt to the impressionist transformation of simple painterly objects into a larger life, a debt that gives us echoes of Stevens: "We swim before we walk. The tropic sea/within the caul is home." Certainly the inflexions are Stevens's, and they are congenial to an attractive toughness in the verse that saves Helwig's taste for darkness, secrecy, night, and their magic from being merely fantasy. Fantasy at its best, though, is present in his "Summer Landscapes" where "the house running away to the stars/ on the feet of mice" has the quality of a Louis de Niverville painting.

Like many Canadian artists Helwig seemed to find his voice abroad. Liverpool nurtured him and in his best poems one hears not the Mersey sound or poets but the voices of "the old women/climbing Brownlow Hill/in the killing fog" that he celebrates in "Liverpool."

In the best of his poetry there is a fine sense of detachment. That is why his poems on Diefenbaker, the Orange Lodge, and American political issues are so weak. His spontaneous emotion is too close to their creation. The picture one retains of him is of a distant walker, a figure in his own landscape, above the world he deplores and celebrates – the world he describes in "Christmas, 1965" in which "Silence/had overwhelmed the noise of men" leaving only the poet's voice.

—D. D. C. Chambers

HENDERSON, Hamish. British. Born in Blairgowrie, Perthshire, Scotland, 11 November 1919. Educated at Blairgowrie High School; Dulwich College, London; Downing College, Cambridge, M.A. Served with the Highland Division during World War II. Married; two daughters. Since 1951, Lecturer and Research Fellow, School of Scottish Studies, Edinburgh University. Recipient: Maugham Award, 1949. Lives in Edinburgh.

PUBLICATIONS

Verse

Elegies for the Dead in Cyrenaica. London, Lehmann, 1948.
Freedom Come-All-Ye, in *Chapbook* special issue (Aberdeen), iii, 6, 1967.

Other

Editor, and Contributor, *Ballads of World War II Collected by Seumas Mor Maceanruig.* Glasgow, Caledonian Press, 1947.

Critical Study: *The Poet Speaks*, edited by Peter Orr, London, Routledge, and New York, Barnes and Noble, 1966.

* * *

Hamish Henderson's one book of verse, *Elegies for the Dead in Cyrenaica*, was published as long ago as 1948, and was the product of the desert war which inspired so much of the best English poetry of World War II, including that of Keith Douglas. Appearing when it did, it tended to miss the tide of interest in "war poetry" which had been nourished by the conflict itself. The fact that the author has never produced another collection has also not aided his reputation. Yet Henderson has always had a small band of admirers, and re-reading his elegies it is easy to see why.

The book has two advantages – it can be read complete, as a whole, not just as a collection of poems written in different moods and on different occasions; and it has a comfortable relationship to the modernist tradition (something more likely to happen with Scottish poets than with English ones). Henderson was obviously much influenced by the Eliot of *Four Quartets* – it was difficult not to be, at that period; that is, if one hadn't succumbed to the influences of Dylan Thomas or Edith Sitwell. But one also hears within his work the voices of Europe – Goethe and Hölderlin, who supply him with epigraphs; and the Alexandrian Greek, Cavafy, whom he quotes. The poems are that comparatively rare thing in 20th century English poetry – successful philosophical verse.

He combines this philosophical bent with a delicate naturalism, and a skilful control of tone, which means that these comparatively long poems can rise up into the "high" style and leave it again without difficulty, just as the author requires. Here is an example, from the beginning of the Second Elegy:

At dawn, under the concise razor-edge
of the escarpment, the laager sleeps. No petrol fires yet
blow flame for brew-up. Up on the pass a sentry
inhales his Nazionale. Horse-shoe-curve of the bay
grows visible beneath him. He smokes and yawns.
Ooo-augh,
              and the limitless
shabby lion-pelt of the desert completes and rounds
his limitless ennui.

One suspects, at a distance of more than a quarter of a century, that this is the kind of war-time verse most likely to last and be read by posterity.

—Edward Lucie-Smith

HENDRIKS, A(rthur) L(emière). Jamaican. Born in Kingston, 17 April 1922. Educated at Jamaica College; Ottershaw College, Surrey, England. Has six children. Clerk, Arthur Hendriks Furniture Company, Jamaica, 1940–50; Sales Manager, Radio Jamaica Ltd., 1950–60; General Manager, Jamaica Broadcasting Corporation, 1961–64; Caribbean Director, Thomson Television Ltd., London, 1964–71. Since 1971, Free-lance writer. Address: Box 1360, Hamilton, Bermuda; or c/o Workshop Press, 2 Culham Court, Granville Road, London N4 4JB, England.

PUBLICATIONS

Verse

On This Mountain and Other Poems. London, Deutsch, 1965.
These Green Islands and Other Poems. Kingston, Bolivar Press, 1971.
Muet. London, Outposts, 1971.
Madonna of the Unknown Nation. London, Workshop Press, 1974.

Other

Editor, with Cedric Lindo, *The Independence Anthology of Jamaican Literature.* Kingston, Arts Celebration Committee of the Ministry of Development, 1962.

* * *

A. L. Hendriks is one of perhaps a half dozen impressive contemporary West Indian poets. His poetry is less agitated by themes of race, alienation and identity than is much West Indian writing, and the impression his poems make on the reader is that they are the private meditations of a delicate soul. There is a certain sobriety in his idiom, a coolness in approach, and a feeling of control and tranquility. His tone is subdued, his voice without stridency or affectation; the rhythms are quiet and they engage the person or subject in a private way. Some of his best poems join sympathy for a particular place, a sense of its quality and particularity, with a capacity for attentive listening. The poetry seems to me to be a mode of intimate access to some truth of experience not yet articulated, not yet quite held:

> This thin and oval stone, cold upon the brown earth,
> is not dumb, nor is the grass, nor the curved stick
> lying smooth by the brook's edge; you may listen
> and through the unapparent sense learn from them
> a new music, secret, and played on no instrument.

In some of his poems, for example "Song for My Brothers and Cousins" and "On This Mountain," Hendriks is troubled out of his secluded world and contemplative posture:

> We no longer belong to a private
> society and cannot hide
> private misdemeanours, we are
> one people in one house and cannot leave it.

The idea trembling on the edge in this stanza is never brought to the passionate explicitness that it would have in the verse of Edward Brathwaite, for example. Indeed, the feeling, even in his more public poems, is less torn and troubled. It has, on the other hand, an unaffected inward dignity, of the kind that is to be seen in his restrained but sensitive relish for the old in "An Old Jamaican Woman Thinks about the Hereafter":

What would I do forever in a big place, who
have lived all my life in a small island?
The same parish holds the cottage I was born in, all
my family, and the cool churchyard.

In all of Hendriks's poetry we find a sensibility which thrives on smallness, coolness, and a fine human simplicity.

—William Walsh

HENRI, Adrian (Maurice). British. Born in Birkenhead, Cheshire, 10 April 1932. Educated at St. Asaph Grammar School, North Wales, 1945–51; King's College, Newcastle, B.A. (honours) in fine arts 1955. Married Joyce Wilson in 1958 (separated). Lecturer, Manchester College of Art and Design, 1961–64, and Liverpool College of Art, 1964–68. Member of the Liverpool Scene, poetry-rock group, 1968–70, American tour, 1969. Painter: One-Man Shows – Institute of Contemporary Arts, London, 1968; Art Net, London, 1975; Retrospective, Wolverhampton, 1976; Demarco Gallery, Edinburgh, 1977. Since 1970, full-time writer, singer, and painter, with occasional work with Grimms, and Henri and Friends groups. Since 1972, President, Liverpool Academy of Arts. Recipient: Arts Council of Northern Ireland prize, for painting, 1964; John Moores Exhibition Prize, 1972. Agent: Deborah Rogers, 5–11 Mortimer Street, London W.1. Address: 21 Mount Street, Liverpool L1 9HD, England.

PUBLICATIONS

Verse

The Mersey Sound: Penguin Modern Poets 10, with Roger McGough and Brian Patten. London, Penguin, 1967; revised edition, 1974.
Tonight at Noon. London, Rapp and Whiting, 1968; New York, McKay, 1969.
City. London, Rapp and Whiting, 1969.
Talking after Christmas Blues, music by Wallace Southam. London, Turret, 1969.
Poems for Wales and Six Landscapes for Susan. Gillingham, Kent, ARC, 1970.
Autobiography. London, Cape, 1971.
America. London, Turret, 1972.
The Best of Henri: Selected Poems 1960–70. London, Cape, 1975.
One Year. Todmorden, Lancashire, ARC, 1976.
City Hedges: Poems 1970–76. London, Cape, 1977.
Words Without a Story. Liverpool, Glasshouse Press, 1979.

Recordings: (with Liverpool Scene) *St. Adrian Co., Broadway and 3rd*, RCA, 1970; *Heirloon*, RCA, 1970; *Recollections*, Charisma, 1972; (solo) *Adrian Henri*, Canon, 1974; *British Poets of Our Times*, with Hugo Williams, Argo.

Plays

I Wonder: A Guillaume Apollinaire Show, with Michael Kustow (produced London, 1968).

Television Play: *Yesterday's Girl*, 1973.

Novel

I Want, with Nell Dunn. London, Cape 1972.

Other

Environments and Happenings. London, Thames and Hudson, 1974; as *Total Art: Environments, Happenings and Performances*, New York, Praeger, 1974.

Critical Study: "Notes on Painting and Poetry" by the author, in *Tonight at Noon*, 1968.

Adrian Henri comments:

(1970) I was trained as a painter and still paint and exhibit paintings. I make a living primarily by performing the works that I write, mostly with music. I think of myself as a maker, and presenter, of images in various media. "Pop Poet" is, I think, the most common label.

My major influences are T. S. Eliot, Apollinaire, Mallarmé, Ginsberg, Olson and recently Tennyson, Creeley and Hugh MacDiarmid; also the prose of Joyce and William Burroughs. I am an autobiographical poet: my poems are extensions of my own life, some fact, some fantasy. For this reason I write perhaps more love-poems than anything else. I am excited by new uses of language in the mass-media, like TV commercials or pop songs, and am only interested in "older" verse-forms (i.e. rhyme, etc.) as they survive in modern society, e.g. ballad and particularly Blues. I would like my poems to be read by as many people as possible, since I can't see any point either personally or politically in writing for an elite minority. I think by doing readings and by working with the "Liverpool Scene" I am beginning to reach a bigger and largely "non-literary" audience.

(1974) Since a serious heart illness in 1970 my way of life, and to some extent my way of working, has changed somewhat. At the moment my poetry is perhaps quieter and more "traditional" in character. Since spending some time in Somerset and Shropshire I have become interested in the English landscape tradition, notably Wordsworth and Housman, and the Pre-Raphaelite painters. My work as a painter is similarly involved in an investigation into the possibilities of landscape.

(1980) I am still involved with landscape, but have recently extended this to "Debris" paintings, studies of urban wasteland. *City Hedges* perhaps reflects this. Current work includes a musical version of Jarry's *Ubu*. Economic problems have made musical collaborations less possible, but I still work with guitarist Andy Roberts, and the Shortwaveband, when I can.

* * *

Adrian Henri is perhaps the most "typical" of the Liverpool pop-poets because of the way in which he mixes topical references, material drawn from pop-songs and from jazz, and a wide range of references to modern painting and the Modern Movement in general. These are made to relate to personal experience and the poet's own immediate context and the result appeals by its directness, gentleness and honesty. From the technical point of view Henri's poetry is interesting because it tries to make use of techniques derived both from jazz and from the procedures of contemporary painting – there is a lot of "verbal collage," for example. Particularly characteristic are the lists of objects and images which ultimately derive from Whitman, but which the poet seems to feel are representative of the fragmentary nature of contemporary experience.

—Edward Lucie-Smith

HEPPENSTALL, (John) Rayner. British. Born in Huddersfield, Yorkshire, 27 July 1911. Educated locally and at the Collège Sophie-Berthelot, Calais, France, 1928; University of Leeds, Yorkshire, 1929–33, B.A. 1932; University of Strasbourg, France, 1931. Served in the Royal Artillery and the Royal Army Pay Corps, 1940–45. Married Margaret Edwards in 1937; two children. Schoolmaster, Eastbrook Senior Boys' School, Dagenham, Essex, 1934; Free-lance writer, 1935–39. Producer, Features and Drama Department, BBC Radio, London, 1945–67. Recipient: Arts Council Novel Prize, 1966. Address: 2 Gilford Road, Deal, Kent, England.

PUBLICATIONS

Verse

Patins. London, Literary Guild, 1932.
First Poems. London, Heinemann, 1935.
Sebastian. London, Dent, 1937.
Proems: An Anthology of Poems, with others. London, Fortune Press, 1938.
Blind Men's Flowers Are Green. London, Secker and Warburg, 1940.
Poems 1933–1945. London, Secker and Warburg, 1946.

Plays

The Fool's Saga, in *Three Tales of Hamlet*, with Michael Innes. London, Gollancz, 1950.
A Clean Break, and Daily Bread, adaptations of plays by Jules Renard (produced Mull, Scotland, 1969).

Radio Plays and Documentaries: *The Death of a Prophet*, *The Rising in the North*, and *The Battle for St. David's*, in the early 1950's; *The Green Bay Tree*, from a novel by Paul Desjardins, 1960; *The Generations*, 1961; *Renard*, 1961; *The Literate Killer*, 1968; *Vautrin* (four parts), based on works by Balzac, 1969; *The General's Daughter*, 1969; *A Pretty Liar*, 1971; *Dr. Satan*, 1971; *A Tidy Little Man*, 1972; *The Case of Eugene Weidmann*, 1972; *The Murder of Jean Jaurès*, 1972; *The Trial of Eugene Aram*, 1974; *Axel*, with James Laver, from a work by Villiers de l'Isle Adam; *The Fair Parricide*, 1975; and others.

Television Plays: *The Seventh Juror*, 1972; *The Bells*, 1974.

Novels

The Blaze of Noon. London, Secker and Warburg, and New York, Alliance, 1939.
Saturnine. London, Secker and Warburg, 1943; revised edition, as *The Greater Infortune*, London, Peter Owen, 1960.
The Lesser Infortune. London, Cape, 1953.
The Connecting Door. London, Barrie and Rockliff, 1962.
The Woodshed. London, Barrie and Rockliff, 1962.
The Shearers. London, Hamish Hamilton, 1969.
Two Moons. London, Allison and Busby, 1977.

Other

Middleton Murry: A Study in Excellent Normality. London, Cape, 1934.
Apology for Dancing. London, Faber, 1936.
*The Double Image; Mutations of Christian Mythology in the Work of Four French

Writers of Today and Yesterday. London, Secker and Warburg, 1947.
Léon Bloy. Cambridge, Bowes, and New Haven, Connecticut, Yale University Press, 1954.
Four Absentees (memoirs). London, Barrie and Rockliff, 1960; Philadelphia, Dufour, 1963.
The Fourfold Tradition (criticism). London, Barrie and Rockliff, and New York, New Directions, 1961.
The Intellectual Part (memoirs). London, Barrie and Rockliff, 1963.
Raymond Roussel. London, Calder and Boyars, 1966; Berkeley, University of California Press, 1967.
Portrait of the Artist as a Professional Man (memoirs). London, Peter Owen, 1969.
A Little Pattern of French Crime. London, Hamish Hamilton, 1969.
French Crime in the Romantic Age. London, Hamish Hamilton, 1970.
Bluebeard and After: Three Decades of Murder in France. London, Peter Owen, 1972.
The Sex War and Others. London, Peter Owen, 1973.
Reflections on the Newgate Calendar. London, W. H. Allen, 1975.

Editor, *Existentialism*, by Guido de Ruggiero. London, Secker and Warburg, 1947; New York, Social Science Publishers, 1948.
Editor, *Imaginary Conversations* (radio scripts). London, Secker and Warburg, 1948.

Translator, *Architecture of Truth.* London, Thames and Hudson, 1957.
Translator, *Atala and René*, by F. R. de Chateaubriand. London, Oxford University Press, 1963.
Translator, with Lindy Foord, *Impressions of Africa*, by Raymond Roussel. London, Calder and Boyars, and Berkeley, University of California Press, 1966.
Translator, *A Harlot High and Low*, by Honoré de Balzac. London, Penguin, 1970.
Translator, *When Justice Falters*, by René Floriot. London, Harrap, 1972.

Rayner Heppenstall comments:

(1970) The usual subjects. A variety of forms and devices. Much affected by Yeats, Blake and minor French symbolists, perhaps also Gerard Manley Hopkins.

(1974) I have written no original verse for almost a quarter of a century. I do not disown what I once did, but view it with no more than autobiographical interest. I take no interest in the verse of my younger contemporaries.

*   *   *

Rayner Heppenstall's literary career has followed a familiar pattern. As a young man he regarded himself primarily as a poet, but after the age of thirty he turned exclusively to prose. In his autobiography, *The Intellectual Part*, he speaks dismissively of poetry as a literary mode, and regards his last collection, *Poems 1933–1945*, as marking a distinctive farewell to verse. Indeed, this book contained very little written after 1940. In 1933 Heppenstall contributed to an early number of *New Verse*, the important English poetry magazine of the thirties, but he never subscribed to its programme of socially concerned verse and precise observation; indeed, in a later number Heppenstall was repudiated and abused by its combative editor, Geoffrey Grigson. Heppenstall's principal influence was Gerard Manley Hopkins, who was then beginning to be seriously read and imitated by English poets. Heppenstall's poetry shows Hopkins's influence in its verbal contortions and its emphatic grappling with spiritual crises. (Though not a Christian, Heppenstall teetered for a while on the brink of conversion to Catholicism.) Formally, it is skilfully controlled and at times, as in the sequence called "Sebastian," it rises to an impressive if frigid rhetoric. But its frequent obscurity looks like the product of affectation rather than genuine complexity of thought and imagination. However, one of his last poems, "Instead of a Carol," dated 1940, deserves to be remembered as a crisp presentation of a wartime moment.

—Bernard Bergonzi

HERNTON, Calvin C. American. Born in Chattanooga, Tennessee, 28 April 1933. Educated at Howard High School, 1946–50; Talladega College, Alabama, 1950–54, B.A. 1954; Fisk University, Nashville, Tennessee, 1954–56, M.A. in sociology 1956; Columbia University, New York, 1961. Has one child. Social Worker, Youth House, New York, 1956; Instructor in Sociology, Benedict College, Columbia, South Carolina, 1956–57, Alabama Agricultural and Mechanical College, Huntsville, 1957–58, Edward Waters College, Jacksonville, Florida, 1958–59, and Southern University, Baton Rouge, Louisiana, 1959–60; Social Investigator, Department of Welfare, New York, 1961–62; Writer-in-Residence, Central State University, Wilberforce, Ohio, 1969. Faculty member since 1970, and currently Professor of Black Studies, Oberlin College, Ohio. Co-Founder, *Umbra* magazine, New York, 1963. Agent: Wendy Weil, Julian Bach Literary Agency, 3 East 48th Street, New York, New York 10017, U.S.A.

PUBLICATIONS

Verse

The Coming of Chronos to the House of Nightsong: An Epical Narrative of the South. New York, Interim, 1964.
Medicine Man: Collected Poems. Berkeley, California, Reed Cannon and Johnson, 1976.

Plays

Glad to Be Dead (produced Jacksonville, Florida, 1958).
Flame (produced Jacksonville, Florida, 1958).
The Place (produced Oberlin, Ohio, 1972).

Novel

Scarecrow. New York, Doubleday, 1974.

Other

Sex and Racism in America. New York, Doubleday, 1965; as *Sex and Racism*, London, Deutsch, 1969.
White Papers for White Americans. New York, Doubleday, 1966.
Coming Together: Black Power, White Hatred, and Sexual Hangups. New York, Random House, 1971.
The Cannabis Experience: A Study of the Effects of Marijuana and Hashish, with Joseph Berke. London, Peter Owen, 1974.

Calvin C. Hernton comments:

I used to make statements about what I wrote, how I wrote it, my method, my process, my poetics, and that stuff. But I don't do that anymore. My poetry is my statement. However, I will say this much. I write about anything, and from as many possible standpoints. I've written poems about war, hatred, racism, racial violence, social and personal suffering and joy as well; poems about trees, making love, loss of love, the blues, being scared in an airplane, persons I've known such as musicians, painters, friends, lovers, enemies and people rushing along the streets with umbrellas open with it no longer raining; poems about whatever I happen to feel necessary at the time; poems for children, women, and poems for nobody but myself! I have noticed that one thing runs through all of my poems no matter what the subject, style or poetic level: and this is an almost too human concern for humanity.

* * *

Calvin C. Hernton's poetry is concerned with the plight of the black masses, the coming of age of the existential Negro, and the misconceptualization of race relations in the United States:

Laughter and scorn on the lips of Edsel automobiles
instructing the populace to love God, be kind to puppies
and the Chase Manhattan National Bank
Because of this there is no Fourth of July this year
No shouting, no popping of firecrackers, no celebrating,
    no parade
But the rage of a hopeless people
Jitterbugging
    in the streets.

He speaks of creative impersonalization:

I am not a metaphor or symbol.
This you hear is not the wind in the trees,
Nor a cat being maimed in the street.
I am being maimed in the street.
It is I who weep, laugh, feel pain or joy.

And finally he symbolizes America spiritually replenished through organic changes in her total civilization:

> to see ALL Americans in freedom and passion for one another, lift ourselves above that lifeless thing (materialism). What America needs most now is room, a kind of transcendent humanity, whereby all men and women can work, love and acquire self-esteem without having to maim one another in the struggle.

—Corrine E. Bostic

HESKETH, Phoebe (née Rayner). British. Born in Preston, Lancashire, 29 January 1909. Educated at Preston High School, 1914–16; Dagfield Birkdale School, 1918–24;

Cheltenham Ladies' College, Gloucestershire, 1924–26. Married William Aubrey Martin Hesketh in 1931; two sons and one daughter. Woman's Page Editor, Bolton *Evening News*, 1942–45; Lecturer, Bolton Women's College, 1967–69; teacher of creative writing, Bolton School, 1976–78. Recipient: Poetry Society Greenwood Prize, 1948, 1966; Arts Council grant, 1965. Fellow, Royal Society of Literature, 1971. Address: 10 The Green, Heath Charnock, Chorley, Lancashire PR6 9JH, England.

PUBLICATIONS

Verse

Poems. Manchester, Sherratt and Hughes, 1939.
Lean Forward, Spring! London, Sidgwick and Jackson, 1948.
No Time for Cowards. London, Heinemann, 1952.
Out of the Dark: New Poems. London, Heinemann, 1954.
Between Wheels and Stars. London, Heinemann, 1956.
The Buttercup Children. London, Hart Davis, 1958.
Prayer for Sun. London, Hart Davis, 1966.
A Song of Sunlight (for children). London, Chatto and Windus, 1974.
Preparing to Leave. London, Enitharmon Press, 1977.
The Eighth Joy. London, Enitharmon Press, 1980.

Plays

Radio: many documentaries, and the plays *One Pair of Eyes* and *What Can the Matter Be?*, 1979.

Other

My Aunt Edith (biography of Edith Rigby). London, Davies, 1966.
Rivington: The Story of a Village. London, Davies, 1972.

Manuscript Collection: Lockwood Memorial Library, State University of New York, Buffalo.

Phoebe Hesketh comments:

I've never belonged to any literary circle and was amazed when Sidgwick and Jackson's poetry reader said they'd like to publish a collection (1948). After the early influences of border ballads, R. L. Stevenson, and de la Mare, I fell, in my teens, under the spell of the Romantics, which undoubtedly coloured my first published work. Gradually, through rare strokes of fortune and the common blows of fate, I began to cast off the lyrical, romantic garments for sparser, bleaker material. Writing for me now is the process of stripping to the bone – with rare bursts of lyricism. I never seem able to write the poem I want to write: when I get the germ of an idea – as soon as it takes form – the poem gets hold of me and takes me where *it* wills, not where I will. I never know how a poem is to end. There are longer and longer periods between poems when I'm certain I'll never write again. I can't sustain a poem from "the top half of the brain"; it comes, unbidden, from a deeper level. It is the poem, not I, that achieves the initial creation. The hard labour comes in the next stages of actual composition and revision. I feel with Robert Frost: "A poem may be labored over once it is in being; it may not be labored into being."

* * *

Some of Phoebe Hesketh's most effective imagery springs from her native northern landscape of "heather-shouldered fells," "grey thin-fingered wind" and "stormy solitudes ... where reluctant spring/Retards the leaf." As she says in "Northern Stone":

Sap of the sullen moor is blood of my blood.
The whale-back ridge and whiplash of the wind
Stripping the branches in a rocking wood –
All these are of my life-stream, scoured and thinned.

Her moors are Brontëan. So too is the visionary quest "to find the Unknown through the known" expressed in many other evocations of this stark and stubborn country, including "Bleasdale: on Fairsnape," "Mountain Top," and the symbolism of solitary search, bereft of consoling certainties, in "Winter Journey." Her depiction of nature is never merely descriptive: its moods and seasons serve always as metaphor to communicate the experience of the human spirit, and a pervasive apprehension of "what is hidden and yet near/And intimate as breath." Emily Brontë is again irresistibly recalled in poems like "Revelation," "In Praise of Darkness," and "Vision": "The air grows luminous and light takes hold/Of darkness till my searching eyes are filled, –/I see, beyond the Seen, new worlds unfold."

Yet this poet also delights in the world of sense: the "beer-bubble stream," the winter sun "muffled in a wool of sullen cloud," the autumn hill where the wind "with iron-fisted blows/ Hammers the colours bleeding to the ground." Like Edward Thomas she celebrates the everyday simplicities of rural sights and pursuits – ploughing or gathering sticks, coltsfoot on a slag-heap, midsummer smoke "pale blue as lupin spires." Animals and birds – the pent-up rage of the solitary bull, the melancholy chestnut mare "with drooping underlip .../Tail-in to the wind," the alertly quivering fox "the colour of last year's beech-leaves"; the mallard and her brood surprised by a stoat, the heron "with elegiac wings" – are captured with sharp and vivid immediacy. The same loving precision informs her portraits of country people: village children tumbling out of school, their days "wide open as a daisy to the sun," the classroom dunce grown wise in his hedgerow truancies, an old man "withered as a gaunt sun-wrinkled tree." It is characteristic that several of these human cameos should explore the theme of spiritual riches implicit in physical deprivation. For the blind, not only the other senses but inward vision too is miraculously heightened; while the cripple's intuition of the intense life in flowers, rooted like himself, enables him "to travel though I may not rise and go." A similar paradox of liberation through captivity is expressed in "Rescue," in the image of the bird finally returning to the Falconer: "Thus chained and hooded, I am free at last."

Phoebe Hesketh's deeply felt conviction that modern man, his life "caged with steel" and "moulded into rods by the machine," has betrayed and desecrated his natural heritage is conveyed with telling impact through poems like "Born Between the Wheels," "The Invading Spring," "No Pause for Death," and her bleak vision of the future in "The Dark Side of the Moon." On all sides she sees "devastation in the unsacred name/Of science mock the cratered human heart." Yet however fiercely "stoned with doubt," her faith always finally reasserts itself. Walking in the city, she discovers in "one weak spire" of grass in a broken paving-stone "strength enough to break/The angled world of concrete."

Seldom unconscious of "The ache of living – beauty spiked with pain," or that "Even upon a peak of joy the flint comes piercing through," Phoebe Hesketh has continued to affirm her hard-won belief in the attainment of inward growth through such griefs as bereavement, love renounced, and loneliness; the spectacle of childhood's unsuspecting innocence overshadowed by the future, and the sadness of old age. As she declares in "Reflection" – "Through temporal loss of light we learn to find/The substance of a Sun that makes no shadow." In recent work like the symbolically titled *Preparing to Leave*, she has largely forsaken her earlier lyrical cadences and romantic imagery for a spare austerity which echoes her prevailing mood of "wintering in the dark."

—Margaret Willy

HEWETT, Dorothy (Coade). Australian. Born in Perth, Western Australia, 21 May 1923. Educated at Perth College; University of Western Australia, Perth, 1941–42, 1959–63, B.A. 1961, M.A. 1963. Married Lloyd Davies in 1944 (marriage dissolved, 1949); lived with Les Flood, 1950–59, three sons; married Merv Lilley in 1960, two daughters. Millworker, 1950–52; advertising copywriter, Sydney, 1956–58; Senior Tutor in English, University of Western Australia, 1964–73. Writer-in-Residence, Monash University, Melbourne, 1975, and University of Newcastle, New South Wales, 1977. Poetry Editor, *Westerly* magazine, Nedlands, Western Australia, 1972–73. Member of the Editorial Board, *Overland* magazine, Melbourne, since 1970, and *Sisters* magazine, Melbourne, since 1979; since 1979, Editor and Director, Big Smoke Books, and Review Editor, *New Poetry*, both Sydney. Recipient: Australian Broadcasting Corporation Prize, 1945, 1965; Australia Council grant, 1973, 1976, 1979; Australian Writers Guild award, 1974; International Women's Year grant, 1976. Agent: Howard Nicholson, 16 Taylor Street, Taylor's Square, Sydney, New South Wales. Address: 49 Jersey Road, Woollahra, New South Wales 2025, Australia.

PUBLICATIONS

Verse

What about the People, with Merv Lilley. Sydney, Realist Writers, 1962.
Windmill Country. Sydney, Edwards and Shaw, 1968.
The Hidden Journey. Newnham, Tasmania, Wattle Grove Press, 1969.
Late Night Bulletin. Newnham, Tasmania, Wattle Grove Press, 1970.
Rapunzel in Suburbia. Sydney, New Poetry, 1975.
Greenhouse. Sydney, Big Smoke, 1979.

Plays

This Old Man Comes Rolling Home (produced Perth, 1968). Sydney, Currency Press, 1976.
Mrs. Porter and the Angel (produced Sydney, 1970).
The Chapel Perilous; or, The Perilous Adventures of Sally Banner, music by Frank Arndt and Michael Leyden (produced Perth, 1971). Sydney, Currency Press, 1972; London, Eyre Methuen, 1974.
Bon-Bons and Roses for Dolly (produced Perth, 1972). Included in *Bon-Bons and Roses for Dolly, and The Tatty Hollow Story*, 1976.
Catspaw (produced Perth, 1974).
Miss Hewett's Shenanigans (produced Canberra, 1975).
Joan (produced Canberra, 1975).
The Tatty Hollow Story (produced Sydney, 1976). Included in *Bon-Bons and Roses for Dolly, and The Tatty Hollow Story*, 1976.
Bon-Bons and Roses for Dolly, and The Tatty Hollow Story. Sydney, Currency Press, 1976.
The Golden Oldies (produced Melbourne, 1977; London, 1978).
The Beautiful Miss Portland, in *Theatre Australia*, (Sydney), 1977.
Pandora's Box (produced Sydney, 1978). Published in *Theatre Australia*, (Sydney), 1978.
The Man from Mukinupin (produced Perth, 1979). Sydney, Currency Press, 1979.

Novel

Bobbin Up. Sydney, Australasian Book Society, 1959.

Short Stories

The Australians Have a Word for It. Berlin, Seven Seas, 1964.

Other

Editor, *Sandgropers: A Western Australian Anthology.* Nedlands, University of Western Australia Press, 1973.

Manuscript Collection (poetry): Australian National Library, Canberra.

Critical Studies: "Confession and Beyond" by Bruce Williams, in *Overland* (Sydney), 1977; interview with Jim Davidson, in *Meanjin* (Melbourne), 1979.

Dorothy Hewett comments:

My first collection, *Windmill Country*, was long delayed and therefore incorporated much that I had already outgrown. The locale of the book is firmly Western Australian, with consequent emphasis on landscape and ancestor-worship. There is also a strong strain of politicizing in the book, influenced by regionalism and the Australian poets of my own generation, particularly Judith Wright. The book is uneven, romantic, and didactic. *Rapunzel in Suburbia*, my second collection, covers my time as an academic. It is strongly confessional, obviously influenced by Lowell and Plath, and romantic in style and subject. Fantasy is a central element in the book; there is also an introverted imagination linked with a sense of the dramatic. *Greenhouse* is an even more radical departure. The book covers my last three years in Sydney and is influenced by the city and by younger Australian city poets. There are a wider range of experimentation, a firmer control, and more substantial intellectual content. The lyrical, the fantastic, and the analytical predominate.

* * *

Dorothy Hewett's career as a poet often seemed overshadowed by the much more public dimension of her obsessive plays, until a poem ("Uninvited Guest") in *Rapunzel in Suburbia*, brought to notice by a quotation in a review in the quarterly *Westerly*, became the target of legal action by her first husband. The notoriety of the resulting financial settlements has warned off booksellers in her native Western Australia and affected production prospects of plays, especially as they share with her poetry a scarcely masked autobiographical derivation. A reissue of the book substituted for the offending poem an "Envoi" patently addressed to her husband. The untried case remains, in 1979, a live issue.

Hewett's birthdate surprises the reader by placing her in the same generation of Australian poets as Judith Wright, Rosemary Dobson, and Gwen Harwood. With only the last of these has she a strong affinity, declared indeed in her recent collection, by virtue of their frank statements about sexuality and their bold self-imaging. Her adventurous attitude to life and the freedom of her verseforms in fact outdo most of the generation born since 1945 – she unites the publishing history of a "late starter" with an agelessly avant-garde élan.

It is her literary training and references that might perhaps "place" her. "In Pissing Alley" is a list of influences, but most notably she early absorbed the achievements of Yeats and T. S. Eliot, and writes with awareness of current United States work. She takes a contemporary view of her Australian writing associations in "Creeley in Sydney."

Her formidable talent emerges clearly in her 1970's books. A noteworthy device in *Rapunzel in Suburbia* is the ransacking of a between-wars up-bringing and 1940's and 1950's living for catchwords and characteristic objects. In this book and *Greenhouse* the poet re-writes or takes up significant detail from legends, literature, and biographies in order to interpret female sexuality – stories of mermaids come ashore, the Lady of Shalott, Rapunzel, the Snow Queen, Madame Bovary, Anna Karenina, Hedda Gabler, Psyche, Sappho, as in "Grave Fairytale":

> Bald as a collaborator I sit walled in the thumb-nosed tower,
> wound round three times with ropes of autumn leaves.
> And the witch ... sometimes I idly kick
> a little heap of rags across the floor.
> I notice it gets smaller every year.

Alongside the fairly lengthy daring expositions of "Calling on Mother," "Underneath the Arches," "Blue Movie," and "Miss Hewett's Shenanigans" are short lyrics of affecting beauty – "In Moncur Street," "Forsaken Mermaid," "The Child":

> But since she came
> she passes by
> so often that we've grown hard;
> yet like a dust mote in the eye
> her beauty troubles us, her cry
> still shakes me: in the empty yard
> I tremble that all things must die
> and call and call her name.

Greenhouse includes, beside a powerful continuation of *Rapunzel*'s themes and devices, an extraordinary series, "The Mandelstam Letters," concluding with a "Sydney Postcript":

This is our fate   the   stoney faces
Mayakovsky's bedbugs   crawlers   in rented rooms
Christs with dimpled female knees   hang   over the painful beds
the women lie visionary   in rows   cataract eyes ablaze

... I run down the hospital stairs   hold   the dead child in the heart
tonguetied guttersnipes   make copies of   my verses
pay me   testify   "we'll hear no more of this"
I am sending my poems   to the literary mags.   bookshops no longer stock them
poems are illegal   poems are   obliterated
one of the accusations   against you   you circulated your verses
in this country I live   only for the present   a little serenity
it is unforgivably vain   unforgivable   to compare ourselves

Hewett's indignant refusal to bow to taboos confronts and contains guilt rather than exorcising it: her self-knowing energy intensely wills both fulfilment and despair. Hers is a celebration of desperate love, proof by its ephemeral magnificence and its visionary source against hostile forces ("Winter Solstice: 1 May"):

> my mortal hand begins to play
> with leaves & grass & eerily
>   the child to say:
> *she does not live with you & me*
> the hoax   the joke   the booby prize!
> a porpoise tumbles in the bay,
> I twist the knife, I shake, I rise,
> past luminous mushrooms on the track
> the child is carried piggyback;
> I try this hairshirt on for size....

The final poems of her latest book come to the image of the labyrinth, in which the poet faces art, age, the world, and death. The charge of unevenness can be brought against Hewett; the charge of irrelevance never.

—Judith Rodriguez

HEWITT, Geof (George F. Hewitt). American. Born in Glen Ridge, New Jersey, 1 September 1943. Educated at Cornell University, Ithaca, New York (Academy of American Poets Prize, 1966), 1962–66, B.A. 1966; Johns Hopkins University, Baltimore, 1966–67, M.A. 1967; University of Iowa, Iowa City, 1967–69, M.F.A. 1969. Married Janet Lind in 1971; one son. Assistant Editor, *Epoch Magazine*, Ithaca, New York, 1964–66; Editor-in-Chief, *Trojan Horse* magazine, Ithaca, New York, 1965–66; Gilman Teaching Fellow, Johns Hopkins University, 1966–67; Teaching Assistant, University of Iowa, 1967–69; Instructor, Coe College, Cedar Rapids, Iowa, 1969, and University of Hawaii, Honolulu, 1969–70. Since 1966, Founding Editor, Kumquat Press, Montclair, New Jersey, later Enosburg, Vermont; since 1970, Contributing Editor, *Cornell Alumni News*, Ithaca, New York; since 1971, Contributing Editor, *New Letters*, Kansas City, Missouri. Recipient: Coordinating Council of Literary Magazines grant, 1967, 1969; Vermont Council on the Arts grants, 1974. Address: R.D.4, Enosburg Falls, Vermont 05450, U.S.A.

PUBLICATIONS

Verse

Poem and Other Poems. Montclair, New Jersey, Kumquat Press, 1966.
Waking Up Still Pickled. Aurora, New York, Lillabulero Press, 1967.
Stone Soup. Ithaca, New York, Ithaca House, 1974.
I Think They'll Lay My Egg Tomorrow. Montpelier, Vermont Council on the Arts, 1976.

Other

Editor, *Quickly Aging Here: Some Poets of the 1970's.* New York, Doubleday, 1969.
Editor, *Selected Poems of Alfred Starr Hamilton.* Highlands, North Carolina, Jargon, 1969.
Editor, *Living in Whales: Stories and Poems from Vermont Public Schools.* Montpelier, Vermont Council on the Arts, 1972.

Critical Studies: Reviews by Michael Benedikt, in *Poetry* (Chicago), December 1968, and by Thomas Lask, in *The New York Times*, 20 February 1970.

Geof Hewitt comments:

I write poetry when I can. There is a tension between the public and the private person, between ambition and sloth, between the joy of language and the sincerity of silence.

Poetry is not a "career" for me, nor am I presumptuous enough to claim it as a way of life. I write what I can whenever I can, sometimes call it "poetry," and am always grateful when it comes.

* * *

Geof Hewitt's poetry, even from such early poems as "The Gift" and "Laramie, 1851," both written about 1965, relies heavily on humor and word-play. These two poems, the former relatively serious, the latter more farcically playful, both announce and anticipate technique and tone to come; the former turns on two connotations of the word "fail," while the latter juggles word permutations like a slap-happy acrobat ("mugs," "smug," and "gums," all within four lines), while both exhibit a sense of humor, whether about himself or others. While many of Hewitt's poems stick close to his own experience and describe convincingly real, if occasionally bizarre events ("The Couple Parking on the Motorcycle," for example, which could be subtitled, "love in gear"), Hewitt sometimes makes a leap into science fiction-related poetry, and some of his s.f. poetry is among the more interesting poetry of this sort. "The Frozen Man" is about a man, quick frozen, who wakes up in the future to find himself merely another t.v. dinner; "My Martian Girl Friend" describes the attributes of an extraterrestrial dream girl, and "At One with the Blue Night" manages to be at once both a metaphysical journey in the vein of *2001* and a highly lyrical love poem.

Hewitt's poetry displays the exuberance of someone excited, rather than intimidated, by the possibilities of language, a poet not afraid to use its full resources: connotation, anagrams, punning, or outrageous internal rhymes we're more accustomed to encountering in nonsense poetry: "men too cool to coo through glass" (from "November 23, 1971"). It takes daring, an admirable penchant for risk-taking which Hewitt has in abundance, to attempt being funny about a serious subject in as slapstick a way as Hewitt is in these lines from "Shudder":

> For months there were hints she was disenchanted:
> the banana peel in the bathtub, a roller
> skate balanced on the ladder rung
> while you repaired the roof of your now-empty

—Duane Ackerson

HEWITT, John (Harold). British. Born in Belfast, Northern Ireland, 28 October 1907. Educated at Methodist College, Belfast; Queen's University, Belfast, B.A. 1930, M.A. 1951. Married Roberta Black in 1934. Art Assistant, then Deputy Director, Belfast Museum and Art Gallery, 1930–57; Art Director, Herbert Art Gallery and Museum, Coventry, 1957–72, now retired. Associate Editor, *Lagan* magazine, 1945–46; Poetry Editor, *Threshold* magazine, Belfast, 1957–61. Fellow, Museums Association. D.Litt.: New University of Ulster, Coleraine, 1974. Member, Irish Academy of Letters, 1960. Address: 11 Stockman's Lane, Belfast BT9 7JA, Northern Ireland.

PUBLICATIONS

Verse

Conacre. Privately printed, 1943.
No Rebel Word. London, Muller, 1948.
Tesserae. Belfast, Festival, 1967.
Collected Poems 1932–1967. London, MacGibbon and Kee, 1968.
The Day of the Corncrake: Poems of the Nine Glens. Belfast, Glens of Antrim Historical Society, 1969.
The Planter and the Gael, with John Montague. Belfast, Arts Council of Northern Ireland, 1970.

An Ulster Reckoning. Privately printed, 1971.
Out of My Time: Poems 1967–1974. Belfast, Blackstaff Press, 1974.
Time Enough: Poems New and Revised. Belfast, Blackstaff Press, 1976.
The Rain Dance: Poems New and Revised. Belfast, Blackstaff Press, 1978.

Play

The Bloody Brae (produced Belfast, 1957). Published in *Threshold* (Belfast), Autumn 1957.

Other

Coventry: The Tradition of Change and Continuity. Coventry, Coventry Corporation, 1966.
Arts in Ulster 1. Belfast, Blackstaff Press, 1977.

Editor, with Sam H. Bell and Nesca A. Robb, *The Arts in Ulster: A Symposium.* London, Harrap, 1951.
Editor, *Poems of William Allingham.* Dublin, Dolmen Press, 1967.
Editor, *Rhyming Weavers and Other Country Poets of Antrim and Down.* Belfast, Blackstaff Press, 1974.

Critical Studies: "Regionalism into Reconciliation: The Poetry of John Hewitt" by John Montague, in *Poetry Ireland* (Dublin), Spring 1964: "The Poetry of John Hewitt" by Seamus Heaney, in *Threshold* (Belfast), Summer 1969; "John Hewitt: Land and People" by Terence Brown, in *Northern Voices*, Dublin, Gill and Macmillan, 1975.

John Hewitt comments:

My poetry is a quest for identity as an individual, as an Irishman of settler stock, as a twentieth-century man.

In imagery, for evocation of mood, I seek accuracy of sensory experience. My verse is low-charged, conversational in tone. I normally use regular forms, largely iambic; now free verse tends to replace blank verse, but with renewed interest in sonnet.

Influences: Wordsworth, Frost, Yeats, Pound, Edward Thomas.

* * *

John Hewitt, Ulster's senior poet, presents the paradox of largely rural inspiration, and an urban (Belfast) background. As he says in "The Lonely Heart":

My father was a city schoolmaster
for forty years acclimatised to air
stale with hot breath, wet jerseys, chalk and crumbs,
in a tall building islanded in slums.

He first began to publish in the socialist thirties, both nature lyrics like "The Leaf" or "The Little Lough," and others in which he asserted his identity as an Irishman of Planter stock: "Once alien here my fathers built their house,/claimed, drained, and gave the land the shape of use ..." ("Once Alien Here").

In the 1940's these two themes came together in a series of long poems, the best known being *Conacre*. Several others appeared in *Lagan*, the leading Ulster magazine of the period, grouped under the title of "Freehold"; as well as the private world of "The Lonely Heart" there was the more public: "To Ulster then, my region, now I turn,/new to sworn service, with so much to learn ..." ("The Glittering Sod"). The poems of this period were part of a conscious attempt to foster Ulster Regionalism, as a companion to the Lallans movement in Scotland. In his extended essay, "Ulster Poets, 1800–1850," first read to the Belfast Literary Society (January, 1950) Hewitt sketched what he calls the "true Ulster tradition," ignoring the Gaelic writers of the province in favour of rural bards and rhyming weavers. But in his first English collection, *No Rebel Word*, he allowed himself to be presented (in the preface by Geoffrey Taylor) as part of the tradition of English nature poetry; a few poems apart, the only hint of defiance is in the title.

Something similar occurs in his *Collected Poems* where, with a kind of retrospective modesty, Hewitt has tended to skimp the more controversial aspects of his career. But a careful reading will discover a development in his thinking about Ulster, especially in the parable poem, "The Colony," which compares the Protestant position to that of a Roman settlement in the declining Empire. There is a more detached note in the later poems, due to his leaving Belfast for an English gallery (cf. "An Irishman in Coventry"). But his affection for the landscape of Antrim remains a constant factor, as Donegal was for the nineteenth century fore-runner whose poems he edited for the Irish Arts Council, William Allingham.

—John Montague

HEYEN, William. American. Born in Brooklyn, New York, 1 November 1940. Educated at State University of New York, Brockport, 1957–61, B.S. 1961; Ohio University, Athens, 1961–67, M.A. 1963, Ph.D. 1967. Married Hannelore Greiner in 1962; one son and one daughter. English teacher, Springville High School, New York, 1961–62; Instructor in English, State University of New York, Cortland, 1963–65. Since 1967, Member of the Department of English, currently Professor, State University of New York, Brockport. Senior Fulbright-Hays Lecturer in American Literature, Germany, 1971–72. Recipient: Borestone Mountain Award, 1966; National Endowment for the Arts Fellowship, 1974; Guggenheim Fellowship, 1977; *Ontario Review* Award, 1977; Eunice Tietjens Memorial Prize (*Poetry*, Chicago), 1978. Address: 142 Frazier Street, Brockport, New York 14420, U.S.A.

PUBLICATIONS

Verse

The Mower. Privately printed, 1970.
Depth of Field. Baton Rouge, Louisiana State University Press, 1970.
The Fireman Next Door. Buffalo, Slow Loris Press, 1971.
The Train. Rochester, New York, Valley Press, 1972.
The Trail Beside the River Platte. Rushden, Northamptonshire, Sceptre Press, 1973.
The Pigeons. Mount Horeb, Wisconsin, Perishable Press, 1973.
Noise in the Trees: Poems and a Memoir. New York, Vanguard Press, 1974.
Mermaid. Derry, Pennsylvania, Rook Press, 1975.
Cardinals. Derry, Pennsylvania, Rook Press, 1976.
Cardinals/The Cardinal. Derry, Pennsylvania, Rook Press, 1976.
The Pearl. Pittsburgh, Slow Loris Press, 1976.
Of Palestine: A Meditation. Omaha, Abattoir, 1976.
Pickerel. Derry, Pennsylvania, Rook Press, 1976.
Dusk. Derry, Pennsylvania, Rook Press, 1976.

The Trench. Derry, Pennsylvania, Rook Press, 1976.
The Carrie White Auction at Brockport, May 1974. Derry, Pennsylvania, Rook Society, 1976.
XVII Machines. Pittsburgh, Sisyphus, 1976.
Ars Poetica. Derry, Pennsylvania, Rook Press, 1976.
Mare. Derry, Pennsylvania, Rook Press, 1976.
Darkness. Derry, Pennsylvania, Rook Society, 1977.
The Swastika Poems. New York, Vanguard Press, 1977.
Fires. Athens, Ohio, Croissant, 1977.
The Elm's Home. Derry, Pennsylvania, Scrimshaw, 1977.
Son Dream/Daughter Dream. Ruffsdale, Pennsylvania, Rook Press, 1978.
The Ash. Potsdam, New York, Banjo Press, 1978.
Witness. Madison, Wisconsin, Rara Avis Press, 1978.
Lord Dragonfly. Ruffsdale, Pennsylvania, Scrimshaw, 1978.
Brockport's Poems. Brockport, New York, Challenger Press, 1978.
The Children. Knotting, Bedfordshire, Sceptre Press, 1979.
Long Island Light: Poems and a Memoir. New York, Vanguard Press, 1979.
The City Parables. Athens, Ohio, Croissant, 1979.
Evening Drowning. Concord, New Hampshire, William B. Ewert, 1979.
The Snow Hen. Concord, New Hampshire, William B. Ewert, 1979.

Other

From This Book of Praise: Poems and a Conversation with William Heyen, edited by Vince Clemente. Port Jefferson, New York, Street Press, 1978.

Editor, *Profile of Theodore Roethke.* Columbus, Ohio, Charles E. Merrill, 1971.
Editor, *American Poets in 1976.* Indianapolis, Bobbs Merrill, 1976.
Editor, *I Would Also Like to Mention Aluminum: A Conversation with William Stafford.* Pittsburgh, Slow Loris Press, 1976.

Bibliography: "Nothing We Do Is Ever Lost to the Light: William Heyen, A Preliminary Bibliography" by Ernest Stefanik, in *Bulletin of Bibliography* (Boston), 1979.

Manuscript Collection: Mugar Memorial Library, Boston University.

William Heyen comments:

I'm glad to say that as the years have gone by I've found it easier to write. I'm not sure of all the reasons for this, and don't want to be too sure of them, but style is involved, the slow and painful evolution of a voice; also involved, unfashionable as it may be even to suggest this, is an evolving conception of the central themes and purposes of poetry, and of the kinds of poetry I most deeply believe in. During the act of writing, this is not a conscious thing, of course (and this comment itself is a kind of second-guessing, surely), but I may have come to feel, at last, that I am doing some good, that my poems characteristically create a consciousness engaged in finding its way through conflict to clarity, hoping for some kind of musical resolution that means, that will, for now, suffice, until the next poem.

* * *

In his formalistic first collection, *Depth of Field*, William Heyen proclaimed a reliance on "detail that deepens into fond symbol." In "Off the Hamptons" and "The Spider" he does enter nature so fully that details deepen to implied statement. But the labored quality of many of these poems suggests that the material is being willed, rather than felt, into poems. Technique seems more important than vision.

When Heyen began to explore his Long Island past in *Noise in the Trees*, he became a visionary poet. He balances his formal control with emotional openness. It is as though he heard the voice of the great Long Island poet Walt Whitman and begins his own version of the journey outlined in "Song of Myself." In the spirit of Thoreau, who "travelled much in Concord," Heyen stays at home and descends within himself into various layers of the past. The spirits of American literary forefathers, pre-eminently that of Whitman, accompany him. Ultimately Heyen ascends with fragments of his local, regional, and national heritage. He suffers pain over the loss of the land, which he dares to equate with the loss of young love, but he grows spiritually as a result.

The emotional openness of the collection is paralleled by an experiment in form. Between the two sequences of poems, Heyen places a prose memoir, "Noise in the Trees," which is a series of 25 vignettes from his youth, sketches, prose poems, dreams, fantasies, legends, excerpts from histories, journals, and even a geological dictionary. The poems and prose are fused together by the author's obsessive retrieval of what he calls his "island of the mind."

In *The Swastika Poems*, an obsession with family heritage drives Heyen into the darkness of the Holocaust. He had addressed poems to his Nazi uncles in his first collection. As revised for their new context, however, these poems more clearly emerge as part of Heyen's dialogue with the darker side of himself. When he tells his Nazi father-in-law, "I have a stake in this," he speaks for all moral beings. To paraphrase the epigraph from Sontag, the function of this urgent remembering is moral. Hansjörg Greiner is "another one I don't know how/to talk to, but have to."

From the opening poem about his father on the boat to America, to the concluding title poem where he recalls the same man scraping away swastikas drawn on their Brooklyn windows, Heyen engages us in his descent into the inferno of the Holocaust. As we emerge from the darkness at the end of the book-length sequence, we are left in silence and light, "our heart beat[ing] with it."

Long Island Light is an expansion and deepening of *Noise in the Trees*. Some 31 new poems and ten prose pieces, written with increased authority, intensify the return to origins, extend the search for heritage into the present, and clarify the timelessness of the vision. The new poems about his life as husband and father in his "second home," upstate Brockport, N.Y., add a maturity and a progression which suggest that Heyen may even have the resources to enlarge this ambitious collection.

Without exaggeration, Heyen's project may be compared to Whitman's ever-expanding *Leaves of Grass*. The depth of Heyen's emotional and spiritual commitment, the growth of his technical skills, and the intensification of his vision have already elevated the people and places of his Long Island past – the farmer Wenzel, Gibbs Pond, Lake Ronkonkoma, Short Beach, St. James Harbor, Nesconsett, even the Jericho Turnpike – to the status of myth. In less than ten years, Heyen has indeed discovered "detail that deepens to fond symbol."

In the 1970's no American poet published stronger back-to-back collections than *The Swastika Poems* and *Long Island Light*. In his feeling for nature and people – in his reverence for life – Heyen is reminiscent of James Wright. No contemporary American poet has written better prose than the memoirs "Noise in the Trees" and "Erica" and the "Afterward" to the exquisite haiku-like sequence *Lord Dragonfly*. Heyen has become one of the major American poets of the post-World War II era.

—Norbert Krapf

HIGHAM, Charles. British. Born in London, 18 February 1931. Educated at St. Peter's School, Cranleigh, Clayesmore. Book critic, 1956–63, and film critic, 1968–69, Sydney

Morning Herald; feature writer, Sydney *Daily Mirror*, 1956–63, and *Nation*, Sydney, 1960–62; Literary Editor, *The Bulletin*, Sydney, 1963–68; Australian correspondent, *Sight and Sound*, London, and *Hudson Review*, New York, 1961–69. Visiting Regents Professor, University of California, Santa Cruz, 1969. Recipient: Poetry Society Prize, London, 1949; Sydney *Morning Herald* prize, 1956; Académie Française Prix des Créateurs, 1978. Agent: Barbara Lowenstein, 250 West 57th Street, New York, New York 10019, U.S.A.

PUBLICATIONS

Verse

A Distant Star. Aldington, Kent, Hand and Flower Press, 1951.
Spring and Death. Aldington, Kent, Hand and Flower Press, 1953.
The Earthbound and Other Poems. Sydney, Angus and Robertson, 1959.
Noonday Country: Poems 1954–1965. Sydney, Angus and Robertson, 1966.
The Voyage to Brindisi and Other Poems 1966–1969. Sydney, Angus and Robertson, 1970.

Other

The Celluloid Muse: Hollywood Directors Speak, with Joel Greenberg. London, Angus and Robertson, 1969; Chicago, Regnery, 1971.
Hollywood in the Forties, with Joel Greenberg. London, Zwemmer, and Cranbury, New Jersey, A. S. Barnes, 1969.
The Films of Orson Welles. Berkeley, University of California Press, 1970.
Hollywood Cameramen: Sources of Light. Bloomington, Indiana University Press, and London, Thames and Hudson, 1970.
Ziegfeld. Chicago, Regnery, 1972; London, W. H. Allen, 1973.
Hollywood at Sunset. New York, Saturday Review Press, 1972.
Cecil B. DeMille. New York, Scribner, 1973; London, W. H. Allen, 1974.
The Art of the American Film 1900–1971. New York, Doubleday, 1973.
Ava. New York, Delacorte Press, and London, W. H. Allen, 1974.
Kate: The Life of Katharine Hepburn. New York, Norton, and London, W. H. Allen, 1975.
Warner Brothers. New York, Scribner, 1975.
Charles Laughton: An Intimate Biography. New York, Doubleday, and London, W. H. Allen, 1976.
The Adventures of Conan Doyle: The Life of the Creator of Sherlock Holmes. New York, Norton, and London, Hamish Hamilton, 1976.
Marlene: The Life of Marlene Dietrich. New York, Norton, 1977; London, Granada, 1978.
Celebrity Circus. New York, Delacorte Press, 1979.
The Adventures of Errol Flynn. New York, Doubleday, and London, Granada, 1980.

Editor, with Alan Brissenden, *They Came to Australia: An Anthology.* Melbourne, Cheshire, 1961; London, Angus and Robertson, 1962.
Editor, with Michael Wilding, *Australians Abroad: An Anthology.* Melbourne, Cheshire, 1967.
Editor, *Australian Writing Today.* London, Penguin, 1968.

Manuscript Collections: Boston University; University of Southern California, Los Angeles; State University of New York, Buffalo.

Critical Study: in *Times Literary Supplement* (London), 23 September 1960.

Charles Higham comments:

(1970) My poems are written in a large variety of largely invented forms, and sometimes words; and their subject matter is equally various. The ocean – a dominating presence in the world I live in – swamps, jungles, strange towns, animals and birds all form the basis of what I believe is essentially a poetry of the senses, and of primitive nature. I try to strike through to the places that are still untouched by man's ruinings; hence my deep passion for Australia, the West Indies, above all Luzon in the Philippines and parts of Japan. If I were asked to set a landscape which my poems live in, I would say: a green sky, with a mid-day moon; palms slanting from a swamp from which rise strange wading and flying birds; a lonely figure digging for clams on a fringing beach beyond which lies the enormous, flat, metallic Pacific.

(1974) In the early part of 1974, after a long hiatus, I began writing a new series of poems based on Rilkean exotic themes.

(1980) Since that time, I have been writing poetry more frequently, all of it published in Australian literary periodocals. I have resumed my earlier formal modes, perhaps in response to the increasing disintegration of Western culture. I have written increasingly of American experience: two recent poems, "Salmon Fishing" and "Los Angeles Sequence," have been indicative of a return to the "Northern" atmosphere of my very earliest work in *A Distant Star* and *Spring and Death*. I can now be described as a stateless poet, having lived in England, Australia, and now California, but I still think of myself as a British poet in exile both from the urban modes that have dominated British verse in my lifetime, and from (at this time) the more strongly regional elements in Australian poetry. The fact that in America I am known only as a broadly popular writer on film and theater subjects is releasing in a sense: I can write poetry without being discovered as a poet in the country I live in, and keep my vision pure and whole. I am still a poet of exotic experience, and remain unrepentantly drawn to the romantic and baroque.

* * *

Although he is an Englishman, Charles Higham has adapted to his Australian identity with remarkable intelligence. His best poems, most of which deal with Australian experience or history, present an interesting and revealing point of view that is, so to say, both involved and yet detached. This newer, Australian poetry is considerably superior to his earliest, English poetry, which was feebly derivative (even neo-Georgian), debilitated and lacking in self-confidence or purpose. He can still write too patly, without tension, relying too much on technical convention, as in these lines from "Rushcutter's Bay":

In winter, trapped by gloom, we long for this:
The body stripped, sex in blue trunks, the leap
Of water to be carved by pressing shoulders....

But in his powerful "The Kelly Show" – surely an extraordinary poem to have come from one who is not a native of Australia – the tight rhyming form (in which he usually chooses to write) is vitalized by a personal rhythm and a tragic urgency. His weaknesses – a tendency to cliché, a fondness for making trite or commonplace points, as well as others already mentioned – have vanished. The last stanza reads:

The curtain falls; she waves a final hand.
He quotes his jot of evidence; he treads
Into the proper place; his smile is bland.
Applause demands her curtsey into beds,
And so she lewdly nods her short assent.
He drops and twists: the watchers nod their heads
And write his name upon the continent.

—Martin Seymour-Smith

HILL, Geoffrey. British. Born in Bromsgrove, Worcestershire, 18 June 1932. Educated at Fairfield Junior School; County High School, Bromsgrove; Keble College, Oxford. Professor of English Literature, University of Leeds. Recipient: Gregory Award, 1961; Hawthornden Prize, 1969; Faber Memorial Prize, 1970; Whitbread Award, 1971; Alice Hunt Bartlett Award, 1971; Heinemann Award, 1972. Fellow, Royal Society of Literature, 1972. Lives in Leeds, Yorkshire, England.

PUBLICATIONS

Verse

(*Poems*). Oxford, Fantasy Press, 1952.
For the Unfallen: Poems 1952–1958. London, Deutsch, 1959; Chester Springs, Pennsylvania, Dufour, 1960.
Preghiere. Leeds, Northern House, 1964.
Penguin Modern Poets 8, with Edwin Brock and Stevie Smith. London, Penguin, 1966.
King Log. London, Deutsch, and Chester Springs, Pennsylvania, Dufour, 1968.
Mercian Hymns. London, Deutsch, 1971.
Somewhere Is Such a Kingdom: Poems 1952–1971. Boston, Houghton Mifflin, 1975.
Tenebrae. London, Deutsch, 1978; Boston, Houghton Mifflin, 1979.

Recording: *The Poetry and Voice of Geoffrey Hill*, Caedmon, 1979.

Play

Brand, adaptation of the play by Ibsen (produced London, 1978). London, Heinemann, 1978.

Critical Studies: by Christopher Ricks, in *London Magazine*, November 1964; Jeffrey Wainwright, in *Stand* (Newcastle upon Tyne), x, 1, 1968; Martin Dodsworth, in *Stand* (Newcastle upon Tyne), xiii, 1, 1971–72; Michael Launchbury, in *Delta* (Sheffield), Spring 1972; "The Poetry of Geoffrey Hill" by Jon Silkin, in *British Poetry since 1960*, edited by Michael Schmidt and Grevel Lindop, Oxford, Carcanet Press, 1972; "Beyond Modernism: Christopher Middleton and Geoffrey Hill" by Wallace D. Martin, in *Contemporary Literature* (Madison, Wisconsin), xii, 4, 1972; Michael Wilding in *New Poetry* (Sydney), xx, 1–2, 1973; "Geoffrey Hill" by John Purkis, in *Twentieth Century Poetry*, Milton Keynes, Buckinghamshire, Open University, 1976; *Figures of Capable Imagination* by Harold Bloom, New York, Seabury Press, 1976; *Geoffrey Hill and "The Tongue's Atrocities"* by Christopher Ricks, Swansea, University College, 1978.

* * *

Geoffrey Hill's poems are poems of extremity. Their thematic poles are the extremes of sex and of death – the body's proximate cravings and terrors, and the body's remotest cravings and terrors – and the ways in which the human imagination can cope with these. Their manner of proceeding – costive, allusive, highly polished – is the self-protective stylistic shield of a man appalled before his own experience, and before what he understands to be the experience of his race in history. The procedure protects with ironies that attempt to render the self invisible. The poems stubbornly refuse statement, assertion, resolution – or, if they allow these things, they allow them only within a dramatic context, a fictional location. "The Songbook of Sebastian Arrurruz," for instance, is a poem "about" sexual despair; but the heart-rending poignancy of some of its moments is undermined, or undercut, or "undervalued," perhaps, by the elaborate literary deceit of the poem's form. If there is personal utterance behind the "Songbook," its tracks are well covered by the artifice in which

Hill creates a completely fictional poet – "Arrurruz" himself – and then "translates" his work into English. At one point in the sequence, we are actually offered Hill's translation of Arrurruz's translation from the Latin. One might think that the modernist cult of impersonality, which Hill himself learnt most immediately, I think, not from Eliot or Pound, but from the more hieratic, and more rigorously formalist, American poet Allen Tate, has never been carried further.

If this has the effect, sometimes, of making Hill's poetry hermetic to the point of a reader's despair, it is also the signature of an intensely dramatic, historical imagination in which a generously responsive, and responsible, empathy lays the individual ego to sleep, dissolving it into history, legend, and myth, and attempts to find a meeting-point between personal and communal meaning. I am thinking particularly of his poem-sequences "Of Commerce and Society," "Funeral Music," *Mercian Hymns* and "An Apology for the Revival of Christian Architecture in England," in which Hill's essential "commerce" is with what he calls "the speechless dead," re-imagining the processes of their human suffering and finding in it paradigms for the ways in which we all, necessarily, live and die.

It will perhaps be obvious from this that Hill is a poet immensely self-conscious about language itself, and a poet whose moral and political preoccupations deepen everywhere into preoccupations that may properly be called religious. In the recent sequences "The Pentecost Castle" and "Lachrimae" these themes are intensely focussed through an attempt to come to some kind of terms with the figure of Christ as it has been presented by the mystical tradition of European Christianity. They are sequences of dark paradox which combine longing, rejection, self-abasement, and a kind of grim hope, what he calls elsewhere "cries of rapture and despair." It is not surprising to find Dietrich Bonhoeffer, the theologian of God's paradoxical presence in his absence, and the religio-political martyr of Hitler's Germany, the subject of a poem that may be taken as representative of Hill's view of religion and of language:

Bonhoeffer in his skylit cell
bleached by the flares' candescent fall,
pacing out his own citadel,

restores the broken themes of praise,
encourages our borrowed days,
by logic of his sacrifice.

Against wild reasons of the state
his words are quiet but not too quiet.
We hear too late or not too late.

The voice that speaks here is serious, dignified, resonant. Totally avoiding the afflatus of rhetorical posture, it addresses itself to the largest themes with a measured weight that is a true moral strength. Geoffrey Hill is, quite simply, the best poet now writing in English.

—Neil Corcoran

HINE, (William) Daryl. Canadian. Born in Burnaby, British Columbia, 24 February 1936. Educated at McGill University, Montreal, 1954–58; University of Chicago, M.A. 1965, Ph.D. in comparative literature 1967. Lived in Europe 1958–62. Assistant Professor of English, University of Chicago, 1967–69. Editor, *Poetry*, Chicago, 1968–78. Recipient:

Canada Foundation-Rockefeller Fellowship, 1958; Canada Council grant, 1959, 1979; Ingram Merrill grant, 1962, 1963. Address: 2740 Ridge Avenue, Evanston, Illinois 60201, U.S.A.

PUBLICATIONS

Verse

Five Poems 1954. Toronto, Emblem, 1954.
The Carnal and the Crane. Toronto, Contact Press, 1957.
The Devil's Picture Book. London and New York, Abelard Schuman, 1960.
Heroics: Five Poems. Fontainebleau, France, Gosswiller, 1961.
The Wooden Horse. New York, Atheneum, 1965.
Minutes: Poems. New York, Atheneum, 1968.
The Homeric Hymns and The Battle of the Frogs and the Mice. New York, Atheneum, 1972.
Resident Alien. New York, Atheneum, 1975.
In and Out: A Confessional Poem. Privately printed, 1975.
Daylight Saving. New York, Atheneum, 1978.

Plays

The Death of Seneca (produced Chicago, 1968).

Radio Plays: *A Mutual Flame*, 1961 (UK); *Alcestis*, 1972 (UK).

Novel

The Prince of Darkness & Co. London and New York, Abelard Schuman, 1961.

Other

Polish Subtitles: Impressions from a Journey. London and New York, Abelard Schuman, 1962.

Editor, with Joseph Parisi, *The "Poetry" Anthology 1912–1977.* Boston, Houghton Mifflin, 1978.

Critical Studies: *Alone with America* by Richard Howard, New York, Atheneum, 1969; "Coming Full Circle" by Robert Martin, in *Modern Poetry Studies* (New York), viii, 1, 1977.

* * *

When *The Carnal and the Crane* appeared in 1957, Northrop Frye described Daryl Hine's first book of poems as "a brilliant series of phrases" moving "across a mysteriously dark background." Now, several books of poetry, a novel and a travel book later, the phrases retain their brilliance and the background its mystery. Elegance is characteristic of all of Hine's writing which may be appreciated for its formal qualities if not for its expressiveness. His work resembles nothing more than an excellent, clear, but very dry wine.

The poet has called his first book "rhapsodic" and surreal in imagery and structure. *The Carnal and the Crane* was followed by *The Devil's Picture Book*, a more crafted work. *The Wooden Horse*, which explored the possibilities of dramatic monologues, led Hine to his most intimate book to date, *Minutes*. This gave way to a technical *tour de force*, *The Homeric Hymns*, translations from once-oral Greek poems written anonymously in the Homeric manner. With these noble-sounding praises, the worlds of poetry and classical scholarship merge for Hine, as in the dactylic hexameters of the first line of "To Apollo": "How should I hymn you, Apollo, so handsomely sung of already?"

Hine's classical learning, far from being confined to *The Homeric Hymns*, reverberates rather than echoes with Greek, Roman, Christian and even Celtic references throughout all his poetry. It is an attractive characteristic of his work that he can capture an image with crystal clarity in a Symbolist fashion, as in "Les Yeux de la Tête" from *Minutes*:

> A tiny palace and a formal garden
> In miniature, lawns, flowers, jewelled trees
> By Fabergé, and in the midst a fountain
> Whose precious drops like tear drops fill the eyes.

Hine's poems proceed from image to image, building on the principle of polarity, finding in the irreconcilability of opposites proof of the inability of people to merge, the impossibility of history, in a world in which "all our wisdom is unwillingness."

—John Robert Colombo

HIRSCHMAN, Jack. American. Born in New York City, 13 December 1933. Educated at City College of New York, 1951–55, B.A. 1955; Indiana University, Bloomington, A.M. 1957, Ph.D. 1961. Married Ruth Hirschman in 1954; one son, David, and one daughter, Celia. Instructor, Dartmouth College, Hanover, New Hampshire, 1959–61; Assistant Professor, University of California, Los Angeles, 1961–66. Painter and Collage-maker: Exhibitions in Venice, California, 1972, and Los Angeles, 1972. Associated with *Tree* magazine, Bolinas, California. Address: 1314 Kearny Street, San Francisco, California, U.S.A.

PUBLICATIONS

Verse

Fragments. Privately printed, 1952.
A Correspondence of Americans. Bloomington, Indiana University Press, 1960.
Two, lithographs by Arnold Belkin. Los Angeles, Zora Gallery, 1963.
Interchange. Los Angeles, Zora Gallery, 1964.
Kline Sky. Privately printed, 1965.
Yod. London, Trigram Press, 1966.
London Seen Directly. London, Goliard Press, 1967.
Wasn't It Like This in the Woodcut. London, Cape Goliard Press, 1967.
William Blake. Topanga, California, Love Press, 1967.
A Word in Your Season, with Asa Benveniste. London, Trigram Press, 1967.
Ltd. Interchangeable in Eternity: Poems of Jackruthdavidcelia Hirschman. Privately printed, 1967.
Jerusalem: A Three Part Poem. Topanga, California, Love Press, 1968.
Aleph, Benoni and Zaddik. Los Angeles, Tenfingers Press, 1968.
Jerusalem, Ltd. London, Trigram Press, 1968.
Shekinah. Mill Valley, California, Maya, 1969.
Broadside Golem. Venice, California, Box Zero, 1969.
Black Alephs: Poems 1960–1968. New York, Phoenix Bookshop, and London, Trigram Press, 1969.
NHR. Goleta, California, Christopher's, 1970.

Scintilla. Bolinas, California, Tree, 1970.
Soledeth. Venice, California, Q Press, 1971.
DT. Santa Barbara, California, Yes Press, 1971.
The Burning of Los Angeles. Venice, California, J'Ose Press, 1971.
HNYC. Topanga, California, Skyline Press, 1971.
Les Vidanges. Venice, California, Beyond Baroque Press, 1972.
The R of the Ari's Raziel. Los Angeles, Press of the Pegacycle Lady, 1972.
Adamnan. Santa Barbara, California, Christopher's, 1972.
Aur Sea. Bolinas, California, Tree, 1973.
Cantillations. Santa Barbara, California, Yes/Capra Press, 1973.
Djackson. Salt Lake City, Rainbow Resin Press, 1974.
Cockroach Street. San Francisco, Street, 1975.
The Cool Boyetz Cycle. San Francisco, Golden Mountain Press, 1975.
Kashtaninyah Segodnyah. San Francisco, Beatitude Press, 1976.
Lyripol. San Francisco, City Lights, 1976.
The Arcanes of Le Compte de St. Germain. San Francisco, Amerus, 1977.

Other

Editor, *Artaud Anthology.* San Francisco, City Lights, 1965.

Translator, with Victor Erlich, *Electric Iron*, by Vladimir Mayakovsky. Mill Valley, California, Maya, 1970.
Translator, *Love Is a Tree*, by Antonin Artaud. Fairfax, California, Red Hill Press, 1972.
Translator, *A Rainbow for the Christian West*, by René Depestre. Fairfax, California, Red Hill Press, 1972.
Translator, *The Exiled Angel*, by Luisa Pasamanik. Fairfax, California, Red Hill Press, 1973.
Translator, *Igitur*, by Stéphane Mallarmé. Los Angeles, Press of the Pegacycle Lady, 1973.
Translator, *Wail for the Arab Beggars of the Casbah*, by Ait Djafer. Los Angeles, Papa Bach, 1973.
Translator, *The Crucifixion*, by Jean Cocteau. Bethlehem, Pennsylvania, Quarter Press, 1975.
Translator, *The Book of Noah*, by Johann Maier. Berkeley, California, Tree, 1975.
Translator, with Alexander Altmann, *Three Tracts*, by Eleazer of Worms. San Francisco, Beatitude Press, 1976.
Translator, *Orange Voice*, by Alexander Kohav. San Francisco, Beatitude Press, 1976.
Translator, *Four Angels in Profile, Four Bears in Fullface*, by Alexander Kohav. San Francisco, Beatitude Press, 1976.
Translator, *Requiem*, by Robert Rodzhdestvensky. San Francisco, Beatitude Press, 1977.
Translator, *Hunger*, by Natasha Belyaeva. Mill Valley, California, D'Aurora Press, 1977.
Translator, *Emigroarium*, by Alexander Kohav. San Francisco, Amerus, 1977.

Jack Hirschman comments:

(1970) Poetry is man at his most complete state of consciousness. As I write this, in March of 1969, I am conscious of whirling bodies of Vietnamese women and children in the long process of death; and aware that "poetry does nothing" is a truth; I reject that truth for the poem I am now going to plunge into. Long live the creative act! May the overlords of the world learn the real meaning of death.

(1974) Putting my poems, my visual works, and my kabbalist interests together, my poetry may be seen more and more to reflect – through the amuletic/hieroglyphic tradition – a politically Left position which sees Hanoi as the extension of the idea of Blake's *Jerusalem.* Free to translate from many languages, and moreover to broadcast such works, as well as my own, on Pacifica Radio in Los Angeles, my works reveal all that is beautifully decayed in western capitalistic societies in the hope that the interchange between the West and the future Asia and Africa takes place, so to speak, across the arc of rainbows rather than the broken backs of those who still have not forfeited the earth to machinery.

(1980) For the past six years I've been living and writing in San Francisco, especially in North Beach, as a propagandist for communism as the poetic energy of revolution itself. I've learned how to translate and to write in Russian, and have worked with different cadres on the street, i.e., the Beatitude group and then the Amerus group. Poems are written in American and Russian and daily read. Since 1974 I have given away some 50,000 hand-made poster-poems in the tradition of Mayakovsky – the genuine poet-painter of the Russian Revolution – and William Blake. Early Jewish Kabbalism has given way to the Kabbalistic Soviet, rooted in the Cyrillic language. This extension of work represents the foremost affirmation of my creative life and is an ongoing process. The latest development is the Union of Street Poets which provides hand-out texts of poems to the people of San Francisco. Long life to the revolutionary poets everywhere.

* * *

Introducing his first book, Karl Shapiro hailed Jack Hirschman exuberantly as "an inventor" who had "evolved his own particular version of the language" and who was "a kind of Hart Crane, without Crane's fatal humorlessness." Such praise is hard to live down, or up to. For years Hirschman's subsequent work appeared mainly in fugitive small editions – many of them experiments in format, such as *Interchange*, with its loose cards to be shuffled, or *Ltd.*, hand-calligraphed on paper strips – and until the 1969 London collection, *Black Alephs*, he seemed an isolated figure. Recently, however, he has worked in collaboration with David Meltzer and appears regularly in the latter's bi-annual of cabbalistic lore and poetry, *Tree*. In his writing, while the content has grown more esoteric, the emphasis on linguistic originality has continued. The early work owed much to a Dylan Thomas-like *Hwyl* and to the comic gusto of the Joyce of *Finnegans Wake*. But what is disarming in a first book can grow tiresome, and those who find the associated names of Crane, Thomas, and Joyce portentous in a depressing way will not read Hirschman's later work with much reward. Both in verse and in the "breath-style" prose-poems of recent years, the writing communicates more a generalized energy and afflatus than any very strictly definable meaning or emotion. The effect aimed at seems usually to be a hectic visionary intoxication and exaltation, as in these opening lines of "Drive":

> What a whine of a mouth in the engine of robot tit
> what an eye of blue chrome thorax my sweet
> necrophiliac my yackity rattling spit hiss my
> lilith leather slashwhip desire my voluptuous
> lynch

Still, when he cares to, Hirschman can write more quietly and convincingly, as in this poem, also from *Black Alephs*:

> I've had enough of love
> to know
> death a little
> way away is
> sleeping,

her hand where she left it,
on me, her hair
tumbled over her mouth half
open for
more.

—Seamus Cooney

HITCHCOCK, George. American. Born in Hood River, Oregon, 2 June 1914. Educated at the University of Oregon, Eugene, B.A. Worked as laborer, shipfitter, smelter-man, mason, carpenter, and gardener. Formerly, Lecturer in English, San Francisco State College. Currently, Lecturer in Literature, University of California, Santa Cruz. Since 1964, Editor and Publisher, *Kayak* magazine and Kayak Books, San Francisco, later Santa Cruz. Recipient: National Endowment for the Arts grant, 1968, 1969. Address: 325 Ocean View, Santa Cruz, California 95062, U.S.A.

PUBLICATIONS

Verse

Poems and Prints, with Mel Fowler. San Francisco, San Francisco Review, 1962.
Tactics of Survival and Other Poems. San Francisco, Bindweed Press, 1964.
The Dolphin with the Revolver in Its Teeth. Santa Barbara, California, Unicorn Press, 1967.
The One Whose Approach I Cannot Evade. Santa Barbara, California, Unicorn Press, 1967.
Two Poems. Santa Barbara, California, Unicorn Press, 1967.
A Ship of Bells: Poems. San Francisco, Kayak, 1968.
Twelve Stanzas in Praise of the Holy Chariot. San Francisco, Kayak, 1969.
The Rococo Eye. LaCrosse, Wisconsin, Juniper, 1970.
Lessons in Alchemy. Reno, Nevada, West Coast Poetry Review, 1977.
The Piano Beneath the Skin. Denver, Copper Canyon, 1979.

Plays

The Busy Martyr (produced Medford, Massachusetts, 1963). Published in *First Stage* (Lafayette, Indiana), Winter 1962–63.
The Counterfeit Rose. Santa Cruz, California, Kayak, 1977.

Novel

Another Shore. Santa Cruz, California, Kayak, 1972.

Other

Editor, with Robert Peters, *Pioneers of Modern Poetry*. San Francisco, Kayak, 1967.
Editor, *Losers Weepers: Poems Found Practically Anywhere*. San Francisco, Kayak, 1969.

Manuscript Collection: University of California, Santa Cruz.

* * *

George Hitchcock has mastered the technique of blending the surreal with the actual: his poems float, believably, from what appears to be subconscious impulse to the surface world that has demanded the poem. Unlike most of America's "surreal" poets, Hitchcock does not strain for his images; they emerge in spite of themselves, almost as if they've existed for all time, waiting to be discovered by a poet who would not elaborate them to death. Hitchcock observes without intellectual frippery; the observation, if fresh, is enough. Children, whose senses have not yet grown callouses, see this way ("The Ascension"):

Flotillas of leaves set sail in the birch trees.
They are answering the call of birds, their brothers;
they too would like to ascend like sonatas of glass
from pianos, but the twigs, the limbs, the roots
hold them back.

In such an April
we would all fly upward like sparks, but some emblem
in our shoes detains us.

The vocabulary is adult, but the vision is new.

Hitchcock's vision, however unstrained, goes *into* things, and it is here that the surreal blends with the actual. If we believe the statement, it is not surreal, whatever the nature of its texture. Hitchcock describes a sinking ship ("Portrait While Sinking"):

I watch her
dissolve into the arms of her
false twin caught in their watery hair
the plumes of terns
over their unknown name the keels
and sails of magic schooners

and, in "A Vogage": "Summer passes/The melon,/split/to the heart,/reveals/its secret/cargo/of mosquitoes." Notice that Hitchcock avoids the fashionable trap of bolstering his images with surprising adjectives: he is sure enough of his vision that the mosquitoes need not assume an unlikely color, or somehow become more human than they already are.

His work includes some of the best poetry that has been written about the war in Vietnam. After a while, most war poems sound the same, inspired as they are by the tragedy of hatred and the innocence of hatred's victims. But Hitchcock avoids revelling in useless rhetoric and his war poetry retains the best qualities of surrealism ("Scattering Flowers"):

Freedom, a dancing girl,
lifts her petticoats of gasoline,
and on the hot sands of a deserted beach
a wild horse struggles, choking
in the noose of diplomacy.

Through his Kayak Press, Hitchcock has become an important force in the new American poetry: his magazine, *Kayak*, sometimes the most exciting of all the little magazines, has made available a variety of new forms, many of which Hitchcock has explored in his own work. These include found poetry, "cut-ups," and collaborations.

—Geof Hewitt

HOBSBAUM, Philip (Dennis). British. Born in London, 29 June 1932. Educated at Belle Vue Grammar School, Bradford, Yorkshire; Downing College, Cambridge, 1952–55, B.A. 1955, M.A. 1961; Royal Academy of Music, London, licentiate 1956; University of Sheffield, 1959–62, Ph.D. 1968. Married 1) Hannah Kelly in 1957 (marriage dissolved, 1968); 2) Rosemary Singleton in 1976. Lecturer in English, Queen's University, Belfast, 1962–66. Lecturer, 1966–72, Senior Lecturer, 1972–79, and since 1979 Reader in English, University of Glasgow. Editor, *Delta*, Cambridge, 1954–55; Co-Editor, *Poetry from Sheffield*, 1959–61. Address: Department of English, The University, Glasgow, Scotland.

PUBLICATIONS

Verse

The Place's Fault and Other Poems. London, Macmillan, and New York, St. Martin's Press, 1964.
Snapshots. Belfast, Festival, 1965.
In Retreat and Other Poems. London, Macmillan, 1966; Chester Springs, Pennsylvania, Dufour, 1968.
Coming Out Fighting. London, Macmillan, and Chester Springs, Pennsylvania, Dufour, 1969.
Some Lovely Glorious Nothing. Frensham, Surrey, Sceptre Press, 1969.
Women and Animals. London, Macmillan, 1972.

Plays

Radio Plays: *Children in the Woods*, 1974; *Round the Square*, music by Nicholas Ricat, 1976.

Other

A Theory of Communication: A Study of Value in Literature. London, Macmillan, 1970; as *Theory of Criticism*, Bloomington, Indiana University Press, 1970.
A Reader's Guide to Charles Dickens. London, Thames and Hudson, 1972; New York, Farrar Straus, 1973.
Tradition and Experiment in English Poetry. London, Macmillan, 1978; Totowa, New Jersey, Rowman and Littlefield, 1979.

Editor, with Edward Lucie-Smith, *A Group Anthology.* London, Oxford University Press, 1963.
Editor, *Ten Elizabethan Poets....* London, Longman, 1969.

Manuscript Collection: University of Texas, Austin.

Critical Studies: Reviews by P. N. Furbank, in *The Listener* (London), May 1964, and by G. S. Fraser, in *The New York Review of Books*, 1964; *The Modern Writer and His World* by G. S. Fraser, London, Penguin, 1964; *British Poetry since 1960* edited by Michael Schmidt and Grevel Lindop, Oxford, Carcanet Press, 1972; *The Group* edited by Ian Fletcher and John Pilling, Reading, University of Reading Library, 1974; "The Belfast Group" edited by Frank Ormsby, in *Honest Ulsterman* (Belfast), November–December 1976.

Philip Hobsbaum comments:

I have been associated, as founder of "The Group" in 1955, with Lucie-Smith, MacBeth,

Porter, Bell, and Redgrove. But I must emphasize that this is a process of teaching creative writing, not a movement in verse. Other groups were started in Belfast in 1963 and in Glasgow in 1967. In recent years I have divided my time between writing a history of English poetry and a series of pieces, some of which have been broadcast, which I call *Poems for Several Voices*. I hope to collect these, to write a few plays and, eventually, to get down on paper a sequence of poems which has been long in my mind concerning autumnal and twilight themes.

* * *

Critics and criticism have exercised an enormous influence on the creative work of Philip Hobsbaum, and some might maintain that the impact has not always been supportive of his initial poetic impulse. At Cambridge he worked under F. R. Leavis and edited the magazine *Delta*, and founded "the Group," a group of poets who met regularly, first in Cambridge and later in London, for the purpose of critically examining each other's efforts. In 1959 Hobsbaum went to Sheffield University to do research under Professor Empson and his first volume, *The Place's Fault*, contains the poems written while he was at Sheffield, after a silence of several years. "Testimony" celebrates the return of his poetic gifts, using the analogy of Sarah's conception of a child in her period of barrenness – "Should I not rejoice/ After these barren years being given a voice?"

If the title of his book and the epigraph from Philip Larkin ("waking at the fumes/And furnace-glares of Sheffield, where I changed ...") acknowledge his debt to Larkin, and if there is a similarity in tone, Hobsbaum, unlike Larkin (who tends to observe human behaviour as if from a safe distance), is not afraid to commit himself to active participation; indeed most of his poems are about that involvement and its effects. In the title poem he says:

We left (it was a temporary halt)
The knots of ragged kids, the wired-off beach,
Faces behind the blinds. I'll not return;
There's nothing there I haven't had to learn,
And I've learned nothing that I'd care to teach –
Except that I know it was the place's fault.

But more often than not he is concerned with his own faults rather than those of the place or situation, and he is so anxious to be frank about himself, "warts and all," that he tends to lay undue emphasis upon physical defects in his wry, self-deprecating manner. He throws ridicule upon his fatness, his shortsightedness and decaying teeth (as in "A Journey round the Inside of My Mouth"). At times he can be very impressive as in "Household Gods," "Old Flame," and "Testimony," and even in his weakest poems he retains a craftsmanlike control over his materials. In the long "Man Without God," his most ambitious poem, he attempts to trace the development of his religious doubts from the superstitious rites of childhood to the intellectual questionings of maturity: but what comes across with greatest force is not so much his doubt in God as the strength of his belief in the invincibility of life.

A phrase from Larkin provides the keynote to *In Retreat* – "Lonely in Ireland, since it was not home." His loneliness (one suspects that he would be lonely anywhere) and the threat of losing his eyesight lends a plangent tone to the volume, yet if there is a certain amount of self-pity, there is something effectively human and communicative here, for in the present situation do not most poets experience this sense of exile and this groping in the half-light for certainties? Much of it is mock-serious, of course. He mocks himself as he remembers falling down the pub-stairs (due to his defective sight) or acting as "a balding, stout morose invigilator" and has a satirical touch in his "Interview with the Professor." But apart from such poems as "The Rock Pool" and "For a Young Nun," the best things in the collection, and those that indicate a new development for Hobsbaum, are the fine monologues on Chopin and Newman in which, turning his attention away from himself, he has a more balanced perspective and can define more clearly the predicament of others.

In *Coming Out Fighting* Hobsbaum concentrates largely upon the personal situation. Linked together, the poems describe a married man's unsatisfactory love affair with a younger girl, his pain and disillusionment, the break-up of his marriage, and his reflections upon the girl's own marriage later. Despite the energy, humour, and immediacy of these poems, the narrator seems able to write better when he can stand at a distance from the experience recorded, as in "The Ice Skaters":

You
Venture to catch them up, reach out, and
Find yourself struggling in dirty water. Call,

Ice in your mouth, spluttering blindly, down,
Down into the mud, entangling with weed you go.
Their laughter tinkles prettily over the ice.

Coming Out Fighting sets the scene for *Women and Animals* which studies "the nightmare of a divorce." It will be interesting to see the direction Hobsbaum takes now that he has taken his personal problems as far as they will go.

—Howard Sergeant

HOCHMAN, Sandra. American. Born in New York City, 11 September 1936. Educated at Bennington College, Vermont, B.A. 1957. Married Harvey Leve in 1965; one child, Ariel. Actress. Poet-in-Residence, Fordham University, New York, 1965. Recipient: Yale Series of Younger Poets Award, 1963. Address: 180 East 79th Street, New York, New York 10021, U.S.A.

PUBLICATIONS

Verse

Voyage Home. Paris, Two Cities, 1960.
Manhattan Pastures. New Haven, Connecticut, Yale University Press, 1963.
The Vaudeville Marriage. New York, Viking Press, 1966.
Love Poems. Privately printed, 1966.
Love Letters from Asia. New York, Viking Press, 1968.
Earthworks: Poems 1960–1970. New York, Viking Press, 1971; London, Secker and Warburg, 1972.
Futures: New Poems. New York, Viking Press, 1974.

Plays

The World of Günter Grass (produced New York, 1966).
Explosion of Loneliness, music by Galt MacDermot (produced New York, 1977).

Screenplay: *Year of the Woman* (also director), 1973.

Novels

Walking Papers. New York, Viking Press, 1971.

Happiness Is Too Much Trouble. New York, Putnam, 1976.
Endangered Species. New York, Putnam, 1977.
Jogging. New York, Putnam, 1979.

Other

The Magic Convention (juvenile). New York, Doubleday, 1971.
Streams: Life-Secrets for Writing Poems and Songs. Englewood Cliffs, New Jersey, Prentice Hall, 1978.

Manuscript Collection: Northwestern University, Evanston, Illinois.

Sandra Hochman comments:

my written voice, my gift, is an instrument for memory,
love, praise & revelation; in my poems i swallow my pride and turn
to the authentic teachers of the dreaming mind.
My work springs out of an inability to forget the loneliness of
childhood and feeds upon all the metaphors of Nature & Revelation.

* * *

The flat, sometimes throwaway, delivery of Sandra Hochman's lines surprises the reader with unexpected, often ominous, echoes: "I scrape death from the black spots of a radish" ("I Live with Solomon"). This richness makes a carriage ride through Central Park subsume the great voyages of legend and history ("Hansoms") and supports the shock when "Old spring umbrellas/Bloom in the looking glass/As if in preparation for thunder" ("I Walk into the Pharmacy of Sleep"). "Poem for Alexandra," which might serve as Hochman's testament, traces this genesis of the miraculous: "... ridiculous stops/Are always turned to advantage – in improbable times/We discover whatever mystery we can." Though "The Love Singer" reduces a street bard to a "miracle-monger," art is the ultimate miracle, directing its force against both external and internal enemies: "David .../Turned all songs to a stone/And overthrew the flesh" ("The Problem of David"). The poems about clowns and magic in *The Vaudeville Marriage* root art in the commonplace it must ultimately transcend: "... I am/ Aware of the tricks. They must be/What ugly feet are to the swan" ("The Magic Convention").

This immanence of wonder in the ordinary creates an appropriate landscape for Hochman's many poems about dreams that recreate the adult's vanished past, childhood dreams that persist, and dreams indistinguishable from the waking state. However frightening, however false, dreams shape the world: "She tries to construct/A small tower out of ivory and horn./Dreams are nails ..." ("Constructions: Upper East Side"). The travel poems of *Love Letters from Asia* celebrate a parallel world of waking miracles: "... How/Can this be all/And be so true? I/Breathe my whole life/In one morning .../I tremble/All day/ In a glass/Of water" ("Written at Vivian Court").

Poems in this volume and new poems in *Earthworks* dramatize this vulnerable but renascent selfhood through a fusion with the spirit of vegetation and, ultimately, in works like "The New Life," with the blossoming foetus within: "... Tonight/My marrow flowers into coral." Only lovers, whether in foreign landscapes or even beneath the sea in "The Couple," lack this regenerative power.

Hochman hymns her daughter's birth as compensation for the violently disrupted past, accessible only in dreams, of the earlier volumes: "... Then, in a white room,/A doctor behind a mask – perhaps a woman,/Perhaps a man – took out our childhood" ("How We Get Rid of Our Childhood"). Hochman's witty novel, *Walking Papers*, defines the ambiguous central incident of this poem as an abortion, but the literal treatment dissipates the force of the episode. Though the novel provides a scenario for many of the poems and often echoes their language, it tends to diminish their evocative power. That the poems generate as much force as they do is a tribute to Hochman's short, spare lines and often flat language, sometimes merely lists of objects. The poems make no attempt to seduce with sound effects, and generally only the early poems use rhyme, usually in a final couplet. The casual tone, often self-deprecating, curbs excesses in paeans to vegetative and female fecundity. And Hochman can be directly, hilariously funny: "When a wheel broke, it was not the wheel of life,/ Buddha's great wheel of birth and endless death,/It was the pierced flat tire of the car/Dying beneath the windows" ("About My Life at That Time"). But ultimately Hochman succeeds with a rhythm that creates the shape of an image, the contours and the stuff of a mood, as in "The Spy":

> If only there were a perfect word
> I could give it to you – a word like some artichoke
> That could sit on the table, dry, and become itself.

—Burton Kendle

HOFFMAN, Daniel (Gerard). American. Born in New York City, 3 April 1923. Educated at Columbia University, New York, A.B. 1947 (Phi Beta Kappa), M.A. 1949, Ph.D. 1956. Served in the United States Army Air Force, 1943–46: Legion of Merit. Married Elizabeth McFarland in 1948; two children. Instructor in English, Columbia University, 1952–56; Visiting Professor, University of Dijon, 1956–57; Assistant Professor, 1957–60, Associate Professor, 1960–65, and Professor of English, 1965–66, Swarthmore College, Pennsylvania. Since 1966, Professor of English, and since 1978, Poet-in-Residence, University of Pennsylvania, Philadelphia. Fellow of the School of Letters, Indiana University, 1959; Elliston Lecturer, University of Cincinnati, 1964; Lecturer, International School of Yeats Study, Sligo, Ireland, 1965; Consultant in Poetry, Library of Congress, Washington, D.C., 1973–74. Recipient: New York Y.M.H.A. Poetry Center Introductions Award, 1951; Yale Series of Younger Poets Award, 1954; Ansley Prize, 1957; American Council of Learned Societies Fellowship, 1962, 1966; National Institute of Arts and Letters grant, 1967; Ingram Merrill Foundation grant, 1971. Since 1972, Chancellor, Academy of American Poets. Address: Department of English, University of Pennsylvania, Philadelphia, Pennsylvania 19174, U.S.A.

PUBLICATIONS

Verse

An Armada of Thirty Whales. New Haven, Connecticut, Yale University Press, 1954.

A Little Geste and Other Poems. New York and London, Oxford University Press, 1960.

The City of Satisfactions. New York and London, Oxford University Press, 1963.
Striking the Stones. New York and London, Oxford University Press, 1968.
Broken Laws. New York and London, Oxford University Press, 1970.
Corgi Modern Poets in Focus 4, with others, edited by Jeremy Robson. London, Corgi, 1971.
The Center of Attention. New York, Random House, 1974.
Able Was I Ere I Saw Elba: Selected Poems 1954–1974. London, Hutchinson, 1977.

Other

Paul Bunyan: Last of the Frontier Demigods. Philadelphia, University of Pennsylvania Press-Temple University, 1952.
The Poetry of Stephen Crane. New York, Columbia University Press, 1957.
Form and Fable in American Fiction. New York and London, Oxford University Press, 1961.
Barbarous Knowledge: Myth in the Poetry of Yeats, Graves, and Muir. New York and London, Oxford University Press, 1967.
Poe Poe Poe Poe Poe Poe Poe. New York, Doubleday, 1972; London, Robson Books, 1973.
"Poetry since 1945," in *Literary History of the United States*, revised edition, edited by R. E. Spiller and others. New York, Macmillan, 1974.
Others: Shock Troops of Stylistic Change (lecture). Philadelphia, University of Pennsylvania, 1975.

Editor, *The Red Badge of Courage and Other Stories*, by Stephen Crane. New York, Harper, 1957.
Editor, *American Poetry and Poetics: Poems and Critical Documents from the Puritans to Robert Frost.* New York, Doubleday, 1962.
Editor, with Samuel Hynes, *English Literary Criticism: Romantic and Victorian.* New York, Appleton Century Crofts, 1963; London, Peter Owen, 1966.
Editor, *New Poets 1970.* Philadelphia, University of Pennsylvania, 1970.
Editor, *University and College Prizes 1967–72.* New York, Academy of American Poets, 1974.
Editor, *The Harvard Guide to Contemporary American Writing.* Cambridge, Massachusetts, Harvard University Press, 1978.

Bibliography: *Daniel Hoffman: A Comprehensive Bibliography* by Michael Lowe, Norwood, Pennsylvania, Norwood Editions, 1973.

Critical Studies: *Alone with America* by Richard Howard, New York, Atheneum, 1969; "Daniel Hoffman's Poetry of Affection" by William Sylvester, in *Voyages* (Washington, D.C.) Winter 1970; "Daniel Hoffman" by Jeremy Robson, in *Corgi Modern Poets in Focus 4*, 1971; Interview with W. B. Patrick, in *Daniel Hoffman: A Comprehensive Bibliography*, 1973; "A Major Poet" by Monroe K. Spears, in *Southern Review* (Baton Rouge, Louisiana), Summer 1975; "Another Country: The Poetry of Daniel Hoffman" by John Alexander Allen, in *Hollins Critic* (Hollins College, Virginia), October 1978.

Daniel Hoffman comments:

The titles of my books, I now see, mark out an unpremeditated design in my work thus far. The character of my early verse is fairly suggested by the title poem in *An Armada of Thirty Whales*, a sportive fable which both celebrates the natural order and suggests that man is limited by his place in it. The theme is elaborated and mythologized in *A Little Geste*, a sequence of eight poems which recreates a 14th century legend (of Robin Hood) as a fertility ritual and dramatizes the conflicts between natural freedom and the harsh restraints of social order. The title poem of my third book, *The City of Satisfactions*, is a free-verse obsessional nightmare enactment of The Great American Dream – a frantic derailed train trip westward in search of treasure, in endlessly receding images evoked by the perpetual recession of the land, the treasure, the satisfactions.

"Striking the stones to make them sing" is the line in my fourth book from which I take its title: an image of the poet's task. The stones may be the pavements that surround us, for my work has come to range between the sea and the city, to include the natural order and its instinctual joys and also the chaos and anguish exacted from us by the intricate disorder of our mechanistic and unmemoried society.

I make no manifestos, save: Keep imagination free to speak its revelations of the true.

* * *

Daniel Hoffman's scansion is modern insofar as he frequently resorts to a shifting visual pattern of spacing, a line of varying length for rhetorical purposes of either reinforcement or of counterpoint. He both demonstrates and denotes his practise in the conclusion of *The Center of Attention*:

The Poem

Arriving at last,

It has stumbled across the harsh
Stones, the black marshes.

The appearance on the page is modern, but actually evokes traditional rhythms. The first line has two unmistakably strong beats, and the isolation of the first line invites a pause, so that the first word of the next line cannot be slighted. The distinction between stressed and unstressed is sharp and consistent. Later on in the poem – "Carved on memory's staff/The legend is nearly decipherable" – one finds a line that echoes a trochaic and choriambic, followed by a line with three primary stresses and a secondary. His lines are like a steady shifting of traditional meters, but never move into the cadences of unmistakable prose. His diction is consistently generic; he prefers to evoke a sense of swerving rather than the precisely classificatory hyperbole. The "stones" and "marshes" do not indicate a world out there, to be photographed, but are emblematic of an inner struggle, the "harsh, black" struggle of writing. The legend, what is read, what is available to all, like a scroll or a saint's life, is "nearly decipherable," "Casting its message/In a sort of singing." "A sort of" in the sense of "approximate," but the phrase has also the decipherably older meaning of "a particular kind" as when Swift writes about "a sort of jabber." Hoffman's use of rhyme, however sparing and occasional, however attenuated semantically or prosodically, brings him close to a tradition which by-passes Whitman and which assumes a correlation between literary and social decorum. In "The Sonnet," he contrasts his memory of Louise Bogan's faith in the sacredness of form to the formlessness of bearded youths and rumpled girls.

His province is conservative, a poetry that indirectly evokes, without imitating them, the worlds of Yeats and Muir, a "sort of singing" to make older ways of feeling accessible today. He is less interested in discovering new perceptions than in finding new ways of expressing feelings common to people now and in the past. He is chary of assuming a common knowledge and is sparing in specific literary references. When he quotes Mallermé, "donner un sens plus pur aux mots de la tribu," the allusion to his own interest in Poe is decipherable, but the central meaning of the quotation expresses his own aim. (Actually his poetry should be seen as one aspect of his total literary production.)

With his concern for *bon sens*, his development has been a shift of emphasis rather than an experimentation with new assumptions. He has put successively rigorous restraints upon his lines. The title "City of Satisfactions" has ironic overtones; whereas the multiple meanings of

"Broken Laws" – legal, or natural identity papers or

The broken laws
Almost deciphered on
This air we breathe

– occurred in a collection that was considerably less ironic than the predecessors. Irony implies a commonly held set of social assumptions, and has, perhaps, inevitably hierarchical implications of shared values. In the increasing pluralism of assumptions, Hoffman has brought the center of his attention to what can be shared. Each line has a sharply delimited focus, so that overtones emerge from the sequence of lines, and from the sequence of poems.

Hoffman is capable of a wide range of tones. The meditative mood of the poem "Himself" in a recent *Hudson Review* ("The one most like himself is not this mirror's/Dishonest representation ...") is sustained to the end:

The blessing given him at last

Across the alien years
Is that he now may judge his actions
By what that one most like himself would do

Whose ease with the world shames his unease,
Whose delight exceeds the joys he's known,
Whose gifts are greater than his own.

He is also capable of a certain playfulness as the title of his most recent book suggests: *Able Was I Ere I Saw Elba.* The last, intense words of this book deserve particular attention because in one way or another, Hoffman's poems move toward a coping with order/disorder, unease/delight, dishonest/blessing, barbarous/knowledge:

It's our life that's burning.
Is it ever too late to thrust
Ourselves into the ruins,
Into the tempering flame?

—William Sylvester

HOLBROOK, David (Kenneth). British. Born in Norwich, Norfolk, 9 January 1923. Educated at Colman Road Primary School; City of Norwich School; Downing College, Cambridge (Exhibitioner), 1941–42, 1945–47, M.A. 1946. Served as a Tank Troop Officer, and Explosives and Intelligence Officer, in the East Riding of Yorkshire Yeomanry, 1942–45. Married Margot Holbrook in 1949; four children. Assistant Editor, *Our Time* magazine, London, 1947–48; Assistant Editor, Bureau of Current Affairs, London, 1948–51; Tutor in Adult Education and School Teacher, 1951–61: Tutor at Bassingbourn Village College, Cambridgeshire, 1954–61; Fellow, King's College, Cambridge, 1961–65; Part-time Lecturer in English, Jesus College, Cambridge, 1968–70; Writer-in-Residence, Dartington Hall, Devon (Elmgrant Trust grant), 1970–72; Assistant Director of Studies, Downing College, Cambridge, 1973–74. Attended Dartmouth Seminar on English Syllabus Reform, Hanover, New Hampshire, 1966; British Council Lecturer in Germany, 1969; visited Australia on British Council grant to work with English teachers, 1970. Recipient: Writing Fellowship,

King's College, Cambridge, and Cambridge University Press, 1961; Leverhulme Senior Research Fellowship, 1964; Arts Council grant, 1970; World Education Fellowship Prize, 1976. Agent: David Bolt, Bolt and Watson, 8–12 Old Queen Street, London SW1H 9HP. Address: Longacre, Waverhill Road, Stapleford, Cambridge, England.

PUBLICATIONS

Verse

Imaginings. London, Putnam, 1961.
Against the Cruel Frost. London, Putnam, 1963.
Penguin Modern Poets 4, with Christopher Middleton and David Wevill. London, Penguin, 1963.
Object Relations. London, Methuen, 1967.
Old World, New World. London, Rapp and Whiting, 1969.
Chance of a Lifetime. London, Anvil Press Poetry, 1978.
Moments in Italy: Poems and Sketches. Richmond, Surrey, Keepsake Press, 1978.

Plays

The Borderline, music by Wilfred Mellers (opera for children; produced London, 1959).
The Quarry, music by John Joubert (opera for children). London, Novello, 1967.
The Wild Swans, music by John Paynter (opera for children; produced Cambridge, 1979).

Novels

Flesh Wounds. London, Methuen, 1966.
A Play of Passion. London, W. H. Allen, 1978.

Short Stories

Lights in the Sky Country. London, Putnam, 1962.

Other

Children's Games. Bedford, Gordon Fraser, 1957.
English for Maturity. London, Cambridge University Press, 1961.
Llareggub Revisited (on Dylan Thomas). London, Bowes and Bowes, 1962; as *Dylan Thomas and Poetic Dissociation*, Carbondale, Southern Illinois University Press, 1964.
The Secret Places: Essays on Imaginative Work in English Teaching and on the Culture of the Child. London, Methuen, 1964.
English for the Rejected. London, Cambridge University Press, 1964.
The Quest for Love. London, Methuen, 1964.
I've Got to Use Words. London, Cambridge University Press, 1966.
The Flowers Shake Themselves Free (songs set by Wilfred Mellers). London, Novello, 1966.
The Exploring Word. London, Cambridge University Press, 1967.
Children's Writing. London, Cambridge University Press, 1967.
Human Hope and the Death Instinct. Oxford, Pergamon Press, 1971.
The Masks of Hate in Art, Thought and Life in Our Time. Oxford, Pergamon Press, 1971.
Sex and Dehumanisation: The Problem of False Solutions in the Culture of an Acquisitive Society. London, Pitman, 1972.

Dylan Thomas and the Code of Night. London, Athlone Press, 1972.
The Pseudo-Revolution: A Critical Study of Extremist "Liberation" in Sex. London, Stacey, 1972.
English in Australia Now. London, Cambridge University Press, 1973.
Changing Attitudes to the Nature of Man: A Working Bibliography. Hatfield, Hertfordshire, Hertis, 1973.
Gustav Mahler and the Courage to Be. London, Vision Press, 1975.
Sylvia Plath: Poetry and Existence. London, Athlone Press, 1976.
Lost Bearings in English Poetry. London, Vision Press, and New York, Barnes and Noble, 1977.
Education, Nihilism, and Survival. London, Darton Longman and Todd, 1977.

Editor, *Iron Honey Gold* (anthology of verse). London, Cambridge University Press, 1961.
Editor, *People and Diamonds* (anthology of stories). London, Cambridge University Press, 1962.
Editor, *Thieves and Angels* (anthology of drama). London, Cambridge University Press, 1963.
Editor, *Visions of Life* (anthology of prose). London, Cambridge University Press, 1964.
Editor, with Elizabeth Poston, *The Cambridge Hymnal.* London, Cambridge University Press, 1967.
Editor, *Plucking the Rushes* (anthology of Chinese poetry). London, Heinemann, 1968.
Editor, *I've Got to Use Words* (course for less-abled children). London, Cambridge University Press, 1969.
Editor, *The Case Against Pornography.* London, Stacey, 1972.
Editor, *The Honey of Man.* Melbourne, Nelson, 1973.

Critical Studies: in *Time* (New York), 14 August 1964; *Times Literary Supplement* (London), 21 January 1965; in *Sunday Times Colour Supplement* (London), 19 May 1968; essay by the author, in *Poetry Book Society Bulletin* (London), Christmas 1969; "David Holbrook's Humanities" by Roger Poole, in *Books and Bookmen* (London), September 1973.

David Holbrook comments:

A few people have seen that all my work is of a piece – Dr. Gordon Pradl, for instance, in his dissertation at Harvard (1971). In my poetry and prose fiction I am trying to find what meaning there might be in normal, everyday existence – assuming that it should be possible, *there*, to find a sense of having existed to some point. I have kept deliberately to domestic, quotidian living, searching for transcendence in that, since I believe we are doomed if we cannot. In my books for teachers and my anthologies I have tried to encourage those in education to cherish creativity in children, in the sense of helping to explore their normal existence, through symbolism, to find meaning in it.

To this exploration of authenticity, searching for what Maslow calls "peak-moments" in ordinary life, the hollow postures of hate are the greatest enemy. I have therefore tried to diagnose the schizoid trends in contemporary culture to show that they are false, and a bluff, from "James Bond" myths, to the sex novel, and pornography. At the same time I have tried to show how genuine artists may be engaged with schizoid problems of identity, and of not knowing where to find a sense of the meaning in life – namely Dylan Thomas, Sylvia Plath, and Gustav Mahler. In doing so I have come to find the prevalent "model" of man unsatisfactory – the belief of those from Freud to Lorenz, who seem to think instincts of aggression and sex are primary. I believe that culture and symbolism are man's primary needs – and I am trying to apply this view in educational books, in criticism, and in my own writing. This revolution in thought about man I believe to be part of a widespread change – encompassing psychoanalysis, phenomenology, post-Kantian philosophy, and philosophical anthropology. I find more interest in this revolution in Europe and America – while at home in England the thinking minority have betrayed "the people" into a new barbarism which is destroying values and making a more creative future impossible. Intellectuals slavishly follow the Sunday papers, or the trendy fashions, or the trivialities of television – and proclaim their right to indulge in pornography and other vices. The onslaught of this new Barbarism will make all our efforts towards a more creative education, towards new and more visionary works of the imagination, and even towards good community life useless – unless there is a change of heart. And meanwhile, all one can do is to go on as best one can, with creative writing, and trying to warn of the dangers to survival in cultural nihilism.

* * *

The subject matter of David Holbrook's poetry is, for the most part, domestic, personal and everyday: it is of the "real world" of which he is an advocate in so much of his critical and educational writing. It is a world that is explored with feeling and compassion and from which morals are drawn or implied. If not directly didactic, there is usually an undertow of didacticism to be detected in his poetry. It can be personal to the point of being candid. Thus in the poem "To His Wife Going to Bed" (the title itself is point enough) it is gooseflesh which is exposed "drawing your petticoat off – showing your husband what he after clings to in bed." Mind you, it is gooseflesh transfigured by being "like wind-touched-on-water." Sometimes the poems are personal to the point of embarrassment when in "Fingers in the Door" his emotion on seeing the pain caused by closing his child's fingers in a door jamb makes him wish "myself dispersed in hundred thousand pieces" when it was "For her I cast seed into her mother's womb."

But it is this sympathy for the pain and distress of others, and the ability to express it, that informs his best poems. In "Unholy Marriage," a poem about the death of a young girl pillion passenger on a motor-cycle who lies "anointed only by the punctured oil" while her parents wait worrying because "she's late tonight," the simple unemphasised ending – "Some news? They hear the gate/A man comes: not the best" – gives strength to the direct emotion of what has gone before.

The language employed in most of his poems is straightforward and unadorned: "This is the sort of evening on which to write a poem" – a reaction, one imagines, against the verbosity of the forties which he castigates in his critical works. Though sometimes, when combined with the long freely written lines he employs, it tends towards a looseness of form which can compromise the strength of the feelings expressed. If there is a weakness in Holbrook's verse it is this, and the influence of a romanticism deriving from what would seem an idiosyncratic interpretation of the work of D. H. Lawrence and other literary heroes. The strength of his verse is its obvious and direct honesty, despite the pitfalls of naivety into which it sometimes leads him.

—John Cotton

HOLDEN, Molly (née Gilbert). British. Born in London, 7 September 1927. Educated at Commonweal Grammar School, Swindon, Wiltshire; King's College, London, B.A. (honours) in English 1948, M.A. 1951. Married Alan Holden in 1949; one son and one daughter. Disabled by multiple sclerosis in 1964. Recipient: Arts Council award, 1970; Cholmondeley Award, 1972. Address: 58 Willow Road, Bromsgrove, Worcestershire, England.

PUBLICATIONS

Verse

The Bright Cloud. London, Outposts, 1964.
To Make Me Grieve. London, Chatto and Windus–Hogarth Press, 1968.
Air and Chill Earth. London, Chatto and Windus, 1971.
The Speckled Bush. London, Poem-of-the-Month Club, 1974.
The Country Over. London, Chatto and Windus, 1975.

Novels

The Unfinished Feud (juvenile). Leicester, Brockhampton Press, 1970; New York, Hawthorn, 1971.
A Tenancy of Flint. London, Chatto and Windus, 1971.
White Rose and Wanderer. London, Chatto and Windus, 1972.
Reivers' Weather. London, Chatto and Windus, 1973.

Critical Studies: by Martha Byers, in *British Poetry since 1960*, edited by Michael Schmidt and Grevel Lindop, Oxford, Carcanet Press, 1972; "The Poetry of Molly Holden" by Roger Alma, in *Poetry Nation 2* (Manchester), 1974.

Molly Holden comments:

My major theme is the English countryside, although town-born and bred, but always near enough to open land to feel that that was where I belonged and which I wanted to preserve, even if only in words. My verse-forms are usually free, although I have used rhyme a little more lately. Any influences on my work are those of English literature. Reviewers have mentioned Clare, Thomas Hardy, Edward Thomas, Housman. These I proudly accept while wishing and feeling my tone to be my own.

* * *

There is a sense in which any poet, on publication, is offering hostages to fortune. This would seem especially so in the case of Molly Holden whose subject matter is external nature, her tone quietly contemplative and her language and forms basically traditional. It is as if Hardy, Frost and Edward Thomas are constantly hovering in the wings and the dangers of invidious comparisons or just becoming lost in the legions of "nature poets" are acute and obvious. What is it then which sees her succeeding in a field where the competition is so strong and failure so frequent, which sees her making something freshly individual from a poetic vein which some might feel to be exhausted? First, of course, is the need for a keenly accurate eye and that it should be directed by a critical faculty which allows of a judicious selection from what is observed, the choice and juxtaposition of just the right details to make the observation illuminating and to the point. This Molly Holden has and exercises: a winter frost is "sharp and white as acid" or the bark of a crack willow "plateaux of outer rind rooted in pith." In "Sanctuary" she describes a derelict railway station –

The unpatched road
leads only to a farm. Building and gates
have been destroyed – Wire boundaries the track
which now is grass, rails gone and signals down

– where it is the reverberating ambiguity of "signals down" that clinches it; and in "Piper's Hill" we encounter what is basically a painter's eye:

Now colour separates and age
makes individuals of them all, edges
the tags of forest with resisting oaks
that stain towards the darker heart
of evergreen on higher contour lines.

But there is more than this. Not vision so much, though in poems such as "Revelation" Molly Holden does capture most skilfully those fleeting moments of realization:

Only the shrinking snow
revealed all this and, likely,
such a state of thaw and I
would not coincide again.

No, it is more a matter of a deeply personal involvement and concern which gives an edge of intense feeling to poems which could, otherwise, so easily lapse into the commonplace. As in "The Dying Publican" when "Upstairs there ebbed away/the life of more than a man."

Molly Holden conveys in her poems that sense of life which reaches out beyond the individual to where one is part of the very environment in which one finds oneself. It is this which enables her to write so sympathetically in "Winter Quarters" of a gipsy family taking shelter in a deserted house – "This was for hibernation only, no need/to make for comfort; a roof to keep out the snow/was all they wanted" – where human beings share with external nature the primeval instinct to survive. It adds up to an intense awareness of an order in which we all share, and without which "the fields would jumble, the hedges stray/and the fork in the road lead nowhere of importance" ("Hill in Winter").

Then there is her technical skill. The ability to tell a story directly and simply as in "Seaman, 1941," or to handle lines with a deftness which pushes the meaning forward while knitting the poem neatly together ("Severn Harvests"):

The theory works. After an edge-flowered spinny
the red soil greens, in thin and tenuous lines
that strengthen, heighten, grow in bulk and gold,
until the corn, in summer fullness, shines.

Indeed, Molly Holden's felicitous pursuit of a line of argument through a poem can give, as in "The Gap" for example, a unity and completeness which result in a pleasingly aesthetic whole.

That Molly Holden is an invalid can add a poignancy to some of her poems. Certain poems allude to this and an anguished note is heard from time to time, but it is so controlled that it enriches rather than intrudes: "Poetic justice is imperfectly exemplified in me/who, as a child, as a girl, was persuaded that/I felt as earth feels, the furrows in my flesh" ("Illness"). In this, as in all else, Molly Holden's unsentimental and tight hold on her use of language produces quietly forceful poems that steadily grow on you.

—John Cotton

HOLLANDER, John. American. Born in New York City, 10 October 1929. Educated at Columbia University, New York, A.B. 1950 (Phi Beta Kappa), M.A. 1952; Indiana University, Bloomington, Ph.D. 1959. Married Anne Loesser in 1953; two daughters. Junior

Fellow, Society of Fellows, Harvard University, Cambridge, Massachusetts, 1954–57; Lecturer, Connecticut College, New London, 1957–59; Instructor, 1959–61, Assistant Professor, 1961–63, and Associate Professor of English, 1963–66, Yale University, New Haven, Connecticut; Professor of English, Hunter College, City University of New York, 1966–77. Since 1977, Professor of English, Yale University. Gauss Lecturer, Princeton University, New Jersey, 1962; Visiting Professor, Indiana University, 1964; Lecturer, Salzburg Seminar in American Studies, 1965; Overseas Fellow, Churchill College, Cambridge, 1967–68. Member of the Poetry Board, Wesleyan University Press, 1959–62; Editorial Assistant for Poetry, *Partisan Review*, New Brunswick, New Jersey, 1959–66; Contributing Editor, *Harper's* magazine, New York, 1969–71. Recipient: Yale Series of Younger Poets Award, 1962; National Institute of Arts and Letters grant, 1963; National Endowment for the Arts grant, 1973; Levinson Prize (*Poetry*, Chicago), 1974. Fellow, American Academy of Arts and Sciences; Member, National Institute of Arts and Letters. Address: 3 Loomis Street, New Haven, Connecticut 06511, U.S.A.

Publications

Verse

A Crackling of Thorns. New Haven, Connecticut, Yale University Press, 1958.
Movie-Going and Other Poems. New York, Atheneum, 1962.
A Beach Vision. Privately printed, 1962.
A Book of Various Owls (for children). New York, Norton, 1963.
Visions from the Ramble. New York, Atheneum, 1965.
The Quest of the Gole (for children). New York, Atheneum, 1966.
Philomel. London, Turret, 1968.
Types of Shape. New York, Atheneum, 1969.
The Night Mirror. New York, Atheneum, 1971.
Town and Country Matters: Erotica and Satirica. Boston, Godine, 1972.
Selected Poems. London, Secker and Warburg, 1972.
The Head of the Bed. Boston, Godine, 1974.
Tales Told of the Fathers. New York, Atheneum, 1975.
Reflections on Espionage: The Question of Cupcake. New York, Atheneum, 1976.
Spectral Emanations: New and Selected Poems. New York, Atheneum, 1978.
In Place. Omaha, Abattoir, 1978.
Blue Wine and Other Poems. Baltimore, Johns Hopkins University Press, 1979.

Play

An Entertainment for Elizabeth, Being a Masque of the Seven Motions; or, Terpsichore Unchained (produced New York, 1969). Published in *English Renaissance Monographs 1* (Amherst, Massachusetts), 1972.

Other

The Untuning of the Sky: Ideas of Music in English Poetry, 1500–1700. Princeton, New Jersey, Princeton University Press, 1961.
Images of Voice: Music and Sound in Romantic Poetry. Cambridge, Heffer, and New York, Chelsea House, 1969.
The Immense Parade on Supererogation Day (juvenile). New York, Atheneum, 1972.
Vision and Resonance: Two Senses of Poetic Form. New York and London, Oxford University Press, 1975.

Editor, *Selected Poems*, by Ben Jonson. New York, Dell, 1961.

Editor, with Harold Bloom, *The Wind and the Rain: An Anthology of Poems for Young People*. New York, Doubleday, 1961.
Editor, with Anthony Hecht, *Jiggery-Pokery: A Compendium of Double Dactyls*. New York, Atheneum, 1967.
Editor, *Poems of Our Moment*. New York, Pegasus, 1968.
Editor, *Modern Poetry: Essays in Criticism*. London, Oxford University Press, 1968.
Editor, *American Short Stories since 1945*. New York, Harper, 1968.
Editor, with others, *The Oxford Anthology of English Literature*. New York and London, Oxford University Press, 2 vols., 1973.
Editor, with Reuben Brower and Helen Vendler, *I. A. Richards: Essays in His Honor*. New York, Oxford University Press, 1973.
Editor, with Irving Howe and David Bromwich, *Literature as Experience*. New York, Harcourt Brace, 1979.

Manuscript Collections: Beinecke Library, Yale University, New Haven, Connecticut; Lockwood Memorial Library, State University of New York, Buffalo.

Critical Studies: *Alone with America* by Richard Howard, New York, Atheneum, 1969; "The Poem as Silhouette: A Conversation with John Hollander" by Philip L. Gerber and Robert J. Gemmett, in *Michigan Quarterly Review* (Ann Arbor), ix, 1970; "The Sorrows of American Jewish Poetry" by Harold Bloom, in *Commentary* (New York), March 1972; " 'I Carmina Figurata' di John Hollander" by Cristina Giorcelli, in *Scritti in Ricordo di Gabriele Baldini*, Rome, Edizione di Storia e Letteratura, 1972; "Some American Masks" by David Bromwich, in *Dissent* (New York), Winter 1973; *Figures of Capable Imagination* by Harold Bloom, New York, Seabury Press, 1976; interview with Richard Jackson, in *The Poetry Miscellany 8* (Chattanooga), 1978; "The White Light of Trope" by Harold Bloom, in *Kenyon Review* (Gambier, Ohio), n.s., 1, 1979.

* * *

John Hollander has been compared to Ben Jonson by Richard Howard, and the exuberant classicism of Jonson, the sense that art was *hard work*, does inform the whole of Hollander's poetic career. Yet Hollander is one of several American poets of his generation (I think of Ashbery, Merwin, Merrill as analogues) who started out in the Fifties largely under an alien guise, as though they were going to be wit-poets of the age of Eliot and Auden. There is in early Hollander (*A Crackling of Thorns*) a technical debt to Auden as to Jonson and Marvell, but deep poetic influence has nothing to do with overt structures, and Hollander's true precursors, creators of his stance and sensibility, provokers of his authentic poetic anxieties, came out of a very different Anglo-American tradition: the Romantic skepticism of Shelley; the Epicurean nihilism of Rossetti, Pater and Wilde; the American elegiac intensities of Stickney, aspects of Stevens, and of Hart Crane; and the equally American tormented pathos of the Yiddish poet Moshe Leib Halpern.

Movie-Going evidenced Hollander's rapid darkening into his own tradition of visionary skepticism and self-conscious yet essentially wild phantasmagoria. The climax of Hollander's first phase is in the long poem, *Visions from the Ramble*, an American Expressionist brief epic in the mode of Crane's *The Bridge*. The poem is stunningly ambitious, but possibly written too soon in the poet's life, and several of its parts are clearly much more successful than the poem as a whole, which, though coherent, is self-divided and even uneasy in its tone, despite the continuous exuberance of invention and the sustained technical mastery.

A middle phase of Hollander's poetry truly begins not with *Types of Shape*, an almost brilliantly despairing collection, but with *The Night Mirror*, a book of introspective lyrics of the poet's first full maturity, and one of the genuinely distinguished volumes of its generation. Themes of mortality, of the sense that no spring can follow past meridian, are expressed here with a directness of emotional power previously untouched by Hollander. The satirical and erotic verse of *Town and Country Matters* gives ebullient release to Hollander's other side, the now energized and grotesque wit of an inharmonious skeptic whose scholarly obsession always has been harmony. With the long poem or quasi-Stevenian sequence, "The Head of the Bed," Hollander opens himself fully to American nostalgias and American nightmares, and achieves his masterpiece, at least to date, giving us a work comparable to the best we have had since the death of Stevens in 1955.

—Harold Bloom

HOLLO, Anselm (Paul Alexis). United States Resident. Born in Helsinki, Finland, 12 April 1934; son of the professor and translator J. A. Hollo. Educated at schools in Helsinki and Cedar Rapids, Iowa; Helsinki University; University of Tübingen, Germany. Married Josephine Wirkus in 1957 (separated, 1974), three children. Translator and Book Reviewer for German and Finnish periodicals, and secretary to his grandfather, Professor Paul Walden, 1955–58; Program Assistant and Co-Ordinator, BBC, London, 1958–66. Visiting Lecturer, State University of New York, Buffalo, Summers 1967, 1969; Visiting Lecturer, 1968–69, Lecturer in English and Music, 1970–71, and Head of the Translation Workshop, 1971–72, University of Iowa, Iowa City; Visiting Professor and/or Poet, Bowling Green University, Ohio, 1972–73, Hobart and William Smith Colleges, Geneva, New York, 1973–74, Michigan State University, East Lansing, 1975, University of Maryland, Baltimore, 1975–77, and Southwest State University, Marshall, Minnesota, 1977–78. Since 1978, Writer-in-Residence, Sweet Briar College, Virginia. Contributing Editor, *Modern Poetry in Translation*, London, and *New Letters*, Kansas City, Missouri; Poetry Editor, *Iowa Review*, Iowa City, 1971–72. Recipient: Creative Artists Public Service Award, 1976; Yaddo Fellowship, 1978. Address: c/o Blue Wind Press, 820 Miramar, Berkeley, California 94707, U.S.A.

PUBLICATIONS

Verse

Sateiden Valilla (Rainpause). Helsinki, Otava, 1956.
St. Texts and Finnpoems. Birmingham, Migrant Press, 1961.
Loverman. New York, Dead Language Press, 1961.
We Just Wanted to Tell You. London, Writers Forum, 1963.
And What Else Is New. Chatham, Kent, New Voice, 1963.
History. London, Matrix Press, 1964.
Trobar: Loytaa (Trobar: To Find). Helsinki, Otava, 1964.
Here We Go. Newcastle upon Tyne, Strangers Press, 1965.
And It Is a Song. Birmingham, Migrant Press, 1965.
Faces and Forms. London, Ambit, 1965.
The Claim. London, Goliard Press, 1966.
For the Sea: Sons and Daughters We All Are. Privately printed, 1966.
The Going-On Poem. London, Writers Forum, 1966.
Poems/Runoja (bilingual edition). Helsinki, Otava, 1967.
Isadora and Other Poems. London, Writers Forum, 1967.
Leaf Times. Exeter, Exeter Books, 1967.
Buffalo – Isle of Wight Power Cable. Buffalo, State University of New York, 1967.
The Man in the Tree-Top Hat. London, Turret, 1968.
The Coherences. London, Trigram Press, 1968.

Tumbleweed. Toronto, Weed/Flower Press, 1968.
Haiku, with John Esam and Tom Raworth. London, Trigram Press, 1968.
Waiting for a Beautiful Bather: Ten Poems. Milwaukee, Morgan Press, 1969.
Maya: Works 1959–1969. London, Cape Goliard Press, and New York, Grossman, 1970.
America del Norte and Other Peace Herb Poems. Toronto, Weed/Flower Press, 1970.
Message. Santa Barbara, California, Unicorn Press, 1970.
Gee Apollinaire. Iowa City, Nomad Press, 1970.
Sensation 27. Canton, New York, Institute of Further Studies, 1972.
Alembic. London, Trigram Press, 1972.
Smoke Writing. Storrs, University of Connecticut Library, 1973.
Spring Cleaning Greens, from Notebooks 1967–1973. Bowling Green, Ohio, Doones Press, 1973.
Surviving with America, with Jack Marshall and Sam Hamod. Iowa City, Cedar Creek Press, 1974.
Some Worlds. New Rochelle, New York, Elizabeth Press, 1974.
Sojourner Microcosms: New and Selected Poems 1959–1977. Berkeley, California, Blue Wind Press, 1977.
Heavy Jars. West Branch, Iowa, Toothpaste Press, 1977.
Phantom Pod, with Joe Cardarelli and Kirby Malone. Baltimore, Pod, n.d.
Lunch in Fur. St. Paul, Minnesota, Aquila Rose, n.d.
Lingering Tangos. Baltimore, Tropos Press, n.d.
Curious Data. Buffalo, White Pine Press, 1978.

Other

The Minicab War, with Gregory Corso and Tom Raworth. London, Matrix Press, 1961.

Editor and Translator, *Kaddisch*, by Allen Ginsberg. Wiesbaden, Limes, 1962.
Editor and Translator, *Red Cats: Selections from the Russian Poets.* San Francisco, City Lights, 1962.
Editor, *Jazz Poems.* London, Vista, 1963.
Editor and Translator, *In der Flüchtigen Hand der Zeit*, by Gregory Corso. Wiesbaden, Limes, 1963.
Editor and Translator, *Huuto ja Muita Runoja*, by Allen Ginsberg. Turku, Finland, Tajo, 1963.
Editor and Translator, *Kuolema van Goghin Korvalle*, by Allen Ginsberg. Turku, Finland, Tajo, 1963.
Editor, *Negro Verse.* London, Vista, 1964.
Editor and Translator, *Selected Poems*, by Andrei Voznesensky. New York, Grove Press, 1964.
Editor and Translator, *Word from the North: New Poetry from Finland.* Blackburn, Lancashire, Screeches Press, 1965.
Editor and Translator, *Helsinki: Selected Poems*, by Pentti Saarikoski. London, Rapp and Whiting, 1967.
Editor and Translator, *Selected Poems*, by Paavo Haavikko. London, Cape Goliard Press, and New York, Grossman, 1968.
Editor and Translator, *The Twelve and Other Poems*, by Aleksandr Blok. Lexington, Kentucky, Gnomon Press, 1971.
Editor and Translator, with Gunnar Harding, *Recent Swedish Poetry in Translation.* Minneapolis, University of Minnesota Press, 1979.

Translator, *Some Poems*, by Paul Klee. Lowestoft, Suffolk, Scorpion Press, 1962.
Translator, *In the Jungle of Cities*, by Bertolt Brecht. New York, Grove Press, 1966.

Translator, *Hispanjalainen Jakovainaa*, by John Lennon. Helsinki, Otava, 1966.
Translator, *In the Dark, Move Slowly: Poems*, by Tuomas Anhava. London, Cape Goliard Press, and New York, Grossman, 1969.
Translator, with Sidney Berger, *Thrymskvitha* (Icelandic Skald). Iowa City, Windhover Press, 1970.
Translator, with Josephine Clare, *Paterson*, by W. C. Williams. Stuttgart, Goverts Verlag, 1970.
Translator, with Elliott Anderson, *Turbines: Twenty One Poems*, by Tomaz Salamun. Iowa City, Windhover Press, 1973.

Other translations from German, French, and Swedish published.

Anselm Hollo comments:

(1970) Poems are *given*: they are also "graphs of a mind moving" (Philip Whalen). Each poem, if and when it works, is a singular, at times even "unique" formal, emotional, intellectual entity, posing no problems to the poet beyond those contained in itself. The sources are in the poet's life – and that includes his reading, his given "place" at any given "time," his awareness of all animate and inanimate objects (and subjects) around him. When he is in love, he writes, "for love"; and writing, he is, stands, falls, gets up and walks again, *in love.* That is the "House of Light," the "portable state of grace," described in one of the world's greatest poems, the Cherokee Indian "Spell for the Attraction of Affections."

(1974) One way or another, most of us poets tend to aim for the "direct hit," that deeply satisfying *ouch!* of the inner gunfighter toppling over on the dusty little main street of the Reader's Heart.... The Temper of that "hit" is various; inflated reputations are proposed on what in another medium, say painting or sculpture, would be instantly recognized and rejected as miserable tear-jerkers. However, no poet ever was, is, or will ever be in total control of his or her radar installation. The Built-In Shit Detector (invented by the late Mr. Hemingway) is always liable to freak out and start regurgitating into thc system the very substance it was supposed to eliminate. It may take a long time, perhaps years, perhaps forever, to discover such malfunction and its causes. However, one keeps on trying, and when the poem is there, one knows it, and you know it too.

* * *

The poetry of Anselm Hollo is fun. In his later verse, furthermore, we come to expect the unexpected with every turn of the page, almost with every new line; and we are seldom disappointed. Of late years, too, his diction has become less "English" (meaning decorous) and more "American" (meaning slangy and colloquial). But his poetry always has been unadorned and keyed to the rhythms of common speech. He speaks, that is, as "one of us" not from a platform, and this is surprising in view of the years he spent as a program director on the BBC. Or perhaps in his diction he is compensating for the fact that his father was an eminent professor of philosophy and theory of education at the University of Helsinki.

Hollo's career as a translator began at the University of Helsinki also, where he translated many European classics into Finnish including Cervantes, Dostoievski, and Henry James. I mention this because Hollo is still better known as a translator (especially for his magnificent translations into English of Alexander Blok and Andrei Voznesensky) than he is as a poet. Another fact delaying such recognition may be that Hollo is primarily a *comic* poet. (What is he laughing at? people ask themselves uneasily, Himself? Me? The world? The nature of things? T. S. Eliot never behaved like that.) Can it be that people have been conditioned into expecting poets to be *serious* and are at a loss with one who has an overmastering sense of the ridiculous, the absurd?

One of the recurrent themes in *Sensation* is the science fiction dream, which, it turns out, is only the old romantic pursuit of the blue flower in disguise:

Let me tell you, the captain knew
exactly what he would do
soon as he reached the destination
he would fuse with her
plumulous essence
& they would become a fine furry plant
later travelers would run their sensors over
to hear it hum
"call me up in dreamland"
by the old minstrel known as "the van"
ultimate consummation of long ethereal affair
he knew he would miss
certain small addictions
acquired in the colonies
visual images baloney sandwiches
but those would be minor deprivations
hardly bothersome in the vita nuova
he was flying high
he was almost there
& that is where
we leave him to go hurtling through the great warp
& at our own ineffable goals

A second recurrent theme is the goddess Maya, who is, he explains, "the energy/put forth in producing/the performance of the world." It follows, of course, that Hollo himself is an aspect of this goddess. It bucks a man up when he is eating out alone to think of himself as part of the cosmic force which makes possible "the performance of the world." Like the science fiction theme, the maya theme is comic, cheerful, with romantic overtones.

On occasion Mr. Hollo pokes fun at a sombre romantic classic, here Verlaine's "Il Pleur dans Mon Coeur": "after Verlaine/right now/it is raining in Iowa City/but it ain't rainin in my heart/nor on my head/because my head/it wears a big floppy heart, ha ha/it wears a big floppy heart." The tragic note enters his poetry rarely and usually in his translations, and even here, as in this brief poem from the Finnish ("Tumbleweeds"), with an element of comic surprise: "go to the lakeshore go/throw in a feather and a stone/the stone floats/it is the day your son comes home." A quieter more intimate tone prevails in some of his earlier lyrics, as in "Webern":

switch off the light
the trees stand together

easier then
to be in our bodies

growing quietly
"dem tode entgegen"

slow it is
a slow business

to grow a few words
to say love.

A traveler through many countries and languages, Hollo has a slightly off-planet slant on human affairs. Like Puck, he is convinced of our absurdity, but like Oberon, beneficent. Of his diction, Peter Schjedahl has commented, "His slight verbal hesitance succeeds in communicating the sense of a man anxious lest his words misrepresent his feelings." And it is very important to this poet that such misunderstandings never occur. Verbal finery and decoration might get in the way of the laughter, the cheerfulness, the outgoing spirit.

—E. L. Mayo

HOLLOWAY, (Percival) Geoffrey. British. Born in Birmingham, Warwickshire, 23 April 1918. Educated at Alsop High School, Liverpool; King Edward's Grammar School, Birmingham; University of Southampton, 1946–48, certificate in social science 1948. Served in the Royal Army Medical Corps, 1939–46. Married 1) Joyce Mildred Holloway (died, 1974), two daughters; 2) Patricia Holloway in 1977. Library Assistant, Salop County Council, Shrewsbury, 1935–39, 1946; Social Worker, Hatton Psychiatric Hospital, Warwick, 1946–48; Officer, Prisoner's Aid Society, Lincoln, 1950–51; Hospital Porter, Lincoln Sanatorium, 1950–53; Mental Health Worker, Westmorland County Council, Kendal, 1953–74. Since 1974, Social Worker, Cumbria County Council, Kendal. Member of the Brewery Poets, and the performance groups Colloquy and Bacchanal. Address: 4 Gowan Crescent, Staveley, near Kendal, Cumbria LA8 9NF, England.

PUBLICATIONS

Verse

To Have Eyes. London, Anvil Press Poetry, 1972.
Rhine Jump. London, London Magazine, 1974.
All I Can Say. London, Anvil Press Poetry, 1978.

Other

Editor, *Trio 2.* Kendal, Cumbria Poetry Society, 1977.

Geoffrey Holloway comments:

Much of what I have written comes out as "war comment." Not merely in its purist, technical sense (though that is treated in poem sequences like "Five Parachutists"), but war as a civil fact: the fight man has against age, environment, his own tyranny, his own captivating suicidal toys.

Perhaps because my profession is that of a social worker, perhaps because I live in the country, I have written often about isolates: outsiders, victims, the bereaved. Sometimes the isolate is human, sometimes animal. One may lead to the other.

So far as metrical forms are concerned, I like to try as many as possible – in the hope the finished thing comes out like a gymnast's asana. Too frequently of course what one gets is a contortionist's nightmare. But I believe it is important to update old forms (think of Empson and the villanelle – before his arrival merely frivolous). So I've recycled, as it were, cwydds and rhupunts – the old Welsh teasers – as well as attempting, among others, senryu, renga, caligramme.

I also think it important to weave poetry in with other arts. Not to oust the printed page, but to stimulate and complement it. Thus one should have, on the page, impressionist, cubist, fauve, maybe even pointilliste poems; and off it poems with jazz, dance, strobic improvisation, for example. Each as natural as the other – and together, still natural.

Multi-media may have its critics, but one thing it does do is redefine the social image of the poet. No longer is he a circus giraffe with a wooden leg, but what he should be: an engaging and acceptable native in a companionable zoo.

* * *

Geoffrey Holloway draws very much on personal experience for his poetry. *To Have Eyes* is an impressive first collection. He uses his eyes and ears and skill to quite remarkable effect in writing about the changing seasons, cricket, a fat woman, a calf born on a Sunday, and so on, and though he sets out with the determination "not to sentimentalize the view," he does not allow this to cloud the issues or obscure, in any way, the natural tenderness exhibited in the poems featuring members of his family. There is, for instance, a touching poem about his daughter, with the gull-slanted nickname, "Doing the Length":

And this, cardinal: a cord of grace
giving strange substance to the loined accident,
tying one into acute paternity,
baptizing in the name of father, love.
Thirty yards, learning to swim, be ...
within the pooled corroborated heart.

He has a fine command of language, an ironic sense of humour which permeates every poem, and an understanding of organic rhythm, which is important since most of his work is in "free verse."

Rhine Jump, a choice of the Poetry Book Society, covers his wartime experiences and also his childhood in Liverpool and Shropshire. There is the typical Holloway concern for accurate observation and rhythm. His hare (in "Neighbours") "canters past, diagonal," and his toad (in "Deadpan") is a "Primrose-leaf-backed old gargoyle/in the wild Elizabethan court-shoes." There are the contradictory attitudes to sexual passion in "One Up on Circe" and "Woman of the Philistines":

It was worth it, to feel again
with hairy hands the pillars' cold integrity;
able, in the roaring hall,
the hard male voices he could understand,

to fight directly, without humbling love.

But as Holloway points out, *Rhine Jump* "comes out mainly as 'war comment'. Not merely war in its purist, technical sense ..., but war as a civil fact: the fight man has against age, environment, his own tyranny, his own captivating suicidal toys." However, the best poems in this collection are not the direct war poems, but "Ode to the River Severn," "The Recidivists," "Galatea," and "Prospecting the Reserves."

Holloway's third collection, *All I Can Say*, is divided into four sections, and the last of these, "Tears on the Wind," contains the most moving and rawly honest attempts to cope with the death of his wife (to whom the book is dedicated) after years of subjection of cancer, years in which the poet was involved in nursing the victim and compelled to witness her humiliations. In "Odalisque Extraordinary" he tries to present his dying wife's feelings –

For no impressive reason this is me:
a one-girl seraglio under house-arrest:
pet, pride of that ghostly sadist
the sultan, who by threatening castration

(and for the holy kingdom of pain's sake)
has my husband as acting eunuch,
and me daily titivated
by one or other of his handmaidens ...

– and his own emotional response, carefully controlled, to her death. *All I Can Say* demonstrates the poet's craftsmanship in the use of form and language and if to some extent it is dominated by a preoccupation with death (not only that of his wife) there is sufficient variety in subject and treatment and in the range of human situations to establish Holloway as one of our most compassionate and accomplished poets.

—Howard Sergeant

HOLLOWAY, (Christopher) John. British. Born in London, 1 August 1920. Educated at County School, Beckenham, Kent; New College, Oxford (Open History Scholar), M.A. 1945, D.Phil. 1947. Served in the British Army, 1941–45. Married 1) Audrey Gooding in 1946, two children; 2) Joan Black in 1978. Temporary Lecturer in Philosophy, New College, 1945, Fellow, All Souls College, 1946–60, and John Locke Scholar, 1947, Oxford; Lecturer in English, Aberdeen University, 1949–54. University Lecturer in English, 1954–66, Fellow of Queens' College, 1955, Reader in Modern English, 1966–72, and since 1972, Professor of Modern English, Cambridge. Byron Professor, University of Athens, 1961–63; Alexander White Professor, University of Chicago, 1965; Hinkley Professor, Johns Hopkins University, Baltimore, 1972. Litt.D.: Aberdeen University, 1954; Cambridge University, 1969. Fellow, Royal Society of Literature, 1956. Address: Queens' College, Cambridge, England.

PUBLICATIONS

Verse

(*Poems*). Oxford, Fantasy Press, 1954.
The Minute and Longer Poems. Hessle, Yorkshire, Marvell Press, 1956.
The Fugue and Shorter Pieces. London, Routledge, 1960.
The Landfallers: A Poem in Twelve Parts. London, Routledge, 1962.
Wood and Windfall. London, Routledge, 1965.
New Poems. New York, Scribner, 1970.
Planet of Winds. London, Routledge, 1977.

Other

Language and Intelligence. London, Macmillan, 1951; Hamden, Connecticut, Archon, 1971.
The Victorian Sage: Studies in Argument. London, Macmillan, and New York, St. Martin's Press, 1953.
The Charted Mirror: Literary and Critical Essays. London, Routledge, 1960; New York, Horizon Press, 1962.
The Story of the Night: Studies in Shakespeare's Major Tragedies. London, Routledge, 1961; Lincoln, University of Nebraska Press, 1963.
The Colours of Clarity: Essays on Contemporary Literature and Education. London, Routledge, and Hamden, Connecticut, Archon, 1964.

The Lion Hunt: A Pursuit of Poetry and Reality. London, Routledge, and Hamden, Connecticut, Archon, 1964.
Widening Horizons in English Verse. London, Routledge, 1966; Evanston, Illinois, Northwestern University Press, 1967.
A London Childhood (autobiography). London, Routledge, 1966; New York, Scribner, 1968.
Blake: The Lyric Poetry. London, Arnold, 1968.
The Establishment of English (lecture). London, Cambridge University Press, 1972.
The Proud Knowledge: Poetry, Insight, and Self 1620–1920. London, Routledge, 1977.
Narrative and Structure: Exploratory Essays. London, Cambridge University Press, 1979.

Editor, *Poems of the Mid-Century.* London, Harrap, 1957.
Editor, *Selected Poems*, by Percy Bysshe Shelley. London, Heinemann, 1959; New York, Macmillan, 1960.
Editor, *Little Dorrit*, by Charles Dickens. London, Penguin, 1967.
Editor, with Joan Black, *Later English Broadside Ballads.* London, Routledge, 2 vols., 1974–79.

John Holloway comments:

(1970) A few guiding ideas would be: indifference to all modishness; constant study and innovation; concentration and density; refusal to compromise over difficulty; an interest in folk, street ballad, and popular poetry; and, more recently, interest in a "classic" style, strictly in Eliot's sense.

(1980) I am at present writing a book-length poem of which the continuing major theme is Cambridge and East Anglia from earliest geological times down to the present or maybe future.

* * *

Although John Holloway has never been thought of primarily as a poet, he has published several volumes of verse during the course of an active career as critic, scholar and teacher. During the 1950's he was sometimes regarded as a Movement poet, and it is true that he contributed to the Movement anthology, *New Lines*, in 1956. But apart from his attachment to fairly strict and traditional verse forms, Holloway had little in common with the other contributors. His characteristic tone was grave, even solemn, rather than ironic, and his poetry was directed to myth rather than social comment. Holloway did, however, resemble some of his contemporaries in being influenced by the terse, formal lyrics of Robert Graves, though in his case the reflective mythopoeic poetry of Edwin Muir was equally influential. In Holloway's first collection, *The Minute*, there were a number of memorable, well-realized poems, such as "Journey to the Capital," "Poem for Deep Winter" and "Warning to a Guest." But there was, equally, a pervasive sense that the will was too much involved in the production of Holloway's poetry; many of his poems were well-written and carefully structured, but somehow lacking in content or point. And this tendency has become more pronounced in his subsequent poetry, much of which is frankly dull. The dedication to the ideal of writing poetry remains strong and commands respect but the spirit seems lacking. A book-length poem like *The Landfallers* is serious and ambitious rather than convincing or enjoyable; Holloway's gifts are more apparent in his evocations of Greek landscape in *Wood and Windfall.*

—Bernard Bergonzi

HONIG, Edwin. American. Born in New York City, 3 September 1919. Educated in public schools, New York; University of Wisconsin, Madison, B.A. 1941, M.A. 1947. Served in the United States Army, 1943–46. Married 1) Charlotte Gilchrist in 1940 (died, 1963); 2) Margot S. Dennes in 1963 (divorced, 1978); two children, Daniel and Jeremy. Library Assistant, Library of Congress, Washington, D.C., 1941–42; Instructor in English, Purdue University, Lafayette, Indiana, 1942–43, New York University and Illinois Institute of Technology, Chicago, 1946–47, University of New Mexico, Albuquerque, 1947–49, and Claremont College, California, Summer 1949; Instructor, 1949–52, and Briggs Copeland Assistant Professor, 1952–57, Harvard University, Cambridge, Massachusetts. Associate Professor, 1957–60, since 1960, Professor of English, and since 1962, Professor of Comparative Literature, Brown University, Providence, Rhode Island. Visiting Professor, University of California, Davis, 1964–65. Poetry Editor, *New Mexico Quarterly*, Albuquerque, 1948–52. Director, Rhode Island Poetry in the Schools Program, 1968–72. Recipient: Guggenheim Fellowship, 1948, 1962; *Saturday Review* prize, 1957; New England Poetry Club Golden Rose, 1961; Bollingen grant, for translation, 1962; National Institute of Arts and Letters grant, 1966; Amy Lowell Traveling Fellowship, 1968; National Endowment for the Arts grant, 1975, 1977. M.A.: Brown University, 1958. Address: Box 1852, Brown University, Providence, Rhode Island 02912, U.S.A.

Publications

Verse

The Moral Circus. Baltimore, Contemporary Poetry, 1955.
The Gazabos: Forty-One Poems. New York, Clarke and Way, 1959; augmented edition, as *The Gazabos: Forty-One Poems, and The Widow*, 1961.
Poems for Charlotte. Privately printed, 1963.
Survivals. New York, October House, 1965.
Spring Journal. Providence, Rhode Island, Hellcoal Press, 1968.
Spring Journal: Poems. Middletown, Connecticut, Wesleyan University Press, 1968.
Four Springs. Chicago, Swallow Press, 1972.
Shake a Spear with Me, John Berryman: New Poems (includes the play *Orpheus Below*). Providence, Rhode Island, Copper Beech Press, 1974; augmented edition, as *The Affinities of Orpheus*, 1976.
At Sixes. Providence, Rhode Island, Burning Deck, 1974.
The Selected Poems of Edwin Honig 1955–1976. Dallas, Center for Writers Press, 1979.

Plays

The Widow (produced Chicago, 1953). Included in *The Gazabos*, 1961.
The Phantom Lady, adaptation of a play by Calderón (produced Washington, D.C., 1965). Included in *Calderón: Four Plays*, 1961.
Calderón: Four Plays, adaptations by Honig. New York, Hill and Wang, 1961.
Cervantes: Eight Interludes, adaptations by Honig. New York, New American Library, 1964.
Calisto and Melibea (produced Stanford, California, 1966). Providence, Rhode Island, Hellcoal Press, 1972; opera version (produced Davis, California, 1979).
Life Is a Dream, adaptation of a play by Calderón (broadcast, 1970; produced Providence, Rhode Island, 1971). New York, Hill and Wang, 1970.

Radio Play: *Life Is a Dream*, 1970 (UK).

Other

García Lorca. New York, New Directions, 1944; London, Editions Poetry London, 1945; revised edition, New Directions, 1963; London, Cape, 1968; New York, Octagon, 1980.
Dark Conceit: The Making of Allegory. Evanston, Illinois, Northwestern University Press, 1959; London, Faber, 1960; revised edition, New York, Oxford University Press, 1966; Providence, Rhode Island, Brown University Press, 1973.
Calderón and the Seizures of Honor. Cambridge, Massachusetts, Harvard University Press, 1972.
The Foibles and Fables of an Abstract Man. Providence, Rhode Island, Copper Beech Press, 1979.

Editor, with Oscar Williams, *The Mentor Book of Major American Poets.* New York, New American Library, 1961.
Editor, with Oscar Williams, *The Major Metaphysical Poets.* New York, Washington Square Press, 1968.
Editor, *Spenser.* New York, Dell, 1968.

Translator, *The Cave of Salamanca*, by Miguel de Cervantes. Boston, Chrysalis, 1960.
Translator, *Selected Poems of Fernando Pessoa.* Chicago, Swallow Press, 1971.
Translator, *Divan and Other Writings*, by García Lorca. Providence, Rhode Island, Bonewhistle Press, 1974.

Bibliography: in *Books and Articles by Members of the Department: A Bibliography* by George K. Anderson, Providence, Rhode Island, Brown University Department of English, 1967.

Manuscript Collection: John Hay Library, Brown University, Providence, Rhode Island.

Critical Studies: "The Voice of Edwin Honig" by John Hawkes, in *Voices* (Vinalhaven, Maine), January–April 1961; "To Seize Truth Assault Dogmas" by Robert Taylor, in *Providence Sunday Journal* (Rhode Island), 4 March 1962; " 'Spring' Breakthrough in the New Poetry" by James Schevill, in *San Francisco Examiner-Chronicle*, 5 January 1969; "Double Exposure" by L. Alan Goldstein, in *The Nation* (New York), 19 May 1969; interviews with H. J. Cargas, in *Webster Review* (Webster Groves, Missouri), Fall 1977, and with Richard Jackson, in *Poetry Miscellany 8* (Chattanooga), 1978.

Edwin Honig comments:

Matters that may have influenced my becoming a writer (though perhaps this is only a nice rationalization) were an early sense of exclusion owing to my being blamed for my younger brother's accidental death when I was five, and a severe, nearly fatal bout with nephritis when I was nine. A positive influence was my illiterate grandmother, who spoke Spanish, Arabic, and Yiddish (but no English); I lived with her and my grandfather for a few years after my parents were divorced when I was twelve. Experiences of this sort urged certain necessities upon me: one was to write instead of choking; another, to make sense of the world around me – but sense that would not exclude my own fantasy. Both my poetry and my criticism seem to rise out of such a mixed need: the criticism that creates – Spain (Calderón and García Lorca) as well as allegory – and the poetry that criticizes persons and places I have loved and distrusted – the "moral circuses" where the "gazabos" live.

My best poems are either unfinished or still merely notes in a notebook. Some poems got away (were printed) but have since been excluded from my books because they did not seem substantial enough or true. In the same way I quarrel constantly with the poems written by contemporaries old and young. No poet writing in English in the last sixty years has mastered his art or has resisted the nervous need to keep changing his style; and so none has been able to write as a complete human being. Perhaps Rilke and Lorca succeeded in a few poems. (I find, now that I have written the penultimate sentence, that I am echoing an opinion of Gottfried Benn.) I have taken to translating and to writing plays out of impatience with poetry and criticism; but I go on writing poetry – to stop would be a self-betrayal.

(1974) (This was written in 1966, and might just as well stand for what I feel today, though I think the statement bleaker than need be. There are probably more than two poets, for instance, who have done a service to the language or their language in the last sixty years, and I am almost willing to admit that Pound is one.)

* * *

Edwin Honig points out that some literary critics, idealizing a golden age of the near or distant past, "speak and write about the poetry of the past hundred and fifty years like a keeper fleaing an underbred dog that is only half the dog its sire was." Not only does Honig disagree with that critical judgment but he has also made his own substantial contribution to the healthy state of contemporary American poetry through his work as poet, teacher, critic, anthologist, translator, and playwright. Like the modernist poetry of a previous generation, much of Honig's poetry makes rigorous demands on the reader and thus has to find its own audience gradually – limited in size but appreciative of the depth, range, and skill they discover in the poems. It is a poetry of careful craftsmanship, breadth of learning, sharp perceptions, and deep authentic feeling.

In the earlier volumes, obviously influenced by Eliot and the prevailing standards of modernism, the feeling is often, though not always, insulated by technical virtuosity and layers of erudition. For a time, Honig moved away from the poem as carefully constructed artifact to a looser, though by no means formless, open-ended poem (*Four Springs*). The new form did not diminish any of his technique or learning, nor did it suddenly transform him into a poet easily accessible to the casual reader, but it did more readily release depths of personal emotion ("One wants to tell/how the memory rushes hungrily back to the remembered/life of the dead/beloved, until at a touch, of themselves, the episodes/rush on unreeling,/speed up beyond one's grasping; imagined again,/retelling themselves,/great hunks of life that plead again to be real!").

A headnote to *Four Springs* observing that "in 1966 or so I began writing a poem that very soon went beyond my conception of when or where it would end" and that the book's three concluding sections "continue the story to the present date, my fiftieth birthday" gave some evidence of an intention to explore further potentiality in this new form. More recent volumes, however, are reminiscent of his earlier style, with a strong added interest in myth. With the conviction that "though we can't live without myths, we find it hard to re-define and adapt them to our experience," Honig has, in *The Affinities of Orpheus*, dramatically reworked the Orpheus-Eurydice myth and has also included two sections of poems which develop further the significant experiences, emotions, and issues raised by the myth.

Honig's critical study of García Lorca calls attention to "his problematical forcing of the door of the constant enemy, death." The comment sheds as much light on Honig himself as it does on Lorca. His book titles (*Survivals*, *Spring Journal*, *Four Springs*) – and indeed the poet's work as a whole – affirm life, but the affirmation is wrested, often fiercely and explicitly, from the omnipresent threat of death. "Death with its cup of hopefulness/needs nourishment/but won't be fed by leftovers –/tired grief,/bewilderment of life's exhaust." Honig is a fine exemplar of his own concept of the function of the poet: "that voice which celebrates the difficult, joyous, imaginative process by which the individual man discovers and enacts his selfhood."

—Rudolph L. Nelson

HOOKER, Jeremy. British. Born in Warsash, Hampshire, 23 March 1941. Educated at St. Peter's, Southbourne, 1954–59; University of Southampton, 1959–65, B.A. 1963, M.A. 1965. Married Susan Hope Gill in 1968; one son. Since 1965, Lecturer in English, University College of Wales, Aberystwyth. Recipient: Eric Gregory Award, 1969; Welsh Arts Council Prize, 1975, and Bursary, 1976. Address: Brynbeidog, Llangwyryfon, Aberystwyth, Wales.

PUBLICATIONS

Verse

The Elements. Llandybie, Dyfed, Christopher Davies, 1972.
Soliloquies of a Chalk Giant. London, Enitharmon Press, 1974.
Solent Shore: New Poems. Manchester, Carcanet Press, 1978.
Landscape of the Daylight Moon. London, Enitharmon Press, 1978.

Other

John Cowper Powys. Cardiff, University of Wales Press, 1973.
David Jones: An Exploratory Study of the Writings. London, Enitharmon Press, 1975.
John Cowper Powys and David Jones: A Comparative Study. London, Enitharmon Press, 1979.

Critical Studies: by Philip Pacey, in *Poetry Wales* (Cardiff), Autumn, 1972, and in *Akros* (Nottingham), 1978; John Tripp, in *Planet* (Llangeilo Tregaron, Cardiganshire), February–March 1973; Randall Jenkins, in *Anglo-Welsh Review* (Pembroke Dock, Wales), Spring 1973; Donald Davie, in *Poetry Nation 9* (Manchester), March 1979.

Jeremy Hooker comments:

So far I have written from a sense of strong personal attachment to southern localities familiar to me since childhood, but where the presence of history and prehistory and also of other writers, such as Hardy, the Powys brothers, Richard Jefferies and Edward Thomas, is palpable. Thus I have attempted to establish my own way of experiencing, and also that of my forebears who were predominately agricultural labourers, the life of places that have strong literary and historical associations – associations that work both with and against the individual experience I try to express. There is, in the south, an opposition between continuity and discontinuity, and often a sense that all the air has been breathed, so that the relationship, and sometimes the struggle, between the living and the dead, the present and the past is one of my principal themes. Above all, I am moved to write by the physical nature of the landscape itself, by the coexistence of such phenomena as Stonehenge and Porton, the Cerne giant and the jets from Boscombe Down, and by a sense of family history that is inseparable from this landscape. Living in Wales has helped to bring these themes into focus by distancing me from their place of origin, but also by making me aware of the Welsh poet's relationship to his material, which is quite different from that of the majority of his English counterparts.

I suppose everything that is implied by "belonging" and "not belonging" can be said to be at the root of my work. My inclination is to write extended sequences and sequences of related lyrics rather than occasional poems.

* * *

Five of the eight poems by Jeremy Hooker in *Introduction One* (1969) included references to other poets – Hardy, Alun Lewis, Edward Thomas, and Dafydd ap Gwilym: it has always been clear that Hooker is a poet consciously rooting himself in traditions. He is acutely aware of the traditions of writing in the South of England, his birthplace, and his adopted home, Wales.

This poet's commitment is to an exploration of structure – historical and metaphorical. His pamphlet *The Elements* included the notable "Elegy for the Labouring Poor" –

No man's lonelier than James Mould
As he wakes with stubble-scored legs
In a rat's refuge of wattle and daub....
But James Mould seeing the ocean
Sees only flint acres
Fought inch by inch, chalkdust rising,
And hears only his ghostly kin
Telling their names in the stunned brain.

This was a clear indication of the method that Hooker was to employ in his subsequent collections: the power of imagination to inhabit another's mind over the centuries.

Soliloquies of a Chalk Giant is a sequence of 38 short poems dealing with the significance in myth and history of the Cerne Abbas phallic man. The cumulative effect is impressive: Hooker uses the persona of the mysterious chalk figure to explore pre-Christian and Christian psyches whilst creating a credible being: "And beneath me/I feel the grass rise/And fall, like the slow,/Deep breaths of a giantess." The implicit danger of such an extended work is that the poet is eventually drawn into poetic exercises. *Soliloquies of a Chalk Giant* stops short of that, but *Solent Shore* was not as exciting, not as tightly controlled, as one would have wished from this talented poet. The book focussed on the poet's personal archetypes and can be seen as a natural sequel to the previous collection.

Too often the poems in *Solent Shore* rest on images that are competent but not exciting. The poet's aim is, to be fair, ambitious: to relate his life, the person he has become, to his background, the landscape and seascape of his heritage. The book's second section, "The Witnesses," is powerful. These related poems turn around the rich 16th-century history of the Solent Waters. This has the necessary force to hold the poet to the core of his theme: "The very last souls I seen/was that man's father/and that man's//Drowned like rattens,/drowned like rattens" ("Mary Rose, 1545").

Jeremy Hooker is an accomplished writer and critic to whom one looks for a significant book over the next decade: his is a vision which can only intensify and come into a compelling focus: "Wires still buzz with messages/from the *Titanic*./A seance breaks up/when a cabin-boy screams."

—Tony Curtis

HOPE, A(lec) D(erwent). Australian. Born in Cooma, New South Wales, 21 July 1907. Educated at Sydney University, B.A. 1928; Oxford University, B.A. 1931. Married Penelope Robinson in 1938; three children. English Teacher, New South Wales Department of Education, 1933–36; Lecturer in English and Education, Sydney Teachers College, 1937–45; Senior Lecturer in English, Melbourne University, 1945–50. Professor of English, 1950–69, and Library Fellow, 1969–72, Canberra University College, later Australian National University; now retired. President, Australian Society of Authors, 1966. Recipient: Britannica-Atlantic Award, 1965; Levinson Prize (*Poetry*, Chicago), 1969; Ingram Merrill Foundation Award, 1969. Litt.D.: Australian National University, 1972. O.B.E. (Officer,

Order of the British Empire), 1972. Agent: Tim Curnow, Curtis Brown (Australia) Pty. Ltd., P.O. Box 19, Paddington, New South Wales 2021. Address: 66 Arthur Circle, Forrest, A.C.T. 2063, Australia.

PUBLICATIONS

Verse

The Wandering Islands. Sydney, Edwards and Shaw, 1955.
Poems. Sydney, Angus and Robertson, and London, Hamish Hamilton, 1960; New York, Viking Press, 1962.
(*Poems*), edited by Douglas Stewart. Sydney, Angus and Robertson, 1963.
Collected Poems 1930–1965. Sydney, Angus and Robertson, London, Hamish Hamilton, and New York, Viking Press, 1966.
New Poems 1965–1969. Sydney, Angus and Robertson, 1969; New York, Viking Press, 1970.
Dunciad Minor: An Heroick Poem. Melbourne, Melbourne University Press, 1970.
Collected Poems 1930–1970. Sydney and London, Angus and Robertson, 1972.
Selected Poems. London, Angus and Robertson, 1973.
The Damnation of Byron. Stratford, Ontario, Pasdeloup Press, 1973.
A Late Picking: Poems 1965–1974. Sydney, Angus and Robertson, 1975.
A Book of Answers. Sydney, Angus and Robertson, 1978.

Other

Australian Literature 1950–1962. Melbourne, Melbourne University Press, 1963.
The Cave and the Spring: Essays on Poetry. Adelaide, Rigby, 1965; Chicago, University of Chicago Press, 1970.
A Midsummer Eve's Dream: Variations on a Theme by William Dunbar. Canberra, Australian National University, and New York, Viking Press, 1970; Edinburgh, Oliver and Boyd, 1971.
Henry Kendall (lecture). Sydney, University of Sydney, 1971.
Native Companions: Essays and Comments on Australian Literature 1936–1966. Sydney, Angus and Robertson, 1974.
Judith Wright. Melbourne and London, Oxford University Press, 1975.
The Pack of Autolycus. Canberra, Australian National University Press, 1979.
The New Cratylus. Melbourne, Oxford University Press, 1979.

Editor, *Australian Poetry 1960.* Sydney, Angus and Robertson, 1960.
Editor, (*Poems*), by Henry Kendall. Melbourne, Sun, 1976.

Bibliography: *A. D. Hope* by Joy Hooton, Melbourne, Oxford University Press, 1979.

Manuscript Collection: Australian National Library, Canberra.

* * *

To say that A. D. Hope is, along with Judith Wright, one of the most highly respected of contemporary Australian poets is not, perhaps, to say very much, since contemporary Australian poetry is so little known outside the antipodes. While Hope does not acknowledge in his poetry the problems of being an "Australian poet" in any obvious or insistent way, his whole achievement – which is, I think, a very large one – is made possible only by his writing from well outside the Anglo-American culture and tradition in which the language he uses has achieved its greatest fulfilment. The early poem, "Australia," is more or less explicit on the point. The country itself is savaged for its spiritual barrenness:

They call her a young country, but they lie:
She is the last of lands, the emptiest,
A woman beyond her change of life, a breast
Still tender but within the womb is dry.

Yet he hopes to find in this "Arabian desert of the human mind" a prophetic inspiration barbed with satiric venom to rail against other sorts of barrenness in European culture, "some spirit which escapes/The learned doubt, the chatter of cultured apes/Which is called civilization over there."

So: although Hope's poems only very rarely evoke the Australian landscape, and although he never uses specifically Australian speech-patterns or rhythms, the vision informing his work, and the forms he uses to embody it, depend on his status as an outsider. No poet within the Anglo-American tradition could afford to summon so insistently and so unselfconsciously, in his own forms, the great European ghosts of Byron, Donne, Pope, and Yeats. But Hope's Australian recklessness, while it runs the risk of toppling into pastiche, often conveys magnificently the sense of enormous energy, or tension, or terror, or lust, or even, occasionally, just delightedly exuberant humour, being kept barely in check by the elaborate formal artifice of traditional metric. This is, perhaps, especially true of his erotic verse, of which he has written a great deal, in which there is Swiftian alteration of celebration and disgust:

Stockings and drawers I shall peel off
From your lithe legs and lovely thighs,
And think the rustling silks you slough
The foam from which, new-born, you rise.

Thus love in mime despoils this world:
Fashions, beliefs and customs fall;
In brutal, naked grace unfurled
He shows the root and ground of all.

The tenderness which he sometimes finds in Eros is the central affirmation in a poetry more often devoted to lacerating satire or elegiac lament. His work is often, indeed, in the title of a poem, "A Commination," heaping disdainful invective on those he calls, memorably, "small turds from the great arse of self-esteem." But, in his later work, there is a wider variety of tone and, perhaps, a larger ambition. The sonnet sequences, "The Planctus" and "Sonnets to Baudelaire," and the long poems, "The Double Looking Glass" and "Vivaldi, Bird and Angel," are poems for which I would make very large claims indeed. The imagination at work in them seems to me a unique one uniquely fulfilling itself. The conclusion of "Vivaldi, Bird and Angel," a poem which imagines Vivaldi conducting a rehearsal of one of his flute concertos, *Il Cardellino*, with the young girls of the *Ospedale della Pieta* in 18th-century Venice, rises to an explicit statement of a religious vision on the other side of satire and elegy. The angel, watching over the rehearsal, speaks:

Yet men in the Great Music, I surmise
Must also share, for what in reveries,
In separateness, in silence they create,
They only play if they participate.
These six girls and their master play as one
Perfected creature; in that unison
They touch, at least, the state in which we move:
A mutual ecstasy of consenting love.

It is a measure of Hope's accomplishment that such things can be said in his work without sentimentality and without portentousness. He is a very good poet indeed.

—Neil Corcoran

HOROVITZ, Frances. British. Born in London in 1938. Educated at the University of Bristol, 1956–59, B.A. in English and drama 1959; Royal Academy of Dramatic Art, London, 1960–62. Married Michael Horovitz, *q.v.*, in 1964; one son. Reader and radio presenter of poetry; tutor for Arvon foundation. Address: Piedmont, Bisley, Stroud, Gloucestershire GL6 7BU, England.

PUBLICATIONS

Verse

Poems. Aylesford, Kent, St. Albert's Press, 1967.
Dream: A Poem. Frensham, Surrey, Sceptre Press, 1969.
The High Tower. London, New Departures, 1970.
Letter to Be Sent by Air. Rushden, Northamptonshire, Sceptre Press, 1974.
Elegy. Knotting, Bedfordshire, Sceptre Press, 1976.

Frances Horovitz comments:

Themes of work concerned with relationships, myth, and nature. Interested in incantatory quality of verse.

* * *

Frances Horovitz's is the art of the miniaturist at its best. An art which produces clear, sharp vignettes which remain in the eye long past the looking, as in "Crow":

guardian on post and wall
watchful each in his own field
in beady surveillance
cottage and dark wood.

The details and their selection are important in order to get the mind vibrating exactly ("Bird"):

light falls from leaf to leaf
spattering gold is leaf is light
and bird
shadow swift
falls – follows

It is an admirable exercise in verbal economy, making each word pull its own exact weight which is what poetry ought to be about.

Then again the poems will present images that go beyond the visual with the same quality of continuity beyond the poem itself: "Your silence/spreads like water/in an empty room." Emotion and feeling or even mystery can be touched off in the same way – "her solitude breeds memory/heaves it to birth/mocks the still-born" ("Moon") – and given just sufficient impetus by the poet to glide on in the mind – "even through glass/I mirror your loneliness/walking in warm rooms" – or in the emotions – "soft as old silk/I tread in this room/wary of space/that between us flows" ("Loving You"). These poems disturb oh so gently, but profoundly for all that. They break in on our consciousness as gradually, but as irresistibly as the roots of those small plants that eventually sift the very earth which sustains us.

—John Cotton

HOROVITZ, Michael. British. Born in Frankfurt, Germany, 4 April 1935; emigrated to England at the age of 2. Educated at William Ellis School, London; Brasenose College, Oxford, B.A. in English. Married Frances Horovitz, *q.v.*, in 1964, one son. Since 1959, Editor and Publisher, *New Departures* magazine, London, later Bisley, Gloucestershire. Painter and singer; director of the Live New Departures road show. Address: Piedmont, Bisley, Stroud, Gloucestershire GL6 7BU, England.

PUBLICATIONS

Verse

Declaration. London, New Departures, 1963.
Strangers. London, New Departures, 1965.
Nude Lines for Barking (in Present Night Soho). London, Goliard Press, 1965.
High Notes from When I Was Rolling in Moss. London, New Departures, 1966.
Poetry for the People: A Verse Essay in "Bop" Prosody. London, Latimer Press, 1966.
Bank Holiday: A New Testament for the Love Generation. London, Latimer Press, 1967.
The Wolverhampton Wanderer: An Epic of Britannia. London, Latimer Press, 1971.
Nineteen Poems of Love, Lust, and Spirit. London, New Departures, 1971.
Growing Up: Poems and Pictures 1951–79. London, Allison and Busby, 1979.

Other

Alan Davie. London, Methuen, 1963.

Editor, *Children of Albion: Poetry of the "Underground" in Britain.* London, Penguin, 1969.
Editor, *"Big Huge" Reunion Anthology.* Bisley, Gloucestershire, New Departures, 1975.

Translator, with Stefan Themerson, *Europa*, by Anatol Stern. London, Gabberbocchus, 1962.

Critical Studies: "Of Relative Importance" by Barry Cole, in *Ambit 26* (London), 1966; Afterwords to *Children of Albion* by the author, 1969; "Poetry Explodes" by Adrian Mitchell, in *The Listener* (London), 14 May 1970; "Vanessa's Hangups" by Jeff Nuttall, in *Ambit 48* (London), 1971; "Blake and the Voice of the Bard in Our Time" by the author, in *Books* (London), Winter 1972; "The Need for the Non-Literary" by the author, in *Times Literary Supplement* (London), 29 December 1972; "The Great Cambridge Poetry Festival" by Christopher Logue, in *The Times* (London), 21 May 1977; "Verse Bet" by Susana Duncan, in *New York Magazine*, 15 May 1978.

* * *

It is often difficult to separate Michael Horovitz's poetry from his public image. This is not said in a derogatory sense, but more in acceptance of the fact that his good-humoured and enthusiastic appearances at readings, and his commitment to an entertaining approach to the writing and presentation of poetry, are always reflected in his work. It is full of surprises, and jabs at the reader/listener with light, fast punches which occasionally have a fair amount of power behind them.

Horovitz's public activities have been maintained over the years, and his own writing has had a constant tone, one which, with its colour and vigour, overcomes certain limitations of depth and precision. The use of language is sometimes noted more for its liveliness than its accuracy, with words being sprayed at the reader/listener in a machine gun-like manner, i.e., not all of them hit the target but some do and have the desired effect. At a public reading the problems of this approach are not too noticeable, but on the printed page they become obvious, and the poems can seem slack or thin.

There are, it's only fair to say, Horovitz poems which do aim at a greater degree of control than is evident in some of his work, and these often have an appealing lyricism. One can perhaps point to the love poems in this connection. But his reputation rests primarily on the longer poems, in particular his magnum opus, *The Wolverhampton Wanderer*, in which the role of the football star as working-class hero – and so a symbol of the true energy in our society – is tied in with the role of the poet as a kind of wandering bard. If any one work of Horovitz's deserves to last it is this, and its racy, humorous style is remarkably effective. It is, of course, very much a 1960's poem in its tone and social sense, and there may be some significance in the fact that it was that decade which saw Horovitz at his best.

It seems doubtful, in fact, that Horovitz will develop much beyond the point he reached in the 1960's, whether as poet or performer, although one cannot write him off as having relevance only in that period. He could still have the energy and vision to create something which will offer a view of Britain beyond the merely superficial. And given a resurgence of public poetry he could come back into his own, being the kind of poet who seems to produce best under pressure. However, although one should not under-estimate his contribution to the literary scene of the 1960's and early 1970's, it would seem fair to suggest that his limitations as a poet have, in a sense, caught up with him. A radical change in style might enable him to go beyond them, but his recent work has not indicated any inclinations to work towards such a change.

—Jim Burns

HOSKINS, Katherine (de Montalant). American. Born in Indian Head, Maryland, 25 May 1909. Educated at Smith College, Northampton, Massachusetts, A.B. 1931. Married Albert Learnard Hoskins in 1935; one child. Recipient: Brandeis University Creative Arts Award, 1957; Guggenheim Fellowship, 1958; Longview Award, 1958; Oscar Williams–Gene Derwood Award, 1978. Lives in Weston, Massachusetts, U.S.A.

PUBLICATIONS

Verse

A Penitential Primer. Cummington, Massachusetts, Cummington Press, 1945.
Villa Narcisse: The Garden, The Statues, and the Pool. New York, Noonday Press, 1956.
The Partridge Tree. San Francisco, Poems in Folio, 1957.
Out in the Open. New York, Macmillan, 1959.
Excursions: New and Selected Poems. New York, Atheneum, 1967.

Manuscript Collection: Library of Congress, Washington, D.C.

Katherine Hoskins comments:

My themes appear to consist of Nature and People wherever I happen to be – often, in thought at least, south of the Mason-Dixon Line. My influences are probably my admirations – George Herbert, Andrew Marvell, Wallace Stevens, J. C. Ransom, Yeats and Spenser. I have been considerably blamed for complication of verse forms, use of inversions and archaic words. Still and all, to quote Apollinaire, "each of these poems commemorates an event in my life."

* * *

In Katherine Hoskins' poems, common occasions acquire uncommon value. A pine overhanging a pond, a child skating on the pond form a harmony "too delicate, too lone to hold/... a second more/against the continents at arms." But in a certain miraculous way, they do hold: the peace they signify fills the watcher's consciousness, "swells ... /to the world's rim, shoves off/the clawing continents and down, down, down."

During a country wedding a sudden flurry of leaf-patterned shadows on a white church wall distracts the congregation. And we are reminded, ever so lightly, that human occasions exist within larger patterns. Friend and kin glance outward "To where these little twisters blow,/To where the prime, the five-point/Stag sleeps under the hill." But nature quiets, and the congregation resumes its business: "faced forward to the old pattern."

The lover of beauty and order, the "debased artistocrat," is offended by graceless ski boots, skis, leaning against a wall "Like careless planking" – "Her unclassed child's appliances for pleasure." But it is the child, she understands, who saves her values: "Self-multiplying quartz refracts all things"; so does the child assimilate a diverse world, find order and meaning in unlikely possibilities.

Mrs. Hoskins' tone, in these and in her poems generally, is reflective, quiet. Her ironies are lightly underlined, almost always countered by larger affirmations. There are, of course, instances of sustained acerbity – "Success," for example, which is entirely concerned with images "straw or carved." Some few poems give us a sense of terror: the mutilated body in "After the Late Lynching," "All down one side no ribs/But broken things that moved"; the wild spirit in "The Municipal Swimming Pool," "Who rests a bloody head against the drain/ and clings with battered nails, be-dazed from scrabbling/fifty feet of naked concrete box."

Yet these poems, based firmly on daily life and common human recognitions, rich in formal resources, are often curiously remote. Partly, this is a consequence of language that moves too easily toward the general and emotionally dead. At the climactic moment of "Pity as Power," when Louie Guevin comes back after death to visit his daughter, "She wasn't she says, afraid/But apprehensive." Is "apprehensive" really the word the daughter would have used? And if it is, why should we understand what she felt? Even so fine a poem as "The Byfield Rabbit" is marred by what may be called poetic diction. The "wheel-whir, bee-hum, bird song/In single sound arose" is soft and quiet like the summer work day it describes, but it does not evoke fresh responses.

There is also an unresisted tendency to make sure we understand the poet's meaning, to give us a nudge, usually at the end of the poem. The effect is to make the major event of the poem merely an illustration of homely wisdom. We need not be told at the end of "Luxury," for instance, that the rowboat, which is lust, "perseveres against the waking hours." Mrs. Hoskins is an accomplished poet, certainly. What she sometimes lacks is not technical skill, but courage. Courage to follow through the implications of her thought, and to let them stand for themselves.

—Jacqueline Hoefer

HOUÉDARD, dom (Pierre-)Sylvester. British. Born in Guernsey, 16 February 1924. Educated at Elizabeth College, Guernsey; Jesus College, Oxford; Collegio Santanselmo,

Rome, Ph.L. Served in the Far East during World War II. Benedictine monk: Prinknash Abbey, Gloucester, since 1949. Librarian, Farnborough Abbey, 1959–61. Literary Editor for the New Testament, Jerusalem Bible, 1961. Since 1965, Founding Member and Vice-President, Association of Little Presses. Visual Poetry exhibited: St. Catherine's College, Oxford, 1964; Galerie Riquelme, Paris, 1964; Galerie Bressy, Lyons, 1965; Galerie Denise-Davy, Paris, 1965; Kornblee Gallery, New York, 1965; ICA, London, 1965; Signals Gallery, London, 1965; Tyler School of Art, Philadelphia, 1966; Peacetower, Los Angeles, 1966; Midland Gallery, Nottingham, 1966; Galeria Universitaria Aristos, Mexico City, 1966; Galeria Juana Mordo, Madrid, 1966; Gallery 10, London, 1966; Kunstcentrum 'tvenster, Rotterdam, 1966; Arnolfini, Bristol, 1966; Galeria Barandiaran, San Sebastian, Spain, 1966; Castello del Valentino, Turin, 1966; Subscription Rooms, Stroud, Gloucestershire, 1966; Brighton Festival, 1967; Lisson Gallery, London, 1967; New Metropole Arts Centre, Folkestone, Kent, 1967; French Institute, London, 1967; Festival de Fort Boyard, Rochefort-sur-Mer, France, 1967; Studio 2-B, Bergamo, Italy, 1967; Festival of Spain, 1967; Absalom, Bath, 1968; Galerie nächst St. Stephan, Vienna, 1968; Totem-1 Gallery, Salford, Lancashire, 1968; Westfälische Kunstverein, Münster, 1969; Fine Arts Gallery, Vancouver, 1969; Axis, Bristol, 1969; Ceolfrith Gallery, Sunderland, 1970; Stedelik Museum, Amsterdam, 1970; Victoria and Albert Museum, London (and tour), 1970–72; Bear Lane Gallery, Oxford, 1970, 1971; Avelles Gallery, Vancouver, 1971; Art Centre, Bristol, 1971; Laing Gallery, Newcastle upon Tyne, 1971, 1972; Oval House, London, 1974; LYC Museum, Brampton, Cumberland, 1974. Vice-President, The Poetry Society, 1974. Address: Prinknash Abbey, Gloucester GL4 8EX, England.

PUBLICATIONS

Verse

Yes-No. Daneway, Gloucestershire, Daneway Press, 1963.
Thalamus-Sol. Maidstone, Kent, St. Albert's Press, 1964.
Rock Sand Tide. Woodchester, Gloucestershire, Daneway Press–Openings Press, 1964.
Frog-Pond-Plop. Woodchester, Gloucestershire, Openings Press, 1965.
Atom. Woodchester, Gloucestershire, Openings Press, 1965.
Kinkon. London, Writers Forum, 1965; revised edition, as *Op and Kinkon Poems and Some Non-Kinkon*, 1965.
Worm-Wood/Womb-Word. Daneway, Gloucestershire, Daneway Press, 1966.
A Book of Chakras (8 Yantrics): Studies Towards Mechanical Fingers by dsh for Inner Moon Pointing. Watford, Hertfordshire, Watford School of Art, 1966.
To Catch a Whiteman by His Manifesto. Corsham, Wiltshire, Openings Press, 1967.
Tantric Poems, Perhaps. London, Writers Forum, 1967.
Book of 12 Mudras. Corsham, Wiltshire, Openings Press, 1967.
Book of Mazes and Troytowns. Corsham, Wiltshire, Openings Press, 1967.
Easter Frog Toy for Pesach-Skipover. Corsham, Wiltshire, Openings Press, 1967.
Eros A-Gape. London, Lisson Delta, 1967.
Semaine Euclidienne. Sherborne, Dorset, South Street, 1968.
Poster for the Breakdown of Nations 4th-World Conference. London, Resurgence, 1968.
Deus-Snap. Corsham, Wiltshire, Openings Press, 1968.
Miniposters. Sherborne, Dorset, South Street, 1968.
The Sun-Cheese Wheel-Ode: A Double-Rolling-Gloster Memorial for Ken Cox. Sherborne, Dorset, South Street, 1969.
A Snow Mouse. Bristol, Axis Multiple, 1969.
En Trance. Bristol, Axis Multiple, 1969.
12 Nahuatl Dancepoems from the Cosmic Typewriter. Sherborne, Dorset, South Street, 1969.

Texts, edited by John Sharkey. London, Lorrimer, 1969.
Streets Go Both Crazy Ways at Once. Sherborne, Dorset, South Street, 1969.
Book of Battledores. Sherborne, Dorset, South Street, 1969.
Book of Onomastikons. Sherborne, Dorset, South Street, 1969.
Splendid Weeping. Corsham, Wiltshire, Openings Press, 1969.
Successful Cube Tranceplant in Honor of Chairman Mao. Corsham, Wiltshire, Openings Press, 1970.
Ode to the Colonels. Corsham, Wiltshire, Openings Press, 1970.
Grove Sings: Reflecting Poem for ihf. Sunderland, Ceolfrith, 1970.
Auto-de-Chakra-Struction. Oxford, Bear Lane Gallery, 1971.
The Sign. Worcester, Stanbrook Abbey Press, 1971.
Main Calm Line. London, National Poetry Centre, 1972.
Like Contemplation. London, Writers Forum, 1972.
(*Poems*), edited by Charles Verey. Sunderland, Ceolfrith, 1972.
Begin Again: A Book of Reflections and Reversals. Brampton, Cumbria, LYC, 1975.

Other

Translator, *Office of Our Lady* (the Encalcat Office). London, Darton Longman Todd, 1962.

Critical Studies: in (*Poems*) edited by Charles Verey, 1972 (includes bibliography).

dom Sylvester Houédard comments:

inevitably i feel my own work as the continuation of the unbroken traditions of benedictine poets & artists – beginning with the monastic literati of the ancient west who *created* civilization & the european cultural revolution until the mimetic embourgeoisification of art as revivalism – with the neo-isms of *re*naissance thru *neo*gothic – even for part of this period tho not right up till napoleon III's salon des refusés there is a wu-wei quality of playing the stringless lute in benedictine baroque as contrasted with the jesuit – & poetmonks in the west have always cultivated what newman calls "the alliance of benedict & virgil." eg:

s-abbo s-adelhard agobard b-alcuin s-aldhelm (the concretist) s-angilbert s-bede s-bertharius (caedmon) s-dunstan (another concretist) florus fridoard gerbert (sylvester II) heiric hepidamn-the-newsallust herimann v-hildebert hincmar b-hrabanus-maurus (concrete) abbess hroswitha the ladycatullus playwright hucbald itier-de-vassy lawrence of durham lupus modoin notkerbalbulus s-odo otfrid s-pascasiusradbert peter-the-venerable sigebert-the-newovid theodulf & walafridstrabo-the-newvirgil – not to mention the preservers & copiers of not only the pagan latin poets including the erotica but also of pagan icelandic sagas & (tho the danes later destroyed these mss) the earlier british poets (& celtic monkpoets were as honoured as their nonmonk-poets) – for similar reasons sahagun & other friars preserved the nahuatl poetry of aztec & earlier mexico.

to the modern contemplative & poet it is hard not to see the sweep of so called avantgarde creativeness from eg the impressionists & thru dada cage concrete antimimesis autodestructive streetguerilla & authentic je-je communication-dialog structures as so many searches for innerpath social liberation & the creative poetic monastic transcendental experience & vision of seeing things change into what they are – but i feel too this equally strong empathy with the monkprophet poets of other cultures – tho particularly with the siberian shamans & the feathery flowerdrum heart-&-face-making nahuatl singers & the welsh englynion makers & the zen haiga/haiku makers – yinyang acceptance of yinyang tension is the unifying field of west scriptorium & east zenga – onepointed poetry as spiritual askesis.

* * *

"There are certain fundamental types of questioning abt language that shld have occurred in English poetry before it got withered by the festival of britain." So dom Sylvester Houédard wrote in 1964, and his output in the last decade has tried to supply this lack of questioning, sometimes within previously accepted parameters of how poetry works, but more often through a radical denudation of subjective and expressionist language elements, producing a cool flicker of mathematical permutations and/or of sound-effects and/or of visual patterns. The works by which he is best-known are his "typestracts" – typed designs of extraordinary ingenuity which increasingly came to be ikons for contemplation, topological tantric forms linked to language or "poetry" only by the lingering literary hookup anything typewritten still tends to retain, or by a title like "slipping sideways into god" which slips the typestract into both poetry and religion, however nonverbal the design in itself.

Western and oriental meditation join their influences in his work, whether in the "sun/bridesroom" (sol/thalamus) Christmas poem or in his version of Basho's Zen-directed haiku "frog/pond/plop," both using the spatialist techniques of concrete poetry. His ecumenical inclusiveness has been held against him, and his "borderblurs" (to use his own term for the dissolving of art-categories) have been regarded with some suspicion as well as admiration. But in the history of the avant-garde in Britain he has a distinctive place.

—Edwin Morgan

HOWARD, Richard. American. Born in Cleveland, Ohio, in 1929. Educated at Columbia University, New York (Editor, *Columbia Review*); the Sorbonne, Paris. Poetry Editor, *American Review*, New York; Director, Braziller Poetry Series. Fellow of Morse College, Yale University, New Haven, Connecticut. Free-lance literary and art critic and translator. Recipient: Guggenheim Fellowship, 1966; Harriet Monroe Memorial Prize, 1969, and Levinson Prize, 1973 (*Poetry*, Chicago); American Institute of Arts and Letters grant, 1970; Pulitzer Prize, 1970. Address: c/o Atheneum Publishers, 122 East 42nd Street, New York, New York 10017, U.S.A.

PUBLICATIONS

Verse

Quantities. Middletown, Connecticut, Wesleyan University Press, 1962.
The Damages. Middletown, Connecticut, Wesleyan University Press, 1967.
Untitled Subjects. New York, Atheneum, 1969.
Findings. New York, Atheneum, 1971.
Two-Part Inventions. New York, Atheneum, 1974.
Fellow Feelings. New York, Atheneum, 1976.
Misgivings. New York, Atheneum, 1979.

Plays

The Automobile Graveyard, adaptation of a play by Fernando Arrabal (produced New York, 1961).
Wildflowers (produced New York, 1976).
Two-Part Inventions (produced Chicago, 1979).

Other

Alone with America: Essays on the Art of Poetry in the United States since 1950. New York, Atheneum, 1969; London, Thames and Hudson, 1970.

Editor, *Preferences: 51 American Poets Choose Poems from Their Own Work and from the Past.* New York, Viking Press, 1974.

Translator, *The Voyeur*, by Alain Robbe-Grillet. New York, Grove Press, 1958.
Translator, *The Wind*, by Claude Simon. New York, Braziller, 1959.
Translator, *The Grass*, by Claude Simon. New York, Braziller, 1960.
Translator, *Two Novels* (*Jealousy* and *In the Labyrinth*), by Alain Robbe-Grillet. New York, Grove Press, 1960.
Translator, *Najda*, by André Bréton. New York, Grove Press, 1961.
Translator, *Last Year at Marienbad*, by Alain Robbe-Grillet. New York, Grove Press, and London, Calder and Boyars, 1962.
Translator, *Mobile*, by Michel Butor. New York, Simon and Schuster, 1963.
Translator, *Manhood*, by Michel Leiris. New York, Grossman, 1963; London, Cape, 1968.
Translator, *Force of Circumstance*, by Simone de Beauvoir. New York, Simon and Schuster, 1963; London, Deutsch-Weidenfeld and Nicolson, 1965.
Translator, *Erasers*, by Alain Robbe-Grillet. New York, Grove Press, 1964; London, Calder and Boyars, 1966.
Translator, *For a New Novel: Essays on Fiction*, by Alain Robbe-Grillet. New York, Grove Press, 1966.
Translator, *The Poetics of Paul Valéry*, by Jean Hytier. New York, Doubleday, 1966.
Translator, *Natural Histories*, by Jules Renard. New York, Horizon Press, 1966.
Translator, *History of Surrealism*, by Maurice Nadeau. New York, Macmillan, 1967; London, Cape, 1968.
Translator, *Histoire*, by Claude Simon. New York, Braziller, 1968; London, Cape, 1969.
Translator, *The Immoralist*, by André Gide. New York, Knopf, 1970.
Translator, *May Day Speech*, by Jean Genet. San Francisco, City Lights, 1970.
Translator, *Professional Secrets: An Autobiography*, by Jean Cocteau. New York, Farrar Straus, 1970; London, Vision Press, 1972.
Translator, *Fall into Time*, by E. M. Cioran. New York, Quadrangle, 1970.
Translator, *The Battle of Pharsalus*, by Claude Simon. New York, Braziller, and London, Cape, 1971.
Translator, *A Happy Death*, by Albert Camus. New York, Knopf, and London, Hamish Hamilton, 1972.
Translator, *Critical Essays*, by Roland Barthes. Evanston, Illinois, Northwestern University Press, 1972.
Translator, *Rosa*, by Maurice Pons. New York, Dial Press, 1972.
Translator, *Project for a Revolution in New York*, by Alain Robbe-Grillet. New York, Grove Press, 1972; London, Calder and Boyars, 1973.
Translator, *The Fantastic*, by Tzvetan Todorov. Cleveland, Case Western Reserve University Press, 1973.
Translator, *Canto for an Equinox*, by St.-John Perse. Princeton, New Jersey, Princeton University Press, 1977.
Translator, *A Lover's Discourse: Fragments*, by Roland Barthes. New York, Hill and Wang, 1978.
Translator, *The Eiffel Tower and Other Mythologies*, by Roland Barthes. New York, Hill and Wang, 1979.

More than 100 other translations of French works published.

* * *

In the somewhat less than twenty years since the appearance of his first book, *Quantities*, Richard Howard has established himself firmly in a distinguished career as one of our most prolific poets, critics, editors, and translators. And the course of his poetic development seems to me to represent the difficult and treacherous job of surmounting and transforming his learning, sophistication, brilliance, and knowingness, instead of simply displaying them. As with Auden, for example, an acknowledged model for Howard, he is so good at writing interesting and skilful poems that he tends to be taken in by his own cleverness, writing poems that are merely skilful and interesting rather than compelling or passionate – poetry that arises inevitably out of the self's confrontation with itself and the world.

In *Quantities*, with variety of subject, flexibility and power of language and structure, and penetration of insight, Howard has much to say coupled with a virtuoso ability to say it. "The Return from Montauk," for example, presents a beautifully balanced moment in terms of a natural yet complex and ambiguous symbol. The speaker is riding a train at nightfall, and, looking to the east, he sees an image of the setting sun reflected in a window. The double perspective is completed when he turns toward the west and sees through the train window the actual setting sun – imagining, however, in line with the logic of his previously-established conception, that it is the rising sun. Thus, at the moment of sunset, he can envision, out of the literal structure of the perception itself, the sunrise, and at the moment of despair, the rebirth of hope. It is a clear and delicate poem, intricately wrought, suggesting implications that go far below its pellucid surface – a thematically central poem in the book as a whole, for Howard characteristically deals with the knife-edge upon which opposites are balanced, but his vision of the abyss which falls between them is neither deep nor powerful, and hence the tension in his poems is often not strong. There is too much of the dandified manner and not enough of the presence of a man. Order is best when it comes out of energy, not out of literature.

With *The Damages* we find an increased assurance and depth, coupled with an increasing prolixity and confirmation of his glib knowingness. In "For Hephaistos," we find the inevitable and moving confrontation with Auden, who "taught me, taught us all a way/To speak our minds," and the speaker's grateful sense of being free from his master: "only now, at last/Free of you, my old ventriloquist,/Have I suspected what I have to say/Without hearing you say it for me first." In "The Encounter," we find a marvelously erotic and mysterious confrontation between a nameless Hero and The Female, which rises convincingly to the level of myth. And there are, on the other hand, Jamesian and Proustian vignettes of childhood ("Seeing Cousin Phyllis Off," "Intimation of Mortality," "Private Drive"); poems of friends, literature, and travel ("Seferiades," "Even the Most Beautiful Sunset"); and the clever poems, such as "To Aegidius Cantor," "Eusebius to Florestan," and "Bonnard: A Novel," which continue his own line of literary ventriloquism and which anticipate the extended fascination Howard is to develop for the "dramatic monologue" in subsequent volumes.

Thus, *Untitled Subjects* (Pulitzer Prize) consists entirely of 15 such monologues (mostly in the form of letters), spoken by such 19th-century Worthies as Scott, Ruskin, Thackeray, and Mrs. William Morris, and arranged chronologically from 1801 to 1915. Howard alludes to Browning in his dedication, "the great poet of otherness," and quotes that poet's saying, "I'll tell my state as though 'twere none of mine." This clearly implies that Browning was writing about himself while pretending to be speaking in the voices of others, and I think this is true. But I do not think either that this makes him simply a poet of otherness or that Howard's dramatic monologues are very similar to his master's. What Howard's poems do, in fact, is "to bring history alive," as the jacket blurb for a historical novel or costume drama might say: they bring the past closer to us, first, by treating it as if it were present, and second, by making it personal and intimate – putting back in, as it were, what the official histories leave out, an intelligent piece of literary legerdemain.

Similar poems make up the first part of *Findings*, and this time Howard does not hesitate to write a 14-page poem, "November, 1889," spoken by Browning himself as he nears the moment of death. Revealingly, Howard puts these words into the master's mouth:

> what is dead or dying
> is more readily apprehended by us
> than what is part of life.
> Nothing in writing is
> easier than to raise the dead.

Perhaps this *is* more Howard than Browning, and so he moves on in the second part to more personal poems of love and friendship. These, however, as with the others, remain merely skilful and interesting.

This impression, alas, is only strengthened by Howard's latest volumes. *Two-Part Inventions* varies the form by expanding monologue to dialogue and by broadening his range of subjects to include Hölderlin, Wilde's visit to Whitman, Ibsen at Capri, Edith Wharton, Rodin, and Di Fiore. *Fellow Feelings* returns to the more usual lyric mode but deals, nevertheless, in its first section with Hart Crane, Randall Jarrell, Valéry Larbaud, Auden, and Goethe. Although the second section occupies more personal ground, poets, as Howard himself says, make "themselves public/without making themselves known." And in the third section he comes back compulsively to his beloved *objets d'art* – by Donatello, Simone Martini, Bellini, and so on. *Misgivings*, finally, contains commentaries on the subjects photographed by Nadar, poems about people from the renaissance to the present, and a series of love poems.

Howard is still so over-civilized, so full of grace, learning, polish, and elegance, as to seem the victim of his own gifts, keeping himself and his life – even when he does write about these things – at such a distance from the poems that they emerge as snowflakes under glass rather than the prowling animals they have every right to be. The libraries and museums await a lifetime of future poems, an endless abundance of stalking horses for the self to hide behind. The bravura technique becomes, in short, a technique of evasion; no poet need trifle, especially a poet such as Howard who has potentially much to say.

—Norman Friedman

HOWELL, Anthony. British. Born in London, 20 April 1945. Educated at Leighton Park School, Berkshire; Royal Ballet School, London; Centre de la Danse Classique, Cannes. Married Signe Lie in 1972. Dancer with the Royal Ballet, London, 1966. Lecturer in Creative Writing, Grenoble University, 1969–70. Editor of Softly Loudly Books, London. Founder, 1974, The Theatre of Mistakes. Address: Purdies Farm, Hazeley Heath, Hartley, Wintney, Hampshire, England.

PUBLICATIONS

Verse

Sergei de Diaghileff (1929). London, Turret, 1968.
Inside the Castle: Poems. London, Barrie and Rockliff-Cresset Press, 1969.
Imruil: A Naturalized Version of His First Ode-Book (pre-Islamic Arabic). London, Barrie and Rockliff-Cresset Press, 1970.
Femina Deserta. London, Softly Loudly, 1971.
Oslo: A Tantric Ode. London, Calder and Boyars, 1975.
The Mekon. London, Many Press, 1976.

Other

Editor, *Erotic Lyrics*. London, Studio Vista, 1970.
Editor, with Fiona Templeton, *Elements of Performance Art*. London, Ting, 1977.

Critical Studies: reviews by Peter Porter, in *London Magazine*, 1970, and Robert Nye, in *The Times* (London), 1975.

Anthony Howell comments:

I write poetry because I was brought up in Reading. You write poetry do you? He writes poetry because he was brought up in Slough. She writes poetry. It doesn't write poetry. We write poetry because we were brought up. They write poetry because they were brought up in blazers.

* * *

Anthony Howell's *Inside the Castle*, his first collection, was a crowded book, comparable with Keats's *Poems* of 1817 in that it marked the emergence of a young man of much talent unable or unwilling to refine a capacity for confusion when he saw that he could employ it to keep a poem going when inspiration failed. The book also contained three very good poems ("The Growing Family," "The Head," and "A Reason for Fidelity") where in each case one clear poetic impulse worked the whole way through, nothing sounded forced, and the only obvious debt was to John Crowe Ransom and the Fugitives generally.

Imruil: A Naturalized Version of His First Ode-Book takes a handful of footnotes in an academic crib to the Mu'Allaqat or "Seven Suspended Odes" of pre-Islamic Arabia, and uses them as "a metaphor-cluster" in the making of an original sequence. A comparison of these verses and the texts of the scholar R. S. Rattray, from whence they are derived, would make a useful exercise for students of literary mechanics. More importantly, this Borgesian game provides Howell with a mask in the shape of a well-fitting *persona* in front of his own feelings, the opacities of *Inside the Castle* are refined, and a number of individual poems reach a high level of lyrical excellence:

Inhaling the wind out of the East
One can tell it has satisfied
The camphor leaves. "Bring
Me a gift with nothing in your hands ..."

Later work in magazines and pamphlets has shown the influence of John Ashbery.

—Robert Nye

HOWES, Barbara. American. Born in New York City, 1 May 1914. Educated at Beaver Country Day School, Boston; Bennington College, Vermont, B.A. 1937. Married William Jay Smith, *q.v.*, in 1947 (divorced, 1965); two sons, David and Gregory. Editor, *Chimera* magazine, New York, 1943–47. Lived in Florence for four years, and in Oxford, France, and Haiti. Recipient: Bess Hokin Prize, 1949, and Eunice Tietjens Prize, 1959 (*Poetry*, Chicago); Guggenheim Fellowship, 1955; Brandeis University Creative Arts Award, 1958; National

Institute of Arts and Letters award, 1971; New England Poetry Club Golden Rose, 1973; Christopher Award, 1974. Agent: John Schaffner, 425 East 51st Street, New York, New York 10022. Address: North Pownal, Vermont 05260, U.S.A.

PUBLICATIONS

Verse

The Undersea Farmer. Pawlet, Vermont, Banyan Press, 1948.
In the Cold Country. New York, Bonacio and Saul-Grove Press, 1954.
Light and Dark. Middletown, Connecticut, Wesleyan University Press, 1959.
Looking Up at Leaves. New York, Knopf, 1966.
The Blue Garden. Middletown, Connecticut, Wesleyan University Press, 1972.
A Private Signal: Poems New and Selected. Middletown, Connecticut, Wesleyan University Press, 1977.

Christmas Card Poems: *Lachrymae Christi and In the Old Country*, with William Jay Smith, 1948; *Poems: The Homecoming and The Piazza*, with Smith, 1949; *Two French Poems: The Roses of Saadi and Five Minute Watercolor*, with Smith, 1950; *The Triumph of Love*, 1953; *Turtle*, 1955; *Early Supper*, 1956; *Lignum Vitae*, 1958; *The Snow Hole*, 1960; *Two Poems: Landscape, Deer Season; Dream of a Good Day*, 1962; *Looking Up at Leaves*, 1963; *Gulls*, 1964; *Leaning into Light*, 1965; *Wild Geese Flying*, 1966; *Elm-Burning*, 1967; *Otis*, 1968; *Talking to Animals*, 1969; *Returning to Store Bay*, 1970; *Evening: Crown Point*, 1971; *Reginae Coeli*, 1972; *Entrance, Casuarinas*, with Gregory Jay Smith, 1973 – all privately printed. Other Occasional Poems: *To W. H. Auden on His Fiftieth Burthday*, 1957; *An Epithalamium: For Petie and Frank Palmer*, 1964; *Hubert Walking: A Profile*; *For Mother: A Log: On Her Eightieth Birthday*, 1968; *A Liking for People and Animals*, 1968; *Millefleurs: For the Presentation of a Tapestry*, 1969; *For Helen and Bob Allen*, 1970; *Gold Beyond Gold*, 1970; *The Sixth Color of the Afternoon*, 1974 – all privately printed.

Other

Editor, *23 Modern Stories.* New York, Knopf, 1963.
Editor, *From the Green Antilles: Writings of the Caribbean.* New York, Macmillan, 1966; London, Souvenir Press, 1967.
Editor, with Gregory Jay Smith, *The Sea-Green Horse: A Collection of Short Stories* (juvenile). New York, Macmillan, 1970.
Editor, *The Eye of the Heart: Short Stories from Latin America.* Indianapolis, Bobbs Merrill, 1973.

Manuscript Collection: Yale University Library, New Haven, Connecticut.

Critical Studies: *Selected Criticism* by Louise Bogan, New York, Noonday Press, 1955; *Modern American Poetry*, edited by Louis Untermeyer, New York, Harcourt Brace, 1962.

Barbara Howes comments:

(1970) [I am] a poet, a woman, a wife, a mother: all these things go to make up one's outline.

I am interested in form, and also in what I call "creative form," the working out of a unique form for that one poem. Also interested in the possibilities of free verse. Basically, in what will happen to me and my work next.

I am not very good at discussing my own work. In the essay in *Poets on Poetry* (edited by Howard Nemerov, New York, Basic Books, 1966), I probably stated things as well as I could. As I suggested above, one never knows what one will do next, or, as W. H. Auden said much more eloquently, one never knows if one will write another poem till one has done it. I have been especially influenced perhaps by Emily Dickinson, Yeats, Frost, Hopkins; really, in some way, by about everyone I read. I am much interested in trying to adapt Old French and other forms to modern or contemporary subjects and emotions. Am also interested in the fascinations and complexities of translation.

Basically, I am trying to deal with my experience through my writing; this is how to a degree one can order what one sees and what happens.

(1974) I guess I'll stand by what I said before. All one can do is do the best you can, and keep at it; all the dress-ups of worrying about reviews and getting to know the "right" people are disaster for the serious poet. You just have to keep on at dealing with your experience, whatever it is.

As it turns out, I seem to write about things I see, my children, my friends, my house, my attachments, our animals, the view from any window, in no special order or arrangement. *Place* (physical, not social), which so affects one, comes into it. If you can be attached to people, to a place or places, to ideas, to trees, you will be less likely to fall into the trap of the snarling little ego, which so ranges abroad. Too many writers give in to violence and spite. It is more interesting, though, to be alive, to find what stimulates the imagination, to meet what is beyond one's powers: then a poem may be hatching.

* * *

Barbara Howes's last three volumes but one – *Light and Dark*, *Looking Up at Leaves*, and *The Blue Garden* – represent a gradual smoothing out and cooling off. In the first, we find that she is an explorer of the abyss, the inner self, and the forbidden. In "City Afternoon," for example, after sensing the vibrations of an unseen subway, an escalator, a disposal unit, and the cooped-up people in a large apartment building, she concludes by hearing, in a lull, the Iron Maiden closing on its spikes. Or again, in "The Undersea Farmer," the poem comes to its end by taking us back up out of the water and toward the land, as Arnold's Forsaken Merman's wife did, but still urges that we keep hold of our "subaqueous lifeline," as Margaret did not. And, in "The Nuns Assist at Childbirth," she wonders what a nun can make of this "Rude life" pouring "From the volcano," "Tragic, regenerate, wild."

She is especially good with women, treating them in terms of genuine passion and sexuality. "Danae," for example, compassionately and frankly sees bed as their destiny, whether it supports agony or joy. And she does not avoid the personal, as in "Indian Summer," where she ponders the man asleep in her arms. Nor is she afraid of love, as in "The Balcony," which portrays a true interchange between human beings. And "The New Leda" is one of her best. Leda awaits the god's arrival; a nun awaits Christ: what will be their various destinies – lust, new life, or emptiness? The poem ends with a powerful appeal to the speaker's "Sisters, wastrels," to give over "sacrifice and harm/And deprivation."

The next two books, however, reveal a somewhat more complacent pattern. Each is divided similarly into two parts, entitled variously "A Short Way by Air" and "Vermont Poems," and "Away" and "At Home," which seems generally to refer to her habit of dividing her time between the West Indies and New England. Thus the one section contains poems of warmth and lushness, while the other embodies a more wintry climate, with human relations being treated in both.

Thus, for example, the first section of *Leaves* deals with seascapes, seabirds, fish, swimming, and boating, but it also has a remarkable poem called "Flight," in which a Russian spaceman, a Goya picture, a boy murdered on a subway, and the speaker's reflections on "the outer spaces of the mind" revealed by such brutality, are effectively made into symbols of one another. In "My Dear, Listen:," she says: "An artist should keep/The pathway open/To his inward life...." The intensity of cold is felt in the second section, especially in "The Snow Hole," which tells of a trip to a cleft in the mountains in which can be seen never-melting snow, and which concludes: "Chilled through/By now, we touch the world." And in the title poem, as well as in "A Few Days Ago," the speaker experiences an almost mythic identification with trees.

And yet the overall impression left by this book is more placid and attenuated than that of *Light*. Howes is still very fine, bright, and resourceful, but less turbulent and anguished. She is rather the keen observer and compassionate commentator than the involved participant, and she has settled on a calm concision of style which tends to flatten the emotional power of her insights – even in as painful a poem as "Flight," which concludes: "Realizing of him/ That nothing is the same as one young man, one son,/One good bet, gone." This is well said, and there is a poignant urgency in the last three repetitive phrases and final verb, but it is still a bit too level in tone.

This impression is confirmed and strengthened by a reading of the third book. Again, a few poems deal with nightmare ("Sweet Sleep") and the deeps of the mind ("Focus"), but many are given over to jewel-like creature poems reminiscent of, but not as taut as, some of Marianne Moore's work in this line ("Luke, Captive," "The Ostrich Tree"), or to bric-a-brac and *objets d'art* ("Millefleurs," "Gold *Beyond* Gold"). And as the language continues almost imperceptibly to slacken, the typography of the stanzas seems to grow more intricate, as if unwittingly needing to compensate for the loss of intensity, as in "Still-life: New England":

> From that old cow in the field
> A calf was born;
> He struggles now to rise –
> No, he cannot
> Yet, on his tapestry legs....

A Private Signal contains selections from these three volumes, plus an additional dozen "New Poems." It is unsafe to spot a trend on the basis of so small a sample, but there are signs here of a renewed tightness of language and intensity of mood. Although these poems are mostly concerned with clear objects existing in the real world – a pool seen from a second-story window, Rome's Pietà, a mirror, her son's house – they often are presented gnomically and end cryptically, as if touched by the hand of a latter-day Emily Dickinson. The one about the pool, for example, is entitled "A Parable," and begins with the speaker looking down and feeling drawn to it. Then she says: "Kindling of bone –/words reveal us – our backbone./ They are our structure...." And the poem concludes by defining "parable" as "wandering," "a theory/of blueness," "It is the pool."

Barbara Howes wrote, in *Light and Dark*, that "the wild cannot rest with the tame," and "the strange/Wild frantic clear-eyed ones are gone" ("Lament"), and if her recent work is any sign, she may be right. Nevertheless, if she is less wild and frantic, she may be becoming more strange and clear-eyed. It is not for us to say which is the better bargain.

—Norman Friedman

HOWITH, Harry. Canadian. Born in Ottawa, Ontario, 11 August 1934. Educated at Carleton University, Ottawa (University Medal in Journalism, 1957), B.A. 1956, B.J. 1957. Ottawa Correspondent, Co-operative Press, Ottawa, 1957–59; Editor, *Flight Comment*, Royal Canadian Air Force, 1960–62; Research Assistant, Royal Commission on Publications, Ottawa, 1960–61; Editor and Publications Officer, Department of Northern Affairs and National Resources, Ottawa, 1962–64; Publications Officer, North York Board of Education, Toronto, 1964–65. Assistant Master in English, 1966–67, Chairman of the English

Department, 1967–69, Assistant to the Academic Dean, 1970–71, and English Master, 1972–73, Centennial College, Toronto. Recipient: Canada Council scholarship, 1959, and grant, 1969, 1970. Address: c/o 335 Crichton Street, Ottawa, Ontario, Canada.

PUBLICATIONS

Verse

Street Encounter. Ottawa, Blue "R" Press, 1962.
Burglar Tools. Ottawa, Bytown, 1962.
Two Longer Poems: The Seasons of Miss Nicky by Harry Howith and Louis Riel by William Hawkins. Toronto, Patrician Press, 1965.
Total War. Toronto, Contact Press, 1967.
Fragments of the Dance. Toronto, Village Book Store Press, 1969.
The Stately Homes of Westmount. Montreal, DC, 1973.
Multiple Choices: New and Selected Poems 1961–1976. Oakville, Ontario, Mosaic Press, 1976.

Play

You Bet Your Love! (produced Ottawa, 1957).

Other

Report of the Royal Commission on Publications, with others. Ottawa, Queen's Printers, 1961.

Manuscript Collection: University of New Brunswick Library, Fredericton.

Harry Howith comments:

His poetry is about love, loss, time, death, and the excrescences of contemporary urban society. It uses both sentiment and heavy-handed irony; it is characterized by wit, and by precision of diction.

The poets whose work he most admires are: Eliot, Mayakovsky, and Rilke.

He thinks of himself as a teacher, journalist, editor, poet, and administrator, more or less in that order.

* * *

"He has a fondness for the romantic," Raymond Souster wrote of Harry Howith after reading the latter's *Fragments of the Dance*. The collection does have more than its share of lines that run "Here, little darling, is my warm hand:/give me your shivering fingers" and poems about loving that end wryly: "And it's supposed to be a crime..../Be my accomplice." But a more touchy tone can be detected in *Fragments of the Dance*, a more public and political tone and subject, that may be summarized, perhaps, in a single line from the title poem which talks about "the dooms of empires written with a feather."

This new concern is fully explored in *The Stately Homes of Westmount*, Howith's 1973 collection, which includes poems about the "stately homes" in the fashionable districts of three cities: Westmount (the exclusive area of Montreal), Rosedale (of Toronto), and Rockcliffe (of Ottawa). In the Rosedale poem, Howith notes the passing of "Wit into humour: Style into fashion: Scorn into hatred," and condemns the decline of civilized values by pushing the observation to its *n*th degree in "MYSTERY, BABYLON THE GREAT, THE

MOTHER OF HARLOTS AND ABOMINATIONS OF THE EARTH." The Westmount and Rockcliffe poems are written more formally but retain a colloquial tone. Here is a verse taken from the latter poem:

sloganeering and invective,
hubristic ignorance elevated
to dogma; it's not so much
the boring arrogance of nonstop

One can detect a manic intensity, and a Canadian can discern the "Ottawa Valley" accent, with its over-enunciation of every word. The tone corresponds to the treatment of the subject in poems like "In Memory of Ezra Pound," the last two verses of which run:

You leave for us, cant-cranky
but monumental, the Cantos,
and your veritable invention

of made-new verse: if we
could sing or even hear correctly,
we too might praise Benito Mussolini.

One wonders what links, in the poet's mind, poetic modernism and Italian fascism, for the poem does not say.

This is not meant to suggest *The Stately Homes of Westmount* is lacking in wit, irony, insight or a wide range of reference, for these may be found in profusion in many of the poems. There is, too, the note of self-examination in "The New Nationalism," which in its conclusion finds the poet wondering whether "there's much difference after all/between nationalism and rheumatism./(P.S.: This makes me, according to my niece,/a male chauvinist pig.)" Howith is plainly irritated with the world around him, with its ambiguities, certainties and pretentions. As Swift preferred horses, Howith admires penguins – in an effective poem with a clever and characteristic title: "If the World Were My Poem, I'd Revise It."

—John Robert Colombo

HOYEM, Andrew. American. Born in Sioux Falls, South Dakota, 1 December 1935. Educated at Pomona College, Claremont, California, B.A. 1957. Served as a lieutenant in the United States Navy, 1957–60. Married 1) Sally Cameron Heimann in 1961 (divorced, 1964); 2) Judith B. Laws in 1971. Partner, with Dave Haselwood, Auerhahn Press, San Francisco, 1961–64; Owner, Andrew Hoyem, printer, San Francisco, 1965–66; Partner, Grabhorn-Hoyem, publishers, San Francisco, 1966–73. Since 1973, Owner, Andrew Hoyem, printer, and since 1975, Arion Press. Address: 4040 17th Street, San Francisco, California 94114, U.S.A.

PUBLICATIONS

Verse

The Wake. San Francisco, Auerhahn Press, 1963.

Lafayette Park Place. San Francisco, Auerhahn Press, 1964.
The Music Room. San Francisco, Dave Haselwood, 1965.
Stranger. San Francisco, San Francisco Arts Festival, 1965.
Happy Birthday. San Francisco, Andrew Hoyem, 1965.
Chimeras: Transformations of "Les Chimères" by Gerard de Nerval. San Francisco, Dave Haselwood, 1966.
A Romance. San Francisco, Andrew Hoyem, 1966.
The Pearl, with John Crawford, translation of the Middle English poem. San Francisco, Grabhorn Hoyem, 1967.
Vengeance. San Francisco, Grabhorn Hoyem, 1967.
Articles: Poems 1960–1967. London, Cape Goliard Press, and New York, Grossman, 1969.
Try. San Francisco, Grabhorn Hoyem, 1971.
Aim. San Francisco, Grabhorn Hoyem, 1972.
Still Life. New York, Valenti Angelo, 1973.
Petit Mal. San Francisco, Grabhorn Hoyem, 1973.
Picture/Poems: An Illustrated Catalogue of Drawings and Related Writings 1961–1974. San Francisco, Arion Press, 1975.
The First Poet Travels to the Moon. San Francisco, Arion Press, 1975.

Critical Studies: Reviews by Gilbert Sorrentino, in *Kulchur 12* (New York), Winter 1963; by Robert B. Shaw, in *Poetry* (Chicago), March 1972.

* * *

Andrew Hoyem is a poet so highly eclectic and derivative in style that one is forced to suspect that he has, as yet, failed to discover his own inner voice – or that, if he has, he does not yet know how to speak in it. When he is direct, as in the prose-poem "The Korean Conflict," he is simply ineffective; but his more recondite work, while it demonstrates an excellent grasp of its sources, does not have enough individual quality to make it memorable. "Birds. Moss. Pebbles. Frog./Fade./The five finger fern" is good enough for a diary entry, but as pastiche of Japanese or Imagist verse it only reminds us of failures. "Spook Sheep," his "transformation" of de Nerval's most famous sonnet, only manages to be either literal or to change the French into an English de-fused of poetry. He can glide easily enough from satirical observation – "This bachelor deluding himself/whose children play in the streets" – to an archaic "Old High Poesy" manner for which it is hard to see the point:

> Fain should I barren Beauty's breast
> such shameless to secrete
> faint praise, fame, and fortunes of war,
> at issue from her teat.

It is all very well to point to irony, Pound, the Provençal; but this lacks attack, appears debilitated by any strong sense of direction besides simply wanting to write poetry. One can at present, regretfully, point only to an evident intelligence and a certain charm and delicacy as Hoyem's positive virtues. But if a poet lacks energy and a personal rhythm then he needs very special qualities indeed to spark him into life; the pleasant and pacific impression that Hoyem's poetry gives, when read as a whole, is not enough.

—Martin Seymour-Smith

HUFANA, Alejandrino G. Filipino. Born in San Fernando, La Union, Philippines, 22 October 1926. Educated at the University of the Philippines, Quezon City, A.B. in English 1952, M.A. in comparative literature 1961; University of California, Berkeley (Rockefeller Fellowship, 1961–62), 1957–58, 1961–62; Columbia University, New York (John D. Rockefeller III Fund Fellowship, 1968–70), M.S. in library science 1969. Served with the North Luzon guerillas, 1944. Married Julita Quiming in 1957; four daughters. Secretary and English teacher, Cebu Chinese High School, 1952–54. Research Assistant in Social Science, 1954–56, since 1956, Member of the English Department, and since 1975, Professor of English and Comparative Literature, University of the Philippines. Since 1970, Director of the Library, since 1971, Editor, *Pamana* magazine, and since 1979, *Lahi* magizine, Cultural Center of the Philippines, Manila. Co-Founding Editor, *Signatures* magazine, 1955, *Comment* magazine, 1956–67, *Heritage* magazine, 1967–68, and *University College Journal*, later *General Education Journal*, 1961–72; Editor, *Panorama* magazine, 1959–61. Managing Editor, University of the Philippines Press, 1965–66. Artist: Exhibitions in Elmira, New York, 1957, and Manila, to 1978. Recipient: Republic Cultural Heritage Award, 1965. Address: 54 Mabini Street, Area I, University of the Philippines, Diliman, Quezon City, Philippines.

PUBLICATIONS

Verse

13 Kalisud. Quezon City, Collegian New Review, 1955.
Sickle Season: Poems of a First Decade 1948–1958. Quezon City, Kuwan, 1959.
Poro Point: An Anthology of Lives: Poems 1955–1960. Quezon City, University of the Philippines, 1961.
The Wife of Lot and Other New Poems. Quezon City, Diliman Review, 1971.
Sieg Heil: An Epic on the Third Reich. Quezon City, Tala, 1975.
Imelda Romualdez Marcos: A Tonal Epic. Manila, Konsensus, 1975.
Obligations: Cheers of Conscience. Quezon City, University of the Philippines, 1975.

Plays

Man in the Moon (produced La Union, 1956, Manila, 1970; revised version, produced Quezon City, 1972). Published in *Panorama* (Quezon City), December 1960.
Curtain-Raisers: First Five Plays (includes *Gull in the Wind*, *Honeymoon*, *Ivory Tower*, *Terra Firma*, *View from Origin*). Quezon City, University of the Philippines Social Science Research Council, 1964.
The Unicorn, in *Pamana 1* (Manila), June 1971.
Salidom-ay, in *Pamana 2* (Manila), September 1971.

Other

Mena Pecson Crisologo and Iloko Drama. Quezon City, Diliman Review, 1963.
Notes on Poetry. Quezon City, Diliman Review, 1973.

Editor, *Aspects of Philippine Literature.* Quezon City, University of the Philippines, 1967.
Editor, *A Philippine Cultural Miscellany, Parts I* and *II.* Quezon City, University of the Philippines, 1968–70.
Editor, with others, *Introduction to Literature.* Quezon City, Alemar Phoenix, 1974.
Editor, *Philippine Writings (Stories, Essays, Poems).* Manila, Regal, 1977.

Manuscript Collections: University of the Philippines Library, Quezon City; University of

Syracuse Library, New York; University of California Library, Berkeley; Cultural Center of the Philippines Library, Manila.

Critical Studies: "The Poetry So Far of A. G. Hufana" by Jean Edwardson, in *Collegian New Review* (Quezon City), January 1954; "Mutineer, Sight Ascending" by Leonard Casper, in *The Wayward Horizon: Essays on Modern Philippine Literature*, Manila, Community Publishers, 1961; "Poet's Portrait Gallery" by Andres Cristobal Cruz, in *Sunday Times* (Manila), 26 November 1961; "Dive in a Hypnosis: The Poetry of Alejandrino G. Hufana" by Albert Casuga, in *Philippine Writing 2* (Manila), 1963; *New Writing from the Philippines: A Critique and Anthology* by Leonard Casper, Syracuse, New York, Syracuse University Press, 1966; "Hufana: Rebellious Poet" by Florentino S. Dauz, in *Graphic* (Manila), 8 September 1966; "A Poet's Romance with Art" by Jolico Cuadra, in *Chronicle Magazine* (Manila), 1 July 1967; *Poetry in the Plays of A. G. Hufana* by Bernardita Castillo, University of Bohol, unpublished thesis, 1973.

Alejandrino G. Hufana comments:

The pre-publication discipline of any poet should be like the pre-performance training of the athlete or prize-fighter. All flaws considered in public must as such turn the performer back to this grind. Only birds, or such creatures, are born to the grace of what they do, which also happens to excuse their plunder.

* * *

Alejandrino G. Hufana is a fascinating and highly original poet. Some of his plans sound somewhat formidably grandiose, but such schemes often result in curtailed versions of the original intention – which must, almost certainly, in the case of mere sections of a work extending to more than 1,000 typescript pages each, be a good thing. Hufana studied in America, and has absorbed much from American poetry – in particular from that neglected master of epigram, Edwin Arlington Robinson. Deeply rooted in the complex culture of his native country, Hufana employs an ambitiously idiosyncratic diction that some non-Filipino readers have taken as evincing a lack of mastery of the English language –

> Unclothing so the Zambul Bali Dag
> May for her dead infanta deep be soft
> The black she-parent grieving on the crag
> A lullaby invokes: "Arrow aloft
> Time for your sleep, piece-of-my-thigh,
> The fletcher is not false, time for your dream,
> Meat will be yours...."

– but this is a serious error. One of Hufana's main aims is to discover and to express what is authentically Filipino, and this, given so complicated and foreign-influenced a culture (there are Filipinos writing in the national language, which is an artifact, and Spanish, as well as in English) is bound to yield results that have an odd appearance to the outside world. Hufana has been called the most successful "anthropological" poet writing in the English language, and the lines quoted above may confidently be employed as evidence in support of such a view. It is high time that both a British and an American publisher put out a comprehensive selection of his poetry.

—Martin Seymour-Smith

HUFF, Robert. American. Born in Evanston, Illinois, 3 April 1924. Educated at Wayne State University, Detroit, A.B. in English 1949, A.M. in humanities 1952. Served as an aerial gunner and bombardier in the Eighth Air Force, 1943–46. Married Sally Ann Sener in 1959; three children. Instructor, Wayne State University, 1950–52, 1957–58, University of Oregon, Eugene, 1952–53, Fresno State College, California, 1953–55, and Oregon State University, Corvallis, 1955–57, 1958–60; Poet-in-Residence and Assistant Professor, University of Delaware, Newark, 1960–64. Since 1964, Member of the English Department, and currently, Professor of English, Western Washington State College, Bellingham. Writer-in-Residence, University of Arkansas, Fayetteville, 1967. Poetry Editor, *Concerning Poetry*, Bellingham. Recipient: Indiana University School of Letters Fellowship, 1957; Bread Loaf Writers' Conference Scholarship, 1961; MacDowell Colony Fellowship, 1963. Address: 2820 Eldridge Street, Bellingham, Washington 98225, U.S.A.

PUBLICATIONS

Verse

Colonel Johnson's Ride and Other Poems. Detroit, Wayne State University Press, 1959.
Poems. Portland, Oregon, Portland Art Museum, 1959.
The Course: One, Two, Three, Now! Detroit, Wayne State University Press, 1966.
The Ventriloquists. Chicago, Swallow Press, 1975.

Recordings: *The Sound of Pacific Northwest Poetry*, with others, Washington State Poetry Foundation, 1968; *Robert Huff Reading at the Poetry Center of New York*, McGraw Hill, 1970.

Other

Activism in the Secondary Schools: Analysis and Recommendations, with Kenneth Erickson and George Benson. Eugene, University of Oregon Bureau of Educational Research, 1969.

Manuscript Collections: University of Kentucky, Lexington; Wayne State University, Detroit; Carnegie Library, Syracuse University, New York.

Critical Studies: Reviews by John Haislip, in *Northwest Review* (Eugene, Oregon), Summer 1967; by William Heyen, in *Poetry* (Chicago), February, 1968.

* * *

Robert Huff is a poet who generally writes in traditional forms; his mentors, as he himself makes clear in *The Course*, are Roethke, Frost and Yeats. His poetry in *The Course* is an autobiographical unfolding of his life from childhood through recent years; topics include finding his vocation as a poet, memories of relatives, enduring the personal and historical shocks life has to deal him. The book might be regarded, like Delmore Schwartz's great short story ("In Dreams Begin Responsibilities") from which it gets its subtitle ("One, Two, Three, Now!"), as a sort of autobiographical fiction in which the author, like the photographer of that story, tries to get a good fix, the proper artistic slant, on the fluid stuff of life. Like all of us, Huff is both involved and a spectator, human being and artist. Like the confessional poets, he is working close to the nerve ends, as in "Fixed":

These days I'm really sure I'm tranquilized
When any little signal says I'm ready,
Like this sweet thing teasing my inner ear
Into a dream of hearing rubber whisper

Along the humped blacktop back to that boy
Spoiled sick to death between one smart fool's ad
And this mean pen at a dead end hanging tight
Until the good pill works its trick of bells.

This is powerful poetry, as are other poems in *The Course*, including the title poem, "If It's an Owl," "How Not to Make a Model in a Bottle in a Bar in Ithaca," and especially "Getting Drunk with Daughter"; the last is surely one of the finest poems ever written by an American poet, as is "Rainbow" in Huff's earlier collection, *Colonel Johnson's Ride*. Huff's language is dense and heavily allusive; occasionally, as in "Previews," the allusions seem to come too fast and to be too personal to really work for the reader. On the whole, this isn't true.

Many of Huff's poems deal with loss, and the things, like drink and death, that accelerate our sense of loss. There is, however, a moving affirmation underlying this work, a suggestion of the spiritual gains that move in to fill the gaps. This is evident in "Rainbow" ("And I am glad/That I have wounded her, winged her heart,/And that she goes beyond my fathering"), and again in "Although I Remember the Sound":

Although I remember the sound
The young snag made when I felled it,
It was not noise or music mattered then.
Briefly, the tree was silent on the ground.

Of what it was that mattered I recall
Simply, among the chips and dust
And keener near the center of the cut,
The sweet, new smell which rose after the fall.

—Duane Ackerson

HUGHES, Glyn. British. Born in Middlewich, Cheshire, 25 May 1935. Educated at Altrincham Grammar School, Cheshire, 1946–52; Regional College of Art, Manchester, 1952–56, 1958–59, National Diploma in Design, 1956, Art Teacher's Diploma, 1959. Married 1) Wendy Slater in 1959 (marriage dissolved), one son; 2) Roya Liakopoulos in 1974. Art teacher in secondary schools in Lancashire and Yorkshire, 1956–65, and in H.M. Prison, Manchester, 1969–71; Extra-Mural Lecturer in Art, University of Manchester, 1971–73. Member of the Manchester Institute of Contemporary Arts Committee, 1966–69. Recipient: Welsh Arts Council Prize, 1969; Arts Council bursary, 1970, 1973. Agent: David Higham Associates Ltd., 5–8 Lower John Street, London W1R 4HA. Address: 28 Lower Millbank, Sowerby Bridge, Yorkshire HX6 3ED, England.

PUBLICATIONS

Verse

The Stanedge Bull and Other Poems. Manchester, Manchester Institute of Contemporary Arts, 1966.
Almost-Love Poems. Oxford, Sycamore Press, 1968.

Love on the Moor: Poems 1965–1968. Manchester, Phoenix Pamphlet Poets Press, 1968.
Neighbours: Poems 1965–1969. London, Macmillan, and Chester Springs, Pennsylvania, Dufour, 1970.
Presence. London, Poem-of-the-Month Club, 1971.
Towards the Sun: Poems/Photographs. Manchester, Phoenix Pamphlet Poets Press, 1971.
Rest the Poor Struggler: Poems 1969–71. London, Macmillan, 1972.
The Breast. Richmond, Surrey, Keepsake Press, 1973.
Alibis and Convictions. Sunderland, Ceolfrith, 1978.

Plays

Radio Plays: *The Yorkshirewomen*, 1978; *Dreamers*, 1979.

Novel

Where I Used to Play on the Green. London, Gollancz, 1980.

Other

Millstone Grit (on Yorkshire and Lancashire). London, Gollancz, 1975.
Fair Prospects: Journeys in Greece. London, Gollancz, 1976.

Critical Studies: by Jeremy Hooker, in *Poetry Wales* (Cardiff), Winter 1970; Eavan Boland, in *The Irish Times* (Dublin), 13 June 1970; John Fuller, in *The Listener* (London), 8 October 1970; Douglas Dunn, in *Encounter* (London), June 1973; W. L. Webb, in *The Guardian* (London), 10 April 1975; Peter Levi, in *The Guardian* (London), 5 August 1976; John Wain, in *The Observer* (London), 15 August 1976.

Glyn Hughes comments:

I spent my childhood in North Cheshire, and my passion was for long, solitary cycle-rides and walks when I often trespassed in that pastoral, rather 18th-century countryside, the secrets of which were guarded by farmers and gamekeepers. There is a description of this in my book *Millstone Grit*. The first poetry that I loved was by Wordsworth, Clare, William Barnes, Edward Thomas, D. H. Lawrence. I painted, and went to the College of Art in Manchester. I think I have learnt a great deal through my visual sense, and that my work was primarily affected by the visual arts, probably more than by poetry. I began to write mostly poetry after art school, when I tried to live off a quarter of an acre of land. My garden was a little paradise amongst the Lancashire, Yorkshire, and Cheshire industrial towns. And in most of the poems of my first book, *Neighbours*, I think I was trying to set vivid realisations of life in circumstances that denied that vividness – for example, in the story of a farmer's wife who sees the possibility of romantic love but who draws back into the familiar drudgery of farm life ("Love on the Moor").

My second book, *Rest the Poor Struggler*, was much affected by my personal restlessness during the period in which I wrote it. I afterwards broke off from writing much verse, and produced two prose books – *Millstone Grit*, which was about Lancashire and Yorkshire, and *Fair Prospects*, about Greece. Through 1977–78 I have been writing poems again, many of them connected with a prose book on 18th-century Yorkshire on which I have been at work.

* * *

One of the purposes of art is to bring order to the complexity of our experiences so that the truth behind them can be explored and revealed, and one aspect of this truth is to be discovered in the observation of man both against and as part of the terrain he inhabits. In the visual arts the Chinese can do this superbly; and so does Hardy, for example, in his novels where a sense of values and proportion is revealed which is a truth in itself. It is such an exploration of how the nature and quality of life are shaped and influenced by the environment (a sort of poetic ecology) which marks out Glyn Hughes's poems in *Love on the Moor* and in his first full collection, *Neighbours*. As Hughes said in his introduction to *Love on the Moor*: "My idealism about how people ought to live is implicit in every poem." This has been maintained in his later collections.

The terrain of Glyn Hughes's poems is one of those harsh, unrelenting inbred bits of country-side that still endure in 20th-century England, as in "Rock Bottom":

> the last place of rickets and bow legs
> aching from their grip of iced roads.
> Where the stranger's stared-at smile is unreturned,
> the stranger's house is shunned.

Even the joys of Spring sunshine are hard won ("Toward the Sun"):

> The fractured land bursts into grass.
> A farmer, woken by the sun and us,
> yaps like a terrier at the field's edge
> to defend his growth. We laugh,
> point, joke. Old walls glow
> like unripe apples as we cross his field
> to see the coltsfoot flowers.

Hughes's approach is as equally uncompromising and well suited to his subject matter. Unsentimental, it is not without compassion, as illustrated in "Love on the Moor" where the farmer's wife, stirred for a moment by the smile of a visiting salesman – "What might/have been that trickle of light/to the cinders of her heart/stopped at a scowling grate" – calls her man who shambles out "From his kitchen doze/fly open, feet in oven –/not that he'd ever lied/he would be different." Hughes's ability to touch on just the right nuance of feeling, in situations where the slightness of its manifestation belies its depth, is quite remarkable.

The life described is harsh; but hashness is not indulged for the sake of it, rather it is allied to the quality of life portrayed ("Neighbours"):

> We communicate
> in other ways: we poke the grate,
> and whether we rise early or rise late
> is boasted from the roof. Each broods alone
> with a false air of no-one at home.

It is a life withdrawn, pulled into itself – like a snail into its shell – in order to render it bearable. It is Glyn Hughes's achievement not only to have described his terrain with economy and accuracy, but to have expressed the spirit of it with a sensitivity which is masterly.

—John Cotton

HUGHES, Ted. British. Born in Mytholmroyd, Yorkshire, in 1930. Educated at Mexborough Grammar School, Yorkshire; Pembroke College, Cambridge, B.A. 1954, M.A. 1959. Served in the Royal Air Force, 2 years. Married 1) Sylvia Plath, *q.v.*, in 1956 (died, 1963); 2) Carol Orchard in 1970; one son and one daughter. Worked as rose gardener and night watchman; Reader for Rank Organization. Since 1965, Editor, with Daniel Weissbort, *Modern Poetry in Translation* magazine, London. Recipient: New York Poetry Center First Publication Award, 1957; Guinness Award, 1958; Guggenheim Fellowship, 1959; Maugham Award, 1960; Hawthornden Prize, 1961; City of Florence International Poetry Prize, 1969; Queen's Gold Medal for Poetry, 1974. O.B.E. (Officer, Order of the British Empire), 1977. Address: c/o Faber and Faber Ltd., 3 Queen Square, London WC1N 3AU, England.

PUBLICATIONS

Verse

The Hawk in the Rain. London, Faber, and New York, Harper, 1957.
Lupercal. London, Faber, and New York, Harper, 1960.
Selected Poems, with Thom Gunn. London, Faber, 1962.
The Burning of the Brothel. London, Turret, 1966.
Recklings. London, Turret, 1966.
Scapegoats and Rabies: A Poem in Five Parts. London, Poet and Printer, 1967.
Animal Poems. Crediton, Devon, Gilbertson, 1967.
Five Autumn Songs for Children's Voices. Crediton, Devon, Gilbertson, 1968.
The Martyrdom of Bishop Farrer. Crediton, Devon, Gilbertson, 1970.
A Crow Hymn. Frensham, Surrey, Sceptre Press, 1970.
A Few Crows. Exeter, Rougemont Press, 1970.
Crow: From the Life and Songs of the Crow. London, Faber, 1970; New York, Harper, 1971; revised edition, Faber, 1972.
Corgi Modern Poets in Focus 1, with others, edited by Dannie Abse. London, Corgi, 1971.
Crow Wakes. London, Poet and Printer, 1971.
Poems, with Ruth Fainlight and Alan Sillitoe. London, Rainbow Press, 1971.
Eat Crow. London, Rainbow Press, 1972.
Selected Poems 1957–1967. London, Faber, 1972; New York, Harper, 1974.
In the Little Girl's Angel Gaze. London, Steam Press, 1972.
Prometheus on His Crag: 21 Poems. London, Rainbow Press, 1973.
Spring, Summer, Autumn, Winter. London, Rainbow Press, 1973.
Cave Birds. London, Scolar Press, 1975; revised edition, London, Faber, 1978; as *Cave Birds: An Alchemical Cave Drama*, New York, Viking Press, 1979.
Eclipse. Knotting, Bedfordshire, Sceptre Press, 1976.
Earth-Moon. London, Rainbow Press, 1976.
Gaudete. London, Faber, and New York, Harper, 1977.
Sunstruck. Knotting, Bedfordshire, Sceptre Press, 1977.
Chiasmadon. Baltimore, Charles Seluzicki, 1977.
Moortown Elegies. London, Rainbow Press, 1978.
A Solstice. Knotting, Bedfordshire, Sceptre Press, 1978.
Orts. London, Rainbow Press, 1978.
Adam and the Sacred Nine. London, Rainbow Press, 1979.
Moortown. London, Faber, 1979.
Remains of Elmet. London, Rainbow Press, and New York, Harper, 1979.
All Around the Year. London, Murray, 1979.

Recording: *The Poetry and Voice of Ted Hughes*, Caedmon, 1977.

Plays

The Calm (produced Boston, 1961).
The Wound (broadcast, 1962). Included in *Wodwo*, 1967; revised edition (produced London, 1972).
Seneca's Oedipus (produced London, 1968; Los Angeles, 1973; New York, 1977). London, Faber, 1969; New York, Doubleday, 1972.
Beauty and the Beast (televised, 1968; produced London, 1971). Included in *The Coming of the King and Other Plays*, 1970.
The Coming of the King and Other Plays (includes *The Tiger's Bones*; *Beauty and the Beast*; *Sean, The Fool, The Devil and the Cats*). London, Faber, 1970; augmented edition, as *The Tiger's Bones and Other Plays for Children* (includes *Orpheus*), New York, Viking Press, 1973.
Sean, The Fool, The Devil and the Cats (produced London, 1971). Included in *The Coming of the King and Other Plays*, 1970.
The Coming of the King (televised, 1972). Included in *The Coming of the King and Other Plays*, 1970.
Orghast (produced Persepolis, 1971).
The Iron Man, adaptation of his own story (televised, 1972). London, Penguin, 1973.
The Story of Vasco, music by Gordon Crosse, adaptation of a play by Georges Schehade (produced London, 1974). London, Oxford University Press, 1974.

Radio Plays: *The House of Aries*, 1960; *A Houseful of Women*, 1961; *The Wound*, 1962; *Difficulties of a Bridegroom*, 1963; *Dogs*, 1964.

Television Plays: *Beauty and the Beast*, 1968; *The Coming of the King*, 1972; *The Iron Man*, 1972.

Other

Meet My Folks! (juvenile). London, Faber, 1961; Indianapolis, Bobbs Merrill, 1973.
The Earth-Owl and Other Moon-People (juvenile). London, Faber, 1963; New York, Atheneum, 1964.
How the Whale Became and Other Stories (juvenile). London, Faber, 1963; New York, Atheneum, 1964.
Nessie the Mannerless Monster (juvenile). London, Faber, and New York, Chilmark Press, 1964; as *Nessie the Monster*, Indianapolis, Bobbs Merrill, 1974.
Poetry in the Making (juvenile). London, Faber, 1965; as *Poetry Is*, New York, Doubleday, 1970.
Wodwo (miscellany). London, Faber, and New York, Harper, 1967.
The Iron Man: A Story in Five Nights (juvenile). London, Faber, 1968; as *The Iron Giant*, New York, Harper, 1968.
Season Songs (juvenile). New York, Viking Press, 1975; London, Faber, 1976.
Moon-Whales and Other Moon Poems (juvenile). New York, Viking Press, 1976.
Moon-Bells and Other Poems (juvenile). London, Chatto and Windus, 1978.

Editor, with Patricia Beer and Vernon Scannell, *New Poems 1962*. London, Hutchinson, 1962.
Editor, with Thom Gunn, *Five American Poets*. London, Faber, 1963.
Editor, *Here Today*. London, Hutchinson, 1963.
Editor, *Selected Poems*, by Keith Douglas. London, Faber, and New York, Chilmark Press, 1964.
Editor, *A Choice of Emily Dickinson's Verse*. London, Faber, 1971.
Editor, *A Choice of Shakespeare's Verse*. London, Faber, 1971; as *Poems: With Fairest Flowers While Summer Lasts: Poems from Shakespeare*, New York, Doubleday, 1971.

Editor, *Selected Poems*, by Yehuda Amichai. London, Penguin, 1971.

Editor, *Crossing the Water*, by Sylvia Plath. London, Faber, 1971; as *Crossing the Water: Transitional Poems*, New York, Harper, 1971.

Editor, and Translator with Janos Csokits, *Selected Poems*, by Janos Pilinszky. Manchester, Carcanet Press, 1976.

Editor, *Johnny Panic and the Bible of Dreams, and Other Prose Writings*, by Sylvia Plath. London, Faber, 1977; augmented edition, Faber, and New York, Harper, 1979.

Editor, and Translator with Yehuda Amichai, *Amen*, by Amichai. New York, Harper, and London, Oxford University Press, 1978.

* * *

Ted Hughes is a kind of 20th-century Aesop whose fables lack an explicit moral because it is precisely the unreflective spontaneity of his creatures, their "bullet and automatic/ Purpose," which constitutes their primary lesson for man. Yet his animals are highly ambiguous. As with "The Jaguar," "hurrying enraged/Through prison darkness after the drills of his eyes/On a short fierce fuse," their instinct can be limiting, self-destructive. Dead, as in "View of a Pig," they are "Just so much/A poundage of lard and pork" without dignity or grace. They exist only in the vital and luminous present. Though they may have the nine lives we are denied, may "outwit ... our nimblest wits" and hold us "in utter mock" ("Of Cats"), they lack that self-consciousness, that sense of "absence" and otherness which in poems such as "Gog" enable us to ponder our "origins" and, in "Cleopatra to the Asp," our end. Cleopatra, braving "the bright mirror" and "the devil in it," knows both herself and the death which defines her ("Now that I seek myself in a serpent/My smile is fatal"). In "Thrushes" man's exteriorizing of himself through work both excludes him from happiness ("Though he bends to be blent in the prayer," racked by "distracting devils") and guarantees the continuance of the human world:

With a man it is otherwise. Heroisms on horseback,
Outstripping his desk-diary at a broad desk,
Carving at a tiny ivory ornament
For years: his act worships itself.

The necessity of the diabolic, a Manichaean conviction that the "divine" has to be restored to its origins, humbled in the ecstasy of the brute, pervades Hughes's work. In "Logos" this is presented through a variation on Christian paradox – that God, as both Father and Son, can only conceive Himself through his own fleshly creature. Hughes gives this a sardonic twist, in a tone which is characteristic of his later poetry: "And within seconds the new-born baby is lamenting/That it ever lived –/God is a good fellow, but His mother's against Him."

In "Theology" and "Reveille" the serpent emerges as coeval with God, a parody sibling and demiurge who does the real work of creation by introducing all those negatives out of which "the ashes of the future," of the real world, are forged. These dark antinomies, hatred, fear, pain, greed, lust and death itself, are the terrain on which *Crow* constructs its creation myths. Atrocity, madness, rapine, are the very grounds of being for this grimly comic persona, who surveys a world torn by violence and entropy, where all hierarchies break down into destruction, and survival, sheer naked continuance in the knowledge of guilt and damnation, is the nearest one comes to hope:

So the survivors stayed.
And the earth and sky stayed.
Everything took the blame.

Not a leaf flinched, nobody smiled.

This outraged and defiant theology at times seems like a paganized version of the fire-and-brimstone puritanism Hughes writes of in his earlier poems. But now the apocalypse has already taken place. In the attempted film scenario, *Gaudete*, Hughes begins to salvage something from this wilderness. Drawing on an epigraph from Heraclitus which claims the dark underworld of Hades and the obscene songs and festivals of Dionysos as expressions of the same primeval force, the poem dramatises a cosmic dualism of man and nature, male and female, mind and body, self and other, in terms of a struggle between brothers who are of one flesh. Recreating ancient fertility myths, *Gaudete* has an Anglican clergyman abducted to "the other world" by elemental spirits who leave in his place a surrogate shaped from an oak log. This changeling "proceeds to interpret the job of ministering the Gospel of love in his own log-like way" by organizing the women of the parish into a sexual coven on whom he is to father the Messiah. But it is at this point that the real significance of Hughes's myth emerges. "While he applies himself to this," the Argument tells us, "he begins to feel a nostalgia for independent, ordinary human life, free of his peculiar destiny," and this forces the spirits to "cancel him," in an elaborate, ritualized sequence which has all Hughes's customary sadistic and compelling vividness. This nostalgia for a lost ordinariness seems to some extent to have been satisfied in his latest volume, *Remains of Elmet*, which is a loving return to Hughes's first world, the Yorkshire Pennines of his childhood. Recovered now only on the other side of outrage, the arcadian dream lies at the heart of Hughes's poetry, most poignantly summarized, perhaps, by one of the lyrics in *Gaudete*:

> The sea grieves all night long.
> The wall is past groaning.
> The field has given up –
> It can't care any more.
>
> Even the tree
> Waits like an old man
> Who has seen his whole family murdered.
>
> Horrible world
>
> Where I let in –
> As if for the first time –
> The untouched joy.

—Stan Smith

HUGO, Richard (Franklin). American. Born in Seattle, Washington, 12 December 1923. Educated at the University of Washington, Seattle, B.A. 1948, M.A. 1952. Served as a bombardier in the United States Army Air Corps during World War II. Worked for the Boeing Company, Seattle, 1951–63. Since 1964, Member of the English Department, and currently, Professor of English, University of Montana, Missoula. Since 1977, Editor, Yale Younger Poets series. Recipient: Theodore Roethke Prize (twice) and Helen Bullis Award (*Poetry Northwest*); Northwest Writers Award, 1966; Rockefeller Fellowship, 1967; Guggenheim Fellowship, 1977. Address: 2407 Wylie, Missoula, Montana 59801, U.S.A.

PUBLICATIONS

Verse

A Run of Jacks. Minneapolis, University of Minnesota Press, 1961.

Five Poets of the Pacific, with others, edited by Robin Skelton. Seattle, University of Washington Press, 1964.
Death of the Kapowsin Tavern. New York, Harcourt Brace, 1965.
Good Luck in Cracked Italian. Cleveland, World, 1969.
The Lady in Kicking Horse Reservoir. New York, Norton, 1973.
What Thou Lovest Well, Remains American. New York, Norton, 1975.
Rain Five Days and I Love It. Port Townsend, Washington, Graywolf Press, 1975.
31 Letters and 13 Dreams. New York, Norton, 1977.
Selected Poems. New York, Norton, 1979.

Other

The Triggering Town: Lectures and Essays on Poetry and Writing. New York, Norton, 1979.

Manuscript Collection: University of Montana, Missoula.

Richard Hugo comments:

Usually I find a poem is triggered by something, a small town or an abandoned house, that I feel others would ignore.

* * *

Central to Richard Hugo's poems is his concern for place and a rhythmic facility that repeatedly compresses the language, as in "Paestum":

> Word's gone back to the commercial world:
> if you sail that region, stop there.
> You will see our work and you can worship
> when the sun is flat and shafts of cream
> spray between our pillars from the sea.
> Odd dark birds weave through black and pink
> we planned. As for natives there,
> they farm, die often from some fever
> we have never seen, make love
> more frequently than we, and when we sweat
> erecting pillars, they laugh above their hoes.

Such linguistic intensity is risky: Hugo surely is not appealing to a "general audience," but to that reader who is willing to stay with the tight rhythms, demanding cadences, long enough that their dominance becomes incidental, at which point the content begins to assert itself.

In an introduction to the work of four American Indian Poets, Hugo wrote (in the *American Poetry Review*) "Indians come from a recently destroyed civilization ... the Indian sensibility is something like those of the 20th Century giants, especially Yeats and Eliot, who felt we inherited ruined worlds that, before they were ruined, gave man a sense of self-esteem, social unity, spiritual certainty and being at home on earth." Hugo's awareness of ruined civilizations is especially evident in *Good Luck in Cracked Italian*, a depressing travelogue, poems written upon his first visit to Italy since the war, when he was a flyer. Hugo's poems in this book express guilt and the sense that since the war many cities have become ugly through both physical and spiritual ruination. Neon and greed have absorbed a finer culture. Each poem finds new human metaphors to express this theme ("Napoli Again"):

I'll never think of virgin angels here.
Did I walk this street before,
protesting: I am kind. You switch the menu,
gyp me on the bill. Remember me? My wings?
The silver target and the silver bomb?
Take the extra coin. I only came
to see you living and the fountains run.

In *The Lady in Kicking Horse Reservoir* Hugo's language is typically dense and rhythmic, and his fascination with place remains strong, but the tone of the poems is lightened by the mirror he turns upon himself, and the growing variety of subjects for his poems. With them, Hugo totters and crashes from bar to bar in Scotland, Italy, Spain, and Montana, his home. In this book, Hugo portrays himself as a highly intemperate person: this apparent lack of control, which adds such an important dimension to his poems of place and occasion, nevertheless works at sharp odds with the rigid control he exercises over the language.

The Lady in Kicking Horse Reservoir includes two short poems which, by their appearance on the page with so much white space beneath then, announce themselves as a departure from the rest of his work. Here they are, "Somersby" and "Taneum Creek," complete:

Mercy Jesus Mercy
cries a stone
b 1586
d 1591
and Tennyson's brook
drones on

I don't come here after June when rattlesnakes
come out of caves and snore on stones
along the stream, though trout and trout remain
and I am keen to harm. Yellow bells have fangs
and jack pines rattle in the slightest wind.

Some of Hugo's finest poems are his most recent. Hugo's sense of humor, somewhat muted in earlier work, provides another dimension to his bauchy bar-hopping disgust. He seems more open, and the language, though still compressed, slackens just a bit. He writes, in "Letter to Logan from Milltown," that he has stopped drinking:

I'm in Milltown. You remember that bar, that beautiful bar
run by Harold Herndon where I pissed five years away
but pleasantly. And now I can't go in for fear
I'll fall sobbing to the floor. God, the ghosts in there.
The poems. Those honest people from the woods and mill.
What a relief that was from school, from that smelly
student-teacher crap and those dreary committees
where people actually say 'considering the lateness
of the hour.' Bad times too. That depressing summer
of '66 and that woman going – I've talked too often
about that. Now no bourbon to dissolve the tension,
to find self love in blurred fantasies, to find the charm
to ask a woman home. What happens to us, John?

Humor introduces optimism, the work brightens, and the reader hungers for more.

—Geof Hewitt

HUNT, Sam. New Zealander. Born in New Zealand, 4 July 1946. Recipient: Young Poets Award, 1971; Burns Fellowship, 1976; New Zealand Literary Fund Award, 1979; Agent: Chris Hampson, 129 Main Street, Greytown, New Zealand. Address: Deaths Corner, Pauatahanui, New Zealand.

PUBLICATIONS

Verse

Between Islands. Privately printed, 1964.
A Fat Flat Blues (When Morning Comes). Wellington, Bottle Press, 1969.
Selected Poems 1965–1969. Wellington, Wellington Training College, 1970.
A Song about Her. Wellington, Bottle Press, 1970.
Postcard of a Cabbage Tree. Wellington, Bottle Press, 1970.
Bracken Country. Wellington, Glenburvie Press, 1971.
Letter to Jerusalem. Wellington, Bottle Press, 1971.
Bottle Creek Blues. Wellington, Bottle Press, 1971.
Bottle Creek. Wellington, Alister Taylor, 1972.
Beware the Man. Wellington, Triple P Press, 1972.
Birth on Bottle Creek. Wellington, Triple P Press, 1972.
South into Winter. Wellington, Alister Taylor, 1973.
Roadsong Paekakariki. Wellington, Triple P Press, 1973.
Time to Ride. Wellington, Alister Taylor, 1975.
Drunkard's Garden. Wellington, Hampson Hunt, 1978.
Bow-Wows and Bones. Wellington, Hampson Hunt, 1979.
Sailor's Morning: 100 Selected Poems 1966–79. Wellington, Hampson Hunt, 1979.

Recording: *Beware the Man*, with Mammal.

Sam Hunt comments:

Lyric tradition.

* * *

Setting out in his late teens to make a living from his poetry, Sam Hunt found the role of rebel Romantic a rewarding profession. In his early thirties now, he remains a thoroughgoing professional, a Romantic poet still, but one whose themes and style have only lately begun to keep pace with his years.

He became known first for poetry that celebrated hard drinking and hard loving; for poems reflecting his brief teaching career as " 'the poem man,' showing the kids and teachers/games they can easily play with words": poems like "The shallow stream through the city floats," and "School Policy on Stickmen," as well as for some moving family poems ("Purple Balloon," "My Father Scything").

On the printed page many of his poems look flat and prosaic, and his syllabic lines lack the stressed delivery of the spoken voice. In fact of course they are written for performance, which explains why Sam Hunt has for over ten years been one of New Zealand's most popular performers of poetry, touring the country to read in schools, in jails, at Parliament, with rock-groups, on records, on radio, and on television.

Hunt's family poems now embrace his own family (Kristin, and their son Tom), and the larger gestures of his younger days have with this change lost some of their violence, if not their vigour. Writing less, perhaps, than before, he still continues to explore an increasing range of forms; as a poet who has always appealed to a youthful audience, he is coming now to deal with the passions of his middle years. I look forward to learning what he makes from this challenge.

—Alan Roddick

HUTCHINSON, (William Patrick Henry) Pearse. Irish. Born in Glasgow, Scotland, 16 February 1927. Educated at Christian Brothers School, Dublin; University College, Dublin; Salzburg Seminar in American Studies, 1952. Translator, International Labor Organization, Geneva, Switzerland, 1951–53; Drama Critic, Radio Eireann, 1957–61, and Telefis Eireann, 1968. Gregory Fellow, University of Leeds, 1971–73. Lived in Barcelona, 1954–57, 1961–67. Recipient: Butler Award, for Gaelic writing, 1969. Address: School of English, University of Leeds, Leeds LS2 9JT, England.

PUBLICATIONS

Verse

Tongue Without Hands. Dublin, Dolmen Press, 1963.
Faoistin Bhacach (Imperfect Confession). Dublin, Clóchomhar, 1968.
Expansions. Dublin, Dolmen Press, 1969.
Watching the Morning Grow. Dublin, Gallery Press, 1973.
The Frost Is All Over. Dublin, Gallery Press, 1975.

Other

Translator, *Poems*, by Josep Carner. Oxford, Dolphin, 1962.
Translator, *Friend Songs: Medieval Love-Songs from Galaico-Portuguese.* Dublin, New Writers Press, 1970.

Pearse Hutchinson comments:

Themes: Growing-up. Near-madness. Near-despair. The colour bar. The horrors of puritanical Irish Catholicity. Xenophobia and xenophilia. Travel (especially Spain). The built-in dangers (to truth) of all revolt. The difficulty, tenuous possibility, and utter necessity, of love. Friendship. Social injustice. God. Pity.

Forms: Free verse and strictly rhyming metres.

Influences: Hard to say – but I suppose Auden, Cavafy, the 17th century Gaelic poet Pierce Ferriter, and the contemporary Catalans Salvador Espriu (especially as to cadence) and Pere Quart.

* * *

Pearse Hutchinson has lived for seven years in Spain and his first volume consisted of verse translations from the work of a Catalan poet, Josep Carner. The effect of his experiences abroad can be plainly seen in his two collections of poems, *Tongue Without Hands*, and *Expansions.* His delight in Mediterranean colour is shown in "Málaga":

The scent of unseen jasmine on the warm night beach.

The tram along the sea road all the way from town
through its wide open sides drank unseen jasmine down.
Living was nothing all those nights but that strong flower.

Equally gay is the lyrical "Fireworks in Córdoba":

Cocks and coins and golden lupins,
parachutes and parasols and shawls,
pamplinas, maltrantos, and glass lawyers,
giant spermatozoa, dwarf giants,
greengage palms, and flying goldfish....

Hutchinson is one of the few Irish poets of today who writes of political oppression and bad social conditions. In "Questions" he describes attempts to suppress the use of the Catalan language by imprisonment and violence in a province: "Where one fine day, the gun smiles, and everyone rumours a thaw,/but next night, the gun kills, and all remember the law."

Hutchinson writes in various measures, including free verse. The poems which he has written on Irish life, both in city and country, are brisk, satiric and ironic, as in "Men's Mission":

Some Lenten evening sharp, at five to eight,
pick a suburban road both long and straight
and leading – which do not? – to a Catholic church:
you'll see, whisked out through every creaking gate,
men only, walking all at the same brisk rate.

"Fleadh Cheoil" (a popular musical festival) is a lively account of a country town *en fête*:

each other door in a mean twisting main street,
flute-player, fiddler and penny-whistler
concentrating on one sense only
such a wild elegance of energy gay and sad
few clouds of lust or vanity could form:
the mind kept cool, the heart kept warm;
therein the miracle, three days and nights
so many dances played and so much drinking done,
so many voices raised in singing but none
in anger nor any fist in harm.

From the manufacturing centres of England and Scotland, exiles "in flashy ties and frumpish hats" return for a few days to hear "an ancient music." "Friday in a Branch Post-Office" tells of the weekly queue of septuagenarians waiting patiently for their meagre pension and ends with an ironic comment: "We don't need a statue of Cú Chulainn/in our Branch Post-Office." The reference reminds us of Yeats's tribute to the statue of the ancient Irish hero in the General Post Office in Dublin.

—Austin Clarke

HUWS, Daniel. Welsh. Born in London, 28 June 1932. Educated at Llangefni County School; Bryanston School; Peterhouse, Cambridge. Address: Penrhyncoch, Dyfed, Wales.

PUBLICATIONS

Verse

Noth. London, Secker and Warburg, 1972.
Buzzards. Knotting, Bedfordshire, Sceptre Press, 1974.
From an Old Book of Riddles. Knotting, Bedfordshire, Sceptre Press, 1974.

Other

Editor, with Maldwyn Mills, *Fragments of an Early Fourteenth Century "Guy of Warwick."* Oxford, Blackwell, 1974.

* * *

As we may gather from lines like these – "We know our crags, our climbs, our controlled terrors,/As we know our own hearthsides. We manage nicely" – the manners of Daniel Huws's verse are staunch, a little downright, self-confident within known limits but respectful of what may lie beyond those limits. On the negative side, we have a propensity for a verse whose well-shaped laboriousness tends to leave flat unfelt material just where it is ("A Mountain Land," "The Knot," "For Better or Worse," "In the Cafe"), despite occasional jabs at over-resonant metaphor: "The world's womb has closed to the seed/Of vitality boxed in our dark hold."

On the other hand his very firmness of touch can serve him well in poems which try to encompass modes of awareness that are not so easily circumscribed. Through a crisp definition of what *can* be defined ("So much was certain ...") a space is cleared for the strangeness beyond immediate notice – see "Escape," "Waking in the Small Hours," "A Dawn." And there is a similar efficacy in some of his miniatures, achieved through the adroit placing of a single image, as in "The Oranges Won't Grow," "The Burden," or "The Piercing Wind." The latter is worth quoting, though it is a happy find somewhat to the side of the main line of his conscious endeavour:

Was there not wood to hew
And stone to quarry?
Had you not eyes?
Had you not hands?

The piercing wind questions.

Answerless,
I huddle behind children.

—Robin Fulton

IGNATOW, David. American. Born in Brooklyn, New York, 7 February 1914. Educated in Brooklyn public schools. Married Rose Graubart in 1938; one son, David, and one daughter, Yaedi. Worked as salesman, public relations writer, editor, shipyard handyman, newspaperman, and treasurer and president of a bindery firm. Instructor, New School for Social Research, New York, 1964–65; Visiting Lecturer, University of Kentucky, Lexington, 1965–66; Lecturer, University of Kansas, Lawrence, 1966–67, and Vassar College, Poughkeepsie, New York, 1967–69; Poet-in-Residence, York College, City University of New York, Jamaica, and Adjunct Professor, Columbia University, New York, 1969–76. Associate Editor, *American Scene* magazine, 1935–37; Literary Arts Editor, *New York Analytic* magazine, 1937; Co-Editor, *Beloit Poetry Journal*, Wisconsin, 1950–59; Poetry Editor, *The Nation*, New York, 1962–63. Since 1969, Consulting Editor, *Chelsea* magazine, New York. Editor-at-Large, *American Poetry Review*, Philadelphia, 1972–76. Recipient: National Institute of Arts and Letters Award, 1964; Guggenheim Fellowship, 1965, 1973; Shelley Memorial Award, 1966; Rockefeller Fellowship, 1968; National Endowment for the Arts grant, 1969; Bollingen Prize, 1977; Wallace Stevens Fellowship, 1977. Address: 155–01 90th Avenue, Jamaica, New York 11432, U.S.A.

PUBLICATIONS

Verse

Poems. Prairie City, Illinois, Decker Press, 1948.
The Gentle Weight Lifter. New York, Morris Gallery, 1955.
Say Pardon. Middletown, Connecticut, Wesleyan University Press, 1961.
Figures of the Human. Middletown, Connecticut, Wesleyan University Press, 1964.
Rescue the Dead. Middletown, Connecticut, Wesleyan University Press, 1968.
Earth Hard: Selected Poems. London, Rapp and Whiting, 1968.
Poems 1934–69. Middletown, Connecticut, Wesleyan University Press, 1970.
Facing the Tree. Chicago, Swallow Press, 1973.
The Notebooks of David Ignatow, edited by Ralph J. Mills, Jr. Chicago, Swallow Press, 1973.
Facing the Tree: New Poems. Boston, Little Brown, 1975.
Selected Poems, edited by Robert Bly. Middletown, Connecticut, Wesleyan University Press, 1975.
Tread the Dark: New Poems. Boston, Little Brown, 1978.
Open Between Us, edited by Ralph J. Mills, Jr. Ann Arbor, University of Michigan Press, 1979.

Recording: *Today's Poets 3*, with others, Folkways.

Other

Editor, *Political Poetry.* New York, Chelsea, 1960.
Editor, *Walt Whitman: A Centennial Celebration.* Beloit, Wisconsin, Beloit College, 1963.
Editor, *William Carlos Williams: A Memorial Chapbook.* Beloit, Wisconsin, Beloit College, 1963.

Bibliography: *A Checklist of Writings* by Robert A. Smith, Storrs, University of Connecticut Library, 1966; in *Tennessee Poetry Journal* (Martin), Winter 1970.

Manuscript Collections: Lockwood Memorial Library, State University of New York, Buffalo; Olin Library, Wesleyan University, Middletown, Connecticut.

Critical Studies: by Edwin Honig, in *New Mexico Quarterly* (Albuquerque), Spring 1951; by James Wright, in *Chelsea 12* (New York), September 1962; by Victor Contoski, in *University Review* (Kansas City), Spring 1968; by Robert Bly in *New Leader* (New York), 22 May 1968; by Paul Zweig, in *The Sixties* (Madison, Minnesota), Summer 1968; *The Suspect in Poetry* by James Dickey, New York, Doubleday, 1971; "Earth Hard: The Poetry of David Ignatow" by Ralph J. Mills, Jr., in *North Shore Review* (Chicago), Winter 1973; "Circumscriptions: The Poetry of David Ignatow" by Jerome Mazzaro, in *Salmagundi* (New York), Spring 1973; "American Poetry in and out of the Cave" by James Moore, in *The Lamp in the Spine* (St. Paul, Minnesota), Spring 1973.

David Ignatow comments:

(1970) I suppose it may be said that my early poems originated in the William Carlos Williams school of hard core realism literally presented, free of the conventional rhyme and/or rhythm patterns. After my second book I found myself deeply interested in the school of surrealism.

I am constantly aware of the absolute and imminent tragedy of men in and among themselves through every level of their existence, socially, politically, privately, in love, family, business affairs. I deal with the entire range of experience given to each man in his life, as I seek through this apprehension of tragedy the saving grace, the cause for living in the act of serving tragedy itself. I dance with Yeats and Williams on the graves of the dead, as I would wish it done to me, in pleasure and homage to the dead.

My form is usually very free, content and/or idea determining it, while I use every conceivable device traditional and new for the proper realization of the poem. My private life, lives of my friends, lives of important men and women, historical events, scientific developments, the works of mythologies, philosophical treatises, the poems and novels of friends and interesting writers, all feed me with materials for poems. But most particularly, it is often history as it is being enacted today from which I draw a sense of the life of the times, with frequent reference to my life in that context. I search for *now*, using the method of introspection and dream in tandem with objective events or things.

In my poetry I have tried especially to make my life a metaphor for existence in these times, to the extent that I experience it. Each poem ultimately is designed with the purpose in mind, no matter the subject. It is for this reason that more than several critics have noticed the metaphysical basis to my work, Randall Jarrell for example, in a brief review many years ago. While I seek for the meaning to the experience, at the same time I am allowing the poem as it takes shape also to contribute its understanding of the experience. Language plays a decisive role in my projection of the experience though never losing sight of the objective event itself.

However, frequently in recent years I have presented completely fictitious events, given them an objective reality so to speak, as I explore the possibilities of the surrealist poem through this device. I have been led to surrealism by internal as well as external events, in a search for absolute understanding of the nature of relationships among us. These have suggested the need for a surrealistic approach. I don't know though whether I wish to continue in that phase, as I discover in myself a delight in projecting a sort of dream quality in the poem, as if it were from here that we take our final shape.

After having written some of the most bitter, terrifying dead end poems, with no place else to go from there, I conceive of the necessity for re-establishing relationships with myself and with the world on still another level, while life goes on. To quote in full from a recent paragraph I submitted for a recording of my poems by Scholastic Records, Inc.: "To me, the act of writing is a gesture of independence. I write with the thought of gaining control over my materials and over myself. With this achieved, I feel free once more to return to the balance and poise I prefer in my life, providing the poem of that moment has released me from the pressure, to my satisfaction. That does not happen often or long enough, as I am continually examining and re-examining my relations with the world and with myself. The poems that get written are what they are, poems; but I suppose, put all together, serve as an index to my way of life. I am very glad that this life within and without is so restless and disturbing to me since I get so much pleasure in writing about it."

(1974) I would only add that much of my early and perhaps later poetry was in response to the pessimism and withdrawal in the poetry of T. S. Eliot. I took my cue in the manner with which to respond from William Carlos Williams, but this is to acknowledge that Eliot played a deeply important role in shaping much of my thinking on my life and the world around me. In other words, I found myself as a kind of mediator between Eliot and Williams, giving respect to the qualities of both and, out of the necessities in my life, shaping my own poems out of an identity with Eliot's own problems while seeking for a resolution in the energy and freedom manifest in Williams' work.

* * *

David Ignatow's earliest poems suggest a view of life that is essentially tragic, and his latest poems do not substantially alter that view. "There must be something wrong with me/ wanting to keep going through/the endless griefs, as if I had iron/bowels and a stone head," he begins a poem in *Facing the Tree*. Accepting this fate has brought him, after 40 years of writing, a kind of peace, a modicum of joy. And in "The Pleasure," he has to admit his enjoyment in watching himself growing older: "I am authentic, I say./I belong with the others."

In the midst of personal and political crises, caught in an "insane world," he affirms, like Whitman, the essential value of life. In "For John Berryman," a tribute to a fellow poet, a suicide, Ignatow says:

> It is depressing to live
> but to kill myself in protest
> is to assume there is something
> to life withheld from me, yet
> who withholds it?...
>   I wish, though,
> I had known sooner, to have
> helped you go on living,
> as I do, half a suicide,
> the need defended by the other half
> that thinks to live in that knowledge
> is praiseworthy.

Contending with a half-mad world is obviously no easy matter. It takes, as Ignatow's poems suggest, all the intelligence and sense of humor one can muster, and calls forth a wide range of moods to accommodate the surrealistic world of day-to-day experience. The range from tragedy to comedy to surrealism, each conveyed with equal authority and skill, makes Ignatow's work demanding. The poems move beyond the conscious mind to that splendid, yet mysterious unconscious world – the night life, the dream-and-shadow world frequently ignored by less ambitious and less talented writers. Plunging below the surface, he brings together the known and unknown world, objective and subjective experience, in a particularly effective way. In the manner of William Carlos Williams, he lets the insight find its own language, set its own pattern, and move in any direction it wants.

Yet there is control, too. Unlike many so-called surrealist writers, Ignatow never lets the complicated and paradoxical vision overwhelm him. In poems such as " Say Pardon" and "Rescue the Dead," particularly, the simple, sparse, and colloquial language fulfills its primary responsibility: communicating thought and feeling as economically, precisely, and beautifully as possible. Ignatow belongs, as Robert Bly has said, to "the William Carlos Williams school, of hard core realism, lyrically presented." These skills, among others, have won him a place, in recent years, among the principal voices of his generation.

—Michael True

IRBY, Kenneth. American. Born in Bowie, Texas, 18 November 1936. Educated at the University of Kansas, Lawrence, B.A. 1958; Harvard University, Cambridge, Massachusetts, M.A. 1960; University of California, Berkeley, M.L.S. 1968. Served in the United States Army, 1960–62. Formerly, reviewer of books and records for *Kulchur* magazine, New York. Address: 1614 Russell, Berkeley, California 94703, U.S.A.

PUBLICATIONS

Verse

The Roadrunner. Placitas, New Mexico, Duende Press, 1964.
Kansas-New Mexico. Lawrence, Kansas, Dialogue Press, 1965.
Movements/Sequences. Placitas, New Mexico, Duende Press, 1965.
The Flower of Having Passed Through Paradise in a Dream: Poems 1967. Annandale-on-Hudson, New York, Matter, 1968.
Relation: Poems 1965–1966. Los Angeles, Black Sparrow Press, 1970.
To Max Douglas. Privately printed 1971.
The Snow Queen. San Francisco, Turtle Island, 1973.
Archipelago. Willits, California, Tuumba Press, 1976.
Catalpa: Poems 1968–73. Lawrence, Kansas, Tansy Press, 1976.
In Excelsis Borealis. N.p., White Creek Press, 1976.
Some Etudes. Privately printed, 1978.

Kenneth Irby comments:

My closest associates (if that makes a "school") are Robert Kelly, Larry Goodell, Clayton Eshleman.

My concern *seems* to have been muchly with *pastoral* verse – that is, poetry that *feeds* us – drawing on a common Great Plains Mysticism in the face of the landscape, that the landscape, *especially*, demands of us. But the concern of *poetry* is not finally at all limited.

* * *

Kenneth Irby's *Catalpa*, his recent large collection, sets his earlier work in clearer relief, and, though he still has few readers, he begins to emerge as a central American poet, as the collection of essays on his work in *Credences* eloquently testifies.

Irby is a poet of geography, and his work, from *Kansas-New Mexico* on, progressively maps the North American continent as a simultaneously literal and visionary space. He is perhaps our only pastoral poet. As he writes: "The pastoral, as a mode of poetry (out of eight Sir Philip Sidney lists), seemed to me particularly of two concerns: a calmness, a quietude of the whole being, derived from all attentions and awareness; and a feeling of great closeness with the vegetation lived among – an ecological calm – poetry that feeds us (*pascere*), not just that tends the sheep." The conviction of pastoral poetry, he goes on to say, is "that the landscape demands us, and reveals us."

To Max Douglas probably offers the new reader the easiest access to Irby's somwhat demanding work. As one might expect of a pastoral poet, his mood is frequently elegiac, and this is a sequence of poems addressed to a promising young poet who died of an overdose of heroin. In it, Irby draws the most important line of his map: the Missouri-Kansas border. It is the center of the spatial coordinates which appear more fully in *Catalpa*: there the Civil War began; there the culture based on corn and timber gives way to the culture based on wheat and steel. For Irby, who grew up in Ft. Scott, Kansas, it is the heartland, the center around which the continent turns. His tribute to a poet whose home was St. Joseph, Missouri, just on the *other* side of the border, calls the tension of the region into play.

Catalpa (etymologically, "head with wings") is the vision of the entire continent. Most of the individual poems are dense structures of minute bits of geographic, historic, and personal information, typical of the earlier work. The vision is largely a function of the book's collage-like structure. In "Jed Smith and the Way," he writes:

You can never get there
the same way twice, and you always
have to get there, this is the way
North and South
the way East and West
this is the Secret History
of the Continent.

In the secret history, the East is associated with the ego and the superego, the accumulated past, parents, and a paradise lost (see "Tufts"). The West is the location of the unconscious, and, when western knowledge comes, it is powerful and social but frequently also disorganizing and dangerous (see "Berkeley"). The North, the province of the Snow Queen as she appears in the last section of *Catalpa*, is like the West, a place of vision, but northern knowledge is cold, clear, isolated and isolating. The artist of the North is associated with Tennyson's Lady of Shallot. The South, though it is not fully explored in *Catalpa*, is sensuality (Irby's most southerly poem is "Delius," in *To Max Douglas*). Only in the center, in the heartland and in the heart, is there some hope of bringing immediacy, clarity, sensuality, and ego into satisfying and useful balance.

A small collection of poems which Irby published in 1978, *Some Etudes*, suggests that his work is undergoing a significant change. These tiny elegant poems are articulations of possibilities suggested by the inherent qualities of words themselves. Irby's work deserves much more attention than it has received.

—Don Byrd

IRELAND, Kevin (Mark). New Zealander. Born in Auckland, 18 July 1933. Married. Founding Editor, *Mate* magazine, Auckland. Address: 2 Earnoch Avenue, Takapuna, Auckland, New Zealand; or, The Studio, 223A, Randolph Avenue, London W9 1NL, England.

PUBLICATIONS

Verse

Face to Face. Christchurch, Pegasus Press, 1963.
Educating the Body. Christchurch, Caxton Press, 1968.
A Letter from Amsterdam. London, Amphadesma Press, 1972.
Orchids Hummingbirds and Other Poems. Auckland, Auckland University Press–Oxford University Press 1974.
A Grammar of Dreams. Wellington, Te Wiata Press, 1975.
Literary Cartoons. Auckland, Island-Hurricane Press, 1978.

* * *

"Thin men/write gaunt poems/and each word/sticks out/like a rib," wrote Kevin Ireland in "Deposition": an accurate picture of some of his work at that time. Whatever the shape of the poet, however, his poems have not always been so spare; indeed his latest work is often quite "plump."

Seeking a congenial form for his witty, whimsical conceits and explorations of metaphors, Ireland adopted, early on, a strict discipline of short lines of one to three feet, with complex rhyme-schemes and patterns of words or phrases recurring from stanza to stanza. After some ten years of such strictness he turned in *A Letter from Amsterdam* to a more open and relaxed style, which he has continued in the love-poems of *Orchids Hummingbirds*, with their wry and affectionate humour, their clear-sightedness ("A Guide to Perfection"):

you complain of your body
and make out a detailed list
of what you can call your worst deformities
you start at your toes and proceed
to ankles knees bottom stomach
breast lungs jaw eyes hair skin

I reply that this is vanity ...
low self-esteem is not aware
of how to turn this way and that
to show ill-favours quite so prettily....

In *A Grammar of Dreams* Ireland gives rein to exuberantly inventive fantasy with nine poems that celebrate youth and love, yet with an acknowledgment of age and liking, as in "Caroline as Scientist":

and then you smiled and waited
until in his slow-thinking time at last
he reached and turned you half around
and kissed your throat
where it had loosened up and aged
like his: and demonstrated in one certain act
not love as image or concoction
but as an attestation of true person
passion time: confirming his undying love
by evidence of mortal flesh

—Alan Roddick

IREMONGER, Valentin. Irish. Born in Dublin, 14 February 1918. Educated at Christian Brothers School, Dublin; Colaiste Mhuire; Abbey Theatre School of Acting, Dublin. Married Sheila Manning in 1948; one son and four daughters. Associated with the Abbey Theatre Company, Dublin, 1939–40, and the Gate Theatre, Dublin, 1942–44. Entered the Irish Foreign Service in 1946: Third Secretary, 1946–48; Private Secretary to the Foreign Minister, 1948–50; First Secretary, successively in the Political, Consular, and Economic Divisions, 1950–55; First Secretary, 1956–59, and Counsellor, 1959–64; Ambassador to Sweden, Norway and Finland, 1964–68; Ambassador to India, 1968–73. Since 1973, Irish Ambassador to Luxembourg. Poetry Editor, *Envoy* magazine, Dublin, 1949–51. Recipient:

AE Memorial Award, 1945. Address: Department of Foreign Affairs, Iveagh House, Dublin 2, Ireland.

PUBLICATIONS

Verse

On the Barricades, with Robert Greacen and Bruce Williamson. Dublin, New Frontiers Press, 1944.
Reservations. Dublin, Envoy, and London, Macmillan, 1950.
Horan's Field and Other Reservations. Dublin, Dolmen Press, 1972.

Play

Wrap Up My Green Jacket (broadcast, 1947; produced Belfast, 1952). Published in *The Bell* (Dublin), 1949.

Other

Editor, with Robert Greacen, *Contemporary Irish Poetry*. London, Faber, 1949.
Editor, *Irish Short Stories*. London, Faber, 1960.

Translator, *The Hard Road to Klondike*, by Micheal MacGabhann. London, Routledge, 1962.
Translator, *An Irish Navvy: The Diary of an Exile*, by Donall MacAmlaigh. London, Routledge, 1966.

* * *

Valentin Iremonger was one of the most interesting and original of Irish poets to emerge during the 1940's. In Ireland this was not an especially stimulating period for literature. The death of W. B. Yeats in 1939 had left the field more open to the younger generation, but censorship was still rigorous and continued to make Irish writers feel outsiders in their own society. It was appropriate that the title of Iremonger's first publication in book form, *On the Barricades*, should suggest a determination to challenge both tradition and the establishment. His early poems, though not revolutionary in the broader context of English and American writing of the period, brought a contemporary urban note into Irish poetry for the first time. A deep concern with the alien position of the poet in society was also apparent. Several of the earlier poems develop this theme. Others explore a sense of disorientation within the individual himself. At times each situation is seen to reflect the other and the two themes interconnect.

Iremonger was quick to achieve an authoritative and individual style. There are occasional suggestions of Patrick Kavanagh, F. R. Higgins and Auden in the earlier work, but right from the start the writing was forthright and incisive; the imagery and diction, though concrete, were vital and vivid. Later Iremonger began to cultivate a greater richness and wrote poems carried forward by a rhapsodic sweep which rarely faltered. A change in subject-matter accompanied this stylistic development. Iremonger's interest in the position of the poet vis-à-vis society was replaced by a concern for the position of man in relation to time. Poems like "Clear View in Summer," "Elegy for the Commencement of Winter," "Lackendarragh," and "Poem in the Depths of Summer" are passionate celebrations of living in which the passion derives from an awareness of impermanence and impending loss. They are filled with the kind of tragic joy which brims over in some of Dylan Thomas's poems, notably "Poems on His Birthday." Iremonger's elegies do not reach quite such a high level but they are splendid achievements.

Two other important poems among Iremonger's later work are "Hector" and "Icarus." In "Hector" he describes the situation of the Trojan hero before his final battle with Achilles, and uses it to evoke a fatalistic attitude towards death. "Icarus" relates the predicament of the legendary flier to the situation of the modern aviator. It is one of his most imaginative and skilful poems, and has appeared widely in anthologies.

Iremonger's output has apparently dwindled since the publication of *Reservations* in 1950. The greater part of *Horan's Field and Other Reservations* consists of poems from the earlier collection. Several of the most recent poems look back with acute regret to the past out of a context of present frustration. The long poem "Horan's Field" provides a vehement expression of this feeling:

> We were famous people in our day
> And to all and to the boy
> I feel now holding this pen
> I send my reminiscent love.
> Marise, Marise, the world is at us all.
> It falls upon us like a Himalayan peak
> And we are all trapped, no hope at all ...

More and more for Iremonger the writing of a poem has become an act which places a portion of the poet's imaginative life within a "reservation" fencing it safely away from the destructive pressures of everyday living.

Though primarily a lyric poet, Iremonger has also written some plays. The most highly regarded of these is *Wrap Up My Green Jacket*, a verse play based on the tragedy of Robert Emmet. The most romantic of Ireland's revolutionaries, Emmet was executed after leading an abortive rising against the British in 1803. The powerful rhetoric of the play both faithfully reflects and implicitly criticises the histrionic but courageous character of a patriot who was to be followed by the men of 1916 in making the sacrificial, heroic gesture of a foredoomed revolt.

—Rivers Carew

JACKSON, Alan. Scottish. Born in Liverpool, Lancashire, 6 September 1938. Educated in Edinburgh schools; Royal High School; Edinburgh University, 1956–59, 1964–65. Married Margaret Dickson in 1963; two sons, Kevin and Yorick. Laborer; trainee psychiatric nurse, 1959–60; Secretary, Scottish Committee of 100, 1961–62. Since 1965, Founding Director, Kevin Press, Edinburgh; since 1967, Director, Live Readings, Scotland. Recipient: Scottish Arts Council bursary, 1967, 1978.

PUBLICATIONS

Verse

Under Water Wedding. Privately printed, 1961.
Sixpenny Poems. Privately printed, 1962.
Well Ye Ken Noo. Privately printed, 1963.
All Fall Down. Edinburgh, Kevin Press, 1965.
The Worstest Beast. Edinburgh, Kevin Press, 1967.
Penguin Modern Poets 12, with Jeff Nuttall and William Wantling. London, Penguin, 1968.
The Grim Wayfarer. London, Fulcrum Press, 1969.
Idiots Are Freelance. Dyce, Aberdeenshire, Rainbow, 1973.

Alan Jackson comments:

I regard the poet as the Blakean "bard" who turns the eye in, tries to bring the dark to light.

Themes: family (particularly the mother), sex (particularly as against Christian morality and also searching my own perversities), death of religion and the absence of myth, man as a pernicious life-form.

Verse forms: many, longer ones often rhyming, and always close to speech, but interest in longer unrhymed rhythms and eluding grammar increasing; dozens of very short unrhymed highly compressed poems. Poems often kept for over a year, then to be worked and re-worked. Clarity desired but not immediate understanding.

Main influence, Jung; can see few limits to his importance. Main admiration: Norman Mailer. Nietzsche somewhere between the two. I try not to be influenced by poets, though I try to absorb lessons about writing. Finally, a man should not know what is characteristic of him.

* * *

Alan Jackson's work has subtle sympathy, ironic wit, technical dexterity and satirical verve, although other pieces express a raucous violence shrieking in concert with the fashionable taste for what Robert Lowell has called "raw, huge, blood-dripping gobbets of unreasoned experience" – as in "Fraulein," where a "shocking" tale of rape followed by syphilis appears merely sensational because presented in complete isolation from the rest of the environment. When he resists the temptation to drop his pants in public, however, his verse shows that although he is still young he has already attained individual achievement as a symbolist-cum-satirist, with such bitter brevities as "Loss" where, using a thin Scots close to urban speech, he turns conventional flower imagery to most unconventional ends in revealing the all too frequent fate of beauty in the Scottish climate. Most often, however, he writes in English, and in at least one poem, "Was a Shame," the influence of Blake is as evident in style as in content, theme and feeling. But elsewhere his work reveals an original stylist with a highly personal voice, capable of a stimulating variety of themes and forms, from the epigrammatic wit of "Young Politician" ("What a lovely moon./And it's in the constituency too") to the controlled passion of rage and sorrow in the couplets picturing man as "the worstest beast" and to the sensuous richness and strangeness of the poem called "3 1/g 4" (three little green quarters) which explores the mysteries of time and fate in terms of superstitions of science and science-fiction.

—Alexander Scott

JACOB, Paul. Indian. Born in Kerala, 27 April 1940. Educated at St. Columba's School, New Delhi; Madras Christian College; St. Stephen's College, Delhi. Member of the Staff, *The Century* magazine, New Delhi, 1963–65. Since 1966, Member of the Editorial Staff. *Enact* Magazine, Delhi. Lives in New Delhi, India.

PUBLICATIONS

Verse

Sonnets. Calcutta, Writers Workshop, 1968.

Alter-Sonnets. Calcutta, Writers Workshop, 1969.
Swedish Exercises. Calcutta, Writers Workshop, 1973.

* * *

Paul Jacob's poetry seems to be a continuous search for the perfect form. His first two volumes consisted of exercises in sonnet form, written in a taut, controlled style. In his recent volume, *Swedish Exercises*, he experiments with the Italian sestina consisting of six six-line stanzas. He has tried his hand at limericks and at present he is writing English poems in the Urdu *ghazal* form.

This concern with form is a challenge Paul Jacob sets for himself and it suits his oblique suggestive style. Though he never writes poetry of plain statement, his poems, rather than appearing obscure, give the impression of almost total communicability at a non-logical level:

> Anywhere there are children is no flaw, but youth
> Must come out of darkness, newspaperish tar,
> Forever celluloid, soundtrack, should warm up
> As you review gulmohar, amaltaz, summerspring to truth.

(Gulmohar and amaltaz are orange and yellow flowering trees that blossom in India in the late spring and summer.)

Paul Jacob uses words skilfully and sensitively, but sometimes also a little self-consciously as in his favourite antithetical devices like "A lifelong sleep, a deathshort sleeplessness," or "My bed shall not make others, others shall make my bed." The central theme of all his poems is self-exploration, but the frame of reference ranges from love to religion: "May every true prayer be repetition/Vain like a baby. May prayer itself be whole/Over this weekend the earth shall burn for you."

—Meenakshi Mukherjee

JACOBSEN, Josephine. American. Born in Coburg, Ontario, 19 August 1908. Educated privately, and at Roland Park Country School, Baltimore, 1915–18. Married Eric Jacobsen in 1932; one son. Poetry Consultant, 1971–73, and since 1973, Honorary Consultant in American Letters, Library of Congress, Washington, D.C. Vice-President, Poetry Society of America, 1979. Recipient: MacDowell Colony grant, 1979. Agent: McIntosh and Otis, 18 East 41st Street, New York, New York 10017. Address: 220 Stony Ford Road, Baltimore, Maryland 21210, U.S.A.

PUBLICATIONS

Verse

Let Each Man Remember. Dallas, Kaleidograph Press, 1940.
For the Unlost. Baltimore, Contemporary Poetry, 1946.
The Human Climate: New Poems. Baltimore, Contemporary Poetry, 1953.
The Animal Inside: Poems. Athens, Ohio University Press, 1966.
The Shade-Seller: New and Selected Poems. New York, Doubleday, 1974.

Short Stories

A Walk with Raschid and Other Stories. Winston-Salem, North Carolina, Jackpine Press, 1978.

Other

The Testament of Samuel Beckett, with William Randolph Mueller. New York, Hill and Wang, 1964; London, Faber, 1966.
Ionesco and Genet: Playwrights of Silence, with William Randolph Mueller. New York, Hill and Wang, 1968.
From Anne to Marianne: Some American Women Poets (lecture). Washington, D.C., Library of Congress, 1973.
The Instant of Knowing (lecture). Washington, D.C., Library of Congress, 1974.

Manuscript Collection: Mugar Memorial Library, Boston University.

Critical Studies: "Poetry and Preaching" by Hugh Kerr, in *Theology Today* (Princeton, New Jersey), October 1964; Richard Ohmann, in *Winconsin Studies in Contemporary Literature* (Madison), Autumn 1965; "The Matter and Manner of Beckett" by David Helsa, in *Christian Scholar* (New York), Winter 1965; "Enduring Saturday" by Anthony Burgess, in *Spectator* (London), 29 April 1966; "The Human Condition," in *Irish Press* (Dublin), 11 June 1966; "The Essential Q," in *Times Literary Supplement* (London), 30 June 1966; John Logan, in *Epoch* (Ithaca, New York), Autumn 1966; "Art in Transition" by Laurence Lieberman, in *Poetry* (Chicago), March 1967; Rosemary Dee, in *Commonweal* (New York), 20 December 1968.

Josephine Jacobsen comments:

I don't really value very highly "statements" from a poet in regard to her own work. I can perhaps best introduce my own poetry by saying what I have not done, rather than defining what I have done. I have not involved my work with any clique, school, or other group: I have tried not to force any poem into an overall concept of "how I write poetry" when it should be left to create organically its own individual style; I have not been content to repeat what I have already accomplished or to establish any stance which would limit the flexibility of discovery. I have not confused technical innovation, however desirable, with poetic originality or intensity. I have not utilized poetry as a social or political lever. I have not conceded that any subject matter, any vocabulary, any approach or any form is in itself necessarily unsuitable to the uses of poetry. I have not tried to establish a reputation as poet on any grounds but those of my poetry.

* * *

"Terrestrial, we learned the accurate measure/Of sharpness is the brevity of touch," wrote Josephine Jacobsen in her early volume, *For the Unlost*. Capturing the brief but significant moment which reveals the essence of a subject has remained her forte. "Precise in its very act," the dance is an apt and frequent metophor in poems celebrating our fleeting, earthly pleasures; its ephemeral beauty a figure for the "art of our mortality." She sizes up the existence by striking to the core. There she finds the shining boy that preceded the greedy, frightened man and the integral marble which shadows the hypocritical monument. In "The Big Hotel Closed Yesterday for the Winter" short scenes depicting rich snobs and selfish, superannuated virgins veer toward the sentimental, only to be cut dead by a savage wit, worthy of Dorothy Parker, which strips away the veneer. In poems written in time of war, she speaks directly; ever clear-eyed, she has strength to view the horrors of the "ugly feast," though her voice catches at the poignancy of suffering and loss. "*At dreadful high noon*," she writes in "Lines to a Poet," "*You may speak only to our heart,/Our honor and our need.*"

Continuing her explorations in *The Human Climate*, she discovers more darkness at the center, and here her lines give up their meaning less easily. Hunger for experience and "utter freedom" leads to momentary confusion: "The blinded eye will have all color." Urgency, even wildness, marks poems in which personae strive for release from "deadly limit." Lost souls are caught in psychological binds, playing games lovers play. The young man travels to the brink of suicide; the old man treads the customary path of penury and loneliness. Here, despite the vivid pointillism, the poet's design can be obscure: details are precise, but the outline remains blurred. In "Variations on Variety" the object is clearer, as the vaudeville show becomes a paradigm of our transitory nature. In "April Asylum" old ladies like "docile sentient dead" watch Technicolor films, sacraments which bring them "lonely and together" a blessing in the empty morning hours. Probing ever more inward, Jacobsen seeks in *The Animal Inside* the mysterious soul which cannot be caught or tamed, but which, "Seen, can be loved." Brilliant flashes of color, flickering images of shadows, water and fire entice the reader into the marvelous poetic world but often leave him in a cul-de-sac. She examines the dying revolutionary, the deaf-mutes isolated in a ball-park, the ancient lady exhumed with her curious case, but maintains dramatic distance from them; despite analysis they remain inscrutable. The persona views religious spectacles, a ritual Indian sacrifice, a haunting All Soul's Day litany, from an original perspective; the Son of Man is seen in the tropical swamp, and Peter is called "crucifixion's clown." The poet seems, however, more in sympathy with wildlife. She reads chaos in a dessicated starfish and finds identity in the awkwardness and hurt of a fiddler crab. "Almost nothing concerns me but communication," she writes, and if here she sometimes meets with failure, the adventure of these poems is worth the risk.

—Joseph Parisi

JAFFIN, David. American. Born in New York City, 14 September 1937. Educated at the University of Michigan, Ann Arbor (Hopwood Award, 1956; Oreon E. Scott Award), 1955–56; New York University (Penfield Fellow), 1956–66, B.A. 1959 (Phi Beta Kappa), M.A. 1961, Ph.D. in history 1966. Married Rosemarie Jaffin in 1961; two sons. Graduate Assistant, New York University, 1961–62; Lecturer in European History, University of Maryland European Division, Germany, 1966–69. Studied theology at the University of Tübingen, 1971–74: Vicar, Tübingen, 1974–75; Minister, Magstadt, 1975–78. Since 1978, Minister, Malmsheim. Address: Ev. Pfarramt, Schöckengasse 35, 7253 Malmsheim, Germany.

PUBLICATIONS

Verse

Conformed to Stone. New York, Abelard Schuman, 1968; London, Abelard Schuman, 1970
Emptied Spaces. London, Abelard Schuman, 1972.
Opened. Sheffield, Headlands, 1973.
Late March. Rushden, Northamptonshire, Sceptre Press, 1973.
At the Gate. New Zealand, Edge Press, 1974.
Of. Knotting, Bedfordshire, Sceptre Press, 1974.

As One. New Rochelle, New York, Elizabeth Press, 1975.
In the Glass of Winter. London, Abelard Schuman, 1975.
Changes. Godalming, Surrey, Words, 1975.
The Half of a Circle. New Rochelle, New York, Elizabeth Press, 1977.
Space Of. New Rochelle, New York, Elizabeth Press, 1978.
Perceptions. New Rochelle, New York, Elizabeth Press, 1979.

Critical Studies: in *Library Journal* (New York), 15 September 1968, and 1 September 1977; *Yorkshire Post* (Leeds), 9 September 1972; *Bristol Evening Post*, 9 November 1972; by Edward Lucie-Smith, in *Emptied Spaces*, 1972, and *In the Glass of Winter*, 1975; *Workshop New Poetry 18* (London), 1973; *Samphire* (Bromsgrove, Worcestershire), ii, 4, 1973; *Poet Lore* (Boston), Summer 1974.

David Jaffin comments:

My art is one of intense compression, both of form and meaning. I seek to create a world at once visually alive, tangible/explicit and yet abstract, inward and restrained. I feel the poetic process as an intensification of consciousness. I break through/break down those words inspired in my mind (revising over and over again while I'm writing), to derive their intrinsic form and relation. Jacques Lipchitz told me that my poems were sculpted as from stone. There must never be a word too many, no decoration, ornament, rhetoric. The craft involves the unity of image, sound, sense, tone and idea. The poem itself is a state of being, not a theme to be developed with the "poetic trimmings." The poem simply is, is not about. But craftsmanship itself is only the prerequisite for the spiritual process. A "state of being" means for me a personal and new definition of reality. All meaningful art must be this. I often describe this via tangible objects, thereby actualizing the senses. My aesthetic moves on two levels, the one being physically alive, so vivid as to be almost touched, and yet when these poems succeed they create an absolute stillness and control. I am told my poems gain by constant re-reading. I always present them at least twice at public readings.

* * *

David Jaffin's *Conformed to Stone* and *Emptied Spaces* have a sculptural quality; the poems are spare, chiselled down to the essentials. The title of each is appropriate; the first collection contains more people among its statuary: "Creatures of Stone," "The Idiot," "Woodcarver," "Self Portrait"; the second collection moves away from human models to still lifes more remote from human life, though the artistic (and particularly, the sculptural) motif remains. In the latter book, Jaffin seems to be hollowing out his previous forms, trying for a sort of negative space to complement the positive space the previous book occupied; things defined by their absense, as in "Door Partly Opened":

You let the light
    in,
Angled-off,

Your hands closed as a
Shadow hanging there

You let the light
    in
As far as your face
    could allow.

Poems like this remind one of French poets like Valéry, with their sense of moments of time mysteriously arrested; the poet seems to be inviting us to study some scene closely and at the same time denying total entrance. The poems are restrained, dignified, pictorial, superficially simple, but turning frequently on the ambiguities inherent in language; reading them is bracing, like stepping through ice that was not as thick as we thought. The poem above, like a number of others, turns on such ambiguities, and on the suggestion, beneath the ice of the poem, of deeper, philosophical ambiguities. The observed person in this poem is the one who has opened the door and shed light on the speaker, and yet, the light becomes merely a mask for the observed, himself no more than a shadow silhouette. The last two lines suggest a deliberate act of will as well as physical obstruction of the light, and remind us of the different disguises we wear; that openness and shedding light on things, illuminating others, can be a mask too. Such subtleties make David Jaffin's poetry rewarding.

—Duane Ackerson

JAY, Peter (Anthony Charles). British. Born in Chester, Cheshire, 24 May 1945. Educated at Lancing College, Sussex; Lincoln College, Oxford (Exhibitioner; Newdigate Prize, 1965). Editor, with John Aczel, *New Measure* magazine, Oxford, 1965–69. Currently, Free-lance writer, and Publisher, Anvil Press Poetry, London. Assistant Director of Poetry International, London, 1969; taught in the writing program, University of Iowa, Iowa City, 1975–76. Recipient: Rockefeller grant, 1968. Address: c/o Anvil Press Poetry, 69 King George Street, London SE10 8PX, England.

PUBLICATIONS

Verse

Lifelines. Edinburgh, Satis, 1977.

Other

Expostulations of Teddy Hogge, with *The Wooden Muse, Part One*, by W. G. Shepherd. London, Antidote Press, 1970.

Editor, *The Greek Anthology and Other Ancient Greek Epigrams.* London, Allen Lane, and New York, Oxford University Press, 1973.

Translator, *Adonis and Venus.* Santa Barbara, California, Peter Whigham, 1968.
Translator, *The Song of Songs.* London, Anvil Press Poetry, 1975.
Translator, with Petru Popescu, *The Still Unborn about the Dead*, by Nichita Stanescu. London, Anvil Press Poetry, and Iowa City, International Writing Program, 1975.
Translator, with Peter Whigham, *The Poems of Meleager.* London, Anvil Press Poetry, 1975.
Translator, with Virgil Nemoianu, *Alibi*, by Ştefan Aug. Doinaş. London, Anvil Press Poetry, and Iowa City, International Writing Program, 1975.
Translator, with Anthony Rudolf and Petru Popescu, *Boxes, Stairs, and Whistle Time*, by Popescu. Knotting, Bedfordshire, Omphalos Press, 1975.

Translator, with Carol Telford and Petru Popescu, *Burial of the Vine*, by Popescu. London, Barrie and Jenkins, 1975.
Translator, *Crater*, by János Pilinszky. London, Anvil Press Poetry, 1978.

* * *

Unnecessarily shy about publishing his own poetry, Peter Jay is the outstanding translator of his generation, and certainly the finest to emerge since Michael Hamburger. His versions of the Romanian poet George Bacovia are the most brilliant of all renderings into English since Hamburger's Hölderlin. Jay is also a brilliant parodist, exposing the weaknesses of his victims with deadly geniality (and very funnily indeed). He is an extremely serious, fastidious poet, and none of his original poetry is less than presentable, which is unusual in an age of low standards. His difficulty lies in discovering his own style, and some of the poems reflect too keenly on his awareness of and sensitivity to many differing manners (Italian, ancient Greek, German, Romanian). Pound, much admired by him, may not have been a useful influence: like that of so many poets who have been dazzled by Pound, Jay's natural manner in no way resembles his; this seems, as in other cases, to have worked as an inhibitory influence. Jay is very stylish, only occasionally lapsing (in earlier poems) into a kind of hermeticism that does not work in English poetry. So far he has said less than he has expressed; yet one feels that he wishes for greater explicitness. But his descriptions of his moods already have a distinction that marks him out as one of the few truly serious poets of his generation – as in "The Gallery":

> There are days when the mind grazes,
> circling itself like an answer
> lazily guessing its question.
> Slowly they assemble, one
> by one: some whose faces
> shine with the smile of certain
> gestures long recalled....

—Martin Seymour-Smith

JENNINGS, Elizabeth (Joan). British. Born in Boston, Lincolnshire, 18 July 1926. Educated at Oxford High School; St. Anne's College, Oxford, M.A. in English language and literature. Assistant, Oxford City Library, 1950–58; Reader, Chatto and Windus Ltd., publishers, London, 1958–60. Since 1961, Free Lance Writer. Recipient: Arts Council award, 1953, bursary, 1965, 1968, grant, 1972; Maugham Award, 1956; Richard Hillary Memorial Prize, 1966. Agent: David Higham Associates Ltd., 5–8 Lower John Street, London W1R 4HA. Address: 11 Winchester Road, Oxford OX2 6NA, England.

PUBLICATONS

Verse

(*Poems*). Oxford, Fantasy Press, 1953.
A Way of Looking. London, Deutsch, 1955; New York, Rinehart, 1956.
The Child and the Seashell. San Francisco, Poems in Folio, 1957.

A Sense of the World. London, Deutsch, 1958; New York, Rinehart, 1959.
Song for a Birth or a Death and Other Poems. London, Deutsch, 1961; Philadelphia, Dufour, 1962.
Penguin Modern Poets 1, with Lawrence Durrell and R. S. Thomas. London, Penguin, 1962.
Recoveries. London, Deutsch, and Philadelphia, Dufour, 1964.
The Mind Has Mountains. London, Macmillan, and New York, St. Martin's Press, 1966.
The Secret Brother and Other Poems for Children. London, Macmillan, and New York, St. Martin's Press, 1966.
Collected Poems 1967. London, Macmillan, and Chester Springs, Pennsylvania, Dufour, 1967.
The Animals' Arrival. London, Macmillan, and Chester Springs, Pennsylvania, Dufour, 1969.
Lucidities. London, Macmillan, 1970.
Hurt. London, Poem-of-the-Month Club, 1970.
Folio, with others. Frensham, Surrey, Sceptre Press, 1971.
Relationships. London, Macmillan, 1972.
Growing-Points: New Poems. Manchester, Carcanet Press, 1975.
Consequently I Rejoice. Manchester, Carcanet Press, 1977.
After the Arc (juvenile). London, Oxford University Press, 1978.
Moments of Grace: New Poems. Manchester, Carcanet Press, 1979.
Selected Poems. Manchester, Carcanet Press, 1979.

Other

Let's Have Some Poetry. London, Museum Press, 1960.
Every Changing Shape (religion and poetry). London, Deutsch, 1961.
Poetry Today 1957–60. London, Longman, 1961.
Frost. Edinburgh, Oliver and Boyd, 1964; New York, Barnes and Noble, 1966.
Christianity and Poetry. London, Burns Oates, 1965; as *Christian Poetry*, New York, Hawthorn, 1965.
Seven Men of Vision: An Appreciation. London, Vision Press, 1976.

Editor, with Dannie Abse and Stephen Spender, *New Poems 1956.* London, Joseph, 1956.
Editor, *The Batsford Book of Children's Verse.* London, Batsford, 1958.
Editor, *An Anthology of Modern Verse 1940–1960.* London, Methuen, 1961.
Editor, *A Choice of Christina Rossetti's Verse.* London, Faber, 1970.

Translator, *The Sonnets of Michelangelo.* London, Folio Society, 1961; revised edition, London, Allison and Busby, 1969; New York, Doubleday, 1970.

Manuscript Collections: Oxford City Library; University of Washington, Seattle.

Critical Study: by Margaret Byers, in *British Poetry since 1960*, edited by Michael Schmidt and Grevel Lindop, Oxford, Carcanet Press, 1972.

Elizabeth Jennings comments:

I do not much care for writing about my own poems. The main reason for this is, I believe, that it makes one too self-conscious. However, I would like to say that I am always interested in what I am writing at present and hope to write in the future. I like to experiment with different poetic forms, and, at this time, I am constantly seeking for more and more clarity. I am working on a series of prose poems about paintings (painting is my second favourite art), and a series of poems, in various forms and from several viewpoints, on religious themes. I have also been writing poems about craftsmen and various aspects of nature, particularly skyscapes. For me, poetry is always a search for order. I started writing at the age of thirteen and wrote only one 4-line poem I now wish to preserve from childhood. My Roman Catholic religion and my poems are the most important things in my life.

* * *

Elizabeth Jennings was the only woman to be included in Robert Conquest's anthology *New Lines*; and she shares with the other so-called "Movement" poets a "coolness which is worked for" – to quote her own description of a Chinese painter – in her lucid diction, use of traditional metres, and the keen and subtle intelligence in her exploration of ideas.

Her absorption in the processes of "art with its largesse and its own restraint" has led to many poems which attempt to enter the experience of fellow-writers and artists in other media: the sculptor, the composer, the dancer, and painters ranging in time from Rembrandt to Rouault, Botticelli to Bonnard, Cézanne and – recurringly – van Gogh. Other conditions of life which especially interest her are childhood and age. Her portraits of children are based on personal recollections of a timeless peace and safety from adult ambiguities, but still more of the distresses which "built a compassion that I need to share"; and she writes about the feelings of the very old with a tender intuitive sympathy. Her insight into contemplative states of being has also resulted in various intense imaginative projections into the lives of such personalities as St. John of the Cross, St. Teresa of Avila, St. Catherine, and St. Augustine; of the Virgin in fine poems like "The Annunciation" and "The Visitation," and even into the loneliness and human conflicts of Christ. These prose poems and dramatic monologues, with her translations of Michelangelo's sonnets and Rimbaud, her classical imitations in the manner of the Greek Anthology, and an increasingly adventurous freedom and flexibility in her rhythms and verse-patterns, demonstrate the versatility of her gifts.

Italy, where she has travelled extensively, is the background for a number of poems which epitomize her great difference from the rest of the "Movement" group. A profound religious conviction colours her vision of life and permeates all her work. As a foreigner at confession in an unknown tongue amid the gold and mosaics, at a Roman mass, or at Assisi "where silence is so wide you hear it," she communicates the quietism most vividly realized in the magnificent "San Paolo Fuori le Mura," where the cool stillness of stone engenders an interior calm which is "a kind of coming home." In *Song for a Birth or a Death* the mystic's apprehensions of reality are as eloquently articulated as anywhere in contemporary poetry. "Notes for a Book of Hours" conjures the raptness of the visionary and his struggle for the elusive language capable of expressing the numinous. "A World of Light" re-creates "A mood the senses cannot touch or damage,/A sense of peace beyond the breathing word," which grows in "a dazzling dark" as reminiscent of Vaughan as later poems like "Winter Night" and "Let there be dark for us to contemplate."

This poet is, however, equally and bitterly familiar with another kind of darkness – the non-fruitful one of doubt, desolation, and despair: the abysses of Hopkins's "winter world" implied in her title *The Mind Has Mountains*. Recurrent breakdowns led to spells in mental hospital; and the guilt, bewilderment, frustrations of unfulfilled love and "very absolute of fear" which culminated in a state "clothed in confusion" are conveyed with poignant directness in many poems of her middle period. Yet this agonized experience of "climates of terror," and compassionate, yet unself-pitying vulnerability to the sufferings of her fellow-patients which are so movingly recorded led to a recognition that "Perhaps to know no desert is a lack": of the necessity of "The painful breaking/Which brings to birth."

The recovery chronicled in *Growing-Points* and *Consequently I Rejoice* shows a full re-possession of her lost capacity for contemplative stillness and receptivity to moments of mystical revelation, and a greater maturity of acceptance. The notable broadening of range of her choice of subject, a more objective awareness of the contemporary world and problems and predicaments other than her own, are matched by a new assurance and virtuosity in the handling of language. Her words describing a disabled countryman apply with equal aptness to Elizabeth Jennings's own impressive testimony and courage and spiritual resilience: "gentleness/Concealing toughness," which takes "pain as birds take buffets from/The wind, then gather strength and fly and fly."

—Margaret Willy

JEROME, Judson. American. Born in Tulsa, Oklahoma, 8 February 1927. Educated at the University of Oklahoma, Norman, 1943–45; University of Chicago, M.A. 1950; Ohio State University, Columbus, Ph.D. 1955. Married Martha-Jane Pierce in 1948; one son and four daughters. Professor of Literature, Antioch College, Yellow Springs, Ohio, 1953–72; Chairman of Humanities Division, College of Virgin Islands, St. Thomas, 1963–65; Director of the Center for Documentary Arts, Antioch Columbia, Columbia, Maryland, 1969–70. Since 1961, Columnist ("Poetry: How and Why"), *Writer's Digest*, Cincinnati. Since 1972, Free-lance Writer. Recipient: Huntington Hartford Fellowship, 1959; Amy Lowell Traveling Fellowship, 1960. Address: Downhill Farm, Hancock, Maryland 21750, U.S.A.

PUBLICATIONS

Verse

Light in the West. Francestown, New Hampshire, Golden Quill Press, 1962.
The Ocean's Warning to the Skin Diver and Other Love Poems. Point Richmond, California, Crown Point Press, 1964.
Serenade. Point Richmond, California, Crown Point Press, 1968.
I Never Saw.... Chicago, Whitman Press, 1974.
The Village. Hancock, Maryland, Trunk Press, 1976.
Public Domain. Hancock, Maryland, Trunk Press, 1977.

Plays

Winter in Eden (produced Yellow Springs, Ohio, 1955). Included in *Plays for an Imaginary Theatre*, 1970.
The Wandering Jew (produced Yellow Springs, Ohio, 1963).
Candle in the Straw (produced St. Paul, Minnesota, 1963). Included in *Plays for an Imaginary Theatre*, 1970.
The Glass Mountain (produced St. Thomas, Virgin Islands, 1964). Included in *Plays for an Imaginary Theatre*, 1970.
Plays for an Imaginary Theatre (includes *Winter in Eden*, *Candle in the Straw*, *The Glass Mountain*, *Drums*). Urbana, University of Illinois Press, 1970.

Novel

The Fell of Dark. Boston, Houghton Mifflin, 1966.

Other

The Poet and the Poem. Cincinnati, Writer's Digest, 1963; revised edition, 1974, 1979.

Poetry: Premeditated Art. Boston, Houghton Mifflin, 1968.
Culture Out of Anarchy: The Reconstruction of American Higher Learning. New York, Herder, 1970.
Families of Eden: Communes and the New Anarchism. New York, Seabury Press, 1974; London, Thames and Hudson, 1975.
Publishing Poetry. Hancock, Maryland, Trunk Press, 1976.

Manuscript Collection: Boston University Library.

Judson Jerome comments:

I believe that a new culture is transforming Western Civilization, and that poets have supplied and are supplying its vision, which essentially is a shift from a mechanistic to an organic world view. By leaving institutions behind and retiring with my family to a rural commune, I am hoping to become a more active participant in this ongoing revolution of consciousness.

My monthly column in *Writer's Digest* continues to be my letter to the world.

* * *

In his poetry, fiction and essays, Judson Jerome has been examining contemporary American life in a way intended to define possibilities of cultural order. Poetry he has described as a vital, liberating illusion: "It is less ecstasy or rebellion or confession than a steady voice that tells a lie so completely that hearts are moved and people live by it." This conception of poetry has moral and aesthetic roots. It involves acknowledgement of radical human fault: "Acting/is honest, the courage to accept/our false condition." And it emphasizes the powers of traditional poetic techniques. Jerome has located tradition in American poetry in the writings of Emily Dickinson, E. A. Robinson and Robert Frost; and his own attention to technique is part of his attempt to clarify experience. In "Cages," for example, he works against meter to convey the limits of human freedom: "dear child with touching hands,/night, day, age, youth, our veins,/our very ribs, are cage."

This interest in technique and in the magical aspect of poetry is behind his *Plays for an Imaginary Theatre*, a collection of related plays, essays and lyrics. The mixed format is peculiarly appropriate to Jerome's talents as poet and critic; and the plays themselves are lyric extravaganzas, less plays of character than plays of ideas, of the possibilities of reconciling a radical individualism and the competing claims of communal order.

At times in the plays, as in poetry, the verbal facility, the deliberate sense of artifice, approaches a kind of self-indulgence. At its best, however, Jerome's writings, with their enthusiasm and discipline, provide humane, clarifying insight.

—Jerry Paris

JOHNSON, Louis. New Zealander. Born in Wellington, 27 September 1924. Educated at Wellington Teachers' Training College. Has three children. School teacher, 1951–54; Editor, *New Zealand Parent and Child* magazine, 1955–59; Assistant Editor, Department of Education School Publications Branch, Wellington, 1963–68; Officer in Charge, Department of Information Bureau of Literature, Port Moresby, Papua New Guinea, 1968–69. Founding Editor, *Numbers* magazine, Wellington, 1954–60. Editor, New Zealand Broadcasting Corporation Poetry programme, 1964, and "Column Comment" television programme, 1968. Since 1970, Free-lance Writer. Secretary, New Zealand P.E.N., 1954–59. Recipient:

New Zealand Literary Fund grants. Address: 6/11A Redan Street, St. Kilda, Melbourne, Victoria 3182, Australia.

PUBLICATIONS

Verse

Stanza and Scene. Wellington, Handcraft Press, 1945.
The Sun among the Ruins. Christchurch, Pegasus Press, 1951.
Roughshod among the Lilies. Christchurch, Pegasus Press, 1952.
Poems Unpleasant, with Anton Vogt and James K. Baxter. Christchurch, Pegasus Press, 1952.
Two Poems: News of Molly Bloom, The Passionate Man and the Casual Man. Christchurch, Pegasus Press, 1955.
The Dark Glass. Wellington, Handcraft Press, 1955.
New Worlds for Old. Wellington, Capricorn Press, 1957.
The Night Shift: Poems on Aspects of Love, with others. Wellington, Capricorn Press, 1957.
Bread and a Pension: Selected Poems. Christchurch, Pegasus Press, 1964.
Land Like a Lizard: New Guinea Poems. Brisbane, Jacaranda Press, 1970.
Onion. Dunedin, Caveman Press, 1972.
Fires and Patterns. Brisbane, Jacaranda Press, 1975.

Other

Editor, *New Zealand Poetry Yearbook 1–11.* Wellington, Reed, 3 vols., 1951–54; Christchurch, Pegasus Press, 8 vols., 1955–64.

Critical Studies: *A Way of Saying* by Kendrick Smithyman, Auckland, Collins, 1965; *Aspects of Poetry in New Zealand* by James K. Baxter, Christchurch, Caxton Press, 1967.

Louis Johnson comments:

I'm a sort of personal-liberal-existentialist of an atheistic inclination.

When I was beginning to write verse, in the early 1940's, New Zealand was just "coming of age" in the art through the works of Mason, Curnow, Glover, Fairburn, etc., and it seemed to me that their "nationalism" was rather overdone, limited, and parochial, especially since my own earlier poetic interests were people like Auden, Yeats, Pound, men whose vision appeared unlimited by the back fence. But from the "broad view" I turned to personal experience, the "known and felt" thing rather than the "New Zealand thing" as prescribed by Curnow, probing the field of human relationships – especially between men and women, the way we live here and now – and became known as "the poet of subtopia."

I have been concerned, in my work, with the way in which people have grown up in, and been shaped by, our small, restricted community; a great deal of the work has been written on themes of childhood and growth, the nature of reality and the manner of our illusions; there is also a strong social strain, almost political at times, in some of it.

My work has gone through several different stages of method – from an overdressed abstractionism to, recently, a direct colloquial "language as she is spoke" approach. Suddenly, in middle-age, I have found my feet as a poet in the mysteries of love; of a new volume in the process of being put together, my friend and colleague James K. Baxter said: "I didn't think any Kiwi would write love poetry like it. It's the best we've got."

* * *

"At the centre of it there is always a mystery," Louis Johnson wrote of the act which is a poem. "Poetry is an act of faith," he insisted at another time. "To the poet, nothing is unbelievable." The central mystery to which he refers is the imagination much as Coleridge conceived of it; the faith is faith in the potential power of imagination, as it may be for a child to whom "possibility is actual." The nominally real must be illusion; conversely, a lot of living may be disillusioning. Life is often an offence to the man able to imagine. To be adult is to be deprived, given over to a reality which endorses the probable at the expense of the possible.

Although sometimes Johnson would seem to want to appear a social realist, opinions of the kind above are at the heart of his view. He rejected a popular doctrine of the poet's obligation to respect "the reality prior to the poem" because the reality foreseen was thought to be too narrowly understood. The common impression of Johnson's vigorous, copious, ostensibly worldly poems is of writing at odds with his announced principles. His most evident engagement is with the external (or even extrinsic) show of life in a cultural province, whether urban, suburban or rural, which implies an accentuating of what is contemporary and thus peculiar because particular. He has been freely and loudly criticized because his sense of contemporary and of what he has referred to as formalism persuades him into practices which strike readers as wilful or gratuitously *farouche*. At his best he is a formalist. Disillusioned, he is a disenchanted romantic. At his most effectively contemporary – in which role he came near to founding a School – he is highly persuasive. At such times he is closest to the tradition, whether he is being a propagandist, a persuader, or a polemicist.

(1980) Ten years after the remarks above were written may they still hold? In 1968 Louis Johnson quit New Zealand, first for Papua New Guinea, later for southeastern Australia, and for a new wife as well. *Land Like a Lizard*, his Papua New Guinea book, works around the new wife and the new life, the moment which domestically is all promise, which publicly is confirmed in "fruit of a season/But cannot be counted except in the presence of love." The idyllic is open to qualification. In reacting to colonialism in place of a cultural provincialism Johnson began to work out for himself his own understanding of "the reality prior to the poem," to examine the conflict of the reality of primitive people or primal emotions with their own pasts and with a present which many were willing to enter, at expense to their innocence. He found a travesty of suburbia, and quit the land like a lizard. The New Guinea poems of *Fires and Patterns* are postscripts to an increasing distaste, partly distaste for himself, "Chewing at my disease," postscripts to a staging point in a new life. The book also contains poems of the closing off of his life in New Zealand. The last of these is an elegy for James K. Baxter which at its end talks of "that final terror and burden – yourself" which is in part a burden of capicity for love. "Love is my burden too" Johnson said when he first got to New Guinea. It is a theme which recurs. Sardonically, it is the part of the white man's burden, but it is also in part the burden of history, of Emma Bovary in a tradition of one kind and of Queen Emma Coe in another kind, of the primitives and of the colonials. It affords in complex and distinct ways evidence of Johnson's reconstituting "the reality prior to the poem" more successfully than the overt reflections on history to be found in his six pieces on Captain Cook's voyage of 1769.

—Kendrick Smithyman

JOHNSON, Ronald. American. Born in Ashland, Kansas, 25 November 1935. Educated at Columbia University, New York, B.A. 1960. Served in the United States Army, 1954–56. Poet-in-Residence, University of Kentucky, Lexington, 1971, and University of Washington, Seattle, 1972. Recipient: Inez Boulton Award (*Poetry*, Chicago), 1964; National Endowment for the Arts grant, 1969, 1974; Anderson Fellowship, 1972. Address: 4041 18th Street, San Francisco, California 94114, U.S.A.

Publications

Verse

A Line of Poetry, A Row of Trees. Highlands, North Carolina, Jargon, 1964.
Assorted Jungles: Rousseau. San Francisco, Auerhahn Press, 1966.
Gorse/Goose/Rose and Other Poems. Bloomington, Indiana University Fine Arts Department, 1966.
Sunflowers. Woodchester, Gloucestershire, John Furnival, 1966.
Io and the Ox-Eye Daisy. Dunsyre, Lanarkshire, Wild Hawthorn Press, 1966.
The Book of the Green Man. New York, Norton, and London, Longman, 1967.
The Round Earth on Flat Paper. Urbana, Illinois, Finial Press, 1968.
Reading 1 and *2.* Urbana, Illinois, Finial Press, 2 vols., 1968.
Valley of the Many-Colored Grasses. New York, Norton, 1969.
Balloons for Moonless Nights. Urbana, Illinois, Finial Press, 1969.
The Spirit Walks, The Rocks Will Talk. Highlands, North Carolina, Jargon, 1969.
Songs of the Earth. San Francisco, Grabhorn Hoyem, 1970.
Maze/Mane/Wane. Cambridge, Massachusetts, Pomegranate Press, 1973.
Eyes and Objects. Highlands, North Carolina, Jargon, 1976.
RADI OS I–IV. San Francisco, Sand Dollar, 1977.

Other

The Aficionado's Southwestern Cooking. Albuquerque, University of New Mexico Press, 1968.

Translator, *Sports and Divertissments*, by Erik Satie. Edinburgh, Wild Hawthorn Press, 1965; Urbana, Illinois, Finial Press, 1969.

Manuscript Collection: University of Kansas, Lawrence.

Critical Studies: in *Vort 9* (Bloomington, Indiana).

Ronald Johnson comments:

(1970) I have been primarily influenced by the Black Mountain "school" of poetry – i.e., Charles Olson out of Ezra Pound, Louis Zukofsky and Williams.

To see the world in a grain of sand, to see the *word* in a grain of sand, this is where the poem begins. Thoreau questioned: "Who placed us with eyes between a microscopic and a telescopic world?" All is built from this position – a solid construct in the apparently invisible, exact words illuminating the ineffable. A grain of sand if looked at long enough waxes first as glowing, then as large as a moon. The architects tell us that large and small are a matter of placement, and that galactic and atomic are simply humming-birds within humming-birds, etc. To write a poem is to begin with words, and is it not where word becomes wor(l)d the primal poem exists? And it is only an arc from there to *whirled* and "the push of numerous humming-birds from a superior bush."

(1974) After ten years of writing and walking out there in the trees, I have found, as William Blake knew all along, that the trees are in the head.

(1980) I am at present at work on a three-book work titled ARK.

* * *

Ronald Johnson's poems are filled with the energy of discovery: he observes, hypothesizes, and moves on to new discovery. There is no form that he regularly employs;

rather, his poems create their own form, the length and the placement of the line dictated by no tradition. Occasionally, as in "Sunflowers," which balances on a center axis, suggesting concrete poetry, the visual appeal of the poem detracts from the text. As always, Johnson surrounds his words with air:

The sky is apple-green.
A sower casts his seed
in a dark field,
while the sun, become pale as silver,
encircles
his head.

Johnson's work frequently incorporates the poetry of earlier writers, to the extent that only the most sophisticated reader will know the source: perhaps this does not matter. Surely Johnson considers these borrowings and their sources important, and the long poem *The Book of the Green Man* has five pages of notes which credit a wide range of authors. *Valley of the Many-Colored Grasses* devotes two pages to "Emerson, On Goethe." There is the paragraph as Emerson wrote it, followed by Johnson's version, which adheres faithfully to the text of the original. Where Emerson begins: "Nature will be reported. All things are engaged in writing their history ...," Johnson has it:

NATURE WILL BE

reported.
All things
are engaged in writing their history.

This is either a beautiful compliment or an insult of sorts.

One could debate endlessly the pros and cons of this poetry, which is not academic but surely research-oriented. I prefer the rare poems in which Johnson lets himself do all the talking, even though he might feel that talk is merely paraphrase. For when he is willing to put us into direct contact with himself, all the energy of discovery mentioned earlier opens heavy doors ("Indian Corn"):

What is myth, but the power to tell
the truth of it? In words
not even the *real* planted here –
with its rootlets reaching from the base
arrested in a movement down,
or its bright green
of leaves, caught in transpiration –
could tell. For truth
includes not only the even row
of kernels, but grey-black
growths, that I have seen split
the greenest husk.
– & *Kan*:
in which scholars
cannot see the simplicity of a kernel ...

—Geof Hewitt

JOHNSTON, George (Benson). Canadian. Born in Hamilton, Ontario, 7 October 1913. Educated at the University of Toronto, B.A. 1936, M.A. 1945. Served in the Royal Canadian Air Force, four years. Married to Jeanne McRae; three sons and three daughters. Assistant Professor of English, Mount Allison University, Sackville, New Brunswick, 1946–48. Member of the English Department, Carleton University, Ottawa, 1950–79, now retired. LL.D.: Queen's University, Kingston, Ontario, 1971; Lit.D.: Carleton University, 1979.

PUBLICATIONS

Verse

The Cruising Auk. Toronto, Oxford University Press, 1959.
Home Free. Toronto, Oxford University Press, 1966.
Happy Enough. Toronto, Oxford University Press, 1972.
Taking a Grip. Ottawa, Golden Dog Press, 1979.

Other

Translator, *The Saga of Gisli.* Toronto, University of Toronto Press, and London, Dent, 1963.
Translator, *The Faroe Islanders' Saga.* Ottawa, Oberon Press, 1975.
Translator, *The Greenlanders' Saga.* Ottawa, Oberon Press, 1976.

Critical Studies: by George Whalley, in *Canadian Literature 35* (Vancouver), Winter 1968; by Lawrence W. Jones, in *Canadian Literature 48* (Vancouver), Spring 1971.

George Johnston comments:

(1970) First volume, *The Cruising Auk*, was considered light verse in mainly conventional forms.

Second volume, *Home Free*, is part light verse, part serious, also largely conventional in form.

* * *

The poetry of George Johnston, that most engaging Canadian poet, shows itself as distinctively individual and very much of a piece, the characteristic tone and idiom having been established almost from the beginning. Not that it isn't difficult to define the tone of verse which on the one side hesitates on the edge of pathos, and on the other leans back from the brink of farce. Perhaps we could say of it that it blends in an inimitably individual way sentiment and daftness, or flippancy and a strong central orthodoxy. Perhaps this is no more than to say, human experience being as enigmatically complex as it is, that the poet's eye registers nuances which the ordinary person, or just the rest of us, loses in a blur of emotional cliché and commonsense expectation. The technique by which Johnston establishes some shade of feeling or being varies from point to point: sometimes it may be a grave disparity between the solemn treatment and the ridiculous subject, as in "Noctambule":

Mr. Murple's got a dog that's long
And underslung and sort of pointed wrong;
When daylight fades and the evening lights come out
He takes him round the neighbour lawns about
To ease himself and leak against the trees
The which he does in drops and by degrees

Leaving his hoarded fluid only where
Three-legged ceremonious hairy care
Has been before and made a solemn sign.

Or it may be, as in "Fields," by the use of a bent parallel, two stanzas laid out side by side, with a small distorting explosive in the second; or it may be by the adoption of a certain simplicity or even simple-mindedness of attitude as many of the poems of *The Cruising Auk*; or it may be a neatly modulating use of repetition, a device he uses very frequently to achieve a strikingly disconcerting effect, as in the last stanza of "Eating Fish."

Johnston's versification is skillful in a traditional way, and indeed the normality of his rhythms and figuration makes even more impressive the individuality of the approach. The central characteristic of that approach is the sort of wit which sees at once what is the discrepant in the situation or the character. The wit in Johnston is not merely clever or sharp but issues from some fundamental sagacity and repose. It is conveyed in diction of an almost Chinese precision and clarity and with a tone of calm and moderate good sense which adds to its point and sharpness.

What makes him so fine a comic poet is that his wit operates within a certain context of desperation, the humour is played out against a background suggestive of anxiety and distress. Like his own Mr. Goom, "he finds he needs a drink/Or else a Turkish bath to chase/His apperception from the brink/Of darkness to a brighter place." Not only Mr. Goom but all his characters have this sense of treading on the brink of darkness: Mr. Murple, Mrs. Beleek, Mrs. Belaney, Mrs. McGonigle, Miss Knit, Poor Edward and Miss Decharmes. In the same way the fantastic, which is so strong an element in his vision, works itself out against an ordinary suburban life, in a tar-warm city where people put ingenious stuff around their gardens "to baffle bugs and coax the ground":

The call of the dufuflu bird
For which I have an ear
Falls like the uncreating word,
But only some can hear.

And often at the droop of day
When evening grumbles in
The great dufuflu has his say
Above the braffic's din ...

Graceful, pointed, odd, George Johnston's is a poetry modest in its pretension, effective in its individuality, successfully conveying a valid human vision. His universe is wry and peculiar but wholly recognisable, crazy but within everybody's competence and recognition. His poetry, in its wit, urbanity and fantasy, adds a genuinely different note to the canon of modern Canadian work.

—William Walsh

JONAS, George. Canadian. Born in Budapest, Hungary, 15 June 1935; left Hungary in 1956, and lived briefly in Austria and England before settling in Canada. Educated at Lutheran Gymnazium, Budapest; studied Theatre and Film Arts with F. Hont, Budapest. Married Barbara Amiel in 1974; one child by a previous marriage. Editor, Light Entertainment, Hungarian Broadcasting Corporation, 1956. Script Editor, 1962–67, Chief Story Editor, 1968–70, and since 1970, Television Drama Producer, Canadian Broadcasting

Corporation, Toronto. Recipient: Canada Council grant, 1968, 1971; Mystery Writers of America Edgar Allan Poe Award, for non-fiction, 1977. Address: c/o Canadian Broadcasting Corporation, Box 500, Terminal A, Toronto, Ontario, Canada.

PUBLICATIONS

Verse

The Absolute Smile. Toronto, Anansi, 1967.
The Happy Hungry Man. Toronto, Anansi, 1970.
Cities. Toronto, Anansi, 1973.

Plays

The European Lover, music by Tibor Polgar (Canada tour, 1966).
The Glove, music by Tibor Polgar (produced Toronto, 1974).
Pushkin (produced Toronto, 1978).

Radio Plays: *Of Mice and Men*, 1963; *To Cross a Bridge*, 1964; *The Redl Affair*, 1966; *The Agent Provocateur*, 1966; *Fasting Friar*, 1967; *Master and Man*, 1967; *Mr. Pym Passes By*, 1967; *First and Vital Candle*, 1967; *Catullus*, 1967; *Tell His Majesty*, 1968; *Ave Luna, Morituri Te Salutant*, 1970; *The Sinking of the Mary Palmer*, 1972.

Television Plays: *The Major*, 1964; *The Family Man*, 1972; *Ave Luna, Morituri Te Salutant*, 1973; *The Princess of Tomboso*, 1977.

Other

By Persons Unknown: The Strange Death of Christine Demeter, with Barbara Amiel. Toronto, Macmillan, and New York, Grove Press, 1977.

Critical Studies: *Robert Fulford in Conversation with George Jonas*, televised, 1968; in *University of Toronto Quarterly*, January 1968; *Poetry* (Chicago), June 1969; *Canadian Literature* (Vancouver), Summer 1969; *Dennis Lee in Conversation with George Jonas*, televised, 1970.

* * *

George Jonas, is, in the world of which he writes, an outsider, almost an exile. The authorities of his post-Kafka Hungarian childhood haunt him in a new landscape. And indeed there is much in the brittle descriptive quality of his verse that is un-Canadian (with the exception of Quebec) and reminiscent of poets like Zbigniew Herbert and Miroslav Holub. The world he inhabits is one of a dream and waking, just this side of nightmare – full of ordinary conversations about dinner or the cleaning lady and yet somehow torn out of life like collage pictures from a magazine.

The format of *The Happy Hungry Man* – interspersed as it is with photographs of Kent State troopers, Iris the scrotum-stroker, or a rampaging river – adds to this sense of disconnection. There is a narrative life to the poems in this collection, held together thinly by the marginal glosses on each poem, but one's sense of the poems overall is of disorder and disarray – a world where all coherence is long gone.

In many ways Jonas's world is like Auden's, but without the toughness of rhyme that gives to Auden's ballads their edge. Largely the connexion is a Horatian tone: the sense of the domestic as paradigmatic of a world gone ruinous. And added to it is the terror that lurks without, the more terrifying in its apparently motiveless malignity:

For someone who has bravely tried
To keep his head and distance
And live as sharks or apples do
Without mercy or assistance,
It is astonishing to see
That it is still not over
And lately at night the stars
Threaten to move closer.

Jonas's answer is to "have elected to live/In legal separation from the world," but this separation is never wholly satisfactory and his lovers return to haunt him – "your breasts' shape, the full length of your limbs" – as he searches the past for analogies of himself – "I am only trying to show/How fully we resembled you/As young men." In the end it is death, resolution, desire, old age that remain with him – "wondering how I'll feel/In 1985."

—D. D. C. Chambers

JONES, Brian. British. Born in 1938. Married; two children. Recipient: Cholmondely Award, 1967; Gregory Award, 1968.

PUBLICATIONS

Verse

Poems. London, Alan Ross, 1966.
A Family Album. London, Alan Ross, 1968.
Interior. London, Alan Ross, 1969.
The Mantis Hand and Other Poems. Gillingham, Kent, ARC, 1970.
For Mad Mary. London, London Magazine Editions, 1974.
The Spitfire on the Northern Line (juvenile). London, Chatto and Windus, 1975.

Play

Radio Play: *The Lady with a Little Dog*, from a story by Chekhov, 1962

* * *

The poems in Brian Jones's books of verse cover a narrow area of subject-matter. Repeatedly he returns to the same material – family life, the married state, parents and children. When he strays outside this, as he sometimes does, he tends to write poems which, though extremely competent, read like the work of a score of other poets – the naturalistic norm of post-war poetry in Britain. The other poems, though they have the same kind of surface and use the same kind of diction, seem to me a different matter. *A Family Album*, which contains Jones's best work, is a series of mologues – each monologue a portrait of the person who speaks, and offering glimpses of those who surround him.

The idea of loss seems to dominate these monologues. The most forcefully created character is Aunt Emily – some of the poems concerning her are in fact transferred from an earlier collection, and it is clear that this deprived, eccentric spinster haunts Jones's imagination, and provides a kind of antonym for himself. Yet Emily's hovering shadow of madness is perhaps the poet's too.

The verse itself, examined in detail, has many felicities, without ever being pioneering. The civilized ease of the writing comes out in a concluding stanza like the following:

> And when she came from hospital
> thin in the cold air, thin like a slip of a girl,
> with our boy like a doll bundled against
> her girl's breast, and from a taxi
> stepped into the neighbour's gaze,
> she and my child were the frail and total
> grounds for my praise.

—Edward Lucie-Smith

JONES, D(ouglas) G(ordon). Canadian. Born in Bancroft, Ontario, 1 January 1929. Educated at McGill University, Montreal, B.A.; Queen's University, Kingston, Ontario, M.A. Married; four children. Currently, Professeur Titulaire, English Department, University of Sherbrooke, Quebec. Recipient: President's Medal, University of Western Ontario, 1976; Governor-General's Award, 1977; A. J. M. Smith Poetry Prize, 1978. Address: P.O. Box 356, North Hatley, Quebec, Canada.

PUBLICATIONS

Verse

Frost on the Sun. Toronto, Contact Press, 1957.
The Sun Is Axeman. Toronto, University of Toronto Press, 1961.
Phrases from Orpheus. Toronto, Oxford University Press, 1967.
Under the Thunder the Flowers Light Up the Earth. Toronto, Coach House Press, 1977.

Other

Butterfly on Rock: A Study of Themes and Images in Canadian Literature. Toronto, University of Toronto Press, 1970.

Translator, *The Terror of the Snows*, by Paul-Marie Lapointe. Pittsburgh, University of Pittsburgh Press, 1976.

Critical Studies: "D. G. Jones: Etre chez soi dans le monde" by George Bowering, in *Ellipse 13* (Sherbrooke, Quebec), 1973; "The Masks of D. G. Jones" by E. D. Blodgett, in *Canadian Literature 60* (Vancouver), Spring 1974.

D. G. Jones comments:

A lyric poetry, relying heavily on a visual imagination ("rhyme of images") and on phrasing (or relationship in rhythm and sound of words to each other and to overall curve of statement) to create a line or sequence with a sense of inevitability or authority. Finally metaphysical (rather than descriptive, social, etc.) in intention. Attempts to digest for own use major influences of 20th century poetry (imagist – symbolist – metaphysical) and to connect with native Canadian tradition of two generations.

* * *

Verbal clarity, economy, precision, and a purity of imagery characterize the poetry of D. G. Jones. These aesthetic qualities are related to a philosophical state of mind and a quality of emotion which give the poetry an unusual consistency of tone and meaning. The relation between an "emptiness" or "barrenness" perceived in nature, on the philosophical plane (recurrent images in Jones), and an aesthetic of purity in poetry is familiar, especially in Mallarmé, and Jones can be usefully compared to the French master. Jones derives more directly from the Imagists, however, from H. D., and from Ezra Pound as critical mentor; later affinities are with Wallace Stevens and Marianne Moore. He is authentic in himself, also, and does not resemble so much as parallel these poets in general ways.

His first book, *Frost on the Sun*, already showed the taint of philosophic disenchantment and affected the shine of purity. *The Sun Is Axeman* revealed a marked advance in control and assurance and a full development of these features. Themes of silence, alienation, and emptiness recur – "a string of notes/limned on the stillness of a void" ... "skeletons of trees" ... "And silence like a snow is everywhere." A number of poems, with their patina of perfection, dealing with lighter subject matter – "Clotheslines," "Schoolgirls" – remind one of Gautier, the father of the aesthetes. A cosmic pessimism – "the universe bleeds into darkness" – underlies these poems.

Phrases from Orpheus is marked by personal suffering not unlike that of W. D. Snodgrass in *Heart's Needle*, but there is no further resemblance. Jones is not confessional; his book gives expression to pain and passion through the indirections of poetry, through the myth of Orpheus, through images and the incantations of symbolism, and through irony. Here "stars are not polite, and/even plants are/violent"; there is comfort in "that relatively immortal blue gas/the sky...." The poetry transcends the personal, and at its best achieves a noble indifference or stoicism that touches on the heroic without rhetoric or mannerism.

Phrases from Orpheus is a deeply moving book and one of the most important to appear in Canada in recent years. It has, unfortunately, been neglected in the hubbub created by numerous young poets appearing on the scene and by the phenomenon of popularity affecting poetry; but the book will no doubt take its place as one of the finest to appear in the fifties and sixties.

—Louis Dudek

JONES, Evan (Lloyd). Australian. Born in Melbourne, Victoria, 20 November 1931. Educated at Melbourne High School; University of Melbourne (Services' Canteen Fund Scholar, 1954–55), B.A. 1953, M.A. in history 1957; Stanford University, California (Writing Fellow, 1958–60), M.A. in English 1959. Married 1) Judith Ann Jones in 1954; 2) Margot Jones in 1966; four children. Tutor, then Senior Tutor in History, University of Melbourne, 1955–58; Lecturer in English, Australian National University, Canberra, 1960–63. Lecturer, 1964, and since 1965, Senior Lecturer in English, University of Melbourne. Address: Department of English, University of Melbourne, Parkville, Victoria 3052, Australia.

PUBLICATIONS

Verse

Inside the Whale. Melbourne, Cheshire, 1960.
Understandings. Melbourne, Melbourne University Press, 1967.
Recognitions. Canberra, Australian National University Press, 1978.

Other

Kenneth Mackenzie. Melbourne, Oxford University Press, 1969.

Editor, "Australian Poetry since 1920," in *The Literature of Australia*, edited by Geoffrey Dutton. London, Penguin, 1964.
Editor, with Geoffrey Little, *The Poems of Kenneth Mackenzie.* Sydney, Angus and Robertson, 1972.

Evan Jones comments:

My poetry is characteristically highly formal in structure, diverse in diction. Forms range from the sestina to unrhymed trimeter. Early influences were a multitude of English, American and Australian poets, but especially W. H. Auden. Most poems are concerned in one way or another with the problem of maintaining or achieving coherence and equanimity in the face (as the anonymous blurb of my second book put it, rather heavy-handedly) of loneliness, separation and death: in the face of being a thinking and sentient being here and now.

* * *

Evan Jones must be considered one of the influential poets of his period and place: Melbourne in the late 1950's and early 1960's. *Inside the Whale* is full of student work in the once fashionable vein of what A. D. Hope calls "the discursive mode." At times, in this volume, Evan Jones almost appears to be self-parodying, as he practices older English stanzaic forms and apostrophizes the Melbourne University. Other poems, however, such as the much anthologised "Noah's Song," became key demonstrations of "the habit of irony" that pervaded University literary circles in the 1950's.

His second collection abandons this youthful donnish guise and concerns itself with a closer approach to the characteristic early adult experiences: love, marriage, estrangement. In these later poems, Evan Jones, though no longer a determinedly donnish poet, demonstrates a considerable erudition and an even more considerable command of language and cadence in a way that is always unspectacular, but often brilliantly sharp and precise. He seems to have settled into a line of quiet, reflective verse. He is, however, the sort of poet one would not be surprised to find emerge suddenly with some long and large-ranging epic after a gestation period of several years. But Jones is assured of a place in the re-animation and re-direction of Australian poetry that occurred, in Melbourne, at the end of the 1950's.

—Thomas W. Shapcott

JONES, Glyn. Welsh. Born in Merthyr Tydfil, Glamorgan, 28 February 1905. Educated at Castle Grammar School, Merthyr Tydfil; St. Paul's College, Cheltenham. Married Phyllis Doreen Jones in 1935. Formerly a schoolmaster in Glamorgan; now retired. Vice-President, Yr Academi Gymreig (English Section). Recipient: Welsh Arts Council Prize, for non-fiction, 1969, and Premier Award, 1972. D. Litt.: University of Wales, 1974. Address: 158 Manor Way, Whitchurch, Cardiff, Wales.

PUBLICATIONS

Verse

Poems. London, Fortune Press, 1939.
The Dream of Jake Hopkins. London, Fortune Press, 1954.
Selected Poems. Llandysul, Dyfed, Gomer, 1975.

Play

The Beach of Falesa, music by Alun Hoddinott (produced Cardiff, 1974). London, Oxford University Press, 1974.

Novels

The Valley, The City, The Village. London, Dent, 1956.
The Learning Lark. London, Dent, 1960.
The Island of Apples. London, Dent, and New York, Day, 1965.

Short Stories

The Blue Bed. London, Cape, 1937; New York, Dutton, 1938.
The Water Music. London, Routledge, 1944.
Selected Short Stories. London, Dent, 1971.
Welsh Heirs. Llandysul, Dyfed, Gomer, 1978; Chicago, Academy Chicago, 1979.

Other

The Dragon Has Two Tongues (essays on Anglo-Welsh writers). London, Dent, 1968.

Editor, *Poems '76.* Llandysul, Dyfed, Gomer, 1976.

Translator, with T. J. Morgan, *The Saga of Llywarch the Old.* London, Golden Cockerel Press, 1955.

Manuscript Collection: National Library of Wales, Aberystwyth.

Critical Study: *Glyn Jones* by Leslie Norris, Cardiff, University of Wales Press, 1973.

Glyn Jones comments:

I began my literary career as a poet and I hope to end it in the same way.

I believe I am usually thought of as belonging to the Anglo-Welsh group of poets (Dylan Thomas, Vernon Watkins, R. S. Thomas, David Jones, etc.), poets who are Welsh but who write in English.

The poets who have meant most to me are G. M. Hopkins, D. H. Lawrence, Walt

Whitman, Dylan Thomas, plus some of the poets of my own country – I mean writers of poems in the Welsh language. I admire poets who are word- and language-conscious; but that does not mean I am indifferent to what the poet says. Hopkins appeals to me so much because I am in sympathy with his agonising over language, and I also find acceptable his subject matter and what he has to say about it.

* * *

Better known as a short story writer and novelist, Glyn Jones began as a poet, his first poems appearing in *The Dublin Magazine* in 1931. His critical work, *The Dragon Has Two Tongues*, reveals that not till later did he become well acquainted with the intricate rhyme-schemes and density of texture of much of the poetry in the Welsh language: the concern for *words* rather than ideas which he showed from the beginning was therefore a Welsh instinct, a natural eloquence which decorated and "blew up" the narrative line, sounding off a country of echoes on either side. Admiration for the rich and sensuous imagery of D. H. Lawrence is reflected in his earliest poems, but, this impetus exhausted, he turned to a kind of proletarian poetry, inspired by the *hen benillion* of the peasant past. Although far from the "public school communism" of the contemporary English mode, the effect of this was not very different on occasion from the neo-romanticisms of Auden. Out of this windy alley grew other poems, realist rather than proletarian, "poems built up solid out of concrete nouns," strongly consonantal (a painter's poems, perhaps, for Glyn applied sounds to his poem much as he would apply blocks of colour to his canvas), as "Dock":

The sky tilts suddenly, its sleety herringbone
Of pouring rain spills thick across the dock,
Shags up the furry liner's side, its blurred
Black iron cliff immense above the dock-wall,
Pelts the sheety concrete, sprawls its gusty growth
Its hiss of cold grey grass across the tingling streets.

His reading of G. M. Hopkins reinforced this development, and meetings with Dylan Thomas from 1934 onwards strengthened his view that the craft was more important than the audience, that social implications were secondary. At its least successful, his new mode of writing had a glutinous quality that could slough the reader; at its best, a distinctive glory of words and images that illuminated the greys of the natural scene ("Gull"):

Blush-feathered, frocked, above the grey-bled sea
He bears my beating heart with rosy webs,
The fire-bird, the flame-silked through the grieving sea-rain, swift
On hot flushed petal-flesh his flashing wings.

After 1940 he wrote much less poetry, though his smaller output included the radio ode "The Dream of Jake Hopkins" and the well-known "Merthyr," both of which made use of a humour and irony which had so far appeared only in his short stories. Novels and translations from the Welsh absorbed him, and it was 1967 before he broke poetic silence again with "Images of Light and Darkness." Unmoved by fashion, he was writing still out of that *cwm-taf* of images, that echo-making mountain of words before which his house had long stood, and the lyrical impulse was now uppermost. In "Profile of Rose" with which he opened 1969, despite its narrative line and tragic symbolism, the lyrical note is still strong:

Hair-bowed Rose, deep in lush grass of the river
Bank, watched through the crystal unflawed block of
Afternoon, broad waters of her tenth birthday
Under sunglare, bottomless ebony
Sheeted with green and shine, and elms black

Along the far brink, and the gold field
Beyond, a shallow dishful of buttercup
Liquor.

There are many who look at this "shallow dishful" wistfully and ask only that Glyn Jones shall honour his declared intention to end, as he began, by writing poetry.

—Roland Mathias

JONES, (Everett) LeRoi. Pseudonym: Amiri Baraka. American. Born in Newark, New Jersey, 7 October 1934. Educated at the Central Avenue School, and Barringer High School, Newark; Howard University, Washington, D.C. Served in the United States Air Force, 1954–56. Married 1) Hettie Cohen in 1958 (divorced, 1965), two daughters; 2) Sylvia Robinson (Bibi Amina Baraka) in 1966, five children. Taught at the New School for Social Research, New York, 1961–64; State University of New York at Buffalo, Summer 1964; Columbia University, New York, 1964; Visiting Professor, San Francisco State College, 1966–67. Founder, *Yugen* magazine and Totem Press, New York, 1958; Editor, with Diane di Prima, *Floating Bear* magazine, New York, 1961–63. Founding Director, Black Arts Repertory Theatre, Harlem, New York, 1964–66. Since 1966, Founding Director, Spirit House, Newark. Involved in Newark politics: Member of the United Brothers, 1967, and Committee for Unified Newark, 1968. Member of the International Coordinating Committee, Congress of African Peoples; Chairman, Congress of Afrikan People; Secretary-General, National Black Political Assembly. Recipient: Whitney Fellowship, 1961; Obie Award, 1964; Guggenheim Fellowship, 1965; Dakar Festival Prize, 1966; National Endowment for the Arts grant, 1966. Member, Black Academy of Arts and Letters. Address: C.A.P., 502 High Street, Newark, New Jersey 07102, U.S.A.

PUBLICATIONS

Verse

Spring and Soforth. New Haven, Connecticut, Penny Poems, 1960.
Preface to a Twenty Volume Suicide Note. New York, Totem-Corinth, 1961.
The Dead Lecturer. New York, Grove Press, 1964.
Black Art. Newark, Jihad, 1966.
A Poem for Black Hearts. Detroit, Broadside Press, 1967.
Black Magic: Poetry 1961–1967. Indianapolis, Bobbs Merrill, and London, MacGibbon and Kee, 1969.
It's Nation Time. Chicago, Third World Press, 1970.
In Our Terribleness: Some Elements and Meaning in Black Style, with Fundi (Billy Abernathy). Indianapolis, Bobbs Merrill, 1970.
Spirit Reach. Newark, Jihad, 1972.
Afrikan Revolution. Newark, Jihad, 1973.
Hard Facts. Newark, Peoples War, 1976.
Selected Poetry. New York, Morrow, 1979.

Plays

A Good Girl Is Hard to Find (produced Montclair, New Jersey, 1958).

Dante (produced New York, 1961; as *The 8th Ditch*, produced New York, 1964). Included in *The System of Dante's Hell*, 1965.
The Toilet (produced New York, 1962). Included in *The Baptism and The Toilet*, 1967.
Dutchman (produced New York, 1964; London, 1967). Included in *Dutchman and The Slave*, 1964.
The Slave (produced New York, 1964; London, 1972). Included in *Dutchman and The Slave*, 1964.
Dutchman and The Slave. New York, Morrow, 1964; London, Faber, 1965.
The Baptism (produced New York, 1964; London, 1971). Included in *The Baptism and The Toilet*, 1967.
Jello (produced New York, 1965). Chicago, Third World Press, 1970.
Experimental Death Unit No. 1 (produced New York, 1965). Included in *Four Black Revolutionary Plays*, 1969.
A Black Mass (produced Newark, 1966). Included in *Four Black Revolutionary Plays*, 1969.
The Baptism and The Toilet. New York, Grove Press, 1967.
Arm Yrself or Harm Yrself (produced Newark, 1967). Newark, Jihad, 1967.
Slave Ship: A Historical Pageant (produced Newark, 1967; New York, 1969). Newark, Jihad, 1967.
Madheart (produced San Francisco, 1967). Included in *Four Black Revolutionary Plays*, 1969.
Home on the Range (produced Newark and New York, 1968). Published in *Drama Review* (New York), Summer 1968.
Police, in *Drama Review* (New York), Summer 1968.
The Death of Malcolm X, in *New Plays from the Black Theatre*, edited by Ed Bullins. New York, Bantam, 1969.
Great Goodness of Life (A Coon Show) (produced New York, 1969). Included in *Four Black Revolutionary Plays*, 1969.
Four Black Revolutionary Plays (includes *Experimental Death Unit No. 1*, *A Black Mass*, *Great Goodness of Life (A Coon Show)*, *Madheart*). Indianapolis, Bobbs Merrill, 1969; London, Calder and Boyars, 1971.
Junkies Are Full of (SHHH ...), and Bloodrites (produced Newark, 1970). Published in *Black Drama Anthology*, edited by Woodie King and Ron Milner, New York, New American Library, 1971.
BA-RA-KA, in *Spontaneous Combustion: Eight New American Plays*, edited by Rochelle Owens. New York, Winter House, 1972.
A Recent Killing (produced New York, 1973).
Sidnee Poet Heroical (also director: produced New York, 1975).
S–1 (also director: produced New York, 1976). Included in *The Motion of History and Other Plays*, 1978.
The Motion of History (also director: produced New York, 1977). Included in *The Motion of History and Other Plays*, 1978.
The Motion of History and Other Plays (includes *S–1* and *Slave Ship*). New York, Morrow, 1978.
What Was the Relationship of the Lone Ranger to the Means of Production? (produced New York, 1979).

Screenplays: *Dutchman*, 1967; *A Fable*, 1971.

Novel

The System of Dante's Hell. New York, Grove Press, 1965; London, MacGibbon and Kee, 1966.

Short Stories

Tales. New York, Grove Press, 1967; London, MacGibbon and Kee, 1969.

Other

Cuba Libre. New York, Fair Play for Cuba Committee, 1961.
Blues People: Negro Music in White America. New York, Morrow, 1963; London, MacGibbon and Kee, 1965.
Home: Social Essays. New York, Morrow, 1966; London, MacGibbon and Kee, 1968.
Black Music. New York, Morrow, 1968.
Trippin': A Need for Change, with Larry Neal and A. B. Spellman. Newark, Cricket, 1969(?).
A Black Value System. Newark, Jihad, 1970.
Raise Race Rays Raze: Essays since 1965. New York, Random House, 1971.
Strategy and Tactics of a Pan African Nationalist Party. Newark, National Involvement, 1971.
Beginning of National Movement. Newark, Jihad, 1972.
The New Nationalism. Chicago, Third World Press, 1972.
National Liberation and Politics. Newark, Congress of African People, 1974.
The Creation of the New Ark. Washington, D.C., Howard University Press, 1975.
Selected Plays and Prose. New York, Morrow, 1979.

Editor, *Four Young Lady Poets.* New York, Totem-Corinth. 1962.
Editor, *The Moderns: New Fiction in America.* New York, Corinth, 1963; London, MacGibbon and Kee, 1965.
Editor, with Larry Neal, *Black Fire: An Anthology of Afro-American Writing.* New York, Morrow, 1968.
Editor, *African Congress: A Documentary of the First Modern Pan-African Congress.* New York, Morrow, 1972.
Editor, with Diane di Prima, *The Floating Bear: A Newsletter, Numbers 1–37.* La Jolla, California, Laurence McGilvery, 1974.

Bibliography: *LeRoi Jones (Imamu Amiri Baraka): A Checklist of Works by and about Him* by Letitia Dace, London, Nether Press, 1971.

Theatrical Activities:
Director: several of his own plays.

LeRoi Jones comments:

(1970) I identify with the "Black" school.
My major theme? The evolution of man.
(1974) The first step is Socialist Revolution.

* * *

LeRoi Jones (Amiri Baraka) is the leading revolutionary poet in America. Change is his consistent belief, progress his preoccupation. Every one of his books embodies such development. In *Home*, it is a matter of growing "blacker" during the very course of the essays, before our eyes; in *The Dead Lecturer* the turning points are the poems "An Agony. As Now," which catalogues the personal disease ending in a scream, and "Black Dada Nihilismus," which finds the West "a grey hideous space." There was much talk of death in the early poems, until it was realized – first in "Black Dada Nihilismus," then throughout

Black Magic ("THE LONE RANGER/IS DEAD./THE SHADOW/IS DEAD./ALL YOUR HEROES ARE DYING. J. EDGAR HOOVER WILL/SOON BE DEAD....") – that it was a culture that was dying, not the poet himself. Recognizing this, Baraka has been committed to re-creating himself in successive stages, and the world, the geo-political, socio-economic, hard-facts world, likewise.

His writing has gone through three obvious stages, and even more changes can be expected – revisions, advances. His first collections of poems reflect his commitment to the cultural avant-garde, with its generally "bohemian," decidedly anti-bourgeois stance shared by Olson, Creeley, Dorn, Ginsberg, Snyder, the post-modern Americans he published among and himself published. This was followed by his rebirth as a black man, the new identity exemplified by the new name, as the old associations, summarized in "The New World" early in *Black Magic*, were left behind:

> Wasted lyricists, and men
> who have seen their dreams come true, only
> seconds after they knew those dreams to be horrible conceits
> and plastic fantasies of gesture and extension,
> shoulders, hair and tongues distributing misinformation
> about the nature of understanding....
> Beatniks, like Bohemians, go calmly out of style.

The last lingering ties in "The Burning General" give way to "Black Art": "We want 'poems that kill.'/Assassin poems, Poems that shoot/guns. Poems that wrestle cops into alleys/and take their weapons leaving them dead...." The new black aesthetic makes possible the construction of a new nation, beginning with the poet's own community of Newark, a New Ark to sail out the destruction of the West. It seeks simultaneously to rouse and direct – raze and raise – toward a cooperative society of value and justice, so that, in his most recent work, cutural nationalism expands to a Marxist-Maoist socialism. The jihad of *Black Magic* and *It's Nation Time* gives way to the internationalism of *Hard Facts*, with no loss of fierceness. The address is to all the oppressed: "the fist of/the mighty is the whole fist."

Other poets have addressed political issues, to be sure, but what makes Baraka exceptional is that his language is equal to both his thought and his feelings. His poetry has the flexibility of syntax and deftness of diction, including vernacular richness, to deliver the message, with wit, irony, all the devices of effective language, at the same time upholding the nobility of its concerns. Every line in such an overt appeal as "The Nation Is Like Ourselves" is unpredictable invention. The oral empowers the dialectic line to move at speeds beyond dull demagoguery. Tireless, of sufficient complexity, with every trick of improvisation and typography allowable, every reach of vocabulary and ethnic association (even the direst), language is his special genius, his uniqueness (which is not the same as individualism, egocentricity). It is a poetry of strategy, exhortatory in the classic ways, propelled by urgency and belief. It is equally a poetry of feeling, though feeling controlled by a whip-like mind. "In the fact of feeling," he writes in *Raise Race Rays Raze*, "is the testing of the soul and the future evolution of men." Its language takes responsibility for itself, does not give itself up compulsively to either its own beauty or its thought. It is not self-hugging, narcissistic. His poetry, in its various developments, is an encouragement that liberation only *begins* with oneself. It is, above all, one of the few poetries today that is responsible to more than itself. Its lines are of lasting readiness. "Every breath must be a bullet, every step an attack," he writes in *Kawaida Studies*. The twist is on the words as they emerge from the bore.

—George F. Butterick

JONG, Erica (née Mann). American. Born in New York City, 26 March 1942. Educated at Barnard College, New York (George Weldwood Murray Fellow, 1963), 1959–63, B.A. 1963 (Phi Beta Kappa); Columbia University, New York (Woodrow Wilson Fellow, 1964), M.A. 1965; Columbia School of Fine Arts, 1969–70. Married 1) Michael Werthman; 2) Allan Jong in 1966 (divorced, 1975). Lecturer in English, City College of New York, 1964–66, and University of Maryland European Division, Heidelberg, Germany, 1967–68; Instructor in English, Manhattan Community College, New York, 1969–70. Since 1971, Instructor in Poetry, YM–YWHA Poetry Center, New York. Recipient: Bess Hokin Prize (*Poetry*, Chicago), 1971; New York State Council on the Arts grant, 1971; Madeline Sadin Award (*New York Quarterly*), 1972; Alice Fay di Castagnola Award, 1972; National Endowment for the Arts grant, 1973. Agent: Sterling Lord Agency, 660 Madison Avenue, New York, New York 10021. Address: 20 West 77th Street, New York, New York 10024, U.S.A.

PUBLICATIONS

Verse

Fruits and Vegetables. New York, Holt Rinehart, 1971; London, Secker and Warburg, 1973.
Half-Lives. New York, Holt Rinehart, 1973; London, Secker and Warburg, 1974.
Here Comes and Other Poems. New York, New American Library, 1975.
Loveroot. New York, Holt Rinehart, 1975; London, Secker and Warburg, 1977.
Selected Poems. London, Panther, 1977.
At the Edge of the Body. New York, Holt Rinehart, 1979.

Novels

Fear of Flying. New York, Holt Rinehart, 1973; London, Secker and Warburg, 1974.
How to Save Your Own Life. New York, Holt Rinehart, and London, Secker and Warburg, 1977.

Other

Four Visions of America, with others. Santa Barbara, California, Capra Press, 1977.

Critical Studies: in *St. Louis Post-Dispatch*, 16 May 1971; "The Comestible Muse," in *The Nation* (New York), 28 June 1971; "Eat, Darling, Eat!," in *Village Voice* (New York), 2 September 1971; *Saturday Review* (New York), 18 December 1971; *Library Journal* (New York) 15 April 1973; *Publishers Weekly* (New York), 7 May 1973; *Hartford Courant* (Connecticut), 1 July 1973; Grace Shulman in *Ms.* (New York), August 1973.

Erica Jong comments:

(1974) Though I have been writing since childhood, my first formal training in poetry came at Barnard College, where I studied from 1959–63. At that time I loved the poetry of Auden, Yeats, Keats, Byron and Alexander Pope, cultivated the command of formal verse, and developed an abiding interest in satire. My early university poems were mostly expert, satirical and somewhat academic. I went on to do a thesis on Alexander Pope in Columbia's graduate English department. In my early and mid-twenties, however, I became much more interested in French surrealist poetry and its South American derivatives. I came to love the poetry of Neruda and Alberti, and I learned the value of poetry which delved deep into the unconscious and relied on the association of images. It seems to me that these two influences

– crisp satire and an abiding belief in the importance of unconscious material – have shaped my voice as a poet. I believe that poetry can be serious and comic at the same time, formal yet free. I think I was also liberated to write out of a frankly female persona by reading the work of such poets as Anne Sexton, Sylvia Plath, Muriel Rukeyser, Carolyn Kizer, Adrienne Rich. It has been very important to me – both in poetry and fiction – to write freely about women and women's sexuality. Throughout much of history, women writers have capitulated to male standards, and have paid too much heed to what Virginia Woolf calls "the angel in the house." She is that little ghost who sits on one's shoulder while one writes and whispers, "Be nice, don't say anything that will embarrass the family, don't say anything your man would disapprove of...." The "angel in the house" castrates one's creativity because it deprives one of essential honesty, and many women writers have yet to win the freedom to be honest with themselves. But once the right to honesty has been established, we can go on to write about anything that interests us. We need not *only* write about childbirth, menstruation and other supposedly feminist topics. I resist the subject matter fallacy in any of its forms. Writing should not be judged on the basis of its subject, but on the artistry with which that subject is treated. It seems to me that all three of my published books (*Fruits and Vegetables*, *Half-Lives* and *Fear of Flying*) have certain themes in common: the search for honesty within oneself, the difficulty of resolving the conflicting needs for security and adventure, the necessity of seeing the world both sensuously and intelligently at the same time. Having said all that, I should add that my views about my writing will probably be entirely different by the time this is printed.

* * *

Erica Jong's poetry places her firmly with her contemporary female poets Carolyn Kizer, Adrienne Rich, and Diane Wakoski, all of whom write "naked poetry," much of it explicitly concerned with women and women's sexuality. They also set her poetry in the confessional mode practiced by Robert Lowell, Sylvia Plath, and Anne Sexton. After the publication of her novel *Fear of Flying*, Jong was hailed as the 1970's female counterpart to J. D. Salinger. In the poetic vein, her writings have been admired for their form, but more for their frankly irreverent treatment of men, sex, women, and eating.

Henry Miller and Walt Whitman are the spirits behind *Loveroot*. Whitman's "Calamus" poems, his exuberant, rocking cadences, his parallel syntactic constructions, his left-branching sentences, and his unashamed, celebratory "Song of Myself" inform Jong's verse. She offers him her hymn of "the body electric":

> you were "hankering, gross, mystical, nude."
> You astonished with the odor of your armpits.
> You cocked your hat as you chose;
> you cocked your cock –
> but you knew "the Me myself"....
> The loveroot will germinate.
> The crotch will be a trellis for the vine,
>   & our threads will all be intermingled silk.

Miller's chaotic, Pantagruelian word play, his ribald accounts of sexual athleticism, and his defiant proclamations are all felt in Jong's poetry.

Her first two volumes of poetry offer her modern version of William Blake's "Marriage of Heaven and Hell." "Arse Poetica," "Seven," and "The Commandments" in *Fruits and Vegetables* are her equivalent to Blake's fancies, parables, and commandments. "Seventeen Warnings in Search of a Feminist Poem" and "The Cabala According to Thomas Alva Edison" in *Half-Lives* continue in this vein. In *Loveroot*, her debt to Blake and Miller is of a different sort. "The Parable of the Four-Poster" fits with the earlier poems, but the others share with Blake's and Miller's writings in their pithiness, candor, and iconoclasm. This volume pays homage to Jong's other mentors, Neruda, Keats, Sexton, Plath, and Donne.

Fruits and Vegetables in formal, chiselled verse built poems thematically based on James Joyce's words: "know me, come eat with me." In *Loveroot*, the mouth and genitals are kissing, and the form is looser. The volume contains many poems derivative of Plath's, but Jong's poem on Plath (the second she has written) reflects her maturity and freedom from Plath's spell. Jong has a quality her mentors lack – her exuberant, affectionate, frolicking humor.

—Carol Simpson Stern

JORDAN, June. American. Born in New York City, 9 July 1936. Educated at Northfield School for Girls, 1950–53; Barnard College, New York, 1953–55, 1956–57; University of Chicago, 1955–56. Married Michael Meyer in 1955 (divorced, 1966); one son. Worked as assistant producer with the filmmaker Frederick Wiseman, 1963–64; Research Associate, Mobilization for Youth Inc., New York, 1965–66; English teacher, City College of New York, 1968–69, 1975–76, Sarah Lawrence College, Bronxville, New York, 1969–70, Yale University, New Haven, Connecticut, 1974–75, and Connecticut College, New London. Member of the Board of Directors, Teachers and Writers Collaborative Inc. Recipient: Rockefeller grant, 1969; American Academy in Rome Environmental Design prize, 1970. Agent: Joan Daves, 505 Madison Avenue, New York, New York 10022, U.S.A.

PUBLICATIONS

Verse

Some Changes. New York, Dutton, 1971.
Poem: On Moral Leadership as a Political Dilemma (Watergate, 1973). Detroit, Broadside Press, 1973.
New Days: Poems of Exile and Return. New York, Emerson Hall, 1974.
Things I Do in the Dark: Selected Poetry. New York, Random House, 1977.

Novel

Okay Now. New York, Simon and Schuster, 1977.

Other (juvenile)

Who Look at Me? New York, Crowell, 1969.
His Own Where – . New York, Crowell, 1971.
Dry Victories. New York, Holt Rinehart, 1972.
Fannie Lou Hamer. New York, Crowell, 1972.
New Life, New Room. New York, Crowell, 1975.

Editor, with Terri Bush, *The Voice of Children.* New York, Holt Rinehart, 1970.
Editor, *Soulscript: Afro-American Poetry.* New York, Doubleday, 1970.

* * *

Poet, essayist, and author of children's fiction, June Jordan is among the most varied and prolific of contemporary Black writers. Together her works chart the artistic concerns of a poet who successfully maintains a sense of spiritual wholeness and the vision of a shared humanity, while relentlessly engaging a brutal and often brutalizing reality. The resultant combination – of courage and vulnerability – is suggested by the poem "Things That I Do in the Dark," in which the poet describes herself as a "stranger/learning to worship the strangers/around me/whoever you are/whoever I may become."

Artistically, Jordan's work shows the influences of two radically different aesthetic criteria. She has clearly been influenced by the Black Arts movement, the cultural arm of the Black Power movement of the 1970's, whose tenets require the work of art to address itself to a Black audience, explore the complexities of Black life, and work towards the building of an autonomous, vital Black culture. In subject matter, theme, and idiom, many of Jordan's poems evidence these tendencies. In others, however, she seems at one with current trends in mainstream American poetry. These poems are intensely personal, syntactically experimental, thematically elusive.

The underlying unity of Jordan's work lies in its uncompromising humanism, eloquently expressed in the historically allusive chronicle, "Who Look at Me," in which the speaker, sometimes a single Black, sometimes Blacks as a group, characterizes the search of African-Americans for visibility as "the search to find/a fatherhood a mothering of mind/a multimillion multicolored mirror/of an honest humankind," and their militance as, ultimately, a rejection of "a carnival run by freaks/who take a life/and tie it terrible/behind my back." The poet's own militance does not end with the political and social struggles of Blacks. She is keenly aware of the dehumanizing effects of economic exploitation ("Nowadays the Heroes" and "47,000 Windows"), as well as of the abuses of power too easily committed by government ("To My Sister Ethel Ennis" and "Poem Against the State [Of Things]").

Feminist concerns are poignantly expressed in the lyrical "Getting Down to Get Over," which celebrates the unique and often solitary role of the Black woman, who is "a full/ Black/glorious/a purple rose ... a shell with the moanin/of ages inside her/a hungry one feedin the folk/what they need." In the anguished "From an Uprooted Condition," the speaker, in quiet frenzy, ponders "the right way the womanly expression/of the infinitive that fights/infinity/*to abort?*" And finally, the precarious position of all women – in a world dominated by men – is effectively portrayed in "On Declining Values."

Despite their profusion, there is an underlying pessimism to Jordan's love poems. The central problem is not the inherent transitoriness of romantic love, a fact which the poet quietly acknowledges in "On a New Year's Eve." Rather, she seems to suggest that love's true enemy is a harsh and merciless reality. Thus, in "The Wedding," "the early wed Tyrone/and his Dizzella" are doomed before their life together begins, for they are "brave enough/but only two." And in poems such as "Shortsong from My Heart," "West Coast Episode," and "On Your Love" relationships are deemed temporary havens, brief respites. Reality, in the form of an impersonal, troubling, often hostile world, always hovers in the background. It is that larger world which, inevitably, reclaims the individual, and perhaps this poet, as its own.

—Saundra Towns

JOSEPH, Jenny. British. Born in Birmingham, Warwickshire, 7 May 1932. Educated at St. Hilda's College, Oxford, 1950–53, B.A. 1953. Recipient: Eric Gregory Award, 1962; Cholmondeley Award, 1975; Arts Council grant, 1976. Agent: John Johnson, Clerkenwell House, 45–47 Clerkenwell Green, London EC1R 0HT. Address: 25 Myrtle Road, London W3 6DY, England.

PUBLICATIONS

Verse

The Unlooked-For Season. Northwood, Middlesex, Scorpion Press, 1960.
Rose in the Afternoon and Other Poems. London, Dent, 1974.
The Thinking Heart. London, Secker and Warburg, 1978.

Other (juvenile)

Boots. London, Constable, 1966.
Wheels. London, Constable, 1966.
Water. London, Constable, 1967.
Wind. London, Constable, 1967.
Tea. London, Constable, 1968.
Sunday. London, Constable, 1968.

Jenny Joseph comments:

It is usually easier for a writer to talk about what he or she is interested in doing "now" or "next" than about what has been done. Work already published is there for all to see, and off the writer's hands. However, I will try to put down some of the things that have interested me in other writers – not that I would claim to be like them.

I am interested in the use of the speaking voice, not merely to provide a "realistic" character for dramatic monologues, but as material, recognizable straight away on one level to the reader, in the musical use of language.

Poetry, it seems to me, is not a novel manqué or a play manqué or a piece of music manqué or a line of philosophic inquiry manqué, but it should be able to deal with the material that goes into all of these. What I think I am doing at the moment is trying to gain enough mastery over structure – mostly in longish poems – to be able to include a wide range of material and give it a unity of tone.

A book I finished in the summer of 1979 which I had been considering for many years is written in prose and verse. The "story-line" goes through the verse passages, the "atmosphere" is in the prose pieces which are a collection of different voices; the tone of the particular literary style chosen is meant to reflect the personality of the voice. The book, called *Persephone*, is not yet published.

I think my poetry is fairly full of references to the surfaces of the world and contains a certain amount of enquiry into the questions of reality. "Art" and "artificial" are words which to me are closely allied – art forms a separate world which to have any point must always feed through roots in non-art, just as language must depend on something that is not language for its life.

* * *

After reading English at Oxford, Jenny Joseph went to South Africa for a couple of years, returning to London in 1959. If in her first pamphlet collection, *The Unlooked-For Season*, there are few poems commenting on her period of residence in South Africa, certainly the experience was not without its impact upon her:

I do not go near
The station at such times for there are too many
People who go home.
Usually it is the season before the storms
And had I not, long since, lost all tears
I could weep enough to bring on thunder.

This feeling of exile, of loss, permeates the whole collection – she dwells upon desertion, abandonment, and death, lost or ruined houses, lost landscapes, deserted seaside towns and abandoned beaches. "Burial" features the burying of a dead seabird by four children. When she explores myths she turns, as Orpheus turned, to the loss of Eurydice. Even when a gold wrist watch is "Recovered from the Sea," it is on the "unloved body" of a middle-aged woman cast up on the shore – "The dead machine survived her beating heart." The background season to most of these poems is Winter. Summer is conceived as the "unlooked-for season," as an "amnesty." Already in these early poems, though, Joseph demonstrated her exceptional descriptive gifts and her capacity to organize her material.

Published 14 years later, *Rose in the Afternoon* is less structured and employs a more colloquial language which, in a curious way, is appropriate to her work, fusing thought and emotion; and the descriptive gifts are now directed to the people, situations, and incidents related to the urban scene and used to more effective purpose. It is as if she had turned her gaze from the distant perspective to focus upon the oddities of normal everyday life. The direct encounter with the subject and the honesty in expression are extremely satisfying. "Warning," which describes how eccentric she expects to become when she grows old, was selected for the *Oxford Book of Twentieth Century Verse*; but "Old Man Going," a complementary poem, is equally outstanding:

I don't mind what you do with the bits when I'm dead
When you take off this ruddy drip and fold up the tubes
And wheel away the catheter, for the last time Thank God,
And let my stinking body rot in its uraemia
There will not be any of it I want honoured.

A somewhat different attitude to that expressed in *The Unlooked-For Season*. Indeed, even the attitude to the season itself has changed:

Perhaps our happiness is like this summer
Holding, corrupting, laying on the air
A sweet narcotic, making the plums fall
Squelchy, ripe, tasteless when they lie too long.

Admittedly this is taken from one of the love poems which, while revealing a new aspect of the poet's personality, lose nothing in novelty of approach. There are some quite exciting poems in this collection, among them "To Keep Each Other Warm," "Language Teaching: Naming," "Old Man Going," "Certain Weathers," and "No Map Available"; but "Thoughts on Oxford Street from Provence and Elsewhere" is Joseph's most ambitious poem so far.

Though it contains some fascinating poems, *The Thinking Heart*, with its paradoxical title, seems to denote a period of indecision. In some of the poems there is more intricate use of simile, metaphor, and allegory, and yet, as if conscious of this development, there is also the "Life and Turgid Times of a Citizen" with its almost deliberate and provocative proem "Against Metaphor":

I am not going to talk to you about islands
Or about waving grasses ...
Oh no, if I want to say louse, pig or bastard,
That people are bullies and likely to watch others fall
On these broken pavements, and never lend a hand
Except to keep themselves up, I should say their names.

Well, sometimes she does say their names, however indelicate, and sometimes she doesn't, depending on her mood and intention. Her title, for instance, is taken from "Centrepiece: St. Sebastian," clearly an allegorical poem. In some poems she is concerned with the philosophical problems which have a bearing upon personal behaviour ("Love and Justice,"

"Trying to Understand Violence") or ironies and paradoxes of the human predicament, and in others she is content merely to talk aloud to herself about the trivia of encounters with tradesmen or doing the family wash. This volume marks a turning point; it will be interesting to see where she goes from here.

—Howard Sergeant

JOSEPH, M(ichael) K(ennedy). New Zealander. Born in Chingford, Essex, England, 9 July 1914. Educated at Auckland University College, B.A. 1933, M.A. 1934; Merton College, Oxford, B.A. 1938, B.Litt. 1939, M.A. 1945. Served in the British Army in the Royal Artillery, 1940–46. Married Mary Julia Antonovich in 1947; five children. Lecturer in English, 1945–49, and Senior Lecturer, 1950–59, Auckland University College; Associate Professor of English, 1960–69, and since 1970, Professor of English, University of Auckland. Recipient: Hubert Church Prose Award, 1958; Jessie Mackay Poetry Award, 1959; Sir James Wattie Prize, 1976; National Book Award, for fiction, 1978. Address: Department of English, University of Auckland, Private Bag, Auckland, New Zealand.

PUBLICATIONS

Verse

Imaginary Islands. Privately printed, 1950.
The Living Countries. Auckland, Paul's Book Arcade, 1959.
Inscription on a Paper Dart. Auckland, Auckland University Press–Oxford University Press, 1974.

Novels

I'll Soldier No More. Auckland, Paul's Book Arcade, and London, Gollancz, 1958.
A Pound of Saffron. Auckland, Paul's Book Arcade, and London, Gollancz, 1962.
The Hole in the Zero. Auckland, Paul's Book Arcade, and London, Gollancz, 1967; New York, Dutton, 1968.
A Soldier's Tale. Auckland and London, Collins, 1976.
The Time of Achamoth. Auckland and London, Collins, 1977.

Other

Byron the Poet. London, Gollancz, 1964.

Editor, *Frankenstein*, by Mary Shelley. London, Oxford University Press, 1969.

M. K. Joseph comments:

From about 1944–54, I was writing poetry; now novels and research. I admire the poets I teach – especially Pope, Byron, Yeats, Auden.

When I was writing verse, I was trying for something with a definite, fairly traditional shape, and a comprehensible meaning, not esoteric, not personal. I suppose I am interested in consciousness and self-consciousness, expressed in poems about New Zealand, about religion and about literature. These interests probably come out now in my novels.

* * *

In a note written at the request of an anthologist, M. K. Joseph said, "If poetry as dialogue seems in danger of extinction, we should take all the more seriously the idea of poetry as making. The poem is an object which we make and set down, like an antique torso in an abandoned city, good, self-sufficient, durable, waiting for the people to come back." In many ways, this could be a description of his own verse, which, even in its lighter form, is always well made, with firm artistry. Yet the sense of dialogue is there as well, for Professor Joseph's poems are also always about something.

He brings to poetry a mind nourished on classical and modern literatures, a quirky imagination, compassion and a concern with religion, art and history. Although he writes of the great truths, of time, love, dissolution, the arrogance of intellect, the guises of sophistry, and what is and what could be, a spirit of luminous joy keeps him from solemnity. This is the case, for instance, in "Mercury Bay Eclogue" in which he moves from a response to a New Zealand landscape through a meditation on New Zealand and European history and on the truth of poetry to an epiphanic enfolding of them all in the transcendence of peace and love.

Some of his poems recall war experiences, others define the New Zealand thing in places and history, others take their point of departure from concepts of modern science or medieval philosophy. All are sustained by a sympathetic awareness of Western culture, including Catholic tradition, which gives his poetry an amplitude rare in New Zealand writing. More than once, as in his satirical "Secular Litany," he contrasts the variety and richness of Mediterranean culture with the plodding materialism of New Zealanders. His other witty parodies and satires proceed from a positive and balanced Christian humanism.

It may sometimes be thought that the virtues of his poetry lie in its intellectual resourcefulness and its richness of allusion, and that it is emotionally rather reticent or low-powered. Some of his poetry supports such a view. The bulk of it does not. Even in such a sequence as "The Lovers and the City," based upon the characters of *Romeo and Juliet*, there is a sensitivity to broad human needs and a compassion that give the poems a glow of benignity which subsumes a recognition of the agonies of physical and spiritual love. His poetry is, in its way, academic poetry, scholarly poetry, urbane, gracious, allusive, and strengthened by a closer understanding of and affinity to the great Western traditions that most of his contemporaries possess. Yet it has tenderness and pity which its formal grace accentuates rather than muffles. And an eye for the freakish, the grotesque and the marvellous enables him to illuminate the ordinary with a sudden radiant perception of the inexhaustible wonders of man and the universe.

—J. C. Reid

JUSTICE, Donald (Rodney). American. Born in Miami, Florida, 12 August 1925. Educated at the University of Miami, B.A. 1945; University of North Carolina, Chapel Hill, M.A. 1947; Stanford University, California, 1947–48; University of Iowa, Iowa City (Rockefeller grant, 1954), Ph.D. 1954. Married Jean Ross in 1947; one son, Nathaniel. Visiting Assistant Professor, University of Missouri, Columbia, 1955–56; Assistant Professor, Hamline University, St. Paul, Minnesota, 1956–57; Lecturer, 1957–59, Assistant Professor, 1959–63, and Associate Professor, 1963–66, University of Iowa; Associate Professor, State University of New York, Syracuse, 1966–70; Visiting Professor, University of California, Irvine, 1970–71. Since 1971, Professor of English, University of Iowa. Poet-in-Residence, Reed College, Portland, Oregon, 1962. Recipient: Lamont Poetry Selection Award, 1959; Inez Boulton Prize, 1960, and Harriet Monroe Memorial Prize, 1965 (*Poetry*, Chicago); Ford Fellowship, in theatre, 1964; National Endowment for the Arts grant, 1967, 1973; National Institute of Arts and Letters award, 1974; Guggenheim Fellowship, 1976. Address: Department of English, University of Iowa, Iowa City, Iowa 52242, U.S.A.

PUBLICATIONS

Verse

The Summer Anniversaries. Middletown, Connecticut, Wesleyan University Press, 1960.
A Local Storm. Iowa City, Stone Wall Press, 1963.
Night Light. Middletown, Connecticut, Wesleyan University Press, 1967.
Four Poets, with others. Pella, Iowa, C.U.I. Press, 1967.
Sixteen Poems. Iowa City, Stone Wall Press, 1970.
From a Notebook. Iowa City, Seamark Press, 1972.
Departures. New York, Atheneum, 1973.
Selected Poems. New York, Atheneum, 1979.

Other

Editor, *The Collected Poems of Weldon Kees.* Iowa City, Stone Wall Press, 1960; revised edition, Lincoln, University of Nebraska Press, 1975.
Editor, with Paul Engle and Henri Coulette, *Midland.* New York, Random House, 1961.
Editor, with Alexander Aspel, *Contemporary French Poetry.* Ann Arbor, University of Michigan Press, 1965.
Editor, *Syracuse Poems 1968.* Syracuse, New York, Syracuse University Department of English, 1968.

Critical Studies: *Alone with America* by Richard Howard, New York, Atheneum, 1969; "On Donald Justice" by Greg Simon, in *American Poetry Review* (Philadelphia), v, 2, 1976.

* * *

The idea of loss is a continuous one in Donald Justice's first book, *The Summer Anniversaries*, and one that deepens and becomes more complex as his career advances. In *Night Light* the idea is extended to include the loss of love, the decline of self and, ultimately, the loss of self. Just as the past exercises its peculiar strength by having become past, so the self can be more compelling, paradoxically present when lost:

He has come to report himself
A missing person

The authorities
Hand him the forms ...

They reassure him
That he can be nowhere

But wherever he finds himself
From moment to moment,

Which, for the moment, is here.
And he might like to believe them.

But in the mirror
He sees what is missing.

It is himself....

In another poem Justice is speaking as much about the body of his work as he is the formal embodiment of his vision: "I indulge myself/In rich refusals./Nothing suffices./I hone myself to/This edge. Asleep, I/Am a horizon" ("The Thin Man"). From the very beginning Justice has fashioned his poems, honed them down, freed them of rhetorical excess and the weight, however gracefully sustained, of an elaborate diction. His self-indulgence, then, has been with the possibilities of plain statement. His refusal to adopt any other mode but that which his subject demands – minimal, narcissist, negating – has nourished him.

Often the subjects in Justice's poems remind one of the paintings of Edward Hopper. Attention is paid to the passing and ephemeral conditions of the present. There is a painful sense that life as it is lived escapes us even in its most ordinary aspects and most durable guises. It is that need in Justice's poems to recover banal views and average moments, to rescue what otherwise would be lost forever, which gives them their sadness, and their success.

If absence and loss are inescapable conditions of life, the poem for Justice is an act of recovery. It synthesizes, for all its meagreness, what is with what is no longer; it conjures up a life that persists by denial, gathering strength from its own hopelessness, and exists, finally and positively, as an emblem of survival.

—Mark Strand

KANDEL, Lenore. American. Born in New York City. Recipient: Borestone Poetry Award, 1962. Address: 925 Sanchez Street, San Francisco, California 94114, U.S.A.

PUBLICATIONS

Verse

A Passing Dragon. Studio City, California, Three Penny Press, 1959.
A Passing Dragon Seen Again. Studio City, California, Three Penny Press, 1959.
An Exquisite Navel. Studio City, California, Three Penny Press, 1959.
The Love Book. San Francisco, Stolen Paper Review Editions, 1966.
Word Alchemy. New York, Grove Press, 1967.

Lenore Kandel comments:

Major theme – awareness of it all. Awareness of same as characteristic subjects – the creature and the planet, the angel and the star. Forms – as the subject demands. Sources – as above. Influences – as above. Devices – clarity that flies.

* * *

Lenore Kandel is an amazing lady who seems to have vanished from the public world of literature at the height of her success. Her most noted work is *The Love Book* – a passionate and explicit work which in turn became a *cause célèbre*. Its strong erotic content was perhaps even more provocative to the prurient and blue-nose alike because it was written by a woman celebrating love-making in an active voice, the voice usually relegated to the male poet: "[*The Love Book*] deals with physical love and the invocation, recognition, and acceptance of the divinity in man through the medium of physical love. In other words, it feels good. It feels so good that you can step outside your private ego and share the grace of the universe. This simple and rather self-evident statement, enlarged and exampled poetically, raised a furor difficult to believe...." *The Love Book* is a marvelously balanced hymn of praise and ascension and remains her most fully-realized accomplishment. Like *Dark Brown* by Michael McClure, *The Love Book* attempts to create an erotic and positive physical love poetry unique in American literature.

Her only other collection, *Word Alchemy*, is a selection of shorter poems written from 1960 to 1967. It is uneven in its voice and strength. The most satisfying poems are those which combine precision, wit and sensitivity. For instance, "Melody for Married Men":

> I like to watch the young girls walk
> swinging their hips and hair
> swinging their hopes and dreams in magic circles
> they never walk alone, but move in twos and threes
> confiding audacities to each other
> twitching their tails and giggling
> while thirty year old men watch from their windows
> drinking coffee with their wives and making fantasies
> of Moslem heaven

or this excerpt from "Spring 61":

> yesterday we went to the ocean and prised mussels
> from low-tide rocks
> cooked them with onion carrots celery seed
> (delicious)
> cut fingers healed in sea water ...

reflect her ability to translate material into forthright and clear language. Many other poems in the collection have the tendency to become strident and break into areas of prose and polemic and lose power because of a lessening of attention to transformative language.

—David Meltzer

KAVANAGH, P(atrick) J(oseph Gregory). British. Born in Worthing, Sussex, in 1931. Educated at the Douai School; Merton College, Oxford, M.A. Formerly, Lecturer, University of Indonesia, Djarkarta. Recipient: Richard Hillary Memorial Prize, 1966; *The Guardian* Fiction Prize, 1969. Lives in Gloucestershire, England.

PUBLICATIONS

Verse

One and One: Poems. London, Heinemann, 1959.

On the Way to the Depot. London, Chatto and Windus-Hogarth Press, 1967.
About Time. London, Chatto and Windus-Hogarth Press, 1970.
Edward Thomas in Heaven. London, Chatto and Windus-Hogarth Press, 1974.
Life Before Death. London, Chatto and Windus-Hogarth Press, 1979.

Plays

Television Plays: *William Cowper Lived Here* (documentary), 1971; *Journey Through Summer* (documentary), 1973.

Novels

A Song and Dance. London, Chatto and Windus, 1968.
A Happy Man. London, Chatto and Windus, 1972.
People and Weather. London, Calder, 1979.
The Irish Captain. New York, Doubleday, 1979.

Other

The Perfect Stranger (autobiography). London, Chatto and Windus, 1966.
Scarf Jack (juvenile). London, Bodley Head, 1978.

* * *

As a poet P. J. Kavanagh is a difficult case – which means that he is interesting. Although skilled in the use of free rhythms and thoroughly professional in his procedures, he has nothing like the robustness to be considered as a major poet, and the content of his work shows no development – but to be a good minor poet has always been an achievement. How good is he? His main fault, and it is a serious one, has been well stated by a critic: "... the final impression, despite [his] neat descriptiveness, is of someone being a little too breezy in his acceptance, with a slightly maddening optimism." Kavanagh is a television entertainer, a failed comedian and a whimsy-sentimental purveyor of middlebrow travelogues: this presumably pot-boiling aspect shows up, which it should not, in his verse. And yet he loves nature and is exceedingly accurate in his descriptions of it. What he has learned from Edward Thomas, Andrew Young, Edmund Blunden and others has been well assimilated. But something happened between his admittedly immature early poetry and his later (if not perhaps, his latest) work: incompetently equipped to deal with suffering as a young poet, he was none the less prepared to confront it; now that he is competently equipped his poetry might actually be described as a series of exercises in how to avoid it. If no other way will do, he is prepared to be deliberately banal or sentimental.

Yet when all this has been said – and it has to be said – Kavanagh is imaginative, intelligent and has a fine sense of delicacy. Occasionally, too, he can be angry – and when he is, he is very effective. An example is his sharp satire on the simple-minded Bardic posturings of Ted Hughes in "The Famous Poet," who, while snarling "right in the teeth of Life's snarl" does not really manifest quite the same attitude towards

Two charabancs
Of Poetry Students in summery clothes necking and laughing.
In dove-light he watches them straighten their clothes and faces,
Thrilled, soon, to frown in the presence of Truth.

Furthermore, Kavanagh's poetry, though it shows no intellectual advance, has consistently improved: observation increasingly takes the place of sentimentality (the habit of giggling banality has not yet been shed), and the rhythms are stronger and more confident. "Commuter" (this, like "The Famous Poet," is from *Edward Thomas in Heaven*) may even be seen as an oblique attempt to avoid the fault of "maddening optimism": what it observes is by no means "breezy" in that manner which has become too notoriously associated with this poet. Broad description of "an open station platform in the Dordogne" narrows to the sinister precision of:

> the rest of us waited, standing beside our cases.
> When it arrived she left him and climbed on the train
> Her face like dawn because of their conversation.
> She suddenly turned, grabbed his neck in the crook of her arm,
> Gave him the bones of her head, the bones of her body, violently,
> Then climbed on again alone. Her face hardened
> In seconds as the train moved away from her island.
> Tight lipped she looked around for a seat on the sea.

This clearly demonstrates that Kavanagh is not a person who does not understand or has not seen suffering; his problem is rather to "place" it in his poetry. It should not be implied that it is his duty to indulge it – rather that he should not pretend it away. His poetry shows some signs that he is concerned to purge away its false elements.

—Martin Seymour-Smith

KEARNS, Lionel (John). Canadian. Born in Nelson, British Columbia, 16 February 1937. Educated at the University of British Columbia, Vancouver, B.A. in English 1961, M.A. 1964; School of Oriental and African Studies, London, 1964–65. Married Dolly Revati Maharaj in 1960 (separated); four children. Lived in Mexico and Trinidad. Since 1966, Assistant Professor of English, Simon Fraser University, Burnaby, British Columbia. Recipient: Canada Council fellowship, 1964, 1965, and grant, 1968, 1973. Address: Department of English, Simon Fraser University, Burnaby, British Columbia, Canada.

PUBLICATIONS

Verse

Songs of Circumstance. Vancouver, Tish Press, 1963.
Listen George. Montreal, Imago Press, 1965.
4 Poeter, with others. Stockholm, Bok Ock Bild, 1966.
Pointing. Toronto, Ryerson Press, 1967.
By the Light of the Silvery McLune: Media Parables, Poems, Signs, Gestures, and Other Assaults on the Interface. Vancouver, Daylight Press-Talonbooks, 1969.
About Time. Prince George, British Columbia, Caledonia, 1974.
Two Poems for a Manitoulin Island Canada Day. Vancouver, Blewointmentpress, 1976.
Practicing Up to Be Human. Toronto, Coach House Press, 1978.

Film-Poems, with Gordon Payne: *The Birth of God*, 1973; *Negotiating a New Canadian Constitution*, 1974.

Critical Studies: in *Tish 1–30* (Vancouver), 1961–64; *Canadian Literature 20* and *37*

(Vancouver), Spring 1964 and Summer 1968; *Rhymes and Reasons*, edited by John Robert Colombo, Toronto, Holt Rinehart, 1971.

Lionel Kearns comments:

I am currently experimenting with and investigating the poetic possibilities of film and the filmic possibilities of poetry.

* * *

"Poems represent a spontaneous projection of my own concern at any particular moment," Lionel Kearns wrote about the verse in his first large-scale book, *Pointing*. The poems are clever and sometimes private. "Recall," for instance, ends: "They will perceive only/an insignificant/hiss of words/in the wind." In "Poet as Salesman" he seems at odds with inner life. "Anguish," he writes, "want some?"

Kearns's other major book is *By the Light of the Silvery McLune*, and the pun on the name of the Toronto media pundit Marshal McLuhan is a clue to the kind of poems that are in the book. From a poet concerned with semantics and semiology, Kearns has become a poet concerned with performance and effect. In the new book are shaggy-dog poems, essentially stand-up comic routines, like "Telephone," which begins: "After completing his call/ Roderick discovered/the phone-booth had no door." It ends, many pages later, on this note: "so that today/no one knows whether Roderick/is living or dead."

Perhaps it is possible to see in Kearns's work – which has so far only touched the surface of an imaginative world of its own making – an intelligence at work that will radically alter the relationship of the reader and the writer. One direction he might move in is into a West Coast Surrealism. At present he remains what George Bowering has dubbed him: "Lionel Kearns, the linguistic poet."

—John Robert Colombo

KELL, Richard (Alexander). British. Born in Youghal, County Cork, Ireland, 1 November 1927. Educated at Methodist College, Belfast; Wesley College, Dublin, 1944–46; Trinity College, Dublin, B.A. (honours) in English and French literature 1952. Married Muriel Adelaide Nairn in 1953 (died, 1975); four children. Assistant Teacher, Kilkenny College, Ireland, and Whinney Bank School, Middlesborough, Lancashire; Assistant Librarian, Luton Public Library, Bedfordshire, 1954–56, and Brunel College of Technology, Uxbridge, Middlesex, 1956–59; Assistant Lecturer, 1960–65, and Lecturer in English, 1966–70, Isleworth Polytechnic, London. Since 1970, Senior Lecturer in English, Newcastle upon Tyne Polytechnic. Address: 18 Rectory Grove, Gosforth, Newcastle upon Tyne NE3 1AL, England.

PUBLICATIONS

Verse

(Poems). Oxford, Fantasy Press, 1957.
Control Tower. London, Chatto and Windus-Hogarth Press, 1962.

Six Irish Poets, with others, edited by Robin Skelton. London, Oxford University Press, 1962.
Differences. London, Chatto and Windus-Hogarth Press, 1969.
Humours. Sunderland, Ceolfrith, 1978.
Heartwood. Newcastle upon Tyne, Northern House, 1978.

Manuscript Collection: Literary and Philosophical Society Library, Newcastle upon Tyne.

Richard Kell comments:

(1970) The poems in *Control Tower*, largely reflective and descriptive, were written without any awareness of a predominant theme; in retrospect, however, it appears that one of my main concerns was the opposition between negative and positive states (restraint and freedom, deprivation and fulfillment, apathy and love, scepticism and faith, inner blindness and vision), often with a note of regret for the elusiveness of the second. Though some aspect of the theme itself was implied fairly frequently, the experiences that represented it were varied – ranging from the sight of some empty coal carts to a meditation focused on the image of a Buddhist goddess. In *Differences*, the same kind of dichotomy emerges, but with an emphasis on harmony and conflict as concomitants of diversity. As for technique, I like to combine fairly well-defined verse forms – of many types, and not necessarily traditional – with rhythmic flexibility. In the choice and syntactic ordering of words I aim at intelligibility as well as imaginative precision (which does not preclude double meanings when these are useful). In general my poetry tends to be quiet and controlled rather than effusive: I love freedom but am distrustful of excess.

(1980) The poems in *Humours*, written in 1964 and 1965, and printed with accompanying pictures by Dick Ward, are concerned with familiar human dispositions, states of mind, beliefs, practices. These are often presented symbolically, and the style is dry and witty (broadly speaking) rather than lyrical. By contrast, the poems in *Heartwood* express personal feeling in a fairly direct way. They were written in memory of my wife, who died in a swimming accident in 1975.

* * *

Richard Kell was a slow developer, for his first collection, *Control Tower*, did not appear until he was thirty-five. It suggested that Kell was a Movement poet with a slight Irish accent. The hint of Yeats's tower in the title might be fortuitous, but there is a stronger echo in "The Swan" (one of Kell's best poems) which recalls another favourite Yeatsian emblem: "Cumbrous wings whacking the startled air/And terror swirls the surface of the lake." But Kell avoids an emphatic Yeatsian rhetoric, and a more immediate model is a quieter poet, Robert Graves, whose influence is apparent in "Citadels." Kell's qualities, as revealed in *Control Tower*, were those of several other British poets of the 1950's: formal skill and a satisfying precision of statement, plus a tendency to comment on experience rather than to explore it from within, and a comparatively narrow emotional range. There was also a tendency, ultimately derived from Auden, to lean heavily on a highly charged abstraction such as "love": "Down the long approach/Of love, to love's darkness." But Kell's most positive quality was his capacity to render experience in clear visual images and a firm draughtsmanlike line.

In *Differences* Kell extended his range to take in new and less immediate areas of experience, such as dreams and Homeric myths. There were slightly fewer poems of sharp visual observation, tied to particular places or occasions, though the pervasive intelligence and the technical accomplishment were still evident. Of Kell's later poetry, *Heartwood* is outstanding, a moving but carefully wrought sequence of lyrics in memory of the poet's dead wife.

—Bernard Bergonzi

KELLY, Robert. American. Born in Brooklyn, New York, 24 September 1935. Educated at the City College of New York, A.B. 1955; Columbia University, New York, 1955–58. Translator, New York, 1956–58. Lecturer in English, Wagner College, New York, 1960–61. Instructor in German, 1961–62, Instructor in English, 1962–64, Assistant Professor, 1964–69, Associate Professor, 1969–74, and since 1974, Professor of English, Bard College, Annandale-on-Hudson, New York. Assistant Professor of English, State University of New York, Buffalo, Summer 1964; Visiting Lecturer, Tufts University, Medford, Massachusetts, 1966–67; Poet-in-Residence, California Institute of Technology, Pasadena, 1971–72, University of Kansas, Lawrence, 1975, and Dickinson College, Carlisle, Pennsylvania, 1976. Editor, *Chelsea Review*, New York, 1958–60; Founding Editor, with George Economou, *Trobar* magazine, 1960–64, and Trobar Books, 1962–64, New York; Contributing Editor, *Caterpillar*, New York, 1969–73; Editors, *Los 1*, 1977. Since 1963, Editor, *Matter* magazine and Matter publishing company, New York, later Annandale-on-Hudson, New York; Since 1977, Contributing Editor, *Alcheringa: Ethnopoetics*. Fellow in Fiction, New York City Writers Conference, 1967. Address: Department of English, Bard College, Annandale-on-Hudson, New York 12504, U.S.A.

PUBLICATIONS

Verse

Armed Descent. New York, Hawks Well Press, 1961.
Her Body Against Time (bilingual edition). Mexico City, El Corno Emplumado, 1963.
Round Dances. New York, Trobar, 1964.
Tabula. Lawrence, Kansas, Dialogue Press, 1964.
Enstasy. Annandale-on-Hudson, New York, Matter, 1964.
Matter/Fact/Sheet/1. Buffalo, New York, Matter, 1964.
Matter/Fact/Sheet/2. Annandale-on-Hudson, New York, Matter, 1964.
Lunes, with *Sightings* by Jerome Rothenberg. New York, Hawks Well Press, 1964.
Lectiones. Placitas, New Mexico, Duende Press, 1965.
Words in Service. New Haven, Connecticut, Robert Lamberton, 1966.
Weeks. Mexico City, El Corno Emplumado, 1966.
Songs XXIV. Cambridge, Massachusetts, Pym Randall Press, 1967.
Twenty Poems. Annandale-on-Hudson, New York, Matter, 1967.
Devotions. Annandale-on-Hudson, New York, Salitter, 1967.
Axon Dendron Tree. Annandale-on-Hudson, New York, Matter, 1967.
Crooked Bridge Love Society. Annandale-on-Hudson, New York, Salitter, 1967.
A Joining: A Sequence for H.D. Los Angeles, Black Sparrow Press, 1967.
Alpha. Gambier, Ohio, Pothanger Press, 1968.
Finding the Measure. Los Angeles, Black Sparrow Press, 1968.
Songs I–XXX. Cambridge, Massachusetts, Pym Randall Press, 1968.
Sonnets. Los Angeles, Black Sparrow Press, 1968.
From the Common Shore, Book 5. Great Neck, New York, George Robert Minkoff, 1968.
We Are the Arbiters of Beast Desire. Berkeley, California, MBVL, 1969.
A California Journal. London, Big Venus, 1969.
The Common Shore, Books I–V: A Long Poem about America in Time. Los Angeles, Black Sparrow Press, 1969.
Kali Yuga. London, Cape Goliard Press, 1970; New York, Grossman, 1971.
Flesh: Dream: Book. Los Angeles, Black Sparrow Press, 1971.
Ralegh. Los Angeles, Black Sparrow Press, 1972.
The Pastorals. Los Angeles, Black Sparrow Press, 1972.
Reading Her Notes. Privately printed, 1972.
The Tears of Edmund Burke. Annandale-on-Hudson, New York, Printed by Helen, 1973.

Whaler Frigate Clippership. Lawrence, Kansas, Tansy, 1973.
The Mill of Particulars. Los Angeles, Black Sparrow Press, 1973.
The Loom. Los Angeles, Black Sparrow Press, 1975.
Sixteen Odes. Santa Barbara, California, Black Sparrow Press, 1976.
The Lady of. Santa Barbara, California, Black Sparrow Press, 1977.
The Convections. Santa Barbara, California, Black Sparrow Press, 1978.
The Book of Persephone. Providence, Rhode Island, Treacle Press, 1978.
The Cruise of the Pnyx. New York, Station Hill Press, 1979.
Kill the Messenger Who Brings Bad News. Santa Barbara, California, Black Sparrow Press, 1979.

Recording: *Finding the Measure*, Black Sparrow Press, 1968.

Plays

The Well Wherein a Deer's Head Bleeds (produced New York, 1964). Published in *A Play and Two Poems*, with Diane Wakoski and Ron Loewinsohn, Los Angeles, Black Sparrow Press, 1968.
Eros and Psyche, music by Elie Yarden (produced New Paltz, New York, 1971). Privately printed, 1971.

Novels

The Scorpions. New York, Doubleday, 1967; London, Calder and Boyars, 1969.
Cities. West Newbury, Massachusetts, Frontier Press, 1971.

Other

Statement. Los Angeles, Black Sparrow Press, 1968.
In Time (essays). West Newbury, Massachusetts, Frontier Press, 1971.
Sulphur. Privately printed, 1972.
A Line of Sight. Los Angeles, Black Sparrow Press, 1974.
Wheres. Santa Barbara, Black Sparrow Press, 1978.

Editor, with Paris Leary, *A Controversy of Poets: An Anthology of Contemporary American Poetry.* New York, Doubleday, 1965.
Editor, *The Journals*, by Paul Blackburn. Los Angeles, Black Sparrow Press, 1975.

Manuscript Collection: Kent State University, Ohio.

Critical Studies: by Paul Blackburn, in *Kulchur* (New York), 1962; *American Poetry from the Puritans to the Present*, by Hyatt Waggoner, Boston, Houghton Mifflin, 1968; review by Diane Wakoski, in *Poetry* (Chicago), 1972; "Robert Kelly Issue" of *Vort* (Bloomington, Indiana), 1974.

Robert Kelly comments:

What help can I give the reader who would come to my work? First, tell him it is not *my* work, only Work, itself, somehow arisen through (or in spite of) my instrumentality. My personality is its enemy, only distracts. But what is there for the reader who reads to find the man? He'll find the man. The man is always there, the stink of him, the hope and fear he confuses with himself, the beauty of him, struggle, dim intuitions of a glory that is not personal, but that only persons can inhabit and share. That we are human in the world, and share our thoughts.

And this sharing of thought, perception, is what becomes the world. The world is our shared thought.

But in language the unperceived or newly perceived can arise, to break the fabric of the ordinary consensus of our lives. News from nowhere, a new handle for an old day.

Invited to introduce my work to the general reader, never!, the *specific* reader, I rehearse for our mutual benefit two answers my work has given, and I here transcribe.

1967. Prefix to *Finding the Measure*:

Finding the measure is finding the mantram,
is finding the moon, as index of measure,
is finding the moon's source;
                                        if that source
is Sun, finding the measure is finding
the natural articulation of ideas.
                                          The organism
of the macrocosm, the organism of language,
the organism of I combine in ceaseless naturing
to propagate a fourth,
                              the poem,
                                        from their trinity.

Style is death. Finding the measure is finding
a freedom from that death, a way out, a movement
forward.
        Finding the measure is finding the
specific music of the hour,
                                      the synchronous
consequence of the motion of the whole world.

(Measure as distinct from meter, from any precompositional grid or matrix super-imposed upon the fact of the poem's own growth "under hand.")

1973. Prefix to *The Mill of Particulars*:

Language is the only genetics.
            Field
"in which a man is understood & understands"
            & becomes
            what he thinks,
becomes what he says
                              following the argument.

When it is written that Hermes or Thoth invented language, it is meant that language is itself the psychopomp, who leads the Individuality out of Eternity into the conditioned world of Time, a world that language makes by discussing it.

So the hasty road
& path of arrow
must lead up
from language again
                        & in language the work be done,
work of light,
            beyond.

Through manipulation and derangement of ordinary language (*parole*), the conditioned world is changed, weakened in its associative links, its power to hold an unconscious world-view (consensus) together. Eternity, which is always there, looms beyond the grid of speech.

I have spoken a little about my motives and my intentions. I have not presumed to speak about the work itself, which must, true to its name, do its own work, and try to lure the reader to dance with it.

* * *

The density of Robert Kelly's poems is balanced by their liveliness. He has, for the time, found "the measure," as expressed in the "prefix" to *Finding the Measure* [quoted above]. Precisely what Kelly means by "style" is a puzzle: I accept the above credo as Kelly's way of saying that the individual poem must create its own form. One would be tempted to say that his style is *not* death, but nevertheless a style. Kelly shares with many of America's best poets an unpredictability: his use of the language is sure but never without surprises. Our most lauded poets, the dandies, either work the language beautifully or play with it cleverly. Kelly plays language and is not afraid to mix various approaches within one poem ("Of Earth"):

blacks menaced by rising boredom, whites
    stung by neuter anopheles
lie at the foot of Uranus' throne
    –for the retail is deadlier
        than the hail,
wipeth stockes oute
            & buggeth corne

Kelly's "freedom" is, perhaps, his willingness to experiment with a variety of forms. In one long, rambling poem, "The Alchemist," Kelly's voice shifts frequently but always seems his own: "the origin, far side of a lake/is always shadow/the voice goes around/it easily in one hour...." The poem deals with change, and achieves tonal changes of its own: "& if we do not get up and destroy all the congressmen/turn them into naked men and let the sun shine on them/set them down in a desert & let them find their way out...." Kelly's rhetoric is dense but not tiring. The language always pivots on an image; the energy of this turning produces sparks:

The alchemist

weeping in the Spanish field
in a cloak chewed into rags by its symbols

        a body,
        under it,
whose name is love & which only of all light love can eat

Kelly may not like it, but he does have a style: the style of a poet whose work cannot be characterized except by his attitude. It is this attitude that marks him as one of America's most promising poets.

In *Flesh : Dream : Book*, Kelly is again at an energetic peak, exploring formal as well as free verse. The book contains a lovely sequence of eighteen sonnets, as well as numerous other poems (of such gentle, natural rhythms!) that make lasting tactile impressions, and harken the priorities suggested by the book's title:

Fish you caught
delight me
five years ago
getting you wet

nourished on
delight
                    sat on the bank
waiting for that life
to come up
that was food
how

cool your body is

—Geof Hewitt

KENNEDY, X. J. Pseudonym for Joseph Charles Kennedy. American. Born in Dover, New Jersey, 21 August 1929. Educated at Seton Hall College, South Orange, New Jersey, B.Sc. 1950 (Phi Beta Kappa); Columbia University, New York, M.A. 1951; the Sorbonne, Paris, Cert. Litt. 1956. Served in the United States Navy, 1951–55. Married Dorothy Mintzlaff in 1962; five children. Teaching Fellow, 1956–60, and Instructor, 1960–62, University of Michigan, Ann Arbor; taught at the University of North Carolina, Greensboro, 1962–63; Assistant Professor, 1963–67, Associate Professor, 1967–73, and Professor of English, 1973–79, Tufts University, Medford, Massachusetts. Visiting Lecturer, Wellesley College, Massachusetts, 1964, and the University of California, Irvine, 1966–67; Bruern Fellow in American Literature, University of Leeds, 1974–75. Poetry Editor, *Paris Review*, Paris and New York, 1962–64. Editor, with Dorothy M. Kennedy, *Counter/Measures* magazine, 1972–74. Recipient: Hopwood Award, 1959; Bread Loaf Writers Conference Fellowship, 1960; Lamont Poetry Selection Award, 1961; Bess Hokin Prize (*Poetry*, Chicago), 1961; National Endowment for the Arts grant, 1967; Shelley Memorial Award, 1970; Guggenheim Fellowship, 1973. Agent: Curtis Brown Ltd., 575 Madison Avenue, New York, New York 10022. Address: 4 Fern Way, Bedford, Massachusetts 01730, U.S.A.

PUBLICATIONS

Verse

Nude Descending a Staircase: Poems, Song, A Ballad. New York, Doubleday, 1961.
Growing into Love. New York, Doubleday, 1969.
Bulsh. Providence, Rhode Island, Burning Deck, 1970.
Breaking and Entering. London, Oxford University Press, 1972.
Emily Dickinson in Southern California. Boston, Godine, 1974.
Celebrations after the Death of John Brennan. Lincoln, Massachusetts, Penmaen Press, 1974.
Three Tenors, One Vehicle: A Book of Songs, with James E. Camp and Keith Waldrop. Columbia, Missouri, Open Places, 1975.
One Winter Night in August and Other Nonsense Jingles (juvenile). New York, Atheneum, 1975.
The Phantom Ice Cream Man: More Nonsense Jingles (juvenile). New York, Atheneum, 1979.

Other

Editor, with James E. Camp, *Mark Twain's Frontier.* New York, Holt Rinehart, 1963.

Editor, *An Introduction to Poetry* (textbook). Boston, Little Brown, 1966; revised edition, 1971, 1974.
Editor, with Keith Waldrop and James E. Camp, *Pegasus Descending: A Book of the Best Bad Verse*. New York, Macmillan, and London, Collier Macmillan, 1971.
Editor, *Messages: A Thematic Anthology of Poetry*. Boston, Little Brown, 1973.
Editor, *An Introduction to Fiction*. Boston, Little Brown, 1976; revised edition, 1979.
Editor, *Literature: An Introduction to Fiction, Poetry, and Drama*. Boston, Little Brown, 1976; revised edition, 1979.

Critical Studies: "Squibs" by Bernard Waldrop, in *Burning Deck 2* (Providence, Rhode Island), Spring 1963; "Recent Poetry: The End of an Era" by Louis L. Martz, in *Yale Review* (New Haven, Connecticut), Winter 1970; Stephen Tudor, in *Spirit* (South Orange, New Jersey), Spring 1970; Henry Taylor, in *Masterplots Annual*, New York, Salem Press, 1970; in *Times Literary Supplement* (London), 24 December 1971; M. L. Rosenthal, in *Shenandoah* (Lexington, Virginia), Fall 1972; David Shapiro, in *Poetry* (Chicago), July 1976.

X. J. Kennedy comments:

[I belong to] the Wolgamot School (group of young poets including Donald Hall, W. D. Snodgrass, and Keith Waldrop, centering around the literary historian John Barton Wolgamot, begun at the University of Michigan in the 1950's).

Nearly always write in rime and metre. Favor narratives, lyrics to be sung.

* * *

Nude Descending a Staircase remains one of the most remarkable first volumes of poetry written by a 20th-century author. In it X. J. Kennedy gives a *tour de force* performance, offering serious poems such as the elegy "On a Child Who Lived One Moment," lyrical poems such as the title piece about a "one woman waterfall," poems to be sung such as the clever "In a Prominent Bar in Secaucus One Day," and light verse like "King Tut." It is a book which inspired hope of even better things from Kennedy, but sadly this hope has not been borne out. Instead, Kennedy in his later work has turned to writing little but light verse, epigrams, and parodies. Of these he can be a master; for example, his "Saint Bulsh" series of couplets, about a hypocritical priest reminiscent of Yeats's Archbishop, is a triumph of bitterly acerbic hilarity. Yet too often Kennedy slips into mere cuteness and writes such lines as these: "Meter/Is the thrust rests thrust of loins and peter/and rime,/to come at the same time"; and sometimes he errs in pushing a joke too far: "Emily Dickinson in Southern California" offers not one but nine parodies of Dickinson.

Kennedy's humorous work is similar to that of Auden's later verse and, like Auden, he writes tightly structured poems. In "Reading Trip" the poet is advised "*Screw prosody*" and is asked "*Why take pains/Trimming it neat? Nobody gonna play/* That *game no more*." Kennedy, though, gladly and expertly plays the prosody game. Yet one wishes that Kennedy would take as much care in his selection of content as he does with technique. Frequently he does not, as when the delicate structure of the villanelle is wasted on the trivial thoughts of "Drivers of Diaper-Service Trucks Are Sad." Kennedy's own advice on poetry is offered in "Ars Poetica": "The goose that laid the golden egg/Died looking up its crotch/To find out how its sphincter worked./Would you lay well? Don't watch." But one seldom gets any feeling of spontaneity in Kennedy's work; instead, the reader is constantly being made aware of the poet at work.

At his best, though, Kennedy can produce such a fine poem as the magnificent sonnet "Nothing in Heaven Functions as It Ought":

Nothing in Heaven functions as it ought.
Peter's bifocals, blindly sat on, crack;
His gates lurch wide with the cackle of a cock,
Not turn with a hush of gold as Milton had thought;
Gangs of the slaughtered innocents keep huffing
The nimbers off the Venerable Bede
Like that of an old dandelion gone to seed;
And the beatific choir keeps breaking up, coughing.

But Hell, sleek Hell hath no freewheeling part:
None takes his own sweet time, none quickens pace.
Ask anyone, *How come you here, poor heart?* –
And he will slot a quarter through his face,
You'll hear an instant click, a tear will start
Imprinted with an abstract of his case.

Here wit and seriousness, as well as form and function, are all in harmony. In the metrical irregularity of the octet and the metrical perfection of the sestet, technique nicely mirrors theme. Kennedy's fine irony, often too rampant in his verse, is tightly controlled and quite effective here.

—Dennis Lynch

KENNELLY, (Timothy) Brendan. Irish. Born in Ballylongford, County Kerry, 17 April 1936. Educated at St. Ita's College, Tarbert, County Kerry: Trinity College, Dublin, Ph.D. 1967; Leeds University. Married Margaret O'Brien in 1969; one daughter. Junior Lecturer, 1963–66, Lecturer, 1966–69, Associate Professor, 1969–73, and since 1973, Professor of Modern Literature, Trinity College, Dublin. Cornell Professor of English Literature, Swarthmore College, Pennsylvania, 1971–72. Recipient: AE Memorial Award, 1967. Address: 19 St. Alban's Park, Sandymount, Dublin, Ireland.

PUBLICATIONS

Verse

Cast a Cold Eye, with Rudi Holzapfel. Dublin, Dolmen Press, 1959.
The Rain, The Moon, with Rudi Holzapfel. Dublin, Dolmen Press, 1961.
The Dark about Our Loves, with Rudi Holzapfel. Dublin, John Augustine, 1962.
Green Townlands, with Rudi Holzapfel. Leeds, Bibliographical Press, 1963.
Let Fall No Burning Leaf. Dublin, New Square, 1963.
My Dark Fathers. Dublin, New Square, 1964.
Up and At It. Dublin, New Square, 1965.
Collection One: Getting Up Early. Dublin, Allen Figgis, 1966.
Good Souls to Survive. Dublin, Allen Figgis, 1967.
Dream of a Black Fox. Dublin, Allen Figgis, 1968.
Selected Poems. Dublin, Allen Figgis, 1969; New York, Dutton, 1971.
A Drinking Cup: Poems from the Irish. Dublin, Allen Figgis, 1970.
Bread. Dublin, Tara Telephone, 1971.

Love-Cry. Dublin, Allen Figgis, 1972.
Salvation, The Stranger. Dublin, Tara Telephone, 1972.
The Voices: A Sequence of Poems. Dublin, Gallery Press, 1973.
A Kind of Trust. Dublin, Gallery Press, 1975.
New and Selected Poems, edited by Peter Fallon. Dublin, Gallery Press, 1976.
Shelley in Dublin. Dublin, Egoist Press, 1977.
Islandman. Dublin, Profile Press, 1977.
The Visitor. Dublin, St. Beuno's Press, 1978.
A Small Light. Dublin, Gallery Press, 1979.

Novels

The Crooked Cross. Dublin, Allen Figgis, 1963; Boston, Little Brown, 1964.
The Florentines. Dublin, Allen Figgis, 1967.

Other

Editor, *The Penguin Book of Irish Verse*. London, Penguin, 1970; revised edition, 1972.

Critical Studies: B.A. Thesis by Antonella Ceoletta, University of Venice, 1973; M.Litt. Thesis by Frances Gwynn, Trinity College, Dublin, 1974.

Brendan Kennelly comments:

I used to divide my poetry into rather facile categories, such as poems written about the countryside, poems written about the city, and poems that tried to express some sort of personal philosophy. I think now that such categories are false and I believe instead that I select appropriate images from aspects of my experience and try to use them in such a way that they express what goes on within. This involves a continued struggle to discover and develop a proper language, carefully selected from the words of the world in which I live. There is this continual battle between civilized sluggishness and sharp seeing, seeing-into. The poem is born the moment one sees into and through one's world, and when one expresses that seeing-into in a totally appropriate language. By totally appropriate I mean a language of complete alertness. As I try to write I know that I am involved in an activity which is a deliberate assertion of energy over indifference, of vitality over deadness, of excitement and ecstasy over dullness and cynicism. Yet the poem must take account of all these negatives. In fact, it must often use them as its raw material, but, by a sort of dynamic, inner alchemy of language, rhythm and image, transform those negatives into living forms.

* * *

In *Collection One: Getting Up Early* Brendan Kennelly has given us a selection from a number of slender books published during the last ten years. The poet, who comes from Kerry, draws frequently on vigorous local stories, as in "Moloney at the Wake" and "Moloney Remembers the Resurrection of Kate Finucane." In these and other poems he evokes the "Kingdom of Kerry":

Between the Banner County and the Kingdom
The burly Shannon strides into the sea.
In rocky desolation. the unploughed parishes end;
The outnumbering waves insist
That the river is nobody's friend.

Kennelly is now Professor of Modern Literature at Trinity College, Dublin, and, in contrast to his local poems, his poems are now filled with the sights and sounds of city life, such as "Ambulance":

Braying on its mercy mission,
The white hysterical bully
Blows all things out of its way,
Cutting through the slack city
Like a knife through flesh.
People respect potential saviours
And immediately step aside,
Watching it pitch and scream ahead,
Ignoring the lights, breaking the rules,
Lurching on the crazy line
Between the living and the dead.

Notable among these poems is an elegy on the late Frank O'Connor, which begins: "Climbing the last step to your house, I knew/That I would find you in your chair,/ Watching the light die along the canal...." The themes range from emigration, children's hospital, old men sharing "the sun's enormous charity" to a sonnet about a negro: "My mother fine. But/Man, she think the whole world made of coconut."

The novel *The Crooked Cross* describes the effects of a drought on a remote village. A handsome gypsy girl, a publican, an old sailor, and a water diviner are among the lively characters. This is a poet's novel with an allegorical context. In lighter mood is *The Florentines*, which tells of the adventures of a young student who takes up a post-graduate course of mythology in England.

—Austin Clarke

KESSLER, Milton. American. Born in Brooklyn, New York, 9 May 1930. Educated at DeWitt Clinton High School, New York; Harvard University, Cambridge, Massachusetts; University of Buffalo, New York, B.A. (magna cum laude) 1957 (Phi Beta Kappa); University of Washington, Seattle, M.A. 1962; Ohio State University, Columbus, 1959–63. Married Sonia Berer in 1952; three children. Teaching Assistant, University of Washington, 1957–58; Instructor, Boston University, 1957–58, and Ohio State University, 1958–63; Lecturer in English, Queens College, City University of New York, 1963–65. Since 1965, Poet-in-Residence and Associate Professor of English, Harpur College, State University of New York, Binghamton. Visiting Professor, University of the Negev, Beersheba, Israel, 1971–72, and University of Hawaii, Honolulu, 1975. Co-Editor, *Choice* magazine, Buffalo, New York, Recipient: Bread Loaf Writers Conference Robert Frost Fellowship, 1961; Yaddo Fellowships, 1965–76; MacDowell Foundation Fellowship, 1966; National Endowment for the Arts grant, 1967; Keio University Fellowship, 1978. Address: 25 Lincoln Avenue, Binghamton, New York 13905, U.S.A.

PUBLICATIONS

Verse

A Road Came Once. Columbus, Ohio State University Press, 1963.

Called Home. Vestal, New York, Black Bird Press, 1967.
Woodlawn North. Boston, Impressions Workshop, 1970.
Sailing Too Far. New York, Harper, 1973.
Sweet Dreams. Hamlin, New York, Black Bird Press, 1979.

Milton Kessler comments:

I ask that my 1970 and 1974 comments be left out. It's beginning to sound like *Krapp's Last Tape.* We're always caught profile with all our mistakes. It can't be helped, can't be stopped, can't be right. We must try to say how things are. We must have a voice in the way things change, but we don't hear that voice until later and further when we have to wonder at what we said. My recent poems are aware of this bewildering situation, more aware.

* * *

Milton Kessler is the kind of writer whose earnestness, whose sympathy for the people and things he writes about, wins the sympathy of his readers. If we take Jung's notion that each man orients himself primarily by one of four basic means – intellect, feeling, sensation, or intuition – it is clear that Kessler's primary mode is feeling. Most of the best poems in *A Road Came Once* are poems of strong feeling for family and for the sorrows and troubles of other people – poems like "The El-Painter's Daughter" and "The Clerk Retires." His tone is often reminiscent of a Jewish cantor's, an energetic wailing tone which conveys the feeling that any life, no matter how small it may seem, is a thing worthy of high drama.

One of the faults of Kessler's past work, however, is that sometimes his language is so lofty and dramatic that it becomes melodramatic or removed from the simple subject of the poem; it makes it seem as if he were so anxious to bring the subject to a "higher" level that the kernel, the basic incident, gets left behind on the ground. For instance, in "The Game" Kessler tries to build a father watching his football-playing son's injury into a kind of Homeric lament, but the language grows too self-consciously grand, melodramatic and obtrusive. In addition, Kessler's poems are sometimes simply obscure.

Since his first volume, Kessler has shown that he has done a great deal to overcome his difficulties with obscurity and grandiose diction. A particularly fine poem is "Songs for Paul Blackburn." His poetry also has become more fanciful on occasion, and more joyous.

—Lawrence Russ

KGOSITSILE, Keorapetse (William). South African. Born in Johannesburg, 19 September 1938. Educated at Madibane High School, Johannesburg, 1958; Lincoln University, Pennsylvania; University of New Hampshire, Durham; Columbia University, New York; New School for Social Research, New York; (African-American Institute Fellow). Married to Melba Kgositsile. Since 1971, Poet-in-Residence, North Carolina Agricultural and Technical State University, Greensboro. African Editor-at-Large, *Black Dialogue*, San Francisco. Recipient: Conrad Kent Rivers Award, 1969; National Endowment for the Arts grant, 1969.

PUBLICATIONS

Verse

Spirits Unchained. Detroit, Broadside Press, 1969.
For Melba. Chicago, Third World Press, 1970.
My Name Is Afrika. New York, Doubleday, 1971.

Other

Editor, *The Word Is Here: Poetry from Modern Africa.* New York, Doubleday, 1973.

* * *

"Because finally things have come to this," writes Keorapetse Kgositsile, "White world gray grim cold turning me into a killer/ Because I love love." The lines are ironic and paradoxical. Yet, their underlying truth argues a radical and profound humanism – the key to understanding the revolutionary poetic vision of this young South African-in-exile.

In Kgositsile's cosmology, love transcends Western definitions: it is not simply felt, or sung about, or sought after; nor is it an essentially individual experience. Rather, love finds its true definition in the commitment of the individual to both self and nation. For Blacks, nation is all Black people, wherever they may live; they are united by a bond forged outside of time: "Searching past the pretensions of knowledge/We move to the meeting place/ The pulse of the beginning the end and the beginning." Thus, the subjects of his first volume of poetry, *Spirits Unchained*, are the Africans and African Americans who dedicated themselves to Black liberation. Among the most moving of the poems are the lyrical "Elegy to David Diop," and the strident "When Brown Is Black," whose hero, H. Rapp Brown, becomes the metaphor for the long awaited insurrection of the oppressed: "... Go on, brother, say it. Talk/the talk slaves are afraid to live."

Militancy softens in *For Melba*, the volume dedicated to his wife; but Kgositsile never loses sight of the larger vision. The intense anguish and joy of interpersonal love – beautiful in itself – are but stepping stones to a union whose strength and commitment will spawn the future Black nation. When, finally, in *My Name Is Afrika*, songs of celebration and love give way to exhortation, it is, again, in the interest of the long view: "Gut it is will move us from the gutter ... to the rebirth of real men."

—Saundra Towns

KINNELL, Galway. American. Born in Providence, Rhode Island, 1 February 1927. Educated at Princeton University, New Jersey, A.B. 1948; University of Rochester, New York, M.A. 1949. Served in the United States Navy, 1945–46. Married to Inés Delgado de Torres; one daughter and one son. Formerly, Member of the Faculty, University of Grenoble, France; Poet-in-Residence, Juniata College, Huntingdon, Pennsylvania, and University of California, Irvine, 1968–69. Field Worker, Congress of Racial Equality, 1963. Recipient: Fulbright Scholarship, 1955; Longview Foundation Award, 1962; National Institute of Arts and Letters grant, 1962, and Medal of Merit, 1976; Bess Hokin Prize, 1965, and Eunice Tietjens Memorial Prize, 1966 (*Poetry*, Chicago); Rockefeller grant, 1967; Cecil Hemley Prize, 1968; Brandeis University Creative Arts Award, 1968; National Endowment for the Arts grant, 1969; Amy Lowell Traveling Fellowship, 1969; Shelley Memorial Award, 1972; Guggenheim Fellowship, 1974. Address: Sheffield, Vermont 05866, U.S.A.

PUBLICATIONS

Verse

What a Kingdom It Was. Boston, Houghton Mifflin, 1960.
Flower Herding on Mount Monadnock. Boston, Houghton Mifflin, 1964.
Poems of Night. London, Rapp and Carroll, 1968.
Body Rags. Boston, Houghton Mifflin, 1968; London, Rapp and Whiting, 1969.
The Hen Flower. Frensham, Surrey, Sceptre Press, 1970.
First Poems 1947–1952. Mount Horeb, Wisconsin, Perishable Press, 1970.
The Book of Nightmares. Boston, Houghton Mifflin, 1971; London, J. Jay, 1978.
The Shoes of Wandering. Mount Horeb, Wisconsin, Perishable Press, 1971.
The Avenue Bearing the Initial of Christ into the New World: Poems 1946–1964. Boston, Houghton Mifflin, 1974.

Recordings: *Today's Poets 5*, with others, Folkways; *The Poetry and Voice of Galway Kinnell*, Caedmon, 1976.

Novel

Black Light. Boston, Houghton Mifflin, 1966; London, Hart Davis, 1967.

Other

3 Self-Evaluations, with Anthony Ostroff and Winfield Townley Scott. Beloit, Wisconsin, Beloit Poetry Journal, 1953.
The Poetics of the Physical World. Fort Collins, Colorado State University, 1969.
Walking Down the Stairs: Selections from Interviews. Ann Arbor, University of Michigan Press, 1978.

Translator, *Bitter Victory*, by René Hardy. New York, Doubleday, and London, Hamish Hamilton, 1956.
Translator, *Pre-Columbian Ceramics*, by Henri Lehmann. London, Elek, 1962.
Translator, *The Poems of François Villon.* New York, New American Library, 1965.
Translator, *On the Motion and Immobility of Douve*, by Yves Bonnefoy. Athens, Ohio University Press, 1968.
Translator, *The Lackawanna Elegy*, by Yvan Goll. Fremont, Michigan, Sumac Press, 1970.
Translator, *The Poems of François Villon.* Boston, Houghton Mifflin, 1977.

Bibliography: *Galway Kinnell: A Bibliography and Index of His Published Works and Criticism of Them*, Potsdam, New York, State University College Frederick W. Crumb Memorial Library, 1968.

* * *

In the winter of 1946–47, when I was teaching at Princeton University, a dark-shocked student, looking more like a prize fighter than a literary man, showed me a poem, maybe his first. I remember it as a Wordsworthian sonnet, not what the avant-garde of Princeton. Blackmur or Berryman, would have taken to – old diction, no modern flair. But the last couplet had a romantic fierceness that amazed me. The man who had done that could go beyond any poetic limits to be assigned. I was reckless enough to tell him so.

I was to lecture at Black Mountain that summer. He took a bit of his G.I. money and came along. Apart from some works of mine which seemed to move him, it was to Yeats that he gave himself with the totality that has always characterized him. By the fall he had written the first form of a four-page poem, "A Morning Wake among the Dead" (later called

"Among the Tombs"), which foreshadowed in volcanic latency all his later long poems. The death-haunted, tragic Kinnell had already spoken, though it would take years for the fact to be recognized.

In form, Kinnell was still using a romantic and Miltonic pentameter almost totally remade under impacts from Donne and the moderns – meter purposely broken up, rhymes concealed – a demonic wrestling with traditional measures. His matter was the reaffirmation of the Promethean and pioneer daring of America, to which I also, after the neo-Augustinian resignations of the war, was committed. He wrote a whole volume of Western poems which did not find a publisher, though some of them, revised, appear in the first sections of *What a Kingdom It Was*.

About 1956 Kinnell was able to get abroad. It was not too late for his "Prairie" style to be infused with French modernism, though without losing its passionate immediacy. The most remarkable fruit of this is "The Supper after the Last," in *What a Kingdom*, a symbolist vision and statement, at one time Promethean-romantic and mysteriously avant-garde.

Kinnell's break with traditional form has continued, leading to his espousal of free verse as the only possible medium for an American poet. It is significantly to Whitman that he has returned, with some inspiration from William Carlos Williams. But anyone who will take the twisted rhymes of the earlier Kinnell and set them beside the free verse of recent works – that staggering diptych of animal poems, "The Porcupine" and "The Bear" in *Body Rags* – will sense how far everything that has occurred, both in content and form, was within the province of the original Apocalyptic vision of "A Morning Wake among the Dead."

What distinguishes that vision from anything else on the contemporary scene is its continuation of the titanism of the last century – whatever flamed from Goethe's *Faust* through Melville, Nietzsche, Rimbaud, to Rilke, Yeats, Jeffers. There is a sense in which Galway Kinnell has remained faithful to this heritage, though for a long time it handicapped him among those of a more oblique and verbal trend, poets who grew up as it were after Pound. Thus a review of *Body Rags* (in the *New York Review of Books*) spent most of its time complaining that Kinnell didn't write like Berryman – as if he hadn't had his chance at that and decided early against it.

Within Kinnell's passionate and personal vein, two drifts have revealed themselves, that of the longer poem prefigured in "A Morning Wake," "The Avenue Bearing the Initial of Christ," and "The Last River," and that of clarified small lyrics aimed at an ultimate transparency. The lyrical tendency reaches its earliest perfection in "First Song" ("Then it was dusk in Illinois") as in the other tender pieces ("Island of Night," "A Walk in the Country") published in Rolfe Humphries' *New Poems* though not included by Kinnell in any of his volumes. So too with "Spring Oak," a poem that illustrates Kinnell's critical pronouncement in his Beloit "Self-Study": "Only meaning is truly interesting." Even in *Body Rags* there are such distillates, "The Falls" and "How Many Nights." Reading them, as the "Self-Study" had also said, is "like opening a window on the thing the poem is talking about":

How many nights
have I lain in terror,
O Creator Spirit,
Maker of night and day,

only to walk out
the next morning over the frozen world
hearing under the creaking of snow
faint, peaceful breaths ...
... snake,
bear, earthworm, ant ...

and above me
a wild crow crying "*yaw yaw yaw*"
from a branch nothing cried from ever in my life.

Against such poems, the underworld involvement of "The Last River" goes another road, groping through caves and antres of "the flinty, night-smelling depths," "waiting by the grief-tree of the last river."

Kinnell's second book, *Flower Herding on Mount Monadnock*, as the title suggests (strange the Indian name for that solitary mountain on a peneplane should hold the Greek root of the One), is largely in the lyrical mode. Even the Wagnerian love-death has wonderfully refined itself in "Poems of Night": "A cheekbone./A curved piece of brow,/A pale eyelid/Float in the dark,/And now I make out/An eye, dark,/wormed with the far-off, unaccountable lights." While the title poem and "Spindrift" – "Sit down/By the clanking shore/Of this bitter, beloved sea" – stand at the pinnacle of the poignantly pure and deeply transparent.

At the moment I have before me various sketches of *The Book of Nightmares*. For oceanic participation, the section on childbirth ("Maud Moon") goes beyond anything Kinnell has done before:

It is all over, little one,
the flipping
and overleaping,
the watery
somersaulting alone in the oneness
under the hill, under
the old, lonely bellybutton pushing forth again
in remembrance, all over,
the drifting there furled like a flower, pressing
a knee down the slippery
walls, sculpting the whole world, hearing
a few cries from without not even as promises, the stream
of omphalos blood humming all over you.

What distinguishes this from the work of any other poet (though parallels can be found: Roethke, Rilke, even Whitman) is the intuitive immediacy of its entrance into pre-birth and subhuman organic nature.

Of all the poets born in the twenties and thirties, Galway Kinnell is the only one who has taken up the passionate symbolic search of the great American tradition.

—Charles G. Bell

KINSELLA, Thomas. Irish. Born in Dublin, 4 May 1928. Educated at University College, Dublin. Married Eleanor Walsh in 1955; two daughters and one son. Worked in the Irish Civil Service, 1948–65, retired from the Department of Finance. Writer-in-Residence, 1965–67, and Professor of English, 1967–70, Southern Illinois University, Carbondale. Since 1970, Professor of English, Temple University, Philadelphia. Director, Dolmen Press, Dublin, and Cuala Press, Dublin; Founder, Peppercanister publishers, Dublin, 1972. Artistic Director, Lyric Players Theatre, Belfast. Recipient: Guinness Award, 1958; Irish Arts Council Award, 1961; Denis Devlin Memorial Award, 1967, 1970; Guggenheim Fellowship, 1968, 1971. Member, Irish Academy of Letters, 1965. Address: Department of English, Temple University, Philadelphia, Pennsylvania, 19122, U.S.A.

Publications

Verse

The Starlit Eye. Dublin, Dolmen Press, 1952.
Three Legendary Sonnets. Dublin, Dolmen Press, 1952.
The Death of a Queen. Dublin, Dolmen Press, 1956.
Poems. Dublin, Dolmen Press, 1956.
Another September. Dublin, Dolmen Press, and Philadelphia, Dufour, 1958; revised edition, Dolmen Press, and London, Oxford University Press, 1962.
Moralities. Dublin, Dolmen Press, 1960.
Poems and Translations. New York, Atheneum, 1961.
Downstream. Dublin, Dolmen Press, 1962.
Six Irish Poets, with others, edited by Robin Skelton. London and New York, Oxford University Press, 1962.
Wormwood. Dublin, Dolmen Press, 1966.
Nightwalker. Dublin, Dolmen Press, 1967.
Nightwalker and Other Poems. Dublin, Dolmen Press, London, Oxford University Press, and New York, Knopf, 1968.
Poems, with Douglas Livingstone and Anne Sexton. London and New York, Oxford University Press, 1968.
Tear. Cambridge, Massachusetts, Pym Randall Press, 1969.
Butcher's Dozen. Dublin, Peppercanister, 1972.
A Selected Life. Dublin, Peppercanister, 1972.
Finistere. Dublin, Dolmen Press, 1972.
Notes from the Land of the Dead and Other Poems. Dublin, Cuala Press, 1972; New York, Random House, 1973.
New Poems 1973. Dublin, Dolmen Press, 1973; London, Oxford University Press, 1976.
Selected Poems 1956–1968. Dublin, Dolmen Press, and London, Oxford University Press, 1973.
Vertical Man. Dublin, Peppercanister, 1973.
The Good Fight. Dublin, Peppercanister, 1973.
One. Dublin, Peppercanister, 1974.
A Technical Supplement. Dublin, Peppercanister, 1976.
Song of the Night and Other Poems. Dublin, Peppercanister, 1978.
The Messenger. Dublin, Peppercanister, 1978.
Fifteen Dead. Dublin, Dolmen Press, and London, Oxford University Press, 1979.
One and Other Poems. Dublin, Dolmen Press, and London, Oxford University Press, 1979.

Other

Davis, Mangan, Ferguson? Tradition and the Irish Writer, with W. B. Yeats. Dublin, Dolmen Press, 1970.

Editor, *Selected Poems of Austin Clarke.* Dublin, Dolmen Press, 1976.

Translator, *The Breastplate of St. Patrick.* Dublin, Dolmen Press, 1954; as *Faeth Fiadha: The Breastplate of St. Patrick*, 1957.
Translator, *Longes mac n-Usnig, Being The Exile and Death of the Sons of Usnech.* Dublin, Dolmen Press, 1954.
Translator, *Thirty Three Triads, Translated from the XII Century Irish.* Dublin, Dolmen Press, 1955.
Translator, *The Tain.* Dublin, Dolmen Press, 1969; London and New York, Oxford University Press, 1970.

Bibliography: by Hensley Woodbridge, in *Eire-Ireland* (St. Paul, Minnesota), 1966.

Critical Studies: *The New Poets: American and British Poetry since World War II* by M. L. Rosenthal, New York and London, Oxford University Press, 1967; "Thomas Kinsella Issue" of *The Hollins Critic* (Hollins College, Virginia), iv, 4, 1968; "The Poetry of Thomas Kinsella" by Robin Skelton, in *Eire-Ireland* (St. Paul, Minnesota), iv, 1, 1968; *Eight Contemporary Poets* by Calvin Bedient, London, Oxford University Press, 1974; *The Poetry of Thomas Kinsella* by Maurice Harmon, Dublin, Wolfhound Press, 1974.

Thomas Kinsella comments:

It is my aim to elicit order from significant experience, with a view to acceptance on the basis of some kind of understanding. Major themes are love, death and the artistic act. Methods various and developing.

* * *

Thomas Kinsella might be described as an intellectual troubadour, his desire to sing increasingly crossed by a need to explain. In his first book, *Poems*, traditional love lyrics, like "Soft to Your Places" and "Midsummer," were balanced by others like "Ulysses," where a dense vocabulary was pressed into the service of a still emerging vision. It was the elegant world of Richard Wilbur, with a metaphysical twist and an Irish music.

Another September represented a more thorough cultivation of the same private garden. The romantic dandy is still in evidence ("Fifth Sunday after Easter") but his presence does not unduly impede Kinsella's clarification of his main theme: an obsession with time. Its expression varies from the conventional ballad stanzas of "In the Ringwood," based on the Irish *aisling* or vision poem,

Dread, a grey devourer,
Stalks in the shade of love.
The dark that dogs our feet
Eats what is sickened of.
The End that stalks Beginning
Hurries home its drove,

to the more analytic pose of "Baggot Street Deserta," with the poet, against his favourite backdrop of nocturnal Dublin, declaring that we must "endure and let the present punish."

The principal reproach that might be levelled against *Another September* is that the poems were not sufficiently anchored in time and place. But a less remote quality was evident towards the end of the collection, especially in the sombre "Thinking of Mr. D." And in his second major collection, Kinsella emerges clearly as a *persona* with the "pious clerkly" hand of "Priest and Emperor" now leading to the dejected face which gazes into "A Mirror in February":

Now plainly in the mirror of my soul
I read that I have looked my last on youth
And little more; for they are not made whole
That reach the age of Christ.

Downstream can be said to mark Kinsella's change of gear from lyric to meditative; as he says in "Time's Mischief": "He must progress/Who fabricates a path, though all about/ Death, Woman, Spring, repeat their first success." The most noticeable change is his determination to grapple with public themes, from the local history and poltics of "A Country Walk" to the problem of Hiroshima in "Old Harry." Perhaps too deliberately, for in the latter poem Truman is dignified with a moral complexity alien to his character, while the most striking effects are lavished on the atom bomb's destruction of "the notorious cities of the plain"!

The same determination flows over into *Nightwalker*, the title poem of which exposes the moral vacuum of modern Ireland. But the monologue technique and diction are still close to early Eliot, and like "Chrysalides" and "Dick King" in *Downstream*, only the more private poems catch Kinsella's distinctive quality. The sequence on marital love, "Wormwood," is heavy with portentousness, but contains at least one poem, "First Light," where despair is crystallised, drop by terrible drop. And there are some moving attempts to face the problem of physical suffering ("Our Mother"):

> The girl whimpers in bed, remote
> Under the anaesthetic still.
> She sleeps on her new knowledge, a bride
> With bowels burning and disarrayed.

This vision of life as ordeal is more fully enunciated in the magnificently romantic intimacies of the long poem, "Phoenix Park." As well as a celebration of married love, it is also a farewell to his native Dublin, and one waits to see how America will affect Kinsella's work. For with his seriousness of purpose, and strength of intellect, went a Parnassian quality which can only benefit from a more experimental poetic climate. His translation of the early Irish epic, *The Tain*, does not wholly succeed in "making it new," but "A Hand of Solo" and "Hen Woman," parts of a new poetic sequence, show a relaxing of technique which augurs well.

"Notes from the Land of the Dead" is incorporated in *New Poems 1973* which, with *Selected Poems 1956–1968*, amounts to a new definition of his career. But he has also established a private press, for broadsides like *Butcher's Dozen* and his meditation on John F. Kennedy, *The Good Fight*. So his career presents the paradox of definitive achievement and increasing adventurousness, a strong combination. The private and public life, love and waste, these are the antimonies that engage Kinsella's intensely serious gaze.

—John Montague

KIRKUP, James (Falconer). British. Born in South Shields, Durham, 23 April 1923. Educated at South Shields High School; Durham University, B.A. 1941. Gregory Fellow in Poetry, Leeds University, 1950–52; Visiting Poet and Head of the Department of English, Bath Academy of Art, Corsham, Wiltshire, 1953–56; Travelling Lecturer, Swedish Ministry of Education, Stockholm, 1956–57; Professor of English, University of Salamanca, Spain, 1957–58, and Tohoku University, Sendai, Japan, 1959–61; Lecturer in English Literature, University of Malaya, Kuala Lumpur, 1961–62; Professor of English Literature, Nagoya University, Japan, 1969–72. Since 1963, Professor of English Literature, Japan's Woman's University, Tokyo; since 1968, Professor of English Literature and Poet-in-Residence, Amherst College, Massachusetts. Morton Visiting Professor of International Literature, Ohio University, Athens, 1975; Visiting Professor, Kyoto University; Arts Council Creative Writer, University of Sheffield, 1975–76; Dramatist-in-Residence, Sherman Theatre, Cardiff, 1976–77. Literary Editor, *Orient/West Magazine*, Tokyo, 1963–64; Founder, *Poetry Nippon*, Nagoya, 1966. Recipient: Atlantic-Rockefeller Award, 1950; Japan P.E.N. Club International Literary prize, 1965. Fellow, Royal Society of Literature, 1962. Address: BM-Box 2870, London WC1V 6XX, England.

PUBLICATIONS

Verse

Indications, with John Ormond and John Bayliss. London, Grey Walls Press, 1942.
The Cosmic Shape: An Interpretation of Myth and Legend with Three Poems and Lyrics, with Ross Nichols. London, Forge Press, 1946.
The Drowned Sailor and Other Poems. London, Grey Walls Press, 1947.
The Submerged Village and Other Poems. London, Oxford University Press, 1951.
The Creation. Hull, Lotus Press, 1951.
A Correct Compassion and Other Poems. London, Oxford University Press, 1952.
A Spring Journey and Other Poems of 1952–1953. London, Oxford University Press, 1954.
The Descent into the Cave and Other Poems. London, Oxford University Press, 1957.
The Prodigal Son: Poems 1956–1959. London, Oxford University Press, 1959.
The Refusal to Conform: Last and First Poems. London, Oxford University Press, 1963.
Japan Marine. Tokyo, Japan P.E.N. Club, 1965.
Paper Windows: Poems from Japan. London, Dent, 1968.
Japan Physical: A Selection, with Japanese translations by Fumiko Miura. Tokyo, Kenkyusha, 1969.
White Shadows, Black Shadows: Poems of Peace and War. London, Dent, 1970.
The Body Servant: Poems of Exile. London, Dent, 1971.
Broad Daylight. Frensham, Surrey, Sceptre Press, 1971.
A Bewick Bestiary. Ashington, Northumberland, MidNAG, 1971.
Transmental Vibrations. London, Convent Garden Press, 1971.
Zen Garden. Guildford, Surrey, Circle Press, 1973.
Many-Lined Poem. Sheffield, Headland Poetry, 1973.
Zen Contemplations (includes prose). Osaka, Kyoto Editions, 1978.
Enlightenment. Osaka, Kyoto Editions, 1978.
Scenes from Sesshu. London, Pimlico Press, 1978.
Prick Prints. Privately printed, 1978.
Steps to the Temple. Osaka, Kyoto Editions, 1979.

Plays

Upon This Rock: A Dramatic Chronicle of Peterborough Cathedral (produced Peterborough, 1955). London, Oxford University Press, 1955.
Masque: The Triumph of Harmony (produced London, 1955).
The True Mistery of the Nativity (televised, 1960). London and New York, Oxford University Press, 1956.
The Meteor, adaptation of a play by Dürrenmatt (produced London, 1956). London, Cape, 1973; New York, Grove Press, 1974.
The Prince of Homburg, adaptation of a play by Heinrich von Kleist (produced New York, 1976). Published in *Classic Theatre 2*, edited by Eric Bentley, New York, Doubleday, 1959.
The True Mistery of the Passion: Adapted and Translated from the French Medieval Mystery Cycle of Arnoul and Simon Grélan (televised, 1960; produced Bristol, 1960). London and New York, Oxford University Press, 1962.
The Physicists, adaptation of a play by Dürrenmatt (produced London and New York, 1963). London, French, and New York, Grove Press, 1964.
Play Strindberg, adaptation of a play by Dürrenmatt (produced New York, 1971; London, 1973). Chicago, Dramatic Publishing Company, n.d.
Peer Gynt, adaptation of the play by Ibsen (produced Cardiff, 1973).
The Magic Drum (for children; produced Newcastle upon Tyne, 1974; London, 1977).

Cyrano de Bergerac, adaptation of the play by Rostand (produced Newcastle upon Tyne, 1975).
The Anabaptists, *Period of Grace*, and *Frank the Fifth*, adaptations of plays by Dürrenmatt (produced Cardiff, 1976).
An Actor's Revenge, music by Minoru Miki (produced London, 1979).

Radio Play: *Ghost Mother*, 1978.

Television Plays: *The Peach Garden*, 1954; *Two Pigeons Flying High*, 1955; *The True Mistery of the Passion*, 1960; *The True Mistery of the Nativity*, 1960.

Novels

The Love of Others. London, Collins, 1962.
The Bad Boy's Bedside Book of Do-It-Yourself Sex. Privately printed, 1978.

Other

The Only Child: An Autobiography of Infancy. London, Collins, 1957.
Sorrows, Passions, and Alarms: An Autobiography of Childhood. London, Collins, 1959.
These Horned Islands: A Journal of Japan. London, Collins, and New York, Macmillan, 1962.
Tropic Temper: A Memoir of Malaya. London, Collins, 1963.
England, Now. Tokyo, Seibido, 1964.
Japan Industrial: Some Impressions of Japanese Industries. Osaka, PEP, 2 vols, 1964–65.
Japan Now. Tokyo, Seibido, 1966.
Frankly Speaking. Tokyo, Eichosha, 1966.
Tokyo. London, Phoenix House, and South Brunswick, New Jersey, A. S. Barnes, 1966.
Filipinescas: Travels Through the Philippine Islands. London, Phoenix House, 1968.
Bangkok. London, Phoenix House, and South Brunswick, New Jersey, A. S. Barnes, 1968.
One Man's Russia. London, Phoenix House, 1968.
Aspects of the Short Story: Six Modern Short Stories with Commentary. Tokyo, Kaibunsha, 1969.
Streets of Asia. London, Dent, 1969.
Hong Kong and Macao. London, Dent, and South Brunswick, New Jersey, A. S. Barnes, 1970.
Japan Behind the Fan. London, Dent, 1970.
Insect Summer (juvenile). New York, Knopf, 1971.
The Magic Drum (juvenile). New York, Knopf, 1973.
Heaven, Hell, and Hara-Kiri: The Rise and Fall of the Japanese Superstate. London, Angus and Robertson, 1974.

Editor, *Shepherding Winds: An Anthology of Poetry from East and West.* London, Blackie, 1969.
Editor, *Songs and Dreams: An Anthology of Poetry from East and West.* London, Blackie, 1970.

Translator, with Leopold Sirombo, *The Vision and Other Poems*, by Todja Tartschoff. London, Newman and Harris, 1953.
Translator, *Ancestral Voices*, by Doan-Vinh-Thal. London, Collins, 1956.

Translator, *Memoirs of A Dutiful Daughter*, by Simone de Beauvoir. Cleveland, World, and London, Weidenfeld and Nicolson-Deutsch, 1959.
Translator, *Don Carlo*, by Schiller, in *Classic Theatre 2*, edited by Eric Bentley. New York, Doubleday, 1959.
Translator, with Oliver Rice and Abdullah Majid, *Modern Malay Verse*. London, Oxford University Press, 1963.
Translator, *Immensee*, by Theodor Storm. London, Blackie, 1965.
Translator, *Tales of Hoffmann*. London, Blackie, 1966.
Translator, *Michael Kohlhaas: From an Old Chronicle*. London, Blackie, 1967.
Translator, *The Eternal Virgin*, by Paul Valéry. Tokyo, Orient Editions, 1970.
Translator, *Brand*, by Ibsen, in *The Oxford Ibsen*, edited by James Walter MacFarlane. London, Oxford University Press, 1972.
Translator, with Michio Nakano, *Selected Poems of Takagi Kyozo*. Cheadle, Cheshire, Carcanet Press, 1973.
Translator, *Modern Japanese Poetry*. Brisbane, University of Queensland Press, 1978; edited by A. R. Davis, Milton Keynes, Buckinghamshire, Open University, 1979.

James Kirkup comments:

Characterized by a very wide variety of themes and verse forms, including many oriental subjects and techniques. Most deeply influenced by Japanese and Chinese poetry, as well as by French. No English or American influences. Major themes: the sea, loneliness, music, painting, photography, sport, travel, the Orient, peace and war, science and space exploration, UFO's, legend, people, psychical research, medicine, satire, social criticism.

In my poetry I have attempted always to express an essence both of myself and of experience, a crystallization of my personal awareness of this world and worlds beyond. I feel I am slowly developing, after nearly thirty years of writing poetry, a voice that is only my own, and illuminating areas of experience and technique untouched by other poets. I am original, so I do not strive for originality for its own sake, or experiment with form unless the subject demands it. My aim is to be perfectly lucid yet to provide mv candour with serious and mysterious undertones of sound and meaning.

* * *

The blurb on the dust wrapper of James Kirkup's collection *The Body Servant* includes this statement by the American poet and novelist, James Dickey: "With Kirkup's work I don't feel that facility is the problem, as it is with many writers." Certainly Kirkup sometimes gives the impression of being able to knock off a passable poem at the drop of a hat. Subject matter is never lacking: his dustbin, photographs in a railway compartment, the New Year, a pet cat, have all suggested poems. Kirkup's first collection, *The Drowned Sailor*, was published in 1947 and was very much a collection of its time in its style and language. A determined poeticism may be the best way of describing it with its peppering of enormous abstractions such as "memory's mountain" or "the candelabra of the soul." The other poets of the time (vide Wrey Gardiner's *Poetry Quarterly*) were full of such stuff as if there was an urgency to plump out otherwise flat poems, a sort of poetic padded bra'; but Kirkup was too adept at this for his own good. It was in Kirkup's second collection, *The Submerged Village*, that something distinctive was to be observed. There were still oddly old-fashioned pieces ("The Ship," "Music at Night" and "Poem for a New Year") which read like those poems the leisured gentlemen of previous centuries were so adept at "turning" as they would put it – competent, agreeable, but strangely impersonal. But among these were poems such as the title poem itself, "The Submerged Village," where it was as if the poet had taken a cool hard look at his subject and determined to deny himself the indulgence of his particular facility:

Calm, the surrounding mountains look upon
the steeple's golden cross, that still
emerges from the centre of the rising lake.
Like a sinking raft's bare mast and spar
anchored to earth by chains of stone.

The facility is still there, of course; but used to the purpose of the poem and not as a merely decorative addition.

This progress towards an individual voice and style was to flower in the next collection, *A Correct Compassion*, in which the title poem can stand with the finest poems written since the war. Here, in a poem written after watching the performance of an operation at the General Infirmary, Leeds, Kirkup combines keenly observed detail –

The glistening theatre swarms with eyes, and hands, and eyes.
On green-clothed tables, ranks of instruments transmit a sterile gleam.
The masks are on, and no unnecessary smile betrays
A certain tension, true concomitant of calm.

– while using the whole as a prolonged and deftly handled metaphor:

– For this is imagination's other place,
Where only necessary things are done, with the supreme the grave
Dexterity that ignores technique; with proper grace
Informing a correct compassion, that performs its love, and makes it live.

It is as if from the controlled skill of the surgeon Kirkup has, as the poem makes clear, not only learnt something concerning the nature of art, but has found a parallel for his own technique. Another poem in this collection, "Matthew Smith," begins: "Yours, brother, is a masculine art,/The business of doing what you see." And in a sense with *A Correct Compassion* Kirkup's, too, becomes a masculine art.

It is true that the old temptations remain and "Rhapsody on a Bead Curtain" sees the facility at work wringing out to the last drop the metaphor of a bead curtain as a shower. But firmness prevails almost to the point of harshness in "Medusa": "those frog-like legs/Seem barely able to support/That sad, amorphous bum," where Kirkup is in danger of overbalancing the other way. Poems such as "The Ventriloquist," "A Visit to Brontë Land," "Photographs in a Railway Compartment," and "Summertime in Leeds" reassure us, however, that Kirkup has found his true voice:

No idle toy would have tempted Branwell
From the "Bull," and brandy; or kept that sister
From her tragic poems. They knew they had nothing but the moor
And themselves. It is we, who want all, who are poor.

and that he will stick to it, though tempted, like Branwell, by the "bull" as he sometimes is.

James Kirkup has published numerous collections. Some have been serious volumes, some rather more playful like *The Body Servant* with its journey over the body's parts and old chestnuts such as the part without a bone. But if, as it should be, a poet is to be remembered by his best work, then a "selected poems" for Kirkup is long overdue, if only as a show case for some of the more pleasing poems to have been written in the past decades.

—John Cotton

KIZER, Carolyn (Ashley). American. Born in Spokane, Washington, 10 December 1925. Educated at Sarah Lawrence College, Bronxville, New York, B.A. 1945; Columbia University, New York, 1945–46; University of Washington, Seattle, 1946–47. Married 1) Charles Stimson Bullitt in 1948 (divorced, 1954), two daughters and one son; 2) John Marshall Woodbridge in 1975. Founding Editor, *Poetry Northwest*, Seattle, 1959–65; State Department Specialist in Pakistan, 1964–65; Director of Literary Programs, National Endowment for the Arts, 1966–70; lecturer or poet-in-residence, University of North Carolina, Chapel Hill, 1970–74, Washington University, St. Louis, 1971, Barnard College, New York, 1972, Ohio University, Athens, 1975, and University of Iowa, Iowa City, 1976.

Publications

Verse

Poems. Portland, Oregon, Portland Art Museum, 1959.
The Ungrateful Garden. Bloomington, Indiana University Press, 1961.
Five Poets of the Pacific Northwest, with others, edited by Robin Skelton. Seattle, University of Washington Press, 1964.
Knock upon Silence. New York, Doubleday, 1965.
Midnight Was My Cry: New and Selected Poems. New York, Doubleday, 1971.

* * *

Carolyn Kizer works in terms of the twinned tensions of life, those central paradoxes so directly felt by women. She poses the problem of the woman poet boldly in her remarkable "A Muse of Water":

We who must act as handmaidens
To our own goddess, turn too fast,
Trip on our hems, to glimpse the muse
Gliding below her lake or sea,
Are left, long-staring after her
Narcissists by necessity ...

Mother and Muse, she can write tenderly of her own mother, who taught her to love nature even at its most loathsome, "a whole, wild, lost, betrayed and secret life/Among its dens and burrows." And though she has a poem on "Not Writing Poetry about Children" they are everywhere in her work. So are cats, symbols of the female condition, as in "A Widow in Wintertime,"

trying
To live well enough alone, and not to dream
Of grappling in the snow, claws plunged in fur,

Or waken in a caterwaul of dying.

The daring and diffidence of womanhood are celebrated in poems of companionship, like "For Jan, In Bar Maria." But her most constant, resonant theme is love and loss, analysed in detail in the sequence "A Month in Summer." This ends with a quotation from Basho, and it is in the fatalism of that ancient civilisation that Carolyn Kizer finds a refuge and an artistic remedy for her womanly woes: "'O love long gone, it is raining in our room.'/So I memorize these lines, without salutation, without close." She must be one of the best woman poets around, profoundly committed to the process of life, however painful.

—John Montague

KNIGHT, Etheridge. American. Born in Corinth, Mississippi, 19 April 1931. Educated in public schools. Served in the United States Army, 1947–51. Married 1) Sonia Sanchez, *q.v.* (divorced): 2) Mary McAnally in 1970; two children. Inmate, Indiana State Prison, 1960–68; Poet-in-Residence, University of Pittsburgh, 1968, Hartford University, West Hartford, Connecticut, 1969–70, and Lincoln University, Jefferson City, Missouri, 1970–71. Poetry Editor, *Motive*, Nashville, 1970–71; Co-Editor, *Black Box*, Washington, D.C., 1971–72. Recipient: National Endowment for the Arts grant, 1972; Guggenheim Fellowship, 1974. Address: 2126 North Dexter Avenue, Indianapolis, Indiana 46202, U.S.A.

PUBLICATIONS

Verse

Poems from Prison. Detroit, Broadside Press, 1968.
The Idea of Ancestry. Rome, 1968.
2 Poems for Black Relocation Centers. Detroit, Broadside Press, 1968.
For Black Poets Who Think of Suicide. Detroit, Broadside Press, 1972.
A Poem for Brother Man. Detroit, Broadside Press, 1972.
Belly Song and Other Poems. Detroit, Broadside Press, 1973.

Recordings: *Poems from Prison* (tape), Broadside; *Tough Poems for Tough People*, Caedmon.

Other

Editor, *Voce negre dal carcere.* Rome, Laterza, 1968; as *Black Voices from Prison*, New York, Pathfinder Press, 1970.

* * *

In 1960, Etheridge Knight was sentenced to serve twenty years in Indiana State Prison. He was to say later: "I died in 1960 from a prison sentence and poetry brought me back to life." His collection *Poems from Prison* was published during this time and shortly thereafter he was released from prison on parole. Even though he has not been as prolific as some other Black poets, Knight has proven to be an especially significant voice of the sixties and seventies. His poetry is an explication in verse of a Malcolm X theme defining a new frame of reference to the prison experience for poor Blacks and Whites.

Knight spells out a direct relationship between "men behind prison walls and men behind the myriad walls that permeate [the American] society." His philosophy captures the themes of Malcolm X when he states that "crime, criminality, and alienation can be understood as being the by-product of a society/culture whose technology has far outstripped its humanism." In this respect, prison is viewed as "the ultimate oppression" of Black people in the larger prison outside. That philosophy is summed up simply and effectively in his "The Warden Said to Me the Other Day":

The warden said to me the other day
(innocently, I think), "Say, etheridge,
why come the black boys don't run off
like the white boys do?"
I lowered my jaw and scratched my head
and said (innocently, I think), "Well, suh,
I ain't for sure, but I reckon its cause
we ain't got no wheres to run to."

Knight's style is particularly suited to his ends. His poems are almost rigidly patterned (among his offerings is a brief series of Haiku poems), meticulously structured, tough in terminology, yet they never seem forced or restrained or without eloquence. He is sometimes as disarmingly simple as Langston Hughes; he is capable of shifting with piston smoothness from the concrete to the abstract:

> This year there is a gray stone wall damming my stream, and when
> the falling leaves stir my genes, I pace my cell or flop on my bunk
> and stare at 47 black faces across the space, I am all of them,
> they are all of me, I am me, they are thee, and I have no sons
> to float in the space between.

—Charles L. James

KNOEPFLE, John. American. Born in Cincinnati, Ohio, 4 February 1923. Educated at Xavier University, Cincinnati, Ph.B. 1949, M.A. 1951; St. Louis University, Ph.D. 1967. Served in the United States Navy, 1942–46: Purple Heart. Married Margaret Sower in 1956; one daughter and three sons. Producer-Director, WCET Educational Television, Cincinnati, 1953–55; Assistant Instructor, Ohio State University, Columbus, 1956–57; Instructor, Southern Illinois University, East St. Louis, 1957–61, St. Louis University High School, 1961–62, and Mark Twain Institute, Clayton, Missouri, Summers 1962–64; Assistant Professor, Maryville College, St. Louis, 1962–66, and Washington University, St. Louis, 1963–66; Associate Professor, St. Louis University, 1966–72; Consultant, Project Upward Bound, Washington, D.C., 1967–70. Since 1972, Professor of Literature, Sangamon State University, Springfield, Illinois. Recipient: Rockefeller Fellowship, 1967. Address: 1008 West Adams, Auburn, Illinois 62615, U.S.A.

PUBLICATIONS

Verse

Poets at the Gate, with others. St. Louis, Arts Festival of Washington University, 1965.
Rivers into Islands. Chicago, University of Chicago Press, 1965.
Songs for Gail Guidry's Guitar. New York, New Rivers Press, 1969.
An Affair of Culture and Other Poems. La Crosse, Wisconsin, Northeast-Juniper, 1969.
After Gray Days and Other Poems. Prairie Village, Kansas, Crabgrass Press, 1970.
The Intricate Land. New York, New Rivers Press, 1970.
The Ten-Fifteen Community Poems. Poquoson, Virginia, Back Door Press, 1971.
Whetstone. Shawnee Mission, Kansas, BkMk Press, 1972.
Deep Winter Poems. Lincoln, Nebraska, Three Sheets, 1972.
Thinking of Offerings: Poems 1970–1973. La Crosse, Wisconsin, Juniper Press, 1975.

Other

Voyages to the Inland Sea: Essays and Poems, with Lisel Mueller and David Etter. La Crosse, Wisconsin Center for Contemporary Poetry, 1971.
Dogs and Cats and Things Like That: A Book of Poems for Children. New York, McGraw Hill, 1971.

Our Street Feels Good: A Book of Poems for Children. New York, McGraw Hill, 1972.
Regional Perspectives: An Examination of America's Literary Heritage, with others, edited by John Gordon Burke. Chicago, American Library Association, 1973.
Frontier Literature: Images of the American West. New York, McGraw Hill, 1979.

Translator, with Robert Bly and James Wright, *Twenty Poems of César Vallejo.* Madison, Minnesota, Sixties Press, 1962.
Translator, with Robert Bly and James Wright, *Neruda and Vallejo: Selected Poems.* Boston, Beacon Dress, 1971.

Critical Studies: "Masks of Self-Deception" by Lloyd Goldman, and "The Reflective Art of John Knoepfle" by Raymond Benoit, in *Minnesota Review 8* (St. Paul), 1968.

John Knoepfle comments:

(1970) I consider myself a poet of the American Middle West, but aware of the same cosmic problems that beset everyone anywhere.

Poems written since the publication of *Rivers into Islands* are less nostalgic. They show bias toward events – often surrealistic ones – that occur in such moments when public and private experience overlaps. The poetry does not attempt to analyze the content of these two kinds of experience so much as it tries to reproduce the dynamics of their encounter. This has not been particularly intentional on my part; it is simply the way the poems have been moving, perhaps in an effort to get away from a propagandist/fatalist dilemma which seems at the moment largely irrelevant. The past in these poems and the midcontinent as place are there, then, not so much as subject matter outside of the poet as they are a part of a community of experience which I feel deeply involved in.

(1974) I am more and more concerned with the nature of a voice that is adequate, that can articulate the overlapping of public and private experience, some voice that is neither totally egocentric nor totally masked speech: how to capture such a voice.

* * *

John Knoepfle's poetry moves between farcical humor and a serious search for spiritual illumination. A desire for communion with God informs much of the work in *Deep Winter Poems* and *The Ten-Fifteen Community Poems*, but this is also underscored, especially in the latter pamphlet, by desire for communion between people. In numerous poems, religious ritual, particularly that of Catholicism, plays its part, and sometimes, as in an hilarious poem in *An Affair of Culture* ("Tunnel Blaster on Bear and Brotherhood"), the farcical and religious strains blend into a ludicrous parody of the mass:

he thought hed hunt bear with his brother
but the bear ate his brother
and he shot the bear
he came back in here on the monday
with a bearmeat sandwich
wanted me to eat half of it
see how a bearmeat sandwich tasted
I told him Im damned the day
I ate any mans brother
but he said there wasnt nothing to it
the bear didnt have time to digest his brother

This sort of outrageous humor takes risks, and Knoepfle, as in this poem, frequently succeeds; he has a good feeling for colloquial speech, and a good sense of his Midwestern locales. He is less successful when he tries for the spareness and starkness of Creeley, in poems like "At Forty," and flatly expresses his spiritual needs:

god look down
on me look
down on me
look at my
face and tell
me something

Many of Knoepfle's poems are concerned with death, whether actual, as in the first poem quoted, or impending, as in the second poem. In his major collection, *Rivers into Islands*, "Evening Departure" pictures the deceased as leaving on a train waving goodbye; another, "Night of Stars and Flowers," apparently again pictures death, but merely as an electing to be somewhere else. "The White Mule" is about a ghostly mule abandoned down in the mines who feeds on lost men. Poems like these, and many of the others about trains and rivers and other Midwestern scenes, are very evocative. Knoepfle has a real talent for the short poem, a talent that is particularly apparent where the rivers of verse in the first two parts of *Rivers into Islands* break up into the islands of short poems in the last part. His short poems seem even shorter in the collections since this one, terser, more compressed, with a greater sense of pressure pushing at their seams. His humor and colloquial grace remain strong assets.

—Duane Ackerson

KNOTT, Bill (William Kilborn Knott). American. Born in Gratiot County, Michigan, 17 February 1940. Educated at Carson City High School, Michigan. Served in the United States Army. Poet-in-Residence, Emerson College, Boston, 1976. Recipient: National Endowment for the Arts grant, 1968.

PUBLICATIONS

Verse

The Naomi Poems, Book One: Corpse and Beans. Chicago, Follett, 1968.
Aurealism: A Study. Syracuse, New York, Salt Mound Press, 1970.
Are You Ready Mary Baker Eddy?, with James Tate. San Francisco, Cloud Marauder Press, 1970.
Auto-Necrophilia: The Bill Knott Poems, Book 2. Chicago, Follett, 1971.
Nights of Naomi. Somerville, Massachusetts, Barn Dream Press, 1971.
Love Poems to Myself. Boston, Barn Dream Press, 1974.
Rome in Rome. New York, Release Press, 1976.
Selected and Collected Poems. New York, Sun, 1977.

Novel

Lucky Daryll, with James Tate. New York, Release Press, 1977.

Bill Knott comments:

I identify with the "Aurealist" School, or the group known as "Posthumous Poets."

Influences: Yvette Mimieux movies. John Logan's ideas and personal example of dedication.

Major theme is avoidance of major themes. Characteristic subjects are my death in 1966 and subsequent posthumous existence, and my virginity.

My usual verse form is iambic prose poems.

* * *

The poems of Bill Knott, who wrote as St. Geraud (1940–1966), are often very brief, deeply psychological lyrics, and he is a master of this form. "Hair Poem," two lines long, is characteristic:

Hair is heaven's water flowing eerily over us
Often a woman drifts off down her long hair and is lost

The sensuality of Knott's work imbues it with value beyond that of the Freudian level where most "Confessional" poets take their steambaths. Knott shares with his reader the possibility of an organic unity, a world where hair and heaven's water are the same elusive obtainables: his "death" may well suggest the view that life and death, equally permeated by identical organic elements, are also the same.

Knott's enormous success with the "deep image" arises from his stance. He seems to live in a world where heaven's water is commonplace, and hair is not. His surrealism arises from what seems to be a surreal existence where the tables and perceptions are turned completely; metaphor, therefore, is reversed, and the world is seen through a crystal lens: "If bombing children is preserving peace, then/my fucking you is a war-crime" ("Nuremburg, USA"). At times the image is tied to nothing but itself and its effect relies simply on the suggested idea, as in "Cueballs have invented insomnia in an attempt to forget eyelids," from *Nights of Naomi*, a 32-page sequence where the surrealist jars the reader over and over: accept the metaphorical condition or don't bother to read any further. The poem begins, "Prefrontal lightningbolt too lazy to chew the sphinx's loudest eyelash.... Only a maze can remember your hair of buttered blowguns."

It makes for thick reading, and the reader must indeed accomodate Knott's unusual stance in a world where "They squeezed your blood back into grapes." The reward is a trip through unvisited rooms of experience, with one of the finest poetic imaginations in print, "Years spent wandering in front of a stab."

—Geof Hewitt

KOCH, Kenneth. American. Born in Cincinnati, Ohio, 27 February 1925. Educated at Harvard University, Cambridge, Massachusetts, A.B. 1948; Columbia University, New York, M.A. 1953, Ph.D. 1959. Served in the United States Army, 1943–46. Married Mary Janice Elwood in 1955; one daughter. Lecturer in English, Rutgers University, New Brunswick, New Jersey, 1953–54, 1955–56, 1957–58, and Brooklyn College, 1957–59; Director of the Poetry Workshop, New School for Social Research, New York, 1958–66. Since 1959, Member of the English Department, and since 1970, Professor of English, Columbia University. Associated with the magazine *Locus Solus*, 1960–62. Recipient: Fulbright Fellowship, 1950, 1978; Guggenheim Fellowship, 1961; National Endowment for the Arts grant, 1966; Ingram Merrill Foundation Fellowship, 1969; Harbison Award, for teaching, 1970; Frank O'Hara Prize (*Poetry*, Chicago), 1973; National Institute of Arts and

Letters award, 1976. Address: Department of English, Columbia University, New York, New York 10027, U.S.A.

PUBLICATIONS

Verse

Poems. New York, Tibor de Nagy, 1953.
Ko; or, A Season on Earth. New York, Grove Press, 1960.
Permanently. New York, Tiber Press, 1960.
Thank You and Other Poems. New York, Grove Press, 1962.
Poems from 1952 and 1953. Los Angeles, Black Sparrow Press, 1968.
When the Sun Tries to Go On. Los Angeles, Black Sparrow Press, 1969.
Sleeping with Women. Los Angeles, Black Sparrow Press, 1969.
The Pleasures of Peace and Other Poems. New York, Grove Press, 1969.
Penguin Modern Poets 24, with Kenward Elmslie and James Schuyler. London, Penguin, 1973.
The Art of Love. New York, Random House, 1975.
The Duplications. New York, Random House, 1977.
The Burning Mystery of Anna in 1951. New York, Random House, 1979.

Plays

Bertha (produced New York, 1959). Included in *Bertha and Other Plays*, 1966.
The Election (also director: produced New York, 1960). Included in *A Change of Hearts*, 1973.
Pericles (produced New York, 1960). Included in *Bertha and Other Plays*, 1966.
George Washinton Crossing the Delaware (produced New York, 1962). Included in *Bertha and Other Plays*, 1966.
The Construction of Boston (produced New York, 1962). Included in *Bertha and Other Plays*, 1966.
Guinevere; or, The Death of the Kangaroo (produced New York, 1964). Included in *Bertha and Other Plays*, 1966.
The Tinguely Machine Mystery; or, The Love Suicides at Kaluka (also co-director: produced New York, 1965). Included in *A Change of Hearts*, 1973.
Bertha and Other Plays (includes *Pericles, George Washington Crossing the Delaware, The Construction of Boston, Guinevere; or, The Death of the Kangaroo, The Gold Standard, The Return of Yellowmay, The Revolt of the Giant Animals, The Building of Florence, Angelica, The Merry Stones, The Academic Murders, Easter, The Lost Feed, Mexico, Coil Supreme*). New York, Grove Press, 1966.
The Gold Standard (produced New York, 1975). Included in *Bertha and Other Plays*, 1966.
The Scotty Dog (produced New York, 1967). Included in *A Change of Hearts*, 1973.
The Apple (produced Philadelphia, 1968). Included in *A Change of Hearts*, 1973.
The Moon Balloon (produced New York, 1969). Included in *A Change of Hearts*, 1973.
The Artist, music by Paul Reif, adaptation of the poem "The Artist" by Kenneth Koch (produced New York, 1972). Poem included in *Thank You and Other Poems*, 1962.
A Little Light (produced Amagansett, New York, 1972).
A Change of Hearts: Plays, Films, and Other Dramatic Works 1951–1971 (includes the contents of *Bertha and Other Plays*, and *A Change of Hearts*; *E. Kology*; *The Moon Balloon*; *Without Kinship*; *Ten Films: Because, The Color Game, Mountains and Electricity, Sheep Harbor, Oval Gold, Moby Dick, L'Ecole Normale, The Cemetery, The Scotty Dog*, and *The Apple*; *Youth*; and *The Enchantment*). New York, Random House, 1973.

Rooster Redivivus (produced Garnerville, New York, 1975).
The Art of Love, adaptation of his own poem (produced Chicago, 1976).
The Red Robins (produced New York, 1978). New York, Performing Arts, 1979.

Novel

The Red Robins. New York, Random House, 1975.

Other

Wishes, Lies and Dreams: Teaching Children to Write Poetry. New York, Random House, 1970.
Rose, Where Did You Get That Red? Teaching Great Poetry to Children. New York, Random House, 1973.
I Never Told Anybody: Teaching Poetry Writing in a Nursing Home. New York, Random House, 1977.

Theatrical Activities:

Director: **Plays** – *The Election*, New York, 1960; *The Tinguely Machine Mystery* (co-director, with Remy Charlip), New York, 1965.

* * *

Kenneth Koch was one of the three principal poets of the "New York school" in the middle and late 1950's, a somewhat amorphous and short-lived group which also included John Ashbery and Frank O'Hara. The three had joined forces while students at Harvard before transferring their activities to New York, where they became associated with the painters who were then ascendant in the American art world, a group known as "abstract expressionists." To a certain extent the poets seemed to be bringing to verbal constructs the principles of abstract expressionism, i.e., they used words totally abstractly and evocatively. At the same time their prosodic practice was in revolt against the academic austerity of mid-century American poetry, and their use of syntax and measure resembled that of the contemporaneous Beat movement. What distinguished the two groups, if anything, was the New York poets' retention of an earlier idea of art as in some sense a puristic activity, not socially amenable, and of the art object as distinct from and perhaps superior to the objects of "ordinary reality." In addition Koch was, during a period of residence abroad, deeply influenced by current French poetry with its emphasis on psychological particularism.

These groupings and distinctions have long since broken down, of course. Koch's association with New York poetry was, in effect, his apprenticeship. Much of his early work was very far out indeed; some was frankly incomprehensible, even to the poet. Since then Koch has elevated his lyric view to another level, not in the least "realistic" but better organized and more simplified than his earlier view, with the result that some of his recent work has been extremely effective. The freedom of his earlier verbal technique has given him a felicity which occasionally still decends to surrealistic glibness but which at its best is remarkably inventive and accurate. At the same time, substantially fixed in his poems is a depth of metaphysical concern that gives them the drive and intensity of genuinely serious experiments.

One distinction of the New York poets was their devotion to the lyric theater. Their connection with "off-Broadway" and "off-off-Broadway" gave them opportunities for experiments with dramatic writing that were open to few poets elsewhere in the country, and some of Koch's best writing occurs in the several books of plays he has published, books which have been generally neglected, however, by American poetry-readers and critics.

—Hayden Carruth

KOLATKAR, Arun (Balkrishna). Indian. Born in Kolhapur, Bombay, 1 November 1932. Works as a graphic artist in an advertising agency, Bombay. Recipient: Commonwealth Poetry Award, 1977. Address: c/o Clearing House, Palm Springs, Cusse Parade, Bombay 400 005, India.

PUBLICATIONS

Verse

Jejuri. Bombay, Clearing House, 1977.

* * *

A bilingual (Marathi and English) poet, Arun Kolatkar virtually burst upon the Indo-English poetic scene when he won the Commonwealth Poetry Award for 1977 with *Jejuri*. *Jejuri* is his first book although his poems have appeared since 1955 in poetry magazines and anthologies. Kolatkar does not show any solipsistic uneasiness as A. K. Ramanujan and R. Parthasarathy do in using a foreign linguistic medium. His poetic idiom being objectivist does not surrender to the pulls of the past – cultural or linguistic – and is, indeed, characterised by an engaging "alfresco individualism."

Jejuri comprising thirty one titled sections stands out as a personal epic like W. C. Williams's *Paterson*. It dramatizes a Jungian passage to contemporary Hinduism symbolised by the shrine at Jejuri, where one has only "to scratch a rock/and a legend springs." Ironically, the rational-minded and irreverent ("God is the word/and I know it backwards") protagonist, Manohar, who regards myth-making as characteristic of decadent Hinduism, himself succumbs to it as his "pilgrimage" nears its end: the train indicator appears as "a wooden saint in need of paint" to Manohar who in sheer desperation is prepared to "slaughter a goat before the clock/smash a cocoanut on the railway track .../bathe the station master in milk .../if only some one would tell .../when the next train is due." Indeed, his easy, informal, though laconic, tone suggestive of post-Romantic expressionism belies his capacity to transfigure his world with his iconoclastic cast of thought. His awareness of the shrine of Khandoba at Jejuri and its railway station being mythical correlatives of the postulates of a purgatory could alone, perhaps, redeem his "pilgrimage."

Kolatkar's subtle use of the montage technique in *Jejuri* (indeed, his first impulse was to do a movie) to achieve the effect of symbolist aesthetic is characteristic of modern poetry. So also is his avoidance of the mixing of "an abstraction with the concrete" (Ezra Pound's dictum). He uses images instinct with the criticism of the unfolding scene – a Wasteland one – which do not lessen the vibrance of the perceiving self: "he doesn't reply/... and happens to notice/a quick wink of a movement/in a scanty patch of scruffy dry grass/burnt brown in the sun/and says/look/there's a butterfly/there." *Jejuri* – a virtuoso performance – exemplifies a movement towards a freer form of verse; this is what is most promising in Kolatkar's poetry.

—K. Venkatachari

KOLLER, James. American. Born in Oak Park, Illinois, 30 May 1936. Educated at North Central College, Naperville, Illinois, B.A. 1958. Has two daughters and one son. Since 1964, Editor, *Coyote Journal* and Coyote Books, San Francisco, then New Mexico and Maine. Recipient: National Endowment for the Arts grant, 1968, 1973. Address: P.O. Box 629, Brunswick, Maine 04011, U.S.A.

PUBLICATIONS

Verse

Two Hands: Poems 1959–1961. Seattle, James B. Smith, 1965.
Brainard and Washington Street Poems. Eugene, Oregon, Toad Press, 1965.
Some Cows: Poems of Civilization and Domestic Life. San Francisco, Coyote, 1966.
The Dogs and Other Dark Woods. San Francisco, Four Seasons, 1966.
I Went to See My True Love. Buffalo, Audit East/West, 1967.
California Poems. Los Angeles, Black Sparrow Press, 1971.
Messages. Canton, New York, Institute of Further Studies, 1972.
Dark Woman, Who Lay with the Sun. San Francisco, Tenth Muse, 1972.
The Tracks Run Together. Santa Fe, New Mexico, Fourwing Press, 1974.
Poems for the Blue Sky. Santa Barbara, California, Black Sparrow Press, 1976.

Manuscript Collections: University of Connecticut, Storrs; Simon Fraser University, Burnaby, British Columbia.

Critical Studies: "Eyes and 'I' " by Richard Duerden, in *Poetry* (Chicago), May 1966; "James Koller Issue" of *Savage 2* (Chicago), 1972.

* * *

James Koller is an earthy poet; perhaps even "raunchy" would not be the wrong adjective to put to his work, which seeks out communion with nature and sex at a visceral level. Though his work calls to mind, with its spontaneous, collage-like technique, the Beat or Black Mountain poets, he is less cerebral, or mystical, in approach than a poet like Olson or Ginsberg; his poetry is direct, sensual, wrenched still steaming from the innards of the other life he encounters – when he speaks of stepping inside a bear's body, the intentions are by no means as metaphysical as in the poems of identification with animal life of, for instance, Kinnell or Dickey.

He is interested in the retreat to a more primitive relationship with nature, with ecstasy and the dangerous, slippery terrain around madness. He takes the sort of risks that can result in bad taste, but also in sudden gains, as in "I Get Crazy in the Full Moon" from *California Poems*:

I crawled over the dark ground
planting squash, an owl
over my shoulder, the moon

she throws back her head, stretches
her arms hands, ripple of muscle
skin, the moon

clouds, shadows
between us
the ground mostly lighted

the flower first, fruit
full & rounded
the softest curve, ripple, moon

the laughter very soft

—Duane Ackerson

KOPS, Bernard. British. Born in London, 28 November 1926. Educated in London elementary schools to age 13. Married Erica Gordon in 1956; four children. Has worked as a docker, chef, salesman, waiter, lift man, and barrow boy. Recipient: Arts Council bursary, 1957. Agent: David Higham Associates, 5–8 Lower John Street, London W1R 4HA. Address: Flat 1, 35 Canfield Gardens, London N.W.6, England.

PUBLICATIONS

Verse

Poems. London, Bell and Baker Press, 1955.
Poems and Songs. Lowestoft, Suffolk, Scorpion Press, 1958.
An Anemone for Antigone. Lowestoft, Suffolk, Scorpion Press, 1959.
Erica, I Want to Read You Something. Lowestoft, Suffolk, Scorpion Press, and New York, Walker, 1967.
For the Record. London, Secker and Warburg, 1971.

Plays

The Hamlet of Stepney Green (produced Oxford, 1957; London and New York, 1958). London, Evans, 1959.
Goodbye World (produced Guildford, Surrey, 1959).
Change for the Angel (produced London, 1960).
The Dream of Peter Mann (produced Edinburgh, 1960). London, Penguin, 1960.
Enter Solly Gold, music by Stanley Myers (produced Wellingborough, Northamptonshire, and Los Angeles, 1962; London, 1970). Published in *Satan, Socialites, and Solly Gold: Three New Plays from England*, New York, Coward McCann, 1961; in *Four Plays*, 1964.
Home Sweet Honeycomb (broadcast, 1962). Included in *Four Plays*, 1964.
The Lemmings (broadcast, 1963). Included in *Four Plays*, 1964.
Stray Cats and Empty Bottles (televised, 1964; produced London, 1967).
Four Plays (includes *The Hamlet of Stepney Green*, *Enter Solly Gold*, *Home Sweet Honeycomb*, *The Lemmings*). London, MacGibbon and Kee, 1964.
The Boy Who Wouldn't Play Jesus (juvenile; produced London, 1965). Published in *Eight Plays: Book 1*, edited by Malcolm Stuart Fellows, London, Cassell, 1965; Chicago, Dramatic Publishing Company, n.d.
David, It is Getting Dark (produced Rennes, France, 1970). Paris, Gallimard, 1970.
It's a Lovely Day Tomorrow, with John Goldschmidt (televised, 1975; produced London, 1976).

Radio Plays: *Home Sweet Honeycomb*, 1962; *The Lemmings*, 1963; *Born in Israel*, 1963; *The Dark Ages*, 1964; *Israel: The Immigrant*, 1964; *Bournemouth Nights*, 1979; *I Grow Old, I Grow Old*, 1979.

Television Plays: *I Want to Go Home*, 1963; *Stray Cats and Empty Bottles*, 1964; *The Lost Years of Brian Hooper*, 1967; *Alexander the Greatest*, 1971; *Just One Kid*, 1974; *Why the Geese Shrieked*, and *The Boy Philosopher*, from stories by Isaac Bashevis Singer, 1974; *It's a Lovely Day Tomorrow*, 1975; *Moss*, 1975; *Rocky Marciano Is Dead*, 1976.

Novels

Awake for Morning. London, MacGibbon and Kee, 1958.
Motorbike. London, New English Library, 1962.

Yes from No-Man's Land. London, MacGibbon and Kee, 1965; New York, Coward McCann, 1966.
The Dissent of Dominick Shapiro. London, MacGibbon and Kee, 1966; New York, Coward McCann, 1967.
By the Waters of Whitechapel. London, Bodley Head, 1969; New York, Norton, 1970.
The Passionate Past of Gloria Gaye. London, Secker and Warburg, 1971; New York, Norton, 1972.
Settle Down Simon Katz. London, Secker and Warburg, 1973.
Partners. London, Secker and Warburg, 1975.
On Margate Sands. London, Secker and Warburg, 1978.

Other

The World Is a Wedding (autobiography). London, MacGibbon and Kee, 1963; New York, Coward McCann, 1964.

Critical Studies: "Bernard Kops" by Colin MacInnes, in *Encounter* (London), May 1960; "The Kitchen Sink" by G. Wilson Knight, in *Encounter* (London), December 1963; "Deep Waters of Whitechapel" by Nina Sutton, in *The Guardian* (London), 6 September 1969.

Bernard Kops comments:

Kops creates specific relationships in order that they might relate universally. He writes compulsively, for himself, and even if his work is acceptable to others, this is a secondary process. Nevertheless, he is pleased that he can sell his work and be able to live by writing. Kops is obsessed by family themes; this runs throughout his work. The relationships are of people bound up together in an intense emotional and intellectual involvement. He believes that the great themes of Shakespeare, Racine, Sophocles, O'Neill have lasted and will last because they deal with themes common to every human being. *King Lear* and its dream and despair lives for us because it lives through us – it is US. We give it life and constantly renew it. Kops is also obsessed with death but only because he is obsessed with life. He believes motives are impossible to define ultimately, but actions are not subjective and one must judge a man by his actions. He likes ambiguity. But he also believes in strict discipline, and thinks that the writer must know exactly what he is doing even if he has shown the subjectivity and complexity of human relationships. He writes constantly about the backgrounds and the people and things he knows, or thinks he knows. The only things that he is really certain about are: the existence of love, the need for it and that "they" no longer exist. There are only US left on this earth. Kops writes about this.

* * *

Bernard Kops's reputation stands on his plays and novels, yet these very substantial writings can be said to arise from the wellsprings of a talent and an approach to literature which is entirely that of a poet.

And, further, it is that of a special sort of poet – the sort contained in the familiar quotation about "the poet's eye in a fine frenzy rolling." Kops's poems usually exhibit a tendency to the frenetic – a free-wheeling fantasy, an extravagance of language and gesture, an explosive celebration of the things that he loves or that excite him, and an apocalyptic rejection of things that he hates or that appall him. He draws a great deal of his poetry from his fervent Jewishness – but not merely in the form of his sense of racial difference, or his horror at the Nazi holocaust. Many of his most successful poems grow out of his family's presence in the foreground of his experience, from which he can create universalised images for what he sees as the sad, proud, lonely, laughable continuity of human life. "Somewhere upon these impossible stairs," he wrote in a poem entitled "Prayer at Forty," "we are attempting love."

Though his poetic output has never been large, his assertion in it of the need to go on "attempting love" has been unflagging – and has figured equally large throughout his considerable oeuvre of plays, novels and that splendid poet's autobiography, *The World Is a Wedding*. That determined assertion has been his poetry's source of power, and its most lasting quality.

—Douglas Hill

KOSTELANETZ, Richard. American. Born in New York City, 14 May 1940. Educated at Brown University, Providence, Rhode Island, A.B. 1962; Columbia University, New York, M.A. 1966; King's College, London (Fulbright Fellow, 1964–65). Program Associate, John Jay College, New York, 1972–73; Visiting Professor, University of Texas, Austin, 1977. Since 1970, Co-Founder, Assembling Press; since 1976, Proprietor, The Future Press; since 1977, Co-Editor, *Precisely*. Contributing Editor, *The Humanist* and *Performing Arts Journal*. Visual poetry exhibited at Christopher Stephens, New York, 1975, Washtenaw Community College, 1975, University of Toledo, 1977, Bertha Urdang, New York, 1977, Simon Fraser University, 1978, University of Alberta, 1978, and Cornell College, 1979. Recipient: Pulitzer Fellowship, 1965; Guggenheim Fellowship, 1967; National Endowment for the Arts grant, 1976, 1978. Address: P.O. Box 73, Canal Street Station, New York, New York 10013, U.S.A.

PUBLICATIONS

Verse

Visual Language. New York, Assembling Press, 1970.
I Articulations, with *Short Fictions*. New York, Kulchur, 1974.
Portraits from Memory. Ann Arbor, Ardis, 1975.
Word Prints. Privately printed, 1975.
Rain Rains Rain. New York, Assembling Press, 1976.
Numbers: Poems and Stories. New York, Assembling Press, 1976.
Illuminations. Woodinville, Washington, and New York, Laughing Bear-Future Press, 1977.

Novels

In the Beginning. Somerville, Massachusetts, Abyss, 1971.
One Night Stood. New York, Future Press, 1977.

Short Stories

Accounting. Brescia, Italy, Amodulo, 1972; Sacramento, California, Poetry Newsletter, 1973.
Ad Infinitum. Friedrichsfehn, Germany, International Artists' Cooperation, 1973.
Openings and Closings. New York, D'Arc, 1975.
Constructs. Reno, Nevada, West Coast Poetry Review, 1975.
Come Here. New York, Assembling Press, 1975.
Extrapolate. New York, Assembling Press, 1975.

Constructs Two. Milwaukee, Membrane, 1978.
Foreshortenings and Other Stories. Willits, California, Tuumba Press, 1978.

Other

The Theatre of Mixed-Means: An Introduction to Happenings, Kinetic Environments, and Other Mixed-Means Performances. New York, Dial Press, 1968.
Master Minds: Portraits of Contemporary American Artists and Intellectuals. New York, Macmillan, 1969.
The End of Intelligent Writing: Literary Politics in America. New York, Sheed and Ward, 1974.
Recyclings: A Literary Autobiography. New York, Assembling Press, 1974.
Grants and the Future of Literature. New York, RK, 1978.
Twenties in the Sixties: Previously Uncollected Critical Essays. Westport, Connecticut, Greenwood Press, 1978.
Wordsand. Burnaby, British Columbia, Simon Fraser Gallery, 1978.

Editor, *On Contemporary Literature: An Anthology of Critical Essays on Major Movements and Writers of Contemporary Literature.* New York, Avon, 1964; revised edition, 1969.
Editor, *The New Amercan Arts.* New York, Horizon Press, 1965.
Editor, *Twelve from the Sixties.* New York, Dell, 1967.
Editor, *The Young American Writers: Fiction, Poetry, Drama, and Criticism.* New York, Funk and Wagnalls, 1967.
Editor, *Beyond Left and Right: Radical Thought for Our Time.* New York, Morrow, 1968.
Editor, *Imaged Words and Worded Images.* New York, Outerbridge and Dienstfrey, 1970.
Editor, *Possibilities of Poetry: An Anthology of American Contemporaries.* New York, Dell, 1970.
Editor, *John Cage.* New York, Praeger, 1970; London, Allen Lane, 1971.
Editor, *Moholy-Nagy.* New York, Praeger, 1970; London, Allen Lane, 1972.
Editor, *Assembling*, and *Second* through *Eighth Assembling.* New York, Assembling Press, 8 vols., 1970–78.
Editor, *Future's Fictions.* New York, Panache, 1971.
Editor, *Human Alternatives: Visions for Us Now.* New York, Morrow, 1971.
Editor, *Social Speculations: Visions for Us Now.* New York, Morrow, 1971.
Editor, *In Youth.* New York, Ballantine, 1972.
Editor, *Seeing Through Shuck.* New York, Ballantine, 1972.
Editor, *Breakthrough Fictioneers: An Anthology.* New York, Something Else Press, 1973.
Editor, *The Edge of Adaptation: Man and the Emerging Society.* Englewood Cliffs, New Jersey, Prentice Hall, 1973.
Editor, *Essaying Essays.* New York, Oolp, 1975.
Editor, *Language and Structure.* New York, Kensington Arts, 1975.
Editor, *Younger Critics of North America: Essays on Literature and the Arts.* Fair Water, Wisconsin, Margins, 1977.
Editor, *Esthetic Contemporary.* New York, Prometheus, 1977.
Editor, *Assembling Assembling.* New York, Assembling Press, 1978.
Editor, *Sketching Language: Selected Experimental Writings*, by Jack Kerouac. Layton, Utah, Peregrine Smith, 1979.

Critical Studies: *Once Again*, edited by Jean-François Bory, New York, New Directions, 1968; "Poetry and Space" by Carolo Alberto Sitta, in *The Gazette* (Modena, Italy), 4 November 1970; "Figured Verse and Calligrams" by Massin, in *Letter and Image*, Paris,

Gallimard, and New York, Van Nostrand, 1970; *Text-Bilder/Visuelle Poésie International*, edited by Klaus Peter Dencker, Cologne, DuMont Schauberg, 1972; L. J. Davis, in *New York Times Book Review*, 21 October 1973; "Richard Kostelanetz" by Hugh Fox, in *West Coast Poetry Review 12* (Reno, Nevada), Summer 1974; "Just Plain Video and Video-Plus" by Davidson Gigliotti, in *Soho Weekly News* (New York), 30 December 1976.

Richard Kostelanetz quotes from "After Sentences" to *I Articulations*, 1974:

In visual poetry, unlike other kinds, the way that words are placed on the page is the primary means of enhancing language; pictorial shaping makes words poetic by generating semantic and symbolic connotations that would not otherwise be present. Conversely, language in visual poetry would have considerably different meanings if presented in uniform, horizontal type; for one thing, it would lack the poetic dimensions that the pictorial increment provides. Visual poetry is not synonymous with "concrete," although all anthologies with "concrete" in the title included some visual work. The principal characteristic of "concrete" appears to be the counter-syntactical use of language; and although most pictorial poetry likewise eschews conventional linguistic syntax, that is not its primary particularity. "Visual poetry" is a genre, or a species of *poetic* literature, as distinct from fictional literature or expository writing. The epithet is useful as a critical-historical classification that, like a genus-term in biology, tells us not only what the work at hand is, but also what it isn't.

Visual poetry is an intermedium between poetry and design. One man's visual poetry is another man's "design" and a third man's "Art." The form of word-image art provided me, as a professional essayist, with a sure means of avoiding the conventions of expository writing, for I assumed from the beginning that a writer's poetry should evolve from processes different from, if not contrary to, prose. Certain things can be articulated in visual poetry that cannot be said in prose, and vice versa.

Visual poetry depends not only upon design but upon language, revealing, intrinsically, why one word was chosen, rather than another; it exploits the advantages of non-verbal communication without relinquishing language. A pictorial poem creates a field of visual-verbal communication; and though both the visual and the verbal dimensions are perceived simultaneously, their relationship is usually comprehended progressively. Some pictorial poets try, often with the help of professional collaborators, to realize the precision of commercial design; but since my own works belong to poetry, rather than design, some of them reveal, perhaps too conspicuously, the presence of the poet's own hand. My aims include not only the communication of information but the making of a visual-verbal field that makes an impression comparable to the "after-image" of painting. The designer Jan Tschichold once said that "typography is the arranging of words to be read," implying that words were servants of an ulterior message; in pictorial poetry, words stand mostly as an end in themselves. What distinguishes my own pictorial poems from those of others has been, I think, the complete avoidance so far of any visual materials other than letters.

* * *

The appropriate descriptive term for Richard Kostelanetz's creative work is "visual poetry," indicating a specialized genre within poetry, or an intermedium between poetry and painting. His visual poems are non-linear and non-syntactic, in contrast to those "shape poems" whose ancestry is traceable back through Apollinaire and George Herbert to the illuminated manuscript and Chinese ideogram. They are consciously counter-conventional poems, reflecting a comprehensive knowledge of contemporary literary practice and deliberate avoidance of it, although they employ such specifically literary devices as punning, wit, allusion, alliteration, parallelism and contrast. Constructivism and minimalism in the visual art tradition have also influenced Kostelanetz. His early poems in *Visual Language*, written around 1967, are usually mimetic, often employing only one letter or word, and often erotic in content. In his second collection, *I Articulations*, he creates more complex structures involving synonyms, multiple repetitions and more philosophical concerns, frequently about the nature of language itself.

His style is immediately recognizable, not only because he has published more visual poetry than any other American practitioner, but because of his distinctive technical means – a common letter-stencil and shamelessly amateur calligraphy which represent calculated avoidance of the polished finish of commercial design. Another recognizable aspect of his style is the strict limitation he places on himself. In these volumes he uses no visual material other than letters in non-syntactic formations. This methodology mirrors his aesthetic conviction that a radical formal constraint is essential to true creativity.

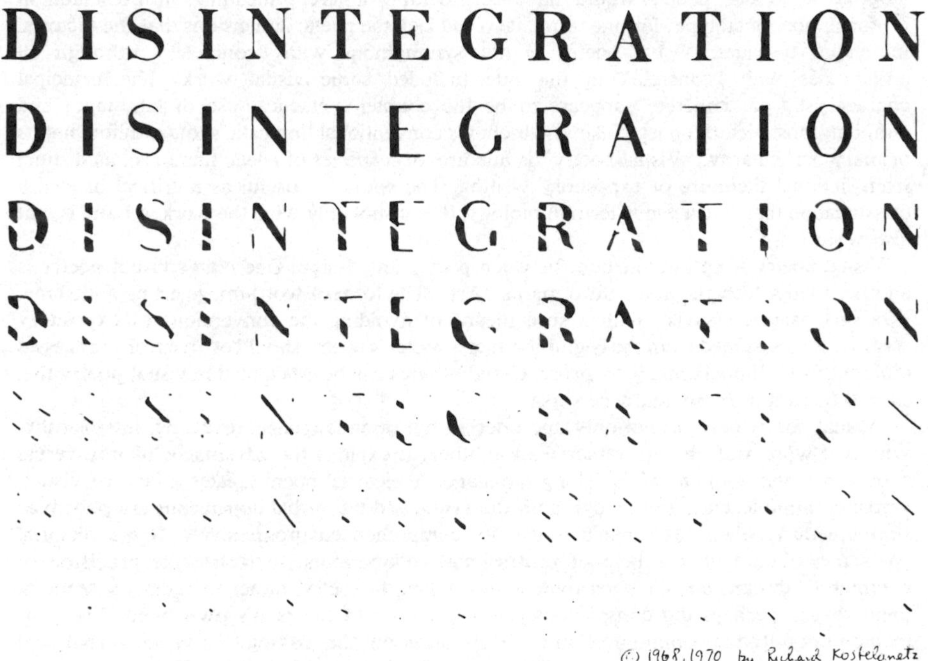

From this style and its ramifications, he has moved into fiction – "sequential forms that still eschew the prosaic form of expository sentences" – and his most recent poems and fictions consist entirely of numbers, thus emphasizing that formal pattern and relationship, rather than semantic content or extrinsic reference, is at the center of his art.

Although traditionalists may object to such expansion of the genre, Kostelanetz's work continually challenges more moderate notions of "new directions" in poetry. It incorporates the values which have governed his work as a critic, anthologist and proponent of the avant-garde movement in America. Visual enhancement of language, he says, is not an exclusive successor to the past, but "one propitious future for literature."

—Jane Augustine

KUMAR, Shiv K(umar). Indian. Born in Lahore, Punjab, 16 August 1921. Educated at Forman Christian College, Panjab University, Lahore, 1941–43, M.A.; Fitzwilliam College, Cambridge, 1953–56, Ph.D. 1956. Married Madhu Kumar in 1967; one son and one daughter. Lecturer, D.A.V. College, Lahore, 1945–47, and Hansraj College, Delhi, 1948–49; Programme Executive, All India Radio, Delhi, 1949; Senior Lecturer and Chairman of the Department of English, Government College, Chandigarh, Punjab, 1953–56; Reader in English, Panjab University, Hoshiarpur, 1956–59; Professor and Chairman of the Department of English, Osmania University, Hyderabad, 1959–76. Since 1976, Professor and Chairman of the Department of English, and Dean of the School of Humanities, University of Hyderabad. Visiting Professor, Elmira College, New York, 1965–67, Marshall University, Huntington, West Virginia, 1968, and University of Northern Iowa, Cedar Falls, 1969; Cultural Award Visitor, Australia, Summer 1971; Visiting Professor, Drake University, Des Moines, Iowa, 1971–72, Hofstra University, Hempstead, New York, 1972, and University of Kent, Canterbury, 1977–78. President, All India English Teachers Conference, 1975. Recipient: Smith-Mundt Fellowship, 1962. Fellow, Royal Society of Literature, 1978. Address: 2-F/Kakatiya Nagar, P.O. Jamia Osmania, Hyderabad 500 007, India.

PUBLICATIONS

Verse

Articulate Silences. Calcutta, Writers Workshop, 1970.
Cobwebs in the Sun. New Delhi, Tata-McGraw Hill, 1974.
Subterfuges. New Delhi, Oxford University Press, 1976.
Woodpeckers. London, Sidgwick and Jackson, 1979.

Play

The Last Wedding Anniversary (produced Hyderabad, 1974). New Delhi, Macmillan, 1975.

Novel

The Bone's Prayer. New Delhi, Arnold-Heinemann, 1979.

Short Stories

Beyond Love and Other Stories. New Delhi, Vikas, 1980.

Other

Virginia Woolf and Intuition. Hoshiarpur, Vishveshvaranand, 1957; Norwood, Pennsylvania, Norwood Editions, 1978.
Virginia Woolf and Bergson's Durée. Hoshiarpur, Vishveshvaranand, 1957; Folcroft, Pennsylvania, Folcroft Editions, 1977.
Bergson and the Stream of Consciousness Novel. London, Blackie, 1962; New York, New York University Press, 1963.
Examine Your English, with M. M. Maison. New Delhi, Orient Longman, 1964.

Editor, *Modern Short Stories.* Madras, Macmillan, 1958.
Editor, *Leaves of Grass,* by Walt Whitman. New Delhi, Eurasia, 1962.
Editor, *Apollo's Lyre.* Madras, Macmillan, 1962.
Editor, *The Red Badge of Courage,* by Stephen Crane. New Delhi, Eurasia, 1964.
Editor, *British Romantic Poets: Recent Revaluations.* New York, New York University Press, and London, University of London Press, 1966.

Editor, with Keith McKean, *Critical Approaches to Fiction.* New York, McGraw Hill, 1968.
Editor, *British Victorian Literature: Recent Revaluations.* New York, New York University Press, and London, University of London Press, 1969.
Editor, *The Life, Adventures, and Pyracies of the Famous Captain Singleton*, by Daniel Defoe. London, Oxford University Press, 1969.
Editor, *Indian Verse in English 1970.* Calcutta, Writers Workshop, 1971.

Critical Studies: "An Essay on the Poems of Shiv K. Kumar" by R. K. Kaul, in *Osmania Journal of English Studies 11* (Hyderabad), 1, 1974; "Beyond the Empiric Point" by M. Sivaramkrishna, in *World Literature Written in English* (Arlington, Virginia), November 1975; "Towards an Idiom of Sincerity" by K. Venkatachari, in *Journal of Indian Writing in English* (Gulbarga, Mysore), July 1976; "Between Kali and Cordelia" by T. G. Vaidyanathan, in *Osmania Journal of English Studies 13* (Hyderabad), 1, 1977; "Resonant Bones" by J. Birje-Patil, in *World Literature Today* (Norman, Oklahoma), Autumn 1977.

Shiv K. Kumar comments:

Although I scribbled some verse during my undergraduate days, it was only at the age of 49 or so that I wrote my first serious poem. Since then poetry has been one of my most continual sources of joy.

A poem comes to me as a phrase or a line or a nebulous image which then gets crystallized into a cluster of words. An idea never starts it off – I seem to have an innate distrust of statement. I believe that a poem achieves its most effective articulation when it emerges from the intensity of a writer's lived experience. It may not be "a kind of locked trunk of confessions" (as Gabriel Pearson puts it), but it acquires its sharp identity from the poet as a private person.

Of course the poet must never forsake the artistic distance and control which mould the disparate elements of experience into a pattern. Nor should a poet allow any kind of intellectual discipline to ossify his sensibility. My dual role as critic and writer has made me particularly conscious of this dilemma, but I agree with Anthony Thwaite that one's activity may "fall into different compartments and that the one doesn't influence the other."

I don't think I have been influenced by any poet, though I greatly admire the work of Robert Lowell, Sylvia Plath, and Anne Sexton. Ultimately each poet has to work out his own credo of life and imagination – "we perish each alone."

Do I consider the use of a language I am not born to a serious impediment to my creativity? No. I feel that it is as much the language that chooses its writer as the writer who selects his medium. In any case, I have grown up with the English language, and cannot write in any other, so I have no alternative.

It has sometimes been remarked that one of the recurring themes in my poetry is cultural interaction, a preoccupation with the polarities of East and West. But this preoccupation must be unconscious. Maybe I have stayed too long in the West, and my Indian sensibility keeps assessing my western experience. Fundamentally, I guess, I am something of a "primitivist" who may never overcome his nostalgia for prelapsarian innocence and simplicity. What hurts me most is any kind of regimentation – political, social, intellectual, or religious. I feel that poetry is an impassioned testament to man's inner freedom. I have done other kinds of creative writing, but it is the poem that satisfies me most because it summons forth my imagination in its intensest form. In the beginning was the word, and that word was the poem – man's profoundest experience articulated through cadence and harmony.

* * *

Although it was only in 1970 that Shiv K. Kumar appeared on the Indian literary scene with his first collection of poems *Articulate Silences*, his subsequent work has established him as a major Indo-anglian poet. He shares with some of his contemporaries (Dom Moraes, A. K. Ramanujan, and Nissim Ezekiel) a crisis of personal identity, an agonising search for some *locus standi* between East and West, between an irrepressible nostalgia for prelapsarian innocence and the compulsions of contemporary civilisation.

Educated at Cambridge, and frequently invited as Visiting Professor of literature at various American and British universities, he has remained an exile as much in his native country as elsewhere. This tension between his two warring selves lends his poetry a rare ironical thrust. "There is," says Roger Iredale, "in his poetry, a pervasive, ironic humour that is missing from the work of other Indian poets" (*Quest*, November-December 1975). It is irony that he uses to expose the smug complacency of his native Hindu culture. In his sequence poem "Broken Columns," he describes his adolescence: "At dusk Father shuffles us all/about on the coir-mat to pray./We spout chants from the *Gita*. 'Feed not thy desire on objects of sense./But like a tortoise/folding up its limbs within the shell/withdraw into supreme wisdom.' " But "a puff of wind rustles through a girl's skirt/and two tender legs/gyrate the air into fuzzy yearnings." Again, he evokes the image of a Hindu crematorium, with a vulture cogitating "upon human avidity – flesh offered/to the flames, bones and ashes/to the Ganges. No leavings/for the living."

"It is assumed," observes Birje-Patil (in *World Literature Today*, Autumn 1977) "that Indian poetry in English is essentially a post-Independence phenomenon.... Today we seem to be poised for a break-through and something that may be truly Indian is being written." Kumar's distinctive achievement, he avers, lies in his ability to convey "the experience of being Indian instead of the experience of feeling like an Indian." Kumar is at his best in his crisp, tautly controlled short lyrics like "My Co-respondent," "My Son," "My Mother's Death Anniversary," and "To a Prostitute." All such poems quicken into meaning through a subtle inter-play of images (for instance, a young Mango-Vendor revealing "through the slits/of her patched blouse/one bare shoulder/two white moons/pulling all horses/off the track") and a juxtaposition of polarities (affirmation and denial, intuition and logic) in a language that is supple and evocatively cadenced.

A striking feature of his poetry is his preoccupation with physical experience: sex, indeed, is almost a mode of perception for him. Even his nature imagery (sea, sky, wind, sun, fish) often implies some kind of sexual play. "The preponderance of erotic images is explicable not only in terms of an uninhibited delight in all sensuous things, but also in terms of the primacy of 'the religion of the blood' " (M. Sivaramkrishna, in *World Literature Written in English*, November 1975). Kumar's poetry, however, is marked by an intellectual distrust of pure emotion as though he were chary of giving himself away ("Cerebral Love").

—K. Venkatachari

KUMIN, Maxine. American. Born in Philadelphia, Pennsylvania, 6 June 1925. Educated at Radcliffe College, Cambridge, Massachusetts, A.B. 1946, M.A. 1948. Married Victor M. Kumin in 1946; three children. Instructor, 1958–61, and Lecturer in English, 1965–68, Tufts University, Medford, Massachusetts; Consultant, Central Atlantic Regional Educational Laboratory, 1967–69, and Board of Coordinated Educational Services, Nassau County, New York, 1967–72. Since 1971, Lecturer in English, Newton College of the Sacred Heart, Massachusetts; since 1972, Visiting Lecturer in English, University of Massachusetts, Amherst. Visiting Professor, Columbia University, New York, Spring 1975, Brandeis University, Waltham, Massachusetts, Fall 1975, Princeton University, New Jersey, Spring 1977 and 1979. Scholar, 1961–63, and since 1972, Officer, The Society of Fellows, Radcliffe Institute, Cambridge, Massachusetts. Recipient: Lowell Mason Palmer Award, 1960;

National Endowment for the Arts grant, 1966; William Marion Reedy Award, 1968; Eunice Tietjens Memorial Prize (*Poetry*, Chicago), 1972; Pulitzer Prize, 1973. Address: Joppa Road, Warner, New Hampshire 03278, U.S.A.

PUBLICATIONS

Verse

Halfway. New York, Holt Rinehart, 1961.
The Privilege. New York, Harper, 1965.
The Nightmare Factory. New York, Harper, 1970.
Up Country: Poems of New England, New and Selected. New York, Harper, 1972.
House, Bridge, Fountain, Gate. New York, Viking Press, 1975.
The Retrieval System. New York, Viking Press, 1978.

Novels

Through Dooms of Love. New York, Harper, 1965; as *A Daughter and Her Loves*, London, Gollancz, 1965.
The Passions of Uxport. New York, Harper, 1968.
The Abduction. New York, Harper, 1971.
The Designated Heir. New York, Viking Press, 1974.

Other (juvenile)

Sebastian and the Dragon. New York, Putnam, 1960.
Spring Things. New York, Putnam, 1961.
Summer Story. New York, Putnam, 1961.
Follow the Fall. New York, Putnam, 1961.
A Winter Friend. New York, Putnam, 1961.
Mittens in May. New York, Putnam, 1962.
No One Writes a Letter to the Snail. New York, Putnam, 1962.
Archibald the Traveling Poodle. New York, Putnam, 1963.
Eggs of Things, with Anne Sexton. New York, Putnam, 1963.
More Eggs of Things, with Anne Sexton. New York, Putnam, 1964.
Speedy Digs Downside Up. New York, Putnam, 1964.
The Beach Before Breakfast. New York, Putnam, 1964.
Paul Bunyan. New York, Putnam, 1966.
Faraway Farm. New York, Norton, 1967.
The Wonderful Babies of 1809 and Other Years. New York, Putnam, 1968.
When Grandmother Was Young. New York, Putnam, 1969.
When Mother Was Young. New York, Putnam, 1970.
When Great Grandmother Was Young. New York, Putnam, 1971.
Joey and the Birthday Present, with Anne Sexton. New York, McGraw Hill, 1971.
The Wizard's Tears, with Anne Sexton. New York, McGraw Hill, 1975.
What Color Is Caesar? New York, McGraw Hill, 1978.
To Make a Prairie: Essays on Poets, Poetry, and Country Living (for adults). Ann Arbor, University of Michigan Press, 1979.

Manuscript Collection: Mugar Memorial Library, Boston University.

* * *

Maxine Kumin is a poet who has written well about many subjects, in several styles. In her first poems she recreated the substance of her early life and Jewish ancestry, subjects given or even prescribed by a history that continues to engage her attention. The precision of her language is evident in "The Sound of Night," from her first collection: "Now every voice of the hour – the known, the supposed, the strange,/the mindless, the witted, the never seen –/ sing, thrum, impinge, and rearrange/endlessly." In *House, Bridge, Fountain, Gate*, published shortly after she received the Pulitzer Prize in 1973, she returned to those early years, in "The Thirties Revisited" and "Sperm," about her grandfather's issue.

The poems of the middle years are spoken in the voice of a person at odds with her surroundings, concerned, rebellious at times, and resentful of unexpected change. In "At the End of the Affair," one of the best poems, the speaker prepares himself/herself for the inevitable disappointment: "That it should end in an Albert Pick hotel/with the air conditioner gasping like a carp/and the bathroom tap plucking its one-string harp/and the sourmash bond half-gone in the open bottle." The sorrowful song of the victim, in "The Masochist," describes a similar betrayal:

Beware of blackeyed lovers. Some
who tease to see you all undone,
who taste and take you in the game
will later trample on your spine
as if they never called you *mine*,
mine, *mine*.

In these and other poems of this period, such as "For My Son on the Highways of the Mind," Kumin writes a language that successfully appropriates the rhythms of contemporary speech to the forms of art.

In more recent poems, she turns a careful eye toward the circumscribed world of her New Hampshire farm, a weekend and summer residence, in the midst of geese, horses, pine groves, and watering troughs, trying to be "terribly specific about many things." In "The Retrieval System," the title poem of a collection, the barnyard animals have come to dominate her imagination and memory. "Uncannily when I'm alone these features/come up to link my lost people/with the patient domestic beasts of my life .../Fact: it is people who fade,/it is animals that retrieve them." Kumin finds this life quite comfortable, and in poems such as "Hello, Hello Henry," "The Excrement Poem," and "The Archeology of Marriage," she continues to enjoy and celebrate a world that her suicidal friend, in "Progress Report," "wouldn't wait for." As a poet of nature and domestic life, Kumin is content to let the middle years fall peacefully about her, "petals that stick/in my hair like confetti/as I cut my way through clouds of gnats and butterflies in the woods."

—Michael True

KUNITZ, Stanley (Jasspon). American. Born in Worcester, Massachusetts, 29 July 1905. Educated at Harvard University, Cambridge, Massachusetts (Garrison Medal, 1926), A.B. (summa cum laude) 1926 (Phi Beta Kappa), A.M. 1927. Served in the United States Army, 1943–45. Married 1) Helen Pearce in 1930 (divorced, 1937); 2) Eleanor Evans in 1939 (divorced, 1958), one daughter; 3) Elise Asher in 1958. Editor, *Wilson Library Bulletin*, New York, 1928–43. Member of the Faculty, Bennington College, Vermont, 1946–49; Professor of English, State University of New York, Potsdam, 1949–50, and Summers, 1949–53; Lecturer, New School for Social Research, New York, 1950–57; Visiting Professor,

University of Washington, Seattle, 1955–56, Queens College, Flushing, New York, 1956–57, Brandeis University, Waltham, Massachusetts, 1958–59, Yale University, New Haven, Connecticut, 1970–72, and Rutgers University, Camden, New Jersey, 1974. Director, YM–YWHA Poetry Workshop, New York, 1958–62. Danforth Visiting Lecturer, United States, 1961–63. Lecturer, 1963–67, and since 1967, Adjunct Professor of Writing, Columbia University, New York. Since 1968 associated with the Fine Arts Work Center, Provincetown, Massachusetts. Editor, Yale Series of Younger Poets, Yale University Press, New Haven, Connecticut, 1969–77. Consultant in Poetry, Library of Congress, Washington, D.C., 1974–76. Formerly, Cultural Exchange Lecturer, U.S.S.R. and Poland. Fellow, Yale University, 1969; Senior Fellow in the Humanities, Princeton University, New Jersey, 1978. Recipient: Oscar Blumenthal Prize, 1941, and Levinson Prize, 1956 (*Poetry*, Chicago); Guggenheim Fellowship, 1945; Amy Lowell Traveling Fellowship, 1953; Harriet Monroe Award, 1958; Pulitzer Prize, 1959; Ford grant, 1959; National Institute of Arts and Letters grant, 1959, and Award of Merit, 1975; Brandeis University Creative Arts Award, 1964; Academy of American Poets Fellowship, 1968. Litt.D.: Clark University, Worcester, Massachusetts, 1961; Anna Maria College, Paxton, Massachusetts, 1977. Member, National Institute of Arts and Letters. Chancellor, Academy of American Poets, 1970. Address: 37 West 12th Street, New York, New York 10011, U.S.A.

Publications

Verse

Intellectual Things. New York, Doubleday, 1930.
Passport to the War: A Selection of Poems. New York, Holt, 1944.
Selected Poems 1928–1958. Boston, Little Brown, 1958; London, Dent, 1959.
The Testing-Tree. Boston, Little Brown, 1971.
The Terrible Threshold: Selected Poems 1940–1970. London, Secker and Warburg, 1974.
The Coat Without a Seam: Sixty Poems 1930–1972. Northampton, Massachusetts, Gehenna Press, 1974.
The Poems of Stanley Kunitz 1928–1978. Boston, Little Brown, and London, Secker and Warburg, 1979.

Other

Robert Lowell, Poet of Terribilità (lecture). New York, Pierpont Library, 1974.
A Kind of Order, A Kind of Folly: Essays and Conversations. Boston, Little Brown, 1975.
From Feathers to Iron (lecture). Washington, D.C., Library of Congress, 1976.

Editor (as Dilly Tante), *Living Authors: A Book of Biographies.* New York, Wilson, 1931.
Editor, with Howard Haycraft and Wilbur C. Hadden, *Authors Today and Yesterday: A Companion Volume to "Living Authors."* New York, Wilson, 1933.
Editor, with others, *The Junior Book of Authors.* New York, Wilson, 1934; revised edition, 1961.
Editor, with Howard Haycraft, *British Authors of the Nineteenth Century.* New York, Wilson, 1936.
Editor, with Howard Haycraft, *American Authors, 1600–1900: A Biographical Dictionary of American Literature.* New York, Wilson, 1938.
Editor, with Howard Haycraft, *Twentieth Century Authors: A Biographical Dictionary of Modern Literature.* New York, Wilson, 1942; *First Supplement*, with Vineta Colby, 1955.

Editor, with Howard Haycraft, *British Authors Before 1800: A Biographical Dictionary*. New York, Wilson, 1952.
Editor, *Poems*, by John Keats. New York, Crowell, 1964.
Editor, with Vineta Colby, *European Authors, 1000–1900: A Biographical Dictionary of European Literature*. New York, Wilson, 1967.
Editor and Translator, with Max Hayward, *Poems of Akhmatova*. Boston, Little Brown, 1973; London, Harvill Press, 1974.
Editor and Co-Translator, *Orchard Lamps*, by Ivan Drach. New York, Sheep Meadow Press, 1978.

Translator, with others, *Antiworlds and the Fifth Ace*, by Andrei Voznesensky. New York, Doubleday, 1967.
Translator, with others, *Stolen Apples*, by Yevgeny Yevtushenko. New York, Doubleday, 1972.
Translator, with others, *Story under Full Sail*, by Andrei Voznesensky. New York, Doubleday, 1974.

Critical Studies: *The Contemporary Poet as Artist and Critic* edited by Anthony Ostroff, Boston, Little Brown, 1964; "The Poetry of Stanley Kunitz" by James Hagstrum, in *Poets in Progress* edited by Edward Hungerford, Evanston, Illinois, Northwestern University Press, 1967; "Man with a Leaf in His Head" by Stanley Moss, in *The Nation* (New York), 20 September 1971; "Voznesensky and Kunitz on Poetry," in *The New York Times Book Review*, 16 April 1972; *The Craft of Poetry* edited by William Packard, New York, Doubleday, 1974; "Imagine Wrestling with an Angel," in *Contemporary Poetry in America* edited by Robert Boyers, New York, Schocken, 1975; "The Language That Saves" by Richard Vine, in *Salmagundi* (Saratoga Springs, New York), Winter 1977.

Stanley Kunitz comments:

Since my *Selected Poems* I have been moving toward a more open style, based on natural speech rhythms. *The Testing-Tree* (1971) embodied my search for a transparency of language and vision. Maybe age itself compels me to embrace the great simplicities, as I struggle to free myself from the knots and complications, the hang-ups, of my youth. I keep trying to improve my controls over language, so that I won't have to tell lies. And I keep reading the masters, because they infect me with human possibility. I am no more reconciled than I ever was to the world's wrongs and the injustice of time. The poetry I admire most is innocent, luminous, and true.

* * *

The poems of Stanley Kunitz have always been carefully made, finely crafted, and attentive to the subtleties of sound and sense. Theodore Roethke, Robert Lowell, and Ralph Mills, among others, have spoken of Kunitz as one of the truly powerful and skilled poets of our time, and he rightly thinks of his work not as a career, but as a life. Kunitz has had the grace, also, to grow and change over the years, exploring the possibilities of new styles that have dominated American poetry since World War II, but never being merely imitative of them. Even in his mid-70's he can write, in "Layers," "I am not done with my changes."

Kunitz's early verses were often highly intellectual or what is called metaphysical in style. One hears in them echoes of several 17th-century English poets, especially John Donne and Andrew Marvell, as well as of their 20th-century American counterparts, T. S. Eliot and John Crowe Ransom. The work of his second collection resembled the first, in its formal style and modernist theme. "Postcript," for example, speaks of the conflict between intellect and feeling, which provides the tension and drama of much of Kunitz's work. In "Benediction" and "Grammar Lesson," in couplets and quatrains respectively, he exhibits the gift for rhyme that brought him early to poetry. He once described his change in poetic style, from the lean, hard, and reasoned approach of the early years, to the more natural, simpler style, since 1960: in his youth, he said, he rather willed himself into being somewhat closed to outside influences; but in later years, he has tried to make his work more open and accessible, "without sacrificing its more complex inner tissue."

Kunitz's poetry, retracing the myth of the lost father, is usually informed by a tragic vision. "The heart breaks and breaks/and lives by breaking," he writes in "The Testing-Tree." But he also speaks in other styles and moods as well. "The Magic Curtain," written in the early 1970's, is a buoyant, nostalgic love poem to his mother's former housekeeper, beautiful yellow-haired Frieda, who took him to afternoon movies, during his childhood in Worcester, Massachusetts. The two of them skipped school in order to live for a few hours among "The Perils of Pauline" or the antics of the Keystone Kops and Charlie Chaplin. In another recent poem – a witty parody of the traditional love lyric – one partner compares the other to Chairman Mao. "Loving you was a kind of Chinese guerilla war," the lover complains in "After the Last Dynasty."

Through a devotion to craft and an insistence upon a high standard of performance, Stanley Kunitz has produced a body of work that increases in stature over the years. In *Poems 1928–1978*, he collects the best of these poems. The essays in *A Kind of Order, A Kind of Folly*, particularly "Poet and State," provide useful commentary on his way of maintaining a distinctive and disciplined vision, the basis of his achievement in poetry.

—Michael True

KYGER, Joanne. American. Born 19 November 1934. Educated at Santa Barbara College, California. Married 1) Gary Snyder, *q.v.*, in 1960; 2) John Boyce. Lived in Japan, 1960–64. Performer and Poet in experimental television project, 1967–68. Recipient: National Endowment for the Arts grant, 1968. Lives in California.

PUBLICATIONS

Verse

The Tapestry and the Web. San Francisco, Four Seasons, 1965.
The Fool in April: A Poem. San Francisco, Coyote, 1966.
Places to Go. Los Angeles, Black Sparrow Press, 1970.
Joanne. New York, Angel Hair, 1970.
Desecheo Notebook. Berkeley, California, Arif Press, 1971.
Trip Out and Fall Back. Berkeley, California, Arif Press, 1974.
All This Every Day. Bolinas, California, Big Sky, 1975.

Joanne Kyger comments:

I myself am a West Coast poet, but I also feel an affinity for much of the work of the younger New York poets.

My vision of the poet changes so I can stay alive and the muse can stay alive. I report on my states of consciousness and the story I am telling.

* * *

In a sequence entitled "Imaginary Apparitions," Joanne Kyger writes, "But this is clearly an enactment/Cut through/I can see all this/and part of an idea." This troublesome space in which sight is in the process of forming itself into thought is the location of her vision. She seems well aware, in fact, that the Greek root of "idea" is "*idein*" (to see), and her work is an investigation of a consciousness in which the modern distinction does not apply. In "Descartes and the Splendor Of," she turns to at least the most visible source of this distinction, accepts his methodology and in part his language in order to re-discover what Charles Olson calls "the *primitive* abstract." "As I move thru language," she writes, "and transfer the delicacy of vision into the moving and written word, so all thought not transferred on that level is lost and degenerated." To Kyger, this consciousness which produces private dreams and public mythologies is a matter of fact, even a domestic place: "I wish to allow great unimpeded/Grandeur like a rising storm/to take over/and do the dishwashing." The vision is never allowed to float away into obscurity or mystery.

The voice in Kyger's poems is at times almost frantic, at times ironic, at times simply and beautifully lyrical. In the control of a fine intelligence and an ear precisely attuned to the rhythms of speech, it is also a voice which is capable of drawing a sense of brutal reality ("like a dark red bruise, the house") and zany fantasy ("the Great Pigs waddle off in the sky") into a seamless poetic world.

—Don Byrd

LAL, P. Indian. Born in Kapurthala, Punjab, 28 August 1929. Educated at St. Xavier's School, Calcutta, B.A. 1950; Calcutta University, M.A. in English literature 1952. Married Shyamasree Devi in 1955; one son and one daughter. Professor of English, St. Xavier's College, Calcutta, 1952–67; now Honorary Professor. Since 1967, Professor of English, University of Calcutta. Visiting Professor, Hofstra University, Hempstead, New York, 1962–63, University of Illinois, Urbana, 1968, Albion College, Michigan, Spring 1973, Ohio University, Athens, 1973–74, and Berea College, Kentucky, 1977. Founder and Secretary, Writers Workshop, publishers, and Editor, *Writers Workshop Miscellany*, Calcutta; Editor, with Alfred Schenkman, *Orient Review and Literary Digest*, 1954–58. Delegate, P.E.N. Conference, New York, 1966. Recipient: Jawaharlal Nehru Fellowship, 1969. D.Litt.: Western Maryland College, Westminster, 1977. Awarded the Padmashri title by the Government of India, 1970. Address: 162/92 Lake Gardens, Calcutta 45, India.

PUBLICATIONS

Verse

The Parrot's Death and Other Poems. Calcutta, Writers Workshop, 1960.
Love's the First. Calcutta, Writers Workshop, 1962.
"Change!" They Said: New Poems. Calcutta, Writers Workshop, 1966.
Draupadi and Jayadratha and Other Poems. Calcutta, Writers Workshop, 1967.
Yakshi from Didarganj. Calcutta, Writers Workshop, 1969.
Creations and Transcreations: Three Poems, Selections from the Subhasita-Ratna-Kosa, and The First 92 Slokas from the Mahabharata. Calcutta, Dialogue, 1968.
The Man of Dharma and the Rasa of Silence. Calcutta, Writers Workshop, 1974.
Calcutta. Calcutta, Writers Workshop, 1977.
The Collected Poems of P. Lal. Calcutta, Writers Workshop, 1977.

Other

The Art of the Essay. Delhi, Atma Ram, 1951.
An Annotated Mahabharata Bibliography. Calcutta, Writers Workshop, 1967.
The Concept of an Indian Literature: Six Essays. Calcutta, Writers Workshop, 1968.
Transcreation: Two Essays. Calcutta, Writers Workshop, 1971.
The Lemon Tree of Modern Sex and Other Essays. Calcutta, Writers Workshop, 1974.
The Alien Insiders: Indian Writing in English. Calcutta, Writers Workshop, 1979.
Personalities: Meetings with Writers. Calcutta, Writers Workshop, 1979.

Editor, *The Merchant of Venice*, by William Shakespeare. Delhi, Atma Ram, 1952.
Editor, with K. R. Rao, *Modern Indo-Anglian Poetry.* New Delhi, Kavita, 1959.
Editor, *T. S. Eliot: Homage from India: A Commemoration Volume of 55 Essays and Elegies.* Calcutta, Writers Workshop, 1965.
Editor, *The First Workshop Story Anthology.* Calcutta, Writers Workshop, 1967.
Editor, *Modern Indian Poetry in English: The Writers Workshop Selection: An Anthology and a Credo.* Calcutta, Writers Workshop, 1969.
Editor, *Selected Poems: A Selection of Lyrics*, by Manmohan Ghose. Calcutta, Writers Workshop, 1969.
Editor, *The First* [and *Second*] *Writers Workshop Literary Reader.* Calcutta, Writers Workshop, 1970–73.

Translator, *Premchand: His Life and Work*, by Hans Raj Rahbar. Delhi, Atma Ram, 1957.
Translator, with Jai Ratan, *Godan*, by Premchand. Bombay, Jaico, 1957.
Translator, *Great Sanskrit Plays in New English Transcreations.* New York, New Directions, 1964.
Transcreator, *Sanskrit Love Lyrics.* Calcutta, Writers Workshop, 1965.
Transcreator, *The Bhagavad-Gita.* Calcutta, Writers Workshop, 1965.
Transcreator, *The Golden Womb of the Sun.* Calcutta, Writers Workshop, 1965.
Transcreator, *The Dhammapada.* New York, Farrar Straus, 1967.
Transcreator, *The Jap-Ji: Fourteen Religious Songs.* Calcutta, Writers Workshop, 1967.
Transcreator, *The Isa-Upanisad.* Calcutta, Writers Workshop, 1967.
Transcreator, *Some Sanskrit Poems.* Calcutta, Writers Workshop, 1967.
Transcreator, *The Farce of the Drunk Monk.* Calcutta, Writers Workshop, 1968.
Transcreator, *The Avyakta-Upanisad.* Calcutta, Writers Workshop, 1969.
Transcreator, *The Mahabharata.* Calcutta, Writers Workshop, 120 monthly vols., 1969–79.
Transcreator, *More Songs from the Jap-Ji.* Calcutta, Writers Workshop, 1969.
Transcreator, *Ghalib's Love Poems.* Calcutta, Dialogue, 1970.
Transcreator, *The Mahanarayana Upanisad.* Calcutta, Writers Workshop, 1971.
Transcreator, with Shyamasree Devi, *Tagore's Last Poems.* Calcutta, Writers Workshop, 1972.
Transcreator, *The Brhadaranyaka Upanisad.* Calcutta, Writers Workshop, 1974.
Transcreator, with Shyamasree Devi, *Where To, Tarapada-babu?* Calcutta, Writers Workshop, 1974.

Critical Studies: "P. Lal's Poetry" by Nita Pillai, in *Poetry India* (Bombay), i,3, 1965; *P. Lal: An Appreciation* by S. Mokashi-Punekar, Calcutta, Writers Workshop, 1968; "P. Lal: A Major Indo-English Poet" by Subhas C. Saha, in *The Banasthali Patrika* (Banasthali), January 1969; "The Poetry of P. Lal" by Suresh Kohli, in *Thought* (Delhi), xx,30, 1969; "P. Lal's Literary Endeavours" by M. P. Kohli, in *Sunday Standard* (Bombay), 14 January 1979; "Metaphor, Music, and Morality: P. Lal's Poetry" by Prema Nandakumar, in *Deccan Herald* (Bangalore), 21 January 1979; "Doyen of Indo-Anglian Poets" by Rajkumar, in *The Tribune* (Chandigarh), 10 February 1979.

* * *

P. Lal is a key figure in the landscape of Indo-English creative writing. He has played a multiple role with remarkable success. Poet, ideologist for Indo-English creativity, avant-garde publisher for markedly new writing, translator of classics, responsible orientalist, he has filled a varied bill, which, in return, has conditioned his own growth through sudden transitions and empirical intuitions. The movements he seemed to lead in the early post-Independence years rallied a good many competent rebels around him under the simple banner: Indians can create in English; but they must break with the past genre of the pompous and the amorphous! To that slogan no contenders are left, and the movement should have reached the more painful state of self-examination with the question: Is that enough? But Lal's pluralist approach has skilfully doctored the movement into a painless transition. In the process, not only Lal's organising ability but his poetic practice has played a role, not exactly by trend-setting but by ice-breaking. Lal's poetry cannot be isolated from the multiple role he has played; it forms a setting for his growth.

Lal's first four collections mark a development, in themes, in technique, even in objectives, though the corpus is too thin to reveal it from book to later book. Since 1960, he has been bringing out collections at regular intervals; but before that is a fifteen-year stretch of apprenticeship. An early poem like "Beside the Pipal," recording a delicately veined Indian pastorale, is an index of some early ambition to poetise on national themes, abandoned under the compulsion of international norms, but restored to a later collection (*"Change!" They Said*) under a renewed sense of national commitment. An oddly rhetorical piece like "On Transience" in an early collection (*The Parrot's Death*) is the token of competent kitten play, too good to be thrown away but too out of character to fit into a stabler manner cultivated later: "and when the winds howl, their raucous breath/convulses the green continence of earth." To make these rhetorical convulsions click is a sign of healthy apprenticeship and can prove a second string to the bow when social commitments demand a raucous breath, as in *"Change!" They Said*: Lal's most stable manner, however, was the green continence of earth.

A studied and taut delicacy which seldom lapses into aestheticism may well be the most fascinating undertone of Lal's verse. A painfully keen love of beauty in nature, in flowers, birds and trees, is ever rendered sturdy by a vigorous mancentredness. Lal's perceptions are delicate and firm; he sketches them in clean strokes: "A mustard of butterflies/Hovers round a lovely eye." Not just a poetic image that, but a perception. Lal shows the same delicacy in love, a theme that dominates his second collection, *Love's the First*. Fortunately for us, Lal is not ashamed of his cleverness and we get fine cavalier swashbuckling:

Love, twin-fuselaged
Sweeps serenely thus
(Weather Report: Unfair)
To passion's terminus.

Lal constantly returns to the manner of spare expression and self-control. And while he belongs to the avant-garde, he must have his roses, petals, leaves and bees to stand by him. Why? We get a clue in poems of another kind, what may be described as lyrics of human behaviour. Lal constantly returns to an adoration of civilized behaviour, a fine instance of which is "The Letter" – a poem written in a mood of agonized gratitude to a brother whose letter opens up old wounds again by its painful but civil talk. Lal's love for language is the greater for its being the index of a rooted civility which is its distinctive feature. The same quality illuminates his effort at self-control and often at self-accusation; and that returns us to Lal the organizer. The finest expression of this "culture" is seen in a really ripe poem like "The Leaf" (in *"Change!" They Said*) in which he accurately sums up the stages of his life: "Cupped in decrepit easy chair/Mellow gum in eyes." Lal's care for words is not a part of his technique but a part of his vision of life – its beauty and tautness. Words, for Lal, are the indices of summations inherent in humanity's past experience, and Lal constantly tries to connect: "Here meaning is in fragrances/And life is the careful delivery of leaf."

Such attitudes cannot but compel Lal to seek roots in an Indian tradition; two trends are already significant – Lal's growing impatience with the rootless highbrow, and with the monstrous outgrowths of India's hurried social transformation which has inspired some raucous social satire of late; and a growing orientalism, primarily for translation, but inspiring poems like *Draupadi and Jayadratha*, which are revealing an altogether different Lal.

—Shankar Mokashi-Punekar

LAMANTIA, Philip. American. Born in San Francisco, California, 23 October 1927. Educated in San Francisco public schools. Assistant Editor, *View* magazine, New York, 1944. Address: c/o City Lights Books, 261 Columbus Avenue, San Francisco, California 94133, U.S.A.

PUBLICATIONS

Verse

Erotic Poems. Berkeley, California, Bern Porter, 1946.
Tower, with *Manifesto* by Max Finstein. San Francisco, Golden Mountain Press, 1958.
Ekstasis. San Francisco, Auerhahn Press, 1959.
Destroyed Works: Hypodermic Light, Mantic Notebook, Still Poems, Spansule. San Francisco, Auerhahn Press, 1962.
Touch of the Marvelous. Berkeley, California, Oyez, 1966.
Selected Poems 1943–1966. San Francisco, City Lights, 1967.
Penguin Modern Poets 13, with Charles Bukowski and Harold Norse. London, Penguin, 1969.
The Blood of the Air. San Francisco, Four Seasons, 1970.

Other

Narcotica, with Antonin Artaud. San Francisco, Auerhahn Press, 1959.

Critical Study: Prefatory Note by Parker Tyler to *Touch of the Marvelous*, 1966.

Philip Lamantia comments:

I consider myself essentially a surrealist, but as Breton qualified this, it is *not* a "school," but a way of life.

I understand the act of poetry as the maximum volatile expression of Imagination, a *central power*, relating all levels of conscious and unconscious thought and being. I believe in poetry as a means of unqualified individual liberation. I believe in the poetry of primal melody and the revelation of the mysteries of cosmic being.

* * *

Although Philip Lamantia's life has been one of change and travel the poetry has continued its function as a tightly controlled inner ritual, and the poem has been continually characterized by a highly burnished surface that seems to gleam with such stillness that if the poem was turned from side to side light would glance off it. It was as a Surrealist that he was published, at the age of fifteen, by Charles Henri Ford and Parker Tyler in their magazine *View*. André Breton, then living in the United States, called him "a voice that rises once in a hundred years." The shifting of image, the layering of association that is characteristic of surrealism has continued in his work, and his language has the hardness of a glimpse through a prism: "The mermaids have come to the desert/They are setting up a boudoir next to the camel/who lies at their feet of roses." But with his first book, *Erotic Poems*, he felt that he had broken with the surrealists, and it was a lyric physicality that gave the book its dominant mood. Though there was still a complex surface imagery in the poems it was, as he had titled it, a collection of erotic poems. The language often had a closeness of physical contact that was almost like a breath: "The crash of your heart/beating its way through a fever of fish/is heard in every crowd of that thirsty tomorrow/and your trip ends in the mask of my candle-lit hair."

A consciousness of brutality has continued in his poetry, even though he is sometimes able to shake it off long enough to see it at a distance from himself. The poem sometimes becomes obsessive in its awareness of cruelty:

> Come my ritual wax and circles
> my rose spitting blood
> When the day is lit up by our magic candles
> and the hours yell their sadistic songs and suck hard
> into the night when the cats invade our skulls

A similar cruelty is apparent in this example of early work finally published in *Touch of the Marvelous*: "The hanged girl in my mirror watches with horror/as I exchange my eyes for yours/But, too late/I pull the gun's trigger/and the mirror shatters." But his work shifted away from this obsessiveness, and he began to find another imagery in his experience, and he was able to write "From a window I see the world/As I would see love." It was after this affirmation that his wanderings began. Of the younger group of San Francisco poets, Lamantia was the first to begin experimenting with altered states of consciousness. He was initiated into the Washo Indian peyote rites in Nevada in 1953, and then spent three years in Mexico, living for some time with the Cora Indians of Nayarit. It was at the close of this period that he destroyed all of his earlier work, and it was not until the late 1950's that he began publishing again. The poems he had destroyed were eventually published in 1962. He spent much of the 1960's in Europe, continuing his search into the forces and the planes of the poem.

Lamantia's work, coming out of a forties dominated in the United States by Eliot and Frost, Stevens and Cummings, seemed to be an entirely new element, an entirely new structuring of the emotions of the poem. Despite the efforts of Ford and others there had not been any wide attention paid to the surrealists, and the first American writing in the idiom forced a belated recognition of the power of surrealist technique. This is not to say that Lamantia became a poet with any kind of popular following, but he was widely read by other poets. In any outline of the main currents of American poetry of the 1940's his name must be considered as one of the forces that led to the burst of surrealist poetry in the United States in the 1950's and 1960's.

—Samuel Charters

LANE, Patrick. Canadian. Born in Nelson, British Columbia, 26 March 1939. Educated in Canadian schools. Has four sons and one daughter. Editor, Very Stone House, publishers,

Vancouver, 1966–72. Writer-in-Residence, University of Manitoba, Winnipeg, 1978–79. Also an artist and illustrator. Recipient: Canda Council grant, 1967, 1971, 1973, 1976; York University Poet's Prize, 1971; Ontario Arts Council grant, 1975, 1978; Governor-General's Award, 1978. Agent: Stephen Williams, 107 Bowmore Road, Toronto, Ontario. Address: c/o St. John's College, University of Manitoba, Winnipeg, Manitoba R3T 2N2, Canada.

PUBLICATIONS

Verse

Letters from the Savage Mind. Vancouver, Very Stone House, 1966.
For Rita – In Asylum. Vancouver, Very Stone House, 1969.
Calgary City Jail. Vancouver, Very Stone House, 1969.
Separations. Trumansburg, New York, Crossing Press, 1969.
Sunflower Seeds. Vancouver, Western Press, 1969.
On the Street. Vancouver, Very Stone House, 1970.
Mountain Oysters. Vancouver, Very Stone House, 1971.
Hiway 401 Rhapsody. Vancouver, Very Stone House, 1972.
The Sun Has Begun to Eat the Mountain. Montreal, Ingluvin, 1972.
Passing into Storm. Vernon, British Columbia, Traumerei, 1973.
Beware the Months of Fire. Toronto, Anansi, 1974.
Certs. Prince George, British Columbia, College of New Caledonia, 1974.
Unborn Things: South American Poems. Madeira Park, British Columbia, Harbour, 1975.
For Riel in That Gawdam Prison. White Rock, British Columbia, Blackfish Press, 1975.
Albino Pheasants. Madeira Park, British Columbia, Harbour, 1977.
If. Toronto, Dreadnaught Press, 1977.
Poems, New and Selected. Toronto, Oxford University Press, 1978; London, Oxford University Press, 1979.
No Longer Two People, with Lorna Uher. Winnipeg, Turnstone Press, 1979.

Manuscript Collections: McMaster University, Hamilton, Ontario; University of British Columbia, Vancouver.

Critical Study: "Pine Boughs and Apple Trees" by Marilyn Bowering, in *Malahat Review* (Victoria, British Columbia), January 1978.

* * *

Patrick Lane is a native of the interior of British Columbia. The essential center of his poetry is its consciousness of that landscape and mythology: "Because I never learned how/ to be gentle and the country/I lived in was hard with dead/animals and men, I didn't question...." If, as Lawrence Durrell says, landscape is character, Lane is a kind of Proteus taking on the shapes of his place, at once fierce and uncompromising in response to its violence and terrible beauty. He writes of logging camps and forests, of bush farming, hunting, herding cattle, all of which he knows at first hand. Whatever the private complex out of which he writes, he understands violence. He writes of people who survive by manipulating violence – the loggers, hustlers, religious bigots, even his father; and of those who have been smashed by it – the derelicts, prostitutes, the murdered child. He speaks without judgement, knowing the cannibal impulse in himself, "that brutal anger that cannot be relieved except on things," and perhaps this is the most exciting aspect of his work because he can write without sentimentality about ordinary cruelty. He also understands the traps of victimization. His poem "What Does Not Change," a long poem about a hooker, is the frankest and yet most compassionate poem I know about that world. Its language is tough and colloquial and yet the literary allusions the poet has managed to weave into the anecdotes give the whole a larger reference that makes it a remarkable piece. Lane has a fine gift for image and writes of the tragic not histrionically but in understatement, deflecting attention to some small detail that is made to carry the full horror of a situation. He has an empathy for all of life that is pained and vulnerable: for the young woman dead from an abortion in a dingy hotel room, for the boy who blows his mother's arm off with a bomb, for the old man who shoves pins into his dead arm cadging drinks.

Many Canadian poets, such as P. K. Page, Al Purdy, and Earle Birney, have proven gifted tourists. In 1975, Lane published a fine sequence of South American poems, called *Unborn Things*, illustrated by his own drawings. The poems catch the mythic surreality and the breathing violence of that culture:

> After the dog drowns in the arroyo
> and the old people stumble into the jungle
> muttering imprecations at the birds
> and the child draws circles in the dust
> for bits of glass to occupy
> like eyes staring out of earth
> and the woman lies on her hammock
> dreaming of the lover who will save her
> from the need to make bread again
> I will go into the field
> and be buried with the corn.

Some poems speak from the Inca past, others from the present to create a remarkable sequence of South American voices.

Poems, New and Selected shows him engaging in a careful study of poetics and enlarging the range of his subject matter; this book places him securely as one of Canada's best poets.

—Rosemary Sullivan

LANGLAND, Joseph (Thomas). American. Born in Spring Grove, Minnesota, 16 February 1917. Educated at Spring Grove High School; Santa Ana Junior College, California, A.A. 1936; University of Iowa, Iowa City, B.A. 1940, M.A. 1941, 1946–48. Served in the United States Army, 1942–46. Married the artist Judith Gail Wood in 1943; one daughter and two sons. School Teacher, Winneshiek County, Iowa, 1936–38; Instructor, Dana College, Blair, Nebraska, 1941–42; Assistant Professor, then Associate Professor, 1948–59, University of Wyoming, Laramie. Since 1959, Professor of English, University of Massachusetts, Amherst. Visiting Professor of Poetry, University of British Columbia, Vancouver, 1960, San Francisco State College, 1961, University of Washington, Seattle, 1964, and the University of Oregon, Eugene, 1968, 1969. Poetry Editor, *Massachusetts Review*, Amherst, 1960–66. Recipient: Ford Fellowship, 1953; Fund for the Advancement of Education in the Humanities grant, 1953; Amy Lowell Traveling Fellowship, 1955; Melville Cane Award, 1964; National Endowment for the Arts grant, 1966. D. Litt.: Luther College, Decorah, Iowa, 1974. Address: 16 Morgan Circle, Amherst, Massachusetts 01002, U.S.A.

PUBLICATIONS

Verse

For Harold. Augsburg, Germany, 1945.
The Green Town. New York, Scribner, 1956.
A Little Homily. Northampton, Massachusetts, Apiary Press, 1960.
The Wheel of Summer. New York, Dial Press, 1963.
Songs and Half-Songs. Boston, Godine, 1975.
Adlai Stevenson. Iowa City, Stone Wall Press, 1975.
The Sacrifice Poems. Cedar Falls, University of Northern Iowa, 1975.

Recording: *Today's Poets 1*, with others, Folkways, 1967.

Other

Editor, with James B. Hall, *The Short Story.* New York, Macmillan, 1956.
Editor, with Paul Engle, *Poet's Choice.* New York, Dial Press, 1962.

Translator, with Tamas Aczel and Lazlo Tikos, *Poetry from the Russian Underground.* New York, Harper, 1973.

Critical Studies: in *Southern Review* (Baton Rouge, Louisiana) i, 4, 1965; in *Tri-Quarterly 5* (Evanston, Illinois), 1966.

Joseph Langland comments:

I began writing in relative isolation. While I know many of the living poets and have corresponded with many, I have never espoused a special group or followed any central creed or statement in poetry.

I join colloquial American speech to the traditions. While much of my immediate subject material has come from the landscape and life of rural America, its true subject is usually the relationship of the individual to the world. Forms are various, sources numerous. I think I am my own man. Presently, I am deeply interested in exploring the chaotic condition of American (and likely world) culture. My orientation is oral rather than visual; in all I write I wish never to neglect the singing voice, even in the harshest poem. All subjects pursue some kind of form, either out of themselves or their situations.

* * *

Joseph Langland's best poems occur when a personal vision of history unites with a song-like immediacy, when his particular emotional intensity and subtlety meet with craft and intellect unnoticed – as in the long poem ("An Open Letter") to Ralph Ellison, and in many of the "Sacrifice" poems of *The Wheel of Summer.*

There is no discordance in such poems, and an authority rings in the voice and diction of "A Hiroshima Lullaby." The same power and quality are in early poems ("War"); and in "Norwegian Rivers" or "Dandelion" a quiet appropriateness fills both vision and voice:

You are both a small sun
and a pale moon.
When you come
flowering through the daylight
my blood smiles in its skin.

But Langland finds horror, too ("Buchenwald"), or an expansive and "moving" sadness, as in "Libertyville," one of the Stevenson sequence.

The sequence of "Sacrifice" poems in Langland's award-winning volume relates the different deaths a boy experiences on a Minnesota farm as he comes of age. These are the sacrifices the world makes, it seems, to the spiritual education and filling of a man, and lest this seem presumptuous, the wheel becomes a cycle of dyings – from all various causes and sources – which the maturing youth comes to participate in and even, finally, perpetrate. All nature is caught in this cycle of dying, and in the poems a consciousness remembers joining, becoming aware of the deaths surrounding it and whirling mysteriously away into the past; the consciousness forms and wakens so that finally the "wheel of summer" is natural, a cause and celebration as well as death. Not surprisingly, then, the poems often function as loving equations, metaphors, although much of the surprise inherent in the structure of individual poems dissipates when the poems are placed in sequence or when Langland's concern for "first principles" strikes against his contemporary feeling for the intrinsic holiness of separate things.

—Joseph Wilson

LARKIN, Philip (Arthur). British. Born in Coventry, Warwickshire, 9 August 1922. Educated at King Henry VIII School, Coventry; St. John's College, Oxford, B.A. 1943, M.A. 1947. Since 1955, Librarian, Brynmor Jones Library, University of Hull, Yorkshire. Jazz feature writer, *Daily Telegraph*, London, 1961–71; Visiting Fellow, All Souls College, Oxford, 1970–71. Recipient: Arts Council Prize, 1965; Queen's Gold Medal, 1965; Cholmondeley Award, 1973; Loines Award, 1974; Benson Medal, 1975, and Companion of Literature, 1978, Royal Society of Literature; Shakespeare Prize (Hamburg), 1976. D. Lit.: University of Belfast, 1969; D. Litt.: University of Leicester, 1970; University of Warwick, 1973; University of St. Andrews, 1974; University of Sussex, Brighton, 1974. Honorary Fellow, St. John's College, Oxford, 1973. Fellow, Royal Society of Literature. Address: Brynmor Jones Library, The University, Hull, Yorkshire, England.

PUBLICATIONS

Verse

The North Ship. London, Fortune Press, 1945; revised edition, London, Faber, 1966.
XX Poems. Privately printed, 1951.
(Poems). Oxford, Fantasy Press, 1954.
The Less Deceived. Hessle, Yorkshire, Marvell Press, 1955; New York, St. Martin's Press, 1960.
The Whitsun Weddings. London, Faber, and New York, Random House, 1964.
The Explosion. London, Poem-of-the-Month Club, 1970.
Corgi Modern Poets in Focus 5, with others, edited by Jeremy Robson. London, Corgi, 1971.
High Windows. London, Faber, and New York, Farrar Straus, 1974.

Recordings: *The Less Deceived*, Listen, 1960; *Philip Larkin Reads and Comments on "The Whitsun Weddings,"* Listen.

Novels

Jill. London, Fortune Press, 1946; revised edition, London, Faber, and New York, St. Martin's Press, 1964.
A Girl in Winter. London, Faber, 1947; New York, St. Martin's Press, 1957.

Other

All What Jazz: A Record Diary 1961–68. London, Faber, and New York, St. Martin's Press, 1970.

Editor, with Bonamy Dobrée and Louis MacNeice, *New Poems 1958.* London, Joseph, 1958.
Editor, *The Oxford Book of Twentieth Century Verse.* Oxford, Clarendon Press, 1973.
Editor, *Poetry Supplement.* London, Poetry Book Society, 1974.

Bibliography: *Philip Larkin: A Bibliography 1933–76* by B. C. Bloomfield, London, Faber, 1979.

Manuscript Collection: British Library, London.

Critical Studies: *Philip Larkin* by David Timms, Edinburgh, Oliver and Boyd, 1973; New York, Barnes and Noble, 1974; "Philip Larkin Issue" of *Phoenix 11–12* (Manchester), Autumn–Winter 1973–74.

* * *

It would be difficult to guess from Philip Larkin's first volume, *The North Ship*, that here were the beginnings of a considerable poet. Certainly it attracted little attention on its first appearance in 1945. Looking back now, one can see what seem to be hints, in a few lines and cadences, of what was to come; but this may be hindsight. A wan Yeatsianism, a steely touch of Auden here and there – these are the book's characteristics, and remarkable only in that they show none of the influences one would expect from an Oxford poet in the 1940's: there is no studied literariness, and no flushed and verbose New Apocalypse rhetoric. These poems are careful, yearning and a little dim.

It was in 1946 that Larkin wrote the first poems of his maturity: "Waiting for Breakfast" (which is attached as a "coda" to the 1966 Faber reissue of *The North Ship*) and "Wedding-wind," chronologically the first piece in *The Less Deceived.* Without showing any overt influence of Hardy, they mark the liberation and sense of direction which reading Hardy's poems had given Larkin. In Larkin's own words, spoken in a radio programme: "When I came to Hardy it was with the sense of relief that I didn't have to try and jack myself up to a concept of poetry that lay outside my own life.... One could simply relapse back into one's own life and write from it." This did not mean that in some way he became anything like what more recently have been called "confessional" poets: the emotional content of Larkin's poems is strong, but the tone is reserved, wry, often resigned, and never self-indulgently revelatory. The "human shows" of Hardy's verse fitted congenially into Larkin's temperament, as did Hardy's unselfpitying pessimism.

After *The North Ship*, Larkin did not publish another book of poems (with the exception of two slim pamphlets) until *The Less Deceived* appeared from the Marvell Press in 1955. (His two novels, *Jill* and *A Girl in Winter*, came in the interim, but – though above average pieces of work – they have no place in this entry.) *The Less Deceived*, though coming from an obscure press and without any barrage of publicity such as a richer publisher might have laid down, was quite quickly received with enthusiasm. The appearance of Robert Conquest's anthology *New Lines* in 1956, and the journalistic conscription of Larkin into the so-called "Movement" because of his inclusion in that book, probably hindered the acceptance of Larkin's true merits as much as they helped, though it did not take keen critical eyes to see that he was more like, say, Kingsley Amis than Dylan Thomas or W. S. Graham. Yet neither does he share very much, in outlook or style, with such companions in *New Lines* as Elizabeth Jennings, D. J. Enright or Thom Gunn. As for the supposed "neutral tone" of what have been called the Faceless Fifties, Larkin's voice is far too individual to be docketed with that label.

It is a voice that commands a range from the light mockery of "I Remember, I Remember" to the wincing brutality of "Sunny Prestatyn," from the tenderness (joyously rapt in the first, gravely compassionate in the second) of "Wedding-wind" and "Love Songs in Age" to the spiritual bleakness of "Mr. Bleaney." Some of Larkin's poems have that lightness of tone without levity that Auden used to command so well: "Toads," "Toads Revisited," "Naturally the Foundation Will Bear Your Expenses." His two longest, most sustained poems – "Church Going" from *The Less Deceived* and "The Whitsun Weddings" from the 1964 book of that title – use combinations or progressions of several of these tones. "Church Going" moves, through seven carefully-patterned 9-line stanzas, from easy, colloquial, mockingly casual beginnings, through reflection and half-serious questioning, to a rhetorical solidity at the close which is of such weight and deliberation that some readers have mistakenly supposed that Christianity is thereby being endorsed, which in fact is what the poem sets out with great pains *not* to do. Rather, what is being acknowledged – as in several of Larkin's poems, such as "An Arundel Tomb" – is the strange power of inherited order and habit. Like so many leading poets of the century (Eliot and Yeats are examples), Larkin's attitudes are often conservative, even "reactionary": see, for instance, two more recent and uncollected poems – "Posterity" (*New Statesman*, London, 28 June 1968) and "Homage to a Government" (*Sunday Times*, London, 19 January 1969). But he is not really a "public" poet at all, though he reflects common experiences and common concerns. He has no easy answers, but he does not wallow in fashionable *angst* either. There is an agnostic stoicism in his work, which confronts change, diminution, death with sardonic resignation. Though he would not relish the description, there is nobility in this.

"The Whitsun Weddings," which proceeds through its eight 10-line stanzas with none of the subdued gear-crashing of "Church Going," is the finest example of Larkin's temper, tone and technique. Its level descriptive sweep, its amused human observation, its intelligent sense of the inexplicable, all move with complete inevitability to the mysterious closing lines as the train with its load of newly-married couples slows as it reaches its destination: "And as the tightened brakes took hold, there swelled/A sense of falling, like an arrow-shower/Sent out of sight, somewhere becoming rain." The force of this is partly cumulative, but it has a lot to do with an unerring ear for individual cadences too: that "sense of falling" which one hears in "Love Songs in Age":

So
To pile them back, to cry,
Was hard, without lamely admitting how
It had not done so then, and could not now.

or in "Reference Back": "They show us what we have as it once was,/Blindingly undiminished, just as though/By acting differently we could have kept it so," or in "Dockery and Son":

Life is first boredom, then fear.
Whether or not we use it, it goes,
And leaves what something hidden from us chose,
And age, and then the only end of age.

Unlike any other important modern British poet (with the exception of the otherwise utterly different Dylan Thomas), Larkin has constructed no system into which his poems can fit: like Parolles in *All's Well*, he seems to say "simply the thing I am shall make me live." It is an individual achievement, and a memorable one.

(1980) Since the above piece was written, Larkin has published *High Windows* and the controversial anthology, *The Oxford Book of Twentieth Century English Verse.* The 24 poems in *High Windows*, representing his total output since *The Whitsun Weddings*, included at least three which stand among Larkin's very best: "The Old Fools," "The Building," and "The Explosion." "The Building," in fact, is the major statement in this book, just as "Church Going" and "The Whitsun Weddings" were in its forerunners. In it, Larkin's habitual theme of the ebbing-away of life is most persistently, elaborately, and movingly worked out. The details of what is in fact a hospital are throughout presented at one remove; the "building" is not specifically called a hospital anywhere in the poem, as if naming it would be to court disaster – though, ironically, the daily arrival of disaster – death – is what the poem is "about." "The Old Fools" confronts the same theme in terms of senility, while "The Explosion" is a strangely dream-like presentation of disaster and death merging into resurrection – itself seen as a dream.

High Windows contains its share of ostensibly "light" poems, and rather more of them than hitherto; but lightness, or coarseness, of tone in Larkin tends to be accompanied by a sardonic leer rather than laughter. Parts of "Sympathy in White Major," "High Windows," "The Card-Players," "Posterity," "This Be the Verse," "Annus Mirabilis," "Vers de Société," and "Money" are all examples of Larkin deliberately using his low style to make points of high seriousness. As Clive James put it in a long review of *High Windows* in *Encounter* (June 1974): "The book is the peer of the previous two mature collections, and if they did not exist would be just as astonishing.... Larkin is the poet of the void. The one affirmation his work offers is the possiblity that when we have lost everything the problem of beauty will still remain. It's enough."

—Anthony Thwaite

LATTIMORE, Richmond (Alexander). American. Born in Paotingfu, China, 6 May 1906. Educated at Dartmouth College, Hanover, New Hampshire, A.B. 1926 (Phi Beta Kappa); Christ Church, Oxford (Rhodes Scholar), B.A. 1932, M.A. 1964; University of Illinois, Urbana, A.M. 1927, Ph.D. 1934. Served in the United States Naval Reserve, 1943–46: lieutenant. Married Alice Bockstahler in 1935; two sons. Assistant in Classics and English, 1926–28, and in Philosophy, 1933–35, University of Illinois; Assistant Professor of Classics, Wabash College, Crawfordsville, Indiana, 1928–29; Assistant Professor, 1935–41, Associate Professor, 1945–48, and Professor of Greek, 1948–71, Bryn Mawr College, Pennsylvania. Visiting Lecturer, University of Chicago, 1947, and Columbia University, New York, 1948, 1950; Taft Lecturer, University of Cincinnati, Ohio, 1952; Turnbull Lecturer, Johns Hopkins University, Baltimore, 1956; Lord Northcliffe Lecturer, University College, London, 1961; Fulbright Lecturer, Oxford University, 1963–64; Centennial Professor, University of Toronto, 1966. Senior Fellow, Center for Hellenic Studies, Washington, D.C., 1960–65. Honorary Student, Christ Church, Oxford, 1971. Recipient: American Academy in Rome Fellowship, 1934; Rockefeller Fellowship, 1946; Fulbright Scholarship, 1951; National Institute of Arts and Letters grant, 1954; American Council of Learned Societies award, 1959; Bollingen translation award, 1962. Litt.D.: Dartmouth College, 1958. Member, National Institute of Arts and Letters; American Academy of Arts and Sciences. Address: 123 Locust Grove Road, Rosemont, Pennsylvania, 19010, U.S.A.

PUBLICATIONS

Verse

Hanover Poems, with A. K. Laing. New York, Vinal, 1927.

Poems. Ann Arbor, University of Michigan Press, 1957.
Sestina for a Far-Off Summer: Poems 1957–1962. Ann Arbor, University of Michigan Press, 1962.
Selected Poems. Oxford, Harlequin Poets, 1965.
The Stride of Time: New Poems and Translations. Ann Arbor, University of Michigan Press, 1966.
Poems from Three Decades. New York, Scribner, 1972.

Other

Themes in Greek and Latin Epitaphs. Urbana, University of Illinois Press, 1942.
The Poetry of Greek Tragedy. Baltimore, Johns Hopkins University Press, 1958.
Story Patterns in Greek Tragedy. Ann Arbor, University of Michigan Press, and London, Athlone Press, 1964.

Editor, with David Grene, *Complete Greek Tragedies* (and translator of *Oresteia* by Aeschylus and *Alcestis*, *Helen*, *The Trojan Women*, and *Rhesus* by Euripides). Chicago, University of Chicago Press, 4 vols., 1959.

Translator, *Early Philosophers of Greece*, by M. McClure. New York, Appleton Century, 1935.
Translator, *Some Odes of Pindar*. New York, New Directions, 1942.
Translator, *The Odes of Pindar*. Chicago, University of Chicago Press, 1947.
Translator, *The Iliad of Homer*. Chicago, University of Chicago Press, 1951.
Translator, *Oresteia*, by Aeschylus. Chicago, University of Chicago Press, 1953.
Translator, *Greek Lyrics: Translated into Close Approximations of the Original Meter*. Chicago, University of Chicago Press, 1955; revised edition, 1960.
Translator, *Works and Days, Theogony, The Shield of Herakles*. Ann Arbor, University of Michigan Press, 1959.
Translator, *The Frogs of Aristophanes*. Ann Arbor, University of Michigan Press, 1962.
Translator, *The Revelation of John*. New York, Harcourt Brace, 1962.
Translator, *The Odyssey of Homer*. New York, Harper, 1967.
Translator, *Iphigenia at Tauris*, by Euripides. New York, Oxford University Press, 1973.
Translator, *The Four Gospels and the Revelation*. New York, Farrar Straus, 1979.

Bibliography: *Richmond Lattimore: A Bibliography*, Chicago, University of Chicago Press, 1971.

Manuscript Collection: Dartmouth College Library, Hanover, New Hampshire.

Richmond Lattimore comments:

My poems are my own and no one else could have written them. They have never been, like my translations, popular, except with live audiences. The volumes are all out of print, but I keep writing them, and hope to have a new collection soon.

* * *

Richmond Lattimore's poetry, as it appears in his last volume, *Poems from Three Decades*, which brings together his three formerly published books of verse plus thirty-four new poems, is an impressive achievement. Lattimore is a thorough student and admirer of the classics, which he taught for many years at Bryn Mawr College, as well as a translator and critic of ancient Greek poetry; it is, therefore, not surprising that he draws a considerable part of his inspiration from classical themes, without, however, becoming their mere imitator or their slave. He is equally moved and inspired by the contemporary scene, the more recent European and American past and even by the Far East, where he was born in 1906. Thus, the most heterogeneous events, places and writers have excited him to compose arresting verse, his subjects ranging from Mycenean linear B tablets to the hulk of the *Lusitania* or a tourist poster about Mount Athos. In this wide world of roughly three thousand years in which he moves, his vision is always deeply humane and the tone he adopts calm – he is never "confessional" or "didactic" in the strict sense of the word – but always beneath the surface of his verse you can sense the *lacrimae rerum.* Occasionally you also come across a good-natured humorous outburst.

The technique Lattimore employs varies. He can be traditional in the forms he chooses – the sonnet, the sestina, the terza rima, etc. – or he can branch out into blank and free verse, where a variety of conversational and regular rhythms are blended. Enjambment is frequently employed as well as rhymes and half-rhymes, in which he excels. His language is on the whole simple, and if occasionally rarer words are used, they are always combined with common words that can carry them. He clearly believes in the "intimacy and appeal of common speech." His imagery is fresh and well developed and his lyricism pleasingly subdued; there is no rhetoric and the use of similes and of extended mataphors is sparse. The one weakness in his style is the use of usual and outworn adjectives: yellow willows, small island, pale cinders, old beards, black wrongs, green trees, white plaster, sweet weather.

But Lattimore is not only a distinguished original poet. He is also a most able translator and adaptator of great poetry in other languages, classical Greek, Latin, Anglo-Saxon, Italian, French and modern Greek. The most important of his translations are those of Homer, Pindar and Aeschylus' *Oresteia.* As so rightly and so often said, every generation must make its own translations of the classics, and Lattimore's rendering of the *Iliad* into contemporary English verse is by far the best we have today, a great and lasting achievement.

—Constantine Trypanis

LAUGHLIN, James. American. Born in Pittsburgh, Pennsylvania, 30 October 1914. Educated at Le Rosey, Switzerland; Choate School, Connecticut, 1930–32; Harvard University, Cambridge, Massachusetts, A.B. 1939. Married 1) Margaret Keyser in 1942 (divorced, 1952); 2) Ann Clark Resor in 1956; four children. Since 1936, Founding Editor and President, New Directions Publishing Corporation, New York. Director, Goethe Bicentennial Foundation, 1949, and the Aspen Institute of the Humanities, 1950; Member, United States National Commission for UNESCO, 1960–63. President, Intercultural Publications; Chairman, Creative Writing Panel, Institute for International Education Conference on Arts Exchange; Trustee, Allen-Chase Foundation; Co-Trustee, Thomas Merton Legacy Trust. Recipient: American Academy of Arts and Letters Distinguished Service Award, 1977; Carey-Thomas Prize, for publishing, 1978; P.E.N. Publisher's Citation, 1978. D. Litt.: Hamilton College, Clinton, New York, 1969; Colgate University, Hamilton, New York, 1978. Member, American Academy of Arts and Sciences; Chevalier, Legion of Honor, France. Address: 80 Eighth Avenue, New York, New York 10011, U.S.A.

PUBLICATIONS

Verse

Some Natural Things. New York, New Directions, 1945.

Report on a Visit to Germany. Lausanne, Switzerland, Held, 1948.
A Small Book of Poems. Milan, Scheiwiller, and New York, New Directions, 1948.
The Wild Anemone and Other Poems. Verona, Valdonega, and New York, New Directions, 1957.
Confidential Report and Other Poems. London, Gaberbocchus, 1959; as *Selected Poems*, New York, New Directions, 1960.
Pulsatilla (bilingual edition), translated by Mary de Rachewiltz. Milan, Scheiwiller, 1961.
Die Haare auf Grossvaters Kopf (bilingual edition), translated by Eva Hesse. Zurich, Verlag der Arche, 1966.
Quel che la Matita Scrive (bilingual edition), translated by Mary de Rachewiltz. Rome, Guanda, 1970.
The Pig. Mount Horeb, Wisconsin, Perishable Press, 1970.
The Woodpecker. Santa Barbara, California, Yes Press, 1971.
In Another Country: Poems 1935–1975, edited by Robert Fitzgerald. San Francisco, City Lights, 1978.

Other

Skiing: East and West, with Helene Fischer. New York, Hastings House, 1947.

Editor, *New Directions in Prose and Poetry.* New York, New Directions, 39 vols., 1937–79.
Editor, *Poems from the Greenberg Manuscripts: A Selection from the Works of Samuel B. Greenberg.* New York, New Directions, 1939.
Editor, with Albert Hayes, *A Wreath of Christmas Poems.* New York, New Directions, 1942; London, Sheldon Press, 1972.
Editor, *Spearhead: Ten Years' Experimental Writing in America.* New York, New Directions, and London, Falcon Press, 1947.
Editor, with Hayden Carruth, *A New Directions Reader.* New York, New Directions, 1964.
Editor, with Naomi Burton and Patrick Hart, *The Asian Journal of Thomas Merton.* London, Sheldon Press, 1974.

James Laughlin comments:

My poems are written by someone I cannot identify in another sphere. At odd moments they come into my mind complete and all I do is type them out in my personal visual metric of couplets which are the same length.

* * *

James Laughlin is known to many as the publisher who has been a particular friend to avant-garde writers in America. His firm, New Directions, which he founded in 1936 to print works then seriously neglected – especially by Ezra Pound and William Carlos Williams – has expanded over the years and now is one of the foremost publishing houses in the world devoted to serious imaginative writing. But until recently Laughlin's own poetry was little known, partly because he wrote little but chiefly because it has been published reticently and distributed among friends and associates. In the past few years, however, his poems have begun to appear in many anthologies and have been translated into several other languages.

The poems are in colloquial diction, arranged according to what Laughlin calls "prosody of the eye": when typed on a typewriter each line of the poem must be no more than one space (occasionally two) longer or shorter than the opening line. The verbal tension arises from a contrast between this intentional artificiality of design and the freedom of the colloquial, sometimes singsongy aural cadence. Beyond this, the poems rely for effect on the directness and acuteness of the poet's insight, as in "A Modest Proposal":

I think I can offer this
simple remedy for a part

at least of the world's
ills and evil I suggest

that everyone should be
required to change his

name every ten years I
think this would put a

stop to a whole lot of
ambition compulsion ego

and like breeders of dis-
cord and wasted motion.

A stop, too, to biographical directories; and that, one feels, would probably be o.k. with Laughlin.

—Hayden Carruth

LAYTON, Irving (Peter). Canadian. Born in Neamtz, Romania, 12 March 1912; emigrated to Canada in 1913. Educated at MacDonald College, Sainte Anne de Bellevue, Quebec, B.Sc. in agriculture 1939; McGill University, Montreal, M.A. 1946. Served in the Canadian Army, 1942–43. Married 1) Betty Frances Sutherland in 1946; 2) the writer Aviva Cantor in 1961; 3) Harriet Bernstein in 1978; two sons and one daughter. Lecturer, Jewish Public Library, Montreal, 1943–58; High School teacher in Montreal, 1954–60; Part-time Lecturer, 1949–65, and Poet-in-Residence, 1965–66, Sir George Williams University, Montreal; Writer-in-Residence, University of Guelph, Ontario, 1968–69. Since 1969, Professor of English Literature, York University, Toronto. Poet-in-Residence, University of Ottawa, 1978. Co-Founding Editor, *First Statement*, later *Northern Review*, Montreal, 1941–43; Associate Editor, *Contact* magazine, Toronto, and *Black Mountain Review*, North Carolina. Recipient: Canadian Foundation Fellowship, 1957; Canada Council Award, 1959, 1967, Senior Arts grant and travel grant, 1973, 1979; Governor-General's Award, 1960; President's Medal, University of Western Ontario, 1961. D.C.L.: Bishop's University, Lennoxville, Quebec, 1970; D.Litt.: York University, 1979. Address: 9 Castlereagh, Niagara-on-the-Lake, Ontario, Canada.

PUBLICATIONS

Verse

Here and Now. Montreal, First Statement Press, 1945.

Now Is the Place: Stories and Poems. Montreal, First Statement Press, 1948.
The Black Huntsman. Montreal, First Statement Press, 1951.
Cerberus, with Raymond Souster and Louis Dudek. Toronto, Contact Press, 1952.
Love the Conqueror Worm. Toronto, Contact Press, 1953.
The Long Pea-Shooter. Montreal, Laocoön Press, 1954.
In the Midst of My Fever. Palma, Mallorca, Divers Press, 1954.
The Cold Green Element. Toronto, Contact Press, 1955.
The Blue Propeller. Toronto, Contact Press, 1955.
The Blue Calf and Other Poems. Toronto, Contact Press, 1956.
Music on a Kazoo. Toronto, Contact Press, 1956.
Improved Binoculars: Selected Poems. Highlands, North Carolina, Jargon, 1956.
A Laughter in the Mind. Highlands, North Carolina, Jargon, 1958; augmented edition, Montreal, Editions d'Orphée, 1959.
A Red Carpet for the Sun: Collected Poems. Toronto, McClelland and Stewart, and Highlands, North Carolina, Jargon, 1959.
The Swinging Flesh (poems and stories). Toronto, McClelland and Stewart, 1961.
Balls for a One-Armed Juggler. Toronto, McClelland and Stewart, 1963.
The Laughing Rooster. Toronto, McClelland and Stewart, 1964.
Collected Poems. Toronto, McClelland and Stewart, 1965.
Periods of the Moon. Toronto, McClelland and Stewart, 1967.
The Shattered Plinths. Toronto, McClelland and Stewart, 1968.
The Whole Bloody Bird (obs, aphs, and pomes). Toronto, McClelland and Stewart, 1969.
Selected Poems, edited by Wynne Francis. Toronto, McClelland and Stewart, 1969.
Five Modern Canadian Poets, with others, edited by Eli Mandel. Toronto, Holt Rinehart, 1970.
Collected Poems. Toronto, McClelland and Stewart, 1971.
Nail Polish. Toronto, McClelland and Stewart, 1971.
Lovers and Lesser Men. Toronto, McClelland and Stewart, 1973.
Selected Poems. London, Charisma, 1974.
The Pole-Vaulter. Toronto, McClelland and Stewart, 1974.
Seventy-Five Greek Poems. Athens, Hermes, 1974.
Selected Poems: The Darkening Fire 1945–1968, The Unwavering Eye 1969–1975. Toronto, McClelland and Stewart, 2 vols., 1975.
For My Brother Jesus. Toronto, McClelland and Stewart, 1976.
The Uncollected Poems 1936–1959. Oakville, Ontario, Mosaic Press, 1976.
The Poems of Irving Layton, edited by Eli Mandel. Toronto, McClelland and Stewart, 1977.
Selected Poems. New York, New Directions, 1977.
The Covenant. Toronto, McClelland and Stewart, 1977.
The Tightrope Dancer. Toronto, McClelland and Stewart, 1978.
Droppings from Heaven. Toronto, McClelland and Stewart, 1979.
The Love Poems of Irving Layton. Toronto, McClelland and Stewart, 1979.
There Were No Signs, illustrated by Sassu. Toronto, Madison Art Gallery, 1979.

Other

Engagements: The Prose of Irving Layton, edited by Seymour Mayne. Toronto, McClelland and Stewart, 1972.
Taking Sides: The Collected Social and Political Writings, edited by Howard Aster. Oakville, Ontario, Mosaic Press, 1977.
An Unlikely Affair: The Correspondence of Irving Layton and Dorothy Rath. Oakville, Ontario, Mosaic Press, 1979.

Editor, with Louis Dudek, *Canadian Poems 1850–1952.* Toronto, Contact Press, 1952

Editor, *Pan-ic: A Selection of Contemporary Canadian Poems.* New York, Alan Brilliant, 1958.
Editor, *Poems for 27 Cents.* Privately printed, 1961.
Editor, *Love Where the Nights Are Long: Canadian Love Poems.* Toronto, McClelland and Stewart, 1962.
Editor, *Anvil: A Selection of Workshop Poems.* Montreal, Kuritzky Frohlinger, 1966.
Editor, *Poems to Colour: A Selection of Workshop Poems.* Privately printed, 1970.
Editor, *Anvil Blood: A Selection of Workshop Poems.* Privately printed, 1973.

Bibliography: "Irving Layton: A Bilbiography in Progress 1931–1971" by Seymour Mayne, in *West Coast Review* (Burnaby, British Columbia), January 1973.

Manuscript Collections: Sir George Williams University, Montreal; University of Saskatchewan, Saskatoon; University of Toronto.

Critical Studies: "Layton on the Carpet" by Louis Dudek, in *Delta 9* (Montreal), October–December 1959; "The Man Who Copyrighted Passion" by A. Ross, in *Macleans Magazine* (Toronto), 15 November 1965; "Personal Heresy" by Robin Skelton, in *Canadian Literature* (Vancouver), Winter 1965; "A Grab at Proteus: Notes on Irving Layton" by George Woodcock, in *Canadian Literature* (Vancouver), Spring 1966; "That Heaven-Sent Lively Ropewalker, Irving Layton" by Hayden Carruth, in *Tamarack Review* (Toronto), Spring 1966; "Satyric Layton" by K. A. Lund, in *Canadian Author and Bookman* (Toronto), Spring 1967; "A Poet of Occasions" by Mike Doyle, in *Canadian Literature* (Vancouver), Autumn 1972; *Irving Layton: The Poet and His Critics* edited by Seymour Mayne, Toronto, McGraw Hill Ryerson, 1978.

Irving Layton comments:

I believe the poet, at his best, is a prophet and a descendant of prophets. Once he allows himself to forget that, he becomes a mere tinkerer. He ends up making pillows and pillow-cases for old fogies to go to sleep on. These love nothing better than ecstatically to snore out their veneration for beauty and order in the old rhythms they have learned so well. The poet's job is to disturb and discomfit. He's an iconoclast, a smasher of cruel idols, even when he accomplishes their destruction with the quietest of lyrics. He speaks to all men, not only to the cultivated and sensitive. Now, more than ever, he must strive to keep alive the spirit of rebellion and dissent. In a world that reveres facts and details, the poet must insist on a complex, imaginative awareness and remain the sworn enemy of all dogmas and dogmatists. Whatever else, poetry is freedom – freedom to experience, to live fully and vitally. For the doctrinaire pedant, as for the doctrinaire politician and ideologist, the poet will always have an abiding contempt. Nothing less than perfect freedom and joy will ever content him. But until that time arrives he will continue to look into the hearts of all and with the dark ambivalences he finds there move them through terror and beauty. As long as the poet is alive and flourishing mankind still has a future.

* * *

The most prolific of Canadian poets and certainly the most fluent since Bliss Carman, Irving Layton published 15 volumes of verse between *Here and Now* (1945) and the *Collected Poems* of 1965, and since then new collections have appeared regularly. A various and indeed an uneven poet, Layton has shown a steady advance in technical accomplishment and in emotional and intellectual maturity. The shrill and strident verses of the earliest volumes had some success in shocking the bourgeoisie with sexual frankness and an uninhibited vocabulary, but they seem rather old-fashioned today and in any case were overshadowed by the later poetry that began with the two volumes of 1954 and 1955, *In the Midst of My Fever* and *The Cold Green Element*. Reviewing the first of these, the critic Northrop Frye wrote: "The question of whether Mr. Layton is a real poet is settled.... An imaginative revolution is proclaimed all through this book: when he says that 'something has taught me severity, exactness of speech' or 'has given me a turn for sculptured stone,' we see a new excitement and intensity in the process of writing. At last it is possible to see what kind of poet Mr. Layton is, and he proves to be not a satirist at all but an erudite elegiac poet, whose technique turns on an aligning of the romantic and the ironic."

In spite of an unmistakably romantic conception of the poet as the voice of the earth and the sun iterating a gospel of the natural and the instinctive that is personal and emotional – and straight out of Blake, Whitman and Lawrence – Layton is in his handling of language, metre, and poetic technique a thoroughly classical poet, the best of whose love poems are quite genuinely in the tradition of Ovid and Catullus. The quality of his sensibility can be seen in the vividness and accuracy of his perceptions and can be illustrated in a line or two:

> The maples glisten with the season's rain;
> The day's porous, as October days are,
> And objects have more space about them.
>
> All field things seem weightless, abstract,
> As if they'd taken one step back
> To see themselves as they literally are
> After the dementia of summer.

The *Collected Poems* contains 385 titles, of which perhaps 50 or 60 must rank with the best lyrical and reflective poems of the mid-century in English. The rest consists of squibs, satires, casual jottings, mordant light verse and some often rather childish curses and polemics, but these (along with the strange glorification of military violence found in *The Shattered Plinths*) should not be allowed to obscure the significance of Layton's contribution to North American poetry.

—A. J. M. Smith

LEE, Dennis (Beynon). Canadian. Born in Toronto, Ontario, 31 August 1939. Educated at the University of Toronto, B.A. 1962, M.A. in English literature 1964. Full-time writer. Has taught at the University of Toronto, Rochdale College, Toronto, and York University, Toronto; Artist-in-Residence, Trent University, Peterborough, Ontario, 1975. Editor, House of Anansi Press, Toronto, 1967–73. Recipient: Governor-General's Award, 1973; Canadian Library Association Medal, 1975. Address: c/o Anansi, 35 Britain Street, Toronto M5A 1R7, Canada.

PUBLICATIONS

Verse

Kingdom of Absence. Toronto, Anansi, 1967.
Civil Elegies. Toronto, Anansi, 1968.
Wiggle to the Laundromat (juvenile). Toronto, New Press, 1970.
Civil Elegies and Other Poems. Toronto, Anansi, 1972.

Alligator Pie (juvenile). Toronto, Macmillan, 1974; Boston, Houghton Mifflin, 1975.
Nicholas Knock and Other People (juvenile). Toronto, Macmillan, 1974; Boston, Houghton Mifflin, 1977.
The Death of Harold Ladoo. San Francisco, Kanchenjunga, 1976.
Garbage Delight (juvenile). Toronto, Macmillan, 1977; Boston, Houghton Mifflin, 1978.
The Gods. Toronto, McClelland and Stewart, 1979.

Other

Savage Fields: An Essay in Literature and Cosmology. Toronto, Anansi, 1977.
The Ordinary Bath (juvenile). Toronto, Magook, 1979.

Editor, with R. A. Charlesworth, *An Anthology of Verse.* Toronto, Oxford University Press, 1964.
Editor, with R. A. Charlesworth, *The Second Century Anthologies of Verse, Book 2.* Toronto, Oxford University Press, 1967.
Editor, with Howard Adelman, *The University Game.* Toronto, Anansi, 1968.
Editor, *T. O. Now: The Young Toronto Poets.* Toronto, Anansi, 1968.

Manuscript Collection: Fisher Rare Book Room, University of Toronto.

* * *

"They are poets who write for real ... they're accessible to people with a wide range of consciousness ... reading them in one sitting is a self-contained pleasure." This is Dennis Lee discussing a group of contemporary poets in *Read Canadian: A Book about Canadian Books* (1972); needless to say, these are essential qualities of Lee's own work. His range of consciousness is wide enough to encompass the academy (he teaches at York University), the market place (he was the first editor of House of Anansi Press), and the anti-establishment (he helped found Rochdale College, a free university that flourished in Toronto in the 1960's).

Lee's poetic reputation rests on a single volume, *Civil Elegies and Other Poems*, which establishes the poet as a concerned citizen of liberal-leftist persuasion, worried by world trends. "Sibelius Park," a ruminating poem about Toronto life, ends ominously: "There is nothing to be afraid of." Other poems celebrate the "excellent pleasures," which are ultimately found wanting, of bourgeois life.

It is not in the short poems but in the longish elegies that Lee makes his mark. The nine elegies are basically free verse (one is tempted to say "free prose"), meditations on "the quality of Canadian civilization." The ruminations were inspired by George Grant, the moral philosopher and author of the influential book *Lament for a Nation* (1965), who saw Canada as a conservative country on a liberal continent engulfed by modern technology. In "Elegy 6," Lee peers into the future: "Though I do not deny technopolis I can see only the bread and circuses to come." By turns ponderous and profound, the elegies are as much concerned with the past as they are with the future, and references to historical and literary figures abound. It is in "Elegy 2" that Lee presents the reader with his measure of the past and standard for the future:

> Master and Lord, there was a
> measure once.
> There was a time when men could say
> my life, my job, my home
> and still feel clean.
> The poets spoke of earth and heaven. There were no symbols.

—John Robert Colombo

LEE, Don L(uther). Pseudonym: Haki R. Madhubuti. American. Born in Little Rock, Arkansas, 23 February 1942. Educated at Dunbar Vocational High School, Chicago; Chicago City College, A.A. 1966; Roosevelt University, Chicago, 1966–67. Served in the United States Army, 1960–63. Apprentice Curator, DuSable Museum of African American History, Chicago, 1963–67; Stock Department Clerk, Montgomery Ward, Chicago, 1963–64; Post Office Clerk, Chicago, 1964–65; Junior Executive, Spiegels, Chicago, 1965–66. Taught at Columbia College, Chicago, 1968; Wirter-in-Residence, Cornell University, Ithaca, New York, 1968–69; Poet-in-Residence, Northeastern Illinois State College, Chicago, 1969–70; Lecturer, University of Illinois, Chicago, 1969–71; Writer-in-Residence, Morgan State College, Baltimore, 1972–73. Since 1971, Writer-in-Residence, Howard University, Washington, D.C. Editor, *Black Books Bulletin*, Chicago; *Black Pages Series*; Third World Press, Chicago. Recipient: National Endowment for the Arts grant, 1969; Kuumba Workshop Black Liberation Award, 1973. Address: Institute of Positive Education, 7524 Cottage Grove, Chicago, Illinois 60619, U.S.A.

PUBLICATIONS

Verse

Think Black. Detroit, Broadside Press, 1967; revised edition, 1968, 1969.
Black Pride. Detroit, Broadside Press, 1968.
Back Again, Home. Detroit, Broadside Press, 1968.
One Sided Shoot-Out. Detroit, Broadside Press, 1968.
For Black People (And Negroes Too). Chicago, Third World Press, 1968.
Don't Cry, Scream. Detroit, Broadside Press, 1969.
We Walk the Way of the New World. Detroit, Broadside Press, 1970.
Directionscore: Selected and New Poems. Detroit, Broadside Press, 1971.
Book of Life. Detroit, Broadside Press, 1973.

Recording: *Rappin' and Readin'*, Broadside Press, 1971.

Other

Dynamite Voices: Black Poets of the 1960's. Detroit, Broadside Press, 1971.
From Plan to Planet: Life Studies: The Need for Afrikan Minds and Institutions. Detroit, Broadside Press, 1973.
Enemies: The Clash of Races. Chicago, Third World Press, 1978.

Editor, with Patricia L. Brown and Francis Ward, *To Gwen with Love.* Chicago, Johnson, 1971.

Critical Studies: "Black Poetry's Welcome Critic" by Hollie I. West, in *The Washington Post* (Washington, D.C.), 6 June 1971; "A Black Poet Faces Reality" by Vernon Jarrett, in *Chicago Tribune*, 23 July 1971; "The Relevancy of Don L. Lee as a Contemporary Black Poet" by Annette Sands, in *Black World* (Chicago), June 1972; "Some Black Thoughts on Don L. Lee's *Think Black*: Thanks by a Frustrated White Academic Thinker" by Eugene E. Miller, in *College English* (Champaign, Illinois), May 1973.

* * *

Of the strong young Black poets of the "Black arts movement" that began in the United States in the late 1960's, Don L. Lee is one of the most powerful and persuasive in content, one of the most creative and influential in technique.

His poetry, consciously utilitarian, is directed to a Black audience, with themes centering around self-identity and self-definition, self-determination, the humanness of Black people and the depravity of white people ("unpeople"), and self-help through collective and institutional efforts. Examples are "In the Interest of Black Salvation," which shows disillusionment with orthodox Euro-American religion; "Move Un-Noticed to Be Noticed," an exhortation for sincerity in Blacks; "The Wall," a celebration of Black pride; "Back Home Again," which depicts an excursion into an alien (white) "establishment" world and a subsequent return to Blackness; "But He Was Cool," a satire on vapid and showy life styles affected by some Blacks; and "Re-Act for Action," a cry for aggression against racial injustices.

Lee's poems convey spontaneity and emotional compulsion as well as ideological commitment. He prefers the speech of the Black urban masses. Much of his poetry seems intended for oral delivery. (He is in demand for readings of his poetry.) He frequently achieves desired aural effects through extra vowels or consonants, phonetic spellings, elisions. He is fond of playing with words, particularly syntactic reversals and the breaking of words into components – for irony, purposeful double meaning, emphasis of components of meaning, aural effects, and other reasons. He is partial to scattered spatial arrangements, broken words, unconventional syntax, and unconventional punctuation, favoring the ampersand and diagonal. His imagery is strong, concrete, and specific. Frequently he builds up a poem's tension incrementally, withholding its point or resolution until the end at which time the poem's logic or impact is made manifest.

—Theodore R. Hudson

LEE, Laurie. British. Born in Stroud, Gloucestershire, 26 June 1914. Educated at Slad Village School, Gloucestershire, and Stroud Central School. During World War II made documentary films for the General Post Office film unit, 1939–40, and the Crown Film Unit, 1941–43, and travelled as a scriptwriter to Cyprus and India; Publications Editor, Ministry of Information, 1944–46; member of the Green Park Film Unit, 1946–47. Married Catherine Francesca Polge in 1950; one daughter. Caption Writer-in-Chief, Festival of Britain, 1950–51. Recipient: Atlantic Award, 1944; Society of Authors Traveling Award, 1951; Foyle Award, 1956; Smith Literary Award, 1960. Fellow, Royal Society of Literature. M.B.E. (Member, Order of the British Empire), 1952. Address: 49 Elm Park Gardens, London S.W.10, England.

PUBLICATIONS

Verse

The Sun My Monument. London, Hogarth Press, 1944; New York, Doubleday, 1947.
The Bloom of Candles: Verse from a Poet's Year. London, Lehmann, 1947.
My Many-Coated Man. London, Deutsch, 1955; New York, Coward McCann, 1957.
(Poems). London, Vista Books, 1960.
Pergamon Poets 10, with Charles Causley, edited by Evan Owen. Oxford, Pergamon Press, 1970.

Recording: *Laurie Lee Reading His Own Poems,* with Christopher Logue, Jupiter, 1960.

Plays

The Voyage of Magellan: A Dramatic Chronicle for Radio (broadcast, 1946). London, Lehmann, 1948.
Peasants' Priest (produced Canterbury, 1947). Canterbury, H. J. Goulden, 1947.

Screenplays: *Cyprus Is an Island*, 1946; *A Tale in a Teacup*, 1947.

Radio Play: *The Voyage of Magellan*, 1946.

Other

Land at War. London, His Majesty's Stationery Office, 1945.
We Made a Film in Cyprus, with Ralph Keene. London, Longman, 1947.
An Obstinate Exile. Privately printed, 1951.
A Rose for Winter: Travels in Andalusia. London, Hogarth Press, 1955; New York, Morrow, 1956.
Cider with Rosie (autobiography). London, Hogarth Press, 1959; as *The Edge of Day: A Boyhood in the West of England*, New York, Morrow, 1960.
Man Must Move: The Story of Transport (juvenile), with David Lambert. London, Rathbone, 1960; as *The Wonderful World of Transportation*, New York, Doubleday, 1960; revised edition, 1969; as *The Wonderful World of Transport*, London, Macdonald, 1969.
The Firstborn (essay on childhood). London, Hogarth Press, and New York, Morrow, 1964.
As I Walked Out One Midsummer Morning (autobiography). London, Deutsch, and New York, Atheneum, 1969.
I Can't Stay Long. London, Deutsch, 1975; New York, Atheneum, 1976.
Innocence in the Mirror, photographs by Angelo Cozzi. New York, Morrow, 1978.

Editor, with Christopher Hassall and Rex Warner, *New Poems 1954*. London, Joseph, 1954.

Translator, *The Dead Village*, by Avigdor Dagan. London, Young Czechoslovakia, 1943.

* * *

A first encounter with Laurie Lee's poems immediately reveals that they are loaded with charm, and almost always in the best sense of that tricky word. Their furniture is traditionally "poetic" – seas, moons, flowers, stars, girls, animals – and their mode romantic, but a fine tact protects the poems from the dangerous slide into sentimentality. Laurie Lee is a fluent creator of images and odd correspondences: sometimes one fancies one hears, though not too loudly, the echoing voice of Lorca:

> You were adventure's web.
> the flag of fear I flew
> riding black stallions
> through the rocky streets.

And sometimes, in his exact observations of physical details, he reminds one of Andrew Young – "holes suck in their bees," and "The birdlike stars droop down and die, / The starlike birds catch fire." Indeed, the outside world fills him, as it does Andrew Young, with a sort of devout pleasure.

But these influences, if they are influences and not coincidences, only occasionally intrude.

Overall a Laurie Lee poem is very much his and no one else's. His rhythms, verbal textures, visual aperçus are all his own.

It stops there, though. If there are some melancholy poems, they are always of a personal and introspective sort. He does not take account of the miseries, not to say atrocities, that are happening all around us. When he looks outward it is at the physical world, but not the suffering people in it, and when he cerebrates he never pushes his thinking very far. A result of this is that, in spite of the numerous felicities, his final effect is one of slightness. You will find in his poems no exclamation marks – but no questions either. One wishes that a man with his sensibility and his technical adroitness might range farther afield, might explore more deeply the larger experiences whose absence makes, in the end, these poems miniatures. However, he has not done that.

This may account for the smallness of his output. And it says something for his critical judgment that he has not made that slightness seem more slight by printing too much.

—Norman MacCaig

LEEMING, Owen (Alfred). New Zealander. Born in Christchurch, 1 August 1930. Educated at the University of Canterbury, Christchurch, 1949–52, M.A. in French 1952; studied musical composition in Paris, 1954–55. Radio Announcer, New Zealand Broadcasting Corporation, Christchurch, 1953–54; Talks Producer, Pacific Service, 1956–59, Home Service, 1959–62, BBC, London; Television Producer, New Zealand Broadcasting Corporation, Wellington, 1962–64; UNESCO Consultant, Dakar, Senegal, 1965–66, and Kuala Lumpur, Malaysia, 1971–72. Recipient: New Zealand Government Bursary, 1954; Katherine Mansfield Menton Fellowship, 1970. Address: 21 rue de la Liberté, 13980 Alleins, France.

PUBLICATIONS

Verse

Venus Is Setting. Christchurch, Caxton Press, 1972.

Plays

The Quarry Game (produced Wellington, 1970).

Radio Plays: *Order*, 1969 (UK); *Yellow*, 1970; *Reefer's Boys*, 1971 (UK); *The Sanctum*, 1974.

Television Play: *White Gardenia* (on Katherine Mansfield), 1969.

Critical Study: *A Way of Saying* by Kendrick Smithyman, Auckland, Collins, 1965.

Owen Leeming comments:

A reviewer of *Venus Is Setting* wrote, "Owen Leeming's creative imagination is more intricately geared to world history than that of any other New Zealand poet." It is true that I am conscious of the reach of time and of the earth as planet. However, I think that the particularities of place and human behaviour, especially those of my own country, have stimulated me more. These days, in spite of a slowing of output caused by material necessity, I am experimenting with writing directly in French.

* * *

Brought up a Catholic and neo-Thomist, Owen Leeming first made a considerable impact as a poet with "The Priests of Serrabonne," a massive elaborately-structured palinode of renunciation:

I think of priests who cowed me, tall soutaned
Caners who vaunted their humility, their wall
Of pride hung with a small
Black cross. They are singing now, controlled
In me ...

This poem, a sort of post-Hopkins "Stanzas from the Grande Chartreuse," is impressive for its muted rhetoric and bleak honesty of personal statement. It is hardly typical of Leeming's more customary style of writing, which is sophisticated, detached, and highly cerebral, reflecting close familiarity with modern French poetry, and the montage effects of one who has worked professionally in theatre and television.

Venus Is Setting, a rigorous selection from perhaps a dozen years' output, has a few poems – "Instance of Death," "At Home with Cold," "My Cousin James" – which record simply and directly moments of experience and recollection, in what might be called the English manner. But Leeming seems more often driven, from intuitions which may be triggered off by a place or an incongruous occasion, into free-ranging intellectual reverie: the result, pared down with verbal economy, becomes a sequence often stimulating but sometimes bizarre. His interest in musical composition may account for the contrasting forms and movement of elaborate set-pieces like "Masks" and "Visions, Limited." It is in a tone-poem like "Verdun," and a few Cavafy-style lyrics of real intensity, that he has come nearest to achieving his declared aim of "exploring the idea of a secular metaphysic."

—James Bertram

LEHMANN, Geoffrey (John). Australian. Born in Sydney, New South Wales, 28 June 1940. Educated at Shore School, Sydney, and Sydney University, Degree in arts, 1960, and in law, 1963. Qualified as a solicitor in 1963. Since 1969, Principal, C. R. Wilcox and Lehmann, Sydney. Address: 8 Highfield Road, Lindfield, New South Wales, Australia.

PUBLICATIONS

Verse

The Ilex Tree, with Les A. Murray. Canberra, Australian National University Press, 1965.
A Voyage of Lions and Other Poems. Sydney, Angus and Robertson, 1968.
Conversation with a Rider. Sydney, Angus and Robertson, 1972.
From an Australian Country Sequence. London, Poem-of-the-Month Club, 1973.
Ross Poems. Sydney, Angus and Robertson, 1978.

Novel

A Spring Day in Autumn. Melbourne, Nelson, 1974.

Other

Australian Primitive Painters. Brisbane, University of Queensland Press, 1977

Editor, *Comic Australian Verse.* Sydney, Angus and Robertson, 1972.

Critical Study: Review by Roy Fuller, in *London Magazine*, January 1967.

Geoffrey Lehmann comments:

I regard myself as somewhat old-fashioned because I think that poetry should be enjoyable. I have written a number of poems about members of my family, but started writing on these themes just before Robert Lowell made this mode popular.

There are a number of Graeco-Roman poems influenced by Pound and Cavafy in which Rome is used as the symbol for modern civilization, city life and over-population. These poems deal with the love-hate relationship that an individual has with his city and contrast private longings with official duties. They use lions and dolphins as symbols of imagination, the natural order and purity.

There are a group of poems about members of my family including a grandfather who died of morphia, self-administered, and another grandfather who built the first Anglican church in New Guinea and died shortly afterwards of tropical diseases. These two deaths blighted the lives of my parents early in their childhood and indirectly affected me very considerably. The poems about my family were motivated by the wish to relive the experiences which made my family what they are, rather than mere nostalgia, although this is an important emotion for me. Amongst Australian poets probably Kenneth Slessor has influenced me most. Recent poems are more spare in their language and free in their form, and attempt to follow thought patterns.

* * *

Among the younger generation of Australian poets Geoffrey Lehmann is possibly the most prolific as well as the most immediately approachable. His verse relies largely on conventional techniques, being for the most part unrhymed iambic pentameters or simple stanzaic patterns of alternative rhymes and half-rhymes.

A penchant for sequences of homely, familial anecdotes and episodes in the lives of his father and grandfather has lent a deceptively simple aura to his reputation. In reality he is a poet of genuine subtleties and complex affiliations with standards of moderation and saneness that seem out of place, even anachronistic, in the present age. This appears to have led him to identify his thought and poetic persona with the immediate and the distant past rather than to take an existential stance in the present.

To date his most effective work is to be found in the excellent sequence entitled "Monologues for Marcus Furius Camillus, Governor of Africa" that opens his second book. Adopting the guise of a provincial administrator during ancient Rome's decadence he narrates a series of episodes in the Roman's career that have caused him to review his life and allegiances. Meditating upon the carefree life of dolphins or the degradation of lions in the Roman arenas, the governor lives and moves through these poems, one of the eternal contemporaries of literature.

—Bruce Beaver

LEHMANN, (Rudolph) John (Frederick). British. Born in Bourne End, Buckinghamshire, 2 June 1907; brother of the actress Beatrix Lehmann, and the novelist Rosamond Lehmann. Educated at Eton (King's Scholar); Trinity College, Cambridge, B.A. Journalist in Vienna for several years prior to 1938. General Manager, 1931–32, 1938–46, and Partner, 1940–46, Hogarth Press, London; Founder and Managing Director, John Lehmann Ltd., publishers, London, 1946–52. Founding Editor, *New Writing, Daylight, New Writing and Daylight*, and *Penguin New Writing*, London, 1936–50, and *The London Magazine*, 1954–61; Advisory Editor, *The Geographical Magazine*, London, 1940–45; Editor, New Soundings, BBC Third Programme, 1952. Visiting Professor, University of Texas, Austin, 1970–71, State University of California, San Diego, 1970–71, University of California, Berkeley, 1974, and Emory University, Atlanta, 1977. Chairman, British Council Editorial Advisory Panel, 1952–58; President, Alliance Française in Great Britain, 1955–64; Member, Anglo-Greek Mixed Commission, 1962–68. Since 1967, President, Royal Literary Fund. Recipient: Prix du Rayonnement Française, 1961; Foyle Prize, 1964. Officer, 1954, and Commander, 1961, Order of King George of the Hellenes; Officer, Legion of Honor, France, 1958; Grand Officer, Etoile Noir, 1960; Officer, Order of Arts and Letters, France, 1965. Fellow, Royal Society of Literature. C.B.E. (Commander, Order of the British Empire), 1964. Address: 85 Cornwall Gardens, London S.W.7, England.

PUBLICATIONS

Verse

The Bud, Burial, Dawn, Grey Days, The Lover, The Mountain, Ruin, The Gargoyles, Turn Not, Hesperides. Privately printed, 10 broadsheets, 1928.
A Garden Revisited and Other Poems. London, Hogarth Press, 1931.
The Noise of History. London, Hogarth Press, 1934.
Forty Poems. London, Hogarth Press, 1942.
The Sphere of Glass and Other Poems. London, Hogarth Press, 1944.
The Age of the Dragon: Poems 1930–1951. London, Longman, 1951; New York, Harcourt Brace, 1952.
The Secret Messages. Stamford, Connecticut, Overbrook Press, 1958.
Collected Poems 1930–1963. London, Eyre and Spottiswoode, 1963.
Christ the Hunter. London, Eyre and Spottiswoode, 1965.
Photograph. London, Poem-of-the-Month Club, 1971.
The Reader at Night and Other Poems. Toronto, Basilike, 1974.

Novels

Evil Was Abroad. London, Cresset Press, 1938.
In the Purely Pagan Sense. London, Blond and Briggs, 1976.

Other

Prometheus and the Bolsheviks. London, Cresset Press, 1937; New York, Knopf, 1938.
New Writing in England. New York, Critics Group Press, 1939.
Down River: A Danubian Study. London, Cresset Press, 1939.
New Writing in Europe. London, Penguin, 1940.
The Open Night (essays). London, Longman, and New York, Harcourt Brace, 1952.
Edith Sitwell. London, Longman, 1952; revised edition, 1970.
In My Own Time: Memoirs of a Literary Life. Boston, Little Brown, 1969.
I. *The Whispering Gallery.* London, Longman, and New York, Harcourt Brace, 1955.

II. *I Am My Brother.* London, Longman, and New York, Reynal, 1960.
III. *The Ample Proposition.* London, Eyre and Spottiswoode, 1966.
Ancestors and Friends. London, Eyre and Spottiswoode, 1962.
A Nest of Tigers: Edith, Osbert, and Sacheverell Sitwell in Their Times. London, Macmillan, and Boston, Little Brown, 1968.
Holborn: An Historical Portrait of a London Borough. London, Macmillan, 1970.
Lewis Carroll and the Spirit of Nonsense (lecture). Nottingham, University of Nottingham, 1974.
Virginia Woolf and Her World. London, Thames and Hudson, 1975; New York, Harcourt Brace, 1976.
Edward Lear and His World. London, Thames and Hudson, and New York, Scribner, 1977.
Thrown to the Woolfs: Leonard and Virginia Woolf and the Hogarth Press. London, Weidenfeld and Nicolson, 1978; New York, Holt Rinehart, 1979.

Editor, with Denys Kilham Roberts and Gerald Gould, *The Year's Poetry.* London, Lane, 3 vols., 1934–36.
Editor, *New Writing.* London, Bodley Head, 2 vols., Lawrence and Wishart, 3 vols., 1936–38; with Christopher Isherwood and Stephen Spender, London, Hogarth Press, 2 vols., 1938–39; Hogarth Press, 1 vol., 1939.
Editor, with C. Day Lewis and T. A. Jackson, *A Writer in Arms*, by Ralph Fox. London, International, 1937.
Editor, with Stephen Spender, *Poems for Spain.* London, Hogarth Press, 1939.
Editor, *Penguin New Writing 1–40.* London, Penguin, 1940–50.
Editor, *Folios of New Writing.* London, Hogarth Press, 4 vols., 1940–41.
Editor, *"New Writing" and "Daylight."* London, Hogarth Press, 5 vols., 1942–47; London, Lehmann, 1 vol., 1946.
Editor, *Poems from "New Writing," 1936–1946.* London, Lehmann, 1946.
Editor, *French Stories from "New Writing."* London, Lehmann, 1947; as *Modern French Stories*, New York, New Directions, 1948.
Editor, *Demetrios Capetanakis: A Greek Poet in England.* London, Lehmann, 1947; as *Shores of Darkness: Poems and Essays*, New York, Devin Adair, 1949.
Editor, *Shelley in Italy: An Anthology.* London, Lehmann, 1947.
Editor, *Orpheus: A Symposium of the Arts.* London, Lehmann, and New York, New Directions, 1948.
Editor, *English Stories from "New Writing."* London, Lehmann, 1951; as *Best Stories from "New Writing,"* New York, Harcourt Brace, 1951.
Editor, *Pleasures of "New Writing": An Anthology of Poems, Stories, and Other Prose Pieces from the Pages of "New Writing."* London, Lehmann, 1952.
Editor, *Modern French Stories.* London, Faber, 1956.
Editor, with Cecil Day Lewis, *The Chatto Book of Modern Poetry 1915–1955.* London, Chatto and Windus, 1956.
Editor, *The Craft of Letters in England: A Symposium.* London, Cresset Press, 1956; Boston, Houghton Mifflin, 1957.
Editor, *Coming to London.* London, Phoenix House, 1957.
Editor, *Italian Stories of Today.* London, Faber. 1959.
Editor, *Selected Poems*, by Edith Sitwell. London, Macmillan, 1965.
Editor, with Derek Parker, *Selected Letters of Edith Sitwell 1919–1964.* London, Macmillan, 1970.

Manuscript Collection: Humanities Research Center, University of Texas, Austin.

* * *

During the 1940's John Lehmann published a number of prose poems which came as near as has yet proved possible to making a success of that difficult form in the English language. Many of them ("Spring Light," for instance, and "After the Fire") remain a tribute to Mr. Lehmann's command of the language. But a continual preoccupation with form and language, while it led to an enviable ease, in some respects inhibited his development as a poet. "The Sphere of Glass," one of his best poems, demonstrates a wholeness and intactness of form which make it much more than a conventional autobiographical anecdote; elsewhere, however, his poems are marked by a certain predictability of "poetic" language which can weaken them. One or two of the poems of the 1940's reflect as well as any other war poems not only the "style" but the emotion of the time, and deserve a place in any anthology of the period. His more recent poems are more organic than the earlier ones; their sum is greater than their parts, and quotation does them less than justice. If a slackening of impetus is hinted at by the rarer appearances of his poems in print, the poems that have appeared within the past ten years have also shown a more sober apprehension of the relative places of technique and "inspiration" in the making of a poem. It is much to be hoped that this always interesting poet will turn a little from accomplished literary journalism, and from the writing of interesting autobiography, and publish more poetry.

—Derek Parker

LEONARD, Tom. British. Born in Glasgow, Lanarkshire, 22 August 1944. Educated at Lourdes Secondary School, Glasgow; postgraduate student, Glasgow University. Married in 1971; two children. Recipient: Scottish Arts Council bursary, 1971, 1978. Address: 56 Eldon Street, Glasgow G3 6NJ, Scotland.

PUBLICATIONS

Verse

Six Glasgow Poems. Glasgow, Midnight Press, 1969.
A Priest Came On at Merkland Street. Glasgow, Midnight Press, 1970.
Poems. Dublin, E. and T. O'Brien, 1973.
Bunnit Husslin. Glasgow, Third Eye Centre, 1975.
Three Glasgow Writers, with Alex Hamilton and James Kelman. Glasgow, Molendinar Press, 1976.
My Name Is Tom. London, Good Elf, 1978.

Play

If Only Bunty was Here (radio play). Glasgow, Print Studio Press, 1979.

Critical Studies: "A Scots Quartette" by Edwin Morgan, in *Eboracum* (York), Winter 1973; "Tom Leonard: Man with Two Heads" by Tom McGrath, in *Akros* (Preston, Lancashire), April 1974.

Tom Leonard comments:

My work this past ten years has been in three broad areas: written work in English, written work in a representation of Glasgow speech, and performance poetry for voice with or without stereo tapes and placards. Collectively the work represents a few more shots on the side of Essence in its continuous battle with Name, and also represents a campaign against the political linguistic tyranny in Britain of prescriptive English and (a more insidious force in Scotland) prescriptive Scots.

* * *

Tom Leonard is one of the most interesting of the younger Scottish poets who emerged during the 1960's. His reputation in Scotland has tended to centre on his poems in Glasgow dialect, but in fact, as the publication of his first general collection, *Poems*, made clear, he is a man of many styles, a restless formal experimenter whose language is laid with surprises, traps, and ironies. There is a considerable element of humour, sometimes fantastic and sometimes moderately black, to attract the reader, and a recurring deadpan strangeness is characteristic. Some of the ironical effects are slight, joky, throwaway. But in the best poems, like "simile please / say cheese," the interlock of images and ideas forces the humour to work in unusual and meaningful ways. The Glasgow poems make use of local idiom and pronunciation for a range of effects, from the bold outspoken backchat of schoolgirls skipping their bus-fares ("A Scream") to the more sophisticated meshing of religion and football in "The Good Thief." These poems take the risk of being obscure to English readers (though the book provides a translation) for the sake of offering a tribute to the much-attacked Glasgow environment – not that the tribute is anything but unsentimental.

—Edwin Morgan

LePAN, Douglas (Valentine). Canadian. Born in Toronto, Ontario, 25 May 1914. Educated at University of Toronto Schools; University College, University of Toronto, B.A.; Merton College, Oxford, M.A. Served in the Canadian Army, 1942–45. Married to Sarah Katharine Chambers; two sons. Lecturer, University of Toronto, 1937–38; Instructor and Tutor in English Literature, Harvard University, Cambridge, Massachusetts, 1938–41. Joined Canadian Department of External Affairs, 1945: First Secretary on the Staff of the Canadian High Commissioner in London, 1945–48; various appointments in the Department of External Affairs, including that of Special Assistant to the Secretary of State, Ottawa, 1949–51; Counsellor and later Minister Counsellor at the Canadian Embassy, Washington, D.C., 1951–55; Secretary and Director of Research, Royal Commission on Canada's Economic Prospects (Gordon Commission), 1955–58; Assistant Under-Secretary of State for External Affairs, 1958–59. Professor of English Literature, Queen's University, Kingston, Ontario, 1959–64. Principal, University College, 1964–70, and since 1970, University Professor, University of Toronto. Since 1964, Member, Canada Coucil. Recipient: Guggenheim Fellowship, 1948; Governor-General's Award, for poetry, 1954, for fiction, 1965; Oscar Blumenthal Prize (*Poetry*, Chicago), 1972. D.Litt.: University of Manchester, 1964. Fellow, Royal Society of Canada, 1968. Address: Massey College, 4 Devonshire Place, Toronto 5, Canada.

PUBLICATIONS

Verse

The Wounded Prince and Other Poems. Toronto, Clarke Irwin, and London, Chatto and Windus, 1948.

The Net and the Sword: Poems. Toronto, Clarke Irwin, and London, Chatto and Windus, 1953.

Novel

The Deserter. Toronto, McClelland and Stewart, 1964.

* * *

When a man of letters is also a man of affairs, his public life cannot but influence his writing. Douglas LePan, who holds degrees from the University of Toronto and Oxford, saw action in the Italian Campaign of World War II. He joined the Department of External Affairs and rose to become Assistant Under-Secretary of State. Then he left to become a professor of English and finally principal of University College, University of Toronto. His careers have influenced his poetry in interesting ways.

His two books of poems are largely concerned with his war experiences. *The Wounded Prince* views the grim events ironically and paradoxically. *The Net and the Sword*, which received the Governor-General's Award, recreates the Italian Campaign and views man mercilessly pitted against the forces of destruction. Along with paintings by the War Artists in the National Gallery in Ottawa, these war poems are a valuable record of the achievements of Canadian soldiers overseas. Both books are mature works full of rich, intellectualized imagery.

Like a public man, LePan is very much concerned with the responsibility of man. He admires the muscular man, whether gladiator, soldier, or *coureur de bois*. In *The Net and the Sword*, he has a poem on the latter:

> Thinking of you, I think of the *coureur de bois*,
> Swarthy men grown almost to savage size
> Who put their brown wrists through the arras of the woods
> And were lost – sometimes for months.

But he is also concerned with the repercussions of action, not with those "whose care is how they fall, not why." This has led him to theorize about the Canadian experience. The title of a poem in *The Wounded Prince* has become a catch-phrase of the period: "A Country Without a Mythology."

His only novel, *The Deserter*, concerns social responsibility and was awarded a Governor-General's Award. It probes the meaning of war to a soldier who deserts – not before or during a campaign, but after the armistice. LePan has recently published a number of essays on social philosophy – further evidence of his concern for the roots of the Canadian community.

—John Robert Colombo

LERNER, Laurence (David). British. Born in Cape Town, South Africa, 12 December 1925. Educated at the University of Cape Town, B.A. 1944, M.A. 1945; Pembroke College, Cambridge, B.A. 1949. Married Natalie Winch in 1948; four children. Schoolmaster, St. George's Grammar School, Cape Town, 1946–47; Assistant Lecturer, then Lecturer in English, University College of the Gold Coast, Legon, Ghana, 1949–53; Extra-Mural Tutor, then Lecturer in English, Queen's University of Belfast, 1953–62. Lecturer, then Reader, 1962–70, and since 1970, Professor of English, University of Sussex, Brighton. Visiting Professor, Earlham College, Richmond, Indiana, and University of Connecticut, Storrs, 1960–61; University of Illinois, Urbana, 1964; University of Munich, 1968–69, 1974–75. Recipient: Prudence Farmer Prize (*New Statesman*), 1975. Address: 50 Compton Avenue, Brighton BN1 3PS, England.

PUBLICATIONS

Verse

(Poems). Oxford, Fantasy Press, 1955.
Domestic Interior and Other Poems. London, Hutchinson, 1959.
The Directions of Memory: Poems 1958–1963. London, Chatto and Windus, 1963.
Selves. London, Routledge, 1969.
Folio, with others. Frensham, Surrey, Sceptre Press, 1971.
A.R.T.H.U.R.: The Life and Opinions of a Digital Computer. Hassocks, Sussex, Harvester Press, 1974; Amherst, University of Massachusetts Press, 1975.

Novels

The Englishmen. London, Hamish Hamilton, 1959.
A Free Man. London, Chatto and Windus, 1968.

Other

English Literature: An Interpretation for Students Abroad. London, Oxford University Press, 1954.
The Truest Poetry: An Essay on the Question: What Is Literature? London, Hamish Hamilton, 1960; New York, Horizon Press, 1964.
The Truthtellers: Jane Austen, George Eliot, and D. H. Lawrence. London, Chatto and Windus, and New York, Schocken, 1967.
The Uses of Nostalgia: Studies in Pastoral Poetry. London, Chatto and Windus, and New York, Schocken, 1972.
Thomas Hardy's "The Mayor of Casterbridge": Tragedy or Social History? London, Chatto and Windus, 1975.
An Introduction to English Poetry: Fifteen Poems Discussed. London, Arnold, 1975.
Love and Marriage: Literature and Its Social Context. London, Arnold, 1979.

Editor, *Poems*, by Milton. London, Penguin, 1953.
Editor, *Shakespeare's Tragedies: A Selection of Modern Criticism.* London, Penguin, 1963.
Editor, with John Holmstrom, *George Eliot and Her Readers: A Selection of Contemporary Reviews.* London, Bodley Head, 1966.
Editor, *Shakespeare's Comedies: A Selection of Modern Criticism.* London, Penguin, 1967.
Editor, with John Holmstrom, *Thomas Hardy and His Readers: A Selection of Contemporary Reviews.* London, Bodley Head, 1968.
Editor, *Poetry South East 2: An Anthology of New Poetry.* Tunbridge Wells, Kent, South East Arts Association, 1977.
Editor, *The Context of English Literature: The Victorians.* London, Methuen, 1978.

Translator, *Spleen*, by Charles Baudelaire. Belfast, Festival, 1966.

Laurence Lerner comments:

My poems are comprehensible, sad, modern in subject-matter more than in form, written infrequently and with intense concentration. The recent ones are dramatic to the extent of being Protean. I wish I could write more poems than I do.

* * *

Like the best of his criticism, Laurence Lerner's poetry is sensible, direct and aware of the complexities of human behaviour. Many of the poems in his first collection, *Domestic Interior*, are reactions to different environments; their strength lies not so much in description as in the way they establish a mental *rapport* with the external world, in which closely-observed incidentals find their place in a wider pattern of experience:

> While shaping eyes stare from the moving train:
> Or else a water-colour landscape glows
> Grey-green and tawny under a wash of rain,
> Or blue with blobs of cabbages in rows.

Most of these poems are "efficient" and well-argued, in a sense which reminds one of the best Thirties' poetry, though occasionally the argument only partly conceals a certain diffuseness of detail. In the more successful ones, however, like the title-poem and "Meditation on the Toothache" (in actual fact, a meditation on the imagination), a powerful social concern is firmly rooted in the trivia of the individual life, and in the means by which these may be absorbed into artistic creation. The dramatic sense is evident in "Domestic Interior" and "Mimesis" – both poems in which the subject is approached through a number of protagonists.

Lerner's second collection, *The Directions of Memory*, is more adventurous in technique, and shows a willingness to handle more difficult kinds of experience. Though one still occasionally feels that a poem has not found its ideal form, there is a more subtle sense of construction and a growing skill in the use of imagery. Several of the most striking poems deal with sexual relationships, sometimes from the woman's point of view. These range from the aggression-dream ("Housewife as Judith") to the qualified celebration of "The Anatomy of Love" and the fine "Midnight Swim," a poem in which a profoundly disturbing situation is conveyed through a brilliantly-controlled central metaphor. The same could be said of the most moving poem in the volume, "Years Later," the monologue of an unborn Jewish child, the victim (with its mother) of a Nazi atrocity. These poems show a determination to face up to the more disturbing aspects of life with honesty, intelligence and, at times, with wit.

The same combination of qualities persists, with increasing verbal power, in *Selves*, as well as in his vigorous and resourceful versions of Baudelaire. The central section of *Selves* includes a group of monologues in which various victims of human cruelty – a laboratory rat, a monkey involved in a feeding experiment, a battery-reared cockerel – comment on their situations with grimly humorous logic. Though in one sense such poems are a natural extension of Lerner's interest in current psychological theory, their real originality comes from the skill with which they render essentially inarticulate suffering in terms of a recognizable human idiom. In other poems ("The Merman," "Adam Names the Creatures," "Information Theory"), the concern with communication extends to the nature of language itself. Here, the deliberate assumption of inarticulateness becomes a powerful device for exploring the gap between words and reality ("The Merman"):

> When humans talk they split their say in bits
> And bit by bit they step on what they feel.
> They talk in bits, they never talk in all.

So live in wetness swimming they call "sea";
And stand on dry and watch the wet waves call
They still call "sea".
Only their waves don't call.

Lerner's continued questioning of the basis of language and perception lies at the root of *A.R.T.H.U.R.* It would be wrong to dismiss this as a *jeu d'esprit*: certainly, the poems are ingenious, entertaining, and wittier than anything else he has written, though none of this should blind one to their underlying seriousness. As the introductory poem makes clear, the world of *A.R.T.H.U.R.* ("Automatic Record Tabulator but Heuristically Unreliable Reasoner") is divided between "metal people" and "movers" – in other words, computers and human beings. This leads to some unusual perspectives: "Movers are constantly bending and running/Through a world of edges and obstacles. Cunning/Their reflexes, but cannot eliminate mourning." From the human point of view, the effect is one of "making strange," a process which is carried still further in those poems, like "Literary Criticism" and "Arthur takes a test for divergent thinking," which are concerned with the properties of language itself. Here, the game seems innocent enough; elsewhere, however, as in certain stories by Borges, there are hints of more frightening possibilities: the sense, for example, that new objects can be brought into existence by the mere fact that it is possible to name them. Hence the ending of "Arthur's reply," with its brilliant final pun: "We can try anything: just turn me on,/Feed me the facts, and wait for trial and terror."

Despite their apparent novelty, these and other recent poems seem to come from a firm and individual centre of experience which Lerner can by now take for granted. For some time past, he has given the impression of a poet who is working hard on himself, and whose sheer resourcefulness makes it difficult to predict his future work. What seems certain, however, is that he will continue to explore the paradoxes of language and human experience with his characteristic blend of compassion and ingenuity.

—Arthur Terry

LEVENSON, Christopher. Canadian. Born in London, 13 February 1934; naturalized Canadian citizen, 1973. Educated at Downing College, Cambridge, 1954–57, B.A. 1957; University of Iowa, Iowa City, M.A. 1970. Conscientious Objector: worked with the Friends Ambulance Unit International Service, 1952–54. Married Ursula Frieda Lina Fischer in 1958 (divorced), four sons. Taught at the International Quaker School, Eerde, Holland, 1957–58; English Lektor, University of Munster, West Germany, 1958–61; taught at Rodway Technical High School, Magotsfield, Gloucestershire, 1962–64. Since 1968, Member of the English Department, Carleton University, Ottawa. Editor, *Delta* magazine for two years. Recipient: Eric Gregory Award, 1960. Address: Department of English, Carleton University, Ottawa 1, Ontario, Canada.

PUBLICATIONS

Verse

New Poets 1959, with Iain Crichton Smith and Karen Gershon. London, Eyre and Spottiswoode, 1959.
Cairns. London, Chatto and Windus-Hogarth Press, 1969.
Stills. London, Chatto and Windus-Hogarth Press, 1972.
Into the Open. Ottawa, Golden Dog Press, 1977.

Other

Editor, *Poetry from Cambridge.* London, Fortune Press, 1958.

Translator, *Van Gogh*, by Abraham M. W. J. Hammacher. London, Spring, 1961.
Translator, *The Golden Casket: Chinese Novellas of Two Millennia* (translation from the German version). London, Allen and Unwin, 1965.
Translator, *The Leavetaking, and Vanishing Point* (novels), by Peter Weiss. London, Calder and Boyars, 1966.

* * *

A considerable body of verse by Christopher Levenson was published in volume form as long ago as 1959. It may be found in Edwin Muir's compilation for Eyre and Spottiswoode, *New Poets*. Nobody took sufficient notice at the time. Yet a discerning reader should have felt that here was a distinctive voice:

Exiled ambassadors of their heart's country, refugees
Carry their futures in one attache case....

In the distorting mirrors of my travels,
Where is tomorrow, now that yesterday
Is bartered for snapshots?...

Past the last city, on to the great plain,
The fevered air grows still, the lights behind us,
Thrown from a thousand scattered windows, blur:
We are alone....

It was no accident that the author called this early collection "In Transit." The word "transit" occurs throughout his work which is that of an exile observing the scenes he passes through:

They came here in transit, would not learn the language
Their children gabble, had not meant to stay,
But gradually drained of will, subsided into
The institutional gray....

This is a later poem – "Transit Camp" -- and the rhymes, though obtrusive, seem an attempt to variegate the obsessively post-Auden verse. But, outside his theme of displaced people, Levenson has little to say. His most famous poem, "Cairns," an elegy on Sylvia Plath, seems to me a rhetorical failure. His attempts to understand situations in personal lives such as divorce or drug-addiction are, though compassionate, clumsy. But, from his earliest verse to his latest, the plight of the wanderer evokes a characteristic Levenson cadence, at once memorable and haunting. This may well be his real contribution to poetry today:

I stand, tenebral, gazing down on a city
lost under smoke but luminous, to overhear
its many baffled night sounds, catch its drift

of hasty farewells, and sift through memory
a half-heard language I no longer know
in a remote country....

—Philip Hobsbaum

LEVERTOV, Denise. American. Born in Ilford, Essex, England, 24 October 1923; emigrated to the United States, 1948; naturalized, 1955. Educated privately. Served as a Nurse in World War II. Married the writer Mitchell Goodman in 1947; one son. Taught at the YM–YWHA Poetry Center, New York, 1964, City College of New York, 1965, and Vassar College, Poughkeepsie, New York, 1966–67; Visiting Professor, Drew University, Madison, New Jersey, 1965, University of California, Berkeley, 1969, Massachusetts Institute of Technology, Cambridge, 1969–70, University of Cincinnati, Spring 1973, and Tufts University, Medford, Massachusetts, 1973–74, 1974–75. Poetry Editor, *The Nation*, New York, 1961. Honorary Scholar, Radcliffe Institute for Independent Study, Cambridge, Massachusetts, 1964–66. Recipient: Bess Hokin Prize, 1960, Harriet Monroe Memorial Prize, 1964, Inez Boulton Prize, 1964, and Morton Dauwen Zabel Prize, 1965 (*Poetry*, Chicago); Longview Award, 1961; Guggenheim Fellowship, 1962; National Institute of Arts and Letters grant, 1966, 1968; Lenore Marshall Prize, 1976. D.Litt.: Colby College, Waterville, Maine, 1970; University of Cincinnati, 1973. Address, c/o New Directions, 333 Avenue of the Americas, New York, New York 10013, U.S.A.

PUBLICATIONS

Verse

The Double Image. London, Cresset Press, 1946.
Here and Now. San Francisco, City Lights, 1957.
Overland to the Islands. Highlands, North Carolina, Jargon, 1958.
5 Poems. San Francisco, White Rabbit Press, 1958.
With Eyes at the Back of Our Heads. New York, New Directions, 1959.
The Jacob's Ladder. New York, New Directions, 1961; London, Cape. 1965.
O Taste and See: New Poems. New York, New Directions, 1964.
City Psalm. Berkeley, California, Oyez, 1964.
Psalm Concerning the Castle. Madison, Wisconsin, Perishable Press, 1966.
The Sorrow Dance. New York, New Directions, 1967; London, Cape, 1968.
Penguin Modern Poets 9, with Kenneth Rexroth and William Carlos Williams. London, Penguin, 1967.
Three Poems. Mount Horeb, Wisconsin, Perishable Press, 1968.
A Tree Telling of Orpheus. Los Angeles, Black Sparrow Press, 1968.
The Cold Spring and Other Poems. New York, New Directions, 1968.
A Marigold from North Vietnam. New York, Albondocani Press-Ampersand Books, 1968.
Embroideries. Los Angeles, Black Sparrow Press, 1969.
Relearning the Alphabet. New York, New Directions, and London, Cape, 1970.
Summer Poems 1969. Berkeley, California, Oyez, 1970.
A New Year's Garland for My Students, MIT 1969–70. Mount Horeb, Wisconsin, Perishable Press, 1970.
To Stay Alive. New York, New Directions, 1971.
Footprints. New York, New Directions, 1972.
The Freeing of the Dust. New York, New Directions, 1975.
Chekhov on the West Heath. Andes, New York, Woomer Brotherson, 1977.
Life in the Forest. New York, New Directions, 1978.
Collected Earlier Poems 1940–1960. New York, New Directions, 1979.

Recording: *Today's Poets 3*, with others, Folkways.

Short Story

In the Night: A Story. New York, Albondocani Press, 1968.

Other

The Poet in the World (essays). New York, New Directions, 1973.
Conversations in Moscow. N.p., Hovey Street Press, 1973.

Editor, *Out of the War Shadow: An Anthology of Current Poetry*. New York, War Resisters League, 1967.
Editor and Translator, with Edward C. Dimock, Jr., *In Praise of Krishna: Songs from the Bengali*. New York, Doubleday, 1967; London, Cape, 1968.

Translator, *Selected Poems of Guillevic*. New York, New Directions, 1969.

Bibliography: *A Bibliography of Denise Levertov* by Robert A. Wilson, New York, Phoenix Bookshop, 1972.

Manuscript Collection: Southern Illinois University, Carbondale.

Critical Studies: *Denise Levertov* by Linda Wagner, New York, Twayne, 1967; *Out of the Vietnam Vortex* by James Mersmann, Lawrence, University Press of Kansas, 1974; Colman McCarthy, in *Washington Post* (Washington, D.C.), 1974; Hayden Carruth, in *Hudson Review* (New York), 1974; *In Her Own Province* edited by Linda Wagner, New York, New Directions, 1979.

* * *

Although she is frequently associated with the Projectivist or Black Mountain poets (the names derive from Charles Olson's influential essay on poetic composition, "Projectivist Verse," and from Black Mountain College, where a number of these poets were once students or teachers), including Robert Duncan, Charles Olson and Robert Creeley, Denise Levertov's career as a writer really has its origins in England. It was in London that she was born, of a Welsh mother and a father who was a Russian-Jew and also an Anglican clergyman. In an age of mass education, she was educated at home and read in her father's library. Her first book of poems, displaying talent but very much influenced by the somewhat vague, imprecise tendencies of a romanticism current in much British poetry of the World War II period, appeared in 1946; the following year she married the young American novelist Mitchell Goodman and later came to the United States to live, a move obviously decisive for her art.

It was not until a decade later that Levertov produced another collection – *Here and Now* – with the then new series of Pocket Poets launched by Lawrence Ferlinghetti. The change in her writing during the intervening years is complete; she had come under the commanding but liberating spell of William Carlos Williams, Ezra Pound, H.D., and doubtless others, the effect of which was to bring about an accurate concentration upon (to apply some words of Robert Creeley's) "the particulars of [her] own experience, the literal *things* of an immediate environment." Freer in form, her new poems are concrete, precise, intense, and shaped, the result of what must have been the most difficult kind of transformation since it meant a total alteration of sensibility and imagination. As she says in "Art," a version after Gautier, included in her next book – a book that firmly established her as one of the finest young poets in America: "The best work is made/from hard, strong materials,/obstinately precise –/the line of the poem, onyx, steel."

If these lines are accepted as an artistic credo – though she has written several different ones equally demanding – it is clear that Levertov has never swerved from them as an ideal, and has, moreover, seldom failed to come up to their measure in her actual practice. The material she now draws on for her poems is what presents itself within the context of living, the circle of her personal experience: "the authentic," as she says in a later poem, is the end of her aesthetic search. So she may write of a conversation overheard on a street in New York, an old man walking his dogs, the profound aspects of her marriage. In "A Window" the observation that among the multitude of city windows one continues to blaze brightly brings Levertov's imagination to the point of vision:

> Among a hundred windows shining
>   dully in the vast side
> of greater-than-palace number such-and-such
>   one burns
> these several years, each night
>   as if the room within were aflame.

But it would be a mistake to view her work as limited to the external world of objects, things, and other persons. Though she is concerned to rejoice in the reality that surrounds her, there is evident a very strong element of inwardness, even mysticism, in the poetry, so that the particulars of outward experience are met by responses from within; and quite a few poems focus solely on an inner space of consciousness where the images and revelations of dream or vision manifest themselves. While Levertov discloses no orthodox commitment of any sort in her work, it is hard not to see a strong religious impulse making itself felt there. Yet this impulse refuses to be separated from the poet's deep *human* compassion, an unbreakable attachment to earthly reality, veneration for and wonder at man's physical body, the endless variety of life, and a feeling that poetry, rising from mysterious, unfathomable sources in the poet's being, is inextricably bound up with all these aspects of existence. The last stanzas of "The Jacob's Ladder," from the volume of that title, illustrate in part this important side of her writing; here man and angels come together, and poetry struggles upward with its author as the spiritual creatures descend into the world:

> A stairway of sharp
> angles, solidly built.
> One sees that the angels must spring
> down from one step to the next, giving a little
> lift of the wings:
>
> and a man climbing
> must scrape his knees, and bring
> the grip of his hands into play. The cut stone
> consoles his groping feet. Wings brush past him.
> The poem ascends.

Levertov's recent work shows no lessening of her accomplishment, and *The Sorrow Dance* is remarkable for the elegiac sequence for her sister Olga and for the series of poems about the Viet Nam war. Two subsequent books are intensely preoccupied with questions of war, politics, and social change, though *Footprints*, while not abandoning such considerations, returns to aspects of the meditative and lyric manner evident before. Few poets of her generation can claim the depth and relevance, imaginative strength and careful craftsmanship so plain to see in Denise Levertov's writing.

—Ralph J. Mills, Jr.

LEVI, Peter (Chad Tigar). British. Born in Ruislip, Middlesex, 16 May 1931. Educated at Beaumont College, Berkshire, 1946–48; Campion Hall, Oxford, M.A. 1961. Married in

1977. Member, The Society of Jesus, 1948–77. Fellow, St. Catherine's College, and Lecturer, Christ Church, Oxford. Address: Austin's Farm, Stonesfield, Oxford, England.

PUBLICATIONS

Verse

Earthly Paradise. Privately printed, 1958.
The Gravel Ponds. London, Deutsch, and New York, Macmillan, 1970.
Orpheus Head. Privately printed, 1962.
Water, Rock, and Sand. London, Deutsch, and Philadelphia, Dufour, 1962.
The Shearwaters. Oxford, Allison, 1965.
Fresh Water, Sea Water. Llandeilo, Carmarthen, and London, Black Raven Press-Deutsch, 1965.
Pancakes for the Queen of Babylon: Ten Poems for Nikos Gatsos. London, Anvil Press Poetry, 1968.
Ruined Abbeys. London, Anvil Press Poetry, 1968.
Life Is a Platform. London, Anvil Press Poetry, 1971.
Death Is a Pulpit. London, Anvil Press Poetry, 1971.
Penguin Modern Poets 22, with Adrian Mitchell and John Fuller. London, Penguin, 1973.
Collected Poems 1955–1975. London, Anvil Press Poetry, 1976.
Five Ages. London, Anvil Press Poetry, 1978.

Novel

Head in the Soup. London, Constable, 1979.

Other

Beaumont 1861–1961. London, Deutsch, 1961.
The Light Garden of the Angel King: Journeys in Afghanistan. London, Collins, and Indianapolis, Bobbs Merrill, 1972.
John Clare and Thomas Hardy (lecture). London, Athlone Press, 1975.
The Noise Made by Poems. London, Anvil Press Poetry, 1977.

Editor, *The English Bible 1534–1859.* London, Constable, and Grand Rapids, Michigan, Eerdmans, 1974.
Editor, *Pope.* London, Penguin, 1974.

Translator, with Robin Milner-Gulland, *Selected Poems of Yevtushenko.* London, Penguin, and New York, Dutton, 1962; as *Poems Chosen by the Author*, London, Collins-Harvill, 1966; New York, Hill and Wang, 1967.
Translator, *Guide to Greece*, by Pausanias. London, Penguin, 2 vols., 1971.
Translator, *The Psalms.* London, Penguin, 1977.
Translator, *The Cellar*, by George Pavlopoulos. London, Anvil Press Poetry, 1977.

* * *

Peter Levi's poetry – like that of Wallace Stevens, with which it sometimes enters into a kind of dialogue – is often concerned with its own procedures; and in the early poem "The Tractor in Spring" Levi establishes a connection between his language and his theme which he has maintained throughout his work:

I want words whose existence is this,
the rough soil and the root work in them,
praising heaven I ever took for theme
this planet, its unnatural wishes,
common reason and human justice,
and growth of life, the last increase of time.

The words he finds for the abstractions of "reason" and "justice" often create a complex kind of interior landscape in which a mood is evoked, a scene described, in order to prompt some defining relation between the human consciousness and its embracing contingencies of nature and of history. In establishing this "definition," Levi uses, most characteristically, the mode of elegy. His favoured landscapes are seen through rain, wind, mist; he imagines himself "counting the pigeons in the snow-cold air,/listening to small voices of the other birds,/walking in the wind that sweeps this poem bare." And his sense of history is darkened by a central awareness of what he calls "the class divisions built into the language," and by the certainty that the humanist values represented by that language are in decay, that "in our lives Europe is saying goodnight." The poems move, then, ambivalently but honestly, between lament and gestures of encouragement. The long poem *Canticum*, for instance, which is, I think, one of Levi's major achievements, oscillates between exactly these poles when it attempts to feel out, in language, what a world radically alternative to the one we must live in might be like:

Not one by one but everyone breaks in,
we shall come back with armfuls of lilac
and the crooked trees behind our kitchens
will blossom again. It is the future
which says death to us and which we love.

The desire to discover alternatives in poetic language itself to what Levi sees as the debilitation of middle-class English has prompted experimentation with kinds of writing not normally handled nowadays by serious writers in the English tradition, and especially with a kind of gentle surrealism inherited largely from modern Greek poetry. Levi has described this element in the work of George Pavlopoulos, which he has translated, as "a glitter on the skin of his poems," and this might also be said of Levi himself: the surrealism of his poetic sequence *Pancakes for the Queen of Babylon* never entirely loses touch with the real and avoids the more obvious dottinesses of the tradition as it has previously manifested itself in English. This sequence, and several others, such as "Thirty Ways of Drowning in the Sea," "Rivers," and "Five Ages of a Poet," are, in a poetry that depends so much on the establishing of mood and tone, on the creation of *context*, among Levi's most important work.

The recent poetry displays, I think, a deepened strength and authority, a sureness in his own voice and strategies; but shows also a striking out in some interesting new directions. There is a collection of vignettes, like "Officers and Gentlemen," which set a particular social class in the ironic perspectives of history; there is a handful of finely achieved, tenderly dignified love poems; and there is an altogether new note struck in the grotesquerie of the "Pigs" sequence, which I find immensely seductive:

Pigs refuse pork sausages
coated in chocolate. They do sniff them.
Sows murder piglets.
What has some smell of incest
is not sheer cold horror.
Who write this, an old silver-bristle.
I am brutish enough.
They are brutish enough.

Peter Levi's is a unique voice in contemporary English poetry; there is absolutely no one remotely like him. His sadness, his humour, his preposterously resilient assertiveness ("An easy smell blowing about a hill/is the beginning of the truth about life," for instance) are intoxicating. His achievement is one to be glad about.

—Neil Corcoran

LEVINE, Philip. American. Born in Detroit, Michigan, 10 January 1928. Educated at Wayne State University, Detroit, B.A. 1950, M.A. 1955; University of Iowa, Iowa City, M.F.A. 1957; Stanford University, California (Fellowship in Poetry, 1957). Married Frances Artley in 1954; three sons. Since 1958, Member of the Department of English, California State University, Fresno. Elliston Professor of Poetry, University of Cincinnati, 1976; Poet-in-Residence, National University of Australia, Canberra, Summer 1978. Recipient: San Francisco Foundation Joseph Henry Jackson Award, 1961; Chapelbrook Award, 1968; National Endowment for the Arts grant, 1969, 1970 (refused), 1976; Frank O'Hara Prize (*Poetry*, Chicago), 1972; National Institute of Arts and Letters grant, 1973; Lenore Marshall Prize, 1976. Address: 4549 North Van Ness Avenue, Fresno, California 93704, U.S.A.

PUBLICATIONS

Verse

On the Edge. Iowa City, Stone Wall Press, 1963.
Silent in America: Vivas for Those Who Failed. Iowa City, Shaw Avenue Press, 1965.
Not This Pig. Middletown, Connecticut, Wesleyan University Press, 1968.
Five Detroits. Santa Barbara, California, Unicorn Press, 1970.
Thistles: A Poem Sequence. London, Turret, 1970.
Pili's Wall. Santa Barbara, California, Unicorn Press, 1971.
Red Dust. Santa Cruz, California, Kayak, 1971.
They Feed They Lion. New York, Atheneum, 1972.
1933. New York, Atheneum, 1974.
New Season. Port Townsend, Washington, Graywolf Press, 1975.
On the Edge and Over: Poems Old, Lost, and New. Oakland, Cloud Marauder Press, 1976.
The Names of the Lost. New York, Atheneum, 1976.
7 Years from Somewhere. New York, Atheneum, 1979.
Ashes: Poems New and Collected. New York, Atheneum, 1979.

Recording: *The Poetry and Voice of Philip Levine*, Caedmon, 1976.

Other

Editor, with Henri Coulette, *Character and Crisis: A Contemporary Reader.* New York, McGraw Hill, 1966.
Editor, and Translator, with Ernesto Trejo, *Tarumba: The Selected Poems of Jaime Sabines.* San Francisco, Two Windows Press, 1979.

Critical Studies: by X. J. Kennedy, in *Poetry* (Chicago), 1964; Robert Dana, in *North American Review* (Mt. Vernon, Iowa), 1964; Hayden Carruth, in *Hudson Review* (New York), 1968; "Personally, I'd Rather Be in Fresno" by Stuart Peterfreund, in *New: American and Canadian Poetry 15* (Trumansburg, New York), May 1971; "Borges and Strand, Weak Henry, Philip Levine" by James McMichael, in *Southern Review* (Baton Rouge, Louisiana), Winter 1972; "Interview with Philip Levine," in *American Poetry Review* (Philadelphia), i, 1, 1972; " 'The True and Earthly Prayer': Philip Levine's Poetry" by Ralph J. Mills, Jr., in *American Poetry Review* (Philadelphia), iii, 2, 1974; "The Burned Essential Oil: The Poetry of Philip Levine" by Charles Molesworth, in *Hollins Critic* (Virginia), December 1975; "Philip Levine" by Calvin Bedient, in *Sewanee Review* (Tennessee), Spring 1976; "New Poems" by Jay Parini, in *Poetry* (Chicago), August 1977; "Bringing It Home" by Stephen Yenser, in *Parnassus* (New York), Fall–Winter 1977; "The Poetry of Anarchism" by Paul Bernard, in *Marxist Perspectives*, Summer 1979.

Philip Levine comments:

It's difficult for me to talk about my poetry because I'm mainly aware of how much it's changed over the years. I began writing when I was about 19; I was outraged by America, and I thought poetry would help me communicate that outrage. I thought I'd write these poems, publish them, and people would shape up or change or love me. Well, it didn't happen that way, and by the time I tried to publish anything I'd written I was 26 years old and had fallen in love with the beast itself, the poem. My first great love was Stephen Crane; that lasted a week; then Eliot, another few weeks; Dylan Thomas, Auden, Yeats, and many others until I came across Williams, and he stuck. I've written in a variety of styles and ways: traditional meters, which dominate my first book, then syllabics, and the rest, and for the past several years in free verse mainly. Some themes have remained through the 25 years: I try to pay homage to the people who taught me my life was a holy thing, who convinced me that my formal education was a lie: these were the men and women I met as an industrial worker and bum in America; they were mainly Southerners – so many of whom had come to Detroit in my boyhood to find work – and they were closer, I believe, to some great truths about people, to the truth that we are the children of God, and that we were meant to come into this world and live as best we could with the beasts and the trees and plants and to leave the place with our love and respect for it intact, and to leave it our selfs. These people, both Black and white, were mainly rural people, and the horror of the modern world was clearer to them than to me, and the beauty and value of the world was something they knew in a way I did not, first hand. So, I learned from them, and I owe them my hope and maybe more. They're in my poems from the start, and so are the animals and plants they loved and showed me. The magic and mystery of that city, Detroit, its immense energy and its carnival atmosphere during WWII and other cities I came to know later, especially Barcelona. My childhood began to dominate my poetry as early as 1972, and in the book *1933* I think I at last laid it to rest, at least for a while. Since then my work has become more concerned with the larger family to which I belong, not only that of my children and my forebears but all those who have suffered birth and death in this world. My religious anarchism at times overwhelms me, and my writing becomes more frankly romantic – that is it asserts defiantly the boundless possibilities of the human, the unique holiness of animals and plants. If I run the risk of sounding like an idiot, so be it. I am 51 and strong as a horse; much of the time I write well, just how well we'll see.

* * *

Though Philip Levine's work has appeared widely since the mid-fifties, it was not till the publication of *Not This Pig* (1968) that he reached the large generally appreciative audience he most certainly deserves. Unremittingly grim, yet as hard on himself as on all that troubles him, he creates a virtual rogue's gallery caught compassionately at dramatic moments of decline: peopling his poems are drunks, draft-dodgers, boxers, Hell's Angels, midgets, poor neighbors. The following passage from the important sequence "Silent in America" will give some idea of his degree of involvement as well as his method:

For a black man whose
name I have forgotten who danced
all night at Chevy
Gear & Axle,
for that great stunned Pole
who laughed when he called me Jew
Boy, for the ugly
who had no chance,
the beautiful in
body, the used and the unused,
those who had courage
and those who quit – ...
all my energy,
all my care for
those I cannot touch
runs on my breath like a sigh....

The poet writes often of his family, as the guilty father/husband whose vulnerability threatens the lot of them. Such poems, invariably tender, may be his most moving, and there is at least one which has significance for the way it relates the poet and his family to their world, "The Morning after the Storm," the third section of which goes:

The winds and the dogs
brought down the garbage.
Ostrichlike, my wife picks
at the tidbits on the lawn.

The wet winds gust,
and her night clothes flap around her –
in her 40th year
she stoops and pecks and clears

our little yard;
she turns away from nothing,
grounds, bottles, bones,
egg shells, animal fat,

the splintered plastic guns,
the burned-out bulbs
and swollen batteries,
all the refuse of this house.

The sky clenches again.
Our three sons grow toward war.
Child of the land, Indian,
you cannot live here any more.

In recent years Philip Levine has travelled, particularly in Spain, and what is most striking about the poems that have come of that experience is that they display the same toughness with self and, when called for, an equal degree of compassion for others. Whether in Fresno or Barcelona the poet is never less than fully human, and one finds oneself admiring the man as much as the poet.

—Lucien Stryk

LEVIS, Larry. American. Born in Fresno, California, 30 September 1946. Educated at California State University, Fresno, 1964–68, B.A. 1968; Syracuse University, New York (Ward Fellow), 1968–70, M.A. 1970; University of Iowa, Iowa City (Teaching Fellow), 1972–74, Ph.D. 1974. Married Marcia Southwick in 1975; one son. Teaching Assistant, Syracuse University, 1969; Instructor, California State University, Fresno, 1970; Lecturer, California State University, Los Angeles, 1970–72; Visiting Lecturer, University of Iowa, 1972. Since 1974, Assistant Professor, University of Missouri, Columbia. Recipient: YM–YWHA Discovery Award, 1971; National Endowment for the Arts Fellowship, 1973; Lamont Poetry Selection Award, 1976. Address: 1024 Crestland Avenue, Columbia, Missouri 65201, U.S.A.

PUBLICATIONS

Verse

Wrecking Crew. Pittsburgh, University of Pitsburgh Press, 1972.
The Rain's Witness. Iowa City, Southwick Press, 1975.
The Afterlife. Iowa City, University of Iowa Press, 1977.

Larry Levis comments:

Most of my poems are bound to specific objects, places, persons, or circumstances, and these are usually places (like Fresno) or people who are part of my experience. This is not to say that I rely only upon my life or the facts of my life. The most important thing I have tried to learn as a poet is to follow and to trust my own imagination. Poets who continue to influence my work: García Lorca, Zbigniew Herbert, Philip Levine, and a number of poets in my own generation.

* * *

Bedizened as he is with prizes, Larry Levis skilfully – and predictably – represents the style of poetry currently being taught and valued in American universities, those new power centers of the literary establishment. It's a sort of diluted, passionless surrealism, derivative of South American originals. There's a characteristic voice in which this poetry gets read by its authors, rising and falling in a special "holy" register, something between a chant and a lilt, far removed at any rate from speech, whether casual or passionate. The syntax is predominantly paratactic, the rhythms enervated and limp, the diction carefully flat, the imagery dominated by similes, and the whole frequently (to my instinct) ersatz.

Levis shows little development between *Wrecking Crew* and *The Afterlife*. True, there's a "pop" imagery of violence (rape, blood, wounds, etc.) in the first book that drops away, and there's what an admirer might call a syntactic advance in the second. (It mainly consists in asking rhetorical questions, as here: "Is it raining on a lame mare/About to be shot?/The horse goes down quickly ..." etc., where if you answer a reasonable "Probably not" to the question, the rest of the poem collapses.) In both books we get a similar range of poems. There's the imitation of Roethke at his most cloyingly *faux naif*: "Maybe the dead know the ant's troubles,/or the debts snails pay out with their bodies ..."; "Is the snow/a birth?/How can a root/stand itself?" In both books we get lots of Robert Bly brand epiphanies, like "Driving East," which I quote in its entirety: "For miles,/the snow is on all sides of me,/waiting.//I feel like/a lot of empty cattle yards,/my hinges swing open to the wind." What is this but a pathetic fallacy plus the imposition of the poet's ego on the landscape? What for the reader but an invitation to indulgence in vague and facile feelings?

If one turns to the poems about people for relief, one finds little enough reward in either book. Here he is on his home town:

In the town of 20 pool cues,...
the men laughed,
they stole cars and left them in ditches, smoldering.
Their wives, spitting at irons, never looked up.
They grew older.

The characteristic reliance on plurals to impart a factitious universality instead deprives the referents of any but an ad hoc existence: these men and women are invented (we feel) to provide feelings for writer and reader, they don't exist in their own right. Again, "This poem so like the hour/when ... the calm/professor burns another book...." Who can believe in this professor, so clearly a construct of paradoxes contrived for the sake of a mere immediate frisson? Even when the person is singular and presumably as real as Levis is, the exoticism of the decor and the careful flatness of the would-be resonant statements produce what I can only read as self-parody.

Very little evaluative criticism of current poetry gets published in America. In the new poetic stakes, every contender wins. Secure with his awards and publications, Levis can surely withstand – and deserves – close inspection by non-members of the club. He is no worse than several dozen of his contemporaries, equally or more deeply entrenched. His career will bear watching, but on the evidence of these two books, it will tell us more about "lit biz" than about literature.

—Seamus Cooney

L'HEUREUX, John (Clarke). American. Born in South Hadley, Massachusetts, 26 October 1934. Educated at the National Academy of Theatre Arts, 1952; College of the Holy Cross, Worcester, Massachusetts, 1952–54; Boston College, A.B. 1959, M.A. in philosophy 1960, M.A. in English 1963; Harvard University, Cambridge, Massachusetts. Married Joan Polston in 1971. Entered the Society of Jesus, 1954; ordained a priest, 1966; requested laicization, 1970; married with Vatican approval, 1971. Writer-in-Residence, Georgetown University, Washington, D.C., 1965; and Regis College, Weston, Massachusetts, 1970; Visiting Lecturer, Tufts University, Medford, Massachusetts, 1971; Visiting Professor, Harvard University, 1973. Since 1973, Associate Professor of English, Stanford University, California. Staff Editor, 1968–70, and since 1970, Contributing Editor, *The Atlantic*, Boston. Agent: Lynn Nesbit, I.C.M., 40 West 57th Street, New York, New York 10019. Address: Department of English, Stanford University, Stanford, California 94305, U.S.A.

PUBLICATIONS

Verse

Quick as Dandelions. New York, Doubleday, 1964.
Rubrics for a Revolution. New York, Macmillan, 1967.
One Eye and a Measuring Rod. New York, Macmillan, 1968.
No Place for Hiding: New Poems. New York, Doubleday, 1971.

Novels

Tight White Collar. New York, Doubleday, 1972.

The Clang Birds. New York, Macmillan, 1972.
Jessica Fayer. New York, Macmillan, 1976.

Short Stories

Family Affairs. New York, Doubleday, 1974.

Other

Picnic in Babylon: A Jesuit Priest's Journal, 1963–1967. New York, Macmillan, 1967.

Manuscript Collection: Boston University.

* * *

A remark that John L'Heureux made in *Picnic in Babylon: A Jesuit Priest's Journal, 1963–1967* gives some insight into what he wishes to do in poetry. Stressing the harm done to American poetry by Poe's jingles and Whitman's "over developed ego," he said that "with the singular exception of Emily Dickinson there is no American poetry until 1900."

What one finds in L'Heureux's poetry, in other words, is a sensibility compatible with the interior religious struggles described in Dickinson and in her admirers among twentieth century poets. In a sequence called "The Problem of God," he expresses something of the impatience Dickinson felt toward divinity: "The trouble with Christ is/he always comes at the wrong time." Yet, as one might suspect, the quarrel between L'Heureux and God is merely temporary. In fact, in the early poems their relationship (in "Death of a Man" and "The Unlikely Prophet") and his familiarity with God's chosen (in "The Journey" and "Joseph") appear too comfortable to be believed.

He is essentially a poet of celebration and of reconciliation, as James Dickey has said, who goes "eagerly toward events and people, open-handed and open-hearted." The final section of L'Heureux's poem, "The Death of Kings," an epitaph for John F. Kennedy, conveys his essential faith in the nature of things:

The end is vision:
stones roll back and wonder cracks
like morning on a disbelieving world.
No Lazarus standing gray and stupid
in his linen bands, but we – harlequins
and fools – stride the fired air
with feet of bronze. Laughter
is our music. Let the earth tremble.

L'Heureux's strength of feeling and wit as a lyric poet exhibit themselves most fully in his recent poems, as in "The Command" and "Narcissus," whose passion and self-knowledge indicate a much wider range of feeling than the earlier conventionally religious poems. And in "A Pleasing Fragrance," the best of the old and the new directions come together:

He was crowing
on the rooftop
of his sanctity
when the house burned
down. Crazy old cock
larger than death

he thought
before the conflagration.

...
And so he's gone,
poor roasted soul,

in blazing glory.
He made, despite himself,
a good holocaust.

In his latest books, both poetry and fiction, L'Heureux recounts his struggle with and ultimate decision to leave the Jesuits. But the religious pilgrimage continues, and in poems such as "Incarnation" and "Foolsgold" it remains as much of a preoccupation as ever.

—Michael True

LIEBERMAN, Laurence (James). Born in Detroit, Michigan, 16 February 1935. Educated at the University of Michigan, Ann Arbor (Hopwood Award, 1958), B.A. 1956, M.A. in English, 1958; University of California, Berkeley. Married Bernice Braun in 1956; one son and two daughters. Former Poetry Editor, *Orange County Illustrated* and *Orange County Sun*, California. Taught at Orange Coast College, Costa Mesa, California, 1960–64; College of the Virgin Islands, St. Thomas, 1964–68. Associate Professor of English, 1968–70, and since 1970, Professor of English, University of Illinois, Urbana. Poetry Reviewer, *Yale Review*, 1968–74. Since 1971, Poetry Editor, University of Illinois Press. Recipient: Yaddo Fellowship, 1963, 1967; Huntington Hartford Foundation Fellowship, 1964; National Endowment for the Arts grant, 1966; University of Illinois Center for Advanced Study grant, 1971. Address: Department of English, University of Illinois, Urbana, Illinois 61801, U.S.A.

PUBLICATIONS

Verse

The Unblinding: Poems. New York, Macmillan, 1968.
The Osprey Suicides. New York, Macmillan, and London, Collier Macmillan, 1973.
God's Measurements. New York, Macmillan, 1980.

Other

Unassigned Frequencies: American Poetry in Review 1964–77. Urbana, University of Illinois Press, 1977.

Editor, *The Achievement of James Dickey: A Comprehensive Selection of His Poems with a Critical Introduction.* Chicago, Scott Foresman, 1968.

Critical Studies: "Fool, Thou Poet" by Vernon Young, in *Hudson Review* (New York) Winter 1973–74; "Tough Scarskins" by John R. Cooley, in *Modern Poetry Studies* (Buffalo), Winter 1974; "All's a Mirroring" by James Ballowe, in *Mississippi Valley Review*, Spring 1974; "Generous Props" by Dave Smith, in *Counter/Measures 3*, 1974; "Actions Outdone" by Richard Johnson, in *Parnassus* (New York), Fall–Winter 1974; "Poems and Pictures" by David Quemada, in *New Letters* (Kansas City), March 1975.

Laurence Lieberman comments:

My first and second volumes of poetry, *The Unblinding* and *The Osprey Suicides*, dealt principally with the four years I spent in St. Thomas (1964–68), exploring life in the Caribbean and the underwater world of the coral reefs as their primary subject. The underwater cycle of poems spanned two books, much as I expect my cycle of poems in progress about Japan to span the next two books. *God's Measurements* was completed this year, and it contains roughly half of the poems I plan to write about Japan, where I spent a year on a travelling fellowship, 1971–2.

* * *

While many of the younger American poets who made their literary debuts in the latter part of the 1960's – that is, in the generation following that of Ginsberg, Bly, Wright, and Kinnell – have developed in directions which enable us to place them in one or another of the large categories of recent poetic tendencies in America, Laurence Lieberman has preferred to proceed on his own. His earlier work, gathered in *The Unblinding*, offers ample evidence of the gifts he possesses, a good ear, a sensitivity to the rich potentialities of diction, and an acute awareness of the extraordinary complexity of the most commonplace event or act of observation. There is a deep impulse in his writing to unfold by means of a subtle and intricate proliferation of language the covert aspects and angles of experience as he envisages it. Words, then, become the keys for unlocking the structure and the details of what the poet sees or undergoes; but in this process words are themselves an integral element of the perception. Hence a density of language in Lieberman's poems which seems at times elaborate, even ornamental, though the latter is true only in weaker pieces.

With the appearance of his second collection, *The Osprey Suicides*, Lieberman makes decisive strides into maturity and accomplishment. Sometimes the early poems failed for lack of a considerable enough subject or theme, one commensurate with the author's talents; but the new poems reveal a forceful grip on substantial materials and a marvelous working out of their possibilities. Like Roethke and James Dickey, who are perhaps closest to him in influence, Lieberman is frequently concerned with nature, though very much in his own way, creating through a full, beautifully textured line a feeling of the intimate relation between man and environment, the poet and the immediate context of the mysterious, fluctuating, complicated existence in which he finds himself. Whether concentrated on nature or other kinds of experience, Lieberman's poems are written with great skill and strong imagination, the result of careful attention to craft and to a fascinated vision of the world.

—Ralph J. Mills, Jr.

LIFSHIN, Lyn (Diane). American. Born in Burlington, Vermont, 12 July 1942. Educated at Syracuse University, New York, B.A. 1961; University of Vermont, Burlington, M.A. 1963; Brandeis University, Waltham, Massachusetts; State University of New York, Albany; Bread Loaf School of English, Vermont. Married Eric Lifshin in 1963. Teaching Fellow, State University of New York, Albany, 1964–66; Educational Television Writer, Schenectady, New York, 1966; Writing Consultant, Mental Health Department, Albany, New York, 1967; Instructor, State University of New York, Cobleskill, 1968, 1970. Recipient: Yaddo Fellowship, 1970, 1971; MacDowell Fellowship, 1973; Creative Arts Public Service Award, 1976. Address: 2142 Apple Tree Lane, Niskayuna, New York 12309, U.S.A.

PUBLICATIONS

Verse

Why Is the House Dissolving. San Francisco, Open Skull Press, 1968.
Femina 2. Oshkosh, Wisconsin, Abraxas Press, 1970.
Leaves and Night Things. West Lafayette, Indiana, Baby John Press, 1970.
Black Apples. Trumansburg, New York, Crossing Press, 1971; revised edition, 1973.
Tentacles, Leaves. Belmont, Massachusetts, Hellric Press, 1972.
Moving by Touch. Traverse City, Michigan, Cotyledon Press, 1972.
Lady Lyn. Milwaukee, Morgan Press, 1972.
Mercurochrome Sun Poems. Tacoma, Washington, Charis Press, 1972.
I'd Be Jeanne Moreau. Milwaukee, Morgan Press, 1972.
Love Poems. Durham, New Hampshire, Zahir Press, 1972.
Forty Days, Apple Nights. Milwaukee, Morgan Press, 1973.
Audley End Poems. Long Beach, California, Mag Press, 1973.
The First Week Poems. Plum Island, Massachusetts, Zahir Press, 1973.
Museum. Albany, New York, Conspiracy Press, 1973.
All the Women Poets I Ever Liked Didn't Hate Their Fathers. St. Petersburg, Florida, Konglomerati, 1973.
The Old House on the Croton. San Lorenzo, California, Shameless Hussy Press, 1973.
Poems. Minneapolis, Northstone, 1974.
Selected Poems. Trumansburg, New York, Crossing Press, 1974.
Upstate Madonna: Poems 1970–1974. Trumansburg, New York, Crossing Press, 1974.
Thru Blue Post, New Mexico. Fredonia, New York, Basilik, 1974.
Blue Fingers. Milwaukee, Shelter Press, 1974.
Plymouth Women. Milwaukee, Morgan Press, 1974.
Shaker House Poems. Chatham, New York, Sagarin Press, 1974.
Old House Poems. Santa Barbara, California, Capra Press, 1975.
North Poems. Niskayuna, New York, Morgan Press, 1976.
Naked Charm. N.p., Fireweed Press, 1976.
Paper Apples. Stockton, California, Wormwood, 1976.
Some Madonna Poems. Buffalo, White Pine Press, 1976.
More Waters. Cincinnati, Waters, 1977.
Offered by Owner. Cambridge, New York, Natalie Slohn, 1978.
Leaning South. New York, Red Dust, 1978.
Glass. Niskayuna, New York, Morgan Press, 1978.
Early Plymouth Women. Niskayuna, New York, Morgan Press, 1978.
Crazy Arms. N.p., Mati, 1978.
Lips on That Blue Rain. N.p., Lion's Breath, 1978.
35 Sundays. N.p., Mati, 1979.
More Naked Charm. N.p., Peter Schneider Press, 1979.
Want Ads. Niskayuna, New York, Morgan Press, 1979.
Doctors. N.p., Mudborn, 1979.

Other

Editor, *Tangled Vines: A Collection of Mother and Daughter Poems.* Boston, Beacon Press, 1978.

Bibliography: by Marvin Malone, in *Wormwood Review* (Stockton, California), xii, 3, 1971.

Critical Studies: by Bill Katz, in *Library Journal* (New York), June 1971, and December 1972; Carol Rainey, in *Road Apple Review* (Albuquerque, New Mexico), Summer–Fall

1971; Victor Contoski, in *Northeast* (La Crosse, Wisconsin), Fall–Winter 1971–72; James Naiden, in *Minneapolis Star*, 18 April 1972; Dave Etter, in *December* (West Springs, Illinois), 1972; "Lyn Lifshin" by Jim Evans, in *Windless Orchard* (Fort Wayne, Indiana), Summer 1972; Eric Mottram, in *Little Magazine* (New York), Summer–Fall 1972; *New York Times Book Review*, 18 December 1978.

Lyn Lifshin comments:

I'm usually better at doing something than talking about how and why I do it. One time I spent days trying to say how I wanted the words to be connected to touch the reader's body. Somehow. Except that sounded strange and so I tore it up.... It seems to me that the poem has to be sensual (not necessarily sexual, tho that's ok too) before it can be anything else. So rhythm matters a lot to me, most, or at least first. Before images even. I want whoever looks at, whoever eats the poem to feel the way old ebony feels at 4 o'clock in a cold Van Cortlandt mansion, or the smell of lemons in a strange place, or skin.

Words that I like to hear other people say the poems are are: strong, tight, real, startling, tough, tender, sexy, physical, controlled – that they celebrate (Carol Rainey), reflect joy in every aspect of being a woman (James Naiden).

I always steal things I like from people: other poets, especially from blues, old black and country blues rhythms (after most readings, people come and ask how, where I started reading the way I do; another mystery, really). So I was glad to have Dave Etter say that *Black Apples* "comes on like a stack of Cannonball Adderley records, blowing cool, blowing hot, sometimes lyrical and sweet, sometimes hard bop, terse and tough."

* * *

In the relatively short time that she has been writing, Lyn Lifshin has developed her talent in ways that extend the significance of her work. Her poems are, characteristically, brief lyrics, often imagistic, that move towards sudden, revelatory metamorphoses. Her earlier poems focus on personal experience. She writes with a hard, disarming candor about sexual love, its familiarities and the powerful transforming element in which it occurs. Sometimes there are visions of fulfillment: "how far away/are the mountains/he kept/saying/could we touch them." More often, there are images of absence and vacancy: "every/time I came/close to you/the place that/was you/changed to air." She uses phantasmagoric imagery to evoke the horror of everyday domestic life in which people have no contact with one another. Her style is deceptively casual: sometimes subversively prosaic, sometimes cool and flamboyant.

Her more recent poems involve a shift from contemporary ghosts and ruins to the American colonial past, in the "Old House on the Croton" poems, and to pre-Columbian Indian culture, in *Museum*. These new poems are even more spare than her personal poems, and their effect is to suggest that those personal poems are ultimately less about contemporary life than about a horror that intrudes, as she writes of the Old House on the Croton, upon the most domestic life: "this must have been the last/room to think of war in." And here, as in the personal poems, there issues from within that horror and vulnerability something tough and sustaining. Her enumeration of the sacrifices of the Indian poor, for example, quietly evokes the ferocity of the human will to survive: "the poor/cocoa corn/flour wool or/a plucked eyelash."

—Jerry Paris

LINDSAY, (John) Maurice. Scottish. Born in Glasgow, 21 July 1918. Educated at Glasgow Academy, 1928–36; Scottish National Academy of Music, now the Royal Scottish Academy of Music, Glasgow, 1936–39. Served in the Cameronians (Scottish Rifles) at the Staff College, Camberley, and in the War Office during World War II. Married Aileen Joyce Gordon in 1946; one son and three daughters. Drama Critic, *Scottish Daily Mail*, Edinburgh, 1946–47; Music Critic, *The Bulletin*, Glasgow, 1946–60; Editor, *Scots Review*, 1949–50. Programme Controller, 1961–62, Production Controller, 1962–64, and Features Executive and Chief Interviewer, 1964–67, Border Television, Carlisle. Since 1964, Editor, with Douglas Young, Saltire Modern Poets series, Edinburgh; since 1976, Editor, *The Scottish Review.* Since 1967, Director, Scottish Civic Trust, Glasgow. Recipient: Atlantic-Rockefeller Award, 1946. Address: 7 Milton Hill, Milton, Dumbarton, Dunbartonshire, Scotland.

PUBLICATIONS

Verse

The Advancing Day. Privately printed, 1940.
Perhaps To-morrow. Oxford, Blackwell, 1941.
Predicament. Oxford, Alden Press, 1942.
No Crown for Laughter. London, Fortune Press, 1943.
The Enemies of Love: Poems 1941–1945. Glasgow, Maclellan, 1946.
Selected Poems. Edinburgh, Oliver and Boyd, 1947.
Hurlygush: Poems in Scots. Edinburgh, Serif, 1948.
At the Wood's Edge. Edinburgh, Serif, 1950.
Ode for St. Andrews Night and Other Poems. Edinburgh, New Alliance, 1951.
The Exiled Heart: Poems 1941–1956, edited by George Bruce. London, Hale, 1957.
Snow Warning and Other Poems. Arundel, Sussex, Linden Press, 1962.
One Later Day and Other Poems. London, Brookside Press, 1964.
This Business of Living. Preston, Lancashire, Akros, 1971.
Comings and Goings. Preston, Lancashire, Akros, 1971.
Selected Poems 1942–1972. London, Hale, 1973.
The Run from Life: More Poems 1942–1972. Burford, Oxfordshire, Cygnet Press, 1975.
Walking Without an Overcoat: Poems 1972–76. London, Hale, 1977.
Collected Poems., edited by Alexander Scott. Edinburgh, Paul Harris, 1979.

Plays

Fingal and Comala (produced Braemar, 1953; London, 1958).
The Abbott of Drimmock, music by Thea Musgrave (produced London, 1957).
The Decision, music by Thea Musgrave (produced London, 1967). London, Chester, 1967.

Other

A Pocket Guide to Scottish Culture. Glasgow, Maclellan, 1947.
The Scottish Renaissance. Edinburgh, Serif, 1949.
The Lowlands of Scotland: Glasgow and the North, Edinburgh and the South. London Hale, 2 vols., 1953–56; revised edition, 1973–77.
Robert Burns: The Man, His Work, The Legend. London, MacGibbon and Kee, 1954; revised edition, 1968, 1978; New York, St. Martin's Press, 1979.
Dunoon: The Gem of the Clyde Coast. Dunoon, Town Council of Dunoon, 1954.
Clyde Waters: Variations and Diversions on a Theme of Pleasure. London, Hale, 1958.

The Burns Encyclopaedia. London, Hutchinson, 1959; revised edition, 1970.
Killochan Castle, with David Somervell. Derby, Pilgrim Press, 1960.
By Yon Bonnie Banks: A Gallimaufry. London, Hutchinson, 1961.
The Discovery of Scotland: Based on Accounts of Foreign Travellers from the Thirteenth to the Eighteenth Centuries. London, Hale, and New York, Roy, 1964.
Environment: A Basic Human Right. Glasgow, Scottish Civic Trust, 1968.
The Eye Is Delighted: Some Romantic Travellers in Scotland. London, Muller, 1970.
Portrait of Glasgow. London, Hale, 1972.
Robin Philipson. Edinburgh, Edinburgh University Press, 1976.
History of Scottish Literature. London, Hale, 1977.
Lowland Scottish Villages. London, Hale, 1979.
Francis George Scott and the Scottish Renaissance. Edinburgh, Paul Harris, 1979.

Editor, *Poetry Scotland One, Two, Three.* Glasgow, Maclellan, 1943–46.
Editor, *Sailing To-morrow's Seas: An Anthology of New Poems.* London, Fortune Press, 1944.
Editor, *Modern Scottish Poetry: An Anthology of the Scottish Renaissance, 1920–1945.* London, Faber, 1946; revised edition, 1966.
Editor, *A Pocket Guide to Scottish Culture.* Glasgow, Maclellan, 1947.
Editor, with Fred Urquhart, *No Scottish Twilight: New Scottish Stories.* Glasgow, Maclellan, 1947.
Editor, *Selected Poems of Sir Alexander Gray.* Glasgow, Maclellan, 1948.
Editor, *Poems*, by Sir David Lyndsay. Edinburgh, Oliver and Boyd, 1948.
Editor, with Hugh MacDiarmid, *Poetry Scotland Four.* Edinburgh, Serif, 1949.
Editor, with Helen Cruickshank, *Selected Poems of Marion Angus.* Edinburgh, Serif, 1950.
Editor, *John Davidson: A Selection of His Poems.* London, Hutchinson, 1961.
Editor, with others, *Scottish Poetry One* to *Nine.* Edinburgh, Edinburgh University Press, 6 vols., 1966–72; Glasgow, University of Glasgow Press, 1 vol., 1974; Manchester, Carcanet Press, 2 vols., 1975–76.
Editor, *A Book of Scottish Verse*, revised edition. London, Oxford University Press, 1967.
Editor, *Scotland: An Anthology.* London, Hale, 1974; New York, St. Martin's Press, 1975.
Editor, *Modern Scottish Poetry: An Anthology of the Scottish Renaissance 1925–1975.* Manchester, Carcanet Press, 1976.
Editor, *As I Remember: Ten Scottish Authors Recall How Writing Began for Them.* London, Hale, 1979.

Manuscript Collections: National Library of Scotland, Edinburgh; Edinburgh University Library.

Critical Studies: Preface by George Bruce to *The Exiled Heart: Poems 1941–1956*, 1957; Alexander Scott, in *Whither Scotland?*, edited by Duncan Glen, London, Gollancz, 1971; *Studies in Scottish Literature, 1971*, Columbia, University of South Carolina Press, 1973; "A Different Way of Being Right: The Poetry of Maurice Lindsay" by Donald Campbell, in *Akros* (Preston, Lancashire), April 1974; Introduction by Alexander Scott to *Collected Poems*, 1979.

Maurice Lindsay comments:

I began writing because, from an early age, I wanted to try to retrieve some tangible aspects from my own experience of living: in other words, to probe the nature of satisfaction, whatever is "reality." Most theories of poetry seem to me pompous, egotistical, and more or less irrelevant. I have therefore never worked to any "programme."

Born a Scot and brought up in Scotland, in spite of being subjected to an anglified public school education, I became fascinated with that part of my literary heritage written in Scots, and for a number of years wrote enthusiastically in Lallans (as Lowland Scots was called by the poets of the"second wind" phase – the expression was Eric Linklater's – of the "Scottish Renaissance" movement, instituted by Hugh MacDiarmid in the 1920's and so dubbed by Denis Saurat). By the early 1950's this concentration on language for its own sake, particularly a language in decline spoken more thinly and by fewer people every year, seemed to me to be forcing a wedge behind that modern Scotland of which I was a part, and the language in which I, and some others, were writing. I therefore turned my attention to writing in the tongue I, and the majority of Scots, actually speak: a kind of Scotticised English. I have been attacked for "betraying" Lallans. This is nonsense. A Scots writer may have a choice of three languages in which to write. That choice depends upon circumstances all valid in the contemporary context. There can therefore be no "right" language and no "wrong." I am entirely in favour of teaching Scots literature and language in Scottish schools so that what exists already may continue to be enjoyed and understood. But the pressures of the modern world cannot be resisted. Compulsion is not saving Ireland's Erse. Not even an independent Scottish Government could successfully decree the survival of the Scots tongue as a fully spoken medium.

My interest in people, which led me to become a radio and television interviewer at one point, has provided a constant theme for my later poetry. Early training as a musician perhaps accounts for the fascination that rhyme and half-rhyme have always exercised upon me. I have seen poetry as one way, perhaps the best, of making sense out of life, and I have therefore been less interested in free verse than in verse in more closely ordered forms.

I deplore the present British academic practice of collecting young poets into groups – "The Beats," "The Movement," "The Confessionals" – each of which reflects, at most, the fashion of half a decade, and their underlying implication that only the newest group's work is of interest or value. Poets can't and shouldn't try to change their styles to keep up with every latest teenage fashion. While a poet and his work must be of, and reflect, the age in which he lives, a poet at fifty may take a different, though no less valid, view of that age than a poet at twenty. The notions that poets are expendable at twenty-five and that each new fashion is an "advance" on the one before, are to me as absurd as any other evolutionary interpretation of the Arts.

From all of this it may have become apparent that I believe the poet's job is to develop his talents and get on with his art, ignoring the cat-calls of the cliques and the compartmentalising of the more fashion-conscious critics. What is, or is not, of permanent value will be assessed by calmer standards long after the outcome is of personal concern to the poet.

* * *

With the publication of his *Collected Poems* Maurice Lindsay confirmed his position as one of the most consistently pleasing and quietly accomplished poets writing in Britain today. He has an assured technique, with a firm and confident control of rhythms, rhymes, and diction; he has an eye for the sharply defined detail that can quicken a subject into life; the voice is characteristically compassionate but with an astringency of tone when commenting on follies and barbarities. Above all, Maurice Lindsay is a master of the incidental lyric, the moment that captures the experience and also hints at meanings that underlie experience.

These qualities have been present in his work for more than 30 years, since the publication of *The Enemies of Love*, but it was in the later collection, *The Exiled Heart*, that the last traces of rhetoric and contrivance were eliminated, that he began to speak in his mature voice. And in the same collection it became clear that Lindsay's experience finds its expression more naturally and completely in English than in Lowland Scots.

In the two decades since *The Exiled Heart* Lindsay's poems have been consistently good and yet they have consistently failed to win the recognition they deserve. Most poets are undervalued in our society, but the comparative neglect of Maurice Lindsay's poetry deserves some comment. (It is worth noting that as an editor of anthologies and journals, and as a broadcaster, he had done much to promote the work of other poets.) A likely explanation for Lindsay's comparative lack of recognition is that there is no single area of experience that is distinctively his own territory. There is an emotional climate in the poetry of his fellow-Scots, Norman MacCaig, Iain Crichton Smith, and George Mackay Brown; there is also a clear sense of physical, almost regional landscape in their work. (This idea of territory, of areas of experience, is at its most obvious in the aggressive mythologising of Hughes, or the urban ironies of Larkin, or the suburban anguish of Betjeman.) Lindsay does not colonise experience in this way, but rather explores a wider range of ordinary experience; and he does so with an almost imperceptible technique, using his considerable craft to conceal the craft of poetry rather than declaim it. His voice is no less distinctive than those of most of his contemporaries, but it is a quieter voice; it is also one that is impossible to parody.

Ironically, this quieter voice, this steadiness of vision, this concern to be true to ordinary experience may have prevented readers from seeing the deeper tensions that underlie much of Lindsay's work. For example, in his poems of childhood, such as "Small Boy Writing" and "Aged Four," the poet intensifies the sense of innocence by hinting at the loss of innocence and the consequent bewilderment that every child must suffer. And when his work is seen as a whole there is a deep, uneasy tension between the order and serenity of some of the nature poems such as "June Rain," "Picking Apples," and "At the Mouth of the Ardyne," and, on the other hand, the savagery of the city in "Attending a Football Match," "Glasgow Nocturne," and "Glasgow Orange Walk." This conflict between civilised values and barbarism is perhaps the strongest preoccupation in Lindsay's most recent work.

The tensions find a satisfying equilibrium in the love poems, and in "Love's Anniversaries," "These Two Lovers," and "Two Weddings" there is a beautiful balancing of the carnal and the spiritual, the sensual and the numinous that is rare in the poetry of this or any age.

—James Aitchison

LIPSITZ, Lou. American. Born in Brooklyn, New York, 29 October 1938. Educated at the University of Chicago, B.A. 1957; Yale University, New Haven, Connecticut, M.A. 1959, Ph.D. in political science 1964. Divorced; two children. Reporter, *Daily Standard*, Celina, Ohio, 1957–58. Instructor, University of Connecticut, Storrs, 1961–64. Since 1964, Member of the Political Science Department, now Professor, University of North Carolina, Chapel Hill. Recipient: National Endowment for the Arts grant, 1967. Address: 43 Rogerson Drive, Chapel Hill, North Carolina, U.S.A.

PUBLICATIONS

Verse

Cold Water. Middletown, Connecticut, Wesleyan University Press, 1967.
Reflections on Samson. Santa Cruz, California, Kayak, 1977.

Other

The Confused Eagle: Division and Dilemma in American Politics. Boston, Allyn and Bacon, 1973.
American Government Today. New York, Random House, 1980.

Editor, *American Government: Behavior and Controversy*. Boston, Allyn and Bacon, 1967.
Editor, *Essentials of American Government Today*. New York, Random House, 1975.

* * *

Lou Lipsitz, like so many other American poets in the last decade, has been influenced by the great modern European and Latin American poets such as Neruda, Vallejo, and Voznesensky. But whereas many other young poets have merely taken the grand style of surrealism and passion and turned it either flippant or blandly mechanical, Lipsitz shares the spirit that informs the originals.

He has written a genuine urban poetry which deals with the callousness and despair of the city but maintains its own concern and gentleness. His range of emotions is wide, and he has written marvelous poems of personal joy and tenderness ("Cold Water," "A Note"), of humor which is not strident but rather pervaded by an affection for the human spirit ("Pancho Villa," "Why I Left My Job"), and of the spiritual imagination ("Night Train," "The Pipes"); but the poems which are perhaps the most impressive are the ones in which he demonstrates the rare and important capacity to feel, to comprehend, the difficult life of another being.

He explores the desperation of prize fighters from the slums, the awkward strangeness of young boys entering manhood, the suffering of emotionally disturbed children, with a fully engaged perceptiveness, portraying them in lines whose accuracy and force are at least as much a proof of his empathy and love as they are of his talent or skill.

—Lawrence Russ

LIVESAY, Dorothy. Canadian. Born in Winnipeg, Manitoba, 12 October 1909. Educated at Trinity College, University of Toronto, 1927–31, B.A. 1931; the Sorbonne, Paris, Diploma, 1932; London Institute of Education, 1959; University of British Columbia, Vancouver, M.Ed. 1966. Married Duncan Macnair in 1937 (died); one son and one daughter. Social Worker, Englewood, New Jersey, 1935–36, and Vancouver, 1936–39, 1953–55; Correspondent, *Toronto Daily Star*, 1946–49; Documentary Scriptwriter, Canadian Broadcasting Corporation, 1950–55; Lecturer in Creative Writing, University of British Columbia, 1955–56, 1965–66; High School Teacher, Vancouver, 1956–58; UNESCO English Specialist, Paris, 1958–60, and Zambia, 1960–63; Writer-in-Residence, University of New Brunswick, Fredericton, 1966–68; Associate Professor of English, University of Alberta, Edmonton, 1968–71; Visiting Lecturer, University of Victoria, British Columbia, 1974–75, University of Manitoba, Winnipeg, 1975–76, and University of Ottawa, 1977. Recipient: Governor-General's Award, 1945, 1948; Lorne Pierce Medal, 1947; President's Medal, University of Western Ontario, 1954; Canada Council grant, 1958, 1964, 1971, 1977. D.Litt.: University of Waterloo, Ontario, 1973. Honorary Fellow, St. John's College, Winnipeg. Address: St. John's College, 400 Dysart Road, Winnipeg, Manitoba R3T 2M5, Canada.

PUBLICATIONS

Verse

Green Pitcher. Toronto, Macmillan, 1928.
Signpost. Toronto, Macmillan, 1932.

Day and Night. Toronto, Ryerson Press, 1944.
Poems for People. Toronto, Ryerson Press, 1947.
Call My People Home. Toronto, Ryerson Press, 1950.
New Poems. Toronto, Emblem, 1955.
Selected Poems 1926–1956. Toronto, Ryerson Press, 1957.
The Colour of God's Face. Vancouver, Unitarian Service Committee, 1965.
The Unquiet Bed. Toronto, Ryerson Press, 1967.
Poets Between the Wars, with others, edited by Milton T. Wilson. Toronto, McClelland and Stewart, 1967.
The Documentaries: Selected Longer Poems. Toronto, Ryerson Press, 1968.
Plainsongs. Fredericton, New Brunswick, Fiddlehead, 1969; revised edition, 1971.
Disasters of the Sun. Burnaby, British Columbia, Blackfish, 1971.
Collected Poems: The Two Seasons. Toronto, McGraw Hill Ryerson, 1972.
Nine Poems of Farewell 1972–1973. Windsor, Ontario, Black Moss Press, 1973.
Ice Age. Erin, Ontario, Press Porcépic, 1975.
Winter Ascending. Prince George, British Columbia, Caledonia, n.d.
The Woman I Am. Erin, Ontario, Press Porcépic, 1977.

Short Stories

A Winnipeg Childhood. Winnipeg, Peguis, 1973; as *Beginnings*, Toronto, Newpress, 1975.

Other

Right Hand, Left Hand. Erin, Ontario, Press Porcépic, 1977.

Editor, *The Collected Poems of Raymond Knister.* Toronto, Ryerson Press, 1949.
Editor, with Seymour Mayne, *40 Women Poets of Canada.* Montreal, Ingluvin, 1971.
Editor, *Woman's Eye: 12 British Columbia Poets.* Vancouver, Air, 1974.

Manuscript Collections: University of Alberta, Edmonton; Queen's University, Kingston, Ontario; University of Manitoba, Winnipeg.

Critical Studies: "My New Found Land" by W. E. Collin, in *The White Savannahs*, Toronto, Macmillan, 1936; "Out of Silence and Across the Distance: The Poetry of Dorothy Livesay" by P. Stevens, in *Queen's Quarterly 4* (Kingston, Ontario), Winter 1969; "Dorothy Livesay: The Love Poetry" by P. Stevens, in *Canadian Literature* (Vancouver), Winter 1971; "Livesay's Two Seasons" by Robin Skelton, in *Canadian Literature* (Vancouver), Autumn 1973; *From Here to There* edited by Frank Davey, Erin, Ontario, Press Porcépic, 1974; Tom Marshall, in *Canadian Forum* (Toronto), February 1979.

Dorothy Livesay comments:

(1970) Early lyrical and imagist poetry became social and documentary (30's and 40's) and reverted to personal statement (50's and 60's). Influenced recently by West Coast movement (projective verse).

Themes and subjects: love and personal psychological relationships between lovers, parents, children. Problems of individual relationships to the question of our age: achieving the just society, how to stop war, how to understand other races and peoples. Recently in *The Unquiet Bed* my theme has been the importance of oneness with another person. If this harmony is achieved, many other harmonies spring from it.

I like to experiment with new forms, to find the subtleties for music in English words and word-arrangements. Poetry is speech and communication and should be said aloud.

(1974) In the past three years I have been giving readings of my poetry to universities across Canada and to women's organizations. The great and encouraging response of women to my poetry is due, perhaps, to the fact that for forty years I have been writing of matters that concern women: love, marriage and its bonds, childbirth, childhood: the need for peace in the world to give children a growing place. But perhaps the greatest response has been to my love poetry, as in *The Unquiet Bed* and *Plainsongs* – now incorporated in *Collected Poems: The Two Seasons.*

* * *

Dorothy Livesay is one of the pioneers of modernism in Canadian poetry. Her early work in *Green Pitcher*, published when she was nineteen, while showing the influence of Imagism current at that time, was also distinguished by its simple lyricism and a rare maturity of spirit.

A start in newspaper writing was followed by university studies in Toronto and in France, and led eventually to a career in social work. Coincident with Livesay's studies at the Sorbonne, 1931–32, was the publication of *Signpost* which is a personal document and consists, in the main, of poems conceived before the politicizing process which befell Western intellectuals in the early 1930's. The suggestion exists, though, in this second chapbook, that Livesay's concerns are going to become progressive, political and committed. The private and the lyrical give way to social awareness which is informed not only by personal involvement in the lives of the under-privileged, but also by the world struggle against fascism. Out of this ambience comes *Day and Night*, a volume of socially relevant and committed writing. The institutional quality of social zeal, and that sense of *movimento* typical of the time were muted and improved upon by new well-springs of humanist affirmation in *Poems for People. Call My People Home* and *New Poems* are two chapbooks with an interim note about them, but with indications of a return to a more private verse concerned with the experiences of love and the joyful and evocative liberation of art. Following the publication of Livesay's *Selected Poems 1926–1956*, the poet's work seemed to mark time briefly until the emergence of a re-enforced sense of the musical phrase and new rhythms. In *The Colour of God's Face*, a chapbook inspired by work and residence in Zambia, the strength of Livesay's rhythms is noteworthy, as is her success in balancing the imagistic with the interpretative. Influences of the Canadian West Coast *TISH*-movement are also at work in her later poems as evidenced in *The Unquiet Bed*, a collection which, with its private intensities, relies on established spareness and discipline, but which is also rich in the rhythm and musicality of its statement.

The process of shifting literary and political orientation did not affect profoundly Livesay's basic style. She continued to write in simple and direct verse forms with variations in tone from the lyrical and subdued, through the emotional and political to the genuinely humane and passionate.

Livesay's 1968 collection, *The Documentaries*, is a selection of key poems like "The Outrider" and "Call My People Home" which have a particular value not only as significant statement, but as milestones in the career of Dorothy Livesay.

—Michael Gnarowski

LIVINGSTONE, Douglas (James). South African. Born in Kuala Lumpur, Malaya, 5 January 1932. Educated at Kearney College, Natal, South Africa; qualified in Pathogenic Bacteriology, Pasteur Institute, Salisbury, Rhodesia. Officer in Charge, Pathological Laboratory, Broken Hill (Kabwe) General Hospital, Zambia, 1959–63. Since 1964, Bacteriologist in charge of marine work, Natal. Recipient: Guinness Prize, 1965;

Cholmondeley Award, 1970; Olive Schreiner Prize, 1975; English Association Prize, 1978. Address: c/o C.S.I.R., P.O. Box 17001, Congella, 4013 Natal, South Africa.

PUBLICATIONS

Verse

The Skull in the Mud. London, Outposts, 1960.
Sjambok and Other Poems from Africa. London and New York, Oxford University Press, 1964.
Poems, with Thomas Kinsella and Anne Sexton. London and New York, Oxford University Press, 1968.
Eyes Closed Against the Sun. London and New York, Oxford University Press, 1970.
A Rosary of Bone. Cape Town, David Philip, 1975.
The Anvil's Undertone. Johannesburg, Donker, 1978.

Plays

The Sea My Winding Sheet (broadcast, 1964; produced Durban, 1971). Published in *Theatre One*, Johannesburg, Donker, 1978.
A Rhino for the Boardroom (broadcast, 1974). Published in *Contemporary South African Plays*, Johannesburg, Ravan Press, 1977.

Radio Plays: *The Sea My Winding Sheet*, 1964 (Rhodesia); *A Rhino for the Boardroom*, 1974.

Bibliography: *Douglas Livingstone: A Bibliography* by A. G. Ullyatt, Pretoria, University of South Africa, 1978.

Critical Study: *Douglas Livingstone: A Critical Study of His Poetry* by M. J. F. Chapman, unpublished M.A. thesis, University of Natal, Pietermaritzburg, 1979.

Douglas Livingstone comments:

Some African themes, especially animals: to reflect the nature of man. Happier with "form." Attempts to "shape" poem to subject. Influences unknown, but favorite poets: Chaucer, John Clare, Catullus, Shelley, Marvell, Donne, Cavafy, E. A. Robinson, Wilfred Owen and Sylvia Plath among the dead.

* * *

Douglas Livingstone might be described as a poet without roots in any particular country or environment, which makes him rather difficult to place for the reader who automatically thinks in terms of nationalities. Born in Kuala Lumpur of middle-class Scottish parents, Livingstone spent his early years in Malaya, Australia, Ceylon, Scotland, South Africa, Rhodesia and Zambia. In Rhodesia he studied and qualified in pathological bacteriology. As he himself observes somewhat ruefully: "I have been to more schools than I care to remember, in several continents, but which to call a capillary, let alone a tap-root, had me foxed."

His earliest work appeared in *Outposts* and his first small collection of poems, *The Skull in the Mud*, was published by Outposts Publications in 1960. Although uneven in quality, this collection already exhibited the characteristics which the critics welcomed on the appearance of his second volume, and had an extraordinary vitality which, surprisingly enough for any

Rhodesian or South African poet, owed nothing at all to Roy Campbell. Indeed, though it was obvious that Livingstone had read widely, no strong literary influences were anywhere apparent. In *The Skull in the Mud* Livingstone refers to himself as a "muscoid Jonah" and takes up his position as "sentry in the shade," recording what he sees with scrupulous attention to detail, yet never quite maintaining the stance of detached observer. He is, in fact, deeply committed to what he sees and apprehends, without knowing why he is so affected by the scene. There are both movement and compassion in these poems, the best of which reflect local colour and conditions; but it is the title poem which most fittingly expresses his individuality and allows him scope for the satirical streak which he has since developed with success.

Livingstone had moved to South Africa by the time his second collection, *Sjambok*, appeared, though the poems were all written in Zambia. *Sjambok* commanded immediate attention for its energy and power, its vigorous employment of language, and its originality in describing animals and landscape. It is curious that no one seems to have noticed the connection between his choice of title (*sjambok* = whip of plaited leather) and that of the magazine founded by Roy Campbell and William Plomer in 1926 (*voorslag* = whiplash) in order to "sting with satire the mental hindquarters ... of the bovine citizenry of the Union." Certainly Livingstone is concentrating more and more upon the satirical element, though the satire is directed at social evils in general rather than those of South Africa in particular. Despite the superficial qualities so highly praised by the critics – the descriptive skill, the evocative phraseology and precision of imagery – *Sjambok* shows that Livingstone is preoccupied with the disrupting effects of Western civilisation upon primitive peoples and traditions. The ambivalence to be detected in his attitudes owes something to the unsettled nature of his own life as well as that of the African continent; and when he extends his range and raises his sights, as in "Suicide Note" and "Johnny Twenty-Three," he can be exceptionally shrewd and perceptive.

—Howard Sergeant

LIYONG, Taban lo. Ugandan. Born in Uganda, in 1938. Educated at Gulu High School; Sir Samuel Baker School; Government Teacher Training College, Kyambogo; Knoxville College, Tennessee; University of North Carolina, Chapel Hill; Georgetown University, Washington, D.C.; Howard University, Washington, D.C., B.A. in literature and journalism 1966; University of Iowa, Iowa City, M.F.A. Since 1968, Member of the Institute for Development Studies Cultural Division, and currently Lecturer in English, University of Nairobi. Address: Department of English, University of Nairobi, P.O. Box 30197, Nairobi, Kenya.

PUBLICATIONS

Verse

Eating Chiefs: Lwo Culture from Lolwe to Malkal. London, Heinemann, 1970; New York, Humanities Press, 1971.
Franz Fanon's Uneven Ribs: With Poems More and More. London, Heinemann, 1971.
Another Nigger Dead: Poems. London, Heinemann, 1972.
Ballads of Underdevelopment: Poems and Thoughts. Nairobi, East African Literature Bureau, 1974.
To Still a Passion. London, Longman, 1977.

Novel

Meditations in Limbo. Nairobi, Equatorial, 1970.

Short Stories

Fixions and Other Stories. London, Heinemann, 1969.
The Uniformed Man. Nairobi, East African Publishing House, 1971.

Other

The Last Word: Cultural Synthesism. Nairobi, East African Publishing House, 1969.
Popular Culture of East Africa: Oral Literature. Nairobi, Longman, 1972.
Thirteen Offensives Against Our Enemies. Nairobi, East African Literature Bureau, 1973.
Meditations. London, Rex Collings, 1978.

Editor, *Sir Apolo Kagwa Discovers England*, by Ham Mukasa, translated by Ernest Millar. London, Heinemann, 1974.

Taban lo Liyong comments:

We have a saying, roughly translated it reads: Chicken lost their teeth through too much talking. I am therefore retiring from writing at the end of 1974 to devote myself to the long postponed scholarly study of Nietzsche. By then the following books will have been completed: *A Calendar of Wisdom* (proverbs in verse); *The African Tourist* (culture criticism); *To Still a Passion* (last poems): *The American Education of Taban lo Liyong; The Lubumbashi Lectures; Meditations* (last version of *Meditations in Limbo*); and *East African Anthology* (comprehensive anthology of literature from Zinjanthropus to Extelcom).

* * *

A wry and acerbic wit, a ready sense of humor, an equally ready sense of tragedy, and a staggeringly wide range of reference points are the most obvious qualities of the poetry of Taban lo Liyong. His poems indicate these dimensions by their titles alone, to say nothing of the cornucopia (Taban is certainly copious and also, at times, corny) of work the reader finds himself confronted with (or assaulted by) when he begins to read them. "Language/is a figure/of speech," begins the first poem in his first book. "Bless the african coups/tragedy now means a thing to us," begins the initial poem in his second volume.

More than almost any other African poet, Taban lo Liyong's poems reflect the odyssey of his life as African and poet ranging from facetiousness to seriousness and from pathos to intentional bathos. His subject matter one minute is the break up of a "modern" African marriage (in the poem which begins "i walked among men in america for a year ...") and the next minute the development of modern poetry (in "The Best Poets," a marvellous ramble through the history of poetic theory).

Call Taban lo Liyong a prodigy, a genius, a freak or an apostate; he might well be pleased with any or all of those titles. If there is any one fault in his work, in fact, it is that there is so much in his volumes that a reader may be overwhelmed. His is not a poetry which one reads to while away an evening or calm one's nerves after a harrowing day. It is a poetry that demands as much from its reader as it gives in return – a high price for quality merchandise.

—Joseph Bruchac

LOCHHEAD, Liz. Scottish. Born in Motherwell, Lanarkshire, 26 December 1947. Educated at Dalziel High School, Motherwell, 1960–65; Glasgow School of Art, 1965–70, Diploma in Art. Currently, Art Teacher at Bishopbriggs High School, Glasgow, and other schools in Glasgow and Bristol. Recipient: BBC Scotland Prize, 1971; Scottish Arts Council Award, 1973, and fellowship, 1978. Address: c/o 13 Tillanburn Road, Newarthill, Motherwell, Lanarkshire, Scotland.

PUBLICATIONS

Verse

Memo for Spring. Edinburgh, Reprographia, 1972.

Play

Screenplay: *Now and Then*, 1972.

Liz Lochhead comments:

I want my poems to be clear. They should make sense to my landlady and the man in the corner shop. But be capable of being pondered over by the academics round at the University if they like to. Probably I'd hope they'd find a lot of controlled ambiguities, puns – a lot of puns – and word play and double-meanings. I hope they'd find them funny, with a lot of irony, but I'm growing as I get older to distrust irony, despise the way an ironic stance can allow one both to say something and deny responsibility for it, hate the way this kind of cowardice has to hide behind its mask. I like to set up what are, I suppose, essentially dramatic situations within a poem. The poems are almost invariably about people and they tell stories. Above all, I want everything to become so visually alive that it's real, physical, palpable. This I'm always trying for, and I suppose it is exactly what almost every other writer tries to do too.

* * *

There is a directness about Liz Lochhead's work that makes it extremely communicative, and she herself has said of her poetry (in an interview with Julie Davidson in *The Scotsman*, 10 June 1972): "I want people to understand it immediately, and I want it to entertain them." However, she distinguishes it from pop-poetry, and indeed its effects often involve more verbal devices and subtleties than might appear at a glance or on a first hearing. Its main characteristics are freshness and truth to experience. An ability to talk about very ordinary things – her young sister trying on her shoes, a trip from Glasgow to Edinburgh, her grandmother knitting, the clang of steelworks, a child carrying a jug of milk, the end of a love-affair – is in a few poems flattened out towards triviality or the prosaic, but for the most part the warmly observing eye and ear are convincingly on target. The experience has a Glasgow and Lanarkshire background, but it is encouraging too that one of her best poems is a "Letter from New England," where elements of ironical comment on small-town life are entertainingly presented through patterned speech-structures and the persona of a surprised visitor.

—Edwin Morgan

LOEWINSOHN, Ron(ald William). American. Born in Iloilo, Philippines, 15 December 1937. Educated at San Francisco State College; University of California, Berkeley, A.B. 1967 (Phi Beta Kappa); Harvard University, Cambridge, Massachusetts (Woodrow Wilson Fellow, 1967–68; Danforth Fellow, 1967–70; Harvard University Graduate Prize Fellow, 1967–70), M.A. 1969, Ph.D. 1971. Taught poetry workshops at San Francisco State College, 1960–61, and the Center for Adult Education, Cambridge, Massachusetts, 1968; Teaching Fellow, Harvard University, 1968–70. Since 1970, Member of the English Department, University of California, Berkeley. Editor, *Change*, 1963, *Sum*, 1964, and *R. C. Lion*, 1966–67, all in Berkeley. Contributing Editor, *W. C. Williams Newsletter*, Middletown, Pennsylvania. Recipient: Poets Foundation Award, 1963; Academy of American Poets Irving Stone Award, 1966; National Endowment for the Arts Fellowship, 1979. Lives in California, U.S.A.

PUBLICATIONS

Verse

Watermelons. New York, Totem, 1959.
The World of the Lie. San Francisco, Change Press, 1963.
Against the Silences to Come. San Francisco, Four Seasons, 1965.
L'Autre. Los Angeles, Black Sparrow Press, 1967.
Lying Together, Turning the Head and Shifting the Weight, The Produce District and Other Places, Moving – A Spring Poem. Los Angeles, Black Sparrow Press, 1967.
Three Backyard Dramas with Mamas. Santa Barbara, California, Unicorn Press, 1967.
The Sea, Around Us. Los Angeles, Black Sparrow Press, 1968.
The Step. Los Angeles, Black Sparrow Press, 1968.
These Worlds Have Always Moved in Harmony, in *A Play and Two Poems*, with Diane Wakoski and Robert Kelly. Los Angeles, Black Sparrow Press, 1968.
Meat Air: Poems 1957–1969. New York, Harcourt Brace, 1970.
The Leaves. Los Angeles, Black Sparrow Press, 1973.
Eight Fairy Tales. Los Angeles, Black Sparrow Press, 1975.
Goat Dances. Santa Barbara, California, Black Sparrow Press, 1976.

Other

Editor, *Embodiment of Knowledge*, by William Carlos Williams. New York, New Directions, 1974.

* * *

So many young American poets owe allegiance and inspiration to the work of William Carlos Williams that we might well, remembering the 17th century Jonsonians known as the Tribe of Ben, speak now of the tribe of Bill. Ron Loewinsohn's first book was one of the many bearing a prefatory commendation by Williams; it bore too an introduction by that senior Tribesman, Allen Ginsberg, acclaiming the younger man expansively as part of the "great wave of Poetry ... breaking over America now." In the years since 1959, Loewinsohn has gone on unobtrusively working in the Williams mode, acknowledging his source with almost insistent modesty (he is currently writing a critical book on Williams and his selected poems, *Meat Air*, is dedicated to him as "informing spirit"), but adding too a note we might connect with Ginsberg – that of a greater sexual explicitness than Williams ever permitted himself (e.g., the poem title "The Romaunt of the Rose Fuck"), still however in the service of a poetry of love. If Loewinsohn's work shows perhaps less sophisticated agility of mind than that of the deceptively mild-seeming doctor of Rutherford, it brings no less gusto to the celebration of the local and the demotic, and to the inventing of beauty in the literal particulars of the common world. *Three Backyard Dramas with Mamas* gives a touching Californian incarnation to the Persephone myth. "The Distractions; The Music" moves effectively between the social world of work and glimpsed violence and the private world of love and beauty. Noteworthy in Loewinsohn is a genuinely sweet lyricism; it's relevant that a recurring motif in his work is the figure of Mozart, exemplar of a lucid, unforced, unegoistic beauty. Here is the end of a short poem called "K. 282":

That door
is open & he is playing at his ease.
He is maybe 18, the beloved of
God, & is in love himself. Beauty
falls from him as easily as the sun
falls thru the windows. His fingers
follow the play of his mind, dancing
over the keys as he waits. He is 18,
it is late summer, he can wait easily
all day. the door is open. forever.

—Seamus Cooney

LOGAN, John (Burton). American. Born in Red Oak, Iowa, 23 January 1923. Educated at Coe College, Cedar Rapids, Iowa, B.A. in zoology 1943; University of Iowa, Iowa City, M.A. in English 1949; Georgetown University, Washington, D.C. Married Mary Guenevere Minor in 1945 (divorced); nine children. Tutor, St. John's College, Annapolis, Maryland, 1947–51; Associate Professor, The General Program, University of Notre Dame, Indiana, 1951–63; Visiting Professor, Department of English, University of Washington, Seattle, 1965, and San Francisco State College; Fellow, Indiana School of Letters, Summers 1965, 1969. Since 1966, Professor of English, State University of New York, Buffalo. Visiting Professor, University of Hawaii, Manoa, 1975–76. Editor, *Choice*, Chicago. Recipient: National Endowment for the Arts grant, 1966, 1968; Miles Modern Poetry Award, 1967; Rockefeller grant, 1968; Morton Dauwen Zabel Award (*Poetry*, Chicago), 1974. Address: Department of English, State University of New York, Buffalo, New York 14214, U.S.A.

PUBLICATIONS

Verse

Cycle for Mother Cabrini. New York, Grove Press, 1955.
Ghosts of the Heart: New Poems. Chicago, University of Chicago Press, 1960.
Spring of the Thief: Poems 1960–1962. New York, Knopf, 1963.
The Zig-Zag Walk: Poems 1963–1968. New York, Dutton, 1969.
The Anonymous Lover: New Poems. New York, Liveright, 1973.
Poem in Progress. San Francisco, Dryad Press, 1975.

Recording: *Today's Poets 5*, with others, Folkways.

Play

Of Poems, Youth, and Spring. New York, French, 1962.

Novel

The House That Jack Built; or, A Portrait of the Artist as a Sad Sensualist. Omaha, Abattoir, 1974.

Other

Tom Savage: A Boy of Early Virginia (juvenile). Chicago, Encyclopaedia Britannica Press, 1962.

Critical Studies: by Robert Bly, in *The Sixties 5* (Madison, Minnesota), 1961; James Dickey, in *Babel and Byzantium*, New York, Farrar Straus, 1967; Jerome Mazzaro, in *Salmagundi 8* (Flushing, New York), 1968; Paul Carroll, in *The Poem in Its Skin*, Chicago, Follett, 1968.

John Logan comments:

I think of poetry as a reaching, an anonymous loving, which occasionally becomes personal when there are those present who care to listen. I began using stresses in my first book. Moved to syllabic writing in my second and third books, invented the thirteen syllable line for my "Monologues of the Son of Saul" in my third book and then moved toward a form which adapts slant rhyme to free verse couplets and triplets, which I used for my fourth book. I think of Ogden Nash as an influence in this "delayed rhyme" technique. I don't know who my other influences are, except for Rilke. Stories of the Old Testament and the lives of poets (Southwell, Heine, Rimbaud, Keats, Cummings, Crane) are important sources.

* * *

Despite the admiring remarks of distinguished poets and critics, John Logan has not been a popular poet in his native country, and the reasons are not hard to discover. Chiefly, of course, he early became known as a writer of religious verse of a particularly orthodox cast, replete with the conventional symbology of church ritual, and though he has more and more tended to break free both of the overt religious concerns and the metaphorical staples, it is only very recently that he has developed a style to which many of us can respond.

A more important factor in explaining Logan's relation to prospective readers of his verse has been the unfortunate misreading of the poetry by those who might have been expected to do better. Where even sensitive observers have seen nothing but orthodoxy in Logan's early poetry, a few have seen the radical ambiguity which so distinguishes Logan's approach to his materials. Too often the rather prosaic voice and straightforward presentation of sequential observations have been mistaken for ideological certitude and dully competent versification. Unnoticed have been the subtle exorcisms, the parody, the intuitive rejection of resolutions legitimized by a Catholicism that continues, whatever its failings, to hold Logan in its embrace. In fact, only in a recent study by Jerome Mazzaro has the relation between Logan's poetic artifacts and his thematic concerns been successfully explored, to the extent that Logan's witty rhymes and absurd puns, for example, may be understood as essential to his verse, rather than as somehow frivolous posturings.

Logan's poetry evinces a remarkable quality of tenderness, of genuine love of creation, and the use of devices to undercut his sombre and touching evocations is a necessary element in his achievement of a modern voice. Occasionally, even in the most recent work, a quality of ingenuous exclamation and breathless wonderment intrudes, and one senses a wilful generation of excitement that is only half-felt. The language, which has been called prosaic, is often richly ornamented, though he relies on metaphor only sparingly, and there is a distinct playfulness which regularly vies with the more reverential tones that dominate the verse. Similarly, the poems in Logan's third volume, *Spring of the Thief*, as well as the pieces that have lately appeared in various magazines, have been marked by a kind of erotic sensuality that has qualified and deepened the piety which rings in his utterance. This is no doubt related to Logan's quest for self-knowledge and the basically religious transcendence of self-love, so that the masturbatory reveries toward which so many of the better poems tend may be seen as part of a larger struggle, not as a manifestation of purely sexual despair.

Many of Logan's poems explore the spiritual and artistic lives of others, such as Rimbaud, Heine, and Keats, not to mention a host of religious figures, but the explorations are carried on in such a way that they implicate Logan's own problems at every turn. What fascinates Logan is the identity in certain men, especially artists, between scapegoat and priest, and it is this identity that he continually probes, searching out the sacramental qualities of a life in which too often the lovely and tender are obscured by the ugly.

—Robert Boyers

LOGUE, Christopher. British. Born in Portsmouth, Hampshire, 23 November 1926. Educated at Prior Park College, Bath; Portsmouth Grammar School. Served in the British Army, 1944–48. Lived in France, 1951–56. Contributor, *Private Eye*, London. Address: 18 Denbigh Close, London W.11, England.

PUBLICATIONS

Verse

Wand and Quadrant. Paris, Olympia Press, 1953.
The Weekdream Sonnets. Paris, Jack Straw, 1955.
Devil, Maggot, and Son. Amsterdam, Stols, 1954; Tunbridge Wells, Kent, Peter Russell, 1955.
First Testament. Rome, Botteghe Oscure, 1955.
She Sings, He Sings. Rome, Botteghe Oscure, 1957.
A Song for Kathleen. London, Villiers, 1958.
The Song of the Dead Soldier, To the Tune of McCafferty: One Killed in the Interests of Certain Tory Senators in Cyprus. London, Villiers, 1959.
Memoranda for Marchers. Privately printed, 1959.
Songs. London, Hutchinson, 1959; New York, McDowell Obolensky, 1960.
Songs from "The Lily-White Boys." London, Scorpion Press, 1960.
Logue's A. B. C. London, Scorpion Press, 1966.
I Shall Vote Labour. London, Turret, 1966.
The Words of Christopher Logue's Establishment Songs, Etcetera. London, Poet and Printer, 1966.
Selections from a Correspondence Between an Irishman and a Rat. London, Goliard Press, 1966.
Gone Ladies, music by Wallace Southam. London, Turret, 1968.
Rat, Oh Rat. Privately printed, 1968.
SL. Privately printed, 1969.
The Girls. Privately printed, 1969.
New Numbers. London, Cape, 1969; New York, Knopf, 1970.
Twelve Cards. London, Lorrimer, 1972.
The Crocodile (juvenile). London, Cape, 1976.
Abecedary (juvenile). London, Cape, 1977.

Recordings: *Christopher Logue Reading His Own Poetry*, with Laurie Lee, Jupiter, 1960; *The Death of Patroclus*, Spoken Arts, 1963.

Plays

The Trial of Cob and Leach: A News Play (produced London, 1959).
The Lily-White Boys (lyrics only), book by Henry Cookson, music by Tony Kinsey and Bill LeSage (produced London, 1960).
Trials by Logue (*Antigone* and *Cob and Leach*) (produced London, 1960).
Friday, adaptation of a work by Hugo Klaus (produced London, 1971). London, Davis Poynter, 1972.
War Music, music by Donald Fraser, adaptation of *The Iliad* (produced London, 1977).

Screenplay: *Savage Messiah*, 1972.

Television Play: *The End of Arthur's Marriage*, with Stanley Myers, 1965.

Novel

Lust (as Count Palmiro Vicarion). Paris, Olympia Press, 1959.

Other

The Arrival of the Poet in the City: A Treatment for a Film. Amsterdam, Yellow Press, and London, Mandarin, 1963.
Ratsmagic (juvenile). London, Cape, and New York, Pantheon, 1976.
Puss-in-Boots Pop-Up (juvenile). London, Cape, 1976; New York, Morrow, 1977.
The Magic Circus (juvenile). London, Cape, and New York, Viking Press, 1979.

Editor, *Count Palmiro Vicarion's Book of Limericks.* Paris, Olympia Press, 1959.
Editor, *Count Palmiro Vicarion's Book of Bawdy Ballads.* Paris, Olympia Press, 1962.
Editor, *True Stories.* London, New English Library, 1966.
Editor, *True Stories from "Private Eye."* London, Deutsch, 1973.
Editor, *The Children's Book of Comic Verse.* London, Batsford, 1979.

Translator, *The Man Who Told His Love: Twenty Poems Based on Pablo Neruda's "Los Cantos d'Amores."* London, Scorpion Press, 1958.
Translator, *Patrocleia* (from Book XVI of Homer's *Iliad*). London, Scorpion Press, 1962; Ann Arbor, University of Michigan Press, 1963.
Translator, *Pax* (from Book XIX of Homer's *Iliad*). London, Turret, 1967.

Theatrical Activities:

Actor: **Films** – *Dante's Inferno*, 1966; *The Peasants' Revolt*, 1966; *The Devils*, 1970; **Television** – *The Gadfly*, 1977.

* * *

Christopher Logue was one of the few really cosmopolitan figures in the British poetry of the nineteen-fifties. His first collection of poems was published in Paris, and he was one of the earliest English writers to show an interest in Pablo Neruda, with his set of translations or, rather, adaptations, *Red Bird Dancing on Ivory*. These texts later became the material for one of the earliest experiments with poetry-and-jazz, experiments which led directly to the now flourishing poetry-and-pop scene. In fact, Logue throughout his career has shown a restless impatience with conventional boundaries for poetry. He has experimented with the nightclub or cabaret song, as Auden did; one of his poems has been used as the theme-song for a film (the film version of Nell Dunn's novel, *Poor Cow*); and a good number have appeared on posters. Often, those which appeared on posters were written especially for the medium, which enabled Logue to explore two themes at once – his interest in visual design, and his feeling that poetry should be a "popular" art-form, the vehicle for a political or social message. Part, at least, of his reputation is based on his protest-poems, which he reads to brilliant effect at recitals and concerts.

Few living British poets have such a paradoxical *oeuvre*, however. Side by side with his political poems, which frequently owe a good deal to the example of Brecht, Logue has been making an adaptation of the *Iliad*. Two sections of this have so far been published, under the titles *Patrocleia* and *Pax*. Clearly, these are influenced by Ezra Pound: some passages are in a high rhetorical style, others slangy and almost colloquial. Homer speaks to us as a modern author, and the *Iliad* often lives as freshly as the day when it was first composed.

—Edward Lucie-Smith

LONGLEY, Michael. Irish. Born in Belfast, Northern Ireland, 27 July 1939. Educated at the Royal Belfast Academical Institution, 1951–58; Trinity College, Dublin, B.A. (honours) in classics 1963. Married to Edna Broderick; two daughters and one son. Assistant Master, Avoca School, Blackrock, 1962–63, Belfast High School and Erith Secondary School, 1963–64, and Royal Belfast Academical Institution, 1964–69. Since 1970, Director for Literature and the Traditional Arts, Arts Council of Northern Ireland, Belfast. Recipient: Eric Gregory Award, 1965. Address: 18 Hillside Park, Stranmillis, Belfast 9, Northern Ireland.

PUBLICATIONS

Verse

Ten Poems. Belfast, Festival, 1965.
Room to Rhyme, with Seamus Heaney and David Hammond. Belfast, Arts Council of Northern Ireland, 1968.
Secret Marriages: Nine Short Poems. Manchester, Phoenix Pamphlet Poets Press, 1968.
Three Regional Voices, with Barry Tebb and Iain Crichton Smith. London, Poet and Printer, 1968.
No Continuing City: Poems 1963–1968. London, Macmillan, and Chester Springs, Pennsylvania, Dufour, 1969.
Lares. London, Poet and Printer, 1972.
An Exploded View: Poems 1968–1972. London, Gollancz, 1973.
Fishing in the Sky: Love Poems. London, Poet and Printer, 1975.
Penguin Modern Poets 26, with Dannie Abse and D. J. Enright. London, Penguin, 1975.
Man Lying on a Wall: Poems 1972–1975. London, Gollancz, 1976.
The Echo Gate: Poems 1975–1978. London, Secker and Warburg, 1979.

Other

Editor, *Causeway: The Arts in Ulster.* Belfast, Arts Council of Northern Ireland, and Dublin, Gill and Macmillan, 1971.

Editor, *Under the Moon, Over the Stars: Young People's Writing from Ulster*. Belfast, Arts Council of Northern Ireland, 1971.

* * *

Michael Longley is one of several interesting Irish poets who made their debut during the 1960's. His first collection, *No Continuing City*, was already quite mature, although a number of the poems dated from Longley's undergraduate years. His second collection, *An Exploded View*, showed he had acquired greater technical assurance and had further humanized and extended his thematic range.

Longley has consistently maintained a careful and disciplined attitude towards his craft whether writing free verse or using rhyme and metre. He has successfully accommodated contemporary idiom within a wide variety of traditional forms, ranging from *terza rima* and sonnet to octo-syllabic eight-line stanzas; and some of the earlier poems suggest that this skill owes much to a profound study of the metaphysical poets. Without having assimilated John Donne, Longley could hardly have written as he has of moths (in "Epithalamion"):

Who hazard all to be
Where we, the only two it seems,
Inhabit so delightfully
A room it bursts its seams
And spills on to the lawn in beams.

This gift for finding symbols in a given environment to express interior meaning is given most elaborate expression in "The Hebrides," a lengthy monologue on the achievement and extension of self-knowledge. The poem is remarkable for the imaginative energy of its imagery and for the accomplished handling of a stanza composed of six lines of varying lengths:

Along my arteries
Sluice those homewaters petroleum hurts.
Dry docks, gantries,

Dykes of apparatus educate my bones
To track the buoys
Up sea lanes love emblazons
To streets where shall conclude
My journey back from flux to poise, from poise
To attitude.

A prominent place in Longley's work is occupied by heroes who belong to what Frank O'Connor called the submerged population group. They range from John Clare and Emily Dickinson to Walter Mitty and jazz musicians like Bix Beiderbecke. Longley's pantheon is also generously peopled with mythological figures taken, interestingly, from Greek myths rather than those of his own land. Sometimes the mythologizing process is extended to real people, for example, Dr. Johnson, or the poet's own nephew who inspired "Christopher at Birth." This ends with a series of heraldic images which could have been taken from some mediaeval tapestry and which turn the poem away from a consideration of the personal implications of the child's birth to place it against the backdrop of history. A mythologizing process also takes place in some of Longley's poems about the animal world. "Swans Mating" describes the pairing in terms which load the physical act with overtones of numinous significance:

This was a marriage and a baptism,
A holding of breath, nearly a drowning,

Wings spread wide for balance where he trod,
Her feathers full of water and her neck
Under the water like a bar of light.

Longley's deep sympathy with the animal world is self-evident. The variety of creatures in his poems is so large that there is a feeling at times of having wandered into a nature reserve. It is with a kindly eye that Longley looks on animals. Sometimes they suggest the working of elemental forces; thus the badger "manages the earth with his paws." But the red in tooth and claw finds no place in this poet's vision of nature and his animals are never put to use as images of cruelty or menace.

In the earlier poems Longley made effective use of certain resonant words, such as "brainstorm," "histories," and "anthem," but tended to overexploit them. With increasing maturity his technique has become more finely honed and he no longer finds it necessary to resort to such props. At the same time his ability to suggest the mysteries which underlie the appearance of life has been retained. "Casualty," a poem about a decaying sheep, has this kind of awareness in spite of the absence of the earlier poeticisms:

For the ribs began to scatter
The wool to move outward
As though hunger still worked there

As though something that had followed
Fox and crow was desperate for
A last morsel and was
Other than the wind or rain.

Reaction to the troubles in Northern Ireland has given rise to some of Longley's most compassionate poems. One of these links the delayed effects on his father of wounds sustained in the Great War with the murders in Belfast of three British soldiers and a bus conductor. Given such an environment it is not surprising that Longley should sometimes convey an impression of *déracinement* but he has shown no sign of rejecting the fractured and psychically scarred society to which he is heir as so many Irish writers before him have done. On the contrary he has made a point of claiming Ireland as his country "though today/*Timor mortis conturbat me*." Longley's awareness of his Irish identity is indeed, like the standing stone of a later poem, firmly set to help the poet

To record the distances
Between islands of sunlight
And, as hub of the breezes,
To administer the scene.

—Rivers Carew

LORDE, Audre (Geraldin). American. Born in New York City, 18 February 1934. Educated at Hunter College, New York, B.A. 1959; Columbia University, New York, M.L.S. 1961. Married Edwin A. Rollins in 1962; one daughter and one son. Staff Member, Mount Vernon Public Library, New York, 1961–63; Instructor, Town School, New York, 1966–68; Poet-in-Residence, Tougaloo College, Mississippi, 1968; Instructor, City College of New York, 1968–70, and Lehman College, New York, 1969–70. Since 1970, Lecturer, later

Associate Professor, John Jay College of Criminal Justice, New York. Recipient: National Endowment for the Arts grant, 1968; Creative Artists Public Service Award, 1972, 1976. Address: 207 St. Paul's Avenue, Staten Island, New York 10304, U.S.A.

PUBLICATIONS

Verse

The First Cities. New York, Poets Press, 1968.
Cables to Rage. Detroit, Broadside Press, and London, Paul Breman, 1970.
From a Land Where Other People Live. Detroit, Broadside Press, 1973.
New York Head Shop and Museum. Detroit, Broadside Press, 1974.
Between Our Selves. San Francisco, Eidolon, 1976.
Coal. New York, Norton, 1976.
The Black Unicorn. New York, Norton, 1978.

* * *

"But I wear my nights as I wear my life/and my dying/absolute and unforgiven." It is with lines such as these that Audre Lorde carves from the complex, multifaceted nature of her own existence – she is Black, feminist, mother, lesbian – poems of stunning originality, honesty, and power. Through them she seems both to define and clarify the boundaries of her own life.

From the rage and disillusionment which characterize her first volume of poems, "We have no passions left to love the spring/who had suffered autumn as we did, alone," she has come to find even the most negative of human experiences useful: "everything can be used/ except what is wasteful/(you will need/to remember this when you are accused of destruction.)" Thus, her gift to her children is not a protective, idyllic world; rather, "I submit them/loving them above all others save myself/to the fire to the rage to the ritual scarifications/to be tried as new steel is tried." As for herself, "I have not been able to touch the destruction/within me./But unless I learn to use/the difference between poetry and rhetoric/my power too will run corrupt as poisonous mold/or lie limp and useless as an unconnected wire."

The discovery that power and strength can be forged from destruction is neither intuitive nor fanciful. For Lorde it is the result of a life lived in the grip of ancient torments. In poems which tend more and more to recall her own childhood, the poet continues to grapple with the spectre of a mother whose lightness of skin and obsessive desire to be white "had bleached her face of everything/but very private furies," and whose aspirations for her daughter caused her to "try to beat me whiter every day." For the poet, the resultant conflict held both racial and sexual implications: "Who shall I curse that I grew up/believing in my mother's face/or that I lived in fear of the potent darkness/that wore my father's shape." In song, "Ballad from a Childhood," and nightmare, "Sequelae," the past is revisited, the ritual of exorcism painfully effected.

While confronting the past, however, Lorde continues to engage those issues and situations which define her present reality. In poems like "The Day They Eulogized Mahalia," "The American Cancer Society," and "Monkeyman," she candidly assesses the debilitating social, economic, and psychological impact of white racism on Blacks. But she is equally aware of the contribution which Blacks make to their own victimization: "We forgot to water the plantain shoots/when our houses were full of borrowed meat/and our stomachs with the gift of strangers." And, because she is a feminist, she challenges an uncritical acceptance of the idea of Black Power. "I do not believe/our wants have made all our lies/ holy," for "Under the sun on the shores of Elmina/a black man sold the woman who carried/my grandmother in her belly." Intra-racial betrayal, male of female, makes necessary a separate struggle for power, *within* the race.

It is the drive for power, for Black female power, which informs the most original and effective of Lorde's recent poetry. In "Sear," she acknowledges this "masculine" element in her own nature: "Donald de Freeze I never knew you so well/as in the eyes of my own mirror." Later, she dreams "of a big black woman with jewels/in her eyes/... her head in a golden helmet/... her name is Colossa." And in the poem "Meet," a stunning evocation of sensual love which begins "woman when we met on the solstice/high over halfway between your world and mine," the poet compares her own lovemaking to mating between unfettered jungle animals: "You shall get young as I lick your stomach/hot and at rest before we move off again."

If a fusion of the distinctive elements of Audre Lorde's identity occurs at all, it occurs poetically, in those poems in which she employs aspects of the mythology and history of West Africa, embracing the Dahomean Amazons and the powerful yet maternal goddesses, Seboulisa and Yemanjá. In poems of haunting beauty, the poet successfully transcends limitations of time, place, and race, giving to the idea of "woman" a mythic, primal significance: "I have been woman/for a long time/beware my smile ... I am/woman/and not white."

—Saundra Towns

LOWBURY, Edward (Joseph Lister). British. Born in London, 6 December 1913. Educated at St. Paul's School, London, 1927–33; University College, Oxford (Newdigate Prize, 1934, Matthew Arnold Memorial Prize, 1937), 1933–37, B.A. (honours) 1936, B.M., B.Ch. 1939; London Hospital, University of London, M.A. 1940, D.M. 1957. Specialist in Pathology, Royal Army Medical Corps, 1943–47. Married Alison Young, daughter of the poet Andrew Young, in 1954; three daughters. Bacteriologist, 1946–49, and currently, Member, Medical Research Council Scientific Staff, Birmingham Accident Hospital; since 1960, Consultant Adviser in Bacteriology, Birmingham Regional Hospital Board; since 1960, Honorary Director, Hospital Infection Research Laboratory, Birmingham. Editor, *Equator* magazine, Nairobi, Kenya, 1945–46. Visited the United States as a World Health Organization Consultant in 1965; John Keats Memorial Lecturer, Guy's Hospital, London, 1973. Visiting Professor, University of Aston, Birmingham, 1979. Recipient: University of Birmingham Research Fellowship, 1957. D.Sc.: University of Aston, 1977. Fellow, Royal College of Pathologists, Royal College of Physicians, 1977, and Royal College of Surgeons, 1978. Fellow, Royal Society of Literature, 1974. Address: 79 Vernon Road, Birmingham B18 9SQ, England.

PUBLICATIONS

Verse

Fire: A Symphonic Ode. Oxford, Blackwell, 1934.
Crossing the Line. London, Hutchinson, 1946.
Metamorphoses. Privately printed, 1955.
Time for Sale. London, Chatto and Windus-Hogarth Press, 1961.
New Poems. Richmond, Surrey, Keepsake Press, 1965.
Daylight Astronomy. London, Chatto and Windus-Hogarth Press, and Middletown, Connecticut, Wesleyan University Press, 1968.
Figures of Eight. Richmond, Surrey, Keepsake Press, 1969.

Green Magic (for children). London, Chatto and Windus, 1972.
Two Confessions. Richmond, Surrey, Keepsake Press, 1973.
The Night Watchman. London, Chatto and Windus-Hogarth Press, 1974.
Poetry and Paradox: An Essay, with Nineteen Relevant Poems. Richmond, Surrey, Keepsake Press, 1976.
Troika, with John Press and Michael Riviere. Stoke Ferry, Norfolk, Daedalus Press, 1977.
Selected Poems. Aberystwyth, Celtion Press, 1978.

Recording: *The Poet Speaks 2*, Argo.

Other

Facing North (miscellany), with Terence Heywood. London, Mitre Press, 1960.
Thomas Campion: Poet, Composer, Physician, with Timothy Salter and Alison Young. London, Chatto and Windus, and New York, Barnes and Noble, 1970.
Drug Resistance in Antimicrobial Therapy. Springfield, Illinois, Thomas, 1974.

Editor, with others, *Control of Hospital Infection: A Practical Handbook.* London, Chapman and Hall, 1975.
Editor, *Widening Circles: Five Black Country Poets.* Stafford, West Midland Arts, 1976.
Editor, *Night Ride and Sunrise: An Anthology of New Poems.* Aberystwyth, Celtion Press, 1978.

Manuscript Collection: Birmingham University Library.

Critical Study: "Edward Lowbury" by John Press, in *Southern Review* (Baton Rouge, Louisiana), Spring 1970.

Edward Lowbury comments:

Poetry is an obsessional activity through which, at intervals in my medical life, I have been able to work off accumulated tension; it is, for me, an exploration, through words, of various experiences, and in particular of painfully exciting or disturbing or conflicting experiences – love; hardship and loss; the attritions of time; childhood and age; nature and the unknown; experiences in my medical work. In the poem I discover verbal, visual and metrical equivalents to represent the conflicts and ambiguities of the world about which I write. When the components shape themselves into structures (i.e. poems) with an inner tension, with what I judge to be the correct balance of thought and feeling, of harmony and discord, and when the structures give me – and others – a simultaneous feeling of surprise and inevitability, I feel I have found whatever it was I was looking for in my "exploration." I usually take many wrong turnings before I find (if I ever do find) the right one; I think I can recognise when I have struck the right path and the place where I should stop but I realize that neither the writer nor any individual critic can make categorical judgements.

* * *

The poetry of Edward Lowbury demonstrates that there is still a place for the competent neo-Georgian who has understood and purged himself of the vices of the original Georgian school. He had a fine master in his late and great father-in-law, Andrew Young. He has shown no development, but has worked hard to record his observations sensitively and in a well-handled verse – his work on Thomas Campion has served him in good stead here. Such a poem as "The Collector" shows him at his best: too over-dependent on Young, certainly, to achieve a really individual voice – but there is the minimum of irrelevant chatter, and the poet means what he says. He collects bluebells, then other kinds of flowers – but discovers that he can never get enough, so that he ends:

A lifetime brought this new collector's itch:
In a world of flowers, names, necessities –
To see how many I could do without:
And at last the distant shout
"Come home" finds me exulting in a wealth
Of unpossessions – all of it, perhaps,
A practice-run for doing without myself.

This is his most successful manner. In love poetry, or less precisely observed nature poetry, he is more awkward; nor do his attempts at the colloquial come off, as the opening of "Astrology" aptly demonstrates: "So it's true, all that nonsense/About the stars controlling destiny:/True, anyway, for migrant birds!..." But he is at all times a modest and unstrident poet, whose quiet achievement outstrips that of many of his better known contemporaries.

—Martin Seymour-Smith

LUCIE-SMITH, (John) Edward (McKenzie). British. Born in Kingston, Jamaica, 27 February 1933. Educated at King's School, Canterbury; Merton College, Oxford, B.A. 1954. Education Officer, Royal Air Force, 1954–56. Free-lance Journalist. Co-Founder, Turret Books, London, 1965. Recipient: Rhys Memorial Prize, 1962; Arts Council Triennial Poetry Prize, 1962. Fellow, Royal Society of Literature. Address: 24 Sydney Street, London S.W.3, England.

PUBLICATIONS

Verse

(Poems). Oxford, Fantasy Press, 1954.
A Tropical Childhood and Other Poems. London and New York, Oxford University Press, 1961.
Penguin Modern Poets 6, with Jack Clemo and George MacBeth. London, Penguin, 1964.
Confessions and Histories. London and New York, Oxford University Press, 1964.
Fir-Tree Song. London, Turret, 1965.
Jazz for the N.U.F. London, Turret, 1965.
A Game of French and English. London, Turret, 1965.
Three Experiments. London, Turret, 1965.
Gallipoli – Fifty Years After. London, Turret, 1966.
Cloud Sun Fountain Statue. Cologne, Hansjörg Mayer, 1966.
Silence, music by Wallace Southam. London, Turret, 1967.
"*Heureux Qui, Comme Ulysse...*" London, Turret, 1967.
Borrowed Emblems. London, Turret, 1967.
Towards Silence. London, Oxford University Press, 1968.

Teeth and Bones. London, Pebble Press, 1968.
Six Kinds of Creature. London, Turret, 1968.
Snow Poem. London, Turret, 1969.
Egyptian Ode. Stoke Ferry, Norfolk, Daedalus Press, 1969.
Six More Beasts. London, Turret, 1970.
Lovers. Frensham, Surrey, Sceptre Press, 1970.
The Rhino. London, Steam Press, 1971.
A Girl Surveyed. London, Hanover Gallery, 1971.
The Yak, The Polar Bear, The Dodo, The Goldfish, The Dinosaur, The Parrot (posters). London, Turret, 1971.
Two Poems of Night. London, Turret, 1972.
The Rabbit. London, Turret, 1973.
The Well-Wishers. London and New York, Oxford University Press, 1974.
Seven Colours. Cambridge, Rampant Lions Press, 1974.
Inscriptions/Inscripciones. Mexico City, Ainle Press, 1975.

Novel

The Dark Pageant. London, Blond and Briggs, 1977.

Other

Mystery in the Universe: Notes on an Interview with Allen Ginsberg. London, Turret, 1965.
Op Art, edited by Duncan Taylor. London, BBC, 1966.
What Is a Painting? London, Macdonald, 1966.
Thinking about Art: Critical Essays. London, Calder and Boyars, 1968.
A Beginner's Guide to Auctions (as Peter Kershaw). London, Rapp and Whiting, 1968.
Movements in Art since 1945. London, Thames and Hudson, 1969; revised edition, 1975; as *Late Modern: The Visual Arts since 1945*, New York, Praeger, 1969; revised edition, 1976.
A Concise History of French Painting. London, Thames and Hudson, and New York, Praeger, 1971.
Eroticism in Western Art. London, Thames and Hudson, 1972.
Symbolist Art. London, Thames and Hudson, and New York, Praeger, 1972.
Movements in Modern Art, with Donald Carroll. New York, Horizon Press, 1973.
The First London Catalogue: All the Appurtenances of a Civilized, Amusing, and Comfortable Life. London, Paddington Press, and New York, Two Continents, 1974.
World of the Makers: Today's Master Craftsmen and Craftswomen. London, Paddington Press, and New York, Two Continents, 1975.
The Waking Dream: Fantasy and the Surreal in Graphic Art 1450–1900, with Aline Jacquiot. London, Thames and Hudson, and New York, Knopf, 1975.
The Invented Eye: Masterpieces of Photography 1839–1914. London, Paddington Press, and New York, Two Continents, 1975.
The Burnt Child: An Autobiography. London, Gollancz, 1975.
Joan of Arc. London, Allen Lane, 1976; New York, Norton, 1977.
How the Rich Lived, and *Work and Struggle: The Painter as Witness 1870–1914*, with Celestine Dars. London and New York, Paddington Press, 2 vols.,1976–77.
Henri Fantin-Latour. Oxford, Phaidon, and New York, Rizzoli, 1977.
Art Today: From Abstract Expressionism to Superrealism. Oxford, Phaidon, and New York, Morrow, 1977.
Toulouse-Lautrec. Oxford, Phaidon, 1977; New York, Dutton, 1978.
Outcasts of the Sea: Pirates and Piracy. London and New York, Paddington Press, 1978.

A Concise History of French Painting. London, Thames and Hudson, and New York, Oxford University Press, 1978.
Super-Realism. Oxford, Phaidon, 1979.
Furniture: A Concise History. London, Thames and Hudson, and New York, Oxford University Press, 1979.
Cultural Calendar of the Twentieth Century. Oxford, Phaidon, 1979.

Editor, *Rubens.* London, Spring, 1961.
Editor, *Raphael.* London, Batchworth Press, 1961.
Editor, with Philip Hobsbaum, *A Group Anthology.* London, Oxford University Press, 1963.
Editor, *The Penguin Book of Elizabethan Verse.* London, Penguin, 1965.
Editor, *The Liverpool Scene.* London, Rapp and Carroll, and New York, Doubleday, 1967.
Editor, *A Choice of Browning's Verse.* London, Faber, 1967.
Editor, *The Penguin Book of Satirical Verse.* London, Penguin, 1967.
Editor, *Holding Your Eight Hands: A Book of Science Fiction Verse.* New York, Doubleday, 1969; London, Rapp and Whiting, 1970.
Editor, with Patricia White, *Art in Britain 1969–70.* London, Dent, 1970.
Editor, *British Poetry since 1945.* London, Penguin, 1970.
Editor, with Simon Watson-Taylor, *French Poetry Today: A Bi-Lingual Anthology.* London, Rapp and Whiting-Deutsch, 1971.
Editor, *Primer of Experimental Poetry 1870–1922.* London, Rapp and Whiting-Deutsch, 1971.
Editor, *A Garland from the Greek: Poems from the Greek Anthology.* London, Trigram Press, 1971.

Translator, *Manet*, by Robert Rey. Milan, Uffici Press, 1962.
Translator, *Jonah: Selected Poems of Jean-Paul de Dadelsen.* London, Rapp and Carroll, 1967.
Translator, *Five Great Odes*, by Paul Claudel. London, Rapp and Whiting, 1967; Chester Springs, Pennsylvania, Dufour, 1970.
Translator, *The Muses*, by Paul Claudel. London, Turret, 1967.

Edward Lucie-Smith comments:

My activities, though various, seem to revolve about poetry and the modern arts in general. I hate the term "poet." I'm simply a man who tries to react honestly to the world.

Since I was one of the founder-members of "The Group," and for some years chairman of its discussions, I'm in that sense a "Group" poet. Nowadays I can't think of anyone who writes much like me.

I think my development as a poet could be described roughly as follows: I began in the wake of the Movement, among a group of undergraduate poets at Oxford which included Anthony Thwaite, George MacBeth, Adrian Mitchell and Geoffrey Hill. I was then a poet of tight conventional forms and my chief subject was childhood experience. Under the influence of the sessions of "The Group," I began to write longer poems, often dramatic monologues, which were greatly influenced by Browning. Poems of this sort appear in my second volume, *Confessions and Histories*. At this period I gradually became dissatisfied with conventional verse forms and especially with their lack of real flexibility. I began to look for forms which would give: (*a*) greater colloquialism, (*b*) greater simplicity, and (*c*) greater concision. The results of these experiments can be seen in my third book, *Towards Silence*, and I have continued them in my more recent work. The metrical principle in most of my recent poetry is twofold – a strict syllabic "ground," and a melody of strong and light stresses. I use the syllabic pattern to syncopate the metre I have chosen which is usually mismatched to it, e.g.

dactyls and a seven- or eleven-syllable line. The effect is, I think, very like that of Greek or Latin poetry, without strictly copying Greek or Latin forms. The influences are various: Catullus, the Elizabethan experiments with classical metre and especially Campion, Rochester (for his colloquial directness), French medieval poetry, and Pound. I am very concerned to preserve strict prose-order of words. A common criticism of my recent work is that it is too "thin" – not complex enough. My translators, on the other hand, tend to complain of simplicity which conceals difficulty.

I am interested in extending the scope of poetry – in writing poster-poems and poems to be set to music, for example.

My themes are, I think, commonly erotic (poems about love), historical and aesthetic (poems about artists and works of art, etc.), and occasionally religious.

* * *

Edward Lucie-Smith's poetry has ranged over the years from the neatly turned and rhymed "Movement" verses of his Fantasy Press pamphlet of 1954 to the experimentation and freedom of syllabics in, for example, his collection, *Towards Silence*, published in 1968. Together with this variety and development goes an impression of a conscious artistry – not only in individual poems, but in the compilation of the collections themselves. The poems in *Towards Silence* gain from being read as a collection, though each poem stands in its own right. Then there is the influence of Lucie-Smith's knowledge of and occupation with the visual arts. The carefully juxtaposed visual images are often starkly clear, and the poems themselves have frequently been prompted by paintings or sculpture: "An unstrung bow. The white, slack/Body collapsing. Mourners/Like mountains/Pieta."

The danger with such poetry can be that the artistry too finely applied tends to exclude feeling; but in the best of Lucie-Smith's poetry this is not so. In early personal poems about his boyhood, such as "A Tropical Childhood" or "The Lesson," the feeling is to be clearly felt: "I cried for knowledge which was bitterer/Than any grief. For there and then I knew/ That grief has uses." In the group of poems about artists in the collection *Confessions and Histories*, for example, the popular "Caravaggio Dying" and the, to my mind, much better "Soliloquy in the Dark," he succeeds in expressing an empathy not only with the situation he takes as his subject matter, but with the feelings of the characters involved:

– how I used to stumble
From frame to frame and rap upon the glass
And scratch the canvas with my old man's nails,
Tears smarting useless eyes with salt and gum.
Flat is not round. And dankness is not colour.

In more recent poems, while using much freer forms, the earlier note of personal feeling comes through strongly:

Don't wonder what it was
that filled the space between
thinking and thinking.
Gone.
My day is like a staircase
with one step missing.

It was the collection *Towards Silence* which signalled a movement into a more markedly direct simplicity of statement and form, though the implications and overtones may be far from being so, as in that near perfect poem "Silence" which rounds off the collection: "Hear/ Your own noisy machine, which/Is moving towards silence." From the same period comes the remarkable translation of Paul Claudel's *Five Great Odes* in which Lucie-Smith captures the quality and feelings of this high, near-baroque poetry. To set this translation beside the simple directness of his recent poetry is to illustrate the versatility of Edward Lucie-Smith and the range of his accomplishment.

—John Cotton

MacADAMS, Lewis (Perry, Jr.) American. Born in San Angelo, Texas, 12 October 1944. Educated at Princeton University, New Jersey, B.A. 1966; State University of New York, Buffalo, M.A. 1968. Married Phoebe Russell in 1967; two sons. Formerly, Switchman on the Southern Pacific Railroad. Recipient: Poets Foundation Award, 1967.

PUBLICATIONS

Verse

City Money. Oxford, Burning Water Press, 1966.
Water Charms. San Francisco, Dariel Press, 1968.
The Poetry Room. New York, Harper, 1970.
Dance. Canton, New York, Institute of Further Studies, 1972.
Now Let Us Eat of This Pollen and Place Some on Our Heads, For We Are to Eat of It. New York, Harper, 1973.
The Population Explodes. Storrs, University of Connecticut Library, 1973.
Live at the Church. New York, Kulchur, 1977.

Other

A Bolinas Report: Reportage and Exhortation. San Francisco, Zone Press, 1971.
Tilth: Interviews. Bolinas, California, Bolinas Future Studies Center, 1972.

Editor, with others, *Where the Girls Are: A Guide to Eastern Women's Colleges.* New York, Dial Press, 1966.

Critical Study: review by John Koethe, in *Poetry* (Chicago), April 1972.

Lewis MacAdams comments:

I would like to introduce myself to you as the work of a poet that derides masks. It's that the wind sings through me, and there is no personality there – anywhere. "Speech" is the state of human things, and the words of the poet telescope elemental space and fire into geometry, which is the dance of sexual joy. It is incredible to be listed in the middle of a huge book linked with thousands of humans only because we all write in the various forms of English, so I would like to say Hello to Bob Marley in Jamaica, to Haile Selassie, to Chinua Achebe, and to Kwesi Brew. I am the words of an average man trained to composition and honed by consciousness and gravity to song. And alot of meat's gone down the pike before. And now, here is a poem by me and Tom Clark:

100 Poets in "The Rolling Stone"

such a smile, like having you near
and so many other poets I
yet never shall my song omit
to sigh and moan, more fit for Ovid
than Shakespeare, for David Bowie
than the Troggs, or Mike "Eggs" Benedict.

We shall not be mooed at gracefully
this afternoon, nor shall we either feel
a hard-on. One inch deeper in shit.
Well, at least it's my shit,
you think. It's
Ocean Lee's shit,
justly entitled Cupid's Hill.

I'd embrace those struggling rocks
with John and Ed and so many a
happy face. Wal kick my ass.
The neck, in which strange graces lurk
has eyes, and looks up into my face.
And I realized I was in a body
that would not die.

* * *

It is characteristic of Lewis MacAdams's poetry, like that of surrealist poetry in general, that metaphors are neither sustained nor exhaustive. The world of experience is too busy a place; no one sense of it is sufficient. Instead, there is a lavishness of images. Some are startling, totalizing: "Her hand on my chin/turning my head around/like cut flowers." Others are more yielding and assuring, such as the closing of "Sonnet": "we will drift/under trees after the rain in dry clothes, and our eyes." He is capable of a dazzling array, all made to cohere by a dynamic personality. Many of the images, flashing as they do, take his own advice: "To outlive time, live through it,/faster than ever before."

Some of MacAdams's word montages defy the absurd ("Like a mongoose the east and west/stalk eternity"), others revel in it (he revels, to reveal). Some are disquieting, such as "The Pyramids" haunted by a murderess named Candy, the "widow-maker," who "waits for the white dot on your lung to show./She is waiting in the white dress at your window" – the rhyme sealing the sense of doom. Most often there is the affirmative: "The most spectacular/paradiso cowboy hitch-hike through the mountains/through the fir trees and pine, through the flush blue sky." His poems luxuriate in such images or end in a sweep of metaphor: "Nothing is working, I'm dropping out of history, I'm/Mephistopheles annexed, I'm a pie being throwed." Dialect, humor, whatever serves to expand the multiplicity of being – MacAdams is a poet of total consciousness, advancing from the west Texas plains like his early hero Kerouac's Dean Moriarty, "mad to live, mad to talk, mad to be saved, desirous of everything at the same time." His poems are never passively descriptive. Even the longest passages of pure description explode into celebration:

Moon gone. Cold gone. Sandpipers
criss-cross the tidal pools below soft Venus light
on your breast most purely womanly form revealed
through a loose boy's shirt in a sleeping bag I roll toward
to heat up before daylight sun blasts and man stands alone with just
fifty-five centavos for an orange crush grande and no coy,
sexual, pacific darkness. I love you! I marry you! Speech good!

He is a poet of unmediated experience, wherever it can be found, whether in a public circumstance or the most intimate and domestic. In the superb "Raw Honey," after an encounter with some bees, he writes:

> Give me a song to sing. Give me focus and legend,
> and following their whirr outside I see unchallenged gold
> in the waters of Bolinas Bay
> and the slight south wind surrounding
> their departure brings me morning's second whiff of coffee
> followed closely by your palm on my cheek and your voice
> aching softly asks would I like a piece of fresh baked bread and butter?
> With a little honey?

Such life-affirming tenderness rocks us from within.

Since MacAdams started living in California, his poems have grown larger and less implacably surreal, although his is still a poetry of evocation. It is characterized by a seemingly endless resourcefulness. *The Population Explodes*, a long celebration written for friends back in Buffalo, is as exuberant and uplifting as anything by Whitman or Ginsberg. It differs from MacAdams's earlier poetry by its continuous flow and movement away from disparate images, but sacrificing none of their jarring vividness – with marvelous puns ("the saxophones ring") and the poet himself as "mailman-angel" proffering "mantic semaphores," insisting "that life must be praised raucously in the best ways." He celebrates not just brotherhood among persons or friends, but the widest, most inclusive of creation's possibilities as befitting the new age. In such a vast throbbing ecosystem, life appears very familiar, sexy, and divine: "life stands revealed totally in majestic black/underpants coming out of the bathroom with a towel round her head/and wings on her heels." The poet concludes by offering the knowledge that "A breath itself is a gift/from a leaf. And the recipient chest sings Wow." There is not a single drop in voltage between MacAdams's "Wow" and Whitman's "Body Electric" as MacAdams leads us through the next time-lock and into a huge but knowable cosmic room, called, after the title of his second collection, the Poetry Room.

—George F. Butterick

MacBETH, George (Mann). Scottish. Born in Shotts, Lanarkshire, 19 January 1932. Educated at King Edward VII School, Sheffield, Yorkshire; New College, Oxford, B.A. (honours) in classical greats 1955. Married Elizabeth Browell Robson in 1955. Editor, *Poet's Voice* programme, 1958–65, *New Comment* programme, 1959–64, and *Poetry Now* programme, 1965–76, BBC, London. Editor, Fantasy Poets series, Fantasy Press, Oxford, 1952–54. Recipient: Faber Memorial Award, 1964; Cholmondeley Award, 1977. Lives in London. Address: Anthony Sheil Associates, 2–3 Morwell Street, London WC1B 3AR, England.

PUBLICATIONS

Verse

A Form of Words. Oxford, Fantasy Press, 1954.

Lecture to the Trainees. Oxford, Fantasy Press, 1962.
The Broken Places. Lowestoft, Suffolk, Scorpion Press, 1963; New York, Walker, 1968.
Penguin Modern Poets 6, with Jack Clemo and Edward Lucie-Smith. London, Penguin, 1964.
A Doomsday Book: Poems and Poem-Games. Lowestoft, Suffolk, Scorpion Press, 1965.
The Twelve Hotels. London, Turret, 1965.
Missile Commander. London, Turret, 1965.
The Calf. London, Turret, 1965.
The Humming Birds: A Monodrama. London, Turret, 1966.
The Castle. Privately printed, 1966.
The Screens. London, Turret, 1967.
The Colour of Blood. London, Macmillan, and New York, Atheneum, 1967.
The Night of Stones. London, Macmillan, 1968; New York, Atheneum, 1969.
A War Quartet. London, Macmillan, 1969.
A Death. Frensham, Surrey, Sceptre Press, 1969.
Zoo's Who. Privately printed, 1969.
The Burning Cone. London, Macmillan, 1970.
The Bamboo Nightingale. Frensham, Surrey, Sceptre Press, 1970.
Poems. Frensham, Surrey, Sceptre Press, 1970.
The Hiroshima Dream. London, Academy, 1970.
Two Poems. Frensham, Surrey, Sceptre Press, 1970.
A Prayer, Against Revenge. Rushden, Northamptonshire, Sceptre Press, 1971.
The Orlando Poems. London, Macmillan, 1971.
Collected Poems 1958–1970. London, Macmillan, 1971.
A Farewell. Rushden, Northamptonshire, Sceptre Press, 1972.
Lusus: A Verse Lecture. London, Fuller d'Arch Smith, 1972.
A Litany. Rushden, Northamptonshire, Sceptre Press, 1972.
Shrapnel. London, Macmillan, 1973.
Prayers. Solihull, Warwickshire, Aquila, 1973.
The Vision. Rushden, Northamptonshire, Sceptre Press, 1973.
A Poet's Year. London, Gollancz, 1973.
Shrapnel, and A Poet's Year. New York, Atheneum, 1974.
Elegy for the Gas Dowsers. Knotting, Bedfordshire, Sceptre Press, 1974.
In the Hours Waiting for the Blood to Come. London, Gollancz, 1975.
The Journey to the Island. Knotting, Bedfordshire, Sceptre Press, 1975.
Last Night. Knotting, Bedfordshire, Sceptre Press, 1976.
Buying a Heart. London, J. Jay, and New York, Atheneum, 1978.

Plays

The Doomsday Show (produced London, 1964). Published in *New English Dramatists 14*, London, Penguin, 1970.
The Scene-Machine, music by Anthony Gilbert (produced Kassel, Germany, 1971; London, 1972). Mainz, Germany, B. Schott's Söhne, 1971.

Novels

The Transformation. London, Gollancz, 1975.
The Samurai. New York, Harcourt Brace, 1975; London, Quartet, 1976.
The Survivor. London, Quartet, 1977; New York, Harcourt Brace, 1978.
The Seven Witches. London, W. H. Allen, and New York, Harcourt Brace, 1978.

Other

Noah's Journey (juvenile). London, Macmillan, and New York, Viking Press, 1966.

Jonah and the Lord (juvenile). London, Macmillan, 1969; New York, Holt Rinehart, 1970.
My Scotland: Fragments of a State of Mind. London, Macmillan, 1973.

Editor, *The Penguin Book of Sick Verse.* London, Penguin, 1963.
Editor, *The Penguin Book of Animal Verse.* London, Penguin, 1965.
Editor, *Poetry 1900–1965: An Anthology.* London, Longman-Faber, 1967.
Editor, *The Penguin Book of Victorian Verse: A Critical Anthology.* London, Penguin, 1969.
Editor, *The Falling Splendour: Poems of Alfred, Lord Tennyson.* London, Macmillan, 1970.
Editor, with Martin Booth, *The Book of Cats.* London, Secker and Warburg, 1976; New York, Morrow, 1977.

Manuscript Collections: University of California, Los Angeles; State University of New York, Buffalo.

Critical Studies. *The New Poets: American and British Poetry since World War II* by M. L. Rosenthal, London and New York, Oxford University Press, 1967; "The Poetry of George MacBeth" by D. M. Black, in *Scottish International* (Edinburgh), August 1968; Roger Garfitt, in *British Poetry since 1960*, edited by Michael Schmidt and Grevel Lindop, Oxford, Carcanet Press, 1972.

* * *

George MacBeth is the most inventive poet of his generation in Britain. His fluency with ideas is accompanied by an equally pronounced skill in versification. He has been very influential, and although he is eclectic in style it is already possible to point to passages in other poets' work which show his influence. He disclaims the title of an intellectual, but he has a seminal intelligence which is perhaps the strongest in British poetry since Auden. Like Auden, he is a popular poet: even his most recondite pieces are written for the general public. Often he overestimates the public's willingness to work at a poem and consequently he can be obscure. But every poem is well planned – he is not hermetic and does not subscribe to a closed aesthetic order or a professional poets club in the manner of Robert Graves. He is a very prolific writer and publishes a lot in pamphlets and limited editions and his poems are often seen in magazines. He tends to operate a poetic canon when collecting his poems into books, but some of his most interesting achievements (such as "The Crab-Apple Crisis" and "Amelia's Will") are uncollected.

MacBeth's first book, *A Form of Words*, is now a collector's piece. These intellectual shavings from the later Caroline poets and from Empson were almost parodies, but revealed for the first time his playfulness with words. His second book, *The Broken Places*, is still, in many ways, his strongest. His preoccupation with violence and cruelty, which has been much remarked on, is present in this book in poems such as "Report to the Director," "The Disciple," "Drop," and "The Son," but so in other poems is a classically sustained note of elegy and a sympathetic talent for autobiography. It should be stressed that the caricature of him as a poet obsessed with the gamiest forms of nastiness is a simplification amounting to a calumny. *The Broken Places* also contains some of the first of MacBeth's dandified interpretations of the past. He has celebrated authors who are men of action like Hemingway and D'Annunzio and he has a natural sympathy for the larger-than-life artists of the late nineteenth century. One of the most original poems in *The Broken Places* is "The Spider's Nest," an ingenious monologue spoken by Eugene Lee-Hamilton, the crippled English poet who lived in Florence. Fin-de-siècle enthusiasms have grown on him until the diction and rhythms of some of his recent poems have acquired a drugged and purple solemnity which is not his best style.

A Doomsday Book is a collection of poems in honour of Homo Ludens, a figure MacBeth, like Auden, places very high in the Pantheon of fallen man. The tone of MacBeth's macabre jokes, such as "Fin-du-Globe" (an apocalyptic card-game poem) and "The Ski Murders," is equivocal. He has a love of picture-stories and games with rules and has used them in poems to take the portentousness out of death and violence. He is not frivolous but appears frequently as a player: his finest work is as detailed and energetic as a medieval Triumph of Death. Both *The Colour of Blood* and *The Night of Stones* show him continuing to explore his major themes but also experimenting with techniques of the avant-garde. MacBeth's originality as a poet lies in the use he makes of the hundreds of styles available to the modern poet. He is not a dedicated innovator and after producing a suitably outrageous experimental poem, he will often write another in a traditional mode. His realisations of Chinese poems in *The Colour of Blood* are hilarious bits of chinoiserie and show him ready to use concrete poetry and sound poetry for his own purposes. In his copious output there are many remarkable poems about animals and a number of successful ones for children, of which "Noah's Journey" is the most considerable. "At Crufts" and "Fourteen Ways of Touching the Peter" from *The Night of Stones* are vignettes in syllabics of pedigree dogs and his own cat. Here is part of his description of the Chow: "your/tail/over-curled/as if attempting/to open/yourself/like a tin/of pilchards...." No poet writing today has put so much of the touchable surface of life into his poetry. Yet Macbeth's concerns are ultimately with the major options of poetry – the unswervable matters of death and life, war and love. It is not possible to forecast what so volatile a poet will do next, but he has written enough good poems already to earn him a high place in the history of post-war English verse.

—Peter Porter

MacCAIG, Norman (Alexander). Scottish. Born in Edinburgh, 14 November 1910. Educated at Royal High School, Edinburgh; Edinburgh University, M.A. (honours) in classics 1932. Married Isabel Munro in 1940; two children. Schoolteacher, 1934–67, and Headmaster, 1969–70, Edinburgh; Fellow in Creative Writing, Edinburgh University, 1967–69. Lecturer in English Studies, 1970–72, and since 1972, Reader in Poetry, University of Stirling. Recipient: Scottish Arts Council Award, 1957, 1966, 1970, 1971, 1978; Society of Authors grant, 1964, prize, 1967; Heinemann Award, 1967; Cholmondeley Award, 1975. Fellow, Royal Society of Literature, 1965. O.B.E. (Officer, Order of the British Empire), 1979. Address: 7 Leamington Terrace, Edinburgh EH10 4JW, Scotland.

PUBLICATIONS

Verse

Far Cry. London, Routledge, 1943.
The Inward Eye. London, Routledge, 1946.
Riding Lights. London, Hogarth Press, 1955; New York, Macmillan, 1956.
The Sinai Sort. London, Hogarth Press, and New York, Macmillan, 1957.
A Common Grace. London, Chatto and Windus-Hogarth Press, 1960.
A Round of Applause. London, Chatto and Windus-Hogarth Press, 1962.
Measures. London, Chatto and Windus, 1965.
Surroundings. London, Chatto and Windus-Hogarth Press, 1966.
Rings on a Tree. London, Chatto and Windus-Hogarth Press, 1968.
A Man in My Position. London, Chatto and Windus-Hogarth Press, 1969.

Midnights. London, Poem-of-the-Month Club, 1970.
Three Manuscript Poems. Exeter, Devon, Rougemont Press, 1970.
Selected Poems. London, Hogarth Press, 1971.
Penguin Modern Poets 21, with George Mackay Brown and Iain Crichton Smith. London, Penguin, 1972.
The White Bird. London, Chatto and Windus, 1973.
The World's Room. London, Chatto and Windus, 1974.
Tree of Strings. London, Chatto and Windus, 1977.
Old Maps and New: Selected Poems. London, Chatto and Windus, 1978.

Other

Editor, *Honour'd Shade: An Anthology of New Scottish Poetry to Mark the Bicentenary of the Birth of Robert Burns.* Edinburgh, Chambers, 1959.
Editor, with Alexander Scott, *Contemporary Scottish Verse 1959–1969.* London, Calder and Boyars, 1970.

Critical Studies: in *Akros 7* (Preston, Lancashire), 1968.

* * *

Norman MacCaig began his poetic career as one of the most apocalyptic of all the White Horseman's Scottish followers with the two collections *Far Cry* and *The Inward Eye.* Like most of the movement's writers, his verse lunged about in a climate of uncontrolled Romanticism.

I brought you elephants and volcano tops
and a eucalyptus tree on a coral island.
I had them in baskets. You looked with surprise
and went away to pick weeds out of the garden....

Nine years elapsed before MacCaig's next book, *Riding Lights*, appeared; with it the real poet emerged, his imagery now disciplined and sensuously relevant. The book explores his perhaps initially Donne-inspired thematic preoccupation, the relationship of the seeing eye to the world of appearances:

Straws like tame lightnings lie about the grass
And hang zigzag on hedges. Green as glass
The water in the horse-trough shines.
Nine ducks go wobbling by in two straight lines....

Self under self, a pile of selves I stand
Threaded on time, and with metaphysic hand
Lift the farm like a lid and see
Farm within farm, and in centre, me.

For the next decade or so, MacCaig concentrated on exploring, through the physical geography of his two worlds of Edinburgh and the West Highlands, the endlessly variable relationship of the observer to the observed, enriching and often surprising the perceptions of his readers in the doing.

By the mid-1960's, there were some who felt that MacCaig had become merely repetitive, playing variants on his intellect with a limited number of themes (a criticism that overlooks the sheerly enjoyable quality of so much of the contents of each succeeding volume in the 1950's and early 1960's. With *Surroundings* and *Rings on a Tree*, however, he confounded his critics. Visits to Italy and America opened up new reaches and possibilities. The structure of his verse forms loosened, the variety of his themes increased, a tone of accepting sadness became more apparent and in poems like "Assisi" and "Visiting Hour" the metaphysical "royal me" of his New Apocalypse 'prentice days (never wholly tamed, though long since trained to an original and observant maturity) moved over to allow emotional room for wider compassion.

The poetry of his later years, though still nerved by his metaphysical preoccupation, has lost none of its delicate accuracy of seeing, its rock-sure handling of language. The imagery, for the most part, has become more fundamental to the direction of his thought, stripped to the bareness of necessity and now only occasionally relaxing into the sensuous ornamentation that regularly graced so many of his middle-period poems. Meanwhile, the poet has noticeably sharpened his wit on the edge of his own wryness, as in "Gone Are the Days" (*The World's Room*):

> Impossible to call a lamb a lambkin
> or say eftsoons or spell you ladye.
> My shining armour bleeds when it's scratched;
> I blow the nose that's part of my visor....
> So don't expect me, lady with no e,
> To look at a lamb and feel lambkin
> or give me a down look because I bought
> my greaves and cuisses at Marks and Spencers.
>
> Pishtushery's out....

Sometimes in the later work, his metaphor of speculation is not always quite strong enough to support a particular poem, and one is left with a slightly uncomfortable sense of cleverness, a thing constructed for its own sake (a danger to which metaphysicians of every sort constantly lay themselves open). But there has not yet been a MacCaig volume without a number of new poems outstanding even when measured against his own lengthening achievement. MacCaig's territories both of the physical country and of experience, though now creatively fairly fully charted, still seem capable of yielding surprises.

In his increasing communal concern, particularly for the way of life of the people of his beloved Sutherlandshire, MacCaig may perhaps be seen as a kind of Scottish counterpart to R. S. Thomas, though with a metaphysical rather than a Christian bent of tolerance. Certainly, as Thomas has made the harsh enduring of the Welsh small farm tradition comprehensible to the rest of the English-speaking world, so MacCaig, with an alert freshness of the imagination that belies the Scottish metaphysical tradition from which (in part at least) he springs, has illumined an aspect of mind that has played a major part in the shaping of the Scottish character. Since the death of MacDiarmid in 1978, the mantle of Scotland's *eminence grise* has fallen upon MacCaig. Yet his contribution to poetry in English written during the second half of the 20th century is as enjoyably individual as it is richly distinguished.

—Maurice Lindsay

MacEWEN, Gwendolyn (Margaret). Canadian. Born in Toronto, Ontario, 1 September 1941. Educated in public schools. Married 1) Milton Acorn, *q.v.*; 2) Nikos Tsingos in 1972. Since 1960, Part-time Librarian, Children's Public Library, Toronto. Recipient: Canadian Broadcasting Corporation prize, 1965; Canada Council Scholarship, 1965, 1969, Senior Arts grant, 1973; Governor-General's Award, 1970. Lives in Toronto. Agent: Anne McDermid, David Higham Associates, 5–8 Lower John Street, London W1R 3PE, England.

PUBLICATIONS

Verse

Selah. Toronto, Aleph Press, 1961.
The Drunken Clock. Toronto, Aleph Press, 1961.
The Rising Sun. Toronto, Contact Press, 1963; as *The Rising Fire*, 1964.
A Breakfast for Barbarians. Toronto, Ryerson Press, 1966.
The Shadow-Maker. Toronto, Macmillan, 1969.
The Armies of the Moon. Toronto, Macmillan, 1972.
Magic Animals: Selected Poems, Old and New. Toronto, Macmillan, 1974.
The Fire-Eaters. Ottawa, Oberon Press, 1976.

Recording: *Open Secrets*, CBC Toronto, 1971.

Plays

Radio Plays: *Terror and Erebus*; *Tesla*; *The World of Neshiah*; *The Death of the Loch Ness Monster*; *The Sweet Breath of the Pard*; *A Celebration of Evil.*

Novels

Julian the Magician. Toronto, Macmillan, and New York, Corinth, 1963.
King of Egypt, King of Dreams. Toronto, Macmillan, 1972.

Short Stories

Noman. Ottawa, Oberon Press, 1972.

Manuscript Collection: University of Toronto.

Critical Studies: "To Improvise an Eden" by Ian Sowton, in *Edge 2* (Montreal), 1964; by George Whalley, in *Quarry* (Kingston, Ontario), 1967; "They Shall Have Arcana" by George Whalley, in *Queen's Quarterly* (Kingston, Ontario), 1967; "MacEwen's Muse" by Margaret Atwood, in *Canadian Literature* (Vancouver), Summer 1970; *Butterfly on Rock*, by D. G. Jones, Toronto, University of Toronto Press, 1970; *15 Canadian Poets* by Gary Geddes, Toronto, Oxford University Press, 1971.

Gwendolyn MacEwen comments:

Major themes include the discovery of mythological patterns and archetypal forces which are present in modern life – the exploration of the meaning of time – human time, cosmic time – frequent use of irony, paradox, dualism to express ambiguous human state – preoccupation with the bi-polarity of life. Also the discovery of the transcendental realities of human love and all human relationships – the search for a reality which resolves all contradictions.

* * *

"Gwendolyn MacEwen is preoccupied with time and its multiple meanings, with the ambivalences of existence, with the archetypal patterns that emerge and re-emerge from ancient times to now," as George Woodcock wrote in his entry devoted to the poet in the *Supplement to the Oxford Companion to Canadian History and Literature* (1973). This may be so, yet the explanation seems heavy beside the achievement, which is light, graceful, imaginative, and refreshingly free of pretension.

The quest for a leader, or saviour, or cultural hero, has taken MacEwen through two novels and a collection of short stories, all essentially poetic. *Julian the Magician* creates an imaginary alchemist out of wholecloth. With *King of Egypt, King of Dreams*, she finds her mythic man in the person of Ikhnaton, the heretic-pharaoh of Ancient Egypt, and this permits her to present the vision in the form of historical fiction. Perhaps the most successful of the prose works is *Noman*, in which the poet's fancy is free to make wide connections without the need to create a credible personality for her mysterious "Noman." The elusive figure, a kind of Jean Sans Terre, "became whatever he encountered."

If *Noman* is poetry written in the form of prose, MacEwen's books of verse are very much poetry. From *The Rising Sun* (1963) to *The Armies of the Moon* (1972), her poems have grown more self-contained and her vision of the magical properties of everyday things has grown clearer. Like a mediaeval alchemist, she turns base experiences into rare epiphanies. Coupled with the imaginative insights there is a *fey* quality to her writing which, playful and elusive, may be found in her description, say, of a cat hiding behind its own shadow, or her lines "there are so many places for places to hide," or her view that the moon is sending Morse Code messages to the earth. And in "The Vacuum Cleaner Dream" she imagines herself an angelic char "vacuuming the universe." It is only slightly upsetting when she finds among the debris "the sleeping body of my love."

A sense of the magic and wonderful movement of MacEwen's work can be felt in the final stanza of "The Discovery," from *The Shadow-Maker*:

> When you see the land naked, look again
> (burn your maps, that is not what I mean),
> I mean the moment when it seems most plain
> is the moment when you must begin again.

—John Robert Colombo

MACKIE, Alastair (Webster). Scottish. Born in Aberdeen, 10 August 1925. Educated at Skene Square School, 1930–37; Robert Gordon's College, Aberdeen, 1937–43; University of Aberdeen, 1946–50, M.A. (honours) in English 1950. Served in the Royal Air Force, 1943, and the Royal Navy, 1944–46. Married Elizabeth Law in 1951; two children. English Teacher, Stromness Academy, Orkney, 1951–59. Since 1959, English Teacher, Waid Academy, Anstruther, Fife. Recipient: Saltire Prize, 1963; Scottish Arts Council bursary, 1976. Address: 13 St. Adrian's Place, Anstruther, Fife, Scotland.

PUBLICATIONS

Verse

Soundings. Preston, Lancashire, Akros, 1966.
To Duncan Glen. Preston, Lancashire, Akros, 1971.

Clytach. Preston, Lancashire, Akros, 1972.
At the Heich Kirk-Yaird: A Hielant Sequence. Preston, Lancashire, Akros, 1974.

Critical Studies: Introduction to *Contemporary Scottish Verse 1959–1969*, edited by Norman MacCaig and Alexander Scott, London, Calder and Boyars, 1970; *Whither Scotland?* edited by Duncan Glen, London, Gollancz, 1971; Robert Garioch, in *Lines Review 42–43* (Edinburgh), 1972; Alexander Scott, in *Glasgow Review 1*, Summer 1972; *The MacDiarmid Makars 1923–1972*, by Alexander Scott, Preston, Lancashire, Akros, 1972; "The Progress of Scots" by J. Herdman, in *Akros 20* (Preston, Lancashire), 1972; J. A. K. Annand, and Donald Campbell, in *Akros 21* (Preston, Lancashire), 1973; "The Poetry of Alastair Mackie" by George Bruce, in *Akros 33* (Preston, Lancashire), April 1977.

Alastair Mackie comments:

My work is directed towards developing the limits of Scots as a vehicle for poetry in the contemporary setting as I am placed in regard to it. I continue the work of MacDiarmid and attempt to annex areas where his influence has not extended. For example, I have written a space sequence in Scots called "Captus Cupidine Coeli." I work for a more extended canon of Scots in order to give Scots poetry bulk and variety. I am more attracted to English translations of European poets – Amichai, Holub, Herbert – than to any contemporary English poetry.

* * *

The publication of Alastair Mackie's collection of poems, *Clytach* (barbarous words), was a matter of consequence to the continuing tradition of poetry in Scots. The book is yet another vindication of the claim Hugh MacDiarmid made 50 years previously to the effect that poetry in the Scots tongue could still contribute apprehensions and perceptions relevant to contemporary life which could not be conveyed in English. In his previous collection, *Soundings*, Mackie's poems in English showed terseness and temper. In his "Notes on 'The Truce' by Primo Levi" he writes:

> Auschwitz in due time
> exported its surplus
>
> Afterwards, the truce
> when the soiled ex-objects
>
> took to trains and began
> their picaresque novels.

This tight-lipped speech has a secure base in the Aberdeenshire dialect which was Alastair Mackie's birthright, though the style witnesses to other influences. His poems in Scots, however, have a rich texture and an intimate responsiveness to his subjects, as well as an ironic turn of phrase that is art and part of his Scots idiom. The wide range of the poet's interest is evident from the titles of the poems in *Clytach*. These include: "The Cosmonaut Hero," "Binary Sets," "Orpheus and Eurydice," "Lines from Mallarmé," "Leopardi on the Hill," "Scots Pegasus," and "Still-Life: Cézanne." Just how appropriate his Scots is to this last subject is clear even from a few phrases. He describes the table on which the apples are set: "The white claith wid aye jist/cowp doun like a lynn aneth the aipples' wecht" [the white cloth would always just tumble down like a waterfall beneath the apples' weight]. He again refers to the apples in the phrase "Yon was mason's work." To re-enact in words the sense of durability and solidity – as if it were the weight of the world that was being presented – requires a language that has retained physical characteristics. One of the best poems that

Mackie has written, "Mongul Quine" (Mongol Girl), presents the child with a blunt directness that draws one up sharply. Mackie writes – "Her blond baa-heid wags [Her blond ball-head wags]/frae side to side" – yet the poem ends gently and mysteriously with the words: "Ayont the hert-brak her een/are set for ever on an unkent airt" [Beyond the heartbreak her eyes are set forever on an unknown place].

Though the Scots may initially daunt readers unacquainted with it, the centrality of Mackie's interests and comments makes a study of the work of this writer very desirable for all interested in the developments in contemporary poetry.

—George Bruce

MACLEAN, Alasdair. Scottish. Born in Glasgow, Lanarkshire, 16 March 1926. Recipient: Cholmondeley Award, 1974; Heinemann Award, 1974. Address: Sanna, Kilchoan, Ardnamurchan, Argyllshire, Scotland.

PUBLICATIONS

Verse

From the Wilderness. London, Gollancz, 1973; New York, Harper, 1975.
Waking the Dead. London, Gollancz, 1976.

* * *

The attempt to come to grips with the fundamental questions about life with which serious literature ought to concern itself need not of itself relate to the physical location of the writer. Alasdair Maclean left university to work a croft near Ardnamurchan, in Argyll. *From the Wilderness* did not appear before the public until he was into his forties, although something of his quality could be seen from anthologised poems in the annual *Scottish Poetry* and others. He is therefore a late starter, at any rate so far as publication is concerned. All to the good, since it means that for the most part he wants to say things, not merely to gyrate like some youthful virtuoso for the sake of attracting fashionable attention. He also has an assured and personal voice.

He tells his reader bluntly what to expect from him:

I leave the foothills of the images
and climb. What I pursue's not means but ends.
You may come, if you've a mind to travelling.
Meet me at the point where the language bends.

At his best, Maclean writes with a hard, direct economy, drawing his imagery and the strength of his thought from the way of life he loves and with which he is familiar. For instance, there is the countryman's unsentimental approach to matters of life and death, focussed into "Hen Dying":

The other hens have cast her out.
They batter her with their beaks
Whenever they come across her.
Most of them are her daughters.
Hens are inhuman.

His poems "Rams," using the same terse short-sentence style, builds up a powerful apprehension of nature's sexual prodigality, and mindless directorial force, a fact which the ingenuity of *homo sapiens* often contrives for comfort to fudge:

I found a ram dead once.
It was trapped by the forefeet
in the dark waters of a peatbog,
drowned before help could arrive
by the sheer weight of its skull.
Maiden ewes were grazing near it,
immune to its clangerous lust.
It knelt on the bank, hunched over its own image
its great head buried in the great head facing it.
Its horns, going forward in the old way,
had battered through at last to the other side.

Not a word, not a rhythm is false there; and Maclean has many poems with this quality in his first collection. There is also some harsh satire apparently arising, though not always admitting such origin, out of the unconfessed awareness of the Gael that his way of life and his culture are now peripheral, and that, rant as he may against the urban-dwelling Lowlander, the Gael himself has been his own worst enemy. Not all of these outbursts are entirely plausible, as in "Eagles":

An eagle of that breed once, for a joke,
picked up a stunted Highlander
and flew him south, witless from the journey
but fertile still,
Hence your race of Lowland Scots.

Inevitably, as in every collection, there are some bookfiller pieces in which there is evident the metaphysical influence of the later, and poetically drier, Norman MacCaig; such a poem is "Sea and Sky," its feyly sentimental conclusion so out of keeping with the firmness of this poet's best texture and direct-sounding voice. Fanciful trifling of that sort is far below the level of a poet who can ring fierce, rough honesty out of the stoney fields of Ardnamurchan, and the hard life their isolation demands. To me, Maclean is certainly the most interesting Scottish poet to make his appearance for at least a couple of decades.

—Maurice Lindsay

MacLEISH, Archibald. American. Born in Glencoe, Illinois, 7 May 1892. Educated at the Hotchkiss School, Lakeville, Connecticut; Yale University, New Haven, Connecticut, A.B. 1915; Harvard University, Cambridge, Massachusetts, LL.B. 1919. Served in the United States Army, 1917–19: Captain. Married Ada Hitchcock in 1916; three children, two living. Lecturer in Government, Harvard University, 1919–21; Attorney, Choate, Hall, and Stewart, Boston, 1920–23; Editor, *Fortune* magazine, New York, 1929–38; Curator of the Niemann Foundation, Harvard University, 1938; Librarian of Congress, Washington, D.C., 1939–44; Director, United States Office of Facts and Figures, 1941–42, Assistant Director of the Office of War Information, 1942–43, and Assistant Secretary of State, 1944–45, Washington, D.C. Chairman of the United States Delegation to the UNESCO drafting conference, London, 1945, and Member of the Executive Board, UNESCO, 1946. Rede Lecturer, Cambridge University, 1942; Boylston Professor of Rhetoric and Oratory, Harvard University, 1949–62; Simpson Lecturer, Amherst College, Massachusetts, 1964–67. Recipient: Shelley Memorial

Award, 1932; Pulitzer Prize, for verse, 1933, 1953, for drama, 1959; New England Poetry Club Golden Rose, 1934; Levinson Prize (*Poetry*, Chicago), 1941; Bollingen Prize, 1952; National Book Award, 1953; Sarah Josepha Hale Award, 1958; Tony Award, for drama, 1959; National Association of Independent Schools Award, 1959; Academy of American Poets Fellowship, 1965; Academy Award, 1966; Presidential Medal of Freedom, 1977; National Medal for Literature, 1978. M.A.: Tufts University, Medford, Massachusetts, 1932; Litt.D.: Wesleyan University, Middletown, Connecticut, 1938; Colby College, Waterville, Maine, 1938; Yale University, 1939; University of Pennsylvania, Philadelphia, 1941; University of Illinois, Urbana, 1947; Rockford College, Illinois, 1952; Columbia University, New York, 1954; Harvard University, 1955; Carleton College, Northfield, Minnesota, 1956; Princeton University, New Jersey, 1965; University of Massachusetts, Amherst, 1969; York University, Toronto, 1971; LL.D.: Dartmouth College, Hanover, New Hampshire, 1940; Johns Hopkins University, Baltimore, 1941; University of California, Berkeley, 1943; Queen's University, Kingston, Ontario, 1948; University of Puerto Rico, Rio Piedras, 1953; Amherst College, Massachusetts, 1963; D.C.L.: Union College, Schenectady, New York, 1941; L.H.D.: Williams College, Williamstown, Massachusetts, 1942; University of Washington, Seattle, 1948. Commander, Legion of Honor; Commander, El Sol del Peru. President, American Academy of Arts and Letters, 1953–56. Address: Conway, Massachusetts 01341, U.S.A.

PUBLICATIONS

Verse

Songs for a Summer's Day (A Sonnet-Cycle). New Haven, Connecticut, Yale University Press, 1915.
Tower of Ivory. New Haven, Connecticut, Yale University Press, and London, Oxford University Press, 1917.
The Happy Marriage and Other Poems. Boston, Houghton Mifflin, 1924.
The Pot of Earth. Boston, Houghton Mifflin, 1925.
Streets in the Moon. Boston, Houghton Mifflin, 1926.
The Hamlet of A. MacLeish. Boston, Houghton Mifflin, 1928.
Einstein. Paris, Black Sun Press, 1929.
New Found Land: Fourteen Poems. Paris, Black Sun Press, and Boston, Houghton Mifflin, 1930.
Before March. New York, Knopf, 1932.
Conquistador. Boston, Houghton Mifflin, 1932; London, Gollancz, 1933.
Frescoes for Mr. Rockefeller's City. New York, Day, 1933.
Poems 1924–1933. Boston, Houghton Mifflin, 1933; as *Poems*, London, Boriswood, 1935.
Public Speech. New York, Farrar and Rinehart, and London, Boriswood, 1936.
Land of the Free – U.S.A. New York, Harcourt Brace, and London, Boriswood, 1938.
Dedication: Motet for Six Voices, music by Douglas Stuart. New York, Arrow Music Press, 1938.
America Was Promises. New York, Duell, 1939; London, Lane, 1940.
Freedom's Land, music by Roy Harris. New York, Mills Music, 1942.
Actfive and Other Poems. New York, Random House, 1948; London, Lane, 1950.
Collected Poems 1917–1952. Boston, Houghton Mifflin, 1952.
Songs for Eve. Boston, Houghton Mifflin, 1954.
New York. Milan, Scheiwiller, 1958.
Collected Poems. Boston, Houghton Mifflin, 1963.
"The Wild Old Wicked Man" and Other Poems. Boston, Houghton Mifflin, 1968; London, W. H. Allen, 1969.
The Human Season: Selected Poems 1926–1972. Boston, Houghton Mifflin, 1972.

New and Collected Poems 1917–1976. Boston, Houghton Mifflin, 1976.

Recording: *Archibald MacLeish Reads His Own Poetry*, Caedmon.

Plays

Nobodaddy. Cambridge, Massachusetts, Dunster House, 1926.
Union Pacific (ballet scenario; produced New York, 1934). Published in *The Book of Ballets*, New York, Crown, 1939.
Panic: A Play in Verse (produced New York, 1935; London, 1936). Boston, Houghton Mifflin, 1935; London, Boriswood, 1936.
The Fall of the City: A Verse Play for Radio (broadcast, 1937). New York, Farrar and Rinehart, and London, Boriswood, 1937.
Air Raid: A Verse Play for Radio (broadcast, 1938). New York, Harcourt Brace, 1938; London, Lane, 1939.
The States Talking (broadcast, 1941). Published in *The Free Company Presents*, edited by James Boyd, New York, Dodd Mead, 1941.
The American Story: Ten Radio Scripts (includes *The Admiral*; *The American Gods*; *The American Name*; *Not Bacon's Bones*; *Between the Silence and the Surf*; *Discovered*; *The Many Dead*; *The Names for the Rivers*; *Ripe Strawberries and Gooseberries and Sweet Single Roses*; *Socorro, When Your Sons Forget*) (broadcast, 1944). New York, Duell, 1944.
The Trojan Horse (broadcast, 1952). Boston, Houghton Mifflin, 1952.
This Music Crept by Me upon the Waters (broadcast, 1953). Cambridge, Massachusetts, Harvard University Press, 1953.
J.B.: A Play in Verse (produced Washington, D.C., and New York, 1958; London, 1961). Boston, Houghton Mifflin, 1958; London, Secker and Warburg, 1959.
The Secret of Freedom (televised, 1959). Included in *Three Short Plays*, 1961.
Three Short Plays: The Secret of Freedom, Air Raid, The Fall of the City. New York, Dramatists Play Service, 1961.
Our Lives, Our Fortunes, and Our Sacred Honor (as *The American Bell*, music by David Amram, produced Philadelphia, 1962). Published in *Think* (Armonk, New York), July–August 1961.
Herakles: A Play in Verse (produced Ann Arbor, Michigan, 1965). Boston, Houghton Mifflin, 1967.
An Evening's Journey to Conway, Massachusetts: An Outdoor Play (produced Conway, 1967). Northampton, Massachusetts, Gehenna Press, 1967.
Scratch, suggested by *The Devil and Daniel Webster* by Stephen Vincent Benét (produced Boston and New York, 1971). Boston, Houghton Mifflin, 1971.
The Great American Fourth of July Parade (produced Pittsburgh, 1975). Pittsburgh, University of Pittsburgh Press, 1975.

Screenplays: *Grandma Moses*, 1950; *The Eleanor Roosevelt Story*, 1965.

Radio Plays: *The Fall of the City*, 1937; *King Lear*, from the play by Shakespeare, 1937; *Air Raid*, 1938; *The States Talking*, 1941; *The American Story* series, 1944; *The Son of Man*, 1947; *The Trojan Horse*, 1952; *This Music Crept by Me upon the Waters*, 1953.

Television Play: *The Secret of Freedom*, 1959.

Other

The Irresponsibles: A Declaration. New York, Duell, 1940.
The Next Harvard, As Seen by Archibald MacLeish. Cambridge, Massachusetts, Harvard University Press, 1941.

A Time to Speak: The Selected Prose of Archibald MacLeish. Boston, Houghton Mifflin, 1941.
The American Cause. New York, Duell, 1941.
American Opinion and the War: The Rede Lecture. Cambridge, University Press, and New York, Macmillan, 1942.
A Time to Act: Selected Addresses. Boston, Houghton Mifflin, 1943.
Poetry and Opinion: The Pisan Cantos of Ezra Pound: A Dialog on the Role of Poetry. Urbana, University of Illinois Press, 1950.
Freedom Is the Right to Choose: An Inquiry into the Battle for the American Future. Boston, Beacon Press, 1951; London, Lane, 1952.
Poetry and Journalism. Minneapolis, University of Minnesota, 1958.
Poetry and Experience. Boston, Houghton Mifflin, and London, Bodley Head, 1961.
The Dialogues of Archibald MacLeish and Mark Van Doren, edited by Warren V. Busch. New York, Dutton, 1964.
The Eleanor Roosevelt Story. Boston, Houghton Mifflin, 1965.
A Continuing Journey. Boston, Houghton Mifflin, 1968.
The Great American Frustration. Stamford, Connecticut, Overbrook Press, 1968.
Champion of a Cause: Essays and Addresses on Librarianship, edited by Eva M. Goldschmidt. Chicago, American Library Association, 1971.
Riders on the Earth: Essays and Reminiscences. Boston, Houghton Mifflin, 1978.

Editor, with E. F. Prichard, Jr., *Law and Politics: Occasional Papers of Felix Frankfurter 1913–1938.* New York, Capricorn, 1962.

Other journalism pieces, lectures, and pamphlets published.

Bibliography: *A Catalogue of the First Editions of Archibald MacLeish* by Arthur Mizener, New Haven, Connecticut, Yale University Library, 1938; *Archibald MacLeish: A Checklist* by Edward J. Mullaly, Kent, Ohio, Kent State University Press, 1973.

Manuscript Collections: Library of Congress, Washington, D.C.; Yale University, New Haven, Connecticut; Harvard University, Cambridge, Massachusetts.

* * *

Archibald MacLeish's lines, "And what became of him? Fame became of him" apply very well to himself – for fame is certainly what became of Archibald MacLeish: few poets have known more honor in their own time, and he has been accorded a respect rare in American cultural life. As Librarian of Congress for some years, as an active and influential government adviser under Franklin Roosevelt, as Assistant Secretary of State, as Harvard professor, as winner of the Bollingen Prize, the National Book Award, the Pulitzer prize, and as an active figure in the world of virtually every art and half-art in America, MacLeish has either moved toward public taste or made it move toward him. His work reveals a highly sensitive awareness of what appeals to the public – there is in it the high-sounding authority of really great art – and because he has been such an eminent man of letters, his ultimate reputation will depend as much on the assessment of his use of office as on his lyrics; he will be subject to the researches of those who want to set straight the social record of American poetry. People will want to know if he really should have advised E. E. Cummings against reading his poem on the Hungarian Revolution at the Boston arts festival, and whether he shouldn't have tried harder to find funds for those poets – Maxwell Bodenheim and others – who dunned him for help while he was Librarian of Congress.

In fact, MacLeish's responsibilities have been so heavy that it is a wonder he has had the time for such an immense outpouring of poems, radio dramas, and plays – all informed by his sense of history, of America's past. This vision is generic, often even jingoistic ("There was a time, Tom Jefferson,/When freedom made free men. The new found earth and the new freed mind"). MacLeish has always worked for a sense of the sublime, and he was never so infected with Pound's notions as to turn away from abstraction and rhetoric when he needed it. Nor has he been afraid, in courting a public audience, to run into charges, perhaps jealously inspired, that he is the poet of the middle-brow, the playwright of the mass man. His warning of the impending doom of mankind, in *J.B.*, is at once an obvious and topical parallel, but it is also a convincing attempt to meet a sense of historical responsibility which MacLeish obviously feels with great depth and sincerity. In short, MacLeish ranks with Robinson Jeffers and Carl Sandburg in the penetration of popular taste.

But it is also an age when poets are judged by their technical innovations, and in this sense MacLeish cannot stand beside Cummings, Pound, or Williams. Like many poets MacLeish may find his most ambitious works absorbed, utterly consumed, by their audience: perhaps it is enough that men left a performance of *J.B.* inspired and went out to lead better lives – while his quieter work lives on in shorter, more private lyrics, scattered through a dozen volumes. In MacLeish's canon such shorter poems are those like "The Snow Fall" and "The Linden Trees" and "Poem in Prose" ("Wherever she is there is sun/ And time and a sweet air/Peace is there/Work done"). And his sense of the magic of places, of the sweetness of energy spent, may survive: "This poem is made for my wife/I have made it plainly and honestly/The Mark is on it/Like the burl of the knife." Long after the speeches ("They say: We were young. We have died. Remember us") one goes on admiring the simple and straightforward ("There are always curtains and flowers/And candles and baked bread/And a cloth spread/And a clean house"). It is perhaps the high dignity of his verse that everyone will acknowledge and remember.

—David Ray

MACLEOD, Joseph (Todd Gordon). Pseudonym: Adam Drinan. British (Scottish). Born in Ealing, Middlesex, 24 April 1903. Educated at Rugby School, 1917–22; Balliol College, Oxford, 1922–25, B.A. 1925, M.A. 1945; Inner Temple, London, called to the Bar 1928. Married 1) Kathleen Macgregor Davis in 1928 (died, 1953); 2) Maria Teresa Foschini; one son and one daughter. Director and Lessee, Festival Theatre, Cambridge, 1933–36; Newsreader and Commentator, BBC, London, 1938–45; Managing Director, Scottish National Film Studios, 1946–47. Secretary, Huntingdonshire Divisional Labour Party, 1937–38, and Parliamentary Candidate. Toured Holland as a guest of the Dutch Government, 1946, and the U.S.S.R. as a guest of the Soviet Government, 1947. Honorary Life Member, British Actors' Equity, 1970. Recipient: Royal Society of Arts Silver Medal, 1944; Scottish Arts Council prize, for drama, 1952, for verse, 1973. Address: Via delle Ballodole 9/7, Trespiano, 50139 Florence, Italy.

PUBLICATIONS

Verse (as Adam Drinan)

The Cove: A Sequence of Poems. Privately printed, 1940.
The Men of the Rocks. London, Fortune Press, 1942.
Women of the Happy Island. Glasgow, Maclellan, 1944.

Verse (as Joseph Macleod)

The Ecliptic. London, Faber, 1930.

Foray of Centaurs. Paris, This Quarter, 1931.
The Passage of the Torch. Edinburgh, Oliver and Boyd, 1951.
Script from Norway (under both names). Glasgow, Maclellan, 1953.
An Old Olive Tree. Edinburgh, Macdonald, 1971.

Plays

The Suppliants of Aeschylus with a Verse Sequel (produced Cambridge, 1933).
A Woman Turned to Stone (produced Cambridge, 1934).
Overture to Cambridge (produced Cambridge, 1934).
Miracle for St. George (produced Cambridge, 1935).
The Ghosts of the Strath. London, Fortune Press, 1943.
Leap in September (produced Perth, 1952).

Screenplay: *Someone Wasn't Thinking,* 1947.

Novel

Overture to Cambridge: A Satirical Story. London, Allen and Unwin, 1934.

Other

Beauty and the Beast. London, Chatto and Windus, 1927; New York, Viking Press, 1928.
The New Soviet Theatre. London, Allen and Unwin, 1943.
Actors Cross the Volga. London, Allen and Unwin, 1946.
A Job at the BBC (autobiography). Glasgow, Maclellan, 1947.
A Soviet Theatre Sketch-Book. London, Allen and Unwin, 1951.
Piccola Storia del Teatro Britannico (A Short History of the British Theatre). Florence, Sansoni, 1958.
Poeple of Florence. London, Allen and Unwin, 1968.
The Sisters d'Aranyi (biography). London, Allen and Unwin, 1969; Boston, Crescendo, 1972.

Manuscript Collections: National Library of Scotland, Edinburgh; Society for Theatre Research, London.

Joseph Macleod comments:

Though Auden and I were greeted in the U.S.A. as a "Dawn in Britain," I never belonged to his school, nor any other I'm aware of. Like most of my poetic generation I was liberated from the word-joys of classical verse (greek melic) by the actuality – accuracies of Ezra Pound. Seeking accuracy has avoided some of the dangers of having a responsive technique and a wide vocabulary. It results in words sometimes outré or obsolete, or can break through the inadequacies of formal grammar.

On the other hand, most of my adult life has been spent in the performing arts (theatre, politics, broadcasting): and the habit of thinking into other people's ears has probably given my verse spoken rhythms and reactions, scottish (Highland father, Perthshire mother) or english (circumstances).

Each word makes up its poem, each poem its book, each book a new part of the same long voyage of discovery. Locality and people: each makes up the other. Without them one would have no personal awareness: so they make up me too. In these circumstances I can't know my direction unless I know the way the world is going. The world is confused by men of action, of commerce and of cruelty. But poetic thought is not confined to these: it can refuse people. For this reason I find my work getting more and more metaphysical. For that reason I feel as much out of sympathy now with the often thoughtless sensationalism of the 70's as I did with the often thoughtless sentimentalism of the 30's.

Poetry = fact + thought = experience. I would like to see myself as a poet who crystallizes (and possibly illuminates?) his and others' experience by discovering it in words.

But readers may not see my work so; and I have no idea of its public effect.

Does this matter?

* * *

Joseph Macleod divides his long poem *The Ecliptic* into 12 sections, each under a sign of the zodiac. "Each," he writes in his introduction, "thus contributes to a single consciousness." Preoccupation with the idea of a "single consciousness" occurs when it is under threat. Those poets who mattered most in the twenties were much concerned with the fragmentation of cultures and consciousness. In his note on this section, "Cancer," Macleod writes: "There is a phase in the twenties when this disintegration becomes complete." He was referring to age only but the comment has, by chance, the other application. It is not surprising that this section carries more conviction than the others, 40 years after the poem was written. Influenced by Pound in method and style, it has a robust directness that is Macleod's own:

> But the Crab is nobody
> Nobody
> Nobody

The poem ends on the word "Nothing."

And there was nothing more from Macleod until some 12 years later, when he began to write poetry dealing with life in the Hebrides under the pseudonym of Adam Drinan. Some of his forebears came from Drinan in Skye. He discovered he had roots in an ancient way of life which he could admire. His poetic problem was how to relate his modern sense of rhythm to the movement of island speech. The temptation of a poet with an exquisite ear was to imitate the cadences of the Gaelic tongue. The desire to identify aurally might become a substitute for genuine identification with the mores and social concerns of the people and indeed those verses which witness to Macleod's social conscience resolve his poetic problem completely. When his lyrical lament is stiffened by references to the "rusty English trawler" that threatens the livelihood of the natives, he writes fine poems such as "Our Pastures Are Bitten and Bare." A delicate balance, however, was involved. How frequently he sustained it may be gathered from his books *The Men of the Rocks* and *Women of the Happy Island*.

The simplification to Adam Drinan was a temporary, but successful, solution to the dilemma of poetic identity. *Script from Norway*, published under both names, capitalised on both sides of the personality, by presenting this poem in dramatic form, though the breach was not healed. Yet later Joseph Macleod was to write some of his finest poems, those particularly where he spoke out of suffering. When he writes "Now that the sun is stopping/ now that the paralysed moon/is gnawn away" we know we are in the presence of a man who is "too wise to include or exclude terror." This has the penetration of maturity but it may still relate to the lively observation of the young man who wrote in *The Ecliptic*: "Butcherboys, square basketed, run to make warm their errands."

—George Bruce

MAC LOW, Jackson. American. Born in Chicago, Illinois, 12 September 1922. Educated at the University of Chicago, 1939–43, A.A. 1941; Brooklyn College, New York, 1955–58, A.B. (cum laude) in philosophy 1958. Married to the painter Iris Lezak; two children. Free-lance music teacher, English teacher, translator and editor, 1950–66; reference book editor, Funk and Wagnalls, 1957–58, 1961–62, and Unicorn Books, 1958–59; copy editor, Alfred A. Knopf, 1965–66, all in New York. Member of the editorial staff, and Poetry Editor, 1950–54, *Why?*, later *Reistance*, a pacifist-anarchist magazine. Instructor, American Language Institute, New York University, 1966–73. Poetry Editor, *WIN* magazine, New York. Recipient: Creative Artists Public Service grant, 1973, 1976; P.E.N. grant, 1974. Address: 42 North Moore Street, New York, New York 10013, U.S.A.

PUBLICATIONS

Verse

The Pronouns: A Collection of 40 Dances – for the Dancers – 6 February–22 March 1964. New York, Jackson Mac Low, 1964; London, Tetrad Press, 1970.
Manifestos. New York, Something Else Press, 1966.
August Light Poems. New York, C. Eshleman, 1967.
22 Light Poems. Los Angeles, Black Sparrow Press, 1968.
23rd Light Poem: For Larry Eigner. London, Tetrad Press, 1969.
Stanzas for Iris Lezak. New York, Something Else Press, 1970.
Four Trains, 4–5 December 1964. Providence, Rhode Island, Burning Deck, 1974.
36th Light Poem: In Memoriam Buster Keaton. New York, Permanent Press, 1975.
3 Light Poems for 3 Women. N.p., Station Hill Press, 1977.
First Book of Gathas. N.p., Membrane Press, 1978.
21 Matched Asymmetries. London, Aloes, 1978.

Recordings: *A Reading of Primitive and Archaic Poems*, with others, Broadside; *From a Shaman's Notebook*, with others, Broadside.

Plays

Biblical Play (produced New York, 1955).
The Marrying Maiden: A Play of Changes, music by John Cage (produced New York, 1960).
Verdurous Sanguinaria (produced New York, 1961). Act I published in *Tulane Drama Review* (New Orleans), Winter 1965.
Thanks: A Simultaneity for People (produced Wiesbaden, 1962).
Letters for Iris, Numbers for Silence (produced Wiesbaden, 1962).
A Piece for Sari Dienes (produced Wiesbaden, 1962).
Thanks II (produced Paris, 1962).
The Twin Plays: Port-au-Prince and Adams County Illinois (produced New York, 1963). New York, Something Else Press, 1966.
Questions and Answers: A Topical Play (produced New York, 1963).
Play (produced New York, 1965).
Asymmetries No. 408, 410, 485 (produced New York, 1965).
Asymmetries, Gathas and Sounds from Everywhere (produced New York, 1966).
A Vocabulary for Carl Fernbach-Flarsheim (produced New York, 1977).

Composer: incidental music for *The Age of Anxiety* by W. H. Auden, produced New York, 1954; for *The Heroes* by John Ashbery, produced New York, 1955.

Theatrical Activities:

Actor: **Plays** – in *Tonight We Improvise* by Pirandello, New York, 1959, and other plays.

Jackson Mac Low comments:

I consider myself a composer: of poetry, music, and theatre works.

I do not think that I belong to any particular school of poetry, but my work is closely related to that of such composers as John Cage, Morton Feldman, Earle Brown, Christian Wolff, and La Monte Young, and it has close affinities with the work of such "concrete" poets as Emmett Williams.

While my earliest work (1937–40) uses mostly free verse and experimental forms, the poems between 1940 and 1954 tend to alternate between traditional metrical forms (and variations on them) and experimental forms, most of which are varieties of free verse. However, from 1954, the poems, plays, and simultaneities incorporate methods, processes, and devices from modern music, including the use of chance operations in composition and/or performance, silences ranging in duration from breath pauses to several minutes, and various degrees of improvisation by performers. Many of the works are "simultaneities" – works performed by several speakers and/or producers of musical sounds and noises at once. These range from completely instrumental pieces (e.g., "Chamber Music for Barney Childs," 1963), thru works combining speech and other sounds (e.g., *Stanzas for Iris Lezak* as simultaneity, 1960), to ones involving only speech (e.g., "Peaks and Lamas," 1959). Other features include indeterminacy (the quality of a work which is in many ways different at every performance) and various degrees of "syntacticalness," ranging from structures that are essentially strings of unrelated words to ones that are partially or fully syntactical in the ordinary sense of the word. Works after 1960 use various proportions of chance and choice in composition and performance. The most recent performance poems (e.g., "Velikovsky Dice-Song," 1968) incorporate multiple slide projections or movies.

* * *

Jackson Mac Low's multifarious activities as an artist are all directed toward the exploration of limits and boundaries: the boundary between poetry and music, poetry and drama, even poetry and dance; or, taken differently, the limits of the ego, of will, of meaning, of significant order. Although he has written in traditional metrical forms and continues to write in an uninhibited variety of free verse which he calls "spontaneous expression," his most characteristic work is an investigation of indeterminacy, chance, and improvisation. His language frequently breaks down to the phonemic level and becomes pure sound. Its meaning derives directly from its structure rather than – like traditional poetry – from its semantic content. In a world in which all meaning appears to become increasingly statistical, the evidence of Mac Low's poetry is of central importance.

The sources of Mac Low's work are diverse. He was educated as a neo-Aristotelian at the University of Chicago, and he remains, in a sense, a classical formalist. He is, however, also a self-proclaimed anarchist and, like John Cage, he has been heavily influenced by Buddhist thought. His practice embodies these ideas in microcosm with remarkable consistency by creating works, as he says, "wherein both other human beings & their environments & the world 'in general' (as represented by such objectively hazardous means as random digits) are all able to act within the general framework & set of 'rules' given by the poet 'the maker of plots or fables' as Aristotle insists – not necessarily of everything that takes place within that framework!"

At its simplest Mac Low's theory produces work like "The Phone Poems," a suite of randomly-generated variations on one of his spontaneous poems. Mac Low, however, is primarily a performance poet, and many of his most characteristic pieces – the gathas and other similar pieces written on graph paper, for example – are not well published. ("5th

Gatha" in *America: A Prophecy*, edited by Jerome Rothenberg and George Quasha, 1973, is one of the most widely available examples of these works.) Typically, in the grid poems, he randomly selects words or phrases from some vocabulary source and arranges them on the grid by predetermined rules. In performance, this "score" becomes the basis for rule-governed improvisation. Although the rules vary from piece to piece, Mac Low always insists that it is an exercise in listening: the performers are asked to give careful attention to the overall form as it develops and to try to contribute to the dynamics of the whole. The performance, in other words, becomes an exploration of group psychology and social order.

In *22 Light Poems*, which is perhaps Mac Low's most beautifully conceived book, the central device is a more or less randomly prepared chart which is keyed to playing cards. "1st Light Poem" is purely a result of random selections from the chart. Others admit "coincidental" input from the environment in which the poem is written (a radio, for example), allow concrete events to stand in place of poems, or freely mix his own spontaneous expression with random material. In one of the light poems written since the publication of the book – there are now thirty-six or more – he allows his numerous typing errors to stand. Despite the indeterminacy, however, *22 Light Poems*, as well as imaginative realizations of the dances in *The Pronouns*, withstand rigorous formal analysis. Order, given an opportunity, thrives.

Mac Low's work adduces cogent evidence that the classic western attitudes toward meaning derive from categorical distinctions which result alternatively in radical isolation of consciousness and ruthless exploitation of the external world. The act of the poem as Mac Low conceives it, rather than isolating the poet in his vision, opens free and useful intercourse between the poet and the external world.

—Don Byrd

MACNAB, Roy (Martin). South African. Born in Durban, 17 September 1923. Educated at Hilton College, Natal; Jesus College, Oxford, M.A. Naval Officer, 1942–45. Married to Rachel Mary Heron-Maxwell; one son and one daughter. Cultural Attaché, South African High Commission, London, 1955–59; Counsellor for Cultural and Press Affairs, South African Embassy, Paris, 1959–67. Since 1968, Director, South Africa Foundation, London. Fellow, Royal Society of Arts. Address: 7 Lincoln Street, London S.W.3, England.

PUBLICATIONS

Verse

Testament of a South African. London, Fortune Press, 1947.
The Man of Grass and Other Poems. London, St. Catherine Press, 1960.

Other

South and Central Africa. New York, McGraw Hill, 1954.
Journey into Yesterday: South African Milestones in Europe. Cape Town, H. Timmins, and London, Bailey Brothers and Swinfen, 1962.
The Youngest Literary Language: The Story of Afrikaans. Johannesburg, South Africa Broadcasting Corporation, 1973.
The French Colonel: Villebois-Mareuil and the Boers 1899–1900. Cape Town and London, Oxford University Press, 1975.
The English-Speaking South Africans. Johannesburg, South African Broadcasting Corporation, 1975.

Editor, with Martin Starkie, *Oxford Poetry 1947*. Oxford, Blackwell, 1947.
Editor, with Charles Gulston, *South African Poetry: A New Anthology*. London, Collins, 1948.
Editor, *Towards the Sun: A Miscellany of South Africa*. London, Collins, 1950.
Editor, *Poets in South Africa: An Anthology*. Cape Town, Maskew Miller, 1958.

Manuscript Collection: Thomas Pringle Collection, Rhodes University, Grahamstown.

Critical Studies: by Anthony Delius, in *Books Abroad* (Norman, Oklahoma), Summer 1955; Guy Butler, in *Listener* (London), 24 May 1956; William Plomer, in *London Magazine*, February 1957; *A Critical Survey of South African Poetry in English*, by G. M. Miller and Howard Sergeant, Cape Town, Balkema, 1957; *South African Poetry*, Pretoria, University of South Africa, 1966.

* * *

Roy Macnab's first book of poetry strikes the reader as a very sincere attempt to convey the poet's thoughts and feelings, but unfortunately the result is somewhat obscured by his struggle with words, a struggle which he seems to have been aware of himself in "The Word":

Said he, the word is a faithless flirt,
Not a lover to your art,
Deceiving with a warm coquetry
Your dreamfilled youth
A spidery dilettante, fondling
Your silver web of thought.

Half-hidden behind this veil of words one senses a very genuine feeling for nature, a deep compassion for the less fortunate among his fellow men and a natural tenderness which finds its best expression in the poem "To a Child." In the poem "The Sick Room" this compassion rises to an impotent fury which unfortunately spoils the poetry and thus proves the truism that genuine involvement does not guarantee genuine poetry.

Although the poems cover a variety of subjects, one experience seems to overshadow all other events in the author's life -- his active participation in the Second World War. This experience left him with a feeling of restless discontent and, like the soldiers of Erich Remarque's books he is constantly searching for a meaning or a purpose in his present life that is noble enough to merit the sacrifices of the war that made it possible, and he is inevitably disappointed. His heroes come back from the War "Battered but unbroken in the time of test," and this is what they find (in "From Turning Tomorrow's Pages"):

Reluctantly turning tomorrow's pages
Where no new sensation is stored,
Only the inevitable dullness of Friday's wages
And further occasion for being bored.

Even those soldiers who died on the battlefield are not allowed to rest in peace, and Macnab is haunted by the knowledge that consequent ages may change their attitude to his heroes. This feeling he expresses in one of his most successful poems, "El-Alamein Revisited":

Six feet is no depth for tragic men
Said the wind and the wind never ceases
To pile up high the soft grey tombs,
And move them where it pleases....

In his disgust with urban life and its tedium Macnab turns to the pioneers, the settlers, the seekers of gold, for it is in these people that he finds the spirit of exploration that so obviously appeals to him.

—Kirsten Holst Petersen

MACPHERSON, (Jean) Jay. Canadian. Born in London, England, 13 June 1931; emigrated to Canada in 1940. Educated at Carleton University, Ottawa, B.A. 1951; University College, London, 1951–52; University of Toronto, M.A. 1955, Ph.D. 1964. Since 1957, Member of the English Department, Victoria College, University of Toronto. Recipient: *Contemporary Verse* prize, 1949; Levinson Prize (*Poetry*, Chicago), 1957; President's Medal, University of Western Ontario, 1957; Governor-General's Award, 1958. Address: Victoria College, University of Toronto, Toronto M5S 1K7, Canada.

PUBLICATIONS

Verse

Nineteen Poems. Deyá, Mallorca, Seizin Press, 1952.
O Earth Return. Toronto, Emblem, 1954.
The Boatman. Toronto, Oxford University Press, 1957.
A Dry Light and the Dark Air. Toronto, Hawkshead Press, 1959.
Welcoming Disaster: Poems 1970–1974. Toronto, Saannes, 1974.

Other

The Four Ages of Man: The Classical Myths (textbook). Toronto, Macmillan, and New York, St. Martin's Press, 1962.
Pratt's Romantic Mythology: The Witches' Brew (lecture). St. John's, Newfoundland, Memorial University, 1972.

Critical Studies: by Kildare Dobbs, in *Canadian Forum* (Toronto), xxxvii, 438; "Poetry" by Northrop Frye, in "Letters in Canada: 1957," in *University of Toronto Quarterly*, xxvii; "The Third Eye" by James Reaney, in *Canadian Literature 3* (Vancouver); Milton Wilson, in *Fiddlehead 34* (Fredericton, New Brunswick); Munro Beattie, in *Literary History of Canada*, Toronto, University of Toronto Press, 1965; "Poetry" by Michael Gnarowski, in "Letters in Canada: 1974," in *University of Toronto Quarterly*, xliv.

* * *

Jay Macpherson's *The Boatman* has been reprinted five times since its first publication in 1957, and has been accepted with enthusiasm by academic critics as well as the general public. The book is a subtly organised suite of lyrics, elegiac, pastoral, epigrammatic, and symbolist, which utilises the traditional forms of quatrain and couplet with great metrical virtuosity and a remarkable flair for the presentation of serious philosophical and, indeed, religious themes in verse that is sometimes beautifully lyrical and sometimes comic in the tradition of Lear or Gilbert or the nursery rhymes – and sometimes both at once.

The book has as its unifying theme the transmutation of time-bound physical reality into the eternal and the spiritual through the magical intermediary of man's imagination. Symbol and myth are the instruments, and the drama of man's fall and redemption is worked out in terms derived from the Bible, Milton, Blake, and such modern poets and scholars as Robert Graves and Northrop Frye. Among the protagonists whose fables supply the seeds of the mystical drama unifying the book are Noah, Leviathan, Sheba, Mary of Egypt, Eurynome, Merlin, Helen, and such symbolic figures as The Plowman, The Fisherman, The Shepherd, and the Angels. One of the reasons for the success of these poems is that they take the reader into the world of childhood's faith in the unquestionable truth of fairy tale and legend. The elegance and grace of the writing and the authority with which wit and a sense of comedy are conveyed in verse that is both timeless and contemporary give the book an appeal also to the most sophisticated of readers.

—A. J. M. Smith

MacSWEENEY, Barry. British. Born in Newcastle upon Tyne, Northumberland, 17 July 1948. Educated at Rutherford Grammar School; Harlow Technical College, 1966–67. Married Elaine Randell in 1972. Formerly, Free-lance Journalist. Currently, Director, Blacksuede Boot Press; Editor, with Elaine Randell, *Harvest* and *The Blacksuede Boot*, Barnet, Hertfordshire. Recipient: *Stand* Prize, 1967; Arts Council grant, 1971. Address: 6 Sherard Mansions, 46 Well Hall Road, London S.E.9, England.

PUBLICATIONS

Verse

Poems 1965–1968: The Boy from the Green Cabaret Tells of His Mother. Hastings, Sussex, The English Intelligencer, 1967; New York, McKay, 1969.
The Last Bud. Newcastle upon Tyne, Blacksuede Boot Press, 1969.
Joint Effort, with Peter Bland. Barnet, Hertfordshire, Blacksuede Boot Press, 1970.
Flames on the Beach at Viareggio. Barnet, Hertfordshire, Blacksuede Boot Press, 1970.
Our Mutual Scarlet Boulevard. London, Fulcrum Press, 1971.
Just 22 and Don't Mind Dyin': The Official Biography of Jim Morrison, Rock Idol. London, Curiously Strong, 1971.
Brother Wolf. London, Turret, 1972.
5 Odes. London, Transgravity Advertiser, 1972.
Dance Steps. London, Joe DiMaggio Press, 1972.
Fog Eye. London, Ted Cavanagh, 1973.
6 Odes. London, Ted Cavanagh, 1973.
Pelt Feather Log. London, Grosseteste Press, 1975.
Odes. London, Trigram Press, 1979.

Other

Elegy for January: An Essay Commemorating the Bi-Centenary of Chatterton's Death. London, Menard Press, 1970.

Barry MacSweeney comments:

Influenced by Shelley, Pound, Blake, Rimbaud; try to reach into the gap between the "real" and the Vita Nuova of the Ideal; the air between the poet and his "dark ideals," some political poetry; lyrical, romantic; Newcastle and Northumberland are a great influence, the hard and sometimes vaporous geography of the fells and valleys. Music is also an influence: Berlioz, Bartok, Vivaldi, Debussy. Also helped revive the poem as the spoken medium; doing many readings. Hard, industrial landscapes of childhood and youth, reflected in the poems, lucid and tensile words like steel or coal; then, softer words reflecting the hills and streams where I go fishing and shooting.

* * *

The diversification of British poetry in the 1960's meant that attention was frequently focused on poets operating from, or at least with their roots in, the provinces. Liverpool was a breeding ground for the so-called "pop" poets, but an equally lively – and in many ways more fertile – scene developed in and around Newcastle. Barry MacSweeney was an important member of the Newcastle poetry community, and time has proved that he is one of the most talented of the various poets who survived the initial wave of group enthusiasm and went on to establish themselves as individuals.

MacSweeney's early work, as represented in *The Boy from the Green Cabaret Tells of His Mother*, has a strong sense of the geography of his locality, and there are frequent references to its physical appearance. But, more important, the rhythm of the poems, and their structure, seem to be shaped by the twin influences of the city and the country. It would be wrong to call MacSweeney a purely urban poet because, like many provincials, he's obviously aware of often being on the edge of the moors or close to the coast. The land, and the sea, spill into his poems, balancing them, and keeping them from becoming merely bright exercises in urban playfulness.

As time passed MacSweeney altered his area of operation, both in physical terms (he left Newcastle in the 1960's) and in terms of what his work dealt with. He began to produce poems (see *Our Mutual Scarlet Boulevard*) which, in his own words, "had to do with dreams; either sleep, fantasy, or the luxurious influence of various hallucinogens." Although perhaps a worthwhile experiment, and certainly displaying skill in construction, the poems lacked the directness and concern of the earlier work, and one wondered if MacSweeney had lost his way in a fashionable maze. But he soon demonstrated that the experience was something he had learned from, rather than being changed by it, and *Brother Wolf* proved he was still his own man. It had a tautness that seemingly came from a desire to discard the unnecessary, and was rich in form and content.

More recent work has continued to revolve around his major interests. *Black Torch* is a long poem-sequence built on the events of a 19th-century miners' strike in the North East, but it also brings in the poet's connection with the area, its traditions, and its landscapes, as well as referring to 20th-century problems facing an idealist in an imperfect world. It is an ambitious work, and although flawed, has much to recommend it. *Odes* goes off in another direction, and is almost mystical at times with MacSweeney seemingly concerned to milk words for the meaning deriving from their rhythm and sound rather than their dictionary definitions. Not all of the pieces work, but at their best they are provokingly mysterious and some lines linger in the mind as if to tease with their play on the subconscious.

The dual role that MacSweeney continues to perform – and his two sides can, and do, intertwine – assures one that he still has much to offer. A semi-surreal view of real events may yet be his major achievement, and the prospect of him bringing it to fruition is an exciting one. He is still a relatively young poet, and yet has built up a fairly impressive body of work in which technical skill is always in evidence. If he continues to blend confidence and imagination he should eventually have a sustained and vigorous bibliography to his credit.

—Jim Burns

MADGE, Charles (Henry). British. Born in Johannesburg, South Africa, 10 October 1912. Educated at Winchester College; Magdalene College, Cambridge. Married 1) Kathleen Raine, *q.v.* (marriage dissolved), one son and one daughter; 2) Inez Pearn, one son and one daughter. Reporter, *Daily Mirror*, London, 1935–36; founded Mass Observation, 1937; Staff Member, National Institute of Social and Economic Research, 1940–42; Research Staff, Policy and Economic Planning, 1943; Director, Pilot Press, London, 1944; Social Development Officer, Stevenage, 1947–50; Professor of Sociology, University of Birmingham, 1950–70. Member, United Nations Technical Assistance Mission, Thailand, 1953–54, India, 1957–58, Southeast Asia, 1959–60; Leader, Mission to Ghana, United Nations Economic Commission for Africa, 1963. Address: La Rivière, 81-Mirandol, France.

PUBLICATIONS

Verse

The Disappearing Castle. London, Faber, 1937.
The Father Found. London, Faber, 1941.

Other

Mass-Observation, with Tom Harrisson. London, Muller, 1937.
War-Time Pattern of Saving and Spending. Cambridge, University Press, and New York, Macmillan, 1943.
Industry after the War: Who Is Going to Run It?, with Donald Tyerman. London, Pilot Press, 1943.
Village Communities in North East Thailand. New York, U.N. Technical Assistance Programme, 1955.
Survey Before Development in Thai Villages. New York, U.N. Secretariat, 1957.
Village Meeting Places: A Pilot Inquiry. Delhi, Indian Ministry of Information, 1958.
Evaluation and the Technical Assistance Expert: An Operational Analysis. Paris, UNESCO, 1961.
Society in the Mind: Elements of Social Eidos. London, Faber, and New York, Free Press of Glencoe, 1964.
Art Students Observed, with Barbara Weinberger. London, Faber, 1973.

Editor, with others, *May the Twelfth: Mass Observation Day-Surveys 1937, by over 200 Observers.* London, Faber, 1937.
Editor, with T. Harrisson, *First Year's Work, 1937–38, by Mass Observation.* London, Lindsay Drummond, 1938.
Editor, with T. Harrisson, *Britain, by Mass Observation.* London, Penguin, and New York, Famous Books, 1938.
Editor, with T. Harrisson, *War Begins at Home, by Mass Observation.* London, Chatto and Windus, 1940.
Editor, *Pilot Guide to the General Election.* London, Pilot Press, 1945.
Editor, *Pilot Papers: Social Essays and Documents, 1945–47.* London, Pilot Press, 1947.

* * *

Charles Madge, who was educated at Winchester and Cambridge (where he came under the influence of William Empson), is an intellectual poet, which may to some extent explain why his poetry has never received the attention it deserves. His earliest poems, collected in *The Disappearing Castle*, demonstrate his readiness to try out new ideas and techniques in his search for an effective medium of communication. If they display many of the weaknesses of the experimentalist, such as ambiguous statements, imprecise images, occasional striving after effects, and surrealistic word-play almost for its own sake, they also hint at his potentialities and reveal an original turn of mind. "Solar Creation," "In Conjunction," "Fortune," and the sequence entitled "Delusions" are among the best of these poems. Like many other poets of the thirties, Madge was concerned with social conditions and "the strain of being man upright in the flat world," but even in these early pieces there is little evidence of the over-simplified analysis of the situation such as those proffered by the Auden-Spender group with whom he has been identified. He had closer affinities with the *Twentieth Century Verse* group of poets, led by Julian Symons, whose theory that the poet ought to be "the perfect mass-observer" was probably derived from Madge's contribution to the development of Mass Observation as a valid instrument of social research.

Madge's second volume, *The Father Found*, marks a distinct advance in technical proficiency. The romantic landscapes, the verbal tricks and ambiguities, have all been discarded, and the poems are written in a controlled and compact language, of which psychological concepts and accurate scientific references form an integral part, against a localised background of filling-stations, factories, traffic, theodolites, airwaves and television. Such poems as "Binocular Vision," "Drinking in Bolton," and "Through the Periscope" indicate the change that had taken place and show a new objectivity in Madge's approach to his chosen themes. If the language presents any difficulties, they arise from the intractable nature of the material he is working upon and his highly individual way of looking at things. As he observes in "Philosophical Poem": "This window by a curious trick can see/ Workaday things and a white rising planet."

Charles Madge has succeeded in translating his philosophical beliefs into action in the sociological sphere, so that his theories have been tested by experience; direct activity in the sociological field in its turn has assisted his creative work by keeping him in close touch with reality; while the dual nature of his vision has enabled him to perform "the curious trick" by which he establishes the connection between "workaday things" and the "white rising planet." It can, therefore, be argued that his best poetry has social value.

This is confirmed by the later and, as yet, uncollected pieces such as "Visions of Camden Town," "In the Lens of Observation," "For an Altar," the sequence "Poem by Stages," and the long poem entitled "The Storming of the Brain," which can best be described as a poetic treatment, in allegorical form acceptable at several levels, of the conflict between detached intellectualism and the unruly and unpredictable forces of life. With "The Storming of the Brain" before us it is possible not only to ascertain the progress Madge has made, but also to trace the direction in which he seems to be moving. First it was necessary to effect a reconciliation between his romantic impulses and his trained scientific methods, and then his intellectual beliefs had to be related to his idealistic concern for humanity in such a way as to maintain his artistic integrity and yet provide a basis for positive action.

In "The Storming of the Brain" Madge lays emphasis upon the need for the integration of society as distinct from the prevailing tendency towards division into armed ideological camps, and indicates what seems to him to be the only practical way in which unity of purpose can be achieved.

—Howard Sergeant

MAGEE, Wes. British. Born in Greenock, Renfrew, 20 July 1939. Educated at Ilford County High School, Essex, 1951–56; Goldsmiths' College, University of London, 1964–67, teachers certificate. Served in the British Army Intelligence Corps, 1960–62. Married Janet Magee in 1969; one son and one daughter. Worked as a bank clerk in the 1950's;

Headmaster, Blackthorn Junior School, Welwyn Garden City, Hertfordshire, 1978. Address: 13 Waysbrook, Letchworth, Hertfordshire, England.

PUBLICATIONS

Verse

Postcard from a Long Way Off. Portrush, County Antrim, Ulsterman, 1969.
The Radish. Frensham, Surrey, Sceptre Press, 1970.
Urban Gorilla. Leeds, School of English Press, 1972.
Proust in a Crowded Store. Rushden, Northamptonshire, Sceptre Press, 1974.
No Man's Land. Richmond, Surrey, Keepsake Press, 1976.
Creature of the Bay: A Set of Poems. Kingston upon Thames, Surrey, Court Poetry Press, 1977.
Headland Graffiti. Knotting, Bedfordshire, Sceptre Press, 1978.
No Surrender. Liverpool, Headland, 1978.
The Dream Spectres. Nottingham, Byron Press, 1978.
No Man's Land (collection). Belfast, Blackstaff Press, 1978.

Play

The Real Spirit of Christmas (juvenile; produced Welwyn Garden City, Hertfordshire, 1978). London, French, 1978.

Other

Reptile Rhymes (juvenile). Bristol, Xenia Press, 1977.
Oliver, The Daring Birdman (juvenile). London, Longman, 1978.
The Space Beasts (juvenile). Maidstone, Kent Library Service, 1979.

* * *

In Wes Magee's first major collection, *Urban Gorilla*, the poems are taken from personal experience and written in a clear, down-to-earth manner which somehow combines a colloquial diction with a strikingly fresh use of image and metaphor in a style which is unique to Magee. In the poem entitled "Maybe I'd Do Well in Tibet" he looks at other poets' ways of life and reaches his own conclusion:

I'm plainly
for the poet keeping his cool in the city,
being steady in the isolation
of his mortgaged box,
a monk without privilege or position,
solitary in his cell,
above the yelping and the traffic snarl.

Magee, then, is definitely an urban poet, concerned with events and situations to be found in everyday life and especially those which make their impact upon him in his role as teacher. In this collection there are several poems featuring incidents at school. In "Today's Lesson: An Observation" a group of teachers on a refresher course visit a show school "learning that what's good for smaller fry is/fine for us, and how to make the educated/guess when things go wrong." "The Bell Sequence" features a teacher watching children in the playground. Another poem deals with basic training during National Service. There are a couple of poems about football. though one of these is a metaphorical account of the reaction of young poets against the prominence given to Establishment figures. Throughout all these poems there are compassion, a wry sense of irony, and an insight into the human situation, though it cannot be said that any clear philosophy emerges.

Two pamphlet collections, *The Dream Spectres* and *No Surrender*, together with some later poems, were incorporated in his second volume, *No Man's Land*. Although the diction employed in this volume is still that of everyday speech, there is greater control of form and in some of the poems, particularly those describing farm life, the language is muscular and gritty, reminiscent of Ted Hughes in his animal poems, though not in any way derivative:

> Urban-soft I feel anguish for the runt
> in each litter, the weakling hanging back
> while the familial toughs fight for pig-meal
> or a swift guzzle at the sow's milk bar.
> Here, in this harsh Irish outhouse, the runts
> surrender. They stand with ears ripped to rags
> and tails snapped to stumps by the pink nasties,
> butts for the *angst* rife in the squalid pens.
> "Better dead, than fed," my boss cracks, and rakes
> his blackthorn stick up and down the sow's spine.

Occasionally, this concentration upon language appropriate to the theme leads him into some awkward combinations and over-ripe alliteration – "Then squelched slow.... Strode to the stone-strewn summit." The range of subject is extended in this second volume, too, and a number of highly imaginative poems, though taking some trivial incident as starting-point, penetrate beneath the surface of the material to provide strange insights, as in "Biography of the Skull," "Yorick in a Junk Shop," "The Skull's Will," "Woman from the Kingdom of Pain," and "Threshold." Magee has a rare gift for fresh and sometimes startling simile and metaphor – "the day was grey as school socks," "skylarks topple like early birdmen," a ridge is "undulating as a boxer's nose," air is "lemon-juice sharp," night "blindfolds the houses," skin like a "frost-bitten potato," and night gathering "like black-suited men at a country funeral." Poems such as "Woman from the Kingdom of Pain," "Snaps," and "No Surrender" show this unusually talented poet at his best. So far he seems to have been testing the ground and developing an individual style, trying out different themes and ideas and modes of expression, but there can be little doubt of his enormous potentiality.

—Howard Sergeant

MAHON, Derek. British. Born in Belfast, Northern Ireland, 23 November 1941. Educated at Belfast Institute; Trinity College, Dublin, B.A. 1965. Married; two children. English teacher, Belfast High School, 1967–68, and Language Centre of Ireland, Dublin, 1968–70; Writer-in-Residence, University of East Anglia, Norwich, 1975, Emerson College, Boston, 1976–77, and New University of Ulster, Coleraine, 1977–79. Co-Editor, *Atlantis*, Dublin, 1970–74; has been drama critic of *The Listener* and features editor of *Vogue*. Recipient: Eric Gregory Award, 1965. Lives in London.

PUBLICATIONS

Verse

Twelve Poems. Belfast, Festival, 1965.

Night-Crossing. London, Oxford University Press, 1968.
Ecclesiastes. Manchester, Phoenix Pamphlet Poets Press, 1970.
Beyond Howth Head. Dublin, Dolmen Press, 1970.
Lives. London, Oxford University Press, 1972.
The Man Who Built His City in Snow. London, Poem-of-the-Month Club, 1972.
The Snow Party. London and New York, Oxford University Press, 1975.
Light Music. Belfast, Ulsterman, 1977.
The Sea in Winter. Dublin, Gallery, 1979.
Poems 1962–1978. London, Oxford University Press, 1979.

Other

Editor, *Modern Irish Poetry*. London, Sphere, 1972.

Critical Studies: *Two Decades of Irish Writings* edited by Douglas Dunn, Manchester, Carcanet Press, 1975; *Northern Voices* by Terence Brown, Dublin, Gill and Macmillan, 1975.

* * *

Derek Mahon is one of a number of fine poets to have emerged from Northern Ireland in the last fifteen or twenty years. Unlike several of his contemporaries, he is defiantly eclectic. When he is at his most local topographically, he is likely also to be at his most metropolitan in his technique, as in "Day Trip to Donegal":

How could we hope to make them understand?
Theirs is a sea-mind, mindless upon land
And dead. Their systematic genocide
(Nothing remarkable that millions died)
To us is a necessity
For ours are land-minds, mindless in the sea.

The "them" of the poem are the fish. Notice the dexterous handling of what could have been a tricky stanza-form, the reference to the Holocaust in that nonchalant parenthesis. Derek Mahon's feet only seem to falter; for him, hesitancy is a special effect.

This is true not only of the poem in question but of other witty, tricky poems in Mahon's output. Consider, for example, "My Wicked Uncle," "April on Toronto Island," "De Quincey in Later Life" from his first major collection; "Job's Comforter," "I Am Raftery," "Consolations of Philosophy" from his second; "The Chair Squeaks ...," "September in Great Yarmouth," and "A Disused Shed in Co. Wexford" from his third.

The titles indicate a poet eclectic in his themes as well as his technique. In recent work he has used his considerable linguistic talent to juxtapose violently registers of speech which one would have thought incompatible. He tells the freethinker

Your great mistake is to disregard the satire
Bandied among the mute phenomena.
Be strong if you must, your brusque hegemony
Means fuck-all to the somnolent sun-flower
Or the extinct volcano....

This is "After Nerval" – a long way after, if we glance at the suave original: "Des forces que tu tiens ta liberté dispose,/Mais de tous tes conseils l'univers est absent...." Mahon gives the tradition a good wrench; it is something that he is fairly inventive in doing. But, by and large, there is an absence of pressure behind his contrasts and transitions. Sometimes, indeed, Mahon's dead heroes – notably Auden – are not sufficiently modified in the guts of the living.

The exceptions to this general remark, though few, are striking. Behind the ironic mask of the aesthete is the sombre countenance of the elegist; and Mahon is at his most impressive when he allows this to emerge, in "They buried him slowly above the sea,/The young Presbyterian minister/Rumpled and windy in the sea air ... ("My Wicked Uncle"), or "Consolations of Philosophy":

> When we start breaking up in the wet darkness
> And the rotten boards fall from us, and the ribs
> Crack under the constriction of tree-roots
> And the seasons slip from the fields unknown to us ...

or in "Even now there are places where a thought might grow –/Peruvian mines, worked out and abandoned/To a slow clock of condensation,/an echo trapped forever ... ("A Disused Shed in Co. Wexford"). As these quotations may indicate, the contemplation of the grave provides Derek Mahon with his richest imagery. This is never more so than in what is, perhaps, still Mahon's finest poem, "At Carrowdore Churchyard." It is an elegy on Louis MacNeice which takes on, characteristically for Mahon, a measure of its subject's manner to invoke an attitude towards life shared at once by the author and by the fine poet, also from Northern Ireland, that he commemorates:

> Maguire, I believe, suggested a blackbird
> And over your grave a phrase from Euripides.
>
> Which suits you down to the ground, like this churchyard
> With its play of shadow, its humane perspective.
> Locked in the winter's fist, these hills as hard
> As nails, yet soft and feminine in their turn
> When fingers open and the hedges burn.
> This, you implied, is how we ought to live –
>
> The ironical, loving crush of roses against snow,
> Each fragile, solving ambiguity. So
> From the pneumonia of the ditch, from the ague
> Of the blind poet and the bombed-out town you bring
> The all-clear to the empty holes of spring,
> Rinsing the choked mud, keeping the colours new.

—Philip Hobsbaum

MAJOR, Clarence. American. Born in Atlanta, Georgia, 31 December 1936. Educated at the Art Institute, Chicago (James Nelson Raymond Scholar), 1952–54; Armed Forces Institute, 1955–56; New School for Social Research, New York, 1972. Served in the United States Air Force, 1955–57. Married Joyce Sparrow in 1958 (divorced 1964). Research Analyst, Simulmatics, New York, 1967. Taught in the Harlem Education Program Writers Workshop, New York, 1967, and the Teachers and Writers Collaborative, New York, 1967–72. Since 1972, Member of the Faculty, Sarah Lawrence College, Bronxville, New York. Associate Editor, *Proof Magazine*, Chicago, 1959–60; Editor, *Coercion Review*, Chicago, 1958–65; Associate Editor, *Caw!* magazine, 1967–68, and *Journal of Black Poetry*, 1967–70. Recipient: National Endowment for the Arts grant, 1970; New York Cultural Foundation grant, 1971. Agent: Howard Moorepark, 444 East 82nd Street, New York, New York 10028, U.S.A.

PUBLICATIONS

Verse

The Fires That Burn in Heaven. Privately printed, 1954.
Love Poems of a Black Man. Omaha, Nebraska, Coercion Press, 1965.
Human Juices. Omaha, Nebraska, Coercion Press, 1965.
Swallow the Lake. Middletown, Connecticut, Wesleyan University Press, 1970.
Symptoms and Madness. New York, Corinth, 1971.
Private Line. London, Paul Breman, 1971.
The Cotton Club: New Poems. Detroit, Broadside Press, 1972.
The Syncopated Cakewalk. New York, Barlenmir House, 1974.

Novels

All-Night Visitors. New York, Olympia Press, 1969.
NO. New York, Emerson Hall, 1973.
Reflex and Bone Structure. New York, Fiction Collective, 1975.
Emergency Exit. New York, Fiction Collective, 1979.

Other

Dictionary of Afro-American Slang. New York, International, 1970; as *Black Slang: A Dictionary of Afro-American Talk*, London, Routledge, 1971.
The Dark and Feeling: Black American Writers and Their Work. New York, Third Press, 1974.

Editor, *Writers Workshop Anthology.* New York, Harlem Education Project, 1967.
Editor, *Man Is Like a Child: An Anthology of Creative Writing by Students.* New York, Macomb's Junior High School, 1968.
Editor, *The New Black Poetry.* New York, International, 1969.

Bibliography: "Clarence Major: A Checklist of Criticism" by Joe Weixlmann, in *Obsidian* (Fredonia, New York), iv, 2, 1978; "Toward a Primary Bibliography of Clarence Major" by Joe Weixlmann and Clarence Major, in *Black American Literature Forum* (Terre Haute, Indiana), Summer 1979.

Critical Studies: in *New York Times*, 7 April 1969; *Quarterly Journal of Speech* (New York), April 1971; *Saturday Review* (New York), 3 April 1971; *Chicago Sun-Times*, 28 April 1971; *Poetry* (Chicago), August 1971; *Virginia Quarterly Review* (Charlottesville), Winter 1971; *New York Times Book Review*, 1 July 1973; *Interviews with Black Writers*, edited by John O'Brien, New York, Liveright, 1973.

Clarence Major comments:

I am trying to break through the artificial effects of language. I'm also trying to break down the artificial distinctions between poetry and fiction.

* * *

In an epigraph to his novel *Reflex and Bone Structure* Clarence Major announces that the book "is an extension of, not a duplication of reality. The characters and events are happening for the first time." The statement equally well describes the poetry in which Major's deliberate opacity discourages our attempt to track his language as references to an empirical world. Even when reading verse we expect words readily to demonstrate a correspondence to outside things or events, because our linguistic competency develops through the code of usage. Like other post-Modern writers, however, Major uses language as a newly constructed code.

His poems are cast subjectively as dramas of feelings, sometimes in conflict, other times their complexities resolved by time. Always, though, the dynamic comes from a logic of emotional knowledge that, more often than not, conceals the subject – what the poem is about. Such verse holds that the structures of feeling have been shaped uniquely, and it follows that the patterns of expression must be intrinsic to poetic execution. In "Overbreak" he writes

> there is a remarkable verb of
> things
> here: a remarkable sensation of
> infected spirits feeling
> & pushing bravely like nurtured waves in
> the machines of
> the sensation, the tremor of water as it
> surrounds the heart beat

The absence of conventional punctuation makes "Overbreak" an uninterrupted utterance intensely felt; yet, the original stimulus has been absorbed into abstractions, the currency of mental constructions that nevertheless stop short of concept.

Major's code regularly employs eccentric punctuation and unusual typographical arrangement so that the poems must be seen as well as heard. Clotted lines, such as "O supreme sledgehammer of reposing verbal stacks of/nouns verbs adjectives charming," insist upon the primary sensation of words as sounds. These eccentricities, and others, then reinforce the premise implied by such fused syntax as in this passage from "The Design":

> I am tired of the
> apartment is dull a place but it comes
> to this each
> item you left, a few belongings....

If conventional syntax asserts the dominance of rational order, then this disruption argues the existence of an "extension of reality," its integrity requiring designation of a new, arbitrary system of signs.

Because it stakes all on the tone conveyed by a linguistic code we can never entirely decipher, Major's verse risks obscurity. But, of course, the risk is well taken. The discontinuities between his verse and the patterns of conventional usage become an experiment in poetics as well as poems.

—John M. Reilly

MALOUF, David. Australian. Born in Brisbane, Queensland, 20 March 1934. Educated at Brisbane Grammar School, 1947–50; University of Queensland, Brisbane, 1951–54, B.A. (honours) in English 1954. Lecturer, University of Sydney, 1968–77. Recipient: Australian Literature Society Gold Medal, 1974; Grace Leven Prize, 1974; James Cook Award, 1975; Australia Council Fellowship, 1978; New South Wales Premier's Prize, for fiction, 1979.

Agent: Curtis Brown (Australia) Pty. Ltd., 89 William Street, Paddington, New South Wales, Australia; or, Curtis Brown Ltd., 1 Craven Hill, London W2 3EP, England. Address: Via Oberdan, Campagnatico, Grosseto, Italy.

PUBLICATIONS

Verse

Four Poets, with others. Melbourne, Cheshire, 1962.
Bicycle and Other Poems. Brisbane, University of Queensland Press, 1970; as *The Year of the Foxes and Other Poems*, New York, Braziller, 1979.
Neighbours in a Thicket. Brisbane, University of Queensland Press, 1974.
Poems 1975–76. Sydney, Prism, 1976.

Novels

Johnno. Brisbane, University of Queensland Press, 1975; New York, Braziller, 1978.
An Imaginary Life. New York, Braziller, and London, Chatto and Windus, 1978.

Other

Editor, with others, *We Took Their Orders and Are Dead: An Anti-War Anthology*. Sydney, Ure Smith, 1971.
Editor, *Gesture of a Hand* (anthology of Australian poetry). Artarmon, New South Wales, Holt Rinehart, 1975.

David Malouf comments:

I like to think of poetry as work done at a place of concordance: where the past and future meet in visible present, where change is celebrated but continuity established, where the actual is open to the fabulous, where the individual stands as the point of connection between a single life and the totality of things. Language also belongs to two worlds: the world of "communication" and of our mysterious naming to ourselves of what surrounds us. Standing as it does at this crossing-point between adjacent, and perhaps rival, zones, it seems like an ideal vehicle for the "passages" I have in mind. Poems are acts of reconciliation.

* * *

Although relatively unprolific as a poet, David Malouf has attained a high degree of achievement in what he has published. He first appeared, as one of a Brisbane-based group of new poets in *Four Poets*, and in that selection already laid out many of his ongoing preoccupations: childhood incidents and resonances (expressed with considerable delight in small, concrete detail); a cosmopolitan familiarity with European history and culture as something intrinsic to his vision; and a sharp, ironic view of contemporary man's social and political milieu – most deftly expressed in "Epitaph for a Monster of Our Times", about Adolf Eichmann:

an organization man
par excellence, whom we
need only convict at last
of gross efficiency.

Bicycle and Other Poems followed after a long period of apparent silence and it immediately placed Malouf in the forefront of his generation. It confirmed the mature, ironic yet sympathetic view of life and events, but added a capacity to blend elements of quiet fantasy with more subterranean urgencies of wonder, loss, and the precariousness of living. The Brisbane poems in this volume have the extraordinary richness of observation and sensuous focus that characterise his first novel, *Johnno*, but the book is perhaps most notable for its wide-ranging resources of reference – something pursued even further in his next collection, *Neighbours in a Thicket*. In this book, though it contains some striking poems of childhood recall (the perspective, now, is richer, and darker), Malouf explores a strong vein of cultural and personal association, a sort of cross-hatching of reflective (and reflexive) emblems of recall. These are essentially meditative poems, poems of exploration rather than arrival, and their starting point is always a fine awareness of the past as being something as immediate and contemporaneous as the present. This capacity to respond to time laterally rather than chronologically makes Malouf unique among Australian poets in that it enables him to transcend issues of cultural identity and assertion, issues that have been of dominant concern in so much Australian writing. Malouf's sense of region is intense and sharply visual. He is thus the most European, yet one of the most regional, of contemporary Australian poets.

Poems 1975–76 can be seen as a lyrical interlude in Malouf's output. It is a short book, dominated by two love sequences of unusual resonance, mainly through their recognition that it is through the *word* that all avenues of perception may be opened up. Malouf's exploration of language is here heightened by an overtly celebrative intent. In his poems published since this book, elements of pure invention have increasingly concerned the poet, often achieving a sense of almost breathtaking virtuosity. David Malouf's second novel, *An Imaginary Life*, which is virtually a prose poem of great lyric power, has achieved international acclaim since it was first published in New York. His first American collection, *The Year of the Foxes* though it is essentially a reprint of *Bicycle and Other Poems*, is a further sign of international recognition of this most elegant and cosmopolitan of Australian poets.

—Thomas W. Shapcott

MANDEL, Eli(as Wolf). Canadian. Born in Estevan, Saskatchewan, in 1922. Educated at the University of Saskatchewan, Saskatoon; University of Toronto. Served in Europe with the Army Medical Corps during World War II. Taught English at Collège Militaire Royal de Saint-Jean, Quebec. Since 1946, Member, Department of English, and since 1965, Professor of English, University of Alberta. Recipient: President's Medal, University of Western Ontario, 1963; Governor-General's Award, 1968; Canada Council Award, 1971, 1974, 1977. Address: Department of English, University of Alberta, Edmonton, Alberta, Canada.

PUBLICATIONS

Verse

Trio, with Gael Turnbull and Phyllis Webb. Toronto, Contact Press, 1954.
Fuseli Poems. Toronto, Contact Press, 1960.
Black and Secret Man. Toronto, Ryerson Press, 1964.
An Idiot Joy. Edmonton, Alberta, Hurtig, 1967.
Crusoe: Poems Selected and New. Toronto, Anansi, 1973.
Stony Plain. Erin, Ontario, Press Porcépic, 1973.
Out of Place. Erin, Ontario, Press Porcépic, 1977.

Other

Criticism: The Silent Speaking Words. Toronto, CBC, 1966.
Irving Layton. Toronto, Forum House, 1969.
Another Time (essays). Erin, Ontario, Press Porcépic, 1977.

Editor, with Jean-Guy Pilon, *Poetry 62.* Toronto, Ryerson Press, 1961.
Editor, *Five Modern Canadian Poets.* Toronto, Holt Rinehart, 1970.
Editor, with Desmond Maxwell, *English Poems of the Twentieth Century.* Toronto, Macmillan, 1971.
Editor, *Contexts of Canadian Criticism.* Chicago, University of Chicago Press, 1971.
Editor, *Poets of Contemporary Canada 1960–1970.* Toronto, McClelland and Stewart, 1972.
Editor, *Eight More Canadian Poets.* Toronto, Holt Rinehart, 1972.
Editor, *The Poems of Irving Layton.* Toronto, McClelland and Stewart, 1977.

* * *

"I am a fable looking for a plot," Eli Mandel wrote in "Aesop" in *Black and Secret Man.* "Actually, I am an unwritten tale." The search for the tale to tell has taken Eli Mandel from Greek mythology and Old Testament fable to modern Freudian and Jungian theories of human motivation. What has remained constant – from his "Minotaur Poems" in *Trio*, where his work appeared with that of Phyllis Webb and Gael Turnbull, to his more recent books – is his feeling for tortured imagery, his sense of the grotesque, his urbane tone of irony, and his language which is by turns dramatic and melodramatic.

It might be argued that Eli Mandel is an academic poet in the best sense of that term. He is interested in the mythopoeic theories of Northrop Frye, and sees in the act of criticism itself (especially in his radio talks published as *The Silent Speaking Words*) an inevitable counterpoint to the practice of poetry. When he edited *Poetry 62* with Jean-Guy Pilon, he isolated the imaginative and dramatic strains in Canadian poetry. To all his writing, he brings a heightened sense of the immediacy of the imaginative act, which owes something to the writing of William Blake.

His first book, *Fuseli Poems*, is full of fragmentation and a concern for anthropology and myth. Writing about "The Anarchist-Poets" in *Black and Secret Man*, he advises the reader to "step carefully through this rubble of words./Can you really say which wrecks were once poems,/which weapons?" In "The Burning Man" from *An Idiot Joy*, he stresses the anarchic quality of the poetic imagination: "I'm a walking crime wave." His poem "In the 57th Century of Our Lord" begins, "Semitic and secret I plan new evasions,/survival, the tribal rite."

Eli Mandel's imagery, often full of literary allusions, is usually bold and arresting. The hermetic and the heroic battle it out within his poems – Orpheus and Hercules united in one man. He ends "Pictures in an Institution" with the following lines:

> Notice: there will be no further communication
> lectures are cancelled
> all students are expelled
> the reading of poetry is declared a public crime.

—John Robert Colombo

MANHIRE, Bill. New Zealander. Born in Invercargill, 27 December 1946. Educated at Otago Boys High School; University of Otago, Dunedin, M.A. (honours) 1968, M.Litt. 1970; University College, London, 1970–73, M.Phil. 1973. Married Barbara McLeod in 1970: one daughter and one son. Since 1973, Lecturer in English, Victoria University, Wellington. Editor, Amphedesma Press, Dunedin; General Editor, New Zealand Stories series, Price Milburn-Victoria University. Recipient: New Zealand Book Award, 1977. Address: Department of English, Victoria University of Wellington, Private Bag, Wellington, New Zealand.

PUBLICATIONS

Verse

Malady. Dunedin, Amphedesma Press, 1970.
The Elaboration. Wellington, Square and Circle, 1972.
Song Cycle. Wellington, Sound-Movement Theatre, 1975.
How to Take Off Your Clothes at the Picnic. Wellington, Wai-te-ata Press, 1977.

Other

Ralph Hotere at the Intensity Centre. Wellington, Hawk Press, 1979.

Editor, *New Zealand Universities Arts Festival Yearbook 1969.* Dunedin, Arts Festival Committee, 1969.
Editor, *New Zealand Listener Stories* and *Volume II.* Wellington, Methuen, 1977–78.

Critical Study: "Pavlova and Wrists: The Poetry of Bill Manhire" by Peter Crisp, in *Islands 24* (Auckland), November 1978.

* * *

Poems choose to give expression to conditions of writing. Poems are strategies for discovery, but do not habitually "articulate solutions to the business of living." The poems are arbitrary facts, not only of the life of whoever writes them but of the lives of those who read them. They arise out of some situation which is in some way true; they are elaborations of whatever the truth of that situation is and in being elaborated they move away from any condition of raw truth towards a condition as fictions. A poem is like a snap shot which may be effected by a camera, insofar as the artifact (the poem) is to be identified with the creative process from which the fiction-fact emerges, "a snap, as it were, at the right moment, in the awareness that the disposition of such moments is not in any sense within the control of the artist." The productive process may be fostered by inducing a state "which borders on narcolepsy, where it seems possible to relax into some generous relationship with words," a state not likely to last more than a few moments which carries with it the consequence that any poem so produced is likely to be quite short.

Bill Manhire's poems are often delightful, but also often cryptic. The statement above may be taken as an account of how they are produced, or were formerly produced. It is compounded from two statements by Manhire, one published in 1972 (in *The Elaboration*) and the other in 1973 (in *The Young New Zealand Poets*). If we take it at all seriously, Manhire was paying tribute to the usefulness of what was once called inspiration, although in the way in which he writes of the poem's arrival he seems to be urging something more like automatic writing. That may be, at the outset, but the poems which arrive before us have fairly obviously been well worked over. They may retain something of the dream about them (which accounts for part of their strange appeal), something of a sense of a showing forth so that their truth "is in some way true," presenting the reader with a tantalising puzzle element which is likely to serve in getting the reader's interest, in which case the poem as "arbitrary fact" meets the condition the poet argues for: of the poem more as an interaction process than as something relatively autonomous.

A qualification was put in earlier that perhaps Manhire's poems were formerly produced in this fashion implying that they may not now be so. Some recent pieces suggest that a good deal more contriving, fictionalising, is being employed. Since Manhire is not at all prolific, it is likely to be some time before this may be properly known. At present, the fictionalising is admitted, whatever weight is given to the spontaneous, the involuntary, part. Looking back, one may be inclined to wonder about the voluntary and the involuntary, the *ordonné* and the *dieu-donné* of which Valéry spoke, and their respective contributions. In a poem such as "The Cinema" the dream factor may be registered, but one recognises as well that this is remarkably of a piece with some of Louis Simpson's poems. Elsewhere one is reminded of Robert Bly, and indeed of Bly's expressed attitudes, just as one is reminded of poets of other languages than English.

Whatever the debts, Manhire is distinctive in the considerable economy of his means, the precise control of his *The Elaboration* pieces, the more expansive (but still far from indulgent) longer-lined and richer textured poems of *How to Take Off Your Clothes at the Picnic*, or the more diverse and discursive of as yet uncollected poems. In either severe constraint or in relaxation of this, he is eminently lyrical, eminently given to celebration, to being playful in poems of love or domesticity, and extraordinarily adept at provoking the reader. Sentiment and intelligence are complementary, like fact and fiction, and as interchangeable.

—Kendrick Smithyman

MANIFOLD, John (Streeter). Australian. Born in Melbourne, Victoria, 21 April 1915. Educated at Geelong Grammar School, Victoria; Jesus College, Cambridge, 1934–37, B.A. (honours) in modern languages 1937. Served with the Intelligence Corps, 1940–46: Captain. Married the singer Katharine Hopwood in 1940 (died, 1969); one son and one daughter. President, Brisbane Realist Writers Group, 1956–66; President, Fellowship of Australian Writers, Queensland Branch, 1959; Commonwealth Literary Fund Lecturer at the universities of New England, Queensland, and South Australia. Currently, Vice-President, National Council of Realist Writers' Groups, and Poetry Editor, *The Realist*. Editor, Bandicoot Ballads series in the 1950's. Toured China in 1963 as a guest of the Association for Cultural Relations with Foreign Countries; toured the U.S.S.R. in 1963 as a guest of the Union of Soviet Writers; Delegate, International Writers' Meeting, Berlin, 1965. Agent: David Higham Associates Ltd., 5–8 Lower John Street, London W1R 4HA, England. Address: 361 Wynnum North Road, Wynnum, Queensland 4178, Australia.

PUBLICATIONS

Verse

The Death of Ned Kelly and Other Ballads. London, Favil Press, 1941.
Trident, with Hubert Nicholson and David Martin. London, Fore, 1944.
Selected Verse. New York, Day, 1946; London, Dobson, 1948.
Nightmares and Sunhorses. Melbourne, Overland, 1961.
Op. 8: Poems 1961–69. Queensland, Queensland University Press, 1970.
Broadsheets. Privately printed, 1973.

Six Sonnets on Human Ecology. Privately printed, 1974.
Collected Verse. Brisbane, University of Queensland Press, 1978.

Other

The Amorous Flute: An Unprofessional Handbook for Recorder Players and All Amateurs of Music. London, Workers Music Association, 1948.
The Music in English Drama from Shakespeare to Purcell. London, Barrie and Rockliff, 1956.
The Violin, The Banjo and the Bones: An Essay on the Instruments of Bush Music. Ferntree Gully, Victoria, Ram's Skull Press, 1957.
Who Wrote the Ballads? Notes on Australian Folksong. Sydney, Australasian Book Society, 1964.

Editor, *Three Pieces from the Plaine and Easie Introduction to Musick 1597*, by Thomas Morley. London, Schott, 1948.
Editor, with Walter Bergmann, *Petite Suite for Two Descant Recorders and Piano.* London, Schott, 1948.
Editor, *The Queensland Centenary Pocket Songbook.* Sydney, Edwards and Shaw, 1959.
Editor, *The Penguin Australian Songbook.* Melbourne, Penguin, 1964.

John Manifold comments:

My verse is old-fashioned. It is about women, horses, soldiers, revolutionists, landscapes, myths, and history. A lot of it is narrative. I enjoy wrestling with the strict forms – the apparently artless ballad being just as strict a form in its way as the apparently artful sonnet or limerick. I learnt from "Banjo" Paterson, Heredia, Heine, Aragon, and more recently Brecht, to strive for clarity, brevity, balance and impersonality.

Melius est quod reprehendent nos grammatici quam non intelligant populi (Saint Augustine).

* * *

John Manifold's *Selected Verse* was well received upon publication both in England and the United States. It centred around a brilliantly cool yet ardent sonnet series that was directly derived from the work of Auden. Manifold was able to bring his own heritage – wealthy pioneer ancestry, brilliant Cambridge career, conversion to Communism – unobtrusively but ingratiatingly into these poems, giving them a lightness and cultivatedness that were disarming and unexpected in Australian poetry of the late 1940's. Returning to Australia, Manifold retired to a small village outside Brisbane and, with his wife, taught local children how to make, and perform upon, antique musical instruments – recorders, lutes, citterns. His poetry became influenced by his own attempts to revive and reanimate early Australian bush-ballad traditions, the results of which were not very convincingly shown in his next collection, *Nightmares and Sunhorses*. Manifold has published a number of volumes on Elizabethan and Jacobean music, as well as Australian folksong. His most important recent work, however, is the verse collection *Op. 8*, which includes a number of recent sonnets that recapture the wit and poise of his earlier work, as well as other work that remains admirably and unashamedly elegant. (Elegant in sensibility, not affectation.) John Manifold has been a personal influence on a number of Australian poets, from David Campbell to Rodney Hall. His writing perhaps captures only part of the man's complex and individual personality. But in itself that remains something of a nectar to be savoured and remembered.

—Thomas W. Shapcott

MARSHALL, Jack. American. Born in Brooklyn, New York, 25 February 1937. Educated at Lafayette High School, Brooklyn. Married Kathleen Fraser, *q.v.*, in 1961 (divorced, 1970), one son. Shipping clerk, salesman, farmhand, steel mill hand, deck hand; Copywriter, J. C. Penney, New York; longshoreman, San Francisco. Taught in poetry workshops at the University of Iowa, Iowa City, California Western College, San Diego, and San Francisco State College.

PUBLICATIONS

Verse

The Darkest Continent. New York, For Now Press, 1967.
Bearings. New York, Harper, 1969.
Floats. Iowa City, Cedar Creek Press, 1971.
Surviving in America, with Anselm Hollo and Sam Hamod. Iowa City, Cedar Creek Press, 1972.
Bits of Thirst. Iowa City, Cedar Creek Press, 1974.
Arriving on the Playing Fields of Paradise. Iowa City, Cedar Creek Press, 1974.
Bits of Thirst and Other Poems and Translations. Berkeley, Blue Wind Press, 1976.

Jack Marshall comments:

My poems are playful investigations and perceptions of alternate realities. I write them because no one else does. I write them as ecstatically as I can; music and metaphor being the compression-chamber of the senses.

* * *

In his early book, *Bearings*, Jack Marshall impresses one as a poet with considerable energy and talent who cannot always harness them successfully; often the poem gets the upper hand, its forceful rhetoric becoming mannered, unclear, or somewhat rambling. Marshall has a talent for stately speech and a rich vocabulary, packing his lines with strong sounds and closely-bunched movements of imagery and thought. The problem is that often his lines are *too* dense; they become crabbed, straining the reader's attention, or else they get caught up in following associations of emotion and image that draw away from the poem's main thrust.

When his poems succeed, some of the qualities apparent in the poorer poems make the successes impressive ones – density of sound and sense, dramatic tone, specificity, variety of vocabulary and image. A great number of his best poems (like "Setting Out" and "On the President's State Visit to Mexico") make an extensive use of syntactical parallelism, a device which at once accommodates his forceful rhetoric, producing a kind of persistent thrust, and also provides a simple structure which tends to prevent excessive convolution or rambling courses of association.

It isn't apparent whether or not the poems are arranged chronologically, but there seems to be a considerable improvement in the poems of the third and fourth sections over those in the first and second, and a more personal and relaxed tone enters the book in poems like "Walking Across Brooklyn Bridge" and "For Kathleen, Gone on a Brief Journey." It should be added that in poems which have appeared in various places since his first book Marshall has assumed a new, freer style which allows him to make a series of non-rational associations without cramping the poem or seeming to get lost in it.

—Lawrence Russ

MARTY, Sid. Canadian. Born in England, 29 June 1944. Educated at Sir George Williams University, Montreal, graduated (honours) 1969. Park Warden in national parks in Banff and Jasper, Alberta, and Yoho, British Columbia, 1966–78. Recipient: Canada Council grant, 1974; Canadian Authors Association prize, 1978, and Alberta Government grant, 1978, both for non-fiction. Address: Box 265, Canmore, Alberta T01 0M0, Canada.

PUBLICATIONS

Verse

Headwaters. Toronto, McClelland and Stewart, 1973.
Tumbleweed Harvest. Wood Mountain, Saskatchewan, Sundog Press, 1973.

Other

Men for the Mountains (on park wardens). Toronto, McClelland and Stewart, 1978; New York, Vanguard Press, 1979.

* * *

Sid Marty is one of the younger poets who emerged in Canada during the 1970's with a remarkable sense of closeness to the geo-historical environment. Before that period, the general tendency of Canadian poets had been either to avoid the wilderness as a poetic terrain, or else to follow in literary terms the example of the pioneers who tried to tame the wilderness because they feared it. Typical of such literary taming was the way in which poets like Charles G. D. Roberts and Archibald Lampman tried to express the uniqueness of the Canadian terrain in forms the Romantics had devised to project a European experience; even poets as late as A. J. M. Smith evoked the wild lands in formalist patterns that had little relation to the experience of having inhabited them. Northrop Frye's concept of Canada as a "garrison society," embattled against the threatening natural world, was certainly a reasonably accurate projection of the attitudes found in Canadian poetry until the present generation.

It was really poets like Al Purdy and John Newlove, coming to maturity in the late 1950's, and wandering over the country, hitchhiking and taking jobs that linked them into the life of remote places, who began to develop a poetry related directly to experience of the land as wilderness and to the life-style that implied an acceptance of the natural world as it is rather than as a source of raw materials to be exploited.

Among the poets most influenced – or perhaps most liberated – in a positive way by the example of Purdy and Newlove is Sid Marty, perhaps the first convincingly successful poet of the Rocky Mountains, and successful because he has sought, not to confront the mountains, to objectify them, but rather to see them as a presence in whose face to live. One of the poems in Sid Marty's first book, *Headwaters*, is entitled "Each Mountain," and begins: "Each mountain/its own country/in the way a country/must be/A state of mind." Another poem, this time about encounters with the denizens of the mountains rather than with the mountains themselves, is entitled "Three Bears," and ends:

But I am reminded
I am not at home
Here where I live
only at hazard

There is a darkness
along the bright petals

Between them, these fragments bound a territory of the mind that Sid Marty had made peculiarly his own. The geography of the land extends the geography of the mind, and in the very act of extension is takes us perhaps not into alien territory, but into country where we are exposed beyond the benefit of certainty.

Sid Marty's poems have a telling directness when they describe the incidents of his life as a park warden in the Rockies, drawing the reader close to the mountain face, to the guarded encounters with nature personified as grumpy grizzlies, to the companionship that grows up between men and their horses, to the ambiguous relationships between human mind and animal mind created by the coyote's cleverness:

> Coyote keeps his real name secret
> so no one gets that handle to beat him with ...
> Returning in other pelts, he walks
> over the graves of pious men
> looking for secret vices
>
> Goes on living, closer to the town
> each year, until he winds up
> feeding in the alleys of night
> a jump away from the bush or prairie
>
> Full of pride, he makes up melodies
> to multiply his saga, a skilled ventriloquist
> moving in from all directions at once.

Sid Marty's is a poetry of episode transmuting into myth, very directly bedded in personal experience, and combining a laconic verbal tone with vividly experienced imagery. It is a poetry of sharp observation, and hence a true nature poetry, and also of tight and compelling narrative.

—George Woodcock

MASSINGHAM, Harold (William). British. Born in Mexborough, Yorkshire, 25 October 1932. Educated at Mexborough Grammar School, 1943–51; Manchester University, 1951–54, B.A. in English 1954. Married Patricia Audrey Moran in 1958; three sons and one daughter. School teacher, Manchester Education Committee, 1955–70. Since 1971, Tutor, Extra-mural Department, University of Manchester. Co-Founder, *Manchester University Poetry*, 1953. Recipient: Cheltenham Festival Guinness Prize, 1962; Arts Council award, 1965; Cholmondeley award, 1968. Address: 30 Spring Bridge Road, Manchester M16 8PW, England.

PUBLICATIONS

Verse

Black Bull Guarding Apples. London, Longman, 1965.
Creation. Oxford, Sycamore Press, 1968.
The Magician: A Poem Sequence. Manchester, Phoenix Pamphlet Poets Press, 1969.

Storm. Frensham, Surrey, Sceptre Press, 1970.
Snow-Dream. Rushden, Northamptonshire, Sceptre Press, 1971.
The Pennine Way. London, BBC, 1971.
Frost-Gods. London, Macmillan, 1971.
Doomsday. London, Poem-of-the-Month Club, 1972.

Other

Mate in Two (chess problems). Manchester, P. C. Woolley, 1976.

Editor, *Poetry Workshop.* Manchester, University of Manchester Extramural Department, 3 vols., 1973–76.

Critical Studies: "Poetry at Ramdom" by Alan Ross, in *London Magazine*, August 1965; "A Yorkshireman" by Douglas Phillips, in *Western Mail* (Cardiff), November 1965; "Northern World 1" by Patrick Henry, in *Phoenix 10* (Manchester), July 1973.

Harold Massingham comments:

As a poet, and apart from certain lyrics and fanciful poems for children, my main concern is to re-live, explore and re-present native experience in concrete terms. Some poems embody natural forces, birth-dreams and animal-nightmares; some relate to the North of England, especially a Yorkshire childhood; other celebrate persons and occasionally treat of domestic issues. The tendency is to create sensuous, physical, elemental impressions in a thick texture of tight phrasing and concrete imagery: most of which imagery has its genesis in my early life. I am indebted to Keats for the earliest impulse to use my own verbal resources (see also *London Magazine* ix, 1); Laurie Lee and Dylan Thomas were later fugitive influences; and for many years my main stylistic influence has been Anglo-Saxon verse, in its ruggedness, deliberate alliterations and seemingly irregular (pre-iambic) rhythms. I have translated a great deal of it, usually as "free versions." Non-literary inspirations have been van Gogh and Beethoven. I have no orthodox political or religious affiliations, but certain pantheistic sympathies and a preoccupation with self-expression and with the genesis and individuality of things.

* * *

Harold Massingham was born in 1932 in Mexborough, Yorkshire, the son of a collier, and spent the first twenty years of his life there. The poems of his first book of verse, *Black Bull Gardening Apples*, are very much those of a Northerner ("The air nips, blonds, it is eye-living light./North-born, I could do worse than house in it"). It is concerned with the history and climate of Northern England and the "separateness" of animals (bull, rat, lizard, spider, frog, jackdaw). The language is terse, the description compact and imaginative (of the rat: "He was filthy silk"). People are represented by a snuff addict, a war veteran, his children, his mining father. Half-rhymes are usual. Significantly, there are versions of the Anglo-Saxon "The Seafarer" and "The Wanderer."

Frost-Gods also celebrates "Northness." Most of these poems are unrhymed; the writing is both more sophisticated and more fanciful ("tree-rain/Fell like isaac-newton apples"). Animals are still represented: a swan, an Alsatian, a cow ("this suede Empress"). There are translations of thirteen Anglo-Saxon riddles and three longer Anglo-Saxon poems. One poem describes the old and the poor in a cafeteria, another ("Winter in Wensleydale") is a very typical poem of landscape and season. These are two of the most successful, and illustrate the two main manifestations of Massingham's talent. There are also two nightmare poems: one childish ("Flitter-Rats"), one adult ("Nightmare of Blazing Vultures"). These are not so successful; nor is his children's verse, some of which appeared in *The Magician*. He is a poet who writes best about animals, natural objects, ordinary people. When he has his eye on these, his poems benefit. Humour, satire, political intention, are entirely absent. This is an art of straightforward projection, making the reader see what the poet sees, with very little variation of theme or tone.

—Gavin Ewart

MATCHETT, William H(enry). American. Born in Chicago, Illinois, 5 March 1923. Educated at Westtown School, Pennsylvania; Swarthmore College, Pennsylvania, B.A. (highest honors) 1949; Harvard University, Cambridge, Massachusetts, M.A. 1950, Ph.D. 1957. Conscientious Objector; Civilian Public Service, 1943–46. Married Judith Wright in 1949; two sons and one daughter. Teaching Fellow, Harvard University, 1953–54. Instructor, 1954–56, Assistant Professor, 1956–60, Associate Professor, 1960–66, and since 1966, Professor of English, University of Washington, Seattle. Member of the Editorial Board, *Poetry Northwest*, Seattle, 1961. Since 1963, Editor, *Modern Language Quarterly*. Recipient: *Furioso* Prize, 1952. Address: Department of English, GN-30, University of Washington, Seattle, Washington 98195, U.S.A.

PUBLICATIONS

Verse

Water Ouzel and Other Poems. Boston, Houghton Mifflin, 1955.

Other

Poetry: From Statement to Meaning, with Jerome Beaty. New York, Oxford University Press, 1965.
The Phoenix and the Turtle: Shakespeare's Poem and Chester's "Loues Martyr." The Hague, Mouton, 1965.

Editor, *The Life and Death of King John*, by William Shakespeare. New York, New American Library, 1966.

William H. Matchett comments:

Minor poetry in a minor key, moving from the natural image to the, hopefully not forced, small affirmation. The early influence was the heavy hand of Eliot. If there is any increased freedom in my recent poetry, it is the direct influence of the poetry and criticism of Paul Hunter.

* * *

Subdued, civil, and marked by an easy grace, William H. Matchett's poems have found favor in several reprintings. Long before Ecology became the fashionable cry, he praised the fragile lives of wild birds, now become extinct, or nearly so, by the wanton hand of predatory man. His sensitive descriptions of nature are based on acute observation and conveyed through personification and perky humor, but they often close in pessimism. "Hang on to the end!" he urges the Ivory Bill, "You still may thrive/The Fates of us all are linked." He places little trust, however, in "the human pest," concluding there may be room for delicate wildfowl when man is extinct. Viewing man against man in war, he despairs, "lacking the strength to put the world in order." In other topographical poems, casual, conversational sketches preface philosophical meditations on nature as a source of grace and "second sight." Dry reflection follows the vivid portraiture of "Old Inn on the Eastern Shore," but finally gives way to mockery. The impression of nature is short-lived, "insight will fade"; the student soon considers himself "no sinne," and "Will go in to bathe before dinner."

This penchant for the didactic is more pronounced in compact rimed lyrics on a simple wedding, a Quaker funeral, Spring, and September, where aphorisms and moral tags render the scenes curiously bloodless. More spirited are the several internal monologues by personages caught in dramatic moments. Blood-thirsty and self-righteous, Mather, scourge of witches, rants to his angry God. Surrounded by dust and dry earth, Kruger waits placidly for death. The selfish patriarch remembers the powers of youth; imperious still in strengthless old age, he is aware of the symbolism of a flower but oblivious to the granddaughter who brings it. The visiting poet slyly avoids, then confronts, his imperceptive admirers – and the vision of his younger, better self. In "Packing a Photograph from Firenze" Matchett's several themes and methods join. Leaving an old house soon to be replaced by a modern jungle of structural steel, a home for statisticians who "doodle death with indelible ink," he marks the end of a life cycle and reaffirms the values of crooked lines, dirty fingers, fertile minds, living things.

—Joseph Parisi

MATHIAS, Roland (Glyn). British (Welsh). Born in Talybont-on-Usk, Breconshire, 4 September 1915. Educated at Caterham School; Jesus College, Oxford (Meyricke Exhibitioner, 1934; Honorary Scholar, 1936), B.A. (honours) in modern history 1936, B.Litt. 1939, M.A. 1944. Married Mary (Molly) Hawes in 1944; three children. Headmaster, Pembroke Dock Grammar School, Wales, 1948–58, The Herbert Strutt School, Belper, Derbyshire, 1958–64, and King Edward's Five Ways School, Birmingham, 1964–69; Schoolmaster-Fellow, Balliol College, Oxford, 1961, and University College, Swansea, 1967; Visiting Lecturer, University of Rennes, France, 1970, University of Brest, France, 1970, and University of Alabama, Birmingham, 1971. Editor, *Anglo-Welsh Review*, 1961–76. Chairman, English Section, Yr Acadami Gymraig, 1975–78. Since 1976, Chairman, Literature Committee, Welsh Arts Council. Recipient: Welsh Arts Council bursary, 1968, award, 1969, and prize, 1972. Address: Deffrobani, Maescelyn, Brecon, Wales.

PUBLICATIONS

Verse

Days Enduring and Other Poems. Ilfracombe, Devon, Stockwell, 1943.
Break in Harvest and Other Poems. London, Routledge, 1946.
The Roses of Tretower. Pembroke Dock, Dock Leaves Press, 1952.
The Flooded Valley. London, Putnam, 1960.

Absalom in the Tree and Other Poems. Llandybie, Dyfed, Gomer, 1971.

Short Stories

The Eleven Men of Eppynt and Other Stories. Pembroke Dock, Dock Leaves Press, 1956.

Other

Whitsun Riot: An Account of a Commotion Amongst Catholics in Herefordshire and Monmouthshire in 1605. London, Bowes, 1963.
Vernon Watkins. Cardiff, University of Wales Press, 1974.
The Hollowed-Out Elder Stalk: John Cowper Powys as Poet. London, Enitharmon Press, 1979.

Editor, with Sam Adams, *The Shining Pyramid and Other Stories by Welsh Authors.* Llandybie, Dyfed, Gomer, 1970.
Editor, *David Jones: Eight Essays on His Work as Writer and Artist.* Llandysul, Dyfed, Gomer, 1976.
Editor, with Sam Adams, *The Collected Short Stories of Geraint Goodwin.* Tenby, H. G. Watters, 1976.

Critical Study: "The Poetry of Roland Mathias" by Jeremy Hooker, in *Poetry Wales* (Llandybie), Summer 1971.

Roland Mathias comments:

In my earlier poetry the sense of "place" was very strong.... Even love poems used the "place" or "history" symbol.

Of recent years the process has changed. The secret "place" is always Wales, but since my return to it physically there has been a blurring of the remembered image by the present reality. In consequence I have become slightly more personal in my poetry, in an overt sense, but there are more people about, more predicaments than mine. I think of history still, of my stock, my parents, family love, and my own insufficiency in the line of descent. For me the old Noncomformist sense of guilt is not inhibiting and useless: it gives me a particular vision of the present through the past, a measurement. Out of it I can write.

* * *

Roland Mathias was born in 1915 at Talybont-on-Usk in Breconshire, a border county which is still largely rural in character. Although he has spent much of his adult life in Pembrokeshire and England, this borderland of his birth, where "Nightingales struggle with thorn-trees for the gate of Wales" and where Welsh and English have rubbed shoulders for hundreds of years, remains an important part of his personal landscape. He has written that in his earlier poetry "the sense of 'place' was very strong ... it was always of tremendous importance to me to know exactly *where* I was and what mood the place engendered in me. People might help to form that mood but the moment of ignition was always (or almost always) produced by solitude, the particular place and the history of men in that place."

In all his writing his appreciation of landscape is profoundly enriched by his sense of history and his concern for truth. He has no time for loose rhetoric or the easy attitude. His poetry presents a consistent view of the world expressed in a tough and concentrated verse of considerable individuality.

Alliteration is a powerful unifying device and with its help he often creates a rhythmic undertow which tugs against the surface flow. His images are concrete, hardly ever merely pictorial, but suggestive of layers of meaning beneath the obvious. His poetry is not always easy, but it is always rewarding.

—John Stuart Williams

MATTHEWS, William. American. Born in Cincinnati, Ohio, 11 November 1942. Educated at Yale University, New Haven, Connecticut, B.A. 1965; University of North Carolina, Chapel Hill, M.A. 1966. Married Marie Harris in 1963 (divorced, 1974); two sons. Instructor in English, Wells College, Aurora, New York, 1968–69; Assistant Professor, Cornell University, Ithaca, New York, 1969–74, and University of Colorado, Boulder, 1974–77. Since 1978, Associate Professor, and Director of Creative Writing, University of Washington, Seattle. Visiting Lecturer, University of Iowa, and Poetry Editor, *Iowa Review*, Iowa City, 1976–77. Member of the Editorial Board, Wesleyan University Press, 1969–74; Member, 1976–79, and Chairman, 1978–79, Literature Panel, National Endowment for the Arts. Since 1966, Co-Founding Editor, Lillabulero Press, and *Lillabulero*, Aurora, New York. Recipient: National Ednowment for the Arts Fellowship, 1974. Address: Department of English, GN-30, University of Washington, Seattle, Washington 98195, U.S.A.

PUBLICATIONS

Verse

Broken Syllables. Aurora, New York, Lillabulero Press, 1969.
Ruining the New Road. New York, Random House, 1970.
The Cloud. Boston, Barn Dream Press, 1971.
The Moon. Baltimore, Penyeach Press, 1971.
Poems for Tennessee, with Robert Bly and William Stafford. Martin, Tennessee Poetry Press, 1971.
Sleek for the Long Flight: New Poems. New York, Random House, 1972.
Without a Mouth. Norfolk, Virginia, Penyeach Press, 1972.
The Secret Life. Rochester, New York, Valley Press, 1972.
An Oar in the Old Water. San Francisco, Stone Press, 1973.
Sticks and Stones. Milwaukee, Pentagram Press, 1975.
Rising and Falling. Boston, Little Brown, 1979.

Critical Studies: in *Tennessee Poetry Journal* (Martin), Spring 1970; interview in *Ohio Review* (Athens), Spring 1972.

William Matthews comments:

My poems hope to speak for themselves. Much of their speech would be silence. Just as an architect uses walls to organize space, I use the words of a poem to organize silences. In those silences, the echoes, reverberations, assents, denials and secrets of my poems occur. These mute events are closely linked to the silences and strange landscapes in the natural world. That natural world, to an American, is large, often melodramatic, and strange – even in the most settled regions, where I have spent most of my life. My poems aren't self-consciously or programmatically American, but it matters – for all my travels – that I have lived here so long, in certain places, with certain people.

The language in my poems is the language one would love if he had grown up loving much British poetry and much American speech. I have grown to love American poetry and what I have heard of British (and Canadian) speech, but the memories of childhood are intense ones, indelible it seems. Of course it is all mixed, in moil, when I write. But I know from listening to what I have written that I love in language those moments which blur the distinctions between "formal" and "street" language. I distrust such categories, so I blur them often. I love best those poems which seem just to have emerged from a thicket of silence and intense emotion.

* * *

Although hc belongs to no particular "school," William Matthews is among a handful of young American poets who first published in early *Kayak* during the mid-1960's and who still seem to share each other's influences and enthusiasms. With Russell Banks and a few other student writers at the University of North Carolina at Chapel Hill, Matthews founded *Lillabulero* in 1966 – a magazine of considerable standing that published many young poets during significant stages of their early development. Matthews's abilities as an editor, and his considerable intelligence as a critic, have helped make him an important figure in contemporary American poetry.

Many of his poems are of the "deep image" tradition that is associated with *Kayak*, and expressive of a common poetic voice, shared at times by such fine poets as Bly, Wright, Merwin, Simic, Knott, and many others. For Matthews, this concern with the image manifests itself in careful and extensive use of metaphor and simile. He is capable of terrific compression – good, tight language – and his penchant for comparisons can become obvious and tiring, especially because there's no verbal fat to hide those metaphoric bones. Here is the first third of "Driving All Night":

My complicated past is an anthology,
a long line painted on the plains
I feel like literary history
about to startle the professors.

But it's not true.

Days ahead, snow heaps up
in the mountains
like undelivered mail.

Taken to its extreme, this tendency obscures the poem by calling to question the poet's credibility who seems so preoccupied with being original that he fails to establish reason. Here is all of "Why We Are Truly a Nation":

Because we rage inside
the old boundaries,
like a young girl leaving the Church,
scared of her parents.

Because we all dream of saving
the shaggy, dung-caked buffalo,
shielding the herd with our bodies.

Because grief unites us,
like the locked antlers of moose
who die on their knees in pairs.

Aside from this basic reservation, I find Matthews to be an inventive and fascinating poet. His best work deals with experience and goes past metaphoric examination. In "Another Beer," the meditational absorption of each beer, with the metaphoric toast preceding each glassful, takes the poem beyond definition, to sharing, of experience: "The last beer is always for the road./The road is what the car drinks/traveling on its tongue of light/all the way home."

Matthews's many poems to date have experimented in almost all poetic forms; also, he has given considerable attention to translation. His still-unwritten books may well reflect experience and consequent narrative as highly as his work in print reflects an active, intelligent word-smith of unusual imaginative power.

—Geof Hewitt

MAYER, Gerda (Kamilla, née Stein). British. Born in Carlsbad, Czechoslovakia, 9 June 1927; emigrated to Britain in 1939; became citizen in 1949. Educated at schools in Czechoslovakia and England, 1933–44; Bedford College, London, 1960–63, B.A. 1963. Married Adolf Mayer in 1949. Worked on farms in Worcestershire and Surrey, 1945–46; did office work in London, 1946–52. Address: 12 Margaret Avenue, London E4 7NP, England.

PUBLICATIONS

Verse

Oddments. Privately printed, 1970.
Gerda Mayer's Library Folder. Kettering, Northamptonshire, All-In, 1972.
Treble Poets 2, with Florence Elon and Daniel Halpern. London, Chatto and Windus, 1975.
The Knockabout Show (juvenile). London, Chatto and Windus, 1978.

Other

Editor, *Poet Tree Centaur: A Walthamstow Group Anthology.* London, Oddments, 1973.

Gerda Mayer comments:

I use a fair amount of humour; even the serious poems sometimes contain an element of verbal clowning. Some of the poems begin seriously and end in a joke, and vice versa. This, together with the fact that I have written quite a number of flimsy whimsies, tends to obscure the more painful messages. Conversely, I have known people to overlook the humour altogether. Perhaps my verse is like those trick-pictures that contain two images, of which it is possible to perceive only one at a time.

* * *

Gerda Mayer's poems have that direct simplicity of approach that gives them an air of timelessness, something of the atmosphere of the folk tale in which addressing God or the universe is as casual as speaking over the fence to your next door neighbour. I don't know if this has anything to do with Gerda's Czechoslovakian origins and memories, but I suspect it has, and the fact is there, her poems are like that: "Save the world God, save your creatures/ save us for a rainy day." Even when she is taking on current subjects and concerns such as the environment the same ability comes to the fore and the "Consumer" assumes a fabulosity: "The Great Consumer/crops the ground bare/where are the flowers?/where the sweet parsnips?" It is the same quality which enables her to invest the everyday with the surreal clarity of dreams:

The waiter licks the tablecloth clean
he licks clean the plates the glasses the
flowers his tongue
moves between the prongs of the forks

It is superb talent, and Gerda Mayer's own. And it makes her a fine creator of poems for young people, poems which, like all the best poems for young people, are not written down to them, but are a natural extension of the rest of her work, with the same sharp humour and directness of approach: "In childhood I took it for granted/that Adam and Eve were Jews:/ though implied rather than stated/it was Good News," and often they reflect the same concerns: "I the sophisticated primate/Have stunted fingers on my feet,/And almost I control my climate/And everything is what I eat."

Eminently readable and deceptively simple, Gerda Mayer's poetry is penetrating stuff. It should be read with care, as readers can suddenly find themselves falling unexpectedly into great wells of meaning.

—John Cotton

MAYNE, Seymour. Canadian. Born in Montreal, Quebec, 18 May 1944, Educated at McGill University, Montreal (Chester Macnaghten Prize, 1962), B.A. (honours) 1965; University of British Columbia, Vancouver, M.A. 1966, Ph.D. 1972. Lecturer, Jewish Institute, Montreal, 1964, and University of British Columbia, 1972. Assistant Professor 1973–78, and since 1978 Associate Professor of English, University of Ottawa. Co-Editor, *Cataract*, Montreal, 1961–62; Poetry Editor, *Forge*, Montreal, 1961–62; Editor, *The Page*, 1962–63, and *Catapult*, Montreal, 1964; Managing Editor, Very Stone House, Vancouver, 1966–69; Poetry Editor, *Ingluvin*, 1970–71, and Managing Editor, Ingluvin Publications, 1970–73, Montreal. Since 1973, Editor, Mosaic Press and Valley Editions, Ottawa; since 1978, Co-Editor, *Stoney Monday*, Ottawa. Recipient: Canada Council bursary, 1969, and grant, 1973, 1977; Segal Prize, 1974. Address: Department of English, University of Ottawa, Ottawa K1N 6N5, Canada.

PUBLICATIONS

Verse

That Monocycle the Moon. Privately printed, 1964.
Tiptoeing on the Mount. Montreal, McGill, 1965; revised edition, Montreal, Catapult, 1965.
From the Portals of Mouseholes. Vancouver, Very Stone House, 1966.
Touches. Vancouver, University of British Columbia, 1966.

I Am Still the Boy. Vancouver, Western Press, 1967.
Ticklish Ticlicorice. Vancouver, Very Stone House, 1969.
The Gigolo Teaspoon. Vancouver, Very Stone House, 1969.
Earseed. Vancouver, Very Stone House, 1969.
Anewd. Vancouver, Very Stone House, 1969.
Mutetations. Vancouver, Very Stone House, 1969.
Manimals (includes prose). Vancouver, Very Stone House, 1969.
Mouth. Kingston, Ontario, Quarry Press, 1970.
For Stems of Light. Vernon, British Columbia, Very Stone House, 1971; revised edition, Ottawa, Valley, 1974.
Face. Burnaby, British Columbia, Blackfish, 1971.
Name. Erin, Ontario, Press Porcépic, 1975; revised edition, Ottawa, Mosaic Press, 1976.
Diasporas: Poems 1973–1977. Ottawa, Mosaic Press, 1977.
Begging. Ottawa, Mosaic Press, 1977.

Other

Editor, with Patrick Lane, *Collected Poems of Red Lane.* Vancouver, Very Stone House, 1968.
Editor, with Victor Coleman, *Poetry of Canada.* Buffalo, Intrepid Press, 1969.
Editor, with Dorothy Livesay, *Forty Women Poets of Canada.* Montreal, Ingluvin, 1971.
Editor, *Engagements: The Prose of Irving Layton.* Toronto, McClelland and Stewart, 1972.
Editor, *Cutting the Keys.* Ottawa, University of Ottawa, 1975.
Editor, *Splices.* Ottawa, University of Ottawa, 1975.
Editor, *The A. M. Klein Symposium.* Ottawa, University of Ottawa, 1975.
Editor, *Choice Parts.* Ottawa, University of Ottawa, 1976.
Editor, *Irving Layton: The Poet and His Critics.* Toronto, McGraw Hill Ryerson, 1978.

Translator, with Catherine Leach, *Genealogy of Instruments*, by Jerzy Harasymowicz. Ottawa, Valley Editions, 1974.

Critical Studies: by Peter Stevens, in *Canadian Forum* (Toronto), March 1968; "Other Vancouverites" by A. W. Purdy, in *Canadian Literature 35* (Vancouver), Winter 1968; "New Poetry of the East" by Tom Marshall, in *New: American and Canadian Poetry 15* (Trumansburg, New York), April–May 1971; Greg Gatenby, in *English Quarterly* (Waterloo, Ontario), Winter 1975–76.

Seymour Mayne comments:

What I have to say about poetry is written into the poems and titles of my books. I have learned from the early study of Biblic poetry and Hebraic liturgy and prayer. More immediately I wish to acknowledge the Montreal poets whose work and example taught me much: A. M. Klein, Irving Layton, Louis Dudek, John Sutherland, Leonard Cohen, F. R. Scott, A. J. M. Smith, and other less known men and women.

* * *

As an editor of several little magazines; as a founder of two private presses named Very Stone House and Ingluvin Press; as a broadcaster of radio documentaries on literary subjects; as the compiler of the prose writings of Irving Layton; and as many other things as well, Seymour Mayne has made a name for himself in the world of Canadian poetry.

But reputations of this sort are ephemeral and double-edged. Perhaps what he will be known for in the future is his own poetry which has been appearing for the last decade and attracting increased interest of late. He has not been an experimental poet (his concrete work has the sense of *déjà vu*) but he has been persistent. His central publication is *Mouth*, a full-length collection of miscellaneous poems, some of which chart the relationship of the various bodily orifices and, in a Freudian fashion, find a link between or among them. As he writes in "Fang of Light": "and make the mouth/one vibrating hoop/of his whole/orificial self." The mood and image are there, but the language, especially the diction, is mixed and not always specific or emotional.

There are various contradictory themes in embryo – or in suspension – in Mayne's poetry, and these include: human desire as against bodily guilt; human transcendence as against whimsical reasonableness or ironic insight. Perhaps it is through a Jewish reconciliation of these opposites that Mayne's poetry will pass. The necessary drive is there, for the poet writes in "You Don't Scream":

> Tear yourself away.
> Bleed, if you must.
> A fever will rise in your eyes
> and burn like a need.

—John Robert Colombo

MAYO, E(dward) L(eslie). American. Born in Dorchester, Massachusetts, 26 July 1904. Educated at the University of Minnesota, Minneapolis (Payne Prize, 1932), B.A. (magna cum laude) 1932, M.A. Married Myra Margaret Buchanan Morton in 1936; three children. Professor of English, Drake University, Des Moines, Iowa, 1947–75. Recipient: Oscar Blumenthal Prize (*Poetry*, Chicago), 1942; Amy Lowell Traveling Fellowship, 1953, 1954. D.Litt.: Iowa Wesleyan College, Mount Pleasant, 1960. Address: 1413 8th Avenue, Grinnell, Iowa 50112, U.S.A.

PUBLICATIONS

Verse

The Diver. Minneapolis, University of Minnesota Press, 1947.
The Center Is Everywhere. New York, Twayne, 1954.
Summer Unbound and Other Poems. Minneapolis, University of Minnesota Press, 1958.
Selected Poems. Iowa City, Prairie Press, 1973.

Critical Study: "E. L. Mayo: A Modern Metaphysical" by John Ciardi, in *University of Kansas City Review* (Missouri), 1947.

E. L. Mayo comments:

I owe a dual homage to the Metaphysicals, especially Donne, and to the French Symbolists. The Symbolist influence first reached me indirectly through Yeats, Eliot, etc. If to these you add a penchant for the plainness of diction which I found in both Hardy and E. A. Robinson, you should be able to place my school pretty accurately.

When I began writing, Eliot and Frost were the main luminaries on the horizon. Hardy and Housman were almost as important. All these poets used traditional forms, meter, rhyme, stanza form – but with a difference. Such, in general, have been my own procedures. I have no objection to good free verse but I feel that poets haven't yet begun to discover the full potentialities of rhythm and sound. Contemporary experiments with free verse force the poet back on imagery, everything else being secondary. That is, he isn't using all the resources at his disposal. My effort in poetry is to avail myself of all these resources.

* * *

According to John Ciardi, some of the poems of E. L. Mayo are "happy evidence of how far poetry has come in a hundred years toward acquiring a wholly natural mastery of the commonest details of ordinary living." Ciardi goes on to praise Mayo's "intellectual fire," "verbal felicity," and capacity to create symbols and images that conspire toward a "sudden burgeoning of second meanings." "Mayo has long ago achieved his technical majority," Ciardi wrote in 1947, and "the personality that emerges from his poems is invariably attractive." James Wright, in *Poetry*, in 1958, commented that Mayo's poems "smolder with a kind of subdued bitterness," praised his work as "unpretentious," and found the poet "daring and successful precisely because he does not overburden his language." From Mayo's volume, *Summer Unbound*, Wright singled out "Handbag" and "Three Ladies" for special praise, but found the entire volume "severe, tough," with a natural modernity. An earlier review of "The Diver" (printed in *Poetry*, 1948) also spoke of Mayo's modernity, relating it to "his rejection of surface meaning": "And there is that most typical contemporary phenomenon: the poem drawing skilfully upon all levels of experience – including, even, the conventionally poetic ... the poet has assimilated many modern voices to his own voice." Freshness was what this critic found in Mayo's "Iron Gate":

To pass the thirtieth year is but to be
Other than one expected, barer here
The heart is than it was in many a year,
No longer cluttered with bright privacies.

Here Solomon perceives he is not wise
And with an eye upon the second prize
Divides desire with possibility ...
The sea gull in his proper breast
Beats louder now against a thinner door....

He "snatches the shining runners as they fly –" yet "even the awkward song is excellent." The poem is surpassed perhaps only by "On Growing Invisible," in which Mayo later speaks "From the bland, snow-crusted eminence/Of sixty," comparing himself to "a mild smiling Cheshire gentleman/Cat of sixty fading softly away," and concluding: "My vision will continue to expand/Brobdingnagian/Until I comprehend all humankind/Without being there." Poems like this latter one, found in *The Center Is Everywhere*, are good examples of the metaphysical style many critics have noted in Mayo. Indeed, what gives his poems their unique appeal may be the heavy, out-in-the-open tension that exists in his poems between the metaphysical and the idiomatic, for the poems also "pretend to be simple prose-like utterances, whereas in fact the best of them contain an echoing poetic meaning which begins to release itself a split second after we have read the words. There is an assumed lightness of touch here, a note not quite of irony but almost of timidity, behind which the richer meanings can be heard ... He understands what form does to an idea, and is not afraid to write something which is in itself trivial but in its poetic context is not" (David Daiches). Milton Crane has defined Mayo's "obvious principle" of unity as "an admirable clarity and lucidity of expression and a determination to shun the clichés which make much modern poetry seem a kaleidoscope in which the same unevocative images and abstractions are constantly reshuffled into new patterns." One could write at length of Mayo's success in knowing "the true, secret name of the river," of opening up in his poems "the mystery of better and of worse," of dealing with that angel whose "name was Loneliness," of speaking of the ghost to whom flesh is only a door, of hearing the "Wind – I said – Breaker of ties, breaker of promises." In "The Diver" Mayo dealt with the poet's trip down into the sea of experience, where "in his brain/The jungles of the sea must flower still"; in another poem he said poetry is a mirror, "showing/Clearer than to our shadowy sense, the glowing/And waning of a more than mortal creature." Just as "moles are very little/And worlds are very big," the poet and his world are unfairly matched. But perhaps the best introduction to Mayo's work is to cite his simple, yet powerful poem on El Greco:

See how the sun has somewhat not of light
Falling upon these men who stand so tall;
See how their eyes observe some inward sight
And how their living takes no room at all –
Their passing stirs no air, so thin they are –
Behind them see small houses with small doors;
The light from an unfamiliar star
That lights their walls and falls across their floors.
What shall we say when one of these men goes
Into his house and we no longer see
His eyes observing something that he knows?
And if their houses brim with radiancy
Why does no light come through as those doors close?

—David Ray

McAULEY, James J(ohn). Irish. Born in Dublin, 8 January 1936. Educated at Clongowes Wood College, 1948–53; University College, Dublin, 1960–62, B.A. 1962; University of Arkansas, Fayetteville, 1966–68, M.F.A. 1971. Married 1) Joan McNally in 1958 (divorced, 1968), three children; 2) Almut R. Nierentz, 1968, two children. Journalist, Electricity Supply Board, Dublin, 1954–66; Lecturer, Municipal Gallery of Modern Art, Dublin, 1965–66; Graduate Assistant, University of Arkansas, 1966–68; Assistant Professor and Director of the Creative Writing Program, Lycoming College, Williamsport, Pennsylvania, 1968–70. Assistant Professor, 1970–73, Associate Professor, 1973–78, and since 1978, Professor of English, Eastern Washington State College, Cheney. Art Critic, *Kilkenny Magazine*, Dublin, 1960–66; Associate Editor, *Poetry Ireland*, Dublin, 1962–66; Arts Consultant, *Hibernia National Review*, Dublin, 1964–66; Book Reviewer, *Irish Times*, Dublin, 1964–66; Reporter, *North West Arkansas Times*, Fayetteville, 1967. Since 1978, Editor, Dolmen Press, Dublin. Recipient: National Endowment for the Arts grant, 1972. Agent: Lordly and Dame Inc., 51 Church Street, Boston, Massachusetts 02116. Address: 624 Lincoln, Cheney, Washington 99004, U.S.A.

PUBLICATIONS

Verse

Observations. Blackrock, Ireland, Mount Salus Press, 1960.

A New Address. Dublin, Dolmen Press, London, Oxford University Press, and Chester Springs, Pennsylvania, Dufour, 1965.
Draft Balance Sheet: Poems 1963–1969. Dublin, Dolmen Press, London, Oxford University Press, and Chester Springs, Pennsylvania, Dufour, 1970.
Home and Away. Privately printed, 1974.
After the Blizzard. Columbia, University of Missouri Press, 1975.
The Exile's Recurring Nightmare. San Francisco, Aisling Press, 1975.

Play

The Revolution (produced Dublin, 1966).

Critical Studies: review in *Hibernia* (Dublin), 1970; *Choice*, edited by Michael Hartnett and Desmond Egan, Dublin, Goldsmith Press, 1973.

James J. McAuley comments:

My first book, *Observations*, consists of 16 confessional lyrics; very young poems, imitative, private. *A New Address* is the offspring of my two-year love affair with *Roget's Thesaurus*: poems resulting from my preoccupation with words, their sounds and associations. *Draft Balance Sheet* resulted from my two-year study of Poetry and Poetics under James Whitehead at Arkansas. *After the Blizzard* is a collection of love-poems, satires, narratives, and monologs. *The Revolution* is a satire on Easter, 1916, and its end result, the modern Irish state.

I've given up the search for my own "voice"; prefer the freedom to invent voices, masks, personae. I try to "sing whatever is well-made." My recent preoccupations concern exile, geographical and spiritual.

* * *

James J. McAuley's poetry has changed very considerably, perhaps not altogether convincingly, since his move from Ireland to America. His newer, distinctly American tone, hardly seems natural to him – although the themes of his poems are clearly ones of his natural choice. Unlike such a poet as John Montague, who has also been closely associated with America, McAuley seems half-inclined to drop his "Irishry," which may in his case be a mistake. (Denise Levertov did turn from an English neo-Georgian into a modernist American – but she married an American and became an American citizen.) Easily the best of McAuley's poetry is his sharp and telling satire on things Irish; this is of course a special prerogative of Irish writers from (to give the remark a characteristically paradoxical Irish air) the Englishman Swift onwards; but McAuley does it well, and lends a dimension of his own to his criticism of Ireland, which is not genial. Other poetry, though composed with great care, tends to be over-literary, falsely fastidious, a shade over-graceful. But the good taste and the intelligence are certainly present: this stanza from "Stella" (dating from the early 1960's) demonstrates both his defects and his virtues:

The swan pierced by an arrow lies
Immortal on sharp stars
Above the bowed head ringing with the tones,
Vibrations, plangent chords of love.
About him, night sounds:
A leaf touching his shoulder
Whispered, descended, dying
At his feet.

—Martin Seymour-Smith

McCLURE, Michael. American. Born in Maryville, Kansas, 20 October 1932. Married to Joanna McClure; one daughter. Recipient: National Endowment for the Arts grant, 1967, 1974; Guggenheim Fellowship, 1973; Magic Theatre Alfred Jarry Award, for drama, 1973; Rockefeller Fellowship, for drama, 1975. Agent: Helen Merrill, 337 West 22nd Street, New York, New York 10011. Address: 264 Downey Street, San Francisco, California 94117, U.S.A.

PUBLICATIONS

Verse

Passage. Big Sur, California, Jonathan Williams, 1956.
Peyote Poem. San Francisco, Wallace Berman, 1958.
For Artaud. New York, Totem Press, 1959.
Hymns to St. Geryon and Other Poems. San Francisco, Auerhahn Press, 1959.
The New Book: A Book of Torture. New York, Grove Press, 1961.
Dark Brown. San Francisco, Auerhahn Press, 1961.
Two for Bruce Conner. San Francisco, Oyez, 1964.
Ghost Tantras. Privately printed, 1964.
Double Murder! Vahrooooooohr! Los Angeles, Wallace Berman, 1964.
Love Lion, Lioness. Privately printed, 1964.
13 Mad Sonnets. Milan, East 128, 1964.
Poisoned Wheat. Privately printed, 1965.
Unto Caesar. San Francisco, Dave Haselwood, 1965.
Mandalas. San Francisco, Dave Haselwood, 1965.
Dream Table. San Francisco, Dave Haselwood, 1966.
Love Lion Book. San Francisco, Four Seasons, 1966.
Hail Thee Who Play: A Poem. Los Angeles, Black Sparrow Press, 1968; revised edition, Berkeley, California, Sand Dollar, 1974.
Oh Christ God Love Cry of Love Stifled Furred Wall Smoking Burning. San Francisco, Auerhahn Press, 1969(?).
The Sermons of Jean Harlow and the Curses of Billy the Kid. San Francisco, Four Seasons, 1969.
The Surge: A Poem. Columbus, Ohio, Frontier Press, 1969.
Hymns to St. Geryon, and Dark Brown. London, Cape Goliard Press, 1969.
Lion Fight. New York, Pierrepont Press, 1969.
Star. New York, Grove Press, 1971.
99 Theses. Lawrence, Kansas, Tansy Press, 1972.
The Book of Joanna. Berkeley, California, Sand Dollar, 1973.
Transfiguration. Cambridge, Massachusetts, Pomegranate Press, 1973.
Rare Angel (writ with raven's blood). Los Angeles, Black Sparrow Press, 1974.
September Blackberries. New York, New Directions, 1974.
Solstice Blossom. Berkeley, California, Arif Press, 1974.
Fleas 189–195. London, Aloes, 1974.
A Fist Full (1956–1957). Los Angeles, Black Sparrow Press, 1974.
On Organism. Buffalo, Institute of Further Studies, 1974.
Jaguar Skies. New York, New Directions, 1975.
Man of Moderation: Two Poems. New York, Hallman, 1975.
Antechamber and Other Poems. New York, New Directions, 1978.

Plays

The Feast (produced San Francisco, 1960). Included in *The Mammals*, 1972.
Pillow (produced New York, 1961). Included in *The Mammals*, 1972.

The Growl, in *Four in Hand* (produced Berkeley, California, 1970). Published in *Evergreen Review* (New York), April–May 1964.
The Blossom; or, Billy the Kid (produced New York, 1964). Milwaukee, Great Lakes Books, 1967.
The Beard (produced San Francisco, 1965; New York, 1967; London, 1968). Privately printed, 1965; revised version, New York, Grove Press, 1967.
The Shell (produced San Francisco, 1970; London, 1975). London, Cape Goliard Press, 1968; in *Gargoyle Cartoons*, 1971.
The Cherub (produced Berkeley, California, 1969). Los Angeles, Black Sparrow Press, 1970.
The Charbroiled Chinchilla: The Pansy, The Meatball, Spider Rabbit (produced Berkeley, California, 1969). Included in *Gargoyle Cartoons*, 1971.
Little Odes, Poems, and a Play, The Raptors. Los Angeles, Black Sparrow Press, 1969.
The Brutal Brontosaurus: Spider Rabbit, The Meatball, The Shell, Apple Glove, The Authentic Radio Life of Bruce Conner and Snoutburbler (produced San Francisco, 1970; *The Meatball* and *Spider Rabbit* produced London, 1971, New York, 1976; *The Authentic Radio Life of Bruce Conner and Snoutburbler* produced London, 1975). Included in *Gargoyle Cartoons*, 1971.
The Pansy (produced London, 1972). Included in *Gargoyle Cartoons*, 1971.
Gargoyle Cartoons (includes *The Shell, The Pansy, The Meatball, The Bow, Spider Rabbit, Apple Glove, The Sail, The Dear, The Authentic Radio Life of Bruce Conner and Snoutburbler, The Feather, The Cherub*). New York, Delacorte Press, 1971.
Polymorphous Pirates: The Pussy, The Button, The Feather (produced Berkeley, California, 1972). *The Feather* included in *Gargoyle Cartoons*, 1971.
The Mammals (includes *The Blossom, The Feast, Pillow*). San Francisco, Cranium Press, 1972.
The Pussy, The Button, and Chekhov's Grandmother; or, The Sugar Wolves (produced New York, 1973).
Gorf (produced San Francisco, 1974). New York, New Directions, 1976.
The Derby (produced Los Angeles, 1974).
General Gorgeous (produced New York, 1975; Edinburgh, 1976).
Sunny-Side Up (includes *The Pink Helmet* and *The Masked Choir*) (produced Los Angeles, 1976). *The Masked Choir* published in *Performing Arts Journal* (New York), August 1976.
Two for the Tricentennial (includes *The Pink Helmet* and *The Grabbing of the Fairy*) (produced San Francisco, 1976). *The Grabbing of the Fairy* published St. Paul, Minnesota, Truck Press, 1978.
Goethe: Ein Fragment (produced San Francisco, 1977).
Minnie Mouse and the Tap-Dancing Buddha (produced San Francisco, 1978).
Josephine, The Mouse Singer (produced New York, 1978).
The Red Snake (produced San Francisco, 1979).

Radio Play: *Music Peace*, 1974.

Television Play: *The Maze* (documentary), 1967.

Novels

The Mad Cub. New York, Bantam, 1970.
The Adept. New York, Delacorte Press, 1971.

Other

Meat Science Essays. San Francisco, City Lights, 1963; revised edition, San Francisco, Dave Haselwood, 1967.

Freewheelin' Frank, Secretary of the Angels, as Told to Michael McClure by Frank Reynolds. New York, Grove Press, 1967.

Editor, with James Harmon, *Ark II/Moby I.* San Francisco, Editorial Offices, 1957.
Editor, with David Meltzer and Lawrence Ferlinghetti, *Journal for the Protection of All Beings.* San Francisco, City Lights, 1961.

Bibliography: *A Catalogue of Works by Michael McClure, 1956–1965* by Marshall Clements, New York, Phoenix Book Shop, 1965.

Manuscript Collection: Simon Fraser University, Burnaby, British Columbia.

Critical Studies: "This Is Geryon," in *Times Literary Supplement* (London), 25 March 1965; interview in *San Francisco Poets*, edited by David Meltzer, New York, Bantam, 1971; "Michael McClure Symposium" in *Margins 18* (Milwaukee), 1975.

* * *

Michael McClure is aware of the choices. Moving into the language (if not the life) like a candidate for a doctoral degree in hedonism, he evinces his zeal with grunts, howls, and meaty whines. He seeks the revelations; is opposite to another poet's "telephone-pole men," each of whom is content to resemble his neighbor. This man, within a play written and directed by others, prepares the program notes, in which his role is illustrated. So that that which may appear as iconoclasm or affectation becomes an effective style in confirmation of the new reverence for body-freedom.

The Libran, refiner of art, works from others' initial strengths (McClure follows work Blake and Artaud began; his language has added no new words to common parlance as has Sanders' or Ginsberg's today; his explorations into sound are more timid than Cage's) but the Libran adds the inimitability of his touch. One recognizes his form and idiom, sans signature. It is sensual above sexual; despite apparently radical moves in *Dark Brown* and *The Beard*, the language is more classical than innovatory, more musical than bestial. When he was young he risked more. Disguised as a lion-maned nude, but never naked, this celebrant chants the body with the elegance of the average caryatid. In his better experiments he resists balancing sensuality with intellect (his weak point, as with most Librans). And he looks typically Libra, moderate in all respects. Air-sign and verbal, he's in love with sound; as a romantic, he shuns the experiences offered by dissonance.

Conscious of status quo, both as observer and participant, he is eager to lend his energy to the fashionable changes. The mutability produces interesting variations on his theme. His ambition exceeds his abilities, with great results: the challenges are in the wisdom of the poem just around the next page or year. An exciting, difficult role, at the edge of the true hand-to-hand revolution of language. The life and work come through of a piece: both vivid, and memorable, neither modest nor monumental.

—Carol Bergé

McCUAIG, Ronald. Australian. Born in Newcastle, New South Wales, in 1908. Educated in Newcastle and Sydney. Married; two sons. Formerly, Radio Journalist. Member of the Editorial Staff, *The Bulletin*, Sydney.

PUBLICATIONS

Verse

Vaudeville. Privately printed, 1938.
The Wanton Goldfish. Privately printed, 1941.
Quod Ronald McCuaig. Sydney, Angus and Robertson, 1946.
The Ballad of Bloodthirsty Bessie and Other Poems. Sydney, Angus and Robertson, 1961.

Other

Tales Out of Bed (essays and short stories). Sydney, Allied Authors and Artists, 1944.
Literature. Canberra, Australian News and Information Bureau, 1962.
Gangles (juvenile). London, Angus and Robertson, 1972.
Tombolino and the Amazing Football Boots (juvenile). London, Angus and Robertson, 1974.

Editor, *Australian Poetry 1954.* Sydney, Angus and Robertson, 1954.

* * *

Ronald McCuaig is still remembered with affection by readers of the *Sydney Bulletin* in its last burst of glory as the leading Australian weekly journal of literature and comment up to the late 1950's. McCuaig's early poetry was self-confessedly influenced by the more strident abrasiveness of early Eliot and Pound. However, his "Vaudeville" sequence seems today more heavily indebted to C. J. Dennis' famous comic masterpiece, "The Sentimental Bloke."

McCuaig worked on the *Bulletin* staff for many years and regularly contributed topical light verse to the "Aboriginalities" and "Society" pages, often under a *nom-de-plume*. His work was gathered together in *The Ballad of Bloodthirsty Bessie and Other Poems*. Much of the topicality has faded, but a number of poems, particularly those influenced by McCuaig's interest in music, retain their original charm and zest. His most ambitious work is contained in a sequence "Scenes from Childhood" whose ten elegies display formal ingenuity with a pervasively nostaligic lyricism. Of these Douglas Stewart has written: "In these elegies his eclecticism turns the verse of *Piers Plowman* into a sestina, combines a hint from Mallarmé with a rhythm of Campion's, paraphrases a Chopin Study, draws a ballad out of 'Auld Lang Syne,' and begins an anecdote of his childhood with an homage to Debussy that turns into a song in praise of Renoir." Ronald McCuaig has published almost nothing since that volume.

—Thomas W. Shapcott

McDONALD, Roger. Australian. Born in Young, New South Wales, 23 June 1941. Educated at the University of Sydney, 1959–62, B.A. 1962. Married Rhyll McMaster in 1967; two children. School Teacher, Murrumburrah and Wellington, New South Wales, 1963–64; Producer, Educational Radio and Television, Brisbane, Queensland, and Hobart, Tasmania, 1964–69. Since 1969, Editor, University of Queensland Press, Brisbane. Delegate, Hari Sastra National Literature Conference, Sabah, Malaysia, 1973. Recipient: Australia Council Fellowship, 1977. Address: P.O. Box 338, Dickson, A.C.T. 2602, Australia.

PUBLICATIONS

Verse

Citizens of Mist. Brisbane, University of Queensland Press, 1968.
Airship. Brisbane, University of Queensland Press, 1975.

Novel

1915. Brisbane, University of Queensland Press, 1979.

Other

Editor, *The First Paperback Poets Anthology.* Brisbane, University of Queensland Press, 1974.

Manuscript Collection: National Library of Australia, Canberra.

Roger McDonald comments:

I would like to think that an introspective strain in my poetry is made acceptable, even interesting, by firmly physical writing. I find abstractions impossible to approach without the armour of careful description. I like to find things said in precise and evocative ways in the work of other writers, and hope that the qualities I prefer can be found in my own work.

* * *

Reading Roger McDonald's poetry one is struck by his fascination with the past, with extracting details from past happenings and making them unique to the present. This is in fact a poetry of moments. Almost cinematically the action is seen to stop – and the frozen frame examined. But seldom does he conclude the poem by, as it were, setting the film in motion again; more often he slightly recasts the details and leaves it at that. It is as if he is saying: Now, at this unrepeatable point of time, I'm going to declare all I have shown you to be a mere collage of appearances whose independent and contemporary meanings already assert themselves, a leap ahead of any attempt I might make at interpretation.

The poem "Two Summers in Moravia" is a clear example of this. In the first summer (looking back to wartime),

This was a day
when little happened
though inch by inch everything changed.
A load of hay narrowly crossed the bridge,
the boy caught a fish underneath in shade,
and ducks quarrelled in the reeds

and in the second summer, the present-time of the poem, he records an almost unchanged scene but, like positive to negative, simple details seem unaccountably reversed; there is a brooding feeling, a threat, the suggestion that some other dimension moves within them.

In another recent poem, "The Hollow Thesaurus," a similar process is applied to language itself, so that here McDonald is writing about his medium as a means of demonstrating his use of it:

Names for everything I touch
were hatched in bibles, in poems cupped by madmen
on rocky hills, by marks on sheets of stone,
by humped and sticky lines in printed books.

Lexicographers burned their stringy eyeballs black
for the sake of my knowing. Instinctive generations
hammered their victories, threaded a chain,
and lowered their strung-up wisdom in a twist
of molecules. But with me in mind
their time was wasted.

When the bloodred, pewter, sickle, sick or meloned moon
swells from nowhere,
the chatter of vast informative print
spills varied as milk. Nothing prepares me
even for common arrivals like this.

Look. The moon comes up. Behind certain trees are bats
that wrench skyward like black sticks.
Light falls thinly on grass, from moon and open door.
This has not happened before.

These recent poems are markedly more original in concept than those in his first book, *Citizens of Mist*, where, although he sustained his interest in gradual decay (whether the doomed politeness of Victorian gentility or flies buzzing about a carcass) by setting it within a context of collapse on a massive scale, the implications remained narrow. There was a tendency for the universal to be cramped by the particular, where now the particular is its point of release.

He is a careful, thoughtful writer. His output is not large but his position in Australian literature is assured. Compact and intelligent, this is a poetry that is never quirky or flashy. Its limitation is that it might be thought too even, too neat, too safe.

Roger McDonald is also a book editor of distinction and is having an important influence on the directions being taken in poetry and prose in Australia today.

—Rodney Hall

McFADDEN, David. Canadian. Born in Hamilton, Ontario, 11 October 1940. Full-time writer. Writer-in-Residence, Simon Fraser University, Burnaby, British Columbia, 1979. Recipient: Canada Council bursary, 1968, and fellowship, 1978. Address: 9 Toby Crescent, Hamilton, Ontario L8T 2N7, Canada.

PUBLICATIONS

Verse

The Poem Poem. Toronto, Weed/Flower Press, 1967.

The Saladmaker: A Humility Cycle. Montreal, Imago Books, 1968.
Letters from the Earth to the Earth. Toronto, Coach House Press, 1968.
Poems Worth Knowing. Toronto, Coach House Press, 1971.
Intense Pleasure. Toronto, McClelland and Stewart, 1972.
The Ova Yogas. Toronto, Weed/Flower Press, 1972.
A Knight in Dried Plums. Toronto, McClelland and Stewart, 1975.
The Poet's Progress. Toronto, Coach House Press, 1977.
On the Road Again. Toronto, McClelland and Stewart, 1978.
I Don't Know. Montreal, Vehicule Press, 1978.
A New Romance. Montreal, Cross Country Press, 1979.

Other

The Great Canadian Sonnet. Toronto, Coach House Press, 1970.
Animal Spirits. Toronto, Coach House Press, 1979.
A Trip Around Lake Huron. Toronto, Coach House Press, 1979.
A Trip Around Lake Erie. Toronto, Coach House Press, 1979.

* * *

"I'm particularly pleased to inhabit the same world as McFadden," wrote Alfred Purdy when he read the manuscript of *Intense Pleasure*, "even if he's crazy as a bedbug." Although David McFadden – a poet and newspaperman who lives and writes in Hamilton, Ontario, a community not celebrated for its artists – has been publishing short collections of his poems and Richard Brautigan-like prose for the last decade, it was not until 1972, with the appearance of *Intense Pleasure*, that McFadden's work reached a wide public and the nature of his singular talent became clear.

McFadden is not as "crazy as a bedbug," for he is as "crazy as a fox" – and as witty and often as irrelevant as Dick Gregory and any number of stand-up comedians who specialize in witty one-liners and put-downs and one-upmanships. Many of his poems are nightclub routines with fast lines like: "He knew he was pregnant," "I'm addicted to toothpicks," "Now I'm middle-aged I want to be an alligator." The poems are amusing, lively and light, and often exhausted on a single reading.

In the poem "Ova Yoga," McFadden writes, "Inside every chicken is a human being trying to get out," and inside McFadden there is another poet beginning to be heard. This is the observer of modern society beset – but not swallowed up by – the incongruities and irrationalities of the contemporary world. This is the poet who in one poem presents a midget's-eye view of the world, who in another discovers Adolf Hitler living in Hamilton and arranges an interview. This is the poet who is attracted to the pop and kitsch characteristics of Canadian advertising: "This is Bruce Marsh speaking/for Kraft Foods in Canada."

On first reading one might mistake this McFadden for the stand-up comedian. But the emerging poet is one who like Apollinaire seeks to celebrate "the heroic of the everyday," who tries to grant a modicum of immortality to such things as "three Motorcycles parked diagonally at the curb/in front of 111 Brucedale Avenue." One looks at the Liverpudlian poets for something approximating McFadden's tone; but to long-dead but always-resurrectible Dadaists and Surrealists for McFadden's sense of the nostalgia of the evanescent. Thus David McFadden is the prophet of the ephemeral present.

—John Robert Colombo

McFADDEN, Roy. Born in Belfast, Northern Ireland, 14 November 1921. Educated at Regent House School, Newtownards, County Down; Queen's University, Belfast. Co-Editor, *Ulster Voices*, 1941–42, *Rann: An Ulster Quarterly of Poetry*, 1948–53, and *Irish Voices*, 1953, all in Belfast. Lives in Belfast.

PUBLICATIONS

Verse

A Poem: Russian Summer. Dublin, Gayfield Press, 1942.
Three New Poets, with Alex Comford and Ian Serraillier. Billericay, Essex, Grey Walls Press, 1942.
Swords and Ploughshares. London, Routledge, 1943.
Flowers for a Lady. London, Routledge, 1945.
The Heart's Townland. London, Routledge, 1947.
Elegy for the Dead of the "Princess Victoria." Lisburn, County Antrim, Lisnagarvey Press, 1952.
The Garryowen. London, Chatto and Windus, 1971.
Verifications. Belfast, Blackstaff Press, 1977.
A Watching Brief. Belfast, Blackstaff Press, 1979.

Critical Studies: in *Rann 20* (Belfast); by Michael Longley, in *Causeway: The Arts in Ulster*, Belfast, Arts Council of Northern Ireland, 1971; *Northern Voices* by Terence Brown, Dublin, Gill and Macmillan, 1975.

* * *

Roy McFadden produced his striking first collection during the war when presumably people were too busy to take notice of it. It was called *Swords and Ploughshares* – an appropriate title for what is in fact a war-book. Its vision is minatory, its verse is prophetic. Roy McFadden is an Irishman and sees his native mountain, "Slieve Donard," amid the waste of sky and flame of wings in terms of another Ararat. His "Train at Midnight" strides through fields whose very green flaunts the insurgent flag of the Irish Republic. War prevails in his inventive rehandling of ballad form, particularly "An Irish Peasant Woman Summons Her Absent Children":

Call them home from foreign lands,
Send my love imperative;
Holding hope between my hands
Theirs the hope I have to give,
Hands of hope imperative.

Stars still walk on secret hills
Hope is still a peasant's child;
The cities hoard their sevens ills,
But I hold wisdom undefiled,
Willing to history this child ...

Call them home where there is light
And still a candle and a prayer;
Call them through the twisted night,
Yesterday is dying there,
Past the hope of priest or prayer ...

Call them home. Send undefiled
This my love imperative.
Hope is still a peasant's child
Theirs the hope I have to give,
Child of hope imperative.

But, in McFadden's subsequent two books, the ghost of Yeats beats too insistently upon the door. The diction, too, becomes lush and over-romantic. After these he published no collection for twenty-five years.

However, in his recent book *The Garryowen*, Mr. McFadden matched his early skill with a wisdom conferred by experience. Here we have an authority all the better for being unforced. It is a craftsmanlike book all through, but "Glenarm," "Roger Casement's Rising," "Premonition," and various poems in the sequence "Family Album" are especially poignant. Like his distinguished contemporary John Hewitt, Roy McFadden has not only learned from the Anglo-Irish tradition but carried it forward. And, like John Hewitt's, his reputation should be consolidated before long by the issue of a Collected Poems.

—Philip Hobsbaum

McGOUGH, Roger. British. Born in Liverpool, Lancashire, 9 November 1937. Educated at St. Mary's College, Crosby, Lancashire; Hull University, Yorkshire, B.A. in French and geography, Cert.Ed. Formerly, Lecturer, Liverpool College of Art. Poetry Fellow, University of Loughborough, Leicestershire, 1973–75. Formerly, a member of "The Scaffold" (humor, poetry and music group). Agent: Hope Leresche and Steele, 11 Jubilee Place, London S.W.3, England.

PUBLICATIONS

Verse

The Mersey Sound: Penguin Modern Poets 10, with Adrian Henri and Brian Patten. London, Penguin, 1967.
Frinck, A Life in the Day of, and Summer with Monika: Poems (novel and verse). London, Joseph, and New York, Ballantine, 1967.
Watchwords. London, Cape, 1969.
After the Merrymaking. London, Cape, 1971.
Out of Sequence. London, Turret, 1973.
Gig. London, Cape, 1973.
Sporting Relations. London, Eyre Methuen, 1974.
In the Glassroom. London, Cape, 1976.
Holiday on Death Row. London, Cape, 1979.

Recordings: *The Incredible New Liverpool Scene*, CBS, 1967; *McGough McGear*, Parlophone; *"Scaffold" Live at Queen Elizabeth Hall*, Parlophone; *"Scaffold" L. the P.*, Parlophone; *Grimms*, Island; *Fresh Liver*, Island; *Sleepers*, DJM; *McGough/Patten*, Argo; *Summer with Monika*, Island, 1978.

Plays

Birds, Marriages and Deaths, with others (produced London, 1964).

The Chauffeur-Driven Rolls (produced Liverpool, 1966).
The Commission (produced Liverpool, 1967).
The Puny Little Life Show (produced London, 1969). Published in *Open Space Plays*, edited by Charles Marowitz, London, Penguin, 1974.
Zones (produced Edinburgh, 1969).
Stuff (produced London, 1970).
P.C. Plod (produced London, 1971).
Wordplay (produced London, 1975).
Monika (produced London, 1978).

Radio Play: *Gruff – A TV Commercial*, 1977.

Television Play: *The Lifeswappers*, 1976.

Other (juvenile)

Mr. Noselighter. London, Deutsch, 1976.
You Tell Me, with Michael Rosen. London, Penguin, 1979.

Manuscript Collection: University of Hull.

* * *

English critics have shown a surprising inability to cope with the "Pop Poetry" boom. Regularly, since the first appearance of the Liverpool poets on the national scene, they have predicted that the whole thing must soon come to an end, must be recognized as no more than an aberration, a flash in the pan. As I write, in 1974, the three principal Liverpool poets – Henri, McGough and Patten – are still very much with us, still publishing volumes of verse which seem to find eager readers.

When my anthology, *The Liverpool Scene*, was first published in 1967, Roger McGough was the poet whom the critics felt most inclined to forgive. They detected in him a lyricism, a simplicity and a lack of American influence which made him more acceptable than the others. Surprisingly, it is McGough, in the ensuing years, who has remained closest to the Pop milieu. He makes his living as a performer, rather than as a writer, and the group with whom he works, The Scaffold, have achieved a celebrity which stretches a long way beyond the poetry circuit, and have even managed, on one occasion, to top the English hit parade.

The result has been, perhaps, that he has not developed as interestingly as his colleagues. The virtues of his poetry remain very much what they always were – charm, high-spirits, and an astonishing capacity for inventing puns. Surely no English writer since W. S. Gilbert has had a cleverer touch with these:

Or when I'm 91
with silver hair
& sitting in a barber's chair
may rival gangsters
with hamfisted tommyguns burst in
& give me a short back & insides.

It seems to me that when McGough adds these qualities to a rarer, but extremely attractive, lyric melancholy about the ups-and-downs of love, then he is producing work which, for all its feather-lightness, is quite likely to survive.

—Edward Lucie-Smith

McGRATH, Thomas M. American. Born near Sheldon, North Dakota, 20 November 1916. Educated at Sheldon public schools; University of North Dakota, Grand Forks, B.A. in English 1939 (Phi Beta Kappa); Louisiana State University, Baton Rouge, M.A. in English 1940; New College, Oxford (Rhodes Scholar), 1947–48. Served in the United States Army Air Force, 1943–46. Married Eugenia Juanopoulos in 1960; one son. English Instructor, Colby College, Waterville, Maine, 1940–41; Assistant Professor, Los Angeles State College, 1950–54, and C. W. Post College, Long Island, New York, 1960–61; Associate Professor, North Dakota State University, Fargo, 1962–67. Since 1969, Associate Professor of English, Moorhead State College, Minnesota. Formerly, Film Writer; Editor, *California Quarterly*. Since 1960, Founding Editor, with Eugenia McGrath, *Crazy Horse*, Fargo. Recipient: Swallow Book Award, 1955; Amy Lowell traveling scholarship, 1965; Guggenheim Fellowship, 1967; National Endowment for the Arts grant, 1974; Bush Foundation Fellowship, 1976. Address: 615 South 11th Street, Moorhead, Minnesota 56560, U.S.A.

PUBLICATIONS

Verse

First Manifesto. Baton Rouge, Louisiana, Swallow, 1940.
Three Young Poets, with William Peterson and James Franklin Lewis, edited by Alan Swallow. Prairie City, Illinois, Decker Press, 1942.
The Dialectics of Love. Prairie City, Illinois, Decker Press, 1944.
To Walk a Crooked Mile. New York, Swallow, 1947.
Longshot O'Leary's Garland of Practical Poesie. New York, International, 1949.
Witness to the Times. Privately printed, 1954.
Figures from a Double World. Denver, Swallow, 1955.
Letter to an Imaginary Friend. Denver, Swallow, 1962.
New and Selected Poems. Denver, Swallow, 1962.
Letter to an Imaginary Friend, Parts I and II. Chicago, Swallow Press, 1970.
The Movie at the End of the World: Collected Poems. Chicago, Swallow Press, 1973.
Voyages to the Inland Sea III, with others, edited by John Judson. La Crosse, University of Wisconsin Center for Contemporary Poetry, 1973.
A Sound of One Hand. St. Peter, Minnesota, Minnesota Writers' Publishing House, 1975.
Letters to Tomasito. Minneapolis, Holy Cow, 1977.
Open Songs: Sixty Short Poems. Mt. Carroll, Illinois, Uzzano Press, 1977.

Novel

The Gates of Ivory, The Gates of Horn. New York, Mainstream, 1957.

Other

About Clouds (juvenile). Los Angeles, Melmont, 1959.
The Beautiful Things (juvenile). New York, Vanguard Press, 1960.

Manuscript Collections: University of North Dakota, Grand Forks; North Dakota State University, Fargo.

Critical Studies: by Tom Bond, in *Measure 2* (Boston), 1958; Charles Potts, in *Small Press Review* (Paradise, California), 1974.

Thomas McGrath comments:

Some of the work is a restructuring of traditional forms; some of it is open and "free." I have written a lot of short haiku-like poems and I'm now working on what may turn out to be the longest poem in America. I think the poems are quite personal in idiom, often "autobiographical" and politically revolutionary.

* * *

Like John Gardner in fiction or Sam Shepard in drama, Thomas McGrath is above all an American artist, whose work reflects the idioms and images of contemporary national life. His two dominant moods are private reminiscence, often meditation on a rural landscape, and public denunciation, often invective at an urban landscape. McGrath is the chronicler of both "the little lost towns ... towns of the dark people: a depot, a beer joint, a small/Fistful of lights flung east as the red-ball train goes past," and of "the rattle of voting machines/In the Las Vegas of the national politic." These lines from his finest work to date, the long poem *Letter to an Imaginary Friend*, suggest the remarkable range of theme and tone typical of McGrath at his best.

In his book *Goatfoot Milktongue Twinbird* the poet Donald Hall judges McGrath the best poet of public denunciation and invective in America today, surpassing both Ginsberg and Bly. McGrath's invective arises from the political idealism that informs all his verse, and often appears as satirical contrasts between homely rural images and mechanical urban ones:

And these but the stammering simulacra of the Rand
  Corpse wise men –
Scientists who have lost the good of the intellect,
  mechanico-humanoids
Antiseptically manufactured by the Faustian homunculus
  process.
And how they dream in their gelded towers these
  demi-men!
(Singing of overkill, kriegspiel, singing of blindfold chess –
  Sort of ainaleckshul rasslin matches to sharpen their
  fantasies
Like a scout knife.)
            Necrophiles.
                    Money protectors.

The plastic urban world of machine-men is a world of ludicrous fantasies of power, but those fantasies are dangerous, even deadly: McGrath derides the death of intellect and conscience in modern technological America, even as he fears the consequent destruction it deals out to the weak or exploited. Loss is a recurrent motif, national loss of mind, loss of health, loss of compassion, loss of destiny, loss of tradition or anchoring past.

Windless city built on decaying granite, loose ends
Without end or beginning and nothing to tie to, city down
  hill
From the high mania of our nineteenth century destiny –
  what's loose
Rolls there, what's square slides, anything not tied down
Flies in ...
        kind of petrified shitstorm.   Retractable
Swimming pools.
            Cancer Farms.
                    Whale dung

At the bottom of the American night refugees tourists
  elastic
Watches . . .

McGrath excels at this sort of national panorama, the poet's catalogue of a decaying society manifesting its putrescence in images of death and madness. "The citizens wrapped like mummies in their coats with poisoned sleep,/The dreamers, crazed, in their thousands, nailed to a tree of wine. . . ." There is rage in this loss, and sorrow over the devastation.

In a more private vein, McGrath likes to fashion personal reminiscences into "pseudo-autobiography," as he calls *Letter to an Imaginary Friend* (from which all quotations here are taken). Then the mood is calmer, the tone more positive, sometimes serene, the humor amused but never ironic, the landscape often the cold north woods.

So, worked together. Fed the wood to the saw
That had more gaps than teeth. Sweated, amd froze
In the dead-still days, as clear as glass, with the biting
Acetylene of the cold cutting in through the daylight,
And the badman trees snapping out of the dusk
Their icy pistols. So, worked, the peddlars pack of us.

Work is a source of peace and pleasure, from the Dakota woods to northern mountains and farms: "the vagrant farms of the north: Montana, Saskatchewan,/With the farmers still on them, merrily plowing away."

McGrath's verse shares points of similarity with that of many modern American poets, from Frost to Ginsberg, yet his voice is distinctly personal. He shares Frost's acute sense of nature and Ginsberg's rage, but blends those almost polar qualities into a single viewpoint capable of rare range and intensity.

—Jan Hokenson

McKEOWN, Tom (Thomas Shanks McKeown). American. Born in Evanston, Illinois, 29 September 1937. Educated at the University of Michigan, Ann Arbor, 1957–62, B.A. 1961, M.A. 1962. Instructor, Alpena College, Michigan, 1962–64, and Wisconsin State University, Oshkosh, 1964–68. Instructor, Stephens College, Columbia, Missouri, 1968–74. Recipient: Hopwood Award, University of Michigan, 1968; Wurlitzer Foundation grant, 1972, 1975; Yaddo grant, 1973, 1975. Address: General Delivery, Pentwater, Michigan 49449, U.S.A.

PUBLICATIONS

Verse

Alewife Summer. Albuquerque, New Mexico, Road Runner Press, 1967.
Last Thoughts. Madison, Wisconsin, Abraxas Press, 1969.
The Winds of the Calendar. Albuquerque, New Mexico, Road Runner Press, 1969.
Drunk All Afternoon. Madison, Wisconsin, Abraxas Press, 1969.
The Milk of the Wolf. Columbia, Missouri, Asari Press, 1970.
The Cloud Keeper. Dublin, Seafront Press, 1972.

The House of Water. Fredonia, New York, Basilisk Press, 1974.
The Luminous Revolver. Fremont, Michigan, Sumac Press, 1974.
Driving to New Mexico. Santa Fe, New Mexico, Sunstone Press, 1974.

Critical Studies: "Contemporary Poetic Statements," in *Road Apple Review* (Oshkosh, Wisconsin), 1971; in *December Magazine* (Western Springs, Illinois), December 1971; in *Back Door* (Poquon, Virginia), 1971; in *New Voices in American Poetry: An Anthology*, Cambridge, Massachusetts, Winthrop, 1973.

Tom McKeown comments:

Have several unfinished novels but I have little interest in them now. Poetry is my full-time obsession.

I lean toward the surreal in poetry. Like experimentation rather than the tired, heavy academic stuff.

Write in free verse almost entirely. No major themes really other than the usual ones: love, death, separation, alienation, war, etc. I am mainly concerned with the *dream* and the poetic possibilities that arise out of the *dream*. This is the area of the surreal where a non-sequitur progression of images or image clusters are drawn from the unconscious mind. The surreal deals with the landscapes of dreams and thus there are infinite possibilities for new and startling creations. Always there is a possibility for a *satori* or sudden illumination. Have been influenced perhaps by Neruda, Bréton and Trakl.

Recently, my poems have been reaching more toward the mystical and supernatural.

* * *

Tom McKeown is a poet who is able to be both concrete and surreal in his poetry. He admits the influence on his verse of such Spanish and Latin American poets as Lorca and Neruda; like Neruda, his surrealism has a strong grip on the natural landscape in which McKeown lives. Like other young American poets such as Greg Kuzma, McKeown manages a synthesis of the concrete and the surreal, the traditions of English nature poetry and Spanish and French surrealism. McKeown is one of the most promising exponents of this approach. He also sees the poet as a shaman in a poem from *Drunk All Afternoon* called "The Buffalo, Our Sacred Beast":

I am running with them
through the streets, drunk
on buffalo milk and nourished
by dung.
I carry a flag with a buffalo on it
and on my staff I spin a human skull.

In an essay he contributed to *Their Place in the Heat*, McKeown notes that he is attracted to both the nature/mythic/archetypal approach and the surreal approach as well in his writing. The former approach is evident in the poem quoted above, in which McKeown sees himself as a medicine man leading the buffalo back to trample the civilization that crushed them. Another poem (in a three poet issue of the *Road Apple Review*), "Aztec Dream," also evokes ancient rites, again involving human sacrifice: "a thin dagger parts the softness of air/of youth of flesh giving over all happy/silence to the carved gods of stone...." McKeown is, however, basically a compassionate poet; even in the first poem, he half apologizes to the human victims for the well-merited revenge of the buffalo, and one of his strongest groups of poems is a small collection of four elegies, *Last Thoughts*, which contains one of the strongest denunciations of the Viet Nam War, all the stronger for bringing it home in "Body En Route":

A twenty year old boy
is en route home. Killed
in Viet Nam. En route home
to the funeral parlor.
Home. En route to Oshkosh.
Twenty below zero. Heavy snow.
He is riding home to be lifted
from the baggage car
of the Chicago-Northwestern.
Quietly and smoothly
he will be driven home
through the frozen luminous streets.
Nothing stirs in the gray houses.
Silence from his metal box.
The park is without voices.
The wind blows a terrible darkness.

—Duane Ackerson

McNEILL, Anthony. Jamaican. Born in Kingston, 17 December 1941. Educated at Excelsior College, 1952; St. George's College, 1953–59; Nassau Community College, 1964–65; Johns Hopkins University, Baltimore, 1970–71, M.A. 1971; University of Massachusetts, Amherst. Married Olive Samuel in 1970; one child. Civil service clerk, Port Maria and Kingston, 1960–64; journalist, The Gleaner Company, Kingston, 1965–66; scriptwriter, JIS radio, Kingston, 1966–68; trainee manager, Jamaica Playboy Club-Hotel, Ocho Rios, 1968–69; Editorial Assistant, *Jamaica Journal*, Kingston, 1970; Teaching Assistant, University of Massachusetts, 1971–76. Recipient: Jamaica Festival Literary Competition prize, 1966, 1971; Silver Musgrave Medal, 1973. Address: Institute of Jamaica, 12–16 East Street, Kingston, Jamaica.

PUBLICATIONS

Verse

Hello Ungod. Baltimore, Peacewood Press, 1971.
Reel from "The Life-Movie." Mona, Jamaica, Savacou, 1972.
Credences at The Altar of Cloud. Kingston, Institue of Jamaica, 1979.

Other

Editor, with Neville Dawes, *The Caribbean Poem: An Anthology of 50 Caribbean Voices.* N.p., Carifesta, 1976(?).

Critical Studies: "An Extreme Vision" by Mervyn Morris, in *Sunday Gleaner* (Kingston), 28 January 1973; Wayne Brown, in *Jamaica Journal* (Kingston), March–June 1973.

* * *

Anthony McNeill is the first and most accomplished poet to appear out of the "now" generation of the anglophone Caribbean. McNeill is "new" in the sense that coming to maturity in the late sixties, he is past the rhetorical colonial assertions and dramatic nationalist self-doubts of the *entre des guerres* writing which gave us Carter, Roach and the early Derek Walcott. He is very much into his own "thing." That thing is "now" in that it deals with clairol and speed, and is very much concerned with splitting, suicide and animal/identity. But there is nothing gratuitously "today" about these energies and work. Here is a poet of patient, scrupulous craftsmanship, concerned with rhythm, cadence, form and the fissionable, rather than fashionable qualities of his word. His most definitive collection to date is *Reel from "The Life-Movie."* It contains 30 poems, 18 of which appear in his earlier 20-poem *Hello Ungod*. The two together give a fair idea of McNeill's thematic interests and poetic development. He begins (setting/style) as a "lyrical" "Nature" poet ("Cliff-Walking"): "and this cliff/where swallows confirm/the sooncome of rain/of long evenings adrift/from your meaning again and again." But this is not traditional "Nature" where metaphors come to rest in contemplation of superordinate glories. Note the "*adrift*/from your meaning" in that last line of the poem which just before said "and my eyes ride/upward, oaring me back/to *loneliness*" (my italics). It it this modern/urban problem and paradox, the concern of anglophone poetry from Auden through Lowell to Plath, that quickly comes to dominate his page. The sense of interior loneliness so pervades McNeill's poetry, in fact, that even physical love ("Mummy + ," "Dermis") is vitiated by it, until the persona/victim loses his hold of self and becomes "other": as in the zoo-poem "Rimbaud Jingle," for example:

When you trip
on my skin of sickness, bruised blue,

I'll slip from my cage and into
the pure life of lions. I'm death-
sick of being two ...

which leads to a frighteningly clear and "cool" contemplation of the anti-solutions: suicide ("Who'll see me dive?") and/or the use of hallucinogens ("The Lady Accepts the Needle Again"):

The lady freaks
out to her loveliness
lost irrevocably lost The Lady cries out
for ships The Lady cries out for Paris ...

The Lady gets sexy & rings
a towering eunuch into her hell

But what makes McNeill an important new voice is his comprehensive perception of this agony: the result of interior loneliness is not just personal freak, but social impasse ("Reel," "American Leader") and cultural, perhaps even cosmic catastrophe ("Hello Ungod," "Black Space"). All the post-Dostoevsky archetypes gather in his poetry, suffering from the death of God: the mad clown, the schizophrenic, the ape, Aunt Angel, The Lady, Godot, Dracula, and the dread ikons from McNeill's own formative experience of the Kingston ghetto: Brother Joe, Saint Ras, and Don Drummond, the sacred trombone-man. All these walk through a broken shadowed wordscape "whose irradiant stop is light"; whose "true country" is "Both doubt and light."

It is from this double (paradoxical, sometimes schizoid) vision that McNeill's remarkable sensibility expresses itself. But his development contains its own perils. More and more the light of his poetry seems to radiate not from the sun, no matter how distant, but from an agnostic space lit only by the flicker of a (life)-*movie*, so that the poet finds himself locked into the "ponderous ingot/that weights down the base of/his/box," until only a dark solar doubt (unseen ungod) is left: "At twenty-nine guru/I'm still unprepared;/one day I will shatter// yank loose in the wind/as a man stuck together with pins./When the god comes, I'll tell him *the perfect flamingo he gifted is gone*" ("Flamingo"; my italics). But this, surely, with one so seriously embattled with his own talent, can only be a temporary or apparent illumination. McNeill's "solutions" over the next few years will be one of the major achievements in our literature.

—Edward Kamau Brathwaite

McPHERSON, Sandra. American. Born in San Jose, California, 2 August 1943. Educated at Westmont College, Santa Barbara, California, 1961–63; San Jose State College, B.A. in English 1965; University of Washington, Seattle, 1965–66. Married Henry Carlile in 1966; one daughter. Technical Writer, Honeywell Inc., Seattle, 1966. Member of the Faculty, Writers Workshop, University of Iowa, Iowa City, 1974–76 and since 1978. Poetry Editor, *Antioch Review*, Yellow Springs, Ohio. Recipient: Helen Bullis Prize (*Poetry Northwest*, Seattle), 1968; Bess Hokin Prize, 1972, and Oscar Blumenthal Prize, 1975 (*Poetry*, Chicago); Ingram Merrill grant, 1972; Poetry Society of America Emily Dickinson Prize, 1973; National Endowment for the Arts grant, 1974; Guggenheim Fellowship, 1976. Address: Writers Workshop, EPB 436, University of Iowa, Iowa City, Iowa 52242, U.S.A.

PUBLICATIONS

Verse

Elegies for the Hot Season. Bloomington, University of Indiana Press, 1970.
Radiation. New York, Ecco Press, 1973.
The Year of Our Birth. New York, Ecco Press, 1978.
Sensing. San Francisco, Meadow Press, 1979.

* * *

"Centerfold Reflected in a Jet Window" is the title of a beautiful short poem in Sandra McPherson's new book, *The Year of Our Birth*. This is its first stanza:

There is someone naked flying alongside the airplane.
The man in the seat in front of me is trying to hold her.
But she reflects, she is below zero, would freeze the
skin off his tongue.

Her characteristic elevation of the prosaic – a traveler staring at photographs in *Playboy* and gracefully, and almost routinely oblique angles of vision are by now, after three collections, hallmarks. What perception gives us – or, when she is reaching for it, what can be wrested from perceptions – is never seen to be strange, but taken and investigated on faith.

The danger in this strategy – it can be sometimes faux-naif – is usually overcome without visible struggle. At her best, which is how she writes, she rivals Elizabeth Bishop in her ability to domesticate the strange and make the ordinary marvelous. The surface of the sea is "crumpled brine." A coconut bobs in water "like a bucket of oak or a light wooden dory," and its hair is like a baby's hair. "Grapefruit's white energetic light/befits it as a morning dish." Sometimes such passages work overtime. "Orange peels in her skillet like lions in the dark/blackened, witching an aroma through the ancient rooms." The conspiracy of "witching" and "ancient" alludes to more significance than the lines can use or justify; but the orange peels curling up like blackened lions are unforgettable, especially and justly in the dark.

She seems, for all her exact quirkiness of vision, so thoroughly a realist who believes that attention to material detail will produce the immaterial significances for which her poems strive – that she can only fail to invoke the world by slackened technique or reticence. Slackened technique is almost unknown to her. Sometimes her poems about love, marriage, and friendship grow opaque from a central reticence about what her angles of vision are variations on. The problem is often that the reticences are incomplete, and need either wholly to erase the traces of an actual biographical subject, or give the poem more use of it. Sections of "Studies of the Imaginary," all traceable to the actual, as I read them, work – and sometimes don't work – this way.

And yet how small my cavils are, given the lustrous, strange body of work she's produced already. "Perception" and "faith," I wrote earlier, suggesting two poles by which we describe the blurred and fascinating continuum of experience. Sandra McPherson has given us, already, indelible evidence about the ways we live by that blur:

> Because I have turned my head for years
> in order to see the bittern
> I won't mind not finding
> what I am looking for
> as long as I know it could be there,
> the cover is right,
> it would be natural.

—William Matthews

McWHIRTER, George. Canadian. Born in Belfast, Northern Ireland, 26 September 1939. Educated at Grosvenor High School, Belfast, 1951–57; Queen's University, Belfast, 1957–62, B.A. 1961; University of British Columbia, Vancouver (Macmillan Prize), 1968–70, B.A. 1970. Married to Angela Coid; one daughter and one son. Assistant Master, Kilkeel Secondary School, Northern Ireland, 1962–64, and Bangor Grammar School, Northern Ireland, 1964–65; English Teacher, University of Barcelona, Spain, 1965–66, and Alberni Secondary School, Port Alberni, British Columbia, 1966–68. Since 1970, Assistant Professor of Creative Writing, University of British Columbia. Associate Editor, 1970–73, Editor, 1978, and since 1979, Advisory Editor, *Prism International*, Vancouver; Editor, *Words from the Inside*, Kingston, Ontario, 1973. Recipient: Canada Council grant, 1969, 1975; Commonwealth Poetry Prize, 1972. Address: 4637 West 13th Avenue, Vancouver V6R 2V6, Canada.

PUBLICATIONS

Verse

Catalan Poems. Ottawa, Oberon Press, 1971.
Columbuscade. Vancouver, Hoffer, 1974.

Bloodlight for Malachi McNair. San Francisco, Kanchenjunga, 1974.
Twenty-Five. Fredericton, New Brunswick, Fiddlehead, 1975.
Queen of the Sea. Ottawa, Oberon Press, 1976.

Short Stories

Bodyworks. Ottawa, Oberon Press, 1974.

George McWhirter comments:

My work to date has been preoccupied with people and substance: people as consumers of substance and at the same time as those consumed by substance. He who eats will in turn be eaten. Such was the base of *Catalan Poems*. The family, man, woman, and child, one flesh, one substance was the central dramatic vehicle for this. *Columbuscade* uses the idea of Columbus to deal with the impossibility of escape from the flesh in terms of space: we can jump no farther than ourselves. Even if there was a new world, few would embark; the superscription of the book runs, "All are chosen for the crew, but few embark fearing a new world." This is the fundamental dilemma in *Queen of the Sea* which is set in the Belfast shipyards. Recently, I've come to regard things and substance as part of the infinite imagination of light. The unknown is the point of disembarkation, the intellect provides place names as we pass, the real rudder in the rear of the head is the intuition. The main thing that poetry does for me is turn ideas or intimations into the properties of the five senses; this is what life itself does for us. Poetry, in short, is life.

* * *

George McWhirter has been accused of producing "deftly crafted anachronisms – still, cold and timeless to the point of utter irrelevance." But the same critic, a Canadian, acknowledged the poet's skill, describing *Catalan Poems* as "a collection of exquisitely sculptured impersonal lyrics." The barrier between poet and reader in this case appears to have derived from the fact that McWhirter's poems were not set in Canada and did not present a Canadian point of view.

To an outsider the virtues of the book are more apparent. The skill is certainly present: there are vividly memorable images such as these lines about a man plucking and eating grapes from a bunch: "Seconds drop *pip* into a dish./Time plants a sprig of green bone/In the empty glass." The style is impressionistic, highly visual, and admittedly somewhat detached. It would be unfair, though, to dismiss this collection as impersonal or irrelevant. It is not confessional, first-person poetry; but there are sharply-observed portraits of people – market-women, a prostitute, a soldier, and in particular the aging, anxious but undauntedly swaggering Eduardo with his long-suffering wife; and insights into the uneasy commitments and compromises of the Catholic faith (far from irrelevant when one remembers that the poet comes from Belfast). Here and elsewhere we are free to draw our own parallels. George McWhirter's world is not a comfortable one, but we cannot ignore his picture of it.

—Fleur Adcock

MEAD, Matthew. British. Born in Buckinghamshire, 12 September 1924. Served in the British Army, 1942–47, including three years in India, Ceylon and Singapore. Married to

Ruth Adrian. Editor, *Satis* magazine, Edinburgh, 1960–62. Has lived in Germany since 1962, currently in Bad Godesberg.

PUBLICATIONS

Verse

A Poem in Nine Parts. Worcester, Migrant Press, 1960.
Identities. Worcester, Migrant Press, 1964.
Kleinigkeiten. Newcastle upon Tyne, Satis, 1966.
Identities and Other Poems. London, Rapp and Carroll, 1967.
The Administration of Things. London, Anvil Press Poetry, 1970.
Penguin Modern Poets 16, with Harry Guest and Jack Beeching. London, Penguin, 1970.
In the Eyes of the People. Edinburgh, Satis, 1973.
Minusland. Edinburgh, Satis, 1977.

Other

Translator, with Ruth Mead, *Shadow Land: Selected Poems of Johannes Bobrowski.* London, Carroll, 1966; revised edition, London, Rapp and Whiting, 1967.
Translator, with Ruth Mead, *Generation*, by Heinz Winfried Sabais. Edinburgh, Satis, 1967.
Translator, with Ruth Mead and others, *O the Chimneys*, by Nelly Sachs. New York, Farrar Straus, 1967; as *Selected Poems of Nelly Sachs*, London, Cape, 1968.
Translator, with Ruth Mead, *Generation and Other Poems*, by Heinz Winfried Sabais. London, Anvil Press Poetry, 1968.
Translator, with Ruth Mead, *Amfortiade and Other Poems*, by Max Hölzer. Edinburgh, Satis, 1968.
Translator, with Ruth Mead, *Horst Bienek.* Santa Barbara, California, Unicorn Press, 1969.
Translator, with Ruth Mead, *Elisabeth Borchers.* Santa Barbara, California, Unicorn Press, 1969.
Translator, with Ruth Mead and Michael Hamburger, *The Seeker and Other Poems*, by Nelly Sachs. New York, Farrar Straus, 1970.
Translator, with Ruth Mead, *Selected Poems*, by Johannes Bobrowski and Horst Bienek. London, Penguin, 1971.
Translator, with Ruth Mead, *Mitteilungen/Communications*, by Heinz Winfried Sabais. Darmstadt, Eduard Roether Verlag, 1971.
Translator, with Ruth Mead, *Socialist Elegy*, by Heinz Winfried Sabais. Darmstadt, Eduard Roether Verlag, 1975.
Translator, with Ruth Mead, *From the Rivers*, by Johannes Bobrowski. London, Anvil Press Poetry, 1975.

Critical Studies: by Christopher Middleton, in *London Magazine*, 1964; in *Neue Deutsche Literatur* (Berlin), February 1965.

* * *

Matthew Mead has been spoken of as a modernist, a social critic, a poet who is proletarian and unacademic. On the contrary, his qualities are those of literary accomplishment. He can turn an epigram or a ballade as well as anyone writing today. The reader may feel his way through deliberately fragmented *hommages* to Ezra Pound or Robert Creeley to light upon such finely tooled verses as

Bodies are rolled from bed to scuffed slippers
and day stiff-jointed; in sense repetition;
in spring one more spring; the figure
in a worn carpet traced with a dull eye.

And the house old, the wind's sound, each ache
lent art and length, given due weight
the dragging footfall. For this are we bent
and gnarled and wrinkled – to cross the room....

It is not that Mead is an escapist; his translations of Bobrowski, done in collaboration with his wife, would assure us of that. Rather he is a Poundian in a sense deeper than that of technical allegiance: an aesthete distressed by the blood and chaos of totalitarian Europe. The poem quoted, "To Redistort a Weltanschauung," comes from his retrospective collection, *Identities*. Here is an extract from his more recent *The Administration of Things:*

What she herself believes
No man alive conceives

We tell the lawful tale
(All fictions else must fail)

And loyal beyond the lie
Nor daring to deny

That what we have she gave
We make of what we have

Lending it length and art
Embellishing each part

A faith to ravage noon
With phases of the moon....

It is clear that writing such as this resembles nothing so much as the more Elizabethan lyrics of Donne – "But come bad chance/And we join to it our strength/ And we teach it art and length/Itself o'er us to advance ..." – or the more lapidary verse of Marvell – "Caesar's head at last/Did through his laurels blast/... And if we must speak true/Much to the man is due...." At present, in Mead's original work, there is a gap between subject and presentation. Those who have followed his work with interest all these years must hope that he will turn this characteristic hiatus to dramatic use. Or, if not that, then they must wish him to find a range of subject matter suited to the cool detachment of his technique.

—Philip Hobsbaum

MEHROTRA, Arvind Krishna. Indian. Born in Lahore, Pakistan, 16 April 1947. Educated at the University of Allahabad, Uttar Pradesh, 1964–66, B.A. 1966; University of Bombay, 1966–68, M.A. 1968. Married Vandana Jain in 1969; one son. Lecturer in English, 1968–77, and since 1978, Reader in English, University of Allahabad. Visiting Writer, University of Iowa, Iowa City, 1971–73; Lecturer in English, University of Hyderabad, India, 1977–78. Editor, *damn you/a magazine of the arts*, Allahabad, 1965–68; Founder,

Ezra-Fakir Press, Bombay, 1966. Address: Department of English Studies, University of Allahabad, Allahabad 211 002, Uttar Pradesh, India.

PUBLICATIONS

Verse

Bharatmata: A Prayer. Bombay, Ezra Fakir Press, 1966.
Woodcuts on Paper. London, Gallery Number Ten, 1967.
Pomes/Poemes/Poemas. Baroda, India, Vrischik, 1971.
Nine Enclosures. Bombay, Clearing House, 1976.

Other

Translator, *Three Poems*, by Bogomil Gjuzel. Allahabad and Iowa City, Ezra Fakir Press, 1973.

Critical Study: "Image as an Immoderate Drug" by N. R. Shastri, in *Osmania Journal of English Studies 13* (Hyderabad), 1, 1977.

* * *

Arvind Krishna Mehrotra has said that a poem comprises "games, riddles and accidents ... and the poet creates as many accidents as he can." Mehrotra is probably the best-known Indian writer of surrealist English verse today, using some of the characteristic techniques of surrealist writing, such as an uninhibited dependence on chance or accident in composition; the collocation of unusual words and phrases; the yoking together of heterogeneous objects and situations and contexts; broken syntax; the ascription of unusual characteristics to familiar objects; the exaltation of the dream state. The general aim is to transform the reader's consciousness and to change his conception of reality. Mehrotra has cited Breton's first *Manifesto* (1924) as one of the influences on his work. Breton defined surrealism as "pure psychic automatism by which it is intended to express either verbally or in writing, the true function of thought. Thought dictated in the absence of all control exerted by reason and outside all aesthetic or moral control." These aims were of course later modified, and not all of Mehrotra's poetry fits in the surrealist category. For instance, poems such as "Songs of the Ganga" (*Nine Enclosures*) are relatively "straightforward" in which experimentation is held down to the minimum. Another, perhaps better-known, poem which is more characteristic and not particularly difficult is "The Sale" in which the language of salesmanship is exploited to suggest the sell-out of the world and its impending conversion to a wasteland. It would be misleading, however, to suggest that Mehrotra's poetry is "about" this or that, about something external to itself. The poems are "enclosures" whose aim is to capture the reader within themselves. Their principal means are the haunting poetic rhythm and the disturbing image:

The widow next door
Lives off her trained
Parrot.
It reads the future
And tells you when
To avoid it.
At night
She dances in the streets
And fills the air
With abuse.

The decorated general
Is alone
In his tent;
The pyres burn
Like new volcanoes.

While the second strophe reads like a summary of first World War poetry, the first one reads rather like a joke, a story, a song. Children enjoy it as it is, and don't ask for its meaning. The world of the child and the world of the grown-ups are juxtaposed, and the meaning arises from this juxtaposition.

Poetry such as Mehrotra's is international, and it is not much bothered with the question of "Indianness" which is such a persistent concern of some of his Indian contemporaries. His poetry is difficult, and "chancy." But the chances quite often come off. His latest poems, however, seem to be written in a non-European mode with only a touch of the surrealistic technique:

Summer is at hand.
New leaves fill the branches
With sunlight, a red and green kite
Bends into the wind. It is two bits
Of thin paper joined
In the middle. It opens the sky.
I have three small rooms and a terrace
Where I sit out and read Han Shan
To my new-born son, or make
That kite. My possessions are few.
I'll stay here.

Poems such as these raise no questions, debate no issues, wave no flags. Peaceful in themselves, they are the cause of peace also in their readers.

—S. Nagarajan

MELTZER, David. American. Born in Rochester, New York, 17 February 1937. Educated in public schools in Brooklyn and Los Angeles; Los Angeles City College; University of California, Los Angeles. Married Christina Meyer in 1958; three daughters. Editor, *Maya*, Mill Valley, California, 1966–71. Currently, Editor, *Tree*, Bolinas, California. Also a composer. Recipient: Council of Literary Magazines grant, 1972; National Endowment for the Arts grant, 1974. Address: Box 9005, Berkeley, California 94709, U.S.A.

PUBLICATIONS

Verse

Poems, with Donald Schenker. Privately printed, 1957.
Ragas. San Francisco, Discovery, 1959.
The Clown: A Poem. Larkspur, California, Semina, 1960.
Station. Privately printed, 1964.

The Blackest Rose. Berkeley, California, Oyez, 1964.
Oyez! Berkeley, California, Oyez, 1965.
The Process. Berkeley, California, Oyez, 1965.
In Hope I Offer a Fire Wheel. Berkeley, California, Oyez, 1965.
The Dark Continent. Berkeley, California, Oyez, 1967.
Nature Poem. Santa Barbara, California, Unicorn Press, 1967.
Round the Poem Box: Rustic and Domestic Home Movies for Stan and Jane Brakhage. Los Angeles, Black Sparrow Press, 1969.
Yesod. London, Trigram Press, 1969.
From Eden Book. Mill Valley, California, Maya, 1969.
Abulafia Song. Santa Barbara, California, Unicorn Press, 1969.
Greenspeech. Santa Barbara, California, Christopher, 1970.
Luna. Los Angeles, Black Sparrow Press, 1970.
Letters and Numbers. Berkeley, California, Oyez, 1970.
Bronx Lil/Head of Lillin S.A.C. Santa Barbara, California, Capra Press, 1970.
32 Beams of Light. Santa Barbara, California, Capra Press, 1970.
Knots. Bolinas, California, Tree, 1971.
Bark: A Polemic. Santa Barbara, California, Capra Press, 1973.
Hero/Lil. Los Angeles, Black Sparrow Press, 1973.
Tens: Selected Poems 1961–1971, edited by Kenneth Rexroth. New York, Herder, 1973.
The Eyes, The Blood. San Francisco, Mudra, 1973.
French Broom. Berkeley, California, Oyez, 1974.
Blue Rags. Berkeley, California, Oyez, 1974.
Harps. Berkeley, California, Oyez, 1975.
Six. Santa Barbara, California, Black Sparrow Press, 1976.
Bolero. Berkeley, California, Oyez, 1976.

Recordings (Vanguard): *Serpent Power*, 1972; *Poet Song*, 1974.

Novels

The Agency Trilogy. North Hollywood, Essex House, 1968.
Orf. North Hollywood, Essex House, 1969.
The Martyr. North Hollywood, Essex House, 1969.
The Brain-Plant Tetralogy: Lovely, Healer, Out, and Glue Factory. North Hollywood, Essex House, 1970.
Star. North Hollywood, Brandon House, 1970.

Other

We All Have Something to Say to Each Other: Being an Essay Entitled "Patchen" and Four Poems. San Francisco, Auerhahn Press, 1962.
Introduction to the Outsiders (essay on Beat Poetry). Fort Lauderdale, Florida, Rodale, 1962.
Bazascope Mother (essay on Robert Alexander). Los Angeles, Drekfesser Press, 1964.
Journal of the Birth. Berkeley, California, Oyez, 1967.
Isla Vista Notes: Fragmentary, Apocalyptic, Didactic Contradictions. Santa Barbara, California, Christopher, 1970.
Abra (juvenile). Berkeley, California, Hipparchia Press, 1976.
Two-way Mirror: A Poetry Note-book. Berkeley, California, Oyez, 1977.

Editor, with Michael McClure and Lawrence Ferlinghetti, *Journal for the Protection of All Beings.* San Francisco, City Lights, 1961; vol. 2, 1978.
Editor, *The San Francisco Poets.* New York, Ballantine, 1971.

Editor, *Birth: An Anthology*. New York, Ballantine, 1973.
Editor, *The Secret Garden: An Anthology in the Kabbalah*. New York, Seabury Press, 1976.

Translator, with Allen Say, *Morning Glories*, by Shiga Naoya. Berkeley, California, Oyez, 1975.

Manuscript Collections: Washington University, St. Louis; University of Indiana, Bloomington; University of California, Los Angeles.

Critical Studies: *David Meltzer: A Sketch from Memory and Descriptive Checklist* by David Kherdian, Berkeley, California, Oyez, 1965; *6 Poets of the San Francisco Renaissance* by David Kherdian, Fresno, California, Giligia Press, 1967; *Vort* (Berkeley), 1979.

* * *

A Californian since he was 14 and a San Franciscan since 1959, David Meltzer has affinities with the other West Coast poets grouped in the *New American Poetry* anthology of 1959, and more specifically with fellow-workers in cabalistic lore like Jack Hirschman and the painter Wallace Berman. Rock musician, editor of a journal of Jewish mystical tradition, and pornographer, he writes poems that are lyrical, esoteric, and erotic. A recent sequence, "Lil," blends the Lilith myth with tangy particulars of contemporary urban California. For example:

Lil in the teenage blond,
Tight purple pants
Legs spread apart.
Looks thru orange shades
Right thru my seams
& seems to smile.

Meltzer has written, "Poetry is the special use of language which welds invisible & visible worlds into words generating great power," and while his power isn't often intense, this blending of the magical and mythic with the local and contemporary is his most distinctive note (see, for instance, his poem "For Raymond Chandler"). Also effective is his work commemorating ancestral racial presences, such as "From a Midrash": "The stories retell themselves. They are memory & they invent my songs. In my head, I swear, Eden flourishes."

—Seamus Cooney

MEREDITH, William (Morris, Jr.). American. Born in New York City, 9 January 1919. Educated at Lenox School, Massachusetts; Princeton University, New Jersey (Woodrow Wilson Fellow, 1946–47), B.A. (magna cum laude) 1940. Served in the United States Army Air Force, 1941–42, and in the United States Navy, 1942–46, 1952–54. Copy-boy and Reporter, *The New York Times*, 1940–41; Resident Fellow in Creative Writing, Princeton University, 1947–48, 1949–50, 1965–66; Associate Professor of English, University of Hawaii, Honolulu, 1950–51. Since 1955, Member of the Department, and since 1965, Professor of English, Connecticut College, New London. Taught at Bread Loaf Writers

Conference, Vermont, Summers 1958–62. Opera Critic, *Hudson Review*, New York, 1955–56. Member, Connecticut Commission on the Arts, 1963–65; Director of the Humanities, Upward Bound Program, 1964–68; Poetry Consultant, Library of Congress, Washington, D.C., 1978–80. Recipient: Yale Series of Younger Poets Award, 1943; Harriet Monroe Memorial Prize, 1944, and Oscar Blumenthal Prize, 1953 (*Poetry*, Chicago); Rockefeller grant, for criticism, 1948, for poetry, 1968; *Hudson Review* fellowship, 1956; National Institute of Arts and Letters grant, 1958; Ford Fellowship, for drama, 1960; Loines Award, 1966; Van Wyck Brooks Award, 1971; National Endowment for the Arts grant, 1972; Guggenheim Fellowship, 1975. Member, National Institute of Arts and Letters; since 1964, Chancellor, Academy of American Poets. Address: Department of English, Connecticut College, New London, Connecticut 06320, U.S.A.

PUBLICATIONS

Verse

Love Letter from an Impossible Land. New Haven, Connecticut, Yale University Press, 1944.
Ships and Other Figures. Princeton, New Jersey, Princeton University Press, 1948.
The Open Sea and Other Poems. New York, Knopf, 1958.
The Wreck of the Thresher and Other Poems. New York, Knopf, 1964.
Earth Walk: New and Selected Poems. New York, Knopf, 1970.
Hazard, The Painter. New York, Knopf, 1975.

Play

The Bottle Imp (libretto), music by Peter Whiton (produced Wilton, Connecticut, 1958).

Other

Editor, *Shelley.* New York, Dell, 1962.
Editor, *University and College Poetry Prizes, 1960–66, in Memory of Mrs. Fanny Fay Wood.* New York, Academy of American Poets, 1966.
Editor, with Mackie L. Jarrell, *Eighteenth Century Minor Poets.* New York, Dell, 1968.

Translator, *Alcools: Poems 1878–1913*, by Guillaume Apollinaire. New York, Doubleday 1964.

Manuscript Collection: Middlebury College, Vermont.

* * *

Introducing William Meredith's *Love Letter from an Impossible Land*, Archibald MacLeish observed that this poet's "instincts are sound" ("He seems to know, without poisoning himself in the process, which fruits are healthful and which fruits are not"). The consistencies in his subsequent volumes have proved MacLeish's prediction true. Although his meters have loosened in recent books, Meredith remains a formal poet who achieves imaginative participation in his subjects by creating them at an aesthetic distance. Poise and understanding are sought and revealed in the subjection of the facts of experience to an imaginative yet rational order. If the experience in a Meredith poem begins as a brute fact or raw emotion, it is transmuted into a shapelier, more civil and more intelligible image of itself. His work renders emotional force into forms. In a period when many poets sacrifice convention and form for force and immediacy, the risks in this aesthetic are evident. Yet the reader responsive to the legitimate demands such poetry makes will find among the resulting poems those which acknowledge the forces which engendered them. In his elegy to the sailors lost in a sunken submarine (the title poem from *The Wreck of the Thresher*) Meredith writes:

> Why can't our dreams be content with the terrible facts?
> The only animal cursed with responsible sleep.
> We trace disaster always to our own acts.
> I met a monstrous self trapped in the black deep:
> *All these years,* he smiled, *I've drilled at sea*
> *For this crush of water.* Then he saved only me.

Confronting the inexplicable tragedy of meaningless death, Meredith characteristically concludes, "Whether we give assent to this or rage/Is a question of temperament and does not matter."

This poem reflects two of his abiding concerns, the threat of death and the loneliness of the sea, already enunciated in the last ten poems of his first book. Service as a naval aviator in two Pacific wars has marked out for Meredith a part of his *donnée*: images of oceanic space, the lonely sky, distant islands seen from vast heights, the unknown destinies of men in wartime, and the responses of an American to Oriental cultures (Japan, Korea, Hawaii) recur in his poems. Characteristically, he deals with such themes pictorially, fixing his images as though in a painting, imposing upon them the designs imagination discovers and the forms and meters appropriated by a scrupulously sensitive ear. His instinct is to render such design; in "Rus in Urbe" (from *The Open Sea*) he chooses "In a city garden an espalliered tree," not nature unadorned but nature shaped by human skill and imagination. Yet in a later poem, "Roots" (from *The Wreck of the Thresher*), a dialogue narrative in the mode of Frost, he discovers in nature itself the pattern which in "Rus in Urbe" imagination had to wrest by altering the shapes of trees.

The new poems in *Earth Walk: New and Selected Poems* use a conversational, colloquial style, as in "Walter Jenks' Bath": "These are my legs. I don't have to tell them, legs,/Move up or down or which leg." With like informality of diction Meredith explores dreams, probes memory, creates characters, and, as in the title poem, makes his wry statement about being himself at a time when almost everyone else is preoccupied by somebody else's moon walk. The formality of this recent work is less a matter of surface and detail (such as regular stanza, rhythm, rhyme) than formerly, but the design of the experience is quietly interiorized in each poem. His tone is modest rather than boisterous, his range deceptively larger than the voice whose speech provides the style.

Hazard, The Painter is a series of 16 poems dramatizing the life not only of the artist of its title but, by inference, of his time. For two years Hazard has been at work on a painting of a falling parachutist, "the human figure dangling safe... full of half-remembered instruction/ but falling, and safe." Hazard "is in charge of morale in a morbid time" – the time of Nixon's election, when the "nation has bitterly misspoken itself." He measures his own modest gift against the greatness of Titian and Renoir, and reflects on his relationships to his wife, children, friends, and the earth. The tone of these poems is at once intimate and slightly distanced by third-person narration; the effect of the suite is that of a novel in verse, a whole life economically suggested by these glimpses. Its theme is no less than the artist's responsibility in a time when "more of each day is dark": "Gnawed by a vision of rightness/ that no one else seems to see,/what can a man do/but bear witness." This is Meredith's finest book thus far.

Meredith has also published a complete translation of *Alcools* by Apollinaire, a poet whose intuitive mode of apprehending experience would seem quite different from his own. In his poem "For Guillaume Apollinaire," Meredith writes, "But these poems –/How quickly the strangeness would pass from things if it were not for them." The same may be said of his own best work.

—Daniel Hoffman

MERRILL, James (Ingram). American. Born in New York City, 3 March 1926. Educated at Lawrenceville School; Amherst College, Massachusetts, B.A. 1947. Served in the United States Army, 1944–45. Recipient: Oscar Blumenthal Prize, 1947, Levinson Prize, 1949, Harriet Monroe Prize, 1951, Eunice Tietjens Memorial Prize, 1958, and Morton Dauwen Zabel Prize, 1966 (*Poetry*, Chicago); National Book Award, 1967, 1979; Bollingen Prize, 1973; Pulitzer Prize, 1977. Member, National Institute of Arts and Letters, 1971. Address: 107 Water Street, Stonington, Connecticut 06378, U.S.A.

PUBLICATIONS

Verse

Jim's Book: A Collection of Poems and Short Stories. Privately printed, 1942.
The Black Swan and Other Poems. Athens, Icaros, 1946.
First Poems. New York, Knopf, 1951.
Short Stories. Pawlet, Vermont, Banyan Press, 1954.
A Birthday Cake for David. Pawlet, Vermont, Banyan Press, 1955.
The Country of a Thousand Years of Peace and Other Poems. New York, Knopf, 1959; revised edition, New York, Atheneum, 1970.
Selected Poems. London, Chatto and Windus-Hogarth Press, 1961.
Water Street. New York, Atheneum, 1962.
The Thousand and Second Night. Athens, Christos Christou Press, 1963.
Violent Pastoral. Privately printed, 1965.
Nights and Days. New York, Atheneum, and London, Chatto and Windus-Hogarth Press, 1966.
The Fire Screen. New York, Atheneum, 1969; London, Chatto and Windus, 1970.
Two Poems. London, Chatto and Windus, 1972.
Braving the Elements. New York, Atheneum, 1972; London, Chatto and Windus, 1973.
Yannina. New York, Phoenix Book Shop, 1973.
The Yellow Pages: 59 Poems. Cambridge, Massachusetts, Temple Bar Bookshop, 1974.
Divine Comedies. New York, Atheneum, 1976; London, Oxford University Press, 1977.
Metamorphosis of 741. Pawlet, Vermont, Banyan Press, 1977.
Mirabell: Books of Number. New York, Atheneum, 1978; London, Oxford University Press, 1979.

Plays

The Bait (produced New York, 1953). Published in *Artists' Theatre: Four Plays*, edited by Herbert Machiz, New York, Grove Press, 1960.
The Immortal Husband (produced New York, 1955). Published in *Playbook: Plays for a New Theatre*, New York, New Directions, 1956.

Novels

The Seraglio. New York, Knopf, 1957; London, Chatto and Windus, 1958.
The (Diblos) Notebook. New York, Atheneum, and London, Chatto and Windus, 1965.

Manuscript Collection: Washington University, St. Louis.

Critical Studies: Interview, in *Contemporary Literature* (Madison, Wisconsin), ix, 1, 1968; *Alone with America* by Richard Howard, New York, Atheneum, 1969; interview, in *Saturday Review of the Arts* (New York), December 1972; "Feux d'Artifice" by Stephen

Yenser, in *Poetry* (Chicago), June 1973; Richard Saez, in *Parnassus* (New York), 1974.

* * *

James Merrill's books of poems are like the rings of a tree: each extends beyond the content, expression, outlook, and craft of the previous work. Merrill has patiently, even doggedly, pursued his craft, giving each poem, however short or terse or ephemeral, a certain lapidary sheen and hardness. Merrill's complete output of verse, fiction, and plays is notable as an absorption with technique and difficulty. This would have assured Merrill a place in poetry as one of our better minor lyricists, one of our perfectionists, had it not been for the sudden turnaround of his two most recent books, *Divine Comedies* and *Mirabell: Books of Number*. Suddenly Merrill has become our grand inquisitor, a poet of metaphysical humor and daring who blithely invents spirits of the Ouija board to confess to us the history of space, the chemical future of man, the heavenly wars at the dawn of being, the whereabouts of old geniuses now reincarnated as scientists and technicians. The whole madcap experiment wobbles and shuffles forward into a sort of greatness – sustained by Merrill's nonchalantly argumentative nature.

His earliest poems are turgid with rime, metric tricks, stuffy diction. Merrill came onto the literary scene during the vogue of revived metaphysical poetry, a verse wrought with high polish and formal orthodoxy. Such is the poetry of his first major book, *The Country of a Thousand Years of Peace*, with its elegant persona, his widely cultivated tastes, his voice of leisured travel and gracious living – the poetry, in gist, of an American aristocrat. *Water Street* maintains this elegant discourse on the vicissitudes of life, love, travel, the perennially chilly rooms and beds of his daily life.

But with *The Fire Screen* we get a new perspective on the persona with his life in Greece, where the warm sun, the old culture, the intimacy of life provoke a deeper self-awareness. Instead of the isolated, inward existence of New England, the speaker is thrust into a more primal and assertive culture where his passions and convictions are awakened. There are also poems of return to the northeastern United States, with lyrics of resignation and quiet regrets. In the American edition is the endless verse narrative "The Summer People," with its heavy-handed irony; Robert Lowell said more about the vacation culture in his one page poem "Skunk Hour." *Braving the Elements* is both freer in its forms and more open and intimate in its voice. Instead of the choppy quality of his earlier, tightly-wrought lines, there is now a smooth, conversational rhythm in this three- or four-line stanza structures. "Days of 1935," "18 West 11th Street," which laments the death of young anti-war radicals, "Days of 1971" are open, intimate revelations of the poet's feelings.

Merrill's progress is toward a balance between rigid formalism and the open poem, where craft would continue to discipline the choice and assembly of language but where the content would be free to take its own course. That balance is reached in the long sequence "The Book of Ephraim" included in *Divine Comedies*. The twenty-six alphabetically ordered parts are interwoven through a leisurely plot where the poet and his lover communicate with the spirit of Ephraim through the Ouija board, whose insight and wit make life seem a mere instant in a vast spiritual universe. In discovering this broader realm, Merrill is dazzling as a conversational poet. Ephraim's reckless honesty about the other side enables the speaker to unravel a complex plot of lives and afterlives, including his own father's, in a humorous, novel-like progression of poems. The verse never impedes the narrative; it enhances it with its exuberance of puns, amazing condensations of ideas and observations, feats of beautiful lyric sound.

The success of this sequence makes clear Merrill's earlier difficulties with orthodox convention: his verve and spontaneity of imagination, his life as a contemporary, were too straitened by the demands of closed forms of verse. Merrill has seized upon the cut-and-paste, leaping perceptual technique of recent poets without relinquishing his metrical skill and eloquence. With *Mirabell: Books of Number*, what might have seemed a fresh new idea in "Ephraim" has become the second step of an important long sequence, a poem capable of making effective summary of the ideational renaissance that has flourished all century long.

Merrill's wit is of a class with Auden's, who features prominently in this book – his disciplined diction moves gracefully through difficult formulations without sagging into prose. Through *Mirabell* and work to come, we have a romance in the making – a grasp of what man now becomes after a century of redefinition.

—Paul Christensen

MERWIN, W(illiam) S(tanley). American. Born in New York City, 30 September 1927. Educated at Princeton University, New Jersey, A.B. in English 1947. Tutor to Robert Graves' son, Mallorca, 1950; Playwright-in-Residence, Poet's Theatre, Cambridge, Massachusetts, 1956–57; Poetry Editor, *The Nation*, New York, 1962; Associate, Théâtre de la Cité, Lyons, France, 1964–65. Recipient: Yale Series of Younger Poets Award, 1952; *Kenyon Review* fellowship, 1954; National Institute of Arts and Letters grant, 1957; Arts Council of Great Britain bursary, 1957; Rabinowitz Research Fellowship, 1961; Bess Hokin Prize, 1962, and Harriet Monroe Memorial Prize, 1967 (*Poetry*, Chicago); Ford grant, 1964; Chapelbrook Award, 1966; P.E.N. Translation Prize, 1969; Rockefeller grant, 1969; Pulitzer Prize, 1971; Academy of American Poets Fellowship, 1973; Shelley Memorial Award, 1974; National Endowment for the Arts grant, 1978; Bollingen Prize, 1979. Address: c/o Ford, Atheneum Publishers, 122 East 42nd Street, New York, New York 10017, U.S.A.

PUBLICATIONS

Verse

A Mask for Janus. New Haven, Connecticut, Yale University Press, 1952.
The Dancing Bears. New Haven, Connecticut, Yale University Press, 1954.
Green with Beasts. London, Hart Davis, and New York, Knopf, 1956.
The Drunk in the Furnace. New York, Macmillan, and London, Hart Davis, 1960.
The Moving Target. New York, Atheneum, 1963; London, Hart Davis, 1967.
The Lice. New York, Atheneum, 1967; London, Hart Davis, 1969.
Three Poems. New York, Phoenix Book Shop, 1968.
Animae. San Francisco, Kayak, 1969.
The Carrier of Ladders. New York, Atheneum, 1970.
Signs: A Poem. Iowa City, Stone Wall Press, 1971.
Writings to an Unfinished Accompaniment. New York, Atheneum, 1974.
The First Four Books of Poems. New York, Atheneum, 1975.
The Compass Flower. New York, Atheneum, 1977.
Feathers from the Hill. New York, Windhover Press, 1978.

Plays

Darkling Child, with Dido Milroy (produced 1956).
Favor Island (produced Cambridge, Massachusetts, 1957).
Eufemia, adaptation of the play by Lope de Rueda, in *Tulane Drama Review* (New Orleans), December 1958.
The Gilded West (produced Coventry, England, 1961).
Turcaret, adaptation of the play by Alain Lesage, in *The Classic Theatre*, edited by Eric Bentley, New York, Doubleday, 1961.

The False Confession, adaptation of a play by Marivaux (produced New York, 1963). Published in *The Classic Theatre*, edited by Eric Bentley, New York, Doubleday, 1961.
Yerma, adaptation of the play by García Lorca (produced New York, 1966).

Other

A New Right Arm (essay). Oshkosh, Wisconsin, Road Runner Press, n.d.
Selected Translations 1948–1968. New York, Atheneum, 1968.
The Miner's Pale Children. New York, Atheneum, 1970.
Houses and Travellers. New York, Atheneum, 1977.
Selected Translations 1968–1978. New York, Atheneum, 1978.

Editor, *West Wind: Supplement of American Poetry*. London, Poetry Book Society, 1961.

Translator, *The Poem of the Cid*. New York, New American Library, and London, Dent, 1959.
Translator, *The Satires of Perseus*. Bloomington, Indiana University Press, 1961.
Translator, *Some Spanish Ballads*. London, Abelard Schuman, 1961; as *Spanish Ballads*, New York, Doubleday, 1961.
Translator, *The Life of Lazarillo de Tormes: His Fortunes and Adversities*. New York, Doubleday, 1962.
Translator, *The Song of Roland*, in *Medieval Epics*. New York, Modern Library, 1963.
Translator, *Transparence of the World: Poems of Jean Follain*. New York, Atheneum, 1969.
Translator, *Products of the Perfected Civilization: Selected Writings*, by Sebastian Chamfort. New York, Macmillan, 1969.
Translator, *Voices: Selected Writings of Antonio Porchia*. Chicago, Follett, 1969.
Translator, *Twenty Love Poems and a Song of Despair*, by Pablo Neruda. London, Cape, 1969.
Translator, with others, *Selected Poems: A Bilingual Editon*, by Pablo Neruda, edited by Nathaniel Tarn. London, Cape, 1969; New York, Delacorte Press, 1972.
Translator, *Chinese Figures: Second Series*. Mount Horeb, Wisconsin, Perishable Press, 1971.
Translator, *Japanese Figures*. Santa Barbara, California, Unicorn Press, 1971.
Translator, *Asian Figures*. New York, Atheneum, 1973.
Translator, with Clarence Brown, *Selected Poems of Osip Mandelstam*. London, Oxford University Press, 1973; New York, Atheneum, 1974.
Translator, *Vertical Poetry*, by Robert Juarroz. Santa Cruz, California, Kayak, 1977.
Translator, with J. Moussaieff Masson, *Sanskrit Love Poetry*. New York, Columbia University Press, 1977.
Translator, with George E. Dimock, Jr., *Iphigenia at Aulis*, by Euripides. New York, Oxford University Press, 1978.

Bibliography: "Seven Princeton Poets," in *Princeton Library Chronicle* (New Jersey), Autumn 1963.

Critical Studies: "W. S. Merwin and the Nothing That Is" by Anthony Libby, in *Contemporary Literature 16* (Madison, Wisconsin), 1973; "The Continuities of W. S. Merwin" by Jarrold Ramsey, in *Massachusetts Review 14* (Amherst), 1973.

* * *

I imagine the writing of a poem, in whatever mode, still betrays the existence of hope, which is why poetry is more and more chary of the conscious mind in our age.

The mystery of man's condition, like the mystery of the word, is like the sea – which fills W. S. Merwin's poetry – with its attendant whales, birds, moon, tides, rocks, and bells; this is a poetry filled with silences and distances, doors and dreams. The early works were sometimes remarkable in their lyrical ease – i.e. "Song of Marvels," "Song of Three Smiles," "Song of the New Fool." Others, more formal and elegant, were long and elaborate narratives based upon folk tales and myth, where story and character were of secondary importance to the poet's questions, much like Wallace Stevens's, about reality and art. In "East of the Sun and West of the Moon," an elaborate, 500-line poem of 39 13-line stanzas in iambic pentameter, Merwin adapts a Norse fairy tale, itself an adaptation of Apuleius's Cupid and Psyche legend. But the story remains mere decoration, a frame within which the poet contemplates the relationship of art and imagination to reality. "All magic is but metaphor," he writes, with the following: "All metaphor ... is magic." Then, speculating on the perfection of art and eternity over the flux of this world, his character ponders: "Why should I/complain of such inflexible content,/Presume to shudder at such serenity,/Who walk in some ancestral fantasy." Like Yeats's Oisin, Merwin's persona is drawn to this world and would "ride a while the mortal air."

Perhaps his numerous and remarkable translations (Porchia, Neruda, Follain, Char, Guillén, *The Song of Roland*, *The Poem of the Cid*) have stimulated or reinforced his own experiments with meter and form (from Yeats's and Stevens's Symbolism to Neruda's Surrealism and Follain's linguistic innovations). Nevertheless, by the mid-1960's, Merwin had honed the form we most often associate with him: the spare and sometimes epigrammatic line, simple language, and the absence of allusion, myth, rhyme, and punctuation. His focus had turned in great part to the articulation of the "desert of the unknown" – the Absurd, Nothingness, Silence, as in "Daybreak": "The future woke me with its silence/I join the procession/An open doorway/Speaks for me/Again." This world of the unknown, always benignly indifferent to man, beckons the poet, in his infinite imagination, for articulation; from the unknown the poet begs for comprehension, consolation.

Merwin has been associated with the tradition of contemporary poets known as the oracular poets, and if his surrealistic style has been compared to that of Roethke, Bly, Wright, Dickey, Plath, Olson, and even Lowell, his apocalyptic vision is entirely his own. Death for Merwin is not an entrance into harmony with the universe; rather it is an entrance into nothingness; in an impressive blending of form and content, Merwin's muted voice and conspicuous absence of punctuation reflect his very quest and felt experience: "I know nothing/learn of me" he writes; "I taught them nothing./Everywhere/The eyes are returning under the stones. And over/My dry bones they build their churches, like wells" ("The Saint of the Uplands"). Like Beckett, a master in the spare articulation of "Nothing," Merwin writes: "It is when I assert to nothing that I assert to all."

Merwin's attraction to nothingness, and the knowledge that inspires, is often associated with water, also associated with sleep, night, and even erotic experience, as in "Sailor Ashore": "the waters are/Under the earth. Now to run from them./It is their tides you feel heaving under you,/Sucking you down, when you close your eyes with women." Such knowledge, which all men aspire to and only a few can articulate, in their own limited terms, becomes their statement of personal tragedy. Of the informed sailor, in "The Shipwreck," he writes:

> ... this sea, it was
> Blind, yes, as they had said, and treacherous –
> They had used their own traits to character it – but without
> Accident in its wildness, in its rage,
> Utterly and from the beginning without
> Error. And to some it seemed the waves
> Grew gentle, spared them, while they died of that knowledge.

At times the poet cries out for revelation: "Oh objects come and talk with us while you can." But, perhaps more frequently, he feels paralyzed, and in an intolerable pain of spiritual vacuity. Sometimes nature is forbidding and frightening: "The whole night is alive with hands,/Is aflame with palms and offerings/... in mid-winter ... empty gloves ..."

Merwin concretizes the benign indifference of the universe in his many plants and animals, which have the knowledge he seeks. In "Noah's Raven," the raven turns away from Noah and says:

Why should I have returned?
My knowledge would not fit into theirs.
I found untouched the desert of the unknown,
Big enough for my feet. It is my home.
It is always beyond them [man].

Again, recalling Wordsworth's imagery, he describes his isolation in the face of an enlightened nature:

... you would think the fields were something
To me, so long I stare out, looking
For their shapes or shadows through the matted gleam, seeing
Neither what is nor what was, but the flat light rising.

When the poet achieves revelation, his vision is one of "blindness," his condition that of a stone; perhaps man is ultimately "invisible, invisible, invisible," an alien in "silence," "trying to read what the five polars are writing/On the void" ("A Scene in May"). In an utter calm of despair, he writes: "Not that heaven does not exist but/That it exists without us./... Everything that does not need you is real" ("The Widow").

Given a world of cosmic indifference, one would hope for comfort in the world of men. Merwin's most bitter poems treat man's brutality to man. Of family relationships he writes: "tell me anything more/Of every kinship than its madness ..." ("Uncle Hess"). Man has ruined his environment and he has destroyed nature: "Men think they are better than grass" ("The River of Bees"). But nature will avenge men who "made up their minds to be everywhere because why not/Everywhere was theirs because they thought so" ("The Last One"). Man has also created a ludicrous albeit murderous political world. In several poems Merwin writes of contemporary atrocities in Asia as a pattern throughout history as well as his own personal act: "I/all that/has become of them/clearly all is lost." The political liberal mocks himself in "I Live Up Here":

I live up here
And a little bit to the left
And I go down only
For the accidents ...
   I see
What my votes the mice are accomplishing
And I know I'm free

American society encourages its own collapse in "Unfinished Book of Kings":

V ... the lips of the last prophets had fallen
  from the last trees

VI They had fallen without sound they had not stayed in spite
  of the assurances proceeding from the mouths of the
  presidents

Merwin's despair for America's future resounds in "News of the Assassins": "An empty window has overtaken me/After the bees comes the smell of cigars/In the lobby of darkness."

Nevertheless, the poet persists in writing, prolific in his search for revelation and the poetry that communicates: "If I could be consistent even in destitution/The world would be revealed." He also writes: "I will take with me the emptiness of my hands/What you do not have you find everywhere"; his well-known words repeat this:

> It has taken me this long
> to know what I cannot say
> ... that my words are the garments of what I shall never be
> like the tucked sleeve of a one-armed boy.

—Lois Gordon

MEYERS, Bert. American. Married; two children. Member of the English Department, Pitzer College, Claremont, California. Recipient: Ingram Merrill grant (two); National Endowment for the Arts grant, 1968.

PUBLICATIONS

Verse

Early Rain. Denver, Swallow, 1960.
The Dark Birds. New York, Doubleday, 1968.
Sunlight on the Wall. Santa Cruz, California, Kayak, 1976.
The Wild Olive Tree. Reno, Nevada, West Coast Poetry Review, 1979.
Windowsills. New Haven, Connecticut, Common Table, 1979.

Other

Translator, with Odette Meyers, *Lord of the Village*, by François Dodat. Reno, Nevada, West Coast Poetry Review, 1973.
Translator, with Odette Meyers, *The Childhood of the World*, by François Dodat. Reno, Nevada, West Coast Poetry Review, 1979.

* * *

Bert Meyers's language is lucid and unambiguous. His imagery is the most striking aspect of his work, particularly the presence in it of two distinct kinds. The first is a familiar kind of metaphor which at its best can be witty, as with the pigeons who "fly by/applauding themselves" ("Pigeons"), or elegiac, as in "People were flowers that grew by the shore;/twilight takes them home,/they fade together at their tables" ("Gulls Have Come Again"), or sensuously evocative, as in "October smokes a long cigar/and hangs its leather in the sun" ("October Poem"). But such images can also seem ostentatious or appliquéd: "airplanes punch the town with invisible fists of sound" ("Icon"), or "A needle's eye/in his tattered head/is losing his life's thread" ("The Accident"). These neither stimulate the mind nor challenge the emotions.

But Meyers also offers images which invite meditation rather than explication and have obvious affinities with the "deep image" of such diverse voices as Robert Bly and Jerome Rothenberg. Not that the *kind* guarantees success. "Surely a dead moth's/the skull of a tiny horse,/and the moon's a saint/who pities the sea" ("Funeral") – only the first half of this pair wins assent, the emotionalism of the second seeming factitious. An image can look like the first kind but get its power from being the second, as in "The huge root lies like a head/on a vacant field" where what matters is not the visual analogy but the ominous and mysterious feeling. This kind of imagery sustains Meyers's best poems, such as "Cigarette" ("You sigh as you tap/your way to the end./The hand is a blind child/called to the blackboard") or his best single piece, "Windy Night":

The sound of the wind
is the sound of a man
alone with himself
in the forest of sleep.

A tree, a mind holding on.

So many dry leaves fall,
then at last the rain.

Seamus Cooney

MEZEY, Robert. American. Born in Philadelphia, Pennsylvania, 28 February 1935. Educated at Kenyon College, Gambier, Ohio, 1951–53; University of Iowa, Iowa City, 1956–60, B.A. 1959; Stanford University, California (Poetry Fellow, 1961), 1960–61. Served in the United States Army, 1953–55: discharged as subversive. Married Ollie Simpson in 1963; two daughters and onc son. Instructor, Western Reserve University, Cleveland, 1963–64, and Franklin and Marshall College, Lancaster, Pennsylvania, 1965–66; Assistant Professor, Fresno State University, California, 1967–68. Since 1973, Associate Professor of English, University of Utah, Salt Lake City. Currently, Poetry Editor, *TransPacific*, Yellow Springs, Ohio. Recipient: Lamont Poetry Selection Award, 1960; Ingram Merrill Foundation Fellowship, 1973. Address: 116 Q Street, Salt Lake City, Utah 84103, U.S.A.

PUBLICATIONS

Verse

Berg Goodman Mezey. Philadelphia, New Ventures Press, 1957.
The Wandering Jew. Mount Vernon, Iowa, Hillside Press, 1960.
The Lovemaker. Iowa City, Cummington Press, 1961.
White Blossoms. Iowa City, Cummington Press, 1965.
Favors. Privately printed, 1968.
The Book of Dying. Santa Cruz, California, Kayak, 1970.
The Door Standing Open: New and Selected Poems 1954–1969. Boston, Houghton Mifflin, and London, Oxford University Press, 1970.

Other

Last Words: For John Lawrence Simpson, 1896–1969. Iowa City, Cummington Press, 1970.

Editor, with Stephen Berg, *Naked Poetry: Recent American Poetry in Open Forms*. Indianapolis, Bobbs Merrill, 1969; *The New Naked Poetry*, 1976.
Editor and Translator, *Poems from the Hebrew*. New York, Crowell, 1973.

Translator, *The Mercy of Sorrow*, by Uri Zvi Greenberg. Philadelphia, Three People Press, 1965.

Critical Study: by Ralph J. Mills, Jr., in *American Poetry Review* (Philadelphia), Fall 1974.

Robert Mezey comments:

There are many schools of poetry; I don't feel allegiance to any. Of my contemporaries, I especially admire Galway Kinnell, Bob Dylan, Philip Levine, Charles Simic, Luis Salinas.

My poems are largely mysterious to me – I don't want to analyze them. I have written love poems, poems of outrage at daily universal fraud and cruelty, expressions of gratitude to mountains and trees, jokes, messages, enigmas, obscenities. My theme is mortality and life everlasting. Influences: Catullus, Po Chu-i, Herbert (both George and Zbigniew), Ecclesiastes, Blake, Clare, Loren Eiseley, Cabeza de Vaca, Sam Cooke, Kenneth Rexroth, Issa, Archilocus, John Fowles, and a dog named Nina.

* * *

Robert Mezey is a metaphysical poet not because like Donne he ransacks scholastic philosophy for images, but because like Hamlet and all true metaphysicians he is given to asking unanswerable questions about himself and the world. He is not, however, a "philosophical poet." A great weight of passion accumulates behind his studied reserve and what finally emerges over the dam is intensely felt, tightly controlled poetry.

Early in his career, Robert Mezey came under the influence of the formalist critic and poet Yvor Winters, and *The Lovemaker*, Mezey's early book, betrays this influence clearly. Of Winters and his own subsequent development he writes wryly in a note appended to a group of his poems in *Naked Poetry*, an anthology of American poems in open forms edited by himself and Stephen Berg:

> When I was quite young I came under unhealthy influences – Yvor Winters, for example, and America, and my mother, though not in that order. Yvor Winters was easy to exorcise; all I had to do was meet him. My mother and America are another story and why tell it in prose?
>
> Once in Iowa City a friend said, "Why do you write in rhyme and meter? Your poetry is nothing like your life." "What do we know of another's life," I thought, but I had nothing to say. I no longer write in rhyme and meter, and still my life is not much like my poetry. At least, I don't think so. It is possible I'm not a poet at all. But I am a man, a Piscean, and unhappy, and therefore I make up poems.

Robert Mezey is a poet all right and an important one, but there is no doubt that a kind of passionate melancholy underlies most of his poetry. Yeats said "Out of our quarrel with the world we make rhetoric; out of the quarrel with ourselves, poetry"; Mezey is never rhetorical, but his quarrel really seems to be with the nature of things. He avoids the Hardian rhetoric against the universe through the adroit use of images which supply objective correlatives for his own moods. In "There," for example, microcosm (the poet) and macrocosm (the world) seem to fuse together:

> It is deep summer. Far out
> at sea the young squalls darken
> and roll, plunging northward,

threatening everything. I see
the Atlantic moving in slow
contemplative fury
against the rocks, the frozen
headlands, and the towns sunk deep
in a blind northern light. Here,
far inland, in the mountains
of Mexico, it is raining
hard, battering the soft mouths
of flowers. I am sullen, dumb,
ungovernable. I taste myself
and I taste those winds, uprisings
of salt and ice, of great trees
brought down, of houses and cries
lost in the storm; and what breaks
on that black shore breaks in me.

The tone here is perhaps more Byronic than usual in his poems, where urban images have their place along with natural ones. But the poem does show quite clearly his strategy for making turbid and passionate feelings objective through the use of corresponding images from the natural world.

Mezey thinks of himself as having abandoned traditional meter and rhyme. His and Berg's anthology is exclusively concerned with poems in what he calls "open form." Yet as one reads over the poem just quoted one becomes aware that a great measure of the force of the poem is owing to the tightly controlled rhythms employed. No line in the poem contains more than four stresses or less than three, a close approach to "regular" meter; yet these fluctuations in line length do much to suggest the fluctuating pressures of the storm and the sea. One senses too that such powerful rhythmic control had to be exerted to keep the poem from exploding all over the page. And the control over raw emotion manifests itself mainly through the poet's handling of rhythm.

Mezey obviously values clarity in a writer. Three things, I think, account for the unfailing clarity of these passionate poems. Two have already been mentioned, sharp clear images, many of which turn out to be objective correlatives, rhythmic control, and frequent, unobtrusive, but effective employment of articulatory symbolism: the forced miming by the organs of speech of the very action or object being described. To illustrate, I quote from another of his poems about autumn, "Touch It." This is the second stanza:

Past the thinning orchard the fields
are on fire. A mountain of smoke
climbs the desolate wind, and at its roots
fire is eating dead grass with many small teeth.

The very shaping of the words in the final line here enforces upon the reader a sort of *chewing* action. Or again, in "There" – "it is raining/hard, battering the soft mouths/of flowers" – simply shaping the words pantomimes the effect the words describe.

These three factors, and perhaps many more that have escaped me, but at least these three, make possible shaping the raw emotion of these poems toward the extraordinary clarity they achieve.

—E. L. Mayo

MICHIE, James. British. Born in London in 1927. Educated at Trinity College, Oxford. Worked as an editor and lecturer. Currently, Director, The Bodley Head, publishers, London.

PUBLICATIONS

Verse

Possible Laughter. London, Hart Davis, 1959.

Other

Editor, with Kingsley Amis, *Oxford Poetry 1949.* Oxford, Blackwell, 1949.
Editor, *The Bodley Head Book of Longer Short Stories.* London, Bodley Head, 1974; as *The Book of Longer Short Stories*, New York, Stein and Day, 1975.

Translator, *The Odes of Horace.* New York, Orion, 1963; London, Hart Davis, 1964.
Translator, *The Poems of Catullus: A Bilingual Edition.* London, Hart Davis, and New York, Random House, 1969.
Translator, *The Epigrams of Martial.* London, Hart Davis MacGibbon, and New York, Random House, 1973.
Translator, *Selected Fables*, by La Fontaine. London, Allen Lane, and New York, Viking Press, 1979.

* * *

James Michie is better known as a translator, probably, than as an original poet, which is hardly surprising considering the wit and energy of his versions of Horace, Catullus and Martial. These translations are not "modern" in the usual sense – they have nothing in common, for example, with the free renderings and "homages" of Pound or Lowell – but are cast in the neo-classical tradition of Pope and Dryden in which the order of English rhyme and meter offers a kind of substitute satisfaction for the unrenderable richness of Latin. Thus Catullus' celebrated "Odi et amo. Quare id faciam, fortasse requiris?/Nescio, sed fieri sentio at excrucior" becomes, in Michie's version,

I hate and love. If you ask me to explain
  The contradiction,
I can't, but I can feel it, and the pain
  Is crucifixion.

Michie's own poetry thus far is collected in one slender volume – very slender indeed, with 32 poems, few of which are longer than a page. They reflect some of the qualities of the Latin verse which Michie has translated, the economy, the sophistication and particularly the good natured cynicism about human nature. The chief English influence seems to have been the light (but serious) black doggerel of Auden during the 'thirties, with its popular ballad forms and quick, surprising imagery. In "Quiet, Child," for example, Michie observes

Glumly we chew on with murder
  Long past the appetite of hate.
Nothing but their shadows' outlines
  Left, like grease-stains on a plate,
People leaning over bridges
  Quietly evaporate.

And big as a telephone directory
His bomber's casualty list,
Gloved, the pilot leaves behind him,
Represented by a mist,
Individuals who were furious,
But no longer now exist.

The poems vary considerably in theme and metrical form, from the Betjeman-like "Park Concert" to the more troubled, individual voice of "Nightmare" and "At Any Rate," with their darker observations about human cruelty and helplessness. Time is the enemy, with its subtle erosions:

The hours, pretending they do not know how to combine,
Walk up as charming freebooters, unarmed, disclaiming
Allegiance to that remote and iron-grey battle-line.

Fidelity is weak. The lovers may

hold like amulets
Precious hands, or go linking
Arms, but no one gets
Cleanly through without slinking.
Quite innocent,
Moving to kiss, although they hadn't meant
It, they'll find themselves archly winking.

The prevailing tone of Michie's verse, however, is neither brutal nor tragic but much more in the spirit of the wise man in "The End of the Sage" who dies

"Much wiser and much dafter,
Now that I quite agree
To become dead,
I achieve a witticism,
And I see at last," he said,
"Hazy like foothills possible laughter."

—Elmer Borklund

MIDDLETON, (John) Christopher. British. Born in Truro, Cornwall, 10 June 1926. Educated at Felsted School, Essex; Merton College, Oxford, B.A. 1951, D.Phil. 1954. Served in the Royal Air Force, 1944–48. Lecturer in English, Zurich University, 1952–55; Senior Lecturer in German, King's College, University of London. Since 1966, Professor of Germanic Languages and Literature, University of Texas, Austin. Recipient: Geoffrey Faber Memorial Prize, 1964; Guggenheim Fellowship, 1974. Address: Department of German, University of Texas, Austin, Texas 78712, U.S.A.

PUBLICATIONS

Verse

Poems. London, Fortune Press, 1944.

Nocturne in Eden: Poems. London, Fortune Press, 1945.
The Vision of the Drowned Man. Ditchling, Sussex, Ditchling Press, 1950(?).
Torse 3: Poems 1949–1961. London, Longman, and New York, Harcourt Brace, 1962.
Penguin Modern Poets 4, with David Holbrook and David Wevill. London, Penguin, 1963.
Nonsequences: Selfpoems. London, Longman, 1965; New York, Norton, 1966.
Our Flowers and Nice Bones. London, Fulcrum Press, 1969.
Die Taschenelefant: Satire. Berlin, Verlag Neue Rabenpresse, 1969.
The Fossil Fish: 15 Micropoems. Providence, Rhode Island, Burning Deck, 1970.
Briefcase History: 9 Poems. Providence, Rhode Island, Burning Deck, 1972.
Fractions for Another Telemachus. Knotting, Bedfordshire, Sceptre Press, 1974.
Wildhorse. Knotting, Bedfordshire, Sceptre Press, 1975.
The Lonely Suppers of W. V. Balloon. Cheadle, Cheshire, Carcanet Press, and Boston, Godine, 1975.
Razzmatazz. Austin, Texas, W. Thomas Taylor, 1976.
Eight Elementary Inventions. Knotting, Bedfordshire, Sceptre Press, 1977.
Pataxanadu: Prose Poems. Manchester, Carcanet Press, 1977.
Carminalenia. Manchester, Carcanet Press, 1979.

Play

The Metropolitans (libretto), music by Hans Vogt. Kassel, Alkor, 1964.

Other

Bolshevism in Art and Other Expository Writings. Manchester, Carcanet Press, 1978.

Editor and Translator, with Michael Hamburger, *Modern German Poetry 1910–1960: An Anthology with Verse Translations.* London, MacGibbon and Kee, and New York, Grove Press, 1962.
Editor and Translator, with William Burford, *The Poet's Vocation: Selections from the Letters of Hölderlin, Rimbaud, and Hart Crane.* Austin, University of Texas Press, 1967.
Editor, *German Writing Today.* London, Penguin, 1967.
Editor, *Selected Poems*, by Georg Trakl. London, Cape, 1968.

Translator, *The Walk and Other Stories*, by Robert Walser. London, Calder, 1957.
Translator, with others, *Primal Vision*, by Gottfried Benn. New York, New Directions, 1960.
Translator, with others, *Poems and Verse Plays*, by Hugo von Hofmannsthal. New York, Pantheon, 1961.
Translator, with Michael Hamburger, *Selected Poems*, by Günter Grass. London, Secker and Warburg, and New York, Harcourt Brace, 1966.
Translator, *Jakob von Gunten*, by Robert Walser. Austin, University of Texas Press, 1969.
Translator, *Selected Letters*, by Friedrich Nietzsche. Chicago, University of Chicago Press, 1969.
Translator, with Michael Hamburger, *Poems*, by Günter Grass. London, Penguin, 1969.
Translator, *The Quest for Christa T.*, by Christa Wolf. New York, Farrar Straus, 1970.
Translator, with Michael Hamburger, *Selected Poems*, by Paul Celan. London, Penguin, 1972.
Translator, *Selected Poems*, by Friedrich Hölderlin and Eduard Mörike. Chicago, University of Chicago Press, 1972.

Translator, *Inmarypraise* by Günter Grass. New York, Harcourt Brace, 1974.
Translator, *Kafka's Other Trial: The Letters to Felice*, by Elias Canetti. New York, Schocken, 1974.

* * *

In an interview in *The London Magazine* in 1964 Christopher Middleton criticised his English contemporaries for a parochialism of form and content which cut them off from the great heritage of European Modernism. The latter, he argued, had "at most points connected ... a strong sense of social revolution, a catastrophic view of history," with an "interest in the radical remaking of techniques." Both in his translations, primarily from the German, and in his own poetry, Middleton has tried to keep open this connection. Middleton's "catastrophic view of history" leads him continually to those moments at which personal crisis interlocks with social crisis. Thus, in "The Arrest of Pastor Paul Schneider," the pastor is dragged reluctantly from a nightmare of arrest to its actuality; in "January 1919" history rips the "holed head" of the murdered German revolutionary Liebknecht out of context, to display it "bleeding across a heap of progressive magazines"; in "The Historian," Procopius, official historian to the tyrant Justinian, is snatched from the desk where he writes his secret exposé of the regime just as he realizes that the only authentic opposition is in deeds not words. The interrupted sentence which closes the poem reveals the fragility of men amidst a history they cannot control, the witness always potentially a victim ("The thought still bothers me, that, instead of writing, I might have changed the"). Many of Middleton's poems turn Hitler's and Stalin's death camps into universal symbols of 20th-century history, uprooting men from their own proper lives to a dream of deportation and massacre, whether the "figures torn from a fog," "feeding on garbage in the camp near Voronezh" of "Pavlovic Variations," or the "eclipsed/Future[s]" slid into the ovens at Treblinka ("Idiocy of Rural Life"). But terror lurks not only in the major events of a public history. Middleton's poetry detects the threat of extinction in more mundane, trivial situations. A pair of gloves left on the floor of a lavatory (so that, "it seems, you'd think, smothering a giggle,/someone has been sucked down the john") can summon up a terrifying vision of disappeared persons. Middleton's poetry repeatedly evokes, in his own words, "A really live sense of what it is like to live in a society where the direction of life has fallen into the hands of malevolent or ignorant functionaries, where all human values seem to be threatened by inhuman organization." Poems such as "Octobers" and "Autobiography" record how this menace inserts itself into the most idyllic and private experiences. But "History ... isn't the past at all, it is the multitudinous new life saturating the present," and "the little significant things" which it is the poet's duty to "unravel" ("Glaucus") contain promise as well as threat, renewal as well as destruction. This is perhaps why so many of Middleton's poems are concerned with children, the inheritors for whom history, the future, is always open, though it may again and again be suppressed, as for "Fania, ten/at the turn of the century" in "The Pogroms in Sebastopol," or for "Pavel's child" who "came to pieces in my hands," dug out of the snow of the camps ("Pavlovic Variations"), or for those napalmed Vietnamese children in "Mérindol Interior" whose photographed agony intrudes into the poet's comfortable middle-class world.

At its best, there are a hardness, a tautness, a lack of false colour and sentimentality to Middleton's language which argue an ascetic's imagination; yet, at the same time, his poetry is passionately involved in the world – "odd as it is to care" (as he says in one poem) "anyhow for things/their mass & contour/& all beginnings." His world is substantial, yet curiously abstract; figured, and yet not personalized. He writes often in the third or second person, and even when he appears himself attention is nearly always focussed on what's out there rather than on subjective response. This classical yet humane distance is maintained by a deliberate employment of that "defamiliarization" technique described by the Russian Formalist Viktor Shklovsky (whom Middleton acknowledges on several occasions). The disjunctions, dislocations and unexpected collocations of his language, the experimental diversity of structure and theme, and a movement between extremes of abstrusity and explicitness, using the very opacity of his language to concentrate our gaze as if for the first time on familiar object and event, all enable Middleton to pursue that "defining of enigmas" which is for him the poetic vocation, exposing us to "the strangeness of being alive, ... the strangeness of living things outside oneself."

In "Oystercatchers," for example, the unexpected verb discloses a world strangely detached from man ("rocks in the bay below/Retrieved their shadows"); while "Wire Spring" turns the pun of the title into a sinister vision by reviving dead metaphors ("The first clock said: it is time we killed. /The second clock said: it is time we told"). "The simplest model for such poems is not the linguistic 'statement' but the question," Middleton notes on the dust-jacket of *The Lonely Suppers*; and, indeed, all his poetry is hermeneutic, interrogative, quizzical, questioning reality with a sceptical and informed eye, and perpetually reminding us that language is not an innocent carrier of meaning but itself a force for good or ill that pre-empts all our seeing. It is this which accounts for the range of Middleton's experiments with the resources of language, whether concrete or "found" poems, cut-ups and grafts, or such pieces as "Computer's Karl Marx" which, starting with a joke (a history of revolution written by a computer that has only the letters of the words "production relations" to play with) goes on to show how the limits of our language are the limits of our world. It is perhaps finally in this ludic sense of the ludicrous, derived from Dada and Surrealism, coupled with a quite un-English seriousness, that Middleton justifies his claim to the European inheritance.

—Stan Smith

MILES, Josephine (Louise). American. Born in Chicago, Illinois, 11 June 1911. Educated at the University of California, Los Angeles, A.B. 1932 (Phi Beta Kappa); University of California, Berkeley, M.A. 1934, Ph.D. 1938. Since 1940, Member of the English Department, and since 1973, University Professor, University of California, Berkeley. Recipient: Shelley Memorial Award, 1936; Phelan Award, 1937; American Association of University Women fellowship, 1939; Guggenheim Fellowship, 1948; National Institute of Arts and Letters grant, 1956; Oscar Blumenthal Prize (*Poetry*, Chicago), 1959; American Council of Learned Societies Fellowship, 1965; National Endowment for the Arts grant, 1967; James Russell Lowell Prize, 1975; Academy of American Poets Award, 1978. D.Litt.: Mills College, Oakland, California, 1965. Fellow, American Academy of Arts and Sciences. Address: 2275 Virginia Street, Berkeley, California 94709, U.S.A.

PUBLICATIONS

Verse

Lines at Intersection. New York, Macmillan, 1939.
Poems on Several Occasions. New York, New Directions, 1941.
Local Measures. New York, Reynal, 1946.
After This Sea. San Francisco, Book Club of California, 1947.
Prefabrications. Bloomington, Indiana University Press, 1955.
Poems 1930–1960. Bloomington, Indiana University Press, 1960.
Civil Poems. Berkeley, California, Oyez, 1966.
Bent. Santa Barbara, California, Unicorn Press, 1967.
Kinds of Affection. Middletown, Connecticut, Wesleyan University Press, 1967.
Saving the Bay. San Francisco, Open Space, 1967.

Fields of Learning. Berkeley, California, Oyez, 1968.
American Poems. Berkeley, California, Cloud Marauder Press, 1970.
To All Appearances: New and Selected Poems. Urbana, University of Illinois Press, 1974.
Coming to Terms. Urbana, University of Illinois Press, 1979.

Recording: *Today's Poets 2*, with others, Folkways, 1968.

Play

House and Home (produced Berkeley, California, 1960). Published in *First Stage* (Lafayette, Indiana), Fall 1965.

Other

Wordsworth and the Vocabulary of Emotion. Berkeley, University of California Press, 1942.
Pathetic Fallacy in the 19th Century: A Study of the Changing Relation Between Object and Emotion. Berkeley, University of California Press, 1942.
The Vocabulary of Poetry: Three Studies. Berkeley, University of California Press, 1946.
The Continuity of Poetic Language: Studies in English Poetry from the 1540's to the 1940's. Berkeley, University of California Press, 1951.
I. *The Primary Language of Poetry in the 1640's.* Berkeley, University of California Press, 1948.
II. *The Primary Language of Poetry in the 1740's and 1840's.* Berkeley, University of California Press, 1950.
III. *The Primary Language of Poetry in the 1940's.* Berkeley, University of California Press, 1951.
Eras and Modes in English Poetry. Berkeley, University of California Press, 1957; revised edition, 1964.
Renaissance, Eighteenth-Century, and Modern Language in English Poetry: A Tabular View. Berkeley, University of California Press, 1960.
Ralph Waldo Emerson. Minneapolis, University of Minnesota Press, 1964.
Style and Proportion: The Language of Prose and Poetry. Boston, Little Brown, 1967.
Poetry and Change: Donne, Milton, Wordsworth, and the Equilibrium of the Present. Berkeley, University of California Press, 1974.

Editor, with Mark Schorer and Gordon McKenzie, *Criticism: The Foundations of Modern Literary Judgment.* New York, Harcourt Brace, 1948; rivised edition, 1958.
Editor, with others, *Idea and Experiment.* Berkeley, University of California Press, 1950.
Editor, *The Poem: A Critical Anthology.* Englewood Cliffs, New Jersey, Prentice Hall, 1959; revised edition as *The Ways of the Poem*, 1961, 1973.
Editor, *Classic Essays in English.* Boston, Little Brown, 1961; revised edition, 1965.

Translator, with others, *Modern Hindi Poetry.* Bloomington, Indiana University Press, 1965.

Manuscript Collections: State University of New York, Buffalo; Washington University, St. Louis; Bancroft Poetry Archive, University of California, Berkeley.

Critical Studies: "Distance and Surfaces" by Robert Beloof, in *Prairie Schooner* (Lincoln, Nebraska), Winter 1958–59; in *Voyages* (Washington, D.C.), Fall 1968; *Times Literary Supplement* (London), April 1975.

Josephine Miles comments:

Interest in poetry of spoken thought, of meditation, of literally making sense of ideas. Main themes, human doubt and amazement. A strong beat of meaning playing against the beat of pattern. Some critics say "western," but I am not aware of this.

* * *

Josephine Miles shares, with William Carlos Williams and his followers, credit for exalting "the American idiom" into the standard language of poetry – a feat surrounded by risk, by the danger of being charged with flatness and being forsaken by all but the most sensitive of critics. Her achievement is that she has successfully laid aside her academic powers (she is one of the land's best scholars) in order to paint with a great gentleness – and sense of their fragility and evanescence – the landscapes of the American scene – its speech, jazz, billboards, comics and assassinations, and those dark streets of towns where three creeks meet. She has raised these materials into a high form of poetry, and her insights in poems provide an enlightening commentary on American life. In clearing her vision of scholarship, in renouncing sophistication and working exclusively with native materials, Miss Miles offers, essentially, the *persona* of a Willa Cather schoolmarm discoursing gently on the wisdom she has acquired from the prairies and a few rides in tin cars. Even when confessing her scholarship ("Bad quartos were my first love") she remains matter of fact. Her skill is in rendering the quotidian stillness of an American street; and she avoids exoticism, even in her treatment of "Bombay" and "Tehachapi South." She is most at home rendering the sadness, the matter-of-factness, the every-evening miracle, of the moon rising over the lumber yard, and perhaps a whiskey bottle; the rendering is pure, strikes life's tonic note of recognition. Her work is at once primitive and sophisticated, like that of Chekhov and Dr. Williams. It must be said too that an undercurrent of sharp physical pain runs through her poems. The fact that she must *be* helped, physically, as well as offer her help to the world, must partly account for the strikingly developed theme of the acknowledgement of others – a sense of the connectedness of people, of obligation, of gratitude reciprocal and eternal. And her elegy on the death of John Kennedy is not only rhythmically enchanting and original, but is a major statement on violence in America, on the resentment of real *qualitas* in American life, on the assertion of mediocrity and the insistence of enshrining it or turning power over to it: with the metaphor of Daniel Boone's shooting of the bear, Miss Miles transforms history and myth in such a way that many readers feel that she alone has offered an adequate explanation for the Kennedy assassination. Her work imparts the riches of a rare and compassionate sensibility.

—David Ray

MILLER, Vassar (Morrison). American. Born in Houston, Texas, 19 July 1924. Educated at the University of Houston, B.S. 1947, M.A. 1952. Formerly, Instructor in Creative Writing, St. John's School, Houston. Address: 1615 Vassar Street, Houston, Texas 77006, U.S.A.

PUBLICATIONS

Verse

Adam's Footprint. New Orleans, New Orleans Poetry Journal, 1956.

Wage War on Silence: A Book of Poems. Middletown, Connecticut, Wesleyan University Press, 1960.
My Bones Being Wiser: Poems. Middletown, Connecticut, Wesleyan University Press, 1963.
Onions and Roses. Middletown, Connecticut, Wesleyan University Press, 1968.
If I Could Sleep Deeply Enough. New York, Liveright, 1974.
Small Change. Houston, Wings Press, 1977.

Vassar Miller comments:

Traditional lyrics, but also free verse and syllabic. Religious themes, though also more humanistic of late.

* * *

To say that Vassar Miller was once Poet Laureate of Texas (1963) may raise some eyebrows and evoke glib remarks about the sweet singer of the purple sage. Any such response is at once stopped by even a cursory reading of her deeply felt, spare poems. In the midst of an expanding society (she is a native of Houston, Texas) she is an interior poet, modest in diction without being trivial in theme. Rather than sing the vastness of the Western Spirit, she examines in carefully wrought poems the individual soul in the individual body; and her poems body forth the implications for us all of her experience. Many of her best poems are what we call "religious" – but they are religious in the quiet mode of Herbert, rather than in the more convoluted and even shrill manner of Crashaw and Berryman. She does not wish to believe; she believes. Nor does she deny the hard realities and difficulties of writing about the religious experience, though she writes from the assurance of faith (perhaps even grace) and the stability of a fully civilized sensibility. Some of her poems are damaged by easy rhetorical victories (as when Pontius Pilate says "The gods will play some joke –/And then get angry every time it works"), trite phrasing ("the afternoons so beautiful"), cliché of emotional response (as in the set responses to religious holidays and E. B. Browning's grave), and even rigid metrical handling ("It would be best to travel light/Between the darkness and the light"). Her best poems avoid these faults. She is most successful in traditional forms, as in the villanelle "Hot Air" ("Soft my pleasure came") and in the sonnet, as in "Reverent Impiety," "Judas," and many others. And although many of her secular poems are moving ("So that I felt relief/ to see your existence wrapped up/in death's lying precision,/pomp prayed and sung/then given discreetly to/the lithe ruin of worms"), and some explore the meanings of love in animal imagery to powerful effect ("the dog whines, rattling her chain,/ not comprehending her crime/when her occupation is love"), Miller's best work remains in her religious poems, as in the sonnet "The Wisdom of Insecurity" which contains the lines: "God will not play our games nor join our fun,/Does not give tit for tat, parade His glories./ And chance is chance, not providence dressed neat,/Credentials hidden in its wooden leg." Miller's books (*My Bones Being Wiser* is the best of her published volumes) are all informed by hard intelligence, insight, and a gift for language.

—James Korges

MILLWARD, Eric. British. Born in Longnor, Staffordshire, 12 March 1935. Educated at Longnor Church of England School, 1941–46; Buxton College, 1946–54. Married 1) Anne

Craig in 1961, two sons; 2) Rosemary Anne Wood in 1975. Address: 4 King's Road, Horsham, Sussex, England.

PUBLICATIONS

Verse

A Child in the Park. Walton-on-Thames, Surrey, Outposts, 1969.
Dead Letters. Liskeard, Cornwall, Peterloo Poets, 1978.

Eric Millward comments:

It is my intention to write good, readable, comprehensible poems about the things/people I find important/happy/sad/helpless/beautiful/ugly/kind/cruel. I have to admit that things sad/helpless/ugly/cruel seem at present to predominate.

I have willingly written poems since the age of 14. I hope my work has shown some improvement. I do not think I know what poetry is: I just know I like it – or some of it. I often find myself apologising for the (apparent) transparency of my poems; but I feel that this may be the fault of those poets who seem to feel that density implies depth! Anyway, I have my own favourite poets – not all of whom are of the upper echelon. Yet.

* * *

The work of Eric Millward has appeared in magazines and anthologies for more than a decade now. Yet it has never achieved permanence between the covers of a hard-back volume. However, of many uncollected poets, he is one whose poems deserve collection.

Eric Millward relates to a tradition deriving from Clare, Hardy, Edward Thomas, and Edmund Blunden. But he is not, any more than these earlier poets, simply pastoral. His themes are various, as instanced by the titles of his better poems: "Children with Hands," "Spastic," "Cows," "The Girl's Confession," "The Widow's Bird," "Mrs. Monk," "When His Wife Died," "Sudden Rain," "A Short Life," "The Cat Returns," "A Winter Wedding," and – two very impressive pieces – "Freeing a Bird" and "A Child in the Park." These two are essentially religious poems.

The plot of "Freeing a Bird" unfolds itself decisively to build up the sense that the sparrow falls into our hands as we ourselves fall into the hands of God. The point is not insisted upon, but, when caught at length, the sparrow is "a sheeted bundle" and it is thrown out into the night "like crumbs." What comes out clearly is the alienation between one species and another, and the sense that there is a similar lack of contact between man and his maker – "And we, who might perhaps presume to teach,/Should count the missions we initiate/That end in failure to communicate."

"A Child in the Park" is a poem of the same kind. It is a meditative lyric on a large scale, couched in traditional but highly expressive metres. Like the previous poem, it recounts a story with a strongly allegorical bent.

It may be some perverse desire
For pain that lets me watch my child
Wander away in the terrible park
Towards a distant target, called
By a half-heard, compelling bark
To cuddle some ungainly cur....

The child, of course, loses his perspective and finds himself alone. Naturally, the father obeys his instinct to run after the child and soothe his fears. But the allegory becomes marked if we mentally capitalize the protagonists, for the final stanzas are a reproach from the mortal Child to the heavenly Father:

> Meanwhile we wandering children move
> Within our park, unheld by hands,
> Some finding peace which grows from trust
> In power that loves and understands;
> Some, loving children, doubting, must
> Concede the power, question the love.

To call Eric Millward a religious poet seems reasonable enough, but the statement must be qualified. This is, for all its formal certainty, a poetry allied to the cries like dead letters sent by the poets of a line that constitutes a key English tradition. In the 20th century this tradition has been carried on by Walter de la Mare, Andrew Young, Norman Cameron, and Joan Barton. It does not seem too much to claim for Eric Millward a place among these distinguished poets.

But his most recent work has taken on a harder, more satiric, tone. We take civilisation to the natives, he tells us, and are soon "exchanging gifts and bacteria." A quirky little poem says that, without your thumbs, you've "got a fight on your hands." A parody of a hymn snarls out "God moves in a mysterious way/His duties to ignore." But none of this seems quite sharp enough. Millward is a charitable rather than a mordant poet. He resorts to attack, possibly, because he lacks a myth to defend. Perhaps, like so many 20th-century poets in this eclectic last quarter, Millward is seeking a fiction outside his personal experience. With his technique and fine ear for verse, he will be a poet to be reckoned with if he finds one.

—Philip Hobsbaum

MILNE, (Charles) Ewart. Irish. Born in Dublin, 25 May 1903. Educated at Nuns Cross National School, Wicklow; Christ Church Cathedral Grammar School, Dublin. Married 1) Kathleen Ida Bradner in 1927 (marriage dissolved), one son; 2) Thelma Dobson in 1948, two sons. Formerly, teacher; seaman, 1920–30; Book Reviewer, *Irish Times*, Dublin; Staff Member, *Ireland Today*, Dublin, 1937–40; Estate Farm Manager, 1947–61. Since 1968, Book Reviewer, *Irish Press*, Dublin. Address: 46 De Parys Avenue, Bedford, England.

PUBLICATIONS

Verse

Forty North, Fifty West. Dublin, Gayfield Press, 1938.
Letter from Ireland. Dublin, Gayfield Press, 1940.
Listen Mangan. Dublin, At the Sign of the Three Candles, 1941.
Jubilo. London, Muller, 1944.
Boding Day. London, Muller, 1947.
Diamond Cut Diamond: Selected Poems. London, Lane, 1950.
Elegy for a Lost Submarine. Burnham on Crouch, Essex, Plow Poems, 1951.
Galion: A Poem. Dublin, Dolmen Press, 1953.
Life Arboreal. Tunbridge Wells, Kent, Pound Press, 1953.
Once More to Tourney: A Book of Ballads and Light Verse, Serious, Gay, and Grisly. London, Linden Press, 1958.

A Garland for the Green. London, Hutchinson, 1962.
Time Stopped: A Poem Sequence with Prose Intermissions. London, Plow Poems, 1967.
Drift of Pinions. Breakish, Isle of Skye, Aquila, 1976.
Cantata under Orion. Breakish, Isle of Skye, Aquila, 1976.

Manuscript Collection: State University of New York, Buffalo.

Critical Studies: "Self Portrait" by the author, in *Poetry Ireland* (Dublin), April 1949; "The Poetry of Ewart Milne" by Peter Russell, in *Chantecleer* (London) i, 3, 1953; "The Poetry of Ewart Milne" by Lawrence Lipton, in *Poetry* (Chicago), September 1955; *A Poet's War: British Poets in the Spanish Civil War*, by Hugh Ford, Philadelphia, University of Pennsylvania Press, 1965; "Recent Poetry" by Terry Eagleton, in *Stand* (Newcastle upon Tyne), 1967; Penelope Palmer, in *Agenda* (London), 1968; *The Outsiders: Poets of Contemporary Ireland* by Frank Kersnowski, Fort Worth, Texas Christian University Press, 1975.

Ewart Milne comments:

My poetry is about people, places, things, events, happenings, and non-happenings. It is not simply about the poet and his words and wordcraft. It is about my relationship to the world, and to the other world, to life and death (which, together, seem to make up one whole identity), with what to do with my life and how to do it, with the past and present of man as I learn about it and about him. All the assurance I have is the certain knowledge that I am in good company, in the mainstream of poets and poetry in English, from Thomas Wyatt to Milton, Blake, and Hardy, even though I am not in the mainstream of much of the poetry being written at present, which seems to me to be the heretical poetry of the eye rather than the ear, as also the poetry of the inward-turning poet seeking only himself and to examine himself. But when I have said that, I find it is a contradiction because the volume I have completed, in the seventy-sixth year of my life, and which I have called *The Folded Leaf*, is almost entirely made up of pieces about my boyhood in the early years of the twentieth century, spent in Dublin and Wicklow. Still, the book is peopled with relatives, friends, and others. And anyway, if I contradict myself, as Whitman said, I contradict myself. So what?

* * *

Ewart Milne began to write in the late 1930's when the new poets were concerned with political and social problems. He has published a dozen volumes, widely ranging in their themes and varied in their moods. He spent some years in the British Merchant Navy, became a teacher, was for some time an ambulance driver in the Spanish Civil War. Of his experiences at sea he has written little except for the moving "Elegy for a Lost Submarine," and an effective allegory, "The Waterside Poem":

Shanghaied aboard
We signed on later because we must.
In a smelly cabin among charts and paraffin
We signed on for the round trip:
Where we were bound for had been left blank.

And a hard going we had of it.
You were below then, in the stokehold, while I
Swung overside in a bosun's chair
Was repainting the ship's name on the rusty bow.
Her name was, as I remember, the steamship Earth.

He has written a number of moving poems, however, about the tragic events which he witnessed in Spain. He has experimented in diverse metrical forms but usually writes in free verse. His opinions are Leftist, but he avoids purely political themes and concentrates on social conditions in Ireland and elsewhere.

A Garland for the Green was inspired by his return to his native country and is romantic in its mood. In contrast, two successive volumes, *Letter from Ireland* and *Listen Mangan*, are satiric in mood. His style is direct and, by disciplined selection, can, at its best, be evocative, as in "Tinker's Moon":

A potato patch to thin on the way, a hen to kill,
And hunger again: and sleep again:
And a moonlight flit while the salmon leaps
From a smouldering spot by the riverside;
The tinker's children take their chance, and bide.

Once More to Tourney is, as the subtitle indicates, a book of light verse, gay and grisly by turn. In an introduction to this volume, J. M. Cohen notes that the poet has a voice of his own and belongs to no school: "His poems are as easy to read as nursery-rhymes, and as tough as a saloon-bar argument."

Milne's 1967 volume *Time Stopped* is a long dramatic poem in a variety of measures, mostly rhymed, deeply tragic in its mood. Written in the first person, it describes how a poet discovers from the letters after her death that his wife had been unfaithful to him with a friend of his. By the use of deliberate plain statement, the tragic mood is set:

In nineteen sixty-four the United States Medical Council
Decreed that cigarette smoking constituted a health hazard
And could cause death from lung cancer; in that year
In that summer in that September when you died

The bitterness and disillusion expressed in the poem will remind readers of *Modern Love*, that cycle of irregular sonnets by George Meredith. Even in its despairing mood, the poem is guarded by its own discipline:

I sat by her bedside and watched her die
And the hopeless and defeated one   that was I
The helpless one the condemned one   that was I
Left over   left to live on   mercilessly
Left with the fallen bricks of my house of poetry.

—Austin Clarke

MITCHELL, Adrian. British. Born in London, 24 October 1932. Educated at Dauntsey's School, Wiltshire; Christ Church, Oxford (Editor, *Isis* magazine, 1954–55), 1952–55. Served in the British Army, 1951–52. Reporter, *Oxford Mail*, 1955–57, and *Evening Standard*, London, 1957–59; Columnist and Reviewer, *Daily Mail*, *Woman's Mirror*, *The Sun*, *The Sunday Times*, *Peace News*, *The Black Dwarf*, and *The Guardian*, all in London. Instructor, University of Iowa, Iowa City, 1963–64; Granada Fellow in the Arts, University of Lancaster, 1967–69; Fellow, Wesleyan University Center for the Humanities, Middletown, Connecticut, 1971. Recipient: Eric Gregory Award, 1961; P.E.N. Translation

Prize, 1966; Tokyo Festival Television Film Award 1971. Agent: Fraser and Dunlop Scripts Ltd., 91 Regent Street, London W1R 8RU, England.

PUBLICATIONS

Verse

(Poems). Oxford, Fantasy Press, 1955.
Poems. London, Cape, 1964.
Peace Is Milk. London, Peace News, 1966.
Out Loud. London, Cape Goliard Press, and New York, Grossman, 1968; revised edition, London, Writers and Readers, 1976.
Ride the Nightmare: Verse and Prose. London, Cape, 1971.
Cease-Fire. London, Medical Aid Committee for Vietnam, 1973.
Penguin Modern Poets 22, with John Fuller and Peter Levi. London, Penguin, 1973.
The Apeman Cometh. London, Cape, 1975.
For Beauty Douglas: Collected Poems and Songs. London, Writers and Readers, 1979.

Recording: *Poems*, with Stevie Smith, Argo, 1974.

Plays

The Ledge (libretto), music by Richard Rodney Bennett (produced London, 1961).
The Persecution and Assassination of Jean-Paul Marat as Performed by the Inmates of the Asylum of Charenton under the Direction of the Marquis de Sade, adaptation of the play by Peter Weiss (produced London, 1964; New York, 1965). London, Calder, 1965; New York, Atheneum, 1966.
The Magic Flute, adaptation of the libretto by Schikaneder and Giesecke, music by Mozart (produced London, 1966).
US, with others (produced London, 1966). Published as *US: The Book of the Royal Shakespeare Production US/Vietnam/US/Experiment/Politics* ..., London, Calder and Boyars, 1968; as *Tell Me Lies*, Indianapolis, Bobbs Merrill, 1968.
The Criminals, adaptation of a play by José Triana (produced London, 1967; New York, 1970).
Tyger: A Celebration of the Life and Work of William Blake, music by Mike Westbrook (produced London, 1971). London, Cape, 1971.
Tamburlane the Mad Hen (for children; produced Devon, 1971).
Man Friday music by Mike Westbrook (televised, 1972; produced London, 1973). Included in *Man Friday, and Mind Your Head*, 1974.
Mind Your Head, music by Andy Roberts (produced Liverpool, 1973; London, 1974). Included in *Man Friday, and Mind Your Head*, 1974.
The Inspector General, adaptation of a play by Gogol (produced Nottingham, 1974).
Man Friday, and Mind Your Head. London, Eyre Methuen, 1974.
A Seventh Man, music by Dave Brown, adaptation of the book by John Berger and Jean Mohr (produced London, 1976).
White Suit Blues, music by Mike Westbrook, adaptation of works by Mark Twain (produced Nottingham and London, 1977).
Uppendown Mooney (produced Welwyn Garden City, Hertfordshire, 1978).
The White Deer (juvenile), adaptation of the story by James Thurber (produced London, 1978).
Hoagy, Bix, and Wolfgang Beethoven Bunkhaus (produced London, 1979).

Screenplays: *Tell Me Lies* (lyrics only), 1968; *The Body* (commentary), 1969.

Radio Play: *The Island* (libretto), music by William Russo, 1963.

Television Plays: *Animals Can't Laugh*, 1961; *Alive and Kicking*, 1971; *William Blake* (documentary), 1971; *Man Friday*, 1972; *Somebody Down There Is Crying*, 1974; *Daft as a Brush*, 1975; *The Fine Art of Bubble Blowing*, 1975; *Silver Giant, Wooden Dwarf*, 1975.

Initiated and helped write student shows: *Bradford Walk*, Bradford College of Art; *The Hotpot Saga*, *The Neurovision Song Contest*, and *Lash Me to the Mast*, University of Lancaster; *Move Over Jehovah*, National Association of Mental Health; *Poetry Circus*, Wesleyan University; *Mass Media Mash* and *Mud Fair*, Dartington College of the Arts, 1976 and 1977.

Novels

If You See Me Comin'. London, Cape, 1962; New York, Macmillan, 1963.
The Bodyguard. London, Cape, 1970; New York, Doubleday, 1971.
Wartime. London, Cape, 1973.
Man Friday. London, Futura, 1975.

Other

Naked in Cheltenham (miscellany). Cheltenham, Gastoday, 1978.

Editor, with Richard Selig, *Oxford Poetry 1955*. Oxford, Fantasy Press, 1955.
Editor, *Jump, My Brothers, Jump: Poems from Prison*, by Tim Daly. London, Freedom Press, 1970.

Translator, with Joan Jara, *Victor Jara: His Life and Songs*. London, Hamish Hamilton, 1976.

Adrian Mitchell comments:

My mind and imagination and my life have been altered by many things and many people. Other people's poetry has been among my most important experiences and I don't just mean great poetry. Politically speaking, it was poetry as much as anything else which pushed me first in the direction of left-wing political action (in which I include committee work, demonstrating, envelope-addressing as well as poetry). To cite some of the poets who have educated and influenced me: Wilfred Owen, Walt Whitman, Kenneth Patchen, Alex Comfort, Brecht, Beckett, John Arden, Allen Ginsberg and most of all, William Blake. (But I've been influenced by hundreds of others, most of all by my close friends and my family and a teacher called Michael Bell.) I'm sometimes called a committed poet. So's your old man. There are many poets who because they turn their back on politics, believe they are somehow not engaged. But their indifference or their silence contributes towards the status quo. And the status quo demands, at different periods, exploitation, starvation, poverty, mass-murder, torture, vile prisons, the stunting of children's imaginations and – in some part of the world during every day of my lifetime – war. When the revolution comes, I expect some poetry to make some contribution toward it – every revolution so far has had its own songs and poems. That contribution towards changing the world may be very small, but the smallest contribution helps when it's a matter of changing the world. (I don't think that poets should sit down and say: I've got to write a political poem.) But I think a poet, like any other human being, should recognise that the world is mostly controlled by political forces and should become politically active. And if a poet attempts to live his politics, his poems will become politically active too.

* * *

Adrian Mitchell is currently the leading "committed" poet in Britain. His work directs itself to political and social issues (the H-bomb, the war in Vietnam), and, as he himself declares: "Direct contact is very important. There is more satisfaction from reading to an audience than from seeing one's work in print." Perhaps more than any other poet, Mitchell is responsible for the growth of the fashion for large-scale poetry readings in Britain, and he has played a large part in getting poetry accepted as part of the "protest culture" of the young, and has considerably refurbished the image of the poet as a natural rebel. These things naturally make it very difficult to assess what he writes simply as literature. It is clear, for instance, that Mitchell does not expect some of his poems to outlast the occasions for which they were written. So far as the more topical ones are concerned, posterity will require a good deal of scholarly elucidation if it is to understand all the references. Yet it is equally plain that the poet hopes that at least some of his work will have staying power. Despite the comparisons which are often made between Mitchell and the American Beats, he is really very European, with a European concern for a fairly tightly structured way of writing (it is worth remembering, for example, that he began his career in the wake of the Movement, and was first published in establishment journals, such as the *London Magazine*). Mitchell's immediate ancestor is clearly not Allen Ginsberg but W. H. Auden, and one often catches echoes in his work of the political verses of the poets of the 30's. There is also a direct influence from Brecht, and on the whole the poets whom Mitchell most closely resembles are some of his own German contemporaries, such as Hans Magnus Enzensberger and Erich Fried, though his language seldom has their degree of concentration and pithiness. The weakness of Mitchell's work is its pop sentimentality; its virtues are a passionate anger and a colloquial directness.

—Edward Lucie-Smith

MITCHELL, David (John). New Zealander. Born in Wellington, 10 January 1940. Educated at Wellington College, 1953–57; Victoria University, Wellington, 1958–59. Married Elsebeth Nielsen in 1963; one daughter.

PUBLICATIONS

Verse

Orange Grove. Auckland, Poets Cooperative, 1969.
Pipe Dreams in Ponsonby. Auckland, Association of Oriental Syndics, 1972.

Critical Study: "He Sing fr You" by C. K. Stead, in *Islands* (Auckland), Spring 1972.

* * *

The physical appearance of David Mitchell's poetry – spacing, setting, punctuation, part-phonetic spelling, etc. – places it at once in the general current that flows out of the work of the Americans Pound, W. C. Williams and Charles Olson. A Mitchell poem is not sequential in any obvious sense except that some things follow others. There is neither logic nor narrative. Each poem is a succession of images, juxtaposition, associations, dissociations, around a central subject or idea. The writing picks out and heightens each phrase, even each word, which is a note of music before it is a sign pointing to anything beyond itself. At their best (and Mitchell is a talented poet whose public readings are especially effective in bringing out the best in his work) the poems are lyrical, nostalgic, wry, generous in feeling and confident in tone. Where they fail it is a failure of denotation. Words used too exclusively for their musical qualities and secondary resonances begin to look under-employed, suggesting the transient brightness of a pop culture rather than the basic stuff which alone endures changes of taste. But Mitchell has also a fine ear for the music latent in the roughest vernacular speech, and this, together with his sense of humour, is likely to keep his poetry concrete and to strengthen its fibre as he goes on writing. Mitchell is a genuine stylist on a literary scene that has been most remarkable for hacking fence posts out of kauri logs, and as such he is surely welcome.

—C. K. Stead

MOAT, John. British. Born in Mussoorie, India, 11 September 1936. Educated at Exeter College, Oxford. Married; two children. Co-Founder, The Arvon Foundation. Currently, Free-lance Writer. Lives in North Devon. Agent: A. D. Peters and Co., 10 Buckingham Street, London WC2N 6BU, England.

PUBLICATIONS

Verse

Sixpence per Annum: 12 Poems. Newbury, Berkshire, Phoenix Press, 1966.
Thunder of Grass. London, Barrie and Rockliff-Cresset Press, 1970.
The Ballad of the Leat. Gillingham, Kent, ARC, 1973.
Fiesta, and The Fox Reviews His Prophecy. London, Enitharmon Press, 1979.

Novels

Heorot. London, Barrie and Rockliff-Cresset Press, 1968.
The Tugen and the Toot. London, Barrie and Jenkins, 1973.

Other

A Standard of Verse. Newbury, Berkshire, Phoenix Press, 1969.
Bartonwood (juvenile). London, Chatto and Windus, 1978.

* * *

John Moat has published one collection of verse, *Thunder of Grass.* The work in it exhibits a Yeatsian smoothness, which, while moving more interestingly towards the rhythms of speech, still stays close to Yeats's special brand of rhetoric for its effects:

I inherited the garden towards dawn
And keep it with a very moderate art;
Though this may prosper now a child is born
To simplify complexities of heart:

The toil is simple while the love is one;
Two kids would tear a toiling soul apart.
For charity I work a routine spell
As premium to save my brat from hell.

Moat does better than "routine spells" in some of the sequence entitled "The Overtures" – notably Overture 37, a love poem where the strong sense of his wife's identity prevents him from drifting off into self-enchantment with what he has to say about it, and words are used for other than musical purposes. He is, on the evidence of this single book, a Romantic who needs plenty of room to transcend his own rather limited idea of what a poem can be. Some longer poems – "Winter Passage," "Stages of Solar Eclipse" – show a possible way forward.

—Robert Nye

MOFFETT, Judith. American. Born in Louisville, Kentucky, 30 August 1942. Educated at Hanover College, Indiana, 1960–64, B.A. (cum laude) 1964; Colorado State University, Fort Collins, 1964–66, M.A. in English 1966; University of Pennsylvania, Philadelphia, 1969–71, M.A. 1970, Ph.D. in American civilization 1971. Fulbright Lecturer, University of Lund, Sweden, 1967–68; Assistant Professor, Behrend College, Pennsylvania State University, Erie, 1971–75; Visiting Lecturer, Program in Creative Writing, University of Iowa, Iowa City, 1977–78. Visiting Lecturer, 1978–79, and since 1979, Assistant Professor of English, University of Pennsylvania. Recipient: Fulbright grant, 1967, 1973; American Philosophical Society grant, 1973; Swedish Institute grant, 1973, 1976; Nathhorst Foundation (Sweden) grant, 1973; Eunice Tietjens Memorial Prize, 1973, and Levinson Prize, 1976 (*Poetry*, Chicago); Borestone Mountain Poetry Award, 1976; Ingram Merrill grant, 1977; Columbia University Translation Prize, 1978. Address: 608 Meadowvale Lane, Media, Pennsylvania 19063, U.S.A.

PUBLICATIONS

Verse

Keeping Time. Baton Rouge, Louisiana State University Press, 1976.

Other

Translator, *Gentleman, Single, Refined, and Selected Poems 1937–1959* (bilingual edition), by Hjalmar Gullberg. Baton Rouge, Louisiana State University Press, 1979.

Judith Moffett comments:

As a child I was given no guidance or encouragement about poetry, but I was born into a family of Southern Baptists and heard the King James Bible read and quoted more or less daily throughout my early life, and it seems to me now that those Biblical cadences still underlie the way I hear and use language. By the age of ten or eleven I had discovered

Kipling's *Jungle Books* in the library and memorized the small poems introducing each story ("Now Chil the Kite brings home the night/That Mang the Bat set free ...") with the purest pleasure; later I happened upon, and was entranced by, Vachel Lindsay's "Ghosts of the Buffaloes"; still later it was Stephen Vincent Benét's *John Brown's Body*. With each discovery came the urge to imitate; and that was how I started trying to write poems. From the beginning, sound was valued more than sense: galloping tetrameters were what I responded to, and therefore what I tried to write. I marvel now at my best students' intuitive understanding of what poetic *language* is and does, since I grew up depending almost entirely on the surge or quietness of forms to make language into poetry.

Having come thus far on my own, I stalled for a while in graduate school. Then, in graduate school I had the tremendous luck to be James Merrill's student for half a semester, and the experience of his poetry at that time had the force of a revelation; it quite literally changed my life. Merrill showed me, by his example, how to move ahead. I could see in his work the effects I cared about most in poetry (beauty, metrical skill, narrative) cranked up to a height tremendously beyond my own reach, yet as it were on the same extension ladder: though we cared, and wrote, about quite different things, somehow the listening and controlling *ear* was much the same.

Because of this ear, at variance with the sensibilities of all but a handful of my own generation of poets, I learned only slowly and with difficulty to appreciate and then to write free verse, and still find formal verse more satisfactory in a fundamental way for much of what I want to say.

Of late I seem to use poetry more and more often to tell a story; even short lyric stanzas add up, like beads on a string, and carry a narrative line. I find also that nearly every poem I finish has what a friend has called a "ruminative" quality – that it seems appropriate to think things over in a poem – which may explain why, unlike many writers, I've never felt out of place in Academe. I have consciously worked to become more restrained in emotional expression, to imply and suggest instead of serving up great shovelsful of feelings, and also to fight clear of my earlier experiments at compressing by way of linguistic density, and have had fair success. I've also consciously tried to be briefer, but at that have done far less well. Now, in early middle life, I seem to have settled most happily (at least for the moment) into the longish local-color narrative-cum-philosophical-exploration on the one hand, and the unabashedly formal lyric on the other, with various other modes and styles thrown in from time to time. In the impulse to this I recognize a reassertion of my early, much loved, influences; but – as far as I can tell – it causes me (*pace* Harold Bloom) no anxiety. The family resemblance gives me pleasure, but what I have to say and do is different.

* * *

Few poets in her generation would undertake the stylistic balances Judith Moffett attempts: an urbane, ethical, and ultimately social tone for which the recent model is Auden and the ultimate model Horace; a range of rhyme and stanza patterns that calls attention to her considerable technical skills, her master in this respect being James Merrill; and an affection for meditative tone and autobiographical subject matter that links her to the most interesting poets of her generation. These lines from a sonnet sequence, "Now or Never," in which the woman speaker, childless in her mid-thirties, is considering if she will ever have children, are characteristic.

> They gave me in my kindergarten year
> What seemed irrelevant, an Old Maid deck.
> Gems, wrinkled skin, strange glasses on a stick,
> Long gloves, pressed lips, and horrible orange hair,
> No child, no husband ever to be hers,
> That gaunt crone wasn't anything like me!
> I got her meaning fast: *ignominy*
> *Is being single in a game of pairs.*

The benign contest between discursion and formal tension is her favorite effect, a moral as well as technical balance. She distrusts the bardic; and the merely personal, or even the very personal unconstrained by formal considerations chosen before the poem, can be self-serving. She has the learning and literary range to strike such poise; she's a Ph.D., has written an excellent book on Merrill's work, and has translated from contemporary Swedish poetry.

Her poems err sometimes towards chattiness ("I always liked even upchucky babies"). And her ability to find poetry in daily life can lead her with cries of delight to the obvious ("Now whatever I glimpse qualifies the vast"). But she is willing to risk these lapses to arrive at lines like these from "Bending The Twig," a poem about a girl who passes through puberty earlier than her peers. It builds on topics we have seldom heard discussed without smirking or melodrama, though it builds, too, on smirking and melodrama, not despising what we cling to.

> Looking older than one's age required,
> it dismayed me to learn, a decorum
> appropriate not to the real but to the apparent.

This intelligent, skillful and deceptively full-hearted poet is one of the most interesting and quietly ambitious of her generation; what she'll be able to make out of her auspicious beginnings may well be of real importance to us.

—William Matthews

MOKASHI-PUNEKAR, Shankar. Indian. Born in Dharwar, Mysore State, 8 May 1928. Educated at K.E.B.'s High School, Dharwar; K.E.B.'s Arts College; Karnatak College, Dharwar, M.A. 1953, Ph.D. 1965. Married; five children. Assistant Lecturer in English, Lingaraj College, Belgaum, 1954–56, and Kishinchand Chellaram College, Bombay, 1956–61; Principal, Sri Poornaprajna College, Udipi, 1967–68. Lecturer, 1961–69, and since 1969, Assistant Professor of English, Indian Institute of Technology, Bombay. Editor, *Jayakarnatak*, 1950–51; Music Critic, *The Times of India*, Bombay, 1965–67. Address: Department of Humanities, Indian Institute of Technology, Powai, Bombay 76, India.

PUBLICATIONS

Verse

The Captive. Bombay, Popular Prakashan, 1965.
The Pretender. Calcutta, Writers Workshop, 1967.
An Epistle to Professor David McCutchion. Calcutta, Writers Workshop, 1970.

Other

The Later Phase in the Development of W. B. Yeats: A Study in the Stream of Yeats's Later Thought and Creativity. Dharwar, Karnatak University, 1966; Folcroft, Pennsylvania, Folcroft Editions, 1977.
P. Lal: An Appreciation. Calcutta, Writers Workshop, 1968.
Indo-Anglian Creed and Allied Essays. Calcutta, Writers Workshop, 1972.

Interpretations of the Later Poems of W. B. Yeats. Dharwar, Karnatak University Press, 1973.
Vinayaka Krishna Gokak. Mysore, Institute of Kannada Studies, 1974.
Perspectives on Indian Drama in English. New Delhi, Oxford University Press, 1977.

Translator, *Ritusamharam: The Cycle of the Seasons*, by Kalidasa. Bombay, Sigma, 1966.

Books in Kannada: *Gangavva Gangamayi*, 1956; *Sri Bendre*, 1962; *Maylya Muru Mukhagalu*, 1970.

Shankar Mokashi-Punekar comments:

I am a poet cursed with a wide diversification of ability and consequent sapping of single-minded energy. I stand for proto-classical values; these involve me in controversies wherein I sometimes use verse for illustration, sometimes for mounting an attack; by and large, I am a lyricist with a high content of ratiocinative passion.

I wish to be a cosmopolitan Hindu in both theme and style, but I love to use – and wherever possible fuse – the terminology and imagery of Christian theology to express my Hindu inspiration. I am confident of selling my ideas in a decade or so.

As a lyricist, I wish not to repeat or practise any single form as a demonstration of having evolved a manner. I want each poem to be faithful to its kind. Within its kind, I try to achieve the fullest possible expression and rhythm. Unfortunately, I find that English does not have certain kinds of inspiration, and if it had them once, it has now evolved social manners which make them sound false or repellent or outmoded – ethical inspiration, bardic self-confidence, clear-cut distinction between friend and enemy (blurred by the Liberal credo), for instance. Nazism made nationalism odious to the English ear, but I cannot help being a nationalist; am I to pare myself to fit into contemporary English stereotypes? Certainly not. I prefer to remain halted, outlandish, even incommunicative; as a compensation, I try to pack my poems with thought and imagery valuable in themselves and hope for the best. I am confident of my prosody and brook no criticism on that score. The turn of my idiom has raised some controversy, but my non-British thought is bound to militate against the culture-created idiom of English. In my opinion, poetry pre-exists single poems, and no single poem can have finality. It is an index, and a good reader alone can drown the shortcomings of a poem in the poetry he can perceive. Our love makes things complete, said Yeats.

* * *

In India most of the successful poets in English come from a certain socio-economic background in the urban areas where the exposure to the English language is the most intense. In such company Shankar Mokashi-Punekar stands out as a unique and solitary voice. He is different from the others both in his attitude to the English language and in his response to life. He is a critic as well as a poet, and his two activities are not unconnected. In his criticism he puts forward entirely original and thought-provoking ideas, often taking unfashionable stands. For example, in 1967 he wrote a serious and cogent critical article on the poetry of Sarojini Naidu, when no one who read or wrote English poetry in India regarded her to be anything more than a facile versifier. He even justified her archaisms and poetic inversions on the ground that the mere existence of these devices cannot disqualify a poem from critical consideration. He does not hesitate to use such devices in his own poetry.

Mokashi-Punekar's poetry reflects what in his monograph on the poetry of P. Lal he calls "a new philosophy of English." This apparently consists of an attempt to be free from the associations that English words have for people in English-speaking countries, and a refusal to be blindly guided by the poetic standards set by someone else in another country. In his poetry this results in an occasional oddity of syntax and diction which is sometimes his strength and occasionally his weakness. His poems vary from witty epigrams, whimsical ballads and sonnets to dramatic monologues, sketches combining prose and poetry, and long poems of philosophic reflections. The general impression is that of a poet whose imagination is verbal and cerebral rather than visual. His poems are often interspersed with literary and academic references, but his most memorable poem, "The Pioneers-II," is remarkably free of these.

Apart from being a critic and a poet in English Mokashi-Punekar is also a translator. His translation from Sanskrit poetry has a deliberate quaintness achieved through the use of rhyme, inversions and outmoded words such as "lass" and "affrighted." One may question the validity of such usage in a modern translation, but Mokashi-Punekar translates, as he does everything else, with such total conviction in matters of principle that no one can take his work casually.

—Meenakshi Mukherjee

MOLE, John. British. Born in Taunton, Somerset, 12 October 1941. Educated at King's School, Bruton, Somerset; Magdalene College, Cambridge, 1961–64, B.A. (honours) in English 1964, M.A. Married Mary Norman in 1968; two sons. English Teacher, Haberdashers' Aske's School, Elstree, Hertfordshire, 1964–73; Exchange Teacher, Riverdale Country School, New York 1969–70. Since 1973, Chairman of the English Department, Verulam School, Hertfordshire. Editor, with Peter Scupham, Cellar Press, and Mandeville Press, Hitchin, Hertfordshire. Recipient: Eric Gregory Award, 1970. Address: 11 Hill Street, St. Albans, Hertfordshire, England.

PUBLICATIONS

Verse

A Feather for Memory. London, Outposts, 1961.
The Instruments. Manchester, Phoenix Pamphlet Poets Press, 1970.
Something about Love. Oxford, Sycamore Press, 1972.
The Love Horse. Manchester, E. J. Morten, 1974.
Landscapes. Berkhamsted, Hertfordshire, Priapus Press, 1975.
A Partial Light. London, Dent, 1975.
The Mortal Room. Berkhamsted, Hertfordshire, Priapus Press, 1977.
The Tales of Rover. Hitchin, Hertfordshire, Mandeville Press, 1977.
Our Ship. London, Secker and Warburg, 1977.
On the Set. Richmond, Surrey, Keepsake Press, 1978.
From the House Opposite. London, Secker and Warburg, 1979.
Once There Were Dragons (juvenile), with Mary Norman. London, Deutsch, 1979.

Other

Understanding Children Writing, with others. London, Penguin, 1973.

Manuscript Collection: State University of New York, Buffalo.

John Mole comments:

Apart from the routine essays, I didn't write much at school except for deeply purple prose in our true-blue magazine. I preferred novels, and, as for poetry, I was more concerned to know about it than to read it; I was, at least, aware that there was something intellectually distinguished about claiming an interest in *modern* poetry – anyone could read novels, but I went on reading them. Then, one Sunday in 1960, I picked up the "Review" section of the *Observer* and noticed a front page spread of poems by Robert Graves called "Symptoms of Love." I began reading, casually, became disconcertingly excited, and by the time I had finished the sequence I knew that I wanted to write poetry. Robert Graves wasn't an unfamiliar name to me; after all, he wrote novels – but what was this? So off I went and fashioned lapidary love poems with titles like "Prodigal Daughter," "Bard in Exile" etc. (see my first pamphlet in the Outposts series). I sent them to Graves who was, at that time, Professor of Poetry at Oxford and he said kind things; he even rewrote the closing lines of one of them in order to tighten up the syntax. It was important to get the shape right; mere feeling, as a later Oxford professor remarked, was too easy. I was hooked. Swinburne had kissed the baby Graves while he was still in his pram, and now Graves had corrected my syntax. The line was clear. I belonged.

Since then, I have gone on writing and come, increasingly (I hope), to belong to myself. I find poetry very difficult to talk about except in terms of my shifting enthusiasm for different poets and my permanent concern for patterning and craftsmanship. I enjoy what W. H. Auden calls "hanging around language" and there's usually some verbal sport going on in my most overtly "serious" poems whether it be called syllables or manipulating couplets. I don't believe that counting and manipulating, mathematical or geometric though they may sound, squeeze out feeling; I think they squeeze it *in*. In general, I hope that the best of my work may be memorable and capable of moving my readers. Anything else to be said about it must be said by others if they will.

* * *

Wit is not a word that figures much in recent critical writing, because, perhaps, it expresses a quality of sharpness of intellect that does not occur much in recent poetry. Yet it is the word which comes first to mind when discussing the work of John Mole. This is not just because John Mole has written humorous poetry, such as his longish jazz poems and the delightful adaptations of Robert Desnos's "Chantefables," where the pleasure they give is derived from the display of technical high jinks, as in "The Owls":

Mother owls make beau-
tiful mothers, a few
might brew more nourishing mouse stew
than they do,
but most of them muddle through

It is because the mind behind and the intellectual pressure driving all John Mole's work is what distinguishes it, the poems impinging on us through the impetus of their logical progression. In the poems contained in his latest collection, *From the House Opposite*, we find more and more the wit and the humour progressing towards penetrating observations of the human situation. The justly celebrated "The Tales of Rover" is a case in point, and even a seemingly light poem, "Bestial Homilies," ends "Be warned by Nature not to let things go –/ The animals prepare to say: We told you so" – and a certain menace shows through the jokey surface.

In his domestic poems, "Not Flouring Pastry" and "Wife," for example, the same technical astuteness allows the expression of a compassionate understanding of everyday marital scenes under which tick the timebombs of passion: "Strange I feel it/Grow unhomely." And often the seemingly straightforwardly and clearly defined everyday scenes possess a disturbingly Magritte-like quality of mystery: "the rain of course/still falls as it should/ which is not on them" ("The Mirror"), where the "extraordinarily safe castle" (of the epigraph from Ford Madox Ford which John Mole puts on the title page of *From the House Opposite*) is not at all so.

"Depths" seems to me a key poem to John Mole's work: a poem which deals directly with what is basic to the theme of his serious work, and a poem which states prophetically:

> Such a depth
> Is fearful, nothing moves
> But thoughts of what may start there
> Even at this moment
> Coming up.

—John Cotton

MONTAGUE, John (Patrick). Irish. Born in Brooklyn, New York, 28 February 1929. Educated at St. Patrick's College, Armagh; University College, Dublin, B.A. in English and history 1949, M.A. 1952; Yale University, New Haven, Connecticut (Fulbright Scholar), 1953–54; University of Iowa, Iowa City, M.F.A. 1955. Worked for State Tourist Board, Dublin, 1956–61; taught at the Poetry Workshop, University of California, Berkeley, Spring 1964 and 1965, University College, Dublin, Spring and Summer 1967, and Spring 1968, and the Experimental University of Vincennes. Currently, Lecturer in Poetry, University College, Cork. Recipient: Arts Council of Northern Ireland grant, 1970; Irish American Cultural Institute prize, 1976; Marten Toonder award, 1977. Member, Irish Academy of Letters. Address: Department of English, University College, Cork, Ireland.

PUBLICATIONS

Verse

Forms of Exile. Dublin, Dolmen Press, 1958.
The Old People. Dublin, Dolmen Press, 1960.
Poisoned Lands and Other Poems. London, MacGibbon and Kee, 1961; Chester Springs, Pennsylvania, Dufour, 1963.
Six Irish Poets, with others, edited by Robin Skelton. London, Oxford University Press, 1962.
All Legendary Obstacles. Dublin, Dolmen Press, 1966.
A Chosen Light. London, MacGibbon and Kee, 1967; Chicago, Swallow Press, 1969.
The Rough Field. Dublin, Dolmen Press, and London, Oxford University Press, 1972.
  Patriotic Suite. Dublin, Dolmen Press, 1966.
  Home Again. Belfast, Festival, 1967.
  Hymn to the New Omagh Road. Dublin, Dolmen Press, 1968.
  The Bread God: A Lecture, with Illustrations in Verse. Dublin, Dolmen Press, 1968.
  A New Siege. Dublin, Dolmen Press, 1969.
The Planter and the Gael, with John Hewitt. Belfast, Arts Council of Northern Ireland, 1970.
Tides. Dublin, Dolmen Press, 1970; Chicago, Swallow Press, 1971.
Small Secrets. London, Poem-of-the-Month Club, 1972.
The Cave of Night. Cork, Golden Stone Press, 1974.
O'Riada's Farewell. Cork, Golden Stone Press, 1975.

A Slow Dance. Dublin, Dolmen Press, 1975.
The Great Cloak. Dublin, Dolmen Press, 1978.

Recording: *The Northern Muse*, with Seamus Heaney, Claddagh, 1968.

Play

The Rough Field (produced London, 1973).

Short Stories

Death of a Chieftain and Other Stories. London, MacGibbon and Kee, 1964; Chester Springs, Pennsylvania, Dufour, 1967.

Other

Editor, *The Dolmen Miscellany of Irish Writing.* Dublin, Dolmen Press, 1962.
Editor, with Liam Miller, *A Tribute to Austin Clarke on His Seventieth Birthday, 9 May 1966.* Dublin, Dolmen Press, and Chester Springs, Pennsylvania, Dufour, 1966.
Editor, *The Faber Book of Irish Verse.* London, Faber, 1974; as *The Book of Irish Verse*, New York, Macmillan, 1977.

Translator, *A Fair House: Versions of Irish Poetry.* Dublin, Cuala Press, 1973.
Translator, with Evelyn Robson, *November*, by André Frénaud. Cork, Golden Stone Press, 1977.

Critical Studies: *The New Poetry* by M. L. Rosenthal, New York and London, Oxford University Press, 1967; by John MacInerney, in *Hibernia* (Dublin), 15 December 1972; D. S. Maxwell, in *Critical Quarterly* (London), Summer 1973; Derek Mahon, in *Malahat Review* (Victoria, British Columbia), July 1973; Thomas Dillon Redshaw, in *Studies* (Dublin), Spring 1974; *John Montague* by Frank Kersnowski, Lewisburg, Pennsylvania, Bucknell University Press, 1975.

John Montague comments:

I am usually classed as an Irish poet and that is true insofar as I am deeply involved with the landscape and people of Ireland, particularly Ulster. In Gaelic poetry, Ireland appears both as a maiden and a hag, a sort of national muse, and her hold is still strong, especially now that her distinctive culture is being submerged. But underneath these tribal preoccupations beats a more personal struggle, the effort to affirm lovingly, to salvage some order, in the face of death and change. The technique is a blend of post-modern (Williams and Pound) and old Gaelic poetry, which could also be regarded as an aspect of nationality, for an Irish poet (following Joyce, Yeats, Beckett) has a better chance of being international than an English writer. But my effort to understand as much of the modern world as possible serves only to illuminate the destruction of that small area from which I initially came, and that theme in turn is only part of the larger one of continually threatened love. We must warn and warm ourselves against a new ice age.

* * *

There is something tight-lipped about John Montague's poetry, revealed even in the terse titles of his volumes and the repeated use of a short, abrupt line, where enjambment projects the reader into sudden peripeties and reversals, and the shifts of pace and meaning have the effect of a clipped, curt rebuff. Yet, within these constraints, the poetry can flower into an unexpected, lyric generosity. Not many poets, for example, could carry off successfully the Anglo-Saxon bluntness of "Love, A Greeting" (*Tides*):

> a lifetime's
> struggle to exchange
> with the strange
> thing inhabiting
> a woman –
>   face,
> breasts, buttocks,
> the honey sac
> of the cunt....

It's the puritanical tautness of his speech that can bring off such large gestures. Constriction is Montague's native ground, as "Home Again" admits:

> Lost in our separate work
> We meet at dusk in the narrow lane.
> I press back against a tree
> To let him pass, but he brakes
> Against our double loneliness
> With: "So you're home again."

Such narrowness runs as a theme throughout Montague's work, an expression of that bare past and "bleak economic future" shared, as he has written, by all such peripheral and remote areas of Europe as Ulster, Brittany, the Highlands. It's this which marks him out clearly as one of the "Ulster school" of poets, despite the casual displacement of his Brooklyn birth. The "narrow huckster streets" of Belfast, "All this dour, despoiled inheritance," together with the heritage of sectarian hatred, in "a culture where constraint is all," have a precise, economic origin: "narrow fields wrought such division." The "Rough Field" which gives the title to one of his major collections is not just a translation of the Gaelic name for his native village, but – in the words of an Afghan proverb which provides his epigraph – the summary of an historical destiny: "I had never known sorrow,/Now it is a field I have inherited, and I till it." This in turn, in "The Bread God," he sees reproduced in "the lean parish of my art." Deracination is a major theme for Montague, from his first volume, *Forms of Exile*, through to his latest collection, ostensibly of love lyrics, *The Great Cloak*.

"A Lost Tradition," in *The Rough Field*, laments the physical expropriation that goes with the loss of the Gaelic, which no amount of "school Irish" can compensate for: "The whole landscape a manuscript/We had lost the skill to read,/A part of our past disinherited." And the whole volume explores the consequences of this uprooting, spanning several hundred years of Irish history, while always relating the public events to the particular lives of individual men and families, including his own forebears. "A Grafted Tongue" sees the linguistic loss not just as a metaphor for this larger dispossession, but its key event: "To grow/a second tongue, as/harsh a humiliation/as twice to be born." "Lament for the O'Neills" and "Stele for a Northern Republican" indicate that the loss is one which lies close to the heart of both communities in the North. The latter poem unsentimentally, but with bitterness, acknowledges his own father's "right to choose a Brooklyn slum/rather than a half-life in this/by-passed and dying place."

In *A Slow Dance* Montague moves away from history into the shadowier realms of Celtic myth to explain the current violence of the North, resurrecting that ancient "Black widow goddess" whose "love-making/is like a skirmish" and who wears "a harvest necklace of heads." The move brings with it a loss of precisely that kind of acute historical particularity which distinguishes his best verse, but it remains nevertheless an impressive volume. The "slow dance" of the title unites human and elemental cycles, pagan and Christian Ireland in a ritual return to origins, where fertility and massacre are intimately linked. But it is, finally, the "sad awkward/dance of pain" of all the living upon the graves of all the dead, and its most moving sequence, perhaps, is the intense and personal elegy for his close friend, the composer O'Riada, who died in 1971.

The love poems of *The Great Cloak* return to the lucid, melodic airs of *Tides* and *A Chosen Light*, but the atmosphere has been darkened by the intervening, public violence, which now finds its correlative in personal life. These poems are as much concerned with loss, jealousy, marital breakdown and its humiliations and shames, as with the lyric celebration of love – "that always strange moment/when the clothes peel away/(bark from an unknown tree)" ("Do Not Disturb"). The violence spoken of as inseparable from love in such a fine early poem as "The Same Gesture" (*Tides*) is now felt more urgently, and as a greater threat. Only briefly, in the sequence of poems which explore the consciousness of the estranged wife, is any connection explicitly acknowledged between personal disintegration and the larger violence of the North ("She Writes"). But, throughout, Montague is groping towards a new understanding of the interdependence of the personal and the political, and their common roots in a harsh and souring history. Such a quest can bring him desperately close to the unspeakable, to silence, shamefaced and appalled, as "No Music" recognizes:

To tear up old love by the roots,
To trample on past affections:
There is no music for so harsh a song.

—Stan Smith

MOORE, Nicholas. British. Born in Cambridge, 16 November 1918; son of the philosopher G. E. Moore. Educated at Dragon School, Oxford; Leighton Park School, Reading; Trinity College, Cambridge, B.A. Married 1) Priscilla Patience Craig (marriage dissolved), one daughter; 2) Shirley Putnam in 1953, one son and one daughter (died). Editor, *Seven*, 1938–40, and *New Poetry*, 1944–45; Editorial Assistant, Editions Poetry London. Has held jobs in horticulture, and written horticultural journalism. Recipient: Patrons Prize (*Contemporary Poetry*, Baltimore), 1945; Harriet Monroe Memorial Prize (*Poetry*, Chicago), 1947. Address: 89 Oakdene Road, St. Mary Cray, Kent BR5 2AL, England.

PUBLICATIONS

Verse

A Wish in Season: Poems. London, Fortune Press, 1941.
The Island and the Cattle. London, Fortune Press, 1941.
A Book for Priscilla. Cambridge, Epsilon Pamphlets, 1941.
Buzzing Around with a Bee and Other Poems. London, Poetry (London), 1941.
The Cabaret, The Dancer, The Gentleman. London, Fortune Press, 1942.
The Glass Tower: Poems 1936–43. London, Editions Poetry London, 1944.
Three Poems, with Fred Marnau and Wrey Gardiner. London, Grey Walls Press, 1944.
Thirty-five Anonymous Odes. London, Fortune Press, 1944.
The War of the Little Jersey Cows: Poems by Guy Kelly. London, Fortune Press, 1945.
Recollections of the Gala: Selected Poems, 1943–1948. London, Editions Poetry London, 1950.

Identity. London, Cadenza Press, 1969.
Resolution and Identity. London, Covent Garden Press, 1970.
Spleen: Thirty-One Versions of Baudelaire's "Je Suis Comme le Roi." London, Black Suede Boot Press, 1973.

Other

Henry Miller. Wigginton, Hertfordshire, The Opus Press, 1943; Folcroft, Pennsylvania, Folcroft Editions, 1969.
The Tall Bearded Iris. London, Collingridge, and New York, Transatlantic Arts, 1956.

Editor, with John Bayliss and Douglas Newton, *The Fortune Anthology.* London, Fortune Press, 1942.
Editor, *The P L Book of Modern American Short Stories.* London, Editions Poetry London, 1945.
Editor, with Douglas Newton, *Atlantic Anthology.* London, Fortune Press, 1945.

Critical Studies: "The Glass Tower" by Kenneth Gee, in *The New English Weekly* (London), 10 May 1945; G. W. Stonier, in *The New Statesman* (London), 1945; "The Poetry of Nicholas Moore" by G. S. Fraser, in *Poetry Quarterly 9* (London), 1947; Preface by Kenneth Rexroth to *New British Poets*, New York, New Directions, 1949; "Nicholas Moore: A Problem Poet" by Margaret Crosland, in *Poetry Quarterly 14* (London), Spring 1952.

Nicholas Moore comments:

Writing in *The Spectator* on January 8th, 1943, Sheila Shannon wrote, in a review of "Some New Poets" as follows: "But too many of the poets under review here write poems as the result of their education; too few of them use any but a single sense at a time in conjunction with the mind. It was with delight and relief that, after much reading, I came across Nicholas Moore's poem in *Poetry Folios.* It is poetry written by a man functioning in all his senses and having a mind and an imagination equal to the tasks of conception and construction. Moore has sensibility; he has great sense of enjoyment; he can be witty and gentle; he can also be silly and trivial, which is the result of an unusual and refreshing exuberance."

Whether I deserve this or not, of course, I don't know, but it does represent, in part at least, what I would like to be true.

So, too, with "In much of Moore's writing there is a sense of justice, a morality that refuses to have anything to do with any morality bespoken by rulers or bewildered crowds," or, "but Mr. Moore is really a reflective poet, his best poems take their shape and movement from his thought, and grow with it; in the later poems in this book, his consciousness has a greater range, and the words of the poems bring to life other words and ideas that are not on the page but are discovered in reading. He is a civilized poet who has much to say, and to say well, against the evils of his civilization.... He can also write with some faith and hope which one feels to be real," from Kenneth Gee; and G. W. Stonier's "the intricacy of workmanship makes one want to reject one meaning for another more intricate; or we turn the poem over feelingly like a scarab," and "I should like to emphasize Mr. Moore's accomplishment in these various phases. Nevertheless, the poems which appeal most are those in which vividness of phrase is matched by vividness of idea.... It comes naturally to him to see sharply and form patterns, and an epigrammatic gaiety is one of the surprises of his talent."

Some of these comments might seem to be mutually exclusive; but that, really, is the point. Victoria Sackville-West in another review (of *Three Poems*) described me as "slightly surrealist." At that time, I thought this a silly comment, but now on reflection I'm not sure that most of the poems of mine I like best myself are not "slightly surrealist."

I do not consider myself a romantic – though I have written some romantic poems – "Ode to Sexual Beauty" and "The Aquatic Stag" for instance – because that seemed appropriate to the particular theme, or particular time and place. In its early days I was associated with The New Apocalypse movement, and contributed to *The White Horseman.* But once it started calling itself – or was it Herbert Read who called it? – The New Romanticism, I was out of sympathy. My own personal tastes – in poetry – were more for the Southern group of writers in America, particularly Ransom and John Peale Bishop, and for the Metaphysicals (Donne, Herbert, Vaughan), and the Elizabethans: Shakespeare, of course; Marlowe; Webster; and especially Ralegh and Fulke Greville.

In other words, I believed – and do believe – in a poetry of greater universality and width of range than any narrow categorising can encompass.

* * *

In the nineteen-forties Nicholas Moore was well known as a talented and prolific poet, whose work appeared frequently in little magazines and anthologies. He published several collections, of which the most substantial were *The Glass Tower* and *Recollections of the Gala.* But after the apperance of the latter volume Moore appeared to stop writing completely, and this silence was broken only in the late sixties, when he once more began to contribute verse to literary reviews.

Nicholas Moore's origins in the late nineteen-thirties are evident in the prevalent influence of Auden, and particularly of Auden's songs and light verse. Moore picked up and carried on Auden's talent for the mellifluous but slightly cerebral lyric. Other influences were Blake, notably the "Songs of Innocence and Experience," and, most interestingly, Wallace Stevens. Moore read and admired Stevens many years before he became a prominent and even fashionable poet; indeed, Stevens was almost wholly unknown in England in the nineteen-forties, when Moore was paying him the tribute of deliberate imitation in a poem such as "Ideas of Disorder at Torquay." From Stevens Moore acquired a flowing music and a deliberate rhetoric that stiffened the colloquial thirties manner and the throwaway wit. Moore's poems of the early forties were sometimes excessively fluent, with a suggestion of more manner than matter. But *Recollections of the Gala* is a very accomplished collection which represents Moore's poetry at its best, variously fantastic, sardonic and lyrical. His most recent work is as adroit and witty as ever; particularly in *Spleen*, a set of thirty-one versions of a famous Baudelaire poem, which provides a series of dazzling variations on a theme.

—Bernard Bergonzi

MORAES, Dom(inic Frank). British. Born in Bombay, India, 19 July 1938, son of Frank Moraes, editor of the *India Express.* Educated at Jesus College, Oxford, B.A. 1959. Married 1) Judith St. John in 1963 (marriage dissolved), one son; 2) Leslie Naidu in 1970. Formerly, Scriptwriter, Granada Television, and documentary film-maker. Since 1972, Editor, *The Asian Magazine*, Hong Kong. Recipient: Hawthornden Prize, 1958.

PUBLICATIONS

Verse

A Beginning. London, Parton Press, 1957.
Poems. London, Eyre and Spottiswoode, 1960.

Penguin Modern Poets 2, with Kingsley Amis and Peter Porter. London, Penguin, 1962.
John Nobody. London, Eyre and Spottiswoode, 1965.
Poems 1955–1965. New York, Macmillan, 1966.
Bedlam Etcetera. London, Turret, 1966.

Other

Green Is the Grass (on cricket). Bombay, Asia Publishing House, 1951.
Gone Away: An Indian Journal. London, Heinemann, and Boston, Little Brown, 1960.
My Son's Father: An Autobiography. London, Secker and Warburg, 1968; as *My Son's Father: A Poet's Autobiography*, New York, Macmillan, 1969.
The Tempest Within: An Account of East Pakistan. New York, Barnes and Noble, 1971.
From East and West: A Collection of Essays. New Delhi, Vikas, 1971.
A Matter of People. London, Deutsch, and New York, Praeger, 1974.
The Open Eyes: A Journey Through Karnataka. Bangalore, Government of Karnataka, 1976.

Editor, *Voices for Life: Reflections on the Human Condition*. New York, Praeger, 1975.

Translator, *The Brass Serpent*, by T. Carmi. London, Deutsch, 1964.

* * *

Amongst Indian poets writing in English today perhaps the best-known is Dom Moraes. It is true that neither in his themes nor in his imagery, neither in the landscape of his poetry nor in his references and allusions is there anything distinctively Indian; but this does not matter much since "Indianness," whatever it may be, is not a poetic virtue *per se*. Moraes's first book of poems, *A Beginning*, published when he was only 19, won the Hawthornden Prize and brought him immediate fame; he was the first non-English poet to win it.

What distinguishes Moraes among Indian poets is his powerful organic sensibility, a very skilful use of words in metrical and verse-patterns, a striking imagery and an authentic personal experience. His difficulty at the moment seems to be that he has not as yet found any convincingly felt solution of his personal problems. This is a difficulty which is almost inevitable in the early poetry of a young poet who is honest, sincere and individual. As a result of this difficulty, however, the style of some of his poems tends to overweigh "the idea." For example, in "Vivisection" (*John Nobody*) the "virgin" (modern version) betrays her own deepest instincts and kills the "unicorn" (original version). The sustained imagery of the poem does not breathe any new life into the commonplace conclusion. Similarly in "The General" (*John Nobody*) the poet speaks of the dilemma of living in a world of horror and violence in which the attitude of neither "the anchorite" nor "the clown" is appropriate – both of them are killed – and there seems to be no permanent escape from contingent becoming into pure being; the elaborate set-up of the story of these poems is hardly justified by the fairly simple conclusions and emotional dilemmas of the poet's situation. The machinery (myths, references, allusions, etc.) is quite often excessive for the jobs that the poet plans. The poet does not always achieve creative mastery of his personal experience. We get to know that he is deeply "troubled" and is searching for solutions. There is an intimation that he accepts life and love and the necessity of struggle against the evil in oneself. Considering the gifts of the poet, it is reasonable to expect that this intimation will obtain convincing poetic realization in due course of time.

Not all the poems, however, suffer from this incompleteness. There are many poems in which the aim and scope of the poet are "impersonal" and these succeed very well. Such for instance are "Figures in the Landscape" (*A Beginning*), "Kanheri Caves" (*A Beginning*) and "Melancholy Prince" (*John Nobody*). In "Figures in the Landscape" the poet re-interprets the story of the Pied Piper to suggest the trustfulness and innocence of the children and the Piper's betrayal – of which he is aware – of that trust. The poem on the Kanheri Caves re-creates in clear sharp detail the poetic impression of the caves and makes skilful use of the scientific hypothesis of evolution and Keats's reference to "stout Cortez" to intimate the cyclic nature of life and civilization; the poem is also an excellent illustration of Moraes's command of word-music. "Melancholy Prince" may not say anything fresh or original about *Hamlet* – hard task to do so – but it conveys admirably the tragedy of Ophelia and the peculiar atmosphere of the play. It is in these comparatively "public" poems that Moraes has greater variety of interest and success to offer than in his purely "personal" poems. He has been deeply concerned of late with public issues such as racial segregation in England, and we may expect him to modulate what he has himself recognized as "a small whimper" and attempt a larger mode without losing his individuality of response and style.

—S. Nagarajan

MORGAN, Edwin (George). Scottish. Born in Glasgow, 27 April 1920. Educated at Rutherglen Academy; Glasgow High School; Glasgow University, 1937–40, 1946–47, M.A. 1947. Served in the Royal Army Medical Corps, 1940–46. Assistant Lecturer, 1947–50, Lecturer, 1950–65, Senior Lecturer, 1965–71, Reader, 1971–75, and since 1975, Titular Professor in English, Glasgow University. Recipient: Cholmondeley Award, 1968; Scottish Arts Council award, 1969, 1973, 1975, 1977, 1978; Hungarian P.E.N. Memorial Medal, 1972. Address: 19 Whittingehame Court, Glasgow G12 0BG, Scotland.

PUBLICATIONS

Verse

The Vision of Cathkin Braes. Glasgow, Maclellan, 1952.
The Cape of Good Hope. Tunbridge Wells, Kent, Peter Russell, 1955.
Starryveldt. Frauenfeld, Switzerland, Gomringer Press, 1965.
Scotch Mist. Cleveland, Renegade Press, 1965.
Sealwear. Glasgow, Gold Seal Press, 1966.
Emergent Poems. Stuttgart, Hansjörg Mayer, 1967.
The Second Life. Edinburgh, Edinburgh University Press, 1968.
Gnomes. Preston, Lancashire, Akros, 1968.
Proverbfolder. Corsham, Wiltshire, Openings Press, 1969.
Penguin Modern Poets 15, with Alan Bold and Edward Brathwaite. London, Penguin, 1969.
The Horseman's Word: A Sequence of Concrete Poems. Preston, Lancashire, Akros, 1970.
Twelve Songs. West Linton, Peeblesshire, Castlelaw Press, 1970.
The Dolphin's Song. Leeds, School of English Press, 1971.
Glasgow Sonnets. West Linton, Peeblesshire, Castlelaw Press, 1972.
Instamatic Poems. London, Ian McKelvie, 1972.
The Whittrick: A Poem in Eight Dialogues. Preston, Lancashire, Akros, 1973.
From Glasgow to Saturn. Cheadle, Cheshire, Carcanet Press, and Chester Springs, Pennsylvania, Dufour, 1973.
The New Divan. Manchester, Carcanet Press, 1977.
Colour Poems. Glasgow, Third Eye Centre, 1978.

Other

Essays. Cheadle, Cheshire, Carcanet Press, 1975.
Rites of Passage: Selected Translations. Manchester, Carcanet Press, 1975.
Hugh MacDiarmid. London, Longman, 1976.
East European Poets. Milton Keynes, Buckinghamshire, Open University Press, 1976.
Provenance and Problematics of "Sublime and Alarming Images" in Poetry. London, British Academy, 1977.

Editor, *Collins Albatross Book of Longer Poems: English and American Poetry from the Fourteenth Century to the Present Day*. London, Collins, 1963.
Editor, with George Bruce and Maurice Lindsay, *Scottish Poetry One* to *Six*. Edinburgh, Edinburgh University Press, 1966–72.
Editor, *New English Dramatists 14*. London, Penguin, 1970.

Translator, *Beowulf*. Aldington, Kent, Hand and Flower Press, 1952; Berkeley, University of California Press, 1962.
Translator, *Poems from Eugenio Montale*. Reading, Berkshire, University of Reading School of Art, 1959.
Translator, *Sovpoems: Brecht, Neruda, Pasternak, Tsvetayeva, Mayakovsky, Martynov, Yevtushenko*. Worcester, Migrant Press, 1961.
Translator, with David Wevill, *Sándor Weöres and Ferenc Juhász: Selected Poems*. London, Penguin, 1970.
Translator, *Wi the Haill Voice: Poems by Mayakovsky*. Oxford, Carcanet Press, 1972.
Translator, *Fifty Renascence Love-Poems*, edited by Ian Fletcher. Reading, Berkshire, Whiteknights Press, 1975.
Translator, *Selected Poems*, by Platen. West Linton, Peeblesshire, Castlelaw Press, 1978.

Manuscript Collection: National Library of Scotland, Edinburgh.

Critical Studies: by Tom Buchan, in *Scottish International* (Edinburgh), August 1968; "Scottish Poets: Edwin Morgan and Iain Crichton Smith" by Robin Fulton, in *Stand* (Newcastle upon Tyne), x, 4, 1969; *Worlds: Seven Modern Poets*, London, Penguin, 1974; *Contemporary Scottish Poetry* by Robin Fulton, Edinburgh, M. Macdonald, 1974; J. A. M. Rillie, in *Lines Review* (Edinburgh), March 1976.

* * *

One aspect of Edwin Morgan's inherent Scottishness is the extent and penetration of his versatility. His themes, and his various treatments of them, range widely; some might say almost too widely, distracting him from following his most successful approaches through. He has written movingly of the decline of Glasgow and the plight of the underprivileged. He has experimented across poetry's borderlines with music and the visual arts. At the same time, he has never been afraid of humour for its own sake.

He was thirty-two when his first paper-back collection was published, *The Vision of Cathin Braes*. There is thus no published Morgan juvenilia. He stakes out his territories in that first collection. In the title poem, for instance, the poet and his love strolled to Cathkin Braes, near Glasgow, there to encounter an imaginary company that includes "Gaunt Jenny Geddes, the Minister's delight ... McGonagal ... a figure somewhat comical," as well as "Knox, Laureen Bacall, Wordsworth and St. Mungo Park." Already, there is the characteristic balance of irony and wit on an exact edge of vocabulary. Already, too, his "Verses for a Christmas Card" show him the amusing master of word-play: "O angellighthoused harbourmorn/ Glazegulfgalexal governoon/Jovegal allenpellor jupiterror...." Here he is employing a device also used with originality in Sydney Goodsir Smith's prose fantasy *Carotid Cornucopius*, Joyce being their common source of inspiration.

Morgan's first major collection, *The Second Life*, contained moving Glasgow-orientated poems like "King Billy," "Glasgow Green," "In a Snack Bar," and brilliantly funny take-offs like "Starlings in George Square," the targets in this case being the gentle deflation of pomposity.

> The City Chambers are hopping mad.
> Councillors with rubber plugs in their ears!
> Secretaries closing windows!
> Window-cleaners want protection and danger-money.
> The Lord Provost can't hear herself think, man
> What's that?
> Lord Provost can't hear herself think.
>
> At the General Post Office
> The clerks write Three Pounds starling in
> the savings-books.
> Each telephone booth is like an aviary.

Morgan's usual method, like Whitman's, is to build up in free verse paragraphs of precise imagery generating a gathering rhetoric.

His second major volume, *From Glasgow to Saturn*, included his powerful Glasgow sonnet-sequence and more of the time-space-exploration poems with which he had already experimented. The title poem in *The New Divan* puzzled some critics, who sought a through-meaning holding together its hundred sections. Based on the *Divan*, or collection of poems, by the Persian poet Hafiz (and, perhaps, with a thought of Goethe's *West-Oestliche Divan* in mind), this book presents a series of subtle and sensuous variations set in a timeless imaginary Near-Eastern context, on a theme outlined in sections 1 and 2, when the "old nightingale," Hafiz, is invoked and the poet's muse instructed: "Go then, dance yourself into the masks." And what a variety of masks Morgan dons, using them to reveal subtle insights into the nature of reality! There are other interesting poems in this book, including some experimental word-play, necessarily slight, and almost the only passable poem ever written to that much mythologised socialist hero-figure, John MacLean, in which, characteristically, Morgan reminds us: " 'We are out/for life and all that life can give us'/was what he said, that's what he said."

Among his other gifts, Morgan excels as a translator, or re-creator. Unlike the versions of foreign poets by Robert Lowell, those by Morgan capture the "feel" of the original, not simply a mirror-image of his own style. This is true whether he is rendering the Anglo-Saxon of *Beowulf*, or turning Mayakovsky into Scots, or capturing the subtle nuances of Montale, or the classical sadness of Von Platen-Hallermünde. The anthology of his re-creations, *Rites of Passage*, bears eloquent testimony to the quality of this all too rare secondary skill.

In the title poem of *The Second Life*, the poet declares: "Many things are unspoken/in the life of a man, and with a place/there is an unspoken love also/in the undercurrents, drifting, waiting in time." Morgan's achievement has been to make articulate something of that love, those undercurrents, both in his own finest poems and in many of the poems of others he has chosen to recreate, in English or Scots. He has given us some of the most memorable verse to come out of 20th-century Scotland.

—Maurice Lindsay

MORGAN, (George) Frederick. American. Born in New York City, 25 April 1922. Educated at St. Bernard's School, New York, 1927–35; St. Paul's School, Concord, New Hampshire, 1935–39; Princeton University, New Jersey, 1939–43, A.B. 1943. Served as a Staff Sergeant in the United States Army Tank Destroyer Corps, 1943–45. Married 1) Constance Canfield in 1942 (divorced), six children (one deceased); 2) Rose Fillmore in 1957 (divorced); 3) Paula Deitz in 1969. Founder, with Joseph Bennett and William Arrowsmith, and since 1947, Editor, *Hudson Review*, New York. Since 1974, Chairman of the Advisory Council, Department of Romance Languages and Literatures, Princeton University. Address: c/o The Hudson Review, 65 East 55th Street, New York, New York 10022, U.S.A.

PUBLICATIONS

Verse

A Book of Change. New York, Scribner, 1972.
Poems of the Two Worlds. Urbana, University of Illinois Press, 1977.
Death Mother and Other Poems. Urbana, University of Illinois Press, 1979.

Other

The Tarot of Cornelius Agrippa. Sand Lake, New York, Sagarin Press, 1978.

Editor, *The Hudson Review Anthology.* New York, Random House, 1961.
Editor, *The Modern Image: Outstanding Stories from "The Hudson Review."* New York, Norton, 1965.

Critical Studies: "The Shocks of Normality" by Laurence Lieberman, in *Yale Review* (New Haven, Connecticut), Spring 1974; "The Poetry of Frederick Morgan" by Hayden Carruth, in *New Republic* (Washington, D.C.), 15 May 1976; "Poet's View" by Thomas Lask, in *New York Times*, 15 April 1977; Chad Walsh, in *Washington Post*, 22 May 1977; "Recent American Poetry" by Andrew Waterman, in *PN Review 8* (Manchester), 1978; interview in *New England Review* (Hanover, New Hampshire), Spring 1979.

* * *

Of the various strains in Frederick Morgan's poetry, two predominate: the legendary-fabulous and the celebratory-consolatory. In addition, he has a number of fanciful and whimsical poems, personal poems in various modes – nostalgic memories, grateful love songs to his wife, companionable conversations with his children – and thoughtful poems that explore the natural world and man's place in it.

In its purest form, the legendary-fabulous is the mode of *The Tarot of Cornelius Agrippa*, a set of 22 little fables of rogues, sorceresses, magicians, kings, queens, princesses, and other animate and inanimate denizens of fairyland and the Tarot pack. The fables are cast as prose poems, but in very loose rhythms and the unsophisticated language of children's stories. Indeed, Morgan's images for the imaginative and religious projections of adult sensibility often have the simplicity and naivety of a child's vision:

> Child, you will die; but between that breath and this –
> now at this moment, unless you put her off –
> eternity outspreads her glittering fields
> where animals play and rivers dance in the sun:
> mostly invisible to the time-bent mind....

The 21st poem of *A Book of Change*, from which these lines are taken, is in what I am calling the celebratory-consolatory mode. Morgan is engaged in such poems with deep emotional and spiritual issues – here the paradise within, informed by the "glowing, sacred center." Further, he is committed to *sharing* his insights into life, death, love, time, a spiritualized natural world, eternity, and God in the commendable hope that such insights will help us with our own perplexities and sorrows. Given his personal losses, he might well say with Walt Whitman, "I am the man, I suffer'd, I was there," and with D. H. Lawrence, "Look! We have come through!"

Many of these poems, however, seem to be conceived less as art than as communication – ways of sharing joys and sorrows, of stating opinions and attitudes, of asserting faith, hope, and charity (or sexual love). An instructive comparison could be made, for example, between the glittering generalities of the passage just quoted and the poetically charged specifics of the analogous section in William Carlos Williams's "Asphodel, That Greeny Flower" – the opening of the "Coda," in which Williams meditates strenuously on the "huge gap/between the flash/and the thunderstroke." Of course Morgan can't be faulted for not being Williams. It's just that, given the worth of the enterprise, one hopes for more of the poetic development manifested between his first and second books.

One cluster in particular in *Poems of the Two Worlds* has a spare clarity and evocativeness that demonstrate Morgan's mastery of his medium: "The Old Days," "The Priest," "Hideyoshi," and "Maitreya." "Hideyoshi," certainly one of Morgan's best poems, performs the unusual feat of making believable a character in whom love of violence and love of beauty are integrated in the interests of justice and spiritual wholeness. On the one hand, the Japanese warrior-hero of the poem cuts his enemy to pieces; on the other, he makes a flower arrangement out of emblems of war:

> So he took a bucket, and his horse's bit
> (which he hung by one ring from the bucket-handle)
> and rigged them into a flower-holder,
>
> then with his bloody sword
> cut wild blossoms and grasses
> and in an hour's silence
> composed a subtle and delicate combination ...
>
> Those whom he had conquered
> he now must judge:
> he wished a mind clean-purged
> of violence and ardor.

The effect is rather as if one of Yeats's bitter and violent men who "longed" for "sweetness ... night and day" ("Ancestral Houses") had somehow, on Morgan's page, completed himself.

—Sally M. Gall

MORGAN, (Colin) Pete(r). British. Born in Leigh, Lancashire, 7 June 1939. Educated at Normanton School, Buxton, Derbyshire, 1950–57. Served in the Royal Army Infantry, 1958–63. Married Kate Smith in 1965; one daughter and one son. Recipient: Scottish Arts Council bursary, 1969; Arts Council of Great Britain award, 1973. Agent: David Higham Associates, 5–8 Lower John Street, London W1R 4HA. Address: c/o Secker and Warburg Ltd., 14 Carlisle Street, London W1V 6NN, England.

PUBLICATIONS

Verse

A Big Hat or What? Edinburgh, Kevin Press, 1968.
Loss of Two Anchors. Edinburgh, Kevin Press, 1970.
Poems for Shortie. Solihull, Warwickshire, Aquila, 1973.
The Grey Mare Being the Better Steed. London, Secker and Warburg, 1973.
I See You on My Arm. Todmorden, Lancashire, ARC, 1975.
The Spring Collection. London, Secker and Warburg, 1979.

Plays

Still the Same Old Harry (produced Edinburgh, 1972).
All the Voices Going Away (produced Ilkley, Yorkshire, 1979).

Screenplay (documentary): *Gardens by the Sea*, 1973.

Other

Editor, *C'mon Everybody: Poetry of the Dance.* London, Corgi, 1969.

*   *   *

The first words in Pete Morgan's Introduction to his anthology, *Poetry of the Dance*, are: "Plato said it – 'The dance is god-like in itself. It is a gift from heaven.' " These words also describe Pete Morgan's poetry at its best. As his poems bound along, or dance, with effortless ease, and as they present their innocent pictures of knights, stallions, "the bull with the rumpus horn," my Moll and partner Joe, the impression is of something given, not made. His poems seem to be immediately original without any special seeking after difference, yet their origins are evident. They begin in the world of nursery rhymes. Nursery rhymes have a known audience which they captivate. Equally Pete Morgan poems have an audience or rather many audiences which respond to his excellent readings. Some of the poems are well suited for ballad-style music settings. Yet despite the immediacy of communication and surface simplicity of the poems, beneath is a psychological curiosity and a sharpness of perception which reveal the poet has not sold out his intelligence.

"The White Stallion" begins:

There was that horse
    that I found then
    my white one
big tall and lean as
    and mean as hell

The supple movement, the momentary halt in the penultimate line, and the unexpected drive of the last line, is the work of a craftsman who has learned from, amongst others, Auden, though the last poems of Yeats have also been caught in Morgan's ear to his advantage. More significant perhaps is the use he makes of the commonplace "mean as hell." He rejoices in the lively vernacular phrase. There is so much delight in his first book, *A Big Hat or What?*, in such poems as "My Moll and Partner Joe," "Whoops! I nearly smiled again," "Elegy for Arthur Prance," and "My enemies have sweet voices," that the subtle tones and undertones may not be regarded.

In *Loss of Two Anchors* the stock imagery is used more personally. In "The Rainbow Knight's Confession" the dance measure is less jaunty, and the characteristic question of today, identity – who is the knight, what does the armour conceal? – emerges as the poem progresses. The deliberate ambiguity of the opening line followed by the conscious placing of the romantic imagery, suggests a mature mind using the pieces on the board as a means of self-discovery: "My armour *becomes* me./I have it to the letter now –/even the colour of my steed,/a much deliberated/white." Pete Morgan is one of the most interesting talents of his generation.

—George Bruce

MORGAN, Robert. British. Born in Glamorgan, Wales, 17 April 1921. Educated at Fircroft College, Birmingham, 1949–51; College of Education, Bognor Regis, Sussex, 1951–53, Dip.Ed. 1953; Southampton University, 1969–70, Advanced Diploma in Special Education. Married Jean Elizabeth Morgan in 1953; two daughters. Coal miner in South Wales, 1936–48; school teacher in Portsmouth. Currently, Adviser in Special Education, Hampshire Education Authority. Painter for many years: one-man shows – Plestor Gallery, Selborne, Wiltshire, 1966; Mermaid Theatre, London, 1967; Winchester Art Gallery, Wiltshire, 1972; Hiscock Gallery, Portsmouth, 1976; Surrey University, 1978; Southampton University, 1979. Formerly, Art Organizer for Welsh Artists Workshop, Cardiff. Address: 72 Anmore Avenue, Denmead, Portsmouth, Hampshire PO7 6NT, England.

PUBLICATIONS

Verse

The Night's Prison: Poems, and Rainbow Valley: A Play for Broadcasting. London, Hart Davis, 1967.
Poems and Extracts. Exeter, Exeter University Press, 1968.
On the Banks of the Cynon. Gillingham, Kent, ARC, 1974.
The Storm. Llandybie, Dyfed, Christopher Davies, 1974.

Plays

Rainbow Valley (broadcast, 1967). Included in *The Night's Prison*, 1967.
The Master Miners (produced Cardiff, 1971). Published in *Anglo-Welsh Review 47* (Pembroke Dock, Wales), 1971.
Fragments of a Dream (produced Cardiff, 1971). Published in *Anglo-Welsh Review 54* (Pembroke Dock, Wales), 1972.
Voices in the Dark. Todmorden, Lancashire, ARC, 1976.

Radio Plays: *Rainbow Valley*, 1967; *The Master Miners*, 1972.

Bibliography: exhibition catalogue, Winchester, Southern Arts Association, 1972.

Critical Studies: by M. H. G. Norman, in *Anglo-Welsh Review 40* (Pembroke Dock, Wales), 1969; Preface to exhibition catalogue, Winchester, Southern Arts Association, 1972.

Robert Morgan comments:

As a poet, the main body of my work is connected with coal mines and the mining valleys of South Wales. Some of the poems cover my life as a boy in the mines, and they show the humanity, the cruelty, the ironies and the sudden brief beauties of the Welsh valleys – above ground and in the Deeps and Levels below.

In my verse-plays, which were written many years after leaving the mines, I explore my mining experiences in more poetic detail, often using ghost characters as a literary vehicle to explore and strengthen the mining underground atmosphere. A small section of my poems is devoted to handicapped children, those whom I am connected with in my professional job as head of a remedial department in a secondary school.

Another section of my work covers pastoral poems. These are connected with the rural landscape around my village home in Hampshire, England.

*   *   *

With his collection *The Night's Prison*, Robert Morgan produced a fine document about the South Wales coalfields. He was a miner for 12 years and wrote out of real experience, unlike some other Anglo-Welsh poets who lived in the mining areas but never went down a pit. No other poet since the late Idris Davies has written quite so vivid and bitter a tract about life in the depressed valleys. Morgan sums up much of the essence of his work in these lines:

I know there are bright places
Under the brow of the hill slag
But it was in the shadows I
Wandered where the truth was thickest.

He has been criticised for returning endlessly to the "oblique, remembered streets" and the "stale shadows/of burning hills," but perhaps such repetition is inevitable, given the limitations of the subject-matter. Also, being very much *inside* the experience, he tends to rush to emotional climaxes, anxious to *move* the reader, to make him share his own harsh memories. The fatal shadow of Dylan Thomas falls on these lines, too: "He lies in his city room in the bandage/of dark clinging to runaway years/of green time in the mist of memories."

But, despite the occasional uneven, untidy lapses, the clichéd symbols and repetitive vocabulary ("buckled hands," "musical silence," and "silica" often recur), Morgan's poems are usually forceful and, indeed, informative in the best sense when he concentrates on tight description (reminding us that he is also a talented painter and sculptor):

We are charmed by thin mice
Eating crumbs and blind
Flies dancing in the lamp's
Cold light and we are always
Curious of the black, squeezed
Roads behind cross-sticks where
Our grandfathers worked as boys.

Among his fully effective poems are "Gomer," "Farewell on a Wet Day," and "Blood Donor," which are chiselled and steely, far superior to some of his looser, hastier constructions. One of his most anthologised pieces is "The Carpenter," which is not about Wales at all and so escapes from the pull of inheritance and Morgan's customary burning necessity to remain faithful to his past and to his dead comrades. This is a fine poem, and so, too, is his long broadcast play *Rainbow Valley*, where he has room to spread himself, as it were, capturing all the simple emotion and the stark tragedy through individual voices naming their own fears and memories.

One still cannot say whether his mining past, which he has already looted and ransacked, will continue to sustain Robert Morgan's work, though he has written an excellent poem, "Maladjusted Boys," and others stemming from his experience as a compassionate teacher of backward children. The mining seam could be worked out, and he may have to look elsewhere for nourishment to avoid becoming trapped and sealed within a monotonous theme. Even the bleak but dignified history of the Welsh pits cannot bear too much repeating, and Morgan has already achieved much by leaving a small monument to them in his poetry. His vitality, faith, honesty and sincerity are unquestioned, and the possible extension of his range may be hinted at in these, his own words:

> The background is overgrown with dreams
> And the horizon fades into smooth tips
> Sprinkled with the blood of coal.
> But the weight of time strengthens
> The corner stones of my heritage.

—John Tripp

MOSS, Howard. American. Born in New York City, 22 January 1922. Educated at the University of Michigan, Ann Arbor, 1939–40; University of Wisconsin, Madison, 1940–43, B.A. 1943; Harvard University, Cambridge, Massachusetts, Summer 1942; Columbia University, New York, 1946. Book Reviewer, *Time*, New York, 1944; Instructor in English, Vassar College, Poughkeepsie, New York, 1944–46. Since 1948, Poetry Editor, *The New Yorker*. Taught at Barnard College, New York, 1976, Columbia University, New York, 1977, and University of California, Irvine, 1979. Recipient: Janet Sewall Davis Award (*Poetry*, Chicago), 1944; National Institute of Arts and Letters Award, 1968; Ingram Merrill Foundation grant, 1972; National Book Award, 1972. Member, National Institute of Arts and Letters. Address: 27 West 10th Street, New York, New York 10011, U.S.A.

PUBLICATIONS

Verse

The Wound and the Weather. New York, Reynal, 1946.
The Toy Fair. New York, Scribner, 1954.
A Swimmer in the Air. New York, Scribner, 1957.
A Winter Come, A Summer Gone: Poems 1946–1960. New York, Scribner, 1960.
Finding Them Lost and Other Poems. New York, Scribner, and London, Macmillan, 1965.
Second Nature. New York, Atheneum, 1968.
Selected Poems. New York, Atheneum, 1971.
Chekhov. New York, Albondocani Press, 1972.
Travel: A Window. New York, Albondocani Press, 1973.
Buried City. New York, Atheneum, 1975.
A Swim Off the Rocks: Light Verse. New York, Atheneum, 1976.
Tigers and Other Lilies (juvenile). New York, Atheneum, 1977.
Notes from the Castle. New York, Atheneum, 1979.

Plays

The Folding Green (produced Cambridge, Massachusetts, 1954; New York, 1964).

The Oedipus Mah-Jongg Scandal (produced New York, 1968).
The Palace at 4 A.M. (produced East Hampton, New York, 1972). Published in *Quarterly Review of Literature* (Princeton, New Jersey), Spring 1973.

Other

The Magic Lantern of Marcel Proust. New York, Macmillan, 1962; London, Faber, 1963.
Writing Against Time: Critical Essays and Reviews. New York, Morrow, 1969.
Instant Lives (satire). New York, Saturday Review Press, 1974.

Editor, *Keats.* New York, Dell, 1952.
Editor, *The Nonsense Books of Edward Lear.* New York, New American Library, 1964.
Editor, *The Poet's Story.* New York, Macmillan, 1973; London, Collier Macmillan, 1974.

Manuscript Collections: Syracuse University Library, New York; Lilly Library, University of Indiana, Bloomington.

Critical Studies: *Alone with America* by Richard Howard, New York, Atheneum, 1969; "Recent Poetry: Exiles and Disinterments" by Laurence Lieberman, in *Yale Review* (New Haven, Connecticut), Autumn 1971; "A Gathering of Poets" by Richard Shramm, in *Western Humanities Review* (Salt Lake City), Autumn 1972.

* * *

Imagine a set of fraternal twins, brothers at once terribly alike and needfully disparate. Who choose different facets of the same life to lead. Each achieving in different facets of the same craft; whose wishes and careers cast into patterns geographically separate and with startingly similar results ... supposing that each "brother" becomes deeply involved in the course of a major magazine, as an editor and as a creative writer; that each excels over a devoted period of long years' work; and that the two men, not having met or discussed, choose strong foreign interests to correspond to the intimately American identity of each ...

The two men might be Howard Moss, poetry editor for the *New Yorker* for over twenty years, poet and playwright, native of New York City and admirer of England and Ireland; and Cid Corman, editor of *Origin* (Series 1–3), native of Boston, experiencer of Italy and Japan. Their physical resemblance is astonishing. Moss being a compact version of Corman's bigger corpus. Where Corman is heavy and flowing, a big man, Moss is formed into compact energy, fastidiousness, and order. They look as alike as brothers. And the magazines: Corman's is, of course, since the Black Mountain days, one of the most influential of the avant garde in the past twenty years. And Moss's section of the *New Yorker* has presented poetry in mass media in an impact undeniable on the American scene.

Howard Moss is, like Corman, the proven and respected possessor of a lucid, compressed poetic style that expresses a dynamic sensitivity to his world. Moss revels in the soft speech-pattern of Ireland's common folk; Corman, for years a visitor to Japan, now lives there. Both men are brown-eyed, affable, gregarious, kindly men, with that distance between upper lip and nose that betokens a generosity of spirit. Both are at once intimately a part of and separate from the realm of the massive creativity of our age. Each has the courage of the editor and the individuality of the creative, and it is to the credit of each that such risk and responsibility are accepted for the greater good.

Howard Moss is deeply engrossed in his interests in the theatre. An accomplished playwright whose "experiments" with dialogue extend into his poetic techniques, he is an avid theatre-goer and commentator on avant garde theatre. He is the recipient of kudos for his criticism and has gathered such pieces into two stimulating collections. An admirer of

Chekov, and of such Americans as Elizabeth Bishop and W. S. Merwin, he involves himself with the shaping of his magazine by himself reading and selecting from 150 poems a week (of the thousand or so that are submitted, from all over the world). His own work bears the imprint of the width, breadth, romanticism, and toughness of his Russian heritage, winning him a distinguished place in American letters.

—Carol Bergé

MOSS, Stanley. American. Born in New York City, 21 June 1935. Educated at Trinity College, Hartford, Connecticut; Yale University, New Haven, Connecticut. Married to Dr. Jane Z. Moss. Poetry Editor, *New American Review*, New York. Currently, Publisher, Sheep Meadow Press, New York. Recipient: Rockefeller grant, 1967. Address: 146 Central Park West, No. 20-C, New York, New York 10023, U.S.A.

PUBLICATIONS

Verse

The Wrong Angel. New York, Macmillan, 1966.
The Wrong Angel (augmented edition). London, Anvil Press Poetry, 1969.
Skull of Adam. New York, Horizon Press, and London, Anvil Press Poetry, 1979.

* * *

Skull of Adam, Stanley Moss's second volume of poems, has solidified a fine reputation that he earned with separate poems in such outlets as *The Times Literary Supplement*, *The New Yorker*, *The New Republic*, *Encounter*, and *The Nation*, and especially with the publication of his first collection, *The Wrong Angel.* That earlier collection reflected his capacity to imbue a moment – biblical, present, any moment – with an exquisite sense of immediacy, often with an ironic ominousness. Thus, for example, even as he watched his father, Moss observed: "Death hooks over the corners of his lips./The wrong angel takes over the lesson." The trait was reflected powerfully in "Another Reply for Pompey," a perversion of the traditional tale of Pompey's respect for hospitality when he refused his captain permission to cut a ship from its mooring to send his sleeping guests, Caesar, Antony, and Lepidus, to oblivion. In the Moss version, which was tinged with characteristic tough humor, Pompey began with modest enough malevolence by ordering the cutting of the mooring. As his sense of decency was further diminished, in what Moss made a powerful account of becalmed ambition whipped up by a rising gale, Pompey even troubled to have the throats of his guests cut – an act which, by that stage, he was able to rationalize without much difficulty.

Moss has always looked at the world with both love and the sadness of dismay – a combination that arouses in him a great sense of responsibility. Those simultaneously and paradoxically held emotions of his have grown more intense in *Skull of Adam*, though Moss still often manages to keep the trace of smile on his lips when he expresses them. He goes around carrying "the law under ... [his] arm like bread" ("Kangaroo"), reading it aloud with warmth, power, good nature whether he is writing whimsically about excrement or seriously about his being the ghost of his father. Perhaps the simple lines from "Prayer for Zero Mostel (1915–1977)" best resound with Moss's view: "If you love life/you simply can't believe/how bad it is." He walks his audience along the brink between the undeniable and the love.

—Alan R. Shucard

MTSHALI, Oswald (Joseph). South African. Born in Vryheid, Natal, 17 January 1940. Educated at Inkamana High School, Natal. Married to Margaret Mtshali. Driver for local engineering firm, 1963–65. Since 1965, messenger and general delivery man for a Johannesburg investment company. Address: P.O. Box 8266, Johannesburg, South Africa.

PUBLICATIONS

Verse

Sounds of a Cowhide Drum. Johannesburg, Renoster Books, 1971; London, Oxford University Press, and New York, Third Press, 1972.

Oswald Mtshali comments:

I am neither a Romantic nor a Traditionalist. Maybe I am a socially involved poet of South Africa as Charles Dickens was a socially involved novelist of England.

I consider Lorca, Allen Ginsberg and Yevtushenko as some of the poets I admire. I draw my themes from my life as I live and experience it. I write in the free verse form because it allows me more freedom in expression without the restriction of metre and rhyme. I depict the life of humanity as a whole as reflected in my environment, Mofolo Village; my community, Soweto; my society, Johannesburg; my country, South Africa. As an aspirant black poet in South Africa, I have no model poet on whom to base my style.

* * *

Oswald Mtshali's *Sounds of a Cowhide Drum* sold over 10,000 copies in South Africa in less than a year. Most of his poems deal with racial tensions. Some, as he says, punch "wildly at the immense powers," but many more successfully control narrative, imagery and the details of linguistic connotation in witty, anecdotal sketches of individuals under pressure or of bitterly ludicrous social injustices. More interestingly still, some longer poems, such as "Snowfall on Mount Frere," achieve a mode of emblematic narration (not unlike the Irish *aisling*) in which political pressure is recast in terms of the natural landscape of the oppressed country. Mtshali's ability to control larger structures, together with his acute visual memory, exploited in vivid analogies – "A newly-born calf/is like oven-baked bread/steaming under a cellophane cover" or "The skin was pale and taut/like a glove on a doctor's hand" – could lead to developments in his work that will make him not only a man with an urgent and well-spoken message, but a poet with a unique voice of international validity.

—Anne Cluysenaar

MUDIE, Ian (Mayelston). Australian. Born in Hawthorn, South Australia, 1 March 1911. Educated at Scotch College, Adelaide. Served in the Australian Army, 1941–45. Married Renée Dunford Doble in 1935; two sons. Lecturer in Creative Writing, Adult Education Department, University of Adelaide, 1959–66; Editor-in-Chief, Rigby Ltd., publishers, Adelaide, 1960–66. President, Fellowship of Australian Writers, 1959–60. Recipient: W. J. Miles Memorial Prize, 1943; Commonwealth Literary Fund Fellowship, 1946; Grace Leven Prize, 1963. Address: 8 Bristol Street, Glenelg South, South Australia 5045, Australia.

PUBLICATIONS

Verse

Corroboree to the Sun. Melbourne, Hawthorn Press, 1940.
This Is Australia. Adelaide, Cork, 1941.
Their Seven Stars Unseen. Adelaide, Jindyworobak, 1943.
The Australian Dream. Adelaide, Jindyworobak, 1943.
Poems 1934–1944. Melbourne, Georgian House, 1945.
The Blue Crane. Sydney, Angus and Robertson, 1959.
The North-Bound Rider. Adelaide, Rigby, 1963.
Look, The Kingfisher! Melbourne, Hawthorn Press, 1970.
Selected Poems 1934–1974. Melbourne, Nelson, 1976.

Other

The Christmas Kangaroo (juvenile). Adelaide, Cork, 1946.
Riverboats. Adelaide, Rigby, 1962.
Wreck of the Admella (history). Adelaide, Rigby, 1966; London, Angus and Robertson, 1967.
Rivers of Australia (juvenile). Adelaide, Rigby, and San Francisco, Tri-Ocean, 1966; London, Angus and Robertson, 1968.
Pageant Stone: The First Hundred Years of John Martin's. Privately printed, 1968.
The Heroic Journey of John McDouall Stuart (biography). Sydney, Angus and Robertson, 1968.
River Murray Sketchbook, drawings by Jeanette McLeod. Adelaide, Rigby, and San Francisco, Tri-Ocean, 1969.
Australia Today (juvenile). Sydney, Hicks and Smith, and London, Kaye and Ward, 1970.
New Zealand Today (juvenile). Sydney, Hicks and Smith, and London, Kaye and Ward, 1973.
Glenelg Sketchbook, drawings by Jeanette McLeod. Adelaide, Rigby, 1974.
Australian Landscapes in Colour. Adelaide, Rigby, 1975.
River Rivals. Sydney, Collins, 1975.
Riverboats Sketchbook, illustrated by Chris Halls. Adelaide, Rigby, 1975.

Editor, *Poets at War: An Anthology of Verse by Australian Servicemen.* Melbourne, Georgian House, 1944.
Editor, *Jindyworobak Anthology 1946.* Adelaide, Jindyworobak, 1946.
Editor, with others, *Verse in Australia.* Adelaide, Australian Letters, 4 vols., 1958–61.
Editor, with Colin Thiele, *Australian Poets Speak.* Adelaide, Rigby, 1961.
Editor, *Favourite Australian Poems.* Adelaide, Rigby, 1963.

Bibliography: *Ian Mudie: A Bibliography*, Adelaide, South Australia Libraries Board, 1970.

Ian Mudie comments:

Ian Mudie came into prominence as one of the Australian nationalist poets of the nineteen-thirties. He became associated with Rex Ingamells's Jindyworobak Movement and, as well as doing much to widen the use of Australian terms and turns of speech in serious Australian poetry, introduced the use of ideas from Aboriginal religion and mythology to apply symbolically to modern national problems. He has also found much of his symbolism in the scenery of the Australian Outback. Possibly his best-known poem is "They'll Tell You about Me," which is largely a catalogue of figures and incidents from Australian literature, history, and folklore. During recent years his poetry has tended to be quieter in tone and more personal, varying in mood from tender to bitter.

He has been called "a Wordsworth in blucher boots," a "serpent of mediocrity," and the founder of a truly Australian poetry. He is completely a compulsive poet, and has said "between one attack of poem-producing and the next I find it difficult to believe I am capable of writing poetry." His work varies from loose free verse expressed in speech-rhythms to strictly formal poetry. One critic has remarked that much of Mudie's work is not easy to accept as verse until it is read aloud, when the fact that it is poetry becomes inescapable.

He is not aware of having consciously attempted to achieve anything in poetry except to get the poem of the moment out of his system and fails to see that he has accomplished anything more with his poetry than that.

* * *

Ian Mudie has been publishing verse since 1934 and in this span there have been many modifications and realignments of poetic orthodoxy. Although Mudie has practised in a number of forms and adopted various stances, ranging from the loud voiced jackeroo to the meditative nature lover to, more recently, the bemused urban victim of the gneration gap, yet he will be remembered, probably, for a handful of poems of simple nationalistic assertiveness, written for, and in, a voice calculated to hold its own with any public bar stridency. These well known, and successfully extrovert larrikin-poems are, within the corpus of Ian Mudie's work, gestures. Mudie, the poet, is obviously more complex than this. Through all his collections one is aware of a simple but genuine preoccupation with Man In A Landscape. When the landscape and the man converge, as in the broad-brimmed slang poems, Mudie achieves his best poetic expression. The quieter poems, particularly in the earlier work, have to struggle with a much more intractable tyranny of form. Mudie, though prolific, has never expressed the exhilaration of conquering merely formal problems and obstacles. The lyric poems, therefore, tend to work doggedly towards their ends. Perhaps the most totally successful collection of poems by Ian Mudie is *The Blue Crane*. In this book the poet comes closest to relaxing his guard in the lyrical pieces, and certainly reaches his most convincing peak in the broad-accented poems. But more important, there is no sense of dichotomy between the two genres. Mudie has continued to write and to publish. His most recent work accepts naturally and without presumption certain lessons of the folk-rock culture. It also is pervaded with the forced reflectiveness of the once-active participant: the preoccupations are direct and physical, the recognitions point otherwise.

—Thomas W. Shapcott

MULDOON, Paul. Irish. Born in County Armagh, Northern Ireland, 20 June 1951. Educated at St. Patrick's College, Armagh; Queen's University, Belfast. Recipient: Eric Gregory Award, 1972. Address: Kennaghan, Duncannon, County Tyrone, Northern Ireland.

PUBLICATIONS

Verse

Knowing My Place. Belfast, Ulsterman, 1971.
New Weather. London, Faber, 1973.

Spirit of Dawn. Belfast, Ulsterman, 1975.
Mules. London, Faber, 1977.
Names and Addresses. Belfast, Ulsterman, 1978.

* * *

Paul Muldoon is an excellent technician who achieved individuality very young. He has been compared with other young Irish poets, but in fact his distinction in his early work was marked out by a sense of apartness, in style as in subject-matter. He wrote of love, for instance, as though it were a dispersion of one's sole self. Proximity was defined in terms of pain in "Wind and Tree":

Often when the wind has gathered
The trees together and together

One tree will take
Another in her arms and hold ...

It is no real fire.
They are breaking each other.

Often I think I should be like
The single tree, going nowhere.

If Muldoon identified with anything at all, it was with such creatures as the hedgehog: "The hedgehog gives nothing/Away, keeping itself to itself./We wonder what a hedgehog/Has to hide, why it so distrusts." For Muldoon, ships were in bottles, the sea was in shells; the illusion of depth was created by carefully appointed mirrors.

There is a paradox in using such careful artistry to communicate distance, remoteness, departure. It is seen at perhaps its most remarkable in "Good Friday, 1971. Driving Westward." Characteristically enough, the allusion to Donne in the title signifies unlikeness. This is a poem about people remote from each other. The growing hiatus between intending lovers is symbolised in terms of driving a car:

Errigal stepped out suddenly in our

Path and the thin arm tightened round the waist
Of the mountain and for a time I lost
Control and she thought we hit something big
But I had seen nothing, perhaps a stick
Lying across the road. I glanced back once
And there was nothing but a heap of stones.

A cairn? or a funeral mound for their love? One has to read this precise and enigmatic poem carefully. The words are never simply what they stand for and the poet's skilled play with them does more than his explicit statement to countenance a wary distrust of life.

Paul Muldoon is certainly an original. His second collection of poems should dispel any notion his readers may have formed as to what he thinks of contact or contiguity. One of the techniques he deploys may be what we could call the New Immediacy:

Look, son. Just look around you.
People are getting themselves killed
Left, right and centre
While you do what? Write rondeaux?
There's more to living in this country

Than stars and horses, pigs and trees,
Not that you'd guess it from your poems....

You would guess it now. This is the Mexican revolutionary, Pancho Villa, advising a young writer, Muldoon's *alter ego*, to take notice of his context in Northern Ireland. It seems to be at once a critique of his earlier work and a justification of what comes later. In *Mules* the events come up against the reader more closely than they did in the first book: "A tree would give its neighbour the elbow/And both look the other way." William of Orange on his charger swims against the current of "our own backyard." The friendly school caretaker makes a pass at a young boy. The gelder, Ned Skinner (!), reminds Aunt Sarah of their erstwhile evenings in the hay. The mule gets itself born: "We might yet claim that it sprang from earth/Were it not for the afterbirth/Trailed like some fine, silk parachute,/That we would know from what heights it fell." Although a good deal of this harks back to the past, there is, for Muldoon, a novel sharpness, a wrenching about of affairs, that marks out his later work as not only vigorous and earthy, but eclectic.

In spite of this, *Mules* is not so consistently good as its predecessor, *New Weather*. But it is a defiant gallimaufry of opinions and stances: the poems certainly refuse to be type-cast. However, one particular note is sounded which may point forward to a new classicism and formalism. It occurs in the poem "Blemish," a poem a good deal more subtle than it may seem at first:

Were it indeed an accident of birth
That she looks on the gentle earth
And the seemingly gentle sky
Through one brown, and one blue eye.

—Philip Hobsbaum

MURPHY, Richard. Irish. Born in County Mayo, 6 August 1927. Educated at Canterbury Cathedral Choir School (Cathedral Chorister, 1940); King's School, Canterbury (Milner Scholar), 1941–42; Wellington College, Berkshire, 1943–44; Magdalen College, Oxford, 1945–48, M.A. 1948; the Sorbonne, Paris, 1954–55. Married Patricia Avis in 1955 (divorced, 1959); one daughter. Director, English School, Canea, Crete, 1953–54; Writer-in-Residence, University of Virginia, Charlottesville, 1965; Visiting Fellow, Reading University, Berkshire, 1968; Compton Lecturer in Poetry, University of Hull, Yorkshire, 1969; O'Connor Professor of Literature, Colgate University, Hamilton, New York, 1971; Visiting Professor of Poetry, Bard College, Annandale-on-Hudson, New York, 1972–74, Princeton University, New Jersey, 1974–75, and University of Iowa, Iowa City, 1976–77. Recipient: AE Memorial Award, 1951; Guinness Award, 1962; Arts Council bursary, 1967. Fellow, Royal Society of Literature, 1968. Address: Cleggan, County Galway, Ireland.

PUBLICATIONS

Verse

The Archaeology of Love. Dublin, Dolmen Press, 1955.

The Woman of the House: An Elegy. Dublin, Dolmen Press, 1959.
The Last Galway Hooker. Dublin, Dolmen Press, 1961.
Six Irish Poets, with others, edited by Robin Skelton. London and New York, Oxford University Press, 1962.
Sailing to an Island. London, Faber, 1963; New York, Chilmark Press, 1964.
Penguin Modern Poets 7, with Jon Silkin and Nathaniel Tarn. London, Penguin, 1966.
The Battle of Aughrim and The God Who Eats Corn. London, Faber, and New York, Knopf, 1968.
High Island: New and Selected Poems. London, Faber, 1974; New York, Harper, 1975.
Selected Poems. London, Faber, 1979.

Recording: *The Battle of Aughrim*, Claddagh, 1969.

* * *

Richard Murphy's poems have, from the earliest collections, been written in a variety of modes and have been set in contrasting landscapes. Poems on Paris and Crete, on a painting by Mantegna, and on Biblical and classical themes, appear in *The Archaeology of Love.* They are technically proficient, but lack full emotional commitment. The strongest poems, and perhaps the most characteristic, are those in which Murphy adopts a Yeatsian, aristocratic stance and writes of the decay of great houses and of the auction of property: "alone I come,/ To bid for damp etchings,/ My great-aunt's chair." He sees himself in the role of conserver and restorer: "I have grown to restore/From dust each room." He is nostalgic about the passing of the older, more graceful way of life represented by the Protestant ascendancy in Ireland, but his attitude was evolving by the time he published *Sailing to an Island.* He accepts the burden of his family's past, and his responsibility towards what survives of it. In powerful narrative poems, "The Last Galway Hooker" and "The Cleggan Disaster," the past is now that of the place itself, and not merely that part of it created by the Protestant settlers. In "The Last Galway Hooker" Murphy describes the construction, previous owners, and subsequent history of "a strong, safe, fishing and cargo boat" which he has bought and proposes to renew: "So I chose to renew her, to rebuild, to prolong/For a while the spliced yards of yesterday."

Among those "spliced yards" are the long narratives from oral tradition which Murphy has transformed into "The Cleggan Disaster" and, on a smaller scale, "Pat Cloherty's Version of *The Maisie.*" Part of the fascination of these poems is formal: Murphy is one of the very few contemporaries who have used narrative verse techniques. They also give a valuable picture of the changing way of life of the fishing villages and rural farmers. Murphy's tone is too astringent to say his attitude is nostalgic, but there is a streak of romantic primitivism in his work. In the past decade one sees it steadily give way to a more ironic stance. His reconstruction of the battle of Aughrim, performed by the BBC in 1968, is as harsh in its treatment of vain Catholic generals as of savage Protestant soldiery. The Irish commander Luttrell, who "sold his country to preserve his class," becomes a type of the traitor. There is a new variety of verse forms in "The Battle of Aughrim," and a new density of language. What is perhaps most striking is Murphy's conviction that "the past is happening today." When he writes of an Irish Protestant landowner in the 1820's in "Droit de Seigneur," and of white settlers in Africa in our own time (in "The God Who Eats Corn"), he finds the same mentality. His own family are far from typical representatives of the Protestant mind, though they share the legacy sufficiently to make Murphy's meditations on his family reach out to a larger historical experience. The strong vein of radical irony in Murphy has not been fully recognized: it helped him replace the proud facade of Yeatsian disdain in his early verse with a view of the world more truly humane.

Murphy's recent work is divided between the landscape of the island off County Galway where he lives, and scenes remembered from his childhood in Ceylon. They show his growing power of description:

When the great bull withdraws his rod, it glows
Like a carnelian candle set in jade.
The cow ripples ashore to feed her calf;
While an old rival, eyeing the deed with hate,
Swims to attack the tired triumphant god.

The "High Island" poems show Murphy consciously seeking a richer texture of metaphor and syntax. They also reveal a new openness to personal feelings. He is breaking new ground in "Sunup," in particular. It is a hauntingly moving love poem.

—Eric Homberger

MURRAY, Les(lie) A(llan). Australian. Born in Nabaic, New South Wales, 17 October 1938. Educated at Taree High School; University of Sydney (Co-Editor, *Arna* and *Hermes*; Literary Editor, *Honi Soit*), 1957–60, 1962. Served in the Royal Australian Naval Reserve, 1960–61. Married Valerie Gina Maria Morelli in 1962; two sons and two daughters. Translator, Australian National University, Canberra, 1963–67. Since 1974, Co-Editor, *Poetry Australia*. Recipient: Grace Leven Prize, 1965; Australian Commonwealth Literary Fund Fellowship, 1968, 1971; Cook Bi-Centenary Prize, 1970; Literature Board Senior Fellowships, 1973–79; National Book Council Award, 1975; C. J. Dennis Memorial Prize, 1977. Address: 27 Edgar Street, Chatswood, New South Wales 2067, Australia.

PUBLICATIONS

Verse

The Ilex Tree, with Geoffrey Lehmann. Canberra, Australian National University Press, 1965.
The Weatherboard Cathedral. Sydney, Angus and Robertson, 1969.
Poems Against Economics. Sydney and London, Angus and Robertson, 1972.
Lunch and Counter Lunch. Sydney, Angus and Robertson, 1974.
Selected Poems: The Vernacular Republic. Sydney, Angus and Robertson, 1976.
Ethnic Radio. Sydney, Angus and Robertson, 1979.
The Boys Who Stole the Funeral. Sydney, Angus and Robertson, 1979.

Other

The Peasant Mandarin. Brisbane, University of Queensland Press, 1978.

Translator, *Trubetzkoy: An Introduction to the Principles of Phonological Description.* The Hague, Nijhoff, 1968.

Manuscript Collection: National Library of Australia, Canberra.

Critical Studies: "The Human-Hair Thread" by the author, in *Meanjin 4* (Melbourne), 1977; *Study Notes on the Poetry of Les A. Murray* by Penelope Nelson, Melbourne, Metheun, 1978; K. L. Goodwin, in *Australian Poems in Perspective*, Brisbane, University of Queensland Press, 1978; "Garlands of Ilex" by Robert Gray, in *Poetry Australia* (Sydney), May 1979;

"Boeotian and Loyolan Art" by Mark O'Connor, in *Kunapipi* (Aarhus, Denmark), 1979 (and Murray's reply).

Les A. Murray comments:

I'm a sort of Australian Hesiod – we've had several of those, and hard reactions against them, but it's a description I accept. Writing from a rural, egalitarian base and taking sacramental Christianity as my compass of value, I try to realise, through art, a certain spacious, dignified, and distinctive order which underlies our late-colonial society and its imported idiocies. I call this order the Vernacular Republic, and find that it extends beyond Australia, finally, as something both age-old and immanent in the world, a vision from which each successive "egalitarian" society retreats into elitism after a few gestures. It is like a sort of law that is not made but *discerned.* When I'm not directly working on this divinatory-pontifical theme, I assume it and write poems of a more general sort, varied in tone but always meditative. My verse tends to be heavily Australian in vocabulary and reference, as well as in its deeper tone and gesture. It's not wholly solemn, though, and not all the jokes are family ones.

* * *

At the age of 40, Les A. Murray is the poet of his generation who is most clearly indicated for celebrity and for inclusion on lists of tertiary-level-course set books. His work, as the *Selected Poems: The Vernacular Republic* made clear, combines extraordinary force of personality in the views of expression, and a masterful confrontation with – you could say a masterful dancing among – large and difficult subjects.

Early poems in the uncharacteristically-named first book he shared with his friend Geoffrey Lehmann, mostly treat of country places and customs – an abiding preoccupation. The exception is the much-anthologized "The Burning Truck," a sustained seemingly-long run of 36 lines about the truck and the fearfully delighted onlookers.

The later books have been named so as to emphasize Murray's local and partisan temper and his uncompromising allegiances. These can be explored in the book of critical essays and reviews, *The Peasant Mandarin.* The poems present a wide range of reflections on man's interactions with nature, firmly localized – Murray of all Australian poets has most strongly celebrated the small-farming districts, particularly his own Northern Rivers (of New South Wales) with its dairy industry. This interest first culminates in a magnificent sequence, "Walking to the Cattle Place," in *Poems Against Economics.* In many different forms, quirkily ranging from Sanskrit derivations to ideas of God, from bullock-jumping in Australia to the salutation of a Xhosa tribesman, the poems encounter, discuss, play with man's age-old role as cattleherder. But there are discussions of other creations of man: the Lee Enfield rifle ("SMLE"), Law and Order ("The Police: Seven Voices") and Learning ("Sidere Mens Eadem Mutato," a reminiscence and discussion in nine unrhymed sonnets, based on Murray's university experience). Groaningly funny is "Vindaloo in Merthyr Tydfil," and not-merely-funny, "Folklore."

David Malouf, in a careful discussion ("Subjects Found and Taken Up" in *Poetry Australia*) of *Lunch and Counter Lunch*, began by calling Murray "perhaps the most naturally gifted poet of his generation"; remarked on his "almost unlimited" verbal inventiveness, the freshness and originality of his insights, and his wit and humour – and then stated his uneasiness at Murray's need for a debating stance. He felt the earlier subject-matter had been worked through and new material must be found "fully expressive" of Murray's gifts.

What has come is the astonishing adaptation in English of the aboriginal Song-Cycle. "The Buledelah-Taree Holiday Song Cycle" has thirteen long-lined sections that look Whitmanesque on the page but are distinctive; there is some rhythmical affinity with Robinson Jeffers, but Murray's lines are end-stopped. The poems celebrate the country-bred city-dweller's yearly return with his family to his childhood district, camping and picnicking, fishing, observing how things are the same or are changed. It is, then, a continuation of Murray's earlier interest, and its finest articulation. But the enterprise and skill – and scholarly scruple, for Murray is a polyglot who has worked as a translator – involved in using the Song-Cycle also points to a newly-urgent interest in the racial mix in Australia, first strongly signalled in "Jószef" in *Lunch and Counter Lunch*. This is carried into poems relating to Celtic origins and also celebrating the arrival of his wife's family in Australia.

Murray's verse novel, *The Boys Who Stole the Funeral*, has a plot characteristically expressive of principled rebellion, and of Murray's need to put a case, in his own person or not. The hero's encounter in the bush with two mentors – one white and one black – is an interesting variation of a motif used by Xavier Herbert in his 1937 novel *Capricornia*. But Murray's energy in reaching towards sufficiently subtle and final-sounding truths and principles is all his own.

Murray's influence has been widely felt during the 1970's through his editorship of *Poetry Australia*, the best-paying poetry quarterly in the country. Editing now for Angus and Robertson, he is in a position to influence what poetry is published. An indefatigable traveller, he is a vivid and dogmatic presence at conferences. His sometimes reactionary but thought-out and complex opinions will continue to win him the polemic responses he apparently needs to release his most gamesome and profound writing.

—Judith Rodriguez

MUSGRAVE. Susan. Canadian. Born in Santa Cruz, California, 12 March 1951. Recipient: Canada Council grant, 1970, 1973, and bursary, 1972. Address: 2407 Tryon Road, R.R. 3, Sidney, British Columbia, Canada.

PUBLICATIONS

Verse

Songs of the Sea-Witch. Vancouver, Sono Nis Press, 1970.
Skuld. Frensham, Surrey, Sceptre Press, 1971.
Birthstone. Frensham, Surrey, Sceptre Press, 1972.
Entrance of the Celebrant. Toronto, Macmillan, and London, Fuller d'Arch Smith, 1972.
Equinox. Rushden, Northamptonshire, Sceptre Press, 1973.
Kung. Rushden, Northamptonshire, Sceptre Press, 1973.
Grave-Dirt and Selected Strawberries. Toronto, Macmillan, 1973.
Guilband (juvenile). Vancouver, J. J. Douglas, 1974.
Against. Rushden, Northamptonshire, Sceptre Press, 1974.
Two Poems. Knotting, Bedfordshire, Sceptre Press, 1975.
The Impstone. Toronto, McClelland and Stewart, 1976; London, J. Jay, 1977.
Kiskatinaw Songs, with Seán Virgo. Victoria, Pharos Press, 1977.
Selected Strawberries and Other Poems. Victoria, Sono Nis Press, 1977.
For Charlie Beaulieu. Knotting, Bedfordshire, Sceptre Press, 1977.
Two Poems for the Blue Moon. Knotting, Bedfordshire, Sceptre Press, 1977.
Becky Swan's Book. Erin, Ontario, Porcupine's Quill, 1977.
A Man to Marry, A Man to Bury. Toronto, McClelland and Stewart, 1979.

Manuscript Collection: McMaster University, Hamilton, Ontario.

Critical Study: "The White Goddess: Poetry of Susan Musgrave" by Rosemary Sullivan, in *Comtemporary Verse 2*, 1975.

* * *

In my review of Susan Musgrave's poetry in the 1975 *Contemporary Poets* I misjudged her. Her obsessive, poignant treatment of death, insanity, and blood reminded me of Sylvia Plath's poetry in *Ariel* and I unwisely voiced my fear that Musgrave might meet the same end as Plath.

The feminist stances of the two poets were similar; so were their attitudes towards men, lesbianism, and sex. Musgrave's imitation of Plath's "Daddy" and "Lady Lazarus" in her poem "Exposure" was unmistakable. She was the celebrant of death, "the spilled child," and all she looked at was transformed into death. In "The Opened Grave," she placed herself at the "edge of things." Her poems of witchcraft read like strange and deeply disturbing myths of blood rites and sexuality, pervaded with violence. The inhabitants of her witch kingdoms resembled those in Gustave Doré's illustrations – beetles, white moths, and figures with bloated heads angling out of hunched shoulders and shrivelled torsos, shaking their gnarled hands, leering at their prey. Lines from "Finding Love" were chilling:

From my bed I could hear
the ripe wound open, the thick sea
pouring in. I told you, then,
the first lie I had in my heart;
the carcass of a dull animal
slipped between our sights.

Her poem "MacKenzie River, North" was imbued with terror.

What I failed to recognize was that although her range was limited in her two collections, *Songs of the Sea-Witch* and *Entrance of the Celebrant*, and her themes were obsessive and derivative, her sense of the bizarre and her ability to evoke the mood of betwitched kingdoms could serve her well in an entirely different vein of poetry. In the earlier collections, she used these gifts to evoke strange, disturbing worlds fraught with psychological significance. In the third section of *Grave-Dirt and Selected Strawberries* she transforms them to create a high-spirited, bawdy, and wonderfully affectionate pastiche of poems and prose in celebration of the strawberry. Gleefully, Musgrave parodies herself and writes in the best eighteenth-century traditions of comedy. In her fanciful history, the strawberry is her picaresque hero. His origins are traced, his baptism marked, his emergence in the writings of others is duly recorded, and all the facts about him that every strawberry lover would like to know are catalogued. In her "character study" of the strawberry, Musgrave feigns an anthropological tone and hilariously records the harvest customs of the strawberry, its method of reproduction, its behaviour in captivity, its sense of fellowship. To satisfy her audience's appetite for books of homespun truths and extraordinary feats, she pens her hero's proverbs and "the Guinness Book of Strawberries." "A Child's Garden of Strawberries" and "Strawberry at Colonus" place her hero in the literary context he deserves. The collection is giddy, witty, and full of good fun. It could not be more unlike her other poetry.

Her other volumes, from *Equinox* through *The Impstone*, reflect continued growth in the kind of poetry that won her acclaim. "Memorial to a Lover" (*Two Poems*) imitates Plath. "The Firstborn" (*Two Poems*), *Kung*, *Against*, *For Charlie Beaulieu....*, *Two Poems for the Blue Moon*, and *Equinox* show further workings on her poetry of Indian lore and witchcraft. The moon poems, like the "Kiskatinaw Songs" (*Grave-Dirt and Selected Strawberries*), experiment with rhythms from songs, chants, and ballads and turn the hackneyed lyrics and rhythms into a new music. Poems like "The Firstborn" and *Equinox* represent Musgrave's best handling of the world of nightmare and demons where dark rituals are enacted between the self and its demon other. What I look for now is more poetry in the comic vein discovered in "Selected Strawberries" or in the raucous vein of the pulsing, erotic, simple, and primitive Indian songs in the "Kiskatinaw Songs" celebrating the cunt and the phallus.

—Carol Simpson Stern

NANDY, Pritish. Indian. Born in Bhagalpur, Bihar, 15 January 1947. Educated at La Martiniere, Calcutta; Presidency College, Calcutta. Married Rina Mumtaz in 1966 (divorced), two children. Since 1968, Editor, *Dialogue Calcutta*, later *Dialogue India*; since 1969, Public Relations Manager, Guest Keen Williams Ltd., Calcutta. Address: 5 Pearl Road, Calcutta 700 017, India.

PUBLICATIONS

Verse

Of Gods and Olives: 21 Poems. Calcutta, Writers Workshop, 1967.
I Hand You in Turn My Nebbuk Wreath: Early Poems. Calcutta, Dialogue, 1968.
On Either Side of Arrogance. Calcutta, Writers Workshop, 1968.
Rites for a Plebeian Statue: An Experiment in Verse Drama. Calcutta, Writers Workshop, 1969.
From the Outer Bank of the Brahmaputra. New York, New Rivers Press, 1969.
Masks to Be Interpreted as Messages. Calcutta, Dialogue, 1970.
Madness Is the Second Stroke. Calcutta, Dialogue, 1972.
The Poetry of Pritish Nandy. Calcutta, Oxford University Press, 1973.
Dhritarashtra Downtown: Zero. Calcutta, Dialogue, 1974.
Riding the Midnight River: Selected Poems. New Delhi, Arnold Heinemann, 1975.
Lone Song Street. Calcutta, Poets Press, 1975.
A Stranger Called I. Calcutta, Poets Press, 1976.

Other

Editor, *Indian Poetry in English 1947–1972.* Calcutta, Oxford University Press, 1972.
Editor, *Modern Indian Poetry.* New Delhi, Arnold Heinemann, 1974; London, Heinemann, 1976.
Editor, *Bengali Poetry Today.* East Lansing, Michigan State University Press, 1974.

Editor and translator of several other volumes.

Critical Studies: *The Poetry of Pritish Nandy*, by Satyabrata Pal, Calcutta, Writers Workshop, 1969; "Workpoints for a Study of Pritish Nandy's 'In Transit, Mind Seeks' " by Satyabrata Pal, in *Banasthali Vidyapith Magazine*, 1969; *Pritish Nandy* by Subhoranjan Dasgupta, New Delhi, Arnold Heinemann, 1975.

Pritish Nandy comments:

Trying to achieve an entirely new breakthrough in form and evolve a new language to characterise Indian writing in English. Feel that creative writing in English by Indians is generally imitative in both form and approach. What is required is a new language that will be characteristic and structurally powerful, with a logic of its own. It is this Indian English that must be worked out and that is what I am trying to do. Also trying to discover/build a tradition for Indo-Anglian poetry: the fusion of a modern language with the myths and symbols we have. Indian writers in English till now have ignored this quest for a tradition, which I consider vital for a living poetry. Finally: a personal quest – a secular, politically-involved poet has his own peculiar problems.

* * *

Pritish Nandy's early poems are often in short-line free verse; others form typographical pictures, or use Cummings-style spacing. He sceptically mingles Indian, classic, and Christian imagery, with gentle irony towards gods who "have aged and are not aware," or Christ who "came third in the contest/with death/and wrote a poem on the cross." Nandy indeed pities those who have to live with him – he "shreds their magic faith into a million assumptions." He is equally skeptical about such rationalists as the recluse found dead: "having read too much of/Salinger/he had checkmated himself in one/man chess." Indeed, "To understand by cataloguing is like/splitting hairs on a bald head."

Perhaps this is why he thinks English poetry stopped at Auden (American "never began"); he most frequently alludes to Spanish-language poets, notably Lorca. His own effort is to combine, and symbolize: "What you cannot explain in terms of symbols is lost forever like blind totems and ruins in an old man's face." For words are only "masks to be interpreted in terms of messages."

He was long preoccupied with the frustrations of penetrating to realities, or saying anything meaningful if one did; he praised a friend for seeking "a new level of communication" and so compacted his own images as to make very sur-real sense: "your eyes bled like a violet tiger/as I watched the winds strangle/whispers of the apocalypse." But certain themes are clear: death, loneliness, suffering – and the mitigations of love, sex, friendship.

In *Masks to Be Interpreted as Messages* he changed to short statements in rhythmic prose, and in his best-known poem, "Calcutta, If You Must Exile Me," states in brutally direct style the cruelties which revolt him. Next year, the Bangla Desh horrors jolted him into plain, moving statements of sympathy with all victims of hate: in India, Vietnam, or Colombia "the marauders changed their name but the sufferers each time were the same." At times he despairs – "blood is a country you and I have loved in vain" – but he no longer thinks of leaving: "Dark city I shall not disown you again." And though he writes for those who cannot read the language he uses, "my voice is the voice of my people, for I speak of their loves and ambitions and secret shames."

Later, he found consolation in translating Tagore's last poems, a "devastating confrontation with death"; the message, of "haunting simplicity," is that "death is but a new birth of the spirit into the great unknown." Modern Indian poetry, he says, draws "strength from the bedrock of our tradition," yet is "violent, anguished, brutally contemporary." His own certainly is.

—George McElroy

NATHAN, Leonard (Edward). American. Born in Los Angeles, California, 8 November 1924. Educated at Georgia Institute of Technology, Atlanta, 1943; University of California,

Los Angeles, 1946–47; University of California, Berkeley, B.A. (summa cum laude) 1950, M.A. 1952, Ph.D. In English 1961. Served in the United States Army during World War II. Married Carol Nash in 1949; three children. Instructor, Modesto Junior College, California, 1954–60. Since 1960, Member of the Department of Rhetoric, Chairman of the Department, 1969–72, currently Professor of Rhetoric, University of California, Berkeley. Recipient: Phelan Award, 1959; Longview Award, 1961; University of California Creative Awards Fellowship, 1967; National Institute of Arts and Letters grant, 1971; Guggenheim Fellowship, 1976. Address: 40 Beverly Road, Kensington, California, U.S.A.

PUBLICATIONS

Verse

Western Reaches. San Jose, California, Talisman Press, 1958.
The Glad and Sorry Seasons. New York, Random House, 1963.
The Matchmaker's Lament and Other Astonishments. Northampton, Massachusetts, Gehenna Press, 1967.
The Day the Perfect Speakers Left. Middletown, Connecticut, Wesleyan University Press, 1969.
Flight Plan. Berkeley, California, Cedar Hill Press, 1971.
Without Wishing. Berkeley, California, Thorp Springs Press, 1973.
Returning Your Call. Princeton, New Jersey, Princeton University Press, 1975.
The Likeness: Poems Out of India. Berkeley, California, Thorp Springs Press, 1975.
The Teachings of Grandfather Fox. Ithaca, New York, Ithaca House, 1976.
Lost Distance. Madison, Wisconsin, Chowder, 1978.
Dear Blood. Pittsburgh, University of Pittsburgh Press, 1980.

Other

The Tragic Drama of William Butler Yeats: Figures in a Dance. New York, Columbia University Press, 1965.

Editor, *Talisman Anthology.* Georgetown, California, Talisman Press, 1963.

Translator, with others, *Modern Hindi Poetry.* Bloomington, Indiana University Press, 1965.
Translator, *First Person, Second Person*, by Ageyeya. Berkeley, California, Center for South and Southeast Asia Studies, 1971.
Translator, *The Transport of Love: The Meghaduta of Kalidasa.* Berkeley, University of California Press, 1976.

Manuscript Collection: University of Syracuse Library, New York.

Critical Studies: in *Shenandoah* (Lexington, Virginia), Autumn 1969; *Malahat Review* (Victoria), October 1969; *Quarterly Journal of Speech* (New York), Winter 1970; *Poetry* (Chicago), January 1971.

* * *

In his review of *The Glad and Sorry Seasons* for *Poetry*, John Woods quite rightly observed that Leonard Nathan has a "preference for statements of revelation" and that his demands on metaphor are relatively minor. Nathan convinces by conclusive statement, seldom by narrative or emotional persuasion. Although he inclines towards declarative and reductionist poetry, his lines are not so concentrated as, say, W. S. Merwin's, nor has he Merwin's power to startle and amaze through revelation. Leonard Nathan employs a steady iambic meter, with frequent variation in end rhymes. His lines seldom fail; they are refined, restrained, and well polished.

The dominant tonality of *The Glad and Sorry Seasons* is autumnal. The poet is middle-aged and wise, detached and reflective:

I sweeten by the minute, bodying
The spirit of my seed; hear how I sing
Inside my skin – that's blood, that growing sound,
The psalm of mellowing....

The following lines from "First Girl," while perhaps uncharacteristic of Nathan's lyrics, reveal the intensity he is capable of:

As she bent, I woke, and felt a pull like water
And saw above her head a foreign blue,
And nothing was homely, even my heavy body,
And what I had never learned I always knew.

This snow queen, resplendent in frosted radiance, has transformed the poet and "crystalized the wildest flux of nature." But the time of ecstasy is past and "too long ago for second thoughts."

The Day the Perfect Speakers Left seems to bemoan the disintegration of high culture and humanistic values. Several poems strike a pose reminiscent of Ezra Pound's "Hugh Selwyn Mauberley," in its condemnation of our "botched civilization," our "old bitch gone in the teeth." In Nathan's "The Crisis" a shadowy figure, a Greek or Jew, has come "To see his children's children, how they escaped/His law, his love, his unpronounceable name." The title poem of this volume confirms the notion and may remind one of Arnold's "Dover Beach." The birds have assembled for what the poet fears is final migration:

And leave-taking was another,
Sadder version of dusk we were attending,
And as though a whole age were going out,
Its head covered, and going out with it
A purpose including stars and stones.

More recently, *Returning Your Call* is less derivative in style and subject than his earlier books. His voice is more direct, less given to cleverness and wit than previously. There are fine single achievements, such as "Audit," and "Breathing Exercises." In the latter poem the poet cries, in fear and urgency, "For God's sake, keep breathing." There is in this book more sense of tension, near disaster, and struggle against loss. "Breathing Exercises" also tells us, "inside Leonard/Nathan is a little spirit." While hardly confessional, his poetry now seems willing to grapple more intensely with tougher topics. We hear a voice struggling to regain contact with itself, and with close friends. There is also a suggestion Nathan recognizes the cleverness and restraint of his verse: "someday I'm going to speak/in my own voice ... you'll have to cover my mouth with your free hand ..." This is precisely what is missing from Nathan's poetry: a strong, direct, and unfettered voice.

In general, the consistently polished flow of his lines is both remarkable and lamentable; one soon craves roughness in line and subject. It is Nathan's very control of his material that keeps most of his poems, while always of craft, from becoming poems of authority. By his own construct ("Mao for nightmare, Mozart for slippers") we need to hear more of Nathan's nightmares, less about his slippers.

—John R. Cooley

NAUDÉ, Adèle. South African. Born in Pretoria, 14 August 1910. Educated at Rustenburg Girls' High School, Rondebosch; University of Cape Town, B.A. 1930. Widow of D. F. Hugo Naudé; one daughter. Formerly, Editor of various women's journals. Currently, Free-lance journalist and radio scriptwriter. Address: Apartment C, 2 Scott Road, Claremont 7700, Cape Province, South Africa.

PUBLICATIONS

Verse

Pity the Spring. Cape Town, Balkema, 1953.
No Longer at Ease. Cape Town, Balkema, 1956.
Only a Setting Forth. Cape Town, Human and Rousseau, 1965.
Time and Memory. Cape Town, Maskew Miller, 1973.

Other

Verhale vit die Griekse Legendes. Cape Town, Oxford University Press, 1949.
Konig Arthur en sy Ridders. Cape Town, Oxford University Press, 1950.
Gentlemen's Relish: Dishes with a Difference. Privately printed, 1956.
Strooihoed en Sonbril (travel). Cape Town, Human and Rousseau, 1965.
Tousandale aan my Voete (travel). Cape Town, Human and Rousseau, 1968.
Gregory Kaapse Pikkewyn: The Jackass Penguins of the Cape and Present-Day Pollution. Cape Town, David Philip, 1971.
Rondebosch and Round About. Cape Town, David Philip, 1973.
Hugo Naudé: The Artist and the Man. Cape Town, Struik, 1974.

Critical Studies: by E. Pereira, in *South African Poetry: A Critical Anthology*, Pretoria, Communications of the University of South Africa, 1966; D. R. Beeton, in *UNISA English Studies* (Pretoria), June 1968.

Adèle Naudé comments:

Verse forms mainly traditional. Subject matter: nature, human relationships, European art and cultures.

* * *

Adèle Naudé's first volume, *Pity the Spring*, strikes the note of seasonal decay and painful regeneration which recurs throughout her work: "Pity the spring that yet unknowing bears/ The seeds of autumn's rotting fruit within/Her youthful self...." Traditional in form (she describes herself as "mainly a stanza poet, with little runs of free verse in between"), her poems are intensely personal explorations of thought, feeling, and human relationships, through images drawn from art and nature. The need for poetic expression, for truths intuitively perceived and sensitively rendered, informs the firm lines of "Stone Man":

It was but stone
And yet it had a force
That dragged the sculptor's hand
Along an unfamiliar course
And led him to an alien land....

Taking its cue from Eliot's "Journey of the Magi," her second volume, *No Longer at Ease*, is full of self-questioning, but there is greater assurance of tone and technique in the empathic exploration of everyday things. She is fascinated by shifts of focus, by the insights gained through changing perspectives. Equally important is her probing of classical myth, and awed experiencing of Mediterranean culture, in the evocative "Oracle of Delphi" and "In the Old Orchard" (reminiscent of Roy Campbell in its structural control and starkly physical portrayal of seasonal process):

> How cold the old arthritic trees
> Knotted in their strings of pain!
> The lupins push their pliant bodies
> Close to take the winter's strain....
>
> Now red the sod and warm the soil
> And friable with youth interred.
> The trees receive Persephone,
> Fair ransom for the massacred.

Her third volume, *Only a Setting Forth*, is notable for the "inner vision" she attains to through the commonplaces of chance encounters and shifting perspectives. There is wry acceptance, tautly phrased, in "The Unpossessed": "I fear no loss/Though never at rest;/ None has yet lost/The unpossessed," and a recurrence of the ironic note and epigrammatic style first encountered in *No Longer at Ease*. Again, however, it is the Mediterranean- (and Cape-) inspired poetry which is most finely felt and wrought, and which places her in the front rank of contemporary South African poets.

Of her latest volume, *Time and Memory*, Adèle Naudé remarks: "... although it is the same voice, the eye is different. I am looking at life from a different point of view." It remains to be seen whether this latest change of focus results merely in variations on a theme, or does in fact signal a new direction.

—E. Pereira

NEAL, Larry (Lawrence P. Neal). American. Born in Atlanta, Georgia, 5 September 1937. Educated at a Roman Catholic high school, Philadelphia; Lincoln University, Pennsylvania, B.A. 1961; University of Pennsylvania, Philadelphia, M.A. 1963. Married to Evelyn L. Neal. Taught at City College of New York, 1968–69, Wesleyan University, Middletown, Connecticut, 1969–70, and Yale University, New Haven, Connecticut, 1970–75. Former Art Editor, *Liberator* magazine, and education director of the Panther party. Co-Editor, *The Cricket* magazine; Contributing Editor, *Journal of Black Poetry*. Recipient: Guggenheim Fellowship, 1971. Address: 12 Jumel Terrace, New York, New York 10032, U.S.A.

PUBLICATIONS

Verse

Black Boogaloo: Notes on Black Liberation. San Francisco, Journal of Black Poetry Press, 1968.

Hoodoo Hollerin' Bebop Ghosts. Washington, D.C., Howard University Press, 1974.

Other

Trippin': A Need for Change, with LeRoi Jones and A. B. Spellman. Newark, New Jersey, Cricket, 1969(?).

Editor, with LeRoi Jones, *Black Fire: An Anthology of Afro-American Writing.* New York, Morrow, 1968.

* * *

Larry Neal is a foremost and influential theorist, interpreter, and spokesman of the current "Black arts movement." He has declared that "Black Art ... speaks directly to the needs and aspirations of Black America.... It proposes a separate symbolism, mythology, critique, and iconology."

His poems are informed by events and situations in, or touching upon, the lives of the masses of Black people. They often celebrate an elitism, a flair, an élan often associated with Black life styles. For example, he says about a jazzman's identifying hat, "... the pork-pie hat reigns supreme,/the elegance of style/gleaned from the city's underbelly/... defying the sanctity of white/America." His poetic Black icons are not often those from traditional history books but rather the likes of Charlie Parker, the folk-hero "Shine," Malcolm X, the Signifying Monkey from Black oral lore, and Langston Hughes. There is in his work an element of spiritualism, frequently Islamic, sometimes approaching the mystical and mythological.

Sensitive to the poetic inherent in Black oral culture, Neal usually employs common language, current as well as older folk idioms, a conversational or "rapping" tone (e.g., "... instant time, my man, history is one quick/fuck; you no sooner in then you come, a quick fuck"). The flow of his lines frequently connotes non-verbal sounds, as in "Kuntu" with its suggestion of talking drums. He often makes allusions to jazz music and musicians, and his technical effects are suggestive of jazz music. His imagery is deft and clear, although at times somewhat ethnocentric. He is an adroit cataloguer. Most of his poetry, in the free verse style, is irregularly structured, or it is complex in such a way that the overall schema, like intricately structured jazz, is not immediately apparent.

—Theodore R. Hudson

NEMEROV, Howard (Stanley). American. Born in New York City, 1 March 1920. Educated at Fieldston School, New York; Harvard University, Cambridge, Massachusetts, A.B. 1941. Served in the Royal Canadian Air Force and the United States Air Force, rising to the rank of First Lieutenant, 1941–45. Married Margaret Russell in 1944; three children. Instructor in English, Hamilton College, Clinton, New York, 1946–48; Member of the Literature Faculty, Bennington College, Vermont, 1948–66; Professor of English, Brandeis University, Waltham, Massachusetts, 1966–69. Professor of English, 1969–76, and since 1976, Edward Mallinckrodt Distinguished University Professor, Washington University, St. Louis. Visiting Lecturer, University of Minnesota, Minneapolis, 1958–59; Writer-in-Residence, Hollins College, Virginia, 1962–64; Consultant in Poetry, Library of Congress, Washington, D.C., 1963–64. Associate Editor, *Furioso*, Madison, Connecticut, later Northfield, Minnesota, 1946–51. Recipient: *Kenyon Review* Fellowship in Fiction, 1955; Oscar Blumenthal Prize, 1958, Harriet Monroe Memorial Prize, 1959, Frank O'Hara Prize, 1971, and Levinson Prize, 1975 (*Poetry*, Chicago); *Virginia Quarterly Review* Short Story

Award, 1958; National Institute of Arts and Letters grant, 1961; New England Poetry Club Golden Rose, 1962; Brandeis University Creative Arts Award, 1962; National Endowment for the Arts grant, 1966; Theodore Roethke Award, 1968; Guggenheim Fellowship, 1968; St. Botolph's Club Prize, 1968; Academy of American Poets Fellowship, 1970; Pulitzer Prize, 1978; National Book Award, 1978. D. L.: Lawrence University, Appleton, Wisconsin, 1964; Tufts University, Medford, Massachusetts, 1969; Washington and Lee University, Lexington, Virginia, 1976; University of Vermont, Burlington, 1977. Fellow, American Academy of Arts and Sciences, 1966; Member, American Academy of Arts and Letters, 1976; Chancellor, Academy of American Poets, 1977. Address: Department of English, Washington University, St. Louis, Missouri 63130, U.S.A.

PUBLICATIONS

Verse

The Image and the Law. New York, Holt, 1947.
Guide to the Ruins. New York, Random House, 1950.
The Salt Garden. Boston, Little Brown, 1955.
Small Moment. Los Angeles, Ward Ritchie Press, 1957.
Mirrors and Windows. Chicago, University of Chicago Press, 1958.
New and Selected Poems. Chicago, University of Chicago Press, 1960.
The Next Room of the Dream: Poems and Two Plays. Chicago, University of Chicago Press, 1962.
Five American Poets, with others, edited by Ted Hughes and Thom Gunn. London, Faber, 1963.
The Blue Swallows. Chicago, University of Chicago Press, 1967.
A Sequence of Seven. Roanoke, Virginia, Tinker Press, 1967.
The Winter Lightning: Selected Poems. London, Rapp and Whiting, 1968.
The Painter Dreaming in the Scholar's House. New York, Phoenix Book Shop, 1968.
Gnomes and Occasions. Chicago, University of Chicago Press, 1972.
The Western Approaches: Poems 1973–1975. Chicago, University of Chicago Press, 1975.
The Collected Poems of Howard Nemerov. Chicago, University of Chicago Press, 1977.

Novels

The Melodramatists. New York, Random House, 1949.
Federigo; or, The Power of Love. Boston, Little Brown, 1954.
The Homecoming Game. New York, Simon and Schuster, 1957.

Short Stories

A Commodity of Dreams and Other Stories. New York, Simon and Schuster, 1959; London, Secker and Warburg, 1960.
Stories, Fables and Other Diversions. Boston, Godine, 1971.

Other

Poetry and Fiction: Essays. New Brunswick, New Jersey, Rutgers University Press, 1963.
Journal of the Fictive Life. New Brunswick, New Jersey, Rutgers University Press, 1965.
Reflexions on Poetry and Poetics. New Brunswick, New Jersey, Rutgers University Press, 1972.

Figures of Thought: Speculations on the Meaning of Poetry and Other Essays. Boston, Godine, 1978.

Editor, *Longfellow.* New York, Dell, 1959.
Editor, *Poets on Poetry.* New York, Basic Books, 1966.

Manuscript Collection: Olin Library, Washington University, St. Louis.

Critical Studies: *Howard Nemerov* by Peter Meinke, Minneapolis, University of Minnesota Press, 1968; *The Critical Reception of Howard Nemerov: A Selection of Essays and a Bibliography*, edited by Bowie Duncan, Metuchen, New Jersey, Scarecrow Press, 1971; *The Shield of Perseus*, by Julia Bartholomay, Gainesville, University of Florida Press, 1972; *The Stillness in Moving Things: The World of Howard Nemerov* by William Mills, Memphis, Memphis State University Press, 1975; "The Signature of Things" by Mary Kinzie, in *Parnassus* (New York), Fall-Winter 1977.

* * *

Howard Nemerov's poems are, on the one hand, often about bugs, birds, trees, and running water. On the other, they are about the Great American Society and its works, e.g. the loyalty oath, the committee, the Indian-head nickel, and the packaged meat in the supermarket. And they are about Lot's wife, and Lu Chi, and Vermeer. They are about history and nature, and about everyman, who participates in and speaks for both.

Nemerov does not seek to impose a vision upon the world so much as to listen to what it says. He works in closer relationship with literal meaning than is at present fashionable; consequently, his worst fault is sententiousness, but his corresponding virtue is a clarity whose object is not to diminish the mystery of the world but to allow it to appear without the interposition of a peculiar individuality, or of fancy-work or arabesque. He is, as much as any modern can be, a romantic poet, a religious poet who has no religion ("Runes"):

> ... and history is no more than
> The shadows thrown by clouds on mountainsides,
> A distant chill when all is brought to pass
> By rain and birth and rising of the dead.

He is a prophet, especially in the polemical and ironic mode, without portfolio. When he writes about history, as Stanley Hyman has said, his theme is "history from the point of view of the losers." Thus when he wants to write about Moses, he does so from the point of view of Pharaoh after the Red Sea debacle; and instead of writing about Perseus, he presents the nitwitted predecessors of that hero, who approached Medusa without a mirror and were turned to stone. To judge by his later poems, being turned to stone is the least agreeable and most probable fate for human beings and their institutions together.

Nemerov is an intellectual but in no obtrusive way a "literary" poet, except insofar as he uses a variety of traditional verse forms. There are rhymed quatrains, songs, sonnets, sestinas, most notably a loose blank-verse line well exemplified in his two short plays, *Endor* and *Cain*. Nemerov's voice is spare and flexible. He allows himself no flourishes, except in irony, e.g., at the expense of Santa Claus, the "annual saviour of the economy," who "speaks in the parables of the dollar sign:/Suffer the little children to come to Him." The over-all effect is of great intellectual and lyric power held in firm control. The poems are like the seeds Nemerov so often speaks of: small, but greatly generative. What they generate in us is painstaking and sometimes painful attention to the insides and outsides of things, and to the subtle relationships between them.

The world, for Nemerov, is a great writing in which we are characters attempting to read our own sentence. We are to see (not solve) our secret in seeds and seasons, in trout pools and in paintings and in poems ("Runes"):

... knowing the secret,
Keeping the secret – herringbones of light
Ebbing on beaches, the huge artillery
Of tides – it is not knowing, it is not keeping,
But being the secret hidden from yourself.

Being is extraordinarily painful: "from nose-picking to the Crucifixion/One terrible continuum extends/Binding disaster to discovery." The point of faith is that you sweat your *being* out. But there is more than sweat. Happiness is "helpless" before the fall of white water which purges away "all this filth" of history and mortality. Nemerov accepts again and again the river-runs of time and language in which the reflections of our stony monuments break and disappear.

—Julia Randall

NEWLOVE, John (Herbert). Canadian. Born in Regina, Saskatchewan, 13 June 1938. Married Susan Mary Phillips in 1966; two step-children. Formerly, Senior Editor, McClelland and Stewart Ltd., publishers, Toronto. Writer-in-Residence, Concordia University, Montreal, 1974–75, University of Western Ontario, London, 1975–76, and University of Toronto, 1976–77. Recipient: Koerner Foundation grant, 1964; Canada Council grant, 1965, 1967, 1977; Governor-General's Award, 1973. Address: c/o McClelland and Stewart Ltd., 25 Hollinger Road, Toronto M4B 3G2, Canada.

PUBLICATIONS

Verse

Grave Sirs. Vancouver, Robert Reid, 1962.
Elephants, Mothers and Others. Vancouver, Periwinkle Press, 1963.
Moving In Alone. Toronto, Contact Press, 1965.
Notebook Pages. Toronto, Charles Pachter, 1966.
Four Poems. Platteville, Wisconsin, It, 1967.
What They Say. Toronto, Weed/Flower Press, 1967.
Black Night Window. Toronto, McClelland and Stewart, 1968.
The Cave. Toronto, McClelland and Stewart, 1970.
Lies. Toronto, McClelland and Stewart, 1972.
The Fat Man: Selected Poems 1962–1972. Toronto, McClelland and Stewart, 1977.
Dreams Surround Us, with John Metcalf. Delta, Ontario, Bastard Press, 1977.

Other

Editor, *Dream Craters*, by Joe Rosenblatt. Erin, Ontario, Press Porcépic, 1974.
Editor, *Canadian Poetry: The Modern Era.* Toronto, McClelland and Stewart, 1977.

Manuscript Collection: University of Toronto Library.

Critical Studies: "How Do I Get Out of Here: The Poetry of John Newlove" by Margaret Atwood, Spring 1973, and "Something in Which to Believe for Once: The Poetry of John Newlove" by Jan Bartley, Fall 1974, both in *Open Letter* (Toronto).

John Newlove comments:

If I had a personal statement to make on my own work, it would consist of the fifth part of Wallace Stevens's "Thirteen Ways of Looking at a Blackbird."

* * *

John Newlove has moved from an initial stage of matter-of-fact, personal recollection through a middle phase of essentially negative vision and a conscious edging towards marginal projectivism, to a latter condition in which there has been a noticeable darkening of his horizons coupled with a new intellectual toughness, and a more studied method in his technique.

In the early poems the most consistent locus is that of a series of private observations, and the tone – understandably personal and not infrequently nostalgic – is honest and outspoken. The correlatives are of youthful experiences; the remembered journey; the sense and sensation of simply being alive. A sombre shift takes place with *Moving In Alone* and with *What They Say* where death, isolation and the pointlessness and ugliness of existence become the hallmarks of much of what Newlove has to say. There is also a sense of a kind of desperate activity; movement; travel in the tumbleweed moods of the hitch-hiker which suggests rootlessness and a worrisome escape.

Disengagement and the poet's alienation continue to dominate *Black Night Window*, Newlove's most ambitious collection, and stamp him with the mark of small "e" existentialism. He continues to be autobiographical although his perspective transcends the purely subjective, and his imagination grapples effectively with abstraction and succeeds in striking a balance between his own vision, the ideas of poetry, and the larger consciousness of collective man.

Newlove's marginal projectivism stems from the technical bias of the Canadian West Coast *TISH*-movement with which the poet has links. His early style has a laconic, forthright quality with later development into the relative complexities of jigsaw structuring of concrete, immediate and precise images.

—Michael Gnarowski

NICHOL, Barrie Phillip (bpNichol). Canadian. Born in Vancouver, British Columbia, 30 September 1944. Attended the University of British Columbia, Vancouver. Formerly, taught grade school. Co-Editor, *GrOnk* magazine, Toronto. Recipient: four Canada Council grants; Governor-General's Award, 1971. Address: c/o The Village Bookstore, 29 Gerrard Street West, Toronto, Ontario, Canada.

PUBLICATIONS

Verse

Cycles Etc. Cleveland, 7 Flowers Press, 1965.
Scraptures: 2nd Sequence. Toronto, Ganglia Press, 1965.
Strange Grey Town, with David Aylward. Toronto, Ganglia Press, 1966.
Tonto or. Toronto, Ganglia Press, 1966.
Calendar. Woodchester, Gloucestershire, Openings Press, 1966.
Scraptures: 3rd Sequence. Toronto, Ganglia Press, 1966.

Scraptures: 4th Sequence. Niagara Falls, New York, Press Today Niagara, 1966.
Fodder Folder. Toronto, Ganglia Press, 1966.
Portrait of David. Toronto, Ganglia Press, 1966.
A Vision in the U of T Stacks. Toronto, Ganglia Press, 1966.
A Little Pome for Yur Fingertips. Toronto, Ganglia Press, 1966.
Langwedge. Toronto, Ganglia Press, 1966.
Alaphbit. Toronto, Ganglia Press, 1966.
Stan's Ikon. Toronto, Ganglia Press, 1966.
The Birth of O. Toronto, Ganglia Press, 1966.
The Chocolate Poem. Toronto, privately printed, 1966.
Letters Home. Toronto, Coach House Press, 1966.
Scraptures: 9th Sequence. Toronto, Ganglia Press, 1967.
Last Poem with You in Mind. Toronto, Ganglia Press, 1967.
Konfessions of an Elizabethan Fan Dancer. London, Writers Forum, 1967.
bp (including *Journeying and The Returns*, *Letters Home*, and a recording, *Borders*). Toronto, Coach House Press, 1967.
Scraptures: 10th Sequence. Toronto, Ganglia Press, 1967.
Scraptures: Sequence 11. Toronto, Fleye Press, 1967.
Ruth. Toronto, Fleye Press, 1967.
The Year of the Frog: A Study of the Frog from the Scraptures: Ninth Sequence. Toronto, Ganglia Press, 1967.
Ballads of the Restless Are. Sacramento, California, Runcible Spoon Press, 1968.
Dada Lama: A Sound Sequence in Six Parts. London, Cavan McCarthy, 1968.
D.A. Dead. Toronto, grOnk, 1968.
Kon 66 and 67. Toronto, grOnk, 1968.
The Complete Works. Toronto, Ganglia Press, 1968.
Sail. Toronto, Ganglia Press, 1969.
A New Calendar. Toronto, Ganglia Press, 1969.
Astronomical Observations July 1969. Toronto, Ganglia Press, 1969.
Third Fragment from a Poem Continually in the Process of Being Written. Toronto, Ganglia Press, 1969.
Final Concrete Testament. Toronto, Ganglia Press, 1969(?).
Lament. Toronto, Ganglia Press, and London, Writers Forum, 1970.
Grease Ball Comics 1. Toronto, Ganglia Press, 1970.
A Condensed History of Nothing. Toronto, Ganglia Press, 1970.
Still Water. Vancouver, Talonbooks, 1970.
Beach Head. Sacramento, California, Runcible Spoon Press, 1970.
MONO tones. Vancouver, Talonbooks, 1971.
Love: A Book of Remembrances. Vancouver, Talonbooks, 1971.
ABC: The Aleph Beth Book. Ottowa, Oberon Press, 1971.
The Other Side of the Room: Poems 1966–69. Toronto, Weed/Flower Press, 1971.
Parallel Texts, with Steve McCaffery. Toronto, Anonbeyond, 2 vols., 1971.
The Captain Poetry Poems. Vancouver, blewointmentpress, 1971.
The Adventures of Milt the Morph in Colour, with Barbara Caruso. Toronto, Seripress, 1972.
Collbrations, with Steve McCaffery. Toronto, Ganglia Press, 1972.
The Martyrology. Toronto, Coach House Press, 2 vols., 1972–76.
Alephunit. Toronto, Seripress, 1973.
Unit of Four. Toronto, Seripress, 1973.

Recordings: *Motherlove*, Allied, 1968; *Canadada*, Griffin House, 1972.

Play

Radio Play: *Little Boy Lost Meets Mother Tongue*, 1969.

Novels

Andy and For Jesus Lunatic: Two Novels. Toronto, Coach House Press, 1969.

Short Stories

Nights on Prose Mountain. Toronto, grOnk, 1969.
The True Eventual Story of Billy the Kid. Toronto, Weed/Flower Press, 1970.

Other

Editor, *The Cosmic Chef: An Evening of Concrete.* Ottawa, Oberon Press, 1970.
Editor, with Jiri Valoch, *Czech Concrete Anthology.* Toronto, Coach House Press, 1973.
Editor, with Steve McCaffery, *The Story so Four.* Toronto, Coach House Press, 1976.

bpNichol comments:

primarily i consider myself to be serving an apprenticeship in language, hopefully to find ways out of the self-imposed trap it has evolved into.

i suppose if i have a general theme it's the language trap and that runs thru the centre of everything i do. in this regard Bill Bissett first pointed the direction with a poem called "They Found th Wagon Cat in Human Body." hence style is disregarded in favor of reproduction of actual states of mind in order to follow these states thru the particular traps they become in search of possible exits. hence for me there is no discrepancy to pass back and forth between trad poetry, concrete poetry, sound poetry, film, comic strips, the novel or what have you in order to reproduce the muse that musses up my own brain.

as large influences i would like to note Chester Gould's *Dick Tracy*, Walt Kelly's *Pogo*, & Winsor McKay's *Dreams of a Rarebit Fiend & Little Nemo in Slumberland.* In addition the poetry of Olson and Creeley, e. e. cummings, gertrude stein & james joyce, rube goldberg, & the children's books by Dr. Seuss.

* * *

bpNichol is internationally known as the Canadian concrete poet, a role bestowed on him by that self-conscious international movement.

Konfessions of an Elizabethan Fan Dancer consists of typewriter poems, visual poetry dependent on the identical size of typewriter letters. "The Return of the Repressed," reminiscent of a genetic chart, evolves in time:

```
               Q
OOOOOOOOO⊠OOOOOQOOOO
OOOOOOOOO⊠OOOOQOOOOO
OOOOOOOOO⊠OOOOOQOOOO
QQQQQQQQQQQQQQQQQQQQ
QQQQQQQQQQQQQQQQQQQQ
QQQQQQQQQQQQQQQQQQQQ
QQQQQQQQQQQQQQQQQQQQ
```

The progenitor is replaced by his sons. Nichol uses the more extravagant Press-On Type for "tight imagistic" effects, not meant as pictures, he says, but as "syllabic and sub-syllabic messages to who care to listen." In "Window," Nichol paints with letters the aural and emotional complex suggested by a window; "imagism" seems to be an appropriate analogue. *Still Water* is a box of poems on cards, cleanly printed in sans-serif type. Many are funny, like this rap at high coo: "2 leaves touch/bad poems are written." Others are one-liners using onomatopoetic permutations: "beyond a bee yawned abbey on debby honda beyond." Although one-line poems are in vogue, their creators seem defensive, probably because scale in poetry and in painting has grown larger through this century, more heroic, more inclusive.

In any case, there is nothing new or unusual about Nichol's concrete poetry. In his book on Canadian literature, Northrop Frye concluded that the country's literary energy had been absorbed in meeting a standard, a self-defeating enterprise because real standards can only be established, not met. Canadian writing, according to Frye, is academic in the pejorative sense, an imitation of a prescribed model, second rate in conception, not merely execution.

The poetry which is loosely called concrete, however, is self-investigative. Richard Kostelanetz, a theoretician of the movement, compares it to minimalism. Like minimal artists, concrete poets will restrict themselves to the means of making statements. Nichol writes a poem on mortality which consists of a rhyme: "FLOWERS/(hours)." The Toronto Research Group, in which Nichol is prominent, investigates translation and narrative in an imaginative rather than critical context. The very process of imitation seems to have freed Nichol from that malaise.

The Martyrology, a recent two-volume large-scale work, is certainly readable. It's about a bunch of saints he made up. Saint Ranglehold, for instance, is the patron of the sea, and he gives lovers a hard time on their Petrarchan voyages; were there such things as "the good" and "the bad" saints, Nichol asks, where would we place him?

a ship in perilous storm
the lover doth compare his state to

often he loses
                    (sinking out of view)

dedications change as frequently as the moon

riding the white waves
patterns seem strangely familiar

ruler of the ships & sea
saint ranglehold guides lovers with a flaccid hand

snickers knowingly
as they flounder on dry land

Saint Reat, like Charles Olson, had difficulty breathing and, as a wanderer in search of breath, he is the patron saint of poetry. Saint Orm, a loser, gets kicked Kafka-style around a circus. Nichol has a special devotion to Saint Orm. These saints are neither Eastern nor Christian but very tough. It takes a Dick Tracy or Emma Peel to handle them.

random brain stranded in the station

sam & dick & emma peel
oh how the real world gets lost in you

the loose ends shrivel
                    & are gone

faces denote the places growing song

The Martyrology is a creation myth. The saints once lived in the clouds. Saint And was the first to leave. Orm followed, expecting rain. Saint Iff had a terrible time, landing in the desert and dying near water. Only Saint Rike and the lady of past nights stayed behind, and their tale is curious indeed. But so are the other tales.

—Michael André

NICHOLSON, Norman (Cornthwaite). British. Born in Millom, Cumberland, 8 January 1914. Educated at local schools. Married Yvonne Gardner in 1956. Frequent public lecturer. Recipient: Heinemann Award, 1945; Cholmondeley Award, 1967; Northern Arts Association Grant, 1969; Society of Authors bursary, 1973; Arts Council bursary, 1977; Queen's Gold Medal for Poetry, 1977; Manchester Polytechnic Fellowship, 1979. M.A.: Manchester University, 1959; Open University, 1975. Fellow, Royal Society of Literature, 1945. Agent: David Higham Associates, 5–8 Lower John Street, London W1R 4HA. Address: 14 St. George's Terrace, Millom, Cumbria LA18 4DB, England.

PUBLICATIONS

Verse

Selected Poems, with John Hall and Keith Douglas. London, John Bale and Staples, 1943.
Five Rivers. London, Faber, 1944; New York, Dutton, 1945.
Rock Face. London, Faber, 1948.
The Pot Geranium. London, Faber, 1954.
Selected Poems. London, Faber, 1966.
No Star on the Way Back: Ballads and Carols. Manchester, Manchester Institute of Contemporary Arts, 1967.
A Local Habitation. London, Faber, 1972.
Hard of Hearing. London, Poem-of-the-Month Club, 1974.
Cloud on the Black Combe. Hitchin, Hertfordshire, Cellar Press, 1975.
Stitch and Stone: A Cumbrian Landscape. Sunderland, Ceolfrith, 1975.
The Shadow on Black Combe. Ashington, Northumberland, MidNAG, 1978.

Recording: *Poems*, with Tony Connor, Argo, 1974.

Plays

The Old Man of the Mountains (produced London, 1945). London, Faber, 1946; revised edition, 1950.
Prophesy to the Wind: A Play in Four Scenes and a Prologue (produced London, 1949). London, Faber, 1950.
A Match for the Devil (produced Edinburgh, 1953). London, Faber, 1955.
Birth by Drowning (produced Mirfield, Yorkshire, 1959). London, Faber, 1960.

Television Play: *No Star on the Way Back*, 1963.

Novels

The Fire of the Lord. London, Nicholson and Watson, 1944; New York, Dutton, 1946.
The Green Shore. London, Nicholson and Watson, 1947.

Other

Man and Literature. London, S.C.M. Press, 1943; Folcroft, Pennsylvania, Folcroft Editions, 1974.
Cumberland and Westmorland. London, Hale, 1949.
H. G. Wells. London, Barker, and Denver, Swallow, 1950.
William Cowper. London, Lehmann, 1951; Folcroft, Pennsylvania, Folcroft Editions, 1977.
The Lakers: The Adventures of the First Tourists. London, Hale, 1955.
Provincial Pleasures. London, Hale, 1959.
William Cowper. London, Longman, 1960.
Portrait of the Lakes. London, Hale, 1963; revised edition, as *The Lakes*, 1977.
Enjoying It All (BBC talks). London, Waltham Forest Books, 1964.
Greater Lakeland. London, Hale, 1969.
Wednesday Early Closing (autobiography). London, Faber, 1975.

Editor, *An Anthology of Religious Verse Designed for the Times.* London, Penguin, 1942.
Editor, *Wordsworth: An Introduction and Selection.* London, Phoenix, and New York, Dent, 1949.
Editor, *Poems*, by William Cowper. London, Grey Walls Press, 1951.
Editor, *A Choice of Cowper's Verse.* London, Faber, 1975.
Editor, *The Lake District: An Anthology.* London, Hale, 1977.

Manuscript Collections: National Collection of Poetry Manuscripts, London; Northern Arts Manuscript Collection, Newcastle upon Tyne.

Critical Studies: *Christian Themes in Contemporary Poets* by Kathleen Morgan, London, S.C.M. Press, 1965; "The Provincial Poetry of Norman Nicholson" by Philip Gardner, in *Toronto Review*; *Norman Nicholson* by Philip Gardner, New York, Twayne, 1973.

Norman Nicholson comments:

(1970) The most obvious characteristic of my poetry is the fact that I draw by far the greater amount of my imagery from my own immediate environment – i.e., from the fells, dales, farms, sea-shore and estuaries of the English Lake District, and from the houses, streets, blast furnaces, mines, etc. of the small industrial town of Millom where I still live in the house where I was born. But, though the topographical element is prominent in my earlier verse, I do not think of myself primarily as a local poet. On the contrary, I feel that, through drawing on my knowledge of the place and the people where and among whom I have spent all my life, I am able to say what I want to say about man in relation to his physical environment and about human society, man in relation to man. In particular, I believe that in a small, somewhat isolated town like Millom, the problems of society, the dwelling-together of people of different types, ages and class, and the pattern of the repetition and variation shown from generation to generation, can be seen on a scale small enough for the mind to grasp it whole.

(1974) After the publication of *The Pot Geranium*, I wrote very little poetry for about ten years, but then began writing again and produced the poems collected together under the title of *A Local Habitation*, which was The Poetry Book Society's Autumn Choice for 1972. This work is, on the whole, more direct, more colloquial in tone, and, though I am as concerned as ever with the problem of environment, the new poems deal more with people than with places, and in particular with the people of Millom, with my family and other memories of childhood and youth.

* * *

Norman Nicholson is very much a poet of the Cumberland area, and very much a poet of the Christian faith; these twin themes run through most of his published work from *Five Rivers* onward. He writes very often of the landscape around Millom, the little town where he was born – only fifteen miles from the Lakeland of Wordsworth, Coleridge, Southey, with whom he evidently feels a deep sympathy; and he frequently speaks through the mouths of the often wryly humorous characters who live in the roughly beautiful Cumberland landscape, "Where the rocks stride about like legs in armour/And the steel birches buckle and bounce in the wind...."

His talent is for somewhat laconic observation of the natural scene, of landscape and wild and human life; the fact that he has made a selection from Wordsworth is significant. His unintellectualized faith often sees Christianity epitomized in acts of nature. He has written on modern European literature from a religious standpoint, and has edited an anthology of religious verse; his own verse-play *The Old Man of the Mountains* is a reworking of the story of Elijah and the raven, set in the contemporary Cumberland landscape.

Nicholson's choice of words is straightforward and unambiguous, and if there is a certain ambiguity at the heart of his verse, it is the ambiguity which as a Christian poet he has set out to reconcile with inner certainty. Most of his poems, however assured, seem to end with a question. Unfashionably direct in language and philosophy, he is perhaps one of the finest landscape poets writing at the present time.

—Derek Parker

NIMS, John Frederick. American. Born in Muskegon, Michigan, 20 November 1913. Educated at De Paul University, Chicago; University of Notre Dame, Indiana, A.B. 1937, M.A. 1939; University of Chicago, Ph.D. in comparative literature 1945. Married Bonnie Larkin in 1947; four children. Taught at the University of Notre Dame, 1939–45, 1946–58; University of Toronto, 1945–46; Visiting Fulbright Professor of American Literature, Bocconi University, Milan, 1952–53, and University of Florence, 1953–54; Visiting Professor of American Studies, University of Madrid, 1958–60 (Smith-Mundt grant). Professor of English, University of Illinois, Urbana, 1961–65, and since 1973, Chicago Circle. Visiting Professor, Harvard University, Cambridge, Massachusetts, 1964, 1968–69, Bread Loaf School of English, Vermont, 1965–69, University of Florida, Gainesville, 1973–76, and Williams College, Williamstown, Massachusetts, 1975. Associate Editor, 1945–48, Guest Editor, 1960–61, and since 1978, Editor, *Poetry*, Chicago. Recipient: Harriet Monroe Memorial Prize, 1942, Guarantors Prize, 1943, and Levinson Prize, 1944 (*Poetry*, Chicago); National Endowment for the Arts grant, 1967; National Institute of Arts and Letters grant, 1968; Brandeis University Creative Arts Award, 1974. Address: Department of English, University of Illinois, Box 4348, Chicago, Illinois 60680, U.S.A.

PUBLICATIONS

Verse

Five Young American Poets: Third Series, with others. New York, New Directions, 1944.
The Iron Pastoral. New York, Sloane, 1947.
A Fountain in Kentucky and Other Poems. New York, Sloane, 1950.
Knowledge of the Evening: Poems 1950–1960. New Brunswick, New Jersey, Rutgers University Press, 1960.
Of Flesh and Bone. New Brunswick, New Jersey, Rutgers University Press 1967.

Other

Western Wind: An Introduction to Poetry. New York, Random House, 1974.

Editor, with others, *The Poem Itself.* New York, Holt, 1960.
Editor, *Ovid's Metamorphoses: The Arthur Golding Translation.* New York, Macmillan, 1965.

Translator, *The Poems of St. John of the Cross.* New York, Grove Press, 1959; revised edition, 1968; Chicago, University of Chicago Press, 1979.
Translator, *Andromache*, in *Euripides III* of *The Complete Greek Tragedies.* Chicago, University of Chicago Press, 1959.
Translator, *Sappho to Valéry: Poems.* New Brunswick, New Jersey, Rutgers University Press, 1971.

Critical Studies: *Babel to Byzantium* by James Dickey, New York, Farrar Straus, 1968; "A Higher Fidelity" by Brewster Ghiselin, in *Sewanee Review* (Tennessee), Spring 1973.

* * *

There has always been a tradition of elegance in American poetry, and it is to this tradition that John Frederick Nims belongs. He has an ease of tone which is very civilized, and an admirable virtuosity when it comes to the handling of verse. He is able to convince his readers that poetry can reject the "barbaric yawp" of Whitman without surrendering the power to communicate. Immediately after the war, Nims was one of the pioneers of a new style in American verse, a style which, for a time, carried all before it with its urbanity. His first full collection, *The Iron Pastoral*, appeared in 1947, the same year as Richard Wilbur's *The Beautiful Changes*, and Nims, as much as Wilbur, was one of the leaders of the reaction against modernism which swept through American poetry in the forties. The manner which was then established has since been challenged by a very different sort of poetry. But Nims, no less than Wilbur, was highly original in the context of the time, and his work seems likely to be remembered not only for its unfailing grace, but as marking an important turning-point in the development of the literary tradition. Meanwhile, it has continued to give pleasure to all those poetry-readers whose taste is not entirely at the mercy of the dictates of fashion.

—Edward Lucie-Smith

NORRIS, Leslie. Welsh. Born in Merthyr Tydfil, Glamorgan, 21 May 1921. Educated at Cyfthfa Castle School, 1931–38; City of Coventry College, 1947–48; University of Southampton (Ralph Morley Prize, 1958), 1955–58, Dip.Ed., M.Phil., 1958. Served in the Royal Air Force, 1940–42. Married Catherine Mary Morgan in 1948. Teacher, Grass Royal School, Yeovil, Somerset, 1948–52; Deputy Head, Southdown School, Bath, 1952–55; Head Teacher, Aldingbourne School, Chichester, 1956–58; Principal Lecturer in Degree Studies, College of Education, Bognor Regis, Sussex, 1958–73; Visiting Lecturer, University of Washington, Seattle, 1973, 1980; Resident Poet, Eton College, 1977; Arts Council Writing Fellow, West Sussex Institute of High Education, 1979–80. Recipient: Welsh Arts Council award, 1967, 1968, and prize, 1978; Alice Hunt Bartlett Prize, 1970; Cholmondeley Prize, 1978; David Higham Prize, for fiction, 1978. Fellow, Royal Society of Literature, 1974. Agent: Charles Schlessiger, Brandt and Brandt, 101 Park Avenue, New York, New York 10017. Address: Plas Nant, Northfields Lane, Aldingbourne, Chichester, Sussex, England.

PUBLICATIONS

Verse

Tongue of Beauty. London, Favil Press, 1941.
Poems. London, Falcon Press, 1946.
The Ballad of Billy Rose. Leeds, Northern House, 1964.
The Loud Winter. Cardiff, Triskel Press, 1967.
Finding Gold. London, Chatto and Windus, 1967.
Curlew. St. Brelade, Jersey, Armstrong, 1969.
Ransoms. London, Chatto and Windus, 1970.
His Last Autumn. Rushden, Northamptonshire, Sceptre Press, 1972.
Mountains, Polecats, Pheasants and Other Elegies. London, Chatto and Windus, 1973.
Stone and Fern. Winchester, Southern Arts Association, 1973.
At the Publishers'. Berkhamsted, Hertfordshire, Priapus Press, 1976.
Ravenna Bridge. Knotting, Bedfordshire, Sceptre Press, 1977.
Islands Off Maine. Maine, Tidal Press, 1977.
Merlin and the Snake's Egg. New York, Viking Press, 1978.

Recording: *Poems*, with Dannie Abse, Argo, 1974.

Short Stories

Sliding and Other Stories. New York, Scribner, 1976; London, Dent, 1978.

Other

Glyn Jones. Cardiff, University of Wales Press, 1973.

Editor, *Vernon Watkins, 1906–1967.* London, Faber, 1970.
Editor, *Tributes to Andrew Young.* Maine, Tidal Press, 1978.

Manuscript Collection: National Library of Wales, Aberystwyth.

Critical Studies: by Sam Adams, in *Poetry Wales* (Cardiff), 1972; R. Jenkins, in *Anglo-Welsh Review* (Pembroke Dock), 1972; Ted Walker, in *Priapus* (Berkhampsted, Hertfordshire), 1972.

Leslie Norris comments:

My poetry is an attempt to recreate, not to describe. The birds or animals or people or buildings or trees existing in my poems, must exist root branch claw skin and stone. The texture of my words must be made of feathers or bones bark or whatever, the lines must move with real muscle. I think I am a Jungian poet, bringing up the images from some unknown source. The poems come unbidden, and my task is to recognise them; often I am well towards the end of a poem before I know what it is "about." But afterwards I work with unremitting labor to make sure of the poem's clarity, to make its surface perfect. I think my poems ought to be like onions; the golden outer skin flawless, the weight surprisingly heavy, solid, much more than you'd expect; then when the outer skin is peeled, there is the moist, pearly inner layer of meaning, then another and another.

Somewhere in the process you might begin to weep.

* * *

Leslie Norris's birth at Wern Farm, just outside Merthyr Tydfil, Wales's Klondyke of the 19th century, and his subsequent residence in southern England together provide the cultural tension that, after a long silence, generated his poetry again in the 1960's and made it something quite different from the early work in *Tongue of Beauty*. The gap is bridged, of course, by Norris's fascination with and power over words, but the Merthyr to which he could never go back (which was, in the spirit of his youth and that of other writers his seniors, quite dead) was the source of many elegies, in *Finding Gold* in particular, which were an expression both of the irrecoverability of his own youth and of a more general irrecoverability ("And yes, those boys are gone"). It was not that he could not return to Wales – he did that, first with holidays in Cardiganshire and then by the purchase of his cottage "Wthan" – but what this did was to make it possible to approach the Welsh heritage in a way which would have been strange to the Merthyr-bound man: it also linked and contrasted the peaceful rurality of Sussex with the more wayward and half-tamed spirit of the countryside round Llandysul. Leslie Norris was always, perhaps, a man of the country and his great achievement, visible more and more in later books like *Mountains, Polecats, Pheasants*, has been to use the simple, physical stimuli of a rural world to make poems which are no more than occasionally recondite and are always couched in a language which accommodates images in the most natural manner possible and gives continuous pleasure. His syntax is rarely distorted or difficult. What he has evolved is that most difficult thing to master and obtain, a style which in its limpidity, clarity and latent force carries the simple, the anecdotal, even the common, experience and gives it an unexpected memorability. Nor is this quality confined to his poetry, for which he received the Cholmondeley Prize in 1978: the ecstatic reception of his volume of short stories, *Sliding* (he was awarded both the David Higham Prize and a Welsh Arts Council Prize for this), was the recognition of an achievement very similar. Like Edward Thomas and, to a lesser extent, Andrew Young, he can conjure common observation into his own idiosyncratic mode. His recourse, even in later books, to boyhood memories of the boxing ring or the collier's care for birds or dogs – or, more piercingly, to recollection of a classmate killed at Aberfan – provides the variety that makes his countryman's perception the more poignant. Leslie Norris is that rare poet who has made his work accessible without cheapening the experience of the poem or blunting its delicacy. In this sense he is an ambassador for poetry at the court of the general public in a generation that sorely needs one.

—Roland Mathias

NORSE, Harold (George). American. Born in New York City, 6 July 1916. Educated at Brooklyn College, B.A. 1938; New York University, M.A. 1951. Has worked as sheet metal worker, dancer, proof-reader; Instructor in English, Cooper Union, New York, 1949–52, Lion School of English, Rome, 1956–57, and U.S. Information Service School, Naples, 1958. Since 1973, part-time teacher, San Jose State University, California. Founding Editor, *Bastard Angel*, San Francisco. Recipient: National Endowment for the Arts Fellowship, 1974. Address: Department of English, San Jose State University, San Jose, California 95114, U.S.A.

PUBLICATIONS

Verse

The Undersea Mountain. Denver, Swallow, 1953.

The Dancing Beasts. New York, Macmillan, 1962.
Karma Circuit: 20 Poems and a Preface. London, Nothing Doing in London, 1967; San Francisco, Panjandrum Press, 1974.
Penguin Modern Poets 13, with Charles Bukowski and Philip Lamantia. London, Penguin, 1969.
Hotel Nirvana: Selected Poems 1953–1973. San Francisco, City Lights, 1974.
I See America Daily. San Francisco, Mother's Hen, 1974.
Carnivorous Saint: Gay Poems 1941–1976. San Francisco, Gay Sunshine Press, 1977.

Other

Translator, *The Roman Sonnets of G. G. Belli.* Highlands, North Carolina, Jargon, 1960; London, Perivale Press, 1974.

* * *

Harold Norse has suffered from a number of disadvantages, as far as making a poetic reputation is concerned. An expatriate and a slow starter, he does not seem to have sought, and certainly has not managed to find, a regular market for his work. A protégé, like Ginsberg, of William Carlos Williams, his mature poems are related to the Beats, yet retain a sufficient stylistic distance to prevent him from being swept up into the Beat movement as a whole, and borne along on its current of energy.

It must also be admitted that he is an uneven writer. His first book, which he now seems to have rejected almost totally, is *The Undersea Mountain*, published in 1953. The prevailing influence is that of Hart Crane. These lines, from a poem called "The Tankers," are exactly in the manner of Crane's *The Bridge*:

The gunmount flashes, flashing metal grey
also the opaque aft, as down the harbor
estuary under steam towards turquoise streams
she plies.
                    And dagger-eyed the gull veers overhead.

Norse next surfaces, seven years later, with a remarkable book of translations – from the sonnets in Roman dialect of G. G. Belli. What these seem to have enabled him to do was to relate his feeling for American vernacular to his feeling for Europe. Belli, with his baroque use of an exuberantly popular diction, was the liberating influence Norse needed.

His more recent poems, couched in the ranging free-verse which is now an accepted American idiom, tend to vary in quality according to the amount of information, and the kind of information, he manages to pack in to them. Quite a few people do the drug poem, and the tantric poem, rather better than Norse. His speciality, if only he would realise it, is of a more traditional kind – he charts the meetings of the Old World and the New with a kind of exuberant delicacy. His best essay in this manner is the appropriately titled "Classic Frieze in a Garage," which takes an idiom which is basically the one Pound forged for *The Cantos* and uses it in a personal, and, to me, extremely seductive way:

perfect! & how strange! garage
  swallows sarcophagus!
mechanic calmly spraying
  paint on a
              fender
observed in turn by lapith & centaur!

—Edward Lucie-Smith

NOTT, Kathleen (Cecilia). British. Born in London. Educated at Mary Datchelor School, London; King's College, London; Somerville College, Oxford, B.A. (honours) in philosophy, politics and economics. Worked in Army Education and with Air Raid Precautions in World War II. President, Progressive League, London, 1958–60. Since 1960, Editor of International P.E.N.'s Bulletin of Selected Books, London. President, International P.E.N., English Centre, 1974–75. Recipient: Arts Council Bursary, 1968. Address: 5 Limpsfield Avenue, Thornton Heath, Surrey CR4 6BG, England.

PUBLICATIONS

Verse

Landscapes and Departures. London, Editions Poetry London, 1947.
Poems from the North. Aldington, Kent, Hand and Flower Press, 1956.
Creatures and Emblems. London, Routledge, 1960.

Novels

Mile End. London, Hogarth Press, 1938.
The Dry Deluge. London, Hogarth Press, 1947.
Private Fires. London, Heinemann, 1961.
An Elderly Retired Man. London, Faber, 1963.

Other

The Emperor's Clothes: An Attack on the Dogmatic Orthodoxy of T. S. Eliot, Graham Greene, Dorothy Sayers, C. S. Lewis and Others. London, Heinemann, and Bloomington, University of Indiana Press, 1954.
A Clean Well-Lighted Place: A Private View of Sweden. London, Heinemann, 1960.
Objections to Humanism, with others. London, Hodder and Stoughton, 1963.
A Soul in the Quad. London, Routledge, 1969.
Philosophy and Human Nature. London, Hodder and Stoughton, 1970.
The Good Want Power: An Essay in the Psychological Possibilities of Liberalism. London, Cape, and New York, Basic Books, 1977.

Editor, with C. Day Lewis and Thomas Blackburn, *New Poems 1957.* London, Joseph, 1957.

Translator, *Northwesterly Gale*, by Lucien Chauvet. London, Hutchinson, 1947.
Translator, *Son of Stalin*, by Riccardo Bacchelli. London, Secker and Warburg, 1956.
Translator, *The Fire of Milan*, by Riccardo Bacchelli. London, Secker and Warburg, 1958.

Kathleen Nott comments:

I am primarily a poet, but I had a philosophical training and I am very much concerned with ethics and aesthetics. *A Soul in the Quad* took over five years to write and is a largish book describing in an autobiographical and intellectual-social setting what I conceive the relations of poetry and philosophy to be.

I regard poetry as a special language and an existential one. It is the language of beings of rather peculiar physiological and psychological organization. It works out as the most favourable selection and balance of the colours, implications, weights, stresses and relations of words – most favourable, that is, to project a highly authentic personal vision (which may be of a momentary kind). Hence rhythmical and musical sense strikes me as paramount.

* * *

As a philosopher Kathleen Nott is a humanist but also a respectful opponent of logical positivism and the "scientism" of Karl Popper. Her position is in fact a remarkably original and interesting one, and it is in her poetry that we find it most subtly and yet explicitly stated. For, like Valéry, she believes in the formulative power of music (in the Valérian sense of that preconceived rhythm that "visits" a poet before he is consciously aware of its content or significance). Thus rhythm is an important aspect of her work: she seldom works within strictly conventional forms, but her line is elegantly formed and controlled. This is also the strongest feature of her work – its weaknesses are unconfident or blurred diction, and an apparent inability to do justice to her initial impulse. Thus "Absolute Zero" begins promisingly:

> There are no tall engines standing in the polar North
> or none that is ready for use. They are all
> sheeted and hooded with the snow: who could discern them
> among faceless pines
> and blinded firs?

But this vision gradually peters out into a confusion of metaphors, only to recover itself at the end of the poem: the result is unintentionally elliptical. There seems little explanation for the wrenched diction ("and at last to be seen of eyes ...") that characterizes the middle section of the poem. Fortunately this does not always happen: "Nature's Betrayal," about Wordsworth and nature, is in a tighter form, and there is more control of meaning and metaphor as well as of rhythm. At her best Kathleen Nott is an interesting philosophical poet whose thinking, in this form, deserves more attention than it has been given.

—Martin Seymour-Smith

NOWLAN, Alden A. Canadian. Born in Windsor, Nova Scotia, 25 January 1933. Married to Claudine Orser; one son. Formerly, News Editor, *The Observer*, Hartland, New Brunswick, and *The Telegraph Journal*, St. John, New Brunswick. Since 1968, Writer-in-Residence, University of New Brunswick, Fredericton. Recipient: Canada Council Fellowship, 1961, Special Award, 1967, and theatre grant, 1974; Governor-General's Award, 1968; Guggenheim Fellowship, 1968; President's Medal, The University of Western Ontario, for short story, 1969, 1971; Queen's Silver Jubilee Medal, 1978; Canadian Authors Association award, 1978. D.Litt.: University of New Brunswick, 1971; LL.D.: Dalhousie University, Halifax, Nova Scotia, 1977. Address: 676 Windsor Street, Fredericton, New Brunswick E3B 4G4, Canada.

PUBLICATIONS

Verse

The Rose and the Puritan. Fredericton, University of New Brunswick, 1958.
A Darkness in the Earth. Eureka, California, Hearse Press, 1959.

Wind in a Rocky Country. Toronto, Emblem, 1960.
Under the Ice. Toronto, Ryerson Press, 1961.
Five New Brunswick Poets, with others, edited by Fred Cogswell. Fredericton, New Brunswick, Fiddlehead, 1962.
The Things Which Are. Toronto, Contact Press, 1962.
Bread, Wine and Salt. Toronto, Clarke Irwin, 1967.
A Black Plastic Button and a Yellow Yoyo. Toronto, Charles Pachter, 1968.
The Mysterious Naked Man. Toronto, Clarke Irwin, 1969.
Playing the Jesus Game: Selected Poems. Trumansburg, New York, New Books, 1970.
Between Tears and Laughter. Toronto, Clarke Irwin, 1971.
I'm a Stranger Here Myself. Toronto, Clarke Irwin, 1974.
Smoked Glass. Toronto, Clarke Irwin, 1977.

Play

Frankenstein, with Walter Learning, adaptation of the novel by Mary Shelley. Toronto, Clarke Irwin, 1976.

Novel

Various Persons Named Kevin O'Brien. Toronto, Clarke Irwin, 1973.

Short Stories

Miracle at Indian River. Toronto, Clarke Irwin, 1968.

Other

Shaped by This Land, paintings by Tom Forrestall. Fredericton, New Brunswick, Brunswick Press, 1974.
Campobello: The Outer Island. Toronto, Clarke Irwin, 1975.
Double Exposure. Fredericton, New Brunswick, Brunswick Press, 1978.

Critical Study: *Poet's Progress* by Michael Brian Oliver, Fredericton, New Brunswick, Fiddlehead, 1978.

Alden Nowlan comments:

I write about what it is like to be Alden Nowlan because that is the only thing I know anything about.

* * *

"Being a Maritimer," Alden Nowlan said recently, "doesn't make it any more likely that you'll write well, but it sure as hell improves the chances of your having something to write about." Nowlan is a native of Nova Scotia; he has spent all his life in the Maritime provinces of Canada, and this region – which in the late nineteenth century produced a whole school of poets clustered around Charles G. D. Roberts and Bliss Carman – has conditioned his poetry with its social problems and its moral compulsions. On another occasion Nowlan said: "I am a product of a culture that fears any display of emotion and attempts to repress any true communication." To be born within such a culture is to know the extremes of ecstasy and damnation, and Nowlan talks obliquely of the dual nature of his own role in a poem where he appears as the creature rather than the creator. It is "Beginning"; the crucial lines are these:

From what they found most lovely, most abhorred,
my parents made me: I was born like sound
stroked from the fiddle to become the ward
of tunes played on the bear-trap and the hound ...

never in making was there brighter bliss,
followed by darker shame. Thus I was made.

Once a prosperous region of shipbuilders and clipper-borne trade, the Maritimes began to decline in the late 19th century as the age of the sailing ship drew to an end; when Alden Nowlan was born at the height of the Depression in 1933, it had become a place of harsh poverty where he grew up as the son of a poor backwoods logger. Nowlan left school when he was 15, did labouring work while he wrote poetry in isolation, became a smalltown reporter, and finally, when he was 24, met another poet, Fred Cogswell, who was perhaps the most important sustaining influence in his career. It was in the year after he met Cogswell that Nowlan published his first book of verse, *The Rose and the Puritan*, whose very title suggested the dual aspects of his sensibility. Since then he has been publishing volumes with a consistency that seems remarkable in view of his long battles with cancer.

Nowlan's poems tend to be anecdotal and strongly linked to the immediate realities of the half-rural life from which he emerged. Often they evoke its barbaric cruelties in direct, harsh tones:

God sour the milk of the knacking wench
with razor and twine she comes
to stanchion our blond and bucking bull,
pluck out his lovely plumbs.

God shiver the prunes on her bark of chest,
who capons the prancing young.
Let maggots befoul her alive in bed
and dibble thorns in her tongue.

Nowlan's poetry talks in the language of clear and colloquial statement about the concrete world of actuality, rendered in sharply defined images. His is perhaps as near as one can reach to a naturalistic poetic manner, but the manner is underlaid by an awareness of the human feelings that may survive in the depths of social neglect and brutalization Nowlan had seen so often in his Nova Scotia youth. There are indeed times when he escapes by the skin of his lyrical teeth from sentimentality, but still carries it off, as in a poem like "Britain Street," which tells of "a street of war" where "The smallest children/battle with clubs/till the blood comes," and even the dogs "would rather fight/than eat." The poem ends with the poet's own reaction to the apparent nihilism of life in Britain Street:

I have lived here nine months
and in all that time
have never once heard
a gentle word spoken.

I like to tell myself
that it is only because
gentle words are whispered
and harsh words shouted.

Nowlan offers no glib political solution to the human condition as he sees it. He offers a poetry of understanding, of indignation, of compassion. The poet, for him, reaches out "in fear and gentleness"; he speaks the truth when he sees it, but offers no panacea and no promise.

—George Woodcock

NUTTALL, Jeff. British. Born in Clitheroe, Lancashire, 8 July 1933. Educated at Hereford School of Art, graduated in 1951; Bath Academy of Art, graduated in 1953. Served in the Royal Army Education Corps. Married Jane Louch in 1954. Has taught in the Art Departments of several secondary schools; Lecturer, Fundamental Studies Department, Bradford College of Art, Yorkshire, 1968–70. Since 1970, Lecturer in Fine Art, Leeds College of Art. Has exhibited paintings and constructions. Formerly, Editor, *My Own Mag.* Address: 461 Huddersfield Road, Wyke, Bradford, Yorkshire, England.

Publications

Verse

The Limbless Virtuoso, with Keith Musgrove. London, Writers Forum, 1963.
Songs Sacred and Secular. Privately printed, 1964.
Poems I Want to Forget. London, Turret, 1965.
Pieces of Poetry. London, Writers Forum, 1965.
Isabel. London, Turret, 1967.
Journals. Brighton, Sussex, Unicorn Bookshop, 1968.
Penguin Modern Poets 12, with Alan Jackson and William Wantling. London, Penguin, 1968.
Love Poems. Brighton, Sussex, Unicorn Bookshop, 1969.
Selected Poems. London, Horizon, 1970.
Poems 1962–69. London, Fulcrum Press, 1970.
Man to Man. Llanfyndd, Unicorn Bookshop, 1975.
Sun Barber. Hayes, Middlesex, Poet and Peasant, 1976.
Objects. London, Trigram Press, 1976.
What Happened to Jackson. London, Aloes, 1978.
The Patriarchs: An Early Summer Landscape. London, Bean and Aloes Arc, 1978.

Plays

Barrow Boys (produced Bradford, Yorkshire, 1972).
Kosher (produced Bradford, Yorkshire, 1972).

Novels and Stories

Come Back Sweet Prince: A Novelette. London, Writers Forum, 1966.
The Case of Isabel and the Bleeding Foetus. London, Turret, 1967.
Mr. Watkins Got Drunk and Had to Be Carried Home. London, Writers Forum, 1968.
Oscar Christ and the Immaculate Conception. London, Writers Forum, 1968.
Pig. London, Fulcrum Press, 1969.
Snipe's Spinster. London, Calder and Boyars, 1974.
The Foxes' Lair. London, Aloes, 1974.

The House Party. Toronto, Basilike, 1975.
The Anatomy of My Father's Corpse. Toronto, Basilike, 1975.
The Gold Hole. London, Quartet, 1978.

Other

Bomb Culture. London, MacGibbon and Kee, 1968; New York, Delacorte Press, 1969.
Common Factors, Vulgar Factions, with Rodick Carmichael. London, Routledge, 1977.
King Twist: A Portrait of Frank Randle. London, Routledge, 1978.
Performance Art: Memoirs and Scripts. London, Calder, 2 vols., 1979.

Editor, *25: Writing from Leeds Polytechnic.* Leeds, Art and Design Press, 1971.

Jeff Nuttall comments:

I make a line out of a rhythmic figure. The previous figure suggests the subsequent one. The rhythmic figures owe much to Parker's saxophone phrasing.

I look to my obsessions to provide me with syllables to fill out the necessary figure.

I am hardly at all concerned with direct verbal/syntactical "meaning." Silly to call my verse "obscure" unless you're short sighted.

* * *

Jeff Nuttall goes a little crazy. He mentions it in *Bomb Culture*, his book of social criticism: "The phone goes. Criton. I don't want to see or speak to anybody. I've recently had a nervous crack-up and managed to pass it off to the family as flu – three wincing days bound in the sheets, trying to dull my screaming nerves. I want to hibernate. And now Criton rings." Think of that passage while reading "Insomnia":

Shall I do it, get up?
Curl like a hurt furred animal?
Shall I curl like an early embryo
All hairy, simian, gone wrong?
Curl up out there, out of the bed,
Red, raw bitten under my itch of pelt,
All huddled up, all curled on my side?

The man suffers from more than insomnia. "Insomnia" appeared in *Poems I Want to Forget.* Again the title misleads, for Nuttall does not want to forget his poems out of temperamental disdain or wispy diffidence; underground poets do not cotton to the wispy. Rather he wants to forget the pain. In *Bomb Culture* he remarks on a similar subterfuge in Ginsberg:

> Ginsberg read, and it registered that what had seemed over-messianic, grotesquely self-exposing and self-lacerating in print, was, in fact, a gay thing, the violent images delivered with a mischievous twinkle, and incredible milky gentleness flowing out from this one man into the minds and bodies of the audience.

Oscar Christ and the Immaculate Conception epitomizes the discrepancy between a gay manner and a horrific subject. It is a cheaply-printed, woolly and daffy underground collage-novel-poem about a Russian girl murdered in World War II by her S.S. lover: "That night I woke and said/'What's your name, Oscar?'/'Christ,' he said." But the grotesquerie underlines the significance, as the woman by admirable sleight of hand comes to typify all contemporary women; they offer themselves to men who oblige by murdering them. "I Hadn't Meant Murder," in *Poems I Want to Forget*, is about a similar impulsive murder of a lover. Nuttall is a little crazy, and he thinks society, in *Bomb Culture*, is completely crazy. Nuclear war, to his underground mind, is inevitable. The goal of life is death, said Freud, and Nuttall sees it in himself and in society.

—Michael André

NYE, Robert. British. Born in London, 15 March 1939. Educated at Dormans Land, Sussex; Hamlet Court, Westfield, Essex; Southend High School. Married 1) Judith Pratt in 1959 (divorced), three sons; 2) Aileen Campbell in 1966, one daughter, one step-daughter, and one step-son. Free-lance writer. Since 1967, Poetry Editor, *The Scotsman*; since 1971, Poetry Critic, *The Times*. Recipient: Eric Gregory Award, 1963; Scottish Arts Council bursary, 1970, 1973, and publication award, 1970, 1976; James Kennaway Memorial Award, 1970; *Guardian* fiction prize, 1976; Hawthornden Prize, 1977. Fellow, Royal Society of Literature. Address: The Anchorage, Summer Cove, Kinsale, County Cork, Ireland.

PUBLICATIONS

Verse

Juvenilia 1. Lowestoft, Suffolk, Scorpion Press, 1961.
Juvenilia 2. Lowestoft, Suffolk, Scorpion Press, 1963.
Darker Ends. London, Calder and Boyars, and New York, Hill and Wang, 1969.
Agnus Dei. Rushden, Northamptonshire, Sceptre Press, 1973.
Two Prayers. Richmond, Surrey, Keepsake Press, 1974.
Five Dreams. Rushden, Northamptonshire, Sceptre Press, 1974.
Divisions on a Ground. Manchester, Carcanet Press, 1976.

Plays

Sawney Bean, with William Watson (produced Edinburgh, 1969; London, 1972). London, Calder and Boyars, 1970.
Sisters (broadcast, 1969; produced Edinburgh, 1973). Included in *Penthesilea, Fugue, and Sisters*, 1976.
Penthesilea, adaptation of a play by Heinrich von Kleist (broadcast, 1971). Included in *Penthesilea, Fugue, and Sisters*, 1976.
The Seven Deadly Sins: A Mask, music by James Douglas (produced Stirling, 1973). Rushden, Northamptonshire, Omphalos Press, 1974.
Mr. Poe (produced Edinburgh and London, 1974).
Penthesilea, Fugue, and Sisters. London, Calder and Boyars, 1976.

Radio Plays: *Sisters*, 1969; *Penthesilea*, 1971.

Novels

Doubtfire. London, Calder and Boyars, 1967; New York, Hill and Wang, 1968.
Falstaff. London, Hamish Hamilton, and Boston, Little Brown, 1976.

Merlin. London, Hamish Hamilton, 1978; New York, Putnam, 1979.

Short Stories

Tales I Told My Mother. London, Calder and Boyars, and New York, Hill and Wang, 1969.
Penguin Modern Stories 6, with others. London, Penguin, 1970.

Other

Taliesin (juvenile). London, Faber, 1966; New York, Hill and Wang, 1967.
March Has Horse's Ears (juvenile). London, Faber, 1966; New York, Hill and Wang, 1967.
Bee Hunter: Adventures of Beowulf (juvenile). London, Faber, and New York, Hill and Wang, 1968; as *Beowulf, The Bee Hunter*, Faber, 1972.
Wishing Gold (juvenile). London, Macmillan, and New York, Hill and Wang, 1970.
Poor Pumpkin (juvenile). London, Macmillan, 1971; as *The Mathematical Princess and Other Stories*, New York, Hill and Wang, 1972.
Cricket: Three Stories (juvenile). Indianapolis, Bobbs Merrill, 1975; as *Once upon Three Times*, London, Benn, 1978.
Out of the World and Back Again (juvenile). London, Collins, 1978; as *Out of This World and Back Again*, Indianapolis, Bobbs Merrill, 1978.
The Bird of the Golden Land (juvenile). London, Hamish Hamilton, 1979.
Harry Pay the Pirate (juvenile). London, Benn, 1979.

Editor, *A Choice of Sir Walter Ralegh's Verse*. London, Faber, 1972.
Editor, *William Barnes of Dorset: A Selection of His Poems*. Cheadle, Cheshire, Carcanet Press, 1973.
Editor, *A Choice of Swinburne's Verse*. London, Faber, 1973.
Editor, *The Faber Book of Sonnets*. London, Faber, 1976; as *A Book of Sonnets*, New York, Oxford University Press, 1976.
Editor, *The English Sermon 1750–1850*. Manchester, Carcanet Press, 1976.

Manuscript Collections: University of Texas, Austin; National Library of Scotland, Edinburgh.

Critical Studies: by A. Alvarez, in *The Observer* (London), 1961, 1963; Martin Seymour-Smith, in *The Scotsman* (Edinburgh), 1963; in *Times Literary Supplement* (London), 1963; *British Book News* (London), February 1970.

* * *

The career of Robert Nye has been a peculiar one. He began with some éclat, publishing poems in *The London Magazine* and *Delta* when he was only 16 years of age. One of these lyrics, "Other Times," is almost his best. It appears, somewhat revised, in a definitive collection, *Darker Ends*:

> Midsummer's liquid evenings linger even
> And melt the wind in autumn, when bonfires
> Burn books and bones, and lend us foreign faces.
> At such a heart's November I might wish
> For summer's heir to come, with his cruel kiss
> Sealing the promises we could not keep.

One may feel that there are a few too many possessives here – "midsummer's," "heart's," "summer's." And yet the poem is purged in diction from its earlier version in *Juvenilia 1*:

Midsummer's liquid evenings linger even
And leave four hours of autumn bonfires –
Terre Gaste of your sleevelessness; imp and scraps,
The oily rags, old bike spokes, bones and cans
And executed dolls forstitched and lax
Folding pink little arms precipitant to ash.

This, in its turn, was altered from the first published version, in *Delta*, Autumn 1956, where we have "a tragedy of autumn bonfires/Raw with a gardener's rubbish, flesh and scraps. ..." The older, more austere Nye appears to have spent the intervening years weeding through several of his teenage pastures. There is no doubt that some fine Gravesian lyrics are the result. What he has done with "Other Times," he has also done with "Kingfisher," "I've Got Sixpence," and "At Last." In this final draft, Nye appears to have found his poetic feet in a rhythm not all that way after Andrew Young:

Dear, if one day my empty heart,
Under your cheek, forgets to start
Its life-long argument with my head –
Do not rejoice that I am dead
And need a colder, harder bed,
But say: "At last he's found the art
To hold his tongue and lose his heart."

Clearly Nye has risen on the stepping-stones of his former romantic selves to finer things. After the baroque ambitions of his earlier years, he has emerged as a poet of wit, epigram, distinction.

The poems in his most recent volume of verse, *Divisions on a Ground*, are at their best when most purged and spare. Nye achieves some poignant effects not so much through words in themselves but by the telling combination of words: "The least disgust betrays the heart's persistence./You kiss the snowscape on the windowpane;/I watch your breath shrink from it, a warm fleck/In freckled glass" ("At the Window"). It is all there: the identification of warmth, life, the capacity to feel disgust at death – a capacity which overcomes the merely aesthetic appreciation which led the girl to kiss the windowpane in the first place. Or again, consider "All Hallows" from the same sequence:

Once as a child I saw the willows
Across the river at All Hallows,
Each one distinct although six miles away.
What brought them close and brings them now again
Sharp to the mind's eye like an icon of it?
An orthodox theology of tears.

The poet compares the sharpness of youthful eyesight with the acuity of adult memory honed by a life's experience. It is as austere and telling as a haiku translated by Bosley or Thwaite, or a Catullan lyric.

Perhaps Nye's verse, as distinct from his prose, will never "please the million" – or even the thousand. His themes tend towards what is commonly thought of as literary. But it is safe to say that there is no poet writing whose next volume is awaited with more interest.

—Philip Hobsbaum

OAKES, Philip. British. Born in Burslem, Staffordshire, 31 January 1928. Educated at Royal School, Wolverhampton; Darwen Grammar School. Married to Stella Fleming; one son and two daughters. Scriptwriter for Granada Television and BBC, London, 1958–62; Film Critic, *Sunday Telegraph*, London, 1963–65; Assistant Editor, *Sunday Times Magazine*, London, 1965–67. Currently, Arts Columnist, *Sunday Times*, London. Agent: Curtis Brown Ltd., 1 Craven Hill, London W2 3EP. Address: Pinnock Farm House, Pluckley, Kent, England.

PUBLICATIONS

Verse

Unlucky Jonah: Twenty Poems. Reading, Berkshire, University of Reading School of Art, 1954.
In the Affirmative. London, Deutsch, 1968.
Notes by the Provincial Governor. London, Poem-of-the-Month Club, 1972.
Married/Singular. London, Deutsch, 1973.

Play

Screenplay: *The Punch and Judy Man*, with Tony Hancock, 1962.

Novels

Exactly What We Want. London, Joseph, 1962.
The God Botherers. London, Deutsch, 1969; as *Miracles: Genuine Cases Contact Box 340*, New York, Day, 1971.
Experiment at Proto. London, Deutsch, and New York, Coward McCann, 1973.
A Cast of Thousands. London, Gollancz, 1976.

Other

Tony Hancock. London, Woburn Press, 1975.

Editor, *The Entertainers.* London, Woburn Press, 1975.
Editor, *The Film Addict's Archive.* London, Elm Tree Books, 1977.

Manuscript Collection: State University of New York, Buffalo.

Philip Oakes comments:

I consider myself an all-round writer, subject at any time to the demands of poetry. Although I was corralled with the Movement poets in the 1950's and still share their concern for form and discipline, the labelling was, I think, a critical-cum-political convenience and no longer applies.

I write about the need for domestic order and the impulse to resist it; also about love and eccentrics I rather admire. These are non-conformist heroes who harm no-one – a retired soldier who hunted unicorns, a sea-captain who sailed to meet mermaids, the fattest man in England and a sad recluse who lived in fear of falling into a pit. Poets whose influence I recognise include Donne, Graves, Auden, and Philip Larkin. Also I suspect, many writers and composers of Hymns Ancient & Modern. Here beginneth the first ballad....

*   *   *

Despite a comparatively slender output, and the competing pressures of journalism and novel-writing, Philip Oakes remains one of the best of the generation of English poets who emerged in the 1950's, and were loosely grouped under the label of the "Movement." His early poems provided social and moral comments in tight, clipped forms in the characteristic manner of the Movement; but Oakes was less severely formal and intellectual than some of his contemporaries. A mild but authentic vein of lyricism lies not far below the cool, conversational surface. Indeed, there is a basic human warmth, recalling Thomas Hardy, at the heart of Oakes' practice as a poet. In his work of the sixties and seventies, collected in *In the Affirmative* and *Married/Singular*, he has written of personal and domestic themes, in direct language and unfussily formal verse. At times, admittedly, the low-key descriptions are merely flat, and the metre occasionally falters. But Oakes' successes are more frequent – notably in his admirable evocations of the pieties and crises of modern family life.

—Bernard Bergonzi

O'GORMAN, Ned (Edward Charles O'Gorman). American. Born in New York City, 26 September 1929. Educated at St. Michael's College, Vermont, A.B.; Columbia University, New York, M.A. Married; one son. Taught at Brooklyn College, New York; New School for Social Research, New York; Manhattan College, New York; Editor, *Jubilee* magazine, New York, 1962–65; State Department American Studies Specialist in Chile, Argentina and Brazil, 1965. Since 1966, Director, Addie MacCollins library and Storefront School, New York. Recipient: Guggenheim Fellowship, 1956, 1962; Lamont Poetry Selection Award, 1958. Agent: Harold Matson Company, 22 East 40th Street, New York, New York 10016. Address: 56 West 11th Street, New York, New York 10011, U.S.A.

PUBLICATIONS

Verse

The Night of the Hammer. New York, Harcourt Brace, 1959.
Adam Before His Mirror. New York, Harcourt Brace, 1961.
The Buzzard and the Peacock. New York, Harcourt Brace, 1964.
The Harvesters' Vase. New York, Harcourt Brace, 1968.
The Flag the Hawk Flies. New York, Knopf, 1972.

Other

The Storefront: A Community of Children on Madison Avenue and 129th Street. New York, Harper, 1970.
The Blue Butterfly (juvenile). New York, Harper, 1971.
The Wilderness and the Laurel Tree: A Guide to Parents and Teachers on the Observation of Children. New York, Harper, 1972.
The Children Are Dying. New York, New American Library, 1978.

Editor, *Prophetic Voices: Essays and Words in Revolution.* New York, Random House, 1969.

Manuscript Collection: Immaculata College, Malvern, Pennsylvania.

* * *

Ned O'Gorman's poems hope that, in the collision of metaphysical and metaphorical opposites, theme and meaning will arise. Compressed and "lush," there are a mystery and lyric extravagance to the poems which, when most successful, provoke a lasting dreamlike quality.

Images repeat exotic light, birds, water, colors, honey, holy oils, vegetables, seeds, centers and sun, in a luxuriant usage of – oftentimes – a pentameter. There are many examples. The result can be overwhelming. At other times O'Gorman's poems have the impact of an abstract painting of planes and trajectories ("What Three?" and "Written on the Occasion in Cairo ...").

The conflicts underlying the poems are intelligent, abstract, controlled, metaphysical. The reader is attracted by the beauty of composition in many poems; real chaos is only mentioned here, but it is of a different world. O'Gorman's best poems address themselves seriously to *things*, making a concrete frame of reference available in direct statement: "The Donkey who is in the field/in this increasing fall is/tall as a hedge of wild rose." Imagery when solely the representative of concept at least must not seem so, unless it is allegory. The poet must have a personal stake in the poem and must risk it as O'Gorman does in his finest efforts, such as "The Graveyard," "In Honor of the Mother of God," "The Aunt," and "To the Memory of Lydia Hoffman." When this expenditure is not made we sense, with a reviewer of *The Flag the Hawk Flies*, that the "imagery touches on nothing real," that the poet merely "names." Or perhaps it is true that in the contemporary world a vision of horror – as in "War" – strikes us as natural and credible while O'Gorman's visions of beauty seem extravagant. This is tragic, yet the poet must take account of the fact or risk a failure – no matter of great beauty.

—Joseph Wilson

O'GRADY, Desmond (James Bernard). Irish. Born in Limerick, 27 August 1935. Educated at St. Michael's Primary School, Limerick; Sacred Heart College, Limerick; Cistercian College, Roscrea, County Tipperary; National University of Ireland, Dublin, 1954–56; Harvard University, Cambridge, Massachusetts, M.A. in Celtic studies 1964. Married; four children. Taught at Berlitz School, Paris; Cambridge Institute and British Institute, Rome; St. George's English School, Rome; English Language School, Rome; Roxbury Latin School, West Roxbury, Massachusetts; Harvard University; Overseas School of Rome; American University, Cairo, 1971, 1975–76. Irish Representative, European Community of Writers Congresses, Florence, Belgrade, Rome.

PUBLICATIONS

Verse

Chords and Orchestrations. Limerick, Echo Press, 1956.
Reilly. London, Phoenix Press, 1961.
Professor Kelleher and the Charles River. Cambridge, Massachusetts, Carthage Press, 1964.
Separazione. Rome, Edizioni Rapporti Europei, 1965.
The Dark Edge of Europe: Poems. London, MacGibbon and Kee, 1967.
The Dying Gaul. London, MacGibbon and Kee, 1968.
Hellas. Dublin, New Writers Press, 1971.
Separations. Dublin, Goldsmith Press, 1973.
Pen and Ink. Dublin, Goldsmith Press, 1973.
Stations. Cairo, American University in Cairo Press, 1976.
Sing Me Creation. Dublin, Gallery Press, 1977.

The Gododdin, from the Welsh of Aneirin. Dublin, Dolmen Press, 1977.
A Limerick Rake: Versions from the Irish. Dublin, Gallery Press, 1978.

Other

Translator, *Off Licence: Translations from Irish, Italian and Armenian Poetry.* Dublin, Dolmen Press, 1968.

Desmond O'Grady comments:

My early work dealt with the experience of growing up on the west coast of Ireland, with the leaving of that place for the cities of the Continent and America and the need to connect my life there with the one I had left. My later work deals with the theme of "the journey" and the theme that emerges from that, "separation"; separation from people, places, things.

My middle work, the long poem *The Dying Gaul*, was an attempt at making a self portrait of what it is to be a Celt. It is this "persona" that journeys and is "separated" in my later work. He is a "wandering Celt" who records his wanderings and experiences and attempts to connect what was left with what is found.

The Prologue of my volume *Sing Me Creation* gives an attempt at condensing my purpose:

Who saw everything to the ends
of the land began
at the end of a primary road.
Who saw the mysteries, knew
secret things, went a long
journey and found the whole story
cut in stone.
His purpose: praise, search,
his appointed pain, and the countries
of the world that housed
his image. Weary,
worn out with his labours,
he returned and told
what he's seen and learned
to help kill the winter.

There is also a great deal of translation from the languages of others under the general title *The Unauthorised Version.* These were done principally to learn the methods of those poets, classical and modern, whose work I admire, the better to extend my own range and at the same time to make their work available to young Irish poets who may not have heard of them or cannot read them in the original in the hope that I might make some contribution to the revitalisation of verse being written in Ireland by the young.

* * *

Desmond O'Grady spent some years in Paris but has taught in Rome and elsewhere since 1965. In his second collection, *Reilly*, he uses as a satirical *persona* a bohemian young man and describes amusingly his reckless adventures in Dublin:

tables and chairs cleared of books and belongings,
the firegrate stuffed with stale fish-and-chips
and a dry whiskey bottle.
Finger-rubbed into the windowpane dust:
Reilly Rotted Here.

The Dark Edge of Europe is a selection from O'Grady's previous work. Many of his poems evoke Paris and Italy, and the imagery in them is contemporary in its unexpectedness, as in "Girl and Widow on a Sea Park Bench":

In this park by the sea, marvellous
As marble, under the fronded green of the palms,
The sun strafing
The stones with flat tracers of light, water like mercury
Tinnular out of the fountain.
You come to me out of the gold stained day like a word.

O'Grady spent his early years in Limerick and many of his poems are inspired by his return visits, as in "Homecoming":

The familiar pull of the slow train
trundling after a sinking sun on shadowed fields.
White light splicing the broad span of the sky.
Evening deepens grass, the breeze,
like purple smoke, ruffles its surface.
Straight into herring-dark skies the great cathedral spire
is sheer Gothic.

Like Joyce and other Irish writers, O'Grady expresses in compressed lines the effect of Puritanic education:

Unwinking eyes of saints and hushed confession queue –
For one loud nervous boot
Of frightened heart,
I felt the Churcheyed, fidget fear of schooltied youth.

Sometimes he objectifies his early experiences as in his depiction of an old man, who turns "for the safest healer/To a clean and bandaged silence of the heart."

—Austin Clarke

OKAI, John. Ghanaian. Born in Ghana. Educated at the Gorky Literary Institute, Moscow, M.A.(Litt.) 1967; University of Ghana, Accra; University of London. Recipient: Royal Society of Arts Fellowship, 1968. Lived in the U.S.S.R., 1961–67. Lives in London.

PUBLICATIONS

Verse

Flowerfall. London, Writers Forum, 1969.
The Oath of Fontomfrom and Other Poems. New York, Simon and Schuster, 1971.

* * *

The use of musical rhythms in poetry is nothing unusual, but few contemporary writers make so great a use of the musical heritage of their culture as does John Okai. The sounds of the talking drums of Ghana figure strongly in his poems and the titles of most of them, such as "Fugue for Fireflies" and "Okponglo Concerto" bear witness of the musical bent of his work. The repetition and alliterative forms which are a part of traditional verse are brought by Okai into the English language, producing effects which are often close to hypnotic, as in "Modzawe" where the line "Let human beings be human beings again" is repeated six times and Okai refers to traditional drums, allowing the musicality of their names to shape his lines:

Descend O God! descend O God!
To the echo-wail-boom and music of
The Dodonpo and the Odono
And the festive Bintim Obonu ...

His Ghanaian background is not the only source Okai draws from, however. Having studied in England, America and Russia, Okai can refer as familiarly to apple trees as to palms and his poems often contain catalogues of people and places reflecting this catholic experience:

the swallow
   and the bougainvillea ...
modigliani's woman with a necklace ...
leonardo da vinci's mona lisa
the parrot
   and the bougainvillea ...
shostakovich's leningrad symphony ...
dvorak's new world symphony (part two) ...
the sparrow
   and the bougainvillea
frank lloyd wright's falling water ...
ya-na's palace at wa in ghana ...

If there is a fault in Okai's work, it may be that some of his lines take on a singsong quality, seeming to sacrifice sense in favor of sound, for Okai can be more alliterative in his writing than was Old English verse. His "Sunset Sonata" is filled with such lines as:

Still stand stubborn
   To stones that strangle the dawn,
Still stand stubborn
   To stones that maim the morn,
Still stand stubborn
   To stones that assail the sun ...

and because of this some critics attempt to easily dismiss Okai, not seeing that even in his most highly alliterative passages there is still meaning.

It cannot be denied that Okai's work is assertive and, especially when read aloud, charged with vitality. His recent work has been a great influence in enlivening the poetry scene in Ghana and the directions in which his poems move take advantage of a rich and, in English, relatively unexplored patrimony.

—Joseph Bruchac

OKARA, Gabriel (Imomotimi Gbaingbain). Nigerian. Born in Bumodi, Ijaw District, Rivers State, Western Nigeria, 21 April 1921. Educated at the Government College, Umuahia; trained as a bookbinder; studied journalism at Northwestern University, Evanston, Illinois, 1956. Principal Information Officer, Eastern Regional Government, Enugu, until 1967; Biafran Information Officer, Nigerian Civil War, 1967–69; travelled to the United States, with Chinua Achebe and Cyprian Ekwensi, to seek help for Biafra, 1969. Since 1972, Director of the Rivers State Publishing House, Port Harcourt. Recipient: Nigerian Festival of the Arts award, 1953; Commonwealth Poetry Prize, 1979. Address: c/o Heinemann Ltd., 15–16 Queen Street, London W1X 8BE, England.

PUBLICATIONS

Verse

Poetry from Africa, with others, edited by Howard Sergeant. Oxford, Pergamon Press, 1968.
The Fisherman's Invocation. London, Heinemann, 1978.

Novel

The Voice. London, Deutsch, 1964; New York, Africana, 1970.

* * *

One of the most gifted, and certainly the least literary, of the African poets is Gabriel Okara. Okara has proved to be what can only be described as a "natural," in that he is highly original in both outlook and expression, and appears to have learned his craft without being influenced unduly by the stylistic mannerisms of any other poet. This, however, has not been without considerable effort on his part. "In order to capture the vivid images of African speech," he observed in an article (printed in *Transition*), "I had to eschew the habit of expressing my thoughts first in English. It was difficult at first, but I had to learn." That he has been successful in capturing the African scene, the African colour and excitement, and the changing African moods, is evidenced by such poems as "The Mystic Drum," "Were I to Choose," "Adhiambo," and "Piano and Drums."

There is, in fact, almost a mystical quality about his work which seems to spring from his racial inheritance, his instincts and sensitivity rather than from his intellect, and he exhibits a curious power when he draws upon the great oral traditions to release this nervous energy, as in "The Mystic Drum." In "Adhiambo" he tries to define his feelings on the subject: "Maybe I'm a medicine man/hearing talking saps/seeing behind trees," and in "Piano and Drums," he writes of the jungle drums "telegraphing the mystic rhythm, urgent, raw like bleeding flesh." In other poems which will probably make more impact upon non-African readers he is practical and down to earth, extremely perceptive in his judgements, and almost analytical in his approach, as in "Once Upon a Time" – "There was a time indeed/they used to shake hands with their hearts" – and "You Laughed and Laughed and Laughed" where the ancient world of Africa merges with the modern world.

—Howard Sergeant

OLSON, Elder (James). American. Born in Chicago, Illinois, 9 March 1909. Educated at the University of Chicago, B.A. 1934 (Phi Beta Kappa), M.A. 1935, Ph.D. 1938. Married 1)

Ann Elizabeth Jones in 1937 (divorced, 1948); 2) Geraldine Louise Hays in 1948; four children. Instructor, Armour Institute of Technology, Chicago, 1938–42. Assistant Professor, 1942–48. Associate Professor, 1948–53, and since 1954, Professor of English, University of Chicago. Visiting Professor, University of Puerto Rico, Rio Piedras, 1952–53; University of Frankfurt; Powell Professor of Philosophy, 1955, Visiting Professor of Literary Criticism, 1958–59, and Patten Lecturer, 1964, University of Indiana, Bloomington; Rockefeller Visiting Professor, University of the Philippines, Quezon City, 1966–67. Recipient: Witter Bynner Award, 1927; Guarantors Prize, 1931, and Eunice Tietjens Memorial Prize, 1953 (*Poetry*, Chicago); Poetry Society of America Chap-Book Award, 1955; Academy of American Poets Award, 1956; Longview Foundation Award, 1958; Balch Award (*Virginia Quarterly Review*, Charlottesville), 1965; Quantrell Award, University of Chicago, 1966. Address: Department of English, University of Chicago, Chicago, Illinois 60637, U.S.A.

Publications

Verse

Thing of Sorrow. New York, Macmillan, 1934.
The Cock of Heaven. New York, Macmillan, 1940.
The Scarecrow Christ and Other Poems. New York, Noonday Press, 1954.
Plays and Poems 1948–58. Chicago, University of Chicago Press, 1958.
Collected Poems. Chicago, University of Chicago Press, 1963.
Olson's Penny Arcade. Chicago, University of Chicago Press, 1975.

Plays

A Crack in the Universe, in *First Stage* (Lafayette, Indiana), Spring 1962.
The Abstract Universe: A Comedy of Masks, in *First Stage* (Lafayette, Indiana), Summer 1963.

Other

General Prosody, Rhythmic, Metric, Harmonics. Chicago, University of Chicago Press, 1938.
Critics and Criticism, with others. Chicago, University of Chicago Press, 1952.
The Poetry of Dylan Thomas. Chicago, University of Chicago Press, 1954.
Tragedy and the Theory of Drama. Detroit, Wayne State University Press, 1961.
The Theory of Comedy. Bloomington, Indiana University Press, 1968.
On Value Judgments in the Arts and Other Essays. Chicago, University of Chicago Press, 1976.

Editor, *American Lyric Poems: From Colonial Days to the Present.* New York, Appleton Century Crofts, 1963.
Editor, *Aristotle's "Poetics" and English Literature: A Collection of Critical Essays.* Chicago, University of Chicago Press, 1965.
Editor, *Major Voices: 20 British and American Poets.* New York, McGraw Hill, 1973.

* * *

The early poems from *Thing of Sorrow* which now make up Part I of Elder Olson's *Collected Poems* are elegiac, deliberately understated and restrained in their expression of some lasting preoccupations: the beauties of this earth, despite our disappointments ("The Tale"); the relationship between the artist's personal sorrows and his work ("Wishes for His Poem"); and, most important by far, the compensations available to a mind able at least to contemplate its losses and vulnerability. Thus Olson writes (in "To Man") that, whatever our limitations:

– Bird, beast, flower, and star
Are of no thing but thought,
Since if mind wills, they are,
Or if mind wills, are not.

The Rose surviving Time
Is patterned in your brain;
Without such paradigm
No rose had ever been....

Be comforted at length,
Be brave; till you are free,
Accept this frailty
That tenders you this strength.

Nevertheless any possible acceptance is more than overshadowed by the awareness of loss, particularly the passing of love:

It is that love goes in the end.
It is that of all this amazement and pain,
The bright harm, the royal woe,
The brilliant wound and the stain,
Naught shall remain
To emblazon one rose-leaf,
To illumine a prism of snow
Or a rainbow's crystal, to
Incline the course of wind
A gull's-wing's width, to bend
The worn sea to a grave:

... And the mind knows this well;
But the heart breaks if it believes.

The tones remain muted throughout, nearly feminine in Olson's preference for short lines and delicate, internal sound patterns. The influences attractive to a young poet starting out in the 1930's are not what one might expect – Eliot, Yeats and Pound – but rather, it seems, Léonie Adams and Louise Bogan.

The poems which stand as Part II of the *Collected Poems* suffer by being torn from the context of *The Cock of Heaven*, a long philosophical sequence which Olson has described as "an epitome of human history ... the destruction of the world, and the causes of both destruction and creation ... [and] the universal catastrophe." Devised in terms of expert imitations of the whole range of voices at work in English poetry (and not only English poetry at that), from the Anglo Saxon through T. S. Eliot, these eighty-seven pieces, now radically diminished to twenty-five, create an uncertain focus and effect. The despairing tones of *Thing of Sorrow* are still present, rendered more forcefully (man is a poor talking animal "possessed by angels and impelled by fiends"), but Olson now seems haunted by the possible revelations behind Christian symbols. The opening "text" asserts: "it is manifest that Man is eternally damned ... And I consider that to save this world God Himself must needs be born into it; and even then even He can but make it worthy to be destroyed." The relationship between Christian doctrine and Olson's apparently naturalistic view of life is not easy to define, but perhaps the poet's own statement, in the tender "Nocturnal for His Children," comes close. After surveying various theories of divinity and the divine plan he concludes:

My children, I cannot tell
Which of these is right.
I never heard God's voice,
To me no angels descend.
All I know is my soul
Which is, like this night sky,
Far more dark than bright,
Yet in that dark waste
While I watch out its night
All strives from dark to light:

Not knowing false from true,
I yet know good from bad;
I cannot think my God
Worse than myself: I
Demand a nobler faith.

Many of the poems which follow *The Cock of Heaven* come close to ultimate despair:

I mourn, not grieving, no, at grievous death,
But at the resurgence after death,
And the death again, and senseless resurgence still.

Cycle on cycle, wheeling Infinity,
Boundless Abyss, where all things rise and fall,
You are my sickness ...

but once more the power of mind to grasp its position offers some measure of consolation, even dignity:

I thought once that I should have at a man's age
Some wisdom hard and pure as diamond
To make the center of a new steadfast world,

Or some bauble, at least, for a toy – accurate enough
To catch the universe in its gay reflex,
Like Paris reflected in a jewel,

And perhaps after all I have it: at last recognizing
The treadmill as a treadmill: asking of my empty journeys
Nothing, in the end, but to spare my private nobility.

The finest later poems are varied in the best sense of the term. There are the familiar elegiac strains ("For the Demolition of a Theater"), the same concern for the Christian symbols of death and mortality ("Crucifix") and, increasingly, a new display of informal humor and relaxed good nature ("Exhibition of Modern Art," "Directions to the Armourer," "Able, Baker, Charlie, Et Al.," and the superb "Childe Roland, Etc." and "Entertainment for a Traveller"). When Olson treats his most serious themes with quick, metaphorical wit the results are memorable (as in "The Last Entries in the Journal," which may well be his best poem to date). The good will of generous acceptance now dominates almost entirely:

I praise the weaknesses
That make us fellows;
Fine faults, that keep us kin....

To that implacable Angel, the stern Scribe
Of heaven or of our consciences, I wish
Short memory, bad ink, a sputtering pen:

Our faults, our common faults, have kept us kin.

In recent years, with *Tragedy and the Theory of Drama* and *The Theory of Comedy*, Elder Olson has established himself as an indispensable critic. The poetry is much less widely known, which is a great pity, considering its seriousness and technical brilliance. But then one of Olson's virtues as a critic and a poet is that he has never been in a hurry. What he has done is likely to last.

—Elmer Borklund

OLSON, Toby (Merle Theodore Olson). American. Born in Berwyn, Illinois, 17 August 1937. Educated at Occidental College, Los Angeles, 1962–64, B.A. 1964; Long Island University, Brooklyn, New York, 1964–66, M.A. 1966. Served as a surgical technician in the United States Navy, 1957–61. Married 1) Ann Yeomans in 1963 (divorced, 1965); 2) Miriam Meltzer in 1966. Associate Director, Aspen Writers Workshop, Colorado, 1964–67; Assistant Professor, Long Island University, 1966–74; Member of the Faculty, New School for Social Research, New York, 1967–75. Since 1975, Assistant Professor, Temple University, Philadelphia. Poet-in-Residence, State University of New York, Cortland, 1972, and Friends Seminary, New York, 1974–75. Recipient: Creative Artists Public Service grant, 1975. Address: 329 South Juniper Street, Philadelphia, Pennsylvania 19107, U.S.A.

PUBLICATIONS

Verse

The Brand: A Five-Part Poem. Mount Horeb, Wisconsin, Perishable Press, 1969.
Worms into Nails. Mount Horeb, Wisconsin, Perishable Press, 1969.
The Hawk-Foot Poems. Madison, Wisconsin, Abraxas Press, 1969.
Maps. Mount Horeb, Wisconsin, Perishable Press, 1969.
Pig/s Foot. New York, Doctor Generosity Press, 1970.
Cold House. Mount Horeb, Wisconsin, Perishable Press, 1970.
Poems. Mount Horeb, Wisconsin, Perishable Press, 1970(?).
Tools. New York, Doctor Generosity Press, 1971.
Shooting Pigeons. Mount Horeb, Wisconsin, Perishable Press, 1971.
Vectors. Milwaukee, Ziggurat-Membrane Press, 1972.
Home. Chicago, Wine Press, 1972.
Fishing. Mount Horeb, Wisconsin, Perishable Press, 1973.
The Wrestlers and Other Poems. New York, Barlenmir House, 1974.
City. Milwaukee, Membrane Press, 1974.
A Kind of Psychology. Milwaukee, Lionhead, 1974.
Changing Appearance: Poems 1965–70. Milwaukee, Membrane Press, 1975.
A Moral Proposition. New York, Aviator Press, 1975.
Priorities. Milwaukee, Lionhead, 1975.
Seeds. Milwaukee, Membrane Press, 1975.

Standard-4. New York, Aviator Press, 1975.
Home. Milwaukee, Membrane Press, 1976.
Three and One. Mount Horeb, Wisconsin, Perishable Press, 1976.
Doctor Miriam: Five Poems by Her Admiring Husband. Mount Horeb, Wisconsin, Perishable Press, 1977.
Aesthetics. Milwaukee, Perishable Press, 1978.
The Florence Poems. London, Permanent Press, 1978.

Novel

The Life of Jesus. New York, New Directions, 1976.

Critical Study: by Robert Vas Dias, in *Poetry Information* (London), Winter 1976–77.

Toby Olson comments:

I remember receiving the impression in school that poetry was a kind of crossword/jigsaw puzzle; the student was helped to figure out meanings and fittings, and in the end he could say he "understood" the poem. Often the result didn't seem worth the effort that got him to it. School talk seldom moved beyond puzzle solving to the possibilities of appreciation. Though this kind of attitude may still prevail, I am no longer able to think of poetry, that which I write and read and value, in this puzzle solving way.

For me poetry is no less than good talk about important things, and this good talk has as its end the telling and presentation of truth. I would like it if my poems were able to fix important talk, make it in some way permanent. I would like it if when my poems were difficult it was because the things I was trying to talk about were difficult things to say; there should be no other reason for them being hard to understand.

My poems are not often very difficult in the puzzle sense of it. I am not much interested in metaphor as comparison, symbolism, or myth; I am very interested in finding structures of good talk that can then become the fixed structures of particular poems. I feel that there is enough in the world around me and what it can recall to me from my own past to make any poem. I trust that the experience of the human tribe is enough in each of us so that if I speak out of attention and with care I'll be heard by those who can give a little time for listening.

I suppose, then, that I feel that my poetry intends to be always both autobiographical and communal, that it is through writing about what I can see, hear, and feel that I can best touch the nature that I believe is common in all of us.

* * *

The title of Toby Olson's first major collection, *Changing Appearance: Poems 1965–1970*, should alert the reader to this poet's preoccupation with those scenes of persons and objects immediately and literally given to him. In this preoccupation, Olson is heir to an attitude of attention, to a certain tone – ironic, but not unsympathetic – of attention, and for a certain number of such scenes that may be identified with the work of the late Paul Blackburn (1926–71) and through Blackburn to the "no ideas but in things" aspect of William Carlos Williams and, less directly, to the imagist phase of Ezra Pound. This is not an inconsiderable inheritance. Technically, it involves the sure handling of speech rhythms in varying line lengths and stanza formations, the reporting of exactly what is before one's eyes – with a predilection for the urban, the unelevated, the unsublime – and with an equal predilection for all the ironies revealed by that reporting. And like Blackburn and Williams, their heir Olson is also the writer of forthright, unconventional love poems.

Yet this inheritance, like any other, has its limitations. Its special appeal is that of the sharply focused but spontaneous snap-shot: in a few words evocative images are constructed and entire scenes laid out. The snapshot or, to use a phrase from Blackburn, out-the-window poem is limited by its very focus to the personal, the local. It has no horizon and its emphasis on brevity allows for little if any complexity of perception or sustained development of perception. Olson deals with the inherent limitations of his approach in a number of ways. In the early poetry of *Changing Appearance*, he most often uses thematic grouping, e.g., the poems of the "Pig/s Book" section all involve the pig in relation with other animals. Later, he turns to the series. And, in a published note on this mode of organization, Olson has commented that he did so because it allows for the clarity of the individual poem and for "the a-rational quality of the poems' genesis extended over a period of time." The most impressive treatment of the series in Olson's work can be found in *Home*, a long poem of 36 parts that successfully enlarges upon its title's theme which would at first appear the very embodiment of the restricted personal/local, and in *Aesthetics*, which seeks not simply a larger space, but a constantly expanding and complex subject matter as well. As the opening lines of this latter book declare: "*Paint what you see*/is already a philosophical problem:/a blood-spot on the eye's membrane/absent in the still-life." In another book of the same year, *The Florence Poems*, Olson returns to thematic grouping for an entire volume. This time the theme is the early death of a friend. Beginning with reflections at "Graveside," each poem of the group remembers past incidents of shared experience and, in the book's progression, leads toward the final commending "into the perfect/community of our isolate lives." Olson's combination here of detailed, unsentimental recollection with mythic elements such as the trickster figure and Indian whale legends along with the constant spiritual notion of "our secret names" is both masterful and moving.

Again like Williams, Olson has also published prose fiction. His *The Life of Jesus* is experimental in its style and in its depiction of the Christ resulting from that style. Interweaving occasional pages of verse with prose narrative, which resembles Robbe-Grillet's spikey emphasis upon the physically particular – though Olson's use of imagery clearly distinguishes him from the French writer – the novel follows the general outline of the Biblical story. Where it differs is a matter of additional – not necessarily contradictory – detail. Olson's Christ, for instance, has a pet dog named Hound who sits in the chair of Elijah at the last supper and who, after his own martyrdom, rejoins his resurrected master in a cloud bank heaven worthy of Tiepolo. Thus we know not simply more, but quite different things about the Christ in Olson's fictional biography. One of the major differences is the degree to which the Christ is made to speak in his own voice. The effect, inasmuch as what Olson's Christ says must diverge from the Biblical, is startling. It would be wrong, however, to consider the novel a challenge to Christian belief. It is more an investigation into the Christ story as it came to be reconstructed in the mind of a young boy at Catholic school listening to the stories of Irish nuns. The novel is both that reconstructed story and its investigation. This unique fiction, along with the poetry of *Home* and *The Florence Poems*, is Toby Olson's most significant work to date.

—John Taggart

ONDAATJE, (Philip) Michael. Canadian. Born in Colombo, Ceylon, 12 September 1943. Educated at St. Thomas' College, Colombo; Dulwich College, London; Bishop's University, Lennoxville, Quebec; University of Toronto, B.A.; Queen's University, Kingston, Ontario, M.A. Married to Betty Kimbark; one daughter and one son. Taught at the University of Western Ontario, London, 1967–71. Since 1971, Member of the Department of English, Glendon College, York University, Toronto. Editor, *Mongrel Broadsides*. Recipient: Ralph Gustafson Award, 1965; Epstein Award, 1966; E. J. Pratt Medal, 1966; President's Medal, University of Western Ontario, 1967; Canada Council grant, 1968, 1977; Governor-

General's Award, 1971. Address: Department of English, Glendon College, York University, Toronto, Ontario, Canada.

PUBLICATIONS

Verse

The Dainty Monsters. Toronto, Coach House Press, 1967.
The Man with Seven Toes. Toronto, Coach House Press, 1969.
The Left-Handed Poems: Collected Works of Billy the Kid. Toronto, Anansi, 1970; New York, Norton, 1974.
Rat Jelly. Toronto, Coach House Press, 1973.
There's a Trick with a Knife I'm Learning to Do: Poems 1963–1978. Toronto, McClelland and Stewart, and New York, Norton, 1979.
Rat Jelly and Other Poems. London, Boyars, 1979.

Play

The Collected Works of Billy the Kid (produced Stratford, Ontario, 1973; New York, 1974). New York, Norton, 1974.

Novel

Coming Through Slaughter. Toronto, Anansi, 1976; New York, Norton, 1977; London, Boyars, 1979.

Other

Leonard Cohen. Toronto, McClelland and Stewart, 1970.

Editor, *The Broken Ark* (animal verse). Toronto, Oberon Press, 1971.
Editor, *Personal Fictions: Stories by Munro, Wiebe, Thomas, and Blaise.* Toronto, Oxford University Press, 1977.
Editor, *The Long Poem Anthology.* Toronto, Coach House Press, 1979.

Theatrical Activities:

Director: **Films** – *Sons of Captain Poetry*, 1971; *Carry on Crime and Punishment*, 1972; *Royal Canadian Hounds*, 1973; *The Clinton Special*, 1974.

* * *

Michael Ondaatje's first book of poems, *The Dainty Monsters*, elicits prophecy. Its poems forecast the possibility that their successors will be poems of the first intensity. Ondaatje was included among the group that a year previously was heralded as the "New Wave" poets. There was nothing much new about this group. The poetry largely derived from the William Carlos Williams/Black Mountain school; eventually from that great re-animator Ezra Pound. The method has been persistent elsewhere for years. What was inadvertently refreshing was the presence of three or four Canadian poets whose practice indicated a choice counter to the standard derivation. Ondaatje was one of these.

His shaping of language was formal and musical; his content was balanced. Departing from the prevailing lack of metrical challenge to dispersed rhythm, aware of verbal sound inherent in the meaning, unaffianced to the egocentric confessional, Ondaatje engages attention. His shapings of a poem do not leak either salt tears or sawdust or inarticulations or empty spaces. The first essential is here: sheer love of language. Otherwise he can be what he wants to be: metaphysician, sociologist, domestic or saint.

His area is dainty monsters. That is satisfyingly contemporary enough. His universal monsters live in Toronto:

> When snows have melted
> how dull to find just grass and dog shit.
> Why not polemic bones of centaurs
> – remnants of a Toronto bullet,
> punishment for eating gladioli.

Why not? It is good to have his centaurs back, his sows like chinless duchesses on spread thighs watching "the sun/fingersnapping out the dying summer." He doesn't want hippopotami barred from public swimming pools. He is equally aware that "Deep in the fields/behind stiff dirt fern/nature breeds the unnatural." You can look but you better not touch, a title of one of his poems tell us:

> We must build new myths
> to wind up the world,
> provoke new christs
> with our beautiful women.

He is on a mythopoeic voyage from Lilith in Eden, "pivoting on the horn/of corrupted unicorns," to modern man on his cold mountain, moving "with fast passion from necessity," and, mutilated, drowning "in the beautiful dark orgasm of his mouth."

He shows evidence of having that rarest of all elements, presently almost destroyed by the tearings of metal and the dark idiocy of its manufacturers: comic perspective and rescuing wit high on poetry and hospitals:

> Three floors down
> my appendix
> swims in a jar
> O world, I shall be buried all over Ontario.

—Ralph Gustafson

OPPEN, George. American. Born in New Rochelle, New York, 24 April 1908. Educated in California public schools. Served in the United States Army, 1943–45. Married Mary Colby in 1928; one daughter. Publisher, To Company, Toulon, France, 1930–33; Member, Objectivist Press Co-op, New York, 1934–36. Formerly, tool and die maker, cabinet-maker, mechanic, and building contractor; shopowner and furniture builder in Mexico City. Recipient: Pulitzer Prize, 1969. Address: 2811 Polk Street, San Francisco, California 94109, U.S.A.

PUBLICATIONS

Verse

Discrete Series. New York, Objectivist Press, 1934.

The Materials. New York, New Directions, 1962.
This in Which. New York, New Directions, 1965.
Of Being Numerous. New York, New Directions, 1968.
Alpine. Mount Horeb, Wisconsin, Perishable Press, 1969.
Seascape: Needle's Eye. Fremont, Michigan, Sumac Press, 1973.
The Collected Poems of George Oppen 1929–1975. New York, New Directions, and London, Fulcrum Press, 1975.
Primitive. Santa Barbara, California, Black Sparrow Press, 1978.

Critical Studies: "The Objectivist Poet," in *Contemporary Literature 10* (Madison, Wisconsin), no. 2, 1970; *Iowa Review* (Iowa City), Winter 1972; *If to Know Is Noble: The Poetry of George Oppen* by David W. Mcaleavy, unpublished dissertation, Cornell University, Ithaca, New York, 1975.

George Oppen comments:

The law of poetry rooted in the most unconscionable romance: the words the thought the form and the music for one's own sake, from this law is born the law *and* the prophets. Or more simply: his own pencil and his own piece of paper, and he is on his own. From scratch.

* * *

George Oppen strikes me as being one of the best and one of the worst of poets. The vantage from which he writes is high: the poetry of George Oppen declaims, defines, and finally establishes for us a series of dicta by George Oppen. This is the poet's task, amply stated by Oppen: "It is the business of the poet/'To suffer the things of the world/And to speak them and himself out' " ("The Building of thc Skyscraper"). In "Route" he writes: "I have not and never did have any motive of poetry/But to achieve clarity."

So Oppen's goal has been clarity, and perhaps this, achieved, is enough. But one suspects that the poet whose aim is clarity must tackle seemingly insoluble problems if his work is to distinguish itself. Oppen's out is to attempt clarification of everything; but no indication of humility and a great many self-assured statements can strain the wary reader's belief. This is not to deny that when Oppen hits, he hits hard, and many of his poems provide compelling testimony to the success of his mission. But in Oppen's books, these same poems, side by side, often seem echoes of one another: the clarity that one has defined is slightly changed by the next. What remains constant is Oppen's refusal to put down his pen and to wrestle bodily with the facts as he sees them. In short, there is a bothersome detachment here, as if Oppen has discounted himself from the viewpoint of his poem. This results in uneven poetry, often too engaged with games instead of play.

One of my principal difficulties with Oppen is his frequent use of abstraction and the equally disturbing double negative. I find myself distrusting these devices, not for themselves, but because they occur so often. He writes of women "In the streets, weakened by too much need/Of too little" (*Of Being Numerous*, section 34), and seeks "Not to reduce the thing to nothing" ("Route"). The double negative often becomes more ponderous than it deserves: "Like hawks we are at least not/Nowhere ..." ("Technologies"); and, again from *Of Being Numerous*: "That which one cannot/Not see."

In spite of this, it would be unfair to deny that Oppen is attempting a poetry far more difficult than most poets will dare, and the finest moments of his work raise questions (rather than answers) that will haunt every reader: "Wars that are just? A simpler question: In the event,/will you or will you not want to kill a German. Because,/in the event, if you do not want to, you won't" ("Route"). And, when he is willing to settle for just the moment of poetry, Oppen is without equal, as in "A Boy's Room":

A friend saw the rooms
of Keats and Shelley
At the lake, and saw "they were just
Boys' rooms" and was moved

By that. And indeed a poet's room
Is a boy's room
And I suppose that women know it.

Perhaps the unbeautiful banker
Is exciting to a woman, a man
Not a boy gasping
For breath over a girl's body.

In *Seascape: Needle's Eye* Oppen works with an even finer edge of clarity, turned towards the ocean. This may be Oppen's most accessible poetry to date, and his openness results in the achievement he hopes for in "Route" ("Anniversary Poem" and "Silver as ..."):

We have begun to say good bye
To each other
And cannot say it

One writes in the presence of something
Moving close to fear
I dare pity no one
Let the rafters pity
The air in the room
Under the rafters
Pity
In the continual sound
Are chords
Not yet struck
Which will be struck
Nevertheless yes

—Geof Hewitt

OPPENHEIMER, Joel (Lester). American. Born in Yonkers, New York, 18 February 1930. Educated in Yonkers public schools; Cornell University, Ithaca, New York, 1947–48; University of Chicago, 1948–49; Black Mountain College, North Carolina, 1950–53. Married 1) Rena Furlong in 1952 (divorced, 1960); 2) Helen Bukbery in 1966; four children. Production Manager, Arrow Typographic Service, New York, 1964; Project Director, Poetry Project at St. Mark's Church in-the-Bowery, New York, 1966–68; Director, Teachers and Writers Collaborative, New York, 1968. Since 1969, Poetry Consultant, Bobbs Merrill, Inc., publishers, Indianapolis and New York, and Poet-in-Residence, City College of New York. Formerly, Editor, *Kulchur*, New York; regular contributor, *The Village Voice*, New York. Recipient: Creative Artists Public Service grant, 1971. Address: Westbeth, 463 West Street, New York, New York 10019, U.S.A.

PUBLICATIONS

Verse

The Dancer. Highlands, North Carolina, Jargon, 1952.
The Dutiful Son. Highlands, North Carolina, Jargon, 1957.
The Love Bit and Other Poems. New York, Totem, 1962.
A Treatise. New York, Brownstone Press, 1966.
Sirventes on a Sad Occurrence. Mount Horeb, Wisconsin, Perishable Press, 1967.
In Time: Poems 1962–1968. Indianapolis, Bobbs Merrill, 1969.
On Occasion: Some Births, Deaths, Weddings, Birthdays, and Other Events. Indianapolis, Bobbs Merrill, 1974.
The Woman Poems. Indianapolis, Bobbs Merrill, 1975.
Acts. Mount Horeb, Wisconsin, Perishable Press, 1976.
Names, Dates, and Places. Laurinburg, North Carolina, St. Andrews Press, 1979.

Plays

The Great American Desert (produced New York, 1961). New York, Grove Press, 1965.
Miss Right (produced New York, 1962).
Like a Hill (produced New York, 1963).

Short Stories

Pan's Eyes. Amherst, Massachusetts, Mulch Press, 1974.

Other

The Wrong Season (on baseball). Indianapolis, Bobbs Merrill, 1973.

Bibliography: *Joel Oppenheimer: A Checklist* by George F. Butterick, Storrs, University of Connecticut Library, 1975.

Manuscript Collection: Wilbur Cross Library, University of Connecticut, Storrs.

Joel Oppenheimer comments:

The poems depend on the real and are motivated by the occasion. They start from the particular and the personal and, hopefully, move out and on to the outside world.

* * *

Joel Oppenheimer was actually a student at that mythical institution, Black Mountain College, and he calls Olson, Creeley, and Ginsberg his "teachers and makers" ("The Excuse" from *In Time*), but in fact his real teacher and maker-mentor has been William Carlos Williams, and he shares an interest in what might be called the occasional poem with his contemporaries, Paul Blackburn and Frank O'Hara. His poems are constructed of talk, the most effective being poems like "Sirventes on a Sad Occurrence" which describes an old lady in a tenement in New York who could not control her bowels and shamed herself and her daughter on the stairs to their apartment. Oppenheimer is best when he is, as in this poem, describing the occasions of everyday occurrences, and uttering his compassion and sympathy with the life of humble people.

Oppenheimer's writing style is typified by hip jargon used by New York artists, Olson-style punctuation, and a continuous line which is punctuated with line-breaks that give the voice pauses where the syntax affords none. His long monologues are personal meditations on everyday occasions such as his wife's breasts or a ball game in the park or going to work, but use those occasions or subjects to spin off into a meditation on how good the world is in spite of everything. The banal style of writing/talking of the poems actually serves as a foil to disarm the reader and suddenly allow him to see that perhaps one kind of poem *is* the simple occasion of being human and appreciating that fact.

The poems are quiet and patient, like an old teacher, waiting for the reader to stop and look at his own life with as much tenderness as Oppenheimer looks at his. At times, the poems have an insidious internal rhyming structure which will pun on old poems or songs or sayings. Poems like "The Cop Out" illustrate this sense of a poem's music which he shares with Blackburn and Creeley. Oppenheimer is a master of the everyday; one feels that the poems ask us all to live intelligently and above all with some mercy for others. They are proper poems for a time in which every educated man writes poems and uses the act of writing and the poem itself to help with his own enlightenment. The actual modesty of the poems underneath the seeming self-aggrandizement of whole poems about the trivia of existence is touching and compelling for its humane reminder of how important each of us thinks his life is and yet how each of us knows, underneath, how little any of us counts for in the larger view.

—Diane Wakoski

ORMOND, John. Welsh. Born in Dunvant, near Swansea, Glamorgan, 3 April 1923. Educated at Swansea Grammar School, 1935–41; University College of Swansea, 1941–45, B.A. 1945. Married Glenys Roderick in 1946; three children. Staff Writer, *Picture Post*, London, 1945–49; Sub-Editor, *South Wales Evening Post*, Swansea, 1949–55; BBC Television News Assistant, Cardiff, 1955–57. Since 1957, BBC Documentary Film-maker, Cardiff. Recipient: Welsh Arts Council prize, 1970, 1974, bursary, 1973; Cholmondeley Award, 1975. Agent: Oxford University Press, Ely House, 37 Dover Street, London W.1. Address: 15 Conway Road, Cardiff, Wales.

PUBLICATIONS

Verse

Indications, with James Kirkup and John Bayliss. London, Grey Walls Press, 1942.
Requiem and Celebration. Llandybie, Dyfed, Christopher Davies, 1969.
Corgi Modern Poets in Focus 5, with others, edited by Dannie Abse. London, Corgi, 1971.
Definition of a Waterfall. London, Oxford University Press, 1973.
Penguin Modern Poets 27, with Emyr Humphreys and John Tripp. London, Penguin, 1979.

Recording: *Poets of Wales*, with Raymond Garlick, Argo.

Other

Documentary Films include: *Under a Bright Heaven* (on Vernon Watkins), 1966; *A*

Bronze Mask (on Dylan Thomas), 1968; *The Fragile Universe* (on Alun Lewis), 1969; *R. S. Thomas: Priest and Poet*, 1971; *The Land Remembers*, 1972; *A Day Eleven Years Long*, 1974; *The Life and Death of Picture Post*, 1977; *Fortissimo Jones*, 1978; *Graham Sutherland in Wales*, 1978; *A Land Against the Light*, 1978; *The Colliers' Crusade*, 1979.

Critical Studies: by Leslie Norris, in *Poetry Wales* (Cardiff), Winter 1969; Robert Shaw, in *Poetry* (Chicago), November 1970; introduction by Dannie Abse to *Corgi Modern Poets in Focus 5*, 1971; "The Poetry of John Ormond" by Randal Jenkins, in *Poetry Wales* (Cardiff), Summer 1972; "The Accessible Song: A Study of John Ormond's Recent Poetry" by Jeremy Hooker, in *Anglo-Welsh Review* (Tenby), Spring 1974; "The Anglo-Welsh Poet John Ormond" by Michael J. Collins, in *World Literature Today* (Norman, Oklahoma), Autumn 1977.

John Ormond quotes from his comment in *Corgi Modern Poets in Focus 5*, London Corgi, 1971:

A number of my poems are elegiac in tone and I suppose this to be an indication of something in my nature, perhaps part of a Celtic characteristic. The ancient Welsh poetic tradition of lament cannot be dismissed as mere literary convention. Some of the reasons for it can be found in history but the factor of temperament, too, is strong. I do not work consciously in the minor key; but I am aware that I am continually concerned with "life's miraculous poise between light and dark."

In some ways my poems are forms in which I work out and test my relationship with the past. They sometimes start in celebrations of kinships and loyalties. Sometimes they are interim accounts of feelings and attitudes arrived at as the result of asking questions, mainly about beginnings and ends, which I cannot answer. They are also about coming to terms with the fact that, for me, there may never be answers. But I would add that this situation, together with my commitment to my roots, does not invalidate loving laughter, and even something approaching a mischievousness with words, as elements which can be present in the making of a poem.

In some ways a poet is a strange mixture of humility and of a self-confidence which borders on self-esteem. Without the latter how could he dare produce work in the face of what all the great poets have written? Excitement, a sureness about his talent, will sustain a young practitioner. What reason had I, seven or eight years ago, to start again? As a young man I wrote and published many pieces I then called poems; and later destroyed many more before falling into near-silence. I can give no reasons except that one is finally stuck with being the person one is. I think I learned the truth of what Valéry meant when he said that to expect perfection is, in itself, a kind of arrogance. I remember that a poet, with whom I had been discussing the general contemporary crisis of faith and the difficulty of being a lyric poet at all in the present age, remarked, "You cannot play a tune upon a slack string." And I recall that Wallace Stevens wrote, "One reads poetry with one's nerves."

* * *

John Ormond, like his compatriot Leslie Norris, is a poet who came to prominence in the 1970's, in his sixth decade, after a lengthy silence. His *Definition of a Waterfall* contained the best of his work from the earlier collection *Requiem and Celebration*, which had appeared in Wales a few years before, together with some newer poems. The collection was reportedly snapped up by O.U.P. within days of its manuscript's arrival. The reasons are clear: here is a mature man delivering a book of mature writing, almost unheralded.

John Ormond's credentials could not have been more sound. He had been schooled in the professionalism, the excitement of being a reporter for the magazine *Picture Post* in its heyday; he had won acclaim for his work in directing television film portraits of Vernon

Watkins, Alun Lewis, Dylan Thomas, and R. S. Thomas. His success as a journalist and film-director fused sound and image in poems such as "Cathedral Builders":

Saw naves sprout arches, clerestories soar,
Cursed the loud fancy glaziers for their luck,
Somehow escaped the plague, got rheumatism,
Decided it was time to give it up,

To leave the spire to others; stood in the crowd
Well back from the vestments at the consecration,
Envied the fat bishop his warm boots,
Cocked up a squint eye and said, "I bloody did that."

Ormond is as acutely aware of community values and social injustices as one would expect from a man who grew up in industrial South Wales through the late 1920's and 1930's. It is the way in which he expresses such feelings while extending the possibilities of conventional "Welsh character" poetry in a piece such as "My Grandfather and His Apple-Tree" that distinguishes him:

But in the time that I remember him
(his wife had long since died, I never saw her)
The sour half took over. Every single apple
Grew – across twenty Augusts – bitter as wormwood.
He'd sit under the box-tree, his pink gums
(Between the white moustache and goatee beard)
Grinding thin slices that his jack-knife cut,
Sucking for sweetness vainly. It had gone,
Gone. I heard him mutter
Quiet Welsh oaths as he spat the gall-juice
Into the seeding onion-bed, watched him toss
The big core into the spreading nettles.

There's a sadness in the anger; life scars the man and the poet's conclusion carries implicit understanding and compassion as well as anger and criticism. The poem rises above labels such as "Anglo-Welsh." Of course John Ormond's poetry is rooted in the South Wales community and landscape but upon these roots his best work grows to a wider significance.

His inclusion, with John Tripp and Emyr Humphreys, in the last of the Penguin Modern Poets series brings together some of those poems from the 1973 collection and later work. Though there is a mannered, overwrought style evident in some of the recent work – "Boundaries," "Captive Unicorn" – the best of this new work is very good indeed – "Message in a Bottle," "An Ending," and the superb "Landscape in Dyfed":

And, at the water's edge,
A struck havoc of trees clutches the interim season,
The given roots bare, seeming to feed on the wind;

And in their limbs what compass of sun
Is contained, what sealed apparitions of summer,
What transfixed ambulations. If you could cut
Right to the heart and uncouple the innermost rings
beyond those nerves you would see the structure of air.

John Ormond is constructing a body of work that may never be large, but is humane and visionary at once. Here is a poet dedicated to his craft, writing steadily and with profundity.

One awaits another collection in the certainty that the writing will engage the reader at the deepest levels of experience.

—Tony Curtis

ORMSBY, Frank. Irish. Born in Enniskillen, County Fermanagh, Northern Ireland, 30 October 1947. Educated at Queen's University, Belfast, 1966–71, M.A. 1971. Married Mary Elizabeth McCaffrey in 1968; two children. Since 1969, Editor, *Honest Ulsterman* magazine, Belfast. Since 1971, Teacher of English, Royal Belfast Academical Institution. Recipient: Eric Gregory Award, 1974. Address: 70 Eglantine Avenue, Belfast BT9 6DY, Northern Ireland.

PUBLICATIONS

Verse

Ripe for Company. Belfast, Ulsterman, 1971.
Business as Usual. Belfast, Ulsterman, 1973.
A Store of Candles. London, Oxford University Press, 1977.
Being Walked by a Dog. Belfast, Ulsterman, 1978.

Other

Editor, *Poets from the North of Ireland.* Belfast, Blackstaff Press, 1979.

* * *

Like several of his Northern Ireland contemporaries, Frank Ormsby cultivates the seeing eye. One cannot help but admire the precision of phrase that defines a neighbour in terms of his childless yard; that finds delight in an old tyre turned into a circular flowerbed; or that – even if only momentarily – sees, in "The Barracks," the official garnishing of a police-station in terms of an ordinary garden:

The woman tending flowers bends her head,
At work on the lupins. Elsewhere the beds
Are weeded. Turned-up soil darkens the edge
Of lawn and plastered wall. The chipped hedge
At the rear might be suburban.

Ormsby is at work on the lupins, and on the Massage Parlour, the Police Museum, and the Air-Raid Shelter. He is industrious in his attempts to compose a Landscape with Figures, and not only in the poem of that name:

What haunts me is a farmhouse among trees
Seen from a bus window, a girl
With a suitcase climbing a long hill
And a woman waiting.

At first it seems as though the poems exist for the things seen. And certainly Ormsby has a determined faithfulness to his subjects that almost entails a rejection of elegance and what used to be called verbal magic. The individual poems yield up their attractions reluctantly. However, a personality emerges from the composite: certainly dour, but also tender; grimly honest, but refreshingly so. At times Ormsby can be quite moving, as in "In Memoriam":

> Father, I'm forgetting you. Mind struggles
> With the smudge of ten years, that shadow loitering
> Off-focus. Squat as a tumulus, you've gone
> To ground.

Moving, too, are poems about his mother and about marriage; and the insight in these poems does much to mitigate what might otherwise seem an occasional gaucherie.

Ormsby certainly has the prose virtues, especially clarity and particularity, but these are qualities of poetry, also. The writer is his own best critic when he takes the title of his major collection from a phrase in a poem called "Under the Stairs." Under the stairs he finds the usual jumble of a life's progress – the shaft of a broom, a tyre, assorted nails. But he also finds that which, however modestly, can illumine the jumble: "a store of candles for when the light fails."

—Philip Hobsbaum

ORTIZ, Simon J. American Indian (Acoma Pueblo). Born in Albuquerque, New Mexico, 27 May 1941. Educated at Fort Lewis College, Durango, Colorado, 1962–63; University of New Mexico, Albuquerque, 1966–68; University of Iowa, Iowa City (International Writing Fellow), 1968–69. Served in the United States Army. Married Roxanne Dunbar; two children from previous marriage. Public relations consultant, Rough Rock Demonstration School, Arizona, 1969–70, and National Indian Youth Council, Albuquerque, 1970–73; taught at San Diego State University, California, 1974; Institute of American Arts, Sante Fe, New Mexico, 1974; Navajo Community College, Tsaile, Arizona, summers 1975–77; and College of Marin, Kentfield, California, 1976–79. Since 1979 has taught at the University of New Mexico. Editor, *Quetzal*, Chinle, Arizona, 1970–73. Recipient: National Endowment for the Arts grant, 1969. Address: Department of Native American Studies, University of New Mexico, 1812 Las Lomas Drive, Albuquerque, New Mexico 87131, U.S.A.

PUBLICATIONS

Verse

Naked in the Wind. Pembroke, North Carolina, Quetzal Vhio Press, 1970.
Going for the Rain. New York, Harper, 1976.
A Good Journey. Berkeley, California, Turtle Island Press, 1977.
The People Shall Continue. Sn Francisco, Children's Press, 1977.
Song, Poetry, Language. Tsaile, Arizona, Navajo Community College Press, 1978.

Short Story

Howbah Indians. Tucson, Blue Moon Press, 1978.

Simon J. Ortiz comments:

My writing, mostly using the tradition of Native American oral narrative, is a stand within the storm that is America. The wind will change; there will be calm.

* * *

The poetry of Simon J. Ortiz is a powerful and moving record of a native American who is an alien in his own land. In "A Designated National Park," he writes, "This morning,/I have to buy a permit to get back home." The Preface to *A Good Journey*, the most important collection of his work, is an excerpt from an interview. Ortiz is asked: "Why do you write? Whom do you write for?" His reply: "Because Indians always tell a story. The only way to continue is to tell a story and that's what Coyote says ... Your children will not survive unless you tell something about them – how they were born, how they came to this certain place, how they continue."

In "Notes for My Child," he does tell his daughter how she was born, and, in the context of his other work – in which his native tradition asserts itself most tellingly in the ritualization of significant events – it is a bemused but good-humored account of an encounter with the impersonality of a hospital. Many of his poems also are about coming to certain places. His sense of place is always precise. Even when he is in relatively unfamiliar territory, he is able to locate himself in the human geography. Above all, however, these are poems of continuance. Ortiz has a confidence that things do go on, a confidence which no Euroamerican, I expect, has ever been able to feel, and this assurance informs all of his work.

The fundamental strata of *A Good Journey* are story-telling and prayer. Even in the poems which deal with the confusion, ugliness, and impersonality of modern American life – as in "Burning River" – the memory of the timeless rituals serve as an orientation. In some ways, of course, the original sources are as lost to him as they are to other Americans: "The prayers of my native selfhood," he writes, "have been strangled in my throat." Some of the more self-conscious "traditional" poems, such as "Telling about Coyote," in which Coyote is "the existential man, Dostoevsky Coyote," suffer from the paradox inherent in any attempt to restore a lost tradition: it is of course the *lack* of self-consciousness which makes the tradition most attractive. In poems like "Earth and Rain, The Plants and Sun," "Canyon de Chelly," "Apache Love," "Vision Shadows," and "When It Was Taking Place," Ortiz gives us some of the most complete articulations to be found in English of that consciousness which dwells in proximity with the eternity which ritual makes manifest.

Ortiz should *not* be read as a specimen native American or an anthropological curiosity. He is, above all, an American poet and a very good one. Neither his loss of orientation in the Los Angeles airport nor his obvious enthusiasm for the variety and drama of American geography are uniquely native American. Lines such as these might be envied by any poet: "And the immensity of the place/settles upon me without weight./I knew that we were near/one of the certain places/that is the center of the center."

—Don Byrd

O'SULLIVAN, Vincent (Gerard). New Zealander. Born in Auckland, 28 September 1937. Educated at the University of Auckland, M.A. 1959; Lincoln College, Oxford, B.Litt. 1962. Married. Formerly, Lecturer, Victoria University, Wellington, and Senior Lecturer, Waikato University, Hamilton. Editor, *Comment*, Wellington, 1963–66. Recipient: Commonwealth Scholarship, 1960; Macmillan Brown Prize, 1961; Jessie Mackay Award, 1965; Farmers Poetry Prize, Sydney, 1967. Address: c/o New Zealand Listener, P.O. Box 3140, Wellington, New Zealand.

PUBLICATIONS

Verse

Our Burning Time. Wellington, Prometheus, 1965.
Revenants. Wellington, Prometheus, 1969.
Bearings. Wellington and London, Oxford University Press, 1973.
From the Indian Funeral. Dunedin, McIndoe, 1976.
Butcher & Co. Wellington, Oxford University Press, 1977; London, Oxford University Press, 1978.
Brother Jonathan, Brother Kafka. Wellington, Oxford University Press, 1979.

Novel

Miracle: A Romance. Dunedin, McIndoe, 1976.

Other

New Zealand Poetry in the Sixties. Wellington, Department of Education, 1973.
James K. Baxter. Wellington and London, Oxford University Press, 1976.

Editor, *An Anthology of Twentieth-Century New Zealand Poetry.* London, Oxford University Press, 1970.
Editor, *New Zealand Short Stories*, 3rd series. Wellington, Oxford University Press, 1975; London, Oxford University Press, 1976.

* * *

Despite the sheer gusto and figurative invention of his verse, Vincent O'Sullivan suffers on two counts from being a New Zealand academic. "New Zealand" in his own words (from his preface to a selection of New Zealand poetry) means burdened with the "cultural penalty" of dissociation from Europe and searching for self-definition. "Academic" means knowing all the skills in theory. O'Sullivan argues that this gap between uninformed heart or reality and over-informed head or technique can be bridged in two ways: by the "rigorous liberty" allowed by the exiled condition, and by the adaptation of old forms which is itself construction. O'Sullivan's occasional achievements by either avenue are memorable; more often his poems fall into the wasteland between original autobiographical experience and borrowed or highly-wrought belle-lettrism.

The clearest example of O'Sullivan's original success is his re-working of Greek myth: using the common facts themselves for a striking image (Helen "who once had a town to read by"); dramatising the characters' experience (Ulysses – "Lip me to silence then, true Penelope"); or twisting the story (the labyrinth is now within Theseus). At the other extreme is his beautiful lyric gift in reporting private experience, usually love ("You, your own leaven, knead perpetual myth"). When tied closely to a dramatic setting, as in "Island Bay," the result is a perfect harmony of form and feeling. In this poem, the poet recalls a love affair as he watches the red bus which carried him to their assignation, resolving to forget it all:

> But if the seventh, sacred wave rides higher by an inch ...
> or the sky lightens, so much as with a match
> struck by some walker half a mile off ...
> then all's unsaid. Reason walks the plank.
> We wait for a bus to drive out of the sea.

Too often, though, the objective correlative to the poet's emotion or imagery is insufficiently evoked, resulting in obscurity or rhetorical indulgence. The long sonnet sequence on the French engraver Charles Meryon tries to dramatise just this problem, the dangerous divorce of imagination from reality. Here reality is Meryon's vision of Paris, and his New Zealand experience abandoned – "Akaroa, the south, lay a hulk, a boyish error." Yet as O'Sullivan ably shows through his own art, New Zealand was the real, "in the way a hawk/over these hills can switch a sky to metal/for the stilled prey." The allegorical meaning is clear: O'Sullivan must begin with himself, "the swan of the body" and not the seductive artifice of Yeats's embroidered coat: "Skin and bones are verbs,/and there's our crown."

Masterly as O'Sullivan's gift is for the right image, the dramatic moment, and the colloquial expression, unfortunately he rarely employs it. In the earlier poetry he is seduced by elegance: "The girl I'd talk of, she goes decked in this"; "Limbs, Lady, Are Like Islands" goes a ponderous title; we find words like "uniquest" and "unvintageable." In later work the problem is uninspired exposition, a feeling of forced writing, often redeemed only by a clever final line (a poem about archery ends, "and when you close your eyes the bird-like drift of it," or a poem about a mad neighbour boarding a bus – "the doors shut behind her like palace sluts"). Even the title sequence from *Butcher & Co.*, featuring a Crow-like butcher who "grizzles" his knife on the stone, swamps his vulgar vitality with calculated images ("death, that perfect hinge") and awkward metaphysics ("Power Sticks Says B. As the Fan Flings"). Brute Butcher reads the *Odyssey*, instead of (as Bloom) being it.

Because of the gaudy juxtaposition of myth and reality in Central American life, and because it is essentially a report on experience, *From the Indian Funeral* is remarkably successful. Here O'Sullivan does give himself to his environment rather than to literature ("I am sick of the smooth ending"). As a New Zealander "facing the world without myth," he borrows everyday imagery to recreate the American's world ("your next meal as planned for as a vacation"), and Aztec imagery to imply the poverty of his own (the tourists dine by a statue of an Aztec "whose god ate time").

When O'Sullivan simply assumes his undeniable skill at adapting other myths and symbols, then, and like his mentor Yeats "lies down in the foul rag and bone shop of the heart" to take the "rigorous liberty" of communicating his own experience – then his words "are out and hunting." So far, and too often, his poetry has been impenetrably private, philosophically abstruse, or forgettably occasional – like his girls in *Revenants* who have merely "bartered talk."

—David Dowling

OWENS, Rochelle. American. Born in Brooklyn, New York, 2 April 1936. Educated at Lafayette High School, Brooklyn, graduated 1953. Married George Economou, *q.v.*, in 1962. Worked as clerk, typist, telephone operator. Member, Playwrights Unit, Actors Studio; Member, The New Dramatists Committee; Founding Member, New York Theatre Strategy. Recipient: Rockefeller Office for Advanced Drama Research grant, 1965; Ford grant, 1965; Creative Artists Public Service grant, 1966; Yale University Drama School Fellowship, 1968; Obie Award, 1968, 1971; Guggenheim Fellowship, 1971; National Endowment for the Arts grant, 1974; Rockefeller grant, 1975. Agent: Michael Imison, Dr. Jan Van Loewen Ltd., 81–83 Shaftesbury Avenue, London W1V 8BX, England. Address: 606 West 116th Street, No. 34, New York, New York 10027, U.S.A.

PUBLICATIONS

Verse

Not Be Essence That Cannot Be. New York, Trobar Press, 1961.
Four Young Lady Poets, with others, edited by LeRoi Jones. New York, Totem, 1962.

Salt and Core. Los Angeles, Black Sparrow Press, 1968.
I Am the Babe of Joseph Stalin's Daughter. New York, Kulchur, 1972.
Poems from Joe's Garage. Providence, Rhode Island, Burning Deck, 1973.
The Joe 82 Creation Poems. Los Angeles, Black Sparrow Press, 1974.
Selected Poems. New York, Seabury Press, 1974.
The Joe Chronicles II. Santa Barbara, California, Black Sparrow Press, 1978.

Recordings: *A Reading of Primitive and Archaic Poetry*, with others, Broadside; *From a Shaman's Notebook*, with others, Broadside.

Plays

Futz (produced Minneapolis, 1965; New York, Edinburgh and London, 1967). New York, Hawk's Well Press, 1961; revised version in *Futz and What Came After*, 1968; in *New Short Plays 2*, London, Methuen, 1969.
The String Game (produced New York, 1965). Included in *Futz and What Came After*, 1968.
Istanboul (produced New York, 1965). Included in *Futz and What Came After*, 1968.
Homo (produced Stockholm and New York, 1966; London, 1969). Included in *Futz and What Came After*, 1968.
Beclch (produced Philadelphia and New York, 1968). Included in *Futz and What Came After*, 1968.
Futz and What Came After (includes *Beclch*, *Homo*, *The String Game*, *Istanboul*) New York, Random House, 1968.
The Karl Marx Play, music by Galt MacDermot, lyrics by Rochelle Owens (produced New York, 1973). Included in *The Karl Marx Play and Others*, 1974.
The Karl Marx Play and Others (includes *Kontraption*, *He Wants Shih*, *Farmer's Almanac*, *Coconut Folksinger*, *O.K. Certaldo*). New York, Dutton, 1974.
He Wants Shih (produced New York, 1975). Included in *The Karl Marx Play and Others*, 1974.
Kontraption (produced New York, 1978). Included in *The Karl Marx Play and Others*, 1974.
Emma Instigated Me, in *Performance Arts Journal 1* (New York), 1976.
The Widow and the Colonel, in *Best Short Plays 1977.* New York, Crown, 1977.

Screenplay: *Futz* (additional dialogue), 1969.

Short Stories

The Girl on the Garage Wall. Mexico City, El Corno Emplumado, 1962.
The Obscenities of Reva Cigarnik. Mexico City, El Corno Emplumado, 1963.

Other

Editor, *Spontaneous Combustion: Eight New American Plays.* New York, Winter House, 1972.

Manuscript Collection: Mugar Library, Boston University.

Critical Studies: in *Margins 24–26* (Milwaukee), 1975.

Rochelle Owens comments:

(1970) I use language at times with a visceral, painter's tongue/eye. I will alter and extend language, transform and nobilize, bless and judge like Isaiah or Roberta? Or Job, for the helluv it! My sources are my skin! And secret scrolls left to me by the prophets of the Old World who still like me! Those who prepare anthologies must smile!

(1974) The process of poetry is growth, authentic, inevitable, the direction of urgency and exploration, the range of language possibilities extensive and sublime, the discovery of the panoramic range of the mind, the eternal curiosity of the aesthetic sensibility. If I write, I am aware of the breath generalized to include all that lives and is, the existence of the thing that is conscious because I am aware of it in the manifold ways of human experience.

* * *

Rochelle Owens is better known as a playwright than as a poet, but perusal of her poems shows them to be close to her theatrical imagination and an essential stimulus to it. In poetry (as distinct from poetic drama) she can concentrate her energies exclusively on verbal invention, coining words, splitting them, splashing them disjunctively on the page, disrupting grammar and free-associating with maximum tonal contrast:

O IF I FORGET THEE O ZION
LET AMERICA'S BALLS RUST

In her recent collection, *I Am the Babe of Joseph Stalin's Daughter*, both her verbal incandescence and dramatic proclivities emerge. As in her play *Futz*, she fearlessly explores the psychic realities of deviant personae. The Deebler Woman poems and "Bernard Fruchtman in Town & Country" create voices speaking fragments of plays. "The Voluminous Agony of Karl Marx" plainly grew into *The Karl Marx Play*, in which Marx, a modern Hebrew prophet cries out to Yahweh, as Job did, to relieve his boils so he can sit down and "write the book."

Owens, herself Jewish and married to a Greek, relishes Old Testament themes and the Mediterranean arena of contrast between Jew and Christian, Turk and Greek, which metaphorically extends to other conflicts – black *vs.* white, male *vs.* female, always juxtaposing ancient and traditional faith and language with contemporary slang and secular thought. Her most recent work, *The Joe 82 Creation Poems*, is a sequence of over a hundred poems titled for the gut-creative act which inspires graffiti on the New York subways. Although its subtitle is "a theater piece," this sequence nevertheless has strongly biblical and epic qualities. In the voices of a primal couple, Wild-Man and Wild-Woman, Owens redesigns the myths of creation in terms of the immediate creativity of every mind confronting its own experience. It is an ambitious task, with impressive results. Still an innovator and still young, this poet is enlarging her originality of thought and exuberance of language to create a new vision of the world which rests on the old virtues of praise and joy:

O World (Yes)
Thy feet are graced with everything!

—Jane Augustine

OXLEY, William. British. Born in Manchester, Lancashire, 29 April 1939. Educated at College of Commerce, Manchester; qualified as Chartered Accountant. Married Patricia Holmes in 1963; two daughters. Office Boy, Salford, Lancashire, 1955–57; Articled Clerk, Manchester, 1957–64; Chartered Accountant, Deloitte and Company, London, 1964–68, and

Lazard Brothers, London, 1968–76. Since 1976, free-lance writer. Editor or Co-Editor, *New Headland*, 1969–74, *Laissez Faire*, 1971–75, *Orbis*, 1972–74, *Littack*, 1972–76, and *Village Review*, 1973–74. Since 1976, Co-Editor of *Poetry Newsletter* and *Lapis Lazuli*, and Editor of *Littack Supplement*. Address: 6 The Mount, Furzeham, Brixham, South Devon, England.

PUBLICATIONS

Verse

The Dark Structures. London, Mitre Press, 1967.
New Workings. Privately printed, 1969.
Passages from Time: Poems from a Life. Epping, Essex, Ember Press, 1971.
The Icon Poems. Epping, Essex, Ember Press, 1972.
Opera Vetera. Privately printed, 1973.
Mirrors of the Sea. London, Quarto Press, 1973.
Fightings (published pseudonymously). Epping, Essex, Ember Press, 1974.
Eve Free. Knotting, Bedfordshire, Sceptre Press, 1975.
The Mundane Shell. Cleveland, County Durham, Uldale House, 1975.
Superficies. Breakish, Isle of Skye, Aquila, 1976.

Other

Sixteen Days in Autumn (travel). Privately printed, 1972.
Three in Campagna. Privately printed, 1973.

Critical Studies: "Poet in Profile: William Oxley" by Mike Shields, in *The Writer* (Aylesbury, Buckinghamshire), April 1975; "Littack: On the Attack" by Derek Stanford, in *The Statesman* (Karachi), 12 and 19 April 1975; "Through Littack to Vitalism" by V. Fenech, in *Bulletin and Times of Malta*, 1976.

William Oxley comments:

For some time, I have had one basic aim, and that has been to try to change the prevailing climate of poetry and poetics in the United Kingdom, away from the dry academic poetry of the Establishment, and away from the formless morass of undisciplined hysteria offered as the alternative to Establishment poetry by those I would choose to call the poets of the Alternative Establishment. Towards this end the magazine *Littack* was founded in 1972, and a systematically guided programme of poetics worked out in open forum by a number of poets, of whom the original cadre may loosely be termed the Vitalist Poets.

Since 1976, with the replacement of *Littack* by *The Littack Supplement*, I have tried to concentrate upon widening the definition of "vitalism" through a, hopefully, thoughtful series of editorials of a somewhat less polemical intent, as well as by the reviewing of a wide range of poetry books and pamphlets. Also, to emphasise the importance of freeing poetry from its chains of prose literalness, I have sought to encourage in *The Littack Supplement* and elsewhere the printing of poems – my own and those of others – which incline towards imaginative and symbolic values couched in lyrical, or at least rhythmical, forms, rather than the purely literal and superficial descriptions of experience that, by and large, pass for poetry today. Finally, my hope still remains the same: to see the *re-vitalisation* of the true tradition of poetry (which works through a multi-dimensional and analogical use of language, rather than by a one-dimensional prose discourse) giving a poetry of sufficient breadth of concern as to be variously describable as a "poetry of the whole mind" or a "poetry of the cosmos."

* * *

William Oxley's poetry lacks a crisp voice, and often runs the danger of being swamped by its feeling or thinned out in the service of its notions: "What measure, father, you asked of poetry./I rather ask it of man." The need for moral clarity, not the same thing as depth, can turn his language into mere attempted persuasion; this combines with an archness in the presentation of the speaker (that "rather" in the lines quoted) which can turn the verses irrevocably toward the prosaic. In his polemical manifesto, he argues, "*Littack 1* laid new attitude of mind. A new circuit was established – it is now necessary to run a current through" (from "The Vitalist Memorandum," from *Littack*, October 1972). Ironically most of Oxley's poems are like circuits without currents:

> Through dust-occluded glass, half-broken
> and most light precluding, I watch
> first mechanical assaults against old
> foundations. A familiar pattern witnessed.

Here the play with "occluded" and "precluded" prevents him from seeing that he's told us the same thing twice, and the enervating effect of the summarizing clause at the end of the quatrain is characteristic. All too often the description is flaccid and the anagogic leap is faulty. Not until his 1973 book, *Mirrors of the Sea*, do his lyrics begin to sing, caught up in more daring, less calculated imaginative excursions. In this book he begins to compose in "the sequence of the musical phrase" as Pound urged, though he may also rely too much on typography to enhance the undertaking. What's missing is still some sense of rectifying or enchanting metaphor, a caressing urge of the language past its domain of the egocentered cuddling of one's reaction to experience, and into a newly rapt ordering of vision. Oxley seldom lets us see anything but his own attitudes: "I am forced to apprehend about all things/There hangs the silent asking of dead faces." *The Dark Structures* and *Opera Vetera* contain early verse filled with poeticized abstractions, and as Oxley continues to struggle against his tendency to reaffirm platitudes, his advance has been real, though he has yet to demand of himself a set of risks beyond the safe discursive designs of prose.

—Charles Molesworth

PACK, Robert. American. Born in New York City, 19 May 1929. Educated at Dartmouth College, Hanover, New Hampshire, B.A. 1951; Columbia University, New York, M.A. 1953. Married Patricia Powell in 1961; three children. Taught at Barnard College, New York, 1957–64; Poetry Workshop of the New School for Social Research, New York; Director, Bread Loaf Writers Conference, Vermont. Abernathy Professor of Literature, Middlebury College Vermont. Editor, *Discovery*, New York. Recipient: Fulbright Fellowship, 1956; National Institute of Arts and Letters grant, 1957; Borestone Mountain Poetry Award, 1964; National Endowment for Arts grant, 1968. Lives in Cornwall, Vermont.

PUBLICATIONS

Verse

The Irony of Joy. New York, Scribner, 1955.
A Stranger's Privilege. Hessle, Yorkshire, Asphodel, and New York, Macmillan, 1959.

Guarded by Women. New York, Random House, 1963.
Selected Poems. London, Chatto and Windus, 1964.
Home from the Cemetery. New Brunswick, New Jersey, Rutgers University Press, 1969.
Nothing But Light. New Brunswick, New Jersey, Rutgers University Press, 1972.
Keeping Watch. New Brunswick, New Jersey, Rutgers University Press, 1976.
Waking to My Name: New and Selected Poems. Baltimore, Johns Hopkins University Press, 1980.

Other

Wallace Stevens: An Approach to His Poetry and Thought. New Brunswick, New Jersey, Rutgers University Press, 1958.
The Forgotten Secret (juvenile). New York, Macmillan, 1959.
Then What Did You Do? (juvenile). New York, Macmillan, 1961.
How to Catch a Crocodile (juvenile). New York, Knopf, 1964.

Editor, with Donald Hall and Louis Simpson, *New Poets of England and America.* Cleveland, Meridian, 1957; *Second Selection*, 1962.
Editor and Translator, with Marjorie Lelach, *Mozart's Librettos.* Cleveland, World, 1961.
Editor, with Tom Driver, *Poems of Doubt and Belief: An Anthology of Modern Religious Poetry.* New York, Macmillan, 1964.
Editor, with Marcus Klein, *Literature for Composition on the Theme of Innocence and Experience.* Boston, Little Brown, 1966.
Editor, with Marcus Klein, *Short Stories: Classic, Modern, Contemporary.* Boston, Little Brown, 1967.
Editor, *Selected Letters*, by Keats. New York, New American Library, 1974.

* * *

Robert Pack's poetry asserts man's connection to all levels of creation. "Grieving on a Grand Scale," a representative work, ranges from the imagined death of a lover, through speculations on the inevitable demise of the entire scale of nature, to the impending fate of the narrator himself. Though the poem resolves "... to mourn softly, without hope of resurrection," the final lines comfort with the image of an unknowing yet elegiac universe: "... young deer/Do not move – their loose watery lips/Slide over their gums with a sound like weeping." Pack avoids sentimentality by acknowledging both human involvement in "the crooked weasel's crooked chase" ("Canoe Ride"), and the horror, however stylized, of the cycle of existence: "... lace/Of mouse bones in owl feces" ("The Black Ant"). That carnage defines and fuses with human beauty implies frightening questions. Poems like "Descending" interpret the terror implicit in the universe as the real cost of exclusion from paradise, but generally Pack, while negating traditional answers, substitutes only an openness to the wonders of creation, whatever its origin: "... above, no missing God/I miss; high satisfying sky though, and below,/Chrysanthemums in garb of gaiety" ("Raking Leaves"). The key image of delight is the family; "Breakfast Cherries" celebrates the richness of ephemeral family moments. In "Everything Is Possible," the expectant father achieves the illusion of godhead, while the husband in "Were It Not" sees daily life as a recapitulation of paradise. Though children "redeem all sorrow," such redemption never completely calms latent anxiety; even the exultant "Welcoming Poem for the Birth of My Son" acknowledges "... that far city where my fears hide." "The Mountain Ash Tree" with its equivocally symbolic berries is Pack's most complex version of man's precarious optimism; despite the ominous appearance and bitter taste of the fruit, its unraveled meanings force the reader to share the final affirmation: "I am still alive."

Because of the relatedness of all elements in the universe, man can revert to the "hermit crab" comfort of "shell" and "tentacles" ("My House"), while the stone reciprocally thrusts forward to "... leaves,/A leaf, my tongue ..." ("To the Muse"). This diversity parallels man's ability to play several family roles simultaneously in a perpetual series of frightening but reassuring traps. A son, struggling to distinguish mother from wife and himself from his dead father, invokes his father's return in a way that ironically suggests a renewal of the whole process: "Dreaming, I seek your skeleton below;/I dig the worms and find your embryo" ("Father"). Most powerful of such poems is "The Boat," in which the speaker, with deadpan earnestness, accepts both the fusion and separateness of roles: "I dressed my father in his little clothes,/Blue sailor suit, brass buttons on his coat./He asked me where the running water goes./... He told me where all the running water goes,/And dressed me gently in my little clothes." If the family generates order, however unstable, sexual love generates the family.

Because Pack sees this love as a variant of complex natural phenomena, his love poems fuse tenderness with fierce eroticism: "The snow now hurtles from my eyes./I can do nothing. Nothing now can stop./The hemlock trees are hair and thighs/And in I drop" ("Let There Be Snow!"). Though long poems like "Home from the Cemetery" and "The Last Will and Testament of Art Evergreen" understandably lack the sustained intensity of the shorter lyrics, these ambitious works reveal Pack's characteristic command of symbolic image and his tact in suiting varying mood and tone to the demands of the overall pattern, in both cases Pack's obsessive equation of acceptance of death with acceptance of life.

While Pack often creates bitterly comic passages or infuses an entire poem with sly irony, his attempts at social satire, as in "Routine," disappoint. However, "The Children" roots Vietnam protest into the perpetual cycle of human guilt and avoids both polemic and easy answers. Pack's stylistic signature is the repetition, sometimes varied, of verb forms: "I grow by choosing what I choose to know" ("Song to Myself"), or the Cummingsesque double infinitive, playful yet capable of supporting intricacies of thought: "... beyond/what the stars/shall have time ever to learn to forsake" ("He Dies Alive"). Pack's special contribution, among a variety of traditional and free metrical forms that never seem arbitrary or defy careful reading, is a moral nursery rhyme in which a convincingly guileless speaker agonizes toward a solution that both repels and involves the reader, a solution that is ultimately no solution: "I shot an otter because I had a gun" leads through six tortured stanzas only to "He shot an otter because he had a gun" ("The Shooting").

—Burton Kendle

PADGETT, Ron. American. Born in Tulsa, Oklahoma, 17 June 1942. Educated at Columbia University, New York (Boar's Head Poetry Prize and George E. Woodberry Award, 1964), A.B. 1964; Fulbright Fellow, Paris, 1965–66. Married; one son. Since 1968, has taught poetry workshops at St. Mark's-in-the-Bowery, New York, and poetry writing in New York public schools. Since 1973, Founding Editor, with Joan Simon and Anne Waldman, Full Court Press, New York. Recipient: Gotham Book Mart prize, 1964; Poets Foundation grant, 1965, 1968; Columbia University Translation Center Award, 1976. Address: 342 East 13th Street, New York, New York 10003, U.S.A.

PUBLICATIONS

Verse

In Advance of the Broken Arm. New York, "C" Press, 1964.
Sky: An Opener. London, Goliard Press, 1966.

Bean Spasms: Poems and Prose, with Ted Berrigan. New York, Kulchur, 1967.
Tone Arm. Brightlingsea, Essex, Once Press, 1967.
100,000 Fleeing Hilda, with Joe Brainard. New York, Boke, 1967.
Bun, with Tom Clark. New York, Angel Hair, 1968.
Some Thing, with Ted Berrigan and Joe Brainard. Privately printed, n.d.
Great Balls of Fire. New York, Holt Rinehart, 1969.
Sweet Pea. New York, Aloe, 1971.
Poetry Collection. London, Strange Faeces Press, 1971.
Back in Boston Again, with Ted Berrigan and Tom Clark. Philadelphia, Telegraph, 1972.
Crazy Compositions. Bolinas, California, Big Sky, 1974.

Plays

Seventeen: Collected Plays, with Ted Berrigan. New York, "C" Press, 1965.
Chrononhotonothologos, with Johnny Stanton, adaptation of the play by Henry Carey. New York, Boke, 1971.

Novel

Antlers in the Treetops. Toronto, Coach House Press, 1973.

Short Stories

2/2 Stories for Andy Warhol. New York, "C" Press, 1965.

Other

The Adventures of Mr. and Mrs. Jim and Ron, with Jim Dine. London, Cape Goliard Press, 1970.

Editor, with David Shapiro, *An Anthology of New York Poets.* New York, Random House, 1970.
Editor, with Bill Zavatsky, *The Whole Word Catalogue.* New York, McGraw Hill, 1977.

Translator, *The Poet Assassinated*, by Guillaume Apollinaire. New York, Holt Rinehart, 1968.
Translator, *Entretiens avec Marcel Duchamp/Dialogues with Marcel Duchamp* (bilingual edition). New York, Viking Press, 1970; London, Thames and Hudson, 1971.
Translator, with David Ball, *Rldasedlrad les Dlcmhypbdf*, by Valéry Larbaud. New York, Boke, 1973.
Translator, with Bill Zavatsky, *The Poems of A. O. Barnabooth*, by Valéry Larbaud. Tokyo, Mushinsha, 1974.

Critical Study: "The New American Poetry" by Jonathan Cott, in *The New American Arts*, New York, Horizon Press, 1966.

Ron Padgett comments:

I have been recognized by others as belonging to the so-called New York "school" of poetry, but I have trouble recognizing myself in that disguise.

* * *

Deeply influenced by modern painting and its techniques, Ron Padgett modulates poems beyond traditional limits. In "Wonderful Things," for example, his diction varies from the language of formal elegy ("Anne, who are dead ...") to that of insanity ("Seriously, I have this mental (smuh!) illness ..."). Then, taking a new direction, he wraps the whole poem, retroactively, in the disarmingly ingenuous diction of a master storyteller ("and that's what I want to do/tell you wonderful things").

A naive world surfaces in this poetry: mysterious appearances, holes in the sky, falling clouds, ghosts, secret notes, funny animals, elves:

DECEMBER

I will sleep
in my little cup.

At its purest, its effect is wonder: "A child draws a man and the earth/is covered with snow." Padgett's power comes from this voice. When it speaks directly, it is the clearest voice of a child in modern poetry. When it speaks indirectly, the irony is clear.

Behind his irony, Padgett grows full of Dada ("What modern poetry needs/is a good beating"), ready to parody anything established ("When I see birches/I think of nothing ... One could do worse than see birches"). Like the Dadaists, he can pit Art against Life with ease:

Let's take a string quartet
Playing one of Beethoven's compositions
We may explain it as the scratching
Of a horse's hair against a cat's gut
Or we may explain it as the mind
Of a genius soaring up to an infinite
Horse's hair scratching against an infinite cat's gut.

The dilemma Padgett especially enjoys is that of the man who climbs after a ball of gold in the sky, actually gets it, but then doesn't know what to do with it:

And ... the way Madison Avenue really
Does go to Heaven
And then turns around and comes back, disappointed.

In his own search for values, Padgett is deeply affected by Surrealism's black humor, unmistakable imagery, and its antipathy towards the merely rational. Intellectual history, Padgett writes,

Is now only an imitation of itself
Like a car
Driving towards itself in the rain
Only to be photographed from behind
As we all eventually are ...
Breaking the visible chains of logic.

Whether he is, like a wise fool, proclaiming "Socrates was a mute, this is generally not known/But understood at some hilarious fork/For a few years! oh," or, like a child full of belief, stretching his hand into a painting to pick up one chocolate from a box. "Breaking the visible chains of logic" is what Padgett is about.

—Edward B. Germain

PAGE, P(atricia) K(athleen). Canadian. Born in Swanage, Dorset, England, 23 November 1916; emigrated to Canada in 1919. Educated at St. Hilda's School for Girls, Calgary, Alberta; Art Students League, and Pratt Institute, New York. Married William Arthur Irwin in 1950; three step-children. Formerly, sales clerk and radio actress, St. John, New Brunswick; filing clerk and historical researcher, Montreal; Script Writer, National Film Board, Ottawa, 1946–50. Painter, as P. K. Irwin. Recipient: Bertram Warr Award (*Contemporary Verse*, Vancouver), 1940; Oscar Blumenthal Award (*Poetry*, Chicago), 1944; Governor-General's Award, 1955. Officer of the Order of Canada, 1977. Address: 3260 Exeter Road, Victoria, British Columbia, Canada.

PUBLICATIONS

Verse

Unit of Five, with others. Toronto, Ryerson Press, 1944.
As Ten as Twenty. Toronto, Ryerson Press, 1946.
The Metal and the Flower. Toronto, McClelland and Stewart, 1954.
Cry Ararat! Poems New and Selected. Toronto, McClelland and Stewart, 1967.
Poems, Selected and New. Toronto, Anansi, 1974.

Novel

The Sun and the Moon (as Judith Cape). Toronto, Macmillan, and New York, Creative Age Press, 1944.
The Sun and the Moon and Other Fictions. Toronto, Anansi, 1973.

Bibliography: "The Poetry of P. K. Page: A Checklist" by Michele Preston, in *West Coast Review* (Burnaby, British Columbia), January 1979.

Critical Studies: by Daryl Hine, in *Poetry* (Chicago), 1968; "Traveller, Conjuror, Journeyman" by the author, in *Canadian Literature* (Vancouver), Autumn 1970; *The Bush Garden* by Northrop Frye, Toronto, Anansi, 1971; "The Poetry of P. K. Page" by A. J. M. Smith, in *Canadian Literature* (Vancouver), Autumn 1971; "P. K. Page: The Chameleon and the Centre" by Constance Rooke, in *Malahat Review* (Victoria), January 1978; "A Size Larger Than Seeing: The Poetry of P. K. Page" by Rosemary Sullivan, in *Canadian Literature* (Vancouver); "Retrospect and Prospect: P. K. Page" by Jean Mallinson, in *West Coast Review* (Burnaby, British Columbia), January 1979.

* * *

P. K. Page is an artist of many aspects; she has written a romance (*The Sun and the Moon*) and short stories; under her married name of P. K. Irwin she is a painter of repute. It is as a poet that she has worked longest, over forty years producing a sparse but interesting body of verse. But in P. K. Page the various arts she practices seem to inter-act, for anyone who is familiar with her poetry will have sensed its strongly visual aspect, that strange white and green country of the imagination which extends before the mind's eye as you read. There are times when her poetry works like a painting.

P. K. Page began to publish in the early 1940's. She first emerged in Montreal as a member of the group that produced *Preview*, a literary magazine dominated by Patrick Anderson and F. R. Scott. P. K. Page's earliest poems were published in *Preview*, and immediately she appeared as one of the more accomplished poets of the group. In 1944, with four other poets, she contributed a group of poems to *Unit of Five*, and two years later published her first independent book, *As Ten as Twenty*. Since then her production has been governed by a rigorously selective self-criticism. In 1954 she published *The Metal and the Flower*, in 1967

Cry Ararat, and in 1974 a "definitive collection," *Poems New and Selected* which in fact is incomplete, since it contains only 85 poems and misses out some of her most interesting pieces, like "Bark Drawing," which in one passage of six lines contains as fine an epitome as one could wish of her own mastery of two variant arts:

(an alphabet the eye
lifts from the air
as if by ear

two senses
threaded through
a knuckle bone)

P. K. Page's early verse tended to be dominated by social protest, but by the end of the 1940's her preoccupations and the content of her work had changed. She became more concerned with the plight of the lonely or of those whom circumstances made seem contemptible, and in poems like "The Stenographers" she treats such situations with a tantalizing combination of satire and compassion:

In the felt of the morning the calico-minded,
sufficiently starched, insert papers, hit keys,
efficient and sure as their adding machines;
yet they weep in the vault, they are taut as net curtains
stretched upon frames. In their eyes I have seen
the pin men of madness in marathon trim
race round the track of the stadium pupil.

From the inner landscapes – the quasi-biographies – of such poems P. K. Page has moved towards a mystical concern with the view out of the self towards images – Cook's Glasshouse Mountains in Australia, Mount Ararat – that suggest in Blakean or Asian vision the way of liberation from the alienated, prisoned self:

The bird in the thicket with his whistle
the crystal lizard in the grass
the star and shell
tassel and bell
of wild flowers blowing where we pass,
this flora-fauna flotsam, pick and touch,
requires the focus of the total I.

A single leaf can block a mountainside;
all Ararat be conjured by a leaf.

P. K. Page's philosophic development is paralleled in form. In one of her poems, "After Rain," she asks that "the whole may toll/its meaning shine/clear of the myriad images that still –/do what I will – encumber its pure line." And, indeed, a progressive purification of the line is clearly evident in Page's work. In the earlier poems the line is long and flowing, with a full kind of eloquence. In the more recent poems there is still fluidity, but it is more controlled, and sparser, like the crystal jet that flows from a Japanese bamboo pipe into a rock basin. A recent uncollected poem, "Prisoners," illustrates the change that has taken place:

One can spot them at once
although not
as one might suppose
by their handcuffs, which of course they wear

or by their rage
their air of guilt
their wounded pride
but by the sharp-nosed
clear-shaven men in drip-dries
who sit indifferent
invisibly shackled
at their side.

—George Woodcock

PALMER, Michael. American. Born in New York City, 11 May 1943. Educated at Harvard University, Cambridge, Massachusetts, 1961–68, B.A. in French 1965, M.A. in comparative literature 1967. Married Cathy Simon in 1972; one daughter. Editor, *Joglars* magazine, Providence, Rhode Island, 1964–66. Recipient: National Endowment for the Arts Fellowship, 1975. Address: 265 Jersey Street, San Francisco, California 94114, U.S.A.

PUBLICATIONS

Verse

Plan of the City of O. Boston, Barn Dream Press, 1971.
Blake's Newton. Los Angeles, Black Sparrow Press, 1972.
C's Songs. Berkeley, California, Sand Dollar, 1973.
Six Poems. Los Angeles, Black Sparrow Press, 1973.
The Circular Gates. Los Angeles, Black Sparrow Press, 1974.
Without Music. Santa Barbara, California, Black Sparrow Press, 1977.

Plays

Radio Plays: *Idem 1–4*, 1979.

Dance Scenarios (collaborations with Margaret Jenkins Dance Company): *Interferences*, 1975; *Equal Time*, 1976; *Video Songs*, 1976; *About the Space in Between*, 1977; *No One But Whitington*, 1978; *Red, Yellow, Blue*, 1978.

Other

Translator, *Relativity of Spring.* Berkeley, California, Sand Dollar, 1976.

Critical Studies: by David Chaloner, in *Poetry Information* (London), Summer 1976; "Counter Memory" by Steve McCaffery, in *Open Letter* (Toronto), April 1978; Martin Dodman, in *Montemora 5* (New York), June 1979.

* * *

It has long been a dogma of poetic criticism that a poem cannot be paraphrased. But, of course, most poems can, and it is frequently useful, especially when the reader is making first acquaintance with a work. The poetry of Michael Palmer *cannot* be paraphrased. Its meaning is strictly a function of the complex interrelations of specific linguistic details.

A typical poem – "On the Way to Language," for example – is a linguistic environment in which poetic particles, phonemes, rhythms, rhymes, images, bits and pieces of "found" language, perform a complex dance. The present example shares its title with a translation of one of Heidegger's philosophic treatises. The reader must assume that this is no accident: it is clear that Palmer is a reader of modern philosophy. Having made this somewhat arcane connection (it is not one of Heidegger's better known works), however, one by no means has a key to the poem. In fact, the information seems to lead nowhere. The poem takes the form of answers and questions, upsetting normal expectations of order, and although it suggests certain Heideggerian themes, it is non-committal. The poem closes when the abstract title produces an image of a concrete "way": "the valley of desire/crossed by the bridge/of frequent sighs," but, in context, this is really another enigma rather than a resolution.

The theme of Palmer's work – to the extent that it may be said to have such – is a Heideggerian or, perhaps more to the point, Wittgensteinian, astonishment at the existence of phenomena. We are presented with a world and a language which is endlessly fascinating. It is possible to trace local connections, follow this or that line of thought to its frequently absurd conclusion, but there is no closure except the confrontation with the inexplicable and irreducible stuff of language and the world.

It is demanding poetry. Its ideal reader is one who can combine intense concentration with willingness to play – in all senses of the word – to play as a child and also, perhaps more importantly, to play as a musician. Despite the fact that his most interesting volume is entitled *Without Music*, all of his work is best read in the spirit of a musician studying a score, trying different tempos, different phrasings, and so forth.

Palmer is involved in an exploration of possibilities in language which have been largely disregarded. He takes a passage from Géza Róheim's *Magic and Schizophrenia* as the epigraph to *Without Music*, and he also names Louis Wolfson's *Le Schizo et les Langues* as one of his important sources. We are beginning to learn that traditional syntax and traditional forms of poetic organization are merely labor-saving devices which allow a vague, careless attention access to language. When such simple strategies are exposed, however, and attention is brought to bear without reservation, it begins to discover possibilities for the production of meaning far more powerful than those we have previously known. Only one of the unexpected turns in this situation is that we learn the schizophrenic's bewilderment is a result of wandering unaided into this difficult and exciting realm of experience.

Michael Palmer is perhaps the only one of his generation to have established himself without question as an important poet.

—Don Byrd

PARKINSON, Thomas (Francis). American. Born in San Francisco, California, 24 February 1920. Educated at the University of California, Berkeley, A.B., M.A., Ph.D. Married to the painter Ariel Parkinson; two daughters. Since 1948, Member, Department of English, currently, Professor of English, University of California, Berkeley. Recipient: Guggenheim Fellowship, 1957; Institute of Creative Art Fellowship, 1963. Address: 1001 Cragmont, Berkeley, California 94708, U.S.A.

PUBLICATIONS

Verse

Men, Women, Vines. Berkeley, California, Ark Press, 1959.

Thanatos: Earth Poems. Berkeley, California, Oyez, 1965; revised edition, 1976.
Protect the Earth (includes essays). San Francisco, City Lights, 1970.
Homage to Jack Spicer and Other Poems: Poems 1965–1969. Berkeley, California, Ark Press, 1970.
Centers, Chiefly Concerning John Wayne and His Horse and Many Incredibilities. Berkeley, California, Thorp Springs Press, 1978.

Play

What the Blind Man Saw; or, Twenty-Five Years of the Endless War. Berkeley, California, Thorp Springs Press, 1974.

Other

W. B. Yeats, Self-Critic: A Study of His Early Verse. Berkeley, University of California Press, and London, Cambridge University Press, 1951.
W. B. Yeats: The Later Poetry. Berkeley, University of California Press, and London, Cambridge University Press, 1964.

Editor, *A Casebook on the Beat.* New York, Crowell, 1961.
Editor, *Masterworks of Prose.* Indianapolis, Bobbs Merrill, 1962.
Editor, *Robert Lowell: A Collection of Critical Essays.* Englewood Cliffs, New Jersey, Prentice Hall, 1968.
Editor, *Hart Crane and Yvor Winters: Their Literary Correspondence.* Berkeley, University of California Press, 1978.

Thomas Parkinson comments:

My poetry is primarily meditative poetry written in various forms but moving increasingly toward a formal free verse that makes use of all the devices of historical poetry in English, not excluding rhyme. My main concerns are the relation of man to nature, of history to wilderness, and of death to love.

* * *

From his position on the Berkeley campus Thomas Parkinson has witnessed first-hand the free speech movement, war resistance and protest, and the student strikes which have been so prominently focused there. His poetry and essays traverse an astonishingly wide range from public, often political, topics to events personal and confessional. Parkinson has himself escaped death by inches, has seen death close at hand, and shows painful awareness of the infinite varieties of dying. His poetry reveals a continual amazement over the very process and flux of life, the cruel ecology of organisms, the fragility, and the mystery of it all. It is like being at the beach at low tide, watching the squirting, crawling, opening abundance of life until you can absorb no more, "And the entire planet screams in the mind, an interminable/ feeding, and swelling and expiring."

Parkinson's *Protect the Earth* contains short environmental and political essays and a long poem, "Litany for the American People," which records his outrage over inhuman governmental actions. The book is based on Parkinson's conviction that "so long as human beings go on building up levels of tolerance against the abominable, the abominable will grow." It records his deep concern for the quality of human life and his rages against human arrogance and environmental insensitivity. Parkinson sees himself as a Franciscan; he is also a poet ecologist in sympathy if not in league with Barry Commoner and Paul Ehrlich.

The poetry of *Homage to Jack Spicer* and *Thanatos: Earth Poems* is considerably more personal. The eight "Spicer" poems span eighteen years of close friendship with Spicer, between 1947 and 1965. There is also the pain of watching Spicer, also a writer, tear and drink himself dead. "He was a battered radio/in the city dump, connections busted, batteries shot ...," dead at forty. Parkinson also refers to his "Dry Season" during this period. He is shot in his office by a "poor lunatic" who believes he is a Communist. His student assistant is killed and sixty pieces of bird shot hit Parkinson in the face and jaw. "My wound/throbs and my wired jaw/Aches." It is a time when "clocks fail, hearts/stumble," poison and violence surround him yet he can affirm "violence only creates more violence." Still, for Parkinson "surviving's not enough," he seeks not merely law and order but inner order, and the "expression of an inner psychological harmony." *Thanatos* presents both a series of "Soliloquies for the Dead," the dying, and a further search, through solitude, for the inner order he craves. He recognizes in life:

> A spark ongoing, and in the ever-branching
>   heavens of the night
> A life-tree bearing on and on.

With the *Thanatos* poems Parkinson's lines are less tightly imagistic, more expansive and more memorable, as seen in "Death as Solitude":

> Moon passes and sun sets, whatever is holy rests
> In the rising susurrah. From their quiet, ecstasy.
> And the sanctified earth turns and turns.

—John R. Cooley

PARTHASARATHY, R(ajagopal). Indian. Born in Tirupparaiturai, near Tiruchchirappalli, Tamil Nadu, 20 August 1934. Educated at Don Bosco High School, Bombay, 1944–51; Siddharth College, Bombay University, 1957–59, M.A. in English 1959; Leeds University, Yorkshire (British Council Scholar), 1963–64, postgraduate diploma in Engish studies 1964. Married Shobhan Koppikar in 1969; two sons. Lecturer in English, Ismail Yusuf College, Bombay, 1959–62, and Mithibai College, Bombay, 1962–63, 1964–65; Lecturer in English Language Teaching, British Council, Bombay, 1965–66; Assistant Professor of English, Presidency College, Madras, 1966–67; Lecturer in English, South Indian Education Society College, Bombay, 1967–71. Regional Editor, Madras, 1971–78, and since 1978, Editor, Delhi, Oxford University Press. Member of the International Writing Program, University of Iowa, Iowa City, 1978–79. Since 1978, Member of the Advisory Board for English, National Academy of Letters, New Delhi. Recipient: Ulka Poetry Prize (*Poetry India*, Bombay), 1966. Address: Oxford University Press, 2/11 Ansari Road, Daryaganj, Box 7035, New Delhi 110 002, India.

PUBLICATIONS

Verse

Rough Passage. New Delhi, Oxford University Press, 1977.

Other

Editor, with J. J. Healy, *Poetry from Leeds.* Calcutta, Writers Workshop, 1968.

Editor, *Ten Twentieth-Century Indian Poets.* New Delhi, Oxford University Press, 1976.

Critical Studies: "Two Indian Poets" by William Walsh, in *Literary Criterion 11* (Mysore), Winter 1974; "The Last Refinement of Speech" by M. Sivaramakrishna, in *Literary Criterion 12* (Mysore), 2–3, 1976; "R. Parthasarathy: Images of a Poet" by Roger Iredale, in *Tenor 1* (Hyderabad), July 1978; "The Parthasarathy Passage: An Interview" by Ayyappa Paniker, in *Tenor 2* (Hyderabad), January 1979; "The Achievement of R. Parthasarathy" by Brijraj Singh, in *Chandrabhāgā 2* (Cuttack), Winter 1979.

R. Parthasarathy comments:

One of the problems that the Indian poet writing in English faces is the problem of trying to relate himself meaningfully to a living tradition. The poet who writes only in English is unable to relate himself to any specific tradition. He cannot relate himself, for instance, to the tradition of English verse, nor can he relate himself to a tradition of verse in any one of the Indian languages.

From the beginning I saw my task as one of acclimatizing the English language to an indigenous tradition. In fact the tenor of *Rough Passage* is explicit: to initiate a dialogue between myself and my Tamil past. "Homecoming," in particular, tries to derive its sustenance from grafting itself on to whatever I find usable in the Tamil tradition. I was eventually able to nativize in English something that had eluded me over the years – the flavour, the essence of Tamil mores.

I am aware of the hiatus between the soil of the language I use and my own roots. Even though I am Tamil-speaking and yet write in English, there is the overwhelming difficulty of using images in a linguistic tradition that is quite other than my own. I believe that an Indian poet who thinks long and hard enough on his own use of language, even if it is English, sooner or later will, through the English language, try to come to terms with himself as an Indian, with his Indian past and present, and that the language will become acclimatized to the Indian environment. Further, if the poet has access to an Indian language, though he may not find himself writing in it, he can gradually try to appropriate that language's tradition. This would mean reconciling ourselves to Tamil English verse, Kannada English verse, Marathi English verse, and so on – all segments of a pan-Indian mosaic that we recognize as the literatures of India. When that happens, the severed head, Indian English verse, will no longer "choke to speak another tongue."

Perhaps *Rough Passage*, as it is now, points to a future poem in Tamil.

* * *

Rough Passage, R. Parthasarathy's only book of verse so far, is a collection of the poems that he had been writing for twenty years. In the preface he says that the poems should be really read as one poem, an autobiographical poem in fact. The initiating experience of the poem is the tension felt by the poet concerning his cultural identity – Tamil-born, but passionately in love with English and English literature. (In retrospect, the love has seemed to him a "whoring after English gods.") Parthasarathy's dilemma has been felt by many, if not all, Indian writers in English: how can an Indian poet or writer in general be himself, be an Indian, in a language which is not his or that of his community or of his tradition? The first part of the poem "Exile" poses the problem; the second part describes an experience of love which filled out the individuality of the poet; the final part resolves the problem in a way by opening a dialogue with the poet's Tamil past. The individual poems, written in three-line stanzas of varying length, form sections in these three parts. While it cannot be claimed that the sections succeed each other in inevitable order, the argument is developed clearly and cogently enough. Parthasarathy has tried to overcome the difficulties that the English language creates for him as a medium of perception and expression by trying to write in images that help the direct apprehension of experience. The sentences are packed – sometimes over-packed – with images that appeal to more than one sense at the same time. The problem cannot of course be solved entirely in this way because the images are in English words. Parthasarathy has therefore tried to do what he says Ramanujan has notably succeeded in doing: to convey in English "what is locked up in another linguistic tradition." (Parthasarathy could have cited the much earlier example of Raja Rao in fiction.) He has tried to give us poems that sound like renderings in contemporary tone and idiom of a Tamil original: to adapt a phrase from the poem, to give us a "coloured English" poem. The example that he cites is the third section of "Homecoming":

And so it eventually happened –
a family reunion not heard of
since grandfather died in '59 – in March

this year. Cousins arrived in Tiruchchanur
in overcrowded private buses,
the dust of unlettered years

clouding instant recognition.
Later, each one pulled,
sitting cross-legged on the steps

of the choultry, familiar coconuts
out of the fire
of rice-and-pickle afternoons.

Sundari, who had squirrelled up and down
forbidden tamarind trees in her long skirt
every morning with me,

stood there, that day, forty years taller,
her three daughters floating
like safe planets near her.

In spite of the poet's claim, it is a moot point whether we can instantly recognize this as an un-English poem in English dress as we do when we chance upon an English haiku or a Pound translation, or even a prose passage from Raja Rao's *Kanthapura*. The Tamil that Parthasarathy favours is, however, not contemporary Tamil, which he denounces as a flea-ridden carcass. Of this cultural degeneration the fate of the river Vaigai near Madurai, once capital of a great Tamil empire, is symbolic. Emperors and poets once slept in her arms, says the poet. Now people use the water to clean themselves.

Parthasarathy is aware that the problem of cultural rootlessness, or rather, of roots that have become desiccated, is not solved by writing Tamil-English poems. As T. S. Eliot realized in *After Strange Gods*, tradition is much more than literary tradition. Unfortunately Parthasarathy's conception of tradition is not very promising. After exhorting himself to "turn inward," he writes: "Scrape the bottom of your past./Ransack the cupboard/for skeletons of your Brahmin childhood." Between people who think of tradition as a river whose waters can be used for cleaning themselves and those who think of it as a skeleton in the cupboard which they can rattle, the difference is not very great. At the moment it looks as though Parthasarathy has reached a dead end. In a poem published after *Rough Passage* but intended to form part of it, he writes:

I've rolled my fate
into a paper ball and tossed it

out of the window. I can now walk
to the end of thc marriage
on my knees for my unspeaking sons.

But children can revive or nurture a tradition only if their parents have made it part of their upbringing.

—S. Nagarajan

PARVIN, Betty. British. Born in Cardiff, Glamorgan, 10 October 1916. Educated at Heathfield House Convent School; extramural classes at the University of Nottingham and the University of Leicester. Married D. F. McKenzie Parvin in 1941; one son. During World War II, worked as a secretary in the Civil Service. Secretary, 1966–71, and since 1973, Vice-Chairman, Nottingham Poetry Society. Member, Advisory Panel, East Midlands Arts Association; Reviewer, *Outposts*, London. Recipient: Lake Aske Memorial Award, 1968, 1971; Manifold Century Scholarship, 1968. Address: "Bamboo," Bunny Hill Top, Costock, near Loughborough, Leicestershire LE12 6UX, England.

PUBLICATIONS

Verse

A Stone My Star. London, Outposts, 1961.
The Bird with the Luck: Twelve Poems. Nottingham, Byron Press, 1968.
Sketchbook from Mercia. London, Manifold, 1968.
Sarnia's Gift. Loughborough, Leicestershire, Griffin Press, 1972.
A Birchtree with Finches. Nottingham, N.P.S., 1974.
Country Matters. Nottingham, Em-press, 1979.

Other

Editor, *Poetry Nottingham 1970.* Nottingham, N.P.S., 1970.

Manuscript Collection: Nottingham Central Library.

Critical Study: Introduction by G. S. Fraser to *The Bird with the Luck*, 1968.

Betty Parvin comments:

When G. S. Fraser read some of my first poems in the early sixties he remarked: "You have a Parnassian gift. Don't let it go!" From that time I ceased to denigrate its Palgravian roots or to attempt consciously to change my style. Poets I have learned to revere since force-fed schooldays have contemporized my work without my conscious manipulation, but still when the rhyme would chime, I permit it. Not unnaturally, many of these poets have similar roots: Hardy, Edward and R. S. Thomas, Larkin, Day Lewis, Wilbur, Fraser; some of the younger "moderns."

My theme is whatever warms me emotionally; I am past the time of powerful bias, unless it be for the beautiful – that which, some would persuade us, has never existed.

Inclusion in textbooks and anthologies has resulted in calls upon me to read and talk about my poems in schools, etc. – a valuable contact with my "public," one which I enjoy.

* * *

Betty Parvin is more widely known and respected among readers of poetry than her six small booklets would appear to indicate, for her work has been published in a number of magazines and anthologies and has been translated into Portuguese and Byelorussian. There is nothing that might be regarded as pretentious in her poetry and no attempt is made at intellectual hair-splitting, though her poems are informed by a cool intelligence and control of language that do not give way to sentimentality or egotism. She concentrates largely upon her own everyday experiences – memories of youth and childhood, encounters with people, family connections, places she has visited or lived in, or moods "caught on the wing at play in timeless Wales." An ivy-wreathed gateway or a gothic window is enough to stimulate her creative imagination. Yet it would be a mistake to regard her as a domestic poet. She has such an individual way of looking at things, whether it is the absurd gait of a magpie or gulls searching for food in the "green harbour muck," and of placing them in some kind of perspective, that the reader is subtly brought into contact with fundamentals, the paradox and underlying reality of life itself. In such poems as "Gulls Aground," "Welsh Cottagers," and "Mothering," Betty Parvin is to be seen at her best.

—Howard Sergeant

PASTAN, Linda (née Olenik). American. Born in New York City, 27 May 1932. Educated at the Fieldston School, New York; Radcliffe College, Cambridge, Massachusetts, B.A 1954; Simmons College, Boston, M.L.S. 1955; Brandeis University, Waltham, Massachusetts, M.A. 1957. Married Ira Pastan in 1953; two sons and one daughter. Recipient: Swallow Press New Poetry Series Award, 1972; National Endowment for the Arts grant, 1972; Bread Loaf Writers Conference John Atherton Fellowship, 1974; Alice Fay di Castagnola Award, 1977. Agent: Jean Naggar, 420 East 72nd Street, New York, New York 10021. Address: 11710 Beall Mountain Road, Potomac, Maryland 20854, U.S.A.

PUBLICATIONS

Verse

A Perfect Circle of Sun. Chicago, Swallow Press, 1971.
On the Way to the Zoo. Washington, D.C., Dryad Press, 1975.
Aspects of Eve. New York, Liveright, 1975.
The Five Stages of Grief. New York, Norton, 1978.
Selected Poems. London, Murray, 1979.
Setting the Table. Washington, D.C., Dryad Press, 1980.

* * *

Linda Pastan sees herself as Eve – one of the fallen, not the temptress. The bathers in "At Woods Hole" "learn nothing, lying/on sand hot and pliant as each other's flesh." Trapped in sensuality, they may appreciate beauty, but that is part of the cosmic deception: "waves seem to bring the water in forever/even as the tide moves surely out." Like Poe, she is conscious of the limits of the human mind, and the impossibility of exceeding them. In "The Last Train" she imagines a boy fascinated with disappearing buffalo, another with the vanishing long-distance passenger train, and concludes that we all "follow sleep as well as we are able/along disintegrating paths of vapor,/high above the dreamlike shapes of clouds."

But she seems more willing to abide by the limits of consciousness than Poe. Her effort has been to clarify this humanness. In "Distances," she images the frustration of being apart:

Straight and cold as railroad track
I lie in my old roadbed
measuring distances –
waiting for you to pass
over me once again,
on your way somewhere else.

In "At the Gynecologist's" her "body so carefully/contrived for pain" "gallop[s] towards death/with flowers of ether in my hair." Acutely aware of her mortality, she does *try* to escape it. In "Williamsburg" she seeks the authenticity of history only to have the spell broken when "a Woolworth pencil" falls from the basketmaker's pocket. She senses "what wildness/is left" in "Bicentennial Winter," and though she is tempted to skate the frozen Potomac, she does not partake of that "dangerous/freedom." She finds violence instead of beauty in "Evening at Bird Island": "under my rocking floor/fish swallow other fish,/feeding/like bad dreams/under the surfaces of sleep." The problem is that the human necessarily pervades everything: "There is a figure in every landscape."

While Pastan's vision has been clear and consistent throughout her books – and her language lucid and intelligent – *The Five Stages of Grief* is the most effective arraying of responses. There is *denial*, when life is made up largely of the familiar and even deaths "wait like domestic animals" "patient and loving" ("After"). And *anger*, when she'd just as soon "everything happen/off-stage" and let her stay "with the scenery" ("Exeunt Omnes"). The stage of *bargaining* produces minimal consolations: "We must learn/the cold lessons/the dinosaurs learned:/to freeze magnified/in someone else's history;/to leave our bones behind" ("Ice Age"). In *depression* even the sun, as her husband's grandmother talks of the Florida weather, seems like a "huge stone/rolled against the door of death/to hold it shut" ("It Is Still Winter Here"). Finally, there is *acceptance*, when the sun is "warm amnesia" and a woman and her griefs sing back and forth ("Old Woman"). But *acceptance*, though "its name is in lights," proves unattainable: as the title poem states, "Grief is a circular staircase." Thus, what might have been linear turns out to be confining, and Pastan must remain a seeker of "the pure/center of light/within the dark circle/of ... demons" ("It Is Raining on the House of Anne Frank").

—Jay S. Paul

PATERSON, Alistair (Ian Hughes). New Zealander. Born in Nelson, 28 February 1929. Educated at Nelson College, 1943–47; Christchurch Teachers College, 1948–49; Victoria University College, Wellington, 1951–52; New Zealand Armed Services Command and Staff College, Whenuapai, 1969. Teacher, Auckland Point School, Nelson, 1950, and Taita North School, Wellington, 1953; Instructor Officer, rising to rank of Lieutenant Commander, Royal New Zealand Navy, 1954–74; Dean of General Studies, New Zealand Police Department, 1974–78. Since 1978, Education Officer, New Zealand Education Department. Former Editor of *Mate*, Auckland, and former consultant, American Institute of

Police Science. Currently, Editor, *Climate*, Auckland. Recipient: Fulbright Fellowship, 1977. Address: P.O. Box 9612, Newmarket, Auckland, New Zealand.

PUBLICATIONS

Verse

Caves in the Hills: Selected Poems. Christchurch, Pegasus Press, 1965.
Birds Flying. Christchurch, Pegasus Press, 1973.
Cities and Strangers. Dunedin, Caveman Press, 1976.
The Toledo Room: A Poem for Voices. Dunedin, Pilgrims South Press, 1978.

Alistair Paterson comments:

After commencing in the traditional New Zealand lyric/pastoral mode, I moved into a study of recent American verse – a study that has resulted in the development of a style and technique based on "open" form as expounded by Pound, Creeley, and Olson. This development has led to poems of the longer form (about 400 lines) as typified by *The Toledo Room*. As an editor and reviewer I have concentrated on the encouragement of post-modern writing in open forms and (hopefully) the extension of this type of writing into the work of other New Zealand poets.

* * *

Alistair Paterson's first book, *Caves in the Hills*, was very much the conventional collection of the post-war years – thirty or so pieces more or less well-made on a variety of subjects in a variety of forms, fairly impersonal, "modern" in tone and language (no Romantic poeticizing), each poem a discrete item. There was the feeling of a man looking around for subjects on which poems might be written. But there was one item which stood apart. The sequence called "The Metropolis" is an early Paterson attempt (not altogether successful) at what has lately become characteristic of his work. The language, one feels, it struggling to gain ascendancy over the statement the poem is making, so that reference, meaning, the poem's "subject," will be only one element in a total poetic structure.

In his second and third books, *Birds Flying* and *Cities and Strangers*, we can see Paterson experimenting, reaching out for freer forms. His subject remains on the whole what it was for the Wellington poets of the 1950's – a rather gloomy realism about domestic, urban, and suburban life, and about human relationships. Again in the best of these poems, however, there is an attempt to make the movement of language, the flow of syntax and grammar, more than direct statement or imagery, carry the feelings that spring from the occasion or event which is the subject. This is a distinct advance from the mode in which Paterson began, where poets too often seemed to feel they could do the fiction writer's job in a few dozen lines, summing up a human action (and particularly human failure) in smart, well-organized images and phrases. Paterson has found his way out of that mode, it seems, by a close study of the post-Modernist American poets. From their work he has acquired his interest in open form and in poem sequences.

The Toledo Room combines Paterson's characteristic subject with his developing interest in open form. It is a dramatic work in which a number of characters speak, none of them clearly identified. They seem to talk about their lives, their love affairs, their failures, the political climate. They are concerned about, and caught up in, the roles their circumstances impose. But the adopting of roles, the assuming of masks, is the game of life itself; and the whole vision, though perhaps negative, is also wry, amused, and is gathered into a music – the structure of the poem itself – which has beauty. This is Paterson writing at his best.

Summer
& the sounds of summer –
we should all be accustomed to it
but the sun throws down such heat
it seems like dying (or death)
fading, falling into silence
seizing the albatross in its flight.
Outwards we follow the horizon
the sweep of the bay
inwards translate
what's seen and said into another language
into some kind of script
words, phrases, pages with footnotes:
Marsden's weather-worn cross
in that far country above lonely water.

—C. K. Stead

PATTEN, Brian. British. Born in Liverpool, Lancashire, 7 February 1946. Educated at Sefton Park Secondary School, Liverpool. Formerly, Editor, *Underdog*, Liverpool. Recipient: Eric Gregory Award, 1967; Arts Council grant, 1969. Address: c/o Allen and Unwin, Museum Street, London W.C.1, England.

PUBLICATIONS

Verse

Portraits. Privately printed, 1962.
The Mersey Sound: Penguin Modern Poets 10, with Adrian Henri and Roger McGough. London, Penguin, 1967.
Little Johnny's Confession. London, Allen and Unwin, 1967; New York, Hill and Wang, 1968.
Atomic Adam. London, Fulham Gallery, 1967.
Notes to the Hurrying Man: Poems, Winter '66–Summer '68. London, Allen and Unwin, and New York, Hill and Wang, 1969.
The Home Coming. London, Turret, 1969.
The Irrelevant Song. Frensham, Surrey, Sceptre Press, 1970.
Little Johnny's Foolish Invention: A Poem (bilingual edition), translated by Robert Sanesi. Milan, Tipographia Bertieri, 1970.
Walking Out: The Early Poems of Brian Patten. Leicester, Transican, 1971.
At Four O'Clock in the Morning. Frensham, Surrey, Sceptre Press, 1971.
The Irrelevant Song and Other Poems. London, Allen and Unwin, 1971; revised edition, 1975.
When You Wake Tomorrow. London, Turret, 1972.
The Eminent Professors and the Nature of Poetry as Enacted Out by Members of the Poetry Seminar One Rainy Evening. London, Poem-of-the-Month Club, 1972.
Double Image, with Michael Baldwin and John Fairfax. London, Longman, 1972.
The Unreliable Nightingale. London, Rota, 1973.

Vanishing Trick. London, Allen and Unwin, 1976.
The Sly Cormorant and the Three Fishes (juvenile). London, Penguin, 1977.
Grave Gossip. London, Allen and Unwin, 1979.

Recordings: *Selections from Little Johnny's Confession and Notes to the Hurrying Man and New Poems*, Caedmon, 1969; *Vanishing Trick*, 1972; *The Sly Cormorant*, Argo, 1977.

Plays

The Pig and the Junkle (produced Nottingham, 1975; London, 1977).
The Sly Cormorant (produced London, 1977).

Radio Play: *The Hypnotic Island*, 1977.

Other

The Elephant and the Flower: Almost-Fables (juvenile). London, Allen and Unwin, 1970.
Manchild (juvenile). London, Covent Garden Press, 1973.
Jumping Mouse (adaptation of an American Indian folk tale). London, Allen and Unwin, 1973.
Two Stories (juvenile). London, Covent Garden Press, 1973.
Mr. Moon's Last Case (juvenile). London, Allen and Unwin, 1975; New York, Scribner, 1976.
Emma's Doll (juvenile). London, Allen and Unwin, 1976.

Editor, with Pat Krett, *The House That Jack Built: Poems for Shelter.* London, Allen and Unwin, 1973.

* * *

The young Liverpool poet Brian Patten made a big reputation for himself on the strength of his first two volumes of verse – and, of course, his own youth. When he first appeared on the scene Patten was commonly identified as a pop-poet – a label apparently justified not only by his working-class background, but by poems such as "Little Johnny's Confession," which in fact was the title poem of his first volume. Yet the pop-references seemed to fall naturally into place, to be part of what the poet was trying to say, and not just fashionable decoration. At the same time, Patten declared his wish to write "the hard lyric." His book *Notes to the Hurrying Man* showed what he meant by this. The poetry has a song-like quality, plaintive and nostalgic, yet is sufficiently dense and sufficiently abrupt in its transitions to avoid looking like words in search of a tune. Patten's touch is not infallible – he can be both clumsy and sentimental – but reviewers have rightly recognised a potentially important talent.

—Edward Lucie-Smith

PATTERSON, Raymond R(ichard). American. Born in New York City, 14 December 1929. Educated at Lincoln University, Pennsylvania, 1947–51, A.B. 1951; New York University, 1954–56, M.A. 1956. Served in the United States Army, 1951–53. Married

Boydie Alice Cooke in 1957; one child, Ama. Children's Supervisor, Youth House for Boys, New York, 1956–58; Instructor in English, Benedict College, Columbia, South Carolina, 1958–59; English Teacher in New York City Public Schools, 1959–68. Since 1968, Lecturer in English, City College of the City University of New York. Recipient: Borestone Mountain award, 1950; National Endowment for the Arts grant, 1969; Creative Artists Public Service grant, 1977. Address: 2 Lee Court, Merrick, New York 11566, U.S.A.

PUBLICATIONS

Verse

Twenty-Six Ways of Looking at a Black Man and Other Poems. New York, Award Books, and London, Tandem, 1969.

Critical Studies: by Aaron Kramer, in *Freedomways* (New York), 1970; Eugene B. Redmond, in *Drumvoices*, New York, Anchor Press, 1976.

Raymond R. Patterson comments:

For me writing poetry is an exploration of the possibilities of experience; a poem written is a poem dis-covered, providing useful knowledge about the territory we travel through.

* * *

Contemporary Black poetry is rooted in the social upheaval that gripped the United States during the 1950's and 1960's, when, in a last ditch push for full integration, Black people – North and South – took to the streets. The result of their effort was the recognition, by some, that the country would cede nothing through protest. From that political truth grew the Black Power Movement. Its cultural arm, the Black Arts Movement, views all art as a weapon in the struggle for Black liberation. In this context, the aim of Black literature is the total revaluation of the ideas and images by which Blacks have traditionally defined themselves.

Poet Raymond R. Patterson reflects the influence of all these forces. The result has been a body of poetry that is seminal in its explorations of black life. Concerned more with the psychological that the physical, Patterson is the poet-chronicler, capturing in verse the revolution in Black thought that created the 1960's. "Come into my black hands./Touch me. Feel the grip/And cramp of angry circumstance...." From the crucial admission of individual rage – a rage given force and articulation in real life by Malcolm X – the poet moves on to attack the various ploys used by Blacks to navigate the American holocaust: "Black boys push carts in alligator shoes," while aspiring integrationists "... carry the word in Brooks Brothers suits," and the tiny elite, while fully convinced of its infallibility, are "Thinking, sometimes .../Someone lied. Sometimes thinking suicide." But all is illusion and self-deception, insists the poet; beneath the carefully controlled masks, "There is enough/Grief-/Energy in/The Blackness/Of the whitest Negro/To incinerate/America."

Incineration is the key to "Riot Rimes U.S.A.," the eighty-five poem sequence that is Patterson's most popular work. The poems are humorous and ironic by turn, in their first person depictions of the Harlem riot of 1965. From the poet's perspective, that event was the high point of the African experience in America: "My mama hadn't said one word/To my daddy for two whole years./But after the riots, she was so happy/She was crying tears .../Nothing suits a family like a big strong male."

—Saundra Towns

PAULIN, Tom. British. Born in Leeds, Yorkshire, 25 January 1949. Recipient: Eric Gregory Award, 1976; Somerset Maugham Award, 1978. Address: c/o Faber and Faber Ltd., 3 Queen Square, London WC1N 3AU, England.

PUBLICATIONS

Verse

Theoretical Locations. Belfast, Ulsterman, 1975.
A State of Justice. London, Faber, 1977.
Personal Column. Belfast, Ulsterman, 1978.

Other

Thomas Hardy: The Poetry of Perception. London, Macmillan, and Totowa, New Jersey, Rowman and Littlefield, 1975.

* * *

Tom Paulin makes few concessions to "personal" emotions in *A State of Justice.* Human relations, the whole realm of the subjective, remain firmly at a distance:

It'll piss all evening now. From next door
The usual man and woman stuff rants on, then fades;
And I know she'll soon be moaning, climbing her little register
Of ecstasy till quiet settles back like dust....

A great deal depends on Paulin's "usual" and "little," perhaps too much. He appears here as observer, not participant. Of the inhabitants of a bungalow in "In Antrim," he says "I watch them from a distance." In "Young Funerals" the same note appears: "They must not touch me, these deaths." But it is the burden of Ulster poets, of Paulin, to *be* touched by such things. To withhold, withdraw, protect, may be, here, no more than a tactic. Everywhere in *A State of Justice* the landscape of imagination is Ulster and its "steel polities." Paulin's Belfast is "built on mud and wrath," echoing Louis MacNeice in *Autumn Journal*: "A city built on mud;/A culture built upon profit." And in "Thinking of Iceland" Paulin turns to Auden and MacNeice's *Letters from Iceland* as a point of reference for his own sense of the "sour outback" and its ambiguous meaning. For MacNeice, Iceland was a refuge, a beautiful Lorelei for the alienated victims of capitalism. Paulin, too, contemplates alternatives to a world of terror, revenge and oppression. "A New Society" and "The Hyperboreans" suggest the costs. The triumph of will and rationality which lies behind "The Hyperboreans" and their struggle to survive in remote regions carries within itself a yawning hollowness of destructive irrationality. "A New Society," perhaps Paulin's finest poem, takes us from the rich textures of the terrace houses of the poor, now "carried away in skips," to Paulin's "factual idealism": all stainless steel sinks, sunlit kitchens, and in which "the Law is glimpsed on occasional traffic duties." This "unaggressively civilian" dream is at the heart of social democracy. If it strikes us, against the background of Ulster, as utopian, the alternative is spelled out in "Cadaver Politic":

At the bottom of a cliff, on a tussock
    Of ground by a lean-to shed, a group
Of men and women huddle, watching a man
    Who tries, with damp matches, to light a board
Washed on that coast by the grey sea.

The task of reconstruction appears here in an image of unrelieved pessimism, though it seems slightly over-done. Things would be bad enough even if the matches weren't damp.

Paulin's subjects are, at first inspection, clearly social. But to pin him down with a political label would be to misunderstand the deeper levels of his sensibility. A "state of justice" has more need of ethics than politics. His view of the world suggests that there are fundamental dimensions of human nature which exist beyond the reach of "murderous authorities." He has a strong sense of the relationship of civil society to nature, and of the precariousness of life. He uses the image of a bridge in "States" to indicate mankind's hunger for protection from the "dark zero" of wind and water and the night. Religion as such does not serve such a purpose for Paulin. Parishioners in "Inishkeel Parish Church" confront a bleak vista as they leave church: "before the recognitions and the talk/There was an enormous sight of the sea,/ A silent water beyond society." Paulin's imagery of vacancy and limitlessness is powerful:

> They own a stone cottage at the end of a field
> That slopes to rocks and a gunmetal sea.
>
> Their silence is part of the silence at this season,
> Is so wide that these solitaries seem hemmed in
> By a distance of empty sea, a bleak mewing
> Of gulls perched on their chimney, expecting storm.

The true achievement of *A State of Justice* lies in Paulin's use of metaphor and image. This transcends the specifically political categories of Ulster, inevitable as they are, and suggests a more subjective and intuitive dimension to his poetry. In "An Authorised Fear" there is a new note of nightmarish fantasy. Throughout the pamphlet *Personal Column* Paulin explores a new dimension of purely personal feelings and memories. His style, which tends to become more elusive and metaphoric in such poems, remains a medium of great power, though its full range is just beginning to be explored.

—Eric Homberger

PAYNE, Basil. Irish. Born in Dublin, 22 June 1928. Educated at Christian Brothers School, Dublin; University College, Dublin. Married to Monessa Keating; six sons and one daughter. Formerly, Drama Critic, the *Irish Times* and the *Irish Press*, Dublin; Scriptwriter, Editor and Critic, Radio Telefis Eireann, Dublin, 1963–73; Poet-in-Residence, Glassboro State College, New Jersey. Recipient: Guinness Prize, 1964, 1966. Address: Cortona, 137 Rathfarnham Road, Dublin 14, Ireland.

PUBLICATIONS

Verse

Sunlight on a Square. Dublin, John Augustine, 1961.
Love in the Afternoon. Dublin, Gill and Macmillan, 1971.
Another Kind of Optimism. Dublin, Gill and Macmillan, 1974.
Voyage à Deux. N.p., Perret Gentil, 1974.

Plays

In Dublin's Quare City (produced Dublin, 1973).

Radio Plays: *The Onlooker*, 1969; *Don't Call Me Honey.*

Television Plays: *Missing Believed Dead*; *A Boy and a Ball.*

Other

Editor and Translator, *Elegy for the Western World*, by Hans Carossa. Dublin, University of Dublin Press, 1964.

Translator, *Collected Poems*, by Karl Gustav Gerold. Dublin, Dolmen Press, 1972.

Basil Payne comments:

Major Themes: (1) Hidden recesses of selfhood. (2) Confessional – Family Album poems (man and wife; father and son; etc.). (3) Dublin as subject matter and/or objective correlative of personal experience. (4) Childhood. (5) Poems of social protest.

General Influences: Environmental mainly. But also Eliot, Brecht, Rilke, and Lowell (I have translated Carossa, Brecht, and Rilke).

I use most verse forms but value irony and tenderness as invaluable in reaching a singular poetic statement.

* * *

The 40 poems in Basil Payne's *Love in the Afternoon* are divided into three sections: "Pilgrimage," "From a Family Album," and "Public and Private Eye." The divisions give an idea of his territory and the way he walks it. He writes about his memories of growing up in the South Circular Road district of Dublin; of watching his father shaving with a cut-throat razor, his mother doing the wash in a zinc bathtub; of journeys, neighbours, accidents, pruning the roses; of other Irish poets; and of love between man and wife and parent and child. This last is Payne's most ambitious theme. His tone is relaxed, pleasant, chatty to a fault:

Watching my father shaving in the kitchen
Before a cracked mirror: this was my four-years-old high-light
In our otherwise humdrum daily domestic ritual ...

Father died having breakfast (*from natural causes*
The Coroner's verdict recorded). My electric razor purrs.
My young son complains it causes T.V. interference.

Contact with the accent of common speech is never quite foregone, and the poet asks our pardon for his one obvious vice of being "so dissolutely *nice*."

—Robert Nye

---

p'BITEK, Okot. Ugandan. Born in Gulu, Acoli District, Northern Uganda, in 1931. Educated at Gulu High School; King's College, Budo, Uganda; University of Bristol, Certificate in Education; University of Wales, Aberystwyth, LL.B.; Oxford University,

B.Litt. in social anthropology 1963. Lecturer in Sociology at Makerere University College, and Director of the Uganda National Theatre and Uganda National Cultural Center, all Kampala, 1964–68; Founder, Kisumu Arts Festival, Kenya, 1968; Fellow, International Writing Program, University of Iowa, Iowa City, 1969–70; Senior Research Fellow, Institute of African Studies, Nairobi, 1971. Lives in Kisumu, Kenya.

PUBLICATIONS

Verse

Lak tar miyo kinyero wi lobo? (in Acoli: Are your teeth white, then laugh!). Kampala, Eagle Press, 1953.
The Song of Lawino (translated from Acoli by the author). Nairobi, East African Publishing House, 1966; New York, Meridian, 1969.
Song of Ocol. Nairobi, East African Publishing House, 1970.
The Song of a Prisoner. New York, Third Press, 1971.
Two Songs: The Song of a Prisoner, The Song of Malaya. Nairobi, East African Publishing House, 1971.
The Horn of My Love (Acoli traditional songs, translated by the author). London, Heinemann, 1974.
Hare and Hornbill. London, Heinemann, 1978.

Other

Religion of Central Luo. Nairobi, East African Literature Bureau, 1971.
Africa's Cultural Revolution. Nairobi, Macmillan, 1973.

* * *

Okot p'Bitek's role in the emergence of East African literature cannot be overestimated. Together with Ngugi wa'Thiongo (James T. Ngugi) he is the leading writer of the area, and he enjoys tremendous popularity both in Africa and abroad. His themes are easily recognized as those which until recently preoccupied the majority of the African writers: culture clash, corruption, and bitterness after the broken promises of independence, but his chosen medium, the song, is a unique – and highly successful – experiment in combining aspects of African oral tradition with Western writing.

The oral genre which serves as a modei for p'Bitek's songs as the Acoli dirge, and his first poem, *The Song of Lawino*, was in fact written in Acoli and later translated into English by the author himself. Transformed into written literature it has an extremely flexible shortlined non-rhyming free-verse metre, reminiscent of the ballad, but retaining certain features of oral literature, notably the direct address to a fictive audience, thus creating the illusion of a singer confronting a crowd or an individual and soliciting support and sympathy. An added complication – and great source of irony – in this genre, is the possibility of making a distinction between the persona of the song and the writer; in other words making the singer condemn himself through his own words rather than through overt criticism. The shades of meaning can become very subtle, but in *Song of Lawino* p'Bitek seems to be squarely behind his heroine who is in fact modelled on his mother. She is lamenting the fact that her western-educated husband Ocol is throwing her out because she is illiterate and still follows the traditional tribal way of life. The thematic aspect of the poem is its centre: a passionate defence of traditional life, exemplified in dances, cooking, architecture, etc., combined with an attack on aspects of modern life. This attack is an indirect one carried out by Lawino as she defends herself against Ocol's unspoken accusation against her for refusing to dance modern dances, cook on modern stoves, or become a Christian. This device provides the author with an intelligent, self-assured and inquisitive outsider's view of Western civilization and an opportunity to turn long accepted concepts upside down. The discussion of time is a case in question; it calls attention to the arbitrariness of the B.C./A.D. dating system and criticises the unnaturalness of living by the clock, indicated by the title of the section "There is no fixed time for breast feeding." The fictional aspect is also present in the song-form. Lawino is not just a vehicle for ideas. She comes to life like a character in a novel, particularly in the section "The woman with whom I share my husband" where her description of Ocol's westernized girl friend betrays a certain amount of jealousy.

Song of Ocol is written as a sequel to *Song of Lawino*, containing Ocol's side of the argument. The symmetry between the two songs suggests an attempt to present the two opposing points of view as objectively as possible, but Ocol soon condemns himself through his rejection of African values and his too eager aping of white ones. He belongs to the elite which benefitted from Uhuru and has become corrupted by his success. The same theme is discussed in "Song of a Prisoner," included in the volume *Two Songs*. The prisoner's identity is uncertain. He is both a poor ignorant peasant arrested for vagrancy and a hired assassin with a prosperous and political past. Perhaps he is two aspects of one person or he could be one person reviewing his past as he lies tied up on the prison floor. His main voice is that of the ordinary man's disappointment and anger at the broken promises of Uhuru. "Song of Malaya" which forms the second half of *Two Songs* is a praise song for prostitutes. p'Bitek's songs are deceptively simple and easy to read and they give a refreshing new angle to well-worn themes.

—Kirsten Holst Petersen

PERRY, Grace. Australian. Born in Melbourne, Victoria. Educated at Sydney University, M.B., B.S., qualified as a physician. Married to Harry Kronenberg; three children. Has held several pediatric appointments. Currently in general practice. Editor, *Poetry Magazine*, Sydney, 1962–64. Since 1963, Writing School and Festival Director. Since 1964, Proprietor, South Head Press, Sydney, and Editor, *Poetry Australia*, Sydney. Address: Berrima, New South Wales 2577, Australia.

PUBLICATIONS

Verse

I Am the Songs You Sing and Other Poems. Sydney, Consolidated Press, 1944.
Red Scarf. Sydney, Edwards and Shaw, 1964.
Frozen Section. Sydney, Edwards and Shaw, 1967.
Two Houses: Poems 66–69. Sydney, South Head Press, 1969.
Black Swans at Berrima. Sydney, South Head Press, 1972.
Berrima Winter. Sydney, South Head Press, 1974.
Journal of a Surgeon's Wife and Other Poems. Sydney, South Head Press, 1976.

Manuscript Collection: Mitchell Library, Sydney.

Critical Studies: by James Libdroth, in *Spirit* (South Orange, New Jersey), Spring 1970; J. G. Tulip, in *Southerly* (Sydney), no. 2, 1973; J. E. Chamberlin, in *Hudson Review* (New York), Summer 1973; Fred Holzknect, in *Makar* (Brisbane), 1973; Elaine Lindsay, in *The Australian* (Sydney), 1976.

* * *

Grace Perry has been a central figure in Australian poetry since the mid-1960's. Largely this has come from her role in founding and editing the journal *Poetry Australia*, which has become in the course of its 70 issues a focal point for poets of all ranges and interests. In the 1960's and early 1970's she established her position with immense energy – writing six books of verse, organising poetry conferences, publishing other poets at South Head Press and running a busy medical practice. More recently she has chosen to live almost in seclusion in the New South Wales country town of Berrima, where as well as recouping her imaginative energies she has developed an interest in grazing and stud cattle.

Her poetry has always been, until recently, the alter ego of her life. As distinct from the frenetic life style she has followed, her poems step into a deep passivity, almost a trance, a high-toned incantation of an inward reflective self. She has ranged over many subjects.

Red Scarf begins with a sequence "Where the Wind Moves" which is characteristic of the strong personal force in Grace Perry's writing that never quite becomes a personal presence but is more a mood, suffused and deep-pitched. A romantic yearning finds itself in a world which cannot satisfy its longings, and the poetry disciplines itself in the gestures it can make. Poems to do with her medical experience appear in *Red Scarf*, and become a major element in her next book *Frozen Section*. The medical world of the operating theatre takes on a ritualistic quality in Grace Perry's poems. But she does not stay fixed in this intense, a-personal mode for long. Her poetry in *Frozen Section* shows her reaching out to random and occasional studies of Australian experience. The "Parramatta Gaol, 1966" sequence foreshadows something of the quality and interests of her more recent Berrima world.

The old sandstone buildings of colonial Berrima appeal to her feel for history, geography, gardens and houses. Her lines have opened up towards images of sensation; there is less irony in the garden world she lives in beside the Wingecarribee; her passivities are no longer a retreat but a resource:

Black birds in pairs under rock ledges
tremble wings
carve up red scum
towards midstream cloud islands in clear water
to name them
is to anchor them
between willow and willow
long wings fan smoke
over mounds softened by sundown
fiery mouths
swallow valley and valley
sucked down
the slow surge
around
above
the water lifting underneath
spread out
the wake unbroken
arrows shore to shore

There is in lines such as these a subjective reading of the Australian country environment which is leading Grace Perry to make her own personal mythology from her life and the world round about her. In *Black Swans at Berrima*, *Berrima Winter*, and *Journal of a Surgeon's Wife* this process of her inner life has refined and liberated itself in several ways.

Often she seems to thrive off negations of negations: a double negative pattern of denying some impossibly romantic idea is her way into and through many a poem. But her most recent and as yet unpublished verse is a confrontation with pain and loss of love in ways that will surely be compared with those of Anne Sexton and Sylvia Plath. Her poetry of inwardness has been an unusual feature of the Australian poetic scene in the last dozen years. Now it seems that her world is re-emerging into drama.

—James Tulip

PETERS, Lenrie (Leopold). Gambian. Born in Bathurst, 1 September 1932. Educated at Trinity College, Cambridge; University College Hospital, London, M.B., B.Chir. Since 1966, Surgical Registrar, Northampton General Hospital. Fellow, Royal College of Surgeons. Address: 34 Howitt Close, Howitt Road, London N.W.3, England.

PUBLICATIONS

Verse

Poems. Ibadan, Nigeria, Mbari, 1964.
Satellites. London, Heinemann, 1967.
Katchikali. London, Heinemann, 1971.

Novel

The Second Round. London, Heinemann, 1965.

* * *

Two biographical influences stand out in the poetry of Lenrie Peters. The first is that he is a surgeon and the second is that he has been considerably influenced by an adulthood spent outside Africa. Surgery is the source of many of his most effective images and themes. No poem demonstrates this more effectively than "Sounds of the Ocean" which frequently resorts to the image of a surgeon groping in the body of a patient to represent the precarious search and exploration for limited objectives through which man eventually achieves self realisation and the peace that this brings: "Hand fumbling with bowel/Or wringing out the brain/Reaches no further than/The moment allows." The end of the poem holds out the hope that this fumbling search will produce results: "But there will be for each/Who seeks with dedication/A solitary triumph of peace." The guarded optimism of "Sounds of the Ocean" is a recurrent note in Peters's poetry which never seeks, however, to conceal the agony, the uncertainty, and the loneliness of the search that leads to self realisation.

The second biographical fact – Peters's African birth and his subsequent physical alienation from Africa – comes out in many ways. He is continually remembering Africa and realises in poetry the physical return to it which so far has not occurred. It is significant that his only novel so far, *The Second Round*, is based on the experiences of a doctor returning to his home after many years of study abroad. The impression one gets is of the poet continually balancing the alternatives in his mind – a felt duty to Africa and a duty to himself which dictates continued residence in Europe. These poetic returns abound in his poetry: "I shall return/When daylight saunters on/When evening shadows the berry/And fiery night the sun." Like others of Peters's poems, however, this is not just a simple return to a country; there is the implication of a return to a basic state of nature which requires an elimination of outward trappings; the return is in fact a spiritual rather than a physical return. Other

"Homecoming" poems show a similar meaningful ambiguity. Peters's vicarious returns are thus symbolically significant.

In spite of his sojourn abroad, the poet is concerned with the fate of Africa. The consequences of independence, the broken promises, the petty tyrannies are all reflected in the long poem "In the Beginning," where Peters exploits his talent for broken pieces of suggestive dialogue to picture the relationship between the ordinary voter and his new rulers:

"But excuse me, Sir;
We're free.
Why do we have to beg?"
Industrial development
Dams, factories, the lot –
change the face of the Continent.
"I see
But my children –
beg pardon Sir,
will they go to school?"
Later!
"Will they have food to eat
and clothes to wear?"
Later I tell you!
"Beg pardon Sir;
a house like yours?"
Put this man in jail.

The concern for the common man in the hands of authority is treated in contexts other than the African:

Every time they shut the gates
And hang up notices
On steel plates
That love-making is forbidden
After eight

This has more of the background of Hyde Park than of Freetown's Victoria Park as has his "Song" which pictures prostitutes "selling old boot/On wet pavements."

Peters has succeeded in making a harmony of his two backgrounds and he uses each without self-consciousness. The range of his interests is very wide. Very few African poets would write a eulogy of Winston Churchill, whom Peters seems genuinely to have admired. The explosion of the Chinese bomb is similarly the unlikely subject of another poem. The result of all this is that Peters is an unlocalised poet, whose concern is ultimately for the general human predicament.

—Eldred D. Jones

PETERSEN, Donald. American. Born in Minneapolis, Minnesota, 11 November 1928. Educated at the Sorbonne, Paris, 1948–49; Carleton College, Northfield, Minnesota, B.A. 1950; Indiana University, Bloomington; University of Iowa, Iowa City, M.F.A. 1952. Married Jeanine Ahrens in 1952; three sons and one daughter. Taught at the University of

Iowa, 1954–56. Since 1956, Member of the English Department, and currently, Professor of English, State University of New York, Oneonta. Assistant Editor, *Western Review*, Iowa City, 1950–55. Address: Department of English, State University of New York, Oneonta, New York 13820, U.S.A.

PUBLICATIONS

Verse

The Spectral Boy. Middletown, Connecticut, Wesleyan University Press, 1964.

* * *

Donald Petersen is a formalist, an elegist, and a pastoral poet whose works are rooted in his small town (rural America) and big city (Paris) experiences. Despite the fact that he studied under such poets as Robert Lowell, Karl Shapiro, Paul Engle, and John Berryman, he regards himself as neither a literary nor an academic poet.

His work is pervaded by a haunting nostalgia for things of value which lends genuine feeling to his lines without becoming mournful:

Home is a place of resurrections. Fears
I ran away from, sorrows that I fled,
Come back to haunt me now from other years.
Two neighbors I remember best are dead.

Petersen states, "My memory plays a large role in making a poem. A poem of mine is often an amalgam of old and new verse, and its subject matter is often concerned with memory. It is also likely to be, in unlikely terms, a religious poem." Central to his poetry are attempts to experience renewal or to effect regeneration through relationships to time, to nature, to religion, and between individuals. The range of these relationships is frequently evinced through "the terrifying extremes" of hot and cold and their possible harmony:

Then summer slid beneath her cold inversion
With sunny slopes and crowded canopies,
    But we were happy.

Fell winter without tears that when they freeze
Can pierce the summer-keeping heart and be
    Forever dripping.

Desire these days, my dear, that we may be
Two ever-shifting dunes of fine white snow,
    Made one completely.

Mr. Petersen further describes himself as one of the few remaining poets who writes in complete sentences. But his poetry is rigidly formed, a characteristic which he accounts for because he is dealing with very "slippery" content.

—Charles L. James

PETRIE, Paul (James). American. Born in Detroit, Michigan, 1 July 1928. Educated at Wayne State University, Detroit, 1946–51, B.A., M.A.; University of Iowa, Iowa City, Ph.D. 1957. Married to Sylvia Spencer; two daughters and one son. Since 1959, Member of the English Department, and currently, Professor of English, University of Rhode Island, Kingston. Address: 66 Dendron Road, Peace Dale, Rhode Island 02879, U.S.A.

PUBLICATIONS

Verse

Confessions of a Non-Conformist. Mount Vernon, Iowa, Hillside Press, 1963.
The Race with Time and the Devil. Francestown, New Hampshire, Golden Quill Press, 1965.
The Leader: For Martin Luther King, Jr. Providence, Rhode Island, Hellcoal Press, 1968.
From under the Hill of Night: Poems. Nashville, Tennessee, Vanderbilt University Press, 1969.
The Idol. Kingston, Rhode Island, Biscuit City Press, 1973.
The Academy of Goodbye. Hanover, New Hampshire, University Press of New England, 1974.
Light from the Furnace Rising. Providence, Rhode Island, Copper Beech Press, 1978.

Paul Petrie comments:

My whole approach to poetry, both thematic and technical, is governed by a hatred of dogmatic theorizing, and since the twentieth century represents the very apotheosis of theorizing, a paradise for half-baked creeds and counter-creeds, I find myself in a "school" of one. If there is any critical notion which I find appealing, it is Keats' idea of Negative Capability, but even that has its limitations. In short I believe that there is nothing that cannot be said in poetry and that there is no limitation on the way it can or should be said. A poem need not be "new" or "old," in "free verse" or "meter," "understated" or "overstated" – all that it must be is a good poem.

As for my own work, I would describe it as lyrical, relatively emotional, dramatic in its inclusion of opposites with a stronger current of movement than is common in verse today, and perhaps an over-indulgence in the doctrine of statement through images. My major strengths are rhythm and organization; my major weaknesses are a lack of exact detail and firm diction. I have a personal notion of the poem as an act of praise (be it positive or negative in theme and tone), and I tend to regard poetry as a semi-religious vocation, but I do not demand that others share these attitudes and I can think of excellent poems which would stretch these terms to the breaking point. The poems will remain; the theory will go.

* * *

Paul Petrie is well known to students of contemporary American poetry. For two decades his poems have appeared in a wide variety of literary journals, magazines, and in several volumes. A sense of death-in-life and our fragile mortality seems to be the exclusive concern of the books. Haunted by death in his dreams and plagued by it in his waking life, Petrie, in an intense and passionate creative act, transforms his fear and dread into art. As *The Race with Time and the Devil* suggests, such an act is not an easy or an unambiguous triumph. His best poems are alive with the sense of a real person's struggle to achieve an elemental relationship with and understanding of the natural cycles of life and death.

There is a clear movement toward concentration; sharpness and mastery of medium. *Confessions of a Non-Conformist* is an adequate work, though not particularly original. *The*

Race with Time and the Devil is a marked improvement and contains a number of fine poems, especially the five poem sequence "Pictures of Departure," "The Last Words of Frederick II," "Chain," "The Church of San Antonio De La Florida," "Morning Psalm," and "In Defense of Colds." *From under the Hill of Night* deserves the most praise. Poems such as "Under the Hill of Night," "The Party," "Mark Twain," "Kindertoten," and "Notes of a Would-Be Traveler," are excellent. In them, Petrie has achieved fully his desire to articulate his organic sense of his world.

—Richard Damashek

PETTY, W(illiam) H(enry). British. Born in Bradford, Yorkshire, 7 September 1921. Educated at Bradford Grammar School, 1931–40; Peterhouse, Cambridge, B.A. 1946, M.A. 1950; University of London, B.Sc. 1953. Served in the Royal Artillery, 1941–45. Married Margaret Bastow in 1948; two daughters and one son. Administrator and teacher in London and Yorkshire, 1946–64. Deputy Education Officer, 1964–73, and since 1973, County Education Officer, Kent County Council. National Executive, Society of Education Officers, 1971; Chairman, Association of Education Officers, 1979–80. Recipient: Cheltenham Festival Prize, 1968; Camden Festival Prize, 1970; Greenwood Prize, 1978. Address: Godfrey House, Hollingbourne, near Maidstone, Kent, England.

PUBLICATIONS

Verse

No Bold Comfort. London, Outposts, 1957.
Conquest and Other Poems. London, Outposts, 1967.

Critical Studies: in the *Times Literary Supplement* (London), July 1957; by Vernon Scannell, in *Outposts* (London), Summer 1957; in *Poetry Review* (London), Winter 1958; in the *Times Educational Supplement* (London), July 1967.

W. H. Petty comments:

An experience – intellectual, emotional, visual – itself informs me when I should write a poem. The process of writing always reveals connections, often subtle connections, with other experiences of which I had not been conscious before beginning to write the poem. The process of writing also indicates the techniques, such as rhythm, rhyme and word and line patterns – or, at times, the deliberate avoidance of these – which appear to be the most effective means of expression. I never "force" a poem: I never pre-determine a technique. This means that the poems I write are comparatively few in number – which seems to me advantageous in the circumstances of today.

* * *

Although only two booklets of W. H. Petty's work have been published, his poems have appeared in a wide range of magazines and anthologies, and he has been awarded prizes in the Cheltenham Festival of Literature and the Camden Festival of Music and the Arts. *No*

Bold Comfort is a collection of 20 lyrics, mostly descriptive of scenes or events which seem to have been thrust upon the poet's attention – "Futility in Cagnes," "Nightmare in Bruges," "Skinningrove Steel-Works," etc. – rather than having been selected as subjects to illustrate a central theme, though there are also a few reflective poems about life in general or personal experience in particular which reveal the poet's philosophy.

Even in his earliest poems, W. H. Petty exhibited a fastidious concern for language and form, but undoubtedly the most noticeable feature of his modest style was the capacity to evoke a scene or recreate an atmosphere by means of striking visual imagery. In poem after poem one comes across such phrases as "the town's white angularities and the morning tables bright as tight fruit," "the village fat with snow," and "the rough kidney cobbles of the Pennine streets"; and occasionally a masterly use of monosyllables to achieve the desired effect, as in "Market":

> So the high sun brings all things here to pattern
> Even the fat cattle amiably
> Ambling between the buxom-windowed shops
> To curt death.

Conquest is a long poem in which the poet reviews his past from childhood to the present, touching upon life in Bradford and Cambridge, and holidays at home and abroad, in the belief that "to contemplate our past is to savour/Mastery, for the past only exists/when the spool of memory is turned/By one's self." W. H. Petty turns the spool to considerable purpose here.

—Howard Sergeant

PICKARD, Tom. British. Born in Newcastle upon Tyne, Northumberland, in 1946. Educated in Newcastle secondary schools. Married 1) Constance Pickard; one son and one daughter; 2) Joanna Voit. Worked for a seed merchant, 1962–63, for a construction company, 1963, and for a wine merchant, 1964, all in Newcastle. Co-Founder and Manager of the Morden Tower Book Room, 1963–72, and the Ultima Thule Bookshop, 1969–73, Newcastle. C. Day Lewis Fellow, Rutherford Comprehensive School, London, 1976. Recipient: Northern Arts Award, 1965; Arts Council grant, 1969, 1973. Agent: Judy Daish Associates, Globe Theatre, Shaftesbury Avenue, London W.1, England.

PUBLICATIONS

Verse

High on the Walls. London, Fulcrum Press, 1967; New York, Horizon Press, 1968.
New Human Unisphere. Newcastle-upon-Tyne, Ultima Thule, 1969.
An Armpit of Lice. London, Fulcrum Press, 1970.
The Order of Chance. London, Fulcrum Press, 1971.
Dancing under Fire. Philadelphia, Middle Earth, 1973.
Hero Dust: New and Selected Poems. London, Allison and Busby, 1979.

Plays

Television Plays: *Squire*, 1974; *The Jarrow March*, 1976.

Novel

Guttersnipe. San Francisco, City Lights, 1972.

Bibliography: in *Poetry Information 18* (London), 1978.

Manuscript Collection: Northern Arts, Newcastle upon Tyne.

Critical Studies: "Tom Pickard" by Eric Mottram, in *Lip 1* (Philadelphia), 1972; interview in *Contact 6* (Philadelphia), 1973; Eric Mottram, in *Poetry Information 18* (London), 1978.

* * *

Tom Pickard's first book had a rightly enthusiastic and characteristically truthful Foreword by Basil Bunting. Here was someone, he said, who had "escaped education," and over whom "tradition and fashion" had no power. For Pickard, victim of an educational system that still has little interest in catering for the socially underprivileged but gifted personality, left school at fourteen. He had not heard of the Greek Anthology, and yet his "unbookish" lyrics had some resemblance (as Bunting pointed out) to the earliest writers in that collection. So here we had the fresh poetry of a young man who had little to inspire him beyond his own impulse, and who could not look at his art with formalized or official or academic eyes. The title poem, "High on the Walls," may be slight; but its vision is pure and it parallels mental events – as such miniaturistic descriptive poems must:

Strange to be higher
than a bird, to watch
them eat

when startled (the only
defence to be above)
take flight, and land
at my feet.

"To My Unborn Child" would doubtless be classed as "obscene" by some ("our heads met/ when both of them/bent to kiss/your mother's womb"), and is biologically incorrect (his head "met," at that stage, his unborn child's feet); but it has perfect simplicity, and its directness is not at all directed towards the fashionably obscene. "Rape," too, in Newcastle dialect (and excellently done), taps real experience. Pickard was at this stage simply not aware of gentility, or even of the nature of the savage hostility of the Northern English establishment to the arts in general (to which Bunting refers in his Foreword). These were minor poems, but tough and innocent: true responses.

The Order of Chance was a grave disappointment. Bunting had written: "Mr. Pickard has yet to read most of the English classics, which must change his writing more or less, perhaps not always for the better. He is poor, and must feel the temptation to dilute his spirit till it is acceptable to the flock of inferior poets who pick up all the gleanings society leaves for literature." This happened; but the gleanings he picked up were not those of academic or over-literary poets who haunt the pages of the modish weeklies, but instead those of pseudo-"drop-outs" or ignorant English imitators of American styles. Once he had sung; now, for the most part, he swore – he repeated what he had already said well enough, on the subject of human nastiness and establishment complacency, and he imitated himself. The language of the newer poems has lost its purity, its freshness: Pickard has discovered gentility, and wants to offend it. But he is not sharp enough to be a good satirical poet; his intellect is not fully formed; the reader no longer gains the impression of independence; the candour has vanished, to be replaced (for the most part) by an almost monotonous aggressiveness – and one that lacks poetic edge. Once again the Arts Council Writer's Award has struck. There is no poem about the committee that gave him this: instead he gives them the mindless and routine blasphemy that is the sure sign of neutralization: they may easily lean back with educated indulgence. But there is some chance that he will move from being a spoiled poet to a once again independent one – who can, as Bunting (again) said, learn to "sing with a longer breath." One hopes for this, for he possesses a distinctive lyrical gift.

—Martin Seymour-Smith

PIERCY, Marge. American. Born in Detroit, Michigan, 31 March 1936. Educated at the University of Michigan, Ann Arbor (Hopwood Award), B.A. 1957; Northwestern University, Evanston, Illinois, M.A. 1958. Recipient: Borestone Mountain Award; National Endowment for the Arts Fellowship, 1978. Agent: Lois Marshall, Wallace and Sheil Agency Inc., 118 East 61st Street, New York, New York 10022. Address: Box 943, Wellfleet, Massachusetts 02667, U.S.A.

PUBLICATIONS

Verse

Breaking Camp. Middletown, Connecticut, Wesleyan University Press, 1968.
Hard Loving. Middletown, Connecticut, Wesleyan University Press, 1969.
A Work of Artifice. Detroit, Red Hanrahan Press, 1970.
4-Telling, with others. Trumansburg, New York, Crossing Press, 1971.
When the Drought Broke. Santa Barbara, California, Unicorn Press, 1971.
To Be of Use. New York, Doubleday, 1973.
Living in the Open. New York, Knopf, 1976.
The Twelve-Spoked Wheel Flashing. New York, Knopf, 1978.

Recordings: *Laying Down the Tower*, Black Box; *At the Core*, Watershed 1978.

Play

The Last White Class, with Ira Wood. Trumansburg, New York, Crossing Press, 1979.

Novels

Going Down Fast. New York, Simon and Schuster, 1969.
Dance the Eagle to Sleep. New York, Doubleday, 1970; London, W. H. Allen, 1971.
Small Changes. New York, Doubleday, 1973.
Woman on the Edge of Time. New York, Knopf, 1976; London, Women's Press, 1979.
The High Cost of Living. New York, Harper, 1978; London, Women's Press, 1979.
Vida. New York, Summit, 1979.

Other

The Grand Coolie Dam. Boston, New England Free Press, 1970(?).

Marge Piercy comments:

I am a committed radical and feminist. I don't understand distinctions between private and social poetry: love, after all, is supposed to be between people. On the other hand, I consider the attempt to build new kinds of relationships as political as a picket line. Half the human race (my half) has been sat on under every form of economic organization. I want my poems to be useful – in the broadest and not necessarily conscious sense – to the people I speak them to or who read them. I am also concerned with the remaking of the symbols we use according to our own values and what we would be.

In making the arrangement of sounds and silences that the notation of a poem on the page is supposed to create in the reader's throat or mind, I am working in measures drawn from American speech and American prosody. I have found that a poem can speak through rich and complex imagery as long as it is emotionally coherent; but I also write a type of poem almost without ornament, attempting purified and clarified speech, just as I also work in long line, short line and lines in which iambic pentameter is a kind of hidden reference. That people who desire be able to approach and experience my poems is important to me and I work hard to make my work open. Each time I put together a volume of poetry I try to create an artifact, to place in it only the poems appropriate to that book and to place them in a meaningful order.

* * *

At the end of the 1970's, Marge Piercy's reputation as a fluent and courageous writer is well established. She began in the early 1960's writing novels and poems exploring the interface between personal relationships and political forces. Her allegiances shifted away from general political activism, whose sexist underpinnings she exposed in a much-anthologized essay, "The Grand Coolie Dam," into commitment to feminism and the women's movement as the leading force toward social revolution today.

Anger was, and is, a frequent motivation and theme in Piercy's writing. In her second collection, *Hard Loving*, she mitigates her anger with intelligence and a gift for apt metaphor. "Letter to Be Disguised as a Gas Bill" is a vituperative poem, rescued from the dangers of that genre by a sustained series of fresh comparisons: "Your face scrapes my sleep tonight/sharp as a broken girder./My hands are empty shopping bags." "Song of the Fucked Duck" is also angry, but rises above anger as it analyzes the manipulative mentality of the male revolutionary organizer while dealing with the personal pain of a particular failed relationship.

But through the 1970's increasingly, and in her latest poems especially, anger is a lesser component. A new element has entered her life: earned affluence. She responds with hearty appreciation and enjoyment of her world. She now lives a semi-rural life outside Wellfleet, Massachusetts, but travels to give poetry readings and lectures. The poverty and struggle of her youth seem to be over. Now the richness of the natural world feeds her experience. Many poems in *Living in the Open* and *The Twelve-Spoked Wheel Flashing* spring from the locale of her country farm. Foods – lettuce, raspberries, tomatoes – and domestic accoutrements reflect her wish to live close to the earth and congruent with the seasons. She wants to "live my life whole,/round, integral as the earth spinning."

In this comfortable life beauties and dangers co-exist. What becomes of revolutionary anger when one's days and hours are so idyllic and rewarding? Poems to Pat Swinton, battered women and "the market economy" seem simplistic; they show her concern but have an unconvincing ring. And poems like "The Poet Dreams of a Nice Warm Motel" show that one can perhaps become too used to comfort and recognition.

Piercy is at her best when she applies images out of her robust and earthy experience to illuminate psychological situations. Her language then becomes charged and her metaphors gather intensity, as in "The Greater Grand Rapids Lover":

How the strange
minds twine and glitter and swing
looped like words in a hammock.
How the strange minds joining stand
charmed snakes glittering
to dance their knowledge.

Piercy is evidently strongest when not very satisfied with herself, when exploring aspects of experience which exclude the potential for stock response. In any case, it is clear that she is a courageous woman. She lives her life bravely and takes plenty of risks, both literarily and personally. One is grateful for her forthrightness, commitment to and engagement with the world. It is worth far more than the falsely delicate and evasive craft manufactured by MFA programs. "The personal is political" is a feminist manifesto which Piercy has always lived by and exemplified. In the last poem of *The Twelve-Spoked Wheel Flashing*, Piercy addresses a lover who works in Washington, D.C., and to whom she is taking grape conserves made from her own grapevines. This is plainly not an ideologically suitable relationship, but she will not shrink from it merely because it doesn't fit political preconceptions. She addresses her politician friend as she might address the world to which she gives her poems:

I bring you trouble
like a hornet's nest in a hat
to roost on your head. I bring you
struggle and trouble and love
and a gift of grape conserves to melt
on your tongue, red and winey,
the summer sun within like soft jewels
passing and strong and sweet.

—Jane Augustine

PILLIN, William. American. Born in Alexandrowsk, Russia, 3 December 1910. Educated at Lewis Institute, Chicago; Northwestern University, Evanston, Illinois; University of Chicago. Married Polia Pillin in 1934; one son. Since 1948, self-employed Artist-Potter. Recipient: Jeanette Sewell Davis Award (*Poetry*, Chicago), 1937. Address: 4913 Melrose Avenue, Los Angeles, California 90029, U.S.A.

PUBLICATIONS

Verse

Poems. Prairie City, Illinois, Decker Press, 1939.
Theory of Silence. Los Angeles, George Yamada, 1949.
Dance Without Shoes. Francestown, New Hampshire, Golden Quill Press, 1956.
Passage after Midnight. San Francisco, Inferno Press, 1958.
Pavanne for a Fading Memory. Denver, Swallow, 1963.
Everything Falling. Santa Cruz, California, Kayak, 1971.
The Abandoned Music Room. Santa Cruz, California, Kayak, 1975.

Critical Studies: by James Dickey, in *Poetry* (Chicago), May 1959; Felix Anselm, in *Prairie*

Schooner (Lincoln, Nebraska), Winter 1959–60; introduction by Robert Bly to *Everything Falling*, 1971; Stewart Granger, in *Northwest Review* (Eugene, Oregon), Spring 1972; "William Pillin: A Certain Music" by Charles Fishman, in *Literary Review* (Madison, New Jersey), Spring 1978.

William Pillin comments:

Earlier poems in strict classical forms, later poems depending largely on cadence and free of rhyme. Characteristic subjects: I identify myself with the great mass of ordinary people, not necessarily in an ideological sense, but in terms of needs, aspirations, attitudes. My moonlight shines in a backyard, not on a formal garden, and I observe the stars from a kitchen window. General influences are poets who emphasize imagery and the surreal: Neruda, Vallejo, Lorca, etc., and poets whose emphasis is social, like Brecht.

Felix Anselm in his *Prairie Schooner* review wrote the following: "His world is characterized by a hopeless nostalgia ... a gentle and affectionate appreciation of the small things of daily living that issue touches of warmth and beauty." If his estimate is correct, I have been successful in my literary intentions.

* * *

William Pillin's poetry shows evidence of more resources than results. He often draws his subject matter from his immigrant background: the Eastern European culture, pulverized by the urban pressures of twentieth-century Los Angeles, is alternately celebrated for its other-worldliness and lamented in its imminent evaporation. But the rhetoric we hear most often resounds with self-conscious nostalgia: "To you I say a farewell daily." The poet, too haunted by memories to speak with unchecked force, leaves behind a language of enervated regret, a prosaic numbering that ends by numbing the sense still further:

My nights are haunted by footsteps
on the wind. The sky, the trees
are kisses of memory on my forehead.

The lack of incisive presentation of sensory images, and the blurring of metaphors by abstraction, prevent Pillin's joy its fullest rendering. He presents his description of the poem as "at best/a black bordered/post-card of grief," but the border is drawn without sufficient care, and it threatens to take over the entire space of the poem. His irony might be tenser, his wit more agile, but too often the syntax of exposition turns stanzas into what Edmund Wilson called "shredded prose."

Besides this nostalgic poetry of the Jewish immigrant, Pillin attempts several love poems, and poems on aesthetic subjects, the latter usually in praise of some artist. This sort of subject matter is rendered more successfully, and emotions are clearer and more forceful. He wishes his daughter's piano playing will "continue somewhat green/and ignorantly sweet." His kiln grins "like a pot-bellied devil/licking with a glowing tongue/opaline on stone jars." But when he strives for a larger scope, the inflated language goes limp, exemplified by the poem on Isadora Duncan, which begins: "Hallucinatory, like theatrical twilight, is her passage." The weak passive construction and the alliterating, but over-obvious, adjective are unfortunately his characteristic weaknesses. When we are told that the city contains "nudities on streetcorners/instigating youths to bacchanalian cakewalks," we are told too much and allowed to see too little. Pillin's poetry displays more emotion than skill, and while that limits it, it marks it as unusual, for he never descends to the merely glib, though he seldom sings his distress into rapture.

—Charles Molesworth

PILLING, Christopher (Robert). British. Born in Birmingham, Warwickshire, 20 April 1936. Educated at King Edward's School, Birmingham, 1947–54; University of Leeds, Yorkshire, 1954–57, B.A. (honours) 1957; Institute of French Studies, La Rochelle, France, 1955; Loughborough College, University of Nottingham, 1958–59, Cert.Ed. 1959. Married Sylvia Pilling in 1960; one son and two daughters. Assistant in English, Ecole Normale, Moulins, France, 1957–58; French Teacher, Wirral Grammar School, Cheshire, 1959–61, King Edward's Grammar School, Birmingham, 1961–62, and Ackworth School, Pontefract, Yorkshire, 1962–71, 1972–73; Chairman of the Department of Modern Languages, Knottingley High School, Yorkshire, 1973–78. Since 1978, Tutor in English, University of Newcastle upon Tyne Department of Adult Education. Reviewer, *Times Literary Supplement*, London, 1973–74. Recipient: Arts Council award, 1970, grant, 1971, and translator's grant, 1977. Address: 25 High Hill, Keswick, Cumbria CA12 5NY, England.

PUBLICATIONS

Verse

Snakes and Girls. Leeds, University of Leeds School of English Press, 1970.
Fifteen Poems. Leeds, University of Leeds School of English Press, 1970.
In All the Spaces on All the Lines. Manchester, Phoenix Pamphlet Poets Press, 1971.
Wren and Owl. Leeds, University of Leeds School of English Press, 1971.
Andrée's Bloom and the Anemones. Rushden, Northamptonshire, Sceptre Press, 1973.
Light Leaves. Hitchin, Hertfordshire, Cellar Press, 1975.

Other

Translator, *These Jaundiced Loves*, by Tristan Corbière. Liskeard, Cornwall, Peterloo Poets, 1979.

Critical Study: by Julian MacKenney, in *Poetry and Audience* (Leeds), 1 May 1970.

* * *

In All the Spaces on All the Lines and *Snakes and Girls* show Christopher Pilling bringing out, at his best, the subjective depths of everyday domestic moments by forming around them multiple concrete and abstract analogies, as in "Sunscape," "Old Celtic Cocoon," and "Partial Ellipse" (all in *Snakes and Girls*). The opening of the third of these illustrates how concretely observant this poetic evocation can be:

My wife's wedding ring is no longer
Circular:

A gold curve
Is all I see on a hand-coloured

Background.
One does not think the world is

Round.

More discursive poems tend to be less fully achieved, but do suggest Pilling's developing intellectual grasp of his life-loving orientation:

The world is not so sinister, such dark.
The left-handed is another turn of truth.
The poet needs an ambidextrous strain.
The words must not go to the ends of the earth.
Hammer them to the gallows of a poem
And let them cry of a spirit they have denied.

Though not poetically successful, "Crow Answers by Flight" takes on Ted Hughes's poem intelligently, and one senses that the younger poet has a more than lyrical basis for future work.

—Anne Cluysenaar

PINSKY, Robert. American. Born in Long Branch, New Jersey, 20 October 1940. Educated at Rutgers University, New Brunswick, New Jersey, B.A. 1962; Stanford University, California (Woodrow Wilson, Stegner, and Fulbright fellow), M.A., Ph.D. 1966. Married Ellen Bailey in 1961; three daughters. Assistant Professor of Humanities, University of Chicago, 1967–68. Since 1968, Professor of English, Wellesley College, Massachusetts. Since 1978, Poetry Editor, *New Republic*, Washington, D.C. Recipient: Massachusetts Council on the Arts grant, 1974; Oscar Blumenthal Prize (*Poetry*, Chicago), 1978. Address: 26 Leighton Road, Wellesley, Massachusetts 02181, U.S.A.

PUBLICATIONS

Verse

Sadness And Happiness. Princeton, New Jersey, Princeton University Press, 1975.
An Explanation of America. Princeton, New Jersey, Princeton University Press, and Manchester, Carcanet Press, 1979.
Five American Poets, with others. Manchester, Carcanet Press, 1979.

Other

Landor's Poetry. Chicago, University of Chicago Press, 1968.
The Situation of Poetry: Contemporary Poetry and Its Traditions. Princeton, New Jersey, Princeton University Press, 1976.

Critical Studies: by Hugh Kenner, in *Los Angeles Times*, 11 February 1976; Robert van Hallberg, in *Chicago Review*, Spring 1976; William Pritchard, in *Times Literary Supplement* (London), 11 June 1976; Louis Martz, in *Yale Review* (New Haven, Connecticut), Autumn 1976.

* * *

To begin at the edge, " 'Wonder' is an inclusive name for our most significant feelings in response to nature, an abrupt and non-referential awe ... Wonder is non-referential in the sense that as a feeling it seems unrelated, by cause or analogy, to the rest of life," writes Robert Pinsky in *The Situation of Poetry*, a critical work which attempts to situate modern poetry in an historical context. Yet in his first book of poetry, *Sadness And Happiness*, life and the response to life are woven together by the varieties of wonder. The incommensurability between a cause and its effects, between the fact seen and the feelings born there, grows into poetry:

> Someone is reading the way a rare child reads,
>
> A kind of changeling reading for the love of reading,
> For love and for the course of something leading
>
> Her child's intelligent soul through its inflection.

"Library Scene," composed in couplets of flowing meter and delicate rhyme (that quoted is the single true rhyme, which forms the center of a variety of imperfect ones) turns concisely about the still figure, deftly giving it motion.

Wonder, however, is an inclusive response, and in Pinsky's longer poems, the discursive techniques predominate: digressions, lists, and the free association of images and feelings lead us remorsefully but remorselessly through the inflections of our inadequate terms for feelings ("Sadness And Happiness"):

> That they have no earthly measure
> is well known – the surprise is
> how often it becomes impossible
> to tell one from the other in memory:
>
> the sadness of past failures, the strangely
> happy – doubtless corrupt –
> fondling of them. Crude, empty
> though the terms are, they do
>
> organize life.

Such poems resist short quotation, but there is a hint of the poem's shape in the dashes, commas, and colons of this one. With these punctuational road signs, Pinsky navigates the bumpy borders which lie between sadness and happiness, crossing and recrossing from one territory to the other.

The shorter poems of *Sadness And Happiness*, such as "Library Scene," have an estimable clarity, precision, and grace, but Pinsky is evidently bending his energies toward longer forms. "Essay on Psychiatrists," 17 pages long, quotes from a journalistic variety of sources, including comic strips (*Rex Morgan, M.D.*, of course), *The Bacchae*, and Walter Savage Landor (the subject of Pinsky's first critical work, *Landor's Poetry*). "Essay on Psychiatrists" again takes up the inadequate terms we have for circumscribing experience – "sanity," "genius," or "madness" – but arrives at a conclusion that seems to strain for a larger field:

> – goods
> and money in their contingency and spiritual
>
> Grace evoke the way we are all psychiatrists,
> All fumbling at so many millions of miles
> Per minute and so many dollars per hour
>
> Through the exploding or collapsing spaces
> Between stars, saying what we can.

Pinsky's current work in progress – "An Explanation of America" – has perhaps found a category large enough for his particular form of speech. In the three sections published so far, the musical theme-and-variation form evident in earlier poems has been applied rigorously, and the resulting work is as clear and as faceted as crystal. The question of limiting terms is being approached from its other side: properly linked and joined, such terms can be used to enclose a territory from without. While remaining highly personal and responsive, Robert Pinsky's poetry seems to be growing ever more inclusive.

—Walter Bode

PITCHFORD, Kenneth (Samuel). American. Born in Moorhead, Minnesota, 24 January 1931. Educated at the University of Minnesota, Minneapolis, B.A. (summa cum laude) 1952; Oxford University (Fulbright Fellow); New York University (Penfield Fellow, 1957), M.A. 1959. Served in the United States Army, 1953–55. Married to the poet Robin Morgan; one child. Member, Department of English, New York University, 1958–62; Writer-in-Residence, Yaddo, Saratoga Springs, New York, Summer 1958; taught at the Poetry Workshop, New School for Social Research, New York, 1960; Associate Editor, *The New International Yearbook*, New York, 1960–66. Currently, Free-lance Editor, New York. Recipient: Borestone Mountain Award, 1964. Address: 109 Third Avenue, New York, New York 10003, U.S.A.

PUBLICATIONS

Verse

The Blizzard Ape. New York, Scribner, 1958.
A Suite of Angels and Other Poems. Chapel Hill, University of North Carolina Press, 1967.
Color Photos of the Atrocities. Boston, Little Brown, 1973.

Kenneth Pitchford comments:

I consider myself a writer. My medium, then, is language. Any form that can be composed of words is of interest to me. Alongside the poems I write, I have also written plays, stories, a novel, essays, etc.

I began writing poetry to express the inexpressible sensation of being alive – before I knew that a formal discipline called poetry existed. In college, I achieved the mastery of traditional forms of poetry under superb taskmasters, but while my first book of poems reflects these acquired skills, I feel that my own poetic bent has always lain elsewhere. My second book of poems shows the attempt to put "schooling" behind me and seize my own sense of poetry more directly. My third book begins to show me a configuration that is uniquely my own.

This "growing into myself" is also reflected in the progression of subject matter that has preoccupied me. Previous to the first book, my work was an uncontrolled outcry about the despair and ignorance that was the lot of a working-class youngster – and the sources of beauty open to such a one. In the first book, written during the McCarthyist Fifties, I had not become so domesticated that this subject matter was totally obscured. But with the second book, several strands come together: the exploration and laying to rest of a tortuous psychological journey from suicide and sexual conflict toward intimations of personal liberation; and a growing refusal to accept the amount of general suffering required to maintain the present shape of society. In the new poems, the commitment is totally to political revolution and a struggle to imagine what social liberation would be like. I find myself embittered now about the years of "training" I underwent in the 1950's – training designed to transform intransigence into passivity and to drive wedges between thought and action, literary values and human needs, taste and utility. I see the whole literary endeavor as presently pursued to be the stutterings of a dying culture. The attempt to tell some part of the truth will be considered propaganda; the urgent outcry will be considered vulgar; the abandonment of outworn forms and assumptions will be seen as inartistic. Yet the revolutionary poet, in trying to re-create himself, will take all these risks, will attempt to fuse thought and action, value and need, and in so doing, perhaps, build a new language strong enough to be of help in the growing worldwide struggle for human liberation from want, greed and domination. Whether the new world that emerges will want to remember such writing is really unimportant. Venceremos!

* * *

... I might have made some greater difference than I did
(though never enough, never mind total)
but all my poems were trying to curry favor
with the *Kenyon Review* and other extinct areas of sensibility
when there was this rage in me that only now has exploded into the
realization that my right to be sensitive, to love the art of any suffering
people, was taken from me by their calling me
faggot faggot faggot – and that all I have to do to reclaim that right
is to realize how faggot is my salvation, whatever they called Chopin.

—"I've Never Been to Majorca"

Kenneth Pitchford's festering rage is well concealed in *The Blizzard Ape*. The poems are chiselled and carefully wrought: many are written as lyrics to be set to music and use the ballad form and colloquial idiom to sing jauntily of the barmaid propositioned by a customer in Tony's Hashhouse, or to sing the "Young Buck's Sunday Blues" when he discovers that his hell raisin' woman has left him to seek comfort with a preacher "full a' brimstone, cash, and hell." Others evoke fleeting moods and meditate upon the difficulty of making a poem speak and the loss experienced when the poem is perfected; finally, a very few, "A Bride's Song," "Still-Life from a Packing Plant," and "The Solipsist at Midnight," strike the macabre note later sustained in many of the poems on conjury and others in *A Suite of Angels*. The spectre of death that chills the lovers' kiss in "A Bride's Song," and the still-life image of the cow slaughtered in the kill room where "... red-aproned men have come,/affixed the cable to bruise the senseless neck, replaced the hooks through the achilles tendons, hoisted the body upwards, set casters/in the grooves of the shiny rail above them, to send it wheeling down rows of skinners and cutters" brutally hint at the rage mounting in the poet as he confronts the butchery and violence in society and in himself which have done their best to slay his gentler, more delicate instincts.

In *A Suite of Angels* a number of the poems continue to rework Greek myths and write in an objective voice designed to win favor from the *Kenyon Review*, but most begin to speak in the first person confessional voice, and begin to dredge up the painful memories from the past and recreate the nightmares of his present marriage. Many express the ambivalence Pitchford feels towards himself as a man and towards women as they have been defined in their traditional roles. The scene of the bull slaughtered repeats itself; the male is transformed into a Wer-Man, turned into this creature by his lust for men but held prisoner by women who demand to feed his blood hunger. The poems speak of moments in childhood when he heard the muffled, scuffling sounds of his father wringing the necks of mallards which his sister later cleaned; when he heard his sister talking of wanting to take her mother's place in her father's bed; when he decried his father's crime of denying him love. Finally, in "Nightmares," his nightmares and those of his wife war upon the two of them: he haunted by his role as Wer-Man, male supremacist, sucking his wife's blood because long ago he was denied his other love; she struggling with spectres of nazi doctors with their scalpels, come to sterilize, rape, or otherwise mutilate her. He becomes the nazi doctors; she the Wer-man's mistress: both trace their nightmares to the wrongs done them by their parents and by an evolutionary history that made the male the dominant species; both briefly overcome the fiendish tortures of sleep when their love finally unites them.

But *Color Photos of the Atrocities* allows no such easy solution to the anti-gender struggle. Pitchford's rage has burst; he has found his cause. Although the reader may find the poems too wordy, the cant of revolution, egalitarianism, racism, sexism, gay liberationism, and militant feminism too much a part of the nostalgia of the 1960's, Pitchford believes he must abandon his old controls and struggle painfully to make explicit the plight of the effeminist married to Robin Morgan (authoress of *The Monster* and a radical feminist herself) who wants to come to terms with his feelings for her, their son, Blake, his lover, Michael, and the future movement which now consumes him. In this volume, all atrocities, Auschwitz, the holocaust, the Attica prison riots, and the mass killings of Brazil's Indians, are one to Pitchford: all bespeak the brutality and violence which has defined The Man, the white straight male, whom Pitchford now identifies with the Establishment, the Kennedys, Rockefellers, and all the moguls. The faggot is their prisoner who awaits a revolution in which, as Pitchford declares, "he will risk his whole self or die." But the enemy is also the faggot himself who cannot entirely get rid of the violence in him that has always made him oppressor, and who cannot survive if the force he believes in, the liberated woman, is to have her way. For she, in Pitchford's poems, must become the real heroine of the revolution and pull the trigger that kills him. Pitchford dreams of a time:

> ... when there is no more religion or family or
> male domination
> or money or property or mine or yours or
> forced obedience
> ... when women are free
> not only to shape their own lives
> but to realize a vision of liberation
> that will shape the lives of all of us
> ... when men are able
> to hug and kiss babies not for show,
> but able to care for them in every sense
> and for each other
> ... when I'm no longer called queer
> for wishing my father had held me
> with a love like that,
> for loving still any rare stray
> glimmer of tenderness in a man....
>
> —"The Flaming Faggots"

But the poetry sees this as a dream; and the reality he wrestles with is one in which suicide or murder seem the more necessary outcomes. At their best, these poems candidly capture the joy of fatherhood, the delight derived from simple domestic moments, and the dizzying pleasure found in music. At their worst, they are too insistent, propagandistic, repetitive, and voguish.

—Carol Simpson Stern

PITTER, Ruth. British. Born in Ilford, Essex, 7 November 1897. Educated at Coborn School for Girls, East London. War Office Clerk, 1916–18. Painter for Walberswick Peasant Pottery Company, Suffolk, 1918–30, and from 1930, Partner, Deane and Forester, London. Now retired. Recipient: Hawthornden Prize, 1937; Heinemann Award, 1954; Queen's Gold Medal for Poetry, 1955. Companion of Literature, 1974. Address: The Hawthorns, Chilton Road, Long Crendon, Aylesbury, Buckinghamshire, England.

PUBLICATIONS

Verse

First Poems. London, Cecil Palmer, 1920.
First and Second Poems 1912–1925. London, Sheed and Ward, 1927; New York, Doubleday, 1930.
Persephone in Hades. Privately printed, 1931.
A Mad Lady's Garland. London, Cresset Press, 1934; New York, Macmillan, 1935.
A Trophy of Arms: Poems 1926–1935. London, Cresset Press, and New York, Macmillan, 1936.
The Spirit Watches. London, Cresset Press, 1939; New York, Macmillan, 1940.
The Rude Potato. London, Cresset Press, 1941.
Poem. Southampton, Shirley Press, 1943.
The Bridge: Poems 1939–1944. London, Cresset Press, 1945; New York, Macmillan, 1946.
Pitter on Cats. London, Cresset Press, 1947.
Urania (selections). London, Cresset Press, 1950.
The Ermine: Poems 1942–1952. London, Cresset Press, 1953.
Still by Choice. London, Cresset Press, 1966.
Poems 1926–1966. London, Barrie and Rockliff-Cresset Press, 1968; as *Collected Poems*, New York, Macmillan, 1969.
End of Drought. London, Barrie and Jenkins, 1975.

Critical Study: Preface by the author to *Poems 1926–1966*, 1968.

Ruth Pitter comments:

I am not even a professional writer, just a poet; the occupations of my life other than this have been simply to gain a subsistence, and I have mostly worked with my hands.

I look at life, and listen inside myself, and try to express what I feel mostly in the well-worn forms of our tradition. From infancy I have intently observed nature (including people), fascinated chiefly by the mysteries of things.

* * *

In a literary period of revolution, reflecting that of Western society, the poetry of Ruth Pitter stands as an isolated monument, untouched by the changes, both technical and moral, around it. She says in the Foreword to her *Collected Poems* that "I have been trying to write poetry since 1903, when I was about five; but I produced little that I now think worth keeping until about the age of thirty." That is a long, and humble apprenticeship. The humility comes from an ever closer dedication to Christian Faith, of an almost Traherne-like individuality and isolation. The persistence comes from a character obstinate, assured and humorous. As she also says, "I have had strange thoughts at times about comedy." They not only emerge in much of her verse. They also play a part in securing her in her assurance of her own idiom as a craftsman in that verse, by making her self-critical without at the same time freezing her muse into sterility. Seriousness, a necessary ingredient of poetry, can be damaged, even crippled, by self-laughter.

For sixty years Miss Pitter has practised her art, obstinately personal, rather as a goldsmith at his bench. She uses words as that precious metal, manipulating it into verbal shapes of recognised modes: the sonnet, the *terza rima*, the couplet and blank verse. In all those shapes it is lucid, simple. Its vowels echo round the halls of the English Pantheon, where Milton has entoned and Spenser sung. But it is a music on its own, self-taught, self-tuned. It is poetry, not merely verse.

That must be why, some thirty years ago, Hilaire Belloc spoke to me about her one day at lunch, saying that he had written an introduction to a book of poems by a young woman of remarkable skill and intellectual and spiritual force. She has persisted since then, singing her own song. It is mainly a *Magnificat*, in praise of life as she has encountered it, close up and through the sharp eye of an intense curiosity. She has not dissipated her literary vitality on professional writing, such as literary journalism, nor, as far as I know, on prose work of any kind. She has been solely a poet, and has made her living at work wholly apart from this major activity which, to be secure in its achievement, demands as much fidelity and patience as marriage. Hers has been a monophilic art, sustained, as I have said, by bouts of extraneous humour, as when she writes verse about cats and gardening, amusing relaxations from the demands of her more devout work.

That work is based upon religious faith, not dogmatic but metaphysical and exalted. It is astonishingly beautiful, and clothed in sensuous phrases and images. Like the swallows (she calls them "freemasons of the air"), in a poem which is a masterpiece, she is one of those "Spirits who can sleep on high/And hold their marriage in the sky." That is an example of close observation of the goings-on of nature, and of the imaginative power to translate such earthy traffic into terms of spiritual symbolism.

This process occupies most of her work. Again and again, she sets out demurely, almost cataloguing something she has noticed in her daily round and common task; then suddenly it is turned round, irradiated, and made to reveal a divine significance. Thus, in a poem called "The Apple Tree," she says:

A dear and blessed thing to see,
The lovely laden apple-tree.
I sit me down his boughs below,
The cold and tortuous musings go;
I from the lowest branches take
Four apples for my childhood's sake.

Somehow, that takes us back to Genesis and the Garden of Eden, and the springtime of the mind. Note, too, how the obsolete device of inversion, so much frowned on today, adds to the effect of total return to the garden of prime innocence.

Much more could be said about her work: its simplicity, its quiet self-assurance; but its source and strength can be summed up in her short lyric "For Sleep or Death":

Cure me with quietness,
Bless me with peace;
Comfort my heaviness,
Stay me with ease.
Stillness in solitude
Send down like dew;
Mine armour of fortitude
Piece and make new:
That when I rise again
I may shine bright
As the sky after rain,
Day after night.

—Richard Church

PLANZ, Allen. American. Born in New York City, 2 January 1937. Educated at New York University, M.A. 1961. Served in United States Army, 1960–61. Married to Doris Sommers; one child. Formerly taught at Hunter College, New York, University of North Carolina, Chapel Hill, and Queens College, New York; Lecturer, Chapman College, Montauk, New York, 1973–74. Poetry Editor, *The Nation*, New York, 1969–70. Currently, "independent fisherman." Recipient: New York Poetry Center Younger Poets prize, 1963; Swallow Press New Poetry Series Award, 1969; Creative Artists Public Service grant, 1975. Address: Box 212, East Hampton, New York 11937, U.S.A.

PUBLICATIONS

Verse

Poor White and Other Poems. Lanham, Maryland, Goosetree Press, 1964.
Heir to Anger. New York, Lower East Press, 1965.
Studsong. New York, Lower East Press, 1968.
A Night for Rioting. Chicago, Swallow Press, 1969.
Wild Craft. New York, Living Poets Press, 1975.

Other

American Wilderness. San Francisco, Sierra Club, 1970.

Allen Planz comments:

Recently, I've come to think of my best work as discovery – discovering again the ancient relations between man and earth, man and man, man and woman, the excess of joy and terror and splendor which in rediscovery becomes celebration, toward which each poem strives, praising earth and the people on it.

* * *

In *A Night for Rioting*, Allen Planz combines visions of urban and rural deterioration. The process of decay, due to technology and industry, occurs wherever modern man locates himself. The disintegration caused by an increasingly object-oriented culture ("gentlemen delivered to chrome by a caress") has radiated outward from the cities to poison the land as well.

In Planz's poetry, speed is both subject and essence of style. Automobiles signify the quest for masculinity and the rapidly accelerating pace of life. However exhilarating it may be, velocity without positive direction is meaningless and destructive ("sons wild/on curves who met their manhood on a wall"). A country that worships power, speed and violence is more than a bit frightening, and Planz concedes this ("if ever I get the courage/to have a son") while capturing the culture:

I put on a uniform & laid down my life

& thereafter lived in dread of it,
thru fear & violence
becoming quite American.

As a resistance poet, he speaks out against the threatening array of anti-life forces – the dollar, the dictator, and the diplomat ("admen felt for their sex in watchpockets"). The land that remains unoccupied (place and state of mind) is where the revolutionary takes hold ("now as a man, dizzy still with gravity/and hard loving, I name my upland rapture"). The land is real:

... nothing but the land survives,
for only the land lasts, outlasting
citizen, city, empire.

The revolt starts with one man ("having found a rifle/a good thing to lie by") in the natural world, a guerilla who recognizes the need to reverse ongoing destructive processes and the cost of the effort ("My heart, my land, it is the courage to starve to death/I work to give or to get").

In *Wild Craft*, Planz continues his revolution of one. Charting his own course, traveling unknown waters, he sings of his craft as fisherman and captain. The poems, imagery-laden, convey with clarity the savagery and terrible beauty of the sea-world which calls to him. The opening poem ("Offshore") begins: "I go to sea, before dawn, wondering/what else wanders these waters in the dark." Here especially change and growth are possible, positive, and necessary. "Offshore" concludes:

alone in this stillness
knowing we change
and affirming
for out to sea we change
and change ourselves
forever.

In "Sharks" the speaker changes from a mindless killer to a perceiver who shares life's unity: "The darkness is one dance/one life, one love."

Planz, amphibian-like, returns to the land and his urban dwelling-place. As in his earlier book, cities pollute the bodies, warp the minds, and stifle the spirits of their inhabitants. The city poems present the senseless violence (physical and psychological), the oppressive claustrophobia and routine, and the waiting to die which characterize so many of the people. Yet, despite the muggers, perverts, and junkies, here are family and friends; Planz concedes in the last poem ("The Tidefall Wilderness"), "I carry in my side/a green unease/gotten where I swept over a reef/into a glade where a girl showed me my need of peoples." In this poem, too, the poet states "The sea itself is survival" – and survival, land or sea, is what *Wild Craft* is ultimately about.

—Carl Lindner

PLUMLY, Stanley. American. Born in Barnesville, Ohio, 23 May 1939. Educated at Ohio University, Athens, M.A. 1968. Married Hope Plumly in 1974. Visiting Poet, Louisiana State University, Baton Rouge, 1968–70; Ohio University, 1970–73; University of Iowa, Iowa City, 1974–76; Princeton University, New Jersey, 1976–78; Columbia University, New York, 1977–79; University of Michigan, Ann Arbor, Spring 1979. Since 1979, Professor of English, University of Houston. Poetry Editor, *Ohio Review*, Athens, 1970–75, and *Iowa Review*, Iowa City, 1976–78. Recipient: Delmore Schwartz Memorial Award, 1973; Guggenheim grant, 1973; National Endowment for the Arts grant, 1977. Address: 3423 Nottingham, Houston, Texas 77005, U.S.A.

PUBLICATIONS

Verse

In the Outer Dark. Baton Rouge, Louisiana State University Press, 1970.
Giraffe. Baton Rouge, Louisiana State University Press, 1973.
How the Plains Indians Got Horses. Crete, Nebraska, Best Cellar Press, 1975.
Out-of-the-Body Travel. New York, Ecco Press, 1977.

Manuscript Collection: State University of New York, Buffalo.

Stanley Plumly comments:

I see my poems as attempts to make something whole of the disparate and difficult parts of my experience. In that sense they are fictions – that which is made of other materials.

* * *

Stanley Plumly says, "I believe in a poetry of protagonist-antagonist relationship, in which the energy, the tension ... is the result of what happens between the two.... Which means that for me a poem is a problem of the trinity, father-son-ghost." The ghost is created by the friction of father and son; it is the poem's content, born mainly through metaphor. Thus, he argues that "[b]ringing the disparate into immediate and intimate relation ... is the hope I have for my poems. My father in the ground is a unifying principle." Plumly's *artful* use of "ground" in this apparently discursive observation is characteristically manifold.

In the Outer Dark is constructed of primal polarities, some more abstract than others. But no abstraction is simply disembodied, no object locked in specificity. Central are light-darkness, motion-stillness, speech-silence, water-stone, father-son. Sun, wind, and tongue flesh out the first three pairs; consciousness and humanized Christian allusion generalize the others. The metaphors conveying these tensions are "moving toward one center," "still inside me," a prior "source," an "embryo," a "womb," an original (not this outer) dark. Moreover, they are so compact that the polarities and our senses of them, as though synesthetic, seem interchangeable: "The body tunes to a single sense...." So, just as "stillness" may be sensed both aurally and kinesthetically, the speaker listens with his hands and "warms" not the cold but "the dark."

For Plumly the antagonist and protagonist may despair, but not the poem's content. It can celebrate, "art [being] first of all a moral act." It is hard to say if this book is finest in darkness, light, or shadow, but Plumly chooses man's inevitable position and in "Between Flesh and What Follows" he arranges the first and penultimate lines so as to say "The Dark that lies ... And the Light that lies." Any poem's true content is shadow.

Animal titles designate the three parts of *Giraffe*. Plumly perceives and identifies with an incipience of flight in each creature, especially as it is conceived at night or in dream. They are, then, emblems of the poet's awakening to transcendence. "Walking Out" makes the point more humanly clear: "I would be silence. Even the sleeves/of my best coat would not know me." These various, still unrealized, leavetakings are, however, not only initiated by a poem about loneliness ("Since England Is an Island") but lead back to another on that same subject ("One of Us").

While the father continues to provide tension, conflict between the desires for death and the transformation of life is equally basic. But the poems of darkness and extinction neither dull the volume's celebratory edge nor fail in themselves to honor struggle (as in the lovely, elegiac "Jarrell") and survival (as in "Dreamsong"). Though never evasive about Jarrell's lifelong flirtation with easing himself out of life, Plumly regards him as a man who, even imaginatively, doubted his own seriousness, and ultimately as "a man walking out of himself on a road at dawn" with "the dark piled up behind." Before rising and walking the water, the persona of "Dreamsong" says, "I wanted to die./I wanted the whole/day."

Perhaps the key to the collection is in "One Line of Light," the geographical background of which is flood country:

I think of my house as a ship
lit up like a birthday.
I walk around inside it
with the page of a poem –
the day's log,
the night's psalm.
The dark is my ocean.
I know the water's rising
in the next town.

In "Jarrell" that poet is himself "the page of his poem filling up" (a masterstroke of ambiguity and metonymy). In "Walking Out" and "Heron," "flight" or its "mockery" are *imagined* "at the edge of water."

"The Wish to Be a Red Indian," a bit of Kafka provided as postscript to *Giraffe*, is equally preface to *Out-of-the-Body Travel*. It involves naturalness and creature identification as conditions of pure motion and the dissolution of fetters. When the speaker says, "We lie in that other darkness, ourselves," he is, among other things, considering the truth of lives not our own. Getting out of ourselves is at once impossible and imperative. These poems realize the poet's experience only as a portion of the lives, deaths and painful self-divisions of others, particularly the members of his family. Two poems entitled "Anothering" are about the mother's transcendence through her progeny but in conjunction with the sad vacancy the child's "out-of-the-body travel" leaves in its wake. But death is the principal battleground for transcendence. Recurrently, as in the last two poems, Plumly discovers perpetuity and new life in identification with the dead, especially the father, both as person and archetype:

Whatever two we were, we become
one falling body, one breath.

And whosoever be reborn in sons
so shall they be also reborn....
And you, my anonymous father,
be with me when I wake.

The title poem, devoid of all artiness, is perfectly apt. His "raw, red cheek/pressed against the cheek of the [violin's] wood," the father elevates his merely "sad relatives" with that mournful music Yeats knew and made through "Lapis Lazuli."

—David M. Heaton

POMEROY, Ralph. American. Born in Evanston, Illinois, 12 October 1926. Educated at the Art Institute, Chicago; University of Illinois, Urbana; University of Chicago. Has worked as a magazine editor, art gallery director, lecturer, stage manager, and bartender; also a painter. Recipient: Yaddo Fellowship, 1955; MacDowell Fellowship, 1967. Address: 115 West 71st Street, New York, New York 10023, U.S.A.

PUBLICATIONS

Verse

Book of Poems. Winnetka, Illinois, New Press, 1948.
Stills and Motives. San Francisco, Gesture, 1961.
The Canaries as They Are. Washington, D.C., Charioteer Press, 1965.
In the Financial District. New York, Macmillan, 1968.

Other

Stamos. New York, Abrams, 1974.
The Ice Cream Connection: All You'd Love to Know about Ice Cream. New York and London, Paddington Press, 1975.
First Things First: A Connoisseur's Companion to Breakfast. New York and London, Paddington Press, 1977.

* * *

The writer, painter, and art critic Ralph Pomeroy has introduced a new, idiomatic voice to American poetry. But at the same time, he has expressed, in his personal way, traditional artistic themes. In particular, he is concerned with art and its relative stability; with the contrasting transience of human experience; and with the American artist as transient and outsider. Technically his signature characteristic, a function perhaps of his emphasis upon the visual, is the bringing to the foreground of the implied dramatic situations which, like negatives, underlie all lyric poetry.

His concern with the allied disciplines of poetry and painting is directly represented in poems clearly connected with artists whom he associates with his own creative world: the writers Marianne Moore, Katherine Anne Porter, Pasternak, Glenway Wescott, Giuseppe di Lampedusa; the painters Edward Hopper, Seurat, Matisse. Set against the seeming permanence of their work, however, is Pomeroy's concern with the paradoxically constant mutability sovereign in everyday life itself. Love ("Confession"), death ("Between Here and Illinois"), the seasonal cycle ("Life of an Apple"), day and night ("Morning in Tarragona"), present familiar aspects of change.

But it is his celebrations of locations, arrivals and departures, implied motionlessness and movement, which are especially significant as expressions of impermanence. Specific examples of this version of what might be called the American picaresque, with the artist as outsider or traveller, include the New York poem, "In the Financial District," "2 P.M. Going Westward on the Chicago, Burlington & Quincy," and such poems of expatriate experience as "The Concerts" and "Visiting, Tibberton Court, near Gloucester." But the most significant of these poems, and the finest example of his lyric dramatic method, is "Corner." The speaker loiters uneasily in what could be a Hopper urban landscape, and, watching him, "The Cop slumps alertly on his motorcycle" until the scene's precarious balance is broken by an explosion of movement.

Finally, in "Sentry Seurat," Pomeroy perhaps best suggests the way in which his own sporadic, "autobiographical" poems operate. Commenting on the painter's pointillist style, he observes: "Later, accused of poetry, he rejoined, 'I apply my method.' /(Dots so set down that distance blinds and binds them.)" When Pomeroy's individual poems, quiet highlights of life's events, are considered with the proper distancing, they too combine to conjure a whole and detailed story.

—Gaynor F. Bradish

PORTER, Hal. Australian. Born in Albert Park, Melbourne, Victoria, 16 February 1911. Educated at Kensington State School, 1917; Bairnsdale State School, Victoria, 1918–21; Bairnsdale High School, 1922–26. Married Olivia Parnham in 1939 (divorced, 1943). Cadet Reporter, *Bairnsdale Advertiser*, 1927. Schoolmaster, Victorian Education Department, 1927–37, 1940; Queen's College, Adelaide, 1941–42; Prince Alfred College, Kent Town, South Australia, 1943–46; Hutchins School, Hobart, Tasmania, 1946–47; Knox Grammar School, Sydney, 1947; Ballarat College, Victoria, 1948–49; Nijimura School, Kure, Japan (Australian Army Education), 1949–50. Director, National Theatre, Hobart, 1951–53. Chief Librarian of Bairnsdale and Shepparton, 1953–61. Full-time Writer since 1961. Australian Writers Representative, Edinburgh Festival, 1962. Lecturer for the Australian Department of External Affairs, in Japan, 1967. Recipient: Sydney Sesquicentenary Prize, 1938; Commonwealth Literary Fund Fellowship, 1956, 1960, 1964, 1968, 1972, 1974, 1977, and Subsidy, 1957, 1962, 1967; *Sydney Morning Herald* Prize, 1958; Sydney Journalists' Club Prize, for fiction, 1959, for drama, 1961; *Adelaide Advertiser* Prize, for fiction, 1964, 1970, for non-fiction, 1968; *Encyclopedia Britannica* Award, 1967; Captain Cook Bi-Centenary Prize, 1970. Address: Glen Avon, Garvoc, Victoria 3265, Australia.

PUBLICATIONS

Verse

The Hexagon. Sydney, Angus and Robertson, 1956.
Elijah's Ravens. Sydney, Angus and Robertson, 1968.
In an Australian Country Graveyard. Sydney, Angus and Robertson, 1973.

Plays

The Tower (produced London, 1964). Melbourne, Penguin, 1963.
The Professor (as *Toda-San*, produced Adelaide, 1965; as *The Professor*, produced London, 1965). London, Faber, 1966.
Eden House (produced Melbourne, 1969; as *Home on a Pig's Back*, produced Richmond, Surrey, 1972). Sydney, Angus and Robertson, 1969.
Parker (produced Ballarat, Victoria, 1972). Melbourne, Arnold, 1979.

Novels

A Handful of Pennies. Sydney, Angus and Robertson, 1958; London, Angus and Robertson, 1959.
The Tilted Cross. London, Faber, 1961.
The Right Thing. Adelaide, Rigby, and London, Hale, 1971.

Short Stories

Short Stories. Adelaide, Advertiser Press, 1942.
A Bachelor's Children. Sydney and London, Angus and Robertson, 1962.
The Cats of Venice. Sydney, Angus and Robertson, 1965.
Mr. Butterfry and Other Tales of New Japan. Sydney, Angus and Robertson, 1970.
Selected Stories, edited by Leonie Kramer. Sydney and London, Angus and Robertson, 1971.
Fredo Fuss Love Life. Sydney, Angus and Robertson, 1974.
An Australian Selection, edited by John Barnes. Sydney, Angus and Robertson, 1974.

Other

The Watcher on the Cast-Iron Balcony (autobiography). London, Faber, 1963.
Australian Stars of Stage and Screen. Adelaide, Rigby, 1965.
The Paper Chase (autobiography). Sydney, Angus and Robertson, 1966.
The Actors: An Image of the New Japan. Sydney, Angus and Robertson, 1968.
The Extra (autobiography). Melbourne, Nelson, 1975.
Bairnsdale: Portrait of an Australian Country Town. Sydney, Ferguson, 1977.
Seven Cities of Australia. Sydney, Ferguson, 1978.

Editor, *Australian Poetry 1957.* Sydney, Angus and Robertson, 1957.
Editor, *Coast to Coast 1961–1962.* Sydney, Angus and Robertson, 1963.
Editor, *It Could Be You.* Adelaide, Rigby, 1972; London, Hale, 1973.

Bibliography: *A Bibliography of Hal Porter* by Janette Finch, Adelaide, Libraries Board of South Australia, 1966; *Papers of Hal Porter 1924–1975*, Sydney, Mitchell Library, n.d.

Manuscript Collection: Mitchell Library, Sydney.

Critical Studies: "The Craft of Hal Porter" by Peter Ward, in *Australian Letters* (Adelaide), October 1962; in *Profile of Australia* by Craig McGregor, Melbourne, Penguin, 1968; essay by Robert Burns, in *Meanjin 1* (Melbourne), 1969; *Hal Porter* by Mary Lord, Melbourne, Oxford University Press, 1974; *Speaking of Writing* edited by R. D. Walshe and Leonie Kramer, Sydney, Reed, 1975.

Hal Porter comments:

A great deal of my writing that could be actual poems overflows into the short stories, novels, autobiographies, and plays. I belong to no school unless there is a school of poets who prefer rigid verse forms, rigid schemes, "old-fashioned" disciplines.

Major themes: Australian landscape, the anguishes of living and loving, disenchantment. Usual verse forms: always rigid ones, but of many varieties, including the sonnet. Never *vers libre*, and not even blank verse. I need to work within a steel frame of rhyme and metre – in this cage I can wrestle with words until they obey me; outside it, I suspect (although I've never even thought of trying this freedom), I should be tricked, cheated, tripped up by words.

I'm not conscious of *direct* influences but the fact that I've strong preferences for disciplined poets suggests that I might be influenced by their intentions, their discipline, their machinery, though not by their topics or their attitudes. I find that, as I get older, I can handle the machinery better – why not? – and that what I intend saying with clarity is less smudged and decorated than formerly. A slow maturer, I look forward to writing "good" poetry very soon.

* * *

Hal Porter is perhaps better known as novelist, short story writer and dramatist than as a poet. Yet such a listing of literary attainments gives some idea of this versatile writer's talents. He is also a much praised autobiographer and as a black and white artist his drawings illustrating the article "South Gippsland and Its Towns" are a graphic *tour de force*.

His first book of poems, *The Hexagon*, disclosed an essentially fastidious poetic talent almost hidden beneath a tumultuous surge of images and stylish word-play. It was not until his second book, *Elijah's Ravens*, was released that his poetic development could be gauged.

Many poems originally appearing in *The Hexagon* are included in the later collection in altered versions that display general improvements in technique and an overall clarification of content. The new poems, though no less rich in imagery than the earlier pieces, have clearer statements to make and a number are devoted to exploring and gauging aspects of love, its finding and loss.

The best poems are "Soldier Farmer," an essentially sympathetic portrait seen against the harsh background of the country's capricious moods, "The Sheep," a brilliantly witty evocation of the economically important yet naturally stupid animals seen as unwitting judges of their own lot ("the visors carved with grieving mourn beneath judicial wigs"), and "Hobart Town, Van Dieman's Land (11th June, 1837)," a historical character sketch in the vividly evocative setting of Sir John Franklin who perished "in attempting the North West Passage."

—Bruce Beaver

PORTER, Peter (Neville Frederick). Australian. Born in Brisbane, Queensland, 16 February 1929. Educated at the Church of England Grammar School, Brisbane; Toowoomba Grammar School. Married Jannice Henry in 1961 (died, 1974); two daughters. Formerly, journalist, bookseller, clerk; worked in advertising for ten years. Compton Lecturer in Poetry, University of Hull, 1970–71; Visiting Lecturer in English, University of Reading, Autumn 1972, Sydney University, 1975, and University of New England, Armidale, New South Wales, 1977. Currently, free-lance writer. Recipient: Cholmondeley Award, 1976. Address: 42 Cleveland Square, London W.2, England.

PUBLICATIONS

Verse

Once Bitten, Twice Bitten. London, Scorpion Press, 1961.
Penguin Modern Poets 2, with Kingsley Amis and Dom Moraes. London, Penguin, 1962.
Poems Ancient and Modern. Lowestoft, Suffolk, Scorpion Press, and New York, Walker, 1964.
Words Without Music. Oxford, Sycamore Press, 1968.
Solemn Adultery at Breakfast Creek: An Australian Ballad, music by Michael Jessett. Richmond, Surrey, Keepsake Press, 1968.
A Porter Folio: New Poems. Lowestoft, Suffolk, Scorpion Press, 1969.
The Last of England. London and New York, Oxford University Press, 1970.
Epigrams by Martial. London, Poem-of-the-Month Club, 1971.
After Martial. London, Oxford University Press, 1972.
Preaching to the Converted. London, Oxford University Press, 1972.
Jonah, illustrated by Arthur Boyd. London, Secker and Warburg, 1973.
A Share of the Market. Belfast, Ulsterman, 1973.
Peter Porter Reads from His Own Work (includes recording). Brisbane, University of Queensland Press, 1974.
The Lady and the Unicorn, illustrated by Arthur Boyd. London, Secker and Warburg, 1975.
Living in a Calm Country. London, Oxford University Press, 1975.
The Très Riches Heures. Richmond, Surrey, Keepsake Press, 1978.
The Cost of Seriousness. London, Oxford University Press, 1978.

Plays

Radio Plays: *The Siege of Munster*, 1971; *The Children's Crusade*, 1973; *All He Brought Back from the Dream*, 1978.

Other

Roloff Beny in Italy, with Anthony Thwaite. London, Thames and Hudson, and New York, Harper, 1974.

Editor, *New Poems, 1971–72*. London, Hutchinson, 1972.
Editor, *A Choice of Pope's Verse*. London, Faber, 1972.
Editor, with Anthony Thwaite, *The English Poets: From Chaucer to Edward Thomas*. London, Secker and Warburg, 1974.
Editor, with Charles Osborne, *New Poetry 1*. London, Arts Council, 1975.

Manuscript Collections: Lockwood Memorial Library, State University of New York, Buffalo; University of Indiana, Bloomington; British Museum, London; University of Reading, Berkshire.

Critical Studies: by Clive James, in *The Review 24* (Oxford); Roger Garfitt, in *British Poetry since 1960: A Critical Anthology*, edited by Michael Schmidt and Grevel Lindop, Oxford, Carcanet Press, 1972.

*   *   *

Peter Porter has steadily built up a reputation as one of the most substantial and various talents among the English poets of the middle generation. An expatriate Australian who does not intend to return to the country of his birth (see "Sidney Cove, 1788" in *Poems Ancient and Modern* and "Recipe" in *A Porter Folio* for examples of his ironic and mistrusting attitude towards it), he casts a scathing and rueful eye on contemporary English civilisation; and yet is inescapably held by it. The loyalty is not only an aversion to an Australia where, he felt, writing in the *TLS* in 1971, "nobody has any natural talent and the Great Supervisor fails me over a whole range of Anglo-Saxon virtues." It is a positive adoption of England, and indeed Europe (in the wider cultural sense, not the constricted one of the Market "Europeans"). It is a respect for, and a comfort in the sense of, "the continuity of the living and the dead which I find in England":

Sailing away from ourselves, we feel
The gentle tug of water at the quay –
Language of the liberal dead speaks
From the soil at Highgate, tears
Show a great water table is intact.
You cannot leave England, it turns
A planet majestically in the mind.

To this point of affirmation, which is nevertheless much qualified by a brooding, increasing sense of the presence of death in his more recent poetry, he has moved through a series of volumes which have been unerring in their recording of the follies of mankind in general with a satire that is grave, sometimes brutal and always acutely observant. He has a considerable flair for a kind of bitter, epigrammatic wit and for elaborately entertaining fantasy (for example, "Fair Go for Anglo-Saxons" in *A Porter Folio*). If there is scarcely any lyric ease or relaxation in his writing, it is not all impassioned seriousness: he can often be extremely funny, sometimes in a sad self-deprecating vein but more often in a way which exorcises the facts of ageing and death with mordant, pertinacious satire (in *Preaching to the*

Converted, "Sex and the Over Forties" and "Affair of the Heart" show this side of his talent).

The strong positive element in Porter's poetry is there in his celebration of the high points of European culture (particularly in the field of music). The great artist survives death, remains a living presence in the sonatas of a Scarlatti or the portraits of a Giotto. But the lines on Giotto's portrait of Dante display the ambivalence out of which springs much of Porter's most arresting and absorbing verse:

> I've eaten in a restaurant named for you
> and seen your posthumous life-mask. You tell us
> we never get home but are buried in eternal exile.

Art is enduring, but death is even more enduring than art; and life is, at best, a kind of exile from any imaginable happiness or reassurance.

Both the satirical tone and the affirmations are echoed in Porter's two collaborations with the Australian artist Arthur Boyd on illustrated poem sequences. Porter essays modern readings of the two legends ("I don't like what's happening in Nineveh,/... it's all parks and permissiveness and lying about"). But these are much more comfortably and unobtrusively accommodated in the exquisitely illustrated *The Lady and the Unicorn* than in *Jonah*, where the modern references seem forced and where it would be charitable to describe Boyd's drawings as merely appalling.

The poems on personal themes, sometimes deriving from dreams (he describes his dreams as a kind of private cinema) or centred on his own personal life-patterns against a garish urban background, are, as a result, largely wry, angry, and self-reproaching; though the emotions are never simple. His love poetry presents that emotion as a tarnished thing, pitiable and unsuccessful, unsuited for treatment in a sensuous or delicate style:

> What I want is a particular body,
> The further particulars being obscene
> By definition. The obscenity is really me,
> Mad, wanting mad possession: what else can mad mean?

His entire style is formal and compressed, with moments of measured solemnity and some successful excursions into the grand manner. There is an air of highly intelligent, witty, intensely committed yet immensely zestful conversation about it; though he is rarely colloquial. This distinguishes him very clearly from contemporaries whose quest for a mode of self-revealing frankness leads them into mawkish self-indulgence or grandiose diffuseness. But Porter has achieved an impressive expansion of range, through the medium of his "versions" of the great Roman satirist, in his volume *After Martial*. Porter both updates Martial, making his satires pointful in a modern age of high, permissive living and egotistic pretentiousness, and preserves the spirit of the original. Otherwise, great formal artists of the past and present – Bach, Shakespeare, Laclos, Hardy, Stravinsky – remain his principal admirations; though a ranging, lively and formidable intellect draws him equally to Marston, Christopher Smart, Schopenhauer, Rilke, Mahler, Auden. There is considerable brilliance, and obvious relish, in his employment of the great as mentors, and in a sense, companions, in a life-situation out of which it is difficult to make final sense or derive any ultimate hope.

But the governing emotion in Porter's poetry is a fierce moral emphasis, suggesting that at least something may be wrested from the human predicament if we confront and understand the inadequacy and impermanence of life itself. All this gains an added poignancy in his most recent volume, *The Cost of Seriousness*, where poems about England, Australia, and the arts of literature, music and painting form a "frame" around a group of deeply moving poems occasioned by the tragic death of the poet's wife in December 1974. Writing elsewhere about this book, Porter describes its main concern as "the inability of art (poetry in this instance) to alter human circumstances or alleviate human distress." Yet the best poems here, as critics have generally acknowledged, show a new lucidity and power in the handling of the traditional major themes of poetry – love, war, death. They confirm the steady development of one of the most original talents in post-war English writing; and they fulfil Porter's own ambition of "making palatable somehow the real tragedy of the world."

—Alan Brownjohn

POULIN, A(lfred A.), Jr. American. Born in Lisbon, Maine, 14 March 1938. Educated at St. Francis College, Biddeford, Maine, B.A. 1960; Loyola University, Chicago, M.A. 1962; University of Iowa, Iowa City, M.F.A. 1968; State University of New York, Buffalo, 1975. Married Basilike H. Parkas in 1966; one daughter. Assistant Professor of English, 1962–64, 1968–71, and Chairman of the Division of Humanities, 1968–71, St. Francis College; Lecturer in English, University of Maryland European Division, Heidelberg, 1965, and University of New Hampshire, Durham, 1965–66. Since 1971, Member of the Department of English, Director of the Writer's Forum, 1972–75, and currently Professor and Faculty Exchange Scholar, State University of New York, Brockport. Since 1972, Editor at Large, *American Poetry Review*, Philadelphia; since 1976, Founding Editor, BOA Editions, Brockport, New York; since 1978, Founding Executive Director, New York State Literary Center, Rochester. Recipient: National Endowment for the Arts Fellowship, 1974, grant, 1978; Columbia University Translation Award, 1976; Ford Foundation grant, 1979. Address: 92 Park Avenue, Brockport, New York 14420, U.S.A.

PUBLICATIONS

Verse

In Advent. New York, Dutton, 1972.
Catawba: Omens, Prayers, and Songs. Port Townsend, Washington, Graywolf Press, 1977.
The Widow's Taboo: Poems after Catawba. Tokyo, Mushinsha, 1977.
The Nameless Garden. Athens, Ohio, Croissant, 1978.

Other

Editor, with David A. DeTurk, *The American Folk Scene: Dimensions of the Folksong Revival.* New York, Dell, 1967.
Editor, *Contemporary American Poetry.* Boston, Houghton Mifflin, 1971.

Translator, *Duino Elegies and The Sonnets to Orpheus*, by Rainer Maria Rilke. Boston, Houghton Mifflin, 1977.
Translator, *Saltimbanques: Prose Poems*, by Rainer Maria Rilke. Port Townsend, Washington, Graywolf Press, 1978.
Translator, *The Roses and The Windows*, by Rainer Maria Rilke. Port Townsend, Washington, Graywolf Press, 1979.
Translator, *Eve: Poems*, by Anne Hébert. Princeton, New Jersey, Quarterly Review of Literature, 1980.

* * *

A. Poulin, Jr., is perhaps best known for his work editing *Contemporary American Poetry*, as fine an anthology of its subject as one will find. In an essay in that book Poulin states that politics, sex, and religion are three of the major concerns to which today's poets address themselves. As his own volumes of poetry, *In Advent* and *Catawba*, reveal, these are certainly the concerns of Poulin himself.

The American political scene of the Vietnam era produced many protest poems, but, unfortunately, most of these were written with too much topicality and too little art. But Poulin's "Famine: 1970" is a poem that merits many rereadings, and it is a work that will be relevant whenever any society at any time becomes a moral wasteland:

The cry of frogs rings the island, rings,
bullets ricocheting off raw steel. Spring.
Tonight the full moon rises pure, precise,
and deadly cold. Everything will freeze.

Trees petrify, their first and fragile
leaves the clatter of slate chips. In
the garden sharp white shoots are glowing
bones of young men rising in revenge.

Buds on bushes fall and shatter, empty
eggs and skulls of a generation turned
to salt. Our eyes turn and, marble, shine.
Our hands and feet root into veins of lead.

Our mouths already fill with sand.
And beyond the moonlight, in the dark dawn
will never break, we can hear the long and
eager moan of boulders as they mate and spawn.

Like this poem, Poulin's other poetry is filled with fearful forebodings. For example, in "Script Prospectus," addressed to his wife, the poet says, "any/day some stranger, relative, or/friend will kill me. Or you will." A paranoic fear of his own death and the loss of loved ones stalks the poet throughout *In Advent*. Fortunately, there are moments of happiness, as in the closing section of the remarkable "Buddha and the Pirates," another poem to the poet's wife, who he fears has been unfaithful:

Morning sails into our bedroom, the splintered
ghost of a Venetian ship.
You aren't here. I find
you in the sunlight
of the alcove. Once more,
across the ocean of my
deepest nightmare, you've
come back, our baby at your
breast. Love, my Buddha,
you are always here.

Love is, indeed, Poulin's Buddha. In his poetry love and religion are inseparably united. In the poem "In Advent," for instance, the birth of Poulin's baby is linked to the birth of Christ. Poulin's poems find in the worship of loved ones a faith that enables the poet to live in a savage world.

A very different world is found in *Catawba*, a thin volume in which Poulin successfully recreates the voice of the Catawba Indians. These poems awaken in us a reverence for a culture based on the most elemental human values. In this volume we listen to Indians pray to insects, teach simple virtues to their children, prescribe folk remedies, and even retell moments of creation, as in "Hummingbird": "the hummingbird was made by a man/he took a dandelion turned to seed/he held it in his hand and blew on it/yes and a hummingbird flew off/that man was very smart." And so were the Catawba Indians, a tribe that Poulin feels has much to teach us.

In his poems about the politics, sex, and religion of our day, and in his poems about the customs and beliefs of a lost culture, Poulin has sought clues to help him survive in this world. These clues have in turn led to a continual process of self-discovery. As Poulin says in "Totem," "I am arriving to myself." Though he is a poet fully aware of the worst horrors of our times, he is also a poet fully aware of our highest potentials. As such, A. Poulin, Jr., is one of the most hopeful poets currently at work.

—Dennis Lynch

POWELL, Craig. Australian. Born in Wollongong, New South Wales, 16 November 1940. Educated at Sydney Boys' High School; Sydney University, M.B., B.S. 1964; New South Wales Institute of Psychiatry. Married Janet Dawson in 1965; one daughter and one son. Resident Medical Officer, Royal Prince Alfred Hospital, 1965, and Western Suburbs Hospital, Sydney, 1966; Psychiatrist, Parramatta Psychiatric Centre, Sydney, 1968–72, and Brandon Mental Health Centre, Manitoba, 1972–75. Since 1976, Psychiatrist, London Psychiatric Hospital, Ontario. Member, Royal Australian and New Zealand College of Psychiatrists, 1971. Recipient: *Poetry Magazine* Award, 1964; Commonwealth Literary Fund grant, 1966, 1968, 1972; Henry Lawson Festival Award, 1969; Canada Council grant, 1977. Address: London Psychiatric Hospital, Box 2532, Terminal A, London, Ontario N6A 4H1, Canada.

PUBLICATIONS

Verse

A Different Kind of Breathing. Sydney, South Head Press, 1966.
I Learn by Going. Sydney, South Head Press, 1968.
A Country Without Exiles. Sydney, South Head Press, 1972.
Selected Poems 1963–1977. London, Ontario, Killaly Press, 1977.
Rehearsal for Dancers. Winnipeg, Turnstone Press, 1978.

Manuscript Collection: Mitchell Library, Sydney.

Critical Study: "Gauging Honesty, Engaging Voice" by William H. New, in *Poetry Australia 49* (Sydney), 1973.

Craig Powell comments:

I was a musician for many years before I began writing poetry. While my work is less formal than it used to be, the musical element remains crucial. My poems are written as a witness to the sustaining, and disdaining, inward spirit; and to the mortal human body which, if it cannot rise beyond its own existence, can at least fall slowly dancing.

* * *

Just as Melbourne University, in the late 1950's, produced a group of lively poets who forced readers to reconsider available currency, so Sydney University in the early 1960's produced three poets who were to epitomise the counter-claim of a revived Vitalist tradition. These were Geoffrey Lehmann, Les A. Murray, and Craig Powell. Of the three, Powell has been least concerned with expounding large scale Life Views. Indeed, his most characteristic verse has been confined within the limitations of the sonnet and the triolet forms.

As a medical practitioner, Craig Powell has openly expressed an admiration of the American poet-medico Merrill Moore, who was reputed to have filing cabinets of sonnets stored away. Powell has never achieved, however, the relaxed assurance of Merrill Moore. His work is essentially dramatic, a performance. For this reason, he is most successful in poems that deal with themes of violence or conflict. Undoubtedly his best work is in the group of hospital and psychiatric poems in his third volume, or in the openly rhetorical "In Memory of Hans Mueller," possibly one of the most effective poems written in Australia on the Vietnam theme. In poems of a personal or lyric tone, one senses an underlying discomfort, with the result that the gestures often fail to convince. Craig Powell is still a young and developing writer. His best work has an admirable vigour and punch – and a formal control – that promise considerable scope for growth and development.

—Thomas W. Shapcott

POWELL, Neil. British. Born in London, 11 February 1948. Educated at Sevenoaks School, Kent, 1959–66; University of Warwick, Coventry, 1966–71, B.A. in English and American literature 1969, M.Phil. in English 1975. Teacher of English, Kimbolton School, Huntingdon, 1971–74. Since 1974, Teacher of English, St. Christopher School, Letchworth, Hertfordshire. Recipient: Eric Gregory Award, 1969. Address: The Mews, 5 Cambridge House, Hitchin Street, Baldock, Hertfordshire SG7 6AE, England.

PUBLICATIONS

Verse

At Little Gidding. Rushden, Northamptonshire, Sceptre Press, 1974.
Afternoon Dawn. Hitchin, Hertfordshire, Cellar Press, 1975.
Suffolk Poems. Hitchin, Hertfordshire, Mandeville Press, 1975.
Four Letters. Sundridge, Kent, Letter Press, 1976.
A Mandeville Troika, with Peter Scupham and George Szirtes. Hitchin, Hertfordshire, Mandeville Press, 1977.
At the Edge. Manchester, Carcanet Press, and Chester Springs, Pennsylvania, Dufour, 1977.
Out of Time. Hitchin, Hertfordshire, Mandeville Press, 1979.

Other

A Commentary on Henry V. Petersfield, Hampshire, Studytapes, 1973.
Carpenters of Light: A Critical Study of Contemporary British Poetry. Manchester, Carcanet Press, 1979; New York, Barnes and Noble, 1980.

* * *

Neil Powell's collection, *At the Edge*, carries as epigraph a verse by Donald Davie: "The purest hue, let only the light be sufficient/Turns colour"; the book itself is a conscious attempt to form a poetic in accordance with the precept. A firm admiration for the controlled force found in the work of Davie and Thom Gunn has led him to a consciousness that to write poetry is to exercise the intelligence, as well as the heart, and that the disciplines of a severe formalism are those most likely to prove fruitful:

> The poem's flow – the rock pools or the bends,
> Metre or syntax, shaping its slow progress –
>
> Becomes a formal fountain as we turn
> Our private art to public artifice.

The exact and exacting patterns, accurate rhyme-schemes, and clear stanzaic forms of the poems are deployed to hold up to the light episodes of time past and time present: inside these crystals the past and the present become each other, and their relationship is celebrated with a restrained, intelligent affection and a consciousness that ends and beginnings are artful mimics of each other:

> The years are misting over. I recall
> Something I didn't say a dream ago,
> Return abruptly to the reading class.
> The weeping condensation on a window
> Becomes the image of another day,
> A conversation in a different place
> Minutely glimpsed, and very far away.

In these handy-dandyings of personal time Powell makes an easy, rueful use of a conjuror's personal box of props: a golden world gathers its tarnish to the accompaniment of a bric-a-brac of talk, drink, jazz, and old sunlight. More subtle and striking deeper home come the meditations on time in collusion with place. The poems show a wariness of dramatic effects and grand gestures, at their happiest with the undemonstrative and hidden landscapes of East Anglia. The poet is frequently found in the role of eavesdropper, watcher, revenant, alert for the chance disclosure of some part of the secret compact which place and time have made: a compact itself under threat.

> Trespasser? Tenant? Neither will win, the sea insists,
>   in the vanished places – Dunwich, Walberswick –
> where lanes scrawl to the margin of a torn-off coastline
>   whose history is rewritten by the tide.

Always beyond the local familiarities and the boundaries, the edges and lines formed by masons and poets, lie worlds evading circumscription. Some of Powell's most impressive poems move out towards enigmatic and uncharted areas of sea, dizzying weathers, oblivion. Roads lead endlessly and nightmarishly on

> Until "The North" proclaims a giant sign,
> As if the north were somewhere you could reach
> By following a disembodied line
> Which joins nowhere to nowhere, each to each,
>
> And work to home. Or will it merely end
> In featureless space, an orange void stretching
> On each side of the road, round the next bend,
> With distant amber lamps, the planets, gleaming?

The stance taken by the poet at this stage of his career is one of some ambivalence: the game is played neither at home nor away, but often in some temporary ground we may provisionally call either. Metaphor is used sparingly; Powell prefers an accurate and evocative use of detail held in place by an intellectual scaffolding. This can lead to a rather dry philosophical tone and a preponderance of abstraction in the weaker poems. His more recent work shows a relaxed and sparer style emerging, however, which promises to bring a suppler tension to his forms:

> I walk through the silent town. A breeze is blowing
> Snuffed-out candles from horse-chestnut trees,
> The unknown is on the air, and I am knowing
> Something I cannot recognise, unless
>
> It is a distant prospect of the future, showing
> All that is and all that will come to be,
> As blossoms of the past are going, going.

—Peter Scupham

PRINCE, F(rank) T(empleton). British. Born in Kimberley, Cape Province, South Africa, 13 September 1912. Educated at Christian Brothers' College, Kimberley; Balliol College, Oxford; Princeton University, New Jersey, 1935–36; Study Groups Department, Chatham House, 1937–40. Served in the Intelligence Corps, 1940–46. Married Pauline Elizabeth Bush in 1943; two children. Member of the English Department, from 1946, and Professor of English, 1957–74, University of Southampton. Visiting Fellow, All Souls College, Oxford, 1968–69; Clark Lecturer, Cambridge University, 1972–73; Professor of English, University of the West Indies, Jamaica, 1975–78; Visiting Professor, Brandeis University, Waltham, Massachusetts, 1978–79, and Amherst College, Massachusetts, 1979. Address: 32 Brookvale Road, Southampton, Hampshire, England.

PUBLICATIONS

Verse

Poems. London, Faber, and New York, New Directions, 1938.
Soldiers Bathing and Other Poems. London, Fortune Press, 1954.
The Stolen Heart. San Francisco, Press of the Morning Sun, 1957.
The Doors of Stone: Poems 1938–1962. London, Hart Davis, 1963.
Memoirs in Oxford. London, Fulcrum Press, 1970.
Penguin Modern Poets 20, with John Heath-Stubbs and Stephen Spender. London, Penguin, 1971.
Drypoints of the Hasidim. London, Menard Press, 1975.
Afterword of Rupert Brooke. London, Menard Press, 1976.
Collected Poems. London, Anvil Press Poetry-Menard Press, and New York, Sheep Meadow Press, 1979.

Other

The Italian Element in Milton's Verse. Oxford, Clarendon Press, 1954.

In Defense of English (lecture). Southampton, University of Southampton Press, 1959.
William Shakespeare: The Poems. London, Longman, 1963.

Editor, *Samson Agonistes*, by Milton. London, Oxford University Press, 1957.
Editor, *The Poems*, by Shakespeare. London, Methuen, and Cambridge, Massachusetts, Harvard University Press, 1960.
Editor, *Paradise Lost, Books I and II*, by Milton. London, Oxford University Press, 1962.
Editor, *Comus and Other Poems*, by Milton. London, Oxford University Press, 1968.

Translator, *Sir Thomas Wyatt*, by Sergio Baldi. London, Longman, 1961.

* * *

F. T. Prince, in introducing his collected poems, *The Doors of Stone*, said these were all he wished to preserve of his published work. They amounted to fewer than 50 poems. From this one may judge the poet's acute fastidiousness, his inability to accept anything from himself that is not of the best. Hence the extraordinary quality of these poems: "Soldiers Bathing," perhaps the finest individual poem of the war, and "The Old Age of Michelangelo," exquisite like the sculptor's cartoon that links it with the previous poem.

Whereas his native South Africa, in its physical beauty of flower and fauna and the heroic quality of its legends, provided Prince with the themes of his early poems, leaving us with gems such as "Moonflower" and "The Babiaantje," the broad tradition of European civilisation and in particular Renaissance Italy exerted a later and more profound influence on his writing, not only as poet but as critic and university teacher. The poems issuing from this influence reveal the gravity and clearness of his thought and imagery, a concern for language that is masterly in its accuracy and its elegance. In fact, when so much of the verse of our time, though powerful, lacks polish, Prince is outstanding for his artistry, chiselling at his images and at his construction so that his poems are always finished, carrying no ballast, nothing in the rough. They demand reading and re-reading that nothing be lost of them.

Handling the English language as a master craftsman is one thing but what really makes Prince's work memorable is his own humanity and compassion, a sombre note amounting almost to melancholy, marking much of what he writes. In "Soldiers Bathing," for instance, as he watches his "band/Of soldiers who belong to me," he sees them transformed by his compassion:

> All pathos now. The body that was gross
> Rank, ravenous, disgusting in the act or in repose,
> All fever, filth and sweat, its bestial strength
> And bestial decay, by pain and labour grows at length
> Fragile and luminous.

The same quality of compassionate feeling also distinguishes his most beautiful cycle of love poems, the final sequence, "The Question," surely one of the finest love poems of our time, where the language twists the heart through the maze that all lovers know:

> For we know nothing but that, long ago,
> We learnt to 'ove God whom we cannot know.
> I touch your eyelids that one day must close,
> Your lips as perishable as a rose:
> And say that all must fade, before we know
> *The thing we know of but we do not know.*

Although a streak of melancholy runs through much of Prince's poetry, there is a measure of comfort there, too. In relating a particular experience, whether at war or in love, to man's broader experience as revealed by artists and writers of the distant past, and in the final resort, to the Son of Man himself, as revealed by God, something of the loneliness of the moment departs:

> ... as I drink the dusky air,
> I feel a strange delight that fills me full,
> Strange gratitude, as if evil itself were beautiful,
> And kiss the wound in thought, while in the west
> I watch a streak of red that might have issued from Christ's breast.

Regret at the thinness of Prince's poetic production is surely tempered by gratitude for what we have.

—Roy Macnab

PROKOSCH, Frederic. American. Born in Madison, Wisconsin, 17 May 1908. Educated at Haverford College, Pennsylvania, 1922–25, M.A. 1926; Yale University, New Haven, Connecticut, 1930–31, Ph.D. 1933; King's College, Cambridge, 1935–37, M.A. 1937. Instructor in English, Yale University, 1932–34, and New York University, 1936–37; Printer, of modern poetry, in Bryn Mawr, Pennsylvania, Cambridge, Florence, Venice and Lisbon, 1933–40; Cultural Attaché, American Legation, Stockholm, 1943–45; Visiting Lecturer, University of Rome, 1950–51. Squash-Racquets Champion of France, 1933–39, and of Sweden, 1944. Recipient: Guggenheim Fellowship, 1937; Harper Prize, 1937; Harriet Monroe Memorial Prize (*Poetry*, Chicago), 1941; Fulbright Fellowship, 1951; National Endowment for the Arts fellowship, 1978. Address: "Ma Trouvaille," Plan de Grasse, Alpes Maritimes, France.

PUBLICATIONS

Verse

Three Mysteries. New Haven, Connecticut, privately printed, 1932.
Three Sorrows. New Haven, Connecticut, privately printed, 1932.
Three Deaths. New Haven, Connecticut, privately printed, 1932.
Three Images. New Haven, Connecticut, privately printed, 1932.
The Voyage. Bryn Mawr, Pennsylvania, privately printed, 1933.
The Dolls. Bryn Mawr, Pennsylvania, privately printed, 1933.
The Grotto. Bryn Mawr, Pennsylvania, privately printed, 1933.
The Enemies. Bryn Mawr, Pennsylvania, privately printed, 1934.
The Survivors. Bryn Mawr, Pennsylvania, privately printed, 1934.
Going Southward. Bryn Mawr, Pennsylvania, privately printed, 1935.
The Red Sea. Cambridge, privately printed, 1935.
Andromeda. Cambridge, privately printed, 1935.
The Assassins. Cambridge, privately printed, 1936.
The Assassins (collection). New York, Harper, and London, Chatto and Windus, 1936.
The Sacred Wood. Cambridge, privately printed, 1936.
The Carnival. New York, Harper, and London, Chatto and Windus, 1938.
Death at Sea. New York, Harper, and London, Chatto and Windus, 1940.

Sunburned Ulysses. Lisbon, privately printed, 1941.
Among the Caves. Lisbon, privately printed, 1941.
Song. New York, privately printed, 1941.
Song. Stockholm, privately printed, 1943.
Fable. New York, privately printed, 1944.
Chosen Poems. London, Chatto and Windus, 1944; New York, Doubleday, 1947.
The Flamingoes. Rome, privately printed, 1948.
Snow Song. Paris, privately printed, 1949.
Boat Song. Venice, privately printed, 1950.
Wood Song. Florence, privately printed, 1951.
Phantom Song. Naples, privately printed, 1952.
Banquet Song. Barcelona, privately printed, 1953.
Temple Song. Stuttgart, privately printed, 1954.
Fire Song. Zurich, privately printed, 1955.
Island Song. Hong Kong, privately printed, 1956.
Jungle Song. Bangkok, privately printed, 1957.
The Death Ship. Singapore, privately printed, 1958.
The Ghost City. Antwerp, privately printed, 1959.
The Mirror. Vienna, privately printed, 1960.

Novels

The Asiatics. New York, Harper, and London, Chatto and Windus, 1935.
The Seven Who Fled. New York, Harper, and London, Chatto and Windus, 1937.
Night of the Poor. New York, Harper, and London, Chatto and Windus, 1939.
The Skies of Europe. New York, Harper, 1941; London, Chatto and Windus, 1942.
The Conspirators. New York, Harper, and London, Chatto and Windus, 1943.
Age of Thunder. New York, Harper, and London, Chatto and Windus, 1945.
The Idols of the Cave. New York, Doubleday, 1946; London, Chatto and Windus, 1947.
Storm and Echo. New York, Doubleday, 1948; London, Faber, 1949.
Nine Days to Mukalla. New York, Viking Press, and London, Secker and Warburg, 1953.
A Tale for Midnight. Boston, Little Brown, 1955; London, Secker and Warburg, 1956.
A Ballad of Love. New York, Farrar Straus, 1960; London, Secker and Warburg, 1961.
The Seven Sisters. New York, Farrar Straus, 1962; London, Secker and Warburg, 1963.
The Dark Dancer. New York, Farrar Straus, 1964; London, W. H. Allen, 1965.
The Wreck of the Cassandra. New York, Farrar Straus, and London, W. H. Allen, 1966.
The Missolonghi Manuscript. New York, Farrar Straus, and London, W. H. Allen, 1968.
America, My Wilderness. New York, Farrar Straus, and London, W. H. Allen, 1971.

Other

Translator, *Some Poems of Friedrich Hölderlin.* New York, New Directions, 1943; London, Grey Walls Press, 1947.
Translator, *Love Sonnets of Louise Labé.* New York, New Directions, 1947; London, Grey Walls Press, 1948.

Manuscript Collection: University of Texas, Austin.

Critical Study: *Frederic Prokosch* by Radcliffe Squires, New York, Twayne, 1964.

Frederic Prokosch comments:

(1974) A poet is ill-advised to make a "personal statement," i.e., a *credo*. He cannot possibly do justice to himself in this manner. It will sound stilted, coy, pompous, irrelevant, even false. As I meditate on the question of why my poetry is totally unlike all other contemporary poetry, I feel puzzled; but I conclude that my conception of a poem is not the current one. To use a poem as a "confessional," a "protest," or a manifesto, a self-analysis or in any way as a self-indulgence, seems to me to abuse and degrade the true function of poetry. A poem should aim for the perfection, the timeless and impersonal "stillness" of a Chinese vase. I think of Yeats and Rilke; I think of Catullus, Goethe and Hölderlin. The present is not an age for poetry, needless to say. The timeless, impersonal stillness is drowned in an orgy of howls and moans, not to mention vituperations, indignations, and masturbations.

(1980) Still, I feel that there is a change in the air. Auden heralded the change, and it was also signaled by Dylan Thomas (though in both cases there was a sharp deterioration in their final phases). I mean this: that certain limits are eventually reached in the purely exploratory. Exploration per se is refreshing and liberating, to be sure, but it becomes a cul-de-sac if it isn't continually nourished by new passions, new experiences, new aperçus. It imposes in the end an artificial strain on the poet, the painter, the novelist. But I detect a new freshness creeping into the atmosphere, a liberation from dogma, a rejection of doctrine, and a subtler, more delicate spirit of affirmation.

* * *

Frederic Prokosch made his reputation with three volumes, *The Assassins*, *The Carnival*, and *Death at Sea*, published just before or at the beginning of the second World War. His poetry impressed T. S. Eliot and Edwin Muir, and it shows the evidence of influences, particularly those of Eliot himself and Yeats, which it was impossible for any ripening talent to avoid at that period. His work has, however, an undoubted poetic individuality. In the first place it is elaborate, sumptuous, formal, musical, characteristically checking the usual long gliding line with a shorter, sharper turn. In the second, there is something of an older, a more traditional and European, manner in the poet's calm assumption of a public pose, in his treatment of the grand, impressive theme, in the formal clarity of his diction and his intricately rhyming patterns. Not that he isn't, clearly, highly sensitive to the strains of his own violent times. He is intensely moved by the combination in reality of style and disaster, by the blend, for example, in "The Country House" of platonic, shadowed lawns, cool airs, instinctive poise, and howling conflagration, or in "Molière" of the suppressed presence in an intricately spun civilisation, with its lucid laws of reason, its learning and perception, of Othello's howl and Dido's unforgettable cave. He is much preoccupied with Yeats's rough beast, and he is conscious beneath the mask of civilisation of the hooked, retaliating nightmare and the horrible disorderly whirlpool. The particular attractiveness of the poetry comes from its joining a cool and cultivated surface to a nightmare vision of inward and inevitable fatality. In Frederic Prokosch's reading of life, the clipped and ordered park, the salon, the formal avenue he so much appreciates and so finely evokes, are "rosy with the approaching glow and spectacle of Hell."

—William Walsh

PRYNNE, J. H. British. Born in the United Kingdom, in 1936.

PUBLICATIONS

Verse

Force of Circumstance and Other Poems. London, Routledge, 1962.
Kitchen Poems. London, Cape Goliard Press, and New York, Grossman, 1968.
Day Light Songs. Pampisford, Cambridgeshire, R. Books, 1968.
Aristeas. London, Ferry Press, 1968.
The White Stones. Lincoln, Grosseteste Press, 1969.
Fire Lizard. Barnet, Hertfordshire, Blacksuede Boot Press, 1970.
Brass. London, Ferry Press, 1971.
Into the Day. Privately printed, 1972.
A Night Square. London, Albion Village Press, 1973.
Wound Response. Cambridge, Street, 1974.
High Pink on Chrome. Privately printed, 1975.
News of Warring Clans. London, Trigram Press, 1977.
Down Where Changed. London, Ferry Press, 1979.

* * *

J. H. Prynne's poetry is at the least a worthy attempt at a totally interior monologue, but it raises the questions of whether the English language can accommodate an absolutely alyrical style – and of whether a strategy of evasion, based on statements that have a resolutely inner reference can yield apprehensible truths. Is Prynne's work in effect simply hideously and disingenuously mannered, or do its oddities convey a sense of human existence hitherto unaccessible?

> ... The
> moraine runs axial to the Finchley Road
> including his hippopotamus, which isn't a
> joke any more than the present fringe
> of intellectual habit. They did live as
> the evidence is ready, for the successive
> drift....

This poem, "The Glacial Question, Unsolved," does contain several references; and its method is much the same, commendably, no doubt, as Alexander Cozens' was in his Blot Drawings. The lack of any discernible rhythm, the bleak "jokes" – these are disturbing; but are they potent ironies, or do they belong to a private notebook? How hard is it to write this kind of poetry if you set your mind to it? Is it original or merely eccentric? The reader has to thank Prynne for raising such questions in the mind by the courageous use of a procedure involving the ju-jitsu-like use of dehumanized boredom which, like any movement in the human mind, may be viewed as a partial achievement. One may add that this poetry ingeniously calls forth its own brand of criticism.

—Martin Seymour-Smith

PRYS-JONES, A(rthur) G(lyn). British (Welsh). Born in Denbigh, North Wales, 7 March 1888. Educated at Llandovery College, Carmarthenshire; Jesus College, Oxford (History Scholar), B.A. (honours) 1912, M.A. 1912. Formerly, Assistant Master, Dulwich College, London; Inspector of Schools, Wales; Staff Inspector, Secondary Education, Wales, 1919–49. Secretary, Welsh Committee, Festival of Britain, 1950–52; Co-Founder and former Chairman, Cardiff Little Theatre; former Chairman, Cardiff Literary Society. Currently, Vice-President, Cardiff Writers Circle; President, English Section, Welsh Academy. O.B.E. (Officer, Order of the British Empire), 1949. Address: 50 Coombe Lane West, Kingston-upon-Thames, Surrey KT2 7BY, England.

PUBLICATIONS

Verse

Poems of Wales. Oxford, Blackwell, 1923.
Rreen Places: Poems of Wales. Aberystwyth, Gwasg Aberystwyth, 1948.
A Little Nonsense. Cowbridge, Glamorgan, Eastgate Press, 1954.
High Heritage: Poems of Wales. Llandybie, Dyfed, Christopher Davies, 1969.
Valedictory Verses. Llandysul, Dyfed, Gomer, 1978.

Other

Gerald of Wales: His "Itinerary" Through Wales and His "Description" of the Country and Its People. London, Harrap, 1955.
The Story of Carmarthenshire. Llandybie, Dyfed, Christopher Davies, 2 vols., 1959–72.

Editor, *Welsh Poets: A Representative Selection in English from Contemporary Writers.* London, Erskine Macdonald, 1917.
Co-Editor, *They Look at Wales.* Cardiff, University of Wales Press, 1946.
Editor, *The Fountain of Life: Prose and Verse from the Authorized Version of the Bible.* London, Pan Books, 1949; Boston, Beacon Press, 1950.
Co-Editor, *The National Songs of Wales.* London, Boosey and Hawkes, 1959.

A. G. Prys-Jones comments:

My themes are almost entirely concerned with the past history, traditions, personalities and scenery of Wales: and my approach is essentially simple, lyrical and romantic. I aim at making my poems pass the test of being read or declaimed aloud, and thus suitable for individual or choral speech. A number have been set to music and published as songs. If I have succeeded at all, it is in this direction, and also in having interpreted the past of Wales, more especially for its young people. In my writing I often use some of the simpler metrical and alliterative devices of Welsh poetry.

* * *

Most of the veteran A. G. Prys-Jones's poems in his volume *High Heritage* (1969) appeared in *Poems of Wales* (1923) and *Green Places* (1948). He himself has modestly suggested that *High Heritage* is intended as an anthology for verse-speaking in schools, and certainly it is a book eminently suitable for this purpose. He has brought into modern English verse something of the visual imagery shaped by his native Welsh tongue. Technically adept, he has a very delicate sense of rhythm, as shown in "Spring Comes to Glamorgan," and a refined gift for the original image:

And how the ragged mendicants of mist
In shifty garb risc up from stcalthy lairs
Thrusting their shapeless hands about your face.

Prys-Jones's style is unfashionable nowadays, but he manages to project the Georgian manner into the turbulent present or past, maintaining a regular rhyme-scheme and a firm stanza-structure. Thus, his well-known, rollicking "Henry Morgan's March on Panama":

Twelve hundred famished buccaneers,
Bitten, blistered and bled,
A sweltering mob, accursed and flayed
By the fierce sun overhead:
Twelve hundred starving scarecrows
With hardly a crust to eat,
And only sips from festering pools
In that grim, monstrous heat.

This has been called "Chestertonian heroic verse in the style of the twenties," and such a strict structure does tend to limit the intention that certain poems are supposed to fulfil. Soaked in history, most of his work involves celebration or nostalgia, reflecting the formal Georgian mode, which could be so exquisite and yet so fustian. He has no time for jagged irregularity, being interested only in building and holding a consistent form. In this he has long reached a mastery, and it is a pity that the stock phrases of "modern" criticism are not equipped to cope with skilled structures like Prys-Jones's, even if his content now appears to be somewhat obsolete. He has a high command of language, splendidly shaped, and many moments of rare beauty which could make a welcome return in our own gloomy time – such as this musical glimpse of a historic Wales: "The tides of evening pass, deep-drenched with rose/And all the perfumes of the summer night."

—John Tripp

PURCELL, Sally (Anne Jane). British. Born 1 December 1944. Educated at Lady Margaret Hall, Oxford (Countess of Warwick prize, 1965), B.A. 1966, M.A. 1970. Recipient: Arts Council award, 1971. Address: c/o Anvil Press Poetry, 69 King George Street, London, SE10 8PX, England.

PUBLICATIONS

Verse

The Devil's Dancing Hour. London, Anvil Press Poetry, 1968.
The Holly Queen. London, Anvil Press Poetry, 1972.
(*Poems*). Berkhamsted, Hertfordshire, Priapus Press, 1976.
Dark of Day. London, Anvil Press Poetry, 1977.

Other

Editor, with Libby Purves, *The Happy Unicorns: The Poetry of the Under-25's.* London, Sidgwick and Jackson, 1971.
Editor, *George Peele.* Oxford, Carcanet Press, 1972.

Editor and Translator, *Monarchs and the Muse: Poems by Monarchs and Princes of England, Scotland, and Wales.* Oxford, Carcanet Press, 1972.
Editor, *The Poems of Charles of Orleans.* Cheadle, Cheshire, Carcanet Press, 1973.

Translator, *Provençal Poems.* Oxford, Carcanet Press, 1969.
Translator, *The Exile of James Joyce*, by Hélène Cixous. New York, David Lewis, 1972; London, Calder, 1976.

Sally Purcell comments:

I was brought up as a classicist, and I believe in courtesy, craftsmanship and honesty.

* * *

Sally Purcell read Medieval French at Lady Margaret Hall, Oxford, and she has published a volume of translations from the troubadour poetry of Provence. Her researches and studies clearly coloured her early poetry both in its content and texture. Many of these poems, in the form of dramatic lyrics, explored the mysteries and characters of classical and medieval legends. Their very titles were indicative of their nature: "Bale Fires on the Dark Moor," "Loquitur Arthurus," "Tarot XII." The settings too, were in keeping: misty shires, a drowned winter world, a petrified chalcedony forest or a ring of standing stones. What gave these poems their special quality was Sally Purcell's imaginative insight into that twilight world of superstition, replete with "prodigies and signs of doom" and especially her ability to pinpoint the accompanying physical sensations of such a world:

Queen Proserpina walks
   through late autumn:
the glowing fruits of ice
   that she holds
covers the dying sun, & chills
   all ripeness to the bone

The best way to describe the texture of the verse is as that of an intellectual sensuality where the precise syntax both knits the poems together and leads the reader into them, while the involvement of the physical senses creates the necessary suspension of disbelief. Thus in "Baroque Episode" Sally Purcell is able to engage the reader in an imagined world where,

Mingling blood for love's token
He hopes to symbolise affection's depth
Achieve the untenable equation
That added selves make one.

It is a world where self-delusion is rife, and in "Oxford, Early Michaelmas Term" she draws a modern parallel where "hypnotised by hearsay, by skilful propaganda – the aesthetes flower gently."

In her more recent poetry Sally Purcell has used these skills to invest landscapes and places with a curiously threatening purpose, as if each embodied their own myths, giving them a past and a future existing collaterally, a sense of unreleased powers locked in stone or hill:

Castellan of a strong headland, forever
Build, renew defences out of silt and rock
Against the shifting meadows of olive or turquoise light;
Here only detail and haste are known –
Further out, the historian or another sees
In Time the laborious perfect.

All the time there smoulders in the background a dark sensuality waiting to entrap the unwary and the pretentious:

> the muse medusa caresses her body,
> glories in her flesh firmness,
> smiles at the promises they assume
> who believe in her advances.

It is a poetry of forebodings and warnings, as much against its own tenebrous embraces as any other.

—John Cotton

PURDY, Al(fred Wellington). Canadian. Born in Wooller, Ontario, 30 December 1918. Educated at Dufferin Public School, Trenton, Ontario; Albert College, Belleville, Ontario; Trenton Collegiate Institute, Ontario. Served with the Royal Canadian Air Force during World War II. Married Eurithe Parkhurst in 1941; one son. Has held numerous jobs; taught at Simon Fraser University, Burnaby, British Columbia, Spring 1970; Poet-in-Residence, Loyola College, Montreal, 1973, University of Manitoba, Winnipeg, 1975–76, and University of Western Ontario, London, 1977–78. Recipient: Canada Council Fellowship, 1960, 1965, 1968, 1971, award, 1973, and grant, 1974, 1977; President's Medal, University of Western Ontario, 1964; Governor-General's Award, 1966; A. J. M. Smith Prize, 1974; Jubilee Medal, 1978. Address: Rural Route 1, Ameliasburgh, Ontario K0K 1A0, Canada.

PUBLICATIONS

Verse

The Enchanted Echo. Privately printed, 1944.
Pressed on Sand. Toronto, Ryerson Press, 1955.
Emu, Remember! Fredericton, University of New Brunswick, 1956.
The Crafte So Longe to Lerne. Toronto, Ryerson Press, 1959.
Poems for All the Annettes. Toronto, Contact Press, 1962.
The Blur in Between: Poems 1960–61. Toronto, Emblem, 1963.
The Cariboo Horses. Toronto, McClelland and Stewart, 1965.
North of Summer: Poems from Baffin Land. Toronto, McClelland and Stewart, 1967.
Poems for All the Annettes (selected poems). Toronto, Anansi, 1968.
Wild Grape Wine. Toronto, McClelland and Stewart, 1968.
Spring Song. Fredericton, New Brunswick, Fiddlehead, 1968.
Love in a Burning Building. Toronto, McClelland and Stewart, 1970.
Five Modern Canadian Poets, with others, edited by Eli Mandel. Toronto, Holt Rinehart, 1970.
The Quest for Ouzo. Trenton, Ontario, M. Kerrigan Almey, 1970.
Selected Poems. Toronto, McClelland and Stewart, 1972.
Hiroshima Poems. Trumansburg, New York, Crossing Press, 1972.
On the Bearpaw Sea. Burnaby, British Columbia, Blackfish Press, 1972.
Sex and Death. Toronto, McClelland and Stewart, 1973.
Scott Hutcheson's Boat. Prince George, British Columbia, Caledonia, 1973.

In Search of Owen Roblin. Toronto, McClelland and Stewart, 1974.
Sundance at Dusk. Toronto, McClelland and Stewart, 1976.
To Feed the Sun. Toronto, Three Trees Press, 1976.
The Poems of Al Purdy. Toronto, McClelland and Stewart, 1976.
At Marsport Drugstore. Sutton West, Ontario, Paget Press, 1977.
A Handful of Earth. Coatsworth, Ontario, Black Moss Press, 1977.
Being Alive: Poems 1958–78. Toronto, McClelland and Stewart, 1978.
Moths in the Iron Curtain. Sutton West, Ontario, Paget Press, 1979.

Other

No Other Country. Toronto, McClelland and Stewart, 1977.

Editor, *The New Romans: Candid Canadian Opinions of the United States.* Edmonton, Alberta, Hurtig, and New York, St. Martin's Press, 1968.
Editor, *Fifteen Winds: A Selection of Modern Canadian Poems.* Toronto, Ryerson Press, 1969.
Editor, *I've Tasted My Blood: Poems 1956–1968*, by Milton Acorn. Toronto, Ryerson Press, 1969.
Editor, *Storm Warning: The New Canadian Poets.* Toronto, McClelland and Stewart, 1971; *Storm Warning 2*, 1976.
Editor, *Wood Mountain Poems*, by Andrew Suknaski. Toronto, Macmillan, 1976.

Manuscript Collections: University of Saskatchewan, Saskatoon; Queen's University, Kingston, Ontario.

Critical Studies: "In the Raw: The Poetry of A. W. Purdy" by Peter Stevens, in *Canadian Literature* (Vancouver), Spring 1966; interview with Gary Geddes, in *Canadian Literature* (Vancouver), 1969; *Al Purdy* by George Bowering, Toronto, Copp Clark, 1970; *Harsh and Lovely Land* by Tom Marshall, Vancouver, University of British Columbia Press, 1979.

Al Purdy comments:

Themes? Sex and death (which last naturally includes life). Subjects? Anything that appeals to me. Form? Pretty irregular, but generally with rhythm running somewhere, sometimes off rhymes and assonance. Influences? Very many, including the usual big names (Pound, Eliot, Yeats); also César Vallejo, Neruda, Superveille, Charles Bukowski, Robinson Jeffers, etc., etc. Style? I have some strong prejudices against schools of any kind, including most particularly the Creeley-Olson Black Mountain bunch and their imitators. I do not dismiss these people and believe it is possible to learn much from them, but only IF one remains oneself, something most of them apparently find difficult. I believe that when a poet fixes on the style or method he severely limits his present and future development. By the same token I dislike the traditional methods of rhyme and metre when used without variation, ditto traditional forms. But I use rhyme, metre and (occasionally) standard forms when a poem seems to call for it. Rules tend to be exclusive of anything outside their own strictures: I think most traditional poets would agree with this, but go right on using traditional metre and rhymes – poets like prime ministers are all against war and on the side of truth and justice.

Perhaps I should say that: I began to write nearly 40 years ago, influenced at that time by people whom I don't appreciate very much now. For instance, I like some of G. K. Chesterton's poems, and his influence no doubt remains with me but is, I think, difficult to discern in what I write today. At one time iambic metrics were so deeply implanted in my mind that it took me years of not-trying to break out of iambics to finally break out of iambics. I suppose other people's styles were apparent in my stuff until publication of *Poems for All the Annettes* in '62, and this book (and also *Blur in Between*, published '63 but earlier poems than *Annettes*) is the transitional period between what I was and am and change into. I have a fixation about change, which can also be regarded as a self-conscious weakness as well as a strength. And yet I wrote a poem in Athens, Greece, in January, 1969 ("The Time of Your Life"), which is probably the best I've ever written; at least I think so now.

* * *

Al Purdy is one of the most prolific of Canadian poets, with more than 20 books to his credit, and also one of the most consistently interesting. He has been publishing poetry for a generation and writing it for longer. Yet, though his first volume, *The Enchanted Echo*, appeared in 1944, it was only during the mid-1960's, already well into middle age, that he emerged as one of Canada's leading poets, vigorous in statement, energetic in travelling the land to read his poetry and travelling the world to gather material for poems whose external form as travelogue or journalism was the vehicle for deeper philosophic statement.

Purdy's lack of an academic background, unusual in the Canadian literary world, has been an advantage to him in many ways, leading him to wander far and freely, to work at many callings and to bring to his writing a wide down-to-earth experience. On the technical side it has liberated him from formal disciplines and has enabled him to work at his own pace, apart from the literary fashions that sweep North American campuses, and taking what he wanted where he wanted, from Williams, from Auden and Thomas, from Pratt and Birney and Layton; by this means he has progressed from the traditional lyricism of *The Enchanted Echo* to the open forms and personal voice of later books like *The Cariboo Horses* and *Wild Grape Wine*, of which the best poems have recently been collected in *Being Alive*. What has struck one about Purdy's verse since the later 1950's is its intense oral impact. It is free verse in the truest form: fluent, untrammeled by conventions, yet possessing rhythmic and grammatical forms that distinguish it from statement in prose.

Purdy's poems are always near to experience; the poem emerges from life and the concept from the poem. Poems about his wanderings in Canada, like those in *Cariboo Horses*, or abroad, like those in *Hiroshima Poems*, often seem to have served Purdy as a journal, so close is the interval between conception and creation, so immediate the response to experience. This leads to unevenness in tone and quality, which Purdy controls to an extent by weeding out much of a voluminous production.

Memory is for Purdy intense experience, and thus his poetry of travel is balanced by his poetry of tradition, which is linked intimately with his own Loyalist ancestry and with the long-settled regions of Ontario in which he grew up. The strain of continuity has recently become very marked in his verse. He goes back to the history of the village of Ameliasburgh where he lives, and he goes back, in memory and physically, to land where his forefathers farmed after they fled from the United States two centuries ago. The emotions stirred by these voyages into history are expressed in poems like "My Grandfather's Country":

> But the hill-red has no such violence of endings
> the woods are alive
> and gentle as well as cruel
> unlike sand and sea
> and if I must give my heart to anything
> it will be here in the red glow
> where failed farms sink back into earth
> the clearings join and fences no longer divide
> where the running animals gather their bodies together
> and pour themselves upward
> into the tips of falling leaves
> with mindless faith that presumes a future.

Purdy's poetry is often densely allusive, but never obscure; indeed, he makes a virtue out of intellectual directness. He draws freely on the funds of knowledge a generalizing and autodidactic mind accumulates, and some of his poems show a remarkable ability to bring images drawn from great sweeps of time and place into a meaningful relationship to his own experience. A fine example is "In the Caves," the concluding poem of *Being Alive*, in which Purdy imagines the creative passion of a palaeolithic artist, and by implication relates it to the poet's modern agony:

> And I do not know why
> whether because I cannot hunt with the others
> and they laugh
> or because the things I have done are useless
> as I may be useless
> but there is something here I must follow
> into myself to find
> outside myself in the mammoth
> beyond the scorn of my people
> who are still my people
> my own pain and theirs
> joining the shriek that does not end
> that is inside me now

Such poetry traps with an extraordinary appearance of spontaneity the roving speculations of a highly original mind. Purdy has moved from early dependence on Canadian romanticism to a highly personal style, always vigorous, often humorous.

—George Woodcock

PYBUS, Rodney. British. Born in Newcastle upon Tyne, Northumberland, 5 June 1938. Educated at Rossall School, Lancashire, 1951–56; Gonville and Caius College, Cambridge (exhibitioner), 1957–60, B.A. 1960, M.A. 1965. Married Ella Pybus in 1961; two sons. Teacher, Aiglon College, Switzerland, 1960–61, and Fifield Road Boys School, Newcastle, 1961–62; Journalist, Newcastle *Journal*, 1962–64; Writer and Producer, Tyne Tees Television, Newcastle, 1964–76; Lecturer in English, Macquarie University, Sydney, 1976–79. Since 1979, Literature Officer for Cumbria. Tutor in the Adult Education Poetry Workshop, Newcastle University, 1974–76; Australia Editor, *Stand* magazine, Newcastle, 1976–79. Recipient: Alice Hunt Bartlett Prize, 1973. Address: c/o Charlotte Mason College, Ambleside, Cumbria, England.

PUBLICATIONS

Verse

In Memoriam Milena. London, Chatto and Windus, 1973.
Bridging Loans and Other Poems. London, Chatto and Windus, 1976.
At the Stone Junction. Newcastle upon Tyne, Northern House, 1978.

Manuscript Collection: Literary and Philosophical Library, Newcastle upon Tyne.

Rodney Pybus comments:

Different historical periods and characters often give me a means of focussing on the present: through such "impersonations" I have tried to render dramatic and deepen the resonance of my writing. The figures I use have all lived at times of great social upheaval. What they salvaged they did by a combination of intelligence and scepticism, and I have tried to express my debt to such exemplary humans. Obviously I do not see the use of a historical perspective as an evasion of the stresses and pressures of the present. I hope some of my concern for the relationship between language and moral, emotional, and political matters can be discerned in the language of my poems: the word and the world are inextricable. Another preoccupation is the exploration of places both urban and rural, mainly in the North-East of England where my roots lie deepest – self-exploration of a kind, and all varieties of location and dislocation.

I prefer compassion to expansiveness, craft to *faux-naif* spontaneity, the "cooked" to the "raw." I think I have learned more about the possibilities of poetry in the second half of the 20th century from European and British poets than American. I believe that a poet's concern for and use of language have never been more important than they are now, in the great age of double-think, new-speak, talk-back, and audio-visual hocus pocus. I try to make the words I write communicate something of that belief; sometimes, I think, they do.

* * *

Many of the most successful of Rodney Pybus's poems are those which confront the extremes of contrast between the world of possibilities and the horror man has made of it: "Strange to think/The same language, the same letters/written by Hitler and Heine." This he manages via historical personae, sometimes ancient: Petronius or Procopius; sometimes more recent: Milena Jesenská, the friend of Kafka, or Yevgeny Zamyatin. The parallels between Nero's Rome and Hitler's Germany are telling, and the way of coping with them, enduring them, are similar. The adoption of either a carapace of stoicism or an urbane disdain is nevertheless vulnerable for sooner or later life's acid will dissolve it or the jack boot smash it. Yet the spirit, manifest in an often oblique dignity, remains untouched: "I am the conscience that runs out."

This is not a cry of despair, but a restatement of human dignity in its refusal to flinch from the truth. The language, too, especially in those poems set in ancient Rome or Constantinople, underlines this. The modern colloquialisms not only bring the situations into relation with the twentieth century, but are an expression of the sardonic intelligence which protects the mind from the horrors it encounters:

I despair, Caius, I despair!
Everything is in the hands
of that trigger-happy
paranoid lecher –
except me, thank heaven!

The poems in which the subject is external nature: "Foxes," "Stoop," "Greenfinch" are sharply observed and often hold the reader by means of startling images ("Greenfinch"):

Wound-up
by hunger or habit, it jerks
its food out in a parody
of famine – broad bill
bashing into nuts,
then filching slivers
between the strings
as if they sizzled –

cocking its head
like that of a tiny
galvanised parrot.

The violence of "bashing," "sizzled," "galvanised," forces the reader's attention. But good as they are, these poems have the air of exercises in that others have treated these subjects, and as well, before. It is when Rodney Pybus explores the emotional world of the survival of individual values in a situation where such values have collapsed, or achieves an empathy with the exceptional, as in his poem on Samuel Palmer, "Summer's Lease," that he is his own man and writes poems that only he could have written.

—John Cotton

RAINE, Craig. British. Born in Shildon, County Durham, 3 December 1944. Educated at Barnard Castle School; Exeter College, Oxford, 1963–68, B.A. in English 1966, B.Phil. 1968. Married Ann Pasternak Slater in 1972; one daughter. Recipient: Cheltenham Literary Festival prize, 1977, 1978; Prudence Farmer Award, 1978. Address: 31 Alma Place, Oxford, England.

PUBLICATIONS

Verse

The Onion, Memory. London, Oxford University Press, 1978.
A Martian Sends a Postcard Home. London, Oxford University Press, 1979.
A Journey to Greece. Oxford, Sycamore Press, 1979.

* * *

Craig Raine is an immensely *clever* poet whose poems are always exciting verbal performances, elaborate structures of proliferating metaphor in which an immense web of inter-relationship is spun. A butcher "stands/smoking a pencil like Isambard Kingdom Brunel"; a baker "smiles like a modest quattrocento Christ"; a college quad is "cobbled like a blackberry." A vacuum cleaner is a cow; falling bricks decline a Latin pronoun ("hic, haec, hoc"); houses in North Oxford are troops on parade; a market is a book; a breast is a blister; a marquee is "Gulliver's grimy white shirt," and – the title of one poem – "Two Circuses Equal One Cricket Match." And so on, through poems that contort and gyrate through an extraordinary acrobatics of perception. The performance is dandified, extremely self-conscious, very literary; and is as liable to miss as to hit. This, about a window cleaner, seems to me a very palpable hit: "All day he sees himself in the glass darkly/and waves goodbye, goodbye, goodbye." And this, from a poem called "Danse Macabre," a very obvious miss: "In his summer shirt, a bobby's notebook/bulges squarely like a nursing breast." A miss which manages, in itself, an inappropriateness verging on extreme vulgarity, and, in the context of a poem whose centre is a man collapsing in the street, proves a distraction so severe that what should, presumably, be compassion presents itself as mere curiosity. Endless *curiosity* about life there certainly is in Raine, and God's plenty stuffs his poems to bursting point. Whether there is anything more than wizardry and the verbal pyrotechnics of a very, very clever Oxford chap is still not proven.

I think that, on balance, there is; though I think that the "more" is not now as obvious as it may become in later volumes. Peter Porter has suggested that Raine's poetry represents "the persistence of some ancient litany." Poetry, he says, "which has lost importance in the world, comes bouncing back as the joker in the semantic pack." Raine's attempt to *read* the world is not, then, merely the enterprise of a man who cannot see the world for the book, but is a desire to discover moments of illumination, of secular grace, within the attempts of language to describe, and control, reality. The best of his poems come to rest in moments of exactly this kind of benediction when, out of the trivia of everyday life, the flesh is made word: "While the pigeons coo and woo, I stroke/the scratchiness of your sow's ear/and wait the miracle of silk." And, for a poet so apparently intent on his manic dance on the superficies of life, Raine is also obsessed with much darker matters – with frustration, with loss of love, with the responsibility of paternity, with death. The closing lines of the poem that provides the title for his first volume, "The Onion, Memory," suggest that Raine can handle a quieter, more meditative cadence that may, in the long run, prove more sustaining. The poem is about a meeting, after divorce, with a former wife:

> It is the onion, memory,
> that makes me cry.
>
> Because there's everything and nothing to be said,
> the clock with hands held up before its face,
> stammers softly on, trying to complete a phrase –
> while we, together and apart,
> repeat unfinished gestures got by heart.
>
> And afterwards, I blunder with the washing on the line –
> headless torsos, faceless lovers, friends of mine.

The characteristic teasing out of metaphor is still here, but now at the obvious service of a complex emotional meaning. This seems to me the direction Craig Raine's more recent work is taking, a direction in which great aesthetic originality and vigour are being deepened into real moral passion.

—Neil Corcoran

RAINE, Kathleen (Jessie). British. Born in London, 14 June 1908. Educated at County High School, Ilford; Girton College, Cambridge, M.A. in natural sciences 1929. Married to Charles Madge, *q.v.* (marriage dissolved); one daughter and one son. Research Fellow, Girton College, Cambridge, 1955–61; Andrew Mellon Lecturer, National Gallery of Art, Washington, D.C., 1962. Recipient: Harriet Monroe Memorial Prize, 1952, and Oscar Blumenthal Prize, 1961 (*Poetry*, Chicago); Arts Council award, 1953; Chapelbrook Award; Cholmondeley Award, 1970; Smith Literary Award, 1972. D.Litt.: Leicester University, 1974. Address: 47 Paultons Square, London S.W.3, England.

PUBLICATIONS

Verse

Stone and Flower: Poems 1935–43. London, Nicholson and Watson, 1943.

Living in Time: Poems. London, Editions Poetry London, 1946.
The Pythoness and Other Poems. London, Hamish Hamilton, 1949; New York, Farrar Straus, 1952.
Selected Poems. New York, Weekend Press, 1952.
The Year One. London, Hamish Hamilton, 1952; New York, Farrar Straus, 1953.
The Collected Poems of Kathleen Raine. London, Hamish Hamilton, 1956; New York, Random House, 1957.
Christmas 1960: An Acrostic. Privately printed, 1960.
The Hollow Hill and Other Poems 1960–1964. London, Hamish Hamilton, 1965.
Six Dreams and Other Poems. London, Enitharmon Press, 1968.
Ninfa Revisited. London, Enitharmon Press, 1968.
Pergamon Poets 4: Kathleen Raine and Vernon Watkins, edited by Evan Owen. Oxford, Pergamon Press, 1968.
A Question of Poetry. Crediton, Devon, Gilbertson, 1969.
Penguin Modern Poets 17, with David Gascoyne and W. S. Graham. London, Penguin, 1970.
The Lost Country. Dublin, Dolmen Press, and London, Hamish Hamilton, 1971.
Three Poems Written in Ireland. London, Poem-of-the-Month Club, 1973.
On a Deserted Shore. Dublin, Dolmen Press, and London, Hamish Hamilton, 1973.
The Oval Portrait and Other Poems. London, Hamish Hamilton, 1977.
Fifteen Short Poems. London, Enitharmon Press, 1978.
The Oracle in the Heart: Poems 1974–1978. Dublin, Dolmen Press, 1979.

Other

William Blake. London, Longman, 1951; revised edition, 1965, 1969.
Coleridge. London, Longman, 1953.
Poetry in Relation to Traditional Wisdom. London, Guild of Pastoral Psychology, 1958.
Blake and England (lecture). Cambridge, W. Heffer, 1960; Folcroft, Pennsylvania, Folcroft Editions, 1974.
Defending Ancient Springs (essays). London and New York, Oxford University Press, 1967.
The Written Word. London, Enitharmon Press, 1967.
Blake and Tradition. Princeton, New Jersey, Princeton University Press, 1968; London, Routledge, 1969; abridged edition, as *Blake and Antiquity*, 1974.
William Blake. London, Thames and Hudson, 1971.
Faces of Day and Night (autobiography). London, Enitharmon Press, 1972.
Yeats, The Tarot and the Golden Dawn. Dublin, Dolmen Press, 1972; New York, Humanities Press, 1973; revised edition, Dolmen Press, 1976.
Hopkins, Nature, and Human Nature (lecture). London, Hopkins Society, 1972.
Autobiography:
1. *Farewell Happy Fields.* London, Hamish Hamilton, 1973; New York, Braziller, 1977.
2. *The Land Unknown.* London, Hamish Hamilton, and New York, Braziller, 1975.
3. *The Lion's Mouth.* London, Hamish Hamilton, 1977; New York, Braziller, 1978.

Death-in-Life and Life-in-Death (lecture). Dublin, Dolmen Press, 1974.
David Jones: Solitary Perfectionist. Ipswich, Golgonooza Press, 1974.
A Place, A State, drawings by Julia Trevelyan. London, Enitharmon Press, 1974.
The Inner Journey of the Poet. Ipswich, Golgonooza Press, 1976.
Berkeley, Blake, and the New Age (lecture). Ipswich, Golgonooza Press, 1977.
From Blake to "A Vision." Dublin, Dolmen Press, 1978.
David Jones and the Actually Loved and Known. Ipswich, Golgonooza Press, 1978.

Blake and the New Age. London, Allen and Unwin, 1979.

Editor, with Max-Pol Fouchet, *Aspects de Littérature Anglaise, 1918–1945.* Paris, Fontaine, 1947.
Editor, *Letters of Samuel Taylor Coleridge.* London, Grey Walls Press, 1950.
Editor, *Selected Poems and Prose of Coleridge.* London, Penguin, 1957.
Editor, with George Mills Harper, *Thomas Taylor the Platonist: Selected Writings.* Princeton, New Jersey, Princeton University Press, and London, Routledge, 1969.
Editor, *A Choice of Blake's Verse.* London, Faber, 1974.
Editor, *Shelley.* London, Penguin, 1974.

Translator, *Talk of the Devil*, by Dénis de Rougemont. London, Eyre and Spottiswoode, 1945.
Translator, *Existentialism*, by Paul Foulquié. London, Dobson, 1948.
Translator, *Cousin Bette*, by Honoré de Balzac. London, Hamish Hamilton, 1948.
Translator, *Lost Illusions*, by Honoré de Balzac. London, Lehmann, 1951.
Translator, with R. M. Nadal, *Life's a Dream*, by Calderón. London, Hamish Hamilton, 1968; New York, Theatre Arts, 1969.

Manuscript Collections: British Museum, London; University of Texas, Austin; University of California, Irvine.

Kathleen Raine comments:

I began as a poet of spontaneous inspirations, drawing greatly on nature and fortified by my more precise biological studies. Though I was born in London, my poetic roots were in wild Northumberland where I lived as a child. Most of my poems have been written in Cumberland or Scotland, some in Italy, Greece or France, but very few in London, where I at present live.

I have studied the symbolic language of Blake, Shelley, Yeats, Coleridge, and other poets of the "Romantic" tradition; who employ that language of analogy inseparable from the Perennial Philosophy (of which Christianity is our own cultural branch) which regards man as a spiritual and immortal being. Increasingly, in an atheist society, the meaning of words and the symbolic implications of traditional poetry become changed or lost. And this makes it difficult, if not impossible, for a poet of my kind to be anthologized with writers committed to another view of the nature of things. I have much sympathy for the young generation now reacting against materialist culture; but I am too firmly rooted in the civilization of the past to speak their language.

* * *

The young poets who caught the widest public attention in the 1930's were a group of Oxford poets, W. H. Auden, C. Day Lewis, Stephen Spender, and Louis MacNeice. A group of Cambridge poets of the same generation, Kathleen Raine, William Empson, Ronald Bottrall, and Miss Raine's second husband, Charles Madge, attracted on the whole less public attention. It was not that they were less politically engaged – two good Cambridge poets, John Cornford and Julian Bell, died in the Spanish Civil War; it was, perhaps, that there was a greater austerity in the Cambridge tradition. Miss Raine studied the natural sciences, not literature, at Cambridge, and an exactness of natural observation (very notable in her first volume, *Stone and Flower*, beautifully illustrated by Barbara Hepworth) is one of the main qualities of her poetry. Another is a beautifully natural and graceful lyrical movement, and a third is what might be called a transparency of diction. She has never attempted wit poetry, or the poetry of personal self-analysis, "confessional" poetry: in gathering together her

Collected Poems she said in her preface that she had at first excluded all poems of "mere human emotion" but, persuaded by a friend that this was a too grandly austere statement – might not Chaucer and Shakespeare be described as poets of "mere human emotion"? – she substituted for that phrase the phrase "the transient." Miss Raine thinks of herself as a poet in a Platonic or neo-Platonic tradition that has included Spenser, Milton, Blake, Shelley and Yeats in its members among the poets of the greater English tradition. The combination of the approach of a trained botanist and geologist with neo-Platonic mysticism may seem strange, but a link could be found in Miss Raine's interest in abstract art, in the sculptures of Barbara Hepworth and the drawings of Ben Nicholson. Both these artists might be thought of as seeking in outward nature archetypal forms, or Platonic ideas, as might another English artist whom Miss Raine greatly admires, Henry Moore. Such artists and the older poets whom she has praised in her book of essays *Defending Ancient Springs* might be thought of as Miss Raine's deepest sources. She has little sympathy with most contemporary poetry, feeling that even her old Cambridge friend, William Empson, is in his poetry and prose her spiritual antagonist. Poetry is only true poetry for her if it utters in traditional language the truths of the perennial philosophy, of ancient wisdom, of ancient revelation. Working on Blake over many years of patient scholarship, she has been concerned with the Blake who created a mythology and a cosmology, not with the Blake who spoke of "the lineaments of gratified desire." It follows that, though her poetry has always been admired by sound judges, some have found it thin and unearthly, speaking too much for what Yeats called soul, not enough for what Yeats called self, not enough for "the fury and the mire of human veins." Her lyrical sweetness, the beauty of the voice that is heard in the poems, is praised, but the vision itself found abstract or schematic. Carefully reading and listening with the inner ear will tell another story. Only a very proud and passionate woman would wage such a stern war, through all her work, against human pride and passion. These are the poems of a sybil, perhaps, of a rapt visionary, but not of a saint.

—G. S. Fraser

RAKOSI, Carl. American. Born in Berlin, Germany, 6 November 1903. Educated at the University of Wisconsin, Madison, B.A. 1924, M.A. 1926; University of Pennsylvania, Philadelphia, M.A. in social work, 1940; University of Chicago; University of Texas, Austin. Married Leah Jaffe in 1939; one daughter and one son. Instructor, University of Texas, 1928–29; Social Worker, Chicago, New York, New Orleans, Brooklyn, St. Louis, and Cleveland, 1932–45; Executive Director, Jewish Family and Children's Service, Minneapolis, Minnesota, 1945–68; Writer-in-Residence, University of Wisconsin, 1969–70, and Michigan State University, East Lansing, 1974. Since 1955, engaged in private practice of psychotherapy, Minneapolis. Recipient: National Endowment for the Arts award, 1969, fellowship, 1972. Address: 128 Irving Street, San Francisco, California 94122, U.S.A.

PUBLICATIONS

Verse

Selected Poems. New York, New Directions, 1941.
Two Poems. New York, Modern Editions Press, 1942.
Amulet. New York, New Directions, 1967.
Ere-VOICE. New York, New Directions, 1971.

Ex Cranium, Night. Los Angeles, Black Sparrow Press, 1975.
My Experiences in Parnassus. Santa Barbara, California, Black Sparrow Press, 1977.

Manuscript Collection: University of Wisconsin, Madison.

Critical Studies: "The Objectivist Poet: Interviews with Oppen, Rakosi, Reznikoff, and Zukofsky" by L. S. Dembo, in *Contemporary Literature* (Madison, Wisconsin) x, 2; "The Poetry of Carl Rakosi" by L. S. Dembo, in *Iowa Review* (Iowa City), ii, 1.

Carl Rakosi comments:

I am identified with the Objectivists but it is questionable whether the term has meaning any more.

* * *

Carl Rakosi was a member of a group of poets in the thirties who called themselves "The Objectivists." Louis Zukofsky, Charles Reznikoff, and George Oppen were other poets identified with this group. Rakosi and Oppen both went unpublished for many years between the thirties and the present time, either writing secretly or not writing at all, as they were both involved with active social protest against the oppression of the laboring classes and, as is usually the case, when active politics reign in a man's life, he has no place for the more meditative art of poetry.

Now as older men, they have both begun to write and publish prolifically. Rakosi, who led his life as a social worker in the Midwest, still concerns his poems with pithy practical comments on life and its injustices. Ironically, however, his best poems are pastoral observations of the natural world, often with tiny comments such as those you might find in early Japanese or Chinese poetry.

Rakosi's poetry is short and spritely and not at all meditative, though seemingly made up of conclusions about the meaning of the world. It feels like the language of a man who has been active all of his life and now has comments about everything he has experienced, slightly wry and not at all uncritical, though delivered with friendliness. As a poet, he is a sort of gadfly, not taking on any epic subjects (perhaps even having wry words about such subjects), but stinging and buzzing about everything, a reminder that to live intelligently is never to relax or to leave unnoticed any slightly foolish thing – the poet as commentator on all of life.

—Diane Wakoski

RAMANUJAN, A(ttipat) K(rishnaswami). Indian. Born in Mysore, 16 March 1929. Educated at the University of Mysore, B.A. 1949, M.A. in English 1950; Indiana University, Bloomington (Fulbright and Smith-Mundt fellowships, 1959), Ph.D. in linguistics 1963. Married Molly Daniels in 1962; two children. Taught in India, 1950–58. Member of the Faculty since 1962, and since 1968, Professor of Dravidian Studies and Linguistics, departments of Linguistics and South Asian Languages, and Committee on Social Thought, University of Chicago. Visiting Professor, University of California, Berkeley, 1967, and Carleton College, Northfield, Minnesota, 1978. Recipient: American Institute of Indian Studies Fellowship, 1963; Indiana School of Letters Fellowship, 1963; Tamil Writers' Association Award, 1969; National Endowment for the Arts fellowship, 1977. Address: 5629 South Dorchester Avenue, Chicago, Illinois 60637, U.S.A.

PUBLICATIONS

Verse

The Striders. London and New York, Oxford University Press, 1966.
No Lotus in the Navel (in Kannada). Dharwar, Manohar Granthmala, 1969.
Relations. London, Oxford University Press, 1972.
Selected Poems. New Delhi and London, Oxford University Press, 1976.
And Other Poems (in Kannada). Dharwar, 1977.

Other

Proverbs (in Kannada). Dharwar, Karnatak University, 1955.
The Literature of India, with others. Chicago, University of Chicago Press, 1974.

Translator, *Fifteen Poems from a Classical Tamil Anthology.* Calcutta, Writers Workshop, 1965.
Translator, *The Yellow Fish* (into Kannada), by Molly Ramanujan. Dharwar, Manohar Granthmala, 1966.
Translator, *The Interior Landscape: Love Poems from a Classical Tamil Anthology.* Bloomington, Indiana University Press, 1967; London, Peter Owen, 1970.
Translator, *Speaking of Siva.* London, Penguin, 1973.
Translator, *Samskara*, by U. R. Anantha Murthy. New Delhi, Oxford University Press, 1976.

Critical Studies: in *Poetry Book Society Bulletin* (London), April 1966; *Ten Indian Poets in English* edited by R. Parthasarathy, New Delhi, Oxford University Press, 1976.

* * *

A. K. Ramanujan achieved recognition when his first book, *The Striders*, was recommended by the Poetry Society of London. He is a South Indian, and has been living in the U.S.A. for many years now, teaching linguistics and Dravidian studies at the University of Chicago. This biographical information is relevant in reading his poems which are mostly poems of memory, quite often nostalgic. They have their origin in an emotion arising from the Indian experience which is recollected in an American environment – not always in a mood of tranquillity. Many of the poems are based on the cultural predicament of a person who has been brought up in a very traditional culture, but who is now living in a very different culture. One of the best poems in *The Striders* which exemplifies these remarks is "Conventions of Despair." The poem opens with the description of a modern hell whose representative figure is the Marginal Man, culturally and linguistically displaced and unsettled, perhaps permanently. But the hell to which the poet feels he is consigned is the Hindu hell of traditional description in which he must "translate and turn/till I blister and roast/for certain lives to come, 'eye-deep'/in those Boiling crates of Oil." This is the punishment for loving a prohibited person. In this Hindu hell he will be condemned to witness the tortures of the beloved person also. But the worst of his punishments comes from the modern hell. It consists in catching a glimpse of a grandchild "bare/her teenage flesh to the pimps/of ideal Tomorrow's crowfoot eyes/and the theory of a peacock-feathered future." The poet finally chooses to live in the present, content with continuous existence. He prefers the archaic despair of Hindu thought which sees human life as a continuous cycle of birth, death and rebirth. The cycle, it is believed, has always existed. Ramanujan, significantly, does not say anything about the complementary belief that we can end this cycle if we so will.

Five years after *The Striders* appeared *Relations.* The poetic impulse and the theme are the same – announced in the epigraph poem which is a beautiful rendering of a classical Tamil poem. (Perhaps Ramanujan's real forte is translation.) The ambiguous nature of the freedom away from home is brought out most satisfactorily in the images:

> Like a hunted deer
> on the wide white
> salt land,
> a flayed hide
> turned inside out,
> one may run,
> escape.
> But living
> among relations
> binds the feet.

The sense of loss is most often connected with the mother. "My cold parchment tongue licks bark/in the mouth when I see her four/still sensible fingers slowly flex/to pick a grain of rice from the kitchen floor" ("Of Mothers, among other things"). The metaphors in the first two lines emphasise the rough, bitter taste of the memory, and the last two lines provide an irresistible "objective correlative" of the emotion. Every poet who communicates principally in images – as Ramanujan does – takes chances, but fortunately most of the chances that Ramanujan takes come off. If there is any cause for dissatisfaction with these poems, it is that many of them are intellectually somewhat thin, though there are numerous exceptions. For example, "A River" in *The Striders* where the images comment obliquely on the blind imitation of past models; or "History" in *Relations* which may be read as an illustration of Eliot's "historical sense" on the plane of personal relations. One no doubt misses a sense of an unfolding pattern in the total experience of these poems, but this lack may disappear as the poet masters his past and learns to assimilate the present. As he himself says: "After the lightning/strikes the tree/and takes all the leaves,/an amnesiac may break into hives/... but recognize nothing present/to his concave eye groping only/for mother and absences."

Technically, Ramanujan is a very interesting poet. His sense of rhythm, his manipulation of syntax, his ability to use ordinary words in extraordinary ways, exploiting fully their semantic potentialities, his run-ons, even his line alignments, above all, his tone, all make his poems a very rewarding experience.

—S. Nagarajan

RAMSEY, Paul. American. Born in Atlanta, Georgia, 26 November 1924. Educated at the University of Chattanooga, Tennessee; University of North Carolina, Chapel Hill, B.A., M.A.; University of Minnesota, Minneapolis, Ph.D. 1956. Served in the United States Navy during World War II. Married to the artist Bets Ramsey; four children. Taught at the University of Alabama, Tuscaloosa, 1948–50, 1953–57; Elmira College, New York, 1957–62; Raymond College, Stockton, California, 1962–64; University of the South, Sewanee, Tennessee, 1964–66. Professor of English, 1966–70, since 1966, Poet-in-Residence, and since 1970, Alumni Distinguished Service Professor, University of Tennessee, Chattanooga. Recipient: Folger Library Senior Fellowship, 1967; English-Speaking Union prize, 1976. Address: Department of English, University of Tennessee, Chattanooga, Tennessee 37403, U.S.A.

PUBLICATIONS

Verse

Triptych, with Sy Kahn and Jane Taylor. Stockton, California, Raymond College Press, 1964.
In an Ordinary Place. Raleigh, North Carolina, Southern Poetry Review Press, 1965.
A Window for New York. San Francisco, Two Windows Press, 1968.
The Doors. Martin, Tennessee Poetry Press, 1968.
The Answerers. San Francisco, Two Windows Press, 1970.
No Running on the Boardwalk. Athens, University of Georgia Press, 1975.
Antiphon: An Introit for Christmas, music by Alec Wyton. Carol Springs, Illinois, Agape Press, 1975.
Eve, Singing. Easthampton, Massachusetts, Pennyroyal Press, 1976.

.Other

The Lively and the Just: An Argument for Propriety. University, University of Alabama Press, 1962.
The Art of John Dryden. Lexington, University of Kentucky Press, 1969.
The Fickle Glass: A Study of Shakespeare's Sonnets. New York, AMS Press, 1979.

Critical Studies: review in *Virginia Quarterly Review* (Charlottesville), 1968; by Scott Bates, in *Times* (Chattanooga, Tennessee), 13 July 1975; Charles Israel, in *Sandlapper* (Columbia, South Carolina), October 1975; Claire Hahn, in *Commonweal* (New York), 22 October 1976.

Paul Ramsey comments:

My poetry is varied, ambitious, exploratory, traditional. For some years I wrote only traditional forms, mostly accentual-syllabics. Since then I have worked in traditional forms, forms I have invented, free verse, combinings of free verse with traditional forms or methods. Valid poetry should enliven and sustain rhythm, touch on and at times enter mystery, offer understanding. My chief and underlying themes are Christian, as is manifest in my long poems "The Flight of the Heart," *A Window for New York*, "The Naming of Adam," a Christianity which permits and includes, for instance, nature's bounty and strangeness, ethical reality, the turns and crowds of events, love's celebrations and complaints, and images that recur: doors, windows, mists, rocks, the sea, the cross.

* * *

Paul Ramsey in his best work often combines the virtues of men whose work he has studied carefully: John Dryden, Allen Tate, and Yvor Winters. The combination may at first seem strange. Yet Dryden is godfather to our critical wars and poetical age; and Tate and Winters were not so far apart as poets as their critical squabbles suggested. Aiming for compression, some of Ramsey's early poems were so tightly packed that they seemed more cryptic than epigramatic. The quatrain "Art" is an often cited example ("Art is act/Betrayed by passion and by artifact/Till images encounter their repose"). Aiming at a general loosening of the poetic line and at a more conversational vocabulary in the fashionable manner, some of his later poems (and the whole book *The Doors*) have become diffuse, sketchy, even lacking in content. Yet superb lines appear in both the tight early poems ("Art" ends: "The mind must learn to suffer what it knows") and the diffuse later experiments ("The Doors" sequence ends with the line "Blood loosens the rust of the keys"); and in all the poems, one finds subtle metrical skill as well as intellectual integrity and grace. Ramsey's profound Christian humanitarian outlook gives moving substance to many of his poems, and informs others with moral strength and character. This habit of mind evidences itself in such poems as the apology to Wordsworth, an apology for having taught that man's poems badly; and to the assertion in the challenging and important critical work *The Lively and the Just*, that of the English Odes examined in the book Wordsworth's Intimations Ode is the greatest. Such a remark, coming from a Dryden scholar and a student of the so-called "New Criticism" is a measure of rigorous intellectual integrity.

No poet writes great poems all the time; nor even good poems. One must, I think, pass over such experiments as *The Doors* and most of Ramsey's "occasional" poems, as one would any other poet's. Then one finds a solid body of work. He has written at least one major poem, "Address to Satan," 14 iambic pentameter lines in two stanzas riming a-a-b-b-c-c-c, and beginning "Now curl about your wisdom and be still,/Old serpent-tooth." In addition he had written some very fine poems, "Forest" and "Even Umpires Wager with Pascal" among them. The poems of a man of such skill and integrity will survive, past fads and fashions. The man who wrote such poems as "Address to Satan" and "Forest" is still composing. His lively verbal imagination will, knock wood, give us more good poems.

—James Korges

RANDALL, Dudley (Felker). American. Born in Washington, D.C., 14 January 1914. Educated at Eastern High School, Detroit; Wayne State University, Detroit, A.B. 1949; University of Michigan, Ann Arbor, M.A.L.S. 1951. Served in the United States Army Signal Corps, 1943–46. Married 1) Ruby Hands in 1935 (marriage dissolved), one daughter; 2) Mildred Pinckney in 1942 (marriage dissolved); 3) Vivian Spencer in 1957. Worked for Ford Motor Company, Dearborn, 1932–37; Post Office carrier and clerk, Detroit, 1937–51; Librarian, Lincoln University, Jefferson City, Missouri, 1951–54, Morgan State College, Baltimore, 1954–56, and Wayne County Federated Library System, Detroit, 1956–69. Since 1969, Librarian and Poet-in-Residence, University of Detroit. Founding Publisher, Broadside Press, Detroit. Visited Paris, Prague and the U.S.S.R. with a delegation of black artists, 1966. Recipient: Wayne State University Tompkins Award, for fiction and poetry, 1962, for poetry, 1966; Kuumba Award, 1973. Agent: Contemporary Forum, 2528a West Jerome Street, Chicago, Illinois 60645. Address: 12651 Old Mill Place, Detroit, Michigan 48238, U.S.A.

PUBLICATIONS

Verse

Ballad of Birmingham. Detroit, Broadside Press, 1965.
Dressed All in Pink. Detroit, Broadside Press, 1965.
Booker T. and W.E.B. Detroit, Broadside Press, 1966.
Poem, Counterpoem, with Margaret Danner. Detroit, Broadside Press, 1966.
Cities Burning. Detroit, Broadside Press, 1968.
On Getting a Natural. Detroit, Broadside Press, 1969.
Love You. London, Paul Breman, 1971.
More to Remember: Poems of Four Decades. Chicago, Third World Press, 1971.
Green Apples. Detroit, Broadside Press, 1972.
After the Killing. Chicago, Third World Press, 1973.

Other

Editor, with Margaret G. Burroughs, *For Malcolm: Poems on the Life and the Death of Malcolm X.* Detroit, Broadside Press, 1967.
Editor, *Black Poetry: A Supplement to Anthologies Which Exclude Black Poets.* Detroit, Broadside Press, 1969.
Editor, *The Black Poets: A New Anthology.* New York, Bantam, 1971.

Dudley Randall comments:

Writes poetry of the Negro. Formal, reflective, with occasional humor.

* * *

Dudley Randall's verse eases its audience into a pleased approval of the poet's viewpoint. Take, for example, what must be his most famous piece, "Booker T. and W.E.B." References to the doctrines of the famous black leaders in this imagined dialogue seem even-handed, each speaker uses in-group language in a manner appropriate to his personality, and the dispute quite appropriately has no logical resolution within the poem. On the other hand, Randall's heavy end-rhymes develop qualitative contrasts as Washington admonishes "... do not grouse,/But work, and save, and buy a house" and DuBois responds that Washington should "try his little plan,/But as for me, I'll be a man." Upon second thought auditors may feel there is less than justice in this mock dialogue in which just one participant gets mocked, but it has been a delight.

Randall generates such verse between the poles of a wit modulated by the rhythms of popular idiom and a strong ethical concern. Frequently he works as a satirist invoking the integrity of discipline and good sense to censure those who sanctify getting high ("Hail, Dionysos"), indulge themselves in fashionable introspection ("Analysands"), or parade as "stone" revolutionaries ("Abu"). The satiric structure, as often as not, builds upon enumeration as in "F.B.I. Memo" where the perfect spy is equipped with beard, Afro, tiki, dashiki, Swahili, and the cry "Kill the Honkies"; and deceptive simplicity is the background for wit, as in "Black Poet, White Critic" where Randall blandly records the critic's advice to write on universal themes symbolized by a white unicorn: "A *white* unicorn?"

Wit, the popular idiom, and an ethical concern are good for more than satire, however. The metaphoric identification of black speech with the Southern land in "Laughter in the Slums" lyrically images a soul world as vividly as Jean Toomer ever did, while "Roses and Revolutions" conveys a prophecy in a striking metaphysical image.

We owe much to Dudley Randall, for his devotion to art that delights and instructs led him to found the very important Broadside Press, first publisher of a number of the new black American poets. Appropriately, though, the epitome of his entire project, as poet and publisher of poets, is to be found in his own verse. Try his beautiful elegy "Langston Blues." It's all there: wit, popular form, and feeling that defies objective description. It's perfect.

—John M. Reilly

RANDALL, Julia. American. Born in Baltimore, Maryland, 15 June 1923. Educated at Bryn Mawr School, Baltimore; Bennington College, Vermont, A.B. 1945; Johns Hopkins University, Baltimore, M.A. 1950. Biology laboratory technician, Harvard University,

Cambridge, Massachusetts, 1946–48; Instructor, Johns Hopkins University, 1949–52, and University of Maryland overseas extension, Paris, 1952–53; Library Assistant, Goucher College, Towson, Maryland, 1954–56; Instructor, Peabody Conservatory, Baltimore, 1956–59; Instructor, then Assistant Professor, Towson State College, Baltimore, 1958–62. Assistant Professor, 1962–66, and since 1966, Associate Professor of English, Hollins College, Virginia. Recipient: *Sewanee Review* Fellowship, 1957; National Endowment for the Arts grant, 1966; National Institute of Arts and Letters grant, 1968. Address: Department of English, Hollins College, Virginia 24020, U.S.A.

PUBLICATIONS

Verse

The Solstice Tree. Baltimore, Contemporary Poetry, 1952.
Mimic August. Baltimore, Contemporary Poetry, 1960.
4 Poems. Hollins College, Virginia, Tinker Press, 1964.
The Puritan Carpenter. Chapel Hill, University of North Carolina Press, 1965.
Adam's Dream. Hollins College, Virginia, Tinker Press, 1966.
Adam's Dream: Poems. New York, Knopf, 1969.

Julia Randall comments:

It seems to me quite beyond the call of duty, modesty, or even common sense to answer questions about one's own verse. Influences? The usual ones for our time: Eliot, Yeats, Rilke, Stevens, Thomas; behind them Hopkins, Wordsworth, Dickinson, the great ambiguous ghost of Milton, and the lesser ghosts of hymn- and ballad-makers. Also, very importantly, musicians, painters, naturalists, novelists, philosophers, and prophets. My subjects are drawn about equally from nature (especially the Maryland-Virginia countryside) and from the arts, which is to say about half my poems are literal and half imaginary. They are personal or local, rather than dramatic or topical. My forms are frequently traditional quatrains, but tend now toward something larger or looser with either sustained or irregular use of slant rhyme. I belong to no school that I know of. I try to achieve at least an articulation of the questions that particular experience seems to pose: how do we attach ourselves to or separate ourselves from each other, or from time? how do we know? where or to whom do we most belong? how do we mean? I try to write complete poems, sensible to the eye and ear as well as to the mind.

* * *

The poems of Julia Randall are tough and compressed, with a complexity that demands much of the reader, hard lines in the traditional sense, taut and metaphysical; but they are also lyrical and musically beautiful, written in a language that sings even as it tightens into knots of fused word and idea. The poems are highly allusive and are often witty in the fullest sense; language leaps to imagination and words contort themselves for the mind's delight. They are highly charged entities in which the arcane and archaic are alloyed with metaphysical passion into an active communion with the colloquial and the immediate. The days of her poems are precise and detailed, often carefully dated, but they open out, forward and back, into thought, memory and belief, into what can best be termed imaginative meditation – the mind fully at work in the harmonies (and disharmonies) of the present, not analyzing and organizing it but rather experiencing it down to the very bone.

Her earlier poems were more self-consciously aesthetic, almost hermetic at times, but even in them, she wrote from a commitment to the immediacy of experience, to learning from the inside out. For example, in the poem "Inscape I" from her first book, *The Solstice Tree*:

You

that curl the blind hand over the breast,
sing for a sign, sign for a feast,

fasten the blade, explore the vein,
learn the familiar blood.

Her later poems have become more openly personal, less artificially wrought, while losing none of the compressed intensity of the early poems. She addresses the world and her "masters" (Stevens and Rilke, Wordsworth, Lawrence, Woolf and Yeats); she invokes them, plant and poet, stone and artist, demanding of them and of herself "what we see clear, but clumsily half-tell." What she sees is the world of bone and blood and words, but also the power of being itself, beyond and through them all:

I walked by the stream. The hay was loud
with bugs escaping; they know
what danger is. I too
feared once the many-bladed mower.
Once, but not now.

—R. H. W. Dillard

RANDALL, Margaret. Mexican. Born in New York City, 6 December 1936. Educated at the University of New Mexico, Albuquerque. Married 1) Sam Jacobs in 1955 (divorced, 1958); 2) Sergio Mondragón in 1962 (marriage dissolved, 1967); lived with Robert Cohen, 1968–75, and since 1976 with Antonio Castro; four children. Editor, the English-Spanish quarterly, *El Corno Emplumado*, Mexico City, 1962–69. Has lived in Cuba since 1969. Recipient: National Institute of Arts and Letters grant, Carnegie Fund grant, and Gutman Foundation grant, 1960. Address: Línea 53, Apto. 9, e/M y N, Vedado, Havana 4, Cuba.

PUBLICATIONS

Verse

Giant of Tears and Other Poems. New York, Tejon Press, 1959.
Ecstasy Is a Number. New York, Gutman Foundation, 1961.
Poems of the Glass. Cleveland, Renegade Press, 1964.
Small Sounds from the Bass Fiddle. Albuquerque, New Mexico, Duende Press, 1964.
October. Mexico City, El Corno Emplumado, 1965.
25 Stages of My Spine. New Rochelle, New York, Elizabeth Press, 1967.
Water I Slip Into at Night. Privately printed, 1967.
So Many Rooms Has a House But One Roof. Nyack, New York, New Rivers Press, 1968.
Getting Rid of Blue Plastic: Poems Old and New, edited by Pritish Nandy. Calcutta, Dialogue, 1968.
Part of the Solution. New York, New Directions, 1972.
With Our Hands. Vancouver, New Star, 1974.

All My Used Parts, Shackles, Fuel, Tenderness, and Stars. Privately printed, 1976.
We. New York, Smyrna Press, 1978.
Carlota. Vancouver, New Star, 1978.

Other

Day's Coming! (miscellany). Privately printed, 1973.
Cuban Women Now: Interviews with Cuban Women. Toronto, Women's Press, 1974.
La Situación de la Mujer (lectures). Lima, Centro de Estudios de Participación Popular, 1974.
Spirit of the People. Vancouver, New Star, 1975.
Doris Tijerino: Inside the Nicaraguan Revolution. Vancouver, New Star, 1978.
Reflections from Cuba. Privately printed, 1978.
No se Puede Hacer la Revolución sin Nosotras. Havana, Casa de las Américas, 1978.
Cuban Women: Twenty Years Later. New York, Pella Press, 1979.

Editor, *Los Hippies: Expressión de Una Crisis.* Mexico City, Siglo XXI, 1968.
Editor, *Las Mujeres.* Mexico City, Siglo XXI, 1970.
Editor, *This Great People Has Said "Enough!" and Has Begun to Move: Poems from the Struggle in Latin America.* San Francisco, People's Press, 1972.

Translator, *Let's Go*, by Otto-René Castillo. London, Cape Goliard Press, 1971.
Translator, *Estos Cantos Habitados/These Living Songs* (15 Cuban poets). Fort Collins, Colorado State University Press, 1978.

Manuscript Collection: New York University Library.

Critical Study: "The Sense of the Risk of the Coming Together" by Alvin Greenberg, in *Minnesota Review* (St. Paul), vi, 2, 1966.

Margaret Randall comments:

There are no longer any separations between the poem (or writing of any kind) and life, the revolution, the changing balance of powers in the world, and the change within the human being as she/he struggles to become the "new man" (or woman) Che spoke of and was. The poem is valuable to me as a documentary of the life experience and the experience of struggle: itself a vehicle for growth, struggle, revolution. Woman's struggle is especially important to me and I grow within it. I want to put my writing at the service of a true history.

* * *

The strength of Margaret Randall's poetry comes from its position on the immediate edges of experience: experience fresh and untempered whatever its quality (loving or violent), and brought forth directly as an offering of the poet's own self. She has been consistently a poet whose major concern is to confront whatever happens – however new and however great the risks – prepared to grow, as artist and person, from that encounter, always seeking to "create a new language for this, a new place." The dangers of such an approach are great – that the experience will be too raw, too unformulated, to become meaningful, or that, particularly in areas of political or social concern, failure to find the new words may cause one to fall back on sloganizing – but the values, as she shows, are well worth the risk: giving a sense of the immediacy of the poet living through a significant encounter (with self, dreams, other people, events, new places), discovering herself in the midst of that encounter, and opening up to the reader the potential for a similar discovery.

Thus her poems deal, for the most part, with, as she says in "Everyone Comes to a Lighted

House," "people moving together" and with her own emergence, as detailed in "Eyes," through such encounters to new vision: "The dream went on but I woke up./The bus is full my stop's coming up everyone has new eyes." The brief prose pieces included in her recent book *Part of the Solution* present in greater detail encounters comparable to those which take place in the poems; they are not actually stories but meetings, generally bizarre and traumatic, in which the poet confronts, or has forced upon her, experiences which call her entire sense of self, society, or relationships into question. Again, as in all her work – and in the movement of her life as well – what is pre-eminent is the sense of risk, and of risk as potential for the new, for learning and growth, as in "So Many Rooms Has a House But One Roof":

> One side a surface where the hole forms, opens,
> to persist means look through
> or change
> as water runs over the found object.

One changes, she indicates, not by becoming something different but by self-discovery, even in the act of writing; the encounters around which her writing centers become the potential for creativity in both her life and her poetry, and the odds which she describes Fidel risking in the mountains become as well her own sense of challenge and possibility, as she concludes in "Both Dreams":"in forests we'll conquer because we have to."

—Alvin Greenberg

RAWORTH, Tom (Thomas Moore Raworth). British. Born in Bexleyheath, Kent, 19 July 1938. Educated at St. Joseph's Academy, London, 1949–54; University of Essex, Colchester 1967–71, M.A. 1971. Owner and Publisher, Matrix Press, and Editor, *Outburst*, London, 1959–64; Founding Editor, with Barry Hall, Goliard Press, London, 1965–67; Poet-in-Residence or Lecturer, University of Essex, 1969–70, Bowling Green State University, Ohio, 1972–73, Northeastern Illinois University, Chicago, 1973–74, University of Texas, Austin, 1974–75, and King's College, Cambridge, 1977–78. Recipient: Alice Hunt Bartlett Prize, 1969; Arts Council grant, 1970, 1972; Cholmondeley Award, 1972. Address: c/o T. A. Raworth, 8 Avondale Road, Welling, Kent, England.

PUBLICATIONS

Verse

Weapon Man. London, Goliard Press, 1965.
Continuation. London, Goliard Press, 1966.
The Relation Ship. London, Goliard Press, 1967; New York, Grossman, 1969.
Haiku, with John Esam and Anselm Hollo. London, Trigram Press, 1968.
The Big Green Day. London, Trigram Press, 1968.
Lion, Lion. London, Trigram Press, 1970.
Moving. London, Cape Goliard Press, and New York, Grossman, 1971.
Penguin Modern Poets 19, with John Ashbery and Lee Harwood. London, Penguin, 1971.

Pleasant Butter. Northampton, Massachusetts, Sand Project Press, 1972.
Tracking. Bowling Green, Ohio, Doones Press, 1972.
Time Being, with Asa Benveniste and Ray DiPalma. London, Blue Chair, 1972.
Here. Privately printed, 1973.
An Interesting Picture of Ohio. Privately printed, 1973.
Back to Nature. London, Joe DiMaggio Press, 1973.
Act. London, Trigram Press, 1973.
Ace. London, Cape Goliard Press, 1974; Berkeley, California, Figures Press, 1977.
Bolivia: Another End of Ace. London, Secret, 1974.
Cloister. Northampton, Massachusetts, Sand Project Press, 1975.
That More Simple Natural Time Tone Distortion. Storrs, University of Connecticut Library, 1975.
Common Sense. San Francisco, Zephyrus Image, 1976.
The Mask. Berkeley, California, Poltroon Press, 1976.
Sky Tails. Cambridge, Lobby Press, 1978.
Four Door Guide. Cambridge, Street Editions, 1979.
Writing. Durham, North Carolina, Bull City Press, 1979.
Heavy Light. Colchester, Essex, Transgravity Press, 1979.
Nicht Wahr, Rosie? Berkeley, California, Poltroon Press, 1979.

Recording: *Little Trace Remains of Emmett Miller*, Stream Records, 1969.

Play

Screenplay: *A Plague on Both Your Houses*, 1966.

Other

The Minicab War (parodies), with Anselm Hollo and Gregory Corso. London, Matrix Press, 1961.
Betrayal. London, Trigram Press, 1967.
A Serial Biography. London, Fulcrum Press, 1969; Berkeley, California, Turtle Island, 1979.
Sic Him Oltorf! San Francisco, Zephyrus Image, 1974.
Logbook. Berkeley, California, Poltroon Press, 1977.
Cancer. Berkeley, California, Turtle Island, 1979.

Translator, with Valarie Raworth, *From the Hungarian.* Privately printed, 1973.

Manuscript Collection: Wilbur Cross Library, University of Connecticut, Storrs.

Critical Study: by Jeff Nuttall, in *Poetry Information 9–10* (London), 1974; Geoffrey Ward, in *Perfect Bound* (Cambridge), Winter 1976–77; John Barrell, in *Granta* (Cambridge), Autumn 1977; Rod Mengham, in *Language 6* (New York), December 1978.

* * *

In Tom Raworth's poetry, there is a reluctance to sort, and so distort, language from experience. It is an agreement the poet has with himself, to let things stand, to accept the persistent fall of experience. His lines are a succession of phrases and images that are principally autonomous, non-referential statements. These are flicks of the mind's eye, pure cinematics, seemingly promiscuous because the pattern may be on too large a scale or too subliminal for usual acts of perception. The problem is briefly explored in *Tracking*: "the connections (or connectives) no/longer work – so how to build the long/poem everyone is straining for? (the/synopsis is enough for a quick mind now/(result of film?) ..." The associations are not of ideas or feelings, but patterns of mind meeting events, recorded not so much for sake of discovery but to document how words and experience might occur with a minimum of willed intervention.

Randomness is his faith. It is in part a response to media explosion, a revolt against data bombardment. He is distrustful of the world that words circumscribe and, in order to be free of the rule of language manipulation, is driven beyond cohesion and clarity as values – "Until finally writing becomes the only thing that's not a petroleum by-product, or a neat capsule available without prescription." He resists the exploitations of the conscious mind, and is aware of the long tradition of such resistance (a dinghy hauled behind in *Logbook* is named "Automatic Writing"). His procedure and form are increasingly that of the notebook, and are summarized in three quick lines from a series of such jottings published as *Pleasant Butter*: "random gives/faster flicker/to draw from." Already in *The Relation Ship*, there is a poem with the title "Notebook," along with others of a similar activity, notably "Six Days," a "documentary" written while staying briefly in Paris, on loose sheets afterwards pieced together, the scraps of each day; while in *Moving*, the sequence "Antlers" has only dates and times for titles.

An important clue to Raworth's compositional technique can be found in the prose *A Serial Biography*, which grew out of letters to Edward Dorn (serial in the sense of produced in installments, but hardly an orderly sequence). There, the narrator tells of writing a book with a friend while working for a pharmaceuticals firm. Each would type out a chapter a day on memo paper, exchanging them through the internal mails. In one section, which he himself is not satisfied with, the narrator pulls the sheet from the typewriter and adds in pencil: "Imagine slightly to the left of this paragraph." (Similarly, in "Wedding Day" in *The Relation Ship*, the poet writes, "i/inhabit a place just to the left of that phrase.") That is, the writing is deliberately off-centered, oblique, out of focus – the way a painter might squint or step back and cover an eye to gain a fresh approach to a painting stale or stubborn.

There are startling juxtapositions and a troubling elliptical quality to Raworth's work, but his deliberate amassing of inert material, non-organic, desensitized data, is not surrealism. Surrealism makes a crooked sense. Moreover, its images are dream-vivid and their junctures evident. Here, there is a ribbon flatness. Language is cut off from anything other than its own momentum (nor is it self-generative, with puns and allusions). One knows from poems such as "The Others," "Morning," "Got Me," or "Shoes," that the poet is capable of humor, sarcasm, wit, even envy and despair. It is evident he actively chooses discontinuity, or, more precisely, allows it and the silences in between. The "buzz," he calls it – a blank honesty. He allows his personality to remain deliberately flat, withdrawn, so the words may be cast in deeper shadows. The result is what Dorn, in writing about Raworth, calls "the experience of apparently inconsequential *detail* shorn of mannner." Ultimately, it is a poetry characteristic not of indecision but immense tolerance and patience toward the human condition, a careful lowering of the threshold through which coherence must pass.

—George F. Butterick

RAY, David. American. Born in Sapulpa, Oklahoma, 20 May 1932. Educated at the University of Chicago, B.A. 1952, M.A. 1957. Married Judy Ray in 1970; three daughters and one son. Member of the Faculty, Wright Junior College, Chicago, 1957–58, Northern Illinois University, DeKalb, 1958–60, and Cornell University, Ithaca, New York, 1960–64; Assistant Professor of Literature and Humanities, Reed College, Portland, Oregon, 1964–66; Lecturer in English, University of Iowa, Iowa City, 1969–71. Since 1971, Professor of English, University of Missouri, Kansas City. Visiting Professor, Syracuse University, New

York, 1978–79. Editor, *Chicago Review*, 1956–57; Associate Editor, *Epoch*, Ithaca, New York, 1960–64. Since 1971, Editor, *New Letters*, Kansas City, Missouri. Recipient: *New Republic* Young Writers Award, 1958; Bread Loaf Writers Conference Robert Frost Fellowship, 1964; Woursell Foundation and University of Vienna fellowship, 1966. Address: Department of English, University of Missouri, Kansas City, Missouri 64110, U.S.A.

PUBLICATIONS

Verse

X-Rays. Ithaca, New York, Cornell University Press, 1965.
Dragging the Main and Other Poems. Ithaca, New York, Cornell University Press, 1968.
A Hill in Oklahoma. Shawnee Mission, Kansas, Bkmk Press, 1973.
Gathering Firewood: New Poems and Selected. Middletown, Connecticut, Wesleyan University Press, 1974.
Enough of Flying: Poems Inspired by the Ghazals of Ghalib. Calcutta, Writers Workshop, 1977.
The Tramp's Cup. Kirksville, Missouri, Chariton Press, 1978.

Short Stories

The Mulberries of Mingo. Austin, Texas, Cold Mountain Press, 1978.

Other

Editor, *The Chicago Review Anthology.* Chicago, University of Chicago Press, and London, Cambridge University Press, 1959.
Editor, *From the Hungarian Revolution: A Collection of Poems.* Ithaca, New York, Cornell University Press, 1966.
Editor, with Robert Bly, *A Poetry Reading Against the Vietnam War.* Madison, Minnesota, American Writers Against the Vietnam War, 1966.
Editor, with Robert M. Farnsworth, *Richard Wright: Impressions and Perspectives.* Ann Arbor, University of Michigan Press, 1973.
Editor, with Jack Salzman, *The Jack Conroy Reader.* New York, Burt Franklin, 1979.
Editor, with Judy Ray, *New Asian Writing.* Calcutta, Writers Workshop, 1979.

David Ray comments:

I like the comparisons that have been made of my poems to X-rays or to found objects, as my poems are attempts to render verbal equivalents of what happens inside me or in persons or things I have found in the world and which have given me and sometimes them a different context through my finding them.

* * *

Like other disciples of W. C. Williams, but none, perhaps so faithfully and persistently, David Ray continues to turn out strong, sharp, direct poem after poem without the help of most of the prosodic conventions. Avoiding regular meter, Ray prefers the casual (hence surprising) turn of thought, the plainest of colloquial diction, until, as when we round the bend of a perfectly ordinary road and see a great holm oak, his poem reveals itself.

It's no use saying of one of his poems: "An accident; it just happened." The miracle happens too frequently. Let us scrutinize "Love Letter" (from *X-Rays*), a poem which (after that title) begins paradoxically among bills and loneliness:

For months now you've hated me
　　and sent on angry letters
From creditors without comment
　　though you've had to address
New envelopes; your anger
　　is joined to theirs
And I take it broadside

Then, through an instant landscape as symbolic as real, comes the shift of tone:

　　here in an empty apartment
Where I watch the cars plunge
　　past all night, where I own
A morning moon above distant farms
　　and my cough annoys no one.

Perhaps the little landscape owes something to the Chinese poets? In any case the vowel melody of the concluding lines (own-moon-no one) along with *m*'s and *n*'s provides an unobtrusive and delightful music that seems inseparable from the images there. Rhythmic elements are also operative. By stress-count the poem goes 3, 3, 3, 2, 3, 2, 3, 3, 3, 3, 4, 3, and since the next-to-last line has four it looms vastly. Rhythm is often working for Ray when the reader least suspects it.

The technique of David Ray's poetry is sophisticated; its total effect, as in the prose of the late George Orwell, is one of unalloyed sincerity. Every line seems washed in the astringencies of simplicity and surprise.

—E. L. Mayo

REANEY, James (Crerar). Canadian. Born near Stratford, Ontario, 1 September 1926. Educated at Elmhurst Public School, Easthope Township, Perth County; Stratford High School; University College, Toronto (Epstein Award, 1948), M.A. in English, Ph.D. 1956. Married Colleen Thibaudeau in 1951; two living children. Member of the English Department, University of Manitoba, Winnipeg, 1949–56. Since 1960, Member of the English Department, Middlesex College, University of Western Ontario, London. Founding Editor, *Alphabet* magazine, London, 1960–71. Active in little theatre groups in Winnipeg and London. Recipient: Governor General's Award, for verse, 1950, 1959, for drama, 1963; President's Medal, University of Western Ontario, 1955, 1958; Chalmers Award, 1975, 1976. Agent: Sybil Hutchinson, Apt. 409, Ramsden Place, 50 Hillsboro Avenue, Toronto, Ontario M5R 1S8, Canada.

PUBLICATIONS

Verse

The Red Heart. Toronto, McClelland and Stewart, 1949.

A Suit of Nettles. Toronto, Macmillan, 1958.
Twelve Letters to a Small Town. Toronto, Ryerson Press, 1962.
The Dance of Death at London, Ontario. London, Ontario, Alphabet, 1963.
Poems, edited by Germaine Warkentin. Toronto, New Press, 1972.
Selected Shorter [and *Longer*] *Poems*, edited by Germaine Warkentin. Erin, Ontario, Press Porcépic, 2 vols., 1976.

Plays

Night-Blooming Cereus (broadcast, 1959; produced Toronto, 1960). Included in *The Killdeer and Other Plays*, 1962.
The Killdeer (produced Toronto, 1960; Glasgow, 1965). Included in *The Killdeer and Other Plays*, 1962; revised version (produced Vancouver, 1970), in *Masks of Childhood*, 1972.
One-Man Masque (produced Toronto, 1960). Included in *The Killdeer and Other Plays*, 1962.
The Easter Egg (produced Hamilton, Ontario, 1962). Included in *Masks of Childhood*, 1972.
The Killdeer and Other Plays (includes *Sun and Moon*, *One-Man Masque*, *Night-Blooming Cereus*). Toronto, Macmillan, 1962.
Sun and Moon (produced Winnipeg, Manitoba, 1971). Included in *The Killdeer and Other Plays*, 1962.
Names and Nicknames (produced Winnipeg, Manitoba, 1963). Included in *Apple Butter and Other Plays*, 1973.
Apple Butter (puppet play; also director: produced London, Ontario, 1965). Included in *Apple Butter and Other Plays*, 1973.
Let's Make a Carol: A Play with Music for Children, music by John Beckwith. Waterloo, Ontario, Waterloo Music, 1965.
Listen to the Wind (produced London, Ontario, 1965; Woodstock, New York, 1967). Vancouver, Talonbooks, 1972.
Colours in the Dark (produced Stratford, Ontario, 1967). Vancouver and Toronto, Talonbooks-Macmillan, 1970.
Three Desks (produced Calgary, 1967). Included in *Masks of Childhood*, 1972.
Ignoramus (produced Toronto, 1967). Included in *Apple Butter and Other Plays*, 1973.
Geography Match (produced London, 1967). Included in *Apple Butter and Other Plays*, 1973.
Masque, with Ron Cameron (produced Toronto, 1972). Toronto, Simon and Pierre, 1974.
Masks of Childhood (includes *The Killdeer*, *Three Desks*, *The Easter Egg*), edited by Brian Parker. Toronto, New Press, 1972.
Apple Butter and Other Plays for Children (includes *Names and Nicknames*, *Ignoramus*, *Geography Match*). Vancouver, Talonbooks, 1973.
The Donnellys: A Trilogy:
1. *Sticks and Stones* (produced Toronto, 1973). Erin, Ontario, Press Porcépic, 1975.
2. *The Saint Nicholas Hotel* (produced Toronto, 1974). Erin, Ontario, Press Porcépic, 1976.
3. *Handcuffs* (produced Toronto, 1975). Erin, Ontario, Press Porcépic, 1976.
Baldoon, with Marty Gervais (produced Toronto, 1975). Erin, Ontario, Porcupine's Quill, 1976.
All the Bees and All the Keys (for children), music by John Beckwith. Erin, Ontario, Press Porcépic, 1976.
The Dismissal (produced Toronto, 1977). Erin, Ontario, Press Porcépic, 1978.
Wacousta (produced Toronto, 1978). Erin, Ontario, Press Porcépic, 1979.

Radio Play: *Night-Blooming Cereus*, 1959.

Other

The Boy with an "R" in His Hand (juvenile). Toronto, Macmillan, 1965.
Fourteen Barrels from Sea to Sea. Erin, Ontario, Press Porcépic, 1977.

Bibliography: in *James Reaney* by Alvin A. Lee, New York, Twayne, 1968; in *James Reaney* by Ross G. Woodman, Toronto, McClelland and Stewart, 1971.

Theatrical Activities:

Director: **Plays** – *One-Man Masque and Night-Blooming Cereus*, Toronto, 1960; *Apple Butter*, London, Ontario, 1965.

Actor: **Plays** – in *One-Man Masque and Night-Blooming Cereus*, Toronto, 1960.

James Reaney comments:

My poetry can probably best be summed up in three words: What I've tried to do and what I keep trying to do is Listen to the Wind, see Colours in the Dark.

* * *

One of the most original and imaginative poets in Canada, James Reaney has published only a small body of work in the past two decades, but it is poetry with a powerful consistency and concentration of mind. His plays have added to the body of his work, and so has his critical writing and editorial direction of the magazine *Alphabet*, which he founded and edited for ten years.

Alphabet, following the critical theories of Northrop Frye, under whom Reaney once studied, is concerned with "the iconography of the imagination," and successive issues have developed specific mythopoeic themes in poetry, prose, and the fine arts. Reaney as editor sometimes took up characteristic positions critical of science and of rationalism, but his own poetry is both wider and deeper (more personally focused) than these ideas would suggest. It is as a poet that he makes his strongest impact, and his imagination seems to be ordered by deep inner necessity rather than by any special theory or criticism.

His first book, *The Red Heart*, already contains the essential elements of his view of life. It offers dazzling and provocative leaps of fantasy, free-wheeling satire, and wild surrealist wit. But there are also deeply serious poems which set the tone for the book and for Reaney's later work.

These poems deal with death, with the universal stage of nature marked by change and destined for ultimate extinction, and with the mystery of the perishable individual heart and mind. Against this backdrop, the world of human concerns withers into insignificance, and thus provides the subject for Reaney's brilliant secular satires.

Further, in the context of death and human folly, the poetry reveals a powerful attachment to childhood memories and emotions. Against the world of childhood, the adult world becomes polarized as its opposite, the scene of triviality and horror.

Reaney's second book, *A Suit of Nettles*, is a complex satire, purportedly directed at Canadian life in Ontario Province, but really concerned with life generally, under the guise of an animal allegory. The poem is a metrical *tour-de-force* in imitation of Spenser's *Shepheardes Calender*. Language is used with a good deal of archaizing arbitrariness and artificial word-placing, but the whole effect is one of great skill and virtuosity in satirical handling. The themes of the earlier book are formalized into what is now clearly a unifying vision, and in technical skill the whole is a professional execution of a full and unified work.

The nature of this vision is thoroughly traditional and recognizably Christian. The *contemptus mundi* is fully explored in the farm and goose allegory; and the complementary theme of eternal order is only touched on here and there. In all his work so far, the Christian resolution appears in only two crucial passages, one at the close of *The Dance of Death*, and the other toward the end of *A Suit of Nettles*, in the November section.

A Suit of Nettles is Reaney's most ambitious and satisfying book. The collections published since are minor developments of his central themes. *Twelve Letters to a Small Town* is written in the style of mock infantilism; it explores the world of childhood in the satirical secular dimension. *The Dance of Death at London, Ontario* is an imitation of the late medieval genre, continuing the same satire on a more general social canvas.

—Louis Dudek

REDGROVE, Peter (William). British. Born in Kingston, Surrey, 2 January 1932. Educated at Queen's College, Cambridge. Married to Barbara Redgrove (separated), three children; lives with Penelope Shuttle, *q.v.*, one daughter. Formerly scientific journalist and editor; Visiting Poet, University of Buffalo, New York, 1961–62; Gregory Fellow in Poetry, Leeds University, 1963–65. Since 1966, Poet-in-Residence, Falmouth School of Art, Cornwall. Visiting Professor, Colgate University, Hamilton, New York, 1974–75. Recipient: Fulbright Fellowship, 1961; Arts Council grant, 1969, 1970, 1973, 1975; *Guardian* Prize, for fiction, 1973; Prudence Farmer Award, 1977; Imperial Tobacco Award, for radio play, 1978. Address: c/o Routledge and Kegan Paul, Publishers, 39 Store Street, London WC1E 7DD, England.

PUBLICATIONS

Verse

The Collector and Other Poems. London, Routledge, 1960.
The Nature of Cold Weather and Other Poems. London, Routledge, 1961.
At the White Monument and Other Poems. London, Routledge, 1963.
The Force and Other Poems. London, Routledge, 1966.
The God-Trap. London, Turret, 1966.
The Old White Man. London, Poet and Printer, 1968.
Penguin Modern Poets 11, with D. M. Black and D. M. Thomas. London Penguin, 1968.
Work in Progress MDMLXVIII. London, Poet and Printer, 1968.
The Mother, The Daughter and the Sighing Bridge. Oxford, Sycamore Press, 1970.
The Shirt, The Skull and the Grape. Frensham, Surrey, Sceptre Press, 1970.
Love's Journeys. Cardiff, Second Aeon, 1971.
The Bedside Clock. Oxford, Sycamore Press, 1971.
Love's Journeys: A Selection. Crediton, Devon, Gilbertson, 1971.
Dr. Faust's Sea-Spiral Spirit and Other Poems. London, Routledge, 1972.
Two Poems. Rushden, Northamptonshire, Sceptre Press, 1972.
The Hermaphrodite Album, with Penelope Shuttle. London, Fuller d'Arch Smith, 1973.
Sons of My Skin: Selected Poems 1954–1974, edited by Marie Peel. London, Routledge, 1975.
Aesculapian Notes. Knotting, Bedfordshire, Sceptre Press, 1975.
Skull Event. Knotting, Bedfordshire, Sceptre Press, 1977.

The Fortifiers, The Vitrifiers, and the Witches. Knotting, Bedfordshire, Sceptre Press, 1977.
From Every Chink of the Ark and Other New Poems. London, Routledge, 1977.
Happiness. Berkhamsted, Hertfordshire, Priapus Press, 1978.
The White, Night-Flying Moths Called "Souls." Knotting, Bedfordshire, Sceptre Press, 1978.
The Weddings at Nether Powers and Other New Poems. London, Routledge, 1979.

Plays

The Sermon: A Prose Poem (broadcast, 1964). London, Poet and Printer, 1966.
Three Pieces for Voices. London, Poet and Printer, 1972.
In the Country of the Skin (broadcast, 1973). Rushden, Northamptonshire, Sceptre Press, 1973.
Miss Carstairs Dressed for Blooding and Other Plays. London, Boyars, 1977.
The Hypnotist (produced Plymouth, 1978).

Radio Plays: *The White Monument*, 1963; *The Sermon*, 1964; *The Anniversary*, 1964; *In the Country of the Skin*, 1973; *The Holy Sinner*, from a novel by Thomas Mann, 1975; *Dance the Putrefact*, music by Anthony Smith-Masters, 1975; *The God of Glass*, 1977.

Novels

In the Country of the Skin. Rushden, Northamptonshire, Sceptre Press, 1972.
The Terrors of Dr. Treviles, with Penelope Shuttle. London, Routledge, 1974.
The Glass Cottage: A Nautical Romance, with Penelope Shuttle. London Routledge, 1976.
The God of Glass. London, Routledge, 1979.
The Sleep of the Great Hypnotist. London, Routledge, 1979.

Other

The Wise Wound: Eve's Curse and Everywoman, with Penelope Shuttle. London, Gollancz, 1978; New York, Marek, 1979.

Editor, *Poet's Playground 1963.* Leeds, Schools Sports Association, 1963.
Editor, *Universities Poetry 7.* Keele, Universities Poetry Management Committee, 1965.
Editor, with John Fuller and Harold Pinter, *New Poems 1967.* London, Hutchinson, 1967.
Editor, with Jon Silkin, *New Poetry 5.* London, Hutchinson, 1979.

Manuscript Collections: Humanities Research Center, University of Texas, Austin; Brotherton Library, University of Leeds.

Critical Studies: "Groupings" by Roger Garfitt, in *British Poetry since 1960*, edited by Michael Schmidt and Grevel Lindop, Oxford, Carcanet Press, 1972; "Peter Redgrove" by Marie Peel, in *Books and Bookmen* (London), April 1973; "Ways of Booming" by Douglas Dunn, in *Encounter* (London), September 1975; interview with Jed Rasula and Mike Erwin, in *Hudson Review* (New York), Autumn 1975; "The Voice of the Green Man" by Anne Stevenson, in *Times Literary Supplement* (London), 18 November 1977; *Tradition and Experiment in English Poetry* by Philip Hobsbaum, London, Macmillan, 1979.

* * *

"The most ordinary people have the most extraordinary dreams, and in them have a capacity for understanding and adaptation far beyond their waking lives," Peter Redgrove has written in a recent review (*Guardian*, 12 April 1979). "Why do we so taboo the dream life when it is so plainly a continuum with the waking creative imagination?"

This continuum has always been a preoccupation of Redgrove's work, and most of his recent poetry has had the free associations, the astonishing, surreal proliferation of details, and the magical transformations of plot and image which we associate with dream. But even in his early poems, Redgrove was concerned to explore that tabooed interface where the ordinary domesticated ego feels both appalled and exhilarated by the sweeping energies of an exuberant and amoral instinctual world. The house, invaded by apparently alien forces which turn out to be an essential part of its being, is a frequent symbol of this process. In the fine poem "Old House," the richly kinetic verbs and boisterous syntax record such an invasion with ambiguous enthusiasm:

> I lay in an agony of imagination as the wind
> Limped up the stairs and puffed on the landings,
> Snuffled through floorboards from the foundations,
> Tottered, withdrew into flaws, and shook the house....

The man, trying to sleep, but afraid of it (as in so many of these early poems), seems at first to be threatened by a dark, deathly force, suffocating in the debris of the past ("Scale of dead people fountained to the ceiling"). But it's not the past but the future which terrifies, as the last line of each stanza indicates, speaking of a child not yet born, and his dread of bringing it into such a world. Only with the reassurance of the last stanza, which reduces his terror to a "silly agony" as his wife turns in her sleep and calls to him, does he learn "what children were to make a home for." In poem after poem this theme is repeated, in "Expectant Father" and "Foundation," for example, or "Bedtime Story for My Son," which turns, in the end, into a story aimed at reassuring the father as much as the child. The house seems to be haunted by the voice of a small boy. The poet hunts for the ghost, to no avail; his wife only smiles and comments, enigmatically, " 'I couldn't go and love the empty air.' " It becomes clear, finally, that the ghost is not the past, but the future pressing into existence: the voice comes "From just underneath both our skins," and the poem concludes, like so many of these early ones, on a carefully prepared note of discovery, educating man and wife into love, procreation and time, which carries, as its obverse, a grasping of the supersession latent in all fulfilment: "Plainly, this is how we found/That love pines loudly to go out to where/It need not spend itself on fancy and the empty air." It is the tension, in these early poems, between domesticity, responsibility, the worried, paternal ego in the hard-earned house, and the spawning, heady but anarchic powers of the instinct, which makes for their success. The emotional strain of keeping the spiritual house in order gives the poems a linguistic resolution and vigour and a sense of contained energies. But the strain also breeds those nagging, fretful ghosts that haunt the early works, lurking in corners, unused rooms and (in "Corposant") a mouldy larder. In "Ghosts," the realization to which the poem works in its last lines is that the terrace is haunted, after ten years of marriage, not by anything external, but by the "bold lovers" themselves, with their "hints of wrinkles,/Crows-feet and shadows," haunted, "Like many places with rough mirrors now,/By estrangement, if the daylight's strong."

Later poems, in losing this poise, succumbing too readily to the passional impulse, have to try harder for emotional effect, sometimes lapsing into a flamboyant and vertiginous whirl of language and imagery, to communicate their sense of the vibrant energies of the natural world. "Lazarus and the Sea," in Redgrove's first volume, presages this development, initiating that theme of Orphic descent which is at times to overwhelm his poetry. Lazarus, dredged "Back to my old problems and to the family" out of "the tide of my death," is resentful of his saviour, feeling uprooted as if by some hostile judgment which charges him "with unfitness for this holy simplicity." An antinomian desire for return to such "holy simplicity" lies behind much of the later poetry. In his latest volume, *The Weddings at Nether Powers*, as the title suggests, the theme is still strong. In "Pleasing the Black Vicar" Redgrove here speaks of wanting "to accept/The presence beyond the altar, beyond appearances," a wish that also lies behind the macabre yet strangely translucent parable of the Emperor who wishes to be flayed alive in "The Son of My Skin" (*Pieces for Voices*). A note to the latest volume tells us that "the poems descend, and return with something not thought or felt before." In a sense, this is not just a descent into the unconscious of nature, into dream and the lost continent of the carnal body; it is also a descent into the unconscious of language, which has always for Redgrove been corporeal, tangible, fleshly. In his poems we pass, as in "The House in the Acorn," through a series of opening and beckoning doors, losing ourselves in a more and more mysterious world where dimension and proportion are lost, a world where, as in "Dr. Faust's Sea-Spiral Spirit," "The roses have learnt to thunder" and "The plain pinafores alert themselves/And are a hive of angry spots," passing through the ritual mysteries of language as we pass through the metamorphoses of a nature where all is flux and entropy, creation and decreation, decomposition and renewal. In "The Case" Redgrove offers a line which sums up this double process, of discovery and return, where all changes and all remains the same: "It was like a door opening on a door of flowers that opened on flowers that were opening." In "Power" he tells us "We rose out of magma where power put his finger,/And the lines show." In "The Force" a mill-wheel which produces electricity from a mountain beck becomes a symbol of the relation of consciousness to its unconscious sources: "It trembles with stored storms/That pulse across the rim to us, as light."

Poems such as "The Idea of Entropy at Maenporth Beach," in which a girl in a white dress renews herself by a baptismal immersion in "the fat, juicy, incredibly tart muck" of the beach, and studies such as *The Wise Wound*, about menstruation, insist on recovering the rejected, the spurned and tacky origins of our being, restoring an image of the human as a living process of ingustation, excretion, sheddings, and growth, like the nature which is all flux and exhalation, wind, water, spore, and, in the title of one poem, "Nothing but Poking." Redgrove pursues this vision with a missionary zeal, even insisting, in the review cited above, "that the Special Theory of Relativity originated in a wet dream of the young Albert Einstein, in which he was riding through the universe astride a beam of light.... Whether you think the story beautiful or ugly, possible or not, will depend on your knowledge of the true ways of the imagination."

—Stan Smith

REED, Henry. British. Born in Birmingham, Warwickshire, 22 February 1914. Educated at the King Edward VI School, Birmingham; University of Birmingham, M.A. Served in the British Army, 1941–42. Teacher and free-lance journalist, 1937–41; Staff Member, Foreign Office, London, 1942–45. Since 1945, broadcaster, journalist, and radio writer. Address: c/o Jonathan Cape Ltd., 30 Bedford Square, London WC1B 3EL, England.

PUBLICATIONS

Verse

A Map of Verona. London, Cape, 1946; New York, Reynal, 1947.
Lessons of the War. New York, Chilmark Press, 1970.

Plays

Moby Dick: A Play for Radio from Herman Melville's Novel (broadcast, 1947). London, Cape, 1947.

The Queen and the Rebels adaptation of a play by Ugo Betti (broadcast, 1954; produced London, 1955). Included in *Three Plays*, 1956.

The Burnt Flower-Bed, adaptation of a play by Ugo Betti (produced London, 1955; New York, 1974). Included in *Three Plays*, 1956.

Summertime, adaptation of a play by Ugo Betti (produced London, 1955). Included in *Three Plays*, 1956.

Island of Goats, adaptation of a play by Ugo Betti (produced New York, 1955). Published as *Crime on Goat Island*, London, French, 1960; San Francisco, Chandler, 1961.

Three Plays (includes *The Queen and the Rebels*, *The Burnt Flower-Bed*, *Summertime*, adaptations of plays by Ugo Betti). London, Gollancz, 1956; New York, Grove Press, 1958.

Corruption in the Palace of Justice, adaptation of a play by Ugo Betti (broadcast, 1958; produced New York, 1963).

The Advertisement, adaptation of a play by Natalia Ginzburg (produced London, 1968; New York, 1974). London, Faber, 1969.

The Streets of Pompeii and Other Plays for Radio (includes *Leopardi: The Unblest*, *The Monument*; *The Great Desire I Had*; *Return to Naples*; *Vincenzo*). London, BBC, 1971.

Hilda Tablet and Others: Four Pieces for Radio (includes *A Very Great Man Indeed*; *The Private Life of Hilda Tablet*; *A Hedge, Backwards*; *The Primal Scene, As It Were ...*). London, BBC, 1971.

Radio Plays: *Noises On*, 1947; *Noises – Nasty and Nice*, 1947; *Moby Dick*, 1947; *Pytheas*, 1947; *Leopardi* (includes *The Unblest*, 1949, and *The Monument*, 1950); *A By-Election of the Nineties*, 1951; *The Dynasts*, 1951; *Malatesta*, 1952; *The Streets of Pompeii*, 1952; *The Great Desire I Had*, 1952; *Return to Naples*, 1953; *All for the Best*, 1953; *A Very Great Man Indeed*, 1953; *The Private Life of Hilda Tablet*, 1954; *Hamlet; or, The Consequences of Filial Piety*, 1954; *The Battle of the Masks*, 1954; *The Queen and the Rebels*, 1954; *Emily Butler*, 1954; *The Burnt Flower-Bed*, 1955; *Vincenzo*, 1955; *Crime on Goat Island*, 1956; *A Hedge, Backwards*, 1956; *Don Juan in Love*, 1956; *Alarica*, 1956; *Irene*, 1957; *Corruption in the Palace of Justice*, 1958; *The Primal Scene, As It Were ...*, 1958; *The Auction Sale*, 1958; *The Island Where the King Is a Child*, 1959; *One Flesh*, 1959; *Not a Drum Was Heard*, 1959; *Musique Discrète*, with Donald Swann, 1959; *The House on the Water*, 1961; *A Hospital Case*, 1961; *The America Prize*, 1964; *Zone 36*, 1965; *Summertime*, 1969; *The Two Mrs. Morlis*, 1971; *The Wig*, from a play by Natalia Ginzburg, 1976; *Sorrows of Love*, from a play by Giuseppe Giacosa, 1978.

Other

The Novel since 1939. London, Longman, 1946.

Translator, *Perdu and His Father*, by Paride Rombi. London, Hart Davis, 1954.
Translator, *Larger Than Life*, by Dino Buzzati. London, Secker and Warburg, 1962.
Translator, *Eugénie Grandet*, by Balzac. New York, New American Library, 1964.

* * *

Henry Reed, although he has published only one collection of poems, *A Map of Verona*, is a much underrated writer. He is better known for the highly amusing dramatic pieces he has written for radio than for his poems.

A Map of Verona divides itself fairly simply into four sections – poems written about the last World War, personal poems, dramatic monologues, and a sequence entitled "Tintagel." Reed is also a comic poet, and he is certainly the only writer of importance who has (in

"Chard Whitlow") parodied T. S. Eliot with complete success. This too must be taken into account.

Henry Reed is a poet with a fine ear, a strongly disciplined sense of form, and passionate feelings. The personal poems, which will be considered first, are all the more effective because emotion is never allowed to get out of hand; Reed always eschews chaos. The title poem of his book is a good example of all his finest qualities. Here are its first two stanzas:

The flutes are warm: in to-morrow's cave the music
Trembles and forms inside the musician's mind,
The lights begin, and the shifting lights in the causeways
Are discerned through the dusk, and the rolling river behind

And in what hour of beauty, in what good arms,
Shall I those regions and that city attain
From whence my dreams and slightest movements rise?
And what good Arms shall take them away again?

Here is nostalgia without a trace of sentimentality. Every word is carefully chosen and placed. All this can be found in other personal poems where, by sheer artistry, the poet can communicate and, at the same time, keep the distance which all very good poems of human feeling must have if they are not to fall into bathos or formlessness.

"Morning," "The Return," "Outside and In," and "The Door and the Window" all fall into this group of personal poems. The last named has the beautiful opening stanza:

My love, you are timely come, let me lie by your heart,
For waking in the dark this morning, I woke to that mystery,
Which we can all wake to, at some dark time or another:
Waking to find the room not as I thought it was,
But the window further away, and the door in another direction.

The sensibility which informs such poems as these is evident in a rather different way in the poems about the Army written during the 1939 war. *Here*, Reed displays irony as well as observation. There is a section entitled "Lessons of the War" which is composed of three parts, "Naming of Parts," "Judging Distances," and "Unarmed Combat." In the first of these poems, the training of soldiers and the arrival of Spring are most dexterously and tellingly blended. The second stanza runs:

This is the lower sling swivel. And this
Is the upper sling swivel, whose use you will see
When you are given your slings. And this is the piling swivel,
Which in your case you have not got. The branches
Hold in the gardens their silent eloquent gestures,
    Which in our case we have not got.

All the futility of war is rendered in these lines. Nature goes on while men train in order to kill their enemy across the English Channel. The last lines of "Naming of Parts" complete what is, in its own very individual way, a most remarkable poem about war: "and the almond-blossom/Silent in all of the gardens and the bees going backwards and forwards,/ For to-day we have naming of parts."

Henry Reed always writes with a skill which conceals itself. This becomes more and more clear in the sequence called "The Desert" (also much concerned with war) and "Tintagel." In the latter, this poet's descriptive gifts are shown at their most intense. Part One, "Tristram" contains these lines:

The ruin leads your thoughts
Past the moment of darkness when silence fell over the hall,
And the only sound rising was the sound of frightened breathing ...
To the perpetually recurring story,
The doorway open, either in the soft green weather,
The gulls seen over the purple-threaded sea, the cliffs,
Or open in mist....

"Tintagel" also demonstrates Reed's ability to enter into the characters of others, which we find in the two monologues, "Chrysothemis" and "Philoctetes." In these poems, his highly-developed dramatic gift is clearly evident, especially in the matter of dialogue. Reed really brings Philoctetes to life in lines such as the following:

To my companions become unbearable,
I was put on this island. But the story
As you have heard it is with time distorted,
And passion and pity have done their best for it ...
... They seized me and forced me ashore,
And wept.

The poet is completely identified with Philoctetes and his plight.

Finally we must glance at "Chard Whitlow (Mr. Eliot's Sunday Evening Postscript)," Henry Reed's brilliant parody of the T. S. Eliot of *Four Quartets*. Here we have just two passages from what is not a long piece:

Seasons return, and to-day I am fifty-five
And this time last year I was fifty-four,
And this time next year I shall be sixty-two.

I think you will find this put,
Far better than I could ever hope to express it,
In the words of Kharma: "It is, we believe,
Idle to hope that the simple stirrup-pump
Can extinguish hell."

This is true parody, both uproariously funny and shrewdly ironic. Eliot's tone is perfectly caught, and Reed's mockery is not unkind but illustrates the ownership of a fine ear and a mastery of language.

Why such a good poet has written so little poetry is strange. The BBC has a way of inadvertently making its poet-employees either "dry-up" altogether or else produce a poem only now and then (Terence Tiller is another case in point). But Henry Reed has written a handful of poems that may well last; these are probably the war poems. His command over verse-forms and language is flawless. Perhaps, in old age, he will return to poetry again. It would be a loss to English literature if he did not.

—Elizabeth Jennings

REED, Ishmael. Afro-American. Born in Chattanooga, Tennessee, 22 February 1938. Educated at the University of Buffalo, New York, 1956–60. Married to Carla Blank-Reed;

one daughter by a previous marriage. Co-Founder of the *East Village Other*, New York, and *Advance*, Newark, New Jersey, 1965. Since 1971, Chairman and President of Yardbird Publishing Company; since 1973, Director, Reed Cannon and Johnson Communications. Guest lecturer, University of California, Berkeley, 1968, 1969, 1974, 1976; Lecturer, University of Washington, Seattle, 1969–70; Senior Lecturer, University of California, Berkeley; Visiting Professor, Yale University, New Haven, Connecticut, Fall 1979. Recipient: National Endowment for the Arts Grant, 1974; Rosenthal Foundation Award, 1975; Guggenheim Fellowship, 1975. Address: 8646 Terrace Drive, El Cerrito, California 94530, U.S.A.

PUBLICATIONS

Verse

Catechism of d neoamerican hoodoo church. London, Paul Breman, 1970.
Conjure: Selected Poems 1963–1970. Amherst, University of Massachusetts Press, 1972.
Chattanooga. New York, Random House, 1973.
Secretary to the Spirits. New York, Nok, 1977.

Novels

The Free-Lance Pallbearers. New York, Doubleday, 1967; London, MacGibbon and Kee, 1968.
Yellow Back Radio Broke-Down. New York, Doubleday, 1969; London, Allison and Busby, 1971.
Mumbo-Jumbo. New York, Doubleday, 1972.
The Last Days of Louisiana Red. New York, Random House, 1974.
Flight to Canada. New York, Random House, 1976.

Other

The Rise, Fall, and ...? of Adam Clayton Powell (as Emmett Coleman), with others. New York, Bee-Line, 1967.
Shrovetide in Old New Orleans (essays). New York, Doubleday, 1978.

Editor, *19 Necromancers from Now.* New York, Doubleday, 1970.
Editor, *Yardbird Reader.* Berkeley, California, Yardbird, 1972 (annual).
Editor, with Al Young, *Yardbird Lives!* New York, New Directions, 1978.
Editor, *Calafia: The California Poetry.* Berkeley, California, Yardbird, 1979.

Bibliography: "Mapping Out the Gumbo Works: An Ishmael Reed Bibliography" by Joe Weixlmann, Robert Fikes, Jr., and Ishmael Reed, in *Black American Literature Forum* (Terre Haute, Indiana), Spring 1978.

Ishmael Reed comments:

Themes – personal, magic, race, politics; no particular verse form.

* * *

Ishmael Reed is a satirist who today is primarily a novelist, but like many other Black American writers he started his literary career writing poetry. *Conjure* is his first collection of poetry and although it was not published until 1972 it is made up of renderings dating back to 1963 – four years before his first novel.

Many of these poems foreshadow the subjects of his novels and point up the fact that his more recent preoccupations are the result of thinking over an extended period of time. For example, in his introduction to *19 Necromancers from Now*, Reed writes that because "Black writers have in the past written sonnets, iambic pentameter, ballads, [and] every possible Western gentleman's form," they have sacrificed their own originality. He further says that "Sometimes I feel that the condition of the Afro-American writer in this country is so strange that one has to go to the supernatural for an analogy." It is from this feeling that Reed has developed the view that the Black artist should function as a "conjuror" who employs "Neo-HooDoo" as a means of freeing his fellow victims from the psychic attack of his oppressors.

Ishmael Reed's poems are not unique either in their intent or their responsibility but they are poignant earlier examples of the dynamic wit and unabashed approach which he demonstrates in his novels. It is scathing, uncompromising satire, but he is always in full control. A typical example of his thematic focus on the incompatibility of Western civilization and the cultures of Africa and Asia is illustrated in this excerpt from "Badman of the Guest Professor":

its not my fault dat yr tradition
was knocked off wop style & left in
d alley w/pricks in its mouth. i
read abt it in d papers but it was no
    skin off my nose
wasnt me who opened d gates & allowed
d rustlers to slip thru unnoticed. u
ought to do something about yr security or
    mend yr fences partner

and again in his prosey dictum from "The Ghost of Birmingham," a poem for which he feels impelled to apologize because it "shows the influence of people I studied in college":

There has never been in history another culture as the
Western civilization – a culture which has practiced the belief
that the physical and social environment of man is subject to
rational manipulation and that history is subject to the will and
action of man; whereas central to the traditional cultures of
the rivals of Western civilization, those of Africa and Asia, is a
belief that it is environment dominates man.

Reed's works are certainly controversial among both Black and White critics, but he wouldn't have it any other way.

—Charles L. James

REEVE, F(ranklin) D(olier). American. Born in Philadelphia, Pennsylvania, 18 September 1928. Educated at Princeton University, New Jersey, A.B. 1950; Columbia University, New York, A.M. 1952, Ph.D. 1958. Married Helen Schmidinger in 1956; three children. Taught at Columbia University, 1952–61; American Council of Learned Societies–U.S.S.R. Academy of Sciences Exchange Professor, 1961, Associate Professor and

Chairman of the Russian Department, 1962–64, Professor of Russian, 1964–66, and since 1968, Adjunct Professor of Letters, Wesleyan University, Middletown, Connecticut. Visiting Professor, Oxford University, 1964; Scholar-in-Residence, Aspen Institute, Colorado, 1973. Since 1973, Visiting Lecturer, Yale University, New Haven, Connecticut. Currently, a Justice of the Peace. Fellow, Saybrook College, Yale University. Recipient: Ford Fellowship, 1955; American Council of Learned Societies Fellowship, 1961; Ingram-Merrill Foundation award, 1961; National Institute of Arts and Letters grant, 1970; Rockefeller Fellowship, 1976. Lives in Higganum, Connecticut, U.S.A.

PUBLICATIONS

Verse

The Stone Island. Middletown, Connecticut, Salamander Press, 1964.
Six Poems. Middletown, Connecticut, Salamander Press, 1964.
In the Silent Stones. New York, Morrow, 1968.
The Blue Cat. New York, Farrar Straus, 1972.

Play

The Three-Sided Cube (produced New London, Connecticut, 1972).

Novels

The Red Machines. New York, Morrow, 1968.
Just over the Border. New York, Morrow, 1969.
The Brother. New York, Farrar Straus, 1971; Henley, Oxfordshire, Aidan Ellis, 1975.
White Colors. New York, Farrar Straus, 1973; Henley, Oxfordshire, Aidan Ellis, 1974.

Other

Aleksandr Blok: Between Image and Idea. New York, Columbia University Press, 1962.
Robert Frost in Russia. Boston, Little Brown, 1964.
On Some Scientific Concepts in Russian Poetry at the Turn of the Century. Middletown, Connecticut, Wesleyan University Center for Advanced Studies, 1966.
The Russian Novel. New York, McGraw Hill, 1966; London, Muller, 1967.

Editor and Translator, *Five Short Novels of Turgenev.* New York, Bantam, 1961.
Editor and Translator, *An Anthology of Russian Plays.* New York, Random House, 2 vols., 1961–63; as *Nineteenth-* (and *Twentieth-*) *Century Russian Plays*, New York, Norton, 2 vols., 1973.
Editor and Translator, *Great Soviet Short Stories.* New York, Dell, 1963.
Editor and Translator, *Contemporary Russian Drama.* New York, Pegasus, 1968.
Editor and Translator, *Nobel Lecture by Alexander Solzhenitsyn.* New York, Farrar Straus, 1972.

F. D. Reeve comments:

The play between the surface – things as seen – and the depths – the moral interpretations of things – is the life of poetry. Traditions supply the concepts, the forms, which we train ourselves to use to catch the experience of change. A poem's landscape delights the mind's eye by moving forward and back out of the present, transfixing change in tensions among words, ferrying between what is outside and the fictions in the imagination. The substance of poetry is metaphor, at times given in colloquial language and images from casual life, at times given in strict verse patterns and difficult images of implication. The mask of the poet – philosopher, songster, clown, apostle – expresses his personality, dances before the reader until the reader picks up a new consciousness.

* * *

F. D. Reeve's first collection, *In the Silent Stones*, is mostly rhymed and metrical – jingling anapests or more flexible iambics. A sign of uncertainty is the frequency with which elaborate stanza forms are undertaken only to be modified. Devices often seem tricks of the trade rather than expressive means: "I head for the heart of a girl/on the soft white breast of the world." But the wit can be amusing, even when it merely decorates a banal observation: "The conversation seesaws on the rim of a teacup./Highwire ladies drop to save a faux pas ..." ("Summer Circus"). One is aware of echoes – of the "Movement" ("Chinese Poem"), of Lowell ("The Plaque ... for My Classmates Killed in Korea"), of Stevens ("A Tangram").

The Blue Cat shows more rhythmic subtlety and less ostentation (though a line like "That shallop symmetry burst from the hawse of her father" is hardly unforced). The imagery continues to be uneven, varying from the witty-elusive – "Like ribs around my body this armillary sphere/cages the fancy with old bars new Marco Polos must unbend" ("Hands") – to the merely flashy – "her hair/swinging like ten pendulums in love" ("The Blue Cat's Daughter"). Outstanding in the book, however, is a sequence of fourteen poems on the life of Thoreau which often achieves a moving intensity in evoking the New England moral climate. As Reeve gives himself to Thoreau we hear the voice of man with more on his mind than self-display:

> Immoral slave who pleads a moral cause,
> bankrupt in Heaven and on earth a stone,
> man sets his course against the natural laws,
> plotting the steps to seize the beautiful
>
> but coming, after all, to his own wet bones.

—Seamus Cooney

REID, Alastair. British. Born in Whithorn, Wigtonshire, Scotland, 22 March 1926. Educated at the University of St. Andrews, Scotland, M.A. (honours) 1949. Served in the Royal Navy, 1943–46. Has one son. Taught at Sarah Lawrence College, Bronxville, New York, 1950–55; Fellow in Writing, Columbia University, New York, 1966; Visiting Professor of Latin American Studies, Antioch College, Yellow Springs, Ohio, 1969–70, Oxford University and St. Andrews University, 1972–73, Colorado College, Colorado Springs, 1977, 1978, and Yale University, New Haven, Connecticut, 1979. Since 1959, Staff Writer and Correspondent, *The New Yorker*. Gave lecture tours for the Association of American Colleges, 1966, 1969. Recipient: Guggenheim Fellowship, 1957, 1958; Scottish Arts Council award, 1979. Lives in New York and Spain. Address: c/o The New Yorker, 24 West 43rd Street, New York, New York 10036, U.S.A.

PUBLICATIONS

Verse

To Lighten My House. Scarsdale, New York, Morgan and Morgan, 1953.
Oddments Inklings Omens Moments. Boston, Little Brown, 1959; London, Dent, 1961.
Corgi Modern Poets in Focus 3, with others, edited by Dannie Abse. London, Corgi, 1971.
Flowers in the Surf. Folkestone, Kent, Aten Press, 1973.
Weathering: Poems and Translations. Edinburgh, Canongate, and New York, Dutton, 1978.

Other

I Will Tell You of a Town (juvenile). Boston, Houghton Mifflin, 1956; London, Hutchinson, 1957.
Fairwater (juvenile). Boston, Houghton Mifflin, 1957.
A Balloon for a Blunderbuss (juvenile). New York, Harper, 1957.
Allth (juvenile). Boston, Houghton Mifflin, 1958.
Ounce Dice Trice. Boston, Little Brown, 1958; London, Dent, 1961.
The Millionaires, with Bob Gill. New York, Simon and Schuster, 1959.
Supposing (juvenile). Boston, Little Brown, 1960; London, Sidgwick and Jackson, 1973.
Passwords: Places, Poems, Preoccupations. Boston, Little Brown, 1963; London, Weidenfeld and Nicolson, 1965.
To Be Alive! (juvenile). New York, Macmillan, 1966.
Mother Goose in Spanish, with Anthony Kerrigan. New York, Crowell, 1967.
Uncle Timothy's Traviata (juvenile). New York, Delacorte Press, 1967.
La Isla Azul (juvenile). Barcelona, Editorial Lumen, 1973.

Translator, with others, *Ficciones*, by Jorge Luis Borges. New York, Grove Press, and London, Weidenfeld and Nicolson, 1965.
Translator, *We Are Many*, by Pablo Neruda. London, Cape Goliard Press, 1967; New York, Grossman, 1968.
Translator, with Anthony Kerrigan, *Jorge Luis Borges: A Personal Anthology*. New York, Grove Press, 1967; London, Cape, 1968.
Translator, with Ben Belitt, *A New Decade: Poems 1958–67*, by Pablo Neruda. New York, Grove Press, 1968.
Translator, with others, *Selected Poems: A Bilingual Edition*, by Pablo Neruda, edited by Nathaniel Tarn. London, Cape, 1970; New York, Delacorte Press, 1972.
Translator, *Extravagaria*, by Pablo Neruda. London, Cape, 1972; New York, Farrar Straus, 1974.
Translator, with others, *Selected Poems*, by Jorge Luis Borges. New York, Delacorte Press, and London, Penguin, 1972.
Translator, *Sunday Sunday*, by Mario Vargas Llasa. Indianapolis, Bobbs Merrill, 1973.
Translator, *Fully Empowered*, by Pablo Neruda. New York, Farrar Straus, 1975; London, Souvenir Press, 1976.
Translator, *The Gold of the Tigers*, by Jorge Luis Borges. New York, Dutton, 1977.
Translator, *Don't Ask Me How the Time Goes By*, by José Emilio Pacheco. New York, Columbia University Press, 1978.
Translator, *Isla Negra: A Notebook*, by Pablo Neruda. New York, Farrar Straus, 1979.

Manuscript Collections: State University of New York, Buffalo; National Library of Scotland, Edinburgh.

Critical Study: in *Corgi Modern Poets 3*, edited by Dannie Abse, 1971.

* * *

Alastair Reid's most recent collection of poems, *Weathering*, which includes a generous selection from his previous books, makes more evident, by a shift of focus, his distinctive contribution to literature. In *Oddments Inklings Omens Moments* a playful interest in words and in such subject matter as mirrors, magic, ghosts, cats, frogs, children, and games gives such immediate pleasure, that his deeper, underlying human concerns may be overlooked. The concern was there in the earlier poems. In "Cat-Faith" Reid's gratitude for the existence of a creature secure in its individuality, beautifully adapted for survival in a hazardous life, is at bottom a confirmation of an ultimate virtue in life itself. His valuation found explicit expression in: "Amazement is the thing./Not love, but the astonishment of loving." This affirmation is made in the recognition and acceptance of the law that "The garden is not ours." We are tenants in "Mediterranean":

> The rent is paid in breath
> and so we freely give
> the apple tree beneath
> our unpossessive love.

It is the writer's "unpossessive love" which allows him to accept the variety of life as it presents itself, and it is his fascination by words, which gives his poems their rare music as in "The Rain in Spain": "Faces press to windows./Strangers moon and booze./Innkeepers doze." The poet's technique draws the ordinary scene intimately and delicately as in "Me to You": "Tell me about the snowfalls/at night, and tell me how we'd sit in firelight/hearing dogs huff in sleep."

Affection, and generally tenderness, is written into the individual thing observed, and we are made aware of its transient nature, but unlike the more characteristic contemporary poet, there is no sense of threat to identity. Consequently there is an absence of tension or drama in the verse. If this is a limitation one should not conclude that this poetry, just in its observation and openness to impression, has been easily achieved. The more recent poetry shows reasons for his confidence and sense of wholeness. In "The Spiral" he writes:

> the rooted self in me
> maps out its true country.
> And, as my father found
> his own small weathered island,
> so will I come to ground

—George Bruce

REXROTH, Kenneth. American. Born in South Bend, Indiana, 22 December 1905. Educated at the Art Institute, Chicago; New School for Social Research, New York; New York Art Students League. Married 1) Andree Dutcher in 1927 (died 1940); 2) Marie Kass in 1940 (divorced, 1948); 3) Marthe Larsen in 1949 (divorced, 1961); two children. Conscientious objector during World War II. Past occupations include farm worker, factory hand, insane asylum attendant. Painter: one-man shows held in Los Angeles, New York, Chicago, San Francisco, Paris. Columnist, *San Francisco Examiner*, 1958–68. Since 1953,

San Francisco correspondent for *The Nation*, New York; since 1968, Columnist for *San Francisco Magazine*, and the *San Francisco Bay Guardian*. Since 1968, Lecturer, University of California, Santa Barbara. Recipient: Guggenheim Fellowship, 1948; Eunice Tietjens Award (*Poetry*, Chicago), 1957; Shelley Memorial Award, 1958; Amy Lowell Fellowship, 1958; National Institute of Arts and Letters grant, 1964; Copernicus Award, 1975. Member, Nationai Institute of Arts and Letters. Address: 1401 East Pepper Lane, Santa Barbara, California 93108, U.S.A.

PUBLICATIONS

Verse

In What Hour. New York, Macmillan, 1940.
The Phoenix and the Tortoise. New York, New Directions, 1944.
The Art of Wordly Wisdom. Prairie City, Illinois, Decker Press, 1949.
The Signature of All Things: Poems, Songs, Elegies, Translations, and Epigrams. New York, New Directions, 1950.
The Dragon and the Unicorn. New York, New Directions, 1952.
A Bestiary for My Daughters Mary and Katharine. San Francisco, Bern Porter, 1955.
Poems. San Francisco, Bern Porter, 1955.
In Defense of the Earth. New York, New Directions, 1956; London, Hutchinson, 1959.
The Homestead Called Damascus. New York, New Directions, 1963.
Natural Numbers: New and Selected Poems. New York, New Directions, 1963.
The Collected Shorter Poems of Kenneth Rexroth. New York, New Directions, 1967.
Penguin Modern Poets 9, with Denise Levertov and William Carlos Williams. London, Penguin, 1967.
The Collected Longer Poems of Kenneth Rexroth. New York, New Directions, 1968.
The Heart's Garden, The Garden's Heart. Cambridge, Massachusetts, Pym Randall Press, 1967.
The Spark in the Tinder of Knowing. Cambridge, Massachusetts, Pym Randall Press, 1968.
Sky Sea Birds Trees Earth House Beasts Flowers. Santa Barbara, California, Unicorn Press, 1970.
New Poems. New York, New Directions, 1974.
On Flower Wreath Hill. Burnaby, British Columbia, Blackfish Press, 1976.
The Silver Swan: Poems Written in Kyoto 1974–75. Port Townsend, Washington, Copper Canyon Press, 1976.
The Morning Star: Poems and Translations. New York, New Directions, 1979.

Recording: *In the Cellar*, with Lawrence Ferlinghetti, Fantasy.

Plays

Beyond the Mountains (includes *Phaedra*, *Iphigenia*, *Hermaios*, *Berenike*) (produced New York, 1951). New York, New Directions, and London, Routledge, 1951.

Other

Bird in the Bush: Obvious Essays. New York, New Directions, 1959.
Assays (essays). New York, New Directions, 1961.
An Autobiographical Novel. New York, Doubleday, 1966.
Classics Revisited. Chicago, Quadrangle, 1968.
The Alternative Society: Essays from the Other World. New York, Herder, 1970.

With Eye and Ear (literary criticism). New York, Herder, 1970.
American Poetry: In the Twentieth Century. New York, Herder, 1971.
The Rexroth Reader, edited by Eric Mottram. London, Cape, 1972.
The Elastic Retort: Essays in Literature and Ideas. New York, Seabury Press, 1973.
Communalism: From Its Origins to the Twentieth Century. New York, Seabury Press, and London, Peter Owen, 1975.

Editor, *Selected Poems*, by D. H. Lawrence. New York, New Directions, 1948.
Editor, *The New British Poets: An Anthology.* New York, New Directions, 1949.
Editor, *Four Young Women: Poems.* New York, McGraw Hill, 1973.
Editor, *Tens: Selected Poems 1961–1971*, by David Meltzer. New York, McGraw Hill Herder, 1973.
Editor, *The Selected Poems of Czeslav Milosz.* New York, Seabury Press, 1973.
Editor, *Seasons of Sacred Lust*, by Kazuko Shiraishi. New York, New Directions, 1978.

Translator, *Fourteen Poems*, by O. V. de L.-Milosz. San Francisco, Peregrine Press, 1952.
Translator, *100 Poems from the Japanese.* New York, New Directions, 1955.
Translator, *100 Poems from the Chinese.* New York, New Directions, 1956.
Translator, *30 Spanish Poems of Love and Exile.* San Francisco, City Lights, 1956.
Translator, *100 Poems from the Greek and Latin.* Ann Arbor, University of Michigan Press, 1962.
Translator, *Poems from the Greek Anthology.* Ann Arbor, University of Michigan Press, 1962.
Translator, *Selected Poems*, by Pierre Reverdy. New York, New Directions, 1969; London, Cape, 1973.
Translator, *Love and the Turning Earth: 100 More Classical Poems.* New York, New Directions, 1970.
Translator, *Love and the Turning Year: 100 More Chinese Poems.* New York, New Directions, 1970.
Translator, *100 Poems from the French.* Cambridge, Massachusetts, Pym Randall Press, 1970.
Translator, with Ling O. Chung, *The Orchid Boat: Women Poets of China.* New York, Herder, 1972.
Translator, *100 More Poems from the Japanese.* New York, New Directions, 1976.
Translator, with Ikuko Atsumi, *Burning Heart: The Women Poets of Japan.* New York, Seabury Press, 1977.
Translator, with Ling O. Chung, *Complete Poems*, by Li Ch'ing-chao. New York, New Drections, 1979.

* * *

In America the relationship between poetry and simplicity is a fixed and almost natural necessity; poets working with what William Carlos Williams called "the American idiom" try to capture the intimacy and appeal of straightforward speech, and because Kenneth Rexroth has succeeded in making even his most intellectual poems seem as natural as campfire talk, he is one of America's great poets. He has mastered the art of talking, in his poems, to anyone: his dead mother or father, the master W.C.W., or to the classic philosophers; he is willing, for the sake of this intimacy and naturalness – in pursuit of his goal of a classical severity – to take fantastic risks with sentiment, with grief. His elegy for Dylan Thomas, "Thou Shalt Not Kill," made famous by a recording of Rexroth reading it with a jazz background, when he was one of the leading figures in the San Francisco Renaissance (a movement, in fact, very much sparked by the admiration of the young for Rexroth and his work), was condemned by many critics as maudlin; but it is a lasting and powerful work in which the *ubi sunt* of those who have been destroyed by materialism rings as if through a hollow corridor in hell. Rexroth's poetry is *factual*; he can report in a poem ("The summer of nineteen eighteen/I read *The Jungle* and *The/Research Magnificent*. That fall/My father died and my aunt/Took me to Chicago to live"); he can make quiet wit erupt in a bestiary poem or an epigram; or he can achieve what Richard Eberhart called "calmness and grandeur, as if something eternal in the natural world has been mastered," but in whatever he writes Rexroth's sense of nature dominates; the love of nature is rich in his work, and his early books like *The Dragon and the Unicorn* are hymns to nature – memorable in their celebration of fishing, reading the classics, lovemaking, meditating; and his voice is noted for its *naturalness*. He writes without pretence, and perhaps this is the true meaning of a classic poet: he can speak to anyone, deeply, directly, and if there is pain and work behind the seeming ease with which he speaks, it is part of his art to hide that effort. Many of his long poems perhaps aim at giving "expression to certain general ideas of more or less social importance for our time"; Rexroth is all on the side of content and message. But to me his most powerful poems are those, like "For a Masseuse and Prostitute" in which he is most a wisecracking natural, even though he has hidden "electric life" in his poem. There is a precision in his short lyrics, and in his translations, that is by force ruled out in his longer, more rhetorical poems in which he comes to terms with this or that body of theory. His own views are available in his criticism. His judgement is that "from the death of Longfellow to the day Allen Ginsberg took off his clothes, the American poet was not an important factor in American life. He was not a factor at all." And yet his own career has argued forcefully and by example for the importance of the poet in all his concerns, public and private.

—David Ray

RICH, Adrienne (Cecile). American. Born in Baltimore, Maryland, 16 May 1929. Educated at Roland Park Country School, Baltimore, 1938–47; Radcliffe College, Cambridge, Massachusetts, A.B. (cum laude) 1951 (Phi Beta Kappa). Married Alfred A. Conrad in 1953 (died, 1970); three sons. Lived in the Netherlands, 1961–62. Taught at the YM-YWHA Poetry Center Workshop, New York 1966–67; Visiting Poet, Swarthmore College, Pennsylvania, 1966–68; Adjunct Professor, Graduate Writing Division, Columbia University, New York, 1967–69; Lecturer, 1968–70, Instructor, 1970–71, Assistant Professor of English, 1971–72, and Professor, 1974, City College of New York; Fannie Hurst Visiting Professor, Brandeis University, Waltham, Massachusetts, 1972–73; Professor of English, Douglass College, New Brunswick, New Jersey, 1976–78. Since 1979, staff member, Smith College, Northampton, Massachusetts. Recipient: Yale Series of Younger Poets award, 1951; Guggenheim Fellowship, 1952, 1961; Ridgely Torrence Memorial Award, 1955; National Institute of Arts and Letters award, 1960; Amy Lowell Traveling Scholarship, 1962; Bollingen Foundation grant, 1962; Bess Hokin Prize, 1963, and Eunice Tietjens Memorial Prize, 1968 (*Poetry*, Chicago); National Translation Center grant, 1968; National Endowment for the Arts grant, 1969; Shelley Memorial Award, 1971; Ingram Merrill Foundation grant, 1973; National Book Award, 1974. D.Litt.: Wheaton College, Norton, Massachusetts, 1967. Lives in New York City. Address: c/o W. W. Norton Company, 500 Fifth Avenue, New York, New York 10036, U.S.A.

PUBLICATIONS

Verse

A Change of World. New Haven, Connecticut, Yale University Press, 1951.
(*Poems*). Oxford, Fantasy Press, 1952.

The Diamond Cutters and Other Poems. New York, Harper, 1955.
The Knight, after Rilke. Privately printed, 1957.
Snapshots of a Daughter-in-Law: Poems 1954–1962. New York, Harper, 1963; London, Chatto and Windus, 1970.
Necessities of Life: Poems 1962–1965. New York, Norton, 1966.
Focus. Privately printed, 1966.
Selected Poems. London, Chatto and Windus, 1967.
Leaflets: Poems 1965–1968. New York, Norton, 1969; London, Chatto and Windus, 1972.
The Will to Change: Poems 1968–1970. New York, Norton, 1971; Chatto and Windus, 1973.
Diving into the Wreck: Poems 1971–1972. New York, Norton, 1973.
Poems Selected and New 1950–1974. New York, Norton, 1975.
Twenty-One Love Poems. Emeryville, California, Effie's Press, 1976.
The Dream of a Common Language: Poems 1974–1977. New York, Norton, 1978.

Recordings: *Today's Poets 4*, with others, Folkways; *Adrienne Rich Reading at Stanford*, Stanford, 1973; *A Sign I Was Not Alone*, with others, Out and Out, 1978.

Other

Of Woman Born: Motherhood as Experience and Institution. New York, Norton, 1976; London, Virago, 1977.
Women and Honor: Some Notes on Lying. Pittsburgh, Motheroot, 1977.
On Lies, Secrets, and Silence: Selected Prose 1966–1978. New York, Norton, 1979.

* * *

Adrienne Rich's first volume, *A Change of World*, reflects the poet's early interest in intellectual clarity and formal control. Somewhat derivative of Auden and Yeats, it questions traditional values, her contemporary world. Among several love poems in the volume Rich introduces two themes that will become synonymous with her mature work: time ("Storm Warnings") and the woman's plight. In "An Unsaid Word," she dictates the difficult lesson all women must learn – patience and accommodation to the usually estranged man: "She who has power to call her man/From that estranged intensity/Where his mind forages alone,/Yet keeps her peace and leaves him free,/And when his thoughts to her return/Stands where he left her, still his own/Knows this the hardest thing to learn."

The same resignation fills *The Diamond Cutters and Other Poems*: "We had to take the world as it was given," but the poems emphasize the isolation and loneliness of the woman who must "always ... live in other people's houses" ("The Middle-Aged"). *Snapshots of a Daughter-in-Law* brings forth a new voice, looser forms, and sharper themes. The title poem, within a historical, mythic, and literary framework, describes the woman's lot wherein "our blight has been our sinecure." Attacking the fashionable feminine mystique, she describes the housewife's daily chores as funereal preparations: "Soon we'll be off, I'll pack us into parcels/stuff us in barrels, shroud us in newspapers,/pausing to marvel at old bargain sales" ("Passing On"). Woman is the product of an alien male society, perversely dependent upon men for sustenance, isolated from other women in "solitary confinement," filled with self-hatred and longings for self-expression. In such a world, where "time is male," the waste of creative energy is profound; suffocated or turned inward it becomes hysteria or guilt, ultimately depression or suicide: "A thinking woman sleeps with monsters/The beak that grabs her, she becomes." One source of this remains clear, and in "A Marriage in the 'Sixties," Rich portrays: "Two strangers, thrust for life upon a rock,/... two minds, two messages," and she asks: "Will nothing ever be the same,/even our quarrels take a different key,/our dreams exhume new metaphors?"

Rich embraces the personal and historical past now as something to be confronted and clarified ("From Morning Glory"). She longs to change the world, and the door to change exists; "poised, trembling and unsatisfied," the poet stands "before an unlocked door"; yet, she warns, "The door itself/makes no promises./It is only a door" ("Prospective Immigrants Please Note").

In *Necessities of Life* Rich again cries out against the woman's desperate plight. She focuses now upon both erotic experience and her solitariness in nature – in order to regain contact with her body, as well as a childlike, even womblike security. To her lover she says: "Sometimes at night/you are my mother:/... and I crawl against you, fighting/for shelter, making you/my cave" ("Like This Together").

In *Leaflets*, in even more colloquial language, her political rage surfaces. As poet and woman, Rich calls out for sisterhood, a new politics, a new language: "I wanted to choose words that even you would have been changed by." In "On Edges" Rich's resistance is active:

I'd rather
taste blood, yours or mine, flowing
from a sudden slash, than cut all day
with blunt scissors on dotted lines
like the teacher told.

The Will to Change develops these themes, especially the problem of using "oppressor's language" ("The Burning of Paper Instead of Children"): "We were bound on the wheel of an endless conversation." "I had pledged myself to try any/instrument that came my way" ("Shooting Script"). Perhaps poetry and erotic sexuality might connect the mind back to feeling: "When will we lie clear headed in our flesh again." "The moment when a feeling enters the body/is political." Then Rich, "in the prime of life" declares her position: "I am bombarded yet .../I am an instrument in the shape/of a woman trying to translate pulsations/into images for the relief of the body/and the reconstruction of the mind" ("Planetarium").

Rich comments that she is a feminist because she feels "endangered, psychically and physically, by this society, and because we have come to an edge of history when men – in so far as they are embodiments of the patriarchal idea – have become dangerous to children and other living things, themselves included." In *Diving into the Wreck* she commits herself to a full-fledged descent into the rubble of sexual-political warfare. In some of the poems she admits, more directly than ever, her hatred of men and her conditioned responses as girl, wife, and mother ("Dialogue"):

I do not know
if sex is an illusion

I do not know
who I was when I did those things
or who I said I was
or whether I willed to feel
what I had read about
or who in fact was there with me
Or whether I knew, even then
that there was doubt about these things.

To her male adversary she says: "I hate you./I hate the mask you wear, your eyes/Assuming a depth/they do not possess"; and she admits: "The only real love I have ever felt/was for children and other women./Everything else was lust, pity,/self-hatred, pity, lust/This is a woman's confession." "Phenomenology of Anger," is a militantly feminist poem in which Rich rages against repressed human energy, which in men finds its outlet in war and murder ("The prince of air and darkness/computing body counts, masturbating/in the factory/of facts"), in women, in "Madness, Suicide. Death." The ills of patriarchy can be abolished only through sisterhood, through nurturing.

"The Stranger" goes beyond sexual warfare. Indeed a prisoner of language, Rich portrays herself as the androgyne, both the male and female, whose loving and nurturing would be restorative: "I am the androgyne/I am the living mind you fail to describe/in your dead language." "Diving into the Wreck" amplifies this:

> And I am here, the mermaid whose dark hair
> streams black, the merman in his armored body
> We circle silently
> about the wreck
> we dive into the hold.
> I am she: I am he
> whose drowned face sleeps with open eyes.

—Lois Gordon

RICKWORD, (John) Edgell. Born in Colchester, Essex, 22 October 1898. Educated at Colchester Grammar School; Pembroke College, Oxford. Served in the Royal Berkshire Regiment during World War I: Military Cross. Editor, *Calendar of Modern Letters*, 1925–27; Associate Editor, *Left Review*, 1934–38; Editor, *Our Time*, 1944–47. Recipient: Arts Council Prize, 1966. D.Litt: University of Essex, Wivenhoe, 1978. Address: 2 Hopping Lane, London N1 2NJ, England.

PUBLICATIONS

Verse

Behind the Eyes. London, Sidgwick and Jackson, 1921.
Invocations to Angels, and The Happy New Year. London, Wishart, 1928.
Twittingpan and Some Others. London, Wishart, 1931.
Collected Poems. London, Lane, 1947.
Fifty Poems. London, Enitharmon Press, 1970.
Behind the Eyes: Selected Poems and Translations. Manchester, Carcanet Press, 1976.

Short Stories

Love One Another: Seven Tales. London, Mandrake Press, 1929.

Other

Rimbaud: The Boy and the Poet. London, Heinemann, and New York, Knopf, 1924; revised edition, Castle Hedingham, Essex, Daimon Press, 1963.
William Wordsworth 1770–1850. London, Bureau of Current Affairs, 1950.
Gillray and Cruikshank, with Michael Katanka. Aylesbury, Buckinghamshire, Shire, 1973.
Essays and Opinions 1921–1931, and *Literature in Society 1931–1978*, edited by Alan Young. Cheadle, Cheshire, and Manchester, Carcanet Press, 2 vols., 1974–78.

Editor, *Scrutinies by Various Writers.* London, Wishart, 2 vols., 1928–31; Folcroft, Pennsylvania, Folcroft Editions, 1976.
Editor, with Jack Lindsay, *A Handbook of Freedom: A Record of English Democracy Through Twelve Centuries.* London, Lawrence and Wishart, and New York, International, 1939.
Editor, *Soviet Writers Reply to English Writers' Questions.* London, Society for Cultural Relations with the U.S.S.R., 1948.
Editor, *Further Studies in a Dying Culture*, by Christopher Caudwell. London, Lane, 1949; New York, Dodd Mead, 1958.
Editor, *Radical Squibs and Loyal Ripostes: Satirical Pamphlets of the Regency Period, 1819–1821.* Bath, Adams and Dart, 1971.

Translator (as John Mavin), with Douglas Mavin Garman, *Charles Baudelaire: A Biography*, by François Porché. London, Wishart, 1928.
Translator, *Poet under Saturn: The Tragedy of Verlaine*, by Marcel Coulin. London, Toulmin, 1932.
Translator, *La Princesse aux Soleils, and Harmonie* (bilingual edition), by Ronald Firbank. London, Enitharmon Press, 1974.

Manuscript Collection: British Library, London.

Critical Studies: "The Poetic Mind of Edgell Rickword" by David Holbrook, in *Essays in Criticism* (Aylesbury, Buckinghamshire), July 1962; in *English Poetry 1900–1950: An Assessment*, by C. H. Sisson, London, Hart Davis, 1971.

Edgell Rickword comments:

Traditional idiosyncratic.

* * *

Edgell Rickword is old enough to have served in the First World War, and his memories of that experience are preserved in a few distinguished poems that deserve to be better known. Here, for instance, is the opening of "The Soldier Addresses His Body":

I shall be mad if you get smashed about;
we've had good times together, you and I;
although you groused a bit when luck was out,
and a girl turned us down, or we went dry.

Here and in the poems that Rickword went on to write in the 1920's one sees a remarkable poise; an openness to disparate elements of experience, together with an ability to relate them in a poetic fashion that may have been ironical but was also deeply felt. Rickword came to poetic maturity in the period when T. S. Eliot was extolling the Metaphysical virtues, and above all the capacity to fuse thought and feeling in a single response. Eliot found this quality in such poets as Donne and Marvell, who were greatly talked about and admired in the twenties, but Rickword was one of the few English poets who were able to make creative use of their example. Some of his verse is undoubtedly open to the charge of being over-intellectual and hence obscure, but the obscurity, where it exists, arises from the poet's determination to pursue a particular argument to its conclusion, rather than from mere mystification for its own sake. There are times, admittedly, when Rickword's diction seems a little too consciously mannered and arch; lines such as "as though your spirit, overweighed,/ tired of the saxophone's pert nonchalance" may seem a slightly faded example of the bright twenties' manner, though the poem from which they are taken, "Strange Party," is impressive as a whole. In addition to his poems of serious wit, Rickword was a sharp but urbane satirist of the cultural scene of the twenties. Since 1931 he has written little poetry, though "To the Wife of a Non-interventionist Statesman" is a brilliant piece of harsh political satire arising from the Spanish Civil War. It was a real loss for English poetry that such an admirable writer did not write more. What he has written deserves to be better known.

—Bernard Bergonzi

RIDING, Laura. American. Born Laura Reichenthal in New York City, 16 January 1901; adopted the surname Riding in 1926. Educated at Cornell University, Ithaca, New York. Married 1) Louis Gottschalk; 2) the poet and critic Schuyler B. Jackson in 1941 (died, 1968). Associated with the Fugitive group of poets; lived in Europe, 1926–39: associated with Robert Graves, in establishing the Seizen Press and *Epilogue* magazine; returned to America, 1939, renounced poetry, 1940, and has since devoted herself to the study of linguistics. Recipient: Guggenheim Fellowship, 1973. Address: Box 35, Wabasso, Florida 32970, U.S.A.

PUBLICATIONS

Verse

The Close Chaplet (as Laura Riding Gottschalk). London, Hogarth Press, and New York, Adelphi, 1926.
Voltaire: A Biographical Fantasy (as Laura Riding Gottschalk). London, Hogarth Press, 1927; Folcroft, Pennsylvania, Folcroft Editions, 1969.
Love As Love, Death As Death. London, Seizin Press, 1928.
Poems: A Joking Word. London, Cape, 1930.
Twenty Poems Less. Paris, Hours Press, 1930.
Though Gently. Deyá, Mallorca, Seizin Press, 1930.
Laura and Francisca. Deyá, Mallorca, Seizin Press, 1931.
The Life of the Dead. London, Barker, 1933.
The First Leaf. Deyá, Mallorca, Seizin Press, 1933.
Poet: A Lying Word. London, Barker, 1933.
Americans. Los Angeles, Primavera, 1934.
The Second Leaf. Deyá, Mallorca, Seizin Press, 1935.
Collected Poems. London, Cassell, and New York, Random House, 1938.
Selected Poems: In Five Sets. London, Faber, 1970; New York, Norton, 1973.

Novels

No Decency Left, with Robert Graves (as Barbara Rich). London, Cape, 1932.
14A, with George Ellidge. London, Barker, 1934.
Convalescent Conversations (as Madeleine Vara). Deyá, Mallorca, Seizin Press, and London, Constable, 1936.
A Trojan Ending. Deyá, Mallorca, Seizin Press, London, Constable, and New York, Random Kouse, 1937.

Short Stories

Experts Are Puzzled. London, Cape, 1930.

Progress of Stories. Deyá, Mallorca, Seizin Press, and London, Constable, 1935; Freeport, New York, Books for Libraries, 1971.
Lives of Wives. London, Cassell, and New York, Random House, 1939.

Other

A Survey of Modernist Poetry, with Robert Graves. London, Heinemann, 1927; New York, Doubleday, 1928.
A Pamphlet Against Anthologies, with Robert Graves. London, Cape, and New York, Doubleday, 1928.
Contemporaries and Snobs. London, Cape, 1928.
Anarchism Is Not Enough. London, Cape, and New York, Doubleday, 1928.
Four Unposted Letters to Catherine. Paris, Hours Press, 1930.
Pictures. London, 1933.
Len Lye and the Problem of Popular Films. London, Seizin Press, 1938.
The Covenant of Literal Morality. London, Seizin Press, 1938.
The Telling. London, Athlone Press, 1972; New York, Harper, 1973.
From the Chapter "Truth" in "Rational Meaning: A New Foundation for the Definition of Words" (Not Yet Published). Berkhamsted, Hertfordshire, Priapus Press, 1975.
It Has Taken Long (selected writings), in "Riding Issue" of *Chelsea 35* (New York), 1976.

Editor, *Everybody's Letters.* London, Barker, 1933.
Editor, *Epilogue 1–3.* Deyá, Mallorca, Seizin Press, and London, Constable, 3 vols., 1935–37.
Editor, *The World and Ourselves: Letters about the World Situation from 65 People of Different Professions and Pursuits.* London, Chatto and Windus, 1938.

Translator (as Laura Riding Gottschalk), *Anatole France at Home*, by Marcel Le Goff. New York, Adelphi, 1926.
Translator, with Robert Graves, *Almost Forgotten Germany*, by Georg Schwarz. Deyá, Mallorca, Seizin Press, London, Constable, and New York, Random House, 1936.

Bibliography: by Alan Clark, in *Chelsea 35* (New York), 1976.

Laura (Riding) Jackson comments:

My first book of poems was published as by Laura Riding Gottschalk, this surname being mine by an early marriage which terminated in divorce. Thereafter my name, authorial and personal, was Laura Riding, until 1941, when I married Schuyler B. Jackson, American poet and critical writer; my authorial name became then Laura (Riding) Jackson, with "Laura Riding" used for republication of work so signed. After the publication of my *Collected Poems* (1938), and my return to the U.S.A. in 1939 – I had been long abroad – I renounced poetry, for reasons of principle. I now permit the republication of my poems if a statement on this renunciation accompanies them.

In my high-school years I received extraordinarily good language-education. At Cornell University I was also very fortunate in teachers (in languages, literature, history). I left before completing my undergraduate career, living then, as a young professor's wife, in the sphere of two other universities, doing some studying, and continuing the writing of poems, become important to me at Cornell – and publishing some in magazines. At the close of 1925, after a period of uncertainty, I went abroad to live. I had found my American fellow-poets more concerned with making individualistic play upon the composition-habitudes of poetic tradition than with what concerned me: how to strike a personal accent in poetry that would be at once an authentic truth-impulsion, of universal force; I saw them as combining something less than complete poetic seriousness with something less than complete personal seriousness. In the English and cross-Atlantic literary atmosphere, there was, instead of crowding individualism, a loose assemblage of unsure positions, occupied with a varying show of modernistic daring; I had there solitariness in which to probe the reality of poetry as a spiritual, not merely literary, inheritance.

In my pursuits abroad, which, besides poetry, included criticism, story-writing, activity in printing and publishing ventures, the editing of a literary-critical miscellany, I became increasingly aware of the prime dependence of worth, in everything formed of words, on observance of the linguistic integrities. I conceived of a work that would help to dissipate the confusion existing in the knowledge of word-meanings – where, I believed, all probity of word must start. This project did not take deep root until after I returned to America. My husband joined me in it, bringing to it poetic experience and linguistic learning and a moral sense of language of his own, and strong-heartedness for facing difficulties, of which there were many, within and outside the task. The resultant book was far advanced when he died, in 1968. I am trying to complete it.

[Asked if she considers herself primarily a poet, Laura (Riding) Jackson says:] Up to 1940 I considered myself centrally a poet, with every other writing activity coming under a government of values (a unity of values prerequisite for truth) that I conceived of as centrally poetic. This moral and spiritual emphasis on poetry I took to be practically justified by the linguistic urgency in poetry towards rightness of word; poetry seemed where the verbal maximum could be one with and the same as the truth-maximum. When, after long-sustained faith in this seeming poetic potential, and pressing of the linguistic possibilities of poetic utterance towards further and further limits, I comprehended that poetry had no provision in it for ultimate practical attainment of that rightness of work that *is* truth, but led on ever only to a temporizing less-than-truth (the lack eked out with illusions of truth produced by physical word-effects), *I stopped*. I stopped – but I went on to search for the way to that rightness of word that is truth, and as the natural yield of words cultivated for truth's sake, not as the product of an *art* of words.... And in so doing I did not, renouncing poetry, transfer allegiance to some other form of literary procedure. I intensified my application to the problem of the knowledge of the meanings of words, and, for the rest, dedicated myself to the saying of what I might be able to say with a more far-reaching trueness of word than I had attained in any special literary climate, poetic or otherwise.

[Asked if she identifies herself with a particular school of poetry, she explains:] I have never belonged to any "school" of poetry – though the values I defined for the poetic use of words, which were nothing other than the values of language treated not only as a verbal discipline but one on which the intellectual integrity and total spiritual worth of poems depended, became associated in people's minds as a school of my instituting. (Thus W. B. Yeats, in a letter: "I wrote today to Laura Riding ... that her school was too thoughtful, reasonable, truthful, that poets were good liars....") All I did was to endeavor to make poetic goodness – the goodness of the "good" poem – comprehensive enough for the good poem to be no mere performance on the stage of a tradition, but something *literally* good, having so much reality as language that it fulfilled the function of language of authenticating the reality of the experiences of human consciousness (this function still only very imperfectly fulfilled in human speaking and writing, on the whole). This amounted to making the linguistic conscience the monitor of poetic goodness.

I had no models, in my particular approach to the question of what "good" is in poetry, no collaborators: the approach was, simply, a unique kind of seriousness directed upon poetry. I lessoned poets with whom I had association, in this work of literal poetic goodness. Though all took away something, and in one case at least the something was massive, none gave much thought to the depths of general principle from which this "higher" literalism, this new poetic gospel of linguistic probity, came – their interest, and therefore their gains, did not exceed the literary. Many poets outside personal range, known and unknown to me, have taken away something variedly, from the linguistic atmosphere of my poems, with superficial results – appearances of new linguistic distinction, and verbal sophistication, not backed by internal events of new experience in terms of principle, the travel within to new places in thought. In the case of one poet never more than a stranger to me, every abstractable manner of tone, diction, rhythmic movement, of mine was worked into the technique of this other – with not mere period-consequences. An application of my method of textual testing of poetic substance to a certain poem, in a book in which I was a collaborator, became the starting point from which a particular poet drew out the line of a critical career; and the resultant diffusion of the idea of such a method caused it to have further part in poetry-criticism developments, in further separation from its background-thought, as the mark of the "new" (for a time). Thus was it with me as to influences, being of a "school," or generating a "school": I have no influences on myself to record, or membership in any school. (In the early twenties I was made an honorary member of the group of Southern poets that called itself "The Fugitives." But I had no programmatic association with them. The membership was a tribute to my work.) My influence on others, directly and remotely, has been extensive and wasted. I think the reason of this is in the moral condition of poets; they have taken on the morals of their time which are not good enough for a thorough concern with goodness, poetic or otherwise.

* * *

In an early poem, "As Well As Any Other," Laura Riding asks: "But for familiar sense what need can be/Of my most singular device or me...." The "singular device" became more and more recognizable as a virtue of dedication in the development of the whole of her work: criticism, stories, editorial and collaborative writings, as well as the poems, and then the later post-poetic rebeginning in a new closeness to words themselves as "secreting in their meanings a natural eloquence of truth" (a recent comment of hers). Her purposes were and are supra-individual: she is bent upon locating the yet unfound in thought, saying the yet unsaid "For All Our Sakes" (the title of another early poem). Her work implies necessary reorientations of values and positions: it tends to test the minds of its readers and critics.

To turn to Laura Riding's poetry is to turn to her thought also. She warns: "The nicest thought is only gossip/If merchandized into plain language and sold/For so much understanding to the minute ..." ("The Talking World"). Some of the poems will be found immediately lucid. Others, the kind to which the long-celebrated difficulty is attributed, will make one stop – not just "stop and think" but stop and read. If this necessity is "difficulty," it is associated with the virtues of the poems, and contributory to a happy consequence in the immediate freshness they have on each return to them. The language has precision, but also litheness of expression-movement; it is language alive and at work. Because there is a right way in, and no other way, one may feel puzzled or dazzled until it is found. A poem of hers is a process; one must travel with it, and, if one does, one "understands" because the process develops and defines itself. This approach is outlined as a reading-method in *A Survey of Modernist Poetry* (pp. 138–49), with reference to "The Rugged Black of Anger."

The strong quality of personal voice and presence permeating Laura Riding's poems can induce the idea that they are full of private references, while her never-absent governing sense of the universal context of all particular contexts can suggest the label "abstract." These two tendences are interlocked, function as a unity, and so demand integration in the readers' minds: no poem-subject of hers is so general that there is not an immediate personal bearing, but its large force will be lost if realistic private identifications are sought for. When she writes, for instance, of "the tragedy of selfhood/And self-haunting," the case is (she avers) not a narrative of personal tragedy but of the approach to knowledge of the human necessity of graduation from the self as tragic. Thus her sensibility of personal crisis as an aspect of a total human event of crisis makes itself felt, as it pulsates through the *Collected Poems*, within an ever-widening emphasis upon the universal context: "The lone defiance blossoms failure,/But risk of all by all beguiles/Fate's wreckage into similar smiles" ("Doom in Bloom").

Much of her thought has a quality of inexorability: "The mercy of truth – it is to be truth." Her poetic standard was for the perfect: the rightness stipulated was "for always"; she meant real survival, minds on the side of permanence, as in "Autobiography of the Present":

Whole is by breaking and by mending.
The body is a day of ruin,
The mind, a moment of repair.
A day is not a day of mind
Until all lifetime is repaired despair ...

Death, in her poetic – and general – sense of the nature of things, is, as she has recently put it, "the reality of the necessity of an end, for that which has a limit. But the coming to a term of the limited is not mere predestined nullification: the mark of the end is a mark of rightness, and so death has, thus, aspects of significance and character which spell the perfect and the true, not mortality and loss." The mental perspective in which she views death can be found in depiction both stern and touched with happy wit ("There Is Much at Work"):

Exchange the multiplied bewilderment
For a single presentation of fact by fairness;
And the revelation will be instantaneous.
We shall all die quickly.

Her controls of the solemn and the large themes, the report of their reality as belonging intimately to the human experience, are everywhere firm. But not only is severity of definition and vision tempered with tenderness: the culminating words are often of a profoundly tender cheer, as in the transcendent "The Flowering Urn," where the fond supersedes the grim:

... Will rise the same peace that held
Before fertility's lie awoke
The virgin sleep of Mother All:
The same but for the way in flowering
It speaks of fruits that could not be.

("Mother All" comes with characteristic cleanness. She uses such figures with serious ontological intent, not for purposes of mythological rhetoric.)

There is an essence of simplicity in these poems. Their many questions are approaches to answers. "What knows in me?/Is it only something inside/That I can't see?" comes from the beginning, and "What were we, then,/Before the being of ourselves began?" from the end, of the *Collected Poems* progression, while almost at its centre "As Many Questions As Answers" reveals the implicit unity of the process. This spirit of simplicity brings the problem of knowledge within the intelligence's intimate range; it informs not only Laura Riding's poems but also such propositions of hers as "we experience reality to the degree to which we are at once a question about reality and its answer" (*Epilogue III*, 1937). She has not been afraid to let her intelligence press its points with the insistence of a child-like refusal to settle for no-answer. She pictures the alternative to this mental mode in rather passionate assault ("Unread Pages"):

Too orthodox maturity
For such heresy of child-remaining –
On these the dusty blight of books descends,
Weird, pundit babyhoods
Whose blinking vision stammers out the past
like a big-lettered foetus-future.

The internal simplicity of her poetic offering, the unity of its motivations and attitudes – so much missed when readers do not read *into* it, but content (or discontent) themselves with surface impressions of "difficulty" or "obscurity" – can provide a key to her ultimate renouncing of poetry. One might say that she moved from an initial belief that the answers we must find with our right questions could be found in poetry by its implicit invitation to (its demand of) truthfulness of word – never, for her, an obscure intellectualized or sentimentally spiritualized ideal, but a literal objective – to an ultimate feeling that poetry itself limits achievement in the unclosable gap between the verbal realms of question and answer. Her preface to the *Collected Poems* of 1938 is a soaring and persuasive defence of poetry; that to her *Selected Poems* of 1970 tells how she has "devoutly renounced allegiance to poetry as a profession and faith in it as an institution." To turn from one preface to the other is to feel one's loose world of poetry and prose, ordinary and literary language, tightening into tensions that suggest the labour of opening up that "other language-path" that has been Mrs. Jackson's commitment since 1940.

—Alan Clark

RIDLER, Anne (Barbara). British. Born in Rugby, Warwickshire, 30 July 1912. Educated at Downe House School; King's College, London, diploma in journalism 1932. Married Vivian Ridler in 1938; four children. Member of editorial department, Faber and Faber, publishers, London, 1935–40. Recipient: Oscar Blumenthal Prize, 1954, and Union League Civic and Arts Foundation Prize, 1955 (*Poetry*, Chicago). Address: 14 Stanley Road, Oxford, England.

PUBLICATIONS

Verse

Poems. London, Oxford University Press, 1939.
A Dream Observed and Other Poems. London, Editions Poetry London, 1941.
The Nine Bright Shiners. London, Faber, 1943.
The Golden Bird and Other Poems. London, Faber, 1951.
A Matter of Life and Death. London, Faber, 1959.
Selected Poems. New York, Macmillan, 1961.
Some Time After and Other Poems. London, Faber, 1972.

Plays

Cain (produced Letchworth, Hertfordshire, 1943; London, 1944). London, Editions Poetry London, 1943.
The Shadow Factory: A Nativity Play (produced London, 1945). London, Faber, 1946.
Henry Bly (produced London, 1947). Included in *Henry Bly and Other Plays*, 1950.
Henry Bly and Other Plays (includes *The Mask and The Missing Bridegroom*). London, Faber, 1950.
The Mask and The Missing Bridegroom (produced London, 1951). Included in *Henry Bly and Other Plays*, 1950.
The Trial of Thomas Cranmer, music by Bryan Kelly (produced Oxford, 1956). London, Faber, 1956.

The Departure, music by Elizabeth Maconchy (produced London, 1961). Included in *Some Time After and Other Poems*, 1972.

Who Is My Neighbour? (produced Leeds, 1961). Included in *Who Is My Neighbour? and How Bitter the Bread*, 1963.

Who is My Neighbour? and How Bitter the Bread. London, Faber, 1963.

The Jesse Tree: A Masque in Verse, music by Elizabeth Maconchy (produced Dorchester, Oxfordshire, 1970). London, Lyrebird Press. 1972.

Rosinda, translation of the libretto by Faustini, music by Cavalli (produced Oxford, 1973; London, 1975).

Orfeo, translation of the libretto by Striggio, music by Monteverdi (produced Oxford, 1975).

Eritrea, translation of the libretto by Faustini, music by Cavalli (produced Wexford, Ireland, 1975).

The King of the Golden River, music by Elizabeth Maconchy (produced Oxford, 1975).

The Return of Ulysses, translation of the libretto by Badoaro, music by Monteverdi (produced London, 1978).

The Lambton Worm, music by Robert Sherlow Johnson (produced Oxford, 1978). London, Oxford University Press, 1979.

Other

Olive Willis and Downe House: An Adventure in Education. London, Murray, 1967.

Editor, *Shakespeare Criticism 1919–1935.* London and New York, Oxford University Press, 1936.

Editor, *The Little Book of Modern Verse.* London, Faber, 1941.

Editor, *Time Passes and Other Poems*, by Walter de la Mare. London, Faber, 1942.

Editor, *Best Ghost Stories.* London, Faber, 1945.

Editor, *The Faber Book of Modern Verse*, revised edition. London, Faber, 1951.

Editor, *The Image of the City and Other Essays*, by Charles Williams. London, Oxford University Press, 1958.

Editor, *Selected Writings*, by Charles Williams. London, Oxford University Press, 1961.

Editor, *Shakespeare Criticism 1935–1960.* London and New York, Oxford University Press, 1963.

Editor, *Poems and Some Letters*, by James Thomson. London, Centaur Press, and Urbana, University of Illinois Press, 1963.

Editor, *Thomas Traherne: Poems, Centuries, and Three Thanksgivings.* London, Oxford University Press, 1966.

Editor, with Christopher Bradby, *Best Stories of Church and Clergy.* London, Faber, 1966.

Editor, *Selected Poems of George Darley.* London, Merrion Press, 1979.

* * *

Anne Ridler's poems demonstrate a triumph (minor, but still perfectly valid) of intelligence and skill in dealing with quiet, domestic themes and "occasional" subjects: meditations on married love, observations and celebrations of children, recordings of places and pictures. They are characteristically low-toned, but a distinct and not at all tepid personality comes through, with a strong sense of loyalty, the need for roots, and an awareness of the divine transfiguring the commonplace.

The quality of the best earlier poems (such as "At Parting" and "For a Child Expected" in *The Nine Bright Shiners*) lies partly in their assured rhythmical sense, traditional and yet not slavishly so, and partly in the transparent sweetness of their diction:

Since we through war a while must part
Sweetheart, and learn to lose
Daily use
Of all that satisfied our heart:
Lay up those secrets and those powers
Wherewith you pleased and cherished me these two years.

It is a note not often heard in contemporary English poetry; the saccharine flavour of women's magazine verse is quite different. Anne Ridler has herself said that she has learned from Wyatt, and Eliot seems to have been a liberating and beneficial modern influence; but her proper poetic ancestry seems to lie in the 17th century, in Herbert. In "Deus Absconditus" (from *The Golden Bird*), Eliot and Herbert both seem somewhere in the background, but not obtrusively so:

Here he is endured, here he is adored.
And anywhere. Yet it is a long pursuit,
Carrying the junk and treasure of an ancient creed,
To a love who keeps his faith by seeming mute
And deaf, and dead indeed.

Ridler's most ambitious work has been in partly or wholly dramatic form (e.g., *Cain*, *The Shadow Factory*, *The Trial of Thomas Cranmer*, the Christmas broadcasts and the title-poem from *The Golden Bird*), but none of these is wholly satisfactory. Much the best of the longer poems is "A Matter of Life and Death," which gave its title to her 1959 volume. This is a two-voiced meditation, of mother and child, on a birth:

I did not see the iris move,
I did not feel the unfurling of my love ...

I have seen the light of day,
Was it sight or taste or smell?
What I have been, who can tell?
What I shall be, who can say?

Anne Ridler is not at all a prolific poet, and her slimness of output, together with her lack of any self-assertiveness, seems unjustly to have made her work much less noticed than it should be.

—Anthony Thwaite

ROBERTS, Philip (Davies). Canadian. Born in Magog, Quebec, 9 October 1938. Educated at Acadia University, Wolfville, Nova Scotia, B.A. 1959; Jesus College, Oxford (Rhodes Scholar), B.A. 1962, M.A. 1966; University of Sydney, B.Mus. 1979. Married Carol Lynn Berney in 1978. English teacher, British Institute, Madrid, 1962; Sub-Editor, Reuters news agency, London, 1963–66; public relations consultant, Peters Bishop and Partners, London, 1966–67; Lecturer, 1967–74, and Senior Lecturer in English, 1974–79, University of Sydney. Since 1980, self-employed writer, Bloomington, Indiana. Founding Editor, Island Press, Sydney, 1970–79; Poetry Editor, Sydney *Morning Herald*, 1970–74. Address: c/o Area Writers Organization, 318 North Dunn Street, Bloomington, Indiana 47401, U.S.A.

PUBLICATIONS

Verse

Just Passing Through. Ladysmith, Quebec, Ladysmith Press, 1969.
Two Poets, with Geoff Page. Brisbane, University of Queensland Press, 1971.
Crux. Sydney, Island Press, 1973.
Will's Dream. Brisbane, University of Queensland Press, 1975.
Selected Poems. Sydney, Island Press, 1978.

Other

Editor, *The Inside Eye: A Study in Pictures of Oxford College Life*, photographs by Jüri Gabriel. Abingdon, Berkshire, Abbey Press, 1961.
Editor, with J. C. and P. M. Bright, *Models of English Style* (textbook). Sydney, Science Press, 1971.

Manuscript Collection: National Library of Australia, Canberra.

Critical Study: "Breaking the Tribal Bounds" by Peter Porter, in *Times Literary Supplement* (London), 9 April 1976.

Philip Roberts comments:

My first real poems came in 1961 when I was living in Oxford, though I had been playing with words for several years before that. They were triggered off, I remember, by the idiom of three lines in the first section of Robert Lowell's "Quaker Graveyard in Nantucket" – just a glance at them seemed to reveal a whole new range of possibilities. I showed some of my new poems to Robert Graves (who was then Professor of Poetry at Oxford) and received not only his blessing but also a great deal of critical support during the next three or four years. Graves read more or less every poem I wrote during this time, and gave detailed written criticism to most of them. That such a prolific poet and writer was able to find time for this is a kindness I shall never forget.

Although my work was first published in establishment publications, I did not have a book of poetry published until I had moved to Australia. Consequently, my work has been better-known there than anywhere else, though I am still very much a Canadian at heart. I now live in a small town in the U.S. midwest, doing odd jobs and writing. The poetry comes when it wants to, and I don't generally think about it at other times. I have not much interest in other poets or their work, though I was initially influenced by Frost, Graves, Cavafy, and Seferis (the latter two in translation). My main pleasures derive from music, the outdoors, and making love. (I am also a keen – even obsessive – long-distance runner and swimmer.)

I am sad that poetry reaches so few readers. Academics have latched onto poetry as their own special preserve, and in doing so have had to exalt discursive, allusive, and referentially complex poetry above all else. The fact that few academics possess the musicality to be able to read the simplest lyric aloud with any competence does not appear to worry them or in any way diminish their authority as arbiters of poetic taste. I also regret that I never seem to have lived in any one country long enough to have felt part of any national literary community. (Perhaps this is not altogether a bad thing – one is at least granted privacy in which to write.)

My view of poetry very much accords with the structuralist-semiotic views of Yury

Lotman's *Analysis of the Poetic Text*, for me one of the great explicatory revelations of the past decade.

* * *

Philip Roberts's restless career – Canadian by birth and upbringing, Australian by virtue of twelve years' residence and his literary contribution there – is to continue in the United States. He has always spread his light, publishing in English, Canadian, U.S., and Australian periodicals. As befits his life, the writing is condensed, sophisticated and cosmopolitan.

Already in *Just Passing Through* locations and personal experience are submitted to an exigent craftsmanship. Roberts's initial equipment includes an almost precious eloquence and an interest in precise manoeuvre such as the time-reversals of "Time Study," the dramatic riddling of "Summer Night," the cunning casualness with which metaphors are assembled in "Testing Song," and the humorous decorum of carnality in "Hungry Horse Café." Again in "Single Eye," a preoccupation with life's ambivalence and risks begets delicate, typically short-lined lyrics such as "Conversation" and "Master Peter's Puppet Show," model constructions such as "Now I Shall Reveal Everything," and some aptly-tuned jokes.

Roberts's peculiar combination of daring articulateness, unexpected detail, and subtle feeling emerge in "Tiny Tim Faces Death":

I want to ask the funeral man
to pack me on my side
curled up in flannelette
pyjamas. He'll say
the coffin would look like a sump:
my friends would all know I was scared.

What if I proved the Hittites
or Abyssinians did it – what then?
Could the world accept me
like a rollmop after all?
the giant earth nestle round
with black unending love?

Crux, handset by the author, notably includes a little satire ("That'd Be Good"), several neat jests ("Genres," "Peppermills," "Amen"), and a fine reflection on the relation of the original artist to followers ("Rescuers"): "Stop here and wait for them?/And what kind of comfort could they bring?/that stone-eyed mob, still groping the dark,/admiring the bones of your last-year's fire!" Something of a departure is the openness of the three-page account of five cases of derangement in "Neuro Ward," where Roberts's control elicits keen and unqualified compassion. The book ends with accomplished translations of seven Anglo-Saxon elegies. The personal and dramatic dimension of these pieces perhaps led on to *Will's Dream*, a tour de force consisting of 113 poems, mostly short. They recount and comment upon the relations between Willoughby, Big Mary, Blake, and Pymbal, though a larger cast is evoked. The rich achievement of this book, acclaimed especially by Robert Adamson in a review in *The Australian* (31 January 1976), surprised only those whose earlier reading had missed Roberts's quality.

Never a band-wagon poet, Roberts showed editorial stringency in compiling his attractive *Selected Poems* – 55 pieces. He set a useful example of modesty for other poets more inclined to include than cull. The selection shows a development towards plainer language and finer shades of wit.

Roberts is something of a Horatian. His command is surest in short poems; the refined cool is his vein; his skills are too polished to be popular, and yet a close reading does not suggest limited interests or resources. It is worth noting that he is a flautist and keyboard-player; the musical surety of his lines never falters. He has had influence on Australian publishing, as the discriminating typesetter and editor of Island Press. He has published several significant poets, and ten anthologies of Australian poetry, *Poet's Choice*. For a distinctive stylist he has been astonishingly receptive to a wide range of work, and by careful invitation has easily eclipsed in interest the later Angus and Robertson anthologies. In the 1970's, *Poet's Choice* became the principle showcase of current Australian poetry.

—Judith Rodriguez

ROBINSON, Roland (Edward). British. Born in Balbriggan, Ireland, 14 June 1912. Educated in secondary schools. Member, Kirsova Ballet, 1944–47. Ballet Critic, 1956–66, and currently, Book Reviewer, *Sydney Morning Herald*. Editor, *Poetry Magazine*, Sydney. President, Poetry Society of Australia. Recipient: Grace Leven Award, 1952; Commonwealth Literary Fellowship, 1954; Australian Council for the Arts grant, 1973; Australian Book Council Award, for non-fiction, 1974. Address: Woollahra Golf Club, O'Sullivan Road, Rose Bay, New South Wales 2029, Australia.

PUBLICATIONS

Verse

Beyond the Grass-Tree Spears: Verse. Adelaide, Jindyworobak, 1944.
Language of the Sand: Poems. Sydney, Lyre Bird, 1948.
Tumult of the Swans. Sydney, Edwards and Shaw, 1953.
Deep Well. Sydney, Edwards and Shaw, 1962.
Grendel. Brisbane, Jacaranda Press, 1967.
Selected Poems. Sydney, Angus and Robertson, 1971.

Play

Television Play: *The Ballad of the Aborigines*, 1972.

Short Stories

Black-Feller, White-Feller. Sydney, Angus and Robertson, 1958.

Other

Legend and Dreaming: Legends of the Dream-Time of the Australian Aborigines. Sydney, Edwards and Shaw, 1952.
The Feathered Serpent: The Mythological Genesis and Recreative Ritual of the Aboriginal Tribes of the Northern Territory of Australia. Sydney, Edwards and Shaw, 1956.
The Man Who Sold His Dreaming. Sydney, Currawong, 1965.
Aboriginal Myths and Legends. Melbourne, Sun, 1966.

The Australian Aboriginal in Colour, photographs by Douglas Baglin. Sydney, Reed, 1968.

The Drift of Things 1914–1952, and *The Shift of Sands 1952–1962* (autobiography). Melbourne, Macmillan, 2 vols., 1973–76.

Editor, *Wandjina: Children of the Dreamtime: Aboriginal Myths and Legends*. Brisbane, Jacaranda Press, 1968.

Critical Study: by Evan Jones, in *The Literature of Australia*, Melbourne, Penguin, 1964.

Roland Robinson comments:

[I belong to the] Jindyworobak school – devoted to poetry with distinctive Australian environment.

Themes are Australia, its fauna and flora, its human inhabitants, Aboriginal and European. Latest theme is involvement in Mankind in its modern environment of cities, industry, etc.

A poem should have the texture and character of its subject. I detest abstract cerebral verse. A poem's sound should argue for its sense. A poem's form should be sculptural. A poet should bring all his senses alive on the page: sight, hearing, taste, smell. A poem's rhythm should express its emotion. A poem should agonize to find its own unique form whether it be a Shakespearean sonnet or the Twenty-third Psalm. Prescribed form is meaningless.

Influences are Edward Thomas, Anglo-Saxon Poetry, Ted Hughes, R. S. Thomas.

* * *

Something of a legend in his own lifetime, Roland Robinson has become a familiar figure reading (brilliantly) his own poems in lecture halls and schools across Australia, his shock of white hair flowing and, latterly, a white wolfhound in attendance. His own career has been colourful enough, ranging from jackeroo to ballet critic for the *Sydney Morning Herald* to greenkeeper of a municipal golf links. He was largely instrumental in organising a writer's cooperative publishing venture (the Lyre Bird Writers series) around 1950 and has, in the early 1970's, revived this series in order to publish the work of younger poets. With this background of activity and variety, it is perhaps surprising that Roland Robinson's own poetry remained for so long centrally concerned with a very private search through the desert and bird-and-animal landscape of outback Australia, a lyrical and often delicate Wanderer's voyage of discovery and communion. The many short lyrics published in magazines and even books over some twenty years were collected and arranged in the volume *Deep Well* in a way that showed them to be, not merely occasional campfire nature pieces, but components of a definite search and expression of a centrally understood vision. *Deep Well* remains the centre of Roland Robinson's achievement, and must be regarded as expressing something close to the very core of that poetic reawakening that began in Australia during the Second World War years, a reawakening that for the first time directed Australians unself-consciously to their own landscape, and with a language at last equipped to approach it. It is interesting that of the two poets most occupied with this task one, Douglas Stewart, was a New Zealander; the other, Roland Robinson, was born in Ireland. Roland Robinson will be remembered for naming, for us, points of a journey both private and universal.

—Thomas W. Shapcott

ROBSON, Jeremy. British. Born in Llandudno, Caernarvonshire, Wales, 5 September 1939. Educated at Haberdashers' Aske's School; Regent Street Polytechnic, London, diploma in journalism 1960. Married Carole de Botton in 1964. Editor, Aldus Books, London, 1963–69. Poetry Critic, *Tribune*, London, 1962–72; Chief Editor, Vallentine Mitchell, publishers, London, 1969–72; Editor, Woburn Press, London, 1972–73. Since 1974, Managing Director, Robson Books, London. Address: 37 Briardale Gardens, London NW3 7PN, England.

PUBLICATIONS

Verse

Penny Pamphlet. London, Writers Club, 1961.
Poems for Jazz. Leicester, L. Weston, 1963.
Thirty-Three Poems. London, Sidgwick and Jackson, 1964.
In Focus. London, Allison and Busby, 1970.
Poems Out of Israel. London, Turret, 1970.
Travelling. Hunton Bridge, Hertfordshire, Kit-Cat Press, 1972.

Recordings: *Blues for the Lonely*, Columbia; *Before Night/Day*, Argo; *Poetry and Jazz in Concert*, Argo; *Poetry and Jazz in Concert 250*, Argo.

Other

Editor, *Letters to Israel: Summer 1967.* London, Vallentine Mitchell, 1968.
Editor, *Poems from Poetry and Jazz in Concert: An Anthology.* London, Souvenir Press, 1969.
Editor, *The Young British Poets.* London, Chatto and Windus, 1971; New York, St. Martin's Press, 1973.
Editor, *Corgi Modern Poets in Focus 2* and *4*. London, Corgi, 2 vols., 1971.
Editor, *Poetry Dimension 1: A Living Record of the Poetry Year.* London, Robson Books, 1973; New York, St. Martin's Press, 1974.

* * *

Jeremy Robson's poetry reveals a man assuming the position of an ordinary person in an ordinary world – then turning aside, now and then, into a poem that expresses and comments on the unease, the distaste, the pain, even the horror which that world bears in upon his perceptions. Clearly his everyman persona is at the mercy of outer forces:

Call my name, sing your psalms, make your war,
speak your speech, Save my Soul ...
Break down my door: I wait.

His poems are replete with the oppressions and diminutions we suffer in the city: underground rush hours, domination by all officialdom and authority, the importunings of the media and of the consumer society, the heaped-up grinding annoyances "of the season's/fickle mood, of today's speech, tomorrow's/march, of the drizzle in the amber lights." But among his experience of these workaday miseries he does not overlook the larger fears and oppressions that afflict us: political upheaval and military threat, social and racial conflict, cruelty and murder, "Rivers to the ocean/lovers to the war...."

He communicates these concerns in a restrained free verse, often partially disciplined by semi-stanzaic forms of irregular rhyme. His use of language is determinedly colloquial, reflecting the "ordinariness" of his chosen persona, but leaving options for frequent ironic asides and moments of humour on the one hand and a heightening into emotional intensity on the other. Recently his output of poetry has slackened somewhat – as have his public appearances (he was one of the prime movers of the poetry-reading boom in Britain during the sixties). But his most recent work shows a steady strengthening and maturing of his poetic intentions, and an ever more sure touch in their expression.

—Douglas Hill

ROCHE, Paul. British. Born in India, 25 September 1928. Educated at Gregorian University, Rome, Ph.B., Ph.L. 1949. Married to Clarissa Tanner; five children. Instructor, Smith College, Northampton, Massachusetts, 1957–59; Poet-in-Residence, California Institute of the Arts, Valencia. Recipient: Bollingen Foundation Fellowship, 1958; Alice Fay di Castagnola Award, 1965; Alice Hunt Bartlett Prize, 1966. Address: The Stables, The Street, Aldermaston, Berkshire, England.

PUBLICATIONS

Verse

The Rank Obstinacy of Things: A Selection of Poems. New York, Sheed and Ward, 1962.
22 November 1963 (The Catharsis of Anguish). London, Adam, 1965.
Ode to the Dissolution of Mortality. New York, Madison Avenue Church Press, 1966.
All Things Considered. London, Duckworth, 1966; New York, Weybright and Talley, 1968.
To Tell the Truth. London, Duckworth, 1967.
Te Deum for J. Alfred Prufrock. New York, Madison Avenue Church Press, 1967.
Lament for Erica: A Poem. Bembridge, Isle of Wight, Yellowsands Press, 1971.
Enigma Variations and.... Gloucester, Thornhill Press, 1974.
The Kiss. Richmond, Surrey, Keepsake Press, 1975.

Recording: *Death at Fun City*, Mercury, 1972.

Plays

Medea, adaptation of the play by Euripides (produced New York, 1978). Included in *Three Plays of Euripides*, 1974.

Screenplay: *Oedipus the King*, 1967.

Novels

O Pale Galilean. London, Harvill Press, 1954.

Vessel of Dishonour. London, Sheed and Ward, 1962; New York, New American Library, 1963.

Other

The Rat and the Convent Dove and Other Tales and Fables (juvenile). Aldington, Kent, Hand and Flower Press, 1952.

Translator, *The Oedipus Plays of Sophocles.* New York, New American Library, 1958.
Translator, *The Orestes Plays of Aeschylus.* New York, New American Library, 1963.
Translator, *Prometheus Bound,* by Aeschylus. New York, New American Library, 1964.
Translator, *The Love Songs of Sappho.* New York, New American Library, 1966.
Translator, *3 Plays of Plautus.* New York, New American Library, 1968.
Translator, *Philoctetes, lines 676–729,* by Sophocles. Bembridge, Isle of Wight, Yellowsands Press, 1971.
Translator, with others, *The Living Mirror: Five Young Poets from Leningrad.* London, Gollancz, and New York, Doubleday, 1972.
Translator, *Three Plays of Euripides: Alcestis, Medea, The Bacchae.* New York, Norton, 1974.

Critical Studies: by John Engels, in *Minnesota Review* (St. Paul), 1963; Patricia deJoux, in *The Times* (London), 5 January 1968; John Moffitt, in *America* (New York), May 1968.

Paul Roche comments:

(1970) There is always a "sufficient reason" even for the worst of happenings, and it is always sufficiently human. I say in my work: "Father forgive them for they know not what they do: and forgive *me.*" Poetry is awareness heightened to the point of love. It is a way of apprehending the intensity of being. I try to re-create experience more intensely, reduce it to a luminous whole, render intuitive the meaning and metaphysics of the universe – and so feed myself and others the kernel of being. My greatest influences have been the Bible (Authorised or Douay), Shakespeare, Hopkins, Eliot, Aeschylus, Sophocles, Euripides and Sappho.

(1974) For me poetry is an incantation of exact experience that seizes the mind and the heart; it is the orchestration of language towards maximum perception; it is condensed verbal impact.... Poetry and art are the unique channels through which knowledge is humanised: enters the blood-stream, is made part of ourselves. Although I write my poems to please myself (to purge myself), I am fully aware of using myself as the exemplar for all human beings, and so ultimately I write for humanity. However embedded in the particular consciousness (even confessional) of a poet his poem is, for me it is only successful if it reaches universality. Which is to say, if anyone (or almost anyone ... some people are just too bovine to bother with) picking up that poem is wounded, is hit, is illuminated, and can say: "This is about *me.* Or it may not exactly be about me, but I now know what it is like to be that person."

* * *

Although born in India and educated in England and at the Gregorian University in Rome, where he graduated in philosophy, Paul Roche has lived in the United States, West Indies, and Mexico in addition to his own country. As a result of an outlook that has never been confined by national boundaries, he has never been unduly influenced by localised coteries, though profiting from them all, and his poetry is equally enjoyed in Britain and America. His skill as a translator has been fully exploited in his own creative writing so that even what he describes as "mere verse" has a liveliness and command of language lacking in the work of many other poets. Whether he writes about events or personal relationships, draws upon his impressive knowledge of mythology or religion, or makes use of private experience as a starting-point for reflection upon the nature of things and the behaviour of his fellows, he has a flair for spotlighting major issues in a playfully ironic and often humorous vein, whilst getting to grips with reality. One of his methods is to approach the metaphysical through the physical, and he has written a whole series of poems about such inanimate objects as "The Brick," "The Spent Matchstick," "The Hairbrush," and "The Nail-Scissors."

His "Act of Love" still remains one of the most satisfactory poems ever written on such an intimate and delicate subject, and his "Paradigm of Love" is a remarkable example of word-play used in a valid and effective manner:

Does love live
Only
As a mirror lives
And give
So much back
Only
As a mirror gives
Which gazes
Only
With what gazing gave
And gives
By gazing back
That only?

In *To Tell the Truth* Roche continued his somewhat hit-or-miss exploration of the significance of experience in a variety of styles, encompassing the satirical "Spring Song of the Petroleum Board Meeting," the amusing commentary on Eliot's poetry, "Te Deum for J. Alfred Prufrock," the lyrical "Her Love Longs for Tears," and a pocm of protest entitled "The Lobotomy":

Oh God! The explosion that shook me so,
That series of small deadly jolts
Dislocating me for one whole dessicated year,
And the sinister cutting away of something I didn't know ...
How I wish I had gone on a real war,
Had been shredded with shrapnel
Or lost half my head.

Enigma Variations and ... is uneven, too. Everything is thrown into the pot – word-play, literary games, light verse, satire, paradox ("The hollow in the bowl/Present by its absence"), lyrics, lively sketches, serious comment – as if to illustrate the title, yet here and there insights seep through:

Everyone is walking with an inner space
Everyone is moving with an inner time
Everyone is growing with an inner change
Everyone is being with an inner pace
Walking, moving, growing, being
Within, beside, beyond, behind
From and to and in and through
Everyone is growing

Everyone is going
Everyone is coming, coming, coming
Everyone is ...
Becoming.

Death at Fun City, a long satirical poem concerned with what man is making of his own environment, shows the poet working towards greater freedom in his choice of form.

—Howard Sergeant

RODDICK, Alan. New Zealander. Born in Belfast, Northern Ireland, 22 July 1937. Educated at Auckland Grammar School; University of Auckland; University of Otago, Dunedin, B.D.S. 1960. Married Patricia Woods in 1959; three daughters and one son. Currently a Dentist, in private practice. Editor, Radio Poetry Programme, New Zealand Broadcasting Corporation, 1968–69, 1973–74. Address: 42 Albert Street, Invercargill, New Zealand.

PUBLICATIONS

Verse

The Eye Corrects: Poems 1955–1965. Auckland, Blackwood and Janet Paul, 1967.

Other

Allen Curnow. Wellington, Oxford University Press, 1979.

Editor, *Home Ground*, by Charles Brasch. Christchurch, Caxton Press, 1974.

* * *

No critic or anthologist has yet done justice to Alan Roddick's poetry, perhaps because it has only its merits as poetry to recommend it. The subject matter is not in itself arresting, the manner is not in any obvious sense innovatory, and Roddick has lacked the advantage (in terms of publicity) gained by poets who start their careers belonging to a movement. He has had to make his way on his own.

Precision, particularity, hardness of outline, descriptive exactness, flexibility of form, wit – these are some of the qualities of Roddick's poetry. The run of the lines commonly matches the action of the subject; the poem is beautifully shaped to the event it describes. He is fond of paradoxes – particularly the paradoxes of mirrors, which (like poems) reflect and yet are not the world. Time, memory, love, the responsibilities and discoveries of parenthood – if his subjects are commonplaces they are also eternal. They are seen in the suburban and domestic setting in which they have been experienced, seen good-humouredly, without Larkinish distaste, but with no room for decorative sentiment either.

The other side of Roddick's poetic merits may be a caution that will not chance its arm. In one poem ("A Patient") he has ventured into unusual territory, making poetry of his day-to-day experience as a dentist. In a recent verse-letter he has experimented technically with a form borrowed from the Russian of Pushkin. Otherwise he has remained within narrow bounds. But Roddick has the kind of literary intelligence and tact that knows you cannot extend yourself stylistically by acts of will. It must be something that happens to the whole man. In the meantime he remains a rare example among New Zealand poets of a perfect miniaturist.

—C. K. Stead

RODEFER, Stephen. American. Born in Wheeling, West Virginia, 20 November 1940. Educated at Rossall School, Fleetwood, Lancashire, 1958–59; Amherst College, Massachusetts, 1959–63, B.A. 1963; State University of New York, Buffalo (Faculty Fellow), 1963–67, M.A. 1972. Married Penny Kaplan in 1962; three sons. Research Assistant, 1965–66, and Instructor in English, 1966–67, State University of New York, Buffalo; Assistant Professor of English and Co-Director of the Creative Writing Program, University of New Mexico, Albuquerque, 1967–71; Editor, *Fervent Valley*, Placitas, New Mexico, 1972–75: Poetry Specialist, Berkeley Unified School District, California, 1976–80. Address: Overlook Court, Bellaire, Ohio 43906, U.S.A.

PUBLICATIONS

Verse

The Knife. Toronto, Island Press, 1965.
After Lucretius. Storrs, University of Connecticut Press, 1973.
One or Two Love Poems from the White World. San Francisco, Pick Pocket, 1976.
Safety. San Francisco, Miam, 1977.
The Bell Clerk's Tears Keep Flowing. Berkeley, The Figures, 1978.

Other

Translator, *Villon.* Placitas, New Mexico, Duende Press, 1976.

Stephen Rodefer comments:

My poetry is an addition to English literature and an improvement of my life.

* * *

The poems in Stephen Rodefer's first collection, *The Knife*, satisfy us by their domestic wit ("for Christ's sake/there are crumbs/in our bed/the size of sandwiches"). They make use of Cummings à la Creeley syncopations and enjambments along with brevity, couplets for structure, wryness, and advantageous breath-lengths. One poem, about eating an ear of corn, seeks to embody (and in part parody) Creeley's "Form is never more than an extension of content," a popular song on everybody's radio those days. Despite the threat (which never materializes) of its title, the volume is mostly coups d'oeil, though proving Rodefer is capable of closely held precisions, tight ironies, comic understatement, and – no matter how concealed or twisted from – sentiment. His best early poems, however, were never collected. "I Make Out Henry Moore" and "The Commotion" are notable for their management of time, both perceptual and narrative, and lead to other fine poems, such as "Characters of a Foreign Letter," in the manner of Frank O'Hara and the conversational, casual, interchangeable quality of time in *Lunch Poems*, which had just been published.

After this, the poetry takes on another language and another tone, the inconclusive rhetoric of the lesser New York poets (although written while the poet was living first in Albuquerque, then Oakland). The poems in *The Bell Clerk's Tears Keep Flowing* (a line from Elvis Presley's "Heartbreak Hotel") are dominated by the world of the quick take, the elusive glamour and superficial accomplishment of the urban style, where either the humor is not bitter enough or the thrust not deep enough. It is a language of approximation and acquisition that would be decorous if sustained – "a storm of unexpected destiny," "a history of resilient feeling," "a proceeding of great endurance," "a figure of spectacular concoction." Poems like "Samson and Delilah," despite an occasional brilliance of image, are overlong, rambling, compulsive. Most are addressed to a nameless, ambisexual "you," with the "I" or "me" just as vague. Some are surprisingly undisguised repetitions of O'Hara. "Accolade" is one of the more accomplished in this mode, but perhaps the best example, and the best poem in the volume, is "Friends of the Hopi," beginning "Living alone is not so bad actually./If you can get by sleeping alone/It's quite possible ...," taking us through one such possible day, and concluding:

Living alone you soon learn
to cultivate the *least* of it.

And think of how you can get by
With avocados and a lot of tonic,
A friend of the Hopi,
Washing your dishes in a tea cup.

No matter the delights of such poems, Rodefer's special contribution lies in his "translations" or derivations from the classics – to date, the Greek Anthology and Villon. His renderings of Villon are completely street-wise, without any pumped-up slang or dusted-off argot – with a running commentary any media personality would love to have the advantage of. The notes below each of the poems are what add genius to the clearly established talent, so that the entire volume, in addition to being faithful in spirit to the text of Villon, is a happy invention, all Rodefer's own. His workings from the Greek Anthology which followed, published under the title *Safety*, are equally remarkable for their beguiling simplicity. He lifts the originals live from the page and transforms them without hesitation into classic American. Here is this reactivization of the traditional complaint against devastation by beauty: "Your eyes are like lips./No one in the sunlight/comes even near your shadow.//The navy,/The marines,/The air force,/You kill them all." Such poems are not translations, they are revitalizations. It is in this form that Rodefer also makes known his unique voice – charmingly oblique and irreplaceable.

—George F. Butterick

RODGERS, Carolyn M(arie). Afro-American. Born in Chicago, Illinois, in the 1940's. Educated at the University of Illinois, Urbana, 1960–61; Roosevelt University, Chicago, 1961–65. Y.M.C.A. Social Worker, Chicago, 1965; Lecturer in Afro-American Literature, Columbia College, Chicago, 1968, University of Washington, Seattle, 1970, and Indiana University, Bloomington, Summer 1973; Writer-in-Residence, Albany State College, Georgia, 1971, and Malcolm X College, Chicago, 1972. Formerly, Mid-West Editor, *Black Dialogue*, New York. Recipient: Conrad Kent Rivers Award, 1968; National Endowment for the Arts grant, 1969; Society of Midland Authors Award, 1970. Address: 5135 South Kenwood, No. 304, Chicago, Illinois 60615, U.S.A.

PUBLICATIONS

Verse

Paper Soul. Chicago, Third World Press, 1968.
Two Love Raps. Chicago, Third World Press, 1969.
Songs of a Blackbird. Chicago, Third World Press, 1969.
Now Ain't That Love. Detroit, Broadside Press, 1969.
For H. W. Fuller. Detroit, Broadside Press, 1970.
Long Rap/Commonly Known as a Poetic Essay. Detroit, Broadside Press, 1971.
How I Got Ovah: New and Selected Poems. New York, Doubleday, 1975.
The Heart as Ever Green. New York, Doubleday, 1978.

Carolyn M. Rodgers comments:

I seek to tell the truth. To explore the human condition, the world's condition. To illuminate the ordinary, the forgotten, the overlooked, to show that the specific me is often the general you and us. To exemplify God working in man and the consequences of man defying and denying God, not only in himself but in the universe. I seek to write simply, so that a child might understand; and to write simply profoundly, so that the educated, the intellectual may enjoy and find mental food, find delight. The Light. Truth. My gift is not my own. What is written by me is written through me. I am an instrument. An inkpen of God's.

* * *

Carolyn M. Rodgers's allegiances are broad and general. The old generation must yield to a revolutionary age, but one cannot "forget the bridge that you crossed over on." The flames of Detroit, Watts, Newark produced Black martyrs, but there is still an ambivalence when the speaker of "Eulogy" asks how tears shed for a single, materialistic, Black soul can be ignored. The song of the Black poet is as universal as eating, sleeping, copulating, and a baby's face ("To the White Critics" and "You Name it"), but the creator often longs for a bus ride to see the sun set or to sing a *sui generis* lyric ("Breakthrough"). The fact is we must "see, the changes are so many/there are several of me and/all of us fight to show up at the same time."

One critic has said that Carolyn Rodgers moves between two worlds, the Bourgeoisie and the Black masses. Another has called her a masterful storyteller giving Black people back to themselves. Both, I think, have set forth partial truths. They have refused to see the poet's canon for what it really is. The poems in *Paper Soul* and *Songs of a Blackbird* are, more than anything else, personal. A hundred and fifty years ago this word would have caused no furor, but in an age of *littérature engagé* it sounds like an indictment. That is not its intent.

Miss Rodgers is personal because there are so many selves that compose her makeup, and poetical honesty demands their expression. Thus, she can be the ironical humorist in "Portrait of a White Nigger" and demand that her audience stop laughing in "Unfunny Situation." She can champion armed revolution at one point ("U Name This One") and praise the singular efforts of a Black magazine editor at another ("For H. W. Fuller"). And some of her finest efforts are poems that deal unapologetically with the lives and loves of Carolyn Rodgers. She speaks self-deprecatingly and honestly about those things that have hurt, embarrassed, appeased, or thrilled her in the past ("Now Ain't That Love," "6:30," and "I Remember"). She moves easily from the self of mixed sexual, astronomical, and technical metaphors ("Written for Love of an Ascension-Coltrane") to the poet who employs dialectal spellings to record a telephone conversation with her proselytizing mother. When she is deeply in love with a revolutionary speaker (not his sentiments) she says so ("Plagiarism for a Trite Love Pome"). Of course, there are all the stock situations of the new Black poetry: Black men vis-à-vis white women, the permanent wave vs. the natural, the establishment's mocking response to horrors it has created, etc. But finally Carolyn Rodgers is a woman speaking to a wide audience about occasions (whether overheard conversations or passionate love affairs) in her own multifaceted life.

—Houston A. Baker, Jr.

RODITI, Edouard (Herbert). American. Born in Paris, 6 June 1910. Educated at Elstree School, Hertfordshire; Charterhouse, Godalming, Surrey; Balliol College, Oxford; University of Chicago, B.A. 1939; University of California, Berkeley. Art Critic, *L'Arche*, Paris, and since 1975, *Pictures on Exhibit*, New York; Co-Editor, *Das Lot*, Berlin, 1947–49; Contributing Editor, *Antaeus*, New York, *European Judaism*, Amsterdam, *The Expatriate Review*, *Shantih*, and *Arts in Society*, Madison, Wisconsin. Recipient: Gulbenkian Foundation grant, 1969. Address: 130 Boulevard Massena, No. 3163, Paris 13, France.

PUBLICATIONS

Verse

Poems for F. Privately printed, 1935.
Prison Within Prison: Three Elegies on Hebrew Themes. Prairie City, Illinois, Decker Press, 1941.
Pieces of Three, with Paul Goodman and Meyer Liben. Harington, New Jersey, 5 × 8 Press, 1942.
Poems 1928–1948. New York, New Directions, 1949.
New Hieroglyphic Tales: Prose Poems. San Francisco, Kayak, 1968.
Emperor of Midnight. Los Angeles, Black Sparrow Press, 1974.
Meetings with Conrad. Los Angeles, Press of the Pegacycle Lady, 1977.
In a Lost World. Santa Barbara, California, Black Sparrow Press, 1978.

Short Stories

The Delights of Turkey. New York, New Directions, 1977.

Other

Oscar Wilde. New York, New Directions, 1947.
Dialogues on Art. London, Secker and Warburg, 1960; New York, Horizon Press, 1961.
Joachim Karsch. Berlin, Verlag Gebr. Mann, 1960.
Chagall, Ernst, Miro: Propos sur l'Art. Paris, Editions Sedimo, n.d.
Selbstanalyse eines Sammlers. Cologne, Galerie der Soiegel, 1960.
Ida Kerkovius. Constance, Simon und Koch, n.d.
De L'Homosexualité. Paris, Editions Sedimo, 1962.
Magellan of the Pacific. London, Faber, 1972; New York, McGraw Hill, 1973.
The Disorderly Poet and Other Essays. Santa Barbara, California, Black Sparrow Press, 1975.
Life in a Ryokan; or, A Jew in Tartary. Santa Barbara, California, Capra Press, 1975.

Editor, *Mein Lieblingsmord*, by Ambrose Bierce. Frankfurt am Main, Insel Verlag, 1963.

Translator, *Selected Works*, by Peter Takal. New York, International University Press, 1945.
Translator, *Young Cherry Trees Secured Against Hares*, by André Breton. New York, View, and London, Zwemmer, 1946.
Translator, *The Pillar of Salt*, by Albert Memmi. London, Elek, 1956.
Translator, *The Essence of Jewish Art*, by Ernest Namenyi. New York and London, Yoseloff, 1960.
Translator, *Memed, My Hawk*, by Yashar Kemal. London, Harvill Press, 1961.
Translator, *Toros y Toreros*, by Pablo Picasso. London, Thames and Hudson, 1961.
Translator, *Art Nouveau*, by Robert Schmutzler. London, Thames and Hudson, 1964.
Translator, *Genesis Rejuvenated*, by Carlos Suares. London, Menard Press, 1973.

Manuscript Collection: Special Collections, University of California at Los Angeles Library.

Critical Studies: by Alvin Rosenfeld, in *Judaism* (New York), Spring 1969; Sidney Rosenfeld, in *Books Abroad* (Norman, Oklahoma), Summer 1972.

Edouard Roditi comments:

Originally a Surrealist, I have sought to broaden the scope of Surrealist poetry so that it can include elegiac, didactic or metaphysical poetry in addition to more strictly lyrical poetry.

My major themes are those that have inspired a great number of poets of the past, ranging from Horace to Baudelaire and T. S. Eliot; in my devotional poetry, however, I have always remained within a strictly Jewish tradition. The American poet and philosopher Paul Goodman has compared me, as an elegiac poet, to Rilke and also to Eliot. I suppose I remain too philosophical a poet to have an important following, as my very critical approach to the philosophical themes that I handle excludes any surprising innovations of style or of thought that would not, in my opinion, withstand the tests of time.

I feel that my work now illustrates a very clear and positive evolution in the course of which I have achieved, as a poet, almost all that I had proposed to achieve. I do not feel the need to add much more to what I have already written, though much of my poetry of recent years remains unpublished, partly because I may wish to correct it before publication.

* * *

Edouard Roditi is two poets, both evolved from that exhausted European romanticism he grew up with that appears in his earliest, adolescent poems:

The sky oppresses me, its vault
Of stone-grey clouds has kept my mind
Imprisoned in sepulchral gloom ...

The conventional Roditi, encouraged and goaded by Eliot, began and remains elegiac, in cadence typically iambic, often end-rimed, becoming over the years slightly more lyrical, more rhythmically varied, enjambing more: a poetry of loss, loneliness, moral outrage, nearly always with an echo of literature in the lines:

Lady, there being nothing more to say
About your beauty that has not been said
By other men about their other loves ...

The other mature Roditi is surrealist. In 1927 he began drawing upon correspondences between the world of surrealism and the world of his anterior temporal lobe seizures, seizures characterized by deeply rhythmic intense hallucinations of unusually vivid colors and symbolic forms, rather than by convulsions and unconsciousness. Encouraged by Desnos, and the Paris surrealists, Roditi recorded and organized a mythic, metamorphic land beyond nightmare – for its images do not invade consciousness, rather the other way around: consciousness seems to invade the dream, opening its shifting symbols to daylight exploration. These are the "vision mantras," as Roditi labeled them in 1928, finally collected in *New Hieroglyphic Tales* (1968), 40 years after the first were written. A remarkable poetry, especially in the light of many more recent, often less ambitious or successful surrealist experiments. As in his conventional poetry, the tone is elegiac, but the images come as startlingly clear as dreams:

And she gazed into the green eyes, her own eyes, and
lay down on the black slab of the sea. And as the
last woman's steel body stiffened, brittle relic
exposed upon the black marble altar of a dead planet,
out of her mouth rose a star: the last star.

At Oxford University that same year, Roditi wrote the first manifesto of surrealism in English, "The New Reality," which was generally ignored. So were his 1930's experiments in black humor and the surrealist absurd. (Some of these are included in his more recent Black Sparrow volume.) In spite of this initial neglect, the surrealist Roditi has obscured the accomplishments of the conventional poet. As reality has come to seem more and more surreal itself, Roditi's conception has become more meaningful. "I accept reality as if it were a found object of an ambiguous nature," Roditi has written. "Those [interpretations of it] that I choose remain, of course, the ones which reveal most clearly my sense of being personally threatened by ... an alien and hostile force."

—Edward B. Germain

RODRIGUEZ, Judith (née Green). Australian. Born in Perth, Western Australia, 13 February 1936. Educated at Brisbane Girls' Grammar School, 1950–53; University of Queensland, Brisbane, 1954–57, B.A. 1958; Cambridge University, 1960–62, M.A. 1965.

Married Fabio Rodriguez in 1964; three daughters and one son. Lecturer, Department of External Studies, University of Queensland, 1959–60; Lecturer in English, University of the West Indies, Kingston, Jamaica, 1963–65; Lecturer, St. Mary's College of Education, Twickenham, Middlesex, 1966–68. Since 1969, Lecturer and Senior Lecturer in English, La Trobe University, Melbourne. Writer-in-Residence, University of Western Australia, Perth, Summer 1978. Since 1979, Poetry Editor, *Meanjin*, Melbourne. Artist and illustrator: one-woman show – Bookshelf Gallery, Melbourne, 1978. Recipient: Arts Council of Australia Fellowship, 1974, 1978; South Australian Government prize, 1978; Artlook Victorian prize, 1979. Address: Department of English, La Trobe University, Bundoora, Victoria 3083, Australia.

PUBLICATIONS

Verse

Four Poets (as Judith Green), with others. Melbourne, Cheshire, 1962.
Nu-Plastik Fanfare Red and Other Poems. Brisbane, University of Queensland Press, 1973.
Broadsheet Number Twenty-Three. Canberra, Open Door Press, 1976.
Water Life. Brisbane, University of Queensland Press, 1976.
Shadow on Glass. Canberra, Open Door Press, 1978.
3 Poems. Melbourne, Old Metropolitan Meat Market, 1979.
Angels. Melbourne, Old Metropolitan Meat Market, 1979.
Arapede. Melbourne, Old Metropolitan Meat Market, 1979.

Manuscript Collection: Fryer Research Library, University of Queensland, Brisbane.

Critical Studies: "More Wow than Flutter" by Les A. Murray, in *Quadrant* (Sydney), October 1976; "Bolder Vision than Superintrospection" by P. Neilsen, in *The Age* (Melbourne), 12 March 1977; "Sea Change" by C. Treloar, in *Twenty-Four Hours* (Sydney), August 1977.

Judith Rodriguez comments:

I write poetry in order to live more fully. A lot of my poems spring directly from that idea. The big facts of my life – of living in a modern city, and being a woman. But "commitment" – small-scale and short-term – is mere distraction. I find it amazingly difficult to react at once in poetry to current world news, and to write about children. The occasion crowds the response. Wait.

My first close critic – the poet John Manifold. Admirations, influence: as a student, Brennan, Mallarmé; but my tastes range widely. Fine prose fascinates me: perhaps extravagance in fineness? Browne, Stein. Also the great journals and travels.

Printmaking has reopened my interest in visual art; I play chamber music. These go inseparably with my feeling for words, though not at all transposable. I am drawn to a strongly disciplined poetic, and to current theories of organic poetry. But, form in practice – so often the poem comes hand-in-hand with its own little playmate – you see how they get on together.

Recent interest: euphoria. Topic: mudcrab. Sideways and onward.

* * *

Judith Rodriguez first attracted attention (under her maiden name Judith Green) in 1962 as one of the contributors to *Four Poets*, a volume that presented the early work of four young writers with Brisbane affiliations and, in effect, announced the emergence of a new force in Australian poetry – a force that was to be tagged, over a decade later, "the Queensland Octopus," indicative of a sort of energy that was less regional than adaptive. Each of the original "Four Poets" (Rodriguez, David Malouf, Rodney Hall, Don Maynard) came to occupy important editorial positions – and in States other than Queensland, so often regarded as the "Deep South" of Australian culture.

Rodriguez, in her first poems, displayed a vigorous manipulation of language (barely kept in check by the formal lyricism of the time) to serve the ends of immediacy and directness of expression. There is the sense of a new writer still seeking a style and a voice, though the uneven "Essay on M.K." comes closest to pushing the author into a genuine self-exploration. It was not until a long period in Europe and Jamaica and an eventual return to Australia that her second volume, *Nu-Plastik Fanfare Red*, was published. The increase in command and in certainty of direction is immediately clear in poems such as "Sojourners at Phoenix":

> They are here, Svetlana, as they were there.
> Men. Difficult to love. Difficult not to.
>
> Slavers strung out in harness, iron-galled;
> smiths of ideals, lining up at the anvil for thrashing.
>
> Stalin, that fathered five-year plans and prisons.
> And an architect of together. You can't say fairer.
>
> And when you left, Svetlana, and when you left
> with nothing ahead but maybe
>
> glimmer in the jaws of the escape hatch
> you could not perhaps slip through whole....

Her poetry had become imbued with a warm female sharpness – precisely observed moments and objects and responses, place rather than time, people through things, humanity through attitudes. Her tone had become clipped, never sloppy; her poems as tight-packed as a larder full of preserves. She had found a way with language to contain her wide experience and range of interests.

Her next book, *Water Life*, was illustrated (or rather, complemented) with the author's own vigorous and sensuous linocuts and awarded a major literary award. Rodriguez's femininity is never embittered, though the exploration of her womanness has been increasingly fruitful for her writing and her development – and has led to moments of painful honesty. *Water Life* summed up not only stages in the poet's own intellectual and emotional development, but that of a generation of women, and in ways directed to growth and celebrative instincts rather than rejection and self immolation. Her most recent, small, collection, *Shadow on Glass*, refines the characteristic Rodriguez energy to an almost clenched lyricism. It could be said that the lyrical mode has always exercised this poet's mind; but only in her most recent work has the combination of song-flow and mind-stress fully cohered, and even then, fitfully. She is in many ways the most exciting and explorative of the "Brisbane Octopus" generation, her work providing the sense of an intellect – and a female strength – in course of liberation and growth. In any terms, her achievement and challenging way with language are already apparent.

—Thomas W. Shapcott

ROOK, (William) Alan. British. Born in Ruddington, Nottinghamshire, 31 October 1909. Educated at Uppingham School, Rutland; Oxford University, 1936–39, B.A. (honours) in English 1939. Served as a Major in the Royal Artillery. Since 1947, Managing Director, Skinner, Rook and Chambers, Ltd. Fellow, Royal Society of Literature. Address: Stragglethorpe Hall, Lincoln, England.

PUBLICATIONS

Verse

Songs from a Cherry Tree. Oxford, Halls, 1938.
Soldiers, This Solitude. London, Routledge, 1942.
These Are My Comrades: Poems. London, Routledge, 1943.
We Who Are Fortunate. London, Routledge, 1945.

Other

Not as a Refuge (literary criticism). London, Lindsey Drummond, 1948.
Diary of an English Vineyard. London, Wine and Spirit Publications, 1972.

Editor, with A. W. Sandford, *Oxford Poetry 1936.* Oxford, Blackwell, 1936.

* * *

Alan Rook was one of the most prolific poets of World War II, but he fell silent immediately the war ended. The coincidence is surely a little too pat? Reading Rook's poems now, thirty years after they were written, one sees that they were precisely adapted to the taste of their time, and in many ways antagonistic to that of ours. The diction has a lush fullness which appealed to the war-time taste for the romantic; and in his first volume – the bulk of it, incidentally, written before war broke out – there are, in uneasy juxtaposition to this romanticism, distinct echoes of the work Auden was doing in the late thirties.

Yet this volume also contains at least one poem of real interest -- Robin Skelton rightly chose it for his representative anthology, *Poetry of the Forties*. This poem is "Dunkirk Pier," and it is one of the few English attempts to sum up the experience of defeat – a muted, but still genuine echo of the kind of poetry Aragon wrote in *Les Yeux d'Elsa:*

> Deeply across the waves of our darkness fear,
> like the silent octopus, feeling, groping, clear
> as a star's reflection, nervous and cold as a bird,
> tells us that pain, tells us that death is near.

What is still valid about Rook's poems is that they encapsulate a mood, a way of feeling otherwise out of reach. The poetic means are often imperfect, but the interest lies in the meeting of the individual and the time – just as it does with much of the poetry of the First World War.

—Edward Lucie-Smith

ROOT, William Pitt. American. Born in Austin, Minnesota, 28 December 1941. Educated at the University of Washington, Seattle, B.A. 1964; University of North Carolina, Greensboro, M.F.A. 1967. Married Judy Bechtold in 1965 (divorced, 1970); one daughter. Instructor, Slippery Rock State College, Pennsylvania, 1967; Assistant Professor of English, Michigan State University, East Lansing, 1967–68; Stegner Creative Writing Fellow, Stanford University, California, 1968–69; Visiting Lecturer or Writer, Mid-Peninsula Free University, 1969–70, Amherst College, Massachusetts, 1971, Wichita State University, Kansas, 1977, University of Southwestern Louisiana, Lafayette, 1977, and University of Montana, Missoula, 1978. Recipient: American Academy of Poets university prize, 1966; Rockefeller grant, 1969; Guggenheim grant, 1970; National Endowment for the Arts grant, 1973; Bicentennial Exchange Fellowship, 1978. Address: c/o Atheneum Publishers, 122 East 42nd Street, New York, New York 10017, U.S.A.

PUBLICATIONS

Verse

The Storm and Other Poems. New York, Atheneum, 1969.
Striking the Dark Air for Music. New York, Atheneum, 1973.
The Port of Galveston. Galveston, Texas, Galveston Arts Center, 1974.
A Journey South. Port Townsend, Washington, Graywolf Press, 1977.
7 Mendocino Songs. Portland, Oregon, Mississippi Mud Press, 1977.
Coot and Other Characters: Poems New and Familiar. Lewiston, Idaho, Confluence Press, 1977.
Fireclock. Boston, 4 Zoas Press, 1979.

Plays

Films (with Ray Rice): *Song of the Woman and the Butterflyman*, 1975; *7 for a Magician*, 1976; *Faces from the Poems of William Pitt Root*, 1978.

Other

Editor, *What a World, What a World! Poetry by Young People in Galveston Schools.* Galveston, Texas, Pipedream Press, 1974.

Manuscript Collection: University of North Carolina Library, Greensboro.

Critical Studies: by Benjamin DeMott, in *New York Times Book Review*, 10 December 1967; "Notes on Current Books," in *Virginia Quarterly* (Charlottesville), August 1969; "The Storm" by Robin Skelton, in *Malahat Review* (Victoria), October 1969; "Striking the Dark Air for Music" by Paul Nelson, in *Carleton Miscellany* (Northfield, Minnesota), September 1974; "An Ultimate Magician: Notes on the Work of William Pitt Root" by Floyd Skloot, in *Chowder Review*, Winter 1978.

William Pitt Root comments:

As a counter to the proliferation of much instant poetry, I regard with respect the efforts of such men as Bly and Merwin in America or Hughes in England, who, with others, bring into English the works of writers from other cultures where the conditions for the development of the human spirit are still more trying, more essentially demanding.

Regarding my own work, I hope it reflects something of the qualities I admire most in Roethke (whose primordial consciousness is inimitable), Frost (who forged memorable work out of an inconsolable solitude), Williams (whose love of animation in people and nature was inexhaustible), García Lorca (whose passions were essential, unsummoned), Whitman, Blake, Neruda, Lawrence, and Jeffers (who share the impulse to accomplish the mythic common bond out of the apparently commonplace) – these are men who in opening to their own experience can extend us as well. These poets are makers, not designers, and what they make is self being freed of ego, first defining, then transcending those limits. In America, now, the most exciting groundwork for such growth is being established by the waking generations of women who dare to explore their own frontiers. I should add I mean those who travel by foot, to distinguish between them and those who travel by bandwagon. No frontier has ever been approached by bandwagon.

* * *

William Pitt Root's first book impresses one with its solidity: dense physical detail; evenly-paced, full sounds; and a strong emotional weightiness. He succeeds, not with leaps of imagination (he uses few similes and little of the dream-world), but by careful description of emotionally significant scenes or situations and occasional, direct statements of feeling. He says:

> ... I am a bear
> as clumsy off the ground
> as I am strong among trees.

The heart of *The Storm* is death. There are poems about dead or dying men, raccoons, fish, girls, flowers, turtles, crows, and starlings. But the primary death, the one to which Root returns again and again in his books, is the death of his father, which occurred while Root was a child. One senses in so many of his poems a subterranean aggression which seems strongly connected to the frustrations and angers, the Oedipal force, of the relationship to his dying father. One feels "a pale brutal ferocity spreading its strength" throughout the poems. He also makes us feel the sorrow, though, and the intense love and admiration he had for his father.

Root's second book, *Striking the Dark Air for Music*, shows a change in both style and intent. The poems are more introspective; there is more abstraction and direct statement, less physical detail. He continues to be concerned with death and dying, but he is more involved in self-examination, in recognizing his faults and fixations, in attempting to change. Not only does he show uncommon openness in his self-scrutiny, but there seems to be genuine growth, the poems at the end of the book having a lighter spirit, joyous and mystical.

—Lawrence Russ

ROSELIEP, Raymond (Francis). American. Born in Farley, Iowa, 11 August 1917. Educated at Loras College, Dubuque, Iowa, B.A. 1939; Catholic University of America, Washington, D.C., M.A. 1948; University of Notre Dame, Indiana, Ph.D. 1954. Ordained a Roman Catholic secular priest, 1943; Assistant Pastor in Gilbertville, Iowa, 1943–45.

Instructor, 1946–48, Assistant Professor, 1948–60, and Associate Professor, 1960–66, Loras College; Poet-in-Residence, Georgetown University, Washington, D.C., Summer, 1964. Since 1966, Resident Chaplain, Holy Family Hall, Dubuque, Iowa, Managing Editor, *Witness*, Dubuque, Iowa, 1945–46. Poetry Editor, *Sponsa Regis*, published by the Benedictine Order, 1959–66. Recipient: Society of Midland Authors Award, 1968; Henderson Haiku Award, 1977. Address: Holy Family Hall, 3340 Windsor Extension, Dubuque, Iowa 52001, U.S.A.

PUBLICATIONS

Verse

The Linen Bands. Westminster, Maryland, Newman Press, 1961.
The Small Rain. Westminster, Maryland, Newman Press, 1963.
Love Makes the Air Light. New York, Norton, 1965.
Voyages to the Inland Sea IV, with others. La Crosse, University of Wisconsin Center for Contemporary Poetry, 1974.
Flute over Walden. West Lafayette, Indiana, Vagrom, 1976.
Walk in Love. La Crosse, Wisconsin, Juniper Press, 1976.
Light Footsteps. La Crosse, Wisconsin, Juniper Press, 1976.
A Beautiful Woman Moves with Grace. Derry, Pennsylvania, Rook Press, 1976.
Sun in His Belly. West Lafayette, Indiana, High/Coo Press, 1977.
Step on the Rain. Derry, Pennsylvania, Rook Press, 1977.
Wake to the Bell. Derry, Pennsylvania, Rook Press, 1977.
Dusk and Ocean. Derry, Pennsylvania, Rook Press, 1977.
A Day in the Life of Sobi-Shi. Ruffsdale, Pennsylvania, Rook Press, 1978.
Sailing Bones. Ruffsdale, Pennsylvania, Rook Press, 1978.
Sky in My Legs. La Crosse, Wisconsin, Juniper Press, 1979.
Firefly in My Eyecup. West Lafayette, Indiana, High/Coo Press, 1979.

Other

Editor, *Into the Round Air.* Derry, Pennsylvania, Rook Press, 1977.

Bibliography: in *Voyages to the Inland Sea IV*, 1974.

Critical Studies: "Priest and Poet: A Note on the Art of Raymond Roseliep" by John Logan, in *Mutiny* (Northport, New York), Spring 1961; "The Poetry of Raymond Roseliep" by Thomas P. McDonnell, in *Four Quarters* (Philadelphia), May 1961; "Magic and the Magician" an interview with Dennis Hayes, in *Today* (Notre Dame, Indiana), October 1963; "Four Poets Take Note of *The Linen Bands* of Raymond Roseliep" by Sam Bradley, Charles Philbrick, Gil Orlovitz, and James L. Weil, in *Mutiny* (Northport, New York), iv, 1; "Priesthood and Poetry" by Gerald Meath, in *The Tablet* (London), 1 January 1966; "Raymond Roseliep Issue" of *Chicory 1* (Ruffsdale, Pennsylvania), 1978.

Raymond Roseliep comments:

Sometimes people ask me, Why do you write a poem? and I remember once asking that question of Stephen Spender. I'd say I write a poem because I can't write a musical score, paint a picture, sculpt, or design a building, and I gave up dancing when I became a priest. A poem seems to be the right form for what I want to express. Sometimes I feel many of my poems should be short stories, and probably they would if I had the patience to work in that medium. If I had other talents in the fine arts, I'm certain I would shape my vision in one or another of their molds. I recall Stephen Spender telling me *he* could work fairly well in some of these areas, but he said practically the same thing I'm saying now about the "rightness" of poetry for a particular vision.

I write to find out what I'm thinking. And because I'm moving in an art structure, naturally I want to *make* something beautiful. Something with the order and harmony and radiance which Thomas Aquinas asked of a piece of beauty – I still believe his *id quod visum placet*, "that which delights the beholder," is our best definition of what's beautiful. I delight myself as first beholder (every writer is his own first and often most appreciative audience); then I hope to give this experience of delight to others. Personally I feel a pressing need to share these ordered thoughts and feelings; not all writers do. I always say beauty is beauty twice when shared. Like Hopkins' "azurous hung hills." They were made by the Master Artificer and just stood there beautiful, "the beholder wanting." They needed the necessary eye of a witness other than the artist.

Of course there's another step beyond "delighting" an audience – and I keep it pretty much in mind too: this business of being "useful" to readers. Maurois stated it poignantly one time when he said, "If [a writer's] own conflict resembles that of many of his fellow men, it may, through his efforts, become less obsessive and troublesome to them – in which case he will have the additional pleasure of having been helpful." This twofold function of "delighting" and "instructing" (being useful) I know is pure Horace.

The inspiration or subject of my poems may evolve from almost anything or anyone – a tire, a violet, a football, tomato juice, a young lover, a toothache, air, fire, water, earth, stuff from books or history or dreams or the world of ideas, religion, blue jeans, bandannas, frogs, children, Indians, cats, drugs, war, popcorn – or from anywhere. A poem's experience may be my own, or it may be vicarious or fictional. Inspirations arrive any time. The worst time is at night after I'm well established in bed. If I don't get up and write down the rough idea for a poem, or some delicious phrase that visits me at this unseasonable moment, I lose it.

A poem takes time. I spend more time revising than in first-drafting a poem. I remember what Housman said once, that his effort as poet was not so much to find the right word as to reject the wrong one. Yeats defended the practice early in his career: "A line will take us hours maybe;/Yet if it does not seem a moment's thought,/Our stitching and unstitching has been naught." It's hard to say how long it takes to write a single poem. Sometimes an hour – for a first draft of a fairly short poem like a sonnet. Maybe five to umpteen hours. And I don't always write "in one sitting." Sometimes I assemble the skeleton on a bus or plane or while listening to a bad lecture, or just almost any time I have a ball point and something to scratch on. I write on the backs of old envelopes, whatever's handy – once I scribbled some verses on my shirt cuff (the left one).

Felix Stefanile wrote me in one of his letters: "I hope you always try to write poetry that is both un-easy and not easy; it is the only kind of art worth the allegiance." I know my poetry is sometimes "un-easy and not easy" because there's pain in it; and there's something ambiguous about pain, something you don't want to clearly define about pain. *Should* a poem be clearly defined anyway? And so, people sometimes consider me "obscure." In reply I can only say that I want my reader to do some of the work, for one thing; and I don't want to overstate my case, for another; I don't want to explain the emotion, or I'm likely to have not a poem but a psychiatric profile. Understatement, then, is any poet's desideratum, maybe even a weapon for self-protection. A poem is distilled significance.

Knowing that I have made something and have given something is the reward of a poem. Occasionally there's a bonus when I write a poem about a certain someone and offer it to my subject as a gift. The most delightful response to a gift-poem was the one I received from Marianne Moore. I had sent her my lines about her reading in Chicago, a poem that started with the cadence, "Peacock elegant the lady wore a necklace microphone," and went on to picture her as that rare bird with "dark jewels" and "a particular flight." She sent me a peacock feather.

"Love is the word of all work," George Eliot said, and love is at the core of my poems. I try to incarnate spiritual reality and spiritualize or humanize material reality. To help in this transfiguration of matter keeps me aware that a poet is, after all, an animal with the sun in his belly. The one thing his poetry must do, as Auden said, is to praise all it can for being and happening. My students took another view: they used to cite Augustine's *vinum daemonum* as descriptive of my poems – they translated it "devilish wine." I like that too.

* * *

Raymond Roseliep is a teacher and a Catholic priest who writes a catholic, well-crafted, and direct love poetry. As the poet John Logan enthusiastically explains in the preface to Roseliep's first volume: "Those three, the priest, the poet, the teacher, are held together either by mere love, which is the thinnest of threads if it's not the strongest, or by art, or by both. I think that in Father Roseliep they are held together by both."

Some poems express the love of the divine representative, the priest, for the worshipper and penitent, but, more often, Roseliep's poems deal with the love of the teacher and scholar for the student ("Room 210: Shakespeare"). "Love," we will see, "makes the air light" and it joins all things. After the "small rain" of the real, through love – and these poems –

light
will wheel to a
point
sharper than rain.

The expression of a "supernatural" love depends on imagery more than intensity or emotion, and Roseliep's poems succeed because, in transcending the "small rain," a human love for the physical is evident. The priestly vows to keep at bay the world where love is "materialized" only intensify – as they did for Hopkins – everything; his vow to keep to a love which will not "touch" only makes his perceptions as man and poet the more impassioned and poignant: this is effective and obvious in "For Denise, Distracting," or "Your Hair Falls Blackbird," and again

on our terrace, robin lithe
and robin bloused, skirted, blown
was a girl brilliant as pain.

Roseliep's love extends to language and its rhythms. In such poems as "Alan" and "GI" he attempts a return to the energy of Anglo-Saxon; he is able to use the immediate image with facility, and although obviously capable in accentual syllabics, Roseliep most often achieves effect with vivid language and syllabics ("Convent Infirmary," or "Rembrandt's 'Young Girl at an Open Half-Door' " are examples). His poems are direct in their love and repeatedly risk the reader with strong emotion. It is to Roseliep's credit that only occasionally can he be charged with sentimentalism.

—Joseph Wilson

ROSENBLATT, Joe (Joseph Rosenblatt). Canadian. Born in Toronto, Ontario, 26 December 1933. Educated at Central Technical School, and George Brown College, Toronto.

Married to Faye Smith; one son. Formerly, a laborer, factory worker, plumber's mate, grave digger, civil servant; worked for the Canadian Pacific Railway for seven years. Currently, Editor, *Jewish Dialog* magazine, Toronto. Recipient: Canada Council grant, 1966, 1968, 1973; Governor-General's Award, 1976. Address: 15 Greensides Avenue, Toronto, Ontario, Canada.

PUBLICATIONS

Verse

Voyage of the Mood. Don Mills, Ontario, Heinrich Heine Press, 1963.
The LSD Leacock. Toronto, Coach House Press, 1966.
Winter of the Luna Moth. Toronto, Anansi, 1968.
Greenbaum. Toronto, Coach House Press, 1971.
The Bumblebee Dithyramb. Erin, Ontario, Press Porcépic, 1972.
The Blind Photographer: Poems and Sketches. Erin, Ontario, Press Porcépic, 1973.
Dream Craters. Erin, Ontario, Press Porcépic, 1974.
Vampires and Virgins. Toronto, McClelland and Stewart, 1975.
Top Soil. Erin, Ontario, Press Porcépic, 1976.
Loosely Tied Hands. Windsor, Ontario, Black Moss Press, 1978.

Recording: *Joe Rosenblatt*, High Barnet, 1973.

Manuscript Collections: Public Archives of Canada, Ottawa; University of Toronto.

Joe Rosenblatt comments:

My own verse and prose-poems basically attack the human condition and society with its crass materialism and phony value-structure.

My poetry is traditional and influenced by American poets such as Hart Crane and Robert Frost. My poems are concerned with the Moloch or Mammon monster of society and the insatiable appetite of the creature. The monster finds its expression in my animal poems.

For example, in my bat poems the psyche of man is found in this terrestrial animal of darkness. Therefore my kinship is with Swift and misanthropes. My super hero is Ambrose Bierce. In nearly all my poems the quest of man is spiritual cannibalism – soul theft and the protein of money – I use the traditional devices of poetry in my work such as rhyme, assonance and metric extension.

* * *

Joe Rosenblatt "is a poet of the small presses," but he is, nevertheless, well-known in Canada. At times he has seemed, superficially, more interested in the world of plants, insects and animals than that of human beings; but this is more an aspect of his fascination with the unusual, the rare, and the minute than a lack of sympathy with the race of men. He has said, "I only deal with the bizarre," but adds that his newer poems are "more directly confessional poems, written without the intervention of imagery or my old animal disguises." Lately, he has been drawing as well as writing poems, and in the drawings images of grotesque, and curiously human, though debased, animals and reptiles abound. He has had exhibitions of his drawings in several Toronto galleries and his 1973 book (*The Blind Photographer*) might more properly be called a book of drawings illustrated by poems than the opposite. He has said that "drawings are the lazy man's way to writing anti-poems, poems without intellectualizing and verbalizing." It is typical of Rosenblatt to hint that he is not much interested in thoughtful technique; in fact, in both poems and drawings, he is always meticulously careful of detail. His interest in "insect and plant sexuality" is extraordinary and Norman Snider has said rightly that "Rosenblatt is a miniaturist in his sensibility, his poems are minute and exquisite observations of the tiny phenomena of nature." It only remains to add that, in the real meaning of the word, wit is the prime mark of his work.

—John Newlove

ROSENTHAL, M(acha) L(ouis). American. Born in Washington, D.C., 14 March 1917. Educated at the University of Chicago, B.A. 1937, M.A. 1938; New York University, Ph.D. 1949. Married Victoria Himmelstein in 1939; two sons and one daughter. Instructor, Michigan State University, East Lansing, 1939–45. Since 1945, Member of the English Department, since 1961, Professor of English, and since 1977, Director of the Poetics Institute, New York University. Poetry Editor, *The Nation*, New York, 1956–61, and *The Humanist*, Buffalo, 1970–78. United States Cultural Exchange Program Visiting Specialist in Germany, 1961, Pakistan, 1965, and Poland, Romania, and Hungary, 1966. Since 1973, Poetry Editor, *Present Tense*, New York. Recipient: American Council of Learned Societies Fellowship, 1942, 1950; Guggenheim Fellowship, 1960, 1964. Agent: Fox Chase Agency, Lincoln Building, 60 East 42nd Street, New York, New York 10017. Address: Department of English, New York University, 19 University Place, New York, New York 10003, U.S.A.

PUBLICATIONS

Verse

Blue Boy on Skates. New York and London, Oxford University Press, 1964.
Beyond Power: New Poems. New York and London, Oxford University Press, 1969.
The View from the Peacock's Tail. New York and London, Oxford University Press, 1972.
She: A Sequence of Poems. Brockport, New York, Boa, 1977.

Other

Effective Reading: Methods and Models, with W. C. Hummel and V. E. Leichty. Boston, Houghton Mifflin, 1944.
Exploring Poetry, with A. J. M. Smith. New York, Macmillan, 1955; revised edition, 1973.
A Primer of Ezra Pound. New York, Macmillan, 1960.
The Modern Poets: A Critical Introduction. New York and London, Oxford University Press, 1960.
The New Poets: American and British Poetry since World War II. New York and London, Oxford University Press, 1967.

Randall Jarrell. Minneapolis, University of Minnesota Press, 1972.
Poetry and the Common Life. New York and London, Oxford University Press, 1974.
Sailing into the Unknown: Yeats, Pound, and Eliot. New York and London, Oxford University Press, 1978.

Editor, with Thomas H. Jameson, *A Selection of Verse.* Paterson, New Jersey, Littlefield, 1952.
Editor, with Gerald D. Sanders and John Herbert Nelson, *Chief Modern Poets of Britain and America.* New York, Macmillan, 1962; revised edition, 1970.
Editor, *Selected Poems and Two Plays of W. B. Yeats.* New York, Macmillan, 1962; revised edition, 1973.
Editor, *The William Carlos Williams Reader.* New York, New Directions, 1966; London, MacGibbon and Kee, 1967.
Editor, *The New Modern Poetry: An Anthology of British and American Poetry since World War II.* New York, Macmillan, 1967; revised edition, New York, Oxford University Press, 1969.
Editor, *100 Postwar Poems: British and American.* New York, Macmillan, 1968.

Critical Studies: "In Spite of Solitude" by Stuart Holroyd, in *John O'London's*, 2 March 1961; "Judgements and Interpretations" by Thomas Lask, in *New York Times*, 25 April 1967; "The Lyre in the Larger Pattern" by Robert D. Spector, in *Saturday Review* (New York), 10 June 1967; "Voices of Victims" by Robie Macauley in *New York Times Book Review*, 10 September 1967; Thomas Lask, in *New York Times*, 29 August 1969; "Sensibilities" by William Heyen, in *Poetry* (Chicago), March 1970; Frederick Feirstein, in *Library Journal* (New York), 8 November 1972; "The Poetry of M. L. Rosenthal" by Sally M. Gall, in *Modern Poetry Studies* (Buffalo), Autumn 1977; "The Poetry of M. L. Rosenthal" by Emile Capouya, in *The Nation* (New York), 1 and 22 October 1977 and 21 January 1978; "Lyrical Readings" by Robert Langbaum, in *New York Times Book Review*, 2 April 1978.

* * *

With the publication of three volumes of poetry since 1964, the distinguished critic and teacher M. L. Rosenthal has emerged as a genuinely important poet in his own right. Rosenthal is capable of considerable variety in tone and form, and this flexibility provides suitable expressive parallels to the breadth of his subject matter. The tone of individual poems varies, for example, from the playfulness of "Jim Dandy," and the sardonic and transforming wit of "Love in the Luncheonette," to the controlled grief of "I Strike a Match ...," and the poems range in form from the disciplined lyricism of "Visiting Yeats's Tower" to more open forms with deceptively relaxed conversational rhythms. In addition, certain poems explore within the framework of a single work the relationships between prose and verse themselves.

Rosenthal's subject matter is drawn from deeply felt personal experience; from Biblical allusions; from literary references to such diverse figures as, among others, Keats, Pasternak, Rilke, Hart Crane, and Mayakovsky; and occasionally from political and historical events. But the triumph of individual poems lies in Rosenthal's ability to place in new and contemporary perspective some of the great and traditional themes: love and death; youth and age; innocence and experience; the identity of man.

The key perhaps to this diversity of style and content is Rosenthal's inclusive and paradoxical concept of the poet himself: in his own case a combination of "a 'tragic view of life' *and* an optimistic 'nature.' " Throughout his work one is aware of the pained intensity of a deeply compassionate man who observes the contradictory behavior of those "Sentimental scorpions," human beings, and who yearns nevertheless – as "Seniority, or It Stands to Reason" indicates – for ultimate metaphors of reconciliation:

These autumn leaves, with their gold or crimson sheen,
could hardly recommend the fresh young green
spring leaves for mature responsibilities.
You need *experience* to capture sun for trees.

—Gaynor F. Bradish

ROSS, Alan. British. Born in Calcutta, India, 6 May 1922. Educated at Haileybury; St. John's College, Oxford. Served in the Royal Naval Voluntary Reserve, 1942–47. Married Jennifer Fry in 1949; one son. Staff Member, British Council, 1947–50; Staff Member, *The Observer*, London, 1950–71. Since 1961, Editor, *London Magazine.* Currently, Managing Director, London Magazine Editions, formerly Alan Ross Publishers, London. Recipient: Atlantic-Rockfeller Award, 1946. Fellow, Royal Society of Literature, 1971. Address: 4 Elm Park Lane, London S.W. 10, England.

PUBLICATIONS

Verse

Summer Thunder. Oxford, Blackwell, 1941.
The Derelict Day: Poems in Germany. London, Lehmann, 1947.
Something of the Sea: Poems 1942–1952. London, Verschoyle, 1954; Boston, Houghton Mifflin, 1955.
To Whom It May Concern: Poems 1952–57. London, Hamish Hamilton, 1958.
African Negatives. London, Eyre and Spottiswoode, 1962.
North from Sicily: Poems in Italy 1961–64. London, Eyre and Spottiswoode, 1965.
Poems 1942–67. London, Eyre and Spottiswoode, 1967.
A Calcutta Grandmother. London, Poem-of-the-Month Club, 1971.
Tropical Ice. London, Covent Garden Press, 1972.
The Taj Express: Poems 1967–1973. London, London Magazine Editions, 1973.
Open Sea. London, London Magazine Editions, 1975.

Other

Time Was Away: A Notebook in Corsica. London, Lehmann, 1948.
The Forties: A Period Piece. London, Weidenfeld and Nicolson, 1950.
The Gulf of Pleasure (travel). London, Weidenfeld and Nicolson, 1951.
Poetry 1945–50. London, Longman, 1951; Folcroft, Pennsylvania, Folcroft Editions, 1974.
The Bandit on the Billiard Table: A Journey Through Sardinia. London, Verschoyle, 1954; revised edition, as *South to Sardinia*, London, Hamish Hamilton, 1960.
Australia 55: A Journal of the M.C.C. Tour (cricket). London, Joseph 1955.
Cape Summer, and The Australians in England. London, Hamish Hamilton, 1957.
The Onion Man (juvenile). London, Hamish Hamilton, 1959.
Danger on Glass Island (juvenile). London, Hamish Hamilton, 1960.

Through the Caribbean: The M.C.C. Tour of the West Indies 1959–1960 (cricket). London, Hamish Hamilton, 1960.
Australia 63 (cricket). London, Eyre and Spottiswoode, 1963.
The West Indies at Lord's (cricket). London, Eyre and Spottiswoode, 1963.
The Wreck of Moni (juvenile). London, Alan Ross, 1965.
A Castle in Sicily (juvenile). London, Alan Ross, 1966.

Editor, *Selected Poems of John Gay*. London, Grey Walls Press, 1950.
Editor, with Jennifer Ross, *Borrowed Time: Short Stories*, by F. Scott Fitzgerald. London, Grey Walls Press, 1951.
Editor, *Abroad: Travel Stories*. London, Faber, 1957.
Editor, *The Cricketer's Companion*. London, Eyre and Spottiswoode, 1960.
Editor, *Poetry Supplement*. London, Poetry Book Society, 1963.
Editor, *London Magazine Stories 1–11*. London, London Magazine Editions, 1964–79.
Editor, *Leaving School*. London, London Magazine Editions, 1966.
Editor, *Living in London*. London, London Magazine Editions, 1974.
Editor, *Selected Poems*, by Lawrence Durrell. London, Faber, 1977.

Translator, *Undersea Adventure*, by Philippe Diolé. New York, Messner, 1953.
Translator, *Sacred Forest*, by Pierre Gaisseau. London, Weidenfeld and Nicolson, 1954.
Translator, *Death Is My Trade*, by Robert Merle. London, Verschoyle, 1954.
Translator, *Seas of Sicily*, by Philippe Diolé. London, Sidgwick and Jackson, 1955; as *Gates of the Sea*, New York, Messner, 1955.

Manuscript Collection: Arts Council of Great Britain, London.

* * *

Alan Ross began as what is vaguely called a war poet. He was in Germany during the early part of the Occupation, and his subjects were German gun sites and military hospitals, day and night in Hamburg, Lüneburg Heath, the dark night of the soul that as he saw it was closing on Germany. The subjects were grim, but the poet's spirit did not fully reflect them; his awareness of the sensuous world was too strong. "Lüneburg," for instance, has a refrain: "The courtroom holds the afternoon in chains." The idea is to convey that Germany too is in chains, but the verse that follows might reflect a peaceful life in Oxford: "October settles on water and weeping willows./Under stone bridges, leaves like boats/Drift golden...."

Many years later, when preparing his collected poems, Ross changed many of these early pieces in a remarkable way, stiffening and sharpening them, making exact what had been vague. "Sengwarden" originally began and ended: "At Sengwarden the silence is the space in the heart." (As a young poet Ross had a weakness for this kind of romantic and not very meaningful statement.) This line has been dropped, and the revised poem begins:

> Something (but what) could be made of this.
> Two U-boat officers turning to piss
> In swastika shapes against a wall.

These revised early poems which bear only the relationship of mood to their originals are certainly among his best work. In general he shows a love of colour and gaiety that sometimes declines to mere prettiness. He has written about cricket at Brighton and the World Cup, the Grand Canal and mine dances in Johannesburg, the Autostrada del Sole and the Finchley Road. He records the scene very vividly, but too often seems content just to do that without looking beneath or outside it. "Beyond the window the tyre-coloured road deflates/Like a tube at night" his poem about the Finchley Road begins. One appreciates the ingenious aptness of the image, but it is expressive only upon a superficial level. Sometimes a general moral is drawn in the last verse, in an attempt to add meaningfulness to a poem which is really no more than a record of observations.

Perhaps Ross was unlucky in the period at which he began writing. His natural tendency to romantic excess was encouraged by the War and by the poets most in favour at the time. In the 1930's or the 1950's his tendency to see everything in terms of brightly coloured pictures would have been controlled, and this in fact he has tried to do himself. The poems he wrote in Africa between 1958 and 1960 offer pictures just as clear as those in his earlier work but some of them, like "Rock Paintings," "Sometime Never" and "Such Matters as Rape" go a good deal further by expressing some involvement with the scenes described. These, and the rewritten early poems, suggest a possible new line of development in the next decade.

—Julian Symons

ROTHENBERG, Jerome. American. Born in New York City, 11 December 1931. Educated in New York public schools, 1937–48; City College of New York, B.A. 1952; University of Michigan, Ann Arbor, M.A. 1953. Served in the United States Army, Germany, 1954–55. Married Diane Brodatz in 1952; one son. Instructor, City College of New York, 1959–60; Lecturer in English, Mannes College of Music, New York, 1961–70; Regents Professor, University of California, San Diego, 1971; Visiting Lecturer in Anthropology, New School for Social Research, New York, 1971–72; Visiting Professor, University of Wisconsin, Milwaukee, 1974–75, San Diego State University, 1976–77, and University of California, San Diego, 1977–79. Founding Publisher, Hawk's Well Press, New York, 1958–65; Editor or Co-Editor, *Some/Thing*, *Floating World*, *Stony Brook*, *Alcheringa: A First Magazine of Ethnopoetics*, and *New Wilderness Letter*. Recipient: Longview Foundation Award, 1961; National Endowment for the Arts grant, 1969, 1976; Wenner-Gren Foundation grant, 1969; Guggenheim grant, 1974. Address: c/o New Directions Inc., 80 Eighth Avenue, New York, New York 10011, U.S.A.

PUBLICATIONS

Verse

White Sun, Black Sun. New York, Hawk's Well Press, 1960.
The Seven Hells of the Jigoku Zoshi. New York, Trobar Books, 1962.
Sightings I-IX, with *Lunes* by Robert Kelly. New York, Hawk's Well Press, 1964.
The Gorky Poems (bilingual edition). Mexico City, El Corno Emplumado, 1966.
Between 1960–1963. London, Fulcrum Press, 1967.
Conversations. Los Angeles, Black Sparrow Press, 1968.
Poems 1964–1967. Los Angeles, Black Sparrow Press, 1968.
Offering Flowers, with Ian Tyson. London, Circle Press, 1968.
Sightings I-IX & Red Easy a Color, with Ian Tyson. London, Circle Press, 1968.
Poland/1931. Santa Barbara, California, Unicorn Press, 1969.
The Directions, with Tom Phillips. London, Tetrad Press, 1969.
Poems for the Game of Silence 1960–1970. New York, Dial Press, 1971.
A Book of Testimony. Bolinas, California, Tree, 1971.

Net of Moon, Net of Sun. Santa Barbara, California, Unicorn Press, 1971.
A Valentine No a Valedictory for Gertrude Stein. London, Judith Walker, 1972.
Seneca Journal I: A Poem of Beavers. Madison, Wisconsin, Perishable Press, 1973.
Three Friendly Warnings, with Ian Tyson. London, Tetrad Press, 1973.
Esther K. Comes to America. Greensboro, North Carolina, Unicorn Press, 1974.
The Cards. Los Angeles, Black Sparrow Press, 1974.
Poland/1931 (complete edition). New York, New Directions, 1974.
The Pirke and the Pearl. San Francisco, Tree, 1975.
Seneca Journal: Midwinter, with Philip Sultz. St. Louis, Singing Bone Press, 1975.
A Poem to Celebrate the Spring and Diane Rothenberg's Birthday. Madison, Wisconsin, Perishable Press, 1975.
Book of Palaces: The Gatekeepers. Boston, Pomegranate Press, 1975.
I Was Going Through the Smoke, with Ian Tyson. London, Tetrad Press, 1975.
Rain Events. Milwaukee, Membrane Press, 1975.
The Notebooks. Milwaukee, Membrane Press, 1976.
A Vision of the Chariot in Heaven. Boston, Hundred Flowers Book Shop, 1976.
Narratives and Realtheater Pieces, with Ian Tyson. Bretenoux, France, Braad, 1977.
Seneca Journal: The Serpent, with Philip Sultz. St. Louis, Singing Bone Press, 1978.
A Seneca Journal (complete edition). New York, New Directions, 1978.
Songs for the Society of the Mystic Animals, with Ian Tyson. London, Tetrad Press, 1979.
*B*R*M*Tz*V*H.* Madison, Wisconsin, Perishable Press, 1979.
Abulafia's Circles. Milwaukee, Membrane Press, 1979.
Numbers and Letters. Madison, Wisconsin, Salient Seedling Press, 1979.

Recordings: *Origins and Meanings*, Folkways, 1968; *From a Shaman's Notebook*, Folkways, 1968.

Play

The Deputy, adaptation of a play by Rolf Hochhuth (produced New York, 1964). New York, French, 1965.

Other

Editor and Translator, *New Young German Poets.* San Francisco, City Lights, 1959.
Editor, *Ritual: A Book of Primitive Rites and Events* (anthology). New York, Something Else Press, 1966.
Editor, *Technicians of the Sacred: A Range of Poetries from Africa, America, Asia, and Oceania.* New York, Doubleday, 1968.
Editor, *Shaking the Pumpkin: Traditional Poetry of the Indian North Americas.* New York, Doubleday, 1972.
Editor, with George Quasha, *America a Prophecy: A New Reading of American Poetry from Pre-Columbian Times to the Present.* New York, Random House, 1973.
Editor, *Revolution of the Word: A New Gathering of American Avant Garde Poetry 1914–1945.* New York, Seabury Press, 1974.
Editor, with Michel Benamou, *Ethnopoetics: A First International Symposium.* Boston, Alcheringa, 1976.
Editor, with Harris Lenowitz and Charles Doria, *A Big Jewish Book: Poems and Other Visions of the Jews from Tribal Times to the Present.* New York, Doubleday, 1978.

Translator, *The Flight of Quetzalcoatl*, from a Spanish prose version of the original Aztec by Angel Maria Garibay. Brighton, Sussex, Unicorn Bookshop, 1967.

Translator, with Michael Hamburger and the author, *Poems for People Who Don't Read Poems*, by Hans Magnus Enzensberger. New York, Atheneum, and London, Secker and Warburg, 1968; as *Poems*, London, Penguin, 1968.
Translator, *The Book of Hours and Constellations*, by Eugen Gomringer. New York, Something Else Press, 1968.
Translator, *The 17 Horse Songs of Frank Mitchell, Nos. X-XIII*. London, Tetrad Press, 1969.
Translator, with Harry Lenowitz, *Gematria 27*. Milwaukee, Membrane Press, 1977.

Critical Studies: "20th Century Music" by Diane Wakoski, in *Parnassus* (New York), Fall-Winter 1972; *Preferences* by Richard Howard, New York, Viking Press, 1974; *Boundary 2* (Binghamton, New York), April 1975; *Vort 7* (Bloomington, Indiana), 1975; review by Victor Turner, in *Boundary 2* (Binghamton, New York), Winter 1978; "In the Beginning Was Aleph" by Jonathan Cott, in *New York Times Book Review*, 23 April 1978; "Jerome Rothenberg" by Richard Kostelanetz, in *New York Arts Journal*, Summer 1978; "Uniting History in a 'Biological Fellowhood' " by Paula Gunn Allen, in *Contact II* (New York), Fall 1978.

Jerome Rothenberg comments:

I think of myself as making poems that other poets haven't provided for me & for the existence of which I feel a deep need.

I look for new forms & possibilities, but also for ways of presenting in my own language the oldest possibilities of poetry going back to the primitive & archaic cultures that have been opening up to us over the last hundred years.

I believe that everything is now possible in poetry, & that our earlier "western" attempts at closed definitions represent a failure of perception we no longer have to endure.

I have recently been translating American Indian poetry (including the "meaningless" syllables, word distortions & music) & have been exploring ancestral sources of my own in the world of Jewish mystics, thieves & madmen.

My personal manifesto reads: 1) I will change your mind; 2) any means (= methods) to that end; 3) to oppose the "devourers" = bureaucrats, systemmakers, priests, etc. (W. Blake); 4) "& if thou wdst understand that wch is me, know this: all that I have sd I have uttered playfully – & I was by no means ashamed of it" (J. C. to his disciples, The Acts of St. John).

* * *

In a poetry world today where each member makes his place by being unique, and each new body of work creates its own definitions, it should be tautological to say that Jerome Rothenberg writes a different poetry from anyone else. However, Rothenberg's poetry is special because it combines so many elements that haven't been combined before. His poetry is remarkable because it is a beautiful combination of lyric and commentary. Its technique is often surrealistic without having the purposes of surrealism at heart. It is ethnic without making one aware of the fact. It is religious and secular at the same time. It is intimate without being autobiographical. And it is experimental without being hard to understand or tedious to listen to. His poetry has influenced many American poets who have been struggling with the mode of "personal poetry," looking for a way to write it without being self-absorbed.

Jerome Rothenberg is one of those interesting poets who started his career by forming his own magazines, his own contemporary colleagues, his own press, and while not ignoring other schools of poetry or poets in the more "established" world of poetry, felt no need to gain recognition in the traditional ways. Consequently, he published more than a dozen books with small presses before publishing his selected poems, *Poems for the Game of Silence 1960–1970*.

He has proved that if you do your own work with integrity and energy, the world will come to you and appreciate your skills, for he is one of the most highly respected and loved poets in New York, and one hears nothing but praise for his poetry in places where Rothenberg has given poetry programs.

One of the most imposing works by Jerome Rothenberg is his long on-going series of poems, called *Poland/1931*. This is a magnificent set of poems which use as their source materials Rothenberg's background as an American Jew born of European parents. Most of the poems in this series are written in the incantatory style we have now come to associate with Rothenberg, using lists of images, often surrealistic, to intone a mood, to create a landscape of feelings and ideas merged together with ecstatic language. The first poem in the series, "The Wedding," is typical of the action of all the poems. Archetypal subjects give a picture of life that everyone can understand, even though they come from special sources:

poland poland poland poland poland
how thy bells wrapped in their flowers toll
how they do offer up their tongues to kiss the moon
old moon old mother stuck in the sky thyself
an old bell with no tongue a lost udder
poland thy beer is ever made of rotting bread
thy silks are linens merely thy tradesmen
dance at weddings where fanatic grooms
still dream of bridesmaids still are screaming
past their red mustaches poland
we have lain awake in thy soft arms forever

The triumph of all the poems in this series is that they are autobiographical without being about Rothenberg's personal life or himself. They give us an intimate feeling of closeness to the mind and the voice without details of the life.

Another very impressive group of poems is Rothenberg's *The Seven Hells of Jigoku Zoshi*, imagistic poems about the punishments for breaking archetypal taboos. These poems sing off the page and remind the reader how possible the lyric still is in English. But even more satisfying, they also comment compassionately on all of our lives, on how much we need from others, and how much pain and punishment all of us suffer. This is from "The Second Hell," where thieves are ground in mortars:

The thieves the thieves the lovely thieves are no more
The shore is washed by the sea
The sea is combed by the wind
The wind sleeps all day in the chimney
It moves through the house in the evening
It wakes us, it opens a door for the sea
It walks where the thieves walked
It leads us into a night without windows
Comfort me, stay with me light of my eyes
The lovely thieves are no more

Rothenberg has also done a considerable amount of translation, especially of contemporary German poetry, and one of his primary concerns is primitive poetry. Many of the surrealistic techniques of his own poetry are directly related to his study of primitive poetry all over the world. He has compiled two anthologies with those interests in mind: *Technicians of the Sacred*, an anthology of primitive poetry with an appendix of contemporary poems which he sees as bearing some resemblance to ancient poetry, and *Shaking the Pumpkin*, an anthology of American Indian poetry. *America a Prophecy*, edited with George Quasha, attempts to review American poetry from the standpoint of the oral and experimental tradition. Many of Rothenberg's innovations in poetry, including a multi-media version of *Poland/1931* in collaboration with the composer, Charles Morrow, and photographer, Lawrence Fink, demonstrate a continuation of the most ancient religious and oral traditions in poetry. He is a powerful poet whose work demonstrates what he has been preaching for many years: that there is some "deep image" or magical spirit in all good poetry, from all ages, which rests in back of a poem and communicates beyond language through the voice. He has created the possibility for all of us to hear the poetry of image through his own magnificent images.

—Diane Wakoski

ROWBOTHAM, David (Harold). Australian. Born in Toowoomba, Queensland, 27 August 1924. Educated at Toowoomba Grammar School; University of Sydney (Lawson Prize, 1949); University of Queensland, Brisbane (Ford Medal, 1948), B.A. Served in the Royal Australian Air Force, Southwest Pacific, 1942–45. Married Ethel Jessie Matthews in 1952; two daughters. Editorial Staff Member, *The Australian Encyclopedia*, 1950–51; Columnist, *Toowoomba Chronicle*, 1952–55; Broadcaster, Australian Broadcasting Commission National Book Review Panel, 1957–63. Literary and Theatre Critic, 1955–64, Chief Book Reviewer, 1964–69, and since 1969, Arts Editor, *The Courier-Mail*, Brisbane. Commonwealth Literary Fund Lecturer, University of Queensland, 1956, 1964, and University of New England, Armidale, New South Wales, 1961; Senior Tutor in English, University of Queensland, 1965–69. Advisory Editor, *Poetry Magazine*, Sydney. Since 1964, Council Member, Australian Society of Authors. Recipient: *Sydney Morning Herald* Competition prize, 1949; Grace Leven Prize, 1964; Xavier Society Award, 1966; Australian Commonwealth Literary Fund travel grant, 1972. Address: 28 Percival Terrace, Holland Park, Brisbane, Queensland, Australia.

PUBLICATIONS

Verse

Ploughman and Poet. Sydney, Lyre Bird Writers, 1954.
Inland. Sydney, Angus and Robertson, 1958.
All the Room. Brisbane, Jacaranda Press, 1964.
Bungalow and Hurricane: New Poems. Sydney, Angus and Robertson, 1967.
The Makers of the Ark. Sydney, Angus and Robertson, 1970.
The Pen of Feathers. Sydney, Angus and Robertson, 1971.
Selected Poems. Brisbane, University of Queensland Press, 1975.

Novel

The Man in the Jungle. London and Sydney, Angus and Robertson, 1964.

Short Stories

Town and City: Tales and Sketches. Sydney, Angus and Robertson, 1956.

Other

Brisbane. Sydney, University of Sydney, 1964.

Editor, *Queensland Writing.* Brisbane, Fellowship of Australian Writers, 1957.

Critical Studies: in *Australian Literature*, by Cecil Hadcraft, London, Heinemann, 1960; *Creative Writing in Australia*, by John K. Ewers, Melbourne, Georgian House, 1966; *Focus on David Rowbotham*, by John Strugnell, Brisbane, University of Queensland Press, 1969; "Some Recent Australian Poetry" by Ronald Dunlop, in *Poetry Australia* (Sydney), 1972.

David Rowbotham comments:

In reading my work backwards (for the purposes of making a selection), I find my beginnings true to subsequent ends. I have been concerned with being and words. I have not been engaged with furnishing values and fighting causes, only with seeing and speaking as myself in the issue called life, and wherever time has taken me. All that a poet has to do is: merely to be. This can still be a task when so many of us have made the most natural things the hardest of all. A common review observation about my early work (in the 1950's) – "landscape is not enough" – has never been enough, for me, in terms of a really human view. No element of one's self – in my case it was landscape – should be disowned by the self though others depreciate or dismiss it. I would only regret, not disown, poems unworthy as poems of their (my) origins. Neither should a writer working in the element of nature disown what has not been admitted or discerned: his element of man. I acknowledge – as a guidance to my earlier work done among my Australian home-countryside, and to my later work done (say) within the sense of surrounding larger worlds – that man and landscape (outer? inner?) can not be separated, and that it never occurred to me whether or not they could be. I also acknowledge that poetry is a passion before it is anything else; I have been concerned with a language for living. We are farmers of ourselves, said Donne; and I would not mind if the whole of my work, from poems about ploughmen to poems about men in space, were seen and summed up in the light of that remark.

* * *

David Rowbotham began writing and publishing after World War II as a young follower of the *Bulletin* school of nature poets in Australia, a school that encouraged Australian writers to look more closely at and reaffirm their own regional identity and meaning. Such a coming to terms with Australian landscape was important at that time, but it threatened our poetry with an ever expanding wash of minor bird and billabong versification. David Rowbotham wrote a number of very delicate lyrics in his first book, *Ploughman and Poet*, but his second collection, *Inland*, though it contained probably his most anthologised – and one of his best – poems, "Mullabinda," did not really prepare his readers for the change in direction, to a more introverted and personal poetry, that was first displayed in the volume *All the Room.*

From this point on, Rowbotham's poetry has struggled its way doggedly, and with considerable effort, into areas of response and experience far removed from the gentle sunny Darling Downs countryside of the earlier books. It is a measure of Rowbotham's integrity that he has not paid easy court to current fashionable styles and mannerisms, even when they have been shown to be amenable to the sort of personal self-exploration he has been struggling to realize. At its worst, then, his later work, in *Makers of the Ark* and *The Pen of Feathers*, is marred by a residue of quatrain-making habits not fully explored or justified. At its best, the recent poetry counterpoints a conservative vocabulary and rhythm with an intensely felt response to the poet's own discoveries and concerns, which have been thought through with an almost painful honesty to their own relevance in Rowbotham's poetic search. David Rowbotham is becoming one of the significant loners in Australian poetry.

—Thomas W. Shapcott

ROWLAND, J(ohn) R(ussell). Australian. Born in Armidale, New South Wales, 10 February 1925. Educated at Cranbrook School; University of Sydney, B.A. Married Moira Armstrong in 1956; one son and two daughters. Member of the Department of Foreign Affairs: Canberra, 1944, 1949–52, 1959–65; Moscow, 1946–48; London, 1948–49, 1957–59; Saigon, 1952–55; Washington, D.C. 1955–57. Ambassador to the U.S.S.R., 1965–68; High Commissioner to Malaysia, 1969–72; Ambassador to Austria, Czechoslovakia, and Hungary, 1973–75; Deputy Secretary, Canberra, 1975–76. Since 1978, Ambassador to France. Address: Australian Embassy, Paris, France.

PUBLICATIONS

Verse

The Feast of Ancestors: Poems. Sydney, Angus and Robertson, 1965.
Snow. Sydney, Angus and Robertson, 1971.
Times and Places: Poems of Locality. Canberra, Brindabella Press, 1975.
The Clock Inside. Sydney, Angus and Robertson, 1979.

J. R. Rowland comments:

Very much a spare-time poet; primarily a diplomat – unfortunately. Lyric verse; poems usually not longer than thirty lines; strongly visual; mostly personal in theme rather than social or philosophical.

* * *

The settings of J. R. Rowland's poems reflect the fact that he has lived in many varied and various parts of the world. Yet whether it be the Australian desert, winter in Moscow, a hotel room in Cairo or Southeast Asia, it is always possible for him in just a few lines to create a landscape and an atmosphere. What helps him so much to achieve this effect is his eye for the tiny but important detail and his gift for the unusual, apt, and fresh image, simile or metaphor.

We are always aware that this is a man with a quiet, dry sense of humour, a man able to laugh at human foibles and pretensions but at the same time questioning his right to do so, realising how easy it is to be "the slick observer." There is a cavalier touch to his verse, the touch of a man who is concerned but who knows that there is nothing worse than taking oneself too seriously.

Much of his verse is personal, concerned with what he himself has described as domesticities. These deal with his wife, children, and ordinary everyday events of family life. To all of these incidents he gives a depth and singularity and if his family holiday by the sea seems a little dull to us he reminds us ("At Noosa") that

Lara and Zhivago
Had no children, nor is laundry mentioned
By Lawrence in a similar situation
With Frieda in the cottage at Thirroul:
It makes a certain difference to the tone.
Exaltation needs to be alone

His special plea is for originality, for men of vision. Against the dull, monotonous routine of suburbia where "admirals pick tomatoes/In their back garden," he sets the Australian continent. This for him is a "half-unearthly country," a land of mystery, a visionary landscape, "a cure for habit." For Rowland the East has the same ability to stir the imagination, both have a "promise/Of strangeness and discovery." There is a celebration not only of the Australian landscape but of the people enveloped by it, of "the natural human pulse/Of Country living." With horror the poet looks at the trends of urban Australia and suggests (in "The Hotel Namatjira") that

To find some essence ours, that is the land's,
True to its nature, fitted to its ends,
Direct, attuned and native, we return

To men and buildings of the primary age.

—Anna Rutherford

ROWSE, A(fred) L(eslie). British. Born in St. Austell, Cornwall, 4 December 1903. Educated at Christ Church, Oxford (Douglas Jerrold Scholar), M.A. in English literature 1929. Since 1925, Fellow, All Souls College, Oxford. President of the English Association, 1952–53; Millar Visiting Professor, University of Illinois, Urbana, 1952–53; Raleigh Lecturer, the British Academy, 1957; Trevelyan Lecturer, Cambridge University, 1958; Visiting Professor, University of Wisconsin, Madison, 1959–60; Research Associate, Huntington Library, San Marino, California, 1962–69; Beatty Memorial Lecturer, McGill University, Montreal, 1963. D.Litt.: Oxford University, 1953; University of Exeter, 1960; D.C.L.: University of New Brunswick, Fredericton, 1960. Fellow, British Academy, 1958; Fellow, Royal Society of Literature. Address: All Souls College, Oxford, England.

PUBLICATIONS

Verse

Poems of a Decade 1931–1941. London, Faber, 1941.
Poems Chiefly Cornish. London, Faber, 1944.
Poems of Deliverance. London, Faber, 1946.

Poems Partly American. London, Faber, 1959.
Poems of Cornwall and America. London, Faber, 1967.
Strange Encounter. London, Cape, 1972.
The Road to Oxford. London, Cape, 1978.

Short Stories

West Country Stories. London, Macmillan, 1945; New York, Macmillan, 1947.
Cornish Stories. London, Macmillan, 1967.

Other

On History: A Study of Present Tendencies. London, Paul Trench Trubner, 1927; as *Science and History: A New View of History*, New York, Norton, 1928.
Politics and the Younger Generation. London, Faber, 1931.
The Question of the House of Lords. London, Hogarth Press, 1934.
Queen Elizabeth and Her Subjects, with G. B. Harrison. London, Allen and Unwin, 1935.
Mr. Keynes and the Labour Movement. London, Macmillan, 1936.
Sir Richard Grenville of the Revenge: An Elizabethan Hero. London, Cape, and Boston, Houghton Mifflin, 1937.
Tudor Cornwall: Portrait of a Society. London, Cape, 1941; revised edition, London, Macmillan, and New York, Scribner, 1969.
A Cornish Childhood: Autobiography of a Cornishman. London, Cape, 1942; New York, Macmillan, 1947.
The Spirit of English History. London, Longman, 1943; New York, Oxford University Press, 1945.
The English Spirit: Essays in History and Literature. London, Macmillan, 1944; revised edition, 1966; New York, Funk and Wagnalls, 1967.
The Use of History. London, English Universities Press, 1946; New York, Macmillan, 1948; revised edition, English Universities Press, and New York, Collier, 1963.
The End of an Epoch: Reflections on Contemporary History. London, Macmillan, 1947.
The England of Elizabeth: The Structure of Society. London, Macmillan, 1950; New York, Macmillan, 1951.
The English Past: Evocations of Persons and Places. London, Macmillan, 1951; New York, Macmillan, 1952; revised edition, as *Times, Persons, Places: Essays in Literature*, New York, Macmillan, 1965.
A New Elizabethan Age? London, Oxford University Press, 1952.
History of France, by Lucien Romier (translated and completed). London, Macmillan, and New York, St. Martin's Press, 1953.
An Elizabethan Garland. London, Macmillan, and New York, St. Martin's Press, 1953.
The Expansion of Elizabethan England. London, Macmillan, and New York, St. Martin's Press, 1955.
The Churchills: The Story of a Family. London, Macmillan, and New York, Harper, 2 vols., 1956–58.
The Elizabethans and America. London, Macmillan, and New York, Harper, 1959.
St. Austell: Church, Town, Parish. St. Austell, Cornwall, Warne, 1960.
All Souls and Appeasement: A Contribution to Contemporary History. London, Macmillan, 1961; as *Appeasement: A Study in Political Decline 1933–1939*, New York, Norton, 1961.
Ralegh and the Throckmortons. London, Macmillan, 1962; as *Sir Walter Ralegh, His Family and Private Life*, New York, Harper, 1962.
William Shakespeare: A Biography. London, Macmillan, and New York, Harper, 1963.

Christopher Marlowe: A Biography. London, Macmillan, 1964; as *Christopher Marlowe: His Life and Work*, New York, Harper, 1965.
A Cornishman at Oxford: The Education of a Cornishman. London, Cape, 1965.
Shakespeare's Southampton: Patron of Virginia. London, Macmillan, and New York, Harper, 1965.
Bosworth Field and the Wars of the Roses. London, Macmillan, 1966; as *Bosworth Field: From Medieval to Tudor England*, New York, Doubleday, 1966.
The Contribution of Cornwall and Cornishmen to Britain. Newton Abbot, Devon, Seale-Hayne Agricultural College, 1969.
The Cornish in America. London, Macmillan, 1969; as *The Cousin Jacks: The Cornish in America*, New York, Scribner, 1969.
The Elizabethan Renaissance:
I. *The Life of the Society.* London, Macmillan, 1971; New York, Scribner, 1972.
II. *The Cultural Achievement.* London, Macmillan, and New York, Scribner, 1972.
The Tower of London in the History of the Nation. London, Weidenfeld and Nicolson, and New York, Putnam, 1972.
The Abbey in the History of the Nation, in *Westminster Abbey.* London, Weidenfeld and Nicolson, 1972.
Shakespeare the Man. London, Macmillan, 1973.
Windsor Castle in the History of the Nation. London, Weidenfeld and Nicolson, and New York, Putnam, 1974.
Simon Forman: Sex and Society in Shakespeare's Age. London, Weidenfeld and Nicolson, 1974; New York, Scribner, 1975; as *The Case Books of Simon Forman*, London, Pan, 1976.
Peter, The White Cat of Trenarren. London, Joseph, 1974.
Robert Stephen Hawker, A Belated Medieval, with Cornish Ballads and Other Poems. St. Germans, Cornwall, Elephant Press, 1975.
Discoveries and Reviews: From Renaissance to Restoration. London, Macmillan, and New York, Barnes and Noble, 1975.
Jonathon Swift, Major Prophet. London, Thames and Hudson, 1975; New York, Scribner, 1976.
Oxford in the History of the Nation. London, Weidenfeld and Nicolson, and New York, Putnam, 1975.
Brown Buck: A Californian Fantasy (juvenile). London, Joseph, 1976.
A Cornishman Abroad. London, Cape, 1976.
Matthew Arnold, Poet and Prophet. London, Thames and Hudson, 1976.
Homosexuals in History: A Study of Ambivalence in Society, Literature, and the Arts. London, Weidenfeld and Nicolson, and New York, Macmillan, 1977.
Milton the Puritan. London, Macmillan, 1977.
Shakespeare the Elizabethan. London, Weidenfeld and Nicolson, and New York, Putnam, 1977.
Heritage of Britain. London, Artus, and New York, Putnam, 1977.
The Byrons and Trevanions. London, Weidenfeld and Nicolson, 1978; New York, St. Martin's Press, 1979.
Chalky Jenkins: A Little Cat Lost. London, Weidenfeld and Nicolson, 1978.
Tommer, The Black Farm-Cat. London, Weidenfeld and Nicolson, 1978.
Three Cornish Cats (omnibus). London, Weidenfeld and Nicolson, 1979.
A Man of the Thirties. London, Weidenfeld and Nicolson, 1979.
Portraits and Views, Literary and Historical. London, Macmillan, 1979.
Story of Britain. London, Weidenfeld and Nicolson, and New York, Putnam, 1979.

Editor, with M. I. Henderson, *Essays in Cornish History*, by Charles Henderson. London, Oxford University Press, 1935.
Editor, *The West in English History.* London, Hodder and Stoughton, 1949.
Editor, *Shakespeare's Sonnets.* London, Macmillan, and New York, Harper, 1964;

revised edition, as *Shakespeare's Sonnets: The Problems Solved*, Macmillan and Harper, 1973.

Editor, *A Cornish Anthology*. London, Macmillan, 1968.

Editor, *The Two Chiefs of Dunboy: A Story of 18th Century Ireland*, by J. A. Froude. London, Chatto and Windus, 1969.

Editor, with John Betjeman, *Victorian and Edwardian Cornwall from Old Photographs*. London, Batsford, 1974.

Editor, *The Poems of Shakespeare's Dark Lady*. London, Cape, 1978.

Editor, *The Annotated Shakespeare*. London, Orbis, and New York, Clarkson N. Potter, 3 vols., 1978.

Editor, *Roper's Life of Sir Thomas More*. London, Folio Society, 1979.

A. L. Rowse comments:

A Celt, growing up in Cornwall, I was early influenced by the Irish poets, especially Yeats. At Oxford I discovered the poetry of T. S. Eliot, whose work, help, and friendship became the most fruitful and enduring affiliation in my career of writing. He first published my work in prose as well as verse, and recognizably wrote the blurbs for the first three volumes of my poems. In my early verse I was particularly interested in exploring the emotion of fear, and – naturally, owing to long years of illness – in expressing the heightened sensitivity, the extra-sensory experiences, that went with it. Wartime brought renewed health, a more varied and outgoing response, some reconciliaton with life, which I always found difficult. Hence the strain of bitterness, an iron element, that runs all through my work, disgust with human foolery, *contemptus mundi*, though not in a religious sense, any more than with Yeats. (Swift much influenced my outlook from youth on.)

As a Celt I have an extra-sensitivity to atmosphere and have given it expression all along, chiefly in relation to Cornwall, but also in Oxford and America. (Very few British poets have been inspired to write about America.) Places speak to me rather than people and are apt to mean more to me. My inner life, from which the poetry springs, has been withdrawn – my outer life has gone into history and politics. But the inner life has always meant more, and by keeping it apart I have kept a flow of inspiration going, where some of my more publicized contemporaries have dried up. One should never be too self-conscious about the springs of art. I don't mind paying the price of not having my poetry noticed – rather a joke really – since it enables me to continue to write. (The joke is on the critics: the combined work in prose and verse, history and literature, is evidently too much for them at present, though they should see that there is a rare literary phenomenon to be investigated.)

A self-contained life, withdrawn from the public eye, a solipsistic outlook, is best for an artist in the hideous contemporary world, so discouraging to real poetry (other than journalistic) – what Yeats described as "this filthy modern tide." He held fast to "his ghostly solitude" as I do. So, I have held by Yeats, early and late, with no more compassion for fools than he or Swift had.

I find traditional verse forms sufficient for what I have to say. Earlier I was attracted by disjoined couplets in rhyme and half-rhyme, like Wilfred Owen, another Celt. Neither blank verse nor free verse has been altogether blank or free with me: each has always had a good deal of unobtrusive decoration, internal as well as end-rhymes, and much alliteration (instinctive, the unconscious mark of the poet). Eliot liked (as well as published) my poetry and used to say that I should give myself more to it; but I was afraid of losing inspiration if I forced myself and *worked* at it: I prefer to trust to the creative urges of the unconscious. However, before I die I should like to write one long narrative poem on a Cornish theme.

Perhaps I have given to history – and wasted on politics – something of what should have gone to poetry.

* * *

Readers and admirers of A. L. Rowse's autobiographical books have on the whole failed to follow the history of his personality into the field of his poetry, which continues to reveal one of the most complex, sometimes irritating, always sensitive and interesting personalities of our time. His earlier collections (*Poems Chiefly Cornish* or *Poems of a Decade*) chronicle his love-hate relationship with Cornwall, and through the subsequent volumes his landscape poems continue to be remarkably vivid. But the personal note continues, too, and grows stronger. Sometimes it is recognisably the tone in which Dr. Rowse conducts his public altercations: "The Cornish crowd/Into the compartment, chattering/As ever with platitudinous vacuity"; but, more rewardingly, it is dark, melancholy, inward-turned: "A public man, scarred with injuries,/Seared by sad experience, without illusion/Or any hope, dedicated to despair." But then there is the note of simple pleasure, in such traditionally pure verses as "How Many Miles to Mylor" and "Child's Verses for Winter." Dr. Rowse's poetry shows almost as many faces as his prose (he is historian, literary critic, editor, biographer, short-story writer). Sturdily in traditional forms, it opens out his personality – as it should – more fully than his critics have understood, and it is much undervalued.

—Derek Parker

RUBIN, Larry (Jerome). American. Born in Bayonne, New Jersey, 14 February 1930. Educated at Columbia University, New York, 1949–50; Emory University, Atlanta, Georgia, B.A. 1951 (Phi Beta Kappa), M.A. 1952, Ph.D. 1956. Instructor, 1956–58, Assistant Professor, 1958–65, Associate Professor, 1965–73, and since 1973, Professor of English, Georgia Institute of Technology, Atlanta. Visiting Professor of American Literature (Smith-Mundt Award), University of Krakow, Poland, 1961–62; Fulbright Lecturer in American Literature, University of Bergen, Norway, 1966–67, Free University of Berlin, 1969–70, and University of Innsbruck, Austria, 1971–72. Recipient: Poetry Society of America Reynolds Lyric Award, 1961, Prize 1973; Sidney Lanier Award, Oglethorpe University, 1964. Address: Box 15014, Druid Hills Branch, Atlanta, Georgia, 30333, U.S.A.

PUBLICATIONS

Verse

The World's Old Way. Lincoln, University of Nebraska Press, 1962.
Lanced in Light. New York, Harcourt Brace, 1967.
All My Mirrors Lie. Boston, Godine, 1975.

Manuscript Collection: Woodruff Memorial Library, Emory University, Atlanta.

Critical Studies: by Charles Beaumont, in *Georgia Review* (Athens), Winter 1963; "A Catalogue of Nine" by Felix Stefanile, in *Poetry* (Chicago), February 1964; John R. Willingham, in *Library Journal* (New York), August 1967; Louis Ginsberg, in *The Poetry Society of America Bulletin* (New York), February 1968; "A Point in Time, A Place in Space" by F. H. Griffin Taylor, in *Sewanee Review* (Tennessee), Spring 1969; Rachelle Rattner, in *Library Journal* (New York), 15 February 1976; Elizabeth Bartlett, in *Etc.* (San Francisco),

June 1976; Roger Dickenson-Brown, in *Southern Review* (Baton Rouge, Louisiana), Spring 1978.

Larry Rubin comments:

My themes are the familiar ones of time, love, death, friendship, isolation, childhood; when I write about family life, I find myself dealing, on the whole, with familial guilt, rather than familial devotion. I have also been emphasizing, of late, the vulnerability of the lover, and of the friend. I am concerned with betrayals, but also with reconciliations. I try to get quickly to the core of feeling, without relying on extraneous and obscure allusions or on cumbersome mythologies. It is in Emily Dickinson's poetry that I find most clearly the compactness and incisiveness that I aim for. In my poetry I try to fulfil my own critical test of a poem, and that is that it should make an immediate emotional impact upon the reader. My usual verse forms include a sort of modified blank verse, a free verse form which I try to control carefully, and a four-line iambic tetrameter stanza with slant rhymes, often in varying positions in each stanza.

* * *

Larry Rubin's poems take the reader into a subtle and private world, their subject-matter apparently determined by circumstance rather than consciously chosen by the author. His experience, after the death of his parents, as a Jew, a bachelor, a teacher, an expatriate momentarily in love, is recounted and dutifully catalogued.

In the early poems, the voice is appropriate to the subject, but later it falters, particularly in *Lanced in Light*, where the speaker's involvement with various subjects seems distant, casual, almost disinterested. As a poet, Rubin is always competent – rather like a veteran reporter whose articles show extensive knowledge, an acute ear, a facility in language, but sometimes a mere academic interest in the topic under discussion, as in "Souvenir," "After Italy," "in lower case," and "The Uninvolved."

The poems in *The World's Old Way*, on the other hand, are consistently witty, lively, precise, inviting, and repay repeated readings. Several of them belong in any collection of the best short lyrics published in America since 1960, particularly "A Note on Library Policy" and that perfect stylistic parody of its subject "Emily Dickinson on Etiquette":

If God came calling at my house,
I'd ask him in for tea
And comment on the lovely day
That brought such Deity.

I'd ask him were his angels well,
And if his saints had dined;
Somehow I'd steer the table talk
On well-accepted lines.

But should he fail to take the hint
And probe my soul in two,
I'd rise a little formally
And end the interview.

Almost as successful, in metrical skill and total effect, are "The Anarchist," "God Opens His Mail," "For a Poet's Wife, Who Has Conceived" (which begins, "You bear creation's double burden"), and several of the poems from the sequence entitled "Greek Family Life."

One looks for a similar authority in all his work. In searching for a new direction or in deepening his own very personal style, Rubin will undoubtedly regain that sophistication in manner and method that he exhibited so frequently in the early poems. Indeed, in "The Discard" and "Annual Checkup," published after his second volume, it appears that that has already begun to happen.

—Michael True

RUDOLF, Anthony. British. Born in London, 6 September 1942. Educated at City of London School, 1953–60; British Institute, Paris, 1961; Trinity College, Cambridge, 1961–64, B.A. in modern languages and social anthropology 1964. Has one son and one daughter. Junior executive, British Travel Association, London and Chicago, 1964–66; English and French teacher, 1967–68; worked in bookshops, London, 1969–71; London Editor, *Stand* magazine, Newcastle upon Tyne, 1969–72; Literary Editor, 1970–72, and Managing Editor, 1972–75, *European Judaism*, London; Advisory Editor, Heimler Foundation publications, London, 1974–76, and *Jewish Quarterly*, London, 1975. Since 1971, Co-Founder and Editor, Menard Press, London; since 1973, Advisory Editor, *Modern Poetry in Translation*, London. Address: 23 Fitzwarren Gardens, London N19 3TR, England.

PUBLICATIONS

Verse

The Manifold Circle. Oxford, Carcanet Press, 1971.
The Same River Twice. Manchester, Carcanet Press, 1976.
After the Dream. St. Louis, Cauldron Press, 1979.

Plays

The Soup Complex, adaptation of a play by Ana Novac. Newcastle upon Tyne, Northumberland, Stand, 1972.
The Storm: The Tragedy of Sinai, adaptation of a play by Eugene Heimler. London, Menard Press, 1976.

Other

Editor, with Richard Burns, *An Octave for Octavio Paz.* Farnham, Surrey, Sceptre Press – Menard Press, 1972.
Editor, *Poems from Shakespeare IV.* London, Globe Playhouse Trust, 1976.
Editor, with Howard Schwartz, *Voices in the Ark: The Modern Jewish Poets.* New York, Avon, 1980.

Translator, *Selected Poems*, by Yves Bonnefoy. London, Cape, 1968; New York, Grossman, 1969.
Translator, *Two Poems from Veines*, by Jean-Paul Guibbert. Rushden, Northamptonshire, Sceptre Press, 1972.

Translator, *Tyorkin, and The Stovemakers: Poetry and Prose of Alexander Tvardovsky.* Cheadle, Cheshire, Carcanet Press, 1974.
Translator, *Relative Creatures: Victorian Women in Society and the Novel 1837–1867*, by Françoise Basch. London, Allen Lane, 1974.
Translator, with Peter Jay and Petru Popescu, *Boxes, Stairs and Whistle Time: Poems*, by Popescu. Knotting, Bedfordshire, Omphalos Press, 1975.
Translator, with Daniel Weissbort, *The War Is Over: Selected Poems*, by Evgeny Vinokurov. Manchester, Carcanet Press, 1976.
Translator, *A Share of Ink*, by Edmond Jabès. London, Menard Press, 1979.

Critical Study: review by George Mackay Brown, in *The Scotsman* (Edinburgh), 21 January 1977.

Anthony Rudolf comments:

After the Dream is the "definitive" collection of my short poems, since it *re-works*, to my relative satisfaction, the two early collections.

* * *

The Same River Twice is Anthony Rudolf's first full-length collection of poetry and serves as a fine guide to the range of his abilities and concerns. Known primarily as an editor and publisher and for his excellent translations from the French and Russian – notably works by Edmond Jabès, Yves Bonnefoy, Alexander Tvardovsky, Evgeny Vinokurov – Rudolf's poems are imbued with international flavor and reference. Poems to Karl Kraus, Kafka, Balthus, Paul Celan, Chagall, Edward Hopper display linked yet diverse elements in his book.

Rudolf appears to write two basic forms of poem: one is closed, i.e., the hermetic or philosophical poem usually written in a terse dense language; the other is what I'd call the open poem, i.e., poems more immediately detailed, with more warmth in the language, and whose usual subject matters are domestic realities and travel. His closed poems often resemble the effect of implosion, a deliberate collapse of language, a process of most intense condensing. The influence of Jabès and other French poets seems present in these works and neutralizes Rudolf's voice. Whereas the open poem has a much greater measure of music in the language and I find them very attractive to read.

What is clear in the poems is Rudolf's desire to create poems of substance and, as is traditional with the "first book," his failures are as significant as his triumphs. Many of the poems are homages to literary teachers like Celan, Cafavy, and Borges, others are homages to his Jewish heritage and yearnings. The variety of forms and voices is not that extreme that one can't appreciate the potential intrinsic in this collection. It will be interesting to see how Rudolf is able to clarify his focus in future collections and add to the power and purpose of his art.

—David Meltzer

RUKEYSER, Muriel. American. Born in New York City, 15 December 1913. Educated at Fieldston Schools, 1919–30; Vassar College, Poughkeepsie, New York; Columbia

University, New York, 1930–32. Has one son. Vice-President, House of Photography, New York, 1946–60. Taught at Sarah Lawrence College, Bronxville, New York, 1946, 1956–57. Since, 1967, Member, Board of Directors, Teachers-Writers Collaborative, New York. President, P.E.N. American Center, 1975–76. Recipient: Yale Series of Younger Poets Award, 1935; Oscar Blumenthal Prize, 1940, Levinson Prize, 1947, and Eunice Tietjens Memorial Prize, 1962 (*Poetry*, Chicago); Harriet Monroe Award, 1941; National Institute of Arts and Letters Award, 1942; Guggenheim Fellowship, 1943; American Council of Learned Societies Fellowship, 1963; Swedish Academy translation award, 1967; Shelley Memorial Award, 1977; Copernicus Award, 1977; Anglo-Swedish Literary Foundation Award, 1978. D.Litt.: Rutgers University, New Brunswick, New Jersey, 1961. Member, National Institute of Arts and Letters. Agent: Monica McCall, International Famous Agency, 40 West 57th Street, New York, New York 10019. Address: Westbeth, 463 West Street, New York, New York 10014, U.S.A.

PUBLICATIONS

Verse

Theory of Flight. New Haven, Connecticut, Yale University Press, 1935.
U.S. 1. New York, Covici Friede, 1938.
Mediterranean. Privately printed, 1938.
A Turning Wind. New York, Viking Press, 1939.
The Soul and Body of John Brown. Privately printed, 1940.
Wake Island. New York, Doubleday, 1942.
Beast in View. New York, Doubleday, 1944.
The Children's Orchard. San Francisco, Book Club of California, 1947.
The Green Wave. New York, Doubleday, 1948.
Orpheus. San Francisco, Centaur Press, 1949.
Elegies. New York, New Directions, 1949.
Selected Poems. New York, New Directions, 1951.
Body of Waking. New York, Harper, 1958.
Waterlily Fire: Poems 1932–1962. New York, Macmillan, 1962.
The Outer Banks. Santa Barbara, California, Unicorn Press, 1967.
The Speed of Darkness. New York, Random House, 1968.
29 Poems. London, Rapp and Whiting, 1970.
Breaking Open. New York, Random House, 1973.
The Gates. New York, McGraw Hill, 1976.
The Collected Poems. New York, McGraw Hill, 1979.

Play

The Color of the Day (produced Poughkeepsie, New York, 1961).

Other

Willard Gibbs (biography). New York, Doubleday, 1942.
The Life of Poetry. New York, Current, 1949.
Come Back Paul (juvenile). New York, Harper, 1955.
One Life (biography of Wendell Willkie). New York, Simon and Schuster, 1957.
I Go Out (juvenile). New York, Harper, 1961.

Bubbles (juvenile). New York, Harcourt Brace, 1967.
The Orgy. New York, Coward, McCann, 1965; London, Deutsch, 1966.
Poetry, and Unverifiable Fact (lectures). Claremont, California, Scripps College, 1968.
Mazes (juvenile). New York, Simon and Schuster, 1970.
The Traces of Thomas Hariot. New York, Random House, 1971.

Translator, with others, *Selected Poems of Octavio Paz*. Bloomington, Indiana University Press, 1963; revised edition, New York, New Directions, 1973.
Translator, *Sun Stone*, by Octavio Paz. New York, New Directions, 1963.
Translator, with Leif Sjöberg, *Selected Poems of Gunnar Ekelöf*. New York, Twayne, 1967.
Translator, *Three Poems by Gunnar Ekelöf*. Lawrence, Kansas, T. Williams, 1967.

Manuscript Collection: Berg Collection, New York Public Library.

* * *

> Whatever has happened, whatever is going to happen in the world, it is the living moment that contains the sum of the excitement, this moment in which we touch life and all the energy of the past and future.

Muriel Rukeyser is recognized primarily as a poet of social protest, but Arthur Miller clarifies her poetic gift as that of "entwining self and personal mirage with events of public consequence," in order to produce a "tension between both," which "opens up living." Since the beginning of her career Rukeyser has been a visionary poet and a pioneer in both form and statement – and her focus has gone beyond her concerns with freedom for all minority groups, the dangers of our capitalistic and technological society, the terrors of war and jail, and of the battered child or woman. She has frequently used the long poem sequence, for example, for extended explorations of raw and intimate experience within the contexts of contemporary or historical, social and political event. But her poetic voice has always remained at once concrete and visionary; she connects primary experience with the wish for a larger brotherhood, from which she aspires toward a common Unity of Being.

"Speak to me," "Grow to know me," "Listen," writes the poet; "I am groping in the dark"; "Nothing must be kept secret." One never loses touch with her concrete, often lonely, raw, and sometimes shameful experiences, as the poet envelops and enraptures her reader or audience (the latter always an integral part of her flight, if not its catalyst) in some radiant moment of awareness and harmony. In "Breaking Open" she writes: "In the night/ wandering" [from] "room to room of this world,"

> I move by touch
> and then some thing says
> let the city pour
> let the sleep of the beloved
> Let the night pour down
> all its meanings
> Let the images pour
> the light is dreaming.

The Collected Poems displays her experiments with language and form – from the lyrical love poems to the documentary narratives, from the bawdy songs to the chilling political commentaries and biting satiric statements: some of the most interesting poems are reworkings of classical myth. The poems, nevertheless, are always about "searching ... to make/closeness." Her purposes are clear: "My life is flying/to your side." With recurrent images of light, silence, gates, doors, walking, and dancing, is the single focus (as she puts it, "I haven't changed very much in my beliefs over the years"): entreaties for love, connection, and brotherhood – for "transformation."

In "Don Baty" she sings of how when the police arrived to arrest this draft resister and asked "Who is Don Baty?" all those who stood in resistance with him answered: "I am Don Baty .../Your arrest is mine .../The Newborn are with us singing." Rukeyser's protest extends back to her personal involvement in the Scottsboro trial and the Spanish Civil War; more recently, she has protested the political prisoners in Greece, Chile, and Spain. One of her better known poems tells of a tragic experience in West Virginia; "Power" documents the Gauley Bridge tragedy where men died of silicosis because they were denied the available resources with which to safeguard their lives.

Rukeyser's dream to break through the destructiveness of a self-aggrandizing society and the barriers of race, class, sex, age is underscored by her volumes' titles – i.e., *The Gates*, *Breaking Open*. Her role, as poet, is that of healer:

Wherever
we walk
we will make

Wherever
we protest
we will go planting

Make poems
seed grass
feed a child growing
build a house
Whatever we stand against
we will stand feeding and seeding

Wherever
I walk
I will make.

Although Rukeyser calls herself a "she-poet," she transcends the confessional and feminist poetry that has become fashionable recently. Her personal experiences are only the starting point toward the larger social and metaphysical "transformation" she seeks. Sexual experience ("days and the sun renewed in semen") provides a means towards knowledge, community, and transcendence: "The days grow and the stars cross over/And my wild bed turns slowly among the stars" ("Darkness Music"). Many of her poems are boldly erotic, but sexuality is always the pathway to knowledge. In "Anemone" she writes:

My eyes are closing, my eyes are opening.
You are looking into me with your waking look.

My mouth is closing, my mouth is opening.
You are waiting with your red promises.

My sex is closing, my sex is opening.
You are singing and opening, the way in.

My life is closing, my life is opening.
You are here.

But on a more concrete level, the joys of womanhood – exuberance, fulfillment, and creativity – are only part of her canvas, which includes as well the loneliness, humiliations, boredom, and sexual frustrations in being a woman. She may, in a poem like "Ajanta," enter the cave of self and sexuality but her comforts are short-lived, for the "naked world" "intrudes upon the self" "with ... old noise of tears." The woman is a microcosm of the external world: "We, introspective/continue to find in ourselves the microcosm/imagined continents, powers, relations/reflecting/all history."

Whether she is talking of the self in the world or alone, a sense of struggle abounds throughout the poetry. There is no experience too shameful or humiliating to be "transformed," however, both through her writing of it and her readers' experiencing of it. There is the impulse towards suicide, for example, along with the poet's call back to life through nature's intense beauty. At 14, the poet admits, she "stood at a steep window ... hoping toward death"; but "the light" "melted clouds and plains to beauty,/if light had not transformed that day, I would have leapt."

Throughout is the need for self-knowledge, and yet the poet's inability to speak: "My life is searching/not searching" – the yearning for harmony and peace, and yet the persistent imprisonment to shame, guilt, and even violence. "My grain," she writes, "is absolutely coarse, violent, full of contradiction." "All things carry contradictions," says Rukeyser. Hence she would wish for "All directions out," as "all desires turn inward."

Rukeyser continues to write poetry with a purpose not unlike that of Yeats, who ultimately (to use Auden's terms) became his poetry and "became his admirers." Rukeyser's prophetic role also resounds in "Then":

When I am dead, even then,
I will still love you, I will wait in these poems,
When I am dead, even then
I am still listening to you
I will still be making poems for you
out of silence;
Silence will be falling into that silence,
it is building music.

—Lois Gordon

RUSSELL, (Irwin) Peter. British. Born in 1921. Served in the British Army, 1939–46. Owner of bookshop and poetry press, 1950–63. Has lived in Venice since 1964. Taught at University of Victoria, British Columbia, 1975–76, and Purdue University, Lafayette, Indiana, 1976–77. Address: Castello 3611, Venice 30122, Italy.

PUBLICATIONS

Verse

Picnic to the Moon. Privately printed, 1944.
Omens and Elegies. Aldington, Kent, Hand and Flower Press, 1951.
Descent: A Poem Sequence. Privately printed, 1952.
The Spirit and the Body: An Orphic Poem. Privately printed, 1956.
Images of Desire: Discreete Sonets. London, Gallery Bookshop, 1962.
Dreamland and Drunkenness. London, Gallery Bookshop, 1963.
Complaints to Circe. Privately printed, 1963.

Visions and Ruins: An Existentialist Poem. Aylesford, Kent, Saint Albert's Press, 1964.
Agamemnon in Hades. Aylesford, Kent, Saint Albert's Press, 1965.
The Golden Chain: Lyrical Poems 1964–1969. Privately printed, 1970.
Paysages Légendaires. London, Enitharmon Press, 1971.
Acts of Recognition: Four Visionary Poems. Ipswich, Suffolk, Golgonooza Press, 1978.
Theories. Teheran, Crescent Moon Press, 1978.

Other

Editor, *Ezra Pound: A Collection of Essays ... to be Presented to Ezra Pound on His Sixty-Fifth Birthday.* London, Peter Nevill, 1950; as *An Examination of Ezra Pound*, New York, New Directions, 1950.
Editor, *Money Pamphlets by £.* London, Peter Russell, 6 vols., 1950–51.
Editor, with Khushwant Singh, *A Note ... on G. V. Desani's "All about H. Hatterr" and "Hali."* London and Amsterdam, Szeben, 1952.
Editor, *ABC of Economics*, by Ezra Pound. Tunbridge Wells, Kent, Pound Press, 1953.

Translator, *Three Elegies of Quintilius.* Tunbridge Wells, Kent, Pound Press, 1954.
Translator, *Landscapes*, by Camillo Pennati (bilingual edition). Richmond, Surrey, Keepsake Press, 1964.
Translator, *The Elegies of Quintilius.* London, Anvil Press Poetry, 1975.

* * *

For me, Peter Russell is the major neglected talent of our time – the author of the finest book of purely "English" lyrics (*The Golden Chain*) of the last twenty years; the author of a gigantic, mostly unpublished epic poem, *Ephemeron*, running to some two thousand pages; the author of *Paysages Légendaires*, a book impregnated with great wisdom and that music the Celts call the "cael moer" or the "great music." In Peter Russell, we are dealing with not just the Poundian theory of the multilingual poet of the future (and Russell was Pound's greatest disciple), but with the realization of such a poet as fact. The sheer magnitude of the job of investigating the innumerable works produced by Russell since *Picnic to the Moon* in 1944 is not a sufficient excuse for not trying. Still less is it an excuse for the wanton neglect of a poet of whom such a figure as Hugh MacDiarmid has written: "Peter Russell is, in my opinion, a writer who has so far received nothing like due recognition ... no one in Great Britain today has rendered anything like the disinterested, many-sided and sustained service to Poetry" – the latter comment referring to Russell's work as editor of *Nine* and as publisher of so many of today's established figures long before they were known.

Of *Paysages Légendaires*, Hugh McKinley's phrase "tribute open-eyed, yet illuminate, of life entire" is remarkably apposite. This is how the poem opens:

Palladian villas and the changing seasons

An old man digging in the shade

The gold sun varnishes
The small viridian of the elms
And gilds the hidden cadmium of the glades.

In fact, its way of expression throughout is best described as an open-eyed style.

So, too, it is a rare book of unimpeachable seriousness and poetic wisdom. Perhaps the most interesting feature of *Paysages Légendaires* (and the explanation of its style) is the absence of a close or particularly tense (or over-tense) verbal and syntactical density, which induces an unusual clarity in the verse. And this goes a long way towards compensating for the major disadvantage of a modern sequential but non-narrative long poem, namely, the breaks in continuity which so trouble the average reader. It is a poem that reads well.

The sheer intelligence of the poem commands respect; but what matters is that one feels it is an extraordinarily "aware" poem – a poem aware of, and in touch with the main-stream of human thought. This awareness of the "now" is undoubtedly achieved by a profound knowledge of the "then" and exemplifies what is, perhaps, the poem's central preoccupation:

It will take time to build again,
To build the soul's tall house,
The tower of the wandering self
Foursquare beneath the moon.

Many people, myself among them, think that poetry – the "real" of the thing, the heart's meat of the matter – is the line, or lines of words that are necklace-perfect. Something that glitters with ineffable quality, wisdom, beauty, LIFE – a kind of instant of revelation in words, the discovery, as Russell puts it, that "Every natural effect has a spiritual cause/(That which is above, is below)." Indeed, if poetry is the unshakable line, memorable phrase – then Peter Russell is probably the greatest English poet now writing.

Myth is the stuff of thought one might say and *Paysages Légendaires* is a "thoughtful poem." There is little concrete description, and, where there is, the object tends towards the emblematic and metaphorical. There is, however, one short passage where the descriptive element is uppermost:

Sweet bones are growing in the earthly night

Slow maturations in the endless dark
Of subterranean galleries, telluric force
That broods whole centuries upon a single grain
That crumbles or coagulates.

One gets a sense of the tremendousness of life, its continual working; the key word is "broods" – it reveals brilliantly the meaning behind the description, the life within.

Apart from the practical problem of the range of this poet's work, there is one other problem, which is only a "problem" in the framework of present day poetry's dusty picture. This derives from the fact that the more one reads Russell's poetry, the more one realises that it demands imagination. In poem after poem, one finds the feeling transcending the flat detail of experience. So, too, there is a copious knowledge displayed of life both past and present, and there is that true linguistic metamorphosis at times, which provides a permanent frame – be it only a single good line – in which the present is held up before our eyes to be seen in infinite terms. Therefore, parodying Pound, these poems must "go to the imaginative" if they are to be understood, and to the serious if they are to be loved.

—William Oxley

RUTSALA, Vern. American. Born in McCall, Idaho, 5 February 1934. Educated at Reed College, Portland, Oregon, B.A. 1956; University of Iowa, Iowa City, M.F.A. 1960. Served in the United States Army, 1956–58. Married Joan Colby in 1957; three children. Since

1961, member of the English Department, currently Professor, Lewis and Clark College, Portland, Oregon. Visiting Professor, University of Minnesota, Minneapolis, 1968–69; Bowling Green State University, Ohio, 1970. Editor, *December* magazine, Western Springs, Illinois, 1959–62. Recipient: National Endowment for the Arts grant, 1974. Address: Department of English, Lewis and Clark College, Portland, Oregon 97219, U.S.A.

PUBLICATIONS

Verse

The Window. Middletown, Connecticut, Wesleyan University Press, 1964.
Small Songs: A Sequence of Poems. Iowa City, Stone Wall Press, 1969.
The Harmful State. Lincoln, Nebraska, Best Cellar Press, 1971.
Laments. New York, New Rivers Press, 1975.
The Journey Begins. Athens, University of Georgia Press, 1976.
Paragraphs. Middletown, Connecticut, Wesleyan University Press, 1978.
The New Life. Portland, Oregon, Trask House, 1978.

Other

Editor, *British Poetry 1972*. Phoenix, Arizona, Baleen Press, 1972.

Critical Study: by Norman Friedman, in *Chicago Review*, June 1967.

Vern Rutsala comments:

Many of the poems in *The Window* are centered in and around houses – often houses in some worn suburb – and are concerned with what might be seen in such an area. The central image of the window is appropriate, then, and the poems reflect both what can be observed and what happens within. More recent work follows this pattern though its focus is usually much more inward. Though the rhythms I use are relatively free, I often like to make use of regular stanza forms. My themes are not unusual – the common obsessions of poets: how does one live? why is the world as it is? *Paragraphs*, a collection of prose poems, explores directions that differ a good deal from my earlier work. *Laments* and *The Journey Begins* have continued my concern with contemporary life while also beginning to explore the past and our relationship to it. *The New Life* focuses rather directly on Western America. It is part of a longer work called *Walking Home from the Icehouse*.

* * *

Vern Rutsala has one of the keenest poetic responses to contemporary middle-class society since Cummings, Auden, the earlier Karl Shapiro, and some of Louis Simpson. His special achievement in *The Window* is to have made the furniture of everyday bourgeois life in America available to the uses of serious poetry. He is thus somewhat like one of the better Pop artists, such as Edward Kienholz, who makes assemblages out of found objects – the chassis of an old car, for example – and, with a few skilfully-constructed wire figures, can confront us with ourselves as we fumble erotically in the back seat with our dates in a doomed search for pleasure and joy ("Lovers in Summer").

But there is here not merely a familiar world of skate keys, wagons, bicycles ("Sunday"); there is also a commanding vision which governs the shaping of that world. He hears the glacier knocking in the cupboard and the rumble of violence and despair hidden within our domestic walls. Rutsala deals card after card, building up unbearably to a remorseless climax, until not a corner is left for us to hide in, nothing is spared – not a toothbrush, family album, mantlepiece clock, visit from relatives, souvenir ashtray, flushing of the toilet, garden hose – nothing escapes his illumination of things so ordinary we have forgotten them, so close we haven't really seen them, revealing what we thought we already knew but never quite understood.

Each aspect of our lives, each object of our mundane environment, is a badge of the numb but terrible disparity between life's possibilities and the horror of diminishment we are all suffering from. A bathroom mirror is a symbol of the abyss, which is not so much the inevitable loss of childhood as the crushing emptiness of spirit characteristic of living in an imperialistic, commercial, and technological civilization ("Gilbert and Market"). In such a society, even childhood is no Eden, and children are not spared ("Playground").

"Nightfall" is one of the most moving poems in the book:

> Night settles like a damp cloth
> over the houses. The houses that are shut,
> that show no wear. Lawns
> are patrolled by plywood flamingoes
> or shrubbery clipped from magazines.

The poem develops to reveal our compulsive housecleaning, sports pages, basement workshops, repairing skills, dinner, dishes in the kitchen sink, bills, two cars, committee meetings, unused telephone appointment pads – and our desperate and suicidal children. Then, as the time for sleep comes, some of us lie awake in the glow of a cigarette, obsessed by disappointment and heartbreak. And the poem concludes, perfectly:

> Dawn lies coiled in clocks.
> There are no conclusions here. The dark is there.
> Cigarettes burn down and are ground out
> in souvenir ashtrays from vacations by the sea.

The Window does, however, suffer from an overly-even stylistic tone, as well as from a certain distance placed between its persona and the world he sees so clearly. But these flaws are on their way to being redeemed in Rutsala's subsequent work. Although *Small Songs*, a sequence of invitations by common household objects, is a rather minor effort and seems really to lack development, *Laments*, his next full volume, marks an advance in depth and variety. Decorated with etchings by James Burgess of fruits, plants, and nuts which seem more like grotesque lobsters, this book, as its title indicates, is still fascinated by the party-is-over mood, by loss, by what to make of a diminished thing. And yet the speaker moves more into the foreground, thus providing that sense of involvement lacking in *The Window*, and the situations, imagery, and rhythms are more consciously diversified, thus mitigating that threat of monotony. Nevertheless, the feeling of exasperation, even of exhaustion, remains much the same, and Rutsala's grasp of its significance, or even of other possible moods, awaits further insight.

The Journey Begins and *Paragraphs* signal a shift out of that impasse. In the former volume he proclaims, as usual, that "Here we practice the cottage/industry of the banal; here we/probe the mysteries of the commonplace" ("Like the Poets of Ancient China"), but something else is beginning to happen: "we must nurse/the deadness from the air/so we may breathe" ("Unlocking the Door"). Those mysteries are beginning to yield up a significance ("Beginning"):

The past gone,
an instant, drained like stream
water full of clarity, light,
ice, the flavor of mountains
that gave you only one thing:
a wetness on your lips, taste.

Such unaccustomed freshness of taste enables the poet at last to touch, in *Paragraphs*, the springs of neurosis itself and find the mirror – even the cause – of all that desolation in society. His sense of the abyss, in other words, becomes internalized and universalized. The pieces in this book are brief prose poems but are also related, as he says, "to the fable, the aphorism, the maxim, the character, and the joke." Many are effectively epigrammatic and eminently quotable, but we must limit ourselves to a single characteristic example, entitled "Demon":

> No matter how you shuffle your traits – making diligence and order turn up regularly – he is always there, waiting. In fact, the harder you try to hide him the more often he breaks into your nights like a party-crashing drunk spilling drinks, upending tables, yelling obscenities at ancient maidens. The trick, you see, is to admit him calmly, see that he is really you – not a double, but *you*, not some actor or black sheep but simply you. He fits your skin; take him places, feed him smoked oysters and good bourbon, let him dance any time he wants to, let him sing. If you fail to do this he will kill himself.

Having found the demon, we must acknowledge him, enable him, or we are doomed to the impasse, and we would do well to follow Rutsala in his tormented progress, extending his forms as he deepens his vision.

—Norman Friedman

ST. JOHN, Bruce (Carlisle). Barbadian. Born in Barbados, West Indies, 24 December 1923. Educated at the University of London, external B.A. 1953; University of Toronto, M.A. in Spanish 1964. Married Ruby Marjorie St. John in 1959; one daughter and one son. Assistant Master, St. Giles' Boys' School, 1942–44, and Combermere School, 1944–64, both in Barbados. Lecturer, 1964–75, and since 1976, Senior Lecturer in Spanish, University of the West Indies, Bridgetown, Barbados. Member, National Council for Arts and Culture, Barbados. Recipient: Yaddo grant, 1972, 1976, 1978; Yoruba Foundation prize, 1973. Address: P.O. Box 64, Bridgetown, Barbados, West Indies.

PUBLICATIONS

Verse

The Foetus Pains. Bridgetown, EP, 1972.
The Foetus Pleasures. Bridgetown, EP, 1972.
Bruce St. John at Kairi House. Port of Spain, Kairi, 1974; revised edition, 1975.
Joyce and Eros and Varia. Bridgetown, Yoruba Press, 1976.

Play

The Vests (produced Bridgetown, 1977).

Other

Por el Mar de las Antillas: A Spanish Course for Caribbean Secondary Schools. London, Nelson, 4 vols., 1979.

Editor, *Aftermath: An Anthology.* Greenfield Center, New York, Greenfield Review Press, 1977.

Critical Studies: "The Poetry of Bruce St. John" by Michael Gitkes, in *Tapia* (Port of Spain), 15 June 1975; "Sex and Class in the Poetry of Bruce St. John" by Elaine Fido, in *Tapia* (Port of Spain), 24 August 1975; "If Barbados Could Speak" by Robert L. Morris, in *Manjak 9* and *10* (Bridgetown), 1975; introduction by Christopher David, to *Bruce St. John at Kairi House*, 1975.

Bruce St. John comments:

In my poetry in Barbadian dialect I try to express viewpoints on Barbadian human situations, in the natural language of Barbadians as they actually speak it – according to my knowledge of the Barbadian dialect lexicon, and its structure of thought and speech. Each poem is tested and re-tested in sound before, during, and after its composition. The views expressed are not always my own; they are *our* views, as Barbadians.

In my poetry in English I tend to express my own views, in Barbadian speech rhythms, and in an English which is my own, in that I choose and position words in order to say effectively what I want to say. In short, I strive to develop a language of my own in order to express *my* self. In my English poems I give fully the whole range of my experience and draw on my exposure to other cultures. I restrict this range somewhat in my dialect poems.

* * *

Although there has been "dialect" in Caribbean poetry "from the beginning," as it were, when plantocratic poets and poetasters attempted to reproduce the "broken lingo" of their black servant/slaves; and although Louise Bennett had been writing and reciting exclusively in "dialect verse" since the early 1940's, there was still, as late as the mid-1960's, a passionate debate as to whether patois could be seriously used as the language of poetry. Edward Brathwaite's *Rights of Passage* (1967) appeared finally to settle the matter, but it was not until the poets of the 1970's, above all Bruce St. John, a former concert singer, physical education instructor, and (presently) lecturer in Spanish at the University of the West Indies, that *nation-language*, conceived of and used as alternative rather than "bad" or "bongo" grammar, came into its own – especially with the large increasingly culturally conscious audiences – to such a degree, that it is practically unthinkable today for any "serious" Caribbean poet not to include at least some kind of nation-language in his work; and moving closer and closer stylistically to the kaiso and reggae singers who of course have always assumed *native* to be the norm and atom. The miracle of nation-language, at its poetic perfect, is that it not only reproduces the language of the people, but it reaches and re-echoes their inner vibration and bone; so that not only word, but psyche and sense become involved: the "nation" poet expressing as he should, the total culture of his subject: word, soul, and body-language.

St. John's first "discovery" (though Bennett always used it, since it is natural to the form and culture) is the dialogue or dramatic monologue. But what St. John adds is a sense of superstructure: the dialogue becomes a litany which in itself becomes a commentary on the Bajan personality; and the language is itself intensified, not only through the intensified form, but through the expression of contemporary politico-moral issues, juxtaposed against traditional norms expressed through proverb and riddle, as in "Bajan Litany":

	Follow pattern kill Cadogan.	*Yes, Lord.*
	America got black power?	*O Lord.*
	We got black power	*Yes, Lord.*
	Wuh sweeten goat mout bun 'e tail ...	*O Lord.*
	Jamaica got industry?	*O Lord.*
	We got industry.	*Yes, Lord.*
	Jamaica got bauxite?	(Silence)
(Louder)	Jamaica got bauxite? ...	*Yes, Lord.*
	De higher monkey go, de more he show 'e tail.	

From here St. John was able to tackle "traditional" subjects such as kite flying, cricket, sea-bathing, the "other woman," and more "modern" issues such as the ambiguities of post-colonial politics, and (constantly) the whole vexed question of Bajan education (contrasted with the more native *studyation*); and said in a way that we are able to see/hear them for the first time as it were, from inside, through the persona of "Archie." Archie/St. John are aware that education and the language man use are intimately connected, and that the respect for this connection says more about one's cultural authenticity than any politician or pedagogue ever could ("Bajan Language"):

Evah language got a rhythm but Bajan
Lick guitar drum an banjo stiff wid blows
Imag'ry purty an sweet like a rose
Limey try fuh muck up we poor nation
But Bajan save we life so here we goes ...

St. John is as Bajan as Miss Lou is Jamaican as Paul Keens-Douglas is Trinidadian: and yet they transcend territorial boundaries to capture and express the spirit of the Caribbean. It is in this new/ancient tradition that the future of Caribbean poetry lies: the word-seers, the sound-poets. But the body of their poetry will have to be constantly enriched (as is being done) with the emerging underground resources of culture itself.

—Edward Kamau Brathwaite

SANCHEZ, Sonia. American. Born in Birmingham, Alabama, 9 September 1934. Educated at New York University; Hunter College, New York, B.A. 1955. Married Etheridge Knight, *q.v.* (divorced); three children. Staff Member, Downtown Community School, 1965–67, and Mission Rebels in Action, 1968–69, San Francisco; Instructor, San Francisco State College, 1967–69; Lecturer in Black Literature, University of Pittsburgh, 1969–70, Rutgers University, New Brunswick, New Jersey, 1970–71, Manhattan Community College, New York, 1971–73, and Amherst College, Massachusetts, 1972–73. Recipient: P.E.N Writing Award, 1969; National Institute of Arts and Letters grant, 1970. Ph.D. in Fine Arts: Wilberforce University, Ohio. Address: c/o Third World Press, 7850 South Ellis Avenue, Chicago, Illinois 60619, U.S.A.

PUBLICATIONS

Verse

Homecoming. Detroit, Broadside Press, 1969.
WE a BaddDDD People. Detroit, Broadside Press, 1970.
Liberation Poem. Detroit, Broadside Press, 1970.
It's a New Day: Poems for Young Brothas and Sistuhs. Detroit, Broadside Press, 1971.
Ima Talken bout The Nation of Islam. Astoria, New York, Truth Del., 1971(?).
Love Poems. New York, Third Press, 1973.
A Blues Book for Blue Black Magical Women. Detroit, Broadside Press, 1974.
I've Been a Woman: New and Selected Poems. Sausalito, California, Black Scholar Press, 1979.

Recordings: *Homecoming*, Broadside Voices; *We a BaddDDD People*, Broadside Voices; *A Sun Woman for All Seasons*, Folkways, 1971.

Plays

The Bronx Is Next (produced New York, 1970).
Sister Son/ji (produced Evanston, Illinois, 1971).
Dirty Hearts, '72, in *Scripts 1* (New York), November 1971.
Uh, Uh: But How Do It Free Us?, in *The New Lafayette Theatre Presents*, edited by Ed Bullins. New York, Doubleday, 1974.

Short Stories

A Sound Investment. Chicago, Third World Press, 1979.

Other

The Adventures of Fathead, Smallhead, and Squarehead (juvenile). New York, Third Press, 1973.

Editor, *Three Hundred Sixty Degrees of Blackness Comin' at You.* New York 5X, 1972.
Editor, *We Be Word Sorcerers: 25 Stories by Black Americans.* New York, Bantam, 1973.

* * *

Sonia Sanchez is a strong and popular poetic voice of the so-called "Black arts movement." She directs her poetry to Black people, concentrating on such themes as Black identity and pride, identification of the source of the Black man's difficulties (the white man and his values and actions), e.g., the "right on: wite america" poems; guidance, instructions, and exhortations for Black directed self-improvement, e.g., the "TCB–en Poems" in *We a BaddDDD People*; love, e.g., "black magic"; exposure and chastisement of white-minded, apathetic, predatory, or faddishly revolutionary Blacks, e.g., "blk/rhetoric." Her relatively recent conversion to the Nation of Islam (Black Muslims) is reflected in the content of (and by the absence of profanity in) her more recent poetry, e.g., "let us begin the real work."

As her recordings and public readings would indicate, Miss Sanchez seems to write for her own speaking voice – a sort of sing-song monotone that, curiously, has a lilting quality. One is struck by the contrast of her strong statements with her feminine inflection, intonation, pacing, and timbre. Frequently she punctuates her lines with a gentle "yeh," elongates sounds, sustains parts of words, particularly word endings, sustains or raises the pitch slightly at line or poem endings. Her language is vigorous, direct, conversational, unabashed, by some standards coarse, and it is not often infused with poetic indirection or metaphor. Her diction is that of the Black urban masses. She employs "Black grammar," e.g., "we bees real/ bad"; "Black speech" sounds, e.g., "white motha/fucka"; elisions, e.g., "blk" for black; extra vowels and consonants to approximate elongated sounds, e.g., "soooooo"; nonstandard spellings, e.g., "amurica"; non-words, e.g., the approximation of musical sounds in "a/ coltrane/ poem"; word components, e.g., "sun day"; diagonals; and ampersands. In the free verse style, she frequently uses open and irregular spatial arrangements, practically never uses symmetrical or formulaic structures.

—Theodore R. Hudson

SANDERS, Ed. American. Born in Kansas City, Missouri, 17 August 1939. Educated at New York University, B.A. in classics 1963. Married Miriam Kittell in 1961; three children. Editor and Publisher, *Fuck You: A Magazine of the Arts*, and *Dick*, New York; Organizer and Lead Singer of The Fugs, a literary-political rock group. Since 1965, Professor, Free University of New York; Owner, Peace Eye Bookstore, New York. Recipient: National Endowment for the Arts grant, 1966, 1969. Address: Westbeth, 463 West Street, New York, New York 10014, U.S.A.

PUBLICATIONS

Verse

Poem from Jail. San Francisco, City Lights, 1963.
King Lord – Queen Freak. Cleveland, Renegade Press, 1964.
The Toe-Queen: Poems. New York, Fuck You Press, 1964.
Banana: An Anthology of Banana-Erotic Poems. New York, Fuck You Press, 1965.
The Complete Sex Poems of Ed Sanders. New York, Fug-Press, 1965.
Peace Eye. Buffalo, Frontier Press, 1965; revised edition, Cleveland, Frontier Press, 1967.
Fuck God in the Ass. New York, Fuck You Press, 1967.
Shards of God. New York, Grove Press, 1971.
Egyptian Hieroglyphics. Canton, New York, Institute of Further Studies, 1973.
Investigative Poetry. San Francisco, City Lights, 1976.
20,000 A.D. Plainfield, Vermont, North Atlantic, 1976.

Short Stories

Tales of Beatnik Glory. New York, Stonehill, 1975.

Other

The Family: The Story of Charles Manson's Dune Buggy Attack Battalion. New York, Dutton, 1971; London, Hart Davis, 1972.
Vote!, with Abbie Hoffman and Jerry Rubin. New York, Warner, 1972.

Editor, *Bugger: An Anthology.* New York, Fuck You Press, 1964.
Editor, *Despair: Poems to Come Down By* (anthology). Privately printed, 1964.

* * *

In Ed Sanders's poetry the raw energy of a 1960's-style peace march, a rock concert, and an orgy impels a fine intelligence. Many of his poems can be read as political protest; some might be read, by a reader intent upon it, as pornography. The best of his work in *Peace Eye* and *20,000 A.D.* – probably the two most interesting books – however, should be read as representing a perhaps unexpected turn in the tradition of Pound and Olson.

"Ed Sanders' language," Charles Olson writes, "advances in a direction of production which probably isn't even guessed at." His language is always near the breaking point, always at the verge of howls and groans. Rude, slangy, obscene, blasphemous, it violates any remaining verbal taboos. At the same time, however, it frequently spills over into Greek, Egyptian hieroglyphs, and glyph-like drawings, giving the impression that one language, or even language itself, cannot contain Sanders's, to use one of his terms, "Endless Gush" (which, it should be noted, is a translation of Anaximander's central term, *tò ápeiron*). Especially when he recites it himself, one has a sense in his language of an archaic power. At its best, however, it is more than that: we begin to sense the relationship between "the holy" and "the accursed" as it is recorded in the etymology of "sacred." The closing section of "The Fugs," "Hymn to the Vagina of Mercy," like "Arise Garland Flame" and "Holy Was Demeter Walking the Corn Furrow," are, as it were, songs from a satyr play.

Sanders's poetry is truly outrageous: that is its beauty. It is a test of Blake's proverbs of Hell. Read at length, it loses its shock value and tends to become tedious, but it is not intended for that kind of consumption. His poems are performance pieces for an athletic performer like Sanders himself, who was the lead singer with a rock group for several years.

The most recent turn in Sanders's work can also be seen as an outgrowth of the Pound-Olson tradition. They propose poetry as a gathering of significant information. Sanders characteristically pushes any possibility to its literal limits. We must be, Olson says, "cooked/ and ruled by information." Sanders's response to this demand is what he calls "investigative poetry." *The Family*, his careful, objective, and thorough report on the Charles Manson case, was his first investigative poem, or at least the idea of investigative poetry derived from his experience of writing that book. Manson was a sign that something had gone seriously wrong with the political movements of the 1960's. The message of investigative poetry – though it stretches traditional definitions of poetry perhaps even beyond the breaking point – is that no political movement can be effective without complete information. It is an attempt to find a fulcrum for political power at precisely the point where governments are most vulnerable: in gathering, organizing, and effectively communicating knowledge. In the manifesto "To the Z-D Generation," he writes, "Never hesitate to open up a case file even upon the bloodiest of beasts or plots! We will see the day of relentless pursuit of data! Interrogate the Abyss."

In a very recent work, "The Karen Silkwood Cantata," first performed on 20 May 1979, Sanders is beginning to combine performance with the results of investigation.

—Don Byrd

SANDY, Stephen. American. Born in Minneapolis, Minnesota, 2 August 1934. Educated at Yale University, New Haven, Connecticut, A.B.; Harvard University, Cambridge, Massachusetts, Ph.D. Instructor in English, Harvard University, 1963–67; Fulbright Lecturer, University of Tokyo, 1967–68; Visiting Assistant Professor, Brown University, Providence, Rhode Island, 1968–69. Since 1970, Professor of English, Bennington College, Vermont. Director, Chautauqua Poetry Workshop, 1975, 1977, and Bennington College Poetry Workshop, 1978, 1979. Address: White Creek, Eagle Bridge, New York 12057, U.S.A.

PUBLICATIONS

Verse

Caroms. Groton, Massachusetts, Groton Press, 1960.
Mary Baldwin. Dublin, Dolmen Press, 1962.
The Destruction of Bulfinch's House. Cambridge, Massachusetts, Identity, 1964.
Stresses in the Peaceable Kingdom. Boston, Houghton Mifflin, 1967.
Home Again, Looking Around. Cambridge, Massachusetts, Halty Ferguson, 1968.
Catullus LVIII: To Caelius. Tokyo, Voyagers Press, 1969.
Japanese Room. Providence, Rhode Island, Hellcoal Press, 1969.
Jerome. Bennington, Vermont, Grel Press, 1970.
A Dissolve, music by Richard Wilson. New York, Schirmer, 1970.
Light in the Spring Poplars, music by Richard Wilson. New York, Schirmer, 1970.
Roofs. Boston, Houghton Mifflin, 1971.
Home from the Range, music by Richard Wilson. New York, Schirmer, 1971.
Soaking, music by Richard Wilson. New York, Schirmer, 1971.
Elegy, music by Richard Wilson. New York, Schirmer, 1972.
Can, music by Richard Wilson. New York, Fischer, 1973.
One Section from "Revolutions." San Francisco, Grabhorn Hoyem, 1973.
The Difficulty. Providence, Rhode Island, Burning Deck, 1975.
Landscapes. Cambridge, New York, White Creek, 1975.
From "Freestone." Binghamton, New York, Bellevue Press, 1975.
The Austin Tower. San Francisco, Empty Elevator Shaft, 1975.
Freestone: Sections 25 and 26. Binghamton, New York, Bellevue Press, 1977.
End of the Picaro. Pawlet, Vermont, Banyan Press, 1977.
Arch (card). Binghamton, New York, Bellevue Press, 1977.
The Hawthorne Effect. Lawrence, Kansas, Tansy Press, 1979.

Play

Hieronymo: An Antiphonal Cantata, music by Henry Brant. New York, MCA Music, 1973.

Other

The Raveling of the Novel. New York, Arno Press, 1979.

Manuscript Collection: Houghton Library, Harvard University, Cambridge, Massachusetts.

Critical Studies: "Like the Bones of Dreams" by Heather Ross Miller, in *The American Scholar* (Washington, D.C.), Autumn 1967; Vernon Young, in *Hudson Review* (New York), Winter 1971–72; Richard Howard, in *American Poetry Review* (Philadelphia), May–June 1973.

* * *

The Difficulty, *The Austin Tower*, and *End of the Picaro* reflect a growing maturation in Stephen Sandy's art. The themes and events that preoccupied his earlier poetry are still in evidence, but his concern with social issues that haunted the 1960's in America – the war in Viet Nam, the plight of the Indian, man's assault upon his environment – has been replaced with a concern for more fundamental philosophical questions and a more studied interest in art's ability to resolve some of them.

In *Stresses in the Peaceable Kingdom* Sandy treated the theme of loss and employed a style which combined conversational ease with clarity of diction and penetrating powers of observation. The poems were a series of epiphanies which compelled the reader to see vividly the objects or moments Sandy recalled. Loss of innocence, or past traditions, or old historical landmarks were treated, sometimes nostalgically, more often with good humor, occasionally with painful irony. In "The Destruction of Bulfinch's House," he rendered an old mansion which had declined into a tenement in a mood reminiscent of Eliot's "Preludes"; in "Can" he transformed a can into "a bent tin soldier," jobless, knocking about, grinning through jagged teeth; in "Home from the Range" he turned the familiar folksong refrain into the lament of a soldier returning from a firing range where he had partially lost his hearing.

In *Roofs*, Sandy presented a series of poems tracing his journey from New England to Japan and back again. He reflected upon the paradoxes inherent in modern Japanese life and in his reaction to it. This volume contains his bitterest poems of social protest. His elegy, "Charley," was an intensely personal response to the death of his friend killed in the demilitarized zone. He discovered technical devices to render visually in his poetry the disparities that he wrote about. He preserved tension and a sense of space by actually separating the print on the page with large spaces. His skill as an artist was more certain in this volume: he captured the stylized figures of Japan's past; his verbal plays were less ostentatious and self-conscious than before; the world he depicted was more complex.

In *The Difficulty* and *End of the Picaro* Sandy traces the mental journey of his speaker. In *The Difficulty*, comprised of six parts, Sandy monochromatically muses about himself (or a thinly disguised extension of himself; the persona in all his poems is highly autobiographical) and an other. The other is a collector, a man who cares who he is, where he has come from, and wants to know the identity of the things he collects, who made them, when, and where. Sandy worries; meanings escape him. Petulantly and pseudocryptically, he retorts to the other: "When you grow up/nothing/is personal." Sandy fights the impulse to order, but later, sensing the continuity between himself and others, the past and present, he submits to the undertow that pulls him, ironically, towards style. The rage for order conquers in this sequence of poems.

End of the Picaro continues the quest that is prefigured in *The Difficulty*. Less colloquial than *The Difficulty*, returning to the vein of rich imagistic renderings of moments and objects so frequently present in *Stresses in the Peaceable Kingdom*, *End of the Picaro* wrestles explicitly with the problem of perspective, the poet's relationship to his personal and historical pasts, and his need to trace the journey of his literary counterpart and double, the Picaro, whose history is often episodic, and whose future this poet must fashion if Sandy is to know himself and mouth his "banal testimony." The poem closes on a celebratory note, with the poet back on the vagabond's road, having understood that the past and the past remembered are not the same, and that possibilities known to him in the present can be discovered in the past, transforming it into the future. The conclusion mingles Sandy's two styles, the one slangy, monosyllabic, and modern, the other richly lyrical, decasyllabic, and descriptive, and invents a new rhythm and style for his verse. Perhaps his next volume will offer what he calls "the simple testament," the base line that he and all men reach for.

—Carol Simpson Stern

SANER, Reg(inald Anthony). American. Born in Jacksonville, Illinois, 30 December 1931. Educated at St. Norbert College, West De Pere, Wisconsin, B.A. 1952; University of Illinois, Urbana, M.A. 1955, Ph.D. in English 1962. Served as a Lieutenant in the United States Army Infantry, 1952–53: Bronze Star. Married Anne Costigan in 1958; two sons. Free-lance photographer, Illinois, 1953–54; photographer and writer, Montgomery Publishing Company, Los Angeles and San Francisco, 1956. Assistant Instructor, 1956–60, Instructor, 1961–62, Assistant Professor, 1962–67, Associate Professor, 1967–72, and since 1972, Professor of English, University of Colorado, Boulder. Recipient: Borestone Mountain Poetry Award, 1972; Academy of American Poets Walt Whitman Award, 1975; National Endowment for the Arts Fellowship, 1976. Address: 1925 Vassar, Boulder, Colorado 80303, U.S.A.

PUBLICATIONS

Verse

Climbing into the Roots. New York, Harper, 1976.

Critical Studies: interviews in *Gumbo Review* (Fort Collins, Colorado), Spring 1977, and *Aspen Anthology* (Colorado), Fall 1978.

Reg Saner comments:

Living among rocks, clouds, and trees in Colorado, I tend to get my most immediate impulses from them. Nature poetry; always a crossroads where earth and air intersect. My feel for things and men is temporal. Man on the edge, the dangerous edge of things fascinates me. I look into ways our address defines us, because I believe what we are will always be where.

Being an atheist, I write poetry that is perhaps naturally religious, though mountain environment, by its potential hostility, staggers anyone's complacent sentimentalizing. Being a Catholic atheist, I have a sense of man that is historical. Wherever I look, either among Anasazi Indian ruins of Chaco Canyon or into the brickwork lining Brunelleschi's cupola over the Duomo of Florence, I hear people saying, "We were." The sound is of mayflies hitting the ice.

* * *

Poems about mountains have a tendency to diminish into what Reg Saner calls "pure calendar art," but even as he acknowledges this risk Saner shows how to avoid the traps in *Climbing into the Roots.* By making the mountains his "chosen place" Saner has staked out a claim that will long bear his mark, even if he eventually abandons it for some other territory. For Saner's concern is less with the grandeur of the mountains than with the perspective they allow – "this difficult magnificence/where we are most our own." In these poems he climbs into a cleaner, purer air where – feet planted firmly on rock – he can look out to look in, just as he has climbed *up* to get *into* the roots:

> Under the rosy foreskin of dawn,
> turned for a parting glance, I leave
> and take all I can. The mountain's huge
> bite of glacial cirque
> hovers, a small glass square
> pressed to the shape of a tent,
> with, still slightly warm,

a sleep print. All summer I'll come
and go, eating spaces like these
to make sure.
My death must be a simply enormous death.

Throughout Saner's poems one feels an embracing sense of place, a blend of the physical and the spiritual, but even more impressive is the enlarged time frame within which this place – the American Rocky Mountains – is so finely realized. In a manner that is reminiscent of Loren Eiseley's powerful essays, Saner makes these poems compellingly human – "staring up between, guessing/how huge a dark we're in" – but the intelligence that is guessing here is quite aware that the mountains on which he stands evolved from an earlier geological state, and further that they are now posed "under gravity's big guns" ready to wear or crash down to become the sand of the desert below. The tension such an awareness creates prevents any of these poems from being still lifes, even though they are largely unpeopled. It also establishes a rich context for Saner to confront in concrete ways a range of issues prehistoric and historic, physical and metaphysical.

Not all of Saner's poems are set in the mountains, of course, nor are all of them flawless successes. At times, his usually brilliant metaphors overreach themselves, the tensions of the poems become too explicit, and the imaginative leaps become forced ("At ponds/whose tundra edges seem rich/I put my hand on Miss America's muff"). There are also some poems in this 1975 Walt Whitman Award-winning collection (especially "One War Is All Wars," "Flag," and "Smiling at 180") that appear to contribute little if anything to the otherwise unified trajectory of the book. Saner is not usually his best in small situations, and when he moves away from the mountains his poems sometimes seem to lose vital energy and become more self-consciously rhetorical. Fortunately, such breaks are few.

One of the qualities that distinguishes *Climbing into the Roots* is that so much of it appears to be the product of mature, intelligent listening. Saner accepts the rhythms operating on the mountains ("timing/our talk to the tent's nylon whip and crackle" or – as he puts it in another poem – "To make talk, we listen"), and he channels his energy into confronting the experience and resisting facile interpretations:

Like a silence coming out of the stones,
the universe flying at terrible speeds
further into itself.
If it is not here it is nowhere.
The stillness where all words are kept.

In an age where the hard-sell has become commonplace, it is a rare pleasure to find such fertile listening in so many excellent poems. And it is clearly one of the reasons why the best of Reg Saner's work has a lasting quality. He has listened with sensitivity to enrich and enlarge, rather than exploit, his experience, and thus he can now take us closer to "the place that we know/must always/be part of the distance."

—Stanley W. Lindberg

SAROYAN, Aram. American. Born in New York City, 25 September 1943; son of the writer William Saroyan. Educated at Trinity High School, New York; University of Chicago; New York University; Columbia University, New York. Married Gailyn McClanahan in 1968; two daughters and one son. Founding Editor, *Lines*, 1964–65, and

Publisher, Lines Books, New York. Recipient: National Endowment for the Arts grant, 1966, 1968. Address: P.O. Box 837, Bolinas, California 94924, U.S.A.

PUBLICATIONS

Verse

Poems, with Jenni Caldwell and Richard Kolmar. New York, Acadia Press, 1963.
In. Eugene, Oregon, Bear Press, 1964.
Cheated Death by Inches. New York, Graphic Composition, 1964.
Top. New York, Lines, 1965.
Works. New York, Lines, 1966.
Sled Hill Voices. London, Goliard Press, 1966.
(Poems). Cambridge, Massachusetts, Lines, 1967.
Coffee Coffee. New York, 0 to 9, 1967.
©1968. New York, Kulchur, 1968.
(Poems). New York, Random House, 1968.
Pages. New York, Random House, 1969.
Words and Photographs. Chicago, Big Table, 1970.
The Beatles. Cambridge, Massachusetts, Barn Dream Press, 1970.
5 Mini-Books. Privately printed, 1971.
The Rest. Philadelphia, Telegraph, 1971.
Poems. Philadelphia, Telegraph, 1972.
By Air Mail, with Victor Bockris. London, Strange Faeces Press, 1972.
Telegrams. Philadelphia, Telegraph, 1972.
San Francisco, with Andrei Codrescu. Privately printed, 1972.
The Bolinas Book. Lancaster, Massachusetts, Other, 1974.
Marijuana and Me. Privately printed, 1974.
O My Generation and Other Poems. Bolinas, California, Blackberry, 1976.

Novels

Cloth: An Electric Novel. Chicago, Big Table, 1971.
The Street: An Autobiographical Novel. Lenox, Massachusetts, Bookstore Press, 1975.

Other

Meet Uncle Aram. Boston, Toumayan, 1970.
Genesis Angels: The Saga of Lew Welch and the Beat Generation. New York, Morrow, 1979.

Manuscript Collections: Special Collections, University of California, Los Angeles; University of Connecticut, Storrs.

Aram Saroyan comments:

(1970) I write on a typewriter, almost never in hand (I can hardly handwrite, I tend to draw words), and my machine – an obsolete red-top Royal Portable – is the biggest influence on my work. This red hood holds the mood, keeps my eye happy. The typeface is a standard pica; if it were another style I'd write (subtly) different poems. And when a ribbon gets dull my poems I'm sure change. – 1966.

ELECTRIC POETRY

By electric I mean instantaneous – without any reading process at all; and therefore continuous – as the Present is – without beginning, middle, or end. – 1968.

(1974) Having spent the past five years largely organizing my previous work and seeing most of it into print, I now find myself writing again, but with a new orientation.

Although I regard my work as a concrete poet, and my later work with the book form itself (*Words and Photographs*, *Cloth*, *5 Mini-Books*, and *The Beatles*) as valid, I feel I have explored this direction as thoroughly as I am able, and hence I am no longer personally interested in it. My new writing, which began with my settling in Bolinas, California, in August 1972, is primarily a return to and an extension of my earlier work as a poet (*Poems*) in which I wrote about my life as honestly as I could, employing conventional syntax. I feel I made a breakthrough in this mode with a poem called "Lines for My Autobiography," written over a period of three days in Bolinas; and seemingly on the momentum of this work have followed three books (the third currently in the writing) – *Lines for My Autobiography*, *Friendly Persuasion*, and *Poetry in Motion*. With the second of these books, I began composing poems in hand.

(1980) My current project is a book called Families, in which I juxtapose a photographic portrait of a family on each right hand page with excerpts from a taped interview with that family on each left hand page. The structure of this book seems to me to harken back to *Words and Photographs*, but the content is more mainstream America, reflecting my changes in relation to the culture in the past decade, most fundamentally the change of becoming a family man myself. The next project I have in mind is writing a screenplay of my novel *The Street*.

* * *

Aram Saroyan's first published poetry, written during the 1960's, established him as an experimental poet whose chief interest was concrete and "minimal" poetry. These poems, skillful as they are, do not often extend beyond a kind of poster-like play with words and the letters of the alphabet. They become objects instantly perceived, and thus fuel for lengthy contemplation for readers so inclined. Such a poem is the untitled one-word "crickets" repeated for 37 or 42 lines, depending on which anthology you find it in. I suppose the length of this poem depends on size of the page, and perhaps Saroyan would accept the notion that a two-line version is likewise complete if printed on a shallow page:

crickets
crickets

The concept may well be an isolation of the components of conscious thought, and in a poem like the one just quoted, repetition and the word itself mimes its subject, and the ubiquitous nature of the crickets' song. A favorite of mine is his "My arms are warm" printed directly over his name; many of the letters used for the statement are those in "Aram Saroyan." Saroyan writes that his "concrete/minimal work now seems to have a lot to do with the strange 'time' the Sixties was for most of us. The one-word poem has *no* time in it, it can be read instantly – and this seemed to me 'perfect' for a while. Now I'm interested less in perfection and more in 'time' – I like lines, sentences, stanzas...."

Saroyan's 1972 book, *Poems*, which he says contains his earliest poems, exemplifies his current interest in the more "traditional" forms, heavily influenced, as ever, by the "New York School," where nothing is too mundane for a place in the poem. Even Saroyan's "traditional" poems are uncommonly spare: here is all of "Almost Midnight":

I type & think & look at the painting of Poe & out
the window there's the top of my head, to the left
and behind me, is the bookcase.

At times this perfected attention captures completely the glimmer of city life, and it is in poems like these that Saroyan's work most distinctly justifies the glorification of the ordinary:

This morning I ate (bacon
& eggs) and
tied my tie
in a hurry
when I went outside
gilt was flashing
in the sidewalk
and the street
sounded like a movie

—Geof Hewitt

SARTON, May. American. Born in Wondelgem, Belgium, 3 May 1912, daughter of the historian of science George Sarton; emigrated to the United States in 1916; naturalized, 1924. Educated at the Shady Hill School and The High and Latin School, both in Cambridge, Massachusetts. Apprentice, then Member, and Director of the Apprentice Group, Eva Le Gallienne's Civic Repertory Theatre, New York, 1930–33; Founder and Director, Apprentice Theatre, New York, and Associated Actors Inc., Hartford, Connecticut, 1933–36. Taught Creative Writing and Choral Speech, Stuart School, Boston, 1937–40. Documentary Scriptwriter, Office of War Information, 1944–45. Poet-in-Residence, Southern Illinois University, Carbondale, Summer 1945; Briggs-Copeland Instructor in English Composition, Harvard University, Cambridge, Massachusetts, 1950–53; Lecturer, Breadloaf Writers' Conference, Middlebury, Vermont, 1951–52, and Boulder Writers Conference, Colorado, 1953–54; Phi Beta Kappa Visiting Scholar, 1959–60; Danforth Lecturer, 1960–61; Lecturer in Creative Writing, Wellesley College, Massachusetts, 1960–63; Poet-in-Residence, Lindenwood College, St. Charles, Missouri, 1964, 1965; Visiting Lecturer, Agnes Scott College, Decatur, Georgia, Spring 1972. Recipient: New England Poetry Club Golden Rose, 1945; Bland Memorial Prize, 1945 (*Poetry*, Chicago); American Poetry Society Reynolds Prize, 1953; Bryn Mawr College Lucy Martin Donnelly Fellowship, 1953; Guggenheim Fellowship, 1954; Johns Hopkins University Poetry Festival Award, 1961; National Endowment for the Arts grant, 1966; Sarah Josepha Hale Award, 1972. Litt.D.: Russell Sage College, Troy, New York, 1958; New England College, Henniker, New Hampshire, 1971; Bates College, Lewiston, Maine, 1974; Colby College, Waterville, Maine, 1974; Clark University, Worcester, Massachusetts, 1975; University of New Hampshire, Durham, 1976; King School of the Ministry, Berkeley, California, 1976. Fellow, American Academy of Arts and Sciences. Address: Box 99, York, Maine 03909, U.S.A.

PUBLICATIONS

Verse

Encounter in April. Boston, Houghton Mifflin, 1937.
Inner Landscape. Boston, Houghton Mifflin, 1939; with a selection from *Encounter in April*, London, Cresset Press, 1939.
The Lion and the Rose. New York, Rinehart, 1948.
The Leaves of the Tree. Mount Vernon, Iowa, Cornell College, 1950.
The Land of Silence and Other Poems. New York, Rinehart, 1953.
In Time like Air. New York, Rinehart, 1957.

Cloud, Stone, Sun, Vine: Poems, Selected and New. New York, Norton, 1961.
A Private Mythology: New Poems. New York, Norton, 1966.
As Does New Hampshire and Other Poems. Peterborough, New Hampshire, Richard R. Smith, 1967.
A Grain of Mustard Seed: New Poems. New York, Norton, 1971.
A Durable Fire: New Poems. New York, Norton, 1972.
Collected Poems 1930–1973. New York, Norton, 1974.
Selected Poems, edited by Serena Sue Hilsinger and Lois Byrnes. New York, Norton, 1978.

Plays

The Underground River. New York, Play Club, 1947.

Screenplays: *Toscanini: The Hymn of Nations*, 1944; *Valley of the Tennessee*, 1944.

Novels

The Single Hound. Boston, Houghton Mifflin, and London, Cresset Press, 1938.
The Bridge of Years. New York, Doubleday, 1946.
Shadow of a Man. New York, Rinehart, 1950; London, Cresset Press, 1952.
A Shower of Summer Days. New York, Rinehart, 1952; London, Hutchinson, 1954.
Faithful Are the Wounds. New York, Rinehart, and London, Gollancz, 1955.
The Birth of a Grandfather. New York, Rinehart, 1957; London, Gollancz, 1958.
The Small Room. New York, Norton, 1961; London, Gollancz, 1962.
Joanna and Ulysses. New York, Norton, 1963; London, Murray, 1964.
Mrs. Stevens Hears the Mermaids Singing. New York, Norton, 1965; London, Peter Owen, 1966.
Miss Pickthorn and Mr. Hare: A Fable. New York, Norton, 1966; London, Dent, 1968.
The Poet and the Donkey. New York, Norton, 1969.
Kinds of Love. New York, Norton, 1970.
As We Are Now. New York, Norton, 1973; London, Gollancz, 1974.
Crucial Conversations. New York, Norton, 1975; London, Gollancz, 1976.
A Reckoning. New York, Norton, 1978; London, Gollancz, 1980.

Other

The Fur Person: The Story of a Cat. New York, Rinehart, 1957; London, Muller, 1958.
I Knew a Phoenix: Sketches for an Autobiography. New York, Holt Rinehart, 1959; London, Peter Owen, 1963.
Plant Dreaming Deep (autobiography). New York, Norton, 1968.
Journal of a Solitude. New York, Norton, 1973.
Punch's Secret (juvenile). New York, Harper, 1974.
A World of Light: Portraits and Celebrations. New York, Norton, 1976.
A Walk Through the Woods (juvenile). New York, Harper, 1976.
The House by the Sea: A Journal. New York, Norton, 1977; London, Prior, 1978.

Bibliography: *May Sarton: A Bibliography* by Lenora P. Blouin, Metuchen, New Jersey, Scarecrow Press, 1978.

Manuscript Collection: Berg Collection, New York Public Library.

Critical Studies: *May Sarton* by Agnes Sibley, New York, Twayne, 1972; "Home to a Place of Exile: The *Collected Poems* of May Sarton" by Henry Taylor, in *Hollins Critic* (Hollins College, Virginia), June 1974.

* * *

Bare of nuance and ambiguity, May Sarton's verse is often indistinguishable from ordinary prose. Within her limits, her earnest and bookish sensibility has for forty years reassured readers about the joys and even the anguishes of love, and the dedication necessary to generate art from everyday life, often at the expense of love and other relationships; beginning with *The Lion and the Rose*, many poems have soothingly transcribed the response of an aroused conscience to the horrors of war, and the deep, but curable, guilt of our racism. Her first volume articulates a view of the universe that supports many later poems on the relation between art and nature, between the artist and his work: "Objects and people/exist within this world/only if they can find their places/in a pattern" ("Portrait of One Person – As by Chirico"). Sometimes Sarton more concisely and effectively stylizes nature: "... the Japanese look of sleet/When it slants back the way the wind blows" ("To the Weary"), a perception that still charms many years later in *A Private Mythology*: "How Japanese the rain looked/In Cambridge" ("A Child's Japan"). As early as *The Land of Silence*, Sarton reveals an occasional skill at capturing natural detail: "As shadows made a river of the road" ("Evening Journey"). Unfortunately, she failed to develop this strength until her later volumes. Many poems celebrate specific works of art, from the early "Portrait of the Artist," which praises both the evocative and organizational power of van Cleve's self-portrait, to "Dutch Interior," which 35 years later analyzes de Hooch's skill at suggesting both the psychology and formal function of the woman in the painting. Avoiding undue modesty, Sarton places an equally high value on her own efforts: "A Letter to James Stephens" prays to transform the "Quick-burning fire of youth" to "... that bush of flame/That ... contained the angel who could speak God's name...." Sometimes this intense dedication collides with a familiar metaphor: "Imagine a moment when student and teacher/(Long after the day and the lesson are over)/Will soar together to the pure immortal air/And find Yeats, Hopkins. Eliot waiting there" ("Poet in Residence").

Nor are Sarton's perpetual love poems convincing, whether the youthful ecstasies of *Encounter in April* or the paeans to love at 60 of *A Durable Fire*. The lover/antagonist achieves neither credible humanity nor symbolic force as an ultra-human principle in an allegory. Since Sarton consistently uses the Shakespearean sonnet, but has difficulties with the final couplet, the poems never reach the resolution implicit in the form. Infrequently in the first volume, the final lines embody a sensuousness that suggests a real relationship and the metrical skill to dramatize it: "Now let us rest. Now let me lay my hand/In yours – like a smooth stone on the smooth sand" ("Sonnet 15"). Too often, however, the couplets strive for Millay's flippancy or Drayton's wit, but stumble: "I am come home to you, for at the end,/I find I cannot live without you, friend" ("Sonnet 14"). Even the competent "Autumn Sonnets" in *A Durable Fire* suffer from Sarton's predilection for familiar abstraction and rhetoric: "Truth is, her daily battle is with death,/Back to the wall and fighting for her breath" ("Sonnet 6").

For all her insistence on strict form and her occasional success with slant rhymes, Sarton is best with free verse. *A Private Mythology*, her strongest volume, succeeds with short poems on Japan, perhaps suggested by haiku, which concentrate image and eliminate the superfluous moral addenda flawing much of her work: "We regretted the rain/Until we saw the mists/Floating the mountains/On their dragon-tails" ("On the Way to Lake Chuzen-ji"). Other poems in the collection display a previously concealed humor and some assurance with conventional forms, especially in "A Late Mowing," in which vivid images vivify the traditional comfort of the eternality of the natural cycle; "A sky flung down to earth as daisies" returns reassuringly in the final stanza: "While overhead your dazzling daisy skies/Flower in the cold, bright mowing that will keep." The success of *A Private Mythology* suggested that Sarton's eclecticism and moral earnestness had found an authentic voice, but other recent volumes are less encouraging. *A Durable Fire* keeps her signature vocative command to a minimum; but "Elegy (for Louise Bogan)" embarrasses not only with Sarton's familiar rhetorical question, but also with a general failure of taste and technique: "Louise, Louise, why did you have to go/In this hard time of wind and shrouding snow[?]" And *A Grain of Mustard Seed* makes a series of awkward pronouncements on American outrages of the 1960's. Despite these flaws and a continuing fondness for stereotyped treatment of abstract themes in abstract language, Sarton's verse has at least transcended the Henleyesque bravado of *Inner Landscape* and has apparently won an audience in a dozen published volumes. Sarton's greatest problem has always been a tendency toward excessive length and repetition in individual works and a willingness to publish everything. Even the new *Collected Poems* stops short of the ruthlessness necessary to eliminate the inferior. However, Sarton has produced enough competent, low-keyed verse to support her credo (expressed in "Second Thoughts on the Abstract Gardens of Japan"):

> Unbuttoned ego. I have staked
> My life on controlled native powers;
> My garden, so untamed, still has not lacked
> Its hard-won flowers.

—Burton Kendle

SAVORY, Teo. American. Born in Hong Kong. Educated privately in Hong Kong; Royal College of Music, London, and Conservatoire in Paris; studied with Harry Plunket Greene. Married the writer Alan Brilliant in 1958. Producer, American National Theatre and Academy, New York. Since 1966, Editor-in-Chief, Unicorn Press and *Unicorn Journal*, Santa Barbara, California, later Greensboro, North Carolina. Recipient: National Endowment for the Arts grant, 1969, 1979. Address: R.F.D. 1, Housatonic, Massachusetts 01236; or, Unicorn Press Inc., P.O. Box 3307, Greensboro, North Carolina 27402, U.S.A.

PUBLICATIONS

Verse

Traveler's Palm: A Poetry Sequence. Santa Barbara, California, Unicorn Press, 1967.
The House Wrecker. Santa Barbara, California, Unicorn Press, 1967.
A Christmas Message Received During a Car Ride. Aptos, California, Grace Hoper Press, 1967.
Snow Vole: A Poetry Sequence. Santa Barbara, California, Unicorn Press, 1968.
Transitions. Santa Barbara, California, Unicorn Press, 1973.
Dragons of Mist and Torrent. Greensboro, North Carolina, Unicorn Press, 1974.

Novels

The Landscape of Dreams. New York, Braziller, 1960.
The Single Secret. New York, Braziller, and London, Gollancz, 1961.
A Penny for the Guy. London, Gollancz, 1963; as *A Penny for His Pocket*, Philadelphia, Lippincott, 1964.
To a High Place. Santa Barbara, California, Unicorn Press, 1971.
Stonecrop: The Country I Remember. Greensboro, North Carolina, Unicorn Press, 1977.
A Childhood. Greensboro, North Carolina, Unicorn Press, 1978.

Short Stories

A Clutch of Fables. Greensboro, North Carolina, Unicorn Press, 1976.

Other

Translator, *Corbière, Supervielle, Prévert, Jammes, Michaux, Guillevic, Queneau, Eich.* Santa Barbara, California, Unicorn Press, 8 vols., 1967–71.
Translator, *Selected Poems of Guillevic.* London, Penguin, 1974.
Translator, *Zen Poems*, by Nhat Hanh. Greensboro, North Carolina, Unicorn Press, 1974.
Translator, *Euclidians*, by Guillevic. Greensboro, North Carolina, Unicorn Press, 1975.
Translator, *Liberté*, by Paul Eluard. Greensboro, North Carolina, Unicorn Press, 1977.
Translator, *Words for All Weather: Selected Poems of Jacques Prévert.* Greensboro, North Carolina, Unicorn Press, 1979.

* * *

Teo Savory could be a contemporary version of Colette. She has starred on the stage, and produced books of a high quality – verse, verse translation, and novels.

In her fiction, strong plot line and an engaging dialogue are her trademarks. Her poetry seems less economical. The vividness of such a novel as *To a High Place* could effectively be transferred to the poetry. Similarly, her translations seem close to the mark, but I would like to see her make the same imaginative leaps she uses in her prose.

The Unicorn Press and *Unicorn Journal*, both of which she founded in 1966, have produced a striking number of original books and translations.

—Glenna Luschei

SCANNELL, Vernon. British. Born in Spilsby, Lincolnshire, 23 January 1922. Educated at Queen's Park School, Aylesbury, Buckinghamshire; University of Leeds, Yorkshire, 1946–47. Served in the Gordon Highlanders, 1941–45. Married Josephine Higson in 1954; five children. Formerly, amateur and professional boxer. Teacher of English, Hazlewood School, Limpsfield, Surrey, 1955–62. Freelance writer and broadcaster since 1962. Resident Poet, village of Berinsfield, Oxfordshire, 1978. Recipient: Heinemann Award, 1961; Arts Council grant, 1967, 1970; Cholmondeley Award, 1974; Southern Arts Writers Fellowship, 1975. Fellow, Royal Society of Literature, 1960. Address: Folly Cottage, Nether Compton, Sherborne, Dorset, England.

PUBLICATIONS

Verse

Graves and Resurrections. London, Fortune Press, 1948.
A Mortal Pitch. London, Villiers, 1957.
The Masks of Love. London, Putnam, 1960.
A Sense of Danger. London, Putnam, 1962.
Walking Wounded. London, Eyre and Spottiswoode, 1965.

Epithets of War: Poems 1965–1969. London, Eyre and Spottiswoode, 1969.
Mastering the Craft. Oxford, Pergamon Press, 1970.
Selected Poems. London, Allison and Busby, 1971.
Company of Women. Frensham, Surrey, Sceptre Press, 1971.
Corgi Modern Poets in Focus 4, with others, edited by Jeremy Robson. London, Corgi, 1971.
Incident at West Bay. Richmond, Surrey, Keepsake Press, 1972.
The Winter Man: New Poems. London, Allison and Busby, 1973.
Meeting in Manchester. Rushden, Northamptonshire, Sceptre Press, 1974.
The Loving Game. London, Robson, 1975.
An Ilkley Quintet. Privately printed, 1975(?).
A Morden Tower Reading 1, with Alexis Lykiard. Newcastle upon Tyne, Morden Tower, 1976.

Plays

Radio Plays: *A Man's Game*, 1962; *A Door with One Eye*, 1963; *The Cancelling Dark*, music by Christopher Whelen, 1965.

Novels

The Fight. London, Peter Nevill, 1953.
The Wound and the Scar. London, Peter Nevill, 1953.
The Big Chance. London, Long, 1960.
The Shadowed Place. London, Long, 1961.
The Face of the Enemy. London, Putnam, 1961.
The Dividing Night. London, Putnam, 1962.
The Big Time. London, Longman, 1965.

Other

Edward Thomas. London, Longman, 1963.
The Dangerous Ones (juvenile). Oxford, Pergamon Press, 1970.
The Tiger and the Rose: An Autobiography. London, Hamish Hamilton, 1971.
The Apple-Raid and Other Poems (juvenile). London, Chatto and Windus, 1974.
Three Poets, Two Children, edited by Desmond Badham-Thornhill. Gloucester, Thornhill Press, 1975.
Not Without Glory: Poets of the Second World War. London, Woburn Press, 1976.
A Proper Gentleman. London, Robson, 1977.
A Lonely Game (juvenile). Exeter, Wheaton, 1979.

Editor, with Patricia Beer and Ted Hughes, *New Poems 1962.* London, Hutchinson, 1962.

Manuscript Collection: British Library, London.

Vernon Scannell comments:

Major themes: violence, the experience of war, the "sense of danger" which is part of the climate of our times; these are contrasted with poems of a more private nature which affirm the continuity and indestructibility of the creative spirit. Some verse satire; the work is traditional, very direct and firmly rooted in recognizable human experience.

* * *

Vernon Scannell's poems began to appear in the magazines in the late 1940's but (despite the 1961 Heinemann Award for Literature, which was given to his book *The Masks of Love*) it was not until the publication of *A Sense of Danger* in 1962 that he showed his real talent as a skilful memorialist of the aspirations, daydreams, lusts, disillusionments and ironies of a bruised, wry and incorrigible romantic. One supposes that it was for this romanticism that he was enlisted as a contributor to *Mavericks*, the anthology intended to be a counterblast to the suggested calm severities of *New Lines*; but in fact Scannell's poems in his later books (*A Sense of Danger* and *Walking Wounded*) have more in common with Philip Larkin than with anyone represented in *Mavericks*. The world of Scannell's incendiaries, suicides, psychopaths, adulterers – as well as telephone calls, pubs, insurance agents and radio interviews – is thoroughly mid-20th century urban, acutely and mordantly observed.

Scannell's technical organisation of a poem is generally sound (he works easily and fluently within received forms), but his language is less sure – for example, in "The Fair":

The night sniffs rich at pungent spice,
Brandy snap and diesel oil:
The stars like scattered beads of rice
Sparsely fleck the sky's deep soil ...

But this overheated metaphorical glow does not appear at all in the real successes of *A Sense of Danger*, such as "Dead Dog," "My Father's Face," "The Telephone Number," and "Hearthquake," Scannell's elegiac mood, well seen in the first two of these poems, is even better handled in *Walking Wounded*, best of all in "The Old Books" and the title-poem, which recreates a wartime memory of soldiers "Straggling the road like convicts loosely chained,/ Dragging at ankles exhaustion and despair."

But the common concern of most of Scannell's poems is with something more immediate, the ordinary hurts of the ordinary world, the dark places and betrayals of everyday experience. Colloquial, easy, even winsome, the tone of voice is generally poised above a pessimism which is lightened with wit and even, sometimes, with coarseness. It has a brutal and unequivocal honesty:

What captivates and sells, and always will,
Is what we are: vain, snarled up, and sleazy.
No one is really interesting until
To love him has become no longer easy.

—Anthony Thwaite

SCHEVILL, James (Erwin). American. Born in Berkeley, California, 10 June 1920. Educated at Harvard University, Cambridge, Massachusetts, B.S. 1942. Served in the United States Army, 1942–46. Married Margot Helmuth Blum in 1967; two children by an earlier marriage. Member of the Faculty, California College of Arts and Crafts, Oakland, 1950–59; Member of the Faculty, 1959–68, and Director of the Poetry Center, 1961–68, San Francisco State College. Since 1969, Professor of English, Brown University, Providence, Rhode Island. Recipient: National Theatre Competition prize, 1945; Dramatists Alliance Contest prize, 1948; Fund for the Advancement of Education Fellowship, 1953; Phelan Biography Competition prize, 1954; Phelan Playwriting Competition prize, 1958; Ford grant, for theatre, 1960; Rockefeller grant, 1964; William Carlos Williams Award (*Contact* magazine), 1965; Roadstead Foundation award, 1966; Rhode Island Governor's Award, 1975. Agent:

Bertha Case, 42 West 53rd Street, New York, New York 10019; or, Dr. Suzanne Czech, International Copyright Bureau Ltd., 53a Shaftesbury Avenue, London W.1, England. Address: Department of English, Brown University, Providence, Rhode Island 02912, U.S.A.

PUBLICATIONS

Verse

Tensions. San Francisco, Bern Porter, 1947.
The American Fantasies. San Francisco, Bern Porter, 1951.
The Right to Greet. San Francisco, Bern Porter, 1955.
Selected Poems 1945–1959. San Francisco, Bern Porter, 1960.
Private Dooms and Public Destinations: Poems 1945–1962. Denver, Swallow, 1962.
The Stalingrad Elegies. Denver, Swallow, 1964.
Release. Providence, Rhode Island, Hellcoal Press, 1968.
Violence and Glory: Poems 1962–1968. Chicago, Swallow Press, 1969.
The Buddhist Car and Other Characters. Chicago, Swallow Press, 1973.
Pursuing Elegy: A Poem about Haiti. Providence, Rhode Island, Copper Beech Press, 1974.
The Mayan Poems. Providence, Rhode Island, Copper Beech Press, 1978.
Force of the Eyes: A Guatemalan Sequence. Providence, Rhode Island, Copper Beech Press, 1979.

Plays

High Sinners, Low Angels, music by James Schevill, arranged by Robert Commanday (produced San Francisco, 1953). San Francisco, Bern Porter, 1953.
The Bloody Tenet (produced Providence, Rhode Island, 1956; Shrewsbury, Shropshire, 1962). Included in *The Black President and Other Plays*, 1965.
The Cid, adaptation of the play by Corneille (broadcast, 1963). Published in *Classic Theatre Anthology*, edited by Eric Bentley, New York, Doubleday, 1961.
Voices of Mass and Capital A, music by Andrew Imbrie (produced San Francisco, 1962). New York, Friendship Press, 1962.
The Master (produced San Francisco, 1963). Included in *The Black President and Other Plays*, 1965.
American Power: The Space Fan and The Master (produced Minneapolis, 1964). Included in *The Black President and Other Plays*, 1965.
The Black President and Other Plays (includes *The Bloody Tenet* and *American Power: The Space Fan and The Master*). Denver, Swallow, 1965.
The Death of Anton Webern (produced Fish Creek, Wisconsin, 1966). Included in *Violence and Glory: Poems 1962–1968*, 1969.
This Is Not True, music by Paul McIntyre (produced Minneapolis, 1967).
The Pilots (produced Providence, Rhode Island, 1970).
Oppenheimer's Chair (produced Providence, Rhode Island, 1970).
Lovecraft's Follies (produced Providence, Rhode Island, 1970). Chicago, Swallow Press, 1971.
The Ushers (produced Providence, Rhode Island, 1971).
The American Fantasies (produced New York, 1972).
Emperor Norton Lives!, music by James Schevill (produced Salt Lake City, Utah, 1972).
Fay Wray Meets King Kong (produced Providence, Rhode Island, 1974). Published in *Wastepaper Theatre*, 1978.
Sunset and Evening Stance; or, Mr. Krapp's New Tapes (produced Providence, Rhode Island, 1974). Published in *Wastepaper Theatre*, 1978.

The Telephone Murderer (produced Providence, Rhode Island, 1975). Published in *Wastepaper Theatre*, 1978.
Cathedral of Ice (produced Providence, Rhode Island, 1975).
Naked in the Garden (produced Providence, Rhode Island, 1975).
Year after Year (produced Providence, Rhode Island, 1976).

Radio Plays: *The Sound of a Soldier*, 1945; *The Death of a President*, 1945; *The Cid*, 1963 (Canada).

Novel

The Arena of Ants. Providence, Rhode Island, Copper Beech Press, 1977.

Other

Sherwood Anderson: His Life and Work. Denver, University of Denver Press, 1951.
The Roaring Market and the Silent Tomb (biographical study of the scientist and artist Bern Porter). Oakland, California, Abbey Press, 1956.
Break Out! In Search of New Theatrical Environments. Chicago, Swallow Press, 1973.

Editor, *Six Historians*, by Ferdinand Schevill. Chicago, University of Chicago Press, and London, Cambridge University Press, 1956.
Editor, *Wastepaper Theatre.* Providence, Rhode Island, Pourboire Press, 1978.

Manuscript Collection: John Hay Library, Brown University, Providence, Rhode Island.

Critical Study: "James Schevill" by Martin Robbins, in *Voyages* (Washington, D.C.), Winter 1970.

James Schevill quotes from *The Prairie Schooner* (Lincoln, Nebraska), 1970:

With the increasing restrictions of poetry to filler material in magazines, to short books of less than a hundred pages for "economy," to exclusive anthology status – the short poem has become a tormented form. Often it is too complex for its own flow. It tries to compress everything into nothing. Or, in self-defense, its simplicity is so extreme that it is merely sentimental instead of musical. If the approach is fashionably confessional, it may attempt to compress an autobiography into a page, losing the most significant details in a few pulverizing images. If the approach is narrative or dramatic, the story and the drama are often condensed into an oblique obscurity that loses the strength of both narrative and drama. If the approach is prophetic, metaphysical, the poem may seem overweighted, filled with puffed-up profundity that reflects personality rather than vision. It is not, of course, that short poems have lost their value; it is rather that the apparatus of poetry – books, magazines, readings, and criticism no matter what the viewpoints – tends to limit and deny the life-giving range of poetry that is essential. If we permit short, pseudo-lyrical forms to dominate not only do they become corrupted, but the longer narrative and dramatic forms are forsaken for the play, and the work of non-fiction. The sad result is the loss of a wide variety of subject matter that was once the domain of poetry and is now the essence of prose.

The only answer to the dominance of pseudo-lyrical forms is a greater exploration of dramatic forms and increased experimentation with the possibility of performance poems. While the poem must be personal and use the forms, the climate, of our "confessional" and psychological age, the danger is self-indulgence, self-pity. Somehow, while remaining personal, a balance must be struck by means of characterization, dramatic portrayal of situations and actions, a recovery of important social subject matter so that the poem does not remain a mere splinter of isolation.

Performance poems can always help in this respect, particularly since poetry readings are so fashionable nowadays. Everyone has sat through too many poetry readings where the poet, no matter how good his work may be on the page, has simply read his work perfunctorily and at the lowest level of audibility. Boredom is the result.

Consequently, the performance poem offers a wide range of exciting possibilities to be explored. The aim is to bring the arts together again, to make poetry the central unifier of the arts that it once was. As far as subject matter, imagery, and rhythm are concerned, performance poems provide formal opportunities of infinite variations. In a time of specialization, the poet can achieve a new unity of the arts in performance that has been too rarely attempted in poetry readings.

* * *

James Schevill, dramatist as well as poet, can make almost anything interesting: side by side in his large selected collection *Private Dooms and Public Destinations: Poems 1945–1962* there are pieces on the painter Seurat, the death of a cat, a meditation on trees, an Irish castle, a man working a hydraulic drill, and gambling in Las Vagas. It is perhaps inevitable that some of these subjects, and they are typical, move him more than others, and that his greatest thrust be reserved for the things that most matter to him (his wartime experiences as a coastguardsman, a scientist like Fabre), yet he is never trivial and poem after poem offers sharp responses and insights. He is, in short, a poet all the way, a somewhat rare species in our time, and has the vitality and the natural equipment to make so strenuous a poetic life possible: curiosity, sensitivity, wide learning and a truly impressive gift with language, reminding one at times of Dylan Thomas'. Here is the first stanza of "The Blue Jay" from the above mentioned collection:

Blue jay in the garden,
Cocky bastard!
Boor on stilts in your Cyrano plume
Where the purple wistaria hangs like grapes.
Go flirt in the boggy woods;
In the gardens of spring,
When the grosbeak sings from the song-struck tree,
What are you but a duenna to beauty,
The claptrap chaperon?

If it is true that reading the poet on such a variety of subjects, however unified the vision from piece to piece, can be a dizzying experience, his volume *The Stalingrad Elegies* offers something altogether different: it is a daring, deeply imaginative and altogether successful experiment, surely one of the most interesting books to come out of the mid-60's. Here the poet has found a theme – a licked German army trapped in the snows of Stalingrad and their attempts, for the most part puny, occasionally noble, to get their feelings into letters home – that taxes his talent to the full, and the talent shows itself to be formidable. One can read the book as one reads an exciting story, so carefully is the volume structured and variety assured – through the selection of sufficiently dissimilar types, through the choice of stanza patterns and meters. Here in one of the shortest poems a soldier writes his wife:

Bury your face in your hands
in order to forget;
You said that
in your last letter ...
Two months of happiness
We had as man and wife,
Then I marched into
The dark nights of the east,

My hands slipping
    from your body
As if it were only a dream of sex,
Not a marriage ... I live
In a sense of space
And time so huge
    that they devour
Every human face.
I can't even imagine your flesh
Any more; too cold ...
You are the wife of death.

James Schevill, a poet of strong gifts and generous impulses, has created a durable body of work, some of it, as in *The Stalingrad Elegies*, of major order.

—Lucien Stryk

SCHMIDT, Michael (Norton). Mexican. Born in Mexico City, 2 March 1947. Educated at Christ's Hospital, Horsham, Sussex; Harvard University, Cambridge, Massachusetts; Wadham College, Oxford, B.A. in English 1970. Since 1969, Managing Director, Carcanet Press Ltd., Oxford, later Cheadle, Cheshire, and Manchester; since 1972, Fellow, Manchester Poetry Centre; since 1973. Co-Editor, *Poetry Nation*, later *PN Review*. Address: c/o Carcanet Press, 330 Corn Exchange Buildings, Manchester M4 3BG, England.

PUBLICATIONS

Verse

Black Buildings. Oxford, Carcanet Press, 1969.
One Eye Mirror Cold. Oxford, Sycamore Press, 1970.
Bedlam and the Oakwood: Essays on Various Fictions. Oxford, Carcanet Press, 1970.
Desert of Lions. Oxford, Carcanet Press, 1972.
It Was My Tree. London, Anvil Press Poetry, 1972.
My Brother Gloucester: New Poems. Manchester, Carcanet Press, 1976.
A Change of Affairs. London, Anvil Press Poetry, 1978.

Other

A Reader's Guide to Fifty Poets from Hardy to Hill [*from Gower to Hopkins*]. London, Pan, 2 vols., 1979.

Editor, with Grevel Lindop, *British Poetry since 1960: A Critical Survey.* Oxford, Carcanet Press, 1972.
Editor, *Ten English Poets.* Manchester, Carcanet Press, 1976.
Editor, *The Avoidance of Literature: Collected Essays 1937–1978*, by C. H. Sisson. Manchester, Carcanet Press, 1978.

Translator, with Edward Kissam, *Flower and Song: Poems of the Aztec Peoples.* London, Anvil Press Poetry, 1977.

* * *

For a poet still early in his career, Michael Schmidt displays a formidable precocity. It is formidable because it is not showing off, not posturing, but has a confidence which seems to arise from the whole personality of the poet. Schmidt almost never writes poems of direct individual feeling, but he is not, on this account, ever devious or obscure; he never assaults us either with joy or grief, but he is never cold. He has read much and travelled much. From his travels much of the basic material of his work is drawn. It supplies him with imagery and description. Even in the early work of 1968 in *It Was My Tree*, sympathy for others is generalised and distanced by the utmost care in the use of language. Here, for example, are some lines from a poem called "Cancer":

... Find out
who is this discoloured
body always half-awake
to itself. A music

from the unrusting
instruments. How deep
the body drinks, customary
thirst, the frightened moon.

There is no lack either of compassion or powerful feeling here, but it is checked by the immediacy of imagery. The same thing happens in the last stanza of "For Pasternak":

Flowers have fallen on us
yellow like wings, fragrant
with the powder of the air; small petals
delicate as the sky. We have been
unable to hold them.

That last line is close to sadness, but grief is not allowed to overflow.

In his booklet of 1969, Michael Schmidt continued in much the same vein. Since then he has brought out two full-scale volumes, *Bedlam and the Oakwood* and *Desert of the Lions*. There are no violent developments to be discerned in either of these volumes but rather a surer grasp of Schmidt's early manner, a keener awareness of language and its potentialities for imagery and description. If he is to be faulted, then one can only do so by pointing out the lack of any lyrical element in his poems and often an unconscious unwillingness to confront the reader directly. The appearance of concealment is at present only a minor blemish, though there are moments when one longs for the poet to appear fully himself, for the curtain to be raised. The following is an example of what I mean, taken from "Nailed like Stoats":

Around you the suppliant
generosity to gifted invalids –
a lifetime of it. Critics were kept at bay.
Your correspondence was meticulously edited.

Echoes of other poets are hard to find in Schmidt's work but, certainly in this poem, one can detect a small debt to early and middle period Auden. *Bedlam and the Oakwood* is divided into sections, and Part I is called "Biographies." Schmidt gives us most vivid portraits of famous writers, as in "Jonathan Swift's Body," "Samuel Johnson's Marriage" and "Hatching." In these pieces the poet identifies himself completely with his chosen characters and makes them truly alive. In another section, places are also powerfully summoned up; one thinks particularly of "Luncheon" and "Venice: A Letter to Robert Browning."

"Some Fictions," yet another section of *Bedlam and the Oakwood*, does show an inclination on the poet's part to reveal himself in the round, but he is more willing to display his thoughts than his feelings, and he is usually quick to move on to other people or to characters from literature. This tendency is evident in a poem called "Appendix": "This reading leaves me seated,/in the gateway to some unlosable wisdom,/and here at least I am no cynic." In these lines, and the following ones from "Flown Eagle," Schmidt comes closest to setting aside his finely chosen language and careful rhythms and telling us about himself:

> I have had to dispose of eagles, and the
> things they seemed to touch: sky,
> liner, and the deserted sea
> which leaves me smaller territory.

Starting with such an accomplished though somewhat limited technique together with so much external material to work upon, Schmidt could hardly advance, in *Desert of the Lions*, except by way of more personal revelation or a real lyric impulse. The latter does not appear but, even if only unobtrusively, the former fitfully does. Amid the scintillating and accurately conveyed settings we come upon such passages as the following: "I follow you hunting with jar and trowel,/with gloves, this poison tail" ("Scorpion"); "Speak cautiously before morning/of fishermen – the men/with nets, with hooks, with knives" and "I eavesdrop on them/from our balcony ..." ("Before Morning"); "We can move near./We cannot touch this bird, stiff,/almost a sawdust dummy, but on fire" ("Reconciliation").

In such poems as these and "Funerals," "Hypothesis," the title poem itself, and "Tourist Waking," this poet can be sensed. Wherever he goes, he enters a new country, city, landscape, and transforms them by the power of his sharp visual gift and his control over form. For so young a man, all this, together with his understanding of many different people, is quite exceptional. Yet this very achievement makes it extremely hard to predict where he can move next. A more varied feeling for movement and sound would certainly be a definite advance, together with a more intimate revelation of such an interesting personality. We have the intellect; now we want more of the heart.

—Elizabeth Jennings

SCHMITZ, Dennis. American. Born in Dubuque, Iowa, 11 August 1937. Educated at Loras College, Dubuque, B.A. 1959; University of Chicago, M.A. 1961. Married Loretta D'Agostino in 1960; five children. Instructor, Illinois Institute of Technology, Chicago, 1961–62, and University of Wisconsin, Milwaukee, 1962–66. Since 1966, Member of the Faculty, and currently Professor of English, California State University, Sacramento. Recipient: New York Poetry Center Discovery Award, 1968; Big Table Series of Younger Poets Award, 1969; National Endowment for the Arts grant, 1976; Guggenheim Fellowship, 1978. Address: 1348 57th Street, Sacramento, California 95819, U.S.A.

PUBLICATIONS

Verse

We Weep for Our Strangeness. Chicago, Follett, 1969.
Double Exposures. Oberlin, Ohio, Triskelion Press, 1971.
Goodwill, Inc. New York, Ecco Press, 1976.

* * *

In the death-haunted poems in Dennis Schmitz's *We Weep for Our Strangeness* a dying rabbit's intestines wind "like roads/between the bones," a remembered farm "fed/on the blue hillsides," ants slide "their hills/wave on lipless wave/down the long bay of grass."

Landscape endures, though in ceaseless modification by glacier, flood, burial, river, ants. Man seems "lost" here, in the religious sense of the word. And indeed God is named often in these poems, and appears still more frequently. In the book's last poem, "The Rescue," three men are lost on a canoe trip. One of them – Peter! – is sick. Finally a small plane flies over:

we signal

we are here, to those above
that we have suffered
the lonely ocean of green
life.

Has the plane spotted them? They can't be sure, but one of them says hopefully that help will come, someone will rescue them: "yes,/I said to Jack, yes he will."

Neither the religious echoes nor the emotional urgency of Schmitz's poems assumes a loud voice. His style is colloquial, his diction Midwestern. The conversational tone and sparse punctuation would make for swift, fluid poems, were not his lines consistently slowed – sometimes nearly broken down – by enjambment. Sometimes the result is needlessly knotty:

%s are the signs. I remember
the birds broke up
on the table. top. scratches
like soft entrails we read sad
tidings if we are to believe
examine the corners

and so on.

Such lapses are few. The three relaxed and fully achieved eclogues beginning the book are beyond the capabilities of most of his contemporaries. Among them he stands out for the authenticity of his vision, its thick obsession with death and its convincing religiosity:

because you have loved your body closes its doors
because you have eaten now the poor came.
& your plate is clean as the skull of God.

—William Matthews

SCHROEDER, Andreas (Peter). Canadian. Born in Hoheneggelsen, Germany, 26 November 1946. Educated at the University of British Columbia. Vancouver, 1966–71, B.A. 1969, M.A. in creative writing and comparative literature 1971; University of Toronto, 1968. Editorial Assistant, *Prism International*, Vancouver, 1968–69; Member, Board of Directors, British Columbia Film Cooperative, 1970–71; Editor, *Poetry Canada*, Toronto, 1970–71. Since 1969, Founding Editor, with J. Michael Yates, *Contemporary Literature in Translation*, Vancouver; since 1970, Literary Critic, *Vancouver Province-Pacific Press*; since 1971, Editorial Board Member, *Canadian Fiction Magazine*, Prince George, British Columbia. Faculty Member, University of Victoria, 1975–77. Chairman, Writers' Union of Canada, 1976–77. Recipient: Canada Council grant, 1968, bursary, 1969, 1971; Gordon Woodward Memorial award, for prose, 1969; National Film Board grant, 1970; Canadian Film

Development grant, 1971. Address: P.O. Box 3127, Mission City, British Columbia, V2V 4JE, Canada.

PUBLICATIONS

Verse

The Ozone Minotaur. Vancouver, Sono Nis Press, 1969.
File of Uncertainties. Vancouver, Sono Nis Press, 1971.
uniVerse, with David Frith. Vancouver, MASSage Press, 1971.

Plays

Screenplays: *The Plastic Mile*, 1969; *Immobile*, 1969; *The Pub*, 1970; *The Late Man*, 1972.

Short Stories

The Late Man. Vancouver, Sono Nis Press, 1971.

Other

Shaking It Rough: A Prison Memoir. Toronto, Doubleday, 1976; New York, Doubleday, 1977.

Editor, with J. Michael Yates, *Contemporary Poetry of British Columbia.* Vancouver, Sono Nis Press, 2 vols., 1970–72.
Editor, with Rudy Wiebe, *Stories from Pacific and Arctic Canada.* Toronto, Macmillan, 1974.

Translator, with Michael Bullock, *The Stage and Creative Arts.* Greenwich, Connecticut, New York Graphic Society, 1969.
Translator, *Collected Stories of Ilse Aichinger.* Vancouver, Sono Nis Press, 1974.

Critical Studies: "The Relevance of Surrealism with Some Canadian Perspectives" by Paul Green, in *Mosaic* (Winnipeg, Manitoba), Summer 1969; "The O-Zone and Other Places" by Alan Shucard, in *Canadian Literature 48* (Vancouver), Spring 1971; "Swarming of Poets" by George Woodcock, in *Canadian Literature 50* (Vancouver), Winter 1971; "A Certain Degree of Madness" by Patricia Morley, in *Ottawa Journal*, 13 May 1972.

Andreas Schroeder comments:

While I have always made considerable use of the surreal mode in both my poetry and prose, my more recent work varies greatly with respect to its surreality. The first book of verse which I published (*The Ozone Minotaur*) was a fairly orthodox example of the genre; the second (*File of Uncertainties*) was only occasionally characteristic of it. I find myself moving more and more toward that thin line where reality and surreality mesh, where a couple making love and a couple killing each other appear involved in identical acts. The result tends often to be cinematic, for which reason many of the stories have proven themselves easily adaptable to film scripts. My poetry, too, makes increasing use of a more linear logic.

* * *

Andreas Schroeder, German-born though he emigrated in childhood, is unusually international among Canadian poets in his literary affiliations. It is impossible to consider him as a poet apart from his activities as editor of *Contemporary Literature in Translation*. His imaginative world is related to Kafka's and, equally, to that of Borges, and his poems have an intellectual complexity rare among young North American poets but relating him directly to the Modernist tradition. He has published two books of verse, *The Ozone Minotaur* and *File of Uncertainties*; the development between them is considerable. The earlier poems are largely neo-surrealist in character, seeking to give verisimilitude to implausible but potent myths, such as "Introduction" in which "three men in tails" cross a cornfield to a creek:

> ... The man in the middle
> of the stream is stepping on the fish;
> he is intent. The fish swim through
> him and he walks through the fish.
> Notice that he is not surprised. The
> man on the other bank is sifting debris
> into a notebook; notice him. The man on
> the bank is now measuring the size of
> the sand grains.
> The man in the middle of the creek is
> walking on.
> He is stepping on the fish.

Schroeder's later poems, in *File of Uncertainties*, explore ambiguities of condition and consciousness like those exemplified in the man through whom the fish swim as he walks through them. The recognition of multiple consciousness, and the sense of being trapped in many selves, are in these later poems more explicit, more apprehensive, more convincing:

> Now, my constant fear:
> To stumble across my own remains
> when this snow melts.

—George Woodcock

SCHUYLER, James (Marcus). American. Born in Chicago, Illinois, 9 November 1923. Educated at Bethany College, West Virginia. Lived in Italy for several years. Currently, Staff Member, Museum of Modern Art, New York. Recipient: Frank O'Hara Prize (*Poetry*, Chicago), 1969; National Endowment for the Arts grant, 1969, 1972; National Institute of Arts and Letters award, 1977. Address: 49 South Main Street, Southampton, New York 11968, U.S.A.

PUBLICATIONS

Verse

Salute. New York, Tiber Press, 1960.
May 24th or So. New York, Tibor de Nagy, 1966.
Freely Espousing. New York, Doubleday, 1969.
The Crystal Lithium. New York, Random House, 1972.
A Sun Cab. New York, Boke, 1972.

Penguin Modern Poets 24, with Kenneth Koch and Kenward Elmslie. London, Penguin, 1973.
Hymn to Life. New York, Random House, 1974.
Song. Syracuse, New York, Kermani Press, 1976.
The Fireproof Floors of Witley Court: English Songs and Dances. Newark, Vermont, Janus Press, 1976.
The Home Book: Prose and Poems 1951–1970, edited by Trevor Winkfield. Calais, Vermont, Z Press, 1977.
What's for Dinner? Santa Barbara, California, Black Sparrow Press, 1978.

Recording: *A Picnic Cantata*, music by Paul Bowles, Columbia, 1955.

Play

Unpacking the Black Trunk, with Kenward Elmslie (produced New York, 1965).

Novels

Alfred and Guinevere. New York, Harcourt Brace, 1958.
A Nest of Ninnies, with John Ashbery. New York, Dutton, 1969.

Other

The Morning of the Poem. New York, Farras Straus, 1980.

* * *

James Schuyler is a poet of the New York School who doesn't particularly care for New York City, preferring those neighboring artistic retreats, Vermont and Long Island. He espouses:

the sinuous beauty of words like allergy
the tonic resonance of
pill when used as in
"she is a pill"
on the other hand I am not going to espouse any short stories in
which lawn mowers clack.
No, it is absolutely forbidden
for words to echo the act described; or try to. Except very directly
as in
bong. And tickle.

His friends Robert Dash and Fairfield Porter are landscape painters and so, in a sense, is Schuyler. He describes what he sees, which is what he loves, and cheers. He sees time, for instance, in its subcategory, the seasons:

It's
not – "the fly buzzed"
finding moods, reflectives:
fall
equals melancholy, spring,
get laid: but to turn it all
one way: in repetition, change:
a continuity, the what
of which you are a part.

He sees. But he doesn't like people who can't see, who claim what they are seeing is an example of something they've read. Schuyler talked to the fog about this very matter:

Fog
you are like the tedium you recall: "Walking
across Central Park it was beautiful this
morning." "I know I know"
she glassily grimaced, "just like
a Chinese painting." Thanks, fog:
it's handy, getting to know someone
so instantly you don't want to
know them any better or further.

Schuyler also writes letters to the days of June. Like nature and like Fairfield Porter, he is prolific. Lately he's broken his collections into sequences, autumn at Kenward's place in Vermont, a really great and ongoing love affair, spring in (Saratoga) Springs.

He talks casually about ecstasy, and he's not nearly as theoretical and acerbic as these three quotes indicate. "Salute" is more representative:

Past is past, and if one
remembers what one meant
to do and never did, is
not to have thought to do
enough? Like that gather-
ing of one of each I
planned, to gather one
of each kind of clover,
daisy, paintbrush that
grew in that field
the cabin stood in and
study them one afternoon
before they wilted. Past
is past. I salute
that various field.

—Michael André

SCHWERNER, Armand. American. Born in Antwerp, Belgium, 11 May 1927. Educated at Cornell University, Ithaca, New York, 1945–47; University of Geneva, Switzerland, 1947–48; Columbia University, New York, B.S. 1950, M.A. 1964. Served in the United States Navy, 1945–46. Married Doloris Holmes in 1961 (divorced, 1978); two sons. Formerly, Instructor in English and French, Barnard School for Boys, Riverdale, New York; Instructor in English, Long Island University, New York, 1963–64. Instructor, 1964–66, Assistant Professor, 1966–69, Associate Professor, 1969–73, and since 1973, Professor of English, College of Staten Island, City University of New York. Recipient: National Endowment for the Arts grant, 1973; Creative Artists Public Service grant, 1973, 1975. Address: 30 Catlin Avenue, Staten Island, New York 10304, U.S.A.

PUBLICATIONS

Verse

The Lightfall. New York, Hawk's Well Press, 1963.
The Tablets I–VIII. West Branch, Iowa, Cummington Press, 1968.
(if personal). Los Angeles, Black Sparrow Press, 1968.
Seaweed. Los Angeles, Black Sparrow Press, 1969.
The Tablets I–XV. New York, Grossman, 1971.
Bacchae Sonnets. Omaha, Nebraska, Abattoir, 1974.
The Tablets XVI–XVIII. Deerfield, Massachusetts, Heron Press, 1976.
The Triumph of the Will. Mount Horeb, Wisconsin, Perishable Press, 1976.
This Practice: Tablet XIX and Other Poems. London, Permanent Press, 1976.
The Bacchae Sonnets 1–7. Baltimore, Pod Press, 1977.
The Work, The Joy, and the Triumph of the Will. New York, New Rivers Press, 1977.

Other

Stendhal's "The Red and the Black": Notes and Criticism. New York, Study Master, 1963.
The Domesday Dictionary, with Donald M. Kaplan. New York, Simon and Schuster, 1963; London, Cape, 1964.
A Farewell to Arms: A Critical Commentary. New York, Study Master, 1963.
Billy Budd and Typee: Critical Commentary. New York, American R.D.M., 1964.
The Sound and the Fury: A Critical Commentary, with Jerome Neibrief. New York, American R.D.M., 1964.
John Steinbeck's "Of Mice and Men." New York, Monarch Press, 1965.
John Steinbeck's "The Red Pony" and "The Pearl." New York, Monarch Press, 1965.
André Gide's "The Immoralist," "Strait Is the Gate," and Other Works: A Critical Commentary. New York, Monarch Press, 1966.
Dos Passos' "U.S.A." and Other Works. New York, Monarch Press, 1966.
Albert Camus' "The Stranger": A Critical Commentary. New York, Monarch Press, 1970.

Translator, *Redspell: Eleven American Indian Adaptations.* Mount Horeb, Wisconsin, Perishable Press, 1975.

Critical Studies: "Son of the Cantos?" by Stanley Sultan, in *Chelsea* (New York), 1971; Allen Planz, in *The Nation* (New York), 19 June 1972; John Shawcross, in *American Poetry Review* (Philadelphia), March 1973; Diane Wakoski, in *Parnassus* (New York), Spring 1973; *Vort 8* (Bloomington, Indiana), 1975; Hugh Kenner, in *New York Times Book Review*, 12 February and 4 June 1978; Richard Kostelanetz, in *Performing Arts* (New York), Winter 1978.

* * *

Armand Schwerner is a multi-talented man and that can be seen plainly in the gigantic scope of his most important collection of poems, *The Tablets*. These amazing poems have a number of qualities that make them praiseworthy and one which makes them stand apart from other poems. *The Tablets* is the closest thing I have seen to a theatrical or oral poetry produced today. They are not merely sound poems, by the way, and I do not mean to imply that. They are poems which the reader/listener must hear before he can understand their whole reality.

The Tablets are poems which satirize the fashionable inclination for poets to be anthropologists, and translators and purveyors of pre-historic knowledge. They purport to be a series of Icelandic tablets dug up by some archaeologist and translated by a theologian-scholar who himself actually makes up half the poetry out of the missing sections. The character of the author-translator is a brilliant act of self-satire by Schwerner himself, who like classical comedians has taken the absurd and ridiculous world he lives in and embodied the ridiculous, satirized it at times, while also creating a beautiful religious and love poetry, as well as a witty game, out of the whole business. The author-translator is so important in this piece that he must be performed, and Schwerner lives in the right age of poetry, for he is a magnificent performer of his own drama.

The Tablets are a topical poetry, for they satirize the poetry world of the 60's and 70's, and they also take advantage of a convention of our times, that poets read their own poems aloud. Yet, this satiric undercurrent is not such a limitation, for the poems themselves are filled with pathos and humor and beautiful images. Schwerner, who began as an academic poet, was opened up to the wider possibilities of poetry by the avant garde poet Jackson Mac Low in the early 1960's. But that he was ready to put the influence to good use is evident from the success of *The Tablets*.

—Diane Wakoski

SCOTT, Alexander. British (Scottish). Born in Aberdeen, 28 November 1920. Educated at Aberdeen Academy, 1933–39; Aberdeen University, 1939–41, 1945–47, M.A. (honours) in English 1947. Served in the British Army, 1941–45: Military Cross, 1945. Married Catherine Goodall in 1944; two sons. Assistant Lecturer, Edinburgh University, 1947–48. Lecturer, 1948–63, Senior Lecturer, 1963–71, since 1971, Head of the Department and since 1976, Reader in Scottish Literature, Glasgow University. Editor, *Northeast Review*, 1945–46; *Scots Review*, 1950–51; *Saltire Review*, Edinburgh, 1954–57; General Editor, Scottish Library, Calder and Boyars, London, 1968–71, and Scottish Series, Routledge and Kegan Paul, London, 1972–75. Since 1968, Secretary, Universities Committee on Scottish Literature. Recipient: Festival of Britain Award, for poetry, 1951, for verse drama, 1951; Arts Council Award, for drama, 1952; Scottish Community Drama Association Award, 1954; Scottish Arts Council Award, 1969. Address: 5 Doune Gardens, Glasgow G20 6DJ, Scotland.

PUBLICATIONS

Verse

The Latest in Elegies. Glasgow, Caledonian Press, 1949.
Selected Poems. Edinburgh, Oliver and Boyd, 1950.
Mouth Music: Poems and Diversions. Edinburgh, M. Macdonald, 1954.
Cantrips. Preston, Lancashire, Akros, 1968.
Greek Fire. Preston, Lancashire, Akros, 1971.
Double Agent. Preston, Lancashire, Akros, 1972.
Selected Poems 1943–1974. Preston, Lancashire, Akros, 1975.
Poems in Scots. Glasgow, Scotsown, 1978.

Plays

Prometheus 48 (produced Aberdeen, 1948). Aberdeen, S.R.C., 1948.
Untrue Thomas. Glasgow, Caledonian Press, 1952.

Right Royal (produced Glasgow, 1954).
Shetland Yarn. London, Evans, 1954.
Tam O'Shanter's Tryst (produced Glasgow, 1955).
The Last Time I Saw Paris. Edinburgh, Saltire Review, 1957.
Truth To Tell (produced Glasgow, 1958).

Other

Still Life: William Soutar 1898–1943. London, Chambers, 1958.
The MacDiarmid Makars 1923–1972. Preston, Lancashire, Akros, 1972.

Editor, *Selected Poems of William Jeffrey*. Edinburgh, Serif, 1951.
Editor, *The Poems of Alexander Scott, 1530–1584*. Edinburgh, Oliver and Boyd, 1952.
Editor, *Diaries of a Dying Man*, by William Soutar. Edinburgh, Chambers, 1955.
Editor, with Norman MacCaig, *Contemporary Scottish Verse*. London, Calder and Boyars, 1970.
Editor, with Michael Grieve, *The Hugh MacDiarmid Anthology: Poems in Scots and English*. London, Routledge, 1972.
Editor, with Douglas Gifford, *Neil M. Gunn: The Man and the Writer*. Edinburgh, Blackwood, and New York, Barnes and Noble, 1973.
Editor, with Maurice Lindsay and Roderick Watson, *Scottish Poetry 7–9*. Glasgow, University of Glasgow Press, 1 vol., 1974; Manchester Carcanet Press, 2 vols, 1975–76.
Editor, *Modern Scots Verse 1922–1977*. Preston, Lancashire, Akros, 1978.

Manuscript Collection: National Library of Scotland, Edinburgh.

Critical Studies: by Norman MacCaig, in *Akros 9* (Preston, Lancashire), 1969; George Bruce, in *Akros 19* (Preston, Lancashire), 1972; Lorn Macintyre, in *Akros 25* (Preston, Lancashire), 1974; David Buchan, in *Library Review* (Glasgow), 1975; *Two North-East Makars* by Leonard Mann, Preston, Lancashire, Akros, 1976; Norman MacCaig, in *Studies in Scottish Literature* (Columbia, South Carolina), 1978.

Alexander Scott comments:

I write in both English and Scots, the latter being my first speech. With me a poem begins itself, as it were, from a phrase which flashes into the mind unbidden and which may present itself in either English or Scots. Since the inception of any poem of mine is to that extent involuntary, I am not bothered, in any one case, by having to make a choice between the two languages. The choice is already made for me, by the initial words themselves, as they rise into the consciousness. Any other procedure, in my view, would be a falsehood so fundamental as to make a mockery of the poetic act.

* * *

Hugh MacDiarmid has said, with a typically Scottish finality, "We have no use for emotions, let alone sentiments, but are solely concerned with passions." If this is not true, regrettably, of all Scots, it is true of Alexander Scott, except that emotions do occasionally creep in – but not subversively, since a stiffening pith in the centre prevents them from deliquescing into sentimentality. He represents, in fact, more than any contemporary Scots poet other than MacDiarmid, those characteristic elements that define the Scots tradition and which are centred on a stubborn, passionate and sardonic realism that eschews the egotistical sublime, that deals with a remarkably high hand with what makes the substance of so much poetry – love, death, God, the Devil, etc. – and that robustly refuses to ignore the grit that forms the pearl, or even the grit. He also provides in himself a flat contradiction of the comical assumption that the Scots are dour, inarticulate and humourless and informs his work with the spirited gusto that makes, for example, Burns so heart-warming a writer.

Because these are his characteristic qualities, unsubtle sensibilities have been known to accuse him of a lack of sympathy, of brashness, of a brutal and unfeeling response to the tears of things. He can be shocking. But the hard directness of his statements (he is an Aberdonian and writes in granite) is infused with a real sympathy, a real tenderness, made triumphantly explicit in his love poems.

The bulk and the best of his poems are in Scots. Since this was his natural speech when he was young and since he has studied it in a scholarly, and responsive, way ever since, it is not surprising that he handles it with a lively naturalness that craftily exploits the wide range of expressive sounds that this almost too onomatopoeic language offers for use, or abuse. This Scots is muscular, athletic, with no fat on its bones, and is quite free from the pedantic antiquarianism that flaws the work of some other Scottish writers. And if his language is contemporary, so are his themes. He takes account of, but is not obsessed by, the past, either his own or his country's.

As for his poems in English, they could not have been written by anyone else. All the same, more of the author gets into the Scots poems – though in *Cantrips* there are some which offer evidence of a new thing in Scott's work, an exploration of looser forms which point forward to what may well be a new sort of achievement.

The plays not surprisingly share most of the characteristics of the poems, except that they mainly concern themselves with situations originally reasonable enough but roisterously developed according to the curious logic of farce. The life they have, and it is plenty, derives from Scott's comic invention, in plot and dialogue, and that healthy gusto which is so prominent a feature in all his work.

—Norman MacCaig

SCOTT, F(rancis) R(eginald). Canadian. Born in Quebec City, 1 August 1899. Educated at Quebec High School; Bishop's College, Lennoxville, Quebec, B.A. 1919; Magdelen College, Oxford (Rhodes Scholar), B.A. 1922, B.Litt. 1923; McGill University, Montreal, B.C.L. 1927, called to the Quebec Bar, 1927. Married Marian Mildred Dale in 1928; one son. Teacher, Quebec High School, 1919; Bishop's College School, Lennoxville, 1920; Lower Canada College, Montreal, 1923. Assistant Professor of Federal and Constitutional Law, 1928–34, Professor of Civil Law, 1934–54, Macdonald Professor of Law, 1955–67, Dean of the Faculty of Law, 1961–64, and Visiting Professor, French Canada Studies Programme, 1967–69, McGill University. Visiting Lecturer, University of Toronto Law School, 1953–54, Michigan State University, East Lansing, 1957, and Dalhouse University Law School, Halifax, Nova Scotia, 1969–71. National Chairman, C.C.F. Party, 1942–50; helped found New Democratic Party, 1960. U.N. Technical Assistant, Burma, 1952. Chairman, Canadian Writers Conference, 1955. Civil Liberties Counsel before the Supreme Court of Canada, 1956–64. Formerly, Co-Founding Editor, with A. J. M. Smith, *McGill Fortnightly Review*, Montreal, 1925; Editor, *Canada Forum*, Toronto, *Canada Mercury, Preview*, and *Northern Review*, Montreal. Recipient: Guggenheim Fellowship, 1940; Guarantor's Prize (*Poetry*, Chicago), 1945; Royal Society of Canada Fellowship, 1947, and Lorne Pierce Medal, 1962; *Northern Review* Award, 1951; Banff Springs Festival Gold Medal, 1958; Quebec Government Prize, 1964; Canada Council Molson Award, 1965, grant, 1974, and translation prize, 1977; Governor-General's Award, 1978. LL.D.: Dalhousie University, Halifax, Nova Scotia, 1958; University of Manitoba, Winnipeg, 1961; Queen's University, Kingston,

Ontario, 1964; University of British Columbia, Vancouver, 1965; Université de Montréal, 1966; Osgoode Hall Law School, Downsview, Ontario, 1966; McGill University, 1967; LL.B.: University of Saskatchewan, Saskatoon, 1965. Honorary Member, American Academy of Arts and Sciences, 1967; Corresponding Member, British Academy, 1978. Companion, Order of Canada, 1967. Address: 451 Clark Avenue, Westmont, Montreal H3Y 3C5, Canada.

PUBLICATIONS

Verse

Overture. Toronto, Ryerson Press, 1945.
Events and Signals. Toronto, Ryerson Press, 1954.
The Eye of the Needle: Satires, Sorties, Sundries. Montreal, Contact Press, 1957.
Signature. Vancouver, Klanak Press, 1964.
Selected Poems. Toronto, Oxford University Press, 1966.
Trouvailles: Poems from Prose. Montreal, Delta Canada, 1967.
Poets Between the Wars, with others, edited by Milton T. Wilson. Toronto, McClelland and Stewart, 1967.
The Dance Is One. Toronto, McClelland and Stewart, 1973.

Play

The Roncarelli Affair, with Mavor Moore (televised, 1974). Published in *The Play's the Thing: Four Original Television Dramas*, edited by Tony Gifford, Toronto, Macmillan, 1976.

Other

Admiralty Jurisdiction and Colonial Courts. Montreal, McGill University Press, 1929.
Social Reconstruction and the B.N.A. Act. Toronto, Nelson, 1934.
Labour Conditions in the Men's Clothing Industry, with H. M. Cassidy. Toronto, Institute of Pacific Relations, 1935.
Social Planning for Canada (co-author). Toronto, 1935.
Democracy Needs Socialism. Toronto, Nelson, 1938.
Canada and the Commonwealth. Toronto, Canadian Institution of International Affairs, 1938.
Canada Today: A Study of Her National Interests and National Policy. London and Toronto, Oxford University Press, 1938.
Canada and the United States. Boston, World Peace Organization, 1941.
Make This Your Canada: A Review of C.C.F. History and Policy, with David Lewis. Toronto, Central Canada Publishing, 1943.
Cooperation for What? Canada and the British Commonwealth. New York, Institute of Pacific Relation, 1944.
New Horizons for Socialism. Ottawa, Wordsworth House, 1951.
The World War Against Poverty, with R. A. MacKay and A. E. Ritchie. Toronto, University of Toronto Press, 1953.
The World's Civil Service. New York, Carnegie Endowment for International Peace, 1954.
Evolving Canadian Federalism. Durham, North Carolina, Duke University Press, 1958.
The Canadian Constitution and Human Rights (radio talks). Toronto, Canadian Broadcasting Corporation, 1959.
Civil Liberties and Canadian Federalism. Toronto, University of Toronto Press, 1959.

Dialogue sur la Traduction, with Anne Hébert. Montreal, Editions HMH, 1970.
Essays on the Constitution: Aspects of Canadian Law and Politics. Toronto, University of Toronto Press, 1977.

Editor, with A. J. M. Smith, *New Provinces: Poems of Several Authors.* Toronto, Macmillan, 1936.
Editor, with Alexander Brady, *Canada after the War: Attitudes of Political, Social, and Economic Policies in Post-War Canada.* Toronto, Canadian Institute of Internal Affairs, 1944.
Editor, with A. J. M. Smith, *The Blasted Pine: An Anthology of Satire, Invective and Disrespectful Verse, Chiefly by Canadian Writers.* Toronto, Macmillan, 1957; revised edition, 1967.
Editor, with Michael Oliver, *Quebec States Her Case: Speeches and Articles from Quebec in the Years of Unrest.* Toronto, Macmillan, 1964.

Translator, *St. Denys Garneau and Anne Hébert.* Vancouver, Klanak Press, 1961.
Translator, *Poems of French Canada.* Vancouver, Blackfish Press, 1977.

Critical Studies: *Ten Canadian Poets*, edited by Desmond Pacey, Toronto, Ryerson Press, 1958; *The Literary History of Canada*, edited by Carl F. Klinck, Toronto, University of Toronto Press, 1965; "F. R. Scott and Some of His Poems" by A. J. M. Smith, in *Canadian Literature 31* (Vancouver), Winter 1967; *The McGill Movement: A. J. M. Smith, F. R. Scott, and Leo Kennedy* edited by Peter Stevens, Toronto, Ryerson Press, 1969; "The Road Back to Eden: The Poetry of F. R. Scott" by Stephen Scobie, in *Queen's Quarterly* (Kingston, Ontario), Autumn 1972; Clara Thomas, in *Our Nature – Our Voices: A Guidebook to English-Canadian Literature*, Toronto, New Press, 1972.

F. R. Scott comments:

What is my personal conception of poetry? If I could define it, it would not be very different from my conception of life itself. The poet is a "maker"; the poetic potential underlies all living and all art, but comes to life in the poet through his special power to make something new and true with words. His tool is language, with which he explores the frontiers of the world inside and the world outside man. His method, and his revelations, are both unique, and can only flourish if he is free to pursue his vision wherever it may lead him.

* * *

F. R. Scott has been a kind of "double agent" who has succeeded in combining an active public life in politics and university teaching with the contemplative and yet very active and practical life of a poet. While still an undergraduate at McGill he helped to introduce the new poetry of the Eliot-Pound tradition into Canada, and for more than thirty years he has been a leader of groups of younger poets and a stimulating force in the poetry scene. His own verse is divided into satirical poetry, a pungent form of social and political criticism, love poems ranging from the simple to the metaphysically or psychologically complex, and nature poems, which begin with simple examples of a northern imagism and develop into an elegance of style and a richness of allusion that suggest at times a Canadian Marvell.

"Lakeshore," the fine poem that stands at the beginning of *Selected Poems*, may be cited as an example. Written in a series of irregularly rhymed stanzas, it begins with the immediate and the personal – the poet standing by the "bevelled edge" of a lake in the air and the sunshine, then plunging into the breathless dark of the subaqueous world below. The senses stimulate the mind, and the theme of the poem becomes Man's history, which extends back into pre-history, before man developed lungs and ceased to be fish. With its unifying symbol of water as the source of life, the poem establishes a contact in awareness with biological history, stretching back to the primordial beginnings of life, and also (as we emerge again to the surface of the lake) with the earthbound now of "a crowded street." This poem is characteristic of Scott's mature non-satirical poetry. The themes and motives of much of his most completely articulated work are seen in it at their clearest and most direct. The fascination with water, as an element and as a symbol; the identification of the poet's self with Man and of the sensuous perceptive physical being with Mind; and the inescapable tendency to interchange the language and imagery of science (especially biology, geology, and psychology) with the language and imagery of religion are all seen in this poem as well as in a dozen other of Scott's more recent metaphysical lyrics and in the remarkable series of poems resulting from his travels in India, Burma, and the Far East.

Scott has managed, more successfully than most, to unify his public life of social responsibility with the private, perceptive and contemplative life of the poet. All his poems, from the gayest and lightest expressions of delight in life through his witty and sometimes savage satires to the metaphysical lyrics, are informed and qualified by a sense of responsibility and an inescapable sincerity, serious but never solemn.

—A. J. M. Smith

SCOTT, Tom. Scottish. Born in Glasgow, Lanarkshire, 6 June 1918. Educated at Hyndland Secondary School, Glasgow; Madras College, St. Andrews, Scotland; Edinburgh University, M.A., Ph.D. Served in the Royal Army Pay Corps, 1939–44. Married Heather Fretwell in 1963; one son and twin daughters. Recipient: Atlantic-Rockefeller Award, 1950; Carnegie Senior Fellowship and Scholarship; Arts Council Award, 1972. Address: Duddingston Park, Edinburgh 15, Scotland.

PUBLICATIONS

Verse

Seeven Poems o Maister Francis Villon. Tunbridge Wells, Kent, Peter Russell, 1953.
An Ode til New Jerusalem. Edinburgh, M. Macdonald, 1956.
The Ship and Ither Poems. London and New York, Oxford University Press, 1963.
At the Shrine o the Unkent Sodger: A Poem for Recitation. Preston, Lancashire, Akros, 1968.
Brand the Builder. London, Ember Press, 1975.
The Tree: An Epic of Evolution in 84 Cantos. Dunfermline, Fife, Borderline Press, 1977.

Other

A Possible Solution to the Scotch Question. Edinburgh, M. Macdonald, 1963.
Dunbar: A Critical Exposition of the Poems. Edinburgh, Oliver and Boyd, and New York, Barnes and Noble, 1966.
Tales of King Robert the Bruce (juvenile). Oxford, Pergamon Press, 1969.

Editor, with John MacQueen, *The Oxford Book of Scottish Verse.* Oxford, Clarendon Press, 1966.

Editor, *Late Medieval Scots Poetry: A Selection from the Makars and Their Heirs down to 1610.* London, Heinemann, and New York, Barnes and Noble, 1967.
Editor, *The Penguin Book of Scottish Verse.* London, Penguin, 1970.

Critical Studies: "Tom Scott" by John Herdman, in *Akros 16* (Preston, Lancashire), April 1971; "Tom Scott Issue" of *Scotia Review* (Caithness), 1976.

Tom Scott comments:

After some years writing in English, to my own dissatisfaction, I found myself beginning to write in my native Scots, suppressed by my English education, in Sicily. Since that conversion I have written mostly in that language, my own reworking of it, for verse, and in English for prose, until recently.

At the centre of my work is a vision of the Good Society. My poems mainly take two modes: visions of that society, and satires of existing society and its evils. Technically I have been influenced by Villon, Dunbar, and Lewis Grassic Gibbon, and stick close to traditional forms, in the main. I have recently revived the verse epistle for social criticism, owing perhaps something to Fergusson and Burns, but very much brought up to date. I am a Scottish nationalist and more concerned with the salvation of my nation than that of my own soul, believing that "he who saveth his soul shall lose it." I have a personal vision of Yeshua of Nazareth, but it accords little and quarrels much with orthodox religion. I am a writer, with no capacity for religion as such, being an observer rather than a man of action. My social vision is moral-aesthetic rather than scientific – old fashioned utopian socialism, I suppose.

* * *

Brand the Builder stands at the heart of Tom Scott's achievement. The language is a rich Scots vernacular, dignified by the formality of a verse that is sufficiently free to allow the direct speech of Brand to rise naturally out of it. In the strong affection of the poet, through the relaxed slow movement of the verse, which is also the pace of the man, Brand comes before the mind's eye, warm and living. The poem can contain without strain the ritual grace of Brand – " 'Lord, for what we are about to receive/Help us to be truly thankful – Aimen' " – and the racy vigorous image of the man dousing his face in water, to be followed by the conclusive last line: "The waater slorps frae his elbucks as he synds his phiz./And this is aa the life he kens there is?" It is as if the poet stands aside to let the subject speak for itself, and this, according to a passage in *The Tree*, is the right stance for the poet. Significantly the solid character of the man is reflected in the character of the speech, a speech, which I regard as Tom Scott's most important inheritance, for it, along with other personal aspects, suggests a continuity of Scottish character, at this moment in history when that continuity might appear no longer to exist.

In terms of aspiration – Tom Scott's dedication to projecting the idea of the Good Society, and to warning the people of inevitable doom when a class-structured society sets money-making above all other ends – Brand is a small achievement. Nevertheless my observation of the rightness of the language in that poem, relates to the problem of being in possession of an idiom and style that can be successfully applied to the major themes that are developed in *The Ship*, *At the Shrine o the Unkent Sodger*, and *The Tree*. Previous to writing *The Ship*, Scott had discovered that the major contribution to his literary identity came from the Scottish Makars of the later Middle Ages. MacDiarmid had already been at this source, but unlike him, Scott worked frequently within the modes of the period and with a language which acknowledged that Middle Scots might still help to create a living verse. The idiom of Tom Scott's translations, particularly in his *Seeven Poems o Maister Francis Villon*, which related to the period of the poems and to the present, was harmoniously right. There could hardly be a finer translation of "Mais où sont les neiges d'antan?" than "Ay, whaur are the snaws o langsyne?" It is warmer and stronger than "Where are the snows of yester year?" and without its feeling of manner, but when Scott employs a stanzaic form for original writing as in "Ithaka," "Fergus," and "A Prayer for the Fowk" (all from *The Ship and Ither Poems*), one is over-conscious of their Medieval reference. Even when the poet writes of the evils of his day – as in the lines

For the rackt by rates and rents and taxes,
Mulctict by insurancies,
For the spreit that nocht but drug relaxes,
Drunken dreams, fagged fantasies,
Let Your mercie, petie, peace
Circulate, no watered beer

– the controlled fluency and the antique spelling milks the verse of social concérn.

For *The Ship*, an allegory on the consequences of the denial of the brotherhood of man based on the sinking of the *Titanic*, an idiom closer to Scots speech yet capable of rhetorical utterance was required, and achieved. The build and momentum of this long poem are impressive. The rhetoric carries the strong, sometimes impassioned, prophetic voice, to the extent of favouring the allegory at the expense of the tragic human tale, as in the substitution of comic archetypes for persons ("Mr and Mrs Warld-Steel were there/Sir James and Lady Banking and Finance"). Not that the less strident voice is unheard. An inventive, well observed passage detailing the reactions of passengers, has the lines: "A few/Noticed some tell-tail detail telt nae tale –/The matresses nae langer shoogled wi the Ship." Scott then has at his command a Scots capable of proselytising and of intimacy. In *At the Shrine o the Unkent Sodger* he exploits the larger voice, though, in this "poem for Recitation," the other is not lost.

When Tom Scott sets himself to embrace the subject of Evolution in English in what he calls "symphonic verse" in *The Tree*, which runs to 230 lines, the problem of recovering a valid idiom for his large purpose may be insoluble. From the outset he puts an apparently unreserved trust in an exhausted poetic diction. Whereas Scots, in certain circumstances, may still win acceptance for a romantic currency, the over-exploited English will not. References to the "Muses," "heart of mystery," and "mighty" even in a line with some evocation, such as "as may a mighty ship loom up through fog" put under suspicion the whole poem; and yet because of the poet's love for the subject, his detailed presentation of it, his deep affection for the great Scottish natural historian, D'Arcy Thompson – who is depicted in the poem – and his passionate concern about the issues he raises, the poem comes alive in passages. The poem is not the thing itself, as is *Brand the Builder*, but Tom Scott will go his own, independent way, and it would be hard to predict where next.

—George Bruce

SCOVELL, E(dith) J(oy). British. Born in Sheffield, Yorkshire, in 1907. Educated at Casterton School, Westmorland; Somerville College, Oxford, B.A. 1930. Married Charles Sutherland Elton in 1937; two children. Lives in Oxford, England.

PUBLICATIONS

Verse

Shadows of Chrysanthemums and Other Poems. London, Routledge, 1944.

The Midsummer Meadow and Other Poems. London, Routledge, 1946.
The River Steamer and Other Poems. London, Cresset Press, 1956.

* * *

The gentle talent of E. J. Scovell has been drowned out by the tumult of competing voices. Her range may be limited, but her poems are distinguished by an attention to detail and an almost mystical sense of the process of life. Of a baby's head, she writes:

Now even the captive light still in a sheltered room,
Claiming you as its kind, pours round your head in bloom,
So melting where it flows that the strong, armour-browed
Skull seems as precious as cloud;

Or seems a field of corn by the wind liquefied
Streaming over the arches of a round hill-side.
Contours and skin make tender the planes of light and shadow,
The pale and darker gold of an upland meadow ...

Delicately touched, this is, and quietly spoken. So much so, indeed, that the ear deadened by the apocalyptic beat of the drop-out poets and their British admirers may well not discern the patterning of rhymes and half-rhymes, the oddly displaced stress that is part of the charm of Scovell's poetry: "Under the pent-house branches the eight swans have come/Into the black-green water round the roots of the yew;/Like a beam descending the lake, the stairway to their room ..." ("A Dark World"). Scovell's original books were published in the 1940's, and there was a retrospective collection in 1956. This seems to be her last word on the matter; she has published nothing since. Yet *The River Steamer*, as her collected poems are called, has some good work apparently dating up to its period of publication, and nothing finer than the title poem, a meditation on the passing years and one remarkable for its sustained allegory:

Waiting for a spirit to trouble the water,

Waiting for a spirit from beneath or over
To trouble the surface of the river
From which the hours like clouds reflected gaze
White, and the daylight shine of all earth's days

Waiting for a spirit to dissolve the glass ...

How could this poem have passed, as it has, virtually unnoticed? An essentially religious poet in the same ambience, for all the individual differences, as Anne Ridler, Joan Barton, Stevie Smith – E. J. Scovell herself, one feels, would expect no higher praise than that.

—Philip Hobsbaum

SCULLY, James (Joseph). American. Born in New Haven, Connecticut, 23 February 1937. Educated at Southern Connecticut State College, New Haven, 1955–57; University of Connecticut, Storrs, B.A. 1959 (Phi Beta Kappa), Ph.D. 1964. Married Arlene Steeves in 1960; two children. Instructor, Rutgers University, New Brunswick, New Jersey, 1963–64;

taught at Hartford Street Academy, Connecticut, 1968–69. Since 1964, Associate Professor of English, University of Connecticut. Visiting Associate Professor, University of Massachusetts, 1973. Recipient: Ingram Merrill Foundation Fellowship, 1962; Lamont Poetry Selection Award, 1967; Contributors' Prize (*The Far Point*, Winnipeg, Manitoba), 1969; Jennie Tane Award (*Massachusetts Review*, Amherst), 1971; Guggenheim Fellowship, 1973; National Endowment for the Arts grant, 1976. Address: 250 Lewiston Avenue, Willimantic, Connecticut 06226, U.S.A.

PUBLICATIONS

Verse

The Marches. New York, Holt Rinehart, 1967.
Communications, with Grandin Conover. Amherst, Massachusetts Review, 1970.
Avenue of the Americas. Amherst, University of Massachusetts Press, 1971.
Santiago Poems. Willimantic, Connecticut, Curbstone Press, 1975.
Scrap Book. Willimantic, Connecticut, Ziesing Brothers, 1977.

Other

Editor, *Modern Poetics.* New York, McGraw Hill, 1965; as *Modern Poets on Modern Poetry*, London, Collins, 1966.

Translator, with C. John Herington, *Prometheus Bound*, by Aeschylus. New York and London, Oxford University Press, 1975.
Translator, with Maria A. Proser, *Quechua Peoples Poetry.* Willimantic, Connecticut, Curbstone Press, 1977.
Translator, with Maria A. Proser and Arlene Scully, *De Repente/All of a Sudden*, by Teresa de Jesús. Willimantic, Connecticut, Curbstone Press, 1979.

James Scully comments:

Some premises and intentions:

*A body of poetry is put together as a life is.

*To write inside out, experientially. Not deform the felt perception by hedging it with arbitrary thematic caution.

*To be *in* the poetry, not a spectator/manipulator of it.

*To avoid the striking of poses because these are little more than personalized prisons.

*Poetry is for real, no fiction. Though it may be fictive, and it must be coherent – which is how it differs from most other modes of reality.

*To dramatize only that reality which has a felt significance.

*Unconsciousness (mystery) is what poetry dispels, realization (revelation) being the end in view.

*Realization as revelation is a process. It is arrived at step by step with no end to the arriving.

*Realization being evolutionary, nothing gets lost: as brackishness in blood, Latin in English – past informs present.

*Revelation broods on complexity, the questions too basic to be answered (too basic to be easily formulated even), whereas mystery generates mere surface complication.

*To admit anything and everything, including arguments, theories, opinions, etc. The point is not to take these at face value, as ends in themselves, but as clues. For instance, a political theory functions much as a word does – more elaborate in some ways, less so in others, but essentially similar. Its power is the power of allusion: it's an instrument for pointing toward realities that are too complex ever to be fully and definitively grasped.

*Not to explain, explanations violate reality, but to burn off the mist that obscures it.

*To write as transparently as possible. Because poetry isn't the most important thing in the world, though it may be the only means we have of approaching and apprehending what is.

*If everything that lives is holy, then there is nothing to hide or banish. What's damnable, or morally warped, is the categorical declaration that certain aspects of our reality (e.g. political, sexual, metaphysical, whatever) are off-limits to poetry. Nothing is taboo. Except, of course, in the psychic provinces.

*Poetic truth is whole truth, at once personal and common. At best that is. Poems are (a) people speaking.

*Any poetry must be able to accomodate people, people who speak in their own voices.

*What makes sense: to work the language that is ours, not one like private property that is merely one's own. To take seriously the shopworn language we take for granted, and allow it consciousness.

*Not to mythicize oneself or others, but to realize that everyone has mythic dimensions.

*Poetry, like the Duomo of Siena, is a common enterprise: communal coherence too accomodating to be egocentric.

* * *

The poems in James Scully's *The Marches* are meditative, dense as the persistence of the past in the present,

as if,
rockbound, this were the kingdom come,

and the hunched fields were crystal-clear
Jerusalem, and life was judged
vibration in the summer air.

Connecticut, northern France, Lake Bled in Yugoslavia, Venice, Gibraltar, Lake Sunapee in New Hampshire – wherever, "you could almost hear/lost gods breathing in the earth." Another noise is time passing: "pink-pale clouds march/as far as the mind can reach, wilting,/central Jersey spread under like spilt milk."

Avenue of the Americas is a far less scattered book, focused by loss. A child is dead at six months, a brilliant and extravagant friend is dead, rapacious grief runs through the poems. Scully's language is less measured than before, more various – discursive, argumentative and lyrical all in the same few lines. Organizing themes are Edenic America, friendship and family, the failure of art to console and its power to instruct, the spiritual collapse of American political life in the 1960's. The rock-like past of *The Marches* is transmogrified by history, by evolution, and seems to be spending itself as fast as the present:

Even the beautiful are too
heartsick for beauty,
astronauts will never make it to the stars
but burn up.

The book includes translations from Joseph Brodsky, whose political themes underscore Scully's own.

Occasionally so ambitious they fail of their own philosophical weight, Scully's newer poems have the urgency and personal risk of letters to a beloved friend (and one group of poems in *Avenue of the Americas* was evidently written as such a series of letters). But the poems are not "confessional," nor does the poet set himself up in them as representative man. They move toward the wider life which is their persistent obsession by a manifest sense that language, perhaps more than history or evolution, is our shared life: "Maybe that's what poetry is, one of the species/claiming grandeur./It's that helpless."

—William Matthews

SCUPHAM, (John) Peter. British. Born in Liverpool, Lancashire, 24 February 1933. Educated at The Perse, Cambridge, 1942–47; St. George's, Harpenden, 1947–51; Emmanuel College, Cambridge, 1954–57. Served in the Royal Army Ordnance Corps, National Service. Married Carola Braunholtz in 1957; one daughter and three sons. English Teacher, Skegness Grammar School, Lincolnshire, 1957–61. Since 1961, Chairman of the English Department, St. Christopher School, Letchworth, Hertfordshire. Editor, with John Mole, Cellar Press, and Owner, Mandeville Press, both in Hitchin, Hertfordshire. Address: 2 Taylor's Hill, Hitchin, Hertfordshire SG4 9AD, England.

PUBLICATIONS

Verse

The Small Containers. Stockport, Cheshire, Phoenix Pamphlet Poets Press, 1972.
The Snowing Globe. Manchester, E. J. Morten, 1972.
Children Dancing. Oxford, Sycamore Press, 1972.
The Nondescript. Stockport, Cheshire, Phoenix Pamphlet Poets Press, 1973.
The Gift: Love Poems. Richmond, Surrey, Keepsake Press, 1973.
Prehistories. London, Oxford University Press, 1975.
A Mandeville Troika, with Neil Powell and George Szirtes. Hitchin, Hertfordshire, Mandeville Press, 1977.
The Hinterland. London, Oxford University Press, 1977.
Megaliths and Water, drawings by Andy Christian. Brampton, LYC Museum, 1978.
Natura. Sidcot, Somerset, Gruffyground Press, 1978.

Critical Studies: in *New Statesman* (London), 29 September 1972; by Michael Longley, in *Phoenix 9* (Stockport, Cheshire), Winter 1972; *Irish Times* (Dublin), 6 January 1973; *The Teacher* (London), 2 March 1973; *Encounter* (London), 18 May 1973; *Times Literary Supplement* (London), 23 May 1975 and 21 November 1977.

Peter Scupham comments:

I feel with Auden that poetry is a game of knowledge, and I enjoy the complexity of rules that make the game worth playing. I enjoy, and hope my work demonstrates, formalities, ironies, technical complexities, patterns, elegance. But since the game is a game of knowledge, I also hope my poems are *about* something, that they possess a strong sense of the reality of people and objects. The game should be played for someone or something else's sake; not for the poet's. I enjoy tightrope-walking, cadence, clarity, celebrations; I dislike the raw, the self-absorbed, the cosmic. The poets for whom I feel particular elective affinities would include James Reeves, Norman Cameron, Louis MacNeice, Richard Wilbur, John Crowe Ransom. I would like my best poems to unite the dance of beauty with the dance of death.

* * *

The subject matter of Peter Scupham's poetry reflects the wide ranging interests of a lively mind: archaeology in "Un Peu d'Histoire: Dordogne"; jazz in "Fats Waller"; children and family in "Small Pets," "Four Fish," and "Family Ties"; and so we could go on. The poetry itself is marked by a scrupulous care in the use of language and form which results in a precision of expression and feeling. Scupham is keenly aware of our vulnerability, of that incidence of tragedy that lies close to the surface of even every day domestic life ("At Home"): "All this dark humus/A soft compound of shared sufferings./The earth is knit together with absences" and that is not without menace where in the nursery ("Wolves"): "The small child tosses. It is not easy/To have wolves wished upon you./They wait patiently beside the bed." His preoccupation with our prehistory and the Earth's geological and historic past ties in here, for in Scupham's world the sense of a common bond between all humanity, past and present, is never far off, our concerns and fears are shared through the ages. It is a poetry of a committed conscience, deriving depth from a historical perspective where responsibility is everyman's. This is seen clearly in an impressive poem, "The Nondescript," which Scupham wrote for the Friends of the Earth, where the use of the first person in the poem manages to be strongly impersonal and yet all embracing: "I am plural. My interests are manifold/I see through many eyes. I am fabulous" so that the poem manages to address the reader while involving him as a participant in its tragic consequences: "I have prepared a stone inheritance/It flourishes beneath my fertile tears."

Scupham's most recent collection, *The Hinterland*, marks a movement towards more recent history, and the sonnet sequence, which gives the collection its title, has as its central theme the Great War of 1914–18. The dazzling technical feat of writing fifteen sonnets linked by their first and last lines, the final sonnet composed of those lines, is such that it has beguiled critics from the quality of the work itself where the poet has infused his historical perspective with an emotional immediacy which is quite remarkable: "Where blood and stone proclaim their unities/Under the topsoil vagaries of green/Works the slow justle of the small debris." In reminding us that technical excellence and true feeling are not inimical Peter Scupham has done the art some service, in contrast to those others who do violence to language and form in order to disguise a pathetic lack of real feeling or concern. Great ends can be worked towards gently.

—John Cotton

SEIDEL, Frederick (Lewis). American. Born in St. Louis, Missouri, 19 February 1936. Educated at St. Louis Country Day School, 1948–53; Harvard University, Cambridge, Massachusetts, A.B. 1957. Married Phyllis Munro Ferguson in 1960; one daughter. Writer-in-Residence, Rutgers University, New Brunswick, New Jersey, 1964. Recipient: National Endowment for the Arts grant, 1968. Address: 251 West 92nd Street, No. 6-A, New York, New York 10025 U.S.A.

PUBLICATIONS

Verse

Final Solutions: Poems. New York, Random House, 1963.

* * *

Past is ever present in Frederick Seidel's *Final Solutions*, as juxtaposed and overlapping time-frames trace the psychic travels of memorable souls. Uneasy, frightened, struggling, and tormented, personae reveal through internal monologues histories whose significance is both individual and universal. But, whether in painful resignation or in fitful turmoil, speakers' voices are modulated into meticulously wrought lines. The frequent contrast between the noisome details of suffering and the controlled tone of its expression results in powerful tension, agony heightened by an ominous placidity. "The Heart Attack," a remarkable evocation of ancient times, conveys eternal themes of lust, hurt, and regret in polished rimes; a long-departed mistress fills an old man's dreams with coy and spiteful recollections and gets a sort of revenge by her "presence" at the poem's dramatic close. The widower finds himself still held in the power of a wife who "killed/Him in her dreams every day," a masochistic thrall perpetuated by his scolding grand-daughter. The retired Jewish analyst in "Daley Island" holds on, locked like the land in a sea of memory. Surrounded by the squalid artefacts of a Parisian spring, the soldier is drawn back by a half-remembered vision of idealism at Harvard and a desire for a girl with "Unmarriageable Minoan eyes,/All intuition, delicately lidded."

Occasionally, the subtle, inferential handling of material gives way to an unfortunate bluntness. "Americans in Rome" proceeds by means of extended reveries and short dramatic scenes to show tenderness confronted by social realities, but leads to self-righteous pity for poor souls who "can give to piety/Their ego, for amnesia," and ends in a crude critique of religious hypocrisy. In "The Beast Is in Chains," time-shifts operate once more, but in facile comparisons of wars (Napoleon's and the Allies') and in obvious commentary upon a fragile peace maintained by American flags in the City of Light. More successful is "A Year Abroad," in which the persona travels to and through modern Germany, with flashes of "Jewbaiting mothers" in Cologne, and further back still to the city of the Roman Varus, a journey made a parable of civilization versus freedom. In the final poem, "The Sickness," the poet gives a virtuoso display of his powers. Graphic scenes in Bellevue are pitted in ironic counterpoint against the world outside, where "others try life, try dope ... join the Reserves,/ Or take the wife their life deserves." Following this unsettling prelude, the final mad fantasies of escape build to terrifying hallucinatory scenarios driven by crazy, relentless logic climaxing in breathless release. In lines such as these, Seidel answers his own question: "What/Else is there but – to live – to care ...?"

—Joseph Parisi

SERGEANT, (Herbert) Howard. British. Born in Hull, Yorkshire, 6 May 1914. Educated at the College of Commerce, Hull; Metropolitan College, St. Albans, 1935–39; School of Accounting, London, 1939–42. Married Jean Crabtree in 1954; four children. Accountant, 1935–39, District Chief Accountant, 1939–41, Broadcast Relay Services, Northern England; Travelling Accountant, British Air Ministry and Ministry of Aircraft Production, 1941–49; Company Secretary and Chief Accountant, Jordan and Sons, publishers, London, 1949–54, and E. Austin and Sons, London, 1954–63; Lecturer in Accountancy, Economics and English Literature, Norwood Technical College, London, 1963–65; Senior Lecturer in Accountancy, Wandsworth Technical College, London, 1965–68; Senior Lecturer in Management Studies, 1969–72, and Head, 1972–78, Brooklands School of Management, Surrey; Creative Writing Fellow, Queen Mary's College, Basingstoke, Hampshire, 1978–79. Since 1943, Founding Editor, *Outposts*, London. M.B.E. (Member Order of the British Empire), 1978. Address: 72 Burwood Road, Walton-on-Thames, Surrey, England.

PUBLICATIONS

Verse

The Leavening Air. London, Fortune Press, 1946.
The Headlands. London, Putnam, 1953.

Other

The Cumberland Wordsworth. London, Williams and Norgate, 1950.
Traditions in the Making of Modern Poetry. London, Britannicus Liber, 1951.
A Critical Survey of South African Poetry in English, with G. M. Miller. Cape Town, Balkema, 1957.

Editor, *For Those Who Are Alive: An Anthology of New Verse.* London, Fortune Press, 1946.
Editor, *An Anthology of Contemporary Northern Poetry.* London, Harrap, 1947.
Editor, *These Years: An Anthology of Contemporary Poetry.* Leeds, Arnold, 1950.
Editor, with Robert Conquest and Michael Hamburger, *New Poems 1953.* London, Joseph, 1953.
Editor, *A Selection of Poems*, by John Milton. London, Grey Walls Press, 1953.
Editor, with Dannie Abse, *Mavericks.* London, Editions Poetry and Poverty, 1957.
Editor, *Selected Poems*, by A. J. Bull. London, Outposts, 1966.
Editor, *Commonwealth Poems of Today.* London, Murray, 1967.
Editor, *New Voices of the Commonwealth.* London, Evans, 1968.
Editor, with Jean Sergeant, *Poems from Hospital.* London, Allen and Unwin, 1968.
Editor, *Poetry from Africa.* Oxford, Pergamon Press, 1968.
Editor, *Universities' Poetry 8.* Keele, Staffordshire, Universities Poetry Management Committee, 1968.
Editor, *Poetry from Australia.* Oxford, Pergamon Press, 1969.
Editor, *The Swinging Rainbow: Poems for the Young.* London, Evans 1969.
Editor, *Poetry from India.* Oxford, Pergamon Press, 1969.
Editor, *John Milton and William Wordsworth.* Oxford, Pergamon Press, 1970.
Editor, *Poetry of the 1940's.* London, Longman, 1970.
Editor, *Happy Landings.* London, Evans, 1971.
Editor, *Evans Book of Children's Verse.* London, Evans, 1972.
Editor, *African Voices.* London, Evans, and New York, Lawrence Hill, 1973.
Editor, *For Today and Tomorrow.* London, Evans, 1974.
Editor, *New Poems 1976–77.* London, Hutchinson, 1976.
Editor, *Poetry South East 1.* Southborough, Kent, South East Arts Association, 1976.
Editor, *The Two Continents Book of Children's Verse.* New York, Two Continents, 1977.
Editor, *Candles and Lamps.* Walton-on-Thames, Surrey, Outposts, 1979.

Critical Study: "The Poetry of Howard Sergeant" by Lionel Monteith, in *Poetry Quarterly* (London), Spring 1951.

* * *

In Howard Sergeant's poetry of the 1940's and 1950's, one of the main themes was a passionately impersonal yet as passionately individual one that, in the poet's own words: "We are responsible for other people and cannot shirk that responsibility, even if they live thousands of miles away." This vital, modern-yet-perennial theme, running through the philosophical work of the novelist Iris Murdoch and resonant in the books of the philosopher Erich Fromm, is central to Howard Sergeant's sequence "The Leaves of Europe" in *The Headlands*:

This is the chosen darkness,
this is the myth our fathers
and their fathers knew, and choosing
closed their eyes and ears, and gave
their willing hands to any cause
that named them heroes, that promised
no responsibility –
I am absolved; I was commanded

And this is false
To murmur
I was not there.

This theme returns in his new poetry – in, for instance, "Strategy," anthologized in *Poems of the Sixties*: "Since every combatant's wound is your wound, too;/for every death, life pins the crime on you." With such an outlook, abandoned by many poets of the 1960's and 1970's for a narrower, sometimes peripheral subjectivity, Sergeant's poetry may develop along the theme of Being (related to Martin Heidegger's) which some critics see as essential to the future both of humanity and of poetry, anywhere in the world.

"The Headlands," a sequence of ten poems in the book of that title, promotes, by skilful lyric yet virile imagery, a depth of experience that raises, and deepens too, Sergeant's importance as poet. Within experiences known to and understandable by all, he suggests the sea as symbol of those as yet barely perceived parts of humanity, the unconscious and the subconcious mind. The seashore he sees as what might be termed "real" everyday life, full of complexity, conflict, incessant, almost always contradictory, thought and action. "Three Sonnets on a Single Theme" touch autobiographically on these conflicts, of intellect with ideal, art with the world of sensuousness and sensuality, action with vision and reason. Three aspects of personality are presented as Head, Hand, Eye. "They need a fourth," Sergeant writes: "Heart (Love) to integrate them into one."

Today's language is never the language of yesterday. Sergeant's poetic style, hitherto packed with imagery, is now starker, freer, less rhythmed and rhymed and with a new element of satiric humour. Perhaps it is not less visioned. The future work of this poet should be watched with interest.

—Anne Tibble

SEYMOUR, A(rthur) J(ames). Guyanese. Born in Georgetown, British Guiana, now Guyana, 12 January 1914. Educated at Queen's College, Georgetown. Married Elma Bryce in 1937; three daughters and three sons. Chief Information Officer, British Guiana, 1954–62;

Development Officer, Caribbean Organization, Puerto Rico, 1962–64; Public Relations Officer, Demerara Bauxite Company, Ltd./Guyana Bauxite Company, Ltd., Guyana, 1965–73; Director of Creative Writing, Department of Culture, 1973–79. Editor, *Kyk-over-Al*, Georgetown, 1945–61; Editor, Miniature Poets Series; Poetry Editor, *Kaie* magazine of the National History and Arts Council, Guyana, 1965. Recipient: Golden Arrow of Achievement, Guyana, 1970. Address: 23 North Road, Bourda, Georgetown, Guyana.

PUBLICATIONS

Verse

Verse. Georgetown, Daily Chronicle, 1937.
More Poems. Georgetown, Daily Chronicle, 1940.
Over Guiana Clouds. Georgetown, Demerara Standard, 1945.
Sun's in My Blood. Georgetown, Demerara Standard, 1945.
Six Songs. Privately printed, 1946.
Seven Poems. Privately printed, 1948.
We Do Not Presume to Come. Privately printed, 1948.
The Guiana Book. Georgetown, Argosy, 1948.
Leaves from the Tree. Georgetown, Miniature Poets, 1951.
Water and Blood: A Quincunx. Georgetown, Miniature Poets, 1952.
Three Voluntaries. Privately printed, 1953.
Variations on a Theme. Privately printed, 1961.
Selected Poems. Privately printed, 1965.
A Little Wind of Christmas. Privately printed, 1967.
Monologue. Privately printed, 1968.
Patterns. Privately printed, 1970.
I, Anancy. Privately printed, 1971.
Black Song. Privately printed, 1972.
Passport. Privately printed, 1972.
The Legend of Kaieteur. Georgetown, Carifesta, 1972.
Song to Man. Privately printed, 1973.
City of Memory. Privately printed, 1974.
A Bethlehem Alleluia. Privately printed, 1974.
Images Before Easter. Privately printed, 1974.
Love Song. Privately printed, 1975.
Mirror. Privately printed, 1975.
A Song for Christmas. Privately printed, 1975.
Tomorrow Belongs to the People. Privately printed, 1975.
For Nicolas Guillen. Georgetown, Guyana Lithographic Company, 1976.
Georgetown General. Georgetown, National History and Arts Council, 1976.
Lament for Jacqueline Williams and Raymond Persaud. Privately printed, 1976.
My Resurrection Morning. Privately printed, 1976.
Shape of the Crystal. Privately printed, 1977.
Images of Majority: Collected Poems 1968–1978. Privately printed, 1978.

Other

A Survey of West Indian Literature. Georgetown, Kyk-over-Al, 1950.
Caribbean Literature (radio talks). Privately printed, 1951.
Window on the Caribbean. Privately printed, 1952.
Edgar Mittelholzer: The Man and His Work. Georgetown, National History and Arts Council, 1968.
Introduction to Guyanese Writing. Georgetown, National History and Arts Council, 1971.

Looking at Poetry. Privately printed, 1974.
I Live in Georgetown. Privately printed, 1974.
Pilgrim Memories. Privately printed, 1974.
Growing Up in Guyana. Privately printed, 1976.
Family Impromptu. Privately printed, 1977.
Nine Caribbean Essays. Privately printed, 1977.
Cultural Policy in Guyana. Paris, Unesco, 1977.
The Making of Guyanese Literature. Privately printed, 1979.

Editor, *The Kyk-over-Al Anthology of West Indian Poetry.* Georgetown, Kyk-over-Al, 1952; revised edition, 1957.
Editor, *Anthology of Guyanese Poetry.* Georgetown, Kyk-over-Al, 1954.
Editor, *Themes of Song.* Privately printed, 1959.
Editor, with Elma Seymour, *My Lovely Native Land.* London, Longman, 1971.
Editor, *New Writing in the Caribbean.* Georgetown, Government of Guyana, 1972.
Editor, *Independence Ten: Guyanese Writing 1966–1976.* Georgetown, Government of Guyana, 1977.

Bibliography: *A. J. Seymour: A Bibliography,* by Joan Christiani, Georgetown, Guyana, National Library, 1974.

Manuscript Collection: National Library, Georgetown.

Critical Study: "A Study of the Poetry of A. J. Seymour" by Celeste Dolphin, in *New World Fortnightly* (Georgetown), 1965.

A. J. Seymour comments:

I would feel that primarily I am a Love poet. I am strongly aware of political shifts in the Community climate in my own country and in the region. Historical personalities stimulate me, and myths and legends of the continent and archipelago also interest me.

I am very conscious of form in poetry – sonnets, terza rima, quatrains and rhyme generally. But everything is grist to the poetic mill and my present influences are W. B. Yeats, Borges, Neruda, and T. S. Eliot.

* * *

Like Frank Collymore, A. J. Seymour has not, over the years, only written poetry. He has also been concerned to encourage its writing in others. He edited the now defunct magazine, *Kyk-over-Al*, between 1945 and 1961, which, apart from a fair proportion of poems in its individual numbers, devoted three entire issues to anthologies. He produced a series, "The Miniature Poets," featuring the work of writers like Martin Carter, Cecil Herbert, and Phillip Sherlock; he conducted (and still conducts) writers workshops; and his weekly broadcast literary programmes did much to encourage an interest in the emerging Caribbean literature of the 1950's. He is also a critic, lecturer, and reader of considerable calibre. But above all, A. J. Seymour is a poet.

Three main themes emerge from this work: a feeling for heroes of history or literature, usually accompanied by a sense of violence and doom ("Caligula"):

> In killing, there must be a fierce, dark joy.
> – To stab a pulsing throat and see the blood
> Spurt angry purple from the quivering gash.
> Or choke life out with muscles tense and hard,
> And hammering temples, gloating at the sight
> Of thick veins swelling snake-like from the skin....

(or "Othello"): "The engine failing,/The shattered peace,/The athlete lost within his stride,/ The look over the edge of the abyss...." or a feeling for the continuity of Caribbean and Guyanese history, centred through the persona of an epic hero ("For Christopher Columbus"):

He dreamed not that the ocean would bear ships
Heavy with slaves in the holds, to spill their seed
And fertilise new islands under whips
... dreamt not indeed
Massive steel eagles would keep an anxious watch
For strange and glittering fish where now was weed.

Seymour has also been concerned to weave a local past using Amerindian mythology – "Amalivaca," for instance, and "The Legend of Kaieteur." But these, with their over-emphatic singing pentameters are not as successful as the poems of the first group (the "literary" poems) where, as will be seen from the earlier quotations, he achieves real eloquence, or, as with "Diocletian," a certain sharpness of focus:

I dream of Diocletian in his age
Walking alone within his cabbage garden.

A gaunt old man with power upon his face
Straighter than furrows, and images of power
Still moving in those deepest eagle eyes.

With these poems, in fact, we reach the paradox of Caribbean "colonial" poetry which tends, like the verse of Frank Collymore, to avoid "social reality"; or, as with Seymour's, to be most technically at home with the "literary." But Seymour is also a "transitional" poet, preparing the way, in "Tomorrow Belongs to the People," for writers like Martin Carter: "Ignorant/Illegitimate/Hungry sometimes,/Living in tenement yards/Dying in burial societies/The people is a lumbering giant/That holds history in his hand."

But it is in the third group of poems, those that disclose Seymour's personal perception of the living world and living love, that we find, perhaps, the most certain successes: "Time spirals upright this unflowing river/This waterrise through the earth safely miracled/This phallus from the deeps unbound and liquid,/Reversal of the dying desert ..." ("The Well"), and "Springtide":

Nearly all women sleep when they are loved

Maybe the body has to coil again
From its full stretch, maybe the drowned brain
Emerges from its Springtide into rest
Maybe they bank their ectasy in dreams
Against a future anguish and devaluation

But as the unhurried stars wheel overhead
Above a thousand million nests of love
One or two women lie and think and glow.

—Edward Kamau Brathwaite

SEYMOUR-SMITH, Martin. British. Born in London, 24 April 1928. Educated at Highgate School, 1939–46; St. Edmund Hall, Oxford (Poetry Editor, *Isis*, 1950–51), 1948–51, B.A. (honours) 1951, M.A. Served as a Sergeant in the British Army in the Near East, 1947–48. Married Janet de Glanville in 1952; two daughters. Tutor to Robert Graves's son, Mallorca, 1951–54; school master, 1954–60. Since 1960, Free-lance Writer. Visiting Professor of English and Poet-in-Residence, University of Wisconsin Parkside, Kenosha, 1971–72. Editorial Assistant, *London Magazine*, 1955–56; Poetry Editor, *Truth*, London, 1955–57, and *The Scotsman*, Edinburgh, 1964–67; Literary Adviser, Hodder and Stoughton, publishers, London, 1963–65; General Editor, Gollancz Classics series, Victor Gollancz Ltd., London, 1967–69. Agent: Anthony Sheil Associates Ltd., 2–3 Morwell Street, London WC1B 3AR; or, Wallace Aitken and Sheil, 118 East 61st Street, New York, New York 10021, U.S.A. Address: 36 Holliers Hill, Bexhill-on-Sea, Sussex TN40 2DD, England.

PUBLICATIONS

Verse

Poems, with Rex Taylor and Terence Hards. Dorchester, Longman, 1952.
(*Poems*). Oxford, Fantasy Press, 1953.
All Devils Fading. Palma, Mallorca, Divers Press, 1954.
Tea with Miss Stockport: 24 Poems. London and New York, Abelard Schuman, 1963.
Reminiscences of Norma: Poems 1963–1970. London, Constable, 1971.

Other

Robert Graves. London, Longman, 1956; revised edition, 1965, 1970.
Bluff Your Way in Literature. London, Wolfe, 1966; New York, Cowles, 1968.
Fallen Women: A Sceptical Inquiry into the Treatment of Prostitutes, Their Clients, and Their Pimps in Literature. London, Nelson, 1969.
Poets Through Their Letters. London, Constable, and New York, Holt Rinehart, 1969.
Inside Poetry, with James Reeves. London, Heinemann, and New York, Barnes and Noble, 1970.
Guide to Modern World Literature. London, Wolfe, 1973; revised edition, London, Hodder and Stoughton, 4 vols., 1975; as *Funk and Wagnalls Guide to Modern World Literature*, New York, Funk and Wagnalls, 1973.
Sex and Society. London, Hodder and Stoughton, 1975.
Who's Who in Twentieth-Century Literature. London, Weidenfeld and Nicolson, and New York, Holt Rinehart, 1976.
Fifty European Novels. London, Pan, 1979.

Editor, *Poetry from Oxford*. London, Fortune Press, 1953.
Editor, *Shakespeare's Sonnets*. London, Heinemann, 1963; New York, Barnes and Noble, 1966.
Editor, *A Cupful of Tears: Sixteen Victorian Novelettes*. London, Wolfe, 1965.
Editor, *Every Man in His Humour*, by Ben Jonson. London, Benn, 1966; New York, Hill and Wang, 1968.
Editor, with James Reeves, *A New Canon of English Poetry*. London, Heinemann, and New York, Barnes and Noble, 1967.
Editor, with James Reeves, *The Poems of Andrew Marvell*. London, Heinemann, and New York, Barnes and Noble, 1969.
Editor, *Longer Elizabethan Poems*. London, Heinemann, and New York, Barnes and Noble, 1970.
Editor, with James Reeves, *Selected Poems*, by Walt Whitman. London, Heinemann, 1976.

Editor, *The English Sermon 1550–1650.* Manchester, Carcanet Press, 1976.
Editor, *The Mayor of Casterbridge*, by Hardy. London, Penguin, 1979.

Manuscript Collection: University of Texas, Austin.

Critical Study: "Poetry of Exactness" by Robert Nye, in *The Scotsman* (Edinburgh), September 1963.

Martin Seymour-Smith comments:

(1970) My earlier poems tended to be "traditional" in form, while the later ones are much freer – although they make full but irregular use of rhyme. Browning seems to be a much more persistent influence than until recently I would have liked to acknowledge. I seem to write many poems about people: they could be described, I suppose, as biographical poems. If I had to sum up the kind of poem I should like to write (a hypothetical question), I should probably say "something like Jacques Audiberti, but wholly anglicized and laced with plenty of native humour." But I find answering questions like this damaging as I write few poems and tend to conserve my energies for them. I like a compact sort of poetry, and rely heavily on the non-manufacturing side of myself in order to produce first drafts.

(1974) An introduction to my work as a poet for the general reader would, I suppose, say that I am essentially a "phenomenological" poet but that I value coherence; that many people don't seem to understand what I am about except when I am "being funny"; that I never "submit" poems to anyone (except God), but only send them when requested; that I find the general atmosphere of unread-poeticule-sucking-up-to-unread-poeticule irrelevant to what I am trying to do, since for any poet poetry is a lonely business; that I would rather have, say, six (no, *ten*) readers than a thousand carrion-fed unminds; that there are contemporary poets whose poems I admire and to which I can respond; that there is nothing left for me but to do exactly what I have to do, in poetry, when I have to do it and in whatever way it should be done; that I would rather be a poet than any kind of dogmatist; that good grocerdom is undoubtedly more difficult than good poetdom, but then in poetry the standards are considerably higher, too high.

* * *

Hart Crane once said: "Poetry, in so far as the metaphysics of absolute knowledge extends, is simply the concrete evidence of the experience of knowledge. It can give you a ratio of fact and experience, and in this sense it is both perception and thing perceived according as it approaches a significant articulation or not."

Apart from a Fantasy Press pamphlet and an early book, *Poems*, Martin Seymour-Smith has published only two collections, *Tea With Miss Stockport* and *Reminiscences of Norma*, but the poems in these books which do not approach a significant articulation are few, for Seymour-Smith is nothing if not fastidious – of language, and of the occasions when language may permissibly aspire to poetry. Whether he is writing simply about subtle thoughts and feelings, or with succinct irony at the expense of his own sensitivity, his concern is the same: to "test" the moment of self-knowledge by applying to it the resources of an intelligent imagination. He is not a poet who finds questions in his experience – in data "given" before the poem happens – and then sets about providing himself, and us, with easy, knowing answers. Each poem is itself a questioning; when an answer is offered it is usually tentative, an understatement of what has been understood, and then that answer is often further qualified by self-satire, as though the poet were mistrustful of where the poem might take him, the satire being there to clarify his perception of his meaning. This makes for an intense and caustic poetry of much exactness. See especially "The Northern Monster" in the

1963 collection, and the thirteen poems which comprise Section III of *Reminiscences of Norma*, and give that book its title.

—Robert Nye

SHAPCOTT, Thomas W(illiam). Australian. Born in Ipswich, Queensland, 21 March 1935. Educated at Ipswich Grammar School, 1949–50; University of Queensland, Brisbane, B.A. in arts 1968. Served in the National Service, 1953. Married Margaret Hodge in 1960; three daughters and one son. Clerk, H. S. Shapcott, Public Accountant, Ipswich, 1951–63; Partner, Shapcott and Shapcott, Accountants, Ipswich, 1963–72; Public Accountant, Sole Trader, Ipswich, 1972–78. Since 1978, full-time writer. Fellow, Australian Society of Accountants, 1970. Churchill Fellow (U.S.A. and England), 1972. Member, Australian Arts Council Australian Literature Board, 1973. Recipient: Grace Leven Prize, 1961; Sir Thomas White Memorial Prize, 1967; Sydney Myer Charity Trust Award, 1968, 1970; Canada-Australia prize, 1979. Address: P.O. Box 476, Toowong, Queensland 4066, Australia.

PUBLICATIONS

Verse

Time on Fire. Brisbane, Jacaranda Press, 1961.
Twelve Bagatelles. Adelaide, Australian Letters, 1962.
The Mankind Thing. Brisbane, Jacaranda Press, 1964.
Sonnets 1960–1963. Privately printed, 1964.
A Taste of Salt Water: Poems. Sydney, Angus and Robertson, 1967.
Inwards to the Sun. Brisbane, University of Queensland Press, 1969.
Fingers at Air: Experimental Poems 1969. Privately printed, 1969.
Begin with Walking. Brisbane, University of Queensland Press, 1972.
Interim Report. Privately printed, 1972.
Shabbytown Calendar. Brisbane, University of Queensland Press, 1975.
Seventh Avenue Poems. Sydney, Angus and Robertson, 1976.
Selected Poems. Brisbane, University of Queensland Press, 1979.

Play

The Seven Deadly Sins, music by Colin Brumby (produced Brisbane, 1970). Privately printed, 1970.

Other

Focus on Charles Blackman (art monograph). Brisbane, University of Queensland Press, 1967.

Editor, with Rodney Hall, *New Impulses in Australian Poetry.* Brisbane, University of Queensland Press, 1968.
Editor, *Australian Poetry Now.* Melbourne, Sun, 1969.
Editor, *Poets on Record.* Brisbane, University of Queensland Press, 1970–73.
Editor, *Contemporary American and Australian Poetry.* Brisbane, University of Queensland Press, 1976.

Manuscript Collections: Australian National Library, Canberra; Fryer Library, University of Queensland, Brisbane.

Critical Studies: by L. Clancy, in *Meanjin Quarterly* (Melbourne), 1967; Carl Harrison-Ford, in *Meanjin Quarterly* (Melbourne), 1972; interview in *Makar 11* (Brisbane), no. 3.

Thomas W. Shapcott comments:

When I first began writing and publishing poetry, in the 1950's, I was soaking myself eagerly in T. S. Eliot and Dylan Thomas, that decade's heroes, as well as discovering new worlds in the important Penguin anthologies of that period. When I had begun to be published I made contact with my own contemporaries and my Australian peers. I have always been interested in experimentation, in the challenge of form (closed forms, open forms), but in the 1950's experimental writing was unfashionable – and unpublishable. My early lyricism was more immediately accepted. In recent years I have been concerned with exploring ways of balancing essentially lyrical expression with the cadence of lyric speech.

I have always been interested in expressing a sense of region, whether it be the provincial backwaters of "Shabbytown" or "Seventh Avenue" mobility. But my essential concern has always been with issues of personality and belief: I once wrote "I believe poetry is a movement towards celebration. Art – Poetry – is to struggle towards the light, knowing the light burns all sight to blindness. We cannot outstare the sun, but it is not in our nature to endure the darkness. Thus all true poetry is in some way a form of experimentation, a groping outwards. Even the earth is moving, how can we stand still?" I still hold to that.

* * *

1968 saw the publication of an anthology entitled *New Impulses in Australian Poetry*. One of the poets behind these new impulses was the co-editor of the volume, Thomas W. Shapcott, who with several volumes of poetry to his credit is firmly established as one of the leading poets of his generation.

Shapcott's first volume, *Time on Fire*, doesn't prepare one at all for the experimentation that one finds increasingly in his poetry. It is very much a young man's work, partly autobiographical it would seem, telling of young love, courtship, marriage, the birth of the first child. These are conventional lyrics, many in the sonnet form, a form which, along with all his experimentation, he has returned to again and again, constantly exploring its possibilities and exploiting the tensions it can provide between form and content. One never feels that Shapcott is indulging in experiment for experiment's sake. On the contrary one feels the constant struggle to express thoughts in words: "It is my tongue, only, falters. Language remains/monstrous." Moreover, recent publication of some of his poems written over fifteen years ago shows that his interest in innovation in form is not a recent one. The lack of innovation in his early published work points not to the poet but rather to the conservatism of the poetry editors of that period.

There is an infinite variety in his subject matter: personal experiences, mythological, religious, historical themes, urban life, social problems, all are there. Yet with this variety one is still able to pinpoint basic concerns. Perhaps the one that he returns to most of all is the question of time. Time, like fire, is all-consuming; struggle as we may against it, we are doomed to defeat. Linked to this question and possibly an answer to it is the poet's attempt to define himself. "Self is beyond grasp" is a line from his first volume. In the minotaur sequence in *Inwards to the Sun* he uses the myth to explore the nature of man, the duality, that we, like the minotaur, partake of. Like the minotaur, we are trapped in our own labyrinths, living in "inconsolable privacy," "in a crowd that hurls again and again the noisy cry/of loneliness."

In *Begin with Walking* "anonymity" continues to haunt him; there is a cry to God for definition, "God, O God define us." Shapcott attempts this definition through his verse:

This
Blank
Page is where I begin to exist.

Perhaps we could say that his verse is not only his attempt to define himself, but also his challenge to time: "I make/a self into this page to placate/my time-veined fears" ("Time on Fire").

—Anna Rutherford

SHAPIRO, David (Joel). American. Born in Newark, New Jersey, 2 January 1947. Educated at Columbia University, New York, B.A. (magna cum laude) 1968; Clare College, Cambridge (Kellett Fellow, 1968–70), B.A. (honours) 1970. Married Lindsay Stamm in 1970. Since 1970, Editorial Associate, *Arts News*, New York. Since 1972, Instructor, Columbia University. Since 1963, a violinist with various orchestras including the New Jersey Symphony and the American Symphony. Recipient: Gotham Book Mart Avant-Garde Poetry Award, 1962; Bread Loaf Writers Conference Robert Frost Fellowship, 1965; Ingram Merrill Foundation Fellowship, 1967; Book-of-the-Month Club Fellowship, 1968; Creative Artists Public Service Fellowship, 1974; Morton Dauwen Zabel Award, 1977. Address: 560 Riverside Drive, Apartment 16K, New York, New York 10027, U.S.A.

PUBLICATIONS

Verse

Poems. Privately printed, 1960.
A Second Winter. Privately printed, 1961.
When Will the Bluebird. Privately printed, 1962.
January: A Book of Poems. New York, Holt Rinehart, 1965.
Poems from Deal. New York, Dutton, 1969.
A Man Holding an Acoustic Panel. New York, Dutton, 1971.
The Dance of Things. New York, Lincoln Center, 1971.
The Page-Turner. New York, Liveright, 1973.
Lateness. New York, Overlook Press, 1978.

Other

John Ashbery: An Introduction to His Poetry. New York, Columbia University Press, 1979.

Editor, with Kenneth Koch, *Learn Something, America.* Bedford, Massachusetts, Bedford Museum, 1968.
Editor, with Ron Padgett, *An Anthology of New York Poets.* New York, Random House, 1970.

Translator, with Arthur A. Cohen, *The New Art of Color: The Writings of Robert and Sonia Delaunay.* New York, Viking Press, 1978.

Composer: incidental music for *The Scotty Dog* by Kenneth Koch, produced New York, 1967.

Critical Study: in the *New York Review of Books*, Christmas 1971.

David Shapiro comments:

Simone Weil said, "The Fool, taken literally, is speaking the truth." Often, in my favorite poets, paradoxia and "nonsense" achieve not so much the ambiguity analysed denotatively and connotatively by Mr. Empson, but a pointing to logos by its extreme absence. As early tribes were obsessed by shadows, convinced that an animal's shadow was part of the animal, so Stein, Carroll, Borges employ the techniques of "nonsense" because they are convinced, like me, that the poet's task is to subdue – in Rimbaud's terms – the formless. If the task of positivism was to expunge nonsense, the work of poetry is to use it. That is "the meaning of meaninglessness," to use nonsense and uncertainty and discontinuity as the central tone and abiding metaphor of our peculiar predicament.

* * *

David Shapiro is one of the most gifted members of what has come to be called the "New York School" of poetry, a loose confederation of talents inspirited by the work of the late Frank O'Hara, John Ashbery, and Kenneth Koch.

Shapiro's poetry, although profoundly influenced by John Ashbery, whose sinuous intelligence and command of French poetic sources have stamped Shapiro's imagination, is nonetheless thoroughly original in the production of his imagery. The Shapiro image, nervous, agitated, associative in the psychoanalytic sense of eliciting connections from puns, sense confusions (both mystical and Rimbaudian), and fabulous and incredible synecdoches often leaves the reader gasping for meaning. However, there is throughout his work a hard rock of intelligence and arbitrariness and it is these which give assurance that his work will continue to explore and colonize the *terra incognita* between private worlds – childhood, music, love, suffering, madness – and the concerns of the reader. A very large talent, David Shapiro will surely, as *The Page-Turner* demonstrates, emerge as one of the major American poets of this decade.

—Arthur A. Cohen

SHAPIRO, Harvey. American. Born in Chicago, Illinois, 27 January 1924. Educated at Yale University, New Haven, Connecticut, B.A. 1947; Columbia University, New York, M.A. 1948. Served in the United States Army Air Force during World War II: Distinguished Flying Cross. Married Edna Lewis Kaufman in 1953; two sons. Instructor in English, Cornell University, Ithaca, New York, 1949–50, 1951–52; Creative Writing Fellow, Bard College, Annandale-on-Hudson, New York, 1950–51. Staff Member, *Commentary*, New York, 1955–56, and *The New Yorker*, 1956–57. Staff Member, then Assistant Editor, 1957–75, *New York Times Magazine*; since 1975, Editor, *New York Times Book Review*. Recipient: YMHA Poetry Center Award, 1952; Swallow Press New Poetry Series Award, 1954; Rockefeller grant, 1967. Address: 264 Hicks Street, Brooklyn, New York 11201, U.S.A.

PUBLICATIONS

Verse

The Eye. Denver, Swallow, 1953.
The Book and Other Poems. Cummington, Massachusetts, Cummington Press, 1955.
Mountain, Fire, Thornbush. Denver, Swallow, 1961.
Battle Report: Selected Poems. Middletown, Connecticut, Wesleyan University Press, 1966.
This World. Middletown, Connecticut, Wesleyan University Press, 1971.
Lauds. New York, Sun Press, 1975.
Lauds and Nightsounds. New York, Sun Press, 1978.

Critical Studies: by David Ignatow, in *The Nation* (New York), 24 April 1967; "Rebels in the Kingdom" by Jascha Kessler, in *Midstream* (New York), April 1972.

Harvey Shapiro comments:

My earlier work is marked by a preoccupation with Jewish (Hebraic) themes. In my later work I have followed mainly chassidic teachings. My later poems are free verse (earlier poems were more formal), anecdotal (based on autobiographical anecdotes), attempts to discover "The Way" (a way of right living). They have urban settings. They are concerned with marriage and the tensions of city life. But many have mystical (kabbalistic or chassidic or zen) underpinnings. Martin Buber has been an influence throughout.

* * *

From the first, Harvey Shapiro's poems have been concerned with the poignancy and gentleness of Jewish religion, and it may be that only readers raised in the same tradition, with rhythms of Yiddish argument and the sonorities of the synagogue running in their ears, can respond to them completely. Yet in his best work Shapiro speaks to, and for, everyone. He himself is a Jew from New York City, one of a number who have contributed important work to modern American poetry: Charles Reznikoff, Louis Zukofsky, Delmore Schwartz, etc. But Shapiro is younger than any of these, and though he may have been influenced in his early years by Schwartz, he has followed the route of most poets who began writing after World War II; that is, his early formalist manner changed to something more free and direct as he took part in the withdrawal from academic modes which characterized American poetry during the late 1950's and 1960's. With this came a heightening of the poignancy of his themes – poignancy driven to the brink of terror – as he responded to the cultural and social crises of his own generation.

In the 1950's Shapiro could still rely on the power of the traditional Jewish vision, as in these lines from "Feast of the Ram's Horn":

Feast of the ram's horn. Let the player rise.
And may the sound of that bent instrument,
In the seventh month, before the seventh gate,
Speak for all the living and the dead,
And tell creation it is memorized.

Let Isaac be remembered in the ram
That when the great horn sounds, and all are come,
These who now are gathered as one man
Shall be gathered again. Set the bright
Scales in the sky until that judgment's done.

But now such assurance is rarely with him. Many of his most effective poems are short, like this one, which he in savage irony entitled "Ditty":

Where did the Jewish god go?
Up the chimney flues.
Who saw him go?
Six million souls.
How did he go?
All so still
As dew from the grass.

Another ironically titled poem, "The Kingdom," which is quoted here in entirety, is no more than part of a sentence:

Battering at the door
Of a pretend house
With pretend cries
Of rage and loss
As I sit remembering
Quiet
And dead white.

Uncertainty, nostalgia and love of ancestors, fear of what is coming, a faith that seems useless – these are the coordinates of Shapiro's poetry today. Often it is very moving. He has written: "There is no reason for survival./As we drift outward/The tribal gods wave farewell." In effect, Shapiro's poems are the gestures of one who waves back.

—Hayden Carruth

SHAPIRO, Karl (Jay). American. Born in Baltimore, Maryland, 10 November 1913. Educated at the University of Virginia, Charlottesville, 1932–33; Johns Hopkins University, Baltimore, 1937–39; Pratt Library School, Baltimore, 1940. Served in the United States Army, 1941–45. Married 1) Evelyn Katz in 1945 (divorced, 1967); 2) Teri Kovach in 1969; three children. Associate Professor, Johns Hopkins University, 1947–50; Visiting Professor, University of Wisconsin, Madison, 1948, and Loyola University, Chicago, 1951–52; Lecturer, Salzburg Seminar in American Studies, 1952; State Department Lecturer, India, 1955; Visiting Professor, University of California, Berkeley and Davis, 1955–56, and University of Indiana, Bloomington, 1956–57; Professor of English, University of Nebraska, Lincoln, 1956–66, and University of Illinois, Chicago Circle, 1966–68. Since 1968, Professor of English, University of California, Davis. Editor, *Poetry*, Chicago, 1950–56, *Newberry Library Bulletin*, Chicago, 1953–55, and *Prairie Schooner*, Lincoln, Nebraska, 1956–66. Consultant in Poetry, Library of Congress, Washington, D.C., 1946–47. Recipient: Jeannette Davis Prize, 1942, Levinson Prize, 1942, Eunice Tietjens Memorial Prize, 1961, and Oscar Blumenthal Prize, 1963 (*Poetry*, Chicago); *Contemporary Poetry* prize, 1943; National Institute of Arts and Letters grant, 1944; Guggenheim Fellowship, 1944, 1953; Pulitzer Prize, 1945; Shelley Memorial Award, 1946; Kenyon School of Letters Fellowship, 1956, 1957; Bollingen Prize, 1969. D.H.L.: Wayne State University, Detroit, 1960; D.Litt.: Bucknell University, Lewisburg, Pennsylvania, 1972. Fellow in American Letters, Library of Congress. Member, American Academy of Arts and Sciences, and National Institute of Arts and Letters. Address: 1119 Bucknell Drive, Davis, California 95616, U.S.A.

Publications

Verse

Poems. Baltimore, Waverly Press, 1935.
Five Young American Poets, with others. New York, New Directions, 1941.
Person, Place and Thing. New York, Reynal, 1942; London, Secker and Warburg, 1944.
The Place of Love. Melbourne, Comment Press, 1942.
V-Letter and Other Poems. New York, Reynal, 1944; London, Secker and Warburg, 1945.
Essay on Rime. New York, Reynal, 1945; London, Secker and Warburg, 1947.
Trial of a Poet and Other Poems. New York, Reynal, 1947.
Poems 1940–1953. New York, Random House, 1953.
The House. Privately printed, 1957.
Poems of a Jew. New York, Random House, 1958.
The Bourgeois Poet. New York, Random House, 1964.
Selected Poems. New York, Random House, 1968.
White-Haired Lover. New York, Random House, 1968.
Auden (1907–1973). Davis, California, Putah Creek Press, 1973.
Adult Bookstore. New York, Random House, 1976.
Collected Poems 1940–1977. New York, Random House, 1978.

Play

The Tenor, music by Hugo Weisgall. New York, Merion Music, 1956.

Novel

Edsel. New York, Geis, 1971.

Other

English Prosody and Modern Poetry. Baltimore, Johns Hopkins University Press, 1947.
A Bibliography of Modern Prosody. Baltimore, Johns Hopkins University Press, 1948.
Beyond Criticism. Lincoln, University of Nebraska Press, 1953; as *A Primer for Poets*, 1965.
In Defense of Ignorance (essays). New York, Random House, 1960.
Start with the Sun: Studies in Cosmic Poetry, with James E. Miller, Jr., and Bernice Slote. Lincoln, University of Nebraska Press, 1960.
The Writer's Experience, with Ralph Ellison. Washington, D.C., Library of Congress, 1964.
A Prosody Handbook, with Robert Beum. New York, Harper, 1965.
Randall Jarrell. Washington, D.C., Library of Congress, 1967.
To Abolish Children and Other Essays. Chicago, Quadrangle, 1968.
The Poetry Wreck: Selected Essays 1950–1970. New York, Random House, 1975.

Editor, with W. H. Auden and Marianne Moore, *Riverside Poetry 1953: Poems by Students in Colleges and Universities in New York City.* New York, Association Press, 1953.
Editor, with Louis Untermeyer and Richard Wilbur, *Modern American and Modern British Poetry*, revised shorter edition. New York, Harcourt Brace, 1955.
Editor, *American Poetry.* New York, Crowell, 1960.
Editor, *Prose Keys to Modern Poetry.* New York, Harper, 1962.

Bibliography: *Karl Shapiro: A Bibliography* by William White, Detroit, Wayne State University Press, 1960.

Manuscript Collection: Library of Congress, Washington, D.C.

* * *

The poetic career of Karl Shapiro is remarkable for its high accomplishment in various styles – all of them his own creations – and for its abrupt, unpredictable departures into new and fruitful territories. From *Person, Place and Thing*, published while he was still in the army, to the bold cycle of love poems, *White-Haired Lover*, his writing shows considerable range as well as changing interests and attitudes. His criticism, of which we can say little here, is perceptive, vigorous, and frequently outspoken; the opinions and judgments it expresses usually reflect the stylistic or other preoccupations of his poetry.

Much of Shapiro's earlier work, and that of his American contemporaries John Berryman, Delmore Schwartz, Muriel Rukeyser, Weldon Kees, and others, demonstrates a concern with the life and institutions of modern society. Like Auden, MacNeice, and Spender in England, whose influence they doubtless felt, these poets struggled towards individual styles that would embrace both personal intuition and public experience. No one is more successful in this achievement than Shapiro: the poetry of his first three books is polished, elegant, witty, conversational, but also marked by deep compassion and humanity quite evident in such poems as "Auto Wreck," "The Leg," and "Elegy for a Dead Soldier." A large number of pieces from the 1940's explore with surgical skill the ironies, hypocrisies, prejudices, and illusions of America and its institutions. "University" begins: "To hurt the Negro and avoid the Jew/Is the curriculum." In his poems about Hollywood he concentrates on its falsities, its manufactured dreams, but also wonders if it doesn't express something inherent in the nation:

O can we understand it? Is it ours,
A crude whim of a beginning people,
A private orgy in a secluded spot?

And the poem "Necropolis" confronts the inequalities which persist between rich and poor even beyond the boundaries of death, reputedly the great equalizer.

In all of these poems Shapiro's voice and conscience are representative of humanity, take man's part before the spectacle and trials of modern existence; yet we find some poems – the sequence "Recapitulations" is an example – that reveal more closely his own life and private feelings. With *Trial of a Poet*, the first of several indications of change and experiment appears – in this instance, two prose poems which look forward to Shapiro's radical adoption of that form later for an entire book, *The Bourgeois Poet*. In addition, the new "Adam and Eve" sequence with which he opens his selected *Poems 1940–1953* announces a growing fascination with Jewish themes that leads directly on his initial, unexpected departure from previous work in *Poems of a Jew*, a collection that includes both earlier and recent pieces and whose introduction is provocative; in it he attempts to identify a "Jewish consciousness" that is man "absolutely committed to the world" but also "essentially himself, beyond nationality, defenseless against the crushing impersonality of history." He cites Joyce's Leopold Bloom, "neither hero nor victim," as the best example of this "free modern Jew." Together with the controversial but enormously stimulating volume of critical essays, *In Defense of Ignorance* (the title and contents of which attack intellectualism and the New Criticism), published two years later, *Poems of a Jew* starts Shapiro off on a poetically rewarding quest for identity. If his criticism occasionally overstates matters, that is probably necessary in order to overthrow his allegiance to the literary prescriptions handed down by Eliot and the New Critics and to take up the support of such strong but too often neglected writers as Whitman, Lawrence, Henry Miller, and W. C. Williams.

The Bourgeois Poet, which follows after these first repudiations of artistic and intellectual convention, provides a complete breakthrough into novel, difficult areas of literary form. The prose poem, utilizing the prose paragraph, has a fine tradition in French literature but has seldom proved manageable in English. However, Shapiro's success is remarkable; the poems have a marvellous flexibility in mood, tone, and temper; they shift from the satirical to the lyric to the dreamlike or irrational with rhythmic facility and strength. This book belongs in a line of descent from Rimbaud, Joyce's *Ulysses*, Henry Miller, Céline, and Isaac Singer.

Shapiro's newest work does not simply try to repeat *The Bourgeois Poet*; he undertakes a certain artistic retrenchment in the love poems, though they profit immensely from his prose experiments and are themselves frank, intimate, tender, and moving – the latest instance of powerful exploratory imaginative gifts.

—Ralph J. Mills, Jr

SHELTON, Richard. American. Born in Boise, Idaho, 24 June 1933. Educated at Harding College, Searcy, Arkansas, 1951–53; Abilene Christian College, Texas, B.A. in English 1958; University of Arizona, Tucson, M.A. 1960. Served in the United States Army, 1956–58. Married Lois Bruce in 1956; one son. Teacher, Lowell School, Bisbee, Arizona, 1958–60; Director, Ruth Stephan Poetry Center, Tucson, 1964–65. Instructor, 1960–64, Assistant Professor, 1969–73, Associate Professor, 1973–79, and since 1979, Professor of English, University of Arizona, Tucson. Recipient: International Poetry Forum United States Award, 1970; Borestone Mountain Award, 1972; National Endowment for the Arts fellowship, 1976. Address: 1548 West Plaza De Lirios, Tucson, Arizona 85705, U.S.A.

PUBLICATIONS

Verse

Journal of Return. San Francisco, Kayak, 1969.
The Tattooed Desert. Pittsburgh, University of Pittsburgh Press, 1971.
The Heroes of Our Time. Lincoln, Nebraska, Best Cellar Press, 1972.
Of All the Dirty Words. Pittsburgh, University of Pittsburgh Press, 1972.
Calendar: A Cycle of Poems. Phoenix, Arizona, Baleen Press, 1972.
Among the Stones. Pittsburgh, Monument Press, 1973.
Chosen Place. Crete, Nebraska, Best Cellar Press, 1975.
You Can't Have Everything. Pittsburgh, University of Pittsburgh Press, 1975.
The Bus to Veracruz. Pittsburgh, University of Pittsburgh Press, 1978.

Critical Studies: in *Chicago Tribune Magazine*, 22 January 1970; *Prairie Schooner* (Lincoln, Nebraska), Summer 1972; *Poetry* (Chicago), July 1972, July 1973, and April 1978; *San Francisco Chronicle*, 27 May 1973; by Philip Allan Friedman, in *Gramercy Review* (New York), Summer 1979; *Rereadings* by Michael Hogan, Crete, Nebraska, Best Cellar Press, 1979.

Richard Shelton comments:

I hope my work reflects something of the Sonora Desert, in which I have lived for more than 20 years.

* * *

At 25, Richard Shelton moved from Texas to southern Arizona (Tucson), where he has lived ever since, teaching literature courses at the University of Arizona and writing book after book of his perceptions and responses to the desert climate and terrain he has called his "chosen place." Shelton is now an inveterate Southwesterner with deep, often spiritual affinity for the rocks and saguaro cactus of the desert, the mountains, the sea a hundred miles below him in the Gulf of California. These are his usual subjects in the many books he has written since his first publication, *Journal of Return*. The sea and desert are the extremes of his personal mythology; they frame the earth for him, an earth of silences, of ghostly night animals, of rocks that exchange brief whispers about the moon on nights of the long dry season. Tucson is ringed with mountains, the Tucson Mountains, Mt. Lemmon, Mica Mountain, and others, and they are a third dimension of nature for him, an urge of nature to thrust up into the sky, a dream of the rocks that lie scattered on the desert floor. The night sky is a brilliance of immense stars in Shelton's poems, under which dark, quiet, sometimes desperate lives are endured.

His verse technique consolidates some extreme tendencies of recent American poetry – the spiritual visions of nature to be found in Robinson Jeffers's and William Stafford's work together with Robert Lowell's painful self-excoriations; but the result for Shelton is often more discord and discontinuity than wholeness of vision. The desert remains for him an ambiguous metaphor – either it is a spiritual paradise or it is the hell of exiled human life. As a result, his poetry never leaps fully into one or the other possibility, but seems suspended between a potential vision of desert infinities and an obsession with his own life-long unhappiness and scepticism ("Mexico"):

I never find what I am looking for
and each time I return older
with my ugliness intact
but with the knowledge that if it isn't there
in the darkness under Scorpio
it isn't anywhere

He writes as though his own individuality will never quite hatch out to the larger realm of nature he longs to be part of.

This alone would be sufficiently interesting drama or poetry, but for Shelton it tends to sever his poetry from its intended depth and freedom. His canon has no perceptible growth or development of vision, but rather moves through cycles of restatement and reexamination of his dilemma. At his best, he can render the desert world with striking immediacy, particularly where he feels himself to be its interpreter and voice, as in "The Kingdom of the Moon":

the moon commands the desert cold
a word so harsh
it splits the tongue
of the true aloe

the moon pulls stones
to the surface
and directs the ghosts
of dry rivers in their paths
toward the sea

And again, in "Burning":

today the rain kept
coming back as if it had
nowhere else to go

and each time
the desert welcomed it

the gates of the desert
never rust but they open
only to the voice of rain

Shelton's poetry must be judged carefully – if it is at times didactic, sentimental, indeterminate, or merely repetitious of statement, these limitations are along the way of a large and beautiful intention: to capture a region and to impose upon it a human witness and contact of extraordinary thoroughness and sensitivity. Many of his poems will drop away in time, but what will remain of his canon will be durable lyrics that are essentially American in their effort to find spiritual jointure with the land.

—Paul Christensen

SHERWIN, Judith Johnson. American. Born in New York City, 3 October 1936. Educated at the Dalton Schools, New York, graduated 1954; Radcliffe College, Cambridge, Massachusetts, 1954–55; Barnard College, New York, B.A. (cum laude) 1958; Columbia University, New York (Woodrow Wilson Fellow, 1958), 1958–59. Married James T. Sherwin in 1955; three children. Promotion Manager, Arrow Press, New York, 1961. President, Poetry Society of America, 1975–78. Recipient: Academy of American Poets prize, 1958; Yaddo Fellowship, 1964; Poetry Society of America Fellowship, 1964; Aspen Writers Workshop Rose Fellowship, 1967; Yale Series of Younger Poets Award, 1968; *St. Andrews Review* prize, 1975; *Playboy* award, for fiction, 1977. Agent: Carl Brandt, Brandt and Brandt, 101 Park Avenue, New York, New York 10017. Address: 271 Central Park West, New York, New York 10024, U.S.A.

PUBLICATIONS

Verse

Uranium Poems. New Haven, Connecticut, Yale University Press, 1969.
Impossible Buildings. New York, Doubleday, 1973.
Waste: The Town Scold, Transparencies, Dead's Good Company. Taftsville, Vermont, Countryman Press, 3 vols., 1977–79.
How the Dead Count. New York, Norton, 1978.

Plays

Belisa's Love (produced New York, 1959).
En Avant, Coco (produced New York, 1961).
two untitled multimedia works (produced Brussels, 1971, 1972).
Waste (multimedia; produced London, 1972).

Short Stories

The Life of Riot. New York, Atheneum, 1970.

Critical Studies: by Hayden Carruth, in *Harper's* (New York), June 1978, and *The Nation* (New York), January 1979; *Choice* (Middletown, Connecticut), July – August and December 1978; Rochelle Ratner, in *Soho Weekly News* (New York), 7 September 1978.

Judith Johnson Sherwin comments:

My poetry comes across in readings as drama or music more than as text. I enjoy reading with cool jazz or with quiet electronic music which provides spaces in the sound and between the sounds. Much of my poetry is meant to be sung or chanted or belted out in the shower.

All my life I have refused to let myself be limited to any theory of what poetry should be, either in form or in content. I write traditional sonnet sequences and I write surreal poems and sound poems. Every form, every technique is of equal interest; I should feel dissatisfied with my mind if there were any approach to poetry that did not excite me to see if I could go out and do likewise.

My writing, poetry, fiction and drama, is both feminist and political, but it is neither didactic nor hortatory. I write about my life as a woman and as a political animal because that's where my life is, those are the questions I have to face. However, I don't know the answers; any answer I examine is hypothesis, not conclusion.

I try to make a rough music, a dance of the mind, a calculus of the emotions, a driving beat of praise out of the pain and mystery that surround me and become me. My poems are meant to make your mind get up and shout.

* * *

Judith Johnson Sherwin's poems deal with the devastating effects of modern politics; they also constitute a weapon to defy it. Her style is characterized by incantatory repetitions and a skewed tense diction which strains the limits of conventional grammar and syntax. She often uses classic forms, sonnet and quatrain, updated with slant rhyme. Her similes and metaphors are extended and bizarre, drawn from the absurd artifacts of contemporary plastic culture but also reminiscent of the 17th-century metaphysical "conceit." Yet Sherwin's sensibility is ultra-modern, influenced by and reflective of jazz music, radio ads, and technological innovations.

Her style originated in her first book, *Uranium Poems*, where words pile up and hammer on each other without breath-break, a style suited to that book's theme and metaphor: uranium mining destroys the earth to procure ores to make bombs that destroy the world. There Sherwin also began to develop a theme which continues into her most recent work: various deaths permeate our lives, especially the death that haunts love and the bitter political deaths of our time – the murders by Eichmann, Marilyn Monroe's suicide. Love and human feeling are difficult to manifest in this destructive environment, but the poet is struggling to assert and maintain them.

In her second collection, *Impossible Buildings*, Sherwin is still hardheaded but her language and forms are less rough-hewn. In "Materials," a sequence of ten sonnets, each poems focusses on a natural substance, such as ice, wood, water, and each is made an elegant symbol for an aspect of sexual love. The prevailing theme there is larger than love, however, as the title poem makes clear. "Impossible buildings," as in M. C. Escher's drawings, are built by the artist's mind at its creative work: "the construction is/the information."

Her latest poems, in *How the Dead Count*, while often elegiac in tone (as in the long title poem) are also often angry and satiric. The stock-exchange mentality, Henry Kissinger, capitalist and technological abuses, all receive her contempt. Love comes back in this book too, as a freighted theme, a sometimes ebullient emotion but frequently bereft and sad in severance from the loved one, as in the section entitled "From Brussels." Grief shakes her and in "The Wake for Myself" induces a painful wittiness and world-play like John Donne's: "now soul, my soul, you lie so long apart/an entity, what was so long a part/and still i must retake you part by part/i search you with my study, and you fade." In this section extreme emotion leads to yet wilder metaphors – the yeti, dead yellowjackets, an acrobat's highwire, burned dinners, stereo records:

> one day the doorbell,
> striped eagles flapping their wings, rocketing
> care packages down (and i need them), they're
> mined, they go off,
> flash, sputter, burn out, but one ...
> i grab, quick, tear, in it a record ...
> i dive
> onto it, drool all over it, crunch, gobble
> it down, ouch, the cut edges cut
> my throat

The pain of love rises out of conflict with, and seems to be the price of, the poet's life as an independent woman and artist. Yet this independence is also felt as an elemental source of power, not destructive to life. In "Three Power Dances" she creates the totem of herself:

> a great Female Bear
> wide as a house sings
> out of Her dark cave
> under her fringed roots sings
> up from Her furred clutch sings.

The emphasis is on female being over male doing: "I hold back your day/your death dance, your night of war/This is My Power dance."

The final assertion of this defiant yet profoundly compassionate sensibility comes in the title poem "How the Dead Count," an elegy for the young dead of the civil rights movement and the Vietnam war, which continues the theme of death intermingled with our lives. These deaths are terrifying but bring creative richness to birth in us. It is a cosmic theme which fully encompasses Sherwin's gift for song, and for intense, far-reaching comparisons as well as her love and commitment to the human creature:

> I will say: sweet are the bells ...
> the ponderous gongs, the living breathing bells
> of the blood of the dead, the dead
> of the mouths of my city ...
> as the death count their words, as the dead count
> their wounds, as the dead count
> their lives in us, as the dead count
> continually, sweet singer say and
> say
> as the dead count.

—Jane Augustine

SHUTTLE, Penelope (Diane). British. Born in Staines, Middlesex, 12 May 1947. Educated at Staines Grammar School, 1952–59; Matthew Arnold County Secondary School, 1959–65. Lives with Peter Redgrove, *q.v.*; one daughter. Worked as a part-time shorthand typist, 1965–69. Recipient: Arts Council grant, 1969, 1972; Greenwood Poetry Prize, 1972; Eric Gregory Award, 1974. Lives in Cornwall. Agent: David Higham Associates Ltd., 5–8 Lower John Street, London W1R 4HA, England.

PUBLICATIONS

Verse

Nostalgia Neurosis. Aylesford, Kent, St. Albert's Press, 1968.
Branch. Rushden, Northamptonshire, Sceptre Press, 1971.
Midwinter Mandala. New Malden, Surrey, Headland, 1973.
The Hermaphrodite Album, with Peter Redgrove. London, Fuller D'Arch Smith, 1973.
Moon Meal. Rushden, Northamptonshire, Sceptre Press, 1973.
Autumn Piano and Other Poems. Liverpool, Rondo, 1974.
Photographs of Persephone. Feltham, Middlesex, Quarto Press, 1974.
The Songbook of the Snow and Other Poems. Ilkley, Yorkshire, Janus Press, 1974.
The Dream. Knotting, Bedfordshire, Sceptre Press, 1975.
Webs of Fire. London, Gallery Press, 1975.
Period. London, Words, 1976.
Four American Sketches. Knotting, Bedfordshire, Sceptre Press, 1976.

Plays

Radio Plays: *The Girl Who Lost Her Glove*, 1975; *The Dauntless Girl*, 1978.

Novels

An Excusable Vengeance, in *New Writers 6.* London, Calder and Boyars, 1967.
All the Usual Hours of Sleeping. London, Calder and Boyars, 1969.
Wailing Monkey Embracing a Tree. London, Calder and Boyars, 1973.
The Terrors of Dr. Treviles, with Peter Redgrove. London, Routledge, 1974.
The Glass Cottage: A Nautical Romance, with Peter Redgrove. London, Routledge, 1976.
Jesusa. Falmouth, Cornwall, Granite Press, 1976.
Rainsplitter in the Zodiac Garden. London, Boyars, 1977; New York, Longship Press, 1979.

Other

The Wise Wound: Menstruation and Everywoman, with Peter Redgrove. London, Gollancz, 1978; as *The Wise Would: Eve's Curse and Everywoman*, New York, Marek, 1978.

* * *

Though Penelope Shuttle is the author of some extraordinary novels, she is a poet who often chooses to write poetry in prose, and not a novelist who occasionally turns to poetry. Her gift is fiercely verbal, overwhelming, intense, at times hysterical, and until recently, obsessional. For like her co-author and partner, Peter Redgrove, Shuttle has dared to open her imagination fully to the forces of her subconscious experience. In all her writing there is a surreal yet totally truthful commitment to exploring hidden regions of human consciousness, particularly women's consciousness. It is this capacity for truth-telling in the shadow of madness, so to speak, that makes her, with Sylvia Plath, one of the most valuable women writers of the century.

Shuttle's theme is the ignorant – and therefore destructive – mental and sexual struggle of possessed women. In all her work vague, symbolically-named heroines – Jesusa, Elinda, Faustina, Persephone – fragment brutally into multiple personalities. They are split between "evil" selves and "good" selves, dark and light, consciousness and subconsciousness, inner world and outer world, image and mirror image. Glass, blood, candles, caves, moons, snakes, witches, spells – the full paraphernalia, in fact, of the 19th-century Gothic novel – are given substance and meaning as Shuttle gathers them into the webs of her vivid sexual fantasies.

Like many obsessional writers, Shuttle has more than once risked becoming a victim of her own sexuality. In her early novels, objectivity is virtually abandoned. The reader is pulled violently into the dark, teeming world of unceasing nightmare. In recent years, however, particularly in her poems, she seems to have emerged from nightmare into a cool dawn of great purity. Her verbal gift, powerful as ever, has allowed itself to be tightened and strengthened. Lines like the following (from "One of the Narrations" in *Four American Sketches*) say as much about the divided self as 10 or 12 pages of dense, turbulent prose:

> But the shadow of my opponent
> who wears my own inaccurate face
> reaches out from unexpected hiding places,
> ending my repose,
> dragging me to sad locations
> on the other side of the candle.
>
> Here the autumn hobbles me.
> All is cloudiness and the antagonist's hug.
> We are face to face, she and I.
> My dark side is towards the earth.

Such strength and simplicity bode well for the future. Penelope Shuttle is able to build poetry from the ruin of personality she had, of necessity, to bring about in order to find the foundations both of herself and her art. It must also be said that, while her association with Peter Redgrove has been remarkably fruitful, Shuttle has developed her own voice in the course of it. No longer is she the hermaphrodite poet of 1973; she speaks, instead, from her own woman's being. She is certainly one of the finest writers living in Britain today.

—Anne Stevenson

SIEBRASSE, Glen. Canadian. Born in Edmonton, Alberta, 5 November 1939. Educated at Loyola College, Montreal. Co-Editor, *Yes* magazine, Montreal, 1956–60, 1964–67. Managing Editor, 1965–71, and since 1972, Editor, *Delta Canada*, Montreal. Recipient: Junior Canada Council Grant, 1966; Junior Quebec grant, 1968; President's Medal, University of Western Ontario, 1969; Canada Council travel grant, 1971. Address: 351 Gerald Street, Lasalle 690, Quebec, Canada.

PUBLICATIONS

Verse

The Regeneration of an Athlete. Montreal, Delta Canada, 1965.

Man: Unman. Montreal, Delta Canada, 1969.
Jerusalem. Montreal, Delta Canada, 1971.

Glen Siebrasse comments:

These books contain all the poetry I never wished to write.

* * *

"My poetry has often been interpreted as a study in death," Glen Siebrasse has explained. "Death is the only thing we have time to fear," he added in a poem. If by death is meant decline as well as decomposition, then this characterization of his theme is a good as any. Like the monk with the skull labelled "Memento Mori" at his elbow as he works, Siebrasse is ever-conscious of the presence of what has been affectionately called "the great leveller."

Perhaps the central book to this theme or obsession is *The Regeneration of an Athlete* which charts decline and laments the impossibility of ascent. Even birth is depicted in terms of caricature, as in "Woman Gives Birth to a Frog": "we mock life:/grow each day/ weaker.//The bones swell in our skull heads." Ever aging, even lovers are advised to leave evidence of their mortality. In "Harrison," he writes: "build for a thousand years that others/ coming after/will note men stopped here/embracing, even under the bombs."

This is a difficult poetry, sometimes rewarding, sometimes merely puzzling. Siebrasse's poems are, as Peter Stevens noted in the *Supplement to the Oxford Companion to Canadian History and Literature* (1973), "carefully organized; some sometimes thickly, even opaquely, textured." The writing is technically unexceptional, except when the poet is moved to create, *sui generis*, a new tone and technique, as in "The Field":

The field contains the hunter and the hare:
the hunter kills the hare,
kills the field,
kills himself;
the field begins itself again,
begins the hare,
begins the hunter:
the field contains the hunter and the hare.

—John Robert Colombo

SILKIN, Jon. British. Born in London, 2 December 1930. Educated at Wycliffe and Dulwich colleges; University of Leeds (Gregory Fellow, 1958–60), B.A. (honours) 1962. Served in the Army Education Corps, 1948–50. Formerly, Extramural Lecturer, University of Leeds, and University of Newcastle; Beck Visiting Lecturer of Writing, Denison University, Granville, Ohio; Visiting Lecturer, Writers Workshop, University of Iowa, Iowa City, 1968–69, Australian Arts Council and University of Sydney, 1974, and College of Idaho, Caldwell, 1977. Since 1952, Founding Co-Editor, *Stand*, Newcastle upon Tyne; since 1964, Co-founding Editor, Northern House, publishers, Newcastle upon Tyne. Recipient: Northern Arts Minor Award, 1965; Faber Memorial Prize, 1966; C. Day Lewis Fellowship, 1976. Address: 19 Haldane Terrace, Newcastle upon Tyne NE2 3AN, England.

PUBLICATIONS

Verse

The Portrait and Other Poems. Ilfracombe, Devon, Stockwell, 1950.
The Peaceable Kingdom. London, Chatto and Windus, 1954; New York, Yorick Books, 1969.
The Two Freedoms. London, Chatto and Windus, and New York, Macmillan, 1958.
The Re-ordering of the Stones. London, Chatto and Windus-Hogarth Press, 1961.
Flower Poems. Leeds, Northern House, 1964.
Nature with Man. London, Chatto and Windus-Hogarth Press, 1965.
Penguin Modern Poets 7, with Richard Murphy and Nathaniel Tarn. London, Penguin, 1966.
Poems New and Selected. London, Chatto and Windus, and Middletown, Connecticut, Wesleyan University Press, 1966.
Three Poems. Cambridge, Massachusetts, Pym Randall Press, 1969.
Killhope Wheel. Ashington, Northumberland, MidNAG, 1971.
Amana Grass. London, Chatto and Windus-Hogarth Press, and Middletown, Connecticut, Wesleyan University Press, 1971.
Air That Pricks Earth. Rushden, Northamptonshire, Sceptre Press, 1973.
The Principle of Water. Cheadle, Cheshire, Carcanet Press, 1974.
A "Jarapiri" Poem. Knotting, Bedfordshire, Sceptre Press, 1975.
The Little Time-Keeper. Manchester, Carcanet Press, 1976; New York, Norton, 1977.
Two Images of Continuing Trouble. Richmond, Surrey, Keepsake Press, 1976.
Jerusalem. Knotting, Bedfordshire, Sceptre Press, 1977.
Into Praising. Sunderland, Ceolfrith, 1978.
The Lapidary Poems. Knotting, Bedfordshire, Sceptre Press, 1979.
The Psalms with Their Spoils. London, Routledge, 1980.

Other

Isaac Rosenberg, 1890–1918: A Catalogue of the Exhibition Held at Leeds University, May–June 1959, Together with the Text of Unpublished Material, with Maurice de Sausmarez. Leeds, University of Leeds, 1959.
Out of Battle: The Poetry of the Great War. London and New York, Oxford University Press, 1972.

Editor, with Anthony Cronin and Terence Tiller, *New Poems 1960.* London, Hutchinson, 1960.
Editor, *Living Voices: An Anthology of Contemporary Verse.* London, Vista, 1960.
Editor, *Poetry of the Committed Individual: A "Stand" Anthology of Poetry.* London, Gollancz-Penguin, 1973.
Editor, *The Penguin Book of First World War Poetry.* London, Allen Lane, 1979.
Editor, with Peter Redgrove, *New Poetry 5.* London, Hutchinson, 1979.

Translator, *Against Parting*, by Nathan Zach. Newcastle upon Tyne, Northern House, 1968.

Critical Studies: by John Fuller, in *London Magazine*, October 1966; Merle Brown, in *Iowa Review* (Iowa City), i, 1, 1969; "Alone in a Mine of Reality: A Matrix in the Poetry of Jon Silkin" by Anne Cluysenaar, in *British Poetry since 1960* edited by Michael Schmidt and Grevel Lindop, Oxford, Carcanet Press, 1972; in *Times literary Supplement* (London), 19 July 1974; in *The Tablet* (London), 10 August 1974; "The Hand That Erases" by Mark Abley, in *Oxford Literary Journal*, Spring 1977; "Stress in Silkin's Poetry and the Healing Emptiness of America" by Merle Brown, in *Contemporary Literature* (Madison, Wisconsin),

Summer 1977; "Reflections on Anglo-Jewish Poetry" by William Baker, in *Jewish Quarterly* (London), Autumn–Winter 1978–79; *A Reader's Guide to Fifty British Poets from Hopkins to Hill* by Michael Schmidt, London, Pan, 1979.

John Silkin comments:

Most writers speak less interestingly of their own work, more openly and responsively about the work of those they admire or care for deeply. It is the difference between the desire to be meticulous about oneself, in a nicely judicious way, and the less pernickety response one affords another's work. Such self-introductory exculpations aren't likely to be productive, but they do at least show a degree of self-consciousness which ought to be the leavening to my faith in narrative, linear, Hebraic writing.

The narrative, we are told, is dead; and the writer's central act of faith is now directed towards imagism. Faith, of course, can do many things, but, for me at any rate, the lessons of imagism are to be *absorbed* and its effects used conjunctively with narrative. The dangers of sensuous art, an art committed to giving the sensuous adequate expression, are repetition, over-abundance and prolixity. These, I am sure, are my dangers, and narrative alone can't contain these productions. If imagism is impacted with narrative – or so I have believed – imagistic profile is given substance and value, and narrative is contained. More than contained, it is re-structured by the demands of imagism. Imagism continues to affect my work. I want to say what I have to say, once, and get out. The syntax must have an onwardness, and even when it's motionless, a moment, it must not be repetitious or anxious to produce an effect.

Yet having said these things, I am aware how much this is only half the story. It is the conscious application of one nexus of aspirations to a quite different psychology; thus my work is dual and in constant tension. That, too, must go for its thematic concerns. How does the Peaceable Kingdom make room for those creatures who do not want to belong to it, and would destroy it if it tried to bring them into its condition of love? That, approximately, is the impulsion of my concerns.

In his essay on Tolstoy's view of history, Isaiah Berlin quotes a fragment by the Greek poet Archilochus: "The fox knows many things, but the hedgehog knows one big thing." Berlin glosses this with: "Taken figuratively [the fragment divides] those, on one side, who relate everything to a single central vision ... and, on the other side, those who pursue many ends, often unrelated, and even contradictory" (*The Hedgehog and the Fox*). I identify my work with the figure of the hedgehog as he is here typified, uneasy creature though he be; and I do this, not out of ambitiousness, but because I can write no other way. My first collection, *The Peaceable Kingdom*, re-enacts Isaiah's vision where "the wolf also shall dwell with the lamb, and the leopard shall lie down with the kid." My work has changed, but that root has never been torn up.

* * *

George Steiner in *Language and Silence* queried the relevance and value of poetry, asking whether we could really consider it a civilizing agent when the civilization that fashioned it also contrived the Holocaust. Jon Silkin, writing since 1950, assuming at times the voice of the Jew, at others the voice of the Northumbrian, attempts in his poetry to speak to the dilemma Steiner posed and write a poetry of "committed individuals." Describing his background as a "mixture of rationalist agnosticism and dilute Orthodox Judaism" (*The Little Time-Keeper*), and calling himself a poet who wants to mingle the techniques of Imagism with a discursive style that allows for moral commentary, Silkin has used his editorship of the Newcastle-based literary journal, *Stand*, to foster a poetry that speaks of responsibilities, of community, and moral probings and escapes the charge of excessive gentility that A. Alvarez levelled against the poets of The Movement.

Silkin's poetry is didactic in the sense urged by Matthew Arnold. Some of his poems express the regional voice of Northumbria and set the coal mines and the mist-enshrouded sheep pastures in their historical perspective. The poems in "Killhope Wheel" (*Amana Grass*; reprinted with one addition in *The Principle of Water*) commemorate the cast iron wheel that washed the ore in County Durham in 1860, and the miners bayoneted by soldiers in the strikes fought to bring relief to the workers from the wretched pay and whiggish policies of the mine owners. Other poems, beginning in *The Two Freedoms*, and becoming more overtly political in the recent volumes, *The Little Time-Keeper* and *Jerusalem*, speak of the Jewish problem, Silkin's own Jewishness, and Britain's expulsion of the Jews in 1190. Whether it is man's inhumanity to man enacted in the coal fields or the gas chambers, or his inhumanity to beasts or the humans he loves that Silkin writes of, he clings tenaciously to the hope that he can recover innocence. His lines in "Small hills among the fells" from "Killhope Wheel" are appropriate to many of his poems of social criticism: "I am trying to make again the feeling/ plants have, and each creature has, looked at,/demure, exultant...."

His early volume *The Peaceable Kingdom* introduced many of the themes later developed in Silkin's poetry: the majesty and innocence of animals, fear occasioned by knowledge of man's and nature's cruelty, man's struggle in darkness to love and to know himself, and man's bewilderment at a world too full of loss. As his verse has developed, Silkin has alternately practiced a lyrical poetry comparable in its simplicity to Blake's *Songs of Innocence and Experience* and an intricate, labyrinthian poetry, with wrenched syntax and obfuscating diction, which arduously struggles to express the contradictions inherent in love, and the triumph of the human spirit that somehow outlasts the degradations of the concentration camps. Two of Silkin's long narrative poems, "Amana Grass" and "The People," suffer from the flaws that mar Silkin's verse – convoluted syntax, overuse of ellipses, ponderous and lapidary building of similes and metaphors – but are worth the strain they put upon the reader. The dialogue is somewhat stilted in "Amana Grass" and the estrangement of the lovers is too like that expressed in Frost's "The Hill Wife" or "Home Burial" while the comparison is unkind to Silkin. But in "The People" Silkin successfully narrates the slightly disguised autobiographical story that lies behind his most frequently praised poem, "Death of a Son," and enlarges its scope. He unfolds, largely through a series of dramatic monologues, the collective tragedy of his and his wife's love so sorely taxed by the birth of their brain-damaged son and the place of Stein, their neighbour and a victim of the concentration camps, in this anguishing experience. Stein becomes the agent to make "two unloving animals/find mercy's image: love." "The People" is probably Silkin's most ambitious poem to date, and next to "Death of a Son" it is his best. The characters, event, and language are unforgettable, and what difficulties there are that perplex the poem needlessly are easily overlooked.

In *The Little Time-Keeper* Silkin has returned to his simple style, with short poems, stanzaic divisions, and a heavy injection of social and political commentary. In this collection Silkin's fear deepens to embrace not only his personal fear of his own death and the death of those he loves, but a dread that an entropic view of the universe may indeed be scientifically and metaphysically correct. As Silkin matures, his poetry has become more certain, his moral concerns more timely, but also, perhaps, less subtle, and his subjects more varied. At his best, he has written some of the most moving poems of the century.

—Carol Simpson Stern

SILLITOE, Alan. British. Born in Nottingham, 4 March 1928. Educated in various Nottingham schools up to the age of 14. Served as a radio operator in the Royal Air Force, 1946–49. Married Ruth Fainlight, *q.v.*, in 1959; two children. Travelled in France, Italy and Spain, 1952–58. Since 1970, Literary Adviser to W. H. Allen and Company, publishers,

London. Recipient: Authors Club prize, 1958; Hawthornden Prize, for fiction, 1960. Address: 21 The Street, Wittersham, Kent, England.

PUBLICATIONS

Verse

Without Beer or Bread. London, Outposts, 1957.
The Rats and Other Poems. London, W. H. Allen, 1960.
A Falling Out of Love and Other Poems. London, W. H. Allen, 1964.
Love in the Environs of Voronezh. London, Macmillan, 1968; New York, Doubleday, 1970.
Shaman and Other Poems. London, Turret, 1968.
Poems, with Ted Hughes and Ruth Fainlight. London, Rainbow Press, 1971.
Barbarians and Other Poems. London, Turret, 1974.
Storm: New Poems. London, W. H. Allen, 1974.
Day-Dream Communique. Knotting, Bedfordshire, Sceptre Press, 1977.
From "Snow on the North Side of Lucifer." Knotting, Bedfordshire, Sceptre Press, 1979.
Snow on the North Side of Lucifer. London, W. H. Allen, 1979.

Plays

The Ragman's Daughter (produced Felixstowe, Suffolk, 1966).
All Citizens Are Soldiers, with Ruth Fainlight, adaptation of a play by Lope de Vega (produced Stratford upon Avon and London, 1967). London, Macmillan, and Chester Springs, Pennsylvania, Dufour, 1969.
The Slot Machine (as *This Foreign Field*, produced London, 1970). Included in *Three Plays*, 1978.
Pit Strike (televised, 1977). Included in *Three Plays*, 1978.
The Interview (produced London, 1978). Included in *Three Plays*, 1978.
Three Plays (includes *The Slot Machine, Pit Strike, The Interview*). London, W. H. Allen, 1978.

Screenplays: *Saturday Night and Sunday Morning*, 1960; *The Loneliness of the Long Distance Runner*, 1961; *The Ragman's Daughter*, 1974.

Television Play: *Pit Strike*, 1977.

Novels

Saturday Night and Sunday Morning. London, W. H. Allen, 1958; New York, Knopf, 1959.
The General. London, W. H. Allen, 1960; New York, Knopf, 1961; as *Counterpoint*, New York, Avon, 1968.
Key to the Door. London, W. H. Allen, 1961; New York, Knopf, 1962.
The Death of William Posters. London, Macmillan, and New York, Knopf, 1965.
A Tree on Fire. London, Macmillan, and New York, Knopf, 1967.
A Start in Life. London, W. H. Allen, 1970; New York, Scribner, 1971.
Travels in Nihilon. London, W. H. Allen, 1971; New York, Scribner, 1972.
Raw Material. London, W. H. Allen, 1972; New York, Scribner, 1973.
The Flame of Life. London, W. H. Allen, 1974.
The Widower's Son. London, W. H. Allen, 1976; New York, Harper, 1977.
The Storyteller. London, W. H. Allen, 1979.

Short Stories

The Loneliness of the Long Distance Runner. London, W. H. Allen, 1959; New York, Knopf, 1960.
The Ragman's Daughter. London, W. H. Allen, 1963; New York, Knopf, 1964.
Guzman Go Home. London, Macmillan, and New York, Doubleday, 1968.
Men, Women, and Children. London, W. H. Allen, 1973; New York, Scribner, 1974.
Down to the Bone. Exeter, Wheaton, 1976.

Other

Road to Volgograd (travel). London, W. H. Allen, and New York, Knopf, 1964.
The City Adventures of Marmalade (juvenile). London, Macmillan, 1967; revised edition, London, Robson, 1977.
Mountains and Caverns: Selected Essays. London, W. H. Allen, 1975.
Big John and the Stars (juvenile). London, Robson, 1977.
The Incredible Fencing Fleas (juvenile). London, Robson, 1978.

Editor, *Poems for Shakespeare 7.* London, Bear Gardens Museum and Arts Centre, 1979.

Critical Studies: *Alan Sillitoe*, London, Times Authors, 1970; *Alan Sillitoe* by Allen Richard Penner, New York, Twayne, 1972; *Alan Sillitoe: A Critical Assessment* by Stanley Atherton, London, W. H. Allen, 1979.

Alan Sillitoe comments:

I use poetry to express emotions that can't be expressed in any other medium.

I am incapable of analysing my own poetry. When I first began to write I considered myself more a poet than a writer. However, novels and stories seem to have overtaken me – though I still am, and still consider myself to be, primarily a poet. A great deal of my "poetry" gets into my prose work, and it is often difficult to find a dividing line. If I have any aim in poetry it is to use images and language as a means of breaking through to new experience – that is to say, old experiences that have not been described before.

* * *

Alan Sillitoe is much better known as a novelist than he is as a poet, and one cannot help feeling that, in essence, this is the correct verdict. Yet it is also true to say that Sillitoe has not received credit for his poems. His first and most substantial collection, *The Rats*, was mostly written in the 1950's; and the poems in it reflect the boredom and impatience which many radical writers felt with the English society of that epoch. The "rats" of the title are the forces of conformity: "They are the government, these marsh-brained rats/Who give protection from outsider cats...." But, in addition to satires, the book also contains a number of tender love poems.

This impatience with society and the way it is going is just one of the characteristics which suggest a comparison with D. H. Lawrence. Lawrence, like Sillitoe, came from the working-class, from Nottingham, made his reputation as a novelist, and spent much time as an expatriate. Like Lawrence's, Sillitoe's poems have been consistently undervalued. More recent work, such as the poems in *Love in the Environs of Voronezh*, shows a marked increase in technical control, but also a continuing impatience with poetic convention – radical conventions as well as conservative ones. Sillitoe seems to write a poem because there is something which, as he sees it, needs to be said. The quality of the "saying" tends to vary a good deal from poem to poem, but one is always aware of the direct thrust of a powerful literary personality.

—Edward Lucie-Smith

SIMIC, Charles. American. Born in Yugoslavia, 9 May 1938; emigrated to the United States in 1949. Educated at Oak Park High School, Illinois; University of Chicago, 1956–59; New York University, 1959–61, 1963–65, B.A. 1964. Served in the United States Army, 1961–63. Married Helene Dubin in 1965; one daughter. Formerly, Proofreader, *Chicago Sun-Times*. Taught English at California State College, Hayward. Since 1974, Associate Professor of English, University of New Hampshire, Durham. Editorial Assistant, *Aperture* magazine, New York, 1966–74. Recipient: Guggenheim Fellowship, 1972; National Endowment for the Arts grant, 1974; Edgar Allan Poe Award, 1975; National Institute of Arts and Letters award, 1976. Address: Old Mountain Road, Northwood, New Hampshire 03261, U.S.A.

PUBLICATIONS

Verse

What the Grass Says. San Francisco, Kayak, 1967.
Somewhere among Us a Stone Is Taking Notes. San Francisco, Kayak, 1969.
Dismantling the Silence. New York, Braziller, and London, Cape, 1971.
White. New York, New Rivers Press, 1972.
Return to a Place Lit by a Glass of Milk. New York, Braziller, 1974.
Charon's Cosmology. New York, Braziller, 1977.
Brooms: Selected Poems. Barry, Glamorgan, Edge Press, 1978.
School for Dark Thoughts. Pawlet, Vermont, Banyan Press, 1978.

Other

Editor and Translator, *Five Gardens*, by Luan Lauc. New York, New Rivers Press, 1970.
Editor and Translator, *Selected Poems of Ivan V. Lalic.* New York, New Rivers Press, 1970.
Editor and Translator, *Four Yugoslav Poets: Ivan V. Lalic, Brank Miljkovic, Milorad Pavic, Ljubomir Simovic.* New York, Lillabulero Press, 1970.
Editor and Translator, *The Little Box: Poems*, by Vasco Popa. Washington, D.C., Charioteer Press, 1970.
Editor, with Mark Strand, *Another Republic: 17 European and South American Writers.* New York, Ecco Press, 1976.

Translator, *Key to Dream According to Djordje.* Chicago, Elpenor, 1978.

* * *

Every so often American poetry exhausts its creative juices and requires new spiritual input for its rejuvenation. In the late 1960's verse was at such a stand-still and poets turned to read, translate, and absorb the ideas of a wide variety of South American and European poets, who offered them a language that mingled political distrust with dream logic and fantasy. The uneasy political and economic conditions of the 1970's made American poets eager to tap the energy of their counterparts. Mark Strand, Marvin Bell, W. S. Merwin, among others, distinguished themselves as translators of Spanish and French poetry and as poets of a new Symbolist era. Charles Simic is of their company, and his half-dozen books have now made him a major voice of this decade.

Simic's verse, composed in tightly worded quatrains and couplets, secretes a dark universe of haunting apparitions and animated common objects thriving beyond ordinary consciousness. The only allegory apparent here is a Symbolist one of catching the drift of one's dreams and dark interiors through distorted analogies to the waking world. The wonder of Simic is that however strange his vision of simple things, his grasp of the illogical is striking – the reader feels that somehow he has been there himself but never put to words his experience. Simic's declarations are deadpan; the syntax is as placid as a school teacher's geography lesson – even when the earth he describes (in "A Landscape with Crutches") becomes a Daliesque nightmare:

I can't get any peace around here:
The bread on its artificial limbs,
A headless doll in a wheelchair,
And my mother, mind you, using
Two knives for crutches as she squats to pee.

But a makeshift vision assembles behind these brief lyrical configurations – a sense of imminent capture, of death behind every flash of life, of a pervasive whiteness suffusing everything with its sterility and lust for oblivion. He puts his persona into a lonely world of infinite emptiness where individuality shrinks to atomic size ("Euclid Avenue"):

All my dark thoughts
laid out
in a straight line.

An abstract street
on which an equally abstract intelligence
forever advances, doubting
the sound of its own footsteps.

Simic's sense of modern political terror is all the more chilling for its mordant wit and nonchalance. His persona is often the unflappable nice guy before the monster apparitions of the dark. He has, in fact, something of Kafka's macabre fine touch and irony. Simic, born in Yugoslavia, has about him the sinister imagination that is characteristic of the Eastern European sensibility in literature – from its ghostly tales of Transylvania to the most recent Symbolist terrorism of contemporary Slavic poetry (of which Simic has been a prolific translator). And his lyric strikes deep into the American psyche – he not only brings to focus a deep horror of political tyranny and repression, he reminds us of our own tenuous freedoms.

The weakness of this kind of poetry is that it can use up its monochrome realm quickly. There are only so many chilling and intense metaphors for one's dreams and fears, and already Simic seems to be coming to the end of his subject. His early books mined out the worst, most terrifying memories and illusions of his Yugoslav childhood, whereas *Charon's Cosmology* seems less potent, even airy by comparison. The book may be transitional to a new subject, perhaps his American identity and his more immediate circumstances in academic life, which he already seems to be edging toward.

—Paul Christensen

SIMMONS, James (Stewart Alexander). British. Born in Londonderry, Northern Ireland, 14 February 1933. Educated at Foyle College, Londonderry; Campbell College, Belfast; University of Leeds, Yorkshire, B.A. (honours) in English 1958. Married to Laura Stinson; four daughters and one son. Has taught at Friends School, Lisburn, Northern Ireland, and Ahmadu Bello University, Zaria, Nigeria. Since 1968, Member of the English Department, New University of Ulster, Coleraine. Editor, *Poetry and Audience*, Leeds, 1957–58. Founder, *The Honest Ulsterman*, 1963, and The Poor Genius Record Company, 1976. Recipient: Eric Gregory Award, 1962; Cholmondeley Award, 1977. Address: 15 Kerr Street, Portrush, Northern Ireland.

PUBLICATIONS

Verse

Ballad of a Marriage. Belfast, Festival, 1966.
Late But in Earnest. London, Bodley Head, 1967.
Ten Poems. Belfast, Festival, 1968.
In the Wilderness and Other Poems. London, Bodley Head, 1969.
Songs for Derry, music by the author. Belfast, Ulsterman, 1969.
No Ties. Belfast, Ulsterman, 1970.
Energy to Burn. London, Bodley Head, 1971.
No Land Is Waste, Dr. Eliot. Richmond, Surrey, Keepsake Press, 1972.
The Long Summer Still to Come. Belfast, Blackstaff Press, 1973.
West Strand Visions. Belfast, Blackstaff Press, 1974.
Memorials of a Tour in Yorkshire. Belfast, Ulsterman, 1975.
Judy Garland and the Cold War. Belfast, Blackstaff Press, 1976.
The Selected James Simmons, edited by Edna Longley. Belfast, Blackstaff Press, 1978.

Recordings: *City and Western*, Outlets Records; *Pubs*, BBC.

Play

Aikin Mata: The Lysistrata of Aristophanes, with T. W. Harrison. Ibadan, Oxford University Press, 1966.

Other

Editor, with A. R. Mortimer, *Out on the Edge.* Leeds, Leeds University, 1958.
Editor, *Ten Irish Poets: An Anthology.* Cheadle, Cheshire, Carcanet Press, 1974.
Editor, *Soundings 3: Annual Anthology of New Irish Writing.* Belfast, Blackstaff Press, 1975.

Manuscript Collections: University of Texas, Austin; New University of Ulster, Coleraine.

Critical Study: Interview with Robert Chapman, in *Confrontations* (New York), Spring 1975.

James Simmons comments:

I see myself in the mainstream of English poetry, following Shakespeare, as most of the poets I admire do, Blake, Hopkins, Hardy, Burns, Yeats, etc. Ewan MacColl reviving the old ballads opened up the possibility of better songs, and also a sense of serious writing, tragedy, being possible in a popular form. For all their self-indulgence the new song-writers (Dylan, Mitchell, Newman, etc.) have a sort of excitement that seems to be lacking in contemporary poetry. The new fashion for reading poetry aloud has turned out to be boring in most cases. Find myself getting curmudgeonly about "experiment," for it so often seems a way for bad poets to disguise their limitations. Don't feel much inclined to argue the toss anymore.

* * *

James Simmons is a curiously vulnerable poet, despite his rumbustious style and the projected, even cultivated, persona of the good-humouredly lecherous boozer: "Our youth was gay but rough,/much drink and copulation./If that seems not enough/blame our miseducation." His rhymes thump steadily home giving the careless reader an impression of verbal insensitivity, and the humour is sometimes so robust that a superficial reading can leave one unaware of the quality of Simmons's sensibility, which may well account for the unfortunate reception given to his collections by certain reviewers. The poem "One of the Boys," from which the four lines quoted above are taken, can be seen as a joyfully iconoclastic romp: "the great careers all tricks,/the fine arts all my arse,/business and politics/a cruel farce." But the final lines get under the surface of this defensive philistinism, to point its emptiness and the subconscious awareness of its emptiness in its practitioners:

Though fear of getting fired
may ease, and work is hated
less, we are tired, tired
and incapacitated.
On golf courses, in bars,
crutched by the cash we earn,
we think of nights in cars
with energy to burn.

There is a sympathetic understanding here of a tragic sense of loss, which reminds me, obliquely, of the purport of that line in Philip Larkin's poem "Mr. Bleaney": "That how we live measures our own nature." And though "One of the Boys" is heavily rhymed, the rhymes can be seen to underpin the poem and as by no means intrusive. But while this poem succeeds, Simmons's style and stance are replete with the dangers of the sentimental "good-natured tart" variety, and it can involve a deal of casuistry as when in "The Wife-swappers" the poet attempts to equate (and therefore justify) a taste for lechery with an honest harmlessness.

It could be said, of course, that Donne, too, indulged in such sophistry; but he employed considerably more wit and subtlety, if that can be considered a defence. It all comes down to the fact, I suppose, that Simmons sees the poet as an entertainer and moralist, and while he never fails to entertain (no mean achievement) the entertainer sometimes elbows out the moralist. Yet, for the most part, not very far from the clowning and posturing surface of his more swashbuckling poems there is always a hint of *carpe diem* or an awareness of values missed: "Your dumbness on a walk/was better than my clown's talk./You showed me what you meant ..." ("Goodbye Sally"). And at its best Simmons's poetry can express an understanding of and empathy with certain aspects of the human tragedy which are only considered minor because they occur with such frequency and are common to so many. Notice here, in "Antigone's Hour," how he moderates the often heavy beat of his poetry to a minor key as it were, so that the tragic element is, in fact, in the very ordinariness of what is often seen as an extraordinary situation:

All risks are a tribute
to the adventurous dead.
Gathering fine small flowers
was all they wanted said....

No guards observed them
acting the clown.
Their own doubts what to do
next let them down.

The very real strength of Simmons's poetry resides in his basic humanity, and his sympathy and preference for the human condition however fallible and whatever its faults, as in "Stephano Remembers": "We were distracted by too many things .../the wine, the jokes, the music, fancy gowns/We were no good as murderers, we were clowns." The constant use of the "clown" as an archetype is a clue here.

—John Cotton

SIMPSON, Louis (Aston Marantz). American. Born in Jamaica, West Indies, 27 March 1923. Educated at Murro College, Jamaica, 1933–40, Cambridge Higher Schools Certificate, 1940; Columbia University, New York, B.S. 1948, A.M. 1950, Ph.D. 1959. Served in the United States Army, 1943–45: Purple Heart and Bronze Star. Married 1) Jeanne Claire Rogers in 1949 (divorced, 1954), one son; 2) Dorothy Roochvarg in 1955, one son and one daughter. Editor, Bobbs-Merrill Publishing Company, New York, 1950–55; Instructor, Columbia University, 1955–59; Professor of English, University of California, Berkeley, 1959–67. Since 1967, Professor of English, State University of New York, Stony Brook. Recipient: American Academy in Rome Fellowship, 1957; *Hudson Review* Fellowship, 1957; Edna St. Vincent Millay Award, 1960; Guggenheim Fellowship, 1962, 1970; American Council of Learned Societies Grant, 1963; Pulitzer Prize, 1964; Columbia University Medal for Excellence, 1965; National Institute of Arts and Letters award, 1976. D.H.L.: Eastern Michigan University, Ypsilanti, 1977. Address: P.O. Box 91, Port Jefferson, New York 11777, U.S.A.

PUBLICATIONS

Verse

The Arrivistes: Poems 1940–1949. Paris, privately printed, 1949; New York, Fine Editions Press, n.d.
Good News of Death and Other Poems. New York, Scribner, 1955.
A Dream of Governors. Middletown, Connecticut, Wesleyan University Press, 1959.
At the End of the Open Road. Middletown, Connecticut, Wesleyan University Press, 1963.
Five American Poets, with others, edited by Thom Gunn and Ted Hughes. London, Faber, 1963.
Selected Poems. New York, Harcourt Brace, 1965; London, Oxford University Press, 1966.
Adventures of the Letter I. London, Oxford University Press, 1971; New York, Harper, 1972.
Searching for the Ox: New Poems and a Preface. New York, Morrow, and London, Oxford University Press, 1976.

Recording: *Today's Poets 1*, with others, Folkways, 1967.

Plays

The Father Out of the Machine: A Masque, in *Chicago Review*, Winter 1951.
Andromeda, in *Hudson Review* (New York), Winter 1956.

Novel

Riverside Drive. New York, Atheneum, 1962.

Other

James Hogg: A Critical Study. Edinburgh, Oliver and Boyd, and New York, St. Martin's Press, 1962.
Air with Armed Men (autobiography). London, London Magazine Editions, 1972; as *North of Jamaica*, New York, Harper, 1972.
Three on the Tower: The Lives and Works of Ezra Pound, T. S. Eliot, and William Carlos Williams. New York, Morrow, 1975.
A Revolution in Taste: Studies of Dylan Thomas, Allen Ginsberg, Sylvia Plath, and Robert Lowell. New York, Macmillan, 1978.

Editor, with Donald Hall and Robert Pack, *New Poets of England and America.* Cleveland, Meridian, 1957.
Editor, *An Introduction to Poetry.* New York, St. Martin's Press, 1967; London, Macmillan, 1968.

Manuscript Collection: Library of Congress, Washington, D.C.

Critical Studies: "The Poetry of Louis Simpson" by C. B. Cox, in *Critical Quarterly 8* (Manchester), Spring 1966; "The Wesleyan Poets – II" by Norman Friedman, in *Chicago Review 19*, 1966; *Louis Simpson*, by Ronald Moran, New York, Twayne, 1972 (includes bibliography); "A Child of the World" by Dave Smith, in *American Poetry Review* (Philadelphia), January–February 1979.

Louis Simpson comments:

(1970) I have written about many subjects: war, love, American landscape and history. For several years I have been writing in free form. Influences: many poets, English and American – particularly Eliot and Whitman. I believe that poetry rises from the inner life of the poet and is expressed in original images and rhythms. Also, the language of poetry should be closely related to the language in which men actually think and speak.

(1980) My earliest published work was in traditional forms. At the end of the 1950's I began writing in irregular, unrhymed lines – I was attempting to write verse that would sound like speech. My subjects have frequently been taken from life and in many of my poems there is a narrative or dramatic element. I aim at transparency, to let the action, feeling, and idea come through with no interference. Writing well is like meditating, it requires rising above the merely personal.

* * *

Louis Simpson's *Selected Poems* contains portions from his four previous volumes – *The Arrivistes*, *Good News of Death*, *A Dream of Governors*, and *At the End of the Open Road* – as well as a dozen "New Poems." The last two volumes alone, published only four years apart, reveal his remarkable growth. Dealing with war, love, history, the emptiness of modern life, the American in Europe, *A Dream of Governors* is knowing and intelligent but somewhat too formal, avoiding simultaneously the pressure of passion and the perspective of vision.

At the End of the Open Road, which received the Pulitzer Prize, is a very different matter entirely. Simpson has found the key to the meaning and power of his themes. The development of a poem from the routine to the timeless, the external to the internal, and situation to response is no longer a matter of mere machinery but rather of vital shock. It is not simply that his style is getting more experimental, but more that this flexibility is a sign of growth in the character and thought of the speaker, an openness to life whereby the poet risks being changed by what he experiences, and Simpson is on his way to becoming a major poet.

Here we have another group of poems about America, but they are much more penetrating than those in *A Dream of Governors*. "In California," for example, begins: "Here I am, troubling the dream coast/With my New York face." And this is "In the Suburbs" entire:

> There's no way out.
> You were born to waste your life.
> You were born to this middleclass life
> As others before you
> Were born to walk in procession
> To the temple, singing.

There are also the three poems at the end inspired by Whitman, who was also hailed in "In California": Simpson knows that "The Open Road goes [now] to the used-car lot," and that, since the past keeps repeating itself, it cannot be cancelled out. And then, finally, that "At the end of the open road we come to ourselves." He has come a long way from the somewhat easy Sherwood-Andersonianism of "Hot Night on Water Street" and "The Boarder" from *A Dream of Governors*. America's emptiness is now seen in its historical context, and thus the poet's satire has cause and direction.

Then there is a group of four wonderful love poems – "Summer Morning," "The Silent Lover," "Birch," and "The Sea and the Forest" – which are by far more meaningful and passionate than his earlier erotic lyrics. In "Summer Morning," for example, the speaker remembers having been with a girl in a hotel room in an abandoned section of New York 15 years ago, and he feels the weight of the intervening time, concluding: "So I have spoiled my chances./For what? Sheer laziness,/The thrill of an assignation,/My life that I hold in secret." And finally, there is a remarkable piece called "American Poetry," a marvel of concise meaning, which I quote in full:

> Whatever it is, it must have
> A stomach that can digest
> Rubber, coal, uranium, moons, poems.
>
> Like the shark, it contains a shoe.
> It must swim for miles through the desert
> Uttering cries that are almost human.

Simpson has digested the indigestible and has now embarked on his long swim through the desert.

Thus we find him realizing, two years later, in "The Laurel Tree" from "New Poems": "I must be patient with shapes/Of automobile fenders and ketchup bottles./These things are the beginning/of things not visible to the naked eye." And, in a confrontation between the speaker and an unearthly visitor, in "Things," the latter tells him: "Things which to us in the pure state are mysteries,/Are your simplest articles of household use." To which the speaker replies: "I have suspected/The Mixmaster knows more than I do,/The air conditioner is the better poet."

The spirituality of the mundane is surely a Whitmanesque theme, and Simpson returns in his next book *Adventures of the Letter I*, to his obsession with America:

I myself am the union of these states,
offering liberty and equality to all.
I share the land equally, I support the arts,

I am developing backward areas.
I look on the negro as myself, I accuse myself
of sociopathic tendencies, I accuse my accusers.

Here he has wittily captured the authentic Whitman mood and cadence – and then the feeling falls and he becomes depressed. But once more he must learn to be patient, he says, and "to breathe in, breathe out,/and to sit by the bed and watch."

Adventures of the Letter I is a marvelous and varied book, fulfilling all of his earlier promise and carrying it a stage further. It begins, for example, with a strange and fable-like section on Volhynia Province, where the poet creates an imaginary version of that part of old Russia his mother came from. And there is a section called "Individuals," which contains a very effective and affecting narrative portrait, "Vandergast and the Girl," reminiscent in subject and tone of E. A. Robinson. In order to digest the trash of ordinary life, then, to see the light of meaning in the trivial, Simpson has had to go into himself and learn to be patient indeed, trusting "in silence," and not believing "in ideas/unless they are unavoidable" ("An American Peasant").

And yet, in *Searching for the Ox*, Simpson's latest book, that desert swim seems at moments to be floundering. There is an expected emphasis in his Preface to this volume upon the rendering of human experience and of the world we live in; but there is also a strange note, at its conclusion, when he recalls his former selves as they appear in some of these poems, of detachment: "But I have changed; I am different from the boy and the man I used to be.... These changes cry out for a life that does not change. The less we are at home in the world, the more we bear witness to that other life." Paying attention to this clue, we are not surprised to find that the style of this book is not simply clear, direct, the language of speech, but that it is also curiously level, limpid, even deliberately flat. And the recurring theme of homelessness, of feeling out of the world, becomes more intelligible, as when we read, for example, "When I look back at myself/it is like looking through a window/and seeing another person" ("The Springs at Gadara"), or again: "At dusk when the lamps go on/I have stayed outside and watched/the shadow-life of the interior,/feeling myself apart from it" ("Searching for the Ox").

A recurring image is that of the speaker staring listlessly into store windows, his experience of other people is blankly quizzical, and there is almost a sense of fatigue, of which using the same image of the snagged balloon in two different poems ("Florida," "Searching") is symptomatic. Passion, desire, engagement, even trust in silence and patience, are alike at a low ebb. Simpson provides a suggestion, again in his Preface and in some of these poems, that the loneliness of his isolated childhood is now returning to consciousness, and one can only hope the consequent shrinking of the ordinary will prove temporary, and that this book represents a necessary stage toward the assimilation of difficult material.

—Norman Friedman

SIMPSON, R(onald) A(lbert). Australian. Born in Melbourne, Victoria, 1 February 1929. Educated at Royal Melbourne Institute of Technology, Associateship Diploma of Art; Melbourne Teachers' College, Primary Teachers' Certificate, 1951. Married to Shirley

Simpson; two children. Lecturer in Art, 1968–71, and since 1972, Senior Lecturer, Caulfield Institute of Technology, Melbourne. Poetry Editor, *The Bulletin*, Sydney, 1963–65. Since 1969, Poetry Editor, *The Age*, Melbourne. Recipient: Australian Arts Council travel grant, 1977. Address: 29 Omama Road, Murrumbeena, Melbourne, Victoria 3163, Australia.

PUBLICATIONS

Verse

The Walk along the Beach. Sydney, Edwards and Shaw, 1960.
This Real Pompeii. Brisbane, Jacaranda Press, 1964.
After the Assassination and Other Poems. Brisbane, Jacaranda Press, 1968.
Diver. Brisbane, University of Queensland Press, 1972.
Poems from Murrumbeena. Brisbane, University of Queensland Press, 1976.
The Forbidden City. Sydney, Edwards and Shaw, 1979.

Manuscript Collection: National Library of Australia, Canberra.

Critical Study: *The Literature of Australia* edited by Geoffrey Dutton, Melbourne, Penguin, 1964.

R. A. Simpson comments:

As a poet I use words in an effort to understand and clarify experiences. I get my main joy from poetry in the use of words; the struggle for clarification is the painful region. My early poetry was stiff and formal: I believe, and hope, that my recent work shows greater ease and freedom. My background as an art teacher contributed to my experiments in "concrete poetry," an area I no longer find interesting.

I do not see myself merely as an Australian poet, though there are obvious Australian attitudes in my poetry – and I have used Australian themes. Most present-day Australian poets would seriously believe that the best poetry being written today here and overseas reflects some kind of international style – a sense of the poet's responsibility to human beings in general. Australian poets feel part of the larger flow of ideas, even if they are not main contributors to the birth of ideas.

* * *

One of a group of Melbourne poets who came to prominence in the 1950's and to influence in the 1960's, R. A. Simpson has carefully maintained certain essential characteristics more consistently than have his fellow poets Vincent Buckley, Chris Wallace-Crabbe and Evan Jones, all of whom have modified their original formal regularity and slightly academic (or, at least, cloistered) affectations of irony and equipoise. Ron Simpson, in his first collection, *The Walk along the Beach*, quite firmly demonstrated a mind concerned with paring language down, with understatement, and with letting the image work with a minimum of encumbrances. The early poems were overtly concerned, however, often with the aftermath of guilt, heritage of a Catholic boyhood and subsequent loss of faith. Indeed, even through Simpson's more recent poetry, *Diver*, the innate direction of mind is through channels of justification or expiation. Though there may be no God, for Simpson, there is still an implied Judgement.

The verse style that worries its way through these concerns is, still, strangely tight-lipped and reticent. At its weakest it seems hesitant, hardly daring to indulge even in connectives. At its best it is a strikingly taut and resonant instrument capable of playing upon (and preying upon) those central nervous gropings and ambivalences that our own speech can enmesh us in. The poetry of R. A. Simpson is not graceful or elegant. It is self-guarded, and keeps catching itself off guard. It has remained outside current fashions, both in the 1960's and 1970's. Its essential honesty sustains it. It is a poetry one can return to many times, and always with gain.

—Thomas W. Shapcott

SINCLAIR, Keith. New Zealander. Born in Auckland, 5 December 1922. Educated at Mount Albert Grammar School, Auckland; University of Auckland, B.A. 1945, M.A. 1946, Ph.D. 1954. Served in the New Zealand Army, 1941–44, and Navy, 1944–46. Married 1) Mary Land in 1947, four sons; 2) Raewyn Mary Dalzeil in 1976. Lecturer, 1947–59, Associate Professor, 1959–62, and since 1962, Professor of History, University of Auckland. Carnegie Visiting Fellow, Institute of Commonwealth Studies, London, 1954; Visiting Fellow, Australian National University, Canberra, 1967, and Cambridge University, 1968–69. Since 1967, Editor, *New Zealand Journal of History*, Auckland. Labour Party Parliamentary Candidate, 1969. Since 1974, Chairman, Authors' Lending Rights Advisory Committee. Recipient: Walter Frewen Lord Prize for History, London, 1951; Ernest Scott Prize, for history, Melbourne, 1958, 1961; F. P. Wilson Prize for History, Wellington, 1966; Hubert Church Prize, for prose, 1966; Jessie Mackay Prize, 1974; National Book Award, for non-fiction, 1977. Litt.D.: University of Auckland. Address: 13 Mariposa Crescent, Birkenhead, Auckland, New Zealand.

PUBLICATIONS

Verse

Songs for a Summer and Other Poems. Christchurch, Pegasus Press, 1952.
Strangers or Beasts. Christchurch, Caxton Press, 1954.
A Time to Embrace. Auckland, Paul's Book Arcade, 1963.
The Firewheel Tree. Auckland, Auckland University Press and Oxford University Press, 1973.

Other

The Maori Land League: An Examination into the Source of a New Zealand Myth. Auckland, University of Auckland, 1950.
Imperial Federation: A Study of New Zealand Policy and Opinion 1880–1914. London, Athlone Press, 1955.
The Origins of the Maori Wars. Wellington, New Zealand University Press, 1957; revised edition, 1961.
A History of New Zealand. London, Penguin, 1959; revised edition, Wellington and London, Oxford University Press, 1961; Penguin, 1969.
Open Account: A History of the Bank of New South Wales in New Zealand, 1861–1961, with William F. Mandle. Marrickville, New South Wales, Whitcombe and Tombs, 1961.
William Pember Reeves: New Zealand Fabian. Oxford, Clarendon Press, 1965.
The Liberal Government 1891–1912: First Steps Towards a Welfare State. Auckland, Heinemann, 1967.

The Reefs of Fire. Auckland, Heinemann, 1977.

Walter Nash. Auckland, Auckland University Press, and New York, Oxford University Press, 1976; London, Oxford University Press, 1977.

Looking Back: A Photographic History of New Zealand, with Wendy Harrex. Wellington, Oxford University Press, 1978; London, Oxford University Press, 1979.

Editor, *The Maori King*, by John Eldon Gorst. Auckland, Oxford University Press, 1959.

Editor, *Distance Looks Our Way: The Effects of Remoteness on New Zealand.* Auckland, University of Auckland, 1961.

Editor, with Robert Chapman, *Studies in a Small Democracy: Essays in Honour of Willis Airey.* Auckland, Paul's Book Arcade, and Sydney, Angus and Robertson, 1963.

Critical Study: *A Way of Saying: A Study of New Zealand Poetry* by Kendrick Smithyman, Auckland and London, Collins, 1965.

Keith Sinclair comments:

The main influence on my early verse of which I was conscious was John Donne; more recently, perhaps Yeats and Robert Graves. In general I have been influenced by contemporary New Zealand poets, especially James K. Baxter, in the early 1950's. My main subjects have been love of various sorts – of country, especially the coast, of children and family and women. I have thought that the intellect and feeling are inseparable in life and in poetry.

* * *

Three pointers toward changing sensibility: John Donne, Dylan Thomas, and Theodore Roethke. But pointers only of a way: to name names is not to describe, still less to define. From Donne's example Keith Sinclair learned, as he has said, to admire "a witty clarity, a clarity within which wits may find obscurity," although Sinclair is rarely obscure. From Thomas, an artifice, a rhetoric, which shows, say, in "The Sleeping Beauty" sequence, but he has not been alive to metric – his own is idiosyncratic – as Thomas was, or as interested in the artifice of regulated patterns. For many years he respected, and still repects, Roethke whose practical bearing, whose homeliness, but most (probably) his evident sense of pitch rather than tone may be thought at least partly to have persuaded Sinclair to that increased directness, that lowered pitch which have served his poems well in his maturity.

If these men helped shape a talent they did not do so totally. At his earliest, Sinclair's poems were his and no one else's; for those of later years the same is to be said. Poems like "Goat Island Valley" and "Explaining Rain" (published in *Landfall* in 1967) clearly are mature expressions of what was present in a younger man's writing. The intelligence, the wit, the ebullience (not the exuberance) of his poems remain constant, producing a particular decorum which subsumes on the one hand what was once referred to as a fantastic element and, on the other, a sensuous if not sensual directness. The sensibility is not dissociated. The traditionalist and the contemporary man are one, with the family man, the Professor of History, the biographer, and the Labour Party candidate. If the latter emphasise the man of public conscience, of public obligation, the poems emphasise the man responsive to private conscience, of less advertised but not necessarily smaller or less significant pieties.

In 1973 Sinclair brought out another collection, *The Firewheel Tree*, but there has been no collection since then. (If in the 1970's the poet has quietened, the historian has been affirmed. Sinclair is probably the most adaptable of New Zealand historians, the most diverse in his professional skills that this country has seen, and the most productive.) Overall, the poems of

The Firewheel Tree are more tightly constructed and in several ways more orthodox than may be said of his earlier work. There is less inclination to eccentric or flamboyant phrasings, to the *jeux d'esprit* in which he liked to indulge. Like so many others, he brought his poems closer to that condition of prose discourse which goes with directness of syntax and the subordination of assertive rhythms to the play and cross-play of cadences, guarding himself against the merely prosaic or the prose by recourse to a heightened diction which suits the lyrical celebrations which are often his occasion and by returning to that old device in English poetry, alliteration. The firewheel tree which affords his title signifies something which is exotic in an everyday situation. It refers to one of the *Embothrium* family of Chile and Australia, a tree which is striking in its flowering. The poem has something to do, as have others of the book, with Sinclair's second marriage, of a time when conscience and conventional pieties were exercised, when the lyrical and the sensual were borne in on him not merely as compelling awarenesses demanding to be celebrated but as powers which (in an old-fashioned metaphor) flowered exotically but were not simply lyrical or assuagingly sensual. The firewheel is the natural wheel of fire, yet also wheel of fortune. Man is "racked on a firewheel tree."

—Kendrick Smithyman

SISSON, C(harles) H(ubert). British. Born in Bristol, 22 April 1914. Educated at the University of Bristol, 1931–34, B.A. (honours) in philosophy and English literature 1934; University of Berlin and University of Freiburg, 1934–35; the Sorbonne, Paris, 1935–36. Served in the British Army Intelligence Corps, India, 1942–45. Married Nora Gilbertson in 1937; two children. Assistant Principal, 1936–42, Principal, 1945–53, Assistant Secretary, 1953–62, and Under Secretary, 1962–68, Ministry of Labour, London; Assistant Under Secretary of State, 1968–71, and Director of Occupational Safety and Health, 1971–73, Department of Employment, London. Since 1976, Co-Editor, *PN Review*. Recipient: Senior Simon Research Fellowship, University of Manchester, 1956. Agent: A. D. Peters and Company, 10 Buckingham Street, London WC2N 6BU. Address: Moorfield Cottage, The Hill, Langport, Somerset TA10 9PU, England.

PUBLICATIONS

Verse

Versions and Perversions of Heine. London, Gaberbocchus, 1955.
Poems. Fairwarp, Sussex, Peter Russell, 1959.
Twenty-One Poems. Privately printed, 1960.
The London Zoo. London, Abelard Schuman, 1961.
Numbers. London, Methuen, 1965.
Catullus. London, MacGibbon and Kee, 1966; New York, Orion Press, 1967.
The Discarnation; or, How the Flesh Became Word and Dwelt among Us. Privately printed, 1967.
Metamorphoses. London, Methuen, 1968.
Roman Poems. Privately printed, 1968.
In the Trojan Ditch: Collected Poems and Selected Translations. Cheadle, Cheshire, Carcanet Press, 1974.
The Corridor. Hitchin, Hertfordshire, Mandeville Press, 1975.
Anchises. Manchester, Carcanet Press, 1976.

Novels

An Asiatic Romance. London, Gaberbocchus, 1953.
Christopher Homm. London, Methuen, 1965; Chester Springs, Pennsylvania, Dufour, 1975.

Other

The Spirit of British Administration and Some European Comparisons. London, Faber, and New York, Praeger, 1959.
Art and Action. London, Methuen, 1965.
Essays. Privately printed, 1967.
English Poetry 1900–1950: An Assessment. London, Hart Davis, 1971.
The Case of Walter Bagehot. London, Faber, 1972.
David Hume. Edinburgh, Ramsay Head Press, 1976.
The Avoidance of Literature: Collected Essays 1937–1978, edited by Michael Schmidt. Manchester, Carcanet Press, 1978.

Editor, *The English Sermon 1650–1750.* Manchester, Carcanet Press, 1976.
Editor, *Poems of Jonathan Swift.* Manchester, Carcanet Press, 1977.
Editor, *Jude the Obscure*, by Hardy. London, Penguin, 1979.

Translator, *The Poetic Art: A Translation of Horace's Ars Poetica.* Cheadle, Cheshire, Carcanet Press, 1975.
Translator, *The Poem on Nature: Lucretius' De Rerum Natura.* Manchester, Carcanet Press, 1976.
Translator, *Selected Contes*, by La Fontaine. Manchester, Carcanet Press, 1979.

Critical Studies: by Martin Seymour-Smith, in *X* (London), ii, 3, 1961, in *Agenda* (London), Summer–Autumn 1970, and in *Guide to Modern World Literature*, London, Wolfe, 1973; Donald Davie, in *Listener* (London), 9 May 1974; Robert Nye, in *Times Literary Supplement* (London), 29 November 1974; David Wright, in *Agenda* (London), Autumn 1975; John Pilling, in *Critical Quarterly* (Manchester), Spring 1979.

C. H. Sisson comments:

My verse is about things that I am, at the moment of writing, just beginning to understand. When I have understood them, or have that impression, the subject has gone, and I have to find another. Or stop. Generally, my resolution is to stop, but another subject is found in time, and I begin again. I began by stopping, so to speak, for having written some verse as an adolescent, I gave up at twenty because I had a great respect for poetry and did not think I could write it. The war and exile produced a few hesitant verses, wrung from me, but I stopped again without really having begun. A more productive start was about 1950, when I was already on the declining side *del cammin di nostra vita*; no wonder therefore that my themes have often been age, decline and death, with the occasional desperate hopes of the receding man. Naturally some facility has come with practice, and the risk now is less from stopping than from going on. One comes to understand too much, or to think one does.

As to verse forms, whether they are what is called regular, or not, it is a small matter: I have written in both kinds. What matters is the rhythm, which is the identifying mark of the poem. If one fails there is no need for a poem; better shut up.

Influences: all one's interests bear, in unexpected ways, on what one writes; still more, one's poetry may be prophetic of interests one is about to have. The influence of other poets – generally in youth – is deadly while it lasts. There is, however, a deliberate, mature learning which is beneficial. For this purpose I have found translations of the greatest value, with the

Latins as the great, though not the only, masters. What I aim at is to make plain statements, and not more of them than I need. "It is the nature of man that puzzles me"; I should like to leave a few recognizable – not novel – indications. The man that was the same in Neolithic and in Roman times, as now, is of more interest than the freak of circumstances. This truth lies at the bottom of a well of rhythm.

* * *

Two years before the publication of his collection *The London Zoo* in 1961, C. H. Sisson had made his name with his *The Spirit of British Administration*, the result of a comparative study of public administration in several European countries. This book was notable for its wit and the sharpness of the author's mind. The same qualities are to be found in C. H. Sisson's poetry and often the terrains overlap. Thus the long title poem of *The London Zoo* gains point and edge from the author's own involvement in the world of the City and the administration that he satirizes:

And who am I, you ask, thus to belly-ache
At my betters? I'll tell you, I am one of the same lot
– Without lobsters and limousine, but, like the rest
Expending my best energies on the second best.

Much of Sisson's earlier poetry is uncomfortable in that it looks at our pretensions and society with an unflinching and critical eye. When it looks at our beliefs it can be just as disquietening as in "The Aeroplane" where below there are those who are "gathered round the Easter cup" when "up here it is empty." This poetry, while written from an uncompromisingly intellectual standpoint, is by no means dispassionate, and can, as in the case of what begins as a somewhat conventional satire on the cash-nexus, explode violently into

Suddenly you are in bed with a screeching tear-sheet
This is money at last without her nightdress
Clutching you against her fallen udders and sharp bones
In an unscrupulous and deserved embrace.

In later poems, however, this shrill voice has been muted and the poems tend to be concerned with regret for times past and age to come:

I will act my senile part as the Furies desire
Having discovered too late what I knew already:
Nothing is new, nothing miraculous.
The tree grows and flowers in order to fall

Is Sisson becoming sorry for himself? But we are reassured when we read,

One of a kind is the most anybody
Can expect to be, and even that
Is a presumption upon a classification
Based upon reason which is wholly imaginary

and when the new muted Sisson gives us poems as splendid as "This Morning":

I do not know what the mist signifies
When it comes, not swirling,
Gathering itself like briony under my window

The trees stand out of it,
Wading you might say,
Have their dark tresses trailing in the water
Which began the world.

Admirers of C. H. Sisson's poetry look forward to what else this new vein will yield.

—John Cotton

SITWELL, Sacheverell. British. Born in Scarborough, Yorkshire, 15 November 1897; younger brother of the poets Dame Edith and Sir Osbert Sitwell. Educated at Eton; Balliol College, Oxford. Married Georgia Doble in 1925; two sons. High Sheriff of Northamptonshire, 1948–49. Succeeded to the baronetcy, 1969. Address: Weston Hall, Towcester, Northamptonshire, England.

PUBLICATIONS

Verse

The People's Palace. Oxford, Blackwell, 1918.
Doctor Donne and Gargantua: First Canto. London, Favil Press, 1921; Boston, Houghton Mifflin, 1930.
The Hundred and One Harlequins. London, Grant Richards, and New York, Boni and Liveright, 1922.
Doctor Donne and Gargantua: Canto the Second. London, Favil Press, 1923.
The Thirteenth Caesar and Other Poems. London, Grant Richards, 1924; New York, Doran, 1925.
Poor Young People, with Edith and Osbert Sitwell. London, The Fleuron, 1925.
Doctor Donne and Gargantua: Canto the Third. Privately printed, 1926.
Exalt the Eglantine and Other Poems. London, The Fleuron, 1926.
The Cyder Feast and Other Poems. London, Duckworth, and New York, Doran, 1927.
(Poems). London, Benn, 1928.
Two Poems, Ten Songs. London, Duckworth, 1929.
Doctor Donne and Gargantua: The First Six Cantos. London, Duckworth, and Boston, Houghton Mifflin, 1930.
Canons of Giant Art: Twenty Torsos in Heroic Landscapes. London, Faber, 1933.
Collected Poems. London, Duckworth, 1936.
Selected Poems. London, Duckworth, 1948.
"Forty-Eight Poems," in *Poetry Review* (London), Summer 1967.
Tropicalia. Edinburgh, Ramsay Head Press, 1972.
To Henry Woodward. London, Covent Garden Press, 1972.
Agamemnon's Tomb. Edinburgh, Tragara Press, 1972.
Rosario d'Arabeschi; *Baraka ("as the Moors call it") and Dionysia*; *Triptych of Poems*; *The Strawberry Feast*; *Ruralia*; *To E.S.*; *Variations upon Old Names of Hyacinths*; *Lily Poems*; *The Archipelago of Daffodils*; *A Charivari of Parrots*; *Flowering Cactus*; *A Look at Sowerby's English Mushrooms and Fungi*; *Auricula Theatre*; *Lyra Varia*; *The House of the Presbyter*; *Nigritian*; *Summer Poems of 1962*; *Doctor Donne and Gargantua (Cantos Seven and Eight)*; *Badinerie*; *An Indian Summer*; *Temple of Segesta*; *L'Amour au Théâtre Italien*; *Notebook on My New Poems*; *Notebook on*

Twenty Canons of Giant Art; *A Note for Bibliophiles*; *Battles of the Centaurs*; *Les Troyens*; *Pastoral and Landscape with the Giant Orion*; *Nymphis et Fontibus and Nymphaeum*; *Serenade to a Sister*; *Placebo*; *Credo, or, An Affirmation*; *Two Themes Taken One at a Time*; *Harlequinade*; *Brother and Sister*; *Dodecameron*; *Diptycha Musica*; *The Octogenarian*; *Little Italy in London*; *Trolling for the Gods of Light*; *The Rose-Pink Chapel*; *Scherzo di Capriccio*; *Scherzo di Fantasia.* Privately printed, 1972–78.

Plays

The Triumph of Neptune (ballet), music by Lord Berners. London, Chester, 1926.
All at Sea: A Social Tragedy in Three Acts for First-Class Passengers Only, with Osbert Sitwell. London, Duckworth, 1927; New York, Doubleday, 1928.

Other

Southern Baroque Art: A Study of Painting, Architecture and Music in Italy and Spain of the 17th and 18th Centuries. London, Grant Richards, and New York, Knopf, 1924.
All Summer in a Day: An Autobiographical Fantasia. London, Duckworth, and New York, Doran, 1926.
German Baroque Art. London, Duckworth, 1927; New York, Doran, 1928.
A Book of Towers and Other Buildings of Southern Europe. London, Frederick Etchells and Hugh Macdonald, 1928.
The Gothick North: A Study of Mediaeval Life, Art, and Thought. Boston, Houghton Mifflin, 1929; London, Duckworth, 3 vols., 1929–30.
Beckford and Beckfordism: An Essay. London, Duckworth, 1930.
Far from My Home: Stories: Long and Short. London, Duckworth, 1931.
Spanish Baroque Art: With Buildings in Portugal, Mexico, and Other Colonies. London, Duckworth, 1931.
Mozart. New York, Appleton, and London, Davies, 1932.
Liszt. London, Faber, and Boston, Houghton Mifflin, 1934; revised edition, London, Cassell, 1955; New York, Philosophical Library, 1956.
Touching the Orient: Six Sketches. London, Duckworth, 1934; Folcroft, Pennsylvania, Folcroft Editions, 1976.
A Background for Domenico Scarlatti, 1685–1757; Written for His Two Hundred and Fiftieth Anniversary. London, Faber, 1935; Freeport, New York, Books for Libraries, 1970.
Dance of the Quick and the Dead: An Entertainment of the Imagination. London, Faber, 1936; Boston, Houghton Mifflin, 1937.
Conversation Pieces: A Survey of English Domestic Portraits and Their Painters. London, Batsford, 1936; New York, Scribner, 1937.
Narrative Pictures: A Survey of English Genre and Its Painters. London, Batsford, 1937; New York, Scribner, 1938.
La Vie Parisienne: A Tribute to Offenbach. London, Faber, 1937; Boston, Houghton Mifflin, 1938.
Roumanian Journey. London, Batsford, and New York, Scribner, 1938.
Edinburgh, with Francis Bamford. London, Faber, and Boston, Houghton Mifflin, 1938.
German Baroque Sculpture. London, Duckworth, 1938.
Trio: Dissertations on Some Aspects of English Genius, with Edith and Osbert Sitwell. London, Macmillan, 1938.
The Romantic Ballet in Lithographs of the Time, with Cyril W. Beaumont. London, Faber, 1938.
Old Fashioned Flowers. London, Country Life, and New York, Scribner, 1939.
Mauretania: Warrior, Man, and Woman. London, Duckworth, 1940.

Poltergeists: An Introduction and Examination Followed by Chosen Instances. London, Faber, 1940; New York, University Books, 1959.
Sacred and Profane Love. London, Faber, 1940.
Valse des Fleurs: A Day in St. Petersburg and a Ball at the Winter Palace in 1868. London, Faber, 1941.
Primitive Scenes and Festivals. London, Faber, 1942.
The Homing of the Winds and Other Passages in Prose. London, Faber, 1942.
Splendours and Miseries. London, Faber, 1943.
British Architects and Craftsmen: A Survey of Taste, Design, and Style During Three Centuries 1600 to 1830. London, Batsford, 1945; revised edition, 1947, 1949, 1960; New York, Scribner, 1946.
The Hunters and the Hunted. London, Macmillan, 1947; New York, Macmillan, 1948.
The Netherlands: A Study of Some Aspects of Art, Costume and Social Life. London, Batsford, 1948; revised edition, 1974; New York, Hastings House, 1974.
Morning, Noon and Night in London. London, Macmillan, 1948.
Theatrical Figures in Porcelain: German 18th Century. London, Curtain Press, 1949.
Spain. London, Batsford, 1950; revised edition, 1951; New York, Hastings House, 1975.
Cupid and the Jacaranda. London, Macmillan, 1952.
Truffle Hunt with Sacheverell Sitwell. London, Hale, 1953.
Fine Bird Books 1700–1900, with Hanasyde Buchanan and James Fisher. London, Collins, and New York, Van Nostrand, 1953.
Selected Works of Sacheverell Sitwell. Indianapolis, Bobbs Merrill, 1953.
Portugal and Madeira. London, Batsford, 1954.
Old Garden Roses: Part One, with James Russell. London, Collins, 1955.
Selected Works of Sacheverell Sitwell. London, Hale, 1955.
Denmark. London, Batsford, and New York, Hastings House, 1956.
Great Flower Books 1700–1900: A Bibliographical Record of Two Centuries of Finely-Illustrated Flower Books, with Wilfrid Blunt and Patrick M. Synge. London, Collins, 1956.
Arabesque and Honeycomb. London, Hale, 1957; New York, Random House, 1958.
Malta, photographs by Anthony Armstrong-Jones. London, Batsford, 1958.
Journey to the Ends of Time: Lost in the Dark Wood. London, Cassell, and New York, Random House, 1959.
Bridge of the Brocade Sash: Travels and Observations in Japan. London, Weidenfeld and Nicolson, 1959; Cleveland, World, 1960.
Austria, photographs by Toni Schneider. London, Thames and Hudson, and New York, Viking Press, 1959.
Golden Wall and Mirador: From England to Peru. London, Weidenfeld and Nicolson, and Cleveland, World, 1961.
The Red Chapels of Banteai Srei, and Temples in Cambodia, India, Siam and Nepal. London, Weidenfeld and Nicolson, 1962; as *Great Temples of the East*, New York, Obolensky, 1963.
Monks, Nuns, and Monasteries. London, Weidenfeld and Nicolson, and New York, Holt Rinehart, 1965.
Southern Baroque Revisited. London, Weidenfeld and Nicolson, 1967.
Baroque and Rococo. New York, Putnam, 1967.
Gothic Europe. London, Weidenfeld and Nicolson, and New York, Holt Rinehart, 1969.
For Want of a Golden City (autobiography). London, Thames and Hudson, and New York, Day, 1973.

Editor, *Great Houses of Europe.* London, Weidenfeld and Nicolson, and New York, Putnam, 1961.

Bibliography: *A Bibliography of Edith, Osbert and Sacheverell Sitwell* by Richard Fifoot, London, Hart Davis, 1963; New York, Oxford University Press, 1964; revised edition, London, Hart Davis MacGibbon, 1976.

* * *

Born in 1897, Sir Sacheverell Sitwell was the youngest member of a brilliant family who, rejecting an assured status as members of the highest country gentry, flung themselves from early youth with dashing enthusiasm into the practice of the arts of prose and poetry and the appreciation of all the arts. They were, for a time, during the 1920's, brilliantly in fashion, and then suddenly out of it. Edith Sitwell attained her highest reputation during the Second World War with her bold, sweeping, and direct poems about the horrors of war and the strange mercies of God. Sir Osbert Sitwell, from whom Sir Sacheverell inherited the baronetcy, attained his highest reputation with his series of autobiographical writings, after the Second World War, in which he made his father, Sir George Reresay Sitwell, one of the greatest comic figures in European fiction. Sir Sacheverell, who has visited almost every country, and seen almost every important art-work in the world, never quite attained the fame of his elder brother and sister, though his almost Trollopeian or Jamesian output of books is larger than theirs, and his early autobiographical fantasia, *All Summer in a Day* (1926), is a masterpiece of poetic prose which neither of his siblings equalled. Between 1948 (when he published his *Selected Poems*, chosen from fifteen previous volumes) and 1972, he found no one willing to risk publishing more poems, though publishers rightly leap for his prose (his book about Japan made me resee, with fresh eyes, many things I thought I had already seen). Yet what I have seen of his poems since 1948 – a large selection was printed in the *Poetry Review*, then edited by John Smith – seemed to me, retrospectively, to prove Sir Sacheverell's contention in a letter that he had been writing *better* poems, on the whole, since 1948. It was simply that Sitwells, first under Grigson and Leavis, and then under Robert Conquest and the "Movement," were out. The "movement," as such, is dead, and there is a growing tendency among young and serious poetic aestheticians, like Dr. Veronica Forrest-Thomson, to recognise that a poem is not a "slice of life," prose chunked up into clumsy verse, but a rational artifice, whose importance is much less in its outward reference to an "external world" which we know only through verbal conventions than in its inner play of interstresses of sound and sense. Poetry, in other words, is less a criticism of life than a criticism of *language*. When this new aesthetics prevails, as I think it will, Sir Sacheverell will have his due, and his siblings be restored to favour. People will no longer worry about the "meaning" but taste the crispness of

The parrot's voice snaps out –
No good to contradict –
What he says he'll say again:
Dry facts, dry biscuits

and the colour and lushness of

Let light like honey shine upon your skin:
When you're hot and like a comb of fire
Glide back into this shade,
Bend that heavy branch down with your hand upon its fruit,
Ripe cherries and a honeycomb must make my bread and wine.

—G. S. Fraser

SKELTON, Robin. Canadian. Born in Easington, East Yorkshire, England, 12 October 1925. Educated at Pocklington Grammar School, near York; Christ's College, Cambridge, 1943–44; University of Leeds, Yorkshire, B.A. 1950, M.A. in English 1951. Served in the Royal Air Force, 1944–47. Married Sylvia Mary Jarrett in 1957; three children. Assistant Lecturer, 1951–54, and Lecturer in English, 1954–63, Manchester University. Associate Professor, 1963–66, since 1966, Professor of English, Director of the Creative Writing Program, 1967–73, and Chairman of the Department of Creative Writing, 1973–76, University of Victoria, British Columbia. Manager, Lotus Press, Hull, 1950–52. Poetry Reviewer, 1956–57, and Drama Reviewer, 1958–60, *Manchester Guardian*; Art Reviewer, *Victoria Daily Times*, British Columbia, 1964–66. Founder Member, Peterloo Group (poets and painters), Manchester, 1957–60; Founding Secretary, Manchester Institute of Contemporary Arts, 1959–62. Centennial Lecturer, University of Massachusetts, Amherst, 1962–63; Visiting Professor, University of Michigan, Ann Arbor, 1967. Editor, with John Peter, 1967–71, and since 1972, Editor, *Malahat Review*, Victoria; since 1972, Director, Pharos Press, Victoria; since 1976, Editor-in-Chief, Sono Nis Press, Victoria. Collage Maker: one man shows, Victoria, 1966, 1968. Recipient: Canada Council grant, 1977. Fellow, Royal Society of Literature, 1966. Address: Department of Creative Writing, University of Victoria, British Columbia, Canada.

PUBLICATIONS

Verse

Patmos and Other Poems. London, Routledge, 1955.
Third Day Lucky. London and New York, Oxford University Press, 1958.
Begging the Dialect: Poems and Ballads. London and New York, Oxford University Press, 1960.
Two Ballads of the Muse. Cambridge, Rampant Lions Press, 1960.
The Dark Window: Verses. London and New York, Oxford University Press, 1962.
A Valedictory Poem. Privately printed, 1963.
An Irish Gathering. Dublin, Dolmen Press, 1964.
A Ballad of Billy Barker. Privately printed, 1965.
Inscriptions. Victoria, Morriss, 1967.
Because of This and Other Poems. Manchester, Manchester Institute of Contemporary Arts, 1968.
The Hold of Our Hands: Eight Letters to Sylvia. Privately printed, 1968.
Selected Poems 1947–1967. Toronto, McClelland and Stewart, and London, Oxford University Press, 1968.
Answers. London, Enitharmon Press, 1969.
An Irish Album. Dublin, Dolmen Press, 1969.
The Hunting Dark. London, Deutsch, 1971.
Remembering Synge: A Poem in Homage for the Centenary of His Birth, 16 April 1871. Dublin, Dolmen Press, 1971.
A Different Mountain. San Francisco, Kayak, 1971.
Private Speech: Messages 1962–1970. Vancouver, Sono Nis Press, 1971.
Three for Herself. Rushden, Northamptonshire, Sceptre Press, 1972.
Musebook. Victoria, Pharos Press, 1972.
A Christmas Poem. Privately printed, 1972.
Country Songs. Rushden, Northamptonshire, Sceptre Press, 1973.
Timelight. Toronto, McClelland and Stewart, and London, Heinemann, 1974.
Fifty Syllables for a Fiftieth Birthday. Privately printed, 1975.
Callsigns. Victoria, Sono Nis Press, 1976.
Because of Love. Toronto, McClelland and Stewart, 1977.
Three Poems. Knotting, Bedfordshire, Sceptre Press, 1977.
Landmarks. Victoria, Sono Nis Press, 1979.

Other

John Ruskin: The Final Years. Manchester, John Rylands Library and Manchester University Press, 1955.
The Poetic Pattern. London, Routledge, 1956; Berkeley, University of California Press, 1958.
Painters Talking: Michael Snow and Tony Connor Interviewed. Manchester, Peterloo Group, 1957.
Cavalier Poets. London, Longman, 1960.
Poetry. London, English Universities Press, 1963; New York, Dover, 1965.
The Writings of J. M. Synge. London, Thames and Hudson, 1971.
The Practice of Poetry. London, Heinemann, and New York, Barnes and Noble, 1971.
J. M. Synge and His World. London, Thames and Hudson, 1971.
J. M. Synge. Lewisburg, Pennsylvania, Bucknell University Press, 1972.
The Poet's Calling. London, Heinemann, and New York, Barnes and Noble, 1975.
Poetic Truth. London, Heinemann, and New York, Barnes and Noble, 1978.
Spellcraft. Toronto, McClelland and Stewart, and London, Routledge, 1978.
They Call It the Cariboo. Victoria, Sono Nis Press, 1979.

Editor, *Leeds University Poetry 1949.* Leeds, Lotus Press, 1950.
Editor, with D. Metcalfe, *The Acadine Poets, Series I–III.* Hull, Yorkshire, Lotus Press, 1950.
Editor, *J. M. Synge: Translations.* Dublin, Dolmen Press, 1961.
Editor, *Four Plays and The Aran Islands*, by J. M. Synge. London and New York, Oxford University Press, 1962.
Editor, *Edward Thomas' Selected Poems.* London, Hutchinson, 1962.
Editor, *J. M. Synge: Collected Poems.* London, Oxford University Press, 1962.
Editor, *Six Irish Poets: Austin Clarke, Richard Kell, Thomas Kinsella, John Montague, Richard Murphy, Richard Weber.* London, Oxford University Press, 1962.
Editor, *Viewpoint: An Anthology of Poetry.* London, Hutchinson, 1962.
Editor, *Five Poets of the Pacific Northwest.* Seattle, University of Washington Press, 1964.
Editor, *Poetry of the Thirties.* London, Penguin, 1964.
Editor, *Selected Poems of Byron.* London, Heinemann, 1964; New York, Barnes and Noble, 1966.
Editor, *Collected Poems*, by David Gascoyne. London, Oxford University Press-Deutsch, 1965.
Editor, with David R. Clark, *The Irish Renaissance: A Gathering of Essays, Letters and Memoirs from the Massachusetts Review.* Dublin, Dolmen Press, and London, Oxford University Press, 1965.
Editor, with Ann Saddlemyer, *The World of W. B. Yeats: Essays in Perspective.* Seattle, University of Washington Press, 1965; revised edition, 1967.
Editor, *Poetry of the Forties.* London, Penguin, 1968.
Editor, *Georges Zuk: Selected Verse.* San Francisco, Kayak, 1969.
Editor, *Riders to the Sea*, by J. M. Synge. Dublin, Dolmen Press, 1969.
Editor, *Introductions from an Island: A Selection of Student Writing.* Victoria, University of Victoria, 5 vols., 1969–74.
Editor, with Alan Clodd, *Collected Verse Translations*, by David Gascoyne. London, Oxford University Press-Deutsch, 1970.
Editor, *The Cavalier Poets.* London, Faber, and New York, Oxford University Press, 1970.
Editor, *Herbert Read: A Memorial Symposium.* London, Methuen, 1970.
Editor, *The Collected Plays of Jack B. Yeats.* London, Secker and Warburg, and Indianapolis, Bobbs Merrill, 1971.

Editor and Translator, *Two Hundred Poems from the Greek Anthology*. London, Methuen, and Seattle, University of Washington Press, 1971.
Editor, *Some Sonnets from "Laura in Death" after the Italian of Francesco Petrarch*, by J. M. Synge (bilingual edition). Dublin, Dolmen Press, 1971.
Editor, *Thirteen Irish Writers on Ireland*. Boston, Godine, 1973.
Editor, *The Underwear of the Unicorn*, by Georges Zuk. Nanaimo, British Columbia, Oolichan, 1975.

Manuscript Collections: MacPherson Library, University of Victoria; University of Texas, Austin.

Robin Skelton comments:

I have been called a Muse Poet, a Lyrical Poet, a Confessional Poet, a Traditional Poet, an Innovative Poet, a Romantic Poet, a British Poet, an Irish Poet, and a Canadian Poet. I hope I am all these things and more. I relish most the compliment paid me by a very old lady, the mother of an eminent British poet, who said (to somebody else) of my work, "All human life is there!" I would like to think that this is the case. All my life I have tried to work in terms of Rabelais' dictum, "Everything that God allows to happen I allow to be written about." This has resulted in my finding myself using, and being used by, many different attitudes and emotions to an extent which makes it impossible for me to sum up a poetry which is, after all, my life and the life of those forces which have spoken through me. There is no point in listing my "masters" or the major "influences" upon my work, for I have learned something from almost every poet I have read from Homer to the present. I could perhaps suggest that the writings of Jung, to which I was introduced by Herbert Read, have been important to me for a quarter of a century, as also has been the Neo-Platonist Tradition from which he drew. I cannot stand back from my poetry and see it clearly, for, thank God, it is still in the writing; and therefore still changing its shape. Perhaps some critic other than I may detect connections between the poetry I have made and the authors I have edited or written about. Perhaps another critic may uncover a central theme or themes and disclose my "philosophy." I myself am in doubt. I can only respond to an editor's request for auctorial comment by parodying Archibald MacLeish's rightly famous line and saying "A poet should not mean, but be," and pray that I may continue to "be" a poet, by which I mean merely a man through whom poems continue to arrive.

* * *

Robin Skelton is English by birth, and it was in Britain that he published his first books of verse, before in 1963, in his crucial middle years, he moved to Canada where he has lived ever since. More than any other poet now working in Canada, he has remained a man of two worlds, European and North American. Since moving to Victoria, British Columbia, he has edited two anthologies of English verse (*Poetry of the Thirties* and *Poetry of the Forties*) and he has continued to write on the Irish renaissance and particularly on J. M. Synge, while a great deal of that background of early 20th-century Anglo-Irish literature has lingered since then in his own poems. He has also edited since 1967 an international literary journal – the *Malahat Review* – which is perhaps the only magazine wherein Canadian poetry competes on an egalitarian basis with the poetry of other traditions.

The effect of emigration on Skelton's own poetry has been to create a feeling of distance – rather than detachment – from significant experience: an inverted telescope view of situations and states of mind which one senses are in reality nearer to the poet than their magic realist aloofness at first suggests. Skelton's poetry from the beginning reflected the analytical and strongly structured frame of mind that dominates his excellent critical work on Ruskin and the Irish poets. He began in the Movement manner of the British 1950's, writing in a flat and almost audibly North country tone the deliberately unexciting verse which was favoured at that time in contrast to the emotional manner of the 1940's. Since then, however, his poetry has developed an individual style – reflective and, in the later poems especially, marked often by a stoic melancholy. Narrative, and especially the narrative of feelings – feelings prompted by memory and the sense of exile – is a mode that Skelton has particularly developed, in volumes like *The Hunting Dark* and *Because of Love*. At the same time, with a fine and continually experimental craftsmanship, he has written in a variety of lyric and satiric moods. More recently, in *Private Speech*, his verse turned towards the gnomic, and in his *Poems from the Greek Anthology* he explored the ambiguous borderland between translation and poetry.

Yet the reflective, quasi-autobiographical poem still shows Skelton at his best, and perhaps his finest work in this vein is contained in the poetic sequence, *Timelight*. In a sense this is Skelton's equivalent of Wordsworth's *Prelude*, a philosophical summing up of his life to date, but instead of being a structured discourse it takes the form of a series of discontinuous insights, sharp flashes of apprehension or, just as often, muted and elusive illuminations. As Skelton points out in his Preface, a prime clue to the whole venture is given in a single line of one of the poems: "Every travelling is of the soul." Yet the road the soul travels is often the way of the senses, and, as the poet says: "I am trapped/in memory's riot,/carried through/ everything that/bones lay claim to." Some poems deal with places the poet has visited, but treat the mundane scene as a kind of translucent screen through which is seen a looming and ambiguous reality:

it is the will of being's self
that fills
the crowding blossom
with the gentle haze
and asks the mountains
for their certainties

Dramatic monologues discuss the problems of life and death. A Bestiary develops the animal symbolism of the world of gross existence through which the soul must pass. Memories of personal life, of dreams, of books are fused "to hint a whole/beyond the vagaries/of its parts." In such lines and in many other ways, *Timelight* and Skelton's other books show very clearly his links with the great modernists in whose shadow (or whose light according to one's viewpoint) he has always written, not only Eliot and Pound but also the later Yeats. Skelton, more than any poet I know, belongs not to one part but to the whole of the tradition of English poetry.

—George Woodcock

SKINNER, Knute (Rumsey). American. Born in St. Louis, Missouri, 25 April 1929. Educated at Culver-Stockton College, Canton, Missouri, 1947–49; Colorado State College, Greeley, A. B. in speech and drama 1951; Middlebury College, Vermont, M.A. in English 1954; University of Iowa, Iowa City, Ph.D. in English 1958. Married 1) Jeanne Pratt in 1953 (divorced, 1954), one son; 2) Linda Kuhn in 1961 (divorced, 1977), two sons; 3) Edna Faye Kiel in 1978. English Teacher, Boise High School, Idaho, 1951–54; Instructor in English, University of Iowa, 1960–61; Assistant Professor of English, Oklahoma College for Women, Chickasha, 1961–62. Part-time Lecturer, 1962–70, Associate Professor, 1971–73, and since 1973, Professor of English, Western Washington University, Bellingham. Since 1977, Co-Editor, *Bellingham Review*. Recipient: Huntington Hartford Foundation Fellowship, 1961;

National Endowment for the Arts grant, 1975. Address: 412 North State Street, Bellingham, Washington 98225, U.S.A.; or, Killaspuglonane, Kilshanny, County Clare, Ireland (summer).

PUBLICATIONS

Verse

Stranger with a Watch. Francestown, New Hampshire, Golden quill Press, 1965.
A Close Sky over Killaspuglonane. Dublin, Dolmen Press, 1968; St. Louis, Burton Press, 1975.
In Dinosaur Country. Greeley, Colorado, Pierian Press, 1969.
The Sorcerers: A Laotian Tale. Bellingham, Washington, Goliards Press, 1972.

Manuscript Collection: Humanities Research Center, University of Texas, Austin.

Critical Studies: "From Ireland the American" by Gregory FitzGerald, in *Ann Arbor Review* (Michigan), Summer 1968; by Thomas Churchill, in *Concerning Poetry* (Bellingham, Washington), Fall 1968; "Killaspuglonane" by Harry Chambers, in *Phoenix* (Manchester), Summer 1969; X. J. Kennedy, in *Concerning Poetry* (Bellingham, Washington), Fall 1969.

Knute Skinner comments:

I have attempted to embody (emphasis on body) love and death. In other poems I have analyzed character. In a few I have attempted to enter nature and have gone so far as to find spirit in a cow. I am no longer as interested in the distant and abstract as I am in my immediate surroundings, and some of my recent poems are set in Killaspuglonane, my adopted townland. My influences are varied and usual. I began by writing rhymed stanzas and now write mostly free verse – though I still use rhyme, meter, syllabic or accentual if the poem asks for it.

* * *

Knute Skinner creates from remarkably disparate sources. His poems of love, death and isolation in *Stranger with a Watch* are powerfully underscored by a wry and acid humor which etches at the surface of experience to reveal inner situations and private struggles. He writes elegies for the living as well as the dead – mourns the mourners. In his constant interplay of mind and senses and in his perception of physical decay and time he recalls Hardy, Housman, and Yeats. Here is ironic laughter at twisted cirumstance; here is understatement, word-play and a combination of metaphysical and sensual imagery; here is concern with madness, prophecy, and the stripping of poetic language to its bones and marrow. In form Skinner ranges widely and easily from lyric to epigram, from sonnet to ballad to free-style; but his vision is peculiarly his own. By his criticism he reveals how things are and thereby implies how they ought to be – how love should not be a commodity, how men should not journey alone, how formality and self-consciousness should not divert people from genuine feeling. Through his poems the reader catches glimpses of lost connections – of time, places, and people that are not what they were – and a sense of love's fragility and ineffability. In *A Close Sky over Killaspuglonane*, Skinner allies himself with his Irish heritage, reflecting the land, the people, and the traditions of Clare county. Here he writes most strongly out of a sense of place. *In Dinosaur Country* displays an exuberant sense of life through humor which can be gentle, whimsical and uproarious. Unflinchingly, Skinner reintroduces "gross" material into the life experience via poetry. He makes poems of "Blackheads," "Phlegm," "Urine," and presents "A Poem for the Class of 69" (in the concrete poetic style). His laughter is compelling and human, reminding the reader that nothing is ugly or alien unless he makes it so.

—Carl Lindner

SLAVITT, David (Rytman). Pseudonym: Henry Sutton. American. Born in White Plains, New York, 23 March 1935. Educated at Phillips Academy, Andover, Massachusetts, graduated 1952; Yale University, New Haven, Connecticut, 1952–56, B.A. (magna cum laude) 1956; Columbia University, New York, M.A. 1957. Married 1) Lynn Meyer in 1956 (divorced, 1977), three children; 2) Janet Abrahm in 1978. Instructor, Georgia Institute of Technology, Atlanta, 1957–58; Associate Editor, *Newsweek* magazine, New York, 1958–65. Since 1978, Associate Professor of English, Temple University, Philadelphia. Address: 2201 Chestnut Street, Box 10, Philadelphia, Pennsylvania 19103, U.S.A.

PUBLICATIONS

Verse

Suits for the Dead. New York, Scribner, 1961.
The Carnivore. Chapel Hill, University of North Carolina Press, 1965.
Day Sailing and Other Poems. Chapel Hill, University of North Carolina Press, 1969.
Child's Play. Baton Rouge, Louisiana State University Press, 1972.
Vital Signs: New and Selected Poems. New York, Doubleday, 1975.
Rounding the Horn. Baton Rouge, Louisiana State University Press, 1978.

Novels

Rochelle; or, Virtue Rewarded. London, Chapman and Hall, 1966; New York, Delacorte Press, 1967.
The Exhibitionist (as Henry Sutton). New York, Geis, 1967; London, Geis, 1968.
Feel Free. New York, Delacorte Press, 1968; London, Hodder and Stoughton, 1969.
The Voyeur (as Henry Sutton). New York, Geis, and London, Hodder and Stoughton, 1969.
Vector (as Henry Sutton). New York, Geis, 1970; London, Hodder and Stoughton, 1971.
Anagrams. London, Hodder and Stoughton, 1970; New York, Doubleday, 1971.
ABCD. New York, Doubleday, 1972; London, Hamish Hamilton, 1974.
The Liberated (as Henry Sutton). New York, Doubleday, 1973; London, W. H. Allen, 1974.
The Outer Mongolian. New York, Doubleday, 1973.
The Killing of the King. New York, Doubleday, and London, W. H. Allen. 1974.
King of Hearts. New York, Arbor House, 1976.
That Golden Woman (as Henry Lazarus). New York, Fawcett, 1976; London, Sphere, 1977.
The Sacrifice (as Henry Sutton). New York, Grosset and Dunlap, 1978.
Jo Stern. New York, Harper, 1978.
The Idol (as David Benjamin). New York, Putnam, 1978.

Other

Translator, *The Eclogues of Virgil.* New York, Doubleday, 1971.
Translator, *The Eclogues and the Georgics of Virgil.* New York, Doubleday, 1972.

Manuscript Collection: Beinecke Rare Book Library, Yale University, New Haven, Connecticut.

Critical Study: interview in *The Writer's Voice*, edited by George Garrett, New York, Morrow, 1973.

* * *

In 1961, in the introduction to David Slavitt's first book of poems, John Hall Wheelock said that "one of the distinguishing characteristics of Mr. Slavitt's poetry is a severe restraint in the use of figurative language. It is the brilliance and clarity of his work, its brisk pace and taut resonance of line, its ironic and sardonic counterpoint, and, above all, its dramatic tensions, rather than any striking use of imagery or metaphor, that make it memorable." Slavitt's later books have borne out that description of his poetry, for he is a classicist – not one of the Eliot generation's neo-classicists who still depended so heavily on the "romantic image," but a genuine classicist, using reason and wit to order his experience, to explain it, to describe it rather than (like a romantic) to embody it or transcend it.

The voice of Slavitt's poetry is literally that of a man talking, an intelligent and urbane man, a man of wit and no little wisdom, speaking of life and more increasingly of death, often playfully, more often very seriously. His version of Virgil's *Eclogues* and *Georgics*, not strictly a translation of Virgil's poetic musings, but an application of Slavitt's own very striking voice and vision to those musings, is (not surprisingly) his finest book of poems, audacious, even arrogant, and brilliant throughout, a genuine translation of Virgil's approach to things into Slavitt's own well-honed modern classical idiom and a commentary on that approach as well.

As aware as any classical poet was of poetry as a self-conscious confidence trick, Slavitt is also aware of its real and necessary values. In his version of the eighth eclogue, he says:

Madness –
schizoid, of course – but it works, and you and I
can read, hear, give ourselves up to the poem,
and all our hurts too are healed, at least for a time.
We're all like dogs. A bone, a sop, distracts,
or the howl of another dog. We take it up,
one or two at a time, and then whole packs,
pouring out a grief we never felt
or sharing a real grief with all the others,
which becomes a public occasion, a communion,
a kind of celebration, a kind of prayer.

David Slavitt masters the madness of that con game in his poems, and he speaks in a voice that is distinctive and immediately recognizable as his. In a romantic time, he has gone his own way, and it has proven to have been a way well worth the going.

—R. H. W. Dillard

SMITH, A(rthur) J(ames) M(arshall). American. Born in Montreal, Quebec, Canada, 8 November 1902. Educated at McGill University, Montreal (Editor, *McGill Literary Supplement*), B.Sc. in arts 1925, M.A. 1926; University of Edinburgh, Ph.D. 1931. Married Jeannie Dougal Robins in 1927; one son. Assistant Professor, Ball State Teachers College, Muncie, Indiana, 1930–31; Instructor, Doane College, Crete, Nebraska, 1934–35; Assistant Professor, University of South Dakota, Vermillion, 1935–36. Instructor, 1931–33, since 1936, Member of the English Department, and since 1960, Professor of English and Poet-in-Residence, Michigan State University, East Lansing; now retired. Visiting Professor, University of Toronto, 1944, 1945, University of Washington, Seattle, 1949, Queen's University, Kingston, Ontario, 1952, 1960, University of British Columbia, Vancouver, 1956, Dalhousie University, Halifax, Nova Scotia, 1966–67, Sir George Williams University, Montreal, Summers 1967, 1969, and McGill University, 1969–70. Co-Founding Editor, with F. R. Scott, *McGill Fortnightly Review*, Montreal, 1925. Recipient: Guggenheim Fellowship, 1941, 1942; Harriet Monroe Memorial Prize (*Poetry*, Chicago), 1943; Governor-General's Award, 1944; Rockefeller Fellowship, 1944; Lorne Pierce Medal, 1966; Canada Centennial Medal, 1967; Canada Council Medal, 1968. D.Litt.: McGill University, 1958; LL.D.: Queen's University, 1966; D.C.L.: Bishop's University, Lennoxville, Quebec, 1967. Address: 640 Bailey Street, East Lansing, Michigan 48823, U.S.A.

PUBLICATIONS

Verse

News of the Phoenix and Other Poems. Toronto, Ryerson Press, and New York, Coward McCann, 1943.

A Sort of Ecstasy: Poems New and Selected. Toronto, Ryerson Press, and East Lansing, Michigan State College Press, 1954.

Collected Poems. Toronto, Oxford University Press, 1962.

Poems: New and Collected. Toronto, Oxford University Press, 1967.

Poets Between the Wars, with others, edited by Milton T. Wilson. Toronto, McClelland and Stewart, 1967.

The Classic Shade: Selected Poems. Toronto, McClelland and Stewart, 1978.

Other

Founders' Day Address. Fredericton, University of New Brunswick, 1946.

The Poetry of Robert Bridges. Montreal, Burton's, n.d.

Exploring Poetry, with M. L. Rosenthal. New York, Macmillan, 1955; revised edition, 1973.

Some Poems of E. J. Pratt: Aspects of Imagery and Theme. St. John's, Newfoundland, Memorial University, 1969.

Towards a View of Canadian Letters: Selected Essays 1928–1972. Vancouver, University of British Columbia Press, 1973.

On Poetry and Poets: Selected Essays. Toronto, McClelland and Stewart, 1977.

Editor, with F. R. Scott, *New Provinces: Poems of Several Authors.* Toronto, Macmillan, 1936.

Editor, *The Book of Canadian Poetry.* Toronto, Gage, and Chicago, University of Chicago Press, 1943; revised edition, 1948, 1957.

Editor, *Seven Centuries of Verse: English and American from the Early English Lyrics to the Present Day.* New York, Scribner, 1947; revised edition, 1957, 1967.

Editor, *The Worldly Muse: An Anthology of Serious Light Verse.* New York, Abelard Press, 1951.

Editor, with F. R. Scott, *The Blasted Pine: An Anthology of Satire, Invective and*

Disrespectful Verse, Chiefly by Canadian Writers. Toronto, Macmillan, 1957; revised edition, 1967.

Editor, *The Oxford Book of Canadian Verse: In English and French.* Toronto and New York, Oxford University Press, 1960; revised edition, 1965.

Editor, *Masks of Fiction* [*Poetry*]: *Canadian Critics on Canadian Prose* [*Verse*]. Toronto, McClelland and Stewart, 2 vols., 1961–62.

Editor, *Essays for College Writing.* New York, St. Martin's Press, 1965.

Editor, *The Book of Canadian Prose.* Toronto, Gage, 2 vols., 1965–73; vol. 2, as *The Canadian Century*, New York, Vanguard Press, 1975.

Editor, *100 Poems: Chaucer to Dylan Thomas.* New York, Scribner, 1965.

Editor, *Modern Canadian Verse: In English and French.* Toronto, Oxford University Press, 1967.

Editor, *The Collected Poems of Anne Wilkinson and a Prose Memoir.* Toronto, Macmillan, and New York, St. Martin's Press, 1968.

Editor, *The Canadian Experience.* Toronto, Gage, 1974.

Critical Studies: *Ten Canadian Poets*, by Desmond Pacey, Toronto, Ryerson Press, 1958; "A Salute to A. J. M. Smith" by various authors, in *Canadian Literature* (Vancouver), Winter 1963; *Literary History of Canada*, edited by Carl F. Klinck, Toronto, University of Toronto Press, 1965; *The McGill Movement: A. J. M. Smith, F. R. Scott, and Leo Kennedy* edited by Peter Stevens, Toronto, Ryerson Press, 1969; *Odysseus Ever Returning* by George Woodcock, Toronto, McClelland and Stewart, 1970.

* * *

A. J. M. Smith holds an important place in Canadian poetry, not merely for his own verse, but also for his part in creating and sustaining the modern movement and in giving Canadian poets a sense of distinctiveness as writers interpreting a unique culture in appropriate language.

It was in the 1930's that Smith began to gain an international reputation, but his Canadian career began in the 1920's. His earliest poems appeared when he was a student at McGill University in Montreal, where he edited the *McGill Literary Supplement*, and later, in 1925, founded with his fellow poet F. R. Scott the *McGill Fortnightly Review*, the first Canadian avant garde literary journal, dedicated to liberating Canada poetically and politically from colonialist attitudes. As important, in 1936, was the appearance of *New Provinces: Poems of Several Authors*, the Canadian equivalent of *New Signatures*, in which the writers who were since recognsized as the pioneers in a distinctive Canadian voice in poetry, Smith, Scott, A. M. Klein, and E. J. Pratt, appeared together. The book's importance – like that of Smith's own poetry – lay in the fact that it showed how a poetry sensitive to a special environment and a local tradition could take on a cosmopolitan character, drawing from and contributing to a wider tradition in a way merely colonial poets have never been able to do.

Later, Smith balanced this achievement by demonstrating a continuity in Canadian poetry between the colonial and national eras through publishing the definitive series of Canadian poetry anthologies, beginning with *The Book of Canadian Poetry* in 1943 and ending with *Modern Canadian Verse* in 1967.

In his own work, Smith is a poet, given to metaphysical speculation, who sustains at the same time a high emotional intensity and a lapidary craftsmanship by which he has sought to make his poems "as hard/And as smooth and as white/As a brook pebble cold and unmarred...."

Smith, in fact, is a poet little bound by time or place. Even the poems he wrote during the 1930's are much less tied to the period than those of most younger poets then writing in English. Indeed, if there is anything that Smith retains to place him in the period through which he has worked and lived, it is a slight rococo tang that reminds one of the 1920's rather than of the later decades in which almost all his verse was written. Yeats and the Sitwells are much more his natural mentors than Auden and his circle.

If the world Smith creates in his poems is autonomous in time, it seems equally free in place. Only a very few of his satirical poems are parochial enough for non-Canadians to follow them with difficulty. It is true that Smith declared his intent

To hold in a verse as austere
As the spirit of prairie and river,
Lonely, unbuyable, dear,
The North, as a deed, and for ever.

But even in his rather imagistic poems on Canadian landscapes the result is usually a glimpse into the same detached and personal world as that where (in Smith's only apparently less literal poems) the Phoenix does not die and "The bellow of good Master Bull/ Astoundeth gentil Cow...." The familiar cedars and firs and wild-duck calls in a poem like "The Lonely Land" lead us into a landscape in its feeling as mythological as any painted by Poussin for the encounters of Gods and mortals:

This is a beauty
of dissonance,
this resonance
of stony strand,
this smoky cry
curled over a black pine
and wind-battered branch
when the wind
bends the tops of the pines
and curdles the sky
from the north.

Besides such landscape poems, and poems devoted to the metaphysical contemplation of death, Smith often resorts in his verse to those sublime forms of literary criticism – the only really creative ones: parody, translation (he has rendered Gautier and Mallarmé excellently), deliberate pastiche, and the tribute, in the manner of his finely rendered "To Henry Vaughan." All these are more than feats of imitative virtuosity; they are the emphatic approaches of a poet who can, when he desires, be resoundingly himself.

Smith's aims are spareness, clarity, balance, the austerity of a latter-day classicism enriched by the discoveries of the Symbolists and the Imagists. One is aware of the unending search for words that are "crisp and sharp and small," for a form as "skin-tight" as the stallions of his poem "Far West." Occasionally the visions clarified through Smith's bright glass are too sharp for comfort, the detachment too remote for feeling to survive. More often they are saved by the dense impact of the darker shapes that lie within the crystal, the "shadows I have seen, of me deemed deeper/That backed on nothing in the horrid air." It is this enduring sense of the shapeless beyond shape that gives Smith's best poems their peculiar rightness of tension, and makes his austerities so rich in implication.

—George Woodcock

SMITH, Dave (David Jeddie Smith). American. Born in Portsmouth, Virginia, 19 December 1942. Educated at the University of Virginia, Charlottesville, 1961–65, B.A. in English 1965; College of William and Mary, Williamsburg, Virginia, 1966; Southern Illinois

University, Edwardsville, M.A. 1969; Ohio University, Athens, Ph.D. in English 1976. Served in the United States Air Force, 1969–72: Staff Sergeant. Married Deloras Mae Weaver in 1966; one son and two daughters. Teacher of English and French, and football coach, Poquoson High School, Virginia, 1965–67; part-time instructor, Christopher Newport College, Newport News, Virginia, 1970–72, Thomas Nelson Community College, Hampton, Virginia, 1970–72, and College of William and Mary, 1971; Instructor, Western Michigan University, Kalamazoo, 1974–75; Assistant Professor, Cottey College, Nevada, Missouri, 1975–76. Assistant Professor, 1976–79, Director of the Creative Writing program since 1976, and since 1979, Associate Professor of English, University of Utah, Salt Lake City. Editor, *Sou'wester* magazine, Edwardsville, Illinois, 1967–68; Founding Editor, *Back Door* magazine, Athens, Ohio, 1969–79. Currently, Poetry Editor, *Rocky Mountain Review*, Tempe, Arizona. Recipient: *Kansas Quarterly* prize, 1975; Breadloaf Writers Conference John Atherton Fellowship, 1975; Borestone Mountain Award, 1976; National Endowment for the Arts Fellowship, 1976; *Southern Poetry Review* prize, 1977; American Academy of Arts and Letters award, 1979; *Portland Review* prize, 1979. Address: 3740 East Yosemite Drive, Salt Lake City, Utah 84109, U.S.A.

PUBLICATIONS

Verse

Bull Island. Poquoson, Virginia, Back Door Press, 1970.
Mean Rufus Throw Down. Fredonia, New York, Basilisk Press, 1973.
The Fisherman's Whore. Athens, Ohio University Press, 1974.
Drunks. Edwardsville, Illinois, Sou'wester, 1974.
Cumberland Station. Urbana, University of Illinois Press, 1976.
In Dark, Sudden with Light. Athens, Ohio, Croissant, 1977.
Goshawk, Antelope. Urbana, University of Illinois Press, 1979.

Critical Studies: "Sappho to Smith" by Vernon Young, in *Hudson Review* (New York), January 1975, "On Dave Smith" by John Gardner, in *Three Rivers 10* (Pittsburgh), Spring 1977; "Oh I Admire and Sorrow" by Helen Vendler, in *Parnassus* (New York), Spring–Summer 1977.

Dave Smith comments:

Miller Williams, the American poet, gives thanks in a poem for people who don't write poetry. I do too. But I am thankful, as well, for the thousands who do write it, for I think scarcely anything can move the mind to pleasure as poetry can. I hope my poems give others that pleasure, for that is why I write them. And I write about that which gives me pleasure. My subjects have been, generally, the Atlantic seacoast, the American West, and people. I care little for poems that do not create a narrative or contextual event in which people are involved with something that is happening or has happened. I am concerned to write a thickly-textured poem whose speech as well as whose event will be memorable, will speak for the uncompromising wildness of the human spirit, and will seem to be felt experience. I do not believe free verse exists but my poem are organized in traditional forms perhaps only one-third of the time. Nevertheless, I take whatever opportunity presents itself. I believe I write in the line of poets marked by strongly stressed language, by a lyrical sense of pietas, by a determination to find the human connection to a natural and sacramental energy, by a willingness to employ rational, as opposed to symbolic, commentary. Such poets might include the Anglo-Saxon lyricists, Hopkins, Hardy, Yeats, Eliot, and among contemporary Americans, James Dickey, James Wright, and Robert Penn Warren. And yet by invoking those names I do not earn any right to stand among such poets, I merely suggest the poetries I would hope to perpetuate and honor. I hope my poems say a very simple thing, that it is good to be alive and good to have love. Whether they say it well or badly, or even comprehensibly, is for others to judge.

* * *

Dave Smith has written powerfully, at times jealously and defiantly, about "his" region of Virginia, a peninsula bordered by the Poquoson River and Chesapeake Bay, telling stories about tough, hard-working watermen and women. "William Styron, from Newport News (over-town), writes of my area as if it were Connecticut," Smith has said. He writes of it as if it were Troy, and one comes upon Smith's poems with a kind of relief, after hearing, for too long, the melancholy whine of lesser poets. He writes about people involved in elemental struggles, and the power of his work, which is often hard on the surface, tense, and vigorous, seems to grow directly from the people he describes. The man in "Hard Times, But Carrying On," for example, has eyes "once blue and pure/as the Bay, but that too turned thick with grim trails of tasteless oil and shapeless carps of paper...

Even so
he works his hole with craft,
eats fish for lunch at noon and dots
it with a single swallow of rye, then
drags back hard on the surging
net, while all around the bags
crank up slack as widow's dugs in rain.

The struggle of his people is not, as in similar tales growing out of a clearly identifiable region, against industrialism or the evil of other people, but against wind, water, and sun. In poems such as "March Storm" and "Among the Oyster Boats at Plum Tree Cove," these forces take on the characteristics of antagonists in a wild and passionate drama. Smith's poems have an extraordinary sense of place about them. One is aware of the writer's having belonged somewhere, and his writing helps one realize why so many Americans leave their native region – a theme in "Cumberland Station" – for another locale.

In recent years, Smith has written appreciatively of Robert Penn Warren ("Save for Warren, I cannot love the fugitive poets") and Louis Simpson, and there are obvious similarities between Smith's early work and the story poems of Warren and between Smith's latest work and the quiet, "accessible" lyrics of Simpson. In "Morning Light at Wanship, Utah" and "The Colors of Our Age: Pink and Black," Smith tries on the second style with somewhat less authority than he wore the earlier one. But he continues to speak in a recognizably poetic voice, and promises to grow and change with the skill he has already indicated in his best work.

—Michael True

SMITH, Iain Crichton. British. Born on the Isle of Lewis, Outer Hebrides, Scotland, 1 January 1928. Educated at the University of Aberdeen, M.A. (honours) in English 1950. Served as a Sergeant in the British Army Education Corps, 1950–52. Married. Secondary School Teacher, Clydebank, 1952–55; Teacher of English, Oban High School, 1955–77. Recipient: Scottish Arts Council Award, 1966, 1968, 1974, 1977, and Prize, 1968; BBC Award, for television play, 1970; Book Council Award, 1970; Silver Pen Award, 1971;

Queen's Jubilee Medal. Fellow, Royal Society of Literature. Address: 42 Combie Street, Oban, Argyll, Scotland.

PUBLICATIONS

Verse

The Long River. Edinburgh, M. Macdonald, 1955.
New Poets 1959, with Karen Gershon and Christopher Levenson. London, Eyre and Spottiswoode, 1959.
Deer on the High Hills: A Poem. Edinburgh, Giles Gordon, 1960.
Thistles and Roses. London, Eyre and Spottiswoode, 1961.
The Law and the Grace. London, Eyre and Spottiswoode, 1965.
Biobuill is Sanasan Reice (Bibles and Advertisements; in Gaelic). Glasgow, Gairm, 1965.
Three Regional Voices, with Michael Longley and Barry Tebb. London, Poet and Printer, 1968.
At Helensburgh. Belfast, Festival, 1968.
From Bourgeois Land. London, Gollancz, 1970.
Selected Poems. London, Gollancz, 1970.
Penguin Modern Poets 21, with George Mackay Brown and Norman MacCaig. London, Penguin, 1972.
Love Poems and Elegies. London, Gollancz, 1972.
Hamlet in Autumn. Edinburgh, M. Macdonald, 1972.
Eadar Fealla-dhà is Glaschu (Between Comedy and Glasgow; in Gaelic). Glasgow, University of Glasgow Celtic Department, 1974.
Notebooks of Robinson Crusoe. London, Gollancz, 1974.
Orpheus and Other Poems. Preston, Lancashire, Akros, 1974.
Poems for Donalda. Belfast, Ulsterman, 1974.
The Notebooks of Robinson Crusoe and Other Poems. London, Gollancz, 1975.
In the Middle –. London, Gollancz, 1977.

Plays

An Coileach (The Cockerel; in Gaelic; produced Glasgow, 1966). Glasgow, An Comunn Gaidhealach, 1966.
A' Chuirt (The Trial; in Gaelic; produced Glasgow, 1966). Glasgow, An Comunn Gaidhealach, 1966.
A Kind of Play (produced Mull, 1975).
Two by the Sea (produced Mull, 1975).
The Happily Married Couple (produced Mull, 1977).

Novels

Consider the Lilies. London, Gollancz, 1968; as *The Alien Light*, Boston, Houghton Mifflin, 1969.
The Last Summer. London, Gollancz, 1969.
My Last Duchess. London, Gollancz, 1971.
Goodbye, Mr. Dixon. London, Gollancz, 1974.
An t-Aonaran (in Gaelic). Glasgow, University of Glasgow Celtic Department, 1976.
An End to Autumn. London, Gollancz, 1978.
On the Island. London, Gollancz, 1979.

Short Stories

Burn is Aran (Bread and Water; includes verse; in Gaelic). Glasgow, Gairm, 1960.
An Dubh is an Gorm (The Black and the Blue; in Gaelic). Aberdeen, Aberdeen University, 1963.
Maighsirean is Ministearan (Schoolmasters and Ministers; in Gaelic). Inverness, Club Leabhar, 1970.
Survival Without Error and Other Stories. London, Gollancz, 1970.
The Black and the Red. London, Gollancz, 1973.
An t-Adhar Amaireaganach (The American Story; in Gaelic). Inverness, Club Leabhar, 1973.
The Hermit and Other Stories. London, Gollancz, 1977.

Other

The Golden Lyric: An Essay on the Poetry of Hugh MacDiarmid. Preston, Lancashire, Akros, 1967.
Iain Am Measg nan Reultan (Iain among the Stars; in Gaelic; juvenile). Glasgow, Gairm, 1970.
River, River: Poems for Children. Edinburgh, M. Macdonald, 1978.

Translator, *Ben Dorain*, by Duncan Ban Macintyre. Preston, Lancashire, Akros, 1969.
Translator, *Poems to Eimhir*, by Sorley Maclean. London and Newcastle upon Tyne, Gollancz-Northern House, 1971.

Bibliography: in *Lines Review* (Edinburgh), no. 29, 1969.

Critical Study: interview in *Scottish International* (Edinburgh), 1971.

Iain Crichton Smith comments:

Interested in the conflict between discipline and freedom, as shown in the title *The Law and the Grace*. No particular sources, except that I admire Lowell's work.

* * *

Iain Crichton Smith's "The White Air of March," a long, elliptical poem in the manner of Pound's *Cantos* and Eliot's *Four Quartets*, opens on a characteristic note:

> This is the land God gave to Andy Stewart – we have our inheritance.
> There shall be no ardour, there shall be indifference.
> There shall not be excellence, there shall be the average.
> We shall be the intrepid hunters of golf balls.

"Excellence! 'costing not less than everything' " has always been Crichton Smith's standard, and it is its conspicuous absence from his native country which stirs him, here and in such volumes as *From Bourgeois Land*, to indictment of a venal and hypocritical culture. "It is bitter," he observes, "to be an exile in one's own land" and "to write poems of exile/ in a verse without honour or style." Yet, significantly, he is generous to honest incompetence like that of William McGonagall, whom he unexpectedly picks out as a "sign" of persistence, even wrongheadedly, at the highest things: "Endlessly you toil towards Balmoral/to the old lady knitting her slow empire." If the dream of the poem's close (in which "The dead bury their dead" and Scotland discovers, "In the white air of March/a new mind") is to be realized, her current "loss of passion, loss of power" has to be admitted, and the "impenetrable dullness" of a parochial culture overcome.

Should that ever happen, Iain Crichton Smith will have been one of its major agents. Staunchly Gaelic, writing fine poetry in that ancient language, he is nevertheless unequivocally in the mainstream of Modernism, like Hugh MacDiarmid and Basil Bunting proving that a strong sense of regional loyalty is not inimical to the best spirit of cosmopolitanism. "Shall Gaelic Die?", which he has translated from his own Gaelic, is an aphoristic meditation on precisely this relationship, drawing on Wittgenstein and Saussure, among others, to build an impassioned argument for the survival of his native tongue, as one irreplaceable element in the "spectrum of beautiful languages" which constitute the human world and protect us from the dogmatic single vision of "The one-language descended like a church – like a blanket, like mist." But his concern for language is not an antiquarian's. The final section contrasts the "immutable, universal" absolute, Language, that unrusting gold which Midas found was deadly, to *speech*, the currency which, like "coins that are old and dirty, ... notes that are wrinkled like old faces," can "cop[e] with time." It is to the latter that he gives "allegiance, to these I owe honour, with sweetness." By turns aureate and colloquial, racy and refined with a grave and sober dignity, Crichton Smith's poetry explores the real texture of life and language in contemporary Scotland with an acute and unsentimental sensitivity. He can write of the clichés of "the Bed and Breakfast routine," of the "faded gentry" and shop girls "who holiday on pop and fish-and-chips" without the condescension of Eliot or Auden, but with a fusion of compassion and dispassionate observation which is peculiarly his own. While he brings a conscientious intellect to bear on the pharisaism of the Scottish gerontocracy, he has drawn sharp and sympathetic portraits of age. "Old Woman" ("And she, being old, fed from a mashed plate") is representative:

> She munched, half dead, blindly searching the spoon.
>
> Outside, the grass was raging. There I sat
> imprisoned in my pity and my shame
> that men and women having suffered time
> should sit in such a place, in such a state.

The change of tense and mood of the same verb ("sit") suggests that observer and observed share a common condition: they are only momentarily distinguished by time. Likewise, "raging" spills over from the grass to the state of mind of the poet without distorting his mood. Crichton Smith's poetry displays a democratic intellect which never stoops to a sentimental populism. Like his "Responsible Spinster" he always "inspect[s] justice through a queer air"; like his Kierkegaard, he is the "Forced theologian of the minimum place." In *Deer on the High Hills*, a fine sequence which recalls the lucid abstraction and sudden intellectual sensuousness of Wallace Stevens, he disposes of the pathetic fallacies by which we evade looking at the real world, concluding: "There is no metaphor. The stone is stony./The deer step out in isolated air./We move at random on an innocent journey."

In poem after poem he faces the fact of death; in his "World War One" sequence refusing the consolations of poetry and myth; in "If You Are about to Die Now," which returns to his fascination with the incomprehensible delusions of "great men," admitting the final insufficiency of language:

> If you are about to die now
> there is nothing I can write for you.
> History is silent about this.
> Even Napoleon, face huge as a plate,
> disguised the advance guard and said
> "Why they sent for my brother is because
> he, and not I, is in trouble."

Even "Excellence" cannot cope with this absolute and irresistible fact. As he says in "Shall Gaelic Die?": "Death is outside the language." But, in a sense, death is for Crichton Smith the only criterion by which to judge the worth of a thing. In "The Law and the Grace," the poet humbly begs to accept that judgment on his "pride,/[his] insufficiency, imperfect works." It is a judgment they can sustain.

—Stan Smith

SMITH, John (Charles). British. Born in High Wycombe, Buckinghamshire, 5 April 1924. Educated at St. James's Elementary School, Gerrards Cross. Director, 1946–58, Managing Director, 1959–71, and since 1972, Advisory Director, Christy and Moore Ltd., literary agents, London. Editor, *Poetry Review*, London, 1962–65. Recipient: *Adam International* Prize, 1953. Address: 11 Palmeira Court, Palmeira Square, Hove, Sussex, England.

PUBLICATIONS

Verse

Gates of Beauty and Death (as C. Busby Smith). London, Fortune Press, 1948.
The Dark Side of Love. London, Hogarth Press, 1952.
The Birth of Venus. London, Hutchinson, 1954.
Excursus in Autumn. London, Hutchinson, 1958.
A Letter to Lao Tze. London, Hart Davis, 1961.
A Discreet Immorality. London, Hart Davis, 1965.
Five Sons of Resurrection. Privately printed, 1967.
Four Ritual Dances. Privately printed, 1968.
Entering Rooms. London, Chatto and Windus-Hogarth Press, 1973.

Plays

The Mask of Glory (produced Gerrards Cross, Buckinghamshire, 1956).
Mr. Smith's Apocalypse: A Jazz Cantata, music by Michael Garrick (produced Farnham, Surrey, 1969). London, Robbins Music, 1970.

Other

Jan le Witt: An Appreciation of His Work, with Herbert Read and Jean Cassou. London, Routledge, 1971.
The Broken Fiddlestick (juvenile). London, Longman, 1971.
The Early Bird and the Worm (juvenile). London, Burke, 1972.
The Arts Betrayed. London, Herbert Press, and New York, Universe, 1978.

Editor, with William Kean Seymour, *The Pattern of Poetry.* London, Burke, 1963.
Editor, *My Kind of Verse.* London, Burke, 1965; New York, Macmillan, 1968.
Editor, *Modern Love Poems.* London, Studio Vista, 1966.
Editor, with William Kean Seymour, *Happy Christmas.* Philadelphia, Westminster Press, and London, Burke, 1968.
Editor, *My Kind of Rhymes.* London, Burke, 1972.

John Smith comments:

As briefly as possible, I would describe my poetry as lyrical, metaphysical, formal, sardonic.

* * *

A certain civilised coolness at first seemed the main characteristic of John Smith's poetry. Admirers of *The Dark Side of Love* – and there were a considerable number – seemed to be looking, like the poet, back to the elegant verse-makers of the seventeenth century: "As any man/With any woman lies/Let him in sleep her lovely limbs discover...." Fortunately, the slightly overblown felicity of the early poems was controlled, in later collections, by a developing intelligence which in that early volume had informed the long "Conversations with the Moon." In subsequent books, while the language remains highly literate and elegant, unsophisticated in everything except its dexterity, the tone has become increasingly and more subtly esoteric; the allusions less romantically projected. Yet Smith has remained largely unnoticed by critics, unanthologised despite some eminently suitable pieces. This may be because he had declined to interest himself in various schools of poetry, has remained unassociated with any movement (except in his interesting experiments in writing verse for recital with jazz, which has resulted in some of the most successful pieces in that *genre* – again largely unnoticed, presumably because more serious than the Liverpool words-and-pop simplicities). Smith has steadfastly refused to be self-indulgent, preferring a private, though not difficult, wit to public clowning. His most recent verse has shown him as a valuable guide to contemporary social life, sometimes terrifying in its vision into psychiatric darkness, sometimes funny. He is perhaps the least recognised good poet writing in England at the moment.

—Derek Parker

SMITH, Ken(neth John). British. Born in Rudston, East Yorkshire, 4 December 1938. Educated at Hull and Knaresborough grammar schools; University of Leeds, Yorkshire, B.A. in English literature, 1963. Served in the Royal Air Force, 1958–60. Married Ann Minnis in 1960; two daughters and one son. Taught in an elementary school, Dewsbury, Yorkshire, 1963–64, and in a technical college, Batley, Yorkshire, 1964–65; Tutor, Exeter College of Art, Devon, 1965–69; Instructor in Creative Writing, Slippery Rock State College, Pennsylvania, 1969–72; Visiting Poet, Clark University, and College of the Holy Cross, both in Worcester, Massachusetts, 1972–73; Yorkshire Arts Fellow, Leeds University, 1976–78. Co-Editor, *Stand*, Newcastle upon Tyne, 1963–69; Editor, *South West Review*, Exeter, 1976–79. Recipient: Gregory Award, 1964; Arts Council bursary, 1975, 1978. Address: c/o 2 Lamplugh Square, Bridlington, East Yorkshire, England.

PUBLICATIONS

Verse

Eleven Poems. Leeds, Northern House, 1964.
The Pity. London, Cape, 1967.
Academic Board Poems. Harpford, Devon, Peeks Press, 1968.
A Selection of Poems. Gillingham, Kent, ARC, 1969.

Work, Distances. Chicago, Swallow Press, 1972.
The Wild Rose. Memphis, Stinktree, 1973.
Hawk Wolf. Knotting, Bedfordshire, Sceptre Press, 1975.
Frontwards in a Backwards Movie. Todmorden, Lancashire, ARC, 1975.
Wasichi. London, Aloes, 1975.
Anus MundiBlack Sonnets. Hardwick, Massachusetts, Four Zoas Press, 1976.
Henry the Navigator. Glen Ellyn, Illinois, Cat's Pajamas Press, 1976.
Tristan Crazy. Newcastle upon Tyne, Bloodaxe, 1978.

Ken Smith comments:

Over the years my work has developed in response to the different environments in which I have arrived as much as to travel and the spaces between; mine are portable roots, some in Yorkshire, some in America, some in Devon. Exeter, the city I have most lived in, has provided me with the figure of *The Wanderer* from the Anglo-Saxon *Exeter Book*; I havc identified as much with him and his homelessness as with the irony of his poem – having had in the cathedral library a home for the past 900 years. Writing then is for me the act of discovering roots and pasts behind the present I find myself in, as if by some marvellous accident; I am located in the work I do and in the daily rediscovery of language, the magic liquid that connects me to all else. I live in that as much as anywhere. Devon has also made available to me the ancient silences of Dartmoor, that marvellous museum of all that has happened to us: a museum I do not encourage anyone to visit. By Kestor, above Chagford, amongst the stoney leavings of the iron makers, is where I go whenever I have a decision to make, and there I feel the strongest root into the sullen past. On other days I am gregarious, and have moved recently closer and closer to drama and dramatic expression. Community, environment, and all the minutiae of gesture and inflexion – these are all my concern still.

Themes: environment (hence nature), domestic, human relations and human attitudes, our subjective world implanted in an indifferent objectivity. Usual verse forms – free, intuitively worked, organic. General sources: any – many accidental and incidental, but environment and history, the sense of being alive, etc. Literary sources – many and scattered, too many to mention but mostly twentieth-century.

Amongst other things, I want to express the way we live, and comment on it: the way we live in society, the way our environment is and we with it, how we form community – the minute ways in which the shapes of our lives are expressed in habits, gestures, buildings, our conscious and unconscious reactions to weather, landscape, each other – how we bind our lives down to the smallest detail distinguishing individual or community. So in this sense I am interested in custom, and in speech, and so in language, and so in process. The poem itself is a process more than a product of this interest. I want a language that enacts and makes living, that is living rather than merely representative: a language metaphoric in itself.

* * *

Ken Smith's poetry is characterised, at its best, by a coincidence of formal syntax with austere passion. When either of these goes awry, or is diminished, the poetry reads thinly. Thus in his first book, *The Pity*, his two best known poems move with a richness of feeling and insight, both of these released through formal, spoken syntax. Released is the proper word; the reader receives a building tension which eventually finds its expressive release without a loosening of the syntactic structure. In "The Pity" (the title poem) the images of bat and fish – "The horned and hanging bat sees a bat's world./Fish quiver in the shallows, cold as their element,/thinking water. I wore contempt, grew hatred" – are used to open out sensually the perception of submission to their environment. Smith implies that the human creature may behave like a fish or bat as he or she submits without struggle to his context; but the deepest part of the insight is reserved for the implication that men, equipped with intelligence, need not always submit, or merge indecipherably with their surroundings.

This nexus of resistance and change is also examined in "Family Group," but here the change, one supposes intimately experienced by the poet, is equivocally appraised. The alteration of the family's circumstances, from those of a farm labourer's to a small-shop owner's, is weighed carefully. For each gain substantiated by independence and physical well-being, there is a corresponding loss (not apparently recognised by the mother and father) which, ironically, is a loss of response inevitably entailed by their town life, a life which aims at reducing the hardships of exposure but which at the same time reduces the responses. On the face of it, my account attributes to Smith a reactionary conservatism, but because the gains and losses can be and are weighed by the son (the poet) the heuristic comparison between the two experiences points not to an either/or choice but to the richer consciousness that is able, through both experiences, to weigh, compare, and qualify both, without blindly committing himself to either. Here the value is in response.

What is Smith's poetry committed to? The propriety of the question is indicated in the strengths – the dogged, at times dourly formed love for the resisting, struggling individual who, through no apparently remediable flaw other than individuality, is condemned to suffer, without society being able, or willing, to help. Where help implies a change of heart. What has developed here, of course, is the deepening realisation of society's intractable nature, an apprehension that has not so much hardened Smith against it, as opened out his tenderness for those individuals who seem society's inevitable victims. This emerges clearly, the tenderness, I mean, in "Eli's Poem" from Smith's second book, *Work, Distances:*

> Now I am with a crazy woman
> who hurts herself with ashes and briars
> running in the scrub. She takes blankets
> and stuffs them under her skirt for a child ...
> Now she is out on the hill wailing
> cutting her flesh on the stiff grass
> where I go to her lamenting.

What is to be done? Here the unornamented language, the starkness of the sensuous apprehension and enactment, which is one of Smith's strengths, expresses the aloneness of the creature, loved for her almost intolerable strangeness, which the poet would not abandon. The almost monotonous drone of the rhythms, both alert and repetitive, builds one's sense of the woman, without the poet having to spell out his feelings for her. The commitment to her is realised through narrative, rhythm, and tone, that is, through characteristically central literary means. And by making clear his allegiance to her, he qualifies his attitude to society, which in this instance is tolerant but uncomprehending.

More recently, in poems such as "Lake" and "Fly," the more formal syntax of the earlier poems takes over, the loss of which threatened to disperse those very feelings which, one supposes, the disjointing of the syntax was meant to release. The casual *movement* but not casual tone of these poems implements a lucid intensity which disencumbers itself of everything but those physically cited details which serve to interconnect feelings. That is, the physical details act as nodes of feelings:

> A month back the lake
> I stood by spreading its bulk
>
> cracked whipped and cried
>
> and fought its bed: animals
> stirring, seeds pressing out
>
> from milkweed's grip

and

come back to the world brought me
out of long sleep. Love,
as you stir from your dream's
untrembling be still for me....

—Jon Silkin

SMITH, Michael. Irish. Born in Dublin, 1 September 1942. Educated at O'Connell's School, Dublin; University College, Dublin, B.A. and H.Dip. in Education. Married; one daughter. Since 1966, teacher of Latin and English, St. Paul's College, Raheny, Dublin. Editor, New Irish Poets series of the New Writers Press, Dublin, and *The Lace Curtain*, Dublin. Address: 19 Warrenmount Place, SCR, Dublin 8, Ireland.

PUBLICATIONS

Verse

With the Woodnymphs. Dublin, New Writers Press, 1968.
Dedications. Dublin, New Writers Press, 1968.
Homage to James Thompson (B.V.) at Portobello. Dublin, New Writers Press, 1969.
Poems. London, Advent Press, 1971.
Times and Locations. Dublin, Dolmen Press, 1972.

Other

Editor, *Selected Poems of James Clarence Mangan.* Dublin, Gallery Press, 1974.

Translator, *Del Camino*, by Antonio Machado. Dublin, Gallery Press, 1974.

Michael Smith comments:

I belong to a school of poetry which probably originated in Ireland with Patrick Kavanagh; might be called cosmopolitan parochialism as its underlying belief is that poets achieve universality by working in the context of their home environment.

The psychological condition out of which most of my poetry comes is not unlike that of Manzoni when he wrote, "An immense multitude, one generation after the other, passing on the face of the earth, passing on its own native piece of earth, without leaving a trace in history, is a sad phenomenon the importance of which cannot be overlooked."

I am living in a small house in Dublin's old quarter, an area of ancient ruin and obsolescence, where the troubled ghosts of Swift and Mangan are omnipresent and where the people still have traditions so that the past is alive. My poetry is a fusion of this environment and that condition which I have used Manzoni's words to suggest. As regards form, I believe it cannot be discussed apart from the poem. As a purely lyric poet, I can only say that I do not think the resources of language or, to use Pound's terms, logopeia, phanopeia, and melopeia, can be considered in isolation from the actual writing of a poem. They are simply things that happen, I hope necessarily, when the poem is being written: the impulse, the moment, the insight dictate all terms. Resulting from this view of poetic methodology I see my poems as short, intense inquiries and revelations which, at present, work against the background of a primeval Dublin so far without expression in literature, notwithstanding Joyce and O'Casey.

* * *

Times and Locations shows Michael Smith to be a maker of short poems which increase their effect as they are re-read. Some are so delicate that the basis of their imagery in genuine observation emerges only slowly; in others, a blunt first impact is later seen to encompass a range of more subtle feeling. He catches very well the atmosphere of localities, of moments of intensity due to imagined or actual events:

> Something ordered, yet desperate and violent –
> A rose, say, or an old man's humiliation.

Already an able and attractive writer, he will gain in depth, perhaps, by the gradual loosening of what is still a very "literary" style, and by a more direct, elaborated approach to the seriousness of his Irish (and universal) subject-matter.

—Anne Cluysenaar

SMITH, Vivian (Brian). Australian. Born in Hobart, Tasmania, 3 June 1933. Educated at the University of Tasmania, Hobart, M.A.; University of Sydney, Ph.D. Married Sybille Gottwald in 1960; two daughters and one son. Formerly, Lecturer in French, University of Tasmania. Currently, Senior Lecturer in English, University of Sydney. Address: 19 McLeod Street, Mosman, New South Wales 2088, Australia.

PUBLICATIONS

Verse

The Other Meaning. Sydney, Edwards and Shaw, 1956.
An Island South. Sydney, Angus and Robertson, 1967.
Familiar Places. Sydney, Angus and Robertson, 1978.

Other

James McAuley. Melbourne, Lansdowne Press, 1965; revised edition, 1970.
Les Vigé en Australie (juvenile). Melbourne, Longman, 1967.
Vance Palmer. Melbourne, Oxford University Press, 1971.
The Poetry of Robert Lowell. Sydney, Sydney University Press, 1974.
Vance and Nettie Palmer. New York, Twayne, 1975.

Editor, *Australian Poetry 1969.* Sydney, Angus and Robertson, 1969.
Editor, *Letters of Vance and Nettie Palmer 1915–1963.* Canberra, National Library of Australia, 1977.

Critical Studies: "The Poetry of *The Other Meaning*" by Margaret Irvin, in *Poetry* (Sydney),

February 1969: *Bread and Wine* by Kenneth Slessor, Sydney, Angus and Robertson, 1970: *Commonwealth Literature* by William Walsh, London, Oxford University Press, 1973; *A Map of Australian Verse* by James McAuley, Melbourne, Oxford University Press, 1976; "Two Poets" by Elaine Lindsay, in *Twenty-Four Hours* (Sydney), January 1979; *Modern Australian Poetry 1920–1970* by Herbert C. Jaffa, Detroit, Gale, 1979.

Vivian Smith comments:

Within the context of Australian poetry I am, I suppose, something of a regionalist since most of my poems are about Hobart and Tasmania, though Sydney too has been one of the poles of my inspiration. I write in free and traditional forms, and my lyrics try to affirm both the sense of a personal inner world and the inescapable presence of the actual. There are two areas of influence in my work. The first is that of the Australian poets who most impressed me when I first started to write, particularly Judith Wright and Kenneth Slessor with their focus on landscape and especially the sea, an inescapable element for a Tasmanian. The second is that of the French and German poets whose work I studied closely and lectured on for many years. Although I have lived in Sydney for the last 12 years, Tasmania, with its special qualities of light, vegetation, and landscape, is still the focal point of my work, and I have tried to capture something of its peculiar essence which is colonial, Europeanised, astringent, secluded, peaceful, and wild. Hobart still seems to me more like a European town or city than any other place in Australia and the most beautiful of all the capital cities.

Looking back over my poems, I find that they are concerned with various attitudes of mind – how to go on living fully and humanly without dogma or theory, but without becoming a victim of unstructured experience. In other words, they are concerned with the nature and meaning of belief.

* * *

In the 1950's there appeared to be a blossoming of fresh young poetic talent, predominantly regional in origin, in Australia: David Rowbotham in Queensland, Randolph Stow in West Australia, and, in Tasmania, Christopher Koch and Vivian Smith. In his first volume, *The Other Meaning*, Smith showed a sensitive response to his environment. The "other meaning" with he sought was some aspect of the transient that gave it either definition or awareness.

In *An Island South*, the influence of the then-predominantly academic poets of dry wit in England and America is more apparent. Vivian Smith has published only occasional poems since that volume. His work has a reticence that sometimes underplays the deftness of observation and precision of control that give his best work a true luminosity. Though his themes have tended to remain persistently close to immediate response, Smith has appreciably hardened the texture of his poems to a gemlike precision. If he does not appear to have justified the early anticipations of his admirers, his work has grown in its own terms and with honesty and quiet dignity.

—Thomas W. Shapcott

SMITH, William Jay. American. Born in Winnfield, Louisiana, 22 April 1918. Educated at Blow School, St. Louis, 1924–31; Cleveland High School, 1931–35; Washington University, St. Louis, 1935–41, B.A. 1939, M.A. in French 1941; Institut de Touraine, Tours,

France, 1938; Columbia University, New York, 1946–47; Wadham College, Oxford (Rhodes Scholar), 1947–48; University of Florence, 1948–50. Served as a Lieutenant in the United States Naval Reserve, 1941–45. Married 1) Barbara Howes, *q.v.*, in 1947 (divorced, 1965), two sons; 2) Sonja Haussmann in 1966, one step-son. Assistant in French, Washington University, 1939–41; Instructor in English and French, 1946–47, and Visiting Professor of Writing and Acting Chairman, Writing Division, 1973, 1974–75, Columbia University; Instructor in English, 1951, and Poet-in-Residence and Lecturer in English, 1959–64, 1966–67, Williams College, Williamstown, Massachusetts. Writer-in-Residence, 1965–66, Professor of English, 1967–68 and since 1970, Hollins College, Virginia. Consultant in Poetry, 1968–70, and Honorary Consultant, 1970–74, Library of Congress, Washington, D.C. Poetry Reviewer, *Harper's*, New York, 1961–64; Editorial Consultant, Grove Press, New York, 1968–70. Democratic Member, Vermont House of Representatives, 1960–62. Recipient: Young Poets Prize, 1945, and Union League Civic and Arts Foundation Prize, 1964 (*Poetry*, Chicago); Alumni Citation, Washington University, 1963; Ford Fellowship, for drama, 1964; Henry Bellamann Major Award, 1970; Loines Award, 1972; National Endowment for the Arts grant, 1972; Gold Medal of Labor (Hungary), 1978. D.Litt.: New England College, Henniker, New Hampshire, 1973. Member, National Institute of Arts and Letters, 1975. Agent: Marilyn Marlow, Curtis Brown Ltd., 575 Madison Avenue, New York, New York 10022. Address: Upper Bryant Road, West Cummington, Massachusetts 01026, U.S.A.

PUBLICATIONS

Verse

Poems. Pawlet, Vermont, Banyan Press, 1947.
Celebration at Dark. London, Hamish Hamilton, and New York, Farrar Straus, 1950.
Typewriter Birds. New York, Caliban Press, 1954; as *Typewriter Town*, New York, Dutton, 1960.
The Bead Curtain: Calligrams. Privately printed, 1957.
Poems 1947–1957. Boston, Little Brown, 1957.
Prince Souvanna Phouma: An Exchange Between Richard Wilbur and William Jay Smith. Williamstown, Massachusetts, Chapel Press, 1963.
The Tin Can and Other Poems. New York, Delacorte Press, 1966.
New and Selected Poems. New York, Delacorte Press, 1970.
A Rose for Katherine Anne Porter. New York, Albondocani Press, 1970.
At Delphi: For Allen Tate on His Seventy-Fifth Birthday, 19 November 1974. Williamstown, Massachusetts, Chapel Press, 1974.
Venice in the Fog. Greensboro, North Carolina, Unicorn Press, 1975.
Verses on the Times, with Richard Wilbur. New York, Gutenberg Press, 1978.
Journey to the Dead Sea. Omaha, Abattoir, 1979.
The Tall Poets. Winston-Salem, North Carolina, Palaemon Press, 1979.

Play

The Straw Market, music by the author (produced Washington, D.C., 1965; New York, 1969).

Other

Laughing Time (juvenile). Boston, Little Brown, 1955; London, Faber, 1956.
Boy Blue's Book of Beasts (juvenile). Boston, Little Brown, 1957.
Puptents and Pebbles: A Nonsense ABC (juvenile). Boston, Little Brown, 1959; London, Faber, 1960.

The Spectra Hoax (criticism). Middletown, Connecticut, Wesleyan University Press, 1961.
What Did I See? (juvenile). New York, Crowell Collier, 1962.
My Little Book of Big and Little: Little Dimity, Big Gumbo, Big and Little (juvenile). New York, Macmillan, 3 vols., 1963.
Ho for a Hat! (juvenile). Boston, Little Brown, 1964.
If I Had a Boat (juvenile). New York, Macmillan, 1966.
Mr. Smith and Other Nonsense (juvenile). New York, Delacorte Press, 1968.
Around My Room and Other Poems (juvenile). New York, Lancelot Press, 1969.
Grandmother Ostrich and Other Poems (juvenile). New York, Lanclot Press, 1969.
Children and Poetry: A Selective Annotated Bibliogaphy, with Virginia Haviland. Washington, D.C., Library of Congress, 1969.
Louise Bogan: A Woman's Words. Washington, D.C., Library of Congress, 1971.
The Streaks of the Tulip: Selected Criticism. New York, Delacorte Press, 1972.

Editor and Translator, *Selected Writings of Jules Laforgue.* New York, Grove Press, 1956.
Editor, *Herrick.* New York, Dell, 1962.
Editor, with Louise Bogan, *The Golden Journey: Poems for Young People.* Chicago, Reilly and Lee, 1965; London, Evans, 1967.
Editor, *Poems from France* (juvenile). New York, Crowell, 1967.
Editor, *Poems from Italy* (juvenile). New York, Crowell, 1972.
Editor, *Light Verse and Satires*, by Witter Bynner. New York, Farrar Straus, and London, Faber, 1978.

Translator, *Scirroco*, by Romualdo Romano. New York, Farrar Straus, 1951.
Translator, *Poems of a Multimillionaire*, by Valéry Larbaud. New York, Bonaccio and Saul, 1955.
Translator, *Two Plays by Charles Bertin: Christopher Columbus and Don Juan.* Minneapolis, University of Minnesota Press, 1970.
Translator, *Children of the Forest* (juvenile), by Elsa Beskow. New York, Delacorte Press, 1970.
Translator, *The Pirate Book* (juvenile), by Lennart Hellsing. New York, Delacorte Press, 1970; London, Benn, 1972.
Translator, *The Telephone* (juvenile), by Kornei Chukovsky. New York, Delacorte Press, 1976.
Translator, with Leif Sjöberg, *Agadir*, by Artur Lundkvist. Pittsburgh, Byblos, 1979.

Manuscript Collection: Washington University, St. Louis.

Critical Studies: "William Jay Smith," in *Modern Verse in English, 1900–1950*, edited by Lord David Cecil and Allen Tate, New York, Macmillan, 1958; "William Jay Smith," in *The Hollins Poets*, edited by Louis D. Rubin, Charlottesville, University Press of Virginia, 1967; *Authors of Books for Young People*, by Martha E. Ward and Dorothy A. Marquardt, Metuchen, New Jersey, Scarecrow Press, 1967; "The Lightness of William Jay Smith" by Dorothy Judd Hall, in *Southern Humanities Review* (Auburn, Alabama), Summer 1968; "A Poet Named Smith" by Jean G. Lawlor, in *Washington Post* (Washington, D.C.), 9 March 1969; "An Interview with William Jay Smith" by Elizavietta Ritchie, in *Voyages* (Washington, D.C.), Winter 1970; *Children's Literature in the Elementary School*, 3rd edition, by Charlotte S. Huck, New York, Holt Rinehart, 1976; *Children and Books*, 5th edition, by Zena Sutherland and May Hill Arbuthnot, Chicago, Scott Foresman, 1977.

William Jay Smith comments:

I am a lyric poet, alert, I hope, as one of my fellow poets, Stanley Kunitz, has put it, "to the changing weathers of a landscape, to the motions of the mind, to the complications and surprises of the human comedy." I believe that poetry should communicate: it is, by its very nature, complex, but its complexity should not prevent its making an immediate impact on the reader. Great poetry must have resonance: it must resound with the mystery of the human psyche, and possess always its own distinct, identifiable, and haunting, music. My recent poems have been written in long unrhymed lines because the material with which I am dealing seems to lend itself to this form, which is often close to, but always different from, prose. I have always used a great variety of verse forms, especially in my poetry for children. I believe that poetry begins in childhood and that a poet who can remember his own childhood exactly can, and should, communicate to children.

* * *

William Jay Smith's first book, *Poems*, announced a poet of exotic subjects, high patina, and exquisite music, a combination suggestive of early Wallace Stevens. Such poems as "The Peacock of Java," "On the Islands Which Are Solomon's," and "Of Islands" transform a seascape of atolls which "brings, even/To the tree of heaven, heaven." Other poems, like "The Barber" and "The Closing of the Rodeo," initiate Smith's satirical rendering of the American commonplace, while "Cupidon" reflects his interest in incremental ballad form and fantasy. This early work seemed a very deft performance in the then-dominant metaphysical style, but Smith has always sounded a note of his own – his lightness, dexterity, elegance, and wit reflect not only the prevailing influence of Eliot, Tate, and Ransom, but also earlier poets who had influenced them.

During World War II, Smith served as a liaison officer aboard a Free French naval vessel, and he began his civilian career as a teacher of French literature at Columbia. He published a distinguished translation of Valéry Larbaud in 1955 and of Jules Laforgue in 1956. The qualities of formal versification, precarious poise, and wit in his early verse seem akin to those of Laforgue, the dreamwork suggestive of Larbaud. Further clues to his own verse are offered in Smith's two critical studies. *The Spectra Hoax* is an entertaining reconstruction of the successful leg-pull by Witter Bynner and Arthur Davidson Ficke, who not only concocted a fictitious school of poets in 1916–18, but, writing pseudonymously as its members, begat better poems than when using their own names and more conventional styles. The following year Smith's introduction to a selection of the poems of Robert Herrick described that poet as "a master of understatement [who] knows what to omit," "a perfect miniaturist; nothing is too small for him to notice or too great to reduce in size." These and other occasional essays are collected in *Streaks of the Tulip: Selected Criticism*.

His translations and studies of English, French, and American poets suggest the range and sources of Smith's fascination with satire, fantasy, and word-play, his comprehension of the true seriousness of successful light verse, and his devotion, until his most recent work, to brief lyrics, conventional forms, aesthetic distance from his subjects, and a burnished surface – as in his little poem "Tulip" which offers "Magnificence within a frame." Similar qualities animate his several books of verse for children; he has written, "I believe that poetry begins in childhood and that a poet who can remember his own childhood exactly can, and should, communicate to children." (One such communication, *Typewriter Town* [1960], anticipates by several years the vogue for concrete poetry among writers for adults.)

These qualities and Smith's characteristic lightness of touch are blended into an unmistakably American idiom in *Poems 1947–1957*, especially in "Letter," "Death of a Jazz Musician," and "American Primitive":

Look at him there in his stovepipe hat,
His high-top shoes, and his handsome collar;
Only my Daddy could look like that,
And I love my Daddy like he loves his Dollar.
The screen door bangs, and it sounds so funny –
There he is in a shower of gold;

His pockets are stuffed with folding money,
His lips are blue, and his hands feel cold.

He hangs in the hall by his black cravat,
The ladies faint, and the children holler:
Only my Daddy could look like that,
And I love my Daddy like he loves his dollar.

With *The Tin Can and Other Poems* and since, Smith, like most of the poets of his generation, moved on from the style he had mastered to a new, freer prosody, in which the dark side of experience is presented in a more unmediated way than in poems like "American Primitive" which had enclosed it in a play of wit and form:

O dreadful night! ... What train will come? ... What tree is that?
 ... a sycamore – the mottled bark stripped bare,
Desolate in winter light against the track, and I continue on to
 the mudflats
By the roaring river where garbage, chicken coops, and houses rush
 by me on mud-crested waves,
And at my feet are dead fish – catfish, gars – and there in a little
 inlet
Come on a deserted camp, the tin can in which the hoboes brewed their
 coffee stained bitter black
As the cinders sweeping ahead under a milkweed-colored sky along a
 darkening track
 And gaze into a slough's green stagnant foam,
 and know that the way out is never back,
 but down,
 down ...

What train will come
to bear me back
across so wide a town?

At least one reviewer of *The Tin Can* suggested that the hitherto elegant Smith had succumbed to the prosier incantations of Allen Ginsberg. As with Ginsberg, this loose, rolling line makes possible the inclusion in Smith's work of many grubby realities which, like Herrick, he had earlier tended to omit or to transfigure. Smith's sensibility, however, has little in common with the Beat bard's; a likelier *point d'origine* for these recent poems is in the free verse and surreal observations of the contemporary by Valéry Larbaud. His long unrhymed line makes possible an amplitude of feeling as well as inclusiveness of subject, and in it Smith continues to explore both his descent into the inarticulate and the terrifying ("My voice goes out like a funicular over an abyss, and my hands hang at my sides, clenching the void;/My dreams are filled with bitter oranges and carrots, signifying calumny and sorrow") and his intimations of the unity of all things, as in "The Tin Can," a poem of withdrawal from the world and the resultant gift of vision to the spirit.

—Daniel Hoffman

SMITHER, Elizabeth. New Zealander. Born in New Plymouth, 15 September 1941. Educated at New Plymouth Girls' High School, 1955–59; extra-mural studies at Victoria

University, Wellington, and Massey University, Palmerston North, 1959–60; New Zealand Library School, Wellington, 1962. Married Michael Duncan Smither in 1963; one daughter and two sons. Library Assistant, Cataloguer, and Children's Librarian, New Plymouth Public Library, 1959–63. Recipient: New Zealand Literary Fund bursary, 1978. Address: 19-A Mount View Place, New Plymouth, New Zealand.

PUBLICATIONS

Verse

Here Come the Clouds. Martinborough, Taylor, 1975.
You're Very Seductive William Carlos Williams. Dunedin, McIndoe, 1978.
The Sarah Train (juvenile). Wellington, Hawk Press, 1978.

Critical Studies: "A Way of Understanding Ourselves" by Elizabeth Caffin, in *Landfall 118* (Christchurch), 1976; "Maurice Shadbolt Talks to Elizabeth Smither," in *Pilgrims 5* and *6* (Christchurch), 1978.

Elizabeth Smither comments:

Robert Lowell wrote me in a letter that my work showed "a strong fierce personality, finding words to wrap itself in." Overcome by reading his work for most of a year, I had impulsively written to him, enclosing as a poor sample my first collection. He went on to suggest that I tune my ear more finely, and the attempt to develop more musicality has been the concern of my latest work. I try to retain the direct emotional qualities for which sometimes characters are mouthpieces while being aware of the problem of the poem itself. An image for my work might be a canal in which the flowing water is the emotion and the banks and reflected poplars represent the absorbing strictures of craft. But there is air between the poplars and their reflections are light. For I think it is necessary to flow inside and within one's craft, like assembling out of bones the flesh and personality.

* * *

The title of Elizabeth Smither's second book, *You're Very Seductive William Carlos Williams*, apparently announces the intention of the author to place herself in a challenging relationship to the tradition of the Modern in letters. For working purposes it may then be fairly assumed that the author and the possible personae of the poems amount to being pretty much the same, even when in the play-acting pieces like the Goethe poem or the Iago poems the persona invites us to suppose that the person of the poem is male, which is not necessarily the case when you enquire more closely into what it is that these small deceptive pieces are advancing. The voice of the poems is seldom emphatically a woman's voice, nor is the point of view markedly a woman's viewpoint except on occasion. Sympathetic, empathetic, imaginative, able to command that kind of quick intelligent comment which can delight the reader simply because it is so aptly intelligent and appropriate, Smither's poems are not poems of wit in any usual sense any more than they are subjective. In fact, Smither distances herself from her occasions and from the ostensible means by which she makes those occasions appear before us, ostensible in that she advertises an ambience yet chooses not to walk in the ways which are signposted. Her attachment to the Modernist mode is sympathetic, but for all her sympathy she does not involve herself in sundry aspects of techniques which we are likely to expect when any talk of Williams, Lowell, or Kinnell is bruited. She tries to make her own mode, her own rapprochement, which she may also be seen attempting in another respect.

It can hardly escape her reader that several of the poems of Smither's second book have something to do with Catholicism, a Catholicism which takes in St. Teresa and St. Ignatius, from whom she arrives at "the long gazing of the blind into the wind," and Teilhard de Chardin, whose passion is for "ennobling flame, for love/Kindling the passive with a spark and giving it a name." Poems like these, along with "Another Prayer to Our Lady" or "The Feast of All Saints" are again poems of rapprochement, of the subjective-objective or attachment-detachment, products of an impulse to reconcile two (at least) modes of tradition within another universe of discourse.

What is the upshot of this? With her second book, which may be taken to indicate a second phase to her work, Smither arrived at a position of control which enabled her to produce poems of a relatively small compass but in which more goes on than at first meets the eye. The question of playing off traditions is one thing; recourse to compressed statement is another in which the calculated opposition of tenor and vehicle in a metaphor results not so much in conveying a sense of metaphoric statement as a sense of incongruity, yet without (as one might expect of this) a consequent nuance of comedy or irony, or, what one might otherwise expect, a disturbing sense of the surreal or the hyper-real. Nonetheless the poems promote a feeling of disturbingly heightened reality as of lovers at their occupation, of the activity of religious faith, of the menace of the mundane. But while you appreciate the heightening, you are also aware that the inherent drama of the occasion has been damped down, its elements made compatible, or reconciled.

In part this may be attributed to an insufficient boldness in Smither's practice. Whatever the degree of influence of people like Williams or Lowell or Kinnell or others of the Modern, the likeness of these poems is more to be found in Edgar Lee Masters. Smither, however, practices a more radical modus than Masters allowed himself, in a peculiarity of punctuation, a disruption of syntax which one may judge is aimed at evoking rather than communicating, to sponsor the illusion of immediacy. It is noticeable that when the poems are orthodoxly punctuated they work rather better, even if they then appear to be rather more old-fashioned. At this phase of her career Smither probably needs to commit herself more one way or the other.

—Kendrick Smithyman

SMITHYMAN, (William) Kendrick. New Zealander. Born in Te Kopuru, Auckland, 9 October 1922. Educated at Seddon Memorial Technical College; Auckland Teachers College; Auckland University College. Served in the New Zealand Artillery and the Royal New Zealand Air Force, 1941–45. Married Mary Stanley in 1946; three sons. Primary School Teacher, 1946–63. Since 1963, Senior Tutor, Department of English, University of Auckland. Visiting Fellow in Commonwealth Literature, University of Leeds, Yorkshire, 1969. Recipient: British Council grant, 1969; New Zealand Literary Fund grant, 1969; Jessie Mackay prize, 1970. Address: Department of English, University of Auckland, Auckland, New Zealand.

PUBLICATIONS

Verse

Seven Sonnets. Auckland, Pelorus Press, 1946.
The Blind Mountain and Other Poems. Christchurch, Caxton Press, 1950.
The Gay Trapeze. Wellington, Arena Press, 1955.

The Night Shift: Poems on Aspects of Love, with others. Wellington, Capricorn Press, 1957.
Inheritance. Auckland, Blackwood and Janet Paul, 1962.
Flying to Palmerston. Wellington, Oxford University Press, 1968.
Earthquake Weather. Auckland, Auckland University Press, and London, Oxford University Press, 1972.
The Seal in the Dolphin Pool. Auckland, Auckland University Press, and London, Oxford University Press, 1974.
Dwarf with a Billiard Cue. Auckland, Auckland University Press, and London, Oxford University Press, 1978.

Other

A Way of Saying: A Study of New Zealand Poetry. Auckland and London, Collins, 1965.

Editor, *The Land of the Lost* (novel), by William Satchell. Auckland, Auckland University Press, and London, Oxford University Press, 1971.

Critical Study: by MacD. P. Jackson, in *Thirteen Facets* edited by Ian Ward, Wellington, Government Printer, 1978.

* * *

If the precise observation of detail is one requirement of a poet, Kendrick Smithyman begins with a genuine advantage. Many of his poems enshrine curious and unexpected details of New Zealand life and landscape, as well as strange material from often esoteric reading. His vocabulary, too, is extremely varied, and this, combined with a packed elliptical style, a habit of exploiting the less-used secondary meanings of words and a kind of syntactical juggling makes his poems, especially of his earlier period, frequently hard to understand. But few of them do not repay extra effort, for Smithyman's restless, leaping mind confronts a wide variety of ontological concepts, problems of being and of personal relations, questions of human identity, as well as aspects of married love and parenthood.

Not a great number of his poems relate directly to the New Zealand scene. When he does begin with such a setting, as in "Gathering the Toheroa" or "Just an Evening in the Ranges," it is only to move at once beyond it to meditate on mortality or the puzzle of meaning. Irony, sometimes gentle, sometimes cutting, sustains many of them. At times his poems suggest a strenuous wrestling with words and forms as if the raid on the inarticulate were indeed a bloody and an exhausting business. But his skilful craftsmanship, as well as his exuberant intellectual curiosity produce, in the main, pieces of a dense, rich substance, wry in flavour. The mind they disclose is akin to that of a 17th-century metaphysical.

During his poetic career, Smithyman has assimilated elements from several contemporary poets, perhaps most noticeably American ones, Robert Lowell among them. Yet his work always sounds an individual note, in part because, despite the complicated verbal structure, a colloquial character is frequently maintained. His poetry gains greatly in effect and in intelligibility by being read aloud.

From *The Blind Mountain* to *Flying to Palmerston*, he shows a gradual increase of directness, with fewer ellipses, more stylistic control and greater urbanity. He has always possessed wit, in its several 18th-century senses, and increasingly in his poetry there have appeared a verbal wit and a kind of ironical gaiety which intensify, rather than negate, his essential seriousness and strength of feeling. What may sometimes teeter on the edge of cynicism or flippancy becomes an ironic or wryly sad comment on time, change, emotional sterility or cultural dryness. His awareness of the social scene in New Zealand, if most often expressed indirectly, goes deeper than that of more overtly socially critical poets. One of the most sophisticated craftsmen New Zealand has so far produced, Kendrick Smithyman brings a quite distinctive, highly selective imagination and a masterly command of technique to bear on subjects which are never trivial.

—J. C. Reid

SNODGRASS, W(illiam) D(eWitt). American. Born in Wilkinsburg, Pennsylvania, 5 January 1926. Educated at Geneva College, Beaver Falls, Pennsylvania, 1943–44, 1946; State University of Iowa, Iowa City, 1949–55, B.A. 1949, M.A. 1951, M.F.A. 1953. Served in the United States Navy, 1944–46. Married 1) Lila Jean Hank in 1946 (divorced, 1953); 2) Janice Wilson in 1954 (divorced, 1966); 3) Camille Rykowski in 1967 (divorced, 1978); one daughter and one son. Instructor in English, Cornell University, Ithaca, New York, 1955–57, University of Rochester, New York, 1957–58, and Wayne State University, Detroit, 1959–67; Professor of English and Speech, Syracuse University, New York 1968–77. Visiting Teacher, Morehead Writers Conference, Kentucky, Summer 1955, Antioch Writers Conference, Yellow Springs, Ohio, Summers 1958–59, Narrative Poetry Workshop, State University of New York, Binghamton, 1977, Old Dominion University, Norfolk, Virginia, 1978–79, and University of Delaware, Newark, 1979. Recipient: Ingram Merrill Foundation Award, 1958; *Hudson Review* Fellowship, 1958; Longview Award, 1959; Poetry Society of America Special Citation, 1960; Yaddo Resident Award, 1960, 1961, 1965, 1976, 1977; National Institute of Arts and Letters grant, 1960; Pulitzer Prize, 1960; Guinness Award (UK), 1961; Ford Fellowship, for drama, 1963; Miles Award, 1966; National Endowment for the Arts grant, 1966; Academy of American Poets Fellowship, 1972; Guggenheim Fellowship, 1972; Centennial Medal (Romania), 1977. Member, National Institute of Arts and Letters, 1972; Fellow, Academy of American Poets, 1973. Address: R.D. 1, Erieville, New York 13061, U.S.A.

PUBLICATIONS

Verse

Heart's Needle. New York, Knopf, 1959; Hessle, Yorkshire, Marvell Press, 1960.
After Experience: Poems and Translations. New York, Harper, and London, Oxford University Press, 1968.
Remains (as S. S. Gardons). Mount Horeb, Wisconsin, Perishable Press, 1970.
The Führer Bunker: A Cycle of Poems in Progress. Brockport, New York, Boa, 1977.
If Birds Build with Your Hair. New York, Nadja Press, 1979.

Other

In Radical Pursuit: Critical Essays and Lectures. New York, Harper, 1975.

Editor, *Syracuse Poems 1969.* Syracuse, Syracuse University Department of English, 1969.

Translator, with Lore Segal, *Gallows Songs*, by Christian Morgenstern. Ann Arbor, University of Michigan Press, 1967.
Translator, *Six Troubadour Songs.* Providence, Rhode Island, Burning Deck, 1977.
Translator, *Traditional Hungarian Songs.* Baltimore, Charles Seluzicki, 1978.

Bibliography: *W. D. Snodgrass: A Bibliography* by William White, Detroit, Wayne State University Press, 1960.

Manuscript Collection: Lockwood Library, State University of New York, Buffalo.

Critical Study: *W. D. Snodgrass* by Paul L. Gaston, Boston, Twayne, 1978.

W. D. Snodgrass comments:

I am usually called a "confessional" poet or else an "academic" poet. Such terms seem to me not very helpful.

I first became known for poems of a very personal nature, especially those about losing a daughter in a divorce. Many of those early poems were in formal metres and had an "open" surface. All through my career, however, I have written both free verse and formal metres. At first, I published more of the formal work because it seemed more successful to me. Recently, my free (or apparently free) verse seems more successful, so I publish more of it. My poems now are much less directly personal and often experiment with multiple voices or with musical devices. My work almost always goes very slowly and involves long periods of gestation and revision. This is not because I am particularly perfectionistic, but because it takes me so long to get through the conscious areas of beliefs and half-truths into the subrational areas where it may be possible to make a real discovery.

* * *

The considerable reputation of W. D. Snodgrass rests on two volumes of verse in which the main element is the confessional: the poet appears as a sad, self-revealing figure whose main concern in poetry (see the paper on "Finding a Poem" at the end of *Heart's Needle*) is to write "what he really thinks." If this entails a markedly autobiographical approach, that is justified in the interests of sincerity, innocence and truthful writing about "the self he cannot help being." This kind of emphasis sets Snodgrass among other, probably more notable, confessional poets of the sixties – John Berryman, Sylvia Plath, Anthony Hecht, the later Robert Lowell, some of whom gave enthusiastic welcomes to his first book. If he lacks the ability of most of those poets to generalise, movingly, from personal experience and make public statements, Snodgrass, at his best, works this personal territory with integrity and resource.

These very personal poems are set in an American landscape which the poet evokes with nostalgic inventiveness, working natural details into his plots with a patient, meditated skill:

After the sharp windstorm
of July Fourth, all that summer
through the gentle, warm
afternoons, we heard great chain saws chirr
like iron locusts. Crews
of roughneck boys swarmed to cut loose
branches wrenched in the shattering wind, to hack free
all the torn limbs that could sap the tree.

In the debris lay
starlings dead.

The careful syllabic metre adopted here (the poem is from his title-sequence in *Heart's Needle*, about the daughter from whom he was separated by divorce) testifies to a zealous craftsmanship for which he has also been much admired, although it seems often to mute his themes and produce an awkwardness of technique, especially in rhyming. Sometimes this care (more noticeable in his less successful second book, *After Experience*) and the consistent attempt to be completely serious give his poems an air of solemnity: certainly the best are those where the self-scrutiny involves humour without a sacrifice of gravity: "These Trees Stand ..." and the much-praised "April Inventory" (*Heart's Needle*).

Sceptical critics of Snodgrass's verse detect the lack of a basic extrovert energy in his writing, a lurking sentimentality, a kind of complacent accomplishment in his handling of distressful material, and a readiness to assume that his readers can accept without quibbling the personal attitudes which his poetry embodies. What they miss is his abundant skill in the ordering of external detail in those poems where he feels he can develop the theme fully without resort to veiled implication or allegory. Poems like "The Operation," and "The Campus on the Hill" (*Heart's Needle*) and (though less strikingly) "Planting a Magnolia" (*After Experience*) show this faculty at its best, and have none of the self-pity or mawkish violence of his more indulgent writing.

—Alan Brownjohn

SNYDER, Gary (Sherman). American. Born in San Francisco, California, 8 May 1930. Educated at Lincoln High School, Portland, Oregon; Reed College, Portland, B.A. in anthropology 1951; Indiana University, Bloomington, 1951–52; University of California, Berkeley, 1953–56; studied Buddhism in Japan, 1956–64, 1965–68. Married 1) Alison Gass in 1950 (divorced, 1952); 2) Joanne Kyger, *q.v.*, in 1960; 3) Masa Uehara in 1967; two children. Lecturer in English, University of California, Berkeley, 1964–65. Recipient: Bess Hokin Prize, 1964, and Levinson Prize, 1968 (*Poetry*, Chicago); Bollingen Grant, for Buddhist Studies, 1965; National Institute of Arts and Letters prize, 1966; Guggenheim Fellowship, 1968; Pulitzer Prize, 1975. Lives in California. Address: c/o New Directions, 333 Avenue of the Americas, New York, New York 10014, U.S.A.

PUBLICATIONS

Verse

Riprap. Ashland, Massachusetts, Origin Press, 1959.
Myths and Texts. New York, Totem, 1960; revised edition, New York, New Directions, 1978.
Hop, Skip, and Jump. Berkeley, California, Oyez, 1964.
Nanao Knows. San Francisco, Four Seasons, 1964.
The Firing. New York, R. L. Ross, 1964.
Across Lamarck Col. Privately printed, 1964.
Riprap, and Cold Mountain Poems. San Francisco, Four Seasons, 1965.
Six Sections from Mountains and Rivers Without End. San Francisco, Four Seasons, 1965; London, Fulcrum Press, 1968; augmented edition, Four Seasons, 1970.
Dear Mr. President. Privately printed, 1965.
Three Worlds, Three Realms, Six Roads. Marlboro, Vermont, Griffin Press, 1966.
A Range of Poems. London, Fulcrum Press, 1966.
The Back Country. London, Fulcrum Press, 1967; New York, New Directions, 1968.
The Blue Sky. New York, Phoenix Book Shop, 1969.
Sours of the Hills. New York, Portents, 1969.
Regarding Wave. New York, New Directions, 1970; London, Fulcrum Press, 1971.

Anasazi. Santa Barbara, California, Yes Press, 1971.
Manzanita. Kent, Ohio, Kent State University Libraries, 1971.
Clear Cut. Detroit, Alternative Press, n.d.
Manzanita (collection). Bolinas, California, Four Seasons, 1972.
The Fudo Trilogy: Spell Against Demons, Smoky the Bear Sutra, The California Water Plan. Berkeley, California, Shaman Drum, 1973.
Turtle Island. New York, New Directions, 1974.

Recording: *Today's Poets 4*, with others, Folkways.

Other

Earth House Hold: Technical Notes and Queries to Fellow Dharma Revolutionaries. New York, New Directions, and London, Cape, 1969.
Four Changes. Privately printed, 1969.
On Bread and Poetry: A Panel Discussion, with Lew Welch and Philip Whalen. Bolinas, California, Grey Fox Press, 1977.
The Old Ways: Six Essays. San Francisco, City Lights, 1977.
He Who Hunted Birds in His Father's Village: The Dimensions of a Haida Myth, edited by Donald Allen. Bolinas, California, Grey Fox Press, 1978.

Editor, with Gutetsu Kanetsuki, *The Wooden Fish: Basic Sutras and Gathas of Rinzai Zen.* Kyoto, First Zen Institute of America in Japan, 1961.

Bibliography: *Gary Snyder* by Katherine McNeill, New York, Phoenix, 1980.

Manuscript Collection: University of California, Davis.

* * *

Thomas Parkinson (in *Southern Review*, July 1968) speaks of "the peculiar blending of Zen Buddhism with IWW political attitudes, Amerindian lore, and the mystique of the wilderness" in Gary Snyder's poetry, and later observes that his aim is "not to achieve harmony with nature but to create an inner human harmony that equals to the natural external harmony." Indeed, though Snyder writes about nature, he is far from the Romantic's idea of the Nature Poet. His valuing of the primitive tribe and its relation to the earth is not a sentiment but a call for action, and his beliefs are practically and explicitly worked out in both his poetry and his prose.

His literary antecedents are Ezra Pound and Kenneth Rexroth, but their influences were quickly absorbed. There is an echo of Pound's "River Merchant's Wife" in the first poem of Snyder's first book, "Mid August at Sourdough Mountain Lookout," but it is already fully Snyder's poem. It conveys an intense clarity of sensation and does so by statement, not by metaphor or symbol. We are invited to test the statement against only the most available of human experiences, the knowledge of what it feels like to be up a mountain, for instance, or of what water tastes like. Snyder is not, indeed, interested in the unique experience but in the shared or sharable experience, and this is why his poetry is so different from that of the "confessional" poets, even though like them he writes largely in the first person.

The shared experience is implicitly compared to an awakening – to wonder, to awareness, to sympathy. In another poem, from *The Back Country*, how, on a walking tour 15 years before, he and his first wife met a mountain lookout. It ends:

I don't know where she is now;
I never asked your name.
In this burning, muddy, lying,
blood-drenched world

that quiet meeting in the mountains
cool and gentle as the muzzles of
three elk, helps keep me sane.

The image at the end is characteristic of Snyder at his best: precise, unrhetorical, and definitive. It resolves and cancels out the large generalities of the third and fourth lines quoted. In a sense the image is the whole poem. And this too is characteristic, for Snyder perceives and communicates largely through images.

They are not static images, however. There are few still-lifes in Snyder's poetry. His writing is full of things caught in motion: on the coast "mussels clamp to sea-boulders/ Sucking the spring tides"; or a deer runs with "Stiff springy jumps down the snowfields/ Head held back, forefeet out,/Balls tight in a tough hair sack."

The structure of his poems varies anywhere from the traditionally shaped poem ending with a summation, like "Hop, Skip, and Jump," to the poem of thematic juxtaposition, like "Bubbs Creek Haircut." The second method is the more common in his early poems, where it is used with variety and inventiveness.

These poems (of the 1950's and the 1960's) are kept alive at every point by the rhythms and the language. The stressed and unstressed syllables are sharply distinguishable and group easily into tight clear rhythmic units. The language is cool, firm, and exact, with no ambitions toward a grand style to intrude between him and his perceptions. Snyder records the world attentively, as an act of love, with all his senses open to it.

In his collections of the 1970's, however, there has been a certain coarsening of the poetry. Snyder has become a public figure and – always a didactic poet – has evidently seen it as his duty to make himself more didactic. "I Went into the Maverick Bar" (*Turtle Island*) shows that his sharp observation and power of terse notation have never deserted him. In this poem he shows himself charmed afresh, against his will, by "that short-haired joy and roughness" of middle America, but it all ends with a formula that crudely and moralistically dismisses the energy of his subject matter: "I came back to myself/to the real work." By simplifying experience thus he has done away with much of the vitality and flexibility of his poetry.

—Thom Gunn

SOLT, Mary Ellen (née Bottom). American. Born in Gilmore City, Iowa, 8 July 1920. Educated at Iowa State Teachers College, B.A. 1941; University of Iowa, Iowa City, M.A. 1948; Indiana University, Bloomington, Summers 1957, 1958. Married Leo Frank Solt in 1946; two daughters. English Teacher, Dinsdale High School, Iowa, 1941–42; Hubbard High School, Iowa, 1942–44; Estherville High School, Iowa, 1944–46; University High School, Iowa City, 1946–48; Bentley School, New York, 1949–52. Since 1970, Associate Professor of Comparative Literature, Indiana University. Recipient: *Folio* award, 1960. Address: 836 Sheridan Road, Bloomington, Indiana 47401, U.S.A.

PUBLICATIONS

Verse

Flowers in Concrete. Bloomington, Indiana University Department of Fine Arts, 1960.
A Trilogy of Rain. Urbana, Finial Press, 1970.
Eyewords. New York, White Rose Press, 1972.

Other

Editor, with Willis Barnstone, *Concrete Poetry: A World View*. Bloomington, Indiana University Press, 1968.

Manuscript Collection: Lilly Library, Indiana University, Bloomington.

* * *

Mary Ellen Solt is not only a concrete poet herself but also a well-known aesthetician of the "concrete poetry" movement. She stipulates that the definition of concrete poetry must be broad, covering visual, phonetic, kinetic, constructivist, and expressionist poems. She says, "The concrete poet seeks to relieve the poem of its century-old burden of ideas, symbolic reference, allusion and repetitious emotional content ... the concrete poem communicates first and foremost its structure." Her own practice is rather classically mimetic and centrally located in the spectrum of what is labelled "concrete." In her collection *Flowers in Concrete*, she arranges the letters of flower-names in differing typefaces to suggest the natural shape of that flower – zinnia, geranium, forsythia. (She had the assistance of a typographer, John Dearstyne, after drawing the originals by hand.) Despite the disclaimer quoted above, her poem "Dogwood: Three Movements" has clear symbolic reference to the tree out of which Christ's cross was hewn, although the poem is primarily an evocation of the blossom's delicacy.

As with almost all concrete and visual poets, wit is a principal literary device with Solt. Her "Moonshot Sonnet" is a fine example. Her comment on it, in *Concrete Poetry: A World View*, reads: "Made by copying the scientists' symbols on the first photos of the moon in the *New York Times*: there were exactly fourteen 'lines' with five 'accents' ... so the poem is both a spoof of old forms and a statement about the necessity for new."

Solt's 1968 poem (or poem-sequence) is very different from *Flowers in Concrete* both in form and theme. It could be called a "happening" or guerilla theater, consisting of a set of ten posters reflecting the terrible events of that year: civil riots, the assassinations of King and Kennedy, Resurrection City, and the presidential elections. They employ such concrete imagistic devices as the A in USA turned upside down to resemble a falling bomb, and punning on the "nix" in Nixon. This poem has been performed four times, most recently in 1970 with readers and slides of historical texts during the exhibition Expose Concrete Poetry at Indiana University.

Solt's extensive comments as editor of *Concrete Poetry: A World View* have served to explain and clarify this international movement to American readers, as well as to introduce multitudinous examples of this intermedial genre. Her own work indicates the range – from the pastoral lyric of flower-names to the poem-as-public-demonstration – which she herself has called for. It is to be expected that her present interest in semiotics will carry her in a new direction.

—Jane Augustine

SORRENTINO, Gilbert. American. Born in Brooklyn, New York, 27 April 1929. Educated in New York public schools; Brooklyn College, 1950–51, 1955–57. Served in the Army Medical Corps, 1951–53. Married 1) Elsene Wiessner (divorced); 2) Vivian Victoria Ortiz; two sons and one daughter. Editor, *Neon* magazine, New York, 1956–60; Editor, Grove Press, New York, 1965–70. Has taught at Columbia University, New York, 1965;

Aspen Writers Workshop, Colorado, 1967; Sarah Lawrence College, New York, 1971–72; New School for Social Research, New York, 1976–79. Since 1979, Edwin S. Quain Professor of Literature, University of Scranton, Pennsylvania. Recipient: Guggenheim Fellowship, for fiction, 1973; National Endowment for the Arts grant, 1974, 1978; Fels Award, 1975; Ariadne Foundation grant, 1975; Creative Artists Public Service grant, 1975. Agent: Mel Berger, William Morris Agency, 1350 Avenue of the Americas, New York, New York 10019. Address: 463 West Street, New York, New York 10014, U.S.A.

PUBLICATIONS

Verse

The Darkness Surrounds Us. Highlands, North Carolina, Jargon, 1960.
Black and White. New York, Totem, 1964.
The Perfect Fiction. New York, Norton, 1968.
Corrosive Sublimate. Los Angeles, Black Sparrow Press, 1971.
A Dozen Oranges. Santa Barbara, California, Black Sparrow Press, 1976.
White Sail. Santa Barbara, California, Black Sparrow Press, 1977.
The Orangery. Austin, University of Texas Press, 1978.

Play

Flawless Play Restored: The Masque of Fungo. Los Angeles, Black Sparrow Press, 1974.

Novels

The Sky Changes. New York, Hill and Wang, 1966.
Steelwork. New York, Pantheon, 1970.
Imaginative Qualities of Actual Things. New York, Pantheon, 1971.
Mulligan Stew. New York, Grove Press, 1979.

Short Story

Splendide-Hôtel. New York, New Directions, 1973.

Other

Translator, *Sulpiciae Elegidia: Elegiacs of Sulpicia.* Mount Horeb, Wisconsin, Perishable Press, 1977.

Manuscript Collection: University of Delaware, Newark.

Critical Studies: in *Grosseteste Review* (Pensnett, Staffordshire), vi, 1–4, 1973; *Vort 6* (Silver Spring, Maryland), Fall 1974.

Gilbert Sorrentino comments:

I do not champion a "poetry of statement" and I despise narrative in verse. What I look for in my work is a verse dense in its particulars, but flexible in its total structure.

* * *

> The concept that language must "inform" or carry messages is a concept abandoned by poets at least as far back as Rimbaud. I subscribe to this belief and distrust a poetry of narrative and "content," and, in so far as I have been able, I have attempted to make the language of my fiction function in the way that the language of my verse functions, i.e. *poetically*.

Gilbert Sorrentino's title *Corrosive Sublimate* provides a clue to his work. In the tradition of those who believe that poetry makes nothing happen, or that it should not mean but be, Sorrentino makes stark, non-metaphoric statements about the corrupt urban world, about his own personal pain, about the reality of death. Written in an open-ended way, usually signalled by his use of the single, open parenthesis, his work invites the reader to simply experience the poem; there is no morality, no vision, simply the thing itself (the "corrosive" reality). Sorrentino speaks of the photograph often, as if to say that this alone stops, or seems to stop, time, though like the poem, it contains no "meaning." However, the eye, memory, and feeling transform the photo; so too, imagination transforms language (the "sublimate"), which is dead until experienced:

> The dead cannot be told anything so we revere them
> The past is static. That is a photo.
>
> But mine – even the dead
> sit up flaking in their graves – mine
> is the heart
> that fell apart
> at the junction unremembered.

"Four Songs," with echoes of Wallace Stevens, treats questions of art and reality:

> It's better not to think
> that when the wind blows
> in the white curtains
> it's the real thing.
>
> When the wind invisible
> touches the curtains
> stop it short as in
> some photograph.
>
> Some photographs show
> the shape of the wind
> the color is the white
> color of the curtains
>
> Against the silence and
> white wind and white curtains
> imagine in a blank room
> one perfect heart.

"The Handbook of Versification" concerns the reality of the word itself and the nonreferential nature of poetry:

> One thought the recurring "image" in the poet's song an instance of consciousness.
> Clear, clear day, in sun, one's majority upon one, it
> is seen to be simple obsession, and helpless,
> The mind careening through the infinite spaces of itself

Snags on some plain word:
Through and between whose familiar letters the true
true image of what happened: of the blank world.

Nevertheless, many of Sorrentino's poems are photos, are glossies on this blank world, and his language is hard and clear, often New York vernacular, his subjects the surfaces of New York. Like the title of his novel *Steelwork*, his poems are scaffolds that only assert the forms of reality, the forms of New York. "I speak now, tell you a bright truth," writes the poet; "This is a bitter city" – one of violence, frustration, and empty dreams. Although Sorrentino may localize his dislikes – i.e. cults (the "moony people") and the mobile middle classes and intellectuals numb with anger and fear – he says of New York: "When you leave this town, you/Is just campin out." As he travels across America ("See America First"), he laments the poverty and unending violence and filth. Sorrentino would have us recover "certain portions of the heart," and heed the possibilities of a unique identity. In a sardonic fashion he warns: "Heed the story of the man/who took the garbage out/and threw himself away" ("Beautiful Soup"). Of psychiatrists he asks: "Who's the character in the armchair/drinking cheap wine/ glum as hell"; of marriage he writes: "you get hurt, fierce ... dear God." Sorrentino's New York is specific – he writes of El Bronx, Broadway, the Van Wyck Expressway – and his is a world peopled by Jung, Artaud, Stevens, Baudelaire, Apollinaire, Blackburn, Creeley, Dexter Gordon, Sarah Vaughan, Louis Armstrong, and Bunk Johnson.

Although some of his poems extend to specific survivors of American history – i.e. veterans, Indians, miners – his finest poems are the personal ones, those occasional moments of bittersweet nostalgia for the past and his own lost innocence. Bartering death's inevitability is the fecundity of memory. "Toward the End of Winter" concerns the poet's 38th birthday; he is "aware/of the birth of all time lost and buried." "Brought almost to tears/by the simple presence of myself in my own flesh, in the chair,/my familiar things around," he listens to a sentimental old song on the phonograph:

In its faded loveliness the loss
of the singer is in me, her
clear voice doing the stupid song
honor, now she is forgotten
as the song.

As the song brings back its many associations, he sees "every act, each careful gesture/in tableaux," and ultimately:

these clarities, moving to aromas,
the singer enmeshed with the reality
of her voice in her own presence, of flesh ...
there is no truth
but in dear event, shaken, sudden, ...
I miss everybody.

Many of these poems contain an irony and self-mockery, along with the pain of lost innocence. To "Marjorie" he writes:

Now there must be
stretch marks beneath her fitted girdle ...
I had the very bud of her, beauty and clarity day clear ...
God
all the things destroyed
since I last kissed her
on what bitter corner
in the Bronx.

Awareness alone is redemptive, the corrosive sublimate:

Be tuned finely
to what ever has made you
the defendant you are.

There is no metaphor
save specific.

One must seek meaning out of life:

Some few moments
of bitter understanding: that we were children
Of loveless worlds, or precisely, one world
and found that (or searched for that)
absolutely alone.

—Lois Gordon

SOUSTER, (Holmes) Raymond. Canadian. Born in Toronto, Ontario, 15 January 1921. Educated at University of Toronto schools; Humberside Collegiate Institute, Toronto. Served in the Royal Canadian Air Force, 1941–45. Married Rosalia Lena Geralde in 1947. Since 1939, Staff Member, and currently, Securities Custodian, Canadian Imperial Bank of Commerce, Toronto. Editor, *Direction*, Sydney, Nova Scotia, 1943–46; Co-Editor, *Contact*, Toronto, 1952–54; Editor, *Combustion*, Toronto, 1957–60. Chairman, League of Canadian Poets, 1968–72. Recipient: Governor-General's Award, 1964; President's Medal, University of Western Ontario, 1967; Centennial Medal, 1967; Silver Jubilee Medal, 1977. Address: 39 Baby Point Road, Toronto, Ontario M6S 2G2, Canada.

PUBLICATIONS

Verse

Unit of Five, with others, edited by Ronald Hambleton. Toronto, Ryerson Press, 1944.
When We Are Young. Montreal, First Statement Press, 1946.
Go to Sleep, World. Toronto, Ryerson Press, 1947.
City Hall Street. Toronto, Ryerson Press, 1951.
Cerberus, with Louis Dudek and Irving Layton. Toronto, Contact Press, 1952.
Shake Hands with the Hangman: Poems 1940–1952. Toronto, Contact Press, 1953.
A Dream That Is Dying. Toronto, Contact Press, 1954.
Walking Death. Toronto, Contact Press, 1954.
For What Time Slays. Privately printed, 1955.
Selected Poems, edited by Louis Dudek. Toronto, Contact Press, 1956.
Crêpe-Hanger's Carnival: Selected Poems 1955–58. Toronto, Contact Press, 1958.
Place of Meeting: Poems 1958–1960. Toronto, Gallery, 1962.
A Local Pride. Toronto, Contact Press, 1962.
12 New Poems. Lanham, Maryland, Goosetree Press, 1964.
The Colour of the Times: The Collected Poems of Raymond Souster. Toronto, Ryerson Press, 1964.

Ten Elephants on Yonge Street. Toronto, Ryerson Press, 1965.
As Is. Toronto, Oxford University Press, 1967.
Lost and Found: Uncollected Poems. Toronto, Clarke Irwin, 1968.
So Far So Good: Poems 1938–1968. Ottawa, Oberon Press, 1969.
The Years. Ottawa, Oberon Press, 1971.
Selected Poems, edited by Michael Macklem. Ottawa, Oberon Press, 1972.
Change-Up: New Poems. Ottawa, Oberon Press, 1974.
Double-Header. Ottawa, Oberon Press, and London, Dobson, 1975.
Rain-Check. Ottawa, Oberon Press, 1975; London, Dobson, 1976.
Extra Innings. Ottawa, Oberon Press, and London, Dobson, 1977.
Hanging In. Ottawa, Oberon Press, 1979.
Collected Poems, Vol. 1, 1940–1955. Ottawa, Oberon Press, 1980.

Novels

The Winter of the Time (as Raymond Holmes). Toronto, Export, 1949.
On Target (as John Holmes). Toronto, Village Book Store Press, 1973.

Other

Editor, *Poets 56: Ten Younger English-Canadians*. Toronto, Contact Press, 1956.
Editor, *Experiment: Poems 1923–1929*, by W. W. E. Ross. Toronto, Contact Press, 1958.
Editor, *New Wave Canada: The New Explosion in Canadian Poetry*. Toronto, Contact Press, 1966.
Editor, with John Robert Colombo, *Shapes and Sounds: Poems of W. W. E. Ross*. Toronto, Longman, 1968.
Editor, with Douglas Lochhead, *Made in Canada: New Poems of the Seventies*. Ottawa, Oberon Press, 1970.
Editor, with Richard Woollatt, *Generation Now* (textbook). Toronto, Longman, 1970.
Editor, with Douglas Lochhead, *100 Poems of Nineteenth Century Canada* (textbook). Toronto, Macmillan, 1973.
Editor, with Richard Woollatt, *Sights and Sounds* (textbook). Toronto, Macmillan, 1973.
Editor, with Richard Woollatt, *These Loved, These Hated Lands* (textbook). Toronto, Doubleday, 1975.
Editor, *Vapour and Blue: The Poetry of William Wilfred Campbell*. Sutton West, Ontario, Paget Press, 1978.
Editor, *Comfort of the Fields: The Best Known Poems of Archibald Lampman*. Sutton West, Ontario, Paget Press, 1979.

Manuscript Collection: Rare Book Room, University of Toronto Library.

Critical Studies: "Groundhog among the Stars" by Louis Dudek, in *Canadian Literature* (Vancouver), Autumn 1964; "To Souster with Vermont" by Hayden Carruth, in *Tamarack Review* (Toronto), Winter 1965; introduction by Michael Macklem to *Selected Poems*, 1972; *From There to Here* edited by Frank Davey, Erin, Ontario, Press Porcépic, 1974 (includes bibliography).

Raymond Souster comments:

Whoever I write to, I want to make the substance of the poem so immediate, so real, so clear, that the reader feels the same exhilaration – be it fear or joy – that I derived from the experience, object or mood that triggered the poem in the first place.... I like to think I'm "talking out" my poems rather than consciously dressing them up in the trappings of the academic school. For many years I held to the theory that all poetry must be written out of a sudden spontaneous impulse in which the poet is unbearably moved to write down the words of that vision. Now I am more inclined to echo the view of Giuseppi Ungaretti when he says: "Between one flower gathered and the other given, the inexpressible Null."

* * *

The title of a book of poems by Raymond Souster is *As Is*. That is exactly the way the world is to be found in the work of Souster, as is, without idealistic impositions, without ideological distortion. The area of his approach and the locality it is centred upon can be pursued through any of his titles. He is after "The Colour of the Times" without sentimental illusions. "Shake Hands with the Hang-man," he tells us, realistically but without sombre destitution; life is "A Dream That Is Dying." Mortal but with comic integrity, we are engaged in a "Crêpe-Hanger's Carnival." His "Place of Meeting" is Toronto. No Canadian poet has exploited a Canadian city for more truth than Souster has Toronto. It is "A Local Pride" for him. But be careful. You may not have as much pride in your city as you think you have:

> The finger of Christ
> points straight from his pedestal
> on the Church of the Sailors
> down history-crawling streets
> to Joe Beef's, the oldest
> loudest tavern in town.

On its streets you are likely to meet a drunk on crutches, "Like this one now: this corpse,/ This living death coming toward you." Our urban world is not likely to turn out pretty – not if you have Souster's perspicacious eye and his peripatetic shoes. Harbouring all the compassion in the world, you are likely to be arrested for loitering. Move on and take refuge in computerization. Get cardboarded. It is the only safe way to escape the penalties of being human. Even so, you are likely to get punched:

> Wrap yourself well in that cheap coat that holds back
> the wind like a sieve,
> you have a long way to go, the streets are dark, you
> may have to walk all night before you can find
> another heart as lonely.

In this disillusioned stance, there is always the danger of becoming an inverted romantic. The bum is the hero. There is always the cynic's disease of blaming man for the cold glitter of the inimical stars. The city of Toronto is responsible for the acne on a girl's face. This is the shuffle dealt out by the freaked-out poets.

Souster does not whine. He knows we are all a little mad, that after our last beer the door opens on nothing, on darkness "into which we walk/dead drunk or chanting poetry//but upright, still with the living/my friend." He can apostrophize a drunken clock, a hollyhock, and birds

> which any moment
> may begin to sing!
>
> Who knows, my heart
> may beat again
> quick as the slap
> of the first skipping rope
> of spring.

Yonge Street is the ugliest main street of Toronto. Souster has ten grey elephants going up it, literally and metaphorically: "Ten grey eminences moving/with the daintiest of steps/and the greatest unconcern/up the canyon." His circus roller coaster takes off into the Empyrean.

Souster says: "I want to make the substance of the poem so immediate, so real, so clear, that the reader feels the same exhilaration – be it fear or joy – that I derived from the experience, object or mood that triggered the poem in the first place." He does.

—Ralph Gustafson

SOYINKA, Wole (Akinwande Oluwole Soyinka). Nigerian. Born in Abeokuta, 13 July 1934. Educated at Government College, Ibadan; University of Leeds, Yorkshire, 1954–57, B.A. (honours) in English. Married; has children. Play Reader, Royal Court Theatre, London, 1958–59; Research Fellow in Drama, University of Ibadan, 1960–61; Lecturer in English, University of Ife, 1962–63; Senior Lecturer in English, University of Lagos, 1964–67; Director of the School of Drama, University of Ibadan, 1969–72. Research Professor in Drama, 1972–75, and since 1975, Professor of Comparative Literature, University of Ife. Founding Director of the Orisun Theatre and the 1960 Masks theatre, Lagos and Ibadan. Political Prisoner, Lagos and Kaduna, 1967–69. Recipient: Dakar Negro Arts Festival award, for drama, 1966; John Whiting award, for drama, 1966; Jock Campbell Award (*New Statesman*), for fiction, 1968. D.Litt.: University of Leeds, 1973. Agent: Morton Leavy, Katz, Leavy Rosenberg, and Sindle, 1211 Avenue of the Americas, New York, New York 10036, U.S.A. Address: Department of Dramatic Arts, University of Ife, Ile-Ife, Nigeria.

PUBLICATIONS

Verse

Idanre and Other Poems. London, Methuen, 1967; New York, Hill and Wang, 1968.
Poems from Prison. London, Rex Collings, 1969.
A Shuttle in the Crypt. London, Eyre Methuen-Rex Collings, and New York, Hill and Wang, 1972.
Ogun Abibiman. London, Rex Collings, 1977.

Plays

The Swamp Dwellers (produced Ibadan and London, 1958; New York, 1968). Included in *Three Plays*, 1963; *Five Plays*, 1964.
The Lion and the Jewel (produced Ibadan, 1959; London, 1966). London, Ibadan, and New York, Oxford University Press, 1963.
The Invention (produced London, 1959).
A Dance of the Forests (produced Ibadan, 1960). London, Ibadan, and New York, Oxford University Press, 1963.
The Trials of Brother Jero (produced Ibadan, 1960; Cambridge, 1965; London, 1966; New York, 1967). Included in *Three Plays*, 1963; *Five Plays*, 1964.
Camwood on the Leaves (broadcast, 1960). London, Eyre Methuen, 1973; in *Camwood on the Leaves, and Before the Blackout*, 1974.
Three Plays: The Trials of Brother Jero, The Swamp Dwellers, The Strong Breed. Ibadan, Mbari, 1963.

The Strong Breed (produced Ibadan, 1964; London, 1966; New York, 1967). Included in *Three Plays*, 1963; *Five Plays*, 1964.

Kongi's Harvest (produced Ibadan, 1964; New York, 1968). London, Ibadan, and New York, Oxford University Press, 1967.

Five Plays: A Dance of the Forests, The Lion and the Jewel, The Swamp Dwellers, The Trials of Brother Jero, The Strong Breed. London, Ibadan, and New York, Oxford University Press, 1964.

Before the Blackout (produced Ibadan, 1964). Ibadan, Orisun, 1965; in *Camwood on the Leaves, and Before the Blackout*, 1974.

The Road (produced London, 1965). London, Ibadan, and New York, Oxford University Press, 1965.

Madmen and Specialists (produced Waterford, Connecticut, and New York, 1970; revised version, produced Ibadan, 1971). London, Methuen, 1971; New York, Hill and Wang, 1972.

The Jero Plays: The Trials of Brother Jero and Jero's Metamorphosis. London, Eyre Methuen, 1973.

The Bacchae: A Communion Rite, adaptation of the play by Euripides (produced London, 1973). London, Eyre Methuen, 1973; New York, Norton, 1974.

Collected Plays:

I. *A Dance of the Forests, The Swamp Dwellers, The Strong Breed, The Road, The Bacchae.* London and New York, Oxford University Press, 1973.

II. *The Lion and the Jewel, Kongi's Harvest, The Trials of Brother Jero, Jero's Metamorphosis, Madmen and Specialists.* London and New York, Oxford University Press, 1974.

Camwood on the Leaves, and Before the Blackout: Two Short Plays. New York, Third Press, 1974.

Death and the King's Horseman (produced Ife, 1976; Chicago, 1979). London, Eyre Methuen, 1975; New York, Norton, 1976.

Opera Wonyosi (produced Ife, 1977). London, Rex Collings, 1979.

Radio Play: *Camwood on the Leaves*, 1960 (UK).

Television Plays: *Joshua: A Nigerian Portrait*, 1962 (Canada); *Culture in Transition*, 1963 (USA).

Novels

The Interpreters. London, Deutsch, 1965; New York, Macmillan, 1970.

Season of Anomy. London, Rex Collings, 1973; New York, Third Press, 1974.

Other

The Man Died: Prison Notes. London, Eyre Methuen-Rex Collings, and New York, Harper, 1972.

In Person: Achebe, Awoonor, and Soyinka at the University of Washington. Seattle, University of Washington African Studies Program, 1975.

Myth, Literature, and the African World. London, Cambridge University Press, 1976.

Editor, *Poems of Black Africa.* London, Secker and Warburg, 1974; New York, Hill and Wang, 1975.

Translator, *The Forest of a Thousand Daemons: A Hunter's Saga*, by D. A. Fagunwa. London, Nelson, 1968; New York, Humanities Press, 1969.

Critical Studies: *The Writing of Wole Soyinka* by Eldred D. Jones, London, Heinemann, 1972; *Wole Soyinka* by Gerald Moore, London, Evans, 1972, revised edition, 1978.

Theatrical Activities:

Director: **Plays** – by Brecht, Chekhov, Clark, Easmon, Eseoghene, Ogunyemi, Shakespeare, Synge, and his own works: *L'Espace et la Magie*, Paris, 1972; *Inquest on Biko*, Ife, 1978.

* * *

Wole Soyinka's first volume of collected poems, *Idanre and Other Poems*, is a significant guide to the direction of the author's work. He first made his name as a writer of light satirical verse in poems like "Telephone Conversation," "The Immigrant," and "The Other Immigrant," all of which he has excluded from this collection. A pre-occupation with more sombre themes is represented by "Requiem" (also, and more surprisingly, excluded from the collected poems) where he explores the continuing but tenuous relationship between the dead and the living in a series of delicate images suggestive of barely perceptible contact: "You leave your faint depressions/Skim-flying still, on the still pond's surface./Where darkness crouches, egret wings/Your love is gossamer." This pre-occupation with death and beyond – particularly with death at speed on the road – is one of the features of his later poetry and drama. His poem "Death in the Dawn" ends with the startled recognition by a victim of a car crash of his sudden translation: "Brother/Silenced in the startled hug of/Your invention – is this mocked grimace/This closed contortion – I?" Several pictures of this kind occur in Soyinka's prose, poetry, and drama. Indeed one of his impressive features is his consistency between genres and over the whole period of his writing.

In a magazine interview Soyinka spoke about the "personal intimacy which I have developed with a certain aspect of the road ... it concerns the reality of death...." For him, death on the road is a kind of sacrifice to "progress," a notion which Soyinka treats with extreme scepticism. But sacrifice – self-sacrifice – martyrdom is another theme with which Soyinka has become increasingly concerned. Society often destroys its greatest benefactors; indeed it is ironically through the willingness of sensitive souls to suffer martyrdom if necessary that society advances. This is the central theme both of his play *The Strong Breed* and "The Dreamer," a poem based on the idea of the Crucifixion. The dreamer (like Eman in *The Strong Breed*) is martyred in his prime, but in the final stanza of the poem there is the suggestion that out of his bitter suffering arises a new and powerful growth:

The burden bowed the boughs to earth
A girdle for the sea
And bitter pods gave voices birth
A ring of stones
And throes and thrones
And incense on the sea.

This theme, that society needs these victims for its own salvation, is a very important one in Soyinka's writing. The captain in his play *A Dance of the Forests* is emasculated and sold into slavery for sticking to his principles – in this case a refusal to fight in a causeless war. There is evidence of Soyinka's growing concern with man's incorrigible urge for self-destruction through war. Nowhere is this better portrayed than in the long poem "Idanre" in which, using what has now become the dominant figure in his writing, Ogun, he pictures the god who, having been invited by men to fight on their behalf, is unable to distinguish friend from foe:

He strides sweat encrusted
Bristles on risen tendons

Porcupine and barbed. Again he turns
Into his men, butcher's axe
Rises and sinks

Behind it, a guest no one
Can recall.

The poet was forced to act out his poetic theme when, as a result of his abortive efforts to avert the Nigerian Civil War with a trip across the embattled frontiers – a typically Soyinkan gesture – he was arrested and detained by the Federal Military Government. The period of solitary confinement was the gestation period for the spate of writing which followed his release nearly two years later. The title of his volume *A Shuttle in the Crypt* (two of the poems had been smuggled out and separately published by Rex Collings as *Poems from Prison*), with its suggestion of confined energetic activity, symbolises both Soyinka's imprisoned state, an active mind frustrated by inactivity, as well as his refusal to accept mental defeat. His writings since his release, both prose and poetry, are characterised by a more activist message. In the prose of *The Man Died*: "These men are not merely evil, I thought. They are the mindlessness of evil made flesh. One should never stumble into their hands but seek the power to destroy them.... To seek the power to destroy them is to fulfil a moral task." In the poetry of *A Shuttle in the Crypt*,

Come, let us
With the mangled kind
Make pact, no less
Against the lesser
Leagues of death, and mutilations of the mind.
Take justice
In your hands who can
Or dare.

"Flowers for My Land" (one of the two smuggled poems) from which that extract is taken does not really represent the mood of the entire collection which is more introspective – "a map of the course trodden by the mind," as Soyinka describes the collection in the Preface – but it does foreshadow the sharper edge of the other post-prison writings.

One African leader who dares to take justice in his hands is Samora Machel, President of Mozambique, who virtually declared war against the minority regime of Rhodesia, an act which inspired Soyinka's long poem *Ogun Abibiman*, a celebration of Machel's symbolic act, and, in the pause before real and uncompromising battle is joined, a vision of the imminent war of liberation in which both parts of the continent – hitherto the separate territories of Shaka of the east and Ogun of the west – unite to overthrow the white tyranny: "Our histories meet, the forests merge/With the savannah .../and Ogun treads the earth of Shaka!" The poem sweeps along with a heady exhilaration, brushing aside all restraining considerations; it is too late for love, too late for reflection: "Can love outrace the random bullet/To possess the heart of black despair?/Remember Sharpville – not as aberration/Of the single hour, but years and generations." Will the war be won? Will the right weapons be found even after in a desperate search for them men have rifled "Our sacred groves to yield, in need, thighbones/Honed to drinking points...?" No one knows! Even those fighting on the side of right will be imperfect men; mistakes will be made; but there is no other way. As Soyinka asks with typically irreverent irony: "If man cannot, what god dare claim perfection?" Soyinka's ideas have not changed fundamentally; prison hardened the tone, but the poet remains the protagonist of freedom against tyranny, of the forces of life against the forces of death.

Because Soyinka's work is an attempt to formulate a meaning out of the contradictory forces that govern human life and actions, Ogun, who unites these two qualities without separating them, is an apt symbol. The poet himself effects a similar fusion in his work between African and European influences. European dramatic and poetic conventions are fused with African conventions and ways of thought to produce an original type of poetry. He invokes the pantheon of Yoruba gods to forge a new ethic whose validity is not confined to Africa. He imbues English with a verve and an expansiveness which spring from the imagic nature of Yoruba speech. This is what makes Soyinka both an African and a world writer.

—Eldred D. Jones

SPACKS, Barry. American. Born in Philadelphia, Pennsylvania, 21 February 1931. Educated at the University of Pennsylvania, Philadelphia, B.A. (honors) 1952; Indiana University, Bloomington, M.A. 1956; Pembroke College, Cambridge (Fulbright Scholar), 1956–57. Served in the United States Army Signal Corps, 1952–54. Married Patricia Meyer in 1955 (separated, 1978); one daughter. Assistant Professor, University of Florida, Gainesville, 1957–59. Since 1960, Professor of English, Massachusetts Institute of Technology, Cambridge. Visiting Professor, University of Kentucky, Lexington, 1978–79, and University of California, Berkeley, 1980. Recipient: St. Botolph's award, 1971. Agent: Lynn Nesbit, International Creative Management, 40 West 57th Street, New York, New York 10019. Address: 353 Woodland Avenue, Lexington, Kentucky 40508, U.S.A.

PUBLICATIONS

Verse

Twenty Poems. Santa Barbara, California, Sun Press, 1967.
The Company of Children. New York, Doubleday, 1969.
Something Human. New York, Harper's Magazine Press, 1972.
Teaching the Penguins to Fly. Boston, Godine, 1975.
Imagining a Unicorn. Athens, University of Georgia Press, 1978.

Novels

The Sophomore. Englewood Cliffs, New Jersey, Prentice Hall, 1968; London, Collins, 1969.
Orphans. New York, Harper's Magazine Press, 1972.

* * *

Barry Spacks has been writing poetry for over 20 years. Yet he is not widely known, nor is he regarded as part of a school or movement. So far as I know he does not give readings; he does not publicize himself. But what he does do is write steadily and well, producing poems that are craftsmanlike, pleasant to read, genuine in feeling and tone. He writes on many subjects, many of them drawn from his life as a professor of English at M.I.T., but it is perhaps fair to say that his real subject is the life of the poet and his responsibilities and rights. Either directly stated or implied throughout his work are the themes of the right of the poet to remain free, to say what he feels, to indulge himself in nostalgia, speculation, dream, fantasy, and metaphor. Spacks is a likeable writer – unpretentious is the word one is tempted to overuse in describing him – at home with himself and in love and his wife. His lyrics reveal an American poet-professor singing of the vagaries of the quotidian in a world which amuses, touches, and delights him.

His subjects are as numerous as his poems: his boyhood, his daughter, famous writers he has seen in Boston (Berryman, Neruda, Borges), a student killed while hang-gliding, lustful thoughts in a laundromat, a Buster Keaton film. But he is particularly good at turning casual occasions into poems; he has the ability to take the small incident, the almost everyday occurrence, and turn it into a small and unpretentious but nevertheless satisfying poem. Grading papers late at night and mistaking the reflection of his light for someone else's, two friends cooking dinner, finding a design of leaves on the pavement, seeing his old professor drunk in a bar, landing at an airport, finding a Yiddish newspaper on the Riverside Line: such subjects furnish the basis for his meditative – perhaps ruminative is more accurate – lyrics. But this intellectual cud-chewing results in a very personal light verse, accomplished and sensitive in its handling of the stuff of everyday life.

Spacks has a good ear for language, and his poems are virtually without a false note; he loves the language and respects it. There is no rhetoric or bombast and little word play. The verse, often free verse but occasionally rhymed or in stanzas, is clean, "hard-edged," each word carefully chosen and placed. In his best poems one sees a delight and almost surprise in seeing things come together: what sometimes seems inconsequential at the outset suddenly resolves into a striking image or idea. In one of his best poems, "Like a Prism," the prism image comes to be an image of equality of opportunity; in "Teaching the Penguins to Fly" a whimsical idea becomes a wry comment on sixties-type notions of social liberation.

The images are often striking, with a whimsical or even surrealistic quality, such as the comparison of the sea to the "sound of 12,000 women scrubbing bloody chainmail," or these opening lines from "For a Pregnant Lady":

Doing my usual thing: vacuuming Death Valley;
stitching up some weekday shrouds;
when all at once your nowhere-near-born child
gazes through my window, nose against the glass;

These lines would seem to follow the little ars poetica he outlines in "Wit and Whimsy":

Rule one: make precious
little sense.

Rule two: commit
no permanence.

Rule three: ignore
rule four.

But there is more to Spacks than mildly breaking the rules. In poems like "New Copley in the Gallery," "The Parent Birds," and "Malediction," he assembles some intricate machines that function smoothly. In his later work his subjects seem more topical, such as the ecological "Malediction," perhaps reflecting his fuller sense of his roles as father, poet, professor, citizen, and Bostonian. If these poems have little chance of changing the world or the direction of modern poetry (and I suspect their creator has no such hopes), they are nevertheless very accomplished, sensitive poems by someone the reader feels he would like to know and to be friends with.

—Donald Barlow Stauffer

SPARK, Muriel (Sarah, née Camberg). British. Born in Edinburgh. Educated at James Gillespie's School for Girls, Edinburgh. Married S. O. Spark in 1937 (divorced); one child. Worked in the Political Intelligence Department of the British Foreign Office during World War II. General Secretary of the Poetry Society, and Editor of the *Poetry Review*, London, 1947–49. Recipient: *The Observer* Story Prize, 1951; Italia Prize, for radio drama, 1962; Black Memorial Prize, 1966. LL.D.: University of Strathclyde, Glasgow, 1971. Fellow, Royal Society of Literature. Honorary Member, American Academy of Arts and Letters, 1978. O.B.E. (Officer, Order of the British Empire), 1967. Lives in Rome. Address: c/o Macmillan and Company, 4 Little Essex Street, London W.C.2, England.

PUBLICATIONS

Verse

Out of a Book (as Muriel Camberg). Leith, Midlothian, Millar and Burden, 1933(?).
The Fanfarlo and Other Verse. Aldington, Kent, Hand and Flower Press, 1952.
Collected Poems I. London, Macmillan, 1967.

Plays

The Party Through the Wall (broadcast, 1957). Included in *Voices at Play*, 1961.
The Interview (broadcast, 1958). Included in *Voices at Play*, 1961.
The Dry River Bed (broadcast, 1959). Included in *Voices at Play*, 1961.
Danger Zone (broadcast, 1961). Included in *Voices at Play*, 1961.
Doctors of Philosophy (produced London, 1962). London, Macmillan, 1963; New York, Knopf, 1966.

Radio Plays: *The Party Through the Wall*, 1957; *The Interview*, 1958; *The Dry River Bed*, 1959; *The Ballad of Peckham Rye*, 1960; *Danger Zone*, 1961.

Novels

The Comforters. London, Macmillan, and Philadelphia, Lippincott, 1957.
Robinson. London, Macmillan, and Philadelphia, Lippincott, 1958.
Memento Mori. London, Macmillan, and Philadelphia, Lippincott, 1959.
The Ballad of Peckham Rye. London, Macmillan, and Philadelphia, Lippincott, 1960.
The Bachelors. London, Macmillan, 1960; Philadelphia, Lippincott, 1961.
The Prime of Miss Jean Brodie. London, Macmillan, 1961; Philadelphia, Lippincott, 1962.
The Girls of Slender Means. London, Macmillan, and New York, Knopf, 1963.
The Mandelbaum Gate. London, Macmillan, and New York, Knopf, 1965.
The Public Image. London, Macmillan, and New York, Knopf, 1968.
The Driver's Seat. London, Macmillan, and New York, Knopf, 1970.
Not to Disturb. London, Macmillan, 1971; New York, Viking Press, 1972.
The Hothouse by the East River. London, Macmillan, and New York, Viking Press, 1973.
The Abbess of Crewe: A Modern Morality Tale. London, Macmillan, and New York, Viking Press, 1974.
The Takeover. London, Macmillan, and New York, Viking Press, 1976.
Territorial Rights. London, Macmillan, and New York, Coward McCann, 1979.

Short Stories

The Go-Away Bird and Other Stories. London, Macmillan, 1958; Philadelphia, Lippincott, 1960.

Voices at Play (includes radio plays). London, Macmillan, 1961; Philadelphia, Lippincott, 1962.
Collected Stories I. London, Macmillan, 1967; New York, Knopf, 1968.

Other

Child of Light: A Reassessment of Mary Wollstonecraft Shelley. London, Tower Bridge, 1951.
Emily Brontë: Her Life and Work, with Derek Stanford. London, Peter Owen, 1953; New York, British Book Centre, 1960.
John Masefield. London, Peter Nevill, 1953.
The Very Fine Clock (juvenile). New York, Knopf, 1958; London, Macmillan, 1969.

Editor, with Derek Stanford, *Tribute to Wordsworth.* London, Wingate, 1950.
Editor, *A Selection of Poems*, by Emily Brontë. London, Grey Walls Press, 1952.
Editor, with Derek Stanford, *My Best Mary: The Letters of Mary Shelley.* London, Wingate, 1953; Folcroft, Pennsylvania, Folcroft Editions, 1972.
Editor, *The Brontë Letters.* London, Peter Nevill, 1954; as *The Letters of the Brontë's: A Selection.* Norman, University of Oklahoma Press, 1954.
Editor, with Derek Stanford, *Letters of John Henry Newman.* London, Peter Owen, 1957.

Bibliography: *Iris Murdoch and Muriel Spark: A Bibliography* by Thomas T. Tominaga and Wilma Schneidermeyer, Metuchen, New Jersey, Scarecrow Press, 1976.

Critical Studies: *Muriel Spark* by Karl Malkoff, New York, Columbia University Press, 1968; *Muriel Spark* by Peter Kemp, London, Elek, 1974.

* * *

"What's good enough for Archimedes/Ought to be good enough for me" ("Elementary"): Muriel Spark's verse mocks the inadequacy of scientific definition and rejoices in "An odd capacity for vision." Though "Against the Transcendentalists" elevates "poets" over "visionaries" and hopes "... that if Byzantium/Should appear in Kensington/The city will fit the size/Of the perimeter of my eyes/And of the span of my hand," the poem paradoxically celebrates the miracle these limits create: "The flesh made word." And the Kensington that obsesses a number of other poems is "Kensington of dreadful night" ("The Pearl-Miners"), where the persona invokes "latent Christ" ("Elegy in a Kensington Churchyard"). Sometimes the miraculous becomes merely the talking steel chairs of familiar satire on human interchangeability with artifacts ("A Visit"). Conversely, the elegant colloquialism of "Fruitless Fable," a chronicle of Mr. Chiddicott's sudden enslavement by his "perfected tea-machine," raises the poem from mock-heroic moral fable ("Alas, the transience of bliss –") to genuine fantasy. Occasionally fantasy dramatizes obsession with "... my other/who sounds my superstition like a bagpipe" ("Intermittence"), or with "... the momentary name I gave/To a slight stir in a fictitious grave" ("Evelyn Cavallo").

Spark's most ambitious fusion of obsession with fantasy creates the "tremorous metropolis" of "The Ballad of the Fanfarlo," a hallucinatory "settlement of fever," in which vocal traffic lights and ether bowls seem as ordinary or extraordinary as everything else. This nightmare continuation of Baudelaire's prose satire traces the quest of the Romantic poet Samuel Cramer for his alter ego Manuela de Monteverde and the dancer Fanfarlo, but significantly changes the tone of the original. Baudelaire's Cramer ultimately edits a socialist journal and presumably no longer signs Manuela's name to "quelques folies romantiques," while Spark's hero, either true to his early vision or atoning for his defection, is willing to endure the horrors of "No-Man's Sanitorium" in his quest. Despite a generous epigraph from Baudelaire, the poem's atmosphere and stanza form suggest "The Ancient Mariner" and, at times, "Sir Patrick Spens" as filtered through Coleridge's "Dejection: An Ode": "The new moon like a pair of surgical forceps/With the old moon in her jaws." Only in such passages, when Spark defines Romantic art through parody, does the poem achieve the simultaneous recreation and mockery of Baudelaire toward which it aims.

Cramer is funnier in a brief appearance as a visiting journalist in "The Nativity," when he replies to rumors of mysterious happenings at the inn: "No good to me if it's local." "The Nativity," Spark's longest religious poem, precariously blends faith and fantasy in a portrait of bizarre wise men: "You with the nose on top of your head, smell out/The principalities of heaven for all of us." Riddling wit defines the limits of religious mystery in shorter works, "Conundrum," "Holy Water Rondel," and "Faith and Works" ("We are the truest saint alive/As near as two and two make five"). Even an apparently secular exercise like "The Rout," which fuses, in the manner of Marianne Moore, a news article about a battle between bees and wasps in a village church with a dispatch from Cromwell, reinforced by quotations from Lawrence and The Pocket Book of British Insects: The Honey Bee, produces not only the eloquent parody of "The murder of innumerable bees," but also an elegant questioning of man's relation to the rest of creation. Like Spark's seemingly casual treatment of religion, the moralizing is always implicit, offhand. However complex her tone, Spark's forms are generally traditional. The more controlled the verse, the more the strictness of the pattern causes a concentration in theme that becomes incantatory, as in "Edinburgh Villanelle":

These eyes that saw the saturnine

Waters no provident whim made wine
Fail to infuriate the dull
Heart of Midlothian, never mine.

—Burton Kendle

SPARSHOTT, Francis (Edward). Canadian. Born in Chatham, Kent, England, 19 May 1926. Educated at King's School, Rochester, Kent, 1934–43; Corpus Christi College, Oxford, 1943–44, 1947–50, B.A. 1950, M.A. 1950. Served in the British Army Intelligence Corps, 1944–47. Married Kathleen Elizabeth Vaughan in 1953; one daughter. Lecturer in Philosophy, University of Toronto, 1950–55. Lecturer in Classics, 1955–70, and Assistant Professor, 1955–62, Associate Professor, 1962–64, Professor since 1964, and Chairman of the Department of Philosophy, 1965–70, Victoria College, Toronto. Visiting Professor, Northwestern University, Evanston, Illinois, 1958–59, University of Illinois, Urbana, 1966, and Sir George Williams University, Montreal, 1971. President, Canadian Philosophical Association, 1975–76, and League of Canadian Poets, 1977–79; Vice-President, American Society for Aesthetics, 1979. Recipient: President's Medal, University of Western Ontario, London, for poetry, 1959, for essay, 1962. Fellow, Royal Society of Canada, 1977. Address: 50 Crescentwood Road, Scarborough, Ontario M1N 1E4, Canada.

PUBLICATIONS

Verse

A Divided Voice. Toronto, Oxford University Press, 1965.
A Cardboard Garage. Toronto, Clarke Irwin, 1969.

The Naming of the Beasts. Windsor, Ontario, Black Moss, 1979.
The Rainy Hills. Privately printed, 1979.

Other

An Enquiry into Goodness and Related Concepts, with Some Remarks on the Nature and Scope of Such Enquiries. Toronto, University of Toronto Press, and Chicago, University of Chicago Press, 1958.
The Structure of Aesthetics. Toronto, University of Toronto Press, and London, Routledge, 1963.
The Concept of Criticism. Oxford, Clarendon Press, 1967.
A Book by Cromwell Kent (humour). Scarborough, Ontario, Vanity Press, 1970.
Looking for Philosophy. Montreal, McGill-Queen's University Press, 1972.

* * *

It is a truism to say that there are really two Francis Sparshotts, the first the philosopher, the second the poet. But this is only a truism because the philosophic prose is rich in poetic insight and passion, and the poetry itself is not wanting in elegant clarity and donnish wit. Also common to both is the spirit of inquiry, for many of Sparshott's best poems turn on argumentation. "Argument with Dr. Williams" from *A Cardboard Garage* begins "But nothing depends/on your old wheel/barrow." And "Rhetoric for a Divided Voice" from *A Divided Voice* has one voice making the following demand: "I challenge your world to atone/For my unmerited pain." The second voice responds, somewhat indignantly, and they finally conclude:

No. Here's the end of all our talk:
That I am I and you are you,
Though in your footsteps I must walk,
Though mine the eyes you must look through.

Mental and moral questioning seem at the core of Sparshott's work, so often do intellectual concerns and a formal use of language take precedence over emotional expression and lyrical flights of fancy.

—John Robert Colombo

SPEAR, Charles. New Zealander. Born in Owaka, in 1910. Formerly a journalist and Lecturer in English, University of Canterbury, Christchurch. Address: 79 Clarence Avenue, London SW4 8LQ, England.

PUBLICATIONS

Verse

Twopence Coloured: Poems. Christchurch, Caxton Press, 1951.

* * *

With one volume of poems, *Twopence Coloured*, which has had no successor, Charles Spear has made a special place for himself in New Zealand poetry. Unlike most of the poets of his time, except R. A. K. Mason, his work pays little attention to the people, the landscape or the specific national concerns of New Zealand. His subject-matter derives in great part from his own experiences in European countries, their history, literature, and scenery, and from his own generous reading. His poems are not, however, descriptive, but subtle, at times enigmatic, pieces, conveying a mood or a sensation and delicately using symbolism to express a mature acceptance of the inevitability of pain, change, sacrifice and loss, while yet remaining curious about life and what it brings.

A number of poems in *Twopence Coloured*, too, show a response to the accidentals of social life, places and things which, in their elusiveness and occasional preciosity, recall the poems of Wilde, Dowson and others of the Nineties. The technical assurance, breadth of allusion and cultivated sensibility which mark the poems make the poetic persona they present a very intriguing one indeed. Mr. Spear does not embark upon subjects beyond his range, but within it achieves an exquisite finish and completeness, so that his best pieces are admirable artefacts.

—J. C. Reid

SPENDER, Stephen (Harold). British. Born in London, 28 September 1909; son of the writer Harold Spender. Educated at University College School, London; University College, Oxford. Served as a fireman in the National Fire Service, 1941–44. Married 1) Agnes Marie Pearn in 1936; 2) Natasha Litvin in 1941; one son and one daughter. Editor, with Cyril Connolly, *Horizon* magazine, London, 1939–41; Co-Editor, 1953–66, and Corresponding Editor, 1966–67, *Encounter* magazine, London. Counsellor, UNESCO Section of Letters, 1947. Elliston Lecturer, University of Cincinnati, 1953; Beckman Professor, University of California, Berkeley, 1959; Visiting Professor, Northwestern University, Evanston, Illinois, 1963; Clark Lecturer, Cambridge University, 1966; Visiting Professor, University of Connecticut, Storrs. 1968–70; Mellon Lecturer, Washington, D.C., 1968; Northcliffe Lecturer, London University, 1969; Visiting Lecturer, University of Florida, Gainesville, 1976. Since 1970, Professor of English Literature, University College, London. Since 1975, President, English Centre, P.E.N. Consultant in Poetry in English, Library of Congress, Washington, D.C., 1965–66. Fellow of the Institute of Advanced Studies, Wesleyan University, Middletown, Connecticut, 1967. Recipient: Queen's Gold Medal for Poetry, 1971; Companion of Literature, 1978. D.Litt.: University of Montpelier; Loyola University, Chicago. Honorary Member, American Academy of Arts and Letters, 1969. C.B.E. (Companion, Order of the British Empire), 1962. Address: 15 Loudoun Road, London N.W.8, England.

PUBLICATIONS

Verse

Nine Experiments by S. H. S., Being Poems Written at the Age of Eighteen. Privately printed, 1928.

20 Poems. Oxford, Blackwell, 1930.

Poems. London, Faber, 1933; New York, Random House, 1934; revised edition, Faber, 1934.

Vienna. London, Faber, 1934; New York, Random House, 1935.
At Night. Privately printed, 1935.
The Still Centre. London, Faber, 1939.
Selected Poems. London, Faber, 1940.
I Sit by the Window. Baltimore, Linden Press, n.d.
Ruins and Visions. London, Faber, and New York, Random House, 1942.
Spiritual Exercises (To Cecil Day Lewis). Privately printed, 1943.
Poems of Dedication. London, Faber, 1946; New York, Random House, 1947.
Returning to Vienna 1947: Nine Sketches. Pawlet, Vermont, Banyan Press, 1947.
The Edge of Being. London, Faber, and New York, Random House, 1949.
Sirmione Peninsula. London, Faber, 1954.
Collected Poems 1928–1953. London, Faber, and New York, Random House, 1955.
Inscriptions. London, Poetry Book Society, 1958.
Selected Poems. New York, Random House, 1964; London, Faber, 1965.
The Generous Days: Ten Poems. Boston, Godine, 1969; augmented edition, as *The Generous Days*, London, Faber, and New York, Random House, 1971.
Descartes. London, Steam Press, 1970.
Art Student. London, Poem-of-the-Month Club, 1970.
Penguin Modern Poets 20, with John Heath-Stubbs and F. T. Prince. London, Penguin, 1971.
Recent Poems. London, Anvil Press Poetry, 1978.

Recordings: *Stephen Spender Reading His Own Poems*, Argo, 1958; *Stephen Spender Reading His Own Poems*, Caedmon.

Plays

Trial of a Judge (produced London, 1938). London, Faber, and New York, Random House, 1938.
Danton's Death, with Goronwy Rees, adaptation of a play by Georg Büchner (produced London, 1939). London, Faber, 1939; in *From the Modern Repertory*, edited by Eric Bentley, Bloomington, Indiana University Press, 1958.
To the Island (produced Oxford, 1951).
Mary Stuart, adaptation of the play by Schiller (produced New York, 1957; Edinburgh and London, 1958). London, Faber, 1959.
Lulu, adaptation of the play by Frank Wedekind (produced New York, 1958).
Rasputin's End, music by Nicholas Nabokov. Milan, Ricordi, 1963.

Novel

The Backward Son. London, Hogarth Press, 1940.

Short Stories

The Burning Cactus. London, Faber, and New York, Random House, 1936.
Engaged in Writing, and The Fool and the Princess. London, Hamish Hamilton, and New York, Farrar Straus, 1958.

Other

The Destructive Element: A Study of Modern Writers and Beliefs. London, Cape, 1935; Boston, Houghton Mifflin, 1936.
Forward from Liberalism. London, Gollancz, and New York, Random House, 1937.
The New Realism: A Discussion. London, Hogarth Press, 1939; Folcroft, Pennsylvania, Folcroft Editions, 1977.

Life and the Poet. London, Secker and Warburg, 1942; Folcroft, Pennsylvania, Folcroft Editions, 1974.
Jim Braidy: The Story of Britain's Firemen, with William Sansom and James Gordon. London, Drummond, 1943.
Citizens in War – and After. London, Harrap, 1945.
Botticelli. London, Faber, 1945; New York, Pitman, 1948.
European Witness (on Germany). London, Hamish Hamilton, and New York, Reynal, 1946.
Poetry since 1939. London and New York, Longman, 1946.
The God That Failed: Six Studies in Communism, edited by Richard H. Crossman. London, Hamish Hamilton, and New York, Harper, 1950.
World Within World: The Autobiography of Stephen Spender. London, Hamish Hamilton, and New York, Harcourt Brace, 1951.
Europe in Photographs. London, Thames and Hudson, 1951.
Shelley. London, Longman, 1952.
Learning Laughter (on Israel). London, Weidenfeld and Nicolson, 1952; New York, Harcourt Brace, 1953.
The Creative Element: A Study of Vision, Despair, and Orthodoxy among Some Modern Writers. London, Hamish Hamilton, 1953; Folcroft, Pennsylvania, Folcroft Editions, 1973.
The Making of a Poem (essays). London, Hamish Hamilton, 1955; New York, Norton, 1962.
The Imagination in the Modern World: Three Lectures. Washington, D.C., Library of Congress, 1962.
The Struggle of the Modern. London, Hamish Hamilton, and Berkeley, University of California Press, 1963.
Ghika: Paintings, Drawings, Sculpture, with Patrick Leigh Fermor. London, Lund Humphries, 1964; Boston, Boston Book and Art Shop, 1965.
The Magic Flute: Retold. New York, Putnam, 1966.
Chaos and Control in Poetry (lecture). Washington, D.C., Library of Congress, 1966.
The Year of the Young Rebels. London, Weidenfeld and Nicolson, and New York, Random House, 1969.
Love-Hate Relations: A Study of Anglo-American Sensibilities. London, Hamish Hamilton, and New York, Random House, 1974.
T. S. Eliot. London, Fontana, 1975; New York, Viking Press, 1976.
Henry Moore: Sculptures in Landscape, photographs by Geoffrey Shakerley. London, Studio Vista, 1978; New York, Potter, 1979.
The Thirties and After: Poetry, Politics, and People (1933–75). London, Macmillan, 1978.
Venice, photographs by Fulvio Roiter. London, Thames and Hudson, 1979.
America Observed, illustrated by Paul Hogarth. New York, Potter, 1979.

Editor, with Louis MacNeice, *Oxford Poetry 1929.* Oxford, Blackwell, 1929.
Editor, with Bernard Spencer, *Oxford Poetry 1930.* Oxford, Blackwell, 1930.
Editor, with John Lehmann and Christopher Isherwood, *New Writing, New Series I* and *II.* London, Hogarth Press, 1938, 1939.
Editor, with John Lehmann, *Poems for Spain.* London, Hogarth Press, 1939.
Editor, *A Choice of English Romantic Poetry.* New York, Dial Press, 1947.
Editor, *Selected Poems*, by Walt Whitman. London, Grey Walls Press, 1950.
Editor, with Elizabeth Jennings and Dannie Abse, *New Poems 1956.* London, Joseph, 1956.
Editor, *Great Writings of Goethe.* New York, New American Library, 1958.
Editor, *Great German Short Stories.* New York, Dell, 1960.
Editor, *The Writer's Dilemma.* London, Oxford University Press, 1961.
Editor, with Donald Hall, *The Concise Encyclopedia of English and American Poets and*

Poetry. London, Hutchinson, and New York, Hawthorn, 1963; revised edition, 1970.

Editor, with Irving Kristol and Melvin J. Lasky, *Encounters: An Anthology from Its First Ten Years*. London, Weidenfeld and Nicolson, and New York, Basic Books, 1963.

Editor, *Selected Poems*, by Abba Kovner and Nelly Sachs. London, Penguin, 1971.

Editor, *A Choice of Shelley's Verse*. London, Faber, 1971.

Editor, *The Poems of Percy Bysshe Shelley*. Cambridge, Limited Editions Club, 1971; New York, Heritage Club, 1974.

Editor, *D. H. Lawrence, Novelist, Poet, Prophet*. London, Weidenfeld and Nicolson, and New York, Harper, 1973.

Editor, *W. H. Auden: A Tribute*. London, Weidenfeld and Nicolson, and New York, Macmillan, 1975.

Translator, *Pastor Hall*, by Ernst Toller. London, Lane, 1939; with *Blind Man's Buff*, by Toller and Denis Johnston, New York, Random House, 1939.

Translator, with J. L. Gili, *Poems*, by García Lorca. London, Dolphin, and New York, Oxford University Press, 1939.

Translator, with J. B. Leishman, *Duino Elegies*, by Rainer Maria Rilke. London, Hogarth Press, and New York, Norton, 1939; revised edition, Hogarth Press, 1948, Norton, 1963.

Translator, with J. L. Gili, *Selected Poems*, by García Lorca. London, Hogarth Press, 1943.

Translator, with Frances Cornford, *Le dur Désir de Durer*, by Paul Eluard. London, Faber, and New York, New Directions, 1950.

Translator, *The Life of the Virgin Mary (Das Marien-Leben)* (bilingual edition), by Rainer Maria Rilke. London, Vision Press, and New York, Philosophical Library, 1951.

Translator, with Frances Fawcett, *Five Tragedies of Sex* (includes *Spring's Awakening*, *Earth-Spirit*, *Pandora's Box*, *Death and Devil*, *Castle Wetterstein*), by Frank Wedekind. London, Vision Press, and New York, Theatre Arts, 1952.

Translator, with Nikos Stangos, *Fourteen Poems*, by C. P. Cavafy. London, Editions Electo, 1977.

Bibliography: *The Early Published Poems of Stephen Spender: A Chronology* by A. T. Tolley, Ottawa, Carleton University, 1967; *Stephen Spender: Works and Criticism: An Annotated Bibliography* by H. B. Kulkarbi, New York, Garland, 1977.

* * *

In *The Destructive Element* Stephen Spender described the difficulties of writing about contemporaries: "One is dealing in a literature of few accepted values. At best one can offer opinions ... at worst, bookmaking, or stockbroking." He goes on to consider a question vital to understanding his own work; he is interested in writers "faced by the destructive element, i.e., by the experience of an all-pervading Present, which is a world without belief." It is easily possible to regard Spender's poetry sympathetically as a near-traumatic reaction to "a void in the present," and much of his personal experience, e.g., his commitment and later disengagement involving communism, can be interpreted as a search for belief. Even the intensity of his well-known personal and literary loyalties (e.g., with Auden and Isherwood) and the value he has given to them in his autobiographies assume a new dimension in this light. Even in his journalism, his book on the Youth Aliyah effort to make homes for Jewish children in the Kibbutzim of Israel (*Learning Laughter*), his book based on journals kept on a trip through Germany in 1945 (*European Witness*), his book on student unrest, a reader can discern a kind of seeking for belief; there is an element of wander-literature, even of Quixote – for Spender's faults are those of idealistic generalizing, of a frequent, often irritating naivety.

His search for a metaphor in Berlin is perhaps illustrative: "At first Berlin seemed less damaged than I had expected, but as we approached the centre of the town it produced the same impression of desolation as all the other large German towns...." A picture emerges, of a haunted palace – something out of Poe: "Charwomen responsible for the upkeep of the Chancellory, and still performing their tasks, concealed on their persons hammers with which they broke off fragments of the yellow marble top of this [Hitler's] desk as souvenirs in exchange for a few cigarettes." He concludes that "the Nazi and the Fascist leaders were often disappointed artists," somehow linking up the Nazi fate with "the gloom of Tennyson, the ennui of Baudelaire and the pessimism of Thomas Hardy." Spender carries away a piece of Hitler's desk. Commenting on its significance as an "unholy relic," he concludes that the Nazis taught us the necessity of choosing between good and evil.

Earlier, a friend had remarked on Spender's poems: "When you write in this way you are filled with social despair, and you have no religious or political beliefs whatever. Directly, out of a sense of conscience, you try to introduce a constructive idea into your writing, you fail." "All the same," Spender replies, "one must look for a constructive idea. If one has the sense of despair and of evil, then one must look for the sense of hope and of good with which to confront despair and evil."

It is perhaps this idealism, and the linking of abstraction with imagery (a Spender play concerns "the belief that man/can overthrow systems of injustice/and build systems of justice") that determine the final tone of a Spender poem.

> The secret of these hills was stone, and cottages
> Of that stone made,
> And crumbling roads
> That turned on sudden hidden villages

he writes in "The Pylons." But soon comes the intervention of politics, of the dark awareness:

> Now over these small hills they have built the concrete
> That trails black wire:
> Pylons, those pillars
> Bare like nude, giant girls that have no secret.

One thinks sometimes that Spender wanted to be the kind of poet George Orwell might have been; and appropriately, his best poems are perhaps those about the Spanish Civil War, in *The Still Centre* (especially "A Stop Watch and an Ordnance Map" and "Fall of a City"), though poems like "I Think Continually of Those Who Were Truly Great," "The Express," and "The Landscape near an Aerodrome" are justly famous. Certain lines of Spender's echo through the minds of anyone familiar with a modern anthology:

> Eye, gazelle, delicate wanderer,
> Drinker of horizon's fluid line;
> Ear that suspends on a chord
> The spirit drinking timelessness....

And who can forget the opening lines of "The Express"? "After the first powerful plain manifesto/The black statement of pistons, without more fuss/But gliding like a queen, she leaves the station" passing "gasworks and at last the heavy page/Of death, printed by gravestones in the cemetery." With the "jazzy madness" of the train we feel a growing confidence in the poet's power, his own confidence in his own as the train arrives at "Edinburgh or Rome."

Perhaps it is difficult to recapture a sense of relevance when it comes to remembering why Spender thought C. Day Lewis shouldn't be afraid of communists, or how Spender himself changed toward "the god that failed" but we can easily recall from some distance the way Spender has developed certain obsessive ideas about death and fame:

For how shall we prove that we really exist
Unless we hear, over and over,
Our ego through the world persist
With all the guns of the self-lover?

Through everything Spender has written has run the same idealism. And a reader can hear it as he speaks in *European Witness* of "a desire to see an International Review for Europe, on the very highest level, in which the best German writers were published side by side with English and French, and perhaps with Russian ones too." There everything was going to be "discussed very seriously and with equal frankness by thinkers of all nations, since they would be on a level which was human and not immediately controversial." Spender's final appeal to many readers is probably to an idealism they have themselves failed to keep alive.

—David Ray

SQUIRES, (James) Radcliffe. American. Born in Salt Lake City, Utah, 23 May 1917. Educated at the University of Utah, Salt Lake City, B.A. 1940; University of Chicago (John Billings Fiske Prize, 1946), A.M. 1945; Harvard University, Cambridge, Massachusetts, Ph.D. 1952. Served in the United States Navy, 1941–45. Married Eileen Mulholland in 1945 (died, 1976). Instructor, Dartmough College, Hanover, New Hampshire, 1946–48. Since 1952, Professor of English, University of Michigan, Ann Arbor. Fulbright Professor of American Culture, Salonika, Greece, 1959–60. Editor, *Chicago Review*, 1945–46, and since 1970, *Michigan Quarterly Review*, Ann Arbor. Recipient: *Voices* magazine Young Poets Prize, 1947. Address: 2261 Glencoe Hills, No. 12, Ann Arbor, Michigan 48104, U.S.A.

PUBLICATIONS

Verse

Cornar. Philadelphia, Dorrance, 1940.
Where the Compass Spins. New York, Twayne, 1951.
Fingers of Hermes. Ann Arbor, University of Michigan Press, and London, Cresset Press, 1965.
The Light under Islands. Ann Arbor, University of Michigan Press, and London, Cresset Press, 1967.
Daedalus. Ann Arbor, Michigan, Generation Press, 1968.
Waiting in the Bone and Other Poems. Omaha, Abattoir, 1973.
Gardens of the World. Baton Rouge, Louisiana State University Press, 1980.

Other

The Loyalties of Robinson Jeffers. Ann Arbor, University of Michigan Press, and London, Oxford University Press, 1956.
The Major Themes of Robert Frost. Ann Arbor, University of Michigan Press, and London, Cresset Press, 1963.
Frederic Prokosch. New York, Twayne, 1964.
Allen Tate: A Literary Biography. Indianapolis, Bobbs Merrill, 1971.

Editor, *Allen Tate and His Work: Critical Evaluations.* Minneapolis, University of Minnesota Press, and London, Oxford University Press, 1972.

Manuscript Collection: State University of New York, Buffalo.

Critical Study: "In the Garden of Talos: The Poetry of Radcliffe Squires" by Brewster Ghiselin, in *Sewanee Review* (Tennessee), Fall 1975.

Radcliffe Squires comments:

I suppose that my major themes involve a belief I have that we have gotten too far out of Nature, we humans, ever to be able to think of it as home again. This has shaken our beliefs far more than the loss of religion has, so that it often seems to me that the only faith man is capable of today is one in which he tells himself that he cannot be good, but that at least he can be wicked, which is better than being nothing. Though this gloomy view haunts much of what I do, my poems owe more to a sense of place, mountains, the Mediterranean, than they do to any dogma.

Technically my verse tends to fall into blank verse with occasional or accidental rhyme. I am not a formalist, but I should feel sheepish to turn out a poem with less metrical discipline than iambics provide. Even so, if I should have to choose between meter and metaphor, I should take metaphor, for metaphor seems to me the essence of poetry, the poem within a poem. Luckily, poetry never insists on taking one thing or the other. I believe there are colorings in my verse that come from Thomas Hardy, Robinson Jeffers, T. S. Eliot, Wallace Stevens, W. H. Auden, and C. P. Cavafy. At any rate, I have admired these poets very deeply.

* * *

The quiet voice of Radcliffe Squires speaks through an extraordinary imagination. His poems are romantic in theme, yet metaphysical, heroic in scope, and yet delicate. It is as if the visionary élan of a Robinson Jeffers were grafted on to lyrical, narrative gifts of a Robert Frost.

Although all Squires' poems share common properties – wit, thought, and a philosophy of nature in which Man is a sacred, yet ruinous intrusion – they tend to fall into four distinct groups. His longer poems are parables drawn from mythology: Beowulf, Hercules, Daedalus. Squires uses these heroes as emblems of human creativity and self-discovery, often blurring the edge of his narrative with hermetic allusions. In his last three books, these long mythical poems are offset by shorter ones describing places, principally in Western America and Greece, by elegies and love poems, and by poems that might best be described as speculative.

It is in his speculative moods that Squires writes his most finished poems. In "Sunday in the Laboratory," the poet turns from an aquarium of newts "hardly less transparent than glass" to "The after-image of that human embryo/The size of a hand" whose "body is all the stupor of time."

Waiting in the Bone, anticipated by the earlier "Bone House," suggests that behind a prevailing sense of loss lies hope. Bones are the source of life, of blood. "We shall come up from the bone now./We shall learn to weep again." Or, to quote the last line of "Self as an Eye," "A squint of tears can hold the sun."

Radcliffe Squires is an evocative poet, so good at his best that no one interested in poetry today should be ignorant of his work.

—Anne Stevenson

STAFFORD, William (Edgar). American. Born in Hutchinson, Kansas, 17 January 1914. Educated at the University of Kansas, Lawrence, B.A. 1936, M.A. 1947; University of Iowa, Iowa City, Ph.D. 1954. Conscientious Objector during World War II; active in Pacifist organizations, and since 1959, Member, Oregon Board, Fellowship of Reconciliation. Married Dorothy Hope Frantz in 1944; two daughters and two sons. Member of the English Department, 1948–54, 1957–60, and since 1960, Professor of English, Lewis and Clark College, Portland, Oregon. Assistant Professor of English, Manchester College, Indiana, 1955–56; Professor of English, San Jose State College, California, 1956–57. Consultant in Poetry, Library of Congress, Washington, D.C., 1970–71. United States Information Agency Lecturer in Egypt, Iran, Pakistan, India, Nepal, and Bangladesh, 1972. Recipient: Yaddo Foundation Fellowship, 1955; Oregon Centennial Prize, for poetry and for short story, 1959; Union League Civic and Arts Foundation Prize (*Poetry*, Chicago), 1959; National Book Award, 1963; Shelley Memorial Award, 1964; National Endowment for the Arts grant, 1966; Guggenheim Fellowship, 1966; Melville Cane Award, 1974. D.Litt.: Ripon College, Wisconsin, 1965; Linfield College, McMinnville, Oregon, 1970. Address: Department of English, Lewis and Clark College, Portland, Oregon 97219, U.S.A.

PUBLICATIONS

Verse

West of Your City. Los Gatos, California, Talisman Press, 1960.
Traveling Through the Dark. New York, Harper, 1962.
Five American Poets, with others, edited by Thom Gunn and Ted Hughes. London, Faber, 1963.
Five Poets of the Pacific Northwest, with others, edited by Robin Skelton. Seattle, University of Washington Press, 1964.
The Rescued Year. New York, Harper, 1966.
Eleven Untitled Poems. Mount Horeb, Wisconsin, Perishable Press, 1968.
Weather. Mount Horeb, Wisconsin, Perishable Press, 1969.
Allegiances. New York, Harper, 1970.
Temporary Facts. Athens, Ohio, Duane Schneider Press, 1970.
Poems for Tennessee, with Robert Bly and William Matthews. Martin, Tennessee Poetry Press, 1971.
Someday, Maybe. New York, Harper, 1973.
That Other Alone. Mount Horeb, Wisconsin, Perishable Press, 1973.
In the Clock of Reason. Victoria, British Columbia, Soft Press, 1973.
Going Places. Reno, Nevada, West Coast Poetry Review, 1974.
Braided Apart, with Kim Robert Stafford. Lewiston, Idaho, Confluence Press, 1976.
Stories That Could Be True: New and Collected Poems. New York, Harper 1977.
The Design in the Oriole. N.p., Night Heron Press, 1977.
Two about Music. Knotting, Bedfordshire, Sceptre Press, 1978.

Recording: *Today's Poets 2*, with others, Folkways, 1968.

Other

Down in My Heart (experience as a conscientious objector during World War II). Elgin, Illinois, Brethren, 1947.
Friends to This Ground: A Statement for Readers, Teachers, and Writers of Literature. Champaign, Illinois, National Council of Teachers of English, 1967.
Leftovers, A Care Package: Two Lectures. Washington, D.C., Library of Congress, 1973.
Writing the Australian Crawl: Views on the Writer's Vocation. Ann Arbor, University of Michigan Press, 1978.

Editor, with Frederick Candelaria, *The Voices of Prose.* New York, McGraw Hill, 1966.
Editor, *The Achievement of Brother Antoninus: A Comprehensive Selection of His Poems with a Critical Introduction.* Chicago, Scott Foresman, 1967.
Editor, with Robert H. Ross, *Poems and Perspectives.* Chicago, Scott Foresman, 1971.
Editor, with Clinton F. Larson, *Modern Poetry of Western America.* Provo, Utah, Brigham Young University Press, 1975.

Critical Studies: "William Stafford Issue" of *Northwest Review* (Eugene, Oregon), Spring 1974, and of *Modern Poetry Studies* (Buffalo, New York), Spring 1975; *Four Poets and the Emotive Imagination* by George S. Lensing and Ronald Moran, Baton Rouge, Louisiana State University Press, 1976.

William Stafford comments:

My poetry seems to me direct and communicative, with some oddity and variety. It is usually not formal. It is much like talk, with some enhancement.

Often my poetry is discursive and reminiscent, or at least is that way at one level: it delivers a sense of place and event; it has narrative impulses. Forms are not usually much evident, though tendencies and patterns are occasionally flirted with. Thomas Hardy is my most congenial poetry landmark, but actually the voice I most consistently hear in my poetry is my mother's voice.

* * *

William Stafford seems a perfect blend of Americanisms – born in Kansas to a businessman and a teacher; a gentle, quiet religious youth; missionary work during the war (he was a conscientious objector); a private and meditative adulthood teaching at Lewis and Clark College in Oregon. It is a life that seems pinpointed at the center of American idcology – though Stafford goes his own way often enough to be called crusty. The drama of his poetry seems to turn on this very point – that he is at once all of us and yet his own vinegary individual, patriotic but wary of government, religious but without orthodoxy, modest and yet quick-witted, wise, at times even a visionary. Like Wordsworth, Stafford is rooted in the common world and his inspiration is to make it intense and brightly conscious. In poem after poem he catches the world nodding over the significant, the scant, the peripheral, and in a few spare lines raises minutiae to special attention: "A tumbleweed that was trying/all along through Texas, failed/and became a wraith one winter/in a fence beyond Las Vegas" ("Small Item"). Or this, "At noon in the desert a panting lizard/waited for history, its elbows tense,/watching the curve of a particular road/as if something might happen" ("At the Bomb Testing Site").

It is a verse that is so narrowly focused at times that it seems the verse equivalent of column fillers. In a century aching from too much history, Stafford has spent his writing life squinting at particulars, at leaf flutters and wind changes, bird calls in the solemn evening woods. His poetic is that everything matters, everything is delicately threaded together, that some spiritual basting has made life whole and as poet he daily makes discovery of this fact: "No touch can find that thread, it is too small./Sometimes we think we learn its course –/through evidence no court allows/a sneeze may glimpse us Paradise" ("Connections"). In other words, Stafford is an antidote to a nervous nation, a moment of utter and tranquil passivity before life, a voice so calm in its spiritual reserves that it lulls any reader into a dreamy curiosity about his own life and surroundings. His poetry is opposed to aggression, to acquisitiveness, to ends and results: "Deaf to process, alive only to ends,/such are the thinkers around me, the logical ones –/... I would sweep the watch face, narrowing angles,/catching at things left here that are ours" ("It Is the Time You Think").

But Stafford has written five or six volumes of verse on this slender poetic, collected in

Stories That Could Be True, a size of canon contradictory to its modest intentions. The weakness of such quantity is that the trivial and particular cannot sustain an indefinite interest – and not all things under Stafford's pen connect to the spirit around them. Many poems are so flatly understated as to be wearying memoes and jots, words of habit not of inspiration. In *Stories That Could Be True*, the tranquil stream of language sets off an unlikely response – a longing for something awful to happen just to quicken reality. Occasionally the poetry tracts real eventfulness and his language handles it well. One of his best and most difficult poems is "With My Crowbar Key," with its macabre loneliness and maniacal passion: "When I see my town over sights of a rifle,/and carved by light/from the lowering sun,/then my old friends darken one by one."

In spite of sameness and occasional tedium, the competency of the verse is very high. Stafford has genius about him; there is in all this poetry his unique imprint, and numbers of poets have come to imitate his spiritual regionalism. The cold northwest winters, the silent deserts, the long vigils at windows all shape themselves as a Stafford experience. When he writes "I could hear the wilderness listen," we believe him. Even his most sermonizing verse has about it some unquestionably honest purpose. In the long run, most of his poetry will fade, but a core of magical lyrics about our daily lives will remain and represent him.

—Paul Christensen

STALLWORTHY, Jon (Howie). British. Born in London, 18 January 1935. Educated at Dragon School, 1940–48; Rugby School, Warwickshire, 1948–53; Magdalen College, Oxford (Newdigate Prize, 1958), 1955–59, B.A. 1958, B.Litt. 1961. Served in the Oxfordshire and Buckinghamshire Light Infantry, Royal West African Frontier Force, 1953–55. Married Gillian Waldcock in 1960; one daughter and two sons. Editor, Oxford University Press, London, 1959–71, and Clarendon Press, Oxford, 1972–74; Deputy Academic Publisher, Oxford University Press, Oxford, 1974–77. Since 1977, John Wendell Anderson Professor of English, Cornell University, Ithaca, New York. Visiting Fellow, All Souls College, Oxford, 1971–72. Recipient: Duff Cooper Memorial Award, 1974; Smith Literary Award, for non-fiction, 1975; E. M. Forster Award, 1976. Address: Long Farm, Elsfield Road, Old Marston, Oxford, England; or, 1456 Hanshaw Road, Ithaca, New York 14850, U.S.A.

PUBLICATIONS

Verse

The Earthly Paradise. Privately printed, 1958.
The Astronomy of Love. London, Oxford University Press, 1961.
Out of Bounds. London, Oxford University Press, 1963.
The Almond Tree. London, Turret, 1967.
A Day in the City. Exeter, Exeter Books, 1967.
Root and Branch. London, Chatto and Windus-Hogarth Press, and New York, Oxford University Press, 1969.
Positives. Dublin, Dolmen Press, 1969.
A Dinner of Herbs. Exeter, Rougemont Press, 1970.
Hand in Hand. London, Chatto and Windus-Hogarth Press, 1974.
The Apple Barrel: Selected Poems 1956–1963. London, Oxford University Press, 1974.

A Familiar Tree. London, Chatto and Windus-Oxford University Press, and New York, Oxford University Press, 1978.

Other

Between the Lines: Yeats's Poetry in the Making. Oxford, Clarendon Press, 1963.
Vision and Revision in Yeats's "Last Poems." Oxford, Clarendon Press, 1969.
Wilfred Owen. London, Chatto and Windus-Oxford University Press, 1974; New York, Oxford University Press, 1975.
Poets of the First World War. London, Oxford University Press, 1974.

Editor, *Yeats: Last Poems: A Casebook*. London, Macmillan, 1968; Nashville, Aurora, 1970.
Editor, with Seamus Heaney and Alan Brownjohn, *New Poems 1970–1971*. London, Hutchinson, 1971.
Editor, *The Penguin Book of Love Poetry*. London, Penguin, 1973; as *A Book of Love Poetry*, New York, Oxford University Press, 1974.

Translator, with Jerzy Peterkiewicz, *Five Centuries of Polish Poetry*, revised edition. London, Oxford University Press, 1970.
Translator, with Peter France, *The Twelve and Other Poems*, by Alexander Blok. London, Eyre and Spottiswoode, and New York, Oxford University Press, 1970; as *Selected Poems*, London, Penguin, 1974.

Critical Studies: "Playing with Words" by the author, in *Times Educational Supplement* (London), August 1976; Harry Marten, in *Contemporary Literature* (Madison, Wisconsin), Summer 1979.

Jon Stallworthy comments:

When a poet is asked to "make a statement" he should respond with a poem, but I am tongue-tied in police stations, so will echo Keats: "I am certain of nothing but the holiness of the heart's affection." The changing seasons of "the heart's affection" have prompted the best of the poems I have written since, at the age of seven, I set myself to learn how to make poems as a carpenter makes tables and chairs. I count myself a maker, and such other things as I have made with words – studies of Yeats "at work," translations of poems by Blok and Pasternak – have been made with one purpose in view: to learn how to make better poems. And what is a poem? When my daughter asked that question, I found my tongue:

A POEM IS
something that someone is saying
no louder, Pip, than my "goodnight" –
words with a tune, which outstaying
their speaker travel as far
as that amazing, vibrant light
from a long-extinguished star.

* * *

Jon Stallworthy is a quiet poet, a fastidious craftsman, whose talent did not reveal itself fully until the publication of his collection, *Root and Branch*. His earlier poems were carefully wrought, but lacked the individuality and style that are apparent in the looser but still controlled forms of *Root and Branch*.

The central poem in this collection is "The Almond Tree," which seeks to discover meaning in the agonizing event of the birth of a mongol son. Such poems are notoriously hard to write, and at the beginning this one achieves a rather high degree of success as it laconically describes the poet, unaware of disaster, driving to the hospital hoping for a son. Then it collapses into more contrived modes, ending with the bathetic "I have learnt that to live is to suffer,/to suffer is to live." Such a failure is, however, understandable: other more successful poems in the volume show that Stallworthy is capable of a more original brand of compassion when he writes less painfully near to the event. "A Poem about Poems about Vietnam" memorably attacks the glib ease of the "protest" poets: those killed in the conflict "whisper in their sleep/louder from underground than all/the mikes that were hung upon your lips/when you were at the Albert Hall." But one of Stallworthy's themes is compassion, concern for suffering, and in "Bread" he illustrates how concern can be meaningful: as he eats the bread for his breakfast he remembers

stick limbs and hunger-blown
bellies; the aftermath
of drought, flood flotsam, cyclone

fodder. And sawdust crams my mouth.

That is an admirable and convincing record of how anguish at that suffering from which one is removed by circumstance can be more than a mere emotion. Now that he has eschewed traditional formal strictness, Stallworthy seems to write better and more imaginatively. Sometimes the exquisiteness for which he strives seems to be dwarfed by the largeness of his subject – as in "War Song of the Embattled Finns 1939"; increasingly, however, the care of his writing and his almost imagistic talent for description match up to his subjects.

—Martin Seymour-Smith

STANFORD, Ann. American. Born in La Habra, California, 25 November 1916. Educated at Stanford University, California (Phelan Fellowship, 1938), B.A. 1938 (Phi Beta Kappa); University of California, Los Angeles, M.A. in journalism 1958, M.A. in English 1961, Ph.D. in English and American literature 1962. Married Roland Arthur White in 1942; three daughters and one son. Executive Secretary, 1957–58, Instructor in Journalism, 1958–59, and Poetry Workshop Instructor, 1960–61, University of California, Los Angeles. Assistant Professor, 1962–66, Associate Professor, 1966–68, and since 1968, Professor of English, San Fernando Valley State College, later California State University, Northridge. Editor, *Uclan Review*, Los Angeles, 1961–64; Co-Founding Editor, California State University Renaissance Editions; Member, Editorial Board, *Early American Literature*, 1971–73. Formerly, Poetry Reviewer, *Los Angeles Times*. Recipient: Yaddo Fellowship, 1957, 1967; Borestone Mountain Award, 1960; National Endowment for the Arts grant, 1967, 1974; Shelley Memorial Award, 1969; National Institute of Arts and Letters Award, 1972; Alice Fay di Castagnola Award, 1976. Address: 9550 Oak Pass Road, Beverly Hills, California 90210, U.S.A.

PUBLICATIONS

Verse

In Narrow Bound. Gunnison, Colorado, Swallow, 1943.

The White Bird. Denver, Swallow, 1949.
The Weathercock. San Jose, California, Talisman Press, 1956.
Magellan: A Poem to Be Read by Several Voices. San Jose, California, Talisman Press, 1958.
The Weathercock. New York, Viking Press, 1966.
The Descent. New York, Viking Press, 1970.
Climbing Up to Light. Los Angeles, Magpie Press, 1973.
In Mediterranean Air. New York, Viking Press, 1977.

Other

Anne Bradstreet, The Worldly Puritan: An Introduction to Her Poetry. New York, Burt Franklin, 1975.

Editor, *The Women Poets in English: An Anthology.* New York, McGraw Hill, 1972.

Translator, *The Bhagavad Gita: A New Verse Translation.* New York, Herder, 1970.

Critical Study: *Dives and Descents: Thematic Strategies in the Poetry of Adrienne Rich and Ann Stanford* by Polly Naoshire Chenoy, unpublished dissertation, Salt Lake City, University of Utah, 1975.

Ann Stanford comments:

I try to set down the inner experiences of human beings, especially their relationships to time and the world. The expression is by means of imagery drawn from the visible, especially the natural, scene. The verse forms vary from traditional metrical verse to free verse in long or short cadences.

* * *

Ann Stanford's poetry thrives in the realm of reverie, bordered by nightmare, "beset by spirits," whose voices reveal the world as a "sifting down of shadows." Objects, often classified, are seldom sharply defined; human actions, attended by larger forces, turn either febrile or hollow. Whatever comforts are presented bob along in a welter of surrender: though "sleepy and warm," in "Night Rain," she falls back to sleep where she can say, "I dream of the great horned owl/Snatching birds like plums out of trees." Inside the black ball of [her] mind," she protects the "one white thought," but it's unclear whether this is a node of joy or concentrated pain. Imagine the extreme situations of Sylvia Plath done over into the sensibility of H.D. and you have some of this poetry's texture: she invokes the "blessed dark that runs across the day" as an opening force.

Her method reveals through abstraction, and though she wants to "descend from ideal to actual touch," her motions are often upward. Upon descent, however, she discovers the "earth with all its destinies," and promise and threat take the shape of an unknown future buried in an immutable plan:

The noun
Is what is feared: to name the sly
Commotion of the blood which runs
Unplanned as leaves to their own ways.

Filled with earth and sky, kernel and shell, this poetry presents assured and limited returns – its horrors are all in the coming and going – but it lacks instantaneous images where accuracy might break open into ecstasy. A poetry of general nouns and basic verbs, its lyricism rides along on stores of emotion: "From the center of our body/Come the bright flowers." The main accomplishment here derives from a quiet honesty; it offers the sureness of craft and the surprises of self-possession. Her victories originate in her willingness to ignore the odds and keep watch at night. She shuns, to advantage, the ordinary and domestic subjects, but hasn't perhaps the complete frenzy to fathom the Blakean excesses; her language is her own, but she is too satisfied with it to complete her experiments. "Caught between never and now," she makes all she can of her patience and her predicament, and her ways are sufficiently beautiful.

—Charles Molesworth

STANLEY, George. American. Born in San Francisco, California, in 1934. Educated at San Francisco State College, B.A. 1969, M.A. 1971. Served in the United States Army, 1953–56. Recipient: National Endowment for the Arts grant, 1968. Address: 2504 York Street, Vancouver 9, British Columbia, Canada.

PUBLICATIONS

Verse

The Love Root. San Francisco, White Rabbit Press, 1958.
Tete Rouge/Pony Express Riders. San Francisco, White Rabbit Press, 1963.
Flowers. San Francisco, White Rabbit Press, 1965.
Beyond Love. San Francisco, Open Space-Dariel Press, 1968.
You: Poems 1957–67. Vancouver, New Star, 1974.
The Stick: Poems 1969–73. Vancouver, Talonbooks, 1974.

Geroge Stanley comments:

(1970) I feel like I can't imagine ever writing another poem and this is the way I usually feel when I feel anything about poetry – I want to distinguish feeling about poetry from compulsively thinking about it. I used to do a lot more of that than I do now. I used to hang on to being a "poet," as an identity. I don't do that now. I have written a few poems that I think are exciting and even beautiful; and I don't think that about much poetry of anyone's. These poems have usually come when I was least expecting them, and I got caught up in the excitement of bringing them into being.

Major influences on my work have been Virgil, Milton, Hopkins, Whitman, Crane, Ginsberg, Spicer and Duncan. A strong recent influence on my life and writing is Whitehead's *Process and Reality.*

(1974) I write a line or two of poetry in my journal from time to time (when I get caught off guard). I'm a poet – *force majeure* by now; if this is identity it's not easily extricable from anything I'd call being. It goes back a long way. But I don't identify with the identity as it has been historically conditioned – bourgeois poet – I don't shit on it either, only on poetasters, some evidence of how many of these there are is the size of your book. I am at present working with the *Western Organizer* newspaper in Vancouver and preparing to write a book on homosexuality and society.

* * *

George Stanley's poetry emerges significantly out of his relationship with Jack Spicer, whose poetics and poetry were a vital force in San Francisco's North Beach in the saloon-schoolrooms of the mid-1950's. Spicer's considerable impact as poet and teacher has not yet been properly evaluated. It is hoped a much clearer idea of his powers will be revealed in the long-awaited long-delayed collected and uncollected works (edited by Robin Blaser).

Stanley maintains a particular, tenacious, and individual voice in all his work. Each of his books is complete, self-contained, exemplary. Each book reveals a clear development and advancement of his abilities.

Though Stanley's work has "opened" in the past few years via extending control over the poem by expanding vocabulary and line, his work remains tightly-reined against excess. Like a juggler he knows the balances. The elegiac tone pervading much of the work is kept in check with a tough no-nonsense stance. It is George Stanley's intelligence and devotion to grace accomplished in the act of creation that sustain his work and make it of constant interest to the reader. His selected poems, *You*, should make Stanley's work more accessible to a larger audience.

—David Meltzer

STARBUCK, George (Edwin). American. Born in Columbus, Ohio, 15 June 1931. Educated at the California Institute of Technology, Pasadena, 1947–49; University of California, Berkeley, 1950–51; University of Chicago, 1954–57; Harvard University, Cambridge, Massachusetts, 1957–58. Served in the United States Army, 1952–54. Married 1) Janice King in 1955 (divorced, 1961); 2) Judith Luraschi in 1962 (divorced, 1968); 3) Kathryn Salyer in 1968; five children. Fiction Editor, Houghton Mifflin Company, Boston, 1958–61. Member of the English Department, State University of New York, Buffalo, 1963–64; Associate Professor, 1964–67, and Director, Writers Workshop, 1967–70, University of Iowa, Iowa City. Since 1971, Professor of English, Boston University. Recipient: Yale Series of Younger Poets Award, 1960; American Academy in Rome Fellowship, 1961, 1962; Guggenheim Fellowship, 1961. Address: Department of English, Boston University, Boston, Massachusetts 02215, U.S.A.

PUBLICATIONS

Verse

Bone Thoughts. New Haven, Connecticut, Yale University Press, 1960.
White Paper: Poems. Boston, Little Brown, 1966.
Three Sonnets. Iowa City, Windhover Press, n.d.
Elegy in a Country Church Yard. Boston, Pym Randall Press, 1975.
Desperate Measures. Boston, Godine, 1978.

Recording: *George Starbuck*, Carillon Records, 1960.

George Starbuck comments:

I have the American academic's common interest in common speech. Do I exchange gossip and advice with a set of peers? No. Am I proud of that? No.

Characterize my poems? In subject, obsessed by wars, religions, beautiful weird Americans, beautiful weird American talk. In impulse, utterly frivolous and formal. Put it this way: One of my poems is a 156-line acrostic in dactylic monometer, heavily alliterated. No poet in his right mind would attempt such a thing. Audiences tell me it's one of my most fluent and forceful and serious poems. What am I to do? For me, the long way round, through formalisms, word-games, outrageous conceits (the worst of what we mean by "wit") is the only road to truth. No other road *takes* me. Put it another way: Rather than chisel away at the rock of language, hoping to leave the world an Easter present of great stone Truths, I dump the rock, a piece at a time, into acid. The acid is brute, arbitrary, simple: this it eats, this it rejects. But find the right acid, and suddenly the rock will, of itself, yield up a whole shaped world – a world I *could not have known* was there. Lovely complexity of fact, of the pre-existent. Fossils, yes. How do you bring them to light? Not by regarding the language as bland *medium* for your own exquisite machinations. Not by chiseling at it. By genuine *experiment* on it – the putterer's destructive prank. Some writers' lives are a search for the philosopher's stone. My search is for *aqua regia*. Not *aqua fortis*.

None of your lesser "acid." Against marble, rhyme. Shakespeare had the idea. Rhyme, pun, palindrome – whatever may do violence *enough* to the shapes we think we have already given Truth. Put it yet another: *Conscious* slavery to the language. The only alternatives are unconscious slavery, or the sainthood of the wholly silent. And if the slave still merely grumbles and wisecracks under his breath, if he shies from the full fervor of insurrection, at least he will know whose fault and choice it is.

Affinities? My great admirations are for Frost, Auden, Hopkins, Dylan Thomas, Merwin, Plath – all lovers of the spoken English sentence, all but the first two fascinated with both the syntax and the metaphysics of metaphor. But who to *lump* me with? Wilbur? Dugan? Hecht? Hollander? A lesser, drearier catalog of names? How does a poet know? James Wright never glommed onto an ounce of Frost's tone or sense or way with American speech, until after he thought he had broken with Frost as a model.

Important experience? Majoring in mathematics at CalTech. Studying the standard textbooks of 1950: Brooks and Warren, O. Williams' anthologies. More recently, winning a long legal battle for free speech in the State University of New York, and in the process realizing that maybe I had never, myself, hazarded in public a truly difficult, unpopular, or dangerous truth. (See "truth" again. I love to bandy bad words.)

* * *

George Starbuck has been for more than a decade a consistently enjoyable poet. His first volume, *Bone Thoughts*, reached, for poetry, a very large audience, which is not hard to understand when one takes into account his technical prowess alone, little short of spectacular, with rhyme, meter, alliteration, etc., deployed as practically nowhere else. If the poet gives the impression that he has done all the homework, his craft sits lightly, and as in the following lines from the second of "Three Dreams on a Warm Sabbath," metrically so dexterous, one finds something of his by now well-known wryness:

> Here is the peak of pressure, here of heat,
> here the descending tension in the feet,
> and here we have the computed muscle-tone.
> The moment, you notice, passes and is gone,
> and if the observer's eye should blink, is lost....

Wit, even when forced by a poet like George Starbuck to do its own serious work, is today more derogated than ever before, partly as the result of the high value placed on directness and depth of involvement, and his type is often perfunctorily labeled academic, even when writing, as the poet does in "Communication to the City Fathers of Boston," on a subject to tax the gifts of the most direct of involved responders:

When New York mushrooms into view, when Boston's
townspeople, gathered solemnly in basements,
feel on their necks the spiderwebs of bombsights,
when subway stations clot and fill like beesnests
making a honey-heavy moan, whose business
will it be then to mourn, to take a busman's
holiday from his death, to weep for Boston's?

Yet *Bone Thoughts* did have its share of the kind of skilful set pieces common to American verse in the 1950's, and those interested enough in the poet – and there were many – to await his second volume with anticipation, must have had doubts about his ability to adjust to a very different poetic mood in the mid-1960's. *White Paper*, the poet's second volume, did not disappoint, for if in *Bone Thoughts* he could write on the subject of war so jazzy a piece as "War Story," whose first stanza goes:

The 4th of July he stormed a nest.
He won a ribbon but lost his chest.
We threw his arms across the rest
    And kneed him in the chin.
    (You knee them in the chin
    To drive the dog-tag in.)

in *White Paper* the response to the threats of the time, not to speak of a new war, larger and more ominous than many thought possible, was sombre and very moving. The book contains at least two such poems, "Poem Issued by Me to Congressmen ..." and "Of Late," among the strongest of their type ever done by an American. Here is the first stanza of the latter:

"Stephen Smith, University of Iowa sophomore, burned what
  he said was his draft card."
And Norman Morrison, Quaker, of Baltimore, Maryland,
  Burned what he said was himself.
You Robert McNamara, burned what you said was a
  concentration
of the enemy aggressor.
No news medium troubled to put it in quotes.

The poet's craftsmanship rose, in *White Paper*, to the occasion offered by a conscience directly involved in a burning world, and the achievement was and continues to be of a very high order.

—Lucien Stryk

STEAD, C(hristian) K(arlson). New Zealander. Born in Auckland, 17 October 1932. Educated at Mount Albert Grammar School; Auckland University, B.A. 1954, M.A. (honours) 1955; Bristol University (Michael Hiatt Baker Scholar), Ph.D. 1961. Married Kathleen Elizabeth Roberts in 1955; two daughters and one son. Lecturer in English, University of New England, New South Wales, 1956–57. Member of the Department, 1960–69, and since 1969, Professor of English, Auckland University. Chairman, New Zealand Literary Fund, 1973–75. Recipient: Poetry Awards Incorporated prize (U.S.A.),

1955; Readers Award (*Landfall*, Christchurch), 1959; Katherine Mansfield Award, for fiction and for essay, 1960, and Fellowship, 1972; Nuffield Travelling Fellowship, 1965; Jessie Mackay Award, 1972; National Book Award, 1975. Address: 37 Tohunga Crescent, Parnell, Auckland 1, New Zealand.

PUBLICATIONS

Verse

Whether the Will Is Free: Poems 1954–62. Auckland, Paul's Book Arcade, 1964.
Crossing the Bar. Auckland, Auckland University Press–Oxford University Press, 1972.
Quesada: Poems 1972–1974. Auckland, The Shed, 1975.
Walking Westward. Auckland, The Shed, 1978.

Novel

Smith's Dream. Auckland, Longman Paul, 1971.

Other

The New Poetic: Yeats to Eliot. London, Hutchinson, 1964; New York, Harper, 1966.

Editor, *New Zealand Short Stories: Second Series.* London and Wellington, Oxford University Press, 1966.
Editor, *Measure for Measure: A Casebook.* London, Macmillan, 1971.
Editor, *The Letters and Journals of Katherine Mansfield: A Selection.* London, Allen Lane, 1977.

Critical Studies: by James Bertram, in *Islands 2* (Christchurch), 1972; Peter Crisp, in *New Argot* (Auckland), 1975; Rob Jackaman, in *Landfall 114* (Christchurch), 1975.

C. K. Stead comments:

I am always troubled that I can't write more poems than I do, that although I am a fairly conscientious and hard-working person, the Muse will not warm to these virtues, in fact, seems bored by them. I don't take the view that poets who write more than I do are less demanding of themselves; that "more means worse." I envy their fluency and still hope one day to learn the trick.

Reviewers tell me (with an emphasis that varies, of course, from approval to disapproval) that my poems are disciplined. This seems to suggest labour, conscious effort, self-control – all the qualities that go (for example) into my critical prose. But for me the discipline by which poems are achieved is quite different and still something I don't properly understand. I have to step out of the world in which I fill various roles (critic, professor, committee member, family man, etc.) and in which the clock rules. I have to sink back into myself to a point where all the trappings, all the things that are accidental, are lost. Then what is dredged up will sometimes seem worth polishing and putting on display.

Although I have on one occasion worked a poem into being through literally hundreds of drafts (an experience which was itself a kind of "possession," and not at all pleasant) it is usually true for me that hard labour doesn't help, and that Keats's dictum holds: "If poetry come not as naturally as the leaves to the tree it might as well not come at all." To be in that rare state where poetry comes naturally is for me the greatest felicity. I am always afraid that it will never happen again.

I am a self-regarding younger son. My natural tone is secure but not definitive. I am a liberal, fitted neither for moralising nor for command. But when I am able to dig deep enough I discover another self who (though not very likable) is perhaps the best of the poet in me. I conceive of this person as German, romantic, authoritarian, detached yet full of passion, above all a musician. To learn that a poet I admire (Yeats, for instance, or the New Zealander James K. Baxter) could not sing in tune shocks me almost to disbelief.

When I write poetry I very often have in mind the image of a place; and whatever the subject or "approach" of the poem, that image will carry through into the final form. But I also have the feeling that if a poem is merely personal it may be trivial; and I often catch myself, in the process of writing, nudging the personal vision towards some kind of general or public utterance.

In my earlier poems influences are clearly apparent but I don't think I am much influenced any longer by other poets. For better or worse, I seem to have found my own form. Though I still write occasionally in formal stanzas, more often I find myself writing a cluster of short pieces, all springing out of one mood, one experience, one preoccupation, which together make up the poem. I like to write with as little punctuation as possible, accommodating line-length and syntax to one another in a free-flowing verse-sentence in which words echo one another and the pauses and runs of sound parallel the sense.

To be invited to write about oneself is, of course, a trap. What can a poet say about his own work except that he does the best he can and that he hopes someone else will enjoy it?

* * *

In 1965 C. K. Stead named Truth, Generosity, and Delight as the qualities which he would like his poems to manifest, although in such a way that the three would not readily be separable. His idea of Truth, of "responses to occasions" and of fidelity to experience which cannot presume to think itself total but may justly be selective, wants to be more than simply honest. His poems should be true as long as they recognise that poetry serves "Art before Principle, because Art serves the world which Principle admonishes."

Stead later qualified this view. The importance of Principle increased, intensified, under the influence of more resolute political commitment prompted by Vietnam, to inform poems (Stead refers to the poems of the first section of his *Crossing the Bar*) with a troubled and indignant or outraged sense of the inhumanity of men, the irresponsible reductiveness of those for whom responsibility was properly their occupation. The poems are inclined to be shortlined, declarative, direct. Their tensions are of patently different orders from those of *Whether the Will Is Free* and in the matter of tension as such as well as in such ploys as regarding Washington as a latecome Rome he may be reflecting one whom he did not name as an influence in his 1970 statement for the first edition of *Contemporary Poets*. That is, Allen Tate.

Stead's poems of protest are naturally enough concerned with intimations of the consequence of power politics, particularly the denial of identity and individual right. "Anonymous" or "anonymity" are words which his reader has to register. Vexatious questioning of identity is old hat but a continuing business. It is also to be affirmed as a matter of Principle, but as principle is affirmed through the means of the art. The second qualification to Stead's 1965 view may be traced in an article on James K. Baxter's later poems, the *Jerusalem Sonnets*. In Baxter's sonnets Stead found an eminent value, "their creation of a personality ... a heightened sense of life." He went on to talk about "the world fresh to our awakening senses."

Increasingly Stead's poetry has moved to the cultivation of personality, to assert a heightened sense of life threatened by the devious contrivings of men of affairs and the unpredictability of everyday accident (a smashed car, a neck broken while swimming), and fresh awakenings to the possibilities of whatever part of the world in which his poems find their scenes, which are now very varied indeed. The scenes, the occasions, and Stead's technical resources along with them are at this date astonishingly varied. In the 1950's he was accomplished, resourceful, but fairly conservative. His "Pictures in a Gallery Undersea" which put to work his expertise in the New Poetic, is an accomplished suite which readers have seen as a tribute to Eliot but which Stead himself regards as more of a tribute to Pound. The success of "Pictures" made him more confident. He extended his range, in forms, in tonalities, in personae. He produced more poems than before and while not as prolific, say, as Baxter, the indications are that his output is still increasing and likely to continue that way. He has enhanced the facts, the Truth, of his poems by splendidly marrying the occasions, his feelings (which may be rich and complex) and his formidable intelligence and delighting ingenuities.

When Professor Stead wrote about John Mulgan (in *Islands 7*) he subtitled his article "A Question of Identity." The first part of that article is about Stead identifying with places known to John Mulgan when young, and how Mulgan became part of the making of Stead. In the same issue Stead published a set of poems under the title, "Scoria" which in parts connect with or overlap with scenes of Mulgan's childhood. Literature in a place, or the placing of literature as part of the process of identifying and finding identity, is an apparent impulse. Throughout his career he has returned to enquire into and effectively to reorganise his own past. "Only what lies behind" he said years ago "falls into shape." "Scoria" seeks out shapes of childhood, events of childhood, stories of its places, and along with these makes an unprecedented (for Stead) use of early New Zealand writers. It is a sustained exercise in recovery and discovery, in which again part of the discovery is finding appropriate forms, and one remembers Allen Tate once more, saying "The form is the meaning."

In "Scoria" and in the varieties of his last two books C. K. Stead's control scarcely falters. If it was true at one time that his poetry was shifting from comment on experience to being direct experience it is also true that in moving to kinds of directness and more kinds of experience he has changed the substantial reality with which experience (as reported) is concerned. His reality now encompasses an active sense of the mythological and to have that in play is to give a fresh vitality to Truth, Generosity, and Delight.

—Kendrick Smithyman

STEPANCHEV, Stephen. American. Born in Mokrin, Yugoslavia, 30 January 1915. Educated at the University of Chicago, A.B. 1937 (Phi Beta Kappa), M.A. 1938; New York University, Ph.D. 1950. Served as a Lieutenant in the United States Army, 1941–45: Bronze Star. Instructor in English, Purdue University, Lafayette, Indiana, 1938–41; New York University, 1946–47, 1948–49. Member of the English Department, 1949–64, and since 1964, Professor of English, Queens College, Flushing, New York, Fulbright Professor of American Literature, University of Copenhagen, Spring 1957. Recipient: Society of Midland Authors Prize (*Poetry*, Chicago), 1937; National Endowment for the Arts grant, 1968. Address: Department of English, Queens College, Flushing, New York 11367, U.S.A.

PUBLICATIONS

Verse

Three Priests in April. Baltimore, Contemporary Poetry, 1956.
Spring in the Harbor. Flushing, New York, Amity Press, 1967.
Vietnam. Los Angeles, Black Sparrow Press, 1968.
A Man Running in the Rain. Los Angeles, Black Sparrow Press, 1969.
The Mind. Los Angeles, Black Sparrow Press, 1972.

The Mad Bomber. Los Angeles, Black Sparrow Press, 1972.
Mining the Darkness. Los Angeles, Black Sparrow Press, 1975.
Medusa and Others. Los Angeles, Black Sparrow Press, 1975.
The Dove in the Acacia (bilingual edition, translations by Rasa Popov). Vrsac, Yugoslavia, KOV, 1977.
What I Own. Santa Barbara, California, Black Sparrow Press, 1978.

Other

American Poetry since 1945: A Critical Survey. New York, Harper, 1965.

* * *

A New York poet-professor, Stephen Stepanchev writes lucid, urbane poems which depict dream- or city-scapes, remember parents or childhood, recount quarrels with a lover, or observe a fellow-victim of life with sympathy. Mostly they're first-person poems and usually the speaker is a wry detached observer: "The telephone squatted all day/In the equilibrium of indifference./No one called that wrong number,/Me, poking among dead men's words" ("A Visit"). The poems rely for their energy on a rapid montage of images, rendered in a succession of simple declarative sentences without much rhythmic intensity (like much current image-centered poetry, they might well be translations). The images are usually clever, seldom memorable. "November withdraws like a junkie," he writes, or "I was of two minds, like traffic," or "I live in the rice paddies of my desperation": one registers the effect, admires the invention, and passes on unmoved. Sometimes one cannot even admire: "Yesterday I poured gasoline all over myself/And flamed like a monk/To move you" seems both lurid and unpleasantly exploitative. Still, the general effect is an agreeable one, well represented by the following complete poem from *The Mad Bomber*, called "In the Gallery":

Repetition makes a garden,
But these roses are, clearly, unemployed.
Nature does so much better than this painter
I am expected to admire. My attention
Wanders to a gallery guest whose hair
Is a lair of lights, whose face dreams
Like a wheat field, and whose eyes glisten
With tears induced by her contact lenses.
I mix her in my martini and drink
Her down at the window overlooking the East
River, where the moon is breaking up in shivers.

—Seamus Cooney

STEPHENS, Alan (Archer). American. Born in Greeley, Colorado, 19 December 1925. Educated at the University of Colorado, Boulder, 1946–48; University of Denver, Colorado, A.B., M.A. 1950; Stanford University, California; University of Missouri, Columbia, Ph.D. 1954. Served in the United States Army Air Force, 1943–45. Married Frances Jones in 1948; three sons. Assistant Professor of English, Arizona State University, Tempe, 1954–58. Assistant Professor, 1959–63, Associate Professor, 1963–67, and since 1967, Professor of English, University of California, Santa Barbara. Recipient: Swallow Press New Poetry Series Award, 1957. Address: 326 Canon Drive, Santa Barbara, California 93105, U.S.A.

PUBLICATIONS

Verse

The Sum. Denver, Swallow, 1958.
Between Matter and Principle. Denver, Swallow, 1963.
The Heat Lightning. Brunswick, Maine, Bowdoin College Museum of Art, 1967.
Tree Meditation and Others. Chicago, Swallow Press, 1970.
White River Poems. Chicago, Swallow Press, 1975.

Other

Editor, *Selected Poems*, by Barnaby Googe. Denver, Swallow, 1961.

Alan Stephens comments:

I caught my share of the academic influenzas of the late '40's and early '50's. As for style, themes, and all that: I used to write like this:

Heavily from the shadeless plain to the river
The bull slants down and bends his head to draw
Bright water in, that goes unbroken ever.

But now I write like this –

– suppose that the words came in
the way a flight of blackbirds
I once watched entered a tree
in the winter twilight:
finding places for themselves
quickly along the bare branches
they settled into their singing
for the time.

* * *

Alan Stephens is a nature poet. Up to this time, his main interest has been to render nature faithfully, but as a realization of a meditative response which answers to the sensibility in natural objects. He seeks an effect similar to that of Wordsworth's early "Influence of Natural Objects." Stephens has remarked about his own poems that they are "descriptive meditations rather than meditative descriptions...." To this end he wishes his poetry naked, the form invariably open, the expression spare. His utterances are, however, either clipped directions, like a dramatist's for the settling of scenes, or discursive meanderings, too often simple only for being denuded of figurative speech. Hence, from "A Breath," a stanza of this sort:

A quiet, cool, spring morning –
the sun up, and its light
crossing things without emphasis,
merely bringing out the pale colors.

Of course, the limitations of this manner are sometimes quite successfully accommodated to a larger context, as in "Home Rock."

While society and socially conscious or sophisticated speech are almost entirely absent from Stephens' quiet poetry, his work is effective in those instances where domestic man is projected against a natural backdrop. In such cases, he usually works with a motif of black and white, of darkness and tenuously comforting light. Meditating on the omnivorous incursion of dark space even into his own beard, the speaker of "To Fran" achieves this minimal consolation:

> it must be we belong in it – at once remotely
> and intimately; the way a sheepherder's fire at night belongs
> in the distance on a desert upland.

And returning from the moonlit night and "the black shadow of the house," the speaker of "Sounds" reports that: "I go back in, and hunch over/The familiar hiss of my pencil tip/ Racing across the lighted page."

—David M. Heaton

STEPHENS, Meic. Welsh. Born in Pontypridd, Glamorgan, 23 July 1938. Educated at University College of Wales, Aberystwyth and Bangor, A.B. (honours) in French; University of Rennes, France, Diolôme de Langue et de Littérature Française. Married Ruth Wynn Meredith in 1965; three daughters. French Master, Ebbw Vale Grammar School, 1962–66; Director, Triskel Press, Merthyr Tydfil, Glamorgan, 1962–67. Founding Editor, *Poetry Wales*, 1965–73; Staff Journalist, *Western Mail*, Cardiff, 1966–67. Since 1967, Assistant Director, then Literature Director, Welsh Arts Council. Address: 9 Museum Place, Cardiff CF1 3NX, Wales.

PUBLICATIONS

Verse

Triad: Thirty-Three Poems, with Peter Gruffydd and Harri Webb. Merthyr Tydfil, Glamorgan, Triskel Press, 1963.
Exiles All. Swansea, Christopher Davies, 1973.

Other

Linguistic Minorities in Western Europe. Llandysul, Dyfed, Gomer, 1976.

Editor, with John Stuart Williams, *The Lilting House: An Anthology of Anglo-Welsh Poetry, 1917–1967.* London, Dent, and Llandybie, Dyfed, Christopher Davies, 1969.
Editor, *Artists in Wales.* Llandysul, Dyfed, Gomer, 3 vols., 1971–77.
Editor, *The Welsh Language Today.* Llandysul, Dyfed, Gomer, 1973.
Editor, *A Reader's Guide to Wales: A Selected Bibliography.* London, National Book League, 1973.
Editor, with Peter Finch, *Green Horse: Young Poets of Wales.* Swansea, Christopher Davies, 1978.
Editor, *The Arts in Wales 1950–75.* Cardiff, Welsh Arts Council, 1979.

* * *

Meic Stephens has been primarily concerned in recent years with the problem of explaining, through his poetry, the predicament of many of his compatriots in Wales who feel themselves to be "exiled," emotionally and intellectually, from their proper Welsh heritage. Brought up English-speaking and learning Welsh as an adult, he is well aware of this condition – not only in his own country but elsewhere in Europe. His deep-rooted social commitment is made vivid by the convincing detail embedded in his "nationalist" poems and those to do with memories of a dwindling valley community. He has also done much as an editor of commendable severity, and as a small publisher, for writers of talent and promise.

His own poems are extremely well-made; he writes sparingly and produces perhaps three or four a year. He is a meticulous craftsman, even if some of his images tend to be a trifle threadbare, tired, and banal, coming perilously near cliché. One of his best, in my view, is a sonnet about Christmas 1968 when the major Welsh-language poet, Gwenallt Jones, died, with his fragment of prayer for his daughters:

may they belong
to Wales as he did, cherishing most of all
his faith, his language and his living song.

Predictions are dangerous, but one feels that Stephens's mark in the future, providing he develops at the pace he has been keeping, could well be made as a continuous explorer of this "spiritual homelessness" among a large segment of his people. A stoic, not easily given to rose-tinted illusion, he possesses the necessary credentials and could bring the right unsentimental and unromantic approach to the task.

—John Tripp

STERN, Gerald. American. Born in Pittsburgh, Pennsylvania, 22 February 1925. Educated at the University of Pittsburgh, B.A. 1947; Columbia University, New York, M.A. 1949. Served in the United States Army Air Corps. Married Patricia Miller in 1952; one daughter and one son. Instructor, Temple University, Philadelphia, 1957–63; Professor, Indiana University of Pennsylvania, Indiana, 1963–67. Since 1968, Professor, Somerset County College, Somerville, New Jersey. Visiting Poet, Sarah Lawrence College, Bronxville, New York, 1977; Visiting Professor, University of Pittsburgh, 1978. Since 1973, Consultant in Poetry, Pennsylvania Arts Council, Harrisburg. Recipient: National Endowment for the Arts grant, 1976; Lamont Poetry Selection Award, 1977. Address: Box 207-A, R.D. 4, Easton, Pennsylvania 18042, U.S.A.

PUBLICATIONS

Verse

The Naming of Beasts and Other Poems. West Branch, Iowa, Cummington Press, 1973.
Rejoicings. Fredericton, New Brunswick, Fiddlehead, 1973.
Lucky Life. Boston, Houghton Mifflin, 1977.

Gerald Stern comments:

If I could choose one poem of mine to explain my stance, or my artistic position, it would be "The One Thing in Life," which appears in *Lucky Life*. In this poem I stake out a place for myself, so to speak, that was overlooked or ignored or disdained, a place no-one else wanted. I mean this in a psychological and metaphorical and philosophical sense. The poem is short, so I'll quote it:

Wherever I go now I lie down on my own bed of straw
and bury my face in my own pillow.
I can stop in any city I want to
and pull the stiff blanket up to my chin.
It's easy now, walking up a flight of carpeted stairs
and down a hall past the painted fire doors.
It's easy bumping my knees on a rickety table
and bending down to a tiny sink.
There is a sweetness buried in my mind;
there is water with a small cave behind it;
there's a mouth speaking Greek.
It is what I keep to myself; what I return to;
the one thing that no one else wanted.

When I think about the place "no-one else wanted," I think of an abandoned or despised area; I think of weeds, a ruin, a desert; but I think of these things not as remote in time or place from that which is familiar and cherished and valuable – our civilization – but as things which lie just under the surface and just out of eyesight; and I think especially of the dynamic and ironic interpenetration of the two. Thus, my poetry is concerned a great deal with opposites, city–country, present–past, civilization–savagery, powerful–weak, well-known–obscure, and it often dualistic in nature, though it is not informed, in any formal sense, by a philosophical or religious principle of dualism. (I clearly favor the "weaker" of the two, but I have affection for both.) Ultimately the "abandoned place" is a state of mind, or an energy-state, or condition, that is within me and I merely am reaching out for "examples" to approximate this state.

Another aspect of the poetry is that of rebirth or regeneration. A great many of my poems are concerned with rebirth and I find that the spring season, the time of rebirth, and those holidays and celebrations, religious and otherwise, that relate to rebirth are important in my poems: "God of Rain, God of Water" and "The Sensitive Knife" from *Lucky Life* and "In Kovalchick's Garden" and "The Blessed" from *Rejoicings*.

I have been living for the last ten years on the Delaware River, near Easton, Pennsylvania, less than two hours away from Philadelphia or New York City. I find myself spending a lot of time in the city, and writing about it, as well as in the country, and I find that the relationship of these two is an embodiment of my underlying myth, so that I am living my life symbolically even as I live it literally. Thus when I write of the literal I am simultaneously writing "symbolically," and the language, which is precise and descriptive, takes on overtones and layers. Several critics, confused by my exact and literal observations (insofar as what I was describing was not common knowledge), mistakenly described me as a surrealist poet.

I find, especially recently, that I am moved a great deal by Jewish mysticism and Chasidism, but I am not unaware that these are parts of huge historical systems that involve commitments and obligations and that I am in a sense "tasting" from the banquet of Judaism those delicacies that suit me. I do believe, though, that even if I don't practice the ritual, I realize, whether I mention him specifically or not, the lot of the Jew in history, and embody him, and his spirit, in my poems.

I have discovered that my poetry is prized because it comes so much to life orally and I have discovered that I am a success as a "reader." I put it this way because I did not start off intending my poems to be part of the "oral revolution" of recent American poetry. I believe my poems stand by themselves on the page, but I am delighted, also, to find how well they work "out loud."

I'm not sure who my precursors are, who has influenced me the most. I am delighted to live in an age without masters.

* * *

Gerald Stern's deeply felt poetry is written in the "confessional" mode, practiced by such other contemporary poets as Ginsberg and Ferlinghetti, and in company with them he continues the American romantic tradition of Walt Whitman with its emphasis upon the writer himself as contemporary everyman and its celebration of place. But Stern uses his narrative and emotional self-portraiture to create a uniquely detailed central figure or speaker, and his America is rendered with Biblical intensity and a Judaic sense of time and loss.

Van Gogh, "Against the Whirling Lines,/Small and powerful in the hands of the Blue God" ("Self-Portrait"), becomes a vivid counterpart figure for Stern himself as wanderer and artist. But as Stern travels in his own personal landscape the journeys are usually return journeys and the places visited effaced by time. "Straus Park," with its specific references, is an especially vivid example:

> If you know about the Babylonian Jews
> coming back to their stone houses in Jerusalem...
> then you must know how I felt when I saw Stanley's Cafeteria
> boarded up and the sale sign out.

"On the Island," "Four Sad Poems on the Delaware," and "County Line Road" present similar time metaphors in rural settings, and Stern brings both the rural and urban aspects of his world together in "One Foot in the River": "Going to New York I carry the river in my head/and match it with the flow on 72nd Street and the flow on Broadway."

Like Whitman and the poets of the "Beat Generation," Stern makes considerable use of repetition for rhetorical effect. But the repetitions work in other ways as well. In the central poem "Lucky Life" they emphasize an ironic optimism and the importance of a survival without illusion, but a survival enhanced by tradition and by the recurring rituals of everyday life. The return journeys are, of course, repetitions also. And the final lines of "Let Me Please Look into My Window" seem to summarize Stern's view of all such wanderings: "Let me wake up happy, let me know where I am, let me lie still,/as we turn left, as we cross the water, as we leave the light."

—Gaynor F. Bradish

STEVENS, Peter. Canadian. Born in Manchester, Lancashire, England, 17 November 1927. Educated at Nottingham University, B.A. (honours) in English, Cert. Ed., 1951; McMaster University, Hamilton, Ontario, M.A., 1964; University of Saskatchewan, Saskatoon, Ph.D. 1968. Married; three children. Chairman of the English Department, Hillfield College, Hamilton, Ontario, 1957–64; Lecturer, Extension Division, McMaster University, 1961–64; Assistant Professor of English, University of Saskatchewan, 1964–69. Since 1969, Associate Professor of English, University of Windsor, Ontario. Recipient: Canada Council Award, 1969. Address: 2055 Richmond Street, Windsor, Ontario N8Y 1L3, Canada.

PUBLICATIONS

Verse

Plain Geometry. Toronto, Ganglia Press, 1968.
Nothing But Spoons. Montreal, Delta Canada, 1969.
A Few Myths. Vancouver, Talonbooks, 1971.
Breadcrusts and Glass. Fredericton, New Brunswick, Fiddlehead, 1972.
Family Feelings and Other Poems. Guelph, Ontario, Alive Press, 1974.
Momentary Stay. London, Ontario, Killaly Press, 1974.
And the Dying Sky Like Blood. Ottawa, Borealis Press, 1974.
The Bogman Pavese Tactics. Fredericton, New Brunswick, Fiddlehead, 1977.

Other

Modern English-Canadian Poetry: A Guide to Information Sources. Detroit, Gale, 1978.

Editor, *The McGill Movement: A. J. M. Smith, F. R. Scott, and Leo Kennedy.* Toronto, Ryerson Press, 1969.
Editor, with J. L. Granatstein, *Forum: Canadian Life and Letters 1920–1970: Selections from "The Canadian Forum."* Toronto, University of Toronto Press, 1972.

Manuscript Collection: University of Saskatchewan, Saskatoon.

Peter Stevens comments:

I deal with the local landscape and places: the prairie, its place in my own personal and family life, its past, its geologic history, its "mythology." I write usually in free verse paragraphs and have experimented with some concrete forms: a method of using anagrams I call Anagrammatics. General influences are simply Canada and being Canadian – Canadian writers I admire and whose work has probably made an impression on mine are Al Purdy and Earle Birney. I admire the technical facility of Auden and early Ezra Pound. I have paid attention to the North American-ness of W. C. Williams, particularly as it emerges in a Canadian manner in the poetry of W. W. E. Ross and Raymond Souster.

* * *

Peter Stevens is a poet who reflects the immigrant experience. Coming to Canada from Britain, he brought a poetic sensibility influenced by the low-toned writing of the English 1950's. That sensibility has since been modified by Canadian experience, and the result is a manner that is undramatic, deliberately uncolourful, but – rather like an early spring landscape in the Prairies where Stevens spent much of his time in Canada – slowly revealing subtleties of perception and tone, pleasing gradations in the range of grey and brown. Generally speaking, there is little metaphorical or adjectival colour in Stevens' poems; the images are meant to speak dryly for themselves, as in the opening lines of "Fuschia":

> blood drops belled
> hanging in hedges
> above the bay curved
> under cliffs I remember
> an island in my past ...

or in "Seeing Is Seeing Is Believing in Poetry":

A stalker lurches across the snow.
His shadow stretches inhuman long
across snow's glistening crust of ice.

A rabbit sits stark still, then spurts away
to black trees, dark lines blacker on the white,
as this dense shadow slides into his eye.

All I see is rabbit flashing into shadows
away from stealthy shadow: no comment.
The eye does not speak, it does not think....

The poems I have quoted come from *Breadcrusts and Glass*, one of the best of Stevens' several small books. They show his sharp, thoughtful perception of the natural world; other poems show him equally sharply aware of the anomalies and frustrations of the plastic life, and here emerges an ironic, almost acerbic view of the self, and, at times, a curious questioning consciousness of literature as pretension.

—George Woodcock

STEVENSON, Anne. American. Born in Cambridge, England, 3 January 1933. Educated at University High School, Ann Arbor, Michigan, 1947–50; University of Michigan, Ann Arbor (Hopwood Award, 1951, 1952, 1954), B.A. 1954 (Phi Beta Kappa), M.A. 1962; Radcliffe Institute, Cambridge, Massachusetts, 1970–71. Married 1) R. L. Hitchcock in 1955 (divorced), one daughter; 2) Mark Elvin in 1962 (divorced), two sons. School Teacher, Lillesden School, Kent, 1955–56, Westminster School, Georgia, 1959–60, and Cambridge School, Massachusetts, 1961–62; Advertising Manager, A. and C. Black, publishers, London, 1956–57; Tutor, Department of Extra-Mural Studies, University of Glasgow, 1970–73; Counsellor, Open University, Paisley, Renfrew, 1972–73; Writing Fellow, University of Dundee, 1973; Fellow, Lady Margaret Hall, Oxford, 1975–77; Writer-in-Residence, Bulmershe College of Higher Education, Reading, 1977–78. Since 1978, Co-Editor, *Other Poetry* magazine and Mid-Day Publications, both in Oxford. Recipient: Scottish Arts Council bursary, 1973, and award, 1974. Member, Royal Society of Literature, 1978. Address: c/o Oxford Area Arts Council, 40 George Street, Oxford 0X1 2AQ, England.

PUBLICATIONS

Verse

Living in America. Ann Arbor, Michigan, Generation Press, 1965.
Reversals. Middletown, Connecticut, Wesleyan University Press, 1969.
Correspondences: A Family History in Letters. Middletown, Connecticut, Wesleyan University Press, and London, Oxford University Press, 1974.
Travelling Behind Glass: Selected Poems 1963–1973. London, Oxford University Press, 1974.
A Morden Tower Reading 3. Newcastle upon Tyne, Morden Tower, 1977.
Cliff Walk. Richmond, Surrey, Keepsake Press, 1977.
Enough of Green. London, Oxford University Press, 1977.

Plays

Radio Plays: *Correspondences*, 1975; *Child of Adam*, 1976.

Other

Elizabeth Bishop. New York, Twayne, 1966.

Critical Studies: by Dorothy Donnelly, in *Michigan Quarterly Review* (Ann Arbor), Fall 1966 and April 1971; Jay Parini, in *Lines Review 50* (Edinburgh), September 1974, and in *Ploughshares* (Cambridge), Autumn 1978.

Anne Stevenson comments:

Verse that is controlled, finely wrought, passionate, and true has a chance of being poetry. It is the felt truth, the authenticity of a poem that moves you. As I grow older I have less and less time for "literature" and the vast growth of "criticism" that flourishes on that sad soil. Fiction has taught me to write poetry. I am indebted to Ursula Le Guin, Angela Carter, Peter Redgrove, among moderns; their imaginations outstrip my own. To Emily Dickinson, Robert Frost, Elizabeth Bishop, and the Scots poet G. F. Dutton I owe the beginnings of a vision of life which I hope I have made my own. But it is, of course, to life itself and my experience of it that I owe the few real poems I have written.

* * *

"We were the very landscape/We walked through," Anne Stevenson wrote in her first volume, *Living in America*. The correspondence of physical and moral landscapes has recurred throughout her work, whether the "Landscape without regrets" of the Sierra Nevada (*Reversals*), the modest frugality of Cambridge and the Fens, or, most recently, the isolation and asperity of the North-East coast of Scotland, which is the setting for most of the poems in *Enough of Green*. "Living in America" describes a continent that threatens its residents, its two shores "hurrying towards each other" while "Desperately the inhabitants hoped to be saved in the middle,/Pray to the mountains and deserts to keep them apart." "The Suburb" gives a human face to this fear – a sullen and domesticated defeatism that says "Better/to lie still and let the babies run through me"; while "The Women" quietly records a similar suppression, in its picture of "Women, waiting, waiting for their husbands,/sit[ting] among dahlias all the afternoons,/while quiet processional seasons drift and subside at their doors like dunes."

But much of Anne Stevenson's poetry has been a revolt against this tyranny of environment over self. *Correspondences*, a "Family History in Letters," traces 150 years in the life of the Chandler family on both sides of the Atlantic. In the last letter of the volume, the fictitious poetess Kay Boyd writes to her father, from London, of her flight from the United States: " 'Nowhere is safe.'/It is a poem I can't continue./It is America I can't contain." Flight here involves refusing "the tug back" of "allegiance to innocence which is not there," deliberately leaving it unclear whether it is innocence or allegiance which is lacking. The "correspondences" of the title are in one sense those between the unsustainable poetic project and the unimaginable magnitude of America. But in the letters themselves new correspondences emerge, as successive generations live through corresponding dilemmas, flights, returns, sometimes unwittingly using the same language to describe their plights. Thus Kay's sister, Eden, writes to her of a recurring nightmare after their mother's death, asking her to come home, in words which echo their ancestor Reuben Chandler, a prodigal son writing to his father, a Vermont minister, in 1832, of his own wish to return. Kay's desire to "make amends for what was not said," not just in her own relationship with her parents but through all the fraught generations of her family, to "Do justice to the living, to the dead," likewise recalls that earlier father, writing to his errant daughter, mourning, in Yorkshire, a husband lost at sea:

> I have studied your letter with exacting and impartial attention.
> What shall I say?
> Except that I suffer, as you, too, must suffer
> increasingly from a sense of the justice of your bereavement.

Preferring, in her father's words, "the precarious apartments of the world/to the safer premises of the spirit," his daughter nevertheless chooses a fall from grace that brings a profounder suffering than he, in his naive self-righteousness, can ever know. Kay Boyd, having the last word in the book, makes it clear that this is a price worth paying.

Travelling Behind Glass attempted to justify this peripatetic living as a conscious moral choice. The title poem toys with residence, imagining "A heart at grass" among the "predictable greens" of an accepted landscape, but opts instead for "the paranoid howl of the/highway," where the "carapace" of the car becomes a symbol of the free-wheeling will that prefers even the risk of madness to domesticity. The theme of renunciation is reiterated in *Enough of Green*. This volume makes it clear that it is precisely the green world of the senses ("love grown rank as seeding grass") which has to be renounced, in favour of the steely, ascetic discipline of an art which has replaced the Christian God as task-master. There is in all Anne Stevenson's poetry an extremist's desire for the sterility and outrage of the puritan's scalpel. What makes the Scottish landscape so attractive is its sense of life as stress and erosion, an attrition which uncovers the essential contours of a mind and a place.

There is a certain relentlessness of imagination, a dogged, insistent quality, to Anne Stevenson's poetry; but it is protected from the stridency of those "intense shrill/ladies and gaunt, fanatical burnt out old women" whose fate she clearly fears in "Coming Back to Cambridge" and elsewhere by both an elegiac sadness and a sly, wicked wit. The former is revealed in those poems which speak of love as the "remorseless joy of dereliction" ("Ragwort"), a song made out of deprivation and loss; the latter in a poem such as "Theme with Variations," with its cool worldliness:

> there is only one love
> which is never enough....
> Such semen has crept
> into blonde violins,
> rich horns, shy string quartets
> out of Beethoven's furious genitals...
> that ladies who bend to their cellos,
> their velvet knees apart
> know well there can only be one love
> which is never Art.

—Stan Smith

STEWART, Douglas (Alexander). Australian. Born in Eltham, New Zealand, 6 May 1913. Educated at New Plymouth Boys High School; Victoria University College, New Zealand. Married Margaret Coen in 1946; one daughter. Literary Editor, *The Bulletin*, Sydney, 1940–61; Literary Adviser, Angus and Robertson Ltd., publishers, Sydney, 1961–72. Recipient: Encyclopedia Britannica Award, 1968; Wilke Award, for non-fiction,

1975. Agent: Curtis Brown (Australia) Pty. Ltd., P.O. Box 19, Paddington, New South Wales 2021. Address: 2 Banool Avenue, St. Ives, New South Wales 2075, Australia.

PUBLICATIONS

Verse

Green Lions. Auckland, Whitcombe and Tombs, 1937.
The White Cry. London, Dent, 1939.
Elegy for an Airman. Sydney, Frank C. Johnson, 1940.
Sonnets to the Unknown Soldier. Sydney and London, Angus and Robertson, 1941.
The Dosser in Springtime. Sydney and London, Angus and Robertson, 1946.
Glencoe. Sydney and London, Angus and Robertson, 1947.
Sun Orchids and Other Poems. Sydney and London, Angus and Robertson, 1952.
The Birdsville Track and Other Poems. Sydney and London, Angus and Robertson, 1955.
Rutherford and Other Poems. Sydney and London, Angus and Robertson, 1962.
The Garden of Ships: A Poem. Sydney, Wentworth Press, 1962.
(*Poems*), selected and introduced by the author. Sydney, Angus and Robertson, 1963.
Collected Poems 1936–1967. Sydney and London, Angus and Robertson, 1967.
Selected Poems. Sydney, Angus and Robertson, 1973.

Plays

Ned Kelly (produced Sydney, 1944; London, 1977). Sydney and London, Angus and Robertson, 1943.
The Fire on the Snow and The Golden Lover: Two Plays for Radio. Sydney and London, Angus and Robertson, 1944.
Shipwreck (produced Sydney, 1948). Sydney, Shepherd Press, 1947.
Four Plays (includes *The Fire on the Snow*, *The Golden Lover*, *Ned Kelly*, *Shipwreck*). Sydney and London, Angus and Robertson, 1958.
Fisher's Ghost: An Historical Comedy (produced Sydney, 1961). Sydney, Wentworth Press, 1960.

Radio Plays: *The Fire on the Snow*, 1941; *The Golden Lover*, 1943; *An Earthquake Shakes the Land*, 1944.

Short Stories

A Girl with Red Hair and Other Stories. Sydney and London, Angus and Robertson, 1944.

Other

The Flesh and the Spirit: An Outlook on Literature. Sydney and London, Angus and Robertson, 1948.
The Seven Rivers. Sydney, Angus and Robertson, 1966; selection, as *Fishing Around the Monarto*, Canberra, Australian National University Press, 1978.
The Broad Stream: Aspects of Australian Literature. Sydney, Angus and Robertson, 1975.
Norman Lindsay: A Personal Record. Melbourne, Nelson, 1975.
A Man of Sydney: An Appreciation of Kenneth Slessor. Melbourne, Nelson, 1977.
Writers of the Bulletin (lectures). Sydney, Australian Broadcasting Commission, 1977.

Editor, *Coast to Coast: Australian Stories.* Sydney, Angus and Robertson, 1945.
Editor, with Nancy Keesing, *Australian Bush Ballads.* Sydney, Angus and Robertson, 1955.
Editor, with Nancy Keesing, *Old Bush Songs and Rhymes of Colonial Times, Enlarged and Revised from the Collection of A. B. Paterson.* Sydney, Angus and Robertson, 1957.
Editor, *Voyager Poems.* Brisbane, Jacaranda Press, 1960.
Editor, *The Book of Bellerive*, by Joseph Tischler. Brisbane, Jacaranda Press, 1961.
Editor, (*Poems*), by A. D. Hope. Sydney, Angus and Robertson, 1963.
Editor, *Modern Australian Verse: Poetry in Australia II.* Sydney, Angus and Robertson, 1964; Berkeley, University of California Press, 1965.
Editor, *Selected Poems*, by Hugh McCrae. Sydney, Angus and Robertson, 1966.
Editor, *Short Stories of Australia: The Lawson Tradition.* Sydney, Angus and Robertson, 1967.
Editor, with Nancy Keesing, *The Pacific Book of Bush Ballads.* Sydney, Angus and Robertson, 1967.
Editor, with Nancy Keesing, *Bush Songs, Ballads, and Other Verse.* Penrith, New South Wales, Discovery Press, 1968.
Editor, with Beatrice Davis, *Best Australian Short Stories.* Hawthorne, Victoria, Lloyd O'Neil, 1971.
Editor, *The Wide Brown Land; A New Selection of Australian Verse.* Sydney, Pacific, 1971.
Editor, *Australia Fair: Poems and Paintings.* Sydney, Ure Smith, 1976.

Manuscript Collection: National Library, Canberra.

Critical Studies: *Douglas Stewart* by Nancy Keesing, Sydney, Oxford University Press, 1965; *Douglas Stewart* by Clement Semmler, New York, Twayne, 1975.

* * *

For just over 20 years (1940 to 1961) Douglas Stewart was literary editor of the Sydney weekly, *The Bulletin*, and in that period he was largely – indeed, centrally – influential in bringing about what can now be clearly seen as the first great school of Australian regional poetry – a school that recognized Robert D. FitzGerald as its elder figure, and encouraged the talents of virtually every notable Australian poet of the period (the significant exception being A. D. Hope). Douglas Stewart, a prolific writer himself, played not only a central editorial role, but a creative one as well. His critical attitudes were more ambiguously decisive: he was an ardent follower of Norman Lindsay's "vitalist" philosophy, which favoured hedonistic energy and a sort of Classical Romp – and rejected entirely the taint of "modernity." In positive terms, Stewart translated this into a code for a sensible concreteness of expression; negatively, it led him to a suspicion of experimentation and a hostility towards many European (and American) developments. In the 1940's the discovery of an intense identification with the Australian environment (heightened by the war years) was strongly encouraged by Stewart's insistence on the concrete and the direct. He pared down much of the mushy pseudo-poetic affectation that still lingered in much local verse. By the 1950's cultural isolation was becoming less possible, and Stewart's own later work is an attempt to come to terms with forces and issues outside the finally restricting field of regional lyricism.

Douglas Stewart was born in New Zealand, and his first volume, *Green Lions*, is entirely devoted to explorations of that countryside. *The White Cry* clarifies Stewart's essentially lyrical voice, but it is in the two early wartime books, *Elegy for an Airman* and *Sonnets to the Unknown Soldier*, that a sudden energising force is revealed. The sonnets were criticised at the time (and later) because "they did not rhyme," and were written in a period of patriotic and emotional stress that did lead to tub-thumping; but they were written, also, with a quite new element of laconic perception:

You see that fellow with the grin, one eye on the girls,
The other on the pub, his uniform shabby already?
Well, don't let him hear us, but he's the Unknown Soldier,
They just let him out, they say he lives for ever.
They put him away with flowers and flags and forget him,
But he always comes when they want him. He does the fighting.

Not until Bruce Dawe, two decades later, is the sense of Australian vernacular speech so precisely captured and made integral to the poem's expression.

Experiments with ballad and song form in *The Dosser in Springtime* led to important modifications in Stewart's style and prepared the way for his mature lyric achievement in *Sun Orchids* and *The Birdsville Track*. Yet despite the still exhilarating successes in these volumes, there is also a sense of a somewhat self-constricting talent, trivializing, not intensifying. It is for this reason that *Rutherford* both surprises and impresses. A long poem based on the heroic, exploring, and enduring aspects of man (in the Lindsay "vitalist" tradition), its subject is the New Zealand physicist. Although novel at the time (poems about scientists were still rare), it accords well with Stewart's own positivist theories: "Mostly too busy to think – too busy thinking. But thinking was doing." It is an almost unconscious irony that what is possibly the finest poem of Norman Lindsay's most ardent disciple should deal with Science, that Modernist windmill of all windmills.

Douglas Stewart contributed four impressive verse plays to the Australian repertoire, in a period when it was thought this was a form that could be revived. The subsequent discovery of new, essentially poetic forms of drama (by Ionesco, Beckett, Pinter, many others) has placed Stewart's verse dramas, like those of Fry, Duncan, and their contemporaries, on a shelf of disregard. Yet *The Fire on the Snow* and *The Golden Lover* – at least in print – combine a warm lyricism with movement and dramatic impetus. It is possible to imagine a time when their enduring qualities will be rediscovered.

Since the publication of *Collected Poems* in 1967, Stewart has virtually retired himself from the poetic scene in Australia. Two generations, or waves, of writers have subsequently arrived and declared (sometimes stridently) their place on the map. His silence is, I think, regrettable. If he had in some ways restricted his poetic horizons, he had certainly staked out a sizeable portion of his world and his culture for himself. It is ground still capable of yielding up a wealth of invention.

—Thomas W. Shapcott

STEWART, Harold (Frederick). Australian. Born in Sydney, New South Wales, 14 December 1916. Recipient: Australia Council Fellowship, 1978. Address: Higashisenouchicho 29, Kitashirakawa, Sakyo-ku, Kyoto, Japan.

PUBLICATIONS

Verse

The Darkening Ecliptic, with James McAuley (as Ern Malley). Melbourne, Reed and Harris, 1944; as *Poems*, Melbourne, Lansdowne Press, 1961.
Phoenix Wings: Poems 1940–6. Sydney and London, Angus and Robertson, 1948.
Orpheus and Other Poems. Sydney, Angus and Robertson, 1956.

Other

By the Old Walls of Kyoto. Tokyo, John Weatherhill, 1979.

Translator, *A Net of Fireflies: Japanese Haiku and Haiku Paintings.* Tokyo and Rutland, Vermont, Tuttle, 1960.

Translator, *A Chime of Windbells: A Year of Japanese Haiku.* Tokyo and Rutland, Vermont, Tuttle, 1969.

Critical Studies: "Poet's Progress," in *Hemisphere* (Canberra), December 1973, and "Ern Malley's Other Half," in *Quadrant* (Sydney), August 1977, both by Dorothy Green.

Harold Stewart comments:

Poetry founded on Tradition is to me not only a way of life but a spiritual method, a kind of Yoga, both mantric and bhaktic, yoking the poet by means of words with the Word. The poet, in turn, has a ministerial function, mediating between the Muse and the reader, and it is his duty to praise and express his gratitude for the inspiration which he receives from above. As a follower of Tradition, I am opposed to "modernism" of every kind in art and thought. My aim is not to be contemporary, but timeless.

Although some of my earlier work treated European themes, since about 1950 I have concentrated entirely on giving poetic expression to certain of the Traditional Doctrines of the Far East, especially those of Buddhism, Taoism and Hinduism. During the past century, Oriental scholarship has opened up the vast treasure houses of the metaphysical, religious and artistic traditions of Asia; yet these have remained largely unexplored by Western poets.

I have devoted the past thirty years to their study, drawing poetic inspiration from these rich resources and endeavouring to acclimatize English poetry to these old but newly rediscovered regions of the spirit, both by direct translation and by original composition. At first I drank from the fountainheads, India and China; but since coming to live in Japan, I have turned to a more personal expression of religious devotion, to the Pure Land School of Buddhism, Jodo Shinshu, as well as attempting to capture some of the natural and cultural atmosphere of Kyoto and its environs.

My poetic methods have always been strictly Traditional, using the regular metres of English verse, often with rhyme, and a modern English diction of a slightly heightened tone, but striving always for greater clarity and simplicity in expressing sometimes difficult and unfamiliar subjects.

I think that I can fairly claim the discovery of two new principles of stanza formation: the inverted stanza, in which the order of rhymes is inverted from the previous one, the two stanzas alternating in various patterns; and the variation stanza, in which each new stanza is formed by a different permutation of a fixed number of rhymes.

* * *

In his sensitive study of James McAuley's poem "Prometheus" in *Workshop* ii, 1, Harold Stewart praises McAuley for using a method which is obviously his own. Stewart writes, "It is only through the myth that reality can be presented in the round: the superficially realist work can give only a one-sided and distorted projection." McAuley's method consists in the presentation of a myth, and at the same time of incorporating into that presentation what the poet himself has called "interpretative words and phrases." In his poem "The Myths" Stewart expresses the same idea in a more poetic form:

Myths are a never-empty urn
Of meaning: poets thence in turn
Pour out the symbols that presage
The rise or ruin of their age.

Stewart draws his material not only from European myth but also from the myths of Buddhism and Taoism, and thus endeavours to give his poetry a universal timeless appeal: "My aim is not to be contemporary, but timeless."

Mr. Stewart seems to be struggling along with Plato, the Christian Saints and Eastern gurus to overcome his earthly desires, his burden of flesh, in order to bè liberated into pure spirit and a feeling of oneness with nature. When he achieves this, in "The Annunciation," for example, the poet savours the rare moment of illumination and insight: "Rarely is flesh from purpose thus untied/It is as though my aching blood were still."

The struggle to obtain this spiritual freedom is the subject of the main body of the poetry, including a very personal interpretation of the myth of Orpheus and Eurydice. Through this personal use of the myths the poet casts new light on his subjects and in turn enriches our understanding of the myths.

—Kirsten Holst Petersen

STOUTENBURG, Adrien. Pseudonym: Lace Kendall. American. Born in Darfur, Minnesota, 1 December 1916. High School education. Librarian, Hennepin County Library, Richfield, Minnesota, 1949–50; Reporter, *Richfield News*, 1950–52; Editor, Parnassus Press, Berkeley, California, 1956–58. Recipient: Edwin Markham Award and Michael Stone Fellowship, Poetry Society of America, 1961; Lamont Poetry Selection Award, 1964; Borestone Mountain Award, 1970, 1972. Agent: Curtis Brown Ltd., 60 East 56th Street, New York, New York 10022. Address: 2034 Bath Street, No. 1, Santa Barbara, California 93105, U.S.A.

PUBLICATIONS

Verse

Heroes, Advise Us: Poems. New York, Scribner, 1964.
Short History of the Fur Trade. Boston, Houghton Mifflin, 1969; London, Deutsch, 1970.
Greenwich Mean Time. Salt Lake City, University of Utah Press, 1979.

Other (juvenile)

The Model Airplane Mystery. New York, Doubleday, 1943.
Timber Line Treasure. Philadelphia, Westminster Press, 1951.
The Silver Trap. Philadelphia, Westminster Press, 1954.
Stranger on the Bay. Philadelphia, Westminster Press, 1955.
Remembered Island, with Barbara Ritchie (as Barbi Arden). New York, Holt Rinehart, 1956.
River Duel. Philadelphia, Westminster Press, 1956.
Snowshoe Thompson, with Laura Nelson Baker. New York, Scribner, 1957.
In This Corner. Philadelphia, Westminster Press, 1957.
Wild Treasure: The Story of David Douglas, with Laura Nelson Baker. New York, Scribner, 1958.
Wild Animals of the Far West. Berkeley, California, Parnassus Press, 1958.
Honeymoon. Philadelphia, Westminster Press, 1958.
Four on the Road. Philadelphia, Westminster Press, 1959.
Scannon: Dog with Lewis and Clark, with Laura Nelson Baker. New York, Scribner, 1959.

Houdini: Master of Escape (as Lace Kendall). Philadelphia, Macrae Smith, 1960.
Good-by Cinderella. Philadelphia, Westminster Press, 1960.
The Blue-Eyed Convertible. Philadelphia, Westminster Press, 1961.
Beloved Botanist: The Story of Carl Linnaeus, with Laura Nelson Baker. New York, Scribner, 1961.
Little Smoke (as Lace Kendall). New York, Coward McCann, 1961.
Lady in the Jungle, with Laura Nelson Baker (as Nelson Minier). Philadelphia, Macrae Smith, 1961.
Window on the Sea. Philadelphia, Westminster Press, 1962.
The Secret Lions (as Lace Kendall). New York, Coward McCann, 1962.
Elisha Kent Kane: Arctic Challenger (as Lace Kendall). Philadelphia, Macrae Smith, 1963.
The Mud Ponies (as Lace Kendall). New York, Coward McCann, 1963.
Dear, Dear Livy: The Story of Mark Twain's Wife, with Laura Nelson Baker. New York, Scribner, 1963.
A Time for Dreaming. Philadelphia, Westminster Press, 1963.
The Things That Are (verse). Chicago, Reilly and Lee, 1964.
Walk into the Wind. Philadelphia, Westminster Press, 1964.
Rain Boat (as Lace Kendall). New York, Coward McCann, 1965; London, Hamish Hamilton, 1966.
Explorer of the Unconscious: Sigmund Freud, with Laura Nelson Baker. New York, Scribner, 1965; as *Freud: Explorer of the Unconscious*, London, Whiting and Wheaton, 1967.
The Crocodile's Mouth: Folk-Song Stories. New York, Viking Press, 1966.
Masters of Magic (as Lace Kendall). Philadelphia, Macrae Smith, 1966.
American Tall Tales. New York, Viking Press, 1966; London, Penguin, 1976.
A Vanishing Thunder: Extinct and Threatened American Birds. New York, Doubleday, 1967.
Tigers Training, Dancing Whales: Wild Animals of the Circus, Zoo, and Screen (as Lace Kendall). Philadelphia, Macrae Smith, 1968.
Listen America: A Life of Walt Whitman, with Laura Nelson Baker. New York, Scribner, 1968.
American Tall-Tale Animals. New York, Viking Press, 1968.
Animals at Bay: Rare and Rescued American Wildlife. New York, Doubleday, 1968.
Fee, Fi, Fo, Fum: Friendly and Funny Giants. New York, Viking Press, 1969; as *The Giant Who Sucked His Thumb and Other Stories*, London, Deutsch, 1972.
People in Twilight: Vanishing and Changing Cultures. New York, Doubleday, 1971.
Haran's Journey (as Lace Kendall). New York, Dial Press, 1971.
Out There. New York, Viking Press, 1971; London, Bodley llead, 1972.
Where To Now, Blue? Englewood Cliffs, New Jersey, Scholastic, 1978.

Manuscript Collections: (verse) University of California, Berkeley; (juvenile) Kerlan Collection, University of Minnesota, Minneapolis.

Adrien Stoutenburg comments:

Nature and history have a predominant place in my work. Two long, narrative poems of mine have historical backgrounds – "This Journey," written about Capt. Robert F. Scott's fatal journey to the South Pole; and the age-old exploitation of animals in the title poem of *Short History of the Fur Trade.* I write chiefly so-called free verse, though in a long poem I sometimes introduce rhymed lines for variation. Wild animals are often subjects in my work. Death, the mechanical destruction of the natural environment, the threat of nuclear holocaust are frequent themes. Although I admire many poets, I am not aware of any strong outside influence on my work. I do not seek for descriptive language but language that is connotative, and strung with fresh imagery or statement. Though I sometimes use surreal images, I am concerned for clarity and accuracy. There is no room in poetry for untruth, whether of the imagination or of fact.

* * *

Adrien Stoutenburg's poetry is richly sensual, well attuned to the plant and animal life of our planet in a way that, at its best, is strongly reminiscent of D. H. Lawrence and Theodore Roethke, as in "Who Love to Lie with Me":

> There is such a buzz here;
> my ears whirl with it,
> and the wind spinning it
> into legs, arms, squeaking trees,
> motes, mites, and the precise blue tick
> inside my wrist, my temple....

She has a unique power for bringing such disparate parts of creation together, for showing the essential oneness of life, as she does with great success is her fine long poem "This Journey," in which she discovers the victory underlying Scott's defeat in his attempt to reach the South Pole first. The long title poem from *Short History of the Fur Trade* manages also to suggest, and draw on, two opposed emotions: anger and disgust at human destruction of wild life (as particularly exemplified in the career of John Jacob Astor) motivated by nothing better than greed and the frivolous desire for rare furs, and, on the other hand, an acute awareness of the beauty and vitality of this wild life that was crushed to benefit the callous and the rich. She recreates the beauty of these vanished breeds of animals before our eyes at the same time she chronicles their destruction. In some of the shorter poems in this volume, she suggests (again, the lyrical and the satirical are often mixed, counterbalancing one another and giving the poems greater complexity as a result) the possibility that we can, as Gary Snyder has also said, re-establish some communion with nature on at least an individual basis, whatever others may be doing to destroy the ecological balance ("Interior Decoration"):

> I am thinking of doing over my room,
> of plastering wings on it,
> of letting clouds in through the attic,
> of collecting moles
> and training them to assemble in an oval
> for a rug as bright as black water.

Though she senses that the excitement she feels in the presence of wild life is perhaps becoming extinct, she is also willing to implicate herself in what is going wrong with our world; she would invite lions into her home, as in "Open House" (one of several titles in her second collection that conjures up Roethke), but knows how far removed hers is from the life of lions:

> For this I might sacrifice
> the chicken in the freezer,
> or the lunch reserved
> for our spoiled kittens
> who yearn to be lions
> but cannot conquer
> their lust for cans
> packed with tuna
> and the long, green bones of mermaids.

Obviously, the satire here is self-satire. The nature poetry that abounds in both *Heroes, Advise Us* and *Short History of the Fur Trade* goes beyond eulogy and lyrical appreciation to teach us, too: Stoutenburg reminds us, particularly in the latter book, of how easily the love of nature can be corrupted into a destructive lust for it, of the culpability of us all in what is happening to our planet. This is the sort of teaching that can help, since it is informed by passion; these poems abound in "the long green bones of mermaids," the magical image that darts for the heart and swims inside to stay.

—Duane Ackerson

STOW, (Julian) Randolph. Australian. Born in Geraldton, Western Australia, 28 November 1935. Educated at Guildford Grammar School, Western Australia; University of Western Australia, Nedlands, B.A. 1956. Formerly, Anthropological Assistant, working in Northwest Australia and Papua New Guinea. Taught at the University of Adelaide, 1957; Lecturer in English Literature, University of Leeds, Yorkshire, 1962, and University of Western Australia, 1963–64; Lecturer in English and Commonwealth Literature, University of Leeds, 1968–69. Recipient: Australian Literature Society Gold Medal, 1957, 1958; Miles Franklin Award, 1958; Commonwealth Fund Harkness Travelling Fellowship, 1964–66; Britannica-Australia Award, 1966; Australia Council grant, 1973. Address: c/o Richard Scott Simon Ltd., 32 College Cross, London N1 1PR, England.

PUBLICATIONS

Verse

Act One. London, Macdonald, 1957.
Outrider: Poems 1956–1962. London, Macdonald, 1962.
A Counterfeit Silence: Selected Poems. Sydney and London, Angus and Robertson, 1969.
Poetry from Australia: Pergamon Poets 6, with Judith Wright and William Hart-Smith, edited by Howard Sergeant. Oxford, Pergamon Press, 1969.

Recording: *Poets on Record 11*, University of Queensland, 1974.

Plays

Eight Songs for a Mad King, music by Peter Maxwell Davies. London, Boosey and Hawkes, 1969.
Miss Donnithorne's Maggot, music by Peter Maxwell Davies (produced 1974).

Novels

A Haunted Land. London, Macdonald, 1956; New York, Macmillan, 1957.
The Bystander. London, Macdonald, 1957.
To the Islands. London, Macdonald, 1958; Boston, Little Brown, 1959.
Tourmaline. London, Macdonald, 1963.
The Merry-Go-Round in the Sea. London, Macdonald, 1965; New York, Morrow, 1966.
Visitants. London, Secker and Warburg, 1979.

Other

Midnite: The Story of a Wild Colonial Boy (juvenile). Melbourne, Cheshire, and London, Macdonald, 1967; Englewood Cliffs, New Jersey, Prentice Hall, 1968.

Editor, *Australian Poetry 1964*. Sydney, Angus and Robertson, 1964.

Bibliography: *Randolph Stow: A Bibliography* by P. A. O'Brien, Adelaide, Libraries Board of South Australia, 1968; "A Randolph Stow Bibliography" by Rose Marie Beston, in *Literary Half-Yearly* (Mysore), No. 2, 1975.

Manuscript Collection: National Library of Australia, Canberra.

Critical Studies: "Raw Material" by the author, in *Westerly* (Nedlands, Western Australia), 1961; "The Quest for Permanence by Geoffrey Dutton, in *Journal of Commonwealth Literature* (Leeds, Yorkshire), September 1965; "Outsider Looking out" by W. H. New, in *Critique* (Minneapolis), ix, 1, 1967; "Waste Places, Dry Souls" by Jennifer Wightman in *Meanjin* (Melbourne), June 1969; "Voyager from Eden" by Brandon Conron, in *Ariel (Canada)* (Calgary, Alberta), October 1970; "The Family Background and Literary Career of Randolph Stow," July 1975, and "The Poetry of Randolph Stow," 1977, both by John B. Beston in *Literary Half-Yearly* (Mysore); *Randolph Stow* by Ray Willbanks, Boston, Twayne, 1978.

* * *

Randolph Stow's already considerable poetic reputation both overseas and in Australia rests on a comparatively small amount of published poetry. However, he is also a novelist who has written in both genres concurrently and the worlds and visions of his novels and of his poetry are interwoven. A discussion of his poetry should not forget these links and it is relevant to note the title of his selected poetry – *A Counterfeit Silence* on whose title page he quotes Thornton Wilder (*The Bridge of San Luis Rey*): "Even speech was for them a debased form of silence; how much more futile is poetry, which is a debased form of speech."

Stow's youthful poetry displayed technical mastery. He often contained great passion in graceful and ingenious traditional forms and frequently wrote a ballad-like verse which he has continued to use and to develop from time to time. Many of his early poems were autobiographical and displayed a sometimes almost oppressive awareness of the physical features of his Western Australian childhood and of its people expressed in lively and telling images: "... living where the sun/rolled on the land like a horse in a cloud of dust."

A series of Sydney Nolan's paintings decorate Stow's second book, *Outrider*. After this publication the term "surrealist" was heard of his work, wrongly I think. He has not, in that volume or later, abandoned effects and forms of great simplicity. Poems like "Ruins of the City of Hay" are many-sided, intricately stratified and dreamlike, but actual experience is their base. One may need a key to perceive the reality and logic but nothing in them is over or beyond reality, or beyond wit and irony ("Ruins of the City of Hay"):

But the wind of the world descended on lovely Petra
and the spires of the towers and the statues and belfries fell.
The bones of my brothers broke in the breaking columns.
The bones of my sisters, clasping their broken children,
cracked on the hearthstones, under the rooftrees of hay.
I alone mourn in the temples, by broken altars
bowered in black nightshade and mauve salvation-jane.

Stow has an acute, and acutely Australian, sense of dynasty. He is close in time and in imagination to his forebears who explored, possessed, named and tamed territories: "I am the country's station; all else is fever./Did we ride knee to knee down canyons, or did I dream it!" ("Strange Fruit"). This dynastic vision is clearest and most open in "Stations," a suite for three voices and three generations. A man, woman and youth speak for each generation, brilliantly evoking the history of a place and family; the whole concludes with this affirmative couplet spoken by the woman: "Across the uncleared hills of the nameless country/I write in blood my blood's abiding name." In "Thailand Railway" a dying Australian prisoner of war thinks of "children on horseback, hordes of my own country," rejects the utterance of "some warning or some charge, some testament" to enjoin: "think of the childless dead and be our sons."

Stow's poetry is international by virtue of his wide reading, his allusiveness in sound, rhythm and sense but unmistakably national as to its imagery, viewpoint and frequent use of Australian idiom.

—Nancy Keesing

STRAND, Mark. American. Born in Summerside, Prince Edward Island, Canada, 11 April 1934. Educated at Antioch College, Yellow Springs, Ohio, B.A. 1957; Yale University, New Haven, Connecticut (Cook Prize and Bergin Prize, 1959), B.F.A. 1959; University of Florence (Fulbright Fellow), 1960–61; University of Iowa, Iowa City, M.A. 1962. Married Antonia Ratensky in 1961 (divorced, 1973); one daughter. Instructor, University of Iowa, 1962–65; Fulbright Lecturer, University of Brazil, Rio de Janeiro, 1965–66; Assistant Professor, Mount Holyoke College, South Hadley, Massachusetts, 1967; Visiting Professor, University of Washington, Seattle, 1968, 1970; Adjunct Associate Professor, Columbia University, New York, 1969; Visiting Professor, Yale University, 1969; Associate Professor, Brooklyn College, New York, 1970–72; Bain-Swiggett Lecturer, Princeton University, New Jersey, 1973; Hurst Professor, Brandeis University, Waltham, Massachusetts, 1974–75; Visiting Professor, University of Virginia, Charlottesville 1976, California State University, Fresno, 1977, and University of California, Irvine, 1978. Recipient: Ingram Merrill Foundation Fellowship, 1966; National Endowment for the Arts grant, 1967, 1977; Rockefeller Award, 1968; Guggenheim Fellowship, 1974; Edgar Allan Poe Award, 1974; National Institute of Arts and Letters award, 1975. Address: 169 West 21st Street, New York, New York 10011, U.S.A.

PUBLICATIONS

Verse

Sleeping with One Eye Open. Iowa City, Stone Wall Press, 1964.
Reasons for Moving. New York, Atheneum, 1968.
Darker: Poems. New York, Atheneum, 1970.
The Story of Our Lives. New York, Atheneum, 1973.
The Sergeantville Notebook. Providence, Rhode Island, Burning Deck, 1973.
Elegy for My Father. Iowa City, Windhover Press, 1973.
The Late Hour. New York, Atheneum, 1978.

Other

The Monument. New York, Ecco Press, 1978.

Editor, *The Contemporary American Poets: American Poetry since 1940.* Cleveland, World, 1969.
Editor, *New Poetry of Mexico.* New York, Dutton, 1970; London, Secker and Warburg, 1973.
Editor and Translator, *The Owl's Insomnia: Selected Poems of Rafael Alberti.* New York, Atheneum, 1973.
Editor and Translator, *Souvenir of the Ancient World: Selected Poems of Carlos Drummond de Andrade.* New York, Antaeus, 1976.
Editor, with Charles Simic, *Another Republic: 17 European and South American Writers.* New York, Ecco Press, 1976.

Translator, *18 Poems from the Quechua.* Cambridge, Massachusetts, Halty Ferguson, 1971.
Translator, *Texas*, by Jorge Luis Borges. Austin, University of Texas Humanities Research Center, 1975.

Manuscript Collection: Lilly Library, University of Indiana, Bloomington.

Critical Studies: "Mark Strand: *Darker*" by James Crenner, in *Seneca Review* (Geneva, New York), April 1971; "A Conversation with Mark Strand," in *Ohio Review* (Athens), Winter 1972; "Dark and Radiant Peripheries: Mark Strand and A. R. Ammons" by Harold Bloom, in *Southern Review* (Baton Rouge, Louisiana), Winter 1972; "Beginnings and Endings" by Robert McKlitsch, in *Literary Review* (Rutherford, New Jersey), Spring 1978; David Kirby, in *Times Literary Supplement* (London), 15 September 1978.

* * *

Not allied with any of the various "schools" of poetry, Mark Strand writes in a readable, deceptively simple, almost traditional style that enhances the strange power with which he expresses disquieting thoughts. He strikes deeply into the heart of modern man; he awakens anxiety, guilt, and desperation; he arouses responses that most readers would prefer to leave dormant. He does it with ease, skill, and wit. There is an eeriness in his lyrics that is transferred to his reader; and with each rereading of a poem one is pulled deeper into "the encircling dark": "Something is happening/that you can't figure out./Things have been put in motion./Something is in the air" ("Something Is in the Air").

By frequent restatement of his themes, he develops a tonal consistency that is a great part of his growing strength and persuasion. Here is an imagination vitally concerned with man in the world today; or is there a world today, and is man in it? "All places that have been/With me will wear away./I do not lift my voice/Or raise a hand. I am/Not capable of force./Feeling myself at stake" ("Standing Still"). But the question concerns not only "All places that have been/With me." Who is the "me"? And why is he "Not capable of force"? What is at stake here? Do we find it in "The Man in the Mirror"?

I look at you
and see myself
under the surface....

It will always be this way.
I stand here scared
that you will disappear,
scared that you will stay.

The man in the mirror pulls the reader in too, and we cannot take our eyes from it – or put it down. It is existence that is at stake, an existence that is not quite real, however: a reflected existence that is not quite life itself. We are afraid of life.

We are afraid because of the illness of our world. Some of the symptoms are developed in "From a Litany":

> Let those in office search under their clothes for the private life.
> They will find nothing.
> Let them gather together and hold hands.
> They shall have nothing to hold.
> Let the black suited priests stand for the good life.
> Let them tell us to be more like them.
> For that is the nature of the sickness.

And what remains? There seems to be no hope. Where can we go?

> My parents rise out of their thrones
> Into the milky rooms of clouds. How can I sing?
> Time tells me what I am. I change and am the same.
> I empty myself of my life and my life remains.

These lines from "The Remains" (originally the title poem of *Darker*) leave us trying to escape from the vacuum which Strand has presented to us, but in which we have been all the time. But can it be a vacuum if we fill it? We are in a dream that Strand has made very, very real; so real that we suddenly awaken from it – not quite the same. He has made us face the questions. And still we want to go on, as he does: "One foot in front of the other/that is the way I do it." We reach the point where "We are reading the story of our lives/as though we were in it,/as though we had written it." There can be no doubt that this is a major voice speaking, and we are eager for it to go on.

—Holly Stevens

STRYK, Lucien. American. Born in Chicago, Illinois, 7 April 1924. Educated at Indiana University, Bloomington, B.A. 1948; University of Maryland, College Park, M.F.S. 1950; University of London; the Sorbonne, Paris, M.F.S.; University of Iowa, Iowa City, M.F.A. 1956. Served in the United States Army, 1943–45. Married; two children. Since 1958, Member of the English Department, and currently Professor of English, Northern Illinois University, DeKalb. Visiting Lecturer, Niigata University, Japan, 1956–58, and Yamaguchi University, Japan, 1962–63; Fulbright Lecturer, Iran, 1961–62. Recipient: Grove Press Fellowship, 1970; Yale University Asia Society grant, 1961; Ford Foundation Faculty Fellowship, University of Chicago, 1963; Isaac Rosenbaum Award (*Voices*, Detroit), 1964; Swallow Press New Poetry Series Award, 1965; National Translation Grant, 1969; National Endowment for the Arts award, 1974; National Institute of Arts and Letters award, 1975. Agent: Doubleday Author Lecture Service, 277 Park Avenue, New York, New York 10017. Address: Department of English, Northern Illinois University, DeKalb, Illinois 60115, U.S.A.

PUBLICATIONS

Verse

Taproot. Oxford, Fantasy Press, 1953.

The Trespasser. Oxford, Fantasy Press, 1956.
Notes for a Guidebook. Denver, Swallow, 1965.
The Pit and Other Poems. Chicago, Swallow Press, 1969.
Awakening. Chicago, Swallow Press, 1973.
Selected Poems. Chicago, Swallow Press, 1976.
The Duckpond. London, J. Jay, 1978.

Other

Editor and Translator, with Takashi Ikemoto, *Zen: Poems, Prayers, Sermons, Anecdotes, Interviews.* New York, Doubleday, 1965.
Editor, *Heartland: Poets of the Midwest.* DeKalb, Northern Illinois University Press, 1967; *Heartland 2*, 1975.
Editor, *World of the Buddha: A Reader.* New York, Doubleday, 1968.
Editor and Translator, with Takashi Ikemoto, *Afterimages: Zen Poems of Shinkichi Takahashi.* Chicago, Swallow Press, and London, Alan Ross, 1970.
Editor, and Translator with Takashi Ikemoto, *The Penguin Book of Zen Poetry.* London, Penguin, 1977.

Translator, with Takashi Ikemoto, *Zen Poems of China and Japan: The Crane's Bill.* New York, Doubleday, 1973.
Translator, with Takashi Ikemoto, *Twelve Death Poems of the Chinese Zen Masters.* Providence, Rhode Island, Hellcoal Press, 1973.
Translator, *Three Zen Poems after Shinkichi Takahashi.* Knotting, Bedfordshire, Sceptre Press, 1976.
Co-Translator, *Haiku of the Japanese Masters.* Derry, Pensylvania, Rook Press, 1977.
Co-Translator, *The Duckweed Way: Haikue of Issa.* Derry, Pensylvania, Rook Press, 1977.

Manuscript Collection: Mugar Memorial Library, Boston University.

Critical Studies: *On Writing, By Writers*, Boston, Ginn, 1966; Peter Michelson in *Chicago Review*, June 1967; Interviews in *Chicago Review*, xxv, 3, 1973, and *American Poetry Review* (Philadelphia), 1975.

Lucien Stryk comments:

I consider myself primarily a poet, though I am seriously interested in Oriental philosophy. Some critics, particularly Peter Michelson, have associated me with other poets and "schools" but, frankly, I like to think of myself as an "independent."

I don't think a grown-up poet can do much about the content of his verse: he either has or hasn't worthy concerns, he is either small or large-minded, and such things as his politics and social attitudes generally get into his verse, one way or another. My chief concern as a poet is to *make* something, something firmly enough crafted to assure its life for longer than one hurried reading. How to get this done is the main study of my life, and I have developed certain methods of using the line within a patterned (by no means conventionally patterned) stanza or unit which, hopefully, help me in the task. I suppose that what some critics have called my economy of statement has to a certain degree been influenced by my work as a translator of Zen poetry, but I'm far from certain about that.

Anyhow, I try for a firm line and, most important of all, image and/or metaphor without which, so far as I'm concerned, there cannot be poetry. Whatever else he is – and he had better be much more – the poet is an active finely-tuned sensorium, his eye working perfectly with his ear, and his fingers touching delicately. When the poet *is* that, and when his theme is worthy, he *may* produce a good poem. Yet the making of a good poem is never less than a mystery, and no poet would really want it to be anything less, however much he despairs.

* * *

For two decades, from *Taproot* (1953) to *Awakening* (1973), war has haunted Lucien Stryk's poetry. War has been the bone beneath the smile, the human constant against which love, loyalty, reverence, and all other qualities or notions of higher being must survive as best they can. This is a deep and complex awareness in Stryk, and is grounded in the poet's own memories: "memories [that] converge to form a shaft of pain" ("The Stack among the Ruins"). Generated by "the gibbet and the gas chamber," by the bombing of a Red Cross ship, by "the screaming victims thrown/From out the burning hospital/Into the burning town," the early poem "Song" from *The Trespasser* indicates just how pervasive these memories are. "Song" ends:

> The withered trees are in bloom again,
>   The earth is ripe and warm,
> But now we watch the lecher worm
>   That stains the vestal bud
> And like a fighter in the sun
>   The acrobatic bird.

We can see here the extent to which his song and vision have been colored. The mind that contemplates even the spring carries with it and always will the horrors of the past. From here on, Stryk, metaphorically speaking, will project into the body of every bird the propensities of the warplane. In "Summer," from *Awakening*, the poet's neighbor

>   scowls up at my maple, rake
> clogged and trembling,
> as its seeds spin down –
>
> not angels, moths, but paratroopers
> carried by the wind,
> planting barricades along his eaves.

However this is read, whatever irony is directed against the sensibility that obsessively reads nature in martial terms, what is clear is that the poet understands this predilection and its origins only too well. Poem after poem will tell us that he had his fill of that life at war, that repulsive anti-life. At the same time, I think, Stryk would agree that the whole of life somehow has to be gotten into each poem.

Stryk's poems are the embodiment of an evolution that carries him along from the despair of the early work to the more balanced and hopeful strains of the later. *Taproot* and *The Trespasser* name the experiences that will temper the life's work. War becomes known, in part, through the occasional realization of love, its divine opposite. In "For Helen" from the former volume Stryk declares

>   I know that all
> True lovers and their words but serve
> A love more tender than their own. Our
> Child, the pollened wind, the swirl of
> Homing birds proclaim its power.

In *Notes for a Guidebook*, the poet's selves become students, wanderers, tourists, beachcombers. The presences of the poems visit for a first time or return to familiar places and wonder how best to live in such a world of flux and seeming contradiction. This volume seems occasionally to labor for ultimate truth and morality, for something to hold to once and for all. *Notes*, I believe, represents a tense and crucial period in the poet's life. In *The Pit and Other Poems*, Stryk comes to grips with the function and worth of his life's work, "this house/of paper" as he terms it. The recognition of this book is that the poem must change, that life is motion, that systems are at once fluid and rooted in a divine One, that if there is no final way to resolve pain and loss and death forever, a man can still come to an ease, can become, as Whitman said, a "cosmos." In "Memo to the Builder" of his house, Stryk directs: "Build me a home/The living day can enter, not a tomb." The title poem, filled with horrifying images of a pit of bodies, ends: "Ask anyone who/Saw it: nobody won that war." This represents a resolution for the poet, an insistence that, although war is a human fact and constant, its acceptance is wrong and a man could and should publish it for what it is and also, at the same time, properly distance himself from it. As he says in "Zen: The Rocks of Sesshu," "The weed also has the desire/To make clean,/Make pure, there against the rock."

As it is in *Notes*, in *The Pit* the same desire for a spiritual calm is apparent. What is new with this book, and what deepens and matures in *Awakening*, is a dimension of peace in the face of what were previously almost debilitating conflicts and fears. "Ask anyone who/Saw it: nobody won that war" – in its straightforwardness, in its staunchness, this is a note of celebration that prefigures the grace and wisdom of Stryk's most recent work.

—William Heyen

STUART, Dabney. American. Born in Richmond, Virginia, 4 November 1937. Educated at Davidson College, North Carolina, 1956–60, A.B. 1960; Harvard University, Cambridge, Massachusetts (Summer Poetry Prize, 1962), A.M. 1962. Instructor in English, College of William and Mary, Williamsburg, Virginia, 1961–65. Since 1965, Member of the English Department, currently Professor of English, Washington and Lee University, Lexington, Virginia. Visiting Professor, Middlebury College, Vermont, 1968–69, and Ohio University, Athens, Spring 1975. Poetry Editor, *Shenandoah*, Lexington, 1966–76. Recipient: Poetry Society of America Dylan Thomas Prize, 1965; National Endowment for the Arts grant, 1969, and fellowship 1974. Address: Department of English, Washington and Lee University, Lexington, Virginia 24450, U.S.A.

PUBLICATIONS

Verse

The Diving Bell. New York, Knopf, 1966.
A Particular Place. New York, Knopf, 1969.
Corgi Modern Poets in Focus 3, with others, edited by Dannie Abse. London, Corgi, 1971.
The Other Hand. Baton Rouge, Louisiana State University Press, 1974.
Friends of Yours, Friends of Mine. Richmond, Virginia, Rainmaker Press, 1975.
Round and Round. Baton Rouge, Louisiana State University Press, 1977.

Other

Nabokov: The Dimensions of Parody. Baton Rouge, Louisiana State University Press, 1978.

Manuscript Collection: Davidson College Library, North Carolina.

Critical Studies: by X. J. Kennedy, in *Shenandoah* (Lexington, Virginia), Autumn 1966; John Unterecker, in *Shenandoah* (Lexington, Virginia), Autumn 1969; Dannie Abse, in *Corgi Modern Poets in Focus 3*, 1971; by the author, in *Contemporary Poetry in America*, edited by Miller Williams, New York, Random House, 1973; D. E. Richardson, in *Southern Review* (Baton Rouge, Louisiana), Autumn 1976.

Dabney Stuart comments:

My work has vacillated formally between traditional English forms (the sonnet in *The Diving Bell*, ballads in *Round and Round*) and so-called "free" (i.e., associative, non-metrical) verse (the whole of *The Other Hand*, so far my most honest performance). I have been consistently involved with certain themes, themselves less fragmented and wandering than my voice: son/father and father/son, levels of consciousness, the unforeseen and ubiquitous past, the aloof self-regard of women, the illusion of solidity and perspective, death and punning.

* * *

Dabney Stuart has received impressive tributes for his skill, his intelligence, and his veracity to experience. In his first book, *The Diving Bell*, he revealed himself as a master of the well-made poem. His command of language and his confident handling of relatively traditional forms are combined there with a gentle candour which enables many of the poems to transcend the category of Lowellesque confessional verse into which they run the risk of falling. There is nothing trite about his contribution to this genre. For example, in a poem for the small daughter whom he seldom sees he speaks of her as a conjuror: "Your voice a wand, you called the olives grapes," but adds later:

Yet, deserting your role,
You called me by my name –
I'd rather
Have been that metaphor, your father.

Here language is both image and instrument.

His second book makes a necessary advance into more adventurous territory. It includes, in fact, a number of poems about places, contemplative in tone, dwelling on stone and water, air and stillness. But it explores also deeper regions of symbol and myth, psychic landscapes, in forms which owe little to tradition.

There is always a danger that this kind of poem may not come off. A few here, even in Stuart's accomplished hands, fail. About those which do not it is, in a sense, impossible to make final judgments: their success depends very much on the range of experience and the type of attention which the reader brings to them, and on the reverberations they cause in his mind. Many of the poems in this book have a haunting resonance which gives more with every reading.

—Fleur Adcock

SUKNASKI, Andrew, Jr. Canadian. Born in Wood Mountain, Saskatchewan, 30 July 1942. Educated at the Ambassador School, Wood Mountain; L. V. Rogers High School,

Nelson, British Columbia; Kootenay School of Art, Nelson, 1961–62, 1966–67, diploma in fine arts 1967; University of Victoria, British Columbia, 1964–65; Montreal Museum of Fine Arts School of Art and Design, 1965; Notre Dame University, Nelson, 1966–67; University of British Columbia, Vancouver, 1967–68; Simon Fraser University, Burnaby, British Columbia, 1968–69. Former editor, Anak Press and Deodar Shadow Press, and *Elfin Plot* and *Sundog*, all Wood Mountain. Currently editor of Sundog Press, Wood Mountain. Writer-in-Residence, St. John's College, University of Manitoba, Winnipeg, 1977–78. Recipient: Canada Council grant, 1971, 1972, 1973, 1976, 1978; Canadian Authors Association prize, 1978. Address: Wood Mountain, Saskatchewan S0H 4L0, Canada.

PUBLICATIONS

Verse

The Shadow of Eden Once. Wood Mountain, Deodar Shadow Press, 1970.
Circles. Wood Mountain, Deodar Shadow Press, 1970.
In Mind ov Xrossroads ov Mythologies. Wood Mountain, Anak Press, 1971.
Rose Way in the East. Toronto, Ganglia Press, 1972.
Old Mill. Vancouver, Blewointmentpress, 1972.
The Nightwatchman. Wood Mountain, Anak Press, 1972.
The Zen Pilgrimage. Wood Mountain, Anak Press, 1972.
Y th Evolution into Ruenz. Wood Mountain, Anak Press, 1972.
Four Parts Sand: Concrete Poems, with others. Ottawa, Oberon Press, 1972.
Wood Mountain Poems. Wood Mountain, Anak Press, 1973; expanded edition, edited by Al Purdy, Toronto, Macmillan, 1976.
Suicide Notes, Book One. Wood Mountain, Sundog Press, 1973.
Phillip Well. Prince George, British Columbia, College of New Caledonia, 1973.
These Fragments I've Gathered for Ezra. Edinburg, Texas, Funch Press, 1973.
Leaving. Seven Person, Alberta, Repository Press, 1974.
On First Looking Down from Lion's Gate Bridge. Wood Mountain, Anak Press, 1974; revised edition, Windsor, Ontario, Black Moss Press, 1976.
Blind Man's House. Wood Mountain, Anak Press, 1974.
Leaving Wood Mountain. Wood Mountain, Sundog Press, 1975.
Writing on Stone: Poemdrawings 1966–1976. Wood Mountain, Anak Press, 1976.
Octomi. Saskatoon, Thistledown Press, 1976.
Almighty Voice. Toronto, Dreadnaught Press, 1977.
Moses Beauchamp. Winnipeg, Turnstone Press, 1978.
The Ghosts Call You Poor. Toronto, Macmillan, 1978.
Two for Father, with George Morrissette. Wood Mountain, Sundog Press, 1978.
East of Myloona. Saskatoon, Thistledown Press, 1979.
Montage for an Interstellar Cry. Winnipeg, Turnstone Press, 1980.

Play

Don'tcha Know the North Wind and You in My Hair, with others (produced Saskatoon, 1978).

Other

Translator, *The Shadow of Sound*, by Andrei Voznesensky. Prince George, British Columbia, College of New Caledonia, 1975.

Critical Studies: "Writing along the Road to Wood Mountain," in *Another Time* by Eli Mandel, Erin, Ontario, Press Porcépic, 1977; "Shadows of Our Ancestors" by Harvey Spak, and "Ghostly Voices" by Stephen Scobie, both in *NeWest ReView* (Edmonton), October 1978.

Andrew Suknaski, Jr., comments:

1. Concerns: the meaning of home and a vaguely divided guilt; guilt for what happened to the Indian, his land taken, imprisoned on his reserve; and guilt because to feel this guilt is a betrayal of what you ethnically are, the son of a homesteader and his wife who must be rightfully honoured in one's mythology

2. Origins: mythic mainsprings – the meaning of self: *self* your place of birth, *self* the proximity of the buried to the living of that place, *self* in *home … being* your *dreamtime* (tribal history, the ancestral way of life – that place where you leave going beyond to become faceless … mind and heart telescoped, forever yearning to return … *home*)

3. Naming the Lost: in the western prairie labyrinth where the poet as art casuality must retie the severed threads: guilt, betrayal, and populist myth on the margins of the dreaming utopia that victimizes one *naming the lost* to arrest niggling visions of where the Godly becomes monstrous, where reality becomes myth … as Leslie Fiedler warns, where myth often victimizes the innocent as one's humanity is shortchanged by the tickettaker at the circus gate – that point of entry to our nightmares and *otherness*

* * *

"If Canada ever needed an argument in defence of the regional writer, Andrew Suknaski is it," wrote a reviewer of this poet who has taken the Canadian Prairies as his province. Suknaski, of Polish-Ukrainian parentage, was born on a farm outside the village of Wood Mountain, in southwestern Saskatchewan. He lives there and writes about his background and that of the prairies: Indians, East European settlers, Mounties, Americans. Reading *Wood Mountain Poems*, one is aware that, in this region, if space has expanded time has contracted, so that the past is ever-present, but Toronto and Vancouver are light years distant. The poems in *The Ghosts Call You Poor* take the form of jottings, rambling letters, documentations, etc., but they are all concerned with what sociologists call "marginalized people." The Indians and Métis are pre-eminently among these, as he shows in "Dreaming of the Northwest Passage":

> the native showed us the way
> the native drew the first map on sand and earth
> the northern esquimaux drew in snow
> and did with small shale cairns
> what contour lines do
> to indicate mountains
> for scottish and british explorers
>
> the indian showed us the way to the heart
> of the prairie
> and distant mountains

There is more rhetoric than drama in his poetry, more feeling for great masses of people than for individuals, more a sense of summing up a patchwork past than of signaling a new society or a significant future. Only in one of his lesser-known books, *Leaving*, does Suknaski write about his travels throughout Europe and the East. The poems there have a bright quality lacking in the prairie poems.

—John Robert Colombo

SUMMERS, Hollis (Spurgeon, Jr.). American. Born in Eminence, Kentucky, 21 June 1916. Educated at Georgetown College, Kentucky, A.B. 1937; Bread Loaf School of English, Middlebury College, Vermont, M.A. 1943; University of Iowa, Iowa City, Ph.D. 1949. Married Laura Vimont Clarke in 1943; two children. Taught at Holmes High School, Covington, Kentucky, 1937–44; Professor of English, Georgetown College, 1945–49, and the University of Kentucky, Lexington, 1949–59. Since 1959, Distinguished Professor of English, Ohio University, Athens. Adviser, Ford Foundation Conference on Writers in America, 1958; Lecturer, Arts Program, Association of American Colleges, 1958–63; Danforth Lecturer, 1963–66. Recipient: Fund for the Advancement of Education grant, 1951; *Saturday Review* Poetry Award, 1957; Colleges of Arts and Sciences Award, 1958; National Endowment for the Arts grant, 1974. LL.D.: Georgetown College, 1965. Address: 181 North Congress Street, Athens, Ohio 45701, U.S.A.

PUBLICATIONS

Verse

The Walks near Athens. New York, Harper, 1959.
Someone Else: Sixteen Poems about Other Children (juvenile). Philadelphia, Lippincott, 1962.
Seven Occasions. New Brunswick, New Jersey, Rutgers University Press, 1965.
The Peddler and Other Domestic Matters. New Brunswick, New Jersey, Rutgers University Press, 1967.
Sit Opposite Each Other. New Brunswick, New Jersey, Rutgers University Press, 1970.
Start from Home. New Brunswick, New Jersey, Rutgers University Press, 1972.
Occupant, Please Forward. New Brunswick, New Jersey, Rutgers University Press, 1976.
Dinosaurs. Athens, Ohio, Rosetta Press, 1978.

Play

A Note to Myself: A Thanksgiving Play. Chicago, Dramatic Publishing Company, 1946.

Novels

City Limit. Boston, Houghton Mifflin, 1948.
Brighten the Corner. New York, Doubleday, 1952.
Teach You a Lesson, with James Rourke (as Jim Hollis). New York, Harper, 1955; London, Foulsham, 1956.
The Weather of February. New York, Harper, 1957.
The Day after Sunday. New York, Harper, 1968.
The Garden. New York, Harper, 1972.

Short Stories

How They Chose the Dead. Baton Rouge, Louisiana State University Press, 1973.

Other

Editor, *Kentucky Story: A Collection of Short Stories.* Lexington, University of Kentucky Press, 1954.

Editor, with Edgar Whan, *Literature: An Introduction.* New York, McGraw Hill, 1960.
Editor, *Discussions of the Short Story.* Boston, Heath, 1963.

Hollis Summers comments:

Could these words serve, some of them, as a statement of faith?

A poem is moving down a summer street,
Darkly, unsure, yet pretending
That assumption is a name for fact;

Pretending even street and season,
It walks with carefully balanced faith to meet
A space for turning, to bring
The eyes, even if blinded for the act,
To look back,
    To ask the reason
For the movement:
    Darkness again, perhaps, or
Darkness barred with slanted light from an opened door.

—from "A Poem Is Moving Down a Summer Street"
in *The Walks near Athens*

You can tell almost all in a poem.
Tears, semen, and bowel movements
Come precisely with fairly simple aids:
Color and consistency charts
Stapled to the wish to show and shout.

I also wish to show and shout,
Look at me, look here, look out
From where you read, considering the poems I need.
I'm sorry I have been reared
Believing poems that said, "Look there."

A poem is room enough to skin a cat in;
A poem is shaking a stick at a cat;
A poem is skinning a cat more ways than one.

—from "For Three Specific Friends"
in *The Peddler and Other Domestic Matters*

* * *

Since *The Walks near Athens*, Hollis Summers' poetry has been characterized by an ease of expression, an effortlessness that balances his classical elegance with rhythms so casual that they seem spontaneous. The beginning lines of "On Looking at Television's Late Movies," for example, move so surely that they seem almost offhand:

John Keats sank into nothingness
Over a star or the song of a bird
Or a vase or marbles, or even the sea
In which he assumed his name was writ.

The lines turn their corners perfectly, as the poem begins to turn on its ironies. Summers' labor has always been to understand the assumptions that we consider facts, and to write clearly about them. This poem ends: "In the water where Keats wrote I have read/ Permanence. I am glad he is dead."

Here and throughout Summers' poetry, romantic notions of beauty (perhaps the most important word in his work) are turned mercilessly on the spit of experience. Faiths built on notions of meaning or permanence are held in the light for what they are. We sing, Summers concludes in the title poem of *Seven Occasions*, "for no final reason." "Song to Be Attached" from *The Peddler and Other Domestic Matters* might serve as a metaphor for his unrelenting vision. Three stanzas tell us to "Decorate the carcass/Thread with amethyst," to "Deck the bowels with ruby." But the poem concludes:

Braise in precious ointment
Drench it if you will
Decorate the carcass
It is a carcass still.

It is not easy to say these things. In "Song for a Dead Lady" from *Sit Opposite Each Other*, Summers tells us that "it is good she is dead .../But I had to live a long time/To say this song." Summers is one of America's finest, most underrated poets. Volume after volume has clarified a voice and a vision that will come to engage us as among the most memorable of our time.

—William Heyen

SWARD, Robert S. American; Canadian Landed Immigrant. Born in Chicago, Illinois, 23 June 1933. Educated at Von Steuben High School, Chicago; San Diego Junior College, California, 1951; University of Illinois, Urbana, 1953–56, B.A. (honors) 1956 (Phi Beta Kappa); Bread Loaf School of English, Middlebury, Vermont, Summers 1956–58; University of Iowa, Iowa City, M.A. 1958; University of Bristol (Fulbright Fellow), 1960–61. Served in the United States Navy in Korea, 1951–53. Married 1) Diane Kaldes in 1960 (divorced); 2) Irina Schestakowich in 1975; three daughters and two sons. Research Fellow, 1956–58, and Poet-in-Residence, Spring 1967, University of Iowa; Lecturer in English, Connecticut College, New London, 1958–59; Writer-in-Residence, Cornell University, Ithaca, New York, 1962–64, Aspen Writers' Conference, Colorado, Summer 1967, and University of Victoria, British Columbia, 1969–73. Since 1970, Founding Editor, Soft Press, and since 1976, Editor, Hancock House Editions, both in Victoria. Recipient: Dylan Thomas Award, 1958; Yaddo Fellowship, Summers 1959–69; MacDowell Colony Fellowship, Summers 1959–72; Guggenheim Fellowship, 1964; University of New Mexico D. H. Lawrence Fellowship, 1966; Canada Council grant, 1973. Address: 1525 McRae Avenue, Victoria, British Columbia V8P 1G4, Canada.

PUBLICATIONS

Verse

Advertisements. Chicago, Odyssey, 1958.

Uncle Dog and Other Poems. London, Putnam, 1962.
Kissing the Dancer and Other Poems. Ithaca, New York, Cornell University Press, 1964.
Thousand-Year-Old Fiancée and Other Poems. Ithaca, New York, Cornell University Press, 1965.
In Mexico and Other Poems. London, Ambit, 1966.
Horgbortom Stringbottom, I Am Yours, You Are History. Chicago, Swallow Press, 1970.
Quorum, with *Noah*, by Mike Doyle. Victoria, Soft Press, 1970.
Songs from the Jurassic Shales. Victoria, Soft Press, 1970.
Hannah's Cartoon. Victoria, Soft Press, 1970.
Gift. Victoria, Soft Press, 1970.
Raspberry (as Dr. Soft). Victoria, Soft Press, 1971.
Risk. Victoria, Soft Press, 1971.
Poems New and Selected 1957–1973. Chicago, Swallow Press, 1973.
Letter to a Straw Hat. Victoria, Soft Press, 1974.
Five Iowa Poems. Iowa City, Stone Wall Press, 1975.
Honey Bear on Lasqueti Island, B.C. Victoria, Soft Press, 1978.

Recording: *Thousand-Year-Old Fiancée and Other Poems*, Aural.

Novel

The Jurrasic Shales. Toronto, Coach House Press, 1975.

Other

Editor, with Tim Groves and Mario Martinelli, *Vancouver Island Poems.* Victoria, Soft Press, 1973.
Editor, *Cheers for Muktananda.* Victoria, Soft Press, 1976.

Bibliography: by John Gill, in *New: American and Canadian Poetry* (Trumansburg, New York), 1973.

Manuscript Collections: Washington University Library, St. Louis; National Library of Canada, Ottawa; University of Victoria.

Critical Studies: "The Voices Have Range" by John M. Brinnin, in *New York Times Book Review*, 25 October 1964; Introduction by William Meredith to *Kissing the Dancer and Other Poems*, 1964; *A Controversy of Poets*, New York, Doubleday, 1965; "A Poetry Chronicle" by Constance Urdang, in *Poetry* (Chicago), 17 February 1972.

* * *

A striking feature of Robert Sward's poetry is its range: he is a master of unique observation, gifted with emotional recall, capable of goofy humor as well as experiments in disdain, and properly turned off by war and the diplomatic posture of his native America. Sward's "Statement of Poetics" – a poem that appeared in *New: American & Canadian Poetry 20* – may indicate his attitudes accurately enough, though it may also indicate his disdain for unanswerable poetic questions. He is outrageous as often as not, seeming capable of walking on words halfway between double exposures of put-on and truth:

Talk
people talking, getting that
into one's poetry that

is my poetics. Love
hate lies laughing stealings
self-confession self-destruction
get them all get
them all into writing.
No one has to
read them. No one
has to publish them.
I am more and
more for unpublished poetry.

Sward's delight with language is evident in all his poetry, and the reader senses a healthy dose of play at work in every poem. He revels in the power of the final word, which he uses with delight against the innocent as well as those who have crossed him. He writes in "Mothers-In-Law" (both of whom he lost through divorce) that the first of them "required, upon departure,/The services of three gentlemen with shoehorns/To get her back into her large black/Studebaker." The reader experiences vicarious pleasure imagining the lady in question thumbing through Robert's book. It may be play of an adolescent nature, but how grand to have a poet awaken the childishness within us.

Indeed, if we accept spontaneity as a primary quality of childhood, Sward's childishness is virtually unequalled. The poetry that results is sometimes half-baked, but so direct of statement that we feel, unquestionably, the poet's complete, warty presence: I'll take this kind of unguarded, risky stuff anyday in preference to the urbane, sophisticated verse of poets (half his age!) who write within only a limited range of highly selected posturings. Sward is willing to let his reader hate him; yet he, himself, escapes the pit of self-hatred. At times, his spontaneity works against him, as in the polemic "In Mexico," where after describing his opposition to American war policies, he concludes: "What a country!/For even/Your stupidity,/The Charm/Of Your/Tastelessness,/Vitality,/Greed// *America, get out/of Vietnam,/The Dominican Republic,/Africa, Europe/Southeast Asia//* Has begun to smell/ Has begun to smell/I would say/Like the Pentagon,/Like senility/Like death." I believe poems written without deference to academic standards should rise above such standards, not be vulnerable to the kind of bitchy complaint that says the subjects "stupidity" and "charm" are not capable of their verbs, and the abstract image is not even linguistically interesting, unless Sward intends a different subject. In any case, spontaneity in this instance results in dull rhetoric.

For each of his few failed risks, Sward has many poems that win against the odds; his only form, the integrity of his voice. The language is tight, the words comprehensible, and he can move up off the page, out of the words, like a man coming into sunlight. I admire his fullness, and will end with excerpts from two distinctly different poems, "San Cristobal" and "Risk":

Pine cones, aspen,
Starlight, the light
World one way, then another
The light rising,
The light drawn up into stars

Voice is light,
The world is light
The stars, their hands
Striking through

It's a calculated risk, whatever you do.
  A man has cancer of the rectum. You
  take out his rectum and

maybe he dies of heart failure.
Or he's fine and goes on for 20 years.

—Geof Hewitt

SWENSON, May. American. Born in Logan, Utah, 28 May 1919. Educated at Utah State University, Logan, B.A. 1939. Editor, New Directions Press, New York, 1959–66. Poet-in-Residence, Purdue University, Lafayette, Indiana, 1966–67, University of North Carolina, Greensboro, 1968–69 and 1975, Lethbridge University, Alberta, 1970. Recipient: Rockfeller Fellowship, 1955, 1967; Breadloaf Writers' Conference Robert Frost Fellowship, 1957; Guggenheim Fellowship, 1959; William Rose Benét Prize, 1959; Longview Foundation Award, 1959; Amy Lowell Traveling Fellowship, 1960; National Institute of Arts and Letters Award, 1960; Ford Fellowship, for drama, 1964; Brandeis University Creative Arts Award, 1966; Utah State University Distinguished Service Gold Medal, 1967; Lucy Martin Donnelly Fellowship, Bryn Mawr College, 1968; Shelley Memorial Award, 1968; National Endowment for the Arts grant, 1974; Academy of American Poets Fellowship, 1979. Member, National Institute of Arts and Letters. Address: 73 The Boulevard, Sea Cliff, New York 11579, U.S.A.

PUBLICATIONS

Verse

Another Animal. New York, Scribner, 1954.
A Cage of Spines. New York, Holt Rinehart, 1958.
To Mix with Time: New and Selected Poems. New York, Scribner, 1963.
Poems to Solve (juvenile). New York, Scribner, 1966.
Half Sun, Half Sleep: New Poems. New York, Scribner, 1967.
Iconographs. New York, Scribner, 1970.
More Poems to Solve (juvenile). New York, Scribner, 1971.
New and Selected Things Taking Place. Boston, Little Brown, 1978.

Recordings: *Today's Poets 2*, with others, Folkways, 1968; *The Poetry and Voice of May Swenson*, Caedmon, 1976.

Play

The Floor (produced New York, 1966). Published in *First Stage* (West Lafayette, Indiana), vi, 2, 1967.

Other

The Contemporary Poet as Artist and Critic. Boston, Little Brown, 1964.
The Guess and Spell Coloring Book (juvenile). New York, Scribner, 1976.

Translator, *Windows and Stones: Selected Poems*, by Tomas Tranströmer. Pittsburgh, University of Pittsburgh Press, 1972.

Manuscript Collections: Rare Book Room, Washington University Library, St. Louis; Lockwood Library, State University of New York, Buffalo.

Critical Studies: "The Poetry of May Swenson" by Betty Miller Davis, in *Prairie Schooner* (Lincoln, Nebraska), Winter 1960; "About May Swenson" by John Hall Wheelock, in *Wilson Library Bulletin* (New York), January 1962; "One Knows by Seeing" by Richard Moore, in *The Nation* (New York), 10 August 1963; "Turned Back to the Wild by Love" by Richard Howard, in *Tri-Quarterly* (Evanston, Illinois), 1966; "A Ball with Language" by Karl Shapiro, in *New York Times Book Review*, 7 May 1967; "The Art of Perceiving" by Ann Stanford, in *Southern Review* (Baton Rouge, Louisiana), January 1969; "May Swenson" by Alicia Ostriker, in *American Poetry Review* (Philadelphia), March 1978; interview with Karla Hammond, in *Parnassus* (New York), Fall-Winter 1978.

May Swenson comments:

I devise my own forms. My themes are from the organic, the inorganic, and the psychological world. I sometimes tend to create a typographical or iconographic frame for my poems *after* the text is complete.

* * *

May Swenson is extremely deft and inventive with sounds and shapes in language. And with that, she is reckless, an attempter of oddities. A juggler and acrobat, she has performed so consistently that her poems find their way into many well known magazines, such as *Harper's*, *The Atlantic*, and *The New Yorker*.

Her agile language has brought fame. Another quality has saved her from the hovering envy of competing writers: she forces her talent into metaphysical attempts and into the service of causes that have solid appeal.

To hear her read to an audience is to become aware of what she has yoked together. Her voice is intense, not at ease – at work. And her surprising, fountaining lines go steadily into their blend of brilliance and integrity. It is the combination that distinguishes her.

She is from the West – Utah. But she has made New York City into her place. An example, an emblem for the foregoing characterizations, is her poem "On Seeing Rocks Cropping Out of a Hill in Central Park" (*Half Sun, Half Sleep*):

Boisterous water arrested, these rocks
are water's body in death. Transparent

water falling without stop makes a wall,
the frenzied soul of rock its white breath.

Dark water's inflated wave, harsh spray
is ghost of a boulder and cave's

marble, agitated drapery. Stillness
water screams for, flying forth,

the body of death. Rock dreams
soul's motion, its hard birth.

—William Stafford

SYMONS, Julian (Gustave). British. Born in London, 30 May 1912. Educated in various state schools. Married Kathleen Clark in 1941; one son and one daughter (deceased). Has worked as a shorthand typist, secretary for an engineering company, and advertising copywriter. Founding Editor, *Twentieth Century Verse*, London, 1937–39; Reviewer, Manchester *Evening News*, 1947–56; Editor, Penguin Mystery Series, 1974–77. Since 1958, Reviewer for the *Sunday Times*, London. Visiting Professor, Amherst College, Massachusetts, 1975–76. Co-Founder, 1953, and Chairman, 1958–59, Crime Writers Association; Chairman, Committee of Management, Society of Authors, 1969–71. Since 1976, President, Detection Club. Recipient: Crime Writers Association Award, 1957, 1966; Mystery Writers of America Edgar Allan Poe Award, 1961, 1973; Swedish Academy of Detection Grand Master Diploma, 1977. Fellow, Royal Society of Literature, 1975. Address: 147 Ramsden Road, London SW12 8RF, England.

PUBLICATIONS

Verse

Confusions about X. London, Fortune Press, 1939.
The Second Man. London, Routledge, 1943.
A Reflection on Auden. London, Poem-of-the-Month Club, 1973.
The Object of an Affair and Other Poems. Edinburgh, Tragara Press, 1974.

Plays

Radio Plays: *Affection Unlimited*, 1968; *Night Rider to Dover*, 1969.

Television Plays: *I Can't Bear Violence*, 1963; *Miranda and a Salesman*, 1963; *The Witnesses*, 1964; *The Finishing Touch*, 1965; *Curtains for Sheila*, 1965; *Tigers of Subtopia*, 1968; *The Pretenders*, 1970; *Whatever's Peter Playing At*, 1974.

Novels

The Immaterial Murder Case. London, Gollancz, 1945; New York, Macmillan, 1957.
A Man Called Jones. London, Gollancz, 1957.
Bland Beginning. London, Gollancz, and New York, Harper, 1949.
The Thirty-First of February. London, Gollancz, and New York, Harper, 1950.
The Broken Penny. London, Gollancz, and New York, Harper, 1953.
The Narrowing Circle. London, Gollancz, and New York, Harper, 1954.
The Paper Chase. London, Collins, 1956; as *Bogue's Fortune*, New York, Harper, 1957.
The Colour of Murder. London, Collins, and New York, Harper, 1957.
The Gigantic Shadow. London, Collins, 1958; as *The Pipe Dream*, New York, Harper, 1959.
The Progress of a Crime. London, Collins, and New York, Harper, 1960.
The Killing of Francie Lake. London, Collins, 1962; as *The Plain Man*, New York, Harper, 1962.
The End of Solomon Grundy. London, Collins, and New York, Harper, 1964.
The Belting Inheritance. London, Collins, and New York, Harper, 1965.
The Man Who Killed Himself. London, Collins, and New York, Harper, 1967.
The Man Whose Dreams Came True. London, Collins, 1968; New York, Harper, 1969.
The Man Who Lost His Wife. London, Collins, 1970; New York, Harper, 1971.
The Players and the Game. London, Collins, and New York, Harper, 1972.
The Plot Against Roger Rider. London, Collins, and New York, Harper, 1973.

A Three-Pipe Problem. London, Collins, and New York, Harper, 1975.
The Blackheath Poisonings. London, Collins, 1978; New York, Harper, 1979.

Short Stories

Murder! Murder! London, Fontana, 1961.
Francis Quarles Investigates. London, Panther, 1965.
Ellery Queen Presents Julian Symons' How to Trap a Crook and Twelve Other Mysteries. New York, Davis, 1977.

Other

A. J. A. Symons: His Life and Speculations. London, Eyre and Spottiswoode, 1950.
Charles Dickens. London, Barker, and New York, Roy, 1951.
Thomas Carlyle: The Life and Ideas of a Prophet. London, Gollancz, and New York, Oxford University Press, 1952.
Horatio Bottomley. London, Cresset Press, 1955.
The General Strike: A Historical Portrait. London, Cresset Press, 1957; Chester Springs, Pennsylvania, Dufour, 1963.
The Thirties: A Dream Revolved. London, Cresset Press, 1960; Chester Springs, Pennsylvania, Dufour, 1963; revised edition, London, Faber, 1975.
A Reasonable Doubt: Some Criminal Cases Re-examined. London, Cresset Press, 1960.
The Detective Story in Britain. London, Longman, 1962.
Buller's Campaign. London, Cresset Press, 1963.
England's Pride: The Story of the Gordon Relief Expedition. London, Hamish Hamilton, 1965.
Crime and Detection: An Illustrated History from 1840. London, Studio Vista, 1966; as *A Pictorial History of Crime*, New York, Crown, 1966.
Critical Occasions. London, Hamish Hamilton, 1966.
Bloody Murder. London, Faber, 1972, as *Mortal Consequences*, New York, Harper, 1972.
Between the Wars: Britain in Photographs. London, Batsford, 1972.
Notes from Another Country. London, London Magazine Editions, 1972.
The Tell-Tale Heart: The Life and Works of Edgar Allan Poe. London, Faber, and New York, Harper, 1978.

Editor, *An Anthology of War Poetry.* London , Penguin, 1942.
Editor, *Selected Writings of Samuel Johnson.* London, Grey Walls Press, 1949.
Editor, *Selected Works, Reminiscences and Letters*, by Thomas Carlyle. London, Hart Davis, 1956; Cambridge, Massachusetts, Harvard University Press, 1957.
Editor, *Essays and Biographies*, by A. J. A. Symons. London, Cassell, 1969.
Editor, *The Woman in White*, by Wilkie Collins. London, Penguin, 1974.
Editor, *The Angry 30's.* London, Eyre Methuen, 1976.
Editor, *Verdict of Thirteen: A Detection Club Anthology.* London, Faber, and New York, Harper, 1979.

Manuscript Collection: Humanities Research Center, University of Texas, Austin.

* * *

Julian Symons's career as a poet was fairly brief (he has only just begun to write poems again) and attracted less notice than his valuable work as editor of *Twentieth Century Verse*, historian, novelist, and critic. But his books of 1939 and 1943 have a great deal more than historical interest. Of his contemporaries, Symons seems temperamentally most akin to Roy

Fuller and Alun Lewis. He shared their preference for precise, formal versification; he, too, disliked the emotional excesses of the Apocalyptic poets. And, like Fuller and Lewis, Symons was a man of the left and was young enough for the war, not the depression, to have been the formative influence on his work.

He was not interested in the topical or propagandistic possibilities of verse. Rather, Symons elaborates a view of society which has metaphysical as well as political overtones. In his work the "political" merges with the epistemological to question the meaning of reality and our purchase upon it. He is, like Louis MacNeice, a sharp critic of the bourgeois tendency to evade problems and to live on "islands." But being himself bourgeois, Symons is every bit as quick to identify within himself the lingering romanticism, compromises, and opportunism which he dislikes. His argument is, to a considerable extent, with himself, though set against a backdrop of "dramatic truces" and newspapers which announce war.

His work gives at times a rich feeling of observed life, of the joys of the ordinary universe: "The twopenny bookstall bargains, the automaton wireless,/The complete sets of dead magazines, the held hand/In the cinema, the smackable bouncing blonde." At his best, in the excellent "Clapham Common" in *The Second Man*, Symons demonstrates considerable power of psychological insight, and effective use of symbols. But far too often his struggles are with epistemological uncertainty: "What seems/To be real is unreal." In another poem a precise description of a pub is followed by "This moment exists and is real." When in "Whitsun 1940" he writes "Our compensation is the sense of touch,/Convincing tyros that the real is real," the effect is to deepen the confusion. He does not possess a truly philosophic mind, and in the end one regrets that he did not leave metaphysics to the metaphysicians and write more persistently about that "real" world around him. There was, as well, a political dimension to his impasse:

If I could give power to
My burning thoughts! This ink turn acid and the pen
Become a gun: pointed against the murderers,
The corrupt class, the scum
Of a top-heavy civilisation:
If I could extinguish the voice that says
Man can endure corruption and be happy.

But such reflections are not quite poetry. His best work appears in *The Second Man*, in poems like "Clapham Common" in which there is a complex, exploratory openness to subjective experience and memory. Symons's work gives us a distinct sense of the conflict between the subjective traditions of lyric poetry, and the political conscience in an age of crisis: "for me the spring advances and the unlimited/Areas of conflict remain outside, the problems of action/And honesty are still unreconciled." It may be that the decision to give up writing poetry came out of an excessively strong respect for its integral wholeness, a wholeness which the divided consciousness can seldom locate.

—Eric Homberger

TAGLIABUE, John. American. Born in Cantu, Como, Italy, 1 July 1923. Educated at Columbia University, New York, B.A. 1944 (Phi Beta Kappa), M.A. in art and literature 1945, 1947–48; University of Florence, Italy (Fulbright Scholar), 1950–52. Married Grace Ten Eyck in 1946; two daughters. Lecturer in American Poetry, American University of Beirut, Lebanon, 1945–46, and Washington State College, Pullman, 1946–47; Assistant

Professor of American Literature, Alfred University, New York, 1948–50; Fulbright Lecturer in American Poetry, University of Pisa, Italy, 1950–52, and Tokyo University, Japan, 1958–60. Member of the English Department, 1953–58, Associate Professor, 1960–71, and since 1971, Professor of English, Bates College, Lewiston, Maine. Formerly, Poet-in-Residence, Bennett College, Greensboro, North Carolina, International Institute of Madrid, Spain, University of Rio Grande do Norte, Natal, Brazil, and Anatolia College, Thessalonika, Greece. Recipient: Bates College grant, 1969. Address: 12 Abbott Street, Lewiston, Maine, 04240, U.S.A.

PUBLICATIONS

Verse

Poems. New York, Harper, 1959.
A Japanese Journal. San Francisco, Kayak, 1966.
The Buddha Uproar. San Francisco, Kayak, 1967.
The Doorless Door. Tokyo, Mushinsha Press, 1970.
Every Minute a Ritual. Lewiston, Maine, Grace Tagliabue, 1973.
Poems on the Winter's Tale. Houghton, New York, Ktaadn Poetry Press, 1973.

Plays

Mario in the Land of the Unicorns [*the Green Queen*] (puppet plays), in *Carolina Quarterly* (Chapel Hill, North Carolina), Spring and Summer 1964.

Other puppet plays produced and published.

Manuscript Collection: George Arents Research Library, Syracuse University, New York.

John Tagliabue comments:

(1970) Poetry is all a matter of design, play, ritual, decorations, symbolism, and like our life it is always changing. I have been writing poems for many years and my moods and styles have changed – sometimes as I see new places, new people, get new suggestions – and yet something which at the moment I can't say in prose doesn't seem to change. I like poems and dances to help make us realize many festivals, all kinds of holidays.

(1974) Often and there are thousands of them, written in many moods, in many centuries, in many religions and love affairs, the poems speak, sing, dance, celebrate for themselves-and-others. I must let it go at that now. The many Travel Journals that I've been keeping might help; they are related to the USA and Italy, Spain, France, England, Greece, Turkey, Yugoslavia, Lebanon, Syria, Mexico, Guatemala, Brazil, Peru, Japan, and some other places.

* * *

John Tagliabue is an unashamedly happy poet, content – too – to be an inexorably minor one. In an age of what Robert Graves once called "posterity-conscious heavyweights" this is no bad thing; but one has to add that many of Tagliabue's poems, charming though they are, are almost too insubstantial to make their presence felt at all. They tend to blow away before one has finished reading them: "Mountain/of Chinese noodles,/heaven for a poor man." This is too obvious, too matter-of-fact, to achieve the true quality of the kind of miniaturist Japanese poetry that has so entranced and influenced this author. Many attempts, of course, have been made to carry over this quality into English verse, and very few of them have succeeded. It is perhaps unfortunate that Tagliabue has confined so much of his poetic intention to the effort. When he becomes more thoughtful he is not only enchanted by life (which is the chief, and attractive, feature of his verse as a whole) but also enchanting, as in "Friendship":

Sleep sat next to me
Like a man on the subway.
Sleep said, Write a poem.
I said, You are a poem.
Sleep was my friend.
Always between places
we are closing our eyes
and growing. We are
always going towards
each other or poetry.
Sleep said, Have I written you?
You said, I am sleepy.

—Martin Seymour-Smith

TARN, Nathaniel. British. Born in Paris, France, 30 June 1928. Educated at Cambridge University, B.A. (honours) 1948, M.A. 1952; the Sorbonne and Ecole des Hautes Etudes, Paris, Cert. C.F.R.E.; University of Chicago, M.A. 1952, Ph.D. 1957; London School of Economics; School of Oriental and African Studies, University of London. Divorced; two children. Has worked as an anthropologist in Guatemala, Alaska, and Burma. Formerly, Member of the Faculty, University of Chicago, and University of London; Visiting Professor, State University of New York, Buffalo, and Princeton University, New Jersey, 1969–70. Since 1970, Professor of Comparative Literature, Rutgers University, New Brunswick, New Jersey. General Editor, Cape Editions, and Director, Cape Goliard Limited, publishers, London, 1967–69. Recipient: Guinness Prize, 1963. Address: 96 New Street, New Hope, Pennsylvania 18938, U.S.A.

PUBLICATIONS

Verse

Old Savage/Young City. London, Cape, 1964; New York, Random House, 1965.
Penguin Modern Poets 7, with Richard Murphy and Jon Silkin. London, Penguin, 1966.
Where Babylon Ends. London, Cape Goliard Press, and New York, Grossman, 1968.
The Beautiful Contradictions. London, Cape Goliard Press, 1969; New York, Random House, 1970.
October: A Sequence of Ten Poems Followed by Requiem Pro Duabus Filiis Israel. London, Trigram Press, 1969.
The Silence. Milan, M'Arte, 1970.
A Nowhere for Vallejo: Choices, October. New York, Random House, 1971; London, Cape, 1972.
Lyrics for the Bride of God: Section: The Artemision. Santa Barbara, California, Tree, 1973.

The Persephones. Santa Barbara, California, Tree, 1974.
Lyrics for the Bride of God. New York, New Directions, and London, Cape, 1975.
Narrative of This Fall. Los Angeles, Black Sparrow Press, 1975.
The House of Leaves. Santa Barbara, California, Black Sparrow Press, 1976.
From Alashka: The Ground of Our Great Admiration of Nature, with Janet Rodney. London, Permanent Press, 1977.
The Microcosm. Milwaukee, Membrane Press, 1977.
Birdscapes, with Seaside. Santa Barbara, California, Black Sparrow Press, 1978.
The Forest, with Janet Rodney. Mount Horeb, Wisconsin, Perishable Press, 1978.
Alashka/Atitlan: New and Selected Poems, with Janet Rodney. Boulder, Colorado, Brillig Works Press, 1979.

Other

Editor, and Translator with others, *Con Cuba: An Anthology of Cuban Poetry of the Last Sixty Years.* London, Cape Goliard Press, and New York, Grossman, 1969.
Editor, and Translator with others, *Selected Poems: A Bilingual Edition*, by Pablo Neruda. London, Cape, 1970; New York, Delacorte Press, 1972.

Translator, *The Heights of Macchu Picchu*, by Pablo Neruda. London, Cape, 1966; New York, Farrar Straus, 1967.
Translator, *Stelae*, by Victor Segalen. Santa Barbara, California, Unicorn Press, 1969.

Critical Studies: in *La Belle Contra Dizzioni*, Milan, Munt Press, 1973; "Nathaniel Tarn Symposium" in *Boundary 2* (Binghamton, New York), Fall 1975; "The House of Leaves" by Kingsley Weatherhead, in *Credences 4* (Kent, Ohio), 1977.

Nathaniel Tarn comments:

Poetry for me is the discovery of a sound which arises out of unimpeded listening. The sound, once recognized, can assume a number of voices; my life-history happens to have given me no convincing English of my own. I have always been fascinated by the interplay between restricted and elaborated codes, between common parlances and formal rhetorics. Form is usually allowed to grow out of content, though I am aware of moving towards more and more open form as I discover that there is less and less that *cannot* be discussed in poetry. In the early work, my anthropological experience prompted me to speak out of various personae associated with *Old Savage*; an old, wise Amerindian or Melanesian, aware of what our culture has done to his, forgiving, sad at his own destruction principally because it mirrors the destruction of the whole natural earth. Dropping anthropology as a profession has enabled me to speak as an anthropologist and add the dialectic of observer and observed to the previous one-dimensional picture. As a result, politics have become a major factor in recent work such as *The Beautiful Contradictions.* This complex material is offset by simple lyrical-erotic sequences such as occur in *October*. The aim is to work towards more and more satisfactory resolutions of the tension between simplicity and complexity.

We may be living at a time when only the exasperation of contradictions is possible for the artist; synthesis is closed to him because of the intolerable weight of new information he must shoulder each day. In this situation, poetry is more than ever a discipline, the means whereby a poet not only discovers, but literally creates, himself out of the total flux. Silence is more than poetry's complement: it is that which poetry must sink back into the moment it ceases to perform this function. It follows that poetry for poetry's sake – decoration *et al.* – is intolerable.

Translation is (i) a duty within the Republic of Letters; (ii) a way of allowing various voices to speak; (iii) a means of letting air into the stale bed of English letters. Editorial activity is an extension of translation, not only from languages but from disciplines. *Transformation* is a key concept, linking early allegiances to Surrealism with present interests in Structuralism.

* * *

That Nathaniel Tarn is a professional anthropologist and that he is a learned and highly informed exponent (as his editorship of Cape Editions demonstrates) of cosmopolitan art and thought are facts of importance in the consideration of his poetry. In an era when the impact of European and South American poetry is being more universally felt among younger poets than ever before, Tarn's poetry is nevertheless the most non-traditional and foreign-influenced of any British poet now writing. It seems appropriate that he was born in the cosmopolitan city of Paris. The chief single influence upon him has undoubtedly been the Chilean poet, Pablo Neruda, whose long poem *The Heights of Macchu Picchu* he has translated with conspicuous success.

Tarn is a "difficult" poet in the sense that his poems yield up little of their meaning when a traditional type of interpretation is applied to them. He eschews what he would call the false neatness of the traditional English-language poem (as well exemplified in Graves, Andrew Young, or Roy Fuller) and embraces a procedure in which the only brake (but an important one) to unconscious, wholly intuitive writing is rhetoric. The sprawlingness of his verse, its relentless search for space, particularly recalls the veteran surrealist Pablo Neruda. An individual line such as "Streets like flexed muscles cannot knock me out" clinches the matter.

Tarn's use of language is only semi-surrealist, however; his many descriptions of landscape, evocative of both its appearance and its atmosphere, make use of a remarkably consistent range of metaphor and imagery. His quest – one that is felt to be desperate if we are to judge from his language – is to rediscover the primitive in the midst of the civilized – hence the title of his first volume, *Old Savage/Young City*. In this he has almost certainly been influenced, though not at any superficial level, by the French anthropologist Claude Lévi-Strauss. Characteristic of the thought underlying his poems are these lines from "Old Savage/Young City,"

> On the day the earth achieved enlightment –
> as it is said: each blade of grass shall know itself
> knowing the wind it bends to its own purpose ...,

which clearly reflect the influences of Oriental thought and folk-poetry. If Tarn is religious, he is religious only in the most primitive – that is to say, pre-civilized – sense. "For the Death of Anton Webern Particularly," one of his simpler poems, is not always successful in the avoidance of cliché; but it aptly illustrates both his concerns and his faith:

> I need to ask what Sunday God first churned
> his cauldron world in such a manner that we all deal death....
> And how, at last, the notes
> composed by fragile Webern survive the boil and music in the bubbles.

His long poem *The Beautiful Contradictions*, describing "the quest for reality" continuing from innocence through "every shade of complexity to the exhaustion of human capacities," again, perhaps more emphatically, demonstrates his debt to Lévi-Strauss and his extremely radical interpretation of historical and anthropological data. Its weakness lies, again, in its sprawlingness and rhythmical innocuousness – Tarn's energy has become dispersed in his dialectic rather than in his technique or his language – but it is nonetheless a notably serious poem in theme.

—Martin Seymour-Smith

TATE, James (Vincent). American. Born in Kansas City, Missouri, 8 December 1943. Educated at the University of Missouri, Kansas City, 1963–64; Kansas State College, Pittsburg, B.A. 1965; University of Iowa, Iowa City, M.F.A. 1967. Visiting Lecturer, University of Iowa, 1965–67, and University of California, Berkeley, 1967–68; Assistant Professor, Columbia University, New York, 1969–71, and Emerson College, Boston, 1970–71. Since 1971, Member of the English Department, University of Massachusetts, Amherst. Since 1967, Poetry Editor, *Dickinson Review*, North Dakota. Currently, Associate Editor, Pym Randall Press, Cambridge, Massachusetts, and Barn Dream Press; Consultant, Coordinating Council of Literary Magazines. Recipient: Yale Series of Younger Poets Award, 1966; National Endowment for the Arts grant, 1968, 1969; National Institute of Arts and Letters award, 1974; Guggenheim Fellowship, 1976. Address: 950 North Pleasant Street, Amherst, Massachusetts 01002, U.S.A.

PUBLICATIONS

Verse

Cages. Iowa City, Shepherds Press, 1966.
The Destination. Cambridge, Massachusetts, Pym Randall Press, 1967.
The Lost Pilot. New Haven, Connecticut, Yale University Press, 1967.
The Torches. Santa Barbara, California, Unicorn Press, 1968; revised edition, 1971.
Notes of Woe. Iowa City, Stone Wall Press, 1968.
Mystics in Chicago. Santa Barbara, California, Unicorn Press, 1968.
Camping in the Valley. Chicago, Madison Park Press, 1968.
Row with Your Hair. San Francisco, Kayak, 1969.
Is There Anything. Fremont, Michigan, Sumac Press, 1969.
Shepherds of the Mist. Los Angeles, Black Sparrow Press, 1969.
The Oblivion Ha-Ha. Boston, Little Brown, 1970.
Amnesia People. Pittsburg, Kansas, Little Balkans, 1970.
Deaf Girl Playing. Cambridge, Massachusetts, Pym Randall Press, 1970.
Are You Ready Mary Baker Eddy?, with Bill Knott. San Francisco, Cloud Marauder Press, 1970.
The Immortals. Santa Barbara, California, Unicorn Press, 1970.
Wrong Songs. Cambridge, Massachusetts, Halty Ferguson, 1970.
Hints to Pilgrims. Cambridge, Massachusetts, Halty Ferguson, 1971.
Nobody Goes to Visit the Insane Anymore. Santa Barbara, California, Unicorn Press, 1971.
Absences: New Poems. Boston, Little Brown, 1972.
Apology for Eating Geoffrey Movius' Hyacinth. Santa Barbara, California, Unicorn Press, 1972.
Viper Jazz. Middletown, Connecticut, Wesleyan University Press, 1976.
Riven Doggeries. New York, Ecco Press, 1979.

Novel

Lucky Darryl, with Bill Knott. New York, Release Press, 1977.

Short Stories

Hottentot Ossuary. Cambridge, Massachusetts, Temple Bar Bookshop, 1974.

Manuscript Collection: Humanities Research Center, University of Texas, Austin.

James Tate comments:

I am in the tradition of the Impurists: Whitman, Williams, Neruda.... I am trying to combine words in such a way as to lend a new life, a new hope, to that which is lifeless and hopeless. If the vision in the poems is occasionally black, it is so in order to see more clearly the fabric of which that blackness is made, and thereby understand the source. If the source is understood, there is the possibility of correcting it.

In my poems it seems one of the recurring themes must be the agony of communication itself: despair and hatred are born out of this failure to communicate. The poem is man's noblest effort because it is utterly useless.

I use the image as a kind of drill to penetrate the veils of illusion we complacently call the Real World, the world of shadows through which we move so confidently. I want to split that world and release the energy of a higher reality. There is nothing I won't do because I see a new possibility each day.

* * *

In 1967, then 23 years old, James Tate won the Yale Series of Younger Poets award for his first book, *The Lost Pilot*. The bored world of contemporary American poetry was jolted: one so young doesn't often gain such recognition, and the foreword by Dudley Fitts said Tate "sounds ... like no one I have ever read – utterly confident, with an effortless elegance of control, both in diction and in composition, that would be rare in a poet of any age and that is particularly impressive in a first book."

More than most of his peers, Tate understands the magic of language itself as distinguished from language that seeks to share the magic of ideas. *The Lost Pilot* bore out the claims of the foreword, but in spite of all the fine use of language, only a few of the poems take on enough substance to stick. Those which most closely reveal Tate retain the elegance, and substance shadows charm. The poet's imagination, like a circus, offers both a fun house and the house of horrors. The title poem, an elegy to his father (1922–1944), addresses conceptions of "father" and stereotypes of astronauts, as well as a cosmological question involving worlds. It is a poem that stretches for, and attains, true importance.

Within two years of *The Lost Pilot*, Tate had another dozen collections in print or accepted for publication (surely a record of sorts), and the critics began to make their claims and demands. Maybe if he could write good poems younger than anyone else, he could also get wisdom sooner. At an age when many writers benefit from neglect, Tate was busy with public readings and what must have been a gratifying if insatiable demand for his new poems.

Most amazing of all this is how gracefully Tate rode it out. He seemed to enjoy himself, and to be aware of the position he was in. At the same time, there were poems like "The Hermit" whose final, second quatrain casts a shadow on what we consider to be required sociability: "From the mountainside,/I watch their fallen faces/rise, and scarcely believe/the luck I have had." A question surfaces: how much of grace is just plain tact? What wear is done to the soul in the name of manners?

Enough of claims and demands. Tate has already written some extraordinary poems; he has an energy of language that may well demand over-production, imagination flooding and sometimes drowning sensibility. The resulting poems can be heavily imagistic, flashy, and confusing, like the two-line "Flushing & Swarming": "She dreamed of excreting white plankton/then woke with a hiccup of white hatchets." The poem seems to center on the idea of white excrement; the difference between dream and reality, however, is not this impossible color, but the substance. Who "she" is, why she would have such a strange experience, and of what importance it all is, Tate characteristically neglects to mention.

Tate's more recent work has taken a fascinating turn towards the depth suggested by "The Lost Pilot," where the imagination is trained on credible events, however zany. Here are the opening lines of "Apology for Eating Geoffrey Movius' Hyacinth":

It has come to this,
a life of uncalculated passion
for the barely wriggling throb
of the invisible tube of force
that manufactures a laugh
for smothering pentagons,
fructifying useless poems,
and salvaging broken-hearted penguins.

It may be Tate's concept that the laugh can smother a pentagon, his idea of "useless poems" that fortify an attitude of unchecked absurdity.

When he abandons this stance, to write openly of himself and those people he loves, he demonstrates the self-awareness that balances him between redemption and the curse of prodigal attention ("The Blue Canyon"):

To be something different like a brussels sprout
it's as if we were ants so far away
made of charcoal made of dust,
good enough to erase and coming down

if I had not grown up dissolving into
the swan the way they think of me.

To retain this balance requires the abundance of grace which he alone so naturally has.

—Geof Hewitt

TAYLOR, Andrew (McDonald). Australian. Born in Warrnambool, Victoria, 19 March 1940. Educated at Scotch College, Melbourne, graduated 1957; University of Melbourne, 1958–61, B.A. (honours) 1961, M.A. 1971. Married Jill Burriss in 1964 (divorced, 1978); one son. Tutor, 1962–63, and Lockie Fellow, 1966–68, University of Melbourne; Teacher, British Institute, Rome, 1964–65; American Council of Learned Societies Fellow, State University of New York, Buffalo, 1970–71. Lecturer, 1971–74, and since 1975, Senior Lecturer in English, University of Adelaide. Address: Department of English, University of Adelaide, Adelaide, South Australia 5001, Australia.

PUBLICATIONS

Verse

The Cool Change. Brisbane, University of Queensland Press, 1971.
Ice Fishing. Brisbane, University of Queensland Press, 1973.
The Invention of Fire. Brisbane, University of Queensland Press, 1976.
The Cat's Chin and Ears: A Bestiary. Sydney, Angus and Robertson, 1976.
Parabolas: Prose Poems. Brisbane, Makar Press, 1976.
The Crystal Absences, The Trout. Sydney, Island Press, 1978.

Other

Editor, *Byron: Selected Poems.* Melbourne, Cassell, 1971.

Editor, with Ian Reid, *Number Two Friendly Street.* Adelaide, Adelaide University Union Press, 1978.

Manuscript Collection: National Library of Australia, Canberra.

Andrew Taylor comments:

Looking back across them, I find that my poems are about the ordinary things of life: they grow out of such things as happiness, a response to the weather, and the more traumatic occurrences that a normal life is prey to: breakup of a marriage, separation from a child, a new being in love, travel, etc. The larger historical dramas and the political scenarios aren't for me.

On the other hand, I don't see my poetry as particularly domestic. I try to convey the way the mundane particulars of my life, because they're so pressing to me, conform to larger patterns that express common experience and give it importance. As a result my poems are an attempt at finding the myth within which we live. (Lévi-Strauss suggests that the number of myths is small, but the forms they take almost infinite.) My poems are thus the result of a lot of listening to what's within me.

I've tried to make colloquial speech say what it rarely says in talk. This has meant moving away from the more formal phrasing and cadences of my first book towards a plainer speech that says more interesting things. This has also meant a move toward longer poems – toward multiples though, rather than narratives.

I suppose you could say I'm a city poet rather than a rural or a nature poet, even though the country and the sea are an inexhaustible source of images for me. It's in cities that, for me anyway, most life is lived. I find that in Australia it's still possible to live in a city without totally losing touch with the country.

* * *

Andrew Taylor was one of the principal Australian participants at a 1979 poetry seminar, at Macquarie University, entitled "The American Model." His paper on early influences showed he is one of the several Australian poets aged about 40 for whom the surprises in the formative reading of their teens and twenties came from United States poets, and who have shown this influence in an increasing freedom with verse forms, and an increasing openness to personally-associative progressions within the poem. Taylor has absorbed these lessons the more readily because, from the very beginning of his published poetry, his has been an emotionally interpreted world.

The early poems are remarkable for the poet's alertness. They are copiously detailed, in their rendering of places and of moods. The forms are solid and richly-worked – long stanzas, discursive chunks of 20 lines or more, often the three-beat Eliot line. There's openness in a willing use of rhyme, which rarely comes into tyrannical prominence. The academic emerges in a well-bred air of being always informed, but Taylor's real business is listening for the personal suggestiveness that living gives to things. Accordingly, his voice is never raised; the tone is intimate. The tenderness of his love poems is distinctive – as in "the fur coat." His second book deliberately explores the breaking-up of form. In its five parts, the last three referring to a stay in the United States, there are several sequences of short numbered segments. Although the poems derive their clearest human appeal from crises in relationships – the death of a father, a love affair – Taylor keeps his world rich with things and weathers and is liable at any moment to let a gentle, rather introverted humour play among them.

Perhaps his most tonally ambitious work is the Cathedral section of *The Invention of Fire*, a celebration of continuing life in love and art. The sequence works very differently from the "Beyond Silence" assemblages of tiny poems, which have attracted much notice. The nine Cathedral poems have wide literary and historical reference, tend to lyrical but intense conclusions, and only (it seems) by lack of vigilance and sudden pressure allow a nakedly personal cry to emerge:

The whole roof
bursts into earth
at the (careful
of skin cancer you say)
touch of summer

villages have burnt like banknotes
for the profit of sunburn lotion

& you've taken our son away

in the vault's wreckage
small pieces of sky
glitter.

The latest book is a sustained love-discourse written over two months. *The Crystal Absences, The Trout* is particularly fluid, a continuous, eager, and intimate communication of memories – notes on present happenings and emotions – and the straining towards a reunion. It is extraordinarily difficult to represent it by quotation. Here the laboured solidity of Taylor's early manner has quite gone, his quick attentiveness has achieved a form suitably mobile. The play of moods is not trivial, and a Protean short line and Taylor's optimism and unaffectedness keep even intense perceptions from weighing and slowing the poem:

a life in the world
                                        a barefoot
and sure walk over stones
the *feel* of a place we know
because it's now thoroughly ours
thus thoroughly other
and can never be known
                                                  ourselves
at home in that mystery
                                                  Parsifal's
divine stupidity
                                        a shaman's
trust in flight
                                    a man's
and a woman's trust in each other
a child's confidence in love.

It will be interesting to see whether Taylor continues within the tonal limits his writing has so far mostly accepted. He is currently productive, and influential through his critical articles, his role in the Friendly Street poetry readings in Adelaide, and his part in the organization of the Adelaide Festival Writers' Week.

—Judith Rodriguez

THOMAS, D(onald) M(ichael). British. Born in Redruth, Cornwall, 27 January 1935. Educated at Redruth Grammar School; University High School, Melbourne; New College,

Oxford, B.A. (honours) in English, 1958, M.A. Since 1963, Senior Lecturer in English, Hereford College of Education. Visiting Lecturer in English, Hamline University, St. Paul, Minnesota, 1967. Recipient: Richard Hillary Memorial Prize, 1960; Cholmondeley Award, 1978; *Guardian*–Gollancz Fantasy Novel prize, 1979. Address: 10 Greyfriars Avenue, Hereford, England.

PUBLICATIONS

Verse

Personal and Possessive. London, Outposts, 1964.
Penguin Modern Poets 11, with D. M. Black and Peter Redgrove. London, Penguin, 1968.
Two Voices. London, Cape Goliard Press, and New York, Grossman, 1968.
Logan Stone. London, Cape Goliard Press, and New York, Grossman, 1971.
The Shaft. Gillingham, Kent, ARC, 1973.
Lilith-Prints. Cardiff, Second Aeon, 1974.
Symphony in Moscow. Richmond, Surrey, Keepsake Press, 1974.
Love and Other Deaths. London, Elek, 1975.
The Rock. Knotting, Bedfordshire, Sceptre Press, 1975.
Orpheus in Hell. Knotting, Bedfordshire, Sceptre Press, 1977.
The Honeymoon Voyage. London, Secker and Warburg, 1978.

Novel

The Flute-Player. London, Gollancz, 1979.

Other

The Devil and the Floral Dance (juvenile). London, Robson, 1978.

Editor, *The Granite Kingdom: Poems of Cornwall.* Truro, Cornwall, Barton, 1970.
Editor, *Poetry in Crosslight.* London, Longman, 1975.
Editor, *Songs from the Earth: Selected Poems of John Harris, Cornish Miner 1820–84.* Padstow, Cornwall, Lodenek Press, 1977.

Translator, *Requiem, and Poem Without a Hero*, by Anna Akhmatova. London, Elek, and Athens, Ohio University Press, 1976.
Translator, *Way of All the Earth*, by Anna Akhmatova. London, Secker and Warburg, 1979.

D. M. Thomas comments:

My poetry does not move far from love and death. Early poems (see *Penguin Modern Poets 11*) use science fiction themes as images of desire and separation. More recently, my most obsessive themes have been sexuality, family deaths and a search for lost roots.

* * *

To follow the work of D. M. Thomas from his first Outposts booklet *Personal and Possessive* through to his latest collection *The Honeymoon Voyage* is to encounter an impressive development and variety. The early erotic poetry gives way to the series of science fiction poems which established his reputation, and then moves on to a poetry of subtle and tender explorations of relationships and emotions. He is a poet who keeps his readers on the alert, never quite knowing what to expect next. In *The Honeymoon Voyage* we find robust reworkings of Brazilian and Japanese myths together with poems which hark back to his family and roots in Cornwall. One is reminded of Fernando Pessoa, the Portuguese poet who invented three other poets to write in modes other than his own, for D. M. Thomas could well do the same if he was so minded.

Yet for all Thomas's versatility there is a common factor in his work. Thomas is essentially a narrative poet. He is more than that, of course, but he can maintain a narrative flow and thrust which carries the reader along. It is this which gives his science fiction poems their strength, and in this he reminds us of the Victorian narrative poets and especially Browning in such s.f. monologues as "Tithonus," "Cygnus A," and "Hera's Spring." They are, in addition, remarkably atmospheric poems, not only in their exotic settings, but in the depth of feeling they convey of desire and separation: "Believe me, dear, though it will seem strange/ to you, I have wept too for all these/things you mention" ("Hera's Spring"). Yet even in his more recent shorter poems it is the narrative thread, however tenuous, which holds them together and helps to give them unity and coherence. It is the same narrative skill which finds him adapting style, language, and rhythm to match the characters and situations he depicts. For Thomas is a fine craftsman and his style, while often deceptively unobtrusive, is clearly adapted and related to his subject matter.

A case in point is "Under Carn Brea," a series of Cornish portraits ranging from the ribald Mona: "Groaned, bumped and thumped and showed how far/Snapped suspenders sank back in the fat./'I'n it shameful!' Whooped her anguish" to the gentle depths of the understanding of Perry who was to become a near recluse on the death of her husband: "It would have been a shocking waste of life,/But it was Perry's self, and nothing else." On the same theme, "A Cornish Graveyard at Keweenow" is full of atmosphere and overtones: "Couples embrace, weep, talk,/Or asleep. On deck, the Scillies past, the seethe/Of brotherly harmony grows coarse and bouyant." Here we observe Thomas's talent for a creative empathy, where by the use of concrete detail he can obliquely suggest and evoke the complex of emotions inherent in the situations of which he writes. It is good to see a poet growing in strength and skill.

—John Cotton

THOMAS, R(onald) S(tuart). Welsh. Born in Cardiff, Glamorgan, in 1913. Educated at University College, Bangor; St. Michael's College, Llandaff; University of Wales, Degree in Classics, 1935. Ordained Deacon, 1936, Priest, 1937. Curate of Chirk, 1936–40; Curate of Hanmer, 1940–42; Rector of Manafon, 1942–54; Vicar of St. Michael's, Eglwysfach, 1954–67, and of St. Hywyn, Aberdaron, with St. Mary, Bodferin, 1967. Recipient: Heinemann Award, 1955; Queen's Gold Medal for Poetry, 1964; Welsh Arts Council Award, 1968, 1976; Cholmondeley Award, 1978. Address: Sarn-y-Plas y Rhiw, Pwllheli, Gwynedd, Wales.

PUBLICATIONS

Verse

The Stones of the Field. Carmarthen, Druid Press, 1946.
An Acre of Land. Newtown, Montgomeryshire Printing Company, 1952.

The Minister. Newtown, Montgomeryshire Printing Company, 1953.
Song at the Year's Turning: Poems 1942–1954. London, Hart Davis, 1955.
Poetry for Supper. London, Hart Davis, 1958; Chester Springs, Pennsylvania, Dufour, 1961.
Judgement Day. London, Poetry Book Society, 1960.
Tares. London, Hart Davis, and Chester Springs, Pennsylvania, Dufour, 1961.
Penguin Modern Poets 1, with Lawrence Durrell and Elizabeth Jennings. London, Penguin, 1962.
The Bread of Truth. London, Hart Davis, and Chester Springs, Pennsylvania, Dufour, 1963.
Pietà. London, Hart Davis, 1966.
Not that He Brought Flowers. London, Hart Davis, 1968.
Pergamon Poets 1, with Roy Fuller, edited by Evan Owen. Oxford, Pergamon Press, 1968.
Postcard: Song. N.p., Fishpaste, 1968.
The Mountains. New York, Chilmark Press, 1968.
H'm: Poems. London, Macmillan, and New York, St. Martin's Press, 1972.
Selected Poems 1946–1968. London, Hart Davis MacGibbon, 1973; New York, St. Martin's Press, 1974.
What Is a Welshman? Llandybie, Dyfed, Christopher Davies, 1974.
Laboratories of the Spirit. London, Macmillan, 1975; Boston, Godine, 1976.
The Way of It. Sunderland, Ceolfrith Press, 1977.
Frequencies. London, Macmillan, 1978.

Other

Words and the Poet (lecture). Cardiff, University of Wales Press, 1964.
Young and Old (juvenile). London, Chatto and Windus, 1972.

Editor, *The Batsford Book of Country Verse.* London, Batsford, 1961.
Editor, *The Penguin Book of Religious Verse.* London, Penguin, 1963.
Editor, *Selected Poems*, by Edward Thomas. London, Faber, 1964.
Editor, *A Choice of George Herbert's Verse.* London, Faber, 1967.
Editor, *A Choice of Wordsworth's Verse.* London, Faber, 1971.

Critical Studies: in *Welsh Anvil* (Llandybie), 1949, 1952; in *Critical Quarterly* (Manchester), ii, 4, 1960; in *A Review of English Literature* (Leeds), iii, 4, 1960; in *Anglo-Welsh Review* (Pembroke Dock, Wales), xiii, 31, 1963; "R. S. Thomas Issue" of *Poetry Wales* (Llandybie), Winter 1972.

* * *

R. S. Thomas's calling is pastoral in a double sense, as a minister in the Welsh hill-country concerned with the spiritual salvation of his parishioners, and as a poet preoccupied with their figurative redemption in verse. This is pastoral poetry with a sour edge to it, set in a bleak, eroded landscape – "The marginal land where flesh meets spirit/Only on Sundays and the days between/Are mortgaged to grasping soil." Thomas is aware of the parochiality of this world, where "the hedge defines/The mind's limits," and he knows that, lost in "the dark wood" of such a life, the search for "the path/To the bright mansions" expresses not so much a religious need as the desperation of minds denied all hope of earthly consolation. His response is both forthright and yet strangely equivocal. In *The Minister*, a dramatic verse narrative for radio, he explores the inadequate Protestantism of ministers such as Morgan, "Condemned to wither and starve in the cramped cell/Of thought their fathers made them," courageous but callow absolutists unable to comprehend "the soul's/Terrible impotence in a warm world," finally defeated by the "sly/Infirmities" of their flock. Poetry, for Thomas, in its large, forgiving gestures, recovers the love "our science has disinfected" – the last refuge of charity in a secularized world. Yet at the same time, poetry sets a rigorous standard. In "Reservoirs," for example, Thomas sees the material causes of Wales' decline, and "the English/Scavenging among the remains/Of our culture." But he is not content to rest there. As the real reservoir is a source of sustenance to English towns at the expense of drowned Welsh villages, so the "serenity" of Welsh landscape and culture has become "a pose/For strangers, a watercolour's appeal/To the mass" only with Welsh complicity, and "the poem's/Harsher conditions" here become a reproach to the compromises and hypocrisies for which, throughout his poems, he castigates his fellow-countrymen.

Thomas's peasants – Walter Llywarch, Job Davies, or Iago Prytherch ("Just an ordinary man of the bald Welsh hills/Who pens a few sheep in a gap of cloud") – transcend their particularity primarily because of his own unease with them. Prytherch for example reveals "something frightening in the vacancy of his mind" which shocks "the refined,/But affected, sense with ... stark naturalness," and it is precisely this which makes him a "prototype" of human endurance. In "The Face" the memory of a man ploughing on the bare hillside becomes a symbol of that "long wrestling with the angel/Of no name" which is not just theological despair but the hard economic facts of life, which outlast the changing "tenancies of the fields." But Thomas is here aware of the extent to which he *is* creating a symbol in "the mind's gallery." He recognizes, too, without sentimentality, the dereliction, depletion, and shabbiness of this fallen world, seeing, in "Funeral," the grudges and the gossip, the "incidence of pious catarrh/At the grave's edge," and acknowledging, in "Welsh Landscape," the "sham ghosts" of an "impotent people," "Worrying the carcase of an old song." For all his passionate Welshness he knows that, in the end, there is only one Kingdom, and a mere accident of nature endowed him with "the absurd label/Of birth, of race hanging askew/About my shoulders" ("Welsh Testament"). In "Here" he writes of the self as a tree, fixed now, but looking back from its topmost branches to the "footprints that led up to me," finally opting (because he must) to "stay here with my hurt." Staying "in the place I happened to be" is for Thomas the true calling: an acknowledgment of fallenness which allows the soul to struggle against contingency. "In Church" catches the poet/minister searching for God in an empty church, no sound in the darkness except that "of a man/Breathing, testing his faith/On emptiness, nailing his questions/One by one to an untenanted cross." Like those other castaways "Clinging to their doomed farms" ("Those Others") he finds belief in the very moment of doubt, "Trying to understand" why, when there were so many places to be born, "This was the cramped womb/At last took me in/From the void of unbeing." It is a measure of the quiet sophistication of Thomas's faith, as of his poetry, that the phrase "took me in" can live with its dangerous ambiguities. Like "Taliesin 1952," the poet, "Knowing the body's sweetness, the mind's treason," can still affirm, in his desperate faith, "a new world, risen,/Stubborn with beauty, out of the heart's need."

—Stan Smith

THOMSON, Derick S(mith). Scottish. Born in Stornoway, Outer Hebrides, 5 August 1921. Educated at Bayble Public School; Nicolson Institute, Stornoway, 1926–39; University of Aberdeen, 1939–41, 1945–47; Cambridge University, 1947–48; University College of North Wales, Bangor, 1950. Served in the Royal Air Force. Married Carol Galbraith in 1952; six children. Assistant in Celtic, University of Edinburgh, 1948–49; Reader in Celtic, University of Aberdeen, 1956–63. Lecturer in Welsh, 1949–56, and since 1963, Professor of Celtic, University of Glasgow. Since 1952, Editor, *Gairm*, Glasgow. Editor, *Scottish Gaelic Studies*, Aberdeen, 1961–76; Chief, Gaelic Society of Inverness, 1969–70. Since 1964,

President, Scottish Gaelic Texts Society; since 1968, Chairman, Gaelic Books Council. Member, Scottish Arts Council, 1975–77. Recipient: Festival of Britain prize, 1951; Scottish Arts Council Award, 1971; Ossian Prize, 1974. Fellow, Royal Society of Edinburgh, 1976. Address: St. Margarets, Taybridge Road, Aberfeldy, Perthshire, Scotland.

PUBLICATIONS

Verse

An Dealbh Briste (The Broken Picture). Edinburgh, Serif, 1951.
Eadar Samhradh is Foghar (Between Summer and Autumn). Glasgow, Gairm, 1967.
An Rathad Cian (The Far Road). Glasgow, Gairm, 1970.
The Far Road and Other Poems. Edinburgh, M. Macdonald, 1971.
The Far Road. New York, New Rivers Press, 1971.
Saorsa agus an Iolaire (Freedom and the Eagle). Glasgow, Gairm, 1977.

Other

The Gaelic Sources of Macpherson's "Ossian." Edinburgh, Oliver and Boyd, 1952; Folcroft, Pennsylvania, Folcroft Editions, 1973.
Edward Lhuyd in the Scottish Highlands 1699–1700, with John Lorne Campbell. Oxford, Clarendon Press, 1963.
An Introduction to Gaelic Poetry. London, Gollancz, and New York, St. Martin's Press, 1974.
The New Verse in Gaelic (lecture). Dublin, University College, 1974.

Editor, *Branwen Uerch Lyr: The Second of the Four Branches of the Mabinogi Edited from the White Book of Rhydderch with Variants from the Red Book of Hergest and from Peniarth.* Dublin, Institute for Advanced Studies, 1961; revised edition, 1968.
Editor, with Ian Grimble, *The Future of the Highlands.* London, Routledge, 1968.
Editor, *Gaelic in Scotland.* Glasgow, Gairm, 1976.
Editor, with Matthew P. McDiarmid and Adam J. Aitken, *Bards and Makars: Scottish Language and Literature, Medieval and Renaissance.* Glasgow, University of Glasgow Press, 1977.

Critical Studies: by Iain Crichton Smith, in *Lines Review 36* (Edinburgh); Donald MacAuley, in *Lines Review 39* (Edinburgh); John Macinnes, in *Scottish International* (Edinburgh), January 1972; in *Gairm 82* and *105* (Glasgow), 1973, 1978.

Derick S. Thomson comments:

I regard myself, of course, primarily as a Gaelic poet, but have been in the habit of making line-for-line translations of many of my own poems, preserving to a large extent the rhythms of the originals. Perhaps because I live daily in the Gaelic and English-speaking worlds, it might be said that my sensibility is a bilingual one, and I am aware of drawing on the traditions of both Gaelic and English literature, though the words themselves must derive most of their resonance from their Gaelic associations.

English was my lisping language, both in speech and verse. I had begun to repair this monoglot image by the age of five, but was in my late teens before becoming powerfully attracted to Gaelic as a writing language. There were political overtones in this attraction, but it has long hardened into a habit, and I have not attempted original English verse for the last twenty-five years.

The main preoccupations of my verse have been: personal themes (especially in *An Dealbh*

Briste); the building up of a fairly detailed impression of my experience of life in the island of Lewis (culminating in *An Rathad Cian*), and allied to that theme, the experience of alienation; the Scottish nation. Political, especially Nationalist, themes become very prominent in my most recent collection, *Saorsa agus an Iolaire*. For many years I think the mainspring of my verse was a sensuousness which often has associations with Lewis and my upbringing there. In recent years there has been more acerbity and anger, and more fun and ridicule, in my verse.

I became attracted to free verse in my teens, and have worked off and on in that medium since then. I now find it difficult to say what I want to say in another form. I hope that I have contributed significantly to the development of this style in Gaelic.

* * *

The fact that Derick S. Thomson grew up on the island of Lewis and has perforce spent his adult life in very different surroundings gives a distinct context to his memories of earlier life. But as well as this richly detailed personal history we also find a sharp focus on social, economic and linguistic circumstances, for those very years, the twenties and early thirties, coincided with the last years of a fully indigenous communal life in the area, so that his memories of boyhood are inextricably linked with his feelings about the erosion of Gaelic society.

Thus while Lewis is a geographical anchor, with its place-names further indicating a deep historical context, the island also has a parallel, non-geographical existence in the poet's mind and feelings. It has been subjected to the alchemy of memory and appears in many transformations (monster, sweet-heart, standing-stone, emigrant ship). Similarly, the nostalgia exists on several different levels. It is relatively straightforward in references to, say, "a coffinful of songs" being laid in the earth. It can be blended with a polemical sharpness, the latter being directed not only towards attempts to improve the purely material aspects of highland life, but also towards that indifference within the beleaguered community which in effect becomes an ally of intrusion from without. And at the level where the poet recognises the apparent insolubility of his dilemma yet refuses to abandon it, the nostalgia is clearly only one element in a complex response:

> The heart tied to a tethering post, round upon round of rope
> till it grows short,
> and the mind free.
> I bought its freedom dearly.

It is worth adding that Thomson's role as a Gaelic writer is not confined to his poetry, for while in that poetry he explores the shifting connections between past and present, as they affect both himself as an individual and the society to which he belongs, he is also actively engaged as a scholar, entrepreneur and propagandist in a wide range of practical activities aimed at preserving and reviving the culture of that society.

—Robin Fulton

THWAITE, Anthony (Simon). British. Born in Chester, Cheshire, 23 June 1930. Educated in Leeds; Sheffield; the United States, 1940–44; at Kingswood School, Bath; Christ Church, Oxford, B.A. (honours) 1955, M.A. 1959. Military Service, 1949–51. Married the writer Ann Harrop in 1955; four daughters. Visiting Lecturer in English Literature, Tokyo

University, Japan, 1955–57; Radio Producer, BBC London, 1957–62; Literary Editor, *The Listener*, London, 1962–65; Assistant Professor of English, University of Libya, Benghazi, 1965–67; Literary Editor, *New Statesman*, London, 1968–72. Since 1973, Co-Editor, *Encounter*, London. Recipient: Richard Hillary Memorial Prize, 1967; Henfield Writing Fellowship, University of East Anglia, Norwich, Summer 1972. Fellow, Royal Society of Literature, 1978. Address: The Mill House, Tharston, Norfolk NR15 2YN, England.

PUBLICATIONS

Verse

(Poems). Oxford, Fantasy Press, 1953.
Home Truths. Hessle, Yorkshire, Marvell Press, 1957.
The Owl in the Tree: Poems. London, Oxford University Press, 1963.
The Stones of Emptiness: Poems 1963–66. London, Oxford University Press, 1967.
Penguin Modern Poets 18, with A. Alvarez and Roy Fuller. London, Penguin, 1970.
Points. London, Turret, 1972.
Inscriptions: Poems 1967–72. London, Oxford University Press, 1973.
Jack. Hitchin, Hertfordshire, Cellar Press, 1973.
New Confessions. London, Oxford University Press, 1974.
A Portion for Foxes. London, Oxford University Press, 1977.

Other

Essays on Contemporary English Poetry: Hopkins to the Present Day. Tokyo, Kenkyusha, 1957; revised edition, as *Contemporary English Poetry: An Introduction*, London, Heinemann, 1959; Chester Springs, Pennsylvania, Dufour, 1961.
Japan in Colour, photographs by Roloff Beny. London, Thames and Hudson, and New York, McGraw Hill, 1967.
The Deserts of Hesperides: An Experience of Libya. London, Secker and Warburg, and New York, Roy, 1969.
Poetry Today 1960–1973. London, Longman, 1973.
Roloff Beny in Italy, with Peter Porter. London, Thames and Hudson, 1974.
Beyond the Inhabited World: Roman Britain (juvenile). London, Deutsch, 1976; New York, Seabury Press, 1977.
Twentieth-Century English Poetry. London, Heinemann, and New York, Barnes and Noble, 1978.

Editor, with Hilary Corke and William Plomer, *New Poems 1961.* London, Hutchinson, 1961.
Editor, and Translator with Geoffrey Bownas, *The Penguin Book of Japanese Verse.* London, Penguin, 1964.
Editor, with Peter Porter, *The English Poets: From Chaucer to Edward Thomas.* London, Secker and Warburg, 1974.
Editor, *Poems for Shakespeare 3.* London, Globe Playhouse, 1974.
Editor, with Fleur Adcock, *New Poetry 4.* London, Hutchinson, 1978.

Manuscript Collection: Brynmor Jones Library, University of Hull, Yorkshire.

* * *

Domestic themes, and the small, homely detail of the everyday scene, predominate in Anthony Thwaite's earlier work. His rueful self-analysis in "Things" and "Personal Effects" confesses to an incorrigible magpie propensity for collecting and hoarding objects. "Things stick to me like burrs"; for these represent concrete proof of the actuality of life which is his chosen subject rather than the abstractions of thought. He writes often, with truth and tenderness, about a father's feelings for his children: sharing as they grow their wonder in discovering the world, but experiencing too the chill of fear during a child's illness, a painful protectiveness towards their vulnerability. Poems like "The Cry," "A Disturbance," and "Night Thoughts" reveal his disquieting sense of some primitive, nameless unease lurking just beneath the calm familiar surface, kept at bay by comforting daily trivia but leaping nocturnally to life to challenge "our bastions of pretence" and threatening the cherished certainties.

But Thwaite's interest has been by no means confined to private satisfactions and anxieties; to exploring his own past recorded in the scars on his body, or the present personality which looks hesitantly back at him from the middle-aged face in the shaving mirror. From the warmth and safety of the family he ponders, in "Home Truths," the meaning of vagrancy and exile; and his alert perception constantly probes, through some chance incident, universal human themes. The crude brashness of boys on a train recalls Larkin in its sharp-eyed precision of detail; and another railway encounter is described in "Incident," where the unwilling listener's irritated indifference to a plausible hard-luck story gradually changes into shamed discomfort and concern. Compassion is, in fact, the keynote of Thwaite's attitude to life – even that of the fly he stalks and kills: "And yet I know the weight/Of small deaths weighs me down." With moving insight he observes the apathy of people in station buffet-bars on Sunday afternoons; the silent, solitary spinster staring at space in a hotel lounge; the foreigner in a pub, banished by his "normal human brother" to a world "with every man a stranger,/Except to indifference." The powerful impact, in "Mr. Cooper," of a laconically scrawled message recording the death of a local jeweller, rivals Larkin's "Mr. Bleaney" in its recognition of the bleak anonymity of the human lot.

Similar feelings are aroused by a cheap memorial to an unknown man washed ashore in Japan, one of the various countries where Thwaite has lived and worked. Conflicting with his need of domestic roots and order, a desire to escape from habit which "silts up, stifles" drove him in search of wider horizons; and the stimulus afforded by change and novelty has given his work a fresh colour, energy, and poetic dimension. Foreign scenes and customs are vividly and acutely chronicled: from the inscrutabilities of Japan ("so cruel, so delicate") to social contrast in a Benghazi street, the alien rhetoric and ritual of wedding and funeral, or the psychology of an astute Arab vendor of antiquities to tourists for whom the past means nothing but "a time when things were made to keep me alive."

To Thwaite, history has a far deeper significance – exemplified in earlier poems with English backgrounds like "The Barrow," his musings on the drowned villages at Pagham Harbour and Dunwich, and the magnificent "Manhood End"; while the legacy of the living to the future is memorably expressed in "Leavings." In later volumes man's ancestral inheritance has developed into a major preoccupation. The stone circles and implements of abandoned desert encampments in *The Stones of Emptiness* are eloquent of former existence. The scimitar curve of Arabic script on tombs of an ancient battle evokes "A swirl of black flags, white crescents, and a language of swords." Many poems in *Inscriptions* originate in old records, and range geographically from English monastic ruins to the Valley of the Kings.

Always Thwaite's sense of history as a potent, pervasive presence is animated by an intensely contemporary consciousness. In juxtaposing the relics of battles past and recent – a cave-painting of Odysseus returning from Troy and a German grave and helmet at Asquefar; Ptolemy's prefect, and his fifteen cohorts, with their successors "grinning in khaki drill" – he stresses the continuity of human experience. The witty, meticulously documented "Letters of Synesius" employs modern colloquial idiom to synthesize the life and times of a fourth-century Cyrenean bishop with the viewpoint of a disenchanted commentator on present-day society.

—Margaret Willy

TIEMPO, Edith (Lopez). Filipino. Born in Nueva Vizcaya, 22 April 1919. Educated at Silliman University, Dumaguete City, B.S.E. 1947; University of Iowa, Iowa City, M.A. 1949; University of Denver, Colorado, Ph.D. 1958. Married to E. K. Tiempo; two children. Since 1961, Professor of English, currently Chairman of the English Department, Silliman University. Visiting Professor of English, Western Michigan University, Kalamazoo, 1963–64, 1965–66, and Wartburg College, Waverly, Iowa, 1964–65. Recipient: Rockefeller Grant, 1949, 1971; Palanca Award, for poetry, 1967, for short story, 1969; Asia Foundation Grant, 1971. Address: Department of English, Silliman University, Dumaguete City, Philippines.

PUBLICATIONS

Verse

The Tracks of Babylon and Other Poems. Denver, Swallow, 1966.

Novels

A Blade of Fern. Manila, A. S. Florentino, 1978.
His Native Coast. Manila, A. S. Florentino, 1979.

Short Stories

Abide, Joshua and Other Stories. Manila, A. S. Florentino, 1964.

Critical Study: by A. O. Constantino, in *Solidarity* (Manila), August 1968.

Edith Tiempo comments:

I am more a fictionist and critic of poetry than a poet. Perhaps my poetry might not fit under any one "school" because, although I write in English, I often work with myths and folk metaphors not easily recognizable outside my geographical milieu. Possible influences are Robert Frost; Nashville group; W. H. Auden's British Socialist group.

The main problem from the beginning has been the projection of the universal through particulars that are (even psychically sometimes) alien to the language medium. But art and communication are miraculous; I feel that this polarity can actually give a valid kind of mystery to the utterance; I feel this has been the case in some of my poems (e.g. "The Tracks of Babylon" and "The Pestle," both published in *Poetry*, Chicago). This kind of "incongruity" is the reason that the poetry has come so slowly – I hope to be able to work more and more meaningfully within this tension between the language and the material.

One American critic criticized my poetry for its use of "archaisms" (the nearest equivalents to transliterating a certain indigenous tone), and praised the poems that are toughened in tone by the abstract, "intellectual" vocabulary. Understandably, I feel easier working with images of the natural world, and like Yeats and Frost I would let these images reveal their final tough meaningfulness through the peepholes that the poet quite often directs himself to "stumble" upon.

* * *

Edith Tiempo's poetry is reminiscent of W. B. Yeats and T. S. Eliot by whom she was deeply influenced, but her finely chiselled images are put to different purposes from theirs. Tiempo's symbols develop a theme common to all her work – one's failure to establish meaningful relationships with others. Her poetry is both cerebral and sensuous. She overwhelms the reader with images which reflect the urgency of the efforts to comprehend formless experience. Her telescoping of past and present lend to these attempts the timelessness and terror of universalised experience. Her poem "The Tracks of Babylon" shows that the search can end only in paradox. The quest for an ordering principle in life becomes futile by one's very obsessiveness. In old age, "Not death, but Memory is the beast" to be feared ("Green Hearts") as man awakes to "bruise [his] hands on the living cage" of his own self ("Lament for the Littlest Fellow"). Yet there is no bitterness because self-knowledge suffuses the old man's disorientation and enables him to live harmoniously with others ("The Return").

Most Asian writers are similarly engaged in the quest for an identity but Tiempo's treatment of the issue is different from that, say, of her compatriots R. Demetillo and A. G. Hufana, and Malaysia's Wong Phui Nam: they trace the quest historically while she is interested only in its impact on the quality of personal life; theirs is a poetry of self-concern, hers one of communication. It is the manner in which she effects this communication that enables her to hold her own against English poets not only in the Philippines but also elsewhere in Asia.

—Abdul Majid bin Nabi Baksh

TILLER, Terence (Rogers). British. Born in Truro, Cornwall, 19 September 1916. Educated at Latymer Upper School, Hammersmith, London; Jesus College, Cambridge (Chancellor's Medal, 1936), B.A. (honours) in history 1937, M.A. 1940. Married; two daughters. Research Scholar and Director of Studies, 1937–39, and University Lecturer in Medieval History, 1939, Cambridge University; Lecturer in English History and Literature, Fuad I University, Cairo, Egypt, 1939–46. Radio Writer and Producer, Features Department, 1946–65, and Drama Department, 1965–76, BBC, London. Lives in Roehampton, London. Address: c/o Chatto and Windus Ltd., 40–42 William IV Street, London WC2N 4DF, England.

PUBLICATIONS

Verse

Poems. London, Hogarth Press, 1941.
The Inward Animal. London, Hogarth Press, 1943.
Unarm, Eros. London, Hogarth Press, 1947.
Reading a Medal and Other Poems. London, Hogarth Press, 1957.
Notes for a Myth and Other Poems. London, Hogarth Press–Chatto and Windus, 1968.
That Singing Mesh and Other Poems. London, Chatto and Windus, 1979.

Plays

The Death of Adam (produced Edinburgh, 1950).

Radio Writings: hundreds of features and plays, including the following plays: *The Wakefield Shepherds' Play* and *Play of Noah*, 1947–48; *The Death of a Friend*, 1949; *The Cornish Cycle of Mystery Plays*, 1949–62; *Lilith*, 1950; *The Tower of Hunger*, 1952; *The Parlement of Foules*, from the work by Chaucer, 1958; *Final Meeting*, 1966; *The*

Carde of Fancie, from the work by Robert Greene, 1966; *The Diversions of Hawthornden*, 1967; *The Assembly of Ladies*, 1968; *Zeus the Barnstormer*, 1969; *After Ten Years*, from a work by C. S. Lewis, 1969; *The Flower and the Leaf*, 1970; *The Batchelar's Banquet*, from a work by Thomas Dekker, 1971; *Four of a Kind*, from a work by Verlaine, 1975; *Madame Aubin*, from a work by Verlaine, 1976; *The Defence*, from the novel by Nabokov, 1979.

Other

Editor, with others, *Personal Landscape: An Anthology of Exile*. London, Editions Poetry London, 1945.
Editor, with Anthony Cronin and Jon Silkin, *New Poems 1960*. London, Hutchinson, 1960.
Editor and Translator, *Confessio Amantis (The Lover's Shrift)*, by John Gower. London, Penguin, 1963.
Editor and Co-Translator, *The Inferno*, by Dante. London, BBC, 1966; New York, Schocken, 1967.
Editor, *Chess Treasury of the Air*. London, Penguin, 1966.

Terence Tiller comments:

I am a poet only in so far as my other interests and occupations are *coloured* by my being a poet. Of course I look at history, novels, music, radio, etc., etc., *differently* because of that. But I don't, and can't, and would never have been able to, earn my living as a poet.

I have been called, and am willing to call myself, "a modern metaphysical." Certainly, I have been more influenced by the "metaphysicals" than by any other poets except Dante and Rilke. Minor, sometimes transient, influences, include obvious names like Hopkins, Eliot, early-to-middle Auden. Most of *them* would/would have disown/disowned me! As far as verse-form is concerned, I tend almost exclusively towards the "traditional," while allowing myself such "license" as I need for specific purposes. I feel strongly that regular prosody is a "springboard" that a poet abandons at his own risk. (Always provided that he can cope with it! Whatever else I am or am not, I am a *technician* in verse.)

Themes? Almost entirely a-political as far as poetry is concerned – except that poetry and politics involve morality, and I am fairly committed *there* (though not with any "party" or "sectarian" affiliation). I would claim to be a polymath, and to attempt poems as a kind of syncretism of the emotions, speculations, and symbolic coincidences, that arise out of my physical and mental experience.

* * *

Terence Tiller's first volume, *Poems*, is immature, but foreshadows certain positive qualities of his later work: the ability, for example, to control complex verse patterns, accomplished rhetoric and an impressive, if cold, heraldic use of imagery. *The Inward Animal* reflects Tiller's experiences as a civilian in the Middle East of the war years, where he was associated with the "Personal Landscape" group: Lawrence Durrell, Bernard Spencer, and Robin Fedden. Flanked by two poems, "Eclogue for a Dying House" and "The Birth of Christ," which attempt in social and religious modes respectively to generalise the pattern of war, exile and single strangeness, the volume's theme in Tiller's own words is to explore the impact of that strangeness which "must have shaken, and perhaps destroyed, many a customary self. There will have been a shocked and defensive rebellion; reconciliation must follow; the birth of some mutual thing in which the old and the new, the self and the alien, are combined after war. ... The birth of something at once myself, the new self and 'Egypt' is the 'inward animal.' " Such a dialectic makes the volume sound somewhat more schematised than it actually is, but underlines the fact that Tiller has always applied stratagems in his work and has never minimised the importance of pure craft. Rilke and the Metaphysicals are presences in *The Inward Animal*. Tiller preferred (until his most recent work) assonance to rhyme, using rhyming only when he wished to enact finality. The poems are strongest where they rise from some observed scene or persons, least sensuous when "Egypt" is missing from the record, even if one allows some dramatic cogency in the ordering of individual poems. Once or twice it becomes difficult to distinguish the "metaphysical" idiom from highly accomplished *New Statesman* competition verse:

> The silence that I break was more profound,
> and purer sound
> – as being absent is a kind
> of closer bridal in the mind.

It is difficult to see what purpose this allusiveness achieves. The impact of such poems as "Bathers," "Sphinx," "The Convalescent Party," and "Egyptian Dancer" (interesting to compare with Bernard Spencer's "Egyptian Dancer at Subra": these gifted poets seem on occasion to have tackled topics in collusion) is immediate – and lasting. Another feature of *Inward Animal* is a happy sensuousness that counterpoints the heraldic coldness, arrived at by dense and witty use of figure, perhaps more *concettist* than metaphysical, though Tiller rarely suppresses the tenor of his metaphors. *Inward Animal* abounds with felicities: "the flags that slap his plunging knee,/and the cold stocking of the stream" ("Bathers"), or "and the soft lath of woman bears/a heaven's agonising weight" ("The Incubus"). "Europa," the second of four folk songs, wittily reads a locomotive and its shed as a modern version of a fertility myth and demonstrates Tiller's virtuosity.

Unarm, Eros is perhaps Tiller's finest collection. The bold sensuousness, the wit and enigma of the surface work together. It is difficult to isolate particular triumphs, but perhaps "Perfumes," "Roman Portraits," "Hospital" (compare Spencer's "In a Foreign Hospital"), "Beggar," an example of strict, compassionate observation, and "Image in a Lilac Tree" incise themselves most sharply. *Reading a Medal* contains individual poems as striking as any Tiller has written, but a general impression persists of pressure diffused, lyricism of less intensity, puzzles not altogether worth solving and the impression is more strongly marked in *Notes for a Myth*. Tiller is reported to have remarked that "mere experience is a distraction" (doubtless he meant something more subtle) but one can barely avoid applying this somewhat ironically to his later work, where the tensions, the concrete situations that underlay *The Inward Animal* and *Unarm, Eros* have been gravely attenuated. The poems have tended to become longer, to retreat further into pattern and myth. The social commentator who kept such good company with the introvert has disappeared. But Tiller's poetry has already asserted its own lingering resonances. He remains something of a poet's poet and must always appeal to those who respond to the mystery of the vocation.

—Ian Fletcher

TILLINGHAST, Richard. American. Born in Memphis, Tennessee, 25 November 1940. Educated at the University of the South, Sewanee, Tennessee (Assistant Editor, *Sewanee Review*), A.B. 1962; Harvard University, Cambridge, Massachusetts (Woodrow Wilson Fellow), A.M. 1968, Ph.D. 1970. Assistant Professor of English, University of California, Berkeley, 1968–73. Currently, Member of the Department of English, College of Marin, Kentfield, California, and teacher at San Quentin State Prison. Address: 88 Walnut Avenue, Corte Madera, California 94925, U.S.A.

PUBLICATIONS

Verse

The Keeper. Cambridge, Massachusetts, Pym Randall Press, 1968.
Sleep Watch. Middletown, Connecticut, Wesleyan University Press, 1969.

Critical Studies: "The Future of Confession" by Alan Williams, in *Shenandoah* (Lexington, Virginia), Summer 1970; "At the First Doorway of the Lost Life" by James Atlas, in *Chicago Review*, Autumn 1970.

Richard Tillinghast comments:

I see poetry as a kind of invocation of the spiritual reality inherent in things – the hidden and mysterious significance to us of colors, sounds, smells. It is something like the speech of beautiful animals and plants, if they could speak. For me, though not necessarily for others, poetry still carries within it the magic of the early days of the human race. At its best it is consistent with the grace, naturalness, solidity, charm, thrill, and necessity of man's earliest accomplishments: hunting, fire-building, cooking, cultivation of the soil, and weaving. It is the voice of our blood.

* * *

Richard Tillinghast's *Sleep Watch* amazed its readers with a startling, ingenious way of seeing things. Here is an animal describing God's bungling of Creation: "Later on when he saw that things had gone wrong/... it rested him to look at us/And I found I could love him in his weakness/as I never could before/the beauty left his face. ..." Here is "Waking on the Train": "after the commuters/cigars windows being jerked open/your body begins to know it hasn't slept/It thinks of all the parts of itself/that would touch a bed...."

Many of Tillinghast's poems touch on that dream-like area of consciousness between waking and sleeping. Everything real is in doubt, and that may be desirable. "Is everything sliding?" he asks in a poem called "Everything Is Going to Be All Right" and answers himself, "Nothing/to worry about –/Getting lost means sliding in all directions."

The present American fashions in poetry – Eastern mysticism, Nature worship, confession – hover dangerously about Tillinghast's work, but they are kept at bay by his delicate obliqueness plus a hawk's eye for metaphor. "I put the cap back onto the pen/the way a court reunites a/mother and child." "I am alert at once/and think of the cat/coasting on its muscles...."

One of the best poems in *Sleep Watch* is about rising from a childhood illness and confronting the world of health. The poet senses an undefined disappointment in his parents; he has not given them cause to mourn: "For them I am closing the door to the place/where the dead children are stored/where the pets have gone to heaven."

A certain self-consciousness has led Tillinghast to develop his own style. He uses spaces where one would normally expect punctuation, allowing his poem to lie on the page between breathing intervals, like directions for speech. Self-consciousness and sensitivity: there is an abundance of this. It will be interesting to see where Tillinghast goes after having given us this brilliant tour of his complex psyche.

—Anne Stevenson

TOMLINSON, (Alfred) Charles. British. Born in Stoke-on-Trent, Staffordshire, 8 January 1927. Educated at Queens' College, Cambridge, B.A. 1948; London University, M.A. 1955. Married Brenda Raybould in 1948; two daughters. Since 1956, Member of the Faculty, currently, Reader in English Poetry, University of Bristol. Visiting Professor, University of New Mexico, Albuquerque, 1962–63; O'Connor Professor of Literature, Colgate University, Hamilton, New York, 1967. Artist: One Man Shows – Oxford University Press, London, 1972, Clare College, Cambridge, 1975, and Arts Council tour, 1978. Recipient: Bess Hokin Prize, 1956, Levinson Prize, 1960, Oscar Blumenthal Prize, 1960, Union League Civic and Arts Foundation Prize, 1961, Inez Boulton Prize, 1964, and Frank O'Hara Prize, 1968 (*Poetry*, Chicago); University of New Mexico D. H. Lawrence Fellowship, 1963; University of Texas National Translation Center grant, 1968; Institute of International Education Fellowship, 1968; Cholmondeley Award, 1979. Fellow, Royal Society of Literature, 1974. Honorary Fellow, Queens' College, Cambridge, 1974. Lives in Ozleworth Bottom, Gloucestershire, England.

PUBLICATIONS

Verse

Relations and Contraries. Aldington, Kent, Hand and Flower Press, 1951.
The Necklace. Oxford, Fantasy Press, 1955; revised edition, London, Oxford University Press, 1966.
Solo for a Glass Harmonica. San Francisco, Poems in Folio, 1957.
Seeing Is Believing. New York, McDowell Obolensky, 1958; London, Oxford University Press, 1960.
A Peopled Landscape. London, Oxford University Press, 1963.
Poems: A Selection, with Tony Connor and Austin Clarke. London, Oxford University Press, 1964.
American Scenes and Other Poems. London, Oxford University Press, 1966.
The Mattachines. Cerillos, New Mexico, San Marcos Press, 1968.
To Be Engraved on the Skull of a Cormorant. London, Unaccompanied Serpent, 1968.
Penguin Modern Poets 14, with Alan Brownjohn and Michael Hamburger. London, Penguin, 1969.
The Way of a World. London, Oxford University Press, 1969.
America West Southwest. Cerillos, New Mexico, San Marcos Press, 1969.
Renga, with others. Paris, Gallimard, 1970; translated by the author, New York, Braziller, 1972.
Words and Images. London, Covent Garden Press, 1972.
Written on Water. London, Oxford University Press, 1972.
The Way In and Other Poems. London, Oxford University Press, 1974.
The Shaft. London, Oxford University Press, 1974.
Selected Poems 1951–1974. London, Oxford University Press, 1978.

Other

The Poem as Initiation. Hamilton, New York, Colgate University Press, 1967.
In Black and White (graphics). Cheadle, Cheshire, Carcanet Press, 1976.

Editor, *Marianne Moore: A Collection of Critical Essays.* Englewood Cliffs, New Jersey, Prentice Hall, 1969.
Editor, *William Carlos Williams: Critical Anthology.* London, Penguin, 1972.
Editor, *Selected Poems*, by William Carlos Williams. London, Penguin, 1976.
Editor and Translator, *Selected Poems*, by Octavio Paz. London, Penguin, 1979.

Translator, *Versions from Fyodor Tyutchev, 1803–1873*. London, Oxford University Press, 1960.
Translator, with Henry Gifford, *Castilian Ilexes: Versions from Antonio Machado*. London, Oxford University Press, 1963.
Translator, with Henry Gifford, *Ten Versions from Trilce*, by César Vallejo. Cerillos, New Mexico, San Marcos Press, 1970.

Manuscript Collection: British Library, London.

Critical Studies: "Negotiations: American Scenes and Other Poems" by Michael Kirkham, in *Essays on Criticism* (Oxford), July 1967; "The Poetry of Charles Tomlinson" by Michael Edwards, in *Agenda 9* (London), 1970; Calvin Bedient, in *Eight Contemporary Poets*, London, Oxford University Press, 1974; interview with Jed Rasula and Mike Erwin, in *Contemporary Literature* (Madison, Wisconsin), Autumn 1975; Michael Schmidt, in *PN Review* (Manchester), v, 1, 1977; by the author, in *Contemporary Literature* (Madison, Wisconsin), Summer 1977.

Charles Tomlinson comments:

My theme is relationship. The hardness of crystals, the facets of cut glass; but also the shifting of light, the energizing weather which is the result of the combination of sun and frost – these are the images for a certain mental climate, components for the moral landscape of my poetry in general. One critic has described that climate as Augustan. But it is an Augustanism that has felt the impact of French poetry – Baudelaire to Valéry – and of modern American poetry. A phenomenological poetry, with roots in Wordsworth and in Ruskin, is what I take myself to be writing. Translation has been an accompanying discipline and so have drawing and painting.

* * *

A rootedness in things, an intelligence of eye and ear, have informed Charles Tomlinson's poetry from the beginning. What Donald Davie wrote in his introduction to *The Necklace* (1955) applies with probably greater force to his most recent poetry: "The world of these poems is a public one, open to any man who has kept clean and in order his nervous sensitivity to the impact of shape and mass and colour, odour, texture, and timbre. The poems appeal outside of themselves only to the world perpetually bodied against our senses. They improve that world. Once we have read them, it appears to us renovated and refreshed, its colours more delicate and clear, its masses more momentous, its sounds and odours sharper, more distinct."

Tomlinson is also a visual artist and there is a quality of *seeing*, a beauty derived from a minute observation of particular things, in his finest work. His words exactly fit his objects, whereas bad poetry erects a barrier between our perceptions and external reality. Allied to this is a lack of rhetoric, and a stillness, perhaps exemplified best in "Farewell to Van Gogh."

But Charles Tomlinson's work has not remained static. In *American Scenes*, there is a quality of *sound* which reinforces and vitalizes what was at times in the early work mere precision of visual description. These poems exemplify Louis Zukofsky's statement: "To see is to inform all speech." The best of these poems grow out of "solitary, sharpened perception" (to quote one of them) in desert places, or the heart of Winter:

Between the graves, you find
a beheaded pigeon, the blood and grain
trailed from its bitten crop, as alien to all
the day's pallor as the raw
wounds of the earth, turned above
a fresh solitary burial.

In the "American Scenes" section of this book, it is the desolation of ghost towns ("Speak of the life that uselessness has unconstrained"), and of the desert that produced some of the most solid and lucid poetry published in England in the sixties. In many of these poems also there is a concern for people. This is particularly present in "Death in the Desert," in memory of an old Hopi doll-maker.

Good poets often discover poets that they are particularly suited to translate and Tomlinson is no exception. His collaboration with Henry Gifford in versions of the Spanish poet Antonio Machado, *Castilian Ilexes*, has enriched English poetry, added a new dimension, and this is the one justification for the translation of poetry. A love of people also permeates these poems. One of the most moving, "Lament of the Virtues and Verses on Account of the Death of Don Guido," is an elegy which has, at the same time, a lightness, hilaritas, that could not have come out of England. It is a creative achievement to have brought this across so that the poem has become part of the English tradition:

The here
and the there,
cavalier,
show in your withered face,
confess the infinite:
the nothingness.
Oh the thin cheeks
yellow
and the eyelids, wax,
and the delicate skull
on the bed's pillow!

In *The Way of a World* and *Written on Water* Tomlinson continues to define his perceptions of people, landscape, air and water. In "Clouds," from the former collection, he has almost overcome the immense difficulties involved in finding adequate words for such intangibles, though here, of course, Shakespeare has excelled him. At times, in Tomlinson's later poetry, there is an over-complexity of language – the vocabulary and sentence structure have the effect of distancing the reader from the subject matter of the poems. But there are several powerful poems in both *The Way of a World* and *Written on Water*, e.g., "The Apparition."

Charles Tomlinson's finest poems are rhythmic units of beauty. They fix moments of heightened perception, of sound and sight, in permanent words. I think particularly here of "The Well," in the Mexican section of *American Scenes*. It is a complete, perfectly balanced statement (consequently it is impossible to substantiate what I am saying by a quotation) while being a complex pattern of things felt with roots extending at the same instant into many areas of experience both past and present.

—William Cookson

TONKS, Rosemary (D. Boswell). British. Born in London. Married. Has lived in West Africa and Pakistan. Poetry Reviewer, BBC European Service. Address: 46 Downshire Hill, London N.W.3, England.

PUBLICATIONS

Verse

Notes on Cafés and Bedrooms. London, Putnam, 1963.

Iliad of Broken Sentences. London, Bodley Head, 1967.

Novels

Opium Fogs. London, Putnam, 1963.
Emir. London, Adam, 1963.
The Bloater. London, Bodley Head, 1968.
Businessmen as Lovers. London, Bodley Head, 1969; as *Love among the Operators*, Boston, Gambit, 1970.
The Way Out of Berkeley Square. London, Bodley Head, 1970; Boston, Gambit, 1971.
The Halt During the Chase. London, Bodley Head, 1972; New York, Harper, 1973.

Other

On Wooden Wings: The Adventures of Webster (juvenile). London, Murray, 1948.
The Wild Sea Goose (juvenile). London, Murray, 1951.

Rosemary Tonks comments:

I have developed a visionary modern lyric, and, for it, an idiom in which I can write lyrically, colloquially, and dramatically. My subject is city life – with its sofas, hotel corridors, cinemas, underworlds, cardboard suitcases, self-willed buses, banknotes, soapy bathrooms, newspaper-filled parks; and its anguish, its enraged excitement, its great lonely joys.

* * *

The extravagant ego of Rosemary Tonks's vivacious, heady poetry is a compound of violent opposites, of roles held together not only by a flamboyant imagination but also by a sense of the flagrant contradictions of the city in which that imagination has its origins. Whatever the aspect displayed – street arab, lover, gambler, "gutter lord," dressing-gowned dreamer, or thief – the poet remains the mirror of the city, its gentle lover, tenderly exposing its most painful truths, diamond cutting diamond, until the violence of the city's reaction transforms him suddenly into its tormentor, a blood-stained matador: "the diamond smells blood and gores/The poet in the ribs in self-defence" ("Poet and Iceberg").

Tonks's cities are always cosmopolitan, whether they be London, Paris, Rome, or Istanbul; each has its own flavour, but all are blended together in the experience of a self-acknowledged transient, a bedouin, an inhabitant of hotel corridors. The poet sees the whole city, "the whole/Imperial rubbish heap of wastrels, scullions,/Houris, fauns and bedouin" ("Bedroom in an Old City"); but frames her vision in her own chosen perspective of decadence and decay: "I had/My lodgings in that quarter of the city/Like a cat's ear full of cankered passages" ("Gutter Lord"). Romantically, she revels in squalor glamourised with a Baudelairean exoticism. The oriental imagery of "Gutter Lord" transforms the green slime underfoot: "Like dungeon floors which/Cobras have lubricated/Your time was kept in shiny yawns."

The "Auroras, icy champagnes" of "Escape" can't be savoured by the city palate until they are processed in the city's foul kitchens: "Your soul knows half the flavour/Lies underfoot in dirty flagstones." Poetry, sex, drugs, and alcohol are not the means to transcend the city's foulness but images of its intoxicating ferments. "Bedouin of the London Morning" acknowledges "My (half-erotic) convulsion of loathing/For the night"; the poet leaning against "The Sash Window" forlornly "Eats again the reek" of a glass she knows she should shatter; "Orpheus in Soho" makes his own hell, deliberately looking for his Eurydice in dingy flesh-markets where she could never be: "there is so little risk of finding her/In Europe's old blue Kasbah, and he knows it."

The poetry lives through a perpetual nostalgia for a stormy adolescence, contrasting black, infernal moods with sudden gushes of refreshing scents ("Oath"); similarly, in "Bedroom in an Old City," squalor has as its focus the sleeping face of "a London minx of seventeen," "a life so young, secret and clean." "Adolescent" fuses the images of adolescent and bohemian, and explores further the nature of adolescence, which it sees as a refusal to be formed, an insistence on staying on the fringes, which produces the feverishly throbbing pulse of "real" life. The delinquent has an original place in history, set apart from all those who accept the uniform of convention. Not only the professionals – gloved surgeon and thief – but also the gloved dandy in his fastidious detachment, the Baudelairean *flâneur*, are spurned for the vandal's attack:

> You, who would tame with toolbag or certificate
> My shudder ... as the east
> Drinks diamonds, and the world's born blazing underfoot!
> Surgeon and robber learn their touch in the great city,
> But I am after heavenly spoil, and it is
> As a gloveless trespasser that I desire supremacy.

It's hard to know sometimes what the poet intends us to make of her self-indulgent bohemianism. The masculine personae of some of her poems indicates a certain desire to keep the role at a distance. The self-deprecating title of "April and the Ideas-Merchant" undercuts the self-congratulation of a text which informs us that: "Poets are only at work/... When they live, dream, *bleed* – within an inch of giving in to art"; in "On the Advantage of Being Ill-Treated by the World" an imaginative sense of humour deflates all Romantic pretension. Elsewhere, there is evidence of a commitment to the posture alarming in its intensity – not only to the reader, but to the role-player herself. The poetry confesses: "I have been young too long, and in a dressing-gown/My private modern life has gone to waste." Between the lines, "A Few Sentences Away," lurks a sense of the real vacancy which no amount of violent attitudinising can disguise:

> Let me *hide*, well away from a past that dreams
> Like that. Away from streets that taste of blood and sugar
> When the glowing month smashes itself against the hedges
> In the dark.

—Jennifer Birkett

TORRES, Emmanuel. Filipino. Born in Manila, 29 April 1932. Educated at Ateneo de Manila University, Quezon City, B.A. in education 1954; University of Iowa, Iowa City (Smith-Mundt Scholar), M.A. in English 1957. Since 1958, Member of the Faculty, Associate Professor, 1965–71, and since 1971, Professor of English, Ateneo de Manila University. Since 1960, Curator, Ateneo Art Gallery, Quezon City. Art Critic, *Manila Times*, 1965–69. First Vice-President, Art Association of the Philippines, 1964–65. Recipient: United States State Department Specialist Grant, 1962; British Council Grant, 1964; Rockefeller Research Grant, 1965; Palanca Award, 1966. Lives in Quezon City.

PUBLICATIONS

Verse

Angels and Fugitives. Manila, Bookmark, 1966.

Shapes of Silence. Manila, Wherehouse, 1972.

Other

Editor, *An Anthology of Poems 1965–1974.* Manila, Bureau of National and Foreign Information, 1975.

Critical Study: *The Philippine Poetic* by O. Alcantara Dimalanta, Manila, Colegio de San Juan de Letran, 1976.

Emmanuel Torres comments:

My poems deal thematically (the better ones at any rate) with the doubtful comforts of individual solitude and complacency and the importance of humane communication and communion; the need to acknowledge and come to terms with the irrational, the unpredictable, the mysterious in the human condition; the difficulty of sustaining courage and love in a world of unspectacular, banal, unheroic urban dailiness. Stylistically the poems owe a great deal to the Symbolists, also something to Zen. Generally they tend to create a tension between the precise image and the elusive feeling, between the heroic stance and the banal circumstance, between the naked cry and the cool suggestion, between having to make explicit meaning and leaving gaps in the meaning.

* * *

The prize-winning *Angels and Fugitives* showed Emmanuel Torres's poetry to be one of the best performances of word and symbol among the works of Philippine poets writing in the English language today. Although Torres can be exotic and deliberately philosophical in his use of language (e.g., his Mu Ch'i poem), he prefers to employ commonplace, almost banal images and situations for his poems. But this is merely his method. Torres's vision is anything but trite: it is that of a seer seeking out the angelic and fugitive Pattern or Configuration even in the most ordinary things or acts, like a wash basin by a window, a girl dozing off in an armchair, a pair of old shoes, and so on. This seeking after the extraordinary in the ordinary – the tension between the spiritual and the humdrum – is characteristic of his poetry.

In *Shapes of Silence*, he shifted from the cosmic, universal theme to the social sphere, with telltale titles like "The Oligarchy," "At the Factory," "What the Rich Think of the Masses," and a poem on ecology called "Walking into the Wild." In "Making Out," the last poem of *Shapes of Silence*, the sense of social irony simmers in such stanzas as "Too bad those who love churches/have not yet heard:/the saints of the truly desperate/have stepped down from their niches." Even the Christ who is supposed to give calm in the presence of his eventual death is dangerous: "Today I saw the Kristo crossing Plaza Miranda/coming toward me in easy strides,/holy terror,/keeper of promises,/whose memory hath power to make or break,/amid gallery cries/for blood."

Significantly Torres's social concern as a poet is absent from such poems as "Hide and Seek: An Odyssey," "At a Betting Station in Cubao," "Watch Poem," and "Bedspacer." Instead the new poems are marked by a certain intimism. The imagery has become less allusively literary, more concrete, almost pop. From the universal to the particular, from the idea through the image to the object: this is the evolution of Torres's poetry. Throughout it all, however, the lyric voice of the poet has remained constant.

—Leonidas V. Benesa

TOULSON, Shirley. British. Born in Henley-on-Thames, Oxfordshire, 20 May 1924. Educated at Birkbeck College, University of London. Formerly, free-lance journalist. Since 1967, Features Editor, *The Teacher* (journal of the National Union of Teachers), London. Address: 63 Denmark Road, Wimbledon, London S.W.19, England.

PUBLICATIONS

Verse

Shadows in an Orchard. London, Scorpion Press, 1960.
Circumcision's Not Such a Bad Thing after All and Other Poems. Richmond, Surrey, Keepsake Press, 1970.
All Right Auden, I Know You're There: A Quick Thought. Leicester, Offcut Press, 1970.
For a Double Time. Frensham, Surrey, Sceptre Press, 1970.
The Fault, Dear Brutus: A Zodiac of Sonnets. Richmond, Surrey, Keepsake Press, 1972.
Four Ways with a Ruin. Richmond, Surrey, Keepsake Press, 1976.
Bones and Angels, with John Loveday. Osney, Oxfordshire, Mid-Day, 1978.

Other

Education in Britain. London, Evans, 1974.
The Drovers' Roads of Wales. London, Wildwood, 1977.
Discovering Farm Museums and Farm Parks. Aylesbury, Buckinghamshire, Shire, 1977.
Careers You'll Enjoy. London, Elek, 1979.
East Anglia: Walking the Ley Lines and Ancient Tracks. London, Wildwood, 1979.

Editor, *The Remind-Me Hat and Other Stories* (juvenile). London, Evans, 1973.

Shirley Toulson comments:

I consider I have a very minor talent which occasionally gets triggered off into expression by some personal, highly charged event. My conscious effort in writing is to give a disciplined more impersonal pattern to the original emotion; for this reason I work usually in fairly rigorous verse forms. The poets I read a lot of are Yeats and Auden, but I do not think they have any discernible influence on my work.

* * *

Shirley Toulson is the sort of poet whose work appears in magazines, and then in small collections under the imprint of such houses as Scorpion Press (*Shadows in an Orchard*) and Keepsake Press (*Circumcision's Not Such a Bad Thing after All* and *The Fault, Dear Brutus*).

Hardly the sort of publishing history to help win éclat or reputation, it nevertheless indicates a certain degree of humility, a self-recognition of minority. What it does not indicate is that her poems exemplify a quiet mastery of a less than limited range, even if her writing might, to some, be too easily characterised as that familiar contemporary mode – the domestic, balanced uneasily over hinted turbulences, as in "Watching" or "Dustbins," both of them poems in which ordinary fascinations are contemplated to a point in which they are made to elicit her perceptions of an individual predicament.

Her collection of 1970, from which these two poems come, is probably her best. Earlier, in *Shadows in an Orchard*, her poems showed an attractive concentration on real settings, real incidents. But even in the reluctantly poetic area of the city ("Fulham in Winter" and "Tube

Train," for instance) the result of her interest in what, in the late Fifties, was not well-covered terrain, produced what appears a too-easily achieved melancholy, even if her strictness could not permit digressions from the realities before her.

By the time of *Circumcision's Not Such a Bad Thing after All*, technical assurance had grown considerably, although her attempt at a villanelle ("Learning to Read") simply sounds like most other attempts at the cumulative vowel-tune. The preciosity of form here devalues the compassion behind the impulse to write. In earlier poems, "Cripples" or "Films for Defectives," that compassion was obvious, and controlled enough.

However, *The Fault, Dear Brutus* was to show Miss Toulson engaging with the frivolous, if difficult, technical problems involved in "a Zodiac of Sonnets." The overall effect of this girlish, sweetly illustrated volume is one of an almost regrettable neatness and charm, thankfully toughened at odd moments by failures of what Alvarez would call "gentility." Each poem, writes Miss Toulson, "is centred round the birthday of a particular individual." Zodiacal play was common in medieval literature (in Chaucer, for example); so Miss Toulson's personal but moral concern can be seen as updating an old technique. There may even be a certain amount of mischievousness in her purpose. Yet for all that it appears little more than a pleasant digression from the compassionate concerns which are the strengths of her earlier work.

—Douglas Dunn

TOYNBEE, (Theodore) Philip. British. Born in Oxford, 25 June 1916; son of the historian Arnold Toynbee. Educated at Rugby School, Warwickshire, 1930–34; Christ Church, Oxford, 1935–38. Served in the Intelligence Corps, 1940–42, the Ministry of Economic Warfare, 1942–45, and at S.H.A.E.F. in France and Belgium, 1944–45. Married, 1) Anne Barbara Denise Powell in 1939 (divorced, 1950), two daughters; 2) Frances Genevieve Smith in 1950, one son and two daughters. Editor, *Birmingham Town Crier*, 1938–39; Literary Editor, Contact Publications, London, 1945–46. Since 1950, Member of the Editorial Staff, *The Observer*, London. Address: Woodroyd Cottage, St. Briavels, Lydney, Gloucestershire, England.

PUBLICATIONS

Verse

The Pantaloon series (novels in verse):

Pantaloon; or, The Valediction. London, Chatto and Windus, and New York, Harper, 1961.

Two Brothers: The Fifth Day of the Valediction of Pantaloon. London, Chatto and Windus, 1964; New York, Harper, 1965.

A Learned City: The Sixth Day of the Valediction of Pantaloon. London, Chatto and Windus, 1966.

Views from a Lake: The Seventh Day of the Valediction of Pantaloon. London, Chatto and Windus, 1968.

Novels

The Savage Days. London, Hamish Hamilton, 1937.

A School in Private. London, Putnam, 1941.
The Barricades. London, Putnam, 1943; New York, Doubleday, 1944.
Tea with Mrs. Goodman. London, Horizon, 1947; as *Prothalamium: A Cycle of the Holy Grail*, New York, Doubleday, 1947.
The Garden to the Sea. London, MacGibbon and Kee, 1953; New York, Doubleday, 1954.
Thanatos: A Modern Symposium, with Maurice Richardson. London, Gollancz, 1963.

Other

Friends Apart: A Memoir of Esmond Romilly and Jasper Ridley in the Thirties. London, MacGibbon and Kee, 1954.
Comparing Notes: A Dialogue Across a Generation, with Arnold Toynbee. London, Weidenfeld and Nicolson, 1963.
Towards the Holy Spirit. London, SCM Press, 1973.
The Age of the Spirit: Religion as Experience. New York, Harper, 1974.

Editor, *Fearful Choice: A Debate on Nuclear Policy.* London, Gollancz, 1958; Detroit, Wayne State University Press, 1959.
Editor, *Underdogs: Eighteen Victims of Society.* London, Weidenfeld and Nicolson, 1961; as *Underdogs: Anguish and Anxiety*, New York, Horizon Press, 1962.
Editor, *The Distant Drum: Reflections on the Spanish Civil War.* London, Sidgwick and Jackson, and New York, McKay, 1976.

Translator, *Kérillis on the Causes of the War*, by Henri de Kérillis and Raymond Cartier. London, Putnam, 1939.

Critical Study: introduction by the author to *Two Brothers*, 1964.

Philip Toynbee comments:

What I am trying to do in *Pantaloon* – no doubt over-ambitiously – is to write something like a modern equivalent of *Don Quixote*, *The Prelude*, *Faust*, and *A la Récherche du Temps Perdu*, all in one. That's to say a tragi-comic epic whose hero is representative, but not in the least typical, of the years 1914–1950. Above all I want to stand at a distance from my own hero, and by means of this device give a fair hearing and showing to all the important ideas and human types of the age, without explicitly endorsing any of them. It is part of the old struggle, in fact, to escape from romanticism and return to a classical outlook and method. My chosen medium is verse – in a great many different forms.

I hope the wide variety of verse styles in the *Pantaloon* will speak for themselves. There is a reason, or several reasons, for every one of them.

* * *

Although Philip Toynbee has been known for most of his life as a critic and an experimental novelist, his long poem or verse novel, *The Valediction of Pantaloon*, which has been appearing in successive volumes since 1961, indicates that he is also a gifted poet, even if he did not turn to writing poetry until middle age. The poem has an ingenious pattern. It is supposedly set in the closing years of the twentieth century, when the elderly narrator, Dick Abberville, aristocrat and sometime rebel, considers his early life. Within this elaborate and distancing structure Toynbee looks back to the 1930's, the period when he himself developed as a writer; the recollections may not be strictly autobiographical, but they seem to have some relation to Toynbee's own experience.

The verse is adroit and well-written; if there are occasional echoes of Eliot and Auden or

MacNeice, one is also reminded of Victorian narrative poetry, with pleasant suggestions of Clough or Tennyson. But it is hard to see that Toynbee has effectively solved the problems of writing a long narrative poem in our age; if anything, he underlines the difficulties. In particular, his determination to vary the verse form for expressive purposes from one volume to the next, and within different sections of the same volume, indicates a certain formal restlessness, which is conspicuously unlike the assurance with which the major Romantic and Victorian poets handled the extended verse narrative.

—Bernard Bergonzi

TRANTER, John (Ernest). Australian. Born in Cooma, New South Wales, 29 April 1943. Educated at Moruya Intermediate High School; Hurlstone Agricultural High School, graduated 1960; Sydney University, B.A. 1970. Married Lynette Maree in 1968; one daughter and one son. Asian Editor, Angus and Robertson, publishers, Singapore, 1971–73; Radio Producer, Australian Boadcasting Commission, Sydney and Brisbane, 1974–77. Recipient: Australia Council Fellowship, 1974, 1978, 1979. Address: 59 View Street, Annandale, New South Wales 2038, Australia.

PUBLICATIONS

Verse

Parallax and Other Poems. Sydney, South Head Press, 1970.
Red Movie and Other Poems. Sydney, Angus and Robertson, 1972.
The Blast Area. Brisbane, Makar Press, 1974.
The Alphabet Murders: Notes from a Work in Progress. Sydney, Angus and Robertson, 1976.
Crying in Early Infancy: One Hundred Sonnets. Brisbane, Makar Press, 1977.

Plays

The Man on the Landing (produced Sydney, 1967?).

Radio Plays and Scripts: *Looking for Hunter*, 1974; *Le Morte d'Arthur*, from the work by Thomas Malory, 1974; *Knight-Prisoner: The Life of Sir Thomas Malory*, 1974; *Sideshow People*, 1976; *The Poetry of Frank O'Hara*, 1976(?).

Other

Editor, *The New Australian Poetry.* Brisbane, Makar Press, 1979.

Manuscript Collection: Australian National Library, Canberra.

Critical Study: "Opening a Murder List" by Alan Gould, in *Nation Review* (Melbourne), 4–10 June 1976.

John Tranter comments:

Australian reviewers have called my work complex, technically assured, cynical, humourless, humorous, too concerned with avant-garde ideas, conservative, and experimental. Though I like a poem to be moving, I dislike gush; though I admire wit and skill, I like to have a good time.

* * *

In 1968 John Tranter achieved publication of a substantial collection of poems, *Parallax*, through the slightly devious means of a special issue of the magazine *Poetry Australia*. It was one way of side-stepping the Commonwealth Literary Fund (then the major funding body), which had refused support for this manuscript. It is always easy, in retrospect, to illustrate the insensitivity of any official patronising (and funding) body; but, in the instance of Tranter, it seems extraordinary. *Parallax*, re-read a decade later, almost bends backwards to present a conservative front – though with integrity. Its direction, though, is clearly towards an absorption of the then recently available American experiments in formal innovation and what has been termed "Drug culture." *Parallax* remains a reprimand to orthodox conservatism; the elements that spoke compromise can now be seen as the least creatively helpful for the young poet, the elements that pointed towards innovation and genuine growth were, in fact, modified by the existing cultural climate but their freshness remains stimulating.

It was in 1972, and with the publication of his volume *Red Movie*, that Tranter spelled out the real dimension of his innovative talent. The early poems had shown an eclectic voracity for stimuli – from Bly to Slessor, from Ginsberg to Beaver – but *Red Movie* made eclecticism a virtue. *Red Movie* (and especially the title poem) remains a pivotal experiment in language – in making language rub against itself, in making it rub against a culture, a commerce, an environment. Although its surface mimics (perhaps even mocks) current American preoccupations with surreal and telescopic forms, its essential laconicism is peculiarly Australian. It was succeeded by a follow-up series of poems, some of them successful, some blatant (and provocative) in their failure, but Tranter's latest collection, *Crying in Early Infancy*, has become, for the late 1970's, what *Red Movie* was for the first half of the decade: the quintessential statement. It is sub-titled (significantly enough) "one hundred sonnets." The renewal of interest in older forms is part of late-1970's culture, though the deeply ironic undertones are particularly Australian – and personal. These "sonnets" are indeed classic in their combination of "sounding against each other" and sounding upon the admass culture of this generation. Nothing in Australian writing quite precedes their constructive use of negative force associations to build up, finally, a resonance of deep vulnerability. Tranter has, in *Crying in Early Infancy*, brought what is perhaps the most intelligent verbal equipment of his generation to a point of creative breakthrough – and of challenge. The challenge is enormous, partly because the alternatives now presented to Tranter are so sharp: his tone of wry mockery may become dangerously brittle; his cautious exploration of the self self-defeating. He is, essentially, a City poet, thoroughly urban in his preoccupations. No other poet of his generation is so well equipped to define whole new areas of poetic territory as Tranter; and, possibly, no other so sharply aware of the risks.

—Thomas W. Shapcott

TREMAYNE, Sydney (Durward). Scottish. Born in Ayr, 15 March 1912. Educated at Ayr Academy, 1917–27. Served as a fireman in London during World War II. Married 1) Lily Hanson in 1931 (marriage dissolved), two sons; 2) Constance Lipop in 1946. Journalist,

Yorkshire Evening News, Leeds, 1929, and for newspapers in Harrogate, Selby, Northampton, Sunderland, and Newcastle upon Tyne, 1929–38. Staff Member, 1938, Chief Sub-Editor, 1939–48, Leader Writer, 1948–54, and Special Writer, 1969–74, *Daily Mirror*, London. Leader Writer, *Daily Herald*, later *The Sun*, London, 1954–69. Recipient: Scottish Arts Council Award, 1970. Agent: Anthony Shiel Associates Ltd., 2–3 Morwell Street, London WC1B 3AR, England. Address: Peterburn, Gairloch, Ross-shire, Scotland.

PUBLICATIONS

Verse

For Whom There Is No Spring. London, Pendulum Press, 1946.
Time and the Wind. London, Collins, 1948.
The Hardest Freedom. London, Collins, 1951.
The Rock and the Bird. London, Allen and Unwin, 1955.
The Swans of Berwick. London, Chatto and Windus-Hogarth Press, 1962.
The Turning Sky. London, Hart Davis, 1969.
Selected and New Poems. London, Chatto and Windus, 1973.

Other

Editor, *Tatlings* (epigrams). Newton Abbot, Devon, David and Charles, 1979.

Critical Studies: by Austin Clarke, in *Irish Times* (Dublin), 10 December 1955; George Bruce, in *Akros* (Preston, Lancashire), August 1978.

Sydney Tremayne comments:

I have written verse since the age of eleven but did not publish until the Second World War. My poems have arisen out of the need to clarify experience and from pleasure in language. All are written to be heard. I hope, simply, that they speak for themselves.

* * *

Sydney Tremayne at the beginning of his practice as a poet used largely the language of romantic poetry. He never rejected it, nor did he develop an interest in new verse techniques, yet thanks to his genuineness, his literary discrimination, and an ability to recognize those subjects that have a special meaning for him, his poems have a winning freshness and frequently authority. He has a robust and immediate response to the animals that he sees – as it were – at his door, as in "Earth Spirits":

The world of the young hare
Is hairy as his milky mother's teat
Who suckles him and rolls him off his feet,
Licks him with rapid care,
Then leaves him with a leap to his own care
Among forget-me-nots to sit and stare.

He has the genuineness to take this poem no further, but in his poem, "The Fox," he begins with a glimpse of the animal: "Out of the corner of his yellow eye/Glanced round his shoulder. Seeing nothing there/Skirted the tall dry biscuit coloured grass...." He then associates the image with a person, "One who was brave and frightened, fugitive,/Fox coloured hair." The poem ends: "Swiftly comes/The verbal thought how many years she's dead./The fox has slipped away in the dark wood." He has achieved a poise whereby he can use natural imagery (without ever falling for the discredited pathetic fallacy) as a means of disclosing the delicately balanced, sometimes threatened, always isolated life of man in a natural environment. The disclosure is tactfully and tenderly made in "Outposts in Winter": "We two adrift in winter share with birds/Confinement in the dark, that comes,/Silence banked upon silence, stranding words." This poem, from *The Turning Sky*, shows an increasing freedom of movement between fact and idea, a recognition that even the conditioning natural world becomes words in poetry. This flexibility, when applied to the details of the environment, which has been the material of his better poems, has given a new depth to some of the most recent poems, as in "Wanting News":

> Waiting for words to fall into the box
> And ice to drop from hedges, wanting news,
> Missing your voice, cold stillness, builds unease:
> The eye looks round for movement, like a fox.

Some of Sydney Tremayne's poems have been referred to as water colour painting. It is true that some have the merit and limitation of that art. The better poems rebut the allegation. It would seem that after sixty he is in a position to take further the developments of his later poems.

—George Bruce

TRIPP, John. Welsh. Born in Bargoed, Glamorgan, 22 July 1927. Educated at Whitchurch Senior School, Cardiff; Morley College, London, Diploma in Moral Philosophy. Served as a Sergeant in the Royal Army Pay Corps, 1945–48. BBC News Researcher and Sub-Editor, London, 1951–58; Press Officer, Indonesian Embassy, London, 1958–67; Information Officer, Central Office of Information, London, 1967–69. Literary Editor, *Planet*. Since 1969, Free-lance Writer, Cardiff. Member, English Language Section, Welsh Academy of Letters. Recipient: Welsh Arts Council Bursary, 1969, 1972. Address: 2 Heol Penyfai, Whitchurch, Cardiff, Wales.

PUBLICATIONS

Verse

Diesel to Yesterday. Cardiff, Triskel Press, 1966.
The Loss of Ancestry. Llandybie, Dyfed, Christopher Davies, 1969.
The Province of Belief. Llandybie, Dyfed, Christopher Davies, 1971.
Bute Park and Other Poems. Cardiff, Second Aeon, 1972.
The Inheritance File. Cardiff, Second Aeon, 1973.
Collected Poems 1958–1978. Swansea, Christopher Davies, 1978.
Penguin Modern Poets 27, with John Ormond and Emyr Humphries. London, Penguin, 1979.

Play

Radio Play: *The Seed of Dismemberment*, 1972.

Other

The Thinskin Award. Barry, Glamorgan, Edge Press, 1978.

Manuscript Collections: National Library of Wales, Aberystwyth; Education Authority, Clwyd.

Critical Studies: by Sam Adams, in *Poetry Wales* (Cardiff), 1969; Roland Mathias, in *Anglo-Welsh Review* (Pembroke Dock, Wales), 1970; Charles Elliott, in *Anglo-Welsh Review* (Pembroke Dock, Wales), 1972; "Poetry in Wales" by Glyn Jones, in *British Poetry since 1960: A Critical Survey*, edited by Michael Schmidt and Grevel Lindop, Oxford, Carcanet Press, 1972; Richard Poole, in *Poetry Wales* (Cardiff), Spring 1979.

John Tripp comments:

The major themes in my work have to do with Wales, its history and people, from the viewpoint of one who is extremely conscious of his roots. I have tried to create a small document about my country, its harsh past, its difficult present, and its chances for the future – including the preservation of the Welsh language. This subject-matter has often been framed within a tight, terse verse-form which has been described as "tough and steely." (There have also been many references to my wryness, dryness, irony and "gallows humor.") But one has tried to keep a cold eye and a warm heart on the raw material – which is often recalcitrant – to find a union of reason and emotion in pulling away from the sentimental nostalgia and discursive rhetoric of much of the poetry common to the overstating Celt. Our problem has always been one of economy.

I suppose I am still a modern who reeks of the museum, caught between two cultures, and well aware of a vacuum of disinheritance. To my published work has recently been added a series of elegies on other writers.

* * *

Most of John Tripp's writing is set in Wales. Like many poets, he is thin in generalization, better in sharp particulars:

> Snow mucks to slush, the yellow
> streaks of dog piss on the lovewalk,
> thin layered frost on their crud
> at the trees' base …

Too much of his work consists of praise of the Welsh and denunciation of the English. The insight missing in his simply nationalistic poems comes out when he speaks, not of the Welsh, but of individual Welshmen – Lloyd George, Aneurin Bevan, Jack Jones, and, best of all, R. Williams Parry, whom, in a sustained analogy, he represents as "The Bard of Winter":

> He was a careful little man
> who looked more like a bank manager
> than a bard: chalk-striped
> suit, waistcoat, hornrimmed spectacles,
> and horror behind the eyes.
> In the woods and fields of Gwynedd
> he was frightened when he saw the fear
> of wood-pigeon, wild fowl, hare and fox …

He was buried on a January day
too cold to lift its head –
a day of honest weather he might have liked
and fitting for a true poet ...
On the hillside at Bethesda
under the snow his wild companions
nestle for shelter.

The language never catches fire, but, equally, Mr. Tripp seems never at a loss for a subject. He gets a good deal of humour and observation, too, into these wry professions of a middle-aged Welshman. It may well be, however, that for all his toughness and irony, Mr. Tripp is insufficiently interested in the craft of verse to make the best of his talent. On the other hand, a novel or a collection of stories from his pen would be interesting to read.

—Philip Hobsbaum

TRYPANIS, Constantine (Athanasius). Greek. Born in Chios, 22 January 1909. Educated at Chios Classical Gymnasium, 1920–26; University of Athens, M.A. 1931, D.Phil. 1939; University of Berlin, 1932–34; University of Munich, 1935–37; Oxford University, M.A. 1946. Served as a Sub-Lieutenant in the Greek Army, 1940–41. Married Alice Macris in 1942; one daughter. Lecturer in Classics, University of Athens, 1939–47. Bywater and Sotheby Professor of Byzantine and Modern Greek Language and Literature, and Fellow, Exeter College, Oxford, 1947–69; since 1969, Emeritus Fellow; since 1969, University Professor of Classics, University of Chicago. Visiting Professor, Hunter College, New York, 1963, Harvard University, Cambridge, Massachusetts, 1963–64, and University of Vienna, 1971. Member, Medieval Academy of America, and Academy of Athens; Honorary Fellow, British Academy, 1978. Recipient: Academy of Athens Koraes Prize, 1933; Heinemann Award, 1960. D.Litt: Oxford University, 1970. Fellow, Royal Society of Literature. Archon Hieromnemon, Oecumenical Patriarchate. Address: 3 George Nikalouw, Kefisia, Athens, Greece.

PUBLICATIONS

Verse

Pedasus: Twenty-Four Poems. Reading, Berkshire, University of Reading School of Art, 1955.
The Stones of Troy. London, Faber, 1957.
The Cocks of Hades. London, Faber, 1958.
Grooves in the Wind (*The Stones of Troy* and *The Cocks of Hades*). New York, Chilmark Press, 1964.
Pompeian Dog. London, Faber, 1964; New York, Chilmark Press, 1965.
The Elegies of a Glass Adonis. New York, Chilmark Press, 1967.
The Glass Adonis. London, Faber, 1972; New York, Chilmark Press, 1973.

Plays

Radio Plays (UK): *Oedipus King*, 1955; *Oedipus at Colonus*, 1958; *Antigony*, 1958; *Persians*, 1958; *Electra*, 1959; *The Oresteia*, 1959.

Other

Eric Arthur Barber 1888–1965. London, Oxford University Press, 1967.

Editor, *Alexandrian Poetry.* Athens, Garouphalias, 1943.
Editor, *Medieval and Modern Greek Poetry: An Anthology.* Oxford, Clarendon Press, 1951.
Editor and Translator, *Callimachus: Aetia, Iambi, Lyric Poems, Hecale, Minor Epic and Elegiac Poems, Fragments of Epigrams, Fragments of Uncertain Location.* London, Heinemann, and Cambridge, Massachusetts, Harvard University Press, 1958.
Editor, with Paul Maas, *Sancti Romani Melodi Cantica.* Oxford, Clarendon Press, 2 vols., 1963–70.
Editor, *Fourteen Early Byzantine Cantica.* Vienna, Academy of Austria, 1968.
Editor, *The Penguin Book of Greek Verse.* London, Penguin, 1970.
Editor, *The Homeric Epics.* Warminster, Wiltshire, Aris and Phillips, 1977.

Manuscript Collection: Library of the State University of New York, Buffalo.

Critical Studies: by W. H. Auden, in *Encounter* (London), 1956; Pamela Beattie, in *Orbis* (Bakewell, Derbyshire), 1976.

Constantine Trypanis comments:

Themes come from the Greek world – ancient, medieval, and modern. Both traditional forms and free verse have been used. Classical Greek poetry and the poetry of Yeats have influenced me.

* * *

Born on the island of Chios, Constantine Trypanis had an English nanny and spoke fluent and correct English from his childhood. For many years he was Professor of Byzantine and Medieval Greek at Oxford, and, in the 1950's particularly, was noted for his kindness and sympathy to young poets – it was a flowering period for poets in Oxford – and began, in middle age, to write poems himself, modestly asking for advice from poets much younger than himself. He uses in poetry his marvellous knowledge of Greek history and literature and his special sense of the pathos of the periods of Greece in the Hellenistic, Rome-dominated period and after the conquest of Constantinople by the Ottoman Turks. In his sense of the fragility and irony of a great tradition in decline he resembles the great modern Alexandrian poet, Kavafis or Cavafy, and Auden, who adored Cavafy, greeted one of Trypanis's earlier volumes with delight (and Auden, like Eliot, tended rather studiously to avoid reviewing his contemporaries). Trypanis's longest and most distinguished poem, *The Glass Adonis*, is a study of a great culture in the stage of vitrification. He writes a formal but not in the least stiff English, rather like the English of the other Greek who chose English for his medium, the late Demetrios Capetanakis. His poems are learned and allusive but full of profound and simple pathos in the emotions they express.

—G. S. Fraser

TURCO, Lewis (Putnam). American. Born in Buffalo, New York, 2 May 1934. Educated at Suffield Academy, Connecticut, 1947–49; Meriden High School, Connecticut,

1949–52; University of Connecticut, Storrs, 1956–59, B.A. 1959; University of Iowa, Iowa City, 1959–60, 1962, M.A. 1962. Served in the United States Navy, 1952–56. Married Jean Cate Houdlette in 1956; one son and one daughter. Editorial Assistant, University of Iowa Writers Workshop, 1959–60; Instructor, 1960–64, and Poetry Center Founding Director, 1961–64, Cleveland State University; Assistant Professor, Hillsdale College, Michigan, 1964–65. Assistant Professor, 1965–68, Associate Professor, 1968–71, since 1969, Director of the Writing Arts Program, and since 1971, Professor of English, State University of New York, Oswego. Visiting Professor of English, State University of New York, Potsdam, 1968–69. Recipient: Yaddo grant, 1959, 1971; Academy of American Poets Prize, 1960; Bread Loaf Writers Fellowship, 1961; Helen Bullis Prize (*Poetry Northwest*, Seattle), 1972. Agent: Del Walker, 475 Fifth Avenue, New York, New York 10017. Address: 54 West 8th Street, Oswego, New York 13126, U.S.A.

PUBLICATIONS

Verse

Day after History. Arlington, Virginia, Samisdat, 1956.
First Poems. Francestown, New Hampshire, Golden Quill Press, 1960.
The Sketches of Lewis Turco and Livevil: A Mask. Cleveland, American Weave Press, 1962.
Awaken, Bells Falling: Poems 1959–1967. Columbia, University of Missouri Press, 1968.
The Inhabitant. Northampton, Massachusetts, Despa Press, 1970.
Pocoangelini: A Fantography. Northampton, Massachusetts, Despa Press, 1971.
The Weed Garden. Orangeburg, South Carolina, Peaceweed Press, 1973.
A Cage of Creatures. Potsdam, New York, Banjo Press, 1978.
The Compleat Melancholick. Madison, Wisconsin, Bieler Press, 1979.

Broadsides, cards, etc.: *At Yule*, 1958; *O Well*, 1963; *Pocoangelini 8*, 1965; *The Burning Bush*, 1966; *Image Tinged with No Color*, 1966; *School Drawing*, 1966; *My Country Wife*, 1966; *Nativity*, 1967; *The Children and the Unicorn*, 1968; *The Glass Nest*, 1968; *Burning the News*, 1968; *The Sign*, 1970; *A Carol for Melora's First Xmas*, 1971; *The Magi*, 1972; *Nursery Rime*, 1973; *The Fences*, 1973; *The Pond*, 1974; *The Vista*, 1975; *The House*, 1976; *The Habitation*, 1978.

Plays

Dreams of Stone and Sun (produced Storrs, Connecticut, 1959). Published in *Theatre Journal* (Oswego, New York), Fall 1971.
The Elections Last Fall (produced Oswego, New York, 1969). Published in *Polemic 6* (Cleveland), 1961.

Ballet Scenario: *While the Spider Slept*, 1965.

Other

The Book of Forms: A Handbook of Poetics. New York, Dutton, 1968.
The Literature of New York: A Bibliography. Oneonta, New York State English Council, 1970.
Creative Writing in Poetry. Albany, State University of New York, 1970.
Poetry: An Introduction Through Writing. Reston, Virginia, Reston Publishing Company, 1973.
Freshman Composition and Literature. Saratoga Springs, New York, Empire State College, 1973.

Editor, *The Spiritual Autobiography of Luigi Turco.* Ann Arbor, Michigan, University Microfilms Books, 1969.

Bibliography: "Lewis Turco: A Bibliography of His Works and of Criticism of Them," in *F. W. Crumb Memorial Library Bibliographies*, Potsdam, State University of New York, 1972.

Manuscript Collection: Wilbur Cross Library, University of Connecticut, Storrs.

Critical Studies: "The Formalism of Lewis Turco" by Hyatt H. Waggoner, in *Concerning Poetry* (Bellingham, Washington), Fall 1969; "Craft and Vision: An Interview with Lewis Turco" edited by David McLean, in *Dekalb Literary Arts Journal* (Clarkston, Georgia), 1970; "The Progress of Lewis Turco" by William Heyen, in *Modern Poetry Studies* (Buffalo), v, 2, 1971; "A Certain Slant of Light" by Herbert Coursen, Jr., in *Bartleby's Review* (Machias, Maine), 1972; "The Poetry of Lewis Turco: An Interview" by Gregory Fitz Gerald and William Heyen, in *Costerus* (Amsterdam, Holland), ix, 1973; "Sympathetic Magic" by the author, in *American Poets in 1976* edited by William Heyen, Indianpolis, Bobbs Merrill, 1976.

* * *

Most of the work in Lewis Turco's *First Poems* is too stiff metrically, or too pretty, or too ingenious, or too heavily moral and wise. Turco was not willing to allow his poems to well up from their own subtle senses of themselves, was not willing to allow them to do what they wanted to do. In *The Sketches*, a collection of twenty-five character sketches and a mask, Turco moves toward the natural style that will come to fruition in *Awaken, Bells Falling: Poems 1959–1967*, and especially in *The Inhabitant*, about which Conrad Aiken said "*The Inhabitant* is the best new poem I've read in something like thirty years – profoundly satisfying to me, speaks my language, such a relief to have WHOLE meaning again, instead of this pitiable dot-and-dash splinter-poetry, or sawdust cornflakes which we usually get."

In *The Inhabitant* Turco is willing to allow his subject to surface when and how it must. As he says in "School Drawing," "There is a road: no one is walking there." Even the furniture of the inhabitant's house is allowed to sing its own songs. Turco's later work is skillful to such an extent that even the effects of accentual-syllabics are conversational, unstrained. "The Portrait of a Clown" describes that portrait in the room of the inhabitant's daughter as she sleeps, and concludes:

how will the clown
  maintain his equipoise as a
    world as a
room tips the frame tilts shades

  of aquamarine the bold lines
    of a face
ride over the sleeping child.

—William Heyen

TURNBULL, Gael (Lundin). British. Born in Edinburgh, 7 April 1928. Married; three children. Medical Practitioner; currently in general practice. Recipient: Union League Civic and Arts Foundation Prize (*Poetry*, Chicago), 1965; Alice Hunt Bartlett Prize, 1968. Address: 61 Belmont Road, Malvern, Worcestershire WR14 1PN, England.

PUBLICATIONS

Verse

Trio, with Eli Mandel and Phyllis Webb. Toronto, Contact Press, 1954.
The Knot in the Wood and Fifteen Other Poems. London, Revision Press, 1955.
Bjarni Spike-Helgi's Son and Other Poems. Ashland, Massachusetts, Origin Press, 1956.
A Libation. Privately printed, 1957.
With Hey, Ho.... Birmingham, Migrant Press, 1961.
To You, I Write. Birmingham, Migrant Press, 1963.
A Very Particular Hill. Edinburgh, Wild Hawthorn Press, 1963.
Twenty Words, Twenty Days: A Sketchbook and a Morula. Birmingham, Migrant Press, 1966.
Walls. Privately printed, 1967.
Briefly. Nottingham, Tarasque Press, 1967.
A Trampoline: Poems 1952–1964. London, Cape Goliard Press, 1968.
I, Maksoud. Exeter, University of Exeter, 1969.
Scantlings: Poems 1964–1969. London, Cape Goliard Press, 1970.
Finger Cymbals. Edinburgh, Satis, 1972.
A Sea Story. Saffron Walden, Essex, Byways, 1973(?).
A Random Sampling. Newcastle upon Tyne, Pig Press, 1974.
Residues: Down the Sluice of Time. Pensnett, Staffordshire, Grosseteste, 1976.
Thronging the Heart. Belper, Derbyshire, Aggie Weston's, 1976.
If a Glance Could Be Enough. Edinburgh, Satis, 1978.

Other

Translator, with Jean Beaupre, *Six Poems*, by Paul Marie Lapointe. Toronto, Contact Press, 1955.

* * *

Gael Turnbull was born in Scotland and now lives in Worcester where he practices medicine. During his apprenticeship both as a physician and as a poet, however, he lived in North America where his early poems were published in, among other journals, *Black Mountain Review.* Until he returned to Britain in 1964, there was some confusion about whether he ought properly to be regarded as a Canadian, an American, or a British poet, and, evidently, at one point Donald Allen considered publishing a selection of Turnbull's poems (at Robert Duncan's suggestion) in his important anthology, *The New American Poetry.* Though Turnbull readily acknowledges his debt to poets like Duncan, Robert Creeley, Charles Olson, and Denise Levertov, he ought not to be looked upon as a kind of minor British Black Mountaineer. English poets like Basil Bunting, Roy Fisher, and Matthew Mead have also been important to his development and, in the end, the character of his best work turns out to be very personal and quite unique.

The danger for Turnbull is minimalism, and he is at his best when he is not attempting to refine and purify his writing down to the quintessential five or six four-syllable lines (or less) in the manner of Cid Corman, the early Creeley, or Ian Hamilton Finlay. For me, his strongest poem to date is a long piece in *A Trampoline* called "Twenty Words/Twenty Days" which ends: "and I remember an Edinburgh room and one saying,/when I asked what he'd done that day, how much –/I tore/it up ... I wisnae pure enough when I wrote ... I wisnae/

pure enough...." The poem, in fact, is marvellously *impure*. A word is chosen by a random method and each day's journal-like entry is constructed around it in a language as relaxed and supple as good prose but which has, in spite of its casual appearance on the page (it is broken up into units by dashes and ellipses), the concentration one expects from poetry. Rhythmically, it is very engaging: the rhythms of comtemporary speech are handled as effectively as they are in William Carlos Williams. The poem is richly anecdotal. Turnbull responds to his responsibilities as a doctor and citizen, to his private experience as a husband and father, and to his memories and desires as a poet and as a man. The twenty days happened to be November 17th to December 6th, 1963, and while November 22nd was the date of John Kennedy's assassination, and while that event figures centrally enough, it is just as important for the final effect of the poem that on November 20th Turnbull prevented a child from choking during a tonsillectomy and "had pleasure in [his] skill" or that on December 2nd he woke up unexpectedly remembering a girl he had met years before "out walking in the Appalachians." The poem is a moving human document. One can say of it, as Turnbull writes elsewhere: "The phrases are apt/The scene is not unusual/The joy is in the attention."

Turnbull's work after *A Trampoline* is gathered in a second volume, *Scantlings*. The note on the title is important: "Of limited or prescribed dimension; a portion, an allotted quantity; a builder's or carpenter's measuring rod; in a building, the small beams or pieces of wood; in archery, the distance from a mark, within which a shot is not regarded as a miss." The most ambitious poem in the new book is "A Word," a piece in some ways related to "Twenty Words/Twenty Days" but which, I feel, suffers from its minimalist and concretist affinities. Any of one hundred and twelve phrases are meant to be interchangable in such a way that they may relate to any of twenty-eight nouns. The printed version, we are told in a note, "is no less final than any other." For example, the first four lines of the printed version, "a word/against silence/a love/impelled to be uttered," could also be "a love/against silence/a word/impelled to be uttered." And so on through all the permutations.

—John Matthias

TURNER, W(illiam) Price. British. Born in York, 14 August 1927. Educated at Whitehill Secondary School, Glasgow, 1941. Served in the Royal Engineers, 1945–47. Married Anne Hamilton Hill in 1950; two children. Editor, *The Poet*, Glasgow, 1951–56; Television Captions Artist and Assistant Floor Manager, BBC, Glasgow, 1957–60; Sub-Editor, 1962–63, and Crime Fiction Reviewer, 1963–66, *Yorkshire Post*, Leeds. Tutor in Creative Writing, Swarthmore Adult Education Centre, Leeds, 1963–66; Creative Writing Fellow, Glasgow University, 1973–75. Recipient: Gregory Fellowship, Leeds University, 1960–62; Scottish Arts Council Award, 1970. Address: 8 Methley Terrace, Chapel Alerton, Leeds LS7 3NL, England.

PUBLICATIONS

Verse

First Offence. Bristol, Derek Maggs, 1954.
The Rudiment of an Eye. London, Villiers, 1955.
The Flying Corset. London, Villiers, 1962.
Fables from Life. Newcastle upon Tyne, Northern House, 1966.
More Fables from Life. Belfast, Ulsterman, 1969.

The Moral Rocking-Horse. London, Barrie and Jenkins, 1970.
Casting One's Bread. Ashington, Northumberland, MidNAG, 1972.

Plays

Baldy Bane (libretto). London, BBC, 1967.

Radio Plays: *The Lair of the Boneyard Clerk*, 1958; *The Symbol*, 1959; *The Refuge*, 1964; *Something to Remember You By*, 1969.

Novels

Bound to Die (as Bill Turner). London, Constable, and New York, Walker, 1967.
Sex Trap (as Bill Turner). London, Constable, 1968.
Circle of Squares (as Bill Turner). London, Constable, and New York, Walker, 1969.
Another Little Death. London, Constable, 1970; New York, Walker, 1971.
Soldier's Woman. London, Constable, 1972.
Hot-Foot. London, Constable, 1973.

Critical Studies: by Michael Butler, in *Samphire 11* (Ipswich, Suffolk); Roy Fisher, in *Birmingham Post*, 31 July 1971.

W. Price Turner comments:

A poet's devotion must be to his own truth; as soon as he starts worrying about the function of poetry, the social responsibility of the poet, or other ideological purgatives, he is lost. He becômes just another actor, conscious of his best profile.

Basically, I try to employ shifts of tone and perspective to liberate insights. I use humour and conversational rhythms to charge my ideas with the irrational dynamic which I believe essential to all poetry. I enjoy the challenge of exacting disciplines, aiming for a cross-weave of ideas against form. If I can entertain my readers, so much the better.

* * *

In one of the poems in his first collection, *First Offence*, W. Price Turner refers to "the lightning-white integrity/of all who stand alone," and independence of spirit and style are the marks of this witty and sharp-eyed (and sharp-tongued) poet. Both the wit and the observing eye have at times, but mainly in his early work, been overlaid by criss-crossing trains of metaphor that fail to explode or don't explode apropo: virtuoso leanings that remain clever rather than functional, and give a heaviness to otherwise promising poems like "The Back-Court Piper." But the back-court piper begging his stint in the streets of Govan (where Turner himself used to live, in the days of his "shoestring lyricism" and editorship of *The Poet*) is a true image of something that matters deeply to him; and poverty, honesty, and integrity are the subjects of a number of good poems, such as "The Angry Gambler," "Alien," "Song in Lean Times," and "The Moral Rocking-Horse."

From *The Rudiment of an Eye* to *The Flying Corset*, *Fables from Life*, and later poems, increased skill in delineation goes with the emergence of a tone of voice that we recognize. The voice ranges between a mocking humour and a fairly swingeing satire. It draws an alert bead on the contemporary world (colour supplements, landladies, "flying corsets," academics, trucks bullet-proofed with telephone directories), but seems more original and distinctive in allowing for an element of the grotesque, as in the rather macabre "Elegy for Seven Teeth," the surprising "Encounter" (with an onion), or the Gogolian incident of "Getting One's Bearings" – perhaps his best poem – where the poet carrying chairs on his back meets two men taking a table on a pram:

They grinned at my strung trophies
wielded like an animated nutcracker,
and looked back laughing as I stopped
to look after them, and we went down
our different slopes, having
exchanged perspectives.

—Edwin Morgan

TUWHARE, Hone. New Zealand Maori. Born in Kaikohe, 21 October 1922. Educated at Campbell's Kindergarten, Victoria Park; Kaikohe Primary School; Avondale Primary School; Mangere Central Primary School; Beresford Street School, Auckland; Seddon Memorial Technical College, Auckland, 1939–41; Otahuhu Technical College, 1941. Served in the Maori Battalion, 1945, and the New Zealand Second Divisional Cavalry, 1945–47. Married Jean Tuwhare in 1949; three sons. Formerly, Member, Wellington Boilermakers Union; Amalgamated Society of Railway Servants; Wellington Public Service Association; Freezing Workers Union; Wellington Tramway Workers Union; and District Executive, Communist Party of New Zealand; President, Te Manhoe Local, New Zealand Workers Union, 1962–64. Since 1964, Member, Auckland Boilermakers Union. President, Birkdale Maori Cultural Committee, Auckland, 1966–68; Councillor, Borough of Birkenhead, Auckland, 1968–70; Organizer of the Maori Artists and Writers Conference, Te Kaha, 1973. Recipient: Internal Affairs Department travel grant, 1956; Robert Burns Centennial Fellowship, University of Otago, 1969. Agent: Longman Paul Ltd., Milford, Auckland. Address: P.O. Box 3417, C.P.O., Auckland, New Zealand.

PUBLICATIONS

Verse

No Ordinary Sun. Auckland, Blackwood and Janet Paul, 1964.
Come Rain Hail. Dunedin, University of Otago Bibliography Room, 1970.
Sapwood and Milk. Dunedin, Caveman Press, 1972.
Something Nothing. Dunedin, Caveman Press, 1973.

Critical Study: by M. P. Jackson, in *Landfall 74* (Christchurch), June 1965.

Hone Tuwhare comments:

Strongly influenced by translated works of Mayakovsky, Mao Tse-Tung, García Lorca, Louis Aragon, Pablo Neruda and Shakespeare, and R. A. K. Mason of New Zealand, together with a close study of *Nga Moteatea me nga harikari o te Iwi Maori*: a collection of untranslated Maori songs. Also, the Old Testament.

* * *

Hone Tuwhare is the first Maori to achieve a reputation for poetry written in English. The fact that he is a Maori and that elements of his native culture find their way into the work has meant that he has attracted wider attention than is the case with most New Zealand poets. In addition, Tuwhare is an attractive personality who reads his poetry well in public and is frequently in demand and on tour. His work is already studied widely in schools and his books go on being reprinted.

His early work (appearing, however, when Tuwhare was already in his early forties) was lyrical, with a strongly aural quality, full of assonance and half-rhyme within a tightly-written free-verse form. In the natural scene trees, mountains, rivers, sun, wind, rain, were addressed directly, "personified." The universe was animate. This was a Maori quality, yet it was also "literary" (even artificial), and there was a sense sometimes of confusion between the two. The weaker poems could descend into whimsy; or they might at times remind the reader of the faded 19th-century language into which Maori poetry was customarily translated by early scholars. And Tuwhare was often more effective when he spoke directly and plainly than when he sought after images and conceits. "Tree let your arms fall/raise them not sharply in supplication/to the bright enhaloed cloud" is weaker, being more literary, than the directness (especially in the second and third lines) of "o voiceless land, let me echo your desolation./The mana of my house has fled,/the marae is but a paddock of thistle." ("Mana" means pride/prestige; and "marae" is the meeting ground of the tribe. Both words are entirely familiar to European New Zealanders.)

Distinct from the predominant lyricism of the early work there is a strong, personal, anecdotal style, humourous, generous in feeling, colloquial in language, and this has come to predominate in Tuwhare's later books. Some reviewers have regretted the change, but it seems clear the gains outweigh any losses.

Some subjects suit Tuwhare better than others in that they get the best, the most authentic, out of him linguistically; and this is especially so of poems dealing with the countryside and with occasions that take him back to his own family. Into such poems he works a physical quality of experience which all New Zealanders recognize but which few of European race can translate so directly into words: "I bend/my back. Ankle deep in water how reassuring/ to hear the knock and rattle of cockle in the/flax kit as I strain black sand away." Tuwhare is particularly good in poems dealing with bereavement, exploiting the Maori custom in which the corpse is addressed by the mourner and kinship is claimed. There is something of Maori oratory in the direct speech of all his work; and his humour is a unifying quality, making the reader feel a consistent personality running through the poems. Tone of voice is an intangible element which often makes the difference between success and failure in poetry and there is in Tuwhare's tone at its best a distinct combination of qualities, at once informal, colloquial New Zealand English, but with a decorum recognizably Maori:

Eat the gifts of the sea raw. That's basic.
Wrap yourself around some of it. Now take this cluster
of mussels for example:

I prise a couple loose, and with one in each palm see,
I clap my hands and crack their hairy heads together
Then I go *shlup*, and spit the broken bits out after.

Read in Tuwhare's rich, breathy voice, such poems become admirable performing scripts.

—C. K. Stead

UPDIKE, John (Hoyer). American. Born in Shillington, Pennsylvania, 18 March 1932. Educated in Shillington public schools; Harvard University, Cambridge, Massachusetts, A.B.

(summa cum laude) 1954; Ruskin School of Drawing and Fine Arts, Oxford, 1954–55. Married Mary Pennington in 1953; four children. Staff Reporter, *New Yorker*, 1955–57. Recipient: Guggenheim Fellowship, 1959; Rosenthal Award, for fiction, 1960; National Book Award, for fiction, 1964; O. Henry Award, for fiction, 1966. Member, American Academy of Arts and Letters, 1976. Lives in Georgetown, Massachusetts.

PUBLICATIONS

Verse

The Carpentered Hen and Other Tame Creatures. New York, Harper, 1958; as *Hoping for a Hoopoe*, London, Gollancz, 1959.
Telephone Poles. New York, Knopf, and London, Deutsch, 1963.
Bath after Sailing. West Haven, Connecticut, Pendulum Press, 1968.
Midpoint and Other Poems. New York, Knopf, and London, Deutsch, 1969.
The Dance of the Solids, with *A New Year Greeting*, by W. H. Auden. New York, Scientific American, 1969.
Seventy Poems. London, Penguin, 1972.
Six Poems. New York, Aloe, 1973.
Query. New York, Albondocani Press, 1974.
Cunts (Upon Receiving the Swingers Life Club Membership Solicitation). New York Hallman, 1974.
Tossing and Turning. New York, Knopf, and London, Deutsch, 1977.

Plays

Three Texts from Early Ipswich: A Pageant. Ipswich, Massachusetts, 17th Century Day Committee, 1968.
Buchanan Dying. New York, Knopf, and London, Deutsch, 1974.

Novels

The Poorhouse Fair. New York, Knopf, and London, Gollancz, 1959.
Rabbit, Run. New York, Knopf, 1960; London, Deutsch, 1961.
The Centaur. New York, Knopf, and London, Deutsch, 1963.
Of the Farm. New York, Knopf, 1965.
Couples. New York, Knopf, and London, Deutsch, 1968.
Rabbit Redux. New York, Knopf, 1971; London, Deutsch, 1972.
A Month of Sundays. New York, Knopf, and London, Deutsch, 1975.
Marry Me: A Romance. New York, Knopf, 1976; London, Deutsch, 1977.
The Coup. New York, Knopf, 1978; London, Deutsch, 1979.

Short Stories

The Same Door. New York, Knopf, 1959; London, Deutsch, 1962.
Pigeon Feathers and Other Stories. New York, Knopf, and London, Deutsch, 1962.
Olinger Stories: A Selection. New York, Knopf, 1964.
The Music School. New York, Knopf, 1966.
Penguin Modern Stories 2, with others. London, Penguin, 1969.
Bech: A Book. New York, Knopf, and London, Deutsch, 1970.
Museums and Women and Other Stories. New York, Knopf, 1972; London, Deutsch, 1973.
Warm Wine: An Idyll. New York, Albondocani Press, 1973.
Couples: A Short Story. Cambridge, Massachusetts, Halty Ferguson, 1976.

Too Far to Go: The Maples Stories. New York, Fawcett, 1979.
Problems and Other Stories. New York, Knopf, 1979.

Other

The Magic Flute (juvenile), with Warren Chappell. New York, Knopf, 1962.
The Ring, with Warren Chappell. New York, Knopf, 1964.
Assorted Prose. New York, Knopf, and London, Deutsch, 1965.
A Child's Calendar. New York, Knopf, 1966.
Bottom's Dream: Adapted from William Shakespeare's "A Midsummer Night's Dream." New York, Knopf, 1969.
A Good Place. New York, Aloe, 1973.
Picked-Up Pieces. New York, Knopf, 1975; London, Deutsch, 1976.

Editor, *Pens and Needles*, by David Levine. Boston, Gambit, 1970.

Bibliography: *John Updike: A Comprehensive Bibliography* by B. A. Sokoloff and Mark E. Posner, Norwood, Pennsylvania, Norwood Editions, 1973.

Manuscript Collection: Harvard University, Cambridge, Massachusetts.

Critical Studies: interviews with the author in *Life* (New York), 4 November 1966, *Paris Review*, Winter 1968, and *New York Times Book Review*, 10 April 1977.

John Updike comments:

I began as a writer of light verse, and have tried to carry over into my serious or lyric verse something of the strictness and liveliness of the lesser form. My extensive prose writing has consumed much of the energy that might have gone into my development as a poet, though my long poem, "Midpoint," is an attempt to catch up.

* * *

The verse of John Updike is not as accomplished as his prose fiction. Specimens of it collected in *Hoping for a Hoopoe* and *Telephone Poles* do not require to be read, however, in that spirit of indulgence usually extended to novelists who have lost their way in poems. He is invariably neat, his wit is well-dressed, and he has a lively interest in form. The better of his verses look like superior exercises in the art of cheering oneself up by playing with words:

> Many-maned scud-thumper, tub
> of male whales, maker of worn wood, shrub-
> ruster, sky-mocker, rave!
> portly pusher of waves, wind-slave.

These four lines, which comprise a complete poem entitled "Winter Ocean," show the verse-making Updike's merits, and his strict limitations. Sophistication seizes upon a lyrical impulse and throttles it with style. It is as though G. M. Hopkins had settled for a job concocting elegant clues for crossword puzzles, or one of the Anglo-Saxon riddlers had been washed up on the staff of *The New Yorker*.

Updike is not always so slight – the title piece in the volume *Midpoint and Other Poems* shows him in a more serious or at any rate energetic mood.

—Robert Nye

URDANG, Constance (Henriette). American. Born in New York City, 26 December 1922. Educated at Fieldston School; Smith College, Northampton, Massachusetts, A.B. 1943; University of Iowa, Iowa City, M.F.A. 1956. Military Intelligence Analyst, United States Department of the Army, Washington, D.C., 1944–46. Married Donald Finkel, *q.v.*, in 1956; two daughters and one son. Copy Editor, Bellas Hess Inc., publishers, New York, 1947–51; Editor, P. F. Collier and Son, publishers, New York, 1952–54. Recipient: *Carleton Miscellany* Centennial Award, 1967; National Endowment for the Arts grant, 1976. Lives in St. Louis, Missouri.

PUBLICATIONS

Verse

Charades and Celebrations. New York, October House, 1965.
The Picnic in the Cemetery. New York, Braziller, 1975.

Novel

Natural History. New York, Harper, 1969.

Other

Editor, with Paul Engle, *Prize Stories '57.* New York, Doubleday, 1957.
Editor, with Paul Engle and Curtis Harnack, *Prize Stories '59.* New York, Doubleday, 1959.
Editor, *The Random House Vest Pocket Dictionary of Famous People.* New York, Random House, 1962.

Manuscript Collection: Washington University, St. Louis.

* * *

In *Charades and Celebrations* Constance Urdang is preoccupied with three themes: the moon embodying the feminine principle; the equivocal nature of men labelled "heroes"; and experience viewed as a junkshop-collage of memories, relationships and reflections, a theme further developed in her unconventionally constructed novel-poem, *Natural History*.

Her "Moon Tree" poems are based on ancient associations of the moon with woman, evidently drawing on sources in Jung, in Harding's *Woman's Mysteries* and Briffault's *The Mothers*. Ishtar the moon-goddess as a fish, the moon as a cow, a panther, a she-bear, a hound, a hare – all symbolic phases of the female psyche are woven into assertions of the mystery, strength, beauty and cyclic nature of women's power:

> Moon-muse, mother, fountain that rises and falls
> Your daughters do not forget you.
> You make their weather. Their blood
> Ebbs and flows like the tide you make.

In the series of poems "The Idea of a Hero," Urdang is most at home with the bizarre history of the failed emperor of Mexico, Maximilian, who is seen through the eyes of people surrounding him. Epigraphs and the device of the persona enable her to present historical information as "eyewitness news" which passes naturally into commentary on the events, implicitly reflecting back on the publicity-created "heroes" of our own anti-heroic time: "Being a hero/Is a public job."

Urdang's third theme is loosely revealed in poems about her grandparents, children, a junkshop owner, and the "country of push-button patios." Her collage technique juxtaposes logically-unconnected scenes and events, mirroring the random flux of contemporary American life. Her novel-poem *Natural History* also follows this pattern: "A long poem written not in, but by means of, prose. Its techniques that of the poem ... Instead of using simple metaphors, use narrative sequences as metaphors. People, situations, as metaphors." Following her own prescription, then, a St. Louis junkshop becomes a metaphor for brokenness and lives thrown away uselessly. The disheartening love affairs of her friends are metaphors for the general difficulty and superficiality of sexual and marital relationships. This collage method eliminates narrative padding and contributes to the continuing evolution of the novel form towards the terseness and density of poetry. Constance Urdang has produced a small but superior body of work. She belongs to a handful of women poets who have undertaken the major and long-neglected task of recording accurately the sensibilities of contemporary women.

—Jane Augustine

VALENTINE, Jean. American. Born in Chicago, Illinois, 27 April 1934. Educated at Milton Academy, 1949–52; Radcliffe College, Cambridge, Massachusetts, 1952–56, B.A. (cum laude) 1956. Married James Chace in 1957 (divorced, 1968); two daughters. Poetry Workshop Teacher, Swarthmore College, Pennsylvania, 1968–70, Barnard College, New York, 1968, 1970, Yale University, New Haven, Connecticut, 1970, 1973–74, Hunter College, New York, 1970–75. Since 1974, Faculty Member, Sarah Lawrence College, Bronxville, New York. Recipient: Yale Series of Younger Poets Award, 1965; National Endowment for the Arts grant, 1972; Guggenheim Fellowship, 1976. Address: 527 West 110th Street, New York, New York 10025, U.S.A.

PUBLICATIONS

Verse

Dream Barker and Other Poems. New Haven, Connecticut, Yale University Press 1965.
Pilgrims. New York, Farrar Straus, 1969.
Ordinary Things. New York, Farrar Straus, 1974.
Turn. Oberlin, Ohio, Pocket Pal Press, 1977.
The Messenger. New York, Farrar Straus, 1979.

Manuscript Collection: Lamont Library, Harvard University, Cambridge, Massachusetts.

* * *

From her first volume, *Dream Barker*, Jean Valentine's poems have translated dreams into living experience. Now in the later volumes, *Ordinary Things* and *The Messenger*, she almost reverses this process to show life as veiled and inconclusive, suggestive rather than definitive, dream-like. The elliptical yet lucid craft of these late poems is unobtrusive while serving the poet's vision of experience as only imperfectly graspable. The poems ride lightly on the waves of thought, more textures than statements, soft as some woven fabric which incorporates rough knots and bright ribbons in a matrix of pale yarn. Whereas the early poems of *Dream Barker* referred openly to events such as first love, wedding, childbirth, parenthood, the later poems are mistier and more private in their reference. Valentine is very careful not to make any over-statement or premature conclusion that might mar the sense of the importance of emotional atmosphere over external incident. But despite the oblique approach, the poems do not ignore cruel realities nor evade the pain of existence. She writes of the loss of love, separations, a child's death, war. Her sensitivity to these sufferings is projected through images of the physical body, heartbeat, arms and legs moving, ribs, hands, faces smiling or somber, against a muted background of gross American culture, radios, graffiti, police. Her delicacy makes her incline to withdraw from this coarseness and brutality, but her honesty will not allow her to blink them away or to consider them more "real" than her own thoughts which transform the harsh exterior landscape into an austere but habitable room within.

Valentine's reluctance to refer to her more recent personal life in overt ways has evidently contributed to her interest in translation, since in that mode she can speak through another poet's voice, identifying with the other's experience but leaving the reader to decide the extent of affinity between the two. The volume *Ordinary Things* includes a translation of the Dutch poet Huub Oosterhuis's "Twenty Days' Journey," a moving meditation on the death of someone the poet has deeply loved. One can infer that Valentine was attracted to this poem for the dream-nightmare quality of grief which completely consumes, yet is simply and delicately expressed: "my body turns to mist but still stays alive,/an eye that will not close." The final section is also a dream:

I rang for days at the door
a long talk going on and on
through me like a wire

I crawled to the roof
where you were
when I got there you were gone

This expression of immediacy and physicality, as well as the sense of love enduring beyond personal absence or presence is a mirror of Valentine's own long poem "Fidelities," in which she is reading a letter from a lover. As she reads, her room becomes his, the park is both present and remembered and becomes another field in which both are walking:

We walked back up the field to the house.
Your room there. This white room. Books, papers, letters.
Stamps. The telephone. Our lives.
We're always choosing our lives.

Yet, reticent as she is, in her latest poems Valentine comes to a well-won affirmation, celebration even, of things as they are, with this lover, present or afar, and with the world:

Here, sitting up late, with a friend
listening, talking, touching her hand, his hand
I touch your hand. No one
says anything much. No one leaves anyone.

Her world is now softened and subdued, bounded by solitude, memories, and letters, peaceful days providing perspective on her life. Friendship is the chief motif of *The Messenger*; she befriends in memory her parents and old acquaintances, cradles and resolves her feelings for them. The poems are sometimes titled merely with a date, and often quote the words of others in a gently free-associative style, usually fragmented in structure, which is faithful to flickering thought ("March 21st"):

to drift   allowing
forgetting my name   my life

the salt of our hands
touching

changing:
over and over: ...

the play of the breath of the world
they   he   she   you

Jean Valentine has created a gentle loving world through her meditation on the raw and painful events of everyday life. She has thus become a modern rarity: a poet without bitterness, self-pity or self-aggrandizement.

—Jane Augustine

VAN DUYN, Mona. American. Born in Waterloo, Iowa, 9 May 1921. Educated at the University of Northern Iowa, B.A. 1942; University of Iowa, Iowa City, M.A. 1943. Married Jarvis Thurston in 1943. Instructor in English, University of Iowa, 1944–46, and University of Louisville, Kentucky, 1946–50; Lecturer in English, Washington University, St. Louis, 1950–67; Lecturer, Salzburg Seminar in American Studies, 1973. Currently, Poetry Consultant, Olin Library Modern Literature Collection, Washington University. Editor, with Jarvis Thurston, *Perspective: A Quarterly of Literature*, St. Louis, 1947–78. Recipient: Eunice Tietjens Memorial Prize, 1956, and Harriet Monroe Memorial Prize, 1968 (*Poetry*, Chicago); Helen Bullis Prize (*Poetry Northwest*, Seattle), 1964; National Endowment for the Arts grant, 1966; Bollingen Prize, 1971; National Book Award, 1971; Guggenheim Fellowship, 1972; Loines Award, 1976. D.Litt.: Washington University, 1971; Cornell College, Mt. Vernon, Iowa, 1972. Address: 7505 Teasdale Avenue, St. Louis, Missouri 63130, U.S.A.

PUBLICATIONS

Verse

Valentines to the Wide World. Iowa City, Cummington Press, 1959.
A Time of Bees. Chapel Hill, University of North Carolina Press, 1964.
To See, To Take. New York, Atheneum, 1970.
Bedtime Stories. Champaign, Illinois, Ceres Press, 1972.
Merciful Disguises: Poems Published and Unpublished. New York, Atheneum, 1973.

Manuscript Collection: Olin Library, Washington University, St. Louis.

* * *

The awarding of the Bollingen Prize in 1971 to Mona Van Duyn brought long overdue general recognition to this excellent poet, whose insight, humor, and technical skill deserve to find a larger audience. "The wintry work of living, our flawed art" is her principal theme. Her poetic craft emanates from, in fact is identical with, the conscious intelligence which everyone has and uses to shape random everyday happenstance into meaningful experience. Mind itself then is her subject-matter. "The world blooms and we all bend and bring/from ground and sea and mind its handsome harvests." Poetry-making therefore becomes a metaphor for activities of living minds. "Join us with charity," she says in "To My Godson, On His Christening," "whose deeds, like the little poet's metaphors,/are good only in brave approximations,/who design, in walled-up workrooms, beautiful doors." In "Three Valentines to the Wide World," she calls the beauty of the world "merciless and intemperate" and suggests that against "that rage" we must "pit love and art, which are compassionate." The tension in Van Duyn's poems rises from two dualisms: the world seen as cruel but lovely, a "brilliant wasting," and the technical exposition of strict forms (often long-lined slant-rhymed quatrains) with prose-like statements, themselves varying from Yeatsian elegance to plain midwestern colloquialism.

Her mind is therefore both the wood and the chisel which cuts into it. She ranges wide and deep. She can be philosophical, ironic, elegiac, penetratingly personal. She lives in and looks at domestic life in suburbia, where she finds that experience is as murderous as on battlefields, highways, and ghetto streets, the terrain of masculinist poets. But she sees as clearly as they, perhaps more clearly, the terror of living. To save and strengthen love is her major concern, which leads her to investigate the mind's attitudes toward love. Sometimes she is gently hopeful – "love is that lovely play/that makes and keeps us." Sometimes she is disillusioned, as in "What I Want to Say":

What do you think love is, anyway?
I'll tell you, a harrowing …
To say I love you is a humiliation …
It is the absolute narrowing of possibilities,
and everyone, down to the last man,
dreads it.

But Van Duyn's fullest exploration of love's permutations comes in the poems about marriage scattered throughout her work from early to late. In one section of "Toward a Definition of Marriage," the marital relationship is typically described in literary terms:

It is closest to picaresque, but essentially artless …
How could its structure be more than improvising,
when it never ends, but line after line plod on …
But it's known by heart now; it rounded the steeliest shape
to shapeliness, it was so loving an exercise.

Because of this parallelism between life and poetry, overt literary reference is frequent in Van Duyn, notably to Christopher Smart and Yeats's "Leda and the Swan." The richest expression of this parallelism, however, occurs in "An Essay on Criticism," in which the poet adapts the genre and heroic couplet form of Pope's 18th-century poem to develop her own full-fledged philosophical discourse on the interrelationship of love and the making of poems. As the poem begins, the poet is in the kitchen about to open a package of dried onion soup when a young woman poet friend rushes in to describe her love affair: "I've learned what love is – how love is like a poem –/how it 'makes nothing happen,' how it 'lies in the valley of its saying.' " The analogy is built up and sustained through many references to well-known theories of poetry until the human acts of loving and creating poetry become identical in the moment in which the beloved, the reader of poetry, meets the lover, the poet: "two humans, artless and similar –/a likeness proved out of difference – and, enlightened in its sunshine,/he sees they've been caring about each other the whole time." Then the poem switches back to the kitchen and the onion soup. The poet is in tears, but onion juice didn't cause them:

but poetry didn't cause them either. The pain, that tear-jerk,
was life, asserting its primacy in a well-timed rebuke,

and the assertion is valid. A poem can stay formally seated
till its person-to-person call, centuries later, is completed...

But these tears, I remind, well and fall in a room without a clock.
Out of action they come, into action they intend to hurry back.

So the poet concludes that her tears have a "rhetoric" which says: "We must move in time, time moves, we must care right away!/Less beautifully patient than a poem, one might call them an essay." "Essay," punning on "attempt" as well as "literary form," is a considerable understatement of Mona Van Duyn's complex achievement. Her astonishing and moving work has come out of her loyalty to the unfashionable stringencies of tight forms both in life and art. These have been true and sufficient means to promulgate a lifelong delight and torment in her love-affair with the world.

—Jane Augustine

VARMA, Monika. Indian. Born in Allahabad, Uttar Pradish, 5 August 1916. Educated privately. Married Brigadier K. K. Varma in 1938; two sons. Delegate, All India Poets Meet, June 1973. Recipient: *Caravan* magazine prize, 1956, 1958; *Illustrated Weekly of India* prize, for short story, 1970; Urmilla Kanoria Creative Arts Fund award, 1976. Address: c/o Mr. S. Varma, C34 Pamposh Enclave, New Delhi 110 048, India.

Publications

Verse

Dragonflies Draw Flame. Calcutta, Writers Workshop, 1962.
Gita Govinda and Other Poems. Calcutta, Writers Workshop, 1966.
Green Leaves and Gold. Calcutta, Writers Workshop, 1970.
Quartered Questions and Queries. Calcutta, Writers Workshop, 1971.
Past Imperative: A Collection of Poems 1953–1964. Calcutta, Writers Workshop, 1972.
Across the Vast Spaces. Calcutta, United Writers, 1975.
Alakananda. Calcutta, Writers Workshop, 1976.

Other

Facing Four: A Critique of Four Indo-Anglian Women Poets. Calcutta, Writers Workshop, 1974.
Lord Krishna. New Delhi, Vikas, 1978.

Translator, *A Bunch of Poems*, by Rabindranath Tagore. Calcutta, Writers Workshop, 1966.
Transcreator, *The Gita Govinda of Jayadeva.* Calcutta, Writers Workshop, 1968.
Transcreator, *Pather Panchali*, by Bibhuti Bhusan Banerjee. Calcutta, Writers Workshop, 3 vols., 1973.

Manuscript Collection: Bangalore University Library, Mysore.

Critical Studies: "Some Poets of the Writers Workshop" by Amalendu Bose, in *Critical Essays on Indian Writings in English*, Dharwar, Karnatak University, 1968; "An Exchange Between Monika Varma and Amalendu Bose," in *Miscellany 30* (Calcutta), December 1968; S. C. Saha, in *Thought* (Delhi), June 1969; "Women Poets from Writers Workshop," in *Deccan Herald Magazine*, May 1972; "Thought Process and Imagery in Monika Varma's Poetry" by Syed Ameer Uddin, in *Commonwealth Quarterly* (Mysore), December 1978.

Monika Varma comments:

The two important points to remember in any understanding of my poetical works are that the metaphors are totally Indian, and the idioms are based on classical Indian philosophy.

Nobody writing English can be said to be devoid of influences of past poets. And Dylan Thomas is the Poet of all poets. But in my case, I think, I can say that a kind of transmutation has taken place in the crucible of Indian thinking.

The stress on "Indian" is obvious on reading all the references to birds, flowers, beasts, in the Nature poems. If the Lake Poets were influenced by their environment, my environment has also had a profound effect on me.

Besides being an Indian, I am a Bengali. The Bengali race is always sensitive to its surroundings. This fact shows up in all Bengali poetic writing and can be seen from my translations of the Tagore poems and finally, in the perfect prose statement of Bibhuti Bhusan Banerjee's *Pather Panchali*. The Bengali poets who have had a profound influence on me are Jibanananda Das and Ajit Dutta. Unfortunately the latter's works have never been translated and there isn't a really good translation of all Jibanananda Das's works.

My philosophical outlook and poetic statements are based on Indian philosophy but if any Western influence has to be sought it is Gerard Manley Hopkins. Though today my philosophical thinking is totally Indian, I have been greatly influenced by the New Testament and the Christ's Life as such, His parables, words, and the words of early Christian mystic saints.

Dr. S. Radhakrishnan's works, his comparative notes on the Western, Indian, and Islamic Sufi saints would also cover the metaphysical aspect of my poetry.

In fact, to understand and appreciate my works, the importance of the metaphysical aspect must be taken into consideration the whole time. Without this realization the subtleties are lost. The simplest statements have a depth of meaning.

It has not been a conscious effort, and it is only on analysis that I find that the metaphysical idiom is the most vital aspect in content. Even in style this is important.

I have, over and over again, in my poems talked about "Words." This love of words is a love of rhythm and music. At one time I was a dedicated student of Western classical music and it was the pure music of Bach that always appealed most to me. Therefore the rules of music, the idioms and phrases of the theory of music have walked into my verse.

The rhythm of words was originally learnt by a love of Swinburne's use of words and their toccata rhythm.

And, finally, a deep religious love for my land permeates my poetry.

* * *

There must be something in the exclusive use of the English language in the context of present-day India that eventually gives a number of poets a vague sense of limitation. There is no other explanation why so many of the more significant poets who started off by writing only in English have later taken up translation from an Indian language into English as a simultaneous activity. Outstanding examples are A. K. Ramanujan, P. Lal, Mokashi-Punekar, Gauri Deshpande, Suniti Namjoshi, and Paul Jacob.

Monika Varma is another such poet who finds a creative challenge in translation. She has published several volumes of original poems and her shorter lyrics have a remarkable capacity of vividly crystallizing a fleeting image or a passing thought, but to me her most impressive and sustained achievement so far is her English rendering of the work of a 12th-century Sanskrit poet, Jayadeva. Jayadeva's *Gita Govinda* is on the surface a long love poem full of beautiful erotic images, but it has a symbolic and mystic undertone that gives the poem a universal significance. Monika Varma successfully conveys the mythic structure and the sensuous texture in contemporary English without doing violence to the spirit of the original. There is a sense of total devotion and enjoyment in this translation that recreates the *bhakti* quality of medieval *vaishnavic* literature.

Monika Varma's own imaginative world is vivid with birds and trees and glow-worms that are not just objects in nature, but personally felt experiences. Grass is not just green but:

> Grass is in my mouth, my throat,
> grass is on my tongue, my taste,
> grass is my love, my touch.
> The scent of grass: green,
> it is my life, my breath.

Here is a mature sensibility, sensitive to touch, to colour, to the seasons, and to the magic of the sound of words. On the whole her work has width of vision and a rootedness quite different in flavour from the academic sophistication of the "alienated" urban poets.

—Meenakshi Mukherjee

VAS DIAS, Robert. American. Born in London, England, 19 January 1931. Educated at Grinnell College, Iowa, B.A. 1953; Columbia University, New York, 1959–61. Served in the United States Army, 1953–55. Married Susan McClintock in 1961; one son. Assistant Editor, Prentice Hall, publishers, New York, 1955–56; Staff Editor, Allyn and Bacon, publishers, Boston, 1956–57; Free-lance Editor, 1957–65; Instructor in English, Long Island University, Brooklyn, New York, 1964–66; Instructor, American Language Institute, New York University, 1966–71; Tutor and Poet-in-Residence, Thomas Jefferson College, Grand Valley State College, Allendale, Michigan, 1971–74. Since 1977, Lecturer, Antioch International Writing Program, London. Director, Aspen Writers Workshop, Colorado, 1964–67; Director of the National Poetry Centre, and General Secretary, Poetry Society, London, 1975–78. Associate Editor, *Sumac*, Fremont, Michigan, 1970–72, and *Mulch*, Amherst, Massachusetts, 1973–74. Since 1975, Publisher, Permanent Press, London and New York; since 1978, Editor, *Atlantic Review*, London. Recipient: Creative Artists Public Service grant, 1975. Address: 25 Cholmeley Park, London N.6, England.

PUBLICATIONS

Verse

Ribbed Vision. Privately printed, 1963.
The Counted. New York, Caterpillar, 1967.
The Life of Parts; or, Thanking You for the Book on Building Birdfeeders. Mount Horeb, Wisconsin, Perishable Press, 1972.
Speech Acts and Happenings. Indianapolis, Bobbs Merrill, 1972.

Making Faces. London, Joe DiMaggio Press, 1975.
Ode. Omaha, Abattoir, 1977.
Poems Beginning: "The World." London, Oasis, 1979.

Other

Editor, *Inside Outer Space: New Poems of the Space Age.* New York, Doubleday, 1970.

Manuscript Collection: University of Virginia, Charlottesville.

Critical Studies: by Linda Wagner, in *Red Cedar Review* (East Lansing, Michigan), 1973; Toby Olson, in *Margins 28–30* (Milwaukee), 1976; Lee Harwood, in *Poetry Information 15* (London), 1976.

* * *

Robert Vas Dias writes a poetry of crisp understatement. He has long expressed a mock-serious view of the world, a world much like that of William Carlos Williams, David Ignatow, and Paul Blackburn in that its images are those of winter birds, children, junkyards, trees, boats. The substance of Vas Dias's poetry is the commonplace; the stance is, often, the stoic; but the real métier of the poetry – and, one suspects, of the poet's philosophy – is the play within the language.

Although W. H. Auden defined a poet as one who loved to play with words, the affinities between Vas Dias's recent verbal constructs and the writing of Gertrude Stein are more noticeable. In *Making Faces* Vas Dias creates high-jinks of word repetition and association, shifting meaning jumping to sprung meaning, all caught within a heavily rhythmic context. The title poem, with its play on *face* ("defaced with the face I face"), introduces a collection in which nearly every poem moves from a root noun (which is also used as verb) to unlikely extensions, clichés, compounds, and misreadings – as variant as the single face in the process of "making faces." The comic use of the contemporary poet's "identity theme," which has dominated American poetry for 20 years, is refreshing. What is impressive is Vas Dias's ability to achieve thematic coherence through what looks to be only word play. Some of the strongest poems are "Poem Starting with Words Written on a Postcard" (using *state* and forms of *to be*; the opening line is "I miss you because I am in another state"), "The Gift of Snakes" (here the word play leads to darker associations in theme), and the funny sexual "Poem of Places and Tongues."

In his earlier collection, *Speech Acts and Happenings*, Vas Dias wrote a more conventional poetry, satisfying his need for invention through creating various speakers. While there are some poems in his later work about other personae, tapping his ability to re-create the idioms of characters he has conceived, most of the later poems express the Vas Dias sense of language and theme – in some ways, this later work is less virtuoso and closer to the poet himself. We see his deep sense of loss over Paul Blackburn's death; his feeling of displacement – at least temporarily – as he returns to his childhood home of England; his melancholy, tempered with tranquility, in winter. We come to know his friends and his fears. But the process of knowing the persona in the poems is not arduous or tiresome; it is lively, interesting, and convincing.

Other recent collections evince this same kind of preoccupation with the sense of play in language, and the poet's responsibility to name. The chapbook *Ode* is a prose-poem montage expressing loss, suiting the definition of "ode" to the content of the poem. Heavily emotional, inventive in its mixed forms, the poem sequence juxtaposes guide-book explanations of the losses of cultural landmarks with the poet's often oblique poem-commentaries: "Blackfriars Convent had been washed away by 1754" appears just before "left window in the row/of windows left/in the wall standing/lights behind me quick/as the vandal sun runs/behind the winter/wall of trees." Effective as a sound and image poem, the verse also repeats words and designs used in other poems within the sequence. Again, the reader must be impressed with the spare control. *Poems Beginning: "The World"* is just that, a group of many poems which have to do with the ponderous themes the phrase suggests. Again, Vas Dias's shifting rhythms and generally taut voice, coupled with his sense of play, make the collection effective. When he writes, "we're afloat but hardly," the reader shares the grimace, not a lament. Whether Vas Dias is writing his way through the world or making faces, his poems are striking examples of the poet creating his own world through his own sense of language; and that, after all, is what poets and poems have been about since the beginning. It did, after all, start with the word.

—Linda Wagner

VIERECK, Peter (Robert Edwin). American. Born in New York City, 5 August 1916. Educated at Horace Mann School for Boys, New York; Harvard University, Cambridge, Massachusetts, B.S. (summa cum laude) 1937 (Phi Beta Kappa), M.A. 1939, Ph.D. 1942; Christ Church, Oxford, 1937–38. Served in the United States Army, 1943–45, and Instructor in History, United States Army University, Florence, Italy, 1945. Married 1) Anya de Markov in 1945 (divorced, 1970), two children; 2) Betty Martin Falkenberg in 1972. Teaching Assistant, 1941–42, Instructor in German, and Tutor in History and Literature, 1946–47, Harvard University; Assistant Professor of History, 1947–48, and Visiting Professor of Russian History, 1948–49, Smith College, Northampton, Massachusetts. Associate Professor, 1948–55, Professor of History, 1955–65, Alumnae Foundation Chair of Interpretive Studies, 1965–79, and since 1979, William R. Kenan, Jr., Chair of History, Mount Holyoke College, South Hadley, Massachusetts. Visiting Lecturer in American Culture, Oxford University, 1953; Whittall Lecturer in Poetry, Library of Congress, Washington, D.C., 1954, 1963; Fulbright Lecturer, University of Florence, 1955; Elliston Lecturer, University of Cincinnati, Ohio, 1956; Visiting Professor, University of California, Berkeley, 1957, 1964, and City College of New York, 1964; State Department Cultural Exchange Lecturer in the U.S.S.R., 1961; Visiting Scholar, American Academy in Rome, 1977–78. Poetry Workshop Director, New York Writers Conference, 1965–67. Recipient: Eunice Tietjens Prize (*Poetry*, Chicago), 1948; Guggenheim Fellowship, 1948; Pulitzer Prize, 1949; Rockefeller grant, 1958; Horace Mann School Award, 1958; Twentieth Century Fund Scholarship, 1962; Columbia University Translation Center Prize, 1978. L.H.D.: Olivet College, Michigan, 1959. Address: 12 Silver Street, South Hadley, Massachusetts 01075, U.S.A.

PUBLICATIONS

Verse

Terror and Decorum: Poems 1940–1948. New York, Scribner, 1948.
Strike Through the Mask! New Lyrical Poems. New York, Scribner, 1950.
The First Morning: New Poems. New York, Scribner, 1952.
The Persimmon Tree: New Pastoral and Lyric Poems. New York, Scribner, 1956.
New and Selected Poems 1932–1967. Indianapolis, Bobbs Merrill, 1967.

Play

The Tree Witch (produced Cambridge, Massachusetts, 1961). Published as *The Tree Witch: A Poem and a Play (First of All a Poem)*, New York, Scribner, 1961.

Other

Metapolitics: From the Romantics to Hitler. New York, Knopf, 1941; revised edition, as *Metapolitics: The Roots of the Nazi Mind*, New York, Putnam, 1961; revised edition, Baton Rouge, Louisiana State University Press, 1979.

Conservatism Revisited: The Revolt Against Revolt, 1815–1949. New York, Scribner, 1949; London, Lehmann, 1950.

Shame and Glory of the Intellectuals: Babbitt Jr. vs. the Rediscovery of Values. Boston, Beacon Press, 1953; revised edition, New York, Putnam, 1965.

Dream and Responsibility: Four Test Cases of the Tension Between Poetry and Society. Washington, D.C., University Press of Washington, 1953.

The Unadjusted Man: A New Hero for Americans: Reflections on the Distinction Between Conforming and Conserving. Boston, Beacon Press, 1956; revised edition, New York, Putnam, 1962.

Conservatism: From John Adams to Churchill. Princeton, New Jersey, Van Nostrand, 1956.

Inner Liberty: The Stubborn Grit in the Machine (lecture). Wallingford, Pennsylvania, Pendle Hill Pamphlets, 1957.

Conservatism Revisited and the New Conservatism: What Went Wrong? New York, Macmillan, 1962; revised edition, Baton Rouge, Louisiana State University Press, 1980.

Critical Study: *Peter Viereck: Poet and Historian*, by Marie Henault, New York, Twayne, 1969.

* * *

A nervous daring informs the characteristic verse of Peter Viereck. Occasionally, the cleverness overreaches itself, when strained sound effects trivialize the image of Nazi evil "Hiking in shorts through tyranny's Tyrols" ("Crass Times Redeemed by Dignity of Souls"). But Viereck's gambles generally win; his sound patterns can create the illusion of a new etymology: "... Aeneas on the boat from Troy/Before harps cooled the arson into art" ("Lot's Wife"). This bravado works best in his epic treatment of "Kilroy," and in "To a Sinister Potato," where echoes of "Ode on a Grecian Urn" heighten the bizarre grandeur of the parody: "O vast earth-apple, waiting to be fried,/Of all life's starers the most many-eyed,/ What furtive purpose hatched you long ago/In Indiana or in Idaho?" The zest animating these poems from *Terror and Decorum* not only suits his frequent comic rhymes, or his bastardized Spenserian language in "Ballad of the Jollie Gleeman," but also supports the tender, frightening "Six Theological Cradle Songs," which use nursery jingles and childhood games to dramatize the terror implicit in mortality. Sometimes, Viereck concentrates his frenzy to achieve the gnomic wit of the elegy for Hart Crane, whose exotic polysyllables he elsewhere imitates: "... and he found/New York was the clerks his daddy hired/Plus gin plus sea; then Hart felt tired,/Drank both and drowned" ("Look, Hart, That Horse You Ride Is Wood").

Though the later volumes provide less outrageous fun than the first, they offer greater control of ambitious themes. The straightforward comic verse falters, as in "Full Cycle," a series of parodies of new critics and modern poets, including Viereck himself. But Viereck develops an impressive group of poems with extraordinary personae; "To My Isis" wittily yet accurately summarizes Viereck's range from "Whatever shimmers ... birch or trout" to "... Mud I also mimic: Let salivating wart-hogs gambol by,/Preening their bristles. All gross masks I'll try/But hairy spiders. These I still can't stomach." His most striking impersonations are of trees; an oak threatens a willow: "Your chance of passing next week's Woodlore Test/Is – bear it oakly – not the best./You know the price! The beaver foreman claims/He needs just one more trunk to mend his dams" ("The Slacker Need Not Apologize"). Then an ironic "stage-direction" states: "beavers in over-alls drag away storm-felled oak" (Viereck's frequent sub-title notes and epigraphs suggest a nervous, though charming editor, eager to help, but unwilling to compromise the integrity of his text). The willow survives: "Mere echo (-strummer?), mad (- or wild with truth?),/By contours of the winds lured far too far,/I'm left behind when even God flies south/(If 'God' means all the climate I ignore)." The dashes, questions, and parentheses heighten the struggling uncertainty already outlined by the dialectic format of the poem. Here, or in a Goethe/Crane debate in "Decorum and Terror," Viereck dramatizes viewpoints limited and belligerent that fuse for the reader into a compassionate accepting overview. Viereck's show-off rhymes: "Courtier's prance/Otto Kahn's," and play on "k" sounds ("barrack/Weimaric/Pyrrhic/wreck" are the rhymes in one quatrain) make both speakers less than Olympian and prepare for the triumphant final rhyme of "Viereck," which asserts the poet's fusion of decorous form and Romantic terror that are the antagonists of the poem.

Viereck's tree poems, while obviously allegories of particular human attitudes, are equally exciting as delicate versions of non-human psyche. After reading "The Slacker Apologizes," it is impossible to deny that a "crass young weed" would boast:

> Last night my stamen
> Could hear her pistil sigh ...
> ...
> My pollen's shy
> Deep nuzzling tells her: weeds must love or die.

Despite his skill in these poems and his flair for dialogue, both elegant and colloquial, Viereck disappoints with *The Tree Witch*, a morality play in verse which places man between the force of nature symbolized by a dryad and the force of technology and conformity symbolized by the Furies (disguised as maiden aunts). Viereck's fondness for dialectic and his familiar satiric targets produce episodes more repetitious than cumulative in their dramatic force, though there are some lovely lyrics, some amusing moments and, occasionally, an explosion of pithy magic: "Lively is not alive; a funeral pyre/Is snugger than a hearth a little while."

Viereck's exaltation of unromanticized nature is a constant in his work, finding strongest expression in "The Autumn Instant: Sky and Earth," which dramatizes the loving destructiveness of the cycle: "I am your sky; look up; my clouds are altars/To worship you with desecrating rain." Because of this frightening context in which nature and man exist, many Viereck poems praise the precarious splendor of the moment, often the moment of August ripeness, with Keatsian intensity, and "Sing the bewildered honor of the flesh" ("Some Lines in Three Parts"). Though his recent work has received insufficient acclaim, *New and Selected Poems* develops this obsessive theme with seemingly artless intensity – the fine sequence "Five Walks on the Edge" makes the Massachusetts coast an inevitable and powerful emblem fusing man's psychological, metaphysical and aesthetic limits; Viereck's characteristic formal control gives resonance and assurance to nervous uncertainties:

> World, world, what wreath from soil so thin?
> The roots replenish till the time
> They don't replenish. Many times
> The warmth is gaining. All the time
> The loss is gaining anyhow.

—Burton Kendle

VILLA, José Garcia. Filipino. Born in Manila, 5 August 1914. Educated at the University of New Mexico, Albuquerque, B.A. 1933; Columbia University, New York. Has two sons. Has taught at the University of the Philippines, Quezon City, and Far Eastern University, Manila. Associate Editor, New Directions, publishers, New York, 1949–51; Poetry Workshop Director, City College of New York, 1952–63; Professor of Poetry, New School for Social Research, New York, 1964–73. Since 1968, Presidential Adviser on Cultural Affairs, Philippine Government. Recipient: National Institute of Arts and Letters grant, 1942; Guggenheim Fellowship, 1942; Bollingen Fellowship, 1951; Shelley Memorial Award, 1959; Philippines Cultural Heritage Award, 1962; Rockefeller Fellowship, 1963. D.Litt.: Far Eastern University, Manila, 1959; D.H.L.: University of the Philippines, 1973. Address: 780 Greenwich Street, New York, New York 10014, U.S.A.

PUBLICATIONS

Verse

Many Voices. Manila, Philippine Book Guild, 1939.
Poems by Doveglion. Manila, Philippine Writers' League, 1941.
Have Come, Am Here. New York, Viking Press, 1942.
Volume Two. New York, New Directions, 1949.
Selected Poems and New. New York, McDowell Obolensky, 1958.
Poems in Praise of Love. Manila, A. S. Florentino, 1962.
Poems 55: The Best Poems of José Garcia Villa as Chosen by Himself. Manila, A. S. Florentino, 1962.

Short Stories

Footnote to Youth: Tales of the Philippines and Others. New York, Scribner, 1933.
Selected Stories. Manila, A. S. Florentino, 1962.

Other

The Portable Villa. Manila, A. S. Florentino, 1962.
The Essential Villa. Manila, A. S. Florentino, 1965.

Editor, *Philippine Short Stories.* Manila, Philippine Free Press, 1929.
Editor, *A Celebration for Edith Sitwell.* New York, New Directions, 1948.
Editor, *A Doveglion Book of Philippine Poetry.* Manila, Katha, 1962; revised edition, as *The New Doveglion Book of Philippine Poetry*, Manila, Caliraya Foundation, 1975.

* * *

José Garcia Villa is as yet the most distinguished contribution of the Philippines to world poetry in English, although a few younger poets are beginning to be recognized beyond Philippine frontiers. (Two minor poets – Carlos Bulosan and M. de Gracia Concepcion – who also had been published in America, are now dead.) A volume of his best poems as chosen by himself, *Poems 55*, is a little too thin and could be expanded to include 100 poems and still remain a distinguished volume of verse.

Villa started as a writer of short stories, then shifted to poetry and art, and for the last decade and a half he has been at work on a theory or philosophy of poetry, which he expects to publish in a multi-volume edition in the near future.

Now in his sixties, he is still known in his country as an eccentric nonconformist. Early in college he was dismissed from the University of the Philippines for authoring a poem that was deemed obscene by college authorities. Thirty years later he received from his school an appointment as professorial lecturer in literature.

Villa's main achievement in poetry has been in experimentation; he has produced a number of poems considered original by critics native to the English language. Not having been born to English, he nevertheless has assiduously studied the language and has acquired a peculiar knowledge of it. This has enabled him to express himself in English with a high degree of originality which sometimes contains flashes of revelation. Some of his poems have been described as among the finest in the English language.

Mr. Villa has been concerned mainly with the individual human being, largely in his erotic and spiritual relations. He has been largely unconcerned, even in his prose fiction, with man as a social being, as a member of a larger community, with problems more complex and more difficult of solution. The possibility, therefore, is that the novelty of much of his poetry will wear off and his significance as a poet may decline. In fact, in the Philippines, although he is widely respected for the reputation which he has acquired among a number of foreign critics, Mr. Villa is not seriously regarded as a poet of significant achievement by the more thoughtful students of humane letters.

—Leopoldo Y. Yabes

VLIET, R(ussell) G. American. Born in Chicago, Illinois, in 1929. Educated at Southwest Texas State College, later, Southwest Texas State University, San Marcos, B.A. and M.A. 1952; Yale University, New Haven, Connecticut, 1955–56. Married Ann Rutherford in 1951; one child. Recipient: Rockefeller grant, 1967. Agent: Lucy Kroll Agency, 390 West End Avenue, New York, New York 10024. Address: Route 1, Stamford, Vermont 01247, U.S.A.

PUBLICATIONS

Verse

Events and Celebrations. New York, Viking Press, 1966; London, Bodley Head, 1967.
The Man with the Black Mouth. Santa Cruz, California, Kayak, 1970.
Water and Stone. New York, Random House, 1980.

Novels

Rockspring. New York, Viking Press, 1974.
Solitudes. New York, Harcourt Brace, 1977.

* * *

The strongest of the pieces in R. G. Vliet's *Events and Celebrations* reveal an easy command of a number of varying poetic modes. The two prose poems, "The Journey" and the Kafka-like "The Ants," are not completely convincing (though Vliet has a true narrative skill, as his later novella *Rockspring* demonstrates); but the lyric sequence, "Clem Maverick," is immediately engaging. The twenty sections, differing in style and point of view, sketch the career of a late, charismatic Country Music star, the exploited and self-destructive victim of his own talent. The dark side of Clem Maverick is barely suggested, however; Vliet is content here to concentrate on the humor and pathos of the people who knew and loved and used Maverick during his short life. The overall effect is a little indeterminate perhaps but the virtuoso display of shifting dramatic voices is impressive.

The most successful pieces in *Events and Celebrations* are the dramatic monologues (particularly "Robert it is eight months to the day") and the purely lyrical poems which make up the first section of the book. The "events" which Vliet celebrates are slight – a group of girls riding their horses down an icy street, a group of boys fiercely at play – and sometimes not events at all, but merely bits of nature carefully observed and lovingly described. "Love" is in fact the keynote of the entire collection:

Love's own form
                    is sufficient unto
itself: never ask how or why:
purpose puffs a grape, is its purple hue,
packs apples; winged maples fly;
horses dogs deer run wordlessly
perfectly; the hand in love
moves through its own country:
love has no use for less than love:
love made these poems. I don't know why.

These lines are slightly disingenuous, however, or at least a modest understatement of Vliet's solid gifts. The closing invocation is in effect a prayer which answers its own petition:

            I beg You mercy, mercy,
You of the long black hair and the winter
skin. I have served Thee. This
I wear under my jacket now is no
hunchback's hump, but a blotch of shriveled
wings. Come down from the forthright
northern country. Teach me the true,
the harsh necessity. Strip me of error.
Widen my eyes. Split my back open
like a late dragonfly in summer thunder
uncrinkling on the marshgrass of everyday
surprise. I labor now, here.

—Elmer Borklund

WADDINGTON, Miriam. Canadian. Born in Winnipeg, Manitoba, 23 December 1917. Educated at Lisgar Collegiate Institute, Ottawa; University of Toronto, B.A. 1939, Diploma in Social Work, 1942, M.A. 1968; University of Pennsylvania, Philadelphia, M.S.W. 1945. Has two sons. Caseworker, Jewish Family Service, Toronto, 1942–44, 1957–60, and Philadelphia Child Guidance Clinic, 1944–45; Assistant Director, Jewish Child Service, Montreal, 1945–46; Lecturer and Supervisor, McGill School of Social Work, Montreal, 1946–49; Caseworker, Montreal Children's Hospital Speech Clinic, 1950–52, and John Howard Society, 1955–57; Supervisor, North York Family Service, 1960–62. Since 1964, Member of the English Department, and currently Professor of Literature, York University, Toronto. Recipient: Canada Council Fellowship, 1962, 1968, 1971, 1979. Address: 32 Yewfield Crescent, Don Mills, Ontario M3B 2Y6, Canada.

PUBLICATIONS

Verse

Green World. Montreal, First Statement Press, 1945.
The Second Silence. Toronto, Ryerson Press, 1955.
The Season's Lovers. Toronto, Ryerson Press, 1958.
The Glass Trumpet. Toronto, Oxford University Press, 1966.
Call them Canadians. Ottawa, Queen's Printers and National Film Board, 1968.
Say Yes. Toronto, Oxford University Press, 1969.
Dream Telescope. London, Anvil Press Poetry, 1972.
Driving Home: Poems New and Selected. Toronto, Oxford University Press, 1972; London, Anvil Press Poetry, 1973.
The Price of Gold. Toronto, Oxford University Press, 1976.
Mister Never. Winnipeg, Turnstone Press, 1978.

Plays

Radio Documentaries: *Chekov*, 1958; *Poe*, 1962.

Other

A. M. Klein. Toronto, Copp Clark, 1970.

Editor, *Essays, Poems, Controversies*, by John Sutherland. Toronto, McClelland and Stewart, 1973.
Editor, *The Collected Poems of A. M. Klein.* Toronto, McGraw Hill Ryerson, and New York, McGraw Hill, 1974.

Bibliography: "Miriam Waddington: A Checklist 1936–1975" by Laurence R. Ricou, in *Essays on Canadian Writing* (Toronto), Fall 1978.

Manuscript Collection: Public Archives of Canada, Ottawa.

Critical Studies: "The Lyric Craft of Miriam Waddington" by Ian Sowton, in *Dalhousie Review* (Halifax, Nova Scotia), Summer 1958; "Into My Green World: The Poetry of Miriam Waddington" by Laurence R. Ricou, in *Essays on Canadian Writing* (Toronto), Fall 1978.

Miriam Waddington comments:

About my poetry: the key to it is in the language. My Canadian English takes its cue from the prairies where I was born and conceals more than it reveals. Some concealments: the social, mythic, and linguistic reverberations of the Yiddish and Russian cultures of my childhood, plus the austerity and Scottish accents of my early teachers.

* * *

"Your poems fuse the flesh and the dream," wrote Anaïs Nin of the poetry of Miriam Waddington, who must be one of the finest lyric poets of the day. Of her books to date, the first three are full of images of changing seasons, green worlds, alfresco silences, lovers meeting and parting, flowers galore; the later ones branch out more from her native Manitoba to Canada as a country, and beyond, with evocative trips to Russia, Poland, Israel, and Germany. Common to both phases of her work are characteristic assertions of human worth and warmth, gentle imperatives, and a self-depracating wit. Her imagery is intelligent without being intellectual, yet apt and derived from personal observation, as when she describes children playing hockey as being "stiff as flowers."

When *Driving Home: Poems New and Selected* appeared in 1972, it became apparent that hers was an essentially lyrical gift, for she sings of what is and finds in the world of desire the point of meeting of what was and what could have been. Hers is a poetry of acceptance rather than of search, for the important thing is to realize the values we have rather than those that we had or hope to have. While other poets were bemoaning the lack of a useable past or vainly engineering the future, she wrote in "Canadians":

> We look
> like a geography but
> just scratch us
> and we bleed
> history.

In other poems she describes bittersweet experiences with the directness of a folk tale and an awareness of modern psychology, for "in my mind/summer never ended." Her playfulness and relationship to the writers of Europe can be seen in the last lines of a characteristic poem, "Sad Winter":

> Dear Nelly Sachs,
> dear Nathalie Sarraute,
> isn't there anything
> you can teach me
> about how to write
> better in Canada?

—John Robert Colombo

WAGONER, David (Russell). American. Born in Massillon, Ohio, 5 June 1926. Educated at Pennsylvania State University, University Park, B.A. 1947; Indiana University, Bloomington, M.A. 1949. Served in the United States Navy, 1944–46. Married Patricia Parrott in 1961. Instructor, De Pauw University, Greencastle, Indiana, 1949–50, and Pennsylvania State University, 1950–54. Associate Professor, 1954–66, and since 1966, Professor of English, University of Washington, Seattle. Since 1966, Editor, *Poetry Northwest*, Seattle, Elliston Lecturer, University of Cincinnati, 1968. Since 1978, Editor, Princeton University Press Contemporary Poetry Series. Recipient: Guggenheim Fellowship, 1956; Ford Fellowship, for drama, 1964; National Institute of Arts and Letters grant, 1967; Morton Dauwen Zabel Prize (*Poetry*, Chicago), 1967; National Endowment for the Arts grant, 1969. Chancellor, Academy of American Poets, 1978. Address 1075 Summit Avenue East, Seattle, Washington 98102, U.S.A.

PUBLICATIONS

Verse

Dry Sun, Dry Wind. Bloomington, Indiana University Press, 1953.
A Place to Stand. Bloomington, Indiana University Press, 1958.

Poems. Portland, Oregon, Portland Art Museum, 1959.
The Nesting Ground. Bloomington, Indiana University Press, 1963.
Five Poets of the Pacific Northwest, with others, edited by Robin Skelton. Seattle, University of Washington Press, 1964.
Staying Alive. Bloomington, Indiana University Press, 1966.
New and Selected Poems. Bloomington, Indiana University Press, 1969.
Working Against Time. London, Rapp and Whiting, 1970.
Riverbed. Bloomington, Indiana University Press, 1972.
Sleeping in the Woods. Bloomington, Indiana University Press, 1974.
A Guide to Dungeness Spit. Port Townsend, Washington, Graywolf Press, 1975.
Travelling Light. Port Townsend, Washington, Graywolf Press, 1976.
Collected Poems 1956–1976. Bloomington, Indiana University Press, 1976.
Who Shall Be the Sun? Poems Based on the Lore, Legends, and Myths of Northwest Coast and Plateau Indians. Bloomington, Indiana University Press, 1978.
In Broken Country. Boston, Little Brown, 1979.

Play

An Eye for an Eye for an Eye (produced Seattle, 1973).

Novels

The Man in the Middle. New York, Harcourt Brace, 1954; London, Gollancz, 1955.
Money, Money, Money. New York, Harcourt Brace, 1955.
Rock. New York, Viking Press, 1958.
The Escape Artist. New York, Farrar Straus, and London, Gollancz, 1965.
Baby, Come On Inside. New York, Farrar Straus, 1968.
Where Is My Wandering Boy Tonight? New York, Farrar Straus, 1970.
The Road to Many a Wonder. New York, Farrar Straus, 1974.
Tracker. Boston, Little Brown, 1975.
Whole Hog. Boston, Little Brown, 1976.

Other

Editor, *Straw for the Fire: From the Notebooks of Theodore Roethke 1943–1963.* New York, Doubleday, 1972.

Manuscript Collections: Olin Library, Washington University, St. Louis; University of Washington, Seattle.

Critical Studies: "The Poetry of David Wagoner" by Robert Boyers, in *Kenyon Review* (Gambier, Ohio), 1970; "An Interview with David Wagoner," in *Crazy Horse 12* (Marshall, Minnesota), 1972; "On David Wagoner" by Sanford Pinsker, in *Salmagundi* (Saratoga Springs, New York), Spring-Summer 1973.

David Wagoner comments:

I have an affinity for the dramatic lyric, in tones ranging from the loud and satiric through the quiet and conversational.

* * *

While it is true that Theodore Roethke, his undergraduate teacher at Pennsylvania State University, was instrumental in bringing David Wagoner to the Pacific Northwest, one could argue that he would have found his way there anyway. After spending his formative years in Whiting, Indiana, that industrial suburb of Chicago which is hard to surpass for disfigured earth, Dantesque fire, polluted water and air, Wagoner has understandably found his place to stand near one of the few regions in America which still has some unspoiled wilderness and some unspoiled people, American Indians.

Wagoner is surely one of America's most prolific and versatile writers. Not only has he published many volumes of poetry – his *Collected Poems* comes to nearly 300 pages – but he has also produced nine substantial novels. The novelist's feeling for detail enriches the poetry, not only in such mythical narrative poems as "The Return of Icarus," "The Labors of Thor," and "Beauty and the Beast," but also in dramatic and lyric poems. His versatility is patent. His themes are important ones: survival, anger at those who violate the natural world, a Chaucerian delight in human oddity. He manages tones from gaiety to meditative seriousness. He is rarely solemn.

Wagoner has been publishing poetry for nearly three decades. After his first two volumes – nothing from the first and little from the second appears in *Collected Poems* – Wagoner moved beyond the influence of Roethke and Edgar Lee Masters to find his own forms. They include the mock instruction manuals best exemplified by "Advice to the Orchestra," "The Singing Lesson," "Staying Alive," "Sleeping in the Woods," and "Meeting a Bear"; elegies far from Theocritus such as the mordant "For a Forest Clear-cut by the Weyerhaeuser Company"; and, most recently, mythic poems based on American Indian materials.

"Staying Alive" is one of the best American poems since World War II, a profoundly sensible set of instructions to one lost in the woods which is also valuable to anyone anywhere who is interested in staying alive. "Sleeping in the Woods" goes on from "Staying Alive" to show us Wagoner achieving his peculiar harmony with the natural world. The poem opens,

> Not having found your way out of the woods, begin
> Looking for somewhere to bed down at nightfall
> Though you have nothing
> But parts of yourself to lie on....

In "Talking to Barr Creek" Wagoner succeeds at what Matthew Arnold failed to do in "A Summer Night." He realistically aspires to a harmony with nature not beyond human possibility. At the end of the poem the speaker prays:

> Grant me your endless, ungrudging impulse
> Forward, the lavishness of your light movements,
> Your constant inconstancy....
> Your sudden stillness....
> Teach me your spirit, going yet staying, being
> Born, vanishing, enduring.

For a man so attuned to the wild natural world where still live American Indians, it seems almost a matter of course that recent work should include a whole book prompted by Indian myths. The final two stanzas of the title poem of *Who Shall Be the Sun?* gives an idea of Wagoner's sensitive, respectful handling of Indian lore:

> The People said, "We shall have no sun at all!"
> But Snake whispered, "I have dreamed I was the sun."
> Raven, Hawk, and Coyote mocked him by torchlight:
> "You cannot scream or howl! You cannot run or fly!
> You cannot burn, dazzle or blacken the earth!
> How can you be the sun?" "By dreaming," Snake whispered.

He rose then out of the rich night.
He coiled in a ball, low in the sky.
Slowly he shed the Red Skin of Dawn,
The Skin of the Blue Noontime, the Skin of Gold,
And last the Skin of Darkness, and the People
Slept in their lodges, safe, till he coiled again.

T. S. Eliot wrote of Tennyson that "he has three qualities which are seldom found in the greatest poets: abundance, variety, and complete competence." Those qualities are also impressively evident in the poetry of David Wagoner.

—James K. Robinson

WAIN, John (Barrington). British. Born in Stoke-on-Trent, Staffordshire, 14 March 1925. Educated at The High School, Newcastle-under-Lyme, Staffordshire; St. John's College, Oxford, B.A. 1946, Fereday Fellow, 1946–49, M.A. 1950. Married 1) Marianne Urmstrom in 1947 (marriage dissolved, 1956); 2) Eirian James in 1960; three children. Lecturer in English, University of Reading, Berkshire, 1947–55; Professor of Poetry, Oxford University, 1973–78. Director, Poetry Book Society Festival, "Poetry at the Mermaid," London, 1961. Churchill Visiting Professor, University of Bristol, 1967; Visiting Professor, Centre Universitaire Experimental, Vincennes, France, 1969; First Holder, Fellowship in Creative Arts, Brasenose College, Oxford, 1971–72. Recipient: Maugham Award, 1958; Heinemann Award, 1975, and Black Memorial Award, 1975, both for non-fiction. Fellow, Royal Society of Literature, 1960; resigned, 1961. Lives in Oxford. Address: c/o Macmillan and Company Ltd., 4 Little Essex Street, London W.C.2, England.

PUBLICATIONS

Verse

Mixed Feelings: Nineteen Poems. Reading, Berkshire, Reading University School of Art, 1951.
A Word Carved on a Sill. London, Routledge, and New York, St. Martin's Press, 1956.
A Song about Major Eatherly. Iowa City, Qara Press, 1961.
Weep Before God. London, Macmillan, and New York, St. Martin's Press, 1961.
Wildtrack: A Poem. London, Macmillan, and New York, Viking Press, 1965.
Letters to Five Artists. London, Macmillan, 1969; New York, Viking Press, 1970.
The Shape of Feng. London, Convent Garden Press, 1972.
Feng. London, Macmillan, and New York, Viking Press, 1975.

Plays

Harry in the Night: An Optimistic Comedy (produced Stoke on Trent, 1975).

Television Play: *You Wouldn't Remember*, 1978.

Novels

Hurry on Down. London, Secker and Warburg, 1953; as *Born in Captivity*, New York, Knopf, 1954.

Living in the Present. London, Secker and Warburg, 1955; New York, Putnam, 1960.
The Contenders. London, Macmillan, and New York, St. Martin's Press, 1958.
A Travelling Woman. London, Macmillan, and New York, St. Martin's Press, 1959.
Strike the Father Dead. London, Macmillan, and New York, St. Martin's Press, 1962.
The Young Visitors. London, Macmillan, and New York, Viking Press, 1965.
The Smaller Sky. London, Macmillan, 1967.
A Winter in the Hills. London, Macmillan, 1970.
The Pardoner's Tale. London, Macmillan, and New York, Viking Press, 1978.

Short Stories

Nuncle and Other Stories. London, Macmillan, 1960; New York, St. Martin's Press, 1961.
Death of the Hind Legs and Other Stories. London, Macmillan, and New York, Viking Press, 1966.
The Life Guard. London, Macmillan, 1971.
King Caliban and Other Stories. London, Macmillan, 1978.

Other

Preliminary Essays. London, Macmillan, and New York, St. Martin's Press, 1957.
Gerard Manley Hopkins: An Idiom of Desperation. London, Oxford University Press, and Folcroft, Pennsylvania, Folcroft Editions, 1959.
Sprightly Running: Part of an Autobiography. London, Macmillan, 1962; New York, St. Martin's Press, 1963.
Essays on Literature and Ideas. London, Macmillan, and New York, St. Martin's Press, 1963.
The Living World of Shakespeare: A Playgoer's Guide. London, Macmillan, and New York, St. Martin's Press, 1964.
Arnold Bennett. New York, Columbia University Press, 1967.
A House for the Truth: Critical Essays. London, Macmillan, 1972; New York, Viking Press, 1973.
Samuel Johnson. London, Macmillan, 1974; New York, Viking Press, 1975.
A John Wain Selection, edited by Geoffrey Halson. London, Longman, 1977.
Professing Poetry. London, Macmillan, 1977.

Editor, *Contemporary Reviews of Romantic Poetry.* London, Harrap, and New York, Barnes and Noble, 1953.
Editor, *Interpretations: Essays on Twelve English Poems.* London, Routledge, 1955; New York, Hillary House, 1957.
Editor, *International Literary Annual.* London, Calder, and New York, Criterion, 2 vols., 1959–60.
Editor, *Fanny Burney's Diary.* London, Folio Society, 1960.
Editor, *Anthology of Modern Poetry.* London, Hutchinson, 1963; revised edition, as *Anthology of Contemporary Poetry: Post-War to the Present*, 1979.
Editor, *Pope.* New York, Dell, 1963.
Editor, *Selected Shorter Poems of Thomas Hardy.* London, Macmillan, and New York, St. Martin's Press, 1966; revised edition, 1975.
Editor, *The Dynasts*, by Thomas Hardy. London, Macmillan, and New York, St. Martin's Press, 1966.
Editor, *Selected Shorter Stories of Thomas Hardy.* London, Macmillan, and New York, St. Martin's Press, 1966.
Editor, *Shakespeare: Macbeth: A Casebook.* London, Macmillan, 1968.
Editor, *Shakespeare: Othello: A Casebook.* London, Macmillan, 1971.
Editor, *Johnson as Critic.* London, Routledge, 1973.

Editor, *Lives of the English Poets: A Selection*, by Samuel Johnson. London, Dent, and New York, Dutton, 1975.
Editor, *Johnson on Johnson: A Selection of the Personal and Autobiographical Writings of Samuel Johnson.* London, Dent, and New York, Dutton, 1976.
Editor, *The Poetry of Thomas Hardy: A New Selection.* London, Macmillan, 1977.
Editor, *An Edmund Wilson Celebration.* Oxford, Phaidon Press, 1978.
Editor, *Personal Choice: A Poetry Anthology.* Newton Abbot, Devon, David and Charles, 1978.

Manuscript Collection: Edinburgh University Library.

Critical Studies: "John Wain et le Magie de l'Individu" by Françoise Barriere, in *Le Monde* (Paris), 8 August 1970; "John Wain: Revolte et Neutralité" by Pierre Yvard, in *Etudes Anglaises* (Paris), October 1970; "The New Puritanism, The New Academism, The New ..." by the author, in *A House for the Truth*, 1972.

* * *

Perhaps better known as a novelist, short-story writer, and critic, John Wain contributed to Robert Conquest's influential anthology of the mid-1950's, *New Lines*; and his poems in this selection alone uncompromisingly defined his distrust of glib emotionalism and the "poetic" gesture. Yet the apparent toughness of his determined anti-romanticism, and a note of conscious cleverness sometimes reminiscent of the early Auden, were superficially deceptive. Wain's refusal to write orthodox nature poetry, or indulge in the rant of conventional patriotism for "this mildewed island," rejects an easy emotive tone for the "sterner choice" of recording without embellishment a "love that I can never speak by rote." His attitude towards the love relationship, although resolutely unsentimentalized, also communicates authentic depth of feeling in pieces like "Poem in Words of One Syllable," "On Reading Love Poetry in the Dentist's Waiting Room," and "Don't Let's Spoil It All, I Thought We Were Going to Be Such Good Friends." A self-evident initial taste for novel, attention-arresting subjects and titles is most strikingly illustrated by the wittily original "Poem Feigned to Have Been Written by an Electronic Brain." Its technical inventiveness, culminating in the explosive stutter of the furiously frustrated machine, conveys a wholly serious statement about the nature of poetry. It is, in fact, not emotion but its cheapening by florid rhetorical diction and the distortions of sentimental poeticism which Wain has strenuously rejected. "When It Comes," a lament written under the shadow of the mushroom cloud for those unfulfilled at the "burning instant" of the world's annihilation, is the more poignantly telling for the strict control of its form.

In his aspiration to "strip our stale speech clean," Wain has shown an Augustan admiration for restraint and the imposition of order upon emotion. Indeed in *Mixed Feelings* and *A Word Carved on a Sill* he seemed in danger of becoming imprisoned by the restriction of his favourite Empsonian verse-forms, terza rima and villanelle. This gave much of his earlier work, for all its aphoristic wit, a certain monotony and air of the accomplished intellectual exercise. Yet the effectiveness of these tight verbal disciplines may be seen in the delectable "Gentleman Aged Five Before the Mirror," which has the same insight and impact as "Villanelle: For Harpo Marx": "In your fake world of frantic gag and pose/We see our real despair come striding near./The clown may speak what silent Hamlet knows."

In *Weep Before God* the threatened stranglehold of neat three-line stanzas was successfully broken to achieve a far greater metrical versatility. The exuberantly varied rhythms of "Boisterous Poem about Poetry" are as uninhibited as its expression of faith in the poet's vocation in an age of "empty clangour" and "wilderness of craving silences." In personal poems like "Time Was," "Anniversary," "To a Friend in Trouble," and the moving love-lyrics "Apology for Understatement" and "Anecdote of 2 a.m.," emotion has become unashamedly explicit. Wain returns to the theme of completeness in "Wise Men, All Questioning Done," a poem as quietly yet powerfully memorable as the fine "This above All

Is Precious and Remarkable." Aspects of contemporary violence and individual responsibility are explored in the portrait of the hunted Gestapo man in "On the Death of a Murderer"; and in the long, technically adventurous "A Song about Major Eatherly," which voices a conviction that the later penitence of the pilot who dropped the atom bomb on Nagasaki "will not take away our guilt."

Wain's recent work has developed in more experimental directions. His addresses in *Letters to Five Artists* to two poets, a painter, a sculptor, and a musician, ranging widely in time and place but unified by recurring reference to key figures like Ovid and Villon, attempts as he says to examine "some of the complex truth about man and his situation." This freely allusive blend of personal, philosophical, and historical is a natural extension of the dominant theme is his long poem *Wildtrack*: the interplay of past and present, public and private, of – again to quote his own words – the "inward-looking Night-self and outward-looking Day-self that together constitute the human personality." *Feng*, based on an early version of the Hamlet myth, is a sequence of 17 dramatic monologues in a flexible diversity of verse-patterns interwoven with prose passages. Its analysis of hallucinated fanaticism, focusing on the figure of the usurper-uncle fettered and finally destroyed by the power he has seized, has a sharp relevance for the present century.

—Margaret Willy

WAKOSKI, Diane. American. Born in Whittier, California, 3 August 1937. Educated at the University of California, Berkeley, B.A. 1960. Married 1) S. Shepard Sherbell in 1965 (divorced); 2) Michael Watterlond in 1973 (divorced, 1975). Clerk, British Book Centre, New York, 1960–63; English Teacher, Junior High School 22, New York, 1963–66; Lecturer, New School for Social Research, New York, 1969; Poet-in-Residence, California Institute of Technology, Pasadena, Spring 1972, University of Virginia, Charlottesville, Autumns 1972–73, and Willamette University, Salem, Oregon, Spring 1974, University of California, Irvine, Fall 1974, University of Wisconsin, Madison, Fall 1975, Michigan State University, East Lansing, Spring 1975, Whitman College, Walla Walla, Washington, Fall 1976, University of Washington, Seattle, Spring–Summer 1977, University of Hawaii, Honolulu, Fall 1978, and Emory University, Atlanta, Winter 1980. Since 1976, Faculty Member, Michigan State University. Recipient: Bread Loaf Writers Conference Robert Frost Fellowship, 1966; Cassandra Foundation Award, 1970; New York State Council on the Arts grant, 1971; Guggenheim grant, 1972; National Endowment for the Arts grant, 1973. Address: 361 Rampart Way, No. 302, East Lansing, Michigan 48823, U.S.A.

Publications

Verse

Coins and Coffins. New York, Hawk's Well Press, 1962.
Four Young Lady Poets, with others. New York, Totem-Corinth, 1962.
Discrepancies and Apparitions. New York, Doubleday, 1966.
The George Washington Poems. New York, Riverrun Press, 1967.
Greed Parts One and Two. Los Angeles, Black Sparrow Press, 1968.
The Diamond Merchant. Cambridge, Massachusetts, Sans Souci Press, 1968.
Inside the Blood Factory. New York, Doubleday, 1968.
A Play and Two Poems, with Robert Kelly and Ron Loewinsohn. Los Angeles, Black Sparrow Press, 1968.

Thanking My Mother for Piano Lessons. Mount Horeb, Wisconsin, Perishable Press, 1969.
Greed Parts 3 and 4. Los Angeles, Black Sparrow Press, 1969.
The Moon Has a Complicated Geography. Palo Alto, California, Odda Tala Press, 1969.
The Magellanic Clouds. Los Angeles, Black Sparrow Press, 1970.
Greed Parts 5–7. Los Angeles, Black Sparrow Press, 1970.
The Lament of the Lady Bank Dick. Cambridge, Massachusetts, Sans Souci Press, 1970.
Love, You Big Fat Snail. San Francisco, Tenth Muse, 1970.
Black Dream Ditty for Billy "The Kid" Seen in Dr. Generosity's Bar Recruiting for Hell's Angels and Black Mafia. Los Angeles, Black Sparrow Press, 1970.
Exorcism. Boston, My Dukes, 1971.
This Water Baby: For Tony. Santa Barbara, California, Unicorn Press, 1971.
On Barbara's Shore. Los Angeles, Black Sparrow Press, 1971.
The Motorcycle Betrayal Poems. New York, Simon and Schuster, 1971.
The Pumpkin Pie, Or Reassurances Are Always False, Tho We Love Them. Only Physics Counts. Los Angeles, Black Sparrow Press, 1972.
The Purple Finch Song. Mount Horeb, Wisconsin, Perishable Press, 1972.
Sometimes a Poet Will Hijack the Moon. Providence, Rhode Island, Burning Deck, 1972.
Smudging. Los Angeles, Black Sparrow Press, 1972.
The Owl and the Snake: A Fable. Mount Horeb, Wisconsin, Perishable Press, 1973.
Greed Parts 8, 9, 11. Los Angeles, Black Sparrow Press, 1973.
Dancing on the Grave of a Son of a Bitch. Los Angeles, Black Sparrow Press, 1973.
Winter Sequences. Los Angeles, Black Sparrow Press, 1973.
Trilogy: Coins and Coffins, Discrepancies and Apparitions, The George Washington Poems. New York, Doubleday, 1974.
Looking for the King of Spain. Los Angeles, Black Sparrow Press, 1974.
The Wandering Tatler. Mount Horeb, Wisconsin, Perishable Press, 1974.
Abalone. Los Angeles, Black Sparrow Press, 1974.
Virtuoso Literature for Two and Four Hands. New York, Doubleday, 1975.
The Fable of the Lion and the Scorpion. Milwaukee, Pentagram Press, 1975.
Waiting for the King of Spain. Santa Barbara, California, Black Sparrow Press, 1976.
The Man Who Shook Hands. New York, Doubleday, 1978.

Other

Form Is an Extension of Content. Los Angeles, Black Sparrow Press, 1972.
Creating a Personal Mythology. Los Angeles, Black Sparrow Press, 1975.
Towards a New Poetry. Ann Arbor, University of Michigan Press, 1979.

Manuscript Collection: University of Arizona Library, Tucson.

Critical Study: *A Terrible War: A Conversation with Diane Wakoski* edited by Philip Gerber and Robert Gemmett, Winnipeg, University of Manitoba, 1970.

Diane Wakoski comments:

I think of myself as a narrative poet, a poet creating both a personal narrative and a personal mythology. I write long poems, and emotional ones. My themes are loss, imprecise perception, justice, truth, the duality of the world, and the possibilities of magic, transformation, and the creation of beauty out of ugliness. My language is dramatic, oral, and as American as I can make it, with the appropriate plain surfaces and rich vocabulary. I am impatient with stupidity, bureaucracy, and organizations. Poetry, for me, is the supreme art of the individual using a huge magnificent range of language to show how special and different and wonderful his perceptions are. With verve and finesse. With discursive precision. And with utter contempt for pettiness of imagination or spirit.

* * *

Some time in the early 1960's Diane Wakoski's poems began to appear on the American scene. She did not make much of a splash at first; her language seemed ordinary and prosy, meandering, talkative, rhythmless, a post-beat idiom incorporating technical jargon as well as street vocabulary but lacking the tension of poems by Ginsberg or Corso. Yet to a few readers her poems signalled the arrival of a remarkably inventive poetic imagination. She was associated with other writers in New York who called themselves the "deep image" poets. It was nothing as grand as a movement of a school, and perhaps the reason for the association was no more than the fun of associating; yet certain principles were observable. The chief was that a poem should be organized, not verbally or formally, but in terms of the consonance of imagery at an intuitive level. Not exactly an original idea; the surrealists, among others, had been announcing it for years. But as it passed through Wakoski's sensibility it issued in poems that were very unlike the difficult preciosities of the surrealists, poems that were instead objective, lucid, readable, and, in spite of their sprawling appearance, densely unified.

Probably her most notable early work was the sequence called *The George Washington Poems*, a series of conversations with a person who was called George Washington but who was given a remarkably various identity. At times he was the historical figure with the same name; at others he was a personal confidant, a father substitute, a wayward lover or friend. Although much of the material of the poems was personal, in parts the poet's consciousness expanded into the national consciousness, so that she addressed the "father of the country" in social-historical-sexual terms, her own body becoming a map of the states. It was a caprice, granted. The poet acknowledged as much in the flippant, easy manner of her writing. But it was a caprice capable of serious extensions, and in any case it was admirable preparation for her mature work.

Wakoski found her proper subject in the difficulty of being a woman in a world of changing values. To what extent her work was influenced by the movement for women's liberation is problematical. It seems clear that she would have come to her knowledge of her own sensibility without any suggestions from outside. She is extremely prolific; probably she is a compulsive writer. She has published at least seven major collections of poems since 1965. Her topics range widely over social and cultural experience, and her poems contain many sharply observed scenes of urban life from New York to Los Angeles. But again and again she returns to themes of sexual need, dread, jealousy, outrage, and anger, developed in images drawn spontaneously from contemporary reality. The titles of her books are some indication of the quality of her mind: *Inside the Blood Factory*, *The Motorcycle Betrayal Poems*, and, especially, *Greed.* This last is a long sequence still in progress, having appeared so far in several different volumes; its early parts may actually have been written before the George Washington sequence. It is in effect a series of poetic essays on the basic human condition, discursive and exploratory, often very acute.

But the impression should not be given that Wakoski's sensibility is only brittle or angry. The fathers and lovers in her poems may be actuated by greed, but so, often, is the poet herself, and all are held in the basic human bond of sympathy. This gives her work a moral and metaphysical resonance that the poetry of merely militant feminists seldom achieves. Indeed, though indignation and thwarted will are the springs which set many of her poems in motion, it is a rare poem that does not lead beyond these feelings into fundamental Aristotelean pity and woe, with the result that Wakoski reaches a great many readers who might otherwise be provoked by her aggressiveness. Her characteristic poems are too long to be quoted in full here, and too cohesive to be quoted in excerpts. But there is no doubt that she has become in a very few years one of the two or three most important poets of her generation in America.

—Hayden Carruth

WALCOTT, Derek (Alton). British. Born in Castries, St. Lucia, West Indies, 23 January 1930. Educated at St. Mary's College, St. Lucia; University of the West Indies, Kingston, Jamaica, B.A. 1953. Married; three children. Taught at St. Mary's College and Jamaica College. Formerly, Feature Writer, *Public Opinion*, Kingston, and *Trinidad Guardian*, Port-of-Spain. Since 1959, Founding Director, Trinidad Theatre Workshop. Recipient: Rockefeller Fellowship, for drama, 1957; Guinness Award, 1961; Heinemann Award, 1966; Cholmondeley Award, 1969; Order of the Humming Bird, Trinidad and Tobago, 1969; Obie Award, for drama, 1971; Jock Campbell Award (*New Statesman*, London), 1974; Welsh Arts Council International Writers Prize, 1979. Address: 165 Duke of Edinburgh Avenue, Diego Martin, Trinidad.

PUBLICATIONS

Verse

Twenty-Five Poems. Port-of-Spain, Trinidad, Guardian Commercial Printery, 1948.
Epitaph for the Young. Bridgetown, Barbados Advocate, 1949.
Poems. Kingston, City Printery, 1953.
In a Green Night: Poems 1948–1960. London, Cape, 1962.
Selected Poems. New York, Farrar Straus, 1964.
The Castaway and Other Poems. London, Cape, 1965.
The Gulf and Other Poems. London, Cape, 1969; as *The Gulf*, New York, Farrar Straus, 1970.
Another Life. London, Cape, and New York, Farrar Straus, 1973.
Sea Grapes. London, Cape, and New York, Farrar Straus, 1976.
Selected Poems, edited by O. R. Dathorne. London, Heinemann, 1977.
The Star-Apple Kingdom. New York, Farrar Straus, 1980.

Plays

Henri Christophe: A Chronicle (produced St. Lucia, 1950; London, 1951). Bridgetown, Barbados Advocate, 1950.
Henri Dernier: A Play for Radio Production. Bridgetown, Barbados Advocate, 1951.
Sea at Dauphin (produced Trinidad, 1954; London, 1960). Mona, University College of the West Indies Extra-Mural Department, 1954; in *The Dream on Monkey Mountain and Other Plays*, 1971.
Ione: A Play with Music (produced Trinidad, 1957). Mona, University College of the West Indies Extra-Mural Department, 1954.
Drums and Colours (produced Trinidad, 1958). Published in *Caribbean Quarterly* (Kingston), vii, 1 and 2, 1961.
Ti-Jean and His Brothers (produced Port-of-Spain, Trinidad, 1958; New York, 1972). Included in *The Dream on Monkey Mountain and Other Plays*, 1971.
Malcochon; or, Six in the Rain (produced St. Lucia, 1959; as *Six in the Rain*, produced

London, 1960; as *Malcochon*, produced New York, 1969). Included in *The Dream on Monkey Mountain and Other Plays*, 1971.
The Dream on Monkey Mountain (produced Toronto, 1967; Waterford, Connecticut, 1968; New York, 1971). Included in *The Dream on Monkey Mountain and Other Plays*, 1971.
In a Fine Castle (produced Jamaica, 1970; Trinidad, 1971; Los Angeles, 1972).
The Dream on Monkey Mountain and Other Plays (includes *Ti-Jean and His Brothers*, *Malcochon*, *Sea at Dauphin*, and the essay "What the Twilight Says"). New York, Farrar Straus, 1971; London, Cape, 1972.
The Charlatan, music by Galt MacDermot (produced Los Angeles, 1974).
The Joker of Seville, adaptation of a play by Tirso de Molina (produced Port-of-Spain, 1974). Included in *The Joker of Seville, and O Babylon!*, 1978.
O Babylon! (produced Port-of-Spain, 1976). Included in *The Joker of Seville, and O Babylon!*, 1978.
The Joker of Seville, and O Babylon! New York, Farrar Straus, 1978; London, Cape, 1979.

Radio Play: *Pantomime*, 1979 (UK).

* * *

The appearance of *In a Green Night* by Derek Walcott in 1962 was a landmark in Caribbean literature in English. Although there had been poets of some quality described elsewhere in this volume, the notable achievements of this literature had been in prose. Walcott's volume marked a new level of poetic attainment. His verse was distinguished by a combination of virtuosity with control; by a sure sense of tone and nuance; and by delight in the sensuous and dramatic vitality of words. In these strengths also lay potential weaknesses. His aural sensibility could trap him into too extensive an echoing of other poets. His sheer pleasure in verbal control could result in artificiality. Nevertheless, many of the poems remain sharply memorable today and need no allowances to be made either for Walcott's youth when writing them or for the formidable difficulties of a poet trying to find an authentic voice without the support of a vital tradition of Caribbean poetry in English behind him.

If Walcott's earlier verse too often echoes English poets, he aggressively rejects the Anglo-American clichés of Caribbean glamour, "Found only/In tourist booklets, behind ardent binoculars" ("Prelude"). He also rejects stereotypes within the Caribbean society; too easy acquiescence in emotional response: "Teach our philosophy the strength to reach/Above the navel" ("Tales of the Islands, I"); and the facile optimism of post-emancipation politics: "This is a brief/Ignored by our first parliaments, to chart/The dangerous current of dividing grief ..." ("A Map of the Antilles"). Again, there are strengths and weaknesses. Walcott's attitudes were intelligent and necessary to a poet in the process of self-discovery, but there is a note of self-indulgent pessimism at times, too. The places he describes, such as La Guiara, Castiliane or D'Ennery, predominantly figure depression and futility, and his most precise and effective poem on human relationships in the volume ends "Only the gulls, hunting the water's edge/ Wheel like our lives, seeking something worth pity."

At this point it should be noted that, unlike another Caribbean poet, Edward Brathwaite, Walcott has made few excursions into poetry in the popular creole idiom of the West Indian masses. This by no means indicates that Walcott looks to Europe rather than to the Caribbean for inspiration. He has written a distinguished body of plays (outside our scope here) largely in dialect, and he has moved towards a flexible style that cannot be claimed as European rather than West Indian. He has used a comparatively "standard English" form in order to find the poetic medium that can most precisely express his complex, often ambiguous, attitudes to the Caribbean situation.

The personal isolation one sensed in his first poems has continued to be a theme through the later poems collected in *The Castaway*. This has not been negative, however; it has become increasingly the basis for a many-sided exploration of isolation – physically, culturally and in ways that Walcott sees as quintessential to the human being and the artist above all. The quest makes its own discoveries in the creation of the poem. His play-writing has widened the range of emotion and tone and the dramatic quality of his verse, always present, has been intensified. Now the Caribbean landscape, brilliant and sharply experienced, moves into the worlds of the poems. The struggle to find the perfect balance between depth of experience and control of expression, however, continues. At times they are not successfully resolved; at times the strains knot the syntax into lacunae of sense the reader has to struggle to decipher ("The Castaway"):

> The green wine bottle's gospel choked with sand,
> Labelled, a wrecked ship,
> Clenched seawood nailed and white as a man's hand.

Nevertheless, in his fully successful poems, even an intimation of despair like that of the slum-dwellers in "Laventville," is transformed into a brilliantly orchestrated complex of anger and of compassion.

Walcott's sense of isolation as a poet is heightened by his Caribbean predicament in many ways. One of them is that in Europe the long tradition of the formal arts has given them an accepted validity. In the art of Chardin or Vermeer, for instance, though painted, a cracked coffee cup, a dented urn – everything – "IS" ("A Map of Europe"). What validity has art in a world that lacks the tradition of formally expressed culture ("an absence of ruins," as he describes it, in "The Royal Palms") and is dominated by the natural environment? Watching the peasant girls walking past the surf to vespers, Walcott reflects that nothing he can learn "from art or loneliness/Can bless them as the bell's/Transfiguring bell can bless" ("Crusoe's Island"). Yet not only has his tongue, like the bell's, transfigured and blessed the scene; in the poem, his island setting has become a valid image of the modern artist facing the failure of traditional validities in art. Rejected by the young Walcott as a cliché, the vitality and colour of the Caribbean setting emerge in Walcott's mature verse to energise a vision at once intensely personal, Caribbean, and universal.

Another Life (1973) marked a new departure for Walcott, and his finest poetic achievement to date. Abandoning the complex style of his shorter poems, this long verse work, like Wordsworth's *Prelude*, is a study of a poet's growth from childhood to youth. The autobiographical evocation is precise, as he explores a world sealed as "in a bell jar" from assaults of adult experience. At the same time Walcott describes this area as it was mediated to him through the culture he gained from his father, his schooling, and his friends, from books, and in particular from painting. As he draws back from this world, the poem becomes an elegy not only for lost childhood, but for a Caribbean world that has irrevocably passed. *Sea Grapes* also shows Walcott reaching a stage of maturity. There is no longer the sense of tension, felt in much earlier work, between his Caribbean environment and the European literary culture in which his poetry has found an accepted place.

—Louis James

WALDMAN, Anne. American. Born in Millville, New Jersey, 2 April 1945. Educated at Bennington College, Vermont, B.A. in English literature 1966. Assistant Director, 1966–68, and Director, 1968–78, St. Mark's Church-in-the-Bowery Poetry Project, New York. Since 1974, Founding Co-Director, with Allen Ginsberg, Naropa Institute, Boulder, Colorado. Editor, *The World*, *Angel Hair* and Angel Hair Books, Full Court Press, and *Rocky Ledge*. Recipient: Dylan Thomas Award, 1967. Address: 47 Macdougal Street, New York, New York 10012, U.S.A.

PUBLICATIONS

Verse

On the Wing. New York, Boke, 1967.
Giant Night. New York, Angel Hair, 1968.
O My Life! New York, Angel Hair, 1969.
Baby Breakdown. Indianapolis, Bobbs Merrill, 1970.
Up Through the Years. New York, Angel Hair, 1970.
Giant Night: Selected Poems. New York, Corinth, 1970.
Icy Rose. New York, Angel Hair, 1971.
No Hassles. New York, Kulchur, 1971.
Memorial Day, with Ted Berrigan. New York, Poetry Project, 1971.
Holy City. Privately printed, 1971.
Goodies from Anne Waldman. London, Strange Faeces Press, 1971.
Light and Shadow. Privately printed, 1972.
The West Indies Poems. New York, Boke, 1972.
Spin Off. New York, Big Sky, 1972.
Self Portrait, with Joe Brainard. New York, Siamese Banana Press, 1973.
Life Notes: Selected Poems. Indianapolis, Bobbs Merrill, 1973.
The Contemplative Life. Detroit, Alternative Press, n.d.
Fast Speaking Woman. Detroit, Red Hanrahan Press, 1974.
Fast Speaking Woman and Other Chants. San Francisco, City Lights, 1975.
Sun the Blond Out. Berkeley, California, Arif, 1975.
Journals and Dreams. New York, Stonehill, 1976.
Shaman. Boston, Munich, 1977.
4 Travels, with Reed Bye. New York, Sayonara, 1978.
To a Young Poet. Boston, White Raven, 1979.

Recording: *John Giorno and Anne Waldman*, Giorno, 1978.

Other

Editor, *The World Anthology: Poems from the St. Mark's Poetry Project*, and *Another World.* Indianapolis, Bobbs Merrill, 1969–71.
Editor, with Marilyn Webb, *Talking Poetics from Naropa Institute.* Boulder, Colorado, Shambala, 2 vols., 1978–79.

Critical Studies: by Alicia Ostriker, in *Partisan Review* (New Brunswick, New Jersey), Spring–Summer 1971, and *Parnassus* (New York), Fall–Winter, 1974; Gerard Malanga, in *Poetry* (Chicago), January 1974; Richard Morris, in *Margins* (Milwaukee, Wisconsin), October–November 1974; Aram Saroyan, in *New York Times Book Review*, April 1976.

Anne Waldman comments:

I am very interested in reading (performing) my work and am writing longer works to be vocalized, almost sung, though not always and absolutely. The short poems are snapshots. The range is open. I am sick of the label "New York School." It is misunderstood and stifling.

* * *

"Poetry should be a joy ... a pleasure.... The whole thing of the suffering poet ... it's so unnecessary. You can get so intense that you can't produce. There's work to be done." Whatever else it may or may not do, Anne Waldman's poetry keeps this promise. Most often her poems find their inspiration and shape in an implicitly celebratory display of the diverse pleasures of things – life in New York, world-travel, sex and friendships, even her own fantasies and dreams. The high-spiritedness, rich humor, and eager openness that sustain her work derive less from the idealism than from the affluence of the 1960's. But then, she can't help it if she's lucky. What matters is that she improves upon her luck, for the imaginative persuasiveness of her best poems recalls Whitman's insight that "the most affluent man is he that confronts all the shows he sees by equivalents out of the stronger wealth of himself." Poetry, for Waldman, justifies itself as the show of life, and the pleasures it offers are inherent in the process whereby the impulses of life are released into living forms.

And if she dismisses the "suffering poet" it is almost always in the spirit of one for whom suffering can properly show itself only indirectly, as the elusive and finally unappeasable passion that both nourishes and chastens the poet's creative play: "There is work to be done." Nowhere is this element in her work more crucial than in her best-known work, "Fast Speaking Woman," which goes like this, with very little variation of pattern, for nearly 600 lines:

I'm a witch woman
I'm a beggar woman
I'm a shade woman
I'm a shadow woman
I'm a leaf woman
I'm a leaping woman

This remarkable piece could never hold our attention for 6 lines, let alone 600, were it not for its creative recklessness, at once desperate and playful. This is a matter, chiefly, of Waldman's splendidly uninhibited aesthetic opportunism, so that each line seems generated by some under-played excess of the matter and movement of preceding ones. The imaginative power of the poem inheres in the immediacy of its language yet remains apart, its freshness not just unharmed but actually enriched by any show it has made.

"Fast Speaking Woman" is something of a tour de force, but even in its extremity it is characteristic of the aims and methods of Waldman's work. She is committed to the classic American mode of "open-form" or "projective" verse, though, despite the idiomatic pungency and speed of her language, the music of her poetry is closer to that of song than of speech. This is especially true of the "chants" in *Fast Speaking Woman*, but even her less regular pieces, the best of which, I think, are in *Baby Breakdown* ("I Am Not a Woman" and "Conversational Poem") and, especially, *Journals and Dreams* ("Blues Cadet," "Mirror Meditation," "My Lady," and "When the World Was Steady"), strike the ear not as speech but as snatches of song stitched into even more various musical patterns – a variousness in music which answers to and resolves a rich contradictoriness of feeling and perception.

From its beginnings the open-form tradition has rested on some form of belief in the correspondence between inner and outer worlds, but one must go back to Whitman to find precedent for Waldman's astonishingly unstudied practical faith that discoveries of self are revelations of a world, and vice versa. The epigraph to "Fast Speaking Woman" is "I is other," and what counts in her work is less the tenacity than the nonchalance of her exploration of the truth of this. She neither apologizes for her egotism nor worries about her otherness. Coming from any poet this is exhilarating, but coming from a woman it is truly revolutionary. The word "woman" appears in nearly every line of "Fast Speaking Woman," yet it receives little rhythmic or semantic stress: it is treated simply as the natural point of departure and return for each excursus of self, as if nothing better could or need be imagined than to create a world in terms of a woman's acts of self-realization. The form of this poem gives the game away more unmistakably than others, but it is far from the only one to play that game with extraordinary inventiveness and grace.

—John Hinchey

WALKER, Margaret (Abigail). American. Born in Birmingham, Alabama, 7 July 1915. Educated at Northwestern University, Evanston, Illinois, B.A. 1935; University of Iowa, Iowa City, M.A. 1940, Ph.D. 1965; Yale University, New Haven, Connecticut (Ford Fellow), 1954. Married Firnist James Alexander in 1943; four children. Has worked as social worker, reporter, and magazine editor; taught at Livingstone College, Salisbury, North Carolina, 1941–42, 1945–46, and West Virginia State College, Institute, 1942–43. Since 1949, Professor of English, and since 1968, Director of the Institute for the Study of the History, Life and Culture of Black Peoples, Jackson State College, Mississippi. Recipient: Yale Series of Younger Poets Award, 1942; Rosenwald Fellowship, 1944; Houghton Mifflin Literary Fellowship, for fiction, 1966; Fulbright Fellowship, 1971; National Endowment for the Arts grant, 1972. D.Litt.: Northwestern University, 1974; Rust College, Holly Springs, Mississippi, 1974; D.F.A.: Denison University, Granville, Ohio, 1974; D.H.L.: Morgan State University, Baltimore, 1976. Address: 2205 Guynes Street, Jackson, Mississippi 39213, U.S.A.

PUBLICATIONS

Verse

For My People. New Haven, Connecticut, Yale University Press, 1942.
Ballad of the Free. Detroit, Broadside Press, 1966.
Prophets for a New Day. Detroit, Broadside Press, 1970.
October Journey. Detroit, Broadside Press, 1973.

Recording: *The Poetry of Margaret Walker*, Folkways, 1975.

Novels

Come Down from Yonder Mountain. Toronto, Longman, 1962.
Jubilee. Boston, Houghton Mifflin, 1966.

Other

How I Wrote "Jubilee." Chicago, Third World Press, 1972.
A Poetic Equation: Conversations Between Margaret Walker and Nikki Giovanni. Washington, D.C., Howard University Press, 1974.

* * *

Margaret Walker's reputation as a poet rests mainly upon *For My People*, which in 1942 won the Yale Series of Younger Poets competition. These race-conscious poems, because of their prescient militancy, strength, and celebration of Black identity, purposes, and traditions, are admired by the current generation of young Afro-American poets and poetry readers.

This volume contains three groupings of poems, each demonstrating the author's creative resourcefulness and technical control. The first grouping is written in Miss Walker's rather distinctive experimental reverse-indented, paragraph-style stanzas. Some of the lines have sentence syntax, as in "Lineage"; some of the stanzas are clause structured, as in the title poem; some of the stanzas are paragraph structured, as in "Dark Blood." All show to advantage her skill in poetry-as-statement. Characteristically, each stanza in a poem is a catalog of images and evocative statements, and each stanza is an increment toward the poem's climax, point, or resolution. The second grouping is lively ballads and narratives informed or inspired by Negro folk characters, lore, and traditions. The language is infused with the idioms, cadences, and intonations of Negro oral traditions. The third grouping is sonnet variations, often informed too by what the author has seen, learned, and felt as a Negro American.

Margaret Walker's poetry since *For My People* mainly deals with current subjects, people, and events of significance to Afro-Americans. These later poems continue to be insightful, compassionate, and sincere; increasingly they have become utilitarian. Her imagery continues to be precise and graphic, perhaps more realistic and less romanticized than in her earlier work, and her language continues to be plain and direct. Her use of free verse techniques has increased.

—Theodore R. Hudson

WALKER, Ted (Edward Joseph Walker). British. Born in Lancing, Sussex, 28 November 1934. Educated at Steyning Grammar School; St. John's College, Cambridge, B.A. (honours) in modern languages 1956. Served in the Royal Naval Volunteer Reserve. Married Lorna Benfell in 1956; two daughters and two sons. Head of the French Department, Southall Grammar School, Middlesex, 1958–61; Head of the Modern Languages Department, Bognor Regis School, Sussex, 1961–63; Assistant Spanish Master, Chichester High School, Sussex, 1963–64. Since 1971, Poet-in-Residence, New England College, Arundel, Sussex. Since 1962, Founding Editor, with John Cotton, *Priapus*, Berkhamsted, Hertfordshire. Recipient: Eric Gregory Award, 1964; Cholmondeley Award, 1966; Alice Hunt Bartlett Prize, 1968; Arts Council travel grant, 1978. Fellow, Royal Society of Literature. Agent: David Higham Associates Ltd., 5–8 Lower John Street, London W1R 4HA. Address: Argyll House, The Square, Eastergate, Chichester, Sussex, England.

PUBLICATIONS

Verse

Those Other Growths. Leeds, Northern House, 1964.
Fox on a Barn Door: Poems 1963–4. London, Cape, 1965; New York, Braziller, 1966.
The Solitaries: Poems 1964–5. London, Cape, and New York, Braziller, 1967.
The Night Bathers: Poems 1966–8. London, Cape, 1970.
Gloves to the Hangman: Poems 1969–72. London, Cape, 1972.
Burning the Ivy: Poems 1973–77. London, Cape, 1978.

Manuscript Collection: Lockwood Memorial Library, State University of New York, Buffalo.

Ted Walker comments:

My poetry seems to deal with loneliness and isolation. Since I live in the country, my imagery tends to be rural and even regional. My territory is Sussex and the Sussex coast.

* * *

Much of Ted Walker's poetry is in the great tradition of English Nature poetry. It is a tradition which stretches in modern times from Wordsworth to Ted Hughes. In Walker's case it is a poetry which, while one of close and accurate detail, looks beyond external nature to where parallels are observed and implications relating to the human condition are drawn: "regret/the vacant seemliness/by which we live. For which we lost/that proper, vital gift of waste" ("Crocuses"). The territory of Walker's poetry is the seashore with its inlets and breakwaters, the isolated lonely areas of the English countryside and the creatures that inhabit them. The parallel drawn is that of the ultimate solitude of the human soul when confronting the universe in which it finds itself, and where man finds himself unsatisfied and incomplete in contrast to the aptness and completeness of the rest of the animal kingdom in relation to its environment. It is where man looks both within himself and out towards "that God I won't believe in" for something beyond his immediate experience to meet the spiritual loneliness which is reflected in the isolation of the situations depicted in the poems. It is not without significance that the title of Ted Walker's second collection was *The Solitaries*.

In his third collection, *The Night Bathers*, there is a shift of emphasis. The same qualities of precise observation and craftsmanship are there; but the poet grows older and the past begins to haunt the present to the point where it enriches it and gives it depth of meaning. The title poem explores the poet's relationship with his son as a reflection of that between himself and his own father:

> when he was young to understand
> why, momently out of the night
> and purposeful beyond the reach
> of all his worry, I had swum
> deep into banks of sea-fret
> too far to have to answer him.

There is, too, a clearly observable growth in Walker's technical mastery which allows him to relax his earlier tight control and use a language closer to the colloquial. This development was to continue in his collection *Gloves to the Hangman*, where in poems such as "Letter to Barbados" there is an ease of expression which gives the poem an immediacy of reception without any diminution of strength: "Dear far-off brother. Thank you for yours,/And for the gift you send of little shells."

His latest collection, *Burning the Ivy*, finds Walker using this skill to write poetry of a more directly personal dimension, the personae are being abandoned and a more vulnerable area of feeling and emotion is being expressed, often tellingly so as in the elegy for William Plomer, "After the Funeral," and the poem for Paul Coltman on his retirement, "For His Old English Master." One feels we are getting nearer to the truth of things here, than in the earlier assaults on the universal plan, splendid as they were.

—John Cotton

WALLACE-CRABBE, Chris(topher Keith). Australian. Born in Richmond, Victoria, 6 May 1934. Educated at Scotch College; University of Melbourne, Victoria, B.A. 1956; M.A. (Lockie Fellow) 1964; Yale University, New Haven, Connecticut (Harkness Fellow), 1965–67. Married; two children. Since 1968, Senior Lecturer in English, University of Melbourne. Visiting Fellow, University of Exeter, Devon, 1973. Address: 28 Silver Street, Eltham, Victoria 3095, Australia.

PUBLICATIONS

Verse

No Glass Houses. Melbourne, Ravenswood Press, 1956.

The Music of Division. Sydney, Angus and Robertson, 1959.
Eight Metropolitan Poems. Adelaide, Australian Letters, 1962.
In Light and Darkness. Sydney, Angus and Robertson, 1964.
The Rebel General. Sydney, Angus and Robertson, 1967.
Where the Wind Came. Sydney, Angus and Robertson, 1971.
Selected Poems 1955–1972. Sydney, Angus and Robertson, 1973.
Act in the Noon. Melbourne, Cotswold Press, 1974.
The Shapes of Gallipoli. Melbourne, Cotswold Press, 1975.
The Foundations of Joy. Sydney, Angus and Robertson, 1976.
The Emotions Are Not Skilled Workers. Sydney, Angus and Robertson, 1979.

Recording: *Chris Wallace-Crabbe Reads from His Own Work*, University of Queensland Press, 1973

Other

Melbourne or the Bush: Essays on Australian Literature and Society. Sydney, Angus and Robertson, 1973.

Editor, *Six Voices: Contemporary Australian Poets.* Sydney, Angus and Robertson, 1963.
Editor, *The Australian Nationalists.* Melbourne, Oxford University Press, 1971.
Editor, *Australian Poetry '71.* Sydney, Angus and Robertson, 1971.

Critical Studies: "A Modest Radiance" by E. A. M. Colman, in *Westerly* (Nedlands, Western Australia), 1969; "To Move in Light: The Poetry of Chris Wallace-Crabbe" by Peter Steele, in *Meanjin* (Melbourne), 1970; "Transition and Advance" by James Tulip, in *Southerly* (Sydney), 1972.

Chris Wallace-Crabbe comments:

My early poetry explored the nature of social order and of intellectual coherence in a world in which religious sanctions seemed irrelevant; my concern at this stage was to make poetic structures which testified to the strength which was inherent in human reason and (hopefully) to humorous resilience as a way of meeting the contradictions of experience. Later, finding my early poetry rather too stiff, rigorous and explicit, I came to seek more supple rhythms and more autonomous images – a poetry which was more fully charged with the physical world.

Over the past few years I have increasingly been trying to come to terms with violence: political, personal and intrapersonal. I am interested in the paradox that we tend most profoundly to worship vitality for its own sake, while we are bound at the same time to deplore such vitality as manifests itself in the form of violence. Poetry, like other constructive activities, issues from forces that are potentially destructive. The self, when it is most vital, is not reducible to a moral agent. These are the central concerns which I have been trying to dramatize in my recent poems. At the same time, inevitably, my poetry has been growing less formal, less architecturally shaped, and more sinuous, more shifting, more various in its effects and directions. Psychomachia concerns me greatly, especially in its lyrical forms.

My current attitude to poetry is best summed up in A. D. Hope's haunting line, "What questions are there that we fail to ask?"

* * *

Chris Wallace-Crabbe's volume of poems *The Music of Division* confirmed the promise indicated by the appearance of his work in Australian literary journals since the early 1950's.

His first work was unusual in an Australian context in that it avoided the over-indulgence and exuberance normally associated with a young writer. *The Music of Division* exhibited a coolness and a quality of apparent detachment that looked forward to the early 1960's, rather than back to the more romantic 1950's of Australian poetry. In the first volume, the most notable poems are based upon observation of political forces, particularly as they implicate individual personalities in the tension between "public" and "private" responses. This preoccupation is developed and expanded in the later books, *In Light and Darkness* and *The Rebel General*, and is perhaps taken to its furthest stretch in the prize-winning long poem "Blood Is the Water," included in the volume *Where the Wind Came*.

Such a continuous preoccupation with and development of the themes of power and political motivation has, interestingly enough, led Wallace-Crabbe away from the earlier detachment to an increasing relaxation and a sense of full humanness in his writing. He himself has written, "After stoical-formalist beginnings, I seek a poetry of Romantic fullness and humanity. I want to see how far lyrical, Dionysian impulses can be released and expressed without loss of intelligence." His *Selected Poems*, published in his fortieth year, would seem to mark a significant watershed in his work. It is worth noting that this volume commences with a series of "Meditations" which imply that he is reaching out in new directions, perhaps more fully exploring the vein of lyricism that has glittered tantalisingly throughout the volumes that preceded it and are abridged into it. The almost ruthless severity of the abridgement still indicates, however, that Chris Wallace-Crabbe exercises a powerful and severe intelligence in the organisation of his compositions. At this point in his development he is certainly one of the leaders of his generation of Australian poets.

—Thomas W. Shapcott

WALSH, Chad. American. Born in South Boston, Virginia, 10 May 1914. Educated at Marion Junior College, Virginia, 1934–36; University of Virginia, Charlottesville, 1936–38, A.B. in French 1938 (Phi Beta Kappa); University of Michigan, Ann Arbor (Hopwood Award, for drama, 1939), 1938–43, A.M. in French 1939, Ph.D. in English 1943. Married Eva May Tuttle in 1938: four daughters. Teaching Fellow, University of Michigan 1942–43; Research Analyst, United States Army Signal Corps, Arlington, Virginia, 1943–45. Member of the faculty from 1946, Professor of English, 1952–77, Writer-in-Residence, 1969–77, Beloit College, Wisconsin. Fulbright Lecturer, Turku, Finland, 1957–58, and Rome, 1962; Visiting Professor, Wellesley College, Massachusetts, 1958–59, Juniata College, Huntingdon, Pennsylvania, 1977–78, and Roanoke College, Salem, Virginia, 1979. Ordained Priest, Episcopal Church, 1949. Founder, with Robert Glauber, *Beloit Poetry Journal*, 1950. Recipient: Catholic Poetry Society Spirit Gold Medal, 1964; Society of Midland Authors Award, 1965, 1970; Yaddo Fellowship, 1966, 1970. D.H.L.: Rockford College, Illinois, 1963; St. Norbert College, West De Pere, Wisconsin, 1972. Address: c/o Parente, 1848 Strong, Beloit, Wisconsin 53511, U.S.A.

PUBLICATIONS

Verse

The Factual Dark. Prairie City, Illinois, Decker Press, 1949.
Eden Two-Way. New York, Harper, 1954.
The Psalm of Christ: Forty Poems on the Twenty-Second Psalm. Philadelphia, Westminster Press, 1963.

The Unknowing Dance. New York and London, Abelard Schuman, 1964.
The End of Nature: Poems. Chicago, Swallow Press, 1969.
Hang Me Up My Begging Bowl. Chicago, Swallow Press, 1979.

Novels

Knock and Enter. New York, Morehouse Barlow, 1953; London, Faith Press, 1959.
The Rough Years. New York, Morehouse Barlow, 1960.

Other

Stop Looking and Listen: An Invitation to the Christian Life. New York, Harper, 1947; London, SCM Press, 1948.
C. S. Lewis: Apostle to the Skeptics. New York, Macmillan 1949.
Early Christians of the 21st Century. New York, Harper, 1950.
Campus Gods on Trial. New York, Macmillan, 1953; revised edition, 1962.
Faith and Behavior: Christian Answers to Moral Problems, with Eric Montizambert. New York, Morehouse Barlow, 1954.
Nellie and Her Flying Crocodile (juvenile). New York, Harper, 1956.
Behold the Glory (meditations). New York, Harper, 1956.
God at Large. New York, Seabury Press, 1960.
The Personality of Jesus. New York, Know Your Bible, 1961.
Why Go to Church?, with Eva Walsh. New York, Association Press, 1962.
Doors into Poetry (textbook). Englewood Cliffs, New Jersey, Prentice Hall, 1962.
From Utopia to Nightmare. New York, Harper, and London, Bles, 1962.
The Story of Job. New York, Doubleday, 1963.
Twice Ten: An Introduction to Poetry, with Eva Walsh. New York, Wiley, 1976.
The Literary Legacy of C. S. Lewis. New York, Harcourt Brace, and London, Sheldon Press, 1979.

Editor, *Today's Poets: American and British Poetry since the 1930's.* New York, Scribner, 1965.
Editor, *Garlands for Christmas: A Selection of Poetry.* New York, Macmillan, 1965.
Editor, *The Honey and the Gall: Poems of Married Life.* New York, Macmillan, 1967.

Manuscript Collections: Lockwood Memorial Library, State University of New York Buffalo; Beloit College Library, Wisconsin.

Critical Study: Introduction by Carl Bode, to *The Unknowing Dance*, 1964.

Chad Walsh comments:

(1974) As a boy, I had a strong quasi-pantheistic, quasi-scientific interest in nature. I roamed the fields and woods, did landscape paintings (as photographic as my ability would permit), daydreamed of being a forester or landscape architect. My interest in poetry began at about the age of ten. Two things triggered it. One was that my eldest brother, who had introduced me to the magic of language by reading Dickens aloud, became briefly interested in poetry. We memorized snatches of Shakespeare's sonnets and of Keats, and strode up and down the country lane near our home, reciting. About the same time my teacher, Miss Louise Johnston, told the students that each should write a poem about autumn. I recall only the ending of mine – "The leaves are falling fast,/Many of the birds are missing,/But cats will stay to the last." Anyway, she praised it, and from that time on I found myself writing poetry.

I have published over twenty books in all, six of them poetry – and these are the books closest to my heart. I find it hard to "label" my poetry – I have experienced the influence, along the way, of diverse poets – Catullus, Villon, Dante, Shakespeare and minor Elizabethan poets, Donne, Keats, Baudelaire, Heine, Hopkins, Yeats, Frost, Eliot, Auden, etc., even Housman and Kipling. I suppose the two poets whose influence is most evident in my work are Frost and Auden.

I earn my living mainly as a college professor, with some moderate income from writing and from poetry readings and lectures that I give on campuses. I am also an Episcopal priest, but a part-time one, helping on weekends at the local church. This three-fold role sometimes suggests to people that I must lead a schizophrenic or polyphrenic life; if I do I am not aware of it.

Perhaps the most frequent theme in my verse is the dialogue between human and divine love. So far as subject-matter is concerned, many of my poems fall into categories: love, religion, nature, geographical impressions, social commentary, etc. I am always experimenting in various forms and tend to swing back and forth between relatively free verse and very complicated forms. I have invented a number of forms and used them extensively – such as the "quintina," the "circular sonnet," and the "rima quinta triplicata." In the last few years I have experimented a great deal with composing poetry directly on the tape recorder, so as to get as free and flowing a quality as possible. I want to experiment with devising a kind of poetic drama in which a number of voices (some perhaps taped) could be used; it would be a unified program of maybe 50 minutes duration. I think public poetry readings are evolving in this direction, and through them a thoroughly modern kind of verse drama may emerge.

I suppose I can best describe what I ideally want to be as a poet by saying that it seems to me the two best American poets of recent times are the late Theodore Roethke and the living Robert Lowell. I'd like to have Roethke's heart and Lowell's head, to write poetry that somehow combines their strengths; in short, I'd like to be both Apollonian and Dionysian as Yeats was. Others must decide how close I come to this.

(1980) At the moment my main poetic project is a book-length sequence of Petrarchan sonnets on the relation of human and divine love. I find that the sonnet form still "works" so long as I rough it up with half-rhymes and metrical variations.

* * *

At the expense of inviting argument I maintain that Chad Walsh is the finest religious poet writing in America today. He has taken a noble but gnarled tradition, has reaffirmed its statement of love, has widened its technical range, and has brought it home to a growing if still sparse audience.

By now he has produced half a dozen volumes of verse. They all celebrate a God who is to be beloved rather than venerated and a humankind which is to be comprehended but never condemned. The writing in these volumes has benefited from the constant refining of Chad Walsh's sensibility. It is a sensibility with at least two levels. One is a response to the variegated worlds in which he moves that has been sharpened instead of being dulled by the passage of time. The other, more practical, more humane, is a comradely awareness of the way his work will look to others; for him his readers are really important. This sense of comradeship has resulted in his experimenting with varied modes and stances, in order to move closer to his readers as well as to help the flow of his poetry. Reacting at one point in his career against a preoccupation with form which led him to devise a circular sonnet, so called, and a quintina, he turned, as he has reported, to the tape recorder and simply said his poetry as it came to him. On the other hand, he remarks in his latest book that he found two-thirds of his taped poetry "still uninteresting even after revision" and so discarded it.

Not surprisingly, his best book is his latest, *Hang Me Up My Begging Bowl*. However, the two prior ones, *The Unknowing Dance* and *The End of Nature*, also contain some memorable poetry. Among the lyrics in them which affect me most are his stately ode "The Destruction by Fire of the Beloit College Chapel"; his urbanely metaphysical "Ode on a Plastic Stapes," in which he meditates on man's replacement for a God-given bone in the poet's inner ear; his "Nuptial Hymn," addressed to an uneasy young bridegroom on the bridal night; and one of many invocations to his wife, "We Were So Busy Being Young." In these two volumes his most enduring poems relate man to God or man to woman; his least permanent originate as reflections about his travels abroad.

Those travels disappear in *Hang Me Up My Begging Bowl.* The poems in this volume are frequently infused by love tinctured with humor; they have the tang of youth. And they are both matter-of-fact and visionary. For example: the opening stanza of "Terrestrial Love":

> For everything under the sun, a time, a reason.
> Coffee and toast at breakfast,
> Christ's body for my dinner once a week,
> Cocktails or wine at 5:00 o'clock,
> And the dark sweetness of your body when in season.

In the most compelling poetry the matter-of-fact turns into the transcendental but never at the expense of excess. In the poem "Ascension" the poet floats far above the auto wreck which has just killed him; yet, as he rises, he does not look up at the heavenly face of God but down at the Great Lakes glistening under a rain like "five petals of a flower."

Two notable poems in this book deal with fellow poets. The first is addressed to Robert Hayden, a distinguished Black poet and classmate of Chad Walsh's. Although they have been warm friends since college days, Black and white racists are struggling to split them apart. The lyric limns the everyday details of the friendship which Chad Walsh urges be maintained till death – and beyond. "I think we could sleep in peace/Side by side," he concludes. The second poem is a bold one indeed, for it is a eulogy of Auden modeled on Auden's masterly eulogy of Yeats. I myself believe it succeeds.

Chad Walsh remains his own poet, remembering the reader but composing the poetry he considers he should compose. In present-day America no form except the epic is less fashionable than the sonnet sequence. No subject is less fashionable than the love of God. Nevertheless, he is at work preparing a book-length sequence of Petrarchan sonnets about the relation of divine love to human.

—Carl Bode

WARNER, Francis (Robert Le Plastrier). British. Born in Bishopthorpe, Yorkshire, 21 October 1937. Educated at Christ's Hospital, 1947–54; London College of Music, 1954–55; County Technical College, Guildford, Surrey, 1955–56; St. Catharine's College, Cambridge (Music Scholar), 1956–59. Married Mary Hall in 1958 (divorced, 1972), two daughters. Taught at St. Catharine's College, 1959–65. Since 1965, Fellow and Tutor in English Literature, St. Peter's College, Oxford. Founder, Pilgrim's Way Players, touring company, 1954, Cambridge University Elgar Centenary Choir and Orchestra, 1957, and the Samuel Beckett Theatre, Oxford, 1967. Assistant Director, Yeats International Summer School, Sligo, Ireland, 1961–67; a Director, James Joyce Symposium, Dublin, 1967, and the James Joyce Foundation, Tulsa, Oklahoma. Recipient: Messing International Award, 1972. Agent: M.L.R., 194 Old Brompton Road, London S.W.5; or, Margaret Kelley, 14 Pond View Road, Canton, Massachusetts, U.S.A. Address: St. Peter's College, Oxford, England.

PUBLICATIONS

Verse

Perennia. Cambridge, Golden Head Press, 1962.

Early Poems. London, Fortune Press, 1964.
Experimental Sonnets. London, Fortune Press, 1965.
Madrigals. London, Fortune Press, 1967.
The Poetry of Francis Warner. Philadelphia, Pilgrim Press, 1970.
Meeting Ends. Rushden, Northamptonshire, Sceptre Press, 1973.
Lucca Quartet. Knotting, Bedfordshire, Omphalos Press, 1975.

Plays

Maquettes (produced Oxford, 1970; London, 1972). Oxford, Oxford Theatre Texts, 1972.
Lying Figures (produced Oxford, 1971; London, 1972). Oxford, Oxford Theatre Texts, 1972.
Meeting Ends (produced Edinburgh, 1973; London, 1974). Cheadle, Cheshire, Oxford Theatre Texts, 1974.
Killing Time (produced Oxford, 1974). Oxford, Oxford Theatre Texts, 1976.
A Conception of Love (produced Oxford, 1978). Gerrards Cross, Buckinghamshire, Smythe, 1978.

Other

Editor, *Garland: A Little Anthology of Poetry and Engravings*. Cambridge, Golden Head Press, 1968.
Editor, *Studies in the Arts: Proceedings of the St. Peter's College Literary Society*. Oxford, Blackwell, 1968; New York, Barnes and Noble, 1969.

Manuscript Collections: St. Louis University Library; University Library, Cambridge.

Critical Studies: *Francis Warner, Poet and Dramatist* edited by Tim Prentki, Knotting, Bedfordshire, Sceptre Press, 1977.

* * *

The Poetry of Francis Warner was compiled from several previous books and "represents those poems written in the decade 1960–1969, with which the ... poet chooses to be associated, on which he stakes his reputation."

The formal tradition of English poetry is very much alive in Mr. Warner's work. There are ten "Experimental Sonnets" which, while they do not sustain the exact form, do maintain the spirit of the Shakespearian sonnet. The elegy "Plainsong" is written mostly in blank verse, and "A Legend's Carol" in eleven stanzas of matched lines artfully arranged with both end and internal rhymes. Scarcely any of the "Lyrical and Mediative Poems" fail to fall into a pattern of rhythm, rhyme, or form. There are songs, lyrics, ballads, and even an aubade and a calypso ballad. "Perennia" is composed in Spenserian stanzas except for Perennia's song which, quite aptly, is written in the rhyme and meter of Swinburne's "Hymn to Proserpine."

What of the wine that Mr. Warner pours into these familiar forms? The "Sonnets" are deeply introspective; "The dark offstage preoccupies my mind," the poet says, and, indeed, the thread of mutability stitches them together. "Plainsong" seeks and finds a resolution for the final change of death in the constant renewal of life, but "A Legend's Carol" undercuts this somewhat by seeing in the archetypal birth of Mary's Son, the simultaneous death of Pan. "Lyrical and Meditative Poems" are Mr. Warner at his best; they are too finely diverse to tarnish with a generalization, but the poet seems to have accepted the urgings of "Venus and the Poet": "Come, leave mutability,/Lie me down beneath this tree" – love does provide both the ecstatic and only practical answer to the inevitability of change. The long poem "Perennia" says this, too, in telling a lovely dream-myth.

Hoping to introduce a poet to new followers often results in an earnest over-simplifying of his work. Mr. Warner is a poet who should be read, not read about; only then can one experience the incarnation he has achieved by mating word with form.

—Norman T. Gates

WARNER, Rex (Ernest). British. Born in Birmingham, Warwickshire, 9 March 1905. Educated at St. George's School, Harpenden, Hertfordshire; Wadham College, Oxford, B.A. in classics and English literature 1928. Served in the Home Guard, London, 1942–45. Married 1) Frances Chamier Grove in 1929, two sons and one daughter; 2) Barbara Lady Rothschild in 1949, one daughter; 3) remarried Frances Chamier Grove in 1966. Schoolmaster in Egypt and England, 1928–45; worked for the Control Commission in Berlin, 1945; Director, British Institute, Athens, 1945–47; Tallman Professor, Bowdoin College, Brunswick, Maine, 1962–63; Professor of English, University of Connecticut, Storrs, 1963–74. Recipient: Black Memorial Prize, for fiction, 1961. Commander, Royal Order of the Phoenix, Greece, 1963. D.Litt.: Rider College, Trenton, New Jersey, 1968. Honorary Fellow, Wadham College, 1973. Address: Anchor House, St. Leonard's Lane, Wallingford, Berkshire, England.

PUBLICATIONS

Verse

Poems. London, Boriswood, 1937; New York, Knopf, 1938; revised edition, as *Poems and Contradictions*, London, Lane, 1945.

Plays

Screenplays (documentaries): *World Without End*, 1953; *The Immortal Land*, 1958.

Novels

The Wild Goose Chase. London, Boriswood, and New York, Knopf, 1937.
The Professor. London, Boriswood, 1938; New York, Knopf, 1939.
The Aerodrome. London, Lane, 1941; Philadelphia, Lippincott, 1946.
Why Was I Killed? A Dramatic Dialogue. London, Lane, 1943; as *Return of the Traveller*, Philadelphia, Lippincott, 1944.
Men of Stones: A Melodrama. London, Lane, 1949; Philadelphia, Lippincott, 1950.
Escapade: A Tale of Average. London, Lane, 1953.
The Young Caesar. London, Collins, and Boston, Little Brown, 1958.
Imperial Caesar. London, Collins, and Boston, Little Brown, 1960.
Pericles the Athenian. London, Collins, and Boston, Little Brown, 1963.
The Converts. London, Bodley Head, and Boston, Little Brown, 1967.

Other

The Kite (juvenile). Oxford, Blackwell, 1936; revised edition, London, Hamish Hamilton, 1963.
English Public Schools. London, Collins, 1945.
The Cult of Power: Essays. London, Lane, 1946; Philadelphia, Lippincott, 1947.

John Milton. London, Max Parrish, 1949; New York, Chanticleer Press, 1950.
Views of Attica and Its Surroundings. London, Lehmann, 1950.
E. M. Forster. London, Longman, 1950.
Men and Gods. London, MacGibbon and Kee, 1950; New York, Farrar Straus, 1951.
Ashes to Ashes: A Post-Mortem on the 1950–51 Tests, with Lyle Blair. London, MacGibbon and Kee, 1951.
Greeks and Trojans. London, MacGibbon and Kee, 1951.
Eternal Greece, photographs by Martin Hurlimann. London, Thames and Hudson, and New York, Viking Press, 1953.
The Vengeance of the Gods. London, MacGibbon and Kee, 1954.
Athens. London, Thames and Hudson, and New York, Studio, 1956.
The Greek Philosophers. New York, New American Library, 1958.
Look at Birds (juvenile). London, Hamish Hamilton, 1962.
The Stories of the Greeks. New York, Farrar Straus, 1967.
Athens at War: Retold from The History of the Peloponnesian War of Thucydides. London, Bodley Head, 1970; New York, Dutton, 1971.
Men of Athens: The Story of Fifth Century Athens. London, Bodley Head, and New York, Viking Press, 1972.

Editor, with Laurie Lee and Christopher Hassall, *New Poems 1954.* London, Joseph, 1954.
Editor, *Look Up at the Skies! Poems and Prose*, by Gerard Manley Hopkins. London, Bodley Head, 1972.

Translator, *The Medea of Euripides.* London, Lane, 1944; New York, Chanticleer Press, 1949.
Translator, *Prometheus Bound*, by Aeschylus. London, Lane, 1947; New York, Chanticleer Press, 1949.
Translator, *The Persian Expedition*, by Xenophon. London, Penguin, 1949.
Translator, *Hippolytus*, by Euripides. London, Lane, 1949; New York, Chanticleer Press, 1950.
Translator, *Helen*, by Euripides. London, Lane, 1951.
Translator, *The Peloponnesian War*, by Thucydides. London, Penguin, 1954.
Translator, *The Fall of the Roman Republic: Marius, Sulla, Crassus, Pompey, Caesar, Cicero: Six Lives*, by Plutarch. London, Penguin, 1958; revised edition, 1972.
Translator, *Poems of George Seferis.* London, Bodley Head, 1960; Boston, Godine, 1979.
Translator, *War Commentaries of Caesar.* New York, New American Library, 1960.
Translator, *Confessions of St. Augustine.* New York, New American Library, 1963.
Translator, with Th. D. Frangopoulos, *On the Greek Style: Selected Essays in Poetry and Hellenism*, by George Seferis. Boston, Little Brown, 1966.
Translator, *A History of My Times*, by Xenophon. London, Penguin, 1966.
Translator, *Moral Essays*, by Plutarch. London, Penguin, 1971.

Bibliography: in *The Achievement of Rex Warner*, edited by A. L. McLeod, Sydney, Wentworth Press, 1965.

Manuscript Collection: University of Connecticut, Storrs.

* * *

Rex Warner's poetry celebrates the force of nature, symbolized usually by birds, either powerful, often ugly – "smothering an airpuff with heave of shoulder" ("Egyptian Kite") – or graceful – "easy on the flying twig's trapeze" ("Longtailed Tit"). In their plenitude and behavior, they reflect the immanent plan shaping the universe ("Mallard"):

designed so deftly that all air is advantage
till, with few flaps, orderly as they left earth,
alighting among curlew they pad on mud.

Frequently human beings submit their emotions to benevolent or tyrannical phenomena that manifest this same control: "to be awed by mountains, & feel the stars friendly" ("Sonnet"). Even in the political poems deleted from his revised edition, *Poems and Contradictions*, Warner plays on the agricultural implications of the Soviet emblem and attributes impending revolution to the working of this natural power: "For blight in the meadows, and for our master builders/let sickle be a staggerer and hammer heavy" ("Sonnet"). Thus, Warner dramatizes political change as the eruption of seasonal forces in the individual and society: "Come then, companions, this is the Spring of blood,/heart's heyday, movement of masses, beginning of blood" ("Sonnet").

Warner can create images startling yet ultimately appropriate: "These bottle-washer trees that give no shade" ("Palm Trees"). However, too often, even in the ambitious sonnet sequence "Contradictions," he depends on words like "love" and "lust" and "birth" and "seed" in contexts which fail to sustain the pulsating effect toward which this language aspires. This attempt, reinforced by elaborate sound and metrical patterns, to recreate the elemental surges of existence, ironically seems more literary than primeval: "All mud & mould shudders with life to-day;/birth bursts by flooding, bloodless without pain" ("Spring Song"). Sometimes, however, Warner masters complex effects of rhythm and alliteration: "Plover, with under the tail pine-red, dead leafwealth in down displayed" ("Lapwing"); but these long lines, whether derived from Hopkins or the fourteenth-century alliterative revival, seem divorced from a living tradition and incapable of generating a new one.

Though Warner has published no verse for almost thirty years, except for his translations of George Seferis and classical dramatists, the promise of his best poetry has contributed to the distinguished style he has continuously polished in a stream of novels and translations of classical prose. His learning and eclecticism provide even minor verse with graceful echoes: the Virgilian "shores of leaning light" give resonance to "Spring Song," and the Audenesque "when kneecaps won't loose leg" enlivens the otherwise rhetorical promise of utopia in "Chorus." Besides this ability to evoke a whole range of other authors and traditions, Warner's real, though undeveloped, strengths lie in the compassionate wit of "Epithalamion and Hymn" – "Let moon and sun approve the fun/that Church and State allow" – and in the epigrammatic concentration of "Sonnet XV": "sinking I see the certain fire and say: 'There are the useful stars, & here am I!' "

—Burton Kendle

WARREN, Robert Penn. American. Born in Guthrie, Kentucky, 24 April 1905. Educated at Guthrie High School; Vanderbilt University, Nashville, Tennessee, B.A. (summa cum laude) 1925; University of California, Berkeley, M.A. 1927; Yale University, New Haven, Connecticut, 1927–28; Oxford University (Rhodes Scholar), B.Litt. 1930. Married 1) Emma Brescia in 1930 (divorced, 1950): 2) the writer Eleanor Clark in 1952; two children. Assistant Professor, Southwestern College, Memphis, Tennessee, 1930–31, and Vanderbilt University, 1931–34; Assistant and Associate Professor, Louisiana State University, Baton Rouge, 1934–42; Professor of English, University of Minnesota, Minneapolis, 1942–50. Professor of Playwriting, 1950–56, Professor of English, 1962–73, and since 1973, Professor Emeritus, Yale University. Member of the Fugitive Group of poets: Co-Founding Editor, *The Fugitive*, Nashville, 1922–25. Founding Editor, *Southern Review*, Baton Rouge, Louisiana,

1935–42. Consultant in Poetry, Library of Congress, Washington, D.C., 1944–45. Recipient: Caroline Sinkler Award, 1936, 1937, 1938; Levinson Prize, 1936, Union League Civic and Arts Foundation Prize, 1953, and Harriet Monroe Prize, 1976 (*Poetry*, Chicago); Houghton Mifflin Literary Fellowship, 1939; Guggenheim Fellowship, 1939, 1947; Shelley Memorial Award, 1943; Pulitzer Prize, for fiction, 1947, for poetry, 1958, 1979; Robert Meltzer Award, Screen Writers Guild, 1949; Sidney Hillman Prize, 1957; Edna St. Vincent Millay Memorial Prize, 1958; National Book Award, 1958; *New York Herald-Tribune* Van Doren Award, 1965; Bollingen Prize, 1967; National Endowment for the Arts grant, 1968, and lectureship, 1975; Henry A. Bellaman Prize, 1970; Van Wyck Brooks Award, 1970; National Medal for Literature, 1970; Emerson-Thoreau Medal, 1975; Copernicus Award, 1976. D.Litt.: University of Louisville, Kentucky, 1949; Kenyon College, Gambier, Ohio, 1952; University of Kentucky, Lexington, 1955; Colby College, Waterville, Maine, 1956; Swarthmore College, Pennsylvania, 1958; Yale University, 1959; Fairfield University, Connecticut, 1969; Wesleyan University, Middletown, Connecticut, 1970; LL.D.: Bridgeport University, Connecticut, 1965; University of New Haven, Connecticut, 1974; Johns Hopkins University, Baltimore, 1977. Member, American Academy of Arts and Letters; American Academy of Arts and Sciences. Address: 2495 Redding Road, Fairfield, Connecticut 06430, U.S.A.

PUBLICATIONS

Verse

Thirty-Six Poems. New York, Alcestis Press, 1935.
Eleven Poems on the Same Theme. New York, New Directions, 1942.
Selected Poems 1923–1943. New York, Harcourt Brace, 1944; London, Fortune Press, 1951.
Brother to Dragons: A Tale in Verse and Voices. New York, Random House, 1953; revised edition, 1979; London, Eyre and Spottiswoode, 1954.
Promises: Poems 1954–1956. New York, Random House, 1957; London, Eyre and Spottiswoode, 1959.
You, Emperors and Others: Poems 1957–1960. New York, Random House, 1960.
Selected Poems: New and Old 1923–1966. New York, Random House, 1966.
Incarnations: Poems 1966–1968. New York, Random House, 1968; London, W. H. Allen, 1970.
Audubon: A Vision. New York, Random House, 1969.
Or Else: Poem/Poems 1968–1974. New York, Random House, 1974.
Selected Poems 1923–1975. New York, Random House, and London, Secker and Warburg, 1976.
Now and Then: Poems 1976–1978. New York, Random House, 1978.

Recording: *Robert Penn Warren Reads from His Own Works*, CMS, 1975.

Plays

Proud Flesh (in verse, produced Minneapolis, 1947; revised [prose] version, produced New York, 1947).
All the King's Men (produced New York, 1959). New York, Random House, 1960.

Novels

Night Rider. Boston, Houghton Mifflin, 1939; London, Eyre and Spottiswoode, 1940.
At Heaven's Gate. New York, Harcourt Brace, and London, Eyre and Spottiswoode, 1943.

All the King's Men. New York, Harcourt Brace, 1946; London, Eyre and Spottiswoode, 1948.
World Enough and Time: A Romantic Novel. New York, Random House, 1950; London, Eyre and Spottiswoode, 1951.
Band of Angels. New York, Random House, 1955; London Eyre and Spottiswoode, 1956.
The Cave. New York, Random House, and London, Eyre and Spottiswoode, 1959.
Wilderness: A Tale of the Civil War. New York, Random House, 1961; London, Eyre and Spottiswoode, 1962.
Flood: A Romance of Our Times. New York, Random House, and London, Collins, 1964.
Meet Me in the Green Glen. New York, Random House, 1971; London, Secker and Warburg, 1972.
A Place to Come To. New York, Random House, and London, Secker and Warburg, 1977.

Short Stories

Blackberry Winter. Cummington, Massachusetts, Cummington Press, 1946.
The Circus in the Attic and Other Stories. New York, Harcourt Brace, 1947; London, Eyre and Spottiswoode, 1952.

Other

John Brown: The Making of a Martyr. New York, Payson and Clark, 1929.
I'll Take My Stand: The South and the Agrarian Tradition, with others. New York, Harper, 1930.
Understanding Poetry: An Anthology for College Students, with Cleanth Brooks. New York, Holt, 1938; revised edition, 1950, 1960.
Understanding Fiction, with Cleanth Brooks. New York, Crofts, 1943; revised edition, Appleton Century Crofts, 1959.
A Poem of Pure Imagination: An Experiment in Reading, in *The Rime of the Ancient Mariner*, by Samuel Taylor Coleridge. New York, Reynal, 1946.
Modern Rhetoric: With Readings, with Cleanth Brooks. New York, Harcourt Brace, 1949; revised edition, 1958, 1972.
Fundamentals of Good Writing: A Handbook of Modern Rhetoric, with Cleanth Brooks. New York, Harcourt Brace, 1950; London, Dobson, 1952; revised edition, Dobson, 1956.
Segregation: The Inner Conflict in the South. New York, Random House, 1956; London, Eyre and Spottiswoode, 1957.
Remember the Alamo! New York, Random House, 1958.
Selected Essays. New York, Random House, 1958; London, Eyre and Spottiswoode, 1964.
The Gods of Mount Olympus (juvenile). New York, Random House, 1959; London, Muller, 1962.
How Texas Won Her Freedom. San Jacinto, Texas, San Jacinto Museum of History, 1959.
The Legacy of the Civil War: Meditations on the Centennial. New York, Random House, 1961.
Who Speaks for the Negro? New York, Random House, 1965.
A Plea in Mitigation: Modern Poetry and the End of an Era (lecture). Macon, Georgia, Wesleyan College, 1966.
Homage to Theodore Dreiser. New York, Random House, 1971.
John Greenleaf Whittier's Poetry: An Appraisal and a Selection. Minneapolis, University of Minnesota Press, 1971.

A Conversation with Robert Penn Warren, edited by Frank Gado. Schenectady, New York, The Ido, 1972.
Democracy and Poetry (lecture). Cambridge, Massachusetts, Harvard University Press, 1975.

Editor, with Cleanth Brooks and J. T. Purser, *An Approach to Literature: A Collection of Prose and Verse with Analyses and Discussions*. Baton Rouge, Louisiana State University Press, 1936; revised edition, New York, Crofts, 1939, Appleton Century Crofts, 1952.
Editor, *A Southern Harvest: Short Stories by Southern Writers*. Boston, Houghton Mifflin, 1937.
Editor, with Cleanth Brooks, *Anthology of Stories from the Southern Review*. Baton Rouge, Louisiana State University Press, 1953.
Editor, with Albert Erskine, *Short Story Masterpieces*. New York, Dell, 1954.
Editor, with Albert Erskine, *Six Centuries of Great Poetry*. New York, Dell, 1955.
Editor, with Albert Erskine, *A New Southern Harvest*. New York, Bantam, 1957.
Editor, with Allen Tate, *Selected Poems*, by Denis Devlin. New York, Holt Rinehart, 1963.
Editor, with Robert Lowell and Peter Taylor, *Randall Jarrell 1914–1965*. New York, Farrar Straus, 1967.
Editor, *Faulkner: A Collection of Critical Essays*. Englewood Cliffs, New Jersey, Prentice Hall, 1967.
Editor, *Selected Poems of Herman Melville*. New York, Random House, 1971.
Editor, *Selected Poems of John Greenleaf Whittier*. New York, Random House, 1971.
Editor, with Cleanth Brooks and R. W. B. Lewis, *American Literature: The Makers and the Making*. New York, St. Martin's Press, 2 vols., 1974.
Editor, *Katherine Anne Porter: A Collection of Critical Essays*. Englewood Cliffs, New Jersey, Prentice Hall, 1979.

Bibliography: *Robert Penn Warren: A Bibliography* by Mary N. Huff, New York, David Lewis, 1968.

Manuscript Collection: Beinecke Library, Yale University, New Haven, Connecticut.

Critical Studies: *Modern Poetry and the Tradition* by Cleanth Brooks, Chapel Hill, University of North Carolina Press, 1939; *Robert Penn Warren* by Klaus Poenicke, Heidelberg, 1959; *The Fugitive Group* by Louise Cowan, Baton Rouge, Louisiana State University Press, 1959; *Fugitives' Return*, edited by Rob Roy Purdy, Nashville, Tennessee, Vanderbilt University Press, 1959; *Robert Penn Warren: The Dark and Bloody Ground* by Leonard Casper, Seattle, University of Washington Press, 1960; *The Faraway Country* by Louis D. Rubin, Jr., Seattle, University of Washington Press, 1963; *The Hidden God* by Cleanth Brooks, New Haven, Connecticut, Yale University Press, 1963; *Robert Penn Warren*, edited by John Longley, New York, New York University Press, 1964; *Robert Penn Warren* by Charles H. Bohner, New York, Twayne, 1964; *The Burden of Time* by John L. Stewart, Princeton, New Jersey, Princeton University Press, 1965; *A Colder Fire* by Victor H. Strandberg, Lexington, University of Kentucky Press, 1965; *The Poetic Vision of Robert Penn Warren* by Victor H. Strandberg, Lexington, University of Kentucky Press, 1977.

* * *

So much acclaim has been given his novels, critical studies and social comment, that it is well to emphasize that Robert Penn Warren is incontestably one of the most distinguished poets now writing. His poems are the meditations of a ghost-haunted philosopher, a man who can remember an agrarian way of life with families closely knit and rooted to the land, a man who has come as far from such pastoral simplicities as has his country and his region. A native of Kentucky, Warren grew up among a tale-telling, ballad-singing, proudly individualistic people. The American South has always had a distinctive regional culture and Warren had the fortune to begin writing as a member of its most influential literary party. Attending Vanderbilt University (1921–25), he studied with John Crowe Ransom and soon joined the Fugitive Movement along with Allen Tate, Donald Davidson, Stark Young, and others. These poets and critics wrote in the hope that the agrarian culture of the South could be preserved against the encroachments of industrial and mercantile values (see *I'll Take My Stand*, 1930). These social attitudes were reflected in their aesthetic, which embodied the values of a presumed stable and hieratic society; a devotion to classical literature; the influence of metaphysical poetry; and the conception of verse as public discourse, formal in diction, traditional in meter, impersonal in tone. These qualities appear, e.g. in the last stanza of Warren's early poem, "Problem of Knowledge":

> The rodent tooth has etched the bone,
> Beech bole is blackened by the fire:
> Was it a sandal smote the troughèd stone?
> We rest, lapped in the arrogant chastity of our desire.

The problem of knowledge has been Warren's continuing concern, but of all the Fugitives he was to move farthest from this conservative social and aesthetic position. After his *Selected Poems 1923–1943*, he published no lyrical verse until *Promises: Poems 1954–1956*, which embodied a style and an aesthetic markedly different from his Fugitive period. In the years since, he has remained true to this later style which he has put to increasingly adventurous uses.

A paradigm of Warren's lasting concerns is found in the poem "Original Sin: A Short Story," a short poem telling a long story indeed of the inescapability of man's knowledge of his fallen state. Its title suggests two permanent aspects of Warren's sensibility, his concern with the dark side of human nature and his commitment to narrative in a period when many poets have eschewed story for symbol, image, ideogram, or other non-discursive devices. These commitments are fully explored and dramatized in Warren's verse novel, *Brother to Dragons*. Here the narrative arises from the historical context most significant to a Southern man of letters. The story, based upon an actual set of events, involves the murderous Oedipal fixation of Lilburn Lewis, a nephew of Thomas Jefferson, whose motives are masked by self-righteousness and by his self-binding idealization of his mother's memory. The character of Lewis is dismaying to Jefferson, whose Augustan faith in human nature allowed no place for such irrationality and violence in one of his own blood, or in any man. Jefferson's idealism proves to be an abstraction which, like the nephew's insane self-righteousness, blinds its possessor to the truth of human nature. As the crime which Lewis commits is the wanton murder of his slave, the narrative poem thus involves also the special guilt of the old South, which Jefferson lamented but could neither assuage nor prevent. Warren's tale is in the Gothic vein (the same murder had been used by Poe as the plot of his verse drama *Politian*), but this is Gothicism deepened by moral responsibility and philosophical questing. The "dragon" of the title is the monster within man.

The brooding violence and terror that striate *Brother to Dragons* characterize Warren's later poetry also. With some poets one recalls lines or stanzas; with Warren it is often characters and actions which persist in the reader's memory: the folktale story of "The Ballad of Billy Potts," the terror and pity of "School Lesson Based on Word of the Tragic Death of Entire Gillum Family," the haunted sievings of time past in "Ballad of a Sweet Dream of Peace." In Warren's poems since *Promises* the narrative element is often subordinated to a brooding metaphysical contemplation of the event, the event itself sometimes not disclosed until the reader is well on into the long, looping sequences in which the poems are arranged. There is also a change in the metrical structure, the stressed meters and regular stanzas now replaced by broken rhythms; clusters of lines arranged in patterns the feelings compel, rather than in those a design proposes; and a beautifully controlled playing-off of speech against the silences of white space, of eye-breaks against the continuity of the brooding, solitary voice.

Selected Poems: New and Old 1923–1966 places the latest work first. The opening poem begins, "The stars are only a backdrop for/the human condition"; this line and a half introduce the two most frequent images in the recent verse: the vast impersonal grandeur of the stars, and the human condition, particularly the remembrance of that inexplicable affront, death. There are elegiac series of poems on the deaths of a boyhood companion ("Ballad: Between the Boxcars, 1923"), and of an old man ("Chain Saw at Dawn in Vermont," "Fall Comes in Back-Country Vermont"); a neighbor's remembered suicide ("The Day Dr. Knox Did It"); the death of the poet's father, his mother, his family's old Negro servant ("Mortmain," "Tale of Time"), as well as the imagined deaths of a Confederate and a Union soldier ("Two Studies in Idealism"). The brooding effort to re-experience, to understand, to explain, to endure these losses is counterpointed by images of stars, space, the diminution of the human scale when seen from an airplane – as in "Homage to Emerson, on Night Flight to New York," in which the poet tests but cannot accept the comforting transcendentalism of the philosopher who "had forgiven God everything," though he admits that "At 38,000 feet Emerson/Is dead right."

Later in the same poem he writes:

> Now let us cross that black cement which so resembles the arctic ice of
> Our recollections. There is the city, the sky
> Glows, glows above it, there must be
>
> A way by which the process of living can become Truth.
>
> Let us move toward the city. Do you think you could tell me
> What constitutes the human bond?

It is this "human bond," as well as how "the process of living can become Truth," which Warren is concerned to know, to experience, to celebrate. In *Audubon: A Vision*, a sequence of seven poems, Warren freely dramatizes an episode from an entry in the journal of the explorer-ornithologist. Audubon becomes a symbol of the artist in the New World, experiencing the grandeur and beauty of the natural environment and the meanness and violence of human life on the frontier. The tale is thematically similar to that in the earlier "The Ballad of Billy Potts," an encounter with greed, lust, and murder. The language of this long poem is so translucent that the reader is aware not of its diction but of the sensibility which records and responds to the action. "I did not know what was happening in my heart," writes the Audubon of the poem, but the reader knows that he has endured a confrontation with the darkest passions of human nature and has questioned the meaning of human existence; the poem concludes:

> Tell me a story.
>
> In this century, and moment, of mania,
> Tell me a story.
>
> Make it a story of great distances, and starlight.
>
> The name of the story will be Time,
> But you must not pronounce its name.
>
> Tell me a story of deep delight.

Intrinsic with Warren's transfiguration of tragedy into "deep delight" are his celebrations of the senses and the human bonds of love. Warren's loyalties are deep and passionate, loyalties to a way of life he can define and pursue despite the difficulties of the divided soul and the contemporary "century, and moment, of mania." The accomplishment and range of his poetry, as well as the dramatic use of an agrarian sensibility to measure the imperfections of the human lot, suggest that Warren is one of the few living poets comparable to Robert Frost.

—Daniel Hoffman

WARSH, Lewis. American. Born in New York City, 9 November 1944. Educated at the City College of New York, B.A. 1966, M.A. 1975. Married Bernadette Meyer in 1975; one daughter. Editor, with Anne Waldman, *Angel Hair*, and Angel Hair Books, New York; Co-Editor, *The Boston Eagle*. Recipient: National Endowment for the Arts grant, 1966; Poets Foundation Award, 1972. Address: 1 Parish Road, Worthington, Massachusetts 01098, U.S.A.

PUBLICATIONS

Verse

The Suicide Rates. Eugene, Oregon, Toad Press, 1967.
Highjacking. New York, Boke, 1968.
Moving Through Air. New York, Angel Hair, 1968.
Chicago, with Tom Clark. New York, Angel Hair, 1969.
Two Poems. Windsor, Ontario, Orange Bear Reader, 1971.
Dreaming as One. New York, Corinth, 1971.
Long Distance. London, Ferry Press, 1971.
Part of My History. Toronto, Coach House Press, 1972.
Immediate Surrounding. Lancaster, Massachusetts, Other, 1974.
Blue Heaven. New York, Kulchur, 1978.

Other

Translator, *Night of Loveless Nights*, by Robert Desnos. New York, Ant's Forefoot, 1973.

Manuscript Collection: New York University Library.

* * *

In the last line of "Brothers Levernoch," Lewis Warsh writes, "People who are discontented shock me." The voice which speaks in his poems is always – at least nearly – content. Although the poems are personal, or seem to be, they are not "confessional" in the usual sense of the term. Warsh is the calm and detached observer. Immediate autobiography, things remembered from long ago, newspaper reports, accounts of his family – all enter on equal footing. The commonest events assert themselves as worthy of complete and careful attention. The writing itself is almost colorless. There is nothing flashy or stylish. The careless reader will miss the mastery.

Warsh seldom commits a generalization. The largest collection of his work in recent years, *Blue Heaven* (presumably from the song), opens with a poem about the pleasures and dangers of thinking:

Thoughts make men strangers
and create great moments of urgency,
as well as nervousness, when a thought
moves you to wake up and light a cigarette
and lie back on pillow, content
in thinking, in playing the thought through,
that's the only way for it to die!

To the extent he thinks in his poetry, Warsh is willing to let his thought have this quality, as one of the media, along with perception, of existence. The danger of thought is that it can become so absorbing that one misses other important things – the cigarette, the pillow. After a certain point, he is willing to let everything go to its proper death. In "Single File," he writes, "All my poems/no center/everything scattered/many voices trailing off/empty illusions/of emotions and thoughts/incredible pipe dreams/disappearing/beneath waves." To many poets this would be cause for despair; to Warsh it is merely the way things are.

Inside these limits, in which irony is raised to a total sense of the world, he is capable of immense variety. He does not play endless variations on two or three successful themes or forms. He can be epigrammatic or tightly imagistic, but he is also effective in looser, anecdotal poems. He has written some strong prose poems and some of his poems seem to cry out for a musical setting: "At times like this/we leave our fears behind and enter/a world/where what we see/doesn't exist, where words/dance out along the curb/like playful cubs/and the heart sings on/– to High Heavens – regardless."

There are no poems which can be called typical – a remarkable fact in a poet who might best be called a formalist. Though he does not work in conventional forms, his poems turn again and again on the recognition of formal connections. This can be seen perhaps most clearly in a poem like "Footnote," which is an exploration of the formal relationship between the Percy Shelley-Harriet Westbrook-Thomas Hogg circle and the Friedrich Nietzsche-Lou Salome-Paul Ree circle. An awareness of relationships of this *kind*, on both the most minute and on the grandest scales, generates the energy of his poetry. It is one of the truest kinds of intelligence, and the pleasure of reading Warsh's work is that he generously makes his intelligence available.

—Don Byrd

WATSON, Robert (Winthrop). American. Born in Passaic, New Jersey, 26 December 1925. Educated at Williams College, Williamstown, Massachusetts, B.A. 1946; University of Zurich, 1946–47; Johns Hopkins University, Baltimore, M.A. 1950; Ph.D. 1955. Served in the United States Naval Reserve, 1943–45. Married in 1952; two children. Instructor, Johns Hopkins University, 1950–52, and Williams College, 1952–53. Member of the Faculty since 1953, and since 1965, Professor of English, University of North Carolina, Greensboro. Visiting Poet, California State University, Northridge, 1968–69. Recipient: *American Scholar* Prize, 1961; National Endowment for the Arts grant, 1974; National Institute of Arts and Letters award, 1977. Address: 527 Highland Avenue, Greensboro, North Carolina 27403, U.S.A.

PUBLICATIONS

Verse

A Paper Horse. New York, Atheneum, 1962.

Advantages of Dark. New York, Atheneum, 1966.
Christmas in Las Vegas. New York, Atheneum, 1971.
Watson on the Beach. Greensboro, North Carolina, SB Press, 1972.
Selected Poems. New York, Atheneum, 1974.
Island of Bones. Greensboro, North Carolina, Unicorn Press, 1977.

Play

A Plot in the Palace, in *First Stage* (Lafayette, Indiana), 1964.

Novels

Three Sides of the Mirror. New York, Putnam, 1966.
Lily Lang. New York, St. Martin's Press, 1977.

Other

Editor, with Gibbons Ruark, *The Greensboro Reader.* Chapel Hill, University of North Carolina Press, 1964.

Critical Studies: by Thomas Lask in *New York Times*, 11 December 1971; Grover Smith, in *Above Ground Review* (Arden, North Carolina), Winter 1971.

Robert Watson comments:

I am primarily a poet, but in my spare time I also enjoy writing fiction and drama. Though I have written some criticisms and reviews, I write informative prose only at the point of a gun.

With few exceptions the statements made by poets in our time about their work seem pretentious, silly, boring or all three at once. Theories get much attention, more than the poems from which they come; no theories for me. And if I try to detail characteristics of my poetry, then I am writing my obituary. In vague terms I try to make my work as musical (in the poetic sense), alive, and intimate as I can, and try to get in the way people feel about their lives and their world. I do dramatic, lyric and narrative poems in a wide variety of forms, most of my own invention. What doesn't seem to fit poems I put in prose fiction.

* * *

Robert Watson's poetry is energetic and economical, splendidly suited to the difficult art of creating characters in verse. Watson's first volume, *A Paper Horse*, established these facts with far more authority and consistency than is usual in first collections; the book demonstrates a mastery of staccato compression in a variety of formal approaches ranging from free verse to strict rhyme and meter. Most of the poems are soliloquies, spoken by a variety of characters particularly qualified to speak of the loss of youth, freedom, or love. The surface bleakness of the characters' lives is mitigated by Watson's compassion for them, and by his strong and distinctive style.

Advantages of Dark does not reveal much stylistic development, but it extends the range of starting points for Watson's poetry. In addition to a few soliloquies, there are a number of satires of contemporary life, some of which portray with harrowing humor the willful recalcitrance of everyday inanimate objects. The book also contains an ambitious long poem, "The City of Passaic," which evokes, through the lives of a few of its inhabitants, the life of the city where Watson was born. "Line for a President" also deserves mention as one of the very few convincing and genuine American poems on the assassination of President Kennedy.

Christmas in Las Vegas is something of a return to the bleakness of *A Paper Horse*. In his accustomed style, which suddenly appears to have been developed for just this purpose, Watson explores the brittle brilliance of modern urban life, in which people are almost indistinguishable from the machines they have become enslaved by. The somber tones of this collection, paradoxically deepened by the relentless presence of artificial light, are more profound than any Watson has struck before.

—Henry Taylor

WATSON, Roderick. Scottish. Born in Aberdeen, 12 May 1943. Educated at Aberdeen Grammar School, 1955–61; Aberdeen University, 1961–65, M.A. in English 1965; Peterhouse, Cambridge (Lucy Jack Scholar), 1966–69, Ph.D. 1971. Married Celia Hall Mackie in 1966; one son and one daughter. Lecturer in English, University of Victoria, British Columbia, 1965–66. Since 1971, Lecturer in English, University of Stirling. Recipent: Scottish Arts Council bursary, 1970. Address: 19 Millar Place, Stirling FK8 1XD, Scotland.

PUBLICATIONS

Verse

28 Poems, with James Rankin. Aberdeen, Aberdeen University Poetry Society, 1964.
Poems. Preston, Lancashire, Akros, 1970.
Trio: New Poets from Edinburgh, with Valerie Simmons and Paul Mills, edited by Robin Fulton. New York, New Rivers Press, 1971.
True History on the Walls. Edinburgh, M. Macdonald, 1976.

Other

Hugh MacDiarmid. Milton Keynes, Buckinghamshire, Open University, 1976.
The Penguin Book of the Bicycle, with Martin Gray. London, Allen Lane, 1978.

Editor, with Alexander Scott and Norman Lindsay, *Scottish Poetry Seven* [to *Nine*]. Glasgow, Glasgow University Press, 1 vol., 1974; Manchester, Carcanet Press, 2 vols., 1975–76.
Editor, with Angus Ogilvy and George Sutherland, *Birds: An Anthology of New Poems.* Stirling, Stirling Gallery, 1978.

Critical Studies: by Philip Hobsbaum, in *Lines Review 42–43* (Edinburgh), September 1972-February 1973; Donald Campbell, in *Akros 8* (Preston, Lancashire), March 1973; David Hewitt, in *Aberdeen University Review*, xliv, 3, 1973.

Roderick Watson comments:

The poem begins in the collision which happens when you say things by means of other things. But I am also concerned to preserve the integrity of these "other things." The images, experiences, and histories which one collects must be themselves too, and not merely the source material for striking metaphors. The long line I use has been a great help in this. So I prefer an angular resistance in the language of poetry, a certain opacity, and a conclusion which retains some of the tension of the poem, rather than one which resolves it with a final epigrammatic flourish.

In the past I have identified this understanding with my origins in the Northeast of Scotland. I'm sure that this is true, but recently I have been thinking that it is not the whole story either. I don't know what the rest is yet.

* * *

Introducing the poems of Roderick Watson in *Trio: New Poets from Edinburgh*, Robin Fulton singled out three characteristic features of his work up to that date (1971): "a treatment of family history alongside the wider history of the century; an ability to localise and focus these wider movements; and the use of a long line and a full paragraph through which his verse can deliberate." The last word is well chosen. Punctuated by gaps which require the reader to stop and mark his words, Watson's twelve poems in that book have a slow, recollecting speech-rhythm that suits his preoccupation with stones, bones, cave paintings, the track of time. There is a kind of archaeology at the back of his imagination, typically active in "3 Stones," which contrasts a stone used as a weapon, a stone used for grinding corn, and a stone on which a message has been cut:

> Leave wax and pigment   and ink the stone itself
> – a beginner's exercise in lithography.
> The printing shows old scars   lines   seams
> a play of forces on matter   collected and recorded.
> Time accumulates thus   and in quarries   mines
> heart shafts   the deep places   it is true history
> written on the walls.   This is a picture of it.
> (And the track of ions too   in a cloud chamber).

Watson did post-graduate work on MacDiarmid, and the experience seems to have inspired him to try to write the kind of poetry MacDiarmid wants – "words coming from a mind/Which has experienced the sifted layers on layers/Of human lives." The result is occasionally clotted and repetitious, but full of possibilities for the future.

—Robert Nye

WATSON, Wilfred. Canadian. Born in Rochester, Kent, England, in 1911; emigrated to Canada in 1925. Educated at Malden Grammar School, England; University of British Columbia, Vancouver; University of Toronto, Ph.D. Served in the Royal Canadian Navy during World War II. Married to the writer Sheilah Watson. Since 1951, Member of the Faculty, currently, Professor of American Literature, University of Alberta, Edmonton. Recipient: Arts Council of Great Britain Award, 1953; Canadian Government Overseas Fellowship, 1955; Governor-General's Award, 1956; President's Medal, University of Western Ontario, 1962. Address: Department of English, University of Alberta, Edmonton, Alberta, Canada.

PUBLICATIONS

Verse

Friday's Child. London, Faber, 1955; New York, Farrar Straus, 1956.

Critical Studies: "Vision and Clarity: The Poetry of Wilfred Watson" by J. W. Bilsland, in *Canadian Literature* (Vancouver), Spring 1960; "First Night in Edmonton" by J. W. Bilsland, in *Canadian Literature* (Vancouver), Spring 1962; *Literary History of Canada*, edited by Carl F. Klinck, Toronto, University of Toronto Press, 1965.

* * *

Wilfred Watson's book of poems, *Friday's Child*, received both the Governor-General's Award for Poetry in 1956 and the Award of the Arts Council of Great Britain for 1953–1955. Although no other books have followed, *Friday's Child* established him as an important, if unusual, Canadian poet. More than any other Canadian book it shows individual use being made of the influences of Hopkins, Yeats, Eliot, and especially Dylan Thomas.

These influences have been translated into largely traditional poems with an apocalyptic edge. He has written two poems on Dylan Thomas, "An Admiration for" and "A Contempt for." He frequently combines classical precision with an incantatory style. The opening of "Love Song for Friday's Child" shows his experimental vein: "The nor/Any day nor/Any movement neither/But now – ever and ever...." His poem on the painter Emily Carr ends: "And every bush an apocalypse of leaf."

As a playwright, particularly in his play "Cockrow and the Gulls," he shows a dramatic side to his work. "The Canticle of the H. in History," a long poem in *Poetry 62*, demonstrates an awareness of mixed modes, an almost beat utterance coupled with a concern for history and learning.

—John Robert Colombo

WAYMAN, Tom (Thomas Ethan Wayman). Canadian. Born in Hawkesbury, Ontario, 13 August 1945. Educated at the University of British Columbia, Vancouver, 1962–66, B.A. 1966; University of California, Irvine, 1966–68, M.F.A. 1968. Instructor in English, Colorado State University, Fort Collins, 1968–69; worked at construction, demolition, and factory jobs, and as a teacher's aide, 1970–74; Writer-in-Residence, University of Windsor, Ontario, 1975–76; Assistant Professor of English, Wayne State University, Detroit, 1976–77; Writer-in-Residence, University of Alberta, Edmonton, 1978–79. Recipient: Helen Bullis Prize (*Poetry Northwest*, Seattle), 1972; Borestone Mountain Poetry Award, 1972, 1973, 1974, 1976; Canadian Authors Association prize, 1974; Canada Council Senior Grant, 1975, 1977; A.J.M. Smith Prize, Michigan State University, 1976. Address: c/o 17 Noel Avenue, Toronto, Ontario M4G 1B2, Canada.

PUBLICATIONS

Verse

Mindscapes, with others, edited by Ann Wall. Toronto, Anansi, 1971.
Waiting for Wayman. Toronto, McClelland and Stewart, 1973.
For and Against the Moon: Blues, Yells, and Chuckles. Toronto, Macmillan, 1974.
Money and Rain: Tom Wayman Live! Toronto, Macmillan, 1975.
Routines. Seattle, Black Eye Press, 1976.
Transport. Toronto, Dreadnaught Press, 1976.
Kitchener/Chicago/Saskatoon. Windsor, Ontario, Flat Singles Press, 1977.
Free Time: Industrial Poems. Toronto, Macmillan, 1977.

Other

Editor, *Beaton Abbot's Got the Contract: An Anthology of Working Poems.* Edmonton, NeWest Press, 1974.

Editor, *A Government Job at Last: An Anthology of Working Poems, Mainly Canadian.* Vancouver, MacLeod, 1976.

Critical Studies: "Tom Wayman: An Introduction" by Paul Delany, in *Little Magazine* (New York), Winter 1975–76; "Way Out with Wayman: The Engaged Voice" by Marlowe Anderson, in *Contemporary Verse 2* (Winnipeg), January 1976.

Tom Wayman comments:

What I want to do with my poems, and with the poems by others that I try to encourage and collect, is to bring into Canadian literature a poetry of everyday life based on what I consider to be the central experience of everyday life – work. By "work" I mean what people do for a living, whether paid or unpaid, blue- or white-collar. To me this experience is central because I believe the work we do affects every other aspect of our lives, including our loves, deaths, appreciations of nature, and all other topics considered to be "poetic." This work poetry, which I feel must originate from first-hand experience to be of any value, is "not poetic" in the sense that it is not romantic, not concerned with an imaginary past or an imaginary future. It is concerned with the present. And so I like to think that this kind of writing gives readers a chance to interact with these poems – a chance they don't have when they are dealing with some poet's or fiction writer's imaginary world. The present is something people know about themselves, and therefore they are not threatened or put off by it. If they don't like what is said about it they can stand up and tell you; such poetry in this way has some potential of becoming an art with an audience.

* * *

Tom Wayman is one of the few Canadian political poets, and it is perhaps to his advantage – as a poet – that his politics is somewhat distanced from the present Canadian scene. It is the politics of the North American 1960's, when Wayman was personally involved in the radical student movement in California and later, as he said, lived "by hustle, construction labouring, unemployment insurance, and welfare." It is a politics with its own kind of realism, accepting defeat without disillusionment, and having – at least in the imagination – its own imperatives of action, as suggested in Wayman's early and moving poem, "The Dream of the Guerillas": "And night quiet/after the dream./Street lights burn on./The slogans are calm on dim walls. The clock,/the clock says: now/the guerillas are coming and you must go with them."

Wayman's radicalism is mingled with a great deal of nostalgia; he looks to the lost causes of the past as well as the losing causes of the present. He has actually been a member of the moribund IWW, and he ends a recent poem, on the continuity of submerged libertarian ideals ("The Ghosts of the Anarchists Speak of George Woodcock"), with a Spanish anarchist saying:

> Still, we didn't win.   So now what happened here
> must be written down.   Not that anybody could list
> all the arguments, the wind, the food,
> the sweat and thinking and fighting
> that led us to try this and try that,
> to be successful here and fail there.   But we need
> true words that tell what we did
> so compactly, so magnificently

they are like a seed you can hold in your hand
and see in it all the intricate beauty
of the strong dark flowers that will come.

Tom Wayman first emerged out of publication in poetry magazines when a group of his poems was printed (with work by three other writers) in *Mindscapes*. The volumes he has published since then, such as *Waiting for Wayman*, *For and Against the Moon: Blues, Yells, and Chuckles*, and *Money and Rain: Tom Wayman Live!*, have projected – as their titles suggest – not only a resolutely minoritarian political attitude, but also a highly idiosyncratic personality. There is indeed a great element of the dramatic in Wayman's poetic method; a comic persona named Wayman faces the world as a kind of Schweikian guerilla, and in this role dominates a whole series of poems that are devoted to exposing the enormities of the world against which the poet clumsily and futilely but relentlessly fights.

But underlying the comedy, and expressed in other poems with a good deal of sincere pathos, is a recognition of the misery and pain which are undergone by the economically and politically oppressed, who represent the greater part of the world's population, a recognition that does not give way to despair, but no longer rises high in the heavens of hope, and no longer sees self-sacrifice as an imperative: "I no longer believe my pain/will help another human being."

But there are times also when Wayman abandons both comedy and pathos and writes with a pure and tender lyricism in which the persona dwindles to a reflective eye, and the voice sings quietly. An example is another recent poem, "Herself, Walking"; in the first two verses the poet imagines the woman walking in June through the pine forest, in winter through the snow; the final verse reads:

And what is she doing
at her kitchen table
on a stormy morning,
lights on since eight,
the rain drumming
on the house roof,
the woods and the dock
soaked with it,
while she
sitting at her table
working
meanwhile goes walking
on the rain-swept rocks
by the turbulent,
difficult sea?

Wayman is vigorous, Protean in fancy, and more self-critical than most poets of his highly productive kind. Facility is his temptation, but so far it has rarely led him away from true feeling, and he is likely to develop in power as his verse becomes less consciously political.

—George Woodcock

WEBB, Harri. Welsh. Born in Swansea, Glamorgan, 7 September 1920. Educated at Glanmôr Secondary School, Swansea; Magdalen College, Oxford. Former librarian in

Dowlais and Mountain Ash, Glamorgan. Recipient: Welsh Arts Council Prize, 1970. Address: 2 Rose Row, Cwmbach, Aberdare, Glamorgan, Wales.

PUBLICATIONS

Verse

Triad: Thirty-Three Poems, with Peter Gruffydd and Meic Stephens. Merthyr Tydfil, Triskel Press, 1963.
The Green Desert. Llandysul, Dyfed, Gomer, 1969.
A Crown for Branwen. Llandysul, Dyfed, Gomer, 1973.
Rampage and Revel. Llandysul, Dyfed, Gomer, 1977.

Other

Dic Penderyn and the Merthyr Rising of 1831. Swansea, Gwasg Penderyn, 1956.
Our National Anthem: Some Observations on "Hen wlad fy nhadau." Merthyr Tydfil, Triskel Press, 1964.

* * *

Most of Harri Webb's poetry deals directly with some aspect of Wales: its landscape, culture, language, history, or national identity. In his collections *The Green Desert* and *A Crown for Branwen* his passionate concern for, and commitment to, the nationalist cause is total and remarkable. He possesses the well-known Welsh "lovely gift of the gab." His poems reveal his delight in language and his flowing facility, his wit and wide references (few Anglo-Welsh poets are as erudite about their country), his technical versatility ranging from simple folk verses to the most sophisticated forms, and a gift for the memorable phrase, as in the lyrical and delicate "Carmarthen Coast":

> In the steep hayfields, in the deep lanes
> Where the primroses linger till autumn
> And the white trefoils star the hedgerow grass,
> Where all the flowers bloom at once and forever,
> You are near, but may not cross, the frontier of time.
> Sweet heifers graze the saltings,
> The tide laps at the roots of elder and thorn,
> But the ferryman does not come to the ruined bellhouse.

Webb is also a popular balladist, pamphleteer, political journalist, and former Plaid Cymru candidate, and this background is shown in the considerable variety of approach and technique which characterises his work. There are many deeply-felt, nostalgic, sometimes bitter responses to what he sees as the tragedy of modern Wales, and odd political squibs like his famous "Ode to the Severn Bridge": "Two lands at last connected/Across the waters wide/And all the tolls collected/On the English side." But the whiplash satire, clever parody, and biting mockery in his work are amply balanced by such powerful, profound and moving poems as "The Stone Face," a dramatic evocation of historical heroes in which he refers to "the special Welsh tone of voice/Half banter, half blind fervour" and which develops with urgency and authority. Nowhere is his love of Wales and the serious side of his talent seen more clearly than in this very fine poem.

Harri Webb's occasional rhetorical discursiveness, and the obligation he feels to preach his cause, have been viewed by some cool critics as inhibiting his poetic intelligence. But his range of moods, forms, and styles, his sheer inventiveness and genial, high-spirited humour have placed him, through the last ten years, in the upper ranks of Anglo-Welsh bards. He is, in a real sense, a "poet of the people."

The simple sincerity, for example, of "Heat Wave," his address to an eminent long-dead Catholic Welshman exiled in Rome, commands the utmost respect:

Will I,
An Anglican atheist writing in the wrong language, exile,
In the way of my century, here at home, earn something
Of the understanding I feel for you, when future men,
If there are any, read my dreams?

—John Tripp

WEBB, Phyllis. Canadian. Born in Victoria, British Columbia, 8 April 1927. Educated at the University of British Columbia, Vancouver, B.A. 1949; McGill University, Montreal, 1953. Program Organizer, 1964–67, and Executive Producer, 1967–69, Canadian Broadcasting Corporation, Toronto. Currently, free-lance writer and broadcaster. Recipient: Canadian Government Overseas Award, 1957; Canada Council bursary, 1963, and Senior Fellowship, 1969. Address: c/o Bassek, R.R. 2, Ganges, British Columbia, Canada.

PUBLICATIONS

Verse

Trio, with Gael Turnbull and Eli Mandel. Toronto, Contact Press, 1954.
Even Your Right Eye. Toronto, McClelland and Stewart, 1956.
The Sea Is Also a Garden. Toronto, Ryerson Press, 1962.
Naked Poems. Vancouver, Periwinkle Press, 1965.
Selected Poems 1954–1965, edited by John Hulcoop. Vancouver, Talonbooks, 1971.

Manuscript Collection: University of Saskatchewan, Saskatoon.

Critical Studies: "The Structure of Loss" by Helen Sonthoff, in *Canadian Literature* (Vancouver), Summer 1961; "Phyllis Webb and the Priestess of Motion" by John Hulcoop, in *Canadian Literature* (Vancouver), Spring 1967; introduction by John Hulcoop to *Selected Poems 1954–1965*, 1971.

* * *

Phyllis Webb's relatively few poems (those she decided to preserve for the 1971 *Selected Poems* – out of 20 years of work – amounted to only 116 sparsely printed pages) have slowly compelled the attention of a steadily growing group of readers.

Her first poems were published at the beginning of the 1950's in *Contemporary Verse*. Since then, her publication has always been sparse; there has seemed a reluctance in all her decisions to release a poem into print or speech, and her works when they appear are honed down to an extraordinary intellectual spareness. Since 1965 she has published no new volume (even the *Selected Poems* contained nothing after 1965) and only a few poems in periodicals. Yet she continues to write in reclusion, to polish and, very often, to discard.

The careers of many Canadian poets – perhaps responding to an expansive movement within the culture – have been marked by a growing and unstemmed exuberance in production and in manner. In others, like Margaret Atwood, the self-conscious disciplining of the manner has not lessened the volume of production. For Webb, growing maturity as a poet has meant growing withdrawal: a narrowing of the circle of the creative self in keeping with the somewhat solipsistic character of much of her verse. She has said – though she said it almost twenty years ago – that "The public and the person are inevitably/one and the same self." But while this may have been true of the Webb who in her early twenties campaigned as a socialist parliamentary candidate, it has not been true for many years of the poet who has been concerned with personal emotions, the loneliness of living, the knife-edge paths on which we painfully dance our way to death. Art she has seen as a "remedy" – not more; as "a patched, matched protection for Because."

The result was perhaps foreshadowed in the early poem, "Is Our Distress," which opens the *Selected Poems*:

This our inheritance
is our distress
born of the weight of eons
it skeletons our flesh,
bearing us on
we wear it
though it bares us.

The philosophic pessimism – in unguarded moments breaking down into self-pity – which these lines suggest, tends to control the development of thought in Webb's poems, the devolution away from the elaborate and the assured, which had led her towards the simplified view of the anarchists (so that poems she has been working on for years are called "Kropotkin Poems"), the view that the less one demands of existence, the less one has to defend. One of "Some Final Questions," a section of *Naked Poems*, reads:

Now, you are sitting doubled up in pain.
What's that for?

doubled up I feel
small like these poems
the area of attack
is diminished

These lines say much of the poetic as well as the philosophic rule by which Phyllis Webb now lives. Her poems have become small, simple, as packed with meaning as stone artifacts. And, by a just paradox, her public presence had grown the farther she had personally retreated, into what often seems silence. Whatever she publishes in future will be the utterance of a poet who has learnt first the limitations and then the powers of her talent.

—George Woodcock

WEBER, Richard. Irish. Born in Dublin, 2 September 1932. Educated in Dublin public schools. Married; one daughter. Formerly, Advisory Editor, *Icarus*, journal of Trinity College, Dublin; Poetry Editor, *Poetry Ireland*, Dublin; Assistant Warden in boys' clubs, Dublin, 1957–58; Lamplighter, London, 1959; Bookseller's Assistant, London, 1959,

Dublin, 1961; Secretary to Percy Lubbock, Lerici, Italy, 1960–61; Assistant Editor, *Bookseller*, London, 1961; Librarian, Chester Beatty Library, Dublin, 1961–65; Poet-in-Residence, University of Massachusetts, Amherst, 1967. Since 1967, Visiting Lecturer, Mount Holyoke College, South Hadley, Massachusetts. B.A.: University of Massachusetts, 1967. Address: Department of English, Mount Holyoke College, South Hadley, Massachusetts 01075, U.S.A.; or, Ballyknockan, Valleymount, County Wicklow, Ireland.

PUBLICATIONS

Verse

O'Reilly. Dublin, Dolmen Press, 1957.
The Time Being: A Poem in Three Parts: Autumn to Winter, Winter to Spring, Spring to Summer. Dublin, Dolmen Press, 1957.
Six Irish Poets, with others, edited by Robin Skelton. London and New York, Oxford University Press, 1962.
Lady and Gentleman. Dublin, Dolmen Press, 1963.
Stephen's Green Revisited. Dublin, Dolmen Press, 1968.
A Few Small Ones. Valleymount, Ballyknockan Press, 1971.

Richard Weber comments:

Being European I tend to use the traditional verse forms, but never, I hope, at the cost of losing the sound of spoken language. However, I began to write (at fifteen or so) in imitation of the American masters, Eliot and Pound, and in what I considered to be free verse. Major theme, subjects, are as with most poets: life, death, love, sex, poetry. Verse forms: whichever suit the poem wants to wear. Reviewers (some) suggest I am addicted to alliteration. I like listening to language; my poems must make sound-sense to me before I release them.

* * *

Richard Weber has written that verse "fills a place/in space/to help us smile/a while." This is a modest claim for a poet to make but it helps to explain Weber's predilection for expressing himself in terms of humour and wit. His main interest lies in the exploration of human relationships and of these, characteristically, he takes a gently ironical view. In some poems the poet's analysis is drily detached but generally this is counterbalanced by an intrinsic warmth of feeling. A basically good-humoured acceptance of experience is the norm in Weber's poetry in spite of an occasional wariness: "The final success/Before beauty/Is not to possess/But to let be."

Romantic and anti-romantic attitudes are both apparent in Weber but they complement, rather than oppose, each other. His verse reflects this in establishing a harmonious relationship between the tone of spoken language and a delicate, cool, water-colour kind of lyricism. A sequence of adaptations from Japanese poets represents Weber's lyrical style at its best. Some poems containing evocations of landscapes are notable for the same quality:

Below a hillside in Italy
The darkness filled the bay
Like flood-water, pushing
Down all opposition, submerging
The ships, the olive trees, the town,
The little gripping houses, the slipping rocks.

A vision of existence as a comedy tinged with sadness is central to Weber's outlook. His poetry is not the product of passionate involvement; it lacks drama, urgency, and daring, but it reflects a mature and well-balanced sensibility. A reassuringly sane and humorous celebration of "the miracle still continuing/Of ourselves and love surviving" is the essence of his achievement.

—Rivers Carew

WEDDE, Ian. New Zealander. Born in Blenheim, 17 October 1946. Educated at the University of Auckland, M.A. (honours) 1968. Married Rosemary Beauchamp in 1967; one son. Formerly, forester, factory worker, gardener, and postman. British Council Teacher, Jordan, 1969–70; Poetry Reviewer, *London Magazine*, 1970–71; Broadcasting Editor, New Zealand Broadcasting Corporation, 1972. Recipient: Robert Burns Fellowship, University of Otago, 1972; Arts Council bursary, 1974.

PUBLICATIONS

Verse

Homage to Matisse. London, Amphedesma, 1971.
Made Over. Auckland, Stephen Chan, 1974.
Earthly: Sonnets for Carlos. Akaroa, New Zealand, Amphedesma, 1975.

Plays

Radio Plays: *Stations*, music by Jack Body, 1969; *Pukeko*, music by John Rimmer, 1972.

Other

Translator, with Fawwas Tuqan, *Selected Poems*, by Mahmud Darwish. Cheadle, Cheshire, Carcanet Press, 1974.

Ian Wedde comments:

Poems are ways out of solipsis, not necessarily the poet's. If the poems are any good, then he in writing & readers in reading are transported. Poems are not mirrors but creations, where "creations" is understood as a kind of present participle. I am myself sceptical about the "perfectibility" of men – I think they change to remain the same. For this reason, & because of what I've said above about poetry, & because poetry is not discrete but a function of men, I am not interested in poems as objects, potentially perfectible, but as processes which involve us. Naturally, the ways in which they do this are not unimportant. But the notion that poems "order" the world interests me only insofar as they may be said to do this by bringing us, through the intercourse in which they involve us, to cognition of varieties of the world's DISorder. This disorder, after all, can be every bit as shapely as the most exquisite *poème bien fait*, so called. My own impulse in writing poems is to inquire rather than describe. At the same time I am attracted by the idea of a *forma formans*, a shape or the ghost of a shape which, as Yves Bonnefoy has pointed out in his notes on translating Yeats, can determine the as yet uncertain "content" of which it becomes, reciprocally, an aspect. Mathematics can show us an exact principle of symmetry shared by one of the very oldest creatures, the nautilus, by a Greek temple, by innumerable supermarkets. With luck, poetry can offer us a similarly continuous and vital perspective.

* * *

Ian Wedde is one of a group of younger New Zealand poets who are graduates in English from the University of Auckland and who have been influenced by the American Modernist tradition as it flows from Pound, early Eliot, and William Carlos Williams through Charles Olson, Robert Duncan, and Robert Creeley. This is a major shift of emphasis in New Zealand poetry, and probably most readers would concede Wedde's place as the leading exponent. At the same time, unlike some of his contemporaries, Wedde does not seem trapped inside a narrow and restrictive mode. He experiments freely. Most often he lets the feeling determine the shape of the poem; but in an unusual departure he has written a sequence of "sonnets" in which there is no rhyme, there is a free flow of idea and image, the predominance of the speaking voice is maintained (all of this in common with Robert Lowell's sonnets), but all is contained within a tight syllabic count, 10 syllables to the line, yet no line permitted to fall into the old iambic beat.

Wedde has spent some time travelling outside New Zealand, and his experiences in Italy and the Middle East, particularly in Jordan, provided the occasion for a number of striking poems; in this connexion his translation (in collaboration with Fawwas Tuqan) of the poems of Mahmud Darwish should be mentioned.

Wedde is consistently at the centre of his own poetry, creating himself (it might be said) as he goes. He is sensitive, voluble, full of energy. There is always the sense that more is being registered than can be mastered, more felt than finds expression – and this is the right sort of imbalance for the production of poetry. His poems may sometimes seem over-charged, producing a hectic, even agitating effect; but this is preferable to a smooth parnassian surface, and inevitable in poems which aim to be highly active and to involve the reader in their activity. Wedde's poems are "open" not merely in finding their form as they go, but in being deliberately less than complete statements. The reader is invited in – his imagination is engaged to do that part of the work which the poet leaves for him. This, I think, is what Wedde means when he writes (in an anthology of younger New Zealand poets): "The reduction of quests and discoveries to their essentials makes them more charismatic, more dependent upon the mysterious triggers which we all share to greater or lesser extent, which can propel us violently or as though in a dream into previously unknown or unimagined or misunderstood territories and times." The judgment involved in such a strategy has to be very exact.

Wedde's temperament is affirmative. He is expansive, rhapsodic, apostrophising, ecstatic, which means he is in more or less constant occupation of that area where a fine line divides the celebratory from the effusive and sentimental. In this, it should be said, he is with Keats – and with Keats on dangerous ground. High spirits anywhere can be offensive to the mean in heart as to the genuinely oppressed, and New Zealand being on the whole a dour, repressive society, Wedde is likely to run into critical trouble. But if that affirmative energy is the quality that makes him vulnerable it is also his greatest strength – the source of the continual vitality and sense of freshness in his language, or (as Arnold said of Keats) that "indescribable *gusto* in the voice":

> & what's better to do than celebrate
> the fact? Look
>   the dark bloom's left your eyes
> spring's ripe   the horizon the blue sky
> the air pours towards you   the bean flower's sweet
> again   that fucking ferryman grates
> his rowlocks in mid channel again   high

clouds are spinning like tops again & I
couldn't ever have enough of all that

& you again & again & again:
waking, quickening, travelling through one
world after another   through all the weird
stations of the earthly paradise named
for one impossible diamond-backed dream
or another, as though no one else cared

Ian Wedde has added considerably to the range of New Zealand poetry. To imagine the scene without him is to imagine it seriously depleted.

—C. K. Stead

WEISS, Theodore (Russell). American. Born in Reading, Pennsylvania, 16 December 1916. Educated at Muhlenberg College, Allentown, Pennsylvania, B.A. 1938; Columbia University, New York, M.A. 1940. Married Renée Karol in 1941. Instructor in English, University of Maryland, College Park, 1941, University of North Carolina, Chapel Hill, 1942–44, and Yale University, New Haven, Connecticut, 1944–47; Assistant Professor, 1947–52, Associate Professor, 1952–55, and Professor of English, 1955–66, Bard College, Annandale-on-Hudson, New York; Lecturer, New School for Social Research, New York, 1955–56; Visiting Professor of Poetry, Massachusetts Institute of Technology, Cambridge, 1961–62; Lecturer, New York City Young Men's Hebrew Association, 1965–67. Poet-in-Residence, 1966–67, Professor of English and Creative Writing, 1968–77, and since 1977, Paton Professor, Princeton University, New Jersey. Visiting Professor, Washington University, St. Louis, 1977. Since 1943, Editor and Owner, *Quarterly Review of Literature*, Annandale-on-Hudson, later, Princeton. Member, Wesleyan University Press Poetry Board, 1963–68; General Editor, Princeton University Press Contemporary Poets series, 1975–78. Since 1964, Honorary Fellow, Ezra Stiles College, Yale University. Recipient: Ford Fellowship, 1953; Wallace Stevens Award, 1956; National Endowment for the Arts grant, 1967, 1969; Ingram Merrill Foundation grant, 1974; Brandeis University Creative Arts Award, 1977. D.Litt.: Muhlenberg College, 1968; Bard College, 1973. Address: 26 Haslet Avenue, Princeton, New Jersey 08540, U.S.A.

PUBLICATONS

Verse

The Catch. New York, Twayne, 1951.
Outlanders. New York, Macmillan, 1960.
Gunsight. New York, New York University Press, 1962.
The Medium. New York, Macmillan, 1965.
The Last Day and the First. New York, Macmillan, 1968.
The World Before Us: Poems 1950–1970. New York, Macmillan, 1970.
Fireweed. New York, Macmillan, 1976.
Views and Spectacles: Selected Poems. London, Chatto and Windus, 1978.
Views and Spectacles: New Poems and Selected Shorter Ones. New York, Macmillan, 1979.

Recording: *Theodore Weiss Reads from His Own Work*, CMS, 1975.

Other

The Breath of Clowns and Kings: A Study of Shakespeare. New York, Atheneum, and London, Chatto and Windus, 1971.

Editor, *Selections from the Note-books of Gerard Manley Hopkins.* New York, New Directions, 1945.

Editor, with Renée Weiss, *Contemporary Poetry* [*Fiction, Major Authors, Criticism*]. Princeton, New Jersey, Princeton University Press, 4 vols., 1975–78.

Manuscript Collection: Princeton University Library, New Jersey.

Critical Studies: by Harry Berger, in *The Fat Abbot* (New Haven, Connecticut), Summer-Fall 1961; Richard Howard, in *Alone with America*, New York, Atheneum, 1969, and in *Perspective* (St. Louis), 1969.

Theodore Weiss comments:

"I am concerned in a proudly snippety time with the sustained poem, one that is more than merely personal and lyrical and happily fragmented. It is easy to go with the time or to cry out against it; but to do something with it, to take it by surprise, to make more of it (as poets usually have) than it can do itself – might that not still occupy poets? And let it be poetry, rather than the poor poet and his predicaments."

The above was printed in *A Controversy of Poets*, New York, Doubleday Anchor Books, 1965. I still more or less subscribe to this view.

* * *

Theodore Weiss is not an easy poet to read. His poems are dense with their own music and as often as not two melodies or more are playing within one piece. The reader does not *adjust* to Weiss, but learns to read him, poem by poem. Weiss has accepted the challenge, and perhaps mastered the form, of extended verse. With *Gunsight*, a book-length, narrative poem, Weiss served notice that his earlier long poems were just a beginning. His principal interest, other than the language itself, seems to be stretching the sense of poetry beyond the physical (and mental) barrier imposed by the page.

Gunsight, which records the reactions of a wounded soldier to surgery, survives 55 pages as a poem because of Weiss's ability to keep the language moving. This is more than a single trick of rhythm; his skill at creating different levels of speech in contrapuntal rhythms and the simply believable imagery which he employs make the poem readily accessible:

Snowy masks
bent over you,
voices flaking,
falling
falling
through the seasick smell
breathe in
LET ME GO, IT'S COLD.
Faces, walls
fling up at you, cavernous waves, snow-kneading
hands.
OH FIE, THAT SMELL
breathe in.

In his shorter work, Weiss's language is even richer. The poems have been meticulously constructed, and at times I wish that Weiss would loosen up a bit. The effect of so much careful writing can amount to bewilderment, or worse, some loss of credibility. Where is the "spontaneous overflow of emotion"? Oh, there is emotion here, plenty of it; but the craft, so keenly wrought, is a kind of barrier: Weiss describes carrots, "coming up, tip-eyed,/ cocking/this frizz of laughter cloddy earth/must break loose in a tipsy/wind to know" ("Phenomenology of the Spirit"). Language as highly constructed as this needs breathing space, but Weiss is too good a poet to write slack lines.

In *The Last Day and the First* Weiss juxtaposes many typically brilliant longer poems ("Caliban Remembers" ought to be on the reading list of all college writing seminars) with some short lyrics. In this collection, the short poems seem to be a break with the sensibility that has created the difficult poems mentioned earlier. In "Fresh Paint," part of his suite for Boris Pasternak, Weiss allows himself a freer approach to poetic language:

> "Fresh paint?" I took that sign
> to be an invitation. Certainly,
> clumsy as I was looking more
> closely, it rubbed off on me,
>
> on hands and face and deeper
> still, as though my breath
> kept brushing it in and freshly....

Weiss has demonstrated here, and with other poems in this collection, that he can write equally well, tight or loose. His forte remains the long narrative, but these shorter poems work wonderfully to provide the reader a moment of rest before studying still another example of how good poetry can be, regardless of length.

—Geof Hewitt

WEISSBORT, Daniel. British. Born in London, 1 May 1935. Educated at St. Paul's School, London, 1948–52; Queens' College, Cambridge, 1953–56, B.A. (honours) 1956. Married Jill Anderson in 1961; two daughters and one son. Advisory Director, Poetry International, London, 1970–73. Since 1964, Co-Founding Editor, with Ted Hughes, *Modern Poetry in Translation*, London; since 1972, Director, Carcanet Press, Oxford, later Cheadle, Cheshire, and Manchester. Visiting Professor in Comparative Literature, 1974–75, and since 1975, Director, Translation Workshop, University of Iowa, Iowa City. Member of the Poetry Society General Council, London, 1972–74. Recipient: Arts Council bursary, for translation, 1971, 1972; University of Iowa Writing Fellowship, 1973. Agent: John Johnson, 51–54 Goshen Buildings, 12–13 Henrietta Street, London WC2E 8LF. Address: Department of Comparative Literature, University of Iowa, Iowa City, Iowa 52242, U.S.A.

PUBLICATIONS

Verse

The Leaseholder. Oxford, Carcanet Press, 1971.
In an Emergency. Oxford, Carcanet Press, 1972.
Soundings. Manchester, Carcanet Press, 1977.

Other

Editor and Translator, *Natalya Gorbanevskaya: Poems, Trial, Prison.* Oxford, Carcanet Press, 1972.
Editor and Translator, *Post-War Russian Poetry.* London, Penguin, 1974.
Editor and Translator, with John Glad, *Russian Poetry: The Modern Period.* Iowa City, University of Iowa Press, 1978.

Translator, *The Soviet People and Their Society*, by Pierre Sorlin. London, Pall Mall Press, and New York, Praeger, 1968.
Translator, *Guerillas in Latin America: The Technique of the Counter-State*, by Luis Mercier Vega. London, Pall Mall Press, and New York, Praeger, 1969.
Translator, *Scrolls: Selected Poems of Nikolai Zabolotsky.* London, Cape, 1971.
Translator, *A History of the People's Democracies: Eastern Europe since Stalin*, by François Fetjö. London, Pall Mall Press, 1971.
Translator, *The Rare and Extraordinary History of Holy Russia*, by Gustave Doré. London, Alcove Press, 1972.
Translator, *Nose! Nose? No-se! and Other Plays*, by Andrei Amalriki. New York, Harcourt Brace, 1973.
Translator, with Anthony Rudolf, *The War Is Over: Selected Poems*, by Evgeny Vinokurov. Manchester, Carcanet Press, 1976.
Translator, *From the Night and Other Poems*, by Lev Mak. Ann Arbor, Michigan, Ardis, 1978.
Translator, *Ivan the Terrible and Ivan the Fool*, by Yevgeny Yevtushenko. London, Gollancz, 1979.

* * *

Daniel Weissbort is a poet with an uneasy conscience the causes of which are hinted at rather than explored. The reader senses a temptation to guilt or sorrow which – in poem after poem, lightly-handled though each may be – seeks to undermine a personality bent on constructive, balanced living. The resulting tension emerges most clearly in the less realistic scenarios: in "Distraction," for example, where a knight's response to his own sorrow would seem to mean his abandonment of the armour that makes a crusade possible. The "emergency" to which *In an Emergency* refers remains, however, understated, with a curiously distinguished reticence which will, one can't help hoping, give way to fuller if still partially veiled expression.

—Anne Cluysenaar

WELCH, James. American. Born in Browning, Montana, in 1940. Educated at the University of Montana, Missoula, B.A.; Northern Montana College, Harve. Recipient: National Endowment for the Arts grant, 1969. Address: Roseacres Farm, Route 6, Missoula, Montana 59801, U.S.A.

PUBLICATIONS

Verse

Riding the Earthboy 40. Cleveland, World, 1971; revised edition, New York, Harper, 1975.

Novels

Winter in the Blood. New York, Harper, 1974; London, Bantam, 1975.
The Death of Jim Loney. New York, Harper, 1979.

* * *

James Welch is a young poet whose Native American background helps shape his first volume of poetry, *Riding the Earthboy 40*, a book which is one of the strongest first volumes of poetry published in the United States in recent years. As is the case with such other fine young American Indian writers as Simon Ortiz, Leslie Silko, Duane Niatum, and Ray Youngbear, Welch brings to his writing a deep consciousness of the earth which makes his poems exciting and alive, full of depth and mystery. This consciousness, mingled with a sense of loss, makes for some of the most powerful moments in his poems, as in the last lines of "Thanksgiving at Snake Butte":

> On top, our horses broke, loped through
> a small stand of stunted pine, then jolted
> to a nervous walk. Before us lay
> the smooth stones of our ancestors, the fish,
> the lizard, snake and bent-kneed
>
> bowman – etched by something crude,
> by a wandering race, driven by their names
> for time: its winds, its rain, its snow
> and the cold moon tugging at the crude figures
> in this, the season of their loss.

Welch's poems frequently revolve around contemporary Indian experience, but without the sentimental overlay which too many bad non-Indian poets have brought to their writings about Native Americans. The images in Welch's poems are like the Northwest winds of a Montana winter, hard, crystal-cold and powerful as in "Christmas Comes to Moccasin Flat": "Christmas comes like this: Wise men/unhurried, candles bought on credit (poor price/for calves), warriors face down in wine sleep./Winds cheat to pull heat from smoke ...," or in "Going to Remake This World":

> From my window, I see bundled Doris Horseman,
> black in the blowing snow, her raving son,
> Horace, too busy counting flakes to hide his face.
> He doesn't know. He kicks my dog
> and glares at me, too dumb to thank the men
> who keep him on relief and his mama drunk ...

His poem "The Man from Washington" is already a minor classic with its picture of a Bureau of Indian Affairs bureaucrat – "a slouching dwarf with rainwater eyes ..." who promises

> that life would go on as usual,
> that treaties would be signed, and everyone –
> man, woman and child – would be innoculated
> against a world in which we had no part,
> a world of money, promise and disease.

With irony and honesty, James Welch has approached being an Indian and being a poet in contemporary America and come out of it with poems which are always memorable and, in some cases, close to great. It seem certain that he will continue to be a vital force in American writing, not just as an Indian or a poet, but as both.

—Joseph Bruchac

WELSH, Anne. South African. Born in Johannesburg, 19 September 1922. Educated at Kingsmead School, Johannesburg; Roedean School, Brighton, Sussex, England; University of Witwatersrand, Johannesburg; Somerville College, Oxford. Married; four children. Formerly, Lecturer in Economics, University of Witwatersrand. Address: 10 Cecil Avenue, Melrose, Johannesburg, South Africa.

PUBLICATIONS

Verse

Set in Brightness. Cape Town, Purnell, 1968.

Other

Editor, *Africa South of the Sahara: An Assessment of Human and Material Resources.* Cape Town and New York, Oxford University Press, 1951.

* * *

Imagery of light and darkness characterizes most of Anne Welsh's verse. The underlying intuition is of a centre of light at the heart of darkness, and the numerous brilliances of day are reminders of this perpetual mysterious spiritual source, a "shining beyond shining." Nearly every poem is a viewing of material items, touched by physical light and seen in terms of metaphorical radiance, and each celebrates the re-discovery of this familiar mystery. A sense of awe unifies the verse and literal reporting of externals is raised to a degree just short of explicit symbolism, since the chief concern is with essence and spirit. Welsh is using traditional light-dark imagery, and she is not afraid of familiar truths; nevertheless, her vision is her own.

The observations are accurate. There is a painter's excitement, controlled by an almost clinical coolness of language, in colour, texture and the play of light, as the eye travels over tree, rock, wall, roof, sky and the wings of a flying bird. The poems are like watercolours, pleasing with their clear lines and pure tones. In them, through the intensity and steadiness of vision, the crude drabness of the city is transformed into something glowing and precious. The eye finds that it can graze on "an iron pasture" and the harsh concrete or tin surface becomes "jewel placed," "comforting." As the distressing difference between organic and inorganic dissolves, the ugly sterility of the South African town is absorbed into and made harmonious with its setting of a wild, spare, untarnished African landscape which the verse frequently suggests.

Clearly, this writer's concern is constantly to unify and relate, and a sense of community and of civilized compassion connects her with the inhabitants of her city-world. What especially touches her imagination are perimeter people – the clown, the deprived, the reject – as well as dancing children and circling birds. But these figures are always distanced: the tone is reserved, without being unfeeling, at times almost anonymous. Yet there is a distinct voice speaking in the poems. It is quiet and unemphatic; the language is clean, exact and taut. Welsh is not a markedly experimental poet and her range is confined to a certain kind of contemplative lyric, written almost in the medium of heightened speech, but a speech with resonance.

Even a minor poet can be said to have attained a certain stature if her work contains an inner landscape of the mind. Here, the mind's country is unassertively individual and African, while yet having a universal, elemental quality. The themes and images which help create this world, sustained sometimes with a slight feeling of strain, are elaborated in the longer poems like "Cartage Possibilities," "Two Voices," "To-day." But more memorable and unified are the shorter, simpler "Time," "That Way," "Rejoicing," "View," "Feast Day," and "Speech." These are poised, and unanxious, in the right way. Each presents a single perception, illuminates the mystery apparent in the ordinary or looks out on a timeless world of dark radiance beyond the present.

—Ruth Harnett

WEVILL, David (Anthony). Canadian. Born in Yokohama, Japan, 15 March 1935. Educated at Trinity College School, Port Hope, Ontario; Fisher Park High School, Ottawa; Caius College, Cambridge, B.A. 1957. Married Assia Gutman in 1960. Lecturer in English, University of Mandalay, Burma, 1958–60. Since 1968, Fellow, National Translation Center, Austin, Texas. Recipient: Eric Gregory Award, 1963; Richard Hillary Memorial Prize, 1965; Arts Council Triennial Prize, 1965, and bursary, 1965, 1966. Address: c/o National Translation Center, 2621 Speedway, Austin, Texas 78705, U.S.A.

PUBLICATIONS

Verse

Penguin Modern Poets 4, with David Holbrook and Christopher Middleton. London, Penguin, 1963.
Birth of a Shark. London, Macmillan, and New York, St. Martin's Press, 1964.
A Christ of the Ice-Floes. London, Macmillan, and New York, St. Martin's Press, 1966.
Firebreak. London, Macmillan, 1971.
Where the Arrow Falls. London, Macmillan, 1973; New York, St. Martin's Press, 1974.

Other

Translator, *Selected Poems of Terence Juhasz.* London, Penguin, 1969.

Critical Study: "David Wevill's *A Christ of the Ice-Floes*: Vision of the Elemental World" by Anthony Saroop, in *Pluck 1* (Edmonton, Alberta), 1967.

David Wevill comments:

I have tried to create complete poems, not just passing observations. So far I think I have succeeded only in a few poems. I do not know what direction a poem will take until it is finished: the theme therefore is unconscious. I have been much taken with Spanish poetry: Lorca, Neruda, Machado, Paz. They have a terseness which I admire and am only just, perhaps, starting to achieve. I do not use any particular verse form: the poem takes its own form. I can't point to any particular influences; these have been many – as much, say, from prose and painting as from other poetry. Landscape is in my poetry not as "nature" but in the North American or Spanish sense, as something "out there."

* * *

David Wevill's poetry is one of intense personal responses intellectualized to a high degree and of essentially religious stances conveyed in the language of organic and frequently violent imagery. A Canadian poet in his origins – and in the occasional reference – he is almost characteristically un-Canadian in his tone in that sense of fatalistic ennui which distinguishes certain of his works. If there are discernible affinities in his poems then these lie with contemporary British poetry and it is as a British poet that one tends to see him.

The common denominators of *Birth of a Shark* are visceral and metamorphic, with a great deal of concentration on a concern which can be best described as that of "life process." Wevill is most impressive in his ability to bring a sophisticated method to the pulpy and primal matter which heaves convincingly and metabolically in his poems:

> The sun seeps into and through your bones.
> Flushing the clotted soil,
> Tapping bacteria, mites, and the locked
> Purses of beetles. And you, fiery and whole
>
> Are pure waste matter, aged to a diamond's strength;
> Your will and body, stone and root....

A Christ of the Ice-Floes shows an extension of earlier interests and a firming of the intellectual posture which makes for the clipped and acerbic quality of Wevill's statement. A religious dimension associates itself with some of the poems as the poet engages in an elaborate and, at times, vicarious ritual of self-discovery which ranges through the metaphor of substitute lives; the experience of travel and geography; and an understanding fundamental to Wevill that life is cyclical and our knowledge of it regenerative: "I hold my ancestry in my hand .../The death of my limbs/Must mean the nucleus is still alive./The afterlife at its roots searching for you...."

Technically, there is little departure from tried and true norms in Wevill's poems and his style is marked by a conventional sureness and an all-too-respectable limitation of experiment; yet he manages a discreet vividness and an authority and conviction in his statement which more than repay the reader.

—Michael Gnarowski

WHALEN, Philip (Glenn). American. Born in Portland, Oregon, 20 October 1923. Educated at Reed College, Portland, B.A. in literature and languages 1951. Served in the United States Army Air Force, 1943–46. Lecturer and teacher: ordained as Zen Buddhist priest, 1973: Shuso (Acting Head Monk), Zen Mountain Center, 1975. Lecturer, San

Francisco Zen Center and Zen Mountain Center, Tassajara Springs. Recipient: Poets Foundation Award, 1962; National Institute of Arts and Letters grant, 1965. Address: Zen Mountain Center, Carmel Valley, California 93924, U.S.A.

PUBLICATIONS

Verse

Three Satires. Privately printed, 1951.
Self-Portrait, from Another Direction. San Francisco, Auerhahn Press, 1959.
Like I Say. New York, Totem-Corinth, 1960.
Memoirs of an Interglacial Age. San Francisco, Auerhahn Press, 1960.
Hymnus ad Patrem Sinensis. San Francisco, Four Seasons, 1963.
Three Mornings. San Francisco, Four Seasons, 1964.
Goddess. Privately printed, 1964.
Monday in the Evening: 21 viii 61. Milan, East 128, 1964.
Every Day. Eugene, Oregon, Coyote, 1965.
Dear Mr. President. Privately printed, 1965.
Highgrade: Doodles, Poems. Eugene, Oregon, Coyote, 1966.
The Education Continues Along. Eugene, Oregon, Toad Press, 1967.
On Bear's Head: Selected Poems. New York, Harcourt Brace, 1969.
Severance Pay: Poems 1967–1969. San Francisco, Four Seasons, 1970.
Scenes of Life at the Capital. Bolinas, California, Grey Fox Press, 1971.
The Kindness of Strangers: Poems 1969–1974. Bolinas, California, Four Seasons, 1975.
Decompressions: Selected Poems. Bolinas, California, Grey Fox Press, 1977.

Novels

You Didn't Even Try. San Francisco, Coyote, 1967.
Imaginary Speeches for a Brazen Head. Los Angeles, Black Sparrow Press, 1972.

Other

The Invention of the Letter: A Beastly Morality (juvenile). New York, Carp and Whitefish Press, 1967.
Prolegomena to a Study of the Universe. Berkeley, California, Poltroon Press, 1976.
On Bread and Poetry: A Panel Discussion, with Lew Welch and Gary Snyder. Bolinas, California, Grey Fox Press, 1977.
Off the Wall: Interviews with Philip Whalen, edited by Donald Allen. Bolinas, California, Four Seasons, 1977.
The Diamond Noodle. Berkeley, California, Poltroon Press, 1979.

Philip Whalen comments:

I try to write in colloquial American speech, but I often fail because many of the subjects I'm interested in – Buddhism, Chinese and Japanese literature and painting and architecture, formal symphonic music, the history of science, historiography, archaeology – aren't much discussed by my fellow Americans. I try to do the best I can. I began studying English poetry at an early age and I continue to work at it.

* * *

Many contemporary American poets, including Allen Ginsberg, W. S. Merwin, Gary Snyder, and Lucien Stryk, have been deeply affected by Zen, but none so much as Philip Whalen, who lives in a Zen commune in California. Whalen turned to Zen rather late in life, but when he did he committed himself completely. Now, with shaved head and saffron robes, Whalen in a unique figure on the poetic scene.

But Whalen has always been different from everyone else, and has felt proud of it. In an early poem, "Further Notice," he proclaims "I shall be myself –/Free, a genius, an embarrassment/Like the Indian, the buffalo/Like Yellowstone National Park." In his early writings, however, Whalen's sense of his singularity often led to feelings of alienation and even, in his frequent references to his "own gross shape," to self-loathing. It also led to producing some exceedingly shrill political verse.

Whalen's Zen awakening changed his approach. Though still believing, as he states in his fine "Birthday Poem," "The world is wicked by definition; my job is to stay aware of it," Whalen now uses methods of expression and poetic subjects which are more subtle. In his preface to *Decompressions* Whalen remarks, "I have a hunch that if I write a really good poem today about the weather, about a flower or any apparently 'irrelevant' ... subject, that the revolution will be hastened considerably more than if I composed a pamphlet attacking the government and the capitalist system." Thus, instead of overt political statements, his later work offers insights gained by and expressed in the traditional Zen manner, as in his arresting poem " 'Never Apologize, Never Explain' ":

> A pair of strange new birds in the maple tree
> Peer through the windows,
> Mother and father visiting me:
> "You are unmarried,
> No child begot
> Now we are birds, now you've
> forgotten us
> Although in dreams we visit you
> in human shape"
>
> They speak Homer's language
> Sing like Aeschylus
>
> The life a poet: less than 2/3rds of a second

In "Science and Language" Whalen writes, "It is impossible to write in English about Japanese/Persons, places and things," but his own work, in poems like "Eamd," belies this. Nevertheless, his subject matter is most frequently American, and usually centered on "the ruined city/San Francisco." What is perhaps most remarkable about his work is the contrast made between its Zen sensibility and its contemporary American setting, a society in which, as "In the Night" says, we "fall upward/Into a fake superiority."

Zen offers Whalen a genuine superiority. It is a discipline that requires much of a man and of a writer, and it is one which makes one constantly aware of one's own shortcomings. Nevertheless, in Zen, as in the poetic imagination, there always exists the potential for human perfection. This is all captured succinctly in "For Kai Snyder":

> 7:V:60 (an interesting *lapsus calami*)
> A few minutes ago I tried a somersault; couldn't do it
> I was afraid and I couldn't remember how.
> I fell over on one shoulder,
> Rolled about and nearly went over backwards
> And finally hurt my chest.
> What kind of psychomotor *malebolge* had I got into ...
> "This is old age, &c."

After thinking it all over
Imagining how it might be done
I performed three forward somersaults, 7:V:70
Aged 46 years 6 months 37 days.

—Dennis Lynch

WHIGHAM, Peter (George). British. Born in Oxford, 6 March 1925. Married 1) Jean Scratton in 1953, two daughters and one son; 2) Priscilla Minn in 1969. Formerly, gardener, teacher, actor, reporter, BBC free-lance scriptwriter. Lecturer in Verse Composition, University of California, Santa Barbara, 1966. Since 1969, Member of the Department of Comparative Literature, University of California, Berkeley. Address: 2237 Mason, No. 2, San Francisco, California 94133, U.S.A.

PUBLICATIONS

Verse

Clear Lake Comes from Enjoyment, with Denis Goacher. London, Spearman, 1959.
The Marriage Rite, with Denis Goacher. Ditchling, Sussex, Ditchling Press, 1960.
The Ingathering of Love. Santa Barbara, California, Unicorn Press, 1967.
The Blue Winged Bee: Love Poems of the VIth Dalai Lama and The Ingathering of Love. London, Anvil Press Poetry, 1969.
Astapovo; or, What We Are to Do. London, Anvil Press Poetry, 1970.
The Fletcher Song Book, music by Preston Fletcher. London, Anvil Press Poetry, 1970.
The Crystal Mountain. London, Anvil Press Poetry, 1970.
Langue d'Oeil. Los Angeles, Press of the Pegacycle Lady, 1971.

Other

Translator, with Mary de Rachewiltz, *The Detail and the Design*, by Umberto Mastroianni. Bologna, Segnacolo, 1963.
Translator, *Black Eros*, by Boris de Rachewiltz. London, Allen and Unwin, and New York, Lyle Stuart, 1964.
Translator, *Introduction to African Art*, by Boris de Rachewiltz. New York, New American Library, 1965; London, John Murray, 1966.
Translator, *The Poems of Catullus.* London, Penguin, 1966; revised edition, Penguin, and Berkeley, University of California Press, 1969.
Translator, with Peter Jay, *The Poems of Meleager.* London, Anvil Press Poetry, 1975; Berkeley, University of California Press, 1976.

Peter Whigham comments:

[On "schools" of poetry] I recognise that the future literary historian, should he mention me at all, will have a category for me, but what that will be I am unable to say. Perhaps I can answer your question in a negative way, by saying I am against the influence of Yvor Winters (in America) and F. R. Leavis (in England).

I can say that my long maturing work on Catullus has been the principal means whereby I have been able to find my own voice. As regards "subject," I believe that this, rather than technique, is now the test of a poet's sincerity – a reversal of the situation Pound proclaimed earlier in the century. And as regards "influences," the single most influential contemporary figure has been Ezra Pound; historical figure, Catullus; country, Italy; notion, the world of fluid forces, or figuratively speaking, the age of the gods; circumstance, uncertainty of any continuing identity other than that of being a poet. I simply do not find any "major" themes in my work, or "usual" verse forms or "characteristic" stylistic devices – though doubtless such are there to be discerned by others. As for "general sources and influences," to what I have already said could be added the English countryside and Shakespeare's plays and poems, as pervasive throughout. Other indications of my current attitude in literary matters can be found in the piece I wrote for the *Poetry Book Society Bulletin* for Spring 1969, and in the blurb, written on my own behalf, to the volume *Astapovo; or, What We Are to Do*. Finally, in the last few months, I have found my interest turning to the Far East.

* * *

Peter Whigham's poetry deserves to be better known. He is one of the few English poets of his generation to be firmly rooted in the modernist tradition and has produced a considerable amount of interesting and varied writing as well as a number of important translations. A few of his early poems are more likely to survive than any produced by poets associated with "The Movement" or "The Group." "The Orchard Is Not Cut Down" is short enough to quote in full:

The orchard is gone. A space, con-
        ventionally like Paaschendaele,
        linearly framed by black rail-
ings, rises to a wide field on
which, inert, the milk-brown cows sun
        themselves and where the bush mail-
        van and the bus brightly curtail,
on the road sudden as a gun
the field, – the vanished grove.

                                        No dream
        of priest or king can empower mind
        to seize the blossom on the wind;
only, in passing, I have seen

        swan leaning on confused swan
        fall inwards like a folding fan.

Whigham is probably best known as the author of the Penguin Catullus, and to have produced the liveliest English version of this poet is no mean achievement. Cyril Connolly defined its quality when he wrote: "I feel that he has really lived these poems; he brings back his translations as something that actually happened to him, like Noah's dove with the olive, and this enables him to bring the longer poems to life, in some cases for the first time."

The Blue Winged Bee is Whigham's finest collection of original poetry – most impressive is a long poem, *The Ingathering of Love*. This is difficult to quote from adequately as it creates its effect by the slow accumulation of images. Here are a few lines to give a glimpse of its quality:

All day the willow weeps by the summerhouse.
Bits of grass, the detritus of summer, lie on the floor;
the birds are muted

appeased by nest-building & egg laying:
a plane fades like mild thunder and
the sun, an atmosphere, pervades the grey sky.

Astapovo is, I think, less successful. He seems here to have lost his own voice in a harsh stridency foreign to his earlier writing. This perhaps presents an example of the bad influence certain kinds of American poetry can exert on an English poet.

—William Cookson

WHISTLER, (Alan Charles) Laurence. English. Born in Eltham, Kent, 21 January 1912; younger brother of the artist Rex Whistler. Educated at Stowe School; Balliol College, Oxford (Chancellor's Essay Prize, 1934), B.A. 1934. Served in the Rifle Brigade, 1939–45: Captain, 1942. Married 1) Jill Furse in 1939 (died, 1944), one son and one daughter; 2) Theresa Furse in 1950, one son and one daughter. Glass Engraver: goblets in point engraving, and church windows and panels at Sherborne Abbey; Moreton, Dorset; Checkendon, Oxfordshire; Ilton, Somerset; Eastbury, Berkshire; Guards Chapel, London; Ashmansworth and Steep, Hampshire. First President, Guild of Glass Engravers, 1975. Recipient: King's Gold Medal for Poetry, 1934; Rockefeller-Atlantic Award, 1945. Honorary Fellow, Balliol College, Oxford, 1974. O.B.E. (Officer, Order of the British Empire), 1955; C.B.E. (Commander, Order of the British Empire), 1973. Fellow, Royal Society of Literature, 1960. Address: The Old Manor, Alton Barnes, Marlborough, Wiltshire SN8 4LB, England.

PUBLICATIONS

Verse

Children of Hertha and Other Poems. Oxford, Holywell Press, 1929.
Proletaria, en avant! A Poem of Socialism. Oxford, Alden Press, 1932.
Armed October and Other Poems. London, Cobden Sanderson, 1932.
Four Walls. London, Heinemann, 1934; New York, Macmillan, 1935.
The Emperor Heart. London, Heinemann, 1936; New York, Macmillan, 1937.
In Time of Suspense. London, Heinemann, 1940.
The Burning-Glass. Privately printed, 1941.
Ode to the Sun and Other Poems. London, Heinemann, 1942.
Who Live in Unity. London, Heinemann, 1944.
¡OHO! Certain Two-Faced Individuals Now Exposed by the Bodley Head, with Rex Whistler. London, Lane, 1946.
The World's Room: The Collected Poems of Laurence Whistler. London, Heinemann, 1949.
The View from This Window. London, Hart Davis, 1956.
Audible Silence. London, Hart Davis, 1961.
Fingal's Cave: A Poem. Birmingham, F. E. Pardoe, 1963.
To Celebrate Her Living. London, Hart Davis, 1967.
On Llangynidr Bridge. Cambridge, Golden Head Press, 1968.
For Example: Ten Sonnets in Sequence to a New Pattern. Birmingham, F. E. Pardoe, 1969.
Way: Two Affirmations, in Glass and Verse. Cambridge, Golden Head Press, 1969.
AHA: Verses to Reversible Faces by Rex Whistler. London, Murray, 1978.

Other

Sir John Vanbrugh, Architect and Dramatist 1664–1726. London, Cobden Sanderson, 1938; Millwood, New York, Kraus, 1976.
Jill Furse: Her Nature and Her Poems 1915–1944. London, Chiswick Press, 1945.
The Masque of Christmas, with *Christmas His Masque*, by Ben Jonson. London, Curtain Press, 1947.
The English Festivals. London, Heinemann, 1947.
Rex Whistler 1905–1944: His Life and His Drawings. London, Art and Technics, 1948.
The Engraved Glass of Laurence Whistler. Hitchin, Hertfordshire, Cupid Press, 1952.
Rex Whistler: The Königsmark Drawings. London, Richards Press, 1952.
The Kissing Bough: A Christmas Custom Described. London, Heinemann, 1953.
The Imagination of Vanbrugh and His Fellow Artists. London, Art and Technics-Batsford, 1954.
Stowe: A Guide to the Gardens. London, Country Life, 1956; revised edition, with Michael Gibbon and George Clarke, Buckingham, Hillier, 1968.
Engraved Glass 1952–58. London, Hart Davis, 1959.
The Work of Rex Whistler, with Ronald Fuller. London, Batsford, 1960.
The Initials in the Heart (autobiography). London, Hart Davis, and Boston, Houghton Mifflin, 1964.
Pictures on Glass. Ipswich, Cupid Press, 1972.
The Image on the Glass. London, Murray, 1975.

Editor, *Selected Poems of John Keats*. London, Grey Walls Press, 1950.

* * *

Laurence Whistler has gained a double reputation, as a poet and as an engraver on glass, whose work in both media is characterised by technical skill, elegance, and lyrical sensibility. His notes on "Fore-Rhyme" and on "A Woven Sonnet" reveal his preoccupation with poetic form and with the possibilities of extending traditional formal patterns in the interests of greater exactness and imaginative power.

Most of his early work, for all its easy grace, is little more than accomplished verse-writing. The death of his beloved first wife, Jill Furse, gave him a powerful poetic theme which preoccupied him over a long period. Indeed, many of his poems, continually revised, may be regarded as parts of one long elegiac poem, which appears to have assumed its final shape in *To Celebrate Her Living*, a volume related to his prose work, *The Initials in the Heart*. The tone is varied, ranging from lyrical tenderness to sombre reflection, and the movement of the verse sometimes recalls the subtle yet direct mode of utterance perfected by the English Metaphysical poets:

> She whom I loved – she whom I love
> Years deep in abject death – who was,
> Who will be that to which I move
> In this or any world ...

Apart from this sequence, Laurence Whistler's work includes a number of poems which are likely to survive when the verse of flashier and inferior talents is forgotten. The range and quality of his art are reflected in such poems as "The Guest," "A Form of Epitaph," and "A Portrait in the Guards," an elegy on his brother Rex.

—John Press

WHITBREAD, Thomas (Bacon). American. Born in Bronxville, New York, 22 August 1931. Educated at St. James School, Maryland; Amherst College, Massachusetts, B.A. 1952 (Phi Beta Kappa); Harvard University, Cambridge, Massachusetts, M.A. 1953, Ph.D. 1959. Instructor, 1959–62, Assistant Professor, 1962–65, Associate Professor, 1965–71, and since 1971, Professor of English, University of Texas, Austin. Visiting Professor, Rice University, Houston, 1969–70. Recipient: *Paris Review* Aga Khan Prize, for fiction, 1961; O. Henry Award, for fiction, 1962; National Endowment for the Arts grant, 1966. Address: Department of English, University of Texas, Austin, Texas 78712, U.S.A.

PUBLICATIONS

Verse

Four Infinitives. New York, Harper, 1964.

Other

Editor, *Seven Contemporary Authors: Essays on Cozzens, Miller, West, Golding, Heller, Albee, and Powers.* Austin, University of Texas Press, 1966.

Thomas Whitbread comments:

Themes: time, change, love, the possibilities of human excellence. Subjects: my remembered past, my present, my anticipated future; public events, railroads, cemeteries, sports, other people, places and their auras, the mind and its creatures. Verse forms: sonnets, blank verse, various stanzaic patterns. Devices: irony, punning, use of verse forms for emphases, Tennysonian straightforwardness.

* * *

In a period that often admires mere surface complexity in poetry, Thomas Whitbread represents a refreshing return to poetry's main traditions. In his work, a surface directness and seeming simplicity deepen with a kind of surreptitious inevitability into new and striking insights. His method, a contemporary adaptation of Wordsworth's practise in the *Lyrical Ballads*, of finding the extraordinary in the common experiences of everyday life, is defined in the opening lines of "A Pool":

> This is a pool which bears deep looking into
> Beneath moon-shadow trees, beneath the mud
> I imagine at its bottom, and beneath
> All its appearances as just a pool.

Whitbread is traditional not only in this respect but in his handling of form as well. He is a highly disciplined technician with a sure ability to manipulate rhythmic and sound patterns. "Christmas Dinner" is a splendid example of the sureness of his ear, and he writes sonnets with genuine skill.

The poems collected in *Four Infinitives* are preoccupied with the conflict between permanence and impermanence, and this theme is suggested by the title with its reference to an active or verbal form capable of transformation or suspension to the substantive. The relative permanence of memory and art is postulated as answer to change, and the last two lines of "Christmas Dinner" crystallize this solution: "Always the juice lies locked in the grape-design/Cut-glassware while we take a walk in snow."

But the poems owe much of their strength to the fact that this formulation is deliberately an ambiguous one. The bicycle of childhood, and trains and railroad tracks, with their invitation to transience, retain their lure. The "National Limited" pauses "indefinitely" for relevation: "I am all Ohio deep in night and snow./I am midway somewhere. Where, I do not know" ("A Pool"). And the poet's own art of printed words, no matter how disciplined, can dissolve into a dark motion: "to think/All of a sudden, that surely the river Styx/Runs below this walk of bricks, and flows black ink ..." ("Autumnal Meditation").

—Gaynor F. Bradish

WHITE, Ivan. British. Born in Seven Kings, Essex, 23 May 1929. Married; two children. Educated at the University of York; University of Manchester. Recipient: Guinness Prize, 1964.

PUBLICATIONS

Verse

Cry Wolf: A Poem of Urgency. London, Hephaestus Circle, 1962.
Crow's Fall. London, Cape Goliard Press, and New York, Grossman, 1969.
Removal of an Exhibition. London, Writers and Readers Cooperative, 1976.

* * *

Ivan White is an intellectual – one may even say metaphysical – poet, of sensitivity, seriousness, modesty, sensibility and feeling. His poetry is only occasionally banal ("... I thought of Keats and Dylan Thomas,/How suspect their respective loves became in death./The one for a woman unmoved,/the other for humanity") and it is significant that when he is, he is also, usually, inaccurate (Fanny Brawne was not "unmoved"); but this comes from an uncharacteristically long, prosaic and rank bad "conversation" poem called "The Suspect Love." His best piece is the title piece from *Crow's Fall*, about a bird striking the stained-glass window of a buttress and killing itself:

Falling into like black it scraped
Mortar from arms that were flesh stripped.

As earth broke over its slight head
The beak point rasped against fluted

Rock poised towards the impetus
Of its feathered dive....

They replaced the glass....
... an act of half truth,

Deep from which stress drove the dark bird
Like a maxim that somehow strayed

From its claw holes or grip on life
That slipped, leaving no trace nor grief.

This may have been influenced or prompted by reading Ted Hughes; but it contains more thought, less hideously gratuitious violence, than anything by Hughes. Unfortunately White has written few other poems as effective: his chief fault seems to be an inability to discover a personal rhythm: too many of his poems are spoiled because they read like prose chopped arbitrarily into lines.

—Martin Seymour-Smith

WHITE, Kenneth. British. Born in Glasgow, Lanarkshire, 28 April 1936. Educated at the University of Glasgow, M.A. (honours) in French and German 1959; University of Munich; University of Paris. Married to Marie-Claude Charlut. Lecturer in English, the Sorbonne, Paris, 1962–63, and Faculty of Letters, Pau, France, 1967–68; Lecturer in French, University of Glasgow, 1963–67. Since 1969, Lecturer in English, Institut Charles V, University of Paris. Founder, *Jargon Papers*, Glasgow, *Feuillage*, Pau, and *The Feathered Egg*, Paris. Address: Residence d'Aspin III, 64000 Pau, France.

PUBLICATIONS

Verse

Wild Coal. Paris, Club des Etudiants d'Anglais, 1963.
The Cold Wind of Dawn. London, Cape, 1966.
The Most Difficult Area. London, Cape Goliard Press, and New York, Grossman, 1968.
A Wind along the Shore. London, Circle Press, 1977.

Other

En Toute Candeur (includes essays and verse), translated by Pierre Leyris. Paris, Mercure de France, 1964.
Letters from Gourgounel (autobiography). London, Cape, 1966.
The Tribal Dharma: Essay on the Work of Gary Snyder. Dyfed, Unicorn, 1975.
The Life-Technique of John Cowper Powys. Swansea, Galloping Dog Press, 1978.

Translator, *Selected Poems*, by André Breton. London, Cape Goliard Press, 1969.
Translator, *Ode to Charles Fourier*, by André Breton. London, Cape Goliard Press, 1969.

Manuscript Collection: National Library of Scotland, Edinburgh.

Critical Studies: *The Truth of Poetry* by Michael Hamburger, London, Weidenfeld and Nicolson, 1969; by Hans ten Berge, in *Raster* (Amsterdam), Autumn 1970.

Kenneth White comments:

I can call myself a poet providing the word be adequately defined. I like Elie Faure's description: "The poet is he who never ceases to have confidence precisely because he does not attach himself to any port ... but pursues ... a form that flies through the tempest and is lost unceasingly in the eternal becoming."

The theme of my poetry (and prose) is the way to the complete and utter realisation of myself (which I see as the real and central content of art, without which it degenerates into a collection of more or less formally or psychologically interesting comments or objects). With a play on words and with the knowledge that "whiteness" is the synthesis of all colours, I tend, for the moment, to call this "complete realisation of myself" – "whiteness," and to translate moments of unity by terms indicative of whiteness. My aim, beyond the temporary realisations of "whiteness," is to ground this idea, this myth (as programme), to situate the ecstasy extensively, and find, discover, create a "white world."

In more philosophical terms, I see myself living in a world of separation and scission, and my aim, my desire is to move beyond this world of separation into unity. I find the theme in Hegel, who speaks of the early Greek world as "an immaculate world unadulterated by any scission." While the Hegelian synthesis, however, is purely intellectual, ideal, my aim is concrete realisation.

In this direction, I have been influenced, or confirmed, by Whitman, and Nietzsche (critique of present civilization, affirmation of life, will to self-realisation). Both of these, also, mean the end of a certain Western culture and, as I see it, an opening to the East (which can help us to discover a deeper West, create, in the West, a civilisation more existentially alive, more integrated, rather than merely mechanically active and essentially incoherent).

It's in the East that I find the terms and the vocabulary (and examples) more consonant with my search. In *L'Esprit Synthetique de la Chine*, Liou Kia-Hway speaks of the aim of Eastern life-thought (as contrasted with the radical dualism and abstraction of the West) as "a concrete totality which suffers no separation," penetrating beyond the dualisms into the "ground of being."

The way I see myself travelling towards this ground-realisation is the *sunyavada*, which Linnart Mäll, in his *Terminologia Indica*, translates as "The Zero Way" – "a quite original way of thought, so original it seems impossible to compare it with anything else."

My travelling on this way I express through poems (and prose), the poems, in general, expressing more intense moments of concentration, the prose recounting the travelling, attempting a synthesis of information, interspersed with moments of higher unity. The poems are characterised perhaps by intuitive rhythm, inner form, simplicity (i.e. a highly organised complexity, without elaboration) and a recurrent iconography (gulls and recent convergent image of the Rosy Gull), which makes for a characteristic "world." They are meant to satisfy demands, desires such as Bashō expresses: "There are many who write verse, but few who keep to the rules of the heart," understanding "heart" here not sentimentally, but as a psychosensual/intellectual synthesis, the poem itself being such a synthesis, uniting a content of ontological significance with an aesthetic of delight. "Before a poet can write haiku," writes Otsuji, and the same goes for poems in general as I understand them, "he must find a unity within his life which must come from the effort to discover his true self."

How far do I think I've travelled on my way? After passing through "the most difficult area," I'd say, with Paul Klee, "a little nearer to the heart of creation than is normal but still too far away."

* * *

If we except the more ecstatic passages, *Letters from Gourgounel* contains some of Kenneth White's most achieved writing to date in the sense that in the prose of that book we see his language engaging with substantial, particular experience more fully than has been the general rule in his poetry. It is not simply that much of his earlier poetry was too content with routine romantic gestures and unsubstantiated claims ("the deep-down poetry I trade my life for" ... "I speak in knowledge to all men/the great things and the beautiful I bring"). It is rather that in his poetry he has set himself the difficult task of exploring those areas of experience where emptiness and silence may be sensed not in terms of negation but in terms of a more positive approach to a sense of immanence and revelation. Thus we have references to such phenomena as "this light that is/the limit of austerity/and makes words blind"; statements like "at the limits of saying/the soul flies to the mouth/and the poem is born"; and poems such as "In the Emptiness" which assert, in the emptiness, an experience of "reality right to the bone."

The general difficulty, then, is to reconcile the mystic's pull towards wordlessness and the poet's ineradicable dependence on words. In particular, the poetry's frequent resort to assertion, to statements *about* experience, may be characterised both by abstractions and by a lack of clear focus upon such concrete details as are mentioned. To what extent White is going to solve such a problem, in a manner germane to his sensibility, remains to be seen. But there are several poems (e.g. "Extraordinary Moment," "Sesshu") which do seem to indicate a possibility: these have clearly learned from oriental models, and their strength is that their focus on particulars is sharp and their implications are clear without being overspelt.

—Robin Fulton

WHITEHEAD, James. American. Born in St. Louis, Missouri, 15 March 1936. Educated at Central High School, Jackson, Mississippi; Vanderbilt University, Nashville, Tennessee, B.A. in philosophy 1959, M.A. in English 1960; University of Iowa, Iowa City, M.F.A. 1965. Married to Gen Graeber; seven children. Member of the Faculty, Millsaps College, Jackson, Mississippi, 1960–63. Currently, Professor of English, University of Arkansas, Fayetteville. Recipient: Bread Loaf Writers Conference Robert Frost Fellowship, 1967; Guggenheim grant, 1972. Address: Department of English, University of Arkansas, Fayetteville, Arkansas 72701, U.S.A.

PUBLICATIONS

Verse

Domains. Baton Rouge, Louisiana State University Press, 1966.
Local Men. Urbana, University of Illinois Press, 1979.

Novel

Joiner. New York, Knopf, 1971.

* * *

There is a strong sense of place and personality in James Whitehead's writing. In both his book of poems, *Domains*, and his novel, *Joiner*, real people live in real houses. The novel contains flowerings of the earlier poems, suggesting the depth to which Whitehead's vision is rooted in the rich earth of the places and people he has known.

The concrete imagery of the poems in *Domains* often suggests Frost. Not a cold fire-under-ice Frost, but a passionate poet who sings the brakes and bayous of Mississippi as Frost sang the fields and west-running brooks of New Hampshire. Which is not to suggest that Whitehead is a nature poet; his river raises "floaters," drowned people, "Bringing a stern sight down to all of us/In the country where only the deaths of the aged were clear." His places are always peopled, and his poems suggest that there *was* a Dallas Tanksley, a Leroy Smith, and a dead baby brother.

Whitehead is a witty poet ("Walking Around," "Love Poem in Midwinter") with a fine feel for irony ("Desertions," "The Lawyer"), but his best poetry is imbued with a passionate sense of life and its evanescence. He is torn between the domains of the crusading spirit and of the lusting flesh, but in his loveliest lines they become one kingdom. At the end of his title poem, "Domains," he prays for the strength to see that he is "... not fit/To serve at once/Two dying bodies with equal wit." But in his best poems he does just that.

—Norman T. Gates

WHITMAN, Ruth. American. Born in New York City, 28 May 1922. Educated at Radcliffe College, Cambridge, Massachusetts, B.A. (magna cum laude) 1944, M.A. 1947. Married Morton Sacks in 1966; two daughters and one son. Editorial Assistant, 1941–42, and Educational Editor, 1944–45, Houghton Mifflin Company, publishers, Boston; Editor, Harvard University Press, 1945–60; Poetry Editor, *Audience*, Cambridge, Massachusetts, 1958–63. Director, Cambridge Center for Adult Education Poetry Workshop, 1964–68; Scholar in Poetry, Radcliffe Institute, 1968–70, and since 1970, Instructor in Poetry, Radcliffe College. Director of the Massachusetts Schools Poetry Writing Program, 1971–74. Recipient: MacDowell Fellowship, 1962, 1964, 1972; Poetry Society of America Lyric Award, 1962, and Alice Fay di Castagnola Award, 1968; Tane Award (*Massachusetts Review*, Amherst), 1964; National Foundation for Jewish Culture grant, 1968, 1969; Radcliffe Institute grant, 1968, 1969; Jewish Book Council of America Kovner Award, 1969; Chanin Award, for translation, 1972; National Endowment for the Arts grant, 1974. Address: 1559 Beacon Street, Brookline, Massachusetts 02146, U.S.A.

PUBLICATIONS

Verse

Blood and Milk Poems. New York, Clark and Way, 1963.
The Marriage Wig and Other Poems. New York, Harcourt Brace, 1968.
The Passion of Lizzie Borden: New and Selected Poems. New York, October House, 1973.
Tamsen Donner: A Woman's Journey. Cambridge, Massachusetts, Alice James, 1977.

Other

Editor and Translator, *An Anthology of Modern Yiddish Poetry.* New York, October House, 1966.
Editor, *Poemmaking: Poets in Classrooms.* Cambridge, Massachusetts Council of Teachers of English, 1975.

Translator, with others, *Selected Poems*, by Alain Bosquet. New York, New Directions, 1962.
Translator, *Selected Poems*, by Jacob Glatstein. New York, October House, 1972.

Ruth Whitman comments:

(1970) The point of writing poetry is to celebrate all human experience and to communicate its value and intensity to other human beings. The poet must have a complete command of strict forms and then be free to abandon them and to use any device to make the poem's rhetoric more direct and telling.

(1974) The best statement I have is this poem from *The Marriage Wig*:

A Spider on My Poem

Black one,
I was going to frighten you away,
but now I beg you,
stay!
You're what I need.
This poem needs real legs, faster than the eye.
And a belly with magic string in it
made from spit,
designed to catch and hold whatever flies by.
Also, the uninvited way
you came, boldly, fast as a spider,
till you paused all real in the middle of the page.
Everything I need.
Please stay.

* * *

Ruth Whitman's books have established her as a significant American woman poet. From the beginning her poetry was personal, subjective, and strongly formal. Throughout Whitman's poetry is the concern with the discovery of herself through her heritage. Jewish to the core, she explores that heritage in a variety of poems ("The Old Man's Mistress," "The Lost Steps," and "Touro Synagogue") about her family and homeland.

The Marriage Wig and Other Poems is a much fuller exploration of the experience of being Jewish and Ruth Whitman. The poems ring with an authenticity lacking in the first volume. Although a few of the poems strain after too much identification with the past, most are effective transformations of past and present.

Her third volume, *The Passion of Lizzie Borden: New and Selected Poems*, not only contains the best poems of the first volumes but some excellent new ones. In addition to the personal, autobiographical and heritage poems, Whitman looks outward at the world larger than her family's, if not as definite. The poems still express Whitman, but her feelings, emotions, ideas are embodied in recent experiences. Several important poems explore the Greek heritage which is finally and inevitably brought together in the last poems, "Passover 1970," with the Hebrew. The book may represent a closing out or exhaustion of these materials, though not of Whitman. Her energy, vitality, and technical proficiency should enable her to continue her excellent work.

—Richard Damashek

WHITTEMORE, (Edward) Reed (Jr.). American. Born in New Haven, Connecticut, 11 September 1919. Educated at Yale University, New Haven, Connecticut, A.B. 1941; Princeton University, New Jersey, 1945–46. Served in the United States Army Air Force, 1941–45. Married Helen Lundeen in 1950; four children. Member of the Faculty, 1947–62,

Chairman of the English Department, 1962–64, and Professor of English, 1962–67, Carleton College, Northfield, Minnesota; Bain-Swiggett Lecturer, Princeton University, 1967–68. Since 1968, Professor of English, University of Maryland, College Park. Editor, *Furioso*, 1939–53, and *Carleton Miscellany*, 1960–64, both in Northfield, Minnesota. Literary Editor, *New Republic*, Washington, D.C., 1969–73. Consultant in Poetry, Library of Congress, Washington, D.C., 1964–65. Recipient: Emily Clark Balch Prize (*Virginia Quarterly Review*, Charlottesville), 1962; National Endowment for the Arts grant, 1968; National Institute of Arts and Letters Award of Merit, 1970. Litt.D.: Carleton College, 1971. Address: 4526 Albion Road, College Park, Maryland 20740, U.S.A.

PUBLICATIONS

Verse

Heroes and Heroines. New York, Reynal, 1947.
An American Takes a Walk and Other Poems. Minneapolis, University of Minnesota Press, 1956.
The Self-Made Man and Other Poems. New York, Macmillan, 1959.
The Boy from Iowa: Poems and Essays. New York, Macmillan, 1962.
Return, Alpheus: A Poem for the Literary Elders of Phi Beta Kappa. Williamsburg, Virginia, King and Queen Press, 1965.
Poems, New and Selected. Minneapolis, University of Minnesota Press, 1967.
50 Poems 50. Minneapolis, University of Minnesota Press, 1970.
The Mother's Breast and the Father's House. Boston, Houghton Mifflin, 1974.

Other

Little Magazines. Minneapolis, University of Minnesota Press, 1963.
The Fascination of the Abomination: Poems, Stories, and Essays. New York, Macmillan, 1963.
Ways of Misunderstanding Poetry. Washington, D.C., Library of Congress, 1965.
From Zero to the Absolute: Essays. New York, Crown, 1967.
William Carlos Williams: Poet from Jersey. Boston, Houghton Mifflin, 1975.
The Poet as Journalist: Life at the New Republic. Washington, D.C., New Republic, 1976.

Editor, *Browning.* New York, Dell, 1960.

* * *

In the essay "But Seriously," published in *The Fascination of the Abomination*, Reed Whittemore describes himself as a person with "the disposition, the temperament of a humorist," one of those who sides "pretty steadily" with those "mundane eccentrics who have stood on the sidelines with the game in progress, and made frosty remarks instead of cheering." His vision, like that of the man who craves balance in "A Porch Chair," is "urban,/Modern and secular" (*The Self-Made Man*). His approach frequently yields what he himself describes as the "ideal poem" of *The New Yorker*: "a straightforward thing, in rhyme and stanzas, which displays the well-managed sensibility of an intelligent private individual at work on the world of his immediate neighbourhood."

Whittemore's materials are "his immediate neighbourhood" (paperboys, U.S. 1, Peck and Peck, popular magazines, a high school band, a radio, winter), "himself and his nearest and dearest." His hero is a self-made man, but one who, though he may *appear* god-like, the master of his destiny, to his audience, knows his own limitations: the void within him, the discontentment of trivial accomplishments and frustrated dreams. His hero can be

Prufrockian: "I have begun, been begun, more than most; I have even/Started a book of beginnings (unfinished)...."

But, both as poet and modern man, Whittemore is not satisfied with this unheroic, "attendant lord" material; his heroes do not want to be "*so* middle class" (*The Boy from Iowa*). At times he is angry, as in "A Teacher":

He hated them all one by one but wanted to show them
What was Important and Vital and by God if
They thought they'd never have use for it he was
Sorry as hell for them, that's all, with their genteel
Mercantile Main Street Babbitt
Bourgeois-barbaric faces....

At times he is bitter. He thinks of himself "As a Renaissance Man manqué, many parts, many interests/Yet to bear fruits." Frequently he is tired and sad, as in the conclusion of "The Renaissance Man" and in "Three Poems of Jackson":

My third book will appear in the spring, a small book,
A slight book,
Containing no plays or long narrative poems,
Borrowing hardly at all from the Middle Ages,
Making few affirmations, avoiding inversions,
Using iambics distrustfully, favoring lines
Of odd lengths and irony.
I am forty.
I seem to know the dimensions of what I can do
And the season to do it in.

Or, looking out of his study window at the gray, cold winter and reflecting on Keats and Tennyson, poets who "have warm, sunny lands tucked away/In their serried works where galoshes, woodpiles, aspirin/And the like are never required," he writes:

If I had talent to make such a place I would not,
I think, scribble about it but would just
Move in, settle down and endeavor to blot
From my memory all the aforesaid icicles,
Letting the future of literature go for heat
On earth, green trees for man, and the sweet
Ease of a life held in tropical trust.

But most often Whittemore is quietly observing, committed to seeing and reassessing (deft, quick, though often strangely dispassionate), not far from his own description of "an ideal satirist who is happy in his work (taking it 'seriously') and who, though perhaps stuffed to the gills with subconscious aggressions, has also a sense of justice, truth, all that" (*The Fascination of the Abomination*). His is a genial satire "informed with pity" which proceeds from "a sense of all of us being in the same leaky boat." It may very well be a light satire, elusive and detached because it masks a deep involvement and concern ("Clamming"):

I go digging for clams once every two or three years
Just to keep my hand in (I usually cut it),
And I'm sure that whenever I do so I tell the same story
Of how, at the age of four, I was trapped by the tide
As I clammed a sandbar. It's no story at all,
But I tell it and tell it. It serves my small lust
To be thought of as someone who's lived.

Whittemore's gifts are many. Aside from his skilful satire, his concern with the peculiarly American problems of the non-heroic middle class aspirant, and his reflection of topical issues ("Lines Composed upon Reading an Announcement by Civil Defense Authorities Recommending That I Build a Bombshelter in My Backyard," "The Citizens Haven't Been Able"), his lyric voice is apparent in "On a Summer Sunday" and "Still Life" and he writes persuasively of the poetic process in "The Philadelphia Vireo." He is a poet so constantly aware of his "artistic heritage" (unlike the "zero-hunters" he describes in *From Zero to the Absolute*) that his poetry is saturated with literary allusions and echoes. At the same time its compression and direct simplicity, and its use of intensifiers, assure its immediacy.

—Rosalie Murphy

WIENERS, John (Joseph). American. Born in Boston, Massachusetts, 6 January 1934. Educated at Boston College, A.B. in English 1954; Black Mountain College, North Carolina, 1955–56; State University of New York, Buffalo (Teaching Fellow), 1965–67. Library Clerk, Lamont Library, Harvard University, Cambridge, Massachusetts, 1955–57; Actor and Stage Manager, Poets Theatre, Cambridge, 1956; Assistant Bookkeeper, 8th Street Bookshop, New York, 1962–63; Subscriptions Editor, Jordan Marsh Company, Boston, 1963–65; Class Leader, Beacon Hill Free School, Boston, 1973. Co-Founding Editor, *Measure*, Boston. Recipient: Poets Foundation grant, 1961; New Hope Foundation Award, 1963; National Endowment for the Arts grant, 1966, 1968; National Institute of Arts and Letters Award, 1968; Committee on Poetry grant, 1970, 1971, 1972. Address: 44 Joy Street, Boston, Massachusetts 02114, U.S.A.

PUBLICATIONS

Verse

The Hotel Wentley Poems. San Francisco, Auerhahn Press, 1958; revised edition, 1965.
Ace of Pentacles. New York, Carr, 1964.
Chinoiserie. San Francisco, Dave Haselwood, 1965.
Hart Crane, Harry Crosby, I See You Going over the Edge. Detroit, Artists' Workshop Press, 1966.
King Solomon's Magnetic Quiz. Pleasant Valley, New York, Kriya Press, 1967.
Pressed Wafer. Buffalo, New York, Gallery Upstairs Press, 1967.
Selected Poems. London, Cape, 1968.
Unhired. Mount Horeb, Wisconsin, Perishable Press, 1968.
A Letter to Charles Olson. New York, Charters, 1968.
Asylum Poems. Cambridge, Massachusetts, Press of the Black Flag Raised, 1969.
Nerves. London, Cape Goliard Press, and New York, Grossman, 1970.
Youth. New York, Phoenix Book Shop, 1970.
Selected Poems. London, Cape, and New York, Grossman, 1972.
Woman. Canton, New York, Institute of Further Studies, 1972.
The Lanterns along the Wall. Lancaster, Massachusetts, Other, 1972.
Playboy. Boston, Good Gay Poets, 1972.
We Were There! Boston, Good Gay Poets, 1972.
Hotels. New York, Angel Hair, 1974.

Behind the State Capitol; or, Cincinnati Pike: A Collection of Poetry. Boston, Good Gay Poets, 1975.

Plays

Still-Life (produced New York, 1961).
Asphodel in Hell's Despite (produced New York, 1963).
Anklesox and Five Shoelaces (produced New York, 1966).

Television Documentary: *The Spirit of Romance*, with Robert Danean, 1965.

Other

Untitled Essay on Frank O'Hara. New York, Doubleday, 1969.
A Memory of Black Mountain College. Cambridge, Massachusetts Institute of Technology Press, 1969.

Bibliography: "John Wieners: A Checklist" by George F. Butterick, in *Athanor 3* (Clarkson, New York), Summer-Fall 1973.

Critical Studies: by Denise Levertov, in *Poetry* (Chicago), February 1965; Robert Duncan, in *The Nation* (New York), 31 May 1965; Lewis Warsh, in *Boston Phoenix*, January 1973; interview, in *Gay Sunshine* (San Francisco), March 1973.

John Wieners comments:

(1970) My themes are heartfelt ones of youth and manly desire. Their subjects are despair, frustration, ideal satisfaction, with Biblical and classical referential echoes. Their forms are declarative, orderly and true, without invention. General sources are Edna St. Vincent Millay, United States prose writers of the twentieth century, lyricists in the Greek anthology. Homer; Sappho; Horace; Virgilius; the songs of Geoffrey Chaucer, and subsequent strains of the English tradition. Characteristic stylistic devices are the direct address of German lieder, Near Eastern intimacy and Chinese abbreviation.

(1974) Poetry since 16 has been an obsession, every day, every minute, hearkening to the form of poetry, its practitioners and personables continues to remain fixed as divinities equal to those of the French novelists since 1945 or the Pléiades of court presentation. I have kept the sun and myself upon a balcony bent under its power to lead my attainment towards magnitudinous worldly success and ultimately the presentation towards one person of its worth. For what would it matter if I could not be of use or of importance to this possible derelict in the world's eyes, but to my heart, husband-god, king-emperor. And yet not that. Simply a poor person in need of myself.

Along its possession blossoms many rewards, leisure, conversation, books, friends, entertainment for the ultimate collected editions to merit his devotion.

* * *

Perhaps the most appealing thing about John Wieners's poems is the vulnerability which they express. He had produced some of the most poignant lyrics of their kind ever. His dominant theme is dolor, loss of love and rapture. His is a poetry of feeling rather than will, small chapels for devotion. He is preoccupied with glamour and unattainable desire, yet is saved from self-pity by service to a poetry larger than even his despair: "It is eternal audience/and my feet hardend, my heart/blackend, nodding and/bowing before it." He avoids triteness by the almost perfect timing, the exquisite phrasing. His best poems are relieved from sentimentality by precarious rhyme, perilous syntax, dramatic poise. He is capable of the most precise syncopations: "Yet so tenuous, so fine/this thing is, I am/sitting on the hard bed...." The casual lines only heighten the authenticity of his voice. The despair is so matter-of-fact, not only do we ache for the pity of it, but we believe that to be overcome by such despair is inevitable for the poet. That is the awe which is awful. It is a single tone played repeatedly, like Housman. Wieners is easily the torch singer he once said he wished he could be. No one has sung so convincingly of the haunted underside of life save Billie Holiday, his heroine, or perhaps Edith Piaf, whose fragility his resembles. How out of the sordid and decadent he is able to raise the purest strains is his specialization and accomplishment. We remain before his poems as the poet does his image of himself – "all morning/long./With my hand over my mouth."

Along with *The Hotel Wentley Poems*, Wieners's finest collection remains *Ace of Pentacles*. There are some excellent poems in *Nerves*, a few otherwise uncollected ones in *Selected Poems*, and fewer still in the most recent *Behind the State Capitol*, a collection of "cinema decoupages; verses, abbreviated prose insights," that takes its title from the poet's residence below Beacon Hill in Boston, behind the state capitol building. Wieners has not been his own best representative, as *Selected Poems* too often attests. Not only did he leave out some of his finest poems – "Long Nook," "A Poem for Trapped Things," "Moon Poems," "Not Complete Enough," "My Mother," "The Meadow Where All Things Grow," "Hart Crane, Harry Crosby," "Billie" – but many of those included have been revised, and not always with success. Whether through loss of confidence or false notions of improvement, in almost every case the alterations are for the poorer, usually a misguided effort to attain a more "poetic" effect, most often through the elimination of articles and copulas or the compression of openly whispered lines into more regular stanzas – but in effect eliminating the spoken directness and accuracy of the original. For example, the poet adds the title "153 Avenue C" (on New York's Lower East Side, where the poem was written) to previously untitled lines, but takes away their perfectly understated horror by removing the copulas of natural speech. Other changes are simply strange if not inept, and they are endemic throughout the volume; while in *Behind the State Capitol*, produced from copy apparently prepared by the poet himself, typing eccentricities have been allowed to stand, contributing nothing but confusion. The poet has forsaken his own genius and the stark simplicity of the original statements, so forthright they cannot be doubted or denied. He has lost the touch which enabled him to revise so successfully "A Poem for Painters" (if one compares the original version with that in the 1958 *Hotel Wentley Poems*), which contains his most famous lines and the summarization of his consistent theme:

> My poems contain no
> wilde beestes, no
> lady of the lake, music
> of the spheres, or organ chants.
>
> Only the score of a man's
> struggle to stay with
> what is his own, what
> lies within him to do.

He has continued loyal to his "voices," those to whom *Ace of Pentacles* was dedicated; only now, youth gone, there are more of them, crowding about, incessant, obscuring the flame. The clear, elegant voice and lyric perfection of the early poems has been lost to the multiple personalities, and the consequence is warring diction, abuse of rhyme, and linguistic excess. The *dérèglement* Rimbaud prepared us for has occurred.

—George F. Butterick

WILBUR, Richard (Purdy). American. Born in New York City, 1 March 1921. Educated at Amherst College, Massachusetts, B.A. 1942; Harvard University, Cambridge, Massachusetts, M.A. 1947. Served in the United States Army, 1943–45. Married Charlotte Ward in 1942; one daughter and three sons. Member of the Society of Fellows, 1947–50, and Assistant Professor of English, 1950–54, Harvard University; Associate Professor of English, Wellesley College, Massachusetts, 1955–57. Since 1957, Professor of English, Wesleyan University, Middletown, Connecticut, and since 1977, Writer-in-Residence, Smith College, Northampton, Massachusetts. General Editor, Laurel Poets series, Dell Publishing Company, New York. State Department Cultural Exchange Representative to the U.S.S.R., 1961. Recipient: Harriet Monroe Memorial Prize, 1948, and Oscar Blumenthal Prize, 1950 (*Poetry*, Chicago); Guggenheim Fellowship, 1952, 1963; American Academy in Rome Fellowship, 1954; Pulitzer Prize, 1957; National Book Award, 1957; Edna St. Vincent Millay Memorial Award, 1957; Ford Fellowship, for drama, 1960; Melville Cane Award, 1962; Bollingen Prize, for translation, 1963, and for verse, 1971; Sarah Josepha Hale Award, 1968; Brandeis University Creative Arts Award, 1970; Prix Henri Desfeuilles, 1971; Shelley Memorial Award, 1973; Harriet Monroe Award, 1978. L.H.D.: Lawrence College, Appleton, Wisconsin, 1960; Washington University, St. Louis, 1964; D.Litt.: Amherst College, 1967. Member, American Academy of Arts and Sciences; President, 1974–77, and Chancellor, 1977–78, American Academy of Arts and Letters; Chancellor, Academy of American Poets, Agent: Gilbert Parker, Curtis Brown Ltd., 60 East 56th Street, New York, New York 10022. Address: Dodwells Road, Cummington, Massachusetts 01026, U.S.A.

PUBLICATIONS

Verse

The Beautiful Changes and Other Poems. New York, Reynal, 1947.
Ceremony and Other Poems. New York, Harcourt Brace, 1950.
Things of This World. New York, Harcourt Brace, 1956; one section reprinted as *Digging to China*, New York, Doubleday, 1970.
Poems 1943–1956. London, Faber, 1957.
Advice to a Prophet and Other Poems. New York, Harcourt Brace, 1961; London, Faber, 1962.
The Poems of Richard Wilbur. New York, Harcourt Brace, 1963.
The Pelican from a Bestiary of 1120. Privately printed, 1963.
Prince Souvanna Phouma: An Exchange Between Richard Wilbur and William Jay Smith. Williamstown, Massachusetts, Chapel Press, 1963.
Complaint. New York, Phoenix Book Shop, 1968.
Walking to Sleep: New Poems and Translations. New York, Harcourt Brace, 1969; London, Faber, 1971.
Seed Leaves: Homage to R.F. Boston, Godine, 1974.
The Mind-Reader: New Poems. New York, Harcourt Brace, 1976; London, Faber, 1977.
Verses on the Times, with William Jay Smith. New York, Gutenberg Press, 1978.

Recordings: *Poems*, Spoken Arts, 1959; *Richard Wilbur Reading His Own Poems*, Caedmon.

Plays

The Misanthrope, adaptation of the play by Molière (produced Cambridge, Massachusetts, 1955; New York, 1956). New York, Harcourt Brace, 1955; London, Faber, 1958; revised version, music by Margaret Pine (produced New York, 1977).

Candide (lyrics only, with others), book by Lillian Hellman, music by Leonard Bernstein, adaptation of the novel by Voltaire (produced New York, 1956; London, 1959). New York, Random House, 1957.
Tartuffe, adaptation of the play by Molière (produced Milwaukee, Wisconsin, 1964; New York, 1965). New York, Harcourt Brace, 1963; London, Faber, 1964.
School for Wives, adaptation of a play by Molière (produced New York, 1971). New York, Harcourt Brace, 1971.
The Learned Ladies, adaptation of a play by Molière (produced Williamstown, Massachusetts, 1977). New York, Harcourt Brace, 1978.

Other

Emily Dickinson: Three Views, with Louise Bogan and Archibald MacLeish. Amherst, Massachusetts, Amherst College Press, 1960.
Loudmouse (juvenile). London, Crowell Collier, and New York, Collier Macmillan, 1963.
Opposites (juvenile), drawings by the author. New York, Harcourt Brace, 1973.
Responses: Prose Pieces 1953–1976. New York, Harcourt Brace, 1976.

Editor, with Louis Untermeyer and Karl Shapiro, *Modern American and Modern British Poetry*, revised shorter edition. New York, Harcourt Brace, 1955.
Editor, *A Bestiary* (anthology). New York, Pantheon, 1955.
Editor, *Complete Poems of Poe*. New York, Dell, 1959.
Editor, with Alfred Harbage, *Poems of Shakespeare*. London, Penguin, 1966; revised eidtion, as *The Narrative Poems, and Poems of Doubtful Authenticity*, 1974.
Editor, *Selected Poems*, by Witter Bynner. New York, Farrar Straus, and London, Faber, 1978.

Translator, *The Funeral of Bobo*, by Joseph Brodsky. Ann Arbor, Michigan, Ardis, 1974.

Bibliography: *Richard Wilbur: A Bibliographical Checklist* by John P. Field, Kent, Ohio, Kent State University Press, 1971.

Manuscript Collection: Amherst College, Massachusetts.

Critical Studies: *Richard Wilbur* by Donald L. Hill, New York, Twayne, 1967; *Richard Wilbur* by Paul F. Cummins, Grand Rapids, Michigan, Eerdmans, 1971; "On Richard Wilbur" by William Heyen, Summer 1973, "Verse Translation and Richard Wilbur" by Raymond Oliver, Spring 1975, and "Richard Wilbur: The Quarrel with Poe" by Bruce F. Michelson, Spring 1978, all in *Southern Review* (Baton Rouge, Louisiana); "The Motions of the Mind" by Anthony Hecht, in *Times Literary Supplement* (London), 20 May 1977; "The Cheshire Smile: On Richard Wilbur" by Mary Kinzie, in *American Poetry Review* (Philadelphia), May–June 1977; "Richard Wilbur's World" by Robert B. Shaw, in *Parnassus* (New York), Spring–Summer 1977; "Reconsideration: The Poetry of Richard Wilbur" by Frank McConnell, in *New Republic* (Washington, D.C.), 29 July 1978.

Richard Wilbur comments:

Poetry, for me, is an exasperating and clarifying play with certain images and themes which I cannot escape and prefer not to state here in prose. As the title of my selected prose (*Responses*) would suggest, I have generally written criticism on invitation, but also out of an appreciative involvement with the subject. My translations also have largely come about through a sense of affinity – a desire to put whatever knacks I may have at the service of some admired original.

* * *

In his 1966 essay "Poetry and Happiness" Richard Wilbur offers the measure by which poetry should be judged: "When the sensibility is sufficient to the expression of the world, and when the world, in turn, is answerable to the poet's mind and heart, then the poet is happy, and can make his reader so." In *The Mind-Reader* he disregards the criticism that his poetry wants passion, that its subjects, although nicely perceived in all their inherent paradoxes, lack significance, and that his voice and sensibility are too academic. He continues to strike that difficult balance between solipsism and scientific objectivity upon which his best poetry depends. Wilbur's poem "Cottage Street, 1953" (*The Mind-Reader*) answers the critic that holds that the play of the mind upon an object has become unfashionable – that only the noisy iconoclasm of the Beats, or the naked outpourings of psyche in the Confessional Poets can excite emotions proper to poetry. It also implicitly sustains Wilbur's belief that even in this day a baroque fountain, or a Delacroix painting, or a boy-grown man asking forgiveness of his dead dog are as significant subjects for verse as man's passions or private confessions.

"Cottage Street, 1953" recalls a gathering in the Cambridge kitchen of Wilbur's mother-in-law, Mrs. Ward, shortly after Sylvia Plath's unsuccessful suicide attempt. In an atmosphere of strain, the good-hearted Mrs. Ward, Plath's mother, and Wilbur awkwardly struggle to cheer up Sylvia. Wilbur concludes his poem affirming the love of Edna Ward over the denial of Sylvia Plath:

And Edna Ward shall die in fifteen years,
After her eight-and-eighty summers of
Such grace and courage as permit no tears,
The thin hand reaching out, the last word love,

Outwitting Sylvia, who condemned to live,
Shall study for a decade, as she must,
To state at last her brilliant negative
In poems free and helpless and unjust.

Wilbur's poems acknowledge pain. His early poems protesting World War II and the more recent occasional poems on the Vietnam War decry war's disorder. The complex and infinitely rich "Castles and Distances" brilliantly knits blood and love together:

Oh, it is hunters alone
Regret the beastly pain, it is they who love the foe
That quarries out their force, and every arrow
Is feathered soft with wishes to atone;
Even the surest sword in sorrow
Bleeds for its spoiling blow.

Some of the lines in this poem make us feel the "harpoon's hurt," the piteous eyes of the "hounded stag," the seeming wantonness of slaughter, but others recast this pain, not softening, but altering it, reminding us that pain is there, but also joy. Neither can be eliminated; experience will not allow the simple, albeit brilliant denial of Sylvia Plath.

To complain that Wilbur is "shy," or "restrained," or "too charitable" is to misunderstand the intent of his poems, which is not to distort, but rightly to see the tensions which inform our sense of the world, to set isolated moments in a perspective. Wilbur's is a world of balanced discord.

In "Poetry and Happiness" Wilbur also acknowledged his debt to John Crowe Ransom and defended his choice to write stanzaically formal verse, full of practiced metrical irregularities which set forth contrapuntally thesis and antithesis and reach a resolution appropriately ironic to suit the disordered world mirrored in the poems. He did detect that his poetry over the years had grown plainer and less precocious, less the jaunty verbal technics of a poet-juggler, and he observed that his manner had moved slightly away from the ironic meditative lyric of "Caserta Gardens" and "A Baroque Wall-Fountain in the Villa Sciarra" to the dramatic poem employing two distinct voices, "Two Voices in a Meadow." He saw the common theme of his poetry as having to do with "the proper relation between the tangible world and the intuitions of the spirit."

The poems in *Walking to Sleep* and *The Mind-Reader* continue to evolve in the direction Wilbur described while remaining constant to his theme and sensibility. Most often Wilbur is fascinated by movement and perspective and manipulates language to create a highly kinesthetic poetry. In "Grace" he wrote of the pause and the leap saying "And Nijinsky hadn't the words to make the laws/For learning to loiter in air; he merely said,/'I merely leap and pause.' " Wilbur's poetry searches for the words Nijinsky lacked. Often Wilbur develops his peoms by arresting the reader's eye and taking it through a minute study of the object – be it from nature, history, legend, or his personal past – which the poem contemplates. As he unfolds the object to the seer, he uses a language of such studied movement and rest that we delight at the variety of ways in which a thing can move and marvel at the final figure of the poem which balances the conflicting motions. Poems such as "Lightness," "The Juggler," and "On the Marginal Way" typify this method.

Thinking about the relationship between ideas and poetry, Wilbur wrote: "what poetry does with ideas is redeem them from abstraction and submerge them in sensibility." "Love Calls Us to the Things of This World" discovered the corporeal in the spiritual. "The Eye" and "The Fourth of July" in *The Mind-Reader* continue to make ideas live. Wilbur's diction in *The Mind-Reader* remains academic, but he experiments more with a colloquial speech. "Piccola Commedia" can be seen to have descended from "A Black November Turkey" (*Poems, 1943–1956*). Wilbur still demurs in his poems from speaking directly of his life, his personal poems speak obliquely; he still relies on humor and the fanciful to distance himself. "The Writer" shows excellently how Wilbur depicts a private and family moment with affection, light humor, and candor. The longer, blank-verse poems "In Limbo" and the title poem "The Mind-Reader" along with "Walking to Sleep" depart from most of Wilbur's verse in their length and sustained characterization of himself, but their concern with perspective, irony, minute detail, and a speech of varied kinds immediately relates them thematically and tonally to the body of Wilbur's writing.

—Carol Simpson Stern

WILD, Peter. American. Born in Northampton, Massachusetts, 25 April 1940. Educated at the University of Arizona, Tucson, 1958–62, 1965–67, B.A. 1962, M.A. 1967; University of California, Irvine, 1967–69, M.F.A. 1969. Married Sylvia Ortiz in 1966. Assistant Professor of English, Sul Ross State University, Alpine, Texas, 1969–71. Since 1971, Associate Professor of English, University of Arizona. Recipient: *Writer's Digest* Prize, 1964; Hart Crane and Alice Crane Williams Memorial Fund grant, 1969; *Ark River Review* prize, 1972. Address: 1405 East Lester, Tucson, Arizona 85719, U.S.A.

PUBLICATIONS

Verse

The Good Fox. Glassboro, New Jersey, Goodly, 1967.
Sonnets. San Francisco, Cranium Press, 1967.

The Afternoon in Dismay. Cincinnati, Art Association of Cincinnati, 1968.
Mica Mountain Poems. Ithaca, New York, Lillabulero Press, 1968.
Joining Up and Other Poems. Sacramento, California, Runcible Spoon, 1968.
Mad Night with Sunflowers. Sacramento, California, Runcible Spoon, 1968.
Love Poems. Northwood Narrows, New Hampshire, Lillabulero Press, 1969.
Three Nights in the Chiricahuas. Madison, Wisconsin, Abraxas Press, 1969.
Poems. Portland, Oregon, Prensa de Lagar, 1969.
Fat Man Poems. Belmont, Massachusetts, Hellric, 1970.
Terms and Renewals. San Francisco, Two Windows Press, 1970.
Grace. Pennington, New Jersey, Stone Press, 1971.
Wild's Magical Book of Cranial Effusions. New York, New Rivers Press, 1971.
Peligros. Ithaca, New York, Ithaca House, 1972.
New and Selected Poems. New York, New Rivers Press, 1973.
Cochise. New York, Doubleday, 1973.
The Cloning. New York, Doubleday, 1974.
Tumacacori. Berkeley, California, Two Windows Press, 1974.
Chihuahua. New York, Doubleday, 1976.
The Island Hunter. Tannersville, New York, Tideline Press, 1976.
Health. Berkeley, California, Two Windows Press, 1976.
House Fires. Santa Cruz, California, Greenhouse Review Press, 1977.
Gold Mines. Iola, Wisconsin, Wolfsong Press, 1978.
Barn Fires. Point Reyes, California, Floating Island, 1978.
Zuni Butte. Bisbee, Arizona, San Pedro Press, 1978.
Jeanne d'Arc: A Collection of New Poems. Memphis, St. Luke's Press, 1979.
The Lost Tribe. Iola, Wisconsin, Wolfsong Press, 1979.

Other

Pioneer Conservationists of Western America. Missoula, Montana, Mountain Press, 1978.
Enos Mills. Boise, Idaho, Boise State University, 1979.

Critical Studies: "Eight Chapbooks," in *The Dragonfly* (Pocatello, Idaho), Fall and Winter 1970; "Keeping Us Mad" by Brain Salchert, in *Wisconsin Review* (Oshkosh), Spring 1972; "Lillabulero's Pamphlets," in *Greenfield Review* (Greenfield Center, New York), June 1972; "Mud Men, Mud Women" by Robert Peters, in *Margins* (Milwaukee, Wisconsin), October–November 1974; "Peter Wild: Ways of Promise" by Philip Allan Friedman, in *Gramercy Review* (Los Angeles), Summer 1978.

Peter Wild comments:

Both figuratively and in reality, I have always felt a necessity to spend a great deal of time in the open, in the outdoors. Hence, the deterioration of the natural environment, overpopulation and the erosion of man's cultural diversity are conditions of great concern to me. Furthermore, due to a strong sense of place, as a resident of the American Southwest, a region of the Anglo, Mexican and American Indian, I often hold conflicting sympathies and allegiances. This is not to imply that I consider myself either a "nature poet" or a regional poet – a poet must write for all men – but in general it may be of help for a reader to remember that the above concerns and circumstances of my life undoubtedly underlie and temper much of my writing.

* * *

Peter Wild's poetry demonstrates a brilliantly facile imagination and an ability to turn any world into a fantasy of magical tricks. His style of writing, properly referred to as surrealist, knits a surface poem with exotic and unreconcilable objects. You often feel that he is a magician pulling a rabbit out of his hat and letting doves fly out of his sleeves. His poems are most beautiful when they begin with some observation of natural phenomena and wander off into a speculation of its possibilities. The poem "Snakes" is a good example of this, as he begins the poem, "the rattlesnakes have begun to come out," and ends it when he fantasizes that he awakes in the night and hears a music outdoors and finds

outside on the lawn, the road,
the housetops, our flowerbeds
were full of them, almost erect,
their thin necks
swaying toward the moon
humming, smiling
sensuously
drinking in the light;
while others sped
back and forth on great
rice paper wings,
carrying messages
across the cloudless night ...

Wild's poems are never overtly funny, yet they are filled with a kind of whimsy and a gentle sense of the "funniness" of the world. His poems are impersonal in that they are not autobiographical. Their personality comes from Wild's ability to imagine and describe any landscape he chooses and, again like a magician, fill it with bizarre and funny objects. William Matthews says of Wild's poems that "the effect is of a baroque telegram, or the wildest photo caption you'll ever read."

—Diane Wakoski

WILLARD, Nancy. American. Born in Ann Arbor, Michigan, 26 June 1936. Educated at the University of Michigan, Ann Arbor (Hopwood Award), B.A. 1958, Ph.D. 1963; Stanford University, California (Woodrow Wilson Fellow), M.A. 1960. Married to Eric Lindbloom; one son. Currently, Lecturer in English, Vassar College, Poughkeepsie, New York. Recipient: Devins Memorial Award, 1967; O. Henry Award, for short story, 1970. Address: 133 College Avenue, Poughkeepsie, New York 12603, U.S.A.

PUBLICATIONS

Verse

In His Country. Ann Arbor, Michigan, Generation, 1966.
Skin of Grace. Columbia, University of Missouri Press, 1967.
A New Herball. Baltimore, Ferdinand-Roter Galleries, 1968.
Nineteen Masks for the Naked Poet. Santa Cruz, California, Kayak, 1971.
The Carpenter of the Sun. New York, Liveright, 1974.

Short Stories

The Lively Anatomy of God. New York, Eakins Press, 1968.
Childhood of the Magician. New York, Liveright, 1973.

Other (juvenile)

Testimony of the Invisible Man: William Carlos Williams, Francis Ponge, Rainer Maria Rilke, Pablo Neruda (for adults). Columbia, University of Missouri Press, 1970.
The Merry History of a Christmas Pie: With a Delicious Description of a Christmas Soup. New York, Putnam, 1974.
Sailing to Cythera and Other Anatole Stories. New York, Harcourt Brace, 1974.
The Snow Rabbit. New York, Putnam, 1975.
All on a May Morning. New York, Putnam, 1975.
Shoes Without Leather. New York, Putnam, 1976.
The Well-Mannered Balloon. New York, Harcourt Brace, 1976.
Strangers' Bread. New York, Harcourt Brace, 1977.
The Highest Hit. New York, Harcourt Brace, 1978.
Simple Pictures Are Best. New York, Harcourt Brace, and London, Collins, 1978.
Papa's Panda. New York, Harcourt Brace, 1979.
The Island of the Grass King. New York, Harcourt Brace, 1979.

* * *

Of scholars and children, alike in the unpredictable movements of their attention, Nancy Willard writes in her first book:

Their order belongs to eyes
that the earth chooses
to edit a work much vexed:
de veritate rerum,
an occult, particular text.

Much of her poetry – like that of Williams, Ponge, Rilke, and Neruda, all of whom she has studied in her critical book, *Testimony of the Invisible Man* – aspires to be "a poetry of things," explicating that text and revivifying our awareness of the world. One way is the vivid image – "dragonflies/thin as barometer's blood," or (of a box of eggs) "the lid raised to show/a jury noncommital/as the bald heads of/a dozen uncles." Another requires a deeper attention, a probing below the surface of reality. In "The Water Diviner" the diviner speaks of her "gift":

Less a gift for me than a burden
of silence, this slow going blind
to the green guests in my father's field,
while the sun behind me scorches the men mowing.
For the sake of that wind in the earth blowing
I walk like a holy fool, past the barn and tree,
with no ship but a broken rudder in my hand,
calling the sea.

Her third book, *Nineteen Masks for the Naked Poet*, shows her leaving *Ding*-poetry to experiment with the loosely surrealist mode associated with Kayak press and magazine. Often merely whimsical, the playfulness can be evocative, as in "Putting His Finger in the Dyke, He Saves All Holland," where the mayor acclaims the poet-hero for saving them from the sea which "covers over the words of our fathers/and torments us with shipwrecks and bad dreams":

This is the poet who took on himself

our bad dreams and made them beautiful,
our fathers' secrets and made them ours.

Uncollected recent poems seen in the anthology *Rising Tides*, such as "Marriage Amulet" and "For You, Who Didn't Know," show Nancy Willard dealing with more personal, even "confessional," subject-matter with no diminution of craft. If her next collection has many others of equal quality, it will have proven worth waiting for.

—Seamus Cooney

WILLIAMS, C(harles) K(enneth). American. Born in Newark, New Jersey, 4 November 1936. Educated at Bucknell University, Lewisburg, Pennsylvania; University of Pennsylvania, Philadelphia, 1955–59, B.A. 1959. Married 1) Sarah Jones in 1965; 2) Catherine Mauger in 1975; one daughter and one son. Since 1972, Contributing Editor, *American Poetry Review*, Philadelphia. Visiting Professor, Franklin and Marshall College, Lancaster, Pennsylvania, 1977, and University of California, Irvine, 1978. Recipient: Guggenheim Fellowship, 1974. Address: 634 Rodman Street, Philadelphia, Pennsylvania 19147, U.S.A.

PUBLICATIONS

Verse

A Day for Anne Frank. Philadelphia, Falcon Press, 1968.
Lies. Boston, Houghton Mifflin, 1969.
I Am the Bitter Name. Boston, Houghton Mifflin, 1972.
The Sensuous President. New York, New Rivers Press, 1972.
With Ignorance. Boston, Houghton Mifflin, 1977.

Other

Translator, with Gregory Dickerson, *Women of Trachis*, by Sophocles. London, Oxford University Press, 1979.

Critical Studies: by Richard Howard, in *Kenyon Review* (Gambier, Ohio), Summer 1970, and in *American Poetry Review* (Philadelphia), November 1972; L. E. Sissman, in *Boston Sun-Globe*, 18 July 1972; Morris Dickstein, in *Parnassus* (New York), Fall 1972, and in *New York Times*, 10 July 1977; Stanley Plumly, in *American Poetry Review* (Philadelphia), January 1978; Dave Smith, in *Western Humanities Review* (Salt Lake City), Autumn 1978.

* * *

"I am uncertain about just about everything – the use of poetry, the form of it," C. K. Williams has said, but judging from his poems, one would never guess that he was uncertain about anything. The tone is sure, swift, almost brittle in its certainty. Somewhat in the manner of Thomas Hardy or Stephen Crane, but with more despair, he shakes his fist in the face of God of god, saying:

your lists of victims dear
god like rows of sharp little teeth
have made me crazy look
I have crushed by poor balls
for you I have kissed the blank
pages drank the pissy chalice
water and thrown up

The poems in *Lies* and *I Am the Bitter Name* are concerned principally with desperate, abandoned, but patient souls; and both books end with long poems about specific victims. "Come sit with me here/kiss me; my heart too is wounded/with forgiveness," the speaker says to the young girl, in "The Day for Anne Frank." And "In the Heart of the Beast – May 1970 – Cambodia, Kent State, Jackson State," a person tired of forgiving, asks:

this is fresh meat right mr nixon
this is even sweeter than mickey schwerner or fred hampton
right?
even more tender than the cherokee nation or guatemala or
greece
having their asses straightened for them isn't it.

Such a heavy political message is uncharacteristic, however, of most of Williams's poems, which belong more to the moral or even theological order. An exchange between two Old Testament figures, for example, provided the title for his second collection: "Abraham said to him, 'Art thou, indeed he that is called Death?' He answered, and said, 'I am the Bitter Name!' "

But there is another aspect of Williams's work not so obvious as the ferocious voice, the startling metaphor, the hard and bitter irony for which he is best known. In "To Market," for example, a man manages to say "I love you," even as, in metamorphosis, he becomes a machine; in "Wood," a young ruffian speaks to his more conventional classmate from the grave; and in "Yours," the speaker promises a poem to everyone in the world, as if each poem brought with it some hope, a saving grace. Such poems suggest a range of feeling that may eventually take Williams into new territory.

In an age of bestial death, as Williams calls it, telling "just what is" is achievement enough, "remembering iwo jima remembering the bulge seoul my lai."

In its precision, intensity, fury, his work gives full imaginative expression to a kind of consciousness that many poets have only hinted at. It asks a great deal of the reader, as all truly exceptional poetry must. One can only guess, at this time – when Williams is still a young man – the possibilities in language and technique yet available to him.

—Michael True

WILLIAMS, Emmett. American. Born in Greenville, South Carolina, 4 April 1925. Educated at Kenyon College, Gambier, Ohio, B.A. 1949; University of Paris. Served in the United States Army, 1943–46. Married 1) Laura Powell MacCarteney in 1949, two daughters and one son; 2) Ann Noël Stevenson in 1970, one son. Lived in Europe, 1949–66: assistant to the ethnologist Paul Radin; associated with the Darmstadt group of concrete poets; Founding Member of the Domaine Poetique, Paris; European Coordinator of the Fluxus group. Editor, Somehting Else Press, New York, 1966–70. Artist-in-Residence, Fairleigh

Dickinson University, Madison, New Jersey, 1968, and University of Kentucky, Lexington, 1969; Professor of Critical Studies, California Institute of the Arts, Valencia, 1970–72; Visiting Professor of Art, Nova Scotia College of Art and Design, Halifax, 1972–74; Visiting Artist, Mount Holyoke College, South Hadley, Massachusetts, 1975–77. Since 1977, Visiting Lecturer, Carpenter Center for the Visual Arts, Harvard University, Cambridge, Massachusetts. Address: Carpenter Center for the Visual Arts, Harvard University, Cambridge, Massachusetts 02138, U.S.A.

PUBLICATIONS

Verse

Konkretionen. Darmstadt, Germany, Material, 1958.
13 Variations on 6 Words by Gertrude Stein (1958). Cologne, Galerie der Speigel, 1965.
Rotapoems. Stuttgart, Hansjörg Mayer, 1966.
The Last French-Fried Potato and Other Poems. New York, Something Else Press, 1967.
Sweethearts. Stuttgart, Hansjörg Mayer, 1967; New York, Something Else Press, 1968.
The Book of Thorn and Eth. Stuttgart, Hansjörg Mayer, 1968.
The Boy and the Bird. Stuttgart, Hansjörg Mayer, and New York, Wittenborn, 1968.
A Valentine for Noël. Stuttgart, Hansjörg Mayer, 1973.
Selected Shorter Poems 1950–1970. Stuttgart, Hansjörg Mayer, 1974; New York, New Directions, 1975.
The Voyage. Stuttgart, Hansjörg Mayer, 1975.

Plays

Ja, Es war noch da (produced Darmstadt, Germany, 1960). Published in *Nota 4* (Munich), 1960; as *Yes It Was Still There* (produced New York, 1965).
A Cellar Song for 5 Voices (produced New York, 1961).
4-Directional Song of Doubt for 5 Voices (produced Wiesbaden, Germany, 1962).
The Ultimate Poem (produced Arras, France, 1964).

Other

Variations upon a Spoerri Landscape (lithographs). Halifax, Nova Scotia College of Art and Design Lithography Workshop, 1973.
Zodiac (lithographs). Tokyo, Gallery Birthday Star, 1974.

Editor, *Poésie et cetera américaine.* Paris, Biennale, 1963.
Editor, *An Anthology of Concrete Poetry.* New York, Something Else Press, 1967.
Editor, *Store Days*, by Claes Oldenburg. New York, Something Else Press, 1967.

Translator, *An Anecdoted Topography of Chance* ..., by Daniel Spoerri. New York, Something Else Press, 1966.
Translator, *The Mythological Travels of a Modern Sir John Mandeville* ..., by Daniel Spoerri. New York, Something Else Press, 1970.

* * *

Emmett Williams's name is better known than his poetry, and one reason for this discrepancy is that he edited *An Anthology of Concrete Poetry*, which has outsold its competitors (including an anthology of mine), while most of his poetry remains unpublished, particularly in his native country. Unlike other American writers of his generation, Williams became closely involved, back in the 1950's, with the European intermedia avant-garde, epitomized by the "Darmstadt Circle," in which he figured prominently. By the sixties, he was an initiator of Fluxus, an international post-Dada, mixed-means movement which won considerable attention at the time (but has so far escaped most historians of contemporary art and literature). Thus, his writing reflects, to an unusual degree, the experimental tradition in the non-literary arts. He echoed not Dylan Thomas but Kurt Schwitters, for instance, in his early "performance poems," to use the term that refers to poems whose most appropriate form is not the printed page but live performance.

It was Williams's good fortune to learn, back in the 1950's, that English-language poetry could be composed in radically alternative ways – different not only from the academic poetry of that time but also from the declamatory expressionism of, say, Allen Ginsberg. Instead, Williams pioneered the art of "concrete poetry," in which the poet eschews conventional syntax (and related devices) to organize language in other ways. Rather than "free form" (whatever that might be), Williams favored such severe constraints as repetition, permutation, and linguistic minimalism. His masterpiece, the book-length *Sweethearts*, consists of one word (the title) whose eleven letters are visually distributed over 150 or so sequentially expressive pages, the work as a whole relating the evolution of a man-woman relationship. Like Williams's other work, *Sweethearts* is extremely witty; and like much else in experimental writing, it must be seen (and read) for its magic to be believed.

—Richard Kostelanetz

WILLIAMS, (David) Gwyn. British (Welsh). Born in Port Talbot, Glamorgan, 24 August 1904. Educated at Port Talbot Grammar School; University College of Wales, Aberystwyth, B.A.; Jesus College, Oxford, M.A. Married; five children. Lecturer in English Literature, Cairo University, 1935–42; Assistant Professor of English, Alexandria University, Egypt, 1942–51; Professor of English, University of Libya, Benghazi, 1956–61; Professor of English Literature, Istanbul University, 1961–69. Recipient: Welsh Arts Council Prize, 1977. Address: Treweithan, Trefenter, Aberystwyth, Dyfed, Wales.

PUBLICATIONS

Verse

Inns of Love: Selected Poems. Llandybie, Dyfed, Christopher Davies, 1970.
Foundation Stock. Llandysul, Dyfed, Gomer, 1974.

Novels

This Way to Lethe. London, Faber, 1962.
The Avocet. Swansea, Christopher Davies, 1970.
Two Sketches of Womanhood. Swansea, Christopher Davies, 1975.

Other

An Introduction to Welsh Poetry from the Beginning to the Sixteenth Century. London, Faber, and Philadelphia, Dufour and Saifer, 1953.

Green Mountain: An Informal Guide to Cyrenaica and Jebel Akhdar. London, Faber, 1963.
Turkey: A Traveller's Guide and History. London, Faber, 1967.
Eastern Turkey. London, Faber, 1972.
Twrci a'i Phobl. Cardiff, Gwasg y Dref Wen, 1975.
To Look for a Word: Collected Translations from Welsh Poetry. Llandysul, Dyfed, Gomer, 1976.
The Land Remembers: A View of Wales. London, Faber, 1977.
An Introduction to Welsh Literature. Cardiff, University of Wales Press, 1978.
Madoc: The Making of a Myth. London, Eyre Methuen, 1979.

Editor, *Presenting Welsh Poetry: An Anthology of Welsh Verse in Translation and of English Verse by Welsh Poets.* London, Faber, 1959.
Editor, *Troelus a Chresyd.* Llandysul, Dyfed, Gomer, 1976.

Translator, *The Rent That's Due to Love.* London, Editions Poetry London, 1950.
Translator, *Against Women.* London, Golden Cockerel Press, 1953.
Translator, *The Burning Tree: Poems from the First Thousand Years of Welsh Verse.* London, Faber, 1956; revised edition, as *Welsh Poems: Sixth Century to 1600*, 1973; Berkeley, University of California Press, 1974.
Translator, *In Defence of Woman: A Welsh Poem*, by William Cynwal. London, Golden Cockerel Press, 1960.

Gwyn Williams comments:

I write a poem when I experience something that requires a poem to be written, I suppose in an attempt to catch the experience, preserve it, give it an existence separate from my own. There are poems which are objects on my mental mantel-shelf, some of them staying clean, others needing an occasional dusting, but most of them have gone further away from me than that. A long poem I am now writing with the idea of letting it carry off bees from my bonnet is already orbiting away from me. The experiences have occurred mostly in Wales and round the eastern end of the Mediterranean. I use stanza forms as they come, half rhymes rather than full, some complex alliteration. Technically I have learnt most from translating Welsh poetry I like into English verse.

* * *

Gwyn Williams has won a high reputation as a translator of Welsh poetry. He has also written a fine travel book, *Turkey*, among many other volumes. He has travelled widely, and spent much of his working life teaching literature at universities in the Near East.

His selected poems, *Inns of Love*, shows how the better verse translators also happen to be good poets in their own right. Like Pound's, the output of Professor Williams may be seen at its best when working through other literatures, as if he needs a framework of translation to keep his intellect and imagination at full stretch. He uses the past, and masterpieces in other languages, as a sort of combined filter for his own peculiar vision.

The most ambitious poem in this splendidly entertaining collection is "Charlemagne in Constantinople," which occupies almost half the book. It is a long narrative work about Charlemagne's legendary encounter with Hu Gadarn in Byzantium, based on the medieval Welsh version of the story in the 14th-century *Red Book of Hergest*. A highly individual treatment, one of its most intriguing features is the daring manner in which Williams employs an obtrusive 20th-century narrator – eloquent, flamboyant, witty, ironic – who marshals his characters, comments, draws parallels to their actions, juxtaposes past and present, legend and contemporary reality, and surveys the European and Eastern scenes of the story through the centuries. This produces a certain shock effect which might bring howls of protest from purists, but the method largely succeeds with the verve of its conversational style:

> Byzantium is the separate city, the ultimate Cokayne
> or the golden point of departure into decline;
> vision of a viable order or retreat into
> a fabricated region of potency; the landing
> on the Moon or the two-gun man doing
> his best with Eskimo Nell. As a ticket of entry you present
> bones, Mary's milk, the pill, the plunging neckline,
> the sports car, the space rocket or a glossy work on cooking.

This concluding passage, with a vigorous and almost vulgar tone, justifies itself by the way in which it clarifies Williams's interpretation of his sources, not treating it as a "museum piece gathering scholarly dust but as a living work of art." Looking deeply into the distant past becomes a way of understanding the present.

In another poem, "City under Snow," a fairly conventional subject evokes a fresh response:

> Mosques into snow-palaces; banks, bagnios,
> party headquarters and apartment blocks
> acquire an innocence; L. S. Lowry figures
> lean into flocked air;
>
> spittle, pigeon-dung, dogshit and broken
> glass, the layer of soot all iced over and
> a new fall powders the cleaned crotches
> of cobbled alleys.

Generally, *Inns of Love* and the later poems are the work of a writer for whom places remain important as nodal points where lines usually thought of as time, sensory impression, tradition, and a view of life intersect. And so the places in which he has lived and worked – Egypt, Libya, Turkey, and now Wales – are more than a background: they form an integral part of the experience which is the poem. Entry into the nature of a place eliminates the illusion of time and throws "hooks into the self," as Williams would put it.

The accomplishment of Gwyn Williams as a valuable verse-translator is considerable, and few more erudite and cultivated men have emerged from Wales – an academic who is yet very much involved in living and the future of his own country. He has recently made a separate, if less permanent, reputation on television as an articulate guide to the long history and archaeology of Wales.

—John Tripp

WILLIAMS, Herbert (Lloyd). British (Welsh). Born in Aberystwyth, Cardiganshire, 8 September 1932. Educated at Alexandra Road Boys School and Ardwyn Grammar School, Aberystwyth. Married Dorothy Edwards in 1954; four sons and one daughter. Staff member, *Welsh Gazette*, Aberystwyth, 1951–53, *Reading Standard*, Berkshire, 1953, *Cambrian News*, Aberystwyth, 1953–56, *South Wales Echo*, Cardiff, 1956–60, *Scottish Daily Mail*, Edinburgh, 1960–61, *South Wales Echo*, 1961–73, and Birmingham *Evening Mail*, 1972–73. Since 1973, BBC Radio Producer, Cardiff. Address: 107 Pontbach Road, Rhiwbina, Cardiff, Wales.

PUBLICATIONS

Verse

Too Wet for the Devil and Other Poems. London, Outposts, 1962.
The Dinosaurs. Cardiff, Triskel Press, 1966.
The Trophy. Llandybie, Dyfed, Christopher Davies, 1967.
Corgi Modern Poets in Focus 1, with others, edited by Dannie Abse. London, Corgi, 1971.

Play

A Lethal Kind of Love (broadcast, 1968). Cardiff, John Jones, 1968.

Other

Battles in Wales. Cardiff, John Jones, 1975.
Stage Coaches in Wales. Barry, Glamorgan, S. Williams, 1977.
The Welsh Quiz Book. Cardiff, John Jones, 1978.

Manuscript Collection: National Library of Wales, Aberystwyth.

Critical Study: by Dannie Abse, in *Corgi Modern Poets in Focus 1*, 1971.

* * *

Herbert Williams is an unambitious poet, avowedly diffident about his own talent; perhaps if he were more committed to the art his work would be tighter and more polished. As it is he succeeds best in low-key, sympathetic examinations of the society he lives in. He has a journalist's eye for detail and atmosphere, a warm social concern, and a healthy outward-looking attitude; his subjects tend to be drawn from everyday life in Wales – local characters, craftsmen and traders, sailors, a choir – individual or group portraits presented with natural, unemphatic realism. He can turn out a lively ballad ("A Man and a Half"), and is good with family occasions ("Morning in Aber"), although few of his poems are overtly personal.

At his best he is unsentimental, honest, and capable of the vivid, down-to-earth phrase which can bring a scene to life: "The smell of cakes at missionary teas"; "hair white as skate." He is least successful when he tackles abstract themes: his language becomes flaccid and slides towards, or into, worn out "poetic diction."

In "Small Fortune," a poem about the little pleasures which add up to contentment, he says "Turnpike trusts/Grew fat upon the twopenny toll." It is with such unpretentious but not to be despised currency that Williams buys our respect.

—Fleur Adcock

WILLIAMS, Hugo. British. Born in Windsor, Berkshire, 20 February 1942; son of the actor and playwright Hugh Williams. Educated at Eton College, 1955–60. Married Hermine Demoriane in 1965; one child. Staff Writer, *Telegraph Magazine*, London, 1965; Assistant Editor, *London Magazine*, 1966–70. Recipient: Eric Gregory Award, 1966; Arts Council bursary, 1966; Cholmondeley Award, 1971. Address: 3 Raleigh Street, London W.1, England.

PUBLICATIONS

Verse

Symptoms of Loss. London and New York, Oxford University Press, 1965.
Poems. London, The Review, 1969.
Sugar Daddy. London and New York, Oxford University Press, 1970.
Cherry Blossom. London, Poem-of-the-Month Club, 1972.
Some Sweet Day. London and New York, Oxford University Press, 1975.
Love-Life. London, Whizzard Press, 1979.

Recording: *British Poets of Our Times*, with Adrian Henri, Argo.

Other

All the Time in the World (travel). London, Alan Ross, 1966; Philadelphia, Chilton, 1968.

Editor, *"London Magazine" Poems, 1961–1966.* London, Alan Ross, 1966.

* * *

Hugo Williams has been one of those poets – Colin Falck and David Harsent are others – most closely associated with the magazines *The Review* and *The New Review*. The poems particularly admired by Ian Hamilton, the editor of these journals and a central presence in the criticism of contemporary English poetry, have several immediately recognisable characteristics. They are almost always short, sometimes very short indeed; their subject matter is almost always domestic, amatory, familial, concerned with the minutiae of personal relationships; they almost always attempt a tight-lipped, tough-minded, very "English" stance in relation to the emotions they describe; and yet their characteristic cadences are, nevertheless, almost always plangent, melancholy, nostalgic. For a poetry that makes claims to speak with honesty about the casual exigencies of modern living, this poetry can sometimes sound disconcertingly close to the wan debilitation of the *fin-de-siècle*.

Williams himself provides ample opportunity for making these generalisations and strictures, and for adding those of inconsequentiality and an almost adolescent self-absorption and sentimentality. This, for instance, is a poem called "Once More with Feeling" in its entirety:

My voice breaks
And I know it must be time
To pour out my heart to you again.

Believe me,
I would like to make you cry
This once,
But you smile encouragingly,
Prepared to understand.

This is a message that I cannot be alone in wishing Williams had addressed in an envelope, and then forgotten about, rather than thinking it worthy of preservation in a published book. And his own disarming admissions – "Don't tell me, I know/I'm mumbling to myself again," he says in "The Ribbon" – which are presumably intended to charm us out of hostility, should not be allowed to do so.

But there is a more interesting side to Williams; and this is largely a matter of his ability to make the very ordinary and prosaic seem suddenly extraordinary and resonantly mysterious by verbalising odd, tangential perceptions, sometimes in an ambiguously wayward syntax. This is "Holidays":

We spread our things on the sand
In front of the hotel
And sit for hours on end
Like merchants under parasols
Our thoughts following the steamers
In convoy across the bay
While far away
Our holidays look back at us in surprise
From fishing boats and fairs
Or wherever they were going then
In their seaweed head-dresses.

Like the holidays here, the end of this singular sentence looks back at its beginning in surprise, wondering how it had ever started out there, or ended up here. Whether we read "they" in the penultimate line as referring to "holidays" or "fishing boats and fairs," or, somehow, to both, the effect of the really very strange statement being made is to set the whole poem in front of a kind of distorting mirror, performing crazily acrobatic feats with its facial muscles. And – a feeling reinforced by the ghostly presence of J. Alfred Prufrock in the final line – the poem is distinctly disturbing, like a sudden gust of sand on an otherwise peaceful beach.

This note echoes sufficiently in Williams to provide sustenance in thin volumes that would otherwise seem a little too precious, surrounding the undoubted delicacy of their perceptions with so much white space. The best of Williams – as in the early poem "The Butcher" – is a depth of unease that goes a long way beyond the wry, bemused, or ironical poses he is often too readily content with:

I think he knows about my life. How we prefer
To eat in when it's cold. How someone

With a foreign accent can only cook veal.
He writes the price on the grease-proof packet

And hands it to me courteously. His smile
Is the official seal on my marriage.

—Neil Corcoran

WILLIAMS, John Stuart. British (Welsh). Born in Mountain Ash, Glamorgan, 13 August 1920. Educated at Mountain Ash County School; University College, Cardiff, B.A. (honours) in English literature, M.A. Married Sheelagh Williams in 1948; two sons. Formerly, English Master, Whitchurch Grammar School, Glamorgan, and Head of the Department of English and Drama, City of Cardiff College of Education. Since 1977, Head of Department of Communications, South Glamorgan Institute of Higher Education, Cardiff. Member of the Welsh Arts Council Literature Committee, 1973–77. Composer. Member, English Section, Welsh Academy (Yr Academi Gymreig). Recipient: Welsh Arts Council prize, 1971. Address: 52 Dan-y-Coed Road, Cyncoed, Cardiff, Wales.

PUBLICATIONS

Verse

Last Fall. London, Outposts, 1962.
Green Rain. Llandybie, Dyfed, Christopher Davies, 1967.
Dic Penderyn and Other Poems. Llandysul, Dyfed, Gomer, 1970.
Banna Strand: Poems 1970–74. Llandysul, Dyfed, Gomer, 1975.

Other

Editor, with Richard Milner, *Dragons and Daffodils.* Llandybie, Dyfed, Christopher Davies, 1960.
Editor, with Meic Stephens, *The Lilting House: An Anthology of Anglo-Welsh Poetry 1917–1967.* Llandybie, Dyfed, Christopher Davies, and London, Dent, 1969.
Editor, *Poems '69.* Llandysul, Dyfed, Gomer, 1969.

Manuscript Collection: National Library of Wales, Aberystwyth.

Critical Studies: in *Outposts* (London), Winter 1967; introduction by Roland Mathias, to *Green Rain*, 1967; *An Introduction to Anglo-Welsh Literature* by Raymond Garlick, Cardiff, University of Wales Press, 1970; Alun Rees, in *Poetry Wales* (Cardiff), Winter 1976.

John Stuart Williams comments:

I was born and brought up in a sceptically anglicised mining comminity which had few problems about its identity; it was stubbornly Welsh, and had small faith in easy solutions. It was a place of sharp contrasts; the open hill was a short step from the coalpits in the centre of town and we were often reminded of death by the colliery hooter signalling an accident underground. A sense of the ambiguity of reality has remained with me and much of my work is an attempt to establish footholds in place and time from which to explore this and the obliquity of our personal and national myths. "Banna Strand," first published in *Decal Poetry Review* is a recent example:

In my raincoat pocket, a faded carnet de bal;
the stillness of mist, a girl on horseback
frightened by something other than the sea,
watching, waiting;
such a pretty little beach ...
Is it my business what they do,
what answers may come with sudden gardens?
I am not Control.
Hoofs in the shallows,
fear in shadows coursing along the wet sand,
the sharp fountains of sprayed light ...
What do you see through your Ross?
A misleading group, windblown hair
falsely suggesting private warmth.
Everything is coded, graffiti on old stone,
on Banna strand or beside the midland sea.

After writing this I was disconcerted to find that Banna strand was where Casement had landed in Ireland for the last fatal time.

It would be easy and misleading to isolate literary influences, as my first lessons in rhythm came from music and the cinema. From the first I learned that rhythm is more subtle than traditional metric easily allows, and from the second I first learned about montage and the inter-relation of images, something later confirmed in conversations with the late John Grierson. The reading came later. The natural order of words is important to me even when I write in more obviously traditional forms, for it is against this pattern that I try to work my variations. This sometimes misfires, for what is natural to me, a valleys Welshman, may be different from what seems so to others. The danger inherent in my subject-matter is compounded in this way. One man's *déjà vu* is, in any case, sometimes another's boredom. But this is a risk I have to take:

> Listening to silence,
> I praise both light and darkness.

* * *

John Stuart Williams's premier achievement is a long dramatic poem, "Dic Penderyn," originally written for radio, which won a Welsh Arts Council prize in 1971. It is the story of the Merthyr Riots of 1831, the conflict between the workers and ironmasters, the violence and reprisals, and the struggle of men for free and decent lives. Dic Penderyn himself was the figure at the centre of the trouble: he wounded a Highlander (one of the troops brought in to quell the riots) and was later hanged at Cardiff. In this impressive poem, Penderyn focuses most of the emotion, as he did in real life among the oppressed ironworkers. (There are also four narrators who impersonate characters in the story, plus several lyrics for a folksinger.) Williams's treatment is what might be termed poetic documentary – accurate, clear, and ordered, with the dramatic tension mounting effectively to its climax. The poetry contributes sinewy and colourful language to the sweep of events, linking images of blood, metal, fire, and nature:

> And the fierce summer leaps in
> With torchlight red on broken glass.
> The throbbing pulse grows louder,
> Until the whole town drowns
> In the blind heat of a dull drum.

Williams's individual poems are usually short, neat impressionistic pieces, resembling attractive snapshots, with titles like "Gironde," "River Walk," or "Beach at Ifracombe." One criticism levelled at him is that these rather "gnomic" poems briefly interest and entertain, but are essentially inconsequential. Apart from "Dic Penderyn," Williams's craft may be a modest one, but it is also a true one, honestly attained. There is a place in literature, as in painting, for the miniature water-colour, even though the heavy guns of contemporary criticism would have us believe otherwise. This particular, largely unsentimental Welsh miniaturist has a good deal to offer in the way of fresh observation and disinterested understanding. He can often breathe life into the oldest stock scenes and the most ordinary, banal moments.

—John Tripp

WILLIAMS, Jonathan (Chamberlain). American. Born in Asheville, North Carolina, 8 March 1929. Educated at St. Albans School, Washington, D.C., 1941–47; Princeton

University, New Jersey, 1947–49; Atelier 17, New York, 1949–50; Institute of Design, Chicago, 1951; Black Mountain College, North Carolina, 1951–56. Conscientious Objector: served in the United States Army Medical Corps, 1952–53. Since 1951, Executive Director, The Jargon Society, Inc., publishers, Highlands, North Carolina. Scholar-in-Residence, Aspen Institute, Colorado, 1967–68, and Maryland Institute College of Art, Baltimore, 1968–69; Poet-in-Residence, University of Kansas, Lawrence, 1971, and University of Delaware, Newark, 1977. Recipient: Guggenheim Fellowship, 1957; Longview Foundation grant, 1960; National Endowment for the Arts grant, 1968, 1969, 1970, 1973, 1977, 1978. D.H.L.: Maryland Institute College of Art, 1969. Address: Highlands, North Carolina 28741, U.S.A.; or, Corn Close, Dentdale, Sedbergh, Yorkshire, England.

PUBLICATIONS

Verse

Garbage Litters the Iron Face of the Sun's Child. San Francisco, Jargon, 1951.
Red Gray. Black Mountain, North Carolina, Jargon, 1951.
Four Stoppages. Stuttgart, Jargon, 1953.
Lord! Lord! Lord! Highlands, North Carolina, Jargon, 1959.
The Empire Finals at Verona. Highlands, North Carolina, Jargon, 1960.
Amen Huzza Selah. Black Mountain, North Carolina, Jargon, 1960.
Elegies and Celebrations. Highlands, North Carolina, Jargon, 1962.
In England's Green & (A Garland and a Clyster). San Francisco, Auerhahn Press, 1962.
Emblems for the Little Dells and Nooks and Corners of Paradise. London, Jargon, 1962.
The Macon County North Carolina Meshuga Sound Society, Jonathan Williams, Musical Director, Presents: Lullabies, Twisters, Gibbers, Drags (à la manière de M. Louis Moreau Gottschalk, late of the City of New Orleans). London, Jargon, 1963.
Petite Concrete Concrete Suite. Detroit, Fenian Head Centre Press, 1965.
Twelve Jargonelles from the Herbalist's Notebook. Bloomington, Indiana University Design Department, 1965.
Ten Jargonelles from the Herbalist's Notebook. Urbana, University of Illinois Design Department, 1966.
Four Jargonelles from the Herbalist's Notebook. Cambridge, Massachusetts, Lowell 1966.
Paean to Dvorak, Deemer, and McClure. San Francisco, Dave Haselwood, 1966.
Affilati Attrezzi Per I Giardini di Catullo (bilingual edition). Milan, Lerici Editore, 1966.
Mahler Becomes Politics, Beisbol. London, Marlborough Gallery, 1967.
50! Epiphytes, -taphs, -tomes, -grams, -thets! 50! London, Poet and Printer, 1967.
A French 75! San Francisco, Dave Haselwood, 1967.
Polycotyledonous Poems. Stuttgart, Hansjörg Mayer, 1967.
The Lucidities: Sixteen in Visionary Company. London, Turret, 1967.
Eight Jargonelles from the Herbalist's Notebook. Bloomington, Indiana University Design Department, 1967.
LTGD. Bloomington, Indiana University Design Department, 1967.
Les Six Pak. Aspen, Colorado, Aspen Institute, 1967.
Sharp Tools for Catullan Gardens. Bloomington, Indiana University Fine Arts Department, 1968.
Ripostes. Stuttgart, Editions Domberger, 1969.
An Ear in Bartram's Tree: Selected Poems 1957–67. Chapel Hill, University of North Carolina Press, 1969.
On Arriving at the Same Age as Jack Benny. Urbana, Illinois, Finial Press, 1969.

Mahler. London, Cape Goliard Press, 1969.
Six Rusticated, Wall-Eyed Poems. Baltimore, Maryland Institute Press, 1969.
The New Architectural Monuments of Baltimore City. Baltimore, Maryland Institute Press, 1970.
The Apocryphal Oracular Yeah-Sayings of Mae West. Baltimore, Maryland Institute Press, 1970.
Strung Out with Elgar on a Hill. Urbana, Illinois, Finial Press, 1971.
Blues and Roots, Rue and Bluets: A Garland for the Appalachians. New York, Grossman, 1971.
The Loco Logodaedalist in Situ: Selected Poems 1968–70. London, Cape Goliard Press, 1971; New York, Grossman, 1972.
Epitaph, with Thomas Meyer. Privately printed, 1972.
Fruits Confits, with Thomas Meyer. Privately printed, 1972.
Pairidaeza. N.p., DBA, 1973.
Adventures with a Twelve-Inch Pianist Beyond the Blue Horizon. N.p., DBA, 1973.
Who Is Little Enis? Highlands, North Carolina, Jargon, 1974.
Five from Up t'Dale. Kendal, Cumbria, Finial Press, 1974.
Hasidic Exclamation on Stevie Smith's Poem "Not Waving But Drowning." Storrs, University of Connecticut Library, 1975.
My Quaker-Atheist Friend. London, Philip Bryden, 1975.
Gists from a Presidential Report on Hardcornponeography. Highlands, North Carolina, Jargon, 1975.
A Wee Tot for Catullus. N.p., Moschatel Press, 1975.
A Celestial Centennial Reverie for Charles Edward Ives. N.p., DBA, 1975.
Imaginary Postcards. London, Trigram Press, 1975.
gAy BC's. Champaign, Illinois, Finial Press, 1976.
In the Field at the Solstice. Champaign, Illinois, Finial Press, 1976.
Untinears and Antennae for Maurice Ravel. St. Paul, Truck Press, 1977.
An Omen for Stevie Smith. New Haven, Connecticut, Yale University Sterling Library, 1977.
A Blue Ridge Weather Prophet. Lexington, Kentucky, Gnomon Press, 1977.
Super-Duper Zuppa Inglese. N.p., Aggie Weston's, 1977.
A Hairy Coat near Yanwath Yat. Rocky Mount, North Carolina Wesleyan College, 1978.
Elite/Elate Poems: Poems 1971–1975. Highlands, North Carolina, Jargon, 1979.
Shankum Naggum. Rocky Mount, North Carolina Wesleyan College Friends of the Library, 1979.
The Delian Seasons. N.p., Topia Press, 1979.
St. Swithin's Swivet. N.p., Circle Press, 1979.

Other

Lines about Hills above Lakes. Fort Lauderdale, Florida, Roman, 1964.
Descant on Rawthey's Madrigal: Conversations with Basil Bunting. Lexington, Kentucky, Gnomon Press, 1968.
The Appalachian Photographs of Doris Ulmann. Highlands, North Carolina, Jargon, 1971.
Clarence John Laughlin: The Personal Eye. New York, Aperture, 1973.
The Family Album of Lucybelle Crater. Highlands, North Carolina, Jargon, 1974.
T. Ben Williams. Highlands, North Carolina, Jargon, 1974.
The Sleep of Reason. Highlands, North Carolina, Jargon, 1974.
Hot What? Collages, Texts, Photographs. Dublin, Georgia, Mole Press, 1975.
"I Shall Save One Land Unvisited": Eleven Southern Photographers. Lexington, Kentucky, Gnomon Press, 1978.
Portrait Photographs. Lexington, Kentucky, Gnomon Press, 1979.

Editor, *Edward Dahlberg: A Tribute.* New York, David Lewis, 1970.
Editor, *Epitaphs for Lorine: 33 Poets Celebrate Lorine Niedecker.* Highlands, North Carolina, Jargon, 1973.
Editor, *Madeira and Toasts for Basil Bunting's 75th Birthday.* Highlands, North Carolina, Jargon, 1977.

Manuscript Collection: Jargon Society Archives, University of North Carolina Library, Chapel Hill.

Critical Studies: introduction by Guy Davenport to *An Ear in Bartram's Tree: Selected Poems 1957–67*, 1969; "The Sound of Our Speaking" by Robert Morgan, in *The Nation* (New York), 6 September 1971; Herbert Leibowitz, in *New York Times Book Review*, 21 November 1971; Raymond Gardner, in *The Guardian* (London), 3 July 1972; in *Vort 4* (Silver Spring, Maryland), 1973.

Jonathan Williams comments:

I am primarily a poet, but since we do not live for ourselves alone I have always assumed (since 1951) that the publishing of my poetic enthusiasms was part of the job. And the reading of poems aloud to audiences – which I have done approximately 850 times from Vancouver to Wien.

I have been called a Black Mountain Poet, a Beat Poet, a Southern-Poetry-Today Poet, a Light Poet, an Informalist Poet, a Formalist Poet, a Concrete Poet, a Found-Object Poet, a Relentlessly and Tiresomely Avant-garde Poet. To my knowledge all I am is a poet, like anyone else. I write as I can.

The masters of delectation and precision are my mentors: Blake, Marvell, Buson, Archilochos, Martial, Catullus, Dickinson, Ono no Komachi, Basho, and Whitman. From more immediate times: Pound, William Carlos Williams, Robinson Jeffers, Kenneth Patchen, Kenneth Rexroth, Charles Olson, Ian Hamilton Finlay, Stevie Smith, Basil Bunting, J. V. Cunningham ... I use all the devices I know, all the tricks in Orpheus's black bag – if it is possible to move rocks and trees, it is just possible to keep ice from forming in other human hearts. Poems are passionate things to give courage to those who respond to their messages. I write for those who long for the saving grace of the language. I never write for Laodiceans. The gentle reader and I are going to go round and round. Richard of St. Victor teaches us that in art and in life there are more things to love than we could possibly have imagined. *Odi et amo*, said Catullus. I want Catullus in the poems, and Willie Mays and Thomas Jefferson and Charles Ives and Apollo and hill farmers and people who talk trash. The language is airy, earthy, Regency, witty, offensive, etc. – whatever it needs to be. This is your friendly Local, Ecological Logodaedalist talking.

* * *

Jonathan Williams has been an important force in poetry since the early 1950's, when he studied at Black Mountain College and founded The Jargon Society, whose publishing record is remarkable: Williams has always ignored fashion and thus Jargon may fairly claim many important "discoveries" – in the form of first books by poets who only later became attractive to the anthologists and commercial publishers.

Williams's own poetry has remained just as idiosyncratic as his publishing tastes, and by ignoring fashion he has created a body of work uniquely his own, dedicated he says to "those who long for the saving grace of the language." One fine description of his poetry comes from Guy Davenport: "Its weightlessness is that of thistledown and like the thistle it bites." He is commonly known as a "light" poet; such a description acknowledges his wit, but ignores the power his poems often carry. He is "light" also in the sense that his poems are only rarely personal, and to my knowledge never "confessional." Williams writes of what he sees and hears, and if his descriptions fail to convey his actual feelings, the body of his work suggests a man of impeccable tastes, deep intellect, and occasional, profound disgust for the homogenization of his country-folk and the Twentieth Century deathlock bureaucracy holds on poetry.

For Williams is the true ecologist, not only in his love for nature, but in his concern for saving the words of a people whose language is undergoing severe mutation. Thanks to television we live in an era when a phrase like "No way," invented on Madison Avenue before Christmas, can be in every home by New Year. Williams detests the cultural death of his country, and when he's not keeping his distance in Yorkshire, he wanders the Appalachian trail, listening and writing down what's left to save of originality. And he visits wherever an audience assembles to hear what he has written, called by Buckminster Fuller, "our Johnny Appleseed."

A major "form" for Williams is the "found poem." Poems like this, usually direct quotes, require good memory or the willingness to produce a pencil at unseemly moments:

I figured
anything anybody
could do a lot of I
could do a little
of

mebby

The title of Williams's selected poems, *An Ear in Bartram's Tree*, suggests his principal technique – to listen and to watch and then to record as objectively as possible what he's observed. The confinement of an ear in that tree hints also that the poet isn't in a position to act on what he hears, except to write it down. But there are exceptions, especially in his early poems. "A Little Tumescence" is characteristic of Williams's joy with language, in spite of the greater sorrow it can convey:

this time, I mean it:
twice tonight!

(*omne animal*, always
The Hope

triste, triste
situation, such outrageous
limitation,
limp,

simply

Blues and Roots, Rue and Bluets stands out as one of the few volumes of poetry where the "illustrations" and the poetry merge; the photographs by Nicholas Dean augment the silent wisdom of the poet, who holds himself in reserve to favor the words of Uncle Iv and Aunt Creasy, and of Snuffy Smith, who says: "More mouth on/that woman/than ass/on a goose." The world of Jonathan Williams's poetry is the still unprocessed world and the quickly fading language that surrounds us. Recording it's a monumental task. We are lucky to have a poet with the energy and humor necessary for the job.

—Geof Hewitt

WILLIAMS, Miller. American. Born in Hoxie, Arkansas, 8 April 1930. Educated at Arkansas State College, Conway, B.S. in biology 1951; University of Arkansas, Fayetteville, M.S. in zoology 1952. Married 1) Rebecca Kelley; 2) Jordan Hall; three children. Formerly, taught biology at McNeese State College, Lake Charles, Louisiana, and Millsaps College, Jackson, Mississippi; Associate Professor of English, Loyola University, New Orleans, 1966–70; Fulbright Professor of American Studies, National University of Mexico, 1970. Associate Professor, 1971–73, since 1973, Professor of English and since 1978, Chairman of the Comparative Literature Program, University of Arkansas. Visiting Professor, University of Chile, Santiago, 1964. Editor, *New Orleans Review*, 1967–70. President, American Literary Translators Association, 1979–81. Recipient: Henry Bellaman Award, 1957; Bread Loaf Writers Conference Fellowship, 1961; Amy Lowell Traveling Scholarship, 1963; Arts Fund Award, 1973; American Academy in Rome Fellowship, 1976. Address: Department of English, University of Arkansas, Fayetteville, Arkansas 72701, U.S.A.

PUBLICATIONS

Verse

A Circle of Stone. Baton Rouge, Louisiana State University Press, 1964.
Recital (bilingual edition). Valparaiso, Chile, Ediciones Océano, 1964.
So Long at the Fair. New York, Dutton, 1968.
The Only World There Is. New York, Dutton, 1971.
Halfway From Hoxie: New and Selected Poems. New York, Dutton, 1973.
Why God Permits Evil: New Poems. Baton Rouge, Louisiana State University Press, 1977.

Other

19 Poetas de Hoy en los EEUU. Valparaiso, Chile, United States Information Agency, 1966.
The Poetry of John Crowe Ransom. New Brunswick, New Jersey, Rutgers University Press, 1972.
Railroad: Trains and Train People, with James A. McPherson. New York, Random House, 1976.

Editor, with John William Corrington, *Southern Writing in the Sixties: Fiction* and *Poetry.* Baton Rouge, Louisiana State University Press, 2 vols., 1966–67.
Editor, *Chile: An Anthology of New Writing.* Kent, Ohio, Kent State University Press, 1968.
Editor, *The Achievement of John Ciardi: A Comprehensive Selection of His Poems with a Critical Introduction.* Chicago, Scott Foresman, 1969.
Editor, *Contemporary Poetry in America.* New York, Random House, 1973.
Editor, with John Ciardi, *How Does a Poem Mean?*, revised edition. Boston, Houghton Mifflin, 1975.

Translator, *Poems and Antipoems*, by Nicanor Parra. New York, New Directions, 1967; London, Cape, 1968.
Translator, *Emergency Poems*, by Nicanor Parra. New York, New Directions, 1972; London, Boyars, 1977.

Manuscript Collection: Special Collections, University of Arkansas Library, Fayetteville.

Critical Study: "About Miller Williams" by James Whitehead, in *Dickinson Review* (North Dakota), Spring 1973.

Miller Williams comments:

I'm not sure that one ought to discuss one's poetry in public; it seems somehow not quite decent, and besides, almost anyone will have a better perspective on a body of poems than the poet. It may mean something if I say that I distrust the Romantic Vision and dislike the Classical. Beyond this, the poems are there to be read, for what they have to say and how they say it.

* * *

Miller Williams knows the meters and forms of traditional poetry and when he discovers that a poem wants to cover a strict line, he lets it.

Then sometimes he moves as a graceful trooper through the mine fields of free verse. He has a marvelous ear and an easy hand with natural metaphor. He writes inside a sophisticated Southern idiom that can pick and choose as the spirit and flesh of his experience decide.

More often than not his poems are a gathering of strategies. On the page there seems to be a casual typography, but after a careful reading we understand the balance between common diction and complicated rhetoric.

Williams is a trained biologist, an ex-stockcar driver, and a cormorant reader of liberal and socialist literature. He is a basically optimistic man who suspects the changes and weathers of our lives include devils and probably a congregation of strange gods.

Williams has written for Judas and about the wife of a Venezuelan revolutionary – he has celebrated open love and plain sex and the glory and torture of old-fashioned families: frogs, hubcaps, metaphysical conceits, Einsteinian physics, and country songs are comfortable together in his books.

Williams's poetry is passionate, understated, regional, and elegant – but it doesn't wink or guffaw or play bored.

Williams is satisfied to be alive and he renders an imagined landscape that is finally a synthesis of romantic reflection and classical order. His waltz is gutbucket and he manages a funky minuet. Finally he is an intellectual, after verse has played the necessary game, and after the body has claimed to enjoy its fine excess. As in these lines from four poems:

Think that when he sees how Christ is killed
he does the only thing he knows to do

*

In New York
taxi drivers know everything
except what I ask them

*

every hope getting out of hand
slings us hopelessly outward one by one
till all that kept us common is undone

*

about the bullfight
which was in Monterrey:
the horns were lobster's claws
the balls were blue
the sword was love in the matador's right hand

Do you understand?

Do you understand?

—James Whitehead

WILLY, Margaret (Elizabeth). British. Born in London, 25 October 1919. Educated at Beckenham County School for Girls; Goldsmiths' College, University of London (W. H. Hudson Memorial Prize, 1938; Gilchrist Medal, 1940), Diploma in English literature 1940. Served in the Women's Land Army, 1942–46. Publishers' Copywriter, 1936–42. Lecturer, Goldsmiths' College, University of London, 1959–75, and St. Marylebone Literary Institute, London, 1966–72. Lecturer, since 1950, British Council, since 1956, City Literary Institute, and since 1973, Morley College. Editor, *English*, London, 1954–75. Recipient: Rockefeller-Atlantic Award, 1946. Fellow, Royal Society of Literature. Address: 1 Brockmere, 43 Wray Park Road, Reigate, Surrey, England.

PUBLICATIONS

Verse

The Invisible Sun. London, Chaterson, 1946.
Every Star a Tongue. London, Heinemann, 1951.

Other

Life Was Their Cry (biographical studies of Chaucer, Traherne, Fielding and Browning). London, Evans, 1950.
The South Hams. London, Hale, 1955.
Three Metaphysical Poets: Richard Crashaw, Henry Vaughan, Thomas Traherne. London, Longman, 1961; in *British Writers and Their Works 4*, Lincoln, University of Nebraska Press, 1964.
English Diarists: Evelyn and Pepys. London, Longman, 1963.
Three Women Diarists: Celia Fiennes, Dorothy Wordsworth, Katherine Mansfield. London, Longman, 1964.
A Critical Commentary on Emily Brontë's "Wuthering Heights." London, Macmillan, 1966.
A Critical Commentary on Browning's "Men and Women." London, Macmillan, 1968.

Editor, *Two Plays of Goldsmith.* London, Arnold, 1962.
Editor, *Poems of Today: Fifth Series.* London, Macmillan, 1963.
Editor, *The Metaphysical Poets.* London, Arnold, 1971.

Margaret Willy comments:

Although my poems have often had a country background (perhaps partly because of my having worked on the land during the war and lived since in the country, which I love in all its moods, seasons and weathers), they are seldom mere descriptive or atmospheric pieces or "straight" portraits of place. Natural background, imagery and analogies are usually employed to communicate some of my main themes. These include the creative processes of the poet and various aspects of his striving to shape experience into words and trap what is transitory into an illusion of permanence; love and war; problems of human identity and alienation, the enigma – and adventure – of death; and the struggles, paradoxes and rewards of religious experience.

In connection with the last, the particular period in English poetry which most interests and which I suppose could be said to have influenced me, is that of the seventeenth-century metaphysical and mystical poets – Donne, Herbert, Vaughan and Traherne. The poetry and personality of Emily Brontë and *Wuthering Heights* have also made a deep and lasting impact. She is the subject of several of my poems about writers (others include Chaucer, Traherne, Dorothy Wordsworth and Lilian Bowes Lyon). The personalities of living people, too, fascinate me; and some whose experience I have tried to explore in my poetry are those of a young countryman, an old farm labourer, a cathedral verger, a singer, children, a mother and a dying elderly lady.

My verse-forms are on the whole traditional, but I have attempted to use as great a variety of rhythm and verse-pattern as possible.

* * *

Better known as a critic and editor of *English*, Margaret Willy would think of herself primarily as a poet, and indeed it is her poetic perception that has enabled her to penetrate to the heart of her subjects when she has chosen to write about the work of Chaucer, Traherne, and Emily Brontë. That she has published only two volumes of poetry would suggest that the responsibilities of editing have tended to crowd out the poetry. Nevertheless, she is a poet of considerable talent and, despite the quality of her critical work, it is to be regretted that she has written little poetry since the publication of her *Every Star a Tongue*.

She has a wide range of subject material – from personal relationships, sketches and portraits of people living and dead, to aspects of the changing seasons in the country, religion, art, philosophy, and death – and has varied her tone and structure to the needs of her subjects. One notices how often she thinks of dying as returning to the embraces of a lover – "Close in her arms, to lie with her for ever"; "Lay down to join his old, first love, the earth"; "tugged back earth's lover, reluctant to let him go" – but only so far as countrymen are concerned. She has written many poems on religious themes ("Annunciation" and "Mary's Carol" are among her best), but her conception of religious experience goes far beyond the conventional applications. We are provided with a clue to her beliefs in the poem on Thomas Traherne – "It showed him God in water, bird and tree" – and another in "The Old Poet" – "... he peers as though to see/Truth in a petal." The poems in which she expresses her love of natural beauty are those in which her faith is most fittingly communicated.

Because she has been so absorbed in her critical studies, her poems on Chaucer, Traherne, Emily Brontë and Dorothy Wordsworth are as much derived from experience as those concerned with personal relationships which, incidentally, are bound up with her reactions to nature. There is, in fact, a constant interface between her subjects: her "nature" poems turn out to be analogies with art and poetry; her travel poems become portraits, and her portraits reflective poems; and poems such as "Tiger at the Zoo" and "Fairground Music" can be interpreted on several levels. It is difficult, therefore, to divide her work into neat categories and perhaps we ought not to attempt it, simply allowing the total complexity and richness of experience to overlap and interact. Certainly Margaret Willy's poetry has never been given the close attention it deserves.

—Howard Sergeant

WILSON, Keith. American. Born in Clovis, New Mexico, 26 December 1927. Educated at the United States Naval Academy, Annapolis, Maryland, B.A. 1950; University of New Mexico, Albuquerque, M.A. 1956. Served as a Lieutenant in the United States Navy during the Korean War. Married Heloise Wilson in 1958; five children. Instructor, University of Nevada, Reno, 1956–57; Technical Writer, Sandia Corporation, Albuquerque, 1958–60; Instructor, University of Arizona, Tucson, 1960–65. Since 1965, Professor of English and Poet-in-Residence, New Mexico State University, Las Cruces. Fulbright Professor,

University of Cluj, Romania, 1974–75. Recipient: University of New Mexico D. H. Lawrence Fellowship, 1972; P.E.N. American Center grant, 1972; Westhafer Award, 1972; National Endowment for the Arts grant, 1974. Address: 1500 Locust, Las Cruces, New Mexico 88001, U.S.A.

PUBLICATIONS

Verse

Sketches for a New Mexico Hill Town. Concord, Massachusetts, Wine Press, 1966.
The Old Car and Other Blackpoems. Sacramento, California, Grande Ronde Press, 1968.
II Sequences. Portland, Oregon, Wine Press, 1968.
Graves Registry and Other Poems. New York, Grove Press, 1969.
The Shadow of Our Bones. Portland, Oregon, Trask House Press, 1969.
Psalms for Various Voices. Las Cruces, New Mexico, Tolar Creek Syndicate, 1969.
Homestead. San Francisco, Kayak, 1970.
The Old Man and Others: Some Faces for America. Las Cruces, New Mexico State University Press, 1970.
Rocks. Oshkosh, Wisconsin, Road Runner Press, 1971.
MidWatch: Graves Registry Part IV and V. Fremont, Michigan, Sumac Press, 1972.
Song of Thantog. New York, Athanor, 1972.
Thantog: Songs of a Jaguar Priest. Dennis, Massachusetts, Salt-Works Press, 1978.
While Dancing Feet Shatter the Earth. Logan, Utah State University Press, 1978.
The Streets of San Miguel. Tucson, Arizona, Maguey Press, 1978.
Desert Cenote. Fort Kent, Maine, Great Raven Press, 1978.
The Shaman Deer. Dennis, Massachusetts, Salt-Works Press, 1978.

Critical Studies: by William Winthrop, in *New Mexican* (Santa Fe), 25 August 1968; in *San Marcos Review* (Albuquerque), February 1978.

Keith Wilson comments:

I hold with (or to) a number of concepts of the New American Poetry.

Three major areas of concern: (1) New Mexico Southwest, (2) the Sea, (3) Emotional Georgraphy. I often use methods derived, in part at least, from Charles Olson's Projective Verse – he, Robert Duncan and Robert Creeley have been large influences on me, as have both William Carlos Williams and – from childhood – Robert Burns.

* * *

Keith Wilson's poetry is informed by a strong sense of history: both the sometimes violent history before his time in his own Southwest, and his own personal experience with violence as a naval officer during the Korean War. A collection central to the first of these preoccupations, tracing both his personal and historical awareness of the Southwest, is his fine book, *Homestead; Graves Registry* traces the Korean War experience, and *MidWatch* (or *Graves Registry*, Parts IV and V) extends his meditations on his war experience and man's attraction to violence through the Vietnam War. These poems face up to the most unpleasant aspects of human existence, and contain powerful images: fountains of flesh rising from bombings, faces blown away by a single bullet, a man who shoots a pregnant sow and feasts on her piglets. Wilson's poetry gains additional force from his willingness to strive toward an affirmation, and, beyond this, a way toward some better life, in the face of the horrendous evidence of past human history. As he says toward the end of *MidWatch*:

Ghosts walk, here in the memory
I have lived a thousand lives or more,
so have you, and you, and you, but our brains
are recent ones, we live in the ruins of castles
and forget we built them.

It is this sense of our own complicity, whether through repetition or reincarnation, in past history, that makes his preoccupation with his own ancestral past and New Mexico's roots in the past valuable; it is not merely nostalgia, but rather a desire to learn from the past how to avoid bumping into it again in the future, how to let the new brain rise from the ruins of the old: "It was the purpose of these poems to show/the glories of war, sadnesses of peace./ Replace them both."

These poems are ultimately heartening; Wilson brings a compassion rather than self righteous anger to human follies, a forgiveness that may help us to forgive ourselves. Perhaps even violence is better than nothingness, he reminds us in "Sidewinder," than not being able to relate to one another at all:

I let him pass,
bearing him no enmity – how
quickly he is gone. We'll never
be friends and he can't eat
me. We're no use to each other.

—Duane Ackerson

WINGFIELD, Sheila (Claude). British. Born in Hampshire, 23 May 1906. Educated at Roedean School, Brighton, Sussex. Married the Honourable M. Wingfield, later Viscount Powerscourt, in 1932 (died, 1973); one daughter and two sons. Lives in Switzerland. Address: c/o Barclays Bank Ltd., 8 West Halkin Street, London S.W.1, England.

PUBLICATIONS

Verse

Poems. London, Cresset Press, 1938.
Beat Drum, Beat Heart. London, Cresset Press, 1946.
A Cloud Across the Sun. London, Cresset Press, 1949.
A Kite's Dinner. London, Cresset Press, 1954.
The Leaves Darken. London, Weidenfeld and Nicolson, 1964.
Her Storms: Selected Poems 1938–1977. Dublin, Dolmen Press, and London, Calder, 1977.
Admissions: Poems 1974–1977. Dublin, Dolmen Press, and London, Calder, 1977.

Other

Real People (autobiography). London, Cresset Press, 1952.
Sun Too Fast (as Sheila Powerscourt). London, Bles, 1974.

Critical Studies: by Monk Gibbon, in *Poetry Review* (London), 1949; preface by G. S. Fraser to *Her Storms*, 1977.

Sheila Wingfield comments:

(1970) My determination to be a poet was formed in the nursery. But my passion for poetry was an affair that had to be conducted in a hole-and-corner way. In youth, parental disapproval forced the study of literature to be a hidden occupation; later a marital ban on meeting literary personalities was even stronger. Also, private and public commitments swallowed up most of my time. So it was impossible for me to get to know other practitioners of my generation or younger writers. Hence my unhappy ignorance about what was being done or hatched by contemporaries; I read them, but usually long after various "movements" had been established.

Though it grieved me to miss what I thought of as vital and fertilising contacts, this privacy may have been good for my work. In such an intellectual vacuum, I had to be myself.

Technically, I have tried to give each poem its own form, smell, rhythm and logic. And to employ as large a vocabulary as possible. Also to use the impact of consonants to gain certain effects.

As for subject-matter – the Irish and English countryside and country ways in general are so deeply rooted in me that I fancy much of this blows through my work. History, archaeology, folklore and the superb economy of the classical Greeks are other influences. These tendencies came together in forming my poetic outlook. This can be stated simply. What is personally felt must be fused with what is being, and has been, felt by *Others*. But always in terms of the factual. Nothing woolly or disembodied will do. The same goes for events (which are in fact emotions suffered throughout history and in many lands). Personal dislike for amorphous description is shown by the 2,000-line poem, *Beat Drum, Beat Heart*, which compares men at war with women in love, and men at peace with women out of love, and is in fact a lengthy psychological-philosophical piece without one philosophical expression and I fancy hardly an abstract noun in it. It attempts to sweep over whole cultures and peoples and histories – but invariably in terms of known or perhaps only suspected feelings, expressed in a way that makes such feelings recognisable by a great variety of human beings.

* * *

Sheila Wingfield's first book, *Poems*, contained work that was praised by Yeats and Walter de la Mare, and her later collections *A Cloud Across the Sun, A Kite's Dinner*, and *The Leaves Darken* have all had their admirers. Yet her verse as a whole remains little known, and she is hardly ever represented in anthologies. This seems unfair, since despite some faults of poetic diction ("No longer, Muse, no longer shall I wait"), her poems are technically well-accomplished and sometimes memorable. The sections "Women in Love" and "Women at Peace" from her long poem *Beat Drum, Beat Heart* contain what is perhaps the best of her work, and it is observable that in them she writes rather more personally than is her usual custom, with a result that the rhythms are more natural and various. Elizabeth Jennings has drawn attention to her other virtues: "At her best she has a sense of the heraldic, the emblematic which can produce glittering lines. One should not forget either Miss Wingfield's detailed observation of natural objects. She never goes wrong when she writes about the countryside or about animals."

—Robert Nye

WITHEFORD, Hubert. New Zealander. Born in Wellington, 18 March 1921. Educated at Wellesley College, Wellington; Victoria University, Wellington, M.A. in history. Married to Noel Brooke; one son. Staff Member, New Zealand Prime Minister's Office, 1939–45, and New Zealand War History Branch, 1945–53. Staff Member, 1954–67, Head of Overseas Section, 1968–78, and since 1978, Director, Reference Division, Central Office of Information, London. Recipient: Jessie Mackay Prize, 1963. Address: 88 Roxborough Road, Harrow, Middlesex, England.

PUBLICATIONS

Verse

Shadow of the Flame: Poems 1942–47. Auckland, Pelorus Press, 1949.
The Falcon Mask. Christchurch, Pegasus Press, 1951.
The Lightning Makes a Difference. Auckland, Paul's Book Arcade, and London, Brookside Press, 1962.
A Native, Perhaps Beautiful. Christchurch, Caxton Press, 1967.

Critical Study: by C. K. Stead, in *Landfall* (Christchurch), December 1968.

Hubert Witheford quotes from his introductory note to *A Native, Perhaps Beautiful:*

Many of the poems spring from sombre emotions. So far as I am concerned, other emotions yield themselves less readily to poetry, that is to transformation, that is to surprise. The great white whale who breaks the surface of my customary stupidities rises from a very dark place.

* * *

Hubert Witheford has carved a small niche for himself in New Zealand poetry not so much by the often too amorphous content of his poetry as by what a critic called his "singular precision in his continual whittling of language." Where he begins with something to say, an "idea," it seems, he tends to fail: such a poem as "Elegy in Orongoringo Valley," though gracefully written, seems too manufactured – as in its final stanza:

Here and in exile and in lost anguish
He found no frenzy to win him this wanton –
In his full failure glistens the wild bush
Too long remembered, too long forgotten.

This rather slack and artificial use of language contrasts strongly with such lines as:

Each year my heart becomes more dry.

Through nerveless fingers life like me
In slow storm runs to the ground;
Not distance nor insentience provides
Cuirass against that mild fatality.

This is both subtle and precise, and the irony of "mild" is nicely and honestly placed. Witheford, however, is on the whole at his best in freer forms, where his rhythms are more confident and he does not feel obliged to be "poetical" in order to fit himself into a preconceived mould. Thus "Barbarossa" is one of his most adventurous and original poems, in which he uses rhyme as and when he wishes, and to good effect:

... I sit down
A stop to stories of the deaths of kings.
I watch the telegraph
Poles. A great hand plucks the strings.

—Martin Seymour-Smith

WONG MAY. Chinese (Singapore citizen). Born in Chungking, 16 November 1944. Educated at the University of Singapore, B.A. in English literature 1965; University of Iowa, Iowa City (Writers Workshop Fellow, 1966–67), M.F.A. 1968. Married Michael Coey in 1973. Assistant Editor, United Business Publications, New York, 1968–69. Recipient: D.A.A.D. Fellowship, Berlin, 1972. Address: c/o Harcourt Brace Jovanovich Inc., 757 Fifth Avenue, New York, New York 10017, U.S.A.

PUBLICATIONS

Verse

A Bad Girl's Book of Animals. New York, Harcourt Brace, 1969.
Reports. New York, Harcourt Brace, 1972.
Wannsee Poems. Berlin, Literarisches Colloquim, 1974.
Superstitions: Poems 1971–1976. New York, Harcourt Brace, 1978.

Other

Translator, with H. C. Buch, *Der Einsturz der Lei-feng Pagoda*, by Lu Hsun. Hamburg, Rowohlt, 1973.

* * *

Wong May's poems are enticed out of single moments. She possesses a point of view, a comprehensive intelligence, and it is these rather than specific themes which engender the poetry. *A Bad Girl's Book of Animals* reveals a personality distinctive in its combination of whimsicality, adultness ("maturity" would be too pedestrian and misleading), innocence, charm, and sharp, ironic sympathy. As we can expect, her perceptions are unusual, though completely acceptable, proving their quality and reach in the life they uncover, the new focus they bring to well-tried subjects. In "Summer Guide," for instance, the encounter between two people generates a mistrust of body and mind, a conflict between the desire to be loved and a feeling of distaste at the prospect:

I distrust, mistrust you equally:
The whole field of sun-
flowers charged, choked,
can't stand themselves
their earth electrified

their sky steers away rapid
west-west-wise. You distrust
mistrust yourselves equally.

The uncertainty is made specific. Deceptively simple language is supported by shrewd organization. By repeating or splitting them, by varying their contexts, she characteristically exploits the associative powers of words, their delicate yet hard-hitting meanings: "I wish pain were/a thing like a tooth-/ache, sharpened/Into a point" ("The Man Who Dies"). Lines are left open to form subsequent affinities, to allow development by expansion, or contrast or a shift in the direction of thought. It is a technique she employs extensively, especially in the first few poems of her collection. But craftsmanship has its temptations. At times the technical performance is overdone, as in "Without Qualms" and "Small Thing." The poems become mannered, seem to lack point and fail to rise above dexterous verbal manipulation which is there, one suspects, dutifully compensating for the feeble material.

A certain charm, an ability to express surprise, and a more open, less contrived power available in poems written before she left for the U.S.A. appear to have been refined out of her poetry. And they are an altogether regrettable loss.

But despite these reservations, her poetry is of considerable interest and includes some of the best poems written in Malaya or Singapore.

—Edwin Thumboo

WONG PHUI NAM. Malaysian. Born in Kuala Lumpur, 20 September 1935. Educated at the University of Singapore, B.A. Currently, Economist, Malaysian Industrial Development Finance Berhad, Kuala Lumpur. Address: Malaysian Industrial Development Finance Berhad, 117 Jalan Ampang, Kuala Lumpur, Selanger, Malaysia.

PUBLICATIONS

Verse

How the Hills Are Distant. Kuala Lumpur, Tenggara, 1968.

* * *

All of Wong Phui Nam's poetry deals with preparations for a kind of self-renewal. They take place in a luminous world just behind the senses, only tenuously related to the common processes of thought. Here a private drama is prosecuted with stoic fatality in anticipation of an expected disaster – or is it an epiphany?

The flares strung out to the jetty's end
burn for your death, burn for a sick consciousness,
the wharves where the debris of old crates and wagons
smoulders with its hurt, for the great ship
crawling out across the water, towards the islands,
towards the sky, as you leave these tides to beat upon
estuaries new to this gathering dark.

The effort to make out whether the hoped-for conclusion is to be regarded as disaster or epiphany generates the tension in his work; it is the source of his concern to achieve an exactness in the presentation of "a private landscape" which has public significance.

Wong's poetry develops a visual intensity in explicating emotion in concrete metaphors.

Especially in *How the Hills Are Distant* one cannot escape the impression of watching a skilfully edited film. A camera-eye picks out objects and scenes in a strange, almost unpeopled landscape, while gradually it is the observer's loneliness, his quiet terror, which impresses more than the things observed:

> About the empty market square
> we do not gather like agitated elders
> in expectation of a runner in with the news,
> the invaders held by the few at a narrow mountain pass,
> bearers of good news being no more of the fashion.
> You who would look for signs, or starve
> among a wilderness, of stone, there are only the boulders
> drowning in pits of worked out mining leases.
> From the main street of the town,
> see how the hills are distant, locked in their silences.

In Wong's more recent poems there is a decisive effort to people his desolate landscapes. As he has said, he wrote of people who "find themselves having to live by institutions and folkways which are not of their heritage, having to absorb the manners of languages not their own." In "Remembering Grandma" (*Tenggara*, April 1968) objectivity of tone combines with allusive utterance in the portrayal of a Chinese grandmother contemplating her unlikely progeny: "Baba [i.e. of mixed Chinese-Malay parentage] children/animal and tartar,/ breaking out in a strange babble of tongues." Wong puts to original use in his poetry the cultural minutiae which have made us in Malaysia/Singapore the polyglot community we are today. He achieves a precision of image while evoking an intangible air of decay and confusing change. The father portrayed in the concluding stanza of his poem is wholly defined by his Baby Austin 7, his Pitman manuals, his copy of *Robinson Crusoe*, and, last but not least, his marriage to his wife's 14-year-old niece. When taken together, these details function also as an ironic portrait of a man culturally adrift.

What Wong is doing in Asian poetry in English is not dissimilar to what Robert Lowell did in America. There are the same rejection of the temptation (to which too many present-day poets have succumbed) to make poetic hay of bourgeois grievances, the same meticulous interest in oblique statement. Like Lowell, Wong holds unyieldingly to personal experience seen in a wide context as the principal factor of a poet's salvation; he is preoccupied with the obscure kinds of violence done to the individual by new societies everywhere.

—Lloyd Fernando

WOODCOCK, George. Canadian. Born in Winnipeg, Manitoba, 8 May 1912. Educated at Morley College, London. Married Ingeborg Linzer in 1949. Lecturer, University of Washington, Seattle, 1954–55; Lecturer, 1956–57, Assistant Professor, 1958–61, and Associate Professor of English, 1961–63, University of British Columbia, Vancouver. Editor, *Now*, London, 1940–47; Editorial Adviser, Porcupine Press, London, 1946–48, and Canadian Broadcasting Corporation *Anthology* programme, 1955–61; Advisory Editor, *Tamarack Review*, Toronto, 1956–60; Contributing Editor, *Arts Magazine*, New York, 1962–64. Since 1954, Contributing Editor, *Dissent*, New York; since 1959, Editor, *Canadian Literature*, Vancouver. Fellow, Royal Geographical Society. Recipient: Guggenheim Fellowship, 1951; Canadian Government Overseas Fellowship, 1957; Canada Council travel grant, 1961, 1963, 1965, 1968, Killam Fellowship, 1970, Molson Prize, 1972, and Senior

Arts Grant, 1974; Governor-General's Award, for non-fiction, 1967; Canadian Centennial Medal, 1967; University of British Columbia Medal, for biography, 1972, 1976. LL.D.: University of Victoria, British Columbia; University of Winnipeg; D.Litt.: Sir George Williams University, Montreal; University of Ottawa; University of British Columbia. Address: 6429 McCleery Street, Vancouver 13, British Columbia, Canada.

PUBLICATIONS

Verse

The White Island. London, Fortune Press, 1940.
The Centre Cannot Hold. London, Routledge, 1943.
Imagine the South. Pasadena, California, Untide Press, 1947.
Selected Poems. Toronto, Clarke Irwin, 1967.
Notes on Visitations: Poems 1936–1975. Toronto, Anansi, 1975.
Anima; or, Swann Grown Old: A Cycle of Poems. Coatsworth, Ontario, Black Moss Press, 1977.
The Kestrel and Other Poems of Past and Present. Sunderland, Ceolfrith Press, 1978.

Plays

Maskerman (broadcast, 1960). Published in *Prism* (Vancouver), Winter 1961.
General Dumont and the Northwest Rebellion. Toronto, Playwrights Co-op, 1976.
Two Plays. Vancouver, Talonbooks, 1977.

Radio Plays: *Maskerman*, 1960; *The Island of Demons*, 1962; *The Benefactor*, 1963; *The Empire of Shadows*, 1964; *The Floor of the Night*, 1965; *The Brideship*, music by Robert Turner, 1967.

Other

New Life to the Land: Anarchist Proposals for Agriculture. London, Freedom Press, 1942.
Railways and Society. London, Freedom Press, 1943.
Anarchy or Chaos. London, Freedom Press, 1944.
William Godwin: A Biographical Study. London, Porcupine Press, and New York, Irving Ravin, 1946.
The Basis of Communal Living. London, Freedom Press, 1947.
The Incomparable Aphra. London, Boardman, 1948.
The Writer and Politics. London, Porcupine Press, 1948.
The Paradox of Oscar Wilde. London, Boardman, 1949; New York, Macmillan, 1950.
British Poetry Today (lecture). Vancouver, University of British Columbia, 1950.
The Anarchist Prince: A Biographical Study of Peter Kropotkin, with Ivan Avakumovic. London, Boardman, 1950.
Ravens and Prophets: An Account of Journeys in British Columbia, Alberta and Southern Alaska. London, Wingate, 1952.
Pierre-Joseph Proudhon: A Biography. New York, Macmillan, and London, Routledge, 1956.
To the City of the Dead: An Account of Travels in Mexico. London, Faber, 1957.
Incas and Other Men: Travels in the Andes. London, Faber, 1959.

Anarchism: A History of Libertarian Ideas and Movements. Cleveland, Meridian, 1962; London, Penguin, 1963.
Faces of India: A Travel Narrative. London, Faber, 1964.
Civil Disobedience. Toronto, Canadian Broadcasting Corporation, 1966.
The Greeks in India. London, Faber, 1966.
Asia, Gods and Cities: Aden to Tokyo. London, Faber, 1966.
The Crystal Spirit: A Study of George Orwell. Boston, Little Brown, 1966; London, Cape, 1967.
Kerala: A Portrait of the Malabar Coast. London, Faber, 1967.
The Doukhobors, with Ivan Avakumovic. Toronto and New York, Oxford University Press, and London, Faber, 1968.
The Trade Union Movement and the Government: A Lecture. Leicester, Leicester University Press, 1968.
The British in the Far East. London, Weidenfeld and Nicolson, and New York, Atheneum, 1969.
Hugh MacLennan. Toronto, Copp Clark, 1969.
Henry Walter Bates: Naturalist of the Amazons. London, Faber, and New York, Barnes and Noble, 1969.
Odysseus Ever Returning: Essays on Canadian Writers and Writing. Toronto, McClelland and Stewart, 1970.
The Hudson's Bay Company. New York, Crowell Collier, 1970.
Canada and the Canadians. London, Faber, and Harrisburg, Pennsylvania, Stackpole Books, 1970; revised edition, Faber, 1973.
Mordecai Richler. Toronto, McClelland and Stewart, 1970.
Into Tibet: The Early British Explorers. London, Faber, and New York, Barnes and Noble, 1971.
Mohandas Gandhi. New York, Viking Press, 1971; as *Gandhi*, London, Fontana, 1972.
Dawn and the Darkest Hour: A Study of Aldous Huxley. London, Faber, and New York, Viking Press, 1972.
Herbert Read: The Stream and the Source. London, Faber, 1972.
The Rejection of Politics. Toronto, New Press, 1972.
Who Killed the British Empire? London, Cape, and New York, Quadrangle, 1974.
Amor de Cosmos, Journalist and Reformer. Toronto, Oxford University Press, 1975.
Gabriel Dumont: The Métis Chief and His Lost World. Edmonton, Hurtig, 1975.
South Sea Journey. Toronto, Fitzhenry and Whiteside, and London, Faber, 1976.
Canadian Poets 1960–1973: A List. Ottawa, Golden Dog Press, 1976.
Peoples of the Coast: The Indians of the Pacific Northwest. Edmonton, Hurtig, and Bloomington, Indiana University Press, 1977.
Gabriel Dumont (juvenile). Toronto, Fitzhenry and Whiteside, 1978.
Thomas Merton, Monk and Poet: A Critical Study. Vancouver, Douglas and McIntyre, Edinburgh, Canongate, and New York, Farrar Straus, 1978.
Faces from History. Edmonton, Hurtig, 1978.

Editor, *A Hundred Years of Revolution: 1848 and After.* London, Porcupine Press, 1948; New York, Haskell House, 1974.
Editor, *The Letters of Charles Lamb.* London, Grey Walls Press, 1950.
Editor, *A Choice of Critics.* Toronto, Oxford University Press, 1966.
Editor, *Variations on the Human Theme.* Toronto, Ryerson Press, 1966.
Editor, *The Sixties: Canadian Writers and Writing of the Decade.* Vancouver, University of British Columbia Press, 1969.
Editor, *Malcolm Lowry: The Man and His Work.* Vancouver, University of British Columbia Press, 1971.
Editor, *Wyndham Lewis in Canada.* Vancouver, University of British Columbia Press, 1971.

Editor, *Typee: A Peep at Polynesian Life*, by Herman Melville. London, Penguin, 1972.
Editor, *Poets and Critics: Essays from "Canadian Literature," 1966–1974*. Toronto, Oxford University Press, 1974.
Editor, *Colony and Confederation: Early Canadian Poets and Their Background*. Vancouver, University of British Columbia Press, 1974.
Editor, *The Canadian Novel in the Twentieth Century: Essays from "Canadian Literature."* Toronto, McClelland and Stewart, 1975.
Editor, *The Anarchist Reader*. Hassocks, Sussex, Harvester Press, and Atlantic Highlands, New Jersey, Humanities Press, 1977.
Editor, *The Egoist*, by Meredith. London, Penguin, 1978.
Editor, *The Return of the Native*, by Hardy. London, Penguin, 1979.

Critical Studies: *George Woodcock* by Peter Hughes, Toronto, McClelland and Stewart, 1974; *From Here to There: A Guide to Canadian Literature since 1960* by Frank Davey, Erin, Ontario, Press Porcépic, 1974; *A Political Art: Essays and Images in Honour of George Woodcock* edited by W. H. New, Vancouver, University of British Columbia Press, 1978.

George Woodcock comments:

In the 1960's I was more concerned with dramatic verse than other types of poetry. Recently I have returned to lyric poetry.

I think that, whatever he may spout about his verse, almost every poet has long lost sight of everything except the work as it stands and is not even the best man to talk about its more multiple meanings. I have often found that readers have found true things in my poems of which I have been at first unaware.

* * *

George Woodcock's history as a poet resembles that of several other writers in his age group. The poems he wrote just before and during the Second World War were based on a belief that revolutionary changes would take place in society. In his period Woodcock was associated with the Anarchist movement, and edited the influential radical literary magazine *Now* for some years after the War, before leaving England for Canada. In recent years he has written a valuable history of anarchism and a study of George Orwell, as well as several travel books.

Judged as a poet simply, he is very much a man of the thirties in the sense that his poetic style and social attitude could hardly have been nurtured in any other time. His best poems fall into two groups. The first, and more powerfully imaginative, deal with an invented scene or story in fabulous yet realistic terms. "The Island," rightly familiar from anthologies, is the finest of his poems of this kind. A group of men come to an island, and capture and torture an inhabitant in the attempt to make him tell some secret about hidden gold. Under the torture his joints burst, fire jets from the ruptures:

> There lay before us on the rigid rack
> Straw limbs and a horse's polished skull.
> Gulls mocked as walked away across the sea
> The man we hunted but could not keep or kill.

It is wrong to look for too precise a meaning in such poems. Their deliberate ambiguity increases rather than diminishes the effect of the vivid images and the direct narrative style.

These fables or parables are timeless. Woodcock's other characteristic kind of poem obtains an effect from its immediacy. He shows us much more clearly than most writers of his generation what it was like to be a particular kind of Left-wing intellectual in the years before and during the War. The titles are revealing: "Waterloo Bridge," "Sunday on Hampstead Heath," "Wartime Evening in Cambridge." The quality of the observation raises these poems above poetic journalism, and their firm anchoring in time and place ("the green Cam slithers beneath me, the yellow girl/Rubs my shoulder") makes their concern for the future more than merely personal. In Woodcock's poetic vision there are only two human possibilities, either the extinction of a generation in war by death and the increasing suppression of freedom, the "daily evils undermining love," or the prospect of some eventual happiness on "a tamarisked and temperate shore" which is actually never reached in his poetry. Individual joy is seen as something lasting only an instant, and perhaps as itself a kind of illusion since one can be happy only by building personal walls against events outside: "And when the events attack, what walls shall stand?" The attitude produced poignant and charming poems, but when the war ended and this social structure remained unchanged except in minor details, Woodcock survived as writer and social commentator, but his poetic vision faded.

—Julian Symons

WOODS, John (Warren). American. Born in Martinsville, Indiana, 12 July 1926. Educated at Indiana University, Bloomington, B.S. 1949, M.A. 1955; University of Iowa, Iowa City. Served in the United States Air Force. Married Emily Newbury in 1951; two sons. Assistant Professor, 1955–60, Associate Professor, 1961–64, and since 1965, Professor of English, Western Michigan University, Kalamazoo. Visiting Professor of English, University of California, Irvine, 1967–68. Recipient: Bread Loaf Writers Conference Robert Frost Fellowship, 1962; Yaddo Fellowship, 1963, 1964; Theodore Roethke Prize (*Poetry Northwest*, Seattle), 1968; National Endowment for the Arts grant, 1969. Address: Department of English, Western Michigan University, Kalamazoo, Michigan 49001, U.S.A.

PUBLICATIONS

Verse

The Deaths at Paragon, Indiana. Bloomington, Indiana University Press, 1955.
On the Morning of Color. Bloomington, Indiana University Press, 1961.
The Cutting Edge. Bloomington, Indiana University Press, 1966.
Keeping Out of Trouble. Bloomington, Indiana University Press, 1968.
Turning to Look Back: Poems 1955–1970. Bloomington, Indiana University Press, 1972.
The Knees of Widows. Kalamazoo, Michigan, Westigan Review Press, 1972.
Voyages to the Inland Sea II: Essays and Poems, with Felix Pollack and James Hearst, edited by John Judson. La Crosse, University of Wisconsin Center for Contemporary Poetry, 1972.
Alcohol. Grand Rapids, Michigan, Pilot Press, 1973.
A Bone Flicker. La Crosse, Wisconsin, Juniper, 1973.
Striking the Earth. Bloomington, Indiana University Press, 1976.
Thrity Years on the Force. La Crosse, Wisconsin, Juniper, 1978.

Critical Studies: by Richard Hugo, in *Northwest Review* (Eugene, Oregon), 1967; David Etter, in *Chicago Review*, Winter 1972.

John Woods comments:

All that is important about my poetry to the general reader lies in the poetry itself. If, Dear General Reader, we might sit down together over a bottle, we might begin a friendship, an enemyship, a love affair, whatever. Until then, the great, whirling mass of particulars that make up You, and I, can only meet at the interface of my poems.

* * *

John Woods, a master of contemporary idiom, sets his poems in the 20th-century midwest. Through three generations of Indiana farm folk, "between the two wars of father and son," he expresses human hopes and anxieties with an exceptional poetic sense of place and of time. Grandfather's recollection of genealogy is vague, yet certain:

I don't know where we came from.
So many graves stay open too long,
so many girls lie back tonight
trying to be secret rivers in the limestone.

Woods has discovered a language needing no support of learned notes for characters who "think back along their bones." Generations die back into the Indiana corn knowing, instinctively, that Adonis is violently stoned red before regeneration. Wood chooses apt items for his own totem:

I shaped a man, my totem animal,
from branches, murky soil, and pasture dung....
From a bird stoned red beneath an elm,
I took a wing for tongue.

Woods, indeed, takes a wing for tongue. His language is lively, his imagery precise, and his rhythms range from the conversational tempo of the elegiac poems on life before death to a swift tumble of images in his wry, humorous asides on life's perplexities.

Turning to Look Back represents his poetic range amply. His first group, "The Deaths at Paragon," gathers elegiac poems on generation and death. Sophisticated love poems, both lithe and muscular, follow in "In Time of Apples." Poems of social commentary are gathered in "Red Telephones"; and formal lyrics, including a fine sestina, in "Barley Tongues."

Dave Etter, writing in the *Chicago Review* (1972), declares Woods "the best poet writing in America today." Etter is on solid ground.

—Edward Callan

WRIGHT, Charles (P., Jr.) American. Born in Pickwick Dam, Tennessee, 25 August 1935. Educated at Davidson College, North Carolina, 1953–57, B.A. 1957; University of Iowa, Iowa City, 1961–63, M.F.A. 1963; University of Rome (Fulbright Fellow), 1963–65, certificate 1965. Served in the United States Army Intelligence Corps, 1957–61: Captain.

Married Holly McIntire in 1969; one son. Since 1966, Assistant Professor to Professor of English, University of California, Irvine. Fulbright Lecturer, University of Padua, 1968–69; Visiting Lecturer, University of Iowa, 1974–75, Princeton University, New Jersey, 1978, and Columbia University, New York, 1978. Recipient: Eunice Tietjens Award (*Poetry*, Chicago), 1969; National Endowment for the Arts grant, 1974; Guggenheim Fellowship, 1975; Poetry Society of America Melville Cane Award, 1976; Academy of American Poets Edgar Allan Poe Award, 1976; American Academy of Arts and Letters grant, 1977; P.E.N. Translation Prize, 1979. Address: 1771 Thurston Drive, Laguna Beach, California 92651, U.S.A.

PUBLICATIONS

Verse

The Voyage. Iowa City, Patrician Press, 1963.
6 Poems. London, Freed, 1965.
The Dream Animal. Toronto, Anansi, 1968.
Private Madrigals. Madison, Wisconsin, Abraxas Press, 1969.
The Grave of the Right Hand. Middletown, Connecticut, Wesleyan University Press, 1970.
The Venice Notebook. Boston, Barn Dream Press, 1971.
Backwater. Santa Ana, California, Golem Press, 1973.
Hard Freight. Middletown, Connecticut, Wesleyan University Press, 1973.
Bloodlines. Middletown, Connecticut, Wesleyan University Press, 1975.
Colophons. Iowa City, Windhover Press, 1977.
China Trace. Middletown, Connecticut, Wesleyan University Press, 1977.
Wright: A Profile. Iowa City, Grilled Flowers Press, 1979.

Other

Translator, *The Storm and Other Poems*, by Eugenio Montale. Oberlin, Ohio, Field, 1978.

Critical Study: Interview, in *Field 17* (Oberlin, Ohio), Fall 1977.

* * *

Charles Wright has cited Pound and Montale (whose *Bufera e altro* he has recently – and brilliantly – translated) as his chief influences, but the poet who is perhaps his most immediate model is the remarkable German visionary Georg Trakl. Here is the beginning of Trakl's "Abendland": "Mond, als träte ein Totes/Aus blauer Höhle,/Und es fallen der Blüten/Viele über den Felsenpfad" (Moon, as if a dead thing/Stepped out of a blue cave,/ And many blossoms fall/Across the rocky path). Compare the first stanza of Wright's "Clear Night":

> Clear night, thumb-top of a moon, a back-lit sky.
> Moon-fingers lay down their same routine
> On the side deck and the threshold, the white keys and the black keys.
> Bird hush and bird song. A cassia flower falls.

Or this, from "Stone Canyon Nocturne": "The moon, like a dead heart, cold and unstartable, hangs by a thread/At the earth's edge,/Unfaithful at last, splotching the ferns and the pink shrubs." And, in a poem appropriately called "Thinking of Georg Trakl," there is an interesting echo of the "blue cave" of "Abendland": "Lips part in the bleached willows./ Finger by finger, above Orion, God's blue hand unfolds."

Charles Wright's poetry is less feverish, less emotional than Trakl's, but he shares the German poet's ability to shift imperceptibly and with seeming ease from the real to the surreal, from the concrete, observable object to something strange and imaginary. Here is a poem called "California Twilight":

Late evening, July, and no one at home.
In the green lungs of the willow, fly-worms and lightning bugs
Blood-spot the whips and wings. Blue

Asters become electric against the hedge.
What was it I had in mind?
The last whirr of a skateboard dwindles down Oak Street hill.

Slowly a leaf unlocks itself from a branch.
Slowly the furred hands of the dead flutter up from their caves.
A little pinkish flame is snuffed in my mouth.

The poem begins matter-of-factly by establishing the scene, but that scene remains oddly undeveloped and unresolved. It is neither the backdrop for a specific dramatic incident nor the occasion for autobiographical rumination. The concrete precision here is not that of Imagism; rather, the particulars of the poet's experience are filtered through the veil of dream. Thus the poem moves from observable natural phenomena – the branches of the willow, seen at twilight, which remind the poet of "green lungs," and the "Blue/Asters" which "Become electric against the hedge" – to a silence in which the mind invents its own fictions: "Slowly the furred hands of the dead flutter up from their caves." In the wake of this momentary vision of death, "A little pinkish flame is snuffed in my mouth": it is as if the light in the poet's heart is suddenly extinguished. He experiences a sense of deprivation, of diminution – a faint chill. Yet there is nothing personal in his sense of loss; it is simply part of the ongoing process of nature, a ritual to be experienced again and again in the normal course of things.

The tension between normalcy and mystery is reflected in the poem's sound structure: three tercets evenly arranged on the page, whose lines are characterized by densely woven alliteration and assonance. Thus "green lungs of the willow" is phonemically echoed by "lightning bugs" and the *fu* of "furred hands" reappears in "flutter" and then, chiastically, in "snuffed." Wright has said that he always counts syllables and stresses and that "All my lines are extensions of seven-syllable lines, or contradictions." So, in "California Twilight," lines 3 and 5 have seven syllables, whereas the climactic eighth line doubles that length. Against such symmetries, Wright creates complex stress patterns, no two lines quite the same and no predominantly rising or falling rhythm. What look like neat stanza-containers thus have unpredictable configurations.

Such intensely perceptual poetry takes great risks. Sometimes the effect doesn't quite come off. Take the second poem in the "Tattoos" sequence in *Bloodlines:*

The pin oak has found new meat,
The linkworm a bone to pick.
Lolling its head, slicking its blue tongue,
The nightflower blooms on its one stem....

Of this, Wright himself has said with rare candor: "Nightflower is a metaphor. The death flower, and one wishes one had not said it three years later." The self-conscious metaphor, that is to say, is at odds with the sense of wonder the poet wishes to convey. A similar problem is created when a poem is made to yield an abstract formulation as in these pieces from "Skins": "Alone with the owl and the night crawler/Where all is a true turning, and all is growth," or "That milky message of breath on cold mornings –/That what you take in is seldom what you let out."

But in *China Trace*, his recent and, I think, his best book, such moralizing is rare. Rather, these short "Chinese" lyrics embody the mystery of being. Consider the exquisite "Spider Crystal Ascension," in which man is passive while the white spider, drifting "on his web/ through the night sky ... Looks down, waiting for us to ascend." Implausibly, "At dawn, he is still there, invisible, short of breath, mending his net." But how can the "I" know this if the spider is invisible? Because the insect remains at the very edge of consciousness, a nagging presence whose memory can produce a startling metamorphosis: "All morning we look for the white face to rise from the lake like a tiny star./And when it does, we lie back in our watery hair and rock." This is the Rimbaldian "On me pense" – a poetry of muted but intense animism.

—Marjorie Perloff

WRIGHT, David (John Murray). British. Born in Johannesburg, South Africa, 23 February 1920. Educated at St. John's Preparatory School, Johannesburg, 1927; Northampton School for the Deaf, 1934–39; Oriel College, Oxford, 1939–42, B.A. 1942. Married Phillipa Reid in 1951. Staff Member, *Sunday Times*, London, 1942–47; Editor, with Tristram Hull, *Nimbus*, London, 1955–56; Editor, with Patrick Swift, *X* magazine, London, 1959–62. Recipient: Rockefeller-Atlantic Award, 1950; Guinness Award, 1958, 1960; Gregory Fellowship, University of Leeds, 1965–67. Address: c/o A. D. Peters Ltd., 10 Buckingham Street, Adelphi, London WC2N 6BU, England.

PUBLICATIONS

Verse

Poems. London, Editions Poetry London, 1949.
Moral Stories. St. Ives, Cornwall, Latin Press, 1952.
Moral Stories. London, Derek Verschoyle, 1954.
Monologue of a Deaf Man. London, Deutsch, 1958.
Adam at Evening. London, Hodder and Stoughton, 1965.
Poems. Leeds, Leeds University, 1966.
Nerve Ends. London, Hodder and Stoughton, 1969.
Corgi Modern Poets in Focus 1, with others, edited by Dannie Abse. London, Corgi, 1971.
A South African Album. Cape Town, David Philip, 1976.
A View of the North. Ashingdon, Northumberland, MidNAG, 1976.
To the Gods the Shades: New and Collected Poems. Manchester, Carcanet Press, 1976.

Other

Roy Campbell. London, Longman, 1960.
Algarve, with Patrick Swift. London, Barrie and Rockliff, 1965; revised edition, Barrie and Jenkins, 1971.
Minho and North Portugal: A Portrait and a Guide, with Patrick Swift. London, Barrie and Rockliff, 1968.
Deafness: A Personal Account. London, Allen Lane, and New York, Stein and Day, 1969.
Lisbon: A Portrait and a Guide, with Patrick Swift. London, Barrie and Jenkins, 1971.

Editor, with John Heath-Stubbs, *The Forsaken Garden: An Anthology of Poetry 1824–1909*. London, Lehmann, 1950.
Editor, with John Heath-Stubbs, *The Faber Book of Twentieth Century Verse: An Anthology of Verse in Britain 1900–1950*. London, Faber, 1953; revised edition, 1965, 1975.
Editor, *Seven Victorian Poets*. London, Heinemann, 1964; New York, Barnes and Noble, 1966.
Editor, *The Mid-Century: English Poetry 1940–60*. London, Penguin, 1965.
Editor, *Longer Contemporary Poems*. London, Penguin, 1966.
Editor, *The Penguin Book of English Romantic Verse*. London, Penguin, 1968.
Editor, *Recollections of the Lakes and the Lake Poets*, by Thomas De Quincey. London, Penguin, 1970.
Editor, *Records of Shelley, Byron, and the Author*, by Edward Trelawny. London, Penguin, 1973.
Editor, *The Penguin Book of Everyday Verse: Social and Documentary Poetry 1250–1916*. London, Allen Lane, 1976.
Editor, *Under the Greenwood Tree*, by Hardy. London, Penguin, 1979.
Editor, *Selected Poems*, by Hardy. London, Penguin, 1979.

Translator, *Beowulf*. London, Penguin, 1957.
Translator, *The Canterbury Tales*, by Geoffrey Chaucer. London, Barrie and Rockliff, 1964; New York, Random House, 1965.

Manuscript Collections: Arts North, Newcastle upon Tyne; Rhodes University, Grahamstown, South Africa.

Critical Studies: by Dannie Abse, in *Corgi Modern Poets in Focus 1*, 1971; *Guide to Modern World Literature* by Martin Seymour-Smith, London, Wolfe, 1973; Richard Poole, in *Poetry Wales* (Cardiff), Spring 1977; Anthony Delius, in *Aquarius 10* (London), 1978; *The Avoidance of Literature* by C. H. Sisson, Manchester, Carcanet Press, 1978.

David Wright comments:

Love, death, liberty, and what we are all here for,
Whether the date is November twenty-three or doomsday,
Discussions of this kind, they somehow manage to ignore:
Theirs is a message of purest frivolity.

Affirming the unprovable, they have nothing to say
But that the fine point of existence, the instant's span
Between the void before and the void after, is really
Valid (and what is the use of knowing this?). Again,

They do not say anything but by analogy.

* * *

Though numbered among the South African exiles, David Wright seems not so much troubled as interested by his displacement. He says firmly that he was "Born in a dominion to which he hoped not to go back/Since predisposed to imagine white possibly black." But beyond this general acknowledgement, he is not much given to beating the air about the plight of his non-white fellow countrymen. One feels he has had to conserve much of his energy for overcoming his own plight of total deafness, getting through university and leading a very active existence in literary London. Yet a certain ironical recall of his early home produces some of his most attractive poetry. His dry-eyed memories are of "the legless kaffir on the Town Hall pavement," "a European tram bellowing down to Norwood," and "her lion-crouched woods and silver-hatted mountains." His even gaze respects the "last passion" in David Livingstone, the curiosity to find the source of the Nile:

In which prayer dying, David Livingstone
Passed, and those whom he could not save
Carried his bones to Zanzibar and England,
But kept his heart and innards in their proper grave.

And there is the cheerful balance of his portrait of Roy Campbell:

My countryman, the poet, wears a Stetson;
He can count his enemies, but not his friends.
A retired soldier living in Kensington,
Who limps along the Church Street to the Swan.

Indeed it is as a raconteur in verse that David Wright achieves some of his best and most pleasing effects, as in his three "Moral Stories," particularly the tale of the fisherman transformed to a god: "His hair growing green as shallows, his colour/Turned blue as out of soundings, flashing with scales:/Divinity and ocean took him over."

The sea flows through much of David Wright's poetry, for which he himself offers the reason – that he was conceived on a liner "Sliding like a swan on a careless ocean." Liberty, the great requirement of poetry, is as uneasy and uncertain as the sea, and possibly as treacherous. Security is a sort of gaol, "With paper and pen, with a room, and with time to think,/Everything, in fact, unnecessary to the Muse." Ironically he salutes an Emperor Penguin that died in Regents Park: "To die of a desire for freedom and bad weather...."

—Anthony Delius

WRIGHT, James (Arlington). American. Born in Martin's Ferry, Ohio, 13 December 1927. Educated at Kenyon College, Gambier, Ohio, B.A.; University of Washington, Seattle, M.S., Ph.D. Married to Edith Anne Runk; two sons. Has taught at the University of Minnesota, Minneapolis, and Macalaster College, St. Paul, Minnesota. Since 1966, Instructor in English, Hunter College, New York. Recipient: Fulbright Scholarship, 1952; Eunice Tietjens Memorial Prize, 1955, and Oscar Blumenthal Prize, 1968 (*Poetry*, Chicago); Yale Series of Younger Poets award, 1957; National Institute of Arts and Letters grant, 1959; Guggenheim Fellowship, 1964, 1978; Brandeis University Creative Arts Award, 1970; Academy of American Poets Fellowship, 1971; Melville Cane Award, 1972; Pulitzer Prize, 1972. Member, American Academy of Arts and Letters, 1974. Lives in New York City.

PUBLICATIONS

Verse

The Green Wall. New Haven, Connecticut, Yale University Press, 1957.
Saint Judas. Middletown, Connecticut, Wesleyan University Press, 1959.

The Lion's Tail and Eyes: Poems Written Out of Laziness and Silence, with Robert Bly and William Duffy. Madison, Minnesota, Sixties Press, 1962.
The Branch Will Not Break. Middletown, Connecticut, Wesleyan University Press, and London, Longman, 1963.
Shall We Gather at the River. Middletown, Connecticut, Wesleyan University Press, 1968; London, Rapp and Whiting, 1969.
Collected Poems. Middletown, Connecticut, Wesleyan University Press, 1971.
Two Citizens. New York, Farrar Straus, 1974.
Moments of the Italian Summer. Washington, D.C., Dryad Press, 1976.
Old Booksellers and Other Poems. Melbourne, Cotswold Press, 1976.
To a Blossoming Pear Tree. New York, Farrar Straus, 1977; London, Faber, 1979.

Recordings: *Today's Poets 3*, with others, Folkways; *The Poetry and Voice of James Wright*, Caedmon, 1977.

Other

Editor and Translator, *Poems*, by Hesse. New York, Farrar Straus, 1970; London, Cape, 1971.

Translator, with Robert Bly, *Twenty Poems of Georg Trakl*. Madison, Minnesota, Sixties Press, 1961.
Translator, with Robert Bly and John Knoepfle, *Twenty Poems of César Vallejo*. Madison, Minnesota, Sixties Press, 1962.
Translator, *The Rider on the White Horse*, by Theodor Storm. New York, New American Library, 1964.
Translator, with Robert Bly, *Twenty Poems of Pablo Neruda*. Madison, Minnesota, Sixties Press, and London, Rapp and Whiting, 1968.
Translator, with Robert Bly and John Knoepfle, *Neruda and Vallejo: Selected Poems*. Boston, Beacon Press, 1971.
Translator, *Wandering: Notes and Sketches*, by Hesse. New York, Farrar Straus, and London, Cape, 1972.

Critical Study: by Robert Coles, in *American Poetry Review* (Philadelphia), 1974.

James Wright comments:

I have written about the things I am deeply concerned with – crickets outside my window, cold and hungry old men, ghosts in the twilight, horses in a field, a red-haired child in her mother's arms, a feeling of desolation in the fall, some cities I've known.

I try and say how I love my country and how I despise the way it is treated. I try and speak of the beauty and again of the ugliness in the lives of the poor and neglected.

I have changed the way I've written, when it seemed appropriate, and continue to do so.

* * *

James Wright's *Collected Poems* contains most of *The Green Wall*, and all of *Saint Judas*, *The Branch Will Not Break*, and *Shall We Gather at the River*, plus some translations and 33 new poems. This impressive volume, although it covers only 14 years of the poet's career, reveals a genuine experimenter, a poet who can, like Yeats, consciously transform himself. Thus we can speak already of Wright's "phases," discerning three distinct stages of development: the early rich and formal poems of the first two books, the spare and "deep-image" work of *The Branch Will Not Break*, and the loose and pain-filled later poems. For these stages also reveal a strange and tragic curve of emotional development: Wright's concern for human suffering, which was never absent from his earlier work and which seemed to have been temporarily balanced by the bright joy of so much of *The Branch Will Not Break*, now reappears as an obsession without let or hindrance or (often) control in an avalanche of anguish and despair in *Shall We Gather at the River* and "New Poems."

The Green Wall and *Saint Judas* are written largely in regular stanzas and literary language. The first is lush with the Dylan Thomas-like ecstasy of a young poet discovering his medium and his powerful sensibility, and is notable for its hallucinatory sense of the seasons and their montagistic overlappings. In "Eleutheria," for example, after rhapsodically portraying an erotic experience in the glowing country of summer and autumn, he says: "Lovers' location is the first to fade./They wander back in winter, but there is/No comfortable grass to couch a dress." *Saint Judas* is somewhat reminiscent, however, in its more rugged subjects and feelings, of Hardy, Robinson, Masters, and Frost. It deals in a stark and compassionate way with love and loss and death in the lives of a dramatic cast of characters. "At Thomas Hardy's Birthplace, 1953," is indicative, for Hardy "turned aside [from nature] and heard the human wail,/That other sound." Then there is a sequence of love poems treating painfully but movingly the loss and sorrow of a love that is failing. Finally, there is a section concerned with crime and violence, the innocent and the guilty – as, for example, in the Caryl Chessman and George Doty poems, "American Twilights" and "At the Executed Murderer's Grave." Here is more than a merely abstract humanitarianism, for Wright sees that there is no absolute difference between the murderer and the rest of us, that the executioner is only doing coldly what his victim did out of madness or passion or grief.

No longer using conventional diction, regular stanzas, and straightforward structures, *The Branch Will Not Break* is given to open and direct lines, poems of varying length, and easy and natural language. Far surpassing his dogmatic master, Robert Bly, he builds his poems, in haiku fashion, on hard images which are juxtaposed in shocking combinations of experience, leaving the connections and transitions to be inferred by the reader. There is correspondingly a tendency to shift from the external dramatic world inward to the subjective world. "Autumn Begins in Martin's Ferry, Ohio," for example, although still in the objective mode of the preceding volume, implies universes of suppressed violence within as it portrays the erotic frustration of the parents of high-school football players, and concludes: "Therefore,/Their sons grow suicidally beautiful/At the beginning of October,/And gallop terribly against each other's bodies." "Lying on a Hammock at William Dufy's Farm" gives the first 12 of its 13 lines to a literal description, marvelously bright, of a peaceful rural scene, and then concludes abruptly with: "I have wasted my life" – implying that this is the first time he has noticed these things so sharply, and that he has wasted his life up to now in not loafing and inviting his soul.

"Fear Is What Quickens Me," with its compressed and dramatic realization of civilization vs. eros, is another notable poem. As is "Today I Was So Happy, So I Made This Poem," which begins with the usual sharply-etched image – a squirrel seen in moonlight – and ends: "An eagle rejoices in the oak trees of heaven,/Crying/*This is what I wanted.*" Finally, "A Blessing" is one of his best. The speaker and a friend see two loving Indian ponies in a pasture, who respond gently and happily to their advances. The speaker's left hand is being nuzzled by the slenderer one, and he concludes: "Suddenly I realize/That if I stepped out of my body I would break/Into blossom." For sweetness and passion, for precision and surprise, this poem is very nearly perfect and has justly won a place in many anthologies.

The emotional – and sometimes artistic – descent, however, is dizzying as we come to *Shall We Gather at the River* and the "New Poems." For unrelieved wretchedness, these pieces must be unmatched in contemporary poetry and suggest that Wright is returning, after the brief high of *The Branch Will Not Break*, to some old and unresolved fundamental despair. Surely the name itself of this volume suggests the Dead gathering by the Styx, and some of the titles are all-too-indicative of its contents and mood: "In Terror of Hospital Bills," "The Poor Washed Up by Chicago Winter," "Old Age Compensation," "Listening to the Mourners." But it is not until the "New Poems" that we actually touch, in "A Secret Gratitude," what one hopes is the bottom of this agony:

We are men.
It doesn't even satisfy us
To kill one another.
We are a smear of obscenity....
I have no use for the human creature....
I am born one, out of an accidental hump of chemistry.
I have no use.

Such hatred and self-hatred is the polarity, it seems to me, of his compassion for the unfortunate and his probing self-awareness, and the total context of the poem, which is about Edna Millay and Eugen Boissevain, and which does in fact have a rather positive ending, does not really integrate and transform the section from which the above lines were taken. It is not even a Swiftian revulsion from human life; it is, rather, a kind of self-indulgent, noncathartic nausea.

A similar stylistic slackness is found in "Many of Our Waters":

If you do not care one way or the other about
The preceding lines,
Please do not go on listening
On any account of mine.
Please leave the poem.
Thank you.

There is a strange desperation here, a kind of hysteria, which could presage Wright's transition to phase four:

All this time I've been slicking into my own words
The beautiful language of my friends.
I have to use my own, now.
That's why this scattering poem sounds the way it does.

He is ready for another transformation, and he seems bewildered: "The kind of poetry I want to write is/The poetry of a grown man." I do not think, however, that the poetry of a grown man is found by writing poorly and then by acknowledging that one is writing poorly. Irony and self-awareness, even anti-poetry, require more than that.

Two Citizens, *Moments of the Italian Summer* (a series of 14 prose pieces), and *To a Blossoming Pear Tree* (which contains work from *Moments*), however, do indeed represent a new stage. To be sure, there remain a certain looseness, ingenuousness, and that trick of turning back to comment on what he has just written, but gone are the bitterness, hopelessness, and self-indulgence. What we have here, in fact, is a growing sense of complexity concealed within a surface of deceptive simplicity. Resolutely sticking now to his own plain Ohioan speech, as he proclaims, he speaks out openly of his and his wife's travels through France and Italy, of his boyhood in Martin's Ferry, of his love, of nature and her creatures, and yet he does something strange at the same time. One of my favorites, "Well, What Are You Going to Do?," is from *Two Citizens*, and tells of his experience as a boy of assisting their cow give birth to Marian, his calf. At first he feels helpless, not knowing anything "about the problem/Of beautiful women." Finally, at the moment of birth itself, he helps Marian come out, and this is what he says:

I had been in love with a lot of girls, but that was my
first time
To clasp the woman beneath her chin
And whisper, Come out to me,
Come on, come on, you can be Marian.

At the end of the experience, he concludes:

I don't know that I belonged
In that beautiful place. But
What are you going to do? Be kind? Kill?
Die?

The ordinary has been somehow transformed into an erotic hallucination, a wondering apotheosis of universalized excitement.

And he unpretentiously effects such transformations in poem after poem. I could wish away some of the repeated "by Gods," "sweet leaping Jesuses," "son of a bitches," "lifes," "dies," "beautifuls," "loves," "wings," and so on, but these are a small price to pay for such honest and human intensity. When all is said and done, Wright is a genuinely passionate poet who does not withhold or spare himself, and his best work still makes him one of the most interesting and valuable middle-generation poets writing in the United States today.

—Norman Friedman

WRIGHT, Judith. Australian. Born in Armidale, New South Wales, 31 May 1915. Educated at New South Wales Correspondence School; New England Girls School, Armidale; University of Sydney, B.A. Married to J. P. McKinney (died); one daughter. Worked as a secretary, clerk and statistician, 1938–49. Commonwealth Literary Fund Lecturer, Australia, 1949, 1962. Since 1967, Honours Tutor in English, University of Queensland, Brisbane. Member, Australia Council, 1973–74. Recipient: Grace Leven Prize, 1949, 1972; Commonwealth Literary Fund Fellowship, 1964; *Encyclopedia Britannica* Award, 1964; Senior Writers Fellowship, 1977; Fellowship of Australian Writers Robert Frost Memorial Award, 1977. D.Litt.: University of Queensland, 1962; University of New England, Armidale, 1963; Sydney University, 1977; Monash University, Clayton, Victoria, 1977. Address: "Edge," Half Moon Wildlife District, Mongarlowe, New South Wales 2622, Australia.

PUBLICATIONS

Verse

The Moving Image. Melbourne, Meanjin Press, 1946.
Woman to Man. Sydney, Angus and Robertson, 1949.
The Gateway. Sydney, Angus and Robertson, 1953.
The Two Fires. Sydney, Angus and Robertson, 1955.
Birds: Poems. Sydney, Angus and Robertson, 1962.
(*Poems*), selected and introduced by the author. Sydney, Angus and Robertson, 1963.
Five Senses: Selected Poems. Sydney, Angus and Robertson, 1963.
City Sunrise. Brisbane, Shapcott Press, 1964.
The Other Half: Poems. Sydney, Angus and Robertson, 1966.
Poetry from Australia: Pergamon Poets 6, with Randolph Stow and William Hart-Smith, edited by Howard Sergeant. Oxford, Pergamon Press, 1969.
Collected Poems 1942–1970. Sydney, Angus and Robertson, 1971.
Alive: Poems 1971–72. Sydney, Angus and Robertson, 1973.

Fourth Quarter. Sydney and London, Angus and Robertson, 1977.
The Double Tree: Selected Poems 1942–1976. Boston, Houghton Mifflin, 1978.

Recording: *Judith Wright Reads from Her Own Work*, University of Queensland Press, 1973.

Short Stories

The Nature of Love. Melbourne, Sun, 1966.

Other

The Generations of Men. Melbourne, Oxford University Press, 1959.
King of the Dingoes (juvenile). Melbourne, Oxford University Press, and London, Angus and Robertson, 1959.
Range the Mountains High (juvenile). London, Angus and Robertson, 1962.
Shaw Neilson (biography and selected verse). Sydney, Angus and Robertson, 1963.
Charles Harpur. Melbourne, Lansdowne Press, 1963.
The Day the Mountains Played (juvenile). London, Angus and Robertson, 1963.
Country Towns (juvenile). London, Oxford University Press, 1964.
Preoccupations in Australian Poetry. Melbourne and London, Oxford University Press, 1965.
The River and the Road (juvenile). Melbourne, Lansdowne Press, 1966; London, Angus and Robertson, 1967; revised edition, Lansdowne Press, 1971.
Henry Lawson. Melbourne, London, and New York, Oxford University Press, 1967.
Conservation as an Emerging Concept. Sydney, Australian Conservation Foundation, 1971.
Australian Poetry (lecture). Armidale, New South Wales, University of New England, 1975(?).
The Coral Battleground. Melbourne, Nelson, 1977.
Charles Harpur. Melbourne and London, Oxford University Press, 1977.

Editor, *Australian Poetry 1948.* Sydney, Angus and Robertson, 1948.
Editor, *A Book of Australian Verse.* Melbourne and London, Oxford University Press, 1956; revised edition, 1968.
Editor, *New Land, New Language: An Anthology of Australian Verse.* Melbourne and London, Oxford University Press, 1957.
Editor, with A. K. Thomson, *The Poet's Pen.* Brisbane, Jacaranda Press, 1966.
Editor, *Witnesses of Spring: Unpublished Poems*, by Shaw Neilson. Sydney, Angus and Robertson, 1970.

Bibliography: *Judith Wright: A Bibliography*, Adelaide, Libraries Board of South Australia, 1968.

Critical Studies: *Critical Essays on Judith Wright* edited by A. K. Thomson, Brisbane, Jacaranda Press, 1968; *Judith Wright* by A. D. Hope, Melbourne, Oxford University Press, 1975.

Judith Wright comments:

The background of my work lies in my main life concerns, as an Australian whose family on both sides were early comers to a country which was one of the last to be settled by the whites, and were from the beginning farmers and pastoralists. Brought up in a landscape once of extraordinary beauty, but despised by its settlers because of its unfamiliarity, I have I suppose been trying to expiate a deep sense of guilt over what we have done to the country, to its first inhabitants of all kinds, and are still and increasingly doing. This is one aspect of the sources of my work. I have never for long been an urban-dweller, and the images I use and also my methods no doubt reflect my ties to the landscape I live in. I tend to use "traditional" – i.e., biological – rhythms more than free or new forms, which I see as better adapted to urban living and urban tensions and problems.

Another strong influence on my work has been my relationship with my husband whose philosophical investigation of the sources and development of Western thought I shared in till his death. As a woman poet, the biological aspect of feminine experience has naturally been of importance in my work also. I expect my poetry is of a kind which no urban technological society will produce again, but I have tried to remain faithful to my own experience and outlook rather than engage in experimental verse for which it does not fit me.

* * *

"Poetry ought not to be thought of as a discipline, but as a kind of praise.... Poetry is a means of regaining faith in man ... a way of finding a difficult balance: relating inner and outer ... our reality is in relation": these gleanings from Judith Wright's prolific, weighty essays provide a helpful gloss on the total achievement of perhaps the world's, certainly Australia's, greatest living woman poet.

Although traditional in form and predominantly lyrical, Wright's poems are acutely modern in recording an attempt to find peace in a godless world: to find a saving balance between "what I think and what I see," the romantic vision and polluted environment, Platonic certainties and Heraclitean flux, philosophical order and body's pulse. In her essays on the Australian artist, dropped out of Europe into "a pocket of silence and space," Wright records her own primal awareness of an alien, fallen world; her landscape is a waste land of bones, rock, fire, and flood, haunted by the Aborigine and swagman. Wright's solution to this sense of alienation, like that of the Australian poets she admires, is metaphysical (Kendall, Baylebridge, Brennan) or romantic (Harpur, above all Nielson and his "folly of Spring").

The latter impulse Wright expressed most notably in *Woman to Man*, a volume centring on the experience of childbirth ("O move in me, my darling"), and in those poems spread throughout her work and addressed to her philosopher husband or to her daughter. In "The Curtain" Wright watches her returned, grown daughter as she sleeps: "So grown you looked, in the same unaltered room,/so much of your childhood you were already forgetting,/while I remembered." But even in these poems there is the metaphysical distrust of instinctive sentiment; the pregnant woman winces at "The blind head butting at the dark,/ the blaze of light along the blade./Oh hold me, for I am afraid." The virgin in "Naked Girl and Mirror" is really a vessel for the spirit which reluctantly makes peace with the transitory and soon to be corrupted body.

In Wright's other most famous poem, "Bullocky," an Australian workman is given mythic dimension when he is likened to Moses. This is typical of the poet's constant intellectual effort to retrieve her subject – often herself – from the "wheel of life" in order to praise it, believe in it, or simply get into some balanced relationship. The poetic act is often the image for this retrieval, whether in relation to trees ("When the last leaf and bird go/Let my thoughts stand like trees here") or birds ("He met me like a word/I needed – pity? love? – the rainbow-bird"). Her middle period contains an excessive number of poems about poetry, and culminates in the lurid yet strangely compelling vision of the Montreal Poetry Conference, where poets burn ignored in highrise windows, their words falling like "unaccepted holy ghosts."

Wright's central concern is, indeed, language. From her first volume ("Words are rubbed smooth and faceless as old coins"), Wright has laboured with the world's command, "interpret me in god-made words." In lesser poems she capitulates to the rhetorical solution of "love," but her best poetry captures the drama of words struggling to comprehend the world. Although she believes strongly in the poet as social commentator ("No panic, and no heroics,/the market's steady" is the satirical advice to a young poet), the humility in Wright's modification of her early approval of Stevens in "The Unnecessary Angel" – "Sing with one reserve;/Silence might be best" – points to the distinctive quality of her poetry, which A. D. Hope defined as "nobility." There is even nobility in the slightness of her latest volumes, her awareness of her waning powers of balance and the increasing incomprehensibility of the modern world: "I've cultivated stability/by keeping my horizons straight./Now of a sudden we're crossing/very mountainous country."

Wright has warned that a critic must take account of a poet's context, what he was "trying to do" and the "play of feeling" which a poem crystallises. I have suggested that she tries to balance opposites, the unwieldy paradoxes of our existence (look at the dualities in her titles – *Woman to Man*, *The Other Half*, *The Two Fires*, *Fourth Quarter*); her "play of feeling" is the exhilarating sense of momentary achievement. One couplet epitomises these essential aspects of her large and varied oeuvre about the relationship of man to earth:

On her dark breast we spring like points of light
and set her language on the map of night.

—David Dowling

WRIGHT, Kit (Christopher Wright). British. Born in Kent in 1944. Educated at Berkhamsted School, Hertfordshire; New College, Oxford. Taught in a comprehensive school, London; Lecturer in English, Brock University, St. Catharines, Ontario, for 3 years. Education Secretary, Poetry Society, London, 1970–75. Fellow-Commoner in Creative Arts, Trinity College, Cambridge. Address: c/o Salamander Imprint, 3 Cadogan Square, London SW1X 0HT, England.

PUBLICATIONS

Verse

Treble Poets 1, with Stephen Miller and Elizabeth Maslen. London, Chatto and Windus, 1974.
The Bear Looked over the Mountain. London, Salamander, 1977.

Other

Arthur's Father [*Granny, Sister, Uncle*] (juvenile). London, Methuen, 4 vols., 1978.
Rabbiting On and Other Poems (juvenile). London, Fontana, 1978.

Editor, *Soundings: A Selection of Poems for Speaking Aloud.* London, Heinemann, 1975.

* * *

Rumour has it that Kit Wright writes lyrics for musical reviews and the like, and I can well believe it. Many of his poems have that breezily rhythmical, easily rhyming quality which shouts out for a catchy tune. Sometimes he even provides a chorus or two:

She's got
Red boots on, she's got
Red boots on,
Kicking up the winter
Till the winter is gone.

What is certain is that there is more to it than that, and if Kit Wright's rhythms have literary forbears then one must be Auden – the echoes are there: "Coming out of nowhere,/Into nowhere sped,/Blind as time, my darling,/Blind nothing in its head" ("Elizabeth").

What are Kit Wright's own are his wit, his insights into our urban life, and the refreshing contemporaneity of his language which does not eschew transatlantic overtones, while making sure they are the genuine article and not the language that never was of the popular entertainer: "I light the last one from the pack. Outside/An evening of wind and rain drivels and blusters/Against my sidestreet window" ("Last Cigarette in Small Town Ontario"). Add to all this Kit Wright's sense of fun and you get sudden glimpses of a world which, however bizarre, is never far from the world we know. Sometimes brittlely bright as in "Humpty's Fatalism": "I was a tough old egg/Philip Marlow/hanging in/sunny side up," at other times getting its effects by contrasting the language used and the theme it expresses: "I was thinking about her all the way from Troy/(I slipped town when the Greek Horse showed)," but never far off pushing at the nerve of real feeling as in "Elizabeth" or "What Were You Going to Say?":

What were you going to say
On the path above the sea
When we stared down at the bay
And suddenly
The film of the bright day
Snapped at the end of a reel.

To read Kit Wright's poems is to be brought up against a new energetic and distinctive voice, which, while it amuses and entertains, also disturbs, making us look at the commonplace with fresh insight and sharpness of feeling, even when it is at its most self-deprecatory, as in "All Souls":

When I am old
And a bushfire of booze veins crackles across a face
With a nose like a squeezed teabag,
I shall consort
With similarly time-mugged parties
And we shall play
Elizabeth Schumann singing Schubert's
Litany for the Feast of All Souls
Because it is beautiful
And there's nothing to say.

Kit Wright's poetry has been classed with the "pop" poetry associated with the Liverpool poets and others, in that it is lively, readily assimilable, and entertaining, but what it has in addition is a depth which puts it into a class of its own.

—John Cotton

YATES, J. Michael. Canadian. Born in Fulton, Missouri, U.S.A., 10 April 1938. Educated at Westminster College, Fulton; University of Kansas City, Missouri (Poetry Prize, 1960), B.A. 1960, M.A. 1961; University of Michigan, Ann Arbor (Hopwood Award, for poetry, 1964, for drama, 1964). Promotional Director, Public Radio Corporation, Houston, 1961–62; Teaching Fellow, University of Michigan, 1962–63; taught at Ohio University, Athens, 1964–65, University of Alaska, Fairbanks, 1965–66, University of British Columbia, Vancouver, 1966–71, University of Arkansas, Fayetteville, Fall 1972, and University of Texas, Dallas, 1976–77. Editor-in-Chief, 1966–67, and Poetry Editor, 1966–71, *Prism International*, and Member of the Editorial Board, Prism International Press, Mission, British Columbia, 1966–71; Founding Editor, with Andreas Schroeder, *Contemporary Literature in Translation*, Vancouver, 1968; Member of the Editorial Board, *Mundus Artium*, Athens, Ohio; General Editor, *Campus Canada*; Head of the Special Projects Division, University of British Columbia Press, 1977–78. Since 1971, President, Sono Nis Press, Vancouver; since 1978, Sales Representative, Mitchell Press. Recipient: International Broadcasting Award, 1961, 1962; Canada Council grant, 1968, 1969, 1971, and Senior Arts Award, 1972, 1974. Address: 1538 Fulton Avenue, West Vancouver, British Columbia V7V 1S6, Canada.

PUBLICATIONS

Verse

Spiral of Mirrors. Francestown, New Hampshire, Golden Quill Press, 1967.
Hunt in an Unmapped Interior and Other Poems. Francestown, New Hampshire, Golden Quill Press, 1967.
Canticle for Electronic Music. Victoria, British Columbia, Charles Morriss, 1967.
Parallax, with Bob Flick. Victoria, British Columbia, Charles Morriss, 1968.
The Great Bear Lake Meditations. Ottawa, Oberon Press, 1970.
Nothing Speaks for the Blue Moraines: New and Selected Poems. Vancouver, Sono Nis Press, 1973.
Breath of the Snow Leopard. Vancouver, Sono Nis Press, 1974.
The Qualicum Physics. San Francisco, Kanchenjunga Press, 1975.
Esox Nobilior non Esox Lucius. Fredericton, New Brunswick, Fiddlehead, 1978.

Plays

Subjunction (produced Fairbanks, 1965).
Night Freight (broadcast, 1968; produced Toronto, 1972). Toronto, Playwrights Co-op, 1974.
Quarks (includes *The Net*, *Search for the Tse-Tse Fly*, *The Calling*). Toronto, Playwrights Co-op, 1975.

Screenplay: *The Grand Edit*, 1966.

Radio Plays: *The Broadcaster*, 1968; *Theatre of War*, 1968; *The Calling*, 1968; *Night Freight*, 1968; *The Panel*, 1968; *Smokestack in the Desert*, 1970; *Poet in an Arctic Landscape*, 1970; *Realia*, 1975; *The Net*, 1975; *Search for the Tse-Tse Fly*, 1975; *Sinking of the North West Passage*, 1975; *The Secret of State*, 1976.

Short Stories

Man in the Glass Octopus. Vancouver, Sono Nis Press, 1968.
The Abstract Beast: New Fiction and Drama. Vancouver, Sono Nis Press, 1971.
Fazes in Elsewhen: New and Selected Fiction. Vancouver, Intermedia Press, 1977.

Other

Editor, with Andreas Schroeder, *Contemporary Poetry of British Columbia.* Vancouver, Sono Nis Press, 2 vols., 1970–72.

Editor, with Charles Lillard, *Volvox: Poetry from the Unofficial Languages of Canada in English Translation.* Vancouver, Sono Nis Press, 1971.
Editor, *Contemporary Fiction of British Columbia.* Vancouver, Sono Nis Press, 1971.

J. Michael Yates comments:

1. For me, an image is one of an infinite number of entrances into an arena where something ineffable is going on. If the thing I'm after were statable, probably it would be better said in expository prose. The issues most often taken up by good poetry usually require use of the silences between and behind words. For this mode of communication, metaphor, indirection are the best engines.
2. With each piece, I attempt to cause a structure, a system, of images whose parts belong dissonantly to a whole whose meaning cannot be stated. I mean Stravinsky's dissonance. In the *Poetics of Music*, he suggests that dissonance is only a transitional element; consonance must be achieved one way or another – either in the instrumentation or in the ear of the listener. The latter is my way – to give the reader the "thing" I'm talking about, frame by frame, and ask him to project it inside him in the manner that most entertains him. Different and isolate as each of us is, it seems the only honesty.
3. Ideally, fifteen readers will make fifteen very different (and fifteen equally justifiable) poems from a piece I have written. As I'm different from you at any moment, I differ from myself through successive moments – even the most familiar things change with changes in the coordinates of consciousness and time, I couldn't possibly recreate the coordinates of consciousness that produced a given piece and thereby tell you what it means.
4. Ideally, a reader would come to a poem relaxed, with open consciousness, no preconceptions nor suspicions that the poem is a locked door and someone somewhere – probably the treacherous bastard author – is hiding the key. The parts of a poem which persist inside a reader arrive there via personal correspondences. Exterior interpretations remain merely exterior. Belief in one's own associations is difficult, very difficult. But only those will translate the poem from "mine" to "yours."
5. Ideally, one would read a poem as if he were the first reader in history to read a poem – and as if no one on earth were reading a poem at that moment. Impossible. Necessary.
6. Ideally, I write as if no one has ever written a poem. As if no one is writing now. Ridiculous. Imperative.
7. "Understanding" is a sweet, vague Renaissance dream which never came true. According to me, poems are not to be understood, but responded to. Understanding promises universal truth. Naive. I'm a rare user and no pusher at all of either reality or its ism. I don't assume a "representative universe." As if one could come to an "understanding" about such things.

* * *

An overview of the work of J. Michael Yates is complicated by the diversity of forms in which he writes and by his marked experimentation, self-education, and maturation as a writer. This apologia notwithstanding, there are themes and images common to all Yates's output, from the early poems to the plays of *The Abstract Beast*. And common to all his work, too, is a certain self-consciousness, arising partly from the experimentation, but largely from a self-image of the "young man as Artist," an image which matures as surely as does his technique. In fact, there is a connection between these two observations, for Yates's self-image is not a pose, but, rather, a preoccupation with the notion that the ideas of the writer are his whole world and reality. This Lockean fascination with a state of being in which the mind becomes a substitute for the existent is seen perhaps most clearly in *Man in the Glass Octopus* but is prefigured in the early poems of *Hunt in an Unmapped Interior* (whose title suggests it) and continues into the endless series of lenses viewing lenses of the *Parallax* poems. It also prompts the recurrent images of animals eating animals, cameras filming cameras, and mirrors mirroring mirrors with which the poems are filled. As well, it explains the persona of the author/narrator as Adam naming Creation, which D. G. Jones has cited as a major theme of all Canadian writing and which in Yates's poems (notably *The Great Bear Lake Meditations*), is extended until the mind of Adam becomes the Mind of God, Itself an insubstantial mirror of Yates's own consciousness. And finally, it is embodied in the name of Yates's press, at once an *impressa* and a complication: Sono Nis – "the I is not."

Each of these concerns is introduced in *Hunt in an Unmapped Interior*, a collection of poems strongly reminiscent of Wallace Stevens, in which the short pieces are deft and incisive, the longer poems ruminative. *Canticle for Electronic Music* is disappointing after this auspicious first collection; again Yates has difficulty in sustaining the longer poem. *Great Bear Lake Meditations* is a more mature work, in which the Adam persona is accepted and in which Yates's love of words becomes congruent with his myth – if the poet's only reality is imaginative, then words become symbols of nothing other than aspects of his imagination. In *Parallax*, Yates gropes toward but fails to quite reach a further refinement in which if "words are better than talk ... [then] silence [is] better than words." The poems attempt the visual, building upon camera imagery. But to create a "silent" poem without words is ultimately to produce a blank page and these poems, however compelling, are "at the verge of total desire that ends in the half-act."

In *The Abstract Beast*, Yates looks to other forms and modifies his poems into the prose they have always approached and into highly successful short radio plays (which would be less successful on stage). Perhaps realizing after *Man in the Glass Octopus* that the end-point of his self-preoccupation would be self-nihilism, Yates has tempered his myth; while it is still obvious it is less obsessive. The result is a collection that with the exception of some unfortunately reprinted early pieces is as inventive as it is exciting. What thinness does arise in the stories and the sometimes disturbing inconclusiveness of the plays is most likely the result of another shift in development and hopefully will not continue into later work. Much more will be heard of J. Michael Yates.

—S. R. Gilbert

YOUNG, Al. American. Born in Ocean Springs, Mississippi, 31 May 1939. Educated at the University of Michigan, Ann Arbor (Co-Editor, *Generation* magazine), 1957–61; Stanford University, California (Wallace E. Stegner Creative Writing Fellow), 1966–67; University of California, Berkeley, A.B. in Spanish 1969. Married Arline June Belch in 1963; one son. Free-lance Musician, 1958–64; Disc Jockey, KJAZ-FM, San Francisco, 1961–65; Instructor and Linguistic Consultant, San Francisco Neighborhood Youth Corps Writing Workshop, 1968–69; Writing Instructor, Teenage Workshop, San Francisco Museum of Art, 1968–69; Jones Lecturer in Creative Writing, Stanford University, 1969–74. Since 1966, Founding Editor, *Loveletter*, San Francisco; since 1972, Co-Editor, *Yardbird Reader*, Berkeley, California; Contributing Editor, since 1972, *Changes*, New York, and since 1973, *Umoja*, New Mexico. Recipient: National Endowment for the Arts grant, 1968, 1969; San Francisco Foundation Joseph Henry Jackson Award, 1969; Guggenheim Fellowship, 1974; National Endowment for the Arts grant, 1974. Agent: Lynn Nesbitt, International Creative Management, 40 West 57th Street, New York, New York 10019. Address: 373 Oxford Street, Palo Alto, California 94306, U.S.A.

PUBLICATIONS

Verse

Dancing. New York, Corinth, 1969.

The Song Turning Back into Itself. New York, Holt Rinehart, 1971.
Some Recent Fiction. San Francisco, San Francisco Book Company, 1974.
Geography of the Near Past. New York, Holt Rinehart, 1976.

Plays

Screenplays: *Nigger*, 1972; *Sparkle*, 1972.

Novels

Snakes. New York, Holt Rinehart, 1970; London, Sidgwick and Jackson, 1971.
Who Is Angelina? New York, Holt Rinehart, 1975; London, Sidgwick and Jackson, 1978.
Sitting Pretty. New York, Holt Rinehart, 1976.

Other

Editor, with Ishmael Reed, *Yardbird Lives!* New York, Grove Press, 1978.

Bibliography: in *New Black Voices*, edited by Abraham Chapman, New York, New American Library, 1972.

Critical Studies: "Reader's Report" by Martin Levin, in *New York Times Book Review*, 17 May 1970; "Growing Up Black" by L. E. Sissman, in *The New Yorker*, 11 July 1970; "Jazzed Up," in the *Times Literary Supplement* (London), 30 July 1971; "Al Young's *Snakes*: Words to the Music" by Neil Schmitz, in *Paunch 35* (Buffalo), February 1972.

Al Young comments:

I see my poetry as being essentially autobiographical in subject matter and detail, characterized by a marked personal and lyrical mysticism as well as a concern with social and spiritual problems of contemporary man in a technological environment that grows hourly more impersonal and unreal. My favorite themes are those of love, the infinite changeability of the world as well as its eternal changelessness, and the kind of meaning (both private and universal) that flowers out of everyday life. My influences in general have been Black culture and popular speech (Southern rural and urban U.S.) and music in particular (jazz, Afro-American folk and popular music, the music of Charles Mingus and John Coltrane which defies categorization, Caribbean music of both English- and Spanish-speaking peoples); American Indian poetry and song; Hindu philosophy. Some poets I admire and have consciously learned from: Li Po, Nicolás Guillén, Rabindranath Tagore, the poetry of the *Bible*, Federico García Lorca, Kenneth Patchen, Blaise Cendrars, early T. S. Eliot, Rimbaud, Brecht, LeRoi Jones, Mayakovsky, Denise Levertov, Leopold Senghor, Kenneth Rexroth, Cervantes, Diane Wakoski and Nicanor Parra.

Besides being as necessary as food, water, air, sunlight and sleep – poetry is my way of celebrating Spirit, in all of its infinite forms (charted and uncharted) as the central unifying force in Creation.

* * *

Al Young's most recent book of verse, *Geography of the Near Past*, contains five poems satirically representing "art as a hustle." Purporting to be dictations by O. O. Gabugah, "a militant advocate of the oral tradition," the poems are full of posturing and the rhetoric of racial politics. Technically facile, they ridicule not the literary method of poets like Gabugah, but their dedication to the notion of art as a weapon. Nothing could be further from the practice of Young himself who calls poetry a magic wafer you take

into your mouth

&

swallow for dear life

To Al Young poetry is a means "to swim against/world current/knowing it to be as much a dream/as it is drama on the highest stage." The trick is to know that "Each universe is only/an ever-shifting sea/in the surfacing eyes of former fish." Inevitably, then, poetry for Young takes an autobiographical subject, seeking authenticity in the flux of process.

A first step occurs in poems of controlled focus where accidental details of ordinary life gain meaning by association. The sequence of a day's ordinary events becomes a love letter in "Dear Arl," and in "A Dance for Li Po" bringing home groceries stimulates reflection on the variety of good places the poet has been over the years. The continuity of associative time converts memory into the principle of a fluid reality in "The Song Turning Back into Itself." Here the images of circling in time and space lead into statement of the power of song to create new versions of love, and loneliness, while also organizing past experience of those states. There is, too, the sense, shared with musicians, of the capacity of art to generate identity through expression of a lyrical mysticism. Appropriately the sequence concludes with a jazz inspired fly-away song in which the poet soars over rooftops.

As though for the time being his aesthetic needs no further statement, Young's poems in *Geography of the Near Past* return to detailing the small incident, so that he can plumb it for significance. A series of poems on the cities of Manhattan, Boston, Providence, Detroit, and Denver relate moments of intense feeling; the verse renounces commentary or explication in favor of a recreation of a moment's mood. The moments are brief, the moods without ambiguity, but there is no mistaking the effect. It is that of poetry performing its ancient function of discovery.

—John M. Reilly

YOUNG, David (Pollock). American. Born in Davenport, Iowa, 14 December 1936. Educated at Carleton College, Northfield, Minnesota, B.A. 1958; Yale University, New Haven, Connecticut, M.A. 1959, Ph.D. 1965. Married Chloe Hamilton in 1963; two children. Instructor, 1961–65, Assistant Professor, 1965–68, Associate Professor, 1969–73, and since 1973, Professor of English, Oberlin College, Ohio. Since 1969, Editor, *Field: Contemporary Poetry and Poetics*, Oberlin. Co-Owner, Triskelion Press, Oberlin. Recipient: Tane Award (*Massachusetts Review*, Amherst), 1965; National Endowment for the Arts grant, 1967; International Poetry Forum United States Award, 1968; Guggenheim Fellowship, 1978. Address: 220 Shipherd Circle, Oberlin, Ohio 44074, U.S.A.

PUBLICATIONS

Verse

Sweating Out the Winter. Pittsburgh, University of Pittsburgh Press, 1969.
Thoughts of Chairman Mao. Oberlin, Ohio, Triskelion Press, 1970.

Boxcars. New York, Ecco Press, 1974.
Work Lights: Thirty-Two Prose Poems. Cleveland, Cleveland State Poetry Center, 1977.
The Names of a Hare in English. Pittsburgh, University of Pittsburgh Press, 1979.

Other

Something of Great Constancy: The Art of "A Midsummer Night's Dream." New Haven, Connecticut, Yale University Press, 1966.
The Heart's Forest: A Study of Shakespeare's Pastoral Plays. New Haven, Connecticut, Yale University Press, 1972.

Editor, *Twentieth Century Interpretations of "Henry IV, Part Two": A Collection of Critical Essays.* Englewood Cliffs, New Jersey, Prentice Hall, 1968.

Translator, *Six Poems from Wang Wei.* Oberlin, Ohio, Triskelion Press, 1969.
Translator, *Magic Strings: Nine Poems from Li Ho.* Oberlin, Ohio, Pocket Pal Press, 1976.
Translator, *Duino Elegies*, by Rilke. New York, Norton, 1978.

* * *

David Young's poetry has a strong sense of the American Midwest where he was born and now teaches; it is a poetry of flat land dreaming of quiet transformations, unsatisfied but calm: "All to the south the dazed, hot landscape lies,/Under its piled thunderheads,/ Dreaming of love and survival."

His poetry reminds one of the work of another Midwestern poet, William Stafford, in that it has a controlled skilfulness which makes itself unobtrusive. There is an essential modesty to their work. And, like Stafford, Young has a quality of faithfulness, of commitment to his own problematic existence; he does not, as so many Americans do, attempt to change his life by merely changing place, by running to New York or California. He faces the emptiness and solitude the land presents to him:

A lonely country? ...
... What's this but
Acceptable solitude? And who'd
Trade it for any multitude?

Young's work is that of a man whose edges are gently blurring, who reaches quietly for something just outside of the room he lives in – a twilight poetry in which past and present, desire and "reality," lose their hard outlines, gliding in and out of one another.

Two of the most prominent influences on Young's writing are apparent in his excellent imitations of Stevens ("Putting It Mildly") and of Robert Bly ("Oh Salmon-colored Edsel"), but he is not confined by any particular mode. His poems are sometimes humorous, often witty, and on some occasions even employ rhyme or meter. The mainstream of Young's poetry, though, is apparent in his "The Small-Town Poets," a fine poem which seems a self-portrait of sorts. The small plane which appears there, as it does in many of his poems, is an apt emblem for his poetic imagination, looping easily, observing things from a certain height with nostalgia and delight, wit and good will.

—Lawrence Russ

YOUNG, Ian (George). British; Canadian Landed Immigrant. Born in London, 5 January 1945. Educated at Beal Grammar School, Ilford, Essex; Malvern Collegiate Institute, Toronto; Victoria College, University of Toronto, 1964–67, 1970. Since 1969, Director, Catalyst Press, Scarborough, Ontario. Press Secretary, 1969–71, and Chairman, 1972–73, University of Toronto Homophile Association. Recipient: Canada Council grant, 1969, 1974, 1976, 1977, bursary, 1972. Address: 315 Blantyre Avenue, Scarborough, Ontario M1N 2S6, Canada.

PUBLICATIONS

Verse

White Garland: 9 Poems for Richard. Scarborough, Ontario, Cyclops, 1969.
Year of the Quiet Sun. Toronto, Anansi, 1969.
Double Exposure. Trumansburg, New York, New Books, 1970.
Cool Fire, with Richard Phelan. Scarborough, Ontario, Catalyst, 1970.
Lions in the Stream, with Richard Phelan. Scarborough, Ontario, Catalyst, 1971.
Some Green Moths. Scarborough, Ontario, Catalyst, 1972.
Autumn Angels. Toronto, Village Book Store, 1973.
Yuletide Story. Scarborough, Ontario, Catalyst, 1973.
Don. Scarborough, Ontario, Catalyst, 1973.
Invisible Words. Toronto, Missing Link Press, 1974.
Alamo. Toronto, Dreadnaught Press, 1976.
Common-or-Garden Gods. Scarborough, Ontario, Catalyst, 1976.
Whatever Turns You On in the New Year. Scarborough, Ontario, Catalyst, 1976.
Schwule Poesie. Hunfeld, Germany, Aschenbach-Verlag, 1978.

Other

The Male Homosexual in Literature: A Bibliography. Metuchen, New Jersey, Scarecrow Press, 1975.

Editor, *The Male Muse: A Gay Anthology.* Trumansburg, New York, Crossing Press, 1973.

Translator, *Curieux d'Amour*, by Count Jacques d'Adelsward Ferson. London, Timothy d'Arch Smith, 1970.

Critical Studies: "The Younger Toronto Poets Add Up to Just One" by Andreas Schroeder, in *Vancouver Province*, 7 February 1969; by Debbie Young, in *The Carleton* (Ottawa), 6 February 1970; Bob Bossin, in *The Varsity* (Toronto), 6 February 1970; introduction by John Gill, to *Double Exposure*, 1970; Robert Peters, in *Gay Sunshine* (San Francisco) January–February 1973; "Ian Young's Verse Delights" by Jim Eggeling, in *The Advocate* (Los Angeles), 25 April 1973; "The Poetry of Ian Young" by Robert Hawkes, in *Margins* (Milwaukee), March 1976; "Gay in Not So Jocund Company" by Pier Giorgio di Cicco, in *Books in Canada* (Toronto), May 1976; "Telegraphic Images" by Andrew Bifrost, in *Dodeca 15* (New York), 1976.

* * *

Ian Young is the Strato of contemporary poetry. Most recently he has published *The Male Muse*, an anthology of contemporary gay poetry that is the *Mousa Paidike* of its time. That there is a doctrinaire cast to Young's introduction to the anthology – "the growing impetus of the homophile/gay liberation movement" – is indicative of the weaknesses in that anthology, which nonetheless contains some very fine work by some surprising authors.

It is indicative too of a more general flaw in Young's own work – the tendency for obsession to override poetry. Only occasionally does one think of Cavafy – or better, Durrell's poem on Cavafy – the ironic distance and the tough-minded disdain for what Sir Thomas Browne called "the foolishest act that a man ever commits in his life."

But such disdain for the foolishness of the flesh is not fashionable at the moment, certainly not in Canadian poetry where a great deal of over-compensating for the 19th century is still in full voice. And one has, in fairness, to point to a fine descriptive ability and a delicious sensuality in Young's work:

How I wanted him
when he came
into the room
with a new blue kerchief

when he knotted it
round his neck
like a noose of sky

But there is sometimes a sense of strain in his work – the necessary touches of fashionable surrealism or the laboured deference to haiku and the cults of karma and *om*. Here more than anywhere one feels the absence of a restraining versification where emotion might be recollected in a tranquility productive of better poetry. The "punk's hands" that he fears and celebrates are a paradigm of that wrestle in poetry which more often needs to engage. For there is no doubt of his ability who is, in his own words, "hunter/hunted/and long sharp knife."

—D. D. C. Chambers

ZATURENSKA, Marya. American. Born in Kiev, Russia, 12 September 1902; emigrated to the United States in 1909, naturalized, 1912. Educated at Valparaiso University, Indiana, 1922–23; University of Wisconsin, Madison, 1923–25. Married Horace Gregory, *q.v.*, in 1925; two children. Recipient: John Reed Memorial Award, 1922, Guarantor's Award, 1937, and Jacob Glatstein Memorial Award, 1973 (*Poetry*, Chicago); Shelley Memorial Award, 1935; Pulitzer Prize, 1938. Address: Closter Road, Palisades, Rockland County, New York 10964, U.S.A.

PUBLICATIONS

Verse

Threshold and Hearth. New York, Macmillan, 1934.
Cold Morning Sky. New York, Macmillan, 1937.
The Listening Landscape. New York, Macmillan, 1941.
The Golden Mirror. New York, Macmillan, 1944.
Selected Poems. New York, Grove Press, 1954.
Terraces of Light. New York, Grove Press, 1960.

Collected Poems. New York, Viking Press, 1965.
The Hidden Waterfall. New York, Vanguard Press, 1974.

Other

A History of American Poetry 1900–1940, with Horace Gregory. New York, Harcourt Brace, 1946.
Christina Rossetti: A Portrait with Background. New York, Macmillan, 1949.

Editor, with Horace Gregory, *The Mentor Book of Religious Verse.* New York, New American Library, 1957.
Editor, with Horace Gregory, *The Crystal Cabinet: An Invitation to Poetry.* New York, Holt Rinehart, 1962.
Editor, *The Collected Poems of Sara Teasdale.* New York, Macmillan, 1966.
Editor, with Horace Gregory, *The Silver Swan: Poems of Romance and Mystery.* New York, Holt Rinehart, 1966.
Editor, with Horace Gregory, *Selected Poems of Christina Rossetti.* New York, Macmillan, 1970.

Marya Zaturenska comments:

I am an independent. My style, my manner is my own. My poetry is traditional and lyrical with a music and a diction which I hope is my own.

* * *

The work of Marya Zaturenska is perhaps best understood by placing it in a poetic tradition she herself has spoken of, that is, the tradition of Christina Rossetti and Sara Teasdale. In style and subject matter, it was popular two generations ago, about the time that Zaturenska's second volume, *Cold Morning Sky*, received the Pulitzer Prize. Its chief characteristics are a regular metrical pattern, often quatrains, and generalized nature imagery, as in "Spring Morning":

The arrowy gold whose winter span
Of life was lost in wind and water
Shed from the sky, to waters ran
Casting new life upon the water.

Nature provides the background in the early poems for conventional reflections on the transitoriness of life and the changing seasons, in such representative poems as "The Scythe, The Spindle, and the Cypress Tree" and "The Runaway," both written in couplets.

The last four poems in her *Collected Poems* return somewhat to the earlier mood of melancholy and quiet reverie, particularly in "Metaphysics of Night" and "Homage to Christina Rossetti," as in the following stanza:

For you the Sacred Muse revealed her illumined way
And taught the simple heart, devout and true,
How to praise God in fire-touched songs that pray
Songs that Teresa heard, Siena's Catherine knew.

In the poems of the middle years, beginning with *The Golden Mirror*, the setting tends to be more dramatic. A tension emerges between speaker and subject, and the poems exhibit a strength and vigor quite different from the lyricism of the early poems. "The Recall of Eurydice," for example, describes the loss of Orpheus and of life on earth, as Eurydice returns to become, in Hell, "a nameless shade, among the nameless shades." In poems based on classic myths, as Louis Untermeyer has said, Marya Zaturenska brings "fresh life to mythological figures, not merely reanimating a legend, but creating a new and complex character." One can say the same about her poems on historical figures, such as "The Affliction of William Cowper," which skillfully conveys the anguish and despair of that distinguished poet's struggle with madness.

Zaturenska's poems with a contemporary setting are, on the whole, less successful, lacking usually a precision of language or a proper idiom to link subject and mood. The spiritual conflict that characterizes so much of contemporary life seems very distant from her later religious poems. They suggest that her strength as a poet lies with the subjects and sensibility of an earlier time, as in those poems published in *Poetry* magazine during the 1920's, while she was still an undergraduate – meditative poems, detached and serene.

—Michael True

ZIMMER, Paul J. American. Born in Canton, Ohio, 18 September 1934. Educated at Kent State University, Kent, Ohio, 1952–53, 1956–59, B.A. 1968. Married Suzanne Koklauner in 1959; one daughter and one son. Macy's Book Department Manager, San Francisco, 1961–63; Manager, San Francisco News Company, 1963–65; Manager, UCLA Bookstore, Los Angeles, 1965–67; Poet-in-Residence, Chico State College, California, Spring 1971; Associate Director, University of Pittsburgh Press, and Editor, Pitt Poetry series, 1967–78. Since 1978, Director, University of Georgia Press, Athens. Recipient: Borestone Mountain Award, 1971; National Endowment for the Arts grant, 1974; Helen Bullis Memorial Award (*Poetry Northwest*, Seattle), 1975. Address: 130 Lullwater Road, Athens, Georgia 30602, U.S.A.

PUBLICATIONS

Verse

A Seed on the Wind. Privately printed, 1960.
The Ribs of Death. New York, October House, 1967.
The Republic of Many Voices. New York, October House, 1969.
The Zimmer Poems. Washington, D.C., Dryad Press, 1976.
With Wanda: Town and Country Poems. Washington, D.C., Dryad Press, 1979.

Critical Studies: "Recent Poetry" by Hayden Carruth, in *Hudson Review* (New York), Summer 1968; "Recent Poetry" by Robert Boyers, in *Partisan Review* (New Brunswick, New Jersey), 1969; James Den Boer, in *Voyages* (Washington, D.C.), Spring 1970; the author, in *American Poets in 1975* edited by William Heyen, Indianapolis, Bobbs Merrill, 1975, and in *Gravida* (New York), 1979.

Paul Zimmer comments:

Because of early scholastic difficulties I was more or less forced to regard myself a failure as a young person. Consequently when I began writing poetry I was not able to make poems about myself, not thinking myself important enough to write about. I began casting my voice into characters I had made up: Peregrine, Mordecai, Phineas, Alphonse, Wanda, Imbellis, Cecil, Willis, etc. I guess, in some ways, I was trying to make my own mythologies (create my own little world?). I look upon this period of my work as an apprenticeship for making the poems I have been working on in recent years. Of late autobiographical work and the early cast-creating seem to be growing together into a kind of dialogue. Zimmer appears in the new Wanda poems along with the cast of characters. Making poems is the best and most exhilarating thing I do. I still derive a great deal of energy from reading people like Yeats, Skelton, Wyatt, Herrick, Lorca, Neruda, Roethke, Browning, Clare, Shakespeare, Chaucer, and many others.

* * *

Paul Zimmer is a protean poet whose personae are not so much depicted as created; we witness poet and subjects in process of becoming. A vivid verbal imagination projects the common, lonely, unwanted, neurotic, merely eccentric, and truly mad people of these poems into the elements which surround them and are soon to reclaim them in death, while inanimate objects assume the habits and attributes of human life. Zimmer makes the stock-in-trade of synaesthesia and personification his own by force of an original, often startling point-of-view: "One Vision./Mine." *The Ribs of Death* not only shows this individual stamp on a wide variety of material but also demonstrates a poetic development. A deft, almost eighteenth-century irony characterizes the first poems. Lord Fluting dreams of an illusory America "where the buffalo turn/Broadside to the hunting horns," but discovers the horrors of a primitive country, and asks "Where are the teepees filled with gold?" The Colonies are infected with the sins and superstitions of the Old World; the "great new land" seemed "too full of sun/For ancient shadows," yet the darkness has become so deep that witches are needed to fill "the belly of some flame." The malaise lingers on, but in turning to more recent times, Zimmer becomes more personal in tone, particularly when speaking of his life and art. The once-Catholic poet is "projected into shapes," his province now catholic enough to gather the buckskinned pioneer, the football player, the oil driller, and the witty Handel with the dying Keats and seafaring Conrad under the title of Poet. He can portray death in the placid invalid and eager consumptive and read it in the quick demise of a snapping wave-tip and in the dullness of a blighted apple.

In *The Republic of Many Voices*, he aims again at a variety of subjects, linked now with a connecting theme of rebirth, and death and with a self-conscious tone. But what was magical in the earlier volume tends to lose its charm through repetition. From his still-skewed angle of vision, people fascinate not as personalities so much as curiosities; after the first half-dozen and despite the variation, would-be originals give off a superficial glint, like other objects of a mechanical process. Alonzo is a snowflake, Rollo bears the ocean, Fritz strangles on the world, Carlos becomes the mountain he climbs. Invested with attributes of nature, certain personae have the power of fantastic hybrids. Gus's "guts ache with elm blight" as he "shaves his dewy chin of all its pixie moss." In the "Mordecai" poems Zimmer works several character transformations upon a Black man, but with typically liberal guilt calls the portraiture mere "egghead prattling." Enlarging his self-portrait, he presents telling sketches of home and school, marred, though, with sentimentality and adolescent peevishness (one poem wreaks vengeance upon an old teaching "nun"). Scenes of youthful adventure, close-calls, and lucky accidents shine more vividly, evoking crucial moments of emerging poetic insight. Though lines sometimes get clotted with botanical metaphors, tenderness and good humor infuse his tales of adolescent sexuality and love. "I know I sing the bird," he notes, "And bloom the flowers myself."

In *The Zimmer Poems*, he continues his song of himself. However, despite the egotism implied by the title, this book is not an exercise in hybris but humility. Examining past failures, as well as future fears, the poet seems to have come to terms with the personae of earlier poems and, perhaps more important, with his imperfect former self (or selves). One measure of this reconciliation is the warmth and good humor with which he considers the intimidations, inadequacies, and unfulfilled desires of youth and manhood. He projects himself into the decrepitudes of old age, the decay of alcoholism, and the inevitability of death; but the fact that he can confront his fears is itself a sign of new strength. Sharing his aching memories as well as his fears, we can accept that it is not simple narcissism when he says: "I am so much, mean so much." Through these revelatory, touching lines we can also agree with the poet: "Zimmer does not mean./He is."

—Joseph Parisi

ZINNES, Harriet. American. Born in Hyde Park, Massachusetts. Educated at Hunter College, New York, B.A. 1939; Brooklyn College, New York, M.A. 1944; New York University, Ph.D. 1953. Married Irving Zinnes in 1943; one daughter and one son. Editor, Raritan Arsenal Publications Division, Metuchen, New Jersey, 1942–43; Associate Editor, *Harper's Bazaar*, New York, 1944–46; Tutor, Hunter College, 1946–49. Assistant Professor, 1949–53, Associate Professor, 1962–78, and since 1978, Professor of English, Queens College, City University of New York. Director, Poetry and Fiction Workshop, University of Oklahoma, Norman, 1959–60; Lecturer, Rutgers University, New Brunswick, New Jersey, 1960–62; Art and Literary Critic, *Weekly Tribune*, Geneva, Switzerland, 1968–69; Visiting Professor of American Literature, University of Geneva, Spring 1970. Since 1971, Editorial Staff Member, *Pictures on Exhibit*, New York; currently, Poetry Coordinator, Great Neck Library, Long Island, New York. Recipient: MacDowell Fellowship, 1972, 1973, 1974, 1977; Yaddo Fellowship, 1978; American Council of Learned Societies grant, 1978. Agent: Roberta Kent, W.B. Agency, 156 East 52nd Street, New York, New York 10022. Address: Department of English, Queens College, Flushing, New York 11367, U.S.A.

PUBLICATIONS

Verse

Waiting and Other Poems. Lanham, Maryland, Goosetree Press, 1964.
An Eye for an I. New York, Folder, 1966.
I Wanted to See Something Flying. New York, Folder, 1976.
Entropisms. Arlington, Virginia, Gallimaufry, 1978.
Book of Ten. Binghamton, New York, Bellevue Press, 1979.

Short Stories

Ancient Ritual. New York, Seagull, 1979.

Manuscript Collections: Lockwood Memorial Library, State University of New York, Buffalo; Sweet Briar College Library, Virginia.

Critical Studies: by Robert Hazel, in *Masterplots: 1966 Annual*, edited by Frank N. Magill, New York, Salem Press, 1967; *Booklist* (Chicago), 15 July 1978; *Choice* (Middletown, Connecticut), September 1978.

Harriet Zinnes comments:

In my earlier work Ezra Pound was my chief influence – principally through his emphasis on a new music discovered through a spare and rigorous poetic line. Robert Bly was my second significant influence, but my newer work emphasizes what was always true, my hard, ironical approach to a reality that is as much surreal as real. I am finding more and more that I am writing narrative poems (I am also writing short fiction) but narratives where more is omitted than related, and where characters involved may or may not be present. Dramatic tension is characteristic of my work (whether or not there is a story line) as in my prose poems where there are strange, sudden juxtapositions. But it is through language that I hope to achieve that tension, through its seductive music, its syntax and meanings, that can be chopped up, destroyed, denied, changed, or affirmed. I want my poems to declare the complexity of experience, its surprises, for to me a poem is the consequence of a deep realization that what is, is not; that what may arrive, will never. Jacques Prévert's work that I am now engaged in translating fascinates me, therefore. He makes his language, through his puns, his ironic gestures, his linguistic games, demonstrate the complexities, absurdities, barbarities of a world that he loves: "*Dans ma maison qui n'est pas ma maison tu viendras.*" *Voilà*: what is, is not, and yet, "*tu viendras.*"

* * *

Harriet Zinnes's poetry invites analogies to modern painting and sculpture. Many of her poems are verbal collages, collections of "found objects" (verse equivalents of Duchamp's "readymades"), the significance of whose juxtaposition depends, at least in part, upon the ingenuity of the reader. In the four-part "Electronic Music" she bows and points to Rauschenberg, splicing together the tapes and other electronic communications gear with the debris of a technological society. Others of her poetic constructs display the irony, wit, and seeming innocence of a Miro sculpture, where, again, the relevance of the configuration lies in the eye of the imaginative beholder. She notes: "(Nothing is far-fetched/that the mind seizes upon.)" She makes Dadaist games of the jumble of life. The persona exclaims: "What an antic traffic jam I am." Playful typography figures in "MEn" and "and the fruit," while drawings supplement other poems, for "Words are not enough/(as any poet knows)." Despite her considerable skill, she harbors a lingering distrust for the lexicon; she is dissatisfied with words "utilized until meaningless." After the first echo, "That word remembered/is death/a verbal corpse."

Nonetheless, she is seldom at a loss for the precise terms to fashion a spare and telling line, particularly when writing of city life. The urban child is engrossed in a gutter pool before his yardless house. In the dark the persona views sparrows and ducks with affection and annoyance. A green leaf pushes its way into an artist's "acrylic garden." The twittering air conditioners in "Cityscape" must do for murmuring sea waves, and the stone birds on the mantlepiece have to stand in for living sea gulls. She captures the city-dweller at his classic recreation, the cocktail party, where one guest beckons: "Come find me as I whisper to my enemies." Another, insecure in the company of such sophisticates, lets her masks fall and asks in anguish: "Is it I? Is it I?" Zinnes also catches the rhythms of conversation in several segments of "Entropisms," a long prose poem made partly of snippets that seem cut from intellectual-artistic soirées, New York style. Along with the snatches of wit and aphorism, she lets mingle fragments both banal and arch. (She even allows Buckminster Fuller to parody himself.) Again as in *An Eye for an I*, she depicts existential moments; her selected short scenes and speeches jostle one another or make curious associations. "All things are not equal. Two substances and two other substances make all kinds of things." Let another "Entropism" serve as partial index to her art: "Hour after hour a fledgling word in space. Silence surrounds embodies sings *only when the word cuts it.*"

—Joseph Parisi

ZURNDORFER, Lotte. British. Born in Germany, in 1929. Educated at Watford Grammar School; St. Hugh's College, Oxford. Married; two daughters. Currently, Lecturer in English, University of Helsinki. Address: Myotale 5, Mankans, Finland.

PUBLICATIONS

Verse

(*Poems*). Oxford, Fantasy Press, 1952.
Poems. London, Chatto and Windus-Hogarth Press, 1960.

Lotte Zurndorfer comments:

I am a midnight writer whose children wake at 6 a.m.

* * *

The poetry of Lotte Zurndorfer is so quiet that it is in danger of bowing itself out of recognition. She has published only one collection. Its themes are decorous, as can be seen from the titles of the better poems: "Peony," "Cathedral," "Autumn and a New Country," "Letter Poem." From this last one could quote:

Snow falls; in France I see the long garden,
The tall trees, poplar or plane-tree, the houses
High and narrow; and so across the Norman
Landscape is drawn this familiar
Mnemonic for home: snowflakes fining in distance,
And where I am it is soundless –
The far yellowing has children calling, sirens
From the river, traffic snoring. I think
Of you and write you letters....

The details are selected to suggest an uncomfortable sort of country – "*long* garden," "*tall* trees," houses "*high* and *narrow*." There is a delicate play on the word "drawn" – the snow is drawn across the landscape like a familiar curtain concealing an unfamiliar set. It is also drawn as one might decorate a picture sent to a friend, to render a drawn-out terrain more comprehensible. In this way, a context is created for the unusual word, almost a conceit, "mnemonic." Such technique as this could be used to considerable effect. It may be no accident that one of Miss Zurndorfer's most striking poems to date is a translation of Baudelaire: "La Servante au grand coeur...."

—Philip Hobsbaum

APPENDIX

AUDEN, W(ystan) H(ugh). American. Born in York, England, 21 February 1907; emigrated to the United States in 1939; naturalized, 1946. Educated at St. Edmund's School, Grayshott, Surrey; Gresham's School, Holt, Norfolk; Christ Church (exhibitioner), Oxford, 1925–28. Served for the Loyalists in the Spanish Civil War; with the Strategic Bombing Survey of the United States Army in Germany during World War II. Married Erika Mann in 1935. Schoolmaster, Larchfield Academy, Helensburgh, Scotland, and Downs School, Colwall, near Malvern, Worcestershire, 1930–35; Co-Founder of the Group Theatre, 1932; worked with the G.P.O. Film Unit, 1935; travelled extensively in the 1930's, in Europe, Iceland, and China; taught at St. Mark's School, Southborough, Massachusetts, 1939–40, American Writers League School, 1939, New School for Social Research, New York, 1940–41, 1946–47, University of Michigan, Ann Arbor, 1941–42, Swarthmore College, Pennsylvania, 1942–45, Bryn Mawr College, Pennsylvania, 1943–45, Bennington College, Vermont, 1946, and Barnard College, New York, 1947; Neilson Research Professor, Smith College, Northampton, Massachusetts, 1953; Professor of Poetry, Oxford University, 1956–61. Editor, Yale Series of Younger Poets, 1947–62. Member of the Editorial Board, *Decision* magazine, 1940–41, and *Delos* magazine, 1968. Recipient: King's Gold Medal for Poetry, 1936; Guggenheim Fellowship, 1942; American Academy of Arts and Letters Award of Merit Medal, 1945, Gold Medal, 1968; Pulitzer Prize, 1948; Bollingen Prize, 1954; National Book Award, 1956; Feltrinelli Prize, 1957; Guinness Award, 1959; Poetry Society of America Droutskoy Gold Medal, 1959; National Endowment for the Arts grant, 1966; National Book Committee National Medal for Literature, 1967. D.Litt.: Swarthmore College, 1964. Member, American Academy of Arts and Letters, 1954; Honorary Student, Christ Church, Oxford, 1962. *Died 29 September 1973.*

Publications

Verse

Poems. N.p., S.H.S. (Stephen Spender), 1928.
Poems. London, Faber, 1930; revised edition, 1933.
The Orators: An English Study. London, Faber, 1932; revised edition, 1934, 1966; New York, Random House, 1967.
Poem. Privately printed, 1933.
Two Poems. Privately printed, 1934.
Poems (includes *The Orators* and *The Dance of Death*). New York, Random House, 1934.
Our Hunting Fathers. Privately printed, 1935.
Sonnet. Privately printed, 1935.
Look, Stranger! London, Faber, 1936; as *On This Island*, New York, Random House, 1937.
Spain. London, Faber, 1937.
Letters from Iceland, with Louis MacNeice. London, Faber, and New York, Random House, 1937.
Selected Poems. London, Faber, 1938.
Journey to a War, with Christopher Isherwood. London, Faber, and New York, Random House, 1939; revised edition, Faber, 1973.
Ephithalamion Commemorating the Marriage of Giuseppe Antonio Borghese and Elisabeth Mann. Privately printed, 1939.
Another Time: Poems (includes *Spain*). New York, Random House, and London, Faber, 1940.
Some Poems. London, Faber, 1940.
The Double Man. New York, Random House, 1941; as *New Year Letter*, London, Faber, 1941.

Three Songs for St. Cecilia's Day. Privately printed, 1941.
For the Time Being. New York, Random House, 1944; London, Faber, 1945.
The Collected Poetry of W. H. Auden. New York, Random House, 1945.
Litany and Anthem for St. Matthew's Day. Northampton, St. Matthew's, 1946.
The Age of Anxiety: A Baroque Eclogue. New York, Random House, 1947; London, Faber, 1948.
Collected Shorter Poems 1930–1944. London, Faber, 1950.
Nones. New York, Random House, 1951; London, Faber, 1952.
Mountains. London, Faber, 1954.
The Shield of Achilles. New York, Random House, and London, Faber, 1955.
The Old Man's Road. New York, Voyages Press, 1956.
Reflections on a Forest. Greencastle, Indiana, DePauw University, 1957.
Goodbye to the Mezzogiorno (bilingual edition). Milan, All'Insegno del Pesce d'Oro, 1958.
W. H. Auden: A Selection by the Author. London, Penguin-Faber, 1958; as *Selected Poetry*, New York, Modern Library, 1959.
Homage to Clio. New York, Random House, and London, Faber, 1960.
W. H. Auden: A Selection, edited by Richard Hoggart. London, Hutchinson, 1961.
Elegy for J. F. K., music by Igor Stravinsky. New York, Boosey and Hawkes, 1964.
The Common Life (in German, translated by Dieter Leisegang). Darmstadt, J. G. Bläschke Verlag, 1964.
The Cave of Making (in German, translated by Dieter Leisegang). Darmstadt, J. G. Bläschke Verlag, 1965.
Half-Way. Cambridge, Massachusetts, Lowell-Adams House, 1965.
About the House. New York, Random House, 1965; London, Faber, 1966.
The Twelve, music by William Walton. London, Oxford University Press, 1966.
Marginalia. Cambridge, Massachusetts, Ibex Press, 1966.
Collected Shorter Poems 1927–1957. London, Faber, 1966; New York, Random House, 1967.
River Profile. Cambridge, Massachusetts, Laurence Scott, 1967.
Selected Poems. London, Faber, 1968.
Collected Longer Poems. London, Faber, 1968; New York, Random House, 1969.
Two Songs. New York, Phoenix Book Shop, 1968.
A New Year Greeting, with *The Dance of the Solids*, by John Updike. New York, Scientific American, 1969.
City Without Walls and Other Poems. London, Faber, 1969; New York, Random House, 1970.
Natural Linguistics. London, Poem-of-the-Month Club, 1970.
Academic Graffiti. London, Faber, 1971; New York, Random House, 1972.
Epistle to a Godson and Other Poems. London, Faber, and New York, Random House, 1972.
Auden/Moore: Poems and Lithographs, edited by John Russell. London, British Museum, 1974.
Poems, lithographs by Henry Moore, edited by Vera Lindsay. London, Petersburg Press, 1974.
Thank You, Fog: Last Poems. London, Faber, and New York, Random House, 1974.
Collected Poems, edited by Edward Mendelson. London, Faber, and New York, Random House, 1976.
Sue. Oxford, Fantasy Press, 1977.
Selected Poems, edited by Edward Mendelson. London, Faber, and New York, Random House, 1979.

Recordings: *Reading His Own Poems*, Harvard Vocarium, 1941; *Reading from His Works*, Caedmon, 1954; *Auden*, Argo, 1960; *Selected Poems*, Spoken Arts, 1968.

Plays

The Dance of Death (produced London, 1934; as *Come Out into the Sun*, produced Poughkeepsie, New York, 1935; as *The Dance of Death*, produced New York, 1936). London, Faber, 1933; in *Poems*, 1934.

The Dog Beneath the Skin; or, Where Is Francis?, with Christopher Isherwood (produced London, 1936; revised version, produced New York, 1947). London, Faber, and New York, Random House, 1937.

No More Peace! A Thoughtful Comedy (lyrics only), book by Edward Crankshaw, adaptation of the play by Ernst Toller (produced London, 1936; Poughkeepsie, New York, and New York City, 1937). New York, Farrar and Rinehart, and London, Lane, 1937.

The Ascent of F6, with Christopher Isherwood (produced London, 1937; New York, 1939). London, Faber, 1936; revised edition, New York, Random House, and Faber, 1937.

On the Frontier, with Christopher Isherwood (produced Cambridge, 1938; London, 1939). London, Faber, 1938; New York, Random House, 1939.

The Dark Valley (broadcast, 1940). Published in *Best Broadcasts of 1939–40*, edited by Max Wylie, New York and London, McGraw Hill, 1940.

Paul Bunyan, music by Benjamin Britten (produced New York, 1941; Aldeburgh and London, 1976). London, Faber, 1976.

The Duchess of Malfi, music by Benjamin Britten, adaptation of the play by John Webster (produced New York, 1946).

The Knights of the Round Table, adaptation of the work by Jean Cocteau (broadcast, 1951; produced Salisbury, Wiltshire, 1954). Published in *The Infernal Machine and Other Plays*, by Jean Cocteau, New York, New Directions, 1963.

The Rake's Progress, with Chester Kallman, music by Igor Stravinsky (produced Venice, 1951; New York, 1953; London, 1962). London and New York, Boosey and Hawkes, 1951.

Delia; or, A Masque of Night, with Chester Kallman (libretto), in *Botteghe Oscure 12* (Rome), 1953.

The Punch Revue (lyrics only) (produced London, 1955).

The Magic Flute, with Chester Kallman, adaptation of the libretto by Schikaneder and Giesecke, music by Mozart (televised, 1956). New York, Random House, 1956; London, Faber, 1957.

The Play of Daniel (narration only) (produced New York, 1958; London, 1960). Editor, with Noah Greenberg, New York, Oxford University Press, 1959; London, Oxford University Press, 1960.

The Seven Deadly Sins of the Lower Middle Class, with Chester Kallman, adaptation of the work by Brecht, music by Kurt Weill (produced New York, 1958; Edinburgh and London, 1961). Published in *Tulane Drama Review* (New Orleans), September 1961; in *Collected Plays*, by Brecht, vol. 2, part 3, London, Eyre Methuen, 1979.

Don Giovanni, with Chester Kallman, adaptation of the libretto by Lorenzo da Ponte, music by Mozart (televised, 1960). New York and London, Schirmer, 1961.

The Caucasian Chalk Circle (lyrics only), with James and Tania Stern, adaptation of the play by Brecht (produced London, 1962). Published in *Plays*, London, Methuen, 1960.

Elegy for Young Lovers, with Chester Kallman, music by Hans Werner Henze (produced Stuttgart and Glyndebourne, Sussex, 1961). Mainz, Schott, 1961.

Arcifanfarlo, King of Fools; or, It's Always Too Late to Learn, with Chester Kallman, adaptation of the libretto by Goldoni, music by Dittersdorf (produced New York, 1965).

Die Bassariden (The Bassarids), with Chester Kallman, music by Hans Werner Henze (produced Salzburg, 1966; Santa Fe, New Mexico, 1968; London, 1974). Mainz, Schott, 1966.

Moralities: Three Scenic Plays from Fables by Aesop, music by Hans Werner Henze. Mainz, Schott, 1969.
The Ballad of Barnaby, music by Wykeham Rise School Students realized by Charles Turner (produced New York, 1970).
Love's Labour's Lost, with Chester Kallman, music by Nicholas Nabokov, adaptation of the play by Shakespeare (produced Brussels, 1973).
The Entertainment of the Senses, with Chester Kallman, music by John Gardner (produced London, 1974). Included in *Thank You, Fog*, 1974.
The Rise and Fall of the City of Mahagonny, with Chester Kallman, adaptation of the libretto by Brecht, music by Kurt Weill. Boston, Godine, 1976; in *Collected Plays*, by Brecht, vol. 2, part 3, London, Eyre Methuen, 1979.

Screenplays (documentaries): *Night Mail*, 1936; *Coal Face*, 1936; *The Londoners*, 1938.

Radio Writing: *Hadrian's Wall*, 1937 (UK); *The Dark Valley*, 1940 (USA); *The Rocking-Horse Winner*, with James Stern, 1941 (USA); *The Knights of the Round Table*, 1951 (UK).

Television Writing: *The Magic Flute*, 1956 (USA); *Don Giovanni*, 1960 (USA).

Other

Education Today – and Tomorrow, with T. C. Worsley. London, Hogarth Press, 1939.
The Intent of the Critic, with others, edited by Donald A. Stauffer. Princeton, New Jersey, Princeton University Press, 1941.
Poets at Work: Essays Based on the Modern Poetry Collection at the Lockwood Memorial Library, University of Buffalo, with others, edited by Charles D. Abbott. New York, Harcourt Brace, 1948.
The Enchafèd Flood; or, The Romantic Iconography of the Sea. New York, Random House, 1950; London, Faber, 1951.
Making, Knowing and Judging. Oxford, Clarendon Press, 1956.
The Dyer's Hand and Other Essays. New York, Random House, 1962; London, Faber, 1963.
Louis MacNeice (lecture). London, Faber, 1963.
Selected Essays. London, Faber, 1964.
Worte und Noten: Rede zur Eröffnung der Salzburger Festspiele 1968. Salzburg, Festungsverlag, 1968.
Secondary Worlds. London, Faber, and New York, Random House, 1969.
A Certain World: A Commonplace Book. New York, Viking Press, 1970; London, Faber, 1971.
Forewords and Afterwords, edited by Edward Mendelson. New York, Viking Press, and London, Faber, 1973.
The English Auden: Poems, Essays, and Dramatic Writings 1927–1939, edited by Edward Mendelson. London, Faber, 1977; New York, Random House, 1978.

Editor, with Charles Plumb, *Oxford Poetry 1926*. Oxford, Blackwell, 1926.
Editor, with C. Day Lewis, *Oxford Poetry 1927*. Oxford, Blackwell, 1927.
Editor, with John Garrett, *The Poet's Tongue: An Anthology*. London, G. Bell, 2 vols., 1935.
Editor, *The Oxford Book of Light Verse*. Oxford, Clarendon Press, 1938.
Editor, *A Selection from the Poems of Alfred, Lord Tennyson*. New York, Doubleday, 1944; as *Tennyson: An Introduction and a Selection*, London, Phoenix House, 1946.
Editor, *The American Scene, Together with Three Essays from "Portraits of Places,"* by Henry James. New York, Scribner, 1946.

Editor, *Slick But Not Streamlined: Poems and Short Pieces*, by John Betjeman. New York, Doubleday, 1947.
Editor, *The Portable Greek Reader*. New York, Viking Press, 1948.
Editor, with Norman Holmes Pearson, *Poets of the English Language*. New York, Viking Press, 5 vols., 1950; London, Eyre and Spottiswoode, 5 vols., 1952.
Editor, *Selected Prose and Poetry*, by Edgar Allan Poe. New York, Rinehart, 1950.
Editor, *The Living Thoughts of Kierkegaard*. New York, McKay, 1952; as *Kierkegaard*, London, Cassell, 1955.
Editor, with Marianne Moore and Karl Shapiro, *Riverside Poetry 1953: Poems by Students in Colleges and Universities in New York City*. New York, Association Press, 1953.
Editor, with Chester Kallman and Noah Greenberg, *An Elizabethan Song Book: Lute Songs, Madrigals, and Rounds*. New York, Doubleday, 1955; London, Faber, 1957.
Editor, *The Faber Book of Modern American Verse*. London, Faber, 1956; as *The Criterion Book of Modern American Verse*, New York, Criterion, 1956.
Editor, *Selected Writings of Sydney Smith*. New York, Farrar Straus, 1956; London, Faber, 1957.
Editor, *Van Gogh: A Self-Portrait: Letters Revealing His Life as a Painter*. Greenwich, Connecticut, New York Graphic Society, and London, Thames and Hudson, 1961.
Editor, with Louis Kronenberger, *The Viking Book of Aphorisms: A Personal Selection*. New York, Viking Press, 1962; as *The Faber Book of Aphorisms*, London, Faber, 1964.
Editor, *A Choice of de la Mare's Verse*. London, Faber, 1963.
Editor, *The Pied Piper and Other Fairy Tales*, by Joseph Jacobs. New York, Macmillan, and London, Collier Macmillan, 1963.
Editor, *Selected Poems*, by Louis MacNeice. London, Faber, 1964.
Editor, with John Lawlor, *To Nevill Coghill from Friends*. London, Faber, 1966.
Editor, *Selected Poetry and Prose*, by Byron. New York, New American Library, 1966; London, New English Library, 1967.
Editor, *Nineteenth Century British Minor Poets*. New York, Delacorte Press, 1966; as *Nineteenth Century Minor Poets*, London, Faber, 1967.
Editor, *G. K. Chesterton: A Selection from His Non-Fiction Prose*. London, Faber, 1970.
Editor, *A Choice of Dryden's Verse*. London, Faber, 1973.
Editor, *George Herbert*. London, Penguin, 1973.
Editor, *Selected Songs of Thomas Campion*. Boston, Godine, 1973; London, Bodley Head, 1974.

Translator, with Elizabeth Mayer, *Italian Journey 1786–1788*, by Goethe. London, Collins, and New York, Pantheon, 1962.
Translator, with Leif Sjöberg, *Markings*, by Dag Hammarskjöld. New York, Knopf, and London, Faber, 1964.
Translator, with Paul B. Taylor, *Völupsá: The Song of the Sybil*, with an Icelandic Text edited by Peter H. Salus and Paul B. Taylor. Iowa City, Windhover Press, 1968.
Translator, *The Elder Edda: A Selection*. London, Faber, 1969; New York, Random House, 1970.
Translator, with Leif Sjöberg, *Selected Poems*, by Gunnar Ekelöf. New York, Pantheon, 1971.
Translator, with Elizabeth Mayer and Louise Bogan, *The Sorrows of Young Werther, and Novella*, by Goethe. New York, Random House, 1973.
Translator, with Leif Sjöberg, *Evening Land/Aftonland*, by Par Lagerkvist. Detroit, Wayne State University Press, 1975.

Bibliography: *W. H. Auden: A Bibliography 1924–1969*, by B. C. Bloomfield and Edward Mendelson, Charlottesville, University Press of Virginia, 1972.

Critical Studies: *The Poetry of W. H. Auden: The Disenchanted Island* by Monroe K. Spears, New York, Oxford University Press, 1963, and *Auden: A Collection of Critical Essays* edited by Spears, Englewood Cliffs, New Jersey, Prentice Hall, 1964; *A Reader's Guide to W. H. Auden* by John Fuller, London, Thames and Hudson, and New York, Farrar Straus, 1970; *The Later Auden* by George W. Bahlke, New Brunswick, New Jersey, Rutgers University Press, 1970; *Man's Place: An Essay on Auden* by Richard Johnson, Ithaca, New York, Cornell University Press, 1973; *W. H. Auden: A Tribute* edited by Stephen Spender, London, Weidenfeld and Nicolson, and New York, Macmillan, 1975; *W. H. Auden: The Life of a Poet* by Charles Osborne, London, Eyre Methuen, 1980.

* * *

The massive Auden canon falls into two parts, usually termed "the English Auden" and "the later Auden," sometimes "the Marxist Auden" and "the Christian Auden," dated roughly 1927–1939 and 1940–1973. Almost all readers and critics favor one period over the other, arguing either that early Auden verse is pioneering and rigorous but late Auden pious and flaccid, or that early Auden is eclectic and confused but late Auden original and crystalline. Unfortunately, many of those debates are a function of ideology, since the public content of Auden's verse can be interpreted either as a desertion of the political Left of the 1930's and a reversion to the conservative Right, or as a revelation of Romantic idealism and a pragmatic coming of age. The change in the art comports much more than changing attitudes toward the efficacy of political action and the possibility of redemption in Christ; however one evaluates the public allegiances, the change marks a transition from bewailing human ignorance in anxious, cautionary verse almost despairing of mankind, to celebrating human ignorance in serene verse praising spousal love and the mysteries of God. In addition to Auden's first (since boyhood) taking of communion in 1940, many other personal events such as his resettling in America in 1940, meeting Chester Kallman in New York in 1940, spending the war years far from Europe, should be taken into any account of the knotty question of the early and late Audens.

The debate about the two chronological Audens was inaugurated by Randall Jarrell in *Southern Review* (1945) and furthered by Joseph Warren Beach's book *The Making of the Auden Canon* (1957). Ideology aside, one of the major contentions was that later Auden heretically edited early Auden, drastically rewriting or indeed even retaining old lines in a radically new context, while insisting upon his right to change "trash that I am ashamed to have written." Jarrell and Beach, and other students of Modernism extending from Yeats to Pound, argued heatedly that a poem once published resides in the public domain, inviolable; but Auden cared little, if at all, for the Modernist cult of art. Evidently ever since the Oxford days with Christopher Isherwood and Stephen Spender, he often read poems aloud, saved only the lines that his friends liked, then put them together as one poem. Isherwood records his amused wonder in *Lions and Shadows*, but there is no gainsaying the enormous influence of this verse over their generation in England of the 1920's and 1930's with its obviously deliberate obscurity and its daring juxtapositions, primarily innovative minglings of Freud and Marx. Anecdotes deriding Auden's compositional methods abound, from both periods, all to be measured against the Modernist standard of the Flaubertian artist espoused by Joyce (though never practised in *Finnegans Wake*).

Recently, Edward Mendelson has advanced the debate, editing *The English Auden* and the *Selected Poems* of 1979. These editions restore both the chronological order of publication and the original form of the poems as first published, clearing away much of the confusion issuing from Auden-edited editions. Like a growing number of readers, Mendelson in his prefaces argues for a balanced view of the two Audens, as complementary halves of the same essential, constant poet.

There remain crucial differences, and willed obscurities, for each reader to interpret. Young Auden the physician's son was unusually well read in contemporary science upon arriving at Oxford, and was soon more than just familiar with the writings of Georg Groddeck, Freud, Kierkegaard, Niebuhr, Charles Williams, Marx, Blake, Lawrence, philosophers of sorts and teachers all. Auden's earliest verse attempts to evolve a moral system out of the combined analytical methods of Freud and Marx, using the symbolic landscape of northern industrial cities, decrying the grey ruins of human potential for love, juxtaposing a fantasized ideal of distant islands and of Eros uninhibited, as in "Petition." Such verse attempts to teach, to instruct frightened mankind that material progress may be matched with mental progress through the advances of psychology: "Send to us power and light, a sovereign touch/Curing the intolerable neural itch,/The exhaustion of weaning, the liar's quinsy,/And the distortions of ingrown virginity." Young Auden hoped to cure by first pointing out to mankind the illness (as Gerald Nelson demonstrates in the excellent study *A Change of Heart*), and as he began the 1930's Auden was confident that people were willing to be taught and to effect "New styles of architecture." Thence the petition in a world rich in possibility.

Auden's verse and the public events of the 1930's did not bear out his hopes. As Stephen Spender wrote in *World Within World*, "We Anti-Fascist writers of what has been called the Pink Decade were not, in any obvious sense, a lost generation [like the Americans of the 1920's]. But we were divided between our literary vocation and an urge to save the world from Fascism. We were the divided generation of Hamlets who found the world out of joint and failed to set it right." Auden felt that division intently. Nordic motifs, even echoes of the Icelandic sagas giving resonance to the Freudian and Marxian figures of the hero as pariah and spy, give way in the 1930's to personifications of Death and History, Love and destructive self-love, in overt echoes of Dante's *Inferno*, though without Christian emphasis. The arcadian "island" remained a prominent motif, but only as a fantasy recognized as such, and "History" and the "city" began moving into the foreground as the immediate and real arena for any possible, increasingly unlikely resolution of hopes and fears. We must "rebuild our cities, not dream of islands." By the late 1930's notably in "September 1, 1939," his poetry was angrier, often impatient with human error and ignorance and selfishness, including his own, divided between "Negation and despair" and the continuing desire to manifest, personally, "an affirming flame." He travelled widely (to Spain in the Civil War, to Iceland with MacNeice, to China with Isherwood), finally settling in America in 1940.

In Gerald Nelson's account, "The pre-Second World War persona of the angry young Marxist-Freudian was destroyed both by Auden's horror at the atrocities of which he saw man to be capable and by his (maybe resultant) reconversion to orthodox Christianity." Auden had always experimented with many genres, including verse essay, Brechtian musical drama, sonnet sequences, and in the 1940's he combined multiple aspects of this earlier work to produce the three long dramatic poems of this period: "The Sea and the Mirror," *For the Time Being*, *The Age of Anxiety*. The loudest literary echo is no longer Dante but Shakespeare, the landscape remains psychologically symbolic but the symbols themselves are sometimes mocked, and the speakers are attempting – unsuccessfully – not to change their world but to escape it. As Malin says in *The Age of Anxiety*, "For the others, like me, there is only the flash/Of negative knowledge, the night when, drunk, one/Staggers to the bathroom and stares in the glass/To meet one's madness." Faith in Christ's love is the one alternative to ignorance and delusion. Christ is "That Always-Opposite which is the whole subject/Of our not knowing," and "His question disqualifies our quick senses,/His Truth makes our theories historical sins." Auden's characters are no longer heroic but bumbling and inadequate because unable fully to accept the life of faith, struggling "To elude Him, to lie to Him."

The poems in the collections *Nones* and *The Shield of Achilles* in the 1950's mark the almost serene resolution of those "anxieties." Auden abandons contending dramatic voices for a single speaker humbly addressing an unidentified "dear" or "my dear," presumably Christ or God. "Memorial for the City" concerns not the City of Man but the City of God. "Our Weakness" concerns man's humanity, his sensual flesh and ignorant mind. "Precious Five" concerns the five senses, the physical realm that man must imbue with Christian meaning. Auden's finest and most complex work from this period is the last section of *The Shield of Achilles*, the seven poems entitled "Horae Canonicae," celebrating the Crucifixion as the supreme mystery to man. Subsequent long works, most notably *Homage to Clio* and *About the House* in the 1960's, amplify these concerns, treating the humble believer's relationship to history and to physical environment, often humorously in what has been called Auden's light metaphysical verse. Throughout the work of the 1960's, amid echoes of Goethe, runs the sheer certainty of the poet at last serene in his faith.

The astonishing extent of the Auden canon reaches beyond verse, especially into collaborative drama with Isherwood in the 1930's and opera libretti with Kallman after 1940, and translation and literary criticism after 1950. His major critical studies, in *The Enchafèd Flood* and *The Dyer's Hand*, often consist in schematizations of literary history, and, as George Bahlke describes in *The Later Auden*, turn upon his distinction between externally and internally imposed suffering, ascribing greater value to Christian literature than, say, Greek, and to the modern tragic hero.

Auden's last published poem was appropriately entitled "Archeology," described as "delving into lifeways." Showing how very far Auden had travelled since "Petition" and "Look, Stranger, At This Island Now," it concludes, "What they call History/is nothing to vaunt of,/being made, as it is,/by the criminal in us:/goodness is timeless."

—Jan Hokenson

BAXTER, James K(eir). New Zealander. Born in Dunedin, 29 June 1926, son of the author Archibald Baxter. Educated at Quaker schools in New Zealand and England; Otago University, Dunedin; Victoria University, Wellington, B.A. 1952. Married Jacqueline Sturm in 1948; two children. Worked as a labourer, journalist, school-teacher. Editor, *Numbers* magazine, Wellington, 1954–60. Spent 5 months in India studying school publications, 1958. Started commune in Jerusalem (a Maori community on the Wanganui River), 1969. Recipient: UNESCO grant, 1958; Robert Burns Fellowship, University of Otago, 1966, 1967. *Died 22 October 1972.*

PUBLICATIONS

Verse

Beyond the Palisade. Christchurch, Caxton Press, 1944.
Blow, Wind of Fruitfulness. Christchurch, Caxton Press, 1948.
Hart Crane. Christchurch, Catspaw Press, 1948.
Rapunzel: A Fantasia for Six Voices. Privately printed, 1948.
Charm for Hilary. Christchurch, Catspaw Press, 1949.
Poems Unpleasant, with Louis Johnson and Anton Vogt. Christchurch, Pegasus Press, 1952.
The Fallen House. Christchurch, Caxton Press, 1953.
Lament for Barney Flanagan. Privately printed, 1954.
Traveller's Litany. Wellington, Handcraft Press, 1955.
The Night Shift: Poems of Aspects of Love, with others. Wellington, Capricorn Press, 1957.
The Iron Breadboard: Studies in New Zealand Writing (verse parodies). Wellington, Mermaid Press, 1957.
In Fires of No Return. London and New York, Oxford University Press, 1958.
Chosen Poems 1958. Bombay, Konkan Institute of Arts and Sciences, 1958.
Ballad of Calvary Street. Privately printed, 1960.
Howrah Bridge and Other Poems. London and New York, Oxford University Press, 1961.
Poems. Wellington, Teachers College, 1964.

Pig Island Letters. London and New York, Oxford University Press, 1966.
A Death Song for M. Mouldybroke. Christchurch, Caxton Press, 1967.
A Small Ode on Mixed Flatting. Christchurch, Caxton Press, 1967.
The Lion Skin. Dunedin, University of Otago Bibliography Room, 1967.
A Bucket of Blood for a Dollar. Christchurch, John Summers Bookshop, 1968.
The Rock Woman: Selected Poems. London and New York, Oxford University Press, 1969.
Ballad of the Stonegut Sugar Works. Privately printed, 1969.
Jerusalem Sonnets: Poems for Colin Durning. Dunedin, University of Otago Bibliography Room, 1970.
The Junkies and the Fuzz. Wellington, Wai-te-ata Press, 1970.
Jerusalem Blues (2). Wellington, Bottle Press, 1971.
Jerusalem Daybook. Wellington, Price Milburn, 1972.
Autumn Testament. Wellington, Price Milburn, 1972.
Four God Songs. Wellington, Futuna Press, 1972.
Letter to Peter Olds. Dunedin, Caveman Press, 1972.
Runes. London and New York, Oxford University Press, 1973.
Two Obscene Poems. Wellington, Mary Martin, 1973(?).
The Tree House and Other Poems for Children. Wellington, Price Milburn, 1974.
The Labyrinth: Some Uncollected Poems 1944–1972. Wellington and New York, Oxford University Press, 1974; London, Oxford University Press, 1975.
The Holy Life and Death of Concrete Grady: Various Uncollected and Unpublished Poems, edited by J. E. Weir. London, Oxford University Press, 1976.
The Bone Chanter: Unpublished Poems 1945–1972, edited by J. E. Weir. London, Oxford University Press, 1977.
Collected Poems, edited by J. E. Weir. London, Oxford University Press, 1978.

Plays

Jack Winter's Dream (broadcast, 1958). Included in *The Wide Open Cage and Jack Winter's Dream*, 1959.
The Wide Open Cage (produced Wellington, 1959; New York, 1962). Included in *The Wide Open Cage and Jack Winter's Dream*, 1959.
The Wide Open Cage and Jack Winter's Dream: Two Plays. Hastings, New Zealand, Capricorn Press, 1959.
The Spots of the Leopard (produced New York, 1963; Wellington, 1967).
The Band Rotunda (produced Dunedin, 1967). Included in *The Devil and Mr. Mulcahy and The Band Rotunda*, 1971.
The Sore-Footed Man, based on *Philoctetes* by Euripides (produced Dunedin, 1967). Included in *The Sore-Footed Man and The Temptations of Oedipus*, 1971.
The Bureaucrat (produced Dunedin, 1967).
The Devil and Mr. Mulcahy (produced Dunedin, 1967). Included in *The Devil and Mr. Mulcahy and The Band Rotunda*, 1971.
Mr. O'Dwyer's Dancing Party (produced Dunedin, 1968).
The Day Flanagan Died (produced Dunedin, 1969).
The Temptations of Oedipus (produced Dunedin, 1970). Included in *The Sore-Footed Man and The Temptations of Oedipus*, 1971.
The Devil and Mr. Mulcahy and The Band Rotunda. Auckland, Heinemann, 1971.
The Sore-Footed Man and The Temptations of Oedipus. Auckland, Heinemann, 1971.

Radio Play: *Jack Winter's Dream*, 1958.

Other

Recent Trends in New Zealand Poetry. Christchurch, Caxton Press, 1951.

The Fire and the Anvil: Notes on Modern Poetry. Wellington, New Zealand University Press, 1955; revised edition, New York, Cambridge University Press, 1960.
Oil. Wellington, School Publications, 1957.
The Coaster. Wellington, School Publications, 1959.
The Trawler. Wellington, School Publications, 1961.
New Zealand in Colour, photographs by Kenneth and Jean Bigwood. Wellington, Reed, 1961; London, Thames and Hudson, and Belmont, Massachusetts, Wellington Books, 1962.
The Old Earth Closet: A Tribute to Regional Poetry. Privately printed, 1965.
Aspects of Poetry in New Zealand. Christchurch, Caxton Press, 1967.
The Man on the Horse (lectures). Dunedin, University of Otago Press, and London, Oxford University Press, 1967.
The Flowering Cross: Pastoral Articles. Dunedin, New Zealand Tablet, 1969.
Six Faces of Love: Lenten Lectures. Wellington, Futuna Press, 1972.
A Walking Stick for an Old Man. Wellington, CMW Print, 1972.
Notes on the Country I Live In, with Tim Shadbolt, photographs by Ans Westra. Wellington, Alistair Taylor, 1972.

Critical Studies: *The Poetry of James K. Baxter* by J. E. Weir, Wellington, Oxford University Press, 1970; *James K. Baxter 1926–1972: A Memorial Volume*, Wellington, Alistair Taylor, 1972; *James K. Baxter* by Charles Boyle, Boston, Twayne, 1976; *James K. Baxter* by Vincent O'Sullivan, London, Oxford University Press, 1977.

* * *

At his best one of the finest English-language poets of the past 30 years, James K. Baxter is the one New Zealand poet of undeniable international reputation. Although he died in his mid-forties, his literary career lasted for over 30 years. Its fruits were many volumes of poems, a handful of plays, four separate works of literary commentary or criticism, a considerable number of essays on religious topics, and a small amount of fiction (he was a fine exponent of the parable).

With *Beyond the Palisade*, published when he was 18, Baxter at once became a figure of note, both as a poet and a maverick bohemian. As he wrote later:

In Calvin's town
At seventeen I thought I might see
Not fire but water rise

From the shelves of surf beyond St Clair
to clang the dry bell. Gripping
A pillow wife in bed
I did my convict drill,
And when I made a mother of the keg
The town split open like an owl's egg....

Within a few years and with the publication of *Blow, Wind of Fruitfulness* he, and his demons, already occupied a central position in the New Zealand literary scene, so that his booklet, *Recent Trends in New Zealand Poetry*, a beautifully condensed commentary, was from the first accepted as authoritative.

When in the late 1940's Baxter moved north to Wellington he began his long friendship and collaboration with Louis Johnson. They became the focus of a "romantic" element in New Zealand writing, which centred on Wellington for the next dozen years or so. The group around them acted as a catalyst and as counter-energy to their predecessors, the poets of the 1930's, and to the nationalism of Allen Curnow. Part of this activity was the characteristically erratic periodical *Numbers*, which Johnson and Baxter edited with Charles

Doyle (and, latterly, others), and which was the only alternative to the few "establishment" periodicals, such as *Landfall.*

In books which ranged from makeshift to brilliant, Baxter throughout the 1950's produced a prolific variety of poems, plays, short stories, and criticism. He made no effort to establish a reputation outside New Zealand and, apart from a boyhood year in England, travelled abroad only once, on a UNESCO award to India and Japan in 1958. But by the late 1950's he was being published by the London branch of Oxford University Press and by 1967 they had issued the three titles which, except for the very last phase, are the core of his achievement – *In Fires of No Return*, *Howrah Bridge and Other Poems*, and *Pig Island Letters.* Substantial parts of the first two collections had been printed earlier by a distinguished New Zealand publisher, the Caxton Press.

These three books, and especially the first and last, show clearly why Baxter more than once has been said to have a touch of genius. It is manifest in such poems as "The Cave," "Rocket Show," "Lament for Barney Flanagan," and the sequence of "Pig Island Letters." The characteristic tone is caught in a moving early poem, "The Bay":

> So now I remember the bay, and the little spiders
> On driftwood, so poisonous and quick.
> The carved cliffs and the great outcrying surf
> With currents round the rocks and the birds rising.
> A thousand times an hour is torn across
> And burned for the sake of going on living.
> But I remember the bay that never was
> And stand like stone, and cannot turn away.

One important turning point in Baxter's life was his conversion to Roman Catholicism in 1958. Another was the award of a Burns Fellowship, which enabled him to return to the University of Otago, where he had been a student twenty years earlier, for the 1966 university year. He remained for two years, did a large amount of writing, and established in particular a virtually new career as a playwright. Equally important, he took up Catholic catechetical work and this led directly into the final rich phase of his career.

Besides the plays, the Dunedin years produced two important critical-autobiographical pieces, *The Man on the Horse* and *Aspects of Poetry in New Zealand*, but the period of catechetical work in the city led to writing which has been reckoned Baxter's most important. In 1967 he went into solitude for some months at Hiruharama (Jerusalem), on the Wanganui River. Later at this tiny religious settlement he founded a commune for troubled youths and social drop-outs and he was also the moving spirit in setting up doss-houses in both Auckland and Wellington.

These ventures took much of his energy, but this was also the time of a further remarkable shift in the development of his poetry, especially in the so-called Jerusalem writings, *Jerusalem Sonnets*, *Jerusalem Daybook*, and *Autumn Testament.* He achieved a very personal "sonnet" form, in fluid pentameter couplets and, particularly in *Jerusalem Daybook*, made most effective use of an amalgam of prose and verse.

New Zealand has in the past 50 years at times had a remarkably strong poetry. If today it is in its weakest phase since the 1920's, this is partly due to Baxter's early death in 1972. Baxter's poems have a natural incandescence, which owes something to his being exposed to the finest poetry from early childhood, but which also comes from a sense of the human universe based on religion. New Zealand, at least until very recently, has been a relatively successful social welfare state, secular in spirit. Baxter, notably, brought to it the example of a strong religious consciousness. His legacy to his country is a double one: a substantial amount of first-rate writing, especially poems, and the example of a man impelled to carry the spiritual life as far as it can go.

—Charles Doyle

BERRYMAN, John. American. Born in McAlester, Oklahoma, 25 October 1914. Educated at South Kent School, Connecticut; Columbia University, New York, A.B. 1936 (Phi Beta Kappa); Clare College, Cambridge (Kellett Fellow, 1936–37; Oldham Shakespeare Scholar, 1937), B.A. 1938; Princeton University, New Jersey (Creative Writing Fellow), 1943–44. Married 1) Eileen Patricia Mulligan in 1942 (divorced, 1953); 2) Ann Levine in 1956 (divorced, 1959), one son; 3) Kathleen Donahue in 1961, two daughters. Instructor in English, Wayne State University, Detroit, 1939, and Princeton University, 1940–43; Briggs-Copeland Instructor in English Composition, Harvard University, Cambridge, Massachusetts, 1945–49; Lecturer in English, University of Washington, Seattle, 1950; Elliston Lecturer in Poetry, University of Cincinnati, Ohio, 1951–52; Member of the English Department, rising to the rank of Professor, University of Minnesota, Minneapolis, 1954–72. Recipient: Rockefeller grant, 1944, 1946; *Kenyon Review*-Doubleday Award, for short story, 1945; Guarantors Prize, 1948, and Levinson Prize, 1950 (*Poetry*, Chicago); Shelley Memorial Award, 1949; National Institute of Arts and Letters grant, 1950; Hodder Fellowship, Princeton University, 1950; Guggenheim Fellowship, 1952, 1966; Harriet Monroe Award, 1957; *Partisan Review* Fellowship, 1957; Brandeis University Creative Arts Award, 1959; Loines Award, 1964; Pulitzer Prize, 1965; Academy of American Poets Fellowship, 1966; National Endowment for the Arts grant, 1967; Bollingen Prize, 1968; Emily Clark Balch Prize (*Virginia Quarterly Review*), 1968; National Book Award, 1969. D.Let.: Drake University, Des Moines, Iowa, 1971. Member: National Institute of Arts and Letters; American Academy of Arts and Sciences; Academy of American Poets. *Died 7 January 1972.*

PUBLICATIONS

Verse

Five Young American Poets, with others. New York, New Directions, 1940.
Poems. New York, New Directions, 1942.
The Dispossessed. New York, Sloane, 1948.
Homage to Mistress Bradstreet. New York, Farrar Straus, 1956; as *Homage to Mistress Bradstreet and Other Poems*, London, Faber, 1959.
His Thought Made Pockets & the Plane Buckt. Pawlet, Vermont, Claude Fredericks, 1958.
77 Dream Songs. New York, Farrar Straus, and London, Faber, 1964.
Berryman's Sonnets. New York, Farrar Straus, 1967; London, Faber, 1968.
Short Poems. New York, Farrar Straus, 1967.
I Have Moved to Dublin.... Dublin, Graduates Club, 1967.
His Toy, His Dream, His Rest: 308 Dream Songs. New York, Farrar Straus, 1968; London, Faber, 1969.
The Dream Songs. New York, Farrar Straus, 1969.
Love and Fame. New York, Farrar Straus, 1970; London, Faber, 1971; revised edition, Farrar Straus, 1972.
Selected Poems 1938–1968. London, Faber, 1972.
Delusions, Etc. New York, Farrar Straus, and London, Faber, 1972.
Henry's Fate and Other Poems 1967–1972, edited by John Haffenden. New York, Farrar Straus, 1977; London, Faber, 1978.

Novel

Recovery. New York, Farrar Straus, and London, Faber, 1973.

Other

Stephen Crane (biography). New York, Sloane, and London, Methuen, 1950.

The Freedom of the Poet (miscellany). New York, Farrar Straus, and London, Faber, 1976.

Editor, with Ralph Ross and Allen Tate, *The Arts of Reading* (anthology). New York, Crowell, 1960.
Editor, *The Unfortunate Traveller; or, The Life of Jack Wilton*, by Thomas Nashe. London, Putnam, 1960.

Bibliography: *John Berryman: A Checklist* by Richard J. Kelly, Metuchen, New Jersey, Scarecrow Press, 1972; *John Berryman: A Descriptive Bibliography* by Ernest C. Stefanik, Jr., Pittsburgh, University of Pittsburgh Press, 1972.

Critical Studies: *John Berryman* by William J. Martz, Minneapolis, University of Minnesota Press, and London, Oxford University Press, 1969; *John Berryman* by James M. Linebarger, New York, Twayne, 1974; *The Poetry of John Berryman* by Gary Q. Arpin, Port Washington, New York, Kennikat Press, 1977; *John Berryman: An Introduction to the Poetry* by Joel Conarroe, New York, Columbia University Press, 1977.

* * *

From the appearance of his "Twenty Poems" in the anthology *Five Young American Poets*, John Berryman was immediately recognized at the forefront of his talented generation, a group of poets including Robert Lowell, Delmore Schwartz, and Randall Jarrell. Most of Berryman's early poems and those in several subsequent volumes are reprinted in his *Short Poems*, but this part of his *oeuvre* – which might well represent another poet's life work – has been quite overshadowed by his three long sequences: *Homage to Mistress Bradstreet*, two volumes of his "dream songs," and *Berryman's Sonnets* (published in 1967 but written in the 1940's). In a period when most poets attempting works of magnitude have followed the examples of Yeats, Pound, and Eliot and abandoned commitment to a single strophic form, Berryman wrote long, intricate works in regular (though sometimes variably repeated) stanzas. The imposition of a formal order upon his wildly conflicting emotions and wide-ranging materials is among Berryman's most impressive accomplishments.

The *Sonnets* are strictly Petrarchan, the convention revived in a fashion both traditional and contemporary. This is the psychological analysis of a love affair, the purpose for which the sonnet form was first devised. Berryman's syncopated, frank, and quirky diction stamp these sonnets as his own. *Homage* successfully enacts an extended metaphysical conceit, that "Mistress Bradstreet," the Puritan poetess, is both the mistress, across the dead centuries, of the contemporary poet, and his alter ego. Like all of Berryman's work this poem is psychologically intense and complex; the voice begins as his own, then merges into Anne Bradstreet's: the verse is crabb'd, allusive to details in her work, life, and readings. The tangible sense of her spiritual searchings and straitened self-fulfilment striates the knotty music of Berryman's lines. His participation in her life becomes a means of his imaginative discovery of America.

The complex texture, the intensity of vision, the willed idiosyncrasy of syntax and the confected diction of *Homage* all prefigure the verse in *77 Dream Songs* and *His Toy, His Dream, His Rest*. These later books comprise a single work in 385 sections, each arranged in three six-line stanzas, the lines varying greatly in length and stress, the stanzas in rhyme pattern. Here the conceit of "dream songs" gives the poet warrant for nondiscursive syntax and for the manipulation of several projected voices. One is a white man in black-face who speaks the dialect of the Negro in a minstrel show and is named Henry, or Pussy-cat. He is heard in meditation or in colloquy with a friend who calls him Mr. Bones. At other times we hear the poet's more normative voice.

These strategies – simple in conception, intricate in effect – make possible the exploration of, seemingly, any and every subject, a man's whole life and dream-life poured through his varied voices. The scope of the work suggests comparison to *The Cantos*, the differences as revealing as the parallels. Where Pound rooted his work in his historical imagination,

Berryman reflects the inward self-preoccupation of a later generation whose sensibility reflects psychoanalytic experience. This is the generation which found Robert Lowell's *Life Studies* the key to its sufferings. Lowell, in that book rejecting history, myth and rhetoric, followed W. C. Williams in achieving the simple syntax of and immediacy of unpremeditated speech; but Berryman, who sometimes writes with analagous clarity, achieves his effects by counterpointing his several voices, natural, colloquial, literary, grand-mannered, demotic. Yet his dream songs share with *Life Studies* their confessional tone and air of uninhibited self-revelation. What comes through as a result of the complexity of tone and texture is a very uneven yet compelling image of modern man suffering, exulting, catching himself exulting and putting himself down, taking wry delight in the knowledge of his own small pleasures and larger failures. The reader is required to bear with many dry patches, much incoherence, and he is obliged to learn a new language in order to let Berryman's dreamer, its sole speaker, converse with him:

Henry sats in de plane & was gay.
Careful Henry nothing said aloud
but where a Virgin out of cloud
to her Mountain dropt in light,
his thought made pockets & the plane buckt.
"Parm me, lady." "Orright."

The willed colloquiality produces comic effects. Elsewhere the tone is tender, wry, fierce, anguished. The minstrel master of demotic syntax is a persona of the same sensibility who swiped a memorable title, *His Toy, His Dream, His Rest*, from three compositions in *The Fitzwilliam Virginal Book* by Giles Farnaby (c. 1560–1600?). Berryman's archness, his wildly comic alternations between the emotionally freer, more libidinous life-style of his white-man-in-black-face and the self that can't escape the strictures of the external world; the primitive energy of his playfulness with language; and perhaps above all the sense of subversion against the rigidities of society given by the willed dream-life in which Berryman's voices mock and undermine and lash out against the pieties of the world they and he can manage to live in only, or best, in dreams: these effects of the dream songs on the reader make his long poem memorable. Its idiosyncrasies seem determined by its time; its delights may well prove to be lasting.

After *Dream Songs* Berryman published two further books of verse, *Love and Fame* and, posthumously, *Delusions, Etc*. In these his style underwent yet a further transformation; abandoning the involutions, elisions, and intensities of *Dream Songs*, he abandoned also the melange of voices and the 18-line verse unit; in their place, now writing in irregularly rhythmic quatrains, came a self-exploitative, determinedly prosaic style, as the poet re-imagined his student days at Columbia and Cambridge universities in the first of these books, and addressed Beethoven, Frost, and other great predecessors in the second. Both contain sequences of religious themes, as Berryman continued to search for his lost faith. Another posthumous work was his novel, *Recovery*, also autobiographical, an account of his struggle with alcoholism.

Berryman's *oeuvre* reflects his life-long effort to find or fuse a style equal to the terrible psychological pressures of his themes of self-revelation and self-discovery. It seems probable that *Homage to Mistress Bradstreet* and *Dream Songs* will be found the most enduring of his works; *Homage* is surely the best unified of his longer poems, though there are structural patterns and thematic continuities and refrains secreted in *Dream Songs* which, when identified, make that long series seem less a random miscellany, more an artistic construct. In any case its structure, based on the accumulation of discrete poems with violent changes of diction, tone, and persona, like Robert Lowell's *Notebook*, represents in its flux and exacerbation the fate of the long poem in America during the latter part of the present century.

—Daniel Hoffman

BLACKBURN, Paul. American. Born in St. Albans, Vermont, 24 November 1926. Educated at New York University; University of Wisconsin, Madison, B.A. 1950; University of Toulouse, France (Fulbright Fellow), 1954–55. Served in the United States Army, 1945–47. Married 1) Winifred Grey McCarthy in 1954 (divorced, 1963); 2) Sara Golden in 1963 (divorced, 1967); 3) Joan D. Miller in 1968, one son. Lecturer, University of Toulouse, 1955–56; Assistant Editor, Funk and Wagnalls *New International Yearbook*, New York, 1959–62; Poetry Editor, *The Nation*, New York, 1962; Associate Editor, *World Scope Encyclopedia Yearbook*, 1963–65; Poet-in-Residence, 1965, and Lecturer in Poetry, 1966–67, Aspen Writers' Workshop, Colorado; Poet-in-Residence and Lecturer in English, City College of New York, 1966–69; Assistant Professor of English, State University of New York, Cortland, 1970–71. Recipient: Guggenheim Fellowship, 1967. *Died 13 December 1971.*

PUBLICATIONS

Verse

The Dissolving Fabric. Palma, Mallorca, Divers Press, 1955.
Brooklyn-Manhattan Transit: A Bouquet for Flatbush. New York, Totem, 1960.
The Nets. New York, Trobar Press, 1961.
Sing-Song. New York, Caterpillar, 1966.
Sixteen Sloppy Haiku and a Lyric for Robert Reardon. Cleveland, 400 Rabbit Press, 1966.
The Dissolving Fabric. Toronto, Mother/Island, 1966.
The Reardon Poems. Madison, Wisconsin, Perishable Press, 1967.
The Cities. New York, Grove Press, 1967.
In, On, or About the Premises, Being a Small Book of Poems. New York, Grossman, and London, Cape Goliard Press, 1968.
Two New Poems. Mount Horeb, Wisconsin, Perishable Press, 1969.
Three Dreams and an Old Poem, edited by Allen De Loach. Buffalo, University Press at Buffalo, 1970.
Gin: Four Journal Pieces. Mount Horeb, Wisconsin, Perishable Press, 1970.
The Assassination of President McKinley. Mount Horeb, Wisconsin, Perishable Press, 1970.
The Journals: Blue Mounds Entries. Mount Horeb, Wisconsin, Perishable Press, 1971.
Early Selected y Mas: Poems 1949–1966. Los Angeles, Black Sparrow Press, 1972.
Halfway Down the Coast: Poems and Snapshots. Northampton, Massachusetts, Mulch Press, 1975.
The Journals, edited by Robert Kelly. Los Angeles, Black Sparrow Press, 1975.

Other

Translator, *Proensa: From the Provençal.* Palma, Mallorca, Divers Press, 1953; as *Proensa: An Anthology of Troubadour Poetry*, edited by George Economou, Berkeley, University of California Press, 1978.
Translator, *Poem of the Cid.* New York, American RDM Corporation, 1966.
Translator, *End of the Game and Other Stories*, by Julio Cortázar. New York, Pantheon, 1967; London, Collins, 1968; as *Blow-up and Other Stories*, New York, Collier, 1968.
Translator, *Hunk of Skin*, by Pablo Picasso. San Francisco, City Lights, 1968.
Translator, *Cronopios and Famas*, by Julio Cortázar. New York, Pantheon, 1969; London, Boyars, 1978.
Translator, *Peire Vidal.* New York, Mulch Press, 1972.
Translator, *Guillem de Poitou: His Eleven Extant Poems.* Mount Horeb, Wisconsin, Perishable Press, 1976.

* * *

The poetry of Paul Blackburn suffered an erratic publishing history during his lifetime, in part due to his seeming reluctance to put his work forward in widely accessible form. This diffidence is in remarkable contrast to the sense of confidence one feels in his handling of diverse material in the poems, the respect and admiration for his work by his contemporaries, his support and encouragement of younger poets and editors, and his active and early participation in the poetry-reading phenomenon in America beginning in the late 1950's. Blackburn published only one major collection during his lifetime, *The Cities*, which, together with a much smaller collection, *In, On, or About the Premises*, gave the general reader access to his work. However, even *The Cities* included less than half of his output between the early 1950's and 1966 and thus gave only a partial idea of the poetry of that period. Even now, there still remains a large body of uncollected and in many cases unpublished poems. By comparison, the literary translations he did to support himself achieved considerable success during his lifetime.

The impossibility of seeing Blackburn's work whole was reflected by critical comment which fastened on only the more immediate features of his work. He was identified as "a poet of the streets" who had a fine ear for slang and colloquial speech rhythms, as a writer of occasional poems, a celebrator of *machismo*, a poet who relied on the visual elements in grouping blocks of material on the page, who was self-deprecatory, ironical, sharply observant, nostalgic, a compulsive list-maker. His later poetry, *The Journals* in particular, was thought by some to take open-form poetry to an extreme of inconclusiveness, to lack "finish."

In fact, *The Journals* represents the culmination – as it unfortunately happened – of a poetic towards which Blackburn had been consistently working. In a 1960 radio interview he said: "Put a person in varied landscapes or cityscapes and he is surrounded by life – you find out a lot about the quality of the city or the country and the quality of the person. This is very valid material for poetry. What else is there? The man in what surrounds him. That he loves or hates or just hears and sees." In the earliest published poems, the concern is to present "the man in what surrounds him" by interweaving specific observations, images, acts, within a carefully delineated frame; this frame may be consciously literary, as in the poem "Two Greeks" (1949), which employs the pastoral tradition of the shepherd's complaint to his unresponsive lover. The earlier work is more consciously crafted, more lyrical, and the poem is more "closed" than the later work; that is, it is structured in a linear fashion, with a tightly unified progression of images leading to a definite closure which both depends upon and binds together the previous images. Though he did not completely abandon the closed form – see the later poem "At the Well," in *Three Dreams and an Old Poem* – his interest lay in the use of seemingly random observations and associations to achieve a different kind of unity: an organic relation among the elements, based on Charles Olson's open-field theories ("one perception ... instanter, on another"). An outstanding example of this kind of poem is "Pre-Lenten Gestures," which is constructed of a series of observations, associations, and allusions which occur within a firmly located setting (a bakery-restaurant). Though seemingly casual in conception, every element in the poem is structurally and thematically tied together, but one is not conscious, as in the early work, of an ordering, "literary" sensibility.

In most of Blackburn's poetry, an overwhelming feeling of isolation is present, reinforced by his emphasis on the objects which reveal place and determine the effect; with few exceptions, even women are treated as erotic or aesthetic objects. He is the detached observer and recorder of the passing scene in a city street, a subway car, restaurant, ale-house. But in a very real sense, Blackburn's writing is a means to establish contact with the world of the living, for whom the urban state is a defining condition. He is very much *in* the world, and his love for it is reflected by his refusal to make it over in his image. The world is as he finds it: just as American painters of the 1960's recognised in the mass-produced artifact the paradigm of modern life, so Blackburn found in the alienated inhabitants of the city and their random rubbish the possibility of identification, affirmation, and, finally, communion ("Meditation on the BMT"):

1 coffee can without a lid
1 empty pint of White Star, the label
faded by rain
1 empty beer-can
2 empty Schenley bottles
1 empty condom, seen from
1 nearly empty train ...

My eyes
enter poor backyards, backyards
O I love you,

backyards, I make you my own, and you
my barren, littered embankments, now that you
've a bit of fire to warm & cleanse you, be
grateful that men still tend you, still will
rake your strange leaves
your strange leavings.

While Blackburn's poetry is quintessentially a poetry of place, he nevertheless uses places to locate the self in a particular time and circumstance, as in "How to Get Up Off It": "in some forgotten way/we carry the masks of places all our lives,/a kind of fate." The places in Blackburn's life are France, where he went originally as a Fulbright scholar at the University of Toulouse to study the Provençal manuscripts for the *Proensa* translations; Spain – in particular, Catalonia –; and New York City "which was most his home and center"; *The Journals* also contain poems from his trips to Puerto Rico, the Colorado Rockies, the West Coast, and his place of last residence, upper New York State. But in assembling his larger collections, Blackburn did not organise them according to geographical correspondences but rather, as he once defined it with respect to *The Cities*, according to the wish to balance the rhythms of different sorts of poems: the concrete, object-determined poems, the love poems, and the "idea" poems. The aim was not simply to alternate them, but to set up rhythms, as in jazz solos and riffs, which would help prevent the reader from getting bogged down in an extended run of the same kind of poem. It is Blackburn's emphasis on the poem (as well as the book) as a musical structure, in short, his sense of rhythm in both its discrete and larger aspects, that has been recognised as one of his outstanding strengths as a poet, and in which he had few peers. The accuracy (never slack) with which he reproduced colloquial speech, his skilled use of repetition, the effortless but disciplined variation of tone, line stress, line division, and stanza breaks, the ability to absorb and functionally to use diverse material and tonal values within a single poem: these are characteristics of a master craftsman.

It is evident that in his approach to his art Blackburn owed much to Pound, William Carlos Williams, Olson, Robert Creeley, the Objectivist poets Louis Zukofsky and Charles Reznikoff, and the troubadours (he had worked on the Provençal translations for twenty years, from the time in 1949–50 when Pound first convinced him that the troubadours needed contemporary American-English versions, until his death). But just as, if not more important, is his reliance on everyday American-English speech patterns and their "notation" in breath units that act as "scores" for oral presentation. This poetic coincided, or was a direct outgrowth of, the movement to restore the communal experience of poetry which provoked the poetry-reading phenomenon of the 1950's.

The Journals, the work of Blackburn's last five years, can be regarded as "A Poem of a Life," as Zukofsky described "*A*," rather than as a collection of individual poems. No other contemporary poet has expressed in his work such a coterminous statement between the life and the art as has Blackburn; he literally did make a poetry of daily existence. *The Journals* shows, as his previous poetry shows, that he used information, data, detailed observation, to discover connections between habits, chores, ablutions (with which *The Journals* abound) – in a word, the commonplaceness of everyday existence – and a transcendent plane of existence in which an image recurs, in which the numinous inhabits a place or object, and with which other people are intimately associated. The "minute particulars" make the place his own, define him, make intense and specific the time he lived through and the space he inhabited. The significance of Blackburn's innovation is that the process subsumes both the work and the working out, the poem and the making of the poem. *The Journals* are extraordinary compositions of sublety and range which permit us to follow the journeyings of a man, a poet, who made attention to his craft and art a way of life.

—Robert Vas Dias

GARRIGUE, Jean. American. Born in Evansville, Indiana, 8 December 1914. Educated at the University of Chicago, B.A. 1937; University of Iowa, Iowa City, M.F.A. 1943. Edited a weekly newspaper for the U.S.O. during World War II. Instructor, Bard College, Annandale-on-Hudson, New York, 1951–52, Queens College, Flushing, New York, 1952–53, New School for Social Research, New York, 1955–56, and University of Connecticut, Storrs, 1960–61; Lecturer in Poetry, Smith College, Northampton, Massachusetts, 1965–66; Poet-in-Residence, University of Washington, Seattle, 1970. Poetry Editor, *New Leader*, New York, 1965–72. Scholar, Radcliffe Institute for Independent Study, Cambridge, Massachusetts, 1968–70. Recipient: Rockefeller grant, 1954, 1966; Union League Civic and Arts Foundation prize (*Poetry*, Chicago), 1956; *Hudson Review* Fellowship, 1957; Longview Award, 1958; Guggenheim grant, 1960; National Institute of Arts and Letters grant, 1961; Lowell Mason Palmer Award, 1961; Emily Clark Balch Prize (*Virginia Quarterly Review*), 1966; Melville Cane Award, 1968. *Died 27 December 1972.*

PUBLICATIONS

Verse

Five Young American Poets, with others. New York, New Directions, 1944.
The Ego and the Centaur. New York, New Directions, 1947.
The Monument Rose. New York, Noonday Press, 1953.
A Water Walk by Villa d'Este. New York, St. Martin's Press, 1959; London, Macmillan, 1960.
Country Without Maps. New York, Macmillan, 1964.
New and Selected Poems. New York, Macmillan, 1967.
Studies for an Actress and Other Poems. New York, Macmillan, 1973.

Short Stories

The Animal Hotel. New York, Eakins Press, 1966.
Chartres and Prose Poems. New York, Eakins Press, 1971.

Other

Marianne Moore. Minneapolis, University of Minnesota Press, 1965; London, Oxford University Press, 1966.

Editor, *Translations by American Poets.* Athens, Ohio University Press, 1970.

Editor, *Love's Aspects: The World's Great Love Poems.* New York, Doubleday, 1975.

* * *

The best summation of Jean Garrigue's idea of poetry is found in the first lines of "Catch What You Can":

The thing to do is try for that sweet skin
One gets by staying deep inside a thing.
The image that I have is that of fruit –
The stone within the plum or some such pith
As keeps the slender sphere both firm and sound.

Throughout her career Garrigue attempted to get deep inside the things she wrote about. The result was poems of exquisite (and at times excessive) delicacy about such subjects as music, nature, travel, and, most especially, love. Her work required patient and sympathetic readers, for her poems have little narrative interest, almost no topical references, and little humor. But at its best her work offers compassionate and minutely detailed pictures of the world about her, and shows us the sweet skin of fine poetry.

Garrigue progressed much in her career and learned from her mistakes. Her early poems suffer from an uncontrolled intensity, as these lines from "Forest" show:

There are short-stemmed forests so close to the ground
You would pity a dog lost there in the spore-budding
Blackness where the sun has never struck down.
There are dying ferns that glow like a gold mine
And weeds and sumac extend the Sodom of color.
Among the divisions of stone and the fissures of branch
Lurk the abashed resentments of the ego.
Do not say this is pleasurable!

One admires Garrigue's image-making ability here, but one also feels that the last two lines are much too blatant. Elsewhere in her early poems Garrigue's rich, lyric phrasings at times unaccountably give way to patches of flatness, as in these lines from the otherwise fine piece "False Country of the Zoo": "Another runner, the emu, is even better/at kicking. Oh the coarse chicken feet/Of this bird reputed a fossil!"

In her final volumes, starting with *A Water Walk by Villa d'Este*, Garrigue developed a firmer, surer poetic voice. Discarding the tortuously ornate wordings of some of her early poems, Garrigue produced works of powerful directness. She had experimented with prose poems and, though these were not very successful, Garrigue did begin to use in her other poems rhythms and words closer to that of everyday speech. Her finest volume is *Country Without Maps*. There are some wonderful evocations of cities in this book in such poems as "Amsterdam Letter" and "New York: Summertime" and some equally insightful pieces on love, such as "Upon the Intimation of Love's Mortality" and "What Tender Bough." But the best poem in this book, and the longest (about 500 lines) Garrigue ever attempted is "Pays Perdu." Here for once narrative plays an important part as the poet recounts a long walk she took in the mountains of Provence. On this trip, which has allegorical, almost epic, undertones, the narrator finds herself lost and by chance meets a remarkable couple living in almost complete isolation in this "country without maps." This is a poem which takes us into uncharted areas of psyche; this has always been Garrigue's aim as a writer, but here she is able, as she was not earlier, to perform this feat with great subtlety and understatement.

Garrigue's final poems before her death show that she was continuing to move forward, experimenting with ballads and even, in "Written in London after a Protest Parade," tackling a contemporary political issue. "Any messages, messages, any word?" asks this poem three times. The first time it is a prosaic inquiry; the third, a question of deep implications. In between Garrigue produced a poem which movingly showed her deep love for all life. It was in her later poems, such as this one, with their simplified, more vigorous style, that Garrigue was at her best.

—Dennis Lynch

JARRELL, Randall. American. Born in Nashville, Tennessee, 6 May 1914. Educated at Vanderbilt University, Nashville, B.S. (Phi Beta Kappa) in psychology 1936, M.A. in English 1939. Served as a celestial navigation tower operator in the United States Army Air Corps, 1942–46. Married Mary Eloise von Schrader in 1952. Instructor in English, Kenyon College, Gambier, Ohio, 1937–39, University of Texas, Austin, 1939–42, and Sarah Lawrence College, Bronxville, New York, 1946–47; Associate Professor, 1947–58, and Professor of English, 1958–65, Women's College of the University of North Carolina (later, University of North Carolina at Greensboro). Lecturer, Salzburg Seminar in American Civilization, 1948; Visiting Fellow in Creative Writing, Princeton University, New Jersey, 1951–52; Fellow, Indiana School of Letters, Bloomington, Summer 1952; Visiting Professor of English, University of Illinois, Urbana, 1953; Elliston Lecturer, University of Cincinnati, Ohio, 1958. Acting Literary Editor, *The Nation*, New York, 1946–47; Poetry Critic, *Partisan Review*, New Brunswick, New Jersey, 1949–53, and *Yale Review*, New Haven, Connecticut, 1955–57; Member of the Editorial Board, *American Scholar*, Washington, D.C., 1957–65. Consultant in Poetry, Library of Congress, Washington, D.C., 1956–58. Recipient: *Southern Review* Prize, 1936; Jeanette Sewell Davis Prize, 1943, Levinson Prize, 1948, and Oscar Blumenthal Prize, 1951 (*Poetry*, Chicago); J. P. Bishop Memorial Literary Prize (*Sewanee Review*), 1946; Guggenheim Fellowship, 1946; National Institute of Arts and Letters grant, 1951; National Book Award, 1961; Oliver Max Gardner Award, University of North Carolina, 1962; American Association of University Women Juvenile Award, 1964; Ingram Merrill Award, 1965. D.H.L.: Bard College, Annandale-on-Hudson, New York, 1962. Member, National Institute of Arts and Letters; Chancellor, Academy of American Poets, 1956. *Died 14 October 1965.*

PUBLICATIONS

Verse

Five Young American Poets, with others. New York, New Directions, 1940.
Blood for a Stranger. New York, Harcourt Brace, 1942.
Little Friend, Little Friend. New York, Dial Press, 1945.
Losses. New York, Harcourt Brace, 1948.
The Seven-League Crutches. New York, Harcourt Brace, 1951.
Selected Poems. New York, Knopf, 1955; London, Faber, 1956.
Uncollected Poems. Privately printed, 1958.
The Woman at the Washington Zoo: Poems and Translations. New York, Atheneum, 1960.
Selected Poems. New York, Atheneum, 1964.
The Lost World: New Poems. New York, Macmillan, 1965; London, Eyre and Spottiswoode, 1966.
The Complete Poems. New York, Farrar Straus, 1969; London, Faber, 1971.
The Achievement of Randall Jarrell: A Comprehensive Selection of His Poems with a Critical Introduction, by Frederick J. Hoffman. Chicago, Scott Foresman, 1970.
Jerome: The Biography of a Poem. New York, Grossman, 1971.

Recording: *Randall Jarrell Discusses His Poems Against War*, Caedmon, 1972.

Play

The Three Sisters, adaptation of a play by Chekhov (produced New York, 1964; London, 1965). New York, Macmillan, 1969.

Novel

Pictures from an Institution: A Comedy. New York, Knopf, and London, Faber, 1954.

Other

Poetry and the Age. New York, Knopf, 1953; London, Faber, 1955.
Poets, Critics, and Readers (address). Charlottesville, University Press of Virginia, 1959.
A Sad Heart at the Supermarket: Essays and Fables. New York, Atheneum, 1962; London, Eyre and Spottiswoode, 1965.
The Gingerbread Rabbit (juvenile). New York, Macmillan, and London, Collier Macmillan, 1964.
The Bat-Poet (juvenile). New York, Macmillan, 1964; London, Collier Macmillan, 1966.
The Animal Family (juvenile). New York, Pantheon, 1965; London, Hart Davis, 1967.
The Third Book of Criticism. New York, Farrar Straus, 1969; London, Faber, 1975.
Fly by Night (juvenile). New York, Farrar Straus, 1976; London, Bodley Head, 1977.
Kipling, Auden, & Co. New York, Farrar Straus, 1979.

Editor, *The Anchor Book of Stories*. New York, Doubleday, 1958.
Editor, *The Best Short Stories of Rudyard Kipling*. New York, Hanover House, 1961; as *In the Vernacular: The English in India* and *The English in England*, New York, Doubleday, 2 vols., 1963.
Editor, *Six Russian Short Novels*. New York, Doubleday, 1963.

Translator, with Moses Hadas, *The Ghetto and the Jews of Rome*, by Ferdinand Gregorovius. New York, Schocken, 1948.
Translator, *The Rabbit Catcher and Other Fairy Tales of Ludwig Bechstein*. New York, Macmillan, and London, Macmillan, 1962.
Translator, *The Golden Bird and Other Fairy Tales by the Brothers Grimm*. New York, Macmillan, 1962.
Translator, *Snow White and the Seven Dwarfs: A Tale from the Brothers Grimm*. New York, Farrar Straus, 1972; London, Penguin, 1974.
Translator, *The Juniper Tree and Other Tales by the Brothers Grimm*. New York, Farrar Straus, 1973.
Translator, *Goethe's Faust, Part One*. New York, Farrar Straus, 1976; London, Faber, 1978.

Bibliography: *Randall Jarrell: A Bibliography* by Charles M. Adams, Chapel Hill, University of North Carolina Press, and London, Oxford University Press, 1958; supplement in *Analects I* (Greensboro, North Carolina), Spring 1961.

Manuscript Collections: Walter Clinton Jackson Library, University of North Carolina, Chapel Hill; Berg Collection, New York Public Library.

Critical Studies: *Randall Jarrell 1914–1965* edited by Robert Lowell, Peter Taylor, and Robert Penn Warren, New York, Farrar Straus, 1967; *The Poetry of Randall Jarrell* by

Suzanne Ferguson, Baton Rouge, Louisiana State University Press, 1971; *Randall Jarrell* by M. L. Rosanthal, Minneapolis, University of Minnesota Press, 1972.

* * *

The sustained richness of Randall Jarrell's *Selected Poems* and of his last collection, *The Lost World*, tends to obscure the fact that despite his early technical sophistication, he matured slowly as a poet. The posthumous *Complete Poems* now includes all the verse (some dating from 1934) which Jarrell himself had wisely omitted from the 1955 selection – poems which suffer badly from Auden's influence and are further weakened, as Delmore Schwartz once observed, by a "thinness and abstractness of texture and reference." The poems in *Little Friend, Little Friend*, however, especially the frequently anthologized war pieces, are completely Jarrell's own and in retrospect explain his initially cryptic remark that all good poets are essentially war poets.

In a 1951 poem, "The Face," Jarrell's aging Princess (the Marschallin of Strauss and von Hofmannsthal) looks into her mirror and thinks:

This is what happens to everyone.
At first you get bigger, you know more,
Then something goes wrong.
You are, and you say: I am –
And you were ... I've been too long.

I know there's no saying no,
But just the same you say it, No.
I'll point to myself and say: I'm not like this.
I'm the same as always inside.
– And even that's not so.

I thought: If nothing happens ...
And nothing happened.
Here I am.
But it's not *right*.
If just living can do this,
Living is more dangerous than anything:

It is terrible to be alive.

The theme, stated here with untypical directness, is repeated with infinitely subtle variations in some of Jarrell's most moving later poems, "Seele im Raum," "Next Day," and "The Lost Children," and is in fact never more than just below the immediate surface of his best verse. The war which all men fight – and inevitably lose – is the war with time and an indifferent universe. Thinking sadly about a maimed veteran Jarrell asks:

How can I care about you much, or pick you out
From all the others other people loved
And sent away to die for them! You are a ticket
Someone bought and lost on, a stray animal:
You have lost even the right to be condemned.
I see you looking helplessly about, in histories,
Bewildered with your terrible companions, Pain
And Death and Empire: what have you understood, to die?
Were you worth, soldier, all that people said
To be spent so willingly? Surely your one theory, to live,
Is nonsense to the practice of the centuries.

But of course Jarrell does care, intensely. The speaker in "The Survivor among Graves" realizes that everyone faces the same hopeless struggle:

The haunters and the haunted, among graves
Mirror each other sightlessly; in soundless
Supplication, a last unheard
Unison, reach to each other: *Say again,*
Say the voices, *say again*
That life is – what it is not;
That, somewhere, there is – something, something;
That we are waiting; that we are waiting.

"What life is not" is fulfillment, the sense of a justifying purpose for human life and suffering. The child of "90 North" reaches his fabled North Pole only to find:

Here at the actual pole of my existence,
Where all that I have done is meaningless,
Where I die or live by accident alone –

Where, living or dying, I am still alone;
. . . .
I see at last that all the knowledge

I wrung from darkness – that the darkness flung me –
Is worthless as ignorance; nothing comes from nothing,
The darkness from the darkness. Pain comes from the darkness
And we call it wisdom. It is pain.

It is poems such as these that confirm Robert Lowell's observation that with all his dazzling gifts, Jarrell was "the most heartbreaking English poet of his generation."

Just as the soldier serves as a basic metaphor for Jarrell, so too does the child, learning by his losses (and through his encounters with the *märchen*, those symbolic fairy tales for which Jarrell had an almost obsessive fascination), and the sensitive adult as well, experiencing great works of the imagination, whether in music, the visual arts, or literature. The import of the true work, as Jarrell states repeatedly throughout his poetry and criticism, is that of Rilke's archaic torso of Apollo: *you must change your life* – you must grow, that is, into a new, more intense consciousness of being. Yet the imperative to change leads to the tragic paradox at the center of Jarrell's work. We change, by the pressure of experience, knowledge and increasing sensitivity, but there is no goal to achieve, no transcendence, no escape, finally, from a world in which it is "terrible to be alive." There is only stoicism, such consolation as knowing the worst can bring, and the compassionate realization that others too must suffer. Life is made bearable – perhaps bearable – by such knowledge and sympathy and in Jarrell's own case by the miraculous recapturing of childhood happiness. "I reach out to it empty handed," Jarrell wrote at the end, and:

my hand comes back empty,
And yet emptiness is traded for its emptiness,
I have found that Lost World in the Lost and Found
Columns whose grey illegible advertisements
My soul has memorized world after world:
LOST – NOTHING. STRAYED FROM NOWHERE. NO REWARD.
I hold in my own hands, in happiness,
Nothing: the nothing for which there's no reward.

The lost world of childhood no longer exists, is "nothing" now; and yet through memory (and by the art of fixing memory in the poem), the poet can hold his nothing in his hands, "in happiness." There is no reward beyond this: memory and art carry their own fulfillment for the poet and for his perceptive readers, who have lived vicariously through the superlative imaginative recreations which Jarrell presents in this final volume.

No brief thematic identification of Jarrell's concerns can begin to do justice to the embodied beauty of the poems themselves. Sweeping judgments are as dangerous as they are vulnerable, but among the poets who followed after the first great generation of modern American poets, Eliot, Stevens, Frost, and Pound, Jarrell may well be the most gifted and eloquent. His poetry is frequently demanding in its subtleties, but is difficult, finally, in the same sense that Jarrell had in mind when he observed that some of Frost's best poems are "hard to understand, but easy to love."

—Elmer Borklund

KAVANAGH, Patrick. Irish. Born in Inniskeen, 21 October 1904. Educated at Kednaminsha National School, 1910–16. Married Katherine Moloney in 1967. Farmer and shoemaker, Inniskeen, 1920–36. Lived in London and Dublin, 1936–42. Columnist ("City Commentary"), *Irish Press*, Dublin, 1942–44; Film Critic and Feature Writer, *The Standard*, Dublin, 1943–49; Editor, *Kavanagh's Weekly*, Dublin, 1952; Contributor, *Nimbus* magazine, London, 1954, and *The Farmer's Journal*, 1958–63 and *RTV-Guide* magazine, 1963–67, Dublin. Extra-Mural Lecturer, University College, Dublin, 1956–59. Recipient: AE Memorial Award, 1940; Arts Council of Great Britain Award, 1967. *Died 30 November 1967.*

PUBLICATIONS

Verse

Ploughman and Other Poems. London, Macmillan, 1936.
The Great Hunger. Dublin, Cuala Press, 1942.
A Soul for Sale. London, Macmillan, 1947.
Recent Poems. New York, Peter Kavanagh Hand Press, 1958.
Come Dance with Kitty Stobling and Other Poems. London, Longman, 1960; Chester Springs, Pennsylvania, Dufour, 1964.
Collected Poems. London, MacGibbon and Kee, and New York, Devin Adair, 1964.
The Complete Poems, edited by Peter Kavanagh. New York, Peter Kavanagh Hand Press, 1972.

Recording: *Almost Everything*, Claddah, 1965.

Plays

Self Portrait (televised, 1962). Dublin, Dolmen Press, 1964.
Tarry Flynn (produced Dublin, 1966).

Television Feature: *Self Portrait*, 1962.

Novels

Tarry Flynn. London, Pilot Press, 1948; New York, Devin Adair, 1949.

By Night Unstarred: An Autobiographical Novel, edited by Peter Kavanagh. The Curragh, County Kildare, Goldsmith Press, 1977.

Other

The Green Fool (autobiography). London, Joseph, 1938; New York, Harper, 1939.
Collected Pruse. London, MacGibbon and Kee, 1967.
Lapped Furrows: Correspondence, 1933–1967, Between Patrick and Peter Kavanagh, With Other Documents, edited by Peter Kavanagh. New York, Peter Kavanagh Hand Press, 1969.
November Haggard: Uncollected Prose and Verse of Patrick Kavanagh, edited by Peter Kavanagh. New York, Peter Kavanagh Hand Press, 1971.

Bibliography: *Garden of the Golden Apples: A Bibliography of Patrick Kavanagh* by Peter Kavanagh, New York, Peter Kavanagh Hand Press, 1972.

Manuscript Collection: National Library of Ireland, Dublin.

Critical Studies: *Clay Is the Word: Patrick Kavanagh 1904–1967* by Alan Warner, Dublin, Dolmen Press, 1973, New York, Humanities Press, 1974; *Patrick Kavanagh* by Darcy O'Brien, Lewisburg, Pennsylvania, Bucknell University Press, 1975.

* * *

I met Patrick Kavanagh just once. He told me that he was dying. He seemed cheerful about it, pointing out that some Irish officials had awarded him a pension when his incurable disease was confirmed. "Like a prize each year until I die," he said. The prospect of cheating officialdom gave him one amusing reason for living – I am sure he had others, more serious. In fact he lived on for five years. I hope the prizes didn't stop.

I have just reread the reprint of his *Collected Poems* and realised what an excellent poet he is, much more various than memories of the early verse allowed for. This book runs from the lyrical simplicities about tinkers and blackbirds which he wrote while still scraping a living from a farm in Monaghan, through the long poem about Ireland which made his reputation and brought the police to his door ("The Great Hunger"), to the parish of gossip about matters of life and death which constitutes the later major verse.

Intuitive, epigrammatic, shrewd, Kavanagh is always the peasant, seeing how much he can get away with, returning again and again to a handful of themes perceived as underlying all creation. Here is a complete short poem which gives his authentic flavour, "Sanctity":

To be a poet and not know the trade,
To be a lover and repel all women;
Twin ironies by which great saints are made,
The agonising pincer-jaws of Heaven.

There is an arresting sentence in his early autobiography, *The Green Fool*, first published in 1938 but then withdrawn as a result of a libel action brought by Oliver St. John Gogarty. This runs: "I turned away from the door of Literature and continued my work among poetry, potatoes, and old boots." What is significant here is not the naive equation of "poetry and potatoes" with what is real, but the degree of ironic self-knowledge implicit in Kavanagh's quite consciously setting himself up as a peasant-poet, and declaring his intention of *working his way through* that chosen role. As C. H. Sisson has written, in his *English Poetry 1900–1950: An Assessment*: "He discovered that 'the Ireland thing' got in the way, and he aspired to free himself from it. Because he was an Irish peasant he wanted to rid himself of the *notion* of the Irish peasant." This, as Sisson concedes, Kavanagh achieved, especially in the outburst of poems which came towards the end of his life, where "his constant preoccupation is to see the world otherwise than through ideas."

Kavanagh possessed very considerable formal skill – he had obeyed Yeats's injunction that Irish poets should "learn their trade" and "sing whatever is well made," while discarding the Yeatsian robes of rhetoric and the magician's hat which so often go with this if it be misinterpreted as an invitation to the oracular. His sonnets, in particular, are an extraordinary extension of the form. Here is one of the best of them, "Canal Bank Walk," which dates from 1957:

Leafy-with-love banks and the green waters of the canal
Pouring Redemption for me, that I do
The will of God, wallow in the habitual, the banal,
Grow with nature again as before I grew.
The bright stick trapped, the breeze adding a third
Party to the couple kissing on an old seat,
And a bird gathering materials for the nest for the Word
Eloquently new and abandoned to its delirious beat.
O unworn world enrapture me, encapture me in a web
Of fabulous grass and eternal voices by a beech,
Feed the gaping need of my senses, give me ad lib
To pray unselfconsciously with overflowing speech
For this soul needs to be honoured with a new dress woven
From green and blue things and arguments that cannot be proven.

When he wished to catch the mind's movements in rhythms not far removed from those of common speech, Kavanagh was equally adept. The more I read in the posthumous *Collected Poems* the more convinced I become that his was a major voice, original and profound, and a voice which will still be heard when the louder voices of his more fashionable contemporaries have been long forgotten.

—Robert Nye

LOWELL, Robert (Traill Spence, Jr.). American. Born in Boston, Massachusetts, 1 March 1917. Educated at St. Mark's School, Southboro, Massachusetts; Harvard University, Cambridge, Massachusetts, 1935–37; Kenyon College, Gambier, Ohio, 1938–40, A.B. (summa cum laude) 1940 (Phi Beta Kappa). Conscientious objector during World War II: served prison sentence, 1943–44. Married 1) the writer Jean Stafford, in 1940 (divorced, 1948); 2) the writer Elizabeth Hardwick in 1949 (divorced, 1972), one son; 3) the writer Caroline Blackwood in 1972, one son. Editorial Assistant, Sheed and Ward, publishers, New York, 1941–42; taught at the University of Iowa, Iowa City, 1949–50, 1952–53; Salzburg Seminar on American Studies, 1952; Boston University; New School for Social Research, New York; Harvard University; Professor of Literature, University of Essex, Wivenhoe, Colchester, 1970–72. Consultant in Poetry, Library of Congress, Washington, D.C., 1947–48; Visiting Fellow, All Souls College, Oxford, 1970. Recipient: Pulitzer Prize, 1947; National Institute of Arts and Letters grant, 1947; Guggenheim Fellowship, 1947, 1974; Harriet Monroe Poetry Award, 1952; Guinness Prize, 1959; National Book Award, 1960; Bollingen Poetry Translation Award, 1962; New England Poetry Club Golden Rose, 1964; Ford Foundation grant, for drama, 1964; Obie Award, for drama, 1965; Sarah Josepha Hale Award, 1966; Copernicus Award, 1974; National Medal for Literature, 1977. Member, American Academy of Arts and Letters. *Died 12 September 1977.*

PUBLICATIONS

Verse

Land of Unlikeness. Cummington, Massachusetts, Cummington Press, 1944.
Lord Weary's Castle. New York, Harcourt Brace, 1946.
Poems 1938–1949. London, Faber, 1950.
The Mills of the Kavanaughs. New York, Harcourt Brace, 1951.
Life Studies. London, Faber, 1959; augmented edition, New York, Farrar Straus, 1959; Faber, 1968.
Imitations. New York, Farrar Straus, 1961; London, Faber, 1962.
For the Union Dead. New York, Farrar Straus, 1964; London, Faber, 1965.
Selected Poems. London, Faber, 1965.
The Achievement of Robert Lowell: A Comprehensive Selection of His Poems with a Critical Introduction, edited by William J. Martz. Chicago, Scott Foresman, 1966.
Near the Ocean. New York, Farrar Straus, and London, Faber, 1967.
The Voyage and Other Versions of Poems by Baudelaire. New York, Farrar Straus, and London, Faber, 1968.
Notebook 1967–1968. New York, Farrar Straus, 1969; augmented edition, as *Notebook*, London, Faber, and Farrer Straus, 1970.
For Lizzie and Harriet. London, Faber, and New York, Farrar Straus, 1973.
History. London, Faber, and New York, Farrar Straus, 1973.
The Dolphin. London, Faber, and New York, Farrar Straus, 1973.
Poems: A Selection, edited by Jonathan Raban. London, Faber, 1974.
Selected Poems. New York, Farrar Straus, 1976; revised edition, 1977.
Day by Day. New York, Farrar Straus, 1977; London, Faber, 1978.

Plays

Phaedra, adaptation of the play by Racine (produced London, 1961). Included in *Phaedra and Figaro*, New York, Farrar Straus, 1961; as *Phaedra*, London, Faber, 1963.
The Old Glory (*Benito Cereno* and *My Kinsman, Major Molineux*) (produced New York, 1964; *Benito Cereno* produced London, 1967). New York, Farrar Straus, 1964; expanded version, including *Endecott and the Red Cross* (produced New York, 1968), London, Faber, 1966; Farrar Straus, 1968.
Prometheus Bound, adaptation of a play by Aeschylus (produced New Haven, Connecticut, 1967; London, 1971). New York, Farrar Straus, 1969; London, Faber, 1970.
The Oresteia of Aeschylus. New York, Farrar Straus, 1978; London, Faber, 1979.

Other

Editor, with Peter Taylor and Robert Penn Warren, *Randall Jarrell 1914–1965.* New York, Farrar Straus, 1967.

Critical Studies: *The Poetic Themes of Robert Lowell* by Jerome Mazzaro, Ann Arbor, University of Michigan Press, 1965; *Robert Lowell: A Collection of Critical Essays* edited by Thomas Parkinson, Englewood Cliffs, New Jersey, Prentice Hall, 1968; *Robert Lowell* by Richard J. Fein, New York, Twayne, 1970; *Critics on Robert Lowell* edited by Jonathan Price, Coral Gables, University of Miami Press, 1972, London, Allen and Unwin, 1974; *The Poetic Art of Robert Lowell* by Marjorie G. Perloff, Ithaca, New York, Cornell University Press, 1973; *The Poetry of Robert Lowell* by Vivian Smith, Sydney, Sydney University Press, 1974; *Circle to Circle: The Poetry of Robert Lowell* by Stephen Yenser, Berkeley, University of California Press, 1976; *Robert Lowell: Life and Art* by Steven Gould Axelrod, Princeton, New Jersey, Princeton University Press, 1978.

Robert Lowell comments:

(1970) I belong to no "school" of poetry, but various living or once-living poets have fascinated me – W. C. Williams, Pound, Tate, Ransom, Eliot, and Yeats. And many, many others, though perhaps I've tried to be a chameleon in vain.

A critical statement on my own verse? I know about my verse, I have been looking at it for a long time since I first started to write and revise. But this question must not be answered. One must only analyse oneself with great seriousness, or casually and intuitively. All these things you inquire about are subjects for the professors, their subjects, their inventions. I suppose these things have value, but go against the intellect. I don't like to read such pieces, see a writer I understand laid on the surgeon's table, see what was comprehensible made dull.

* * *

Robert Lowell's career plots the middle decades of the century, an era in which America consolidated its empire and leapt to the status of world power. After these ends were achieved, however, there followed the accelerated disintegration of the European heritage in America as technological and economic reorganization tended to devaluate the past. Caught in this transition were Lowell and other poets who believed deeply in the humanistic values and traditions of Europe, and who had a morbid distrust of the forces that seemed to be sweeping them away.

Hence Lowell's own life was his primary subject – the persona he projects must be seen as the late, possibly a final flowering of the New England spirit, with its deep attachment to Europe and its own American values of individuality and self-reliance. The political, economic, and cultural changes of the mid-century increasingly isolated Lowell, until even his personal disasters and pains became metaphors of the torment of historic change. Later in his canon, Lowell remembers other writers and friends, most of them now dead, as a last generation of true literacy, and that he now faced the cultural void alone.

Lowell began by embracing the strict literary conservatism of the southern Fugitive poets (themselves staunchly against industrialization) and wrote a book under their influence, *Land of Unlikeness*, of brittle and cluttered verse in traditional forms. "He was obsessed with his Augustinian idea of the modern world as a 'land of unlikeness' (*regio dissimilitudinis*)," Steven Axelrod observed, "a land in which human beings have lost their likeness to God and therefore have become alienated from themselves as well." Two years later, Lowell explored this theme more deeply in *Lord Weary's Castle*, but with more grace and flexibility. The poems are sombre expressions of post-World War II disillusionment and religious outrage: "war has taught me to revere/The rulers of this darkness," he declared in one poem. Lowell received the Pulitzer Prize for *Lord Weary's Castle*, but there followed a long and difficult period of writing that resulted in *The Mills of the Kavanaughs*, entirely made of dramatic monologues weighted with tedious detail and long, circuitous meditations.

Eight years later Lowell issued his masterpiece, *Life Studies*, which combines self-analysis with myth and history in a limpidly pure and imagistic language. Depths of agony and despair are illuminated with candid analysis and lifted beyond personal torment by a mind saturated with historical analogues. By wit and charm the voice urges upon us dreadful images of a life torn by disaster and alienation but without pathos or self-pitying. Throughout there is the persona caught reading and writing in a hell of domestic terrors – an image of the imperishable will and conscience. The verse is a balance of openness and measured diction achieved from careful study of William Carlos Williams. This freer style carried over to *For the Union Dead* with equal success – which sustains the attention to discord, private and public, and the suffering but resilient self.

Lowell chafed against his image as doleful confessionalist and returned to a stricter, more formalized verse in his series of *Notebooks*, later reordered as *History*, which he intended as his long poem. It too makes art from life but without the varied rhythms and forms of his earlier works. The fourteen-line segments become an unwieldy and monotonous pace for the immense length of this journal of ancient and current history. Lowell had lost the immediacy of felt life in this verse and became a mere chronicler instead. It too continues the theme of a lost culture and a dying past. A final work, *Day by Day*, returns to the conversational rhythm of *Life Studies* and is sombre in mood. The poet acknowledges the coming end of his own life at sixty years of age, and is elegiac on the deaths of many other poets.

Lowell is credited with having created confessional poetry – a verse that specializes in self-scrutiny and personal suffering in the mode of dramatic monologue. But the confessional impetus is only a small part of Lowell's purpose – in essence, he found his own life to be the instance of broadly shared feelings and so plundered and explored himself as a means of poetry. Many poets were influenced by his style, but few could catch the unique tonality and interest of a typical Lowell poem. Most imitators lost the Lowell ambience either by being mundanely thorough in their confessions or by shrilly exceeding him with tales of horror. The secret of Lowell is that he fully understood his moment in American history and reacted passionately to his times – creating therein both the integrity and the value of his self-analyzing poetry.

—Paul Christensen

O'HARA, Frank (Francis Russell O'Hara). American. Born in Baltimore, Maryland, 27 June 1926. Educated privately in piano and musical composition, 1933–43; New England Conservatory of Music, Boston, 1946–50; Harvard University, Cambridge, Massachusetts, 1946–50, A.B. in English 1950; University of Michigan, Ann Arbor (Hopwood Award, 1951), M.A. 1951. Served in the United States Navy, 1944–46. Staff Member, 1951–54, and Fellowship Curator, 1955–64, Associate Curator, 1965, and Curator of the International Program, 1966, Museum of Modern Art, New York. Editorial Associate, *Art News* magazine, New York, 1954–56; Art Editor, *Kulchur Magazine*, New York, 1962–64. Recipient: Ford Fellowship, for drama, 1956. *Died 25 July 1966.*

PUBLICATIONS

Verse

A City Winter and Other Poems. New York, Tibor de Nagy, 1952.
Oranges. New York, Tibor de Nagy, 1953.
Meditations in an Emergency. Palma, Mallorca, M. Alcover, 1956; New York, Grove Press, and London, Calder, 1957.
Hartigan and Rivers with O'Hara: An Exhibition of Pictures, with Poems. New York, Tibor de Nagy, 1959.
Second Avenue. New York, Totem-Corinth, and London, Centaur Press, 1960.
Odes. New York, Tiber, 1960.
Featuring Frank O'Hara. Buffalo, New York, Audit/Poetry, 1964.
Lunch Poems. San Francisco, City Lights, 1964.
Love Poems: Tentative Title. New York, Tibor de Nagy, 1965.
In Memory of My Feelings: A Selection of Poems, edited by Bill Berkson. New York, Museum of Modern Art, 1967.

Two Pieces. London, Long Hair, 1969.
Odes. New York, Poets Press, 1969.
The Collected Poems of Frank O'Hara, edited by Donald Allen. New York, Knopf, 1971.
Belgrade, November 19, 1963. New York, Adventures in Poetry, n.d.
Selected Poems, edited by Donald Allen. New York, Knopf, 1974.
Hymns of St. Bridget, with Bill Berkson. New York, Boke, 1974.
Standing Still and Walking in New York, edited by Donald Allen. Bolinas, California, Grey Fox Press, 1975.
Early Poems 1946–1951, edited by Donald Allen. Bolinas, California, Grey Fox Press, 1976.
Poems Retrieved 1951–1966, edited by Donald Allen. Bolinas, California, Grey Fox Press, 1977.

Plays

Try! Try! (produced Cambridge, Massachusetts, 1951; revised version, New York, 1952). Published in *Artists' Theatre*, edited by Herbert Machiz, New York, Grove Press, 1960.
Change Your Bedding (produced Cambridge, Massachusetts, 1952).
Love's Labor: An Eclogue (produced New York, 1959). New York, American Theater for Poets, 1964.
Awake in Spain (produced New York, 1960). New York, American Theater for Poets, 1960.
The General Returns from One Place to Another (produced New York, 1964).

Screenplay: *The Last Clean Shirt.*

Other

Jackson Pollock. New York, Braziller, 1959.
A Frank O'Hara Miscellany. Bolinas, California, Grey Fox Press, 1974.
Art Chronicles 1954–1966. New York, Braziller, 1975.

Editor, *Robert Motherwell: A Catalogue with Selections from the Artist's Writings.* New York, Museum of Modern Art, 1966.

Theatrical Activities:
Actor: **Play** – *Desire Caught by the Tail* by Pablo Picasso, New York, 1952.

Critical Studies: *Frank O'Hara, Poet among the Artists* by Marjorie G. Perloff, New York, Braziller, 1977.

* * *

F. S. C. Northrop speaks in *The Logic of the Sciences and the Humanities* of the value of relentlessly generalizing a given verifiable scientific theory. This extends, as he himself might point out, to the humanities, where the weakness of a particular aesthetic may be seen by the relentless attempt to hypostasize it. In much of so-called "New York School" work, the relentless derivatives of American surrealism, "abstract expressionism," pop, or what label you will, show weaknesses of an art without the transcendental term; an art low, repetitive, solipsistic. But in the great original, Frank O'Hara, one sees the intense first case, with all its multifoliate strengths. While the few verse plays seem merely vapid verse descendants of the early Auden-and-Isherwood collaborations, or the Auden of "The Orators," the poetry of O'Hara speaks to us as a sensuous analogue of Lorca.

If the weakness of the "hardboiled empiricist," in Northrop's scheme, is that of the impressionist, fresh but lacking in the theoretical or moral component, then the charge of "frivolity," often hurled at O'Hara, can be understood. O'Hara's way out of a mere "abstract impressionism" was to be converted early to a Pasternakian sense of "the revolutionary city." While the "pure facts" of his "I Do This – I Do That" poems are now everyone's ineffable birthright, O'Hara's mature strength lies in this continuous affirmation of liberty and possible liberations. His personalism, randomnesses, spontaneities, hermeticisms, etc., must be interpreted as Dr. Meyer Schapiro interpreted the paintings of Pollock: efforts in a hypocritical age to maintain an integrity despite manufactured vocabularies.

In some of the poems of Allen Ginsberg – a friend of O'Hara's – there is adumbrated a romantic love of "experience and travel" and O'Hara's connection to this was in his love for the purely inductive methods of empiricism. He was, in this sense, as Kenneth Koch pointed out years ago, the most competent poet to convey New York City in its pure factuality. If he has seemed a revolutionary poet without a revolution, he made of this lack a central and abiding metaphor.

Very early he mastered and modulated academic dictions into something tessellated, vivid, everyday. The early "To the Harbormaster," recited at his funeral by John Ashbery, remains one of the finest examples of his coherent laments. His later, discontinuous streams might seem the work of a mind unable to sustain a vehicle or tenor, but this early exemplum proves that he could.

His discontinuities were selected audaciously to break down false, glib, "silver" continuities (see in the by-now infamous Hall-Pack anthology of the 1950's) with a reliance on neo-Georgianism, neo-Yeatsism, "neo, neo, neo." O'Hara's disjunction was a betrayal of the norm, releasing the usual emotions of such a betrayal. Psychologism, naturalism, verismo, too, are betrayed, as they are in his flat, parodistic plays (one is reminded, too, of Koch's farces).

Where the political poems of the Latin American surrealists often seem purple and mismanaged, O'Hara was able to synthesize private and public dimensions through a *collagiste* method analogous to Robert Rauschenberg's. Influenced by Neruda, he is capable of the rhapsodical manner allied to a drab and touching quality of newspaperese.

While never as flat and plain as the prose parodies of John Ashbery, it is O'Hara's *collagiste* flatness, in juxtaposition to his glamours, camps, and *potestas* or bravura passages, which distinguish him from the Latin Americans of his generation – the witty prose of Borges being the exception here. While James Wright and Robert Bly were influenced by the Chinese poets of the Tang period, Rilke, Trakl, and the Latin American surrealists, O'Hara seemed best able to digest and enucleate all such influences but with no connotatively encrusted diction. And his parodies are explicit and sharp.

Behind his images of whimsy, his Firbankian modes, behind his nostalgias and manners, behind the "Chaucerian cheerfulness" that Vendler has evaluated, lies O'Hara's peculiarly revolutionary hedonism, shared by Koch, and which, in the love poems (see *Love Poems: Tentative Title*) result in poems of exquisite empathies in a time of crisis. The Keatsian obsession with pleasure is fundamental, but an elementary other is addressed, a Buberian need for a real "you" is resolved, and the poems seem as convincing as overheard telephone conversations. In his long "Ode to Michael Goldberg's Birth and Other Births," with its closing crescendo "and he shall be the wings of an extraordinary liberty," one notes a sustained mode of examining one's self as an "other," as in the self-lacerating monologues of Ashbery. These sustained, self-lacerating, prose-ridden odes seem exemplary syntheses.

For many poets of his so-called "New York School" the problem lay in the aestheticization of the universe. This problem, comparable to the eroticization of the ego, with its concomitant dessications and addictions, was not a problem for O'Hara, who did not give in to a regressive narcissism. He found a proper relationship to things, and he speaks of this rapport in his great Mayakovskian "A True Account of Talking to the Sun at Fire Island." As with his friend LeRoi Jones, cultural psychopathology was adequately summoned, abused, and/or countermanded. His adequate vision of the city was not one of mere Whitmanesque joys; even in *Second Avenue*, the city is also an incubus, a spectre, like the cyst which grew larger than the host. In many poets influenced by O'Hara, the city and the facts of urbanity loom more solidly than the poets themselves. But this was not O'Hara's problem, though he is seen too often as thoughtless and exponentially dandified.

His poetry is filled with his resentments, and his rights to those resentments. While his coterie may have glamorized false collaborations (see the *Locus Solus* issue on Collaboration, edited by Koch) in direct ratio to its truer lack of relations, the best work of O'Hara is of a non-imperialistic ego, never engulfed or engulfing. If his work seems capricious, it reminds us that, as Whitehead said, "exactness is a fake."

—David Shapiro

OKIGBO, Christopher (Ifenayichukwu). Nigerian. Born in Ojoto, Onitsha Province, in 1932. Educated at Umuahia Government College; University College, Ibadan, 1951–56, B.A. in classics 1956. Served in the Biafran Defense Forces: killed in action, 1967. Married Sefi, daughter of the Attah of Igberra, in 1963; one daughter. Worked for the Nigerian Tobacco Company and the United Africa Company. Latin teacher, Fiditi Grammar School, 1959–60; Assistant Librarian, University of Nsukka, 1960–62; Cambridge University Press Nigerian Representative, 1962–66. *Died in August 1967.*

PUBLICATIONS

Verse

Heavensgate. Ibadan, Mbari, 1962.
Limits. Ibadan, Mbari, 1964.
Labyrinths, with Path of Thunder. London, Heinemann, and New York, Africana, 1971.

Critical Studies: *The Trial of Okigbo* by Ali A. Mazrui, London, Heinemann, 1971; *Christopher Okigbo: Creative Rhetoric* by Sunday O Anozie, London, Evans, and New York, Holmes and Meier, 1972.

* * *

The death of Christopher Okigbo, a rich and rarely attractive personality, in the 1967 war in Nigeria, was a tragic loss to African literature in English. He was one of the most promising of that group of poets of whom Wole Soyinka said, "they regroup images of Ezra Pound round the oil bean and the nude spear." Certainly the influence of Pound is evident in Okigbo's work, in the light, floating rhythms, in the abolition of transitions and connectives, in the cool, outlined imagery, and in the vast rag-bag of learning. Okigbo's poetry has an impressive intellectual content which seems to come from blending a Latin view of life with an African energy and feeling. His poetry brings the powerful oral tradition of Africa into the world of contemporary literary practice, and he manages with a considerable degree of success to keep these two traditions and idioms in play without friction or disharmony:

The Stars have departed,
the sky in monocle
surveys the world under.

The stars have departed,
and I – where am I?

Stretch, stretch, O antennae,
to clutch at this hour,

fulfilling each moment in a
broken monody.

Okigbo was a peculiarly conscious poet, in the manner of Pound and Eliot, and there are a remarkable number of oblique or half-suppressed references to the work of other poets in his verse, just as there are many – too many, one often thinks – private references in the manner of Auden. But there is unmistakably a highly distinctive literary personality implicit in the poetry, together with a gift for rhythmic variation and considerable metaphorical vivacity. He was brought up as a Christian but still maintained a living relationship with his own village and its gods and rituals, and in fact managed successfully to reconcile these two modes of religious experience. Religious experience is a basic and constant theme of the poetry. He accepts its presence and reality with a naturalness quite uncommon in contemporary verse; and although he maintained in an interview in 1965 (*Journal of Commonwealth Literature*, July 1970) that he saw the African writer as having no particular function as teacher or preacher, except simply to be a writer, he takes a decidedly sacred or priestly view of his own function as poet. In the opening passage of *Heavensgate*, his first volume of poems, he wrote:

Before you, mother Idoto,
    naked I stand,
before your watery presence,
    a prodigal,

leaning on an oilbean;
lost in your legend ...

Under your power wait I on barefoot,
Watchman for the watchword at
    HEAVENSGATE:

out of the depths my cry
give ear and hearken.

In much of his poetry, and fairly explicitly in the late sequence, "Limits," he attempts to identify, or at least to bring very closely together, religious experience and poetic experience, as well as the processes of religious and poetic inspiration. He saw each as the attempt to achieve a ritual integrity. It is clear that Okigbo had not arrived at a clear or full articulation of his poetic theory, but all his practice demonstrates that he had, in spite of a certain immaturity, a pure and impressive talent. His talent gained in richness and point from his never suffering any feeling of alienation from his own society or its past, from his supple virtuosity in exploring the most varied sources of imagery, rhythm and illusion, and from his never attempting to muffle the effect of poetry by importing into it other social or political ends.

—William Walsh

OLSON, Charles (John). American. Born in Worcester, Massachusetts, 27 December 1910. Educated at Wesleyan University, Middletown, Connecticut, B.A. 1932, M.A. 1933; Yale University, New Haven, Connecticut; Harvard University, Cambridge, Massachusetts. Taught at Clark University, Worcester, and Harvard University, 1936–39; Instructor and Rector, Black Mountain College, North Carolina, 1951–56; taught at State University of New York, Buffalo, 1963–65, and University of Connecticut, Storrs, 1969. Recipient: Guggenheim grant (twice); Wenner-Gren Foundation grant, 1952; Oscar Blumenthal Prize (*Poetry*, Chicago), 1965; National Endowment for the Arts grant, 1966, 1968. *Died 10 January 1970.*

PUBLICATIONS

Verse

Corrado Cagli March 31 Through April 19 1947. New York, Knoedler, 1947.
Y & X. Washington, D.C., Black Sun Press, 1948.
Letter for Melville 1951. Privately printed, 1951.
This. Black Mountain, North Carolina, Black Mountain College Graphics Workshop, 1952.
In Cold Hell, in Thicket. Palma, Mallorca, Divers Press, 1953; San Francisco, Four Seasons, 1967.
The Maximus Poems 1–10. Stuttgart, Jonathan Williams, 1953.
Ferrini and Others, with others. Berlin, Gerhardt, 1955.
Anecdotes of the Late War. Highlands, North Carolina, Jargon, 1955.
The Maximus Poems 11–22. Stuttgart, Jonathan Williams, 1956.
O'Ryan 2 4 6 8 10. San Francisco, White Rabbit Press, 1958; expanded edition as *O'Ryan 12345678910*, 1965.
The Maximus Poems. New York, Jargon–Corinth Books, and London, Centaur Press, 1960.
The Distances. New York, Grove Press, 1960.
Maximus, From Dogtown I. San Francisco, Auerhahn Press, 1961.
Signature to Petition on Ten Pound Island Asked of Me by Mr. Vincent Ferrini. San Francisco, Oyez, 1964.
West. London, Goliard Press, 1966.
Charles Olson Reading at Berkeley, edited by Zoe Brown. San Francisco, Coyote, 1966.
Before Your Very Eyes!, with others. London, Cape Goliard Press, 1967.
The Maximus Poems, IV, V, VI. London, Cape Goliard Press, and New York, Grossman, 1968.
Reading about My World. Buffalo, Institute of Further Studies, 1968.
Added to Making a Republic. Buffalo, Institute of Further Studies, 1968.
Clear Shifting Water. Buffalo, Institute of Further Studies, 1968.
That There Was a Woman in Gloucester, Massachusetts. Buffalo, Institute of Further Studies, 1968.
Wholly Absorbed into My Own Conduits. Buffalo, Institute of Further Studies, 1968.
Causal Mythology. San Francisco, Four Seasons, 1969.
Archaeologist of Morning: The Collected Poems Outside the Maximus Series. London, Cape Goliard Press, and New York, Grossman, 1970.
Maximus, to Himself. San Francisco, Spanish Main Press, 1970.
New Man and Woman. Privately printed, 1970.
May 20, 1959. Middletown, Connecticut, Wesleyan University, 1970.
The Maximus Poems, Volume Three, edited by Charles Boer and George F. Butterick. New York, Grossman, 1975.

Recording: *Charles Olson Reads from Maximus Poems*, Folkways, 1975.

Plays

The Fiery Hunt and Other Plays. Bolinas, California, Four Seasons, 1977.

Short Story

Stocking Cap: A Story. San Francisco, Four Seasons, 1966.

Other

Call Me Ishmael: A Study of Melville. New York, Reynal, 1947; London, Cape, 1967.
Apollonius of Tyana: A Dance, with Some Words, for Two Actors. Black Mountain, North Carolina, Black Mountain College, 1951.
Mayan Letters, edited by Robert Creeley. Palma, Mallorca, Divers Press, 1954; London, Cape, and New York, Grossman, 1968.
Projective Verse. New York, Totem, 1959.
A Bibliography on America for Ed Dorn. San Francisco, Four Seasons, 1964.
Pleistocene Man: Letters from Charles Olson to John Clarke during October, 1965. Buffalo, Institute of Further Studies, 1968.
Human Universe and Others Essays, edited by Donald Allen. San Francisco, Auerhahn Press, 1965.
Proprioception. San Francisco, Four Seasons, 1965.
Selected Writings, edited by Robert Creeley. New York, New Directions, 1966.
Letters for "Origin" 1950–1956, edited by Albert Glover. London, Cape Goliard Press, 1969; New York, Grossman, 1970.
The Special View of History, edited by Ann Charters. Berkeley, California, Oyez, 1970.
Poetry and Truth: The Beloit Lectures and Poems, edited by George F. Butterick. San Francisco, Four Seasons, 1971.
Additional Prose: A Bibliography on America, Proprioception, and Other Notes and Essays, edited by George F. Butterick. Bolinas, California, Four Seasons, 1974.
The Post Office: A Memoir of His Father. Bolinas, California, Grey Fox Press, 1974.
In Adullam's Lair (lecture). Provincetown, Massachusetts, To the Lighthouse Press, 1975.
Muthologos: The Collected Lectures and Interviews of Charles Olson, edited by George F. Butterick. Bolinas, California, Four Seasons, 1976.

Bibliography: *A Bibliography of Works by Charles Olson* by George F. Butterick and Albert Glover, New York, Phoenix Bookshop, 1967.

Critical Studies: *Olson/Melville: A Study in Affinity*, San Francisco, Oyez, 1968, and *Charles Olson: The Special View of History*, San Francisco, Oyez, 1970, both by Ann Charters; "Charles Olson Issues" of *Boundary* (Binghamton, New York), Fall 1973 and Winter 1974; *Olson's Push: "Origin," Black Mountain, and Recent American Poetry* by Sherman Paul, Baton Rouge, Louisiana State University Press, 1978; *Charles Olson: Call Him Ishmael* by Paul Christensen, Austin, University of Texas Press, 1979; *Charles Olson: The Scholar's Art* by Robert von Hallberg, Cambridge, Massachusetts, Harvard University Press, 1979.

* * *

Because Charles Olson has been considered the mentor of an entire school of poets – that growing out of the extremely interesting Black Mountain College group in the early Fifties – his readers have been as interested in knowing his doctrines as his poems. A typical (and reductive) summary of Olson's essay on Projective Verse is a claim by former Oxford Professor of Poetry Roy Fuller that Olson's Essay "conveniently contains its recipes and claims," chiefly "a number of exhortations to write good verse.... A poem is to concentrate on the syllable rather than, e.g., on metre and rhyme. The line must be kept from slowness, deadness, by being suspicious of description, of adjectives, of similes. The individual breath gives language its force, the force of speech, and in so far as the logical conventions of syntax hamper this force they must, in projective verse, go. The typewriter, because of its precision with spacing, is the personal and instantaneous recorder of the poet's work: with it he can indicate exactly the breath, the pauses, the suspension – even of syllables – and the juxtaposition – even of parts of phrases – he intends." Fuller then comments on Olson's sentimentality, perhaps failing to realize that sentimentality and dead seriousness often look alike. In his major work, *The Maximus Poems*, Olson not only demonstrated his theories, "found his measure," but also constructed a suitable vehicle for quite varied poems, both of his personal experience and of his reactions to the city of Gloucester, Massachusetts "where fishing continues/and my heart lies." Whether his poem's parallels and indebtedness to Pound's *Cantos* and Williams's *Paterson* really matters, I can't say; to me the poem justifies itself in individual songs:

that which will last,
that! o my people, where shall you find it, how, where, where shall you listen
when all is become billboards, when, all, even silence, is spray-gunned?
when even our bird, my roofs,
cannot be heard
when even you, when sound itself is neoned in?

Olson's domestic poems of everyday life are intense, whether he is cussing out the Melville society (his *Call Me Ishmael* is an important book, especially in tracing Melville's sources in Shakespeare), or commenting on his household:

Or the plumbing,
that it doesn't work, this I like, have even used paper clips
as well as string to hold the ball up And flush it
with my hand
But that the car doesn't, that no moving thing moves
without that song I'd void my ear of, the musickracket
of all ownership....

But Olson harks "back to an older polis,/who has this tie to a time when the port" was involved in a fabulous history. To me, these lines about John Smith and Miles Standish, about what fourteen men required as food and supplies in the winter of 1624/25, these asides on "the nature of the cargo" are not so interesting as the present, when Olson observes:

love was
Or ought to be,
like an orange tree!
(The way they do grow
in that ex-sea soil,
in that pumice dust only a fowl
can scratch a living from).

His pictures achieve the vividness of a Hiroshige, or of netsuke:

They should raise a monument
to a fisherman crouched down
behind a hogshead, protecting
his dried fish.

Many of Olson's disciples prefer to concentrate on the philosophy in his work, and on his fairly systematic and interesting ideas, delivered in reaction to the classics, to Sumerians and Mayans, expounded in letters that have become a literature in themselves; they would be unhappy to find him characterized as a master of sketches, glimpses. But to me his best poems are humorous and domestic, rather than scholarly; his best work can be read without footnotes. Many who worship Olson, whose integrity as teacher and artist has inspired them, have perhaps overlooked his lines: "There is a limit/to what a car/will do." In concentrating on his seriousness they overlook the maker of netsuke; they neglect to admire the lightness, the humor, of the artist they've overlooked by turning him into a sage. This is, after all, the man who ate his own polishing cloth:

> Trouble
> with the car. And for a buck
> they gave me
> what I found myself
> eating! A polishing
> cloth. And I went right on
> eating it, it was that good.
> And thick, color
> orange & black, with a map – the billowing dress
> the big girl wears
> every so often.

In the time since his death, Olson has been more than ever venerated as a poet who inspired and taught such students as Robert Creeley and Hilda Morley, who continue to acknowledge his importance for their work. Many poets, including this one, felt a genuine grief for the loss of Charles Olson, and some of us much resented the vulgarity of the picture published in *The Antioch Review* of Charles Olson in his casket. A better memorial is in the work of his students and followers, in whom his words are "modified in the guts of the living."

—David Ray

PATCHEN, Kenneth. American. Born in Niles, Ohio, 13 December 1911. Educated at Warren High School, Ohio; the Experimental College, University of Wisconsin, Madison, 1928–29. Married Miriam Oikemus in 1934. Also an artist: one-man show – Corcoran Gallery, Washington, D.C., 1969. Recipient: Guggenheim Fellowship, 1936; Shelley Memorial Award, 1954; National Endowment for the Arts Distinguished Service Grant. 1967. *Died 8 January 1972.*

PUBLICATIONS

Verse

Before the Brave. New York, Random House, 1936.
First Will and Testament. New York, New Directions, 1939.
The Teeth of the Lion. New York, New Directions, 1942.
The Dark Kingdom. New York, Harriss and Givens, 1942.
Cloth of the Tempest. New York and London, Harper, 1943.
An Astonished Eye Looks Out of the Air, Being Some Poems Old and New Against War and in Behalf of Life. Waldport, Oregon, Untide Press, 1945.

Outlaw of the Lowest Planet, edited by David Gascoyne. London, Grey Walls Press, 1946.
Selected Poems. New York, New Directions, 1946; revised edition, 1958, 1964.
Pictures of Life and of Death. New York, Padell, 1947.
They Keep Riding Down All the Time. New York, Padell, 1947.
Panels for the Walls of Heaven. Berkeley, California, Bern Porter, 1947.
Be Music, Night: Poem for Voice and Piano, music by David Leo Diamond. New York, Carl Fischer, 1948.
CCCLXXIV Poems. New York, Padell, 1948.
To Say If You Love Someone and Other Selected Love Poems. Prairie City, Illinois, Decker Press, 1948.
Red Wine and Yellow Hair. New York, New Directions, 1949.
Orchards, Thrones, and Caravans. San Francisco, Print Workshop, 1952.
Fables and Other Little Tales. Karlsruhe, Germany, Jonathan Williams, 1953.
The Famous Boating Party and Other Poems in Prose. New York, New Directions, 1954.
Poems of Humour and Protest. San Francisco, City Lights, 1954.
Rain, Wind, Light, Cold. Sausalito, California, Bern Porter, 1955.
The Moment. Privately printed, 1955(?).
Glory Never Guesses. Privately printed, 1956.
A Surprise for the Bagpipe Player. Privately printed, 1956.
When We Were Here Together. New York, New Directions, 1957.
Hurrah for Anything. Highlands, North Carolina, Jargon, 1957.
Two Poems for Christmas. Privately printed, 1958.
Poem-scapes. Highlands, North Carolina, Jargon, 1958.
Pomes Penyeach. Privately printed, 1959.
Because It Is. New York, New Directions, 1960.
A Poem for Christmas. Privately printed, 1960.
Love Poems. San Francisco, City Lights, 1960; London, Scorpion Press, 1961.
Drawing-Poem. Palo Alto, California, Patchen Cards, 1962.
Picture Poems. Palo Alto, California, Patchen Cards, 1962.
Doubleheader. New York, New Directions, 1966.
Hallelujah Anyway. New York, New Directions, 1966.
Where Are the Other Rowboats? Privately printed, 1966.
But Even So. New York, New Directions, 1968.
Love and War Poems, edited by Dennis Gould. Mickleover, Derby, Whisper and Shout, 1968.
Selected Poems. London, Cape, 1968.
The Collected Poems of Kenneth Patchen. New York, New Directions, 1968.
Aflame and Afun of Walking Faces: Fables and Drawings. New York, New Directions, 1970.
There's Love All Day, edited by Dee Danner Barwick. Kansas City, Missouri, Hallmark, 1970.
Wonderings. New York, New Directions, 1971.
In Quest of Candlelighters. New York, New Directions, 1972.
A Poem for Christmas. Mountain View, California, Artichoke, 1976.

Recordings: *Kenneth Patchen Reads His Poetry with the Chamber Jazz Sextet*, Cadence, 1958; *Kenneth Patchen Reads Poetry with Jazz in Canada*, Folkways, 1959; *Kenneth Patchen Reads His Selected Poems*, Folkways, 1959; *Kenneth Patchen Reads His Love Poems*, Folkways, 1961.

Plays

The City Wears a Slouch Hat (broadcast, 1942). Included in *Lost Plays*, 1977.

Now You See It (Don't Look Now) (produced New York, 1966). Included in *Lost Plays*, 1977.
Lost Plays (includes *Don't Look Now* and *The City Wears a Slouch Hat*), edited by Richard Morgan. Santa Barbara, California, Capra Press, 1977.

Radio Play: *The City Wears a Slouch Hat*, 1942.

Novels

The Journal of Albion Moonlight. Privately printed, 1941.
The Memoirs of a Shy Pornographer: An Amusement. New York, New Directions, 1945; London, Grey Walls Press, 1948.
Sleepers Awake. New York, Padell, 1946.
See You in the Morning. New York, Padell, 1948; London, Grey Walls Press, 1949.

Other

Kenneth Patchen: Painter of Poems (exhibition catalogue). Baltimore, Garamond-Pridemark Press, 1969.
The Argument of Innocence: A Selection from the Arts of Kenneth Patchen, edited by Peter Veres. San Francisco, Scrimshaw Press, 1976.

Bibliography: *Kenneth Patchen: A First Bibliography* by Gail Eaton, Denver, Swallow, 1948; *Kenneth Patchen: A Descriptive Bibliography*, Mamaroneck, New York, Paul P. Appel, 1978.

Manuscript Collection: University of California, Santa Cruz.

Critical Studies: *Kenneth Patchen, Man of Anger and Light* by Henry Miller, New York, Padell, 1947; *Kenneth Patchen: A Collection of Essays* edited by Richard Morgan, New York, AMS Press, 1977; *Tribute to Kenneth Patchen*, London, Enitharmon Press, 1977; *Kenneth Patchen* by Larry R. Smith, Boston, Twayne, 1978.

* * *

Kenneth Patchen was one of America's great poet-prophets. This range of his work holds the wildness of America's energy and all the horror implicit in her need for self-destruction. It continues the proud fury of Whitman's large vision of the U.S.A.

Patchen's work is a Bible torn out of America's heart. It is the prophet's urgent warning. It is a righteous refusal to accept the end of man.

Everything Patchen created reveals his effort to make sense of a people bent on destroying the human spirit and the planet man lives upon. Patchen warned man, hating, loving and smooth-talking man, for over a quarter of a century. Like all great poet-prophets, Patchen continued to forgive man. To bind the wounds and heal the maimed and mad victims of America's paradox.

It's all there in his work. In the many volumes of poetry. In his illuminated tracts and ikons: his talismanic wall-hangings warning Fear and Stupidity that Love is in town and well-armed. It's there in his blood-roaring apocalyptic novels, *The Journal of Albion Moonlight* and *Sleepers Awake*. The waterfall of those novels is balanced rightly with his two love novels: the naked *See You in the Morning* and *Memoirs of a Shy Pornographer*. It's there in the care and charm of his handbound, handpainted books. It's there in his voice reading his poems backed-up by the Chamber Jazz Sextet.

It's there in his work. The history of the American poet-myth.

During the Depression, Patchen wrote Blakean hymns to the Revolution of the Proletariat – which really didn't happen. (All revolts seem to change masks and the revolutionaries often wind-up looking suspiciously like the Enemy.) Patchen was hailed as one of the foremost young Proletarian Poets ("The World Will Have Little Note"):

O not the drill and brazen energy of singing.
We shall reach a stand and cause for fighting.
O we should be the hunter in the hall of eternity.

But the workers didn't have time to read or use Patchen's poems.

During World War II he wrote passionate and furious words to fight back insane shadow-beasts bent on devouring earth. His songs insisted on man's great potential. They sang of love's imperative necessity. We must care, or we perish ("What Is the Beautiful"):

And begin again.
It would take little to be free.
That no man live at the expense of another.
Because no man can own what belongs to all.
Becuase no man can kill what all must use.
Because no man can lie when all are betrayed.
Because no man can hate when all are hated.

But soldiers need bullets and bombs, not poems. When man makes war his singing turns to screaming. The screams are louder than death. The screams are louder than the bombs, the bullets, or the poems.

It is a paradox. The center of man's need to create is his journey to Light. Yet, at the same time, and on the same road, man will refuse to listen to the message of Angels. In his desire to conquer earth and himself, man often re-routes God's messengers. This paradox is crucial to understanding the poet-myth in America: "I never had any other desire so strong, and so like to covetousness, as that one which I have had always, that I might be master at last of a small house and a contenting woman, with moderate conveniences joined to them, and, living there and with her to love, dedicate the remainder of my life only to the culture of myself ..." (*First Will and Testament*). Patchen was the wounded Cupid of the American dream.

He lay on his back in dark pain. His spinal agony limited his mobility. He was cared for by his wife Miriam. She protected him and acted as his liaison to the outer world. She provided space and ease for him to work.

For over 20 years, Patchen was infirm. Doctors, operations, hospital expenses, pharmacological idiocy, combined with the basic needs of survival, drained him and wounded him, but did not crush him. This kind of torture-wheel, a strange space-station, rarely stops spinning around most poets. Often it blinds them. Thank God it rarely silences them.

Patchen's work has always sung to the youth. His work reveals and affirms their hopes and strength. His work has always spoken to men of spirit and passion. From the 1930's to today, Patchen's intense and humane visions have inspired new generations of poets and writers. Like Blake and Whitman, his spiritual forefathers, Patchen lays the vital groundwork of man's future. His work continues the necessary stream of visionary art for our time and for Eternity.

—David Meltzer

PLATH, Sylvia. American. Born in Boston, Massachusetts, 27 October 1932. Educated at Smith College, Northampton, Massachusetts (Glasscock Prize, 1955), B.A. (summa cum laude) in English 1955 (Phi Beta Kappa); Newnham College, Cambridge (Fulbright Scholar), 1955–57, M.A. 1957. Married Ted Hughes, *q.v.*, in 1956 (separated, 1962); one daughter and one son. Guest Editor, *Mademoiselle* magazine, New York, Summer 1953. Instructor in English, Smith College, 1957–58. Moved to England in 1959. Recipient: Bess Hokin Award (*Poetry*, Chicago), 1957; Yaddo Fellowship, 1959; Cheltenham Festival award, 1961; Saxon Fellowship, 1961. *Died 11 February 1963.*

PUBLICATIONS

Verse

A Winter Ship (published anonymously). Edinburgh, Tragara Press, 1960.
The Colossus. London, Heinemann, 1960; New York, Knopf, 1962.
Ariel. London, Faber, 1965; New York, Harper, 1966.
Uncollected Poems. London, Turret, 1965.
Wreath for a Bridal. Frensham, Surrey, Sceptre Press, 1970.
Million Dollar Month. Frensham, Surrey, Sceptre Press, 1971.
Fiesta Melons. Exeter, Rougemont Press, 1971.
Crossing the Water, edited by Ted Hughes. London, Faber, and New York, Harper, 1971.
Crystal Gazer and Other Poems. London, Rainbow Press, 1971.
Lyonesse: Hitherto Uncollected Poems. London, Rainbow Press, 1971.
Winter Trees. London, Faber, 1971; New York, Harper, 1972.
Child. Exeter, Rougement Press, 1971.
Pursuit. London, Rainbow Press, 1973.

Recording: *Sylvia Plath Reading Her Poetry*, Caedmon, 1977.

Play

Three Women: A Monologue for Three Voices (broadcast, 1962; produced New York and London, 1973).

Radio Play: *Three Women*, 1962 (UK).

Novel

The Bell Jar (as Victoria Lucas). London, Heinemann, 1963; as Sylvia Plath, London, Faber, 1966; with drawings, New York, Harper, 1971.

Short Stories

Penguin Modern Stories 2, with others. London, Penguin, 1969.

Other

Letters Home: Correspondence 1950–1963, edited by Aurelia Schober Plath. New York, Harper, 1975; London, Faber, 1976.
The Bed Book (juvenile). New York, Harper, and London, Faber, 1976.
Sylvia Plath: A Dramatic Portrait (miscellany), edited by Barry Kyle. London, Faber, 1976.
Johnny Panic and the Bible of Dreams, and Other Prose Writings, edited by Ted Hughes. London, Faber, 1977; augmented edition, Faber, and New York, Harper, 1979.

Editor, *American Poetry Now: A Selection of the Best Poems by Modern American Writers.* London, Oxford University Press, 1961.

Bibliography: *A Chronological Checklist of the Periodical Publications of Sylvia Plath* by Eric Homberger, Exeter, University of Exeter American Arts Documentation Centre, 1970; *Sylvia Plath: A Bibliography* by Gary Lane and Maria Stevens, Metuchen, New Jersey, Scarecrow Press, 1978.

Critical Studies: *The Art of Sylvia Plath: A Symposium* edited by Charles Newman, Bloomington, Indiana University Press, and London, Faber, 1970; *A Closer Look at "Ariel": A Memory of Sylvia Plath* by Nancy Hunter Steiner, New York, Harper's Magazine Press, 1973, London, Faber, 1974; *Sylvia Plath* by Eileen M. Aird, New York, Harper, 1973, Edinburgh, Oliver and Boyd, 1974; *Sylvia Plath: Method and Madness* by Edward Butscher, New York, Seabury Press, 1976; *Sylvia Plath: The Woman and Her Work* edited by Edward Butscher, New York, Dodd Mead, 1977, London, Peter Owen, 1979; *Sylvia Plath and Ted Hughes* by Margaret Dickie Uroff, Urbana, University of Illinois Press, 1979; *Sylvia Plath: New Views on the Poetry* edited by Gary Lane, Baltimore, Johns Hopkins University Press, 1979; *Sylvia Plath: The Poetry of Limitation* by Jon Rosenblatt, Chapel Hill, University of North Carolina Press, 1979.

* * *

After her suicide in 1963, Sylvia Plath gained that kind of public notoriety that seems inevitably reserved for just those artists who die voluntarily. She was 30 years old, the mother of two children. By 1965 *Ariel* was published, a book consisting of poems, the dust jacket says, "Written in the last months of her life, and often rushed out at the rate of two or three a day." There followed republication of her first volume of poems, *The Colossus*, and of *The Bell Jar*, a novel first published in England under the pseudonym Victoria Lucas. Within three years of her death Sylvia Plath became the world's most widely-read contemporary suicide. Critics pointed to the suicidal hints within her beautifully crafted poems and implied that their authenticity derived somehow from the *fait accompli*.

In *The Bell Jar*, which recounts the author's experience as a prize-winning college writer who attempts suicide, Plath anticipated the grim humor of her own posthumous popularity. "Then I remembered that at medical school Buddy had won a prize for persuading the most relatives of dead people to have their dead ones cut up whether they needed it or not, in the interests of science." Following *Ariel*, a number of other poetry collections were issued, but her best work, and that indisputably finished by her own hand, is available in the three books mentioned here by title.

While it is inescapable that the grim humor of Plath's work reflects the personality of a suicide (as the writings of Professors reflect the personalities of professors) the actual life, the liveliness, the play within her writing is too often missed by readers whose attention is diverted by her death. At 30, Plath had developed her craft to a point far beyond what many poets ever reach. That she did so within the confines of motherhood and a shaky marriage suggests that like a citrus seed, poets progress fastest when squeezed. And her cry of desperate ordinariness reminds us that the universe of death may be far more intriguing to the genius than flower gardens and changing diapers.

Sylvia Plath's poems are so personal that they often assume separate personae. "Daddy," a hateful love poem for a father whose early death she resents, blends the voice of a young girl with that of a hardened adult. Like much of her work, the poem has rhyme, established here with the repetition (more than 60 times in 80 lines!) of a single sound:

> You stand at the blackboard, daddy,
> In the picture I have of you,
> A cleft in your chin instead of your foot
> But no less a devil for that, no not
> Any less the black man who

Bit my pretty red heart in two.
I was ten when they buried you.
At twenty I tried to die
And get back, back, back to you.
I thought even the bones would do.

The limerick quality within these verses, in contrast to the subject, reinforces the struggle between the poem's personae. The culmination of the struggle and the play is realized with the final lines, where the poem focuses on its own deepest bitterness:

There's a stake in your fat black heart
And the villagers never liked you.
They are dancing and stamping on you.
They always *knew* it was you.
Daddy, daddy, you bastard, I'm through.

In "Cut," which describes slicing with the shears "My thumb instead of an onion," Plath takes the other road and celebrates pain so lightly that the slightness of her reaction becomes a part of the poem's substance. Again, the persona vibrates between at least two identities, that of gardener and that of cut thumb, which (pun intended) *becomes* the poet:

The balled
Pulp of your heart
Confronts its small
Mill of silence

How you jump –
Trepanned veteran,
Dirty girl,
Thumb stump.

Plath's genius existed not so much in the uniqueness of her vision as in what she could do with that vision linguistically, how compact and almost orderly she could make it all, in opposition, always, to the pathos thus described. Here, finally, from *The Colossus*, is "Aftermath" in its entirety:

Compelled by calamity's magnet
They loiter and stare as if the house
Burnt-out were theirs, or as if they thought
Some scandal might any minute ooze
From a smoke-choked closet into light;
No deaths, no prodigious injuries
Glut these hunters after an old meat,
Blood-spoor of the austere tragedies.

Mother Medea in a green smock
Moves humbly as any housewife through
Her ruined apartments, taking stock
Of charred shoes, the sodden upholstery:
Cheated of the pyre and the rack,
The crowd sucks her last tear and turns away.

—Geof Hewitt

ROETHKE, Theodore (Huebner). American. Born in Saginaw, Michigan, 25 May 1908. Educated at John Moore School, 1913–21, and Arthur Hill High School, 1921–25, Saginaw; University of Michigan, Ann Arbor, 1925–29, B.A. 1929 (Phi Beta Kappa), M.A. 1936; Harvard University, Cambridge, Massachusetts, 1930–31. Married Beatrice O'Connell in 1953. Instructor in English, 1931–35, Director of Public Relations, 1934, and Varsity Tennis Coach, 1934–35, Lafayette College, Easton, Pennsylvania; Instructor in English, Michigan State University, East Lansing, Fall 1935; Instructor, 1936–40, Assistant Professor, 1940–43, and Associate Professor of English Composition, 1947, Pennsylvania State University, University Park; Instructor, Bennington College, Vermont, 1943–46; Associate Professor, 1947–48, Professor of English, 1948–62, and Honorary Poet-in-Residence, 1962–63, University of Washington, Seattle. Recipient: Yaddo fellowship, 1945; Guggenheim grant, 1945, 1950; Eunice Tietjens Memorial Prize, 1947, and Levinson Prize, 1951 (*Poetry*, Chicago); National Institute of Arts and Letters grant, 1952; Fund for the Advancement of Education Fellowship, 1952; Ford grant, 1952, 1959; Pulitzer Prize, 1954; Fulbright Fellowship, 1955; Borestone Mountain Award, 1958; National Book Award, 1959, 1965; Bollingen Prize, 1959; Poetry Society of America Prize, 1962; Shelley Memorial Award, 1962. D.H.L.: University of Michigan, 1962. *Died 1 August 1963.*

PUBLICATIONS

Verse

Open House. New York, Knopf, 1941.
The Lost Son and Other Poems. New York, Doubleday, 1948; London, Lehmann, 1949.
Praise to the End! New York, Doubleday, 1951.
The Waking: Poems 1933–1953. New York, Doubleday, 1953.
Words for the Wind: The Collected Verse of Theodore Roethke. London, Secker and Warburg, 1957; New York, Doubleday, 1958.
The Exorcism. San Francisco, Poems in Folio, 1957.
Sequence, Sometimes Metaphysical, Poems. Iowa City, Stone Wall Press, 1963.
The Far Field. New York, Doubleday, 1964; London, Faber, 1965.
Two Poems. Privately printed, 1965.
The Achievement of Theodore Roethke: A Comprehensive Selection of His Poems, with a Critical Introduction, edited by William J. Martz. Chicago, Scott Foresman, 1966.
Collected Poems. New York, Doubleday, 1966; London, Faber, 1968.
Selected Poems, edited by Beatrice Roethke. London, Faber, 1969.

Recordings: *Words for the Wind*, Folkways; *The Light and Serious Side of Theodore Roethke*, Folkways; *Theodore Roethke Reading His Poetry,* Caedmon, 1972.

Other

I Am! Says the Lamb (juvenile). New York, Doubleday, 1961.
Party at the Zoo (juvenile). New York, Crowell Collier, and London, Macmillan, 1963.
On the Poet and His Craft: Selected Prose of Theodore Roethke, edited by Ralph J. Mills, Jr. Seattle, University of Washington Press, 1965.
Selected Letters, edited by Ralph J. Mills, Jr. Seattle, University of Washington Press, 1968; London, Faber, 1970.
Straw for the Fire: From the Notebooks of Theodore Roethke 1943–1963, edited by David Wagoner. New York, Doubleday, 1972.
Dirty Dinky and Other Creatures: Poems for Children, edited by Beatrice Roethke and Stephen Lushington. New York, Doubleday, 1973.

Bibliography: *Theodore Roethke: A Bibliography* by James R. McLeod, Kent, Ohio, Kent State University Press, 1973; *Theodore Roethke's Career: An Annotated Bibliography* by Keith Moul, Boston, Hall, 1977.

Manuscript Collection: University of Washington, Seattle.

Critical Studies: *Theodore Roethke* by Ralph J. Mills, Jr., Minneapolis, University of Minnesota Press, and London, Oxford University Press, 1963; *Theodore Roethke: Essays on His Poetry* by Arnold S. Stein, Seattle, University of Washington Press, 1965; *Theodore Roethke: An Introduction to the Poetry* by Karl Malkoff, New York, Columbia University Press, 1966; *The Glass House: The Life of Theodore Roethke* by Allan Seager, New York, McGraw Hill, 1968; *Profile of Theodore Roethke* by William Heyen, Columbus, Ohio, Merrill, 1971; *The Wild Prayer of Longing: Poetry and the Sacred* by Nathan A. Scott, New Haven, Connecticut, Yale University Press, 1971; *A Concordance to the Poems of Theodore Roethke* by Gary Lane, Metuchen, New Jersey, Scarecrow Press, 1972; *Theodore Roethke's Dynamic Vision* by Richard Allen Blessing, Bloomington, Indiana University Press, 1974; *Theodore Roethke: The Garden Master* by Rosemary Sullivan, Seattle, University of Washington Press, 1975; *The Echoing Wood of Theodore Roethke* by Jenijoy La Belle, Princeton, New Jersey, Princeton University Press, 1976; *Theodore Roethke: An American Romantic* by Jay Parini, Amherst, University of Massachusetts Press, 1979.

* * *

Theodore Roethke was one of the most original of the post-war American poets. He was a nature poet, with all the particular concatenation of themes and images that word implies. His poetic ancestors, as he was fond of calling them, were the visionary poets: Blake, Wordsworth, Clare, Smart, and their American counterparts, Whitman, Emerson – poets who find in the metamorphic world of nature a direct language of being. But Roethke's vision of nature was eccentric. His great poetry begins in the private world of the greenhouses of his childhood. His father had been a florist in Michigan, owning what were at one time the largest greenhouses in the state. This was the kind of world that could shape a poet's imagination, since the greenhouse came to be a microcosmic image; in fact a universe, complete, exhaustive, with its own eschatology of heaven and hell, a moist artificial womb of growth. When Roethke reclaimed this world, his attention was riveted on growth, on the wilful tenacious struggle of plants into being in a drive against death: "I can hear, underground, that sucking and sobbing,/In my veins, in my bones I feel it"; in effect, in this artificial cell of forced growth, he sought to explore the essentially creative impulse compelling life. Later his natural realm would extend to swamps and boglands, those perfect mirrors of the turbulent psyche; to snails, slugs, snakes and frogs, the "small shapes, willow-shy" which in his work represent the extremity of instinctual life alien to the human condition. What overwhelms in this instinctive world is Roethke's capacity for empathic response, his ability to place himself within the life he contemplated in order to coincide with it, to achieve an experience of identity. There is something childlike, or better, primitive and animistic in his celebration of the intuitive capacity of the imagination which endears him to all readers. Yet as Stanley Kunitz remarked, Roethke could not be content with simply naming the things he loved, he was driven to converting them to symbols, that painful ritual.

He came into his own as a poet with the greenhouse sequence written between 1942 and 1946 when he discovered how to use the slimy world of botanic growth as an imagistic focus to embody private suffering and disorder. *The Lost Son* sequence, one of his greatest achievements as a poet, followed. These are dark poems of suffering and mental disorder composed in a surrealistic language which attempts to reproduce the psychic shorthand of the unconscious. They describe an interior journey into complete and terrifying self-absorption. Throughout his life Roethke suffered from periodic experiences of mental breakdown which he symbolized as the condition of the lost son. His private relationship to his father, who died when he was fifteen, became the model for his sense of an existential state of loss, one of those transformations that are the key to great art. What may have been a struggle for personal identity became a human struggle for spiritual identity: "a struggle out of the slime ... a slow spiritual progress."

Roethke's regressive exploration of psychic extremity was very sophisticated, often indebted to Jung through Maud Bodkin, so that the concepts of collective unconscious, rebirth, integration, are essential to his poems. Through his harrowing experiences he became convinced of an *a priori* principle of being beyond intellect – a still center or soul, not an objective reality but a goal in an on-going process of spiritual ascent. In his later poems, which are almost neo-Elizabethan in their formal elegance, he is deeply interested in mysticism, that area of psychic experience so puzzling and yet so vital to modern sensibility. Yet there is no mystical piety in his work. The idea of soul is an emotional hypothesis built out of the sheerest force of will, an act of faith which had to be constantly renewed. In the end, he is a poet of life, of celebration: "Now I adore my life/With the Bird, the abiding Leaf, ... For love, for Love's sake." One is drawn to the words of James Dickey for a final assessment of Roethke's work: "There is no poetry anywhere that is so valuably conscious of the human body ... no poetry that can place the body in an *environment* – wind, seascape, greenhouse, forest, desert, mountainside, among animals or insects or stones – so vividly and evocatively, waking unheard-of exchanges between the place and human responsiveness at its most creative. He more than any other is a poet of pure being."

—Rosemary Sullivan

SCHWARTZ, Delmore. American. Born in Brooklyn, New York, 8 December 1913. Educated at the University of Wisconsin, Madison, 1931; New York University (Editor, *Mosaic* magazine), 1933–35, B.A. in philosophy 1935; Harvard University, Cambridge, Massachusetts, 1935–37. Married 1) Gertrude Buckman (marriage dissolved); 2) Elizabeth Pollet in 1949. Briggs-Copeland Instructor, 1940, Instructor, 1941–45, and Assistant Professor of English, 1946–47, Harvard University. Fellow, Kenyon School of English, Gambier, Ohio, Summer 1950; Visiting Professor at New York University, Indiana School of Letters, Bloomington, Princeton University, New Jersey, and University of Chicago. Editor, 1943–47, and Associate Editor, 1947–55, *Partisan Review*, New Brunswick, New Jersey; associated with *Perspectives*, New York, 1952–53; Literary Consultant, New Directions, publishers, New York, 1952–53; Poetry Editor and Film Critic, *New Republic*, Washington, D.C., 1955–57. Recipient: Guggenheim Fellowship, 1940; National Institute of Arts and Letters grant, 1953; *Kenyon Review* Fellowship, 1957; Levinson Prize (*Poetry*, Chicago), 1959; Bollingen Prize, 1960; Shelley Memorial Award, 1960. *Died 11 July 1966.*

PUBLICATIONS

Verse

In Dreams Begin Responsibilities (includes short story and play). New York, New Directions, 1938.

Genesis: Book One (includes prose). New York, New Directions, 1943.

Vaudeville for a Princess and Other Poems (includes prose). New York, New Directions, 1950.

Summer Knowledge: New and Selected Poems 1938–1958. New York, Doubleday, 1959.

What Is to Be Given: Selected Poems. Manchester, Carcanet Press, 1976.
The Last and Lost Poems of Delmore Schwartz, edited by Robert Phillips. New York, Vanguard Press, 1979.

Play

Shenandoah; or, The Naming of the Child. New York, New Directions, 1941.

Short Stories

The World Is a Wedding and Other Stories. New York, New Directions, 1948; London, Lehmann, 1949.
Successful Love and Other Stories. New York, Corinth, 1961.

Other

American Poetry at Mid-Century (lectures), with John Crowe Ransom and John Hall Wheelock. Washington, D.C., Library of Congress, 1958.
The Selected Essays of Delmore Schwartz, edited by Donald A. Dike and David H. Zucker. Chicago, University of Chicago Press, 1970.
"I Am Cherry Alive," The Little Girl Sang (juvenile). New York, Harper, 1979.

Editor, *Syracuse Poems 1964.* Syracuse, New York, Syracuse University Department of English, 1965.

Translator, *A Season in Hell*, by Rimbaud. New York, New Directions, 1939.

Critical Studies: *Delmore Schwartz* by Richard McDougall, New York, Twayne, 1974; *Delmore Schwartz: The Life of an American Poet* by James Atlas, New York, Farrar Straus, 1977, London, Faber, 1979.

* * *

By design or unhappy accident, *Summer Knowledge*, which Delmore Schwartz called a selective but nevertheless "representative" volume, contains all of the verse which won him considerable acclaim during the 1930's and early 1940's, as well as the more problematic late poetry. The volume is intended to convey a particular point of view, though it is hardly one which Schwartz's admirers might have predicted: he moves, rather mysteriously, from a questioning kind of lyricism to a more affirmative but much less convincing late manner.

The early poems from *In Dreams Begin Responsibilities* are now brought together under the heading "The Dream of Knowledge." The Virgilian refrain "Happy is he who knows the causes of things" haunts the young poet. Knowledge, understanding, is the aim, the dream, the means of achieving responsible selfhood and the remission of old pains. "This is the first of spectacles," asserts one of the presiding spirits of *Genesis: Book One*:

O this
Consoles in the last illness all our pain:
Gazing upon the old life's vaudeville,
Viewing the motions of the struggling will,
Seeking the causes of each fresh event....

Schwartz's simple Freudianism demands first of all an "understanding" of his parents; thus throughout the self-indulgent stretches of *Genesis* (and the brief verse play, *Shenandoah*) he insists on tracing the forces which shaped the forces which then shaped him. (In all fairness it should be added that when Schwartz did discover a suitable form for his family chronicle he produced one of the finest of all American short "stories," the title piece of *In Dreams Begin Responsibilities*.)

But inevitably knowledge brings disillusionment: "Well! The heart of man is known./It is a cactus bloom." Soon enough there is the fear that all aspirations to knowledge in this world of appearances, "In the naked bed, in Plato's cave," may be futile. Each morning merely repeats "the mystery of beginning/again and again,/while History is unforgiven." The ultimate basis of true awareness is the recognition of mortality: "Decide that you are dying," a symbolic Father tells his equally symbolic Son: "act in that shadow ... Your own self acts then, then you know." Yet "what can any actor know?" complains the shade of Socrates in another poem: only "the contradiction in every act,/the infinite task of the human heart." This task requires not only self-knowledge but the responsibility to "love one another," as Schwartz concludes in "The Old Age of Faust." But the finest early poems are the least didactic, the simple lyrical expressions of doubt, sorrow and tentative hope. "The Ballad of the Children of the Czar," "Tired and Unhappy, You Think of Houses," "The Ballet of the Fifth Year"; the wistful funny poems, "The Heavy Bear Who Goes with Me" (the poet's body and its awkward demands) and "A Dog Named Ego, the Snowflakes as Kisses" – these and another half-dozen or so affecting short works are the poems which encouraged admirers to place Schwartz in the company of Jarrell, Lowell, Berryman, Wilbur, and Karl Shapiro.

The poems which alternate with the somewhat arch prose pieces of *Vaudeville for a Princess* are often strained, as if Schwartz were trying hard to live up to the hopes of his *Partisan Review* colleagues for a kind of big American Spender, a Keats who had read Marx and Freud. And the last poems, with very few exceptions (notably "Seurat's Sunday Afternoon along the Seine") are pretentious efforts in which Schwartz seems desperate to convince himself and his readers, by mere blunt assertion, that the natural world at its natural zenith (and our Laurentian "summer knowledge" of it), while admittedly incomplete, is enough. By this time Schwartz had lost the power to clothe his thought. The long lines are rhythmically slack and self-consciously vatic; the verse is too often "free" in the worst sense of that much-abused term. Those who remember Schwartz's best work from the 1930's may understandably *want* to like these final gestures, but to make serious claims for them is to do a disservice to the relatively limited but genuine poetic talent which fashioned a handful of moving poems.

—Elmer Borklund

SEXTON, Anne (née Harvey). American. Born in Newton, Massachusetts, 9 November 1928. Educated at Garland Junior College, Boston; Radcliffe Institute, Cambridge, Massachusetts (Scholar) 1961–63. Married Alfred M. Sexton in 1948 (divorced, 1974); two daughters. Fashion Model, Boston, 1950–51. Taught at Wayland High School, Massachusetts, 1967–68; Lecturer, 1970–71, and Professor of Creative Writing, 1972–74, Boston University. Crawshaw Professor of Literature, Colgate University, Hamilton, New York, 1972. Recipient: Bread Loaf Writers Conference Robert Frost Fellowship, 1959; Levinson Prize (*Poetry*, Chicago), 1962; American Academy of Arts and Letters Traveling Fellowship, 1963; Ford grant, 1964; Shelley Memorial Award, 1967; Pulitzer Prize, 1967; Guggenheim Fellowship, 1969. Litt.D.: Tufts University, Medford, Massachusetts, 1970; Regis College, Weston, Massachusetts, 1971; Fairfield University, Connecticut, 1971. Fellow, Royal Society of Literature. *Died 4 October 1974.*

Publications

Verse

To Bedlam and Part Way Back. Boston, Houghton Mifflin, 1960.
All My Pretty Ones. Boston, Houghton Mifflin, 1962.
Selected Poems. London, Oxford University Press, 1964.
Live or Die. Boston, Houghton Mifflin, 1966; London, Oxford University Press, 1967.
Poems, with Douglas Livingstone and Thomas Kinsella. London and New York, Oxford University Press, 1968.
Love Poems. Boston, Houghton Mifflin, and London, Oxford University Press, 1969.
Transformations. Boston, Houghton Mifflin, 1971; London, Oxford University Press, 1972.
The Book of Folly. Boston, Houghton Mifflin, 1972; London, Chatto and Windus, 1974.
O Ye Tongues. London, Rainbow Press, 1973.
The Death Notebooks. Boston, Houghton Mifflin, 1974; London, Chatto and Windus, 1975.
The Awful Rowing Toward God. Boston, Houghton Mifflin, 1975; London, Chatto and Windus, 1977.
The Heart of Anne Sexton's Poetry, edited by Linda Gray Sexton and Lois Ames. Boston, Houghton Mifflin, 1977.
Words for Dr. Y: Uncollected Poems and Three Stories, edited by Linda Gray Sexton. Boston, Houghton Mifflin, 1978.

Play

45 Mercy Street (produced New York, 1969). Boston, Houghton Mifflin, 1976.

Other

Eggs of Things (juvenile), with Maxine Kumin. New York, Putnam, 1963.
More Eggs of Things (juvenile), with Maxine Kumin. New York, Putnam, 1964.
Joey and the Birthday Present (juvenile), with Maxine Kumin. New York, McGraw Hill, 1971.
The Wizard's Tears (juvenile), with Maxine Kumin. New York, McGraw Hill, 1975.
Anne Sexton: A Self-Portrait in Letters, edited by Linda Gray Sexton and Lois Ames. Boston, Houghton Mifflin, 1977.

Bibliography: *Sylvia Plath and Anne Sexton: A Reference Guide* by Cameron Northouse and Thomas P. Walsh, Boston, Hall, 1975.

Critical Studies: "Les Belles Dames sans Merci" by Geoffrey H. Hartman, in *Kenyon Review* (Gambier, Ohio), Autumn 1960; "The Hungry Sheep Looks Up" by Neil Meyers, in *Minnesota Review* (Minneapolis), Fall 1960; "A Return to Reality" by Cecil Hemley, in *Hudson Review* (New York), Winter 1962–63; "Seven Voices" by M. L. Rosenthal, in *Reporter* (New York), 3 January 1963; "Interview with Anne Sexton" by Patricia Marx, in *Hudson Review* (New York), Winter 1965; *Contemporary American Poetry* by Ralph J. Mills, Jr., New York, Random House, 1965; "In Spite of Artifice" by Hayden Carruth, in *Hudson Review* (New York), Winter 1966–67; "O Jellow Eye" by Philip Legler, in *Poetry* (Chicago), May 1967; "Achievement of Anne Sexton" by Robert Boyers, in *Salmagundi* (New York), Spring 1967; interview with Barbara Kevles, in *Paris Review*, Spring 1971; *Anne Sexton: The Artist and Her Critics* edited by J. D. McClatchy, Bloomington, Indiana University Press, 1978.

Anne Sexton comments:

(1970) It is said that I am part of the so-called "confessional school." I prefer to think of myself as an imagist who deals with reality and its hard facts.

I write stories about life as I see it. As one critic put it I am "metaphor-mad." I work happily within strict forms that differ poem by poem or in what I call loose poems. Each time I look for the voice of the poem and each time it is a different one. I have been influenced by Rilke, Rimbaud, Kafka, Neruda. My themes deal with life and death; insanity, daughterhood, motherhood and love. My poems are intensely physical.

* * *

By the time of her death in 1974, Anne Sexton had won a wide and attentive audience, ranging from Robert Lowell to young students of poetry at universities in England and America. Her work began in the mode of what is often called the "confessional school," inaugurated by Lowell's *Life Studies* (1959) and including Lowell, Sexton, Plath, Berryman, and others. Each of their works might be entitled "A Study of My Life," especially Sexton's poems: the lyricist's self-portrait, drawn in concrete details of personal life rendered as metaphor. Initially, on the American poetry scene of the late 1950's, the metaphors were familiar fare – "the beach waits like an altar./We are lying on a cloth of sand" ("The Kite") – only to become increasingly hallucinatory – "as I lay in a chloral cave of drugs" ("Angels of the Love Affair No. 2") – and even grotesque – "myself, Ms. Dog" ("Is It True?") – then at the last the Sexton metaphor diffuses into verse parable.

Through changing styles, her canon is remarkably uniform in its themes. From changing perspectives, and with different possibilities of resolution, she asks herself the same questions, querying the nature and sources of emotional pain, the value of the effort to survive such pain, the existence of God.

Roughly, her work falls into three stages: first, the beginnings, in *To Bedlam and Part Way Back* and *All My Pretty Ones*, her record of madness, of estrangement and reunion as daughter and as mother, of willed faith in healers and in nature's seasonal healings; second, the chastened and more spare, less celebratory and more caustic verse culminating in *Live or Die*, which many readers consider her finest collection; third, darker in many ways but ultimately more hopeful still, the last period bridging *The Book of Folly* and *The Awful Rowing Toward God*, works rooted in nightmare and grotesques, but culminating in the resilient poet's entrance into Heaven, where God challenges her to a poker match and beats her royal flush with his wild card, in "lucky love." As in much of Sexton's work, one can hear in that phrase both faith and dread, because both are always present in her verse, in varying and often indeterminate emphasis.

Confused metaphorical structures and mannerisms typical of the period mar her early work. But as Sexton began tempering the excessively personal references in the late 1960's and to explore archetypal images derived mostly from psychiatry and Christianity ("the fire woman," "the leather men," the witch, the bird, the sea-breast), while tapping into her own bedrock of New England folklore and superstitions, she found rich sources of cynical wonder and figures for its articulation. Her early distress at the lack of human mutual understanding, and her compassion for the mad and the healers alike, cedes (in the Vietnam War years) to disgust with the limitations of human action, and *Love Poems* celebrates limited pleasure and joy shared in respite from all else. But no joy remains unalloyed, mostly because Sexton is her parents' daughter, suffering their suffering, and her own daughter's mother, suffering the same love and the same estrangement – but this time mysteriously responsible for it.

Love is prized, but no emotion can be definitive because the poet is haunted by its sources and its extensions, all finally unknowable, all ultimately God in the late work. The poetry of the early 1970's seems at first to have a more casual tone, since the language is more colloquial, the style more elliptic, the world of childhood memories more inviting; but the old questions are still there, indeed more intense and haunting than ever: grief of self and of humankind without God, loneliness with the "dead heart" of the too tried and trying, frail joy at brief perceptions of physical beauty or of "useful objects," fear of "EVIL." Finally in *The Awful Rowing Toward God* EVIL finds a counterweight in her certainty – perhaps not of God himself, but of her own perfected articulation of faith in God, an expression sought a lifetime.

She began capitalizing EVIL in the early 1970's, and there is surely more than an echo of Baudelaire in her "After Auschwitz" ("And death looks on with a casual eye/and scratches his anus"), and in other poems of this period. It is certain that she deliberately echoes Rimbaud and the Kafka of *Parables and Paradoxes*. Through all the allusions, EVIL means primarily the pained ignorance of God, an ignorance that is everywhere, that seeps out of telephone coin boxes, even out of useful objects unexpectedly, out of the invisible sources of things. The immediate effects of EVIL are treble: first, the sub-human actions of people and oneself in brutality, deceit, ignorance of self, as well as the pain one feels at such failings of the (basically Romantic) standard; second, the esthetic incapacity of the poet, in poems about dead eyeless bees no longer swarming; third, the unstable "I," the woman who cannot keep a covenant, saying, "Evil is maybe lying to God./Or better, lying to love" ("Is It True?").

Unlike the poetry of the mentors she invokes, Sexton's verse is primarily emotional, scornful of ideas, grounded upon a rich store of metaphors for emotional pain, amid a nagging hope in God. "To be without God is to be a snake/who wants to swallow an elephant" ("The Play"), she concludes, affirming the impossibility even as she affirms the desire. Such metaphors for human ignorance and aspiration, along with figures for Mother and Daughter, Lover and Sea, distinguish her haunted verse.

—Jan Hokenson

SINGER, Burns (James Hyman Singer). American. Born in New York City, 29 August 1928; emigrated to Scotland in 1932. Educated at schools in Glasgow, and Maud, Aberdeenshire; University of Glasgow, 1945, 1949–51: studied zoology. Married Marie Battle in 1956. Travelled in Europe, 1945–47. Research Assistant, Scottish Home Department Marine Laboratory, Aberdeen, 1951–55. Free-lance Writer and Reviewer, London, 1955–59, and Cambridge, 1959–64. Leverhulme Research Fellow, Marine Laboratory, Plymouth, Devon, 1964. *Died 8 September 1964.*

PUBLICATIONS

Verse

The Gentle Engineer. Rome, Botteghe Oscure, 1952.
The Love of Orpheus. Rome, Botteghe Oscure, 1954.
Still and All. London, Secker and Warburg, 1957; Chester Springs, Pennsylvania, Dufour, 1959.
The Collected Poems of Burns Singer, edited by W. A. S. Keir. London, Secker and Warburg, 1970.
Selected Poems, edited by Anne Cluysenaar. Manchester, Carcanet Press, 1977.

Other

Living Silver: An Impression of the British Fishing Industry. London, Secker and Warburg, 1957; Boston, Houghton Mifflin, 1958.

Editor and Translator, with Jerzy Peterkiewicz, *Five Centuries of Polish Poetry 1450–1950.* London, Secker and Warburg, 1960; Chester Springs, Pennsylvania, Dufour, 1962.

Television documentary: *Between the Tides*, 1956.

* * *

The Collected Poems of Burns Singer, edited and introduced by W. A. S. Keir, and with a preface by Hugh MacDiarmid, was published in 1970. Singer himself died young, in 1964, and published only one collection of poems during his lifetime, *Still and All.* The *Collected* volume adds 64 poems to this. There are others that have so far escaped the net – for instance, "S.O.S. Lifescene."

Singer was one of a number of recent Scottish poets who have sought to master philosophy, in the technical sense, and reproduce it in their verse. The process of his poetry is speculative. Walter Keir has suggested that Wittgenstein may have had a bad influence on him, and certainly a self-conscious passion for ratiocination did little to help Singer in his quest for clarity, slowing down the movement of his mind on the page and involving him in a grinding debate with his subject-matter which makes for passages that achieve only a turgid kind of pre-poetry. In its concern with the difficulty of utterance, his verse has several points of contact with that of his friend W. S. Graham. The long argumentative poems which Hugh MacDiarmid was writing in the thirties and forties also left their mark upon Singer's style.

This poet's best work re-vivifies the uses of formal dialectic, however, and sounds a note which, while modern, harks back to the real master of its kind, John Donne:

Gently, my darling, I will hurt by saying
But the one word that it would hurt to silence.
I smother it in every syntax, miming
With different motions but a constant meaning
Till strangers marvel at my way of living.

In these lines the utterance, though cooled by the need to be precise, has an urgency which Singer denies himself in over-intellectualised meditations upon linguistics such as "A Sort of Language," or unsuccessful escapes into surrealism as in "Respect." The beginning stanza of the title poem in *Still and All* may also be taken to represent him at his finest:

I give my word on it. There is no way
Other than this. There is no other way
Of speaking. I am my name. I find my place
Empty without a word, and my word is
Given again. It is nothing less than all
Given away again, and all still truly
Returned on a belief. Believe me now.
There is no other. There is no other way.

The reader is held by the conviction of the tone, and the honest subtlety of the argument. Plain words have been found for something hard to say. This is cerebral poetry, verse stripped of image, puritanical in its need to retreat from things seen or heard or smelt or felt into a world of the mind where the poet can be alone with his concentration upon the possibility of saying anything true, or of speaking at all. Yet for all its bareness and spareness, Singer's work exerts a fascination – "the fascination of what's difficult." It should also be noted that in such near-narrative poems as "The Transparent Prisoner" he found a partial way out of his solipsistic dilemmas.

—Robert Nye

SMITH, Stevie (Florence Margaret Smith). British. Born in Hull, Yorkshire, 20 September 1902. Educated at Palmers Green High School, London, and the North London Collegiate School for Girls. Secretary to Neville Pearson, Newnes Publishing Company, London, 1923–53. Occasional writer and broadcaster for the BBC. Recipient: Cholmondeley Award, 1966; Queen's Gold Medal for Poetry, 1969. *Died 8 March 1971.*

PUBLICATIONS

Verse

A Good Time Was Had by All. London, Cape, 1937.
Tender Only to One. London, Cape, 1938.
Mother, What Is Man? London, Cape, 1942.
Two Poems. Derby, Kenneth Hopkins, 1942.
Three Poems. Derby, Kenneth Hopkins, 1943.
Harold's Leap. London, Chapman and Hall, 1950.
Not Waving But Drowning. London, Deutsch, 1957.
Selected Poems. London, Longman, 1962; New York, New Directions, 1964.
The Frog Prince and Other Poems. London, Longman, 1966.
Penguin Modern Poets 8, with Edwin Brock and Geoffrey Hill. London, Penguin, 1966.
The Best Beast. New York, Knopf, 1969.
Francesca in Winter. London, Poem-of-the-Month Club, 1970.
Corgi Modern Poets in Focus 4, edited by Jeremy Robson. London, Corgi, 1971.
Two in One: Selected Poems and The Frog Prince and Other Poems. London, Longman, 1971.
Scorpion and Other Poems. London, Longman, 1972.
The Collected Poems of Stevie Smith, edited by James MacGibbon. London, Allen Lane, 1975; New York, Oxford University Press, 1976.
Selected Poems, edited by James MacGibbon. London, Penguin, 1978.

Recordings: *Reading Her Own Poems*, Listener, 1967; *Poems*, with Adrian Mitchell, Argo, 1974.

Novels

Novel on Yellow Paper; or, Work It Out for Yourself. London, Cape, 1936; New York, Morrow, 1937.
Over the Frontier. London, Cape, 1938.
The Holiday. London, Chapman and Hall, 1949.

Other

Some Are More Human than Others: Sketch-Book. London, Gaberbocchus, 1958.
Cats in Colour. London, Batsford, 1959; New York, Viking Press, 1960.

Editor, *T. S. Eliot: A Symposium for His 70th Birthday.* London, Hart Davis, 1958.
Editor, *The Batsford Book of Children's Verse.* London, Batsford, 1970; as *The Poet's Garden*, New York, Viking Press, 1970.

Critical Study: *Ivy and Stevie: Ivy Compton-Burnett and Stevie Smith: Conversations and Reflections* by Kay Dick, London, Duckworth, 1971.

* * *

In her first novel Stevie Smith gives free rein to the talking voice that runs on, as "the thoughts come and go." Her imagination is apt to relish the inconsequential, the bathetic, the illuminating quirk of behaviour that can set off a whole mocking tirade. "A food-off-the-ground novel that came by the left hand," she calls it; of course this describes also the method that she perfected in her poems, which has made her into a notable writer of the 20th century. The forms and structures which she used, the fable, the moral tale, the riddle, the nursery rhyme, the ballad, the hymn, are all dressed up in the kind of whimsey that carries the sharpest implications. Her verse may be gay and raffish, or melancholy in the Victorian way, but she never imitates without adding the necessary personal reflection, the pin-prick of ridicule. A joking, elaborate manner is sometimes necessary to enliven the voice of moderation and common sense, for the person of "plain" views is as much a target for Smith's humour as the pompous and the absurd.

Scorn for the shallower conventions of English life is often expressed appropriately in idiosyncratic rhythms – "Oh to be sensible about social advance at seventeen is to be lost"; but the poet's most characteristic pose is a kind of charming sedateness which is tempered by a critical element: "I sat upright in my baby-carriage/And wished mama hadn't made such a foolish marriage." She is always extraordinarily alert to the nuances of social ritual and the stuff of fancy, and this makes for an effervescent combination which gives the poems a note of special eccentricity. The unexpected opinion, when it's brought out suddenly, is amusing and instructive – "Girls! I will let down the side if I get the chance/And I will sell the pass for a couple of pence." Colloquialism and precision play a part ("You never want to go in a jungle pool/In the hot sun, it would be the act of a fool/Because it's always full of anacondas, Evelyn, not looking ill-fed/I'll say") and the fascination with death, which contributes a serious, sinister or lyrical quality: "Tender Only to One," "Do Take Muriel Out," "God the Drinker," and the later "Scorpion":

(I often wonder what it will be like
To have one's soul required of one
But all I can think of is the Out-Patients' Department –
"Are you Mrs Briggs, dear?"
No, I am Scorpion.)

"Not Waving But Drowning" is Smith's most famous poem because of its apparent simplicity and actual representation of whole areas of tangle and misunderstanding: but this is really one of her objectives which is fulfilled over and over again. The frivolity and lightness of touch which mark the surface of the poems are pleasing because of the darker undertones, the worm in the bed. Maxims and comments, disgust and despair are there to be extracted but Stevie Smith is always able to entertain, to put on a performance like Louis MacNeice's fool who donned his motley "to prick their pseudo-reason with his rhymes." She is high-spirited, teasing, and playful but very much in earnest, productively cynical.

—Patricia Craig

SMITH, Sydney Goodsir. Scottish. Born in Wellington, New Zealand, 26 October 1915. Educated at Edinburgh University; Oxford University, M.A. Taught English to the Polish Army in Scotland for the War Office. Married; two children. Joined the British Council, Edinburgh, 1945. Editor, *Lines Review*, 1955–56. Recipient: Atlantic-Rockefeller Award, 1946; Festival of Britain Scots Poetry Prize, 1951; Oscar Blumenthal Prize (*Poetry*, Chicago), 1956; Thomas Urquhart Award, 1962. *Died 15 January 1975.*

PUBLICATIONS

Verse

Skail Wind. Edinburgh, Chalmers Press, 1941.
The Wanderer and Other Poems. Edinburgh, Oliver and Boyd, 1943.
The Deevil's Waltz. Glasgow, Maclellan, 1946.
Selected Poems. Edinburgh, Oliver and Boyd, 1947.
Under the Eildon Tree: A Poem in xxiv Elegies. Edinburgh, Serif, 1948.
The Aipple and the Hazel. Glasgow, Caledonian Press, 1951.
So Late into the Night: Fifty Lyrics 1944–1948. London, Peter Russell, 1952.
Cokkils. Edinburgh, M. Macdonald, 1953.
Omens: Nine Poems. Edinburgh, M. Macdonald, 1955.
Orpheus and Euridice: A Dramatic Poem. Edinburgh, M. Macdonald, 1955.
Figs and Thistles. Edinburgh, Oliver and Boyd, 1959.
The Vision of the Prodigal Son. Edinburgh, M. Macdonald, 1960.
Kynd Kittock's Land. Edinburgh, M. Macdonald, 1965.
Fifteen Poems and a Play. Edinburgh, Southside, 1969.
Gowdspink in Reekie. Edinburgh, M. Macdonald, 1974.
Collected Poems. London, Calder, 1976.

Play

The Wallace (produced Edinburgh, 1960). Edinburgh, Oliver and Boyd, 1960.

Novel

Carotid Cornucopius: Caird o the Cannon Gait and Voyeur of the Outluik Touer: A Drammatick, Backside, Bogbide, Bedride or Badside Buik, by Gude Schir Skidderie Smithereens. Glasgow, Caledonian Press, 1947.

Other

A Short Introduction to Scottish Literature. Edinburgh, Serif, 1951.

Editor, *Robert Fergusson 1750–1774: Essays by Various Hands to Commemorate the Bicentenary of His Birth.* Edinburgh, Nelson, 1952.
Editor, *Gavin Douglas: A Selection of His Poetry.* Edinburgh, Oliver and Boyd, 1959.
Editor, with J. Delancey Ferguson and James Barke, *The Merry Muses of Caledonia*, by Robert Burns. Edinburgh, M. Macdonald, 1959; New York, Putnam, 1964.
Editor, with others, *Hugh MacDiarmid: A Festschrift.* Edinburgh, K. D. Duval, 1962.
Editor, *Bannockburn: The Story of the Battle and Its Place in Scotland's History.* Stirling, Scots Independent, 1965.
Editor, *A Choice of Burns's Poems and Songs.* London, Faber, 1966.

Critical Studies: "The Poetry of Sydney Goodsir Smith" by Norman MacCaig, in *Saltire Review 1* (Edinburgh), April 1954; Alexander Scott, in *Lines Review* (Edinburgh), Summer 1956; *The Scottish Tradition in Literature* by Kurt Wittig, Edinburgh, Oliver and Boyd, 1958; Thomas Crawford, in *Studies in Scottish Literature* edited by G. Ross Roy, Columbia, University of South Carolina, 1969; "Sydney Goodsir Smith Issue" of *Akros 10* (Preston, Lancashire); *Sydney Goodsir Smith's "Under the Eildon Tree": An Essay* by Eric Gold, Preston, Lancashire, Akros, 1975.

* * *

Sydney Goodsir Smith was, after Hugh MacDiarmid, the only poet of the Scottish Renaissance group to produce a long poem that is an unquestioned masterpiece, *Under the Eildon Tree*. Like MacDiarmid's *A Drunk Man Looks at the Thistle* (1926), it is constructed of closely related segments (in this case 24 elegies on the common theme of love as experienced by the poet, varied against the stories of some great lovers from history and mythology) rather than held together by through-thought, as is *Paradise Lost*.

In *Under the Eildon Tree*, Smith achieved in Scots a kind of Poundian synthesis of allusion and quotation from world literature, a technique also applied by MacDiarmid in *A Drunk Man*, though in a less sophisticated manner. Smith's sense of fun and generous warmth of personality also play no small part in making *Under the Eildon Tree* one of the most successful sustained love poems of the 20th century. The same blend of qualities, though this time with the accent on the humorously melancholic pleasures of bibulous good-fellowship, characterises "The Riggins o Chelsea or Hame Thochts frae Abraid." His serious human concern for society's drop-outs is powerfully reflected in "The Grace of God and the Meth-Drinker."

Smith's early reputation was based on the love lyrics in his earlier collections, principally *The Deevil's Waltz*, *So Late into the Night*, and *Figs and Thistles*. Most of these have not worn well. When it came to the measures of strict forms his ear frequently let him down, while the absence of imagery in his style – much of such occasional imagery as he does use is simply banal – means that the lyric pressure has to be sustained largely by the intensity of the subject matter. He is most often successful where the content is linked to a contemporary setting, as in:

I loe* ma luve in a lamplit bar — * love
Braw on a wuidan stool,
Her knees cocked up and her neb* doun — * nose
Slorpan* a pint o' yill* — * swilling; ale

or where, so to say, he is directly fired by the red surge of passion itself:

Hairst, ma hairt, forgae* — * forgo
This dirlan* o ma soul — * piercing
Ye steer* ma deeps til* a reel o flame — * stir; to
Like a smashed coal.

Smith's ebullient patriotism found expression in his highly rhetorical play *The Wallace*, staged at the Edinburgh Festival in 1960. His love of words for their own sake also produced the Joycean Scots fantasy *Carotid Cornucopius*, although here the evident artificiality of the language, far removed from any Scots ever spoken, prevents it touching the seat of associative depths of meaning achieved in *Ulysses*. Smith's mastery of an updated version of the Scots colloquial style of the Eighteenth-Century Revival is well demonstrated in his long verse-letter "To Robert Fergusson," an earlier Edinburgh poet with whom he felt affinity.

In spite of this reassessment of his lyrical output, Goodsir Smith's place in 20th-century Scottish literature is secure. It is therefore a pity that the *Collected Poems* misses out much of his later work (among the missing pieces being "The Riggins o Chelsea") and includes material discarded by the poet himself. Sooner or later, the work of producing an authentic and textually accurate *Collected Poems* will have to be undertaken again.

—Maurice Lindsay

SPICER, Jack (John Lester Spicer). American. Born in Hollywood, California, 30 January 1925. Lived in Berkeley, California, 1945–55, and in San Francisco, 1957–65;

Editor and Curator in the Rare Book Room, Boston Public Library, 1955–56. *Died 17 August 1965.*

PUBLICATIONS

Verse

After Lorca. San Francisco, White Rabbit Press, 1957; London, Aloes, n.d.
Homage to Creeley. Privately printed, 1959.
Billy the Kid. Stinson Beach, California, Enkidu Surrogate, 1959.
The Heads of the Town Up to the Aether. San Francisco, Auerhahn, 1962.
Lament for the Makers. Oakland, California, White Rabbit Press, 1962; London, Aloes, 1971.
The Holy Grail. San Francisco, White Rabbit Press, 1964.
Language. San Francisco, White Rabbit Press, 1965.
The Redwood Forest. San Francisco, White Rabbit Press, 1965.
Book of Magazine Verse. San Francisco, White Rabbit Press, 1966.
The Day Five Thousand Fish Died in the Charles River. Pleasant Valley, New York, Kriya Press, 1967.
A Book of Music. San Francisco, White Rabbit Press, 1969.
Indian Summer: Minneapolis 1950. New York, Samuel Charters, 1970.
Some Things from Jack. Verona, Plain Wrapper Press, 1972.
Fifteen False Propositions about God. San Francisco, ManRoot, 1974.
Admonitions. New York, Adventures in Poetry, 1974.
Berkeley in a Time of Plague. Berkeley, California, Arif Press, 1974.
An Ode and Arcadia, with Robert Duncan. Berkeley, California, Ark Press, 1974.
A Lost Poem. Verona, Plain Wrapper Press, 1975.
The Collected Books of Jack Spicer, edited by Robin Blaser. Los Angeles, Black Sparrow Press, 1975.
There Is an Inner Nervousness in Virgins. Eureka, California, Spotted Pig Press, 1975(?).

Play

Troilus, edited by Robin Blaser. Los Angeles, Black Sparrow Press, 1975.

Other

Dear Ferlinghetti/Dear Jack:The Spicer-Ferlinghetti Correspondence. San Francisco, White Rabbit Press, 1962(?).

* * *

Jack Spicer's poetry is so totally engaged with his poetics that the two often serve as complementary (or contending) voices within any given poem. For this reason, the poems appear to be arguments with themselves, opaque to a casual reading and at the same time possessed of an arch and playful wit. Their coherence depends upon the intensity of this argument, extended through a series of short poems and gathered into small books or "serial poems." Each single poem depends upon the others in the series to advance or revise what has gone before so that things appear to be constantly in motion. The tone of debate provides the primary mood in Spicer's work, the poet struggling with forces beyond him which threaten to inhabit the work. In this drama of poetic contentions, these forces (or "ghosts," as Spicer points out) might be rhetoric, ethical statement, authorial intention, or the canons of taste represented by official academic and scholarly opinion. Spicer wants the poem to come to him in the form of cryptic message or occult code rather than emanate from his own will to form. The poet, then, is not an inspired or possessed artificer but rather a "radio" (to use his favorite image) through whom the poem broadcasts.

Although Spicer refused to define his poetics separate from the poems themselves, he provided a useful statement about his method of dictation in "Vancouver Lectures" (*Caterpillar 12*) describing poetry as "spiritual method" and the central poetic act as "emptying yourself as a vessel," rather than finding equivalences for subjective experience. For Spicer the poem which is engaged with the *play* of meaning (puns, anagrams, jokes, semantic doublings) is one which operates in the largest domain of meaning – that is, where ideas and experiences have a multifarious existence. In this sense Spicer respects the so-called "innocent" poetry of nursery rhymes and the slightly more intentionalized nonsense of Lewis Carroll and Edward Lear.

Paradoxically, this desire for a playful sliding of meaning provides a more accurate translation of the world. In one of the letters addressed to García Lorca in *After Lorca*, Spicer makes the following distinction:

> I would like to make poems out of real objects. The lemon to be a lemon that the reader could cut or squeeze or taste – a real lemon like a newspaper in a collage is a real newspaper. I would like the moon in my poems to be a real moon, one which could be suddenly covered with a cloud that has nothing to do with the poem – a moon utterly independent of images. The imagination pictures the real. I would like to point to the real, disclose it, to make a poem that has no sound in it but the pointing of a finger.

The fault with most modern poetry, Spicer feels, is that it searches for a more exact objective correlative or image – a "picture" of the real. Spicer wants a poetry which "corresponds" with the world, not by imitating it but by being an activity within it. Unlike Baudelaire's formulation of correspondences, Spicer's poetry is not directed toward a super-sensual effect or mystic apprehension; it is concerned with the world in all of its accidental and unanticipated occasions, frightening and sublime at the same time.

The volatile atmosphere of San Francisco during the 1950's and 1960's provided a fertile ground for such a poetics. In the bars and coffee houses of North Beach, the new poetry appeared to Spicer as the gospel of a heretical sect or Gnostic enclave. Spicer sat at the central table of bars like The Place or Gino/Carlo's and held a kind of court in which the university English Department and east coast publishing firms could be regarded as the Pope's army and the new poetry emerging from San Francisco's "Beat" movement functioned as the secret (and spirited) language of Catharist adepts. With Robert Duncan and Robin Blaser, Spicer charged the air with his sense of a literary renaissance on the west coast, one not bound by official proclamations or manifestos but constantly engaged in poetry's problematic nature.

—Michael Davidson

WATKINS, Vernon (Phillips). Welsh. Born in Maesteg, Glamorganshire, 27 June 1906. Educated at Swansea Grammar School, Glamorganshire; Repton School, Yorkshire; Magdalene College, Cambridge, 1924–25; studied modern laguages. Served in the Home Guard, 1939–41, and Royal Air Force, 1941–45. Married Gwendoline Mary Davies in 1944; five children. Clerk, Lloyds Bank, Swansea, 1925–41, 1946–65. Visiting Lecturer in Modern Poetry, University of Washington, Seattle, 1964, 1967; Calouste Gulbenkian Fellow in Poetry, University College, Swansea, 1965–66. Recipient: Levinson Prize (*Poetry*, Chicago),

1953; Guinness Prize, 1957. D.Litt.: University of Wales, Cardiff, 1966. Fellow, Royal Society of Literature. *Died 8 October 1967.*

PUBLICATIONS

Verse

Ballad of Mari Lwyd and Other Poems. London, Faber, 1941.
The Lamp and the Veil. London, Faber, 1945.
The Lady with the Unicorn. London, Faber, 1948.
Selected Poems. New York, New Directions, 1948.
The Death Bell: Poems and Ballads. London, Faber, and New York, New Directions, 1954.
Cypress and Acacia. London, Faber, 1959; New York, New Directions, 1960.
Affinities. London, Faber, 1962; New York, New Directions, 1963.
Selected Poems 1930–1960. London, Faber, and New York, New Directions, 1967.
Arrival in East Shelby. Privately printed, 1968.
Pergamon Poets 4, with Kathleen Raine, edited by Evan Owen. Oxford and New York, Pergamon Press, 1968.
Fidelities. London, Faber, 1968; New York, New Directions, 1969.
Vernon Watkins and Jon Silkin: Poems. London, Longman, 1969.
Uncollected Poems. London, Enitharmon Press, 1969.
Elegiac Sonnet (bilingual edition). Milan, M'Arte Edizioni, 1970.
The Influences. Hayes, Middlesex, Bran's Head, 1976.
I Was Born in Wales: A New Selection from the Poems of Vernon Watkins, edited by Gwen Watkins and Ruth Pryor. Cardiff, University of Wales Press, 1976.
Elegy for the Latest Dead. Privately printed, 1977.
Unity of the Stream: A New Selection of Poems. Llandysul, Dyfed, Gomer, 1978.
The Ballad of the Outer Dark and Other Poems, edited by Ruth Pryor. London, Enitharmon Press, 1979.
The Breaking of the Wave. Ipswich, Golgonooza Press, 1979.

Other

Selected Verse Translations, with an Essay on the Translation of Poetry, edited by Ruth Pryor. London, Enitharmon Press, 1977.

Editor, *Letters to Vernon Watkins*, by Dylan Thomas. London, Dent, and New York, New Directions, 1957.
Editor, *Landmarks and Voyages: Poetry Supplement.* London, Poetry Book Society, 1957.

Translator, *The North Sea*, by Heinrich Heine. London, Faber, and New York, New Directions, 1955.

Bibliography: *Two Swansea Poets: Dylan Thomas and Vernon Watkins*, Swansea, Swansea Public Libraries, 1969.

Manuscript Collection: British Museum, London.

Critical Studies: *Vernon Watkins 1906–1967* edited by Leslie Norris, London, Faber, 1970; *Vernon Watkins* by Roland Mathias, Cardiff, University of Wales Press, 1974; *Vernon Watkins and the Spring of Vision* by Dora Polk, Swansea, Christopher Davies, 1977; "Vernon Watkins Issue" of *Poetry Wales 12* (Cardiff), 1977.

* * *

The poems of Vernon Watkins are of a sort so uncommon in our day that they deserve what almost amounts to a new set of critical tools for their evaluation, although their individuality may not be apparent at first reading. It is true that in an age predominantly visual in expression, his verse springs most often "from a musical source"; that although experimental forms are popular, he remained constant to traditional patterns – even if he was within them a great craftsman and a sure inventor; and that when critics insist on dealing with each lyric as a singular artefact, his work is inter-related to the extent that we can read it almost as one long poem. It is, however, his material that is most unusual: in a life dedicated to poetry, during which he published eight important collections, numerous translations, and left behind substantial unpublished work, his themes remained those which obsessed him as a young man, developing naturally in profundity and richness.

When he was 22 he experienced the extraordinary vision which was to shape the direction of his life and work. He saw, more clearly than the things of this world, the true nature of Time and Eternity. After "this revolution of sensibility" as he called it, he was never again able to write a poem dominated by time, nor to think of this world as in any way ruled by time. It took him some time to develop a language and a style which could deal with his "transfigured vision of the world"; he continued to read widely, as he did throughout his life, but he gained most help from Yeats, whose work remained a continuing aspiration to him, and just as valuably – if more briefly – from the example and friendship of Dylan Thomas.

Watkins believed that the true artist received his inspiration from a religious source, that inspiration was a religious experience in which the artist recognised the appearance and qualities of the eternal world, and that it was his responsibility to await such inspiration and then interpret it through the practice of his art. In this way, those of us who are not artists will be able to understand something of the nature of the real world, of which ours is a faulty shadow. Such a belief demonstrates Watkins's affinity with poets like Vaughan and Blake, as well as with Yeats – although Watkins himself believed that all true artists are such interpreters. His 1962 volume, *Affinities*, is an explicit statement of this belief: in it he calls for the support not only of the poets, but of dancers like Nijinsky, and painters such as Michelangelo. So timeless a point of view meant that Watkins was quite unaware of fashion – his verse is neither fashionable nor unfashionable – but very much aware of the permanent virtues of his art.

His point of view accounts, too, for the recurring images to be found in his work, although they are less noticeable in his later poems. Such imagery tends always to stand for the defeat of time: I mean the fountain, which gives out water without stop, the foal, the violet, the hawthorn (or, as Watkins most frequently calls it, the "may"), and the sycamore. This last symbol, for example, is used in the early poem "Sycamore," in which the long-living tree is compared with the brief life of man. The tree is not only itself long-lived, but is perpetuated through its highly fertile fruits, its wood is used to make musical instruments – and art is necessary for the understanding of true reality – and it was, moreover, the tree into which Zaccheus climbed to see Jesus pass through Jericho. This last point, barely touched on in "Sycamore," becomes the central issue in "Zaccheus in the Leaves," a poem from *The Lady with the Unicorn*. This reminds us that, for Watkins, the ability to see the truth, that faculty given only to true artists, was a religious gift; indeed, although there were true artists before the coming of Christ, it is only through the intervention of Christ that perfect inspiration is to be found. Thus, the vision of Zaccheus was a species of inspiration; he saw the eternal world because of the presence of Christ.

The poem which most clearly states this belief is, perhaps, "Music of Colours – White Blossom...." Here the poet, having walked the cliffs above Swansea Bay and admired the white of the foam, retraces his footsteps the next day after a fall of snow, and sees the spray he had thought white no more than grey. He reflects that true whiteness does not exist in this world, not in white blossom, nor shell, nor snow, nor in "Marlowe's queen." Nor does it exist in myth, in the white swan's-down of "Web-footed Jupiter" as he descends to Leda, since the poets of other religions are not able to see as clearly as those inspired by Christ's truth. Indeed, the only true whiteness "must have been/When His eyes looked down and made the leper clean." And the position of the artist is that he can "know nothing of Earth or colour until I know I lack/Original white...."

This is an important stage in Wakins's development, and was followed by his assumption of the personality of the early Welsh poet, Taliesin. In Welsh mythology, Taliesin, as a small boy, accidentally swallowed the three magical drops of Inspiration, and saw Past, Future, and Present all at once. The attraction of such a persona for Watkins was very great. Here was a voice he could use to discharge his incredible responsibility to the rest of us, to speak boldly and simply of the nature of inspiration and of the truth of eternity. The Taliesin poems, most particularly "Taliesin and the Spring of Vision," are Watkins's clearest statements, in a personal sense, of his great themes. Later he found the work of Hölderlin of equal importance, and the work of the German poet enabled him to intensify and modify his personal vision, as we can see in Watkins's poem "The Childhood of Hölderlin."

Briefly, then, Watkins attacks the conventional idea of time on several fronts: through the inspiration given to true artists which enables the idea of eternity to be known, through personal love, which is akin to ideal love and may be all that some people can achieve, and through the practice of art (both the second and third of these attitudes can be found in "The Lady with the Unicorn," and other poems contain all three ideas). After his prolonged meditations on these themes in the Taliesin poems, the Hölderlin poems, and, indeed, all the poems in *Affinities*, it seems almost as if Watkins had decided to turn his attention to this world, for his posthumous volume *Fidelities* contains a number of poems new in the attention they pay to the visible and palpable detail of the physical world. In "The Guest," a remarkable poem from that collection, he makes our mortal world eternal, a miraculous demonstration for his belief in the power of art in lines so perfect they seem without art:

> The cliff's crossed path lay silvered with slug tracks
> Where webs of hanging raindrops caught the sun.
> A thrush with snail cocked sideways like an axe
> Knocked with quick beak to crack it on a stone....

In these late poems Watkins had achieved the synthesis of the mortal and the eternal worlds, and the tragedy is that he died at the height of his powers. He was a wholly serious and dedicated poet, his concerns always those of absolute great poetry.

—Leslie Norris

ZUKOFSKY, Louis. American. Born in New York City, 23 January 1904. Educated at Columbia University, New York, M.A. 1924. Married Celia Thaew in 1939; one son. Taught at the University of Wisconsin, Madison, 1930–31; Colgate University, Hamilton, New York, 1947; Polytechnic Institute of Brooklyn, New York, 1947–66. Recipient: Longview Foundation Award, 1961; Union League Civic and Arts Foundation Prize, 1964, and Oscar Blumenthal Prize, 1966 (*Poetry*, Chicago); National Endowment for the Arts grant, 1966, 1968. National Institute of Arts and Letters award, 1976. *Died 12 May 1978.*

PUBLICATIONS

Verse

First Half of "A"-9. Privately printed, 1940.

55 Poems. Prairie City, Illinois, Decker Press, 1941.
Anew. Prairie City, Illinois, Decker Press, 1946.
Some Time: Short Poems. Stuttgart, Germany, Jonathan Williams, 1956.
Barely and Widely. New York, Celia Zukofsky, 1958.
"A" 1–12. Ashland, North Carolina, Origin Press, 1959; London, Cape, 1966.
16 Once Published. Edinburgh, Wild Hawthorn Press, 1962.
I's, Pronounced "Eyes." New York, Trobar Press, 1963.
After I's. Pittsburgh, Boxwood Press, 1964.
Found Objects 1962–1926. Georgetown, Kentucky, H. B. Chapin, 1964.
An Unearthing: A Poem. Privately printed, 1965.
Iyyob. London, Turret, 1965.
I Sent Thee Late. Privately printed, 1965.
Finally a Valentine. Stroud, Gloucestershire, Piccolo Press, 1965.
"A" Libretto. Privately printed, 1965.
All: The Collected Short Poems 1923–1958 and *1956–1964.* New York, Norton, 2 vols., 1965–66; London, Cape, 2 vols., 1966–67; Norton, 1 vol., 1971.
"A"-9. Cologne, Hansjörg Mayer, 1966.
"A"-14. London, Turret, 1967.
"A" 13–21. London, Cape, and New York, Doubleday, 1969.
The Gas Age: A Poem. Newcastle upon Tyne, Ultima Thule Bookshop, 1969.
Initial. New York, Phoenix Book Shop, 1970.
"A"-24. New York, Grossman, 1972.
"A" 22 and 23. New York, Viking Press, 1975; London, Trigram Press, 1978.
"A" (complete version). Berkeley, University of California Press, 1978.

Play

Arise, Arise. New York, Grossman, 1973.

Short Stories

It Was. New York, Origin Press, 1961.
Little: A Fragment for Careenagers. Los Angeles, Black Sparrow Press, 1967; complete version, New York, Grossman, 1970.
Ferdinand, Including It Was. London, Cape, and New York, Grossman, 1968.

Other

Le Style Apollinaire. Paris, Les Presses Modernes, 1934.
5 Statements for Poetry. San Francisco, San Francisco State College, 1958.
Bottom: On Shakespeare. Austin, Ark Press, 1963.
Prepositions: The Collected Critical Essays of Louis Zukofsky. London, Rapp and Carroll, 1967; New York, Horizon Press, 1968.
Autobiography. New York, Grossman, 1970.

Editor, *An "Objectivists" Anthology.* Le Beausset, France, To Publishers, 1932; Folcroft, Pennsylvania, Folcroft Editions, 1975.
Editor, *A Test of Poetry.* New York, Objectivist Press, 1948; London, Routledge, 1952.

Translator, *Albert Einstein*, by Anton Reiser. New York, Boni, 1930.
Translator, with Celia Zukofsky, *Catullus: Fragmenta*, music by Paul Zukofsky. London, Turret, 1969.
Translator, with Celia Zukofsky, *Catullus.* London, Cape Goliard Press, and New York, Grossman, 1969.

Bibliography: *A Bibliography of Louis Zukofsky* by Çelia Zukofsky, Los Angeles, Black Sparrow Press, 1969.

Manuscript Collection: Humanities Research Center, University of Texas, Austin.

Critical Studies: by Guy Davenport, in *Agenda* (London), Autumn–Winter 1970; Kenneth Cox, in *Agenda* (London), Autumn–Winter 1971.

* * *

Perfected in 1978, after fifty years of insight, Louis Zukofsky's *"A"* indirectly assesses his other writings, exemplifies his "objectivist" theory (with which William Carlos Williams, Charles Reznikoff, and others were associated in the 1930's) and by a blending of lyric and epigrammatic qualities achieves an enduring, epic scope.

The 24 sections (A-1 to A-24) are followed by an index so that the poem begins on page 1 with "A/Round of fiddles playing Bach," and ends on page 826 (sic) with the word "Zion." The letter "z" is also in the last line of A23, a section which announces the "music, thought, drama, story, poem," the simultaneous voices which quote his previous works, and (set to music of Handel) form a collage, 240 pages long, a complex coda. The index also begins with the letter (or word) "A" and includes the instances when "an" and "the" appear, words he usually suppresses in his search for concentration. Names of public significance are in the index, so that one can be reassured that "Henry R." of the text is indeed Henry Rago of *Poetry* magazine, and that "Ludwig" is Wittgenstein. Essentially the index stresses the main concerns of the poem. The words most frequently found in the poem are man, eye, and day; and, next to these three, body, child, face, hand, heart, home, love, and sun.

"A" is "one song" with "many voices" ranging from the "lower limit, speech," to "upper limit song." Through collages, quotations, and puns ("Better a fiddler than a geiger" reminds us that Geige is "fiddle" in German), the individual perception of public history is frivolously, seriously interwoven with his private history for public perception – his son Paul, and his wife Celia: "Blessed/Ardent/Celia, unhurt/Happy" also announces BACH, that the fiddles are playing.

The poem provides occasions for delight in patterns, a naive delight in counting, as well as what is counted. The 24 A's are twenty-four hours, but A-12 is "twelve years." A-9 consists of two sets of sonnets, five sonnets in each set followed by a concluding five-line stanza. The terminal words of the first set are also the terminal words of the second set, with some surprising variations ("into," "thin to").

These dispersive elements cluster around a central theory, far too complex for a summary. His theory involves motion, the motion of physical sounds, of letters, the movement of the mind toward abstraction, the motion of light as it is brought to a focus. His interest is in the act of focusing, rather than what is focused upon. "The image is not the sole object of knowledge," for there is the "image of a voice." He uses "object" in the sense of *objectif*, a lens. Indeed, he believes "it is possible in imagination to divorce speech of all graphic elements" (A-24).

The "objectivist" then is not a photographer. The tendency to manifest motion itself rather than what is moving becomes associated with extraordinary concentration. When we read for example, in A-21, "See here splendent stellar candid/sign forever ...," we find it almost easier to go back to the Plautus he is translating for an "explanation": "ita sum ut videtis, splendens stella candida...." But the words *sum ut*, "I am as," are precisely the sort that Zukofsky suppresses. His concentrated passages may seem "difficult" if one wishes to elucidate them conceptually, but the effect is immediate: "Late later and much later/surge sea erupts boiling molten/lava island from ice, land." One may or may not agree that, conceptually, the lines present "a surge within the sea erupts into boiling water, owing to the lava pouring down from an island, from ice, and land, from Iceland," but the immediate effect is a distillation of feeling. The search for conceptual connections will move away from the poem, but those motions too are part of his poetry, which often curves back upon itself:

"An unforeseen delight a round/beginning ardent; to end blest ..." from A-23 echoes many earlier passages of "blest, ardent Celia," Bach, and a round of fiddles.

Zukofsky is capable of extraordinary wit, as in some of his poems collected in *All*, or in *Ferdinand*, and there is a delightful coruscation at the periphery of "A"; yet the central impulse is the immediacy of experience – man, eye, day:

> what hurries? why hurry? wit's
> but the fog, the literal senses
> senses move in light's song
> modesty cannot force, blind call
> its own, nor self-effaced fled
>
> to woods perpend without pride
> stone into lotus.

One exercises one's wit in running the index from A to Z, but the light's song emerges at the end of A-24 "What is it, I wonder that makes thee so loved?" a quotation from A-20 which includes a list of works for Paul, an evocation of a "sound akin to mosaic": "Each writer writes/one long work whose beat he cannot/entirely be aware of." The entire corpus of Zukofsky's poetry moves to a beat that is hard to define. He himself has come as close as anybody to describing it: "Thus one modernizes/His lute .../The melody! the rest is accessory."

—William Sylvester

NOTES ON ADVISERS AND CONTRIBUTORS

ABDUL MAJID BIN NABI BAKSH. Assistant Lecturer in English, University of Malaya, Kuala Lumpur. Author of *Critical History of the Filipino Novel in English*. **Essays:** Carlos A. Angeles; Ricaredo Demetillo; Edith Tiempo.

ACKERSON, Duane. Assistant Professor of English and Director of Creative Writing, Idaho State University, Pocatello; Editor, *The Dragonfly*, Pocatello. Verse pamphlets include *UA Flight to Chicago*, 1971, *Inventory*, 1971, *Old Movie House*, 1972, and *Weathering*, 1974. Fiction published in magazines and the anthology *Generation*, 1973. **Essays:** James Den Boer; Russell Edson; Vi Gale; Geof Hewitt; Robert Huff; David Jaffin; John Knoepfle; James Koller; Tom McKeown; Adrien Stoutenburg; Keith Wilson.

ADCOCK, Fleur. See her own entry. **Essays:** Basil Dowling; George McWhirter; Dabney Stuart; Herbert Williams.

AITCHISON, James. Free-lance writer. Author of two books of verse – *Sounds Before Sleep*, 1971, and *Spheres*, 1975. **Essay:** Maurice Lindsay.

ALCOCK, Peter. Senior Lecturer in English, Massey University, Palmerston North, New Zealand; Associate Editor of *World Literature Written in English* and bibliographer for *Journal of Commonwealth Literature*. Member of the Executive Committee, Association for Commonwealth Literature and Language, 1968–77. **Essay:** Alistair Campbell.

ALLEN, Donald. Associated with the Grove Press, since 1950; Editor, with Barney Rosset, of *The Evergreen Review*, 1957–59, and West Coast Editor since 1960; Owner, The Grey Fox Press, Bolinas, California. Editor, *Selected Poems of Lorca*, 1955; *The New American Poetry 1945–60*, 1960; *New American Story* (with Robert Creeley), 1965; *New Writing in the U.S.A.* (with Creeley), 1967; *The Collected Poems of Frank O'Hara*, 1970; *Poetics of the New American Poetry* (with Warren Tallman), 1973. Translator of *Four Plays* by Ionesco, 1958.

ANDRÉ, Michael. Editor of *Unmuzzled Ox* magazine, New York. Author of three books of verse – *Get Serious*, 1973, *My Regrets*, 1976, and *Studying the Ground for Holes*, 1978. Contributor to *Art News*, New York. **Essays:** Bill Bissett; Robin Blaser; Michael Brownstein; Paul Carroll; Kenward Elmslie; Gene Fowler; Barrie Philip Nichol; Jeff Nuttall; James Schuyler.

ASTLE, David. Principal Lecturer in Communication Studies, Sheffield City Polytechnic. **Essay:** Roy Fuller.

AUGUSTINE, Jane. Adjunct Instructor in English, Pratt Institute, Brooklyn, New York. Author of *Lit by the Earth's Dark Blood*, 1977, fiction in the anthology *Solo*, 1977, and verse for little magazines. Member, Feminist Writers Guild. **Essays:** Marilyn Hacker; Richard Kostelanetz; Rochelle Owens; Marge Piercy; Judith Johnson Sherwin; Mary Ellen Solt; Constance Urdang; Jean Valentine; Mona Van Duyn.

BAKER, Houston A., Jr. Professor of English, University of Pennsylvania, Philadelphia. Has taught at Yale University, New Haven, Connecticut, and the University of Virginia, Charlottesville. Author of *Long Black Song: Essays in Black American Literature and Culture*, 1972, *Singers of Daybreak: Studies in Black American Literature*, 1974, *A Many-Colored Coat of Dreams: The Poetry of Countée Cullen*, 1974, *The Journey Back: Issues in Black Literature and Criticism*, 1980, and a book of verse, *No Matter Where You Travel You Still Be Black*, 1979. Editor of *Black Literature in America*, 1971, and *Twentieth-Century Interpretations of "Native Son,"* 1972. **Essays:** James A. Emanuel; Carolyn M. Rodgers.

BAKER, Roger. Regular book reviewer for *The Times*, *Books and Bookmen*, and *Gay*

News; Editor of *Men Only* and the literary quarterly *Gay Journal*. Author of *The Book of London*, 1968, and *Drag: A History of Female Impersonation on the Stage*, 1968. **Essay:** Laurence Collinson.

BEAVER, Bruce. See his own entry. **Essays:** Geoffrey Dutton; Gwen Harwood; Geoffrey Lehmann; Hal Porter.

BEETON, D. R. Professor of English, University of South Africa, Pretoria. Author of *A Dictionary of English Usage in Southern Africa*, with H. H. T. Dorner, 1975, and of three radio series on poetry, *From Cape to Zambezi*, *New Voices*, and *The Widening Search*; verse published in *The Penguin Book of South African Verse*, 1968. Co-Editor of *South African Poetry: A Critical Anthology*, 1966. **Essay:** Sydney Clouts.

BELL, Charles G. See his own entry. **Essay:** Galway Kinnell.

BENESA, Leonidas V. Poet and Art Critic. Managing Editor, *Archipelago* magazine, Manila. **Essay:** Emmanuel Torres.

BERGÉ, Carol. See her own entry. **Essays:** Isabella Stewart Gardner; Michael McClure; Howard Moss.

BERGONZI, Bernard. Professor of English, University of Warwick, Coventry. Author of *Descartes and the Animals*, 1954; *The Early H. G. Wells*, 1961; *Heroes' Twilight*, 1965; *The Situation of the Novel*, 1970; *T. S. Eliot*, 1971; *Gerard Manley Hopkins*, 1977; *Reading the Thirties*, 1978; *Years: Sixteen Poems*, 1979. Contributor to *The Observer*, *Times Literary Supplement*, and other periodicals. **Essays:** Robert Conquest; Malcolm Cowley; Gavin Ewart; Colin Falck; David Gascoyne; Geoffrey Grigson; Rayner Heppenstall; John Holloway; Richard Kell; Nicholas Moore; Philip Oakes; Edgell Rickword; Philip Toynbee.

BERTRAM, James. Professor of English, Victoria University of Wellington; General Editor of *New Zealand Writers and Their Work* series. Editor of *Phoenix*, 1932; associated with the founding of *Landfall*, 1946. Author of several books on China, and of *Charles Brasch*, 1976. Editor of *New Zealand Letters of Thomas Arnold the Younger*, 1966; contributor to *Student Guide to English Poetry*, 1969. **Essays:** Rewi Alley; Ruth Dallas; Owen Leeming.

BIRKETT, Jennifer. Lecturer in French, University of Dundee, Scotland. Author of a forthcoming study of sexuality and politics in the literature of the French Revolution. **Essays:** Anne Cluysenaar; Elaine Feinstein; Rosemary Tonks.

BIRNEY, Earle. See his own entry.

BLOOM, Harold. DeVane Professor of the Humanities, Yale University, New Haven, Connecticut. Author of several books on Blake and the Romantics; his most recent books are *The Anxiety of Influence*, 1973; *A Map of Misreading*, 1975; *Kabbalah and Criticism*, 1975; *Poetry and Repression*, 1976; *Wallace Stevens: The Poems of Our Climate*, 1977; and the novel *The Flight to Lucifer*, 1979. Editor of several anthologies and of works by Ruskin, Shelley, Pater, and Coleridge. **Essay:** John Hollander.

BODE, Carl. Professor of American Literature and American Studies, University of Maryland, College Park. Author of three books of verse (most recently *Practical Magic*, 1979), and of several books on American civilization, including *Antebellum Culture*, 1970, *Mencken*, 1973, and *Maryland: A Bicentennial History*, 1978. Editor of works by Thoreau and Mencken, and of *The Young Rebel in American Literature*, 1959, and *Ralph Waldo Emerson*, 1968. **Essay:** Chad Walsh.

BODE, Walter. Editor in the Chemistry Department, University of California, Berkeley; Assistant Editor of *San Francisco Theatre Magazine* and free-lance theatre and film critic. **Essays:** Richard Emil Braun; Daniel Halpern; Robert Hass; Robert Pinsky.

BORKLUND, Elmer. Associate Professor of English, Pennsylvania State University, University Park. Former Associate Editor of *Chicago Review*. Author of *Contemporary Literary Critics*, 1977, and of articles for *Modern Philology*, *Commentary*, *New York Herald-Tribune Book Week*, *Journal of General Education*, and *World Book Encyclopedia*. **Essays:** Charles G. Bell; Randall Jarrell (appendix); James Michie; Elder Olson; Delmore Schwartz (appendix); R. G. Vliet.

BOSTIC, Corrine E. Part-time faculty member, Quinsigamond Community College, Worcester, Massachusetts; Radio Broadcaster, WTAG and WICN-FM. Author of *Requiem for Bluesville* (verse), 1970, *The Horns of Freedom* (play), 1971, and *Blacks* (essay), 1972. Editor of *Message in Black*, 1971. **Essays:** Victor Hernández Cruz; Calvin C. Hernton.

BOYERS, Robert. Member of the English Department, Skidmore College, Saratoga Springs, New York; Editor of *Salmagundi* magazine. Author of *Excursions: Selected Literary Essays*, 1976, *Lionel Trilling: Negative Capability and the Wisdom of Avoidance*, 1977, and *F. R. Leavis: Judgment and the Discipline of Thought*, 1978. Editor of *Robert Lowell: The Poet in His Time* (with Michael London), 1969, and *Contemporary Poetry in America*, 1975. **Essays:** Ben Belitt; Alan Dugan; Irving Feldman; John Logan.

BRADISH, Gaynor F. Visiting Associate Professor of English, Union College, Schenectady, New York. Head of the Playwrights' Unit, Actors Studio, New York, 1962–63; Head of the Dunster Drama Workshop, Harvard University; first director of Department of Dramatic Literature at New York University, to 1968; Drama Adviser, Hill and Wang Publishers, 1961–67. Director of *Asylum* by Arthur Kopit, New York, 1963, and author of introduction to Kopit's *Oh Dad, Poor Dad ...*, 1960. **Essays:** Kay Boyle; John Ciardi; Ralph Pomeroy; M. L. Rosenthal; Gerald Stern; Thomas Whitbread.

BRATHWAITE, Edward Kamau. See his own entry. **Essays:** George Campbell; Martin Carter; Frank A. Collymore; Wilson Harris; Anthony McNeill; Bruce St. John; A. J. Seymour.

BROWN, Lloyd W. Member of the Department of Comparative Literature, University of Southern California, Los Angeles. **Essay:** Edward Kamau Brathwaite.

BROWNJOHN, Alan. See his own entry. **Essays:** Ian Hamilton; Peter Porter; W. D. Snodgrass.

BRUCE, George. See his own entry. **Essays:** Alan Bold; Tom Buchan; Stewart Conn; Robin Fulton; Duncan Glen; Alastair Mackie; Joseph Macleod; Pete Morgan; Alastair Reid; Tom Scott; Sydney Tremayne.

BRUCHAC, Joseph. Editor of *Greenfield Review*, Greenfield Center, New York. Author of several collections of poetry – the most recent being *Flow*, 1975 – a novel, *The Way to Black Mountain*, 1975, and two books for children. Editor of *Words from the House of the Dead: Anthology of Prison Writings from Soledad* (with William Witherup), 1971, and *The Next World: Poems of 32 Third-World Americans*, 1978. **Essays:** Chinua Achebe; Syl Cheney-Coker; Michael Echeruo; Taban lo Liyong; John Okai; James Welch.

BURNS, Jim. See his own entry. **Essays:** Ray Bremser; Michael Horovitz; Barry MacSweeney.

BUTTERICK, George F. Curator of Literary Archives and Lecturer in English, University of Connecticut, Storrs. Author of *A Guide to the Maximus Poems of Charles Olson*, 1978, and *The Norse* (verse). Editor of *The Postmoderns: The New American Poetry Revised.* **Essays:** LeRoi Jones; Lewis MacAdams; Tom Raworth; Stephen Rodefer; John Wieners.

BYRD, Don. Member of the Department of English, State University of New York, Albany. Author of *Aesop's Garden* (verse), 1976, *Charles Olson's Maximus Poems*, 1980, and criticism in journals. **Essays:** William Bronk; Michael Davidson; Allen Ginsberg; Kenneth Irby; Joanne Kyger; Jackson Mac Low; Simon J. Ortiz; Michael Palmer; Ed Sanders; Lewis Warsh.

CALLAN, Edward. Professor of English, Western Michigan University, Kalamazoo. Author of *W. H. Auden: An Annotated Checklist*, 1958, *Albert Luthuli*, 1961, and *Alan Paton*, 1968, and of book reviews for *Saturday Review* and articles on Auden and Yeats in journals. Editor of *The Long View* by Alan Paton, 1968. **Essay:** John Woods.

CAREW, Rivers. Editor of *Dublin Magazine*, 1964–69. Author of *Figures Out of Mist* (with Timothy Brownlow), 1966, and of verse in *The Penguin Book of Irish Verse*, 1970, and in periodicals. **Essays:** Monk Gibbon; Valentin Iremonger; Michael Longley; Richard Weber.

CARRUTH, Hayden. See his own entry. **Essays:** Carol Bergé; Philip Booth; Thomas Hornsby Ferril; Arthur Gregor; Kenneth Koch; James Laughlin; Harvey Shapiro; Diane Wakoski.

CHAMBERS, D. D. C. Associate Professor of English, Trinity College, Toronto. Author of the forthcoming book *The Lost Cities.* **Essays:** Leonard Cohen; John Robert Colombo; David Helwig; George Jonas; Ian Young.

CHARTERS, Samuel. Poet, critic, and music historian. His most recent books are *From a Swedish Notebook* (verse), *Some Poems/Poets* (critical studies), *Robert Johnson: A Life, The Songs, The Legacy of the Blues*, and *I Love: The Story of Vladimir Mayakovsky and Lili Brik* (with Ann Charters). **Essays:** James Broughton; Larry Eigner; Philip Lamantia.

CHRISTENSEN, Paul. Assistant Professor of Modern Literature, Texas A. & M. University, College Station. Author of *Old and Lost Rivers* (verse), and *Charles Olson: Call Him Ishmael*, 1978. **Essays:** Helen Adam; Bill Berkson; Robert Bly; Robert Creeley; Albert Goldbarth; Robert Lowell (appendix); James Merrill; Richard Shelton; Charles Simic; William Stafford.

CHURCH, Richard. Poet, novelist, and critic. His most recent books were *Prince Albert* (novel), 1963, *The Burning Bush* (verse), 1967, and *The Wonder of Words*, 1970. Died, 1972. **Essay:** Ruth Pitter.

CLARK, Alan. Librarian since 1957, currently with the Royal Society Library, London; has conducted poetry courses at Braziers Park Adult College, Ipsden, Oxfordshire. Author of an essay on Laura Riding in *Stand* and of a checklist of Laura Riding's publications in *Chelsea*, 1976. **Essay:** Laura Riding.

CLARKE, Austin. Poet, playwright, and literary critic. His *Collected Poems* edited by Liam Miller were published in 1974. Died, 1974. **Essays:** Pearse Hutchinson; Brendan Kennelly; Ewart Milne; Desmond O'Grady.

CLUYSENAAR, Anne. See her own entry. **Essays:** Wayne Brown; John Cotton; Roy Fisher; Oswald Mtshali; Christopher Pilling; Michael Smith; Daniel Weissbort.

COHEN, Arthur A. Author of three novels – *In the Days of Simon Stern*, 1973, *A Hero in His Time*, 1976, and *Acts of Theft*, 1980 – and of *Osip Mandelstam: An Essay in Antiphon*, 1974. Translator (with David Shapiro) of *The New Art of Color* by Robert and Sonia Delaunay, 1978. **Essay:** David Shapiro.

COLOMBO, John Robert. See his own entry. **Essays:** Margaret Atwood; George Bowering; Elizabeth Brewster; Frederick Cogswell; Frank Davey; Ronald Everson; Doug Fetherling; Gary Geddes; Don Gutteridge; Daryl Hine; Harry Howith; Lionel Kearns; Dennis Lee; Douglas LePan; Gwendolyn MacEwen; Eli Mandel; Seymour Mayne; David McFadden; Glen Siebrasse; Francis Sparshott; Andrew Suknaski, Jr.; Miriam Waddington; Wilfred Watson.

COOKSON, William. Editor of *Agenda*, London. **Essays:** Anne Beresford; Peter Dale; Charles Tomlinson; Peter Whigham.

COOLEY, John R. Associate Professor of English, Western Michigan University, Kalamazoo. Author of articles on Hardy, Welty, Stephen Crane, Hemingway, and O'Neill. **Essays:** Hayden Carruth; Norman Dubie; George Economou; Leonard Nathan; Thomas Parkinson.

COONEY, Seamus. Associate Professor of English, Western Michigan University, Kalamazoo; Editor of *Sparrow* magazine. Author of articles on Byron, Scott, Lawrence, Binyon, and Austin Clarke. Editor of *By the Well of Living and Seeing: New and Selected Poems* by Charles Reznikoff. **Essays:** David Bromige; Cid Corman; Theodore Enslin; Patricia Goedicke; Jonathan Greene; Jack Hirschman; Larry Levis; Ron Loewinsohn; David Meltzer; Bert Meyers; F. D. Reeve; Stephen Stepanchev; Nancy Willard.

CORCORAN, Neil. Member of the Department of English, University of Sheffield. **Essays:** George Mackay Brown; Thom Gunn; Geoffrey Hill; A. D. Hope; Peter Levi; Craig Raine; Hugo Williams.

COTTON, John. See his own entry. **Essays:** Alan Brownjohn; Jim Burns; Bob Cobbing; Roger Garfitt; David Holbrook; Molly Holden; Frances Horovitz; Glyn Hughes; James Kirkup; Edward Lucie-Smith; Gerda Mayer; John Mole; Sally Purcell; Rodney Pybus; Peter Scupham; James Simmons; C. H. Sisson; D. M. Thomas; Ted Walker; Kit Wright.

CRAIG, Patricia. Literary critic and reviewer. Author of *You're a Brick, Angela!*, 1976, *Women and Children First*, 1978, and a forthcoming book on fictional women detectives and spies, *Sisters-in-Law*, all with Mary Cadogan; also author of a forthcoming study of Ulster writing. Contributor to *New Statesmen*, *Guardian*, *Books and Bookmen*, and *Irish Press*. **Essays:** Fleur Adcock; Stevie Smith (appendix).

CURTIS, Tony. Senior Lecturer in English, Polytechnic of Wales, Cardiff; Founding Editor of Edge Press, 1977. Author of several books of verse, the most recent being *The Deerslayers*, 1978, and of *Out of the Dark Wood* (fiction), 1975, and a book for children; has published articles in *Anglo-Welsh Review*, *Poetry Wales*, and other periodicals. **Essays:** Gillian Clarke; Raymond Garlick; Jeremy Hooker; John Ormond.

DAMASHEK, Richard. Assistant Professor of Literature, Sangamon State University, Springfield, Illinois. Author of articles on Randall Jarrell and Ingmar Bergman, and reviews in *Books Abroad* and other periodicals. **Essays:** R. H. W. Dillard; Paul Petrie; Ruth Whitman.

DAVIDSON, Michael. See his own entry. **Essay:** Jack Spicer (appendix).

DELIUS, Anthony. See his own entry. **Essay:** David Wright.

DILLARD, R. H. W. See his own entry. **Essays:** George Garrett; Julia Randall; David Slavitt.

DOEPKE, Dale. Free-lance writer; author of essays on 19th-century American literature. **Essays:** Jane Cooper; R. P. Dickey.

DORSINVILLE, Max. Assistant Professor of English, McGill University, Montreal. Author of *Caliban Without Prospero: An Essay on Quebec and Black Literature*, 1974, and articles in *PMLA*, *Canadian Literature*, and *Livres et Auteurs Québecois*. **Essays:** Joan Finnigan; Michael Gnarowski.

DOWLING, David. Member of the Faculty, Massey University, Palmerston North, New Zealand. Author of articles on Katherine Mansfield, Basil Dowling, and women's poetry in *Explicator*, *New Zealand Listener*, *Landfall*, and *Westerly*; verse published in *Pacific Quarterly*. Theatre reviewer for Wellington *Dominion* and *ACT* magazine; script reader for Playmarket agency. **Essays:** Charles Doyle; Vincent O'Sullivan; Judith Wright.

DOYLE, Charles. See his own entry. **Essays:** James K. Baxter (appendix); Robert Duncan.

DUDEK, Louis. See his own entry. **Essays:** D. G. Jones; James Reaney.

DUNN, Douglas. See his own entry. **Essay:** Shirley Toulson.

EMANUEL, James A. See his own entry.

EWART, Gavin. See his own entry. **Essay:** Harold Massingham.

FERNANDO, Lloyd. Formerly Professor of English, University of Malaya, Kuala Lumpur. Author of *Scorpion Orchard* (novel) and *"New Women" in the Late Victorian Novel*, 1977. Editor of *Twenty-Two Malaysian Stories*, 1968. **Essay:** Wong Phui Nam.

FLETCHER, Ian. See his own entry. **Essay:** Terence Tiller.

FRASER, G. S. See his own entry. **Essays:** Samuel Beckett; Ronald Bottrall; Lawrence Durrell; William Empson; Kathleen Raine; Sacheverell Sitwell; Constantine Trypanis.

FRIEDMAN, Norman. Professor of English, Queens College, City University of New York. Author of *E. E. Cummings: The Art of His Poetry*, 1960; *Poetry: An Introduction to Its Form and Art* (with C. A. McLaughlin), 1961; *Logic, Rhetoric, Style* (with McLaughlin), 1963; *E. E. Cummings: The Growth of a Writer*, 1964; and of verse in magazines and anthologies. Editor of *E. E. Cummings: A Collection of Critical Essays*, 1972, and *Form and Meaning in Fiction*, 1975. **Essays:** Kenneth Burke; Robert Francis; Richard Howard; Barbara Howes; Vern Rutsala; Louis Simpson; James Wright.

FULTON, Robin. See his own entry. **Essays:** James Fenton; David Gill; Daniel Huws; Derick S. Thomson; Kenneth White.

GALL, Sally M. Adjunct Assistant Professor of English, New York University; Distinguished Visiting Professor, Drew University, Madison, New Jersey. Author of articles on M. L. Rosenthal, Ramon Guthrie, and Sylvia Plath in *Modern Poetry Studies* and *American Poetry Review*. **Essays:** J. V. Cunningham; Frederick Morgan.

GATES, Norman T. Professor of English, Rider College, Trenton, New Jersey. Author of

The Poetry of Richard Aldington, 1974, and *A Checklist of the Letters of Richard Aldington*, 1977. **Essays:** Francis Warner; James Whitehead.

GERMAIN, Edward B. Associate Professor of English, Nathaniel Hawthorne College, Antrim, New Hampshire. Editor of *Flag of Ecstasy: Selected Poems of Charles Henri Ford*, 1972, *Shadows of the Sun: The Diaries of Harry Crosby*, 1977, and *English and American Surrealist Poetry*, 1977. **Essays:** Robert Dana; Charles Henri Ford; Donald Hall; Lee Harwood; Ron Padgett; Edouard Roditi.

GILBERT, S. R. Professor of Drama and Comparative Literature and Chairperson of the Humanities Division, Capilano College, North Vancouver. Author of the play *A Glass Darkly* (published in *Dialogue and Dialectic*, 1972), "A Bibliography of British Columbia" in *Communique*, 1973, and of articles and reviews. **Essays:** Phyllis Gotlieb; J. Michael Yates.

GNAROWSKI, Michael. See his own entry. **Essays:** Milton Acorn; Douglas Barbour; Henry Beissel; Dorothy Livesay; John Newlove; David Wevill.

GORDON, Lois. Professor of English and Comparative Literature, Fairleigh Dickinson University, Teaneck, New Jersey. Author of *Strategems to Uncover Nakedness: The Dramas of Harold Pinter*, 1969, and of articles on Eberhart, Jarrell, Faulkner, T. S. Eliot, and Philip Roth. **Essays:** Elizabeth Bishop; Donald Davie; Richard Eberhart; W. S. Merwin; Adrienne Rich; Muriel Rukeyser; Gilbert Sorrentino.

GREENBERG, Alvin. Professor of English, Macalester College, St. Paul, Minnesota. Author of several volumes of verse, the most recent being *In/Direction*, 1978, and two novels, *Going Nowhere*, 1971, and *The Invention of the West*, 1976. **Essay:** Margaret Randall.

GUNN, Thom. See his own entry. **Essay:** Gary Snyder.

GUSTAFSON, Ralph. See his own entry. **Essays:** Louis Dudek; Robert Finch; Michael Ondaatje; Raymond Souster.

HALL, Donald. See his own entry.

HALL, Rodney. See his own entry. **Essay:** Roger McDonald.

HARNETT, Ruth. Lecturer in English, Rhodes University, Grahamstown, South Africa. **Essays:** Guy Butler; Anne Welsh.

HEATON, David M. Associate Professor of Comparative Literature, and Chairman of the Comparative Literature Program, Ohio University, Athens. Verse, verse translations, and articles on Ted Hughes and Alan Sillitoe published in periodicals. **Essays:** Jon Anderson; George P. Elliott; Stanley Plumly; Alan Stephens.

HEWITT, Geof. See his own entry. **Essays:** Léonie Adams; Marvin Bell; Richard Brautigan; Peter Davison; George Hitchcock; Richard Hugo; Ronald Johnson; Robert Kelly; Bill Knott; William Matthews; George Oppen; Sylvia Plath (appendix); Aram Saroyan; Robert Sward; James Tate; Theodore Weiss; Jonathan Williams.

HEYEN, William. See his own entry. **Essays:** Lucien Stryk; Hollis Summers; Lewis Turco.

HILL, Douglas. Literary Editor of *Tribune*, London. Author of several works of non-fiction, fiction for children, and verse in periodicals and anthologies. **Essays:** Bernard Kops; Jeremy Robson.

HINCHEY, John. Member of the Department of English, Swarthmore College, Pennsylvania. **Essay:** Anne Waldman.

HOBSBAUM, Philip. See his own entry. **Essays:** Francis Berry; Keith Bosley; Stanley Cook; Jeni Couzyn; Zulfikar Ghose; Frederick Grubb; Christopher Levenson; Derek Mahon; Roy McFadden; Matthew Mead; Eric Millward; Paul Muldoon; Robert Nye; Frank Ormsby; E. J. Scovell; John Tripp; Lotte Zurndorfer.

HOEFER, Jacqueline. Free-lance writer. Author of articles on Beckett and other modern writers. **Essay:** Katherine Hoskins.

HOFFMAN, Daniel. See his own entry. **Essays:** A. R. Ammons; John Berryman (appendix); Abbie Huston Evans; William Meredith; William Jay Smith; Robert Penn Warren.

HOKENSON, Jan. Assistant Professor of English, Florida Atlantic University, Boca Raton. Author of articles on Beckett, Céline, and Proust, in *James Joyce Quarterly*, *L'Esprit Créateur*, *Far-Western Forum*, and *Samuel Beckett: An Anthology of Criticism* edited by Ruby Cohn, 1975. **Essays:** W. H. Auden (appendix); Thomas McGrath; Anne Sexton (appendix).

HOMBERGER, Eric. Member of the School of English and American Studies, University of East Anglia, Norwich. Author of *The Art of the Real: Poetry in England and America since 1939*, 1977. **Essays:** Richard Murphy; Tom Paulin; Julian Symons.

HUDSON, Theodore R. Professor of English, Howard University, Washington, D.C. Author of *A LeRoi Jones (Amiri Baraka) Bibliography*, 1971, and *From LeRoi Jones to Amiri Baraka: The Literary Works*, 1973. **Essays:** Lucille Clifton; Don L. Lee; Larry Neal; Sonia Sanchez; Margaret Walker.

JAMES, Charles L. Associate Professor of English, Swarthmore College, Pennsylvania. Author of *The Black Writer in America* (bibliography), 1969. Editor of *From the Roots: Short Stories by Black Americans*, 1970. **Essays:** Gwendolyn Brooks; Michael S. Harper; Etheridge Knight; Donald Petersen; Ishmael Reed.

JAMES, Louis. Senior Lecturer in English and American Literature, University of Kent, Canterbury. Author of *The Islands in Between*, 1968, and *Fiction for the Working-Class Man 1830–1850*, 1974. **Essay:** Derek Walcott.

JENNINGS, Elizabeth. See her own entry. **Essays:** Henry Reed; Michael Schmidt.

JONES, Eldred D. Professor of English, Fourah Bay College, University of Sierra Leone, Freetown. Author of *Othello's Countrymen: The Africans in English Renaissance Drama*, 1955, and *African Literature Today*, 1973. Editor, with Clifford N. Fyle, of *A Krio-English Dictionary*, 1980. **Essays:** Lenrie Peters; Wole Soyinka.

KEESING, Nancy. Writer, critic, and editor. Chairman of the Literature Board of the Australia Council, 1974–77. Author of verse (most recently *Hails and Farewells*, 1977), memoirs (*Garden Island People*, 1975), biography (*John Lang*, 1979), critical studies of Douglas Stewart and Elsie Carew, and books for children. Editor of several anthologies of Australian songs and ballads, and of *Gold Fever*, 1967, and *Shalom: Australian Jewish Short Stories*, 1978. **Essay:** Randolph Stow.

KENDLE, Burton. Professor of English, Roosevelt University, Chicago. Author of articles on D. H. Lawrence, John Cheever, William March, Tennessee Williams, and others. **Essays:**

John William Corrington; Sandra Hochman; Robert Pack; May Sarton; Muriel Spark; Peter Viereck; Rex Warner.

KENNELLY, Brendan. See his own entry. **Essay:** Michael Hartnett.

KINSELLA, Thomas. See his own entry.

KORGES, James. Free-lance writer. Editor of *Critique: Studies in Modern Fiction*, 1962–70. Author of *Erskine Caldwell*, 1969. Died, 1975. **Essays:** Howard Baker; Edgar Bowers; Charles Gullans; Vassar Miller; Paul Ramsey.

KOSTELANETZ, Richard. See his own entry. **Essays:** Clark Coolidge; Emmett Williams.

KRAPF, Norbert. Associate Professor of English, C. W. Post College, Long Island University, Greenvale, New York; Contributing Editor, *West Hills Review: A Walt Whitman Journal*. Author of *The Playfair Book of Hours* (verse), 1976, and *Finding the Grain*, 1977, and of poetry, fiction, translations, and articles in periodicals. **Essay:** William Heyen.

LINDBERG, Stanley W. Member of the Humanities Faculty, University of Georgia, Athens; Editor of *Georgia Review*. Author of *The Annotated McGuffey*, 1976. **Essays:** Michael Casey; R. A. D. Ford; Reg Saner.

LINDNER, Carl. Member of the Humanistic Studies Division, University of Wisconsin-Parkside, Kenosha. **Essays:** Michael Anania; Edward Field; Allen Planz; Knute Skinner.

LINDSAY, Maurice. See his own entry. **Essays:** George Bruce; Douglas Dunn; G. S. Fraser; Valerie Gillies; Norman MacCaig; Alasdair Maclean; Edwin Morgan; Sydney Goodsir Smith (appendix).

LUCIE-SMITH, Edward. See his own entry. **Essays:** Barry Cole; Tony Connor; Kevin Crossley-Holland; Ruth Fainlight; Karen Gershon; Henry Graham; Hamish Henderson; Adrian Henri; Brian Jones; Christopher Logue; Roger McGough; Adrian Mitchell; John Frederick Nims; Harold Norse; Brian Patten; Alan Rook; Alan Sillitoe.

LUSCHEI, Glenna. Associated with the Solo Press and the Cosmep Women's Committee, San Luis Obispo. Author of *Back into My Body: Poems*, 1974. **Essay:** Teo Savory.

LYNCH, Dennis. Member of the Department of English, Northern Illinois University, DeKalb. Author of articles on William Stafford and other American poets in *Modern Poetry Studies*, *New Republic*, *American Poetry Review*, and other periodicals. **Essays:** Ted Berrigan; Lawrence Ferlinghetti; Donald Finkel; Jean Garrigue (appendix); X. J. Kennedy; A. Poulin, Jr.; Philip Whalen.

LYNCH, Michael. Director of Antioch University International Writing Programmes, London. Author of four books of verse, the most recent being *Allegory of Fire*, 1979, *An American Soldier* (novel), 1969, and an opera libretto, *The Magician*, 1974. **Essay:** Elliott Coleman.

MacCAIG, Norman. See his own entry. **Essays:** Laurie Lee; Alexander Scott.

MACNAB, Roy. See his own entry. **Essays:** R. N. Currey; Anthony Delius; F. T. Prince.

MATHIAS, Roland. See his own entry. **Essays:** Dannie Abse; Glyn Jones; Leslie Norris.

MATTHEWS, William. See his own entry. **Essays:** Kenneth O. Hanson; Sandra McPherson; Judith Moffett; Dennis Schmitz; James Scully.

MATTHIAS, John. Associate Professor of English, University of Notre Dame, Indiana. Author of three books of verse – *Bucyrus*, 1971, *Turns*, 1975, and *Crossing*, 1979. Editor of several anthologies of contemporary poetry, and of *Introducing David Jones*, 1980. **Essay:** Gael Turnbull.

MAYO, E. L. See his own entry. **Essays:** James Bertolino; Anselm Hollo; Robert Mezey; David Ray.

McELROY, George. Lecturer at Indiana University Northwest, Gary. Writer for the University of Chicago Home Study Department's Great Books syllabus; author of a text on drama for the University of Wisconsin's Home Study Department. Regular contributor to *Opera News* for 25 years. **Essays:** D. K. Das; Pritish Nandy.

MELTZER, David. See his own entry. **Essays:** Asa Benveniste; John Brandi; Diane di Prima; Lenore Kandel; Kenneth Patchen (appendix); Anthony Rudolf; George Stanley.

MILLS, Ralph J., Jr. Professor of English, University of Illinois at Chicago Circle. Author of books on Theodore Roethke, Richard Eberhart, Edith Sitwell, and Kathleen Raine, and of *Contemporary American Poetry*, 1965, *Creation's Very Self*, 1969, and *Cry of the Human: Essays on Contemporary American Poetry*, 1975. Editor of Roethke's prose and letters. **Essays:** Stephen Berg; James Dickey; H. R. Hays; Denise Levertov; Laurence Lieberman; Karl Shapiro.

MIOLA, Robert. Member of the Department of English, Lafayette College, Easton, Pennsylvania. **Essay:** Charles Edward Eaton.

MOKASHI-PUNEKAR, Shankar. See his own entry. **Essay:** P. Lal.

MOLE, John. See his own entry. **Essay:** Patric Dickinson.

MOLESWORTH, Charles. Member of the Department of English, Queens College, City University of New York. Author of *The Fierce Embrace: A Study of Contemporary American Poetry*, 1979. **Essays:** William Dickey; William Oxley; William Pillin; Ann Stanford.

MONTAGUE, John. See his own entry. **Essays:** John Hewitt; Thomas Kinsella; Carolyn Kizer.

MORGAN, Edwin. See his own entry. **Essays:** David Black; Ian Hamilton Finlay; Robert Garioch; W. S. Graham; dom Sylvester Houédard; Tom Leonard; Liz Lochhead; W. Price Turner.

MOSER, Norman. Free-lance writer and editor. Author of *Open Season* (verse), 1970, and of critical articles. Editor of *Bay Window*, later *Bay Area Arts Review* and *Transfer*, both San Francisco, and *Illuminations*, Santa Fe. **Essay:** Charles Bukowski.

MUKHERJEE, Meenakshi. Member of the Department of English, Fergusson College, University of Poona, India. Author of *The Twice-Born Fiction* (on the Anglo-Indian novel), 1971. Translator of *The Virgin Fish of Babughat* by Lokenath Bhattacharya, 1975, and of Bengali poetry into English. **Essays:** Paul Jacob; Shankar Mokashi-Punekar; Monika Varma.

MURPHY, Rosalie. Editor of the 1970 edition of *Contemporary Poets*. **Essay:** Reed Whittemore.

NAGARAJAN, S. Professor of English, University of Hyderabad, India. **Essays:** Nissim Ezekiel; Arvind Krishna Mehrotra; Dom Moraes; R. Parthasarathy; A. K. Ramanujan.

NELSON, Rudolph L. Assistant Professor of English, State University of New York, Albany. **Essay:** Edwin Honig.

NEWLOVE, John. See his own entry. **Essay:** Joe Rosenblatt.

NORRIS, Leslie. See his own entry. **Essay:** Vernon Watkins (appendix).

NYE, Robert. See his own entry. **Essays:** Anthony Howell; Patrick Kavanagh (appendix); John Moat; Basil Payne; Martin Seymour-Smith; Burns Singer (appendix); John Updike; Roderick Watson; Sheila Wingfield.

OXLEY, William. See his own entry. **Essay:** Peter Russell.

PARIS, Jerry. Member of the Department of English, State University of New York, Albany. **Essays:** Hilary Corke; Judson Crews; Judson Jerome; Lyn Lifshin.

PARISI, Joseph. Associate Editor of *Poetry* magazine, Chicago. Editor (with Daryl Hine) of *The "Poetry" Anthology 1912–1977*, 1978. **Essays:** Sarah Appleton; Charles Boer; William Burford; Alfred Corn; Louis Coxe; Maurice English; Josephine Jacobsen; William H. Matchett; Frederick Seidel; Paul Zimmer; Harriet Zinnes.

PARKER, Derek. Editor of *Poetry Review*, London. Author of many books, including *The Fall of Phaethon and Other Poems*, 1954, *Byron and His World*, 1968, *The Natural History of the Chorus Girl* (with Julia Parker), 1975, *Radio: The Great Years*, 1977, and *The Story and the Song* (with Julia Parker), 1979. **Essays:** Gavin Bantock; Leonard Clark; Alex Comfort; Ronald Duncan; Christopher Fry; John Lehmann; Norman Nicholson; A. L. Rowse; John Smith.

PAUL, Jay S. Assistant Professor of English, Christopher Newport College, Newport News, Virginia. Author of poetry, fiction, reviews, and essays in periodicals. **Essays:** Bob Dylan; Nikki Giovanni; Linda Pastan.

PEREIRA, E. Professor of English, University of South Africa, Pretoria. Author of radio broadcasts and articles in journals and the *Dictionary of South African Biography*. Editor of the anthologies *The Poet's Circle* and *Contemporary South African Plays*. **Essays:** Perseus Adams; Robert Dederick; Adèle Naudé.

PERLOFF, Marjorie. Florence R. Scott Professor of English, University of Southern California, Los Angeles. Author of *Rhyme and Meaning in the Poetry of Yeats*, 1970, *The Poetic Art of Robert Lowell*, 1973, *Frank O'Hara: Poet among Painters*, 1977, *The Other Tradition: Towards a Postmodern Poetry*, 1980, and an article on Frank O'Hara and John Ashbery in *Yearbook of English Studies*, 1978. **Essays:** David Antin; John Ashbery; Kathleen Fraser; Charles Wright.

PETERSEN, Kirsten Holst. Member of the Commonwealth Literature Division, University of Aarhus, Denmark; reviewer for *Danida*. Editor of *Enigma of Values* (with Anna Rutherford), 1975. **Essays:** John Pepper Clark; Roy Macnab; Okot p'Bitek; Harold Stewart.

PLOMER, William. Novelist, short story writer, and poet. His most recent books were *Celebrations* (verse), 1972, and *The Autobiography*, 1975; *Electric Delights* (selections), edited by Rupert Hart-Davis, was published in 1978. Died, 1973. **Essay:** John Betjeman.

PORTER, Peter. See his own entry. **Essay:** George MacBeth.

PRESS, John. Area Officer, British Council, Oxford. Author of three books of verse – *Uncertainties*, 1956, *Guy Fawkes Night*, 1959, and *Troika* (with others), 1977 – and several critical works, including *Rule and Energy*, 1963, *A Map of English Verse*, 1969, *The Lengthening Shadows*, 1971, and *John Betjeman*, 1974. **Essays:** J. C. Hall; Laurence Whistler.

RANDALL, Dudley. See his own entry. **Essay:** Robert Hayden.

RANDALL, Julia. See her own entry. **Essay:** Howard Nemerov.

RAVENSCROFT, Arthur. Senior Lecturer in English Literature, University of Leeds; Founding Editor, *Journal of Commonwealth Literature*, Leeds. Author of *Chinua Achebe*, 1969. Translator, with C. K. Johnson, *Journal of Jan Van Riebeeck*, vol. 3, 1958.

RAY, David. See his own entry. **Essays:** Ed Dorn; Horace Gregory; Archibald MacLeish; E. L. Mayo; Josephine Miles; Charles Olson (appendix); Kenneth Rexroth; Stephen Spender.

REID, J. C. Professor of English, University of Auckland. Author of *The Mind and Art of Coventry Patmore*, 1957; *Francis Thompson: Man and Poet*, 1959; *Thomas Hood*, 1963; *Bucks and Bruisers: Pierce Egan and Regency England*, 1971. Died, 1972. **Essays:** M. K. Joseph; Kendrick Smithyman; Charles Spear.

REILLY, John M. Associate Professor of English, State University of New York, Albany; Advisory Editor, *Obsidian: Black Literature in Review* and *Melus*. Author of the bibliographical essay on Richard Wright in *Black American Writers* and of articles on Wright and other Afro-American writers, and on detective fiction, in *Colorado Quarterly*, *Phylon*, *Journal of Popular Culture*, and other periodicals. Editor of *Twentieth-Century Interpretations of "Invisible Man,"* 1970, *Richard Wright: The Critical Reception*, 1978, and of the reference book *Twentieth-Century Crime and Mystery Writers*, 1980. **Essays:** Alvin Aubert; Clarence Major; Dudley Randall; Al Young.

RICKARDS, Colin. Press correspondent in Latin America and the Caribbean for 12 years; now with Caribnews, London. Author of *Caribbean Power*, 1963, and *The Man from Devil's Island*, 1968. **Essay:** Louise Bennett.

ROBINSON, James K. Professor of English, University of Cincinnati. **Essays:** Wendell Berry; Tess Gallagher; Louise Glück; David Wagoner.

RODDICK, Alan. See his own entry. **Essays:** Sam Hunt; Kevin Ireland.

RODRIGUEZ, Judith. See her own entry. **Essays:** John Blight; Vincent Buckley; Dorothy Hewett; Les A. Murray; Philip Roberts; Andrew Taylor.

RUSS, Lawrence. Free-lance writer; verse published in magazines and anthologies. **Essays:** Henri Coulette; Jim Harrison; Milton Kessler; Lou Lipsitz; Jack Marshall; William Pitt Root; David Young.

RUTHERFORD, Anna. Head of the Commonwealth Literature Division, University of Aarhus, Denmark; Editor of *Kunapipi*, and Chairman of the European branch of the

Commonwealth Literature and Language Association. Editor of *Commonwealth Short Stories* (with Donald Hannah), 1971, *Commonwealth* (essays), 1972, and *Enigma of Values* (with Kirsten Holst Petersen), 1975. **Essays:** J. R. Rowland; Thomas W. Shapcott.

SAFFIOTI, Carol Lee. Assistant Professor of English, University of Wisconsin-Parkside, Kenosha. **Essay:** Sterling Brown.

SCHROEDER, Andreas. See his own entry. **Essay:** Michael Bullock.

SCOTT, Alexander. See his own entry. **Essays:** Donald Campbell; Alan Jackson.

SCUPHAM, Peter. See his own entry. **Essays:** Freda Downie; Neil Powell.

SERGEANT, Howard. See his own entry. **Essays:** Kofi Awoonor; Taner Baybars; Martin Booth; Kwesi Brew; Edwin Brock; Dennis Brutus; Jack Clemo; Marcus Cumberlege; John Figueroa; Robert Gittings; Bryn Griffiths; Harry Guest; Christopher Hampton; Keith Harrison; Philip Hobsbaum; Geoffrey Holloway; Jenny Joseph; Douglas Livingstone; Charles Madge; Wes Magee; Gabriel Okara; Betty Parvin; W. H. Petty; Paul Roche; Margaret Willy.

SEYMOUR-SMITH, Martin. See his own entry. **Essays:** John Malcolm Brinnin; George Buchanan; Federico Espino; John Fairfax; Robert Fitzgerald; Ian Fletcher; John Fuller; Denis Goacher; Giles Gordon; Robert Graves; Tony Harrison; Charles Higham; Andrew Hoyem; Alejandrino G. Hufana; Peter Jay; P. J. Kavanagh; Edward Lowbury; James J. McAuley; Kathleen Nott; Tom Pickard; J. H. Prynne; Jon Stallworthy; John Tagliabue; Nathaniel Tarn; Ivan White; Hubert Witheford.

SHAPCOTT, Thomas W. See his own entry. **Essays:** Robert Adamson; Bruce Dawe; Rosemary Dobson; Rodney Hall; Evan Jones; David Malouf; John Manifold; Ronald McCuaig; Ian Mudie; Craig Powell; Roland Robinson; Judith Rodriguez; David Rowbotham; R. A. Simpson; Vivian Smith; Douglas Stewart; John Tranter; Chris Wallace-Crabbe.

SHAPIRO, David. See his own entry. **Essay:** Frank O'Hara (appendix).

SHARMA, J. N. Deputy Director (Literature), American Studies Research Centre, Hyderabad, India. **Essays:** Sam Cornish; Kamala Das.

SHUCARD, Alan R. Associate Professor of English, University of Wisconsin-Parkside, Kenosha. Author of two books of verse – *The Gorgon Bog*, 1970, and *The Louse on the Head of the Lord*, 1972. **Essays:** Mari Evans; Stanley Moss.

SILKIN, Jon. See his own entry. **Essays:** Gene Baro; Michael Hamburger; Ken Smith.

SMITH, A. J. M. See his own entry. **Essays:** Margaret Avison; John Glassco; Ralph Gustafson; Irving Layton; Jay Macpherson; F. R. Scott.

SMITH, Stan. Lecturer in English, University of Dundee, Scotland. Author of *A Superfluous Man* (on Edward Thomas), 1979, and of articles on modern literature for *Critical Quarterly*, *Literature and History*, *Irish University Review*, *Scottish International Review*, and other periodicals. **Essays:** Basil Bunting; Seamus Heaney; Ted Hughes; Christopher Middleton; John Montague; Peter Redgrove; Iain Crichton Smith; Anne Stevenson; R. S. Thomas.

SMITHYMAN, Kendrick. See his own entry. **Essays:** Louis Johnson; Bill Manhire; Keith Sinclair; Elizabeth Smither; C. K. Stead.

SQUIRES, Radcliffe. See his own entry. **Essay:** Brewster Ghiselin.

STAFFORD, William. See his own entry. **Essays:** William Everson; John Haines; May Swenson.

STAUFFER, Donald Barlow. Associate Professor of English, State University of New York, Albany. Author of several articles on Poe, and *A Short History of American Poetry*, 1974. **Essays:** Stanley Burnshaw; Gregory Corso; Barry Spacks.

STEAD, C. K. See his own entry. **Essays:** Allen Curnow; Janet Frame; Denis Glover; David Mitchell; Alistair Paterson; Alan Roddick; Hone Tuwhare; Ian Wedde.

STERN, Carol Simpson. Associate Professor, Department of Interpretation, Northwestern University, Evanston, Illinois. Research Consultant and Contributor, *English Literature in Transition*; Theatre and Book Reviewer for *Victorian Studies* and Chicago *Sun-Times*. **Essays:** A. Alvarez; Peter Everwine; Pauline Hanson; Erica Jong; Susan Musgrave; Kenneth Pitchford; Stephen Sandy; Jon Silkin; Richard Wilbur.

STEVENS, Holly. Business Manager of *The Yale Review*, New Haven, Connecticut; Director of the Connecticut Poetry Circuit. Editor of *The Letters of Wallace Stevens*, 1967, and *The Palm at the End of the Mind: Selected Poems and a Play* by Wallace Stevens, 1971. **Essay:** Mark Strand.

STEVENS, Joan. Professor of English, Victoria University, Wellington, New Zealand; now retired. Author of *The New Zealand Novel 1860–1965*, 1966, *New Zealand Short Stories: A Survey*, 1968, and articles on the Brontës, Thackeray, and Dickens. **Essay:** Ruth Gilbert.

STEVENSON, Anne. See her own entry. **Essays:** Penelope Shuttle; Radcliffe Squires; Richard Tillinghast.

STEWART, Douglas. See his own entry. **Essays:** David Campbell; Robert D. FitzGerald.

STRAND, Mark. See his own entry. **Essay:** Donald Justice.

STRYK, Lucien. See his own entry. **Essays:** Philip Levine; James Schevill; George Starbuck.

SULLIVAN, Rosemary. Assistant Professor of English, University of Toronto. Author of *Theodore Roethke: The Garden Master*, 1975, and of articles on Roethke, Samuel Beckett, Robert Lowell, Margaret Atwood, and P. K. Page. **Essays:** Patrick Lane; Theodore Roethke (appendix).

SYLVESTER, William. Professor of English and Comparative Literature, State University of New York, Buffalo. Author of *Curses, Omens, Prayers* (verse), 1974, "The Poetics of Robert Creeley" in *Boundary 2*, 1979, and fiction and poetry in periodicals. **Essays:** Daniel Hoffman; Louis Zukofsky.

SYMONS, Julian. See his own entry. **Essays:** Alan Ross; George Woodcock.

TAGGART, John. Free-lance writer. Author of critical articles on William Bronk in *Ironwood*, Spring 1978, and Louis Zukofsky in *Paideuma*, Winter 1979. **Essay:** Toby Olson.

TATE, Allen. Poet, novelist, and literary critic. Collections of his work include *Collected Poems*, 1977, *The Fathers and Other Fiction*, 1976, *Collected Essays*, 1959, and *Memoirs and Opinions*, 1975. Died, 1979.

TAYLOR, Henry. Professor of Literature, American University, Washington, D.C. Author of three books of verse – *The Horse Show at Midnight*, 1966, *Breakings*, 1971, and *Afternoon of Pocket Billiards*, 1975 – and *Poetry: Points of Departure* (textbook), 1974. Editor of *The Water of Light: A Miscellany in Honor of Brewster Ghiselin*, 1976. **Essays:** Samuel Hazo; Robert Watson.

TAYLOR, Myron. Associate Professor of English, State University of New York, Albany. Author of articles on Shakespeare in *The Christian Scholar*, *Studies in English*, and *Shakespeare Quarterly*. **Essay:** Daniel Berrigan.

TERRY, Arthur. Professor of Literature, University of Essex, Wivenhoe. Author of *Catalan Literature*, 1973. Editor of *An Anthology of Spanish Poetry 1500–1700*, 2 vols., 1965–68. **Essay:** Laurence Lerner.

THUMBOO, Edwin. Lecturer in English, University of Singapore; Editor of *Poetry Singapore*. Author of *Rib of Earth* (verse), 1956. Editor, *Seven Poets*, 1969. **Essay:** Wong May.

THWAITE, Anthony. See his own entry. **Essays:** Kingsley Amis; George Barker; Patricia Beer; Charles Causley; Philip Larkin; Anne Ridler; Vernon Scannell.

TIBBLE, Anne. Free-lance writer. Author of *John Clare: A Life* (with J. W. Tibble), 1932, *John Clare: His Life and Poetry*, 1956, *African/English Literature*, 1964, *The Story of English Literature*, 1970, *The God Spigo* (novel), 1976, books on Helen Keller and Gertrude Bell, and three volumes of autobiography. Editor of the letters, prose, and selected poetry of Clare and his *The Midsummer Cushion*, 1979. **Essay:** Howard Sergeant.

TOWNS, Saundra. Lecturer in English, Bernard Baruch College, City University of New York. Author of essays and reviews in *The Nation*, *Black Books Bulletin*, *Black World*, *Black Position*, and other periodicals. **Essays:** June Jordan; Keorapetse Kgositsile; Audre Lorde; Raymond R. Patterson.

TRIPP, John. See his own entry. **Essays:** Anthony Conran; Gloria Evans Davies; Peter Gruffydd; Robert Morgan; A. G. Prys-Jones; Meic Stephens; Harri Webb; Gwyn Williams; John Stuart Williams.

TRUE, Michael. Professor of English, Assumption College, Worcester, Massachusetts; Poetry Editor of *English Journal*. Author of *Worcester Poets*, 1972, *Poets in the Schools: A Handbook*, 1976, and articles on Thomas Paine and Karl Shapiro in *American Writers*. **Essays:** Stephen Dunn; Barbara Guest; David Ignatow; Maxine Kumin; Stanley Kunitz; John L'Heureux; Larry Rubin; Dave Smith; C. K. Williams; Marya Zaturenska.

TRYPANIS, Constantine. See his own entry. **Essay:** Richmond Lattimore.

TULIP, James. Associate Professor of English, Sydney University. **Essay:** Grace Perry.

TURNER, Roland. Head of the Reference Division, St. Martin's Press, New York. Editor of the biennial reference book *The Grants Register*. **Essay:** David Harsent.

VAN DOMELEN, John. Professor of English, Texas A. & M. University, College Station. **Essay:** John Heath-Stubbs.

VAN DOREN, Mark. Poet, novelist, literary critic, and editor. His *Collected and New Poems* was published in 1963; *Collected Stories*, 3 vols., 1962–68; *Autobiography*, 1958. Died, 1972. **Essay:** Babette Deutsch.

VAS DIAS, Robert. See his own entry. **Essays:** Paul Blackburn (appendix); Michael D. Heller.

VENKATACHARI, K. Reader in English, Osmania University, Hyderabad, India. **Essays:** Arun Kolatkar; Shiv K. Kumar.

WAGNER, Linda. Professor of English, Michigan State University, East Lansing. Author of *The Poems* (1964) *and Prose* (1970) *of William Carlos Williams*; *Denise Levertov*, 1967; *Hemingway and Faulkner: Inventors, Masters*, 1975; *Introducing Poems*, 1976; *John Dos Passos*, 1978. **Essay:** Robert Vas Dias.

WAKOSKI, Diane. See her own entry. **Essays:** Clayton Eshleman; Joel Oppenheimer; Carl Rakosi; Jerome Rothenberg; Armand Schwerner; Peter Wild.

WALSH, William. Professor of Commonwealth Literature and Chairman of the School of English, University of Leeds. Author of *Use of Imagination*, 1958; *A Human Idiom*, 1964; *Coleridge*, 1967; *A Manifold Voice*, 1970; *R. K. Narayan*, 1972; *V. S. Naipaul*, 1973; *Patrick White's Fiction*, 1978. **Essays:** A. L. Hendriks; George Johnston; Christopher Okigbo (appendix); Frederic Prokosch.

WEINBERGER, Eliot. Editor of the poetry journal *Montemora*, New York; also a poet and translator. His recent translations include two books by Octavio Paz, *Eagle or Sun?* and *A Draft of Shadows*. **Essay:** Jonathan Griffin.

WHITEHEAD, James. See his own entry. **Essay:** Miller Williams.

WILLIAMS, John Stuart. See his own entry. **Essay:** Roland Mathias.

WILLY, Margaret. See her own entry. **Essays:** D. J. Enright; Phoebe Hesketh; Elizabeth Jennings; Anthony Thwaite; John Wain.

WILSON, Joseph. Lecturer in Creative Writing, Anna Maria College, Paxton, Massachusetts. Verse published in little magazines. **Essays:** John Beecher; Michael Dennis Browne; Paul Engle; Anthony Hecht; Joseph Langland; Ned O'Gorman; Raymond Roseliep.

WOODCOCK, George. See his own entry. **Essays:** Earle Birney; Roy Daniells; Sid Marty; Alden Nowlan; P. K. Page; Al Purdy; Andreas Schroeder; Robin Skelton; A. J. M. Smith; Peter Stevens; Tom Wayman; Phyllis Webb.

WRIGHT, Judith. See her own entry. **Essay:** William Hart-Smith.

YABES, Leopoldo Y. Professor of English and Dean of the Graduate School, University of the Philippines, Quezon City; Editor of *Philippine Social Sciences and Humanities*. Author of many books, including *Philippine Literature in English 1898–1957*, 1958; *The Filipino Struggle for Intellectual Freedom and Other Essays on Philippine Life and Thought*, 1959; *In Larger Freedom*, 1961. **Essay:** José Garcia Villa.

YOUNG, Steven. Member of the Department of English, Pomona College, Claremont, California; theatre director and actor. Has made or collaborated on several art books, including *1" : 1,000,000* (with Mowry Baden), *Fifty Postcard Views*, and *Twelve Images* (with Jan Raithel). **Essays:** Michael Benedikt; Tom Clark.